CONTRACT LAW

CONTRACT LAW

TEXT, CASES, AND MATERIALS

SECOND EDITION

EWAN McKENDRICK

OXFORD

UNIVERSITY PRESS

OXFORD
UNIVERSITY PRESS

Great Clarendon Street, Oxford OX2 6DP

Oxford University Press is a department of the University of Oxford.
It furthers the University's objective of excellence in research, scholarship,
and education by publishing worldwide in

Oxford New York

Auckland Cape Town Dar es Salaam Hong Kong Karachi
Kuala Lumpur Madrid Melbourne Mexico City Nairobi
New Delhi Shanghai Taipei Toronto

With offices in

Argentina Austria Brazil Chile Czech Republic France Greece
Guatemala Hungary Italy Japan Poland Portugal Singapore
South Korea Switzerland Thailand Turkey Ukraine Vietnam

Oxford is a registered trade mark of Oxford University Press
in the UK and in certain other countries

Published in the United States
by Oxford University Press Inc., New York

British Library Cataloguing in Publication Data

Data available

ISBN 0–19–927480–0   9–78–019927480–2

3 5 7 9 10 8 6 4 2

Typeset in Adobe Minion with Bell Gothic
by RefineCatch Limited, Bungay, Suffolk
Printed in Great Britain by
Ashford Colour Press, Gosport, Hampshire

PREFACE TO THE SECOND EDITION

This book has three principal aims. The first is to provide an exposition of the rules that make up the law of contract. To this end it seeks to describe and to analyse the central doctrines of the modern law of contract and to explore the principal controversies associated with these doctrines. It seeks to fulfil this aim through a combination of text, cases, and materials. The function of the text is both to explain and to evaluate the principal rules and doctrines of contract law and to provide a commentary on the leading cases and statutes. The cases chosen for inclusion in the book are the leading cases on the law of contract. The 'materials' consist of statutes, statutory instruments, re-statements of contract law, extracts from textbooks, and academic articles. Secondly, the book aims to explore the law of contract in its transactional context. It is not confined to an analysis of the doctrines that make up the law of contract but extends to the terms that are to be found in modern commercial contracts and the principles that are applied by the courts when seeking to interpret these contracts. The third aim is to explore English contract law in a transnational and comparative perspective. This is not a book on comparative contract law but it does attempt to take account of documents such as the Unidroit Principles of International Commercial Contracts and the Principles of European Contract Law.

The book is supported by a companion web site. The principal purposes of the web site will be to provide critical summaries of recent developments in the law and to provide links to helpful web sites where further information can be obtained. The web site will be updated twice per year and can be accessed at **www.oup.com/uk/best .textbooks/law/mckendrick**.

I would like to thank Rachel Kapila for her assistance in the preparation of this edition of the book. In preparing the first edition I benefited from the assistance of Felicity Maher, Ryan Beckwith, Catherine Button, Jamie Edelman, Emily Elford, Martin Graham, Wenying Li, Vanessa Mak, Danny Priel, Aimee Daruwala, and Tim Akkouh I am grateful to Andrew Burrows for his willingness to allow me in Chapters 18–21 and 23 to draw on material which first appeared in our book, *Cases and Materials on the Law of Restitution*, published by Oxford University Press, 1997. I am also grateful to the publishers for their assistance and encouragement at every stage. Finally, I would like to thank my wife, Rose, and our children, Jenny, Sarah, Rachel, and Katie for their encouragement and support. My greatest debt is to my wife, Rose, without whose help and support in so many ways, this book would never have been written. This book is dedicated to her with my love and thanks.

The law is stated on the basis of the information available to me as at 1 November 2004.

Ewan McKendrick
Lady Margaret Hall
Oxford

ACKNOWLEDGEMENTS

Grateful acknowledgement is made to all the authors and publishers of copyright material which appears in this book, and in particular to the following for permission to reprint material from the sources indicated:

Extracts from Law Commission Reports, Consultation Papers, and Discussion Papers are Crown copyright material and are reproduced under Class Licence Number C01P0000148 with the permission of the Controller of HMSO and the Queen's Printer for Scotland.

The Executors of Peter Birks: extracts from Equity in Modern Law: An Exercise in Taxonomy, 26 *University of Western Australia Law Review* 1 (1996).

The Butterworths Division of Reed Elsevier (UK) Limited: extracts from Michael Furmston (Ed): *Butterworths Common Law: The Law of Contract* 2e, 2003.

Cambridge University Press: extracts from H Collins: *The Law of Contract* (3e, 1997).

Cambridge Law Journal and the authors: extracts from *Cambridge Law Journal* (CLJ), S Smith: 'Contracting under Pressure: A Theory of Duress', 343 *CLJ* (1997), and J R Spencer: 'Signature, Consent, and the Rule in *L'Estrange v Graucob*', 104 *CLJ* (1973).

Cardiff Law School and the authors: extracts from *Legal Studies*, J Adams and R Brownsword: 'The Ideologies of Contract Law', 7 *Legal Studies* 205 (1987); S Bright: 'Winning the Battle Against Unfair Contract Terms', 20 *Legal Studies* 331 (2000); and P Luther: extract from 'Campbell, Espinasse and the Sailors: Text and Context in the Common Law', 19 *Legal Studies* 526 (1999).

Hart Publishing Ltd: extract from M Spence: *Protecting Reliance: The Emergent Doctrine of Equitable Estoppel* (Hart, 1999).

Informa Professional Publishing and the authors: extracts from *Lloyd's Maritime and Commercial Law Quarterly (LMCLQ)*: N Bamforth: 'Unconscionability as Vitiating Factor', *LMCLQ* 538 (1995); A Burrows: 'The Contracts (Rights of Third Parties) Act and its Implications for Commercial Contracts', *LMCLQ* 540 (2000); and R Halson: 'The Offensive Limits of Promissory Estoppel', *LMCLQ* 257 (1999).

LexisNexis Butterworths Australia and the author: extract from R Brownsword: 'Retrieving Reasons, Retrieving Rationality? A New Look at the Right to Withdraw for Breach of Contract', 5 *Journal of Contract Law* 83 (1992).

J C B Mohr (Paul Siebeck): extracts from H Kotz and A Flessner: *European Contract Law Volume 1: Formation, Validity, and Content of Contracts: Contract and Third Parties* (1997).

Oxford University Press: extracts from P S Atiyah: *An Introduction to the Law of Contract* (5e, 1995); P S Atiyah 'Consideration: A Re-statement' in P S Atiyah: *Essays on Contract* (1986); P S Atiyah: *The Rise and Fall of Contract* (1979); J Beatson (ed): *Anson's Law of Contract* (28e, 2002); R Brownsword: *Contract Law: Themes for the Twenty First Century* (2000); A W B Simpson: 'Quackery and Contract Law: *Carlill v Carbolic Smoke Ball Company* (1893)', and 'The Beauty of Obscurity: *Raffles v Wichelhaus and Busch* (1894)' in A W B Simpson: *Leading Cases in the Common Law* (1995); and G Treitel: *Some Landmarks of Twentieth Century Contract Law* (2002); also the authors for extracts from *Oxford Journal of Legal Studies*: S Gardner: 'Trashing the Trollope: A Deconstruction of the Postal Rules in Contract', 12 *OJLS* 170 (1992); S Smith: 'Reconstructing Restraint of Trade', 15 *OJLS* 565 (1995); and S A Smith: 'Contracts for the Benefit of third Parties: In Defence of the Third-Party Rule', 7 *OLJS* 643 (1997).

Penguin Books Ltd: extracts from Roy Goode: *Commercial Law* (Penguin Books, 2004) copyright © Roy Goode 2004.

Sweet & Maxwell Ltd: extracts from R Christou: *Boilerplate: Practical Clauses* (3e, 2002); B Coote: *Exception Clauses* (1964); G H Treitel: *Frustration and Force Majeure* (1994); and G H Treitel: *The Law of Contract* (11e, 2003); also extracts from *Law Quarterly Review*: D Capper: 'Undue Influence and Unconscionability: A Rationalisation', 114 *LQR* 479 (1998); D Friedmann: 'The Performance Interest in Contract Damages', 111 *LQR* 628 (1995); S A Smith: 'In Defence of Substantive Unfairness', 112 *LQR* 138 (1996); Lord Steyn: 'Contract Law: Fulfilling the Reasonable Expectations of Honest Men', 119 *LQR* 433 (1997); and J Vorster: 'A Comment on the Meaning of Objectivity in Contract', 103 *LQR* 174 (1987).

The Yale Law Journal Company and William S Hein Company: extract from L L Fuller and William R Perdue Jr: 'The Reliance Interest in Contract Damages', 46 *The Yale Law Journal* 52 (1995).

Every effort has been made to clear the necessary permissions. If notified, the publisher will undertake to rectify any errors or omissions at the earliest opportunity.

CONTENTS

PART II   TERMS

PART III SETTING THE CONTRACT ASIDE

TABLE OF CASES

Cases and page references in **bold** indicate that the case is discussed significantly

TABLE OF STATUTES

Page references in **bold** indicate that the text is reproduced in full

TABLE OF STATUTORY INSTRUMENTS

Page references in **bold** indicate that the text is reproduced in full

TABLE OF TREATIES, CONVENTIONS, AND EUROPEAN LEGISLATION

Page references in **bold** indicate that the text is reproduced in full

1

INTRODUCTION

1. THE AIMS OF THIS BOOK

This book has three principal aims. The first is to provide an exposition of the rules that make up the law of contract. To this end it seeks to describe and to analyse the central doctrines of the modern law of contract and to explore the principal controversies associated with these doctrines. It seeks to fulfil this aim through a combination of text, cases, and materials. The function of the text is both to explain and to evaluate the principal rules and doctrines of contract law and to provide a commentary on the leading cases and statutes. The cases chosen for inclusion in the book are the leading cases on the law of contract. I have chosen to rely on longer extracts from a smaller range of cases rather than try to include short extracts from every case that can claim to have made an important contribution to the development of the law of contract. The decision to restrict the number of cases was made for two reasons. First, it is important to allow the judges to speak for themselves. Too great a willingness on the part of an editor to use scissors and paste can create a misleading picture, particularly where the extract consists of the conclusions reached by the judge without setting out the reasoning that led him or her to that conclusion. Secondly, it is important that law students get used to reading cases. The ability to read judgments and to extract from them the principle that is to be applied to the facts of the case at hand is an important skill that lawyers must acquire. They will not acquire that skill if their legal education does not expose them to judgments and instead provides them with books that do all the editing for them. The 'materials' consist of statutes, statutory instruments, restatements of contract law, extracts from textbooks, and academic articles. I have used the extracts from academic articles largely for the purpose of illustrating particular points or different interpretations of a case. It has not been possible, for reasons of space, to include lengthy extracts from major theoretical writings on the law of contract.

Secondly, the book aims to explore the law of contract in its transactional context. It is not confined to an analysis of the doctrines that make up the law of contract but extends to the terms that are to be found in modern commercial contracts and the principles that are applied by the courts when seeking to interpret these contracts. Many of the 'rules' that regulate modern contracts are to be found, not in the rules of law, but in the terms of the contract itself. The rules of law are often 'default' rules, that is to say, they apply unless they have been excluded by the terms of the contract. Many modern commercial contracts do displace the rules that would otherwise be applicable, especially in the case of contracts concluded between substantial commercial entities. These are often substantial documents that make elaborate provision for various eventualities. It is therefore important to have regard to the standard terms that are to be found in modern commercial contracts (often referred to as 'boilerplate clauses'). The book does not attempt to provide detailed guidance on the drafting of contract clauses. But nor does it ignore drafting issues. On a number of occasions I have included the text of the clause that was in issue between the parties for the purpose of trying to identify the issues that can and do confront lawyers in practice. This is particularly so in relation to the drafting of clauses such as exclusion clauses (see Chapter 13 below), force majeure clauses (see pp. 434–436 below), entire agreement clauses (see pp. 440–441 below), and liquidated damages clauses (see pp. 1124–1131 below). It is important to understand why it is that lawyers insert such clauses into their contracts and why, in the case of clauses such as exclusions and limitations of liability, they can be the subject of vigorous negotiation between the parties (or their lawyers).

The third aim is to explore English contract law in a transnational and comparative perspective. This is not a book on comparative contract law but it is no longer possible to ignore the fact that transactions in the modern world are frequently entered into on a cross-border basis. As the Lord Chancellor's Advisory Committee on Legal Education stated in its *First Report on Legal Education and Training* (HMSO, 1996) at paragraph 1.13:

Legal transactions are increasingly international in character. An understanding of the different ways that civilian lawyers approach common law problems can no longer be regarded as the preserve of a few specialists. Legal education in England and Wales must be both more European and more international.

It should not, however, be thought that the mere fact that the parties to the contract are from different jurisdictions has the inevitable consequence that their contract is regulated by rules that differ from those applicable to purely domestic transactions. The law affords to contracting parties considerable freedom to choose the law that is to govern their contract (see further pp. 436–437 below) and they will generally select as the applicable law the law of a nation state (usually, but not always, the domestic law of one of the parties to the contract). In the 'choice of law' stakes English law has done remarkably well. The volume of international trade that has been done on contracts governed by English law is enormous. A glance at the law reports will tell you that some of the leading contract cases have been litigated between parties who had no connection with England other than the fact that their contract was governed by English law. The explanation for this undoubtedly lies in this country's great trading history, which has been of great profit to the City of London and to English law, if not to other parts of the United Kingdom. Some commodities markets have had their centres in England and many standard form commodity contracts are governed by English law. London has also been, and continues to be, a major centre for international arbitration. However, it can no longer be assumed that international contracts will continue to be governed exclusively by the laws of a nation state. Developments are taking place at a number of different levels.

In the first place there is the impact of our membership of the European Union. European law has had a significant impact on the law relating to certain particular types of contract (especially in the context of public procurement) but its impact on the general principles of contract law has, until recently, been relatively small. This may be about to change. The Unfair Terms in Consumer Contracts Regulations 1999, enacted in implementation of a European Directive on Unfair Terms in Consumer Contracts, are beginning to bite (see further Chapter 14). The Regulations have now been the subject of analysis by the House of Lords in *Director General of Fair Trading* v. *First National Bank* [2001] UKHL 52; [2002] 1 AC 481 (p. 521 below) and the Regulations have also been the catalyst for a re-examination by the Law Commissions of the Unfair Contract Terms Act 1977, one effect of which may be to give the courts greater powers to control unfair terms in commercial contracts that have been concluded on standard terms (see pp. 535–540 below). More far-reaching measures may be on the horizon. On 13 July 2001, the European Commission issued a Communication on European Contract Law to the Council and the European Parliament. In February 2003 the Commission issued an 'Action Plan' which sets out for discussion a possible mix of non-regulatory and regulatory measures which might help to produce a 'more coherent European Contract Law' and resolve the problems presented by the existing divergences between national contract laws. A further Communication, issued by the Commission on 11 October 2004, is discussed in more detail below (see pp. 12–13).

At the second level we have internationally agreed conventions such as the United Nations Convention on Contracts for the International Sale of Goods ('the Vienna Convention'). The Convention has been ratified by most of the major trading nations in the world but not by the United Kingdom. While the present Government has indicated its intention to ratify the Convention at some future time, it has not, as yet, found the Parliamentary time to do so. The Convention is obviously confined to international contracts for the sale of goods and so is not of general application throughout the law of contract. But it is nevertheless an extremely significant document and it has exercised, and will continue to exercise, considerable influence on the development of the law of contract in various jurisdictions around the world.

At a third level there have been attempts to draft statements of non-binding principles of contract law. There are two notable examples in this category. The first is the Unidroit Principles of International Commercial Contracts and the second is the Principles of European Contract Law. It is important to stress that neither of these documents is legally binding in the sense that it is intended to be ratified by States and incorporated into their law (although the Principles of European Contract Law may at some future time form the basis for the Contract chapter of a European Code). Rather, in the short- to medium-term these Principles are intended for use by contracting parties and can be incorporated into their contract as a set of terms or, possibly, as the applicable law (at least in the case of arbitration). We shall encounter both sets of Principles at various points in this book.

This introduction is divided into five further parts. Part 2 explores the limits of the subject and in particular the fact that English law does not have a formal definition of a contract. The third part turns to consider some transactional elements of contract law. The fourth part moves on to consider in more detail some aspects of the creation of a European contract law, while the fifth part moves on to consider the possible development of an international contract law. The final part consists of a brief examination of some of the conflicting policies that can be seen at work in the law of contract.

2. THE SCOPE OF THE LAW OF CONTRACT

English law has no formal definition of a contract. In the absence of a Code it has not needed one. Textbook writers frequently commence their books with a definition of the law of contract but the definition is not part of the law itself. Such definitions are indicative or illustrative; they do not purport to be definitive or comprehensive. Two examples suffice to illustrate the point. First, Sir Jack Beatson states in the opening chapter of *Anson's Law of Contract* (28th edn, Oxford University Press, 2002), p. 1 that:

The law of contract may be provisionally described as that branch of the law which determines the circumstances in which a promise shall be legally binding on the person making it.

The tentative nature of this statement can be seen from the fact that it is expressly stated to be 'provisional' and it does not attempt to explain why it is that the law regards some promises as legally binding and others not. A second example is provided by Sir Guenter Treitel in his textbook *The Law of Contract* (11th edn, Sweet & Maxwell, 2003), p. 1 which begins with the following words:

A contract is an agreement giving rise to obligations which are enforced or recognised by law. The factor which distinguishes contractual from other legal obligations is that they are based on the agreement of the contracting parties.

Professor Treitel notes that, while this proposition 'remains generally true', it is subject to 'a number of important qualifications'. First, the law is 'often concerned with the objective appearance, rather than the actual fact, of agreement' (see further Chapter 2). Secondly, the proposition that contractual obligations are based on agreement must be qualified because 'contracting parties are normally expected to observe certain standards of behaviour' so that, for example, terms are implied into many contracts as a matter of law rather than as a product of the agreement of the parties (see further Chapter 10). Thirdly, the idea that contractual obligations are based on agreement must be qualified 'in relation to the scope of the principle of freedom of contract'. For example, the judges and Parliament have, in recent years, qualified the scope of the principle of freedom of contract in an attempt to protect the weaker party to a contract.

The lack of an agreed definition of a contract is a product of the way in which contract law in England has evolved. English contract law is unusual in that it did not develop from some underlying theory or conception of a contract but rather developed around a form of action known as the action of assumpsit. What mattered was the procedure, or the form of action, not the substance of the claim. With the abolition of the forms of action by the Common Law Procedure Act 1852, the grip of procedural considerations over substantive law began to decline. At about the same time the practice of writing treatises on the law of contract began to increase and the authors of these texts sought to rationalize the existing mass of case-law in principled terms. In so doing they relied heavily on the works of continental jurists (see generally AWB Simpson, 'Innovation in Nineteenth Century Contract Law' (1975) 91 *LQR* 247). The outcome of this process was a number of influential books, written most notably by Sir Frederick Pollock and Sir William Anson, which sought to set out the general principles of the law of contract. While these authors succeeded in establishing a series of general principles that commanded almost universal acceptance it was still not necessary to frame a precise definition of a contract.

While there is no universally agreed definition of a contract, the basic principles of the law of contract can be set out with a large degree of certainty. To conclude a contract the parties must reach agreement, the agreement must be supported by consideration and there must be an intention to create legal relations. The courts generally decide whether an agreement has been reached by looking for an offer made by one party to the other, which has been accepted by that other party: the acceptance, if it is to count, must be a mirror image of the offer (see Chapter 3). The rule that the agreement must be supported by consideration perhaps requires further explanation. The doctrine of consideration is a distinctive, if somewhat elusive, feature of English law (see further Chapter 5). The essence of consideration is that something must be given in return for a promise in order to render that promise enforceable. It does not matter how much has been given in return for the promise; that is a matter for the parties to decide. All that matters is that *something* which the law recognizes as being of value has been given. Thus if I agree to sell my house for £1 that is an enforceable promise because it is supported by consideration. On the other hand a promise to give you my house for nothing is not enforceable, unless contained in a deed (on which see pp. 284–285 below). In essence therefore the law of contract does not enforce gratuitous promises, although it will occasionally provide protection for a party who has acted to his detriment upon a gratuitous promise via the doctrine of estoppel (see pp. 236–271 below). While the doctrine of consideration has excited considerable academic interest, it gives rise to few practical problems because it can be avoided either by the provision of nominal consideration or by including the promise in a deed (see further p. 284 below). The requirement that there be an intention to create legal relations similarly gives rise to few practical problems. This is because there is a heavy presumption in a commercial context that the parties intended to create legal relations. The function of the doctrine is, essentially, to keep the law of contract out of domestic and social relations (see further Chapter 7).

The scope of the contract is generally limited to the parties to it, unless the contracting parties agree to confer a right to enforce a term of the contract on a third party and that agreement satisfies the requirements of the Contracts (Rights of Third Parties) Act 1999. The 1999 Act has made a significant change to the shape of English contract law in that, prior to its enactment, the general rule was that a third party could neither take the benefit of, nor be subject to a burden by, a contract to which he was not a party. This is the doctrine of privity of contract. The rule has been heavily modified in relation to the ability of contracting parties to confer rights of action upon third parties but the 1999 Act has not altered the general rule that a third party cannot be subjected to a burden by a contract to which he is not a party.

The law also polices the terms of contracts and the procedures by which a contract is concluded. Thus a contract may be set aside where it has been entered into under a fundamental mistake (Chapter 16), where it has been procured by a misrepresentation (Chapter 17), duress (Chapter 18), or undue influence (Chapter 19), where its object or method of performance is illegal or contrary to public policy (Chapter 22) or where an event occurs after the making of the contract which renders performance impossible, illegal, or something radically different from that which was in the contemplation of the parties at the time of entry into the contract (Chapter 23). Assuming that a valid contract has been made, a failure to perform an obligation under the contract without a lawful excuse is a breach of contract (Chapter 24). A breach of contract gives to the innocent party a claim for damages, the aim of which is to put the innocent party in the position in which he would have been had the contract been performed according to its terms (Chapter 25). Where the breach is of an important term of the contract the innocent party may also be entitled to termi- nate further performance of the contract without incurring any liability for doing so (Chapter 24). But the law does not generally require the party in breach to perform his obligations under the contract: specific performance is an exceptional remedy, not the primary remedy (Chapter 26). The law is committed to give a money substitute for performance, not performance itself.

Two points should be noted about this outline. The first is that it purports to be of general application; that is to say, the propositions outlined above purport to be applicable to all contracts and not just to some. In this sense they claim to be of general application. This claim must not be taken too seriously. The reality today is that many contracts are the subject of specific regulation, so that the general prin- ciples of the law of contract are either excluded or are of marginal significance. Thus employment contracts, contracts between landlords and tenants, contracts of mar- riage, and consumer credit contracts are the subject of distinct regulation. While this regulation builds on the foundation laid by the general principles of the law of contract, the detailed rules applicable to these contracts depart from the general principles in significant respects. This book does not purport to deal with the law relating to specific contracts, such as contracts of employment. That must be left to specialist textbooks. The aim of this book is to provide a foundation for the study of the law of particular contracts by examining the principles that are applicable to all contracts, unless they have been excluded.

The second point to note about this outline is that it would generally be recognized by authors of contract textbooks in the late nineteenth century. The formal structure of the law has not changed a great deal. There is less emphasis on matters such as contractual capacity (see Chapter 21) and requirements of form (Chapter 6) but Sir William Anson, who published the first edition of his book on contract law in 1879, would not have dissented a great deal from the outline given above (with, perhaps, the exception of the law relating to third party rights of action). A feature of the develop- ment of English contract law is that the pace of change has been slow: English law favours incremental rather than revolutionary change. The gradual nature of the change should not be allowed to hide the extent of the changes that have taken place. Some, such as Professor Hugh Collins (see *The Law of Contract* (4th edn, Butterworths, 2003)) have argued that the law of contract has undergone a transformation from the ideals of the classical law of contract set out by Anson and others. Any such transformation is not reflected in the formal doctrines of the law of contract. Freedom of contract and freedom from contract remain the underlying norms and doctrines such as consideration (but not privity) remain as central doctrines of the law of contract. Nevertheless significant changes have taken place. The modern law of contract pays more overt attention to the fairness of the bargain (both in procedural and substantive terms) than did the law in the nineteenth century. Thus doctrines such as economic duress (see pp. 724–744 below) and undue influence (see Chapter 18 below) flourished in the last quarter of the twentieth century. Statute has intervened more widely to regulate the fairness of the bargain (see, for example, the Unfair Terms in Consumer Contracts Regulations 1999 (Chapter 14), the Unfair Contract Terms Act 1977 (see pp. 460–485 below), and the Consumer Credit Act 1974 (see pp. 810–812 below). The commitment to freedom from contract (that is to say, the principle that, as long as a contract has not been concluded, the parties are free to withdraw from negotiations without incurring liability for doing so) has also been eroded. The extent of the departure is not at first sight apparent. English law still refuses to recognize the existence of a duty to negotiate with reasonable care, nor does it formally recognize a doctrine of good faith (see Chapter 15). But careful examination of recent cases demonstrates that the courts have been able to place not insignificant limits on the ability of parties to withdraw from negotiations without incurring any liability for doing so. They have done so largely by drawing upon doctrines from outside the law of contract by, for example, imposing a restitutionary obligation to pay for work done in anticipation of a contract which does not materialize (see, for example, *British Steel Corporation* v. *Cleveland Bridge and Engineering Co Ltd* [1984] 1 All ER 504, p. 105 below). Occasionally, the courts have been able, by a benevolent interpretation of the facts, to find that those who appear to be negotiating parties have in fact concluded a contract (see, for example, *Blackpool and Fylde Aero Club Ltd* v. *Blackpool Borough Council* [1990] 1 WLR 1195, p. 78 below). Via such covert means the courts have been able to give the appearance that formal contract doctrine has not changed. The reality is otherwise. There can be little doubt that freedom from contract has been whittled away to the extent that the law should now consider whether it has reached the point where it ought to recognize openly what it appears to be doing surreptitiously, namely recognize that negotiating parties can, in some circumstances, be subject to a duty to exercise reasonable care or to act in good faith.

　　The subtle, incremental nature of the changes that have taken place is important. It raises the question of the extent of the changes that have taken place in the law of contract and the impact that these changes should have on the structure of the law. It would be possible to organize a book around the ideals or principles that are said to influence the modern law of contract and thus give greater emphasis to ideas such as fairness, co-operation, and autonomy. The approach taken in this book is more conservative. It adheres to the formal structure of the law that we have inherited from our predecessors (both judicial and academic) but at the same time endeavours to reflect the nature of the changes that are taking place both in terms of contract doctrine (for example, the increasing significance of doctrines such as duress (Chapter 18) and undue influence (Chapter 19) and the questions that have been raised over the future of the doctrine of consideration (Chapter 5)) and in relation to the content of modern contracts (see Chapter 12).

3. TRANSACTIONS

To my knowledge there has been no attempt to engage in a systematic analysis of contract forms and styles of drafting in use in this country. One must therefore proceed largely by way of impression. Two points seem worthy of comment by way of introduction.

The first is the growth in the use of standard form contracts. Standard form contracts assume different forms (see, for example, the judgment of Lord Diplock in *A Schroeder Music Publishing Co Ltd* v. *Macaulay* [1974] 1 WLR 1308, p. 857 below). These standard forms may be industry wide, an example being the JCT contracts which are in wide use within the construction industry. These contract forms perform useful functions in so far as they lay down industry-accepted standards which save valuable negotiation time. And they give rise to few legal problems, apart from difficulties of interpretation and these depend largely on the quality of the drafting of the contract form itself. Standard form contracts produced by individual businesses have given rise to greater legal difficulties. In the case of inter-business transactions, the use of standard terms of business has given rise to 'battles of the forms' as each business seeks to ensure that its standard terms prevail in the transactions which it concludes (on which see pp. 91–110 below). Standard form contracts under which businesses seek to impose their terms upon consumers have given rise to greater problems because these terms can be one-sided. A particular problem has been the sweeping exclusion clauses which these contracts frequently contain. The common law largely failed to deal with this problem. Lord Denning did his best but he could not persuade his colleagues to give themselves the power to strike down unreasonable exclusion clauses (see p. 445 below). Although the courts were sometimes able to protect the weaker party by applying stringent rules of interpretation (see p. 446 below) or by refusing to incorporate the exclusion clause into the contract (see Chapter 9 below), the general picture was one of the impotence of the common law. Instead it was left to Parliament to intervene to control the excesses of these standard form contracts. Parliament was slow to intervene. It was not until 1977 that it found the time to enact the Unfair Contract Terms Act 1977, and even then it was via a private member's Bill. Consumers have recently been given greater protection, courtesy of Europe. The Unfair Terms in Consumer Contracts Regulations 1999, passed in response to a European Directive, give consumers much broader protection from unfair terms in standard form contracts (see Chapter 14). The law has finally adjusted to the existence of these standard form contracts. But it has done so slowly and it may continue to evolve. The Law Commissions have provisionally proposed that the controls over standard form contracts in business-to-business transactions should be increased (see pp. 535–540 below). These proposals are bound to cause some controversy on account of the uncertainty that they will generate, but the point has been made that many small businesses are in a similar bargaining position to consumers and also need protection from the standard terms imposed upon them by big business. The debate on the legal regulation of standard form contracts is set to continue.

The second point to note is that the form and the content of modern contracts have become increasingly complex. Contracts today often include a vast array of clauses which seek to provide for various eventualities which may have an impact upon the performance of the contract. Some of these clauses are designed to take away rights which the law would otherwise give, as in the case of exclusion and limitation clauses (see Chapter 13) and entire agreement clauses (see pp. 440–441 below). Other clauses are a response to the perceived rigidities of the common law. The common law has generally set its face against court adjustment of contract terms and is reluctant to conclude that hardship can discharge a contract: to meet this problem parties have included within their contracts complex hardship and force majeure clauses which enable the contract to be adjusted, suspended, or terminated in the event of hardship or the dislocation of performance (see pp. 434–436 and 439–440 below). Some clauses are examples of attempts to exploit opportunities which the common law affords, as in the case of retention of title clauses (see pp. 432–433 below) and liquidated damages clauses (see pp. 1124–1131 below). It is no easy matter to draft these clauses. On the one hand, they must be wide enough in order to achieve their purpose but on the other hand they must not be over-broad because then they may fall foul of legislative or judicial controls over the content of clauses (for example, in the case of exclusion clauses see the powers given to the courts under the Unfair Contract Terms Act 1977, pp. 460–485 below, and for an example of the role of the courts see the regulation of restraint of trade clauses in cases such as *Mason* v. *Provident Clothing & Supply Co Ltd* [1913] AC 724, p. 846 below).

4. EUROPEAN CONTRACT LAW

Legislation in certain specific areas of contract law at EC level to date has covered an increasing number of issues. The EC legislator has so far followed a selective approach, adopting directives on specific contracts or specific marketing techniques (such as package travel and distance selling) where a particular need for harmonization was identified.

However, on 13 July 2001 the European Commission issued a Communication on European Contract Law to the European Parliament and the Council. The purpose of the Communication was to broaden the debate by encouraging contributions from consumers, businesses, professional organizations, public administrations and institutions, the academic world, and all interested parties. The Commission was concerned with possible obstacles and problems encountered in cross-border trade within the Internal Market that may result from divergences of national contract law. The Communication also discussed options for the future of contract law in the EC, setting out an inexhaustive list of four options to stimulate discussion:

• *Option I: No EC action,* leaving interest groups and others to advise on cross-border trade and solve problems encountered in it.

- *Option II: Promote the development of common contract law principles leading to more convergence of national laws*, encouraging the development of non-binding restatements of principles.

- *Option III: Improve the quality of legislation already in place*, concentrating attention on reviewing existing Directives, modernizing, extending, and simplifying them, so as to produce a more rational and coherent set of laws.

- *Option IV: Adopt new comprehensive legislation at EC level.* This could take the form of a Directive, a Regulation, or a Recommendation, and could range from an optional set of rules to be incorporated by the parties to rules that apply unless excluded or even a mandatory code. The level of harmonization that would be effected would depend very much on the form and extent of the model chosen.

Following the publication of the Communication on European Contract Law, the Commission received contributions from some 180 stakeholders, the largest number coming from the academic and business communities, with a considerable number from governments and legal practitioners. In addition, the European Council, European Parliament, and the Economic and Social Committee each produced responses to the Communication. This interest of the Community Institutions and stakeholders shows the importance of the debate launched by the Communication. In relation to future directions the majority of contributors rejected option I on the ground that it was unrealistic and inadequate and it failed to give sufficient protection to weaker parties. By contrast option II attracted more favourable comment, although a number of respondents saw this as merely a step on the way to a new legal instrument at Community level (option IV). Under this head, the European Parliament's Resolution proposed that a database of national contract legislation and case law in all Community languages be set up by the end of 2004 to promote comparative law research with a view to finding common legal concepts, solutions, and terminology that could be applied on a voluntary basis. The Parliament also proposed a longer-term plan involving dissemination and implementation of the results of the research. Option III seemed to be the most favoured solution, receiving support from governments, business, consumer organizations, legal practitioners, and academic lawyers. Opinions varied on option IV. Some respondents saw a uniform and comprehensive European civil code as the best solution to the problems identified, whereas others were strongly opposed to the creation of a civil code. The creation of such a code would seem to be very much a long-term strategy. It should be noted that the UK government was opposed to option IV in any of its forms and considered it to be disproportionate and likely to cut across the principle of subsidiarity. In its opinion, EC legislation should continue to focus on specifically identified problems on a case-by-case basis.

In 2003 the Commission produced a further communication in the form of an Action Plan.[1] In this document, following on from the responses to the earlier Communication (which are summarized in the second half of the Action Plan

---

[1] Communication from the Commission to the European Parliament and the Council on A More Coherent European Contract Law: An Action Plan, COM(2003) 68 final, http://europa.eu.int/comm/consumers/cons_int/safe_shop/fair_bus_pract/cont_law/com_2003_68_en.pdf.

communication), the Commission identifies areas in which problems may undermine the proper functioning of the internal market and the uniform application of Community law. It notes support for option II and that the 'overwhelming majority' supported option III, and thus proposes to continue a broad strategy of sector-specific legislation as well as non-regulatory measures. Steps to promote standard EU-wide cross-border contract terms were launched immediately. Such steps consist mainly of the creation of a web site and other means (such as a conference which was held at the start of 2004) to facilitate the exchange of information about existing terms and relevant initiatives.

However the central plank of the Action Plan is more ambitious, and consists of the production, after three or so years of heavy consultation through a pan-European network of stakeholders, of a Common Frame of Reference (CFR) document. The CFR is to consist of a delineation of fundamental principles of European contract law (such as the principle of freedom of contract) and when such principles are to be derogated from, definitions of legal terms (the examples given are 'contract' and 'damage'), and possibly model rules. The CFR is intended to be used directly when existing legislation is being reviewed and new legislation drawn up, so as to improve consistency in Community legislation; it is also hoped that the CFR will be taken into account in the drafting of national legislation and so further encourage convergence of contract legal rules throughout Europe; finally, the CFR will provide the foundation for the development of an optional instrument, should that option be pursued. Extensive research into national and Community laws, contractual practice, and relevant binding international instruments must take place, although the Action Plan emphasizes the need to take advantage of existing research activities as well as commencing new ones.

Over 120 responses to the Action Plan have been received and published on the web site, again from a wide range of stakeholders. There was some scepticism about the efficacy and desirability of measures intended to increase the use of EU-wide standard contract terms. With regard to the CFR, there was broad support, although perhaps some confusion as to what exactly it entailed. The Council and European Parliament were in favour of the CFR becoming an optional body of rules; the Parliament in particular asking for early creation of optional instruments governing consumer transactions and insurance sectors, and envisaging the general CFR becoming mandatory at a later date. The UK was again opposed to any general instrument of this kind, optional or mandatory. Further, the European Parliament asked for the timetable to be tightened up so as to require completion of the CFR by 2006 and implementation soon afterwards. Parliament also reiterated its request, first made in response to the 2001 Communication, to set up by 2004 a data bank of national contractual legal provisions and case law, a request the Commission seemed to have ignored in its Action Plan.

It is noteworthy that the Principles of European Contract Law, discussed in the next section, were not mentioned in the Commission Action Plan, although more than one response to the Action Plan noted that the CFR seems likely to reproduce much of the work done and conclusions reached in those Principles. The European Commission Director-General for Health and Consumer Protection, in a recent conference held to discuss the CFR, said that he saw the CFR as 'a kind of European contract law toolkit' that 'would draw together in one place best solutions based on the common principles underpinning national contract laws'.

On 11 October 2004 the Commission issued a further Communication on a European Contract Law and the Revision of the *Acquis*: The Way Forward (COM (2004) 651 Final). In this document the Commission states that it will 'pursue the elaboration of the CFR'. It is clear that the CFR will play a crucial role in the development of a European Contract Law. At present, the Commission considers that 'the CFR would be a non-binding instrument', although it acknowledges that this is an issue on which divergent views have been expressed and which it may be necessary to re-visit. The main role of the CFR will lie, at least initially, in the improvement of the existing *acquis*. To this end, there will be a review of eight consumer Directives in order to determine whether the Directives meet the Commission's consumer protection and internal market goals. But the CFR will not be confined to the present and future acquis: a more extensive role is envisaged for the CFR. Thus it is suggested that the CFR could: (i) be taken into account by national legislators 'when transposing EU directives in the area of contract law into national legislation'; (ii) be used in arbitration to 'find unbiased and balanced solutions to resolve conflicts arising between contractual parties'; (iii) be developed 'into a body of standard contract terms to be made available to legal practitioners'; and (iv) 'inspire the European Court of Justice when interpreting the *acquis* on contract law.' The preparation of the CFR will be undertaken, at least initially, by a group of researchers who will be expected to deliver a final report to the Commission in 2007. This research 'will aim to identify best solutions, taking into account national contract laws (both case law and established practice), the EC *acquis* and relevant international instruments, particularly the UN Convention on Contracts for the International Sale of Goods.' The proposed structure of the CFR bears a remarkable resemblance to the structure of the Principles of European Contract Law (although the Communication does not expressly acknowledge this) with the addition of chapters on sales contracts and insurance contracts. Once the report has been received by the Commission, it will consider the report and subject it to a 'practicability test on the basis of concrete examples of the anticipated uses of the CFR' and will consult with a wide range of interested parties. It is hoped that the adoption of the CFR will take place in 2009, when it will be published in the Official Journal of the European Union and reviewed as necessary.

The Communication of 11 October 2004 also deals with the promotion of the use of EU-wide standard terms and conditions. There is, however, little here that is new. The Commission confirms that it will 'host a website, on which market participants can exchange information' about EU-wide standard terms and conditions 'which they are currently using or plan to develop.' However the Commission will not accept responsibility for the content of the web site, nor will it issue 'separate guidelines' relating to the development and use of standard terms and conditions. The responsibility for the content of the web site will lie with the parties posting the information and publication 'will not constitute any recognition of the legal or commercial validity' of those standard terms and conditions.

Finally, the Communication raises the more difficult issue of 'an optional instrument in European contract law'. Here the Commission states that it intends 'to continue this process in parallel with the work on developing the CFR'. But the message which emerges from this section of the document is ambiguous. On the one hand the document states that 'it is premature to speculate about the possible outcome of this reflection' but on the other hand it states that 'it is neither the Commission's intention to propose a "European Civil Code" which would harmonise contract laws of Member States, nor should the reflections be seen as in any way calling into question the current approaches to promoting free circulation on the basis of flexible and efficient solutions'. Nevertheless, the linkage of the optional instrument to the progress of the CFR suggests that it would be premature to dismiss the possibility of a European Civil Code at some time in the medium to long term. Quite what will emerge from this process is hard to predict, but in hindsight the CFR, when it is completed, may (together with the Principles of European Contract Law) turn out to have been one of the first significant steps on a road that will end with a European Code of Contract Law.

5. TRANSNATIONAL CONTRACT LAW

Rather than seek to impose uniform solutions on nation states, an alternative is to formulate uniform rules or principles that can be adopted by contracting parties. In this connection the Unidroit Principles of International Commercial Contracts and the Principles of European Contract Law assume considerable significance. What are the aims of these documents? The Preamble to the Unidroit Principles states:

These Principles set forth general rules for international commercial contracts.

They shall be applied when the parties have agreed that their contract be governed by them.

They may be applied when the parties have agreed that their contract be governed by general principles of law, the *lex mercatoria* or the like.

They may be applied when the parties have not chosen any law to govern their contract.

They may be used to interpret or supplement international uniform law instruments.

They may be used to interpret or supplement domestic law.

They may serve as a model for national and international legislators.

Article 1:101 of the Principles of European Contract Law provides:

(1) These Principles are intended to be applied as general rules of contract law in the European Communities.

(2) These Principles will apply when the parties have agreed to incorporate them into their contract or that their contract is to be governed by them.

(3) These Principles may be applied when the parties:

(a) have agreed that their contract is to be governed by 'general principles of law', the 'lex mercatoria' or the like; or (b) have not chosen any system or rules of law to govern their contract.

(4) These Principles may provide a solution to the issue raised where the system or rules of law applicable do not do so.

Professors Lando and Beale, in their editorial introduction to *Principles of European Contract Law: Parts I and II* (Kluwer, 2000), set out a number of purposes for which the Principles are designed. First, they state that the Principles may form a foundation for European legislation, including a possible European Code of Contracts. Secondly, they are suitable for express adoption by contracting parties, who can 'declare that the contract is to be governed by the Principles of European Contract Law'. Thirdly, they are a 'modern formulation of a *lex mercatoria* (in other words, they can be applied by arbitrators in the case where a contract is stated to be governed by "general principles of law" or "the *lex mercatoria*", rather than the law of a nation state)'. Fourthly, they are a model for judicial and legislative development of the law of contract and, finally, they may form the basis for the harmonization of contract law among the Member States of the European Union. Professors Lando and Beale conclude (at p. xxiv):

Thus the Principles have both immediate and longer-term objectives. They are available for immediate use by parties making contracts, by courts and arbitrators in deciding contract disputes and by legislators in drafting contract rules whether at the European or the national level. Their longer-term objective is to help bring about the harmonisation of general contract law within the European Union.

Three points are worth noting about these Principles. First, they are not legally binding. They are intended for incorporation into contracts by contracting parties. The type of situation in which use may be made of the Principles is the case where parties who come from different parts of the world cannot agree upon which law is to govern their contract. In such a case they may agree to use the Principles as a set of neutral terms. While the parties can incorporate the Principles as a set of contract terms, they may not be able to incorporate them into the contract as the applicable law. Within Europe, parties to litigation must choose the law of a nation state as the applicable law (see pp. 436–437 below) so that the choice of the Principles will take effect subject to the national law that is found to be applicable to the contract applying the usual conflict of law rules. Secondly, the Principles may possibly have a role to play when developing national rules of contract law. To date courts have not made use of the Principles in this way. But this may change. One example, discussed at a later point in the book (see p. 425 below), is the possible use of the Principles of European Contract Law in the development of the rules or principles relating to the interpretation of contracts. Thirdly, the Principles may have an important role to play in terms of the production of a European or international code of contract law. If the Principles are found to work in arbitration and litigation when used by the parties on a voluntary basis, it may be that in time they will then go on to form the basis for a binding Code.

6. CONFLICTING POLICIES

The aim of this final section is to sketch out some of the conflicting policies that underpin the law of contract. The classical law of contract is based upon freedom of contract and sanctity of contract; that is to say, it is up to the parties to decide for themselves the terms of their contract and the task of the court is to give effect to the agreement that the parties have reached. But the law of contract was never committed to freedom of contract to the exclusion of all other policies. The law has always had a concern for the fairness of the bargain and the protection of the weak. Thus children have very little contractual capacity and the courts have refused to enforce contracts that are illegal. In the former case the demands of freedom of contract give way to the need to protect the inexperienced and the vulnerable, whereas in the case of illegal contracts freedom of contract has to bow to public policy considerations. The law attempts to strike a balance between the conflicting demands of freedom of contract, on the one hand, and fairness on the other hand. These conflicting policies have been labelled 'market-individualism' and 'consumer-welfarism' by Professors Adams and Brownsword. The following extract sets out the essence of these two policies. It also draws on cases that will be discussed at later points in the book. The reason for including this extract at this stage in the book is to convey the general idea that conflicting policies are at work in the law of contract. The aim is not to descend into the details of that conflict and its resolution.

J Adams and R Brownsword, 'The Ideologies of Contract Law'

(1987) 7 *Legal Studies* 205, 206–213

I THE IDEOLOGIES OF THE CONTRACT RULE-BOOK

There is an important academic debate about just where the boundaries of the law of contract lie, about which mix of statutes and cases constitutes the law of contract. Functionalists will argue that the law of contract is about the regulation of agreements, and so any legal materials concerned with the regulation of agreements should belong within the law of contract. Traditionalists, however, take a narrower view, the view implicit in the standard contract text-books. Here, a well-known litany of cases (together with a few statutes), organised in a very similar way from one book to another, is taken to represent the law of contract. Without entering into this debate, let us follow the narrower view and assume that the contract rule-book comprises just those materials which traditionalists take for the law of contract.

Our contention, as we have said, is that these materials are to be interpreted in the light of two basic ideologies, Market-Individualism and Consumer-Welfarism. Accordingly, we devote this part of the article to mapping out the salient features of these two contractual ideologies, and to illustrating their linkage to particular doctrines and ideas current in the contract rule-book.

1. Market-Individualism

The ideology of Market-Individualism has both market and individualistic strands. The strands are mutually supportive, but it aids exposition to separate them. We can look first at the market side of this ideology and then at its individualistic aspect.

(1) The market ideology

According to Market-Individualism, the market place is a site for competitive exchange. The function of contract is not simply to facilitate exchange, it is to facilitate *competitive* exchange. Contract establishes the ground rules within which competitive commerce can be conducted. Thus, subject to fraud, mistake, coercion and the like, bargains made in the market must be kept. In many ways, the line drawn between (actionable) misrepresentation and mere non-disclosure, epitomises this view. There are minimal restraints on contractors: the law of the market is not the law of the jungle, and this rules out misrepresentations. However, non-disclosure of some informational advantage is simply prudent bargaining—contractors are involved in a competitive situation and cannot be expected to disclose their hands. In line with these assumptions, the market-individualist philosophy attaches importance to the following considerations.

First, security of transactions is to be promoted. This means that where a party, having entered the market, reasonably assumes that he has concluded a bargain, then that assumption should be protected. This interest in security of contract receives doctrinal recognition in the objective approach to contractual intention, the traditional caution with respect to subjective mistake, and the protection of third party purchasers. Ideally, of course, security of transactions means that a party gets the performance he has bargained for, but, as the market reveals an increasing number of transactions where performance is delayed, the opportunities for non-performance increase. To protect the innocent party, contract espouses the expectation measure of damages (it is the next best thing to actual performance), and in the principle of sanctity of contract (which we will consider under the individualistic side of Market-Individualism) it takes a hard line against excuses for non-performance.

Secondly, it is important for those who enter into the market to know where they stand. This means that the ground rules of contract should be clear. Hence, the restrictions on contracting must not only be minimal (in line with the competitive nature of the market), but also must be clearly defined (in line with the market demand for predictability, calculability etc). The postal acceptance rule is a model for Market-Individualism in the sense that it is clear, simple, and not hedged around with qualifications which leave contractors constantly unsure of their position. Similarly, the traditional classification approach to withdrawal encapsulates all the virtues of certainty, which are dear to Market-Individualism.

Thirdly, since contract is concerned essentially with the facilitation of market operations, the law should accommodate commercial practice, rather than the other way round. Deference to commercial practice is evident in the market-individualist doctrine of incorporation of terms by reasonable notice, as it is in the *Hillas* v. *Arcos* [p. 142 below] approach to certainty of terms and the re-alignment of the law in *The Eurymedon* [p. 1223 below]. Also, we should not overlook the import of the commonplace that many of the rules concerning formation (e.g. the rules determining whether a display of goods is an offer or an invitation to treat) simply hinge on convenience. This may well be a statement of the obvious, but the obvious should never be neglected. Contract's concern to avoid market inconvenience is a measure of its commitment to the market-individualist policy of facilitating market dealing.

(2) The Individualistic Ideology

A persistent theme in Market-Individualism is that judges should play a non-interventionist role with respect to contracts. This distinctive non-interventionism derives from the individualistic side of the ideology. The essential idea is that parties should enter the market, choose their fellow-contractors, set their own terms, strike their bargains and stick to them. The linchpins of this individualistic philosophy are the doctrines of 'freedom of contract' and 'sanctity of contract'.

The emphasis of freedom of contract is on the parties' freedom of choice. First, the parties should be free to choose one another as contractual partners (i.e. partner-freedom). Like the tango, contract takes two. And, ideally the two should consensually choose one another. Secondly, the parties should be free to choose their own terms (i.e. term-freedom). Contract is competitive, but the exchange should be consensual. Contract is about unforced choice.

In practice, of course, freedom of contract has been considerably eroded. Anti-discrimination statutes restrict partner-freedom; and term-freedom has been restricted by both the common law (e.g. in its restrictions on illegal contracts) and by statute (e.g. the Unfair Contract Terms Act 1977—UCTA) [p. 460 below]. Moreover, the development of monopolistic enterprises, in the public and private sector alike, has made it impossible for the weaker party actually to *exercise* the freedoms in many cases. For example, if one wants a British family car, a railway ride, telephone services etc. the other contractual partner is virtually self-selecting. Similarly, where the other side is a standard form or a standard price contractor, the consumer has no say in setting the terms. Nevertheless, none of this should obscure the thrust of the principle of freedom of contract, which is that one should have the freedoms, and that the law should restrict them as little as possible—indeed, it is consistent with the principle (in a widely held view) that the law should facilitate the freedoms by striking down monopolies.

Although the principle of partner-freedom still has some life in it (e.g. in defending the shopkeeper's choice of customer), it is the principle of term-freedom which is the more vital. Term-freedom can be seen as having two limbs:

(i) The free area within which the parties are permitted, in principle, to set their own terms should be maximised; and,

(ii) Parties should be held to their bargains, i.e. to their agreed terms (provided that the terms fall within the free area).

. . .

The second limb of term-freedom is none other than the principle of sanctity of contract. By providing that parties should be held to their bargains, the principle of sanctity of contract has a double emphasis. First, if parties must be held to *their* bargains, they should be treated as masters of their own bargains, and the courts should not indulge in *ad hoc* adjustment of terms which strike them as unreasonable or imprudent. Secondly, if parties must be *held* to their bargains, then the courts should not lightly relieve contractors from performance of their agreements. It will be appreciated that, while freedom of contract is the broader of the two principles, it is sanctity of contract which accounts for the distinctive market-individualistic stand against paternalistic intervention in particular cases.

The law is littered with examples of the principle of sanctity of contract in operation. It is the foundation for such landmarks as the doctrine that the courts will not review the adequacy of consideration; the principle that the basis of implied terms is necessity not reasonableness; the hard-line towards unilateral 'collateral' mistake, common mistake and frustration; the cautious reception of economic duress; the anxiety to limit the doctrine of inequality of bargaining power; the resistance to the citation of relatively unimportant uncertainty as a ground for release from a contract and the reluctance to succumb to arguments of economic waste or unreasonableness as a basis for release from a bargain. The principle of sanctity of contract is a thread which runs through contract from beginning to end, enjoining the courts to be ever-vigilant in ensuring that established or new doctrines do not become an easy exit from bad bargains.

2. Consumer-Welfarism

The consumer-welfarist ideology stands for a policy of consumer-protection, and for principles of fairness and reasonableness in contract. It does not start with the market-individualist premise that all contracts should be minimally regulated. Rather, it presupposes that consumer contracts are to be closely regulated, and that commercial contracts, although still ordinarily to be viewed as competitive transactions, are to be subject to rather more regulation than Market-Individualism would allow. The difficulties with Consumer-Welfarism appear as soon as one attempts to identify its particular guiding principles (i.e. its operative principles and conceptions of fairness and reasonableness).

Without attempting to draw up an exhaustive list of the particular principles of Consumer-Welfarism, we suggest that the following number amongst its leading ideas:

(1) The principle of constancy: parties should not 'blow hot and cold' in their dealings with one another, even in the absence of a bargain. A person should not encourage another to act in a particular way or to form a particular expectation (or acquiesce in another's so acting or forming an expectation) only then to act inconsistently with that encouragement (or acquiescence). . . .

(2) The principle of proportionality: an innocent party's remedies for breach should be proportionate to the seriousness of the consequences of the breach. . . . We can also see this principle at work in regulating contractual provisions dealing with the amount of damages. Thus, penalty clauses are to be rejected because they bear no relationship to the innocent party's real loss (they are disproportionately excessive) and exemption clauses are unreasonable because they err in the opposite direction.

(3) The principle of bad faith: a party who cites a good legal principle in bad faith should not be allowed to rely on that principle. . . .

(4) The principle that no man should profit from his own wrong: . . .

(5) The principle of unjust enrichment: no party, even though innocent, should be allowed unfairly to enrich himself at the expense of another. Accordingly, it is unreasonable for an innocent party to use another's breach as an opportunity for unfair enrichment: hence, again, the prohibition on penalty clauses, the anxiety about the use made of cost of performance damages, and perhaps the argument in *White & Carter* [p. 995 below] which (unsuccessfully) pleaded the unreasonableness of continued performance. Equally, frustration should not entail unfair financial advantage.

(6) The better loss-bearer principle: where a loss has to be allocated to one of two innocent parties, it is reasonable to allocate it to the party who is better able to carry the

loss. As a rule of thumb, commercial parties are deemed to be better loss-bearers than consumers.

(7) The principle of exploitation: a stronger party should not be allowed to exploit the weakness of another's bargaining situation; but parties of equal bargaining strength should be assumed to have a non-exploitative relationship. The first part of this principle, its positive interventionist aspect, pushes for a general principle of unconscionability, and justifies the policy of consumer-protection. The latter (qualifying) aspect of the principle, however, is equally important, for it invites a non-interventionist approach to commercial contracts.

(8) The principle of a fair deal for consumers: consumers should be afforded protection against sharp advertising practice, against misleading statements, against false representations, and against restrictions on their ordinary rights. Moreover, consumer disappointment should be properly compensated.

(9) The principle of informational advantage: representors who have special informational advantage must stand by their representations; but representees who have equal informational opportunity present no special case for protection. The positive aspect of the principle of informational advantage is protective, but its negative aspect offers no succour to representees who are judged able to check out statements for themselves.

(10) The principle of responsibility for fault: contractors who are at fault should not be able to avoid responsibility for their fault. This principle threatens both exemption clauses which deal with negligence; and indemnity clauses which purport to pass on the risk of negligence liability.

(11) The paternalistic principle: contractors who enter into imprudent agreements may be relieved from their bargains where justice so requires. The case for paternalistic relief is at its most compelling where the party is weak or naïve. Although the consumer-welfarist line on common mistake and frustration suggests a general concern to cushion the effects of harsh bargains, it is an open question to what extent Consumer-Welfarism would push the paternalistic principle for the benefit of commercial contractors.

As we have seen, some of these ideas can generate novel doctrines such as equitable estoppel and unconscionability. However, Consumer-Welfarism also attempts to feed reasonableness into such existing contractual categories as implied terms, mistake, and frustration (thereby opening the door to the employment of the particular principles of the ideology). Whilst Lord Denning's attempts to make such a move in respect of implied terms and frustration have failed, the equitable doctrine of common mistake continues to enjoy support [that support has since been withdrawn, see p. 642 below]. The most spectacular doctrinal success, however, has been with exemption clauses which are, of course, generally regulated now under a regime of reasonableness by UCTA.

Consumer-Welfarism suffers from its pluralistic scheme of principles. Where a dispute clearly falls under just one of its principles, there is no difficulty; but, as soon as more than one principle is relevant, there is potentially a conflict. Without a rigid hierarchy of principles, the outcome of such conflicts will be unpredictable, as different judges will attach different weights to particular principles. It follows that Consumer-Welfarism is unlikely ever to attain the unity and consistency of its market-individualist rival.

7. FURTHER READING

ADAMS, J, and BROWNSWORD, R, 'The Ideologies of Contract Law' (1987) 7 *Legal Studies* 205.

BROWNSWORD, R, *Contract Law: Themes for the Twenty-First Century* (Butterworths, 2000).

MCKENDRICK, E, 'English Contract Law: A Rich Past, An Uncertain Future' (1997) 50 *Current Legal Problems* 25.

SIMPSON, AWB, 'Innovation in Nineteenth Century Contract Law' (1975) 91 *LQR* 247.

PART I

FORMATION

2

AGREEMENT: OBJECTIVE
OR SUBJECTIVE?

1. CENTRAL ISSUES

1. When deciding whether or not parties have in fact reached agreement the law could either seek to examine the subjective intentions of the parties or it could have regard to their intention, objectively ascertained.

2. English law has chosen to adopt an objective approach. The reasons for this choice will be examined in this chapter, together with the different forms that the objective test can take. It will be suggested that the approach adopted by the judges is to attempt to put themselves in the position of a reasonable person in the position of the parties (principally, but not exclusively, the promisee of the disputed promise). The judges do not adopt the perspective of the reasonable detached observer.

3. Finally the chapter concludes by considering whether or not the law adopts a subjective approach in the case where one party attempts to 'snap up' an offer which he knew that the offeror did not intend and in the case where one party was at fault in failing to notice that the other party's offer contained a mistake or he was himself responsible for inducing that mistake in the other party. The conclusion that will be reached is that it is not necessary to resort to a subjective approach in order to explain these cases and that they can be analysed in terms consistent with the objective test that is generally applied by the courts.

2. INTRODUCTION

A party who wishes to establish that a legally binding contract has been formed between himself and another party must prove a number of matters. The first is that the parties have reached agreement. This is usually done by demonstrating that one party has made an offer that the other has accepted. The rules relating to offer and acceptance are discussed in Chapter 3. Secondly, the agreement must be expressed in a form that is sufficiently certain for the court to be able to enforce. The tests applied by the courts when deciding whether a term has been expressed in a form that is too vague, incomplete, or uncertain to be enforced are discussed in Chapter 4. Thirdly, the agreement must be supported by consideration (although it is possible that effect may be given to a promise that is unsupported by consideration via an estoppel). The doctrine of consideration and the role that estoppel can play in giving effect to promises that are unsupported by consideration are discussed in Chapter 5. Fourthly, the law may only recognize the validity of the agreement if it is entered into in a particular form (such as writing). The significance of requirements of form has diminished in recent years but they have not been entirely abolished. Requirements of form are discussed in Chapter 6. Finally, the parties must have had an intention to create legal relations. This intention is presumed in commercial transactions but in the case of domestic and social agreements the law initially presumes that the parties did not intend to be legally bound by their agreement. The doctrine of intention to create legal relations is discussed in Chapter 6.

The function of this chapter is to discuss a preliminary matter, namely the approach adopted by the courts when seeking to ascertain the intention of the parties. Many of the rules of contract law are said to rest on the intention of the parties. But how does the court ascertain their intention? Does it seek to examine the actual, subjective state of mind of the parties or does it look to the outward manifestation of their intention (as expressed in the words used, their appearance, conduct, etc.)? The general rule is that the existence and content of an agreement are objective questions that must be answered by reference to the intention of the parties, objectively ascertained. John Cartwright has helpfully set out the general rule as follows (*Unequal Bargaining* (Oxford University Press, 1991), p. 5):

The test whether there has been correspondence between offer and acceptance is not subjective, but objective. Therefore, it is not simply a question of whether both parties actually understood that there would be a contract and that it would contain a particular set of terms. There may still be a contract if, objectively tested, the parties can be said to have agreed (even though they did not in fact agree).

The proposition that the test for the existence and content of an agreement is objective rather than subjective raises three issues. The first relates to the justification for the adoption of an objective approach. If contract is about the enforcement of promises voluntarily made, why does the law not place primary emphasis on the subjective intentions of the parties? The reasons for the adoption of an objective approach are, essentially, the need to encourage certainty in commercial transactions and the desire to avoid the evidential difficulties associated with an inquiry into the actual state of mind of a party to the contract. Lord Steyn, writing extra-judicially ('Contract Law: Fulfilling the Reasonable Expectations of Honest Men' (1997) 113 *LQR* 433), put the matter as follows:

It is a defensible position for a legal system to give predominance to the subjective intentions of the parties. Such a policy can claim to be committed to the ideal of perfect individualised justice. But that is not the English way. Our law is generally based on an objective theory of contract. This involves adopting an external standard given life by using the concept of the reasonable man. The commercial advantage of the English approach is that it promotes certainty and predictability in the resolution of contractual disputes. And, as a matter of principle, it is not unfair to impute to contracting parties the intention that in the event of a dispute a neutral judge should decide the case applying an objective standard of reasonableness.

A similar point has been made by Professor Friedmann ('The Objective Principle and Mistake and Involuntariness in Contract and Restitution' (2003) 119 *LQR* 68, 69) when he stated that the purpose behind the objective theory is 'generally limited to protecting the performance interest of the party who acquired in good faith the other party's promise while being unaware that the promise is not in accord with the genuine will of the party who made it'.

The second issue relates to the definition or the scope of this 'objective theory of contract'. Lord Steyn's definition is a broad one in that it places considerable emphasis on the concept of 'reasonableness' (more than one might, perhaps, expect from an English judge). There are in fact different variants of the objective theory of contract. Howarth ('The Meaning of Objectivity in Contract' (1984) 100 *LQR* 265) identifies three varieties. The first he terms 'promisor objectivity' (that is to say, the promise is to be understood in the way in which it would have been understood by a reasonable person in the position of the promisor); the second is 'promisee objectivity' (according to which the promise is to be understood in the way in which it would have been understood by a reasonable person in the position of the promisee); and the third is 'detached objectivity' (in which case the perspective adopted is that of the reasonable man who is independent of the two parties to the contract). Howarth is himself an advocate of 'detached objectivity'. The distinction that he draws between 'promisor' and 'promisee' objectivity is, however, a troublesome one in application because in an ordinary bilateral contract the parties are both promisors and promisees (for criticism of Howarth's analysis along these lines see J Vorster, 'A Comment on the Meaning of Objectivity in Contract' (1987) 103 *LQR* 274). Thus in the case of a contract for the sale of goods the seller is a promisor in relation to the promise to sell the goods but a promisee in relation to the buyer's promise to pay for them, while the buyer is a promisor in relation to his promise to pay for the goods but a promisee in relation to the seller's promise to deliver the goods. What does Howarth himself mean by the use of the labels 'promisor' and 'promisee'? He defines his concepts in footnote 5 of his article where he states:

The use of promisor/promisee terminology, rather than plaintiff/defendant or offeror/offeree, serves as a convenient means of distinguishing the party wishing to enforce a contract or contractual promise (the promisee) from the party wishing to avoid the enforcement of that promise (the promisor).

As we shall see (pp. 30, 41, and 48–49 below) this distinction gives rise to considerable difficulty in terms of application and should, for that reason, be rejected. Nevertheless, despite these terminological difficulties, Howarth's insight is a useful one because it points out that the objective test can be viewed from different perspectives. Generally, there are two parties to a contract and the law could adopt the perspective of the reasonable person in the position of either party to the contract or it could adopt the position of the reasonable independent observer.

The third issue relates to the role of the subjective intentions of the parties to the contract. Are they irrelevant (at least to the extent that they do not coincide with the result reached by the application of the objective test) or do they have some residual significance? Cases in which it has been argued that the courts have resorted to a subjective approach are cases in which one party attempts to snap up an offer which she knows the other party did not intend (see *Hartog* v. *Colin & Shields* [1939] 3 All ER 566, p. 38 below) and where one party was at fault in not realizing that the other party had made a mistake (see *Scriven Brothers & Co* v. *Hindley & Co* [1913] 3 KB 564,

p. 45 below). We shall examine these cases and consider whether they do in fact adopt a subjective approach after we have discussed two leading cases that consider the scope of the objective test, namely *Smith* v. *Hughes* (1871) LR 6 QB 597 and *Centrovincial Estates plc* v. *Merchant Investors Assurance Company Ltd* [1983] Com LR 158.

3. THE OBJECTIVE THEORY ILLUSTRATED

Smith v. Hughes

(1871) LR 6 QB 597, Court of Appeal

The facts are set out in the judgment of Cockburn CJ

Cockburn CJ

This was an action brought in the county court of Surrey, upon a contract for the sale of a quantity of oats by plaintiff to defendant, which contract the defendant had refused to complete, on the ground that the contract had been for the sale and purchase of old oats, whereas the oats tendered by the plaintiff had been oats of the last crop, and therefore not in accordance with the contract.

The plaintiff was a farmer, the defendant a trainer of racehorses. And it appeared that the plaintiff, having some good winter oats to sell, had applied to the defendant's manager to know if he wanted to buy oats, and having received for answer that he (the manager) was always ready to buy good oats, exhibited to him a sample, saying at the same time that he had forty or fifty quarters of the same oats for sale, at the price of 35s. per quarter. The manager took the sample, and on the following day wrote to say he would take the whole quantity at the price of 34s. a quarter.

Thus far the parties were agreed; but there was a conflict of evidence between them as to whether anything passed at the interview between the plaintiff and defendant's manager on the subject of the oats being old oats, the defendant asserting that he had expressly said that he was ready to buy old oats, and that the plaintiff had replied that the oats were old oats, while the plaintiff denied that any reference had been made to the oats being old or new.

The plaintiff having sent in a portion of the oats, the defendant, on meeting him afterwards, said, 'Why, those were new oats you sent me', to which the plaintiff having answered, 'I knew they were; I had none other'. The defendant replied, 'I thought I was buying old oats: new oats are useless to me; you must take them back'. This the plaintiff refused to do, and brought this action.

It was stated by the defendant's manager that trainers as a rule always use old oats, and that his own practice was never to buy new oats if he could get old. But the plaintiff denied having known that the defendant never bought new oats, or that trainers did not use them; and, on the contrary, asserted that a trainer had recently offered him a price for new oats. Evidence was given for the defendant that 34s. a quarter was a very high price for new oats, and such as a prudent man of business would not have given. On the other hand, it appeared that oats were at the time very scarce and dear.

The learned judge of the county court left two questions to the jury: first, whether the word 'old' had been used with reference to the oats in the conversation between the plaintiff and the defendant's manager; secondly, whether the plaintiff had believed that the defendant believed, or was under the impression, that he was contracting for old oats; in either of which cases he directed the jury to find for the defendant.

It is to be regretted that the jury were not required to give specific answers to the questions so left to them. For, it is quite possible that their verdict may have been given for the defendant on the first ground; in which case there could, I think, be no doubt as to the propriety of the judge's direction; whereas now, as it is possible that the verdict of the jury—or at all events of some of them—may have proceeded on the second ground, we are called upon to consider and decide whether the ruling of the learned judge with reference to the second question was right.

For this purpose we must assume that nothing was said on the subject of the defendant's manager desiring to buy old oats, nor of the oats having been said to be old; while, on the other hand, we must assume that the defendant's manager believed the oats to be old oats, and that the plaintiff was conscious of the existence of such belief, but did nothing, directly or indirectly, to bring it about, simply offering his oats and exhibiting his sample, remaining perfectly passive as to what was passing in the mind of the other party. The question is whether, under such circumstances, the passive acquiescence of the seller in the self-deception of the buyer will entitle the latter to avoid the contract. I am of opinion that it will not.

[he set out his reasons and continued]

It only remains to deal with an argument which was pressed upon us, that the defendant in the present case intended to buy old oats, and the plaintiff to sell new, so the two minds were not ad idem; and that consequently there was no contract. This argument proceeds on the fallacy of confounding what was merely a motive operating on the buyer to induce him to buy with one of the essential conditions of the contract. Both parties were agreed as to the sale and purchase of this particular parcel of oats. The defendant believed the oats to be old, and was thus induced to agree to buy them, but he omitted to make their age a condition of the contract. All that can be said is, that the two minds were not ad idem as to the age of the oats; they certainly were ad idem as to the sale and purchase of them. Suppose a person to buy a horse without a warranty, believing him to be sound, and the horse turns out unsound, could it be contended that it would be open to him to say that, as he had intended to buy a sound horse, and the seller to sell an unsound one, the contract was void, because the seller must have known from the price the buyer was willing to give, or from his general habits as a buyer of horses, that he thought the horse was sound? The cases are exactly parallel.

The result is that, in my opinion, the learned judge of the county court was wrong in leaving the second question to the jury, and that, consequently, the case must go down to a new trial.

Blackburn J

In this case I agree that on the sale of a specific article, unless there be a warranty making it part of the bargain that it possesses some particular quality, the purchaser must take the article he has bought though it does not possess that quality. And I agree that even if the vendor was aware that the purchaser thought that the article possessed that quality, and would not have entered into the contract unless he had so thought, still the purchaser is bound, unless the vendor was guilty of some fraud or deceit upon him, and that a mere abstinence from disabusing the purchaser of that impression is not fraud or deceit; for, whatever may be the case in a court of morals, there is no legal obligation on the vendor to inform the purchaser that he is under a mistake, not induced by the act of the vendor. And I also agree that where a specific lot of goods are sold by a sample, which the purchaser inspects instead of the bulk, the law is exactly the same, if the sample truly represents the bulk; though, as it is more probable that the purchaser in such a case would ask for some further warranty, slighter evidence would suffice to prove that, in fact, it was intended there should be such a warranty . . .

But I have more difficulty about the second point raised in the case. I apprehend that if one of the parties intends to make a contract on one set of terms, and the other intends to make a contract on another set of terms, or, as it is sometimes expressed, if the parties are not ad idem, there is no contract, unless the circumstances are such as to preclude one of the parties from denying that he has agreed to the terms of the other. The rule of law is that stated in *Freeman* v. *Cooke* 2 Ex 663. If, whatever a man's real intention may be, he so conducts himself that a reasonable man would believe that he was assenting to the terms proposed by the other party, and that other party upon that belief enters into the contract with him, the man thus conducting himself would be equally bound as if he had intended to agree to the other party's terms.

The jury were directed that, if they believed the word 'old' was used, they should find for the defendant—and this was right; for if that was the case, it is obvious that neither did the defendant intend to enter into a contract on the plaintiff's terms, that is, to buy this parcel of oats without any stipulation as to their quality; nor could the plaintiff have been led to believe he was intending to do so.

But the second direction raises the difficulty. I think that, if from that direction the jury would understand that they were first to consider whether they were satisfied that the defendant intended to buy this parcel of oats on the terms that it was part of his contract with the plaintiff that they were old oats, so as to have the warranty of the plaintiff to that effect, they were properly told that, if that was so, the defendant could not be bound to a contract without any such warranty unless the plaintiff was misled. But I doubt whether the direction would bring to the minds of the jury the distinction between agreeing to take the oats under the belief that they were old, and agreeing to take the oats under the belief that the plaintiff contracted that they were old.

The difference is the same as that between buying a horse believed to be sound, and buying one believed to be warranted sound; but I doubt if it was made obvious to the jury, and I doubt this the more because I do not see much evidence to justify a finding for the defendant on this latter ground if the word 'old' was not used. There may have been more evidence than is stated in the case; and the demeanour of the witnesses may have strengthened the impression produced by the evidence there was; but it does not seem a very satisfactory verdict if it proceeded on this latter ground. I agree, therefore, in the result that there should be a new trial.

Hannen J

I think there should be a new trial in this case, not because the ruling of the county court judge was incorrect, but because, having regard to the evidence, I think it doubtful whether the jury sufficiently understood the direction they received to enable them to take it as their guide in determining the question submitted to them. . . .

It is essential to the creation of a contract that both parties should agree to the same thing in the same sense. Thus, if two persons enter into an apparent contract concerning a particular person or ship, and it turns out that each of them, misled by a similarity of name, had a different person or ship in his mind, no contract would exist between them: *Raffles* v. *Wichelhaus* 2 H & C 906.

But one of the parties to an apparent contract may, by his own fault, be precluded from setting up that he had entered into it in a different sense to that in which it was understood by the other party. Thus in the case of a sale by sample where the vendor, by mistake, exhibited a wrong sample, it was held that the contract was not avoided by this error of the vendor: *Scott* v. *Littledale* 8 E & B 815.

But if in the last-mentioned case the purchaser, in the course of the negotiations preliminary to the contract, had discovered that the vendor was under a misapprehension as to the sample he was offering, the vendor would have been entitled to shew that he had not intended to enter into the contract by which the purchaser sought to bind him. The rule of law applicable to such a case is a corollary from the rule of morality which Mr Pollock [counsel for the plaintiff] cited from Paley, *Moral and Political Philosophy*, Book III, ch. V, that a promise is to be performed 'in that sense in which the promiser apprehended at the time the promisee received it', and may be thus expressed: 'The promiser is not bound to fulfil a promise in a sense in which the promisee knew at the time the promiser did not intend it'. And in considering the question, in what sense a promisee is entitled to enforce a promise, it matters not in what way the knowledge of the meaning in which the promiser made it is brought to the mind of the promisee, whether by express words, or by conduct, or previous dealings, or other circumstances. If by any means he knows that there was no real agreement between him and the promiser, he is not entitled to insist that the promise shall be fulfilled in a sense to which the mind of the promiser did not assent.

If, therefore, in the present case, the plaintiff knew that the defendant, in dealing with him for oats, did so on the assumption that the plaintiff was contracting to sell him old oats, he was aware that the defendant apprehended the contract in a different sense to that in which he meant it, and he is thereby deprived of the right to insist that the defendant shall be bound by that which was only the apparent, and not the real bargain.

This was the question which the learned judge intended to leave to the jury; and, as I have already said, I do not think it was incorrect in its terms, but I think that it was likely to be misunderstood by the jury. The jury were asked, 'whether they were of opinion, on the whole of the evidence, that the plaintiff believed the defendant to believe, or to be under the impression that he was contracting for the purchase of old oats? If so, there would be a verdict for the defendant'. The jury may have understood this to mean that, if the plaintiff believed the defendant to believe that he was buying old oats, the defendant would be entitled to the verdict; but a belief on the part of the plaintiff that the defendant was making a contract to buy the oats, of which he offered him a sample, under a mistaken belief that they were old, would not relieve the defendant from liability unless his mistaken belief were induced by some misrepresentation of the plaintiff, or concealment by him of a fact which it became his duty to communicate. In order to relieve the defendant it was necessary that the jury should find not merely that the plaintiff believed the defendant to believe that he was buying old oats, but that he believed the defendant to believe that he, the plaintiff, was contracting to sell old oats.

I am the more disposed to think that the jury did not understand the question in this last sense because I can find very little, if any, evidence to support a finding upon it in favour of the defendant. It may be assumed that the defendant believed the oats were old, and it may be suspected that the plaintiff thought he so believed, but the only evidence from which it can be inferred that the plaintiff believed that the defendant thought that the plaintiff was making it a term of the contract that the oats were old is that the defendant was a trainer, and that trainers, as a rule, use old oats; and that the price given was high for new oats, and more than a prudent man would have given.

Having regard to the admitted fact that the defendant bought the oats after two days' detention of the sample, I think that the evidence was not sufficient to justify the jury in answering the question put to them in the defendant's favour, if they rightly understood it; and I therefore think there should be a new trial.

COMMENTARY

Smith was decided at a time when juries were still in common use in civil disputes. As Cockburn CJ states in his judgment, the judge left two questions for the jury. Had he required the jury to answer these questions separately the appeal to the Court of Appeal might have been avoided. The jury entered a verdict for the defendant but, as a consequence of their failure to answer the two questions separately, the plaintiff was able to secure a new trial because of the possibility that the jury had misunderstood the second question and had entered judgment for the defendant only as a result of that misapprehension.

There are two points of importance that emerge from *Smith*. The first relates to the scope of the doctrine of mistake. This is a topic to which we shall return in Chapter 16. Here it suffices to note that the Court of Appeal distinguished between the case where the plaintiff believed that the defendant thought he was buying old oats and the case where the plaintiff believed that the defendant thought that he was buying oats which the plaintiff had promised were old. In the former case the defendant is liable to take the oats and must take the consequences of his own mistake, whereas in the latter he is not liable to take the oats on the ground that the parties were at cross-purposes as to the terms of the contract.

The second point, and the issue with which we are here concerned, relates to the submission that the parties were not 'ad idem' and that, consequently, no contract had been concluded between the parties. In considering whether or not the parties had reached agreement, the Court of Appeal clearly did not adopt a subjective approach because the fact that the defendant mistakenly believed that the oats were old oats was not sufficient to persuade the court to conclude that no contract had been concluded. So the court applied an objective approach.

But which variant of the objective test did the Court of Appeal apply? The judgments do not appear to offer any support for 'detached objectivity'. Howarth interprets the judgment of Hannen J as support for 'promisor objectivity' and the judgment of Blackburn J as support for 'promisee objectivity' (at (1984) 100 *LQR* 265, 268, and 271 respectively). But here we encounter the problem, alluded to above (p. 25), of the identification of the 'promisor' and the 'promisee'. The seller was the promisor in relation to his promise to sell the oats, while the buyer was the promisor in relation to his promise to pay for them. Was the subject matter of the dispute the buyer's promise to pay or the seller's promise to sell? There is a real sense in which the dispute was about the buyer's promise to pay in that the seller was suing for the price and so was attempting to enforce the buyer's promise to pay. But neither the buyer nor the seller disputed that the buyer had promised to pay for the oats at 34s per quarter. The dispute between the parties related to the seller's promise to sell the oats and, in particular, the buyer's understanding of that promise. In relation to that promise, the seller was the promisor and the buyer was the promisee. But it is unlikely that either Blackburn J or Hannen J thought it necessary to distinguish between 'promisor objectivity' on the one hand and 'promisee objectivity' on the other. It seems more likely that they intended to examine the case from the perspective of the reasonable person in the position of both parties.

Applied to the facts of *Smith* this approach works out as follows. The seller sues for the price. The buyer cannot deny that he promised to pay for the oats. But he denies that he is liable to pay for them because he alleges that the seller promised to sell him old oats. This focuses attention on the seller's promise. Does the court attempt to put itself in the position of the reasonable man in the position of the buyer or the reasonable man in the position of the seller? It starts with the reasonable man in the position of the buyer (who is the promisee in relation to the seller's promise to sell). How would a reasonable man in the position of the buyer understand the seller's offer? Assuming that the seller did not use the word 'old' to describe the oats the reasonable man would understand it to be an offer to sell oats. This being the case, the contract was for the sale of oats and the buyer was liable to pay the price to the seller. But it does not follow from this that the court has no concern with the position of the seller (or, more accurately, the reasonable person in the position of the seller). On the facts of *Smith* the court gave little overt attention to the position of the seller because the reasonable man in the position of the seller would understand the buyer's promise as a promise to buy oats. But suppose that the seller knew that the buyer had mis-understood the terms of his offer and, further, he knew that the buyer believed that the seller had offered to sell him old oats. In such a case the seller would not be entitled to rely on the objective appearance created by the buyer's promise to pay for the oats because of his knowledge that the buyer did not intend to buy the new oats. The law does not allow a party to snatch at a bargain which he knew was not intended (see *Hartog* v. *Colin & Shields* [1939] 3 All ER 566, p. 38 below). This, indeed, is the point that was made by Hannen J in the context of his quotation from the work of Paley.

Suppose a further variation of the facts of *Smith* (based on the example given by Hannen J in the third paragraph of his judgment). Assume that the seller did not in fact intend to sell oats. He intended to sell barley but took along oats as his sample because he was unable to distinguish between oats and barley. When he delivers the barley the buyer refuses to take delivery or to pay for it. Again the buyer does not deny that he promised to pay for the goods. His defence is that the goods delivered were not those he contracted to buy. He states that he contracted to buy oats and not barley. The seller maintains that he intended to sell barley and not oats. So, once again, it is the subject-matter of the seller's promise that is in dispute. How would a reason-able person in the position of the buyer understand the seller's offer? He would understand it as an offer to sell oats and, this being the case, the buyer would not be liable to pay for the barley. Any argument by the seller to the effect that he did not intend to offer oats for sale would be dismissed by the court on the ground that a reasonable person in the position of the buyer would understand his offer as an offer to sell oats and the seller would be bound by the appearance created by his conduct.

It is therefore suggested that the court does not have to choose between adopting the position of the reasonable person in the position of one party or the other. In relation to the promise, the meaning of which is disputed, the law starts from the position of the reasonable person in the position of the promisee but it does not stop there. It then goes on to examine the transaction from the perspective of the reasonable person in the position of the other party to the contract.

Centrovincial Estates plc v. Merchant Investors Assurance Company Ltd

[1983] Com LR 158, Court of Appeal

The plaintiffs let premises to the defendants for a term running from 1 December 1978 to 24 December 1989 at a yearly rental of £68,320, payable from 25 December 1978 and subject to a rent review from 25 December 1982. The agreement between the parties contained the following rent review clause:

'PROVIDED ALWAYS and it is hereby agreed that the rent hereby reserved shall on the Twenty-fifth day of December One thousand nine hundred and eighty-two be increased to the then current market rental value of the demised premises and in this connection the following procedure shall be adopted namely—

A. At least six months before the Twenty-fifth day of December One thousand nine hundred and eighty-two the Lessor and the Lessee or their duly authorised preresentatives (sic) will endeavour to reach agreement on the then current market rental value of the demised premises and if they are able to agree such current market rental value within a period of three months they shall certify the amount of the then current market rental value as agreed between them—

B. In the event of the parties hereto failing to reach agreement as to the then current market rental value within the said period of three months by sub-clause A hereof

PROVIDED then the matter shall be referred to an independent surveyor or valuer (to be appointed within a further period of one month by the President for the time being of the Royal Institution of Chartered Surveyors) for assessment and not by way of arbitration and the assessment of such independent surveyor shall be communicated to the parties hereto in writing and shall be final and binding upon them

C. A memorandum of such current market rental value so agreed or assessed as aforesaid shall be endorsed on these presents and signed by the duly authorised officers of the parties hereto.

D. Upon the signing of the Certificate by the duly authorised representative of the Lessor and Lessee respectively or the receipt by the Lessor and the Lessee of the independent surveyor's or valuer's written communication as to the then current market rental value the rent hereby reserved shall as from the twenty-fifth day of December One thousand nine hundred and eighty-two be increased to the amount so certified or assessed

  E. Under no circumstances shall this proviso operate to effect a reduction in the rent below that which was payable immediately before the particular date of any rent revision hereunder

  F. The fees payable to the independent surveyor or valuer hereinbefore referred to in respect of such assessment of rental shall be borne by the parties hereto in equal shares.'

On 22 June 1982 a letter was written to the defendants on behalf of the plaintiffs by their solicitors which invited the defendants to agree that the 'current market rental value' of the premises was £65,000. The defendants' company secretary replied to this letter on the following day and he agreed that £65,000 was the appropriate figure. The plaintiffs received this letter on 28 June and immediately one of their partners telephoned the defendants to inform them that the letter of 22 June 1982 contained an error and that they had intended to propose a current market rental value of £126,000, not £65,000. The plaintiffs' solicitors wrote to the defendants in similar terms on the following day. But the defendants refused to accept the amended terms and insisted that the parties had concluded a binding agreement at a rental of £65,000.

The plaintiffs issued a writ against the defendants and sought a declaration that no legally binding agreement had been made between the parties in respect of the reviewed rent payable by the defendants to the plaintiffs from 25 December 1982 and a declaration that the plaintiffs were entitled to refer the assessment of the current market rental value to an independent surveyor or valuer in accordance with sub-clause B of the rent review clause.

The trial judge held that the plaintiffs were entitled to summary judgment. The defendants appealed to the Court of Appeal who allowed the appeal and gave the defendants unconditional leave to defend the action.

Slade LJ [giving the judgment of the court]

The essence of the plaintiffs' case is, and has at all times been, that the parties have failed to reach 'agreement' as to the 'current market rental value' of the demised premises within the meaning of sub-paragraphs A and B of the rent review provision and that the plaintiffs are accordingly entitled to have matters referred to an independent surveyor pursuant to sub-paragraph B. To establish this claim, it was and is necessary for them to satisfy this Court that the two letters of the 22nd and 23rd June did not result in the conclusion of any 'agreement' within the meaning of those sub-paragraphs.

So far as their affidavit evidence revealed, the two grounds upon which the plaintiffs intended to argue the latter proposition were in effect:

  (1) that not even an apparent binding agreement was concluded by these two letters, because, on the true construction of the rent review provision, there could be no binding agreement until the parties had signed the contemplated certificate;

  (2) that even if the two letters did evidence an apparent binding agreement, there was in fact no binding agreement in law, on the grounds that the defendants, in responding as they did to the letter of the 22nd June, were trying to take advantage of what they knew, or ought reasonably to have known, was an error on the part of the plaintiffs' solicitors.

When the Order XIV[1] summons came on for hearing before Mr Justice Harman, the plaintiffs shifted their position. They did not attempt to pursue the first of these two points. As to the second, they accepted that there was a substantial disputed issue of fact as to whether the defendants on the 23rd June 1982, knew, or ought reasonably to have known, of the alleged error on the part of the plaintiffs. Correspondingly, they conceded that they could not expect to obtain summary judgment on the basis of any such alleged knowledge on the part of the defendants since the disputed issue as to the defendants' state of knowledge is one that can only be appropriately resolved at the trial.

This concession having been made, in our opinion correctly, the plaintiffs were confronted with at least formidable difficulties on their application for summary judgment. On the face of it, the letter of the 22nd June 1982 constituted a formal, unequivocal and unambiguous offer made to the defendants on behalf of the plaintiffs, with an intent to create legal relations, to agree that the 'current market rental value' of the demised premises, for the purpose of sub-paragraph A of the rent review provision, was £65,000 per annum. On the face of it, the letter of the 23rd June 1982 constituted a formal, unequivocal and unambiguous acceptance of that offer by the defendants. The plaintiffs' solicitors indeed assert that they erroneously inserted the figure of £65,000 in the letter of the 22nd June 1982 in substitution for the figure of £126,000, which they had intended to insert; and like the learned Judge we are prepared to accept the truth of this assertion for the purpose of dealing with the present application. But in the absence of any proof, as yet, that the defendants either knew or ought reasonably to have known of the plaintiffs' error at the time when they purported to accept the plaintiffs' offer, why should the plaintiffs now be allowed to resile from that offer? It is a well-established principle of the English law of contract that an offer falls to be interpreted not subjectively by reference to what has actually passed through the mind of the offeror, but objectively, by reference to the interpretation which a reasonable man in the shoes of the offeree would place on the offer. It is an equally well-established principle that ordinarily an offer, when unequivocally accepted according to its precise terms, will give rise to a legally binding agreement as soon as acceptance is communicated to the offeror in the manner contemplated by the offer, and cannot thereafter be revoked without the consent of the other party. Accepting, as they do, that they have not yet proved that the defendants knew, or ought reasonably to have known, of their error at the relevant time, how can the plaintiffs assert that the defendants have no realistic hope of establishing an agreement of the relevant nature by virtue of the two letters of the 22nd and 23rd June 1982?

Mr Richard Scott [counsel for the plaintiffs] in answer has submitted an argument to the following effect. The 'agreement' envisaged by sub-paragraphs A and B of the rent review provision is a genuine agreement, a real meeting of the minds. In the present case there was no real meeting of the parties' minds because of the plaintiffs' error. True it is that their intentions would have fallen to be judged objectively, according to their external manifestation, if the defendants had not only purported to accept the offer but had further altered their position as a result. However, so the argument runs, the general rule that the intentions of an offeror must be judged objectively is based on estoppel. Accordingly, if the person who has accepted the offer has not altered his position in reliance on the offer, no such estoppel arises. In the present case, it is submitted, the critical fact is that the figure of £65,000 was lower than the rent currently payable under

---

[1] The terms of Order 14 are set out at p. 36 below.

the Lease immediately before the 25th December 1982. In these circumstances, it is said, the defendants in agreeing that figure, did not alter their position in any way. Because of sub-paragraph E of the rent review provision, the current rent of £68,320 would have continued to be payable after the 25th December 1982, notwithstanding the agreement. In all the circumstances, it is submitted, the plaintiffs, having proved their error at the relevant time, were at liberty to withdraw the offer contained in the letter of the 22nd June 1982, even after it had been accepted, and they duly did so at the end of June 1982.

We understand from the learned Judge's judgment that an argument on much the same lines was submitted to him on behalf of the plaintiffs and that, though he regarded it as novel and surprising, he was in the end convinced by it.

As will have appeared, Mr Scott's submissions based on mistake involve the implicit proposition (among other propositions) that the defendants have given no consideration for the agreement on which they now rely; we understood him to accept that if the defendants had altered their position in any material respect in agreeing the figure of £65,000, the argument based on mistake could not avail the plaintiffs. Since, for reasons which we will explain later in this judgment, we have come to the clear conclusion that the defendants did give consideration, the argument based on mistake must in our opinion fail for this reason, if no other, and any further reference to the issue of mistake is not strictly necessary. Furthermore, it is right to record that Mr Scott, in an argument which brevity rendered no less forceful, did not burden (and indeed was not pressed to burden) the Court with citations of authority on this issue. In all the circumstances this judgment on an Order XIV summons is not an appropriate occasion to embark on a lengthy discussion on the law relating to mistake in contract. Nevertheless, we should perhaps attempt to explain briefly (albeit obiter) why, quite apart from questions of consideration, we respectfully differ from the learned Judge on the question of mistake, as a matter of broad principle.

The nature of the apparent contract concluded by the two letters of the 22nd and 23rd June 1982 is what is sometimes called a 'bilateral contract'. It was concluded by

(a) an offer by the plaintiffs to treat £65,000 as the 'current market rental value' of the premises for the purpose of the Lease if the defendants would promise to accept that figure as that value, followed by

(b) the giving of a promise by the defendants in those terms.

Where the nature of an offer is to enter into a bilateral contract, the contract becomes binding when the offeree gives the requested promise to the promisor in the manner contemplated by the offer; the mutual promises alone will suffice to conclude the contract. In our opinion, subject to what is said below relating to consideration, it is contrary to the well established principles of contract law to suggest that the offeror under a bilateral contract can withdraw an unambiguous offer, after it has been accepted in the manner contemplated by the offer, merely because he has made a mistake which the offeree neither knew nor could reasonably have known at the time when he accepted it. And in this context, provided only that the offeree has given sufficient consideration for the offeror's promise, it is nothing to the point that the offeree may not have changed his position beyond giving the promise requested of him.

For these reasons we think that the plaintiffs' submissions based on mistake cannot, as matters stand, suffice to negative the existence of the apparent agreement of the parties to treat £65,000 as the current market rental value for the purpose of the Lease and to deprive the defendants of the right to defend this action on the basis of such agreement, though we are not, of course, saying that the plea of mistake as formulated in the statement of claim will not succeed at the trial . . .

This is a case where the defendants clearly ought to be given leave to defend this action, unless the plaintiffs can satisfy the Court that the defendants have no realistic prospect of establishing an agreement of the relevant nature at the trial. The plaintiffs have not so satisfied us on the evidence now before the Court.

For these reasons, respectfully differing from the learned Judge, we have allowed this appeal and given the defendants unconditional leave to defend the action, coupled with certain ancillary directions for a speedy trial.

COMMENTARY

It is important to note that the plaintiffs in this case were seeking summary judgment against the defendants under what was Order 14 of the Rules of the Supreme Court (see now Part 24 of the Civil Procedure Rules). Order 14 rule 1 provided:

Where in an action to which this rule applies a statement of claim has been served on a defendant and that defendant has given notice of intention to defend the action, the plaintiff may, on the ground that the defendant has no defence to a claim included in the writ, or to a particular part of such a claim, or has no defence to such a claim or part except as to the amount of any damages claimed, apply to the Court for judgment against that defendant.

The court in an Order 14 case could either give judgment for the plaintiff or give the defendant leave to defend. The Court of Appeal in the present case gave the defendants unconditional leave to defend the action. All this means is that the defendant is entitled to defend the claim so that the plaintiff must proceed to trial if he is to succeed in his claim. This being the case, the plaintiffs' claim in *Centrovincial* would proceed to trial unless the parties were able to settle it before trial.

What would the plaintiffs have to prove in order to win their claim at trial? According to Slade LJ they would have to prove that the 'defendants either knew or ought to have known of the plaintiffs' error at the time when they purported to accept the plaintiffs' offer'. One might think that the fact that the proposed rental was lower than the existing rental (and that sub-clause E stated that effect could not be given to a proposal to lower the rent) would have alerted the defendants to the fact that the proposed reduction in the rental value was a mistake. But Mr Evans, a chartered surveyor who acted for the defendants and who drafted the defendants' letter of 23 June, swore an affidavit in which he 'strongly denied that he either knew or ought reasonably to have known of any such error and supported this denial by a number of reasons'. The state of the defendants' knowledge was therefore a matter of dispute and, as Slade LJ stated, that dispute could 'only be appropriately resolved at the trial'.

The decision of the Court of Appeal in *Centrovincial* establishes a number of points of importance. First, it affirms the general rule that the intentions of the parties are to be ascertained objectively and not subjectively. Secondly, it rejects the proposition that this general rule is based on estoppel.[2] It is a rule of contract law and is not confined to

---

[2] Estoppel is discussed in more detail at pp. 236–271 below.

estoppel. Thus it was not necessary for the defendants to establish that they had acted to their detriment in reliance upon the plaintiffs' offer in order to hold the plaintiffs to the terms of their offer. The fact that they had accepted the offer was sufficient to give rise to a binding contract, notwithstanding the fact that the plaintiffs were mistaken and that they pointed out their mistake to the defendants immediately and before the defendants had acted on it in any way. This aspect of the decision has aroused some controversy. Thus Professor Atiyah has asked ('The Hannah Blumenthal and Classical Contract Law' (1986) 102 *LQR* 363, 368–369):

Why should an offeree be entitled to create legal rights for himself by the bare act of acceptance when he has in no way relied upon the offer before being informed that it was made as a result of a mistake and did not in reality reflect the intention of the offeror? Now that liability for misleading statements is an accepted part of tort law, it becomes increasingly anomalous if in a contractual context a party is able to sue upon an unrelied-upon statement, whereas in any other context he is not. A misleading offer is a commercial or perhaps a social nuisance which should be discouraged and for which compensation may be due, if loss is thereby caused, but surely the principles governing such misleading communications ought not to depend upon whether the communication can be classified as an offer or not?

The answer given by the Court of Appeal to Professor Atiyah's questions is that, while a binding promise may render reliance possible, it is not the case that it is the reliance that renders the promise binding. The parties were bound to one another the moment that the defendants accepted the plaintiffs' offer and there was nothing further that the defendants needed to do in order to render the contract binding. Were the law otherwise parties would not be able to have confidence in the security of their transactions unless and until they had acted to their detriment upon the promise made by the other party. The plaintiffs' offer was therefore binding upon them from the moment of acceptance and they could not unilaterally bring that agreement to an end by the assertion that their offer contained within it a mistake. On its facts the decision in *Centrovincial* may seem harsh on the plaintiffs. But any appearance of hardship is mitigated by two factors. The first is that the plaintiffs may well have had an action in negligence against their solicitors who mistakenly inserted the figure of £65,000 in the offer. The second is that the need to consider the position of the defendants and, more generally, the need for a measure of security in commercial transactions must be balanced against any hardship to the plaintiffs. Assuming that the defendants neither knew or ought reasonably to have known of the plaintiffs' mistake, why should they not be entitled to the benefit of their bargain? Parties need to know where they stand in relation to transactions that have been concluded and, were the law to allow a party to escape from an agreement by the mere assertion that he entered into it under a mistake, such security would be significantly undermined (see further D Friedmann, 'The Objective Principle and Mistake and Involuntariness in Contract and Restitution' (2003) 119 *LQR* 68).

Finally, the Court of Appeal noted that it was open to the plaintiffs to prove at trial that the defendants either knew or ought reasonably to have known of the plaintiffs' mistake at the time they purported to accept the plaintiffs' offer. Cases in which the defendant knew of the plaintiffs' mistake at the time at which he purported to accept the plaintiffs' offer are commonly referred to as examples of 'snapping up'. These cases are discussed in the next section. Cases in which the defendants ought reasonably to have known of the plaintiffs' mistake are slightly more difficult to classify. They could be examples of 'snapping up'. But there is a wider category of case in which one party was at fault in failing to notice that the other party's offer contained a mistake or he was himself responsible for inducing that mistake in the other party. In such a case the party at fault may not be entitled to hold the other party to the terms of his offer. These cases are discussed in the final section of this chapter.

4. THE 'SNAPPING UP' CASES

Hartog v. Colin & Shields

[1939] 3 All ER 566, King's Bench Division

The plaintiff alleged that the defendants had agreed to sell him 30,000 Argentine hare skins and that, in breach of contract, the defendants had failed to deliver them. He accordingly brought an action for damages against the defendants. The defendants denied that any binding contract had been entered into. They maintained that they had made a mistake in offering to sell the hare skins at a price per pound when they had intended to sell the skins at a price per piece (the value of a piece being approximately one third of the value of a pound). Further, the defendants alleged that the plaintiff was well aware of the mistake and had 'fraudulently' accepted an offer which 'he well knew that the defendants had never intended to make'. It was held that the plaintiff was not entitled to recover damages from the defendants on the ground that he must have known that the defendants' offer contained a material mistake.

Singleton J

In this case, the plaintiff, a Belgian subject, claims damages against the defendants because he says they broke a contract into which they entered with him for the sale of Argentine hare skins. The defendants' answer to that claim is: 'There really was no contract, because you knew that the document which went forward to you, in the form of an offer, contained a material mistake. You realised that, and you sought to take advantage of it.'

   Counsel for the defendants took upon himself the onus of satisfying me that the plaintiff knew that there was a mistake and sought to take advantage of that mistake. In other words, realising that there was a mistake, the plaintiff did that which James LJ, in *Tamplin v. James* (1880) 15 Ch D 215, 211, described as 'snapping up the offer'. It is important, I think, to realise that in the verbal negotiations which took place in this country, and in all the discussions there had ever been, the prices of Argentine hare skins had been discussed per piece, and later, when correspondence took place, the matter was always discussed at the price per piece, and never at a price per pound. Those witnesses who were called on behalf of the plaintiff have had comparatively little experience of dealing in Argentine hare skins. Even the expert witness who was called had had very little. One witness, Mr Caytan, I think, had had no dealings in them for some years, though before that he had had some, no doubt. On the whole, I think that the evidence of Mr Wilcox, on behalf of the defendants, is the more likely to be right—namely, that the way in which

Argentine hare skins are bought and sold is generally per piece. That is shown by the discussions which took place between the parties in this country, and by the correspondence. Then on 23 November came the offer upon which the plaintiff relies. It was an offer of 10,000 Argentine hares, winters (100 skins equalling 16 kilos), at 10d per lb; 10,000 half hares at 6d per lb; 10,000 summer hares at 5d per lb. Those prices correspond, roughly, in the case of the winter hares, to 3d per piece, half hares 2d per piece, and summer hares 1d per piece. The last offer prior to this, in which prices were mentioned, was on 3 November from the defendants, and the price then quoted for winter hares was 10d per piece. Even allowing that the market was bound to fall a little, I find it difficult to believe that anyone could receive an offer for a large quantity of Argentine hares at a price so low as 3d per piece without having the gravest doubts of it.

I mention merely the price of the winter hares, because Mr Wilcox told me and I accept his evidence, that at some time the price of Argentine winter hares fell to 9d. I am satisfied, however, from the evidence given to me, that the plaintiff must have realised, and did in fact know, that a mistake had occurred. What did he do? Mr Hartog put it forward as being a bona fide act on his part that he at once went to Mr Caytan and entered into a contract with him. I am not sure that it points to a bona fide act at all. Mr Caytan, who was called before me, apparently entered into an arrangement with him on that same day, 23 November, to buy Argentine winter hares at 11d per lb, so that the price, if there had been a contract at 10d per lb, has risen on the sale of the goods to Mr Caytan to 11d per lb. That is 11/2d up, which is a considerable increase, and much greater than that which he had been offering to pay in the letters which passed earlier. It is a much greater increase.

I cannot help thinking that, when this quotation in pence per pound reached Mr Hartog, the plaintiff, he must have realised, and that Mr Caytan, too, must have realised, that there was a mistake. Otherwise I cannot understand the quotation. There was an absolute difference from anything which had gone before—a difference in the manner of quotation, in that the skins are offered per pound instead of per piece.

I am satisfied that it was a mistake on the part of the defendants or their servants which caused the offer to go forward in that way, and I am satisfied that anyone with any knowledge of the trade must have realised that there was a mistake. I find it difficult to understand why, when Mr Caytan bought in this way at 11d per lb, he could not tell me what the total purchase price was, and I cannot help thinking that there was an arrangement of some sort, amounting rather to a division of the spoil. That is the view I formed, having heard the witnesses. I do not form it lightly. I have seen the witnesses and heard them, and in this case can form no other view than that there was an accident. The offer was wrongly expressed, and the defendants by their evidence, and by the correspondence, have satisfied me that the plaintiff could not reasonably have supposed that that offer contained the offerers' real intention. Indeed, I am satisfied to the contrary. That means that there must be judgment for the defendants.

COMMENTARY

Singleton J attributes the phrase 'snapping up' to the judgment of James LJ in *Tamplin* v. *James* (a case which is discussed at p. 43 below).

Singleton J states that, on the evidence, the plaintiff 'must have realised, and did in fact know, that a mistake had occurred'. This suggests that he found that the plaintiff actually knew that a mistake had been made. But this finding does not appear to have been crucial to the outcome of the case because he also makes it clear in his judgment that it sufficed for the defendants to demonstrate that the plaintiff could not reasonably have supposed that the offer expressed the defendants' real intention. The judgment therefore combined subjective and objective elements. The plaintiff was not entitled to enforce the contract either because he knew that the defendants had made a mistake or on the ground that the reasonable person in the plaintiff's position would have known that the defendants had made a mistake.

What were the factors that led Singleton J to conclude that the plaintiff could not reasonably have supposed that the offer expressed the defendants' real intention? Two factors appear to predominate. The first was that the prior negotiations were conducted on the basis of a price per piece and the second was the extent of the disparity between the price per piece and the price per pound.

A helpful modern illustration of the application of this rule is provided by the facts of *Chwee Kin Keong* v. *Digilandmall.Com Pte Ltd* [2004] SGHC 71; [2004] 2 SLR 594 (affirmed [2005] SGCA 2). The defendants mistakenly altered the price of commercial laser printers on their web site. The price was altered from 3,854 Singaporean dollars to 66 Singaporean dollars. Overnight some 4,000 printers were ordered before the defendants were informed of their mistake. The defendants contacted all the purchasers immediately they became aware of the mistake, informed them of the mistake and stated that they would not be supplying the printers at the price of S$66. The six plaintiffs refused to accept this and claimed that they were entitled to the benefit of their bargain. Between them the six plaintiffs had ordered 1,606 printers and they claimed that they were entitled to the benefit of their good bargain (namely the acquisition of printers with a market value of S$6,189,524 for S$105,996). Rajah JC held that the plaintiffs were not entitled to succeed with their claim. He examined the evidence in relation to all six plaintiffs (one of whom had placed orders for 1,090 printers) and concluded that 'they were fully conscious that an unfortunate and egregious mistake had indeed been made by the defendant'. In reaching this conclusion he had regard to the fact that there was a 'stark gaping difference between the price posting and the market price' of the printers and the fact that the plaintiffs were 'well-educated professionals—articulate, entrepreneurial and, quite bluntly, streetwise and savvy individuals'. A further factor relied upon by Rajah JC was the circumstances in which the printers were purchased. They were placed in the 'dead of night' with 'indecent haste' and the e-mail exchanges between the plaintiffs demonstrated that they were 'clearly anxious to place their orders before the defendant took steps to correct the error'. In these circumstances he held that the plaintiffs were not entitled to enforce 'their purported contractual rights' and so he dismissed their claim.

Is *Hartog* an example of an objective approach to agreement or a subjective approach? It can be argued that it is an example of a subjective approach on the basis that, objectively, the parties did reach agreement. The defendants offered to sell the hare skins at a price per pound and the plaintiff accepted that offer. It was the fact that the plaintiff knew that the defendants were mistaken that led Singleton J to conclude that no contract had been concluded to sell the hare skins at a price per pound. This suggests that the vital factor in persuading Singleton J to conclude that the plaintiff was not entitled to recover damages was his finding that the parties were not subjectively agreed. On the other hand, it is possible to get to the same conclusion via the application of an objective test. Thus Dr Endicott has argued ('Objectivity, Subjectivity and Incomplete Agreements' in J Horder (ed), *Oxford Essays in Jurisprudence*, Fourth Series (Oxford University Press, 2000), p. 157) that '*Hartog* does not depart from the objective approach, because a reasonable person who knew that A had made a blunder in communicating a term would not treat A as having agreed to price hare skins per pound'.

Howarth treats *Hartog* as an example of 'promisee objectivity' ((1984) 100 *LQR* 265, 272), while Vorster points out that the penultimate sentence in the judgment of Singleton J adopts the standard of 'promisor objectivity' ((1987) 103 *LQR* 274, 281 n.42). This further illustrates the terminological confusion which Howarth's approach can cause. The promise which was the subject-matter of the dispute was the defendants' offer to sell the hare skins and the court focused attention on the plaintiff's understanding of that offer. In relation to the promise to sell, the plaintiff was the promisee. The reason for the focus on the position of the plaintiff was that he was seeking to enforce his version of the contract and it was his understanding (or, more accurately, the understanding of the reasonable person in his position) that was in issue. But the position would have been otherwise had the defendants brought a claim against the plaintiff on the basis that the parties had concluded a contract to sell the hare skins at a price per piece. No such claim was brought on the facts. The defendants had not delivered the hare skins to the plaintiff and were content simply to deny the existence of a contract. But suppose that the defendants had attempted to deliver the hare skins and the plaintiff had refused to pay at a price per piece. Would Singleton J have found the existence of a contract to sell the hare skins at a price per piece? This is not an easy question to answer. There seems little point in asking how a reasonable person in the position of the defendants would have understood the plaintiff's promise to pay given that there was no dispute in relation to the promise to pay. It was the promise to sell that was in dispute. Given that the plaintiff knew of the defendants' mistake and must have known that the defendants' intention was to sell at a price per piece, should his acceptance of their offer be regarded as an acceptance of an offer to sell at a price per piece? It is suggested that it should not. Objectively the price agreed was a price per pound and the fact that the plaintiff snapped at a bargain he knew was not intended should not result in him being bound by an offer that was never in fact made. A reasonable person in the position of the defendants, who was aware of the fact that the plaintiff had purported to snap at an offer which he knew was not intended, would be more likely to conclude that no contract had been formed because the parties were at cross-purposes and not that a contract had been concluded on his terms. This appears to have been the view of the defendants in *Hartog*. Their defence was that no contract had been concluded; it was not to assert the existence of a contract on their own terms.

5. THE ROLE OF FAULT

More difficult are the cases in which the mistake in relation to the terms of the contract has been induced or caused by one of the parties to the contract. Three cases will be discussed in this context. In all three the claim was brought by a seller. In the first and third case it was held that the seller was not entitled to the remedy which he sought on the ground that he was responsible for creating in the mind of the buyer a mistake in relation to the terms of the seller's offer. In the second case it was held that the buyer was responsible for his own misapprehension and so the seller was held to be entitled to the remedy that it sought.

Denny v. Hancock

(1870) LR 6 Ch App 1, Court of Appeal

The plaintiffs put up property for sale by auction. Prior to bidding for the land, the defendant inspected the property. He took with him a plan that had been annexed to the particulars of sale. The plan showed that the western side of the property was bounded by a strip of ground that was covered with a mass of shrubs or trees. The defendant discovered an iron fence and three magnificent trees to the west of the property and, in the belief that they represented the western edge of the property, he bid for it. In fact the fence and the three trees belonged to an adjoining property. The actual boundary of the property was in fact concealed by shrubs. Further, the plan represented all the trees on the property in a conspicuous manner but did not show the three trees seen by the defendant. The three trees were found to be a material element in the value of the property. When he discovered the mistake the defendant refused to complete the purchase. The plaintiffs sought a decree of specific performance and they succeeded before Malins VC. The defendant appealed successfully to the Court of Appeal where it was held that the defendant had been misled by the fault of the plaintiffs and that the plaintiffs were not entitled to a specific performance order.

Sir W. M. James LJ

I have no doubt whatever that if I had done exactly what this gentleman did, and taken that plan in my hand, and gone through the property, and found a shrubbery, or ground covered partly with shrubs and partly with thorns, with an iron fence outside, I should have arrived at exactly the same conclusion as this gentleman did, and I should have gone to the sale and bid in the belief that I was buying the belt up to the iron fence with those trees upon it . . .

There is no denial in evidence of this fact, that the plan produced was calculated to induce anybody to believe that the whole of the belt, or shrubbery, or whatever you may call it, was included in the property sold. It is urged, however, that the Defendant was negligent. The substance of the argument seems to be this: that if he had looked at the plan very minutely he would have seen that the trees in the meadows and in the garden were marked, but these three fine trees, which added so much to the value of the property, were not marked; and it is urged that the absence of these remarkable trees from the plan is a thing calculated to put a man so completely on his guard that he ought not to have been misled, and is not to be believed when he says he was misled. But it seems to me that it never would occur to a person who entertained no doubt whatever about what the thing was that had been sold to him, to make any inquiry about the omission of two or three trees in that which appeared on the plan to be a mass of wood. If this gentleman did as he says, buy it under a mistake as to the property, such mistake was caused by the plan which was presented to him, drawn by the vendors' agent, and also caused by this fact, which alone might have been enough to mislead him, that there was on the ground an apparent visible boundary, quite distinct from the almost invisible real boundary. I think that, independently of the plan, and on this latter ground alone, it would have required great consideration before a Court of Equity would have fixed the purchaser with this contract, which he swears he entered into in the belief that the property extended to its apparent boundary; but coupling the state of the property with the representation made by the plan, I am of opinion that it would not be according to the established principles of this Court to compel the purchaser to complete his contract. I am also of opinion that the mistake was occasioned by at least *crassa negligentia* on the part of the vendors in respect to what they sent out to the public. I am, therefore, unable to agree with the Vice-Chancellor, and am of opinion that he ought to have dismissed this bill with costs.

Sir G. Mellish LJ delivered a concurring judgment.

Tamplin v. James

(1880) 15 Ch D 215, Court of Appeal

The plaintiffs put property up for sale under the following description:

> 'All that well-accustomed inn, with the brewhouse, outbuildings, and premises known as *The ship*, together with the messuage, saddler's shop, and premises adjoining thereto, situate at *Newerne*, in the same parish, No 454 and 455 on the said tithe map, and containing by admeasurement twenty perches, more or less, now in the occupation of Mrs *Knowles* and Mr *S. Merrick*.'

> 'This lot is situate close to the *Lydney Town* station, on the *Severn and Wye Railway*, and abuts on other premises of the vendors, on the canal, and on lands now or late of the Rev. W. H. Bathurst.'

The lot was not sold at the auction but the defendant, who was present at the auction, made an offer to buy the property immediately afterwards. His offer was accepted and he signed a contract to purchase the property according to the conditions of sale for £750. The defendant made his offer in the belief that two pieces of garden were included in the sale. The reason for his belief was that he had known the property from the time that he was a boy and he knew that the gardens had always been occupied with the Ship Inn and the saddler's shop. Had he looked at the plans for the sale he would have seen that the gardens were not included in the sale and, further, that they were not included in the description of the sale. When he discovered his mistake the defendant refused to complete the sale unless the gardens were conveyed to him. The plaintiffs brought an action for specific performance. Both at first instance (before Baggallay LJ) and in the Court of Appeal it was held that the plaintiffs were entitled to a specific performance order.

Baggallay LJ
The Defendant insists in his statement of defence that he signed the memorandum in the reasonable belief that the property comprised therein included the whole of the premises in the occupation of Mrs *Knowles* and of Mr *Samuel Merrick*, and not merely the messuages and hereditaments which the Plaintiffs allege to be the only property comprised

therein, and that such his belief was induced and confirmed by the acts and words of the auctioneer at the sale. The Defendant has sworn positively that he had such a belief at the time he signed the memorandum, and I see no reason to doubt the statement so made by him; but was such a belief a reasonable belief?

It is doubtless well established that a Court of Equity will refuse specific performance of an agreement when the Defendant has entered into it under a mistake, and where injustice would be done to him were performance to be enforced. The most common instances of such refusal on the ground of mistake are cases in which there has been some unintentional misrepresentation on the part of the Plaintiff (I am not now referring to cases of intentional misrepresentation which would fall rather under the category of fraud), or where from the ambiguity of the agreement different meanings have been given to it by the different parties. . . . But where there has been no misrepresentation, and where there is no ambiguity in the terms of the contract, the Defendant cannot be allowed to evade the performance of it by the simple statement that he has made a mistake. Were such to be the law the performance of a contract could rarely be enforced upon an unwilling party who was also unscrupulous. I think that the law is correctly stated by Lord Romilly in *Swaisland* v. *Dearsley* 29 Beav 430, 433: 'The principle on which the Court proceeds in cases of mistake is this—if it appears upon the evidence that there was in the description of the property a matter on which a person might *bonâ fide* make a mistake, and he swears positively that he did make such mistake, and his evidence is not disproved, this Court cannot enforce the specific performance against him. If there appears on the particulars no ground for the mistake, if no man with his senses about him could have misapprehended the character of the parcels, then I do not think it is sufficient for the purchaser to swear that he made a mistake, or that he did not understand what he was about.'

Now does it appear, or can it safely be held in this case that the Defendant reasonably entertained a belief that the gardens were included in the property purchased by him? I will consider first the terms of the contract itself, and then the allegations as to the acts and words of the auctioneer and other agents of the Plaintiffs, for it is possible that although the terms of the agreement taken per se may have been free from doubt, enough may have been said or done by the Plaintiffs' agents to lead the Defendant to attribute a different meaning to its terms.

Mr *Pearson* [counsel for the plaintiffs] admitted, and I think he could not well have avoided admitting, that if the vendors had merely referred to the property as being in the occupation of Mrs *Knowles* and Mr *Merrick* without more, there would have been at any rate such an amount of ambiguity that the Defendant might reasonably have understood that he was purchasing the whole of the property in their occupation. But the particulars go on to state that the property sold is Nos. 454 and 455 on the tithe map and contains twenty perches. The additional land which the Defendant claims to have included is about twenty perches more. Therefore, if he is right in his contention, he would be entitled to double the amount which the printed particulars state the lot to contain. There, no doubt, is force in the argument that a person unaccustomed to measuring would not know whether a property contained twenty perches or forty perches, but that does not get rid of the effect of the reference to the tithe map. The Defendant appears to have purchased in reliance upon his knowledge of the occupation of the premises with-out looking at the plans, and probably without paying any attention to the details of the particulars of Lot 1, but is a person justified in relying upon knowledge of that kind when he has the means of ascertaining what he buys? I think not. I think that he is not entitled to say to any effectual purpose that he was under a mistake, when he did not think it worth while to read the particulars and look at the plans. If that were to be allowed, a person might always escape from completing a contract by swearing that he was mistaken as to what he bought, and great temptation to perjury would be offered. Here the description of the property is accurate and free from ambiguity, and the case is wholly unaffected by *Manser* v. *Back* 6 Hare 443 and the other cases in which the Defendant has escaped from performance of a contract on the ground of its ambiguity.

Baggallay LJ therefore made a decree for specific performance. The defendant appealed to the Court of Appeal.

James LJ

In my opinion, the order under appeal is right. The vendors did nothing tending to mislead. In the particulars of sale they described the property as consisting of Nos. 454 and 455 on the tithe map, and this was quite correct. The purchaser says that the tithe map is on so small a scale as not to give sufficient information, but he never looked at it. He must be presumed to have looked at it, and at the particulars of sale. He says he knew the property, and was aware that the gardens were held with the other property in the occupation of the tenants, and he came to the conclusion that what was offered for sale was the whole of what was in the occupation of the tenants, but he asked no question about it. If a man will not take reasonable care to ascertain what he is buying, he must take the consequences. The defence on the ground of mistake cannot be sustained. It is not enough for a purchaser to swear, 'I thought the farm sold contained twelve fields which I knew, and I find it does not include them all', or, 'I thought it contained 100 acres and it only contains eighty'. It would open the door to fraud if such a defence was to be allowed. Perhaps some of the cases on this subject go too far, but for the most part the cases where a Defendant has escaped on the ground of a mistake not contributed to by the Plaintiff, have been cases where a hardship amounting to injustice would have been inflicted upon him by holding him to his bargain, and it was unreasonable to hold him to It. *Webster* v. *Cecil* 30 Benv 62 is a good instance of that, being a case where a person snapped at an offer which he must have perfectly well-known to be made by mistake, and the only fault I find with the case is that, in my opinion, the bill ought to have been dismissed with costs. It is said that it is hard to hold a man to a bargain entered into under a mistake, but we must consider the hardship on the other side. Here are trustees realizing their testator's estate, and the reckless conduct of the Defendant may have prevented their selling to somebody else. If a man makes a mistake of this kind without any reasonable excuse he ought to be held to his bargain.

Brett LJ and **Cotton LJ** delivered concurring judgments.

Scriven Brothers & Co v. Hindley & Co

[1913] 3 KB 564, King's Bench Division

The plaintiffs instructed an auctioneer to sell by auction a large quantity of Russian hemp and tow. The auctioneer prepared a catalogue which did not distinguish between the hemp and the tow. Further, both lots were given the same shipping mark, 'S.L.'. Lots

63–67 were the hemp and consisted of 47 bales and lots 68–79 were the tow and consisted of 176 bales. Prior to the sale, samples of hemp and tow were displayed in the show-rooms in Cutler Street. Opposite the samples of hemp was written in chalk 'S.L. 63 to 67' and opposite the samples of tow was written 'S.L. 68 to 79'. The defendants' manager, Mr Gill, inspected the hemp but not the tow (he was not interested in bidding for the tow). At the auction the defendants' buyer, Mr Macgregor, bid for the 47 bales of hemp and these were knocked down to him. Lots 68–79 were then put up for sale and the defendants' buyer bid £17 per ton for it (an extravagant price for tow). When the defendants discovered their mistake they refused to pay for the tow. The plaintiffs brought an action to recover the price of the tow. The defendants denied that they had agreed to buy the tow and claimed that the tow had been knocked down to them under a mistake of fact.

The jury made the following findings: '(1) That hemp and tow are different commodities in commerce. (2) That the auctioneer intended to sell 176 bales of tow. (3) That Macgregor intended to bid for 176 bales of hemp. (4) That the auctioneer believed that the bid was made under a mistake when he knocked down the lot. (5) That the auctioneer had reasonable ground for believing that the mistake was merely one as to value. (6) That the form of the catalogue and the conduct of Calman [the foreman in charge of the show], or one of them, contributed to cause the mistake that occurred. (7) That Mr Gill's "negligence" in not taking his catalogue to Cutler Street and more closely examining and identifying the bales with lots contributed to cause Macgregor's mistake.'

On this basis of these findings it was held that the plaintiffs were not entitled to recover the price of the tow from the defendants.

A. T. Lawrence J

In this case the plaintiffs brought an action for 476l. 12s. 7d., the price of 560 cwt. 2 qrs. 27 lbs. of Russian tow, as being due for goods bargained and sold. The defendants by their defence denied that they agreed to buy this Russian tow, and alleged that they bid for Russian hemp and that the tow was knocked down to them under a mistake of fact as to the subject-matter of the supposed contract. The circumstances were these.

[he stated the facts and the findings of the jury as set out above, and continued]

Upon these findings both plaintiffs and defendants claimed to be entitled to judgment. A number of cases were cited upon either side. I do not propose to examine them in detail because I think that the findings of the jury determine what my judgment should be in this case.

The jury have found that hemp and tow are different commodities in commerce. I should suppose that no one can doubt the correctness of this finding. The second and third findings of the jury shew that the parties were never ad idem as to the subject-matter of the proposed sale; there was therefore in fact no contract of bargain and sale. The plaintiffs can recover from the defendants only if they can shew that the defendants are estopped from relying upon what is now admittedly the truth. Mr Hume Williams for the plaintiffs argued very ingeniously that the defendants were estopped; for this he relied upon findings 5 and 7, and upon the fact that the defendants had failed to prove the allegation in paragraph 4 of the defence to the effect that Northcott knew at the time he knocked down the lot that Macgregor was bidding for hemp and not for tow.

I must, of course accept for the purposes of this judgment the findings of the jury, but I do not think they create any estoppel. Question No 7 was put to the jury as a supplementary question, after they had returned into Court with their answers to the other questions, upon the urgent insistence of the learned junior counsel for the plaintiffs. It begs an essential question by using the word 'negligence' and assuming that the purchaser has a duty towards the seller to examine goods that he does not wish to buy, and to correct any latent defect there may be in the sellers' catalogue. Once it was admitted that Russian hemp was never before known to be consigned or sold with the same shipping marks as Russian tow from the same cargo, it was natural for the person inspecting the 'S.L.' goods and being shewn hemp to suppose that the 'S. L.' bales represented the commodity hemp. Inasmuch as it is admitted that someone had perpetrated a swindle upon the bank which made advances in respect of this shipment of goods it was peculiarly the duty of the auctioneer to make it clear to the bidder either upon the face of his catalogue or in some other way which lots were hemp and which lots were tow.

To rely upon a purchaser's discovering chalk marks upon the floor of the show-room seems to me unreasonable as demanding an amount of care upon the part of the buyer which the vendor had no right to exact. A buyer when he examines a sample does so for his own benefit and not in the discharge of any duty to the seller; the use of the word 'negligence' in such a connection is entirely misplaced, it should be reserved for cases of want of due care where some duty is owed by one person to another. No evidence was tendered of the existence of any such duty upon the part of buyers of hemp. In so far as there was any evidence upon the point it was given by a buyer called as a witness for the plaintiffs who said he had marked the word 'tow' on his catalogue when at the show-rooms 'for his own protection.' I ought probably to have refused to leave the seventh question to the jury; but neither my complaisance nor their answer can create a duty. In my view it is clear that the finding of the jury upon the sixth question prevents the plaintiffs from being able to insist upon a contract by estoppel. Such a contract cannot arise when the person seeking to enforce it has by his own negligence or by that of those for whom he is responsible caused, or contributed to cause, the mistake.

I am therefore of opinion that judgment should be entered for the defendants.

COMMENTARY

In *Denny* and *Scriven* the seller's claim failed because the seller was at fault in creating the mistake in the mind of the buyer, whereas in *Tamplin* the fault was found to be that of the buyer, not the seller. In this sense *Denny* and *Scriven* belong together. But there is also a sense in which *Denny* and *Tamplin* belong together in that they both concern the remedy of specific performance, whereas in *Scriven* the seller's action was one to recover the price. Specific performance is a discretionary remedy (unlike a claim for damages or the action for the price) and so a court may refuse to grant a specific performance order notwithstanding the fact that a binding contract has been concluded between the parties.[3] This being the case, it does not necessarily follow from the refusal of the Court of Appeal in *Denny* to make a specific performance order that no contract had been concluded between the parties. Had the plaintiffs in *Denny* brought an action for damages then it would have been necessary for the court formally to decide whether or not a contract had been concluded at least on the terms

[3] Specific performance is discussed in more detail in Chapter 26 below.

alleged by the seller. *Scriven* takes matters a stage further in that there Lawrence J did decide that the plaintiffs were not entitled to recover the price of the goods so that it is clear that in that case there was no contract between the parties, at least on the terms alleged by the seller.

Are these cases examples of an objective approach or a subjective approach? Take *Scriven* as an example. Lawrence J uses language that is consistent with a subjective test and it could be argued that, objectively, the parties were in agreement because in the normal case an auctioneer is entitled to assume that a bidder knows what he is bidding for. It was the fact that the parties were not subjectively in agreement and that the plaintiffs were responsible for inducing a mistake in the mind of the defendants that led Lawrence J to dismiss the plaintiff's claim. On the other hand, it is possible to reach the same conclusion by virtue of the application of an objective test. Thus Dr Endicott has argued ('Objectivity, Subjectivity and Incomplete Agreements' in J Horder (ed), *Oxford Essays in Jurisprudence*, Fourth Series (Oxford University Press, 2000), p. 159) that:

to hold that the parties had not reached agreement for the sale of tow, the court did not need to ask what the buyer intended; a reasonable auctioneer who had induced the customer to believe that the lot was hemp would not take the customer to be bidding for tow. The duty that the court identified gave the auctioneer reason not to take the buyer to be bidding for tow, and bidding for a lot of tow in that context does not count as agreeing to buy tow. So on an objective test, there was no agreement for the sale of tow.

W Howarth considers *Denny, Tamplin*, and *Scriven* and states ((1984) 100 *LQR* 265, 270–271):

the conclusion to be abstracted from these three decisions must be that there is a body of judicial support for the principle that contract formation is to be viewed from the perspective of the promisor rather than any other viewpoint. If contract formation is to be objectively ascertained, the stance must be that of a reasonable man in the promisor's position rather than that of the actual promisor.

Vorster disagrees. He states ((1987) 103 *LQR* 274, 277) that Howarth's conclusion is 'misleading' on the basis that:

these three cases are not authority for 'promisor' objectivity in the conventional sense of that term. In all three cases there was disagreement about what exactly, if anything, had been bought and sold. There was, in other words, a dispute about the content of the seller's promise. As it was the seller's promise which had to be interpreted, the seller was the promisor for purposes of the dispute as to whether a binding contract had been concluded. In all three cases it was the seller who was attempting to enforce the buyer's obligation to pay the agreed price. In the terminology of Howarth this made the seller the *promisee*, whereas, according to conventional usage, the seller would be the *promisor* for purposes of the dispute.

In all three cases the court tried to determine what a reasonable man in the position of the buyer (i.e. the promisee) would have thought he was buying. These decisions are, therefore, quite unremarkable. They are wholly in accord with the main stream of authority in their period, as they are examples of 'promisee' objectivity in the conventional meaning of that term.

Once again we encounter our terminological problem. Vorster's view seems the preferable one in that all three cases are concerned to examine the buyer's understanding of the offer that was made and the role of the seller in producing that understanding. But what would have been the position in *Denny* or *Scriven* if the buyer had brought an action for breach of his own version of the contract? For example, in *Scriven* how would the reasonable person in the position of the seller have understood the buyer's offer to buy the lot? It is suggested that the reasonable person would have understood it as an offer to purchase the lot that was being advertised for sale. This being the case there was no contract between the parties as they were at cross-purposes as to the terms of the contract and so neither would be liable to the other in damages.

In conclusion it is suggested that Vorster accurately captures the approach of the courts when he states ((1987) 103 *LQR* 274, 283):

> The only practicable method of dealing with the formation of contracts, is to view the matter from the perspectives of each of the parties concerned. . . . The fact that the courts do not expressly adopt this method in cases dealing with mistake, is not necessarily due to judicial aversion to it. The majority of mistake cases have been pleaded in such a way as to make it unnecessary for the courts to expressly formulate a comprehensive approach to contract formation. In most cases the defendant who is sued for specific performance or damages for breach of an apparent contract, is content to deny liability; accordingly the question whether he is entitled to specific performance or damages for breach of *his version* of the contract does not arise. If the court finds that the plaintiff's understanding of the contract was unreasonable, the claim fails. The same is true if the court finds that the defendant's understanding of the contract was reasonable. These two findings make it unnecessary for the court to enquire into the reasonableness or otherwise of the other party's understanding. Where the court allows the claim for specific performance or damages because it accepts that the plaintiff's understanding of the contract was reasonable, it is at least implicit in this finding that the defendant's understanding was unreasonable. This has to be so, because if the differing understandings of the parties are both reasonable, there is no contract. Where the court allows the claim because it accepts that the defendant's understanding was unreasonable, it is also at least implicit in this finding that the plaintiff's version was reasonable.
>
> In cases where the defendant does not merely deny the plaintiff's claim, but counterclaims for specific performance of his version of the contract it will necessarily be more apparent that the court views the question from the perspectives of both parties.

6. FURTHER READING

ENDICOTT, T, 'Objectivity, Subjectivity and Incomplete Agreements' in HORDER, J (ed), *Oxford Essays in Jurisprudence*, 4th Series (Oxford University Press, 2000), p. 159.

FRIEDMANN, D, 'The Objective Principle and Mistake and Involuntariness in Contract and Restitution' (2003) 119 *LQR* 68.

HOWARTH, W, 'The Meaning of Objectivity in Contract' (1984) 100 *LQR* 265.

VORSTER, J, 'A Comment on the Meaning of Objectivity in Contract' (1987) 103 *LQR* 274.

3

OFFER AND ACCEPTANCE

1. CENTRAL ISSUES

1. When deciding whether or not a contract has been concluded the courts generally look for an offer made by one party that has been accepted by the other. Not every contract can be analyzed in terms of offer and acceptance and indeed the 'offer and acceptance' model has been criticized on the ground that it is too rigid and out of step with commercial practice. These criticisms will be considered in the course of this chapter.

2. An offer is a statement by one party of a willingness to enter into a contract on the terms that he has put forward. An offer is generally contrasted with an invitation to negotiate (or an 'invitation to treat') which is no more than an invitation to the other party to enter into negotiations on the terms proposed. The distinction between an offer and an invitation to negotiate has proved to be a difficult one to draw in certain circumstances, such as

advertisements, the display of goods for sale in shops, tenders, and auction sales. The problems experienced by the courts in these contexts are explored in this chapter.

3. An acceptance is a final and unqualified expression of assent to the terms of an offer. The question whether an offer has been accepted has generated a considerable amount of case-law and these are expressed in the form of a number of different rules that are set out in section 4 of this chapter. Some of these rules have given rise to considerable difficulty in practice, particularly in connection with the 'battle of the forms'.

4. An offer can be terminated by revocation, rejection by the person to whom the offer has been made, lapse of time, the occurrence of a stipulated event and, possibly, the death of one or other party to the contract.

2. INTRODUCTION

It is not always an easy task to decide whether or not a contract has been concluded between two (or more) parties. Uncertainty can exist at a number of different levels. In the first place, it may not be clear whether the parties have entered into a contract at all. For example, the parties may have been involved in protracted negotiations. These negotiations may have produced agreement on many points but there may remain some outstanding issues between the parties. Does the fact of these unresolved or disputed issues preclude the existence of a binding contract? Secondly, there may be uncertainty as to the precise point in time at which the contract was concluded between the parties. At what point in the negotiation process did the parties cross the line from negotiating parties to contracting parties? Or suppose that the parties have been corresponding through the post. At what point in time do postal negotiations result in the conclusion of a contract? Is it when the final letter, the letter of acceptance, is sent through the post or is it when that letter is actually received (and read?) by its recipient? Finally, there may be uncertainty as to the precise terms of the contract. The agreement between the parties may be expressed in terms that are very vague. Does such vagueness prevent the existence of a contract between the parties? Or what is to be done in the case where there is agreement between the parties on the principal issues but there is disagreement on some minor issues? Does such inconsistency mean that there cannot be a contract between the parties? Or does the court have the power to ignore the inconsistency and select the term that it believes is the most appropriate one to govern the relationship between the parties?

This uncertainty should not be over-emphasized. The vast majority of contracts do not give rise to such difficulties (or, if they do, they do not result in litigation). But when they do arise the law must seek to resolve them. In order to do so, the courts have devised a set of rules that they apply in order to determine whether or not the parties have, in fact, concluded a contract. The principal rules applied by the courts can be stated relatively shortly. A contract is created by an offer made by one party that has been accepted by the party to whom the offer was made. There are two vital ingredients of this definition. The first is the 'offer' and the second is the 'acceptance'. Both of these words require further elaboration. An offer can be defined as a statement, whether written or oral, of a willingness to be bound by the terms of the statement. Not every statement made in the course of the negotiation process amounts to an offer. The statement may be no more than a representation made by one party to the other that has induced that other to enter into the contract but which has not been incorporated into the contract itself. This issue will be discussed in more detail later (see Chapter 8 below). The issue that falls to be examined in this chapter is a different one, namely, whether or not the maker of the statement intended to be bound by the terms put forward in his statement (in which case it is an offer) or whether the statement simply reflects his current negotiating position but is not a final commitment to that position (in which case it is an invitation to negotiate or, as lawyers often call it, an 'invitation to treat'). The distinction is easily stated but can be difficult to apply in practice (see further pp. 60–90 below).

The word 'acceptance' also requires further elaboration. Not everything that purports to be an acceptance is, in fact, an acceptance in the eyes of the law. If the acceptance contains terms which differ from those contained in the offer, it is not treated by the courts as an acceptance but as a counter-offer. Thus, far from amounting to an acceptance of the offer, a counter-offer operates as a rejection of the terms contained in the original offer and is instead a fresh offer to be bound on the new terms put forward (see further pp. 91–110 below). These basic concepts of 'offer' and 'acceptance' have been refined by case-law and the courts have, over time, developed a number of rules in response to the facts of the cases that have come before them. Issues that have arisen before the courts include the following:

(i) when can an offer be revoked or withdrawn?

(ii) how do the rules of offer and acceptance apply to transactions concluded through the post?

(iii) can the silence of an offeree amount to an acceptance?

(iv) must an acceptance be communicated to the offeror?

(v) must the person to whom the offer is made comply precisely with the method of acceptance which has been prescribed by the offeror? and

(vi) can a party accept an offer by performing an act which would otherwise amount to an acceptance, when ignorant of the fact that an offer has been made?

These issues will be discussed in greater detail in the course of this chapter. Here it suffices to draw attention to a number of features of the rules that have been laid down by the courts over the years. The first is that the rules claim to be of general application. The second is that the rules purport to give effect to the intention of the parties, albeit their intention objectively ascertained. The third is that the rules in practice are often inter-linked. For example, the question whether or not an offer has been accepted may depend in a particular case on whether or not the offer was revoked before it was accepted; a court deciding such a case must decide both when the acceptance and the revocation took effect. Fourthly, the rules appear to attach considerable significance to the precise moment in time at which the contract was concluded. Finally, the reception of the offer and acceptance rules, as we know them today, is linked with the will theory of contract, a theory that has been the subject of some criticism, particularly in its application to unilateral contracts. Each of these features requires some further elaboration.

(a) GENERAL APPLICATION

The offer and acceptance rules purport to be of general application; that is to say, they are applicable to all contracts and not just to some. The supposed universality of these rules is, in itself, a source of difficulty. Contracts are made in many different ways and it is extremely difficult, if not impossible, to frame rules that can be applied across such a broad spectrum. Contracts can be made in writing or orally; they can be made by letter, fax, or e-mail; they may be the outcome of a period of negotiation or they may not; they may be made by an exchange of promises or they may be made by the conduct of the parties, without any words passing between them. Further, the contract between the parties may be bilateral or unilateral in nature. Most of the contracts discussed in this book are bilateral in nature, that is to say, the two parties to the contract promise to each other that they will carry out their respective obligations under the contract (in other words, they exchange promises). In a unilateral contract, on the other hand, only one party makes a promise to the other. The classic example of a unilateral contract is an offer to pay a reward to someone who finds and returns a piece of lost property. In this situation the promise is made by the party offering to pay the reward but there is no counter-promise made in return. Members of the public do not promise that they will look for and find the lost property. They accept the offer by doing the act stipulated in the offer (in this instance, finding and returning the lost piece of property). As we shall discover (in particular see pp. 68 and 127 below), the rules laid down by the courts require some modification in their application to unilateral contracts.

The attempt by the courts to analyse all contracts in terms of offer and acceptance has been the subject of some criticism. The leading judicial critic has been Lord Denning. In *Gibson* v. *Manchester City Council* [1978] 1 WLR 520, 523 (the facts of which are set out at p. 61 below) he stated:

To my mind it is a mistake to think that all contracts can be analysed into the form of offer and acceptance. I know in some of the textbooks it has been the custom to do so; but, as I understand the law, there is no need to look for a strict offer and acceptance. You should look at the correspondence as a whole and at the conduct of the parties and see therefrom whether the parties have come to an agreement on everything that was material. If by their correspondence and their conduct you can see an agreement on all material terms, which was intended thence-forward to be binding, then there is a binding contract in law even though all the formalities have not been gone through.[1]

This statement elicited the following response from Lord Diplock when *Gibson* was subsequently appealed to the House of Lords. Lord Diplock stated ([1979] 1 WLR 294, 297):

My Lords, there may be certain types of contract, though I think they are exceptional, which do not fit easily into the normal analysis of a contract as being constituted by offer and acceptance; but a contract alleged to have been made by an exchange of correspondence between the parties in which the successive communications other than the first are in reply to one another is not one of these. I can see no reason in the instant case for departing from the conventional approach of looking at the handful of documents relied on as constituting the contract sued on and seeing whether on their true construction there is to be found in them a contractual offer by the council to sell the house to Mr Gibson and an acceptance of that offer by Mr Gibson. I venture to think that it was by departing from this conventional approach that the majority of the Court of Appeal was led into error.

Lord Diplock's remark to the effect that cases can be found which cannot 'easily' be accommodated within the offer and acceptance framework echoes a statement made by Lord Wilberforce in *New Zealand Shipping Co Ltd* v. *A M Satterthwaite & Co Ltd* (*The Eurymedon*) [1975] AC 154. After noting that the relationship between the parties to the case was of a commercial character and that the description of one set of promises as gratuitous seemed 'paradoxical and . . . prima facie implausible', Lord Wilberforce concluded (at p. 167):

It is only the precise analysis of this complex of relations into the classical offer and acceptance, with identifiable consideration, that seems to present difficulty, but this same difficulty exists in many situations of daily life, e. g. sales at auction; supermarket purchases; boarding an omnibus; purchasing a train ticket; tenders for the supply of goods; offers of reward; acceptance by post; warranties of authority by agents; manufacturers' guarantees; gratuitous bailments; bankers' commercial credits. These are all examples which show that English law, having committed itself to a rather technical and schematic doctrine of contract, in application takes a practical approach, often at the cost of forcing the facts to fit uneasily into the marked slots of offer, acceptance and consideration.

---

[1] To similar effect see his judgment in *Butler Machine Tool Co Ltd* v. *Ex-Cell-O Corporation (England) Ltd* [1979] 1 WLR 401, set out at p. 92 below.

The classic example of a case that cannot be analysed in terms of offer and acceptance is *The Satanita* [1895] P 248 (CA), affirmed *sub nom Clarke* v. *Dunraven* [1897] AC 59 (HL). Both the plaintiff and the defendant entered their yachts in a regatta. In doing so they agreed to be bound by the sailing rules of the Yacht Racing Association. One of these rules provided that the owner of any 'yacht disobeying or infringing any of these rules . . . shall be liable for all damages arising therefrom'. In breach of one of the rules of the Yacht Racing Association the defendant's yacht ran into and sank the plaintiff's yacht. The collision occurred without fault on the part of the defendant. It was held that the parties had accepted a contractual obligation not to disobey the sailing rules with the result that the defendant was liable to the plaintiff for the loss suffered as a result of the breach and, further, that the effect of the agreement between the parties was to displace the limitation on liability which would otherwise have been applicable as a result of the application of a statutory provision. It is important to note that the issue in this case was not one between one of the competitors and the organizers of the competition. Rather, it was between two of the competitors and the question for the court was one that related to the terms of the contract concluded between the competitors. How was this contract formed? No clear answer can be given. Different views were expressed in the Court of Appeal. Lord Esher MR stated (at p. 255) that the competitors were bound when they began to sail and not before then. Lopes LJ concluded (at p. 261) that the contract arose 'directly any owner entered his yacht to sail'. Finally, Rigby LJ stated (at p. 262) that the contract was created when the parties 'actually came forward and became competitors'. The House of Lords did not devote much attention to the precise mechanism by which the contract was created. Only Lord Herschell considered the matter and he did so very briefly. He stated (at p. 63):

I cannot entertain any doubt that there was a contractual relation between the parties to this litigation. The effect of their entering for the race, and undertaking to be bound by these rules to the knowledge of each other, is sufficient, I think, where those rules indicate a liability on the part of the one to the other, to create a contractual obligation to discharge that liability.

The difficulty in using the tools of offer and acceptance to explain how the contract between the parties came into being has been expressed by Professor Sir Guenter Treitel (*The Law of Contract* (11th edn, Sweet & Maxwell, 2003), pp. 47–48) in the following terms:

It was held that there was a contract between all the competitors on the terms of the undertaking [to obey certain rules during the race], though it is not clear whether the contract was made when the competitors entered their yachts or when they actually began to race. In either event, it is difficult to analyse the transaction into offer and acceptance. If the contract was made when the yachts were entered, one would have to say that the entry of the first competitor was an offer and that the entry of the next was an acceptance of that offer and (simultaneously) an offer to yet later competitors; but this view is artificial and unworkable even in theory unless each competitor knew of the existence of previous ones. It would also lead to the conclusion that entries which were put in the post together were cross-offers and thus not binding on each other.[2] If the contract was

---

[2] The proposition that cross-offers do not suffice to create a contract was established in *Tinn* v. *Hoffmann & Co* (1873) 29 LT 271 below p. 129.

made when the race began, then it seems that each competitor simultaneously agreed to terms proposed by the officers of the club, and not that each proposed an identical set of terms amounting at the same time to an offer to the others and to an acceptance of the offers at that instant made by them. Even if the second view of the facts could be taken, the 'offers' and 'acceptances' would all occur at the same moment. Thus they would be cross-offers and would not create a contract. The competitors, no doubt, reached agreement, but they did not do so by a process which can be analysed into offer and acceptance.

What conclusion should we draw from the fact that it appears that not all contracts can be (easily) analysed in terms of offer and acceptance? We could decide either to abandon the offer and acceptance model in its entirety or we could recognize that, while offer and acceptance is the usual means by which a contract is created, it is not the only one. The first of these alternatives is a radical one. Nevertheless, it must be conceded that the offer and acceptance model has been the subject of some criticism. For example, Professor Collins states (*The Law of Contract* (4th edn, Butterworths, 2003), p. 159) that:

To decide when consent has been given by both parties to a contract, the authors of traditional textbooks devised an intricate set of rules employing the concepts of 'offer and acceptance' to fix the moment of responsibility. These rules typify the formalist qualities of classical law: they are detailed, technical, and mysterious, yet claim logical derivation from the idea of agreement.

As we shall see, the rules are at times detailed and technical and they are susceptible to criticism on the ground that they appear to be rather mechanical and divorced from commercial reality. In many ways, the difficulty lies in formulating an alternative to the rules that are currently applied by the courts. There have been calls for the adoption of a broader approach which focuses on the question of whether or not the parties have reached agreement (see, for example, the approach of Lord Denning in *Gibson* v. *Manchester City Council* (above)). The problem with the latter suggestion is that it tends to create uncertainty, in that it can often be very difficult to determine whether or not the parties have, in fact, reached agreement. There is a need for clear rules so that lawyers and their clients can know where they stand and do not have to resort to litigation in order to be able to ascertain their rights and liabilities. Thus there is a general reluctance to abandon the old rules in their entirety.

The more likely option is the second one, namely to recognize offer and acceptance as the principal but not the only route by which a contract can be created. This recognition can be either overt or covert. At the moment in England it is probably true to say that it is covert in that the courts continue to employ the offer and acceptance rule-book but, as Lord Wilberforce put it (above), sometimes force the facts to fit uneasily into the marked slots of offer and acceptance. An alternative approach is overt recognition of the fact that offer and acceptance are sufficient but not necessary ingredients of a valid contract. Thus Article 2.1.1 of the Unidroit Principles of International Commercial Contracts states that 'A contract may be concluded *either* by the acceptance of an offer *or by conduct of the parties that is sufficient to show agreement*' (emphasis added). The Principles of European Contract Law arrive at the same conclusion but by a slightly more elaborate route. Article 2:101 provides that:

A contract is concluded if:

(a) the parties intend to be legally bound, and

(b) they reach a sufficient agreement

without any further requirement.

Section 2 of Article 2 then sets out a number of rules relating to offer and acceptance and, in doing so, recognizes that offer and acceptance is the usual model for the creation of a contract. But section 2 concludes with the following provision (Article 2:211):

The rules in this Section apply with appropriate adaptations even though the process of conclusion of a contract cannot be analysed into offer and acceptance.

At first sight this provision seems rather unhelpful in that it does not tell us what constitutes an 'appropriate adaptation' of the rules otherwise applicable. But it is in fact very difficult to provide more concrete guidance, other than to state that the otherwise applicable rules should be applied by way of analogy to the facts of the case. English law can learn at least two important lessons from the provisions on formation of contracts to be found in the Unidroit Principles and the Principles of European Contract Law. The first is that neither rejects the offer and acceptance analysis. On the contrary, they both recognize that it is the usual mode of analysis but also accept the need for provision to be made for agreements that cannot be accommodated within the offer and acceptance framework. The second is that they both inject greater flexibility into the offer and acceptance rules themselves and also provide some tailor-made solutions to well-known and frequently-encountered problems in commercial practice (see, for example, the battle of the forms at pp. 103–104 below).

(b) THE INTENTION OF THE PARTIES

The courts frequently declare that they are seeking to give effect to the intention of the parties when applying the rules of offer and acceptance. It is, however, important to understand that the courts do not generally seek to ascertain the subjective intentions of the parties. It is their intention, objectively ascertained, that counts (on which see further p. 60 below). But there is a problem here and it arises from the fact that the parties may not have had any observable intention one way or the other. Take the case of a couple going into a restaurant for a meal. They look at the menu outside the restaurant and then decide to go in. When they go in a waiter gives them a copy of the menu and awaits their order. They each order their meals. Nothing is said about who is to pay for the meal. At the end of the meal the waiter presents a bill to one or other party and payment is made. At what point in time did a contract come into existence between the customers and the restaurant owner? Was it when the cus-tomers entered into the restaurant, when they ordered the food or when they paid for the meal? Further, how was the contract created? Who made the offer and who accepted it? What is the status of the menu (either outside or inside the restaurant)? Is it an offer or is it simply an invitation to negotiate (or, as it is more commonly put by lawyers, an invitation to 'treat')? Who has concluded the contract? Is the contract between the restaurant owner and the party who pays the bill, or are both customers party to a contract with the restaurant owner? Reference to the intention of the parties is unlikely to yield many answers to these questions. The average customer in a restaurant is unlikely to have given much thought to the precise process by which a contract is created. He or she intends to eat a meal and to pay for it but, beyond this, is unlikely to have any discernible intention as to the means by which or the time at which the contract is created. It falls to the courts to devise a presumptive rule that can then be applied to the facts of the case at hand. In this way uncertainty and inconsistency can be reduced, if not eliminated. In devising the presumptive rule the courts attempt to produce a rule which is workable and consistent with what they believe would have been the intention of the parties had they given the matter some thought. Oddly enough, there is in fact no authority on the contractual status of a menu displayed or handed to a customer in a restaurant. The consensus of academic opinion is that a menu amounts to an invitation to negotiate, not an offer.

(c) THE INTER-RELATED NATURE OF THE RULES

It is easy to get the impression that the courts apply the offer and acceptance rules in a rather mechanical fashion. The court first looks for an offer and, having found that, it then moves on to look for a matching acceptance. If it finds an acceptance then a contract is concluded; if not, no contract has been concluded. But it does not follow from this that the rules applicable to offers and those applicable to acceptances exist in splendid isolation. They are vitally inter-related. A simple example is provided by one of the rules relating to the revocability of an offer. As a general rule, an offer can be revoked at any time before it is accepted. Thus a court asked to determine whether an offer has been validly revoked must first decide whether or not the offer has been accepted. If the offer has been accepted then it cannot be revoked and there is a binding contract in existence between the parties. The readier the court is to find the existence of an acceptance, the less room there is likely to be for the withdrawal of an offer.

A number of cases in this chapter raise issues relating both to the existence of an offer and to the existence of an acceptance. One example is the decision of the Court of Appeal in *Carlill* v. *Carbolic Smoke Ball Company* [1893] 1 QB 256 (see p. 64 below) where the court was asked to decide, first, whether the defendant had made an offer to the plaintiff and, secondly, assuming that such an offer had been made, whether the plaintiff had validly accepted it. The extracts do not attempt to separate out the issues relating to the existence of an offer from those relating to the existence of an acceptance where they arise within a single case. They are treated together and this is done for the purpose of emphasizing the fact that the issues are inter-related in practice.

(d) THE TIME AT WHICH THE CONTRACT WAS CREATED

It has been argued that the rules of contract law, and in particular the offer and acceptance rules, attach undue significance to the precise moment in time at which the contract between the parties was concluded. They appear to posit a world in which parties suddenly transform themselves from negotiating parties into contracting parties. Thus Professor Macneil has argued ('Contracts: Adjustments of Long-Term Economic Relations under Classical, Neoclassical and Relational Contract Law' (1978) 72 *Northwestern Univ L Rev* 854, 864) that:

classical contract law draws clear lines between being in and not being in a transaction; e.g., rigorous and precise rules of offer and acceptance prevail with no half-way houses where only some contract interests are protected or where losses are shared.

This classical model may not fit with the practice of many commercial parties. Relationships evolve rather than suddenly spring into existence. Thus many contracts may not have a clearly defined beginning because the relationship between the parties gradually develops as the negotiation process unfolds. Equally, they may not have a clearly defined duration because the relationship between the parties will continue to evolve after the conclusion of the contract with the result that the contract itself will undergo a process of modification or adaptation. The offer and acceptance model, it is argued, does not capture the dynamic nature of the relationship between the parties. It presents a static model of contracts that attempts to attribute the rights and liabilities of the parties to one particular moment in time, namely the point in time at which the contract was concluded.

While the moment at which the contract is formed is undoubtedly of importance its significance should not be over-emphasized. It is important in the sense that it identifies the moment in time at which the parties became subject to the duty to perform the obligations as set out in their contract. But it does not follow from this that the parties did not owe each other duties while they remained negotiating parties. As we shall see (Chapter 17) the law does regulate the bargaining process and, while the duties owed by negotiating parties to each other are not as extensive as those owed by contracting parties, they cannot be dismissed as insignificant. Thus it is not as if the parties move suddenly from a world in which they owe each other no duties to one in which they owe each other full contractual duties. The law does reflect the different stages in the evolution of the relationship between the parties by imposing on the parties different obligations at the two principal stages in the evolution of their relationship (namely as negotiating parties and then as contracting parties). It is also important to realize that the contract agreed by the parties can have a substantial degree of flexibility built into it. It is not necessarily static. In the case of a long-term contract the parties are unlikely to be able to anticipate all the future events that are likely to impinge upon the performance of the various obligations contained in the contract. Contracting parties who anticipate that their relationship will endure for a long period of time are therefore likely to have to phrase their contractual obligations in rather vague, aspirational terms in order to enable them to deal with future but as yet unanticipated problems. Thus it is not necessarily the case that the parties must take all of their decisions at the moment of entry into the contract. They can build into the contract clauses that will enable them to adjust their relationship in order to reflect the altered circumstances that may later confront them.

(e) OFFER AND ACCEPTANCE AND THE 'WILL THEORY' OF CONTRACT

The offer and acceptance rules, as we know them today, are linked with the will theory of contract, particularly as that theory developed in the nineteenth century. The most influential exponents of the will theory were the French jurist Robert-Joseph Pothier and the German jurist Friedrich von Savigny. They attributed contractual liability to the agreement or the mutual assent of the parties. The introduction of this theory made a significant change to English contract law. Professor Simpson ('Innovation in Nineteenth Century Contract Law' (1975) 91 *LQR* 247, 257) has put the point in the following way:

the formation of a contract today is analysed in terms of offer and acceptance, an intention to create legal relations and the doctrine of consideration. If these requirements are satisfied there is a contract and (subject to various provisos) this gives rise to rights in the contracting parties for whose violation the law provides remedies in the form of actions for damages, injunctions and decrees of specific performance. Now way back in the sixteenth century when it all began the form of action for verbal or parol *agreements* (to use a neutral term) was an action for breach of promise, and the essentials involved were neatly stated In *Goldring's Case* (1856) by the then Solicitor General, Egerton: 'In every action upon the case upon a promise, there are three things considerable, consideration, promise and breach of promise'. You will notice the fact that between then and today we have moved from an essentially one-sided conception—a *promise* broken—to an essentially two-sided notion—a *contract* broken. [Emphasis in the original.]

This perception of a contract in bilateral terms, as a product of the meeting of the minds of the two parties, has not been without its critics. Thus Professor Ibbetson has stated (*A Historical Introduction to the Law of Obligations* (Oxford University Press, 1999), pp. 221–222) that:

the great merit of the Will Theory was that it had a measure of intellectual coherence that the traditional Common law wholly lacked, though this coherence had been to some extent bought at the expense of practical common sense. Its greatest demerit was that it was imposed on the Common law from the outside rather than generated from within. It embodied a model of contract law significantly different from the traditional English exchange model, and there was considerable friction between the two theories. The Common law did not—of course—simply discard elements that did not fit neatly into the theory but strained to squeeze them into it. The result was a mess . . .

 As an intellectual construct, the idea that contractual liability was based on the meeting of the parties' minds was reasonably satisfactory, but in practical terms it was rather more problematical. All too often it might occur that what appeared to be a perfect agreement concealed a more ragged mixture of things on which the parties agreed, things on which they disagreed, and things to which one or both of them had given no thought. This was early recognized by Joseph Chitty, who borrowed from Archdeacon Paley the theory of objective agreement, conveniently ignoring the fact that Paley's whole theory of liability was completely at odds with the Will Theory derived from Pothier. . . . The objective theory obviously sat ill with the theory that contractual liability stemmed from the meeting of the minds of the parties; the difficulty was explained away by treating it as a rule of evidence rather than a rule of substance, parties being estopped from denying that their words meant what they appeared to mean.

The adoption of the will theory posed, and continues to pose, particular challenges for unilateral contracts. Thus Professor Simpson has observed (above, at pp. 261–262) that:

so far as what are now called unilateral contracts are concerned we must note that this category only comes into the limelight when the notion of an action for breach of contract (in *some* sense a two-sided thing) prevails over the older idea of an action for breach of promise—a unilateral thing. When the paradigm becomes bilateral, the one-sided contract attracts notice and attention as anomalous. So it continues to be regarded, and it is easy to find examples of passages in works on contract which seem to deny the existence of contracts binding only one side. The analysis of such transactions in terms of offer and acceptance was first suggested by counsel in *Williams* v. *Carwardine* (1833), a case involving a promise of a reward. Such cases fitted easily into the older model—they were cases involving promises in consideration of an act not yet performed—called a future or executory consideration; the promise to the man who goes to York is first discussed in an assumpsit case in 1572. The application of the offer and acceptance analysis to such promises has never been happy; it only became canonical late in the nineteenth century in the celebrated case of *Carlill* v. *Carbolic Smoke Ball Co* (1892).

The five features of the rules discussed above will surface at various points in this chapter and you should bear them in mind when reading the rest of the chapter. It is now time to turn to a more detailed examination of the rules relating to offer and acceptance. We shall proceed in three stages. At the first stage (section 3) we shall consider whether or not an offer has been made, at the second stage (section 4) we shall discuss what constitutes an acceptance and at the final stage (section 5) we shall consider whether an offer has been validly withdrawn or terminated.

3. HAS AN OFFER BEEN MADE?

The first question that has to be answered when deciding whether or not a contract has been concluded is whether or not an offer was made. The existence or otherwise of an offer will depend upon the intention of the party alleged to have made the offer. Did he intend to be bound by the terms that he has proposed to the other party or not? If he did, then the statement is likely to be an offer. If he did not, then it is likely that he has not made an offer but simply expressed a willingness to negotiate on the terms proposed. The statement that the existence of an offer depends upon the intention of the party alleged to have made the offer must be qualified in two important respects.

The first is that the courts are not generally concerned to ascertain the subjective intention of the party alleged to have made the offer. A judge cannot establish what was actually taking place in the minds of the parties. Rather he will examine the intention of the party alleged to have made the offer, *as that intention appears to others*. In other words, the courts focus attention on the objective intention of the parties, not their subjective intention (on which see further Chapter 2 above).

Secondly, the party making the statement alleged to constitute the offer may not have had in mind the distinction between an offer and an expression of a willingness to negotiate when making his statement. In such a case the court must endeavour to ascertain, as best it can, the intention of the party who made the statement. In some cases this is a matter of examining the correspondence that has passed between the parties with a view to determining whether or not an offer has been made. In other cases, where the fact situation is one of everyday occurrence, such as the purchase of goods in a supermarket, the courts tend to lay down what might be termed a prima facie rule of law that they will apply when deciding whether or not an offer has been made. This is not to say that this prima facie rule is invariably applied: it can be displaced by evidence of contrary intent. The reason for the existence of these prima facie rules is probably the need for certainty in commercial transactions. Parties need to know where they stand and they would not be able to do so if the courts embarked upon a fresh inquiry into the intention of the parties in each case involving a purchase of goods from a supermarket. Much better to establish a prima facie rule so that parties can at least know the general rule that is applicable to their case and can plan accordingly (or, as the case may be, settle disputes that have occurred).

In terms of ascertaining whether or not an offer has been made it is perhaps best to separate out those cases in which the court is asked to examine the correspondence that has passed between the parties from the other cases. In the 'correspondence' cases the courts tend to have more evidence to work from and their task is to examine the correspondence that has passed between the parties with a view to determining whether or not a statement has been made that amounts to an offer. The outcome of such cases very much depends upon the facts of the individual case. Thus in *Harvey* v. *Facey* [1893] AC 552 the plaintiffs sent a telegraph to the defendant phrased as follows: 'will you sell us Bumper Hall Pen? Telegraph lowest cash price'. The defendant replied by telegraph stating: 'Lowest cash price for Bumper Hall Pen £900'. The plaintiffs in turn replied by telegraph in which they stated: 'we agree to buy Bumper Hall Pen for £900 asked for by you'. The defendant did not reply to this last telegraph. It was held that no contract had been concluded between the parties for the sale of Bumper Hall Pen. The first telegraph was a mere inquiry in which the plaintiffs simply sought to ascertain whether or not the defendant was willing to sell and, if so, at what price. The defendant's response was not an offer to sell the property but a precise answer to the question that had been asked of him. The mere statement of the lowest price at which he was prepared to sell did not constitute an implied offer to sell at that price to the person making the inquiry. The final telegraph sent by the plaintiffs was therefore an offer, not an acceptance, and, not having been accepted by the defendant, it could not give rise to a contract between the parties.

Another example of this process at work is provided by the decision of the House of Lords in *Gibson* v. *Manchester City Council* [1979] 1 WLR 294. The plaintiff, a council house tenant, alleged that he had entered into a contract with the defendant city council for the purchase of the house in which he lived. The defendant denied that a contract had been concluded for the sale of the house. There had been a number of communications between the parties. The defendant initially sent out a brochure to council house tenants who had previously expressed an interest in purchasing their homes. The brochures contained a detachable form, to be completed by the tenant, which asked the council to inform the tenant of the price at which the council was willing to sell the house and also asked the council to provide tenants with details

about mortgage facilities. The plaintiff completed the form and sent it to the defendant. The defendant replied to the plaintiff on 10 February 1971 in the following
terms:

I refer to your request for details of the cost of buying your Council house. The Corporation may be
prepared to sell the house to you at the purchase price of £2,275 less 20% = £2,180 (freehold).

The details which you requested about a Corporation mortgage are as follows:-

Maximum mortgage the Corporation may grant: £2,177 repayable over 20 years . . .

This letter should not be regarded as a firm offer of a mortgage.

If you would like to make formal application to buy your Council house, please complete the
enclosed application form and return it to me as soon as possible.

The letter was signed by the City Treasurer. The plaintiff completed the application
form and returned it. However he left the purchase price of the house blank. The
reason for this was that he wanted to know whether or not the council intended to
repair the tarmac paths in the vicinity of the house and, if not, he stated that he was
prepared to carry out the work himself provided that an appropriate deduction was
made from the purchase price. The council replied to the effect that the price quoted
took account of the present condition of the property and that they could not authorize the repair of the paths. The plaintiff replied to this in a letter in which he stated
that 'in view of your remarks I would be obliged if you will carry on with the purchase
as per my application already in your possession'. Before the council was able to reply
to the plaintiff's letter there was a change in the political composition of the council as
a result of local elections and the policy of selling council houses was promptly
stopped by the incoming Labour administration. The plaintiff alleged that the
defendant council was obliged to sell him the council house on the ground that a
contract had been concluded for the sale of the house before the policy of selling
council houses had been stopped. The defendant council denied that a contract had
been concluded. The plaintiff succeeded before the Court of Appeal but failed in the
House of Lords. The judges in the House of Lords undertook a careful examination of
the correspondence which had passed between the parties. Particular attention was
paid to the defendant's letter of 10 February. The plaintiff submitted that it was an
offer but this submission was rejected for two principal reasons. The first was that the
letter did not commit the council to the sale of the property. According to the second
sentence of the letter the position of the council was that it 'may' be prepared to sell.
This did not amount to a commitment to sell. The second was that the final sentence
of the letter invited the plaintiff to make a formal application. It did not invite him to
accept the offer contained in the letter. This being the case the council never offered
to sell the council house to the plaintiff, nor did it accept any offer made by him to
purchase the house. It therefore followed that no contract had been concluded
between the parties. It is possible to criticize the decision on the ground that it
focused unduly on a precise construction of the documentation that passed between
the parties and failed to pay sufficient attention to their conduct (in particular, the fact
that the plaintiff had done 'much work in repairing and improving his house and

premises' and the fact that the council had, at one point in time, taken the house off the list of houses being maintained by them and put it on the list of 'pending sales'). Lord Edmund-Davies did, however, address these points. He stated that it was impossible to conclude on the evidence that improvements had been carried out on the basis that the council had already committed itself to sell the property. He also stated that the plaintiff could not place any reliance on the fact that, unknown to him, the council had at one point taken the property off the list of houses for which it was responsible for maintenance and put it on the list of 'pending sales'.

In other cases the courts have evolved prima facie rules of law to be applied to certain standard types of transaction in order to determine whether or not there has been an offer or an invitation to negotiate. The cases that are discussed in the following sections illustrate four commonplace transactions, namely (a) advertisements, (b) displays of goods in shops, (c) auctions, and (d) tenders.

(a) ADVERTISEMENTS

The general rule applicable to advertisements is that, at least in the case of bilateral contracts, an advertisement constitutes an invitation to negotiate and not an offer. Thus, to take the standard example, suppose that a vendor of goods advertises them for sale in a local newspaper. The advertisement will generally be regarded as an invitation to negotiate and not an offer (see *Partridge* v. *Crittenden* [1968] 1 WLR 1204). The principal reason for this is said to be the need to protect the party placing the advertisement from incurring a liability in contract to every person who is willing to purchase the goods at the stipulated price. Thus in *Grainger & Son* v. *Gough (Surveyor of Taxes)* [1896] AC 325, 334 Lord Herschell considered the case of a price-list distributed by a merchant 'among persons likely to give orders' and concluded that:

[t]he transmission of such a price-list does not amount to an offer to supply an unlimited quantity of the wine described at the price named, so that as soon as an order is given there is a binding contract to supply that quantity. If it were so, the merchant might find himself involved in any number of contractual obligations to supply wine of a particular description which he would be quite unable to carry out, his stock of wine of that description being necessarily limited.

While there is obvious force in the point that there is a need to protect the vendor from potential multiple liability, this could have been done in another way. It did not demand that the advertisement be classified as an invitation to negotiate. It could have been done by treating the advertisement as an offer but then implying into that offer a term to the effect that the offer can only be accepted 'while stocks last'. One consequence of choosing to regard an advertisement as an invitation to negotiate rather than an offer is that the party who responds to the advertisement and is willing to purchase the goods at their advertised price cannot compel the advertiser to sell the goods to him at the stated price. He can only make an offer which the vendor can then choose either to accept or to reject. It has also had unfortunate consequences in the context of the criminal law. For example, in *Partridge* v. *Crittenden* (above) the defendant was charged with an offence of offering wild birds for sale contrary to the Protection of Birds Act 1954. The advertisement placed by the defendant stated 'Quality British A.B.C.R . . . Bramblefinch cocks, Bramblefinch hens, 25s each'. It was held that he had not committed the offence with which he was charged because he had not offered the birds for sale; the advertisement was simply an invitation to negotiate. Legislators who wish to catch those who advertise certain goods for sale must therefore extend the scope of the offence beyond those who 'offer' goods for sale (thus section 10 of the Consumer Protection Act 1987 extends the scope of the general safety requirement contained in that section to someone who 'exposes or possesses any such goods for supply' and does not confine it to someone who 'offers or agrees to supply any such goods').

The conclusion that an advertisement is an invitation to negotiate is not, however, an invariable one. Cases can be found in which the courts have concluded that an advertisement is an offer and not an invitation to negotiate. The leading case, to which we now turn, is an example of a unilateral contract and the inference that an advertisement is an offer rather than an invitation to negotiate will often be more readily drawn in the context of a unilateral contract.

Carlill v. Carbolic Smoke Ball Company

[1893] 1 QB 256, Court of Appeal

The defendants advertised their medicinal product, the now infamous 'carbolic smoke ball', in various newspapers in the following terms:

'100l. reward will be paid by the Carbolic Smoke Ball Company to any person who contracts the increasing epidemic influenza, colds, or any disease caused by taking cold, after having used the ball three times daily for two weeks according to the printed directions supplied with each ball. 1000l. is deposited with the Alliance Bank, Regent Street, shewing our sincerity in the matter.

During the last epidemic of influenza many thousand carbolic smoke balls were sold as preventives against this disease, and in no ascertained case was the disease contracted by those using the carbolic smoke ball.

One carbolic smoke ball will last a family several months, making it the cheapest remedy in the world at the price, 10s., post free. The ball can be refilled at a cost of 5s. Address, Carbolic Smoke Ball Company, 27, Princes Street, Hanover Square, London.'

The plaintiff, in reliance upon this advertisement, purchased and used the product as directed but subsequently caught influenza. She sued for payment of the £100 and succeeded before Hawkins J. The defendants appealed to the Court of Appeal but the appeal was dismissed. It was held that the terms of the advertisement constituted an offer, the terms of which were accepted by the plaintiff with the result that she was entitled to recover the promised £100.

Bowen LJ
. . . We were asked to say that this document was a contract too vague to be enforced.

The first observation which arises is that the document itself is not a contract at all, it is only an offer made to the public. The defendants contend next, that it is an offer the terms of which are too vague to be treated as a definite offer, inasmuch as there is no limit of time fixed for the catching of the influenza, and it cannot be supposed that the advertisers seriously meant to promise to pay money to every person who catches the influenza at any time after the inhaling of the smoke ball. It was urged also, that if you look at this document you will find much vagueness as to the persons with whom the contract was intended to be made—that, in the first place, its terms are wide enough to include persons who may have used the smoke ball before the advertisement was issued; at all events, that it is an offer to the world in general, and, also, that it is unreasonable to suppose it to be a definite offer, because nobody in their senses would contract them-selves out of the opportunity of checking the experiment which was going to be made at their own expense. It is also contended that the advertisement is rather in the nature of a puff or a proclamation than a promise or offer intended to mature into a contract when accepted. But the main point seems to be that the vagueness of the document shews that no contract whatever was intended. It seems to me that in order to arrive at a right conclusion we must read this advertisement in its plain meaning, as the public would understand it. It was intended to be issued to the public and to be read by the public. How would an ordinary person reading this document construe it? It was intended unquestionably to have some effect, and I think the effect which it was intended to have, was to make people use the smoke ball, because the suggestions and allegations which it contains are directed immediately to the use of the smoke ball as distinct from the purchase of it. It did not follow that the smoke ball was to be purchased from the defendants directly, or even from agents of theirs directly. The intention was that the circulation of the smoke ball should be promoted, and that the use of it should be increased. The advertisement begins by saying that a reward will be paid by the Car-bolic Smoke Ball Company to any person who contracts the increasing epidemic after using the ball. It has been said that the words do not apply only to persons who contract the epidemic after the publication of the advertisement, but include persons who had previously contracted the influenza. I cannot so read the advertisement. It is written in colloquial and popular language, and I think that it is equivalent to this: '100l. will be paid to any person who shall contract the increasing epidemic after having used the carbolic smoke ball three times daily for two weeks'. And it seems to me that the way in which the public would read it would be this, that if anybody, after the advertisement was published, used three times daily for two weeks the carbolic smoke ball, and then caught cold, he would be entitled to the reward. Then again it was said: 'How long is this protection to endure? Is it to go on for ever, or for what limit of time?' I think that there are two constructions of this document, each of which is good sense, and each of which seems to me to satisfy the exigencies of the present action. It may mean that the protection is warranted to last during the epidemic, and it was during the epidemic that the plaintiff contracted the disease. I think, more prob-ably, it means that the smoke ball will be a protection while it is in use. That seems to me the way in which an ordinary person would understand an advertisement about medicine, and about a specific against influenza. It could not be supposed that after you have left off using it you are still to be protected for ever, as if there was to be a stamp set upon your forehead that you were never to catch influenza because you had once used the carbolic smoke ball. I think the immunity is to last during the use of the ball. That is the way in which I should naturally read it, and it seems to me that the subsequent language of the advertisement supports that construction. It says: 'During the last epidemic of influenza many thousand carbolic smoke balls were sold, and in no ascertained case was the disease contracted by those using' (not 'who had used') 'the carbolic smoke ball', and it concludes with saying that one smoke ball will last a family several months (which imports that it is to be efficacious while it is being used), and that the ball can be refilled at a cost of 5s. I, therefore, have myself no hesitation in saying that I think, on the construction of this advertisement, the protection was to enure during the time that the carbolic smoke ball was being used. My brother, [Lord Justice Lindley], thinks that the contract would be sufficiently definite if you were to read it in the sense that the protection was to be warranted during a reasonable period after use. I have some difficulty myself on that point; but it is not necessary for me to consider it further, because the disease here was contracted during the use of the carbolic smoke ball.

Was it intended that the 100l. should, if the conditions were fulfilled, be paid? The advertisement says that 1000l. is lodged at the bank for the purpose. Therefore, it cannot be said that the statement that 100l. would be paid was intended to be a mere puff. I think it was intended to be understood by the public as an offer which was to be acted upon.

But it was said there was no check on the part of the persons who issued the advertisement, and that it would be an insensate thing to promise 100l. to a person who used the smoke ball unless you could check or superintend his manner of using it. The answer to that argument seems to me to be that if a person chooses to make extravagant promises of this kind he probably does so because it pays him to make them, and, if he has made them, the extravagance of the promises is no reason in law why he should not be bound by them.

It was also said that the contract is made with all the world—that is, with everybody; and that you cannot contract with everybody. It is not a contract made with all the world. There is the fallacy of the argument. It is an offer made to all the world; and why should not an offer be made to all the world which is to ripen into a contract with anybody who comes forward and performs the condition? It is an offer to become liable to any one who, before it is retracted, performs the condition, and, although the offer is made to the world, the contract is made with that limited portion of the public who come forward and perform the condition on the faith of the advertisement. It is not like cases in which you offer to negotiate, or you issue advertisements that you have got a stock of books to sell, or houses to let, in which case there is no offer to be bound by any contract. Such advertisements are offers to negotiate—offers to receive offers—offers to chaffer, as, I think, some learned judge in one of the cases has said. If this is an offer to be bound, then it is a contract the moment the person fulfils the condition . . .

Then it was said that there was no notification of the acceptance of the contract. One cannot doubt that, as an ordinary rule of law, an acceptance of an offer made ought to be notified to the person who makes the offer, in order that the two minds may come together. Unless this is done the two minds may be apart, and there is not that consensus which is necessary according to the English law—I say nothing about the laws of other countries—to make a contract. But there is this clear gloss to be made upon that doctrine, that as notification of acceptance is required for the benefit of the person who makes the offer, the person who makes the offer may dispense with notice to himself if he thinks it desirable to do so, and I suppose there can be no doubt that where a person in an offer made by him to another person, expressly or impliedly intimates a particular mode of acceptance as sufficient to make the bargain binding, it is only necessary for the other person to whom such offer is made to follow the indicated method of acceptance; and if the person making the offer, expressly or impliedly intimates in his offer that it will be sufficient to act on the proposal without communicating acceptance of it to himself, performance of the condition is a sufficient acceptance without notification.

That seems to me to be the principle which lies at the bottom of the acceptance cases, of which two instances are the well-known judgment of Mellish, LJ, in *Harris' Case* (1872) LR 7 Ch App 587, and the very instructive judgment of Lord Blackburn in *Brogden* v. *Metropolitan Ry Co* (1876) 2 App Cas 666, 691, in which he appears to me to take exactly the line I have indicated.

Now, if that is the law, how are we to find out whether the person who makes the offer does intimate that notification of acceptance will not be necessary in order to constitute a binding bargain? In many cases you look to the offer itself. In many cases you extract from the character of the transaction that notification is not required, and in the advertisement cases it seems to me to follow as an inference to be drawn from the transaction itself that a person is not to notify his acceptance of the offer before he performs the condition, but that if he performs the condition notification is dispensed with. It seems to me that from the point of view of common sense no other idea could be entertained. If I advertise to the world that my dog is lost, and that anybody who brings the dog to a particular place will be paid some money, are all the police or other persons whose business it is to find lost dogs to be expected to sit down and write me a note saying that they have accepted my proposal? Why, of course, they at once look after the dog, and as soon as they find the dog they have performed the condition. The essence of the transaction is that the dog should be found, and it is not necessary under such circumstances, as it seems to me, that in order to make the contract binding there should be any notification of acceptance. It follows from the nature of the thing that the performance of the condition is sufficient acceptance without the notification of it, and a person who makes an offer in an advertisement of that kind makes an offer which must be read by the light of that common sense reflection. He does, therefore, in his offer impliedly indicate that he does not require notification of the acceptance of the offer.

Lindley and **A.L. Smith LJJ** delivered concurring judgments.

COMMENTARY

It should be noted that a number of legal issues arose on the facts of *Carlill*, not all of which were concerned with the question whether or not the advertisement constituted an offer. This is not surprising. Most litigation generates more than one point of law. A number of distinct issues of law were raised by the facts of *Carlill*. These issues are: (i) did the defendants intend to be bound by the terms stated in their advertisement? (ii) did Mrs Carlill validly accept the offer contained in the advertisement? (iii) did Mrs Carlill provide any consideration for the promise contained in the offer? One of the arguments advanced by the defendants in support of their submission that the advertisement did not constitute an offer was that it was too vague to be enforceable. This argument was rejected on the facts. But what would have been the position if Mrs Carlill had caught influenza some six months after using the smoke balls? Would the defendants have been liable to pay the £100? Lindley LJ concluded (at p. 264) that the reward was offered to 'any person who contracts the epidemic or other disease within a reasonable time after having used the smoke ball', while A. L. Smith LJ stated (at p. 274) that he found it unnecessary to resolve this point. What was the opinion of Bowen LJ on this particular issue?

As Professor Simpson has noted ('Quackery and Contract Law: *Carlill* v. *Carbolic Smoke Ball Company*' in *Leading Cases in the Common Law* (Oxford University Press, 1995) p. 259), *Carlill* has achieved the status of a leading case. He attributes this status in part to 'the comic and slightly mysterious object involved'. This is undoubtedly true. Professor Simpson locates the case in the context of the great influenza epidemic of the 1890s and the 'seedy world of the late nineteenth-century vendors of patent medical appliances'. Thus he records (at p. 274) the verdict of the *Lancet* to the decision of the court at first instance:

To those amongst our readers who are familiar with the way of the quack medicine vendor the facts proved the other day by Mrs Carlill in the action she has brought against the Carbolic Smoke Ball Company will occasion no surprise. . . . We are glad to learn that in spite of the ingenuity of their legal advisers the defendants have been held liable to make good their promise.

These factors no doubt played their part in persuading the court to find for Mrs Carlill. However Professor Simpson is careful to point out that the interest in the case does not lie solely in its rather bizarre facts. He adds (at p. 281) that there:

were two reasons of a legal character that suggest that it deserves its place in the firmament. The first, which is not always fully appreciated, is historical; it was the vehicle whereby a new legal doctrine was introduced into the law of contract. The second is that the decision could be used by expositors of the law of contract to illustrate the arcane mysteries surrounding the conception of a unilateral or one-sided contract.

In making the claim that *Carlill* introduced a 'new legal doctrine' into the law of contract, Professor Simpson asserts that the case 'clearly recognized the requirement of an intention to create legal relations'. As we shall see (p. 295 below), the case which is generally cited as authority for the existence of the doctrine of intention to create legal relations is the later case of *Balfour* v. *Balfour* [1919] 2 KB 571. However Professor Simpson points out that counsel for the defendants in *Carlill* submitted that 'the defendants did not by issuing [the advertisement] mean to impose upon themselves any obligations enforceable by law'. Bowen LJ rejected this submission (as did the other judges) on the ground that the advertisement was not a 'mere puff' but was 'intended to be understood by the public as an offer which was to be acted upon'. Professor Simpson then concludes (at p. 282) that 'the fact that the judges found it necessary to make this point entailed their acceptance of the idea that, without an intention to create legal relations, there could be no actionable contract'. This point is perhaps debatable but it is now an academic one given that English contract law clearly recognizes the existence of such a doctrine. But there does appear to be a link between *Carlill* and the doctrine of intention to create legal relations. This can be seen from the more recent case of *Bowerman* v. *Association of British Travel Agents Ltd* [1996] CLC 451. The plaintiffs booked a holiday with a tour operator who was a member of the defendant travel association. After the plaintiffs booked the holiday but before it began, the tour operator became insolvent. A notice displayed in the premises of the tour operator stated:

Where holidays or other travel arrangements have not yet commenced at the time of failure [of the tour operator], ABTA arranges for you to be reimbursed the money you have paid in respect of your holiday arrangements.

The issue before the Court of Appeal was whether or not this notice sufficed to create a direct contractual relationship between the defendant association and the plaintiffs. By a majority, the Court of Appeal concluded that it did. Hobhouse LJ noted (at p. 459) that the arguments of the defendants echoed 'in almost every respect those rejected by the Court of Appeal more than a century ago' in *Carlill* and he concluded that the defendants' arguments in the present case had no greater validity than those advanced in *Carlill*. Further, Waite LJ stated (at p. 457) that 'the central issue in this appeal is whether the ordinary member of the public, reading the notice as a whole, would regard it as intended to create legal relations between ABTA and those who buy tours or holidays through its members'. Thus there is undoubtedly a link between *Carlill* and the doctrine of intention to create legal relations, although it is probably fair to say that the recognition of the doctrine is implicit in the judgments in *Carlill* rather than explicit.

Professor Simpson is perhaps on safer ground with his second claim, namely that *Carlill* illustrates the 'mysteries surrounding the conception of a unilateral or one-sided contract'. Thus he argues (at pp. 282–283) that:

most contracts that concern the courts involve two-sided agreements, two-sided in the sense that the parties enter into reciprocal obligations to each other. A typical example is a sale of goods, where the seller has to deliver the goods and the buyer to pay for them. The doctrines of nineteenth-century contract law were adapted to such bilateral contracts, but the law also somewhat uneasily recognized that there could be contracts in which only one party was ever under any obligation to the other. The standard example was a published promise to pay a reward for information on the recovery of lost property: £10 to anyone who finds and returns my dog. In such a case obviously nobody has to search for the dog, but if they do so successfully, they are entitled to the reward. Such contracts seem odd in another way; there is a promise, but no agreement for the parties never even meet until the reward is claimed. Classified as 'unilateral' contracts, such arrangements presented special problems of analysis to contract theorists, whose standard doctrines had not been evolved to fit them. Thus it was by 1892 orthodox to say that all contracts were formed by the exchange of an offer and an acceptance, but it was by no means easy to see how this could be true of unilateral contracts, where there was, to the eyes of common sense, no acceptance needed.

The analytical problems arose in a particularly acute form in the smoke ball case. Thus it seemed very peculiar to say there had been any sort of agreement between Mrs Carlill and the company, which did not even know of her existence until . . . her husband wrote to them to complain. There were, indeed, earlier cases permitting the recovery of advertised rewards; the leading case here was *Williams* v. *Carwardine*, where a reward of £20 had been promised by handbill for information leading to the conviction of the murderer of Walter Carwardine, and Williams, who gave such information, successfully sued to recover the reward. But this was long before the doctrines which made unilateral contracts problematic had become established, and in any event the case was distinguishable. It concerned a reward, whereas Mrs Carlill was seeking compensation. Furthermore, the Carbolic Smoke Ball Company had no chance of checking the validity of claims, of which there could be an indefinite number; much was made of this point in argument. But the judges were not impressed; their attitude was no doubt influenced by the view that the defendants were rogues. They fitted their decision into the structure of the law by boldly declaring that the performance of the condition—using the ball and getting ill—was the acceptance, thus fictitiously extending the concept of acceptance to cover the facts. And, since 1893, law students have been introduced to the mysteries of the unilateral contract through the vehicle of *Carlill* v. *Carbolic Smoke Ball Company* and taught to repeat, as a sort of magical incantation of contract law, that in the case of unilateral contracts performance of the act specified in the offer constitutes acceptance, and need not be communicated to the offeror.

In relation to the existence of a valid acceptance, two principal problems arose on the facts of *Carlill*. The first related to the identification of the acceptance. How and when did Mrs Carlill accept the offer contained in the advertisement? Did she accept the offer when she purchased the smoke ball, when she used it for the first time, or only when she completed the course? Bowen LJ appeared to take the latter view. This issue is important not only in relation to the existence of an offer, but also for the ability of the defendants to revoke the offer contained in their advertisement. As we shall see (p. 130 below), the general rule is that an offer cannot be revoked once it has been accepted. But if acceptance does not take place until the completion of the course then the defendants may be entitled to revoke the offer even in the case where the purchaser has begun to use the smoke ball. The second problem concerned the communication of the acceptance. As we shall see (p. 110 below) the general rule is that an acceptance, to be valid, must be communicated to the party who made the offer. This rule was held not to be applicable to Mrs Carlill because the terms of the offer demonstrated that the need for communication had been waived by the defendants.

Finally, it should be noted that the defendants argued that there was no consideration for their promise (the doctrine of consideration is discussed in more detail in Chapter 5). In essence the doctrine of consideration requires the existence of a bargain between the parties. In other words, both parties must have contributed something towards the agreement. The Court of Appeal held that there was consideration on two grounds. The first was the benefit that the defendants gained as a result of the use of the smoke ball in response to the advertisements and the sales produced thereby. The second was that the use by Mrs Carlill of the smoke ball three times daily for two weeks constituted a detriment so that she had provided consideration for the defendants' promise.

(b) DISPLAYS OF GOODS FOR SALE IN A SHOP

The general rule in relation to the display of goods for sale in a shop is that the display constitutes an invitation to negotiate and not an offer. The leading case is:

Pharmaceutical Society of Great Britain v. Boots Cash Chemists (Southern) Ltd

[1953] 1 QB 401, Court of Appeal

Section 18(1) of the Pharmacy and Poisons Act, 1933 provided that:

> 'it shall not be lawful—(a) for a person to sell any poison included in Part I of the Poisons List, unless—(i) he is an authorized seller of poisons; and (ii) the sale is effected on premises duly registered under Part I of this Act; and (iii) the sale is effected by, or under the supervision of, a registered pharmacist.'

The plaintiffs brought an action against the defendants in which they alleged that the defendants had infringed section 18(1)(a)(iii) of the Act on the basis that the sale of poisons in the defendants' self-service store was not effected by, nor did it take place under the supervision of, a registered pharmacist. The pharmacist was not present at the cash desk. He was stationed close to the poisons section and in view of the cash desks and he was authorised by the defendants to prevent the sale of any drug (although customers were not aware of the fact that he was so authorised). On 13 April 1951 two customers purchased medicines which fell within the scope of the Act and the issue for the court was whether or not these sales were effected by or under the supervision of a registered pharmacist. The Court of Appeal, affirming the decision of Lord Chief Justice Goddard, concluded that they had been so effected.

Somervell LJ

This is an appeal from a decision of the Lord Chief Justice on an agreed statement of facts, raising a question under section 18(1)(a)(iii) of the Pharmacy and Poisons Act, 1933. The plaintiffs are the Pharmaceutical Society, incorporated by Royal charter. One of their duties is to take all reasonable steps to enforce the provisions of the Act. The provision in question is contained in section 18. [His Lordship read the section and stated the facts, and continued] It is not disputed that in a chemist's shop where this self-service system does not prevail a customer may go in and ask a young woman assistant, who will not herself be a registered pharmacist, for one of these articles on the list, and the transaction may be completed and the article paid for, although the registered pharmacist, who will no doubt be on the premises, will not know anything himself of the transaction, unless the assistant serving the customer, or the customer, requires to put a question to him. It is right that I should emphasize, as did the Lord Chief Justice, that these are not dangerous drugs. They are substances which contain very small proportions of poison, and I imagine that many of them are the type of drug which has a warning as to what doses are to be taken. They are drugs which can be obtained, under the law, without a doctor's prescription.

The point taken by the plaintiffs is this: it is said that the purchase is complete if and when a customer going round the shelves takes an article and puts it in the receptacle which he or she is carrying, and that therefore, if that is right, when the customer comes to the pay desk, having completed the tour of the premises, the registered pharmacist, if so minded, has no power to say: 'This drug ought not to be sold to this customer'. Whether and in what circumstances he would have that power we need not inquire, but one can, of course, see that there is a difference if supervision can only be exercised at a time when the contract is completed.

I agree with the Lord Chief Justice in everything that he said, but I will put the matter shortly in my own words. Whether the view contended for by the plaintiffs is a right view depends on what are the legal implications of this layout—the invitation to the customer. Is a contract to be regarded as being completed when the article is put into the receptacle, or is this to be regarded as a more organized way of doing what is done already in many types of shops—and a bookseller is perhaps the best example—namely, enabling customers to have free access to what is in the shop, to look at the different articles, and then, ultimately, having got the ones which they wish to buy, to come up to the assistant saying 'I want this'? The assistant in 999 times out of 1,000 says 'That is all right', and the money passes and the transaction is completed. I agree with what the Lord Chief Justice has said, and with the reasons which he has given for his conclusion, that in the case of an ordinary shop, although goods are displayed and it is intended that customers should go and choose what they want, the contract is not completed until, the customer having indicated the articles which he needs, the shopkeeper, or someone on his behalf, accepts that offer. Then the contract is completed. I can see no reason at all, that being clearly the normal position, for drawing any different implication as a result of this layout.

The Lord Chief Justice, I think, expressed one of the most formidable difficulties in the way of the plaintiffs' contention when he pointed out that, if the plaintiffs are right, once an article has been placed in the receptacle the customer himself is bound and would have no right, without paying for the first article, to substitute an article which he saw later of a similar kind and which he perhaps preferred. I can see no reason for implying from this self-service arrangement any implication other than that which the Lord Chief Justice found in it, namely, that it is a convenient method of enabling customers to see what there is and choose, and possibly put back and substitute, articles which they wish to have, and then to go up to the cashier and offer to buy what they have so far chosen. On that conclusion the case fails, because it is admitted that there was supervision in the sense required by the Act and at the appropriate moment of time. For these reasons, in my opinion, the appeal should be dismissed.

Birkett and **Romer LJJ** delivered concurring judgments.

COMMENTARY

It should be noted that the claim was not one between a purchaser of goods in a shop and the shop itself. Rather, it was an action between the plaintiffs, the professional association of pharmacists, and the defendant pharmacists and the context was one of an allegation of unlawful conduct by the defendants. Thus the claim made by the plaintiffs was not one of breach of contract but that the defendants had acted in contravention of a duty imposed on them by statute.

In terms of the outcome of the case, the important factor was the place at which the contract was concluded, rather than the precise way in which the contract was concluded. It sufficed for the court to decide that the contract was concluded at the cash-desk and thus under the supervision of the pharmacist. The court could have concluded that the offer was made by the shop in displaying the goods for sale at fixed prices but that the offer was not accepted by the customer until the goods were taken to the cash-desk. In such a case the contract would still have been concluded under the supervision of the pharmacist. But this was not the reasoning that the court chose to employ. It treated the display as an invitation to negotiate and stated that the offer was made by the customer which the defendants could then decide whether to accept or reject. The fullest analysis of the process by which the contract was formed was provided by Lord Goddard CJ at first instance when he said ([1952] 2 All ER 456, 458):

It is a well-established principle that the mere fact that a shop-keeper exposes goods which indicate to the public that he is willing to treat does not amount to an offer to sell. I do not think that I ought to hold that there has been here a complete reversal of that principle merely because a self-service scheme is in operation. In my opinion, what was done here came to no more than that the customer was informed that he could pick up an article and bring it to the shop-keeper, the contract for sale being completed if the shop-keeper accepted the customer's offer to buy. The offer is an offer to buy, not an offer to sell. The fact that the supervising pharmacist is at the place where the money has to be paid is an indication that the purchaser may or may not be informed that the shop-keeper is willing to complete the contract. One has to apply common sense and the ordinary principles of commerce in this matter. If one were to hold that in the case of self-service shops the contract was complete directly the purchaser picked up the article, serious consequences might result. The property would pass to him at once and he would be able to insist on the shop-keeper allowing him to take it away, even where the shop-keeper might think it very undesirable. On the other hand, once a person had picked up an article, he would never be able to put it back and say that he had changed his mind. The shop-keeper could say that the property had passed and he must buy.

It seems to me, therefore, that it makes no difference that a shop is a self-service shop and that the transaction is not different from the normal transaction in a shop. The shop-keeper is not making an offer to sell every article in the shop to any person who may come in, and such person cannot insist on buying by saying; 'I accept your offer'. Books are displayed in a bookshop and customers are invited to pick them up and look at them even if they do not actually buy them. There is no offer of the shop-keeper to sell before the customer has taken the book to the shop-keeper or his assistant and said that he wants to buy it and the shop-keeper has said: 'Yes'. That would not prevent the shop-keeper, seeing the book picked up from saying: 'I am sorry I cannot let you have that book. It is the only copy I have got, and I have already promised it to another customer.' Therefore, in my opinion, the mere fact that a customer picks up a bottle of medicine from a shelf does not amount to an acceptance of an offer to sell, but is an offer by the customer to buy. I feel bound also to say that the sale here was made under the supervision of a pharmacist. There was no sale until the buyer's offer to buy was accepted by the acceptance of the purchase price, and that took place under the supervision of a pharmacist.

In *Fisher* v. *Bell* [1961] 1 QB 394 the defendant was charged with the offence of offering for sale a flick knife, contrary to section 1(1) of the Restriction of Offensive Weapons Act 1959. He had displayed the knife in his shop window with a price ticket behind it which stated 'Ejector knife—4s'. It was held that the defendant had not committed the offence with which he was charged because, in displaying the knife in his shop window, he had not offered it for sale. Lord Parker CJ stated (at p. 400) that he found it 'quite impossible to say that an exhibition of goods in a shop window is itself an offer for sale'.

But it does not follow from these cases that a display of goods in a shop will never be held to amount to an offer. There are cases in which the courts have held that a display of goods, or an advertisement to the effect that goods will be sold at a particular price, constitutes an offer. One such case is the decision of the Supreme

Court of Minnesota in *Lefkowitz* v. *Great Minneapolis Surplus Stores Inc*, 86 NW2d 689 (1957). The judgment of the court was given by Murphy J:

Murphy J
This case grows out of the alleged refusal of the defendant to sell to the plaintiff a certain fur piece which it had offered for sale in a newspaper advertisement. It appears from the record that on April 6, 1956, the defendant published the following advertisement in a Minneapolis newspaper:

'Saturday 9 a.m. sharp
3 Brand New
Fur
Coats
Worth to $ 100.00
First Come
First Served
$ 1
Each'

On April 13, the defendant again published an advertisement in the same newspaper as follows:

'Saturday 9 a.m.
2 Brand New Pastel
Mink 3-Skin Scarfs
Selling for $ 89.50
Out they go
Saturday. Each . . . $ 1.00
1 Black Lapin Stole
Beautiful,
worth $ 139.50. . . . $ 1.00
First Come
First Served'

The record supports the findings of the court that on each of the Saturdays following the publication of the above-described ads the plaintiff was the first to present himself at the appropriate counter in the defendant's store and on each occasion demanded the coat and the stole so advertised and indicated his readiness to pay the sale price of $1. On both occasions, the defendant refused to sell the merchandise to the plaintiff, stating on the first occasion that by a 'house rule' the offer was intended for women only and sales would not be made to men, and on the second visit that plaintiff knew defendant's house rules.

The trial court properly disallowed the plaintiff's claim for the value of the fur coats since the value of these articles was speculative and uncertain. The only evidence of value was the advertisement itself to the effect that the coats were 'Worth to $100.00', how much less being speculative especially in view of the price for which they were offered for sale. With reference to the offer of the defendant on April 13, 1956, to sell the '1 Black Lapin Stole . . . worth $139.50 . . .' the trial court held that the value of this article was established and granted judgment in favor of the plaintiff for that amount less the $1 Quoted purchase price.

The defendant contends that a newspaper advertisement offering items of merchandise for sale at a named price is a 'unilateral offer' which may be withdrawn without notice. He relies upon authorities which hold that, where an advertiser publishes in a newspaper that he has a certain quantity or quality of goods which he wants to dispose of at certain prices and on certain terms, such advertisements are not offers which become contracts as soon as any person to whose notice they may come signifies his acceptance by notifying the other that he will take a certain quantity of them. Such advertisements have been construed as an invitation for an offer of sale on the terms stated, which offer, when received, may be accepted or rejected and which therefore does not become a contract of sale until accepted by the seller; and until a contract has been so made, the seller may modify or revoke such prices or terms . . .

The defendant relies principally on *Craft* v. *Elder & Johnston Co* 38 NE 2d 416. In that case, the court discussed the legal effect of an advertisement offering for sale, as a one-day special, an electric sewing machine at a named price. The view was expressed that the advertisement was (38 NE 2d 417) 'not an offer made to any specific person but was made to the public generally. Thereby it would be properly designated as a unilateral offer and not being supported by any consideration could be withdrawn at will and without notice'. It is true that such an offer may be withdrawn before acceptance. Since all offers are by their nature unilateral because they are necessarily made by one party or on one side in the negotiation of a contract, the distinction made in that decision between a unilateral offer and a unilateral contract is not clear. On the facts before us we are concerned with whether the advertisement constituted an offer, and, if so, whether the plaintiff's conduct constituted an acceptance.

There are numerous authorities which hold that a particular advertisement in a news paper or circular letter relating to a sale of articles may be construed by the court as constituting an offer, acceptance of which would complete a contract . . .

The test of whether a binding obligation may originate in advertisements addressed to the general public is 'whether the facts show that some performance was promised in positive terms in return for something requested'. 1 Williston, Contracts (Rev. ed.) § 27.

The authorities . . . emphasize that, where the offer is clear, definite, and explicit, and leaves nothing open for negotiation, it constitutes an offer, acceptance of which will complete the contract. The most recent case on the subject is *Johnson* v. *Capital City Ford Co* . . . in which the court pointed out that a newspaper advertisement relating to the purchase and sale of automobiles may constitute an offer, acceptance of which will consummate a contract and create an obligation in the offeror to perform according to the terms of the published offer.

Whether in any individual instance a newspaper advertisement is an offer rather than an invitation to make an offer depends on the legal intention of the parties and the surrounding circumstances. . . . We are of the view on the facts before us that the offer by the defendant of the sale of the Lapin fur was clear, definite, and explicit, and left nothing open for negotiation. The plaintiff having successfully managed to be the first one to appear at the seller's place of business to be served, as requested by the advertisement, and having offered the stated purchase price of the article, he was entitled to performance on the part of the defendant. We think the trial court was correct in holding that there was in the conduct of the parties a sufficient mutuality of obligation to constitute a contract of sale.

The defendant contends that the offer was modified by a 'house rule' to the effect that only women were qualified to receive the bargains advertised. The advertisement contained no such restriction. This objection may be disposed of briefly by stating that, while an advertiser has the right at any time before acceptance to modify his offer, he does not have the right, after acceptance, to impose new or arbitrary conditions not contained in the published offer.

How do the courts decide whether or not a display of goods in a shop amounts to an offer or not? Is it a question of fact in each case? Does it depend solely on the intention of the shopkeeper or does it depend upon policy considerations or value judgments? Consider the following argument advanced by Professor Atiyah (*An Introduction to the Law of Contract* (5th edn, Oxford University Press, 1995), pp. 59–60):

the question whether a display of goods in a self-service store amounts to an offer is itself a 'conceptual' question. The answer can have no meaning except in some legal context. The most usual context would be that in which a shopkeeper refused to serve a customer (or perhaps refused to sell the goods at the price indicated) and the real question would be whether he was *entitled* to do this. The conceptual method of answering this is to rephrase the issue in terms of concepts. Instead of asking if the shopkeeper is entitled to refuse to serve a customer, or to refuse to sell at a marked price, the courts ask whether the shopkeeper has made or accepted an offer. And this question is answered with little reference to the consequences. One result is that an important social or moral question is never openly discussed by the courts, namely should a shopkeeper be allowed to refuse to serve a member of the public, or should he be allowed to refuse to sell goods at a marked price?

Another result is that the decisions of the courts often rest on demonstratively faulty reasoning. In this particular area many of the courts' reasons are shown to be unconvincing by other legal decisions dealing with a situation in which the right to refuse to serve a member of the public is *denied*, that is, in the case of 'common inns' or hotels. For example, much has been made of the difficulties which a shopkeeper may encounter if he receives more acceptances than he has goods to sell. If he is deemed to 'offer' his goods for sale, is he then to be liable to all those customers who 'accept' his offer even though he cannot supply them? But this is an unreal difficulty, as is shown by the law relating to hotel-keepers. If a hotel proprietor is asked for a room when he has no room vacant the courts have had no difficulty in adopting the common sense view that he is not liable.

It will be seen that, if it had been desired to impose liability on a shopkeeper who refused to serve a customer, the relevant legal concepts would not have stood in the way of achieving this result. The courts could have said that a shopkeeper 'impliedly' offers to do business with any member of the public, and therefore that a contract is concluded when a customer 'accepts' the offer by intimating that he wishes to buy something in the shop.

Thus in strict logic the way in which a fact or a particular piece of conduct should be conceptualised by having a legal label attached to it should depend on the result which it is desired to achieve. But it must be recognized that lawyers and courts often reason in a way which suggests that they do not accept the strictly logical position. They frequently attach the label first, and give every appearance of thinking that the selection of the correct label is something which must be done without reference to the result.

In the particular case of self-service shops, legal methods of reasoning probably mean that the law is today out of touch with modern social conditions, and also with public attitudes. Most people would probably be surprised to discover that a shop-keeper is not obliged to sell an article at the price indicated if a customer offers to pay for it, and this public attitude is confirmed by the fact that such behaviour by a shopkeeper would today probably constitute an offence under the Consumer Protection Act 1987 or other consumer protection legislation.

There is no clear authority on the question whether an advertisement on a web site is an invitation to treat or an offer. A court asked to decide this issue is likely to draw on the analogy of a display of goods in a shop window or an advertisement in a newspaper. A good example of this process can be found in the judgment of Rajah JC in the Singaporean case of *Chwee Kin Keong* v. *Digilandmall.com Pte Ltd* [2004] SGHC 71; [2004] 2 SLR 594 when he stated (at [93]) that:

Website advertisement is in principle no different from a billboard outside a shop or an advertisement in a newspaper or periodical. The reach of and potential response(s) to such an advertisement are however radically different. Placing an advertisement on the Internet is essentially advertising or holding out to the world at large. A viewer from any part of the world may want to enter into a contract to purchase a product as advertised. Websites often provide a service where online purchases may be made. In effect the Internet conveniently integrates into a single screen traditional advertising, catalogues, shop displays/windows and physical shopping.

Two points emerge from this paragraph. The first is that the effect of the analogy drawn with shop displays and newspaper advertisements is likely to be to create a default rule to the effect that a web site advertisement is an invitation to treat and not an offer. But there may be a need for caution here. The default rule may be displaced rather more easily in the context of internet sales than in the context of the display of goods in a shop window. The range and variety of sales that can take place over the internet may have the consequence that less weight will be placed on a default rule and more on the words used in the particular advertisement. As Rajah JC observed (at [94]),

As with any normal contract, Internet merchants have to be cautious how they present an advertisement, since this determines whether the advertisement will be construed as an invitation to treat or a unilateral contract. Loose language may result in inadvertently establishing contractual liability to a much wider range of purchasers than resources permit

This suggests that the possibility of there being an electronic equivalent of *Carlill* or *Lefkowitz* is a real one. The second point, which tends in the opposite direction, is that the potential range of liability may in fact make judges reluctant to conclude that an advertisement on a web site is an offer. On the other hand, a court could mitigate the possible consequences of such a conclusion by implying into the advertisement a term to the effect that the offer is only open for acceptance while stocks last. However, such an implication was rejected by Rajah JC when he stated that 'the law may not imply a condition precedent as to the availability of stock simply to bail out an Internet merchant from a bad bargain'. This statement is open to the objection that the term is implied not to save the internet merchant from a bad bargain but to give effect to the intention of the parties, objectively ascertained; that is to say, the parties to such an internet transaction would be presumed to have had the intention that the seller was not offering to sell a limitless number of goods but was in fact offering to sell its existing stock only. Rajah JC was on stronger ground when he pointed out that the implied term may not work in all cases because, in some cases, such as the supply of information, the supply is potentially limitless. This is true but the response in such a case may be to place the onus on the seller to insert an appropriate protective clause in order to shield himself from a huge exposure to liability. As Rajah JC stated (at [96]):

It is therefore incumbent on the web merchant to protect himself, as he has both the means to do so and knowledge relating to the availability of any product that is being marketed. As most web merchants have automated software responses, they need to ensure that such automated responses correctly reflect their intentions from an objective perspective.

(c) TENDERS

The practice of inviting parties to tender, or to bid, for a particular project is not an uncommon one. It is, perhaps, most frequently encountered in the context of construction projects. The employer will generally invite various contractors to tender or to quote for the work to be done. What is the status of this invitation to tender? Does it amount to an offer or is it an invitation to negotiate? The answer ultimately depends upon the facts and circumstances of the individual case. At common law, the general rule is that the invitation to tender is not an offer but an invitation to negotiate (*Spencer* v. *Harding* (1870) LR 5 CP 561). But, once again, the rule is not an invariable one. Cases can be found in which the courts have concluded that the invitation to tender did in fact contain within it an offer (see, for example, *Blackpool and Fylde Aero Club Ltd* v. *Blackpool Borough Council* [1990] 1 WLR 1195, discussed below).

It is important to stress in this context that we are here concerned only with the common law rules applicable to invitations to tender. The regulation of the tendering process is not left entirely to the common law (for a consideration of the role of the common law in protecting those who submit tenders see S Arrowsmith, 'Protecting the Interests of Bidders for Public Contracts: The Role of the Common Law' [1994] *CLJ* 104). Statute has increasingly intervened to regulate the tendering process, particularly in the context of public bodies, and, while they are beyond the scope of this book, these regulations assume considerable practical importance for those subject to them (see, for example section 3(1) of the Local Government Act 1999 and, more generally, H Beale, (ed), *Chitty on Contracts* (29th edn, Sweet & Maxwell, 2004), paras 10-026–10-030).

Blackpool and Fylde Aero Club Ltd v. Blackpool Borough Council

[1990] 1 WLR 1195, Court of Appeal

The appellant council invited tenders for a concession to operate pleasure flights from the local airport. Among the recipients of this invitation was the respondent club which in fact had held the concession since 1975. The invitation stated that:

'The council do not bind themselves to accept all or any part of any tender. No tender which is received after the last date and time specified shall be admitted for consideration.'

The date and time stipulated was 17 March 1983 at noon. The club submitted its tender by posting it in the appropriate box on the morning of 17 March. The box was normally checked and cleared each day at noon but on this occasion it was not checked until the following day: 18 March. The council at its meeting later in March refused to consider the club's tender on the ground that it had been received late and the concession was awarded to another party. When the council discovered that the club's bid had in fact been submitted on time it sought to rectify the situation by declaring the initial tenders invalid and by re-scheduling the tendering procedure. But they backed down after being threatened with legal proceedings by the company whose bid had been accepted. The club then brought an action for damages against the council. It was held by the trial judge and by the Court of Appeal that the council was contractually obliged to consider the club's tender and, for breach of that obligation, it was held liable in damages.

Bingham LJ [set out the facts and continued]
The judge resolved the contractual issue in favour of the club, holding that an express request for a tender might in appropriate circumstances give rise to an implied obligation to perform the service of considering that tender. Here, the council's stipulation that tenders received after the deadline would not be admitted for consideration gave rise to a contractual obligation (on acceptance by submission of a timely tender) that such tenders would be admitted for consideration.

In attacking the judge's conclusion on this issue, Mr Toulson [counsel for the appellants] made four main submissions. First, he submitted that an invitation to tender in this form was well established to be no more than a proclamation of willingness to receive offers. Even without the first sentence of the council's invitation to tender in this case, the council would not have been bound to accept the highest or any tender. An invitation to tender in this form was an invitation to treat, and no contract of any kind would come into existence unless or until, if ever, the council chose to accept any tender or other offer. For these propositions reliance was placed on *Spencer* v. *Harding* (1870) LR 5 CP 561 and *Harris* v. *Nickerson* (1873) LR 8 QB 286.

Second, Mr Toulson submitted that on a reasonable reading of this invitation to tender the council could not be understood to be undertaking to consider all timely tenders submitted. The statement that late tenders would not be considered did not mean that timely tenders would. If the council had meant that it could have said it. There was, although [counsel] did not put it in these words, no maxim exclusio unius, expressio alterius.[3]

Third, the court should be no less rigorous when asked to imply a contract than when asked to imply a term in an existing contract or to find a collateral contract. A term would not be implied simply because it was reasonable to do so: *Liverpool City Council* v. *Irwin* [1977] AC 239, 253H. In order to establish collateral contracts, 'Not only the terms of such contracts but the existence of an animus contrahendi[4] on the part of all the parties to them must be clearly shewn': see *Heilbut Symons & Co* v. *Buckleton* [1913] AC 30, 47. No lower standard was applicable here and the standard was not satisfied.

---

[3] The inclusion of the one is the exclusion of the other.   [4] An intention to contract.

Fourth, Mr Toulson submitted that the warranty contended for by the club was simply a proposition 'tailor-made to produce the desired result' (per Lord Templeman in *CBS Songs Ltd* v. *Amstrad Consumer Electronics plc* [1988] AC 1013, 1059F) on the facts of this particular case. There was a vital distinction between expectations, however reasonable, and contractual obligations: see per Diplock LJ in *Lavarack* v. *Woods of Colchester Ltd* [1967] 1 QB 278, 294. The club here expected its tender to be considered. The council fully intended that it should be. It was in both parties' interests that the club's tender should be considered. There was thus no need for them to contract. The court should not subvert well-understood contractual principles by adopting a woolly pragmatic solution designed to remedy a perceived injustice on the unique facts of this particular case.

In defending the judge's decision Mr Shorrock [counsel for the club] accepted that an invitation to tender was normally no more than an offer to receive tenders. But it could, he submitted, in certain circumstances give rise to binding contractual obligations on the part of the invitor, either from the express words of the tender or from the circumstances surrounding the sending out of the invitation to tender or (as here) from both. The circumstances relied on here were that the council approached the club and the other invitees, all of them connected with the airport, that the club had held the concession for eight years, having successfully tendered on three previous occasions, that the council as a local authority was obliged to comply with its standing orders and owed a fiduciary duty to ratepayers to act with reasonable prudence in managing its financial affairs and that there was a clear intention on the part of both parties that all timely tenders would be considered. If in these circumstances one asked of this invitation to tender the question posed by Bowen LJ in *Carlill* v. *Carbolic Smoke Ball Co* [1893] 1 QB 256, 266, 'How would an ordinary person reading this document construe it?', the answer in Mr Shorrock's submission was clear: the council might or might not accept any particular tender; it might accept no tender; it might decide not to award the concession at all; it would not consider any tender received after the advertised deadline; but if it did consider any tender received before the deadline and conforming with the advertised conditions it would consider all such tenders.

I found great force in the submissions made by Mr Toulson and agree with much of what was said. Indeed, for much of the hearing I was of opinion that the judge's decision, although fully in accord with the merits as I see them, could not be sustained in principle. But I am in the end persuaded that [the] argument proves too much. During the hearing the following questions were raised: what if, in a situation such as the present, the council had opened and thereupon accepted the first tender received, even though the deadline had not expired and other invitees had not yet responded? or if the council had considered and accepted a tender admittedly received well after the deadline? Mr Toulson answered that although by so acting the council might breach its own standing orders, and might fairly be accused of discreditable conduct, it would not be in breach of any legal obligation because at that stage there would be none to breach. This is a conclusion I cannot accept, and if it were accepted there would in my view be an unacceptable discrepancy between the law of contract and the confident assumptions of commercial parties, both tenderers . . . and invitors (as reflected in the immediate reaction of the council when the mishap came to light).

A tendering procedure of this kind is, in many respects, heavily weighted in favour of the invitor. He can invite tenders from as many or as few parties as he chooses. He need not tell any of them who else, or how many others, he has invited. The invitee may often, although not here, be put to considerable labour and expense in preparing a tender, ordinarily without recompense if he is unsuccessful. The invitation to tender may itself, in a complex case, although again not here, involve time and expense to prepare, but the invitor does not commit himself to proceed with the project, whatever it is; he need not accept the highest tender; he need not accept any tender; he need not give reasons to justify his acceptance or rejection of any tender received. The risk to which the tenderer is exposed does not end with the risk that his tender may not be the highest (or, as the case may be, lowest). But where, as here, tenders are solicited from selected parties all of them known to the invitor, and where a local authority's invitation prescribes a clear, orderly and familiar procedure (draft contract conditions available for inspection and plainly not open to negotiation, a prescribed common form of tender, the supply of envelopes designed to preserve the absolute anonymity of tenderers and clearly to identify the tender in question and an absolute deadline) the invitee is in my judgment protected at least to this extent: if he submits a conforming tender before the deadline he is entitled, not as a matter of mere expectation but of contractual right, to be sure that his tender will after the deadline be opened and considered in conjunction with all other conforming tenders or at least that his tender will be considered if others are. Had the club, before tendering, inquired of the council whether it could rely on any timely and conforming tender being considered along with others, I feel quite sure that the answer would have been 'of course'. The law would, I think, be defective if it did not give effect to that.

It is of course true that the invitation to tender does not explicitly state that the council will consider timely and conforming tenders. That is why one is concerned with implication. But the council does not either say that it does not bind itself to do so, and in the context a reasonable invitee would understand the invitation to be saying, quite clearly, that if he submitted a timely and conforming tender it would be considered, at least if any other such tender were considered.

I readily accept that contracts are not to be lightly implied. Having examined what the parties said and did, the court must be able to conclude with confidence both that the parties intended to create contractual relations and that the agreement was to the effect contended for. It must also, in most cases, be able to answer the question posed by Mustill LJ in *Hispanica de Petroleos SA v. Vencedora Oceanica Navegacion SA (No 2) (Note)* [1987] 2 Lloyd's Rep 321, 331: 'What was the mechanism for offer and acceptance?' In all the circumstances of this case (and I say nothing about any other) I have no doubt that the parties did intend to create contractual relations to the limited extent contended for. Since it has never been the law that a person is only entitled to enforce his contractual rights in a reasonable way (*White and Carter (Councils) Ltd v. McGregor* [1962] AC 413, 430A per Lord Reid), Mr Shorrock was in my view right to contend for no more than a contractual duty to consider. I think it plain that the council's invitation to tender was, to this limited extent, an offer, and the club's submission of a timely and conforming tender an acceptance.

Mr Toulson's fourth submission is a salutary warning, but it is not a free-standing argument: if, as I hold, his first three submissions are to be rejected, no subversion of principle is involved. I am, however, pleased that what seems to me the right legal answer also accords with the merits as I see them.

I accordingly agree with the judge's conclusion on the contractual issue, essentially for the reasons which he more briefly gave.

Stocker LJ delivered a concurring judgment and **Farquharson LJ** concurred.

COMMENTARY

Given the general rule that an invitation to tender is an invitation to negotiate and not an offer, it is important to identify the factors upon which the Court of Appeal relied in concluding that this particular invitation to tender amounted to an offer to consider tenders submitted on time. The task of identifying these factors is not, however, an easy one. The court relied upon a number of factors and it would appear that it was their combination that was important. No one factor was decisive. The factors considered by the court included the following:

(i)　the invitation to tender was addressed to a small number of interested parties;

(ii)　the tender procedure was 'clear, orderly and familiar'; and

(iii)　the outcome was, in the opinion of the court, consistent with the 'assumptions of commercial parties'.

Other factors which may have been of significance include:

(iv)　the club was the holder of the concession and therefore might be said to have had a legitimate expectation of consideration for renewal; and

(v)　the fact that the invitation was issued by a local authority which, it was argued, owed a 'fiduciary duty to ratepayers to act with reasonable prudence in managing its financial affairs'.

The invitation to tender did not state expressly that the council was subject to a duty to consider all tenders submitted. Indeed, the first sentence of the invitation to tender stated that the council did not bind itself to accept all or any part of any tender. But the fact that the council excluded a duty to accept any tender was held to be insufficient to exclude the duty to consider tenders made. Presumably the council should have gone further and excluded not only a duty to accept a tender but also the duty to consider any tender submitted.

It was not necessary for the Court of Appeal to analyse in any detail the extent of the obligation to consider tenders submitted on time given that the council had not, on the facts, given any consideration to the tender submitted by the club. What would have been the position if the council had considered the tender and rejected it but awarded the tender to a party whose bid was higher than that submitted by the club? Stocker LJ stated that the obligation to consider 'would not preclude or inhibit the council from deciding not to accept any tender or to award the concession, provided the decision was bona fide and honest, to any tenderer'. Thus a bona fide decision to exclude a party from the bidding process (for example, because of a conflict of interest between one of the tenderers and an employee of the party issuing the invitation to tender) may not constitute a breach of the duty to consider tenders submitted on time (see *Fairclough Building Ltd* v. *Borough Council of Port Talbot* (1993) 62 Build LR 82). This duty to consider is not as onerous as a duty to act judicially. Thus the duty to consider tenders does not require the party inviting the tenders to give a hearing to parties who submit a tender (see *Pratt Contractors Ltd* v. *Transit New Zealand* [2003] UKPC 33).

The Court of Appeal was not asked to consider the measure of damages to which the club was entitled. On the facts the tender submitted by the club was larger than the one accepted by the council. Given this fact it is suggested that the loss to the club was not in fact the loss of the contract (because we cannot be sure that the club would have been awarded the concession) but the 'loss of a chance' to participate in the tendering process and to have its tender considered (on damages for loss of a chance see *Chaplin* v. *Hicks* [1911] 2 KB 786 at p. 1055 below).

The proposition that an invitation to tender followed by the submission of a tender can result in the creation of a contract between the party inviting the bid and the party making the bid has implications for both parties. In *The Queen in Right of Ontario* v. *Ron Engineering & Construction Eastern Ltd* (1981) 119 DLR (3d) 267 a bidder discovered shortly after the bids had been opened that it had made a mistake in formulating its bid. It sought to withdraw from the process and recover the deposit which it had paid to the party inviting the bids. The basis on which the deposit had been paid was that it would be forfeited if the tender was withdrawn or the tenderer refused to proceed with the contract. The Supreme Court of Canada held that the plaintiffs were not entitled to recover their deposit. A contract had been created by the parties, one of the terms of which was that bidders were not entitled to recover their deposit if they refused to proceed with the contract.

A factor which may also have been of some significance in *Blackpool Aero* is the fact that the defendant was a public authority. It is possible that in future cases a greater role will be given to public law principles in regulating the tendering process (on which see further J Beatson, 'Public Law Influences in Contract Law' in J Beatson and D Friedmann (eds), *Good Faith and Fault in Contract Law* (Oxford University Press, 1995), p. 263 at pp. 279–288).

A further example of a case in which an invitation to tender was held to contain within it an offer is the decision of the House of Lords in *Harvela Investments Ltd* v. *Royal Trust Company of Canada (CI) Ltd* [1986] AC 207. The first defendants owned a block of shares in a company. The plaintiff (Harvela) and the second defendant (Sir Leonard Outerbridge) were rival bidders for the shares. The reason for their interest in the shares was that ownership of them would give to the successful bidder effective control of the company. The first defendants sent out an invitation to both Harvela and Sir Leonard in which they invited both parties to submit 'any revised offer which you may wish by sealed tender or confidential telex' to the first defendants' solicitors. The first defendants in turn stated that 'we confirm that if any offer made by you is the highest offer received by us we bind ourselves to accept such offer provided that such offer complies with the terms of this telex'. Harvela submitted a bid of $2,175,000, while Sir Leonard submitted a bid of $2,100,000 'or [Canadian] $101,000 in excess of any other offer which you may receive which is expressed as a fixed monetary amount, whichever is the higher'. The first defendants accepted Sir Leonard's offer, treating it as a bid of $2,276,000 and entered into a contract with the second defendant for the sale of the shares. Harvela issued proceedings against both the first defendants and Sir Leonard in which, among other things, it challenged the validity of Sir Leonard's bid. The House of Lords held that Sir Leonard's bid was indeed invalid and that the first defendant was contractually bound to transfer the shares to Harvela in accordance with the terms of its bid.

It is one thing to describe the outcome of the litigation; it is quite another to explain the reasoning that led to this conclusion. At first sight Sir Leonard appeared to have a strong argument, namely that he was invited to make a 'revised offer' for the shares, he made one and the first defendants accepted it. Therefore a contract had been validly concluded for the sale to him of the shares. Lord Templeman (at p. 230) in the House of Lords rejected this submission on the ground that the invitation to bid sent out by the first defendants contained provisions 'which are only consistent with the presumed intention to create a fixed bidding sale and which are inconsistent with any presumed intention to create an auction sale by means of referential bids' (a referential bid being a bid which is not of a fixed amount but one made by reference to another bid). He held that, as a matter of construction, the invitation issued by the first defendants created a fixed bidding sale. Thus he concluded (at p. 233):

The invitation required Sir Leonard to name his price and required Harvela to name its price and bound the vendors to accept the higher price. The invitation was not difficult to understand and the result was bound to be certain and to accord with the presumed intentions of the vendors discernible from the express provisions of the invitation. Harvela named the price of $2,175,000; Sir Leonard failed to name any price except $2,100,000 which was less than the price named by Harvela. The vendors were bound to accept Harvela's offer.

But on what basis could it be said that the vendors were bound to accept Harvela's offer given that the general rule is that an offeree is free to decide whether or not to accept an offer? Lord Diplock used the following analysis. In his view (at p. 224), the legal nature of the invitation sent out by the first defendants was that of:

a unilateral or 'if' contract, or rather of two unilateral contracts in identical terms to one of which the vendors and Harvela were the parties as promisor and promisee respectively, while to the other the vendors were promisor and Sir Leonard was promisee. Such unilateral contracts were made at the time when the invitation was received by the promisee to whom it was addressed by the vendors; under neither of them did the promisee, Harvela and Sir Leonard respectively, assume any legal obligation to anyone to do or refrain from doing anything.

The first defendants did, however, assume a legal obligation to Harvela and Sir Leonard under these two contracts. They assumed an obligation to enter into a contract to sell shares to the promisee who submitted the highest bid in accordance with the terms of the invitation. In this way the unilateral contract concluded with the successful bidder would be transformed into a binding bilateral contract, while the unilateral contract with the unsuccessful bidder would be terminated by the submission of the higher bid. This analysis, involving as it does two unilateral contracts, one of which is transformed into a bilateral contract and the other of which is terminated, is complex, possibly too complex. A simpler analysis might have been to conclude that the invitation was an offer of a unilateral contract. The point has been made by Professor Smith in the following way (JC Smith and JAC Thomas, *A Casebook on Contract* (11th edn, Sweet & Maxwell, 2000), pp. 15–16). He concludes that:

The Royal Trust's telex to Harvela and Sir Leonard was an offer to each of them which could be accepted only by one—the one who made the higher valid bid. The telex was an offer of a unilateral contract, like an offer to give a prize to the one of two entrants for a race who comes first. The 'prize' was a contract for the sale of the shares—the Trust was bound to accept the higher bidder's offer to buy them.

Until that bid was made, no one was under any obligation. The Trust could have withdrawn its offer and the two offerees were under no obligation to bid. While the offer stood, the Trust was, of course, liable to become bound to one of the offerees through the acceptance of its offer, but that is the position of all offerors, so long as their offer remains open to acceptance. When the higher bid was ascertained, the Trust was bound to accept it. At that moment there was just one contract—a contract by the Trust to accept the higher bidder's offer—a unilateral contract. The bidder was free to withdraw his bid until the Trust accepted it, but when they did he became bound to buy the shares.

(d) AUCTION SALES

One battleground for the formulation of the rules relating to offer and acceptance has been the auction-house. Many of the cases were decided in the nineteenth century but uncertainty in relation to the rules applicable to an auction without reserve (that is to say, an auction where no reserve price is stated for the lot that has been put up for sale) persisted until very recently. The legal position is much more straightforward in the case of auctions held with a reserve price. The auctioneer, in inviting bids to be made for the lot offered for sale, makes an invitation to negotiate. The offer is then made by the member of the public who makes a bid for the lot. That bid is not usually accepted immediately. Instead the auctioneer generally invites further bids to be made for the lot. If no other bids are forthcoming the auctioneer will accept the bid on the fall of his hammer (see, for example, *British Car Auctions* v. *Wright* [1972] 1 WLR 1519). It is the case of the auction without a reserve price that has given rise to difficulty. There were dicta in a nineteenth century case, *Warlow* v. *Harrison* (1859) 1 E & B 309, to the effect that, in the case of an auction held without a reserve price, the auctioneer makes an offer to sell the goods and that the offer is accepted by the person who makes the highest bid at the auction. The difficulty lay in accommodating this analysis within the offer and acceptance framework and a considerable amount of academic ink was spilt on the topic. However the issue recently came before the Court of Appeal in the following case:

Barry v. Davies (Trading as Heathcote Ball & Co)

[2000] 1 WLR 1962, Court of Appeal

Customs and Excise put up two engine analyzers for sale by auction, without a reserve price. The price of new machines was £14,521 each. The claimant bid £200 for each machine after the auctioneer tried and failed to get bids of £5,000 and £3,000 for each machine. The auctioneer refused to sell the machines to the claimant for such a low price and they were later sold to a third party for £1,500 each. The claimant brought an action against the auctioneer for breach of contract. The claim succeeded on the ground that there was a collateral contract between the auctioneer and the highest bidder. The contract was constituted by an offer by the auctioneer to sell to the highest bidder and it was accepted when the bid was made. The claimant was held to be entitled to recover

£27,600 by way of damages, being the difference between the amount that the claimant had bid to purchase the machines and the amount he would have been required to pay to obtain the machines in the ordinary way.

Sir Murray Stuart-Smith [set out the facts and continued]
The judge held that it would be the general and reasonable expectation of persons attending at an auction sale without reserve that the highest bidder would and should be entitled to the lot for which he bids. Such an outcome was in his view fair and logical. As a matter of law he held that there was a collateral contract between the auctioneer and the highest bidder constituted by an offer by the auctioneer to sell to the highest bidder which was accepted when the bid was made. In so doing he followed the views of the majority of the Court of Exchequer Chamber in *Warlow* v. *Harrison* (1859) 1 E & E 309.

He also held that this was the effect of condition 1 of the conditions of sale, which was in these terms:

'The highest bidder to be the purchaser; but should any dispute arise between two or more bidders the same shall be determined by the auctioneers who shall have the right of withdrawing lots.'

The judge concluded that the first clause meant what it said and the right of withdrawal was conditioned on there being a dispute between bidders, and there was none.

Mr Moran on behalf of the defendant criticised this conclusion on a number of grounds. First, he submitted that the holding of an auction without reserve does not amount to a promise on the part of the auctioneer to sell the lots to the highest bidder. There are no express words to the effect, merely a statement of fact that the vendor has not placed a reserve on the lot. Such an intention, he submitted, is inconsistent with two principles of law, namely that the auctioneer's request for bids is not an offer which can be accepted by the highest bidder (*Payne* v. *Cave* (1789) 3 Durn & E 148) and that there is no completed contract of sale until the auctioneer's hammer falls and the bidder may withdraw his bid up until that time (Sale of Goods Act 1979, section 57(2), which reflects the common law). There should be no need to imply such a promise into a statement that the sale is without reserve, because there may be other valid reasons why the auctioneer should be entitled to withdraw the lot, for example if he suspected an illegal ring or that the vendor had no title to sell.

Secondly, Mr Moran submitted that there is no consideration for the auctioneer's promise. He submitted that the bid itself cannot amount to consideration because the bidder has not promised to do anything, he can withdraw the bid until it is accepted and the sale completed by the fall of the hammer. At most the bid represents a discretionary promise, which amounts to illusory consideration, for example promising to do something 'if I feel like it'. The bid only had real benefit to the auctioneer at the moment the sale is completed by the fall of the hammer. Furthermore, the suggestion that consideration is provided because the auctioneer has the opportunity to accept the bid or to obtain a higher bid as the bidding is driven up depends upon the bid not being withdrawn.

Finally, Mr Moran submitted that where an agent is acting for a disclosed principal he is not liable on the contract: Bowstead & Reynolds *on Agency*, 16th ed (1996), p. 548, para 9-001 and *Mainprice* v. *Westley* (1865) 6 B & S 420. If therefore there is any collateral contract it is with the principal and not the agent.

These submissions were forcefully and attractively argued by Mr Moran. The authorities, such as they were, do not speak with one voice. The starting point is section 57 of the Sale of Goods Act 1979, which re-enacted the Sale of Goods Act 1893 (56 & 57 Vict. c. 71), itself in this section a codification of the common law. I have already referred to the effect of subsection (2). Subsections (3) and (4) are also important. They provide:

'(3) A sale by auction may be notified to be subject to a reserve or upset price, and a right to bid may also be reserved expressly by or on behalf of the seller.

(4) Where a sale by auction is not notified to be subject to the right to bid by or on behalf of the seller, it is not lawful for the seller to bid himself or to employ any person to bid at the sale, or for the auctioneer knowingly to take any bid from the seller or any such person.'

Although the Act does not expressly deal with sales by auction without reserve, the auctioneer is the agent of the vendor and, unless subsection (4) has been complied with, it is not lawful for him to make a bid. Yet withdrawing the lot from the sale because it has not reached the level which the auctioneer considers appropriate is tantamount to bidding on behalf of the seller. The highest bid cannot be rejected simply because it is not high enough.

The judge based his decision on the reasoning of the majority of the Court of Exchequer Chamber in *Warlow* v. *Harrison*, 1 E & E 309. The sale was of 'the three following horses, the property of a gentleman, without reserve': see p. 314. The plaintiff bid 60 guineas for one of the horses; another person, who was in fact the owner, immediately bid 61 guineas. The plaintiff, having been informed that the bid was from the owner declined to bid higher, and claimed he was entitled to the horse. He sued the auctioneer; he based his claim on a plea that the auctioneer was his agent to complete the contract on his behalf. On that plea the plaintiff succeeded at first instance; but the verdict was set aside in the Court of Queen's Bench. The plaintiff appealed. Although the Court of Exchequer Chamber upheld the decision on the case as pleaded, all five members of the court held that if the pleadings were appropriately amended, the plaintiff would be entitled to succeed on a retrial. Martin B gave the judgment of the majority, consisting of himself, Byles and Watson BB. He said, at pp. 316–317:

'Upon the facts of the case, it seems to us that the plaintiff is entitled to recover. In a sale by auction there are three parties, viz the owner of the property to be sold, the auctioneer, and the portion of the public who attend to bid, which of course includes the highest bidder. In this, as in most cases of sales by auction, the owner's name was not disclosed: he was a concealed principal. The name of the auctioneers, of whom the defendant was one, alone was published; and the sale was announced by them to be "without reserve". This, according to all the cases both at law and equity, means that neither the vendor nor any person in his behalf shall bid at the auction, and that the property shall be sold to the highest bidder, whether the sum bid be equivalent to the real value or not; *Thornett* v. *Haines* (1846) 15 M & W 367. We cannot distinguish the case of an auctioneer putting up property for sale upon such a condition from the case of the loser of property offering a reward, or that of a railway company publishing a timetable stating the times when, and the places to which, the trains run. It has been decided that the person giving the information advertised for, or a passenger taking a ticket, may sue as upon a contract with him; *Denton* v. *Great Northern Railway Co* (1856) 5 E & B 860. Upon the same principle, it seems to us that the highest bona fide bidder at an auction may sue the auctioneer as upon a contract that the sale shall be without reserve. We think the auctioneer who puts the property up for sale upon such a condition pledges himself that the sale shall be without reserve; or, in other words, contracts that it shall be so; and that this contract is made with the highest bona fide bidder; and, in case of breach of it, that he has a right of action against the auctioneer. . . . We entertain no doubt that the owner may, at any time before the contract is legally complete, interfere and revoke the auctioneer's authority: but he does so at his peril; and, if the auctioneer has contracted any liability in consequence of his employment and the subsequent revocation or conduct of the owner, he is entitled to be indemnified.'

The two other members of the court, Willes J and Bramwell B reached the same conclusion, but based their decision on breach of warranty of authority.

Although therefore the decision of the majority is not strictly binding, it was the reasoned judgment of the majority and is entitled to very great respect. In *Mainprice* v. *Westley* (1865) 6 B & S 420 the court distinguished *Warlow* v. *Harrison*, 1 E & E 309 on the basis that in *Mainprice's* case the principal was disclosed, whereas in *Warlow's* case he was not. The judgment of the court, consisting of Cockburn CJ, Blackburn and Shee JJ, was given by Blackburn J. On this basis it was held that the agent was not liable. With all respect to the court, it does not seem to me that this was the basis of the decision in *Warlow's* case; rather that there was a separate collateral contract with the auctioneer; there is no reason why such a contract should not exist, even if the principal is disclosed. It is indeed the basis of an action for breach of warranty of authority. Moreover it was in fact clear in *Warlow's* case that the auctioneer was selling as an agent.

In *Harris* v. *Nickerson* (1873) LR 8 QB 286 the defendant, an auctioneer, advertised a sale by auction of certain lots including office furniture on a certain day and the two following days. But the sale of furniture on the third day was withdrawn. The plaintiff attended the sale and claimed against the defendant for breach of contract in not holding the sale, seeking to recover his expenses in attending. The claim was rejected by the Court of Queen's Bench. In the course of his judgment Blackburn J said, at p. 288:

'in the case of *Warlow* v. *Harrison* 1 E & E 309, 314, 318, the opinion of the majority of the judges in the Exchequer Chamber appears to have been that an action would lie for not knocking down the lot to the highest bona fide bidder when the sale was advertised as without reserve; in such a case it may be that there is a contract to sell to the highest bidder, and that if the owner bids there is a breach of the contract.'

And Quain J said, LR 8 QB 286, 289:

'When a sale is advertised as without reserve, and a lot is put up and bid for, there is ground for saying, as was said in *Warlow* v. *Harrison*, E & E 309, 314, that a contract is entered into between the auctioneer and the highest bona fide bidder . . .'

In *Johnston* v. *Boyes* [1899] 2 Ch 73, 77 Cozens-Hardy J also accepted the majority view in *Warlow's* case as being good law . . .

So far as textbook writers are concerned both Chitty *on Contracts*, 28th ed (1999), vol 1, p. 94, para. 2-010 and Benjamin's *Sale of Goods*, 5th ed (1997), p. 107, para 2-005 adopt the view expressed by the majority of the court in *Warlow's* case.

As to consideration, in my judgment there is consideration both in the form of detriment to the bidder, since his bid can be accepted unless and until it is withdrawn, and benefit to the auctioneer as the bidding is driven up. Moreover, attendance at the sale is likely to be increased if it is known that there is no reserve.

As to the agency point, there is no doubt that, when the sale is concluded, the contract is between the purchaser and vendor and not the auctioneer. Even if the identity of the vendor is not disclosed, it is clear that the auctioneer is selling as agent. It is true that there was no such contract between vendor and purchaser. But that does not prevent a collateral agreement existing between the auctioneer and bidder. A common example of this is an action for breach of warranty of authority which arises on a collateral contract.

For these reasons I would uphold the judge's decision on liability.

Pill LJ delivered a concurring judgment.

COMMENTARY

The contract found to exist on the facts of *Barry* was one between the potential buyer and the auctioneer. It was not a contract of sale between the seller and the buyer. The effect of the auctioneer's action was to prevent a contract coming into being between the seller and the buyer.

At what point in time does the auctioneer make the offer to sell the goods? Is it when the auction is advertised without a reserve price or is it when the auctioneer puts the goods up for sale at the auction? It was not necessary for the Court of Appeal to answer this question on the facts of *Barry*. Academic authority is divided on this issue. Support can be found for the proposition that the offer is made when the auction is advertised (see Gower (1952) 68 *LQR* 238, 241) and for the proposition that the offer is made when the auctioneer puts the goods up for sale (Scott [2001] *LMCLQ* 334, 335).

On the facts of *Barry* it would appear that there were no other bidders for the lots so that the identification of the claimant as the highest bidder was not problematic. But in other cases the issue may give rise to difficulty, given that there is always the possibility that another bidder will emerge before the auctioneer finally brings down his hammer. The courts will probably take a pragmatic approach to the resolution of this issue and equate the highest bidder with the party who made the last bid before the lot was withdrawn by the auctioneer.

While an auctioneer can generally withdraw a lot from the auction where the item has been put up for sale subject to a reserve price, it has been argued that the auctioneer can no longer do so once the reserve price has been reached (see Scott [2001] *LMCLQ* 334, 336–337). In other words, it is argued that the position of a bidder at an auction without a reserve price is in this respect the same as a bidder at an auction with a reserve price, where that price has already been reached. This is so unless the owner has reserved for himself the right to bid for the lot in question.

While an auctioneer cannot withdraw the lot simply because it has not reached the reserve price, he may be able to do so where he suspects that the bidder is not bona fide, in the sense that he is a participant in a group that is attempting to depress the price of the lot.

The analysis of the process by which the offer and the acceptance was made cannot be cleanly separated from the issue of whether or not there is consideration for the promise. One of the difficulties in *Barry* lay in identifying the consideration for the auctioneer's promise to sell the lot to the highest bidder. The answer given by the court was that the consideration was to be found in the fact that the auctioneer obtains the benefit of the fact that the price for the lot might be driven up and the bidder might be bound by the bid he makes. The difficulty with this view is that the bid made is a revocable one and this provides an insecure foundation for the finding of consideration for the promise.

One final issue that arose on the facts of the case concerned the claimant's entitlement to damages. It was held that the claimant was entitled to recover £27,600 by way of damages, being the difference between the amount that the claimant had bid to purchase the machines and the amount he would have been required to pay to obtain the machines in the ordinary way. It should be noted that the claim was for the entire difference between the two measures and not simply for the loss of a chance of purchasing the machines and that, perhaps rather oddly (given that the contract between the auctioneer and the claimant was not a contract for the sale of goods), the court relied on section 51(3) of the Sale of Goods Act 1979 when assessing the damages to which the claimant was entitled.

4. WHAT CONSTITUTES AN ACCEPTANCE?

An acceptance has been defined as 'a final and unqualified expression of assent to the terms of an offer' (H Beale (ed), *Chitty on Contracts* (29th edn, Sweet & Maxwell, 2004), para 2-024). This definition appears straightforward. But initial appearances can be misleading. The question whether an offer has been accepted has generated a considerable amount of case-law. Questions that have been asked of the courts include the following:

  (i)   must the acceptance coincide exactly with the terms of the offer?
 (ii)   must the acceptance be communicated to the offeror in all cases?
(iii)   where an offeror prescribes a particular method of acceptance, can the offer only be accepted by the prescribed method?
 (iv)   can silence ever constitute an acceptance of an offer?
  (v)   when does an acceptance sent through the post take effect?
 (vi)   how and when does acceptance take place in the case of a unilateral contract? and
(vii)   can a party accept an offer if he was unaware of the offer at the time at which he performed the act which constitutes the acceptance?

Thus the law in this area consists of a number of detailed rules. That said, there appear to be two central principles. The first is that the acceptance must be both final and unqualified and the second is that it must generally be communicated to the offeror. We shall consider these central principles together with the more detailed rules of law in the the remainder of this section.

(a) MUST THE ACCEPTANCE COINCIDE EXACTLY WITH THE TERMS OF THE OFFER?

The general answer is that an acceptance must be an 'unqualified expression of assent' to the terms proposed by the offeror. Thus a purported acceptance which attempts to vary the terms contained in an offer is not an acceptance at all. In fact, it will be interpreted by the court as a **rejection** of the offer and as a fresh offer (or a 'counter-offer') which is then open for acceptance or rejection by the original offeror. Thus in *Hyde* v. *Wrench* (1840) 3 Beav 334 the defendant offered to sell his farm to the plaintiff for £1,000. The plaintiff offered to buy it for £950 but the defendant refused to do so. The plaintiff then wrote to the defendant and agreed to pay £1,000 for the farm but the defendant never replied to that letter. It was held that no contract had been concluded for the sale of the farm. Lord Langdale stated (at p. 337) that:

I think there exists no valid binding contract between the parties for the purchase of the property. The Defendant offered to sell it for £1,000, and if that had been at once unconditionally accepted, there would undoubtedly have been a perfect binding contract; instead of that, the Plaintiff made an offer of his own, to purchase the property for £950, and he thereby rejected the offer previously made by the Defendant. I think that it was not afterwards competent for him to revive the proposal of the Defendant, by tendering an acceptance of it; and that, therefore, there exists no obligation of any sort between the parties.

It is, however, important to consider the correspondence between the parties with some care because what appears at first sight to be a counter-offer, and hence a rejection, may turn out on closer inspection to be a mere inquiry or request for information. Such was the case in *Stevenson, Jacques & Co* v. *McLean* (1880) 5 QBD 346. The defendants wrote to the plaintiffs stating that they were willing to sell iron to the plaintiffs and stated that the offer was open for a period of time. On the last day of that period the plaintiffs telegraphed to the defendant: 'Please wire whether you would accept forty for delivery over two months, or if not, longest limit you would give'. Later that day the defendants sold the iron to a third party and they sent a telegram to the plaintiffs to inform them of this. Before they received the telegram from the defendants the plaintiffs found a buyer for the iron and sent a telegram to the defendants in which they accepted the defendants' offer to sell the iron. The defendants refused to deliver the iron to the plaintiffs and so the plaintiffs sued for non-delivery. One of the grounds on which the defendants sought to deny liability was that the plaintiffs' first telegram was a rejection of the defendants' offer so that their offer was no longer open for acceptance when the plaintiffs purported to accept it later in the day. Lush J rejected the defendants' argument and their reliance upon *Hyde* v. *Wrench*. He concluded (at p. 350):

the form of the telegram is one of inquiry. It is not 'I offer forty for delivery over two months,' which would have likened the case to *Hyde* v. *Wrench*. . . . Here there is no counter-proposal. The words are 'Please wire whether you would accept forty for delivery over two months, or if not, longest limit you would give'. There is nothing specific by way of offer or rejection, but a mere inquiry, which should have been answered and not treated as a rejection of the offer. This ground of objection therefore fails.

The defendants' attempted revocation of their offer was held to be ineffective because the plaintiffs had accepted the offer prior to the revocation being brought to their attention. The plaintiffs were therefore entitled to recover damages for the non-delivery of the iron.

A rigid insistence on a precise correspondence between the terms of the offer and the terms of the acceptance gives rise to difficulty in modern trading conditions, where businesses frequently make use of their own standard terms and conditions of business. These standard terms frequently differ in major or minor respects. Do these differences prevent the conclusion of a contract in most business contracts? The leading case on this issue is:

Butler Machine Tool Co Ltd v. Ex-Cell-O Corporation (England) Ltd

[1979] 1 WLR 401, Court of Appeal

The facts of the case are set out in the judgments below.

Lord Denning MR

This case is a 'battle of forms'. The plaintiffs, the Butler Machine Tool Co Ltd, suppliers of a machine, on May 23, 1969, quoted a price for a machine tool of £75,535. Delivery was to be given in 10 months. On the back of the quotation there were terms and conditions. One of them was a price variation clause. It provided for an increase in the price if there was an increase in the costs and so forth. The machine tool was not delivered until November 1970. By that time costs had increased so much that the sellers claimed an additional sum of £2,892 as due to them under the price variation clause.

The defendant buyers, Ex-Cell-O Corporation (England) Ltd, rejected the excess charge. They relied on their own terms and conditions. They said:

'We did not accept the sellers' quotation as it was. We gave an order for the self-same machine at the self-same price, but on the back of our order we had our own terms and conditions. Our terms and conditions did not contain any price variation clause.'

The judge held that the price variation clause in the sellers' form continued through the whole dealing and so the sellers were entitled to rely upon it. He was clearly influenced by a passage in *Anson's Law of Contract*, 24th edn. (1975), pp. 37 and 38, of which the editor is Professor Guest: and also by *Treitel, The Law of Contract*, 4th ed. (1975), p. 15. The judge said that the sellers did all that was necessary and reasonable to bring the price variation clause to the notice of the buyers. He thought that the buyers would not 'browse over the conditions' of the sellers: and then, by printed words in their (the buyers') document, trap the sellers into a fixed price contract.

I am afraid that I cannot agree with the suggestion that the buyers 'trapped' the sellers in any way. Neither party called any oral evidence before the judge. The case was decided on the documents alone. I propose therefore to go through them.

On May 23, 1969, the sellers offered to deliver one 'Butler' double column plane-miller for the total price of £75,535. Delivery 10 months (subject to confirmation at time of ordering) other terms and conditions are on the reverse of this quotation. On the back there were 16 conditions in small print starting with this general condition:

'All orders are accepted only upon and subject to the terms set out in our quotation and the following conditions. These terms and conditions shall prevail over any terms and conditions in the buyer's order.'

Clause 3 was the price variation clause. It said:

'Prices are based on present day costs of manufacture and design and having regard to the delivery quoted and uncertainty as to the cost of labour, materials etc. during the period of manufacture, we regret that we have no alternative but to make it a condition of acceptance of order that goods will be charged at prices ruling upon date of delivery.'

The buyers replied on May 27, 1969, giving an order in these words: 'Please supply on terms and conditions as below and overleaf'. Below there was a list of the goods ordered, but there were differences from the quotation of the sellers in these respects: (i) there was an additional item for the cost of installation, £3,100 and (ii) there was a different delivery date: instead of 10 months, it was 10–11 months.

Overleaf there were different terms as to the cost of carriage: in that it was to be paid to the delivery address of the buyers: whereas the sellers' terms were ex warehouse. There were different terms as to the right to cancel for late delivery. The buyers in their conditions reserved the right to cancel if delivery was not made by the agreed date: whereas the sellers in their conditions said that cancellation of order due to late delivery would not be accepted.

On the foot of the buyers' order there was a tear-off slip headed:

'Acknowledgment: Please sign and return to Ex-Cell-O. We accept your order on the terms and conditions stated thereon—and undertake to deliver by—Date—signed.'

In that slip the delivery date and signature were left blank ready to be filled in by the sellers.

On June 5, 1969, the sellers wrote this letter to the buyers:

'We have pleasure in acknowledging receipt of your official order dated May 27 covering the supply of one Butler Double Column Plane-Miller. This being delivered in accordance with our revised quotation of May 23 for delivery in 10/11 months, i.e., March/April 1970. We return herewith duly completed your acknowledgment of order form.'

They enclosed the acknowledgment form duly filled in with the delivery date March/April 1970 and signed by the Butler Machine Tool Co.

No doubt a contract was then concluded. But on what terms? The sellers rely on their general conditions and on their last letter which said: 'in accordance with our revised quotation of May 23' (which had on the back the price variation clause). The buyers rely on the acknowledgment signed by the sellers which accepted the buyer's order 'on the terms and conditions stated thereon' (which did not include a price variation clause).

If those documents are analysed in our traditional method, the result would seem to me to be this: the quotation of May 23, 1969, was an offer by the sellers to the buyers containing the terms and conditions on the back. The order of May 27, 1969, purported to be an acceptance of that offer in that it was for the same machine at the same price, but it contained such additions as to cost of installation, date of delivery and so forth that it was in law a rejection of the offer and constituted a counter-offer. That is clear from *Hyde* v. *Wrench* (1840) 3 Beav 334. As Megaw J said in *Trollope & Colls Ltd* v. *Atomic Power Constructions Ltd* [1963] 1 WLR 333, 337: '. . . the counter-offer kills the original offer'. The letter of the sellers of June 5, 1969, was an acceptance of that counter-offer, as is shown by the acknowledgment which the sellers signed and returned to the buyers. The reference to the quotation of May 23 referred only to the price and identity of the machine.

To go on with the facts of the case. The important thing is that the sellers did not keep the contractual date of delivery which was March/April 1970. The machine was ready about September 1970 but by that time the buyers' production schedule had to be re-arranged as they could not accept delivery until November 1970. Meanwhile the sellers had invoked the price increase clause. They sought to charge the buyers an increase due to the rise in costs between May 27, 1969 (when the order was given), and April 1, 1970 (when the machine ought to have been delivered). It came to £2,892. The buyers rejected the claim. The judge held that the sellers were entitled to the sum of £2,892 under the price variation clause. He did not apply the traditional method of analysis by way of offer and counter-offer. He said that in the quotation of May 23, 1969, 'one finds the price variation clause appearing under a most emphatic heading stating that it is a term or condition that is to prevail'. So he held that it did prevail.

I have much sympathy with the judge's approach to this case. In many of these cases our traditional analysis of offer, counter-offer, rejection, acceptance and so forth is out of date. This was observed by Lord Wilberforce in *New Zealand Shipping Co Ltd* v. *A. M. Satterthwaite & Co Ltd* [1975] AC 154, 167. The better way is to look at all the documents passing between the parties—and glean from them, or from the conduct of the parties, whether they have reached agreement on all material points—even though there may be differences between the forms and conditions printed on the back of them. As Lord Cairns said in *Brogden* v. *Metropolitan Railway Co* (1877) 2 App Cas 666, 672:

> '. . . there may be a *consensus* between the parties far short of a complete mode of expressing it, and that *consensus* may be discovered from letters or from other documents of an imperfect and incomplete description;. . .'

Applying this guide, it will be found that in most cases when there is a 'battle of forms', there is a contract as soon as the last of the forms is sent and received without objection being taken to it. That is well observed in *Benjamin's Sale of Goods*, 9th ed. (1974), p. 84. The difficulty is to decide which form, or which part of which form, is a term or condition of the contract. In some cases the battle is won by the man who fires the last shot. He is the man who puts forward the latest terms and conditions: and, if they are not objected to by the other party, he may be taken to have agreed to them. Such was *British Road Services Ltd* v. *Arthur V. Crutchley & Co Ltd* [1968] 1 Lloyd's Rep 271, 281–282, per Lord Pearson; and the illustration given by Professor Guest in *Anson's Law of Contract*, 24th ed., pp. 37, 38 when he says that 'the terms of the contract consist of the terms of the offer subject to the modifications contained in the acceptance'. In some cases the battle is won by the man who gets the blow in first. If he offers to sell at a named price on the terms and conditions stated on the back: and the buyer orders the goods purporting to accept the offer—on an order form with his own different terms and conditions on the back—then if the difference is so material that it would affect the price, the buyer ought not to be allowed to take advantage of the difference unless he draws it specifically to the attention of the seller. There are yet other cases where the battle depends on the shots fired on both sides. There is a concluded contract but the forms vary. The terms and conditions of both parties are to be construed together. If they can be reconciled so as to give a harmonious result, all well and good. If differences are irreconcilable—so that they are mutually contradictory—then the conflicting terms may have to be scrapped and replaced by a reasonable implication.

In the present case the judge thought that the sellers in their original quotation got their blow in first: especially by the provision that 'these terms and conditions shall prevail over any terms and conditions in the buyer's order'. It was so emphatic that the price variation clause continued through all the subsequent dealings and that the buyers must be taken to have agreed to it. I can understand that point of view. But I think that the documents have to be considered as a whole. And, as a matter of construction, I think the acknowledgment of June 5, 1969, is the decisive document. It makes it clear that the contract was on the buyers' terms and not on the sellers' terms: and the buyers' terms did not include a price variation clause.

I would therefore allow the appeal and enter judgment for the defendants.

Lawton LJ

The modern commercial practice of making quotations and placing orders with conditions attached, usually in small print, is indeed likely, as in this case to produce a battle of forms. The problem is how should that battle be conducted? The view taken by Thesiger J was that the battle should extend over a wide area and the court should do its best to look into the minds of the parties and make certain assumptions. In my judgment, the battle has to be conducted in accordance with set rules. It is a battle more on classical 18th century lines when convention decided who had the right to open fire first rather than in accordance with the modern concept of attrition.

The rules relating to a battle of this kind have been known for the past 130-odd years. They were set out by Lord Langdale MR in *Hyde v. Wrench*, 3 Beav 334, 337, to which Lord Denning MR has already referred; and, if anyone should have thought they were obsolescent, Megaw J in *Trollope & Colls Ltd* v. *Atomic Power Constructions Ltd* [1963] 1 WLR 333, 337 called attention to the fact that those rules are still in force.

When those rules are applied to this case, in my judgment, the answer is obvious. The sellers started by making an offer. That was in their quotation. The small print was headed by the following words:

'General. All orders are accepted only upon and subject to the terms set out in our quotation and the following conditions. These terms and conditions shall prevail over any terms and conditions in the buyer's order.'

That offer was not accepted. The buyers were only prepared to have one of these very expensive machines on their own terms. Their terms had very material differences in them from the terms put forward by the sellers. They could not be reconciled in any way. In the language of article 7 of the Uniform Law on the Formation of Contracts for the International Sale of Goods (see Uniform Laws on International Sales Act 1967, Schedule 2) they did 'materially alter the terms' set out in the offer made by the plaintiffs.

As I understand *Hyde* v. *Wrench*, 3 Beav 334, and the cases which have followed, the consequence of placing the order in that way, if I may adopt Megaw J's words [1963] 1 WLR 333, 337, was 'to kill the original offer'. It follows that the court has to look at what happened after the buyers made their counter-offer. By letter dated June 4, 1969, the plaintiffs acknowledged receipt of the counter-offer, and they went on in this way:

> 'Details of this order have been passed to our Halifax works for attention and a formal acknowledgment of order will follow in due course.'

That is clearly a reference to the printed tear-off slip which was at the bottom of the buyers' counter-offer. By letter dated June 5, 1969, the sales office manager at the plaintiffs' Halifax factory completed that tear-off slip and sent it back to the buyers.

It is true, as counsel for the sellers has reminded us, that the return of that printed slip was accompanied by a letter which had this sentence in it: 'This is being entered in accordance with our revised quotation of May 23 for delivery in 10/11 months'. I agree with Lord Denning MR that, in a business sense, that refers to the quotation as to the price and the identity of the machine, and it does not bring into the contract the small print conditions on the back of the quotation. Those small print conditions had disappeared from the story. That was when the contract was made. At that date it was a fixed price contract without a price escalation clause.

As I pointed out in the course of argument to counsel for the sellers, if the letter of June 5 which accompanied the form acknowledging the terms which the buyers had specified had amounted to a counter-offer, then in my judgment the parties never were ad idem. It cannot be said that the buyers accepted the counter-offer by reason of the fact that ultimately they took physical delivery of the machine. By the time they took physical delivery of the machine, they had made it clear by correspondence that they were not accepting that there was any price escalation clause in any contract which they had made with the plaintiffs.

I agree with Lord Denning MR that this appeal should be allowed.

Bridge LJ

Schedule 2 to the Uniform Laws on International Sales Act 1967 is headed 'The Uniform Law on the Formation of Contracts for the International Sale of Goods'. To the limited extent that that Schedule is already in force in the law of this country, it would not in any event be applicable to the contract which is the subject of this appeal because that was not a contract of international sale of goods as defined in that statute.

We have heard, nevertheless, an interesting discussion on the question of the extent to which the terms of article 7 of that Schedule are mirrored in the common law of England today. No difficulty arises about paragraph 1 of the article, which provides: 'An acceptance containing additions, limitations or other modifications shall be a rejection of the offer and shall constitute a counter-offer'. But paragraph 2 of the article is in these terms:

> 'However, a reply to an offer which purports to be an acceptance but which contains additional or different terms which do not materially alter the terms of the offer shall constitute an acceptance unless the offeror promptly objects to the discrepancy; if he does not so object, the terms of the contract shall be the terms of the offer with the modifications contained in the acceptance.'

For my part, I consider it both unnecessary and undesirable to express any opinion on the question whether there is any difference between the principle expressed in that paragraph 2 and the principle which would prevail in the common law of England today without reference to that paragraph, but it was presumably a principle analogous to that expressed in paragraph 2 of article 7 which the editor of *Anson's Law of Contract*, 24th ed., Professor Guest, had in mind in the passage from that work which was quoted in the judgment of Lord Denning MR. On any view, that passage goes a good deal further than the principle expressed in article 7 of the Act of 1967, and I entirely agree with Lord Denning MR that it goes too far.

But when one turns from those interesting and abstruse areas of the law to the plain facts of this case, this case is nothing like the kind of case with which either the makers of the convention which embodied article 7 of Schedule 2 or the editor of *Anson*, 24th ed., had in mind in the passages referred to, because this is a case which on its facts is plainly governed by what I may call the classical doctrine that a counter-offer amounts to a rejection of an offer and puts an end to the effect of the offer.

The first offer between the parties here was the plaintiff sellers' quotation dated May 23, 1969. The conditions of sale in the small print on the back of that document, as well as embodying the price variation clause, to which reference has been made in the judgments already delivered, embodied a number of other important conditions. There was a condition providing that orders should in no circumstances be cancelled without the written consent of the sellers and should only be cancelled on terms which indemnified the sellers against loss. There was a condition that the sellers should not be liable for any loss or damage from delay however caused. There was a condition purporting to limit the sellers' liability for damage due to defective workmanship or materials in the goods sold. And there was a condition providing that the buyers should be responsible for the cost of delivery.

When one turns from that document to the buyers' order of May 27, 1969, it is perfectly clear not only that that order was a counter-offer but that it did not purport in any way to be an acceptance of the terms of the sellers' offer dated May 23. In addition, when one compares the terms and conditions of the buyers' offer, it is clear that they are in fact contrary in a number of vitally important respects to the conditions of sale in the sellers' offer. Amongst the buyers' proposed conditions are conditions that the price of the goods shall include the cost of delivery to the buyers' premises; that the buyers shall be entitled to cancel for any delay in delivery; and a condition giving the buyers a right to reject if on inspection the goods are found to be faulty in any respect.

The position then was, when the sellers received the buyers' offer of May 27, that that was an offer open to them to accept or reject. They replied in two letters dated June 4 and 5 respectively. The letter of June 4 was an informal acknowledgment of the order, and the letter of June 5 enclosed the formal acknowledgment, as Lord Denning MR and Lawton LJ have said, embodied in the printed tear-off slip taken from the order itself and including the perfectly clear and unambiguous sentence 'We accept your order on the terms and conditions stated thereon'. On the face of it, at that moment of time, there was a complete contract in existence, and the parties were ad idem as to the terms of the contract embodied in the buyers' order.

Counsel for the sellers has struggled manfully to say that the contract concluded on those terms and conditions was in some way overruled or varied by the references in the two letters dated June 4 and 5 to the quotation of May 23, 1969. The first refers to the machinery being as quoted on May 23. The second letter says that the order has been entered in accordance with the quotation of May 23. I agree with Lord Denning MR and

Lawton LJ that that language has no other effect than to identify the machinery and to refer to the prices quoted on May 23. But on any view, at its highest, the language is equivocal and wholly ineffective to override the plain and unequivocal terms of the printed acknowledgment of order which was enclosed with the letter of June 5. Even if that were not so and if [counsel for the sellers] could show that the sellers' acknowledgment of the order was itself a further counter-offer, I suspect that he would be in considerable difficulties in showing that any later circumstance amounted to an acceptance of that counter-offer in the terms of the original quotation of May 23 by the buyers. But I do not consider that question further because I am content to rest upon the view that there is nothing in the letter of June 5 which overrides the plain effect of the acceptance of the order on the terms and conditions stated thereon.

I too would allow the appeal and enter judgment for the defendants.

COMMENTARY

The decision in *Butler* is helpfully discussed by R Rawlings (1979) 42 *MLR* 715. All three judgments have been set out in full and this is for a particular reason. It can often be difficult to discern the *ratio* of a particular case. There can be a tendency to attach primary significance to the judgment that is given first, particularly when it is given by Lord Denning! This is a temptation which must be resisted because closer analysis of the judgments may reveal that Lord Denning's approach did not in fact command the support of the other judges. Where one judge dissents it is easy to spot the differences between the judgments. But it is much more difficult where, as in *Butler*, the judges actually reach the same result but do so for very different reasons.

The approach adopted by Lawton and Bridge LJJ is the traditional one, according to which the court must ascertain whether or not an offer has been made and then whether there has been an acceptance which mirrors the terms of the offer. The advantage of this approach is its apparent certainty. The court must simply work through the correspondence that has passed between the parties in search of a matching offer and acceptance. The discovery of such a match will result in the conclusion that there is a contract between the parties, whereas a failure to find it will result in there being no contract. One problem with this approach is its tendency to result in the conclusion that there is no contract between the parties. Discrepancies can frequently be found between the respective sets of standard terms and conditions (indeed, in *Butler* itself Bridge LJ identified a number of discrepancies between the terms of the sellers and the terms of the buyers) and the conclusion that no contract has been made may run counter to the expectations of the parties who may have acted (possibly for a period of time) in the belief that their relationship was governed by the terms of a contract. The appearance of certainty can also be deceptive, as *Butler* itself demonstrates. Both Lawton and Bridge LJJ adopted what might be thought to be a rather strained interpretation of the facts in order to reach the conclusion that the parties had in fact reached agreement. An analysis of the documents that passed between the parties appears to suggest a degree of inconsistency in the actions of the sellers. On the one hand, they signed the buyers' tear-off acknowledgement slip (thus indicating their assent to the buyers' terms) but they also referred to their own terms and conditions of business (thus appearing simultaneously to insist that their own terms and conditions governed the parties' relationship). It may be that their intention was to re-instate their own terms and conditions but Lawton and Bridge LJJ were not convinced. In their view, the reference to the sellers' own terms and conditions was no more than a reference to the order. It did not have the effect of over-riding the plain terms of the tear-off acknowledgement slip which the sellers had signed.

Lord Denning took a very different approach from that taken by Lawton and Bridge LJJ. He painted with a broad brush, rejecting as 'out-of-date' the traditional approach based on the need to identify an offer and an acceptance which mirrors the terms of the offer. In his view, the 'better way' was to examine all the documents passing between the parties, to identify whether or not the parties 'have reached agreement on all material points, even though there may be differences between the forms and conditions printed on the back of them'. The advantage of this approach is said to be its flexibility and its commercial practicality. The negotiation process can often be both complex and protracted and it can be difficult to analyse it in terms of offer and acceptance. Much better, it is argued, to ask the question whether the parties have reached agreement and then to work out the terms of the contract. This involves the judiciary in a two-stage process. At the first stage the court must ask itself whether or not the parties have reached agreement and concluded a contract while, at the second stage, the court must ask what are the terms of the contract. The court has some flexibility at this second stage, as Lord Denning recognizes (he acknowledges that, where the differences between the terms are irreconcilable, the conflicting terms may have to be 'scrapped and replaced by a reasonable implication'). The difficulty with this view is that it tends to generate uncertainty. For example, Lord Denning states that it suffices for the parties to reach agreement on all 'material points'. When is a point 'material' and when is it not? The price of the goods would appear to be the most obvious 'material' factor yet the parties in *Butler* failed to agree on the price and were nevertheless held to have concluded a contract (unless it can be argued that the parties did in fact reach agreement on the price and that a distinction must be drawn between the initial agreement as to the price, which is material, and a price-escalation clause, which is not).

Assume that you are a lawyer instructed to act for the sellers in *Butler*. How would you advise them in relation to their conduct in future transactions? Presumably, you would advise them not to sign the tear-off acknowledgement slip, but how, if it all, can they ensure that their own terms and conditions govern the contracts into which they enter? The sellers in *Butler* included in their standard terms and conditions a clause to the effect that the seller's terms and conditions were to prevail over any inconsistent term in the buyer's terms and conditions but this was held not to be effective to incorporate the seller's terms into the contract. Some support for the plight of sellers can be gleaned from the judgment of Leggatt LJ in *Hitchins (Hatfield) Ltd* v. *H Butterworth Ltd*, unreported, Court of Appeal, 25 February 1995 when he stated that 'if express terms are to govern a contract of sale, a buyer would expect to buy goods upon the seller's terms, unless supplanted by the buyer's own'. This clearly suggests that the onus is upon the buyer and that a seller who insists that its terms prevail and refuses to sign the buyer's tear-off acknowledgement slip will generally be in a strong position.

The 'battle of the forms', as it has come to be known, is frequently encountered in commercial practice but it is not easy to resolve. The problem is in large part created by the parties themselves. Commercial parties generally wish to ensure that the contract is made on their own standard terms of business and these standard terms often differ in significant respects. The content of these standard terms differs from industry to industry but the types of clause commonly found in standard terms and conditions of business (using a contract of sale as the typical example) include:

(i) a retention of title clause, under which the seller, in essence, purports to retain title to (or ownership of) the goods until they are paid for by the buyer (on which see further pp. 432–433 below);

(ii) a price-escalation clause, of the type in dispute on the facts of *Butler*;

(iii) a clause making provision for the payment of interest on money owed by the buyer to the seller (on which see further p. 434 below);

(iv) a force majeure clause (on which see further pp. 434–436 below);

(v) a hardship clause (on which see further pp. 439–440 below);

(vi) a choice of law clause, namely a clause which stipulates the law that is to govern the contract. This is a matter of particular importance where the parties to the contract are in different jurisdictions. Both parties are likely to want the contract to be governed by their own law and the negotiations on this particular point can be very difficult (on which see further pp. 436–437 below);

(vii) an arbitration clause. Arbitration is a popular method of dispute resolution and parties who do not wish to litigate a dispute in the courts (for reasons of cost, speed, or publicity) may insert an arbitration clause into the contract (on which see further pp. 437–439 below);

(viii) a general clause which states that every contract of sale is subject to the seller's conditions of sale.

The approach adopted by the common law to the resolution of the battle of the forms has been the subject of some criticism. As *Butler* demonstrates, the traditional approach of the courts has been to focus on the correspondence between the parties. The reason for this is that contracts are said to be about what people promise and not what they do (although one would normally expect their conduct to coincide with their promises). An alternative view is that the courts should place greater emphasis on the conduct of the parties: in other words, if the parties have acted as if a contract has been concluded between them then the law should be slow to turn round and conclude that the parties did not, in fact, conclude a contract. Thus Professor Atiyah has stated (PS Atiyah, *An Introduction to the Law of Contract* (5th edn, Oxford University Press, 1995), pp. 67–70) that *Butler* is a case where:

the truth is that the parties were never really agreed on the terms which were to govern the sale of the machine, but the case illustrates a fact of business behaviour which is difficult to reconcile with the legal rules of offer and acceptance. The theory of the law is that parties first make their agreement and then perform it; but the reality is that sometimes, at least, parties agree in principle on their contract, and then start performing it, while continuing to try to agree on the details. And occasionally no agreement on those details is ever finalized. When this happens, as it seems to have happened in this case, the law appears to offer the judges only two choices. The first choice was the one adopted in this case; it is to pretend that the parties *have* agreed on one or other set of terms. Clearly this is a somewhat fictional exercise . . .

The second option open to the judge . . . is to hold that no agreement was ever reached and that there was in consequence no legal contract at all . . .

Both these alternative approaches appear to be unsatisfactory. They stem from the insistence of the law that, if any of the terms of the bargain are not agreed, there can be no contract. This is an unsatisfactory approach, because it seems wholly unreal to say that where (for instance) goods are manufactured and delivered and accepted, there is *no contract*. Indeed (though others may think differently), it is absurd . . .

It seems obvious that there is sufficient agreement to make a contract in this sort of case: the parties have agreed that the goods should be made and delivered and accepted, and they have also agreed . . . that if there are any arguments they should be solved by the courts. So it would seem better in such circumstances to hold that delivery and acceptance of the machine made a new contract which is on neither set of written terms, but on the ordinary (implied) terms which operate in the absence of agreed express terms, together with any further terms which the judge feels should be implied in the particular circumstances. In the *Ex-cell-O* case that would have led to the same conclusion as the court in fact reached, because there is no general implied term in a contract of sale (or any other contract) that prices are to increase if costs increase . . .

Of course if . . . the parties continue to argue about the terms and, failing agreement, no performance occurs at all, it would seem clear that there would be no contract because there would be no agreement. So these cases may illustrate again the importance of the distinction between executed and executory arrangements. While the arrangements are executory, it might be sensible to hold that there is no contract; but once a machine is made and delivered . . . that result would be absurd.

The proposition that it is absurd to conclude that there is no contract when the machine tool is made, delivered, and accepted is not one that commands universal assent. Cases can be found in which the courts have decided that no contract was concluded between the parties notwithstanding the fact that they had apparently acted on the basis that they were in a contractual relationship. Such was the case in *Mathieson Gee (Ayrshire) Ltd* v. *Quigley*, 1952 SC (HL) 38. The pursuers offered to supply machinery that could be used to remove silt from the defender's pond. The defender replied to this offer saying that he accepted the pursuers' offer to 'remove the silt and deposit from the pond'. The pursuers duly supplied the machinery and some drivers and they removed the deposit from the pond. The defender refused to pay for the work done, claiming that the price was excessive and that the pursuers were in breach of contract. The pursuers sued for £1,129 as being due under the contract. One of the issues before the House of Lords was whether or not the parties had in fact concluded a contract. Lord Reid stated (at p. 43):

Both parties have throughout contended that these letters constitute a contract between them. No other case is made by either party on record. The main issue between the parties has been what are the terms of this contract. But in the Inner House Lord Carmont, who dissented, held that no contract could be found to have existed between the parties, and before this House Counsel for the appellant supported this view as an alternative to his main argument.

It is necessary, therefore, to consider whether it is open to a Court to decide that there was no *consensus in idem* and therefore no contract when neither party has any plea to that effect. In my opinion, it must be open to a Court so to decide. No doubt if an agreement could be spelled out from the documents, the Court in such circumstances would be inclined to do that and proceed to determine what were its terms. But if it clearly appears to the Court that the true construction of the documents is such as to show that there was no agreement, then it is plainly an impossible task for the Court to find the terms of an agreement which never existed. If authority be necessary for this I find it in the speech of Lord Loreburn, LC, in *Houldsworth* v. *Gordon Cumming* [1910] AC 537, 543, where he said: 'It is not enough for the parties to agree in saying there was a concluded contract if there was none, and then to ask a judicial decision as to what the contract in fact was. That would be the same thing as asking us to make the bargain, whereas our sole function is to interpret it'. I must therefore consider whether any agreement can be found in the terms of these two letters.

Lord Reid considered these letters and decided that no contract had been concluded between the parties. The pursuers had offered to supply machinery, while the defender had purported to accept an offer to remove the silt. The fact that the pursuers had supplied drivers to operate the machinery and remove the silt did not demonstrate the existence of a contract on the defender's terms. Rather it was, in the words of Lord Normand (at p. 42), a case of 'conduct by the parties inconsistent with the contract alleged by them'. This will strike some as being excessively formalistic. Why not focus on what people do rather than what they promise to do? The answer to this question is to be found in the fact that the basis of contractual obligations is the agreement of the parties and, where that agreement is absent, there cannot be a liability in contract (although there may be a liability to pay for the work done on some other basis, such as the law of restitution, on which see p. 105 below).

An exclusive focus on the conduct of the parties will not provide a solution to all battle of the forms cases. But it may be possible to produce a more acceptable solution to the problems posed by the battle of the forms via a modification of the general offer and acceptance rules. There have in fact been numerous attempts to modify the rules of offer and acceptance and thereby prescribe a solution to the battle of the forms. In the main, these attempts have sought to provide a more flexible framework that can accommodate within the scope of contract law a degree of inconsistency between the respective sets of standard terms. Thus trivial inconsistencies should not preclude the existence of a contract between the parties, while 'material' or more significant inconsistencies may do so. The difficulty is the obvious one, namely that of distinguishing between an inconsistency which is sufficiently material to prevent a contract from coming into existence and an inconsistency which is not material. The line has been drawn in different places by different people, as can be demonstrated by the provisions dealing with the battle of the forms to be found in the American Uniform Commercial Code, the Vienna Convention on Contracts for the International Sale of Goods, the Unidroit Principles of International Commercial Contracts, and the Principles of European Contract Law (see also the references to Article 7 of the Uniform Law on the Formation of Contracts for the International Sale of Goods in the judgments of Lawton and Bridge LJJ in *Butler*). The different solutions proposed are as follows:

- **Uniform Commercial Code, section 2-207**

   (1) A definite and seasonable expression of acceptance or a written confirmation which is sent within a reasonable time operates as an acceptance even though it states terms additional to or different from those offered or agreed upon, unless acceptance is expressly made conditional on assent to the additional or different terms.

   (2) The additional terms are to be construed as proposals for addition to the contract. Between merchants such terms become part of the contract unless:

   (a) the offer expressly limits acceptance to the terms of the offer;

   (b) they materially alter it; or

   (c) notification of objection to them has already been given or is given within a reasonable time after notice of them is received.

- **Vienna Convention on Contracts for the International Sale of Goods: Article 19**

   (1) A reply to an offer which purports to be an acceptance but contains additions, limitations, or other modifications is a rejection of the offer and constitutes a counter-offer.

   (2) However, a reply to an offer which purports to be an acceptance but contains additional or different terms which do not materially alter the terms of the offer constitutes an acceptance, unless the offeror, without undue delay, objects orally to the discrepancy or dispatches a notice to that effect. If he does not so object, the terms of the contract are the terms of the offer with the modifications contained in the acceptance.

   (3) Additional or different terms relating, among other things, to the price, payment, quality, and quantity of the goods, place and time of delivery, extent of one party's liability to the other, or the settlement of disputes are considered to alter the terms of the offer materially.

- **Unidroit Principles of International Commercial Contracts: Article 2.1.11**

   (1) A reply to an offer which purports to be an acceptance but contains additions, limitations, or other modifications is a rejection of the offer and constitutes a counter-offer.

   (2) However, a reply to an offer which purports to be an acceptance but contains additional or different terms which do not materially alter the terms of the offer, constitutes an acceptance, unless the offeror, without undue delay, objects to the discrepancy. If the offeror does not object, the terms of the contract are the terms of the offer with the modifications contained in the acceptance.

- **Principles of European Contract Law: Article 2:208—Modified Acceptance**

   (1) A reply by the offeree which states or implies additional or different terms which would materially alter the terms of the offer is a rejection and a new offer.

(2) A reply which gives a definite assent to an offer operates as an acceptance even if it states or implies additional or different terms, provided these do not materially alter the terms of the offer. The additional or different terms then become part of the contract.

(3) However, such a reply will be treated as a rejection of the offer if:

(a) the offer expressly limits acceptance to the terms of the offer; or

(b) the offeror objects to the additional or different terms without delay; or

(c) the offeree makes its acceptance conditional upon the offeror's assent to the additional or different terms, and the assent does not reach the offeree within a reasonable time.

- Article 2:209—Conflicting General Conditions

(1) If the parties have reached agreement except that the offer and acceptance refer to conflicting general conditions of contract, a contract is nonetheless formed. The general conditions form part of the contract to the extent that they are common in substance.

(2) However, no contract is formed if one party:

(a) has indicated in advance, explicitly, and not by way of general conditions, that it does not intend to be bound by a contract on the basis of paragraph (1); or

(b) without delay, informs the other party that it does not intend to be bound by such contract.

(3) General conditions of contract are terms which have been formulated in advance for an indefinite number of contracts of a certain nature, and which have not been individually negotiated between the parties.

It can be seen that there are noticeable similarities between these provisions. They tend to build on one another. But there are also differences between them. For example, Article 19 of the Vienna Convention attempts a non-exhaustive definition of a 'material' alteration, while no such attempt is to be found in the other instruments. The Principles of European Contract Law also differ from the others in that they contain an additional provision dealing with 'conflicting general conditions'. Apply these different Articles to the facts of *Butler* v *Ex-Cell-O*. In doing so you will probably find that it is not at all easy to work out how these Articles apply to the facts of *Butler* and, indeed, it may be that they produce different solutions. What lessons can we learn about the utility of these provisions as a result of applying them to the facts of a particular case?

It should not be thought that the answer in all cases must be to find the existence of a contract between the parties. There will be cases where the degree of inconsistency between the sets of terms is such that it is not possible to conclude that there is a contract in existence between the parties. Thus courts may have to resort to other areas of the law, such as the law of restitution, in order to find solutions to some of the cases that come before them. An example of this process at work is to be found in the case of *British Steel Corporation* v. *Cleveland Bridge and Engineering Co Ltd* [1984] 1 All ER 504. The case did not involve a battle of the forms in the traditional sense, but the issue of principle at stake in the case was the same.

British Steel Corporation v. Cleveland Bridge and Engineering Co Ltd

[1984] 1 All ER 504, Queen's Bench Division

The parties were involved in negotiations for the supply of steel components. The defendants ('CBE') sent to the plaintiffs ('BSC') a letter of intent which stated their intention to enter into a contract and to do so on their own standard terms. The plaintiffs did not respond to this, but went ahead with the manufacture of the components required, expecting a formal offer to follow soon. Negotiations continued between the parties over the specifications of the steel components, but no agreement was reached on matters such as progress payments, and liability for loss arising from late delivery. The defendants refused to pay for the work done and instead informed the plaintiffs that they were claiming damages for late delivery and that this claim exceeded the plaintiffs' claim for the contract price. The positions adopted by the parties in the litigation were slightly unusual. The plaintiffs contended that no contract had been concluded but that they were entitled to recover the reasonable value of the work done (referred to as a 'quantum meruit' claim) in 'quasi-contract' (or, to use the terminology more commonly used today, the law of restitution). The defendants, on the other hand, submitted that a contract had been concluded between the parties. It was necessary for the defendants to establish the existence of a contract in order for them to be able to bring a counter-claim for damages for the loss suffered as a result of the alleged late delivery of the components and their delivery out of sequence. Robert Goff J first considered whether or not a contract had been concluded between the parties before turning to consider the plaintiffs' restitutionary claim.

Robert Goff J

There can be no hard and fast answer to the question whether a letter of intent will give rise to a binding agreement: everything must depend on the circumstances of the particular case. In most cases, where work is done pursuant to a request contained in a letter of intent, it will not matter whether a contract did or did not come into existence, because, if the party who has acted on the request is simply claiming payment, his claim will usually be based on a quantum meruit, and it will make no difference whether that claim is contractual or quasi-contractual. Of course, a quantum meruit claim (like the old actions for money had and received and for money paid) straddles the boundaries of what we now call contract and restitution, so the mere framing of a claim as a quantum meruit claim, or a claim for a reasonable sum, does not assist in classifying the claim as contractual or quasi contractual. But where, as here, one party is seeking to claim damages for breach of contract, the question whether any contract came into existence is of crucial importance.

As a matter of analysis the contract (if any) which may come into existence following a letter of intent may take one of two forms: either there may be an ordinary executory contract, under which each party assumes reciprocal obligations to the other or there may be what is sometimes called an 'if' contract, i.e. a contract under which A requests B to carry out a certain performance and promises B that, if he does so, he will receive a certain performance in return, usually remuneration for his performance. The latter transaction is really no more than a standing offer which, if acted on before it lapses or is lawfully withdrawn, will result in a binding contract.

The former type of contract was held to exist by Mr Edgar Fay QC, the Official Referee, in *Turriff Construction Ltd* v *Regalia Knitting Mills Ltd* (1971) 202 EG 169 and it is the type of contract for which counsel for CBE contended in the present case. Of course, as I have already said, everything must depend on the facts of the particular case but certainly, on the facts of the present case (and, as I imagine, on the facts of most cases), this must be a very difficult submission to maintain. It is only necessary to look at the terms of CBE's letter of intent in the present case to appreciate the difficulties. In that letter, the request to BSC to proceed immediately with the work was stated to be 'pending the preparation and issuing to you of the official form of sub-contract', being a sub-contract which was plainly in a state of negotiation, not least on the issues of price, delivery dates, and the applicable terms and conditions. In these circumstances, it is very difficult to see how BSC, by starting work, bound themselves to any contractual performance. No doubt it was envisaged by CBE at the time they sent the letter that negotiations had reached an advanced stage, and that a formal contract would soon be signed but, since the parties were still in a state of negotiation, it is impossible to say with any degree of certainty what the material terms of that contract would be. I find myself quite unable to conclude that, by starting work in these circumstances, BSC bound themselves to complete the work. In the course of argument, I put to counsel for CBE the question whether BSC were free at any time, after starting work, to cease work. His submission was that they were not free to do so, even if negotiations on the terms of the formal contract broke down completely. I find this submission to be so repugnant to common sense and the commercial realities that I am unable to accept it. It is perhaps revealing that, on 4 April 1979, BSC did indeed state that they were not prepared to proceed with the contract until they had an agreed specification, a reaction which, in my judgment, reflected not only the commercial, but also the legal, realities of the situation.

I therefore reject CBE's submission that a binding executory contract came into existence in this case. There remains the question whether, by reason of BSC carrying out work pursuant to the request contained in CBE's letter of intent, there came into existence a contract by virtue of which BSC were entitled to claim reasonable remuneration, i.e. whether there was an 'if' contract of the kind I have described. In the course of argument, I was attracted by this alternative (really on the basis that, not only was it analytically possible, but also that it could provide a vehicle for certain contractual obligations of BSC concerning their performance, e.g. implied terms as to the quality of goods supplied by them). But the more I have considered the case, the less attractive I have found this alternative. The real difficulty is to be found in the factual matrix of the transaction, and in particular the fact that the work was being done pending a formal sub-contract the terms of which were still in a state of negotiation. It is, of course, a notorious fact that, when a contract is made for the supply of goods on a scale and in circumstances such as the present, it will in all probability be subject to standard terms, usually the standard terms of the supplier. Such standard terms will frequently legislate, not only for the liability of the seller for defects, but also for the damages (if any) for which the seller will be liable in the event not only of defects in the goods but also of late delivery. It is a commonplace that a seller of goods may exclude liability for consequential loss, and may agree liquidated damages for delay. In the present case, an unresolved dispute broke out between the parties on the question whether CBE's or BSC's standard terms were to apply, the former providing no limit to the seller's liability for delay and the latter excluding such liability altogether. Accordingly, when, in a case such as the present, the parties are still in a state of negotiation, it is impossible to predicate what liability (if any) will be assumed by the seller for, e.g., defective goods or late delivery, if a formal contract should be entered into. In these circumstances, if the buyer asks the seller to commence work 'pending' the parties entering into a formal contract, it is difficult to infer from the buyer acting on that request that he is assuming any responsibility for his performance, except such responsibility as will rest on him under the terms of the contract which both parties confidently anticipate they will shortly enter into. It would be an extraordinary result if, by acting on such a request in such circumstances, the buyer were to assume an unlimited liability for his contractual performance, when he would never assume such liability under any contract which he entered into.

For these reasons, I reject the solution of the 'if' contract. In my judgment, the true analysis of the situation is simply this. Both parties confidently expected a formal contract to eventuate. In these circumstances, to expedite performance under that anticipated contract, one requested the other to commence the contract work, and the other complied with that request. If thereafter, as anticipated, a contract was entered into, the work done as requested will be treated as having been performed under that contract; if, contrary to their expectation, no contract was entered into, then the performance of the work is not referable to any contract the terms of which can be ascertained, and the law simply imposes an obligation on the party who made the request to pay a reasonable sum for such work as has been done pursuant to that request, such an obligation sounding in quasi contract or, as we now say, in restitution. Consistently with that solution, the party making the request may find himself liable to pay for work which he would not have had to pay for as such if the anticipated contract had come into existence, e.g. preparatory work which will, if the contract is made, be allowed for in the price of the finished work (cf *William Lacey (Hounslow) Ltd* v. *Davis* [1957] 2 All ER 712). This solution moreover accords with authority: see the decision in *Lacey* v. *Davis*, the decision of the Court of Appeal in *Sanders & Forster Ltd* v. *A Monk & Co Ltd* [1980] CA Transcript 35, though that decision rested in part on a concession, and the crisp dictum of Parker J in *OTM Ltd* v. *Hydranautics* [1981] 2 Lloyd's Rep 211 at 214, when he said of a letter of intent that 'its only effect would be to enable the defendants to recover on a quantum meruit for work done pursuant to the direction' contained in the letter. I only wish to add to this part of my judgment the footnote that, even if I had concluded that in the circumstances of the present case there was a contract between the parties and that that contract was of the kind I have described as an 'if' contract, then I would still have concluded that there was no obligation under that contract on the part of BSC to continue with or complete the contract work, and therefore no obligation on their part to complete the work within a reasonable time. However, my conclusion in the present case is that the parties never entered into any contract at all.

In the course of his argument counsel for BSC submitted that, in a contract of this kind, the price is always an essential term in the sense that, if it is not agreed, no contract can come into existence. In support of his contention counsel relied on a dictum of Lord Denning MR in *Courtney & Fairbairn Ltd* v. *Tolaini Bros (Hotels) Ltd* [1975] 1 All ER 716 at 719 to the effect that the price in a building contract is of fundamental importance. I do not however read Lord Denning MR's dictum as stating that in every building contract the price is invariably an essential term, particularly as he expressly referred to the substantial size of the contract then before the court. No doubt in the vast majority of business transactions, particularly those of substantial size, the price will indeed be an essential term, but in the final analysis it must be a question of construction of the particular transaction whether it is so. This is plain from the familiar trilogy of cases which show that no hard and fast rule can be laid down but that the question in each case is whether, on a true construction of the relevant transaction, it was consistent with the intention of the parties that even though no price had been agreed a reasonable price should be paid (*May & Butcher Ltd* v. *R* (1929) [1934] 2 KB 17, *W N Hillas & Co Ltd* v. *Arcos Ltd* (1932) 147 LT 503 and *Foley* v. *Classique Coaches Ltd* [1934] 2 KB 1). In the present case, however, I have no doubt whatsoever that, consistently with the view expressed by Lord Denning MR in *Courtney & Fairbairn Ltd* v. *Tolaini Bros (Hotels) Ltd*, the price was indeed an essential term, on which (among other essential terms) no final agreement was ever reached.

It follows that BSC are entitled to succeed on their claim and that CBE's set-off and counterclaim must fail. But, in case this matter should go further, I propose, having heard the evidence and the submissions of the parties, to express my opinion on the question whether, if BSC were under any obligation to deliver the goods in a reasonable time, they were in breach of that obligation. In this part of my judgment, I do not propose to consider any question of delivery out of sequence; an obligation to deliver in a certain sequence could only have arisen from an express term in a contract between the parties, and I am satisfied that no such express term can possibly be said to have been agreed in the present case and if any court should hereafter form a different view, the difference between the actual and contractual order of delivery can be ascertained without difficulty.

COMMENTARY

Letters of intent are commonly used in commercial practice, particularly in the construction industry where it not infrequently happens that the work has to begin before the contract is concluded. Suppliers in such a case are in a vulnerable position and they often seek to protect their position by requiring the employer to issue a letter of intent, which gives them the security of an assurance of an intention to enter a contract. But the legal status of a letter of intent is uncertain. It may give rise to liability in contract where work has been done pursuant to a letter of intent (see, for example, *Trollope & Colls Ltd* v. *Atomic Power Constructions Ltd* [1963] 1 WLR 333) but that inference is probably an unusual one, as the present case demonstrates. A letter of intent may, however, give rise to a 'simple' contract between the parties. This was the case in *Tesco Stores Ltd* v. *Costain Construction Ltd* [2003] EWHC 1487 (TCC); [2003] All ER (D) 394 (July) where Judge Seymour QC concluded that:

The natural interpretation of a 'letter of intent' of the sort now under consideration is that it is an offer to engage the addressee to commence the execution of work which it is anticipated will, in due course, be the subject of a more formal or detailed contract, but upon terms that, unless and until the more formal or detailed contract is made, the requesting party reserves the right to withdraw the request and its only obligation in respect of the making of payment for work done before the more formal or detailed contract is made is that spelled out in the 'letter of intent'. If an offer in those terms is accepted either expressly, as, for example, it could be by countersigning and returning a copy of the 'letter of intent' to indicate agreement to its terms, or by conduct in acting upon the request contained in the letter, it would seem that a binding contract was thereby made, albeit one of simple content.

On the facts of *British Steel* v. *Cleveland Bridge*, Robert Goff J decided that no contract had been concluded between the parties. He considered, and rejected, two possible routes to a finding that a contract had been concluded between the parties. The first he termed an 'ordinary executory contract'. He rejected the submission that the parties had entered into an executory contract because he found that the parties had failed to reach agreement on important matters, such as the price, delivery dates, and the applicable terms and conditions. The second he termed an 'if' contract. Here the focus was upon the fact that the plaintiffs had carried out work pursuant to the defendants' request. But Robert Goff J found that no 'if' contract had been concluded because of the failure of the parties to reach agreement on issues such as liability for late delivery. The finding that the parties had not in fact concluded a contract has been criticized. For example, Professor Atiyah (*An Introduction to the Law of Contract* (5th edn, Oxford University Press, 1995), p. 154) has argued that 'it is strange to deny that a contract exists when the parties are sufficiently agreed to manufacture and deliver and accept specified goods, even though they have not agreed on all terms'. Indeed, in his view it is 'absurd' to decide that the parties had not concluded a contract. It is important to note that Professor Atiyah focuses attention on the conduct of the parties and seeks to justify the claim that the parties had concluded a contract by reference to their conduct rather than their promises. Robert Goff J, by contrast, examined the conduct of the parties only for the purpose of deciding whether or not they had reached agreement and, finding that they had not reached agreement on a number of issues, held that no contract had been concluded between the parties. The finding that the parties had not concluded a contract was of primary significance for the defendants because it left their counter-claim without foundation. The plaintiffs, by contrast, were held to be entitled to recover the reasonable value of the work done on a *quantum meruit* basis.

The *quantum meruit* claim identified by Robert Goff J is an independent restitutionary claim. In order to succeed with such a claim, a claimant must establish three things: first, that the defendant was enriched; second, that the defendant was enriched at the claimant's expense; and third, that the enrichment of the defendant was unjust. All three factors were held to have been satisfied on the facts of the case. The difficulty that generally confronts a claimant in bringing a restitutionary claim in a case such as *British Steel* v. *Cleveland Bridge* lies in identifying and measuring the extent of the defendant's enrichment. A claimant will generally seek to establish the existence of an enrichment by proving that the defendant requested performance of the particular services and that those services were performed by the claimant. Where the terms of the request are satisfied no particular difficulties should arise. More problematic is the case where the work is done but it does not conform precisely to the terms of the request. In some cases the non-compliance will not diminish the extent of the defendant's enrichment (as was held to be the case in *British Steel* where the allegation that the nodes had been delivered out of sequence did not have an impact on the extent of the enrichment). In other cases, where the extent of the departure from the terms of the request is greater (for example, the goods are defective) then the courts are likely to scale down the value of the defendant's enrichment in order to reflect the fact that the defendant has not received the performance which it requested (*Crown House Engineering Ltd* v. *Amec Projects Ltd* (1990) 48 BLR 32).

Where the work is done on a 'subject to contract' basis then it is unlikely that the party carrying out the work will be able to bring a restitutionary claim in order to recover the reasonable value of the work done (*Regalian Properties plc* v. *London Docklands Development Corporation* [1995] 1 WLR 212). The effect of the 'subject to contract' stipulation will generally be that the loss lies where it falls in the event that the parties fail to conclude a contract. At least this is the case where the work done by one party has not been received by the other party. On the other hand, where, as in *British Steel*, the defendant actually takes possession of the work done by the claimant, the fact that the work was done by the claimant on a 'subject to contract' basis will not generally suffice to relieve the defendant of his liability to pay for the work done.

(b) MUST THE ACCEPTANCE BE COMMUNICATED TO THE OFFEROR?

The general rule is that an acceptance, to be valid, must be communicated to the offeror. The general rule makes good sense. If it were otherwise, an offeror could be bound by an acceptance of which he was blissfully unaware. The rule that an acceptance must be communicated to the offeror is not without its exceptions. Thus the party making the offer can waive the requirement of communication (on which see *Carlill* v. *Carbolic Smoke Ball Co* [1893] 1 QB 256, p. 64 above), the rule does not apply when the reason for the lack of communication is attributable to the fault of the offeror (on which see *Entores Ltd* v. *Miles Far East Corporation*, below) nor does it apply to communications sent by post (see p. 118 below).

The leading case on the rule that acceptance must be communicated to the offeror is:

Entores Ltd v. Miles Far East Corporation
[1955] 2 QB 327, Court of Appeal

The plaintiffs, a company based in London, made an offer by telex (similar to a fax machine) to the defendants, a company based in Amsterdam who acted as agents for an American corporation. The defendants sent their acceptance of the offer by telex. The plaintiffs applied for leave to serve notice of a writ on the American corporation in New York. Their entitlement to do so turned on the answer to the question: where was the contract made? Was the contract made when the defendants sent their acceptance by telex (i.e., in Amsterdam) or was it made when the telex was received on the plaintiffs' machine (i.e., in London)? It was only if the contract was made in England that the court had jurisdiction to grant leave to serve out of the jurisdiction. It was held that the contract was formed when the communication of the acceptance was received by the plaintiffs in London so that the English courts had jurisdiction and that this was a proper case for service out of the jurisdiction.

Denning LJ [after setting out the facts continued]

The question for our determination is, where was the contract made?

When a contract is made by post it is clear law throughout the common law countries that the acceptance is complete as soon as the letter is put into the post box, and that is the place where the contract is made. But there is no clear rule about contracts made by telephone or by Telex. Communications by these means are virtually instantaneous and stand on a different footing.

The problem can only be solved by going in stages. Let me first consider a case where two people make a contract by word of mouth in the presence of one another. Suppose, for instance, that I shout an offer to a man across a river or a courtyard but I do not hear his reply because it is drowned by an aircraft flying overhead. There is no contract at that moment. If he wishes to make a contract, he must wait until the aircraft is gone and then shout back his acceptance so that I can hear what he says. Not until I have his answer am I bound. I do not agree with the observations of Mr Justice Hill in *Newcomb and Another* v. *De Roos*, (1859) 2 E & E 271, at p. 275.

Now take a case where two people make a contract by telephone. Suppose, for instance, that I make an offer to a man by telephone and, in the middle of his reply, the line goes 'dead' so that I do not hear his words of acceptance. There is no contract at that moment. The other man may not know the precise moment when the line failed. But he will know that the telephone conversation was abruptly broken off, because people usually say something to signify the end of the conversation. If he wishes to make a contract, he must therefore get through again so as to make sure that I heard. Suppose next that the line does not go dead, but it is nevertheless so indistinct that I do not catch what he says and I ask him to repeat it. He then repeats it and I hear his acceptance. The contract is made, not on the first time when I do not hear, but only the second time when I do hear. If he does not repeat it, there is no contract. The contract is only complete when I have his answer accepting the offer.

Lastly take the Telex. Suppose a clerk in a London office taps out on the teleprinter an offer which is immediately recorded on a teleprinter in a Manchester office, and a clerk at that end taps out an acceptance. If the line goes dead in the middle of the sentence of acceptance, the teleprinter motor will stop. There is then obviously no contract. The clerk at Manchester must get through again and send his complete sentence. But it may happen that the line does not go dead, yet the message does not get through to London. Thus the clerk at Manchester may tap out his message of acceptance and it will not be recorded in London because the ink at the London end fails or something of that kind. In that case the Manchester clerk will not know of the failure but the London clerk will know of it and will immediately send back a message 'not receiving'. Then, when the fault is rectified, the Manchester clerk will repeat his message. Only then is there a contract. If he does not repeat it, there is no contract. It is not until his message is received that the contract is complete.

In all the instances I have taken so far, the man who sends the message of acceptance knows that it has not been received or he has reason to know it. So he must repeat it. But suppose that he does not know that his message did not get home. He thinks it has. This may happen if the listener on the telephone does not catch the words of acceptance, but nevertheless does not trouble to ask for them to be repeated: or the ink on the teleprinter fails at the receiving end, but the clerk does not ask for the message to be repeated: so that the man who sends an acceptance reasonably believes that his message has been received. The offeror in such circumstances is clearly bound, because he will be estopped from saying that he did not receive the message of acceptance. It is his own fault that he did not get it. But if there should be a case where the offeror without any fault on his part does not receive the message of acceptance—yet the sender of it reasonably believes it has got home when it has not—then I think there is no contract.

My conclusion is that the rule about instantaneous communications between the parties is different from the rule about the post. The contract is only complete when the acceptance is received by the offeror, and the contract is made at the place where the acceptance is received.

In a matter of this kind, however, it is very important that the countries of the world should have the same rule. I find that most of the European countries have substantially the same rule as that I have stated. Indeed, they apply it to contracts by post as well as instantaneous communications. But in the United States of America it appears as if instantaneous communications are treated in the same way as postal communications. In view of this divergence, I think we must consider the matter on principle; and so considered, I have come to the view I have stated, and I am glad to see that Professor Winfield in this country (55 *Law Quarterly Review*, at p. 514) and Professor Williston in the United States of America (Contracts, Vol. I, Sect. 82) take the same view.

Applying the principles which I have stated, I think that the contract in this case was made in London where the acceptance was received. It was therefore a proper case for service out of the jurisdiction.

Birkett LJ

... In my opinion, the cases governing the making of contracts by letters passing through the post have no application to the making of contracts by Telex communications. The ordinary rule of law, to which the special considerations governing contracts by post are exceptions, is that the acceptance of an offer must be communicated to the offeror and that the place where the contract is made is the place where the offeror receives the notification of the acceptance by the offeree.

If a Telex instrument in Amsterdam is used to send to London the notification of the acceptance of an offer, the contract is complete when the Telex instrument in London receives the notification of the acceptance (usually at the same moment that the message is being printed in Amsterdam) and the acceptance is then notified to the offeror, and the contract is made in London.

Parker LJ delivered a concurring judgment.

COMMENTARY

Denning LJ expressly distinguishes between the case of 'instantaneous communications between the parties' and the case where the means of communication chosen by the parties is the post. As we shall see (pp. 118–127 below) the rule that the acceptance must be communicated to the offeror does not apply to postal communications: the general rule being that acceptance takes place when the acceptance is posted, not when it is received.

The reasoning of Denning LJ in the paragraph beginning 'Lastly take the telex' and the next paragraph appears to be equally applicable to faxes, in that the sender of a fax message will usually receive a transmission report which will indicate whether or not the fax has been sent successfully.

The decision of the Court of Appeal in *Entores* has since been approved by the House of Lords in *Brinkibon Ltd* v. *Stahag-Stahl und Stahlwarenhandelsgesellschaft mbH* [1983] 2 AC 34. The issue in *Brinkibon* was the same as that which arose on the facts of *Entores* and the conclusion of the House of Lords was the same, namely that, in the case of communications by telex, the acceptance is effective when it is communicated to the offeror with the result that the contract is concluded in the jurisdiction where the offeror is located (on the facts of *Brinkibon* this was Vienna). Their Lordships expressly declined the invitation to overrule *Entores*. The essence of the reasoning of their Lordships in *Brinkibon* is to be found in the following two passages:

Lord Wilberforce

In this situation, with a general rule covering instantaneous communication inter praesentes, or at a distance, with an exception applying to non-instantaneous communication at a distance, how should communications by telex be categorised? In *Entores Ltd* v. *Miles Far East Corporation* [1955] 2 QB 327 the Court of Appeal classified them with instantaneous communications. Their ruling, which has passed into the textbooks, including Williston on Contracts, 3rd ed. (1957), appears not to have caused either adverse comment, or any difficulty to business men. I would accept it as a general rule. Where the condition of simultaneity is met, and where it appears to be within the mutual intention of the parties that contractual exchanges should take place in this way, I think it a sound rule, but not necessarily a universal rule.

Since 1955 the use of telex communication has been greatly expanded, and there are many variants on it. The senders and recipients may not be the principals to the contemplated contract. They may be servants or agents with limited authority. The message may not reach, or be intended to reach, the designated recipient immediately: messages may be sent out of office hours, or at night, with the intention, or upon the assumption, that they will be read at a later time. There may be some error or default at the recipient's end which prevents receipt at the time contemplated and believed in by the sender. The message may have been sent and/or received through machines operated by third persons and many other variations may occur. No universal rule can cover all such cases: they must be resolved by reference to the intentions of the parties, by sound business practice and in some cases by a judgment where the risks should lie: see *Household Fire and Carriage Accident Insurance Co Ltd* v. *Grant* (1879) 4 Ex D 216, 227 per Baggallay LJ and *Henthorn* v. *Fraser* [1892] 2 Ch 27 per Lord Herschell.

The present case is, as *Entores Ltd* v. *Miles Far East Corporation* [1955] 2 QB 327 itself, the simple case of instantaneous communication between principals, and, in accordance with the general rule, involves that the contract (if any) was made when and where the acceptance was received. This was on May 4, 1979, in Vienna.

Lord Brandon of Oakbrook

My Lords, I am not persuaded that the *Entores* case [1955] 2 QB 327, was wrongly decided and should therefore be overruled. On the contrary, I think that it was rightly decided and should be approved. The general principle of law applicable to the formation of a contract by offer and acceptance is that the acceptance of the offer by the offeree must be notified to the offeror before a contract can be regarded as concluded, *Carlill* v. *Carbolic Smoke Ball Co* [1893] 1 QB 256, 262, per Lindley LJ. The cases on acceptance by letter and telegram constitute an exception to the general principle of the law of contract stated above. The reason for the exception is commercial expediency:

see, for example, *Imperial Land Co of Marseilles, In re (Harris' Case)* (1872) LR 7 ChApp 587, 692 per Mellish LJ. That reason of commercial expediency applies to cases where there is bound to be a substantial interval between the time when the acceptance is sent and the time when it is received. In such cases the exception to the general rule is more convenient, and makes on the whole for greater fairness, than the general rule itself would do. In my opinion, however, that reason of commercial expediency does not have any application when the means of communication employed between the offeror and the offeree is instantaneous in nature, as is the case when either the telephone or telex is used. In such cases the general principle relating to the formation of contracts remains applicable, with the result that the contract is made where and when the telex of acceptance is received by the offeror.

When is a telex message communicated to the offeror? Is it when the message is received on the telex machine or when it is read by the offeror? The difficulty with the latter possibility is that the sender will generally have no way of knowing when the message was in fact read by the offeror. This being the case, a court is more likely to conclude that the message is communicated at the moment of receipt provided that it has been sent during normal business hours. Where the message is sent outside of office hours then one might expect the court to conclude that it was not communicated until the office re-opened for business, or shortly thereafter (such a conclusion was reached in the context of a notice of withdrawal of a ship under a charterparty in *The Brimnes* [1975] QB 929 and could be applied in this context by way of analogy).

In *Entores* Denning LJ stated that 'it is very important that the countries of the world should have the same rule'. Do you agree? Does this suggest that English law should adopt the Unidroit Principles or the Principles of European Contract Law in an attempt to achieve this level of uniformity?

(c) PRESCRIBED METHOD OF ACCEPTANCE

It is open to an offeror to state in the terms of his offer that an acceptance must assume a particular form or be sent to a particular place. In such a case, is the offeror bound by a purported acceptance of the offer that does not comply with the requirements stipulated in the offer? Obviously, it is open to the offeror to waive the requirement that the acceptance assume a particular form provided that the party sending the acceptance is not adversely affected thereby. But what of the case where there has been no waiver by the offeror and the party who submits the purported acceptance has not complied with the strict terms of the offer? Is the purported acceptance inevitably ineffective? The answer depends upon a proper interpretation of the terms of the offer. If the form of the acceptance is mandatory then a purported acceptance that assumes a different form will not be effective. On the other hand, if it is not mandatory and the method of acceptance adopted differs from that stipulated but is no less advantageous to the offeror then the acceptance may be effective to conclude a contract between the parties. In *Manchester Diocesan Council for Education* v. *Commercial and General Investments Ltd* [1970] 1 WLR 242, 246 Buckley J stated:

It may be that an offeror, who by the terms of his offer insists on acceptance in a particular manner, is entitled to insist that he is not bound unless acceptance is effected or communicated in that precise way, although it seems probable that, even so, if the other party communicates his acceptance in some other way, the offeror may by conduct or otherwise waive his right to insist on the prescribed method of acceptance. Where, however, the offeror has prescribed a particular method of acceptance, but not in terms insisting that only acceptance in that mode shall be binding, I am of opinion that acceptance communicated to the offeror by any other mode which is no less advantageous to him will conclude the contract. Thus in *Tinn* v. *Hoffman & Co* (1873) 29 LT 271, 274, where acceptance was requested by return of post, Honeyman J said:

> 'That does not mean exclusively a reply by letter by return of post, but you may reply by telegram or by verbal message, or by any means not later than a letter written and sent by return of post . . .'

If an offeror intends that he shall be bound only if his offer is accepted in some particular manner, it must be for him to make this clear.

On the facts of the case Buckley J concluded that the prescribed form of acceptance was not the only valid method of acceptance with the result that the offeror was bound by a method of acceptance which differed from the prescribed method but was no less advantageous to it. It is therefore incumbent upon an offeror to state in clear terms that an acceptance must assume a particular form. For the avoidance of doubt it may be necessary for the offeror to go further and state that this form is mandatory or that an acceptance in any other form will not be valid. An offeror who fails to do this may be vulnerable to the argument that the form of acceptance chosen is valid because it is equally efficacious from the point of view of the offeror. When considering whether or not the actual form of the acceptance is no less advantageous to the offeror than the prescribed method, it is necessary to ascertain the object that the offeror had in mind when prescribing the form of the acceptance. For example, the object behind a stipulation that the acceptance must be in writing may be to ensure that the acceptance is in permanent form, in which case an oral acceptance will not suffice. Alternatively, where the object behind the stipulation is to ensure that the acceptance is received within a given time frame, an alternative mode of acceptance which is just as quick (for example, e-mail rather than fax) may be effective to conclude a contract.

(d) CAN SILENCE AMOUNT TO ACCEPTANCE?

The general rule is that silence does not amount to an acceptance and the rule is a good one. Were the law otherwise traders would have every incentive to send out offers to sell goods at a particular price accompanied by a statement to the effect that the trader will regard the offer to sell as having been accepted unless the customer informs him to the contrary within a stipulated period of time. The law would be unduly burdensome if it imposed on people an obligation to take positive steps to rejected unwanted offers. Thus it is that the law puts the onus on the person to whom the offer has been made to demonstrate that he has, by some positive conduct on his part, accepted the offer. Silence does not generally constitute such 'positive conduct'. It is, by its nature, equivocal; it could be consistent with a rejection of the offer, indifference to the offer, or acceptance of it.

The issue that must be considered is not the validity of the general rule, but whether or not there should be exceptions to it. Take the following example. X sends an offer to Y and states that he, X, will regard the offer as having been accepted unless Y informs him to the contrary within seven days. Y decides to accept the offer but does not communicate his acceptance to X because he believes that there is no need to do so. X subsequently informs Y that, in his view, no contract has been concluded between the parties as a result of Y's failure to communicate his acceptance to X. Does Y have a claim against X for breach of contract? According to the general rule, he does not because silence does not amount to an acceptance. This seems harsh. If the reason for the general rule is a desire to protect Y from the burden of having to take positive steps to reject the imposition of unwanted contractual obligations, why should we in effect punish Y for this failure to communicate his acceptance when he does in fact wish to conclude a contract? Should the law not recognize an exception to the general rule in order to enable Y to establish the existence of a contract? It would appear that it does not and the reason for this is to be found in the following case.

Felthouse v. Bindley

(1862) 11 CBNS 869, 142 ER 1037, Court of Common Pleas

The plaintiff claimed that he had purchased a horse from his nephew. After some negotiations, the plaintiff wrote to his nephew on 2 January 1862 in which he offered to buy the horse for £30 15s. He concluded his letter by stating: 'If I hear no more about him, I consider the horse mine at £30 15s'. The nephew did not reply to this letter. On 25 February the defendant auctioneer, who had been instructed by the nephew to sell his farming stock, sold the stock at auction. The nephew told the defendant that the horse had already been sold but the auctioneer mistakenly included it in the sale and sold it to a third party. The auctioneer acknowledged his mistake in a letter to the plaintiff written on 26 February and the nephew also wrote to the plaintiff on 27 February in which he acknowledged their 'previous arrangement' in relation to the sale of the horse. The plaintiff brought an action for the conversion of the horse. The claim failed on the ground that the plaintiff could not show that he had acquired title to the horse before it was sold by the auctioneer on 25 February.

Willes J [set out the facts and continued]
It is clear that there was no complete bargain on the 2nd of January: and it is also clear that the uncle had no right to impose upon the nephew a sale of his horse for £30 15s. unless he chose to comply with the condition of writing to repudiate the offer. The nephew might, no doubt, have bound his uncle to the bargain by writing to him: the uncle might also have retracted his offer at any time before acceptance. It stood an open offer: and so things remained until the 25th of February, when the nephew was about to sell his farming stock by auction. The horse in question being catalogued with the rest of the stock, the auctioneer (the defendant) was told that it was already sold. It is clear, therefore, that the nephew in his own mind intended his uncle to have the horse at the price which he (the uncle) had named—£30 15s: but he had not communicated such his intention to his uncle, or done anything to bind himself. Nothing, therefore, had been done to vest the property in the horse in the plaintiff down to the 25th of February, when

the horse was sold by the defendant. It appears to me that, independently of the subsequent letters, there had been no bargain to pass the property in the horse to the plaintiff, and therefore that he had no right to complain of the sale. Then, what is the effect of the subsequent correspondence? The letter of the auctioneer amounts to nothing. The more important letter is that of the nephew, of the 27th of February, which is relied on as showing that he intended to accept and did accept the terms offered by his uncle's letter of the 2nd of January. That letter, however, may be treated either as an acceptance then for the first time made by him, or as a memorandum of a bargain complete before the 25th of February, sufficient within the statute of frauds. It seems to me that the former is the more likely construction: and, if so, it is clear that the plaintiff cannot recover. But, assuming that there had been a complete parol bargain before the 25th of February, and that the letter of the 27th was a mere expression of the terms of that prior bargain, and not a bargain then for the first time concluded, it would be directly contrary to the decision of the Court of Exchequer in *Stockdale* v. *Dunlop*, 6 M & W 224, to hold that that acceptance had relation back to the previous offer so as to bind third persons in respect of a dealing with the property by them in the interim.

Keating J
I am of the same opinion. Had the question arisen as between the uncle and the nephew, there would probably have been some difficulty. But, as between the uncle and the auctioneer, the only question we have to consider is whether the horse was the property of the plaintiff at the time of the sale on the 25th of February. It seems to me that nothing had been done at that time to pass the property out of the nephew and vest it in the plaintiff. A proposal had been made, but there had before that day been no acceptance binding the nephew.

Byles J delivered a short judgment in which he expressed his agreement with Willes J.

COMMENTARY
The claim brought by the uncle was a claim in conversion against the auctioneer. Conversion is a tort that is committed by dealing with goods in a manner inconsistent with the rights of the true owner. In order to be able to bring a claim in conversion the uncle had to prove that he had an immediate right to possession of the horse and this in turn depended upon whether or not he had concluded a contract with his nephew for the purchase of the horse prior to its sale on 25 February. The Court of Common Pleas concluded that no such contract had been concluded and their decision to this effect was subsequently affirmed by the Exchequer Chamber: (1863) 7 LT 835.

The result in *Felthouse* has been criticized by some commentators. The difficulty with the case lies in the fact that the nephew had told the defendant auctioneer, prior to the sale of the horse by the auctioneer to a third party, that it had already been sold. Professor Miller ('*Felthouse* v. *Bindley* Revisited' (1972) 35 *MLR* 489, 491) has criticized *Felthouse* in the following terms:

The Common Pleas held for the auctioneer on the ground that the plaintiff had no title to sue since at the date of the auction the nephew had not effectively accepted the offer. Given that he had admittedly told the auctioneer that the horse was reserved for his uncle and that the latter had equally assumed that this was so, it is not clear why anything further should have been regarded as essential to the formation of a contract. On balance it is submitted that the approach of the

Common Pleas was wrong in principle and that the actual result of the case can only be supported because there had been no delivery, part payment or memorandum in writing to satisfy the requirements of the Statute of Frauds.

Felthouse v. *Bindley* would have been more difficult had the litigation taken place between the nephew and the uncle rather than between the uncle and the auctioneer. Suppose that the nephew had refrained from selling the horse and the uncle then denied that he was bound to purchase the horse. Could the nephew have brought a claim against the uncle for breach of contract? Given that the uncle had himself stated that he did not expect to hear from his nephew, any reliance placed by him on his nephew's failure to communicate his acceptance would have been unmeritorious but his entitlement to do so would appear to follow from a strict application of the rule laid down in *Felthouse*.

While silence generally does not amount to an acceptance, it is clear law that the conduct of the offeree can amount to an acceptance (see, for example, *Brogden* v. *Metropolitan Railway* (1877) 2 App Cas 666). What is the difference between conduct (which can amount to an acceptance) and silence (which cannot)? In other words, how much does the law require by way of positive conduct before the line between silence and conduct is crossed? The answer may be that the law does not require much by way of conduct on the part of the offeree. In *Rust* v. *Abbey Life Assurance Co Ltd* [1979] 2 Lloyd's Rep 334 the issue before the Court of Appeal was whether or not a contract had been concluded between the plaintiff insured and the defendant insurer. On the facts it was held that the defendants had accepted the plaintiff's offer, probably by issuing her with the policy. But, even making the assumption that the policy constituted an offer rather than an acceptance, it was held that the parties were in a contractual relationship. Brandon LJ stated (at p. 340):

the plaintiff had the policy in her possession at the end of October, 1973. She raised no objection to it of any kind until some seven months later. While it may well be that in many cases silence or inactivity is not evidence of acceptance, having regard to the facts of this case and the history of the transaction between the parties . . ., it seems to me to be an inevitable inference from the conduct of the plaintiff in doing and saying nothing for seven months that she accepted the policy as a valid contract between herself and the first defendants.

Rust was later cited with approval by Lord Steyn (who was himself counsel for the defendant insurers in *Rust*) in *Vitol SA* v. *Norelf Ltd* [1996] AC 800, 811 for the proposition that 'while the general principle is that there can be no acceptance of an offer by silence, our law does in exceptional cases recognise acceptance of an offer by silence'. The precise scope of these exceptions has not been judicially established (for further recognition of the fact that there are exceptions to the general rule, albeit that they operate within very narrow limits see *Allied Marine Transport Ltd* v. *Vale do Rio Doce Navegacao SA (The Leonidas D)* [1985] 1 WLR 925, 937).

(e) THE POSTAL RULE

When does an acceptance sent through the post become effective? Is it when the acceptance is posted by the offeree, when it is posted through the letter box of the offeror or when it is opened and read by the offeror? One might have expected the answer to be that acceptance occurs upon communication of the acceptance to the offeror (whether that communication takes place upon receipt or upon actual reading of the letter) but English law has adopted the former view, namely that acceptance takes place upon posting of the letter of acceptance. This rule has been the subject of considerable criticism and it has not been adopted in many other jurisdictions in the world. Yet the rule is one of some antiquity in English law (the case that is commonly cited as authority for the existence of the rule is *Adams* v. *Lindsell* (1818) 1 B & Ald 681 but its place was not secured until the later decision of the House of Lords in *Dunlop* v. *Higgins* (1848) 1 HLC 381) and is now unlikely to be uprooted judicially. Rather, the courts are likely to widen the exceptions to the general rule and not to attempt to abolish the general rule itself. That this is so, can be demonstrated by reference to the following case:

Holwell Securities Ltd v. Hughes

[1974] 1 WLR 155, Court of Appeal

Under a contract with the defendant, the plaintiffs were granted an option to purchase land. Clause 2 of the agreement provided:

> 'THE said option shall be exercisable by notice in writing to the [defendant] at any time within six months from the date hereof . . .'

The plaintiffs purported to exercise that option by a letter sent by their solicitors on 14 April 1972 but the defendant never received the letter. The defendant refused to accept that the option had been validly exercised. The plaintiffs sought specific performance of the option agreement. Their claim was rejected on the ground that the option had not been validly exercised. The plaintiffs had failed to comply with the requirements of clause 2 of the agreement in that they had failed to give the defendant notice that they were exercising the option.

Russell LJ

It is not disputed that the plaintiffs' solicitors' letter dated April 14, 1972, addressed to the defendant at his residence and place of work, the house which was the subject of the option to purchase, was posted by ordinary post in a proper way, enclosing a copy of the letter of the same date delivered by hand to the defendant's solicitors. It is not disputed that the letter and enclosure somehow went astray and never reached the house nor the defendant. It is not disputed that the language of the letter and enclosure would have constituted notice of exercise of the option had they reached the defendant. It is not contended that the handing of the letter to the solicitor constituted an exercise of the option.

The plaintiffs' main contention below and before this court has been that the option was exercised and the contract for sale and purchase was constituted at the moment that the letter addressed to the defendant with its enclosure was committed by the plaintiffs' solicitors to the proper representative of the postal service, so that its failure to reach its destination is irrelevant.

It is the law in the first place that, prima facie, acceptance of an offer must be communicated to the offeror. Upon this principle the law has engrafted a doctrine that, if in any given case the true view is that the parties contemplated that the postal service might be used for the purpose of forwarding an acceptance of the offer, committal of the acceptance in a regular manner to the postal service will be acceptance of the offer so as to constitute a contract, even if the letter goes astray and is lost. Nor, as was once suggested, are such cases limited to cases in which the offer has been made by post. It suffices I think at this stage to refer to *Henthorn* v. *Fraser* [1892] 2 Ch 27. In the present case, as I read a passage in the judgment below [1973] 1 WLR 757, 764D, Templeman J concluded that the parties here contemplated that the postal service might be used to communicate acceptance of the offer (by exercise of the option); and I agree with that.

But that is not and cannot be the end of the matter. In any case, before one can find that the basic principle of the need for communication of acceptance to the offeror is displaced by this artificial concept of communication by the act of posting, it is necessary that the offer is in its terms consistent with such displacement and not one which by its terms points rather in the direction of actual communication. We were referred to *Henthorn* v. *Fraser* and to the obiter dicta of Farwell J in *Bruner* v. *Moore* [1904] 1 Ch 305, which latter was a case of an option to purchase patent rights. But in neither of those cases was there apparently any language in the offer directed to the manner of acceptance of the offer or exercise of the option.

The relevant language here is, 'The said option shall be exercised by notice in writing to the intending vendor . . .', a very common phrase in an option agreement. There is, of course, nothing in that phrase to suggest that the notification to the defendant could not be made by post. But the requirement of 'notice . . . to', in my judgment, is language which should be taken expressly to assert the ordinary situation in law that acceptance requires to be communicated or notified to the offeror, and is inconsistent with the theory that acceptance can be constituted by the act of posting, referred to by *Anson's Law of Contract*, 23rd ed. (1969), p. 47, as 'acceptance *without notification*'.

It is of course true that the instrument could have been differently worded. An option to purchase within a period given for value has the characteristic of an offer that cannot be withdrawn. The instrument might have said 'The offer constituted by this option may be accepted in writing within six months': in which case no doubt the posting would have sufficed to form the contract. But that language was not used, and, as indicated, in my judgment, the language used prevents that legal outcome. Under this head of the case hypothetical problems were canvassed to suggest difficulties in the way of that conclusion. What if the letter had been delivered through the letter-box of the house in due time, but the defendant had either deliberately or fortuitously not been there to receive it before the option period expired? This does not persuade me that the artificial posting rule is here applicable. The answer might well be that in the circumstances the defendant had impliedly invited communication by use of an orifice in his front door designed to receive communications.

Lawton LJ
. . . I turn now to what I have called the roundabout path to the same result. [Counsel for] the plaintiffs submitted that the option was exercised when the letter was posted, as the rule relating to the acceptance of offers by post did apply. The foundation of his argument was that the parties to this agreement must have contemplated that the option

might be, and probably would be, exercised by means of a letter sent through the post. I agree. This, submitted [counsel for the plaintiffs], was enough to bring the rule into operation. I do not agree. In *Henthorn* v. *Fraser* [1892] 2 Ch 27, Lord Herschell stated the rule as follows, at p. 33:

'Where the circumstances are such that it must have been within the contemplation of the parties that, according to the ordinary usages of mankind, the post might be used as a means of communicating the acceptance of an offer, the acceptance is complete as soon as it is posted.'

It was applied by Farwell J in *Bruner* v. *Moore* [1904] 1 Ch 305 to an option to purchase patent rights. The option agreement, which was in writing, was silent as to the manner in which it was to be exercised. The grantee purported to do so by a letter and a telegram.

Does the rule apply in *all* cases where one party makes an offer which both he and the person with whom he was dealing must have expected the post to be used as a means of accepting it? In my judgment, it does not. First, it does not apply when the express terms of the offer specify that the acceptance must reach the offeror. The public nowadays are familiar with this exception to the general rule through their handling of football pool coupons. Secondly, it probably does not operate if its application would produce manifest inconvenience and absurdity. This is the opinion set out in Cheshire and Fifoot, *Law of Contract*, 3rd ed. (1952), p. 43. It was the opinion of Lord Bramwell as is seen by his judgment in *British & American Telegraph Co* v. *Colson* (1871) LR 6 Exch 108, and his opinion is worthy of consideration even though the decision in that case was overruled by this court in *Household Fire and Carriage Accident Insurance Co* v. *Grant* (1879) 4 Ex D 216. The illustrations of inconvenience and absurdity which Lord Bramwell gave are as apt today as they were then. Is a stockbroker who is holding shares to the orders of his client liable in damages because he did not sell in a falling market in accordance with the instructions in a letter which was posted but never received? Before the passing of the Law Reform (Miscellaneous Provisions) Act 1970 (which abolished actions for breach of promise of marriage), would a young soldier ordered overseas have been bound in contract to marry a girl to whom he had proposed by letter, asking her to let him have an answer before he left and she had replied affirmatively in good time but the letter had never reached him? In my judgment, the factors of inconvenience and absurdity are but illustrations of a wider principle, namely, that the rule does not apply if, having regard to all the circumstances, including the nature of the subject matter under consideration, the negotiating parties cannot have intended that there should be a binding agreement until the party accepting an offer or exercising an option had in fact communicated the acceptance or exercise to the other. In my judgment, when this principle is applied to the facts of this case it becomes clear that the parties cannot have intended that the posting of a letter should constitute the exercise of the option . . .

I would dismiss the appeal.

Buckley LJ agreed with the judgment of **Russell LJ.**

COMMENTARY

It can be seen from the judgment of Russell LJ that there are a number of requirements that must be satisfied before the postal rule is applicable. The first is that the parties must have contemplated that the postal service would be used for the purpose of forwarding the acceptance of the offer. In *Henthorn* v. *Fraser* [1892] 2 Ch 27 the plaintiff, who lived in Birkenhead, visited the defendants' offices in Liverpool and, while he was there, the defendants handed to him a written offer to sell to him property in Birkenhead for £750. The offer took the form of an option to purchase within fourteen days. On the following day, between 12.00 and 13.00, the defendants posted a letter to the plaintiff purporting to withdraw their offer to sell. This letter reached the plaintiff's place of business between 17.00 and 18.00 on the same day but not before the plaintiff's solicitor had posted to the defendants a letter accepting the offer to sell the property for £750. The letter of acceptance was posted at 15.50 and was delivered to the defendants' offices at 20.30, after the offices had closed with the result that the letter was not opened until the following morning. The defendants maintained that they were not bound to sell the property to the plaintiff because they had validly withdrawn their offer before it was accepted. In particular, they argued that the rule that the contract is complete as soon as the acceptance is posted had no application to the present facts because they had not sent their offer to the plaintiff through the post; they had handed it to him in person. The Court of Appeal rejected this argument. The applicability of the postal rule depends, not on the medium by which the offer is communicated, but upon whether the parties contemplated that the post might be used as a means of communicating the acceptance. Lord Herschell stated (at p. 33) that:

> although the Plaintiff received the offer at the Defendant's office in Liverpool, he resided in another town, and it must have been in contemplation that he would take the offer, which by its terms was to remain open for some days, with him to his place of business, and those who made the offer must have known that it would be according to the ordinary usages of mankind that if he accepted it he should communicate his acceptance by means of the post.

This being the case, the postal rule was applicable with the result that the defendants' revocation was ineffective because it was received by the plaintiff after the contract had been concluded on the posting of the letter of acceptance at 15.50 (on the revocation of an offer by post, see *Byrne & Co* v. *Van Tienhoven & Co* (1880) 5 CPD 344, p. 130 below, which was applied by the Court of Appeal on the present facts).

Secondly, the parties can, expressly or impliedly, contract out of the rule that acceptance takes place upon posting of the letter of acceptance. Indeed, it was held that the effect of clause 2 of the contract in *Hughes* was to exclude the operation of the postal rule because the meaning of the phrase 'notice in writing' to the defendant was to require communication or notification to the defendant and, for this purpose, posting of the letter did not constitute 'notice'.

It might have been thought that the fact that the letter never in fact reached the defendant would have sufficed to prevent the existence of a valid acceptance. But this was not in fact the case. Indeed, Russell LJ expressly accepted that, where the postal rule is applicable, acceptance takes place 'even if the letter goes astray and is lost'. Authority for the latter proposition can be traced back to the decision of the Court of Appeal in *Household Fire and Carriage Accident Insurance Co Ltd* v. *Grant* (1879) 4 Ex D 216. The defendant applied for shares in a company. He was allotted shares but he never received the letter informing him that shares had been allotted to him. The company subsequently went into liquidation and the liquidator sought to recover from the defendant the unpaid balance of the share price. The defendant denied that he was a shareholder but his defence was unsuccessful. It was held that his offer to buy shares was accepted when the notice of allotment was posted to him and the fact that the letter subsequently went astray in the post did not have the effect of discharging the contract that had already been made for the purchase of the shares. Thesiger LJ stated (at p. 223):

How . . . can a casualty in the post, whether resulting in delay, which in commercial transactions is often as bad as no delivery, or in non-delivery, unbind the parties or unmake the contract? To me it appears that in practice a contract complete upon the acceptance of an offer being posted, but liable to be put an end to by an accident in the post, would be more mischievous than a contract only binding upon the parties to it upon the acceptance actually reaching the offeror, and I can see no principle of law from which such an anomalous contract can be deduced.

Lawton LJ recognizes the existence of a much wider exception to the postal rule. In his view (Russell LJ does not comment on the point) the postal rule 'does not operate if its application would produce manifest inconvenience and absurdity'. In many ways it is difficult to object to the proposition that a rule should not apply when it produces 'manifest inconvenience and absurdity' but much depends on what is meant by the phrase. If adoption of such a principle requires departure from binding precedent then it must be rejected. The fact that Lawton LJ draws support for his proposition from the judgment of Bramwell B in *British & American Telegraph Co* v. *Colson* (1871) LR 6 Exch 108—which, as he acknowledges, was overruled by the Court of Appeal in *Household Fire and Carriage Accident Insurance Co Ltd* v. *Grant* (1879) 4 Ex D 216 (in which Bramwell LJ (as he had then become) dissented)—suggests that the breadth of his proposed exception should be viewed with some suspicion.

Why has English law adopted the postal rule? Why does acceptance take place at the moment of posting the letter and not the moment of receipt? The competing arguments have been neatly summarised as follows by Professor Treitel (*The Law of Contract* (11th edn, Sweet & Maxwell, 2003), pp. 24–25 (footnotes omitted)):

Various reasons for the rule have been suggested. One is that the offeror must be considered as making the offer all the time that his offer is in the post, and that therefore the agreement between the parties is complete as soon as the acceptance is posted. But this does not explain why posting has any significance at all: any other proof of intention to accept would equally well show that the parties were in agreement. Another suggested reason for the rule is that, if it did not exist, 'no contract could ever be completed by the post. For if the [offerors] were not bound by their offer when accepted by the [offerees] till the answer was received, then the [offerees] ought not to be bound till after they had received the notification that the [offerors] had received their answer and assented to it. And so it might go on *ad infinitum*'. But it would be perfectly possible to hold that the acceptance took effect when it came to the notice of the offeror, whether the offeree knew of this or not. Such a rule would not result in an infinity of letters. Yet another suggested reason for the rule is that the Post Office is the common agent of both parties, and that communication to this agent immediately completes the contract. But the contents of a sealed letter cannot realistically be said to have been communicated to the Post Office, which in any case is at most an agent to *transmit* the acceptance, and not to *receive* it. A mere delivery of the acceptance to such an agent does not of itself complete a contract. Finally, it has been suggested that the rule minimises difficulties of proof: it is said to be easier to prove that a letter has been posted than that it has been received. But this depends in each case on the efficiency with which the parties keep records of incoming and outgoing letters.

The rule is in truth an arbitrary one, little better or worse than its competitors. When negotiations are conducted by post, one of the parties may be prejudiced if a posted acceptance is lost or delayed; for the offeree may believe that there is a contract and the offeror that there is none, and each may act in reliance on his belief. The posting rule favours the offeree, and is sometimes justified on the ground that an offeror who chooses to start negotiations by post takes the risk of delay and accidents in the post; or on the ground that the offeror can protect himself by expressly stipulating that he is not to be bound until actual receipt of the acceptance. Neither justification is wholly satisfactory for the negotiations may have been started by the offeree; and the offer may be made on a form provided by the offeree in which case he, and not the offeror, will for practical purposes be in control of its terms. The rule does, however, serve a possibly useful function in limiting the offeror's power to withdraw his offer at will: it makes a posted acceptance binding although that acceptance only reaches the offeror after a previously posted withdrawal reaches the offeree.

The strongest justification for the postal rule is the last one, namely that it places a limit on the offeror's power to withdraw his offer (see *Byrne & Co* v. *Van Tienhoven & Co* (1880) 5 CPD 344, p. 130 below). But even this consideration does not justify the current rule. It would suffice for the law to conclude that, once the offeree has posted his letter of acceptance, the offeror can no longer withdraw his offer. English law goes too far in laying down the rule that acceptance takes place on posting. It would suffice for the law to say that acceptance takes place when the letter of acceptance is received by, or communicated to, the offeror but that the offeror cannot withdraw his offer once the letter of acceptance has been posted or dispatched. This is, in fact, the position adopted by the Vienna Convention on Contracts for the International Sale of Goods (Article 23), the Unidroit Principles of International Commercial Contracts (Article 2.1.6(2)) and the Principles of European Contract Law. Thus Article 2:205(1) of the Principles of European Contract Law provides that 'if an acceptance has been dispatched by the offeree the contract is concluded when the acceptance reaches the offeror' while Article 2:202(1) states that 'an offer may be revoked if the revocation reaches the offeree before it has dispatched its acceptance . . .'

As the House of Lords made clear in *Brinkibon Ltd* v. *Stahag-Stahl und Stahlwaren-handelsgesellschaft mbH* [1983] 2 AC 34 (p. 113 above) the postal rule does not apply to instantaneous forms of communication. As modes of communication become quicker, the practical significance of the postal rule is likely to recede. *Brinkibon* affirmed that the postal rule does not apply to telexes. There is, as yet, no authority on the rule applicable to faxes and e-mails. In the case of faxes, the likelihood is that they will not be governed by the postal rule given that, in many respects, they resemble telexes (see p. 112 above). The position is a little more uncertain in relation to e-mails. When considering the time at which an acceptance is received in the context of contracts concluded electronically, it may be necessary to distinguish between contracts concluded by e-mail and contracts concluded over the worldwide web. The case for making such a distinction was made by Rajah JC in *Chwee Kin Keong* v. *Digilandmall.com Pte Ltd* [2004] SGHC 71; [2004] 2 SLR 594 in the following terms:

97. Different rules may apply to e-mail transactions and worldwide web transactions. When considering the appropriate rule to apply, it stands to reason that as between sender and receiver, the party who selects the means of communication should bear the consequences of any unexpected events. An e-mail, while bearing some similarity to a postal communication, is in some aspects fundamentally different. Furthermore, unlike a fax or a telephone call, it is not instantaneous. E-mails are processed through servers, routers and Internet service providers. Different protocols may result in messages arriving in an incomprehensible form. Arrival can also be immaterial unless a recipient accesses the e-mail, but in this respect e-mail does not really differ from mail that has to be opened. Certain Internet service providers provide the technology to inform a sender that a message has not been properly routed. Others do not.

98. Once an offer is sent over the Internet, the sender loses control over the route and delivery time of the message. In that sense, it is akin to ordinary posting. Notwithstanding some real differences with posting, it could be argued cogently that the postal rule should apply to e-mail acceptances; in other words, that the acceptance is made the instant the offer is sent . . . [The] acceptance would be effective the moment the offer enters that node of the network outside the control of the originator. There are, however, other sound reasons to argue against such a rule in favour of the recipient rule. It should be noted that while the common law jurisdictions continue to wrestle over this vexed issue, most civil law jurisdictions lean towards the recipient rule. In support of the latter it might be argued that unlike a posting, e-mail communication takes place in a relatively short time frame. The recipient rule is therefore more convenient and relevant in the context of both instantaneous or near instantaneous communications. Notwithstanding occasional failure, most e-mails arrive sooner rather than later.

99. Like the somewhat arbitrary selection of the postal rule for ordinary mail, in the ultimate analysis, a default rule should be implemented for certainty, while accepting that such a rule should be applied flexibly to minimise unjustness. In these proceedings . . . the parties did not address me on the issue of when the contract was formed . . . In the absence of proper and full arguments on the issue of which rule is to be preferred, I do not think it is appropriate for me to give any definitive views in these proceedings on this very important issue.

[he then referred to Article 24 of the Vienna Convention and continued]

It appears that in Convention transactions, the receipt rule applies unless there is a contrary intention. Offer and acceptances have to 'reach' an intended recipient to be effective. It can be persuasively argued that e-mails involving transactions embraced by the Convention are only effective on reaching the recipient. If this rule applies to international sales, is it sensible to have a different rule for domestic sales?

101. The applicable rules in relation to transactions over the worldwide web appear to be clearer and less controversial. Transactions over websites are almost invariably instantaneous and/or interactive. The sender will usually receive a prompt response. The recipient rule appears to be the logical default rule. Application of such a rule may however result in contracts being formed outside the jurisdiction if not properly drafted. Web merchants ought to ensure that they either contract out of the receipt rule or expressly insert salient terms within the contract to deal with issues such as a choice of law, jurisdiction and other essential terms relating to the passing of risk and payment. Failure to do so could also result in calamitous repercussions. Merchants may find their contracts formed in foreign jurisdictions and therefore subject to foreign laws.

The proposition that the receipt rule applies to contracts concluded over the worldwide web would seem to be correct and appears to command general assent (albeit that there is little authority on the point). More difficult is the case of contracts concluded by e-mail. The question whether they are caught by the postal rule or not is not an easy question to answer. The judgment of Rajah JC vacillates between the two options. The balance of academic authority would appear to support the view that the postal rule should not apply to contracts concluded by e-mail and that the general rule requiring communication of the acceptance should apply (see generally S Hill, 'Flogging a Dead Horse—The Postal Acceptance Rule and Email' (2001) 17 *Journal of Contract Law* 151). Given that the justifications said to underpin the postal rule are weak, there seems to be little justification for extending the rule to a further category of transactions, namely transactions concluded by e-mail.

An alternative explanation for the adoption of the postal rule has been provided by Simon Gardner ('Trashing with Trollope: A Deconstruction of the Postal Rules in Contract' (1992) 12 *OJLS* 170). He seeks to place the cases in their historical context. He notes that 1840 was the year in which the uniform penny post was introduced and that the general perception at the time of the new postal system was that it was wonderful. He continues (at p. 180):

This contemporary perception may have played a substantial part in the decisions in which the courts established the acceptance rule in the 1840s. In these terms, the basis of the rule might have been not a preference for posting over delivery as the dispositive act. It might have been an idea that delivery was self-evidently important, but that in the newly prevailing conditions posting and delivery were little different: that once posted, a letter was as good as delivered. But there is a certain weakness about this. Despite the great improvements in efficiency . . . equating posting with delivery on purely empirical grounds would have been a little foolish: indeed, the reason why these cases came to court at all was because the equation had failed.

However, some . . . other innovations added a further dimension to this constructive identifica- tion of posting with delivery. One was a dramatic shift towards prepayment of postage. In March 1839, only 14% of letters sent by the London General Post were prepaid, leaving 86% for which payment had to be collected from the addressee. By February 1840 these figures had been precisely reversed. Prepayment was endorsed by none other than Queen Victoria herself, abandon- ing the privilege of free use of the mail. A year later still, the unpaid element had fallen further to 8%. A second was the further facilitation of prepayment by the introduction in 1840 of the self- adhesive postage stamp; another measure which entranced the public. Of the February 1841 prepaid total of 92%, 45% comprised letters for which the payment was by this means. A third important innovation was the cutting of letter-boxes in front doors of houses, so that letters no longer needed to be handed to their addressee; this too captured the public imagination.

Taken together, these measures may have great significance. Until 1840, the delivery of a letter typically required that the addressee should manually receive it and pay for it. This was not, of course, a significant practical hurdle, but it sat in symbolic contrast with the new position, whereby the sender had only to affix his stamp and post the letter, and it would go through to its destination without further subvention from outside the system. So these three innovations of 1840 may be seen as predicating a radically new perception of the nature of the post: the notional equation of the posting of a letter with its delivery. They may thus have been a very powerful influence towards the courts affirming the acceptance rule in the way that they did in that decade.

One of the attractions of this rationalization of the postal rule is that it helps to explain the apparent lack of enthusiasm for the postal rule in cases such as *Henthorn* v.

Fraser (above) and *Byrne* v. *van Tienhoven* (below) towards the end of the nineteenth century. As Gardner notes (at p. 191):

Later decisions . . . have generally drifted away from the equation of posting with delivery. In terms of the present thesis, that would be very understandable. The further one gets from the 1840 reforms, and in particular the more one has access to instantaneous modes of communication such as became available in 1878–80 [the first telephone company began business in London in 1878], the less natural one would find that equation. The development of additional new modes of remote communication has further discredited the old equation of posting with delivery, and it is noticeable that cases dealing with these new technologies increasingly marginalize the postal acceptance rule. The decisions on telex communications, for example, explicitly treat the rule for postal acceptance as artificial, and an exception.

(f) ACCEPTANCE IN UNILATERAL CONTRACTS

The rules relating to acceptance must be modified in their application to unilateral contracts. One modification is that the courts may readily imply, as they did in *Carlill* v. *Carbolic Smoke Ball Co* [1893] 1 QB 256 (p. 64 above), that the offeror has waived the requirement that the acceptance be communicated to him. But further difficulties arise. The first relates to the identification of the act that constitutes the acceptance. The general rule must be that the offeror is entitled to require that the offeree perform the requested act in its entirety. A second issue relates to the time at which the offeror can withdraw his offer. A common example cited in the books is the man who promises to pay a sum of money if another walks from London to York. The offeror must be entitled to insist that the other party complete the walk before he makes his claim for payment. But at what point in time does the offeror lose his right to withdraw the offer? It seems rather harsh to allow him to do so at any time before the other party reaches York. This would be to enable the offeror to behave opportunistic- ally. The better rule might be to say that the offeror cannot withdraw his offer once performance has begun but that he is not obliged to honour his promise to make the payment until the other party has fully performed the act for which payment was promised. This was the view adopted by Goff LJ in *Daulia Ltd* v *Four Millbank Nominees Ltd* [1978] Ch 231, 239:

Whilst I think the true view of a unilateral contract must in general be that the offeror is entitled to require full performance of the condition which he has imposed and short of that he is not bound, that must be subject to one important qualification, which stems from the fact that there must be an implied obligation on the part of the offeror not to prevent the condition becoming satisfied, which obligation it seems to me must arise as soon as the offeree starts to perform. Until then the offeror can revoke the whole thing, but once the offeree has embarked on performance it is too late for the offeror to revoke his offer.

In *Errington* v. *Errington* [1952] 1 KB 290 a father bought a house for his son and daughter-in-law. The house was bought with the assistance of a mortgage. The father told his son and daughter-in-law that the house would be theirs if they paid off the mortgage on the house. The couple began to pay off the mortgage but were not subject to any contractual obligation to continue to pay off the mortgage (the party who was subject to the obligation to pay was the father). The father died before the mortgage had been paid off. In his will he left the house to his widow and in the present action his widow brought an action for possession of the house against the daughter-in-law. It was held that the widow was not entitled to an order for possession. It was necessary for the court to examine the nature of the relationship between the father and the daughter-in-law in order to establish whether or not the daughter-in-law was entitled to remain in possession of the house. Denning LJ analysed the nature of the relationship in the following terms (at p. 295):

It is to be noted that the couple never bound themselves to pay the instalments to the building society, and I see no reason why any such obligation should be implied. It is clear law that the court is not to imply a term unless it is necessary, and I do not see that it is necessary here. Ample content is given to the whole arrangement by holding that the father promised that the house should belong to the couple as soon as they had paid off the mortgage. The parties did not discuss what was to happen if the couple failed to pay the instalments to the building society, but I should have thought it clear that, if they did fail to pay the instalments, the father would not be bound to transfer the house to them. The father's promise was a unilateral contract—a promise of the house in return for their act of paying the instalments. It could not be revoked by him once the couple entered on performance of the act, but it would cease to bind him if they left it incomplete and unperformed, which they have not done. If that was the position during the father's lifetime, so it must be after his death. If the daughter-in-law continues to pay all the building society instalments, the couple will be entitled to have the property transferred to them as soon as the mortgage is paid off, but if she does not do so, then the building society will claim the instalments from the father's estate and the estate will have to pay them. I cannot think that in those circumstances the estate would be bound to transfer the house to them, any more than the father himself would have been.

(g) ACCEPTANCE IN IGNORANCE OF AN OFFER

The general rule is that performance of the requested act does not amount to an acceptance unless the party performing the act did so with knowledge of the existence of an offer. Were it otherwise a party could find himself bound to the terms of a contract of which he was wholly unaware. The difficult case is the unilateral contract. Suppose that a person promises to pay a reward if his lost property is returned to him. The property is subsequently returned by someone who is unaware of the existence of the offer. Can that person claim the reward? The point has not been authoritatively resolved by the courts (the leading English case is probably *Gibbons* v. *Proctor* (1891) 64 LT 594 but the report of that case at 55 JP 616 indicates that the party claiming the reward did have knowledge of the offer of a reward at the time at which the relevant information was passed on to the person named in the advertisement). While the general rule requiring knowledge of the existence of the offer is a sound one, there is a case for making an exception in the case of a unilateral contract, at least where performance of the act cannot subject the performing party to any detriment. Provided that the promisor has obtained the performance for which he promised to pay, it can be argued that the law should impose upon him an obligation to carry out his promise and pay the promised sum.

One further consequence of the need for knowledge of the existence of the offer is that identical cross-offers do not, in themselves, establish the existence of a contract. In *Tinn* v. *Hoffman & Co* (1873) 29 LT 271 Blackburn J stated (at p. 279):

When a contract is made between two parties, there is a promise by one, in consideration of the promise made by the other; there are two assenting minds, the parties agreeing in opinion, and one having promised in consideration of the promise of the other—there is an exchange of promises; but I do not think exchanging offers would, upon principle, be at all the same thing. . . . The promise or offer being made on each side in ignorance of the promise or offer made on the other side neither of them can be construed as an acceptance of the other. Either of the parties may write and say 'I accept your offer, and, as you perceive, I have already made a similar offer to you', and then people would know what they were about, I think either side might revoke. Such grave inconvenience would arise in mercantile business if people could doubt whether there was an acceptance or not, that it is desirable to keep to the rule that an offer that has been made should be accepted by an acceptance such as would leave no doubt on the matter.

More difficult is the question whether or not the act must have been done with the intention of accepting the offer. It has been stated that 'an act which is *wholly* motivated by factors other than the existence of the offer cannot amount to an acceptance; but if the existence of the offer plays some part, however small, in inducing a person to do the required act, there is a valid acceptance of the offer' (H Beale (ed), *Chitty on Contracts* (29th edn, Sweet & Maxwell, 2004), para. 2-041, emphasis in the original). However it has recently been argued (in reliance upon *Williams* v. *Carwardine* (1833) 5 C & P 566) that English law does not inquire into the motive of the person carrying out the act. Hence, provided that the person was aware of the existence of the offer at the time at which he performed the act that is alleged to constitute the acceptance, he should be held to have accepted the offer. This is so unless it is proved affirmatively that he did not intend to accept the offer when carrying out the particular act (see P Mitchell and J Phillips, 'The Contractual Nexus: Is Reliance Essential?' (2002) 22 *OJLS* 115). A case which illustrates these issues is the Australian case of *R* v. *Clarke* (1927) 40 *CLR* 227. The Government of Western Australia publicly offered a reward 'for such information as shall lead to the arrest and conviction of the person or persons who committed the murders' of two police officers. The petitioner was arrested and charged with one of the murders. He gave information that led to the arrest and conviction of those responsible for the murders. In giving this information the petitioner was found to be acting 'exclusively in order to clear himself from a false charge of murder'. He nevertheless brought a claim to recover the reward. His claim failed. The court held that, in providing the information, the petitioner had not acted on or in reliance upon the offer of a reward and so was not entitled to it. This insistence on the need for reliance upon the offer suggests that knowledge of the existence of the offer is not enough, in itself, to amount to acceptance of an offer. On the facts, the petitioner had seen the offer of a reward, although it may not have been present to his mind at the time at which he gave the information that led to the arrest and conviction of the murderers. In many ways the crucial issue may relate to the burden of proof. Once the person who claims that he has accepted the offer demonstrates that he knew of the offer and that he has performed the act requested by the offeror, must he also show that he performed that act with the intention of accepting the offer or is it for the offeror to prove that he had no intention of accepting the offer at the time at which he performed the act? It is suggested that the latter proposition is the correct one and that *Clarke* is not inconsistent with this proposition, because of the finding that the information was provided by the petitioner 'exclusively' in order to clear himself of the charge of murder. It will generally be a difficult task for an offeror to prove that the offeree did not intend to accept the offer at the time at which he performed the requested act. But it is not impossible, as can be demonstrated by reference to the following hypothetical example given by Isaacs ACJ in *Clarke* (at p. 235):

An offer of £100 to any person who should swim a hundred yards in the harbour on the first day of the year, would be met by voluntarily performing the feat with reference to the offer, but would not in my opinion be satisfied by a person who was accidentally or maliciously thrown overboard on that date and swam the distance simply to save his life, without any thought of the offer. The offeror might or might not feel morally impelled to give the sum in such a case, but would be under no contractual obligation to do so.

5. HAS THE OFFER BEEN WITHDRAWN OR OTHERWISE TERMINATED?

The final issue to be considered is whether or not an offer, once made, can be withdrawn or revoked. The general rule is that an offer may be withdrawn at any time before it has been accepted and, for this purpose, the revocation must have been communicated to the offeree prior to his acceptance of that offer. The latter proposition is illustrated by the following case:

Byrne & Co v. Van Tienhoven & Co

(1880) 5 CPD 344, Common Pleas Division

The defendants, who carried on business in Cardiff, offered by letter on October 1 to sell tinplate to the plaintiffs at a fixed price. The plaintiffs were in New York and they did not receive the letter until October 11. They immediately communicated their acceptance by telegram. There was a surge in the price of tinplate in the first week in October and so on October 8 the defendants sent to the plaintiffs a letter in which they withdrew their earlier offer. This second letter was not received in New York until October 20. The plaintiffs sued for damages for non-delivery of the tinplate. The defendants denied liability on a number of grounds, one of which was that they had validly revoked their offer before it was accepted by the plaintiffs.

It was held that the revocation of October 8 was ineffective on that date with the result that the plaintiffs were entitled to accept the offer on October 11 and so they were entitled to recover damages from the defendants.

Lindley J

There is no doubt that an offer can be withdrawn before it is accepted, and it is immaterial whether the offer is expressed to be open for acceptance for a given time or not: *Routledge* v. *Grant* (1828) 4 Bing. 653. For the decision of the present case, however, it is necessary to consider two other questions, viz.: 1. Whether a withdrawal of an offer has any effect until it is communicated to the person to whom the offer has been sent? 2. Whether posting a letter of withdrawal is a communication to the person to whom the letter is sent?

It is curious that neither of these questions appears to have been actually decided in this country. As regards the first question, I am aware that Pothier and some other writers of celebrity are of opinion that there can be no contract if an offer is withdrawn before it is accepted, although the withdrawal is not communicated to the person to whom the offer has been made. The reason for this opinion is that there is not in fact any such consent by both parties as is essential to constitute a contract between them. Against this view, however, it has been urged that a state of mind not notified cannot be regarded in dealings between man and man; and that an uncommunicated revocation is for all practical purposes and in point of law no revocation at all. This is the view taken in the United States: see *Tayloe* v. *Merchants Fire Insurance Co* 9 How Sup Ct Rep cited in Benjamin on Sales, pp. 56–58, and it is adopted by Mr Benjamin. The same view is taken by Mr Pollock in his excellent work on Principles of Contract, ed. ii., p. 10, and by Mr Leake in his Digest of the Law of Contracts, p. 43. This view, moreover, appears to me much more in accordance with the general principles of English law than the view maintained by Pothier. I pass, therefore, to the next question, viz., whether posting the letter of revocation was a sufficient communication of it to the plaintiff. The offer was posted on the 1st of October, the withdrawal was posted on the 8th, and did not reach the plaintiff until after he had posted his letter of the 11th, accepting the offer. It may be taken as now settled that where an offer is made and accepted by letters sent through the post, the contract is completed the moment the letter accepting the offer is posted: *Harris' Case* (1872) LR 7 Ch 587; *Dunlop* v. *Higgins* (1848) 1 HLC 381, even although it never reaches its destination. When, however, these authorities are looked at, it will be seen that they are based upon the principle that the writer of the offer has expressly or impliedly assented to treat an answer to him by a letter duly posted as a sufficient acceptance and notification to himself, or, in other words, he has made the post office his agent to receive the acceptance and notification of it. But this principle appears to me to be inapplicable to the case of the withdrawal of an offer. In this particular case I can find no evidence of any authority in fact given by the plaintiffs to the defendants to notify a withdrawal of their offer by merely posting a letter; and there is no legal principle or decision which compels me to hold, contrary to the fact, that the letter of the 8th of October is to be treated as communicated to the plaintiff on that day or on any day before the 20th, when the letter reached them. But before that letter had reached the plaintiffs they had accepted the offer, both by telegram and by post; and they had themselves resold the tin plates at a profit. In my opinion the withdrawal by the defendants on the 8th of October of their offer of the 1st was inoperative; and a complete contract binding on both parties was entered into on the 11th of October, when the plaintiffs accepted the offer of the 1st, which they had no reason to suppose had been withdrawn. Before leaving this part of the case it may be as well to point out the extreme injustice and inconvenience which any other conclusion would produce. If the defendants' contention were to prevail no person who had received an offer by post and had accepted it would know his position until he had waited such a time as to be quite sure that a letter withdrawing the offer had not been posted before his acceptance of it. It appears to me that both legal principles, and practical convenience require that a person who has accepted an offer not known to him to have been revoked, shall be in a position safely to act upon the footing that the offer and acceptance constitute a contract binding on both parties.

COMMENTARY

It should be noted that at no point in time were the parties actually in agreement. By the time that the plaintiffs posted their letter of acceptance, the defendants had already posted their letter of revocation.

Why is it that a letter of acceptance is effective from the moment of posting but that a letter revoking an offer does not take effect upon posting but only upon actual communication of the revocation to the other party? Note in this respect that the case was decided towards the end of the nineteenth century at a time when the enthusiasm of the courts for the postal rule appeared to be on the wane (see Gardner p. 126 above).

It was not necessary for Lindley J to decide the moment in time at which the revocation was communicated to the offeree. In *Henthorn* v. *Fraser* [1892] 2 Ch 27, 32 Lord Herschell cited *Byrne* with approval and stated that the revocation, to be effective, must be 'brought to the mind of the person to whom the offer is made'. Thus the general requirement is one of actual communication to the offeree. In the case of businesses this general requirement may require some modification. Where a revocation of an offer is received by a business during normal office hours, a court is likely to conclude that the revocation takes effect from the moment in time at which, according to normal business practice, the revocation would be read. Where the revocation is received outside business hours, then it will not take effect until the resumption of normal business hours (*The Brimnes* [1975] QB 929).

The requirement that the revocation must be communicated to the offeree gives rise to difficulty in the case where the offer has been made to the general public. How can such an offer be withdrawn? Article 2:202(2) of the Principles of European Contract Law states that 'an offer made to the public can be revoked by the same means as were used to make the offer'. A similar conclusion was reached by the United States Supreme Court in *Shuey* v. *United States* (1875) 92 US 73. A proclamation was published on 20 April 1865 offering a reward of $25,000 for the apprehension of a particular criminal. A notice was published on 24 November 1865 revoking the offer. The plaintiff discovered the whereabouts of the criminal in 1866 and notified the authorities. At that time the plaintiff was unaware of the revocation of the offer. It was held that he was not entitled to recover the reward. Strong J stated:

The offer of a reward for the apprehension of Surratt was revoked on the twenty-fourth day of November, 1865; and notice of the revocation was published. It is not to be doubted that the offer was revocable at any time before it was accepted, and before any thing had been done in reliance upon it. There was no contract until its terms were complied with. Like any other offer of a contract, it might, therefore, be withdrawn before rights had accrued under it; and it was withdrawn through the same channel in which it was made. The same notoriety was given to the revocation that was given to the offer; and the findings of fact do not show that any information was given by the claimant, or that he did any thing to entitle him to the reward offered, until five months after the offer had been withdrawn. True, it is found that then, and at all times until the arrest was actually made, he was ignorant of the withdrawal; but that is an immaterial fact. The offer of the reward not having been made to him directly, but by means of a published proclamation, he should have known that it could be revoked in the manner in which it was made.

While the revocation must have been communicated to the offeree, it need not have been communicated by the offeror. In an appropriate case, the revocation can be communicated to the offeree by a third party. The following case illustrates the point:

Dickinson v. Dodds

(1876) 2 Ch D 463, Court of Appeal

On Wednesday 10 June 1974 the defendant (Dodds) sent to the plaintiff (Dickinson) a note in which he stated:

> 'I hereby agree to sell to Mr George Dickinson the whole of the dwelling-houses, garden ground, stabling and outbuildings thereto belonging, situate at Croft, belonging to me, for the sum of £800.'

The note was signed by the defendant and it contained the following postscript: 'This offer to be held over until Friday, 9 o'clock a.m., 12th June 1874'. On the following day, the plaintiff was informed by his own agent, Mr Berry, that the defendant had offered to sell the property to another purchaser, Mr Allan. The defendant in fact signed a formal contract to sell the land to Mr Allan on the afternoon of 11 June for £800. The plaintiff communicated his acceptance to the defendant on the morning of the 12th before 9a.m. but the defendant refused to accept it on the ground that he had already sold the property to Mr Allan. The plaintiff brought a bill for specific performance but the action failed on the grounds that the defendant was entitled to revoke his offer before Friday the 12th, and that the plaintiff was aware of the revocation prior to his purported acceptance so that his acceptance was not in fact valid and there was no contract between the parties.

James LJ [after referring to the document of 10 June, 1874, continued]
The document, though beginning 'I hereby agree to sell', was nothing but an offer, and was only intended to be an offer, for the Plaintiff himself tells us that he required time to consider whether he would enter into an agreement or not. Unless both parties had then agreed there was no concluded agreement then made; it was in effect and substance only an offer to sell. The Plaintiff, being minded not to complete the bargain at that time, added this memorandum—'This offer to be left over until Friday, 9 o'clock a.m., 12th June, 1874'. That shews it was only an offer. There was no consideration given for the undertaking or promise, to whatever extent it may be considered binding, to keep the property unsold until 9 o'clock on Friday morning; but apparently Dickinson was of opinion, and probably Dodds was of the same opinion, that he (Dodds) was bound by that promise, and could not in any way withdraw from it, or retract it, until 9 o'clock on Friday morning, and this probably explains a good deal of what afterwards took place. But it is clear settled law, on one of the clearest principles of law, that this promise, being a mere nudum pactum, was not binding, and that at any moment before a complete acceptance by Dickinson of the offer, Dodds was as free as Dickinson himself. Well, that being the state of things, it is said that the only mode in which Dodds could assert that freedom was by actually and distinctly saying to Dickinson, 'Now I withdraw my offer'. It

appears to me that there is neither principle nor authority for the proposition that there must be an express and actual withdrawal of the offer, or what is called a retraction. It must, to constitute a contract, appear that the two minds were at one, at the same moment of time, that is, that there was an offer continuing up to the time of the acceptance. If there was not such a continuing offer, then the acceptance comes to nothing. Of course it may well be that the one man is bound in some way or other to let the other man know that his mind with regard to the offer has been changed; but in this case, beyond all question, the Plaintiff knew that Dodds was no longer minded to sell the property to him as plainly and clearly as if Dodds had told him in so many words, 'I withdraw the offer'. This is evident from the Plaintiff's own statements in the bill. . . . It is to my mind quite clear that before there was any attempt at acceptance by the Plaintiff, he was perfectly well aware that Dodds had changed his mind, and that he had in fact agreed to sell the property to Allan. It is impossible, therefore, to say there was ever that existence of the same mind between the two parties which is essential in point of law to the making of an agreement. I am of opinion, therefore, that the Plaintiff has failed to prove that there was any binding contract between Dodds and himself.

Mellish LJ
I am of the same opinion. . . . If an offer has been made for the sale of property, and before that offer is accepted, the person who has made the offer enters into a binding agreement to sell the property to somebody else, and the person to whom the offer was first made receives notice in some way that the property has been sold to another person, can he after that make a binding contract by the acceptance of the offer? I am of opinion that he cannot. The law may be right or wrong in saying that a person who has given to another a certain time within which to accept an offer is not bound by his promise to give that time; but, if he is not bound by that promise, and may still sell the property to some one else, and if it be the law that, in order to make a contract, the two minds must be in agreement at some one time, that is, at the time of the acceptance, how is it possible that when the person to whom the offer has been made knows that the person who has made the offer has sold the property to someone else, and that, in fact, he has not remained in the same mind to sell it to him, he can be at liberty to accept the offer and thereby make a binding contract? It seems to me that would be simply absurd. If a man makes an offer to sell a particular horse in his stable, and says, 'I will give you until the day after to-morrow to accept the offer', and the next day goes and sells the horse to somebody else, and receives the purchase-money from him, can the person to whom the offer was originally made then come and say, 'I accept', so as to make a binding contract, and so as to be entitled to recover damages for the non-delivery of the horse? If the rule of law is that a mere offer to sell property, which can be withdrawn at any time, and which is made dependent on the acceptance of the person to whom it is made, is a mere nudum pactum, how is it possible that the person to whom the offer has been made can by acceptance make a binding contract after he knows that the person who has made the offer has sold the property to some one else? It is admitted law that, if a man who makes an offer dies, the offer cannot be accepted after he is dead, and parting with the property has very much the same effect as the death of the owner, for it makes the performance of the offer impossible. I am clearly of opinion that, just as when a man who has made an offer dies before it is accepted it is impossible that it can then be accepted, so when once the person to whom the offer was made knows that the property has been sold to some

one else, it is too late for him to accept the offer, and on that ground. I am clearly of opinion that there was no binding contract for the sale of this property by Dodds to Dickinson, and even if there had been, it seems to me that the sale of the property to Allan was first in point of time. However, it is not necessary to consider, if there had been two binding contracts, which of them would be entitled to priority in equity, because there is no binding contract between Dodds and Dickinson.

Baggallay JA concurred with the judgments of James and Mellish LJJ.

COMMENTARY

Mellish LJ stated that 'in order to make a contract, the two minds must be in agreement at some one time, that is, at the time of the acceptance'. Taken literally this is difficult to reconcile with the approach taken in the later case of *Byrne & Co* v. *Van Tienhoven & Co* (1880) 5 CPD 344 (p. 130 above) where there was found to be a contract between the parties but there was no 'one time' at which they were in agreement. The judgment of Mellish LJ is also open to criticism on the ground that he appears to adopt a subjective rather than an objective approach to the existence of an agreement (on the difference between the two approaches see further Chapter 2).

The revocation was communicated to the plaintiff by a third party but was nevertheless effective to withdraw the offer. Does notice by a third party inevitably have the effect of revoking the offer or does this occur only where the third party is a reliable source of information? It was not necessary for the Court of Appeal to consider this point on the facts of *Dickinson* because the information was conveyed by the plaintiff's own agent (who was, presumably, reliable). No clear answer can be given to this question as a matter of authority but it is suggested that the courts ought to take account of the reliability of the source of the information. The more reliable the source of the information, the readier the court should be to conclude that the revocation has been effectively communicated to the offeree.

What was the meaning of the postscript? Did Dodds mean merely that Dickinson had to accept by Friday at the latest but that in the meantime he, Dodds, remained free to accept any better offer that he received or did Dodds promise that he would not revoke the offer before Friday? Does it matter which interpretation is adopted of the postscript? Consider the following claim made by Professor Gilmore (*The Death of Contract* (Ohio State University Press, 1974), p. 32):

It should be noted that the 'restatement' of *Dickinson* v. *Dodds* in terms of consideration theory makes irrelevant what the parties may have intended by the provision that the offer should be 'left over' until Friday. If, apart from the possibility of an offer under seal, all offers are revocable unless supported by what came to be called an 'independent' consideration, then it makes no difference, absent the consideration, in what form of language the offer may be expressed. 'You may have until Friday to accept but I may revoke the offer at any time before acceptance' comes out exactly the same way as 'You may have until Friday to accept and I also promise that I will not revoke the offer before Friday'. Under the new dispensation the offeror is not bound by what he has said or has intended to say or has been understood to say; he is bound if, and only if, he has received a 'consideration'.

Dickinson is therefore regarded as authority for the proposition that a promise to keep an offer open for a particular period of time is not binding unless the offeree has provided consideration for the promise to keep the offer open (the doctrine of consideration is discussed in more detail in Chapter 5). In this respect English law stands out from other jurisdictions where 'firm offers' (as such offers are generally known) are binding. Thus Article 2:202(3) of the Principles of European Contract Law provides:

. . . a revocation of an offer is ineffective if:

(a) the offer indicates that it is irrevocable; or

(b) it states a fixed time for its acceptance; or

(c) it was reasonable for the offeree to rely on the offer as being irrevocable and the offeree has acted in reliance on the offer.

There are other ways in which an offer can be terminated (on which see generally H Beale (ed), *Chitty on Contracts* (29th edn, Sweet & Maxwell, 2004), paras 2-085–2-107). For example, a rejection of an offer operates to terminate the offer (see p. 91 above). An offer may also come to an end as a result of the passage of time. Where the offer is stated to be open for acceptance for a particular period of time, the expiry of that time-period will operate to terminate the offer. Where the offer does not contain a time-limit, it will remain open for acceptance for a reasonable period of time (provided of course that it has not been accepted, rejected, or withdrawn in that period of time). More difficult is the question whether or not the death of the offeror or the offeree operates to terminate the offer. In *Dickinson* v. *Dodds* (above) Mellish LJ stated that an offer cannot be accepted in the case where the offeror dies before the offer is accepted. But his statement does not appear to have been a considered one and he did not cite any authority to support this proposition. His view is probably correct where the contract is a personal one (in the sense that the identity of the parties is a crucial aspect of the contract) but, in other cases, it is not so clear that the death of the offeror should have the automatic effect of rendering the offer incapable of acceptance, especially in the case where the accepting party was, at the time of the acceptance, unaware of the death of the offeror.

6. CONCLUSION

The rules applied by the courts when deciding whether or not the parties have concluded a contract are now rather complex but the complexity is due in large part to the diverse range of factual situations to which the rules must be applied. In essence the approach of the courts is first to seek out an offer and, having found it, see whether or not there has been a matching acceptance. In practice of course the process is much more complex as the facts of cases tend not to fit neatly into the rules that the courts have devised. The 'battle of the forms' cases illustrate this neatly. Yet the difficulty involved in accommodating individual cases within the offer and acceptance framework has not persuaded the judges to throw out the model and seek an alternative (see, for example, *Tesco Stores Ltd* v. *Costain Construction Ltd* [2003] EWHC 1487 (TCC); [2003] All ER (D) 394 (July) where Judge Seymour QC stated that 'the notions of offer and acceptance are . . . of the highest importance in any consideration of the issues whether an agreement has been made and, if so, what were the terms of the agreement and whether the parties intended to be legally bound by those terms'). It is true that Lord Denning did state that the offer and acceptance approach was 'out-of-date' but he failed to persuade his colleagues of the merits of his view. Rather than abandon the offer and acceptance analysis in its entirety, the courts have chosen to apply it with a degree of flexibility to the facts of individual cases (as can be seen from cases such as *Butler* v. *Ex-Cell-O Corporation* (p. 92 above) and *Blackpool and Fylde Aero Club Ltd* v. *Blackpool Borough Council* (p. 78 above)). Finally, it is important to resist the conclusion that the rules of offer and acceptance are rules that are mechanically developed and applied by the courts. For example, there is no obvious answer to the question of the time at which an acceptance sent through the post should take effect. The court must consider the relative advantages and disadvantages of the different options and make its choice. The English courts have chosen the time of posting and not the time of receipt and, as we have seen, this choice has not been universally approved. The initial choice of the rule is not a value-free exercise, even if the application of that rule in subsequent cases can appear to be rather mechanical.

7. FURTHER READING

GARDNER, S, 'Trashing with Trollope: A Deconstruction of the Postal Rules in Contract' (1992) 12 *OJLS* 170.

HILL, S, 'Flogging a Dead Horse – The Postal Acceptance Rule and Email' (2001) 17 *Journal of Contract Law* 151.

MILLER, J, '*Felthouse* v. *Bindley* Revisited' (1972) 35 *MLR* 489.

MITCHELL, P, and PHILLIPS, J, 'The Contractual Nexus: Is Reliance Essential?' (2002) 22 *OJLS* 115.

RAWLINGS, R, 'The Battle of the Forms' (1979) 42 *MLR* 715.

SIMPSON, AWB, 'Quackery and Contract Law: *Carlill* v. *Carbolic Smoke Ball Company* (1893)' in *Leading Cases in the Common Law* (Oxford University Press, 1995), p. 259.

4

UNCERTAIN AND INCOMPLETE AGREEMENTS

1. CENTRAL ISSUES

1. The courts will not generally make the contract for the parties. It is for the parties to make their contract and they must express their agreement in a form that is sufficiently certain for the courts to be able to enforce it.

2. The courts have experienced considerable difficulty in the cases in deciding whether or not an agreement has been expressed in a form that is sufficiently certain for them to enforce. On the one hand, the judges generally do not wish to be seen to be making the contract for the parties. On the other hand, they are reluctant to deny legal effect to an agreement that the parties have apparently accepted as valid and binding. The result has been a degree of tension in the case-law. This is particularly so in relation to 'agreements to agree'. The view taken by the House of Lords in a case decided some seventy years ago is that an agreement to agree is not enforceable. However courts in other jurisdictions have recog-

nized the validity of such agreements and many commentators and commercial practitioners have argued that English law should now do so as well. The competing views in this debate are considered in this chapter.

3. An agreement is less likely to be held to be too vague or too uncertain where it contains within it criteria or machinery that the court can use in order to resolve the uncertainty or to clarify the word or phrase that is expressed in vague terms. For example, the agreement can provide that the uncertainty or doubt is to be resolved by one of the contracting parties or by a third party (provided that the third party is not a judge sitting in a court of law). The court may also be able to imply a term into the agreement in order to fill the gap that was left by the parties or it may be able to cut out (or 'sever') the term that is alleged to be too uncertain or too vague and enforce the rest of the agreement.

2. INTRODUCTION

It sometimes happens that parties to agreements express themselves in terms that are vague, incomplete, or uncertain. Does an agreement expressed in such terms amount to an enforceable contract? This question does not admit of an easy answer, largely because it cannot be answered in black and white terms. A great deal depends on the facts of the individual case. Further, the question which the courts ask themselves is whether or not the agreement is 'sufficiently certain' to be enforced and sufficiency involves questions of degree. The result has been a degree of inconsistency in the case-law, with some judges appearing to be more willing than others to find the existence of a contract notwithstanding the fact that the agreement between the parties was expressed in terms that were in some way vague, incomplete, or uncertain.

The tension in the case-law can be easily stated, if not easily resolved. On the one hand, the courts insist that it is not their function to make the contract for the parties. It is for the parties to make the contract and the task of the courts is simply to interpret the contract and, where necessary, enforce it or grant remedies for its breach. On the other hand, the courts do not wish to incur the reproach of the commercial community by denying legal effect to an agreement that has been reached by commercial parties, was regarded by them as a binding agreement and, possibly, had been acted upon over a period of time. This tension is particularly acute where the parties expressly recognize that they have not reached agreement on a particular issue but have reached agreement on a number of other points. In such a case should a court conclude that the agreement is not enforceable on the ground that the parties have failed to reach agreement or on the ground that it is not the function of the court to make the agreement for the parties? Or should the court nevertheless give legal effect to the agreement concluded between the parties even though it was expressed in the form of an agreement to reach an agreement? An example will illustrate the point. Clause 1 of the contract between the parties in *Foley* v. *Classique Coaches Ltd* [1934] 2 KB 1 provided as follows:

The vendor shall sell to the company and the company shall purchase from the vendor all petrol which shall be required by the company for the running of their said business at a price to be agreed by the parties in writing and from time to time.

A dispute broke out between the parties and one of the issues between them was whether or not the agreement to supply petrol to the purchasers was valid and binding despite their failure to reach agreement on the price at which the petrol was to be sold. The purchasers argued that it was not binding. They submitted that the parties had failed to reach agreement on the price and it was not the function of the courts to make the contract for the parties. The vendors, on the other hand, relied on the fact that the parties had acted on the basis of this agreement for three years and the fact that the agreement contained an arbitration clause which covered a failure to agree the price at which the petrol was to be sold. The Court of Appeal came down on the side of the vendors and held that the agreement was valid and binding. Greer LJ stated (at p. 11) that, 'in order to give effect to what both parties intended the Court is justified in implying that in the absence of agreement as to price a reasonable price must be paid, and if the parties cannot agree as to what is a reasonable price then arbitration must take place'.

The task of the Court of Appeal in *Foley* was made more difficult by the fact that, in the words of Scrutton LJ (at p. 9), 'a good deal of the case turns upon the effect of two decisions of the House of Lords which are not easy to fit in with each other'. The first of these decisions is *May and Butcher Ltd* v. *The King* [1934] 2 KB 17n, a case decided in 1929 but not reported until 1934, while the second is *Hillas & Co Ltd* v. *Arcos Ltd* (1932) 147 LT 503. These two cases remain leading cases and their relationship is an uneasy one. It is therefore important to commence our analysis by considering these two cases and their relationship with each other.

May and Butcher Ltd v. The King

[1934] 2 KB 17n, House of Lords

May and Butcher Ltd, the suppliants[1] (also referred to in the judgments as the appellants), alleged that they had concluded an agreement with the Controller of the Disposals Board under which they agreed to buy the whole of the tentage which might become available in the United Kingdom for disposal up to 31 March 1923. On 29 June 1921, the Controller wrote to the suppliants stating that:

'in consideration of your agreeing to deposit with the [Disposals & Liquidation] Commission the sum of 1000l. as security for the carrying out of this extended contract, the Commission hereby confirm the sale to you of the whole of the old tentage which may become available . . . up to and including December 31, 1921, upon the following terms:

(1.) The Commission agrees to sell and [the suppliants] agree to purchase the total stock of old tentage . . .

(3.) The price or prices to be paid, and the date or dates on which payment is to be made by the purchasers to the Commission for such old tentage shall be agreed upon from time to time between the Commission and the purchasers as the quantities of the said old tentage become available for disposal, and are offered to the purchasers by the Commission.

(4.) Delivery . . . shall be taken by the purchasers in such period or periods as may be agreed upon between the Commission and the purchasers when such quantities of old tentage are offered to the purchasers by the Commission. . . .

(10.) It is understood that all disputes with reference to or arising out of this agreement will be submitted to arbitration in accordance with the provisions of the Arbitration Act, 1889.'

In a second letter, dated 7 January 1922, the Disposals Controller confirmed the sale to the suppliants of the tentage that might become available for disposal up to 31 March, 1923. This letter, which varied in certain respects the earlier terms, stated that 'the prices to be agreed upon between the Commission and the purchasers in accordance with the terms of clause 3 of the said earlier contract shall include delivery free on rail . . . nearest to the depots at which the said tentage may be lying. . . .'

In August 1922, after the suppliants had made proposals to purchase tentage that were not acceptable to the Controller, the Disposals Board wrote to the suppliants and stated that they considered themselves no longer bound by the agreement. The suppliants then filed their petition of right in which they claimed (i) an injunction restraining the Commission from disposing of the remainder of the tentage to anyone other than the suppliants, and (ii) an account of the tentage that had become available and compensation for the damage done to them. Their petition was dismissed by the House of Lords.

Lord Buckmaster

The points that arise for determination are these: Whether or not the terms of the contract were sufficiently defined to constitute a legal binding contract between the parties.

---

[1] In this connection a suppliant is someone who petitions humbly of the King.

The Crown says that the price was never agreed. The suppliants say first, that if it was not agreed, it would be a reasonable price. Secondly, they say that even if the price was not agreed, the arbitration clause in the contract was intended to cover this very question of price, and that consequently the reasonableness of the price was referred to arbitration under the contract . . .

My Lords, those being the contentions, it is obvious that the whole matter depends upon the construction of the actual words of the bargain itself.

[he set out various terms of the correspondence that had passed between the parties and continued]

What resulted was this: it was impossible to agree the prices, and unless the appellants are in a position to establish either that this failure to agree resulted out of a definite agreement to buy at a reasonable price, or that the price had become subject to arbitration, it is plain on the first two points which have been mentioned that this appeal must fail.

In my opinion there never was a concluded contract between the parties. It has long been a well recognized principle of contract law that an agreement between two parties to enter into an agreement in which some critical part of the contract matter is left undetermined is no contract at all. It is of course perfectly possible for two people to contract that they will sign a document which contains all the relevant terms, but it is not open to them to agree that they will in the future agree upon a matter which is vital to the arrangement between them and has not yet been determined. It has been argued that as the fixing of the price has broken down, a reasonable price must be assumed. That depends in part upon the terms of the Sale of Goods Act, which no doubt reproduces, and is known to have reproduced, the old law upon the matter. That provides in s. 8 that 'the price in a contract of sale may be fixed by the contract, or may be left to be fixed in manner thereby agreed, or may be determined by the course of dealing between the parties. Where the price is not determined in accordance with the foregoing provisions the buyer must pay a reasonable price'; while, if the agreement is to sell goods on the terms that the price is to be fixed by the valuation of a third party, and such third party cannot or does not make such valuation, s. 9 says that the agreement is avoided. I find myself quite unable to understand the distinction between an agreement to permit the price to be fixed by a third party and an agreement to permit the price to be fixed in the future by the two parties to the contract themselves. In principle it appears to me that they are one and the same thing . . .

The next question is about the arbitration clause, and there I entirely agree with the majority of the Court of Appeal and also with Rowlatt J. The clause refers 'disputes with reference to or arising out of this agreement' to arbitration, but until the price has been fixed, the agreement is not there. The arbitration clause relates to the settlement of whatever may happen when the agreement has been completed and the parties are regularly bound. There is nothing in the arbitration clause to enable a contract to be made which in fact the original bargain has left quite open.

Viscount Dunedin

I am of the same opinion. This case arises upon a question of sale, but in my view the principles which we are applying are not confined to sale, but are the general principles of the law of contract. To be a good contract there must be a concluded bargain, and a concluded contract is one which settles everything that is necessary to be settled and leaves nothing to be settled by agreement between the parties. Of course it may leave something which still has to be determined, but then that determination must be a determination which does not depend upon the agreement between the parties. In the system of law in which I was brought up[2], that was expressed by one of those brocards of which perhaps we have been too fond, but which often express very neatly what is wanted: 'Certum est quod certum reddi potest'.[3] Therefore, you may very well agree that a certain part of the contract of sale, such as price, may be settled by some one else. As a matter of the general law of contract all the essentials have to be settled. What are the essentials may vary according to the particular contract under consideration. We are here dealing with sale, and undoubtedly price is one of the essentials of sale, and if it is left still to be agreed between the parties, then there is no contract. It may be left to the determination of a certain person, and if it was so left and that person either would not or could not act, there would be no contract because the price was to be settled in a certain way and it has become impossible to settle it in that way, and therefore there is no settlement. No doubt as to goods, the Sale of Goods Act, 1893, says that if the price is not mentioned and settled in the contract it is to be a reasonable price. The simple answer in this case is that the Sale of Goods Act provides for silence on the point and here there is no silence, because there is a provision that the two parties are to agree. As long as you have something certain it does not matter. For instance, with regard to price it is a perfectly good contract to say that the price is to be settled by the buyer. I have not had time, or perhaps I have not been industrious enough, to look through all the books in England to see if there is such a case; but there was such a case in Scotland in 1760, where it was decided that a sale of a landed estate was perfectly good, the price being left to be settled by the buyer himself. I have only expressed in other words what has already been said by my noble friend on the Woolsack. Here there was clearly no contract. There would have been a perfectly good settlement of price if the contract had said that it was to be settled by arbitration by a certain man, or it might have been quite good if it was said that it was to be settled by arbitration under the Arbitration Act so as to bring in a material plan by which a certain person could be put in action. The question then arises, has anything of that sort been done? I think clearly not. The general arbitration clause is one in very common form as to disputes arising out of the arrangements. In no proper meaning of the word can this be described as a dispute arising between the parties; it is a failure to agree, which is a very different thing from a dispute.

Lord Warrington of Clyffe delivered a concurring judgment.

Hillas & Co Ltd v. Arcos Ltd

(1932) 147 LT 503, House of Lords

By an agreement dated 21 May 1930 the appellants agreed to buy from the respondents '22,000 standards of softwood goods of fair specification over the season 1930' subject to a number of conditions, one of which, clause 9, was in the following terms:

---

[2] Lord Dunedin was brought up in Scotland.
[3] If something is capable of being made certain, it should be treated as certain.

'Buyers shall also have the option of entering into a contract with sellers for the purchase of 100,000 standards for delivery during 1931. Such contract to stipulate that, whatever the conditions are, buyers shall obtain the goods on conditions and at prices which show to them a reduction of 5 %. on the f.o.b. value of the official price list at any time ruling during 1931. Such option to be declared before the 1st Jan. 1931.'

The appellants purported to exercise the option on 22 December 1930 but the respondents had already agreed to sell the whole of the output of the 1931 season to a third party. The appellants sued for damages for breach of contract but were met by the defence that the document of 21 May 1930 did not constitute an enforceable agreement because it did not contain a sufficient description of the goods to be sold to enable them to be identified and it contemplated in the future some further agreement upon essential terms. The House of Lords rejected the defence and held that, the option having been exercised, the agreement was complete and binding in itself and was not dependent on any future agreement for its validity.

Lord Tomlin
In the present case one or two preliminary observations fall to be made.

First, the parties were both intimately acquainted with the course of business in the Russian softwood timber trade, and had without difficulty carried out the sale and purchase of 22,000 standards under the first part of the document of the 21st May 1930;

Secondly, although the question here is whether Clause 9 of the document of the 21st May 1930, with the letter of 22nd Dec. 1930, constitutes a contract, the validity of the whole of the document of the 21st May 1930 is really in question so far as the matter depends upon the meaning of the phrase 'of fair specification'; and,

Thirdly, it is indisputable, having regard to clause 11, which provides that 'this agreement cancels all previous agreements', that the parties intended by the document of 21st May 1930 to make, and believed that they had made, some concluded bargain.

The case against the appellants is put on two grounds.

First, it is said that there is in Clause 9 no sufficient description of the goods to be sold; and

Secondly, it is said that clause 9 contemplates a future bargain the terms of which remain to be settled.

As to the first point it is plain that something must necessarily be implied in clause 9. The words '100,000 standards' without more do not even indicate that timber is the subject-matter of the clause. The implication at the least of the words 'of softwood goods' is in my opinion inevitable, and if this is so I see no reason to separate the words 'of fair specification' from the words 'of softwood goods'. In my opinion, there is a necessary implication of the words 'of softwood goods of fair specification' after the words '100,000 standards' in clause 9.

What, then, is the meaning of '100,000 standards of softwood goods of fair specification for delivery during 1931'?

If the words 'of fair specification' have no meaning which is certain or capable of being made certain, then not only can there be no contract under clause 9 but there cannot have been a contract with regard to the 22,000 standards mentioned at the beginning of the document of the 21st May 1930. This may be the proper conclusion, but before it is reached it is, I think, necessary to exclude as impossible all reasonable meanings which would give certainty to the words. In my opinion, this cannot be done.

The parties undoubtedly attributed to the words in connection with the 22,000 stand-ards, some meaning which was precise or capable of being made precise . . .

Reading the document of 21st May 1930 as a whole, and having regard to the admis-sible evidence as to the course of the trade, I think that upon their true construction the words 'of fair specification over the season 1930,' used in connection with the 22,000 standards, mean that the 22,000 standards are to be satisfied in goods distributed over kinds, qualities and sizes in the fair proportions, having regard to the output of the season 1930 and the classifications of that output in respect of kinds, qualities and sizes. That is something which if the parties fail to agree can be ascertained just as much as the fair value of a property.

I have already expressed the view that clause 9 must be read as '100,000 standards of fair specification for delivery during 1931,' and these words, I think, have the same meaning, *mutatis mutandis*,[4] as the words relating to the 22,000 standards. Thus, there is a description of the goods which if not immediately yet ultimately is capable of being rendered certain.

The second point upon clause 9, that it contemplates a future agreement, remains to be considered.

The form of the phrases 'the option of entering into a contract' and 'such contract to stipulate that' upon which stress has been laid by the respondents seems to me unimportant. These phrases are but an inartificial way of indicating that there is no contract till the option is exercised. The sentence that such contract is to stipulate that whatever the conditions are the buyers are to obtain the goods at a certain reduction is more difficult. The words 'whatever the conditions are' being governed by the word 'that' which follows the words 'to stipulate' must be intended to be part of the contract. If so the word 'conditions' cannot mean terms of the contract, but must connote some extrinsic condition of affairs, and the condition of affairs referred to is, I think, the condi-tions as to supply and demand which may prevail during 1931.

Upon this view of the matter it cannot, I think, be said that there is nothing more than an agreement to make an agreement.

It is also urged as a minor point that there was no provision as to shipment, and that this was an essential of such a contract. I am not prepared without further consideration to accept the view that in the absence of a provision in relation to shipment there can be no contract in law in such a case as the present.

In my opinion, however, the point does not arise here. Clause 9 is one of the clauses containing the conditions upon which the sale of the 22,000 standards is made. This fact, together with the presence of the word 'also' in clause 9, satisfies me that upon the true construction of the document the sale conditions in relation to the 22,000 standards are so far as applicable imported into the option for the sale of this 100,000 standards, and in particular that clause 6, relating to shipping dates and loading instructions, is so imported.

Reference was made in the course of the arguments before your Lordships and in the judgments in the Court of Appeal to the unreported[5] case before your Lordships' House of *May & Butcher, Ltd* v. *Rex.*

---

[4] With the necessary changes in points of detail.
[5] The case was in fact subsequently reported in 1934 and is set out at p. 140 above.

In the agreement there under consideration there was an express provision that the price of the goods to be sold should be subsequently fixed between the parties. Your Lordships' House reached the conclusion that there was no contract, rejecting the appellants' contention that the agreement should be construed as an agreement to sell at the fair or reasonable price or alternatively at a price to be fixed under the arbitration clause contained in the agreement.

That case does not, in my opinion, afford any assistance in determining the present case, the result of which must depend upon the meaning placed upon the language employed . . .

It was urged on behalf of the respondents before your Lordships that if there was a contract still it was one upon which only nominal damages should have been awarded . . . because the respondents were free to give to other customers an equal or greater reduction in price. . . . I think the phrase 'the official price list at any time ruling during 1931' makes plain that the reduction given is from the general operative price and not from a merely nominal price which is not being adhered to in actual practice.

Lord Thankerton

My Lords, I have had the privilege of considering the opinion which has been delivered by my noble and learned friend on the Woolsack, and in which he has fully narrated the material facts of this case and the terms of the document of the 21st of May 1930.

Subject to some doubts that I have felt as to the proper construction of the words 'of fair specification,' and as to which I desire to add some observations, I find myself in entire agreement with the construction which my noble and learned friend has put upon the document of May 21, 1930, and I also agree with his conclusion that it is not open to the respondents to maintain that there was no concluded agreement.

The question on which I have had doubt is whether the words 'of fair specification', on their proper construction, will enable the subject to be identified by the Court. In other words, do they provide a standard by which the Court is enabled to ascertain the subject-matter of the contract, or do they involve an adjustment between the conflicting interests of the parties, which the parties have left unsettled and on which the Court is not entitled to adjudicate?

Does the phrase mean a specification which is fair as between the interests, on the one hand, of the seller in respect of the stock of wood, comprising various kinds of wood and various qualities and sizes, available for sale in the season of 1931, and, on the other hand, the interests of the buyer in respect of the requirements of his trade during that season? Or does the phrase mean a fair selection from the seller's stock of wood available for sale in that season? If the former construction be the proper one, I would be of opinion that the Court would not be entitled to adjudicate between the opposing interests of the two parties. If the latter construction be the proper one, the ascertainment of a fair selection from the seller's available stock is within the province of the Court; in that case the Court is applying a standard which is provided by the contract, and is thereby merely identifying the subject- matter of the contract.

While I have had considerable doubt on this question of construction I am affected by the consideration that the contract is a commercial one and that the parties undoubtedly thought that they had concluded a contract, and I have come to the conclusion, in agreement with the noble Lord, that the second alternative construction above stated is the proper one and that there was here a concluded contract. I therefore concur in the motion proposed.

Lord Wright

The document of the 21st May 1930 cannot be regarded as other than inartistic, and may appear repellent to the trained sense of an equity draftsman. But it is clear that the parties both intended to make a contract and thought they had done so. Business men often record the most important agreements in crude and summary fashion; modes of expression sufficient and clear to them in the course of their business may appear to those unfamiliar with the business far from complete or precise. It is accordingly the duty of the court to construe such documents fairly and broadly, without being too astute or subtle in finding defects, but, on the contrary, the court should seek to apply the old maxim of English law *verba ita sunt intelligenda ut res magis valeat quam pereat*.[6] That maxim, however, does not mean that the Court is to make a contract for the parties, or to go outside the words they have used, except in so far as there are appropriate implications of law, as, for instance, the implication of what is just and reasonable to be ascertained by the court as a matter of machinery where the contractual intention is clear but the contract is silent on some detail. Thus, in contracts for future performance over a period the parties may neither be able nor desire to specify many matters of detail, but leave them to be adjusted in the working out of the contract. Save for the legal implication I have mentioned, such contracts might well be incomplete or uncertain; with that implication in reserve they are neither incomplete nor uncertain. As obvious illustrations I may refer to such matters as prices or times of delivery in contracts for the sale of goods, or times for loading or discharging in a contract of sea carriage. Furthermore, even if the construction of the words used may be difficult, that is not a reason for holding them too ambiguous or uncertain to be enforced, if the fair meaning of the parties can be extracted.

[Lord Wright proceeded to consider the construction of the words used in some detail and concluded]

In the result, I arrive at the same conclusion as MacKinnon, J, viz., that the contract is valid and enforceable and that the appellants are entitled to recover damages from the respondents for its repudiation.

Lord Warrington and **Lord Macmillan** concurred in the judgment delivered by Lord Tomlin.

COMMENTARY

The spirit of the judgments in *Hillas* appears to stand in marked contrast to the tenor of the judgments in *May and Butcher*. The modern perception tends to be that the House of Lords in *May and Butcher* adopted an unduly restrictive approach and that it should be kept within narrow confines, if not overruled. This sentiment was recently expressed by Blanchard J, giving the judgment of the Court of Appeal of New Zealand, in *Fletcher Challenge Energy Ltd* v. *Electricity Corporation of New Zealand Ltd* [2002] 2 NZLR 433. He stated (at pp. 446–447):

Something should be said about the place that the controversial decision of the House of Lords in *May and Butcher Ltd* v. *The King* [1934] 2 KB 17n has in the modern law of contract. We take the view that this case is no longer to be regarded as authority for any wider proposition than that

---

[6] Words are to be understood that the object may be carried out and not fail.

an 'agreement' which omits an essential term (or, as Lord Buckmaster called it, 'a critical part'), or a means of determining such a term does not amount to a contract. No longer should it be said, on the basis of that case, that *prima facie*, if something essential is left to be agreed upon by the parties at a later time, there is no binding agreement. The intention of the parties, as discerned by the Court, to be bound or not to be bound should be paramount. If the Court is satisfied that the parties intended to be bound, it will strive to find a means of giving effect to that intention by filling the gap. On the other hand, if the Court takes the view that the parties did not intend to be bound unless they themselves filled the gap (that they were not content to leave that task to the Court or a third party), then the agreement will not be binding.

On its own facts we respectfully doubt that *May and Butcher* would be decided by their Lordships in the same way today. We are now perhaps more accustomed to resort to arbitration in order to settle matters of considerable importance to the contracting parties. We find curious the notion that, in a commercial contract where price is left to be agreed, a reasonable price cannot be fixed and that, even where there is an arbitration clause, that clause cannot be used to determine the price because 'unless the price has been fixed, the agreement is not there'.

We agree with Professor McLauchlan ('Rethinking Agreements to Agree' (1998) 18 *NZULR* 77, 85) that 'an agreement to agree will not be held void for uncertainty if the parties have provided a workable formula or objective standard or a machinery (such as arbitration) for determining the matter which has been left open'. We also agree with him that the court can step in and apply the formula or standard if the parties fail to agree or can substitute other machinery if the designated machinery breaks down.

One feature of this passage from the judgment of Blanchard J is the emphasis that it places upon the issue of whether or not the parties intended to be bound by the agreement they have concluded (on which see further p. 313 below). In other words, instead of asking the question whether or not the agreement reached by the parties was sufficiently certain to constitute an enforceable contract, the court should ask itself whether or not the parties intended to be bound by their agreement. In this way lack of certainty ceases to be a distinct issue in itself and instead is subsumed within a wider inquiry as to the intention of the parties. The difficulty with the latter approach is its lack of precision and this may itself give rise to uncertainty!

The reality appears to be that judges do find it difficult to know where to draw the line. As an illustration of the difficulties involved it is instructive to examine the judgment of Scrutton LJ in the Court of Appeal in *Hillas*. Scrutton LJ had also been one of the judges in the Court of Appeal in *May and Butcher* where, in a dissenting judgment, he had expressed the view that the agreement between the parties was enforceable. He returned to this issue in his judgment in *Hillas* (at p. 506) in the following terms:

I am afraid I remain quite impenitent. I think it was right and that nine out of ten business men would agree with me. But of course I recognise that I am bound as a judge to follow the principles laid down by the House of Lords. But I regret that in many commercial matters the English law and the practice of commercial men are getting wider apart, with the result that commercial business is leaving the courts and is being decided by commercial arbitrators with infrequent reference to the courts. . . . The commercial man does not think there can be no contract to make a contract when every day he finds a policy 'premium to be agreed' treated by the law as a contract.

The force with which this view was expressed might lead us to believe that he would have upheld the validity of the agreement in *Hillas*. But this is not in fact the case. In his view, the agreement was not enforceable. He stated (at p. 506):

In my view, *apart from authority*, considering the number of things left undetermined, kinds, sizes and quantities of goods, times and ports and manner of shipment, as will be seen from the detailed terms in contracts which were agreed, but which had in this case to be determined by agreement after negotiation, the option clause was not an agreement, but . . . 'an agreement to make an agreement' which is not an enforceable agreement. [Emphasis added.]

Thus Scrutton LJ thought that the agreement in *May and Butcher* was enforceable but that the agreement in *Hillas* was not, whereas the House of Lords adopted the opposite view in both cases. This difference of view serves to illustrate the problem of distilling clear and coherent principles from the case-law. Professor Macneil recently described the attempt to find 'coherent principles' in the agreement to agree cases as 'a fool's errand' (Macneil in 'Biographical Statement' in D Campbell (ed), *The Relational Theory of Contract: Selected Works of Ian Macneil* (Sweet & Maxwell, 2001)). In this respect he is probably right. Much will depend on the facts of the individual case. The parties are unlikely to have reached agreement on every single matter and so the court must decide in each case whether there is *sufficient* evidence of agreement to enable it to reach the conclusion that the agreement is valid and binding. On the other hand, while this inquiry is in many respects fact-specific it is nevertheless possible to identify some factors that are taken into account by the courts in deciding whether or not an agreement is valid and enforceable.

The cases will be divided into two groups. The first group consists of cases in which it was held that the agreement was too uncertain or too vague to be enforced, while the second group comprises a number of cases in which the courts have concluded that the agreement was valid and binding.

3. CASES IN WHICH IT HAS BEEN HELD THAT THE AGREEMENT IS TOO VAGUE OR UNCERTAIN TO BE ENFORCED

The leading case in this category is undoubtedly the decision of the House of Lords in *May and Butcher* v. *The King* (above). But there are other examples. It suffices for our purposes to provide one further illustration.

Scammell and Nephew Ltd v. Ouston

[1941] AC 251, House of Lords

The defendants (appellants) wrote to the plaintiffs (respondents) and offered to sell them a Commer van for £268 and to take the plaintiffs' Bedford van in part exchange, allowing them the sum of £100 for the Bedford van. The parties agreed these terms at an interview. The following day the defendants wrote to the plaintiffs and asked them to place the official order for the van in order to enable them to complete their records. The plaintiffs accordingly wrote to the defendants and the letter included the following sentence: 'this order is given on the understanding that the balance of the purchase price can be had on hire-purchase terms over a period of 2 years.' This sentence reflected the plaintiffs' position throughout the negotiations, namely that they could only purchase the van on hire-purchase terms. The relationship between the parties then deteriorated, principally as a result of a disagreement about the condition of the Bedford van that led the defendants to refuse to take it in part-exchange. The plaintiffs claimed that this amounted to a breach of contract and brought a claim for damages. The defendants denied any liability on the ground that no contract had in fact been concluded between the parties. The defence failed at first instance and in the Court of Appeal but succeeded in the House of Lords where it was held that the words 'on hire-purchase terms' could not be given any definite meaning so that the parties had not, in fact, concluded a contract.

Viscount Maugham

My Lords, I have had the advantage of reading the opinion of my noble and learned friend, Lord Russell of Killowen. I entirely agree with it and with his statement of the relevant facts. No less, however, than four judges have come to a different conclusion, and they think that the respondents have succeeded in establishing a contract in this case. I should always be slow to differ from views of those for whom I entertain a very genuine respect, if I could entertain any real doubt about the matter. I am constrained therefore to add some remarks of my own to explain why I am led to an opinion which coincides with that of my noble friend.

It is a regrettable fact that there are few, if any, topics on which there seems to be a greater difference of judicial opinion than those which relate to the question whether as the result of informal letters or like documents a binding contract has been arrived at. Many well known instances are to be found in the books, the last being that of *Hillas & Co v. Arcos, Ltd* (1932) 147 LT 503. The reason for these different conclusions is that laymen unassisted by persons with a legal training are not always accustomed to use words or phrases with a precise or definite meaning. In order to constitute a valid contract the parties must so express themselves that their meaning can be determined with a reasonable degree of certainty. It is plain that unless this can be done it would be impossible to hold that the contracting parties had the same intention; in other words the consensus ad idem would be a matter of mere conjecture. This general rule, however, applies somewhat differently in different cases. In commercial documents connected with dealings in a trade with which the parties are perfectly familiar the court is very willing, if satisfied that the parties thought that they made a binding contract, to imply terms and in particular terms as to the method of carrying out the contract which it would be impossible to supply in other kinds of contract: see *Hillas & Co v. Arcos, Ltd* . . .

We come then to the question as to the effect of the (so-called) purchase being on 'hire-purchase terms', and here we are confronted with a strange and confusing circumstance. The term 'hire-purchase' for a good many years past has been understood to mean a contract of hire by the owner of a chattel conferring on the hirer an option to purchase on the performance of certain conditions: *Helby v. Matthews* [1895] AC 471. There is in these contracts—and this is from a business standpoint a most important matter—no agreement to buy within the Factors Act, 1889, or the Sale of Goods Act, 1893; there is only an option and the hirer can confer on a purchaser from him no better title than he himself has, except in the case of sale in market overt. It is inaccurate and misleading to add to an order for goods, as if given by a purchaser, a clause that hire-purchase terms are to apply, without something to explain the apparent contradiction. Moreover a hire-purchase agreement may assume many forms and some of the variations in those forms are of the most important character, e.g., those which relate to termination of the agreement, warranty of fitness, duties as to repair, interest, and so forth.

Bearing these facts in mind, what do the words as to 'hire-purchase terms' mean in the present case? They may indicate that the hire-purchase agreement was to be granted by the appellants or on the other hand by some finance company acting in collaboration with the appellants; they may contemplate that the appellants were to receive by instalments a sum of £168 spread over a period of two years upon delivering the new van and receiving the old car, or, on the other hand, that the appellants were to receive from a third party a lump sum of £168 and that the third party, presumably a finance company, was to receive from the respondents a larger sum than £168 to include interest and profit spread over a period of two years. Moreover, nothing is said (except as to the two years period) as to the terms of the hire-purchase agreement, for instance, as to the interest payable, and as to the rights of the letter whoever he may be in the event of default by the respondents in payment of the instalments at the due dates. As regards the last matters there was no evidence to suggest that there are any well known 'usual terms' in such a contract; and I think it is common knowledge that in fact many letters though by no means all of them insist on terms which the legislature regards as so unfair and unconscionable that it was recently found necessary to deal with the matter in the recent Act entitled the Hire-Purchase Act, 1938.

These, my Lords, are very serious difficulties, and when we find as we do in this curious case that the trial judge and the three Lords Justices, and even the two counsel who addressed your Lordships for the respondents, were unable to agree upon the true construction of the alleged agreement, it seems to me that it is impossible to conclude that a binding agreement has been established by the respondents.

The appeal must, I think, succeed, and the action for damages must be dismissed with costs here and below.

Viscount Simon LC, Lord Russell of Killowen, and **Lord Wright** delivered concurring speeches.

COMMENTARY

Scammell further evidences the difficulties that the courts experience when deciding whether or not an agreement is too vague or uncertain to be valid and binding. As Viscount Maugham points out at the beginning of his speech, the judges in the lower courts reached a different conclusion from that reached by the House of Lords. Viscount Maugham also makes the point that the courts are 'very willing' to imply a term 'in commercial documents connected with dealings in a trade with which the parties are perfectly familiar' if they are satisfied that the parties thought that they had made a binding contract. In such a case a court may have more to draw upon in order to give a meaning to the vague phrase (for example, the court may be able to have regard to the custom of the trade in which the parties were working: *Shamrock SS Co v. Storey and Co* (1899) 81 LT 413).

One of the problems that confronted the plaintiffs on the facts of *Scammell* lay in explaining the basis on which they alleged that the parties had concluded a contract. Lord Russell of Killowen pointed out that the decisions of the lower courts and the arguments of counsel for the plaintiffs had been put in five different ways. Before their Lordships leading counsel for the plaintiffs argued that the contract was one of sale and purchase, subject to a condition precedent that the balance of the purchase price could be paid on reasonable hire-purchase terms, while junior counsel for the plaintiffs submitted that the contract was not one of sale and purchase at all. Lord Russell of Killowen concluded (at p. 260) that:

the existence of this fivefold choice is embarrassing but eloquent. An alleged contract which appeals for its meaning to so many skilled minds in so many different ways is undoubtedly open to suspicion. For myself I feel no doubt that no contract between the parties existed at all; notwithstanding that they may have thought otherwise.

Scammell is thus a case in which the court felt unable, on the basis of the evidence that had been led, to identify the meaning which the parties had agreed should be given to the words 'hire-purchase'. Such cases tend to be rare and when they do occur they tend to be controversial (another case in this category is the decision of the House of Lords in *Walford* v. *Miles* [1992] 2 AC 128, discussed in more detail at p. 544 below, where it was held that the courts could not give effect to an obligation to negotiate in 'good faith').

Why is it that the House of Lords concluded in both *Scammell* and *May and Butcher* that the agreements were not valid and enforceable? The answer would appear to lie in the fact that their Lordships were of the view that there was no basis in the evidence for a finding that the parties had reached agreement on the point at issue nor was there, in their opinion, criteria or machinery agreed by the parties that the courts could employ in order to fill the gap or resolve the uncertainty.

4. CASES IN WHICH THE COURTS HAVE HELD THE AGREEMENT TO BE VALID AND BINDING

The courts have at their disposal a variety of techniques that they can employ in order to resolve the uncertainty or the lack of clarity that surrounds a particular agreement. In this respect *May and Butcher* and *Scammell* should be seen as the exception rather than the rule. The principal techniques are as follows:

(a) MAKE USE OF THE CRITERIA OR MACHINERY THAT HAS BEEN AGREED BY THE PARTIES IN ORDER TO RESOLVE THE UNCERTAINTY OR TO CLARIFY THE WORD OR PHRASE THAT IS EXPRESSED IN VAGUE TERMS

The main stumbling-block that confronts the courts in these cases is the principle that it is not the function of the courts to make the contract for the parties. This being the case, the parties cannot simply leave it to the courts to resolve issues that the parties themselves have left unresolved. To do so would be to invite the court to make the contract for the parties and the courts will generally decline such an invitation. But the courts will generally make use of criteria or machinery that have been agreed by the parties in order to resolve the uncertainty or clarify the meaning of a particular word or phrase. There are in fact a number of options open to the parties to establish some criteria or machinery to resolve the issue. The two principal options are as follows:

(I) RESOLUTION BY ONE OR OTHER OF THE PARTIES

The parties can agree to entrust the resolution of the issue to one or other party to the contract. Thus in *May and Butcher* (above) Viscount Dunedin stated that 'with regard to price it is a perfectly good contract to say that the price is to be settled by the buyer'. The difficulty with such a clause is that it appears to place the seller at the mercy of the buyer. But the courts may be able to imply a term into the agreement in order to place a limit on the power of the buyer. In *Paragon Finance plc* v. *Nash* [2001] EWCA Civ 1466; [2002] 1 WLR 685 the clause at issue between the parties stated:

The rate of interest applicable to the loan and the monthly payment will be as specified in the offer of loan as varied from time to time in accordance with the applicable mortgage condition indicated in the offer of loan.

One of the issues before the Court of Appeal was whether or not the claimant's power to set the interest rates from time to time was completely unfettered. The Court of Appeal held that it was not. A term was to be implied into the agreement to the effect that the rates of interest would not be set dishonestly, for an improper purpose, capriciously or arbitrarily, or in a way in which no reasonable mortgagee,[7] acting reasonably, would do (the basis upon which the Court of Appeal decided to imply this term is discussed in more detail at p. 399 below). On the facts of *Paragon Finance* it was held that the borrowers had no real prospect of successfully establishing a breach of this implied term. The reason for the increase in interest rates was that the lenders were in financial difficulties and so had to increase their interest rates in order to protect their own financial position. It could not be said that they behaved dishonestly, improperly, capriciously, arbitrarily, or unreasonably in so acting. The protection afforded by such an implied term may be limited but it does at least ensure that one party is not left entirely at the mercy of the other.

(II) RESOLUTION BY A THIRD PARTY

Alternatively, the parties can entrust the resolution of the particular issue to a third party, such as an arbitrator. In *May and Butcher* Viscount Dunedin stated that the parties could have agreed 'that a certain part of the contract of sale . . . may be settled by some one else'. That someone else is often, but not invariably, an arbitrator. In general, the courts have been slower to conclude that an agreement is too uncertain to be enforced where the agreement contains an arbitration clause (with the notable exception of *May and Butcher*). Thus in *Queensland Electricity Generating Board* v. *New Hope Collieries Pty Ltd* [1989] 1 Lloyd's Rep 205, 210 Sir Robin Cooke, delivering the judgment of the Privy Council, stated:

---

[7] A mortgagee is the creditor in a mortgage, usually a bank or a building society.

At the present day, *in cases where the parties have agreed on an arbitration or valuation clause in wide enough terms,* the Courts accord full weight to their manifest intention to create continuing legal relations. Arguments invoking alleged uncertainty, or alleged inadequacy in the machinery available to the Courts for making contractual rights effective, exert minimal attraction. [Emphasis added.]

But there is a need for caution here. Sir Robin Cooke attached considerable significance to the width of the arbitration clause, whereas the House of Lords in *May and Butcher* placed emphasis on the terms of the agreement as a whole. The latter case demonstrates that the presence of an arbitration clause will not inevitably lead to the conclusion that the agreement is valid and binding; for this reason it has been criticized by arbitration lawyers. Further, *May and Butcher* is not easy to reconcile with the later decisions of the Court of Appeal in *Foley* v. *Classique Coaches Ltd* [1934] 2 KB 1 (p. 139 above) and *F & G Sykes (Wessex) Ltd* v. *Fine Fare Ltd* [1967] 1 Lloyd's Rep 53 (p. 158 below) where the presence of an arbitration clause was an important factor in persuading the court to conclude that the agreement was valid and binding. But the proposition that an arbitration clause should operate as a passport to the validity of an agreement is not beyond question. Why should the parties be entitled to leave important matters for the decision of an arbitrator when they cannot leave the same matters to be resolved by a judge in the High Court?

(iii) what happens when the machinery agreed by the parties breaks down?

While the courts will generally make use of the criteria or machinery that have been agreed by the parties, what is to be done in the case where the machinery breaks down or for some other reason does not work? In *May and Butcher* Viscount Dunedin appeared to suggest that the failure of the agreed machinery (in his example it was the determination of a third party) would inevitably result in the conclusion that no agreement had been reached. The modern courts, however, adopt a more flexible approach. The leading modern case on this point is:

Sudbrook Trading Estate Ltd v. Eggleton

[1983] 1 AC 444, House of Lords

Lord Fraser of Tullybelton

My Lords, the appellants are the tenants in four leases, by each of which they were granted an option to purchase the freehold reversion of the leased premises at a valuation. The appellants have exercised the options, but the respondents, who are the landlords, contend that the options are unenforceable. The questions now to be determined, therefore, are whether the options are valid and enforceable, and, if so, how they should be enforced.

The leases relate to adjacent industrial premises in Gloucester. They were granted at different dates, but for terms which all expire on December 24, 1997, at yearly rents which are subject to periodical review. The leases are all in substantially the same form. For reasons that are not now material the option contained in the earliest lease, that dated March 23, 1949, had not been exercised when the writs in these proceedings were issued, but it has been subsequently exercised and there is now no relevant distinction between that option and the other three. The clause in the 1949 lease, clause 11, has been taken as typical of them all. It entitled the appellants to purchase the reversion in fee simple, upon certain conditions which were all satisfied,

> 'at such price not being less than £75,000 as may be agreed upon by two valuers one to be nominated by the lessor and the other by the lessee or in default of such agreement by an umpire appointed by the said valuers. . . .'

The respondents contend that the options are void for uncertainty on the ground that they contain no formula by which the price can be fixed in the event of no agreement being reached, and that they are no more than agreements to agree. The respondents have therefore declined to appoint their valuer. The machinery provided in the leases has accordingly become inoperable.

In these proceedings the appellants seek a declaration that the options are valid, that they have been validly and effectively exercised, and that the contracts constituted by the exercise ought to be specifically performed. As regards the mode of performance, the main argument for the appellants is that the court should order such inquiries as are necessary to ascertain the value of each of the properties. Lawson J decided the question of principle in favour of the appellants, but his decision was reversed by the Court of Appeal which held that the options were unenforceable. Templeman LJ, who delivered the judgment of the Court of Appeal, made a full review of the English authorities and the conclusion which he drew from them was, in my opinion inevitably, adverse to the appellants' contentions. The fundamental proposition upon which he relied was, in his own words:

> 'that where the agreement on the face of it is incomplete until something else has been done, whether by further agreement between the parties or by the decision of an arbitrator or valuer, the court is powerless, because there is no complete agreement to enforce: . . .'

I agree that that is the effect of the earlier decisions but, with the greatest respect, I am of opinion that it is wrong. It appears to me that, on the exercise of the option, the necessary preconditions having been satisfied, as they were in this case, a complete contract of sale and purchase of the freehold reversion was constituted. The price, which was of course an essential term of the contract, was for reasons which I shall explain, capable of being ascertained and was therefore certain. Certum est quod certum reddi potest: see *May and Butcher Ltd* v. *The King (Note)* [1934] 2 KB 17, 21, per Viscount Dunedin.

The courts have applied clauses such as those in the present case in a strictly literal way and have treated them as making the completion of a contract of sale conditional upon agreement between the valuers either on the value of the property, or failing that, on the choice of an umpire. They have further laid down the principle that where parties have agreed on a particular method of ascertaining the price, and that method has for any reason proved ineffective, the court will neither grant an order for specific performance to compel parties to operate the agreed machinery, nor substitute its own machinery to ascertain the price, because either of these clauses would be to impose upon parties an agreement that they had not made . . .

While that is the general principle it is equally well established that, where parties have agreed to sell 'at a fair valuation' or 'at a reasonable price' or according to some similar formula, without specifying any machinery for ascertaining the price, the position is different. . . . The court will order such inquiries as may be necessary to ascertain the fair price: see *Talbot v. Talbot* [1968] Ch 1.

I recognise the logic of the reasoning which has led to the courts' refusing to substitute their own machinery for the machinery which has been agreed upon by the parties. But the result to which it leads is so remote from that which parties normally intend and expect, and is so inconvenient in practice, that there must in my opinion be some defect in the reasoning. I think the defect lies in construing the provisions for the mode of ascertaining the value as an essential part of the agreement. That may have been perfectly true early in the 19th century, when the valuer's profession and the rules of valuation were less well established than they are now. But at the present day these provisions are only subsidiary to the main purpose of the agreement which is for sale and purchase of the property at a fair or reasonable value. In the ordinary case parties do not make any substantial distinction between an agreement to sell at a fair value, without specifying the mode of ascertaining the value, and an agreement to sell at a value to be ascertained by valuers appointed in the way provided in these leases. The true distinction is between those cases where the mode of ascertaining the price is an essential term of the contract, and those cases where the mode of ascertainment, though indicated in the contract, is subsidiary and non-essential. . . . The present case falls, in my opinion, into the latter category. Accordingly when the option was exercised there was constituted a complete contract for sale, and the clause should be construed as meaning that the price was to be a fair price. On the other hand where an agreement is made to sell at a price to be fixed by a valuer who is named, or who, by reason of holding some office such as auditor of a company whose shares are to be valued, will have special knowledge relevant to the question of value, the prescribed mode may well be regarded as essential. Where, as here, the machinery consists of valuers and an umpire, none of whom is named or identified, it is in my opinion unrealistic to regard it as an essential term. If it breaks down there is no reason why the court should not substitute other machinery to carry out the main purpose of ascertaining the price in order that the agreement may be carried out.

In the present case the machinery provided for in the clause has broken down because the respondents have declined to appoint their valuer. In that sense the breakdown has been caused by their fault, in failing to implement an implied obligation to co-operate in making the machinery work. The case might be distinguishable in that respect from cases where the breakdown has occurred for some cause outside the control of either party, such as the death of an umpire, or his failure to complete the valuation by a stipulated date. But I do not rely on any such distinction. I prefer to rest my decision on the general principle that, where the machinery is not essential, if it breaks down for any reason the court will substitute its own machinery . . .

The appropriate means for the court to enforce the present agreements is in my opinion by ordering an inquiry into the fair value of the reversions. That was the method used in *Talbot v. Talbot* [1968] Ch 1. The alternative of ordering the respondents to appoint a valuer would not be suitable because in the event of the order not being obeyed, the only sanction would be imprisonment for contempt of court which would clearly be inappropriate.

Lord Russell of Killowen [dissenting]

My Lords, it appears to be generally accepted that the law as previously understood since at least the early 19th century is in favour of the respondents and of the decision of the

Court of Appeal. It is proposed by the majority of your Lordships to assert that that previous understanding was erroneous. I cannot agree.

Basically the assumption is made that the parties intended that the exercise of the option should involve payment of a 'fair price' or a 'fair value'. Of course parties to such a contract could in terms so agree, and I am not concerned to deny that in such a case a court could enforce the contract by ascertainment of a fair price or fair value, treating specific provisions in the contract for methods (which proved to be unworkable) of ascertaining that fair price or valuation as being inessential. But that is not this case. Why should it be thought that potential vendor and purchaser intended the price to be 'fair'? The former would intend the price to be high, even though 'unfairly' so and the latter vice versa. Vendors and purchasers are normally greedy . . .

In my opinion this case is an example of the long established and quite sound principle that if A agrees to sell Blackacre to B the contract must provide for the price to be paid either in express terms or by the establishment of agreed machinery *which is bound to work* by which the price can be ascertained. If the machinery is not so bound to work the party taking ultimate advantage of its deficiencies is not to be castigated as having taken some unfair advantage, as though he had from the outset plotted to do so. If the tackle is not in order from the start it cannot be assumed that either party then knew it.

The important issue for the court is whether or not the machinery agreed by the parties is essential or not. In *Sudbrook* it was not essential. A case on the other side of the line is *Gillatt* v. *Sky Television Ltd* [2000] 1 All ER (Comm) 461. A clause in a contract between the parties stated that, if the defendant sold or otherwise disposed of the entire issued share capital of a company, the claimant would be entitled to payment of '55% of the open market value of such shares . . . as determined by an independent chartered accountant'. Neither party took any steps to appoint an independent chartered accountant to determine the value of the shares, but the claimant nevertheless sought to recover from the defendant a 'sum equal to 55% of such sum as is found to be the value of the true open market value of the issued share capital' of the company. Relying upon *Sudbrook*, the claimant argued that the reference to an independent chartered accountant was not intended as an essential condition precedent to the existence of any entitlement to payment under the clause and that it was open to the court to determine the extent of his entitlement under the clause. The Court of Appeal rejected the claimant's submission, distinguished *Sudbrook*, and held that the expression 'as determined by an independent chartered accountant' was an integral and essential part of the definition of the payments to which the claimant was entitled; it was not merely a mechanism or permissive procedure for dispute resolution. Nor did the reference to 'open market value' of the shares provide the court with adequate objective criteria because there is more than one possible approach to the valuation of shares in a private company (an earnings basis, an assets basis, a discounted cash flow basis, or some combination of these). Commercial indications also suggested that the parties intended that the determination of the open market value of the shares should be carried out by an independent accountant and not by the court. Finally, there was no question in this case, unlike *Sudbrook*, of the 'breakdown' of machinery for the determination of value. Neither party had attempted to invoke the procedure laid down in the clause and the court refused to substitute something different (its own opinion of the market value of the shares) in place of what the parties had actually agreed. It therefore followed that no payment was due to the claimant under the clause in the contract.

(b) THE INTERVENTION OF STATUTE

Occasionally statute may intervene to provide an answer to the issue that has not been resolved by the parties. The principal example in this category is section 8 of the Sale of Goods Act 1979 which provides:

(1) The price in a contract of sale may be fixed by the contract, or may be left to be fixed in a manner agreed by the contract, or may be determined by the course of dealing between the parties.

(2) Where the price is not determined as mentioned in subsection (1) above the buyer must pay a reasonable price.

(3) What is a reasonable price is a question of fact dependent on the circumstances of each particular case.

Section 8(2) was not applicable on the facts of *May and Butcher* because it only comes into play where the contract is silent as to the price of the goods and the contract in *May and Butcher* was not silent. It purported to make provision for the determination of the price and this was sufficient to exclude the operation of section 8. It may seem odd that section 8 only comes into play when the contract is silent and not where the contract purports to deal with the issue but it is not open to the courts to alter the clear meaning of a statutory provision.

(c) SEVERANCE

The court may be able to sever the term that is alleged to be vague or uncertain and enforce the rest of the contract. An example of this process at work is provided by the case of *Nicolene Ltd* v. *Simmonds* [1953] 1 QB 543. The defendant sent to the plaintiffs an acceptance of the plaintiffs' order which contained the following sentence:

As you have made the order direct to me, I am unable to confirm on my usual printed form which would have the usual force majeure and war clauses, but I assume that we are in agreement and that the usual conditions of acceptance apply.

The plaintiffs replied to this letter, confirming the order. The defendant failed to deliver the goods and so the plaintiffs brought an action for damages for breach of contract. The defendant denied that a contract had been concluded on the ground that there were no 'usual conditions' in operation between the parties. The defence failed. The Court of Appeal held that the reference to 'usual conditions' was meaningless and could be struck out without impairing the rest of the contract. Denning LJ stated (at p. 551):

In my opinion a distinction must be drawn between a clause which is meaningless and a clause which is yet to be agreed. A clause which is meaningless can often be ignored, whilst still leaving the contract good; whereas a clause which has yet to be agreed may mean that there is no contract at all, because the parties have not agreed on all the essential terms.

I take it to be clear law that if one of the parties to a contract inserts into it an exempting condition in his own favour, which the other side agrees, and it afterwards turns out that that condition is meaningless, or what comes to the same thing, that it is so ambiguous that no ascertainable meaning can be given to it, that does not mean that the whole contract is a nullity. It only means that the exempting condition is a nullity and must be rejected. It would be strange indeed if a party could escape every one of his obligations by inserting a meaningless exception from some of them . . .

In the present case there was nothing yet to be agreed. There was nothing left to further negotiation. All that happened was that the parties merely agreed that 'the usual conditions of acceptance apply'. That clause was so vague and uncertain as to be incapable of any precise meaning. It is clearly severable from the rest of the contract. It can be rejected without impairing the sense or reasonableness of the contract as a whole, and it should be so rejected. The contract should be held good and the clause ignored. The parties themselves treated the contract as subsisting. They regarded it as creating binding obligations between them; and it would be most unfortunate if the law should say otherwise. You would find defaulters all scanning their contracts to find some meaningless clause on which to ride free.

The result was that the contract was to be found in the exchange of correspondence between the parties and the defendant's letter was to be read as an unqualified acceptance of the plaintiffs' order.

One of the cases relied upon by the defendant was *Scammell & Nephew* v. *Ouston* (p. 148 above) but Denning LJ distinguished it (at p. 551) on the ground that, in that case, 'there were hire-purchase terms yet to be agreed' and he noted that Lord Wright stated that the 'agreement was inchoate, and never got beyond negotiations'. He also distinguished *Scammell* on the ground that the term in the present case was 'clearly severable from the rest of the contract' while the term in *Scammell* was not. The more important the term to the transaction as a whole, the less likely it is that the court will be able to sever it from the rest of the agreement.

(d) IMPLICATION OF TERMS

Finally, the court may be able to imply a term the effect of which will be to fill the gap that was left by the parties. The courts do not have the power to imply a term into a contract simply on the basis that it would be reasonable to imply such a term into the contract (see pp. 379–400 below). A term will only be implied where it is necessary to do so. Nevertheless, the courts have said on a number of occasions that they are more likely to imply a term into the contract when the parties have acted on the basis of or, as it is often put, in reliance upon their agreement. Thus in *F & G Sykes (Wessex) Ltd* v. *Fine Fare Ltd* [1967] 1 Lloyd's Rep 53 Lord Denning stated (at pp. 57–58):

In a commercial agreement the further the parties have gone on with their contract, the more ready are the Courts to imply any reasonable term so as to give effect to their intentions. When much has been done, the Courts will do their best not to destroy the bargain. When nothing has been done, it is easier to say there is no agreement between the parties because the essential terms have not been agreed. But when an agreement has been acted upon and the parties, as here, have been put to great expense in implementing it, we ought to imply all reasonable terms so as to avoid any uncertainties. In this case there is less difficulty than in others because there is an arbitration clause which, liberally construed, is sufficient to resolve any uncertainties which the parties have left.

To similar effect is the judgment of Steyn LJ in *G Percy Trentham Ltd* v. *Archital Luxfer Ltd* [1993] 1 Lloyd's Rep 25 when he stated (at p. 27) that, 'the fact that the transaction is executed *makes it easier* to imply a term resolving any uncertainty, or, alternatively, it may make it possible to treat a matter not finalized in negotiations as inessential' (emphasis added). Thus the point that is being made is not that action in reliance upon the agreement will inevitably result in the conclusion that the agreement is valid and binding (a case in point being *May and Butcher* where the fact that the suppliants had apparently deposited £1,000 as security was not sufficient to render the agreement between the parties sufficiently certain to be enforced). Rather, the point is that reliance makes it easier for the court to find that the agreement is valid and binding, by providing evidence from which the court can infer that the parties had reached agreement on all essential terms. The courts do not find the existence of an agreement in every case where the agreement has been partially or substantially executed. In *British Steel Corporation* v. *Cleveland Bridge and Engineering Co Ltd* [1984] 1 All ER 504 (discussed at pp. 105–110 above) Robert Goff J refused to find the existence of a contract between the parties, despite the fact that both parties had acted on the agreement, and he looked to the law of restitution to resolve the dispute between the parties.

5. CONCLUSION

English law is often criticized on the ground that it adopts an unduly restrictive approach to these issues and, in this respect, the decision of the House of Lords in *May and Butcher* is often held out as the prime illustration of this restrictive tendency. While cases can be found in which the courts have adopted a more relaxed approach, it can be argued that these are no more than piecemeal interventions which fail to provide a coherent set of principles to guide the courts when seeking to decide whether or not an agreement that is expressed in terms that are uncertain, incomplete, or vague is nevertheless valid and binding. Bearing in mind Professor Macneil's warning that the search for coherent principles in this area is a 'fool's errand' (p. 148 above), would English law be put on a sounder footing if it adopted one or more of the following rules in place of its existing rules?

• Unidroit Principles of International Commercial Contracts: Conclusion of
  contract dependent on agreement on specific matters or in a particular form

2.13.   Where in the course of negotiations one of the parties insists that the contract is not concluded until there is agreement on specific matters or in a particular form, no contract is concluded before agreement is reached on those matters or in that form.

- **Contract with terms deliberately left open**

2.14.   (1) If the parties intend to conclude a contract, the fact that they intentionally leave a term to be agreed upon in further negotiations or to be determined by a third person does not prevent a contract from coming into existence.

(2) The existence of the contract is not affected by the fact that subsequently

(a) the parties reach no agreement on the term, or

(b) the third person does not determine the term,

provided that there is an alternative means of rendering the term definite that is reasonable in the circumstances, having regard to the intention of the parties.

- **Principles of European Contract Law: Article 2:103: Sufficient agreement**

(1) There is sufficient agreement if the terms:

(a) have been sufficiently defined by the parties so that the contract can be enforced, or

(b) can be determined under these Principles.

(2) However, if one of the parties refuses to conclude a contract unless the parties have agreed on some specific matter, there is no contract unless agreement on that matter has been reached.

- **Uniform Commercial Code:[8] section 2:204(3)**

Even though one or more terms are left open a contract for sale does not fail for indefiniteness if the parties have intended to make a contract and there is a reasonably certain basis for giving an appropriate remedy.

All of these provisions are more liberal than the approach taken by the House of Lords in *May and Butcher*. They therefore add further weight to the argument that *May and Butcher* is out of line with the demands of modern commercial practice. That said, it should be noted that these provisions are all expressed in broad terms and so may not provide the clear guidance that English courts and practitioners generally seek.

6. FURTHER READING

FRIDMAN, GHL, 'Construing, Without Constructing a Contract' (1962) 76 *LQR* 521.

McLAUCHLAN, D, 'Rethinking Agreements to Agree' (1998) 18 *NZULR* 77.

---

[8] Applicable in the United States of America.

5
CONSIDERATION AND PROMISSORY ESTOPPEL

1. CENTRAL ISSUES

1. The doctrine of consideration is a feature of English contract law that is not to be found in civilian legal systems. It is now a very technical doctrine and it has been the subject of considerable criticism.

2. The essence of the doctrine of consideration is that a promisee cannot enforce a promise unless he has given or promised to give something in exchange for the promise or unless the promisor has obtained (or been promised) something in return. In other words, there must have been a bargain between the parties.

3. The doctrine of consideration can be explained in outline in the form of three rules: (i) consideration must be sufficient but need not be adequate, (ii) consideration must not be past, and (iii) consideration must move from the promisee.

4. There is an important conflict at the heart of the rules that make up the doctrine of consideration and that relates to the test to be applied when deciding whether or not the promisee has obtained a benefit as a result of the promise made by the promisor. The Court of Appeal in *Williams* v. *Roffey Brothers* looked for the existence of a practical benefit,

whereas the House of Lords in *Foakes* v. *Beer* applied a much stricter test that focused on whether the promisee had, as a matter of law, received a benefit. The relationship between these two cases is a major part of this chapter.

5. A promise which is not supported by consideration may nevertheless be given legal effect as a result of the operation of an 'estoppel'. 'Estoppel' is not a word that is used in everyday language and it is a concept that is difficult to explain, largely because it appears to defy classification. In essence, the effect of an estoppel may be to prevent a party from going back on his promise when the person to whom the promise has been made has acted on it to his detriment. However the scope of estoppel is limited by a number of rules, the most important of which is that estoppel cannot create a cause of action. The scope of these rules, the criticisms made of them, and the justifications offered in support of them are considered in this chapter.

6. Finally, the chapter concludes with a brief discussion of the future of the doctrine of consideration and, in particular, it draws on the critique of consideration developed by Professor Atiyah.

2. INTRODUCTION

One feature of English contract law that readily distinguishes it from the law of contract in civilian jurisdictions is the doctrine of consideration. As we shall see, the scope of the doctrine is the subject of some debate. The orthodox view is that consideration is about reciprocity or bargains. In order to be entitled to enforce a promise a promisee must have given something in return for the promise. The fundamental distinction is therefore between a bargain and a promise to make a gift. The former is enforceable, while the latter is not unless it is made in a deed (on deeds see further Chapter 6). This conception of consideration has been challenged by a number of writers, in particular by Professor Atiyah. We shall return to these criticisms at the end of the chapter after we have examined the current scope of the doctrine of consideration. But it is necessary first of all to outline the principal criticisms that have been levelled against the doctrine because they ought to be borne in mind when reading the cases that seek to determine its scope.

Five principal criticisms can be levelled against the doctrine of consideration. The first is that it is too narrow in its scope and so fails to give effect to promises that ought to have legal effect. Thus Professor Dawson has argued (*Gifts and Promises* (Yale University Press, 1980), pp. 3–4) that

even the most embittered critics of bargain consideration do not really object to the enforcement of bargains. The objection has been to its transformation into a formula of denial, a formula that would deny legal effect to most promises for which there is nothing given or received in exchange.

Secondly, the doctrine has become extremely technical, a point evidenced by the fact that the account of the doctrine contained in the current edition of Professor Treitel's classic textbook on the law of contract runs to some ninety-five pages. Thirdly, it has been argued that the doctrine is divorced from commercial reality. It is much harder to evaluate the merits of this claim because the doctrine is rarely in issue in modern commercial practice. The reason for this is that it is a relatively simple matter for a lawyer to ensure that consideration is provided. The law does not, in general, inquire into the adequacy of the consideration that has been supplied (see further p. 164 below). Provided that some consideration has been provided the requirements of the doctrine are satisfied. Thus one can find transactions, reported in the media, of major businesses being sold for £1. In such cases the company that is acquired is usually debt-ridden and the reason for the payment of £1 is simply to ensure that consideration has been supplied for the promise to sell the company. Where there is doubt about the presence or absence of consideration, lawyers might make use of a deed and so avoid the problem because a promise contained in a deed is enforceable whether or not consideration has been supplied (see further p. 284 below). In this respect the doctrine of consideration is not of major significance in modern commercial transactions. On the other hand, there are some commercial transactions which are difficult to explain in terms that are consistent with the requirements of the doctrine of consideration (an example being, perhaps, the letter of credit, on which see p. 272 below). Fourthly, it is extremely difficult to reconcile the doctrine of consideration with any of the modern theoretical models of contract law (see SA Smith, *Contract Theory*, Oxford University Press, 2004, pp. 215–233). For example, if contract law is based upon the promise principle or upon the will of the parties, why insist upon the presence of consideration in order to render the promise enforceable? Fifthly, it has been argued that the doctrine of consideration is over-broad and that the work that is currently done by the doctrine could be done more effectively by more specific doctrines such as duress and intention to create legal relations which can target with greater precision the reason for the law's refusal to give effect to the promise that has been made.

At this point it is not necessary to reach a final conclusion on the relative strengths and weaknesses of these arguments. It suffices to note that consideration is a doctrine that is under some pressure. While consideration may be said to be a distinctive feature of English contract law, it is probably true to say that it is a feature that many English contract lawyers could live without. Thus Lord Goff stated in *White* v. *Jones* [1995] 2 AC 207, 262 that 'our law of contract is widely seen as deficient in the sense that it is perceived to be hampered by the presence of an unnecessary doctrine of consideration'. But, while the doctrine may 'not be very popular nowadays . . . [it] still exists as part of our law' (*Johnson* v. *Gore Wood & Co (A Firm)* [2001] 1 All ER 481, 507 per Lord Goff) and, as such, it must be applied by the courts.

The principal part of this chapter is devoted to an analysis of the current scope of the doctrine of consideration. This analysis will be followed by a discussion of the role of estoppel, in particular the role of promissory estoppel, in contract cases. The reason for including estoppel at this stage is that the effect of an estoppel is to give (at least limited) effect to a promise that would otherwise be unenforceable. Thus the effect of an estoppel may be to supplement, or even supplant, the doctrine of consideration. It is therefore necessary to consider the scope of estoppel alongside the doctrine of consideration before embarking upon a critical evaluation of the role of the doctrine of consideration in English contract law.

3. CONSIDERATION: ITS SCOPE

Conventional accounts of the doctrine of consideration start with the classic definition of the doctrine adopted by Lush J in *Currie* v. *Misa* (1875) LR 10 Ex 153, 162. He stated:

A valuable consideration, in the sense of the law, may consist either in some right, interest, profit, or benefit accruing to the one party, or some forebearance, detriment, loss, or responsibility, given, suffered, or undertaken by the other.

This definition has been amplified by Professor Treitel in the following terms (*The Law of Contract* (11th edn, Sweet & Maxwell, 2003), p. 68):

The traditional definition of consideration concentrates on the requirement that 'something of value' must be given and accordingly states that consideration is either some detriment to the promisee (in that he may give value) or some benefit to the promisor (in that he may receive value). Usually, this detriment and benefit are merely the same thing looked at from different points of view. Thus payment by a buyer is consideration for the seller's promise to deliver and can be described as a detriment to the buyer or as a benefit to the seller; and conversely delivery by a seller is consideration for the buyer's promise to pay and can be described either as a detriment to the seller or as a benefit to the buyer. These statements relate to the consideration *for the promise of each party* looked at separately. For example, the seller suffers a 'detriment' when he delivers the goods and this enables him to enforce the buyer's promise to pay the price. It is quite irrelevant that the seller has made a good bargain and so gets a benefit from the performance of the contract. What the law is concerned with is the consideration *for a promise*—not the consideration *for a contract*.

Two points should be noted about this definition, as amplified by Professor Treitel. The first is that the requirement of consideration can be satisfied by the presence of benefit **or** detriment. The law does not generally insist that both elements be present (although frequently they are). The second point concerns the use of the phrase 'in the sense of the law' in the judgment of Lush J. This suggests that it is for the law to decide whether or not consideration has been supplied. This has in fact proved to be an issue of some controversy in the cases. While it is no doubt true to say that, in the final analysis, it is for the courts to decide whether or not consideration has been provided, the courts on a number of occasions have given considerable weight to the preferences of the parties to the contract when deciding whether or not something of value has been given or promised (see further pp. 183–203 below).

The rules that make up the doctrine of consideration can be set out in the form of three principal rules. The first is that consideration must be sufficient but need not be adequate. This rule can be further broken down into a number of sub-rules and has proved to be particularly problematic in the case where the consideration is alleged to take the form of a promise to perform or the performance of a pre-existing duty. The second rule is that past consideration is not good consideration and the third is that consideration must move from the promisee. Each rule requires further analysis. Most attention will be given to the first of them.

(a) CONSIDERATION MUST BE SUFFICIENT

The rule that consideration must be sufficient but that it need not be adequate requires that *something* of value must be given in return for a promise but that something need not be an adequate return. In other words, the doctrine of consideration requires the existence of a bargain but it does not demand that the bargain be a good one. The parties, and not the doctrine of consideration, are in general the arbiters of what constitutes a good or a bad bargain. However it does not follow from the fact that the doctrine of consideration is not interested in the fairness of the bargain that the law of contract is similarly disinterested. A number of contractual rules and doctrines, such as duress and undue influence, are concerned with the fairness of the bargain that has been concluded by the parties (these rules are discussed in Chapters 18–20).

What does it mean to say that consideration must be 'sufficient'? Who decides whether or not the consideration is 'sufficient'? Is it the parties or is it the court? In answering these questions it is useful to distinguish the case where the alleged consideration takes the form of a promise to pay money for a service or a product from the case where the promise takes the form of a promise to provide some non-monetary benefit.

Where the promise is one to pay money for a service or a product (here used to encompass both goods and land) the law does not generally encounter any difficulty.

The example has already been given (p. 162 above) of a contract for the sale of a business. In such a case a promise to pay £1 for the business does constitute the provision of sufficient consideration. Such consideration is often described as 'nominal consideration'. The label 'nominal' should not be taken to imply that the law regards such transactions with suspicion. As Professor Atiyah has observed ('Consideration: A Restatement' in *Essays on Contract* (Oxford University Press, 1986), p. 194) a 'promise for nominal consideration is just about the clearest possible indication that the promisor intended his promise seriously and intended to give the promisee a legally enforceable right'. The reason for this is that the parties will generally have been advised by lawyers to make £1 payable precisely in order to render the agreement legally enforceable. Of course if the promise to sell the business for such a small amount of money has been extracted by pressure that amounts in law to duress (on which see p. 200 below) then the promise may not be enforceable but, in the absence of such a vitiating factor, the promise is enforceable. A distinction is sometimes drawn between 'nominal consideration' and consideration which is 'inadequate' but, for most purposes, the distinction does not matter.[1]

The issue is more difficult where the alleged consideration takes a form other than a promise to pay a sum of money. Here we encounter the question whether it is for the courts or the parties to determine what constitutes sufficient consideration. Take an extreme example. Suppose that A promises to pay B £5,000 if B promises in return to stand on one leg for ninety seconds. Does B provide consideration by promising to stand on one leg for ninety seconds? The courts have generally adopted a liberal approach to the identification of consideration and cases can be found in which trifling or apparently insignificant acts have been held to constitute consideration, as can be seen from the following case.

Chappell & Co Ltd v. The Nestlé Co Ltd

[1960] AC 87, House of Lords

The plaintiffs were the owners of the copyright in a musical work entitled 'Rockin' Shoes'. The defendants offered to supply gramophone records which included Rockin' Shoes to anyone sending in a postal order for 1s 6d together with three wrappers from bars of Nestlé milk chocolate. The plaintiffs alleged that the manufacture and sale of this record amounted to an infringement of their copyright in the song. The defendants relied by way of defence on section 8 of the Copyright Act 1956 which, in essence, permitted the making of records of a musical work that the manufacturer intended to sell by retail provided that he gave the owner of the copyright prior notice and paid a royalty of 6¼% of the 'ordinary retail selling price' of the record. The defendants notified the plaintiffs that the ordinary retail selling price of the records would not be greater than 1s 6d. The plaintiffs submitted that this notice did not satisfy the requirements of section 8 because it did not take into account the three wrappers from the chocolate bars. They accordingly

---

[1] In most cases it is not necessary to distinguish between the two categories because both suffice to render a promise enforceable. However in some transactions relating to the disposition of interests in land it may be necessary to distinguish consideration which is nominal from consideration which is not nominal but nevertheless inadequate: see GH Treitel, *The Law of Contract* (11th edn, Sweet & Maxwell, 2003), pp. 75–76.

sought an injunction to restrain the defendants from infringing their copyright. The defendants denied that the wrappers were part of the consideration and they pointed to the fact that the wrappers, when received, were worthless and were in fact thrown away. The House of Lords held by a bare majority (Viscount Somervell and Lord Keith of Avonholm dissenting) that the sending of the wrappers was not simply a condition which had to be fulfilled before a copy of the record could be obtained: it was part of the consideration for the sale of the record. The defendants had therefore not complied with the requirements of section 8 and the plaintiffs were entitled to an injunction restraining the defendants from infringing their copyright.

Viscount Simonds [dissenting]

In my opinion, my Lords, the wrappers are not part of the selling price. They are admittedly themselves valueless and are thrown away and it was for that reason, no doubt, that Upjohn J [the trial judge] was constrained to say that their value lay in the evidence they afforded of success in an advertising campaign. That is what they are. But what, after all, does that mean? Nothing more than that someone, by no means necessarily the purchaser of the record, has in the past bought not from Nestlés but from a retail shop three bars of chocolate and that the purchaser has thus directly or indirectly acquired the wrappers. How often he acquires them for himself, how often through another, is pure speculation. The only thing that is certain is that, if he buys bars of chocolate from a retail shop or acquires the wrappers from another who has bought them, that purchase is not, or at the lowest is not necessarily, part of the same transaction as his subsequent purchase of a record from the manufacturers.

I conclude, therefore, that the objection fails, whether it is contended that (in the words of Upjohn J) the sale 'bears no resemblance at all to the transaction to which the section . . . is pointing' or that the three wrappers form part of the selling price and are incapable of valuation. Nor is there any need to take what, with respect, I think is a somewhat artificial view of a simple transaction. What can be easier than for a manufacturer to limit his sales to those members of the public who fulfil the qualification of being this or doing that? It may be assumed that the manufacturer's motive is his own advantage. It is possible that he achieves his object. But that does not mean that the sale is not a retail sale to which the section applies or that the ordinary retail selling price is not the price at which the record is ordinarily sold, in this case 1s. 6d.

Lord Reid

To determine the nature of the contract one must find the intention of the parties as shown by what they said and did. The Nestlé Co's intention can hardly be in doubt. They were not setting out to trade in gramophone records. They were using these records to increase their sales of chocolate. Their offer was addressed to everyone. It might be accepted by a person who was already a regular buyer of their chocolate; but, much more important to them, it might be accepted by people who might become regular buyers of their chocolate if they could be induced to try it and found they liked it. The inducement was something calculated to look like a bargain, a record at a very cheap price. It is in evidence that the ordinary price for a dance record is 6s. 6d. It is true that the ordinary record gives much longer playing time than the Nestlé records and it may have other advantages. But the reader of the Nestlé offer was not in a position to know that.

It seems to me clear that the main intention of the offer was to induce people interested in this kind of music to buy (or perhaps get others to buy) chocolate which otherwise would not have been bought. It is, of course, true that some wrappers might come from the chocolate which had already been bought or from chocolate which would have been bought without the offer, but that does not seem to me to alter the case. Where there is a large number of transactions—the notice mentions 30,000 records—I do not think we should simply consider an isolated case where it would be impossible to say whether there had been a direct benefit from the acquisition of the wrappers or not. The requirement that wrappers should be sent was of great importance to the Nestlé Co; there would have been no point in their simply offering records for 1s. 6d. each. It seems to me quite unrealistic to divorce the buying of the chocolate from the supplying of the records. It is a perfectly good contract if a person accepts an offer to supply goods if he (a) does something of value to the supplier and (b) pays money: the consideration is both (a) and (b). There may have been cases where the acquisition of the wrappers conferred no direct benefit on the Nestlé Co, but there must have been many cases where it did. I do not see why the possibility that in some cases the acquisition of the wrappers did not directly benefit the Nestlé Co should require us to exclude from consideration the cases where it did; and even where there was no direct benefit from the acquisition of the wrappers there may have been an indirect benefit by way of advertisement . . .

I am of opinion that the . . . notice that the ordinary retail selling price was 1s. 6d. was invalid, that there was no ordinary retail selling price in this case and that the respondents' operations were not within the ambit of section 8. They were therefore infringements of the appellants' copyright and in my judgment this appeal should be allowed.

Lord Somervell of Harrow

My Lords, section 8 of the Copyright Act, 1956, provides for a royalty of an amount, subject to a minimum, equal to 6 1/4 per cent. of the ordinary retail selling price of the record. This necessarily implies, in my opinion, that a sale to be within the section must not only be retail, but one in which there is no other consideration for the transfer of property in the record but the money price. Parliament would never have based the royalty on a percentage of a money price if the section was to cover cases in which part, possibly the main part, of the consideration was to be other than money. This is in no sense a remarkable conclusion, as in most sales money is the sole consideration. It was not argued that the transaction was not a sale.

The question, then, is whether the three wrappers were part of the consideration or, as Jenkins LJ held, a condition of making the purchase, like a ticket entitling a member to buy at a co-operative store. I think they are part of the consideration. They are so described in the offer. 'They,' the wrappers, 'will help you to get smash hit recordings.' They are so described in the record itself—'all you have to do to get such new record is to send three wrappers from Nestlé's 6d. milk chocolate bars, together with postal order for 1s. 6d.' This is not conclusive but, however described, they are, in my view, in law part of the consideration. It is said that when received the wrappers are of no value to Nestlés. This I would have thought irrelevant. A contracting party can stipulate for what consideration he chooses. A peppercorn does not cease to be good consideration if it is established that the promisee does not like pepper and will throw away the corn. As the whole object of selling the record, if it was a sale, was to increase the sales of chocolate, it seems to me wrong not to treat the stipulated evidence of such sales as part of the consideration.

Lord Tucker delivered a speech in which he concluded that the defendants had not complied with the requirements of section 8 so that the plaintiffs were entitled to an injunction in the term sought. **Lord Keith of Avonholm** dissented.

COMMENTARY

The issue that divided the majority and the minority was whether the supply of the chocolate bar wrappers was a condition that had to be satisfied in order to obtain the record but was not part of the consideration or whether it was part of the consideration itself. The distinction is not always an easy one to draw. As Lord Wedderburn has remarked ([1959] *CLJ* 160, 161) it is 'notoriously difficult to set out satisfactory theoretical distinctions between bare promises of gifts subject to contingent conditions, and offers proper, e.g. in regard to statements such as: "if you go to London on Monday, I will give you £10."' On the facts of *Chappell* the majority construction was that the supply of chocolate bar wrappers was part of the consideration (although it should be noted that both sides expressed themselves in strong terms: Viscount Simonds stated that the majority construction was 'quite artificial' while Lord Reid stated that the minority construction was 'quite unrealistic').

The litigation in *Chappell* was not between a purchaser of a chocolate bar and the supplier of the records. So the House of Lords was not actually asked to enforce a contract under which one party promised to sell goods to another in return for payment by chocolate bar wrappers. Nevertheless, the question whether or not the chocolate bar wrappers were part of the consideration for the supply of the record was integral to the decision of their Lordships. It would therefore appear to follow from their decision that a contract to sell a record in return for chocolate bar wrappers is a contract that is supported by consideration. But does it follow from *Chappell* that a promise to supply chocolate bar wrappers will always constitute consideration for a promise given in return? Take the case of a promise to sell a work of art, valued at £2 million, in return for three chocolate bar wrappers. Is the promise to sell the work of art supported by consideration? *Chappell* does not necessarily support such a conclusion. The reason for this is that Nestlé had good commercial reasons for asking for the supply of chocolate bar wrappers. It was an integral part of their marketing strategy in that their purpose was to encourage people to buy their products. In the case of the sale of the work of art there appears to be no objectively good reason for asking for the supply of chocolate bar wrappers; it could be attributable simply to the subjective whim of the vendor. On the other hand it can be argued that it is for the parties to decide what is to constitute good consideration. If a party chooses to ask for a performance which others would regard as bizarre that is no concern of the law.

Nevertheless it would appear that the courts do reserve to themselves the right to decide that a particular act alleged to amount to consideration does not in fact do so. In *Thomas* v. *Thomas* (1842) 2 QB 851, 859 Patteson J stated that 'consideration means something which is of some value in the eye of the law'. This statement is not altogether easy to reconcile with the statement of Lord Somervell in *Chappell* that 'a contracting party can stipulate for what consideration he chooses'. It would appear that the starting point, at least in commercial cases, is that it is for the parties to decide what is or is not of value, but that the court nevertheless retains the right to conclude that the alleged consideration does not in law have any value and so does not amount to consideration. But the courts should be slow to conclude that something which the parties believe to be of value is not in fact of value. Lord Wedderburn, commenting on *Chappell* ([1959] *CLJ* 160, 162), summed the matter up as follows:

if the offer requires a certain act from the offeree, it is not open to the courts to speculate about whether it has any 'real value' in the mind of the offeror. Such an inquiry would approach perilously near to an investigation of motive. Provided that it is not wholly illusory, the act becomes part of the consideration because it is asked for by the offeree.

Of course it may not always be easy to decide whether or not an alleged consideration is 'wholly illusory' but in most cases it will be tolerably clear. In commercial cases the courts have tended to adopt a benevolent approach. This can be seen from a number of cases. The first is *Bainbridge* v. *Firmstone* (1838) 8 A & E 743. The defendant asked for permission to weigh two of the plaintiff's boilers and he promised to return them to the plaintiff in the same condition as they were in when he took possession of them. The plaintiff gave his permission. The defendant took the boilers to pieces but failed to put them together again. When sued by the plaintiff the defendant responded that no consideration had been provided for his promise to restore the boilers. The court held otherwise. Lord Denman CJ stated (at p. 744):

It seems to me that the declaration is well enough. The defendant had some reason for wishing to weigh the boilers; and he could do so only by obtaining permission from the plaintiff, which he did obtain by promising to return them in good condition. We need not inquire what benefit he expected to derive. The plaintiff might have given or refused leave.

Patteson J stated (at p. 744):

The consideration is, that the plaintiff, at the defendant's request, had consented to allow the defendant to weigh the boilers. I suppose the defendant thought he had some benefit; at any rate, there is a detriment to the plaintiff from his parting with the possession for even so short a time.

The finding that consideration took the form of giving up possession of the boilers seems more secure than the finding that the defendant obtained some (unidentified) benefit by being given permission to weigh the plaintiff's boilers.

Other cases can be found in which the consideration supplied took an insignificant form. Thus in *Haigh* v. *Brooks* (1839) 10 A & E 309 it was held that the surrender of a guarantee which turned out to be of doubtful validity was good consideration for a promise to pay certain bills. A more modern example is provided by *Pitt* v. *PHH Asset Management Ltd* [1994] 1 WLR 327. Property was put up for sale by the defendant at an asking price of £205,000. There were two parties interested in the property, the plaintiff and a Miss Buckle. The bids started at £185,000 and increased to £200,000. The plaintiff was the first to bid £200,000 but Miss Buckle matched it. However the defendant accepted the plaintiff's offer subject to contract. Miss Buckle then increased her offer to £210,000 and the defendant informed the plaintiff that acceptance of his offer had been withdrawn. The plaintiff threatened the estate agent acting for the defendant that he would seek an injunction to restrain the sale to Miss Buckle and that he would tell Miss Buckle that he had withdrawn his offer so that she could then lower her offer. The plaintiff and the estate agent then reached an agreement accord-ing to which the defendant would sell the property to the plaintiff for £200,000 and would not consider any further offers provided that the plaintiff exchanged contracts on the property within two weeks of the plaintiff receiving a draft contract (this obligation not to consider other offers is known as a 'lock-out agreement'). The defendant subsequently decided that it would accept the offer of £210,000 made by Miss Buckle, although it did give the plaintiff the opportunity to exchange contracts that day at the price of £210,000. The plaintiff refused to accept these terms and the property was sold to Miss Buckle. The plaintiff then brought an action against the defendant seeking damages for breach of contract. One of the points taken by the defendant by way of defence was that the plaintiff had not provided any consideration for the agreement with the result that it was not enforceable. The Court of Appeal held that the plaintiff did provide consideration. Peter Gibson LJ stated (at p. 332):

On the second point, the consideration moving from the plaintiff, [counsel for the defendant] submitted that in reality there was no consideration provided by the plaintiff. The plaintiff was expressing himself to be ready, willing and able to proceed to exchange contracts, which was, he submitted, simply what he would have to do in any case. Further, he said that the judge rightly described the threat by the plaintiff to issue an injunction as vapid, that is to say of no substance. He accordingly submitted that there was nothing by way of valuable consideration which the defendant received. I cannot accept these submissions either. I accept that the threat of an injunction only had a nuisance value in that I cannot see how the plaintiff could have succeeded in any claim. Nevertheless, that nuisance was something which the defendant was freed from by the plaintiff agreeing to the lock out agreement. Further, the threat of causing trouble with Miss Buckle was again a matter which could have been a nuisance to the defendant and again removal of that threat provided some consideration. But I also believe that the promise by the plaintiff to get on by limiting himself to just two weeks if he was to exchange contracts was of some value to the defendant. The defendant had the benefit of knowing that if it chose to give the plaintiff a draft contract to agree, there would be no delay on the plaintiff's part beyond a maximum of two weeks thereafter. The judge held that these three items constituted valuable consideration sufficient to support the lock out agreement and I respectfully agree with him.

The decision is clearly correct in relation to the finding that the plaintiff provided consideration because the plaintiff's promise to exchange contracts within two weeks did amount to the provision of consideration. More difficult is the proposition that he provided consideration in relation to (i) the withdrawal of his threat to seek an injunction and (ii) his refraining from causing trouble by advising Miss Buckle that she could now lower her offer.

The proposition that he provided consideration by withdrawing his threat to seek an injunction is slightly problematic given that Peter Gibson LJ stated that the threat lacked substance. Consideration is clearly provided in the case where the claim given up is a good one. It is also provided in the case where the claim given up is a doubtful one because in promising to give up a claim which may have substantial value the promisor is clearly providing value. But in what sense can it be said that he has provided consideration where the claim that has been abandoned is one that is inevit-ably doomed to failure? Nevertheless, the courts have concluded that a promise to give up a worthless claim can amount to the provision of consideration provided that the party who gives up the claim is acting in good faith and does not know of the invalidity of his claim. That this is so can be demonstrated by reference to the following two cases, namely *Cook* v. *Wright* (1861) 1 B & S 559 and *Wade* v. *Simeon* (1846) 2 CB 548.

In *Cook* v. *Wright* notice was given to the defendant occupier of a house calling upon him to pay his share of the cost of works done in an adjoining street. The defendant objected that he was not liable to make a contribution to the cost of the works on the ground that he was not the owner of the house. He later promised to pay a reduced contribution in three instalments (by way of three promissory notes) after being threatened with legal action if he did not pay. He paid the first instalment but then refused to make any further payment. The plaintiffs, the Commissioners responsible for carrying out the works, brought an action to recover the outstanding balance. At the trial of the action it transpired that the defendant was not in fact personally liable to make a contribution to the cost of the work. The court summed up the issue before it in the following terms (at p. 568):

it appeared on the evidence that [the defendant] believed himself not to be liable; but he knew that the plaintiffs thought him liable, and would sue him if he did not pay; and in order to avoid the expense and trouble of legal proceedings against himself he agreed to a compromise; and the question is, whether a person who has given a note as a compromise of a claim honestly made on him, and which but for that compromise would have been at once brought to a legal decision, can resist the payment of the note on the ground that the original claim thus compromised might have been successfully resisted.

The Court of Common Pleas concluded that the defendant was not entitled to resist the demand for payment and, for this purpose, it did not matter that the plaintiffs had not in fact commenced suit at the time at which the compromise was reached. Blackburn J stated that the 'real consideration' depends on 'the reality of the claim made and the bona fides of the compromise'. On the facts, the plaintiffs had suffered a detriment in that the compromise had induced them not to take proceedings against the actual owner of the house.

On the other hand, in *Wade* v. *Simeon* the plaintiff brought an action against the defendant to recover £1300 and £700. The defendant promised to pay the sum claimed provided that the plaintiff did not pursue his claim. The plaintiff did not pursue his claim but the defendant refused to honour his promise. The plaintiff sued to recover the promised sum. His action failed. The vital finding of the court was that the plaintiff knew that he had no claim against the defendant at the time at which he issued proceedings. It was held that there was no consideration to support the defendant's promise. Tindal CJ stated (at pp. 564–565):

the plaintiff admits that he had no cause of action against the defendant in the action . . . and that he knew it. It appears to me, therefore, that he is estopped from saying that there was any valid consideration for the defendant's promise. It is almost contra bonos mores, and certainly contrary to all the principles of natural justice, that a man should institute proceedings against another, when he is conscious that he has no good cause of action. In order to constitute a binding promise, the plaintiff must shew a good consideration, something beneficial to the defendant, or detrimental to the plaintiff. Detrimental to the plaintiff it cannot be, if he has no cause of action: and beneficial to the defendant it cannot be; for, in contemplation of law, the defence upon such an admitted state of facts must be successful, and the defendant will recover costs, which must be assumed to be a full compensation for all the legal damage he may sustain. The consideration, therefore, altogether fails.

In the light of *Cook* and *Wade* it must be concluded that in *Pitt* the withdrawal of the plaintiff's threat to seek an injunction could only amount to consideration provided that he was not aware of the fact that he had no entitlement to an injunction. But why does the law attribute such importance to the knowledge of the claimant? Should the presence or absence of consideration turn upon the state of mind of the claimant? One might expect the law to conclude either that a promise to give up a worthless claim is not good consideration (on the basis that nothing of value is given in promising to give up a worthless claim) or that it is good consideration (on the basis that the defendant is freed from the nuisance of having to defend the claim). Instead the law has adopted an uneasy compromise that rests on the knowledge of the claimant. The reason for this is probably to be found in the fact that the compromise of litigation is generally perceived to be in the public interest (hence the general rule that giving up a claim is good consideration) but, at the same time, the courts do not wish to encourage parties to threaten to resort to the courts in pursuit of a claim that is known to be invalid (hence the emphasis on the knowledge of the claimant).

The second difficulty with *Pitt* lies in the proposition that the plaintiff provided consideration by refraining from causing trouble by advising Miss Buckle that she could now lower her offer. In not making a nuisance of himself the plaintiff was held to have provided consideration. This conclusion is more problematic in the domestic sphere than in the context of commercial transactions. The particular difficulty with this conclusion lies in reconciling it with the old case of *White* v. *Bluett* (1853) 23 LJ Ex 36 (discussed in more detail at p. 306 below) in which a son was held not to have provided consideration for his father's promise to release him from liability under a promissory note on condition that he stopped his practice of complaining to his father about his father's intentions in relation to the distribution of his estate. But it may be that *White* would not be decided the same way today (at least on the consideration point). An indication of greater judicial willingness to find consideration in a domestic context is provided by the New York case of *Hamer* v. *Sidway* 124 NY 538 (1891), the facts of which are set out in the judgment of the court which was given by Parker J.

Parker J
The question which provoked the most discussion by counsel on this appeal and which lies at the foundation of plaintiff's asserted right of recovery, is whether by virtue of a contract defendant's testator William E. Story became indebted to his nephew William E. Story, 2d, on his twenty-first birthday in the sum of five thousand dollars. The trial court found as a fact that 'on the 20th day of March, 1869, William E. Story agreed to and with William E. Story, 2d, that if he would refrain from drinking liquor, using tobacco, swearing, and playing cards or billiards for money until he should become 21 years of age then he, the said William E. Story, would at that time pay him, the said William E. Story, 2d, the sum of $5,000 for such refraining, to which the said William E. Story, 2d, agreed,' and that he 'in all things fully performed his part of said agreement.'

The defendant contends that the contract was without consideration to support it, and, therefore, invalid. He asserts that the promisee by refraining from the use of liquor and tobacco was not harmed but benefited; that that which he did was best for him to do independently of his uncle's promise, and insists that it follows that unless the promisor was benefited, the contract was without consideration. A contention, which if well founded, would seem to leave open for controversy in many cases whether that which the promisee did or omitted to do was, in fact, of such benefit to him as to leave no consideration to support the enforcement of the promisor's agreement. Such a rule could not be tolerated, and is without foundation in the law . . . [he set out a number of judicial and textbook definitions of the doctrine of consideration, including a statement by Pollock that 'consideration means not so much that one party is profiting as that the other abandons some legal right in the present or limits his legal freedom of action in the future as an inducement for the promise of the first' and continued]

Now, applying this rule to the facts before us, the promisee used tobacco, occasionally drank liquor, and he had a legal right to do so. That right he abandoned for a period of years upon the strength of the promise of the testator that for such forbearance he would give him $5,000. We need not speculate on the effort which may have been required to give up the use of those stimulants. It is sufficient that he restricted his lawful freedom of action within certain prescribed limits upon the faith of his uncle's agreement, and now having fully performed the conditions imposed, it is of no moment whether such performance actually proved a benefit to the promisor, and the court will not inquire into it; but were it a proper subject of inquiry, we see nothing in this record that would permit a determination that the uncle was not benefited in a legal sense.

It is necessary to take some care with *Hamer* because it is not an English case and there is no guarantee that an English court will follow it. Nevertheless, it is widely cited in English textbooks and it is reasonable to conclude that it is likely that an English court would follow it. It is also consistent with the approach that we have noted in commercial cases such as *Chappell, Bainbridge*, and *Pitt* (above). But in what sense did the uncle obtain a benefit as a result of the promise made by his nephew and did the nephew suffer a detriment in promising to give up activities which his uncle believed to be harmful to him? Has English law now reached the position that the performance of a requested act is consideration for a promise of payment, no matter how absurd the act that is carried out? Consider the following two extracts:

PS Atiyah, 'Consideration: A Restatement' in *Essays on Contract*

(Oxford University Press, 1986), p. 195

[After setting out the facts of *Hamer* v. *Sidway* he continues] the nephew plainly incurs no detriment in fact by forbearing from smoking (indeed, quite the reverse) and it is hard to see that the uncle derives any benefit from the forbearance. Yet such a promise has been held enforceable in America, and it is generally thought that it would be enforceable in England. It may, of course, be argued that in such a case there is some indirect benefit to the uncle. No doubt he has his reasons for wishing the nephew not to smoke or he would not have made the promise; and no doubt he will be gratified if in fact the nephew forbears for the stated period. But here again, this seems to be a matter of motive rather than benefit. If this were a benefit in the sense in which the word is used in the orthodox doctrine, it would seem that many gratuitous promises would become enforceable simply because the promisor derives a sense of satisfaction from his generosity or from the recognition of it by the promisee or the public. Professor Treitel objects that the plaintiff in this case gave up a right; but in a unilateral contract the plaintiff gives up no right except by his behaviour. He just acts in reliance on the promise, and the reward cases suggest that the promise does not have to be a necessary condition for the 'action in reliance'. A promise of a reward to the winner of a race is generally believed to be legally enforceable even if the winner would still have run just as effectively absent the promise. It is hard to see that there is anything here which can sensibly be called a 'detriment'. The truth appears to be once again that a promise of this kind may be enforced because, if the promisee is induced to act on it, it may appear to the courts to be just to enforce it. Although a detrimental change of position is the usual reason for thinking it would be just to enforce the promise, the absence of detriment does not by itself seem fatal.

JC Smith, 'The Law of Contract—Alive or Dead?'

(1979) 13 *The Law Teacher* 73, 77

The language of benefit and detriment is, and I believe long has been, out of date. So is the idea that consideration must be an economic benefit of some kind. All that is necessary is that the defendant should, expressly or impliedly, ask for something in return for his promise, an act or a promise by the offeree. If he gets what he has asked for, then the promise is given for consideration unless there is some vitiating factor. Though lip service has been paid to the notions of benefit and detriment, they have no substantial meaning, in the light of the principle that the court will not inquire into the adequacy of the consideration. If I make a promise to you in return for your supplying me with three, quite useless, chocolate wrappers, which I will instantly throw away, there is a perfectly good contract provided that the promise was seriously intended. I have got what I asked for and that is a sufficient 'benefit'. You have parted with something that you might have kept and that is a sufficient 'detriment'. But the wrappers are of no value to me, and you are perhaps glad to be rid of them. As for economic value, the judges have recognised, for over a century, the validity of the contract to pay £100 if the promisee will walk to York . . . and no one has ever demonstrated what economic value there is in walking to York. Similarly, with promises of reward for not smoking . . .

(b) THE PRE-EXISTING DUTY RULE

Assume that A is promised a sum of money by B if he, A, promises to perform an act that he is already obliged to perform. Does A provide consideration for B's promise of payment? It is not easy to provide an answer to this question because the law is in a state of flux. The answer depends in part on the nature of A's pre-existing obligation. The cases can be divided into three categories, namely (i) performance of a contractual duty owed to a third party, (ii) performance of a contractual duty owed to the promisor, and (iii) performance of a duty imposed by law. If the pre-existing obligation is a contractual duty owed to a third party, then A will have provided consideration for B's promise. If, on the other hand, A's obligation is a contractual duty owed to B, the answer is uncertain. The old case of *Stilk* v. *Myrick* (1829) 6 Esp 129, 2 Camp 317 suggests that A does not provide consideration by promising to perform a contractual duty owed to B but the modern case of *Williams* v. *Roffey Bros & Nicholls (Contractors) Ltd* [1991] 1 QB 1 suggests that A does in fact provide consideration in such a case. The relationship between these two cases is the central issue in this section. Finally, if A's obligation is one that is imposed on him by the law (as opposed to the terms of his contract) then the general rule is that A does not provide consideration for B's promise of payment (although the status of the general rule is uncertain as a result of the decision of the Court of Appeal in *Ward* v. *Byham* [1956] 1 WLR 496 and the possible impact of the decision in *Williams* v. *Roffey Bros*). Thus the traditional account of the law distinguishes between the case where the pre-existing duty is a contractual duty owed to a third party (which clearly constitutes consideration) and the case where the pre-existing duty is either a contractual duty owed to the promisor or a duty imposed by law (where the general rule, subject to *Williams* v. *Roffey Bros*, is that there is no consideration).

A number of important questions have to be answered in this context. The first is whether or not there is any justification for continuing to differentiate between these three different categories. Why, for instance, does the law recognize the existence of consideration where the promise is a promise to perform a pre-existing contractual duty owed to a third party when it has been so reluctant to recognize the existence of consideration where the promise is one to perform a pre-existing contractual duty owed to the promisor or a pre-existing duty that is imposed by law? The second question relates to the role of duress in these cases. As we shall see (p. 200 below), it is possible that the general refusal of the law to recognize the existence of consideration was attributable to a desire to protect the promisor (B) from duress by the party promising to perform his pre-existing duty (A). If duress, or the fear of duress, is indeed the concern that underlies these cases then, it is argued, that concern should be reflected through the development of rules that target behaviour that constitutes duress. Thirdly, there is an issue relating to the conception of benefit and detriment that the law employs. If the conception is of 'legal benefit' and 'legal detriment' then it is more difficult to find the existence of consideration in these cases because A does not suffer a 'legal' detriment in promising to perform a duty that he is already obliged to perform and B does not receive a 'legal benefit' if all that he receives is a performance to which he is already entitled. On the other hand, the picture changes somewhat if we adopt a conception of 'practical' or 'factual' benefit and 'practical' detriment. A party who performs a pre-existing obligation may incur a practical detriment in doing so and a party who receives a performance to which he is already entitled may receive a practical benefit in consequence. One of the most important features of *Williams* v. *Roffey Bros* is the emphasis that it places on 'practical' benefit and detriment. The final issue is whether the law should distinguish between the requirements necessary for the creation of a contract and the requirements necessary for the modification of an existing contract. The traditional view has been that the law does not distinguish between formation and modification; the doctrine of consideration applies in both contexts. But it has been argued that the law should differentiate between contract formation and the modification of a contract and that the doctrine of consideration, if it is to apply to modifications at all, should apply in a much less stringent form.

(I) PERFORMANCE OF A CONTRACTUAL DUTY OWED TO A THIRD PARTY

Performance of a pre-existing contractual duty owed to a third party does constitute consideration for a promise given by another party. This proposition is supported by a number of cases. An old case is *Shadwell* v. *Shadwell* (1860) 9 CB (NS) 159. An uncle wrote to his nephew in the following terms:

My dear Lancey,

   I am glad to hear of your intended marriage with Ellen Nicholl; and, as I promised to assist you at starting, I am happy to tell you that I will pay to you £150 yearly during my life and until your annual income derived from your profession of a Chancery barrister shall amount to 600 guineas; of which your own admission will be the only evidence that I shall receive or require.

   Your ever affectionate uncle,

   Charles Shadwell

The nephew alleged that his uncle failed to honour his promise in full during his life-time and brought a claim for the arrears. One of the points taken by way of defence was that there was no consideration to support this agreement. By a majority, it was held that the promise was enforceable (Byles J dissented on the ground that the letter was 'no more than a letter of kindness, creating no legal obligation'). The consider-ation which the plaintiff claimed that he had supplied was the performance of his contractual obligation to marry Ellen Nicholl (at that time a promise to marry did have legal effect). In finding that the promise to pay was supported by consideration Erle CJ stated (at pp. 173–174):

Now, do these facts shew that the promise was in consideration either of a loss to be sustained by the plaintiff or a benefit to be derived from the plaintiff to the uncle, at his, the uncle's request? My answer is in the affirmative.

   First, do these facts shew a loss sustained by the plaintiff at his uncle's request? When I answer this in the affirmative, I am aware that a man's marriage with the woman of his choice is in one sense a boon, and, in that sense the reverse of a loss: yet, as between the plaintiff and the party promising to supply an income to support the marriage, it may well also be a loss. The plaintiff may have made a most material change in his position, and induced the object of his affection to do the same, and may have incurred pecuniary liabilities resulting in embarrassments which would be in every sense a loss if the income which had been promised should be withheld; and, if the promise was made in order to induce the parties to marry, the promise so made would be in legal effect a request to marry.

   Secondly, do these facts shew a benefit derived from the plaintiff to the uncle, at his request? In answering again in the affirmative, I am at liberty to consider the relation in which the parties stood and the interest in the settlement of his nephew which the uncle declares. The marriage primarily affects the parties thereto; but in a secondary degree it may be an object of interest to a near relative, and in that sense a benefit to him. This benefit is also derived from the plaintiff at the uncle's request. If the promise of the annuity was intended as an inducement to the marriage, and the averment that the plaintiff, relying on the promise, married, is an averment that the promise was one inducement to the marriage, this is the consideration averred in the declaration; and it appears to be expressed in the letter, construed with the surrounding circumstances.

A more modern example of the performance of a pre-existing contractual duty owed to a third party being held to constitute consideration is provided by the decision of the Privy Council in *The Eurymedon* [1975] AC 154. There the Privy Council held that a shipper of goods had made a promise to the defendant stevedores, who unloaded its goods from a ship, that it would not sue them for any damage that was done to the goods while they were being unloaded from the ship. One of the issues before the Privy Council was whether or not the stevedores had provided consideration for the shipper's promise not to sue them. It was held that the performance of their contractual duty to unload the goods (which contractual duty was owed to a third party, the carrier), was good consideration for the shipper's offer not to sue them for any damage done.

More difficult is the case where the consideration is alleged to take the form of a promise to perform, as opposed to performance of, a contractual duty owed to a third party. Initially, in *Jones* v. *Waite* (1839) 5 Bing NC 341 the courts took the view that a promise to perform a contractual duty owed to a third party was not good consideration, but in *Pao On* v. *Lau Yiu Long* [1980] AC 614 (see further p. 227 below) the Privy Council held that such a promise does amount to the provision of consideration. Lord Scarman, delivering the judgment of the Privy Council, stated (at p. 632):

Their Lordships do not doubt that a promise to perform, or the performance of, a pre-existing contractual obligation to a third party can be valid consideration. In *New Zealand Shipping Co Ltd* v. *AM Satterthwaite & Co Ltd (The Eurymedon)* [1975] AC 154, 168 the rule and the reason for the rule were stated:

'An agreement to do an act which the promisor is under an existing obligation to a third party to do, may quite well amount to valid consideration . . . the promisee obtains the benefit of a direct obligation. . . . This proposition is illustrated and supported by *Scotson* v. *Pegg* (1861) 6 H & N 295 which their Lordships consider to be good law.'

It is therefore clear that both performance of, and a promise to perform, a pre-existing contractual duty owed to a third party constitute good consideration for a promise given in return.

(II) PERFORMANCE OF A DUTY IMPOSED BY LAW

When we turn to the case of a duty imposed by law we find a different picture. The traditional rule is that performance of a duty imposed by law, or the promise to perform such a duty, does not, in law, amount to the provision of consideration. In *Collins* v. *Godefroy* (1831) 1 B & Ad 950 an attorney was subpoenaed to give evidence as a witness. He brought a claim for payment, alleging that he had been promised a guinea a day for his attendance. His claim failed. Lord Tenterden CJ stated (at pp. 956–957) that:

if it be a duty imposed by law upon a party regularly subpoenaed, to attend from time to time to give his evidence, then a promise to give him any remuneration for loss of time incurred in such attendance is a promise without consideration. We think that such a duty is imposed by law; and on consideration of the Statute of Elizabeth, and of the cases which have been decided on this subject, we are all of opinion that a party cannot maintain an action for compensation for loss of time in attending a trial as a witness. We are aware of the practice which has prevailed in certain cases, of allowing, as costs between party and party, so much per day for the attendance of professional men; but that practice cannot alter the law. What the effect of our decision may be, is not for our consideration. We think, on principle, that an action does not lie for a compensation to a witness for loss of time in attendance under a subpoena.

But the rule that performance of a duty imposed by law does not constitute consideration was challenged by Lord Denning in the following two cases:

Ward v. Byham

[1956] 1 WLR 496, Court of Appeal

The plaintiff and the defendant were, respectively, mother and father to a child. After they had lived together as partners for several years, and the plaintiff had given birth to an illegitimate child, the defendant turned the plaintiff out of the family home. Initially, the defendant put the child into the care of a neighbour for which he paid £1 per week. When the plaintiff found a new home for herself, she agreed with the defendant that she would care for the child and that he would pay her £1 per week. Subsequently, the plaintiff remarried and the defendant ceased payment. The plaintiff brought an action against the defendant on the basis of his undertaking to pay her £1 per week. The defendant denied that he was liable to make the promised payments on the ground that his promise to pay her was not supported by consideration. The Court of Appeal held that the plaintiff had provided consideration for the defendant's promise with the result that the defendant was liable to make the promised payment.

Denning LJ [set out the facts of the case and continued]
I approach the case, therefore, on the footing that, in looking after the child, the mother is only doing what she is legally bound to do. Even so, I think that there was sufficient consideration to support the promise. I have always thought that a promise to perform an existing duty, or the performance of it, should be regarded as good consideration, because it is a benefit to the person to whom it is given. Take this very case. It is as much a benefit for the father to have the child looked after by the mother as by a neighbour. If he gets the benefit for which he stipulated, he ought to honour his promise, and he ought not to avoid it by saying that the mother was herself under a duty to maintain the child.

I regard the father's promise in this case as what is sometimes called a unilateral contract, a promise in return for an act, a promise by the father to pay £1 a week in return for the mother's looking after the child. Once the mother embarked on the task of looking after the child, there was a binding contract. So long as she looked after the child, she would be entitled to £1 a week . . . I would dismiss the appeal.

Morris LJ
It seems to me . . . that the father was saying, in effect: Irrespective of what may be the strict legal position, what I am asking is that you shall prove that Carol [the child] will be well looked after and happy, and also that you must agree that Carol is to be allowed to

decide for herself whether or not she wishes to come and live with you. If those conditions were fulfilled the father was agreeable to pay. Upon those terms, which in fact
became operative, the father agreed to pay £1 a week. In my judgment, there was ample
consideration there to be found for his promise, which I think was binding.

Parker LJ
I have come to the same conclusion. I think that the letter of July 27, 1954, clearly
expresses good consideration for the bargain, and for myself I am content to adopt the
very careful judgment of the learned county court judge.

Shortly after the decision in *Ward* the Court of Appeal was given another opportunity
to consider whether or not the performance of a duty imposed by law can constitute
consideration and, once again, Lord Denning (but not the other judges) took the
opportunity to lodge an assault on the rule that such performance generally does not
constitute consideration:

Williams v. Williams

[1957] 1 WLR 148, Court of Appeal

The facts of the case are set out in the judgment of Denning LJ.

Denning LJ
In the present case a wife claims sums due to her under a maintenance agreement. No
evidence was called in the court below because the facts are agreed. The parties were
married on Apr. 25, 1945. They have no children. On Jan. 24, 1952, the wife deserted the
husband. On Mar. 26, 1952, they signed the agreement now sued on, which has three
clauses:

'(1) The husband will pay to the wife for her support and maintenance a weekly sum of
£1 10s. to be paid every four weeks during the joint lives of the parties so long as the
wife shall lead a chaste life the first payment hereunder to be made on Apr. 15, 1952.
(2) The wife will out of the said weekly sum or otherwise support and maintain herself
and will indemnify the husband against all debts to be incurred by her and will not in
any way at any time hereafter pledge the husband's credit. (3) The wife shall not so
long as the husband shall punctually make the payments hereby agreed to be made
commence or prosecute against the husband any matrimonial proceedings other than
proceedings for dissolution of marriage but upon the failure of the husband to make
the said weekly payments as and when the same become due the wife shall be at
full liberty on her election to pursue all and every remedy in this regard either by
enforcement of the provisions hereof or as if this agreement had not been made.'

So far as we know, the parties have remained apart ever since. On June 1, 1955, the
husband petitioned for divorce, on the ground of his wife's desertion, and on Oct. 12,
1955, a decree nisi was made against her. On Dec. 2, 1955, the decree was made
absolute. In this action the wife claims maintenance at the rate of £1 10s. a week under
the agreement for a period from October, 1954, to October, 1955. The sum claimed is
£30 5s. 9d., which is the appropriate sum after deduction of tax. The husband disputes

the claim, on the ground that there was no consideration for his promise. Clause 2, he says, is worthless and cl. 3 is unenforceable.

Let me first deal with cl. 3. It is settled law that a wife, despite such a clause as cl. 3, can make application to the magistrates or to the High Court for maintenance. If this wife had made such an application, the husband could have set up the fact of desertion as an answer to the claim, but he could not have set up cl. 3 as a bar to the proceedings. The clause is void, and as such is no consideration to support the agreement: see *Bennett* v. *Bennett* [1952] 1 All ER 413. Now let me deal with cl. 2. The husband relies on the fact that his wife deserted him. If there had been a separation by consent, he agrees that the agreement would have been enforceable. In that case the husband would still be under a duty to maintain, and the sum of 30s. a week would be assumed to be a quantification of a reasonable sum for her maintenance having regard to her own earning capacity. The ascertainment of a specific sum in place of an unascertained sum has always been held to be good consideration. So long as circumstances remained unchanged, it would be treated by the courts as binding on her and she could not recover more from him: see *National Assistance Board* v. *Parkes* [1955] 3 All ER 1. In the present case the husband says that, as the wife deserted him, he was under no obligation to maintain her and she was not entitled to pledge his credit in any way. Clause 2 therefore gives him nothing and is valueless to him. The husband says that *Goodinson* v. *Goodinson* [1954] 2 All ER 255 is distinguishable because there was no finding in that case that the wife was in desertion, and, moreover, the wife promised to maintain the child as well as herself.

Now I agree that, in promising to maintain herself whilst she was in desertion, the wife was only promising to do that which she was already bound to do. Nevertheless, a promise to perform an existing duty is, I think, sufficient consideration to support a promise, so long as there is nothing in the transaction which is contrary to the public interest. Suppose that this agreement had never been made, and the wife had made no promise to maintain herself and did not do so. She might then have sought and received public assistance or have pledged her husband's credit with tradesmen; in which case the National Assistance Board might have summoned him before the magistrates, or the tradesmen might have sued him in the county court. It is true that he would have an answer to those claims because she was in desertion, but nevertheless he would be put to all the trouble, worry and expense of defending himself against them. By paying her 30s. a week and taking this promise from her that she will maintain herself and will not pledge his credit, he has an added safeguard to protect himself from all this worry, trouble and expense. That is a benefit to him which is good consideration for his promise to pay maintenance. That was the view which appealed to the county court judge, and I must say that it appeals to me also.

There is another ground on which good consideration can be found. Although the wife was in desertion, nevertheless it must be remembered that desertion is never irrevocable. It was open to her to come back at any time. Her right to maintenance was not lost by the desertion. It was only suspended. If she made a genuine offer to return which he rejected, she would have been entitled to maintenance from him. She could apply to the magistrates or the High Court for an order in her favour. If she did so, however, whilst this agreement was in force, the 30s. would be regarded as prima facie the correct figure. It is a benefit to the husband for it to be so regarded, and that is sufficient consideration to support his promise.

I construe this agreement as a promise by the husband to pay his wife 30s. a week in consideration of her promise to maintain herself during the time she is living separate from him, whether due to her own fault or not. The wife cannot throw over the agreement and seek more maintenance from him unless new circumstances arise making it reasonable to allow her to depart from it. The husband cannot throw it over unless they resume married life together (in which case it will by inference be rescinded) or they are divorced (in which case it is a post-nuptial settlement and can be varied accordingly), or perhaps other circumstances arise not envisaged at the time of the agreement. Nothing of that kind has, however, occurred here. The husband must honour his promise. I would dismiss the appeal accordingly.

Hodson and **Morris LJJ** delivered concurring judgments but they found for the plaintiff on the basis that clause 2 of the agreement provided consideration for the defendant's promise to maintain her on the basis that her right to maintenance was not forfeited but only in suspension and would be resurrected in the event of her making an offer to return to the defendant.

COMMENTARY

In both *Ward* and *Williams* Lord Denning launched a direct attack on the pre-existing duty rule. The other judges were more circumspect and both cases can be explained on the ground that the plaintiff in both cases had done more than her existing legal duty. In *Ward* the plaintiff did more than her legal duty in promising to keep the child happy, while in *Williams* the plaintiff's right to maintenance had not been lost but was only in abeyance and so she was not simply promising to perform her legal duty when she promised to maintain herself in return for payment by her husband. *Ward* is the more problematic of the two decisions. The proposition that the plaintiff provided consideration by promising to keep the child happy sits rather uneasily with the proposition that a promise to provide love and affection does not in general constitute consideration (see *Bret* v. *JS* (1600) Cr Eliz 755). While it is clear that a promise to do more than one is legally obliged to do does amount to consideration, it can be difficult to tell whether or not the claimant has promised to do more than he was in fact legally obliged to do. This problem is not confined to cases such as *Ward*. It is of more general application. That this is so can be demonstrated by reference to the decision of the House of Lords in *Glasbrook Brothers Ltd* v. *Glamorgan County Council* [1925] AC 270 where their Lordships divided 3–2 on the question whether the police force had done more than their legal duty in providing protection to the owners of a colliery.

In *Glasbrook* a colliery manager, Mr James, applied for police protection for the colliery in the immediate aftermath of the settlement of the national coal strike. While the national strike had been settled, the local situation remained extremely volatile and the men responsible for keeping the mine working had decided to cease work because of fears for their own safety. Mr James informed the police superintendent that it was necessary to have the police billetted in the colliery. The police superintendent was of the view that this was unnecessary; he thought he could protect the colliery without installing a police garrison. The police superintendent eventually agreed to garrison seventy policemen at the colliery after Mr James signed a requisition in which he promised to pay for the agreed level of service. After the dispute had come to an end Glamorgan County Council presented the colliery owners with a bill for some £2,200 which the colliery owners refused to pay. The colliery owners submitted that there was no consideration for their promise to pay for the police protection they had been given. The majority concluded that consideration had been given on the ground that the police had done more than their legal duty. Thus Viscount Cave LC stated (at p. 281) that:

The question for the Court was whether on July 9, 1921, the police authorities, acting reasonably and in good faith, considered a police garrison at the colliery necessary for the protection of life and property from violence, or, in other words, whether the decision of the chief constable in refusing special protection unless paid for was such a decision as a man in his position and with his duties could reasonably take. If in the judgment of the police authorities, formed reasonably and in good faith, the garrison was necessary for the protection of life and property, then they were not entitled to make a charge for it, for that would be to exact a payment for the performance of a duty which they clearly owed to the appellants and their servants; but if they thought the garrison a superfluity and only acceded to Mr James' request with a view to meeting his wishes, then in my opinion they were entitled to treat the garrison duty as special duty and to charge for it.

He concluded on the facts (at p. 282) that the garrison 'formed an additional and not a substituted or alternative means of protection' with the result that the colliery owners were liable to pay for the services provided. Lord Carson and Lord Blanesburgh dissented. Lord Carson expressed his dissent in the following terms (at pp. 297–298):

I cannot, on the facts of this case, myself see that the demands of the colliery owners were for anything in the nature of a luxury. The circumstances speak for themselves, and we must in the calmer atmosphere of this House be quite sure we realize the facts as existing at the time. The safety men had left the colliery under compulsion, owing, as they said themselves, to want of police protection, and it is not to my mind any justification for not protecting them that, to use the words of Superintendent Smith, they were very nervous or unduly nervous. When the protection in the form in which it was asked for had been granted they returned to work, and I cannot help thinking that it was in this way a great disaster was avoided. My Lords, I find great difficulty in trying to define 'special services' in a case where there is actually being carried on an open invasion of the rights of subjects and when riot and violence threaten the destruction of property of such individuals and the right to work of other individuals, and indeed it would, I think, render the law difficult to carry out under similar circumstances if those demanding protection were to be told at any moment in the course of such attacks that the limit of protection had been reached unless they were rich enough to buy further protection by agreeing to pay a sum which in this case amounted to some £3000 to the police authorities.

Given these difficulties that can arise in terms of deciding whether or not the claimant has done more than his legal duty, should the law not take the additional step advocated by Lord Denning and recognize that performance of a legal duty does constitute consideration and that the transaction is enforceable provided that there is nothing in it contrary to the public interest? This raises the question of the rationale that lies behind the rule that performance of a legal duty cannot in general amount to consideration. Why, for example, can the police not generally charge for the public services that they render? Lord Shaw of Dunfermline considered this issue in *Glasbrook* in the following terms (at p. 290):

I clearly am of opinion that no charge can be exacted from a private citizen for the performance of a public duty. Furthermore, I would also add that, on the assumption that a payment is made to induce or secure that the public authority will perform such a duty, moneys paid under such a bargain are recoverable by the private citizen on the double ground, first, that it is against public policy that the performance of public duty shall be a matter of private purchase, and second, that a promise or agreement to pay, accepted from a citizen in times of nervous alarm or anxiety, fails in legality on the ground of duress, and sums paid under it must be restored.

It is important to note the two distinct grounds advanced by Lord Shaw. The second objection is narrower than the first. The second objection is based on duress: absent duress, or, possibly, the fear of duress, a promise to perform an existing legal duty does amount to consideration. The first ground is, however, wider in that the public policy objection takes account of a broader range of factors than simply duress. Take the case where a member of the public freely agrees to pay a policeman for services which the policeman was obliged by law to perform. Should the promise to pay the policeman be enforceable? On the basis of Lord Shaw's first ground it should not, but on the second it seems that it may be enforceable. Does the example of a promise to pay a member of the police force for the performance of a legal duty not suggest that there is good sense behind the general rule that performance of a legal duty is not good consideration and that the public policy objection is more deeply rooted than the fear of duress? On the other hand, does this public policy objection apply with the same force on the facts of either *Ward* or *Williams*? Were the parties in either case seeking to turn the performance of a 'public duty' into a 'matter of private purchase'? While there is obviously a public interest in ensuring that children are cared for and looked after, does this public policy require that the law should refuse to give effect to private bargains between parents in relation to their obligations in respect of the care of their children?

Notwithstanding the views expressed by Lord Denning the formal position in English law remains that performance of a legal duty does not amount to consideration. But the rule is likely to come under pressure as a result of developments that have taken place in our next group of cases.

(III) PERFORMANCE OF A CONTRACTUAL DUTY OWED TO THE PROMISOR
The question whether or not performance of a pre-existing contractual duty owed to the promisor is good consideration for an additional promise of payment made by the promisor has proved to be a vexed one in English law. Take the following example. A enters into a contract with B under which B agrees to build a house for A at a price of £100,000. B finds that he cannot perform the contract for the agreed sum and informs A that he will not be able to complete the works unless he is paid an additional £10,000. A promises to pay the additional sum but, after the works are completed, refuses to honour his promise. Can B recover the additional £10,000 from A? The traditional answer is that he cannot on the ground that he has not provided any consideration for B's promise to pay him £10,000. He has simply performed his existing contractual duty, owed to A, to build the house and performance of an existing contractual duty owed to the promisor (here A) is not good consideration. Authority for such a proposition is to be found in *Stilk* v. *Myrick* (1809) 2 Camp. 317, 6 Esp 129 (p. 184 below) and *Foakes* v. *Beer* (1884) 9 App Cas 605 (p. 204 below). This

view has, however, been challenged by the decision of the Court of Appeal in *Williams* v. *Roffey Bros & Nicholls (Contractors) Ltd* [1991] 1 QB 1 (p. 188 below) where, on facts which resemble our hypothetical, the court held that a promise to perform an existing contractual duty did amount to consideration for a promise of additional payment by the party in the position of A in our hypothetical example. The basis for this conclusion was that A received a practical benefit as a result of the performance by B of his existing contractual duty and, in the absence of duress, there were no public policy objections to giving effect to A's promise to pay B more money for the performance of B's existing contractual obligations.

In terms of authority the central issue at stake in the cases is the relationship between *Williams* v. *Roffey Bros*, on the one hand, and *Stilk* v. *Myrick* and *Foakes* v. *Beer* on the other hand. The relationship between *Williams* and *Foakes* is particularly difficult, given that the latter is a decision of the House of Lords which was not in fact mentioned by the Court of Appeal in their judgments in *Williams*. In terms of principle there are two important points at stake. The first relates to the conception of benefit or detriment to which the court ought to have regard. If the court looks for a benefit or detriment as a matter of law, it will struggle to find such benefit or detriment in these cases because it is difficult to say that A has been benefited as a matter of law when all that he has received is a performance to which he was already entitled, and it is also hard to say that B has suffered a legal detriment in performing a duty that he was already legally obliged to perform as a result of his contract with A. On the other hand, if attention is focused on the existence of a 'practical' or 'factual' benefit or detriment then it can be argued that A has received a 'practical' benefit in obtaining performance which he might not otherwise have obtained and B can be said to have suffered a 'practical' or 'factual' detriment in continuing with performance when he might have simply refused to go on with his contractual obligations. The second issue relates to the role of duress. Is the reason for refusing to give effect to A's promise to pay B more, the fact that B either has, or may have, extracted the promise of additional payment by subjecting A to duress? If duress is the rationale behind the cases then we should give effect to re-negotiations of a contract provided that they are freely entered into. But if duress is not the rationale behind the rule then the courts should refuse to give effect to A's promise to pay B an additional £10,000 even in the case where A freely agreed to pay B the additional sum.

The leading case, at least in historical terms, is *Stilk* v. *Myrick*. Unfortunately, the case was reported twice and the two reports differ in significant respects. The facts of *Stilk* were as follows:

The plaintiff seaman agreed to sail to the Baltic and back at a rate of pay of £5 per month. When the vessel arrived in Cronstadt two of the seamen deserted. The master of the vessel failed in his attempt to find two sailors to replace the deserters and so he entered into an agreement with the rest of the crew, which included the plaintiff, under which he agreed that if the crew worked the ship back to London he would divide the wages of the two deserters between them in equal shares. The crew worked the ship back to London but the master did not pay the plaintiff his share of the deserters' wages. The plaintiff brought an action against the master to recover the wages which he believed were due to him. His claim failed.

The reasons for the failure of the plaintiff's claim are stated differently in the two reports. The first report was prepared by Espinasse ((1809) 6 Esp 129) and is in the following terms:

Lord Ellenborough ruled, That the plaintiff could not recover upon this part of his demand. His Lordship said, That he recognised the principle of the case of *Harris* v. *Watson* as founded on just and proper policy. When the defendant entered on board the ship, he stipulated to do all the work his situation called upon him to do. Here the voyage was to the Baltick and back, not to Cronstadt only; if the voyage had then terminated, the sailors might have made what terms they pleased. If any part of the crew had died, would not the remainder have been forced to work the ship home? If that accident would have left them liable to do the whole work without any extraordinary remuneration, why should not desertion or casualty equally demand it?

Verdict for the monthly wages only.

The second report was prepared by Campbell ((1809) 2 Camp 318) and it states:

Lord Ellenborough I think *Harris* v. *Watson* was rightly decided; but I doubt whether the ground of public policy, upon which Lord Kenyon is stated to have proceeded, be the true principle on which the decision is to be supported. Here, I say, the agreement is void for want of consideration. There was no consideration for the ulterior pay promised to the mariners who remained with the ship. Before they sailed from London they had undertaken to do all that they could under all the emergencies of the voyage. They had sold all their services till the voyage should be completed. If they had been at liberty to quit the vessel at Cronstadt, the case would have been quite different; or if the captain had capriciously discharged the two men who were wanting, the others might not have been compellable to take the whole duty upon themselves, and their agreeing to do so might have been a sufficient consideration for the promise of an advance of wages. But the desertion of a part of the crew is to be considered an emergency of the voyage as much as their death; and those who remain are bound by the terms of their original contract to exert themselves to the utmost to bring the ship in safety to her destined port. Therefore, without looking to the policy of this agreement, I think it is void for want of consideration, and that the plaintiff can only recover at the rate of £5 per month.

COMMENTARY

At the time at which *Stilk* was decided there was no centralized system of law reporting and the quality of the reporting was variable. The two reporters of *Stilk* were Espinasse and Campbell. It is fair to say that Espinasse was not highly regarded as a law reporter. His standing, or lack of it, was summed up by Isaacs J when he said that he did not care for 'Espinasse or any other ass'! On the other hand Espinasse was junior counsel in *Stilk* and so one might have expected him to note down accurately what Lord Ellenborough actually said. But Espinasse's hearing was apparently suspect so we may not be able to rely on his ability to record what was said accurately. Campbell, on the other hand, is an altogether more powerful figure. He rose to become Lord Chancellor and his reputation as a law reporter is much higher, although it might be said that his position as Lord Chancellor insulated him from some of the criticisms that might otherwise have been levelled against the quality of his reporting.

However it is possible to exaggerate the significance of the differences between the two reports. Indeed, Peter Luther notes ('Campbell, Espinasse and the Sailors: Text and Context in the Common Law' (1999) 19 *Legal Studies* 526) that there are substantial similarities between the two reports of the case. Thus he states (at p. 538):

> Bearing in mind that both texts must be treated with caution, it is interesting to compare the two methodically. The surprise is not how different, but how *similar* they are. The best way to do this is to take each sentence of Espinasse's report, as the less full version, and to find its equivalent in Campbell. To the sentence which refers to *Harris* v. *Watson* there is, it appears, no equivalent in Campbell; this is the crux of the case, and to this we will return. But, except for this sentence, there is nothing in Espinasse that does not have its parallel in Campbell. Espinasse's following sentence, beginning 'When the defendant . . .' makes the same point as the sentence in Campbell which begins 'Before they sailed from London . . .'. The next sentence, 'Here the voyage was to the Baltick . . .', corresponds to the first part of Campbell's 'If they had been at liberty to quit the vessel at Cronstadt . . .', though Campbell continues with a point omitted by Espinasse, concerning what might have happened had the master 'capriciously discharged the two men who were want-ing'. This is, of course, not the only point made by Campbell but ignored by Espinasse—the latter's omission of any reference to consideration is another point that must be considered in more detail . . . Espinasse's two closing questions, beginning 'If any part of the crew had died . . .' and 'If that accident would have left them liable . . .' are the equivalent of Campbell's single sentence begin-ning 'But the desertion of the crew . . .'. Leaving aside for the moment the problem references to *Harris* v. *Watson*, each report makes sense as it stands, but Espinasse has produced a report which supports a 'public policy' analysis, and Campbell a report which culminates in an applica-tion of the doctrine of consideration, *by using identical reasoning*. A literary critic would be struck by the consonance between the two reports, not the difference. Perhaps it is in the nature of lawyers—or at least those used to an adversarial system—to assume that if two texts are not identical, they must be diametrically opposed; that one must be wrong, one right.
>
> What about the references to *Harris* v. *Watson*? Surely at this point there is a direct conflict between the two reports? It is suggested—tentatively—that it may be possible to reconcile even these two sentences. This can only be speculation, but it is surely as valid to suggest an answer to the question 'what did the judge mean?' when we have two accounts (or, at least, impressions) of what he said, than it is to ask and answer the question 'what really happened in Cronstadt?', which is what judges and commentators have done when they suppose *Stilk* v. *Myrick* to have been a case of coercion. Could Espinasse's statement that Ellenborough 'recognised the principle of the case of *Harris* v. *Watson* as founded on just and proper policy' be no more than his equivalent of Campbell's 'I think *Harris* v. *Watson* was rightly decided'? Or, to put it another way and to paraphrase the combined text of both reporters, could Ellenborough have been suggesting that Lord Kenyon's decision in the earlier case was indeed based on *a* just and proper policy, but not on *the* policy which is stated in the report of *Harris* v. *Watson*? Such a construction would have the advantage of making perfect sense of Espinasse's report, in which the apparent approval of *Harris* v. *Watson* otherwise looks rather odd, since there is no subsequent reference to any of the reason-ing used in the case. Espinasse, on such an analysis, makes Ellenborough give an *alternative* policy-based reason why he approves of the decision in *Harris* v. *Watson*.

Notwithstanding the similarities noted by Luther, *Stilk* has been analyzed in two different ways by commentators and these two different analyses reflect the two reports of the case. The first analysis is based on duress (and hence on Espinasse's report) and the second on consideration (based on Campbell's report). The difference between the two analyses is important because the latter is much broader in scope than the former in that it refuses to give effect to the promise of additional payment even in the case where no duress has been exercised.

The claim that *Stilk* can be explained on the ground of duress is somewhat problematic. The difficulties are both doctrinal and factual. The doctrinal difficulty relates to the status of the doctrine of duress in 1809. The doctrine of duress, at least that part of it concerned with the application of economic, as opposed to physical, coercion was in a very undeveloped state in 1809 and indeed there are doubts as to its very existence at that point in time (it is common to attribute the recognition of the doctrine of economic duress in English law to Kerr J in 1976 in *The Siboen and The Sibotre* [1976] 1 Lloyd's Rep 293). For present purposes, it suffices to concentrate on the factual difficulty. It is important to note that the context in which the master made his promise of additional pay was not one in which the sailors had refused mid-voyage to continue with the journey unless they were promised extra pay. The vessel was in port at the time at which the promise was made and so there may not have been any pressure on the master at all (at least if there were other sailors looking for work in the port, a point which we can never now resolve). In other words, we need to know more about the facts of the case before we can be in a position to decide whether or not this was a case of duress. There is evidence that duress, or the fear of potential duress, may have been a factor that influenced Lord Ellenborough. Some support for the proposition that duress does have a role to play in understanding these cases can be gleaned from the case of *Harris* v. *Watson* (1791) 1 Peake 102 (although note Peter Luther's comments on *Harris* above). The plaintiff was a seaman on board the vessel The Alexander. The defendant was the master of the vessel and he promised to pay the plaintiff five guineas over and above his common wages if the plaintiff would perform some extra work in navigating the ship. The promise was made at a time when the ship was in danger and it was made in order to induce the seamen to exert themselves. Lord Kenyon held that the plaintiff was not entitled to recover the promised five guineas. He stated (at p. 103):

If this action was to be supported, it would materially affect the navigation of this kingdom. It has been long since determined, that when the freight is lost, the wages are also lost. This rule was founded on a principle of policy, for if sailors were in all events to have their wages, and in times of danger entitled to insist on an extra charge on such a promise as this, they would in many cases suffer a ship to sink, unless the captain would pay any extravagant demand they might think proper to make.

The alternative analysis of *Stilk*, based on Campbell's report, was that it was a case in which there was no consideration for the promise of extra pay. Why was there no consideration on the facts of the case? The plaintiff in all probability had to work harder as a result of the desertion of the two crew-members and it could be argued that the master obtained a benefit as a result of the work done by the sailors. Lord Ellenborough addressed the detriment side of the equation but he did not comment on the benefit issue. In rejecting the submission that the plaintiff had provided consideration as a result of the work he had done on the voyage home Lord Ellenborough did not focus on the question whether, as a matter of fact, the plaintiff had worked harder. Instead he examined the legal obligations of the plaintiff and concluded that he had not, as a matter of law, done more than he was legally required to do. He had accepted a contractual obligation to work the vessel to the Baltic and back and that was what he had done. The absence of any discussion of whether or not the master obtained a benefit as a result of the work done by the sailors is a matter of some significance given the emphasis placed by modern courts upon the question of whether or not the party in the position of the master obtained a 'practical benefit' as a result of the performance of the pre-existing duty (see further p. 198 below).

We have seen in the context of cases concerned with the performance of a duty imposed by law (p. 177 above) that the courts have recognized that a party who does more than his legal duty does provide consideration. The same principle has been applied in the present context. Thus in *Hanson* v. *Royden* (1867) LR 3 CP 47 the plaintiff did more than he was obliged to do in that he was promoted and so performed additional tasks in return for the promise of extra pay. Similarly, in *Hartley* v. *Ponsonby* (1857) 7 E & B 872 the sailors did more than they were contractually bound to do in that the ship was so under-manned as a result of desertions that they would have been entitled to refuse to continue with the voyage. Thus in continuing the voyage when they might lawfully have refused to do so they provided consideration for the promise of extra pay.

The question whether *Stilk* is properly analysed as a duress case or as a case in which no consideration was provided for the defendant's promise of additional pay resurfaced in the case of *Williams* v. *Roffey Bros & Nicholls (Contractors) Ltd* [1991] 1 QB 1, which is now regarded as the leading modern authority on the point.

Williams v. Roffey Bros & Nicholls (Contractors) Ltd

[1991] 1 QB 1, Court of Appeal

The defendant building contractors entered into a contract with the plaintiff carpenter under which the plaintiff agreed to carry out the carpentry work on the refurbishment of 27 flats. The contract price for the carpentry work was agreed at £20,000. After he had completed part of the work, and been paid £16,200 by the defendants, the plaintiff ran into financial difficulties. The trial judge found that there were two principal causes of his difficulties. The first was that the contract price was too low to enable him to operate satisfactorily and make a profit. The second was that he failed to supervise his workmen adequately. The defendants wished to ensure that the plaintiff completed the work on time because a failure to do so would result in them incurring liability under a 'penalty clause' to the employer. The defendants called a meeting with the plaintiff and they promised to pay him a further sum of £10,300 to be paid at the rate of £575 for each flat in which the carpentry work was completed. The plaintiff continued with the work and was paid a further £1,500. The plaintiff then walked off the site. The defendants employed other contractors to finish off the work, albeit that they incurred liability under the 'penalty clause' as a result of their completion of the works one week late. The plaintiff brought a claim against the defendants for damages of £10,847.07. The Assistant Recorder found that before he ceased work the plaintiff had substantially completed the work on 8 flats after the defendants had made their promise of additional payment. He accordingly awarded the plaintiff damages of £4,600 (consisting of 8 x £575) 'less some small deduction for defective and incomplete items' and held that the plaintiff was entitled to a reasonable proportion of the £2,200 outstanding from the original contract price.

The defendants appealed to the Court of Appeal on two principal grounds. The first was that they submitted that there was no consideration for their promise to pay an additional £575 per completed flat. The second was that the money was only payable upon completion of each flat and that, since the work had not been completed on any flat, no payment was due. The Court of Appeal dismissed the appeal and held that the plaintiff was entitled to be paid because he had substantially completed the work on eight of the flats and had provided consideration for the defendants' promise of additional payment.

Glidewell LJ [set out the facts, decided that substantial completion of the eight flats entitled the plaintiff to payment and continued]

Was there consideration for the defendants' promise made on 9 April 1986 to pay an additional price at the rate of £575 per completed flat?

The judge made the following findings of fact which are relevant on this issue. (i) The subcontract price agreed was too low to enable the plaintiff to operate satisfactorily and at a profit. Mr Cottrell, the defendants' surveyor, agreed that this was so. (ii) Mr Roffey (managing director of the defendants) was persuaded by Mr Cottrell that the defendants should pay a bonus to the plaintiff. The figure agreed at the meeting on 9 April 1986 was £10,300.

The judge quoted and accepted the evidence of Mr Cottrell to the effect that a main contractor who agrees too low a price with a subcontractor is acting contrary to his own interests. He will never get the job finished without paying more money. The judge therefore concluded:

'In my view where the original subcontract price is too low, and the parties subsequently agree that additional moneys shall be paid to the subcontractor, this agreement is in the interests of both parties. This is what happened in the present case, and in my opinion the agreement of 9 April 1986 does not fail for lack of consideration.'

In his address to us, Mr Evans [counsel for the defendants] outlined the benefits to his clients, the defendants, which arose from their agreement to pay the additional £10,300 as: (i) seeking to ensure that the plaintiff continued work and did not stop in breach of the subcontract; (ii) avoiding the penalty for delay; and (iii) avoiding the trouble and expense of engaging other people to complete the carpentry work.

However, Mr Evans submits that, though his clients may have derived, or hoped to derive, practical benefits from their agreement to pay the 'bonus', they derived no benefit in law, since the plaintiff was promising to do no more than he was already bound to do by his subcontract, i.e., continue with the carpentry work and complete it on time. Thus there was no consideration for the agreement. Mr Evans relies on the principle of law which, traditionally, is based on the decision in *Stilk* v. *Myrick* (1809) 2 Camp 317 . . .

[he set out the facts of the case and the judgment as reported by Campbell and continued]

In *North Ocean Shipping Co Ltd* v. *Hyundai Construction Co Ltd* [1979] QB 705, Mocatta J regarded the general principle of the decision in *Stilk* v. *Myrick*, 2 Camp 317 as still being good law. He referred to two earlier decisions of this court, dealing with wholly different subjects, in which Denning LJ sought to escape from the confines of the rule, but was not accompanied in his attempt by the other members of the court . . .

[he considered *Ward* v. *Byham* [1956] 1 WLR 496 and, after setting out passages from the judgments of Denning LJ and Morris LJ stated]

As I read the judgment of Morris LJ, he and Parker LJ held that, although in maintaining the child the plaintiff was doing no more than she was obliged to do, nevertheless her promise that the child would be well looked after and happy was a practical benefit to the father which amounted to consideration for his promise.

[he then considered *Williams* v. *Williams* [1957] 1 WLR 148 and continued]

It was suggested to us in argument that, since the development of the doctrine of promissory estoppel, it may well be possible for a person to whom a promise has been made, on which he has relied, to make an additional payment for services which he is in any event bound to render under an existing contract or by operation of law, to show that the promisor is estopped from claiming that there was no consideration for his promise. However, the application of the doctrine of promissory estoppel to facts such as those of the present case has not yet been fully developed: see e.g. the judgment of Lloyd J in *Syros Shipping Co SA* v. *Elaghill Trading Co* [1980] 2 Lloyd's Rep 390, 392. Moreover, this point was not argued in the court below, nor was it more than adumbrated before us. Interesting though it is, no reliance can in my view be placed on this concept in the present case.

There is, however, another legal concept of relatively recent development which is relevant, namely, that of economic duress. Clearly if a subcontractor has agreed to under-take work at a fixed price, and before he has completed the work declines to continue with it unless the contractor agrees to pay an increased price, the subcontractor may be held guilty of securing the contractor's promise by taking unfair advantage of the difficul-ties he will cause if he does not complete the work. In such a case an agreement to pay an increased price may well be voidable because it was entered into under duress. Thus this concept may provide another answer in law to the question of policy which has troubled the courts since before *Stilk* v. *Myrick*, 2 Camp 317, and no doubt led at the date of that decision to a rigid adherence to the doctrine of consideration.

This possible application of the concept of economic duress was referred to by Lord Scarman, delivering the judgment of the Judicial Committee of the Privy Council in *Pao On* v. *Lau Yiu Long* [1980] AC 614. He said, at p. 632:

'Their Lordships do not doubt that a promise to perform, or the performance of, a pre-existing contractual obligation to a third party can be valid consideration. In *New Zealand Shipping Co Ltd* v. *AM Satterthwaite & Co Ltd (The Eurymedon)* [1975] AC 154, 168 the rule and the reason for the rule were stated: "An agreement to do an act which the promisor is under an existing obligation to a third party to do, may quite well amount to valid consideration . . . the promisee obtains the benefit of a direct obliga-tion. . . . This proposition is illustrated and supported by *Scotson* v. *Pegg* (1861) 6 H & N 295 which their Lordships consider to be good law". Unless, therefore, the guarantee was void as having been made for an illegal consideration or voidable on the ground of economic duress, the extrinsic evidence establishes that it was supported by valid consideration. Mr Leggatt for the defendants submits that the consideration is illegal as being against public policy. He submits that to secure a party's promise by a threat of repudiation of a pre-existing contractual obligation owed to another can be, and in the circumstances of this case was, an abuse of a dominant bargaining position and so contrary to public policy. . . . This submission found favour with the majority in the Court of Appeal. Their Lordships, however, considered it misconceived.'

Lord Scarman then referred to *Stilk* v. *Myrick*, 2 Camp 317, and its predecessor *Harris* v. *Watson* (1791) Peake 102, and to *Williams* v. *Williams* [1957] 1 WLR 148, before turning to the development of this branch of the law in the United States of America. He then said, at pp. 634–635:

'Their Lordships' knowledge of this developing branch of American law is necessarily limited. In their judgment it would be carrying audacity to the point of foolhardiness for them to attempt to extract from the American case-law a principle to provide an answer to the question now under consideration. That question, their Lordships repeat, is whether, in a case where duress is not established, public policy may nevertheless invalidate the consideration if there has been a threat to repudiate a pre-existing contractual obligation or an unfair use of a dominating bargaining position. Their Lordships' conclusion is that where businessmen are negotiating at arm's length it is unnecessary for the achievement of justice, and unhelpful in the development of the law, to invoke such a rule of public policy. It would also create unacceptable anomaly. It is unnecessary because justice requires that men, who have negotiated at arm's length, be held to their bargains unless it can be shown that their consent was vitiated by fraud, mistake or duress. If a promise is induced by coercion of a man's will, the doctrine of duress suffices to do justice. The party coerced, if he chooses and acts in time, can avoid the contract. If there is no coercion, there can be no reason for avoiding the contract where there is shown to be a real consideration which is otherwise legal. Such a rule of public policy as is now being considered would be unhelpful because it would render the law uncertain. It would become a question of fact and degree to determine in each case whether there had been, short of duress, an unfair use of a strong bargaining position. It would create anomaly because, if public policy invalidates the consideration, the effect is to make the contract void. But unless the facts are such as to support a plea of "non est factum", which is not suggested in this case, duress does no more than confer upon the victim the opportunity, if taken in time, to avoid the contract. It would be strange if conduct less than duress could render a contract void, whereas duress does no more than render a contract voidable. Indeed, it is the defendants' case in this appeal that such an anomaly is the correct result. Their case is that the plaintiffs, having lost by cancellation the safeguard of the subsidiary agreement, are without the safeguard of the guarantee because its consideration is contrary to public policy, and that they are debarred from restoration to their position under the subsidiary agreement because the guarantee is void, not voidable. The logical consequence of Mr Leggatt's submission is that the safeguard which all were at all times agreed the plaintiffs should have—the safeguard against fall in value of the shares—has been lost by the application of a rule of public policy. The law is not, in their Lordships' judgment, reduced to countenancing such stark injustice: nor is it necessary, when one bears in mind the protection offered otherwise by the law to one who contracts in ignorance of what

he is doing or under duress. Accordingly, the submission that the additional consideration established by the extrinsic evidence is invalid on the ground of public
policy is rejected.'

It is true that *Pao On* is a case of a tripartite relationship that is, a promise by A to
perform a pre-existing contractual obligation owed to B, in return for a promise of payment by C. But Lord Scarman's words, at pp. 634–635, seem to me to be of general
application, equally applicable to a promise made by one of the original two parties to a
contract.

Accordingly, following the view of the majority in *Ward* v. *Byham* [1956] 1 WLR 496
and of the whole court in *Williams* v. *Williams* [1957] 1 WLR 148 and that of the Privy
Council in *Pao On* [1980] AC 614 the present state of the law on this subject can be
expressed in the following proposition: (i) if A has entered into a contract with B to do
work for, or to supply goods or services to, B in return for payment by B; and (ii) at
some stage before A has completely performed his obligations under the contract B
has reason to doubt whether A will, or will be able to, complete his side of the bargain;
and (iii) B thereupon promises A an additional payment in return for A's promise to
perform his contractual obligations on time; and (iv) as a result of giving his promise, B
obtains in practice a benefit, or obviates a disbenefit; and (v) B's promise is not given
as a result of economic duress or fraud on the part of A; then (vi) the benefit to B is
capable of being consideration for B's promise, so that the promise will be legally
binding.

As I have said, Mr Evans accepts that in the present case by promising to pay the
extra £10,300 his client secured benefits. There is no finding, and no suggestion, that
in this case the promise was given as a result of fraud or duress. If it be objected that
the propositions above contravene the principle in *Stilk* v. *Myrick*, 2 Camp 317, I
answer that in my view they do not; they refine, and limit the application of that
principle, but they leave the principle unscathed e.g. where B secures no benefit by his
promise. It is not in my view surprising that a principle enunciated in relation to the
rigours of seafaring life during the Napoleonic wars should be subjected during the
succeeding 180 years to a process of refinement and limitation in its application in
the present day. It is therefore my opinion that on his findings of fact in the present case,
the judge was entitled to hold, as he did, that the defendants' promise to pay the extra
£10,300 was supported by valuable consideration, and thus constituted an enforceable
agreement.

As a subsidiary argument, Mr Evans submits that on the facts of the present case the
consideration, even if otherwise good, did not 'move from the promisee'. This submission is based on the principle illustrated in the decision in *Tweddle* v. *Atkinson* (1861) 1 B
& S 393. My understanding of the meaning of the requirement that 'consideration must
move from the promisee' is that such consideration must be provided by the promisee,
or arise out of his contractual relationship with the promisor. It is consideration provided
by somebody else, not a party to the contract, which does not 'move from the promisee'.
This was the situation in *Tweddle* v. *Atkinson*, but it is, of course, not the situation in the
present case. Here the benefits to the defendants arose out of their agreement of 9 April
1986 with the plaintiff, the promisee. In this respect I would adopt the following passage
from Chitty on Contracts, 26th ed. (1989), p. 126, para. 183, and refer to the authorities
there cited:

'The requirement that consideration must move from the promisee is most generally satisfied where some detriment is suffered by him e.g. where he parts with money or goods, or renders services, in exchange for the promise. But the requirement may equally well be satisfied where the promisee confers a benefit on the promisor without in fact suffering any detriment.'

That is the situation in this case. . . . For these reasons I would dismiss this appeal.

Russell LJ

I find [the] primary argument relating to consideration much more difficult. It is worth rehearsing some of the facts . . .

[he set out an extract from the defendants' pleading and continued]

There is no hint in that pleading that the defendants were subjected to any duress to make the agreement or that their promise to pay the extra £10,300 lacked consideration. As the judge found, the plaintiff must have continued work in the belief that he would be paid £575 as he finished each of the 18 uncompleted flats (although the arithmetic is not precisely accurate). For their part the defendants recorded the new terms in their ledger. Can the defendants now escape liability on the ground that the plaintiff undertook to do no more than he had originally contracted to do although, quite clearly, the defendants, on 9 April 1986, were prepared to make the payment and only declined to do so at a later stage? It would certainly be unconscionable if this were to be their legal entitlement.

The submissions advanced on both sides before this court ranged over a wide field. They went far beyond the pleadings, and indeed it is worth noticing that the absence of consideration was never pleaded, although argued before the assistant recorder, Mr Rupert Jackson QC. Speaking for myself—and I notice it is touched upon in the judgment of Glidewell LJ—I would have welcomed the development of argument, if it could have been properly raised in this court, on the basis that there was here an estoppel and that the defendants, in the circumstances prevailing, were precluded from raising the defence that their undertaking to pay the extra £10,300 was not binding. For example, in *Amalgamated Investment & Property Co Ltd* v. *Texas Commerce International Bank Ltd* [1982] QB 84 Robert Goff J said, at p. 105:

'it is in my judgment not of itself a bar to an estoppel that its effect may be to enable a party to enforce a cause of action which, without the estoppel, would not exist. It is sometimes said that an estoppel cannot create a cause of action, or that an estoppel can only act as a shield, not as a sword. In a sense this is true—in the sense that estoppel is not, as a contract is, a source of legal obligation. But as Lord Denning MR pointed out in *Crabb* v. *Arun District Council* [1976] Ch 179, 187, an estoppel may have the effect that a party can enforce a cause of action which, without the estoppel, he would not be able to do.'

When the case came to the Court of Appeal Lord Denning MR said, at p. 122:

'The doctrine of estoppel is one of the most flexible and useful in the armoury of the law. But it has become overloaded with cases. That is why I have not gone through them all in this judgment. It has evolved during the last 150 years in a sequence of separate developments: proprietary estoppel, estoppel by representation of fact, estoppel by acquiescence, and promissory estoppel. At the same time it has been sought to be limited by a series of maxims: estoppel is only a rule of evidence, estoppel cannot give rise to a cause of action, estoppel cannot do away with the need for consideration, and so forth. All these can now be seen to merge into one general principle shorn of limitations. When the parties to a transaction proceed on the basis of an underlying assumption—either of fact or of law—whether due to misrepresentation or mistake makes no difference—on which they have conducted the dealings between them—neither of them will be allowed to go back on that assumption when it would be unfair or unjust to allow him to do so. If one of them does seek to go back on it, the courts will give the other such remedy as the equity of the case demands.'

Brandon LJ said, at pp. 131–132:

'while a party cannot in terms found a cause of action on an estoppel, he may, as a result of being able to rely on an estoppel, succeed on a cause of action on which, without being able to rely on that estoppel, he would necessarily have failed.'

These citations demonstrate that whilst consideration remains a fundamental require-ment before a contract not under seal can be enforced, the policy of the law in its search to do justice between the parties has developed considerably since the early 19th century when *Stilk* v. *Myrick*, 2 Camp 317 was decided by Lord Ellenborough CJ. In the late 20th century I do not believe that the rigid approach to the concept of consideration to be found in *Stilk* v. *Myrick* is either necessary or desirable. Consideration there must still be but, in my judgment, the courts nowadays should be more ready to find its existence so as to reflect the intention of the parties to the contract where the bargaining powers are not unequal and where the finding of consideration reflects the true intention of the parties.

What was the true intention of the parties when they arrived at the agreement pleaded by the defendants in paragraph 5 of the amended defence? The plaintiff had got into financial difficulties. The defendants, through their employee Mr Cottrell, recognised the price that had been agreed originally with the plaintiff was less than what Mr Cottrell himself regarded as a reasonable price. There was a desire on Mr Cottrell's part to retain the services of the plaintiff so that the work could be completed without the need to employ another subcontractor. There was further a need to replace what had hitherto been a haphazard method of payment by a more formalised scheme involving the pay-ment of a specified sum on the completion of each flat. These were all advantages accruing to the defendants which can fairly be said to have been in consideration of their undertaking to pay the additional £10,300. True it was that the plaintiff did not under-take to do any work additional to that which he had originally undertaken to do but the terms upon which he was to carry out the work were varied and, in my judgment, that variation was supported by consideration which a pragmatic approach to the true relationship between the parties readily demonstrates.

For my part I wish to make it plain that I do not base my judgment upon any reserva-tion as to the correctness of the law long ago enunciated in *Stilk* v. *Myrick*. A gratuitous promise, pure and simple, remains unenforceable unless given under seal. But where, as in this case, a party undertakes to make a payment because by so doing it will gain an advantage arising out of the continuing relationship with the promisee the new bargain will not fail for want of consideration. As I read the judgment of the assistant recorder this was his true ratio upon that part of the case wherein the absence of consideration was raised in argument. For the reasons that I have endeavoured to outline, I think that the assistant recorder came to a correct conclusion and I too would dismiss this appeal.

Purchas LJ [set out the facts and continued]

The point of some difficulty which arises on this appeal is whether the judge was correct in his conclusion that the agreement reached on 9 April did not fail for lack of consideration because the principle established by the old cases of *Stilk* v. *Myrick*, 2 Camp 317 approving *Harris* v. *Watson*, Peake 102 did not apply. Mr Makey, who appeared for the plaintiff, was bold enough to submit that *Harris* v. *Watson*, albeit a decision of Lord Kenyon, was a case tried at the Guildhall at nisi prius in the Court of King's Bench and that *Stilk* v. *Myrick* was a decision also at nisi prius albeit a judgment of no less a judge than Lord Ellenborough CJ and that, therefore, this court was bound by neither authority. I feel I must say at once that, for my part, I would not be prepared to overrule two cases of such veneration involving judgments of judges of such distinction except on the strongest possible grounds since they form a pillar stone of the law of contract which has been observed over the years and is still recognised in principle in recent authority: see the reference to *Stilk* v. *Myrick* to be found in *North Ocean Shipping Co Ltd* v. *Hyundai Construction Co Ltd* [1979] QB 705, 712 per Mocatta J. With respect, I agree with his view of the two judgments by Denning LJ in *Ward* v. *Byham* [1956] 1 WLR 496 and *Williams* v. *Williams* [1957] 1 WLR 148 in concluding that these judgments do not provide a sound basis for avoiding the rule in *Stilk* v. *Myrick*, 2 Camp 317. Although this rule has been the subject of some criticism it is still clearly recognised in current textbooks of authority: see *Chitty on Contracts*, 28th ed. (1989) and Cheshire, Fifoot and Furmston's *Law of Contract*, 11th ed. (1986). By the same token I find myself unable to accept the attractive invitation offered by Mr Makey to follow the decision of the Supreme Court of New Hampshire in *Watkins and Sons Inc* v. *Carrig* (1941) 21 A. 2d 591.

In my judgment, therefore, the rule in *Stilk* v. *Myrick*, 2 Camp 317 remains valid as a matter of principle, namely that a contract not under seal must be supported by consideration. Thus, where the agreement upon which reliance is placed provides that an extra payment is to be made for work to be done by the payee which he is already obliged to perform then unless some other consideration is detected to support the agreement to pay the extra sum that agreement will not be enforceable. The two cases, *Harris* v. *Watson*, Peake 102 and *Stilk* v. *Myrick*, 2 Camp 317 involved circumstances of a very special nature, namely the extraordinary conditions existing at the turn of the 18th century under which seamen had to serve their contracts of employment on the high seas. There were strong public policy grounds at that time to protect the master and owners of a ship from being held to ransom by disaffected crews. Thus, the decision that the promise to pay extra wages even in the circumstances established in those cases, was not supported by consideration is readily understandable. Of course, conditions today on the high seas have changed dramatically and it is at least questionable, as Mr Makey submitted, whether these cases might not well have been decided differently if they were tried today. The modern cases tend to depend more upon the defence of duress in a commercial context rather than lack of consideration for the second agreement. In the present case the question of duress does not arise. The initiative in coming to the agreement of 9 April came from Mr Cottrell and not from the plaintiff. It would not, therefore, lie in the defendants' mouth to assert a defence of duress. Nevertheless, the court is more ready in the presence of this defence being available in the commercial context to look for mutual advantages which would amount to sufficient consideration to support the second agreement under which the extra money is paid. Although the passage cited below from the speech of Lord Hailsham of St. Marylebone LC in *Woodhouse AC Israel Cocoa Ltd SA* v. *Nigerian Produce Marketing Co Ltd* [1972] AC 741 was strictly obiter dicta I respectfully adopt it as an indication of the approach to be made in modern times. The case involved an agreement to vary the currency in which the buyer's obligation should be met which was subsequently affected by a depreciation in the currency involved. The case was decided on an issue of estoppel but Lord Hailsham of St. Marylebone LC commented on the other issue, namely the variation of the original contract in the following terms, at pp. 757–758:

> 'If the exchange of letters was not variation, I believe it was nothing. The buyers asked for a variation in the mode of discharge of a contract of sale. If the proposal meant what they claimed, and was accepted and acted upon, I venture to think that the vendors would have been bound by their acceptance at least until they gave reasonable notice to terminate, and I imagine that a modern court would have found no difficulty in discovering consideration for such a promise. Business men know their own business best even when they appear to grant an indulgence, and in the present case I do not think that there would have been insuperable difficulty in spelling out consideration from the earlier correspondence.'

In the light of those authorities the question now must be addressed: Was there evidence upon which the judge was entitled to find that there was sufficient consideration to support the agreement of 9 April, as set out in the passage from his judgment already set out in the judgment of Glidewell LJ? The references to this problem in *Chitty on Contracts* 26th ed. (1989), are not wholly without some conflict amongst themselves. In paragraph 1601 the editors turn to the question of consideration to support an agreement to vary an existing contract:

> 'In many cases, consideration can be found in the mutual abandonment of existing rights or the conferment of new benefits by each party on the other.'

Reference is made to the *Woodhouse* case to which I have already referred:

> 'For example, an alteration of the money of account in a contract proposed or made by one party and accepted by the other is binding on both parties, since either may benefit from the variation. . . . However, an agreement whereby one party undertakes an additional obligation, but the other party is merely bound to perform his existing obligations, or an agreement whereby one party undertakes an additional obligation, but for the benefit of that party alone, will not be effective to vary the contract as no consideration is present.'

These statements are based upon *Stilk* v. *Myrick*, 2 Camp 317 and *Syros Shipping Co SA* v. *Elaghill Trading Co* [1980] 2 Lloyd's Rep 390. Reference is also made to paragraph 197 earlier in the textbook where *Stilk* v. *Myrick* is considered at some length. On the other hand, at paragraph 183 the editors make this proposition:

> 'The requirement that consideration must move from the promisee is most generally satisfied where some detriment is suffered by him: e.g. where he parts with money or goods, or renders services, in exchange for the promise. But the requirement may

equally well be satisfied where the promisee confers a benefit on the promisor without in fact suffering any detriment. For example, in *De la Bere* v. *Pearson Ltd* [1908] 1 KB 280 the defendants owned a newspaper and invited readers to apply for financial advice on the terms that the defendants should be entitled to publish the readers' letters and their own replies.'

This is an accurate recital of the facts in *De la Bere* v. *Pearson Ltd* [1908] 1 KB 280 but when the argument and judgments are read the case turned on issues other than consideration, namely remoteness of damage, etc. So the case is doubtful support for the proposition made in this paragraph.

The question must be posed: what consideration has moved from the plaintiff to support the promise to pay the extra £10,300 added to the lump sum provision? In the particular circumstances which I have outlined above, there was clearly a commercial advantage to both sides from a pragmatic point of view in reaching the agreement of 9 April. The defendants were on risk that as a result of the bargain they had struck the plaintiff would not or indeed possibly could not comply with his existing obligations without further finance. As a result of the agreement the defendants secured their position commercially. There was, however, no obligation added to the contractual duties imposed upon the plaintiff under the original contract. Prima facie this would appear to be a classic *Stilk* v. *Myrick* case. It was, however, open to the plaintiff to be in deliberate breach of the contract in order to 'cut his losses' commercially. In normal circumstances the suggestion that a contracting party can rely upon his own breach to establish consideration is distinctly unattractive. In many cases it obviously would be and if there was any element of duress brought upon the other contracting party under the modern development of this branch of the law the proposed breaker of the contract would not benefit. With some hesitation and comforted by the passage from the speech of Lord Hailsham of St. Marylebone LC in *Woodhouse AC Israel Cocoa Ltd SA* v. *Nigerian Produce Marketing Co Ltd* [1972] AC 741, 757–758, to which I have referred, I consider that the modern approach to the question of consideration would be that where there were benefits derived by each party to a contract of variation even though one party did not suffer a detriment this would not be fatal to the establishing of sufficient consideration to support the agreement. If both parties benefit from an agreement it is not necessary that each also suffers a detriment. In my judgment, on the facts as found by the judge, he was entitled to reach the conclusion that consideration existed and in those circumstances I would not disturb that finding. . . . For these reasons and for the reasons which have already been given by Glidewell LJ I would dismiss this appeal.

COMMENTARY

Williams v. *Roffey Bros* is the leading modern case on the doctrine of consideration. It has attracted a huge amount of academic commentary but its impact on the world of practice seems small; the case has been cited on only a handful of occasions. But this may simply reflect the point that has already been made, namely the limited practical significance of the doctrine of consideration. Eight points fall to be made in relation to the scope of the case.

The first relates to the basis for the finding that the plaintiff provided consideration for the defendants' promise to pay an extra £10,300. All three judges emphasized the fact that the defendants obtained a 'practical benefit' as a result of the plaintiff's promise to perform his existing contractual duty. What was this 'practical benefit'? Various explanations were offered by the judges in *Williams*. Check back through the judgments and try to identify as many as you can. At one end of the spectrum is the observation of Purchas LJ that the plaintiff could be said to have provided consideration in that he did not break his contract with the defendants. This is a controversial statement in that it gives little or no emphasis to the fact that the defendants had purchased the right to the plaintiff's performance under the original contract. While they may have obtained a practical benefit in the sense that the plaintiff continued with performance when he might not otherwise have done so, they were already entitled to that performance as a matter of law so that, in the eyes of the law, it can be said that they did not obtain a benefit as a result of the performance by the plaintiff of his existing contractual duty. At the other end of the spectrum is the point made by Russell LJ that a 'haphazard method of payment' was replaced by a more formalized payment system which gave the defendants greater control over the order of the plaintiff's performance. The latter does seem to amount to the provision of consideration and so the case was probably correctly decided on its own facts. But the wider dicta which suggest that the plaintiff provided consideration merely by continuing with the work and not breaching his contract are more problematic in so far as they fail to give weight to the defendants' right to performance under the original contract.

The second point concerns the relationship between *Williams* and *Stilk* v. *Myrick*. All three judges discuss *Stilk* but they do not overrule it. Thus the six propositions set out by Glidewell LJ (p. 192 above) are said to 'refine' and 'limit' the application of the principle laid down in *Stilk* but they do not 'contravene' it. Rather oddly, all three judges cite Campbell's report of *Stilk* but their interpretation of the case is much closer to Espinasse's version of it. This suggests that the difference between *Stilk* and *Williams* lies in the absence of duress, or the potential for duress, in the latter case. But there is another possible explanation for the difference between the two cases. The emphasis on 'practical benefit' in *Williams* finds no counterpart in *Stilk*. What would have been the outcome in *Stilk* if Lord Ellenborough had asked himself the question whether the master of the ship had obtained a practical benefit as a result of the performance by the plaintiff of his contractual obligation to work the ship back home? We shall never know the answer to this question but it is important to bear in mind that, post *Williams* v. *Roffey Bros*, there are two possible analyses of *Stilk*. The first is that the plaintiff did provide consideration for the master's promise of additional pay but that the agreement was set aside on the ground of duress (or on the ground that it was contrary to public policy). The second explanation is that the plaintiff did not in fact provide any consideration in promising to carry out his existing contractual obligation. Which interpretation of *Stilk* did the judges in *Williams* adopt? The answer is not clear. But in *Anangel Atlas Compania Naviera SA* v. *Ishikawajima-Harima Heavy Industries Co Ltd (No 2)* [1990] 2 Lloyd's Rep 526 Hirst J appeared to adopt the latter interpretation. Thus he said (at p. 545) that:

the ratio of *Williams'* case is that, whoever provides the services, where there is a practical conferment of benefit or a practical avoidance of disbenefit for the promisee, there is good consideration, and it is no answer to say that the promisor was already bound; where, on the other hand, there is a wholly gratuitous promise *Stilk's* case still remains good law.

The relationship between *Stilk* and *Williams* was further considered by the New Zealand Court of Appeal in *Antons Trawling Co Ltd* v. *Smith* [2003] 2 NZLR 23 (on which see B Coote (2004) 120 *LQR* 16). The defendants employed the plaintiff as the master of one of their fishing vessels on terms that he would be paid a percentage of the catch after deduction of certain costs. The defendants subsequently orally agreed to pay him 10% of any additional quota allocated to the defendants in the event that the plaintiff could prove the existence of a commercial fishery. One of the issues which arose before the court was whether or not the plaintiff had provided consideration for the promise by the defendants to give him a percentage of the additional quota. Baragwanath J examined *Stilk* and *Williams* and noted the 'trenchant criticisms' level-led against the latter case by Professor Coote in which he argued that 'mere perform-ance of a duty already owed to the promisee under a contract cannot constitute consideration and that the only principled way to such a result is to decide that consideration should not be necessary for the variation of a contract'. Baragwanath J noted that the latter approach had been adopted in s. 2-209(1) of the Uniform Com-mercial Code in America and continued (at [93]):

We are satisfied that *Stilk* v. *Myrick* can no longer be taken to control such cases as *Roffey Bros* . . . and the present case where there is no element of duress or other policy factor suggesting that an agreement, duly performed, should not attract the legal consequences that each party must reasonably be taken to have expected. On the contrary, a result that deprived Mr Smith [the plaintiff] of the benefit of what Antons [the defendants] promised he should receive would be inconsistent with the essential principle underlying the law of contract, that the law will seek to give effect to freely accepted reciprocal undertakings. The importance of consideration is as a valuable signal that the parties intend to be bound by their agreement, rather than an end in itself. Where the parties who have already made such intention clear by entering legal relations have acted upon an agreement to a variation, in the absence of policy reasons to the contrary, they should be bound by their agreement. Whatever option is adopted, whether that of *Roffey Bros* or that suggested by Professor Coote or other authorities, the result is in this case the same.

Two observations can be made about *Antons*. The first is that the court did not actually choose between the adoption of a more liberal approach to finding the existence of consideration (the *Roffey* approach) and the abolition of the consider-ation requirement in the context of variations (the view attributed to Professor Coote). While it was not necessary for the court to make a choice between these two views on the facts of the case, a choice must ultimately be made between the liberaliza-tion of the doctrine of consideration in the context of contract modifications and its abolition. The two views will not always lead to the same result. The second observa-tion is that it is not entirely clear what view was taken by the court of *Stilk*. The headnote records that the decision was 'not followed' but this may not be entirely accurate. Baragwanath J actually stated that *Stilk* 'can no longer be taken to control' *Roffey Bros*. This may not be the same thing as saying that the case was incorrectly decided. But it would appear that the view of the court was that the variation in *Stilk* should have been enforced in the absence of 'policy reasons to the contrary'. This leads us to the third point concerning the scope of *Williams*.

The third point relates to the role of duress. The point can be put more widely. In *Antons Trawling Co Ltd* v. *Smith* Baragwanath J referred more broadly to 'policy reasons to the contrary'. These 'policy factors' are nowhere identified but they are presumably doctrines that are related to duress, such as undue influence (on which see Chapter 19) and, in so far as they are recognised as vitiating factors, unconscionability and inequality of bargaining power (on which see Chapter 20). But the essential point to grasp is the argument that the real fear in contract modification cases is that one party will exploit the vulnerability of the other in order to extract a promise of more pay. On this view there is a fundamental distinction to be drawn between a modification that is freely negotiated (which should be enforceable) and a modification extracted as a result of the application of illegitimate pressure (which should not be enforceable). If the concern of the law is to ensure that contract modifications are freely negotiated then duress rather than consideration should be the regulator of contract modifications or re-negotiations. This point was made by Posner CJ in *United States* v. *Stump Homes Specialties Manufacturing Inc*, 905 F 2d 1117 (1990) in the following passage from his judgment (at pp. 1121–1122):

The guarantors' second major argument is that the modification in the loan agreement is unenforceable because it is not supported by consideration. The black-letter rule is indeed that a contract may not be modified without consideration. . . . And yet the cautionary, evidential, and other policies behind the requirement of consideration do not apply, or apply only with much attenuated strength, in the context of written modification. By hypothesis the parties already have a contract, so that the danger of mistaking casual promissory language for an intention to be legally bound is slight; moreover, we deal here with a written, not an oral, modification, so fabrication of a promise is harder.

The requirement of consideration has, however, a distinct function in the modification setting—although one it does not perform well—and that is to prevent coercive modifications. Since one of the main purposes of contracts and of contract law is to facilitate long-term commitments, there is often an interval in the life of a contract during which one party is at the mercy of the other. A may have ordered a machine from B that A wants to place in operation on a given date, specified in their contract; and in expectation of B's complying with the contract, A may have made commitments to his customers that it would be costly to renege on. As the date of scheduled delivery approaches, B may be tempted to demand that A agree to renegotiate the contract price, knowing that A will incur heavy expenses if B fails to deliver on time. A can always refuse to renegotiate, relying instead on his right to sue B for breach of contract if B fails to make delivery by the agreed date. But legal remedies are costly and uncertain, thereby opening the way to duress. Considerations of commercial reputation will deter taking advantage of an opportunity to exert duress on a contract partner in many cases, but not in all.

[he cited a number of examples of duress in the contract-modification setting and continued]

The rule that modifications are unenforceable unless supported by consideration strengthens A's position by reducing B's incentive to seek a modification. But it strengthens it feebly. . . . The law does not require that consideration be adequate—that it be commensurate with what the party accepting it is giving up. Slight consideration, therefore, will suffice to make a contract or a contract modification enforceable. . . . And slight consideration is consistent with coercion. To surrender one's contractual rights in exchange for a peppercorn is not functionally different from surrendering them for nothing.

The sensible course would be to enforce contract modifications (at least if written) regardless of consideration and rely on the defense of duress to prevent abuse. . . . All coercive modifications would then be unenforceable, and there would be no need to worry about consideration, an inadequate safeguard against duress. But we need not decide whether the Indiana Supreme Court is prepared to take the bold step of abolishing the requirement of consideration in modification cases; there was consideration here.

A similar judicial sentiment has been expressed on this side of the Atlantic. In *The Alev* [1989] 1 Lloyd's Rep 138, 147 Hobhouse J stated that

now that there is a properly developed doctrine of the avoidance of contracts on the grounds of economic duress, there is no warrant for the Court to fail to recognise the existence of some consideration even though it may be insignificant and even though there may have been no mutual bargain in any realistic use of that phrase.

The adoption of a duress-based analysis does have significant implications for the doctrine of consideration because it usually carries with it the proposition either that the court should be readier to find the existence of consideration (the view taken by Hobhouse J) or that the court should take the bolder step, suggested by Posner CJ, of abolishing the requirement that contract modifications be supported by consideration. Should English law take the latter step? *Williams* itself does not take it. It retains the consideration requirement, albeit that it makes it much easier for the court to find the existence of consideration in the context of a re-negotiation of a contract. The answer to the question whether or not English law should abolish the consideration requirement in relation to contract modifications depends in large part upon whether consideration is seen as a once-for-all requirement in English law; that is to say it should apply only at the moment of formation of the contract and not subsequently. But is there a difference between a promise to make a gift of £1,000 (which is not enforceable in the absence of consideration) and a promise to pay an extra £1,000 for something to which one is already contractually entitled? The latter could be said to be a form of gift that should be treated in exactly the same way as all other promises to make a gift. On the other hand, as Posner CJ points out, the parties in a modification case have already made a contract 'so that the danger of mistaking casual promissory language for an intention to be legally bound is slight'. Yet there are difficulties with the view that consideration should no longer apply to contract modifications. The most pressing difficulty relates to the current state of the doctrine of duress (on which see further Chapter 18). The doctrine does not, as yet, exhibit a great deal of stability and, as *Stilk* v. *Myrick* demonstrates (see p. 184 above), it can be a difficult task to ascertain whether or not duress has been applied on the facts of a particular case. The doctrine of duress may not be ready for an exalted role as the principal regulator of contract modifications.

The fourth point relates to the reference by Purchas LJ (see p. 195 above) to the American case of *Watkins and Sons Inc* v. *Carrig* (1941) 21 A 2d 591. In that case the court held that there had not been a variation of the initial contract but a consensual abandonment of that contract which was then replaced by a second contract on new terms. In this way the court was able to find that the abandonment of the contract and the entry into a new contract was supported by consideration. *Watkins* has been applied by the Court of Appeal in *Compagnie Noga D'Importation et D'Exportation SA v. Abacha (No 2)* [2003] EWCA Civ 1100; [2003] 2 All ER (Comm) 915. Tuckey LJ stated (at [57]–[60]:

The essential difference between rescission and variation for present purposes is that a contract comes to an end when it is rescinded but continues if it is varied. If the rescinded agreement is replaced by a new agreement containing the same obligations, it is not the old agreement which compels the performance of those obligations but the new agreement. It follows that the principle in *Stilk* v. *Myrick* has no application to this situation because it is premised on the continuation of the obligations in the old agreement. Mr Flint [counsel for the defendant] accepted this analysis in a case where there was an interval between the rescission and replacement, but I do not see that there can be any difference in principle between the two situations. . . . It is not necessary in my judgment to create a scintilla temporis [a moment in time] for there to be a rescission and replacement. It can be achieved concurrently by the same document in the way it was done in this case.

Thus, had the court in *Stilk* decided that the original contract had been abandoned and replaced by a new contract, it would have found that the sailors were entitled to the additional pay because, in such a case, the agreement to abandon the original contract would have been supported by consideration and, equally, the new contract entered into between the parties would have been supported by consideration. The distinction between a rescission of the original contract (and its replacement with a new contract) and the variation of that contract may be difficult to draw on the evidence but it is an important one in terms of the legal consequences which flow from it.

The fifth point relates to the role of estoppel. All three judges in *Williams* make reference to estoppel cases and Russell LJ stated that he would have welcomed the development of an argument to the effect that the defendants were estopped from taking the position that their promise to pay an extra £10,300 was not binding. Estoppel will be discussed in greater detail later in the chapter (see pp. 236–271 below). Here it suffices to note that it was not in fact necessary for the plaintiff to place reliance upon estoppel because he succeeded with his primary submission that he had provided consideration for the defendants' promise of additional payment. A claimant who can establish the existence of consideration does not need to invoke an estoppel. Indeed, the wider the scope of the doctrine of consideration, the less need there is in practice to have resort to estoppel. Conversely, the narrower the scope of the doctrine of consideration, the greater the potential role for estoppel.

The sixth point relates to the willingness of the judges in *Williams* to draw on caselaw concerned with the performance of a contractual duty owed to a third party and the performance of a duty imposed by law. Thus Glidewell LJ drew considerable support for his analysis from *Pao On* v. *Lau Yiu Long* [1980] AC 614, a case concerned with a promise to perform a contractual duty owed to a third party. Of greater interest is the use made of cases concerned with the performance of a duty imposed by law, in particular Glidewell LJ's analysis of *Ward* v. *Byham* [1956] 1 WLR 496 (p. 178 above). He analysed *Ward* as a case in which the consideration was to be found in the fact that the father obtained a 'practical benefit' as a result of the mother's promise that the child would be well looked after and happy. The effect of the 'practical benefit' analysis is to shift attention away from the mother and the question whether or not she had simply performed her existing legal duty. Instead it focuses attention on the father and suggests that the question which the court should ask itself is whether or not the promise to perform, or the performance of, a pre-existing legal duty confers a 'practical benefit' upon the other party. But this analysis may go too far. Suppose that in *Glasbrook Brothers Ltd* v. *Glamorgan County Council* [1925] AC 270 (p. 181 above) the House of Lords had concluded that the police had done no more than their legal duty in providing a garrison for the colliery owners. Would they nevertheless have been entitled to charge the colliery owners for the service they had provided on the basis that the colliery owners had obtained a 'practical benefit' as a result of the performance of their legal duty? The adoption of a 'practical benefit' test in the context of the legal duty cases could largely undermine the general rule that perform-ance of, or a promise to perform, a legal duty does not constitute consideration for a promise given in return.

The seventh point relates to the measure of the plaintiff's recovery. As Professor Treitel has pointed out (*Some Landmarks of Twentieth Century Contract Law* (Oxford University Press, 2002), p. 19) 'the reason for the exact amount of the recovery cannot be deduced from the figures given in the report'. The plaintiff claimed damages of £10,847 but was awarded only £3,500. Damages were calculated by reference to the work done by the plaintiff at the date of the termination of the contract: he was not awarded anything for the loss of profit on the flats he would have finished had the defendants performed their obligations in accordance with the contract. As Mindy Chen-Wishart has pointed out ('Consideration: Practical Benefit and the Emperor's New Clothes' in J. Beatson and D. Friedmann (eds), *Good Faith and Fault in Contract Law* (Oxford University Press, 1995), pp. 123, 134) the award to the plaintiff:

appears to be reliance- and not expectation-based. On an orthodox contractual analysis, the real question on the facts of *Roffey* is not 'why was the plaintiff's claim treated so generously?' . . . but 'why so mean?' The suggestion must be that practical benefits impose a less than expectation right on the promisee. To describe such rights and liabilities as contractual seriously compromises contract as an action which enforces expectations.

The final point relates to the relationship between *Williams* and the decision of the House of Lords in *Foakes* v. *Beer* (1884) 9 App Cas 605. The relationship between these two cases is the subject-matter of the next section.

(IV) PART PAYMENT OF A DEBT
The final aspect of the pre-existing duty rule is the general rule that payment of part of a debt is not good consideration for a promise to discharge the entire debt. The leading case on this general rule is:

Foakes v. Beer

(1884) 9 App Cas 605, House of Lords

In August 1875 the respondent, Mrs Beer, obtained a judgment against the appellant, Dr Foakes, for the sum of £2090 19s. Mrs Beer was entitled to interest on the judgment debt at 4%, arising immediately on the entering of the judgment, until the judgment debt was fully paid. Dr Foakes asked Mrs Beer for more time to pay the debt and so in December 1876 the parties entered into an agreement. The agreement was drawn up by Dr Foakes' solicitor and it recited that:

> 'Whereas the said John Weston Foakes is indebted to the said Julia Beer, and she has obtained a judgment in Her Majesty's High Court of Justice, Exchequer Division, for the sum of £2090 19s. And whereas the said John Weston Foakes has requested the said Julia Beer to give him time in which to pay such judgment, which she has agreed to do on the following conditions. Now this agreement witnesseth that in consideration of the said John Weston Foakes paying to the said Julia Beer on the signing of this agreement the sum of £500, the receipt whereof she doth hereby acknowledge in part satisfaction of the said judgment debt of £2090 19s., and on condition of his paying to her or her executors, administrators, assigns or nominee the sum of £150 on the 1st day of July and the 1st day of January or within one calendar month after each of the said days respectively in every year until the whole of the said sum of £2090 19s. shall have been fully paid and satisfied, the first of such payments to be made on the 1st day of July next, then she the said Julia Beer hereby undertakes and agrees that she, her executors, administrators or assigns, will not take any proceedings whatever on the said judgment.'

In 1882 Mrs Beer sought to recover interest on the judgment debt (Dr Foakes having paid to Mrs Beer the sum of £2090 19s by instalments). Dr Foakes denied that he was liable to pay interest and relied for this purpose on the terms of the agreement. At trial Dr Foakes was successful but the Court of Appeal allowed Mrs Beer's appeal and held that the agreement was no bar to her claim. Two points were in issue before the House of Lords. The first was whether, as a matter of construction, Mrs Beer had agreed to forego her claim to interest on the judgment debt and the second was whether, if she had, that agreement was supported by consideration. The four judges in the House of Lords divided on the question of construction but were unanimous (subject to the doubts of Lord Blackburn) that the agreement was not supported by consideration and that Mrs Beer was entitled to recover interest on the judgment debt.

Earl of Selborne LC [considered the meaning of the agreement and concluded that Mrs Beer had relinquished her claim to interest on the judgment debt and continued]

But the question remains, whether the agreement is capable of being legally enforced. Not being under seal, it cannot be legally enforced against the respondent, unless she received consideration for it from the appellant, or unless, though without consideration, it operates by way of accord and satisfaction, so as to extinguish the claim for interest. What is the consideration? On the face of the agreement none is expressed, except a present payment of £500, on account and in part of the larger debt then due and payable by law under the judgment. The appellant did not contract to pay the future instalments of £150 each, at the times therein mentioned; much less did he give any new security, in the shape of negotiable paper, or in any other form. The promise de futuro was only that of the respondent, that if the half-yearly payments of £150 each were regularly paid, she would 'take no proceedings whatever on the judgment'. No doubt if the appellant had been under no antecedent obligation to pay the whole debt, his fulfilment of the condition might have imported some consideration on his part for that promise. But he was under that antecedent obligation; and payment at those deferred dates, by the forbearance and indulgence of the creditor, of the residue of the principal debt and costs, could not (in my opinion) be a consideration for the relinquishment of interest and discharge of the judgment, unless the payment of the £500, at the time of signing the agreement, was such a consideration. As to accord and satisfaction, in point of fact there could be no complete satisfaction, so long as any future instalment remained payable; and I do not see how any mere payments on account could operate in law as a satisfaction ad interim, conditionally upon other payments being afterwards duly made, unless there was a consideration sufficient to support the agreement while still unexecuted. Nor was anything, in fact, done by the respondent in this case, on the receipt of the last payment, which could be tantamount to an acquittance, if the agreement did not previously bind her.

The question, therefore, is nakedly raised by this appeal, whether your Lordships are now prepared, not only to overrule, as contrary to law, the doctrine stated by Sir Edward Coke to have been laid down by all the judges of the Common Pleas in *Pinnel's Case* 5 Rep. 117a in 1602, and repeated in his note to Littleton, sect. 344 (2), but to treat a prospective agreement, not under seal, for satisfaction of a debt, by a series of payments on account to a total amount less than the whole debt, as binding in law, provided those payments are regularly made; the case not being one of a composition with a common debtor, agreed to, inter se, by several creditors. . . . The doctrine itself, as laid down by Sir Edward Coke, may have been criticised, as questionable in principle, by some persons whose opinions are entitled to respect, but it has never been judicially overruled; on the contrary I think it has always, since the sixteenth century, been accepted as law. If so, I cannot think that your Lordships would do right, if you were now to reverse, as erroneous, a judgment of the Court of Appeal, proceeding upon a doctrine which has been accepted as part of the law of England for 280 years.

The doctrine, as stated in *Pinnel's Case*, is 'that payment of a lesser sum on the day' (it would of course be the same after the day), 'in satisfaction of a greater, cannot be any satisfaction for the whole, because it appears to the Judges, that by no possibility a lesser sum can be a satisfaction to the plaintiff for a greater sum'. As stated in Coke Littleton, 212 (b), it is, 'where the condition is for payment of £20, the obligor or feoffor cannot at the time appointed pay a lesser sum in satisfaction of the whole, because it is apparent that a lesser sum of money cannot be a satisfaction of a greater'; adding (what is beyond controversy), that an acquittance under seal, in full satisfaction of the whole, would (under like circumstances) be valid and binding.

The distinction between the effect of a deed under seal, and that of an agreement by parol, or by writing not under seal, may seem arbitrary, but it is established in our law; nor is it really unreasonable or practically inconvenient that the law should require particular solemnities to give to a gratuitous contract the force of a binding obligation. If the question be (as, in the actual state of the law, I think it is), whether consideration is, or is not, given in a case of this kind, by the debtor who pays down part of the debt presently due from him, for a promise by the creditor to relinquish, after certain further payments on account, the residue of the debt, I cannot say that I think consideration is given, in the sense in which I have always understood that word as used in our law. It might be (and indeed I think it would be) an improvement in our law, if a release or acquittance of the whole debt, on payment of any sum which the creditor might be content to receive by way of accord and satisfaction (though less than the whole), were held to be, generally, binding, though not under seal; nor should I be unwilling to see equal force given to a prospective agreement, like the present, in writing though not under seal; but I think it impossible, without refinements which practically alter the sense of the word, to treat such a release or acquittance as supported by any new consideration proceeding from the debtor. All the authorities . . . which were relied upon by the appellant at your Lord-ships' Bar (such as *Sibree* v. *Tripp* 15 M & W 23, *Curlewis* v. *Clark* 3 Ex 375, and *Goddard* v. *O'Brien* 9 QBD 37) have proceeded upon the distinction, that, by giving negotiable paper or otherwise, there had been some new consideration for a new agreement, dis-tinct from mere money payments in or towards discharge of the original liability. I think it unnecessary to go through those cases, or to examine the particular grounds on which each of them was decided. There are no such facts in the case now before your Lordships. What is called 'any benefit, or even any legal possibility of benefit', in Mr Smith's notes to *Cumber* v. *Wane* 1 Sm L C 8th ed. 366, is not (as I conceive) that sort of benefit which a creditor may derive from getting payment of part of the money due to him from a debtor who might otherwise keep him at arm's length, or possibly become insolvent, but is some independent benefit, actual or contingent, of a kind which might in law be a good and valuable consideration for any other sort of agreement not under seal.

My conclusion is, that the order appealed from should be affirmed, and the appeal dismissed, with costs, and I so move your Lordships.

Lord Blackburn [considered the meaning of the agreement and concluded that Mrs Beer had relinquished her claim to interest on the judgment debt and continued]

I think, therefore, that it is necessary to consider the ground on which the Court of Appeal did base their judgment, and to say whether the agreement can be enforced. I construe it as accepting and taking £500 in satisfaction of the whole £2090 19s., subject to the condition that unless the balance of the principal debt was paid by the instalments, the whole might be enforced with interest. If, instead of £500 in money, it had been a horse valued at £500, or a promissory note for £500, the authorities are that it would have been a good satisfaction, but it is said to be otherwise as it was money.

This is a question, I think, of difficulty.

In Coke, Littleton 212 b, Lord Coke says: 'where the condition is for payment of £20, the obligor or feoffor cannot at the time appointed pay a lesser sum in satisfaction of the whole, because it is apparent that a lesser sum of money cannot be a satisfaction of a greater. . . . If the obligor or feoffor pay a lesser sum either before the day or at another place than is limited by the condition, and the obligee or feoffee receiveth it, this is a good satisfaction'. For this he cites *Pinnel's Case* 5 Rep. 117a. That was an action on a bond for £16, conditioned for the payment of £8 10s. on the 11th of November 1600. Plea that defendant, at plaintiff's request, before the said day, to wit, on the 1st of October, paid to the plaintiff £5 2s. 2d., which the plaintiff accepted in full satisfaction of the £8 10s. The plaintiff had judgment for the insufficient pleading. But though this was so, Lord Coke reports that it was resolved by the whole Court of Common Pleas 'that payment of a lesser sum on the day in satisfaction of a greater cannot be any satisfaction for the whole, because it appears to the judges that by no possibility a lesser sum can be a satisfaction to the plaintiff for a greater sum: but the gift of a horse, hawk, or robe, &c., in satisfaction is good, for it shall be intended that a horse, hawk, or robe, &c., might be more beneficial to the plaintiff than the money, in respect of some circumstance, or otherwise the plaintiff would not have accepted of it in satisfaction. But when the whole sum is due, by no intendment the acceptance of parcel can be a satisfaction to the plaintiff; but in the case at bar it was resolved that the payment and acceptance of parcel before the day in satisfaction of the whole would be a good satisfaction in regard of circumstance of time; for peradventure parcel of it before the day would be more beneficial to him than the whole at the day, and the value of the satisfaction is not material; so if I am bound in £20 to pay you £10 at Westminster, and you request me to pay you £5 at the day at York, and you will accept it in full satisfaction for the whole £10, it is a good satisfaction for the whole, for the expenses to pay it at York is sufficient satisfaction'.

There are two things here resolved. First, that where a matter paid and accepted in satisfaction of a debt certain might by any possibility be more beneficial to the creditor than his debt, the Court will not inquire into the adequacy of the consideration. If the creditor, without any fraud, accepted it in satisfaction when it was not a sufficient satisfaction it was his own fault. And that payment before the day might be more beneficial, and consequently that the plea was in substance good, and this must have been decided in the case.

There is a second point stated to have been resolved, viz.: 'That payment of a lesser sum on the day cannot be any satisfaction of the whole, because it appears to the judges that by no possibility a lesser sum can be a satisfaction to the plaintiff for a greater sum'. This was certainly not necessary for the decision of the case; but though the resolution of the Court of Common Pleas was only a dictum, it seems to me clear that Lord Coke deliberately adopted the dictum, and the great weight of his authority makes it necessary to be cautious before saying that what he deliberately adopted as law was a mistake . . .

[he considered the authorities and continued]

What principally weighs with me in thinking that Lord Coke made a mistake of fact is my conviction that all men of business, whether merchants or tradesmen, do every day recognise and act on the ground that prompt payment of a part of their demand may be more beneficial to them than it would be to insist on their rights and enforce payment of the whole. Even where the debtor is perfectly solvent, and sure to pay at last, this often is so. Where the credit of the debtor is doubtful it must be more so. I had persuaded myself that there was no such long-continued action on this dictum as to render it improper in this House to reconsider the question. I had written my reasons for so thinking; but as they were not satisfactory to the other noble and learned Lords who heard the case, I do not now repeat them nor persist in them.

I assent to the judgment proposed, though it is not that which I had originally thought proper.

Lord Watson and **Lord Fitzgerald** delivered concurring judgments in which they held that, as a matter of construction, Mrs Beer had not promised to forego her claim to recover interest (although Lord Watson added that he assumed that he was wrong on this point) but that, in any event, Mrs Beer was entitled to recover interest because there was no consideration to support any promise to forego interest.

COMMENTARY

Before dealing with the consideration aspect of *Foakes*, it is worth exploring the question of construction because it may shed light on the reasons that led their Lordships to conclude that Mrs Beer was entitled to interest on the judgment debt on the particular facts of the case. Professor Treitel (*Some Landmarks of Twentieth Century Contract Law* (Oxford University Press, 2002), pp. 24–26) neatly sets out the issue as follows:

the question was whether the agreement meant that, if Dr Foakes paid instalments amounting to the principal sum, then Mrs Beer would not claim interest. There is nothing in the reports to indicate that Dr Foakes' liability to pay interest was discussed in the negotiations leading up to the 1876 agreement, and Lord Selborne doubted whether this issue was 'really present to the mind of' Mrs Beer. Nevertheless he held that the operative part of the agreement was 'clear'— it said '£2090 19s' and not '£2019 19s plus interest'—and, that being so, the case was governed by the well-established rule that 'clear' words in the operative part of an agreement could not be controlled by recitals—i.e. here by the recital that Dr Foakes was asking for time. On the issue of construction, Lord Blackburn agreed with Lord Selborne; Lords Fitzgerald and Watson did not agree, but Lord Watson was prepared to assume that he was wrong on the construction point. There being no record of any speech from a fifth Law Lord, we have a majority of sorts in favour of Dr Foakes on the construction issue. But on the issue of legal effect of the agreement the decision went in favour of Mrs Beer. She was not bound by her promise to forego interest: Dr Foakes had provided no consideration for that promise by paying the principal sum since he was already bound to make that payment before the promise was made.

The actual decision in *Foakes* v. *Beer* does not seem to be unjust. What seems to have happened was that Dr Foakes' solicitor dug a technical trap for Mrs Beer and the House of Lords arranged an equally technical rescue. The technical trap was the rule that recitals cannot control 'clear' words in the operative provisions of a contract. The technicality invoked to rescue her was the rule in *Pinnel's* case (as later interpreted) under which payment by Dr Foakes of part of what was due (the principal) could not constitute consideration for Mrs Beer's promise to forego the rest (the interest). I call this a technical rescue because probably she did benefit in fact from the 1876 agreement. Lord Blackburn stressed this aspect of the case and was critical of the rule in *Pinnel's* case. But, being a good judge as well as a great lawyer, he did not dissent: he must have seen that the outcome proposed by the other members of the House was not unjust. Conversely, the reasoning of those others is, with respect, less than wholly convincing. They were not prepared to overturn the 'rule in *Pinnel's* case' because it 'has been accepted as part of the law of England for 280 years'. Sometimes, that would be a strong argument. If a long-established rule is one on which people rely, there is a case for saying that it should not be overturned by judicial decision since such a reversal operates retrospectively and so defeats legitimate expectations, at least in the particular case. But is 'the rule in *Pinnel's* case' really of this kind? Do people rely on this rule, or if they do, should the law encourage them to do so? I doubt whether the antiquity of the rule was an adequate justification for continuing to apply it in the circumstances of *Foakes* v. *Beer*. If there had been evidence of Mrs Beer's intention to exploit the rule as a weapon in the negotiations with Dr Foakes, I should have had little, if any sympathy with her. The fact that does engage my sympathy on her side is that, although she was probably not coerced, she does appear to have been tricked into making a promise which, on its true construction, had an effect not intended by her. The requirement of consideration was a useful tool for protecting her against trickery.

In this passage Professor Treitel provides a defence of the result on the facts of *Foakes* but raises a question-mark against the general rule for which the case stands as authority, namely that payment of part of a debt is not good consideration for a promise to discharge the entire debt. The general rule has been attacked on a number of different grounds.

The first is that a payment of part of a debt can be, and generally is, of benefit to the creditor. This is the point made by Lord Blackburn in the penultimate paragraph extracted from his judgment (above). The second is that the general rule is easy to evade. The simplest way of evading the rule is for the debtor to provide fresh consideration for the promise to accept part payment in full settlement of the debt. For example, the debtor can agree to make payment a day early or make payment at a different place from that agreed in the contract. Why does the law refuse to give effect to a promise to treat payment of £95,000 as good consideration for the discharge of a debt of £100,000 but at the same time give effect to a promise to pay £20,000 in discharge of a debt of £100,000 where the debtor agrees to make payment at a place other than that agreed in the contract? The law should not encourage such artificial behaviour: it should look to the substance of the transaction and not its form. Provided that the creditor intends to be bound by his promise to accept part payment as full satisfaction of the debt, should the law not give effect to the new agreement? Thirdly, it can be argued that the rule in *Foakes* v. *Beer* is out of step with modern developments in the doctrine of consideration, particularly the decision of the Court of Appeal in *Williams* v. *Roffey Bros & Nicholls (Contractors) Ltd* [1991] 1 QB 1 (p. 188 above).

Given these criticisms, why has the general rule survived for as long as it has? There appear to be three answers to this question. The first is that the rule has played a useful role in protecting creditors from unscrupulous debtors. This function is illustrated by *Foakes* and, more clearly, by our next case, the decision of the Court of Appeal in *D & C Builders* v. *Rees* [1966] 2 QB 617. The second reason is precedent. *Foakes* is a decision of the House of Lords and can only be overruled by the House of Lords (a point made by Peter Gibson LJ in *In re Selectmove* [1995] 1 WLR 474, p. 214 below). The third is that *Foakes* is consistent with the general rule at common law that a promise to perform an existing duty owed to the promisor does not generally constitute good consideration for a fresh promise given by the promisor (see p. 183 above). Each of these points requires further elaboration.

(a) *Protection of the creditor*

The following case illustrates the role that the general rule can play in the protection of the creditor from an unscrupulous debtor.

D & C Builders v. Rees

[1966] 2 QB 617, Court of Appeal

The plaintiffs, a small building company, carried out building work for the defendant. The defendant paid £250 on account and a balance of £482 13s. 1d. remained outstanding. The plaintiffs made several requests for payment but received no reply. By this time the plaintiff company was in 'desperate financial straits'. The defendant's wife offered to pay them £300 in settlement of the whole claim. The plaintiffs stated that they would accept £300 straight away and give the defendant a year to find the balance. The defendant's wife refused to agree to this, stating that 'we will never have enough money to pay the balance. £300 is better than nothing'. The plaintiffs stated that they had no choice but to accept. The defendant's wife gave the plaintiffs a cheque for £300 and insisted that they give her a receipt which included the words 'in completion of the account'. The plaintiffs then brought an action for the balance. The defendants relied on a defence of bad workmanship and also claimed that there had been a binding settlement of the claim. The latter issue was ordered to be tried as a preliminary issue. The judge decided that the alleged settlement was not binding on the plaintiffs. The defendant appealed to the Court of Appeal who dismissed the appeal and held that the purported settlement did not bar the plaintiff company from recovering the balance of the debt.

Lord Denning MR
This case is of some consequence: for it is a daily occurrence that a merchant or trades-man, who is owed a sum of money, is asked to take less. The debtor says he is in difficulties. He offers a lesser sum in settlement, cash down. He says he cannot pay more. The creditor is considerate. He accepts the proffered sum and forgives him the rest of the debt. The question arises: Is the settlement binding on the creditor? The answer is that, in point of law, the creditor is not bound by the settlement. He can the next day sue the debtor for the balance: and get judgment. The law was so stated in 1602 by Lord Coke in *Pinnel's Case* (1602) 5 Co Rep 117a—and accepted in 1884 by the House of Lords in *Foakes* v. *Beer* (1884) 9 App Cas 605.

   Now, suppose that the debtor, instead of paying the lesser sum in cash, pays it by cheque. He makes out a cheque for the amount. The creditor accepts the cheque and cashes it. Is the position any different? I think not. No sensible distinction can be taken between payment of a lesser sum by cash and payment of it by cheque. The cheque, when given, is conditional payment. When honoured, it is actual payment. It is then just the same as cash. If a creditor is not bound when he receives payment by cash, he should not be bound when he receives payment by cheque. This view is supported by the leading case of *Cumber* v. *Wane* (1721) 1 Stra 426 which has suffered many vicissitudes but was, I think, rightly decided in point of law.

   Sibree v. *Tripp* 15 & W 23 is easily distinguishable. There the plaintiffs brought an action for £500. It was settled by the defendant giving three promissory notes amounting in all to £250. Those promissory notes were given upon a new contract, in substitution for the debt sued for, and not as conditional payment. The plaintiff's only remedy thenceforward was on the notes and not on the debt.

   Goddard v. *O'Brien* (1882) 9 QBD 37 is not so easily distinguishable. There a creditor was owed £125 for some slates. He met the debtor and agreed to accept £100 in dis-charge of it. The debtor gave a cheque for £100. The creditor gave a written receipt 'in settlement on the said cheque being honoured'. The cheque was clearly given by way of conditional payment. It was honoured. The creditor sued the debtor for the balance of £25. He lost because the £100 was paid by cheque and not by cash. The decision was criticised by Fletcher Moulton LJ in *Hirachand Punamchand* v. *Temple* [1911] 2 KB 330, 340 and by the editors of Smith's Leading Cases, 13th ed. (1929), Vol. 1, p. 380. It was, I think, wrongly decided. In point of law payment of a lesser sum, whether by cash or by cheque, is no discharge of a greater sum.

This doctrine of the common law has come under heavy fire. It was ridiculed by Sir George Jessel in *Couldery* v. *Bartram* (1881) 19 Ch D 394, 399. It was said to be mistaken by Lord Blackburn in *Foakes* v. *Beer* (1884) 9 App Cas 605. It was condemned by the Law Revision Committee (1945 Cmd. 5449), paras. 20 and 21. But a remedy has been found. The harshness of the common law has been relieved. Equity has stretched out a merciful hand to help the debtor. The courts have invoked the broad principle stated by Lord Cairns in *Hughes* v. *Metropolitan Railway Co* (1877) 2 App Cas 439, 448:

'It is the first principle upon which all courts of equity proceed, that if parties, who have entered into definite and distinct terms involving certain legal results, afterwards by their own act or with their own consent enter upon a course of negotiation which has the effect of leading one of the parties to suppose that the strict rights arising under the contract will not be enforced, or will be kept in suspense, or held in abeyance, the person who otherwise might have enforced those rights will not be allowed to enforce them when it would be inequitable having regard to the dealings which have taken place between the parties.'

It is worth noticing that the principle may be applied, not only so as to suspend strict legal rights, but also so as to preclude the enforcement of them.

This principle has been applied to cases where a creditor agrees to accept a lesser sum in discharge of a greater. So much so that we can now say that, when a creditor and a debtor enter upon a course of negotiation, which leads the debtor to suppose that, on payment of the lesser sum, the creditor will not enforce payment of the balance, and on the faith thereof the debtor pays the lesser sum and the creditor accepts it as satisfaction: then the creditor will not be allowed to enforce payment of the balance when it would be inequitable to do so. This was well illustrated during the last war. Tenants went away to escape the bombs and left their houses unoccupied. The landlords accepted a reduced rent for the time they were empty. It was held that the landlords could not afterwards turn round and sue for the balance, see *Central London Property Trust Ltd* v. *High Trees House Ltd* [1947] 1 KB 130. This caused at the time some eyebrows to be raised in high places. But they have been lowered since. The solution was so obviously just that no one could well gainsay it.

In applying this principle, however, we must note the qualification: The creditor is only barred from his legal rights when it would be *inequitable* for him to insist upon them. Where there has been a true *accord*, under which the creditor voluntarily agrees to accept a lesser sum in satisfaction, and the debtor acts upon that accord by paying the lesser sum and the creditor accepts it, then it is inequitable for the creditor afterwards to insist on the balance. But he is not bound unless there has been truly an accord between them.

In the present case, on the facts as found by the judge, it seems to me that there was no true accord. The debtor's wife held the creditor to ransom. The creditor was in need of money to meet his own commitments, and she knew it. When the creditor asked for payment of the £480 due to him, she said to him in effect: 'We cannot pay you the £480. But we will pay you £300 if you will accept it in settlement. If you do not accept it on those terms, you will get nothing. £300 is better than nothing'. She had no right to say any such thing. She could properly have said: 'We cannot pay you more than £300. Please accept it on account'. But she had no right to insist on his taking it in settlement. When she said: 'We will pay you nothing unless you accept £300 in settlement', she was putting undue pressure on the creditor. She was making a threat to break the contract (by paying nothing) and she was doing it so as to compel the creditor to do what he was unwilling to do (to accept £300 in settlement): and she succeeded. He complied with her demand. That was on recent authority a case of intimidation: see *Rookes* v. *Barnard* [1964] AC 1129 and *Stratford (J T) & Son Ltd* v. *Lindley* [1965] AC 269, 283, 284. In these circumstances there was no true accord so as to found a defence of accord and satisfaction: see *Day* v. *McLea* (1889) 22 QBD 610. There is also no equity in the defendant to warrant any departure from the due course of law. No person can insist on a settlement procured by intimidation.

In my opinion there is no reason in law or equity why the creditor should not enforce the full amount of the debt due to him. I would, therefore, dismiss this appeal.

Danckwerts LJ

I agree with the judgment of the Master of the Rolls. *Foakes* v. *Beer* (1884) 9 App Cas 605, applying the decision in *Pinnel's Case* (1602) 5 Co Rep 117a settled definitely the rule of law that payment of a lesser sum than the amount of a debt due cannot be a satisfaction of the debt, unless there is some benefit to the creditor added so that there is an accord and satisfaction.

In *Foakes* v. *Beer* Lord Selborne, while approving *Cumber* v. *Wane* (1721) 1 Stra 426, did not overrule the cases which appear to differ from *Cumber* v. *Wane*, saying:

> 'All the authorities subsequent to *Cumber* v. *Wane*, which were relied upon by the appellant at your Lordships' Bar (such as *Sibree* v. *Tripp*, 15 M & W 23, *Curlewis* v. *Clark* (1849) 3 Exch 375 and *Goddard* v. *O'Brien* 9 QBD 37) have proceeded upon the distinction, that, by giving negotiable paper or otherwise there had been some new consideration for a new agreement, distinct from mere money payments in or towards discharge of the original liability.'

Lord Selborne was distinguishing those cases from the case before the House.

But the giving of a cheque of the debtor for a smaller amount than the sum due is very different from 'the gift of a horse, hawk, or robe, etc.' mentioned in *Pinnel's Case*. I accept that the cheque of some other person than the debtor, in appropriate circumstances, may be the basis of an accord and satisfaction, but I cannot see how in the year 1965 the debtor's own cheque for a smaller sum can be better than payment of the whole amount of the debt in cash. The cheque is only conditional payment, it may be difficult to cash, or it may be returned by the bank with the letters 'R.D.' upon it, unpaid. I think that *Goddard* v. *O'Brien* 9 QBD 37 either was wrongly decided or should not be followed in the circumstances of today.

I agree also that, in the circumstances of the present case, there was no true accord. The Rees really behaved very badly. They knew of the plaintiffs' financial difficulties and used their awkward situation to intimidate them. The plaintiffs did not wish to accept the sum of £300 in discharge of the debt of £482, but were desperate to get some money. It would appear also that the defendant and his wife misled the plaintiffs as to their own financial position. Rees, in his evidence, said: 'In June (1964) I could have paid £700 odd. I could have settled the whole bill.' There is no evidence that by August, or even by November, their financial situation had deteriorated so that they could not pay the £482. Nor does it appear that their position was altered to their detriment by reason of the receipt given by the plaintiffs. The receipt was given on November 14, 1964. On November 23, 1964, the plaintiffs' solicitors wrote a letter making it clear that the payment of £300 was being treated as a payment on account. I cannot see any ground in this case for treating the payment as a satisfaction on equitable principles.

In my view the county court judge was right in applying the rule in *Foakes* v. *Beer*, and I would dismiss the appeal.

Winn LJ

The question to be decided may be stated thus: Did the defendant's agreement to give his own cheque for £300 in full settlement of his existing debt to the plaintiffs of £482 and the plaintiff's agreement to accept it in full payment of that debt, followed by delivery and due payment of such a cheque, constitute a valid accord and satisfaction discharging the debt in law? . . .

In my judgment it is an essential element of a valid accord and satisfaction that the agreement which constitutes the accord should itself be binding in law, and I do not think that any such agreement can be so binding unless it is either made under seal or supported by consideration. Satisfaction, viz., performance, of an agreement of accord, does not provide retroactive validity to the accord, but depends for its effect upon the legal validity of the accord as a binding contract at the time when it is made: this I think is apparent when it is remembered that, albeit rarely, existing obligations of debt may be replaced effectively by a contractually binding substitution of a new obligation.

In my judgment this court should now decline to follow the decision in *Goddard* v. *O'Brien* 9 QBD 37 and should hold that where a debtor's own cheque for a lesser amount than he indisputably owes to his creditor is accepted by the creditor in full satisfaction of the debt, the creditor is to be regarded, in any case where he has not required the payment to be made by cheque rather than in cash, as having received the cheque merely as conditional payment of part of what he was entitled to receive: he is free in law, if not in good commercial conscience, to insist upon payment of the balance of the amount due to him from the debtor.

I would dismiss this appeal.

COMMENTARY

The case is important for a number of reasons. The first is that the Court of Appeal, not without something of a struggle in terms of the authorities, refused to draw a distinction between a payment by cash and a payment by the debtor by his own cheque. This must be right. The defendant in *Rees* asked the plaintiffs whether they wanted payment by cash or by cheque. It would have been absurd to conclude that there was no consideration in the case where the defendant paid cash but that there was consideration in the case where payment was made by cheque. The second point is the significance of the difference between the reasoning of Lord Denning on the one hand and Danckwerts and Winn LJJ on the other. Danckwerts and Winn LJJ reached the conclusion that the agreement was not enforceable by a straightforward application of *Foakes* v. *Beer*. Lord Denning took a different approach. While he did not seek to challenge the authority of *Foakes* v. *Beer* at common law (he could not do so as a matter of authority), he resorted to equity in an attempt to confine, if not undermine, *Foakes*. Thus he was careful to say that the reason why the plaintiffs were entitled to sue for the balance of the price was that the defendant had behaved inequitably. This division of opinion in many ways reflects the debate that has taken place over the true analysis of *Stilk* v. *Myrick* (on which see p. 184 above). The majority judgments adopt traditional reasoning, based on the absence of consideration for the promise to discharge the entire debt, while the minority opinion of Lord Denning attempts to distinguish an agreement that has been freely concluded from one that has been extracted as a result of the application of illegitimate pressure. The third point of significance relates to the basis for the finding made by Lord Denning and Danckwerts LJ that the defendants had behaved 'inequitably' or 'very badly'. Lord Denning relied upon the tort of intimidation (which, at least in its two-party form, is, essentially, the tortious counterpart of economic duress) and emphasized the threat made by the defendant's wife to break the contract unless the plaintiffs agreed to the discharge of the entire debt. Winn LJ adopted a broader approach. He emphasized the fact that the defendants knew of the plaintiffs' financial difficulties and that they had misrepresented their own financial position. Are any of these elements a necessary component of a finding that the debtor acted 'inequitably' or is it the case that no one factor is essential and that the task of the court is to engage in a careful evaluation of the facts and circumstances of the individual case with a view to ascertaining whether or not the conduct of the debtor can be said to be sufficiently 'inequitable' to entitle the creditor to claim the balance of the debt? The former view is the preferable one in that it draws on recognized legal doctrines, such as intimidation and economic duress. But it may be that the courts will adopt the latter approach and will take into account factors such as the debtor's knowledge of the creditor's financial position, any misrepresentation made by the debtor as to his financial position, any threats made by the debtor to break his contract with the creditor, and the options that were reasonably open to the creditor when faced with this threat.

(b) *The role of precedent*

The second reason for the survival of *Foakes* v. *Beer* is that it is a decision of the House of Lords and so can only be overruled by a decision of the House of Lords. The significance of this point is apparent from the following case:

In re Selectmove

[1995] 1 WLR 474, Court of Appeal

In July 1991 Selectmove Ltd owed substantial amounts of income tax (PAYE) and national insurance contributions (NIC) to the Inland Revenue. Mr Ffookes, the managing director of the company, met with Mr Polland, a collector of taxes. At that meeting Mr Ffookes claimed that he put a proposal to Mr Polland to the effect that Selectmove Ltd would pay future tax and national insurance liabilities as they fell due and would pay off the arrears at a rate of £1,000 per month. Mr Ffookes further claimed that Mr Polland stated that he would have to seek approval from his superiors to such a proposal and that he would revert to Mr Ffookes if the proposal was unacceptable. Mr Polland did not get back in touch with Mr Ffookes. In October 1991 the Revenue wrote to the company demanding payment of arrears of £24,650 and threatened a winding-up petition if payment was not made. The Revenue served a statutory demand for payment and presented a winding-up petition in September 1992. On behalf of the company it was submitted that the petition should be dismissed. The judge rejected the submission and compulsorily wound up the company. The company appealed to the Court of Appeal. One of the grounds on which they appealed was that an agreement had been reached with the Revenue in July 1991 and that agreement was supported by consideration. The Court of Appeal held that no such agreement had been reached but that, in any event, there was no consideration to support the alleged agreement.

Peter Gibson LJ

There are two elements to the consideration which the company claims was provided by it to the revenue. One is the promise to pay off its existing liability by instalments from 1 February 1992. The other is the promise to pay future PAYE and NIC as they fell due. Mr Nugee [counsel for Selectmove] suggested that implicit in the latter was the promise to continue trading. But that cannot be spelt out of Mr Ffookes' evidence as to what he agreed with Mr Polland. Accordingly, the second element is no more than a promise to pay that which it was bound to pay under the fiscal legislation at the date at which it was bound to make such payment. If the first element is not good consideration, I do not see why the second element should be either.

The judge held that the case fell within the principle of *Foakes* v. *Beer* (1884) 9 App Cas 605. . . . Although their Lordships were unanimous in the result, that case is notable for the powerful speech of Lord Blackburn, who made plain his disagreement with the course the law had taken in and since *Pinnel's Case* (1602) 5 Co Rep 117a and which the House of Lords in *Foakes* v. *Beer* 9 App. Cas. 605, decided should not be reversed. Lord Blackburn expressed his conviction, at p. 622, that

'all men of business, whether merchants or tradesmen, do every day recognise and act on the ground that prompt payment of a part of their demand may be more beneficial to them than it would be to insist on their rights and enforce payment of the whole.'

Yet it is clear that the House of Lords decided that a practical benefit of that nature is not good consideration in law.

Foakes v. *Beer* has been followed and applied in numerous cases subsequently, of which I shall mention two. In *Vanbergen* v. *St Edmunds Properties Ltd* [1933] 2 KB 223, 231 Lord Hanworth MR said

'It is a well established principle that a promise to pay a sum which the debtor is already bound by law to pay to the promisee does not afford any consideration to support the contract.'

More recently in *D & C Builders Ltd* v. *Rees* [1966] 2 QB 617 this court also applied *Foakes v. Beer*, Danckwerts LJ saying, at p. 626, that the case

'settled definitely the rule of law that payment of a lesser sum than the amount of a debt due cannot be a satisfaction of the debt, unless there is some benefit to the creditor added so that there is an accord and satisfaction.'

Mr Nugee, however, submitted that an additional benefit to the Crown was conferred by the agreement in that the Crown stood to derive practical benefits therefrom: it was likely to recover more from not enforcing its debt against the company, which was known to be in financial difficulties, than from putting the company into liquidation. He pointed to the fact that the company did in fact pay its further P.A.Y.E. and N.I.C. liabilities and £7,000 of its arrears. He relied on the decision of this court in *Williams* v. *Roffey Bros &*

Nicholls (Contractors) Ltd [1991] 1 QB 1 for the proposition that a promise to perform an existing obligation can amount to good consideration provided that there are practical benefits to the promisee.

[he considered the case, noting in particular the six-point summary to be found in the judgment of Glidewell LJ and continued]

Mr Nugee submitted that, although Glidewell LJ in terms confined his remarks to a case where B is to do the work for or supply goods or services to A, the same principle must apply where B's obligation is to pay A, and he referred to an article by Adams and Brownsword, 'Contract, Consideration and the Critical Path' (1990) 53 *MLR* 536, 539–540 which suggests that *Foakes* v. *Beer* might need reconsideration. I see the force of the argument, but the difficulty that I feel with it is that, if the principle of *Williams* v. *Roffey Bros & Nicholls (Contractors) Ltd* [1991] 1 QB 1 is to be extended to an obligation to make payment, it would in effect leave the principle in *Foakes* v. *Beer* without any application. When a creditor and a debtor who are at arm's length reach agreement on the payment of the debt by instalments to accommodate the debtor, the creditor will no doubt always see a practical benefit to himself in so doing. In the absence of authority there would be much to be said for the enforceability of such a contract. But that was a matter expressly considered in *Foakes* v. *Beer* yet held not to constitute good consideration in law. *Foakes* v. *Beer* was not even referred to in *Williams* v. *Roffey Bros & Nicholls (Contractors) Ltd* [1991] 1 QB 1, and it is in my judgment impossible, consistently with the doctrine of precedent, for this court to extend the principle of the *Williams* case to any circumstances governed by the principle of *Foakes* v. *Beer* 9 App Cas 605. If that extension is to be made, it must be by the House of Lords or, perhaps even more appropriately, by Parliament after consideration by the Law Commission.

In my judgment, the judge was right to hold that if there was an agreement between the company and the revenue it was unenforceable for want of consideration.

Stuart-Smith and **Balcombe LJJ** agreed with the judgment of Peter Gibson LJ.

COMMENTARY

Selectmove establishes, as a matter of authority, that *Foakes* v. *Beer* remains good law and that it has not been undermined by *Williams* v. *Roffey Bros.* That said, *Foakes* received a distinctly lukewarm reception in *Selectmove.* Had the matter not been governed by authority it seems clear that Peter Gibson LJ would have reached a contrary conclusion to that reached by the House of Lords in *Foakes.* But he does make one very significant point in relation to the extension of the 'practical benefit' test to a promise to pay part of a debt and that is that its effect will be to leave the principle in *Foakes* 'without any application'. The reason for this is that payment of money will always constitute a 'practical benefit' to the creditor. Thus the consequence of extending *Williams* v. *Roffey Bros* to the case of part payment of a debt will not be to limit or confine *Foakes* but to undermine it.

Given that *Foakes* is presently secure as a matter of authority, what is the status of *Williams* v. *Roffey Bros*? Can it be reconciled with *Foakes*? Here we encounter the problem that the Court of Appeal in *Williams* did not consider *Foakes* and so did not attempt to explain the relationship between the two cases. Peter Gibson LJ in *Selectmove* did not doubt the correctness of *Williams* v. *Roffey Bros* and so it remains binding up to and including the level of the Court of Appeal (unless, which is highly unlikely, a court were to conclude that *Williams* was wrongly decided because it was decided *per incuriam*). Is there a relevant difference between *Williams* and *Foakes*? The short answer is that *Williams* is about a promise to pay more, whereas *Foakes* is about a promise to accept less. Thus there is a clear distinction on the facts between the two cases, but is there a distinction in principle? Peter Gibson LJ does not answer this particular question. His analysis of the relationship between the two cases is conducted in terms of authority rather than principle. This is understandable given that he was bound by the two decisions but it leaves the question of principle unanswered. His suggestion that the relationship between the two cases should be considered by the Law Commission and then by Parliament is unlikely to bear fruit. The issue is not of sufficient practical significance to attract the time and the resources of the Law Commission. It is therefore likely that it will be left to the courts themselves to work out the relationship between the two cases.

(c) *A question of consistency*

Foakes v. *Beer* is consistent with the rule that neither performance of a contractual duty owed to the promisor nor performance of a duty imposed by law amount to good consideration. The latter two rules have, however, been radically qualified, if not undermined, by cases such as *Ward* v. *Byham* and *Williams* v. *Roffey Bros.* If it is the case that the law is moving in the direction indicated by the Court of Appeal in *Williams* v. *Roffey Bros* should it not result in the application of the 'practical benefit' test to the *Foakes* v. *Beer* fact situation? Or is there a difference in principle between a promise to pay more and a promise to accept less? Or, to use the language of Professor Treitel (*Some Landmarks of Twentieth Century Contract Law* (Oxford University Press, 2002)), is there a difference between an 'increasing pact' (the *Williams* v. *Roffey Bros* type case) and a 'decreasing pact' (the *Foakes* v. *Beer* type case)? These questions can be explored by reference to the following Australian case:

Musumeci v. Winadell Pty Ltd

(1994) 34 NSWLR 723, Supreme Court of New South Wales

The plaintiffs were tenants in a shopping centre where they ran a business as fruiterers. The defendants were the landlords of the shopping centre. The defendants subsequently leased another unit in the shopping centre to another fruiterer and the plaintiffs alleged that this caused a drop in their trade and rendered the goodwill of the business valueless. They wrote to the defendants and sought a reduction in their rent. The defendants replied in a letter written on a 'without prejudice' basis in which they offered to reduce the rent payable by one third. The plaintiffs accepted this offer. The defendants later terminated their concession. The plaintiffs nevertheless tendered two thirds of the rent which the defendants initially accepted as 'incomplete payments'. The defendants subsequently changed their mind, entered the premises and changed the locks. The plaintiffs then brought an action for damages. The defendants submitted that their promise to reduce the rent was unenforceable for lack of consideration.

The court held that the promise to reduce the rent was supported by consideration.

The defendants had obtained a practical benefit by promising to reduce the rent because the promise had the effect of increasing the ability of the plaintiffs to remain in occupation of the premises, notwithstanding the competition. The plaintiffs had also suffered a practical detriment in that they had continued under the lease whilst being exposed to the risk of being put out of business by their competitor. The plaintiffs were therefore entitled to recover damages from the defendants.

Santow J

[He set out the facts, considered *Stilk* v. *Myrick*, *Williams* v. *Roffey Bros*, and *Re Selectmove* and noted that 'there has been a continuing trend to side-step the artificial results of a strict doctrine of consideration'. He then asked himself the question whether Australian courts should follow *Roffey*. He answered this question in the affirmative but suggested various amendments to the six-point analysis of Glidewell LJ (see p. 192 above). In particular, he stated that 'conceptually it can make no difference whether B promises A an additional payment for A's promise of performance or grants A the equivalent concession of promising a reduction in A's payment obligations, where these pre-exist'. He then sought to recast the propositions set out by Glidewell LJ in the following terms, using italics to indicate his amendments to the original propositions]

'The present state of the law on this subject can be expressed in the following propositions:

(i) If A has entered into a contract with B to do work for, or to supply goods or services to, B in return for the payment by B, and

(ii) At some stage before A has completely performed his obligations under the contract B has reason to doubt whether A will, or be able to, complete his side of the bargain, and

(iii) B thereupon promises A an additional payment *or other concession (such as reducing A's original obligation)* in return for A's promise to perform this contractual obligation at the time, and

(iv) (a) As a result of giving his promise B obtains in practice a benefit, or obviates a disbenefit *provided that A's performance, having regard to what has been so obtained, is capable of being viewed by B as worth more to B than any likely remedy against A (allowing for any defences or cross-claims), taking into account the cost to B of any such payment or concession to obtain greater assurance of A's performance, or*

(b) *as a result of giving his promise, A suffers a detriment (or obviates a benefit) provided that A is thereby foregoing the opportunity of not performing the original contract, in circumstances where such non-performance, taking into account B's likely remedy against A (and allowing for any defences or cross-claims) is capable of being viewed by A as worth more to A than performing that contract, in the absence of B's promised payment or concession to A, and*

(v) B's promise is not given as a result of economic duress or fraud *or undue influence or unconscionable conduct on the part of A nor is it induced as a result of unfair pressure on the part of A, having regard to the circumstances*, then,

(vi) The benefit to B *or the detriment to A* is capable of being consideration for B's promise, so that the promise will be legally binding.'

Application of Williams v. Roffey to Present Circumstances.

Applying that reasoning to the present circumstances, the practical benefit that the Lessor gained from the concession of lower future rental, was argued to be the enhanced capacity of the Plaintiffs to stay in occupation, able to carry out their future reduced lease obligations, notwithstanding substantial newly introduced competition from the other tenant. What this practical benefit consists of therefore is enhanced capacity for the Lessor to maintain a full shopping centre with another competing tenant, when the original tenant is no longer at so great a risk of defaulting and more likely to stay. That is a practical benefit, even though legally there be no inhibition on the Lessor to introduce new competition . . . there is nothing in the evidence before me to indicate that the Plaintiffs were not genuine at the time the new tenant was introduced, about the serious threat this posed to their viability. Certainly I can infer that the Lessor must have thought so. Landlords are not in the habit of extending such rent concessions for purely altruistic reasons. More likely, there was a strong element of enlightened self-interest.

It must also be remembered that two years have passed, during which the lower rent has been paid and received (though without prejudice to the Lessor's rights). Thus the Plaintiffs' present capacity to pay the original rent . . . is by no means inconsistent with a much more fragile capacity when the new competition was first introduced in 1992. From the Lessor's viewpoint, it evidently came to have other alternatives than the Plaintiffs, as tenants, certainly when it commenced proceedings for possession culminating in the steps of January this year. But none of this precludes a practical benefit to the Defendant from the Plaintiffs' continued possession at the earlier point of time, when those possibilities had yet to emerge.

. . . in a shopping centre it is well known that vacant shops are not in the interests of the landlord whilst a reputation for fairness is. The landlord/owner benefits from uninterrupted, successful trade overall in that shopping centre, even if leases of themselves as here, do not confer on the lessor a share of the tenant's profit. This is particularly when it comes to renewing leases, or when vacancies otherwise arise and the landlord wants to attract tenants.

Thus I find that the particular practical benefit here, was that the Lessor had greater assurance of the Lessees staying in occupation and maintaining viability and capacity to perform by reason of their reduction in their rent, notwithstanding the introduction of a major, much larger competing tenant. The practical detriment to the Lessees lay in risking their capacity to survive against a much stronger competitor, by staying in occupancy under their lease, rather than walking away at the cost of damages, if the Lessees' defences . . . were unsuccessful. From the Lessees' actions, it is evident that without the rent concession, the latter course was viewed as more likely to be in the Lessees' interests than staying in occupation . . .

I am satisfied in the circumstances that the remaining elements set out earlier are made out, including element (v), (or more precisely, absence of any element of extortion in the sense there set out). The Lessees' reaction to the original introduction of a competing, powerful tenant, with the perceived capacity to wipe them out was to threaten redress to legal remedies. In the circumstances that was not coercive, but a simply defensive, if fairly aggressive, reaction designed to elicit a constructive response.

As to element (iv) which, in its proviso, is designed to eliminate 'wholly' gratuitous promises, there is evidence before me that the Plaintiffs' goodwill was at risk of destruction by the introduction of the much stronger competitor on a concessional basis, unless the rent reduction were forthcoming. That makes it a proper inference for me to draw that there was indeed a sufficient practical benefit, procured by maintaining the Plaintiffs as viable tenants on the promise of reduced rental. This is compared to the evidently less attractive alternative of finding another tenant and suing for any rent shortfall, particularly where the Lessees might plead a number of foreshadowed defences and cross-claims.

COMMENTARY

Two points can be made about this refinement of the principles laid down in *Williams*. The first is that it expands their scope, in that it extends them to concessions. The second is that in point (v) it enlarges the defences available to the promisor beyond economic duress. The most significant aspect of the decision is undoubtedly the extension of *Williams* v. *Roffey Bros* to a case in which the consideration takes the form of a grant of a concession. The effect of this approach is to make it more difficult to conclude that there is a difference in principle between a promise to pay more and a promise to accept less. The extension of the practical benefit test to *Foakes* would also undermine the reasoning of the House of Lords in that case. Indeed, it was recognition of the fact that part payment of a debt does constitute a practical benefit to the creditor that was at the root of the doubts expressed by Lord Blackburn in the case itself (see p. 207 above).

The predominant view would appear to be that, in the event of conflict between the two streams of authority, it is *Foakes* v. *Beer* that should give way and that the courts should take the *Williams* v. *Roffey Bros* line and focus on the presence or absence of practical benefit or detriment (subject to defences such as economic duress). Not all are convinced of the wisdom of such a step (see, for example, J O'Sullivan, 'In Defence of *Foakes* v. *Beer* [1996] *CLJ* 219). The concerns surrounding the application of the practical benefit test to the part payment of a debt are that the test is so easy to satisfy and that the defences, such as duress, may not provide sufficient protection for the creditor. Professor Treitel expresses his doubts about the reversal of *Foakes* v. *Beer* in the following terms (*Some Landmarks of Twentieth Century Contract Law* (Oxford University Press, 2002), pp. 45–46):

Would anything be lost if such a reversal took place? The rule no doubt has a protective function in cases such as *D & C Builders Ltd* v. *Rees*, though in that kind of situation the same function could perhaps in many cases be performed by the concept of economic duress. But that concept may not go far enough. There was, I repeat, nothing wrong with the outcome in *Foakes* v. *Beer*; and I do not see how the case could be brought within even the expanding concept of duress; nor is it obvious what other legal machinery could be used to achieve the same end. Rectification has been suggested as a possibility but this would work only if *both* parties had no intention that the interest should be given up or if Dr Foakes *knew* that Mrs Beer had no such intention or if he was guilty of fraud or other unconscionable conduct in procuring the agreement. But there was no evidence of any such circumstances so that the problem cannot be solved in this way. There is much to be said against *Foakes* v. *Beer* but also something in its favour. How the balance will one day, perhaps in the twenty-first century, be struck continues to be a matter of speculation.

(c) PAST CONSIDERATION

The general rule is that past consideration is not good consideration. The rule is linked to the bargain theory of consideration. Take the following example. X washes Y's car. Y later promises to pay X £15 for washing his car but then changes his mind and refuses to pay. Can X sue Y for the promised sum? The answer to this question ultimately depends upon the evidence. If it is the case that there was an unexpressed bargain between X and Y according to which X agreed to wash Y's car in return for payment then the promise will be enforceable (see p. 230 below). On the other hand, if X washed Y's car and Y then separately promised to pay X £15 then X will not be entitled to sue Y for payment because the consideration that he provided for Y's promise of payment, namely washing the car, was in the past. It may be difficult to distinguish these two cases on the facts. But the difference between them is essentially an evidential one relating to the nature of the obligations assumed by the parties. The essence of the distinction is between a bargain, on the one hand, and a gift which is followed by a promise to make a gift, on the other. The former is enforceable while the latter is not. The general rule that past consideration is not good consideration was established in two cases in the nineteenth century, namely *Eastwood* v. *Kenyon* (1840) 11 Ad & E 438 and *Roscorla* v. *Thomas* (1842) 3 QB 234. Both cases have been the subject of criticism.

Eastwood v. Kenyon

(1840) 11 Ad & E 438, Queen's Bench

John Sutcliffe died and left his entire estate to his daughter, Sarah. The plaintiff was Sutcliffe's executor and he acted as Sarah's agent and guardian until she came of full age. Sutcliffe's estate proved to be insufficient to cover the cost of maintaining and educating Sarah and maintaining and improving some cottages that had been left to Sarah. The plaintiff therefore borrowed £140 from Mr Blackburn in order to meet these costs. This money was spent for the benefit of Sarah and, after she came of full age, she promised to repay the £140 which the plaintiff had borrowed and, indeed, she paid the interest to Blackburn for one year. The plaintiff then gave up the control and management of the estate to Sarah's agent. Sarah later married the defendant and he in turn promised that he would discharge the plaintiff's liability to Blackburn. He failed to honour his promise but it was held that he incurred no liability in failing to do so because his promise to pay the debt which the plaintiff had incurred was unenforceable.

Lord Denman CJ [delivering the judgment of the court]
It was . . . argued for the plaintiff that the declaration disclosed a sufficient moral consideration to support the promise.

Most of the older cases on this subject are collected in a learned note to the case of *Wennall* v. *Adney* (3 B & P 249), and the conclusion there arrived at seems to be correct in general, 'that an express promise can only revive a precedent good consideration, which might have been enforced at law through the medium of an implied promise, had it not been suspended by some positive rule of law; but can give no original cause of action, if the obligation, on which it is founded, never could have been enforced at law, though not barred by any legal maxim or statute provision'. Instances are given of voidable contracts, as those of infants ratified by an express promise after age, and distinguished from void contracts, as of married women, not capable of ratification by them when widows; *Loyd* v. *Lee* (1 Stra 94); debts of bankrupts revived by subsequent promise after certificate; and similar cases . . .

The eminent counsel who argued for the plaintiff in *Lee* v. *Muggeridge* (5 Taunt 36), spoke of Lord Mansfield as having considered the rule of *nudum pactum* as too narrow, and maintained that all promises deliberately made ought to be held binding. I do not find this language ascribed to him by any reporter, and do not know whether we are to receive it as a traditional report, or as a deduction from what he does appear to have laid down. If the latter, the note to *Wennall* v. *Adney* (3 B & P 249), shews the deduction to be erroneous. If the former, Lord Tenterden and this Court declared that they could not adopt it in *Littlefield* v. *Shee* (2 B & Ad 811). Indeed the doctrine would annihilate the necessity for any consideration at all, inasmuch as the mere fact of giving a promise creates a moral obligation to perform it.

The enforcement of such promises by law, however plausibly reconciled by the desire to effect all conscientious engagements, might be attended with mischievous consequences to society; one of which would be the frequent preference of voluntary undertakings to claims for just debts. Suits would thereby be multiplied, and voluntary undertakings would also be multiplied, to the prejudice of real creditors. The temptations of executors would be much increased by the prevalence of such a doctrine, and the faithful discharge of their duty be rendered more difficult.

Taking then the promise of the defendant, as stated on this record, to have been an express promise, we find that the consideration for it was past and executed long before, and yet it is not laid to have been at the request of the defendant, nor even of his wife while sole (though if it had, the case of *Mitchinson* v. *Hewson* (7 T R 348), shews that it would not have been sufficient), and the declaration really discloses nothing but a benefit voluntarily conferred by the plaintiff and received by the defendant, with an express promise by the defendant to pay money.

If the subsequent assent of the defendant could have amounted to a ratihabitio[2] the declaration should have stated the money to have been expended at his request, and the ratification should have been relied on as matter of evidence; but this was obviously impossible, because the defendant was in no way connected with the property or with the plaintiff, when the money was expended. If the ratification of the wife while sole were relied on, then a debt from her would have been shewn, and the defendant could not have been charged in his own right without some further consideration, as of forbearance after marriage, or something of that sort; and then another point would have arisen upon the Statute of Frauds which did not arise as it was, but which might in that case have been available under the plea of non assumpsit.

In holding this declaration bad because it states no consideration but a past benefit not conferred at the request of the defendant, we conceive that we are justified by the old common law of England.

Lampleigh v. *Brathwait* (Hob 105), is selected by Mr Smith (1 Smith's Leading Cases, 67), as the leading case on this subject, which was there fully discussed, though not necessary to the decision. Hobart CJ lays it down that 'a mere voluntary courtesy will

---

[2] That is to say, ratification.

not have a consideration to uphold an assumpsit. But if that courtesy were moved by a suit or request of the party that gives the assumpsit, it will bind; for the promise, though it follows, yet it is not naked, but couples itself with the suit before, and the merits of the party procured by that suit; which is the difference'; a difference brought fully out by *Hunt v. Bate* (Dyer, 272 (a)), there cited from Dyer, where a promise to indemnify the plaintiff against the consequences of having bailed the defendant's servant, which the plaintiff had done without request of the defendant, was held to be made without consideration; but a promise to pay £20 to plaintiff, who had married defendant's cousin, but at defendant's special instance, was held binding.

The distinction is noted, and was acted upon, in *Townsend v. Hunt* (Cro Car 408), and indeed in numerous old books; while the principle of moral obligation does not make its appearance till the days of Lord Mansfield, and then under circumstances not inconsistent with this ancient doctrine when properly explained.

Upon the whole, we are of opinion that the rule must be made absolute to arrest the judgment.

COMMENTARY

The language in which the judgment is expressed is not always easy to follow but this is frequently so with reports that date from this period. *Eastwood* is an important decision for a number of reasons. The first relates to the conclusion that the consideration was 'past and executed' long before the express promise to pay was made. The plaintiff performed services that were of value to Sarah and the defendant did promise to pay for them but there was never a bargain between them to the effect that, if the plaintiff performed these services, the defendant would pay for them. Rather, there was one event, the loan taken out by the plaintiff for the benefit of Sarah, followed by a second event, the promise by the defendant to reimburse the plaintiff, but no sufficient connection between the two to constitute a bargain to this effect. The plaintiff had conferred a gift on Sarah and her husband, in gratitude or as a matter of moral obligation (on which see below), had promised to repay the money borrowed, but the latter promise was unenforceable in law. Secondly, Lord Denman recognizes that the rule that past consideration is no consideration is the subject of exceptions. He recognizes an exception, based on *Lampleigh v. Brathwait* (1615) Hob 105 (discussed at p. 229 below), where the earlier act was performed at the request of the promisor. This exception was not applicable on the facts of *Eastwood* because the defendant had not asked the plaintiff to borrow the money. Lord Denman also refers to the possibility of ratification, albeit he rejects it on the facts. A party who ratifies an obligation which, prior to ratification, was not (or no longer) binding on him may incur a liability in respect of that obligation as a result of the ratification. The law in this area is, however, rather uneven. A debtor who promises to pay a debt after it has become statute-barred does not thereby become liable to repay the debt (Limitation Act 1980, section 29(7)). His ratification is ineffective to revive the debt (unless his promise to pay the debt is supported by fresh consideration). But the position is otherwise in the case of a child who ratifies a contract that was not binding on him during his childhood. Children have limited contractual capacity and so many contracts do not bind them during their childhood (see further pp. 825–829). But if a child, on reaching adulthood, ratifies the contract he will generally become liable on it

(*Williams* v. *Moor* (1843) 11 M & W 256). In this way ratification can serve to give legal effect to an obligation that was previously unenforceable. Thirdly, *Eastwood* is of great significance because of its rejection of the proposition, associated with Lord Mansfield, that a promise to perform a pre-existing 'moral obligation' could constitute good consideration. In this respect *Eastwood* is something of a watershed. It provided the court with an opportunity to abandon the doctrine of consideration but instead Lord Denman used it to affirm the existence of the doctrine. The impact of *Eastwood* has been described by Professor Atiyah (*The Rise and Fall of Freedom of Contract* (Oxford University Press, 1979), pp. 491–493) in the following terms:

There is no doubt that this is one of the most puzzling of all nineteenth-century decisions on contract law. Why did the Court go out of its way to overrule decisions representing the law of some seventy years' standing, when the result seemed so unjust? Further, if . . . the whole trend of contract law had been to stress the importance of the promissory basis, is it not passing strange that the Court should have invoked the doctrine of consideration (which elsewhere had been reduced by this time to a bare technicality) to defeat a clear and express promise? Moreover, the idea that this was a conservative decision, a return to the old, true, pre-Mansfield law, does not square with what we know of Denman. For though Denman may not have had any great reputation as a lawyer, he was by no means a conservative figure. He had spent many years as a fairly radical Whig in Parliament, was a close associate of Brougham's, and even while on the Bench, took an active part in many law reform proposals.

I suggest that three factors may have been responsible for the decision. First, there was the growing strength of positivism which stressed the line between law and morality far more than had ever been the case in Mansfield's time. Positivism owed its origins to Bentham's *Fragment on Government*, but was given much greater elaboration and force in Austin's *Province of Jurisprudence Determined*, first published in 1832. Austin, it must be remembered was a member of the Benthamite circle, on the outer fringes of which had been Denman himself before he became Chief Justice. Denman may have been acquainted with Austin, and, more likely, with his work. It does not seem unduly speculative to suggest that the Court was unhappy at the idea of having openly to convert moral obligations into legal ones.

The second factor is less obvious, and more dubious, but I suggest that there is a sense in which the decision was part of the process of downgrading quasi-contractual duties, liabilities not based on consent, which was such a pronounced feature of the times. The fact that in the case itself there was an express promise is no doubt paradoxical, but the point is that the original benefit received by Sarah was not at that time the subject of any promise to pay, either by Sarah or by her husband. If there had been any quasi-contractual duty on Sarah to reimburse the plaintiff for his expenditure, then there is no doubt that she at least would have been subsequently liable on her promise. The Court stressed the rule that where a benefit is rendered in circumstances which create a legal liability to pay without any promise, then a subsequent promise is itself binding and the past consideration is treated as good. In a sense, therefore, the importance of the decision may lie not so much in the denial of liability on the express promise, but in the denial of any pre-existing quasi-contractual duty. . . . Now we have seen how, around 1840, the Courts were cutting down on such [quasi-contractual] liabilities. A man was not to be held liable for some benefit conferred upon his wife or his child, unless authorized by him. And in *Eastwood* v. *Kenyon* the Court appears to be insisting that the authority must be contemporaneous with the conferring of the benefit. Benefits are not to be thrust upon people behind their backs, and then promises afterwards extracted from them.

The third possible factor which may have contributed to the decision in *Eastwood* v. *Kenyon* was the disappearance of the idea that the binding nature of a promise rested upon some pre-existing obligation. This is shown by the fact that Lord Denman rejects the argument that a moral obligation can amount to a consideration by arguing that all promises anyhow give rise to moral obligations, and the doctrine, literally applied, would eliminate the need for consideration altogether.

Roscorla v. Thomas

(1842) 3 QB 234, Queen's Bench

The plaintiff bought a horse from the defendant for £30. The defendant gave to the plaintiff an oral warranty that the horse was sound and free from vice. The plaintiff brought an action against the defendant, alleging a breach of this oral warranty. It was held that the oral warranty was unenforceable for want of consideration. The consideration which supported the contract for the sale of the horse was insufficient to support the subsequent oral warranty.

Lord Denman CJ

It may be taken as a general rule, subject to exceptions not applicable to this case, that the promise must be coextensive with the consideration. In the present case, the only promise that would result from the consideration, as stated, and be coextensive with it, would be to deliver the horse upon request. The precedent sale, without a warranty, though at the request of the defendant, imposes no other duty or obligation upon him. It is clear, therefore, that the consideration stated would not raise an implied promise by the defendant that the horse was sound or free from vice.

But the promise in the present case must be taken to be, as in fact it was, express and the question is, whether that fact will warrant the extension of the promise beyond that which would be implied by law; and whether the consideration, though insufficient to raise an implied promise, will nevertheless support an express one. And we think that it will not.

The cases in which it has been held that, under certain circumstances, a consideration insufficient to raise an implied promise will nevertheless support an express one, will be found collected and reviewed in the note (a) to *Wennall* v. *Adney* (3 Bos & Pul 249), and in the case of *Eastwood* v. *Kenyon* (11 A & E 438). They are cases of voidable contracts subsequently ratified, of debts barred by operation of law, subsequently revived, and of equitable and moral obligations, which, but for some rule of law, would of themselves have been sufficient to raise an implied promise. All these cases are distinguishable from, and indeed inapplicable to, the present, which appears to us to fall within the general rule, that a consideration past and executed will support no other promise than such as would be implied by law.

COMMENTARY

This is another decision of Lord Denman, decided shortly after *Eastwood*. At the time it was decided there was no implied obligation of quality in horse sales (see P Mitchell, 'The Development of Quality Obligations in Sale of Goods' (2001) 117 *LQR* 645, esp. pp. 645–650). Therefore the only basis upon which the plaintiff could bring a claim against the defendant was on the basis of the express oral warranty given by the defendant. But the consideration provided by the plaintiff in entering into the contract of sale was insufficient to support the oral warranty because that consideration was held to be 'past and executed'. There is, however, one problem with the case and that relates to the time at which the oral warranty was given. It would appear from this report that the warranty was given after the conclusion of the contract of sale but Professor Treitel has pointed out (H Beale (ed), *Chitty on Contracts* (29th edn, Sweet & Maxwell, 2004), para 3-026 fn 129) that, according to another report of the case ((1842) 11 LJQB 214, 215), the oral warranty was given at the time of the sale. If this was the case it makes the conclusion that the consideration was past much more difficult to defend (although Professor Treitel states that the result in the case can nevertheless be justified on the ground that the oral warranty was, at the time, void for want of written evidence).

The outcome in *Roscorla* might be thought to be an unsatisfactory one. The court could, perhaps, have taken the view that the oral warranty was part and parcel of one overall transaction. Such a view has been taken in other cases (see, for example, *Thornton* v. *Jenyns* (1840) 1 M & G 166, 188–189). Thus a guarantee given after the conclusion of a contract for the sale of goods is not necessarily unenforceable on the ground that the consideration alleged to support it (entry into the contract of sale) is past. A court is more likely to conclude that there is but one transaction and that entry into the contract of sale is good consideration for the guarantee.

Finally in relation to *Roscorla* it should be noted that Lord Denman, once again, refers to the ratification cases as an exception to the general rule, albeit that they were not applicable on the facts of the case.

Eastwood and *Roscorla* between them established the general rule that past consideration is not good consideration. When deciding whether or not consideration is past the courts have regard to what has actually happened. They do not rely exclusively on the terms of the contract between the parties. Thus in *Re McArdle* [1951] Ch 669 the document stated that payment would be to Mrs McArdle 'IN CONSIDERATION of your carrying out certain alterations and improvements' to some property. The evidence established that all the work had in fact been done prior to the execution of the deed and that this fact was 'well-known to everybody who signed it'. The Court of Appeal held that Mrs McArdle could not show that she had provided consideration for the promise of payment because the 'consideration was wholly past'.

As has been noted, the rule that past consideration is not good consideration is not an absolute rule. There are exceptions. In the first place the court may be able to conclude on the evidence that the consideration was not in fact past because the later promise was part and parcel of one overall transaction. Secondly, section 27(1)(b) of the Bills of Exchange Act 1882 provides that an 'antecedent debt or liability' constitutes valuable consideration for a bill of exchange and the effect of this subsection is, potentially, to render past consideration good consideration (although in most cases involving bills of exchange the consideration is not in fact past). The principal exception consists of a line of cases that originated with the old case of *Lampleigh* v. *Brathwait* (1615) Hob 105 and was re-stated in modern form by the Privy Council in *Pau On* v. *Lau Yiu Long* [1980] AC 614. The facts of this case are rather complex but factual complexity is the hallmark of many modern commercial transactions. It is therefore important that you work through the facts of the case with some care.

Pao On v. Lau Yiu Long

[1980] AC 614, Privy Council

The plaintiffs were the owners of all the shares of a company called Shing On, while the defendants were the majority shareholders in Fu Chip, a company which 'went public' on 9 February 1973. The principal asset owned by Shing On was a building which the defendants wished to acquire. At the same time, the plaintiffs wished to realize the value of the property by selling the shares in Shing On. So the parties agreed that the plaintiffs would sell the shares in Shing On to Fu Chip, the price payable to be met by the allotment to the plaintiffs of 4.2 million ordinary shares of $1 each in Fu Chip. It was agreed that the market value of each Fu Chip share was to be deemed to be $2.50, and the plaintiffs also agreed that they would not, before the end of April 1974, sell or transfer 2.5 million of the shares so transferred. This restriction was imposed in order to prevent a depression in the value of Fu Chip shares caused by heavy selling of the shares. The difficulty which this restriction posed for the plaintiffs was that their inability to sell the shares exposed them to the risk of any drop in their value. In order to reduce this exposure, the parties entered into a subsidiary agreement under which the defendants agreed, on or before the end of April 1974, to buy back the shares at $2.50 per share. However, this agreement operated to the advantage of the defendants because they could require the plaintiffs to sell them the shares for $2.50 even if the market value of the shares had risen beyond $2.50. When the plaintiffs discovered this, they informed the defendants that they would not perform the main agreement unless the subsidiary agreement was cancelled and replaced by a guarantee which only came into operation in the event of the price of the shares falling below $2.50. The defendants were anxious to complete the transaction so that public confidence in the newly formed company was not undermined, and so they agreed to the terms proposed by the plaintiffs and the guarantee was duly executed on 4 May 1973. The price of Fu Chip shares subsequently slumped on the market and the plaintiffs sought to enforce the guarantee against the defendants. The defendants maintained that the guarantee was unenforceable because it was not supported by consideration and had been procured by duress. The Privy Council rejected the defendants' argument and held that the guarantee was supported by consideration and that there had been no operative duress because the defendants could not show that their will had been coerced such as to vitiate their consent. In this extract we are only concerned with the first question which was asked of the Privy Council, namely whether or not the guarantee was supported by consideration.

Lord Scarman [giving the judgment of the Board]

The first question

The first question is whether upon its true construction the written guarantee of May 4, 1973, states a consideration sufficient in law to support the defendants' promise of indemnity against a fall in value of the Fu Chip shares. The instrument is, so far as relevant, in these terms:

'Re: Tsuen Wan Shing On Estate Co Ltd

In consideration of your having at our request agreed to sell all of your shares of and in the above mentioned company whose registered office is situate at 274 Sha Tsui Road Ground Floor, Tsuen Wan New Territories in the colony of Hong Kong for the consideration of $10,500,000: by the allotment of 4,200,000 ordinary shares of $1.00 each in Fu Chip Investment Co Ltd whose registered office is situate at no. 33 Wing Lok Street Victoria in the said colony of Hong Kong and that the market value for the said ordinary shares of the said Fu Chip Investment Co Ltd shall be deemed as $2.50 for each of $1.00 share under an agreement for sale and purchase made between the parties thereto and dated February 27, 1973, we Lau Yiu Long ( ) of no. 152 Tin Hau Temple Road, Flat C1, Summit Court, 14th floor in the colony of Hong Kong merchant and Benjamin Lau Kam Ching ( ) of no. 31 Ming Yuen Street West, basement in the said colony of Hong Kong merchant the directors of the said Fu Chip Investment Co Ltd hereby agree and guarantee the closing market value for 2,520,000 shares (being 60 per cent. of the said 4,200,000 ordinary shares) of the said Fu Chip Investment Co Ltd shall be at $2.50 per share and that the total value of 2,520,000 shares shall be of the sum of HK$6,300,000 on the following marketing date immediately after April 30, 1974, and we further agree to indemnify and keep you indemnified against any damages, losses and other expenses which you may incur or sustain in the event of the closing market price for the shares of Fu Chip Investment Co Ltd according to the Far East Exchange Ltd, shall fall short of the sum of $2.50 during the said following marketing date immediately after April 30, 1974, provided always that if we were called upon to indemnify you for the discrepancy between the market value and the said total value of HK$6,300,000 we shall have the option of buying from you the said 2,520,000 shares of Fu Chip Investment Co Ltd at the price of HK$6,300,000 . . .' . . .

Mr Neill, counsel for the plaintiffs, . . . contends that the consideration stated in the agreement is not in reality a past one. It is to be noted that the consideration was not on May 4, 1973, a matter of history only. The instrument by its reference to the main agreement with Fu Chip incorporates as part of the stated consideration the plaintiffs' three promises to Fu Chip: to complete the sale of Shing On, to accept shares as the price for the sale, and not to sell 60 per cent. of the shares so accepted before April 30, 1974. Thus, on May 4, 1973, the performance of the main agreement still lay in the future. Performance of these promises was of great importance to the defendants, and it is undeniable that, as the instrument declares, the promises were made to Fu Chip at the request of the defendants. It is equally clear that the instrument also includes a promise by the plaintiffs to the defendants to fulfil their earlier promises given to Fu Chip.

The Board agrees . . . that the consideration expressly stated in the written guarantee is sufficient in law to support the defendants' promise of indemnity. An act done before the giving of a promise to make a payment or to confer some other benefit can sometimes be consideration for the promise. The act must have been done at the promisors' request: the parties must have understood that the act was to be remunerated either by a payment or the conferment of some other benefit: and payment, or the conferment of a benefit, must have been legally enforceable had it been promised in advance. All three features are present in this case. The promise given to Fu Chip under the main agreement not to sell the shares for a year was at the first defendant's request. The parties understood at the time of the main agreement that the restriction on selling must be compensated for by the benefit of a guarantee against a drop in price: and such a guarantee would be legally enforceable. The agreed cancellation of the subsidiary agreement left, as the parties knew, the plaintiffs unprotected in a respect in which at the time of the main agreement all were agreed they should be protected.

Mr Neill's submission is based on *Lampleigh* v. *Brathwait* (1615) Hobart 105. In that case the judges said, at p. 106:

> 'First . . . a meer voluntary courtesie will not have a consideration to uphold an assumpsit. But if that courtesie were moved by a suit or request of the party that gives the assumpsit, it will bind, for the promise, though it follows, yet it is not naked, but couples it self with the suit before, and the merits of the party procured by that suit. which is the difference.'

The modern statement of the law is in the judgment of Bowen LJ in *In re Casey's Patents* [1892] 1 Ch 104, 115–116; Bowen LJ said:

> 'Even if it were true, as some scientific students of law believe, that a past service cannot support a future promise, you must look at the document and see if the promise cannot receive a proper effect in some other way. Now, the fact of a past service raises an implication that at the time it was rendered it was to be paid for, and, if it was a service which was to be paid for, when you get in the subsequent document a promise to pay, that promise may be treated either as an admission which evidences or as a positive bargain which fixes the amount of that reasonable remuneration on the faith of which the service was originally rendered. So that here for past services there is ample justification for the promise to give the third share.'

Conferring a benefit is, of course, an equivalent to payment: see *Chitty on Contracts*, 24th ed. (1977), vol. 1, para. 154.

Mr. Leggatt, for the defendants, does not dispute the existence of the rule but challenges its application to the facts of this case. He submits that it is not a necessary inference or implication from the terms of the written guarantee that any benefit or protection was to be given to the plaintiffs for their acceptance of the restriction on selling their shares. Their Lordships agree that the mere existence or recital of a prior request is not sufficient in itself to convert what is prima facie past consideration into sufficient consideration in law to support a promise: as they have indicated, it is only the first of three necessary preconditions. As for the second of those preconditions, whether the act done at the request of the promisor raises an implication of promised remuneration or other return is simply one of the construction of the words of the contract in the circumstances of its making. Once it is recognised, as the Board considers it inevitably must be, that the expressed consideration includes a reference to the plaintiffs' promise not to sell the shares before April 30, 1974—a promise to be performed in the future, though given in the past—it is not possible to treat the defendants' promise of indemnity as independent of the plaintiffs' antecedent promise, given at the first defendant's request, not to sell. The promise of indemnity was given because at the time of the main agreement the parties intended that the first defendant should confer upon the plaintiffs the benefit of his protection against a fall in price. When the subsidiary agreement was cancelled, all were well aware that the plaintiffs were still to have the benefit of his protection as consideration for the restriction on selling. It matters not whether the indemnity thus given be regarded as the best evidence of the benefit intended to be conferred in return for the promise not to sell, or as the positive bargain which fixes the benefit on the faith of which the promise was given—though where, as here, the subject is a written contract, the better analysis is probably that of the 'positive bargain'. Their Lordships, therefore, accept the submission that the contract itself states a valid consideration for the promise of indemnity.

COMMENTARY

In this extract Lord Scarman identifies the three elements that must be satisfied by a claimant who wishes to invoke this exception to the past consideration rule. The claimant must show: (i) that he performed the original act at the request of the defendant, (ii) that it was clearly understood or implied between the parties when the act was requested that the claimant would be paid for doing the act, and (iii) the defendant's promise of payment must have been one which, had it been made prior to or at the time at which the claimant performed the act in question, it would have been enforceable. All three conditions were satisfied on the facts of this case.

Pao On is an important case for a number of other reasons and, indeed, we have already encountered the case on two occasions. First, the case illustrates the rule that a promise to perform, or the performance of, a pre-existing contractual obligation owed to a third party can be valid consideration (see p. 176 above). Thus Lord Scarman stated that 'the consideration for the promise of indemnity, while it included the cancellation of the subsidiary agreement, was primarily the promise given by [the plaintiffs] to [the defendants], to perform their contract with Fu Chip, which included the undertaking not to sell 60% of the shares allotted to them before 30 April 1974'. Fu Chip was a third party for the purposes of this rule notwithstanding the fact that the defendants were the major shareholders in Fu Chip (a company being in law a separate entity from its shareholders). Secondly, the case is notable for its rejection of the plaintiffs' submission that the consideration supplied by the defendants was illegal as being against public policy. The reasons given by Lord Scarman for rejecting this submission are set out in the judgment of Glidewell LJ in *Williams* v. *Roffey Bros* (p. 191 above). Thirdly (and a point that we have not yet encountered), the case is notable for its recognition of the fact that 'there is nothing contrary to principle in recognising economic duress as a factor which may render a contract voidable, provided always that the basis of such recognition is that it must amount to a coercion of the will, which vitiates consent'. However, on the facts of the case it was found that the plaintiffs could not establish that they had entered into the guarantee under duress.

(d) CONSIDERATION MUST MOVE FROM THE PROMISEE

Finally, consideration must move from the promisee and not from a third party; that is to say, the promisee rather than a third party must provide the consideration. The rule does not require that the consideration move to the promisor. It suffices that it moves from the promisee. Thus the rule is satisfied in the case where the promisee agrees to confer a benefit on a third party at the request of the promisor (see *Bolton* v. *Madden* (1873) LR 9 QB 55). This is the rule at common law but it must now be read in the light of the Contracts (Rights of Third Parties) Act 1999 which confers on third parties a limited right to enforce a term in a contract between two (or more) other parties provided that certain conditions have been satisfied (on which see Chapter

27). A third party who is given a right to enforce a term of the contract by the Act does not have to provide consideration in order to be able to enforce his right. The fact that the Act confers a right of action is sufficient to displace the requirement that he provide consideration.

(e) ESTABLISHING THE NECESSARY LINK

What link or connection must there be between the act alleged to constitute the consideration and the promise made by the other party? The link is generally provided by the terms of the promise itself. A simple example will illustrate the point. Suppose that A promises to pay £5 to B if he will take him to the train station. In such a case B's act of taking A to the station is the consideration for A's promise of payment. But suppose that A promises to pay B £5 but makes no mention of a lift to the station. B nevertheless provides A with a lift to the station. In such a case can B claim that he has provided consideration in giving A a lift to the station? Prima facie the answer is no. In order to constitute consideration the act must have been performed at the request, express or implied, of the promisor. Thus B would have to show that A, in making the promise of payment, expressly or impliedly requested B to give him a lift to the station: it would not be enough for B to show that it was reasonably foreseeable that he would give A a lift to the station as a result of the promise of payment. This point is an important one because it bears directly on the scope of the doctrine of consideration. A court that is willing to imply a request by A that B act in a particular way will generally find the existence of consideration and so will not have any need to resort to estoppel. But a finding that there is no sufficient link between the promise of A and the act of B will generally result in a finding that no consideration has been supplied and the court will then be asked to find the existence of an estoppel in order to give effect to A's promise. The following case illustrates these points:

Combe v. Combe

[1951] 2 KB 215, Court of Appeal

The plaintiff (the wife) and the defendant (the husband) were married in 1915 and separated in 1939. On 1 February 1943 a decree nisi of divorce was pronounced on the plaintiff's application. Later that month the defendant's solicitor wrote to the plaintiff's solicitor and stated that the defendant had agreed to allow the plaintiff £100 per annum free of tax. On 11 August 1943 the decree was made absolute. The defendant failed to make any of the promised payments. The plaintiff pressed for payment but made no application to the Divorce Court for maintenance. The plaintiff's annual income was between £700 and £800 per year, while the defendant's annual income was in the region of £650. In July 1950 the plaintiff brought an action against the defendant in which she claimed arrears of £675. Byrne J held that the plaintiff was not entitled to recover the first three instalments of £25 (on the ground that the limitation period had expired and the claim in respect of them was time-barred) but he held that the plaintiff was entitled to recover the remaining £600 from the defendant. He held that, while the plaintiff had not provided any consideration for the defendant's promise of payment, she was entitled to succeed in her claim on the ground that it fell within the scope of the principle laid down by Denning J in *Central London Property Trust Ltd* v. *High Trees House Ltd* [1947] KB 130 [p. 239 below] and *Robertson* v. *Minister of Pensions* [1949] 1 KB 227. The defendant appealed to the Court of Appeal. The Court of Appeal affirmed the decision of Byrne J in so far as he held that the plaintiff had not provided any consideration for the defendant's promise but allowed the appeal on the ground that the *High Trees* principle could not be used so as to confer a cause of action on the plaintiff.

Denning LJ [after stating the facts continued]
Much as I am inclined to favour the principle stated in the *High Trees* case [1947] KB 130, it is important that it should not be stretched too far, lest it should be endangered. That principle does not create new causes of action where none existed before. It only prevents a party from insisting upon his strict legal rights, when it would be unjust to allow him to enforce them, having regard to the dealings which have taken place between the parties. That is the way it was put in *Hughes* v. *Metropolitan Railway* (1877) 2 App Cas 439, 448, the case in the House of Lords in which the principle was first stated, and in *Birmingham, etc., Land Company* v. *London and North-Western Railway Co* (1888) 40 Ch D 268, 286, the case in the Court of Appeal where the principle was enlarged. It is also implicit in all the modern cases in which the principle has been developed. Sometimes it is a plaintiff who is not allowed to insist on his strict legal rights. Thus, a creditor is not allowed to enforce a debt which he has deliberately agreed to waive, if the debtor has carried on business or in some other way changed his position in reliance on the waiver. . . . On other occasions it is a defendant who is not allowed to insist on his strict legal rights. His conduct may be such as to debar him from relying on some condition, denying some allegation, or taking some other point in answer to the claim. Thus a government department, which had accepted a disease as due to war service, were not allowed afterwards to say it was not, seeing that the soldier, in reliance on the assurance, had abstained from getting further evidence about it: *Robertson* v. *Minister of Pensions* [1949] 1 KB 227. . . . In none of these cases was the defendant sued on the promise, assurance, or assertion as a cause of action in itself: he was sued for some other cause, for example, a pension or a breach of contract, and the promise, assurance or assertion only played a supplementary role—an important role, no doubt, but still a supplementary role. That is, I think, its true function. It may be part of a cause of action, but not a cause of action in itself.

The principle, as I understand it, is that, where one party has, by his words or conduct, made to the other a promise or assurance which was intended to affect the legal relations between them and to be acted on accordingly, then, once the other party has taken him at his word and acted on it, the one who gave the promise or assurance cannot afterwards be allowed to revert to the previous legal relations as if no such promise or assurance had been made by him, but he must accept their legal relations subject to the qualification which he himself has so introduced, even though it is not supported in point of law by any consideration but only by his word.

Seeing that the principle never stands alone as giving a cause of action in itself, it can never do away with the necessity of consideration when that is an essential part of the cause of action. The doctrine of consideration is too firmly fixed to be overthrown by a side-wind. Its ill-effects have been largely mitigated of late, but it still remains a cardinal necessity of the formation of a contract, though not of its modification or discharge. I fear that it was my failure to make this clear which misled Byrne J, in the present case. He held that the wife could sue on the husband's promise as a separate and independent cause of action by itself, although, as he held, there was no consideration for it. That is not correct. The wife can only enforce it if there was consideration for it. That is, therefore, the real question in the case: was there sufficient consideration to support the promise?

If it were suggested that, in return for the husband's promise, the wife expressly or impliedly promised to forbear from applying to the court for maintenance—that is, a promise in return for a promise—there would clearly be no consideration, because the wife's promise was not binding on her and was therefore worth nothing. Notwithstanding her promise, she could always apply to the Divorce Court for maintenance—maybe only with leave—and no agreement by her could take away that right: *Hyman* v. *Hyman* [1929] AC 601, as interpreted by this court in *Gaisberg* v. *Storr* [1950] 1 KB 107.

There was, however, clearly no promise by the wife, express or implied, to forbear from applying to the court. All that happened was that she did in fact forbear—that is, she did an act in return for a promise. Is that sufficient consideration? Unilateral promises of this kind have long been enforced, so long as the act or forbearance is done on the faith of the promise and at the request of the promisor, express or implied. The act done is then in itself sufficient consideration for the promise, even though it arises ex post facto. . . . If the findings of Byrne J, were accepted, they would be sufficient to bring this principle into play. His finding that the husband's promise was intended to be binding, intended to be acted upon, and was, in fact, acted on—although expressed to be a finding on the *High Trees* principle—is equivalent to a finding that there was consideration within this long settled rule, because it comes to the same thing expressed in different words. . . . But my difficulty is to accept the finding of Byrne J, that the promise was 'intended to be acted upon'. I cannot find any evidence of any intention by the husband that the wife should forbear from applying to the court for maintenance, or, in other words, any request by the husband, express or implied, that the wife should so forbear. He left her to apply if she wished to do so. She did not do so, and I am not surprised, because it is very unlikely that the Divorce Court would have then made any order in her favour, seeing that she had a bigger income than her husband. Her forbearance was not intended by him, nor was it done at his request. It was therefore no consideration.

It may be that the wife has suffered some detriment because, after forbearing to apply to the court for seven years, she might not now be given leave to apply. . . . The court is, however, nowadays much more ready to give leave than it used to be . . ., and I should have thought that, if she fell on hard times, she would still obtain leave. Assuming, however, that she has suffered some detriment by her forbearance, nevertheless, as the forbearance was not at the husband's request, it is no consideration. . . . The doctrine of consideration is sometimes said to work injustice, but I see none in this case. . . . I do not think it would be right for this wife, who is better off than her husband, to take no action for six or seven years and then come down on him for the whole £600.

The truth is that in these maintenance cases the real remedy of the wife is, not by action in the King's Bench Division, but by application in the Divorce Court. I have always understood that no agreement for maintenance, which is made in the course of divorce proceedings prior to decree absolute, is valid unless it is sanctioned by the court. . . . I know that such agreements are often made, but their only valid purpose is to serve as a basis for a consent application to the court. The reason why such agreements are invalid, unless approved, is because they are so apt to be collusive. Some wives are tempted to stipulate for extortionate maintenance as the price of giving the husband his freedom. It is to remove this temptation that the sanction of the court is required. It would be a great pity if this salutary requirement could be evaded by taking action in the King's Bench Division. The Divorce Court can order the husband to pay whatever maintenance is just. Moreover, if justice so requires, it can make the order retrospective to decree absolute. That is the proper remedy of the wife here, and I do not think she has a right to any other.

Asquith LJ

The judge has decided that, while the husband's promise was unsupported by any valid consideration, yet the principle in *Central London Property Trust Ltd* v. *High Trees House Ltd* [1947] KB 130 entitles the wife to succeed. It is unnecessary to express any view as to the correctness of that decision, though I certainly must not be taken to be questioning it; and I would remark, in passing, that it seems to me a complete misconception to suppose that it struck at the roots of the doctrine of consideration. But assuming, without deciding, that it is good law, I do not think, however, that it helps the plaintiff at all. What that case decides is that when a promise is given which (1.) is intended to create legal relations, (2.) is intended to be acted upon by the promisee, and (3.) is in fact so acted upon, the promisor cannot bring an action against the promisee which involves the repudiation of his promise or is inconsistent with it. It does not, as I read it, decide that a promisee can sue on the promise. On the contrary, Denning, J, expressly stated the contrary. Neither in the *High Trees* case nor in *Minister of Pensions* v. *Robertson* [1949] 1 KB 227 (another decision of my Lord which is relied upon by the plaintiff) was an action brought by the promisee on the promise. In the first of those two cases the plaintiff was in effect the promisor or a person standing in the shoes of the promisor, while in the second the claim, though brought by the promisee, was brought upon a cause of action which was not the promise, but was an alleged statutory right . . .

Finally, I do not think an actual forbearance, as opposed to an agreement to forbear to approach the court, is a good consideration unless it proceeds from a request, express or implied, on the part of the promisor. If not moved by such a request, the forbearance is not in respect of the promise.

Birkett LJ delivered a concurring judgment.

COMMENTARY

There are two central aspects to this decision. The first relates to the finding that the plaintiff did not provide any consideration for the defendant's promise of payment and the second relates to the scope of the principle laid down in *High Trees* (see p. 239 below). We shall explore the second issue in greater detail when we examine *High Trees* in the section on estoppel. Here our focus is confined to the first issue.

Why did the Court of Appeal not conclude that the plaintiff had provided consideration for the defendant's promise? Could the court not have found that the defendant impliedly requested the plaintiff to refrain from applying for maintenance? Professor Goodhart (1951) 67 *LQR* 456, 458 made the following comments in relation to the facts of *Combe*:

To suggest that this might be an offer of a generous gift on the part of a guilty but repentant husband would be to place a considerable burden on one's credulity. It cannot be believed that the husband was promising to pay the wife £100 per year even though she should make an application to the court for maintenance. In *Alliance Bank* v. *Broom* (1864) 2 Dr & Sim 289 the court said that 'although there was no promise on the part of the plaintiff to abstain for any certain time from suing for the debt, the effect was that the plaintiff did, in fact, give, and the defendant receive, the benefit of some degree of forbearance'. It is not unreasonable to suggest that in the present case the husband was offering to pay £100 per year in return for the wife's forbearance.

While it may not be unreasonable to suggest that the husband was offering to pay £100 per year in return for the wife's forbearance, this was not the construction adopted by the Court of Appeal on the facts. It has to be remembered that *Combe* is, essentially, a family law case and it was heavily influenced by the procedure then applicable to divorce proceedings. Thus, writing extra-judicially, Lord Denning stated ('Recent Developments in the Doctrine of Consideration' (1952) 15 *MLR* 1, 2) that the defendant's statement that he would pay £100 per annum to his wife:

did not mean that she should forbear from applying for maintenance. It is well known that agreements of that kind are made as a preliminary to an application for maintenance. They form the basis for a consent order to be approved by the court. The agreement, therefore, so far from being an implied request to forbear from applying to the court, was almost an invitation to her to apply to the court. Her forbearance was therefore no consideration.

An alternative explanation for the court's refusal to imply a request has been provided by Professor Atiyah in the following terms ('Consideration: A Restatement' in Atiyah, *Essays on Contract*, Oxford University Press, 1986, pp. 179, 231). He argues that the court could have implied a request 'without doing the least violence to the facts' but that it did not so because the justice of the case did not require it. The justice of the case did not support the plaintiff for two reasons. The first was that her income was greater than her husband's and the second was that she was attempting to recover a lump sum of £600 from the defendant and not seeking to enforce his promise to pay £100 per annum.

However Professor Goodhart's citation of *Alliance Bank* v. *Broom* demonstrates that cases can be found in which the courts have been prepared to imply a request. In *Alliance Bank* the defendant, who was heavily indebted to the plaintiff bank, promised to provide the bank with security to cover his indebtedness. He failed to provide the promised security and, when sued by the bank, submitted that his promise to provide security was not supported by consideration. It was held that the bank had in fact provided consideration in that it had refrained from taking proceedings against the defendant in relation to his indebtedness. This forbearance was held to be at the implied request of the defendant. The willingness of a court to imply a request will very much depend upon the facts and circumstances of the individual case. The bank in *Alliance Bank* was, in all probability, much more likely to institute proceedings than the wife in *Combe* and, this being the case, the court doubtless found it easier to imply that the defendant had requested the bank not to sue him on the debt provided that he gave the bank security. The readier the court is to find the existence of such a request, the wider will be the doctrine of consideration and, in consequence, the less need there will be to invoke estoppel.

4. ESTOPPEL: ITS SCOPE

We have encountered estoppel at various points in this chapter (in the judgments in *Williams* v. *Roffey Bros & Nicholls (Contractors) Ltd* [1991] 1 QB 1, *D & C Builders* v. *Rees* [1966] 2 QB 617, and *Combe* v. *Combe* [1951] 2 KB 215) but have not as yet sought to define it or to ascertain its scope. Estoppels come in different shapes and sizes. One commentator has identified twelve different types of estoppel (A Leopold, 'Estoppel: A Practical Appraisal of Recent Developments' (1991) 7 *Aust Bar Rev* 47). Our concern in this chapter is not to survey the whole range of estoppels but rather to examine the role which estoppel plays, or can play, in giving legal effect to a promise that is unsupported by consideration. Take *Combe* v. *Combe* as an example. The wife's claim that she had provided consideration for her husband's promise to pay her £100 per year failed. But she had a second string to her bow. She argued that her husband was estopped, or prevented, from going back upon his promise to pay her £100 per year. As it happened, her estoppel claim failed (as indeed did the estoppel claim in *D & C Builders* v. *Rees*) but the case nevertheless illustrates the way in which estoppel is invoked by litigants who are unable to establish that the promise upon which they base their claim, or defence, is supported by consideration. Two cases feature prominently in the development of the doctrine of estoppel. These cases are *Hughes* v. *Metropolitan Railway Company* (1877) 2 App Cas 439 and *Central London Property Trust Ltd* v. *High Trees House Ltd* [1947] 1 KB 130, both of which are cited in *D & C Builders* and in *Combe*. Given their significance in the development of the law we shall examine them in more detail after first giving a brief definition of the meaning of the word estoppel.

(a) ESTOPPEL: A BRIEF DEFINITION

Estoppel is not a word that is used in everyday conversation. What does it mean? A dictionary definition states that it means an obstruction and the example given is of an obstruction of a waterway. In legal terms an estoppel has been described as an impediment or bar to a right of action arising from a man's own act as, for example, where a man is forbidden by law to speak against his own deed. A fuller definition of estoppel has been provided in the following terms:

E Cooke, *The Modern Law of Estoppel*

(Oxford University Press, 2000), pp. 1–2

Estoppel is a mechanism for enforcing consistency; when I have said or done something that leads you to believe in a particular state of affairs, I may be obliged to stand by what I have said or done, even though I am not contractually bound to do so.

It is perhaps easiest to begin with examples. If your bank pays money into your account by mistake, it may be estopped from telling you later that it is not yours and demanding repayment—but only if it has assured you that the money is yours, and you have relied on that by spending the money. The parties to a commercial deal might agree: 'we'll treat clause 2 as meaning such-and-such'; if they go ahead with the deal on that basis, they have to abide by that agreement if the construction of the document is disputed later. A landlord might reassure his tenant: 'I will not insist that you pay for the roof repairs, even though your lease obliges you to do so'; he may then be estopped from going back on that promise and demanding payment. The idea running through these examples is of making the person concerned work on the basis that what he has said is true, even if it is not.

Estoppel has been described as 'a simple and wholly untechnical conception, perhaps the most powerful and flexible instrument to be found in any system of court juris-prudence'. It is not easy to frame a definition of estoppel, in the sense of a neat formula that will tell us whether or not a given set of facts is an instance of estoppel. Lord Denning's description of the doctrine is both informative and brief:

> 'Estoppel . . . is a principle of justice and of equity. It comes to this: when a man, by his words or conduct, has led another to believe in a particular state of affairs, he will not be allowed to go back on it when it would be unjust or inequitable for him to do so.'

A number of features should be noted about this passage. The first is that, as a definition, it is lacking in precision. It makes use of broad standards such as 'justice' and 'equity'. Its emphasis on flexibility echoes a recurrent theme in legal writing, both judicial and academic, on estoppel. Not everyone approves of this flexibility. Professor Birks launched an attack on it in the following terms ('Equity in the Modern Law: An Exercise in Taxonomy' (1996) 26 *University of Western Australia Law Review* 1, 21–22):

'Estoppel' is by origin a common law word. But ever since, in imitation of American law, the *High Trees* case set equity on the path of supplementing the doctrine of consideration by extending the common law notion of estoppel, 'equitable estoppel' has been more prominent in the books than its common law original. The law is at its worst when it refuses to name things in a straight-forward way. It is impossible to understand or place something that is obscurely named. For example, the reason why the tort in *Rylands v. Fletcher* is so puzzling is that it is called just that, *Rylands v. Fletcher*. 'Subrogation' plays the same vanishing trick. Never used in the world and never paraphrased by lawyers, it hides its subject-matter in a cloud of unknowing, tinged with fear. 'Estoppel' is much the same. Out in the shops and restaurants of the city, the word is never heard. Generations of law students have somehow let their teachers escape without making them say how exactly the word works and what exactly it denotes. From the taxonomist's point of view, the consequence is that this entity is difficult to place. A huge case law has developed, and all the time we have never, in a sense, known what we were talking about.

The word 'stop' in the middle gives a clue. The French original means 'bung' or 'stopper'. It was when it came to bottling wines that estoppels had their natural home. The law makes liberal use of the metaphor of binding and being bound. It is in 'obligation' and in 'liable', more obviously in 'bond'. 'Estoppel' is another version of the same metaphor. As a wine bottle is corked, so one is restricted or shut up. In short, one is bound. The phrase 'in pais' is often added. This is evidently thought to give extra dignity. 'In pais' means 'in the country'. In English law the jury was 'the country', and trial by jury was trial 'by the country'. It may be that the phrase 'in pais' originally meant 'before the jury' and referred to the evidential effect of estoppel. However that may be, we see that estoppel names something obliquely, telling us that something binds. The thing or things we need to classify is named by a consequence, the consequence being that, at least for some purposes, one is bound. In most estoppels the thing in question is an undertaking, and in equitable estoppel, it is an undertaking as to the future or, in short, a promise. Demystifying the word does not take us very far, but, subject to more refined argument, it does allow the taxonomist committed to a classification of causative events to see what event he has to classify.

Secondly, three different types of estoppel are referred to in the passage from Cooke. The bank payment illustration is an example of estoppel by representation, the contract interpretation hypothetical is an example of estoppel by convention and the illustration involving the landlord is an example of equitable or promissory estoppel. As we shall see, one of the most contested issues in this area of law is whether or not these different estoppels can be unified into one coherent doctrine. The third point is that the definition does not identify the cause of action that is at the root of an estoppel claim. It tells us that estoppel is a 'mechanism for enforcing consistency' and the reference to the fact that the party is 'not contractually bound' to stand by what he said or did suggests that it is not part of the law of contract. But if it is not part of the law of contract, how do we classify the claim? Is it part of the law of wrongs, the law of unjust enrichment or is it some type of claim that cannot be classified as a matter of law? We shall return to these and other questions after examining two of the leading estoppel cases.

(b) TWO LEADING CASES

The most commonly cited case in the development of estoppel in the twentieth century is the decision of Mr Justice Denning, as he then was, in *Central London Property Trust Ltd* v. *High Trees House Ltd* [1947] 1 KB 130. In his judgment Mr Justice Denning purported to find the foundation for his approach in the judgment of the House of Lords in *Hughes* v. *Metropolitan Railway Company* (1877) 2 App Cas 439. *Hughes* was decided some seventy years before *High Trees* but it had fallen into obscurity prior to its 'rescue' in *High Trees* (see *WJ Alan & Co Ltd* v. *El Nasr Export & Import Co* [1972] 2 QB 189, 212). Given its influence in the development of the law, it is important to start with *Hughes* before turning to *High Trees*.

Hughes v. Metropolitan Railway Company

(1877) 2 App Cas 439, House of Lords

The defendant company (the respondents) was the lessee of property owned by the plaintiff (the appellant). On 22 October 1874 the plaintiff, acting pursuant to its entitlement under the lease, served notice upon the defendants to repair the property within six months. The lease was forfeitable by the plaintiff if the defendants failed to comply with the notice. The defendants replied that the repairs would be carried out but also suggested that the plaintiff might wish to buy the defendants' interest in the property and they therefore proposed to defer carrying out the repairs until they heard from the plaintiff in relation to their offer to dispose of their interest in the property. In November 1874 the plaintiff entered into negotiations with the defendants for the surrender of the lease but made no response to the defendants' statement that they intended to defer carrying out the repairs. The negotiations between the parties broke down on 31 December 1874. There were no further communications between the parties until 19 April 1875 when the defendants wrote to the plaintiff and stated that, in the light of the breakdown in negotiations, 'the company would take in hand the repairs'. The notice issued by the plaintiff expired on 22 April 1875 and on 28 April the plaintiff served a writ of ejectment on the defendants. The defendants completed the repairs in June 1875. The House of Lords held that the defendants were entitled to be relieved against the forfeiture of the lease. The plaintiff's notice to repair the property was in suspension for the duration of the negotiations between the parties and did not revive until 31 December 1874. The repairs were carried out by the defendants within six months of that date and they were entitled to relief against forfeiture.

Lord Cairns, LC

It was not argued at your Lordships' Bar, and it could not be argued, that there was any right of a Court of Equity, or any practice of a Court of Equity, to give relief in cases of this kind, by way of mercy, or by way merely of saving property from forfeiture, but it is the first principle upon which all Courts of Equity proceed, that if parties who have entered into definite and distinct terms involving certain legal results—certain penalties or legal forfeiture—afterwards by their own act or with their own consent enter upon a course of negotiation which has the effect of leading one of the parties to suppose that the strict rights arising under the contract will not be enforced, or will be kept in suspense, or held in abeyance, the person who otherwise might have enforced those rights will not be allowed to enforce them where it would be inequitable having regard to the dealings which have thus taken place between the parties. My Lords, I repeat that I attribute to the Appellant no intention here to take advantage of, to lay a trap for, or to lull into false security those with whom he was dealing; but it appears to me that both parties by entering upon the negotiation which they entered upon, made it an inequitable thing that the exact period of six months dating from the month of October should afterwards be measured out as against the Respondents as the period during which the repairs must be executed.

Lords O'Hagan, Selborne, Blackburn, and **Gordon** delivered concurring judgments.

Central London Property Trust Ltd v. High Trees House Ltd

[1947] 1 KB 130, King's Bench Division

In 1937, the plaintiff company granted a ninety-nine-year lease over a block of flats in London to the defendant company, a subsidiary of the plaintiff, at an annual rent of £2,500. Many people left London on the outbreak of the Second World War and, as a consequence, the defendant was unable to let all the flats. Discussions took place between the directors of the two companies and they resulted in an agreement, made in January 1940, by which the plaintiff agreed to reduce the rent 'as from the commencement of the lease to £1,250 per annum'. In March 1941 a receiver was appointed to the plaintiff company. The defendant paid the reduced rent from 1941 until the beginning of 1945 by which time the flats were fully occupied. In September 1945 the receiver of the plaintiff company wrote to the defendant and informed it that £2,500 was the agreed annual rent and he claimed arrears of £7,916. The receiver then instituted 'friendly proceedings' to test the legal position as between the two companies. The plaintiff claimed £625, being the difference between £2,500 and £1,250 for the last two quarters of 1945. The defendant denied that it was liable to pay the sums claimed. Denning J held that the plaintiff was entitled to recover £625.

Denning J [stated the facts and continued]

If I were to consider this matter without regard to recent developments in the law, there is no doubt that had the plaintiffs claimed it, they would have been entitled to recover ground rent at the rate of 2,500*l.* a year from the beginning of the term, since the lease under which it was payable was a lease under seal which, according to the old common law, could not be varied by an agreement by parol (whether in writing or not), but only by deed. Equity, however stepped in, and said that if there has been a variation of a deed by a simple contract (which in the case of a lease required to be in writing would have to be evidenced by writing), the courts may give effect to it as is shown in *Berry* v. *Berry* [1929] 2 KB 316. That equitable doctrine, however, could hardly apply in the present case because the variation here might be said to have been made without consideration. With regard to estoppel, the representation made in relation to reducing the rent, was not a representation of an existing fact. It was a representation, in effect, as to the future, namely, that payment of the rent would not be enforced at the full rate but only at the reduced rate. Such a representation would not give rise to an estoppel, because, as was said in *Jorden* v. *Money* (1854) 5 HLC 185, a representation as to the future must be embodied as a contract or be nothing.

But what is the position in view of developments in the law in recent years? The law has not been standing still since *Jorden* v. *Money*. There has been a series of decisions over the last fifty years which, although they are said to be cases of estoppel are not really such. They are cases in which a promise was made which was intended to create legal relations and which, to the knowledge of the person making the promise, was going to be acted on by the person to whom it was made and which was in fact so acted on. In such cases the courts have said that the promise must be honoured. The cases to which I particularly desire to refer are: *Fenner* v. *Blake* [1900] 1 QB 426, *In re Wickham* (1917) 34 TLR 158, *Re William Porter & Co, Ld* [1937] 2 All ER 361 and *Buttery* v. *Pickard* [1946] WN 25. As I have said they are not cases of estoppel in the strict sense. They are really promises— promises intended to be binding, intended to be acted on, and in fact acted on. *Jorden* v. *Money* (1854) 5 HLC 185 can be distinguished, because there the promisor made it clear that she did not intend to be legally bound, whereas in the cases to which I refer the proper inference was that the promisor did intend to be bound. In each case the court held the promise to be binding on the party making it, even though under the old common law it might be difficult to find any consideration for it. The courts have not gone so far as to give a cause of action in damages for the breach of such a promise, but they have refused to allow the party making it to act inconsistently with it. It is in that sense, and that sense only, that such a promise gives rise to an estoppel. The decisions are a natural result of the fusion of law and equity: for the cases of *Hughes* v. *Metropolitan Ry Co* (1877) 2 App Cas 439, 448, *Birmingham and District Land Co* v. *London & North Western Ry Co* (1888) 40 Ch D 268, 286 and *Salisbury (Marquess)* v. *Gilmore* [1942] 2 KB 38, 51, afford a sufficient basis for saying that a party would not be allowed in equity to go back on such a promise. In my opinion, the time has now come for the validity of such a promise to be recognized. The logical consequence, no doubt is that a promise to accept a smaller sum in discharge of a larger sum, if acted upon, is binding notwithstanding the absence of consideration: and if the fusion of law and equity leads to this result, so much the better. That aspect was not considered in *Foakes* v. *Beer* (1884) 9 App Cas 605. At this time of day however, when law and equity have been joined together for over seventy years, principles must be reconsidered in the light of their combined effect. It is to be noticed that in the Sixth Interim Report of the Law Revision Committee, pars. 35, 40, it is recommended that such a promise as that to which I have referred, should be enforceable in law even though no consideration for it has been given by the promisee. It seems to me that, to the extent I have mentioned that result has now been achieved by the decisions of the courts.

I am satisfied that a promise such as that to which I have referred is binding and the only question remaining for my consideration is the scope of the promise in the present case. I am satisfied on all the evidence that the promise here was that the ground rent should be reduced to 1,250l. a year as a temporary expedient while the block of flats was not fully, or substantially fully let, owing to the conditions prevailing. That means that the reduction in the rent applied throughout the years down to the end of 1944, but early in 1945 it is plain that the flats were fully let, and, indeed the rents received from them (many of them not being affected by the Rent Restrictions Acts), were increased beyond the figure at which it was originally contemplated that they would be let. At all events the rent from them must have been very considerable. I find that the conditions prevailing at the time when the reduction in rent was made, had completely passed away by the early months of 1945. I am satisfied that the promise was understood by all parties only to apply under the conditions prevailing at the time when it was made, namely, when the flats were only partially let, and that it did not extend any further than that. When the flats became fully let, early in 1945, the reduction ceased to apply.

In those circumstances, under the law as I hold it, it seems to me that rent is payable at the full rate for the quarters ending September 29 and December 25, 1945.

If the case had been one of estoppel, it might be said that in any event the estoppel would cease when the conditions to which the representation applied came to an end, or it also might be said that it would only come to an end on notice. In either case it is only a way of ascertaining what is the scope of the representation. I prefer to apply the principle that a promise intended to be binding, intended to be acted on and in fact acted on, is binding so far as its terms properly apply. Here it was binding as covering the period down to the early part of 1945, and as from that time full rent is payable.

I therefore give judgment for the plaintiff company for the amount claimed.

COMMENTARY

Professor Treitel has stated (*Some Landmarks of Twentieth Century Contract Law* (Oxford University Press, 2002), p. 29) that 'the *High Trees* case is surely one of the most prominent of the landmarks in twentieth century contract law'. He notes that its exalted status is, in many ways, remarkable given that it was apparently argued and decided in one day. The judgment of Denning J was therefore, in all probability, an unreserved judgment. As Professor Treitel has remarked, 'if there was any time for reflection, it could at most have been the luncheon recess'. The facts of the case are rather unusual in that the litigation was conducted between members of the same corporate group and it is not altogether clear why the claim was brought in the first place. The claim may not in fact have been a 'friendly' one but a keenly fought contest between the defendant and the creditors of the plaintiff company.

High Trees is a notable decision for a number of reasons. First it would appear from the first paragraph of the judgment that *High Trees* might not be an estoppel case at all. In this part of his judgment Denning J is attempting to get round the decision of the House of Lords in *Jorden* v. *Money* (1854) 5 HLC 185 in which it was held that an estoppel must relate to a statement of fact and that it could not apply to a case where, in the words of Lord Cranworth LC (at pp. 214–215), 'the representation is not a representation of fact, but a statement of something which the party intends or does not intend to do'. The statement in issue in *High Trees* was clearly a statement of intent, or a promise, and so was vulnerable to the argument that effect could not be given to it consistently with *Jorden* v. *Money*. Denning J attempts to deal with this difficulty in the second paragraph of his judgment where he draws on cases in equity, including *Hughes* v. *Metropolitan Railway*, which he states are 'not cases of estoppel in the strict sense'. Rather, he states that they are cases of 'promises intended to be binding, intended to be acted on, and in fact acted on' and he then distinguishes *Jorden* on the rather dubious ground that the promisor there did not intend to be legally bound by the promise made.

Secondly, it is important to note that the reasoning of Denning J in this second paragraph brings him into an apparent conflict with *Foakes* v. *Beer* in that he recognizes that the 'logical consequence' of the principle that he articulates is that 'a promise to accept a smaller sum in discharge of a larger sum, if acted upon, is binding notwithstanding the absence of consideration'. He then adds the rather curious sentence that this aspect 'was not considered in *Foakes* v. *Beer*'. Professor Treitel points out (*Some Landmarks of Twentieth Century Contract Law* (Oxford University Press, 2002), p. 32) that this sentence is only to be found in the official report of the case; it is not to be found in the other four reports of the case. It is therefore possible that it was inserted as an afterthought by Denning J when the draft judgment was submitted by the editor of the Law Reports for his approval. But what is to be made of his suggestion that the House of Lords in *Foakes* did not consider this aspect of the case? Professor Treitel responds to this suggestion in the following way (*Some Landmarks of Twentieth Century Contract Law* (Oxford University Press, 2002), p. 32)

it is hard to suppose that the House of Lords in *Foakes* v. *Beer* can have been unaware of *Hughes* v. *Metropolitan Railway* which had been decided only seven years previously, particularly as two members of the House of Lords who had decided the *Hughes* case [Lords Selborne and Blackburn] also heard the appeal in *Foakes* v. *Beer*. The most plausible explanation of the fact that 'That aspect was not considered in *Foakes* v. *Beer*' seems to be that it was not thought to be relevant since *Foakes* v. *Beer* was concerned with the argument that legal rights had been *permanently* extinguished while the *Hughes* principle was concerned with their temporary suspension.

It can be argued that the principles that underpin *Hughes* and *Foakes* are very different in nature. Professor Smith (*A Casebook on Contract* (11th edn, Sweet & Maxwell, 2000), p. 256) sets out the principle that was applied in *Hughes* in the following terms:

if A tells B (by words or conduct) that B need not perform a contractual (or other) obligation owed by B to A and B takes A at his word and does not perform that obligation, A cannot treat that non-performance as a breach of contract entitling him to damages or to terminate the contract. It would be entirely wrong that A should be allowed to treat as a legal wrong that to which he has consented.

On the other hand, he formulates the principle in *Foakes* as follows:

If A tells B that B need not perform a contractual (or other) obligation owed by B to A, A can change his mind and require B to perform that obligation in so far as it is still possible to do so. A is not alleging that B has broken his contract—he is simply saying 'Now you must perform—and if you fail to do so, *that* will be a breach of contract'.

The third point to note is that the result of the case was that the plaintiff was entitled to demand the full rent of £2,500 from the time at which the flats became fully let in early 1945. In this sense the effect of the estoppel (albeit that it may not have been an estoppel in the strict sense) was not to deprive the plaintiff of its right to demand the full rent. Rather the right was in suspension for the war-time period when the flats were only partially let. But it is important to note that there is a sense in which the estoppel had extinctive effect. Denning J was careful to state that 'the reduction in rent applied throughout the years down to the end of 1944' and it would therefore seem to follow that, had the plaintiff demanded that the defendants pay the rent in full for the duration of the war years, the claim would have failed. As a result of its promise the plaintiff's right to demand the full rent from 1940 to 1945 was not in suspension. It was lost.

(c) THE INGREDIENTS OF PROMISSORY ESTOPPEL

Notwithstanding the statement of Denning J that *High Trees* is not a case of estoppel in the 'strict sense' it has subsequently been regarded as a landmark case in the development of what has come to be known as 'equitable' or 'promissory' estoppel (see, for example, J Beatson, *Anson's Law of Contract* (28th edn, Oxford University Press, 2002), p 117.) The transition to the language of promissory estoppel can be seen in the following passage from the judgment of Lord Hodson in *Ajayi* v. *R T Briscoe (Nigeria) Ltd* [1964] 1 WLR 1326, 1330:

The principle, which has been described as quasi estoppel and perhaps more aptly as promissory estoppel, is that when one party to a contract in the absence of fresh consideration agrees not to enforce his rights, an equity will be raised in favour of the other party. This equity is, however, subject to the qualifications (i) that the other party has altered his position, (ii) that the promisor can resile from his promise on giving reasonable notice, which need not be formal notice, giving the promisee a reasonable opportunity of resuming his position, (iii) the promise only becomes final and irrevocable if the promisee cannot resume his position.

As a definition of the scope of estoppel this statement cannot be said to be exhaustive. It does not identify all the ingredients of promissory estoppel. In particular, it does not include the requirement that the promise must be 'clear and unequivocal' nor does it provide any clear definition of the remedy available (other than the broad reference to an 'equity'). A fuller account of the elements of promissory estoppel can be provided as follows:

(I) CLEAR AND UNEQUIVOCAL PROMISE

The promise that gives rise to the estoppel must be a clear and unequivocal promise. The promise must have been one that was intended to affect the legal relations between the parties and that clearly demonstrated that the promisor was giving up his strict legal rights (or some of them) against the promisee. In *Woodhouse AC Israel Cocoa SA* v. *Nigerian Produce Marketing Co Ltd* [1972] AC 741, 757 Lord Hailsham of St Marylebone LC stated:

Counsel for the appellants was asked whether he knew of any case in which an ambiguous statement had ever formed the basis of a purely promissory estoppel. . . . He candidly replied that he did not. I do not find this surprising, since it would really be an astonishing thing if, in the case of a genuine misunderstanding as to the meaning of an offer, the offeree could obtain by means of the doctrine of promissory estoppel something that he must fail to obtain under the conventional law of contract.

Notwithstanding its absence from Lord Hodson's description in *Ajayi*, this element is a necessary one for the protection of promisors. Promisors should not be required to insist upon their legal rights in order to protect them and the law does not demand that they do so. Rather the law provides that they will only lose their contractual rights when they clearly and unequivocally promise that they will give them up (either in whole or in part).

(II) THE PROMISEE HAS ALTERED HIS POSITION

The promisor must have altered his position in reliance upon the promise that has been made. In many cases the promisee will alter his position to his detriment. This was the case in *Hughes* v. *Metropolitan Railway* (above) where, as a result of the negotiations with the landlord, the tenants lost the time they otherwise would have had to carry out the repairs. But detrimental reliance is not apparent in all cases. For example, there was no obvious detriment to the tenants in *High Trees* (above) because they were only being asked to pay the rent that they had contracted to pay. Thus it would appear from *High Trees* that the promisee need not have acted to his detriment provided that he has altered his position to the extent that it would be inequitable to allow the promisor to go back on the promise made. In *Societe Italo-Belge pour le Commerce et l'Industrie* v. *Palm and Vegetable Oils (Malaysia) Sdn Bhd (The Post Chaser)* [1982] 1 All ER 19, 26–27 Robert Goff J stated:

I approach the matter as follows. The fundamental principle is that stated by Lord Cairns [in *Hughes* v. *Metropolitan Railway*], viz. that the representor will not be allowed to enforce his rights 'where it would be inequitable having regard to the dealings which have thus taken place between the parties'. To establish such inequity, it is not necessary to show detriment; indeed, the representee may have benefited from the representation, and yet it may be inequitable, at least without reasonable notice, for the representor to enforce his legal rights. Take the facts of *Central London Property Trust Ltd* v. *High Trees House Ltd* [1947] 1 KB 130, the case in which Denning J breathed new life into the doctrine of equitable estoppel. The representation was by a lessor to the effect that he would be content to accept a reduced rent. In such a case, although the lessee has benefited from the reduction in rent, it may well be inequitable for the lessor to insist upon his legal right to the unpaid rent, because the lessee has conducted his affairs on the basis that he would only have to pay rent at the lower rate; and a court might well think it right to conclude that only after reasonable notice could the lessor return to charging rent at the higher rate specified in the lease. Furthermore it would be open to the Court, in any particular case, to infer from the circumstances of the case that the representee must have conducted his affairs in such a way that it would be inequitable for the representor to enforce his rights, or to do so without reasonable notice. But it does not follow that in every case in which the representee has acted, or failed to act, in reliance on the representation, it will be inequitable for the representor to enforce his rights for the nature of the action, or inaction may be insufficient to give rise to the equity, in which event a necessary requirement stated by Lord Cairns LC for the application of the doctrine would not have been fulfilled.

(III) INEQUITABLE FOR THE PROMISOR TO GO BACK ON HIS PROMISE

The requirement that it must be inequitable for the promisor to go back on his promise overlaps to some extent with the requirement that the promisee must have altered his position, as can be seen from the extract from the judgment of Robert Goff J in *The Post Chaser*. The significance of the requirement that it must be inequitable for the promisor to go back on his promise can be seen in *D & C Builders* v. *Rees* (p. 209 above) where both Lord Denning and Danckwerts LJ, albeit for slightly different reasons (p. 213 above), concluded that it was not inequitable for the creditor to go back on his promise to accept part payment in discharge of the entire debt.

(IV) SUSPENSION

The effect of an estoppel is generally suspensory (see *Tool Metal Manufacturing Co Ltd* v. *Tungsten Electric Co Ltd* [1955] 1 WLR 761). Thus in *Hughes* v. *Metropolitan Railway* (above) the landlord did not lose his right to require that the repairs be carried out within six months. It was simply the case that this right was in suspense during the currency of the negotiations between the landlord and the tenants. On the breakdown of the negotiations the landlord could have revived his right by giving notice to the tenants requiring them to effect the repairs within a six month period. The suspensory nature of estoppel is underlined by Lord Hodson in his second 'qualification' in *Ajayi* (above). On the other hand, Lord Hodson's third qualification clearly suggests that an estoppel can, in certain circumstances, be 'final and irrevocable'. When can an estoppel have extinctive effect? Some guidance can be obtained on this point from *High Trees* (p. 238 above) where Denning J held that the plaintiff landlord could revive its right to demand the full rent for the future but that it could not go back and demand the unpaid rent during the war when the flats were only partially let. Thus estoppel is generally suspensory in relation to obligations to be performed in the future (in the sense that the obligation can be revived by the giving of reasonable notice) but it may be extinctive in relation to events that have occurred in the past (so that the promisor cannot go back and retrospectively demand that the promisee perform his obligations in the past or maintain that the promisee was in breach of contract as a result of his failure to perform his contractual obligations to the full when the reason for the promisee's failure to perform was his reliance upon the promisor's promise that he need not perform in accordance with the strict letter of the contract).

(v) ESTOPPEL CANNOT ACT AS A CAUSE OF ACTION

Combe v. *Combe* illustrates the final point to be made in relation to the requirements of promissory estoppel, namely that it cannot create a cause of action. It generally operates, as in *Hughes* v. *Metropolitan Railway* and *High Trees*, as a defence to a claim. However the proposition that estoppel cannot create a cause of action requires some refinement, as the following extract demonstrates:

R Halson, 'The Offensive Limits of Promissory Estoppel'

[1999] *Lloyd's Maritime and Commercial Law Quarterly* 257, 259–261

A.   The estoppel spectrum described

(1) *Estoppel can only be used as a defence*

This is the least ambitious claim that can be made. New legal doctrines often make their first appearance in a truncated and non-threatening guise. Therefore it should occasion no surprise that in both of the seminal cases, *Hughes* v. *Metropolitan Ry* and *Central London Property Trust Co Ltd* v. *High Trees House*, estoppel was relied upon as a defence . . .

(2) *Estoppel can be used by a party seeking to enforce a claim based upon a recognized cause of action to defeat the defence or counter-claim of the other party*

A simple example of this use of promissory estoppel would be provided by a variation of the facts of *High Trees*: the lessor lets directly to an occupying tenant; some time after the representation has been made and reduced rent payments have been accepted, the landlord distrains the tenant's property in order to recover the balance of the rent. Here the tenant could bring an action for conversion; the landlord would reply that he was rightfully distraining, and the tenant could use estoppel to defeat this defence. Academic authority also supports this usage.

(3) *Estoppel can be used by a party seeking to enforce a claim to prove one element of a recognized cause of action*

This appears to be the effect the promissory estoppel was stated to have in *Robertson* v. *Ministry of Pensions*, where the plaintiff was relieved of the burden of having to prove that his injury was attributable to war service in order to qualify for a disablement pension because the Ministry were estopped from denying this causal connection. The plaintiff's cause of action was a recognized one; in this case statutory or at least *sui generis*. Yet it could not be said that the estoppel relieved the colonel of the obligation to prove all the elements of his cause of action, e.g., that he had served long enough and in a sufficient capacity to qualify for a pension, that the injury was serious enough to so qualify etc. The estoppel related solely to the question of causation; was the injury attributable to military service. This usage may have been what Denning LJ was thinking of when, in *Combe* v. *Combe*, commenting upon a number of decisions including the *Robertson* case, he said:

> 'In none of these cases was the defendant sued on the promise, assurance or assertion as a cause of action in itself; he was sued for some other cause, for example a pension . . . and the promise, assurance or assertion only played a supplementary role—an important role, no doubt, but still a supplementary role.'

(4) Estoppel can be used by a party seeking to enforce a claim to prove all the elements of a recognized cause of action

This appears to be the way the promissory estoppel was used in *The Henrik Sif*. The first defendants conducted themselves as if they were a party to a bill of lading, which they were not. This led the plaintiff to allow the limitation period to run out against the second defendant, who was a party to the bill of lading. The judge based his finding for the plaintiff in his action against the first defendants, *inter alia*, upon promissory estoppel. It appears that all the elements (agreement, consideration etc) of a recognized cause of action (contract) were proved by the estoppel . . .

(5) Estoppel has created a new cause of action

This was the effect of the first instance decision in *Combe* v. *Combe*. The judge appeared to have dispensed with the need for consideration in order to enforce a promise, as opposed to giving more limited effect to the promise which the common law and equitable doctrines of waiver and promissory estoppel would allow. This would create a new cause of action and abrogate the requirement of consideration. The Court of Appeal strongly disclaimed this view, Denning LJ saying of promissory estoppel: 'the principle never stands alone as giving a cause of action in itself'.

The rule that promissory estoppel cannot create a cause of action is one to which we shall return, after giving brief consideration to some of the different types of estoppel currently recognized in English law.

(d) THE DIFFERENT TYPES OF ESTOPPEL

The proposition that estoppel cannot create a new cause of action is not, however, universally true in English law. Proprietary estoppel, as we shall see, can create a cause of action. But promissory estoppel cannot (at least at present). This raises the question why it is that English law has different rules for different types of estoppel. This is not the place to embark upon a discussion of the various types of estoppel that exist. The topic is a terminological minefield (especially in relation to words such as 'waiver' and 'forbearance'). For our purposes it suffices to draw attention to the doctrine of waiver and three different types of estoppel.

The word 'waiver' is a difficult one in English law. The cause of the difficulty is that the word has been used in many different situations. Essentially, waiver covers the situation where one party promises to give up some or all of his contractual rights. A waiver that is supported by consideration takes effect as a variation but the type of waiver in which we are interested is a waiver of rights that is not supported by consideration (often referred to as forbearance). This is a topic of some difficulty and the terminology is particularly confusing. While waiver, in the sense of forbearance, enjoys an ancient history, it may be that today it should be seen as a species of estoppel which should be amalgamated within the *High Trees* line of authority. In *Charles Rickards Ltd* v. *Oppenhaim* [1950] 1 KB 616, 623, when considering whether or not a buyer had waived a term in the contract relating to the time of delivery, Denning LJ stated:

Whether it be called waiver or forbearance on his part, or an agreed variation or substituted performance, does not matter. It is a kind of estoppel. By his conduct he made a promise not to insist on his strict legal rights. That promise was intended to be binding, intended to be acted on, and was, in fact, acted on. . . . It is a particular application of the principle which I endeavoured to state in *Central London Property Trust Ltd* v. *High Trees House Ltd*.

Turning now to the estoppels, the first is estoppel by representation. It can be distinguished from promissory estoppel on the ground that estoppel by representation is confined to statements of fact and does not extend to promises. Thus a party who makes a representation of existing fact which induces the other party to act to his detriment in reliance upon the representation may not be permitted subsequently to act inconsistently with that representation. Estoppel by representation is a rule of evidence that has the effect of permanently preventing a representor from asserting or proving facts that are contrary to his own representation.

The second type of estoppel is estoppel by convention. In *Amalgamated Investment & Property Co Ltd* v. *Texas Commerce International Bank Ltd* [1982] QB 84, 130–131 Brandon LJ adopted the following definition of estoppel by convention, taken from the third edition of *Spencer-Bower and Turner, Estoppel by Representation* p. 157:

This form of estoppel is founded, not on a representation of fact made by a representor and believed by a representee, but on an agreed statement of facts the truth of which has been assumed, by the convention of the parties, as the basis of a transaction into which they are about to enter. When the parties have acted in their transaction upon the agreed assumption that a given state of facts is to be accepted between them as true, then as regards that transaction each will be estopped as against the other from questioning the truth of the statement of facts so assumed.

Estoppel by convention is most commonly invoked in the context of the interpretation of documents. For example, in *Amalgamated Investment* the defendant bank provided a loan to a subsidiary company of the plaintiff company and the plaintiff provided the defendants with a guarantee which stated:

The guarantor will pay to you on demand all moneys which now are or shall at any times hereafter be due or owing or payable to you on any account whatsoever by the principal.

But for exchange control purposes the money was advanced not by the defendant bank but by one of the defendant's subsidiaries. The plaintiff claimed that its liability was to the subsidiary and not to the bank so that it could not be liable under the guarantee. The Court of Appeal held that the plaintiff was liable to the defendant both as a matter of interpretation of the guarantee (on the basis that the guarantee was not to be interpreted on its own but in the context of the negotiations between the parties) and, in the alternative, on the ground that the plaintiff was estopped by convention from denying that it was bound to discharge the indebtedness of its own subsidiary company to the subsidiary of the defendant that had advanced the money. The parties had entered into the transaction on the assumption that the plaintiff was so liable and the parties had acted on that assumption when giving effect to the transaction and the effect of the estoppel was to hold them to the validity of that assumption.

The third type of estoppel is proprietary estoppel. Proprietary estoppel has been defined as follows by Professor Treitel (*The Law of Contract* (11th edn, Sweet & Maxwell, 2003), pp. 134–135):

Proprietary estoppel is said to arise in certain situations in which a person has done acts in reliance on the belief that he has, or that he will acquire, rights in or over another's land. Usually, but not invariably, these acts consist of erecting buildings on, or making other improvements to, the land in question. Where the requirements of proprietary estoppel are satisfied, the landowner is precluded from denying the existence of the rights in question, and may indeed be compelled to grant them. Because the estoppel precludes him from denying the existence of rights in property, it has come to be known as 'proprietary estoppel'.

Cases of proprietary estoppel can be divided into two broad categories. The first consists of cases in which a landowner stands by while another person improves his land in the mistaken belief that he, the improver, is the owner of the land. The second is made up of cases in which the promisee relies to his detriment upon the land-owner's promise that he has or will be given an interest in the land. However proprietary estoppel appears to defy exhaustive categorization. Its flexibility is often emphasized and it has recently been stated that 'the fundamental principle that equity is concerned to prevent unconscionable conduct permeates all the elements of the doctrine' (*Gillett* v. *Holt* [2001] Ch 210, 225).

(e) UNIFYING THE ESTOPPELS

At the moment it cannot be said that we have a common set of rules that govern the various different types of estoppel. A number of differences exist. First, in the case of promissory estoppel there must be a clear and unequivocal promise or representation, whereas in the case of proprietary estoppel the understanding between the parties can be much more imprecise (see, for example, *Gillett* v. *Holt* [2001] Ch 210). Secondly, estoppel by representation only applies to statements of fact and cannot apply to representations as to the future, whereas promissory estoppel applies to promises or statements that relate to the future. Estoppel by representation is also permanent in its effects, while promissory estoppel is generally suspensory in effect. Thirdly, there is a need for detrimental reliance in some types of estoppel but not necessarily in others. In the case of estoppel by representation it seems clear that there must be detrimental reliance but in other cases, such as promissory estoppel, there must be reliance but that reliance need not be detrimental. Fourthly, proprietary estoppel can create a cause of action while promissory estoppel presently cannot.

One of the issues that surfaces from time to time in both the case-law and the academic literature is whether or not English law should seek to develop a general principle which is capable of unifying the various estoppels. Cases can be found in which judges have stated that the distinctions drawn between the different types of estoppel are 'unhelpful' (see, for example, the judgment of Scarman LJ in *Crabb* v. *Arun District Council* [1976] Ch 179, 193, below). Other judges have sought to formulate a broad, overarching principle to govern estoppels (see, for example, *Amalgamated Investment & Property Co Ltd* v. *Texas Commerce International Bank Ltd* [1982] QB 84, 122, per Lord Denning (the relevant passage is set out in the judgment of Russell LJ in *Williams* v. *Roffey Bros* at pp. 193–194 above), and *Taylors Fashions Ltd* v. *Liverpool Victoria Trustees Ltd* [1982] QB 133, 151–152, per Oliver J ('whether in particular individual circumstances it would be unconscionable for a party to be permitted to deny that which, knowingly or unknowingly, he has allowed or encouraged another to assume to his detriment')).

The general judicial response to attempts to unify the estoppels has not, however, been positive. Various objections have been put forward. First, some of the differences are established as a matter of authority (for example, the rule that promissory estoppel cannot create a cause of action) and cannot lightly be set aside. Secondly, if we are to unify the rules which rules should prevail? Should it be the rules of estoppel by represesentation, promissory estoppel, or proprietary estoppel? The proposition that estoppel by representation should provide the basis for the unification of the law was rejected by Millett LJ in *First National Bank* v. *Thompson* [1996] Ch 231, 236 in the following terms:

Spencer Bower's valiant attempt in *The Law Relating to Estoppel by Representation* (1923) to demonstrate that all estoppels other than estoppel by record are now subsumed in the single and all-embracing estoppel by representation and that they are all governed by the same requirements has never won general acceptance. Historically unsound, it has been repudiated by academic writers and is unsupported by authority.

Promissory estoppel may be a more suitable candidate as the basis for the articulation of a general principle but would we want to expand the rule that promissory estoppel cannot create a new cause of action to cases of proprietary estoppel? As Professor Treitel points out (*Some Landmarks of Twentieth Century Contract Law* (Oxford University Press, 2002), p. 40) the view that the various estoppels may merge into one general principle 'may encourage cross-fertilization between them, but it can equally encourage cross-infection and even cross-sterilization'. Thirdly, any general principle would have to be stated at a very high level of abstraction and so may give rise to considerable uncertainty. We may want to recognize that at least some of the estoppels are related to one another but it does not follow from this that we should attempt to formulate a general principle that can unite them all. As Lord Goff stated in *Johnson* v. *Gore Wood & Co (A Firm)* [2001] 1 All ER 481, 508:

In the end, I am inclined to think that the many circumstances capable of giving rise to an estoppel cannot be accommodated within a single formula, and that it is unconscionability which provides the link between them.

Fourthly, there may be good reasons for the differences between (at least some of) the different types of estoppel. In *Republic of India* v. *Indian Steamship Co Ltd (No 2)* [1997] 3 WLR 818, 830 Lord Steyn stated:

The question was debated whether estoppel by convention and estoppel by acquiescence are but aspects of one overarching principle. I do not underestimate the importance in the continuing development of the law of the search for simplicity. I, also, accept that at a high level of abstraction such an overarching principle could be formulated. But . . . to restate the law in terms of an overarching principle might tend to blur the necessarily separate requirements and distinct terrain of application, of the two kinds of estoppel.

In *Baird Textile Holdings Ltd* v. *Marks and Spencer plc* [2001] EWCA 274, [2002] 1 All ER (Comm) 737 Mance LJ stated (at paras [83] and [84]):

Speaking generally, I accept that estoppel is a flexible doctrine, that broad equitable principles underlie its application in different fields (the concept of unconscionability being one such general principle) and that one should avoid 'rigid classification of equitable estoppel into exclusive and defined categories'. . . . However, not only are we bound in this court by previous authority on the scope of particular types of estoppel, but it seems to me inherent in the doctrine's very flexibility that it may take different shapes to fit the context of different fields.

Given these statements, the way ahead might be to seek to rationalize the principles underpinning the estoppels whenever it is possible to do so with a view to eliminating any unnecessary differences that exist between the different estoppels. This will not be an easy task. It will require us to justify some of the differences that currently exist between the different estoppels. Why, for example, can proprietary estoppel create a new cause of action when promissory estoppel cannot? What is so special about promises that relate to the creation of an interest in land that demands that they be given special treatment? In an attempt to answer these two questions consideration will be given to two cases. The first is the decision of the English Court of Appeal in *Crabb* v. *Arun District Council* [1976] Ch 179, a case in which proprietary estoppel was held to create a cause of action. The second is the decision of the High Court of Australia in *Waltons Stores (Interstate) Ltd* v. *Maher* (1987) 164 CLR 387 where the High Court took the additional step of recognizing that equitable or promissory estoppel can, in an appropriate case, create a new cause of action. The question for the English courts, which they have yet to answer, is whether or not they should follow *Waltons Stores*.

Crabb v. Arun District Council

[1976] Ch 179, Court of Appeal

The plaintiff owned a piece of land adjoined by a road owned by the defendants. He had a legal right of access to the road at Point A but wished to have an additional right of access at point B so that he could sell the land in two parts. He accordingly approached the defendants with a view to obtaining a right of access at point B. A meeting took place between the plaintiff, his architect (Mr Alford) and a representative of the defendants on 26 July 1967. The trial judge concluded that the outcome of that meeting was that there was an 'agreement in principle' that the plaintiff should have an additional access to the road at point B.

The defendants did not make a formal grant to the plaintiff of access at point B but the parties acted in the belief that he had or would be granted such a right. The defendants erected a fence along the agreed boundary line of the plaintiff's property and put gates in the fence at points A and B. Both gates were substantial and were intended to be permanent. In 1968 the plaintiff sold the front portion of his land to a third party. He assigned his right of access at point A to the third party and did not reserve to himself a right to go over the land for the purpose of obtaining access to the road at A because he believed that he already had a right of access at point B. In 1969 the plaintiff put a padlock on the inside of the gate at point B. The defendants responded by tearing down the gate at point B. They then filled the gap with a fence, thereby closing access at point B entirely with the result that the plaintiff was landlocked.

The plaintiff brought an action against the defendants in which he claimed that he had a right of access at point B and a right of way along the estate road. The trial judge held that the defendants were not estopped from denying the existence of these rights because they had not given the plaintiff a definite assurance that he would be given a right of access at point B at the meeting on 26 July. The plaintiff appealed to the Court of Appeal who allowed his appeal and held that he was entitled to a right of access at point B and a right of way along the estate road and that he was not liable to make any payment to the defendants in return for these rights.

Lord Denning MR [set out the facts and continued]
When Mr Millett, for the plaintiff, said that he put his case on an estoppel, it shook me a little: because it is commonly supposed that estoppel is not itself a cause of action. But that is because there are estoppel and estoppel. Some do give rise to a cause of action. Some do not. In the species of estoppel called proprietary estoppel, it does give rise to a cause of action. . . . The new rights and interests, so created by estoppel, in or over land, will be protected by the courts and in this way give rise to a cause of action . . .

The basis of this proprietary estoppel—as indeed of promissory estoppel—is the interposition of equity. Equity comes in, true to form, to mitigate the rigours of strict law. The early cases did not speak of it as 'estoppel'. They spoke of it as 'raising an equity'. If I may expand what Lord Cairns LC said in *Hughes* v. *Metropolitan Railway Co* (1877) 2 App Cas 439, 448: 'it is the first principle upon which all courts of equity proceed', that it will prevent a person from insisting on his strict legal rights—whether arising under a contract, or on his title deeds, or by statute—when it would be inequitable for him to do so having regard to the dealings which have taken place between the parties.

What then are the dealings which will preclude him from insisting on his strict legal rights? If he makes a binding contract that he will not insist on the strict legal position, a court of equity will hold him to his contract. Short of a binding contract, if he makes a promise that he will not insist upon his strict legal rights—then, even though that promise may be unenforceable in point of law for want of consideration or want of writing—then, if he makes the promise knowing or intending that the other will act upon it, and he does act upon it, then again a court of equity will not allow him to go back on that promise: see *Central London Property Trust Ltd* v. *High Trees House Ltd* [1947] KB 130 and *Charles Rickards Ltd* v. *Oppenhaim* [1950] 1 KB 616, 623. Short of an actual promise, if he, by his words or conduct, so behaves as to lead another to believe that he will not insist on his strict legal rights—knowing or intending that the other will act on that belief—and he does so act, that again will raise an equity in favour of the other; and it is for a court of equity to say in what way the equity may be satisfied. The cases show that this equity does not depend on agreement but on words or conduct [he considered the cases and continued].

The question then is: were the circumstances here such as to raise an equity in favour of the plaintiff? True the defendants on the deeds had the title to their land, free of any access at point B. But they led the plaintiff to believe that he had or would be granted a right of access at point B. At the meeting of July 26, 1967, Mr Alford and the plaintiff told the defendants' representative that the plaintiff intended to split the two acres into two portions and wanted to have an access at point B for the back portion; and the defendants' representative agreed that he should have this access. I do not think the defendants can avoid responsibility by saying that their representative had no authority to agree this. They entrusted him with the task of setting out the line of the fence and the gates, and they must be answerable for his conduct in the course of it . . .

The judge found that there was 'no definite assurance' by the defendants' representative, and 'no firm commitment', but only an 'agreement in principle', meaning I suppose that, as Mr Alford said, there were 'some further processes' to be gone through before it would become binding. But if there were any such processes in the mind of the parties, the subsequent conduct of the defendants was such as to dispense with them. The defendants actually put up the gates at point B at considerable expense. That certainly led the plaintiff to believe that they agreed that he should have the right of access through point B without more ado.

The judge also said that, to establish this equity or estoppel, the defendants must have known that the plaintiff was selling the front portion without reserving a right of access for the back portion. I do not think this was necessary. The defendants knew that the plaintiff intended to sell the two portions separately and that he would need an access at point B as well as point A. Seeing that they knew of his intention—and they did nothing to disabuse him but rather confirmed it by erecting gates at point B—it was their conduct which led him to act as he did: and this raises an equity in his favour against them.

In the circumstances it seems to me inequitable that the council should insist on their strict title as they did; and to take the high-handed action of pulling down the gates without a word of warning: and to demand of the plaintiff £3,000 as the price for the easement. If he had moved at once for an injunction in aid of his equity—to prevent them removing the gates—I think he should have been granted it. But he did not do so. He tried to negotiate terms, but these failing, the action has come for trial. And we have the question: in what way now should the equity be satisfied?

Here equity is displayed at its most flexible, see *Snell's Principles of Equity*, 27th edn. (1973), p. 568, and the illustrations there given. If the matter had been finally settled in 1967, I should have thought that, although nothing was said at the meeting in July 1967, nevertheless it would be quite reasonable for the defendants to ask the plaintiff to pay something for the access at point B, perhaps—and I am guessing—some hundreds of pounds. But, as Mr Millett pointed out in the course of the argument, because of the defendants' conduct, the back land has been landlocked. It has been sterile and rendered useless for five or six years: and the plaintiff has been unable to deal with it during that time. This loss to him can be taken into account and at the present time, it seems to me that, in order to satisfy the equity, the plaintiff should have the right of access at point B without paying anything for it.

I would, therefore, hold that the plaintiff, as the owner of the back portion, has a right of access at point B over the verge on to Mill Park Road and a right of way along that road to Hook Lane without paying compensation. I would allow the appeal and declare that he has an easement, accordingly.

Lawton LJ
In my judgment this appeal turns on the answer to one question. At the meeting on 26th July 1967 between the plaintiff and his architect, Mr Alford, on one side, and the representative of the defendant on the other, did the parties agree that the plaintiff should have access to the land at point B?

[he considered the evidence, concluded that they did so decide and continued]

What are the legal consequences of finding as I do that there had been a firm undertaking by the defendants that access would be granted at point B? This necessitates considering principles of equity and applying them to the facts of this case. Before doing so I have reminded myself of what Harman LJ said in *Campbell Discount Co Ltd* v. *Bridge* [1961] 1 QB 445, 459:

> 'Equitable principles are, I think, perhaps rather too often bandied about in common law courts as though the Chancellor still had only the length of his own foot to measure when coming to a conclusion. Since the time of Lord Eldon the system of equity for good or evil has been a very precise one, and equitable jurisdiction is exercised only on well-known principles.'

I start with a firm agreement between the plaintiff on one side and the defendants' representative on the other to the effect I have already indicated. From then onwards there can be no doubt whatsoever that the plaintiff believed that he had got a firm undertaking from the defendants and he acted as if he had. In so doing he prejudiced his own position greatly by selling off the front portion of his land and failing to retain a right of way over it. It is also clear on the evidence, and was so found by the judge, that when the agreement was made the defendants knew that the plaintiff wanted access at point B because he intended to sell off part of his land.

What did the defendants believe had happened on July 26, 1967? The facts speak for themselves. In 1968 they started to put up the fence between their own land and the plaintiff's land, as they were bound to do under the conveyance by which the land had been transferred to them. When they did put up that fence they left gaps for gates at points A and B. Clearly they intended to provide a point of access at B. This could only have been done because they knew their representative had given an undertaking that the plaintiff could have access at point B. . . . After the gates had been erected at point B the plaintiff altered his position in a way which proved disastrous for him in the short term. Then the defendants behaved in a manner which the judge described in restrained terms as high-handed and discourteous. I am surprised that a local authority should have behaved in the way this local authority did. They had gone back on the firm undertaking which they had given through their representative to the plaintiff on July 26, 1967; and they had so behaved without a word of warning, explanation or apology. Since then they have asked the plaintiff to pay a very substantial sum of money—close on £4,000—in order to provide him with that which their representative had undertaken to provide on July 26, 1967.

I ask myself whether any principle of equity applies. I am grateful to Mr Lightman [counsel for the defendants] for having drawn our attention this morning to *Ramsden* v. *Dyson* (1866) LR 1 HL 129. If there had been any doubt in my mind about the application of principles of equity to the facts as I have recounted them, that case has dissipated it. As was pointed out to Mr Lightman in the course of the argument, if one changes the parties in a passage in the speech of Lord Cranworth LC into the names of the parties in this case, one has a case for the intervention of equity which Lord Cranworth regarded with favour. That passage, at p. 142, is in these terms:

> '. . . if I had come to the conclusion that Thornton, when he erected his building in 1837, did so in the belief that he had against Sir John an absolute right to the lease he claims, and that Sir John knew that he was proceeding on that mistaken notion, and

did not interfere to set him right, I should have been much disposed to say that he was entitled to the relief he sought.'

Mr Lightman's answer was that the plaintiff had not got an absolute right to have the gates put up. For the reasons I have stated, I am of the opinion that he had in the sense that he had been given a firm undertaking. The defendants, knowing that the plaintiff intended to sell part of this land, stood by when he did so and without a word of warning allowed him to surround himself with a useless piece of land from which there was no exit. I would allow this appeal and grant relief in the terms indicated by Lord Denning MR.

In conclusion I should add this: as the result of the defendants resiling from their undertaking, this piece of land which is designated for light industry has stood useless. It might well have been profitable not only to the plaintiff but to other people living nearby. In an area where employment for the young is not always easy to find, we have the spectacle of this piece of land next door to a housing estate being rendered useless at a time when it could have been of value to the community. For that the defendants are solely to blame.

In the circumstances I agree with Lord Denning MR that they should not be paid anything for the right of way which they should have granted as long ago as 1967.

Scarman LJ

I agree that the appeal should be allowed. The plaintiff and the defendants are adjoining landowners. The plaintiff asserts that he has a right of way over the defendants' land giving access from his land to the public highway. Without this access his land is in fact landlocked, but, for reasons which clearly appear from the narration of the facts already given by my Lords, the plaintiff cannot claim a right of way by necessity. The plaintiff has no grant. He has the benefit of no enforceable contract. He has no prescriptive right. His case has to be that the defendants are estopped by their conduct from denying him a right of access over their land to the public highway. If the plaintiff has any right, it is an equity arising out of the conduct and relationship of the parties. In such a case I think it is now well settled law that the court, having analysed and assessed the conduct and relationship of the parties, has to answer three questions. First, is there an equity established? Secondly, what is the extent of the equity, if one is established? And, thirdly, what is the relief appropriate to satisfy the equity? . . . Such therefore I believe to be the nature of the inquiry that the courts have to conduct in a case of this sort. In pursuit of that inquiry I do not find helpful the distinction between promissory and proprietary estoppel. This distinction may indeed be valuable to those who have to teach or expound the law; but I do not think that, in solving the particular problem raised by a particular case, putting the law into categories is of the slightest assistance. . . .

I come now to consider the first of the three questions which I think in a case such as this the court have to consider. What is needed to establish an equity? In the course of an interesting addition to his submissions this morning, Mr Lightman cited *Ramsden* v. *Dyson*, (1866) LR 1 HL 129, 142, to support his proposition that in order to establish an equity by estoppel there must be a belief by the plaintiff in the existence of a right created or encouraged by the words or actions of the defendant. With respect, I do not think that that is today a correct statement of the law. I think the law has developed so that today it is to be considered as correctly stated by Lord Kingsdown in his dissenting speech in *Ramsden* v. *Dyson*. Like Lord Denning MR, I think that the point of dissent in *Ramsden* v.

Dyson was not on the law but on the facts. So what is the effect of looking to Lord Kingsdown's speech for a statement of the law? . . . Lord Kingsdown said, LR 1 HL 129, 170:

> 'The rule of law applicable to the case appears to me to be this: If a man, under a verbal agreement with a landlord for a certain interest in land, or, what amounts to the same thing, *under an expectation, created or encouraged by the landlord,*'—my italics—'that he shall have a certain interest, takes possession of such land, with the consent of the landlord, and upon the faith of such promise or expectation, with the knowledge of the landlord, and without objection by him, lays out money upon the land, a court of equity will compel the landlord to give effect to such promise or expectation.'

That statement of the law is put into the language of landlord and tenant because it was a landlord and tenant situation with which Lord Kingsdown was concerned; but it has been accepted as of general application. While *Ramsden* v. *Dyson* may properly be considered as the modern starting-point of the law of equitable estoppel, it was analysed and spelt out in a judgment of Fry J in 1880 in *Willmott* v. *Barber* (1880) 15 Ch D 96 . . . I agree . . . that the passage from Fry J's judgment, from p. 105, is a valuable guide as to the matters of fact which have to be established in order that a plaintiff may establish this particular equity. Moreover, Mr Lightman for the defendants sought to make a submission in reliance upon the judgment. Fry J said, at pp. 105–106:

> 'It has been said that the acquiescence which will deprive a man of his legal rights must amount to fraud, and in my view that is an abbreviated statement of a very true proposition. A man is not to be deprived of his legal rights unless he has acted in such a way as would make it fraudulent for him to set up those rights. What, then, are the elements or requisites necessary to constitute fraud of that description? In the first place the plaintiff must have made a mistake as to his legal rights. Secondly, the plaintiff must have expended some money or must have done some act (not necessarily upon the defendant's land) on the faith of his mistaken belief. Thirdly, the defendant, the possessor of the legal right, must know of the existence of his own right which is inconsistent with the right claimed by the plaintiff. If he does not know of it he is in the same position as the plaintiff, and the doctrine of acquiescence is founded upon conduct with a knowledge of your legal rights. Fourthly, the defendant, the possessor of the legal right, must know of the plaintiff's mistaken belief of his rights. If he does not, there is nothing which calls upon him to assert his own rights. Lastly [if I may digress, this is the important element as far as this appeal is concerned], 'the defendant, the possessor of the legal right, must have encouraged the plaintiff in his expenditure of money or in the other acts which he has done, either directly or by abstaining from asserting his legal right.'

Mr Lightman, in the course of an interesting and vigorous submission, drew the attention of the court to the necessity of finding something akin to fraud before the equity sought by the plaintiff could be established. 'Fraud' was a word often in the mouths of those robust judges who adorned the bench in the 19th century. It is less often in the mouths of the more wary judicial spirits today who sit upon the bench. But it is clear that whether one uses the word 'fraud' or not, the plaintiff has to establish as a fact that the defendant, by setting up his right, is taking advantage of him in a way which is unconscionable, inequitable or unjust. It is to be observed from the passage that I have quoted from the judgment of Fry J, that the fraud or injustice alleged does not take place during the course of negotiation, but only when the defendant decides to refuse to allow the plaintiff to set up his claim against the defendants' undoubted right. The fraud, if it be such, arises after the event, when the defendant seeks by relying on his right to defeat the expectation which he by his conduct encouraged the plaintiff to have. There need not be anything fraudulent or unjust in the conduct of the actual negotiations—the conduct of the transaction by the defendants.

The court therefore cannot find an equity established unless it is prepared to go as far as to say that it would be unconscionable and unjust to allow the defendants to set up their undoubted rights against the claim being made by the plaintiff. In order to reach a conclusion upon that matter the court does have to consider the history of the negotiations under the five headings to which Fry J referred. I need not at this stage weary anyone with an elaborate statement of the facts. I have no doubt upon the facts of this case that the first four elements referred to by Fry J exist. The question before the judge and now in this court is whether the fifth element is present: have the defendants, as possessor of the legal right, encouraged the plaintiff in the expenditure of money or in the other acts which he has done, either directly or by abstaining from asserting their legal rights?

[he considered the evidence, concluded that the defendants had so encouraged the plaintiff and that an equity was established and continued]

I turn now to the other two questions—the extent of the equity and the relief needed to satisfy it. There being no grant, no enforceable contract, no licence, I would analyse the minimum equity to do justice to the plaintiff as a right either to an easement or to a licence upon terms to be agreed. I do not think it is necessary to go further than that. Of course, going that far would support the equitable remedy of injunction which is sought in this action. If there is no agreement as to terms, if agreement fails to be obtained, the court can, in my judgment, and must, determine in these proceedings upon what terms the plaintiff should be put to enable him to have the benefit of the equitable right which he is held to have. It is interesting that there has been some doubt amongst distinguished lawyers in the past as to whether the court can so proceed. . . . But there can be no doubt that since *Ramsden* v. *Dyson* the courts have acted upon the basis that they have to determine not only the extent of the equity, but also the conditions necessary to satisfy it, and they have done so in a great number and variety of cases.

In the present case the court does have to consider what is necessary now in order to satisfy the plaintiff's equity. Had matters taken a different turn, I would without hesitation have said that the plaintiff should be put upon terms to be agreed if possible with the defendants, and, if not agreed, settled by the court. But, as already mentioned by Lord Denning MR and Lawton LJ, there has been a history of delay, and indeed high-handedness, which it is impossible to disregard. In January 1969 the defendants, for reasons which no doubt they thought good at the time, without consulting the plaintiff, locked up his land. They removed not only the padlocks which he had put on the gates at point B, but the gates themselves. In their place they put a fence—rendering access impossible save by breaking down the fence. I am not disposed to consider whether or not the defendants are to be blamed in moral terms for what they did. I just do not know. But the effect of their action has been to sterilise the plaintiff's land; and for the reasons which I have endeavoured to give, such action was an infringement of an equitable right possessed by the plaintiff. It has involved him in loss, which has not been measured; but, since it amounted to sterilisation of an industrial estate for a very considerable period of time, it must surpass any sort of sum of money which the plaintiff ought reasonably, before it was done, to have paid the defendants in order to obtain an enforceable legal right. I think therefore that nothing should now be paid by the plaintiff and that he should receive at the hands of the court the belated protection of the equity that he has established. Reasonable terms, other than money payment, should be agreed: or, if not agreed, determined by the court.

For those reasons I also would allow the appeal.

COMMENTARY

Crabb is a notable case for a number of reasons. First, it is a case in which the plaintiff was promised an interest in land and so is generally regarded as a case of proprietary estoppel. That said, it should be noted that Scarman LJ stated that he did not find 'helpful the distinction between promissory and proprietary estoppel' and in *Waltons Stores (Interstate) Ltd* v. *Maher* (1987) 164 CLR 387, 403 Mason CJ and Wilson J stated that '*Crabb* was an instance of promissory estoppel' (Professor Atiyah also describes it as a case of promissory estoppel in the extract at p. 259 below). Secondly, the estoppel had the effect of conferring on the plaintiff a cause of action that he would not otherwise have had. Thirdly, the remedy awarded had the effect of protecting the plaintiff's expectation interest, namely his expectation that he would acquire a right of way. Simon Gardner has described the remedy in *Crabb* in the following terms ('Remedial Discretion in Proprietary Estoppel' (1999) 115 *LQR* 438, 445):

The court vindicated the plaintiff's estoppel claim by an expectation award *in specie*, giving him his right of way. Ordinarily, since this was the nature of the deal originally envisaged by the parties, the plaintiff would have had to pay for the right of way. But the court decided that, in the circumstances, no money need change hands after all. The defendant's leaving the plaintiff land-locked for seven years wrongfully infringed the plaintiff's estoppel right throughout that time. Although unquantified, the loss so caused must have been substantial (particularly as the land in question was to be used as an industrial estate), and greater than any price which the parties could reasonably have agreed for the right of way. Lord Denning MR and Scarman LJ regarded relieving the plaintiff from paying for the right of way as a means of giving him compensation for that wrongfully caused loss. Fully explicated, the plaintiff's expectation interest was not merely a right of way for the future, but also the benefit of having had such a right for the previous seven years. So this interest would not have been fully vindicated by an award of such a right and no more, as the plaintiff would then have remained out of pocket to the value of seven years' user of the way. The ruling that the plaintiff need not pay for the right was an attempt to correct that deficiency and give the plaintiff his full expectation after all.

Finally, the case produced a sharp exchange of views between Professor Atiyah ((1976) 92 *LQR* 174) and Mr Millett, now Lord Millett, who was counsel for the plaintiff ((1976) 92 *LQR* 342). In essence Professor Atiyah argued that the Court of Appeal could have decided the case on orthodox contractual reasoning and had no need to resort to equitable estoppel in order to render the agreement enforceable. Mr Millett, on the other hand, pointed out that there were good reasons to support the concession that no enforceable contract had been concluded between the parties and he stated (at p. 346) that *Crabb* is an 'important' case 'precisely because there was no contract, and yet the plaintiff's claim succeeded'. Subsequently Professor Atiyah returned to the issue and stated ('Consideration: A Re-statement' in *Essays on Contract* (Oxford University Press, 1986), p. 239):

I merely protest at the absurdity of a conceptual analysis which states that the agreement in *Crabb* v. *Arun District Council* was not enforceable because the detrimental reliance was not requested, and therefore failed to comply with the requirements of consideration; and then proceeds to add that the 'agreement' was nevertheless enforceable because the element of reliance did satisfy the doctrine of promissory estoppel. Surely, it would be simpler and more sensible if the law made up its mind what kind of detrimental reliance was sufficient to justify the imposition of some kind of obligation without regard to whether the case should be classified as involving consideration or promissory estoppel.

Waltons Stores (Interstate) Ltd v. Maher

(1987) 164 CLR 387, High Court of Australia

In September 1983 Waltons Stores (Interstate) Ltd (referred to in the judgments as 'the appellant') entered into negotiations with Mr and Mrs Maher (referred to in the judgments as 'the respondents') for the lease by Waltons of the Mahers' property. The Mahers proposed to demolish the buildings on their land and erect a new building built to Waltons' specifications. Solicitors acting for Waltons sent a form of lease to the Mahers' solicitors. On 1 November the Mahers' solicitor informed Waltons' solicitor that the Mahers had begun to demolish the old building on the site. On 7 November he further informed them that it was essential that the agreement be concluded within a day or so if the work was to progress and that the Mahers did not want to demolish the 'new brick part of the old building' until it was clear that there would be no problems with the lease. Waltons' solicitor replied to the effect that he had received verbal instructions that the amendments made to the lease were acceptable to his clients but that he would obtain formal instructions from them and inform him if there were any problems. No problems were reported to the Mahers' solicitor. On 11 November the Mahers' solicitor sent to Waltons' solicitor 'by way of exchange' the lease which had been executed by the Mahers. The Mahers then began the demolition of the new part of the old building. On 21 November Waltons began to have second thoughts about the project and they instructed their solicitors to 'go slow'. On 10 December Waltons became aware of the fact that the Mahers had begun the demolition work. In early January the Mahers started to build on the land in accordance with Waltons' specifications until they were told on 21 January that Waltons did not intend to proceed with the lease, by which time 40% of the works were complete.

The Mahers sought a declaration that the parties had concluded a valid and enforceable agreement for a lease. The trial judge found in their favour and awarded them damages in lieu of specific performance. Waltons appealed to the New South Wales Court of Appeal and to the High Court of Australia but on both occasions their appeal was unsuccessful. The High Court held that, although no formal contract had been concluded between the parties, Waltons were estopped from denying that they were bound by such an agreement and that Waltons were therefore liable in damages to the Mahers.

Mason CJ and Wilson J

Promissory estoppel ... extends to representations (or promises) as to future conduct. ... So far the doctrine has been mainly confined to precluding departure from a representation by a person in a pre-existing contractual relationship that he will not enforce his contractual rights, whether they be pre-existing or rights to be acquired as a result of the representation. ... But Denning J in *Central London Property Trust Ltd* v. *High Trees House Ltd* [1947] KB 130, at pp. 134–135, treated it as a wide-ranging doctrine operating outside the pre-existing contractual relationship. ... In principle there is certainly no reason why the doctrine should not apply so as to preclude departure by a person from a representation that he will not enforce a non-contractual right ...

There has been for many years a reluctance to allow promissory estoppel to become the vehicle for the positive enforcement of a representation by a party that he would do something in the future. Promissory estoppel, it has been said, is a defensive equity (*Hughes* v. *Metropolitan Railway Co* (1877) 2 App Cas 439, at p. 448; *Combe* v. *Combe* [1951] 2 KB 215, at pp. 219–220) and the traditional notion has been that estoppel could only be relied upon defensively as a shield and not as a sword. ... *High Trees* itself was an instance of the defensive use of promissory estoppel. But this does not mean that a plaintiff cannot rely on an estoppel. Even according to traditional orthodoxy, a plaintiff may rely on an estoppel if he has an independent cause of action, where in the words of Denning LJ in *Combe* v. *Combe*, at p. 220, the estoppel 'may be part of a cause of action, but not a cause of action in itself'.

But the respondents ask us to drive promissory estoppel one step further by enforcing directly in the absence of a pre-existing relationship of any kind a non-contractual promise on which the representee has relied to his detriment. For the purposes of discussion, we shall assume that there was such a promise in the present case. The principal objection to the enforcement of such a promise is that it would outflank the principles of the law of contract. Holmes J expressed his objection to the operation of promissory estoppel in this situation when he said 'It would cut up the doctrine of consideration by the roots, if a promisee could make a gratuitous promise binding by subsequently acting in reliance on it': *Commonwealth* v. *Scituate Savings Bank* (1884) 137 Mass 301, at p. 302. Likewise, Sir Owen Dixon considered that estoppel cut across the principles of the law of contract, notably offer and acceptance and consideration: 'Concerning Judicial Method' (1956) 29 Australian Law Journal 468, at p. 475. And Denning LJ in *Combe* v. *Combe*, after noting that 'The doctrine of consideration is too firmly fixed to be overthrown by a side-wind', said (at p. 220) that such a promise could only be enforced if it was supported by sufficient consideration ...

There is force in these objections and it may not be a sufficient answer to repeat the words of Lord Denning MR in *Crabb* v. *Arun District Council* [1976] Ch 179, at p. 187, 'Equity comes in, true to form, to mitigate the rigours of strict law'. True it is that in the orthodox case of promissory estoppel, where the promisor promises that he will not exercise or enforce an existing right, the elements of reliance and detriment attract equitable intervention on the basis that it is unconscionable for the promisor to depart from his promise, if to do so will result in detriment to the promisee. And it can be argued (see, for example, Greig and Davis, *The Law of Contract*, p. 184) that there is no justification for applying the doctrine of promissory estoppel in this situation, yet denying it in the case of a non-contractual promise in the absence of a pre-existing relationship. The promise, if enforced, works a change in the relationship of the parties, by altering an existing legal relationship in the first situation and by creating a new legal relationship in the second. The point has been made that it would be more logical to say that when the parties have agreed to pursue a course of action, an alteration of the relationship by non-contractual promise will not be countenanced, whereas the creation of a new relationship by a simple promise will be recognized . . .

The direct enforcement of promises made without consideration by means of promissory estoppel has proceeded apace in the United States. The *Restatement on Contracts* 2d 90 states:

'(1) A promise which the promisor should reasonably expect to induce action or for-bearance on the part of the promisee or a third person and which does induce such action or forbearance is binding if injustice can be avoided only by enforcement of the promise. The remedy granted for breach may be limited as justice requires.'

This general proposition developed from the treatment in particular situations of promissory estoppel as the equivalent of consideration . . .

However, we need to view the development of the doctrine in the United States with some caution. There promissory estoppel developed partly in response to the limiting effects of the adoption of the bargain theory of consideration which has not been expressly adopted in Australia or England. It may be doubted whether our conception of consideration is substantially broader than the bargain theory . . . though we may be willing to imply consideration in situations where the bargain theory as implemented in the United States would deny the existence of consideration. . . . It is perhaps sufficient to say that in the United States, as in Australia, there is an obvious interrelationship between the doctrines of consideration and promissory estoppel, promissory estoppel tending to occupy ground left vacant due to the constraints affecting consideration.

The proposition stated in 90(1) of the Restatement seems on its face to reflect a closer connection with the general law of contract than our doctrine of promissory estoppel, with its origins in the equitable concept of unconscionable conduct, might be thought to allow. This is because in the United States promissory estoppel has become an equivalent or substitute for consideration in contract formation, detriment being an element common to both doctrines. Nonetheless the proposition, by making the enforcement of the promise conditional on (a) a reasonable expectation on the part of the promisor that his promise will induce action or forbearance by the promisee and (b) the impossibility of avoiding injustice by other means, makes it clear that the promise is enforced in circumstances where departure from it is unconscionable. Note that the emphasis is on the promisor's reasonable expectation that his promise will induce action or forbearance, not on the fact that he created or encouraged an expectation in the promisee of performance of the promise.

Some recent English decisions are relevant to this general discussion.

[They considered *Amalgamated Property Co* v. *Texas Bank* [1982] QB 84, *Pacol Ltd* v. *Trade Lines Ltd* [1982] 1 Lloyd's Rep 456, *Crabb* v. *Arun District Council* [1976] Ch 179, *Taylors Fashions Ltd.* v. *Liverpool Victoria Trustees Co Ltd* [1982] QB 133, *Ramsden* v. *Dyson* (1866) LR 1 HL 129, and *Attorney-General of Hong Kong* v. *Humphreys Estate Ltd* [1987] 1 AC 114 and continued]

The foregoing review of the doctrine of promissory estoppel indicates that the doctrine extends to the enforcement of voluntary promises on the footing that a departure from the basic assumptions underlying the transaction between the parties must be unconscionable. As failure to fulfil a promise does not of itself amount to unconscionable conduct, mere reliance on an executory promise to do something, resulting in the promisee changing his position or suffering detriment, does not bring promissory estoppel into play. Something more would be required. *Humphreys Estate* suggests that this may be found, if at all, in the creation or encouragement by the party estopped in the other party of an assumption that a contract will come into existence or a promise will be performed and that the other party relied on that assumption to his detriment to the knowledge of the first party. *Humphreys Estate* referred in terms to an assumption that the plaintiff would not exercise an existing legal right or liberty, the right or liberty to withdraw from the negotiations, but as a matter of substance such an assumption is indistinguishable from an assumption that a binding contract would eventuate. On the other hand the United States experience, distilled in the Restatement (2d 90), suggests that the principle is to be expressed in terms of a reasonable expectation on the part of the promisor that his promise will induce action or forbearance by the promisee, the promise inducing such action or forbearance in circumstances where injustice arising from unconscionable conduct can only be avoided by holding the promisor to his promise.

The application of these principles to the facts of the present case is not without difficulty. The parties were negotiating through their solicitors for an agreement for a lease to be concluded by way of customary exchange. *Humphreys Estate* illustrates the difficulty of establishing an estoppel preventing parties from refusing to proceed with a transaction expressed to be 'subject to contract'. And there is the problem identified in *Texas Bank* (at p. 107) that a voluntary promise will not generally give rise to an estoppel because the promisee may reasonably be expected to appreciate that he cannot safely rely upon it. This problem is magnified in the present case where the parties were represented by their solicitors.

All this may be conceded. But the crucial question remains: was the appellant entitled to stand by in silence when it must have known that the respondents were proceeding on the assumption that they had an agreement and that completion of the exchange was a formality? The mere exercise of its legal right not to exchange contracts could not be said to amount to unconscionable conduct on the part of the appellant. But there were two other factors present in the situation which require to be taken into consideration. The first was the element of urgency that pervaded the negotiation of the terms of the proposed lease. As we have noted, the appellant was bound to give up possession of its existing commercial premises in Nowra in January 1984; the new building was to be available for fitting out by 15 January and completed by 5 February 1984. The respondents' solicitor had said to the appellant's solicitor on 7 November that it would be impossible for Maher to complete the building within the agreed time unless the agreement were concluded 'within the next day or two'. The outstanding details were agreed within a day or two thereafter, and the work of preparing the site commenced almost immediately.

The second factor of importance is that the respondents executed the counterpart deed and it was forwarded to the appellant's solicitor on 11 November. The assumption on which the respondents acted thereafter was that completion of the necessary exchange was a formality. The next their solicitor heard from the appellant was a letter from its solicitors dated 19 January, informing him that the appellant did not intend to proceed with the matter. It had known, at least since 10 December, that costly work was proceeding on the site.

It seems to us, in the light of these considerations, that the appellant was under an obligation to communicate with the respondents within a reasonable time after receiving the executed counterpart deed and certainly when it learnt on 10 December that demolition was proceeding. It had to choose whether to complete the contract or to warn the respondents that it had not yet decided upon the course it would take. It was not entitled simply to retain the counterpart deed executed by the respondents and do nothing. . . . The appellant's inaction, in all the circumstances, constituted clear encouragement or inducement to the respondents to continue to act on the basis of the assumption which they had made. It was unconscionable for it, knowing that the respondents were exposing themselves to detriment by acting on the basis of a false assumption, to adopt a course of inaction which encouraged them in the course they had adopted. To express the point in the language of promissory estoppel the appellant is estopped in all the circumstances from retreating from its implied promise to complete the contract.

Brennan J

In all cases where an equity created by estoppel is raised, the party raising the equity has acted or abstained from acting on an assumption or expectation as to the legal relationship between himself and the party who induced him to adopt the assumption or expectation . . .

Parties who are negotiating a contract may proceed in the expectation that the terms will be agreed and a contract made but, so long as both parties recognize that either party is at liberty to withdraw from the negotiations at any time before the contract is made, it cannot be unconscionable for one party to do so. Of course, the freedom to withdraw may be fettered or extinguished by agreement but, in the absence of agreement, either party ordinarily retains his freedom to withdraw. It is only if a party induces the other party to believe that he, the former party, is already bound and his freedom to withdraw has gone that it could be unconscionable for him subsequently to assert that he is legally free to withdraw.

It is essential to the existence of an equity created by estoppel that the party who induces the adoption of the assumption or expectation knows or intends that the party who adopts it will act or abstain from acting in reliance on the assumption or expectation: see per Lord Denning MR in *Crabb* v. *Arun District Council* [1976] Ch at p. 188. When the adoption of an assumption or expectation is induced by the making of a promise, the knowledge or intention that the assumption or expectation will be acted upon may be easily inferred. But if a party encourages another to adhere to an assumption or expectation already formed or acquiesces in the making of an assumption or the entertainment of an expectation when he ought to object to the assumption or expectation—steps which are tantamount to inducing the other to adopt the assumption or expectation—the inference of knowledge or intention that the assumption or expectation will be acted on may be more difficult to draw.

The unconscionable conduct which it is the object of equity to prevent is the failure of a party, who has induced the adoption of the assumption or expectation and who knew or intended that it would be relied on, to fulfil the assumption or expectation or otherwise to avoid the detriment which that failure would occasion. The object of the equity is not to compel the party bound to fulfil the assumption or expectation; it is to avoid the detriment which, if the assumption or expectation goes unfulfilled, will be suffered by the party who has been induced to act or to abstain from acting thereon.

If this object is kept steadily in mind, the concern that a general application of the principle of equitable estoppel would make non-contractual promises enforceable as contractual promises can be allayed. A non-contractual promise can give rise to an equitable estoppel only when the promisor induces the promisee to assume or expect that the promise is intended to affect their legal relations and he knows or intends that the promisee will act or abstain from acting in reliance on the promise, and when the promisee does so act or abstain from acting and the promisee would suffer detriment by his action or inaction if the promisor were not to fulfil the promise. When these elements are present, equitable estoppel almost wears the appearance of contract, for the action or inaction of the promisee looks like consideration for the promise on which, as the promisor knew or intended, the promisee would act or abstain from acting . . .

But there are differences between a contract and an equity created by estoppel. A contractual obligation is created by the agreement of the parties; an equity created by estoppel may be imposed irrespective of any agreement by the party bound. A contractual obligation must be supported by consideration; an equity created by estoppel need not be supported by what is, strictly speaking, consideration. The measure of a contractual obligation depends on the terms of the contract and the circumstances to which it applies; the measure of an equity created by estoppel varies according to what is necessary to prevent detriment resulting from unconscionable conduct.

In *Combe* v. *Combe* Denning LJ limited the application of promissory estoppel, as he expounded the doctrine, to ensure that it did not displace the doctrine of consideration. His Lordship's solution of the problem was to hold that the promise should not itself be a cause of action, but merely the foundation of a defensive equity. . . . The remedy offered by promissory estoppel has been limited to preventing the enforcement of existing legal rights. . . . If the object of the principle were to make a promise binding in equity, the need to preserve the doctrine of consideration would require a limitation to be placed on the remedy. But there is a logical difficulty in limiting the principle so that it applies only to promises to suspend or extinguish existing rights. If a promise by A not to enforce an existing right against B is to confer an equitable right on B to compel fulfilment of the promise, why should B be denied the same protection in similar circumstances if the promise is intended to create in B a new legal right against A? There is no logical distinction to be drawn between a change in legal relationships effected by a promise which extinguishes a right and a change in legal relationships effected by a promise which creates one. Why should an equity of the kind to which *Combe* v. *Combe* refers be regarded as a shield but not a sword?

Moreover, unless the cases of proprietary estoppel are attributed to a different equity from that which explains the cases of promissory estoppel the enforcement of promises to create new proprietary rights cannot be reconciled with a limitation on the enforcement of other promises. If it be unconscionable for an owner of property in certain circumstances to fail to fulfil a non-contractual promise that he will convey an interest in the property to another, is there any reason in principle why it is not unconscionable in similar circumstances for a person to fail to fulfil a non-contractual promise that he will confer a non-proprietary legal right on another? It does not accord with principle to hold that equity, in seeking to avoid detriment occasioned by unconscionable conduct, can give relief in some cases but not in others.

If the object of the principle of equitable estoppel in its application to promises were regarded as their enforcement rather than the prevention of detriment flowing from reliance on promises, the courts would be constrained to limit the application of the principles of equitable estoppel in order to avoid the investing of a non-contractual promise with the legal effect of a contractual promise. . . . But the better solution of the problem is reached by identifying the unconscionable conduct which gives rise to the equity as the leaving of another to suffer detriment occasioned by the conduct of the party against whom the equity is raised. Then the object of the principle can be seen to be the avoidance of that detriment and the satisfaction of the equity calls for the enforcement of a promise only as a means of avoiding the detriment and only to the extent necessary to achieve that object. So regarded, equitable estoppel does not elevate non-contractual promises to the level of contractual promises and the doctrine of consideration is not blown away by a side-wind. Equitable estoppel complements the tortious remedies of damages for negligent mis-statement or fraud and enhances the remedies available to a party who acts or abstains from acting in reliance on what another induces him to believe . . .

In my opinion, to establish an equitable estoppel, it is necessary for a plaintiff to prove that (1) the plaintiff assumed that a particular legal relationship then existed between the plaintiff and the defendant or expected that a particular legal relationship would exist between them and, in the latter case, that the defendant would not be free to withdraw from the expected legal relationship; (2) the defendant has induced the plaintiff to adopt that assumption or expectation; (3) the plaintiff acts or abstains from acting in reliance on the assumption or expectation; (4) the defendant knew or intended him to do so; (5) the plaintiff's action or inaction will occasion detriment if the assumption or expectation is not fulfilled; and (6) the defendant has failed to act to avoid that detriment whether by fulfilling the assumption or expectation or otherwise. For the purposes of the second element, a defendant who has not actively induced the plaintiff to adopt an assumption or expectation will nevertheless be held to have done so if the assumption or expectation can be fulfilled only by a transfer of the defendant's property, a diminution of his rights or an increase in his obligations and he, knowing that the plaintiff's reliance on the assumption or expectation may cause detriment to the plaintiff if it is not fulfilled, fails to deny to the plaintiff the correctness of the assumption or expectation on which the plaintiff is conducting his affairs.

Deane and **Gaudron JJ** delivered judgments which concurred in the result but reached that result by a different route. They held that the Mahers had acted under a mistaken assumption that a binding agreement had come into existence (as opposed to a mistaken belief that a contract would come into existence) but that Waltons were nevertheless estopped from denying the existence of a contract between the parties so that the Mahers were entitled to bring an action on the 'contract' notwithstanding the fact that no binding contract had actually been made.

COMMENTARY

A number of points should be noted about *Waltons Stores*. The first is that the estoppel clearly operated to confer a cause of action upon the Mahers. The second is that the judges were careful to state that not every act of reliance upon a gratuitous promise will bring promissory estoppel into play. 'Something more' is required. The exact nature of that 'something more' will doubtless depend upon the facts of the case but there must be something which renders it 'unconscionable' for the promisor to go back on his promise. Thirdly, it is not clear how *Waltons Stores* would be decided by an English court. It would probably not fall within the scope of proprietary estoppel because the work was done on the Mahers' land and not Waltons' land and, in relation to promissory estoppel, it would run into the obstacle that promissory estoppel cannot create a cause of action. On the other hand in *Baird Textile Holdings Ltd* v. *Marks and Spencer plc* [2002] 1 All ER (Comm) 737 Mance LJ stated (at para [98]):

There was in *Waltons Stores* complete agreement on the terms of the lease. The agreement was merely unenforceable for want of compliance with the statute. It may be arguable that recognition of an estoppel here would not be to use estoppel 'as giving a cause of action in itself', and it would certainly not be to undermine the necessity of consideration. Rather, it would preclude the potential lessee from raising a collateral objection to the binding nature of the agreed lease.

Such an approach would enable the English courts to reach the same result as that reached in *Waltons Stores* without taking on board the broader jurisdiction asserted by the High Court of Australia. The latter jurisdiction may be too broad for English tastes. Thus Professor Treitel has stated (H Beale (ed), *Chitty on Contracts* (29th edn, Sweet & Maxwell, 2004), para 3-106) that it:

gives rise to the difficulties that there appear to be no clear limits to its scope, and that this lack of clarity is a regrettable source of uncertainty. The doctrine is, moreover, hard to reconcile with a number of fundamental principles of English law, such as the non-enforceability of informal gratuitous promises (even if relied on) and the rule that there is no right to damages for a wholly innocent non-contractual representation.

The fourth point relates to the remedy. Brennan J is clearly of the view that the aim of the remedy is to compensate the promisee for his detrimental reliance on the promise. The judgment of Mason CJ and Wilson J is more equivocal. They state that the doctrine extends to the 'enforcement of voluntary promises' and, in so stating, appear to envisage that the remedy may extend to the protection of the expectation interest. The split between those who see the function of estoppel as being to compensate for detrimental reliance and those who see it as being to fulfil the expectations engendered by the promise was further evident in the decision of the High Court in *Commonwealth of Australia* v. *Verwayen* (1990) 170 CLR 394. In *Giumelli* v. *Giumelli* (1999) 196 CLR 101 the High Court took a step in the direction of recognizing the expectation measure as the presumptive remedy in estoppel cases when they stated that 'often the only way to prevent the promisee suffering detriment will be to enforce the promise'.

Waltons Stores is a difficult case for English lawyers as it raises in stark form the problem that English law has in terms of justifying the difference in principle that currently exists between proprietary and promissory estoppel (in that only proprietary estoppel can create a cause of action). Had the Mahers been promised an interest in Waltons' land they would have had a claim against Waltons on the basis of proprietary estoppel. But the fact that they were not, and that it was Waltons who were promised an interest in their land, has the consequence that the case cannot come within the fold of proprietary estoppel and it may be left in the wilderness of promissory estoppel (which cannot create a cause of action). This difference in treatment cannot be justified. Why does English law continue to differentiate between proprietary estoppel and promissory estoppel in relation to the creation of causes of action? Professor Treitel states (*Some Landmarks in Twentieth Century Contract Law* (Oxford University Press, 2002), p. 40):

Exactly why proprietary estoppel can give rise to a cause of action while promissory estoppel cannot is not made at all clear in the English cases. One possible explanation is that the proprietary estoppel cases originally involved an element of unjust enrichment (though some modern cases apply the doctrine even in the absence of this factor), while promissory estoppel could arise from mere action in reliance by the promisee; and that this was regarded as a less strong ground (than unjust enrichment) for relief.

This is not a convincing explanation for the difference between proprietary and promissory estoppel. Either they both should be able to create a new cause of action or neither of them should be able to do so. The proposition that one can and one cannot is a proposition that can no longer (if it ever could) be justified.

(f) LOCATING ESTOPPELS

One of the real difficulties with estoppel lies in locating its position within the law of obligations. Take the straightforward case of the party who relies to his detriment upon a promise that is not supported by consideration. What legal basis does such a promisee have for maintaining that he or she has a cause of action against the defaulting promisor? The question is not an academic one. It is a profoundly practical question as has become evident in the context of the analysis of the remedies available in estoppel cases. Is the aim of the remedy to protect the claimant's reliance interest or to protect his expectation interest? The answer to this question depends, in large part, upon the nature of the cause of action that the claimant asserts. So what is the legal basis of an estoppel claim? There appear to be six possible bases. It is, however, possible to take the view that estoppel straddles more than one of these bases (in particular, it can be argued that, in certain circumstances, estoppel is contractual in nature but that in other circumstances it operates to provide a remedy for a wrong).

The first view is that the claim is contractual in nature. On this view the effect of the estoppel is to render the promise legally enforceable. Estoppel thus functions as an alternative to consideration in that it renders a promise enforceable once there has been detrimental reliance upon it. Thus Professor Birks has argued ('Equity in the Modern Law: An Exercise in Taxonomy' (1996) 26 *University of Western Australia Law Review* 1, 63) that:

Estoppels have all along been binding promises. . . . Detrimental reliance promises, binding with limited legal effect, have become and are becoming binding with general effect. But, if that is right, there is no point at all in continuing to call them estoppels. In a jurisdiction where detrimental reliance promises are binding with general effect it has become true that promises are contracts when made by deed, supported by consideration or relied on to the detriment of the promisee.

Adoption of this view leads to the conclusion that the remedies available in estoppel cases are the normal contractual remedies, the aim of which is generally to protect the expectation interest.

The second view is that the estoppel acts as a cause of action to enforce promises and that it operates in a manner akin to contract but that it is not the same as a contractual claim. This view has been taken by Dr Edelman ('Remedial Certainty and Remedial Discretion in Estoppel after *Giumelli*' (1999) 15 *Journal of Contract Law* 179). He argues that it is not a contract on the ground that more than a breach of promise is required in order to trigger the operation of an estoppel. There must be some 'unconscionable conduct' or detrimental reliance in order to render the promise binding. It is the reliance that renders the promise binding rather than the promise that renders reliance possible. Thus Dr Edelman argues (at pp. 188–189) that, although:

an estoppel cannot be said to be a 'contract' it is still concerned with the enforcement of promises where not to do so would be unconscionable and where they have caused reliance detriment. It is a different doctrine which enforces promises in different situations.

The third view is that estoppel is part of the law of wrongs. It cannot be a tort because tort is the label used by English law to denote a common law wrong and here we are in the realms of equity. Support for the proposition that estoppel is a wrong can be derived from the numerous references to 'unconscionability' in both judicial and academic analyses of estoppel. On this view estoppel appears to be defendant-sided, in that it attaches primary significance to the conduct of the promisor. But the difficulty with this view lies in identifying the wrong that the defendant has committed. Professor Birks has argued (at p. 64) that 'there is no other kind of unconscionable behaviour involved other than that which consists in failing to honour one's promises'. Adoption of this analysis leads most naturally to the conclusion that the remedy awarded should aim to compensate the promisee for the loss that he has suffered as a result of his reliance upon the promise that has been made.

The fourth view of estoppel is that it is concerned with the reversal of unjust enrichments. Take the case where A owns land and he promises to give some of the land to B as a gift. B builds a house on A's land in reliance upon A's promise to give him the land. A then revokes that promise. To allow A to go back on his word in such a case is to allow A to enrich himself at B's expense because he gets a house built on his land for nothing. In such cases the courts have generally strained to give B a remedy and proprietary estoppel has often been the remedy to which they have resorted. The case for intervention in this example is stronger in that there is both a detriment to B and an enrichment of A. More difficult is the case where there is a loss to B but A has not made a gain. Unjust enrichment may provide a basis for explaining the remedy in cases where there is a gain to the defendant and a loss to the claimant but it cannot explain the remedy in cases where there is a loss to one party but no corresponding gain made by the other.

The fifth view of estoppel is that the cause of action lies in equity and so it is a flexible remedy that is available in the discretion of the court. Thus one can find references in estoppel cases to the 'minimum equity' on the facts of the case and the need to tailor the remedy to fit the facts of the case. Mr Justice Finn, writing extra-judicially ('Equitable Doctrine and Discretion in Remedies' in W Cornish, R Nolan, J O'Sullivan, and G Virgo (eds), *Restitution, Past, Present and Future* (Hart, 1998), pp. 269–270) has argued that 'appropriateness' should be the arbiter of the remedy granted by the court. He picks up on the reference in both *Waltons Stores* v. *Maher* and *Commonwealth of Australia* v. *Verwayen* to the 'minimum equity to do justice to the plaintiff' and the judgment of Scarman LJ in *Crabb* v. *Arun District Council* and argues (at p. 270) that:

The remedies given in estoppel cases can vary widely in character and content—monetary awards, the grants of estates and interests in land, the truncation of the rights arising in or under contracts, etc. But ... the ... remedy is not at large. Its object is detriment averting. What I would emphasise in this is that in selecting the appropriate remedy in the circumstances there must be *proportionality* between the remedy selected and its effects, and the detriment to be avoided. This, I venture, will be found to be an important constraint on the award of relief. And it necessitates that the selection of remedy cannot in the end be left simply to a plaintiff.

Three points should be noted about this approach. The first is that the discretion is founded on the premiss that the aim of the remedy is detriment averting. It is possible to have a different foundation for the exercise of the discretion. In particular, it is possible to start from the assumption that the aim of the remedy should be to give effect to the expectation engendered by the promise but that the court should have the discretion not to fulfil that expectation in certain circumstances. Simon Gardner takes exactly this position (see 'The Remedial Discretion in Proprietary Estoppel' (1999) 115 *LQR* 438) and this view is closer to that taken by the High Court of Australia in *Giumelli* v. *Giumelli* (1999) 196 CLR 101 and by the Court of Appeal in England in *Jennings* v. *Rice* [2002] EWCA Civ 159, a proprietary estoppel case. Secondly, the extent of the discretion given to the court can vary from a totally unstructured discretion, at the one end of the spectrum, to a discretion that can be exercised only within very narrow limits, at the other end. The former view is difficult to defend, given the level of uncertainty it will generate. It may be that the latter approach is the one that is closest to the position taken by the courts. Gardner has put forward the following (((1999) 115 *LQR* 438, 452) as a possible hypothesis for the remedial regime for proprietary estoppel:

The approach is

- to vindicate the plaintiff's expectations (care being taken to achieve the best match between the details of the plaintiff's expectations and the possible legal responses);

- to vindicate those expectations in specie if practicable, but otherwise in a monetary form; but

- to resort to some other quantum, not more generous than the expectation measure, if it is impracticable to give relief in the expectation measure; and

- to resort to some other quantum, with no ceiling at the expectation measure, in the presence of another factor from a limited range recognised as meriting a departure from expectation relief.

This leads us to the third point in relation to the discretionary model and that is that it does not tell us the basis of the claim that is being made. The views advanced by Mr Justice Finn and Simon Gardner are, in many ways, refinements of options 1–3. That is to say, the cause of action remains the contract or the wrong but the court is given a discretion to depart from the basic measure of recovery in certain, limited circumstances. This position has its attractions. Take a case where a claimant is promised a huge sum of money by the defendant and he relies on that promise to his detriment in a relatively minor way. In such a case a court may well baulk at the proposition that it must give the claimant his full expectation as a result of his relatively trivial reliance. In such a case a discretion to commute the basic expectation measure to the reliance measure may not be unwarranted. But it is important to notice that this type of discretion is very different from a discretion which gives the court the ability to award the measure of relief it thinks fit, for whatever reason it thinks fit. It is a structured discretion that operates within an initial commitment to a particular measure of recovery.

Finally it can be argued that the basis of estoppel can be located in a 'duty to ensure the reliability of induced assumptions'. This view has been put forward by Dr Spence in his book, *Protecting Reliance: The Emergent Doctrine of Equitable Estoppel* (Hart, 1999). He argues (at pp. 2–3):

The duty to ensure the reliability of induced assumptions places primary and secondary obligations on a party who (i) induces an assumption in the mind of another party and (ii) induces the other party to rely upon that assumption. The primary obligation is that the inducing party must, in so far as he is reasonably able, prevent harm to the relying party. 'Harm' consists in the extent to which the relying party is worse off because the assumption has proved unjustified than he would have been had it never been induced. The secondary obligation is that, if the relying party does suffer harm of the relevant type, and the inducing party might reasonably have prevented it, then the inducing party must compensate the relying party for the harm he has suffered.

It is inducing reliance, rather than merely inducing an assumption, that attracts the duty to ensure the reliability of induced assumptions. The question of whether reliance has been induced, and if so how strongly, determines whether, and if so how strongly, the duty to ensure the reliability of induced assumptions applies. Seven aspects of the parties' dealings and relationship must be considered in determining whether, and if so how strongly, reliance was induced. Four of these seven considerations concern the parties' dealings. They are (i) the way in which the assumption and reliance upon it were induced (a claim that reliance has been induced and that the duty is owed is more plausible when there has been an express representation, than it is when there has merely been conduct or silence), (ii) the content of the assumption (a claim that reliance has been induced and that the duty is owed is more plausible when the relevant assumption relates to present fact, than it is when it relates to evidently less reliable matters such as another party's intentions), (iii) the relative knowledge of the parties (a claim that reliance has been induced and that the duty is owed is more plausible when the inducing party knew that the relying party would rely upon the relevant assumption) and (iv) the parties' relative interest in the activities undertaken in reliance on the assumption (a claim that reliance has been induced and that the duty is owed is more plausible when the relying party is providing the inducing party with some service in the relevant activities in reliance). Three of the seven considerations concern the parties' relationship. They are: (i) the nature and context of the parties' relationship (the claim that reliance was induced and that the duty is owed is less plausible in contexts in which a high degree of self-reliance might be expected, such as highly competitive contexts), (ii) the parties' relative strength of position (the claim that reliance was induced and that the duty is owed is more plausible in situations in which there is a disparity in the parties' strength of position in favour of the inducing party), and (iii) the history of the parties' relationship (the claim that reliance was induced and that the duty is owed is more plausible as between parties with long-standing relationships of trust). I do not claim that this list of seven considerations is necessarily exhaustive. Nor do I claim that there is no overlap between them. For example, if parties enjoy a longstanding relationship in a context of close co-operation, it might be assumed that one party knew that the other would rely upon an assumption he induced. However, any consideration of the claim that one party induced another to rely upon a particular assumption must involve assessment of at least these seven aspects of the parties' dealings and relationship.

There are a number of difficulties with this view. The first relates to the moral basis for this duty. In the absence of a promise, is there any justification for imposing an obligation on the party said to have induced the assumption? As Professor Fried points out (*Contract as Promise* (Harvard University Press, 1981), p. 10):

Should your expectations of me limit my freedom of choice? If you rent the apartment next to mine because I play chamber music there, do I owe you more than an expression of regret when my friends and I decide to meet instead at the cellist's home? And, in general, why should my liberty be constrained by the harm you would suffer from the disappointment of the expectations you choose to entertain about my choices?

The second difficulty relates to the complexity of the factors identified by Dr Spence. It does not give the appearance of providing a high degree of predictive yield when applied to concrete fact situations. The third is that, while it may be consistent with the results in many of the cases, it does not conform with the language of the courts.

Enough has been said to demonstrate that the theoretical basis of estoppel remains a matter of difficulty and it is, perhaps, for this reason that the courts have had so many problems in terms of working out the appropriate remedy in estoppel cases. The basic choice that has to be made is between a model that aims to protect detrimental reliance (options three and six above) and one that aims to fulfil the expectations engendered by the promise (options one and two above). That choice can be refined through the exercise of a discretion (option five) by which the court can depart from the basic measure of recovery in certain, exceptional circumstances. While English law adheres to the rule that estoppel cannot create a cause of action it is spared the need overtly to answer some of these questions. In the context of proprietary estoppel, the English courts have inclined to the view that the measure of recovery is prima facie the expectation measure but that the courts have a discretion to depart from it in certain circumstances. A similar view would now appear to be emerging in Australia in relation to equitable estoppel. The likelihood is that English courts will adopt this view in the event that they decide that promissory estoppel can create a new cause of action.

5. THE FUTURE OF CONSIDERATION

As was noted at the beginning of this chapter, the doctrine of consideration is a doctrine that is under attack. It does not appear to fit with the demands of commercial practice and it is difficult to explain its existence and content in theoretical terms. Further, as a result of the tension that exists between *Williams* v. *Roffey Bros*, on the one hand, and *Foakes* v. *Beer*, on the other, the doctrine cannot even be said to be internally coherent. Things are not much better when we turn to estoppel. The law exhibits a high degree of uncertainty, particularly in relation to the remedies available, the differences between the various estoppels and in relation to the question whether or not promissory estoppel should be able to create a cause of action.

Yet there are surprisingly few calls for reform from the world of practice. Why is this? Lord Steyn, writing extra-judicially ('Contract Law: Fulfilling the Reasonable Expectations of Honest Men' (1997) 113 *LQR* 433, 437) stated:

I have no radical proposals for the wholesale review of the doctrine of consideration. I am not persuaded that it is necessary. And great legal changes should only be embarked on when they are truly necessary. First, there are a few cases where even in modern times courts have decided that contractual claims must fail for want of consideration. On the other hand, on careful examination it will usually be found that such claims could have been decided on other grounds, e.g. the absence of an intention to create legal relations or the fact that the transaction was induced by duress. Once a serious intention to enter into legal relations and a concluded agreement is demonstrated in a commercial context there is virtually a presumption of consideration which will almost invariably prevail without a detailed search for some technical consideration. On balance it seems to me that in modern practice the restrictive influence of consideration has markedly receded in importance. Secondly, it seems to me that in recent times the courts have shown a readiness to hold that the rigidity of the doctrine of consideration must yield to practical justice and the needs of modern commerce.

Letters of credit provide a useful illustration of the way in which the doctrine of consideration is made to yield to the needs of modern commerce. Letters of credit are often used in the financing of international sales transactions. Sellers generally wish to know that they have a secure right to payment before they ship goods, while buyers are usually reluctant to pay for the goods before receiving them. Letters of credit can break this impasse. The buyer will instruct his bank (the issuing bank, 'IB') to open a letter of credit in favour of the seller under which the bank promises to pay the price to the seller on presentation by the seller of the documents relating to the goods. In this way the seller knows that it has a secure right of payment against the bank when it presents the documents. The buyer is also given some protection in that, if the seller presents non-conforming documents, the bank must reject the documents and refuse to pay unless authorized by the buyer to pay. On what basis is the bank obliged to pay the seller under the letter of credit? Professor Goode has written (*Commercial Law* (3rd edn, Penguin, 2004), pp. 970–971):

In banking usage an irrevocable credit binds IB . . . upon issue of the credit, that is, upon its release from the control of the issuer or confirmer, irrespective of the time it is delivered to or received by the beneficiary, S. If the credit is rejected by S, e.g. because it does not conform to the contract of sale, it ceases to have effect.

Though there is no reported case since the adoption of the 'irrevocable' label [that is to say, that the credit is irrevocable by the bank upon issue] in which the point has directly arisen for determination, there are several dicta indicating judicial acceptance of the binding nature of the credit by virtue of the issue of the document. . . . The problem is to reconcile the binding nature of the bank's undertaking with traditional concepts of general law, which deny legal effect to a simple promise unless consideration is furnished by the promisee, producing a contract, or the promisee is induced to act in reliance on the promise, generating some form of estoppel. The difficulty created by the undertaking embodied in an irrevocable letter of credit is that it appears to be binding on IB, and enforceable by S, despite the fact that S has furnished no consideration for IB's promise and, indeed, may not have taken steps to act upon it nor even have signified his assent to its terms. . . . How, then, can the bank concerned become bound to the beneficiary solely by virtue of the issue of the letter of credit to him?

Various ingenious theories have been advanced designed to accommodate the binding nature of the bank's undertaking within the framework of traditional contract law. All of these fall to the ground because, in an endeavour to produce an acceptable theoretical solution, they distort the character of the transaction and predicate facts and intentions at variance with what is in practice done and intended by the parties. The defects in these various theories show the undesirability of trying to force all commercial instruments and devices into a strait-jacket of traditional rules of law. Professor Ellinger has rightly argued that the letter of credit should be treated as a *sui generis* instrument embodying a promise which by mercantile usage is enforceable without consideration. Professor Kozolchyk takes the description a stage further, treating a letter of credit as a new type of mercantile currency embodying an abstract promise of payment, which . . . possesses a high, though not total, immunity from attack on the ground of breach of duty of S to B.

The adaptability of consideration may be said to be its strength. The ability to find consideration has been described by Professor Treitel as the practice of 'inventing' consideration. Thus he states (GH Treitel, *The Law of* Contract (11th edn, Sweet & Maxwell, 2003), p. 71):

Normally, a party enters into a contract with a view to obtaining the consideration provided by the other: for example, the buyer wants the goods and the seller the price. In the United States it has been said that this is essential, and that 'Nothing is consideration that is not regarded as such by both parties'. But English courts do not insist on this requirement and often regard an act or forbearance as the consideration for a promise even though it may not have been the object of the promisor to secure it. They may also regard the possibility of some prejudice to the promisee as a detriment without regard to the question whether it has in fact been suffered. These practices may be called 'inventing consideration', and the temptation to adopt one or the other of them is particularly strong when the act or forbearance which was actually bargained for cannot be regarded as consideration for some reason which is thought to be technical and without merit. In such cases the practice of inventing consideration may help to make the operation of the doctrine of consideration more acceptable; but the practice may also be criticised on the ground that it gives the courts a wide discretion to hold promises binding (or not) as they please. Thus the argument that the promisee *might* have suffered prejudice by acting in reliance on a promise is in some cases made a basis of decision, while in others precisely the same argument is rejected. The courts have not been very consistent in the exercise of this discretion and its existence is a source of considerable uncertainty in this branch of the law.

But not all writers have adopted such an accommodating approach towards the doctrine of consideration. Its principal critic has been Professor Atiyah. He famously attacked the doctrine of consideration in a lengthy essay, entitled 'Consideration: A Restatement' (contained in *Essays on Contract* (Oxford University Press, 1986), pp. 179–243), the beginning and the conclusion of which are reproduced below:

pp. 180–183

The conventional statement of the doctrine of consideration is not perhaps as easily reduced to a simple set of rules as it is often assumed, but few would disagree with the following propositions. Firstly, a promise is not enforceable (if not under seal[3]), unless the promisor obtains some benefit or the promisee incurs some detriment in return for the promise. A subsidiary proposition, whose claim to be regarded as a part of the orthodox doctrine is perhaps less certain, is sometimes put forward, namely that consideration must be of economic value. Secondly, in a bilateral contract the consideration for a promise is a counter-promise, and in a unilateral contract consideration is the performance of the act specified by the promisor. Thirdly, the law of contract only enforces bargains; the consideration must, in short, be (and perhaps even be regarded by the parties as) the 'price' of the promise. Fourthly, past consideration is not sufficient consideration. Fifthly, consideration must move from the promisee. Sixthly (and this is regarded as following from the first three propositions), the law does not enforce gratuitous promises. Seventhly, a limited exception to these propositions is recognized by the *High Trees* principle which, however, only enables certain promises without consideration to be set up by way of defence.

More generally, it would, I think, be commonly agreed that there is such a concept as a 'doctrine of consideration'. This very phrase carries certain implications. In particular it implies that there is *one* doctrine, and *one* concept. The word 'consideration' is invariably used in the singular. Lawyers do not today inquire what are *the considerations* which lead a court to enforce a promise, but whether *there is* consideration. The word 'doctrine' also appears to carry certain implications. In this particular area of the law, it seems to carry the implication that the 'doctrine' is 'artificial', and has no rational foundation except possibly in so far as it may be argued that gratuitous promises should not necessarily be enforceable.

It is my purpose to suggest that the conventional account of the law is unsatisfactory, and that scarcely one of the propositions set out above accurately represents the law. But it is necessary to start by suggesting that one of the principal reasons for the present divergence between the conventional account of the law and its actual operation arises from the more general beliefs about the existence of a set of artificial and irrational rules termed the doctrine of consideration. The truth is that the courts have never set out to create a doctrine of consideration. They have been concerned with the much more practical problem of deciding in the course of litigation whether a particular promise in a particular case should be enforced. Since it is unthinkable that any legal system could enforce *all* promises it has always been necessary for the courts to decide which promises they would enforce. When the courts found a sufficient reason for enforcing a promise they enforced it; and when they found that for one reason or another it was undesirable to enforce a promise, they did not enforce it. It seems highly probable that when the

---

[3] The requirement of a seal has since been abolished. It now suffices for the promise to be made in the form of a deed: see further Chapter 6.

courts first used the word 'consideration' they meant no more than that there was good 'reason' for the enforcement of a promise. If the consideration was 'good', this meant that the court found sufficient reason for enforcing the promise. All this is not to suggest that the law was ever unprincipled, or that judges ever decided cases according to personal or idiosyncratic views of what promises it was desirable to enforce. As always with the common law, it was the collective view of the judges, based largely on the conditions and moral values of the community, which prevailed over a period of time. The doctrine of precedent, then as now, was always available as an aid to the courts in deciding what promises to enforce.

The notion that consideration means a reason for the enforcement of a promise was largely borrowed in my original essay from Corbin, and although Professor Treitel has objected to this, and insisted that it cannot just be asserted that this is what consideration means, it seems clear to me that it is both a historical and an analytical truth. I will not inquire further into the historical use of the term here, but at least it must be admitted that in modern law the presence of consideration is a necessary condition for the enforceability of a promise, leaving aside the promissory estoppel and other 'non-contractual' means of enforcement. To translate that into saying that consideration means a *reason* for the enforcement of a promise only requires us to make the assumption that the law is a rational enterprise. To assert that the law 'will not do A unless B' surely entails, if law is purposive in its nature, that the presence of B is a *reason* for doing A—unless (which can hardly be suggested here) it is merely a condition for the doing of A. Of course this does not carry the implication that the *reason* is always a good one; nor that sometimes the reason ought not to be outweighed by other reasons. But unless the presence of consideration is regarded, in general terms, as a reason for the enforcement of promises, the whole doctrine would have to be treated as mumbo-jumbo. Doubtless the law is sometimes irrational, but to treat a whole doctrine of the law as irrational implies both an extraordinary lack of faith in the intelligence of former judges, and an astonishing perversity in the erection of a system of precedent which requires that their decisions should be followed. I decline to make either of these assumptions.

Professor Treitel's critique of my original essay (and his textbook on the *Law of Contract*) insists that the courts have power to 'invent' consideration, and that this ability is an important phenomenon which I have overlooked and which explains many otherwise puzzling things about the doctrine. I find this a difficult concept to grasp. Is an 'invented' consideration something different from a 'real' consideration or is it the same thing? If it is the same thing, then it is hard to see in what sense it is invented; and if it is not the same thing, then it either violates the rules of law, or it modifies them. Presumably Professor Treitel does not mean to suggest that when judges invent consideration they are defying the law and violating their judicial oaths, but if an invented consideration modifies the rules governing ordinary consideration, then an invented consideration becomes again an ordinary consideration, though the legal significance of the doctrine has now changed. The only other possibility that occurs to me is that the courts might use the concept of 'invented consideration' rather like an equitable or merciful dispensation from the ordinary law, but it is unthinkable that judges should behave in this way. They have no power to invent a consideration in one case and refuse to do so in a relatively identical case. Thus an invented consideration must in the end be the same thing as an ordinary consideration. I fear that Professor Treitel has himself invented the concept of an invented consideration because he finds it the only way in which he is able to reconcile many decisions with what he takes to be the 'true' or 'real' doctrine. This is, of course, exactly the sort of process against which Corbin warned us, and I give my full allegiance to Corbin on this point.

Nevertheless, I would today wish to qualify the suggestion that consideration 'means' a reason for the enforcement of a promise. It now seems to me to be more accurate to suggest that consideration really was and is a reason for the recognition of an obligation, rather than a reason for the enforcement of a promise. Given that . . . reliance and benefit are often themselves good reasons for the recognition of obligations in law—that we have many non-promissory cases in which the obligation is based upon an element of detrimental reliance or an element of benefit rendered or obtained—and given also that many cases in contract law are based on implied promises which seem more or less fictitious, the wider formulation of the function of consideration seems more accurate. But for the purposes of this essay, I do not think that it matters much whether I proceed on the narrower or wider understanding of what is the general purpose of the doctrine of consideration.

pp. 240–243

The present orthodoxy therefore seems to me unnecessarily cumbrous. It would be a great deal simpler if the courts were willing to treat action in reliance which suffices for estoppel as also sufficient to satisfy the requirements of consideration; but it would at the same time be necessary, of course, for the courts to become more sophisticated about when expectation protection is, and when it is not, justified. If American experience is anything to go by, it may well be necessary to retain considerable flexibility as to when to confine contractual redress to the protection of reliance, and when to go further; it is unwise to try to draw this line by fastening on the absurdly narrow and unreal distinction between an action in reliance which is requested, and one which is not requested, but merely foreseeable. Fortunately, in practice it is so easy for a court to 'imply' a request when it wishes to do so, that no court which wishes directly to enforce a promise in this sort of case need find any difficulty in doing so . . .

. . . there are, I suggest, important conclusions to be drawn from what I have tried to demonstrate. The first is that to talk of abolition of the doctrine of consideration is non-sensical. Consideration means a reason for the enforcement of a promise, or, even more broadly, a reason for the recognition of an obligation. If the broader sense is right, then, of course, talk of abolition is quite absurd. But even if one takes only the narrower sense, it is hard to take seriously talk of abolition. Nobody can seriously propose that all promises should become enforceable; to abolish the doctrine of consideration, therefore, is simply to require the courts to begin all over again the task of deciding what promises are to be enforceable. They will, of course, have to use new technical justifications for this task, and the obvious one that lies to hand is the 'intent to create legal relations'. No doubt there is something to be said for beginning this task all over again, and for using a new technique for this purpose. Changes in social and commercial conditions, and changes in the moral values of the community, mean that the courts will not always find the same reasons for the enforcement of promises to be good today as their forbears did; equally, it is likely that they will often find good reasons for the enforcement of promises where their pre-decessors did not. Moreover, I think there is less likelihood of the 'intent to create legal relations' formula ossifying into a 'doctrine'; though there is the converse danger that its application may create uncertainty as to what promises will be enforceable. But

I question whether the 'intent to create legal relations' formula will in the long run work any better than the rules of consideration.

In particular, I believe that the problems arising from the enforcement of gratuitous promises are too complex to be adequately dealt with by either the rules of consideration or the 'intent to create legal relations' formula. For a start, the 'intent' formula can only be squared with the importance of detrimental reliance by repeated use of fictions. And if it should be suggested that the law should be more willing to enforce gratuitous promises, I believe that it will be necessary to start by asking more about the concept of a 'gratuitous' promise. To be legally enforceable, gratuitous promises will presumably need to be sensible, rational activities. But surely we then need to ask more about the kind of circumstances in which people do rationally make gratuitous promises, and we may need to distinguish various classes of cases. For instance, there are promises made in a commercial context which may appear gratuitous, but where the promisor expects some return in a rather more indirect way than the present doctrine of consideration recognizes. There is a lot to be said for the view that such promises are really bargain promises, and should be fully enforceable, even while executory, to the same extent as ordinary contracts. (But there is also a lot to be said for achieving this result by modification of the present rather rigid view of what kind of benefit constitutes sufficient consideration.) Then there are gratuitous charitable promises, gratuitous family promises, and so on. Above all, of course, there is the distinction between gratuitous relied-upon and unrelied-upon promises.

Whether unrelied-upon gratuitous promises should ever be rendered enforceable seems to me a very dubious proposition, and even if the principle is conceded, such promises are difficult to generalise about in advance, because so much depends upon the context out of which they arise. It may conceivably be found desirable to enforce gratuitous promises in a much wider range of circumstances than exists at the moment, but not to the same extent as ordinary commercial promises. For instance, it may be found wise to render some gratuitous promises enforceable in principle against the promisor, but not necessarily against his executors. Whether this would be just may well depend on his family obligations, and the solvency of his estate. It may be wise to provide for a much wider defence of frustration in the case of gratuitous promises, if they are to become enforceable while yet unrelied upon. A man promises his son an allowance while the latter is at the university; it may be just and equitable to enforce this promise, but would it remain just and equitable if the promisor became incapacitated and lost his job? Perhaps, too, a wider latitude should be allowed to some form of defence based on mistake. Perhaps we need to consider a shorter limitation period. And perhaps after all some gratuitous promises may be better treated as merely giving rise to a defence rather than a course of action. Certainly we shall need to consider whether the same rules will be appropriate for all kinds of gratuitous promises. A promise to render gratuitous services is not necessarily in like case with a promise to make a cash gift; and a promise of money to a charity is not necessarily the same as a promise made to a member of the family. In short we must look to the reasons (or considerations) which make it just or desirable to enforce promises, and also to the extent to which it is just to enforce them.

Professor Atiyah's attack has been the subject of a counter-attack by Professor Treitel ('Consideration: A Critical Analysis of Professor Atiyah's Fundamental Restatement)' (1976) 50 *Australian Law Journal* 439) principally on the ground that his proposal that the courts should look to the reasons which make it just or desirable to enforce promises is too vague to provide a workable standard.

Given all of these criticisms of the doctrine of consideration it is unlikely that English law would adopt the doctrine of consideration were it to be given the opportunity to start afresh. International re-statements on contract law find no role for the doctrine. Thus Article 2.101 of the Principles of European Contract Law states that:

(1) A contract is concluded if:

(a)   the parties intend to be legally bound; and

(b)   they reach a sufficient agreement

without any further requirement.

(2) A contract need not be concluded or evidenced in writing nor is it subject to any other requirement as to form. The contract may be proved by any means, including witnesses.

Article 3.2 of the Unidroit Principles of International Commercial Contracts provides that 'a contract is concluded, modified or terminated by the mere agreement of the parties, without any further requirement'.

But the fact is that English law has not been given, and may never be given, the opportunity to start afresh. This being the case, it is unlikely that the courts will, for the reasons given by Lord Steyn (p. 272 above), abandon the doctrine. They are more likely to continue the process, evident in cases such as *Williams* v. *Roffey Bros*, of being more willing to find the existence of consideration where they believe that the parties intended to be bound by their agreement. One consequence of this may be that greater prominence will be given to the doctrine of intention to create legal relations, to which we shall turn in Chapter 7.

6. FURTHER READING

ATIYAH, PS, 'Consideration: A Re-statement' in Atiyah, PS, *Essays on Contract* (Oxford University Press, 1986), p. 179.

——, 'When is an Enforceable Agreement not a Contract? Answer: When it is an Equity' (1976) 92 *LQR* 174.

CHEN-WISHART, M, 'Consideration: Practical Benefit and the Emperor's New Clothes' in Beatson, J and Friedmann, D (eds), *Good Faith and Fault in Contract Law* (Oxford University Press, 1995), p. 123.

COOKE, E, 'Estoppel and the Protection of Expectations' (1997) 17 *Legal Studies* 258.

EDELMAN, J, 'Remedial Certainty or Remedial Discretion in Estoppel after *Giumelli*' (1999) 15 *Journal of Contract Law* 179.

GARDNER, S, 'Remedial Discretion in Proprietary Estoppel' (1999) 115 *LQR* 438.

HALSON, R, 'The Offensive Limits of Promissory Estoppel' [1999] *Lloyd's Maritime and Commercial Law Quarterly* 257.

Kotz, H and Flessner, A, *European Contract Law Volume One: Formation, Validity, and Content of Contracts; Contract and Third Parties* (Oxford University Press, 1997), Chapter 4.

Luther, P, 'Campbell, Espinasse and the Sailors: Text and Context in the Common Law' (1999) 19 *Legal Studies* 526.

Millett, P, '*Crabb v. Arun DC*—A Riposte' (1976) 92 *LQR* 342.

Nolan, D, 'Following in Their Footsteps: Equitable Estoppel in Australia and the United States' (2000) *King's College Law Journal* 201.

O'Sullivan, J, 'In Defence of *Foakes v. Beer*' [1996] *CLJ* 219.

Robertson, A, 'Reliance and Expectation in Estoppel Remedies' (1998) 18 *Legal Studies* 360.

Spence, M, *Protecting Reliance: The Emergent Doctrine of Equitable Estoppel* (Hart, 1999).

Treitel, GH, 'Consideration: A Critical Analysis of Professor Atiyah's Fundamental Restatement' (1976) 50 *ALJ* 439.

——, *Some Landmarks of Twentieth Century Contract Law* (Oxford University Press, 2002), Chapter 1.

6

FORMALITIES

1. CENTRAL ISSUES

1. Requirements of form (such as writing) are not as important today as they were in the past. As a general rule, contracts can be made in any form and can be proved by any means. Commercial parties generally reduce their contract to written form but this is for reasons of practical convenience, not legal compulsion.

2. However, there remain exceptional cases where the law does insist upon requirements of form. The reasons for continued reliance upon requirements of form are considered in this chapter, together with the criticisms that are advanced against such requirements.

3. The only example in English contract law of a formal requirement which is sufficient in itself to render a promise binding is a promise that is made in a deed. The deed is a useful device in commercial practice. Where there is no consideration for a promise or there is a doubt about the presence of consideration, the promise can be rendered enforceable by the simple device of making use of a deed.

4. There are other cases where the formal requirement is an *additional, necessary* prerequisite that must be satisfied if the contract is to be binding (in other words the agreement must also be supported by consideration, etc.). The formal requirement may take different forms. The principal forms are (i) the contract must be made in writing, (ii) it must be evidenced in writing, or (iii) it must be made by deed.

2. INTRODUCTION

It is an old joke that an oral contract is not worth the paper it is written on. This reflects a general perception, common among laypersons, that they are not bound by a contract until they 'sign on the dotted line'. However this perception is misconceived since an oral contract is generally just as binding as a written one. It may prove advantageous to the parties to record the terms of their agreement in writing in order to minimize the risk of dispute at a later stage. Indeed, because of the desire for certainty, particularly valuable contracts will invariably take written form. But a contract is in general legally binding notwithstanding the lack of written evidence. To this general principle certain exceptions have been made. In some circumstances a contract will be unenforceable unless it is evidenced in writing. In other circumstances a contract will be void unless it is actually made in writing. Finally, there are certain types of transaction which must be made in the form of a deed that is signed before witnesses. These requirements are referred to in this chapter as 'formalities', 'formal requirements', or 'requirements of form' (all three terms being interchangeable).

As Professor Kotz has pointed out (*European Contract Law, Volume 1: Formation,*

Validity, and Content of Contracts; Contract and Third Parties (Oxford University Press, 1997), p. 78):

All legal systems in Europe have rules which invalidate certain contracts if specified formalities are ignored. Such rules are commonly regarded as exceptional, the general principle being that no formalities are required.

This statement is generally true of English contract law. It does have rules that have the effect of invalidating a limited class of contracts in the event of a failure to comply with certain prescribed formal requirements. But these rules are very much the exception. The general rule is that the parties are free to decide for themselves the form that their contract is to assume. If they wish to impose upon themselves a formal requirement they are free to do so. Further, parties can make a requirement of form a condition precedent to the existence of any contractual obligation provided that they use sufficiently clear words to this effect. Thus in *Winn* v. *Bull* (1877) 7 Ch D 29, 32 Jessel MR stated that:

where you have a proposal or agreement made in writing expressed to be subject to a formal contract being prepared, it means what it says; it is subject to and is dependent upon a formal contract being prepared.

But in the absence of such a stipulation the law does not generally impose formal requirements: the parties can make their contract quite informally if they wish to do so.

However it was not always so. Formal requirements were a prominent feature of English contract law until the second half of the twentieth century. The principal source of these formal requirements was the Statute of Frauds 1677. Professor Simpson (*A History of the Common Law of Contract* (Oxford University Press, 1975), pp. 599–600) has stated that the 'broad policy' behind the Statute of Frauds was:

to require written evidence of important legal transactions as a prerequisite to their enforcement, to insist, that is, on a measure of formality in areas in which wholly informal transactions had come to be legally effective. Thereby the bringing of groundless suits would become more difficult, though inevitably at the cost of some injustice to plaintiffs unable to produce written evidence.

But over time it became apparent that the 'cost' of the legislation was greater than the benefits which it brought in terms of preventing parties from bringing groundless or fraudulent claims. The Statute gradually fell into disrepute as it came to be used by those who wished to get out of their agreements on the 'technical' ground that the agreement did not comply with the prescribed formalities and so was not enforceable. It was largely (but not entirely) repealed in 1954 by the Law Reform (Enforcement of Contracts) Act 1954. This repeal is consistent with the modern trend which, with the notable exception of a deed (on which see pp. 284–285), is to place less emphasis on formal requirements in the law of contract. The reduced significance of formal requirements can be seen in both the Principles of European Contract Law and the Unidroit Principles of International Commercial Contracts. Article 2.101(2) of the Principles of European Contract Law provides that:

A contract need not be concluded or evidenced in writing nor is it subject to any other requirement as to form. The contract may be proved by any means, including witnesses.

While Article 1.2 of the Unidroit Principles provides that:

Nothing in these Principles requires a contract, statement or any other act to be made in or evidenced by a particular form. It may be proved by any means, including witnesses.

The similarity between these two provisions is striking and it demonstrates the measure of consensus that currently exists in relation to the declining significance of formal requirements. However, before we consign formal requirements to the dustbin of history, it is important to notice that this consensus is largely confined to the sphere of commercial contracts. When we turn to consumer contracts a very different picture emerges. The point has been well put by Professor Kotz (above p. 79) in the following terms:

it would be a mistake to suppose that formalities are no longer important in modern systems. Quite the contrary. New formal requirements are constantly being imposed everywhere, in the name of consumer protection, to such an extent that in France there has been much discussion of the *renaissance de formalisme*.

A number of examples of formal requirements imposed in the name of consumer protection can be found in English law (see, for example, the Consumer Credit Act 1974, sections 60 and 61, the Package Travel, Package Holidays and Package Tours Regulations 1992 (SI No 1992/3288), regulation 9 and the Timeshare Regulations 1997 (SI No 1997/1081), regulation 6). Before examining the circumstances in which English law imposes formal requirements on contracting parties it is worth considering the reasons that lead legal systems to make use of requirements of form.

3. THE REASONS FOR FORMAL REQUIREMENTS

Why do legal systems impose formal requirements upon contracting parties? The question has to be asked given the obvious disadvantages that attend such requirements. They are open to criticism on a number of grounds. In the first place, they tend to be time-consuming, cumbersome, and bureaucratic. Secondly, it is not easy to decide which out of the millions of contracts that are entered into on a daily basis should be subject to formal requirements. Thirdly, the content of the formal requirement can be difficult to prescribe. In the past the formal requirement was often one of writing but, given the increasing use of electronic means of communication, is it sensible to continue to insist upon writing? Further, should the contract be made in writing or should it suffice that it is evidenced in writing? Finally, difficulties arise where the parties do not comply with the formal requirements, especially in the case where the parties were unaware of their existence. Should the courts always refuse to give effect to a contract that does not comply with a requirement of form?

Powerful though these objections are, they are not conclusive. There does remain a role for requirements of form in the modern law. While recognizing the difficulties that they can bring, the case for a limited role for formal requirements has been made by

Professor Kotz (*European Contract Law Volume 1: Formation, Validity, and Content of Contracts; Contract and Third Parties* (Oxford University Press, 1997), pp. 80–81), in the context of an analysis of the development of contract law in Europe, in the following terms:

It takes time and trouble to meet formal requirements—the text has to be drafted, properly recorded, and signed by the parties. The law therefore imposes such requirements only if there is some good reason for doing so.

One such reason has to do with *proof*, with *evidence*. Parties whose agreement is purely oral are quite apt to find themselves in disagreement over what was agreed and when; if they put their undertakings and agreements in writing, such disputes are still possible, but they are much less likely.

Other formal requirements have the alternative or additional purpose of putting the parties on *notice*. Requiring a person who is about to embark on an important undertaking to go through a formality affords him a final chance to reflect on what he is doing. This is desirable not only when the deal is an important one, but also when it is one-sided: a party giving something for nothing may need to be protected from impulsive generosity or exposure to unconsidered risks. This is why donative promises and guarantees are always subjected to formal requirements. The requirement of writing does not necessarily afford much time for reflection since it does not take long to draw up and sign a guarantee agreement, yet people, especially laymen, have the impression that when a pen is put in their hand they are entering the sphere of obligation, and this concentrates the mind on the question whether they really want to engage in a legally enforceable transaction.

Sometimes formalities are required in order to mark the *transition* from negotiation to contract. In cases where precontractual negotiations tend to be prolonged, as in sales of land, the parties can easily disagree on whether the negotiations have reached the stage of agreement and legal obligation, but if the contract has to be in writing, the answer is clear. Both parties know that nothing they say or write during the negotiations is binding in law so that they may break off the negotiations without liability; they also know that they should not rely on what the other party has said until it is put in writing.

Modern legislation increasingly requires that a contract be put in writing when one of the parties to it needs special protection. To give but a few examples,[1] this is true of contracts for consumer credit, residential leases, sales of dwellings yet to be built, and articles of apprenticeship. Since all these contracts are put into writing anyway, it may seem superfluous for the legislator to insist on it, but in fact the law is not so much concerned with the writing as such: it wants to ensure that the party needing protection is provided with certain information before or at the time the contract is concluded. The purpose of this requirement of writing is to *give information*. . . . Such regulation is doubtless well-intentioned but it is doubtful whether it is effective: a consumer in urgent need of money will hardly be deterred from accepting credit by the mass of information he has to be given, though it will prevent his saying afterwards that he did not know what he was letting himself in for. Good deeds overdone can be a bane. Man's ability to process information thrust on him is limited. The costs of such paternalistic legislation are sometimes underestimated. They consist not only in the cost of paper and printing, but also in the legal uncertainty which results from the courts forever having to deal with the question of the sanctions to be applied, in particular whether the protected party can withdraw from the contract just by

---

[1] The examples given by Professor Kotz are drawn from EC Directives and French law and they are used for illustrative purposes only. It is important to note that they are not necessarily drawn from English law.

founding on a breach of the duty to give this information when he may have quite other reasons for wanting to get out of his engagement. [Emphasis in the original.]

4. FORMAL REQUIREMENTS IN ENGLISH CONTRACT LAW

When considering the role of formal requirements in English contract law it is important to distinguish two different types of case. The first is the case where the formal requirement is both necessary and sufficient to render the promise binding. This is the case of a gratuitous promise made in a deed: such a promise is binding notwithstanding the fact that it is not supported by consideration. The second is the case where the formal requirement is necessary but not sufficient to render a promise binding. In other words, the formal requirement is an additional hurdle to the usual requirements of a binding contract that must be overcome by the parties.

(a) FORMAL REQUIREMENTS WHICH ARE SUFFICIENT TO RENDER THE PROMISE BINDING

The only example in English contract law of a formal requirement which is sufficient in itself to render a promise binding is a promise that is made in a deed. Until recently, the deed had to be made under seal but the requirement of sealing was abolished by the Law of Property (Miscellaneous Provisions) Act 1989. The rules applicable to deeds are to be found in section 1 of the Law of Property (Miscellaneous Provisions) Act 1989, the principal provisions of which provide:

Deeds and their execution

1.—(1)   Any rule of law which—

(a) restricts the substances on which a deed may be written;

(b) requires a seal for the valid execution of an instrument as a deed by an individual; or

(c) requires authority by one person to another to deliver an instrument as a deed on his behalf to be given by deed,

is abolished.

(2) An instrument shall not be a deed unless—

(a) it makes it clear on its face that it is intended to be a deed by the person making it or, as the case may be, by the parties to it (whether by describing itself as a deed or expressing itself to be executed or signed as a deed or otherwise); and

(b) it is validly executed as a deed by that person or, as the case may be, one or more of those parties.

(3) An instrument is validly executed as a deed by an individual if, and only if—

(a) it is signed—

    (i) by him in the presence of a witness who attests the signature; or

    (ii) at his direction and in his presence and the presence of two witnesses who each attest the signature; and

(b) it is delivered as a deed by him or a person authorised to do so on his behalf.

    (4) In subsections (2) and (3) above 'sign', in relation to an instrument, includes making one's mark on the instrument and 'signature' is to be construed accordingly . . .

The principal requirements that must be complied with if a deed is to be validly executed are set out in subsections (2) and (3) above. Most of them, such as signature and attestation, are relatively straightforward. The only requirement that requires some elaboration is the concept of 'delivery' as found in section 1(3)(b). In *Vincent* v. *Premo Enterprises (Voucher Sales) Ltd* [1969] 2 QB 609, 619 Lord Denning stated that:

'Delivery' in this connection does not mean 'handed over' to the other side. It means delivered in the old legal sense, namely, an act done so as to evince an intention to be bound. Even though the deed remains in the possession of the maker, or of his solicitor, he is bound by it if he has done some act evincing an intention to be bound, as by saying: 'I deliver this my act and deed'.

Deeds have an important role to play in legal practice. They provide a relatively simple means by which a unilateral gratuitous promise can be rendered binding. Take the example of a company that wishes to provide financial support to a university in order to endow a university lectureship. The company may be unwilling to pay all the money up front: it would rather pay an annual sum to the university over a fixed period of time. But the university will want to know that the money will be paid as a matter of legal obligation before it commits itself to employing a new member of staff in reliance upon the promise of payment. The simplest way to make the promise binding is to use a deed in which the company will undertake to pay a stipulated sum of money to the university for a defined period of time. The other circumstance in which deeds play an important role is where there is doubt about whether or not consideration has been provided for a particular promise. Rather than invite litigation over whether or not consideration has been provided, the parties may choose to eliminate the doubt by including the promise in a deed, thus rendering it binding.

(b) FORMAL REQUIREMENTS WHICH ARE NECESSARY IN ORDER TO RENDER A CONTRACT BINDING

The second group of cases differs from the first in that the formal requirement does not suffice to render the promise binding. In these cases the formal requirement is an **additional, necessary** pre-requisite that must be satisfied if the contract is to be binding. Thus the parties must show that there has been an offer, acceptance, consideration, and intention to create legal relations in the usual way and, in addition, they must demonstrate that the formal requirement has been satisfied. The formal requirement may take different forms: it may be that the contract must be (i) made in writing, (ii) evidenced in writing, or (iii) made by deed. Brief consideration will be given to these three different formal requirements, to the consequences that may flow from a failure to comply with them, and to the problems to which these requirements have given rise.

(1) CONTRACTS WHICH MUST BE MADE IN WRITING

An example of a contract that must be made in writing is a contract for the sale or disposition of an interest in land. Section 2 of the Law of Property (Miscellaneous Provisions) Act 1989 provides:

(1) A contract for the sale or other disposition of an interest in land can only be made in writing and only by incorporating all the terms which the parties have expressly agreed in one document or, where contracts are exchanged, in each.

(2) The terms may be incorporated in a document either by being set out in it or by reference to some other document.

(3) The document incorporating the terms or, where contracts are exchanged, one of the documents incorporating them (but not necessarily the same one) must be signed by or on behalf of each party to the contract.

(4) Where a contract for the sale or other disposition of an interest in land satisfies the conditions of this section by reason only of the rectification of one or more documents in pursuance of an order of a court, the contract shall come into being, or be deemed to have come into being, at such time as may be specified in the order.

(5) This section does not apply in relation to—

    (a) a contract to grant such a lease as is mentioned in section 54(2) of the Law of Property Act 1925 (short leases);

    (b) a contract made in the course of a public auction; or

    (c) a contract regulated under the Financial Services Act 1986;

and nothing in this section affects the creation or operation of resulting, implied or constructive trusts.

(6) In this section—

'disposition' has the same meaning as in the Law of Property Act 1925;

'interest in land' means any estate, interest or charge in or over land.

(7) Nothing in this section shall apply in relation to contracts made before this section comes into force.

(8) Section 40 of the Law of Property Act 1925 (which is superseded by this section) shall cease to have effect.

Section 2 has generated a considerable amount of litigation in its short life-time as parties who have failed, for one reason or another, to comply with its requirements have sought to escape from the consequences of non-compliance. In general, the courts have not been sympathetic to their plight. The reason for this is that the courts have discerned in section 2 an intention by Parliament to 'introduce new and strict requirements as to the formalities to be observed for the creation of a valid disposition of an interest in land' (per Neill LJ in *McCausland* v. *Duncan Lawrie Ltd* [1997] 1 WLR 38, 44 and see to similar effect *Firstpost Homes Ltd* v. *Johnson* [1995] 1 WLR 1567). Section 2 is stricter than its statutory predecessor, section 40 of the Law of Property Act 1925, in a number of respects. First, section 40 only required that the contract be evidenced in writing, whereas section 2 requires that the contract be 'made' in writing (section 2(1)). Secondly, non-compliance with section 40 did not render the contract void[2] but only unenforceable,[3] whereas an agreement which does not comply with section 2 is a nullity (this is not expressly stated in section 2(1) but, given that the subsection states that the contract must be made in writing, it follows that a contract that does not comply with this requirement is ineffective as a matter of law). Thirdly, under section 40 the written evidence could be contained in more than one document, whereas under section 2(1) only one document is allowed. Fourthly, section 40 did not require the memorandum or note to contain every term of the contract, whereas section 2(1) does require that all the terms must be contained in the document in question. Finally, section 40(2) of the Law of Property Act 1925 preserved a role for the doctrine of part performance which was used by the courts in order to mitigate the hardships that would otherwise flow from the conclusion that the contract was unenforceable. The essence of the doctrine of part performance was summed up in H Beale (ed), *Chitty on Contracts* (29th edn, Sweet & Maxwell, 2004), para 4-042) as follows:

Where the claimant has partly performed an oral contract required by the statute to be evidenced in writing, in the expectation that the defendant would perform the rest of the contract, the court will not allow the defendant to escape from his contract upon the strength of the statute, but may order specific performance of the oral contract. The principle is that the defendant may not set up the statute where the claimant has been induced, or allowed, by the defendant to alter his position on the faith of the contract, so that it would be fraud on the part of the defendant to rely on the statute.

The doctrine of part performance has not survived the enactment of section 2 (section 2(8)). This further evidences the fact that the pendulum has swung away from the prevention of hardship in favour of the promotion of certainty. But do the courts have at their disposal any techniques that they can employ in order to prevent section 2 giving rise to undue hardship?

The answer to this question is to be found in large part in section 2(5) which expressly preserves a role for resulting and constructive trusts[4]; the courts are likely to turn to this subsection in order to ensure that section 2 is not used as a cloak to hide unconscionable conduct or fraud. In *Yaxley* v. *Gotts* [2000] Ch 162 Beldam LJ said (at p. 193):

I do not think it inherent in a social policy of simplifying conveyancing by requiring the certainty of a written document that unconscionable conduct or equitable fraud should be allowed to prevail.

In *Yaxley* Mr Gotts decided that he would buy a property for the purpose of refurbishing it. He made an oral offer to Mr Yaxley (a builder) of the ground floor flat, which

---

[2] A contract which is void has, in general, no legal effect.

[3] A contract which is unenforceable is valid in all respects except that it cannot be enforced by one or other party (possibly, both).

[4] A constructive trust is generally regarded as a trust that is imposed by law, whereas a resulting trust is a trust where the beneficial interest jumps back, or returns, to the settlor. See further P Birks (ed), *English Private Law* (Oxford University Press, 2000), paras 4.247–4.256.

Mr Yaxley was to turn into two flats, in return for carrying out work on the four flats on the middle and top floors and then agreeing to act as the landlord's managing agent for the whole property. Mr Yaxley accepted the offer. The property was then purchased by Mr Gotts' son, rather than Mr Gotts himself, but the son knew of, and adopted, the arrangement that had been made between Mr Yaxley and his father. After Mr Yaxley had spent some £9,000 renovating the entire property, including the ground floor flat, the son refused to honour the agreement. Mr Yaxley brought a claim against both Mr Gotts senior and Mr Gotts junior in which he claimed that he was entitled to a long lease of the ground floor flat. The defendants resisted the claim on various grounds, one of which was that the oral agreement made with Mr Yaxley was a nullity because it did not comply with the requirements of section 2. The Court of Appeal held that, while the oral agreement was indeed void and unenforceable as a result of the operation of section 2, effect could nevertheless be given to the agreement on the basis of a constructive trust so that Mr Yaxley was entitled to a leasehold interest in the ground floor flat for ninety-nine years. The reasoning of the Court of Appeal in *Yaxley* was complex. The judges found it necessary to consider in some detail whether the relief arose by way of a constructive trust or as a result of the operation of the doctrine of proprietary estoppel.[5] The essence of their reasoning was that a clear promise had been made to Mr Yaxley that he would be given a beneficial interest in the ground floor flat and he had been allowed to work on the flats in the belief that he had such an interest in the ground floor flat. It would therefore be unconscionable to allow the defendants to resile from the promise that had been made. However *Yaxley* is likely to be the exception rather than the rule. The courts will probably be reluctant to find the existence of a constructive or a resulting trust because, were it otherwise, the purpose of the statute would be subverted. The dominant policy underpinning the section is the promotion of certainty in conveyancing transactions and any exception to that policy must be kept within narrow bounds. The judicial approach to the interpretation of section 2 was perhaps best summed up by Robert Walker LJ in *Yaxley* when he stated (at p. 175) that section 2:

can be seen as embodying Parliament's conclusion, in the general public interest, that the need for certainty as to the formation of contracts of this type must *in general* outweigh the disappointment of those who make informal bargains in ignorance of the statutory requirement. If an estoppel would have the effect of enforcing a void contract and subverting Parliament's purpose it may have to yield to the statutory law which confronts it, except so far as the statute's saving for a constructive trust provides a means of reconciliation of the apparent conflict. [Emphasis added.]

However it should not be thought that such a strict approach is an inevitable consequence of a statutory requirement that a contract be made in writing. The strict approach to the interpretation of section 2 is a product of the policy that underpins the section. But the aim of a statute may not be to promote certainty; it may be to protect one party to the transaction. An example in the latter category is provided by the Consumer Credit Act 1974, section 61(1) of which states that a 'regulated agreement' is not 'properly executed' unless it complies with the requirements of sections 60 and 61. In this instance the consequence of non-compliance is not inevitable

---

[5] On which see p. 248 above.

nullity because such a conclusion would frustrate the policy behind the legislation. The aim of the Act is to protect the consumer and this is reflected in section 65(1) which states that 'an improperly-executed regulated agreement is enforceable *against the debtor or hirer* on an order of the court only' (emphasis added). The court is thus interposed as the protector of the consumer. The jurisdiction of the court to make an enforcement order notwithstanding the fact that the agreement has been improperly executed is regulated by section 127 of the Act. Section 127 instructs the court to respond to improper execution in one of two ways. In the first category (those agreements falling within section 127(1) and (2)) the court is given a discretion to make an enforcement order notwithstanding the infringement. But in the second category (those agreements falling within section 127(3) and (4)) the court is not given a discretion: it must refuse the creditor an enforcement order.

The validity of a blanket refusal to make an enforcement order, as found in section 127(3), has been challenged on the ground that it amounts to a violation of the creditor's human rights. This challenge succeeded in the Court of Appeal (*Wilson* v. *First County Trust Ltd (No 2)* [2001] EWCA Civ 633; [2002] QB 74) but failed before the House of Lords (*Wilson* v. *First County Trust Ltd (No 2)* [2003] UKHL 40; [2004] 1 AC 816). The House of Lords held that section 127(3) of the Consumer Credit Act 1974 was not incompatible with Article 6(1) of the European Convention for the Protection of Human Rights and Fundamental Freedoms (Article 6(1) contains the right to a 'fair and public hearing within a reasonable time by an independent and impartial tribunal established by law'). In so concluding, their Lordships emphasized that Article 6(1) cannot be used in order to create a substantive civil right of action which otherwise has no basis in national law. The target of Article 6(1) is procedural bars on bringing claims to court. As Lord Nicholls recognized (at [35]) 'the distinction between the substantive content of a right and an unacceptable procedural bar to its enforcement by a court can give rise to difficulty in distinguishing the one from the other in a particular case'. But on the present facts no such difficulty arose. Thus Lord Nicholls concluded:

36. In the present case the essence of the complaint is that section 127(3) of the Consumer Credit Act has the effect that a regulated agreement is not enforceable unless a document containing all the prescribed terms is signed by the debtor. In my view, thus framed, the complaint does not bring article 6(1) into play. In terms of labels, that is a restriction on the scope of the rights a creditor acquires under a regulated agreement. It does not bar access to court to decide whether the case is caught by the restriction. It does bar a court from exercising any discretion over whether to make an enforcement order. But in taking that power away from a court the legislature was not encroaching on territory which ought properly to be the province of the courts in a democratic society.

Section 127(3) was also challenged on the ground that it was incompatible with Article 1 of the First Protocol to the European Convention. Article 1 provides that: 'Every natural or legal person is entitled to the peaceful enjoyment of his possessions.' Lord Nicholls stated that the word 'possessions' in Article 1 is 'apt to embrace contractual rights as much as personal rights'. This is an important point in so far as it recognizes that the deprivation of contractual rights may give rise to a claim under

Article 1 of the First Protocol. On the facts of the case, their Lordships divided on whether or not Article 1 was triggered. Lord Hope and Lord Scott in the minority concluded that Article 1 was not engaged on the basis that Article 1 only guarantees the peaceful enjoyment of the possessions that a person already owns and First County Trust acquired its contractual rights subject to the restrictions on the contract's execution set out in section 127(3). The majority disagreed. In their view, section 127(3) was 'more readily and appropriately characterised as a statutory deprivation of the lender's rights of property in the broadest sense of that expression than as a mere delimitation of the extent of the rights granted by a transaction' (at [44]). While the majority concluded that Article 1 had been engaged, they did not find that it had been breached. Lord Nicholls noted the criticisms levelled against the blanket prohibition on enforcement contained in section 127(3) and continued:

74. Despite this criticism I have no difficulty in accepting that in suitable instances it is open to Parliament, when Parliament considers the public interest so requires, to decide that failure to comply with certain formalities is an essential prerequisite to enforcement of certain types of agreements. This course is open to Parliament even though this will sometimes yield a seemingly unreasonable result in a particular case. Considered overall, this course may well be a proportionate response in practice to a perceived social problem. Parliament may consider the response should be a uniform solution across the board. A tailor-made response, fitting the facts of each case as decided in an application to the court, may not be appropriate. This may be considered an insufficient incentive and insufficient deterrent. And it may fail to protect consumers adequately. Persons most in need of protection are perhaps the least likely to participate in court proceedings. They may well let proceedings go by default: see, in relation to money lending agreements, the Crowther report, p 236, para 6.1.19.

To similar effect is the following passage from the speech of Lord Hobhouse:

138. On the basis that Article 1 was engaged, does the Consumer Credit Act 1974 go beyond what is justifiable under that Article? For the reasons already given by your Lordships, I consider that it did not. The relevant provisions of the Act are a legitimate exercise in consumer protection. Borrowers are vulnerable and not on an equal footing with lenders. The Act legitimately regulates the transparency and recording of the terms of the loan transaction and makes provision for the clear obtaining of the borrower's informed consent to those terms. Any such Act would have to provide effective sanctions against the lender for any failure to comply with the requirements of the Act otherwise they will be liable to be flouted, as occurred in the instant case. The values to which the legislative provisions were applied were appropriate to consumer legislation, indeed arguably low, and the rates of interest chargeable, so far as your Lordships were told, unlimited. (In the instant case—a secured loan of some £5,000—the rate of interest claimed worked out at 99.66% pa.) The Act, as a matter of policy, places a strong emphasis on the clarity and transparency of the actual transaction and, although in respect of other infringements a degree of latitude is allowed and the sanctions are discretionary, for the infringement involved in the instant case the sanction is automatic, as the statute makes plain. It is argued that the legislature could have made the sanction discretionary. Maybe. But it does not follow that the view that the sanction should here be automatic was not a permissible view. There was no breach of Article 1. The Court of Appeal was wrong to hold the contrary.

(II) CONTRACTS WHICH MUST BE EVIDENCED IN WRITING

Secondly, the law may state that the contract must be **evidenced** in writing (rather than made in writing). An example in this category is provided by section 4 of the Statute of Frauds 1677 which states:

Noe action shall be brought . . . whereby to charge the defendant upon any speciall promise to answere for the debt default or miscarriages of another person . . . unlesse the agreement upon which such action shall be brought or some memorandum or note thereof shall be in writeing and signed by the partie to be charged therewith or some other person thereunto by him lawfully authorized.

Section 4 is another provision that has given rise to a substantial amount of litigation. In many ways it is the classic illustration of the problems that can arise in terms of identifying the type of contract that should be the subject of the formal requirement. The critical phrase when determining the scope of the section is 'debt, default or miscarriages of another person'. Thus the section applies only where a primary liability has been assumed by 'another person' and the defendant has assumed a secondary liability to answer for that debt (a secondary liability is a liability that arises upon default by the debtor of a primary obligation). If the defendant's liability proves to be primary rather than secondary in character, section 4 will not be applicable. The problem is that it can, in some cases, be difficult to tell whether the liability that has been assumed by the defendant is primary or secondary in nature. The courts have in fact experienced considerable difficulty in deciding whether the liability of the defendant is secondary (a guarantee) or primary (an indemnity) and the difficulty in drawing this distinction once led Harman LJ to state that this 'barren controversy' has 'raised many hair-splitting distinctions of exactly that kind which brings the law into hatred, ridicule and contempt by the public' (*Yeoman Credit Ltd* v. *Latter* [1961] 1 WLR 828, 835).

The effect of non-compliance with section 4 is to render the contract unenforceable. In *Actionstrength Ltd* v. *International Glass Engineering IN.GL.EN SpA* [2003] UKHL 17; [2003] 2 AC 541 sub-contractors on a construction project threatened to withdraw their labour because they were not being paid for their work by the main contractor (notwithstanding the fact that the main contractor had been paid by the employer). The sub-contractors withdrew this threat after reaching an oral agreement with the employer under which the employer agreed to ensure that the sub-contractors received the sums due to them by the main contractor and that, if necessary, the employer would do this by making payments directly to the sub-contractors rather than to the main contractor. The sub-contractors returned to work but the main contractor's indebtedness to them continued to increase until it reached £1.3 million. It being clear that the main contractor was unable to pay this amount, the sub-contractors brought a claim against the employer. The employer argued that its promise to pay was unenforceable on the ground that it did not satisfy the requirements of section 4. The sub-contractors argued that the agreement did not fall within the scope of section 4 but this submission was rejected. It was held that the employer's liability was secondary in nature rather than primary so that it fell within the scope of section 4 and, being an oral promise that was not evidenced in writing, it was not enforceable. Further, it was held that the employers were not estopped from invoking section 4 in order to deny the efficacy of the promise made. On the facts the only assurance given by the employers to the sub-contractors was the oral promise itself (which was unenforceable) and this was held to be insufficient to give rise to an estoppel. The House of Lords did not conclude that estoppel can never be invoked in order to prevent reliance upon the Statute of Frauds. But they stated that 'something more' was required than reliance upon the unenforceable promise itself. The precise nature of that 'something more' was not established but it is likely to take the form of an express assurance that reliance will not be placed upon the Statute of Frauds.

Actionstrength therefore illustrates the serious consequences that can flow from a failure to comply with formal requirements. The decision must have caused significant hardship to the sub-contractors in that they were left with no enforceable claim against the employer and a worthless claim for £1.3 million against the main contractor who was in liquidation. This point was noted by their Lordships. Thus Lord Woolf stated that he reached the decision to dismiss the appeal with 'regret'. Lord Bingham was more forthright. He stated:

6. While section 4 of the Statute of Frauds has been repealed or replaced in its application to the other four classes of contract originally specified, it has been retained in relation to guarantees. In 1937 the Law Revision Committee (in its Sixth Interim Report, *Statute of Frauds and the Doctrine of Consideration*, Cmd 5449, paragraph 16) recommended the repeal of so much as remained of section 4. But a minority headed by Goddard J dissented in relation to guarantees, on the grounds

> (1) that there was a real danger of inexperienced people being led into undertaking obligations which they did not fully understand, and that opportunities would be given to the unscrupulous to assert that credit was given on the faith of a guarantee which the alleged surety had had no intention of giving;
>
> (2) that a guarantee was a special class of contract, being generally one-sided and disinterested as far as the surety was concerned, and the necessity of writing would give the proposed surety an opportunity for thought;
>
> (3) that the requirement of writing would ensure that the terms of the guarantee were settled and recorded;
>
> (4) that Parliament had imposed a requirement of writing in other contractual contexts;
>
> (5) that judges and juries were not infallible on questions of fact, and in the vast majority of cases the surety was getting nothing out of the bargain;
>
> (6) that it was desirable to protect the small man; and
>
> (7) that the necessity for guarantees to be in writing was generally understood.

No action was taken on the 1937 report. In 1953 the Law Reform Committee (First Report, *Statute of Frauds and Section 4 of the Sale of Goods Act 1893*, Cmd 8809) endorsed the recommendation of its predecessor that section 4 of the Statute of Frauds should be largely repealed but, agreeing with those who had earlier dissented, unanimously recommended that the section should continue to apply to guarantees. Effect was given to this report by enactment of the 1954 Act. Whatever the strength of the reasons given . . . for retaining the old rule in relation to conventional consumer guarantees, it will be apparent that those reasons have little bearing on cases where the facts are such as those to be assumed here. It was not a bargain struck between inexperienced people, liable to misunderstand what they were doing. St-Gobain [the employers], as surety, had a very clear incentive to keep the Actionstrength workforce on site and, on the assumed facts, had an opportunity to think again. There is assumed to be no issue about the terms of the guarantee. English contract law does not ordinarily require writing as a condition of enforceability. It is not obvious why judges are more fallible when ruling on guarantees than other forms of oral contract. These were not small men in need of paternalist protection. While the familiar form of bank guarantee is well understood, it must be at least doubtful whether those who made the assumed agreement in this case appreciated that it was in law a guarantee. The judge at first instance was doubtful whether it was or not. The Court of Appeal reached the view that it was, but regarded the point as interesting and not entirely easy . . . Two members of the court discussed the question at a little length, with detailed reference to authority.

7. It may be questionable whether, in relation to contracts of guarantee, the mischief at which section 4 was originally aimed, is not now outweighed, at least in some classes of case, by the mischief to which it can give rise in a case such as the present, however unusual such cases may be. But that is not a question for the House in its judicial capacity. Sitting judicially, the House must of course give effect to the law of the land of which (in England and Wales) section 4 is part.

Reform of the law is therefore a matter for Parliament, not the judges.

(III) CONTRACTS WHICH MUST BE MADE BY DEED

Thirdly, the law may state that the contract must be made by deed. This is an exceptional requirement and it is now confined to conveyancing transactions. Thus section 52(1) of the Law of Property Act 1925 provides:

All conveyances of land or of any interest therein are void for the purpose of conveying or creating a legal estate unless made by deed.

Section 52(2) provides for a number of exceptions to the requirement laid down in section 52(1). One of these exceptions is a lease for a term not exceeding three years (see section 52(2)(d) and section 54(2)).

5. THE FUTURE OF FORMAL REQUIREMENTS

Requirements of form are likely to continue to play a prominent role in transactions involving consumers. In the commercial sphere it is unlikely that there will be a further significant role for requirements of form. The nature of formal requirements will also have to be given further thought. This is true both for consumer and for commercial contracts. Writing remains the prominent requirement of form but this may require reconsideration as a result of the increasing use of electronic means of communication. Article 9(1) of the EC Directive on Electronic Commerce (2000/31 OJ L178/1) states that:

Member States shall ensure that their legal system allows contracts to be concluded by electronic means. Member States shall in particular ensure that the legal requirements applicable to the contractual process neither create obstacles for the use of electronic contracts nor result in such contracts being deprived of legal effectiveness and validity on account of their being made by electronic means.

Section 8 of the Electronic Communications Act 2000 gives to Ministers the authority
to review statutes and related legislation that require documents to be in writing and
to amend them by way of secondary legislation 'in such manner as [the Minister] may
think fit for the purpose of authorising or facilitating the use of electronic communications or electronic storage'. Further, section 91(4) of the Land Registration Act 2002
provides that a document properly made in electronic form is to be treated as if it were
in writing and property executed, while section 91(5) further provides that a document properly made in electronic form is to be regarded 'for the purposes of any
enactment as a deed'. The section thus paves the way for the introduction of electronic conveyancing. Gradually, we can expect to see further modifications to existing
legislation to reflect the fact that, in the modern world, requirements of form can be
satisfied by electronic means in addition to more traditional formal requirements,
such as writing.

6. FURTHER READING

KOTZ, H and FLESSNER, A, *European Contract Law Volume One: Formation, Validity,
    and Content of Contracts; Contract and Third Parties* (Oxford University Press, 1997),
    Chapter 5.

7

INTENTION TO CREATE LEGAL RELATIONS

1. CENTRAL ISSUES

1. In order to create a valid and binding contract the parties must have had an intention to create legal relations. This rule does not generally give rise to any difficulties in the context of commercial transactions because the courts presume that parties to a commercial agreement do intend to create legal relations. The presumption is not an irrebuttable one but it is not an easy one to rebut.

2. The doctrine of intention to create legal relations plays its most important role in the context of domestic and social agreements. In both contexts the courts presume that the parties to the agreement did not intend to create legal relations. Once again this presumption is not an irrebuttable one and the factors relied upon by the courts in order to rebut the presumption are considered in this chapter.

3. It is important to consider the basis of this doctrine. Does it rest on the intention of the parties or is it based on a rule of law or public policy? It will be suggested that the initial presumption rests on a rule of law or public policy and that the intention of the parties is relevant to the rebuttal of that presumption. The policy that is articulated in the presumption is that the law should, in general, keep out of the regulation of domestic and social agreements.

4. But this leads on to another, more difficult question and that relates to the role of the presumptions and the doctrine of intention to create legal relations more generally. Should the law of contract continue to keep out of family life or is the presumption that the parties to domestic agreements do not intend to create legal relations one that is out of step with modern family life?

2. INTRODUCTION

A further essential ingredient of a binding contract is that the parties must have had an intention to create legal relations. In other words, they must have had an intention to be bound by the terms of their agreement. The doctrine of intention to create legal relations is a relatively late arrival in English contract law. As has already been noted (see p. 68 above), Professor Simpson gives the credit for the first recognition of the doctrine to the Court of Appeal in *Carlill* v. *Carbolic Smoke Ball Co Ltd* [1893] 2 QB 256. It was not, however, until the judgment of Atkin LJ in *Balfour v. Balfour* [1919] 2 KB 571 (p. 296 below) that its place was firmly established in English contract law.

The impact of this doctrine is greatest outside the sphere of commercial transactions. In the case of ordinary commercial transactions the law presumes that the parties did intend to create legal relations. The presumption that the parties to a commercial transaction intended to create legal relations is not an irrebuttable one. It can be rebutted but clear evidence is required in order to do so (*Edwards* v. *Skyways Ltd* [1964] 1 WLR 349, 355). The picture is otherwise when we turn to domestic and social agreements. In these contexts the presumption operates the other way. The presumption is that the parties to domestic and social agreements do not intend to create legal relations. This presumption is not as difficult to rebut as the presumption in favour of intention to create legal relations in the context of commercial transactions. But evidence must be led in order to establish that the parties did in fact intend to create legal relations.

We shall start by considering cases concerned with agreements made in a domestic and a social context before turning to analyse the role of intention to create legal relations in the commercial environment.

3. DOMESTIC AGREEMENTS

In the case of agreements entered into in a domestic context the presumption is that the parties did not intend to create legal relations. The leading case is:

Balfour v. Balfour

[1919] 2 KB 571, Court of Appeal

The defendant and plaintiff were husband and wife. They were married in 1900 and went to live in Ceylon (now Sri Lanka). They returned to England in 1915 when the defendant (the husband) had some leave from his work. When his leave came to an end he returned to Ceylon but his wife remained in England, on the advice of her doctor. Shortly before the defendant set sail for Ceylon in August 1916 the plaintiff alleged that they made an oral agreement, according to which he promised to pay her £30 per month until she returned to Ceylon. Differences then arose between them and the defendant wrote to the plaintiff suggesting that they should live apart. The plaintiff commenced divorce proceedings in 1918 and she obtained an order for alimony.

In the present proceedings the plaintiff sought to enforce the alleged agreement by which the defendant had promised to pay her £30 per month. The first instance judge, Sargant J, held that the defendant was under an obligation to support his wife and that effect should be given to the agreement reached by the parties. The defendant appealed to the Court of Appeal. His appeal was allowed and it was held that he was not liable to make the promised payments to the plaintiff.

Warrington LJ [set out the facts and continued]
Those being the facts we have to say whether there is a legal contract between the parties, in other words, whether what took place between them was in the domain of a contract or whether it was merely a domestic arrangement such as may be made every day between a husband and wife who are living together in friendly intercourse. It may be, and I do not for a moment say that it is not, possible for such a contract as is alleged in the present case to be made between husband and wife. The question is whether such a

contract was made. That can only be determined either by proving that it was made in express terms, or that there is a necessary implication from the circumstances of the parties, and the transaction generally, that such a contract was made. It is quite plain that no such contract was made in express terms, and there was no bargain on the part of the wife at all. All that took place was this: The husband and wife met in a friendly way and discussed what would be necessary for her support while she was detained in England, the husband being in Ceylon, and they came to the conclusion that £30 a month would be about right, but there is no evidence of any express bargain by the wife that she would in all the circumstances treat that as in satisfaction of the obligation of the husband to maintain her. Can we find a contract from the position of the parties? It seems to me it is quite impossible. If we were to imply such a contract in this case we should be implying on the part of the wife that whatever happened and whatever might be the change of circumstances while the husband was away she should be content with this £30 a month, and bind herself by an obligation in law not to require him to pay anything more; and on the other hand we should be implying on the part of the husband a bargain to pay £30 a month for some indefinite period whatever might be his circumstances. Then again it seems to me that it would be impossible to make any such implication. The matter really reduces itself to an absurdity when one considers it, because if we were to hold that there was a contract in this case we should have to hold that with regard to all the more or less trivial concerns of life where a wife, at the request of her husband, makes a promise to him, that is a promise which can be enforced in law. All I can say is that there is no such contract here. These two people never intended to make a bargain which could be enforced in law. The husband expressed his intention to make this payment, and he promised to make it, and was bound in honour to continue it so long as he was in a position to do so. The wife on the other hand, so far as I can see, made no bargain at all. That is in my opinion sufficient to dispose of the case . . .

I think the judgment of Sargant J cannot stand, the appeal ought to be allowed and judgment ought to be entered for the defendant.

Duke LJ

I agree. This is in some respects an important case, and as we differ from the judgment of the Court below I propose to state concisely my views and the grounds which have led me to the conclusion at which I have arrived. Substantially the question is whether the promise of the husband to the wife that while she is living absent from him he will make her a periodical allowance involves in law a consideration on the part of the wife sufficient to convert that promise into a binding agreement. In my opinion it does not. I do not dissent, as at present advised, from the proposition that the spouses in this case might have made an agreement which would have given the plaintiff a cause of action. . . . But we have to see whether there is evidence of any such exchange of promises as would make the promise of the husband the basis of an agreement. It was strongly urged by [counsel for the plaintiff] that the promise being absolute in form ought to be construed as one of the mutual promises which make an agreement. It was said that a promise and an implied undertaking between strangers, such as the promise and implied undertaking alleged in this case would have founded an action on contract. That may be so, but it is impossible to disregard in this case what was the basis of the whole communications between the parties under which the alleged contract is said to have been formed. The basis of their communications was their relationship of husband and wife, a relationship which creates certain obligations, but not that which is here put in suit. There was a discussion between the parties while they were absent from one another, whether they should agree upon a separation. In the Court below the plaintiff conceded that down to the time of her suing in the Divorce Division there was no separation, and that the period of absence was a period of absence as between husband and wife living in amity. An agreement for separation when it is established does involve mutual considerations . . .

But in this case there was no separation agreement at all. The parties were husband and wife, and subject to all the conditions, in point of law, involved in that relationship. It is impossible to say that where the relationship of husband and wife exists, and promises are exchanged, they must be deemed to be promises of a contractual nature. In order to establish a contract there ought to be something more than mere mutual promises having regard to the domestic relations of the parties. It is required that the obligations arising out of that relationship shall be displaced before either of the parties can found a contract upon such promises. The formula which was stated in this case to support the claim of the lady was this: In consideration that you will agree to give me £30 a month I will agree to forego my right to pledge your credit. . . . What is said on the part of the wife in this case is that her arrangement with her husband that she should assent to that which was in his discretion to do or not to do was the consideration moving from her to her husband. The giving up of that which was not a right was not a consideration. The proposition that the mutual promises made in the ordinary domestic relationship of husband and wife of necessity give cause for action on a contract seems to me to go to the very root of the relationship, and to be a possible fruitful source of dissension and quarrelling. I cannot see that any benefit would result from it to either of the parties, but on the other hand it would lead to unlimited litigation in a relationship which should be obviously as far as possible protected from possibilities of that kind. I think, therefore, that in point of principle there is no foundation for the claim which is made here, and I am satisfied that there was no consideration moving from the wife to the husband or promise by the husband to the wife which was sufficient to sustain this action founded on contract. I think, therefore, that the appeal must be allowed.

Atkin LJ
The defence to this action on the alleged contract is that the defendant, the husband, entered into no contract with his wife, and for the determination of that it is necessary to remember that there are agreements between parties which do not result in contracts within the meaning of that term in our law. The ordinary example is where two parties agree to take a walk together, or where there is an offer and an acceptance of hospitality. Nobody would suggest in ordinary circumstances that those agreements result in what we know as a contract, and one of the most usual forms of agreement which does not constitute a contract appears to me to be the arrangements which are made between husband and wife. It is quite common, and it is the natural and inevitable result of the relationship of husband and wife, that the two spouses should make arrangements between themselves—agreements such as are in dispute in this action—agreements for allowances, by which the husband agrees that he will pay to his wife a certain sum of money, per week, or per month, or per year, to cover either her own expenses or the necessary expenses of the household and of the children of the marriage, and in which the wife promises either expressly or impliedly to apply the allowance for the purpose for which it is given. To my mind those agreements, or many of them, do not result in

contracts at all, and they do not result in contracts even though there may be what as between other parties would constitute consideration for the agreement. The consideration, as we know, may consist either in some right, interest, profit or benefit accruing to one party, or some forbearance, detriment, loss or responsibility given, suffered or undertaken by the other. That is a well-known definition, and it constantly happens, I think, that such arrangements made between husband and wife are arrangements in which there are mutual promises, or in which there is consideration in form within the definition that I have mentioned. Nevertheless they are not contracts, and they are not contracts because the parties did not intend that they should be attended by legal consequences. To my mind it would be of the worst possible example to hold that agreements such as this resulted in legal obligations which could be enforced in the Courts. It would mean this, that when the husband makes his wife a promise to give her an allowance of 30s. or £2 a week, whatever he can afford to give her, for the maintenance of the household and children, and she promises so to apply it, not only could she sue him for his failure in any week to supply the allowance, but he could sue her for nonperformance of the obligation, express or implied, which she had undertaken upon her part. All I can say is that the small Courts of this country would have to be multiplied one hundredfold if these arrangements were held to result in legal obligations. They are not sued upon, not because the parties are reluctant to enforce their legal rights when the agreement is broken, but because the parties, in the inception of the arrangement, never intended that they should be sued upon. Agreements such as these are outside the realm of contracts altogether. The common law does not regulate the form of agreements between spouses. Their promises are not sealed with seals and sealing wax. The consideration that really obtains for them is that natural love and affection which counts for so little in these cold Courts. The terms may be repudiated, varied or renewed as performance proceeds or as disagreements develop, and the principles of the common law as to exoneration and discharge and accord and satisfaction are such as find no place in the domestic code. The parties themselves are advocates, judges, Courts, sheriff's officer and reporter. In respect of these promises each house is a domain into which the King's writ does not seek to run, and to which his officers do not seek to be admitted. The only question in this case is whether or not this promise was of such a class or not. For the reasons given by my brethren it appears to me to be plainly established that the promise here was not intended by either party to be attended by legal consequences. I think the onus was upon the plaintiff, and the plaintiff has not established any contract. The parties were living together, the wife intending to return. The suggestion is that the husband bound himself to pay £30 a month under all circumstances, and she bound herself to be satisfied with that sum under all circumstances, and, although she was in ill-health and alone in this country, that out of that sum she undertook to defray the whole of the medical expenses that might fall upon her, whatever might be the development of her illness, and in whatever expenses it might involve her. To my mind neither party contemplated such a result. I think that the parol evidence upon which the case turns does not establish a contract. I think that the letters do not evidence such a contract, or amplify the oral evidence which was given by the wife, which is not in dispute. For these reasons I think the judgment of the Court below was wrong and that this appeal should be allowed.

COMMENTARY

The judgment of Atkin LJ is the one that is most commonly quoted in the textbooks and in subsequent cases. His judgment clearly recognizes the existence of the doctrine of intention to create legal relations and he applies it to the facts of the case. The judgments of Warrington and Duke LJJ are more equivocal. The central question for Warrington LJ was whether or not it was possible to imply a contract on the facts of the case and, while he made reference to the question of whether or not the parties intended to make a bargain which could be enforced in law, he did not expressly articulate an independent requirement that the parties must intend to create legal relations. The judgment of Duke LJ seems to be based rather more on the doctrine of consideration. As the law then stood, a wife had authority, under certain circumstances, to pledge her husband's credit for suitable necessaries. In essence this was the common law remedy available to a wife who was not supported financially by her husband. Thus it was argued on behalf of Mrs Balfour that she had supplied consideration for the promise to pay her £30 a month by refraining from pledging her husband's credit for necessaries. However Duke LJ held that she had not supplied consideration for her husband's promise. His reason for so concluding appears to have been simply that the parties were still husband and wife at the time the promise was made and this brings us back to the point that the reason for the failure of the claim is to be found in the fact that the parties were husband and wife, and had not separated, at the time the promise was made.

This diversity in the reasoning of the court in *Balfour* makes it difficult to discern the precise *ratio* of the case. That said, courts in subsequent cases have not been unduly concerned by this point and have turned to the judgment of Atkin LJ for support for the proposition that English law recognizes the existence of a doctrine of intention to create legal relations. The existence of this doctrine is now clearly established by authority, whatever doubts we may harbour about the *ratio* of the case that is usually cited as the origin of the doctrine in English law. We must now turn to consider the scope of the presumption that parties to domestic agreements do not intend to create legal relations, the factors that have been used by the courts in order to rebut the presumption, the rationale of the presumption and, finally, the relationship, in the domestic context, between the doctrine of intention to create legal relations and the doctrine of consideration.

(a) THE SCOPE OF THE PRESUMPTION

As *Balfour* demonstrates the presumption that parties to domestic agreements do not intend to create legal relations is applicable as between husbands and wives, at least where they have not separated and are living together 'in amity'. The position is otherwise where they have separated at the time at which the agreement is made. Thus in *Merritt* v. *Merritt* [1970] 1 WLR 1211 the Court of Appeal held that an agreement between a husband and wife who had separated was enforceable as a contract. Lord Denning MR stated (at p. 1213):

I do not think that [*Balfour* v. *Balfour* has] any application here. The parties there were living together in amity. In such cases their domestic arrangements are ordinarily not intended to create legal relations. It is altogether different when the parties are not living in amity but are separated, or about to separate. They then bargain keenly. They do not rely on honourable understandings. They want everything cut and dried. It may safely be presumed that they intend to create legal relations.

In this respect *Balfour* may be thought to be close to the margins because the parties agreed to separate shortly after Mr Balfour promised to pay £30 per month to Mrs Balfour. But Duke LJ records in his judgment that Mrs Balfour conceded that there was no separation at the time at which the agreement was made and that 'the period of absence was a period of absence as between husband and wife living in amity'. Had she not made that concession and had there been evidence to prove that a separation was imminent, *Balfour* might have been decided differently (indeed in *Pettitt* v. *Pettitt* [1970] AC 777, 816 Lord Upjohn stated that the facts of *Balfour* stretched the doctrine of intention to create legal relations to 'its limits'). It is unlikely that *Balfour* only applies as between married couples who are living together 'in amity'. It must also apply by analogy to parties who cohabit, whether or not they are married.

The presumption that parties to a domestic agreement do not intend to create legal relations has also been applied to an agreement between a mother and her daughter. In *Jones* v. *Padavatton* [1969] 1 WLR 328 a mother promised to maintain her daughter if she gave up her job in Washington and went to London to read for the Bar with a view to practising as a lawyer in Trinidad. The mother lived in Trinidad and her promise was made in 1962. Initially, the promise took the form of a promise of a monthly allowance but subsequently that arrangement was varied and the mother bought a house for her daughter in 1964, on the understanding that the daughter could live there rent free, rent out rooms in the house to lodgers and use the rent to provide for her maintenance. The daughter entered on her studies for the Bar in November 1962 but by November 1968, the date of the hearing before the Court of Appeal, she had not completed the course successfully (she had passed all but one of her Part I papers but had not yet embarked upon Part II). In 1967 the mother issued a summons in which she claimed possession of the house. The daughter resisted her attempt to do so on the ground that she had a contractual entitlement to live in the house. The Court of Appeal held that the mother was entitled to possession of the house. The reasons given for the rejection of the daughter's claim differed. Danckwerts LJ stated (at p. 332):

There is no doubt that this case is a most difficult one, but I have reached a conclusion that the present case is one of those family arrangements which depend on the good faith of the promises which are made and are not intended to be rigid, binding agreements. *Balfour* v. *Balfour* was a case of husband and wife, but there is no doubt that the same principles apply to dealings between other relations, such as father and son and daughter and mother. This, indeed, seems to me a compelling case. Mrs Jones and her daughter seem to have been on very good terms before 1967. The mother was arranging for a career for her daughter which she hoped would lead o success. This involved a visit to England in conditions which could not be wholly foreseen. What was required was an arrangement which was to be financed by the mother, and was such as would be adaptable to circumstances, as it in fact was. The operation about the house was, in my view, not a completely fresh arrangement, but an adaptation of the mother's financial assistance to the daughter due to the situation which was found to exist in England. It was not a stiff contractual operation any more than the original arrangement.

Fenton-Atkinson LJ adopted a similar approach. In his view neither party intended to enter into a contract at any stage in this saga: rather, they placed trust in one another to honour their promises. Salmon LJ took a rather different view. He concluded that there was, initially, a binding agreement between the mother and the daughter. Thus he stated (at p. 333) that he could not think that 'either intended that if, after the daughter had been in London, say, for six months, the mother dishonoured her promise and left her daughter destitute, the daughter would have no legal redress'. On the 'very special circumstances of this case' he concluded that 'the true inference must be that neither the mother nor the daughter could have intended that the daughter should have no legal right to receive, and the mother no legal obligation to pay, the allowance of $200 a month'. But the problem which he identified was one relating to the certainty of the agreement itself, particularly in relation to its duration. Thus he concluded (at p. 334) that:

the promise was to pay the allowance until the daughter's studies were completed, and to my mind there was a clear implication that they were to be completed within a reasonable time. . . . It may not be easy to decide, especially when there is such a paucity of evidence, what is a reasonable time. The daughter, however, was a well educated intelligent woman capable of earning the equiva-lent of over £2,000 a year in Washington. It is true that she had a young son to look after, and may well . . . have been hampered to some extent by the worry of this litigation. But, making all allowances for these factors and any other distraction, I cannot think that a reasonable time could possibly exceed five years from November 1962, the date when she began her studies.

Jones v. Padavatton is, in many ways, a difficult case. The daughter initially gave up a great deal on the strength of her mother's promise and that factor pointed in the direction of the promise being legally enforceable. But, in the end, the Court of Appeal concluded that that factor was outweighed by the presumption that the parties did not intend to create legal relations combined with the vague terms in which the agreement was expressed.

(b) REBUTTING THE PRESUMPTION

The presumption that the parties to domestic agreements do not intend to create legal relations can be rebutted in a number of different ways. There is no finite list of methods by which the presumption can be rebutted. There are, however, one or two restrictions on the type of evidence that can be led. In particular, the parties cannot lead evidence of their own subjective intentions (see p. 416) but that is a general proposition of contract law and is not confined to the present context.

While the question whether or not the presumption has been rebutted ultimately depends upon the facts of the case, the cases in which the presumption has been rebutted exhibit some common features. In the first place the context in which the agreement was concluded has often been a factor in persuading the court to rebut the presumption. For example, where the relationship between the parties is approaching the point of break-down the courts are more likely to conclude that there was an intention to create legal relations (see *Merritt* v. *Merritt* (above)). Similarly, where the context in which the agreement is reached is a commercial one, as in the example of an agreement made in connection with the running of a family business, a court is more likely to conclude that the presumption has been rebutted (see, for example, *Snelling* v. *John G Snelling Ltd* [1973] 1 QB 87).

Secondly, the presumption may be rebutted where the parties have acted to their detriment in reliance upon the agreement that has been concluded between the parties. This factor does not always suffice to rebut the presumption, as can be seen from *Jones* v. *Padavatton* (above). But cases can be found in which it has operated to rebut the presumption. An example is *Parker* v. *Clark* [1960] 1 WLR 286. The plaintiffs, a married couple, agreed to give up their own home in order to move in and share the home of the defendants, an elderly couple. The parties reached an agreement under which they agreed to share the household expenses and the defendants promised to leave the house in their will for the benefit of the plaintiffs and their relatives. In reliance upon the agreement, the plaintiffs sold their home and lent part of the proceeds to their daughter in order to enable her to buy a flat. The plaintiffs moved in to the defendants' home in March 1956 and they did most of the work around the house. However the relationship between the parties soon began to deteriorate and in December 1957 the plaintiffs, in order to avoid being evicted, left the house. They brought an action for damages against the defendants. One of the grounds on which the defendants denied that they were liable to the plaintiffs was that the parties had not concluded a contract because they had no intention to create legal relations. Devlin J concluded that there was a contract between the parties and that the defendants were liable in damages to the plaintiffs. He stated:

I cannot believe . . . that the defendant really thought that the law would leave him at liberty, if he so chose, to tell the plaintiffs when they arrived that he had changed his mind, that they could take their furniture away and that he was indifferent whether they found anywhere else to live or not. Yet this is what the defence means. . . . I am satisfied that an arrangement binding in law was intended by both parties.

However, the position may well have been different had the parties fallen out before the plaintiffs acted to their detriment by selling the house and moving in with the defendants. On such facts a court may well have concluded that the parties did not intend to enter into a binding contract. This suggests that there may be a difference between executed and executory agreements. In this context, consider the following claim made by Hedley (see S Hedley, 'Keeping Contract in its Place: *Balfour* v. *Balfour* and the Enforceability of Informal Agreements' (1985) 5 *OJLS* 391, 408):

The fallacy to be avoided . . . consists of asking the question 'Is there a contract?', but forgetting that a court is almost invariably faced with a particular claim based on an alleged contract. The perspective given by the claim made alters everything. Take a variation of the classic academic conundrum in this area: Jack and Jill agree to go out to dinner and to split the bill. By asking the academic question 'Is there a contract?' we are immediately in the realm of the abstract. If, however, we approach the matter from a practical standpoint, we must know what claim is being made. If Jill is suing Jack because Jack has refused to go to dinner at all, the arguments against liability are compelling. Surely, Jack cannot be taken as giving an outright commitment to go to dinner—what if he is ill, or they cannot agree on a suitable restaurant? But imagine that the two already had their dinner, for convenience Jill pays the bill in full, but Jack subsequently refuses to pay his half. The perspective changes. It is no longer so obvious that the contract cannot be enforced. *If it is the 'reasonable man' we are consulting, then the 'reasonable man's' opinion may change in the course of the transaction.* Jack's contention that there was no intention to form a binding contract is likely to receive little sympathy. Blanket statements in cases that there is no 'intention to contract' on the facts before the court should therefore be treated with suspicion; it is vital to note whether this was being said in relation to an executed or an executory contract. [Emphasis in the original.]

(c) THE RATIONALE BEHIND THE PRESUMPTION

What is the basis of the presumption that the parties to domestic agreements do not intend to create legal relations? Is it to be found in the actual, albeit unexpressed intention of the parties or is its basis to be found in a rule of law or of public policy? The judgment of Atkin LJ in *Balfour* suggests that the initial presumption is derived from the law (or, if one prefers, public policy) rather than the intention of the parties. The reasons he gave in support of the conclusion that the parties did not intend to create legal relations did not relate specifically to the position of Mr and Mrs Balfour but were of general application. Thus he advanced the floodgates argument ('the small courts of this country would have to be multiplied one hundredfold if these arrangements were held to result in legal obligations') and also reasons of policy about the role of the law in the regulation of family relationships ('the common law does not regulate the form of agreements between spouses. . . . The consideration that really obtains for them is that natural love and affection which counts for so little in these cold Courts'). This is not to say that the intention of the parties is irrelevant. Their intention is relevant but it is relevant to the rebuttal of the presumption rather than its formulation.

   Are the reasons given in support of this presumptive exclusion of contract law from the regulation of family life valid? Professor Michael Freeman, a leading family lawyer, has recently concluded that they are not (see 'Contracting in the Haven: *Balfour* v. *Balfour* Revisited' in R Halson (ed), *Exploring the Boundaries of Contract* (Dartmouth, 1996), p. 68). Professor Freeman argues (at pp. 75–77):

The Balfours was a Victorian marriage. The ideals of Victorian marriages and values concerning the family lasted until perhaps a generation ago. But where the emphasis was on status, it is now on autonomy. For role identification we have now substituted role distance. The 'self' and individual choice have replaced role and obligation as central organising concepts. . . . Modern family law, responding to this trend, has embraced contract as its governing principle. Despite the ruling orthodoxy of *Balfour* v. *Balfour*, private ordering, rather than public regulation, has become the preferred means of organising and governing relationships within the family. . . . Thus, entry into marriage is less regulated than it was and is more dependent upon individual choice. . . . The law is also more willing to let those who are married define the terms of their relationship. Husbands and wives can sue each other, in contract and in tort. . . . In addition to greater control over entry into marriage and its terms, husbands and wives have been given greater powers to determine for themselves when to leave the marital relationship. . . . The conceptualisation of marriage as a private matter is emphasised also by the trend to define marital fault very narrowly in property and money determinations and in disputes about children . . .

Marriage has become 'a personal rather than a social institution', fit for private ordering rather than state regulation. And yet the official version of the truth is that husbands and wives do not subject their arrangements to the law of contract. If *Balfour* v. *Balfour* was a 'wise' decision based on the 'realities' of life, then wisdom dictates that we rethink the doctrine it embodies. It no longer reflects realities nor is it in line with developments taking place in family law. Once the fiction is rejected we will be in a position to assess the role of contract in intimate relationships and to examine the relevance of the modern law of contract on the family.

Professor Freeman's thesis has its attractions in that it recognizes the changes that have taken place in family life since Victorian times. But it has not commended itself to all family lawyers (see, for example, G Douglas, *An Introduction to Family Law* (Oxford University Press, 2001), pp. 67–68). It also gives rise to the floodgates problem identified by Atkin LJ in *Balfour*. Once the law of contract is admitted into family life, how far do we allow it to go? That there is a real problem here can be demonstrated by reference to the following radical proposal made by Professor Anthony Giddens in his book *The Third Way* (Polity Press, 1998). When discussing the problem of how to ensure that children are protected and cared for in a society where marriage and parenthood are becoming increasingly disentangled, he writes (at p. 95):

Contractual commitment to a child could . . . be separated from marriage, and made by each parent as a binding matter of law, with unmarried and married fathers having the same rights and the same obligations. Both sexes would have to recognize that sexual encounters carry the chance of life-time responsibilities, including protection from physical abuse.

In what may be thought to be something of an under-statement he notes (at p. 96) that 'enforcing parenthood contracts wouldn't be without its problems'. It is clear that there is a vital interest at stake in ensuring that children are properly cared for, but is the creation of binding contracts between parents and children really the best way to do this? The presence at the birth of a child of the family lawyer, ready and willing to draw up a contract between each parent and the child, is not a prospect to be viewed with enthusiasm. The policy values underpinning *Balfour* seem preferable to those advocated by both Professor Freeman and Professor Giddens. As Professor Kahn Freund stated back in 1952, '*Balfour* v. *Balfour* is one of those wise decisions in which the courts allow the realities of life to determine the legal norm which they formulate' ('Inconsistencies and Injustices in the Law of Husband and Wife' (1952) 15 *MLR* 133, 138).

(d) THE RELATIONSHIP WITH CONSIDERATION

Balfour v. *Balfour*, in particular the judgment of Duke LJ, demonstrates that there is a link between the doctrine of intention to create legal relations and the doctrine of consideration. But they are nevertheless doctrinally distinct. Intention to create legal relations is an additional hurdle which a claimant must overcome. That is to say, even if Mrs Balfour had been successful in proving that she had provided consideration for her husband's promise to pay her £30 per month, her claim would still have failed (at least on the reasoning of Atkin LJ, on the ground that she could not prove that she and her husband had intended to create legal relations, see p. 299 above).

While consideration and intention to create legal relations are doctrinally distinct they can overlap, in the sense that it is not always entirely clear whether the basis of the court's decision is the absence of consideration or the absence of an intention to create legal relations. A helpful illustration of this point is provided by the case of *White* v. *Bluett* (1853) 23 LJ Ex 36. A father lent money to his son and the son in return gave his father a promissory note by which he promised to repay the money. After the father's death his executor sought to recover from the son the money that had not been repaid. The son defended the claim on the basis that his father had promised to discharge him from his liability to repay provided that he stopped his practice of complaining about his father's distribution of his estate. His defence failed. Pollock CB said this (at p. 37):

The plea [of the son] is clearly bad. By the argument a principle is pressed to an absurdity, as a bubble is blown until it bursts. Looking at the words merely, there is some foundation for the argument, and, following the words only, the conclusion may be arrived at. It is said, the son had a right to an equal distribution of his father's property, and did not complain of his father because he had not an equal share, and said to him, I will cease to complain if you will not sue upon this note. Whereupon the father said, if you will promise me not to complain I will give up the note. If such a plea as this could be supported, the following would be a binding promise: A might complain that another person used the public highway more than he ought to do, and that other might say, do not complain, and I will give you five pounds. It is ridiculous to suppose that such promises could be binding. . . . In reality, there was no consideration whatever. The son had no right to complain, for the father might make what distribution of his property he liked; and the son's abstaining from doing what he had no right to do can be no consideration.

The language of the court is the language of the doctrine of consideration but it may be that it is the doctrine of intention to create legal relations that best captures the spirit of the decision to reject the son's defence. The difficulty with the argument based on consideration is that the son did have a right to complain, in the sense that he was entitled to complain, even if he was not entitled to an equal distribution of his father's estate. Thus, in giving up his right to complain, he did give up something that he was entitled to do (although whether that something was something of value in the eyes of the law is another matter, on which see p. 172 above). The better view may be that the basis of the decision was that there was no intention to create legal relations. But this proposition is not entirely straightforward either. In the first place the court did not use the language of intention to create legal relations. But that is not a conclusive objection given that the doctrine had not been recognized in 1853. A modern court might well invoke the doctrine of intention to create legal relations on the facts of *White*. A second difficulty is that the parties did intend to create legal relations in the sense that it was accepted that the son was in principle liable to repay the debt. And, if the son was subject to a liability to repay the debt, why should the father not be liable on his promise to waive the debt? This is a difficult question to which there are at least two possible answers. The first is that the father was not liable because the son's promise was too vague to be enforceable (and the vagueness may be relevant either to the doctrine of consideration or to the doctrine of intention to create legal relations). The second is that, as Parke B commented (at p. 37), it was 'not immaterial . . . to observe, that the [father] did not give the [promissory] note up'. Thus it may well be that he did not intend to discharge his son from his liability to repay the debt and so he retained the promissory note in order to evidence the fact that he did not intend to waive the debt and release his son from his liability to pay.

4. SOCIAL AGREEMENTS

A similar presumption operates in the context of social agreements, where the courts presume that the parties did not intend to create legal relations. In his judgment in *Balfour* v. *Balfour* (above) Atkin LJ provided two examples of social agreements that are not generally intended to give rise to legal relations, namely an agreement between two people to take a walk together and an offer and acceptance of hospitality. A further example is provided by the case of *Lens* v. *Devonshire Club, The Times*, 4 December 1914 where it was held that the winner of a golf competition was not entitled to sue in order to recover the prize (although many competitions, for example those in national newspapers, do now give rise to legal relations between the competitors and the organizers of the competition: see *O'Brien* v. *MGN Ltd* [2002] CLC 33, discussed in more detail at p. 362 below).

The presumption is a rebuttable one and the factors relevant to the rebuttal of the presumption in a domestic context (see pp. 302–304 above) are also applicable to social agreements. An example of a case in which the presumption was held to have been rebutted is provided by the case of *Simpkins* v. *Pays* [1955] 1 WLR 975. The plaintiff lived with the defendant as her lodger. Each week the plaintiff, the defendant and the defendant's granddaughter entered a competition in a Sunday newspaper. The plaintiff filled out the coupon in the defendant's name. They shared the entry fee and the postage between themselves. One week they won the prize and the sum of £750 was paid to the defendant. The defendant refused to pay to the plaintiff a one-third share of the prize. One of the grounds on which the defendant refused to pay was that she alleged that the agreement made between them was not intended to be legally binding. Sellers J held that the plaintiff was entitled to payment of a one-third share of the prize. He concluded (at p. 979):

It may well be there are many family associations where some sort of rough and ready thing is said which would not, on a proper estimate of the circumstances, establish a contract which was contemplated to have legal consequences, but I do not so find here. I think that there was here a mutuality in the arrangement between the parties. It was not very formal, but certainly in effect it was agreed that every week the forecast should go in in the name of the defendant, and that if there was success, no matter who won, all should share equally. That seems to be the implication from or the interpretation of what was said, that this was in the nature of a very informal syndicate so that they should all get the benefit of success.

The reference to 'mutuality' is a puzzling one and it has been argued (Unger (1956) 19 *MLR* 96, 98) that it refers to the presence of consideration rather than the presence of an intention to create legal relations. This point is made as part of a wider argument to the effect that 'absence of consideration . . . provides a simpler and more realistic explanation of the special quality of domestic agreements' than does the doctrine of intention to create legal relations. While it is true that Sellers J does not nail his colours to the doctrinal mast, counsel for the defendant submitted that the agreement was not binding because there was no intention to create legal relations and the judgment of Sellers J appears to be directed principally towards the rebuttal of that submission. The case is therefore probably best regarded as a case in which the court held that there was an intention to create legal relations notwithstanding the fact that the agreement was reached in a social or a domestic context (no formal distinction is drawn between these two categories and they can overlap). The reasons for the rebuttal of the presumption are probably to be found in the fact that the parties had acted in reliance upon the agreement in relation to the sharing of the expenses of entering into the competition and the agreement was not one made in connection with the running of the household (had the dispute been about whose turn it was to do the ironing, the court may well have concluded that there was no intention to create legal relations).

The courts have also experienced some difficulty in deciding whether or not an agreement between workmates to share the cost of travelling to work by car is intended to be legally binding. The issue arose in a line of cases concerned with the meaning of the words 'hire or reward' in the Road Traffic Act 1930. The relevant provisions have since been repealed so that the particular point at issue in these cases is no longer a live one. One of the issues discussed by the courts when deciding whether or not a passenger had been carried for 'reward' was whether a contract had been concluded for the carriage of the passenger. For example, in *Coward* v. *Motor Insurers Bureau* [1963] 1 QB 259 Mr Cole regularly gave a lift to his work colleague Mr Coward on the pillion seat of his motorcycle. Mr Coward made a contribution to Mr Cole's expenses. One of the issues before the court was whether or not Mr Cole had carried Mr Coward 'for reward'. The Court of Appeal concluded that he had not. Sellers LJ stated (at p. 271):

The practice whereby workmen go to their place of business in the motor-car or on the motor cycle of a fellow-workman upon the terms of making a contribution to the costs of transport is well known and widespread. In the absence of evidence that the parties intended to be bound contractually, we should be reluctant to conclude that the daily carriage by one of another to work upon payment of some weekly (or it may be daily) sum involved them in a legal contractual relationship. The hazards of everyday life, such as temporary indisposition, the incidence of holidays, the possibility of a change of shift or different hours of overtime, or incompatibility arising, make it most unlikely that either contemplated that the one was legally bound to carry and the other to be carried to work. It is made all the more improbable in this case by reason of the fact that alternative means of transport seem to have been available to Coward.

On the probabilities of the case . . . we reach the conclusion that . . . neither party intended to enter into a legal contract.

In the later case of *Albert* v. *Motor Insurers' Bureau* [1972] AC 301 Lord Cross adopted a different approach. In his view, there may be a contract, at least in relation to completed journeys. Thus he stated (at p. 340):

It is not necessary in order that a legally binding contract should arise that the parties should direct their minds to the question and decide in favour of the creation of a legally binding relationship. If I get into a taxi and ask the driver to drive me to Victoria Station it is extremely unlikely that either of us directs his mind to the question whether or not we are entering into a contract. We enter into a contract not because we form any intention to enter into one but because if our minds were directed to the point we should as reasonable people both agree that we were in fact entering into one. When one passes from the field of transactions of an obviously business character between strangers to arrangements between friends or acquaintances for the payment by the passenger of a contribution towards expenses the fact that the arrangement is not made purely as a matter of business and that if the anticipated payment is not made it would probably never enter into the head of the driver to sue for it disposes one to say that there is no contract; but in fact the answer to the question 'contract' or 'no contract' does not depend on the likelihood of an action being brought to enforce it in case of default.

Suppose that when one of Mr Quirk's fellow workers [Mr Quirk being the driver of the car] got in touch with him and asked him whether he could travel in his car to Tilbury and back next day, an 'officious bystander' had asked 'Will you be paying anything for your transport?' the prospective passenger would have answered at once 'Of course I will pay'. If the officious bystander had gone on to ask Mr Quirk whether, if he was not paid, he would sue the man in the county court, Mr Quirk might well have answered in the words used by the driver in *Connell's* case—'Not bloody likely'. But the fact that if default was made Mr Quirk would not have started legal proceedings but would have resorted to extra-judicial remedies does not mean that an action could not in theory have been brought to recover payment for the carriage. If one imagines such proceedings being brought a plea on the part of the passenger that he never meant to enter into a contract would have received short shrift and so, too, would a plea that the contract was void for uncertainty because no precise sum was mentioned. If the evidence did not establish a regular charge for the Tilbury trip the judge would have fixed the appropriate sum.

5. COMMERCIAL AGREEMENTS

Commercial agreements differ from domestic and social agreements in that the presumption operates the other way. In the case of commercial transactions the courts presume that the parties did intend to create legal relations and that presumption is not an easy one to displace. The strength of the presumption is such that the issue rarely arises in commercial litigation. One case in which it did arise, and which produced a division of judicial opinion, is the decision of the House of Lords in *Esso Petroleum Ltd* v. *Commissioners of Customs and Excise* [1976] 1 WLR 1. Esso devised a sales promotion scheme for its petrol under which it offered to give away a World Cup coin to every motorist who purchased four gallons of Esso petrol (each coin bore the likeness of one member of the England football squad for the 1970 World Cup competition in Mexico). The Customs and Excise Commissioners claimed that the coins were chargeable to a purchase tax on the ground that they had been 'produced in quantity for general sale'. The House of Lords held that the coins were not subject to the purchase tax on the ground that they had not been 'sold'. A contract of sale is one under which goods are transferred to a buyer in return for a money consideration called the price. But the consideration supplied by the motorists for the coins was not a money payment but entry into a collateral contract to purchase the appropriate quantity of petrol. Given that the supply of the coins did not fall within the scope of the taxation legislation, it was not strictly necessary for their Lordships to consider whether or not the coins were supplied by Esso as a matter of legal obligation or by way of gift. Nevertheless, the issue was considered by their Lordships. By a bare majority they concluded that there was an intention to create legal relations. Lord Wilberforce, Lord Simon of Glaisdale, and Lord Fraser of Tullybelton were of the view that the coins were supplied as a matter of contractual obligation (albeit that Lord Fraser dissented on the ground that he was of the view that the coins had been sold and thus were chargeable to the purchase tax), whereas Viscount Dilhorne and Lord Russell of Killowen concluded that the coins were not supplied as a matter of contractual obligation. In considering whether or not there was an intention to create legal relations much reliance was placed on Esso's advertising campaign in which they stated 'Collect the full set of thirty coins. One coin given when you buy four gallons of petrol'. Lord Simon of Glaisdale concluded that the parties did intend to create legal relations. He stated (at pp. 5–6):

I am . . . not prepared to accept that the promotion material put out by Esso was not envisaged by them as creating legal relations between the garage proprietors who adopted it and the motorists who yielded to its blandishments. In the first place, Esso and the garage proprietors put the material out for their commercial advantage, and designed it to attract the custom of motorists. The whole transaction took place in a setting of business relations. In the second place, it seems to me in general undesirable to allow a commercial promoter to claim that what he has done is a mere puff, not intended to create legal relations (cf. *Carlill* v. *Carbolic Smoke Ball Co* [1893] 1 QB 256). The coins may have been themselves of little intrinsic value; but all the evidence suggests that Esso contemplated that they would be attractive to motorists and that there would be a large commercial advantage to themselves from the scheme, an advantage to which the garage proprietors also would share. Thirdly, I think that authority supports the view that legal relations were envisaged . . .

[he considered *Rose and Frank Co* v. *JR Crompton and Brothers Ltd* (below) and *Edwards* v. *Skyways Ltd* (below) and continued]

And I venture to add that it begs the question to assert that no motorist who bought petrol in consequence of seeing the promotion material prominently displayed in the garage forecourt would be likely to bring an action in the county court if he were refused a coin. He might be a suburban Hampden who was not prepared to forgo what he conceived to be his rights or to allow a tradesman to go back on his word.

Viscount Dilhorne, on the other hand, concluded that the parties did not have an intention to create legal relations. He said (at pp. 3–4):

True it is that the respondents are engaged in business. True it is that they hope to promote the sale of their petrol, but it does not seem to me necessarily to follow or to be inferred that there was any intention on their part that their dealers should enter into legally binding contracts with regard to the coins; or any intention on the part of the dealers to enter into any such contract or any intention on the part of the purchaser of four gallons of petrol to do so.

If in this case on the facts of this case the conclusion is reached that there was any such intention on the part of the customer, of the dealer and of the respondents, it would seem to exclude the possibility of any dealer ever making a free gift to any of his customers however negligible its value to promote his sales.

If what was described as being a gift, which would be given if something was purchased, was something of value to the purchaser, then it could readily be inferred that there was a common intention to enter into legal relations. But here, whatever the cost of production, it is clear that the coins were of little intrinsic value.

I do not consider that the offer of a gift of a free coin is properly to be regarded as a business matter . . . I see no reason to imply any intention to enter into contractual relations from the statements on the posters that a coin would be given if four gallons of petrol were bought.

Nor do I see any reason to impute to every motorist who went to a garage where the posters were displayed to buy four gallons of petrol any intention to enter into a legally binding contract for the supply to him of a coin. On the acceptance of his offer to purchase four gallons there was no doubt a legally binding contract for the supply to him of that quantity of petrol, but I see no reason to conclude that because such an offer was made by him, it must be held that, as the posters were displayed, his offer included an offer to take a coin. The gift of a coin might lead a motorist returning to the garage to obtain another one, but I think the facts in this case negative any contractual intention on his part and on the part of the dealer as to the coin and suffice to rebut any presumption there may be to the contrary.

It is important to note that *Esso* is a tax case. It is not a case in which a motorist was bringing a claim against a garage that had refused to give him a coin. The issue was whether or not the supply of the coins was chargeable to a purchase tax. This required their Lordships to focus on the obligations of the garage in relation to the supply of the coin and not their obligations in relation to the supply of petrol. The fact that the coins had little intrinsic value (although they may now have value as collectors' items) is often used by commentators to demonstrate the strength of the presumption in favour of legal relations in a commercial context.

Two principal issues remain to be discussed in terms of the application of the doctrine of intention to create legal relations to commercial transactions. The first relates to the circumstances in which the presumption may be rebutted and the second concerns the relationship between the doctrine of intention to create legal relations and the question of whether or not the parties intended to contract. We shall consider each issue in turn.

(a) REBUTTAL OF THE PRESUMPTION

The presumption in favour of legal relations in commercial transactions can be rebutted but the cases in which it has been rebutted are few. It can be rebutted by the express stipulation of the parties. In *Rose and Frank Co* v. *JR Crompton and Bros Ltd* [1925] AC 445 the agreement between the parties contained the following clause:

This arrangement is not entered into, nor is this memorandum written as a formal and legal agreement, and shall not be subject to legal jurisdiction in the Law Courts either of the United States or England, but it is only a definite expression and record of the purpose and intention of the three parties concerned, to which they each honourably pledge themselves with the fullest confidence—based on past business with each other—that it will be carried through by each of the three parties with mutual loyalty and friendly co-operation.

The plaintiffs had been appointed as sole agents of the defendants. The agreement was entered into in 1913 for a three-year period with an option to extend it for a further period of time. The agreement was extended to March 1920 but in 1919 the defendants terminated it without giving notice. The plaintiffs sued for breach of contract but the House of Lords held that the effect of the 'honour' clause was to prevent a contract coming into existence between the parties. Is such a clause contrary to public policy? Scrutton LJ addressed this particular issue in the Court of Appeal in *Rose and Frank* [1923] 2 KB 261 and concluded it was not. He stated (at p. 288):

I can see no reason why, even in business matters, the parties should not intend to rely on each other's good faith and honour, and to exclude all idea of settling disputes by any outside intervention, with the accompanying necessity of expressing themselves so precisely that outsiders may have no difficulty in understanding what they mean. If they clearly express such an intention I can see no reason in public policy why effect should not be given to their intention.

An important distinction must be drawn here. On the one hand, it is contrary to public policy for parties to a legally binding contract to attempt to oust the jurisdiction of the court. On the other hand, it is not contrary to public policy for parties to an agreement to insert into their agreement a clause the effect of which is to prevent their agreement from amounting to a contract in law.

In every case the court must consider, as a matter of construction, whether or not the effect of the words used is to rebut the presumption that the parties intended to create legal relations. In *Edwards* v. *Skyways Ltd* [1964] 1 WLR 349 the defendant employers promised to make an 'ex gratia payment' to employees who were made redundant. The defendants subsequently sought to go back on their promise, alleging that it was not legally binding. Megaw J rejected their submission. He stated (at p. 356):

the words 'ex gratia' do not, in my judgment, carry a necessary, or even a probable, implication that the agreement is to be without legal effect. . . . The words . . . are used simply to indicate . . . that the party agreeing to pay does not admit any pre-existing liability on his part; but he is certainly not seeking to preclude the legal enforceability of the settlement itself by describing the contemplated payment as 'ex gratia'. So here, there are obvious reasons why the phrase might have been used by the defendant company in just such a way. It might have desired to avoid conceding that any such payment was due under the employers' contract of service. It might have wished—perhaps ironically in the event—to show, by using the phrase, its generosity in making a payment beyond what was required by the contract of service. I see nothing in the mere use of the words 'ex gratia', unless in the circumstances some very special meaning has to be given to them, to warrant the conclusion that this promise, duly made and accepted, for valid consideration, was not intended by the parties to be enforceable in law.

Exceptionally, the presumption may be rebutted notwithstanding the absence of an express stipulation to this effect by the parties. An example is a collective agreement between a trade union and an employer (or an employer's association) which is presumed not to be legally enforceable as between the parties to the agreement. This was held to be the case at common law in *Ford Motor Co Ltd* v. *Amalgamated Union of Engineering and Foundry Workers* [1969] 2 QB 303. Statute has now intervened in order to strengthen the common law position. Thus section 179(1) of the Trade Union and Labour Relations (Consolidation) Act 1992 states that:

A collective agreement shall be conclusively presumed not to have been intended by the parties to be a legally enforceable contract unless the agreement—

(a) is in writing, and

(b) contains a provision which (however expressed) states that the parties intend that the agreement shall be a legally enforceable contract.

Section 179(2) of the Act further provides that a 'collective agreement which does not satisfy those conditions shall be conclusively presumed to have been intended by the parties to be a legally enforceable contract'.

(b) DID THE PARTIES INTEND TO CONTRACT?

Rather than seek to rebut the presumption that the parties intended to create legal relations, a defendant may take the point that the parties did not intend to contract or otherwise lacked contractual intent. What is the difference, if any, between the submission that the parties lacked contractual intent and the submission that the parties did not intend to create legal relations? The answer would appear to be that the former submission is much wider in scope, in that it can encompass issues such as whether the parties have in fact reached agreement. The latter submission, by contrast, accepts that the parties *have* reached agreement and is restricted to the issue of whether the agreement was intended to create legal obligations.

While it is possible to separate out these two issues in theory, it may not be so easy to do this in practice. The issues may overlap. This is particularly so in the case where the agreement between the parties is expressed in vague or uncertain terms. In such a case a defendant may argue that there is no contract on two grounds: (i) the agreement is too vague or uncertain to amount to a contract; and (ii) the parties did not intend to create legal relations. The two grounds are inter-related in that the vagueness or uncertainty of the agreement may suggest both that the parties did not reach sufficient agreement on essential matters, and that they lacked an intention to create legal relations.

It may, however, be important to distinguish between the two issues in relation to the location of the burden of proof. First, it is for the claimant to prove that a contract has been concluded. But, secondly, once the existence of an otherwise enforceable contract has been established and the defendant wishes to take the point that the agreement apparently concluded by the parties was not intended to give rise to legal obligations, the onus of proof switches to the defendant to prove that the parties did not intend to create legal relations, at least in the case where the agreement is made in a commercial context. The relationship between these two issues was considered in more detail by Mance LJ in *Baird Textile Holdings Ltd* v. *Marks & Spencer plc* [2001] EWCA Civ 274; [2002] 1 All ER (Comm) 737 when he stated (at paras [59]–[61]) that:

for a contract to come into existence, there must be both (a) an agreement on essentials with sufficient certainty to be enforceable and (b) an intention to create legal relations.

Both requirements are normally judged objectively. Absence of the former may involve or be explained by the latter. But this is not always so. A sufficiently certain agreement may be reached, but there may be either expressly (i.e. by express agreement) or impliedly (e.g. in some family situations) no intention to create legal relations.

An intention to create legal relations is normally presumed in the case of an express or apparent agreement satisfying the first requirement. . . . It is otherwise, when the case is that an implied contract falls to be inferred from parties' conduct. . . . It is then for the party asserting such a contract to show the necessity for implying it . . . [I]f the parties would or might have acted as they did without any such contract, there is no necessity to imply any contract. It is merely putting the same point another way to say that no intention to make any contract will then be inferred.

The order of the two requirements identified by Mance LJ should be noted. He expressly rejected a submission that the order should be reversed. In his view it was 'more appropriate to take the requirements in the order in which I have set them out, and to recognise their potential inter-relationship'. This ordering is significant because it puts the initial onus of proof on to the party alleging the existence of an enforceable contract. At the same time Mance LJ recognizes that the two issues are inter-related in that an absence of sufficient agreement on essential matters may well also reflect an absence of an intention to create legal relations.

6. THE FUTURE OF THE DOCTRINE OF INTENTION TO CREATE LEGAL RELATIONS

The doctrine of intention to create legal relations has not lacked its critics. Some, such as Professor Freeman (p. 304 above), are critical of the way in which it has been used to deny legal effect to agreements made in a family context. Others point out that the doctrine rests on a fiction in that the parties to the alleged agreements frequently have no discernible intention one way or the other.

In the light of these and other arguments it has been argued that the doctrine of intention to create legal relations is, in fact, unnecessary. The case for the elimination of the doctrine of intention to create legal relations has been put in the following terms (M Furmston (ed), *Butterworths Common Law Series: The Law of Contract* (Butterworths, 2nd edn, 2003), para 2.169):

The existence of a separate requirement of intention to create legal relations has . . . been criticised by a number of commentators. It is submitted that there is much force in these criticisms and that it is unnecessary to impose a separate requirement of 'intention to create legal relations' over and above those of offer, acceptance and consideration. A proposal cannot properly be regarded as an offer unless it indicates an intention to undertake a legal obligation if its terms are accepted and the requested consideration is furnished by the offeree. Thus a proposal in which the maker indicates, expressly or impliedly, that he does not intend to undertake a legal obligation cannot properly be regarded as an offer. Similarly, if an offer is made and the offeree responds agreeing to the terms of the offer but indicating that he does not intend to create a legal relationship, the offeree's response cannot properly be regarded as an acceptance of the offer. Where the offer is of a bilateral contract the offeror requests a promise from the offeree as the consideration for his offer. That counter-promise must necessarily be legally binding if it is to be regarded as consideration for the offeror's promise, so that if the offeree makes the requested promise but expressly or impliedly indicates that he does not intend to be legally bound by his promise (i) his response does not meet the conditions of the offer and therefore cannot be regarded as an acceptance of it and (ii) his counter-promise cannot be regarded as consideration for the offeror's promise. Thus if either offeror or offeree does not intend a legal relationship there is in fact no offer or acceptance, as the case may be. If the parties agree but neither intends a legal relationship there is neither offer nor acceptance. If this view is accepted, 'intention to create legal relations' is not a separate, additional requirement, but an aspect of the rules relating to offer, acceptance and consideration. There is some support for this approach in *Carlill* v. *Carbolic Smoke Ball Co* where the defendants argued that their advertisement was not intended to be legally binding and there- fore could not be regarded as an offer, and indeed the cases concerning the classification of proposals as 'offers' or 'invitations to treat' are effectively concerned with the question whether the proposal in question is intended to be legally binding.

The difficulty with this argument is that it does not in fact eliminate the doctrine of intention to create legal relations; rather it imports it as an element into the rules relating to offer, acceptance, and consideration. Such a step is likely to make the law more complex and, for this reason, it is unlikely that the courts will go down this road. They are more likely to increase the role of the doctrine of intention to create legal relations. The reduction of the practical significance of the doctrine of consideration (in the sense that the requirements of the doctrine appear to be easier to satisfy as a result of the decision of the Court of Appeal in *Williams* v. *Roffey Bros & Nicholls (Contractors) Ltd* [1991] 1 QB 1, on which see pp. 183–203 above) is likely to bring the doctrine of intention to create legal relations into play to a greater extent than before. Thus in *Williams*, Russell LJ stated that 'the courts nowadays should be more ready to find [the existence of consideration] so as to reflect the intention of the parties'. In this way it may fall to the doctrine of intention to create legal relations to distinguish those promises intended to be binding from those that are not intended to be binding (see to similar effect the judgment of Rajah JC in *Chwee Kin Keong* v. *Digilandmall.com Pte Ltd* [2004] SGHC 71; [2004] 2 SLR 594, 634: 'the time may have come for the common law to shed the pretence of searching for consideration to uphold com- mercial contracts. The marrow of contractual relationships should be the parties' intention to create a legal relationship').

But this is not to say that the doctrine of intention to create legal relations will remain in its present form. For example, the utility of the presumptions has recently been doubted by the High Court of Australia. In *Ermogenous* v. *Greek Orthodox Community of SA Inc* (2002) 209 CLR 95, 106, Gaudron, McHugh, Hayne, and Callinan JJ made the following observations in the context of considering whether or not the appellant, a minister of religion, was employed under a contract of employment:

In this context of intention to create legal relations there is frequent reference to 'presumptions'. It is said that it may be presumed that there are some 'family arrangements' which are not intended to give rise to legal obligations and it was said in this case that it should not be presumed that there was an intention to create legal relations because it was a matter concerning the engagement of a minister of religion. For our part, we doubt the utility of using the language of presumptions in this context. At best, the use of that language does no more than invite attention to identifying the party who bears the onus of proof. In this case, where issue was joined about the existence of a legally binding contract between the parties, there could be no doubt that it was for the appellant to demonstrate that there was such a contract. Reference to presumptions may serve only to distract attention from that more basic and important proposition.

The effect of this approach is to shift attention away from the presumptions and towards the elements that the claimant must prove in order to establish the existence of a binding contract between himself and the defendant. But it may not prove to be much of an advance because the presumptions are likely to re-emerge in relation to the rules regarding the onus of proof. In commercial cases the onus of proof is likely to be on the defendant to show that the parties did not intend to create legal relations, whereas in other contexts the onus is likely to be on the claimant. This may prove to be very similar in practical effect to the presumptions and, for this reason, it must be doubted whether the English courts will follow the approach taken by the High Court of Australia in *Ermogenous*.

7. FURTHER READING

ALLEN, D, 'The Gentleman's Agreement in Legal Theory and in Modern Practice' (2000) *Anglo-American Law Review* 204.

FREEMAN, M, 'Contracting in the Haven: *Balfour v Balfour* Revisited' in R Halson (ed), *Exploring the Boundaries of Contract* (Dartmouth, 1996), p. 68.

HEDLEY, S, 'Keeping Contract in its Place: *Balfour* v. *Balfour* and the Enforceability of Informal Agreements' (1985) 5 *OJLS* 391.

HEPPLE, B, 'Intention to Create Legal Relations' [1970] *CLJ* 122.

SIMPSON, AWB, 'Innovation in Nineteenth Century Contract Law' (1975) 91 *LQR* 247, 263–265.

PART II
TERMS

8

THE TERMS OF THE CONTRACT

1. CENTRAL ISSUES

1. The answer to the question whether a statement made by one contracting party to another, prior to the conclusion of the contract, has been incorporated into the contract as a term or is merely a representation that has induced that party to enter into the contract depends upon the intention of the parties, objectively ascertained. In seeking to discern the intention of the parties the courts have regard to a variety of factors that are considered in this chapter.

2. While the distinction between a term and a representation remains one of some importance today it is not as important as it was prior to changes to the law of misrepresentation made by the judiciary in 1963 and by Parliament in 1967. Before these changes were made damages could be recovered for a fraudulent misrepresentation but not for an innocent or for a negligent misrepresentation. Thus a plaintiff who wished to recover damages in respect of an innocent or a negligent misstatement had to prove that the statement had been incorporated into the contract as a term in order to recover damages. Now that damages for misrepresentation are more widely avail-

able the distinction between a term and a representation tends to be of importance not to the *existence* of the jurisdiction to award damages but to the *measure* of damages recoverable.

3. In the case where the parties have reduced their contract to writing an issue can arise as to whether or not one of the parties is entitled to lead evidence of the existence of a term not to be found in that written document. The 'parol evidence' rule was thought to exclude such evidence where its effect was to add to, vary, or contradict the written document. But the status of this rule is the subject of some controversy. On one view the rule is a 'circular statement' on the basis that it only applies where the written document is intended by the parties to contain all the terms of the contract. The other view is that the rule is not circular because it applies where the document *looks* like a complete contract (even if it was not so intended by both parties) and, in such a case, the court will presume that the written document contains the whole contract in the absence of evidence to the contrary.

2. INTRODUCTION

A contract is composed of a number of terms. The number of terms will obviously depend upon the importance of the transaction. Large-scale transactions often produce contracts of considerable length and complexity and some of the standard form clauses, such as exclusion and limitation clauses, are likely to have been the subject of protracted negotiation between the parties (or at least between their lawyers). The terms of the contract are obviously of great significance to the parties because they define their rights and liabilities. English law gives the parties considerable freedom to define for themselves the terms of their contract: freedom of contract remains a fundamental part of English law. Many commercial parties have their own standard terms of business which they seek to incorporate into the contracts they conclude (hence the so-called 'battle of the forms' discussed at pp. 92–110 above). However the freedom of the parties is not unlimited. Parliament has in recent years intervened to regulate the use of certain types of contract terms. Initially the regulation was confined principally to exclusion and limitation clauses but it was extended in 1994, in the case of contracts that have not been individually negotiated between a seller or a supplier and a consumer, to a much wider range of terms (see further pp. 504–521 below). The Law Commissions have recently provisionally proposed that the scope of the latter controls should be extended beyond consumer contracts to business-to-business contracts that have been concluded on 'standard' terms or on terms that have not been individually negotiated (the scope of these proposals is discussed in more detail at pp. 535–540 below). Not all terms are, however, agreed expressly by the parties. Some are implied into the contract either by the courts or by Parliament. Implied terms form an important part of many contracts, particularly contracts for the sale of goods.

This Part of the book is divided up in the following way. This chapter is devoted to two issues. The first relates to the identification of the express terms of the contract and the second concerns written contracts and the extent to which it is permissible to lead evidence of the existence of terms not found in the written contract. Chapter 9 deals with the subject of the incorporation of terms into a contract. This is an important issue in practice. Many companies spend substantial sums of money on legal advice in relation to the drafting of their standard terms of business but then fail to take adequate steps to ensure that these terms are incorporated into the contracts which they conclude. The subject-matter of Chapter 10 is implied terms. Here the principal difficulty relates to the legal basis upon which courts imply terms into contracts. Chapter 11 deals with the principles applied by the courts when interpreting contracts. Many cases that come before the courts raise issues of interpretation or construction. Indeed, the most cited contract case in recent years is the decision of the House of Lords in *Investors Compensation Scheme Ltd* v. *West Bromwich Building Society* [1998] 1 WLR 896 where Lord Hoffmann (at pp. 912–913) re-stated the principles by which contract documents are to be interpreted. Chapter 12 moves on to consider some standard clauses that are to be found in commercial contracts today (often known as 'boilerplate clauses'). The subject-matter of Chapter 13 is one particular type of boilerplate clause, namely the exclusion or limitation clause. These clauses have been the subject of a considerable amount of judicial analysis and the Unfair Contract Terms Act 1977 was passed in order to regulate their use. Much of Chapter 13 is concerned with the statutory control of contract terms and this theme is developed in Chapter 14 which is devoted to the Unfair Terms in Consumer Contracts Regulations 1999. The Regulations give to the courts much broader powers to regulate terms in contracts which have not been individually negotiated and which have been concluded between sellers or suppliers, on the one hand, and consumers on the other hand. Chapter 15 draws this Part of the book to a close with a discussion of the role of good faith in contract law. The location of any discussion of good faith is a matter of real difficulty in English law. The courts have so far refused to recognize the existence of a general principle of good faith and fair dealing in contract law (see *Walford* v. *Miles* [1992] 2 AC 128) yet, on the other hand, it may be said that notions of good faith and fair dealing permeate all parts of the law of contract (see, for example, *First Energy (UK) Ltd* v. *Hungarian International Bank Ltd* [1993] 2 Lloyd's Rep 194, 196). The principle of good faith and fair dealing is a fundamental part of the law of contract in most civilian legal systems and it is declared to be a mandatory principle by both the Principles of European Contract Law and the Unidroit Principles of International Commercial Contracts. Given that English law presently refuses to recognize the existence of a doctrine of good faith and fair dealing, it may seem odd to give it its own chapter. But the reality is that it is an issue that does require analysis and, a notion of good faith having been introduced into English law via the Unfair Terms in Consumer Contracts Regulations 1999, this seems to be an appropriate point to discuss the issue. The question which English law has to answer can be shortly stated, even if it cannot be answered easily. The question is: is the role of good faith in English law confined to those cases that fall within the scope of the 1999 Regulations or will its influence extend beyond these cases and into transactions, particularly commercial transactions, that do not fall within the scope of the Regulations?

3. TWO PRELIMINARY ISSUES

The purpose of this chapter is not to consider the substantive content of the express terms of a contract. The content of the most important standard clauses found in commercial contracts is considered later in Chapter 12. Here we are concerned with two preliminary issues. The first relates to the identification of the terms of the contract. How do the courts decide what is and what is not a term of the contract? In the case where the parties reduce their agreement to the form of a written contract, the answer is fairly obvious, namely that the content is to be found in the terms set out in the document. But what about oral statements made prior to the conclusion of the contract? Are they also terms or are they merely representations which, while they may have induced one party to enter into the contract, are not part of the contract itself? The second issue concerns the entitlement of the parties to lead evidence of terms not to be found in their written contract. Where the parties take the time, trouble, and expense of reducing their agreement to writing, are they still entitled to adduce evidence of terms other than those found in the written document or is the written document the sole source of the terms of their contract? We shall explore each issue in turn.

4. TERMS AND REPRESENTATIONS

The question whether or not a statement made by one party to the other prior to the conclusion of the contract has been incorporated into the contract as a term is one of some importance. If the statement has been incorporated into the contract as a term then a failure to comply with it will amount to a breach of contract. On the other hand, if the statement has not been so incorporated then any liability cannot be for breach of contract but must be for misrepresentation. The distinction between a term and a representation is an important one but it is not as significant as it used to be. The primary significance of the distinction lies in the different remedial responses to a breach of contract and a misrepresentation. We shall deal with the different remedial responses in more detail in the chapter on misrepresentation (see Chapter 17). Here it suffices to use one remedial difference for illustrative purposes. Every breach of contract gives rise to a claim for damages (in the case where the claimant suffers no loss as a result of the breach, she will still be entitled to recover damages but they will be nominal). But not every misrepresentation gives rise to a claim for damages. Indeed, prior to the decision of the House of Lords in *Hedley Byrne & Co Ltd* v. *Heller & Partners Ltd* [1964] AC 465 and the subsequent enactment of the Misrepresentation Act 1967 damages could only be recovered for fraudulent misrepresentations[1] and fraud is not an easy matter to prove (*Derry* v. *Peek* (1889) 14 App Cas 337). The fact that damages could not be recovered in respect of negligent or innocent misrepresentations prior to *Hedley Byrne* and the enactment of the 1967 Act had a significant impact on cases decided prior to these developments. In these cases a plaintiff who wished to recover damages had either to prove fraud (in order to recover damages for fraudulent misrepresentation) or prove that the statement had been incorporated into the contract as a term (in order to recover damages for breach of contract). In cases where the defendant had clearly not been fraudulent the only hope for a plaintiff who wished to recover damages was therefore to prove that the statement had been incorporated into the contract as a term. Cases can be found in which the courts adopted what appears to be a rather benevolent approach to the identification of a term in order to give a deserving plaintiff a remedy in damages (see, for example, *De Lassalle* v. *Guildford* [1901] 2 KB 215). But cases can also be found in which the courts took a stricter view. Thus in *Heilbut, Symons & Co* v. *Buckleton* [1913] AC 30, 51 Lord Moulton stated that 'it is . . . of the greatest importance, in my opinion, that this House should maintain in its full integrity the principle that a person is not liable in damages for an innocent misrepresentation, no matter in what way or under what form the attack is made'.

How then do the courts decide whether or not a statement has been incorporated into a contract as a term? The answer is that the distinction turns upon the intention of the parties, objectively ascertained. As John Cartwright has pointed out (*Misrepresentation* (Sweet & Maxwell, 2002), para 6.05):

The question, in general terms, is whether the parties intended the statement to be incorporated into the contract as one of its terms; whether, therefore, the defendant intended to make a contractually binding promise about the accuracy of his statement.

When seeking to ascertain whether the defendant intended to make a contractually binding promise about the accuracy of his statement, no one factor predominates. As Lord Moulton stated in *Heilbut, Symons* (at p. 51), 'the intention of the parties can only be deduced from the totality of the evidence, and no secondary principles . . . can

---

[1] Here leaving to one side the decision of the House of Lords in *Nocton* v. *Lord Ashburton* [1914] AC 932.

be universally true'. It is therefore necessary to examine the cases in order to identify the range of issues to which the courts have regard when seeking to ascertain the intention of the parties. The approach that will be adopted here is to examine three illustrative cases and then seek to draw the threads together by setting out the range of factors taken into account by the courts in their decision-making.

(a) THREE ILLUSTRATIVE CASES

Oscar Chess Ltd v. Williams

[1957] 1 WLR 370, Court of Appeal

The plaintiff car dealers bought a car from the defendant in a part-exchange deal under which the defendant bought a new car from the plaintiffs' garage (the defendant in fact purchased the car from a finance company to which the plaintiffs had sold the car, but nothing turns on this for present purposes). The events that led up to the purchase of the car by the plaintiffs were as follows. The defendant had told one of the plaintiffs' salesmen that he wished to buy a new car. The salesman was a neighbour of the defendant and he had been given a lift in the car on a number of occasions. He thought that the car was a 1948 Morris and indeed the defendant described the car to him as a 1948 10 h.p. Morris and produced the registration book for it. The salesman checked the registration book and it showed that 1948 was the date of first registration. He then consulted a book (known as 'Glass' Guide'), which gave him the current prices for second-hand cars according to the year of their manufacture. On this basis he offered the defendant an allowance of £290 against the purchase of a new car. The defendant agreed and the transactions were completed. Eight months later the plaintiffs discovered that the car was not in fact a 1948 Morris but a 1939 model. If the plaintiffs had known that it was a 1939 model they would have offered the defendant only £175 for the car. The defendant honestly believed that the car was a 1948 model. The car had previously been bought by his mother and she had bought it on the basis that it was a 1948 model. The car's registration book showed that it had been first registered in 1948 and that it had changed hands five times between 1948 and 1954.

The plaintiffs sought to recover from the defendant damages of £115, based on the difference in value between £290 and £175. The trial judge held that the defendant was liable in damages but the Court of Appeal allowed the defendant's appeal by a majority (Morris LJ dissenting) on the basis that the statement by the defendant as to the age of the car was not a term of the contract but an innocent misrepresentation that had induced the plaintiffs to enter into the contract.

Denning LJ

I entirely agree with the judge that both parties assumed that the Morris car was a 1948 model and that this assumption was fundamental to the contract. This does not prove, however, that the representation was a term of the contract. The assumption was based by both of them on the date given in the registration book as the date of first registration. They both believed that the car was a 1948 model, whereas it was only a 1939 one. They were both mistaken and their mistake was of fundamental importance.

The effect of such a mistake is this: It does not make the contract a nullity from the beginning, but it does in some circumstances enable the contract to be set aside in equity. If the buyer had come promptly, he might have succeeded in getting the whole transaction set aside in equity on the ground of this mistake: see *Solle* v. *Butcher* [1950] 1 KB 671; but he did not do so and it is now too late for him to do it: see *Leaf* v. *International Galleries* [1950] 2 KB 86. His only remedy is in damages, and to recover these he must prove a warranty.

In saying that he must prove a warranty, I use the word 'warranty' in its ordinary English meaning to denote a binding promise. Everyone knows what a man means when he says, 'I guarantee it', or 'I warrant it', or 'I give you my word on it'. He means that he binds himself to it. That is the meaning which it has borne in English law for 300 years from the leading case of *Chandelor* v. *Lopus* (1603), Cro Jac 4 onwards. During the last hundred years, however, the lawyers have come to use the word 'warranty' in another sense. They use it to denote a subsidiary term in a contract as distinct from a vital term which they call a 'condition'. In so doing they depart from the ordinary meaning, not only of the word 'warranty', but also of the word 'condition'. There is no harm in their doing this, so long as they confine this technical use to its proper sphere, namely, to distinguish between a vital term, the breach of which gives the right to treat the contract as at an end, and a subsidiary term which does not. The trouble comes, however, when one person uses the word 'warranty' in its ordinary meaning and another uses it in its technical meaning. When Holt CJ, in *Crosse* v. *Gardner* (1869) Carth 90, as glossed by Buller J in *Pasley* v. *Freeman* (1789) 3 Perm Rep 51, 57 and *Medina* v. *Staughton* (1699) 1 Salk 210, made his famous ruling that an affirmation at the time of the sale is a warranty, provided it appear on evidence to be so intended, he used the word 'warranty' in its ordinary English meaning of a binding promise: and when Lord Haldane LC and Lord Moulton in 1913, in *Heilbut, Symons & Co* v. *Buckleton* [1913] AC 30, adopted this ruling (*ibid.*, at pp. 38, 49), they used it likewise in its ordinary meaning. These different uses of the word seem to have been the source of confusion in the present case. The judge did not ask himself, 'Was the representation (that the car was a 1948 Morris car) intended to be a warranty?' He asked himself, 'Was it fundamental to the contract?' He answered it by saying that it was fundamental, and, therefore, it was a condition and not a warranty. By concentrating on whether it was fundamental, he seems to me to have missed the crucial point in the case which is whether it was a term of the contract at all. The crucial question is: Was it a binding promise or only an innocent misrepresentation? The technical distinction between a 'condition' and a 'warranty' is quite immaterial in this case, because it is far too late for the buyer to reject the car. He can, at best, only claim damages. The material distinction here is between a statement which is a term of the contract and a statement which is only an innocent misrepresentation. This distinction is best expressed by the ruling of Lord Holt: Was it intended as a warranty or not?, using the word warranty there in its ordinary English meaning: because it gives the exact shade of meaning that is required. It is something to which a man must be taken to bind himself.

In applying Lord Holt's test, however, some misunderstanding has arisen by the use of the word 'intended'. It is sometimes supposed that the tribunal must look into the minds of the parties to see what they themselves intended. That is a mistake. Lord Moulton made it quite clear, in *Heilbut, Symons & Co* v. *Buckleton* [1913] AC at p. 51, that 'The intention of the parties can only be deduced from the totality of the evidence'. The question whether a warranty was intended depends on the conduct of the parties, on their words and behaviour, rather than on their thoughts. If an intelligent bystander would reasonably infer that a warranty was intended, that will suffice. And this, when the facts are not in dispute, is a question of law. That is shown by *Heilbut, Symons & Co* v. *Buckleton* itself, where the House of Lords upset the jury's finding of a warranty.

It is instructive to take some recent instances to show how the courts have approached this question. When the seller states a fact which is or should be within his own knowledge and of which the buyer is ignorant, intending that the buyer should act on it, and he does so, it is easy to infer a warranty; see *Couchman* v. *Hill* [1947] KB 554, where the farmer stated that the heifer was unserved, and *Harling* v. *Eddy* [1951] 2 KB 739, where he stated that there was nothing wrong with her. So also if the seller makes a promise about something which is or should be within his own control; see *Birch* v. *Paramount Estates Ltd* (1956) 16 Estates Gazette 396, decided on October 2, 1956, in this court, where the seller stated that the house would be as good as the show house. But if the seller, when he states a fact, makes it clear that he has no knowledge of his own but has got his information elsewhere, and is merely passing it on, it is not so easy to imply a warranty. Such a case was *Routledge* v. *McKay* [1954] 1 All ER 855, where the seller 'stated that it was a 1942 model, and pointed to the corroboration found in the book', and it was held that there was no warranty.

Turning now to the present case, much depends on the precise words that were used. If the seller says: 'I believe the car is a 1948 Morris. Here is the registration book to prove it', there is clearly no warranty. It is a statement of belief, not a contractual promise. If, however, the seller says: 'I guarantee that it is a 1948 Morris. This is borne out by the registration book, but you need not rely solely on that. I give you my own guarantee that it is', there is clearly a warranty. The seller is making himself contractually responsible, even though the registration book is wrong.

In this case much reliance was placed by the judge on the fact that the buyer looked up 'Glass' Guide' and paid £290 on the footing that the car was a 1948 model: but that fact seems to me to be neutral. Both sides believed the car to have been made in 1948 and in that belief the buyer paid £290. That belief can be just as firmly based on the buyer's own inspection of the log-book as on a contractual warranty by the seller.

Once that fact is put on one side, I ask myself: What is the proper inference from the known facts? It must have been obvious to both that the seller had himself no personal knowledge of the year when the car was made. He only became owner after a great number of changes. He must have been relying on the registration book. It is unlikely that such a person would warrant the year of manufacture. The most that he would do would be to state his belief, and then produce the registration book in verification of it. In these circumstances the intelligent bystander would, I suggest, say that the seller did not intend to bind himself so as to warrant that the car was a 1948 model. If the seller was asked to pledge himself to it, he would at once have said 'I cannot do that. I have only the log-book to go by, the same as you'.

The judge seems to have thought that there was a difference between written contracts and oral contracts. He thought that the reason why the buyer failed in *Heilbut, Symons & Co* v. *Buckleton* and *Routledge* v. *McKay* was because the sales were afterwards recorded in writing, and the written contracts contained no reference to the representation. I agree that that was an important factor in those cases. If an oral representation is afterwards recorded in writing, it is good evidence that it was intended as a warranty. If it is not put into writing, it is evidence against a warranty being intended; but it is by no means decisive. There have been many cases where the courts have found an oral warranty collateral to a written contract such as *Birch* v. *Paramount Estates Ltd*. But when the purchase is not recorded in writing at all it must not be supposed that every representation made in the course of the dealing is to be treated as a warranty. The question then is still: Was it intended as a warranty? In the leading case of *Chandelor* v. *Lopus* in 1603 a man by word of mouth sold a precious stone for £100 affirming it to be a bezar stone whereas it was not. The declaration averred that the seller *affirmed* it to be a bezar stone, but did not aver that he *warranted* it to be so. The declaration was held to be ill because (Cor Jac at p. 4): '. . . the bare affirmation that it was a bezar stone, without warranting it to be so, is no cause of action . . .' That has been the law from that day to this and it was emphatically re-affirmed by the House of Lords in *Heilbut, Symons & Co* v. *Buckleton* [1913] AC at pp. 38, 50.

One final word: It seems to me clear that the motor dealers who bought the car relied on the year stated in the log-book. If they had wished to make sure of it, they could have checked it then and there, by taking the engine number and chassis number and writing to the makers. They did not do so at the time, but only eight months later. They are experts, and, as they did not make that check at the time, I do not think that they should now be allowed to recover against the innocent seller who produced to them all the evidence which he had, namely, the registration book. I agree that it is hard on the plaintiffs to have paid more than the car is worth, but it would be equally hard on the seller to make him pay the difference. He would never have bought the Hillman car unless he had received the allowance of £290 for the Morris. The best course in all these cases would be to 'shunt' the difference down the train of innocent sellers until one reached the rogue who perpetrated the fraud; but he can rarely be traced, or if he can, he rarely has the money to pay the damages. Therefore, one is left to decide between a number of innocent people who is to bear the loss. That can only be done by applying the law about representations and warranties as we know it: and that is what I have tried to do. If the rogue can be traced, he can be sued by whosoever has suffered the loss: but, if he cannot be traced, the loss must lie where it falls. It should not be inflicted on innocent sellers, who sold the car many months, perhaps many years before, and have forgotten all about it and have conducted their affairs on the basis that the transaction was concluded. Such a seller would not be able to recollect after all this length of time the exact words which he used, such as whether he said 'I believe it is a 1948 model', or 'I warrant it is a 1948 model'. The right course is to let the buyer set aside the transaction if he finds out the mistake quickly and comes promptly before other interests have irretrievably intervened, otherwise the loss must lie where it falls: and that is, I think, the course prescribed by law. I would allow this appeal accordingly.

Hodson LJ

I am of opinion that there was no evidence to support the conclusion that the statement that the Morris car was a 1948 car was a term of the contract. The registration book, showing that the car was first registered in 1948, was produced by the defendant to the plaintiffs' representative, a motor salesman, who was familiar with the car, having often had lifts in it, thought it looked like a 1948 car, and checked up on the registration book.

The defendant was stating an opinion on a matter of which he had no special knowledge or on which the buyer might be expected also to have an opinion and to exercise his judgment.

This is not a decisive test, as was pointed out by Lord Moulton (in *Heilbut, Symons & Co*

v. *Buckleton* [1913] AC at p. 50), but it is a feature which he said may be a criterion of value in guiding a jury in coming to a decision whether or not a warranty was intended.

There is, in my opinion, nothing in this case to set against the criterion to which I have referred. That is to say, there is nothing to indicate that the statement as to the date of the car amounted to a promise or guarantee that the information given was accurate.

Morris LJ [dissenting]

In the present case, on a consideration of the evidence that he heard, the judge came to the conclusion that the statement which he held to have been made by the defendant at the time of the making of the contract was a statement made contractually. It seems to me that the totality of the evidence points to that view. The statement related to a vitally important matter: it described the subject-matter of the contract then being made and the statement directed the parties to, and was the basis of, their agreement as to the price to be paid or credited to the defendant. In the language of Scott LJ [in *Couchman* v. *Hill* [1947] KB 554, 559], it seems to me that the statement made by the defendant was 'an item in the description' of what was being sold and that it constituted a substantial ingredient in the identity of the thing sold.

It is with diffidence that I arrive at a conclusion differing from that of my Lords, but I cannot see that the learned judge in any way misdirected himself or misapplied any principle of law, and I see no reason for disturbing his conclusion.

COMMENTARY

In order to be able to recover damages the plaintiffs had to show that the defendant's statement that the car was a 1948 model was a term of the contract. The word that is used in the judgments is generally not 'term' but 'warranty'. The difficulty with the latter word is, as Denning LJ points out, that it also has a technical meaning in that it can refer to a lesser, subsidiary term of the contract, the breach of which gives to the innocent party the right to claim damages but does not give him the right to terminate further performance of the contract (the technical meaning of 'warranty' is discussed in more detail at p. 958 below). In this chapter the word 'term' will be used in preference to 'warranty' for the reason that it describes more clearly the issue that is at stake in the cases. We are not here concerned with the status of a term of the contract (that is, whether it is important or not) but with the prior question of whether the statement made has been incorporated into the contract as a term or not. The central question may be formulated as follows: has the statement been incorporated into the contract as a term or is it simply a statement that has induced the other party to enter into the contract but does not form part of the contract itself?

The Court of Appeal concluded, by a majority, that the defendant's statement was not a term but only an innocent misrepresentation. This conclusion was fatal to the plaintiffs' claim for damages. But it is important to note that the plaintiffs' claim for damages would not necessarily fail today. As has been noted, the law has moved on since *Oscar Chess* was decided in November 1956. In 1963 the House of Lords in *Hedley Byrne & Co Ltd* v. *Heller & Partners Ltd* [1964] AC 465 held that there is a tort of negligent misrepresentation which gives rise to a liability in damages (see further

p. 703 below). Section 2 of the Misrepresentation Act 1967 takes matters further. Section 2(1) imposes a liability in damages on a misrepresentor whose misrepresentation induces the claimant to enter into a contract with him unless the misrepresentor can show that he had reasonable grounds to believe and did believe in the truth of his statement up to the time that the contract was made (see further p. 691 below). Section 2(2) goes still further and gives to the court a discretionary power to award damages in lieu of rescission in cases of entirely innocent misrepresentation (see further p. 705 below). In the light of these developments it cannot be assumed that *Oscar Chess* would be decided the same way today. But, equally, it does not follow that all differences between terms and representations have been eliminated. In the days of *Oscar Chess* the difference between a term and a representation was relevant to the *existence* of the jurisdiction to award damages, whereas today it is relevant to the *measure* of damages recoverable. As we shall see, the amount recoverable in a misrepresentation claim is generally less than the sum recoverable in a breach of contract claim. The amount recoverable in a misrepresentation claim is the claimant's reliance loss, that is to say, the aim of the award of damages is to compensate the claimant for the loss that he has suffered as a result of relying to his detriment upon the truth of the statement made. In a breach of contract claim, on the other hand, the aim of the award of damages is to protect the claimant's expectation interest, that is to say, the aim is to put the claimant in the position which he would have been in had the contract been carried out according to its terms (the difference between the reliance measure and the expectation measure is discussed in more detail at pp. 1006–1017 below).

Denning LJ applied an objective test (on which see further Chapter 2) in order to distinguish between a term and a representation. The distinction therefore depends on the words used by the parties and their behaviour; it does not depend upon their innermost thoughts. What factors persuaded the majority in the present case to conclude that the statement was a representation and not a term? The crucial factor would appear to have been the knowledge, or rather the lack of it, of the defendant. Both Denning and Hodson LJJ concluded that it was unlikely that the defendant, given the state of his knowledge, would have guaranteed that the car was in fact a 1948 model. Denning LJ also placed emphasis on the fact that the plaintiffs were experts and that they failed to take appropriate steps to check the vintage of the car. Morris LJ, in his dissenting judgment, emphasized the importance to the parties of the age of the car (in the sense that it had a considerable impact on the value of the car) and he also expressed his unwillingness to interfere with the finding of the trial judge. Denning LJ acknowledged the significance of the age of the car when he stated that both parties had made a mistake of 'fundamental importance' in relation to the age of the car, but he held that this was not enough of itself to turn the defendant's statement into a term of the contract. In his view, the significance of the importance of the statement was outweighed by the fact that the defendant lacked specialist knowledge and the fact that the plaintiffs were experts. The combination of these factors persuaded him to conclude that the statement was a representation and not a term. The significance of the knowledge of the parties becomes even more apparent when *Oscar Chess* is contrasted with the following case:

Dick Bentley Productions Ltd v. Harold Smith (Motors) Ltd

[1965] 1 WLR 623, Court of Appeal

The plaintiff, Dick Bentley, told the defendant, Harold Smith, that he was on the look-out for a 'well vetted Bentley car'. Mr Smith found one and bought it for £1,500. He then informed Mr Bentley of his acquisition. Mr Bentley then went to see the car. Mr Smith told him that the car had been fitted with a replacement engine and gearbox and that it had done only 20,000 miles since the work had been carried out. The speedometer on the car showed only 20,000 miles. Mr Bentley agreed to buy the car for £1,850 but the car proved to be a 'considerable disappointment to him'. He brought an action for damages for breach of warranty. Mr Smith admitted that he had made a statement that, to the best of his belief, the car had done only 20,000 miles since the replacement of the engine and the gear box but he denied that these statements amounted to warranties or representations and averred that the statements were made honestly in the belief that they were true. The trial judge found that certain representations, including the state-ment as to mileage, were untrue and amounted to warranties. He accordingly awarded Mr Bentley damages of £400. Mr Smith appealed to the Court of Appeal who dismissed his appeal.

Lord Denning MR
The first point is whether this representation, namely, that [the car] had done 20,000 miles only since it had been fitted with a replacement engine and gearbox, was an innocent misrepresentation (which does not give rise to damages), or whether it was a warranty. It was said by Holt CJ and repeated in *Heilbut, Symons & Co* v. *Buckleton* [1913] AC 30 at p. 49, that: 'An affirmation at the time of the sale is a warranty, provided it appear on evidence to be so intended'. But that word 'intended' has given rise to difficul-ties. I endeavoured to explain in *Oscar Chess, Ltd* v. *Williams* [1957] 1 WLR 370 that the question whether a warranty was intended depends on the conduct of the parties, on their words and behaviour, rather than on their thoughts. If an intelligent bystander would reasonably infer that a warranty was intended, that will suffice. What conduct, then? What words and behaviour, lead to the inference of a warranty?

   Looking at the cases once more, as we have done so often, it seems to me that if a representation is made in the course of dealings for a contract for the very purpose of inducing the other party to act on it, and actually inducing him to act upon it, by entering into the contract, that is prima facie ground for inferring that it was intended as a warranty. It is not necessary to speak of it as being collateral. Suffice it that it was intended to be acted upon and was in fact acted on. But the maker of the representation can rebut this inference if he can show that it really was an innocent misrepresentation, in that he was in fact innocent of fault in making it, and that it would not be reasonable in the circum-stances for him to be bound by it. In the *Oscar Chess* case the inference was rebutted. There a man had bought a second-hand car and received with it a log-book, which stated the year of the car, 1948. He afterwards resold the car. When he resold it he simply repeated what was in the log-book and passed it on to the buyer. He honestly believed on reasonable grounds that it was true. He was completely innocent of any fault. There was no warranty by him but only an innocent misrepresentation. Whereas in the present case it is very different. The inference is not rebutted. Here we have a dealer, Smith, who was in a position to know, or at least to find out, the history of the car. He could get it by writing to the makers. He did not do so. Indeed it was done later. When the history of this car was examined, his statement turned out to be quite wrong. He ought to have known better. There was no reasonable foundation for it.

[he summarized the history of the car, and continued]

The judge found that the representations were not dishonest. Smith was not guilty of fraud. But he made the statement as to 20,000 miles without any foundation. And the judge was well justified in finding that there was a warranty. He said: 'I have no hesitation [in saying] that as a matter of law the statement was a warranty. Smith stated a fact that should be within his own knowledge. He had jumped to a conclusion and stated it as a fact. A fact that a buyer would act on'. That is ample foundation for the inference of a warranty. So much for the first point . . .

[he then dealt with an issue on the counterclaim and on the county court judge's award of damages and concluded]

I hold that the appeal fails and should be dismissed.

Danckwerts LJ
I agree with the judgment of Lord Denning MR.

Salmon LJ
I agree. I have no doubt at all that the learned county court judge reached a correct conclusion when he decided that Smith gave a warranty to the plaintiff and that that warranty was broken. Was what Smith said intended and understood as a legally binding promise? If so, it was a warranty and as such may be part of the contract of sale or collateral to it. In effect, Smith said: 'If you will enter into a contract to buy this motor car from me for £1,850, I undertake that you will be getting a motor car which has done no more than 20,000 since it was fitted with a new engine and a new gearbox'. I have no doubt at all that what was said by Smith was so understood and was intended to be so understood by Bentley . . .

I accordingly agree that the appeal should be dismissed.

COMMENTARY
Lord Denning expressly distinguished *Oscar Chess* on the ground that the defendant in that case had no knowledge of the age of the car and had made his statement in all innocence. On the present facts Lord Denning had no hesitation in concluding that Mr Smith was a dealer who was in a position to know, or at least to find out, the history of the car. Given his knowledge, he was not entitled to turn round and assert that his statement in relation to the mileage done by the car since the repairs had been carried out was a mere representation on his part. It was a warranty, for the breach of which he was liable in damages. It would seem to follow from this case that a statement made by a dealer in relation to the goods sold will generally be held to be a term of the contract. Indeed, it may be possible to go further. Professor Atiyah states of *Dick Bentley* (*An Introduction to the Law of Contract* (5th edn, Oxford University Press, 1995), p. 195) that it is a 'good illustration of the point that the courts tend to place the responsibility on the person who they think reasonably ought to bear the responsibility, rather than on the person who has agreed to bear it,

for the simple reason that it is often not apparent whether anybody has agreed to bear it'.

Lord Denning in both *Oscar Chess* and *Dick Bentley* uses the language of fault, in that he concluded that Mr Smith in *Dick Bentley* 'ought to have known better' while the plaintiffs in *Oscar Chess* could have checked the vintage of the car by 'taking the engine number and chassis number and writing to the makers'. But, while fault may be a relevant consideration when deciding whether a statement is a term or representation, liability for breach of contract does not generally depend upon fault so that, even if Mr Smith had taken all reasonable care to discover whether the car had done more than 20,000 miles since the repair work had been carried out, he would still, presumably, have been liable to Mr Bentley in damages when it transpired that the car had, in fact, done more than 20,000 miles.

Esso Petroleum Co Ltd v. Mardon

[1976] QB 801, Court of Appeal

In 1961 Esso found a site for a filling station on a busy main road. One of Esso's employees, Mr Leith, who had forty years' experience in the petrol trade, estimated that the throughput of petrol at the station would be 200,000 gallons per year by the third year of operation. After Esso had bought the site and started to build the station the local planning authority refused permission for the pumps to front onto the road, so that the station had to be built back to front. Nonetheless when in 1963 Esso interviewed Mr Mardon, a prospective tenant of the station, Mr Leith stated that the estimated throughput of the station was 200,000 gallons per year. On that basis Mr Mardon entered into a tenancy agreement with Esso for three years at a rent of £2,500 for the first two years and £3,000 for the third year. Despite Mr Mardon's best efforts, which included raising an overdraft with his bank and putting all his available capital into the business, in the first fifteen months the throughput of petrol was only 78,000 gallons. The trial judge found that the lack of throughput was due to the inability of passing traffic to see the pumps. In June 1964 Mr Mardon terminated the tenancy agreement by notice. However Esso offered him a new tenancy agreement for one year at a rent of £1,000 plus a surcharge on petrol sold. Mr Mardon entered into the agreement on these terms in September 1964. But the losses continued. When Mr Mardon failed to pay for petrol supplied, Esso cut off his supplies and brought an action for moneys owed. Mr Mardon counterclaimed for damages for breach of warranty as to the throughput of petrol and for negligent misrepresentation. The trial judge held that Mr Leith's statement as to the throughput was not a warranty such as to give Mr Mardon a cause of action for breach of warranty but that Esso was liable for negligent misrepresentation. The Court of Appeal held that Mr Leith's statement was a warranty which Esso had breached. In addition the statement was a negligent misrepresentation, for which they were also liable.

Lord Denning MR

Collateral warranty

Ever since *Heilbut, Symons & Co v. Buckleton* [1913] AC 30, we have had to contend with the law as laid down by the House of Lords that an innocent misrepresentation gives no right to damages. In order to escape from that rule, the pleader used to allege—I often did it myself—that the misrepresentation was fraudulent, or alternatively a collateral warranty. At the trial we nearly always succeeded on collateral warranty. We had to reckon, of course, with the dictum of Lord Moulton, at p. 47, that 'such collateral contracts must from their very nature be rare'. But more often than not the court elevated the innocent misrepresentation into a collateral warranty: and thereby did justice—in advance of the Misrepresentation Act 1967. I remember scores of cases of that kind, especially on the sale of a business. A representation as to the profits that had been made in the past was invariably held to be a warranty. Besides that experience, there have been many cases since I have sat in this court where we have readily held a representation— which induces a person to enter into a contract—to be a warranty sounding in damages. I summarised them in *Dick Bentley Productions Ltd* v. *Harold Smith (Motors) Ltd* [1965] 1 WLR 623, 627, when I said:

> 'Looking at the cases once more, as we have done so often, it seems to me that if a representation is made in the course of dealings for a contract for the very purpose of inducing the other party to act upon it, and actually inducing him to act upon it, by entering into the contract, that is prima facie ground for inferring that it was intended as a warranty. It is not necessary to speak of it as being collateral. Suffice it that it was intended to be acted upon and was in fact acted on.'

Mr. Ross-Munro [counsel for Esso], retaliated, however, by citing *Bisset* v. *Wilkinson* [1927] AC 177, where the Privy Council said that a statement by a New Zealand farmer that an area of land 'would carry 2,000 sheep' was only an expression of opinion. He submitted that the forecast here of 200,000 gallons was an expression of opinion and not a statement of fact: and that it could not be interpreted as a warranty or promise.

Now I would quite agree with Mr Ross-Munro that it was not a warranty—in this sense—that it did not *guarantee* that the throughput *would* be 200,000 gallons. But, nevertheless, it was a forecast made by a party—Esso—who had special knowledge and skill. It was the yardstick (the estimated annual consumption) by which they measured the worth of a filling station. They knew the facts. They knew the traffic in the town. They knew the throughput of comparable stations. They had much experience and expertise at their disposal. They were in a much better position than Mr Mardon to make a forecast. It seems to me that if such a person makes a forecast, intending that the other should act upon it—and he does act upon it, it can well be interpreted as a warranty that the forecast is sound and reliable in the sense that they made it with reasonable care and skill. It is just as if Esso said to Mr Mardon: 'Our forecast of throughput is 200,000 gallons. You can rely upon it as being a sound forecast of what the service station should do. The rent is calculated on that footing'. If the forecast turned out to be an unsound forecast such as no person of skill or experience should have made, there is a breach of warranty. Just as there is a breach of warranty when a forecast is made—'expected to load' by a certain date—if the maker has no reasonable grounds for it: see *Samuel Sanday and Co* v. *Keighley, Maxted and Co* (1922) 27 Com Cas 296; or bunkers 'expected 600/700 tons': see *Efploia Shipping Corporation Ltd* v. *Canadian Transport Co Ltd (The Pantanassa)* [1958] 2 Lloyd's Rep 449, 455–457 by Diplock J. It is very different from the New Zealand case where the land had never been used as a sheep farm and both parties were equally able to form an opinion as to its carrying capacity: see particularly *Bisset* v. *Wilkinson* [1927] AC 177, 183–184.

In the present case it seems to me that there was a warranty that the forecast was sound, that is, Esso made it with reasonable care and skill. That warranty was broken. Most negligently Esso made a 'fatal error' in the forecast they stated to Mr Mardon, and on which he took the tenancy. For this they are liable in damages. The judge, however, declined to find a warranty. So I must go further.

Negligent misrepresentation

Assuming that there was no warranty, the question arises whether Esso are liable for negligent misstatement under the doctrine of *Hedley Byrne & Co Ltd* v. *Heller & Partners Ltd* [1964] AC 465 . . .

It seems to me that *Hedley Byrne & Co Ltd* v. *Heller & Partners Ltd* [1964] AC 465, properly understood, covers this particular proposition: if a man, who has or professes to have special knowledge or skill, makes a representation by virtue thereof to another—be it advice, information or opinion—with the intention of inducing him to enter into a contract with him, he is under a duty to use reasonable care to see that the representation is correct, and that the advice, information or opinion is reliable. If he negligently gives unsound advice or misleading information or expresses an erroneous opinion, and thereby induces the other side to enter into a contract with him, he is liable in damages. This proposition is in line with what I said in *Candler* v. *Crane, Christmas & Co* [1951] 2 KB 164, 179–180, which was approved by the majority of the Privy Council in *Mutual Life and Citizens' Assurance Co Ltd* v. *Evatt* [1971] AC 793, and the judges of the Commonwealth have shown themselves quite ready to apply *Hedley Byrne* [1964] AC 465, between contracting parties: see in Canada, *Sealand of the Pacific Ltd* v. *Ocean Cement Ltd*. (1973) 33 DLR (3d) 625; and in New Zealand, *Capital Motors Ltd* v. *Beecham* [1975] 1 NZLR 576.

Applying this principle, it is plain that Esso professed to have—and did in fact have—special knowledge or skill in estimating the throughput of a filling station. They made the representation—they forecast a throughput of 200,000 gallons—intending to induce Mr Mardon to enter into a tenancy on the faith of it. They made it negligently. It was a 'fatal error'. And thereby induced Mr Mardon to enter into a contract of tenancy that was disastrous to him. For this misrepresentation they are liable in damages.

The measure of damages

Mr Mardon is not to be compensated here for 'loss of a bargain'. He was given no bargain that the throughput *would* amount to 200,000 gallons a year. He is only to be compensated for having been induced to enter into a contract which turned out to be disastrous for him. Whether it be called breach of warranty or negligent misrepresentation, its effect was *not* to warrant the throughput, but only to induce him to enter the contract. So the damages in either case are to be measured by the loss he suffered. Just as in *Doyle* v. *Olby (Ironmongers) Ltd* [1969] 2 QB 158, 167 he can say: '. . . I would not have entered into this contract at all but for your representation. Owing to it, I have lost all the capital I put into it. I also incurred a large overdraft. I have spent four years of my life in wasted endeavour without reward: and it will take me some time to re-establish myself'.

For all such loss he is entitled to recover damages. It is to be measured in a similar way as the loss due to a personal injury. You should look into the future so as to forecast what would have been likely to happen if he had never entered into this contract: and contrast it with his position as it is now as a result of entering into it. The future is necessarily problematical and can only be a rough-and-ready estimate. But it must be done in assessing the loss.

Shaw LJ

Mr Mardon complained that 'he had been sold a pup'. I think he had; but it was a warranted pup, so that Esso are in breach of warranty and liable in damages accordingly. . . . Mr Mardon is entitled in my view to damages for breach of warranty or for negligent misrepresentation.

Ormrod LJ delivered a concurring judgment.

COMMENTARY

Esso were found liable to Mr Mardon on two grounds, namely breach of warranty and negligent misrepresentation. We can see that the law of misrepresentation has moved on since *Oscar Chess* was decided because Lord Denning in his judgment draws upon the decision of the House of Lords in *Hedley Byrne.* Thus the distinction between a term and a misrepresentation was not on the facts significant in terms of the *existence* of the right to recover damages. Nor does it appear to have been significant for the *measure* of recovery. The same sum was recoverable by Mr Mardon whether his claim was one for breach of a term of the contract or for negligent misrepresentation. The reason for this was that the warranty found on the facts by the Court of Appeal was a promise that Esso had used reasonable care and skill in making their forecast as to the likely throughout of petrol. It was not a case in which Esso had actually guaranteed that the throughput would reach a given level. Therefore the appropriate measure of recovery for breach of the term was not the profit Mr Mardon would have made had the projected throughput been reached, but the losses he had suffered as a result of relying to his detriment on the exercise by Esso of reasonable care and skill in making the projection. This formulation of the warranty given by Esso has been criticized. Thus Professor Taylor argues ('Expectation, Reliance and Misrepresentation' (1982) 45 *MLR* 139, 142) that:

Esso v. *Mardon* provides a good illustration of the court limiting the plaintiff to reliance damages precisely because the gist of his claim is that he has relied on a representation rather than that his expectations have been disappointed. Of course Mr Mardon's expectations were *in fact* disappointed but the Court of Appeal clearly did not think that his was a case where his expectations ought to be legally protected in damages but rather felt that compensation for reliance incurred because of expectations aroused by the forecast was more appropriate. It would have been better to express this by denying that the forecast made by Esso was a warranty, rather than by finding a warranty and then denying that expectation damages were available for it.

(b) DRAWING THE THREADS TOGETHER

We can see from the decisions in *Oscar Chess, Dick Bentley,* and *Esso* v. *Mardon* that the knowledge of the parties is an important factor when seeking to decide whether or not a statement has been incorporated into a contract as a term. We can also see from the dissenting judgment of Morris LJ in *Oscar Chess* that the importance of the statement is also a relevant factor (in the sense that the more important the statement, the more likely it is that it will be incorporated into the contract as a term). Morris LJ cited as authority for this proposition the decision of the Court of Appeal in *Couchman* v. *Hill* [1947] KB 554. There the plaintiff purchased at an auction a heifer which was described in the sale catalogue as 'unserved'. At the auction the plaintiff asked the defendant vendor and the auctioneer whether the heifer was in fact unserved and was informed by both that she was. The plaintiff then bought the heifer. He later discovered that the heifer was in calf and she died as a result of the strain of carrying a calf at too young an age. The plaintiff brought an action against the defendant claiming damages for breach of warranty. One of the issues in the case was whether the defendant's oral representation at the auction was a warranty or not. The Court of Appeal concluded that it was and, in doing so, had regard to the importance to the plaintiff of the assurance given to him by the defendant that the heifer was unserved.

The range of factors taken into account by the courts extends beyond those we have already identified. The authorities have been helpfully summarized by Sir Jack Beatson (in *Anson's Law of Contract* (28th edn, Oxford University Press, 2002), pp. 129–130) in the following terms:

First, [the courts] may have regard to the time which elapsed between the time of making the statement and the final manifestation of agreement; if the interval is a long one, this points to a representation. Secondly, they may consider the importance of the statement in the minds of the parties; a statement which is important is likely to be classed as a term of the contract. Thirdly, if the statement was followed by the execution of a formal contract in writing, it is more likely to be regarded as a representation where it is not incorporated in the written document. Finally, where the maker of the statement is, *vis-à-vis* the other party, in a better position to ascertain the accuracy of the statement or has the primary responsibility for doing this, the Courts will tend to regard it as a contractual term unless it relates to a process, such as a medical procedure, the results of which are inherently unpredictable.

But even this list is not complete. A further factor taken into account by the courts is whether or not the maker of the statement asks the other party to verify the truth of his statement. Where he does ask the other party to verify its truth it is unlikely that the statement will amount to a term (*Ecay* v. *Godfrey* (1947) 80 Ll LR 286). Conversely, where he states expressly that there is no need to verify its truth, it is more likely that the statement will amount to a term (*Schawel* v. *Reade* [1913] IR 64). It is not possible to define exhaustively the list of factors to which the courts will have regard. But we have been able to identify the principal factors taken into account by the courts. Whether or not a statement is incorporated into a contract as a term depends ultimately upon the facts of the individual case and, as *Oscar Chess* demonstrates, judges can and do differ in the conclusions which they reach in individual cases.

5. THE PAROL EVIDENCE RULE

The second issue that arises for consideration concerns the situation where the parties have reduced their contract to writing. In such a case is it possible for them to lead

evidence of terms other than those contained in their written contract or does the
written contract constitute the sole repository of the terms of their contract? This is
not an easy question to answer. The answer depends upon the scope of what is
generally referred to as the 'parol evidence rule'. The scope of this rule is a matter of
some controversy. One view is that the rule amounts to no more than this: that in the
case where the parties intend that the written document shall contain all the terms of
their contract it is not possible to lead evidence for the purpose of adding to, varying,
subtracting from, or contradicting the terms contained in that document. An alternative view is that the rule does not rest on the intention of both parties but consists of a
presumption made by the court that a document that looks like the whole contract is
in fact the whole contract so that it is not possible to lead evidence for the purpose of
adding to, varying, subtracting from, or contradicting the terms contained in the
written document. The first view is held by the Law Commission, while the second is
held by Professor Treitel. Their views are set out in the following passages:

Law Commission No 154, *Law of Contract: The Parol Evidence Rule* (1986)

Nature of the parol evidence rule

2.6.   So far as we are aware, no English or Commonwealth court has ever found it
necessary to analyse the parol evidence rule in detail as to its applicability, width and
effect. In the cases in which the rule has been mentioned, it has generally been in terms
which seem to indicate that the judge thought it was both obvious and well known. For
the purpose of deciding whether the parol evidence rule should be abolished or
amended by statute, it has been necessary to analyse the rule in detail. We had to be clear
as to what the rule was which might be abolished, amended or declared.

2.7.   We have now concluded that although a proposition of law can be stated which
can be described as the 'parol evidence rule' it is not a rule of law which, correctly
applied, could lead to evidence being unjustly excluded. Rather, it is a proposition of law
which is no more than a circular statement: *when it is proved or admitted that the parties
to a contract intended that all the express terms of their agreement should be as recorded in
a particular document or documents, evidence will be inadmissible (because irrelevant) if it
is tendered only for the purpose of adding to, varying, subtracting from or contradicting the
express terms of that contract.* We have considerable doubts whether such a proposition
should properly be characterised as a 'rule' at all, but several leading textbook writers and
judges have referred to it as a 'rule' and we are content to adopt their terminology for the
purposes of this report.

2.8.   Our conclusion as to the nature of the parol evidence rule is no new theory. The
opinions of some leading textbook writers, who reached a similar conclusion long before
we approached the subject, confirm us in our view that the parol evidence rule is no more
than as we have stated above . . .

2.9.   The two principal reasons which have led us to our conclusion on the nature of
the parol evidence rule are, in substance, two aspects of the same process of reasoning.

2.10.   The first relates to the circumstances in which the rule is to be applied. In our view, some statements of the rule may have given rise to misunderstandings because they have concentrated on the *effect* of the rule rather than *when it is to be applied*. The effect of the rule is to exclude evidence or to cause the judge to ignore the evidence if given. As to the application of the rule, Lord Morris' statement in *Bank of Australasia* v. *Palmer* refers to the inadmissibility of parol evidence to 'contradict, vary, add to or subtract from the terms of a *written contract*' (emphasis added). Thus, the rule can only be applied where the parties have entered into a written contract when 'the writing is intended by the parties as a contractual document which is to contain all the terms of their agreement'. When the parties have set down *all* the terms of their contract in writing, extrinsic evidence of other terms must be ignored. If the contract is not entirely in writing, it is not a written contract. . . . If it is proved or admitted that all the terms of the contract have been set out in a particular document or documents, then evidence of other terms must be irrelevant and therefore inadmissible, because inconsistent with the finding that the parties have entered into a written contract.

2.11.   The second reason for our conclusion as to the nature of the parol evidence rule is exemplified by the concept of the contract which is made partly orally and partly in writing . . .

2.12.   Because a contract can be made partly orally and partly in writing, the mere production of a contractual document, however complete it may look, cannot as a matter of law exclude evidence of oral terms if the other party asserts that such terms were agreed. If that assertion is proved, evidence of the oral terms cannot be excluded because the court will, by definition, have found that the contractual terms are partly to be found in what was agreed orally as well as in the document in question. No parol evidence rule could apply. On the other hand, if that assertion is not proved, there can be no place for a parol evidence rule because the court will have found that all the terms of the contract were set out in the document in question and, by implication, will thereby have excluded evidence of terms being found elsewhere . . .

2.13.   Of course, the more the parties have done to create what appears to be a written contract, the greater are the probabilities that the court will conclude that they did indeed make such a contract. In this connection, in considering the parol evidence rule in 1959, Professor Lord Wedderburn concluded that,

'What the parol evidence rule has bequeathed to the modern law is a presumption— namely that a document which *looks* like a contract is to be treated as the *whole* contract.'

While we have no doubt that this statement accurately reflects the practical effect of the parol evidence rule as we now believe it to be, the presumption (which can be displaced by evidence) is not a rule of law laying down whether a particular type of evidence should be admitted or, if it is admitted, whether the court should give effect to it. Moreover, we do not think that in this context it is strictly correct to refer to a 'presumption'. In reaching a conclusion as to whether a document which looks like a complete contract was the whole contract, the court does not apply any presumption of law. Rather, it will reach its conclusion on the evidence tendered, applying to its judgment the prima facie probability derived from its experience of how people normally behave in a given situation. For example, if the plaintiff proves that the parties signed a document, such as a complicated lease of a commercial chattel, which document appears to be a complete contract and which is in a form generally adopted for setting out all the contractual terms, it may be difficult in practice for the defendant to prove, on the balance of probabilities, that terms were orally agreed in addition to those set out in the document.

2.14.   The issue whether parties intended that the whole of their agreement should be as recorded in a particular document or documents is to be judged objectively. The court is not concerned with whether both parties, in their minds, intended the writing to contain the whole of the agreement between them but whether, having regard to what was said or done, and to what documents were signed and exchanged, and when, a reasonable person would have understood the writing to contain the whole of the agreement. A party is not permitted to give evidence of his private but uncommunicated intention as to what was to be agreed, or as to what the written agreement was to mean.

2.15.   Sometimes parties may include in their contracts a clause to the effect that the whole contract is contained in the document and that nothing was agreed outside it (sometimes called a 'merger' or 'integration' clause). In particular, it may be provided that nothing said during negotiations is intended to be of any contractual effect unless recorded in the document. Without legislative provision such a clause cannot, we think, have conclusive effect. It may have a very strong persuasive effect but if it were proved that, notwithstanding the clause, the parties actually intended some additional term to be of contractual effect, the court would give effect to that term because such was the intention of the parties. If the parties intended that the additional term should have been recorded in the document, the contract could be rectified. If it had been their intention that the term should be of contractual effect but not be included in the document, the analysis likely to be adopted by the court is that the parties agreed a collateral contract alongside the written one. But if it were proved that the intention of the parties was to make one contract partly in writing and partly orally, the court would give effect to that contract. The parties might have been aware of the integration clause when they agreed the additional terms but have agreed to ignore it, or they might have forgotten about the clause or never read it. Whatever the reason for there being an integration clause and additional terms, the court will give effect to the intention of the parties as it is proved or admitted to have been.

2.16.   The same analysis should, we think, be applied to the situation where it is proved that the parties intended that their transaction was partly as recorded in a document and party as agreed orally, although the oral terms conflict with the written terms. Such a situation is no different in principle from that in which the parties agree two inconsistent terms both of which are set out in the same document. The court will have to decide which of the inconsistent terms more nearly represents the intention of the parties. If it is impossible to resolve this issue the court may be driven to the conclusion that no contract came into existence because it is impossible to say what the terms of the contract were.

2.17.   The conclusion which emerges from the discussion above is that there is no *rule of law* that evidence is rendered inadmissible or is to be ignored solely because a document exists which looks like a complete contract. Whether it is a complete contract depends upon the intention of the parties, objectively judged, and not on any rule of law.

Professer Treitel states by way of reply:

GH Treitel, *The Law of Contract*

(11th edn, Sweet & Maxwell, 2003), pp. 193–195

It has been argued [by the Law Commission] that the right of a party to rely on extrinsic evidence . . . turns the parol evidence rule (as applied to contracts) into 'no more than a circular statement'. For if the rule applies only where the written document is intended to contain *all* the terms of the contract, evidence of other terms would be useless even if admitted (since they would not form part of the contract); while the rule never prevents a party from relying on evidence of terms which *were* intended to be part of the contract. Accordingly, on this view, no injustice is caused by the operation of the rule. There is much force in this view in cases in which, at the time of contracting, both parties actually shared a common intention with regard to the term in question. But in most cases in which the rule is invoked this is not the position: the dispute arises precisely because the parties had different intentions, and one alleges, while the other denies, that terms not set out in the document were intended to form part of the contract. In such cases, the court will attach importance to the appearance of the document: if it *looks* like a complete contract to one of the parties taking a reasonable view of it, then the rule will prevent the other party from relying on extrinsic evidence to show that the contract also contained other terms. This result has been described as being simply an application of the objective test of agreement; but, even if it can be so regarded, it is such a common and frequently recurring application of this test as to amount to an independent rule. In cases of the present kind, moreover, the law goes beyond the normal objective test. That test normally requires the party relying on it to prove that he reasonably believed that the other party was contracting on the terms alleged. Where a document *looks* like a complete contract, the party relying on it does not have to prove that he had such a belief: he can rely on a presumption to that effect which it is up to the other party to rebut. As laymen are known to attach greater importance than the law does to writing in a contractual context, it will be hard for the party relying on the extrinsic evidence to rebut the presumption that the written document was an exclusive record of the terms agreed. Moreover, the objective test normally prevents a party from relying on his 'private but uncommunicated intention as to what was to be agreed'. The presumption which applies in the case of an apparently complete contractual document goes beyond this: it prevents a party from relying on evidence of intention that was not 'private and uncommunicated' at all, but simply not recorded in the document. For these reasons, it is submitted that the admissibility of extrinsic evidence, where it is proved that the document was not in fact intended to contain all the terms of the contract, does not turn the rule into a merely 'circular statement'. Whether it also supports the conclusion that the rule is not one that 'could lead to evidence being unjustly excluded' is perhaps more doubtful. The primary purpose of the rule, like that of the objective test of agreement, is to promote certainty, sometimes even at the expense of justice. Where the parties have brought into being an apparently complete contractual document, the rejection of evidence of extrinsic terms that were actually agreed may cause injustice to the party relying on those terms, while the reception of such evidence may cause injustice to the other party, if he reasonably believed that the document formed an exclusive record of the contract. The question is which, on balance, is the greater injustice. Where the evidence is rejected because the party relying on it cannot overcome the presumption arising from the fact that the document *looks* like a complete contract, the greater injustice would appear to lie in the exclusion of the evidence; for the presumption seems to be based on the nature and form of the document, rather than on any actual belief of the party relying on it, that it formed an exclusive record of the contract.

COMMENTARY

The difference between these two views is not as stark as might at first sight appear. The reason for this is that any presumption that a document that looks like the whole contract is the whole contract does not appear to be a particularly strong one. This brings Professor Treitel's view much closer to that of the Law Commission in the sense that it seems unlikely that the presumption will preclude a party from leading evidence of terms which it is argued were intended to be part of the contract. The modern court is more likely to admit the evidence and evaluate its significance than declare it to be inadmissible.

In any event, it is clear that the parol evidence rule, whatever its true scope, is the subject of a number of exceptions. For example, evidence is admissible to prove a custom (*Hutton* v. *Warren* (1836) 1 M & W 466, p. 377 below), to show that the contract is invalid on a ground such as misrepresentation, to show that the document should be rectified, and to prove the existence of a collateral agreement (*City and Westminster Properties (1934) Ltd* v. *Mudd* [1959] Ch 129).

The final point to be made relates to the wisdom of this drift towards the admissibility of such evidence and the desirability of leaving it to the court to evaluate its significance. There has been a commercial reaction against this trend, largely because it is said to promote uncertainty. The Law Commission at paragraph 2.15 of their report (above) refer to 'merger' or 'integration' clauses. These clauses are often referred to today as 'entire agreement clauses'. We shall encounter them in more detail in Chapter 12 (see pp. 440–441 below). Here it suffices to note that the purpose of these clauses is generally to shut out evidence that the parol evidence rule would probably have excluded in the past. So evidence that is now admissible as a matter of law is sought to be excluded from judicial consideration by contractual stipulation. The Law Commission state that such provisions cannot have 'conclusive effect'. As we shall see, the modern courts have taken a more benevolent approach towards the construction of entire agreement clauses so that they can have the effect of preventing a party from leading evidence of terms other than those contained in the written contract (see, in particular, *Watford Electronics Ltd* v. *Sanderson CFL Ltd* [2001] All ER (D) 290, discussed in more detail at pp. 441 and 473 below). But the drafting of entire agreement clauses is a matter of great difficulty and the time and expense that is devoted by commercial parties and their lawyers to the drafting of such clauses tends to suggest that the relaxation of the parol evidence rule that has taken place over the last 100 years or more might not necessarily have been a desirable development.

6. FURTHER READING

CARTWRIGHT, J, *Misrepresentation* (Sweet and Maxwell, 2002), Chapter 6.

LAW COMMISSION, Report No 154, *Law of Contract: The Parol Evidence Rule* (1986).

9

INCORPORATION OF TERMS

1. CENTRAL ISSUES

1. In order to be effective a term must have been incorporated into the contract between the parties. Incorporation can be a surprisingly difficult issue in commercial practice. Many businesses spend significant sums of money on legal advice in relation to the drafting of their standard terms of business but then adopt what appears to be a surprisingly lax approach when it comes to ensuring that these standard terms are incorporated into the contracts they conclude. It is a noticeable feature of litigation concerning standard form clauses, such as exclusion clauses and retention of title clauses, that the defendant frequently takes the point that the term in issue between the parties has not been incorporated into the contract. Incorporation issues are not, however, confined to exclusion clauses or retention of title clauses. They can arise in relation to any contract term.

2. The simplest method of incorporation is signature. A party is generally bound by terms he has signed, whether or not he has read them. This rule can produce harsh results and it has been criticized on this basis. The justification that is usually offered in support of the rule is that it promotes certainty and protects the interests of third parties who may rely to their detriment upon the validity of the signature.

3. Terms can also be incorporated into a contract by notice. In order to be effective the notice must have been given at or before the time of contracting, in a document that was intended to have contractual effect and reasonable steps must have been taken to bring the terms to the notice of the other party. Where the term is 'onerous' or 'unusual' greater steps must be taken to bring it to the attention of the other party. This rule is firmly established in English law but it is open to criticism on the ground that it gives rise to uncertainty (in terms of defining a clause that is 'onerous' or 'unusual') and on the basis that no convincing justification has been offered for differentiating between different terms in relation to their incorporation. Attempts to regulate the fairness of the terms of a contract should be done directly and not by the backdoor of the rules relating to the incorporation of terms.

4. Finally terms can be incorporated into a contract by virtue of a course of dealing or as a result of the custom of the trade. In order to constitute a 'course of dealing' there must have been a series of transactions between the parties that was both 'consistent' and 'regular'.

2. INTRODUCTION

The incorporation of terms into a contract can be a contentious issue in practice. A failure by a claimant to take adequate steps to ensure that its standard terms are incorporated into the contracts it concludes can be an expensive mistake. A simple illustration of this point is provided by the facts of *Poseidon Freight Forwarding Co Ltd*

v. *Davies Turner Southern Ltd* [1996] 2 Lloyd's Rep 388. A fax was sent by the defendants to the plaintiff. At the bottom of the fax appeared the words 'NOTE: The only
conditions on which we transact business are shown on the back'. Unfortunately, it
would appear that no one had informed the employee of the defendants who was
operating the fax machine that it was necessary to fax the back page as well as the
front page. So the terms on the back were never sent to the plaintiff. The Court of
Appeal held that, in these circumstances, the defendants' terms had not been
incorporated into the contract so that the defendants were unable to rely on an
exemption clause contained in their standard terms. Leggatt LJ stated (at p. 394):

[t]his is not a case where a party declares that the terms are available for inspection. It is a case
where, on documents sent by fax, reference is made to terms stated on the back, which are,
however, not stated or otherwise communicated. Since what was described as being on the back
was not sent, it was a more cogent inference that the terms were not intended to apply.

How can a party take adequate steps to ensure that its terms are incorporated into
the contracts it concludes? Three principal options are available. The first is to ensure
that the other party to the contract signs the document that contains all the relevant
terms. The general rule in English law is that a party is bound by his signature and this
rule applies whether or not the party signing the document has read it. The second is
to take reasonable steps to bring the terms to the notice of the other party. This is a
less reliable method of incorporation than signature because of the need to persuade
the court that 'reasonable steps' have been taken (and, as we shall see, it is not always
an easy task to persuade a court that reasonable steps have been taken). The third
option is incorporation by course of dealing or by custom. The last option is the least
satisfactory option, largely because of the difficulties involved in establishing the
existence of a course of dealing that is sufficiently consistent and regular for it to
amount in law to a 'course of dealing'. Incorporation by custom is easier to establish
where both parties transact in a particular market or trade: in such a case the court
may be relatively willing to infer that the customary trade terms have been incorporated into the parties' contract. It is, however, the case that it is safer to take more active
steps to ensure that terms are incorporated into a contract, whether these active steps
take the form of obtaining the signature of the other party or taking reasonable steps
to bring the terms to the notice of the other party.

3. INCORPORATION BY SIGNATURE

A party is, in general, bound by his signature. This being the case, a party who signs a
contract will, in principle, be bound by its terms. This is so, whether the party signing
the document has actually read it or not. A party who does not want to be bound by
the terms contained in the document should not sign it. The law does not in general
allow him to sign the document and afterwards claim that he is not bound by its terms
on the basis that he had not read or understood its terms. The general rule that a party
is bound by his signature can lead to harsh results, as the following case demonstrates:

L'Estrange v. F. Graucob Ltd

[1934] 2 KB 394, Divisional Court

Two of the defendants' representatives visited the plaintiff and asked her to buy an automatic slot machine for cigarettes. The plaintiff was the owner of a café in Llandudno. She agreed to buy the machine and signed a 'Sales Agreement' produced by one of the defendants' representatives. The document, so far as relevant, provided:

'Sales Agreement. Date Feb. 7, 1933. To F. Graucob, Ltd, . . . Please forward me as soon as possible: One Six Column Junior Ilam Automatic Machine . . . which I agree to purchase from you on the terms stated below . . . and to pay for the same in the following manner: Instalments 8l. 15s. 0d. down. 18 payments of 3l. 19s. 11d.'

Then after some other formal matter came certain clauses in small print which, so far as material, were as follows:

'I agree to take delivery of the machine upon receiving notice that it is ready for delivery, and to make the first monthly payment 30 days after the date following that of the posting of such notice and all subsequent payments on the corresponding date of each succeeding month. . . . If any payment shall not have been received by you within a fortnight after it has become due, all the remaining payments shall fall due for immediate payment, and I agree to pay interest on these remaining payments at the rate of ten per cent. per annum as from the date of their so falling due. In consideration of your undertaking to put in hand at once work on this machine I agree not to countermand this order. . . . This agreement contains all the terms and conditions under which I agree to purchase the machine specified above, and any express or implied condition, statement, or warranty, statutory or otherwise not stated herein is hereby excluded. . . . (sgd.) H. M. L'Estrange.'

The machine was delivered to the plaintiff some six weeks later but the machine did not work satisfactorily and after a few days became jammed and unworkable. The plaintiff brought an action against the defendants. One of the claims advanced by the plaintiff was that the machine was not fit for the purpose for which it had been sold. The defendants denied liability on the basis that the agreement expressly provided for the exclusion of this and all other implied warranties. The plaintiff in turn contended that she was induced to sign the contract by the misrepresentation that it was an order form and that at the time when she signed she knew nothing of the conditions. The county court judge held that the defendants were not entitled to rely upon the clause which excluded implied warranties from the contract on the ground that they had not done what was reasonably sufficient to give the plaintiff notice of the conditions. The defendants appealed to the Court of Appeal who allowed the appeal. It was held that the plaintiff had not been induced to sign the contract by any misrepresentation and that she was bound by her signature. She was therefore bound by the terms of the contract, including the exclusion clause, and judgment was entered for the defendants.

Scrutton LJ [set out the facts and continued]

As to the defence that no action would lie for breach of implied warranty, the defendants relied upon the following clause in the contract: 'This agreement contains all the terms and conditions under which I agree to purchase the machine specified above and any express or implied condition, statement, or warranty, statutory or otherwise not stated herein is hereby excluded'. A clause of that sort has been before the Courts for some time. The first reported case in which it made its appearance seems to be *Wallis, Son & Wells* v. *Pratt & Haynes* [1911] AC 394, where the exclusion clause mentioned only 'warranty' and it was held that it did not exclude conditions. In the more recent case of *Andrews Brothers (Bournemouth), Ltd* v. *Singer & Co* [1934] 1 KB 17, where the draftsman had put into the contract of sale a clause which excluded only implied conditions, warranties and liabilities, it was held that the clause did not apply to an express term describing the article, and did not exempt the seller from liability where he delivered an article of a different description. The clause here in question would seem to have been intended to go further than any of the previous clauses and to include all terms denoting collateral stipulations, in order to avoid the result of these decisions.

The main question raised in the present case is whether that clause formed part of the contract. If it did, it clearly excluded any condition or warranty.

In the course of the argument in the county court reference was made to the railway passenger and cloak-room ticket cases. . . . These cases have no application when the document has been signed. When a document containing contractual terms is signed, then, in the absence of fraud, or, I will add, misrepresentation, the party signing it is bound, and it is wholly immaterial whether he has read the document or not.

The plaintiff contended at the trial that she was induced by misrepresentation to sign the contract without knowing its terms, and that on that ground they are not binding upon her. The learned judge in his judgment makes no mention of that contention of the plaintiff, and he pronounces no finding as to the alleged misrepresentation. There is a further difficulty. Fraud is not mentioned in the pleadings, and I strongly object to deal with allegations of fraud where fraud is not expressly pleaded. I have read the evidence with care, and it contains no material upon which fraud could be found . . .

In this case the plaintiff has signed a document headed 'Sales Agreement', which she admits had to do with an intended purchase, and which contained a clause excluding all conditions and warranties. That being so, the plaintiff, having put her signature to the document and not having been induced to do so by any fraud or misrepresentation, cannot be heard to say that she is not bound by the terms of the document because she has not read them.

Maugham LJ

I regret the decision to which I have come, but I am bound by legal rules and cannot decide the case on other considerations.

The material question is whether or not there was a contract in writing between the plaintiff and the defendants in the terms contained in the brown paper document . . .

In the present case on February 7, 1933, an order form, for such I consider the brown paper document to be, was signed by the plaintiff. It was an elaborate form containing a number of clauses, and among them certain terms and conditions in regrettably small print but quite legible. The plaintiff having signed that document gave it to a canvasser of the defendants, who took it away. It had been filled up in ink by the canvasser before she signed it. Another document called an order confirmation dated February 9, 1933, was sent to her by the defendants. In my opinion the contract was concluded not when the brown order form was signed by the plaintiff but when the order confirmation was signed by the defendants. If the document signed by the plaintiff was a part of a contract in writing, it is impossible to pick out certain clauses from it and ignore them as not binding on the plaintiff . . .

I deal with this case on the footing that when the order confirmation was signed by the defendants confirming the order form which had been signed by the plaintiff, there was then a signed contract in writing between the parties. If that is so, then, subject to certain contingencies, there is no doubt that it was wholly immaterial whether the plaintiff read the small print or not . . .

There are, however, two possibilities to be kept in view. The first is that it might be proved that the document, though signed by the plaintiff, was signed in circumstances which made it not her act. That is known as the case of Non est factum. . . . The written document admittedly related to the purchase of the machine by the plaintiff. Even if she was told that it was an order form, she could not be heard to say that it did not affect her because she did not know its contents.

Another possibility is that the plaintiff might have been induced to sign the document by misrepresentation. She contended that she was so induced to sign the document inasmuch as (i.) she was assured that it was an order form, (ii.) that at the time when she signed it she knew nothing of the conditions which it contained. The second of these contentions is unavailing by reason of the fact that the document was in writing signed by the plaintiff. As to the first contention it is true that the document was an order form. But further, if the statement that it was an order form could be treated as a representation that it contained no clause expressly excluding all conditions and warranties, the answer would be that there is no evidence to prove that that statement was made by or on behalf of the defendants.

In this case it is, in my view, an irrelevant circumstance that the plaintiff did not read, or hear of, the parts of the sales document which are in small print, and that document should have effect according to its terms. I may add, however, that I could wish that the contract had been in a simpler and more usual form. It is unfortunate that the important clause excluding conditions and warranties is in such small print. I also think that the order confirmation form should have contained an express statement to the effect that it was exclusive of all conditions and warranties.

I agree that the appeal should be allowed.

COMMENTARY

Three points should be noted about *L'Estrange*. The first is that the Court of Appeal recognized that the rule that a person is bound by his signature is not an absolute one. Two exceptions were acknowledged on the facts of the case and a third has been recognized subsequently. The first exception arises where the party signing the document can invoke the defence of *non est factum*. The scope of this defence is discussed in more detail in a subsequent chapter (see pp. 651–656 below). Here it suffices to note that it is a defence that operates within narrow confines. In essence it allows a party to deny that the document which he has signed is his deed on the basis that he was unable, through no fault of his own, to have any real understanding of a document, without being given an explanation of it. The causes of the lack of understanding can be 'defective education, illness or innate incapacity' (see *Saunders* v. *Anglia Building Society* [1971] AC 1004, 1016). The second arises where the person is induced to sign the document as the result of a misrepresentation made to him. In *Curtis* v.

Chemical Cleaning and Dyeing Co Ltd [1951] 1 KB 805 the plaintiff took a white satin wedding dress to the defendants for cleaning. She was asked to sign a document that contained a clause which stated that the dress was 'accepted on condition that the company is not liable for any damage howsoever arising'. Prior to signing the document the plaintiff inquired why it was that she was being asked to sign the document. She was told that it was because the defendants did not accept liability for damage done to beads or sequins on the dress. The plaintiff then signed the document but did not take the time to read its terms. When the dress was returned to her there was a stain on it. She brought a claim against the defendants who attempted to rely on the exclusion clause by way of defence. The Court of Appeal held that they could not do so in the light of the representation made by the defendant's employee prior to the plaintiff signing the document. Denning LJ stated (at pp. 808–809):

If the party affected signs a written document, knowing it to be a contract which governs the relations between him and the other party, his signature is irrefragable evidence of his assent to the whole contract, including the exempting clauses, unless the signature is shown to be obtained by fraud or misrepresentation: see *L'Estrange* v. *Graucob*. . . . What is a sufficient misrepresentation for this purpose? . . .

In my opinion, any behaviour by words or conduct is sufficient to be a misrepresentation if it is such as to mislead the other party about the existence or extent of the exemption. If it conveys a false impression, that is enough. If the false impression is created knowingly, it is a fraudulent misrepresentation; if it is created unwittingly, it is an innocent misrepresentation. But either is sufficient to disentitle the creator of it to the benefit of the exemption. It was held in *R* v. *Kylsant (Lord)* [1932] 1 KB 442 that a misrepresentation might be literally true but practically false, not because of what is said, but because of what it left unsaid. In short, because of what it implied. This is as true of an innocent misrepresentation as it is of a fraudulent misrepresentation. When one party puts forward a printed form for signature, failure by him to draw attention to the existence or extent of the exemption clause may in some circumstances convey the impression that there is no exemption at all, or, any rate, not so wide an exemption as that which is in fact contained in the document. The present case is a good illustration. The customer said in evidence:

'When I was asked to sign the document I asked why. The assistant said I was to accept any responsibility for damage to beads and sequins. I did not read it all before I signed it.'

In those circumstances, by failing to draw attention to the width of the exemption clause, the assistant created the false impression that the exemption clause related to the beads and sequins only, and that it did not extend to the material of which the dress was made. It was done perfectly innocently, but, nevertheless, a false impression was created . . . [I]t was a sufficient misrepresentation to disentitle the cleaners from relying on the exemption, except in regard to the beads and sequins.

The third exception, acknowledged in *Grogan* v. *Robin Meredith Plant Hire* [1996] CLC 1127 is that the document which has been signed must have been a document which purports to have contractual effect and not an administrative document, such as a time-sheet. The latter does not purport to constitute the contract; rather, it records or gives effect to a part of the contract that has already been concluded (for example, by recording the number of hours for which a piece of machinery has been hired out, so that the price payable can be calculated). Whether a document amounts to a contractual document or not is a decision that must be reached in the light of all the facts and circumstances of the case.

The second point to note is that the Unfair Contract Terms Act 1977 (see pp. 460–485 below) would now regulate the validity of the exclusion clause found in the contract between the parties in *L'Estrange*. But at the time at which *L'Estrange* was decided the court did not have the power at common law to strike down exclusion clauses on the ground that they were unreasonable or unfair. In so far as the criticisms of *L'Estrange* are based on the unfairness of the result, it can be argued that any such unfairness is best addressed by giving to the courts the power to control unreasonable or unfair terms and not by modifying the rule that a party is bound by his own signature.

The third point relates to the criticisms that have been levelled against the decision in *L'Estrange*. Maugham LJ expressed his regret at the outcome but was of the view that he was bound by authority so to conclude. Others have challenged the view that the court was in fact bound and, in doing so, have invoked cases discussed in Chapter 2 (see pp. 38–49 above) concerned with the objective approach adopted by the courts when seeking to ascertain whether or not the parties have reached agreement. In his article 'Signature, Consent, and the Rule in *L'Estrange* v. *Graucob*' [1973] *CLJ* 104, JR Spencer has this to say of *L'Estrange* (at pp. 114–115):

When Miss L'Estrange signed the order form on which were written various terms, she gave the appearance of agreeing to everything that was written on the document. To borrow the words from *Smith* v. *Hughes* itself, she so conducted herself 'that a reasonable man would believe that she was assenting to the terms proposed by the other party'. It would usually follow from this that she was bound by her apparent consent to all those terms. However, a person is not bound by apparent consent where the other party knew that his mind did not go with his apparent consent, or where the other party is responsible for the mistake which has been made. Didn't the facts of the case bring Miss L'Estrange within the scope of these exceptions to apparent consent?

The order form which Graucob Ltd provided seems to have been drawn up in a most confusing way. Maugham LJ said '... I could wish that the contract had been in a simpler and more usual form. It is unfortunate that the important clause excluding conditions and warranties is in such small print'. Not only was the clause printed in small print, but it was also printed on brown paper, which must have made the small print even harder to read. The general layout of the form also appears to have been confusing, too, the exemption clause being in a part of the document where it easily escaped notice. Then was this not one of those cases where although A apparently consented to B's terms, he did so because B had earlier confused him as to what those terms should be? In principle, the case is surely the same as *Scriven* v. *Hindley*, where A was allowed to deny his apparent consent to a contract to buy tow, because the auction catalogue had been confusing, and had contributed to form A's belief that he was offering to buy, not tow, but hemp.

Perhaps Miss L'Estrange could have gone even further than this, and also denied her apparent consent to the exemption clause on the ground that the company either knew or ought to have known that her mind did not go with her apparent consent. Why did Graucob Ltd use order forms printed on brown paper containing obscure exemption clauses in minute print in unexpected places? Was it because it knew that if it said what it meant more plainly, its customers would understand the document they were being asked to sign, and would refuse to do so? Who in their right mind would sign a document headed 'I agree to pay for your goods even if they are useless, and not to sue you even if they injure me?' Even if Graucob Ltd had used the words it did use—

'any express or implied condition, statement or warranty, statutory or otherwise, not stated herein is hereby excluded'—Miss L'Estrange might still have refused to sign if those words had been printed clearly where they could be seen. She would not have understood them, of course, but . . . she might have asked the salesmen what the words meant. If the salesman had explained correctly, presumably she would not have signed. If he had explained incorrectly, then the company would have misrepresented the legal effect of the form, and . . . would have been unable to rely on the exemption clause.

The truth is that whatever may have been Graucob Ltd's intentions disreputable companies put harsh exemption clauses in minute print in order to 'put one over' people like Miss L'Estrange. Then why should people in her position not be allowed to deny their apparent consent to the clause because the company either *knew* or *ought to have known* that their mind did not go with their apparent consent?

Yet the Divisional Court, which felt sorry for Miss L'Estrange, did not allow her to deny her assent to the exemption clause by alleging either that Graucob Ltd were to blame for her mistake, as in *Scriven* v. *Hindley* [see p. 45 above], or that they had actual or constructive knowledge of the mistake she had made, as in *Hartog* v. *Colin and Shields* [see p. 38 above]. Why not? . . .

The reason why the [court in *L'Estrange v. Graucob*] . . . refused to admit the usual defences based on *Smith* v. *Hughes*, and restricted the range of available defences to fraud, misrepresentation and *non est factum*, appears to be that [the court] thought that there was something special about a signed document. Where there is a signed document, the courts thought that some kind of magic operated to take the contract out of the usual rules that govern the formation of contracts, and to bind the signatory almost absolutely.

An approach similar to that advocated in the penultimate paragraph of Professor Spencer's article was adopted by the Court of Appeal of Ontario in *Tilden Rent-A-Car Co* v. *Clendinning* (1978) 83 DLR (3d) 400. The defendant, Mr Clendinning, rented a car from Tilden Rent-A-Car at Vancouver airport. He was asked whether or not he wished to have additional insurance cover and he replied that he did. He was given a form to sign which he signed without reading, as would have been apparent to the clerk. The question for the court was whether or not the defendant was bound by an exemption clause in the policy which had the effect of imposing liability upon him for damage done to the car. The Court of Appeal concluded that he was not bound by the term. Dubin JA stated (at pp. 403–409):

It was urged that the rights of the parties were governed by what has come to be known as 'the rule in *L'Estrange* v. *F Graucob Ltd*' . . . *Consensus ad idem* is as much a part of the law of written contracts as it is of oral contracts. The signature to a contract is only one way of manifesting assent to contractual terms . . .

The justification for the rule in *L'Estrange* v. *F Graucob Ltd* appears to have been founded upon the objective theory of contracts, by which means parties are bound to a contract in writing by measuring their conduct by outward appearance rather than what the parties inwardly meant to decide . . .

Even accepting the objective theory to determine whether Mr Clendinning had entered into a contract which included all the terms of the written instrument, it is to be observed that an essential part of that test is whether the other party entered into the contract in the belief that Mr Clendinning was assenting to all such terms. In the instant case, it was apparent to the employee of Tilden-Rent-A-Car that Mr Clendinning had not in fact read the document in its entirety before he signed it. It

follows under such circumstances that Tilden-Rent-A-Car cannot rely on provisions of the contract which it had no reason to believe were being assented to by the other contracting party.

As stated in Waddams, *The Law of Contracts*, p. 191:

'One who signs a written document cannot complain if the other party reasonably relies on the
signature as a manifestation of assent to the contents, or ascribes to words he uses their
reasonable meaning. But the other side of the same coin is that only a reasonable expectation
will be protected. If the party seeking to enforce the document knew or had reason to know of
the other's mistake the document should not be enforced.'

In ordinary commercial practice where there is frequently a sense of formality in the transaction, and where there is a full opportunity for the parties to consider the terms of the proposed
contract submitted for signature, it might well be safe to assume that the party who attaches his
signature to the contract intends by so doing to acknowledge his acquiescence to its terms, and
that the other party entered into the contract upon that belief. This can hardly be said, however,
where the contract is entered into in circumstances such as were present in this case.

A transaction, such as this one, is invariably carried out in a hurried, informal manner. The speed
with which the transaction is completed is said to be one of the attractive features of the services
provided.

The clauses relied on in this case . . . are inconsistent with the over-all purpose for which the
contract is entered into by the hirer. Under such circumstances, something more should be done by
the party submitting the contract for signature than merely handing it over to be signed . . .

In modern commercial practice, many standard form printed documents are signed without
being read or understood. In many cases the parties seeking to rely on the terms of the contract
know or ought to know that the signature of a party to the contract does not represent the true
intention of the signer, and that the party signing is unaware of the stringent and onerous provisions which the standard form contains. Under such circumstances, I am of the opinion that the
party seeking to rely on such terms should not be able to do so in the absence of first having taken
reasonable measures to draw such terms to the attention of the other party, and, in the absence of
such reasonable measures, it is not necessary for the party denying knowledge of such terms to
prove either fraud, misrepresentation or *non est factum*.

In the case at bar, Tilden Rent-A-Car took no steps to alert Mr Clendinning to the onerous
provisions in the standard form contract presented by it. The clerk could not help but have known
that Mr Clendinning had not in fact read the contract before signing it. Indeed the form of the
contract itself with the important provisions on the reverse side and in very small type would
discourage even the most cautious customer from endeavouring to read and understand it.
Under such circumstances, it was not open to Tilden Rent-A-Car to rely on those clauses, and it
was not incumbent on Mr Clendinning to establish fraud, misrepresentation or *non est factum*.
Having paid the premium, he was not liable for any damage to the vehicle while being driven
by him.

The English courts have not as yet embraced such a broad exception to the general
rule (see *Peninsula Business Services Ltd* v. *Sweeney* [2004] IRLR 49 at [22]). The
exceptions currently recognized are much narrower in scope. Why is this? The answer
lies in the significance that is attached to a signature. Why do we generally treat a
signature as conclusive? Professor Atiyah has stated ('Form and Substance in Contract
Law' in *Essays on Contract* (Oxford University Press, 1986), p. 109) that:

A signature is, and is widely recognized even by the general public as, a formal device, and its value would be greatly reduced if it could not be treated as a conclusive ground of contractual liability at least in all ordinary circumstances.

New forms of technology may in time challenge this perspective of the value of a signature. Will an electronic signature count as a signature for the purposes of the rule in *L'Estrange*? If it does, will the courts continue to follow *L'Estrange* or will they adopt the approach taken in *Clendinning*? In time the English courts may well go down the road taken by the Canadian courts. But an alternative, and possibly preferable, approach might be to adhere to the rule, subject to its existing exceptions, but to give the courts greater power to deal with unreasonable terms contained in contracts. In this way the value of a signature as a formal device will be retained but the courts will be given the power to deal with what seems to be the real evil in these cases, namely the presence of unfair terms in contracts (but contrast the approach taken by the courts in cases concerned with the incorporation by notice of terms, where the courts take a stricter approach in the case of terms that are 'onerous' or 'unusual', p. 361 below).

4. INCORPORATION BY NOTICE

A party who wishes to incorporate terms into a contract by giving his contracting party notice of them must satisfy three requirements. First, notice must have been given at or before the time of contracting. This may require the courts to apply the rules of offer and acceptance in order to ascertain the moment in time at which the contract was concluded. Two cases illustrate this point. The first is *Olley* v. *Marlborough Court Ltd* [1949] 1 KB 532. Here the notice was located in a hotel bedroom. It was held that it was ineffective to exclude liability towards a guest of the hotel on the basis that the contract between the hotel and the guest had been concluded before she set foot in the hotel bedroom. It was therefore too late to be effective. A further example is provided by the case of *Thornton* v. *Shoe Lane Parking* [1971] 2 QB 163. There the exemption clause was to be found inside a car park. The Court of Appeal held that the defendants had not taken reasonable steps to bring the clause to the attention of the customer (this aspect of the case is analysed by Bingham LJ in his judgment in *Interfoto Picture Library Ltd* v. *Stiletto Visual Programmes Ltd* [1989] QB 433, p. 358 below). But Lord Denning also held that the clause was too late to be incorporated into the contract. The car park was described as a 'multi-storey automatic car park' and a ticket was issued to a customer when he drove up to the machine at the entrance to the car park. Lord Denning held that the contract was concluded at the moment of entry into the car park so that the notice contained inside the car park and the terms printed on the ticket were too late to be included. He analysed the nature of the transaction between the parties in the following terms (at p. 169):

The customer pays his money and gets a ticket. He cannot refuse it. He cannot get his money back. He may protest to the machine, even swear at it. But it will remain unmoved. He is committed beyond recall. He was committed at the very moment when he put his money into the machine. The contract was concluded at that time. It can be translated into offer and acceptance in this way: the offer is made when the proprietor of the machine holds it out as being ready to receive the money. The acceptance takes place when the customer puts his money into the slot. The terms of the offer are contained in the notice placed on or near the machine stating what is offered for the money. The customer is bound by those terms as long as they are sufficiently brought to his notice beforehand, but not otherwise. He is not bound by the terms printed on the ticket if they differ from the notice, because the ticket comes too late. The contract has already been made.

The second requirement is that the terms must have been contained or referred to in a document that was intended to have contractual effect. So, for example, where the terms are contained in a document that is a receipt rather than a contractual document, the receipt will not be effective to incorporate the terms into the contract (see, for example, *Chapelton* v. *Barry UDC* [1940] 1 KB 532 where a ticket given to someone who hired a deckchair was held not to be a contractual document and so was not effective to give the hirer notice of the terms).

The third requirement is that reasonable steps must have been taken to bring the terms to the attention of the other party. This requirement has generated a considerable amount of case-law which dates back to the decision of the Court of Appeal in *Parker* v. *South Eastern Railway* (1877) 2 CPD 416. This case-law was helpfully reviewed by the Court of Appeal in the following case:

Interfoto Picture Library Ltd v. Stiletto Visual Programmes Ltd

[1989] QB 433, Court of Appeal

The defendant advertising agency wanted some photographs for a presentation for a client. On 5 March 1984 Mr Beeching, a director of the agency, telephoned the plaintiffs who ran a library of photographic transparencies and inquired whether they had any photographs of the 1950s which would be suitable for the defendants' purpose. The plaintiffs responded that they would look into the matter and, later the same day, they sent forty-seven transparencies to the defendants in a jiffy bag together with a delivery note which contained a number of terms. The delivery note stated that the date for the return of the transparencies was 19 March 1984. At the bottom of the delivery note, under the heading 'Conditions' which was 'fairly prominently printed in capitals', there were nine conditions, printed in four columns. Condition 2 provided:

> 'All transparencies must be returned to us within 14 days from the date of posting/delivery/collection. A holding fee of £5 plus VAT per day will be charged for each transparency which is retained by you longer than the said period of 14 days save where a copyright licence is granted or we agree a longer period in writing with you.'

On receipt of the transparencies Mr Beeching telephoned the plaintiffs to say that the defendants were very impressed with the speed of the service, that one or two of the transparencies could be of interest and that they would get back to the plaintiffs on the matter. The defendants did not, however, use the transparencies for the presentation. Instead they put them to one side and forgot about them. The plaintiffs attempted to contact Mr Beeching on 20 and 23 March but were only able to speak to his secretary. In the event, the transparencies were not returned until 2 April. The plaintiffs then sent an invoice to the defendants for £3,783.50, which represented the holding charge in respect of their retention of the transparencies. The defendants refused to pay. The plaintiffs brought an action to recover the £3,783.50. The trial judge gave judgment for the plaintiffs. The defendants appealed to the Court of Appeal where it was held that condition 2 had not been incorporated into the contract. The defendants' appeal was therefore allowed and the defendants were ordered to pay £3.50 per transparency per week on a quantum meruit basis for the retention of the transparencies beyond a reasonable period, which was fixed at fourteen days from the date of their receipt by the defendants.

Dillon LJ [set out the facts and continued]
The primary point taken in the court below was that condition 2 was not part of the contract between the parties because the delivery note was never supplied to the defendants at all. That the judge rejected on the facts; he found that the delivery note was supplied in the same jiffy bag with the transparencies, and that finding is not challenged in this court. He made no finding however that Mr Beeching or any other representative of the defendants read condition 2 or any of the other printed conditions, and it is overwhelmingly probable that they did not.

An alternative argument for the defendants, in this court as below, was to the effect that any contract between the parties was made before the defendants knew of the existence of the delivery note viz. either in the course of the preliminary telephone conversation between Mr Beeching and Miss Fraser, or when the jiffy bag containing the transparencies was received in the defendants' premises but before the bag was opened. I regard these submissions as unrealistic and unarguable. The original telephone call was merely a preliminary inquiry and did not give rise to any contract. But the contract came into existence when the plaintiffs sent the transparencies to the defendants and the defendants, after opening the bag, accepted them by Mr Beeching's phone call to the plaintiffs at 3.10 on 5 March. The question is whether condition 2 was a term of that contract.

There was never any oral discussion of terms between the parties before the contract was made. In particular there was no discussion whatever of terms in the original telephone conversation when Mr Beeching made his preliminary inquiry. The question is therefore whether condition 2 was sufficiently brought to the defendants' attention to make it a term of the contract which was only concluded after the defendants had received, and must have known that they had received the transparencies *and* the delivery note . . .

[he considered *Parker* v. *South Eastern Railway Co* (1877) 2 CPD 416 and *Thornton* v. *Shoe Lane Parking Ltd* [1971] 2 QB 163 and continued]

Condition 2 of these plaintiffs' conditions is in my judgment a very onerous clause. The defendants could not conceivably have known, if their attention was not drawn to the clause, that the plaintiffs were proposing to charge a 'holding fee' for the retention of the transparencies at such a very high and exorbitant rate.

At the time of the ticket cases in the last century it was notorious that people hardly ever troubled to read printed conditions on a ticket or delivery note or similar document. That remains the case now. In the intervening years the printed conditions have tended to become more and more complicated and more and more one-sided in favour of the party who is imposing them, but the other parties, if they notice that there are printed conditions at all, generally still tend to assume that such conditions are only concerned with ancillary matters of form and are not of importance. In the ticket cases the courts held that the common law required that reasonable steps be taken to draw the other parties' attention to the printed conditions or they would not be part of the contract. It is, in my judgment, a logical development of the common law into modern conditions that it should be held, as it was in *Thornton v. Shoe Lane Parking Ltd* [1971] 2 QB 163, that, if one condition in a set of printed conditions is particularly onerous or unusual, the party seeking to enforce it must show that that particular condition was fairly brought to the attention of the other party.

In the present case, nothing whatever was done by the plaintiffs to draw the defendants' attention particularly to condition 2; it was merely one of four columns' width of conditions printed across the foot of the delivery note. Consequently condition 2 never, in my judgment, became part of the contract between the parties.

I would therefore allow this appeal and reduce the amount of the judgment which the judge awarded against the defendants to the amount which he would have awarded on a quantum meruit on his alternative findings, i.e. the reasonable charge of £3.50 per transparency per week for the retention of the transparencies beyond a reasonable period, which he fixed at 14 days from the date of their receipt by the defendants.

Bingham LJ

In many civil law systems, and perhaps in most legal systems outside the common law world, the law of obligations recognises and enforces an overriding principle that in making and carrying out contracts parties should act in good faith. This does not simply mean that they should not deceive each other, a principle which any legal system must recognise; its effect is perhaps most aptly conveyed by such metaphorical colloquialisms as 'playing fair', 'coming clean' or 'putting one's cards face upwards on the table'. It is in essence a principle of fair and open dealing. In such a forum it might, I think, be held on the facts of this case that the plaintiffs were under a duty in all fairness to draw the defendants' attention specifically to the high price payable if the transparencies were not returned in time and, when the 14 days had expired, to point out to the defendants the high cost of continued failure to return them.

English law has, characteristically, committed itself to no such overriding principle but has developed piecemeal solutions in response to demonstrated problems of unfairness. Many examples could be given. Thus equity has intervened to strike down unconscionable bargains. Parliament has stepped in to regulate the imposition of exemption clauses and the form of certain hire-purchase agreements. The common law also has made its contribution, by holding that certain classes of contract require the utmost good faith, by treating as irrecoverable what purport to be agreed estimates of damage but are in truth a disguised penalty for breach, and in many other ways.

The well known cases on sufficiency of notice are in my view properly to be read in this context. At one level they are concerned with a question of pure contractual analysis, whether one party has done enough to give the other notice of the incorporation of a term in the contract. At another level they are concerned with a somewhat different question, whether it would in all the circumstances be fair (or reasonable) to hold a party bound by any conditions or by a particular condition of an unusual and stringent nature.

In the leading case of *Parker v. South Eastern Railway Co* (1877) 2 CPD 416, Baggallay LJ plainly thought on the facts that the plaintiffs were right, Bramwell LJ that they were wrong; Mellish LJ thought that there had been a misdirection and there should be a re-trial, a view in which the other members of the court concurred. The judgments deserve to be re-read. Mellish LJ said, at pp. 422–423:

> 'Now, I am of opinion that we cannot lay down, as a matter of law, either that the plaintiff was bound or that he was not bound by the conditions printed on the ticket, from the mere fact that he knew there was writing on the ticket, but did not know that the writing contained conditions. I think there may be cases in which a paper containing writing is delivered by one party to another in the course of a business transaction, where it would be quite reasonable that the party receiving it should assume that the writing contained in it no condition, and should put it in his pocket unread. . . . The railway company, as it seems to me, must be entitled to make some assumptions respecting the person who deposits luggage with them: I think they are entitled to assume that he can read, and that he understands the English language, and that he pays such attention to what he is about as may be reasonably expected from a person in such a transaction as that of depositing luggage in a cloak-room. The railway company must, however, take mankind as they find them, and if what they do is sufficient to inform people in general that the ticket contains conditions, I think that a particular plaintiff ought not to be in a better position than other persons on account of his exceptional ignorance or stupidity or carelessness. But if what the railway company do is not sufficient to convey to the minds of people in general that the ticket contains conditions, then they have received goods on deposit without obtaining the consent of the persons depositing them to the conditions limiting their liability.'

Baggallay LJ's analytical approach was somewhat similar. He said, at pp. 425–426:

> 'Now as regards each of the plaintiffs, if at the time when he accepted the ticket, he, either by actual examination of it, or by reason of previous experience, or from any other cause, was aware of the terms or purport or effect of the endorsed conditions, it can hardly be doubted that he became bound by them. I think also that he would be equally bound if he was aware or had good reason to believe that there were upon the ticket statements intended to affect the relative rights of himself and the company, but intentionally or negligently abstained from ascertaining whether there were any such, or from making himself acquainted with their purport. But I do not think that in the absence of any such knowledge or information, or good reason for belief, he was under any obligation to examine the ticket with the view of ascertaining whether there were any such statements or conditions upon it.'

Both Mellish LJ and Baggallay LJ were, as it seems to me distinguishing the case in which it would be fair to hold a party bound from the case in which it would not. But this approach is made more explicit in the strongly worded judgment of Bramwell LJ, at p. 427:

> 'The plaintiffs have sworn that they did not know that the printing was the contract, and we must act as though that was true and we believed it, at least as far as entering the verdict for the defendants is concerned. Does this make any difference? The plaintiffs knew of the printed matter. Both admit they knew it concerned them in some way, though they said they did not know what it was; yet neither pretends that he knew or believed it was not the contract. Neither pretends he thought it had nothing to do with the business in hand; that he thought it was an advertisement or other matter unconnected with his deposit of a parcel at the defendants' cloak-room. They admit that, for

anything they knew or believed, it might be, only they did not know or believe it was, the contract. Their evidence is very much that they did not think, or, thinking, did not care about it. Now they claim to charge the company, and to have the benefit of their own indifference. Is this just? Is it reasonable? Is it the way in which any other business is allowed to be conducted? Is it even allowed to a man to 'think', 'judge', 'guess', 'chance' a matter, without informing himself when he can, and then when his 'thought', 'judgment', 'guess', or 'chance' turns out wrong or unsuccessful, claim to impose a burthen or duty on another which he could not have done had he informed himself as he might?'

He continued in the same vein, at p. 428:

'Has not the giver of the paper a right to suppose that the receiver is content to deal on the terms in the paper? What more can be done? Must he say, 'Read that?' As I have said, he does so in effect when he puts it into the other's hands. The truth is, people are content to take these things on trust. They know that there is a form which is always used—they are satisfied it is not unreasonable, because people do not usually put unreasonable terms into their contracts. If they did, then dealing would soon be stopped. Besides, unreasonable practices would be known. The very fact of not looking at the paper shews that this confidence exists. It is asked: What if there was some unreasonable condition, as for instance to forfeit £1,000 if the goods were not removed in 48 hours? Would the depositor be bound? I might content myself by asking: Would he be, if he were told 'our conditions are on this ticket', and he did not read them. In my judgment, he would not be bound in either case. I think there is an implied understanding that there is no condition unreasonable to the knowledge of the party tendering the document and not insisting on its being read—no condition not relevant to the matter in hand. I am of opinion, therefore, that the plaintiffs, having notice of the printing, were in the same situation as though the porter had said, 'Read that, it concerns the matter in hand'; that if the plaintiffs did not read it, they were as much bound as if they had read it and had not objected.'

This is not a simple contractual analysis whether an offer has been made and accepted.

In *Hood* v. *Anchor Line (Henderson Brothers) Ltd* [1918] AC 837, an appeal from the Court of Session, the question was whether a steamship company had effectively protected itself against liability for injury to a passenger. Lord Finlay LC, at p. 842, posed the simple question: 'What more could have been done to bring the conditions to the notice of the passenger?' Viscount Haldane approached the matter in a more general way, at p. 843:

'There is a large and varied class of cases where the legal duty of a member of society to his neighbour cannot be laid down a priori or without examining the special circumstances of the situation. The duty in these instances is ascertained by a standard which depends, not on mere general principles fashioned by the jurist, for no such general principles can provide for all the concrete details of which account must be taken, but on the opinion of reasonable men who have considered the whole of the circumstances in the particular instance and can be relied on to say how, according to accepted standards of conduct, a reasonable man ought to behave in these circumstances towards the neighbour towards whom he is bound by the necessities of the community to act with forbearance and consideration.'

And he added, at p. 845:

> 'It is true that Mr May did not look at the envelope closely or refer to the condition. He took the contract away and put it in a safe, and ultimately gave it to the appellant, who did not read it either. But I am of opinion that the real question was not whether they did read it, but whether they can be heard to say that they did not read it. If it had been merely a case of inviting people to put a penny into an automatic machine and get a ticket for a brief journey, I might think differently. In such a transaction men cannot naturally be expected to pause to look whether they are obtaining all the rights which the law gives them in the absence of a special stipulation. But when it is a case of taking a ticket for a voyage of some days, with arrangements to be made, among other things, as to cabins and luggage, I think ordinary people do look to see what bargain they are getting, and should be taken as bound to have done so and as precluded from saying that they did not know.'

Lord Dunedin said, at pp. 846–847:

> 'Accordingly it is in each case a question of circumstance whether the sort of restriction that is expressed in any writing (which, of course, includes printed matter) is a thing that is usual, and whether, being usual, it has been fairly brought before the notice of the accepting party.'

These authoritative passages appear to base the law very firmly on consideration of what is fair in all the circumstances.

J Spurling Ltd v. *Bradshaw* [1956] 1 WLR 461 concerned an exemption clause in a warehousing contract. The case is now remembered for the observations of Denning LJ, at p. 466:

> 'This brings me to the question whether this clause was part of the contract. Mr Sofer urged us to hold that the warehousemen did not do what was reasonably sufficient to give notice of the conditions within *Parker* v. *South Eastern Railway Co* 2 CPD 416. I quite agree that the more unreasonable a clause is, the greater the notice which must be given of it. Some clauses which I have seen would need to be printed in red ink on the face of the document with a red hand pointing to it before the notice could be held to be sufficient.'

Here, therefore, is made explicit what Bramwell LJ had perhaps foreshadowed, that what would be good notice of one condition would not be notice of another. The reason is that the more outlandish the clause the greater the notice which the other party, if he is to be bound must in all fairness be given.

McCutcheon v. *David MacBrayne Ltd* [1964] 1 WLR 125 is a case out of the common run because the document containing the contractual exemption was neither issued nor signed. The interest of the case for present purposes lies in two passages in the speeches of Lord Reid and Lord Pearce. Lord Reid said, at p. 128:

> 'If it could be said that when making the contract Mr McSporran knew that the respondents always required a risk note to be signed and knew that the pursuer was simply forgetting to put it before him for signature, then it might be said that neither he nor his principal could take advantage of the error of the other party of which he was aware. But counsel frankly admitted that he could not put his case as high as that.'

Lord Pearce expressed a similar opinion, at page 138:

> 'This is not a case where there was any bad faith on the part of the pursuer or his agent. Had the pursuer's agent snatched at an offer that he knew was not intended, or deliberately taken advantage of the defenders' omission to proffer their usual printed form for his signature, the situation would be different and other considerations would apply.'

Here again, as it seems to me, one finds reference to a concept of fair dealing that has very little to do with a conventional analysis of offer and acceptance.

Lastly I would mention *Thornton* v. *Shoe Lane Parking Ltd*. [1971] 2 QB 163. Lord Denning MR said, at pp. 169–170:

> 'Assuming, however, that an automatic machine is a booking clerk in disguise—so that the old fashioned ticket cases still apply to it. We then have to go back to the three questions put by Mellish LJ in *Parker* v. *South Eastern Railway Co*, 2 CPD 416, 423, subject to this qualification: Mellish LJ used the word "conditions" in the plural, whereas it would be more apt to use the word "condition" in the singular, as indeed the Lord Justice himself did on the next page. After all, the only condition that matters for this purpose is the exempting condition. It is no use telling the customer that the ticket is issued subject to some "conditions" or other, without more: for he may reasonably regard "conditions" in general as merely regulatory, and not as taking away his rights, unless the exempting condition is drawn specifically to his attention. (Alternatively, if the plural "conditions" is used, it would be better prefaced with the word "exempting", because the exempting conditions are the only conditions that matter for this purpose.) Telescoping the three questions, they come to this: the customer is bound by the exempting condition if he knows that the ticket is issued subject to it; or, if the company did what was reasonably sufficient to give him notice of it.
>
> Mr Machin admitted here that the company did not do what was reasonably sufficient to give Mr Thornton notice of the exempting condition. That admission was properly made. I do not pause to inquire whether the exempting condition is void for unreasonableness. All I say is that it is so wide and so destructive of rights that the court should not hold any man bound by it unless it is drawn to his attention in the most explicit way. It is an instance of what I had in mind in *J Spurling Ltd* v. *Bradshaw* [1956] 1 WLR 461, 466. In order to give sufficient notice, it would need to be printed in red ink with a red hand pointing to it—or something equally startling.'

The judgment of Megaw LJ was to similar effect, at pp. 172–173:

> 'So I come to the third of the three questions. That question, if I may return to the speech of Lord Dunedin in *Hood* v. *Anchor Line (Henderson Brothers) Ltd* [1918] AC 837, 846, 847 was posed by him in this way: "Accordingly it is in each case a question of circumstance whether the sort of restriction that is expressed in any writing (which, of course, includes printed matter) is a thing that is usual, and whether, being usual, it has been fairly brought before the notice of the accepting party".
>
> That, though it is more fully stated by Lord Dunedin, is essentially the same question, I think, as was formulated by Mellish LJ in *Parker's* case, 2 CPD 416, 424 at the very end of his judgment, where he said that the question which ought to have been left to the jury was: whether the railway company did what was reasonably sufficient to give the plaintiff notice of *the condition*. (I emphasise the use by Mellish LJ of the definite article

and of the word "condition" in the singular.) I agree with Lord Denning MR that the question here is of the particular condition on which the defendants seek to rely, and not of the conditions in general.

When the conditions sought to be attached all constitute, in Lord Dunedin's words [1918] AC 846, 847, "the sort of restriction . . . that is usual", it may not be necessary for a defendant to prove more than that the intention to attach *some* conditions has been fairly brought to the notice of the other party. But at least where the particular condition relied on involves a sort of restriction that is not shown to be usual in that class of contract, a defendant must show that his intention to attach an unusual condition of that particular nature was fairly brought to the notice of the other party. How much is required as being, in the words of Mellish LJ, 2 CPD 416, 424, "reasonably sufficient to give the plaintiff notice of the condition", depends upon the nature of the restrictive condition.'

The tendency of the English authorities has, I think, been to look at the nature of the transaction in question and the character of the parties to it; to consider what notice the party alleged to be bound was given of the particular condition said to bind him; and to resolve whether in all the circumstances it is fair to hold him bound by the condition in question. This may yield a result not very different from the civil law principle of good faith, at any rate so far as the formation of the contract is concerned.

Turning to the present case, I am satisfied for reasons which Dillon LJ has given that no contract was made on the telephone when the defendants made their initial request. I am equally satisfied that no contract was made on delivery of the transparencies to the defendants before the opening of the jiffy bag in which they were contained. Once the jiffy bag was opened and the transparencies taken out with the delivery note, it is in my judgment an inescapable inference that the defendants would have recognised the delivery note as a document of a kind likely to contain contractual terms and would have seen that there were conditions printed in small but visible lettering on the face of the document. To the extent that the conditions so displayed were common form or usual terms regularly encountered in this business, I do not think the defendants could successfully contend that they were not incorporated into the contract.

The crucial question in the case is whether the plaintiffs can be said fairly and reasonably to have brought condition 2 to the notice of the defendants. The judge made no finding on the point, but I think that it is open to this court to draw an inference from the primary findings which he did make. In my opinion the plaintiffs did not do so. They delivered 47 transparencies, which was a number the defendants had not specifically asked for. Condition 2 contained a daily rate per transparency after the initial period of 14 days many times greater than was usual or (so far as the evidence shows) heard of. For these 47 transparencies there was to be a charge for each day of delay of £235 plus value added tax. The result would be that a venial period of delay, as here, would lead to an inordinate liability. The defendants are not to be relieved of that liability because they did not read the condition, although doubtless they did not; but in my judgment they are to be relieved because the plaintiffs did not do what was necessary to draw this unreasonable and extortionate clause fairly to their attention. I would accordingly allow the defendants' appeal and substitute for the judge's award the sum which he assessed upon the alternative basis of quantum meruit.

In reaching the conclusion I have expressed I would not wish to be taken as deciding that condition 2 was not challengeable as a disguised penalty clause. This point was not argued before the judge nor raised in the notice of appeal. It was accordingly not argued before us. I have accordingly felt bound to assume, somewhat reluctantly, that condition 2 would be enforceable if fully and fairly brought to the defendants' attention.

COMMENTARY

It is important to get the focus of attention right. The focus is not upon the recipient of the notice. The test applied by the court is not whether the recipient has read the terms or taken reasonable steps to discover their existence (although where the recipient has actual knowledge of the existence of the terms it would appear that, in principle, he is bound by them: *Parker* v. *South Eastern Railway* (1877) 2 CPD 416, 421). Instead, the courts focus attention upon the party relying upon the terms and ask themselves whether that party has taken reasonable steps to bring notice of the term or terms to the attention of the other party. The case-law can be traced back to the old 'ticket cases', of which *Parker* v. *South Eastern Railway* (1877) 2 CPD 416 is a leading example, where the issue between the parties was generally whether or not a sweeping exclusion clause had been incorporated into the contract with the passenger.

In determining whether or not reasonable steps have been taken in order to draw the term to the attention of the other party, the courts have regard to obvious factors such as the location of the notice and its prominence. A notice which is located on the back of a document is unlikely to be incorporated in the absence of a reference on the front of the document alerting the reader to the presence of terms, or a reference to terms, on the back (see *Henderson* v. *Stevenson* (1875) LR 2 HL (Sc) 470). Similarly, a notice that has been obliterated by a stamp is unlikely to be incorporated (*Sugar* v. *London, Midland and Scottish Railway Co* [1941] 1 All ER 172). On the other hand, where the term, or the reference to the terms, is located prominently on the front of the document then the likelihood is that the term will be incorporated (*Thompson* v. *London, Midland and Scottish Railway Co Ltd* [1930] 1 KB 41).

However, as the judgment of Bingham LJ in *Interfoto* makes clear, the inquiry undertaken by the courts in this connection is no mere mechanical exercise. It requires the court to evaluate the nature of the term that one party is seeking to incorporate into the contract. The more onerous or unusual the term, the greater the steps that must be taken in order to draw its existence to the other party's attention. Bingham LJ in his judgment endeavours to demonstrate that this approach has a sure foundation in the authorities. Its foundation in terms of principle is perhaps more debatable. Why seek to differentiate between different terms in relation to their incorporation into a contract? If the law's concern is with the unfairness of the term itself, would this not be better expressed by conferring on the court a direct power to regulate unfair terms? One answer to this question is that the law does not presently confer upon the courts such a broad power and, in its absence, the courts have to make use of what might be said to be the 'second-best alternative' of regulating the incorporation of terms into contracts. While the Unfair Contract Terms Act 1977 does confer a limited power upon courts to regulate certain clauses which seek to exclude or restrict liability (on which see pp. 460–485 below), the Act does not extend to the type of clause in issue in *Interfoto*. In the absence of a power directly to control the substantive content of the clause, the court chose to regulate it by concluding that it had not been incorporated into the contract.

Post-*Interfoto* the courts have had some difficulty in identifying which terms are 'onerous' or 'unusual' and which are not. It should be noted that the term need not be 'onerous' in order to attract this more rigorous scrutiny. It suffices that it is 'unusual'. Presumably, therefore, a party who changes his terms in significant respects may be under an obligation to take greater steps to draw these changes to the attention of the other party. Two cases illustrate the difficulties that the courts are currently experiencing.

The first is the decision of the Court of Appeal in *AEG (UK) Ltd* v. *Logic Resource Ltd* [1996] CLC 265. The plaintiffs sold goods to the defendants and the defendants in turn sub-sold them to their customers in Iran. The goods proved to be defective when they were inspected by the sub-buyers in Iran. Arrangements were made to air freight the goods back to the plaintiffs' factory in the UK at a cost of some £4,230 so that the necessary modifications could be carried out. The defendants refused to pay the £4,230. The plaintiffs sued to recover the sum on the basis of clause 7.5 of the contract which stated: 'the purchaser shall return the defective parts at his own expense to the supplier immediately upon request by the latter'. One of the issues before the court was whether or not this term had been incorporated into the contract between the parties and this depended upon whether or not the term was 'particularly onerous or unusual'. The majority, Hirst and Waite LJJ, concluded that it was both 'extremely onerous . . . and also unusual in the absence of any evidence that it is a standard or common term'. The basis for their conclusion was that the only right available to the purchasers under the contract in the event of the goods proving to be defective was to exercise their right to return the goods to the plaintiffs. To append to this right the requirement that the purchaser pay for the cost of returning the goods was held to be both onerous and unusual. The position would probably have been different had the purchasers had available to them a range of rights in the event of the goods being defective. In such a case a seller might legitimately attach to the exercise of the right to return the goods for repair a condition that the purchaser meet the cost of returning the goods. Hobhouse LJ dissented and he did so in forthright terms. He stated:

The problem in the present case arises from the fact that these clauses have been unreasonably drafted. As is almost inevitable in printed standard terms, they are not related to the particular circumstances of the case and, furthermore, they stipulate for a greater protection of the seller than is reasonable, or anyway is reasonable without some special justification. In my judgment, and this is where I part company from Hirst and Waite LJJ, it is necessary before excluding the incorporation of a clause *in limine* to consider the type of clause it is. Is it a clause of the type which you would expect to find in the printed conditions? If it is, then it is only in the most exceptional circumstances that a party will be able to say that it was not adequately brought to his notice by standard words of incorporation. If a party wishes to find out precisely how a clause of a normal sort has been worded, he should ask for the actual text of the clause. This case is not analogous to either of the two cases upon which the appellant founds. The *Interfoto* case involved an extortionate clause which did not relate directly to the expected rights and obligations of the parties. In the *Shoe Lane Parking* case, it related to personal injuries and the state of the premises and not to the subject matter of the car parking contract, which would, in the view of the Court of Appeal, have been concerned with damage to property.

Therefore, in my judgment, it is necessary to consider the type of clause, and only if it is a type of clause which it is not to be expected will be found in the printed conditions referred to then to go on to question its incorporation. These conditions do include clauses which, in my judgment, do fall foul of the *Interfoto* principle, but I do not consider that clause 7 comes into that category. In my judgment, it is desirable as a matter of principle to keep what was said in the *Interfoto* case within its proper bounds. A wide range of clauses are commonly incorporated into contracts by general words. If it is to be the policy of English law that in every case those clauses are to be gone through with, in effect, a toothcomb to see whether they were entirely usual and entirely desirable in the particular contract, then one is completely distorting the contractual relationship between the parties and the ordinary mechanisms of making contracts. It will introduce uncertainty into the law of contract.

In the past there may have been a tendency to introduce more strict criteria but this is no longer necessary in view of the Unfair Contract Terms Act. The reasonableness of clauses is the subject matter of the Unfair Contract Terms Act and it is under the provisions of that Act that problems of unreasonable clauses should be addressed and the solution found. In the present case, it is my opinion that the Act provides the answer to the question which has been raised.

The second case is *O'Brien* v. *MGN Ltd* [2002] CLC 33. The claimant thought that he had won a prize in a scratchcard game in the defendants' newspaper. Unfortunately for him, a mistake had been made by the defendants in that they had failed to notice that a number of cards had been issued with the winning numbers on them. Instead of there being two winners of the £50,000 prize some 1,472 people rang up to claim the prize. In these circumstances the defendants refused to pay out to all the 'winners'. They relied upon rule 5 of the competition rules which provided that, if more prizes were claimed than were available in any prize category for any reason, a separate draw would then take place for the prize. The question for the court was whether or not rule 5 had been incorporated into the contract between the parties. The trial judge found that a contract was concluded between the parties on 3 July 1995, the day on which the claimant bought the paper. The offer was contained in the paper that day and the claimant accepted the offer when he telephoned the hotline in order to claim his prize. Alongside the instructions relating to the telephone hotline were the words: 'Normal Mirror Group rules apply'. Was this reference to the rules sufficient to incorporate them into the contract? The Court of Appeal held that it was.

This time the Court of Appeal held that the clause was neither 'onerous' nor 'unusual'. It was not onerous because it did not seek to impose a burden on the claimant, nor did it attempt to exclude liability for negligently caused personal injury. It simply deprived 'the claimant of a windfall for which he has done very little in return'. Nor could it be said that the clause was 'unusual' given that other games and competitions had similar rules.

Hale LJ concluded (at para. [23]):

the words 'onerous or unusual' are not terms of art. They are simply one way of putting the general proposition that reasonable steps must be taken to draw the particular term in question to the notice of those who are bound by it and that more is required in relation to certain terms than to others depending on their effect. In the particular context of this particular game, I consider that the defendants did just enough to bring the rules to the claimant's attention. There was a clear reference to rules on the face of the card he used. There was a clear reference to rules in the paper containing the offer of a telephone prize. There was evidence that those rules could be discovered either from the newspaper offices or from back issues of the paper. The claimant had been able to discover them when the problem arose.

Sir Anthony Evans was much more hesitant. He held that the rule had been incorporated but only because he was not prepared to interfere with the finding of fact by the trial judge that the rule had been incorporated. In his view 'the promise of significant riches' deserved more and he stated that a rule which gave the 'winner' no more than a further chance to obtain the prize was sufficiently onerous, if not unusual, to require greater prominence than was given to this one. While the result in the case was ultimately unanimous, the judgments nevertheless display a degree of unease about the meaning of the words 'onerous or unusual' and about the application of this test to any given fact situation.

Where a term is held to be 'onerous' or 'unusual', what steps are required in order to incorporate it into the contract? In *Interfoto* it does not appear that the plaintiffs attempted to hide their conditions on the delivery note and the defendants were presumably capable of reading them. Yet condition 2 was not incorporated. What should they have done to ensure that it was incorporated? In *J Spurling Ltd* v. *Bradshaw* [1956] 1 WLR 461 (referred to in the judgment of Bingham LJ in *Interfoto* at p. 357 above) Denning LJ famously referred to the need for a 'red hand' pointing to the clause. While his comment may have made its mark on the judicial memory and on textbook writers, it has not been translated into commercial practice. Little red hands are not to be found in commercial contracts in the UK. A more realistic step to take is to put the clause in bold print or specifically to draw the other party's attention to the existence of the clause in a letter. A court may be more likely to conclude that reasonable steps have been taken where there has been 'an express acknowledgement in the contractual documents that the terms and conditions in question were incorporated' (*Ocean Chemical Transport Inc* v. *Exnor Craggs Ltd* [2000] 1 Lloyd's Rep 446, 454).

5. INCORPORATION BY COURSE OF DEALING AND BY CUSTOM

Finally, a term may be incorporated into a contract as a result of a course of dealing between the parties or as a result of the custom of the trade in which the parties work. The leading case on incorporation by course of dealing is the following decision of the House of Lords:

McCutcheon v. David MacBrayne Ltd

[1964] 1 WLR 430, House of Lords

Mr McCutcheon, the appellant, asked his brother-in-law, Mr McSporran, to arrange for his car to be shipped from Islay to the mainland. Mr McSporran took the car to the respondents' office in Port Askaig where he was quoted a price for a return journey for the car. He paid the fare and was given a receipt. He delivered the car into the possession of the respondents. The vessel sank on the journey as a result of the negligence of the respondents' employees and the car was a total loss. The appellant brought an action in negligence against the respondents, who sought to rely on the terms of an exclusion clause contained in their conditions of carriage.

The usual practice of the respondents was to ask the person sending the goods to sign a risk note by which the person sending the goods agreed to be bound by the respondents' terms and conditions. But on this occasion Mr McSporran was not asked to sign the risk note and so did not sign one. He gave evidence to the effect that he had shipped goods before with the respondents and had sometimes been asked to sign a risk note but had never read it. The appellant himself had consigned goods with the respondents on four occasions. On three of them he had been acting on behalf of his employer and on the other occasion he had shipped his own car. On all four occasions he had signed a risk note. He admitted that he knew of the existence of the conditions but stated that he was not aware of their content. The House of Lords held that the respondents' terms had not been incorporated into the contract with the consequence that the respondents had not excluded their liability in negligence.

Lord Reid

The only other ground on which it would seem possible to import these conditions is that based on a course of dealing. If two parties have made a series of similar contracts each containing certain conditions, and then they make another without expressly referring to those conditions it may be that those conditions ought to be implied. If the officious bystander had asked them whether they had intended to leave out the conditions this time, both must, as honest men, have said 'of course not'. But again the facts here will not support that ground. According to Mr McSporran, there had been no consistent course of dealing; sometimes he was asked to sign and sometimes not. And, moreover, he did not know what the conditions were. This time he was offered an oral contract without any reference to conditions, and he accepted the offer in good faith.

The respondents also rely on the appellant's previous knowledge. I doubt whether it is possible to spell out a course of dealing in his case. In all but one of the previous cases he had been acting on behalf of his employer in sending a different kind of goods and he did not know that the respondents always sought to insist on excluding liability for their own negligence. So it cannot be said that when he asked his agent to make a contract for him he knew that this or, indeed, any other special term would be included in it. He left his agent a free hand to contract, and I see nothing to prevent him from taking advantage of the contract which his agent in fact made.

> 'The judicial task is not to discover the actual intentions of each party; it is to decide what each was reasonably entitled to conclude from the attitude of the other.' [WM Gloag on Contract (2nd edn, W Green, 1929), p. 7.]

In this case I do not think that either party was reasonably bound or entitled to conclude from the attitude of the other as known to him that these conditions were intended by the other party to be part of this contract. I would, therefore, allow the appeal and restore the interlocutor of the Lord Ordinary.

Lord Guest

All that the previous dealings in the present case can show is that the appellant and his agent knew that the previous practice of the respondents was to impose special conditions. But knowledge on their part did not and could not by itself import acceptance by them of these conditions, the exact terms of which they were unaware, into a contract which was different in character from those in the previous course of dealing. The practice of the respondents was to insist on a written contract incorporated in the risk note. On the occasion in question a verbal contract was made without reference to the conditions.

Lord Devlin

In my opinion, the bare fact that there have been previous dealings between the parties does not assist the respondents at all. The fact that a man has made a contract in the same form 99 times (let alone three or four times which are here alleged) will not of itself affect the 100th contract in which the form is not used. Previous dealings are relevant only if they prove knowledge of the terms, actual and not constructive, and assent to them. If a term is not expressed in a contract, there is only one other way in which it can come into it and that is by implication. No implication can be made against a party of a term which was unknown to him. If previous dealings show that a man knew of and agreed to a term on 99 occasions, there is a basis for saying that it can be imported into the 100th contract without an express statement. It may or may not be sufficient to justify the importation—that depends on the circumstances; but at least by proving knowledge the essential beginning is made. Without knowledge there is nothing . . .

If a man is given a blank ticket without conditions or any reference to them, even if he knows in detail what the conditions usually exacted are, he is not, in the absence of any allegation of fraud or of that sort of mistake for which the law gives relief, bound by such conditions. It may seem a narrow and artificial line that divides a ticket that is blank on the back from one that says 'For conditions see time-tables', or something of that sort, that has been held to be enough notice. I agree that it is an artificial line and one that has little relevance to everyday conditions. It may be beyond your Lordships' power to make the artificial line more natural: but at least you can see that it is drawn fairly for both sides and that there is not one law for individuals and another for organizations that can issue printed documents. If the respondents had remembered to issue a risk note in this case, they would have invited your Lordships to give a curt answer to any complaint by the appellant. He might say that the terms were unfair and unreasonable, that he had never voluntarily agreed to them, that it was impossible to read or understand them and that anyway if he had tried to negotiate any change the respondents would not have listened to him. The respondents would expect him to be told that he had made his contract and must abide by it. Now the boot is on the other foot. It is just as legitimate, but also just as vain, for the respondents to say that it was only a slip on their part, that it is unfair and unreasonable of the appellant to take advantage of it and that he knew perfectly well that they never carried goods except on conditions. The law must give the same answer: they must abide by the contract they made. What is sauce for the goose is sauce for the gander. It will remain unpalatable sauce for both animals until the Legislature, if the Courts cannot do it, intervenes to secure that when contracts are made in circumstances in which there is no scope for free negotiation of the terms, they are made upon terms that are clear, fair and reasonable and settled independently as such. That is what Parliament has done in the case of carriage of goods by rail and on the high seas.

Lord Pearce

The defenders rely on the course of dealing. But they are seeking to establish an oral contract by a course of dealing which always insisted on a written contract. It is the consistency of a course of conduct which gives rise to the implication that in similar circumstances a similar contractual result will follow. When the conduct is *not* consistent, there is no reason why it should still produce an invariable contractual result. The defenders having previously offered a written contract, on this occasion offered an oral one. The pursuer's agent duly paid the freight for which he was asked and accepted the oral contract thus offered. This raises no implication that the conditions of the oral contract must be the same as the conditions of the written contract would have been had the defenders proferred one.

Recourse is then sought to knowledge and intention. This is not a case where there was any bad faith on the part of the pursuer or his agent. Had the pursuer's agent snatched at an offer that he knew was not intended, or deliberately taken advantage of the defenders' omission to proffer their usual printed form for his signature, the situation would be different and other considerations would apply. But neither the pursuer nor his agent gave any thought to conditions. Nor had they any knowledge that Clause 11 would contain, wrapped in 30 lines of small print and in language intelligible only to a lawyer or a person of education and perspicacity, a total exclusion of liability for almost every conceivable act of the defenders that might damage the pursuer's goods.

The defenders never intended to offer or make any oral contract on the terms of the printed conditions. They intended to offer a written contract and by mistake they offered an oral one. The pursuer was unaware of the mistake. He accepted an oral contract but he never intended to accept an oral contract on the printed conditions. He knew that he usually had to sign a form which he supposed contained some conditions. When he was offered an oral contract without conditions he accepted with no thought about its terms. Why should such intentions or knowledge on the part of the contracting parties lead the Court to create a contract which neither intended? The furthest to which this argument of the defenders could lead is to the conclusion that the parties were never ad idem; in which case there was no special contract and the common-law contract prevails.

Some reliance was placed on the fact that the pursuer and his agent were in no wise misled nor suffered from the absence of the written form since they would not have read it or paid any attention to it in any event. This argument has a cynical flavour. It really amounts to saying that because the pursuer would have been bound by a harsh condition, of which he did not know, if the defenders had taken the proper legal steps, he should be likewise bound when they neglected to take those steps. The law inflicts some hardship on ignorant or careless plaintiffs who accept a ticket or sign a printed form in that it holds them bound by printed conditions which they have not read and of which they know nothing. The reasons for this are given in *Parker* v. *South Eastern Railway Company* (1877) 2 CPD 416. If the defenders are to have the benefit of the reasoning in *Parker's Case*, they must take the necessary steps. To decide in the defenders' favour on the facts of this case would be a further extension of the protection afforded to defendants by the ticket cases. Such an extension seems to me very undesirable.

Lord Hodson delivered a concurring judgment.

COMMENTARY

In order to establish the existence of a course of dealing there must be both a regularity and a consistency of dealing between the parties. The downfall of the respondents in *McCutcheon* was the lack of consistency in their previous dealings with the appellant and Mr McSporran. But the consistency point should not be taken too far. Both Lord Guest and Lord Pearce emphasized the fact that the respondents were attempting to establish an oral contract by reference to a course of dealing which always required a written contract. This should not have been a decisive factor. A party will generally only rely on a 'course of dealing' argument where he has, for some reason, failed to comply with his standard practice and, if this failure also had the effect of negativing the consistency of dealing, incorporation by course of dealing would be almost an impossibility. So the mere fact that the contract in the present case was an oral contract should not, of itself, have prevented the respondents from establishing a course of dealing on the basis of written contracts. The better reason for the failure of the respondents to incorporate their terms into the contract was given by Lord Reid, namely that past practice was itself inconsistent. As Mr McSporran stated in evidence 'sometimes he was asked to sign [a risk note] and sometimes not'. The extent of the consistency required must ultimately depend upon the facts of the case. In essence the courts are looking for a consistency of dealing which is such as to lead both parties reasonably to believe that the standard terms have been incorporated into their contract.

It can also be difficult to prove a sufficient regularity of dealing, especially where the contract is concluded between a consumer and a business. In *Hollier* v. *Rambler Motors (AMC) Ltd* [1972] 2 QB 71 the plaintiff brought an action for damages against the defendant garage after his car had been badly damaged in a fire at the defendants' garage. The car had been left with the defendants so that repair work could be undertaken. The defendants sought to rely on an exclusion clause contained in an invoice which stated that 'The Company is not responsible for damage caused by fire to customers' cars on the premises'. The plaintiff had signed this invoice on at least two previous occasions when the defendants repaired his car but he was not asked to sign it on this occasion. The plaintiff had had his car repaired by the defendants on three or four occasions over a five-year period. The defendants submitted that the exclusion clause contained in the invoice had been incorporated into the contract as a result of the course of dealing between the parties. The Court of Appeal rejected this submission. It was held that 'not quite one dealing a year' was insufficient to constitute a course of dealing. A greater degree of regularity is required (see, for example, *Henry Kendall & Sons (A Firm)* v. *William Lillico & Sons Ltd* [1969] 2 AC 31, where there were three or four transactions between the parties per month over a three-year period).

The position may, however, be different where the parties to the transaction are in the same trade or industry. In such a case the court may be able to incorporate the term into the contract either on the basis of a course of dealing between the parties or on the basis of the 'common understanding' of the parties derived from the practice of the trade. This point is demonstrated by the following case:

British Crane Hire Corporation v. Ipswich Plant Hire Ltd

[1975] QB 303, Court of Appeal

The defendants being in urgent need of a dragline crane agreed to hire one from the plaintiffs. Both parties were in the business of hiring out heavy earth-moving equipment. Given the urgency of the situation, the agreement was reached over the telephone. Agreement was reached on the price but nothing was said about the general conditions of hire. The plaintiffs did send their conditions of hire to the defendants but before the defendants signed it the crane sank into the marshy ground on which the defendants were working (although the accident occurred without negligence on the part of the defendants). The plaintiffs sought to recover from the defendants the cost of recovering the crane from the marshy ground. The defendants denied that they were liable to meet this cost. The Court of Appeal held that the defendants were liable to meet this cost on the basis that the plaintiffs' terms contained a clause which required the defendants to indemnify them against such losses and such a term was, as the defendants knew, in standard use in the trade.

Lord Denning MR
In support of the course of dealing, the plaintiffs relied on two previous transactions in which the defendants had hired cranes from the plaintiffs. One was February 20, 1969; and the other October 6, 1969. Each was on a printed form which set out the hiring of a crane, the price, the site, and so forth; and also setting out the conditions the same as those here. There were thus only two transactions many months before and they were not known to the defendants' manager who ordered this crane. In the circumstances I doubt whether those two would be sufficient to show a course of dealing.

In *Hollier* v. *Rambler Motors (AMC) Ltd* [1972] 2 QB 71, 76 Salmon LJ said he knew of no case

> 'in which it has been decided or even argued that a term could be implied into an oral contract on the strength of a course of dealing (if it can be so called) which consisted at the most of three or four transactions over a period of five years.'

That was a case of a private individual who had had his car repaired by the defendants and had signed forms with conditions on three or four occasions. The plaintiff there was not of equal bargaining power with the garage company which repaired the car. The conditions were not incorporated.

But here the parties were both in the trade and were of equal bargaining power. Each was a firm of plant hirers who hired out plant. The defendants themselves knew that firms in the plant-hiring trade always imposed conditions in regard to the hiring of plant: and that their conditions were on much the same lines . . .

[he considered the evidence and continued]

From that evidence it is clear that both parties knew quite well that conditions were habitually imposed by the supplier of these machines: and both parties knew the substance of those conditions. In particular that if the crane sank in soft ground it was the hirer's job to recover it: and that there was an indemnity clause. In these circumstances, I think the conditions on the form should be regarded as incorporated into the contract. I would not put it so much on the course of dealing, but rather on the common understanding which is to be derived from the conduct of the parties, namely, that the hiring was to be on the terms of the plaintiffs' usual conditions.

As Lord Reid said in *McCutcheon* v. *David MacBrayne Ltd* [1964] 1 WLR 125, 128 quoting from the Scottish textbook, Gloag on Contract, 2nd ed. (1929), p. 7:

'The judicial task is not to discover the actual intentions of each party; it is to decide what each was reasonably entitled to conclude from the attitude of the other.'

It seems to me that, in view of the relationship of the parties, when the defendants requested this crane urgently and it was supplied at once—before the usual form was received—the plaintiffs were entitled to conclude that the defendants were accepting it on the terms of the plaintiffs' own printed conditions—which would follow in a day or two. It is just as if the plaintiffs had said: 'We will supply it on our usual conditions', and the defendants said 'Of course, that is quite understood'.

Applying the conditions, it is quite clear that nos. 6 and 8 cover the second mishap. The defendants are liable for the cost of recovering the crane from the soft ground.

Megaw LJ concurred and **Sir Eric Sachs** delivered a concurring judgment.

6. FURTHER READING

CLARKE, M, 'Notice of Contractual Terms' [1976] *CLJ* 51.

MACDONALD, E, 'Incorporation of Contract Terms by a "Consistent Course of Dealing"' (1988) 8 *Legal Studies* 48.

—— 'The Duty to Give Notice of Unusual Contract Terms' [1988] *JBL* 375.

SPENCER, JR, 'Signature, Consent, and the Rule in *L'Estrange* v. *Graucob*' [1973] *CLJ* 104.

10

IMPLIED TERMS

1. CENTRAL ISSUES

1. Terms may be implied into contracts from three principal sources, namely statute, custom, and the courts.

2. Terms are frequently implied into contracts by Parliament. These terms can be very important in practice. For example, terms are implied into contracts for the sale of goods which give buyers important rights against sellers. These terms were first enacted in the Sale of Goods Act 1893 and are now to be found in the Sale of Goods Act 1979.

3. Terms can also be implied into contracts by custom where the custom is certain, reasonable, and notorious. Customs and usages are an important source of obligation in commercial contracts.

4. Courts also imply terms into contracts. The jurisdiction of the court to imply terms into a contract is a source of considerable controversy. The difficulty which the courts have experienced lies in locating both the basis and the extent of their jurisdiction to imply terms into a contract. The traditional justification for the implication of terms is that the court is giving effect to the presumed intention of the parties. Terms were therefore implied on the basis that it was necessary to do so. However it is difficult, if not impossible, to justify the implication of all terms on the basis of necessity. In some cases the courts take account of a wider range of considerations than the presumed intention of the parties and apply a test that is less stringent than necessity. On the other hand, the courts have rejected the proposition that they can imply a term into a contract simply on the basis that it is reasonable to do so.

5. Implied terms are customarily divided into two categories, namely terms implied in law and terms implied in fact. In the case of terms implied in fact it is possible to ascribe the implied term to the intention of the parties, but it is much more difficult to do this where the term is implied in law. In the latter case a term is implied as an incident of every contract of that kind and the courts take account of a wide range of considerations when deciding whether or not to imply such a term into the contract.

2. INTRODUCTION

Implied terms are important both in practice and in theory. They are important in practice because a number of important terms in contracts today are there as a result of implication rather than express agreement. The implied terms contained in sections 12–15 of the Sale of Goods Act 1979 impose important obligations upon sellers of goods. The word 'impose' is important. These terms can no longer be attributed to the intention of the parties because Parliament has intervened to establish very strict limits within which these terms can be excluded (in the case of consumer contracts they cannot be excluded at all). One of the important terms to be found in contracts of employment is a term to the effect that the parties must not conduct themselves in such a way as to undermine the relationship of 'trust and confidence' that exists between an employer and an employee. Again, this implied term does not owe its origin to the express agreement of the parties. Its source is to be found in the willingness of the courts to imply such a term into contracts of employment (*Mahmud* v. *Bank of Credit and Commercial International SA* [1998] AC 20, see further pp. 398–399 below).

Two issues of particular significance arise in relation to implied terms. The first relates to the justification for implying terms into contracts. On what basis do the courts and Parliament imply terms into a contract? Is it to give effect to the presumed intention of the parties or is the search for an implied term based on wider considerations of policy? The second issue relates to the test to be applied by the courts when deciding whether or not to imply a term into a contract. This issue is related to the first one. If the justification for implying a term into a contract is to give effect to the presumed intention of the parties then the likelihood is that the test will be based on necessity. A term will only be implied where it is necessary to give effect to the presumed intention of the parties. On the other hand, if the justification for implying a term is to be located in broader issues of policy, then one would expect the test applied by the court to reflect these broader policy issues: in short, one would expect a test based upon criteria such as the reasonableness of the implication on the facts of the case.

3. TERMS IMPLIED BY STATUTE

Parliament has, on a number of occasions, implied terms into contracts. The precise reason for the implication of the term obviously depends upon the particular statute. It may be to give effect to the presumed intention of the parties; it may be to reduce uncertainty by enacting a default rule out of which the parties can contract if they do not like the term that Parliament has seen fit to imply; or it may be to protect one party to the transaction from the superior bargaining power of the other party. Terms have been implied by Parliament into a wide range of transactions: for example, contracts for the sale of goods, hire-purchase contracts, other contracts for the supply of goods, contracts for the supply of services, and contracts for the construction of a dwelling. We shall use contracts for the sale of goods as our example. Sections 12–15 of the Sale of Goods Act 1979 imply a number of terms into contracts for the sale of goods. These terms are as follows:

Implied terms about title, etc.

12.—(1) In a contract of sale, other than one to which subsection (3) below applies, there is an implied term on the part of the seller that in the case of a sale he has a right to sell the goods, and in the case of an agreement to sell he will have such a right at the time when the property is to pass.

(2) In a contract of sale, other than one to which subsection (3) below applies, there is also an implied term that—

(a) the goods are free, and will remain free until the time when the property is to pass, from any charge or encumbrance not disclosed or known to the buyer before the contract is made, and

(b) the buyer will enjoy quiet possession of the goods except so far as it may be disturbed by the owner or other person entitled to the benefit of any charge or encumbrance so disclosed or known.

(3) This subsection applies to a contract of sale in the case of which there appears from the contract or is to be inferred from its circumstances an intention that the seller should transfer only such title as he or a third person may have.

(4) In a contract to which subsection (3) above applies there is an implied term that all charges or encumbrances known to the seller and not known to the buyer have been disclosed to the buyer before the contract is made.

(5) In a contract to which subsection (3) above applies there is also an implied term that none of the following will disturb the buyer's quiet possession of the goods, namely—

(a) the seller;

(b) in a case where the parties to the contract intend that the seller should transfer only such title as a third person may have, that person;

(c) anyone claiming through or under the seller or that third person otherwise than under a charge or encumbrance disclosed or known to the buyer before the contract is made.

(5A) As regards England and Wales and Northern Ireland, the term implied by subsection (1) above is a condition and the terms implied by subsections (2), (4) and (5) above are warranties.

Sale by description

13.—(1) Where there is a contract for the sale of goods by description, there is an implied term that the goods will correspond with the description.

(1A) As regards England and Wales and Northern Ireland, the term implied by subsection (1) above is a condition.

(2) If the sale is by sample as well as by description it is not sufficient that the bulk of the goods corresponds with the sample if the goods do not also correspond with the description.

(3) A sale of goods is not prevented from being a sale by description by reason only that, being exposed for sale or hire, they are selected by the buyer.

Implied terms about quality or fitness

14.—(1) Except as provided by this section and section 15 below and subject to any other enactment, there is no implied term about the quality or fitness for any particular purpose of goods supplied under a contract of sale.

(2) Where the seller sells goods in the course of a business, there is an implied term that the goods supplied under the contract are of satisfactory quality.

(2A) For the purposes of this Act, goods are of satisfactory quality if they meet the standard that a reasonable person would regard as satisfactory, taking account of any description of the goods, the price (if relevant) and all the other relevant circumstances.

(2B) For the purposes of this Act, the quality of goods includes their state and condition and the following (among others) are in appropriate cases aspects of the quality of goods—

(a) fitness for all the purposes for which goods of the kind in question are commonly supplied,

(b) appearance and finish,

(c) freedom from minor defects,

(d) safety, and

(e) durability.

(2C) The term implied by subsection (2) above does not extend to any matter making the quality of goods unsatisfactory—

(a) which is specifically drawn to the buyer's attention before the contract is made,

(b) where the buyer examines the goods before the contract is made, which that examination ought to reveal, or

(c) in the case of a contract for sale by sample, which would have been apparent on a reasonable examination of the sample.

(2D) If the buyer deals as consumer or, in Scotland, if a contract of sale is a consumer contract, the relevant circumstances mentioned in subsection (2A) above include any public statements on the specific characteristics of the goods made about them by the seller, the producer or his representative, particularly in advertising or on labelling.

(2E) A public statement is not by virtue of subsection (2D) above a relevant circumstance for the purposes of subsection (2A) above in the case of a contract of sale, if the seller shows that—

(a) at the time the contract was made, he was not, and could not reasonably have been, aware of the statement,

(b) before the contract was made, the statement had been withdrawn in public or, to the extent that it contained anything which was incorrect or misleading, it had been corrected in public, or

(c) the decision to buy the goods could not have been influenced by the statement.

(2F) Subsections (2D) and (2E) above do not prevent any public statement from being a relevant circumstance for the purposes of subsection (2A) above (whether or not the buyer deals as consumer or, in Scotland, whether or not the contract of sale is a consumer contract) if the statement would have been such a circumstance apart from those subsections.

(3) Where the seller sells goods in the course of a business and the buyer, expressly or by implication, makes known—

(a) to the seller, or

(b) where the purchase price or part of it is payable by instalments and the goods were previously sold by a credit-broker to the seller, to that credit-broker, any particular purpose for which the goods are being bought, there is an implied term that the goods supplied under the contract are reasonably fit for that purpose, whether or not that is a purpose for which such goods are commonly supplied, except where the circumstances show that the buyer does not rely, or that it is unreasonable for him to rely, on the skill or judgment of the seller or credit-broker.

(4) An implied term about quality or fitness for a particular purpose may be annexed to a contract of sale by usage.

(5) The preceding provisions of this section apply to a sale by a person who in the course of a business is acting as agent for another as they apply to a sale by a principal in the course of a business, except where that other is not selling in the course of a business and either the buyer knows that fact or reasonable steps are taken to bring it to the notice of the buyer before the contract is made.

(6) As regards England and Wales and Northern Ireland, the terms implied by subsections (2) and (3) above are conditions.

. . .

Sale by sample

Sale by sample

15.—(1) A contract of sale is a contract for sale by sample where there is an express or implied term to that effect in the contract.

(2) In the case of a contract for sale by sample there is an implied term

(a) that the bulk will correspond with the sample in quality;

. . .

(c) that the goods will be free from any defect, making their quality unsatisfactory, which would not be apparent on reasonable examination of the sample.

(3) As regards England and Wales and Northern Ireland, the term implied by subsection (2) above is a condition.

COMMENTARY

These implied terms are of considerable significance for buyers of goods because they give them a number of important rights against sellers of goods. The rule at common law was generally believed to be '*caveat emptor*' (let the buyer beware). Under such a rule the onus was put upon the buyer to seek a specific undertaking from the seller in relation to the quality of the goods. Now that the implied terms have been enacted the need for buyers to seek express undertakings from sellers has been significantly reduced. The implied terms contained in sections 12–15 of the Sale of Goods Act 1979 provide buyers with a minimum floor of rights and, as we shall see, the law has placed considerable limits on the ability of sellers to contract out of these implied terms.

The aim of section 12 is to give a buyer a remedy against a seller in the event that the seller does not have title to sell the goods that he has contracted to sell to the buyer. In such a case the buyer will generally be entitled to recover from the seller the price which he has paid for the goods. This is so even in the case where the buyer has been able to make use of the goods over a period of time prior to discovery of the fact that the seller did not have title to the goods that have been sold to the buyer (see, for example, *Rowland* v. *Divall* [1923] 2 KB 500). Section 12(2) also implies two warranties into contracts for the sale of goods. The function of the warranties of freedom from encumbrances and quiet possession is, essentially, to enable the buyer to enjoy the use of the goods without interference by third parties. The implied term as to title is a condition, whereas the implied terms relating to freedom from encumbrances and quiet possession are warranties. The difference between a condition and a warranty will be explained in more detail in a later chapter (see pp. 941–958 below). Here it suffices to note that breach of a condition entitles a buyer to reject the goods and terminate the contract, whereas breach of a warranty does not. The only remedy for breach of a warranty is damages.

Section 13 provides protection for the buyer who receives goods that do not correspond with the description. The section is, however, more difficult than it looks at first sight and it has generated a considerable amount of case-law. The section only comes into play where there has been a contract for sale 'by' description. In order for the contract to be by description the buyer must have entered into the contract in reliance upon the description provided by the seller (*Harlingdon and Leinster Enterprises Ltd* v. *Christopher Hull Fine Art Ltd* [1991] 1 QB 564). In order to amount to a 'description' the words used must identify the subject-matter of the contract (*Reardon Smith Line Ltd* v. *Yngvar Hansen-Tangen* [1976] 1 WLR 989).

Section 14 implies two very important conditions into contracts for the sale of goods. The first, contained in section 14(2), (2A), and (2B), is that the goods must be of 'satisfactory quality' (formerly 'merchantable quality'). The definition of 'satisfactory quality' was inserted into the 1979 Act by the Sale and Supply of Goods Act 1994 and was further amended by the Sale and Supply of Goods to Consumers Regulations 2002 (SI 2002 No 3045). It provides a check-list of factors to be taken into account when deciding whether or not goods are of satisfactory quality. The list is applicable to all contracts of sale but it seems to have been drafted with consumer sales particularly in mind. The second condition, to be found in section 14(3), is that the goods must be reasonably fit for their purpose. A buyer who wishes to make some unusual use of the goods must disclose that use to the seller prior to entry into the contract of sale if he wishes to be able to invoke the fitness for purpose implied term. The seller does not provide a guarantee that the goods will be fit for all purposes. The goods need only be 'reasonably fit' for their purpose. So, where the goods cannot be used for their intended purpose because of some idiosyncrasy, not made known to the seller, of the buyer or in the circumstances of the use of the goods by the buyer, the seller will not be liable to the buyer under section 14(3) (*Slater* v. *Finning Ltd* [1997] AC 473). These two conditions only come into play where the 'seller sells goods in the course of a business'. The test applied by the court when deciding whether or not the seller sold in the course of a business does not depend upon the regularity of the sale or whether it was integral to the seller's business. In *Stevenson* v. *Rogers* [1999] QB 1028 the Court of Appeal held that, unless the sale was 'a purely private sale of goods outside the confines of the business (if any) carried on by the seller' it is within the course of the seller's business so as to attract the implied terms relating to satisfactory quality and fitness for purpose.

Section 15 implies two conditions in the case of a sale of goods by sample. The first is that the bulk will correspond with the sample in quality and the second is that the goods will be free from any defect making their quality unsatisfactory, which would not be apparent on reasonable examination of the sample (see *Godley* v. *Perry* [1960] 1 WLR 9).

The importance of these implied terms is demonstrated by the fact that Parliament has intervened to place restrictions upon the ability of sellers to exclude their operation. In the case of consumer sales, the implied terms cannot be excluded as against the consumer. In commercial sales the implied terms can be excluded provided that it is reasonable to do so (except in the case of section 12 where it is not possible to exclude liability for breach of this term, even in the case of a commercial sales contract). Statutory controls on exclusion and limitation of liability are discussed in more detail below (see pp. 460–485).

What is the basis of these implied terms? Are they based on the presumed intention of the parties? There is some support for this proposition in the authorities. In *Philips Electronique Grand Publique SA* v. *British Sky Broadcasting Ltd* [1995] EMLR 472 Lord Bingham MR stated (at p. 481) that:

quite apart from statute, the courts would not ordinarily hesitate to imply into a contract for the sale of unseen goods that they should be of merchantable quality and answer to their description and conform with sample. It is hard to imagine trade conducted, in the absence of express agreement, on any other terms.

While it may be 'hard to imagine' trade being conducted on any other terms, it is not impossible. There is still in English law no general implied term that a house is fit for any particular purpose or even for human habitation. Further, as a general rule a landlord does not give an implied undertaking that leased premises will be fit for habitation or for any particular purpose, although in the case of a lease of furnished premises there is an implied condition that the premises are fit for human habitation at the beginning of the tenancy. If contracts for the sale of real property can be concluded without the benefit of extensive implied terms for the benefit of the purchaser, can the same not be said of contracts for the sale of personal property, such as goods? Support for the proposition that contracts for the sale of goods can be concluded without the benefit of such implied terms can be derived from the law of sale in the nineteenth century, where *caveat emptor* played a much more dominant role than it does today. This being the case, the claim that the implied terms are based on the presumed intention of the parties seems very doubtful. It is much more likely that the function of the implied terms is to protect what are perceived to be the legitimate or reasonable expectations of buyers when they enter into contracts for the sale of goods. That this is so is evidenced by the fact that Parliament has intervened to limit the ability of sellers to contract out of these terms. The fact that it is impossible to contract out of some of these implied terms demonstrates that they are not based on the presumed intention of the parties. They are part of a legislative policy to protect the expectations of buyers, especially consumer buyers.

4. TERMS IMPLIED FROM USAGE OR CUSTOM

Terms may be implied into a contract from the usage or custom of the industry or market in which the parties transact. In *Hutton* v. *Warren* (1836) 1 M & W 466 Parke B stated (at p. 475) that

It has long been settled, that, in commercial transactions, extrinsic evidence of custom and usage is admissible to annex incidents to written contracts, in matters with respect to which they are silent. The same rule has also been applied to contracts in other transactions of life, in which known usages have been established and prevailed; and this has been done upon the principle of presumption that, in such transactions, the parties did not mean to express in writing the whole of the contract by which they intended to be bound, but a contract with reference to those known usages. Whether such a relaxation of the strictness of the common law was wisely applied, where formal instruments have been entered into, and particularly leases under seal, may well be doubted; but the contrary has been established by such authority, and the relations between landlord and tenant have been so long regulated upon the supposition that all customary obligations, not altered by the contract, are to remain in force, that it is too late to pursue a contrary course; and it would be productive of much inconvenience if this practice were now to be disturbed.

Two points emerge from this statement. The first is that the usage must be a 'known' usage. This does not mean that the parties must actually have been aware of its existence. It suffices that it was so well known that 'an outsider who makes reasonable enquiries could not fail to be made aware of it' (*Kum* v. *Wah Tat Bank Ltd* [1971] 1 Lloyd's Rep 439, 444). The requirement that the custom be 'known' is often expressed in the formula that the custom or usage must be 'notorious, certain and reasonable'. In *Cunliffe-Owen* v. *Teather & Greenwood* [1967] 1 WLR 1421 Ungoed-Thomas J stated (at p. 1438–1439) that:

For the practice to amount to such a recognised usage, it must be certain, in the sense that the practice is clearly established; it must be notorious, in the sense that it is so well known in the market in which it is alleged to exist that those who conduct business in that market contract with the usage as an implied term, and it must be reasonable. The burden lies on those alleging usage to establish it . . . The practice that has to be established consists of a continuity of acts, and those acts have to be established by persons familiar with them, although, as is accepted before me, they may be sufficiently established by such persons without a detailed recital of instances. Practice is not a matter of opinion of even the most highly qualified expert as to what it is desirable that the practice should be. However, evidence of those versed in a market, so it seems to me, may be admissible and valuable in identifying those features of any transaction that attract usage and in discounting other features which for such purpose are merely incidental and if there is conflict of evidence about this it is subject to being resolved like other conflicts of evidence. Arrangements or compromises to the same effect as the alleged usage do not establish usage; they contradict it. They may be the precursors of usage, but usage presupposes that arrangements and compromises are no longer required. It is, in my view, clearly not necessary that a practice should be challenged and enforced before it can become a usage as, otherwise, a practice so obviously universally accepted and acted on as not to be challenged could never be a usage. However, enforcement would be valuable and might be conclusive in establishing usage. What is necessary is that for a practice to be a recognised usage it should be established as a practice having binding effect.

The last sentence is important because it demonstrates that repetitive behaviour in the market is not sufficient, of itself, to establish a custom: 'it must also be shown that this pattern of behaviour is observed from a sense of legally binding obligation, not from mere courtesy, convenience or expediency' (R Goode, 'Usage and its Reception in Transnational Commercial Law' (1997) 46 *ICLQ* 1, 8). In *General Reinsurance Corp* v. *Forsakringsaktiebolaget Fennia Patria* [1983] QB 856, 874 Slade LJ stated:

There is, however, the world of difference between a course of conduct that is frequently, or even habitually, followed in a particular commercial community as a matter of grace and a course which is habitually followed because it is considered that the parties concerned have a legally binding right to demand it.

The distinction between courtesy and obligation, while easy to state in theory, can be difficult to draw in practice (see, for example, *Libyan Arab Foreign Bank* v. *Bankers Trust Co* [1989] QB 728). It is nevertheless a distinction of considerable importance.

The second point that can be derived from the judgment of Parke B in *Warren* is that the custom must not have been 'altered by the contract'. A term will therefore not be implied into a contract by custom where the custom is inconsistent with the express terms of the contract (*Palgrave, Brown & Son Ltd* v. *SS Turid (Owners)* [1922] 1 AC 397).

Custom and usage play an important role in commercial law generally as the following extract demonstrates:

R Goode, *Commercial Law*

(3rd edn, Penguin, 2004), pp. 13–14

Of great importance as a source of obligation in commercial contracts are the unwritten customs and usages of merchants. The impact of these on the content and interpretation of contract terms cannot be overstated. It is, perhaps, this feature above all which distinguishes commercial from other contracts, a distinction not formally adopted by the law. The fertility of the business mind and the fact that a practice which begins life by having no legal force acquires over time the sanctity of law are key factors to which the commercial lawyer must continually be responsive. Is a particular document a document of title? The House of Lords may have said no, possibly more than once. But how long ago was the ruling given? Cannot it now be said, in another time, that the acceptance of this document as a document of title in mercantile usage is so entrenched as to justify according it legal recognition as such? . . .

What is it that gives binding force to unwritten mercantile usage? Is it the express or implied adoption of the usage by the parties in their contract? Or does mercantile usage have independent normative force? The question has been much debated in the context of international commercial arbitration and the controversy as to the existence of an international *lex mercatoria*. In some legal systems the binding force of mercantile usage does not depend on adoption by contract, but in the theory of English law usage takes effect as an express or implied term of the contract between the parties . . .

It is in the nature of unwritten custom or usage that its meaning and content may be understood differently by different people; indeed, the very existence of an alleged usage may be challenged. In areas of business or finance with a highly developed and widely used body of custom or usage it is particularly important to avoid disputes of this kind. To that end, national and international trade associations and clearing houses may find it convenient to formulate the relevant usages in a published code or set of rules. These will rarely reflect existing usage in every particular, since the opportunity will usually be taken to make improvements to established practice and procedures, but the intended effect of the code or rules is to state or restate best practice. They may be given effect either by making adherence to them a condition of membership of the relevant association or clearing house or by incorporation into individual contracts. At the international level the prime mover in the codification of international trade usage is the International Chamber of Commerce (ICC), an international non-governmental organization serving world business. Working through its specialist Commissions, the ICC has produced numerous uniform rules which are adopted by incorporation into contracts. These fall broadly into three groups: banking and insurance, international trade and international transport. The most long-standing and successful of the various ICC formulations is the Uniform Customs and Practice for Documentary Credits (UCP), first promulgated by the ICC in 1933. Bankers throughout the world have adopted the UCP, which is now used almost universally in documentary credit transactions.[1] Other ICC uniform rules in banking and insurance are the Uniform Rules for Collections, the Uniform Rules for Demand Guarantees and the Uniform Rules for Contract Bonds. In the field of international trade extensive use is made of Incoterms [a set of rules for the interpretation of commonly used price and delivery terms in international trade], while in relation to transport the ICC has collaborated with the United Nations Commission on Trade and Development (UNCTAD) in producing the UNCTAD/ICC Rules for Multimodal Transport Documents. The ICC has also instantly endorsed the ISP 98 on International Standby Practices.

In English law codified customs and usages, like those which are uncodified, depend for their operation on express or implied adoption in the contract.

As Professor Goode makes clear in the last sentence of the extract, customs, at least in English law, depend for their operation on 'express or implied' incorporation into the contract. Very often that incorporation will be express (and so might properly be said to fall within the scope of Chapter 9). Thus banks will generally incorporate the UCP expressly into their contracts with their customers. The reason for this is that the matter is too important to be left to implication by a court. However, should a bank fail, for some reason, to incorporate the UCP into a contract with one of its customers, it is likely that a court would conclude that it was incorporated into the contract either on the basis of custom or on the basis of a course of dealing between the parties (on which see pp. 363–369 above).

5. TERMS IMPLIED BY THE COURTS

It is customary to divide terms implied by the courts into two groups, namely terms implied in fact and terms implied in law. A term is implied in fact when it is implied into the contract in order to give effect to what is deemed by the court to be the

---

[1] Letters of credit are discussed in more detail at p. 272 above, where their essential nature is described.

unexpressed intention of the parties. It is generally, but not always, a term that is specific to the particular transaction between the parties. Terms implied in law 'are those terms that are consistently implied into all contracts of a particular type because of the nature of the contract, rather than the supposed intentions of the parties' (E Peden, 'Policy Concerns Behind Implication of Terms in Law' (2001) 117 *LQR* 459). For example, the courts have held that there is an implied term of 'trust and confidence' in contracts of employment (see pp. 398–399 below). The existence of this term is not dependent upon it being representative of the unexpressed intention of the parties to the particular employment contract. It is a term that is implied into all contracts of employment unless it has been expressly excluded by the parties.

The importance of the distinction between a term implied in fact and a term implied in law is that the test for the implication of a term as a matter of law appears to be less stringent than that applicable to terms implied in fact. Traditionally, the courts have insisted that they will only imply a term into a contract as a matter of fact where it is 'necessary' to do so. In the case of terms implied in law, however, it would appear that the test is not one of necessity, although the precise nature of the test remains unclear. It appears to be somewhere in between 'reasonableness' and 'necessity'. Thus it might be said that it must be 'reasonably necessary' to imply the term into the contract.

One of the difficulties with the distinction between terms implied in fact and terms implied in law is that the distinction between the two is not always easy to draw. The one tends to shade into the other. Therefore, rather than seek to divide the cases formally into two groups we shall take a chronological approach to the development of the law. The advantage of doing so is that we can see the law unfold as judges have grappled with the difficulty of working out when it is appropriate to imply a term into a contract. Two tensions will become apparent. The first is whether the test for the implication of terms should be based on 'necessity' or upon 'reasonableness' and the second is whether a distinction ought to be drawn between terms implied in law and terms implied in fact and, if so, where the line of distinction ought to be drawn.

We shall start with the first leading case on the implication of terms into a contract, namely the decision of the Court of Appeal in *The Moorcock* (1889) 14 PD 64. It is a case concerned with a term implied in fact and it articulates a test which is based on 'necessity' rather than 'reasonableness'. We shall then move on to the leading case of *Liverpool City Council* v. *Irwin* [1976] QB 319 (CA); [1977] AC 239 (HL). This case is principally concerned with terms implied in law, although it also raised much wider issues relating to the basis upon which terms are implied by the courts into contracts. In this respect it produced a difference of opinion between Lord Denning (who applied a test based upon reasonableness) and the House of Lords (who re-stated the traditional test based on necessity). Lord Denning then attempted to re-state the law, dividing the cases into two broad categories, in *Shell UK Ltd* v. *Lostock Garage Ltd* [1976] 1 WLR 1187. After noting the judgment of Lord Simon of Glaisdale in *BP Refinery (Westernport) Pty Ltd* v. *Shire of Hastings* (1978) ALJR 20, 26 we shall conclude this section with an analysis of two leading modern cases concerned with terms implied in law (namely *Scally* v. *Southern Health and Social Services Board* [1992] 1 AC 294 and *Mahmud* v. *Bank of Credit and Commerce International SA* [1998] AC 20).

The Moorcock

(1889) 14 PD 64, Court of Appeal

The defendants agreed to allow the plaintiff to discharge his vessel at their wharf so that the vessel could discharge and load her cargo. In order for the vessel to be able to discharge her cargo it was necessary for the vessel to be moored alongside the jetty (which was also owned by the defendants). The jetty extended in to the River Thames and the bed of the river adjoining the jetty was vested in the Conservators of the River Thames. While the vessel was moored at the end of the jetty, the tide ebbed so that the vessel was no longer waterborne and she suffered damage as a result of the uneven condition of the river bed. The plaintiff brought an action for damages against the defendants. The defendants admitted that they had not taken any steps to ascertain whether or not the ground was level and suitable for the vessel. The trial judge, Butt J, held that the defendants were liable in damages to the plaintiff on the ground that they were in breach of an implied undertaking to take 'reasonable care to ascertain that the bottom of the river at the jetty was in such a condition as not to endanger the vessel using their premises in the ordinary way'. The defendants appealed to the Court of Appeal but the appeal was dismissed.

Bowen LJ

The question which arises here is whether when a contract is made to let the use of this jetty to a ship which can only use it, as is known by both parties, by taking the ground, there is any implied warranty on the part of the owners of the jetty, and if so, what is the extent of the warranty. Now, an implied warranty, or, as it is called, a covenant in law, as distinguished from an express contract or express warranty, really is in all cases founded on the presumed intention of the parties, and upon reason. The implication which the law draws from what must obviously have been the intention of the parties, the law draws with the object of giving efficacy to the transaction and preventing such a failure of consideration as cannot have been within the contemplation of either side; and I believe if one were to take all the cases, and they are many, of implied warranties or covenants in law, it will be found that in all of them the law is raising an implication from the presumed intention of the parties with the object of giving to the transaction such efficacy as both parties must have intended that at all events it should have. In business transactions such as this, what the law desires to effect by the implication is to give such business efficacy to the transaction as must have been intended at all events by both parties who are business men; not to impose on one side all the perils of the transaction, or to emancipate one side from all the chances of failure, but to make each party promise in law as much, at all events, as it must have been in the contemplation of both parties that he should be responsible for in respect of those perils or chances.

Now what did each party in a case like this know? For if we are examining into their presumed intention we must examine into their minds as to what the transaction was. Both parties knew that this jetty was let out for hire, and knew that it could only be used under the contract by the ship taking the ground. They must have known that it was by grounding that she used the jetty; in fact, except so far as the transport to the jetty of the cargo in the ship was concerned, they must have known, both of them, that unless the ground was safe the ship would be simply buying an opportunity of danger, and that all consideration would fail unless some care had been taken to see that the ground was safe. In fact the business of the jetty could not be carried on except upon such a basis. The parties also knew that with regard to the safety of the ground outside the jetty the shipowner could know nothing at all, and the jetty owner might with reasonable care know everything. The owners of the jetty, or their servants, were there at high and low tide, and with little trouble they could satisfy themselves, in case of doubt, as to whether the berth was reasonably safe. The ship's owner, on the other hand, had not the means of verifying the state of the jetty, because the berth itself opposite the jetty might be occupied by another ship at any moment.

Now the question is how much of the peril of the safety of this berth is it necessary to assume that the shipowner and the jetty owner intended respectively to bear—in order that such a minimum of efficacy should be secured for the transaction, as both parties must have intended it to bear? Assume that the berth outside had been absolutely under the control of the owners of the jetty, that they could have repaired it and made it fit for the purpose of the unloading and the loading. If this had been the case, then the case of *The Mersey Docks Trustees* v. *Gibbs* Law Rep 1 HL 93 shews that those who owned the jetty, who took money for the use of the jetty, and who had under their control the locus in quo, would have been bound to take all reasonable care to prevent danger to those who were using the jetty—either to make the berth outside good, or else not to invite ships to go there—either to make the berth safe, or to advise persons not to go there. But there is a distinction in the present instance. The berth outside the jetty was not under the actual control of the jetty owners. It is in the bed of the river, and it may be said that those who owned the jetty had no duty cast upon them by statute or common law to repair the bed of the river, and that they had no power to interfere with the bed of the river unless under the licence of the Conservators. Now it does make a difference, it seems to me, where the entire control of the locus in quo—be it canal, or be it dock, or be it river berth—is not under the control of the persons who are taking toll for accommodation which involves its user, and, to a certain extent, the view must be modified of the necessary implication which the law would make about the duties of the parties receiving the remuneration. This must be done exactly for the reason laid down by Lord Holt in his judgment in *Coggs* v. *Bernard* Ld Raym 909, where he says 'it would be unreasonable to charge persons with a trust further than the nature of the thing puts it in their power to perform'. Applying that modification, which is one of reason, to this case, it may well be said that the law will not imply that the persons who have not the control of the place have taken reasonable care to make it good, but it does not follow that they are relieved from all responsibility. They are on the spot. They must know that the jetty cannot be used unless reasonable care is taken, if not to make it safe, at all events to see whether it is safe. No one can tell whether reasonable safety has been secured except themselves, and I think if they let out their jetty for use they at all events imply that they have taken reasonable care to see whether the berth, which is the essential part of the use of the jetty, is safe, and if it is not safe, and if they have not taken such reasonable care, it is their duty to warn persons with whom they have dealings that they have not done so. This is a business transaction as to which at any moment the parties may make any bargain they please, and either side may by the contract throw upon the other the burden of the unseen and existing danger. The question is what inference is to be drawn where the parties are dealing with each other on the assumption that the negotiations are to have some fruit, and where they say nothing about the burden of this kind of unseen peril, leaving the law to raise such inferences as are reasonable from the very nature of the transaction. So far as I am concerned I do not wish it to be understood that I at all consider this is a case of any duty on the part of the owners of the jetty to see to the access to the jetty being kept clear. The difference between access to the jetty and the actual use of the jetty seems to me, as Mr Finlay [counsel for the defendants] says it is, only a question of degree, but when you are dealing with implications which the law directs, you cannot afford to neglect questions of degree, and it is just that difference of degree which brings one case on the line and prevents the other from approaching it. I confess that on the broad view of the case I think that business could not be carried on unless there was an implication to the extent I have laid down, at all events in the case where a jetty like the present is so to be used, and, although the case is a novel one, and the cases which have been cited do not assist us, I feel no difficulty in drawing the inference that this case comes within the line.

Lord Esher MR and **Fry LJ** delivered concurring judgments.

COMMENTARY

The Moorcock is an important case for two reasons. The first relates to the source of the implied term. Bowen LJ attributed it to the 'presumed intention of the parties'. In this way he avoided the conclusion that the court was making the contract for the parties. Instead, the court stated that it was giving effect to the intention of the parties, albeit that the intention was presumed rather than express. However it should be noted that Bowen LJ does not rest the implication of terms solely upon the 'presumed intention of the parties'. He adds that it is also based 'upon reason'. This appears to suggest a wider basis for the implication of terms, a point to which we shall return. The second point relates to the test put forward by Bowen LJ. It is one based on the need to give 'business efficacy' to the transaction. This has been interpreted subsequently as a test that is based on necessity rather than reasonableness. In other words, the court does not imply a term into the contract on the basis that it is, in the opinion of the court, reasonable to do so. The court implies a term into the contract on the basis that it is necessary to do so in order to make the contract work. That said, was the term implied in *The Moorcock* one that was necessary to give efficacy to the contract? Could the contract not have worked without such a term? The issue before the court was, in essence, who was to take the risk of the bed of the river being unsuitable for the vessel. Business efficacy does not seem to require that the risk be allocated to one party or the other. Nevertheless, the court took the view that business efficacy supported the implication of a term to the effect that the defendants had undertaken to exercise reasonable care to ascertain that the river bed adjoining the jetty was in such a condition as not to cause injury to the vessel.

In the years following *The Moorcock* the necessity test established itself in the case-law. Two famous judicial statements demonstrate this. The first is taken from the judgment of Scrutton LJ in *Reigate* v. *Union Manufacturing Co (Ramsbottom) Ltd* [1918] 1 KB 592 when he stated (at p. 605):

A term can only be implied if it is necessary in the business sense to give efficacy to the contract; that is, if it is such a term that it can confidently be said that if at the time the contract was being negotiated some one had said to the parties, 'What will happen in such a case', they would both have replied, 'Of course, so and so will happen; we did not trouble to say that; it is too clear'.

Unless the Court comes to some such conclusion as that, it ought not to imply a term which the parties themselves have not expressed.

The second example is a passage from the judgment of MacKinnon LJ in *Shirlaw* v. *Southern Foundries (1926) Ltd* [1939] 2 KB 206 when he said (at p. 227):

I recognize that the right or duty of a Court to find the existence of an implied term or implied terms in a written contract is a matter to be exercised with care; and a Court is too often invited to do so upon vague and uncertain grounds. Too often also such an invitation is backed by the citation of a sentence or two from the judgment of Bowen LJ in *The Moorcock* (1889) 14 PD 64. They are sentences from an extempore judgment as sound and sensible as all the utterances of that great judge; but I fancy that he would have been rather surprised if he could have foreseen that these general remarks of his would come to be a favourite citation of a supposed principle of law, and I even think that he might sympathize with the occasional impatience of his successors when *The Moorcock* is so often flushed for them in that guise.

For my part, I think that there is a test that may be at least as useful as such generalities. If I may quote from an essay which I wrote some years ago, I then said: 'Prima facie that which in any contract is left to be implied and need not be expressed is something so obvious that it goes without saying; so that, if, while the parties were making their bargain, an officious bystander were to suggest some express provision for it in their agreement, they would testily suppress him with a common "Oh, of course!" '

At least it is true, I think, that, if a term were never implied by a judge unless it could pass that test, he could not be held to be wrong.

This test has become known as the 'officious bystander test' and it emphasizes the fact that the test to be applied by the court is one of necessity, not reasonableness. The standard was therefore a high one and many plaintiffs failed to satisfy it. In *Spring* v. *National Amalgamated Stevedores and Dockers Society* [1956] 1 WLR 585, for example, the court refused to imply the Bridlington Agreement into a contract of membership between an individual union member and a trade union. Had the plaintiff been asked whether the Bridlington Agreement had been incorporated into the contract, he would not have replied 'Of course' but would have asked 'What's that?' His ignorance of the existence of the agreement was sufficient to prevent it being implied into his contract with the union.

It therefore appeared that 'necessity' was firmly established as the test to be applied when deciding whether or not a term was to be implied into a contract. But the proposition that a term can only be implied into a contract when it is necessary to do so in order to give business efficacy to the contract was challenged by Lord Denning in *Liverpool City Council* v. *Irwin* [1976] QB 319. This case is an important one for two reasons. First, it explores the question whether 'necessity' or 'reasonableness' should be the basis for the implication of terms and, secondly, it raises issues relating to the distinction between a term implied in law and a term implied in fact.

Liverpool City Council v. Irwin

[1976] QB 319, Court of Appeal; [1977] AC 239, House of Lords

The defendant tenants lived in Haigh Heights, a tower block in the district of Everton in Liverpool. The plaintiffs, Liverpool City Council, were their landlords. The defendants stopped paying rent for their maisonette on the ninth and tenth floors of the tower block. The plaintiffs brought an action for possession. The defendants counterclaimed for nominal damages of £10 for (i) breach of the landlord's duty to repair and maintain the common parts of the building retained by the plaintiffs, namely the lifts, staircases, passages, rubbish chutes, playground, etc. and in relation to the maisonette itself, (ii) breach of the covenant for quiet enjoyment, and (iii) breach of the implied covenant in section 32(1) of the Housing Act 1961, specifying defects in and disrepair of the water closet cisterns, damp, defective door frames, and related matters. The plaintiffs denied the existence of any implied obligation to keep the common parts of the building in repair and they also denied breaches of the covenant for quiet enjoyment and of the covenant implied under section 32(1). The trial judge held that the plaintiffs were in breach of all three duties and, while he granted the council an order for possession, he awarded the defendants nominal damages of £10.

The plaintiffs appealed to the Court of Appeal. The Court of Appeal allowed their appeal. It held by a majority (Lord Denning MR dissenting) that the plaintiffs were not under any contractual duty to keep the common parts in repair and, further, that they were not in breach of the implied covenant in section 32(1) of the Housing Act 1961. The majority refused to imply a term into the tenancy contract to the effect that the plaintiffs would keep the common parts in repair on the ground that it was not necessary to imply such an onerous obligation into the tenancy agreement in order to give it business efficacy. Lord Denning took a different approach. He held that the plaintiffs were subject to an implied duty to take reasonable care to keep the common parts reasonably fit for use by the tenants but that the tenants had failed to prove that the plaintiffs had not exercised reasonable care. He therefore concurred in the result, namely that the defendants were not entitled to recover damages from the plaintiffs.

The defendants appealed to the House of Lords. The House of Lords allowed their appeal in part. Their appeal was successful in relation to their claim pursuant to section 32(1) of the Housing Act 1961 and it was held that they were entitled to nominal damages of £5. In relation to their claim that the plaintiffs were in breach of their duty to keep the common parts of the building in repair, the House of Lords held that the plaintiffs were subject to an obligation to take reasonable care to do so but that, on the facts, they had not breached that duty.

Two extracts from the case are set out below. The first is taken from the dissenting judgment of Lord Denning MR in the Court of Appeal and the second from the speech of Lord Wilberforce in the House of Lords. The extracts do not deal with the scope of section 32(1) of the Housing Act 1961. They deal only with the defendants' submission that the plaintiffs were in breach of their implied duty to keep the common parts of the building in repair.

Lord Denning MR

It is often said that the courts only imply a term in a contract when it is reasonable and necessary to do so in order to give business efficacy to the transaction: see *The Moorcock*

(1889) 14 PD 64, 68. (Emphasis is put on the word 'necessary': *Reigate* v. *Union Manufacturing Co (Ramsbottom) Ltd* [1918] 1 KB 592, 605.) Or when it is obvious that both parties must have intended it: so obvious indeed that if an officious bystander had asked them whether there was to be such a term, both would have suppressed it testily: 'Yes, of course': see *Shirlaw* v. *Southern Foundries (1926) Ltd* [1939] 2 KB 206, 227.

Those expressions have been repeated so often that it is with some trepidation that I venture to question them. I do so because they do not truly represent the way in which the courts act. Let me take some instances. There are stacks of them. Such as the terms implied by the courts into a contract for the sale of goods—*Jones* v. *Just* (1868) LR 3 QB 197: or the hire of goods—*Asley Industrial Trust Ltd* v. *Grimley* [1963] 1 WLR 584: into a contract for work and materials—*Young & Marten Ltd* v. *McManus Childs Ltd* [1969] 1 AC 454: or into a contract for letting an unfurnished house—*Hart* v. *Windsor* (1843) 12 M & W 68: or a furnished house—*Collins* v. *Hopkins* [1923] 2 KB 617: or into the carriage of a passenger by railway: see *Readhead* v. *Midland Railway Co* (1869) LR 4 QB 379: or to enter on premises: see *Francis* v. *Cockrell* (1870) LR 5 QB 501: or to buy a house in course of erection: see *Hancock* v. *B W Brazier (Anerley) Ltd* [1966] 1 WLR 1317.

If you read the discussion in those cases, you will see that in none of them did the court ask: what did both parties intend? If asked, each party would have said he never gave it a thought: or the one would have intended something different from the other. Nor did the court ask: Is it necessary to give business efficacy to the transaction? If asked, the answer would have been: 'It is reasonable, but it is not necessary'. The judgments in all those cases show that the courts implied a term according to whether or not it was reasonable in all the circumstances to do so. Very often it was conceded that there was some implied term. The only question was: 'What was the extent of it?' Such as, was it an absolute warranty of fitness, or only a promise to use reasonable care? That cannot be solved by inquiring what they both intended, or into what was necessary. But only into what was reasonable. This is to be decided as matter of law, not as matter of fact. Lord Wright pulled the blinkers off our eyes when he said in 1935 to the Holdsworth Club:

> 'The truth is that the court . . . decides this question in accordance with what seems to be just or reasonable in its eyes. The judge finds in himself the criterion of what is reasonable. The court is in this sense making a contract for the parties—though it is almost blasphemy to say so.' (*Lord Wright of Durley, Legal Essays and Addresses* (1939), p. 259.)

In 1956, Lord Radcliffe put it elegantly when he said of the parties to an implied term:

> 'their actual persons should be allowed to rest in peace. In their place there rises the figure of the fair and reasonable man. And the spokesman of the fair and reasonable man, who represents after all no more than the anthropomorphic conception of justice, is and must be the court itself': see *Davis Contractors Ltd* v. *Fareham Urban District Council* [1956] AC 696, 728.

In 1969, Lord Reid put it simply when he said: '. . . no warranty ought to be implied in a contract unless it is in all the circumstances reasonable,' see *Young & Marten Ltd* v. *McManus Childs Ltd* [1969] 1 AC 454, 465: and Lord Upjohn echoed it when he said, at p. 471, that the implied warranty was 'imposed by law'.

Is there a term to be implied in this tenancy about the lifts and staircases and other common parts? . . .

[he considered the case-law and other authorities and concluded]

It is clearly the duty of the landlord, not only to take care to keep the lifts and staircase safe, but also to take care to keep them reasonably fit for the use of the tenant and his visitors. If the lifts break down, the landlord ought to repair them. If the lights on the staircase fail, the landlord ought to replace them.

[he then considered whether or not there had been a breach of the duty and concluded that, on the facts, there had been no breach].

Lord Wilberforce

We have then a contract which is partly, but not wholly, stated in writing. In order to complete it, in particular to give it a bilateral character, it is necessary to take account of the actions of the parties and the circumstances. As actions of the parties, we must note the granting of possession by the landlords and reservation by them of the 'common parts'—stairs, lifts, chutes, etc. As circumstances we must include the nature of the premises, viz., a maisonette for family use on the ninth floor of a high block, one which is occupied by a large number of other tenants, all using the common parts and dependent upon them, none of them having any expressed obligation to maintain or repair them.

To say that the construction of a complete contract out of these elements involves a process of 'implication' may be correct; it would be so if implication means the supplying of what is not expressed. But there are varieties of implications which the courts think fit to make and they do not necessarily involve the same process. Where there is, on the face of it, a complete, bilateral contract, the courts are sometimes willing to add terms to it, as implied terms: this is very common in mercantile contracts where there is an established usage: in that case the courts are spelling out what both parties know and would, if asked, unhesitatingly agree to be part of the bargain. In other cases, where there is an apparently complete bargain, the courts are willing to add a term on the ground that without it the contract will not work—this is the case, if not of *The Moorcock* (1889) 14 PD 64 itself on its facts, at least of the doctrine of *The Moorcock* as usually applied. This is, as was pointed out by the majority in the Court of Appeal, a strict test—though the degree of strictness seems to vary with the current legal trend—and I think that they were right not to accept it as applicable here. There is a third variety of implication, that which I think Lord Denning MR favours, or at least did favour in this case, and that is the implication of reasonable terms. But though I agree with many of his instances, which in fact fall under one or other of the preceding heads, I cannot go so far as to endorse his principle; indeed, it seems to me, with respect, to extend a long, and undesirable, way beyond sound authority.

The present case, in my opinion, represents a fourth category, or I would rather say a fourth shade on a continuous spectrum. The court here is simply concerned to establish what the contract is, the parties not having themselves fully stated the terms. In this sense the court is searching for what must be implied.

What then should this contract be held to be? There must first be implied a letting, that is, a grant of the right of exclusive possession to the tenants. With this there must, I would suppose, be implied a covenant for quiet enjoyment, as a necessary incident of the letting. The difficulty begins when we consider the common parts. We start with the fact that the demise is useless unless access is obtained by the staircase; we can add that, having regard to the height of the block, and the family nature of the dwellings, the demise would be useless without a lift service; we can continue that, there being rubbish chutes built into the structures and no other means of disposing of light rubbish, there must be a right to use the chutes. The question to be answered—and it is the only question in this case—is what is to be the legal relationship between landlord and tenant as regards these matters.

There can be no doubt that there must be implied (i) an easement for the tenants and their licensees to use the stairs, (ii) a right in the nature of an easement to use the lifts, (iii) an easement to use the rubbish chutes.

But are these easements to be accompanied by any obligation upon the landlord, and what obligation? There seem to be two alternatives. The first, for which the council contends, is for an easement coupled with no legal obligation, except such as may arise under the Occupiers' Liability Act 1957 as regards the safety of those using the facilities, and possibly such other liability as might exist under the ordinary law of tort. The alternative is for easements coupled with some obligation on the part of the landlords as regards the maintenance of the subject of them, so that they are available for use.

My Lords, in order to be able to choose between these, it is necessary to define what test is to be applied, and I do not find this difficult. In my opinion such obligation should be read into the contract as the nature of the contract itself implicitly requires, no more, no less: a test, in other words, of necessity. The relationship accepted by the corporation is that of landlord and tenant: the tenant accepts obligations accordingly, in relation inter alia to the stairs, the lifts and the chutes. All these are not just facilities, or conveniences provided at discretion: they are essentials of the tenancy without which life in the dwellings, as a tenant, is not possible. To leave the landlord free of contractual obligation as regards these matters, and subject only to administrative or political pressure, is, in my opinion, inconsistent totally with the nature of this relationship. The subject matter of the lease (high rise blocks) and the relationship created by the tenancy demand, of their nature, some contractual obligation on the landlord.

I do not think that this approach involves any innovation as regards the law of contract. The necessity to have regard to the inherent nature of a contract and of the relationship thereby established was stated in this House in *Lister* v. *Romford Ice and Cold Storage Co Ltd* [1957] AC 555. That was a case between master and servant and of a search for an 'implied term'. Viscount Simonds, at p. 579, makes a clear distinction between a search for an implied term such as might be necessary to give 'business efficacy' to the particular contract and a search, based on wider considerations, for such a term as the nature of the contract might call for, or as a legal incident of this kind of contract. If the search were for the former, he says, '. . . I should lose myself in the attempt to formulate it with the necessary precision'. (p. 576.) We see an echo of this in the present case, when the majority in the Court of Appeal, considering a 'business efficacy term'—i.e., a 'Moorcock' term (*The Moorcock*, 14 PD 64)—found themselves faced with five alternative terms and therefore rejected all of them. But that is not, in my opinion, the end, or indeed the object, of the search.

We have some guidance in authority for the kind of term which this typical relationship (of landlord and tenant in a multi-occupational dwelling) requires in *Miller* v. *Hancock* [1893] 2 QB 177. There Bowen LJ said, at pp. 180–181:

'The tenants could only use their flats by using the staircase. The defendant, therefore, when he let the flats, impliedly granted to the tenants an easement over the staircase, which he retained in his own occupation, for the purpose of the enjoyment of the flats so let. Under those circumstances, what is the law as to the repairs of the staircase? It was contended by the defendant's counsel that, according to the common law, the person in enjoyment of an easement is bound to do the necessary repairs himself. That may be true with regard to easements in general, but it is subject to the qualification that the grantor of the easement may undertake to do the repairs either in express terms or by necessary implication. This is not the mere case of a grant of an easement without special circumstances. It appears to me obvious, when one considers what a flat of this kind is, and the only way in which it can be enjoyed, that the parties to the demise of it must have intended by necessary implication, as a basis without which the whole transaction would be futile, that the landlord should maintain the staircase, which is essential to the enjoyment of the premises demised, and should keep it reasonably safe for the use of the tenants, and also of those persons who would necessarily go up and down the stairs in the ordinary course of business with the tenants; because, of course, a landlord must know when he lets a flat that tradesmen and other persons having business with the tenant must have access to it. It seems to me that it would render the whole transaction inefficacious and absurd if an implied undertaking were not assumed on the part of the landlord to maintain the staircase so far as might be necessary for the reasonable enjoyment of the demised premises.'

Certainly that case, as a decision concerning a claim by a visitor, has been overruled: *Fairman* v. *Perpetual Investment Building Society* [1923] AC 74. But I cite the passage for its common sense as between landlord and tenant, and you cannot overrule common sense.

There are other passages in which the same thought has been expressed . . .

These are all reflections of what necessarily arises whenever a landlord lets portions of a building for multiple occupation, retaining essential means of access.

I accept, of course, the argument that a mere grant of an easement does not carry with it any obligation on the part of the servient owner to maintain the subject matter. The dominant owner must spend the necessary money, for example in repairing a drive leading to his house and the same principle may apply when a landlord lets an upper floor with access by a staircase: responsibility for maintenance may well rest on the tenant. But there is a difference between that case and the case where there is an essential means of access, retained in the landlord's occupation, to units in a building of multi-occupation, for unless the obligation to maintain is, in a defined manner, placed upon the tenants, individually or collectively, the nature of the contract, and the circumstances, require that it be placed on the landlord.

It remains to define the standard. My Lords, if, as I think, the test of the existence of the term is necessity the standard must surely not exceed what is necessary having regard to the circumstances. To imply an absolute obligation to repair would go beyond what is a necessary legal incident and would indeed be unreasonable. An obligation to take reasonable care to keep in reasonable repair and usability is what fits the requirements of the case. Such a definition involves—and I think rightly—recognition that the tenants themselves have their responsibilities. What it is reasonable to expect of a landlord has a clear relation to what a reasonable set of tenants should do for themselves.

I add one word as to lighting. In general I would accept that a grant of an easement of passage does not carry with it an obligation on the grantor to light the way. The grantee must take the way accompanied by the primeval separation of darkness from light and if he passes during the former must bring his own illumination. I think that *Huggett* v. *Miers* [1908] 2 KB 278 was decided on this principle and possibly also *Devine* v. *London Housing Society Ltd* [1950] WN 550. But the case may be different when the means of passage are constructed, and when natural light is either absent or insufficient. In such a case, to the extent that the easement is useless without some artificial light being provided, the grant should carry with it an obligation to take reasonable care to maintain adequate lighting—comparable to the obligation as regards the lifts. To impose an absolute obligation would be unreasonable; to impose some might be necessary. We have not sufficient material before us to see whether the present case on its facts meets these conditions.

I would hold therefore that the landlords' obligation is as I have described and in agreement, I believe, with your Lordships I would hold that it has not been shown in this case that there was any breach of that obligation. On the main point therefore I would hold that the appeal fails.

My Lords, it will be seen that I have reached exactly the same conclusion as that of Lord Denning MR, with most of whose thinking I respectfully agree. I must only differ from the passage in which, more adventurously, he suggests that the courts have power to introduce into contracts any terms they think reasonable or to anticipate legislative recommendations of the Law Commission. A just result can be reached, if I am right, by a less dangerous route.

COMMENTARY

The term sought to be implied into the tenancy agreement was one which related to the obligation of the landlord to keep the common parts of the tower block in repair and properly lit. Two principal issues arose in relation to this term. The first was whether or not such an obligation should be implied into the tenancy agreement at all and the second was, if such a term was to be implied, what was its scope? Was it an obligation to take reasonable care to keep the tower block in repair or was it a stricter obligation? The House of Lords concluded that a term was to be implied, that it required the plaintiffs to exercise reasonable care, and that, on the facts, the plaintiffs had not breached their duty.

Two further points are worthy of note. The first relates to the test to be applied when deciding whether or not to imply a term into the contract. Lord Denning advocated a test based on reasonableness but the House of Lords rejected his analysis. Lord Wilberforce did so in a rather restrained fashion in the final extracted paragraph of his speech. Some of the other judges in the House of Lords were more robust. Thus Lord Salmon stated (at p. 262):

I cannot go so far as Lord Denning MR and hold that the courts have any power to imply a term into a contract merely because it seems reasonable to do so. Indeed, I think that such a proposition is contrary to all authority. To say, as Lord Reid said in *Young & Marten Ltd* v. *McManus Childs Ltd* [1969] 1 AC 454, 465, that '. . . no warranty ought to be implied in a contract unless it is in all the circumstances reasonable' is, in my view, quite different from saying that any warranty or term which is, in all the circumstances, reasonable ought to be implied in a contract. I am confident that Lord Reid meant no more than that unless a warranty or term is in all the circumstances reasonable there can be no question of implying it into a contract, but before it is

implied much else besides is necessary, for example that without it the contract would be inefficacious, futile and absurd.

Lord Edmund-Davies stated (at p. 266) that the 'touchstone is always *necessity* and
not merely *reasonableness*'. The difficulty with the 'necessity' analysis relates to its
application to the facts. Was it really 'necessary' to imply such a term into the tenancy
agreement? The reality would appear to be that the House of Lords was deciding a
matter of social policy in relation to the extent of the obligations that are to be
imposed upon landlords. Are they expected to keep the common parts in repair and
to provide facilities to their tenants? If they are, what is the scope of their duty? Are
they liable even in the case where the problems were caused by vandals who damaged
the lifts and removed the light bulbs from the stairs? It is by no means clear that there
is a 'necessary' answer to these questions. The point has been well made by Professor
Atiyah (*An Introduction to the Law of Contract* (5th edn, Oxford University Press,
1995), p. 207) in the following terms:

the difference in opinion between the judges on this point seems, however, to have been somewhat
unreal. For it is evident that the formula that implications can only be made when necessary is
not to be taken too literally. It is not *necessary* to have lifts in blocks of flats ten storeys high
(indeed high rise buildings existed long before lifts were invented), though it would no doubt be
exceedingly inconvenient not to have them. So 'necessary' really seems to mean 'reasonably
necessary', and that must mean, 'reasonably necessary having regard to the context and the
price'. So in the end there does not seem to be much difference between what is necessary and
what is reasonable.

There is a second aspect to *Liverpool City Council* v. *Irwin* which merits further
consideration and that relates to the question whether the term implied into the
contract was a term implied in law or a term implied in fact. The case is generally
regarded as an authority on terms implied in law, on the basis that the term that the
landlord was under an obligation to take reasonable care to keep the common parts in
repair was to be implied into all tenancy contracts between occupants of flats in tower
blocks and their landlords. It was not a term that was peculiar to the relationship
between this particular landlord and this particular tenant. However it would appear
that counsel for the defendants put his case on two different bases. First, he argued
that such a term ought to be implied into all contracts of this type (in other words, it
was a term implied in law) but he also relied upon the 'officious bystander' test. Lord
Cross of Chelsea rejected (at p. 258) the submission that the term satisfied the 'officious bystander' test but nevertheless agreed (at p. 259) that the term was to be
implied as a general incident of all contracts of this type. Thus Lord Cross seems to
have concluded that a term could not be implied as a matter of fact but that it was
appropriate to imply a term as a matter of law. If this is correct, it demonstrates that
there is a difference between the test to be applied for terms implied in fact and the
test applicable to terms implied in law.

The difficulty is that not all of the judges were as clear as Lord Cross on the
distinction between terms implied in law and terms implied in fact. This point can be
made in relation to Lord Denning's advocacy of the reasonableness test. While he

stated that 'stacks' of cases cannot be reconciled with the necessity test most, if not all of the cases that he cites in support of the proposition that reasonableness is the test applied by the courts, are cases concerned with terms implied in law (that is to say, they are terms that are generally implied into all contracts of a particular type). Indeed, his failure to address the distinction between terms implied in law and terms implied in fact was criticized by Lord Cross of Chelsea (at pp. 257–258) in the following:

When it implies a term in a contract the court is sometimes laying down a general rule that in all contracts of a certain type—sale of goods, master and servant, landlord and tenant and so on—some provision is to be implied unless the parties have expressly excluded it. In deciding whether or not to lay down such a prima facie rule the court will naturally ask itself whether in the general run of such cases the term in question would be one which it would be reasonable to insert. Sometimes, however, there is no question of laying down any prima facie rule applicable to all cases of a defined type but what the court is being in effect asked to do is to rectify a particular— often a very detailed—contract by inserting in it a term which the parties have not expressed. Here it is not enough for the court to say that the suggested term is a reasonable one the presence of which would make the contract a better or fairer one; it must be able to say that the insertion of the term is necessary to give—as it is put—'business efficacy' to the contract and that if its absence had been pointed out at the time both parties—assuming them to have been reasonable men—would have agreed without hesitation to its insertion. The distinction between the two types of case was pointed out by Viscount Simonds and Lord Tucker in their speeches in *Lister* v. *Romford Ice and Cold Storage Co Ltd* [1957] AC 555, 579, 594, but I think that Lord Denning MR in proceeding—albeit with some trepidation—to 'kill off' MacKinnon LJ's 'officious bystander' (*Shirlaw* v. *Southern Foundries (1926) Ltd* [1939] 2 KB 206, 227) must have overlooked it. Counsel for the appellant did not in fact rely on this passage in the speech of Lord Denning.

Evidence in support of the proposition that there was some confusion in the judgments in *Irwin* between terms implied in law and terms implied in fact can be drawn from the judgment of Lord Denning MR in *Shell UK Ltd* v. *Lostock Garage Ltd* [1976] 1 WLR 1187. One of the issues between the parties in that case was whether or not a term was to be implied into a contract between a petrol supplier and a garage owner to the effect that the petrol supplier would not discriminate between different garages in relation to the provision of price support. Lord Denning refused to imply such a term and stated (at pp. 1195–1197):

Implied terms

It was submitted by Mr Kemp on behalf of the garage that there was to be implied in the solus agreement a term that Shell, as the supplier, should not abnormally discriminate against the buyer and/or should supply petrol to the buyer on terms which did not abnormally discriminate against him. He said that Shell had broken that implied term by giving support to the two Shell garages and refusing it to Lostock; that, on that ground, Shell were in breach of the solus agreement; and that Lostock were entitled to terminate it.

This submission makes it necessary once again to consider the law as to implied terms. I ventured with some trepidation to suggest that terms implied by law could be brought within one comprehensive category, in which the courts could imply a term such as was just and reasonable in the circumstances: see *Greaves & Co (Contractors) Ltd* v. *Baynham Meikle & Partners* [1975] 1 WLR 1095, 1099–1100; *Liverpool City Council* v. *Irwin* [1976] QB 319, 331–332. But, as I feared, the House of Lords in *Liverpool City Council* v. *Irwin* [1976] 2 WLR 562 have rejected it as quite unacceptable. As I read the speeches, there are two broad categories of implied terms.

(i) *The first category*

The first category comprehends all those relationships which are of common occurrence, such as the relationship of seller and buyer, owner and hirer, master and servant, landlord and tenant, carrier by land or by sea, contractor for building works, and so forth. In all those relationships the courts have imposed obligations on one party or the other, saying they are implied terms. These obligations are not founded on the intention of the parties, actual or presumed, but on more general considerations: see *Luxor (Eastbourne) Ltd* v. *Cooper* [1941] AC 108, 137 by Lord Wright; *Lister* v. *Romford Ice and Cold Storage Co* [1957] AC 555, 576 by Viscount Simonds, and at p. 594 by Lord Tucker (both of whom give interesting illustrations); and *Liverpool City Council* v. *Irwin* [1976] 2 WLR 562, 571 by Lord Cross of Chelsea and at p. 579 by Lord Edmund-Davis. In such relationships the problem is not solved by asking: what did the parties intend? Or, would they have unhesitatingly agreed to it, if asked? It is to be solved by asking: has the law already defined the obligation or the extent of it? If so, let it be followed. If not, look to see what would be reasonable in the general run of such cases (see by Lord Cross of Chelsea at p. 570H): and then say what the obligation shall be. The House in *Liverpool City Council* v. *Irwin* [1976] 2 WLR 562 went through that very process. They examined the existing law of landlord and tenant, in particular that relating to easements, to see if it contained the solution to the problem; and, having found that it did not, they imposed an obligation on the landlord to use reasonable care. In these relationships the parties can exclude or modify the obligation by express words, but unless they do so, the obligation is a legal incident of the relationship which is attached by the law itself and not by reason of any implied term.

Likewise, in the general law of contract, the legal effect of frustration does not depend on an implied term. It does not depend on the presumed intention of the parties, nor on what they would have answered, if asked, but simply on what the court itself declares to amount to a frustration: see *Davis Contractors Ltd* v. *Fareham Urban District Council* [1956] AC 696, 728 by Lord Radcliffe and *The Eugenia* [1964] 2 QB 226, 238, 239.

(ii) *The second category*

The second category comprehends those cases which are not within the first category. These are cases, not of common occurrence, in which from the particular circumstances a term is to be implied. In these cases the implication is based on an intention imputed to the parties from their actual circumstances: see *Luxor (Eastbourne) Ltd* v. *Cooper* [1941] AC 108, 137 per Lord Wright. Such an imputation is only to be made when it is necessary to imply a term to give efficacy to the contract and make it a workable agreement in such manner as the parties would clearly have done if they had applied their mind to the contingency which has arisen. These are the 'officious bystander' type of case: see *Lister* v. *Romford Ice & Cold Storage Co* [1957] AC 555, 594 per Lord Tucker. In such cases a term is not to be implied on the ground that it would be reasonable, but only when it is necessary and can be formulated with a sufficient degree of precision. This was the test applied by the majority of this court in *Liverpool City Council* v. *Irwin* [1976] QB 319, and they were emphatically upheld by the House on this point; see [1976] 2 WLR 562, 571D–H by Lord Cross of Chelsea; p. 578G–579A by Lord Edmund-Davies.

There is this point to be noted about *Liverpool City Council* v. *Irwin*. In this court the argument was only about an implication in the second category. In the House of Lords that argument was not pursued. It was only the first category.

Into which of the two categories does the present case come? I am tempted to say that a solus agreement between supplier and buyer is of such common occurrence nowadays that it could be put into the first category; so that the law could imply a term based on general considerations. But I do not think this would be found acceptable. Nor do I think the case can be brought within the second category. If Shell had been asked at the beginning: 'Will you agree not to discriminate abnormally against the buyer?' I think they would have declined. It might be a reasonable term, but it is not a necessary term. Nor can it be formulated with sufficient precision. On this point I agree with Kerr J. It should be noticed that in *Esso Petroleum Co Ltd* v. *Harper's Garage (Stourport) Ltd* [1966] 2 QB 514, 536–541 Mocatta J also refused to make such an implication and there was no appeal from his decision. In the circumstances, I do not think any term can be implied.

In this passage Lord Denning affirms that the arguments advanced in *Irwin* encompassed both categories but he suggests that, in the House of Lords, the arguments were confined to the first category. *Shell* v. *Lostock* also demonstrates that it can be difficult to distinguish between the two categories of case. Where the relationship between the parties is one of a particular type but the term that is sought to be implied is, perhaps, an unusual one, does the case fall within category one or category two? In *Shell* it was held that the term fell within neither category so that no term was to be implied.

Where then did the decision of the House of Lords in *Liverpool City Council* v. *Irwin* leave the law? In the first place it re-affirmed that the test to be applied when deciding whether or not to imply a term is based on necessity and not simply on reasonableness. But it left some uncertainty in relation to terms implied in law because the term implied into the tenancy contract did not seem to be a necessary ingredient of all contracts of this type. It might have been 'reasonably necessary' but not 'necessary'. That the test for the implication of terms as a matter of law might be slightly less stringent than that applicable to terms implied in fact is evidenced by the fact that Lord Cross concluded that a term was not to be implied on the basis of the officious bystander test but that it was nevertheless appropriate to imply a term as a matter of law into all contracts of this type.

The Privy Council returned to the test to be applied when deciding whether or not to imply a term into a contract the following year in *BP Refinery (Westernport) Pty Ltd* v. *Shire of Hastings* (1978) ALJR 20. Lord Simon of Glaisdale, giving the judgment of the majority stated (at p. 26):

Their Lordships do not think it necessary to review exhaustively the authorities on the implication of a term in a contract which the parties have not thought fit to express. In their view, for a term to be implied, the following conditions (which may overlap) must be satisfied: (1) it must be reasonable and equitable; (2) it must be necessary to give business efficacy to the contract, so that no term will be implied if the contract is effective without it; (3) it must be so obvious that 'it goes without saying'; (4) it must be capable of close expression; (5) it must not contradict any express term of the contract.

Lord Simon referred to three cases, namely *The Moorcock*, *Reigate* v. *Union Manufacturing Co (Ramsbottom) Ltd* and *Shirlaw* v. *Southern Foundries (1926) Ltd*. No mention was made of *Liverpool City Council* v. *Irwin*. The impression gleaned from the judgment is that this is no more than an amalgamation of the various tests that have been formulated over the years, that it draws in particular on cases concerned with terms implied in fact, and that it makes no attempt to consider whether or not a distinction is to be drawn, in terms of the applicable test, between terms implied in law and terms implied in fact.

The next significant case to come before the House of Lords on implied terms was:

Scally v. Southern Health and Social Services Board

[1992] 1 AC 294, House of Lords

The plaintiffs brought an action against the defendants, their employers, for damages for breach of contract, negligence, and breach of statutory duty in failing adequately to advise and inform them about their contractual and statutory rights in relation to the superannuation[2] scheme of which they were members. In order to qualify for a full pension under the original scheme it was necessary for an employee to complete forty years of contributory service. In 1975 a change was made to the scheme which entitled employees to purchase additional years of contributing service at advantageous rates. However this right was only exercisable within twelve months of the change coming into force. The Department of Health and Social Services were initially given a discretion to extend the twelve-month period but that discretion was taken away in 1983 and replaced by a right given to the employee to purchase added years at any time until two years before an employee's retirement on fixed and progressively less favourable terms.

The defendants failed to inform the plaintiffs of their right to purchase additional years of service at advantageous rates. The plaintiffs alleged that the defendants' failure to do so amounted to a breach of an implied term of the contract of employment, breach of a duty of care owed to the plaintiffs, and a breach of statutory duty. The House of Lords held that the defendants had not breached their statutory duty but that they were in breach of an implied term to take reasonable steps to inform the employees of the existence of their right to take steps to enhance their pension entitlement on advantageous terms. The defendants were therefore liable in damages to the plaintiffs and the case was remitted to the trial judge so that the losses suffered by the plaintiffs could be assessed.

Lord Bridge of Harwich

Leaving aside the claim based on breach of statutory duty . . . it seems to me that the plaintiffs' common law claims can only succeed if the duty allegedly owed to them by their employers arose out of the contract of employment. If a duty of the kind in question was not inherent in the contractual relationship, I do not see how it could possibly be derived from the tort of negligence.

---

[2] A superannuation scheme is a form of pension scheme.

[he quoted from the judgment of Lord Scarman in *Tai Hing Cotton Mill* v. *Liu Chong Hing Bank Ltd* [1986] AC 80, 107 and continued]

In the instant case I believe that an attempt to analyse the issue in terms of the law of tort may be positively misleading. If the question is framed in terms of the law of negligence, it takes the form: did the employers owe a duty of care to employees to save them from economic loss consequent on a failure to purchase added years of pensionable entitlement in due time? The strong trend of recent authority has been to narrow the range of circumstances which the law of tort will recognise as sufficient to impose on one person a duty of care to protect another from damage which consists in purely economic loss . . .

But if the issue is analysed in contract, the starting point is quite different. Here the express terms of the contract of employment confer a valuable right on the employee which is, however, contingent upon his taking certain action. Where that situation is known to the employer but not to the employee, will the law imply a contractual obligation on the employer to take reasonable steps to bring the existence of the contingent right to the notice of the employee? It is true that such an implication may have the consequence of sustaining a claim for purely economic loss. But this consideration would not furnish the essential reason for making the implication. If there is a basis for making the implication, it must lie rather in the consideration that the availability of the contingent right was intended by those who drew up the terms of the contract for the benefit of the employee; but if the existence of the contingent right never comes to his attention, he cannot profit by it and it might, so far as he is concerned, just as well not exist.

The problem is a novel one which could not arise in the classical contractual situation in which all the contractual terms, having been agreed between the parties, must, ex hypothesi, have been known to both parties. But in the modern world it is increasingly common for individuals to enter into contracts, particularly contracts of employment, on complex terms which have been settled in the course of negotiations between representative bodies or organisations and many details of which the individual employee cannot be expected to know unless they are drawn to his attention. The instant case presents an example of this phenomenon arising in the context of the statutory provisions which regulate the operation of the health services in Northern Ireland . . .

[he set out the terms of these statutory provisions, rejected a submission made by the defendants that the obligation to notify the plaintiffs lay with the Department of Health and Social Services and not themselves and continued]

It seems to me beyond question that the legal obligation, if there was one, to notify the plaintiffs of their rights in relation to the purchase of added years rested in each case on the board, not on the department.

Will the law then imply a term in the contract of employment imposing such an obligation on the employer? The implication cannot, of course, be justified as necessary to give business efficacy to the contract of employment as a whole. I think there is force in the submission that, since the employee's entitlement to enhance his pension rights by the purchase of added years is of no effect unless he is aware of it and since he cannot be expected to become aware of it unless it is drawn to his attention, it is necessary to imply an obligation on the employer to bring it to his attention to render efficacious the very benefit which the contractual right to purchase added years was intended to confer. But this may be stretching the doctrine of implication for the sake of business efficacy beyond its proper reach. A clear distinction is drawn in the speeches of Viscount Simonds in *Lister* v. *Romford Ice and Cold Storage Co Ltd* [1957] AC 555 and Lord Wilberforce in *Liverpool City Council* v. *Irwin* [1977] AC 239 between the search for an implied term necessary to give business efficacy to a particular contract and the search, based on wider considerations, for a term which the law will imply as a necessary incident of a definable category of contractual relationship. If any implication is appropriate here, it is, I think, of this latter type. Carswell J accepted the submission that any formulation of an implied term of this kind which would be effective to sustain the plaintiffs' claims in this case must necessarily be too wide in its ambit to be acceptable as of general application. I believe however that this difficulty is surmounted if the category of contractual relationship in which the implication will arise is defined with sufficient precision. I would define it as the relationship of employer and employee where the following circumstances obtain: (1) the terms of the contract of employment have not been negotiated with the individual employee but result from negotiation with a representative body or are otherwise incorporated by reference; (2) a particular term of the contract makes available to the employee a valuable right contingent upon action being taken by him to avail himself of its benefit; (3) the employee cannot, in all the circumstances, reasonably be expected to be aware of the term unless it is drawn to his attention. I fully appreciate that the criterion to justify an implication of this kind is necessity, not reasonableness. But I take the view that it is not merely reasonable, but necessary, in the circumstances postulated, to imply an obligation on the employer to take reasonable steps to bring the term of the contract in question to the employee's attention, so that he may be in a position to enjoy its benefit. Accordingly I would hold that there was an implied term in each of the plaintiffs' contracts of employment of which the boards were in each case in breach.

Lord Roskill, Lord Goff of Chieveley, Lord Jauncey of Tullichettle, and **Lord Lowry** concurred.

COMMENTARY

The implied term, as set out in the last paragraph of the speech of Lord Bridge, is narrowly drawn. As Professor Freedland has pointed out ((1992) 21 *ILJ* 135, 139):

the implied term was confined to the case where a particular term of the contract makes available to the employee a valuable right contingent upon action being taken by him to avail himself of its benefit, and where the employee cannot reasonably be expected to be aware of the term unless it is drawn to his attention. There are few if any other situations where this would occur in an employment context, except when the employee is in the position of an investor, for example in relation to employee share purchase schemes.

While the implied term recognized is narrow in scope, Lord Bridge does acknowledge that it is based 'on wider considerations' than whether the term is 'necessary to give business efficacy to a particular contract'. This being the case, there must be a difference between a term implied in law, at least in the sense of a term that is implied as a 'necessary incident of a definable category of contractual relationship' and a term that is implied as a matter of fact into a particular contractual relationship. That this is so can be demonstrated by reference to the cases concerned with the obligation of 'trust and confidence' that is implied into contracts of employment. The existence of this implied term was approved by the House of Lords in *Mahmud* v. *Bank of Credit and Commerce International SA* [1998] AC 20 where Lord Steyn stated (at pp. 45–46):

The implied term of mutual trust and confidence

The applicants do not rely on a term implied in fact. They do not therefore rely on an individualised term to be implied from the particular provisions of their employment contracts considered against their specific contextual setting. Instead they rely on a standardised term implied by law, that is, on a term which is said to be an incident of all contracts of employment: *Scally* v. *Southern Health and Social Services Board* [1992] 1 AC 294, 307B. Such implied terms operate as default rules. The parties are free to exclude or modify them. But it is common ground that in the present case the particular terms of the contracts of employment of the two applicants could not affect an implied obligation of mutual trust and confidence.

The employee's primary case is based on a formulation of the implied term that has been applied at first instance and in the Court of Appeal. It imposes reciprocal duties on the employer and employee. Given that this case is concerned with alleged obligations of an employer I will concentrate on its effect on the position of employers. For convenience I will set out the term again. It is expressed to impose an obligation that the employer shall not:

> 'without reasonable and proper cause, conduct itself in a manner calculated and likely to destroy or seriously damage the relationship of confidence and trust between employer and employee.'

. . . A useful anthology of the cases applying this term, or something like it, is given in *Sweet & Maxwell's Encyclopedia of Employment Law* (looseleaf ed.), vol. 1, para. 1.5107, pp. 1467–1470. The evolution of the term is a comparatively recent development. The obligation probably has its origin in the general duty of co-operation between contracting parties: *Hepple & O'Higgins, Employment Law*, 4th ed. (1981), pp. 134–135, paras. 291–292. The reason for this development is part of the history of the development of employment law in this century. The notion of a 'master and servant' relationship became obsolete. Lord Slynn of Hadley recently noted 'the changes which have taken place in the employer–employee relationship, with far greater duties imposed on the employer than in the past, whether by statute or by judicial decision, to care for the physical, financial and even psychological welfare of the employee': *Spring* v. *Guardian Assurance plc* [1995] 2 AC 296, 335B. A striking illustration of this change is *Scally's* case [1992] 1 AC 294, to which I have already referred, where the House of Lords implied a term that all employees in a certain category had to be notified by an employer of their entitlement to certain benefits. It was the change in legal culture which made possible the evolution of the implied term of trust and confidence.

There was some debate at the hearing about the possible interaction of the implied obligation of confidence and trust with other more specific terms implied by law. It is true that the implied term adds little to the employee's implied obligations to serve his employer loyally and not to act contrary to his employer's interests. The major importance of the implied duty of trust and confidence lies in its impact on the obligations of the employer: Douglas Brodie, 'Recent Cases, Commentary, The Heart of the Matter: Mutual Trust and Confidence' (1996) 25 ILJ 121. And the implied obligation as formulated is apt to cover the great diversity of situations in which a balance has to be struck between an employer's interest in managing his business as he sees fit and the employee's interest in not being unfairly and improperly exploited.

The evolution of the implied term of trust and confidence is a fact. It has not yet been endorsed by your Lordships' House. It has proved a workable principle in practice. It has not been the subject of adverse criticism in any decided cases and it has been welcomed in academic writings. I regard the emergence of the implied obligation of mutual trust and confidence as a sound development.

In the light of *Scally* and *Mahmud* it seems appropriate to conclude that the test applied by the courts in cases of terms implied in law is not based on necessity alone. It seems to be based on a slightly lower standard which entitles the court to take account of 'wider considerations'. That this is so can be demonstrated by reference to the following two decisions.

The first is the decision of the Court of Appeal in *Paragon Finance plc* v. *Nash* [2001] EWCA Civ 1466; [2002] 1 WLR 685. The claimant made secured loans to the defendants in 1987 and 1990. Both agreements contained variable interest clauses. The claimant claimed possession from the defendants on the ground that the defendants were in arrears with their mortgage payments. The defendants defended the claim on a number of grounds. One of the issues before the Court of Appeal was whether or not the claimant's power to set the interest rates from time to time was completely unfettered. The Court of Appeal held that it was not. A term was to be implied into both agreements to the effect that the rates of interest would not be set dishonestly, for an improper purpose, capriciously or arbitrarily, or in a way in which no reasonable mortgagee, acting reasonably, would do. *Paragon Finance* is a fascinating case because it demonstrates the willingness of the courts in a private law claim to draw on the analogy of public law for the purpose of placing limits on the discretionary power of a contracting party. On what basis did the Court of Appeal see fit to imply this term into the contract? Was it on the basis of necessity? While some limit on the power of the creditor to vary interest rates is clearly highly desirable it is not clear that it can be said to be necessary. Dyson LJ, on the other hand, stated (at para [36]) that the implied term was 'necessary to give effect to the reasonable expectations of the parties'. However it would appear that the driving force behind the recognition of the implied term was the 'reasonable expectations of the parties' (on which see below) rather than necessity.

The second case is the decision of the Court of Appeal in *Crossley* v. *Faithful & Gould Holdings Ltd* [2004] EWCA Civ 293; [2004] 4 All ER 447. The issue before the court was whether or not there was an 'implied term of any contract of employment that the employer will take reasonable care for the economic well-being of his employee'. In answering this question Dyson LJ stated (at [36]):

It seems to me that, rather than focus on the elusive concept of necessity, it is better to recognise that, to some extent at least, the existence and scope of standardised implied terms raise questions of reasonableness, fairness and the balancing of competing policy considerations: see Peden (2001) *LQR* 459, 467–475.

Dyson LJ concluded, after a review of the authorities, that the implied term proposed on behalf of the employee should be rejected. He relied on two principal considerations in reaching this conclusion. First, after referring to *Scally*, he stated that 'it is not for this court to take a big leap to introduce a major extension of the law in this area when only comparatively recently the House of Lords declined to do so'. As we have noted (p. 395 above), the implied term recognized in *Scally* was drawn in very narrow terms and so it was thought to be inappropriate for the Court of Appeal now to imply a term cast in much broader terms. Secondly, he concluded that such an implied term 'would impose an unfair and unreasonable burden on employers'. He continued:

It is one thing to say that, if an employer assumes the responsibility for giving financial advice to his employee, he is under a duty to take reasonable care in giving that advice...It is quite a different matter to impose on an employer the duty to give his employee financial advice in relation to benefits accruing from his employment, or generally to safeguard the employee's economic well-being.

Dyson LJ pointed out that the interests of employers and employees can and do conflict and, in such cases, he stated that it would be 'unreasonable' to require the employer 'to have regard to the employee's financial circumstances when he takes lawful business decisions which may affect the employee's economic welfare'. Further, it was held not be the function of an employer to 'act as his employee's financial adviser' on the ground that it 'is simply not part of the bargain that is comprised in the contract of employment'. This being the case, it was held that there were 'no obvious policy reasons to impose on an employer the general duty to protect his employee's economic well-being'. In this way the conclusion that no term should be implied into the contract of employment obliging the employer to take reasonable care for the economic well-being of an employee was based, not on the need for such a term, but on the appropriateness of the term having regard to the court's perception of the nature of the relationship that exists between an employer and an employee.

While the test applied by the courts in cases of terms implied in law may no longer be based solely on necessity it does not follow that the judges have a free-hand to imply terms into contracts when they see fit. They do not. As Lord Bingham MR observed in *Philips Electronique Grand Publique SA* v. *British Sky Broadcasting Ltd* [1995] EMLR 472, 481, 'it is because the implication of terms is so potentially intrusive that the law imposes strict constraints on the exercise of this extraordinary power'. In the case of terms implied in fact the test is probably still based on necessity and the courts will in general be slow to imply a term into a contract, particularly where the parties have entered into a lengthy and carefully-drafted contract but have failed to make provision for a particular issue. And, while the courts take a less stringent approach in the case of a term implied in law, cases such as *Scally, Mahmud*, and *Paragon Finance* demonstrate that the threshold for the implication of a term remains a high one.

6. CONCLUSION

What is the justification for implying terms into a contract? This issue is considered in the following two extracts. In the first extract Professor Collins considers a range of possible justifications, while in the second extract Lord Steyn, writing extra-judicially, surveys the different categories of implied terms. Interestingly, they reach a similar conclusion, albeit by different routes, namely that the justification for implied terms is to be found in the court's view of the reasonable expectations of the contracting parties.

H Collins, *The Law of Contract*

(4th edn, Butterworths, 2003), pp. 245–246

How can we explain and justify the . . . use of implied terms to supplement contractual obligations? In some instances it is apparent that the reference to the joint intention of the parties, as evidenced by the need to give business efficacy to their transaction, supports the implication of terms on grounds which merely complement the traditional justification of contractual obligations based upon the will of the parties. It is true that the will of the parties was never expressed, but the evidence supporting the claim that the term represents a presupposition or necessary implication of the words used can be so overwhelming that few could doubt that the term represents their original intention. But it is clear that the use of implied terms extends beyond any sort of justification of the type that the term merely states expressly what was silently understood by the parties.

Economic analysis of law suggests a good reason why the courts should provide a set of default rules to govern contractual relations in the absence of express terms. Default rules save transaction costs by permitting the parties to avoid the costs of negotiating every detail of their arrangement every time they make a contract, because they know that the courts will fill in the gaps in the usual way. This makes good sense, but it is arguable whether or not participants in the market deliberately avail themselves of this opportunity to save transaction costs. On the contrary, the proliferation of the standard form contract suggests that any party with sufficient resources is likely to devise a standard set of express terms to suit his or her purposes exactly. Many cases we have discussed so far concerning implied terms, such as . . . *Liverpool City Council* v. *Irwin*, comprise instances where the claim that an implied term exists is used to combat the one-sided standard form contract of the other party.

Nor does the economic analysis suggest a satisfactory account of the grounds for the selection of terms by the courts. Under the efficiency analysis, the court should select those implied terms to which the parties would have agreed but for the presence of transaction costs. Although this criterion makes sense for terms which give a contract business efficacy, it is far from clear that it provides an intelligible guide in other cases. Consider the bargaining situation in *Liverpool City Council* v. *Irwin*. The council was presumably reluctant to agree to an obligation to maintain the common premises, so it would have held out against such an obligation, and, depending upon the local forces of supply and demand for tower block local authority housing, it might or might not have been successful. But even if it had agreed to the obligation, it could have insisted upon an increased rent to cover those costs, so to imply a term requiring a maintenance obligation without adjusting the rent produces a contract to which the parties never would have agreed.

Further this economic analysis does not appear to correspond to the reasons ventured by the courts for the selection of implied terms. What seems to be at the heart of the model reasoning surrounding the implication of terms is the courts' endeavour to structure contracts so that they incorporate a fair and practical allocation of risks. The court imposed the duty to maintain the premises upon Liverpool City Council almost certainly because this was the most practical and efficient means of achieving the result. In the context of the employment relationship, the recent introduction of implied terms which impose obligations upon employers surely reflects changing views about the fair treatment of employees and the risk of losing a job. Similarly, the duty imposed upon professional sellers of goods to ensure that they are of satisfactory quality cannot be justified as the term which would have been agreed in the absence of transaction costs, for sellers would almost certainly seek to avoid such liability for latent defects. The reason for this allocation of risk is surely that it fits both the purpose of consumer protection and it places the risk of defects on the person in the better position to avoid the advent of such risks occurring.

The notion of a default rule is therefore a misleading description of the use of implied terms. Through the implication of terms the courts can achieve what they regard as a fair and practical allocation of risks between the contracting parties, a view which may alter over time as illustrated by the changing implied terms inserted into the contract of employment. In this process the courts can seek to equalise the obligations of the parties, even in the teeth of express terms of standard form contracts, and so pursue ideas of fairness. The justification for implied terms therefore rests ultimately not on the intentions of the parties but rather the court's view of the reasonable expectations of the parties to the transaction.

Lord Steyn, 'Contract Law: Fulfilling the Reasonable Expectations of Honest Men'

(1997) 113 *LQR* 433, 441–442

In systems of law where there is a general duty of good faith in the performance of contracts the need to supplement the written contract by implied terms is less than in the English system. In our system, however, the implication of terms fulfils an important function in promoting the reasonable expectations of parties. Three categories of implied terms can be identified. First, there are terms implied by virtue of the usages of trade and commerce. The assumption is that usages are taken for granted and therefore not spelled out in writing. The recognition of trade usages protects the reasonable expectations of the parties. Secondly, there are terms implied in fact, *i.e.* from the contextual scene of the particular contract. Such implied terms fulfil the role of ad hoc gap fillers. Often the expectations of the parties would be defeated if a term were not implied, *e.g.* sometimes a contract simply will not work unless a particular duty to co-operate is implied. The law has evolved practical tests for the permissibility of such an implication, such as the test of whether the term is necessary to give business efficacy to the contract or the less stringent test whether the conventional bystander, when faced with the problem, would immediately say 'yes, it is obvious that there is such an implied term'. The legal test for the implication of a term is the standard of strict necessity. And it is right that it should be so since courts ought not to supplement a contract by an implication unless it is perfectly obvious that it is necessary to give effect to the reasonable expectations of parties. It is, however, a myth to regard such an implied term as based on an inference of the actual intention of the parties. The reasonable expectations of the parties in an objective sense are controlling: they sometimes demand that such terms be imputed to the parties. The third category is terms implied by law. This occurs when incidents are impliedly annexed to particular forms of contracts, *e.g.* contracts for building work, contracts of sale, hire etc. Such implied terms operate as default rules. By and large such implied terms have crystallised in statute or case law. But there is scope for further development. In such new cases a broader approach than applied in the case of terms implied in fact must necessarily prevail. The proposed implication must fit the generality of cases. Indeed, despite some confusion in the authorities, it is tolerably clear that the court may take into account considerations of reasonableness in laying down the scope of terms to be implied in contracts of common occurrence. This function of the court is essential in providing a reasonable and fair framework for contracting. After all, there are many incidents of contracts of common occurrence which the parties cannot always be expected to reproduce in writing. This type of supplementation of contracts also fulfils an essential function in promoting the reasonable expectations of the parties.

7. FURTHER READING

GOODE, R, 'Usage and its Reception in Transnational Commercial Law' (1997) 46 *ICLQ* 1.

KRAMER, A, 'Implication in Fact as an Instance of Contractual Interpretation' [2004] 63 *CLJ* 384.

PEDEN, E, 'Policy Concerns Behind Implication of Terms in Law' (2001) 117 *LQR* 459.

RAKOFF, T, 'The Implied Terms of Contracts: Of "Default Rules" and "Situation-Sense" ' in BEATSON, J and FRIEDMANN D (eds), *Good Faith and Fault in Contract Law* (Oxford University Press, 1995), p. 191.

11

THE INTERPRETATION OF CONTRACTS

1. CENTRAL ISSUES

1. The principles applicable to the interpretation of contracts were re-stated in 1998 by Lord Hoffmann in *Investors Compensation Scheme Ltd* v. *West Bromwich Building Society*. The aim of this re-statement is, subject to one important exception, to assimilate the way in which contractual documents are interpreted to the common sense principles by which any serious utterance would be interpreted in ordinary life. A major component of this chapter consists of an examination of the principles enunciated by Lord Hoffmann. The significance of these principles should not be under-estimated. Many contract cases that come before the courts raise issues of interpretation.

2. In his speech in *Investors Compensation Scheme* Lord Hoffmann referred to the 'fundamental change' that has taken place in this area of contract law. The essence of the change is that the courts have gradually moved away from a literal approach to interpretation towards an approach that favours the adoption of a 'commercially sensible construction' of the term that is in dispute.

3. Lord Hoffmann's re-statement has aroused a degree of controversy, principally because it is said to generate too much uncertainty and on the ground that it threatens to add to the cost and complexity of litigation.

It is said to generate uncertainty because it widens the circumstances in which the judges can depart from the 'natural and ordinary meaning' of the words used by the parties. In particular, it is no longer necessary for there to be an ambiguity in the words used by the parties before the courts can have regard to the circumstances surrounding the conclusion of the contract. A court that is persuaded that the parties have used the wrong words or syntax is no longer required to attribute to the parties an intention that they did not have. The re-statement has also been criticized on the ground that it will add to the cost and complexity of litigation because it permits the courts to have regard to a very wide range of materials when interpreting contracts (the 'matrix of fact'). The cost of admitting this material in evidence may exceed any benefits derived from its admission.

4. However, there continue to be limits on the evidence to which the courts can have regard when seeking to interpret a contract. Evidence of pre-contractual negotiations and of conduct subsequent to the making of the contract remain generally inadmissible. The reasons for their exclusion will be considered in this chapter. The general exclusionary rule is the subject of some exceptions, albeit their scope remains uncertain.

2. INTRODUCTION

The principles applied by the courts when interpreting contracts are of enormous significance for contracting parties and their lawyers. This is so for a number of reasons. The first is that a significant number of the disputes that come before the courts raise issues of interpretation. The second is that many commercial parties make use of standard terms of business (or use industry-wide standard forms) and the precise meaning of these terms is a matter of considerable importance to them. The third is that many lawyers spend a considerable amount of time drafting contracts and the drafting process must be carried out against the backdrop of the principles applied by the courts to the interpretation of contracts. An example will illustrate the point. Suppose that a client instructs a lawyer to draft an exclusion clause that will have the effect of excluding the client's liability for negligence in the course of the performance of any contract that it concludes. Drafting such a clause is not a straightforward matter because the courts have adopted restrictive principles which are to be applied when interpreting exclusion clauses that purport to exclude liability in negligence (see *Canada Steamship Lines Ltd* v. *The King* [1952] AC 192, discussed in more detail at pp. 449–457 below). The clause must therefore be drafted in the light of these principles and the courts are unlikely to show much sympathy to a commercial party whose lawyer has not complied with them. This view was classically expressed by Hobhouse J in *EE Caledonia Ltd* v. *Orbit Valve Co Europe* [1993] 4 All ER 165, 173 when he said:

it has to be borne in mind that commercial contracts are drafted by parties with access to legal advice and in the context of established legal principles as reflected in the decisions of the courts. Principles of certainty, and indeed justice, require that contracts be construed in accordance with the established principles. The parties are always able by the choice of appropriate language to draft their contract so as to produce a different legal effect. The choice is theirs.

3. THE EVOLUTION FROM LITERALISM TOWARDS CONTEXTUALISM

Traditionally, the English courts adopted a literal approach to the interpretation of contracts. In *Lovell and Christmas Ltd* v. *Wall* (1911) 104 LT 85 Cozens-Hardy MR stated (at p. 88):

If there is one principle more clearly established than another in English law it is surely this: It is for the court to construe a written document. It is irrelevant and improper to ask what the parties, prior to the execution of the instrument, intended or understood. What is the meaning of the language that they have used therein? That is the problem, and the only problem. In saying that, I do not mean to assert that no evidence can be admitted. Indeed, the contrary is clear. If a deed relates to Black Acre, you may have evidence to show what are the parcels. If a document is in a foreign language, you may have an interpreter. If it contains technical terms, an expert may explain them. If, according to the custom of a trade or the usage of the market, a word has acquired a secondary meaning, evidence may be given to prove it. A well-known instance is where in a particular trade 1000 rabbits meant 1200. But unless the case can be brought within some or one of these exceptions, it is the duty of the court, which is presumed to understand the English language, to construe the document according to the ordinary grammatical meaning of the words used therein, and without reference to anything which has previously passed between the parties to it. When we come to the question of rectification,[1] wholly different considerations apply. The essence of rectification is to bring the document which was expressed and intended to be in pursuance of a prior agreement into harmony with that prior agreement.

The meaning of a document was therefore to be found within its four corners. This approach was not without its merits. A court that was called upon to interpret a contract did not have to listen to evidence about the commercial purpose of the clause or the circumstances surrounding the conclusion of the contract. Its task was to rule on the meaning of the words used by the parties and it could do that on the basis of the documents alone. It was therefore possible for the parties to obtain a quick and relatively inexpensive ruling on the meaning of a disputed term in a contract. However the drawbacks of this approach have been deemed to exceed its merits. In particular, it was argued that it was unrealistic to engage in a process of interpretation that was divorced from the context in which the parties found themselves. In other contexts, such as the interpretation of statutes, there has been a shift from 'a literalist to a purposive approach' to interpretation (see the dissenting speech of Lord Steyn in *Deutsche Genossenschaftsbank* v. *Burnhope* [1995] 1 WLR 1580, 1589) and this shift in emphasis has penetrated into the interpretation of contractual documents.

In retrospect the turning point can be seen to be the decision of the House of Lords in *Prenn* v. *Simmonds* [1971] 1 WLR 1381. The dispute between the parties related to the meaning of the word 'profit' in an agreement concluded under seal on 6 July 1960. Lord Wilberforce, giving the only reasoned judgment in the House of Lords, stated (at pp. 1383–1384):

> In order for the agreement of July 6, 1960, to be understood, it must be placed in its context. The time has long passed when agreements, even those under seal, were isolated from the matrix of facts in which they were set and interpreted purely on internal linguistic considerations. There is no need to appeal here to any modern, anti-literalist tendencies, for Lord Blackburn's well-known judgment in *River Wear Commissioners* v. *Adamson* (1877) 2 App Cas 743, 763 provides ample warrant for a liberal approach. We must, as he said, inquire beyond the language and see what the circumstances were with reference to which the words were used, and the object, appearing from those circumstances, which the person using them had in view. Moreover, at any rate since 1859 (*Macdonald* v. *Longbottom* 1 E & E 977) it has been clear enough that evidence of mutually known facts may be admitted to identify the meaning of a descriptive term.

The change in emphasis is clearly discernible. Contract documents are no longer to be interpreted 'purely' on internal linguistic considerations. Rather, they are to be placed in their 'context'. In other words, the court must have regard to the wider circumstances surrounding the conclusion of the contract. Lord Wilberforce returned to the

---

[1] Rectification is discussed in more detail at pp. 646–650 below. Rectification only comes into play once the meaning of the words used by the parties has been ascertained. A contract can be rectified if there has been a defect in the recording of the contract so that the written agreement does not reflect the agreement which the parties intended to make. In such a case it may be possible for a court to rectify the document so as to bring it into line with the intention of the parties. One reason why rectification has always been treated differently in the context of interpretation of contracts is that the court can have regard to a wider range of materials in a rectification case than it can in a case concerned solely with the interpretation of the contract. In particular, the court can have regard to pre-contractual negotiations in a rectification case, on which see pp. 416–417 below.

issue in *Reardon Smith Line Ltd* v. *Yngvar Hansen-Tangen* [1976] 1 WLR 989, 995–997 when he said:

No contracts are made in a vacuum: there is always a setting in which they have to be placed. The nature of what is legitimate to have regard to is usually described as 'the surrounding circumstances' but this phrase is imprecise: it can be illustrated but hardly defined. In a commercial contract it is certainly right that the court should know the commercial purpose of the contract and this in turn presupposes knowledge of the genesis of the transaction, the background, the context, the market in which the parties are operating . . .

It is often said that, in order to be admissible in aid of construction, these extrinsic facts must be within the knowledge of both parties to the contract, but this requirement should not be stated in too narrow a sense. When one speaks of the intention of the parties to the contract, one is speaking objectively—the parties cannot themselves give direct evidence of what their intention was—and what must be ascertained is what is to be taken as the intention which reasonable people would have had if placed in the situation of the parties. Similarly when one is speaking of aim, or object, or commercial purpose, one is speaking objectively of what reasonable persons would have in mind in the situation of the parties . . . [w]hat the court must do must be to place itself in thought in the same factual matrix as that in which the parties were.

4. LORD HOFFMANN'S RE-STATEMENT

The shift from a literal to a contextual approach to the interpretation of contracts, evident in the speeches of Lord Wilberforce in *Prenn* and *Reardon Smith*, culminated in the speech of Lord Hoffmann in *Investors Compensation Scheme Ltd* v. *West Bromwich Building Society* [1998] 1 WLR 896 in which he sought to re-state the principles according to which contractual documents are to be interpreted. He set out these principles in the following terms (at pp. 912–913):

My Lords . . . I should preface my explanation of my reasons with some general remarks about the principles by which contractual documents are nowadays construed. I do not think that the fundamental change which has overtaken this branch of the law, particularly as a result of the speeches of Lord Wilberforce in *Prenn* v. *Simmonds*, [1971] 1 WLR 1381 at 1384–1386 and *Reardon Smith Line Ltd* v. *Hansen-Tangen, Hansen-Tangen* v. *Sanko Steamship Co* [1976] 1 WLR 989, is always sufficiently appreciated. The result has been, subject to one important exception, to assimilate the way in which such documents are interpreted by judges to the common sense principles by which any serious utterance would be interpreted in ordinary life. Almost all the old intellectual baggage of 'legal' interpretation has been discarded. The principles may be summarised as follows.

(1) Interpretation is the ascertainment of the meaning which the document would convey to a reasonable person having all the background knowledge which would reasonably have been available to the parties in the situation in which they were at the time of the contract.

(2) The background was famously referred to by Lord Wilberforce as the 'matrix of fact', but this phrase is, if anything, an understated description of what the background may include. Subject to the requirement that it should have been reasonably available to the parties and to the exception to be mentioned next, it includes absolutely anything which would have affected the way in which the language of the document would have been understood by a reasonable man.

(3) The law excludes from the admissible background the previous negotiations of the parties and their declarations of subjective intent. They are admissible only in an action for rectification. The law makes this distinction for reasons of practical policy and, in this respect only, legal interpretation differs from the way we would interpret utterances in ordinary life. The boundaries of this exception are in some respects unclear. But this is not the occasion on which to explore them.

(4) The meaning which a document (or any other utterance) would convey to a reasonable man is not the same thing as the meaning of its words. The meaning of words is a matter of dictionaries and grammars; the meaning of the document is what the parties using those words against the relevant background would reasonably have been understood to mean. The background may not merely enable the reasonable man to choose between the possible meanings of words which are ambiguous but even (as occasionally happens in ordinary life) to conclude that the parties must, for whatever reason, have used the wrong words or syntax (see *Mannai Investment Co Ltd* v. *Eagle Star Life Assurance Co Ltd* [1997] 2 WLR 945).

(5) The 'rule' that words should be given their 'natural and ordinary meaning' reflects the commonsense proposition that we do not easily accept that people have made linguistic mistakes, particularly in formal documents. On the other hand, if one would nevertheless conclude from the background that something must have gone wrong with the language, the law does not require judges to attribute to the parties an intention which they plainly could not have had. Lord Diplock made this point more vigorously when he said in *Antaios Cia Naviera SA* v. *Salen Rederierna AB, The Antaios* [1985] AC 191 at 201:

'. . . if detailed semantic and syntactical analysis of words in a commercial contract is going to lead to a conclusion that flouts business common sense, it must be made to yield to business common sense.'

On its facts, *Investors Compensation Scheme* was a case concerned with the construction of a claim form. Investors submitted a claim to the Investors Compensation Scheme Ltd ('ICS') for compensation in respect of negligent advice given to them by brokers who had sold them home income plans in contravention of the provisions of the Financial Services Act 1986. The plans proved to be a disastrous investment and rendered the investors' homes vulnerable to re-possession by the building societies to whom the investors had mortgaged their homes as part of the home income plan. The building society involved in this particular case was the West Bromwich Building Society (referred to in the speech of Lord Hoffmann as 'WBBS'). The claim form was drafted by ICS and it required the investors to assign to ICS all their rights arising out of the sale to them of the home income plans. However the claim form, in section 3(b) expressly excluded from the assignment

any claim (whether sounding in rescission for undue influence or otherwise) that you [the investor] may have against [the building society] in which you claim an abatement of sums which you would otherwise have to pay to that Society in respect of sums borrowed by you from that Society in connection with the transaction and dealings giving rise to the claim.

The investors subsequently brought proceedings against the West Bromwich Building Society seeking damages for negligence and misrepresentation and the rescission of their mortgages. ICS also instituted proceedings against the building society in which it asserted that the investors had assigned to it all their claims, with the exception of their claims for rescission. The claims brought by the investors and ICS against the building society therefore overlapped. The issue of interpretation that arose between the parties related to the construction of the claim form, in particular the scope of the provisions relating to the assignment of the investors' rights against the building society.

Applying his principles to the facts of the case, Lord Hoffmann concluded that all claims for damages and compensation had been validly assigned to ICS (so that ICS and not the investors could bring a claim for damages) but that the investors had retained the right to claim rescission of the mortgages. Thus he concluded that the phrase 'Any claim (whether sounding in rescission for undue influence or otherwise)' was actually used by the parties to mean 'Any claim sounding in rescission (whether for undue influence or otherwise)'. In this respect he approved of the analysis of the trial judge, Evans-Lombe J. In the Court of Appeal Leggatt LJ had rejected the reasoning of Evans-Lombe J on the basis that it was 'not an available meaning of the words'. Lord Hoffmann approved the reasoning of Evans-Lombe J in the following terms:

If one applies these principles [that is, the five principles set out above], it seems to me that the judge must be right and, as we are dealing with one badly drafted clause which is happily no longer in use, there is little advantage in my repeating his reasons at greater length. The only remark of his which I would respectfully question is when he said that he was 'doing violence' to the natural meaning of the words. This is an over-energetic way to describe the process of interpretation. Many people, including politicians, celebrities and Mrs Malaprop, mangle meanings and syntax but nevertheless communicate tolerably clearly what they are using the words to mean. If anyone is doing violence to natural meanings, it is they rather than their listeners.

I shall, however, make four points supplemental to those of the learned judge. First, the claim form was obviously intended to be read by lawyers and the explanatory note by laymen. It is the terms of the claim form which govern the legal relationship between the parties. But in construing the form, I think that one should start with the assumption that a layman who read the explanatory note and did not venture into the claim form itself was being given an accurate account of the effect of the transaction. It is therefore significant that paragraph 4 of the note says categorically and without qualification that the investor gives up all his rights against anyone else and transfers them to the ICS. If the effect of the claim form was that the investor retained his claim against the building society, paragraph 4 of the note was very misleading. Secondly, this leads to the conclusion that section 3(b) was intended only to deal with the possibility that a lawyer might argue that some right was a 'claim' when it would not be regarded as a claim by a layman. This is a fair description of the possibility of a reduction of the mortgage debt as part of the equitable taking of accounts upon rescission, which would not result in the investor receiving any money but merely having to pay less to WBBS. Thirdly, any lawyer would think it extremely odd for the ICS to take an assignment of the investor's claim for damages against the solicitors and leave the investor with a claim for the same damages against WBBS. He would be likely to wonder whether this was conceptually possible and, as I shall explain, I think that his doubts would be well founded. The investor and the ICS could not between them recover more than the loss which the investor had actually suffered. As a matter of common sense, one would therefore expect that the ICS either had a right to the damages or it did not. It would seem eccentric to leave this question to be decided (if such a thing were possible) by a race to judgment. Fourthly, no lawyer in his right mind who intended simply to say that all claims against the WBBS were reserved to the investor would have used the parenthesis. Nor, unless he intended to limit the reservation to the amount, if any, which happened to be outstanding on the mortgage, would he have described them as claims 'in which you claim an abatement of the sums which you would otherwise have to repay'. And it is difficult to think of any reason for such an arbitrary limitation.

Finally, on this part of the case, I must make some comments upon the judgment of the Court of Appeal. Leggatt LJ said that his construction was 'the natural and ordinary meaning of the words used'. I do not think that the concept of natural and ordinary meaning is very helpful when, on any view, the words have not been used in a natural and ordinary way. In a case like this, the court is inevitably engaged in choosing between competing unnatural meanings. Secondly, Leggatt LJ said that the judge's construction was not an 'available meaning' of the words. If this means that judges cannot, short of rectification, decide that the parties must have made mistakes of meaning or syntax, I respectfully think he was wrong. The proposition is not, I would suggest, borne out by his citation from Alice Through the Looking Glass. Alice and Humpty Dumpty were agreed that the word 'glory' did not mean 'a nice knock-down argument'. Anyone with a dictionary could see that. Humpty Dumpty's point was that 'a nice knock-down argument' was what he meant by using the word 'glory'. He very fairly acknowledged that Alice, as a reasonable young woman, could not have realised this until he told her, but once he had told her, or if, without being expressly told, she could have inferred it from the background, she would have had no difficulty in understanding what he meant.

Lord Lloyd dissented and he did so in robust terms. He stated (at p. 904) that he knew of 'no principle of construction' which enabled a court 'to take words from within the brackets, where they are clearly intended to underline the width of "any claim", and place them outside the brackets where they have the exact opposite effect'. What the parties meant was to be derived from the words they had used. He continued:

purposive interpretation of a contract is a useful tool where the purpose can be identified with reasonable certainty. But creative interpretation is another thing altogether. The one must not be allowed to shade into the other.

We shall return to Lord Lloyd's speech in the final section of this chapter, which is devoted to an evaluation of the relevant advantages and disadvantages of the modern approach to the interpretation of contracts. Before we do that, it is important to ascertain the scope of the principles set out by Lord Hoffmann.

5. THE SCOPE OF LORD HOFFMANN'S PRINCIPLES

Lord Hoffmann's re-statement merits careful evaluation. The re-statement can be broken down into six units consisting of the first paragraph extracted above (p. 407) followed by the five principles which he identifies.

(a) REVOLUTIONS, DISCARDING THE 'OLD BAGGAGE', AND THE ROLE OF PRECEDENT

Three principal points can be deduced from the first paragraph of Lord Hoffmann's re-statement. The first is that it does not purport to be revolutionary. Rather, it attempts to build on the principles established by Lord Wilberforce in *Prenn* v.

Simmonds and *Reardon Smith Line Ltd* v. *Hansen-Tangen.* While it is true that Lord Hoffmann notes that there has been a 'fundamental change' in the applicable legal principles, he attributes that change to Lord Wilberforce and not to himself. Indeed in *New Hampshire Insurance Co* v. *Philips Electronics North America Corporation (No 2)* [1999] LRLR 66, 70 Clarke J stated that, in his view, Lord Hoffmann had not 'intended to alter the principles of construction which have been developed in recent years'. His speech is therefore perceived as an affirmation of a change that had already taken place, rather than as an initiator of change. The law thus appears to be in a process of evolution rather than revolution. It is evolving slowly both in relation to the range of materials which the court is willing to admit into evidence and in relation to the extent to which it is prepared to depart from the literal meaning of the words used by the parties and adopt a construction which leads to a commercially sensible construction.

The second point relates to the significance of Lord Hoffmann's phrase that 'almost all the old intellectual baggage of "legal" interpretation has been discarded'. At first sight this does not appear to be a particularly significant statement. But first appearances can deceive. Its true significance was explained by Lord Hoffmann in *Bank of Credit and Commerce International SA* v. *Ali* [2001] UKHL 8; [2002] 1 AC 251 (see further pp. 412–413 below) when he explained that the baggage that had been discarded included the 'artificial rules' relating to the construction of exemption (or exclusion) clauses. After referring to the judgments of Lord Denning in *George Mitchell (Chesterhall) Ltd* v. *Finney Lock Seeds Ltd* [1983] QB 284, 296–297 and Lord Wilberforce in *Photo Production Ltd* v. *Securicor Transport Ltd* [1980] AC 827, 843 Lord Hoffmann concluded (at para [62]) that

the disappearance of artificial rules for the construction of exemption clauses seems to me in accordance with the general trend in matters of construction which has been to try to assimilate judicial techniques of construction to those which would be used by a reasonable speaker of the language in the interpretation of any serious utterance in ordinary life.

As we shall see (pp. 446–460 below), matters are not quite so straightforward. Some of the cases concerned with the interpretation of exemption clauses, in particular the line of cases represented by the decision of the Privy Council in *Canada Steamship Lines Ltd* v. *The King* [1952] AC 192 (on which see pp. 449–457 below), have been approved on a number of occasions both by the Court of Appeal and by the House of Lords. These cases are too well entrenched to be uprooted by a passing remark of Lord Hoffmann in the House of Lords. Nevertheless, cases can be found in which the courts have applied the principles set out in *Investors Compensation Scheme* to the interpretation of exemption clauses (see, for example, *British Fermentation Products Ltd* v. *Compair Reavell Ltd* [1999] BLR 352 and *National Westminster Bank* v. *Utrecht-America Finance Company* [2001] EWCA Civ 658; [2001] 3 All ER 733). The result is a degree of uncertainty in the law. Many of the old cases in which a restrictive approach was adopted towards the interpretation of an exemption clause have not been overruled but the likelihood of their long-term survival seems rather low. They cannot survive the drift towards the assimilation of the way in which contractual documents are interpreted by judges to the common sense principles by which any serious utterance would be interpreted in ordinary life.

This takes us to the third point, which is the impact of Lord Hoffmann's re-statement on cases decided prior to it and, more generally, the role of precedent in cases concerned with the interpretation of contracts. What impact does Lord Hoffmann's re-statement have on previous case-law? In *NLA Group Ltd* v. *Bowers* [1999] 1 Lloyd's Rep 109 Timothy Walker J stated (at p. 112) that 'Lord Hoffmann was simply overruling old and outdated cases by reference to an approach on construction which has been followed in the Commercial Court for many years'. The obvious difficulty is that neither Lord Hoffmann nor Timothy Walker J make clear which 'old and outdated cases' have in fact been overruled.

This lack of clarity may not be of great significance if the precedent value of a case concerned with the interpretation of a contract is low. If it is, then courts will be able to free themselves from the dead-hand of the old cases with relative ease. There is authority to support the proposition that cases concerned with the interpretation of contracts have very little value as precedents. Thus in *Surrey Heath Borough Council* v. *Lovell Construction Ltd* (1990) 48 Build LR 113 Dillon LJ stated (at p. 118) that 'a decision on a different clause in a different context is seldom of much help on a question of construction'. Further, in *Midland Bank plc* v. *Cox McQueen* [1999] 1 FLR 1002 Mummery LJ stated (at p. 1012):

Detailed comparisons of one document with another and of one precedent with another do not usually help the court to reach a decision on construction. Indeed, that exercise occupies a disproportionate amount of valuable time which would be better spent on the arguments that really count: those which focus on the precise terms of the relevant documents and the illuminating environment of the transaction.

However, the authorities are not all one way. A rather different approach was taken by the House of Lords in *Bank of Credit and Commerce International SA* v. *Ali* [2001] UKHL 8; [2002] 1 AC 251. The case concerned the interpretation of a release that was drafted in the following terms:

The applicant agrees to accept the terms set out in the documents attached in full and final settlement of all or any claims whether under statute, common law or equity of whatsoever nature that exist or may exist and, in particular, all or any claims, rights or applications of whatsoever nature that the applicant has or may have or has made or could make on or to the industrial tribunal, except the applicant's rights under [the bank's] pension scheme.

Such clauses are generally used when parties settle or compromise a dispute. The aim of the clause is to draw a line under the dispute. As Lord Nicholls stated (at para [22]) the parties want 'to wipe the slate clean'. The particular issue that arose in *Ali* was whether or not the release was effective to exclude a claim, the existence of which neither party could have been aware at the time of entry into the release. At first sight, the clause does appear to be effective to encompass such a claim. It is drafted in wide terms. As Lord Hoffmann noted (at para [38]):

the draftsman meant business. He has gone to some trouble to avoid leaving anything out. He uses traditional style: pairs of words like 'full and final settlement', 'all or any claims', 'that exist or may exist' and phrases like 'whether under statute, Common law or in Equity' and 'of whatsoever nature'.

But the majority held that the clause was not effective to exclude unknown claims. In reaching this conclusion the majority placed considerable emphasis on a line of cases going back to the eighteenth century. While Lord Bingham accepted (at para [17]) that 'the authorities must be read in the context of their peculiar facts', he nevertheless had regard to them for the purpose of establishing the principle that the courts are reluctant to infer that a party intended to give up something which neither he, nor the other party, knew or could have known that he had. Lord Hoffmann dissented. He adopted a stance similar to that taken by Dillon LJ and Mummery LJ (above). He asked (at para [51]):

If interpretation is the quest to discover what a reasonable man would have understood specific parties to have meant by the use of specific language in a specific situation at a specific time and place, how can that be affected by authority? How can the question of what a reasonable man in 1990 would have thought BCCI and Mr Naeem meant by using the language of an ACAS form be answered by examining what Lord Keeper Henley said in 1758 . . . ? I can understand that if parties in a legal context use words in what appears to have been a technical sense, it may be necessary to ascertain that technical meaning from authorities. But there is nothing of that kind here.

There is much to be said for the approach of Lord Hoffmann. The authorities are obviously important in the situation where parties have chosen to use words that have acquired an established technical meaning. In such a case the courts are likely to give the words the meaning that they have been given in the case-law. Thus in *British Sugar plc* v. *NEI Power Projects Ltd* (1997) 87 BLR 42, 50 Waller LJ stated, when considering the meaning of the words 'consequential loss', that

once a phrase has been authoritatively construed by a court in a very similar context to that which exists in the case in point, it seems to me that a reasonable businessman must more naturally be taken to be having the intention that the phrase should bear the same meaning as construed in the case in point. It would again take very clear words to allow a court to construe the phrase differently.

However Lord Hoffmann's approach did not commend itself to the majority. They were prepared to have regard to the precedents for a wider range of purposes than simply to ascertain the technical meaning of the words used by the parties. In particular, they were able to deduce from the cases a 'cautionary principle' that 'in the absence of clear language, the court will be very slow to infer that a party intended to surrender rights and claims of which he was unaware and could not have been aware' (see paras [10] and [22]). It is important to note that the latter principle is stated at a fairly high level of abstraction. It may therefore be that the courts can deduce broad principles of general application from the case-law but that the precedents themselves are unlikely to shed much light on detailed points of construction that arise in individual cases. In the latter context, the approach of Mummery LJ in *Midland Bank plc* v. *Cox McQueen* (above) is likely to prevail, namely that the authorities are unlikely to be of much assistance to the courts.

(b) THE OBJECTIVE NATURE OF THE TEST

Lord Hoffmann's first principle is, or appears to be, relatively uncontroversial. It emphasizes the objective nature of the test applied by the courts. The 'methodology' of the common law is 'not to probe the real intentions of the parties but to ascertain the contextual meaning of the relevant contractual language. Intention is determined by reference to expressed rather than actual intention' (per Lord Steyn in *Deutsche Genossenschaftsbank* v. *Burnhope* [1995] 1 WLR 1580, 1587). This principle has been cited on a number of occasions by the judges but it does not seem to have given rise to any difficulty. The judges have understood it as an affirmation of the traditional, objective approach to the interpretation of contracts.

(c) THE 'FACTUAL MATRIX'

Lord Hoffmann's second principle has proved to be more controversial. It is the breadth of his principle that has attracted criticism. The use of the language of 'matrix of fact' can be traced back to the speech of Lord Wilberforce in *Prenn* v. *Simmonds* [1971] 1 WLR 1381. However its use has been attacked, in particular by Sir Christopher Staughton who was, until recently, a judge in the Court of Appeal (see 'How Do the Courts Interpret Commercial Contracts?' [1999] *CLJ* 303, 306–308 and his judgment in *Scottish Power plc* v. *Britoil (Exploration) Ltd, The Times*, 2 December 1997, referred to at p. 423 below). He has criticized the use of language such as 'the matrix of fact' on the ground that 'counsel have wildly different ideas as to what a matrix is and what it includes'. Particularly difficult was the use by Lord Hoffmann of the words 'absolutely anything' which appeared to encourage lawyers to trawl through all the documentation relating to the transaction and then seek to introduce it all in evidence as part of the 'matrix of fact'. Lord Hoffmann has now qualified his second principle. In *Bank of Credit and Commerce International* v. *Ali* [2001] UKHL 8; [2002] 1 AC 251 he stated (at para [39]) that:

> I did not think it necessary to emphasise that I meant anything which a reasonable man would have regarded as *relevant*. I was merely saying that there is no conceptual limit to what can be regarded as background. It is not, for example, confined to the factual background but can include the state of the law (as in cases in which one takes into account that the parties are unlikely to have intended to agree to something unlawful or legally ineffective) or proved common assumptions which were in fact quite mistaken . . . I was certainly not encouraging a trawl through 'background' which could not have made a reasonable person think that the parties must have departed from conventional usage.

This qualification is very limited in its scope. It does not purport to fix a formal limit to the scope of the 'factual matrix'. Rather, it attempts to send a message out to the legal community that they should resist the temptation to swamp the court with evidence of dubious value. Counsel have sometimes been guilty of giving in to this temptation. In *NLA Group Ltd* v. *Bowers* [1999] 1 Lloyd's Rep 109 the issue between the parties was stated to be a 'short point of construction of a few words'. Nevertheless, counsel for the plaintiff 'originally had in mind to adduce the factual evidence of no fewer than five witnesses, with subpoenas served on two further witnesses' together with an expert's report. Timothy Walker J decided the point of construction against the plaintiff and stated (at p. 113) that the decision to attempt to adduce this amount of evidence was 'wholly unreasonable'. Judges can to some extent control these excesses by an award of costs and this was the course of action taken by Timothy Walker J. *NLA Group Ltd* v. *Bowers* was decided soon after Lord Hoffmann's restatement, at a time when they were still bedding down. Now that it is more firmly established, there is little evidence that the judges have experienced difficulty in ascertaining what does and what does not fall within the 'matrix of fact' or in restraining the excesses of counsel. The point was well put by Arden LJ in *Static Control Components (Europe) Ltd* v. *Egan* [2004] EWCA Civ 392; [2004] 2 Lloyd's Rep 429 when she stated:

When the principles in the *ICS* case were first enunciated, there were fears that the courts would on simple questions of the construction of deeds and documents be inundated with background material. Lord Hoffmann recognised this risk by emphasising in *BCCI* v. *Ali* [2002] 1 AC 251 at 269 that his reference to 'absolutely anything' in his second proposition was to anything that a reasonable man would have regarded as relevant. Speaking for myself, I am not aware that the fears expressed as to the opening of floodgates have been realised. The powers of case management in the Civil Procedure Rules could obviously be used to keep evidence within its proper bounds. The important point is that the principles in the *ICS* case lead to a more principled and fairer result by focusing on the meaning which the relevant background objectively assessed indicates that the parties intended.

To the extent that uncertainty persists it would appear to relate to the weight to be given to the evidence once it has been admitted rather than to the decision whether to admit the evidence or not.

(d) THE EXCLUSIONARY RULES

Lord Hoffmann's third principle is his exception to the rule that documents are to be interpreted in accordance with the common sense principles by which any serious utterance would be interpreted in ordinary life. It is a principle that declares certain types of evidence to be inadmissible. In so far as it states that 'declarations of subjective intent' are inadmissible it has not given rise to debate. The first principle establishes that the test to be applied by the court is an objective one and so the exclusion of statements of subjective intent does not occasion surprise. More difficult is the exclusion of 'previous negotiations'. Lord Hoffmann, while he recognized the existence of only one exception to this exclusionary rule (namely rectification), acknowledged that the boundaries of this exclusion are 'in some respects unclear'. In *Bank of Credit and Commerce International* v. *Ali* [2001] UKHL 8; [2002] 1 AC 251 Lord Nicholls noted the debate on this issue and stated (at para [31]) that he wished 'to keep the point open for careful consideration on a future occasion'.

The issue of the admissibility of pre-contractual negotiations has in fact arisen in a number of cases post-*Investors Compensation Scheme*. The courts have usually been content to affirm the general exclusionary rule. The issue was considered by the Privy

Council, on appeal from the Court of Appeal of New Zealand, in *Canterbury Golf International Ltd* v. *Yoshimoto* [2002] UKPC 40. The judgment of the Privy Council was delivered by Lord Hoffmann. In the Court of Appeal of New Zealand Thomas J had expressed the view that his construction of the contract was supported by two provisions in earlier drafts of the contract and he further stated that the rule that excluded evidence of pre-contractual negotiations should be departed from or relaxed. In the Privy Council Lord Hoffmann stated that the case did not provide a 'suitable occasion' for a re-examination of the law in relation to the admissibility of pre-contractual negotiations because, on the facts, the evidence of the pre-contractual negotiations was 'unhelpful'. He stated [at para [28]) that:

Their Lordships do not think that it is helpful to try to construe the earlier version of clause 6.3 because it was dropped and the present clause 6.3 substituted. It seems to them pointless to try to speculate upon why the change was made. No doubt each party had their reasons for proposing it on the one hand and accepting it on the other. All a court can do is decide what the final contract means.

Why does the law generally declare inadmissible evidence of pre-contractual negotiations? A number of possible reasons can be given. The first is that the test to be applied by the courts when seeking to ascertain the meaning of a term in a contract is objective, not subjective. This being the case, the courts should not concern themselves with subjective statements by either party as to the meaning to be ascribed to a particular term. The law does not wish to encourage parties to make self-serving statements in the course of negotiations and then produce them in evidence when a dispute breaks out in relation to the meaning of that particular term. Secondly, it is claimed that evidence of pre-contractual negotiations is not helpful on the basis that the parties' positions are in a state of flux pending the conclusion of the contract and the court should not be asked to speculate upon the reasons that led the parties to make changes to the various drafts that were produced before agreement was finally reached. The task of the court is to ascertain the meaning of the contract, not the process that led up to the formation of the contract. It was this justification that was invoked by the Privy Council in *Canterbury Golf International Ltd* v. *Yoshimoto*. But the arguments are not all one way. In the first place it can be argued that the second objection is one that relates to the weight to be given to the evidence, not its admissibility. While it may be the case that evidence of pre-contractual negotiations will, in many cases, be 'unhelpful' this should not prevent it being admissible in those cases in which it is helpful. Secondly, in so far as the courts state that they seek to adopt an interpretation that is commercially sensible (on which see p. 420 below), the pre-contractual negotiations may provide very good evidence of the commercial aims of the parties, in the sense that they will provide evidence of what the parties were bargaining about and where the conflicts between them arose.

The exclusion of pre-contractual negotiations is not, however, absolute. Where there is an ambiguity in the final written document, evidence of pre-contractual negotiations may be admissible to show that the parties had attached a particular meaning to that phrase (*The Karen Oltman* [1976] 2 Lloyd's Rep 708). Similarly, as

Lord Hoffmann acknowledged, such evidence is admissible in an action for rectification. Further, it would appear that evidence of the background and of the object and genesis of the transaction is admissible but that evidence of the parties' previous negotiating positions is not. This distinction is not an easy one to draw. As Judge MacDuff QC stated in *Sykes* v. *Pannell Kerr Forster*, unreported, QBD, 30 March 2001:

there is . . . a very fine borderline between the admissible and the inadmissible. One may look at the facts and circumstances surrounding the negotiation and that about which the parties were negotiating, but not at what the parties said during negotiations nor at previous drafts. The rationale, at least in part, appears to be a wish on the part of the courts to encourage open negotiations and to discourage the creation of self-serving documents or utterances.

Similarly, in *The 'Tychy' (No 2)* [2001] EWCA Civ 1198; [2001] 2 Lloyd's Rep 403 Lord Phillips of Worth Matravers MR stated (at para [29]):

It is . . . important, though not always easy, to identify what is extrinsic to the agreement and what forms an intrinsic part of it. When a formal contract is drawn up and signed, care must be taken to distinguish between admissible background evidence relating to the nature and object of the contractual venture and inadmissible evidence of the terms for which each party was contending in the course of negotiations. Where, as in the present case, an agreement is alleged to have been reached in the course of dealings which do not culminate in the drawing up of a formal contract, the task is to identify whether, and if so which, terms proposed in the course of negotiations have become the subject of a joint agreement.

Judges have on a number of occasions noted the difficulty in distinguishing between admissible facts and inadmissible negotiations. Now that the courts give more weight to the adoption of an approach that seeks to give a commercially sensible construction to the clause in dispute, the justification for excluding pre-contractual negotiations from evidence appears suspect. They may in fact provide very good evidence of the issue that was at stake between the parties and, to that extent, should be admissible in evidence. The courts should continue to exclude from evidence 'self-serving utterances' but the reason for this exclusion is that it is for the court, not the parties, to decide what the contract means. Evidence of the subjective state of mind of the parties is irrelevant and this is so whether the evidence relates to their state of mind during the negotiations or at the time at which the contract was concluded. Evidence of pre-contractual negotiations should therefore be admissible in evidence unless that evidence relates to the subjective state of mind of the negotiating parties. This is not to say that a great deal of weight should necessarily be given to evidence of pre-contractual negotiations. The weight will very much depend upon the facts of the case. But in principle evidence of pre-contractual negotiations should be admitted, even if, in many cases, it ultimately proves to be 'unhelpful'.

Lord Hoffmann made no express reference in his speech in *Investors Compensation Scheme* to the admissibility of evidence of conduct subsequent to the making of the contract. Pre-*Investors Compensation Scheme* authority establishes that such evidence is inadmissible (*Schuler AG* v. *Wickman Machine Tool Sales* [1974] AC 235), although it may be relevant to a plea of estoppel, including estoppel by convention (*James Miller & Partners Ltd* v. *Whitworth Street Estates (Manchester) Ltd* [1970] AC 583;

Mannai Investment Co Ltd v. *Eagle Star Life Assurance Co Ltd* [1997] AC 749, 768 (Lord Steyn) and 779 (Lord Hoffmann)) and to the question whether a contract has been subsequently varied (*Philip Collins Ltd* v. *Davis* [2000] 3 All ER 808, 822). The reason given for the exclusion of this evidence is that, were it admissible, the contract could mean one thing on the day on which it was signed but mean something completely different six weeks after it was signed by virtue of the subsequent conduct of the parties. The exclusion of this evidence has been affirmed in a number of cases post-*Investors Compensation Scheme* (see, for example, *The 'Tychy' (No 2)* [2001] EWCA Civ 1198; [2001] 2 Lloyd's Rep 403, para [33]).

(e) THE MEANING IS NOT A MATTER OF DICTIONARIES

The fourth principle has given rise to some disquiet, particularly when taken in combination with the fifth principle. While the meaning which a document would convey to a reasonable man may not be the same thing as the meaning of its words, it does not of course follow that the meaning of its words is irrelevant. Lawyers often draft documents using a finely tuned linguistic fork (see, for example, *Kleinwort Benson Ltd* v. *Malaysia Mining Corporation Berhad* [1989] 1 WLR 379, p. 421 below) and, when they do, they expect the courts to give effect to them according to their terms and not to re-write them under the guise of interpretation. In such cases the parties expect the court to interpret the words and give them their ordinary, natural (dictionary) meaning. Having said that, there are cases in which the parties do use language in a much looser way or attribute a meaning to a word that it would not ordinarily bear. In such a case the courts are not bound to give the word or words their dictionary meaning. They are entitled to give the words or the document the meaning which the parties intended.

In the abstract this sounds entirely reasonable. In practice, however, it can be more problematic. The problem arises in the case where the meaning of the words is clear (at least in their dictionary sense) but one party alleges that they did not use the words in their ordinary sense but attributed to them some special meaning. For example, in *Tucker* v. *Tucker*, unreported, Chancery Division, 19 March 1999 it was argued that the word 'gave' meant 'received'. Park J rejected the argument and stated that he was unable 'to construe the agreement as if it said the opposite of what it actually says'. The problem is that Lord Hoffmann's fourth principle could be said to give to the parties an incentive to raise this type of argument. In the past the courts could only resort to evidence of the surrounding circumstances where the meaning of the words used by the parties was obscure or ambiguous. This is no longer the case. As Lord Steyn stated in *Westminster City Council* v. *National Asylum Support Service* [2002] UKHL 38; [2002] 1 WLR 2956 para [5], Lord Hoffmann has made it 'crystal clear that an ambiguity need not be established before the surrounding circumstances may be taken into account'. Indeed, it is the fact that the court can have regard to the surrounding circumstances even where the meaning of the words used is clear that has attracted criticism. It generates uncertainty. In what circumstances will the courts be prepared to depart from the dictionary meaning of the words used by the parties? The answer is not clear. One suspects that the courts will not lightly depart from the dictionary or accepted meaning of the words used by the parties. But there is no formal limit on their ability to do so.

(f) SOMETHING HAS GONE WRONG WITH THE LANGUAGE

The fifth principle comes into play in the case where 'something must have gone wrong with the language'. In such a case the law 'does not require the judges to attribute to the parties an intention which they plainly could not have had'. There is, however, an initial hurdle that must be overcome by a party who wishes to submit that something has 'gone wrong with the language'. That hurdle is that the courts 'do not easily accept that people have made linguistic mistakes'.

In this context it may be important to recall that *Investors Compensation Scheme* was itself a case in which something had gone wrong with the language in that the parties were held to have used words in an unnatural sense. As Lord Hoffmann noted, the court was 'inevitably engaged in choosing between competing unnatural meanings'. This being the case, the court had to have regard to the surrounding circumstances in order to ascertain the intention of the parties in relation to the words they had used. Given that the words had not been used by the parties in their ordinary, natural sense it was not necessary for Lord Hoffmann to address his mind to the case in which the parties have used words in their ordinary, natural meaning but one party wishes to adduce evidence of surrounding circumstances in order to demonstrate that the parties in fact used the words in a secondary or unnatural sense. In cases where it is not apparent that the parties have used words in an unnatural sense, and the document has been drawn up with professional advice, there is some evidence of judicial reluctance to have regard to the surrounding circumstances. Thus in *Breadner v. Granville-Grossman* [2001] Ch 523 Park J stated (at p. 536):

Although I appreciate that the modern approach to construction of a legal document has loosened to quite some degree from a formal syntactical approach . . . it remains the case that the starting point, and usually the finishing point as well, is to identify the natural and ordinary meaning of the words which the draftsman has used . . .

[he referred to Lord Hoffmann's fifth principle and continued]

It is of course true that Lord Hoffmann was mainly concerned to bring out that there are circumstances where it is appropriate to depart from the natural and ordinary meaning of words, but he had particularly in mind cases where it was realistic to acknowledge that the draftsman had made a 'linguistic mistake'. In this case . . . I do not think that the draftsman . . . made a linguistic mistake. He said what he intended to say. So why should not the 'natural and ordinary meaning' of his words be adopted?

The document that was in issue in *Breadner* was a formal legal document that one would expect to be drawn up by a lawyer. In such a case the court is likely to be very slow to infer that something has gone wrong with the language (and even in the case where something has 'gone wrong' with the language, the more appropriate way to deal with the issue might be by a professional negligence action against the draftsman rather than by giving the words in the document a meaning which they do not seem to be capable of bearing in order to rescue the draftsman from his mistake).

Two final points must be made in relation to this fifth principle. The first relates to its scope. When is it likely to be invoked? In *Tucker* v. *Tucker*, unreported, Chancery Division, 19 March 1999, Park J distinguished three different types of case. The first is where 'the natural meaning of the words is ambiguous and obscure'. This is the most straightforward case in which a court may give the words used a secondary meaning. The second is where the 'draftsman has chosen the right words but his grammatical use of them is inept'. *Investors Compensation Scheme* is a case that falls into this category. The third is where the 'ordinary meaning of the words would defeat the whole agreement or would be unworkable'. This third category may be too narrowly drawn in that a court may be persuaded that something has gone wrong with the language even in the case where the ordinary meaning of the words would not render the agreement unworkable.

The difficult case is the one in which the agreement does not fit together particularly well or appears to contain a drafting mistake. Given the speed with which major contracts are often put together today, the likelihood of such cases arising is rather high. What is a court to do in such cases? The problem for the courts is that they are not entitled to re-write the contract for the parties but the line between a commercial construction (which is permissible) and re-writing a contract (which is not) is a difficult one to draw (see, for example, S Gee, 'Construing Contracts with Mistakes in Them' [2001] *Lloyd's Maritime and Commercial Law Quarterly* 214). The problem was highlighted by Mance LJ in *Sinochem International Oil (London) Co Ltd v. Mobil Sales and Supply Corporation* [2000] 1 Lloyd's Rep. 339, 340 when he said that the case was 'on the border between . . . "commercial construction" . . . and re-writing the parties' contract'. The Court of Appeal divided 2–1 on the construction of the clause. The majority made some allowance for the 'vicissitudes of drafting' (p. 345) in order to give effect to the 'general aim' of the contract. Thorpe LJ stated (at p. 346) that the cases 'allowed a sufficient latitude in construction to justify the rejection of what [was] claimed to be the literal meaning of the disputed clause'. Similarly it has been stated that the court may 'require what appear to be errors or inadequacies in the choice of language to yield to [the intention of the parties] and be understood as saying what (in the light of that purpose) that language must reasonably be understood to have been intended to mean' (*Don King Productions Ltd* v. *Warren* [1998] 2 All ER 608, 624, cited with approval by Morritt LJ in the Court of Appeal, [1999] 2 All ER 218, 229–230).

The distinction between a 'commercial construction' and re-writing the contract is one of degree rather than kind. As Lord Mustill stated in *Charter Reinsurance Co Ltd* v. *Fagan* [1997] AC 313, 388 there:

comes a point at which the court should remind itself that the task is to discover what the parties meant from what they have said, and that to force upon the words a meaning which they cannot fairly bear is to substitute for the bargain actually made one which the court believes could better have been made. This is an illegitimate role for a court.

The difficulty is that different judges seem to draw the line between interpretation and re-writing the contract in different places. Some are more willing than others to smooth over the rough edges of the contract in order to reach a conclusion which they perceive to be commercially sensible. The most that can be said with any confidence is that the courts are generally unwilling to adopt a construction that leads to a very unreasonable result (see *Schuler AG* v. *L Wickman Machine Tool Sales* [1974] AC 235, discussed in more detail at p. 944 below). This approach to interpretation reflects the ordinary perception that contracting parties are unlikely to have agreed to something absurd.

The final point to note in relation to Lord Hoffmann's fifth principle is his reference to the speech of Lord Diplock in *The Antaios*. This links Lord Hoffmann's restatement with a theme that has underpinned some of Lord Steyn's recent speeches in the House of Lords where he has emphasized the shift towards an approach to the interpretation of contracts which favours the adoption of a 'commercially sensible construction'. Thus in *Lord Napier and Ettrick* v. *R F Kershaw Ltd* [1999] 1 WLR 756, 763 Lord Steyn stated:

Loyalty to the text of a commercial contract, instrument, or document read in its contextual setting is the paramount principle of interpretation. But in the process of interpreting the meaning of the language of a commercial document the court ought generally to favour a commercially sensible construction. The reason for this approach is that a commercial construction is likely to give effect to the intention of the parties. Words ought therefore to be interpreted in the way in which a reasonable commercial person would construe them. And the reasonable commercial person can safely be assumed to be unimpressed with technical interpretations and undue emphasis on niceties of language.

The drift is clear but whether it is a wholly desirable development is less clear cut. The last sentence is problematic. Is Lord Steyn's assumption about the 'reasonable commercial person' correct? What about the case in which our 'reasonable commercial person' consults a lawyer before entering into a transaction? Is a lawyer also assumed to be unimpressed with 'technical interpretations and undue emphasis on niceties of language'. Take *Kleinwort Benson Ltd* v. *Malaysia Mining Corporation Berhad* [1989] 1 WLR 379 as an example. A parent company gave a letter of comfort to a bank that had agreed to provide a £10 million credit facility to a subsidiary of the parent company. The bank asked the parent company to provide a guarantee of the subsidiary's debts. The parent company refused. Instead the parent company gave the bank a letter of comfort which stated that: 'it is our policy to ensure that the business of [the subsidiary company] is at all times in a position to meet its liabilities to you under the above arrangements'. The subsidiary defaulted under the credit facility and the bank brought a claim against the parent company. The parent company denied any liability to the bank. The crucial question was: did the parent company promise that it would continue to ensure that its subsidiary would remain in a position to meet its liabilities? The Court of Appeal held that it did not. It reached this conclusion on the basis of a careful evaluation of the terms of the letter of comfort. Given the significance of the letter of comfort to the parties we can be certain that the lawyers fought hard over its precise wording. The letter bears the hallmarks of a carefully drawn document. It conspicuously stops short of a promise by the parent company to continue its policy. It sets out the current policy of the parent company but refrains from making any commitment as regards the future. In other words there is a difference between a document which states 'it is our policy' (which makes no commitment in relation to the future) and one which states 'it is and will at all times continue to be our policy' (which clearly does make such a commitment). A different result to that reached in *Kleinwort Benson* was reached by Rogers CJ in the Supreme Court of New South Wales in *Banque Brussels Lambert SA* v. *Australian National Industries Ltd* (1989) 21 NSWLR 502. He held that the letter of comfort was promissory in nature. In reaching his conclusion he stated (at p. 524) that 'it is inimical to the effective administration of justice in commercial disputes that a court should use a finely tuned linguistic fork'. Further, after referring to the fact that the Court of Appeal in *Kleinwort Benson* had subjected the letter of comfort to minute textual analysis, stated (at p. 523) that 'courts will become irrelevant in the resolution of commercial disputes if they allow this to dominate their consideration of commercial documents'. Many English commercial practitioners will recoil in horror at the latter statements. In their view it is the function of the judge to give effect to the agreement as it stands and not to re-write it in accordance with his own perception of what 'commercial good sense' requires.

Has Lord Hoffmann begun to take English law down a road that will lead to the approach taken by Rogers CJ? Probably not. Lord Hoffmann is in fact concerned to ensure that the courts give effect to the intention of the parties and that they do not attribute to them an intention that they did not have. This being the case, where the parties intend to use a finely tuned linguistic fork, a judge applying Lord Hoffmann's re-statement should use such a fork. Conversely, where the parties do not so intend, a judge should resist the temptation to get out his finely tuned linguistic fork because the effect of doing so would be to impose upon the parties an agreement they did not intend to conclude.

6. JUDICIAL REACTION TO LORD HOFFMANN'S RE-STATEMENT

How have the judges responded to Lord Hoffmann's re-statement? Initial judicial response was distinctly cool. The first case to consider *Investors Compensation Scheme* was the decision of the Court of Appeal in *National Bank of Sharjah* v. *Dellborg*, unreported, Court of Appeal, 9 July 1997. In fact, *Investors Compensation Scheme* was cited to the court after the conclusion of argument. Saville LJ only made a passing reference to the case at the end of his judgment when he stated that nothing in the case caused him to alter the conclusion that he had reached on the facts. He nevertheless launched an attack on the state of the law relating to the interpretation of contracts. He concluded that 'what appears to be the present law does no service to the international or domestic commercial community'. In particular, he stated that 'where the words used have an unambiguous and sensible meaning as a matter of ordinary language, I see serious objections in an approach which would permit the surrounding circumstances to alter that meaning'. He identified two principal objections in the following terms:

Firstly, such an approach would seem to entail that even where the words that the parties have chosen to use have only one meaning; and that meaning (bearing in mind the aim or purpose of the agreement) is not self-evidently nonsensical, the court will not be allowed to adopt that meaning without an examination of the surrounding circumstances, which could involve discovery, inter-rogatories, cross-examination and the like; for a party seeking to challenge that meaning could assert with great force that until the circumstances are fully examined, it is impossible to decide whether or not they should override the plain words of the agreement. This would do nothing but add to the costs and delays of litigation and indeed of arbitration, much of which is concerned with interpreting agreements.

Secondly, the position of third parties (which would include assignees of contractual rights) does not seem to have been considered at all. They are unlikely in the nature of things to be aware of the surrounding circumstances. Where the words of the agreement have only one meaning, and that meaning is not self evidently nonsensical, is the third party justified in taking that to be the agreement that was made, or unable to rely on the words used without examining (which it is likely to be difficult or impossible for third parties to do) all the surrounding circumstances? If the former is the case, the law would have to treat the agreement as meaning one thing to the parties and another to third parties, hardly a satisfactory state of affairs. If the latter is the case, then unless third parties can discover all the surrounding circumstances and are satisfied that they make no difference, they cannot safely proceed to act on the basis of what the agreement actually says. This again would seem to be highly unsatisfactory.

Judge LJ gave greater consideration to *Investors Compensation Scheme*. After setting out excerpts from Lord Hoffmann's fourth and fifth principles he stated:

It therefore appears that if one party to the written contract wishes to dispute the obvious meaning of the words actually used in the document, as I understand it, he is entitled to do so by canvassing all the permitted matters of background—'absolutely anything'—which will serve to undermine the conclusion that the contract means what it apparently says. If this is the correct conclusion then I am bound to say expressly that I share the concerns expressed by Saville LJ in his judgment.

Further judicial criticism of Lord Hoffmann's speech followed when, on 18 November 1997, the Court of Appeal gave judgment in the case of *Scottish Power plc v. Britoil (Exploration) Ltd, The Times*, 2 December 1997. Staughton LJ was particularly critical of the width of Lord Hoffmann's second principle and his use of the phrase 'factual matrix'. He stated:

it is often difficult for a judge to restrain the enthusiasm of counsel for producing a great deal of evidence under the heading of matrix, which on examination is found to contribute little or nothing to the true understanding of the parties' contract. All, or almost all, judges are now concerned about the huge cost of litigation. I have to say that such a wide definition of surround-ing circumstances, background or matrix seems likely to increase the cost, to no very obvious advantage.

There are at least four aspects to these criticisms of Lord Hoffmann's re-statement. The first is the claim that it will add to the already extremely high cost of litigation. It is difficult to assess the strength of this argument. It was certainly a concern of Timothy Walker J in *NLA Group Ltd v. Bowers* [1999] 1 Lloyd's Rep 109 (pp. 414–415 above) but it may be that the courts' powers of case management and their ability to use the sanction of costs will suffice to keep the length and cost of litigation under control. The second and related point is that it will generate uncertainty. Uncertainty is said to arise at a number of points, namely in relation to the scope of the 'factual matrix', the possibility that the courts can resort to the surrounding circumstances even in the case where the words used clearly have a natural and ordinary meaning and in terms of the impact of the decision on older authorities. The claim that the modern approach has produced too much uncertainty may draw some support from the fact that the House of Lords has recently found it very difficult to reach agreement in cases concerned with the interpretation of contracts (for example, in *Mannai Investment Co Ltd* v. *Eagle Star Life Assurance Co Ltd* [1997] AC 749 their Lordships divided 3–2, while in *Investors Compensation Scheme, Deutsche Genossenschaftsbank* v. *Burnhope* [1995] 1 WLR 1580 and *BCCI* v. *Ali* they divided 4–1). The extent of the unpredictability in the present law can be demonstrated by reference to *BCCI* v. *Ali* where the majority and the minority both applied Lord Hoffmann's principles but reached very different results (and, indeed, Lord Hoffmann was himself in a minority of one!). The third point is that the re-statement has the potential to cause unfairness, particularly in its application to third parties who may have no knowledge of the commercial purpose of the transaction and who rely solely on the words used by the parties. Finally it may tempt judges to engage in the re-writing of contracts under the guise of the adoption of a commercial construction. The courts have, however, been alive to this difficulty and have not, as yet, sought to engage in extensive re-writing of contracts.

While these criticisms have their force, they have not won the day. Lord Hoffmann's re-statement has been cited on over 200 occasions and is now regularly applied by the courts. Both *National Bank of Sharjah* v. *Dellborg* and *Scottish Power plc* v. *Britoil (Exploration) Ltd* were decided in the early days of the life of Lord Hoffmann's re-statement, before it had time to bed down in the case-law. Now that the principles are well-established, criticisms are much more muted. There remains a concern about the amount of material that can be introduced in evidence under cover of the 'matrix of fact' but this does not require a wholesale re-evaluation of Lord Hoffmann's re-statement. At most it requires judicial caution in relation to the scope of the 'matrix of fact'.

7. FUTURE DEVELOPMENTS?

How will the law develop in the future? It is, of course, impossible to tell. There are three principal choices open to the courts. The first is to return to the old days and to resurrect the traditional, literal approach to the interpretation of contracts. This is unlikely to happen, although it is possible that the courts will try to curb the scope of Lord Hoffmann's re-statement, particularly through a restrictive interpretation of the 'matrix of fact'. The second is to keep the law as it is now. On this view evidence of pre-contractual negotiations and conduct subsequent to the making of the contract would continue to be generally inadmissible. The third view is that the law should continue to evolve and that the courts should continue to expand the range of materials to which they have regard when interpreting contracts. The model here might be Article 5-102 of the Principles of European Contract Law which states:

In interpreting a contract, regard shall be had, in particular, to:

  (a) the circumstances in which it was concluded, including the preliminary negotiations;

  (b) the conduct of the parties, even subsequent to the conclusion of the contract;

  (c) the nature and purpose of the contract;

  (d) the interpretation which has already been given to similar clauses by the parties and the practices they have established between themselves;

  (e) the meaning commonly given to terms and expressions in the branch of activity concerned and the interpretation similar clauses may already have received;

  (f) usages; and

  (g) good faith and fair dealing.

This Article has not, as yet, been referred to in any of the cases concerned with the interpretation of contracts in the English courts. Paragraphs (a) and (b) clearly go beyond the current limits of English law, although it has been argued that English law should develop along these lines provided that evidence of the subjective intentions of the parties continues to be inadmissible on the ground that it is irrelevant. Paragraph (g) also raises difficult issues for English lawyers because, as we shall see (Chapter 15), English law does not currently recognize the existence of a doctrine of good faith and fair dealing in contract law. But these may not prove to be insuperable obstacles. For those who wish to see English law continue to evolve, Article 5-102 may prove to be a useful tool in persuading others that English law on the interpretation of contracts has not yet reached its final destination.

8. FURTHER READING

GEE, S, 'Construing Contracts with Mistakes in Them' [2001] *Lloyd's Maritime and Commercial Law Quarterly* 214.

KRAMER, A, 'Common Sense Principles of Contract Interpretation (and how we've been using them all along)' (2003) 23 *Oxford Journal of Legal Studies* 173.

McKENDRICK, E, 'The Interpretation of Contracts: Lord Hoffmann's Re-Statement' in S Worthington (ed), *Commercial Law and Commercial Practice* (Hart, 2003), p. 139.

McLAUCHLAN, DW, 'The New Law of Contract Interpretation' (2000) 19 *New Zealand Universities Law Review* 147.

McMEEL, G, 'The Rise of Commercial Construction in Contract Law' [1998] *Lloyd's Maritime and Commercial Law Quarterly* 382.

McMEEL, G, 'Prior Negotiations and Subsequent Conduct—the Next Step Forward for Contractual Interpretation' (2003) 119 *LQR* 272.

STAUGHTON, C, 'How do the Courts Interpret Commercial Contracts?' [1999] *CLJ* 303.

12

BOILERPLATE CLAUSES

1. CENTRAL ISSUES

1. Contracting parties frequently have a set of standard terms and conditions which they seek to incorporate into all the contracts which they conclude. In the case of more complex contracts they will also have a set of clauses (generally referred to as 'boilerplate clauses') which they will attempt to incorporate into these contracts. Some of these standard terms can be the subject of protracted negotiations between the parties. These standard terms therefore assume considerable significance in commercial practice.

2. The aim of this chapter is not to examine the content of these standard terms in detail. Rather, it is to identify, and briefly examine, some of the standard terms and to outline the structure of modern commercial contracts.

2. INTRODUCTION

The aim of this chapter is not to examine contracting practices as such. Such an enterprise would require not only a separate book but a major research project to examine the diverse contracting practices that exist throughout the country. While there have been some extremely valuable analyses of contracting practices in certain sectors of the economy or certain geographical areas (see, for example, H Beale and A Dugdale, 'Contracts Between Businessmen: Planning and the Use of Contractual Remedies' (1975) 2 *British Journal of Law and Society* 45 and R Lewis, 'Contracts Between Businessmen: Reform of the Law of Firm Offers and an Empirical Study of Tendering Practices in the Building Industry' (1982) 9 *Journal of Law and Society* 153), there remains a great deal to be done in terms of obtaining information about the way in which contracts are concluded and their content. The study carried out by Beale and Dugdale in the early 1970s consisted of interviews with 'representatives of nineteen firms of engineering manufacturers, mainly in Bristol, about their firm's contracts of purchase and sale'. One of the principal points that emerged from this study was the relatively limited use that was made by the parties of the law of contract in the regulation of their relationship. But it would be dangerous to generalize from this study and conclude that contracting parties generally make little use of the rules of law. Thus Beale, Bishop and Furmston (*Contract Cases and Materials* (4th edn, Butterworths, 2001)) conclude (at p. 87):

although this study suggests that some businesses make only limited use of contract law, it must be remembered that it was studying only a small sample from one industry. Other trades may well demonstrate a much more 'legalistic' approach: for instance, a glance into Lloyd's Reports, which concentrate on commercial cases, suggests that businesses in some commodity trades and in the charter markets litigate much more regularly—frequently taking points that lack any real merit in order to escape unprofitable contracts . . . The contracts seem to have been planned in quite some detail . . .

The aim of the chapter is to examine some of the principal standard terms used in commercial contracts today. The examination is limited in two important respects. First, it is confined to commercial contracts. Contracts concluded informally between members of the public are not examined at all. Contracts between businesses and consumers also fall largely outside the scope of this chapter. They are included to the extent that many businesses seek to incorporate their standard terms and conditions into contracts with consumers as well as with other businesses. But the regulation of these standard terms as they apply to consumer contracts raises distinct issues which are examined in Chapter 14. Secondly, this chapter is confined to terms that will, in all probability, have been drafted by lawyers. It therefore examines the clauses very much through the lens of a lawyer. It does not purport to examine more informal methods of contracting that may be developed by businesses (important though these methods may be in practice).

3. BOILERPLATE CLAUSES AND STANDARD TERMS

Standard terms can be divided into two broad groups. The first consists of standard terms that are inserted into a written contract which has been drawn up by the contracting parties (more usually, their lawyers). These are often known as 'boiler-plate clauses'. The second consists of a set of standard terms and conditions which a business attempts to incorporate into all of its contracts. These terms are often appended to an order form or are incorporated into the standard documentation sent out on behalf of the business whenever a transaction is concluded. The distinction between these two groups is a very loose one. A term can be both a boilerplate clause inserted into a written contract and a term that is included in a standard set of terms and conditions. The distinction that is drawn relates not to the substance of the term itself but to the process by which the contract is concluded. The first group consists of cases where two parties negotiate a contract and then draw up a formal written contract which records the agreement that the parties have reached. The second group is made up of those cases in which one party sends out an order form on his own standard terms of business and the other party 'accepts' the order and in doing so often sends back his own terms and conditions (the so-called 'battle of the forms' discussed at pp. 91–110 above). In the first situation it is important to see the boiler-plate clauses in their context. The first extract, taken from a book by Richard Christou, does this by locating the discussion of boilerplate clauses within the structure of the agreement as a whole. The second extract, taken from *Schmitthoff's Export Trade*, sets out a list of commonly used standard form clauses. These are particularly suitable for incorporation in a set of standard terms and conditions but they can also be incorporated into a written contract as one of the boilerplate clauses. The section that follows these two extracts is devoted to a brief examination of the standard clauses listed in *Schmitthoff* and will also include one or two other boilerplate clauses not included in that list.

R Christou, *Boilerplate: Practical Clauses*

(3rd edn, Sweet & Maxwell, 2002), pp. 1–2 and 4–8

The term 'boilerplate' is most properly used in its widest sense to describe the clauses, common to nearly all commercial contracts, which deal with the way in which the contract itself operates, as opposed to the rights of the parties under the particular transaction that they have agreed upon and embodied in the substantive clauses. Boilerplate clauses regulate, control, and in some cases modify, these substantive rights and their operation and enforcement. They are thus a vital part of every contract, without which the substantive rights of the parties embodied in the agreement would have little meaning.

If one can take the analogy from the field of computing, boilerplate is like the operating system of a computer, while the substantive content of the contract relating to the particular transaction could be likened to the application of software. All commercial contracts have an underlying 'operating system' that is (at least in the jurisdictions based on common law and even in some others) approximately the same.

In the absence of boilerplate the parties must rely on the general system of law applicable to the contract, and ask the court to apply this in settling disputes. In extreme cases, however, even the systems of law to be applied, and the question of which court has jurisdiction, would have to be decided by reference to some system of private international law. This approach defeats the whole aim of commercial contracts: to create certainty in dealings between the parties, and an easy method of enforcement of rights where necessary.

The different parts of a commercial contract

(a) *Designation of the parties*

At the head of the contract it is usual to set out the names and identifying details of each of the parties. Although it is not uncommon to preface this section with a statement such as 'This Agreement is made the. . . . . date of 20. . . . . . .', this is not legally necessary. It is vital, however, that the agreement states from what date it is effective. The actual date upon which the agreement is signed (if this is different to the effective date) is therefore desirable but not essential.

(b) *Recitals*

After the details of the parties, a set of paragraphs called recitals will usually appear. They set out the background to the transaction and the purpose for which the parties are entering into the transaction. It is not legally necessary to include recitals in a contract, but it is customary to do so. However . . . current practice is to keep recitals as short as possible. Without express words later on in the agreement, recitals are not regarded as a part of the agreement which actually gives rise to legal obligations, and yet they will, at the least, be taken into account by a court which has to interpret the substantive portion of the agreement. Even worse, a court may regard them as, or as evidence of, pre-contract representations, the breach of which would ground an action for misrepresentation . . .

(c) Definitions

Although it is possible to insert definitions in any of the foregoing or in substantive parts of the agreement, where there are a great many definitions it is usual to arrange them together in a separate section straight after the recitals. As a drafting tip, it can be easier to insert definitions throughout the agreement, as drafting the clauses throws up the need for them, and then to remove these definitions at the end, collect and edit them, and arrange them in a suitable order (either alphabetical or logical) in the initial definition section.

The definitions form part of the substantive agreement because they prescribe that certain terms *shall* mean certain things. This prescriptive language can take various forms. The most unambiguous, and therefore the most desirable, is: 'In this Agreement A shall mean B'. A less desirable style, but still often used, is: 'Where the context so admits, in this Agreement A shall mean B'. The following approach, which is even more undesirable, is a partial definition: 'In this Agreement [where the context so admits] A includes B'. An example of this is: 'In this Agreement taxation includes income tax, corporation tax and value added tax'. We do not have a complete definition of 'taxation', but do know some items which are included in the term. The parties are left free to argue, by reference to the ordinary dictionary meaning of taxation, whether other items such as stamp duty or inheritance tax fall within the definition or not.

Besides pure definitions, this section will also contain general interpretation clauses . . .

(d) Substantive clauses

After the definitions follow the main clauses of the agreement—the substantive provisions. These clauses are sometimes introduced by: 'Now it is hereby agreed as follows . . .' Although customary, this phrase does not appear to serve any legal purpose, since the substantive clauses will obviously be seen as matters upon which the parties are agreeing.

(e) Schedules

To ensure that the logical flow of the substantive clauses is not interrupted and obscured with a great deal of detail, it is useful to put many of the more detailed substantive provisions into schedules. A clause in the substantive part of the agreement could then read: 'All orders for the Products placed by the Buyer with the Seller shall be upon the terms and conditions set out in Schedule . . .' The schedule concerned could then carry a detailed set of conditions of sale which, had they been left within the main clauses, would have completely disrupted the sequence.

Another use for schedules is to remove transaction-specific details so that the main document can be more easily used as a standard form. Standard form distributor or agency agreements, for example, usually place details of the products, territories covered and sales targets within the schedules.

Schedules are a substantive and integral part of the agreement, and there should always be a specific provision in the main clauses stating that this is so.

(f) Appendices

Where documents are referred to in an agreement they are often attached as appendices so that they can be easily referred to. Such appendices are usually signed by the parties by way of identification of the document concerned.

Such documents are not necessarily part of the agreement. For instance, a warranty can be given that a set of accounts, or a copy of a memorandum and articles attached as an appendix, is true and correct. The document is then attached for reference but its provisions are not incorporated in the agreement. Where a document is actually incorporated by reference (for example a set of standard conditions of sale or a technical specification) the document is sometimes also attached as an appendix. However, even in this case, the *provisions* of the document are incorporated by reference in the main clause, but the appended copy of the document only serves as a record of those terms and is not itself a part of the agreement.

(g) *Signature section*

This section should come after the schedules and before the appendices. It is often, but need not be, introduced with wording such as: 'The duly authorised representatives of the parties hereto have hereunto set their hands, the day and year first above written'. A shorter and equally acceptable method is 'Signed by X for and on behalf of ABC Ltd' followed by X's signature.

Commercial agreements do not normally need witnesses to the signatures: they are certainly not necessary under English law.

Most commercial agreements are just signed . . . and not executed as deeds . . . One great advantage (or drawback depending upon which party is concerned) to the use of a deed under English law, is that the statute of limitations prescribes 12 years for an action on a deed, but only six years for a document under hand.

Deeds are also used by bodies such as local authorities in England and Wales whose processes for authorisation of signature of contracts are very complicated . . .

Mention should also be made of the new possibilities for the electronic signature of contracts provided by section 7 of the Electronic Communications Act 2000 . . .

(h) *Counterparts and copies*

Copies of commercial documents are usually supplied for each of the parties: these are signed by all the parties and include a special counterpart clause inserted to make each of them fully signed original copies for purposes of enforcement. As an alternative to counterparts, there is sometimes only one original, with the other parties being given certified copies which are regarded as equivalent to the originals.

Conformed copies are sometime produced. These are copies of documents which contain manuscript amendments made at the last minute, or illegible signatures. The manuscript (including the signatures) is reproduced in the documents in typed form. Such copies are obviously not originals and are often just used for ease of reference, but they may also, of course, be certified copies.

(i) *Headings and contents pages*

Headings to clauses, sections and schedules, and contents pages are often introduced into long documents for ease of reference. Such matters should not be part of the agreement or their drafting becomes too complicated and they no longer serve the purpose of providing easy reference guides. Usually a provision appears in the substantive clauses stating that this is the case.

(j) *Contract numbering systems*

Numbering systems can vary. Traditionally, they consist of hierarchical mixtures of arabic and roman numerals and letters of the alphabet. In a long document one spends more time than it is worth working out and adjusting such hierarchies and keeping them consistent. The aim of all numbering systems is to provide a unique and easy way of referring to each part of each clause of the contract.

C Schmitthoff, *Export Trade: The Law and Practice of International Trade*

(10th edn, Sweet & Maxwell, 2000), paras 32-014 and 32-015

The importance, for international sales, of well-drafted general terms of business can hardly be exaggerated. They are particularly important where neither uniform conditions of export sales nor standard contract forms are used. Litigation can often be avoided when the seller is able to refer the buyer to a clause in his printed terms of business which was embodied in the quotation or acceptance, and the fact that these terms apply to all transactions concluded by the seller adds persuasive force to his argument.

Some important clauses

The most important clauses which the exporter should incorporate in his general terms of business are:

(a) *General clause* which subjects every contract of sale to the seller's conditions of sale;

(b) *Retention of title clause* which provides that until the seller receives the purchase price fully in cash,

  (i) the seller retains the legal property in the goods and is given the irrevocable right to enter into the premises of the buyer at any time and without notice in order to retake possession of the goods; and

  (ii) the buyer may resell the goods only as an agent of the seller and only in the ordinary course of business to a bona fide repurchaser and, if he does so, shall receive the proceeds of the resale as an agent of and trustee for the seller and shall place the proceeds of sale in a separate account in the name of the seller.

(c) *Price escalation clause* which provides that unless firm prices and charges are agreed upon, the seller shall be entitled to increase the agreed prices and charges in the same proportion in which the prices or charges of the goods or their components, including costs of labour to be paid or borne by the seller, have been increased between the date of the quotation and the date of the delivery;

(d) *Interest* which provides where payment is made after the agreed date, interest shall be paid at a specified rate;

(e) *Force majeure clause* . . .;

(f) *Choice of law clause* which specifies that the contract be governed by English law;

(g) *Arbitration* which provides that any disputes between the parties are to be settled by arbitration; or

(h) *Jurisdiction*, providing for the jurisdiction of the English courts.

4. BOILERPLATE CLAUSES — SOME ILLUSTRATIONS

This section is devoted to an analysis of some standard or boilerplate clauses. It takes as its starting point the clauses listed in Schmitthoff. But it also adds one or two additional clauses. Schmitthoff's list is directed towards export sellers and it is therefore necessary to supplement it by reference to standard terms that are found in other types of contract.

(a) GENERAL CLAUSE

While many sellers include such a 'general clause' in their standard terms, it by no means follows that it will be effective. The sellers in *Butler Machine Tool Co Ltd* v. *Ex-Cell-O Corporation (England) Ltd* [1979] 1 WLR 401 (p. 92 above) included such a clause in their standard terms. The clause there stated:

All orders are accepted only upon and subject to the terms set out in our quotation and the following conditions. These terms and conditions shall prevail over any terms and conditions in the Buyer's order.

The clause was not effective to achieve its goal because the sellers, in signing the buyer's tear-off acknowledgement slip, were held to have entered into a contract on the buyer's standard terms of business. While the clause may not work in a given fact situation, it is nevertheless included in standard terms and conditions.

(b) RETENTION OF TITLE CLAUSES

The aim of this type of clause is to protect the seller in the event of the insolvency of the buyer. While such a clause is commonly found in sellers' standard terms and conditions it is by no means certain that it will achieve its goal. The case-law on this issue is difficult. Retention of title clauses came to prominence as a result of the decision of the Court of Appeal in *Aluminium Industrie Vaasen BV* v. *Romalpa Aluminium Ltd* [1976] 1 WLR 676, where a retention of title clause was held to be effective not only to reserve to the sellers property in the goods sold to the buyer but also to trace into the proceeds of sub-sales which had been entered into by the buyer, where the goods the subject-matter of the sub-sales included goods supplied by the sellers to the buyers. The clause stated:

The ownership of the material to be delivered by A.I.V. will only be transferred to purchaser when he has met all that is owing to A.I.V., no matter on what grounds. Until the date of payment, purchaser, if A.I.V. so desires, is required to store this material in such a way that it is clearly the property of A.I.V. A.I.V. and purchaser agree that, if purchaser should make (a) new object(s) from the material, mix this material with (an) other object(s) or if this material in any way whatsoever becomes a constituent of (an) other object(s) A.I.V. will be given the ownership of this (these) new object(s) as surety of the full payment of what purchaser owes A.I.V. To this end A.I.V. and purchaser now agree that the ownership of the article(s) in question, whether finished or not, are to be transferred to A.I.V. and that this transfer of ownership will be considered to have taken place through and at the moment of the single operation or event by which the material is converted into (a) new object(s), or is mixed with or becomes a constituent of (an) other object(s). Until the moment of full payment of what purchaser owes A.I.V. purchaser shall keep the object(s) in question for A.I.V. in his capacity of fiduciary owner and, if required, shall store this (these) object(s) in such a way that it (they) can be recognized as such. Nevertheless, purchaser will be entitled to sell these objects to a third party within the framework of the normal carrying on of his business and to deliver them on condition that—if A.I.V. so requires—purchaser as long as he has not fully discharged his debt to A.I.V. shall hand over to A.I.V. the claims he has against his buyer emanating from this transaction.

Two points are worth noting about this clause. The first is its length and the second is the fact that it is not very well drafted. Notwithstanding its obvious shortcomings the Court of Appeal held that it was effective to entitle the seller to claim the proceeds of the sub-sales entered into by the buyer in priority to the secured and unsecured creditors of the insolvent buyer. The result was to confer a right of enormous value on the sellers in the insolvency of the buyers. It is not surprising, in the light of this decision, that sellers immediately began to insert retention of title clauses into their standard terms. Since *Romalpa* was decided, however, the courts have taken a more restrictive view of the efficacy of retention of title clauses. While they continue to be effective where the goods which have been sold to the buyers have not been mixed irrevocably with other goods (*Hendy Lennox (Industrial Engines) Ltd* v. *Graham Puttick Ltd* [1984] 1 WLR 485; *Armour* v. *Thyssen Edelstahlwerke* [1991] 2 AC 339) they are generally not effective where the goods have been mixed irrevocably (*Borden (UK) Ltd* v. *Scottish Timber Products Ltd* [1981] Ch 25) nor in relation to attempts to trace into the proceeds of sub-sales (*Compaq Computer Ltd* v. *Abercorn Group Ltd* [1991] BCC 484). The drafting of the clause in the example given by Schmitthoff is based on *Romalpa* but, in the light of cases such as *Compaq* v. *Abercorn*, it is probably ineffective to enable the sellers to claim the proceeds of any sub-sales. It is necessary to take great care when drafting a retention of title clause but even a well drafted clause may be held to be ineffective to entitle a seller to trace into the proceeds of sub-sales (see *Compaq* v. *Abercorn*).

(c) PRICE ESCALATION CLAUSES

Price escalation clauses are of considerable importance to sellers in long-term contracts and in cases where there is a time-lag between entry into the contract and the time at which the buyer is to pay for the goods or services supplied by the seller. The clause that was in issue between the parties in *Butler Machine Tool Co Ltd* v. *Ex-Cell-O Corporation (England) Ltd* [1979] 1 WLR 401 was a price variation or a price escalation clause (see clause 3 of the sellers' terms and conditions, set out at p. 93 above). As *Butler* demonstrates it is important not only to ensure that standard terms are properly drafted but to ensure that they are incorporated into the contracts that the sellers conclude.

(d) INTEREST

The reason for inserting a clause into the contract dealing with interest is that the common law rule was that interest could not be recovered as damages in respect of a failure to pay a debt when it fell due (see *President of India* v. *Lips Maritime Corporation* [1988] AC 395). In the absence of a general common law rule entitling a party to recover interest, it was necessary to create a contractual right to interest by an appropriately drafted term of the contract. The need for a contractual term entitling a party to recover interest has been reduced but not eliminated by the enactment of the Late Payment of Commercial Debts (Interest) Act 1998. Section 1(1) of the Act provides that:

It is an implied term in a contract to which this Act applies that any qualifying debt created by the contract carries simple interest subject to and in accordance with this Part.

Section 2(1) of the Act states that the Act applies to:

a contract for the supply of goods or services where the purchaser and the supplier are each acting in the course of a business, other than an excepted contract.

A debt is a 'qualifying debt' unless it consists of a sum to which a right to interest or to charge interest arises by virtue of some other enactment. The parties remain free to make their own provision for the payment of interest, although any attempt to exclude the right to statutory interest in relation to the debt is void unless the contract provides a 'substantial contractual remedy for late payment of the debt' (see sections 8 and 9 of the Act).

(e) FORCE MAJEURE CLAUSES

A force majeure clause is a clause which entitles a party to suspend or terminate the contract on the occurrence of an event which is beyond the control of the parties and which prevents, impedes, or delays the performance of the contract. The precise scope of the clause will depend upon its wording and the details of the clause may be the subject of difficult negotiations between the parties. Force majeure clauses are generally inserted into contracts because the doctrine of frustration operates within very narrow limits (see pp. 867–878 below). Given that the courts are unwilling to adjust the contract in the event that performance becomes more onerous for one party, contracting parties who wish to preserve to themselves a degree of flexibility in the performance of a contract may agree to insert a force majeure clause into their contract. An example of a force majeure clause is provided by clause 17 of the contract between the parties in *J Lauritzen AS* v. *Wijsmuller BV (The 'Super Servant Two')* [1990] 1 Lloyd's Rep 1 (a case discussed in more detail at pp. 885–894 below). The clause provided:

17. Cancellation

17.1. Wijsmuller has the right to cancel its performance under this Contract whether the loading has been completed or not, in the event of force majeur [sic], Acts of God, perils or danger and accidents of the sea, acts of war, warlike-operations, acts of public enemies, restraint of princes, rulers or people or seizure under legal process, quarantine restrictions, civil commotions, blockade, strikes, lockout, closure of the Suez or Panama Canal, congestion of harbours or any other circumstances whatsoever, causing extra-ordinary periods of delay and similar events and/or circumstances, abnormal increases in prices and wages, scarcity of fuel and similar events, which reasonably may impede, prevent or delay the performance of this contract.

A rather more complex force majeure clause was the version of clause 22 of GAFTA 100 that was litigated in *Toepfer* v. *Cremer* [1975] 2 Lloyd's Rep 118. It provided:

Sellers shall not be responsible for delay in shipment of the goods or any part thereof occasioned by any Act of God, strike, lockout, riot or civil commotion, combination of workmen, breakdown of machinery, fire or any cause comprehended in the term 'force majeure'. If delay in shipment is likely to occur for any of the above reasons, Shippers shall give notice to their Buyers by telegram, telex or teleprinter or by similar advice within 7 consecutive days of the occurrence, or not less than 21 consecutive days before the commencement of the contract period, whichever is later. The notice shall state the reason(s) for the anticipated delay. If after giving such notice an extension to the shipping period is required, then Shippers shall give further notice not later than 2 business days after the last day of the contract period of shipment stating the port or ports of loading from which the goods were intended to be shipped, and shipments effected after the contract period shall be limited to the port or ports so nominated. If shipment be delayed for more than one calendar month, Buyers shall have the option of cancelling the delayed portion of the contract, such option to be exercised by Buyers giving notice to be received by Sellers not later than the first business day after the additional calendar month. If Buyers do not exercise this option, such delayed portion shall be automatically extended for a further period of one month. If shipment under this clause be prevented during the further one month's extension, the contract shall be considered void. Buyers shall have no claim against Sellers for delay or non-shipment under this clause provided that Sellers shall have supplied to Buyers, if required, satisfactory evidence justifying the delay or non-fulfilment.

There are three principal components of a force majeure clause. The first and most important component is the description of the events that trigger the operation of the clause. There is no doctrine of force majeure in English law and so the phrase 'force majeure' is not a term of art (see *Thomas Borthwick (Glasgow) Ltd* v. *Faure Fairclough Ltd* [1968] 1 Lloyd's Rep 16, 28). It is therefore for the parties to define the list of events which they intend should fall within the scope of the clause. The events included in the list are generally events that are beyond the control of the parties, such as Acts of God and war. Not much significance tends to be attached to the words 'force majeure' themselves. Either the event will fall within the list of specific events listed in the clause or it will fall within the general words at the end of the clause. But it is rare for any dispute between the parties to focus explicitly on the words 'force majeure'. The description of the force majeure events is generally divided into two parts. The first part consists of a list of specific events. The length of the list can vary enormously. Sometimes it is very short; at other times, it can be very long. The second part consists of a general provision which is intended to cover events not included in the specific list. Views differ as to the utility of the specific list. Some draftsmen are of the view that it is largely useless and that it suffices to use general words only. Others prefer the list on the ground that it can help reduce disputes over whether events, such as strikes, fall within the scope of the clause (although in the case of internal industrial action it can be difficult to persuade a court that it falls within the scope of a force majeure clause: see *B & S Contracts and Design Ltd* v. *Victor Green Publications Ltd* [1984] ICR 419).

The second component of a force majeure clause consists of the obligations of the parties in relation to the reporting of the occurrence of a force majeure event. Not all force majeure clauses set out the obligations of the parties in this regard. The clause in *Super Servant Two* does not, whereas the more elaborate clause in *Toepfer* does set out the procedure to be followed by the parties. The reporting obligations of the parties should cover matters such as the person to whom the report is to be made, the time at which the report is to be made, the form it should take, and the consequences of a failure to make a report in the prescribed fashion.

The third component consists of the remedial consequences of the occurrence of a force majeure event. Once again, the clause in *Super Servant Two* is in a simple form in that it only provides for a right to cancel the contract. The clause in *Toepfer* is a little more elaborate in that it makes provision for the extension of the contract as well as the possibility of cancellation. Force majeure clauses in fact give to the parties a high degree of remedial flexibility. Thus provision can be made for the granting of extensions of time, the suspension or variation of the contract, or even the termination of the contract. It is common for parties to make provision for the initial suspension of the contract which can lead to termination should the force majeure event continue to prevent or impede performance for a considerable period of time (such as twenty-eight days). The remedial flexibility that a force majeure clause potentially affords to the parties compares favourably with the remedial rigidity of the doctrine of frustration (on which see p. 902 below).

(f) CHOICE OF LAW CLAUSES

A choice of law clause assumes considerable significance when dealing with a contracting party from another jurisdiction. Take the example of a contract concluded between a seller in England and a buyer in France. The seller is likely to wish to have the contract governed by English law, whereas the buyer will, in all probability, wish to ensure that the contract is governed by French law. This gives rise to what is known as the conflict of laws. What is to happen in such a case? The answer depends upon the parties. The law allows the parties to choose the law that is to govern the transaction. Article 3 of the Rome Convention on the Law Applicable to Contractual Obligations, which is applicable in the European Union, provides:

A contract shall be governed by the law chosen by the parties. The choice must be express or demonstrated with reasonable certainty by the terms of the contract or the circumstances of the case. By their choice the parties can select the law applicable to the whole or a part only of the contract.

The significance of this provision has been described in the following terms (A Briggs, *An Introduction to the Conflict of Laws* (Oxford University Press, 2002), p. 159):

The Convention . . . broadly adopts the principle of party autonomy, allowing a choice to be decisive except only in relation to limited and clearly specified matters; but it requires two things: the choice to be made, and that choice to be expressed or demonstrable, and this will preclude the argument that the parties (as reasonable people) must have chosen a particular law but did not express that choice or suggest that they had made it.

A choice expressed in the form 'this contract shall be governed by the law of France' will therefore be effective to make French law the governing law; and a less artful choice, such as 'this contract shall be construed in accordance with French law', will probably be taken as a choice of governing law. In advising clients, one hopes that a legal adviser will recognize the freedom to choose, but also the responsibility to express that choice clearly, which is afforded by Article 3. But one could be forgiven for thinking that some draftsmen regard a clear expression of choice as being too easy, rejecting it for something more challenging. An expression of choice of the law of the United Kingdom, or of British law, for example, cannot be given literal effect, because there is no such law to be chosen; and to interpret this as an express choice of English law is to make an assumption which is probably factually correct but politically incorrect. Again, a choice of the *lex mercatoria*, or of the law of Mars, not being the law of a country, cannot be upheld, because the Convention sanctions only the choice of the law of a country and in such a case Article 3 cannot apply.

Where the parties fail to make a choice, Article 4 provides:

To the extent that the law applicable to the contract has not been chosen in accordance with Article 3, the contract shall be governed by the law of the country with which it is most closely connected. Nevertheless, a severable part of the contract which has a closer connection with another country may by way of exception be governed by the law of that other country.

The difficulty with this provision is that it is not always easy to work out which law is most 'closely connected' with the contract. It is in order to avoid such difficulties that contracting parties who deal with foreign parties should wherever possible insert a choice of law clause into their contracts and into their standard terms and conditions of business.

(g) ARBITRATION CLAUSES

Parties frequently make provision in their contracts for the dispute resolution mechanism that is to apply in the event of a dispute between them arising out of their contract. The principal choice which the parties must make is between arbitration and litigation (although mediation and alternative dispute resolution ('ADR') are becoming increasingly common in commercial practice). Arbitration is commonly associated with international contracts. Arbitration is claimed to have a number of advantages. First, it is private. It does not take place in a public court and the result of the arbitration is not publicly available. Secondly, it can have the appearance of neutrality in that it can take place at a neutral venue (unlike litigation which will often take place in the courts of the country of one of the parties to the contract). Thirdly, arbitration is more flexible in that the parties can choose where and when to arbitrate, they can often choose their arbitrators, and they can also decide, albeit within limits, the form that the arbitration is to assume. Party autonomy is a very important principle in international arbitration. Fourthly arbitration is said to be speedier than litigation and finally it is often claimed to be cheaper.

These arguments are not, however, conclusive. Arbitration does have its disadvantages. It can be very expensive and it is not necessarily quick. A party who loses an arbitration may decide to appeal to the courts and, if the courts accept that they have jurisdiction to hear the appeal, the parties' privacy is lost as may be all hope of a quick and relatively inexpensive conclusion to the proceedings. Some of the awards issued by arbitrators are also of rather doubtful pedigree. The quality control in litigation appears to be much higher than in the case of arbitration. The parties therefore have to make a choice as to the form of dispute resolution mechanism that they wish to utilize. There is no requirement that they make that choice at the moment of entry into the contract. They can defer the decision until such time as a dispute occurs between the parties. But many parties do make the decision at the time of entry into the contract.

Parties who wish to ensure that disputes arising out of their contract are referred to arbitration rather than litigation must draft a suitably worded arbitration clause and the clause must be drafted with care. It is not necessary to go into the drafting details here. It suffices to give two examples of an arbitration clause, one taken from an international arbitral institution and the other from a clause in the contract between the parties in one of the leading contract cases in recent years. The clause taken from the international arbitral institution is the UNCITRAL Model Arbitration clause which provides:

any dispute, controversy or claim arising out of or relating to this contract, or the breach, termination or invalidity thereof, shall be settled by arbitration in accordance with the UNCITRAL Arbitration Rules as at present in force.

The clause taken from the leading case is the opening part of the arbitration clause agreed between the parties in *Alfred McAlpine Construction Ltd* v. *Panatown Ltd* [2001] 1 AC 518 (discussed in more detail at pp. 1029–1054 below). Clause 39.1 of the contract provided:

When the Employer or the Contractor require a dispute or difference as referred to in Article 5 to be referred to arbitration then either the Employer or the Contractor shall give written notice to the other to such effect and such dispute or difference shall be referred to the arbitration and final decision of a person to be agreed between the parties as the Arbitrator, or, upon the failure so to agree within 14 days after the date of the aforesaid written notice, of a person to be appointed as the Arbitrator on the request of either the Employer or the Contractor by the person named in Appendix 1 to the Conditions.

One of the interesting features of the litigation between Panatown and McAlpine was that the corporate group of which Panatown was a member had a choice between litigating the dispute with McAlpine in the courts or invoking the arbitration clause in the contract between Panatown and McAlpine. They chose the latter option. With the benefit of hindsight it can be seen that the choice was a dubious one because McAlpine exercised its rights under the contract to appeal to the High Court against the provisional award of the arbitrator. So, in the event, the parties found themselves embroiled in complex litigation as well as arbitration (see further E McKendrick, 'The Common Law at Work: The Saga of *Alfred McAlpine Construction Ltd* v. *Panatown Ltd*' (2003) 3 *OUCLJ* 145). The choice between arbitration and litigation is an important one that must be made with some care.

(h) JURISDICTION CLAUSES

If litigation is the preferred method of dispute resolution then consideration ought to be given to the jurisdiction in which the dispute is to be litigated. Within Europe the law gives the parties considerable freedom of choice in relation to the selection of the appropriate jurisdiction. Article 23 of Council Regulation (EC) No 44/2001 of 22 December 2000 provides:

If the parties, one or more of whom is domiciled in a Member State, have agreed that a court or the courts of a Member State are to have jurisdiction to settle any disputes which have arisen or which may arise in connection with a particular legal relationship, that court or those courts shall have jurisdiction. Such jurisdiction shall be exclusive unless the parties have agreed otherwise. Such an agreement conferring jurisdiction shall be either:

(a) in writing or evidenced in writing;

(b) in a form which accords with practices which the parties have established between themselves; or

(c) in international trade or commerce, in a form which accords with a usage of which the parties are or ought to have been aware and which in such trade or commerce is widely known to, and regularly observed by, parties to contracts of the type involved in the particular trade or commerce concerned.

Jurisdiction is a complex issue and it is beyond the scope of this book (see more generally A Briggs, *The Conflict of Laws* (Oxford University Press, 2002), Chapter 3). We shall, however, encounter jurisdiction clauses in the context of the important decision of the Privy Council in *The Mahkutai* [1996] AC 696, a case which is discussed at some length at pp. 1214–1223 below.

Some other standard terms not mentioned in Schmitthoff are as follows:

(i) HARDSHIP CLAUSES

A clause which is frequently inserted into a contract to deal with unforeseen events which make performance of the contract more onerous than originally anticipated is a hardship clause. An example of such a clause can be found in *Superior Overseas Development Corporation* v. *British Gas Corporation* [1982] 1 Lloyd's Rep 262, 264–265 in the following terms:

(a) If at any time or from time to time during the contract period there has been any substantial change in the economic circumstances relating to this Agreement and (notwithstanding the effect of the other relieving or adjusting provisions of this Agreement) either party feels that such change is causing it to suffer substantial economic hardship then parties shall (at the request of either of them) meet together to consider what (if any) adjustments(s) in the

prices . . . are justified in the circumstances in fairness to the parties to offset or alleviate
the said hardship caused by such change.

(b) If the parties shall not within ninety (90) days after any such request have reached agreement on the adjustments (if any) in the said prices . . . the matter may forthwith be referred
by either party for determination by experts . . .

(c) The experts shall determine what (if any) adjustments in the said prices or in the said price
revision mechanism shall be made . . . and any revised prices or any change in the price
revision mechanism so determined by such experts shall take effect six (6) months after the
date on which the request for review was first made.

Such a clause should define the circumstances in which 'hardship' exists and should
then lay down a procedure to be adopted in the event that these circumstances occur.
Care must be taken when drafting hardship clauses because the House of Lords in
Walford v. *Miles* [1992] 2 AC 128 (discussed in more detail at pp. 544–554 below)
refused to recognize the validity of an obligation to negotiate in good faith. Hardship
clauses not infrequently employ the language of good faith in order to describe the
obligations of the parties in any re-negotiation of the contract. The clause in *Superior
Overseas Development Corporation* manages to avoid the use of the language of good
faith. The vitally important matter is to ensure that the clause provides a mechanism
or a sanction to be applied in the event that the parties fail to reach agreement or
refuse to enter into negotiations with a view to adjusting the contract. A common
sanction, employed in *Superior Overseas Development Corporation*, is to provide for
the intervention of a third party expert or arbitrators (but not a judge sitting in a
court of law) should the parties fail to reach agreement themselves.

The advantage of a hardship clause is that it is designed to enable the relationship
between the parties to continue, albeit on different terms. Given that the courts at
common law have no power to adjust the terms of a contract to meet changed
circumstances (see p. 902 below), this can be a useful clause to incorporate should the
parties wish to make provision for the adjustment (rather than the suspension or
termination) of the contract.

(j) ENTIRE AGREEMENT CLAUSES

Entire agreement clauses are frequently relied upon in an attempt to prevent one
party from asserting that the written contract is not the sole repository of the terms of
the contract and that there is in fact another term of the contract which has been
broken by the other party. The aim is thus to prevent liability arising for breach of
contract outside of the terms of the written agreement. Entire agreement clauses can
also be utilized for another purpose, namely the attempt to eliminate any possible
liability for misrepresentation. Not all entire agreement clauses attempt to fulfil this
second function. For example, in *Deepak Fertilisers and Petrochemicals Corporation* v.
ICI Chemicals & Polymers Ltd [1999] 1 Lloyd's Rep 387 the entire agreement clause
consisted of the following:

This contract comprises the entire agreement between the parties, as detailed in the various
Articles and Annexures and there are not any agreements, understandings, promises or conditions,

oral or written, expressed or implied, concerning the subject matter which are not merged into this contract and superseded hereby. This contract may be amended in the future only in writing executed by the parties.

It was held that this clause was effective to exclude liability in respect of a collateral warranty. But it does not attempt to exclude liability for misrepresentation. A slightly more elaborate entire agreement clause is illustrated by *Watford Electronics Ltd* v. *Sanderson CFL Ltd* [2001] All ER (D) 290 where the entire agreement clause was drafted in the following terms:

The parties agree that these terms and conditions (together with any other terms and conditions expressly incorporated in the Contract) represent the entire agreement between the parties relating to the sale and purchase of the Equipment and that no statement or representations made by either party have been relied upon by the other in agreeing to enter into the Contract.

The addition of the words 'and that no statement or representations made by either party have been relied upon by the other in agreeing to enter into the Contract' were inserted in an attempt to exclude liability for misrepresentation. Whether such words are effective to exclude liability for misrepresentation is a difficult matter to which we shall return (at pp. 711–713 below). The modern practice of inserting entire agreement clauses into contracts is in many ways a reaction to the relaxation of the parol evidence rule (on which see pp. 335–340 above).

(k) TERMINATION CLAUSES

Contracting parties frequently produce standard form termination clauses which they insert into their contracts. Termination tends to be seen as an important right (or, if one prefers, remedy) in English contract law. The drafting of termination clauses is a difficult matter (on which see *Rice (t/a Garden Guardian)* v. *Great Yarmouth Borough Council, The Times*, 26 July 2000, at pp. 977–985 below). We shall examine termination clauses in more detail in a subsequent chapter (see pp. 977–985 below).

(l) ASSIGNMENT

The law allows parties, within prescribed limits, to assign their rights under the contract to another party. Standard terms of contract frequently regulate the entitlement of contracting parties to assign their rights. For example, clause 17(1) of the contract between the parties in *Linden Gardens Trust Ltd* v. *Lenesta Sludge Disposals Ltd* [1994] 1 AC 85 provided:

The Employer shall not without the written consent of the Contractor assign this Contract.

This clause is, in fact, drafted rather loosely in that it is the rights under the contract that are assigned and not the contract itself (see further pp. 1205–1207 below). But the House of Lords nevertheless gave effect to the clause and held that an attempted assignment of contractual rights in breach of the prohibition contained in clause 17 was ineffective to transfer any such contractual rights to the assignee.

(m) EXCLUSION AND LIMITATION CLAUSES

Exclusion and limitation clauses are both extremely important boilerplate clauses and they constitute the subject-matter of the next chapter.

5. FURTHER READING

CHRISTOU, R, *Boilerplate: Practical Clauses* (3rd edn, Sweet & Maxwell, 2002).

13

EXCLUSION CLAUSES

1. CENTRAL ISSUES

1. One of the most contentious boilerplate clauses in practice is an exclusion or limitation clause. This is particularly so in relation to liability for consequential losses. These losses can be enormous. Contracting parties generally wish both to contain and to control that risk. The clause that is generally used for this purpose is an exclusion or limitation clause (in this chapter the general term 'exclusion clause' will be used to refer to both exclusion and limitation clauses unless it is necessary to draw a distinction between an exclusion clause and a limitation clause in relation to the matter that is under discussion).

2. In order to perform its function an exclusion or limitation clause must (i) be validly incorporated into the contract, (ii) cover the loss which has been suffered, and (iii) survive scrutiny under the Unfair Contract Terms Act 1977, where that Act is applicable.

3. An exclusion or limitation clause must be drafted in clear terms if it is to be effective. In the past the courts interpreted exclusion clauses particularly strictly. The modern approach is to subject exclusion clauses to the ordinary rules of interpretation but it remains necessary for a lawyer drafting an exclusion clause to proceed with caution because remnants of the old restrictive rules remain.

4. The Unfair Contracts Terms Act 1977, despite its rather misleading title, does not apply to all unfair terms in contracts. It applies to exclusion, limitation, and indemnity clauses.

5. Two fundamental issues arise when seeking to apply the 1977 Act to a contract term. The first may be termed a jurisdictional question, that is to say, whether the Act applies to the term at all. Thus the court may be asked whether the clause is truly an exclusion clause or whether it is a clause that simply defines the obligations of the parties but does not purport to exclude liability for breach of an obligation. The second issue relates to the type of control that is applicable under the Act. Where the Act declares that the term is void no particular difficulty arises. On the other hand, where the clause is subject to a reasonableness test, then it can be a difficult matter to decide whether or not a term satisfies that test.

6. The final matter relates to the justification for subjecting exclusion, limitation, and indemnity clauses to distinct regulation. Why has Parliament chosen to intervene in order to regulate these clauses? If we think that unfair contract terms should be the subject of legislative control, why confine that control to one particular type of contract term? This issue will be explored briefly at the end of this chapter and in the following chapter.

2. INTRODUCTION

Exclusion clauses can be portrayed as a social nuisance on the basis that they are a means by which contracting parties can seek to avoid the consequences of their failure to perform their contractual obligations. Exclusion clauses provided an easy means by which a powerful party could exempt itself from any liability towards its contracting party. This was particularly so in relation to consumers. The infamous ticket cases in the late nineteenth century and the early part of the twentieth century (see, for example, *Parker* v. *South Eastern Railway* (1877) 2 CPD 416, at p. 354 above) demonstrated the willingness of business enterprises to make use of sweeping exemption clauses in their dealings with consumers. The problems presented by big business systematically excluding liability towards consumers continued well into the twentieth century, as can be demonstrated by cases such as *McCutcheon* v. *David MacBrayne Ltd* [1964] 1 WLR 125 (p. 363 above) and *Thornton* v. *Shoe Lane Park*ing *Ltd* [1971] 2 QB 163 (p. 358 above). It is, however, a mistake to see exclusion and limitation clauses entirely in this negative light. They can play an important (and positive) role in the regulation of risk.

An example of the role played by exclusion clauses in the regulation of risk is provided by the case of *British Fermentation Products Ltd* v. *Compair Reavell Ltd* [1999] BLR 352. The defendant sellers agreed to supply and install a centrifugal air compressor at the purchaser's premises. The contract price was 'a little under £300,000'. The purchasers alleged that the compressor did not perform to its contractually agreed level. Further, they alleged that, while the sellers had attempted to remedy the fault, they had been unable to do so and that, in consequence, they had suffered loss. That loss took the form of increased operating costs for the life of the machine of £1,168,584 and also loss of capacity and/or downtime. Here it can be seen that the consequential losses were almost four times the size of the contract price. Some businesses cannot afford to bear that type of loss and so rely on exclusion or limitation clauses in order to contain their potential liability. The defence of the sellers in *British Fermentation Products* depended upon the relationship between three clauses in the contract. The first was condition 4 which made provision for the testing of the compressor and stated that, if the compressor failed to pass the test, the purchaser was entitled 'by notice in writing to reject the goods or such part thereof as shall have failed' the test. Secondly, condition 5 gave to the purchasers the right to replace goods which were rejected and, in such a case, the defendants agreed to pay to the purchasers 'any sum by which the expenditure reasonably incurred by the Purchaser in replacing the rejected goods exceeds the sum deducted' in order to reflect the value of the rejected goods. The claimants decided not to exercise their rights under either condition 4 or condition 5. The third clause relied upon by the defendants was condition 11 which stated:

The Vendor's liability under this condition or under condition 5 (Rejection and Replacement) shall be accepted by the Purchaser in lieu of any warranty or condition implied by law as to the quality or fitness for any particular purpose of the goods and save as provided in this condition the Vendor shall not be under any liability to the Purchaser (whether in contract, tort or otherwise) for any defects in the goods or for any damage, loss, death or injury (other than death or personal injury caused by the negligence of the Vendor as defined in section 1 of the Unfair Contract Terms Act 1977) resulting from such defects or from any work done in connection therewith.

Judge Bowsher QC held that this clause was effective to exclude the vendors' liability to the purchasers. In reaching this conclusion Judge Bowsher was heavily influenced by his perception of the commercial purpose of condition 11 seen in the context of the contract as a whole. He stated (at p. 358):

It seems to me that the business common sense intention of the agreement as a whole is that the vendors undertake to supply a machine of the specification warranted, and if they fail in that undertaking the purchasers have an initial right to withdraw from the contract and reject the machine on terms that the vendors pay for them to buy from other suppliers a machine that is up to specification. If the purchasers so choose, there will be a period when the vendors will try to bring the machine up to specification, and those efforts again may be terminated by the purchasers by rejecting on the same agreed terms. If the purchasers still do not reject when the machine fails to come up to specification, the purchasers keep the machine but on terms that they do not complain thereafter of the failure to come up to specification. The amount of the damages claimed in this action compared with the purchase price shows the good business common sense of the contract. If the project is not successful, the purchasers have two opportunities to withdraw and buy a substitute machine of the standard warranted from another supplier at the vendor's expense, but they are not to be allowed to stand on the deal and charge the vendors enormous sums for their loss continuing for the life of the machine.

In the light of cases such as *British Fermentation Products* it is difficult to defend the view that exclusion clauses do not have a legitimate role to play in modern contract law. They clearly do play an important and valuable role in regulating and containing risk. The difficulty lies in determining when they perform a legitimate function and when they do not. In other words, exclusion and limitation clauses need to be regulated, not outlawed.

The nature of this regulation has changed over time. Prior to the enactment of the Unfair Contract Terms Act 1977 the courts did not have the power, at common law, to invalidate an exclusion or limitation clause on the ground that it was unreasonable. Lord Denning did attempt to formulate such a jurisdiction but his attempts in this regard were firmly rejected by the House of Lords. In the absence of a direct power to regulate unreasonable exclusion clauses the courts resorted to indirect means. The principal indirect means were the rules relating to the incorporation and interpretation of exclusion clauses. In cases such as *J Spurling Ltd* v. *Bradshaw* [1956] 1 WLR 461 (p. 357 above) and *Thornton* v. *Shoe Lane Parking Ltd* [1971] 2 QB 163 (p. 358 above) the courts were able in effect to regulate an unreasonable exclusion clause by concluding that it had not been incorporated into the contract. The other device which the courts used was to apply to exclusion clauses particularly restrictive rules of interpretation so as to enable them to conclude that the clause did not in fact exempt the defendant from the particular loss that the plaintiff had suffered. Now that the Unfair Contract Terms Act 1977 has been enacted, the need for these indirect methods of control has largely disappeared. The Act can now do the job. While there are signs in the case-law that these old restrictive rules are on the way out (see, for example, *Bank of Credit and Commerce International SA* v. *Ali* [2001] UKHL 8; [2002] 1 AC 251, p. 447 below) it cannot be said that they have disappeared (see, for example, *AEG (UK) Ltd* v. *Logic Resource Ltd* [1996] CLC 265, p. 361 above and note, in particular, the dissenting judgment of Hobhouse LJ). The law is currently in a state of transition. The status of some of the old cases, which adopt a restrictive approach to the interpretation of exclusion clauses, is presently uncertain.

A contracting party which wishes to rely on an exclusion or limitation clause in order to exclude or limit its liability towards its contracting party must prove two matters and may be subject to challenge on a third issue. The first matter which the party relying on the exclusion clause must prove is that the clause has been validly incorporated into the contract. Incorporation has been discussed in Chapter 9. It is not necessary to go over this ground again. It suffices to note that many (but not all) of the cases discussed in Chapter 9 are cases concerned with the incorporation of exclusion clauses into a contract and that the courts have often been reluctant to conclude that an exclusion clause has been so incorporated. Exclusion clauses are generally regarded as 'onerous' or 'unusual' and so attract the more stringent rules relating to the incorporation of terms into a contract (see generally *Interfoto Picture Library Ltd* v. *Stiletto Visual Programmes Ltd* [1989] QB 433, p. 351 above). The second matter which a party relying upon an exclusion clause must prove is that the exclusion clause, as a matter of construction, is effective to exclude liability for the loss that the claimant has suffered. The principles applied by the courts when interpreting contract terms have been discussed in Chapter 11 but it is necessary here to examine some of the particular principles of interpretation that have been formulated in the context of cases concerned with the interpretation of exclusion clauses. The future of these principles is a matter of some doubt. But it cannot yet be said that they have disappeared. The third matter relates to the Unfair Contract Terms Act 1977. A party relying on an exclusion clause does not have to prove that the clause is valid under the Act. It is for the party challenging the validity of the clause to prove that it falls within the scope of the Act but, once he does so, the onus of proof switches to the party relying upon the clause to prove that it is reasonable (at least in those cases in which the clause is subject to the reasonableness test).

3. INTERPRETATION

In the past the courts applied extremely restrictive rules to the interpretation of exclusion and limitation clauses. In essence what the courts did was to apply the *contra proferentem* principle with particular venom to exclusion clauses. *Contra proferentem* is a principle of general application in contract law. It is not confined to exclusion clauses (see *Tan Wing Chuen* v. *Bank of Credit and Commerce Hong Kong Ltd* [1996] 2 BCLC 69, 77). The principle itself is not an unreasonable one; it provides that, in the event of there being an ambiguity in a contract term, the ambiguity is to be resolved against the party relying upon the term. Thus an ambiguously drafted exclusion clause is ineffective to exclude liability, at least in the case where it is not clear whether the clause covers the loss that has been suffered. This is not an unreasonable result. But the principle was applied in an unreasonable way in an attempt to create an ambiguity in order to apply the rule (see, for example, *Wallis, Son and Wells* v. *Pratt and Haynes* [1911] AC 394 and *Andrews Bros (Bournemouth) Ltd* v. *Singer and Co Ltd* [1934] 1 KB 17). These old cases may now have been overruled. In *Investors Compensation Scheme Ltd* v. *West Bromwich Building Society* [1998] 1 WLR 896, 912 (see pp. 407–408 above) Lord Hoffmann stated that 'almost all the old intellectual baggage of "legal" interpretation has been discarded'. The significance of this sentence for the interpretation of exclusion and limitation clauses was explained by Lord Hoffmann in his dissenting speech in *Bank of Credit and Commerce International SA* v. *Ali* [2001] UKHL 8; [2002] 1 AC 251 in the following terms:

57. It was however unusual, even in the 19th century, for commercial documents to be interpreted according to rules of construction. The quest for certainty, which still dominated the construction of wills and deeds, was thought less important than the need to give effect to the actual commercial purpose of the document. There was however one remarkable example in the 20th century of a rule of construction being evolved by the courts in a commercial context. This was the rule for construing exemption clauses. But the purpose was different from that of most of the rules applied to wills and deeds. It was not to promote certainty of construction but to remedy the unfairness which exemption clauses could create. As Mr Allen [counsel for Mr Naeem] also contended for a rule of construction on grounds of fairness, I think that the story of the rise and fall of the rule of construction for exemption clauses may be instructive.

58. A vivid account of what happened was given by Lord Denning MR in *George Mitchell (Chesterhall) Ltd* v. *Finney Lock Seeds Ltd* [1983] QB 284, 296–297:

'None of you nowadays will remember the trouble we had—when I was called to the Bar—with exemption clauses. They were printed in small print on the back of tickets and order forms and invoices. They were contained in catalogues or timetables. They were held to be binding on any person who took them without objection. No one ever did object. He never read them or knew what was in them. No matter how unreasonable they were, he was bound. All this was done in the name of "freedom of contract". But the freedom was all on the side of the big concern which had the use of the printing press. No freedom for the little man who took the ticket or order form or invoice. The big concern said, "Take it or leave it". The little man had no option but to take it. The big concern could and did exempt itself from liability in its own interest without regard to the little man. It got away with it time after time. When the courts said to the big concern, "You must put it in clear words", the big concern had no hesitation in doing so. It knew well that the little man would never read the exemption clauses or understand them . . .

Faced with this abuse of power—by the strong against the weak—by the use of the small print of the conditions—the judges did what they could to put a curb upon it. They still had before them the idol, "freedom of contract". They still knelt down and worshipped it, but they concealed under their cloaks a secret weapon. They used it to stab the idol in the back. This weapon was called "the true construction of the contract". They used it with great skill and ingenuity. They used it so as to depart from the natural meaning of the words of the exemption clause and to put upon them a strained and unnatural construction. In case after case, they said that the words were not strong enough to give the big concern exemption from liability; or that in the circumstances the big concern was not entitled to rely on the exemption clause. If a ship deviated from the contractual voyage, the owner could not rely on the exemption clause. If a warehouseman stored the goods in the wrong warehouse, he could not pray in aid the limitation clause. If the seller supplied goods different in kind from those contracted for, he could not rely on any exemption from liability. If a shipowner delivered goods to a person without production of the bill of lading, he could not escape responsibility by reference to an exemption clause. In short, whenever the wide words—in their natural meaning—would give rise to an unreasonable result, the judges either rejected them as repugnant to the main purpose of the contract, or else cut them down to size in order to produce a reasonable result.'

59. Lord Denning went on, at pp. 298–299 to explain that everything had now changed as a result of the passing of the Unfair Contract Terms Act 1977. 'We should no longer have to go through all kinds of gymnastic contortions to get round them'. A few years earlier, in *Photo Production Ltd* v. *Securicor Transport Ltd* [1980] AC 827, 843 Lord Wilberforce had said much the same thing:

'There was a large number of problems, productive of injustice, in which it was worse than unsatisfactory to leave exception clauses to operate. Lord Reid referred to these in *Suisse Atlantique Société d'Armement Maritime SA* v. *NV Rotterdamsche Kolen Centrale* [1967] 1 AC 361, 406, pointing out at the same time that the doctrine of fundamental breach was a dubious specific. But since then Parliament has taken a hand: it has passed the Unfair Contract Terms Act 1977. This Act applies to consumer contracts and those based on standard terms and enables exception clauses to be applied with regard to what is just and reasonable. It is significant that Parliament refrained from legislating over the whole field of contract. After this Act, in commercial matters generally, when the parties are not of unequal bargaining power, and when risks are normally borne by insurance, not only is the case for judicial intervention undemonstrated, but there is everything to be said, and this seems to have been Parliament's intention, for leaving the parties free to apportion the risks as they think fit and for respecting their decisions.'

60. My Lords, the lesson which I would draw from the development of the rules for construing exemption clauses is that the judicial creativity, bordering on judicial legislation, which the application of that doctrine involved is a desperate remedy, to be invoked only if it is necessary to remedy a widespread injustice. Otherwise there is much to be said for giving effect to what on ordinary principles of construction the parties agreed.

61. Whether such a rule of construction is necessary in this case can best be considered after I have dealt with the second point, namely whether BCCI is precluded on grounds of fairness and equity from relying upon the ordinary meaning of the release. It will then be possible to say whether the law is adequate to deal with cases of unfairness, so as to make it unnecessary to approach the matter by an artificial rule of construction. When judges say that 'in the absence of clear words' they would be unwilling to construe a document to mean something, they generally mean (as they did in the case of exemption clauses) that the effect of the document is unfair. It will therefore be essential to examine whether this is true of the present case.

62. The disappearance of artificial rules for the construction of exemption clauses seems to me in accordance with the general trend in matters of construction, which has been to try to assimilate judicial techniques of construction to those which would be used by a reasonable speaker of the language in the interpretation of any serious utterance in ordinary life. In *Investors Compensation Scheme Ltd* v. *West Bromwich Building Society* [1998] 1 WLR 896, 912, I said with the concurrence of three other members of the House: 'Almost all the old intellectual baggage of "legal" interpretation has been discarded'. But if Mr Allen's submissions on the rules of construction are accepted, a substantial piece of baggage will have been retrieved. Lord Keeper Henley's ghost (*Salkeld* v. *Vernon*, 1 Eden 64) will have struck back. I think it would be an unfortunate retreat into formalism if the outcome of this case were to require employers using the services of Acas to add verbiage to the form of release in order to attain the comprehensiveness which it is obviously intended to achieve.

Two factors may be said to cast doubt over the authority of this passage. The first is that it is clearly *obiter* because *BCCI* v. *Ali* was a case concerned with the interpretation of a release, not the interpretation of an exemption clause. The second is the fact that Lord Hoffmann's speech was a dissenting speech. However it is suggested that this factor cannot be decisive because Lord Hoffmann was in fact providing a gloss on his own speech in *Investors Compensation Scheme* and there he was speaking for the majority of their Lordships.

The crucial question that must now be answered by the courts is this: has Lord Hoffmann's statement in *Investors Compensation Scheme* that 'almost all the old intellectual baggage of "legal" interpretation has been discarded' had the effect of overruling all the old cases in which 'artificial rules' for the interpretation of exclusion clauses were adopted? The cases post-*Investors Compensation Scheme* do provide some support for a more relaxed approach to the interpretation of exclusion clauses and judges have cited *Investors Compensation Scheme* when adopting a more clement approach (see, for example, *National Westminster Bank* v. *Utrecht-America Finance Co* [2001] EWCA Civ 658; [2001] 3 All ER 733 and *British Fermentation Products Ltd* v. *Compair Reavell Ltd* [1999] BLR 352, p. 444 above). But it may be too soon to write the obituary for the old rules applicable to the interpretation of exclusion clauses. Some of the cases in which these rules were enunciated have been approved by appellate courts and cannot easily be swept aside.

There is one particular context in which the old rules may have survived and that is in the case where one party relies on an exclusion clause in order to exclude or limit liability for his own negligence. The rules or, more accurately, the principles applied by the courts when deciding whether or not a party has effectively excluded liability for his own negligence or the negligence of his employees was authoritatively stated by Lord Morton of Henryton in *Canada Steamship Lines Ltd* v. *The King* [1952] AC 192, 208 in the following terms:

Their Lordships think that the duty of a court in approaching the consideration of such clauses may be summarized as follows:-

(1) If the clause contains language which expressly exempts the person in whose favour it is made (hereafter called 'the proferens') from the consequence of the negligence of his own servants, effect must be given to that provision . . .

(2) If there is no express reference to negligence, the court must consider whether the words used are wide enough, in their ordinary meaning, to cover negligence on the part of the servants of the proferens. If a doubt arises at this point, it must be resolved against the proferens . . .

(3) If the words used are wide enough for the above purpose, the court must then consider whether 'the head of damage may be based on some ground other than that of negligence', to quote again Lord Greene in the *Alderslade* case [1945] KB 189, 192. The 'other

ground' must not be so fanciful or remote that the proferens cannot be supposed to have desired protection against it; but subject to this qualification, which is no doubt to be implied from Lord Greene's words, the existence of a possible head of damage other than that of negligence is fatal to the proferens even if the words used are prima facie wide enough to cover negligence on the part of his servants.

The first of these three principles is not problematic. If a clause 'expressly exempts' a party from the consequences of his or his employees' negligence then the clause is effective, as a matter of interpretation, to exclude liability for negligence. In order to constitute an express reference to negligence it does not suffice for a party to use general words such as 'loss however caused' or 'damage howsoever arising'. The word 'negligence' or a synonym for negligence (such as carelessness) must be used (see *Shell Chemicals UK Ltd* v. *P & O Roadtanks Ltd* [1995] 1 Lloyd's Rep 297, 301). The problem lies with the second and the third principles because they rest on the dubious assumption that parties do not intend to use general words such as 'loss howsoever caused' to cover both negligently inflicted loss and non-negligently inflicted loss. One would have thought that the natural inference to be drawn from the use of such general words is that the precise cause of the loss is irrelevant so that the clause is apt to encompass loss whether or not it is caused by negligence. But this is not the approach taken by the courts. According to the third principle, general words will only be effective to exclude liability for negligently inflicted loss in the case where the only realistic loss likely to be suffered by the claimant is loss suffered as a result of the negligence of the defendants. Where there is a realistic possibility that the defendant might be liable to the claimant either in negligence or on some other basis then the scope of the exclusion clause will generally be confined to the non-negligent source of liability and leave the defendant with no protection at all in the event that the claimant suffers loss as a result of the negligence of the defendant. The impact of these rules at work can be demonstrated by reference to the following case:

Hollier v. Rambler Motors (AMC) Ltd

[1972] 2 QB 71, Court of Appeal

The plaintiff brought an action for damages against the defendant garage after his car had been badly damaged in a fire at the defendants' garage. The fire was caused by the defendants' negligence. The car had been left with the defendants so that repair work could be undertaken. The defendants sought to rely on an exclusion clause contained in an invoice which stated that 'The company is not responsible for damage caused by fire to customers' cars on the premises'. The Court of Appeal held that the exclusion clause had not been validly incorporated into the contract with the plaintiff and for that reason it was ineffective to exclude liability to the plaintiff (see p. 367 above). This sufficed to decide the case but the judges nevertheless went on to consider whether the clause was effective, as a matter of construction, to exclude the defendants' liability in negligence. They concluded that it was not.

Salmon LJ [held that the clause had not been incorporated into the contract and continued]

That really disposes of this appeal, but in case I am wrong on the view that I have formed, without any hesitation, I may say, that the course of dealing did not import the so-called exclusion clause, I think I should deal with the point as to whether or not the words on the bottom of the form, had they been incorporated in the contract, would have excluded the defendants' liability to compensate the plaintiff for damage caused to the plaintiff's car by a fire which in turn had been caused by the defendants' own negligence. It is well settled that a clause excluding liability for negligence should make its meaning plain on its face to any ordinarily literate and sensible person. The easiest way of doing that, of course, is to state expressly that the garage, tradesman or merchant, as the case may be, will not be responsible for any damage caused by his own negligence. No doubt merchants, tradesmen, garage proprietors and the like are a little shy of writing in an exclusion clause quite so bluntly as that. Clearly it would not tend to attract customers, and might even put many off. I am not saying that an exclusion clause cannot be effective to exclude negligence unless it does so expressly, but in order for the clause to be effective the language should be so plain that it clearly bears that meaning. I do not think that defendants should be allowed to shelter behind language which might lull the customer into a false sense of security by letting him think—unless perhaps he happens to be a lawyer—that he would have redress against the man with whom he was dealing for any damage which he, the customer, might suffer by the negligence of that person.

The principles are stated by Scrutton LJ with his usual clarity in *Rutter* v. *Palmer* [1922] 2 KB 87, 92:

> 'For the present purposes a rougher test will serve. In construing an exemption clause certain general rules may be applied: First the defendant is not exempted from liability for the negligence of his servants unless adequate words are used; secondly, the liability of the defendant apart from the exempting words must be ascertained; then the particular clause in question must be considered; and if the only liability of the party pleading the exemption is a liability for negligence, the clause will more readily operate to exempt him.'

Scrutton LJ was far too great a lawyer, and had far too much robust common sense, if I may be permitted to say so, to put it higher than that 'if the only liability of the party pleading the exemption is a liability for negligence, the clause will more readily operate to exempt him'. He does not say that 'if the only liability of the party pleading the exemption is a liability for negligence, the clause will necessarily exempt him'. After all, there are many cases in the books dealing with exemption clauses, and in every case it comes down to a question of construing the alleged exemption clause which is then before the court. It seems to me that in *Rutter* v. *Palmer*, although the word 'negligence' was never used in the exemption clause, the exemption clause would have conveyed to any ordinary, literate and sensible person that the garage in that case was inserting a clause in the contract which excluded their liability for the negligence of their drivers. The clause being considered in that case—and it was without any doubt incorporated in the contract—was: 'Customers' cars are driven by your staff at customers' sole risk'. Any ordinary man knows that when a car is damaged it is not infrequently damaged because the driver has driven it negligently. He also knows, I suppose, that if he sends it to a garage and a driver in the employ of the garage takes the car on the road for some purpose in connection with the work which the customer has entrusted the garage to do, the garage could not conceivably be liable for the car being damaged in an accident unless the driver was at fault. It follows that no sensible man could have thought that the words in that case had any meaning except that the garage would not be liable for the negligence of their own drivers. That is a typical case where, on the construction of the clause in question, the meaning for which the defendant was there contending was the obvious meaning of the clause.

The next case to which I wish to refer is the well-known case of *Alderslade* v. *Hendon Laundry Ltd* [1945] 1 KB 189. In that case articles were sent by the plaintiff to the defendants' laundry to be washed, and they were lost. In an action by the plaintiff against the defendants for damages, the defendants relied on the following condition to limit their liability: 'The maximum amount allowed for lost or damaged articles is 20 times the charge made for laundering'. Again, this was a case where negligence was not expressly excluded. The question was: what do the words mean? I have no doubt that they would mean to the ordinary housewife who was sending her washing to the laundry that, if the goods were lost or damaged in the course of being washed through the negligence of the laundry, the laundry would not be liable for more than 20 times the charge made for the laundering. I say that for this reason. It is, I think, obvious that when a laundry loses or damages goods it is almost invariably because there has been some neglect or default on the part of the laundry. It is said that thieves break in and steal, and the goods (in that case handkerchiefs) might have been stolen by thieves. That of course is possible, but I should hardly think that a laundry would be a great allurement to burglars. It is a little far-fetched to think of burglars breaking into a laundry to steal the washing when there are banks, jewellers, post offices, factories, offices and homes likely to contain money and articles far more attractive to burglars. I think that the ordinary sensible housewife, or indeed anyone else who sends washing to the laundry, who saw that clause must have appreciated that almost always goods are lost or damaged because of the laundry's negligence, and therefore this clause could apply only to limit the liability of the laundry, when they were in fault or negligent.

But Mr Tuckey [counsel for the defendants] has drawn our attention to the way in which the matter was put by Lord Greene MR in delivering the leading judgment in this court, and he contends that Lord Greene MR was in fact making a considerable extension to the law as laid down by Scrutton LJ in the case to which I have referred. For this proposition he relies on the following passage in Lord Greene MR's judgment, at p. 192:

'The effect of those authorities can I think be stated as follows: Where the head of damage in respect of which limitation of liability is sought to be imposed by such a clause is one which rests on negligence and nothing else, the clause must be construed as extending to that head of damage, because it would otherwise lack subject matter.'

If one takes that word 'must' au pied de la lettre that passage does support Mr Tuckey's contention. However, we are not here construing a statute, but a passage in an unreserved judgment of Lord Greene MR, who was clearly intending no more than to re-state the effect of the authorities as they then stood. It is to be observed that MacKinnon LJ, who gave the other judgment in this court, set out the rule or principle which he said was very admirably stated by Scrutton LJ in *Rutter* v. *Palmer* [1922] 2 KB 87. He said, at p. 195:

'Applying that principle to the facts of the case, I think that the clause in question does avail to protect the proprietors of the laundry in respect of liability for negligence which must be assumed to be the cause of these handkerchiefs having disappeared.'

And clearly it did, for the reasons that I have already given. I do not think that Lord Greene MR was intending to extend the law in the sense for which Mr Tuckey contends. If it were so extended, it would make the law entirely artificial by ignoring that rules of construction are merely our guides and not our masters; in the end you are driven back to construing the clause in question to see what it means. Applying the principles laid down by Scrutton LJ, they lead to the result at which the court arrived in *Aldersdale* v. *Hendon Laundry Ltd* [1945] 1 KB 189. In my judgment these principles lead to a very different result in the present case. The words are: 'The company is not responsible for damage caused by fire to customers' cars on the premises'. What would that mean to any ordinarily literate and sensible car owner? I do not suppose that any such, unless he is a trained lawyer, has an intimate or indeed any knowledge of the liability of bailees in law. If you asked the ordinary man or woman: 'Supposing you send your car to the garage to be repaired, and there is a fire, would you suppose that the garage would be liable?' I should be surprised if many of them did not answer, quite wrongly: 'Of course they are liable if there is a fire'. Others might be more cautious and say: 'Well, I had better ask my solicitor', or, 'I do not know. I suppose they may well be liable'. That is the crucial difference, to my mind, between the present case and *Aldersdale* v. *Hendon Laundry Ltd* and *Rutter* v. *Palmer* [1922] 2 KB 87. In those two cases, any ordinary man or woman reading the conditions would have known that all that was being excluded was the negligence of the laundry, in the one case, and the garage, in the other. But here I think the ordinary man or woman would be equally surprised and horrified to learn that if the garage was so negligent that a fire was caused which damaged their car, they would be without remedy because of the words in the condition. I can quite understand that the ordinary man or woman would consider that, because of these words, the mere fact that there was a fire would not make the garage liable. Fires can occur from a large variety of causes, only one of which is negligence on the part of the occupier of the premises, and that is by no means the most frequent cause. The ordinary man would I think say to himself: 'Well, what they are telling me is that if there is a fire due to any cause other than their own negligence they are not responsible for it'. To my mind, if the defendants were seeking to exclude their responsibility for a fire caused by their own negligence, they ought to have done so in far plainer language than the language here used.

Stamp LJ
On the question of construction, I reach the same conclusion as Salmon LJ, but by, I think, a slightly different route. As I understand the law, it is settled that where in a contract such as this you find a provision excluding liability capable of two constructions, one of which will make it applicable where there is no negligence by the defendant, and the other will make it applicable where there is negligence by the defendant, it requires special words or special circumstances to make the clause exclude liability in case of negligence: see, for example, *Price & Co* v. *Union Lighterage Co* [1904] 1 KB 412. Similarly, I would hold that, where the words relied upon by the defendant are susceptible either to a construction under which they become a statement of fact in the nature of a warning or to a construction which will exempt the defendant from liability for negligence, the former construction is to be preferred. The words here, 'the company is not responsible for damage caused by fire to customers' cars on the premises', are, in my

judgment, certainly susceptible to a construction which would regard them as a mere statement in the nature of a warning, and reinforced by the principle that I have stated, I would hold that that is how they ought to be construed in this case. If this be correct, I do not find it necessary to consider the cases which have been decided upon the footing that the clause under consideration was a term of the contract excluding some liability: for on the view that I have formed, the clause on its true construction is not a clause of that nature.

Latey J delivered a concurring judgment.

COMMENTARY

The first paragraph from the judgment of Salmon LJ emphasizes the importance of using clear words. A party who wishes to exclude liability for negligence should say so expressly and then effect will be given to the clause (subject now to the Unfair Contract Terms Act 1977, on which see pp. 460–485 below). On the other hand, a party who is 'shy' of making express reference to negligence in his exclusion clause runs the risk that his clause will be held to be ineffective, as a matter of construction, to exclude liability for negligence. This may be a reasonable conclusion to reach if the aim of the law is to require parties wishing to exclude liability for their own negligence to use the word 'negligence' expressly in their clause. But it seems unreasonable if the aim is to give effect to the intention of the parties because it denies to parties the ability to use words such as 'loss howsoever arising' if they wish to be sure that they have excluded liability for negligently inflicted harm. The law does not conclude that such general words are always ineffective to exclude liability for negligence because liability was effectively excluded in both *Rutter* v. *Palmer* and *Alderslade* v. *Hendon Laundry Ltd* (both of which are discussed in the judgment of Salmon LJ). But it is very difficult to have any confidence in the effectiveness of such general words. This can be demonstrated by contrasting the facts of *Rutter* v. *Palmer* with *Hollier*. What would have been the position in *Hollier* if the car had gone on fire after being involved in a crash caused by the negligence of one of the defendants' employees? Would such a case fall within the scope of *Rutter* or *Hollier*? It is impossible to be sure.

The basic flaw in the *Canada Steamship* rules is the assumption that contracting parties do not intend to use general words of exclusion to cover both negligently inflicted loss and non-negligently inflicted loss. This 'assumption' does not take the form of a rule of law. As Salmon LJ stated in *Hollier* 'rules of construction are merely our guides and not our masters'. It is therefore open to a court to conclude that a clause is effective to exclude liability for negligence under the third limb of *Canada Steamship* notwithstanding the fact that it was possible to envisage some other possible source of liability to which the clause might potentially apply (see *The Raphael* [1982] 2 Lloyd's Rep 42). But the more realistic the alternative source of liability, the less likely it is that the court will conclude that general words are effective to exclude liability for negligently inflicted loss (see *EE Caledonia Ltd* v. *Orbit Valve Co Europe* [1994] 1 WLR 1515).

The *Canada Steamship* rules cannot be easily cast aside. They have been applied by the House of Lords (*Smith* v. *South Wales Switchgear Ltd* [1978] 1 WLR 165) and by the Court of Appeal on numerous occasions (see, for example, *EE Caledonia Ltd* v.

Orbit Valve Co Europe [1994] 1 WLR 1515 and *Dorset County Council* v. *Southern Felt Roofing Co Ltd* (1989) 48 Build LR 96). It is therefore highly unlikely that a single sentence expressed in general terms in *Investors Compensation Scheme,* combined with Lord Hoffmann's elaboration in *BCCI* v. *Ali,* will suffice to overrule the *Canada Steamship* line of authority. Yet the relationship between *Investors Compensation Scheme* and *Canada Steamship* is an uneasy one. This can be demonstrated by reference to the decision of the Court of Appeal in *National Westminster Bank* v. *Utrecht-America Finance Company* [2001] EWCA Civ 733; [2001] 3 All ER 733. The issue before the Court of Appeal was whether or not the *Canada Steamship* rules applied to a clause (clause 8.2(d)) that, in essence, purported to exclude liability for both negligent and fraudulent non-disclosure. Clarke LJ referred to the *Canada Steamship* rules and stated, at paragraph [47], that Lord Morton's rules 'are essentially rules or principles of construction'. He stated that they remained 'valuable tools' in the construction of the contract but then attempted to link them with the principles of construction set out by Lord Hoffmann in *Investors Compensation Scheme* (p. 408 above) by stating (at para [48]) that 'like any clause, cl. 8.2(d) must be construed in its context and in the context of the contract as a whole having regard to its factual matrix or surrounding circumstances'. Clarke LJ concluded (at para [49]) that clause 8.2(d) was 'a far cry from the kind of clause which the courts have had in mind in the kind of case in which they have applied Lord Morton's tests'. The background to clause 8.2(d) was that the parties were two large banks, dealing at arm's length and advised by skilled commercial lawyers. The terms of the contract demonstrated that they had agreed that neither party was under a duty to disclose information to the other. He concluded (at para [52]), applying Lord Hoffmann's approach in *Investors Compensation Scheme,* that in these circumstances there was 'no room for the application of Lord Morton's tests' and that effect should be given to the 'clear and unambiguous' terms of the clause which were that 'neither bank can be liable for breach of a duty to disclose, whether the failure to disclose is categorised by a foreign law as negligent, fraudulent or otherwise' (however it should be noted that the case was concerned with liability for non-disclosure and that the Court of Appeal expressly recognized that the position would have been different had the clause purported to exclude liability for misrepresentation).

There is a tension in the judgment of Clarke LJ. On the one hand, he acknowledged that Lord Morton's tests remained 'valuable tools' but on the other hand he concluded that there was 'no room' for their application to the clause in issue between the parties. Why was there this reluctance to apply the tests? The only possible answer seems to be that the *Canada Steamship* tests can fail to give effect to the intentions of the parties. This is particularly so in relation to a clause that excludes liability for damage 'howsoever caused'. As has been noted, this does not count as an express reference to negligence within limb one of the *Canada Steamship* tests and so will only be effective to exclude liability for negligence where there is no other realistic source of liability that can fall within the scope of the clause. In other words the tests are based on the assumption that the parties did not intend to encompass more than one type of loss within the same clause. Yet where the parties use the words 'howsoever caused' surely this is their intention. The Australian courts have departed from the

Canada Steamship rules. In *Schenker & Co (Aust) Pty Ltd* v. *Malpas Equipment and Services Pty Ltd* [1990] VR 834 McGarvie J concluded (at p. 846) that

> to construe commercial contracts as they would be understood by business people serves primary aims of both the law and commerce. The law serves the community best if citizens understand it and are able to resolve their dispute themselves by reference to it, without resorting to lawyers.

The first sentence from this quotation very much reflects the sentiments of Lord Hoffmann's re-statement in *Investors Compensation Scheme* and, in principle, there is much to be said for it. But it is an approach that must lead to the overruling of the *Canada Steamship* line of authority and, if this is to be done, it should be done explicitly and not left to implication. This would leave the regulation of exclusion clauses largely to the control of the Unfair Contract Terms Act 1977. Support for such a proposition can be derived from the speech of Lord Diplock in *Photo Production Ltd* v. *Securicor Transport Ltd* [1980] AC 827, 851 when he stated:

> My Lords, the reports are full of cases in which what would appear to be very strained constructions have been placed upon exclusion clauses, mainly in what to-day would be called consumer contracts and contracts of adhesion. As Lord Wilberforce has pointed out, any need for this kind of judicial distortion of the English language has been banished by Parliament's having made these kinds of contracts subject to the Unfair Contract Terms Act 1977. In commercial contracts negotiated between business-men capable of looking after their own interests and of deciding how risks inherent in the performance of various kinds of contract can be most economically borne (generally by insurance), it is, in my view, wrong to place a strained construction upon words in an exclusion clause which are clear and fairly susceptible of one meaning only.

Adoption of this approach must surely lead to the demise of the *Canada Steamship* rules. They are part of the 'intellectual baggage' which Lord Hoffmann is seeking to discard on the basis that they are 'artificial' or, in the words of Lord Diplock, 'strained'.

However the House of Lords has refused to discard the *Canada Steamship* rules. Instead they have retained them while emphasizing that the paramount task of the court is to give effect to the intention of the parties (see *HIH Casualty and General Insurance Ltd* v. *Chase Manhattan Bank* [2003] UKHL 6; [2003] 2 Lloyd's Rep 61 at [11], [61]–[63], [95], and [116]). The approach of their Lordships was best summed up by Lord Bingham in the following passage (at [11]):

> There can be no doubting the general authority of [Lord Morton's principles], which have been applied in many cases, and the approach indicated is sound. The courts should not ordinarily infer that a contracting party has given up rights which the law confers upon him to an extent greater than the contract terms indicate he has chosen to do; and if the contract terms can take legal and practical effect without denying him the rights he would ordinarily enjoy if the other party is negligent, they will be read as not denying him those rights unless they are so expressed as to make clear that they do.

On this basis Lord Morton's rules may express no more than a judicial reluctance to conclude that one party has agreed to exempt the other party from the consequences of his negligence. This reluctance is understandable but it does not justify the *Canada Steamship* rules, in particular the operation of the second and the third rules. These rules should be discarded and the courts should instead be left free to give the words in the contract their natural and ordinary meaning. This being the case, words such as 'howsoever caused' or 'howsoever arising' should ordinarily be effective to exclude liability in negligence.

Three points remain to be made in relation to the interpretation of exclusion clauses. The first relates to the doctrine of fundamental breach. This doctrine gave rise to a considerable amount of difficulty in the 1960s and 1970s. It was, essentially, a device that was used by the courts in order to control unreasonable exclusion clauses before they were given statutory jurisdiction to do so in the Unfair Contract Terms Act 1977. The principal architect of the doctrine was Lord Denning. In *Harbutt's Plasticine Ltd* v. *Wayne Tank and Pump Co Ltd* [1970] 1 QB 447, 467 Lord Denning MR stated:

> when one party has been guilty of a fundamental breach of the contract, that is, a breach which goes to the very root of it, and the other side accepts it, so that the contract comes to an end—or if it comes to an end anyway by reason of the breach—then the guilty party cannot rely on an exemption or limitation clause to escape from his liability for the breach.

The importance of this statement lies in the assertion that, as a matter of law, a party cannot rely on an exclusion or limitation clause where he has committed a fundamental breach of the contract. In making this statement Lord Denning was purporting to summarize the decision of the House of Lords in *Suisse Atlantique Société d'Armement Maritime SA* v. *NV Rotterdamsche Kolen Centrale* [1967] 1 AC 361. His summary was demonstrably faulty. The House of Lords in *Suisse Atlantique* laid down no such rule. It is admittedly not entirely easy to extract a clear ratio from the lengthy judgments of the House of Lords in that case but it is tolerably clear that their conclusion was that fundamental breach was a rule of construction not a rule of law. In other words, it was a rule that stated, the more serious the breach, the clearer the words that have to be used in order to exclude liability for the breach. This reflects the ordinary, common sense perception that one party is unlikely to agree that the other party can breach the contract in a fundamental respect without incurring any liability for doing so. The House of Lords did not state that, as a matter of law, one party cannot exclude or limit liability for a fundamental breach of contract.

That this was so was confirmed by the House of Lords in *Photo Production Ltd* v. *Securicor Transport Ltd* [1980] AC 827. The House of Lords overruled *Harbutt's Plasticine* and held that the question whether or not an exclusion or limitation clause is effective to exclude or limit liability is, in all cases, a question of construction. In doing so, their Lordships did not deny that Lord Denning's version of fundamental breach had performed a useful function in the past, but they concluded that it was no longer necessary in the light of the enactment of the Unfair Contract Terms Act 1977. Thus Lord Wilberforce acknowledged (at p. 843) that the 'doctrine of "fundamental breach" in spite of its imperfections and doubtful parentage [had] served a useful purpose' but went on, in the passage quoted by Lord Hoffmann in *BCCI* v. *Ali* (p. 447 above) to state that there was no longer any need for the doctrine in the light of the enactment of the Unfair Contract Terms Act.

In *George Mitchell (Chesterhall) Ltd* v. *Finney Lock Seeds Ltd* [1983] 2 AC 803 Lord Bridge stated (at p. 813) that *Photo Production* 'gave the final quietus to the doctrine that a "fundamental breach" of contract deprived the party in breach of the benefit of clauses in the contract excluding or limiting his liability'. Further, as Neill LJ stated in *Edmund Murray Ltd* v. *BSP International Foundations Ltd* (1993) 33 Con LR 1, 16:

it is always necessary when considering an exemption clause to decide whether as a matter of construction it extends to exclude or restrict the liability in question, but, if it does, it is no longer permissible at common law to reject or circumvent the clause by treating it as inapplicable to 'a fundamental breach'.

The second point to note is that there is authority to the effect that limitation clauses are not interpreted as restrictively as exclusion clauses. In *Ailsa Craig Fishing Co Ltd* v. *Malvern Fishing Co Ltd* [1983] 1 WLR 964 Lord Fraser of Tullybelton stated (at p. 970):

There are . . . authorities which lay down very strict principles to be applied when considering the effect of clauses of exclusion or of indemnity . . . In my opinion these principles are not applicable in their full rigour when considering the effect of clauses merely limiting liability. Such clauses will of course be read contra proferentem and must be clearly expressed, but there is no reason why they should be judged by the specially exacting standards which are applied to exclusion and indemnity clauses. The reason for imposing such standards on these clauses is the inherent improbability that the other party to a contract including such a clause intended to release the proferens from a liability that would otherwise fall upon him. But there is no such high degree of improbability that he would agree to a limitation of the liability of the proferens, especially when . . . the potential losses that might be caused by the negligence of the proferens or its servants are so great in proportion to the sums that can reasonably be charged for the services contracted for. It is enough in the present case that the clause must be clear and unambiguous.

The justification put forward in support of this difference in treatment between exclusion clauses and limitation clauses is not particularly convincing. The improbability of a party agreeing to an exclusion clause is not necessarily much greater than the improbability of a party agreeing to a limitation clause. Much depends upon the size of the limitation clause. A limitation clause of £1 is very similar to a total exclusion of liability. In *BHP Petroleum Ltd* v. *British Steel plc* [2000] 2 Lloyd's Rep 277 Evans LJ stated (at p. 285):

I think it is unfortunate if the present authorities cannot be reconciled on the basis that no categorization is necessary and of a general rule that the more extreme the consequences are, in terms of excluding or modifying the liability which would otherwise arise, then the more stringent the Court's approach should be in requiring that the exclusion or limit should be clearly and unambiguously expressed. Indeed, if the requirement is of a clear and unambiguous provision, then it is not easy to see why degrees of clarity and lack of unambiguity should be recognized.

The third point relates to the meaning of the phrase 'indirect or consequential loss'. As has been noted (p. 444 above), claims for consequential losses can be enormous. This being the case, parties frequently wish to exclude liability for consequential losses and they often do so by excluding liability for 'indirect or consequential loss' in order to keep liability within acceptable bounds. But what does this phrase mean? Its meaning has been considered by the Court of Appeal on a number of occasions. One such case is *Hotel Services Ltd* v. *Hilton International Hotels (UK) Ltd* [2000] BLR 235. The parties entered into a contract under which the defendants agreed to supply the claimants with 'Robobars' for their hotels. A 'Robobar' was a hotel minibar which automatically recorded any removal of its contents and at the same time electronically registered the item concerned on the account of the guest. The attraction for the claimants was the obvious one, namely that it was hoped that it would reduce the incidence of theft from hotel minibars. Unfortunately, the Robobars proved to be defective in that their chillers leaked ammonia which corroded the equipment and also created a very small risk of injury to guests in the hotel. The claimants therefore removed the Robobars from their hotels and brought an action for damages against the defendants, in which they claimed the cost of removal and storage of the chiller units and cabinets and their loss of profit on the minibars. The defendants relied on an exclusion clause in the following terms:

The Company will not in any circumstances be liable for any indirect or consequential loss, damage or liability arising from any defect in or failure of the System or any part thereof or the performance of this Agreement or any breach hereof by the Company or its employees.

The issue before the Court of Appeal was whether or not this clause was effective to exclude liability for the losses claimed by the claimants. The Court of Appeal held that it was not. The important distinction that must be drawn in this context is between a 'direct' loss (which is outside the scope of the exclusion clause) and an 'indirect' loss (which is within its scope). As a matter of authority the line between direct and indirect or consequential losses is drawn along the boundary between the first and second limbs of the rule in *Hadley* v. *Baxendale* (1854) 9 Exch 341 (discussed in more detail at pp. 1079–1082 below). In other words, if the loss is such as may fairly and reasonably be considered as arising naturally from the breach of contract ('limb one'), it is a direct loss. On the other hand, if the loss is such as may reasonably be supposed to have been in the contemplation of both parties at the time of entry into the contract ('limb two'), it is an indirect or consequential loss. Although the task of distinguishing between limb one of *Hadley* v. *Baxendale* and limb two is not always an easy one (see further p. 1080 below), the Court of Appeal did not experience any difficulty in applying it to the facts of the present case. Thus Lord Justice Sedley stated (at p. 241) that:

we prefer . . . to decide this case . . . on the direct ground that if equipment rented out for selling drinks without defalcations turns out to be unusable and possibly dangerous, it requires no special mutually known fact to establish the immediacy both of the consequent cost of putting it where it can do no harm and—if when in use it was showing a direct profit—of the consequent loss of profit. Such losses are not embraced by the exclusion clause, read in its documentary and commercial context.

The loss of profit claim on the facts of the case amounted to £127,000, yet it was all held to be a direct consequence of the breach and so not within scope of the exclusion clause. The clause was only effective to exclude liability for losses of profit that were not direct but were nevertheless recoverable because they were within the contemplation of both parties at the time of entry into the contract (as in *Victoria Laundry (Windsor) Ltd* v. *Newman Industries Ltd* [1949] 2 KB 528, p. 1082 below). This being the case, a clause which excludes liability for 'indirect or consequential losses' will provide very little protection for a defendant because many sizeable loss of profit claims will fall within the category of 'direct' rather than 'indirect' losses. If the intention of the defendant is to exclude liability for loss of profits suffered by the claimant then the exclusion or limitation clause should make express reference to the exclusion of loss of profit claims and not rely on general words of uncertain scope, such as 'indirect or consequential loss'. That said, there may be some hope for defendants who rely on such clauses. In *Caledonia North Sea Ltd* v. *British Telecommunications plc* [2002] UKHL 4; [2002] 1 Lloyd's Rep 553, Lord Hoffmann stated (at para [100]) that he wished to 'reserve the question of whether, in the context of the contracts in the *Hotel Services* and similar cases, the construction adopted by the Court of Appeal was correct'. This remark is not sufficient to overturn the line of authority represented by *Hotel Services*. These cases therefore remain good law. But they may not survive scrutiny in the House of Lords. The current uncertainty surrounding the meaning of the phrase 'indirect or consequential loss' is unfortunate given the widespread reliance upon the phrase in practice and the size of many consequential loss claims. Contracting parties, and their lawyers, need to have clearer guidance on this point from the courts. At the moment it is extremely difficult, if not impossible, to advise with any degree of confidence as to the meaning of the words 'indirect or consequential loss'. The best advice is probably not to use the phrase but to spell out, if possible, which losses of profit are included within the exclusion clause and which are not.

4. THE UNFAIR CONTRACT TERMS ACT 1977

The Unfair Contract Terms Act 1977 made major changes to the law relating to exclusion clauses in that it declared certain exclusion clauses ineffective and subjected others to a reasonableness test. The Act was based on a report prepared by the Law Commission for England and Wales and the Scottish Law Commission. The impact of the Act has been considerable but it is now under review by both Law Commissions. The immediate cause of this revision of the Act is the enactment of the Unfair Terms in Consumer Contracts Regulations 1994, later revoked and replaced by the Unfair Terms in Consumer Contracts Regulations 1999. The scope of these Regulations is discussed in Chapter 14. The relationship between the Act and the Regulations has been an uneasy one. The two pieces of legislation overlap and the provisional proposal of the Law Commissions in their Consultation Paper (Law Commission Consultation Paper No 166 and Scottish Law Commission Discussion Paper No 119, discussed in more detail at pp. 535–540 below) is to replace the Act and the Regulations by a unified regime. We shall return to these proposals for reform after we have discussed both the Act and the Regulations. The remainder of this chapter will focus exclusively upon the Act and the case-law which it has generated.

The approach that will be taken is to set out the Act section by section. Each section will be followed by a brief commentary. It will then conclude with consideration of two illustrative cases.

Before examining the first section of the Act it is necessary to make two preliminary points. The first is that the Act is divided into three parts. Part I applies to England, Wales, and Northern Ireland. Each section in this Part, with the exception of section 8 (which is discussed at pp. 711–713 below) will be given brief consideration. Part II applies to Scotland. We shall not examine Part II, except for a comparison between section 17 and section 3. Part II has many similarities with Part I but it is not identical. The failure to produce a unified regime for the whole of the United Kindgom is an unfortunate feature of the 1977 Act and it is a defect which the Law Commissions intend to rectify in their current review of the Act. Part III consists of a miscellany of provisions which apply to the whole of the United Kingdom. We shall examine some but not all of the sections in this Part. The second point to note is that the Act only comes into play where it has been demonstrated that the defendant is in some way liable to the claimant. This being the case, it is important first of all to identify the basis upon which the defendant is liable to the claimant before proceeding to apply the Act to the facts of the case. If, for example, the liability of the defendant is in negligence, then the applicable section will be section 2 of the Act. If, on the other hand, the liability is for breach of contract it will be section 3 or, in the case of a contract for the sale of goods, section 6. The Act does not regulate liability in the abstract; it regulates liability in respect of recognized causes of action and it is vital first to identify the basis upon which the defendant is liable to the claimant.

The text of Part I of the Act is as follows:

Scope of Part I

1.—(1) For the purposes of this Part of this Act, 'negligence' means the breach—

(a) of any obligation, arising from the express or implied terms of a contract, to take reasonable care or exercise reasonable skill in the performance of the contract;

(b) of any common law duty to take reasonable care or exercise reasonable skill (but not any stricter duty);

(c) of the common duty of care imposed by the Occupiers' Liability Act 1957 or the Occupiers' Liability Act (Northern Ireland) 1957.

(2) This Part of this Act is subject to Part III; and in relation to contracts, the operation of sections 2 to 4 and 7 is subject to the exceptions made by Schedule 1.

(3) In the case of both contract and tort, sections 2 to 7 apply (except where the contrary is stated in section 6(4)) only to business liability, that is liability for breach of obligations or duties arising—

(a) from things done or to be done by a person in the course of a business (whether his own business or another's); or

(b) from the occupation of premises used for business purposes of the occupier;

and references to liability are to be read accordingly but liability of an occupier of premises for breach of an obligation or duty towards a person obtaining access to the premises for recreational or educational purposes, being liability for loss or damage suffered by reason of the dangerous state of the premises, is not a business liability of the occupier unless granting that person such access for the purposes concerned falls within the business purposes of the occupier.

(4) In relation to any breach of duty or obligation, it is immaterial for any purpose of this Part of this Act whether the breach was inadvertent or intentional, or whether liability for it arises directly or vicariously.

COMMENTARY

This section provides us with two important definitions and it also draws attention to the fact that certain contracts are excluded from the scope of the Act. The first definition is the definition of 'negligence' in subsections (1) and (4). Three points should be noted about this definition. The first is that it assumes that a liability has arisen on the part of the defendant because it refers to a 'breach' of an obligation to use reasonable care. This being the case, an exclusion clause which has the effect of negating the existence of the duty of care would appear to be outside the scope of the Act because the effect of such a clause is to prevent a duty from arising in the first place. A defendant who does not owe a duty of care to a claimant cannot be liable to that claimant. And, if he is not liable, there appears to be nothing on which the Act can bite because there has been no 'breach' of any 'duty of care'. As we shall see (p. 489 below), the courts have not been receptive to a submission that the effect of a clause is to prevent a duty of care from arising with the consequence that the Act is inapplicable (see *Smith* v. *Eric S Bush* [1990] 1 AC 831 and *Phillips Products Ltd* v. *Hyland* [1987] 1 WLR 659, p. 489 below). Secondly, 'negligence' encompasses both contractual negligence (that is to say, breach of a contractual duty to exercise reasonable care) and tortious negligence (that is to say, liability which has arisen in tort rather than contract). Notwithstanding the title of the Act it is not confined to liability for breach of contract. It can apply to notices which purport to exclude liability, even in the absence of a contract between the parties (see section 2 of the Act below). Thirdly, subsection (4) expands the definition of negligence by making it clear that it does not matter whether the breach was inadvertent or intentional or whether liability for it arose directly or vicariously. Vicarious liability arises where one party is held liable for the wrongdoing of another. The principal example of vicarious liability in this context is the liability of an employer for the negligence of his employee.

The second definition is located in subsection (3), which makes it clear that the Act only applies to attempts to exclude or restrict business liability as defined in the subsection. An attempt by one party to exclude liability towards another in the context of a purely private sale (for example, the sale by one member of the public to another of a motor car or some other item) is generally outside the scope of the Act. 'Business' is defined in section 14 (p. 481 below).

The third point to note is the exclusion, referred to in subsection (2), of certain contracts from the scope of the Act. These contracts are referred to in Schedule 1 (p. 484 below).

Avoidance of liability for negligence, breach of contract, etc

Negligence liability

2.—(1) A person cannot by reference to any contract term or to a notice given to persons generally or to particular persons exclude or restrict his liability for death or personal injury resulting from negligence.

(2) In the case of other loss or damage, a person cannot so exclude or restrict his liability for negligence except in so far as the term or notice satisfies the requirement of reasonableness.

(3) Where a contract term or notice purports to exclude or restrict liability for negligence a person's agreement to or awareness of it is not of itself to be taken as indicating his voluntary acceptance of any risk.

COMMENTARY

A number of points arise in relation to the scope of section 2. The first is that it applies both to contract terms and to notices. Notice is defined in section 14 (p. 481 below). The principal point to note in this context is that it encompasses non-contractual notices so that the Act is not confined in its application to contract terms. A notice on land purporting to exclude liability for damage caused by negligence can be subject to the Act (at least if the liability that is sought to be excluded falls within the definition of business liability in s. 1(3), above). Secondly section 2 only applies to attempts to exclude liability for 'negligence' and negligence is defined in section 1. Here it is important to recall that negligence means the 'breach' of an obligation to exercise reasonable care. The section cannot therefore apply to attempts to exclude or restrict strict liability. Thirdly, the section only applies to clauses which 'exclude or restrict' liability. It does not apply to a clause that simply 'transfers' a liability from one party to another (*Thompson* v. *T Lohan (Plant Hire) Ltd* [1987] 1 WLR 649). The distinction between a clause which 'excludes or restricts' a liability and a clause which 'transfers' a liability is discussed further below (at pp. 497–498).

Fourthly, any attempt to exclude liability for death or personal injury caused by negligence is ineffective (section 2(1)). The court is not given a choice in the matter: the Act states that it is not possible to exclude liability for such losses. Personal injury is defined in section 14 (p. 481 below). Fifthly, in the case of other loss or damage a term or notice which purports to exclude liability in negligence is valid only if it satisfies the requirement of reasonableness (s. 2(2)). Reasonableness is defined in section 11 (p. 472 below). Finally, section 2(3) has been enacted in order to prevent the protection of section 2 being outflanked by a party relying on the term or notice for the purpose of establishing the defence of *volenti non fit injuria*. Reliance cannot be placed on the term or notice in order to establish that the claimant consented to the risk of suffering injury and, consequently, has no claim. A defendant who wishes to rely on the defence of *volenti* must do more than point to the existence of the term or notice and the claimant's awareness of it or agreement to it. This being the case, section 2(3) makes it extremely difficult for a defendant to make out the defence of *volenti*.

Liability arising in contract

3.—(1) This section applies as between contracting parties where one of them deals as consumer or on the other's written standard terms of business.

(2) As against that party, the other cannot by reference to any contract term—

(a) when himself in breach of contract, exclude or restrict any liability of his in respect of the breach; or

(b) claim to be entitled—

   (i) to render a contractual performance substantially different from that which was reasonably expected of him, or

   (ii) in respect of the whole or any part of his contractual obligation, to render no performance at all,

except in so far as (in any of the cases mentioned above in this subsection) the contract term satisfies the requirement of reasonableness.

COMMENTARY

Section 3 regulates attempts to exclude or restrict liability for breach of contract. Once again, a number of points must be noted. First, it is vital to note that the section only applies to two types of contract and these are defined in subsection (1). The phrase 'deals as consumer' is defined in section 12 and we shall discuss its meaning there (p. 478 below). Here it is necessary to explore the meaning of the phrase 'deals . . . on the other's written standard terms of business'. This phrase is of considerable importance because it is the gateway to the application of the Act to commercial contracts. Commercial contracts concluded on terms which are not 'the other's written standard terms of business' are not regulated by this section. The meaning of this phrase has been explored in three principal cases.

The first is *Chester Grosvenor Hotel Co Ltd* v. *Alfred McAlpine Management Ltd* (1991) 56 Build LR 115, where the word in issue between the parties was 'standard'. Judge Stannard concluded (at p. 131) that:

what is required for terms to be standard is that they should be so regarded by the party which advances them as its standard terms and that it should habitually contract in those terms. If it contracts also in other terms, it must be determined in any given case, and as a matter of fact, whether this has occurred so frequently that the terms in question cannot be regarded as standard, and if on any occasion a party has substantially modified its prepared terms, it is a question of fact whether those terms have been so altered that they must be regarded as not having been employed on that occasion.

The second case is *St Albans City and District Council* v. *International Computers Ltd* [1996] 4 All ER 481 where the word at stake was 'deals'. In that case counsel for the defendants submitted that 'you cannot be said to deal on another's standard terms of business if, as was the case here, you negotiate with him over those terms before you enter into the contract'. Nourse LJ rejected this submission. He stated (at p. 491):

In my view that is an impossible construction for two reasons: first, because as a matter of plain English 'deals' means 'makes a deal', irrespective of any negotiations that may have preceded it; secondly, because s 12(1)(a) equates the expression 'deals as consumer' with 'makes the contract'. Thus it is clear that in order that one of the contracting parties may deal on the other's written standard terms of business within s.3(1) it is only necessary for him to enter into the contract on those terms.

On the other hand, where there has been meaningful negotiation about the terms of the contract which has resulted in alterations to the standard terms then it is much less likely that the requirements of section 3 will have been satisfied (see *The Flamar Pride* [1990] 1 Lloyd's Rep 434).

The third case on section 3(1) is *British Fermentation Products Ltd* v. *Compair Reavell Ltd* [1999] BLR 352. This time the word in issue was 'other's'. The contract between the parties was concluded on the Institution of Mechanical Engineers Model Form of General Conditions of Contract. One of the issues between the parties was whether or not this Model Form of contract fell within the scope of section 3(1). Judge Bowsher QC concluded that it did not. He did not attempt to lay down any general principle as to when 'Model Forms drafted by an outside party' fall within the scope of section 3 but stated (at p. 361) that:

> if the Act ever does apply to such Model Forms, it does seem to me that one essential for the application of the Act to such forms would be proof that the Model Form is invariably or at least usually used by the party in question. It must be shown that either by practice or by express statement a contracting party has adopted a Model Form as his standard terms of business. For example, an architect might say, 'My standard terms of business are on the terms of the RIBA Form of Engagement'. Without such proof, it could not be said that the Form is, in the words of the Act, '*the other's*' standard terms of business. I leave open the question what would be the position where there is such proof, and whether such proof either alone or with other features would make section 3 of the Act applicable. [Emphasis in the original.]

On the facts of the case it had neither been alleged nor proved that the defendants either invariably or usually used the Model Form. Nor did the defendants state that they would only be prepared to contract on the Model Form; they may well have been prepared to contract on other terms. In the absence of proof of the practice of the defendants, the vital question related to the burden of proof. Judge Bowsher QC stated that it was for the claimants to show that the Act applied and this they had not done. This being the case, the Model Form had not been shown to be the defendants' standard terms of business and section 3 did not apply to the contract between the parties.

One word in section 3(1) which has not, as yet, been litigated is 'written'. Does section 3 apply to a contract that is partly written and partly oral? The Scottish case of *McCrone* v. *Boots Farm Sales Ltd*, 1981 SLT 103 is sometimes cited in support of the proposition that section 3 applies to such a contract. But *McCrone* was concerned with the interpretation of Part II of the Act and the wording of section 17 differs from the wording of section 3. Section 17 uses the phrase 'standard form contract'. The absence of the word 'written' from section 17 made it easy for Lord Dunpark to conclude that the section applied to contracts which are partly oral. It is much more difficult to reach this conclusion in relation to section 3 given the use of the word 'written'.

The second point to note in relation to section 3 is that section 3(2)(a) applies to clauses that seek to exclude or restrict liability for breach of contract. Such clauses are subject to the reasonableness test, on which see section 11 below (pp. 472–278).

The third point relates to the subject-matter of section 3(2)(b). This is a much more difficult provision than section 3(2)(a). Given that the latter provision regulates attempts to exclude liability for breach of contract, the former must regulate something other than cases of breach because otherwise the two provisions overlap. So what is the subject-matter of section 3(2)(b)? It applies in two cases. The first is where one party claims to be entitled to render a 'contractual performance substantially different from that which was reasonably expected of him' and the second is where he claims to be entitled to render 'no performance'. An example in the latter category might be the case where a defendant seeks to rely on a widely drafted force majeure clause (on which see pp. 434–436 above) in order to justify his failure to perform his obligations under the contract. There is, as yet, no case on this issue and so the question whether section 3(2)(b)(ii) applies to force majeure clauses remains a matter of some doubt. In practice it may be that the issue will never be litigated because, even if the subsection is held to extend to force majeure clauses, the likelihood of such a clause passing the reasonableness test is high.

Section 3(2)(b) has been the subject of some judicial analysis. The leading case is the decision of the Court of Appeal in *Timeload Ltd* v. *British Telecommunications plc* [1995] EMLR 459. The plaintiffs sought an interlocutory injunction to restrain the defendants, BT, from terminating the contract between them under clause 18 of the contract which provided that BT had the right 'at any time' to terminate the contract between the parties on the giving of one month's notice. The reason why the plaintiffs wanted an injunction to prevent termination was that they wanted to keep their telephone number and termination of the contract would have deprived them of their ability to do so. The plaintiffs sought to challenge the validity of clause 18 under section 3 of the Act. The application was for an interlocutory injunction and so it was not necessary for the Court of Appeal to resolve definitively the scope of section 3(2)(b)(i). Sir Thomas Bingham MR set out the submission of counsel for BT, Mr Hobbs, and his response to that submission as follows (at p. 468):

Mr Hobbs submits that the subsection cannot apply where, as here, the clause under consideration defines the service to be provided and does not purport to permit substandard or partial performance. He says that the customer cannot reasonably expect that which the contract does not purport to offer, namely enjoyment of a telephone service under a given number for an indefinite period. That may indeed be so, but I find the construction and ambit of this subsection by no means clear. If a customer reasonably expects a service to continue until BT has substantial reason to terminate it, it seems to me at least arguable that a clause purporting to authorise BT to terminate it without reason purports to permit partial or different performance from that which the customer expected. If, however, s 3(2) does not in its precise terms cover this case, I do not myself regard that as the end of the matter. As I ventured to observe in *Interfoto Picture Library Ltd* v. *Stiletto Visual Programmes Ltd* [1989] QB 433, 439, the law of England, while so far eschewing any broad principle of good faith in the field of contract, has responded to demonstrated problems of unfairness by developing a number of piecemeal solutions directed to the particular problem before it. It seems to me at least arguable that the common law could, if the letter of the statute does not apply, treat the clear intention of the legislature expressed in the statute as a platform for invalidating or restricting the operation of an oppressive clause in a situation of the present, very special, kind. I say no more than there is, I think, a question here which has attracted much attention in Commonwealth jurisdictions and on the continent and may well deserve to be further explored here.

This is an adventurous decision. But it has to be remembered that it is a decision on an interlocutory application and so cannot be regarded as the last word on the scope of the subsection.

A more conservative approach was adopted in *Peninsula Business Services Ltd* v. *Sweeney* [2004] IRLR 49. A term in a contract of employment stated that 'an employee has no claim whatsoever to any commission payments that would otherwise have been generated and paid if he is not in employment on the date when they would normally have been paid'. The claimant resigned his post with the defendants and, as a consequence, he had to forgo substantial commission payments to which he would have been entitled had he remained in employment. He challenged the decision to withhold commission on the ground that the clause purported to entitle his employers to render a contractual performance substantially different from that which was reasonably expected of them. His claim failed on the ground that the defendants were simply operating the contract in accordance with its terms so that section 3(2)(b) was not applicable on the facts. Rimer J stated that the clause 'simply defined the limits' of the claimant's rights and did not purport to 'cut down or restrict his rights in any way'. This reasoning is very different to that adopted by the Court of Appeal in *Timeload* and it is open to criticism on the basis that it appears to ignore the fact that the aim of the subsection is to extend the scope of the Act to certain duty-defining contract terms. Thus the fact that the term assisted in the definition of the claimant's rights should not, of itself, have had the effect of taking the term outside the scope of the subsection. A better ground for rejecting the claimant's reliance on section 3(2)(b) was that there was 'no basis on which [the claimant] could ever have reasonably expected any rights greater than' those that the contract conferred on him. On this basis it would appear that the distinction between *Peninsula* and *Timeload* lies principally in the weight given by the court to the terms of the contract when seeking to ascertain the reasonable expectations of the parties. It is suggested that the approach of the court in *Peninsula* is the preferable one and that a court ought to attach considerable weight to the terms of the contract when identifying the reasonable expectations of the parties unless it can be demonstrated that the party relying on the term of the contract either knew, or ought to have known, that the other party to the contract was unaware of the term of the contract and could not reasonably be expected to have been familiar with it.

The easier case to accommodate within the subsection is the case in which a service provider purports to be entitled to offer the customer an alternative performance that is of a lower standard than the service originally offered. Take the case of a holiday company which reserves the right to offer its customer an alternative holiday should the one which the customer originally booked turn out, for some reason, to be unavailable. In offering an alternative holiday the company is not in breach of contract because it has reserved the right to do so. But the customer may be able to challenge the validity of such a term under section 3(2)(b), at least where the clause purports to entitle the holiday company to offer a holiday of a lower standard than that originally offered.

Unreasonable indemnity clauses

4.—(1) A person dealing as consumer cannot by reference to any contract term be made to indemnify another person (whether a party to the contract or not) in respect of liability that may be incurred by the other for negligence or breach of contract, except in so far as the contract term satisfies the requirement of reasonableness.

(2) This section applies whether the liability in question—

(a) is directly that of the person to be indemnified or is incurred by him vicariously;

(b) is to the person dealing as consumer or to someone else.

COMMENTARY

The subject-matter of section 4 is indemnity clauses. An indemnity clause is a clause by which one party is obliged to pay a sum of money to the other in respect of a liability which that other party has incurred. Section 4 only applies where the party required to make the indemnity is a consumer. Take the case of a consumer who hires a car from a car hire company. The company may insert into its terms of business a term to the effect that the consumer must indemnify the car hire company in respect of any liability it may incur to a third party as a result of the consumer's use of the car. Such an indemnity is caught by section 4 and is subject to the requirement of reasonableness (on which see section 11, below). Matters are otherwise where the car is hired out, not to a consumer, but to a business. In such a case the indemnity will not fall within the scope of section 4. Commercial indemnities are outside the scope of the section and, if they are regulated at all, they fall within the scope of section 2 (see *Phillips Products Ltd* v. *Hyland* [1987] 1 WLR 659 and *Thompson* v. *T Lohan (Plant Hire) Ltd* [1987] 1 WLR 649, discussed in more detail at pp. 489–498 below).

Liability arising from sale or supply of goods

'Guarantee' of consumer goods

5.—(1) In the case of goods of a type ordinarily supplied for private use or consumption, where loss or damage—

(a) arises from the goods proving defective while in consumer use; and

(b) results from the negligence of a person concerned in the manufacture or distribution of the goods,

liability for the loss or damage cannot be excluded or restricted by reference to any contract term or notice contained in or operating by reference to a guarantee of the goods.

(2) For these purposes—

(a) goods are to be regarded as 'in consumer use' when a person is using them, or has them in his possession for use, otherwise than exclusively for the purposes of a business; and

(b) anything in writing is a guarantee if it contains or purports to contain some promise or assurance (however worded or presented) that defects will be made good by complete or partial replacement, or by repair, monetary compensation or otherwise.

(3) This section does not apply as between the parties to a contract under or in pursuance of which possession or ownership of the goods passed.

COMMENTARY

This section deals with a rather different matter, namely the relationship between a manufacturer or a distributor of goods and a consumer and it restricts the ability of a manufacturer or distributor to exclude liability by reference to such a guarantee. It provides that the manufacturer or distributor cannot by reference to the terms of a 'guarantee' exclude or restrict liability for loss or damage that arises from defects in the goods while they are 'in consumer use'. But it only does so where the loss or damage results from the negligence of a person concerned in the manufacture or distribution of the goods.

Liability arising from sale or supply of goods

Sale and hire-purchase

6.—(1) Liability for breach of the obligations arising from—

(a) section 12 of the Sale of Goods Act 1979 (seller's implied undertakings as to title, etc.);

(b) section 8 of the Supply of Goods (Implied Terms) Act 1973 (the corresponding thing in relation to hire-purchase),

cannot be excluded or restricted by reference to any contract term.

(2) As against a person dealing as consumer, liability for breach of the obligations arising from—

(a) section 13, 14 or 15 of the 1979 Act (seller's implied undertakings as to conformity of goods with description or sample, or as to their quality or fitness for a particular purpose);

(b) section 9, 10 or 11 of the 1973 Act (the corresponding things in relation to hire-purchase),

cannot be excluded or restricted by reference to any contract term.

(3) As against a person dealing otherwise than as consumer, the liability specified in subsection (2) above can be excluded or restricted by reference to a contract term, but only in so far as the term satisfies the requirement of reasonableness.

(4) The liabilities referred to in this section are not only the business liabilities defined by section 1(3), but include those arising under any contract of sale of goods or hire-purchase agreement.

COMMENTARY

This section regulates attempts to exclude liability for breach of the implied terms in contracts for the sale of goods (ss. 12–15 of the Sale of Goods Act 1979, on which see pp. 371–376 above) and contracts of hire-purchase (sections 8–12 of the Supply of Goods (Implied Terms) Act 1973). The fundamental distinction that has to be drawn is between the case where the buyer is, and the case where he is not, dealing as consumer. Where the buyer is dealing as consumer liability for breach of the implied terms cannot be excluded but where the buyer is not dealing as consumer liability can be excluded provided that the term satisfies the requirement of reasonableness (except in the case of an attempt to exclude liability for a breach of section 12 of the Sale of Goods Act 1979 or section 8 of the Supply of Goods (Implied Terms) Act 1973, both which are inevitably void). The phrase 'dealing as consumer' is defined in section 12 (p. 478 below) and reasonableness is defined in section 11 (p. 472 below). This section applies to any attempt to exclude or restrict liability for breach of one of the implied terms, even if the liability sought to be excluded is not a business liability within the meaning of section 1(3) of the 1977 Act (s. 6(4)). This extension of the scope of the Act is not as big as it might at first sight appear because the 'satisfactory quality' and 'fitness for purpose' implied terms only operate where the seller sells the goods in the course of a business (see p. 375 above).

Miscellaneous contracts under which goods pass

7.—(1) Where the possession or ownership of goods passes under or in pursuance of a contract not governed by the law of sale of goods or hire-purchase, subsections (2) to (4) below apply as regards the effect (if any) to be given to contract terms excluding or restricting liability for breach of obligation arising by implication of law from the nature of the contract.

(2) As against a person dealing as consumer, liability in respect of the goods' correspondence with description or sample, or their quality or fitness for any particular purpose, cannot be excluded or restricted by reference to any such term.

(3) As against a person dealing otherwise than as consumer, that liability can be excluded or restricted by reference to such a term, but only in so far as the term satisfies the requirement of reasonableness.

(3A) Liability for breach of the obligations arising under section 2 of the Supply of Goods and Services Act 1982 (implied terms about title, etc. in certain contracts for the transfer of the property in goods) cannot be excluded or restricted by reference to any such term.

(4) Liability in respect of—

(a) the right to transfer ownership of the goods, or give possession; or

(b) the assurance of quiet possession to a person taking goods in pursuance of the contract,

cannot (in a case to which subsection (3A) above does not apply) be excluded or restricted by reference to any such term except in so far as the term satisfies the requirement of reasonableness.

(5) This section does not apply in the case of goods passing on a redemption of trading stamps within the Trading Stamps Act 1964 or the Trading Stamps Act (Northern Ireland) 1965.

COMMENTARY

This section performs a similar function to section 6 but it applies to contracts other than contracts for the sale of goods and contracts of hire-purchase under which possession or ownership of goods passes to another party. Thus it applies to contracts of hire, contracts for work and materials, and contracts of exchange. The distinction between the case where one party deals as consumer and the case where one party does not is once again of crucial significance because liability cannot be excluded as against a person who deals as consumer but the parties generally have greater liberty to exclude or restrict liability as against a person who does not deal as consumer. The requirement of reasonableness is discussed below (pp. 472–478).

Effect of breach

9.—(1) Where for reliance upon it a contract term has to satisfy the requirement of reasonableness, it may be found to do so and be given effect accordingly notwithstanding that the contract has been terminated either by breach or by a party electing to treat it as repudiated.

(2) Where on a breach the contract is nevertheless affirmed by a party entitled to treat it as repudiated, this does not of itself exclude the requirement of reasonableness in relation to any contract term.

COMMENTARY

This section confirms that the fact that the contract has been terminated does not, of itself, prevent a party from relying upon an exclusion or limitation clause contained in the contract. In this way it confirms the fact that the 'rule of law' version of fundamental breach (on which see p. 457 above) is not good law. Section 9(2) provides that affirmation of the contract (on which see p. 991 below) does not of itself exclude the requirement of reasonableness.

Evasion by means of secondary contract

10. A person is not bound by any contract term prejudicing or taking away rights of his which arise under, or in connection with the performance of, another contract, so far as those rights extend to the enforcement of another's liability which this Part of this Act prevents that other from excluding or restricting.

COMMENTARY

This section gives rise to a number of interpretative difficulties. The effect of the section has been summed up in H Beale (ed), *Chitty on Contracts* (29th edn, Sweet & Maxwell, 2004), para 14-081) in the following terms:

The purpose of this provision has been said to be to prevent rights arising in favour of A under a contract between A and B from being affected by the terms of a secondary contract between A and C which take away or inhibit the exercise of those rights, as, for example, where a term in a contract between a manufacturer of goods and the buyer purports to affect the rights of the buyer under the Sale of Goods Act against the retailer from whom he purchases the goods. The scope of the section is, however, enigmatic. It employs the words 'prejudicing or taking away rights' instead of the usual 'excludes or restricts liability'. The extended interpretation of the latter phrase therefore does not apply. Also the reference to 'the enforcement of another's *liability*' would preclude the application of section 10 to a case where the terms of the secondary contract purported to entitle a party to another contract to render a performance substantially different from that reasonably expected of him, or to render no performance at all.

It has been held that the section does not apply to the compromise or waiver of an existing contractual claim (*Tudor Grange Holdings Ltd* v. *Citibank NA* [1992] Ch 53).

Explanatory provisions

The 'reasonableness' test

11.—(1) In relation to a contract term, the requirement of reasonableness for the purposes of this Part of this Act, section 3 of the Misrepresentation Act 1967 and section 3 of the Misrepresentation Act (Northern Ireland) 1967 is that the term shall have been a fair and reasonable one to be included having regard to the circumstances which were, or ought reasonably to have been, known to or in the contemplation of the parties when the contract was made.

(2) In determining for the purposes of section 6 or 7 above whether a contract term satisfies the requirement of reasonableness, regard shall be had in particular to the matters specified in Schedule 2 to this Act; but this subsection does not prevent the court or arbitrator from holding, in accordance with any rule of law, that a term which purports to exclude or restrict any relevant liability is not a term of the contract.

(3) In relation to a notice (not being a notice having contractual effect), the requirement of reasonableness under this Act is that it should be fair and reasonable to allow reliance on it, having regard to all the circumstances obtaining when the liability arose or (but for the notice) would have arisen.

(4) Where by reference to a contract term or notice a person seeks to restrict liability to a specified sum of money, and the question arises (under this or any other Act) whether the term or notice satisfies the requirement of reasonableness, regard shall be had in particular (but without prejudice to subsection (2) above in the case of contract terms) to—

(a) the resources which he could expect to be available to him for the purpose of meeting the liability should it arise; and

(b) how far it was open to him to cover himself by insurance.

(5) It is for those claiming that a contract term or notice satisfies the requirement of reasonableness to show that it does.

COMMENTARY

This section is one of the most important provisions in the Act. The reasonableness test applies to clauses that fall within the scope of sections 2(2), 3, 4, 6(3), 7(3), 7(4), and 8. It is therefore of wide application. A number of points can be made in relation to the scope of this section. The first is that subsection (1) establishes that the time at which the reasonableness test is to be applied is the time of entry into the contract. It is not the time at which the breach of contract occurred. The aim of the reasonableness test is therefore to examine the reasonableness or the fairness of the allocation of the rights and responsibilities between the parties at the moment of entry into the contract.

The second point is that, in the case of contracts that fall within sections 6 and 7, the court is expressly directed by subsection (2) to take into account the matters listed in Schedule 2 to the Act (p. 485 below). However the significance of the factors listed in Schedule 2 transcends cases that fall within the scope of sections 6 and 7. In practice, the courts have regard to these factors even in cases that do not fall within the scope of sections 6 and 7.

The third point relates to the application of the reasonableness test to notices. It differs from the test applicable to contract terms. Subsection (3) provides that it must have been fair and reasonable to rely on the notice and that the court is to have regard to the circumstances obtaining when the liability arose or when, but for the notice, it would have arisen.

Subsection (4) requires the court to take into account two matters in the case of clauses that seek to limit rather than exclude liability. It does not follow that these matters are irrelevant in the case of total exclusions of liability; it is simply that they are particularly relevant in the context of limitation clauses, in the sense that the court must have regard to these factors. As we shall see (p. 476 below), availability of insurance has proved to be an important factor in deciding whether or not a clause is reasonable.

Subsection (5) is an important provision because it puts the onus of proof in relation to reasonableness upon the party who asserts that the term or notice is reasonable. It is therefore unnecessary for a claimant to state in his statement of claim that he intends to challenge the reasonableness of a clause (*Sheffield* v. *Pickfords Ltd* [1997] CLC 648).

In deciding whether or not a particular clause is reasonable, the courts have regard to a range of factors. Judges have a considerable degree of discretion in the application of the reasonableness test to the facts of individual cases. The balancing of the different factors is left largely to the decision of the trial judge. The appellate courts have been extremely reluctant to review the findings of trial judges on the issue of whether a particular clause is or is not reasonable (see *George Mitchell (Chesterhall) Ltd* v. *Finney Lock Seeds Ltd* [1983] 2 AC 803, p. 485 below), unless the judge has had regard to some factor which was irrelevant or has adopted an interpretation of the exclusion clause which is incorrect (see, for example, *Watford Electronics Ltd* v. *Sanderson CFL Ltd* [2001] All ER (D) 290).

When deciding whether or not the requirement of reasonableness has been satisfied, the courts have had regard to factors such as the following:

(i) **The meaning of the clause.** This is clearly a very important factor. In *Watford Electronics Ltd* v. *Sanderson CFL Ltd* [2001] All ER (D) 290 the Court of Appeal emphasized the need to ascertain the meaning of a clause before deciding whether or not it satisfies the requirement of reasonableness. The clause in dispute in *Watford Electronics* was clause 7.3 which provided:

Neither the Company nor the Customer shall be liable to the other for any claims for indirect or consequential losses whether arising from negligence or otherwise. In no event shall the Company's liability under the Contract exceed the price paid by the Customer to the Company for the Equipment connected with any claim.

The Court of Appeal held that it was necessary to ascertain the meaning of this clause before applying the reasonableness test to it. Chadwick LJ stated (at para [35]):

In order to decide whether the relevant contract term was a fair and reasonable one to be included having regard to the circumstances which were, or ought reasonably to have been, known to or in the contemplation of the parties when the contract was made it is necessary, as it seems to me, to determine, first, the scope and effect of that term as a matter of construction. In particular, it is necessary to identify the nature of the liability which the term is seeking to exclude or restrict.

Whether or not a contract term satisfies the requirement of reasonableness within the meaning of section 11 of the Unfair Contract Terms Act 1977 does not fall to be determined in isolation. It falls to be determined where a person is seeking to rely upon the term in order to exclude or restrict his liability in some context to which the earlier provisions of the 1977 Act (or the provisions of section 3 of the Misrepresentation Act 1967) apply.

When ascertaining the meaning of clause 7.3 the Court of Appeal broke it down into its two sentences. It held that the purpose of the first sentence was to exclude contractual claims for indirect and consequential losses: that is to say, to exclude liability in contract for cases which fall within the second limb of the rule in *Hadley* v. *Baxendale* (1854) 9 Exch 341 (on the meaning of 'indirect or consequential loss' see pp. 458–460 above). Contrary to the view taken by the trial judge, Judge Thornton QC, it was held that the first sentence did not purport to exclude claims in respect of pre-contractual misrepresentations (this point is discussed in more detail below at pp. 712–713). The purpose of the second sentence of clause 7.3 was held to be to restrict the seller's liability under the contract with the customer to a specified sum of money, namely the price paid by the customer for the equipment. The meaning of the clause has an obvious bearing on the likelihood of it passing the reasonableness test. The wider the scope of the clause, the less likelihood there is that it will pass the reasonableness test.

(ii) **Equality of bargaining power.**   The greater the equality of the bargaining power of the parties, the more likely it is that the clause will pass the reasonableness test. The Court of Appeal in *Watford Electronics Ltd* v. *Sanderson CFL Ltd* (above) took a particularly robust line in this respect. Chadwick LJ stated (at para [55]):

Where experienced businessmen representing substantial companies of equal bargaining power negotiate an agreement, they may be taken to have had regard to the matters known to them. They should, in my view be taken to be the best judge of the commercial fairness of the agreement which they have made; including the fairness of each of the terms in that agreement. They should be taken to be the best judge on the question whether the terms of the agreement are reasonable. The court should not assume that either is likely to commit his company to an agreement which he thinks is unfair, or which he thinks includes unreasonable terms. Unless satisfied that one party has, in effect, taken unfair advantage of the other or that a term is so unreasonable that it cannot properly have been understood or considered—the court should not interfere.

In so far as this statement suggests there must be some form of 'advantage taking' or a failure to comprehend the clause before courts will intervene to declare exclusion or limitation clauses unreasonable in contracts between 'experienced businessmen representing substantial companies of equal bargaining power' it goes too far. Cases can be found in which the courts have not attached such weight to the ability of businessmen to look after themselves in the market-place. For example, Tomlinson J (whose judgment was affirmed by the Court of Appeal) in *Britvic Soft Drinks Ltd* v. *Messer UK Ltd* [2002] 1 Lloyd's Rep 20, 57–58 placed less emphasis on the fact that the parties were of equal bargaining power than did Chadwick LJ. He concluded that the laissez faire approach adopted by Chadwick LJ must be seen against the background of the facts of that particular case and such an approach was not necessarily of general application. On the facts of *Britvic* Tomlinson J stated (at p. 58):

In my judgment it is wholly unreasonable for a supplier of a bulk commodity such as CO_2 for a food application to seek to exclude liability for the commodity not being of satisfactory quality or being unfit for its purpose where that had come about as a result of a breakdown in the manufacturing process allowing the inadvertent introduction of a redundant carcinogen.

This was so notwithstanding the fact that both parties were substantial companies who presumably had access to skilled legal advice. Similarly, in *George Mitchell (Chesterhall) Ltd* v. *Finney Lock Seeds Ltd* [1983] 2 AC 803 (p. 485 below) the limitation clause was held to be unreasonable but there does not appear to have been any evidence of 'advantage taking' on the facts of the case.

(iii) **Regard must be had to the clause as a whole.**   The clause must be tested at the moment of entry into the contract, not the moment of breach. This being the case, the court cannot simply have regard to that part of the clause that is in issue between the parties on the facts as they have turned out. It must have regard to the clause in its entirety and the range of events to which the clause could realistically apply and decide whether or not it is reasonable. This has important implications for the drafting of an exclusion or limitation clause. There is a temptation to draft the clause as widely as possible in order to protect the client to the greatest extent possible. This is a temptation which, in general, should be resisted. The reason for this is that the validity of the clause can be tested at its weakest point. Suppose that in a contract for the sale of goods a clause states that a buyer can only reject goods if he does so within seven days of the date of purchase and all other implied conditions in the Sale of Goods Act are excluded. Such a clause may be entirely reasonable in relation to a patent defect but it is probably unreasonable in relation to a latent defect. A commercial buyer faced by such a clause can challenge it on the ground that it is unreasonable in its application to latent defects. It should not matter that the actual defect in the goods was patent because the validity of the clause is to be tested at the time of entry into the contract (when the nature of the defect will be unknown) not the date of breach.

A further factor which suggests the need for caution is that the courts have held that they do not have the power to sever the unreasonable parts of an exclusion clause so as to render the clause reasonable (see *Stewart Gill Ltd* v. *Horatio Myer & Co Ltd* [1992] QB 600). It can be argued that the courts should in fact have this power because of the presence of the words 'in so far as' in, for example, sections 2(2) and 3(2) (pp. 463 and 464 above). These words might be thought to suggest that, to the extent that the clause is reasonable, effect should be given to it. But the courts have thus far declined to embark upon the modification of clauses with a view to saving as much of the clause as possible. The clause will generally either stand or fall; it will not be re-written by the courts. This has important consequences for the drafting of limitation clauses. A limitation clause that is unreasonable because it is too low is ineffective to place any limit on the liability of the party in breach. The court cannot insert into the limitation clause a sum which it believes to be fair and reasonable. This being the case, a limitation clause should always be set at a realistic level because the consequences of it being held to be unreasonable as a result of it being set too low may be disastrous.

Given that the courts declare that they have no general power to separate out the unreasonable parts of an exclusion clause from the reasonable parts, draftsmen frequently carry out the task themselves and separate out an exclusion clause into different constituent parts in the hope that, if one part is held to be invalid, its invalidity will not spread throughout the clause. There are signs that the courts will respect this drafting device and not spread the infection. For example in *Watford Electronics Ltd* v. *Sanderson CFL Ltd* (above) the Court of Appeal considered the two sentences in clause 7.3 separately when seeking to ascertain the meaning of the clause and the reasonableness test should also be separately applied to each sentence. This being the case, any invalidity in the first sentence should not necessarily result in the second sentence being held to be invalid.

(iv) **The importance of insurance.**   The court will have regard to the availability of insurance but not to the actual insurance position of the parties (see *The Flamar Pride* [1990] 1 Lloyd's Rep 434). It is expressly directed to take account of the availability of insurance in relation to limitation clauses (see s. 11(4)). In *Moores* v. *Yakeley Associates Ltd* (1999) 62 Con LR 76 the defendant agreed to provide architectural services for the plaintiff. The defendant limited his liability to £250,000. The defendant, a one man company, had taken out insurance cover of £500,000. When asked why he had not chosen £500,000 as the limitation figure, Mr Yakeley responded that (i) he considered the figure of £250,000 to be reasonable having regard to the estimated cost of the project (between £225,000 and £274,000) and (ii) he was concerned to leave some allowance in case he had to meet any legal costs. Dyson J accepted the first of these explanations and did not consider the second. But, given that it is the availability of insurance that matters, the fact that the defendant was actually insured for a sum in excess of the sum stipulated in the limitation clause should not suffice, of itself, to establish that the limitation was an unreasonable one.

(v) **The dangers of relaxation of the clause in practice.**   A party to a contract may have good commercial reasons for not wishing to enforce an exclusion or limitation clause against a customer, particularly a well-established customer. The fear of losing business may lead it not to enforce the clause according to its letter. But such conduct may lead a court to conclude that the term is unreasonable. Non-enforcement of the clause was 'the decisive factor' that led the House of Lords in *George Mitchell (Chesterhall) Ltd* v. *Finney Lock Seeds Ltd* [1983] 2 AC 803 (p. 485 below) to conclude that the term was unreasonable. In other cases the courts have taken a more relaxed view. In *Schenkers Ltd* v. *Overland Shoes Ltd* [1998] 1 Lloyd's Rep 498 Pill LJ stated (at p. 508):

In present circumstances, I see little merit in the defendants' argument that the clause had not in practice been relied upon. The give and take practised by the parties in the course of substantial dealings upon the running account was admirable and conducive to a good business relationship but did not in my judgment prevent the plaintiffs, when the dispute arose, relying upon the term agreed. In *George Mitchell*, there was evidence that neither party expected the limitation of liability clause to [be] applied literally and a recognition that reliance on the clause was unreasonable. While there was evidence in the present case that there was no ready or frequent resort to the clause, there was no such recognition. I cannot find conduct which permits the defendants to claim that reliance on the clause would be unfair or unreasonable.

This suggests that it is important to examine the reason for the non-enforcement of a particular clause. If it is attributable to the 'give and take' of business life it will do little in terms of establishing the unreasonableness of the clause. But where the reason for the non-enforcement of the clause is general recognition of the fact that the clause does not operate reasonably it will provide very good evidence from which a court can infer that the clause is unreasonable (as in the *George Mitchell* case where Lord Bridge regarded this as the 'decisive factor'—see p. 488 below).

(vi) **Two different losses within the same clause.** It is not generally advisable to include two very different types of loss within the same limitation clause. In *Overseas Medical Supplies Ltd* v. *Orient Transport Services Ltd* [1999] 2 Lloyd's Rep 273 the defendant freight forwarders failed to insure the plaintiffs' goods as they were required to do under the terms of the contract. The defendants limited their liability, both for any damage suffered during transit and in respect of their failure to take out insurance, to £600. The trial judge held that a limitation of £600 would have been reasonable for a claim for direct loss suffered by the plaintiffs while the goods were in transit, but it was not reasonable for a failure to insure. He therefore held that the clause was unreasonable and the Court of Appeal affirmed his decision. The two losses subject to the £600 limitation were very different in nature. Had the goods been damaged in transit the defendants' liability would have been limited to £600 but the plaintiffs would have been able to look to their insurers for the rest of their loss. But in the case of a failure to insure there was no one else to whom the plaintiffs could look in relation to the loss in excess of £600. Potter LJ stated (at p. 280):

The burden of proof of reasonableness was upon the [defendants] in the case. Their position was that of a trading organisation which, under a single contract had agreed to combine at least two activities or functions in respect of which the nature of the work undertaken, the incidence of risk as between the parties, and the effect of a breach of duty by the [defendants] were all of different character, yet were treated without distinction as subject to a single limitation of liability of only £600. Whereas it may be that, in relation to certain 'package' services, a broad brush approach to limitation of liability will be reasonable, and indeed may largely be dictated by the type of insurance cover available in the market to the supplier, the Judge held that, in this case, such an approach was unjust and inappropriate for reasons which he clearly and comprehensively stated.

In my view, the judgment of Judge Kenny was a careful one in which he considered and weighed the various considerations in a manner which is not open to any substantial criticism.

(vii) **The advantage of limitation clauses.** In many cases a sensibly drawn limitation clause is more likely to pass the reasonableness test than a total exclusion of liability. This proposition was thrown into some doubt by the decision of the Court of Appeal in *St Albans City and District Council* v. *International Computers Ltd* [1996] 4 All ER 481 where it was held that a limitation clause of £100,000 in a contract to supply a computer system to a local authority was unreasonable. The case generated a considerable amount of concern in commercial practice but its impact has not proved to be great. Indeed, there is very little discussion of the reasonableness of the clause in the judgments of the Court of Appeal. The judges were content to conclude (at p. 492) that the trial judge had not 'proceeded upon some erroneous principle or was plainly and obviously wrong'. In reaching his conclusion that £100,000 was unreasonable on the facts of the case the trial judge, Scott Baker J, attached importance to the facts that the parties were of unequal bargaining power (the plaintiffs being a local authority), the defendants had not justified the figure which they had inserted into the contract, and the defendants were insured; and to the view that the party who stood to make the profit (here the defendants) should also take the risk. The conclusion of Scott Baker J is perhaps questionable but it was not, in the opinion of the Court of Appeal, 'plainly and obviously wrong'.

Other cases can be found in which limitation clauses have failed the reasonableness test (most notably *George Mitchell (Chesterhall) Ltd* v. *Finney Lock Seeds Ltd* [1983] 2 AC 803, p. 485 below) but it remains the case that they are likely to pass the reasonableness test provided that the figure chosen is a realistic one (see, for example, *Britvic Soft Drinks Ltd* v. *Messer UK Ltd* [2002] 1 Lloyd's Rep 20). The onus of proof of showing that the clause is reasonable lies on the party relying upon the limitation clause. This being the case, that party must be able to lead evidence to show why it was that this particular figure was chosen as the limit of liability. A figure that is simply plucked out of the air will struggle to pass the reasonableness test. But a figure that is supported by some objective justification, such as the turnover of the party relying on the clause, the insurance cover available, or the value of the contract, will provide good evidence from which a court can infer that the clause was in fact reasonable.

These factors do not purport to be exhaustive. Other factors are listed in Schedule 2 to the Act (p. 485 below). The task of the court in any given case is first to identify the factors to be taken into account when deciding whether or not the clause is reasonable and it must then balance these factors in a sensible fashion. A judge who carries out both of these tasks is unlikely to be overturned by the Court of Appeal, should an appeal be lodged against his decision.

'Dealing as consumer'

12.—(1) A party to a contract 'deals as consumer' in relation to another party if—

(a) he neither makes the contract in the course of a business nor holds himself out as doing so; and

(b) the other party does make the contract in the course of a business; and

(c) in the case of a contract governed by the law of sale of goods or hire-purchase, or by section 7 of this Act, the goods passing under or in pursuance of the contract are of a type ordinarily supplied for private use or consumption.

(1A) But if the first party mentioned in subsection (1) is an individual paragraph (c) of that subsection must be ignored.

(2) But the buyer is not in any circumstances to be regarded as dealing as consumer—

(a) if he is an individual and the goods are second hand goods sold at public auction at which individuals have the opportunity of attending the sale in person;

(b) if he is not an individual and the goods are sold by auction or by competitive tender.

(3) Subject to this, it is for those claiming that a party does not deal as consumer to show that he does not.

COMMENTARY

Two requirements must be satisfied before a person can 'deal as consumer' within the meaning of this section. First, the person who asserts that he is dealing as a consumer must not make the contract in the course of a business, nor hold himself out as doing so. Secondly, the other party to the contract must make the contract in the course of a business. It therefore follows that a contract between two parties, neither of whom is acting in the course of a business, does not constitute a 'consumer' contract for the purposes of the Act. When, for this purpose, is a contract made 'in the course of a business'? In *R & B Customs Brokers Co* v. *United Dominions Trust Ltd* [1988] 1 WLR 321 the plaintiff, a private company, purchased a car from the defendant finance company. The car had been supplied by a third party dealer. The car was bought for the personal and business use of one of the plaintiff's directors. The plaintiff rejected the car after discovering that the roof of the car leaked and the dealer had failed to rectify the problem. The terms of the contract between the defendant and the plaintiff purported to exclude any implied condition as to the condition or quality of the car or its fitness for any particular purpose. The plaintiff submitted that the exclusion was invalidated by section 6(2) of the 1977 Act (p. 469 above) on the basis that it was dealing as consumer in entering into the contract to purchase the car. The Court of Appeal held that the plaintiff company was dealing as consumer with the result that the implied term could not be excluded. In reaching this conclusion the Court of Appeal adopted a rather narrow construction of 'in the course of a business'. It held that, in order to be 'in the course of a business', the transaction must either be integral to the business or, if not integral, must be entered into as part of the regular course of dealing of the business. On the facts the purchase of a car was not integral to the plaintiff's business. Nor was the contract entered into as a regular part of the business of the company. While the plaintiff had acquired two or three vehicles on credit terms this was held to be insufficient to establish the requisite degree of regularity. The conclusion that the plaintiff company dealt as a consumer is not one that could have been reached under the Unfair Terms in Consumer Contracts Regulations 1999 (see p. 504 below) because a company cannot be a consumer under the Regulations. The result in *R & B Customs* is, in many ways, a surprising one (but it was followed by the Court of Appeal in *Feldaroll Foundry Plc* v. *Hermes Leasing (London) Ltd* [2004] EWCA Civ 747). The effect of the decision was to deprive the defendants of any opportunity to prove that their exclusion clause was reasonable because the effect of concluding that the plaintiff was dealing as consumer was to render the exclusion clause void. This seems a rather generous degree of protection for small businesses and the case has been the subject of a considerable degree of criticism (note also the much broader interpretation given to 'in the course of a business' by the Court of Appeal in *Stevenson* v. *Rogers* [1999] QB 1028 (p. 375 above) in the context of section 14(2) of the Sale of Goods Act 1979).

Varieties of exemption clause

13.—(1) To the extent that this Part of this Act prevents the exclusion or restriction of any liability it also prevents—

(a) making the liability or its enforcement subject to restrictive or onerous conditions;

(b) excluding or restricting any right or remedy in respect of the liability, or subjecting a person to any prejudice in consequence of his pursuing any such right or remedy;

(c) excluding or restricting rules of evidence or procedure;

and (to that extent) sections 2 and 5 to 7 also prevent excluding or restricting liability by reference to terms and notices which exclude or restrict the relevant obligation or duty.

(2) But an agreement in writing to submit present or future differences to arbitration is not to be treated under this Part of this Act as excluding or restricting any liability.

COMMENTARY

Section 13 is another section which seeks to regulate attempts to evade the clutches of the Act. Section 13(1)(a) can catch a clause which puts a very short time-limit on the availability of a particular remedy or any remedy; 13(1)(b) might catch a clause which excludes or restricts a right of set-off; and 13(1)(c) would potentially catch a conclusive evidence clause (a clause which states that acceptance of the goods shall constitute conclusive evidence that the goods conform with the requirements of the contract). These extensions of the scope of the Act are useful in so far as they reduce the possibility of evasion by well-advised commercial parties. It is important to note that section 13 does not have an independent role; that is to say, section 13 cannot be used to invalidate a particular clause. The function of section 13 is to extend the scope of sections 2 and 5–7 and it is to these sections that a court ought to look for jurisdiction to invalidate a clause. Section 13 cannot be used to extend the scope of section 3 but it is probably unnecessary to expand the scope of that section given the width of section 3(2)(b) (p. 464 above).

Section 13(1) does, however, give rise to one very considerable interpretative difficulty. It relates to the meaning of the words 'terms and notices which exclude or restrict the relevant obligation or duty' at the end of the subsection. The effect of the addition of these words is to extend the scope of sections 2 and 5–7 of the Act beyond clauses which exclude or restrict a liability to clauses that define the relevant 'obligation or duty'. The problem is that all terms of a contract have a role to play in defining the obligations of the parties. Once the step is taken of recognizing that some duty-defining clauses fall within the scope of the Act, how can the courts decide which duty-defining clauses fall within the scope of the Act and which do not? The difficulties involved in this extension of the Act are neatly noted in the following passage from H Beale (ed), *Chitty on Contracts* (29th edn, Sweet & Maxwell, 2004), para 14-063):

It may be difficult, however, to differentiate between contractual provisions which exclude or restrict the relevant obligation or duty, and those which define the scope of the obligation or which specify the duties of the parties. For example, a seller of kitchen utensils may expressly state that they are suitable to be used only on electric cookers and not with gas, or a surveyor may stipulate that he undertakes to carry out a valuation of the property and not a full structural survey. Further, there may be difficulty in distinguishing between provisions which exclude or restrict the relevant obligation or duty, and those which prevent it from arising, such as a clause limiting the ostensible authority of an agent to give undertakings.

We shall return to this issue, and the scope of section 13, when examining the decision of the Court of Appeal in *Phillips Products Ltd* v. *Hyland* [1987] 1 WLR 659 (p. 489 below).

Interpretation of Part I

14. In this Part of this Act—

'business' includes a profession and the activities of any government department or local or public authority;

'goods' has the same meaning as in the Sale of Goods Act 1979;

'hire-purchase agreement' has the same meaning as in the Consumer Credit Act 1974;

'negligence' has the meaning given by section 1(1);

'notice' includes an announcement, whether or not in writing, and any other communication or pretended communication; and

'personal injury' includes any disease and any impairment of physical or mental condition.

COMMENTARY

This section provides a number of important definitions. Particularly important are the definitions of 'business' and 'personal injury'. It should be noted that the definition of business does not purport to be exhaustive. A business need not necessarily be carried on with a view to making a profit.

PART III
PROVISIONS APPLYING TO THE WHOLE OF UNITED KINGDOM

Miscellaneous

International supply contracts

26.—(1) The limits imposed by this Act on the extent to which a person may exclude or restrict liability by reference to a contract term do not apply to liability arising under such a contract as is described in subsection (3) below.

(2) The terms of such a contract are not subject to any requirement of reasonableness under section 3 or 4: and nothing in Part II of this Act shall require the incorporation of the terms of such a contract to be fair and reasonable for them to have effect.

(3) Subject to subsection (4), that description of contract is one whose characteristics are the following—

(a) either it is a contract of sale of goods or it is one under or in pursuance of which the possession or ownership of goods passes; and

(b) it is made by parties whose places of business (or, if they have none, habitual residences) are in the territories of different States (the Channel Islands and the Isle of Man being treated for this purpose as different States from the United Kingdom).

(4) A contract falls within subsection (3) above only if either—

(a) the goods in question are, at the time of the conclusion of the contract, in the course of carriage, or will be carried, from the territory of one State to the territory of another; or

(b) the acts constituting the offer and acceptance have been done in the territories of different States; or

(c) the contract provides for the goods to be delivered to the territory of a State other than that within whose territory those acts were done.

COMMENTARY

Section 26 of the Act provides that the limits imposed by the Act on the extent to which a person may exclude or restrict liability by reference to a contract term do not apply to liability arising under an international supply contract, nor are the terms of such a contract subject to the reasonableness requirement under sections 3 or 4. An international supply contract is defined in section 26(3) and (4). The phrase 'made by parties' is a reference to the principals to the contract in question and not to the agents (*Ocean Chemical Transport Inc* v. *Exnor Craggs Ltd* [2000] 1 Lloyd's Rep 446, 453). Given the volume of cross-border transactions that are concluded in the modern economy this is a very important provision. The requirement in section 26(4)(c) that the contract must provide for the goods to be delivered to the territory of a State other than that within whose territory those acts were done has been strictly interpreted. In particular, it is not enough to show that the goods have been delivered 'in' the territory of a State other than the State within whose territory the acts constituting the offer and acceptance were done. The goods must be delivered 'to' that country; in other words, the goods must have been delivered from a country which was outside of that territory (*Amiri Flight Authority* v. *BAE Systems plc* [2003] EWCA Civ 1447; [2004] 1 All ER (Comm) 385).

Choice of law clauses

27.—(1) Where the law applicable to a contract is the law of any part of the United Kingdom only by choice of the parties (and apart from that choice would be the law of some country outside the United Kingdom) sections 2 to 7 and 16 to 21 of this Act do not operate as part of the law applicable to the contract.

(2) This Act has effect notwithstanding any contract term which applies or purports to apply the law of some country outside the United Kingdom, where (either or both)—

(a) the term appears to the court, or arbitrator or arbiter to have been imposed wholly or mainly for the purpose of enabling the party imposing it to evade the operation of this Act; or

(b) in the making of the contract one of the parties dealt as consumer, and

he was then habitually resident in the United Kingdom, and the essential steps necessary for the making of the contract were taken there, whether by him or by others on his behalf.

COMMENTARY

Section 27(1) of the Act states that where the law applicable to a contract is the law of any part of the United Kingdom only by the choice of the parties, sections 2–7 of the Act do not operate as part of the law applicable to the contract. Thus foreign parties who choose English law as the law applicable to the contract do not thereby subject themselves to sections 2–7. Section 27(2) seeks to prevent evasion of the Act by resort to a choice of foreign law. Essentially, the controls contained in the Act cannot be evaded by the choice of a law outside the United Kingdom as the governing law if it appears that the choice of law was imposed wholly or mainly to enable the party imposing it to evade the operation of the Act or where one of the parties dealt as a consumer, was then habitually resident in the UK, and the essential steps for the making of the contract were taken in the UK. This is an important provision in terms of consumer protection.

Saving for other relevant legislation

29.—(1) Nothing in this Act removes or restricts the effect of, or prevents reliance upon, any contractual provision which—

(a) is authorised or required by the express terms or necessary implication of an enactment; or

(b) being made with a view to compliance with an international agreement to which the United Kingdom is a party, does not operate more restrictively than is contemplated by the agreement.

(2) A contract term is to be taken—

(a) for the purposes of Part I of this Act, as satisfying the requirement of reasonableness; and

(b) for those of Part II, to have been fair and reasonable to incorporate,

if it is incorporated or approved by, or incorporated pursuant to a decision or ruling of, a competent authority acting in the exercise of any statutory jurisdiction or function and is not a term in a contract to which the competent authority is itself a party.

(3) In this section—

'competent authority' means any court, arbitrator or arbiter, government department or public authority;

'enactment' means any legislation (including subordinate legislation) of the United Kingdom or Northern Ireland and any instrument having effect by virtue of such legislation; and

'statutory' means conferred by an enactment.

COMMENTARY

The Act does not purport to regulate any contractual provision which is authorized or required by the express terms or necessary implication of an enactment, nor any contractual provision which is necessary in order to secure compliance with an international agreement to which the United Kingdom is a party (s. 29(1)). Relevant statutes and international conventions include those relating to carriage of goods by sea and carriage of passengers, goods, and luggage by air and by land. Furthermore, a contract term will be assumed to have satisfied the requirement of reasonableness if it is incorporated or approved by, or incorporated pursuant to a decision or ruling of, a competent authority (that is, any court, arbitrator, or arbiter, government department or public authority) acting in the exercise of any statutory jurisdiction or function and is not a term in a contract to which the competent authority is itself a party.

SCHEDULE 1

SCOPE OF SECTIONS 2 TO 4 AND 7

1. Sections 2 to 4 of this Act do not extend to—

(a) any contract of insurance (including a contract to pay an annuity on human life);

(b) of any contract so far as it relates to the creation or transfer of an interest in land, or to the termination of such an interest, whether by extinction, merger, surrender, forfeiture or otherwise;

(c) any contract so far as it relates to the creation or transfer of a right or interest in any patent, trade mark, copyright or design right registered design, technical or commercial information or other intellectual property, or relates to the termination of any such right or interest;

(d) any contract so far as it relates—

(i) to the formation or dissolution of a company (which means any body corporate or unincorporated association and includes a partnership), or

(ii) to its constitution or the rights or obligations of its corporators or members;

(e) any contract so far as it relates to the creation or transfer of securities or of any right or interest in securities.

2. Section 2(1) extends to—

(a) any contract of marine salvage or towage;

(b) any charterparty of a ship or hovercraft; and

(c) any contract for the carriage of goods by ship or hovercraft;

but subject to this sections 2 to 4 and 7 do not extend to any such contract except in favour of a person dealing as consumer.

3. Where goods are carried by ship or hovercraft in pursuance of a contract which either—

(a) specifies that as the means of carriage over part of the journey to be covered, or

(b) makes no provision as to the means of carriage and does not exclude that means,

then sections 2(2), 3 and 4 do not, except in favour of a person dealing as consumer, extend to the contract as it operates for and in relation to the carriage of the goods by that means.

4. Section 2(1) and (2) do not extend to a contract of employment, except in favour of the employee.

5. Section 2(1) does not affect the validity of any discharge and indemnity given by a person, on or in connection with an award to him of compensation for pneumoconiosis attributable to employment in the coal industry, in respect of any further claim arising from his contracting that disease.

COMMENTARY

Schedule 1 to the Act exempts a number of different types of contract from the controls contained in sections 2–4 of the Act. In particular, it should be noted that these sections do not apply to (i) any insurance contract, (ii) any contract so far as it relates to the creation or transfer of an interest in land, or the termination of such an interest, and (iii) any contract so far as it relates to the creation or transfer of a right or interest in any patent, trade mark, copyright, registered design, or any other intellectual property. It should also be noted that section 2(1) and (2) do not extend to contracts of employment, except in favour of the employee.

SCHEDULE 2

'GUIDELINES' FOR APPLICATION OF REASONABLENESS TEST

The matters to which regard is to be had in particular for the purposes of sections 6(3), 7(3) and (4), 20 and 21 are any of the following which appear to be relevant—

(a) the strength of the bargaining positions of the parties relative to each other, taking into account (among other things) alternative means by which the customer's requirements could have been met;

(b) whether the customer received an inducement to agree to the term, or in accepting it had an opportunity of entering into a similar contract with other persons, but without having to accept a similar term;

(c) whether the customer knew or ought reasonably to have known of the existence and extent of the term (having regard, among other things, to any custom of the trade and any previous course of dealing between the parties);

(d) where the term excludes or restricts any relevant liability if some condition is not complied with, whether it was reasonable at the time of the contract to expect that compliance with that condition would be practicable;

(e) whether the goods were manufactured, processed or adapted to the special order of the customer.

COMMENTARY

While a court is expressly directed to have regard to these factors where the validity of the clause is challenged under sections 6 and 7 of the Act, the influence of these factors is not confined to these contracts. The courts have regard to them in all cases where it is appropriate to do so.

5. TWO ILLUSTRATIVE CASES

George Mitchell (Chesterhall) Ltd v. Finney Lock Seeds Ltd

[1983] 2 AC 803, House of Lords

The facts are set out in the speech of Lord Bridge.

Lord Bridge of Harwich

My Lords, the appellants are seed merchants. The respondents are farmers in East Lothian. In December 1973 the respondents ordered from the appellants 301b. of Dutch winter white cabbage seeds. The seeds supplied were invoiced as 'Finney's Late Dutch Special'. The price was £201.60. 'Finney's Late Dutch Special' was the variety required by the respondents. It is a Dutch winter white cabbage which grows particularly well in the area of East Lothian where the respondents farm, and can be harvested and sold at a favourable price in the spring. The respondents planted some 63 acres of their land with seedlings grown from the seeds supplied by the appellants to produce their cabbage crop for the spring of 1975. In the event, the crop proved to be worthless and had to be ploughed in. This was for two reasons. First, the seeds supplied were not 'Finney's Late Dutch Special' or any other variety of Dutch winter white cabbage, but a variety of autumn cabbage. Secondly, even as autumn cabbage the seeds were of very inferior quality.

The issues in the appeal arise from three sentences in the conditions of sale endorsed on the appellants' invoice and admittedly embodied in the terms on which the appellants contracted. For ease of reference it will be convenient to number the sentences. Omitting immaterial words they read as follows:

1. 'In the event of any seeds or plants sold or agreed to be sold by us not complying with the express terms of the contract of sale . . . or any seeds or plants proving defective in varietal purity we will, at our option, replace the defective seeds or plants, free of charge to the buyer or will refund all payments made to us by the buyer in respect of the defective seeds or plants and this shall be the limit of our obligation.

2. We hereby exclude all liability for any loss or damage arising from the use of any seeds or plants supplied by us and for any consequential loss or damage arising out of such use or any failure in the performance of or any defect in any seeds or plants supplied by us or for any other loss or damage whatsoever save for, at our option, liability for any such replacement or refund as aforesaid.

3. In accordance with the established custom of the seed trade any express or implied condition, statement or warranty, statutory or otherwise, not stated in these conditions is hereby excluded.'

I will refer to the whole as 'the relevant condition' and to the parts as 'clauses 1, 2 and 3' of the relevant condition.

The first issue is whether the relevant condition, on its true construction in the context of the contract as a whole, is effective to limit the appellants' liability to a refund of £201.60, the price of the seeds ('the common law issue'). The second issue is whether, if the common law issue is decided in the appellants' favour, they should nevertheless be precluded from reliance on this limitation of liability pursuant to the provisions of the modified section 55 of the Sale of Goods Act 1979 which is set out in paragraph 11 of Schedule 1 to the Act and which applies to contracts made between May 18, 1973, and February 1, 1978 ('the statutory issue').

[he first dealt with 'the common law issue' and concluded that 'the relevant condition' was effective, as a matter of construction, to limit the appellants' liability to the replacement of the seeds or the refund of the price paid. He then turned to 'the statutory issue'.]

The statutory issue turns, as already indicated, on the application of the provisions of the modified section 55 of the Sale of Goods Act 1979, as set out in paragraph 11 of Schedule 1 to the Act . . .

'(4) In the case of a contract of sale of goods, any term of that or any other contract exempting from all or any of the provisions of section 13, 14 or 15 above is void in the case of a consumer sale and is, in any other case, not enforceable to the extent that it is shown that it would not be fair or reasonable to allow reliance on the term.

(5) In determining for the purposes of subsection (4) above whether or not reliance on any such term would be fair or reasonable regard shall be had to all the circumstances of the case and in particular to the following matters—(a) the strength of the bargaining positions of the seller and buyer relative to each other, taking into account, among other things, the availability of suitable alternative products and sources of supply; (b) whether the buyer received an inducement to agree to the term or in accepting it had an opportunity of buying the goods or suitable alternatives without it from any source of supply; (c) whether the buyer knew or ought reasonably to have known of the existence and extent of the term (having regard, among other things, to any custom of the trade and any previous course of dealing between the parties); (d) where the term exempts from all or any of the provisions of section 13, 14, or 15 above if some condition is not complied with, whether it was reasonable at the time of the contract to expect that compliance with that condition would be practicable; (e) whether the goods were manufactured, processed, or adapted to the special order of the buyer . . .'

The statutory issue . . . turns on the words in subsection (4) 'to the extent that it is shown that it would not be fair or reasonable to allow reliance on' this restriction of the appellants' liabilities, having regard to the matters referred to in subsection (5).

This is the first time your Lordships' House has had to consider a modern statutory provision giving the court power to override contractual terms excluding or restricting liability, which depends on the court's view of what is 'fair and reasonable'. The particular provision of the modified section 55 of the Act of 1979 which applies in the instant case is of limited and diminishing importance. But the several provisions of the Unfair Contract Terms Act 1977 which depend on 'the requirement of reasonableness', defined in section 11 by reference to what is 'fair and reasonable', albeit in a different context, are likely to come before the courts with increasing frequency. It may, therefore, be appropriate to consider how an original decision as to what is 'fair and reasonable' made in the application of any of these provisions should be approached by an appellate court. It would not be accurate to describe such a decision as an exercise of discretion. But a decision under any of the provisions referred to will have this in common with the exercise of a discretion, that, in having regard to the various matters to which the modified section 55(5) of the Act of 1979, or section 11 of the Act of 1977 direct attention, the court must entertain a whole range of considerations, put them in the scales on one side or the other, and decide at the end of the day on which side the balance comes down. There will sometimes be room for a legitimate difference of judicial opinion as to what the answer should be, where it will be impossible to say that one view is demonstrably wrong and the other demonstrably right. It must follow, in my view, that, when asked to review such a decision on appeal, the appellate court should treat the original decision with the utmost respect and refrain from interference with it unless satisfied that it proceeded upon some erroneous principle or was plainly and obviously wrong.

Turning back to the modified section 55 of the Act of 1979, it is common ground that the onus was on the respondents to show that it would not be fair or reasonable to allow the appellants to rely on the relevant condition as limiting their liability. It was argued for the appellants that the court must have regard to the circumstances as at the date of the contract, not after the breach. The basis of the argument was that this was the effect of section 11 of the Act of 1977 and that it would be wrong to construe the modified section 55 of the Act as having a different effect. Assuming the premise is correct, the conclusion does not follow. The provisions of the Act of 1977 cannot be considered in construing the prior enactment now embodied in the modified section 55 of the Act of 1979. But, in any event, the language of subsections (4) and (5) of that section is clear and unambiguous. The question whether it is fair or reasonable to allow reliance on a term excluding or limiting liability for a breach of contract can only arise after the breach. The nature of the breach and the circumstances in which it occurred cannot possibly be excluded from 'all the circumstances of the case' to which regard must be had.

The only other question of construction debated in the course of the argument was the meaning to be attached to the words 'to the extent that' in subsection (4) and, in particular, whether they permit the court to hold that it would be fair and reasonable to allow partial reliance on a limitation clause and, for example, to decide in the instant case that the respondents should recover, say, half their consequential damage. I incline to the view that, in their context, the words are equivalent to 'in so far as' or 'in circumstances in which' and do not permit the kind of judgment of Solomon illustrated by the example. But for the purpose of deciding this appeal I find it unnecessary to express a concluded view on this question.

My Lords, at long last I turn to the application of the statutory language to the circumstances of the case. Of the particular matters to which attention is directed by paragraphs (a) to (e) of section 55 (5), only those in (a) to (c) are relevant. As to paragraph (c), the respondents admittedly knew of the relevant condition (they had dealt with the appellants for many years) and, if they had read it, particularly clause 2, they would, I think, as laymen rather than lawyers, have had no difficulty in understanding what it said. This and the magnitude of the damages claimed in proportion to the price of the seeds sold are factors which weigh in the scales in the appellants' favour.

The question of relative bargaining strength under paragraph (a) and of the opportunity to buy seeds without a limitation of the seedsman's liability under paragraph (b) were inter-related. The evidence was that a similar limitation of liability was universally embodied in the terms of trade between seedsmen and farmers and had been so for very many years. The limitation had never been negotiated between representative bodies but, on the other hand, had not been the subject of any protest by the National Farmers' Union. These factors, if considered in isolation, might have been equivocal. The decisive factor, however, appears from the evidence of four witnesses called for the appellants, two independent seedsmen, the chairman of the appellant company, and a director of a sister company (both being wholly-owned subsidiaries of the same parent). They said that it had always been their practice, unsuccessfully attempted in the instant case, to negotiate settlements of farmers' claims for damages in excess of the price of the seeds, if they thought that the claims were 'genuine' and 'justified'. This evidence indicated a clear recognition by seedsmen in general, and the appellants in particular, that reliance on the limitation of liability imposed by the relevant condition would not be fair or reasonable.

Two further factors, if more were needed, weight the scales in favour of the respondents. The supply of autumn, instead of winter, cabbage seeds was due to the negligence of the appellants' sister company. Irrespective of its quality, the autumn variety supplied could not, according to the appellants' own evidence, be grown commercially in East Lothian. Finally, as the trial judge found, seedsmen could insure against the risk of crop failure caused by supplying the wrong variety of seeds without materially increasing the price of seeds.

My Lords, even if I felt doubts about the statutory issue, I should not, for the reasons explained earlier, think it right to interfere with the unanimous original decision of that issue by the Court of Appeal. As it is, I feel no such doubts. If I were making the original decision, I should conclude without hesitation that it would not be fair or reasonable to allow the appellants to rely on the contractual limitation of their liability.
I would dismiss the appeal.

Lord Diplock delivered a short concurring speech. **Lord Scarman**, **Lord Roskill**, and **Lord Brightman** concurred.

COMMENTARY

A number of points should be noted about this case. First, the case is concerned with the construction of the now repealed section 55 of the Sale of Goods Act 1979. The factors listed in section 55(4) are, however, very similar to those listed in Schedule 2 to the Unfair Contract Terms Act 1977 and so the case is one of some significance for the interpretation of the 1977 Act. Secondly, Lord Bridge sets out a very limited role for appellate courts when reviewing decisions of lower courts on the reasonableness or otherwise of a particular clause. An appellate court should 'refrain from interference . . . unless satisfied that [the original decision] proceeded upon some erroneous principle or was plainly and obviously wrong'. Thirdly, Lord Bridge notes the issue relating to the meaning of to the extent that' (see p. 475 above). While he states that, in his view, the court does not have jurisdiction to make an order to the effect that a party is entitled to recover half his consequential losses, he is careful to say that it is 'unnecessary to express a concluded view on this question'. Finally, the 'decisive factor' which led Lord Bridge to conclude that the term was unreasonable was the 'recognition by seedsmen in general . . . that reliance on the limitation of liability . . . would not be fair or reasonable' (see further on this point, p. 476 above).

Phillips Products Ltd v. Hyland

[1987] 1 WLR 659, Court of Appeal

The second defendants, Hamstead Plant Hire Co Ltd, hired an excavator to the plaintiffs, Phillips Products Ltd. The excavator was driven by the first defendant, Mr Hyland, who was also hired out to the plaintiffs. The contract of hire incorporated the Contractors' Plant Association ('CPA') conditions, Condition 8 of which stated:

'When a driver or operator is supplied by the owner to work the plant, he shall be under the direction and control of the hirer. Such drivers or operators shall for all purposes in connexion with their employment in the working of the plant be regarded as the servants or agents of the hirer who alone shall be responsible for all claims arising in connexion with the operation of the plant by the said drivers and operators. The hirer shall not allow any other person to operate such plant without the owner's previous consent to be confirmed in writing.'

Considerable damage was done to the plaintiffs' buildings as a result of Mr Hyland's negligence while operating the excavator. The plaintiffs brought an action for damages against both defendants in respect of the loss that they had suffered as a result of the negligence of Mr Hyland. The claim succeeded before the trial judge. The second defendants appealed to the Court of Appeal and relied upon condition 8 by way of defence. The Court of Appeal dismissed the appeal and held that condition 8 fell within the scope of section 2(2) of the Unfair Contract Terms Act 1977 and that the trial judge's conclusion that the clause was unreasonable was neither plainly and obviously wrong nor based on an erroneous principle. This being the case, condition 8 did not provide the second defendants with a defence to the plaintiffs' claim and they were, accordingly, liable in damages to the plaintiffs.

Slade LJ [delivered the judgment of the court]

The issues arising on the appeal

The principal question arising on this appeal concerning the applicability or otherwise of the Act . . . itself gave rise to three issues. The first two do not appear to have been argued before the learned Judge . . . No objection, however, was raised on behalf of Phillips to these points being taken . . . These three issues are:

(i)   On the admitted facts of the present case, was there on the part of Hamstead 'negligence' within the definition of that word contained in section 1(1) of the Act?

(ii) If the answer to (i) is 'yes', is condition 8 a contract term which, apart from the effect of the Act, can properly be said to 'exclude or restrict' Hamstead's liability for negligence within the meaning of these words in section 2(2) of the Act? In considering this issue, it is necessary to bear in mind the concluding words of section 13(1) which bring within the ambit of section 2(2) terms 'which exclude or restrict the relevant obligation or duty'.

(iii) If the answers to (i) and (ii) are both 'Yes', does condition 8 satisfy the requirement of reasonableness, within the meaning of that phrase as used in the Act?

Issue (i)

As to (i), the argument for Hamstead is simple, and runs on these lines. If a claim is based on contract, 'negligence' within the definition of section 1(1)(a) can have occurred only if there has been a breach of 'any obligation, arising from the express or implied terms of a contract, to take reasonable care or exercise reasonable skill in the performance of the contract'. So, it is said, if in the case of such a claim the contract has by its express terms excluded liability for negligence, there can ex hypothesi have been no breach of any obligation of the nature referred to in section 1(1)(a).

The claim in the present case, as it happens, is of the nature referred to in section 1(1)(b); the breach of a common law duty to take reasonable care is alleged. Here again a similar argument is advanced. It is suggested that there can be no breach of a common law duty to take reasonable care within the meaning of section 1(1)(b), by a party to a contract which contains a condition which purports to absolve him from liability for negligence.

These arguments, though superficially attractive, are in our judgment fallacious. If correct, they would make nonsense of the 1977 Act. They would mean that the very contractual term which pre-eminently is suitable to be subject to review for reasonableness under the Act would be taken out of its scope. The Act, however, is not nonsensical. Its purpose is not defeated by the wording of its first section. In our judgment, in considering whether there has been a breach of any obligation of the nature referred to in (a) or of any duty of the nature referred to in (b) or (c), the court has to leave out of account, at this stage, the contract term which is relied on by the defence as defeating the plaintiffs' claim for breach of such obligation or such duty, and section 1(1) should be construed accordingly.

If any support were necessary for this construction of section 1(1), it is to be found in the concluding words of section 13(1) of the Act. For these words make it clear that section 2 is capable of negating the effect of contract terms which purport to exclude or restrict 'the relevant obligation or duty'.

Section 1(4), by its reference to 'vicariously', defeats a further argument which counsel for Hamstead at one stage sought to raise on issue (i): namely, that the admitted negligence of Mr Hyland was not sufficient and that there had to be shown personal negligence on the part of Hamstead.

Accordingly, though the validity of condition 8 still remains to be considered, on the admitted facts of this case there was 'negligence' on the part of Hamstead falling within section 1(1)(b) of the Act. This took the form of a breach (subject to the effect, if any, of condition 8) of Hamstead's common law duty to take reasonable care, by reason of the fact that Mr Hyland who, subject to condition 8, was Hamstead's servant, had caused the loss to Phillips by his negligence in the performance of his duties as such servant.
Issue (i) therefore has to be answered 'Yes'.

Issue (ii)

Issue (ii) brings us to section 2(2). Subsection (1) does not apply because there was, fortunately, no death or personal injury. Section 2(2), set out as incorporating the relevant wording of subsection (1), provides that in case of other loss or damage a person cannot by reference to any contract term exclude or restrict his liability for negligence except in so far as the term satisfies the requirement of reasonableness. The argument for Hamstead is that they do not, by reference to condition 8, 'exclude or restrict' their liability for negligence. Condition 8, it is stressed, is not an 'excluding' or 'restricting' clause. It may have an effect on the liability for negligence which would otherwise have existed if there were, as there was in the present case, negligence. (For 'may' we would substitute 'must' assuming that Hamstead's submission as to the validity of condition 8 is correct). Nevertheless, the condition does not, it is said, amount to an attempt by either party to the contract to 'exclude or restrict' liability: it is simply an attempt on their part to divide and allocate the obligations or responsibilities arising in relation to the contract by transferring liability for the acts of the operator from the plant owners to the hirers. A transfer, it is suggested, is not an exclusion; hence the hirers fail at the section 2(2) hurdle.

We were referred by counsel for Hamstead to the House of Lords' case *Arthur White (Contractors) Ltd* v. *Tarmac Civil Engineering Ltd* [1967] 1 WLR 1508 in which the construction and effect of a clause ('clause 8') in more or less identical terms to that of condition 8 was considered. In that case, which concerned a contract of hire, a driver had been supplied by the owners with a crane excavator. During the period of hire an accident occurred due to the driver's negligence in which the plaintiff, an engineer on the site, was severely injured. The question on the appeal was whether the hirers were, as between themselves and the owners, solely responsible for the amount recovered by the plaintiff in damages, judgment having been entered against both of them. It was held that as between the hirers and the owners the responsibility was placed on the hirers by clause 8. It was argued on behalf of the hirers that on the basis of the *Alderslade* principle (a reference to the judgment of Lord Greene MR in *Alderslade* v. *Hendon Laundry Ltd* [1945] KB 189) a clause of exception or exemption against loss by one contracting party is presumed not to apply to a case where the loss is occasioned by the negligence of that party unless the clause expressly covers that event, or there is no other liability to which the clause could reasonably refer. This argument was rejected, essentially on the grounds that clause 8 was not an exemption clause but was intended to allocate the responsibility for claims as between the hirers and the owners: (see at p. 593E per Lord Pearce, at p. 597F per Lord Upjohn and at p. 599 H–I per Lord Pearson). If we may respectfully say so, it is readily intelligible that the House of Lords should have concluded that the *Alderslade* presumption could not possibly have applied to a clause such as clause 8.

However, the question for this court is not whether the *Alderslade* presumption applies to condition 8. It is whether or not the provisions of condition 8 'exclude or restrict' Hamstead's liability for negligence within the meaning of section 2(2) of the Act. We see nothing in the *Arthur White* decision or in the speeches in that case which have any relevant bearing on this point. Certainly there is nothing which leads to the conclusion that a plant-owner who uses the general conditions is not excluding his liability for negligence in the relevant sense by reference to the contract term condition 8. We are unable to accept that in the ordinary sensible meaning of words in the context of section 2 and the Act as a whole, the provisions of condition 8 do not fall within the scope of section 2(2). A transfer of liability from A to B necessarily and inevitably involves the exclusion of liability so far as A is concerned. Mr Thompson pointed out that in other circumstances liability for the acts of the operator might well have fallen on the hirers at common law in any event: see, for example, *Mersey Docks and Harbour Board* v. *Coggins and Griffiths (Liverpool) Ltd* [1947] AC 1 per Lord Simon at p. 10 and per Lord Macmillan at p. 13. This, in our judgment, is immaterial. On the particular facts of this case the effect of condition 8, if valid, is to negate a common law liability in tort which would otherwise admittedly fall on the plant-owner. The effect of condition 8 making 'the hirer alone responsible for all claims' necessarily connotes that by the condition the plant-owner's responsibility is excluded: In applying section 2(2), it is not relevant to consider whether the form of a condition is such that it can aptly be given the label of an 'exclusion' or 'restriction' clause. There is no mystique about 'exclusion' or 'restriction' clauses. To decide whether a person 'excludes' liability by reference to a contract term, you look at the effect of the term. You look at its substance. The effect here is beyond doubt. Hamstead does most certainly purport to exclude its liabilities for negligence by reference to condition 8. Furthermore, condition 8 purports to 'exclude or restrict the relevant obligation or duty' within the provisions of section 13(1) of the Act.

Issue (ii) has to be answered 'Yes'.

Issue (iii)

Issue (iii) is the issue which alone it would seem, apart from the construction of condition 8 itself, the learned Judge was asked to decide. Does the condition, on the evidence and in the context of the contract as a whole, satisfy the 'requirement of reasonableness', as defined by section 11(1) and elsewhere in the Act?

Under section 11(5) the onus falls on Hamstead to show that condition 8 satisfies the condition of reasonableness. For this purpose having regard to section 11(1), it has to show that that condition was 'a fair and reasonable one to be included, having regard to the circumstances which were, or ought reasonably to have been, known to or in the contemplation of the parties when the contract was made'. As the learned Judge pointed out, all the relevant circumstances were known to both parties at that time. The task which he therefore set himself was to examine all the relevant circumstances and then ask himself whether, on the balance of probabilities, he was satisfied that condition 8, in so far as it purported to exclude Hamstead's liability for Mr Hyland's negligence, was a fair and reasonable term. As to these matters, his conclusions as set out in his judgment were as follows:

'What then were the relevant circumstances? First, the second defendants carried on the business of hiring out plant and operators. In contrast the plaintiffs were steel stockholders, and as such had no occasion to hire plant except on the odd occasions when they had building work to be done at their premises. There had been apparently only three such occasions: one in 1979, one in July 1980 when the drainage trench was dug and the final occasion when the drainage was done in August 1980.

Secondly, the hire was to be for a very short period. It was arranged at very short notice. There was no occasion for the plaintiffs to address their mind to all the details of the hiring agreement, nor did they do so. The inclusion of condition 8 arose because it appeared in the second defendants' printed conditions. It was not the product of any discussion or agreement between the parties.

Thirdly, there was little if any opportunity for the plaintiffs to arrange insurance cover for risks arising from the first defendant's negligence. Insofar as the first defendant was to be regarded as the plaintiffs' servant it might have been an easy matter to ensure that the plaintiffs' insurance policies were extended, if necessary, to cover his activities in relation to third party claims. Any businessman customarily insures against such claims. He does not usually insure against damage caused to his own property by his own employees' negligence. Thus to arrange insurance cover for the first defendant would have required time and a special and unusual arrangement with the plaintiffs' insurers.

Fourthly, the plaintiffs played no part in the selection of the first defendant as the operator of the JCB. They had to accept whoever the second defendant sent to drive the machine. Further, although they undoubtedly would have had to, and would have had the right to tell the JCB operator what job he was required to do, from their previous experience they knew they would be unable in any way to control the way in which the first defendant did the job that he was given. They would not have had the knowledge to exercise such control. All the expertise lay with the first defendant. I do not think condition 8 could possibly be construed as giving control of the matter of operation of the JCB to the plaintiffs. Indeed in the event the first defendant made it perfectly plain to Mr Pritchard, the plaintiffs' builder, that he would brook no interfer-ence in the way he operated his machine.

Those being the surrounding circumstances, was it fair and reasonable that the hire contract should include a condition which relieved the second defendants of all responsibility for damage caused, not to the property of a third party but to the plain-tiff's own property, by the negligence of the second defendants' own operators? This was for the plaintiffs in a very real sense a "take it or leave it" situation. They needed a JCB for a simple job at short notice. In dealing with the second defendants they had the choice of taking a JCB operator under a contract containing some 43 written condi-tions or not taking the JCB at all. The question for me is not a general question whether any contract of hire of the JCB could fairly and reasonably exclude such liability, but a much more limited question as to whether this contract of hire entered into in these circumstances fairly and reasonably included such an exemption.

I have come to the conclusion that the second defendants have failed to satisfy me that condition 8 was in this respect a fair and reasonable term.'

Before reverting to the conclusions and reasoning of the learned Judge, it is unfortunately necessary to deviate from the arguments as they were presented to us. Schedule 2 of the Act contains what are called '"guidelines" for Application of Reason-ableness Test'. These guidelines state:

[he set out the guidelines (on which see p. 485 above) and continued]

We were told that the guidelines in Schedule 2 of the Act were not applicable in this case. It would seem, on a study of the provisions of the Act to which we were not referred in argument, that this may have been wrong. The contract here was a contract of hire. Normally in such a contract, and it would seem consistently with the provisions of the general conditions in this case, the hirer takes possession of the article hired. Therefore, it appears to us that subsection (3) of section 7 (which we do not think it necessary to quote) would apply and thus render Schedule 2 applicable. On this basis the guidelines would fall to be considered. Fortunately, however, in view of the way in which the case has been argued on both sides, no difficulty arises on this account. Guideline (d) is, on any footing, irrelevant. Guidelines (a), (b) and (c) were argued as factors properly to be taken into account, even though not because of the guidelines themselves. Guideline (e) would no doubt have been mentioned in argument if counsel on either side had thought that it affected their decision as to 'fair and reasonable' in this case.

In approaching the learned Judge's reasons and conclusions on this issue, four points have, in our judgment, to be borne in mind.

First, as the learned Judge himself clearly appreciated, the question for the court is not a general question whether or not condition 8 is valid or invalid in the case of any and every contract of hire entered into between a hirer and a plant owner who uses the relevant CPA Conditions. The question was and is whether the exclusion of Hamstead's liability for negligence satisfied the requirement of reasonableness imposed by the Act, in relation to this particular contract.

Secondly, we have to bear in mind that the relevant circumstances, which were or should have been known to or contemplated by the parties, are those which existed when the contract was made. Section 11(1) is specific on that point. Hence, evidence as to what happened during the performance of the contract must, at best, be treated with great caution. As we have indicated, such evidence was adduced at the trial, apparently without objection. At best, it could probably be used to show, by evidence of conduct and absence of objection to that conduct, what the attitude of the parties would have been in that respect, what they would have contemplated, at the time when they made the contract.

Thirdly, the burden of proof falling upon the owner under section 11(5) of the Act is, in our judgment, of great significance in this case in the light, or rather in the obscurity, of the evidence and the absence of evidence on issues which were, or might have been, relevant on the issue of reasonableness. One particular example is the matter of insurance. The insurance position of all the parties was canvassed to some extent in oral evidence at the trial, but such evidence seems to us to have been singularly imprecise and inconclusive.

Finally, by way of approach to the issue of reasonableness, it is necessary to bear in mind, and strive to comply with, the clear and stern injunction issued to appellate courts by Lord Bridge in his speech, concurred in by the other members of their Lordships' House, in *Mitchell (George) (Chesterhall) Ltd* v. *Finney Lock Seeds Ltd* [1983] 2 AC 803 at pp. 815–816:

[he set out a passage from the speech of Lord Bridge which is extracted above at p. 487 and continued]

In the context of issue (iii), criticism has been made by Hamstead's counsel of some parts of the learned Judge's reasoning. It is said that in some respects he misunderstood or mis-recollected the evidence. Some of the evidence was indeed confused and not easy to follow. It is, in some passages, difficult to be confident what was really meant. It may be that the learned Judge placed more stress than we would think right on the lack of opportunity of Mr Phillips to study and understand the conditions, and in particular condition 8. But this is the very sort of point to which Lord Bridge referred in saying that there is room for a legitimate difference of judicial opinion.

Against this, there is to be set the fact, as it appeared at the trial, that the general conditions with their 43 clauses were adopted by and used by all the members of the Trade Association to which Hamstead belonged. (Counsel has told us that there is other material which might alter the picture, but we cannot go beyond the evidence which was in fact before the Judge). Thus, we think he was justified in saying that in dealing with Hamstead this was for Phillips in a very real sense a 'take it or leave it situation'. As he said, they needed a JCB for a simple job at short notice and, in dealing with Hamstead, had the choice of taking a JCB operator under the general conditions or not taking the JCB at all. Even if Mr Phillips had understood and had been worried by the effect of condition 8 before he arranged for the conclusion of the earlier contracts or before he authorized Mr Pritchard to conclude the contract in August 1980 now in question, it is reasonable to assume, on the evidence as it stood, that he would not have thought that there was much that he could do about it, except to take the conditions offered. It is fair to say that we were told that various changes had been made, including the alterations to some of the general conditions since the coming into force of the Act and that the position today might be very different. But counsel for Hamstead necessarily and realistically accepts that we have to deal, as the learned Judge had to deal, with the contractual terms as they were and with the facts as to relevant considerations as they were given in evidence at the trial, not as the terms are now or as the relevant facts might have appeared to be if further evidence had been given.

As appears from the passage which we have cited, other matters which influenced the

Judge in his decision on unreasonableness, and which we think were clearly relevant factors to be weighed in the balance, were that the hirers could play no part in the selection of the operator who was to do the work. Nor did the general conditions contain any warranty by Hamstead as to his fitness or competence for the job. Furthermore, despite the words in condition 8 'he shall be under the direction and control of the hirer', we think it reasonable to infer that the parties, when they made the contract, would have assumed that the operator would be the expert in the management of this machine and that he would not, and could not be expected to, take any instructions from anyone representing the hirers as to the manner in which he would operate the machine to do the job, once the extent and nature of the job had been defined to him by the hirers; in short they would tell him what to do but not how to do it. If such evidence is admissible, which we do not find it necessary to decide, this inference would be strongly supported by the evidence of what actually happened on the site before the accident occurred.

It may be that in several respects this is a very special case on its facts, its evidence and its paucity of evidence. But on these facts and on the available evidence, we are wholly unpersuaded that the learned Judge proceeded upon some erroneous principle or was plainly and obviously wrong in his conclusion that Hamstead had not discharged the burden upon them of showing that condition 8 satisfied the requirements of reasonableness in the context of this particular contract of hire. It is important therefore that our conclusion on the particular facts of this case should not be treated as a binding precedent in other cases where similar clauses fall to be considered but the evidence of the surrounding circumstances may be very different.

Issue (iii) accordingly has to be answered 'No' and we dismiss this appeal.

COMMENTARY

There were two principal issues at stake in *Phillips*. The first was a jurisdictional issue, namely whether or not the Act applied to condition 8, and the second was the application of the reasonableness test to the clause. The jurisdictional issue is the more difficult of the two. It had two aspects to it, being issues (i) and (ii) in the judgment. In issue (i) the second defendants submitted that they had not been negligent while in issue (ii) they denied that condition 8 was a clause that attempted to 'exclude or restrict' liability. The essence of the defence was the same in both issues, namely that condition 8 had the effect of defining the obligations of the parties and did not provide the defendants with a defence to a breach of an obligation. The Court of Appeal rejected both arguments. Slade LJ held that, when deciding whether or not a defendant has been negligent, the court must leave out of account, at least initially, the contract term which is relied on by the defendant in order to defeat the plaintiff's claim for damages for breach of the duty to take reasonable care. The reasoning here is difficult. Why choose to leave the exclusion clause out of account when seeking to identify the obligations that have been assumed by the parties when the exclusion clause may be an integral part of the definition of the obligations of the parties? The Court of Appeal gave two answers to this question. First, the conclusion that there had been no negligence on the part of the defendants would have made 'nonsense of the Act' because it would have taken condition 8, and many other clauses, outside the scope of the Act. There is obvious force in this point but it can be countered by the argument that the Act is itself based on a false premiss. The Act generally assumes that the function of an exclusion clause is to provide the defendant with a defence to a breach of duty, whereas it can be argued that the true function of an exclusion clause is to assist in the definition of the obligations which the parties have assumed (see Coote, p. 499 below). The second answer given by the Court of Appeal was that section 13(1) of the Act extends the scope of section 2 to clauses that purport to exclude or restrict 'the relevant obligation or duty'. The House of Lords in *Smith* v. *Eric S Bush* [1990] 1 AC 831 also relied upon section 13 when rejecting an argument advanced on behalf of the defendant surveyor that his disclaimer fell outside the scope of section 2 because its effect was to negate the duty of care rather than provide him with a defence in respect of his breach of duty. It is true that section 13 extends the scope of the Act to certain duty-defining clauses, as does section 3(2)(b), but the problem with the section lies in identifying which duty-defining clauses fall within its scope and which do not.

The jurisdictional issue raised in issue (ii) is also a difficult one. Here the second defendants submitted that condition 8 did not seek to 'exclude or restrict' a liability. They submitted that the effect of the clause was to 'transfer' a liability from themselves to the plaintiffs and that 'a transfer . . . is not an exclusion'. The Court of Appeal rejected this submission stating that 'a transfer of liability from A to B necessarily and inevitably involves the exclusion of liability as far as A is concerned'. The subsequent decision of the Court of Appeal in *Thompson* v. *T Lohan (Plant Hire) Ltd* [1987] 1 WLR 649 demonstrates that matters are not quite so straightforward. The case is factually similar to *Phillips* but the conclusion was different. An excavator and a driver, Mr Hill, were hired out by the first defendants, T Lohan (Plant Hire) Ltd, to a third party. The plaintiff's husband was killed in an accident caused by the negligence of the driver of the excavator. The plaintiff brought an action in negligence against the first defendants. The claim succeeded and the first defendants then sought an indemnity from the third party pursuant to condition 8 (which was in substance the same condition 8 as was in issue in *Phillips*). The third party denied any liability to indemnify the first defendants on the basis that condition 8 was an exclusion clause which was invalidated by section 2(1) of the 1977 Act. The Court of Appeal rejected this submission and held that the Act had no application to condition 8. Fox LJ stated (at pp. 656–657) that there was a 'sharp distinction' between the present case and *Phillips* and that the distinction was that:

whereas in the *Phillips* case there was a liability in negligence by Hamstead to Phillips (and that was sought to be excluded), in the present case there is no exclusion or restriction of the liability sought to be achieved by reliance on the provisions of condition 8. The plaintiff has her judgment against Lohan and can enforce it. The plaintiff is not prejudiced in any way by the operation sought to be established of condition 8. All that has happened is that Lohan and the third party have agreed between themselves who is to bear the consequences of Mr Hill's negligent acts. I can see nothing in section 2(1) of the 1977 Act to prevent that. In my opinion, section 2(1) is concerned with protecting the victim of negligence, and of course those who claim under him. It is not concerned with the arrangements made by the wrongdoer with other persons as to the sharing or bearing of the burden of compensating the victim. In such a case it seems to me there is no exclusion or restriction of the liability at all. The liability has been established by Hodgson J. It is not in dispute and is now unalterable. The circumstance that the defendants have between themselves chosen to bear the liability in a particular way does not affect that liability; it does not exclude it, and it does not restrict it. The liability to the plaintiff is the only relevant liability in the case, as it seems to me, and that liability is still in existence and will continue until discharged by payment to the plaintiff. Nothing is excluded in relation to the liability, and the liability is not restricted in any way whatever. The liability of Lohan to the plaintiff remains intact. The liability of Hamstead to Phillips was sought to be excluded.

In those circumstances it seems to me that, looking at the language of section 2(1) of the 1977 Act, this case does not fall within its prohibition.

While the Court of Appeal in *Phillips* refused to draw a distinction between a clause that 'excluded or restricted' a liability and a clause which 'transferred' a liability, the Court of Appeal in *Thompson* drew a distinction between a clause that 'shared' a liability and one which 'excluded or restricted' a liability. It did so by reading the words 'to the victim of the negligence' into section 2(1) so that the subsection only regulates attempts to exclude or restrict a liability towards the *victim of the negligence*. This reading of section 2 can, however, have some bizarre consequences. Suppose that Mr Hyland in *Phillips* had damaged the property of a third party instead of the property of the plaintiffs. If the third party sued and recovered damages from Phillips in respect of the property damage, Phillips would have been entitled to an indemnity from Hamstead under condition 8 because, on these facts, there would be no attempt to exclude or restrict a liability towards the victim of the negligence (the third party). But why should the application of the Unfair Contract Terms Act 1977 to condition 8 depend upon whose property has been damaged? Either it is a reasonable condition or it is not. This is not, however, the view of the Court of Appeal. The validity of the clause will turn upon such fortuitous circumstances as the identity of the person who suffers loss as a result of the negligence of the driver.

The second issue at stake in *Phillips* was the application of the reasonableness test to condition 8 (issue (iii) in the judgment). Once again we can see the deference shown by the Court of Appeal to the decision of the trial judge. The Court of Appeal did appear to have some sympathy with the criticisms levelled against 'some parts of the learned Judge's reasoning' but their reservations were not sufficiently strong to lead them to intervene. But they did confine the precedent value of the case by stating that 'in several respects this is a very special case on its facts, its evidence and its paucity of evidence'. This being the case, it cannot be assumed that condition 8 of the CPA conditions will be unreasonable in all cases: much will depend on the facts of the individual cases. Given the widespread use of the CPA conditions, this conclusion is unlikely to be a welcome one.

6. CONCLUSION: DEFENCE OR DEFINITION?

One of the issues that has surfaced from time to time in this chapter relates to the nature of an exclusion clause. Is the function of the clause to assist in the definition of the obligations that the parties have assumed or is its function to provide a defendant with a defence to a breach of an obligation? The judges have tended to adopt the latter view and have conceived of exclusion clauses in defensive rather than definitional terms. The Unfair Contract Terms Act 1977, with the exceptions of section 3(2)(b) and 13(1), makes the same assumption. This assumption has been challenged, most notably, by Professor Coote. The essence of his analysis of the nature of an exclusion clause is to be found in the following extract:

B Coote, *Exception Clauses*

(Sweet & Maxwell, 1964), pp. 9–11 and 17–18

A suggested classification of exception clauses

All exception clauses . . . fall within one or other of the two following classes, which it is proposed to call 'Type A' and 'Type B' respectively:

Type A: exception clauses whose effect, if any, is upon the accrual of particular primary rights.

Thus, where words relating to quality have been employed by a vendor of goods, an exclusion of conditions, warranties, or undertakings as to quality, helps determine the extent to which those words are contractually binding as, by the same token, would a stipulation by the vendor that he should not be required to make compensation for poor quality.

Type B: Exception clauses which qualify primary or secondary rights without preventing the accrual of any particular primary right.

Examples would be limitations on the time within which claims might be made, and limitations as to the amount which might be recovered on a claim. By contrast, a clause which purported to take away a buyer's right to reject goods would belong to Type A.

To bring it within Type A, an exception may operate either directly or indirectly. The direct effect requires little elaboration. If we suppose, for example, a promise in general terms, and a series of particular exceptions from that promise, we have a case where an exception clause is directly limiting the substantive contractual content of a promise, or more technically, perhaps, is negativing any primary right to performance of those matters excluded from the promise. Thus, where a horse is sold warranted sound 'except for hunting', a purchaser will have no primary right to call for a horse sound for hunting. An exception may have the same effect indirectly, through the operation of the proposition that it is impossible to create valid contractual rights while at the same time agreeing that they shall be at all times unenforceable. A total exclusion, either of sanctioning rights or of procedural rights of enforcement, would have the effect of making the apparent primary right unenforceable. In so far as the 'unenforceable right' would be illusory (that is, would have no existence as a contractual right), exceptions of this type would, accordingly, have the effect on primary rights of preventing their accrual. Thus, if the vendor of a horse should represent that the animal is sound but stipulate that he shall not be required to make compensation if it should prove to be unsound, then unless he is merely contradicting himself, he is indicating thereby that his representation is a 'mere' representation and that he refuses to contract as to the horse's soundness. In other words, by excluding sanctioning rights he is indirectly preventing the purchaser from acquiring any contractual primary right as to soundness. Similarly, if the vendor should exclude sanctioning rights by providing that 'this agreement shall not be justiciable in the courts of any place or in any circumstances' then, either that provision is void as ousting the jurisdiction of the courts, or it indicates that the agreement is an 'honour' agreement which does not give rise to contractual rights and duties and which is binding in the moral sense only.

By contrast, exceptions of type B do not affect the question of whether particular primary rights shall accrue, but merely qualify rights which *ex hypothesi* do accrue. There are three ways in which they can do this. First, they may act directly on a primary right, as by placing a limit on its duration. To take again the sale of a horse 'warranted sound', a provision that unless the horse were returned within three days it would be deemed sound would be an exception clause to this second Type. It would not prevent a valid primary right to soundness from arising. Secondly, they may act directly on sanctioning rights, as by placing a limit on the amount recoverable for breach of particular primary rights. The carrier's notice limiting his liability to £5 in respect of any one package is a familiar example. Again, a valid primary right to performance arises despite the exception. Finally, the exception may lay down a time limit within which an action may be brought. Whether such limitations act directly on sanctioning rights, or only indirectly by controlling procedural rights, the result is the same. Once the time-limit has expired, the primary rights concerned become unenforceable and are extinguished or fulfilled. But, until that time, they subsist as valid contractual rights. In other words, the exception does not prevent particular primary rights accruing.

It ought, perhaps, to be emphasised that both types of exception clause help define and delimit the rights to which they apply. One result of this is that rights affected by exceptions of Type B are qualified from their inception by the exception clause just as much as are the rights affected by clauses of Type A. What makes the distinction between the two types significant and important is that if the effect of clauses of Type A is upon whether particular primary rights shall arise from a promise, they are directly relevant to the existence or otherwise, in that promise, of substantive contractual content. Since promises are ordinarily expressed in a number of words, or may have more than one aspect, the Type A exception may help to determine how many of the words used give rise to rights and duties, or in how many aspects the promise has contractual force. In the ordinary way a contractual promise may give rise to a whole complex of rights. It can be the function of an exception clause to show how many of these rights do in fact come into existence. Where the question is, 'has the promisor contracted to do this or this?' an exception of Type A will have a direct bearing on the answer . . .

Conclusion

If the argument so far has been accepted, it follows that the true juristic function and effect of exception clauses are quite different from those currently ascribed to them by the courts. Instead of being mere shields to claims based on breach of accrued rights, exception clauses substantively delimit the rights themselves. A large class of them prevent those rights from ever arising in the first place. As it has been put in an American publication: 'the ordinary function of an exception is to take out of the contract that which otherwise would have been in it, or to guard against misinterpretation'.

So regarded, the exception clause of Type A is seen to fulfil a function not unlike that of an exception from grant, an analogy which, incidentally, did not escape lawyers of the early nineteenth century. Just as an exception from grant operates immediately to prevent its subject passing to the grantee, so an exception clause of Type A operates immediately to prevent its subject forming part of the rights and duties created by the contract.

It may seem feasible that the parties should have intended a contractual duty to remain when they excluded liability for its breach, but this is in reality a juristic impossibility. A duty of sorts there may be, but it will be a duty of honour, not a contractual one.

It would follow, then, that the current approach to exception clauses is based on a fallacy.

The analysis is a powerful one. But it has been attacked by Professors Adams and Brownsword (1988) 104 *LQR* 94, 95 on the ground that it is 'elegantly formalistic' and that it 'ignored both the historical development of the problem, and the realities of the situation. Its implicit rejection by the draftsmen of UCTA was both realistic and right'. The objection that the Coote thesis is 'elegantly formalistic' is an interesting one but it can be countered by pointing out that the source of the formalism could be said to be the Unfair Contract Terms Act itself and not Professor Coote. That this is so is demonstrated by cases such as *Thompson* v. *T Lohan (Plant Hire) Ltd* (above) and *Phillips Products Ltd* v. *Hyland* [1987] 1 WLR 659 (above) where the issue before the Court of Appeal was whether or not a distinction should be drawn between a clause which 'excludes or restricts' a liability and a clause which either 'transfers' or 'shares' a liability. Any attempt to regulate clauses which 'exclude or restrict' liability but not other clauses is bound to throw up questions relating to the meaning of 'exclude or restrict'. To use one of Coote's examples, is there a difference between a case where a horse is sold warranted sound 'except for hunting' and a horse which is sold warranted sound but the warranty is followed by a clause which provides that 'no liability is accepted for any injury or loss suffered when using the horse for hunting'? The latter would appear to be an exclusion clause but what about the former? The reason that we have to ask the question whether or not a contract term which states that a horse that is warranted sound 'except for hunting' is an exclusion clause is not because of Coote's thesis but because the Act requires us to ask the question. Had the Act enacted a general control over all unreasonable terms in standard form contracts these jurisdictional issues would not have arisen (except in relation to the definition of a 'standard form contract'). In this connection it is worth noting that the Law Commissions have provisionally proposed that the scope of the Unfair Contract Terms Act should be extended into a more general control over unreasonable terms which have not been individually negotiated (see further pp. 535–540 below). This provisional proposal is likely to be a source of some controversy on the basis that it will generate additional uncertainty in commercial transactions but one of its distinct advantages is that a more broadly based jurisdiction to regulate unfair terms will largely eliminate the practical significance of debates about the true nature of an exclusion clause.

7. FURTHER READING

ADAMS, J and BROWNSWORD, R, 'The Unfair Contract Terms Act: A Decade of Discretion' (1988) 104 *LQR* 94.

COOTE, B, *Exception Clauses* (Sweet & Maxwell, 1964).

PALMER, N and YATES, D, 'The Future of the Unfair Contract Terms Act 1977' [1981] *CLJ* 108.

14

UNFAIR TERMS IN CONSUMER CONTRACTS REGULATIONS 1999

1. CENTRAL ISSUES

1. The Unfair Terms in Consumer Contracts Regulations 1999 implement an EC Directive on Unfair Terms in Consumer Contracts (93/13/EC) into English law. The Regulations make far-reaching changes to English contract law in that they give to the courts (and, in particular, to the Director General of Fair Trading) broad powers to regulate unfair terms in standard form consumer contracts. The reach of the Regulations is much broader than the Unfair Contract Terms Act 1977.

2. The aim of the Regulations is to regulate unfair terms rather than unfair contracts. Consequently, terms which relate to the definition of the main subject-matter of the contract and terms which relate to the adequacy of the price do not fall within the scope of the Regulations. Consumers tend, on the whole, to be aware of these terms and they can decide for themselves whether or not to accept them. Matters are otherwise in relation to the 'small print' that often accompanies consumer contracts. Consumers tend to be unaware of the content of these terms and, consequently, are taken by surprise when they discover their content. The Regulations seek to protect consumers against such 'unfair surprise'.

3. The definition of an unfair term in Regulation 5(1) is a complex one. It consists of two principal elements. The first is that the term must be 'contrary to the requirement of good faith' and the second is that the term must 'cause a significant imbalance in the parties' rights and obligations arising under the contract' to the detriment of the consumer. When

interpreting these phrases it is necessary to bear in mind the European origin of the Regulations. This is particularly so in relation to the definition of 'good faith'. It must be interpreted from a European and not an English perspective.

4. Schedule 2 to the Regulations sets out an indicative and non-exhaustive list of terms that may be regarded as unfair (the so-called 'grey list'). The reach of this Schedule is extremely broad.

5. The key role in the enforcement of the Regulations has been played by the Unfair Contract Terms Unit of the Office of Fair Trading and not by the courts. Consumers tend to be reluctant to resort to the courts for the purpose of vindicating their rights. The Unfair Contract Terms Unit has made considerable progress in terms of persuading businesses to withdraw or re-draft unfair terms. The 1999 Regulations extend the range of representative bodies that are entitled to seek redress on behalf of consumers and this may further strengthen the impact of the Regulations.

6. The relationship between the Unfair Terms in Consumer Contracts Regulations 1999 and the Unfair Contract Terms Act 1977 is an uneasy one. There are a number of differences between the two regimes. In August 2002 the Law Commissions proposed that the two pieces of legislation should be replaced by a unified regime. The most significant (and controversial) recommendation made by the Law Commissions is that the range of controls over unfair terms in business-to-business contracts should be extended so that, in effect, the controls presently to be found in the 1999 Regulations should apply to commercial contracts concluded on standard terms.

2. INTRODUCTION

The EC Directive on Unfair Terms in Consumer Contracts (93/13/EC) was the first major European intervention into the heartland of domestic contract law. As such, it has attracted a considerable amount of academic comment. The Directive was initially implemented into English law by the Unfair Terms in Consumer Contracts Regulations 1994 (SI No 1994/3159). The 1994 Regulations came into force on 1 July 1995 but were revoked and replaced by the Unfair Terms in Consumer Contracts Regulations 1999 (SI No 1999/2083) which came into effect on 1 October 1999. The fact that the Regulations seek to implement an EC Directive is a matter of some importance. In the first place, it helps to explain the structure of the Regulations. The legislative technique that has been employed is one of 'copy-out', that is to say the Regulations use the same, or virtually the same, language as the Directive itself. The principal motivation behind the copy-out approach is the desire to avoid liability on the part of the State for a failure to implement the Directive properly. The 1994 Regulations did endeavour in one or two places to elaborate upon the Directive but these elaborations have largely disappeared in the 1999 Regulations which adhere more closely to the text of the Directive. The 'copy-out' technique does have its drawbacks. In particular, it has the effect of discouraging national Parliaments from taking steps to improve the quality of the drafting of the Directive or to clarify any obscurities. The EC Directive on Unfair Terms has been criticized for the poor quality of its drafting (see generally T Hartley, 'Five Forms of Uncertainty in European Community Law' [1996] *CLJ* 265) and some of these criticisms can be levelled against the Regulations as well. Secondly, the fact that the origins of the Regulations lie in a Directive has important consequences for the interpretation of the Regulations. This is particularly so in relation to phrases such as 'good faith'. The court must have regard to the European origin of the Directive and not interpret the Regulations as if they were a domestic statute. Thus far it would appear that the courts have been sensitive to the European origins of the Regulations (although the House of Lords in the leading case of *Director General of Fair Trading* v. *First National Bank* [2001] UKHL 52; [2002] 1 AC 481 has been criticized for failing to make a reference to the European Court of Justice, see below).

This chapter is divided into four sections. The first section consists of an analysis of the Regulations. The text of the Regulations will be set out and annotated. The second section is devoted to an analysis of the decision of the House of Lords in *Director General of Fair Trading* v. *First National Bank* [2001] UKHL 52; [2002] 1 AC 481. The third section draws on work done by Susan Bright in relation to the role of the Unfair Contract Terms Unit in the enforcement of the Regulations. The fourth and final section consists of a brief summary of the provisional recommendations made by the Law Commissions for reform of this area of law, in particular their proposal to produce a unified regime that will replace both the Unfair Contract Terms Act 1977 and the Unfair Terms in Consumer Contracts Regulations 1999.

3. UNFAIR TERMS IN CONSUMER CONTRACTS REGULATIONS 1999

The text of the Regulations is set out in full. Most articles are the subject of brief explanatory comment but, where the meaning of the particular regulation is clear, no commentary has been provided.

Citation and commencement

1.   These Regulations may be cited as the Unfair Terms in Consumer Contracts Regulations 1999 and shall come into force on 1st October 1999.

Revocation

2.   The Unfair Terms in Consumer Contracts Regulations 1994 are hereby revoked.

COMMENTARY

There are a number of differences between the 1994 Regulations and the 1999 Regulations. In general the 1999 Regulations follow more closely the wording of the Directive than was the case with the 1994 Regulations. Secondly, the 1999 Regulations expand the category of bodies who are entitled to take steps to enforce the Regulations (see pp. 512–515 below).

Interpretation

3.—(1) In these Regulations—

'the Community' means the European Community;

'consumer' means any natural person who, in contracts covered by these Regulations, is acting for purposes which are outside his trade, business or profession;

'court' in relation to England and Wales and Northern Ireland means a county court or the High Court, and in relation to Scotland, the Sheriff or the Court of Session;

'Director' means the Director General of Fair Trading;

'EEA Agreement' means the Agreement on the European Economic Area signed at Oporto on 2nd May 1992 as adjusted by the protocol signed at Brussels on 17th March 1993;

'Member State' means a State which is a contracting party to the EEA Agreement;

'notified' means notified in writing;

'qualifying body' means a person specified in Schedule 1;

'seller or supplier' means any natural or legal person who, in contracts covered by these Regulations, is acting for purposes relating to his trade, business or profession, whether publicly owned or privately owned;

'unfair terms' means the contractual terms referred to in regulation 5.

COMMENTARY

The most important definitions for our purposes are the definitions of 'consumer' and 'seller or supplier'. These definitions were all amended by the 1999 Regulations. A consumer must be a natural person. In this respect the definition of a consumer is narrower than the definition of a consumer in section 12 of the Unfair Contract Terms Act 1977 (see p. 478 above), where it is possible for a limited liability company to be a consumer. The Regulations apply only to consumer contracts. They have no application to business-to-business contracts and in this respect they differ from the Unfair Contract Terms Act 1977. The most significant definitional change between the 1994 and the 1999 Regulations relates to the definitions of 'seller' and 'supplier'. In the 1994 Regulations a seller was defined as a 'person who sells goods' and a supplier as a 'person who sells goods or services'. The words 'goods' and 'goods and services' have been dropped from these definitions in the 1999 Regulations. The use of the word 'goods' in the 1994 Regulations caused considerable confusion because 'goods' do not normally encompass land in English law, yet it would appear that the intention behind the Directive was to include within its scope contracts relating to the creation or the transfer of an interest in land. While the English version of the Directive does contain the word 'goods' in the preamble, the word that appears in the other language versions of the Directive is a word that applies to property generally and so would ordinarily include land. This being the case, the deletion of the word 'goods' from the 1999 Regulations brings English law into line with the Directive with the consequence that the Regulations do apply to contracts for the sale of land where the contract otherwise falls within the scope of the Regulations (see *London Borough of Newham* v. *Khatun* [2004] EWCA Civ 55). One further point which should be noted is that the seller or supplier must be 'acting for purposes relating' to his trade, business, or profession when concluding the contract. It is not enough that he is in business. There must be a sufficient connection between the contract and his business.

Terms to which these Regulations apply

4.—(1) These Regulations apply in relation to unfair terms in contracts concluded between a seller or a supplier and a consumer.

(2) These Regulations do not apply to contractual terms which reflect—

(a) mandatory statutory or regulatory provisions (including such provisions under the law of any Member State or in Community legislation having effect in the United Kingdom without further enactment);

(b) the provisions or principles of international conventions to which the Member States or the Community are party.

COMMENTARY

Regulation 4(2) is a curiously worded provision. The intention behind the provision would appear to be to make clear that contract terms inserted into a contract in order to give effect to a statutory requirement or an international convention cannot be challenged under the Regulations. The wording chosen to give effect to this policy is, however, rather unusual. The first point relates to the meaning of the word 'mandatory'. It would appear that it does not mean 'mandatory' in the sense of a rule of law out of which the parties cannot contract. Recital 13 to the Directive states that the words 'mandatory statutory or regulatory provisions' also 'covers rules which, according to the law, shall apply between the contracting parties provided that no other arrangements have been established'. The latter appear to be 'default' rules rather than 'mandatory' rules and, this being the case, the word 'mandatory' in the Regulations appears misleading and possibly redundant. It would appear to suffice that the term in question is permitted or authorized by statute: it need not be required by statute. Secondly, regulation 4(2)(a) refers to the law of 'any' Member State. On a strict reading it appears to mean that compliance with a relevant statutory provision in 'any' Member State will take the term outside the scope of the Regulations even if the contract has no connection with that State. Such a provision would be haphazard in its operation and it is unlikely that a literal interpretation of the word 'any' would be consistent with the Directive. Thirdly, the word 'reflects' is rather vague. But it may be important. Take the case of a regulator who approves contract terms while acting in the course of a statutory jurisdiction. Is such a term exempt from the Regulations? The term itself is not 'authorised' by the statute but the Directive in Recital 13 refers to 'statutory or regulatory provisions . . . which directly or indirectly determine the terms of consumer contracts' and the reference to indirect authorization may be sufficient to catch our regulator example. Finally, the word 'principles' in regulation 4(2)(b) has given rise to some difficulty. Professor Treitel (*The Law of Contract* (11th edn, Sweet & Maxwell, 2003), p. 277) states that 'a term based on the principles of a relevant convention would not be governed by the Regulations even though the contract in which the term was contained was not governed by the convention: *e.g.* where a term in a contract for the domestic carriage of goods was based on the principles of a convention which in terms governed only international carriage'. The difficulty with this suggestion is that a clause which has been agreed to be fair and reasonable in one context (international carriage) may not be fair and reasonable in another context (domestic carriage). For this reason it is suggested that the mere fact that the term reflects an international convention should not suffice to take it outside the scope of the Regulations where the relevant convention does not apply to the contract that has been concluded between the parties.

Unfair Terms

5.—(1) A contractual term which has not been individually negotiated shall be regarded as unfair if, contrary to the requirement of good faith, it causes a significant imbalance in the parties' rights and obligations arising under the contract, to the detriment of the consumer.

(2) A term shall always be regarded as not having been individually negotiated where it has been drafted in advance and the consumer has therefore not been able to influence the substance of the term.

(3) Notwithstanding that a specific term or certain aspects of it in a contract has been individually negotiated, these Regulations shall apply to the rest of a contract if an overall assessment of it indicates that it is a pre-formulated standard contract.

(4) It shall be for any seller or supplier who claims that a term was individually negotiated to show that it was.

(5) Schedule 2 to these Regulations contains an indicative and non-exhaustive list of the terms which may be regarded as unfair.

COMMENTARY

This provision lies at the heart of the Regulations. A number of points arise here. The first is that the Regulations apply only where the term has 'not been individually negotiated'. In other words, the Regulations are aimed at what might be termed 'standard form contracts'. The meaning of the phrase 'not been individually negotiated' is elaborated in regulation 5(2)–(4). It is for the seller or supplier to establish that the term was individually negotiated. Regulation 5(3) is important because it makes it very difficult for sellers or suppliers to avoid the scope of the Regulations by the device of ensuring that one term of the contract is always individually negotiated. The court must have regard to the substance and not the form so that if, on an overall assessment of the contract, the court decides that it is a 'pre-formulated standard contract' then the regulations are applicable.

Secondly, there must have been a 'significant imbalance' in the rights and obligations arising under the contract and that imbalance must be to the detriment of the consumer. The precise meaning of 'significant imbalance' is elusive. It would appear to involve an examination of the content of the term rather than the procedure which led to the conclusion of the contract (in other words, it is directed at 'substantive' rather than 'procedural' unfairness—the difference between these two categories is explored in more detail at p. 793 below). But this appearance may be misleading to the extent that it cannot be assumed that the courts will not have regard to procedural matters when deciding whether or not a term is unfair.

The third point relates to the phrase 'contrary to the requirement of good faith'. There are two problems here. The first relates to the relationship between 'good faith' and 'significant imbalance'. Are these two entirely separate requirements, two related requirements, or only one requirement? It can be argued that there is only one requirement on the basis that the crucial test is whether or not there has been a 'significant imbalance' to the detriment of the consumer and that the conclusion that the requirements of good faith have not been satisfied follows inevitably from a finding that there has been a significant imbalance. On this view good faith has no independent role to play at all and is practically redundant. A second view is that 'significant imbalance' operates as a threshold requirement which serves to exclude cases where the imbalance is insignificant. On this view good faith becomes the predominant test to be applied by the courts. A third view is that 'good faith' and 'significant imbalance' are both important and that one should not be subordinated to the other. The difficulty with this view lies in distinguishing between 'good faith' and 'significant imbalance'. What is the difference between the two tests? Does 'significant imbalance' focus on the substantive content of the term, while 'good faith' looks to the procedure by which the contract was concluded? The second problem relates to the meaning of 'good faith'. This is not an easy issue for the English courts because English contract law does not, as yet, recognize a doctrine of good faith (see further Chapter 15). There is therefore no national law from which the English courts can draw. The courts must therefore draw upon the European origin of 'good faith'. These issues are explored in more detail in the speeches of the House of Lords in *Director General of Fair Trading* v. *First National Bank* [2001] UKHL 52; [2002] 1 AC 481 (pp. 521–531 below).

Fourthly, the Regulations are silent in relation to the location of the burden of proof of unfairness. However Schedule 2 gives what is called an 'indicative and non-exhaustive list' of terms that may be regarded as unfair (see pp. 515–521 below). Inclusion on the list does not therefore entail a finding that the term is unfair. The precise status of the list is unclear. It could be said to raise a presumption that the term is unfair. On the other hand, it has been said that the list is only a 'guide' and that it does not create rebuttable presumptions of unfairness (see *Zealander & Zealander* v. *Laing Homes Ltd*, unreported, 19 March 1999). In the case of a term that is not listed in Schedule 2, the onus of proof of establishing that the term is unfair is likely to be on the consumer. Where the term is listed in Schedule 2 the position is less clear. The answer probably depends upon the status of the list in Schedule 2. If it creates a rebuttable presumption that the term is unfair then the burden of proof is likely to shift to the seller or supplier to show that the term is fair. On the other hand, if the list is no more than a guide, then the burden of proof will probably remain with the consumer, although the fact that the term is included in the list will doubtless make it easier for the consumer to establish that the term is unfair.

The fifth point relates to the range of clauses that have been found to be unfair. As we shall see (p. 531 below) the principal role in the enforcement of the Regulations has been played by the Unfair Contract Terms Unit in the Office of Fair Trading ('OFT'). A study of the operation of the Regulations (S Bright, 'Winning the Battle Against Unfair Terms' (2000) 20 *Legal Studies* 329, 349–350) demonstrates that a wide range of contract terms have been found to be unfair:

The OFT Bulletins contain numerous examples of clauses that have been found unfair. Common examples are terms that limit or restrict liability for shortcomings in the quality of goods and services (particularly those that exclude liability for delay), clauses that exclude liability for oral statements made by employees and agents, price variation clauses, and clauses requiring full payment in advance of the consumer receiving the goods or services being purchased. The variety of clauses investigated is huge and it is only by reading the Bulletins that it is possible to appreciate the extent of the activity of and the width of the jurisdiction assumed by the Office of Fair Trading.

Finally, in deciding whether or not a term is unfair, regard is to be had to the matters listed in regulation 6(1) below.

Assessment of unfair terms

6.—(1) Without prejudice to regulation 12, the unfairness of a contractual term shall be assessed, taking into account the nature of the goods or services for which the contract was concluded and by referring, at the time of conclusion of the contract, to all the circumstances attending the conclusion of the contract and to all the other terms of the contract or of another contract on which it is dependent.

(2) In so far as it is in plain intelligible language, the assessment of fairness of a term shall not relate—

(a) to the definition of the main subject matter of the contract, or

(b) to the adequacy of the price or remuneration, as against the goods or services supplied in exchange.

COMMENTARY

Regulation 6(1) makes the point that it is the time of entry into the contract that is crucial when deciding whether or not a term is unfair. It is the fairness of the allocation of rights and liabilities at the moment of entry into the contract that is subject to scrutiny. This being the case, the question that has to be answered is whether or not the clause is potentially fair or unfair, not whether on the facts of the particular case it operated in a fair or unfair manner. Regulation 6(1) also provides a non-exhaustive list of the factors to be taken into account when deciding whether or not a particular term is unfair. These factors appear to resemble the factors taken into account by the courts when deciding whether or not a clause is reasonable under the Unfair Contract Terms Act 1977 (on which see pp. 472–478 above). The factors listed are very broad in scope. Indeed, they are so broad that it can be said with some justification that they are likely to be of little assistance in resolving individual cases.

Regulation 6(2) is particularly important because of the exclusion from review of terms that define the main subject-matter of the contract or the price term (the so-called 'core terms'). An example of a core term is given by Recital 19 of the Directive which states that:

in insurance contracts, the terms which clearly define or circumscribe the insured risk and the insurer's liability shall not be subject to such assessment since these restrictions are taken into account in calculating the premium paid by the consumer.

The reason for this exclusion is that consumers tend to be aware of the existence of the core terms of a contract. They are therefore able to decide for themselves whether or not to accept these terms. But this is generally not the case in relation to the 'small print' that is often found in consumer contracts. While consumers are often aware of the existence of these terms, they tend to be unaware of their content. Discovery of the true content of the small print can come as a nasty surprise to consumers when they discover that the effect of a particular term is to take away what they thought were their rights. The Regulations aim to protect consumers against such 'unfair surprises'.

Regulation 6(2) is therefore a crucial element in the definition of the scope of the Regulations. The House of Lords in *Director General of Fair Trading* v. *First National Bank* [2001] UKHL 52; [2002] 1 AC 481 adopted a narrow construction of this provision and they did so precisely in order to avoid the emasculation of the Regulations in jurisdictional wrangles over whether or not a term defines the main subject matter of the contract (this point is discussed in more detail at p. 529 below). Some examples of the difficulties that can arise in attempting to ascertain what constitutes a 'core term' can be seen from the following extract (S Bright, 'Winning the Battle Against Unfair Terms' (2000) 20 *Legal Studies* 329, 344–347):

In determining whether or not a term is a core provision, the Office of Fair Trading has asked whether the clause is a core term that the consumer would have concentrated on in deciding whether or not to enter the contract. There have not been many case studies involving paragraph (a) but two reports in the OFT Bulletins describe core terms which, as they do not relate to the price paid, presumably come within paragraph (a): an insurance clause which prevented a claim on the policy if the loss was also covered by any other policy, and the expiry date on gift vouchers. It is surprising that both of these are viewed as core terms, especially on a view of the Regulations which excludes core provisions from assessment for fairness at all. It is generally thought that the core terms exemption should be interpreted in a very restrictive way. One way of interpreting paragraph (a) (but clearly not the approach which the OFT followed) would be to ask what the consumer would say she had bought if asked, and this will be the main subject matter of the contract. In relation to the gift vouchers, for example, she would have said, 'I have bought some gift vouchers'. This is the main subject matter; the expiry date is a subsidiary term. Non-core terms will be subjected to the fairness test and, as will be seen, this may require the term to be brought to the attention of the consumer. If, therefore, a subsidiary term apparently limits the main subject matter, this limitation must be made clear to the consumer, and reflected in the price paid.

In relation to paragraph (b) the price/quality ratio is excluded, but not other terms relating to the price. The OFT Bulletins report numerous cases of price variation clauses being amended or deleted, drawing support for the intervention from para 1(l) in the illustrative list of potentially unfair terms . . .

On the whole there has been a 'consumer-oriented' approach to Regulation 6(2), especially paragraph (b). A term is seen as 'core' only if the consumer would have treated it as such and it relates to the price or defining the subject matter. This means that even a provision that does relate to the price or subject matter will not be excluded from review if it was not brought to the consumer's attention, and therefore could not have been something which the consumer focused on. Even a core term will not survive intact if it is not written in plain, intelligible language.

The scope of Regulation 6(2)(b) is explored further in the context of the discussion of *Director General of Fair Trading* v. *First National Bank* [2001] UKHL 52; [2002] 1 AC 481 (pp. 521–531 below).

Written contracts

7.—(1) A seller or supplier shall ensure that any written term of a contract is expressed in plain, intelligible language.

(2) If there is doubt about the meaning of a written term, the interpretation which is most favourable to the consumer shall prevail but this rule shall not apply in proceedings brought under regulation 12.

COMMENTARY

Regulation 7(1) only applies to written terms and it applies to all written terms, even to those that define the subject-matter of the contract or the price. Thus 'core terms' must be expressed in plain, intelligible language. One difficulty with this provision is that it does not appear to provide a remedy for a breach of its requirements. However it is likely that a failure to ensure that the term is in plain, intelligible language will be taken into account by the court when deciding whether or not a term is unfair. This has been the approach taken by the Office of Fair Trading. Thus Susan Bright has noted ('Winning the Battle Against Unfair Terms' (2000) 20 *Legal Studies* 329, 346):

Even core terms can be reviewed if they are not written in plain, intelligible language. This is clearly required by the Regulations. The Office of Fair Trading has also been willing to review core terms when the term has been hidden away in the contract and not brought to the attention of the consumer, revealing a keenness to deal not only with issues of substantive fairness but also procedural fairness:

'Recital 20 of the relevant Directive (93/13) makes clear that the aim is not just the substitution of plain words for legal jargon but rather that consumers are given a real chance to read and understand contracts before becoming bound by them.' [A quotation from *Unfair Contract Terms*, OFT Bulletin, Issue No 6, April 1999, OFT 262.]

This 'purposive' approach is entirely appropriate in the context of Community law with its teleological approach to the interpretation of legislation and the principle of *effet utile* which provides that preference should be given to the construction which gives it fullest effect and maximum practical value.

Regulation 7(2) should be a familiar provision to English lawyers because *contra proferentem* is a general rule of construction in English law. According to this rule any ambiguity in a term must be resolved against the party who is relying upon it. In so far as regulation 7(2) provides that the consumer must be given the benefit of any doubt about the meaning of a written term, it would appear to be no more than a statutory form of the *contra proferentem* rule.

Effect of unfair term

8.—(1) An unfair term in a contract concluded with a consumer by a seller or supplier shall not be binding on the consumer.

(2) The contract shall continue to bind the parties if it is capable of continuing in existence without the unfair term.

COMMENTARY

This regulation sets out the consequences of a finding that a term is unfair. An unfair term is not binding on the consumer. But it does not follow from this that the contract is not binding. In most cases the contract will continue to bind the parties with the exception of the unfair term. The regulation does not, however, confer on the court a power to re-write the term of the contract in order to make it conform with the requirement of fairness. If the term is fundamental to the contract and it is held to be unfair, the consequence may be that the contract will cease to bind the parties on the basis that the contract is not capable of continuing in existence without such a fundamental term (see regulation 8(2)).

Choice of law clauses

9. These Regulations shall apply notwithstanding any contract term which applies or purports to apply the law of a non-Member State, if the contract has a close connection with the territory of the Member States.

COMMENTARY

The aim of this provision is to prevent sellers or suppliers avoiding the application of the Regulations by inserting a choice of law clause into the contract. Take the case where a seller inserts into its standard form contract a choice of law clause and the law chosen is the law of an African or a South American country. Such a choice of law is not effective where the contract has a close connection with the territory of the Member States. It is, however, open to the seller to insert a choice of law clause in the contract where the law chosen is a law that would or might have applied to the contract even in the absence of a choice of law clause.

Complaints—consideration by Director

10.—(1) It shall be the duty of the Director to consider any complaint made to him that any contract term drawn up for general use is unfair, unless—

(a) the complaint appears to the Director to be frivolous or vexatious; or

(b) a qualifying body has notified the Director that it agrees to consider the complaint.

(2) The Director shall give reasons for his decision to apply or not to apply, as the case may be, for an injunction under regulation 12 in relation to any complaint which these Regulations require him to consider.

(3) In deciding whether or not to apply for an injunction in respect of a term which the Director considers to be unfair, he may, if he considers it appropriate to do so, have regard to any undertakings given to him by or on behalf of any person as to the continued use of such a term in contracts concluded with consumers.

Complaints—consideration by qualifying bodies

11.—(1) If a qualifying body specified in Part One of Schedule 1 notifies the Director that it agrees to consider a complaint that any contract term drawn up for general use is unfair, it shall be under a duty to consider that complaint.

(2) Regulation 10(2) and (3) shall apply to a qualifying body which is under a duty to consider a complaint as they apply to the Director.

Injunctions to prevent continued use of unfair terms

12.—(1) The Director or, subject to paragraph (2), any qualifying body may apply for an injunction (including an interim injunction) against any person appearing to the Director or that body to be using, or recommending use of, an unfair term drawn up for general use in contracts concluded with consumers.

(2) A qualifying body may apply for an injunction only where—

(a) it has notified the Director of its intention to apply at least fourteen days before the date on which the application is made, beginning with the date on which the notification was given; or

(b) the Director consents to the application being made within a shorter period.

(3) The court on an application under this regulation may grant an injunction on such terms as it thinks fit.

(4) An injunction may relate not only to use of a particular contract term drawn up for general use but to any similar term, or a term having like effect, used or recommended for use by any person.

Powers of the Director and qualifying bodies to obtain documents and information

13.—(1) The Director may exercise the power conferred by this regulation for the purpose of—

(a) facilitating his consideration of a complaint that a contract term drawn up for general use is unfair; or

(b) ascertaining whether a person has complied with an undertaking or court order as to the continued use, or recommendation for use, of a term in contracts concluded with consumers.

(2) A qualifying body specified in Part One of Schedule 1 may exercise the power conferred by this regulation for the purpose of—

(a) facilitating its consideration of a complaint that a contract term drawn up for general use is unfair; or

   (b) ascertaining whether a person has complied with—

   (i) an undertaking given to it or to the court following an application by that body, or

   (ii) a court order made on an application by that body, as to the continued use, or recommendation for use, of a term in contracts concluded with consumers.

(3) The Director may require any person to supply to him, and a qualifying body specified in Part One of Schedule 1 may require any person to supply to it—

(a) a copy of any document which that person has used or recommended for use, at the time the notice referred to in paragraph (4) below is given, as a pre-formulated standard contract in dealings with consumers;

(b) information about the use, or recommendation for use, by that person of that document or any other such document in dealings with consumers.

(4) The power conferred by this regulation is to be exercised by a notice in writing which may—

(a) specify the way in which and the time within which it is to be complied with; and

(b) be varied or revoked by a subsequent notice.

(5) Nothing in this regulation compels a person to supply any document or information which he would be entitled to refuse to produce or give in civil proceedings before the court.

(6) If a person makes default in complying with a notice under this regulation, the court may, on the application of the Director or of the qualifying body, make such order as the court thinks fit for requiring the default to be made good, and any such order may provide that all the costs or expenses of and incidental to the application shall be borne by the person in default or by any officers of a company or other association who are responsible for its default.

Notification of undertakings and orders to Director

14.   A qualifying body shall notify the Director—

(a) of any undertaking given to it by or on behalf of any person as to the continued use of a term which that body considers to be unfair in contracts concluded with consumers;

(b) of the outcome of any application made by it under regulation 12, and of the terms of any undertaking given to, or order made by, the court;

(c) of the outcome of any application made by it to enforce a previous order of the court.

Publication, information and advice

15.—(1) The Director shall arrange for the publication in such form and manner as he considers appropriate, of—

(a) details of any undertaking or order notified to him under regulation 14;

(b) details of any undertaking given to him by or on behalf of any person as to the continued use of a term which the Director considers to be unfair in contracts concluded with consumers;

(c) details of any application made by him under regulation 12, and of the terms of any undertaking given to, or order made by, the court;

(d) details of any application made by the Director to enforce a previous order of the court.

(2) The Director shall inform any person on request whether a particular term to which these Regulations apply has been—

(a) the subject of an undertaking given to the Director or notified to him by a qualifying body; or

(b) the subject of an order of the court made upon application by him or notified to him by a qualifying body;

and shall give that person details of the undertaking or a copy of the order, as the case may be, together with a copy of any amendments which the person giving the undertaking has agreed to make to the term in question.

(3) The Director may arrange for the dissemination in such form and manner as he considers appropriate of such information and advice concerning the operation of these Regulations as may appear to him to be expedient to give to the public and to all persons likely to be affected by these Regulations.

COMMENTARY

Regulations 10–15 are particularly important because they set out the responsibilities and rights of the Director General of Fair Trading in the enforcement of the Regulations. The Unfair Contract Terms Unit of the Office of Fair Trading has played a key role in the enforcement of the Regulations (see the extract from the article by Susan Bright, p. 531 below). The 1999 Regulations set out the powers of the Director General of Fair Trading in more elaborate form than was the case in 1994. A duty is imposed on the Director to consider complaints made to him (regulation 10) and he is also subject to various duties in relation to the dissemination of information (regulation 15). The Director is given the power to apply to court for an injunction to restrain the continued use of unfair terms (regulation 12), and he is given considerable powers to obtain documents and information in relation to the use of unfair terms (regulation 13). One further change in the enforcement proceedings made by the

1999 Regulations is the increase in the range of bodies that have an enforcement role. The Regulations now recognize the existence of various 'qualifying bodies' (regulation 11 and see Schedule 1 below) who are given enforcement powers (see regulations 12(2), 13(2), and 14). The addition of these 'qualifying bodies' may not necessarily operate in the best interests of consumers. As we shall see (p. 531 below), the Unfair Contract Terms Unit of the Office of Fair Trading has been very effective in policing unfair terms and there have been fears expressed that the addition of these 'qualifying bodies' will inhibit rather than enhance the enforcement of the Regulations. Much will depend on the ability of these bodies to organize and implement a coherent strategy to combat the use of unfair terms in consumer contracts.

SCHEDULE 1

QUALIFYING BODIES

Regulation 3

Part One

1   The Information Commissioner.
2   The Gas and Electricity Markets Authority.
3   The Director General of Electricity Supply for Northern Ireland.
4   The Director General of Gas for Northern Ireland.
5   The Director General of Telecommunications.
6   The Director General of Water Services.
7   The Rail Regulator.
8   Every weights and measures authority in Great Britain.
9   The Department of Enterprise, Trade and Investment in Northern Ireland.
10   The Financial Services Authority.

Part Two

11   Consumers' Association

COMMENTARY

Schedule 1 contains the list of 'qualifying bodies' who are given rights and responsibilities under regulations 10–15 The bodies listed in Part One are regulatory organizations that already perform 'watchdog' functions in particular sectors of the economy. The addition of the Consumers' Association in Part Two is significant because it is a private body which seeks to protect the interests of consumers and so may have a different perspective from the regulators. The potential impact of the addition of these qualifying bodies is discussed in more detail at pp. 531–534 below.

SCHEDULE 2

INDICATIVE AND NON-EXHAUSTIVE LIST OF TERMS WHICH MAY BE REGARDED AS UNFAIR

Regulation 5(5)

1   Terms which have the object or effect of—

(a)   excluding or limiting the legal liability of a seller or supplier in the event of the death of a consumer or personal injury to the latter resulting from an act or omission of that seller or supplier;

(b) inappropriately excluding or limiting the legal rights of the consumer vis-a-vis the seller or supplier or another party in the event of total or partial non-performance or inadequate performance by the seller or supplier of any of the contractual obligations, including the option of offsetting a debt owed to the seller or supplier against any claim which the consumer may have against him;

(c) making an agreement binding on the consumer whereas provision of services by the seller or supplier is subject to a condition whose realisation depends on his own will alone;

(d) permitting the seller or supplier to retain sums paid by the consumer where the latter decides not to conclude or perform the contract, without providing for the consumer to receive compensation of an equivalent amount from the seller or supplier where the latter is the party cancelling the contract;

(e) requiring any consumer who fails to fulfil his obligation to pay a disproportionately high sum in compensation;

(f) authorising the seller or supplier to dissolve the contract on a discretionary basis where the same facility is not granted to the consumer, or permitting the seller or supplier to retain the sums paid for services not yet supplied by him where it is the seller or supplier himself who dissolves the contract;

(g) enabling the seller or supplier to terminate a contract of indeterminate duration without reasonable notice except where there are serious grounds for doing so;

(h) automatically extending a contract of fixed duration where the consumer does not indicate otherwise, when the deadline fixed for the consumer to express his desire not to extend the contract is unreasonably early;

(i) irrevocably binding the consumer to terms with which he had no real opportunity of becoming acquainted before the conclusion of the contract;

(j) enabling the seller or supplier to alter the terms of the contract unilaterally without a valid reason which is specified in the contract;

(k) enabling the seller or supplier to alter unilaterally without a valid reason any characteristics of the product or service to be provided;

(l) providing for the price of goods to be determined at the time of delivery or allowing a seller of goods or supplier of services to increase their price without in both cases giving the consumer the corresponding right to cancel the contract if the final price is too high in relation to the price agreed when the contract was concluded;

(m) giving the seller or supplier the right to determine whether the goods or services supplied are in conformity with the contract, or giving him the exclusive right to interpret any term of the contract;

(n) limiting the seller's or supplier's obligation to respect commitments undertaken by his agents or making his commitments subject to compliance with a particular formality;

(o) obliging the consumer to fulfil all his obligations where the seller or supplier does not perform his;

(p) giving the seller or supplier the possibility of transferring his rights and obligations under the contract, where this may serve to reduce the guarantees for the consumer, without the latter's agreement;

(q) excluding or hindering the consumer's right to take legal action or exercise any other legal remedy, particularly by requiring the consumer to take disputes exclusively to arbitration not covered by legal provisions, unduly restricting the evidence available to him or imposing on him a burden of proof which, according to the applicable law, should lie with another party to the contract.

2   Scope of paragraphs 1(g), (j) and (l)

(a) Paragraph 1(g) is without hindrance to terms by which a supplier of financial services reserves the right to terminate unilaterally a contract of indeterminate duration without notice where there is a valid reason, provided that the supplier is required to inform the other contracting party or parties thereof immediately.

(b) Paragraph 1(j) is without hindrance to terms under which a supplier of financial services reserves the right to alter the rate of interest payable by the consumer or due to the latter, or the amount of other charges for financial services without notice where there is a valid reason, provided that the supplier is required to inform the other contracting party or parties thereof at the earliest opportunity and that the latter are free to dissolve the contract immediately.

Paragraph 1(j) is also without hindrance to terms under which a seller or supplier reserves the right to alter unilaterally the conditions of a contract of indeterminate duration, provided that he is required to inform the consumer with reasonable notice and that the consumer is free to dissolve the contract.

(c) Paragraphs 1(g), (j) and (l) do not apply to:

—transactions in transferable securities, financial instruments and other products or services where the price is linked to fluctuations in a stock exchange quotation or index or a financial market rate that the seller or supplier does not control;
—contracts for the purchase or sale of foreign currency, traveller's cheques or international money orders denominated in foreign currency.

(d) Paragraph 1(l) is without hindrance to price indexation clauses, where lawful, provided that the method by which prices vary is explicitly described.

COMMENTARY

Schedule 2 contains the so-called 'grey list' of terms which may be regarded as unfair. As has been noted (p. 508 above), there is some uncertainty as to whether the list is for guidance only or whether it creates a rebuttable presumption that a term included in the list is unfair. Whatever its precise legal status, it is clear that Schedule 2 will play an important role when deciding whether or not a particular term is unfair. It is therefore necessary to explain, albeit briefly, the likely scope of the different paragraphs set out in this Schedule.

Paragraph 1(a) overlaps with the Unfair Contract Terms Act 1977 in that it applies to terms that purport to exclude or limit liability for death or personal injury. There is one very important difference between the two regimes which is that clauses that purport to exclude or limit liability for death or personal injury caused by negligence are declared void by section 2(1) of the Unfair Contract Terms Act 1977 (see p. 462 above), whereas they are only indicatively unfair under the Regulations. This is an example of the uneasy relationship between the Regulations and the Act. The Act will undoubtedly take precedence over the Regulations. It is inconceivable that an English court would conclude that the Regulations had impliedly repealed section 2(1) of the 1977 Act (see FMB Reynolds (1994) 110 *LQR* 1, 3). Nevertheless, it is untidy law and it illustrates the need for the creation of a unified regime, as advocated by the Law Commissions (see p. 535 below). The Regulations do not attempt to define 'personal injury' (contrast in this respect section 14 of the 1977 Act).

Paragraph 1(b) has wide potential application, yet its scope is uncertain. There is no definition of 'inappropriately', notwithstanding its importance to the paragraph as a whole. This paragraph also overlaps with the Unfair Contract Terms Act 1977. The paragraph appears to be in the nature of a wrap-up or catch-all provision.

Paragraph 1(c) applies to conditional service provisions. Terms which purport to bind one party to the contract before binding the other are now indicatively unfair. What will be the effect of a finding that such a term is unfair? It will not be binding on the consumer (regulation 8(1)). But will the contract continue to bind the parties? One possibility is that the invalidity of the term will have the effect of making the contract binding on both parties to the contract from the same point in time. This paragraph will have considerable impact on hire-purchase transactions and leasing agreements, where it was not uncommon for the contract to provide for the consumer to be bound before the supplier was bound to the transaction.

Paragraph 1(d) applies to deposits. Attempts by sellers or suppliers to retain deposits are already regulated by the common law (see pp. 1132–1137 below) and, in the case of consumer contracts, by the Consumer Credit Act 1974. The novelty in this particular provision is the requirement that the consumer receive equal protection through being entitled to compensation of an 'equivalent amount' from the seller or supplier in the event of the seller or supplier cancelling the contract. Professor Treitel states (*The Law of Contract* (11th edn, Sweet & Maxwell, 2003), pp. 1012–1013) that this provision is based on 'the civil law institution (which has no counterparty in the common law) by which a contract can, in effect, be dissolved on forfeiture of a deposit or on the return by the payee of double the amount'. He also suggests (at p. 1013) that the consumer will have the right to the return of any sum paid on the basis that the use of the word 'retain' suggests the availability of a remedy for the recovery of the pre-payment. Finally, Professor Treitel notes (at p. 1013) that the paragraph does not apply to rights of forfeiture conferred by law: the scope of the Regulations being confined to 'contract terms'.

Paragraph 1(e) overlaps with the existing common law rules relating to penalty clauses (which are discussed at pp. 1124–1131 below), but it is not clear to what extent, if at all, this paragraph differs from the common law rules. The word 'disproportionately' is not defined. At what time is the disproportion to be assessed: is it the time of formation or the time of breach? Professor Treitel points out (at p. 1007) that this paragraph may be wider than the penalty clause rules because the regulations may not be confined to sums payable on breach: a consumer who 'fails to fulfil his obligation' might not be in breach of contract because he may have an excuse for his non-performance. It may also catch a clause requiring payment of a holding charge, of the type used in *Interfoto Picture Library Ltd* v. *Stiletto Visual Programmes Ltd* [1989] QB 433 (p. 352 above).

Paragraph 1(f) is likely to have considerable impact because many suppliers give themselves the right to dissolve the contract where the consumer does not have the same right. Such a term will be indicatively unfair unless it gives the consumer an identical right to dissolve the contract. The latter part of the paragraph overlaps with paragraphs (d) and (e) but this paragraph only applies to the retention of sums paid for 'services not yet supplied'.

The subject-matter of paragraph 1(g) is terms which purport to entitle a seller or supplier to terminate a contract without notice. There are three critical phrases in this provision: (i) 'indeterminate duration', (ii) 'reasonable notice', and (iii) 'serious grounds'. None of these phrases is defined. Professor Treitel points out (p. 781) that the fact that the Schedule is non-exhaustive 'would not preclude the court from holding that a cancellation clause in a fixed-term contract was also unfair'. The reference to 'serious grounds' may catch force majeure clauses which purport to bind consumers. The scope of this paragraph is limited by paragraphs 2(a) and 2(c) of Schedule 2 which make particular provision for the financial services industry.

Paragraph 1(h) applies to terms which purport to give to sellers the right unilaterally to extend contracts of fixed duration and will probably have the greatest impact on long-term hire contracts. In this way the Regulations appear to introduce a test of fairness into the renewal period for certain contracts. This paragraph may also catch a holding-fee of the type used in *Interfoto Picture Library Ltd* v. *Stiletto Visual Programmes Ltd* [1989] QB 433 (p. 352 above). The effect of a finding that such a term is unfair will be that it is not binding on the consumer so that the contract will not be extended in the manner contemplated by the term.

Paragraph 1(i) is important, albeit that its scope is rather unclear. It applies to a contract term which purports to incorporate the terms of other documents not accessible to the consumer. But it does not appear to challenge the rule in *L'Estrange* v. *Graucob* [1934] 2 KB 394 (p. 344 above) because the subject-matter of this paragraph is the term which seeks to incorporate the other terms into the contract rather than the term which it is sought to incorporate into the contract.

Paragraph 1(j) applies to unilateral alteration clauses. Such clauses may also be vulnerable to challenge under the Unfair Contract Terms Act 1977 (see section 3, discussed at p. 463 above). The scope of this paragraph is limited by paragraphs 2(b) and 2(c) of Schedule 2 which make particular provision for the financial services industry. Paragraph 2(b) also provides that a seller or supplier can reserve the right unilaterally to alter the conditions of a contract of indeterminate duration, provided that he is required to inform the consumer with reasonable notice and that the consumer is free to dissolve the contract.

Paragraph 1(k) applies to terms which enable the seller or supplier to alter without a valid reason any characteristics of the product or service to be provided. This paragraph only applies where the seller or supplier does not have a 'valid reason' for making the alteration. 'Valid reason' is not defined in the Regulations.

Paragraph 1(l) applies to terms which purport to entitle the seller to make uni-lateral changes to the price of goods or services. Thus, while the adequacy of the price cannot be challenged as an unfair term provided that it is in plain, intelligible lan-guage (see regulation 6(2)), the same cannot be said of terms which purport to entitle one party to make changes to the agreed price of the goods or services. Such terms are susceptible to challenge under the Regulations. It is not entirely clear what will happen in the event that such a term is found to be unfair. While the term will not bind the consumer, what price will be payable for the goods or services? Is there no contract, a contract to pay for the goods or services at a 'reasonable price', or a contract to pay for the goods or services at the originally agreed price? The scope of this paragraph is also limited by paragraphs 2(c) and 2(d) of Schedule 2. The former makes special provision for the financial services industry, while the latter states that paragraph 1(l) is without hindrance to price indexation clauses, where lawful, pro-vided that the method by which prices vary is 'explicitly' described. In other words, the emphasis is placed on the clarity and quality of the information given in relation to the price index.

Paragraph 1(m) catches unilateral interpretation terms. It is possible that such terms could also fall within the scope of the Unfair Contract Terms Act 1977, but the point is doubtful. No such doubt arises under the Regulations.

Paragraph 1(n) applies to formality requirements. This paragraph would appear not to apply to exclusion clauses because it opens with the word 'limiting'. On the other hand, the fact that the list does not purport to be exhaustive may enable a court to conclude that an exclusion clause cast in these terms is also unfair. Professor Treitel notes (p. 275, n.18) that 'it is not clear whether the concluding words of this illustration are limited to commitments undertaken by agents'.

Paragraph 1(o) applies to terms obliging the consumer to fulfil all of his obligations where the seller or supplier does not perform his. This paragraph could apply to a rental agreement under which the hirer is obliged to pay the hire, when the owner is not under an obligation to repair the goods hired.

Paragraph 1(p) applies to a term which purports to entitle the seller or supplier to transfer his rights and obligations under the contract and the effect of this is to reduce the guarantees for the consumer without the consumer's consent. The refer-ence to the transfer of obligations in this paragraph is a little puzzling to an English lawyer because English law does not allow one party to transfer his obligations under a contract to a third party without the consent of his contracting party. This being the case, an attempt by a seller to transfer his obligations to a third party without the consent of the consumer would be invalid irrespective of this particular provision.

Paragraph 1(q) applies to terms which seek to restrict the availability of legal remedies. Professor Treitel (at p. 274) analyses this provision in the following terms:

Terms 'excluding or hindering' the consumer's right to take legal action or exercise any other legal remedy are included in the list of prima facie unfair terms. In this context, the list refers, in particular, to terms 'requiring the consumer to take disputes exclusively to arbitration not covered by legal provisions' . . . The reference to arbitration clauses . . . is, however, restricted by the words 'not covered by legal provisions' and the purpose of this restriction may be to narrow the category of prima facie unfair arbitration clauses to those in which the parties have agreed to exclude the powers of the courts to control the arbitrator's decision.

4. DIRECTOR GENERAL OF FAIR TRADING v. FIRST NATIONAL BANK

The leading case on the Unfair Terms in Consumer Contracts Regulations is the decision of the House of Lords in *Director General of Fair Trading* v. *First National Bank* [2001] UKHL 52; [2002] 1 AC 481. The case is actually concerned with the interpretation of the 1994 rather than the 1999 Regulations but the differences between the two sets of Regulations are immaterial for the purposes of the case. Therefore the decision is relevant to the interpretation of the 1999 Regulations and, indeed, it establishes a number of points of considerable importance in relation to the scope of the Regulations.

Director General of Fair Trading v. First National Bank

[2001] UKHL 52; [2002] 1 AC 481, House of Lords

The Director General of Fair Trading applied for an injunction to restrain First National Bank from using or relying upon a sentence in their standard terms of business on the ground that it was an 'unfair term' within the meaning of regulation 4(1)[1] of the Unfair Terms in Consumer Contracts Regulations 1994. First National Bank provides consumer finance and is regulated by the Consumer Credit Act 1974. Clause 8 of its standard terms of business stated that, should the customer default on repayments to it, it was to be entitled to recover from the customer the whole of the balance on the customer's loan account together with outstanding interest and the costs of seeking judgment. The portion of clause 8 which was challenged by the Director General of Fair Trading was in the following terms:

> 'Interest on the amount which becomes payable shall be charged in accordance with Condition 4, at the rate stated in paragraph D overleaf (subject to variation) until payment as well as before any judgment (such obligation to be independent of and not to merge with the judgment).'

The effect of this clause was to extend the liability of customers of First National Bank in the case where they paid off an outstanding loan pursuant to an instalment scheme that had been approved by a court. In such a case payment pursuant to the instalment scheme did not necessarily have the effect of discharging the debt because interest continued to accrue on the unpaid balance of the debt by virtue of clause 8. Thus many customers were faced with a demand for further payment in relation to the interest which had accrued under clause 8 on completion of their payments pursuant to the instalment scheme that had been approved by the court.

On behalf of the Director General of Fair Trading it was submitted that clause 8 was an

---

[1] Regulation 5(1) in the 1999 Regulations.

unfair term under the Regulations. The trial judge, Evans-Lombe J, held that the term was not unfair. The Court of Appeal allowed the Director General's appeal and concluded that the term was unfair. The House of Lords in turn allowed First National Bank's appeal and held that the term was not unfair. The speech of Lord Steyn is set out in full in the extracts that follow. In his speech are to be found the reasons for the conclusion that clause 8 was not an unfair term. The extracts from the other speeches deal with the more general conclusions of their Lordships in relation to the interpretation of the Regulations and do not deal in any detail with the application of these principles to the particular facts of the case.

Lord Bingham

8.   . . . It should . . . be noted that the regulations were made to give effect in the United Kingdom to Council Directive 93/13/EEC (OJ 1993, L95, p 29) on unfair terms in consumer contracts ('the Directive'). (They were superseded by further regulations in 1999, but these are to very much the same effect, do not govern this case and need not be further considered). It is common ground that the regulations should be construed so as to give effect to the directive, to which resort may properly be made for purposes of construction . . .

[he set out what is now regulations 8 and 6(2) of the 1999 Regulations, together with the 19th Recital to the Directive and continued]

12.   . . . The regulations, as Professor Sir Guenter Treitel QC has aptly observed (*The Law of Contract*, 10th ed, 1999, p. 248) 'are not intended to operate as a mechanism of quality or price control' and regulation 3(2)[2] is of "crucial importance in recognising the parties' freedom of contract with respect to the essential features of their bargain" (*ibid*, at p 249). But there is an important 'distinction between the term or terms which express the substance of the bargain and "incidental" (if important) terms which surround them' (*Chitty on Contracts*, 28th ed, 1999, 'Unfair Terms in Consumer Contracts', p 747, para 15–025). The object of the regulations and the Directive is to protect consumers against the inclusion of unfair and prejudicial terms in standard-form contracts into which they enter, and that object would plainly be frustrated if regulation 3(2)(b)[3] were so broadly interpreted as to cover any terms other than those falling squarely within it. In my opinion the term, as part of a provision prescribing the consequences of default, plainly does not fall within it. It does not concern the adequacy of the interest earned by the bank as its remuneration but is designed to ensure that the bank's entitlement to interest does not come to an end on the entry of judgment . . .

[he set out what is now Regulation 5 of the 1999 Regulations, what was Schedule 2 to the 1994 Regulations and the 15th and 16th Recitals to the Directive and continued]

17.   The test laid down by regulation 4(1),[4] deriving as it does from article 3(1) of the Directive, has understandably attracted much discussion in academic and professional circles and helpful submissions were made to the House on it. It is plain from the recitals to the Directive that one of its objectives was partially to harmonise the law in this important field among all member states of the European Union. The member states have no common concept of fairness or good faith, and the Directive does not purport to

---

[2] Regulation 6(2) in the 1999 Regulations.   [3] Regulation 6(2)(b) in the 1999 Regulations.
[4] Regulation 5(1) in the 1999 Regulations.

state the law of any single member state. It lays down a test to be applied, whatever their pre-existing law, by all member states. If the meaning of the test were doubtful, or vulnerable to the possibility of differing interpretations in differing member states, it might be desirable or necessary to seek a ruling from the European Court of Justice on its interpretation. But the language used in expressing the test, so far as applicable in this case, is in my opinion clear and not reasonably capable of differing interpretations. A term falling within the scope of the regulations is unfair if it causes a significant imbalance in the parties' rights and obligations under the contract to the detriment of the consumer in a manner or to an extent which is contrary to the requirement of good faith. The requirement of significant imbalance is met if a term is so weighted in favour of the supplier as to tilt the parties' rights and obligations under the contract significantly in his favour. This may be by the granting to the supplier of a beneficial option or discretion or power, or by the imposing on the consumer of a disadvantageous burden or risk or duty. The illustrative terms set out in Schedule 3[5] to the regulations provide very good examples of terms which may be regarded as unfair; whether a given term is or is not to be so regarded depends on whether it causes a significant imbalance in the parties' rights and obligations under the contract. This involves looking at the contract as a whole. But the imbalance must be to the detriment of the consumer; a significant imbalance to the detriment of the supplier, assumed to be the stronger party, is not a mischief which the regulations seek to address. The requirement of good faith in this context is one of fair and open dealing. Openness requires that the terms should be expressed fully, clearly and legibly, containing no concealed pitfalls or traps. Appropriate prominence should be given to terms which might operate disadvantageously to the customer. Fair dealing requires that a supplier should not, whether deliberately or unconsciously, take advantage of the consumer's necessity, indigence, lack of experience, unfamiliarity with the subject matter of the contract, weak bargaining position or any other factor listed in or analogous to those listed in Schedule 2[6] of the regulations. Good faith in this context is not an artificial or technical concept; nor, since Lord Mansfield was its champion, is it a concept wholly unfamiliar to British lawyers. It looks to good standards of commercial morality and practice. Regulation 4(1)[7] lays down a composite test, covering both the making and the substance of the contract, and must be applied bearing clearly in mind the objective which the regulations are designed to promote.

Lord Steyn
My Lords,

30. This is the first occasion on which the House has had the opportunity to examine an important branch of consumer law. It is therefore appropriate to consider the framework in which the questions before the House must be considered.

31. As between the Directive and the domestic implementing regulations, the former is the dominant text. Fortunately, the 1994 Regulations, and even more so the 1999 Regulations, appear to have implemented the Directive in domestic law in a manner which ought not to cause serious difficulty. The purpose of the Directive is twofold, viz the promotion of fair standard contract forms to improve the functioning of the European

---

[5] Schedule 2 to the 1999 Regulations.
[6] Schedule 2 to the 1994 Regulations has not been re-enacted in the 1999 Regulations.
[7] Regulation 5(1) in the 1999 Regulations.

market place and the protection of consumers throughout the European Community. The Directive is aimed at contracts of adhesion, viz 'take it or leave it' contracts. It treats consumers as presumptively weaker parties and therefore fit for protection from abuses by stronger contracting parties. This is an objective which must throughout guide the interpretation of the Directive as well as the implementing regulations. If contracting parties were able to avoid the application of the Directive and regulations by exclusionary stipulations the regulatory scheme would be ineffective. The conclusion that the Directive and regulations are mandatory is inescapable.

32.   The Directive is not an altogether harmonious text. It reflects the pragmatic compromises which were necessary to arrive at practical solutions between member states with divergent legal systems. But, despite some inelegance and untidiness in the text, the general principle that the construction must be adopted which promotes the effectiveness and practical value of the system ought to overcome difficulties. And the concepts of the Directive must be given autonomous meanings so that there will be uniform application of the Directive so far as is possible.

33.   The Directive made provision for a dual system of ex casu challenges and pre-emptive or collective challenges by appropriate bodies: see article 7. This system was domestically enacted in the 1994 Regulations, with the Director General of Fair Trading as the administering official to investigate and take action on complaints: see regulation 8.[8] The 1999 Regulations extended the system of enforcement by including other bodies as qualified to undertake pre-emptive challenges. The system of pre-emptive challenges is a more effective way of preventing the continuing use of unfair terms and changing contracting practice than ex casu actions: see Susan Bright, 'Winning the battle against unfair contract terms', (2000) 20 *Legal Studies* 331, 333–338. It is, however, to be noted that in a pre-emptive challenge there is not a direct lis between the consumer and the other contracting party. The Directive and the Regulations do not always distinguish between the two situations. This point is illustrated by the emphasis in article 4.1 of the Directive and regulation 4(2)[9] on the relevance of particular circumstances affecting a contractual relationship. The Directive and the regulations must be made to work sensibly and effectively and this can only be done by taking into account the effects of contemplated or typical relationships between the contracting parties. Inevitably, the primary focus of such a pre-emptive challenge is on issues of substantive unfairness.

34.   Under the Regulations, a term in a standard form contract that is unfair is not binding on the consumer. But certain provisions, sometimes called core terms, have been excepted from the regulatory regime. Regulation 3(2)[10] so provides:

'In so far as it is in plain, intelligible language, no assessment shall be made of the fairness of any term which—(a) defines the main subject matter of the contract, or (b) concerns the adequacy of the price or remuneration, as against the goods or services sold or supplied.'

Clause 8 of the contract, the only provision in dispute, is a default provision. It prescribes remedies which only become available to the lender upon the default of the consumer. For this reason the escape route of regulation 3(2) is not available to the bank. So far as the description of terms covered by regulation 3(2) as core terms is helpful at all, I would

---

[8] Regulation 10 in the 1999 Regulations.   [9] Regulation 6(1) in the 1999 Regulations.
[10] Regulation 6(2) in the 1999 Regulations.

say that clause 8 of the contract is a subsidiary term. In any event, article 3(2) must be given a restrictive interpretation. Unless that is done article 3(2)(a) will enable the main purpose of the scheme to be frustrated by endless formalistic arguments as to whether a provision is a definitional or an exclusionary provision. Similarly, article 3(2)(b) dealing with 'the adequacy of the price or remuneration' must be given a restrictive interpretation. After all, in a broad sense all terms of the contract are in some way related to the price or remuneration. That is not what is intended. Even price escalation clauses have been treated by the Director as subject to the fairness provision: see Susan Bright, loc. cit., at pp 345 and 349. It would be a gaping hole in the system if such clauses were not subject to the fairness requirement. For these further reasons I would reject the argument of the bank that regulation 3(2), and in particular 3(2)(b), take clause 8 outside the scope of the regulations . . .

36. It is now necessary to refer to the provisions which prescribe how it should be determined whether a term is unfair. Implementing article 3(1) of the Directive regulation 4(1)[11] provides:

' "unfair term" means any term which contrary to the requirement of good faith causes a significant imbalance in the parties' rights and obligations under the contract to the detriment of the consumer.'

There are three independent requirements. But the element of detriment to the consumer may not add much. But it serves to make clear that the Directive is aimed at significant imbalance against the consumer, rather than the seller or supplier. The twin requirements of good faith and significant imbalance will in practice be determinative. Schedule 2[12] to the Regulations, which explains the concept of good faith, provides that regard must be had, amongst other things, to the extent to which the seller or supplier has dealt fairly and equitably with the consumer. It is an objective criterion. Good faith imports, as Lord Bingham has observed in his opinion, the notion of open and fair dealing: see also *Interfoto Picture Library Ltd* v. *Stiletto Visual Programmes Ltd* [1989] QB 433. And helpfully the commentary to the 2000 edition of Principles of European Contract Law, prepared by the Commission of European Contract Law, explains that the purpose of the provision of good faith and fair dealing is 'to enforce community standards of fairness and reasonableness in commercial transactions': at 113; A fortiori that is true of consumer transactions. Schedule 3[13] to the Regulations (which corresponds to the Annex to the Directive) is best regarded as a check list of terms which must be regarded as potentially vulnerable. The examples given in Schedule 3 convincingly demonstrate that the argument of the bank that good faith is predominantly concerned with procedural defects in negotiating procedures cannot be sustained. Any purely procedural or even predominantly procedural interpretation of the requirement of good faith must be rejected.

37. That brings me to the element of significant imbalance. It has been pointed out by Hugh Collins that the test 'of a significant imbalance of the obligations obviously directs attention to the substantive unfairness of the contract': 'Good Faith in European Contract Law,' (1994), 14 *Oxford Journal of Legal Studies* 229, 249. It is however, also

---

[11] Regulation 5(1) in the 1999 Regulations.
[12] This Schedule was not re-enacted in the 1999 Regulations.
[13] Schedule 2 to the 1999 Regulations.

right to say that there is a large area of overlap between the concepts of good faith and significant imbalance.

38. It is now necessary to turn to the application of these requirements to the facts of the present case. The point is a relatively narrow one. I agree that the starting point is that a lender ought to be able to recover interest at the contractual rate until the date of payment, and this applies both before and after judgment. On the other hand, counsel for the Director advanced a contrary argument. Adopting the test of asking what the position of a consumer is in the contract under consideration with or without clause 8, he said that the consumer is in a significantly worse position than he would have been if there had been no such provision. Certainly, the consumer is worse off. The difficulty facing counsel, however, is that this disadvantage to the consumer appears to be the consequence not of clause 8 but of the County Courts (Interest on Judgment Debts) Order 1991. Under this Order no statutory interest is payable on a county court judgment given in proceedings to recover money due under a regulated agreement: see regulation 2. Counsel said that for policy reasons it was decided that in such a case no interest may be recovered after judgment. He said that it is not open to the House to criticise directly or indirectly this legal context. In these circumstances he submitted that it is not legitimate for a court to conclude that fairness requires that a lender must be able to insist on a stipulation designed to avoid the statutory regime under the 1991 Order. Initially I was inclined to uphold this policy argument. On reflection, however, I have been persuaded that this argument cannot prevail in circumstances where the legislature has neither expressly nor by necessary implication barred a stipulation that interest may continue to accrue after judgment until payment in full.

39. For these reasons as well as the reasons given by Lord Bingham I agree that clause 8 is not unfair.

Lord Hope of Craighead
44. The primary reason which the Director has given for maintaining that the term is unfair is the uncertainty, confusion and hardship which has been shown to result from the bank's practice of claiming contractual interest from its borrowers after judgment has been given for the principal. Particular unfairness is said to arise where an order is made to pay the debt by instalments, whether under section 71 of the County Courts Act 1984 or a time order under section 129 of the 1974 Act, and where no consideration has been given to making an order under section 136 of the 1974 Act to amend the agreement so as to prevent the accrual of contractual interest on instalments which are paid when they fall due. The fact that it is commonplace for no consideration to be given to the use of section 136 when payment by instalments is being ordered is not in dispute. So it is not surprising that borrowers, on finding that they are liable for further amounts in addition to the instalments provided for in judgments obtained against them by the bank, have complained to the Director.

45. I am not persuaded that, despite these consequences, the term is unfair. The meaning to be given to the word 'unfair' in this context is laid down in regulation 4(1)[14] of the 1994 Regulations. Guidance as to how the words used in that paragraph are to be understood is to be found in the sixteenth recital to the directive. The recital explains

---

[14] Regulation 5(1) of the 1999 Regulations.

what 'constitutes the requirement of good faith'. It states that an assessment of the unfair character of unfair terms must be supplemented by an overall evaluation of the different interests involved. Regulation 4(2)[15] indicates the wide range of circumstances to be taken into account in the assessment. It provides that the assessment is to be done as at the time of the conclusion of the contract. But an appreciation of how the term will affect each party when the contract is put into effect must clearly form part of the exercise. It has been pointed out that there are considerable differences between the legal systems of the member states as to how extensive and how powerful the penetration has been of the principle of good faith and fair dealing: Lando and Beale, Principles of European Contract Law, Parts I and II (Combined and Revised, 2000), p 116. But in the present context there is no need to explore this topic in any depth. The Directive provides all the guidance that it needed as to its application.

46.   Following this approach it does not seem to me that there is a significant imbalance to the detriment of the borrower in the stipulation that the interest which is payable in terms of the first part of the last sentence is to be charged after as well as before any judgment and that this obligation is not to merge in the judgment. The primary obligation in condition 4 is to pay interest on the outstanding balance due to the bank. The plain fact is that, in the event of a default by the borrower, the bank will not have recovered all of its money until the entire balance on the borrower's account has been paid. The main purpose of the last sentence is to ensure that the borrower does not enjoy the benefit of the outstanding balance after judgment without fulfilling the corresponding obligation which he has undertaken to pay interest on it as provided for in the contract. While the working out of that purpose may give rise to uncertainty in practice, the term itself does not seem to me to be unfair.

Lord Millett

54.   A contractual term in a consumer contract is unfair if 'contrary to the requirement of good faith [it] causes a significant imbalance in the parties' rights and obligations under the contract to the detriment of the consumer'. There can be no one single test of this. It is obviously useful to assess the impact of an impugned term on the parties' rights and obligations by comparing the effect of the contract with the term and the effect it would have without it. But the inquiry cannot stop there. It may also be necessary to consider the effect of the inclusion of the term on the substance or core of the transaction; whether if it were drawn to his attention the consumer would be likely to be surprised by it; whether the term is a standard term, not merely in similar non-negotiable consumer contracts, but in commercial contracts freely negotiated between parties acting on level terms and at arms' length; and whether, in such cases, the party adversely affected by the inclusion of the term or his lawyer might reasonably be expected to object to its inclusion and press for its deletion. The list is not necessarily exhaustive; other approaches may sometimes be more appropriate.

55.   The substance of the transaction in the present case is self-evident. It is a loan repayable by instalments with interest on the balance from time to time outstanding until the whole of the principal is repaid. The borrower would have no difficulty in understanding this. Nor would he think it unfair. If his attention were drawn to the impugned term, ie that interest should continue to be paid on the outstanding balance after as well as

---

[15] Regulation 6(1) in the 1999 Regulations.

before judgment, he might well be surprised at the need to spell this out, but he would surely not be at all surprised by the fact. It is what he would expect. The term does not affect the substance of the transaction, which is that the borrower should continue to pay interest on the principal from time to time outstanding, nor does it impose any further or unexpected liability upon him not inherent in the basic transaction. It is included only to protect the lender from the (to modern eyes artificial) meaning placed on a covenant to pay interest by the Court of Appeal in *In re Sneyd, Ex p Fewings* (1883) 25 Ch D 338, where a covenant to pay interest on the balance of the principal sum from time to time remaining unpaid was construed as meaning remaining due under the covenant, so that it fell when the covenant was subsumed in the judgment.

56.   The term is not only a standard term in non-negotiable loans to consumers, but in commercial loans freely negotiated between parties on equal terms and acting with professional advice. I venture to think that no lawyer advising a commercial borrower would dream of objecting to the inclusion of such a term, which merely reinforces and carries into effect what the parties themselves would regard as the essence of the transaction.

57.   I am satisfied, therefore, that the term is not unfair. It does not cause an imbalance in the parties' rights and obligations; and the lender did not act in bad faith by taking advantage of the borrower's weakness of bargaining power or lack of professional advice to insist upon a term which would otherwise have been omitted.

58.   This is not to say that the many complaints which the Director General has received from borrowers are without substance . . .

61.   But this unfairness does not arise from any inherent unfairness of the term. It is due to the limited nature of the judgment and the fact that it does not cover the whole of the borrower's indebtedness to the lender.

Lord Rodger of Earlsferry

64.   At first sight the language of both the regulation and the Directive is somewhat strange since it might seem to suggest that the court is not to consider the fairness of a term which concerns 'the adequacy', in its usual sense of 'the sufficiency', of the price or remuneration as against the goods or services sold or supplied. But it is obvious from the context that this cannot be what is intended. In his opinion Evans-Lombe J accepted a submission to the effect that 'adequacy' must be read 'as meaning the equivalent of "the extent of the remuneration"': *Director General of Fair Trading* v. *First National Bank PLC* [2000] 1 WLR 98, at p 107 B–C. That interpretation seems to me to risk watering down what the directive may have intended. While the point was not explored before us and I therefore express no concluded view on it, I note that the French text of the Directive uses the word 'adéquation' and the German text the word 'Angemessenheit'. Both may suggest that what is in issue is the 'appropriateness' of the price or remuneration as compared with the services or goods—in other words whether there is an equivalence between the services or goods and the consideration for them. This would seem to be consistent with the reference to 'the price/quality ratio' in the nineteenth recital. It may therefore be that 'adequacy' in both the Directive and the regulations should be interpreted in that spirit. Which is indeed how I understand your Lordships to have approached the matter.

COMMENTARY

As Lord Bingham pointed out, there were two principal issues in this case. The first was whether the regulations were applicable to the term or not. The second was, if they were, whether or not the term was unfair.

In relation to the first point, their Lordships took a narrow approach to the interpretation of what is now regulation 6(2) of the 1999 Regulations. They rejected the bank's submission that receipt of interest was part of its remuneration so that the court was not entitled to scrutinize the term in the name of fairness. Particularly important is Lord Steyn's observation in paragraph [34] that what is now regulation 6(2) should be interpreted 'restrictively' otherwise it would 'enable the main purpose of the scheme to be frustrated by endless formalistic arguments as to whether a provision is a definitional or an exclusionary provision'. This conservative approach was followed by Gross J in *Bairstow Eves London Central Ltd* v. *Smith* [2004] EWHC 263. The case concerned a claim by estate agents that they were entitled to recover commission at a rate of 3%. The contract provided that 3% was to be the 'standard commission rate' and further provided for an 'early payment discounted commission rate of 1.5%.' The 1.5% commission rate was payable if it was paid in full within 10 working days of completion. The defendants failed to pay the 1.5% commission within 10 days as a result of a failure by their solicitors to pay the money (as they were authorised by the defendants to do). The defendants maintained that the clause providing for payment of a commission rate of 3% was an unfair contract term but the claimant submitted that the clause did not fall within the scope of the Unfair Terms in Consumer Contracts Regulations 1999 because it fell within the scope of regulation 6(2). Gross J held that regulation 6(2) must be 'given a restrictive interpretation' because 'otherwise a coach and horses could be driven through the Regulations'. He continued:

while it is not for the Court to re-write the parties' bargain as to the fairness or adequacy of the price itself, regulation 6(2) may be unlikely to shield terms as to price escalation or default provisions from scrutiny under the fairness requirement contained in regulation 5(1).

The critical question for the court was whether the commission rate of 3% was the default rate or not. If it was not, then it was not subject to review. On the other hand, if it was then it was subject to review. Gross J concluded that, notwithstanding the use of the words 'standard commission rate', the rate of 3% was a default rate. He reached this conclusion for three reasons. The first was that a standard rate of 3% would not have attracted much business on the market; secondly, the negotiations between the parties focused on a commission rate of 1.5%; and, thirdly, both parties proceeded on the assumption that the 1.5% commission would be paid within 10 working days so that the operative commission rate was 1.5% and the 3% would only be payable in the unlikely event that the defendants failed to honour their obligation to pay the 1.5% commission within 10 days.

A further point worth noting about *First National Bank* is Lord Steyn's comments in relation to what is now regulation 6(2)(b) and his affirmation of the fact that price escalation clauses fall within the scope of the Regulations (see p. 510 above). Lord Bingham distinguished in paragraph [12] between a term which expresses the substance of the bargain and a term which is incidental. In his opinion clause 8 was not a term which expressed the substance of the bargain between the parties. It was an incidental (possibly an important incidental) term of the agreement between the parties.

Turning to the fairness of the term, the House of Lords focused on the twin requirements of 'good faith' and 'significant imbalance'. Their Lordships did not appear to have particular difficulties with the meaning of good faith. They equated it with the 'notion of fair and open dealing' (see, in particular, paras [17] and [36]). Lord Steyn also stated that a purely procedural or even predominantly procedural interpretation of the requirement of good faith must be rejected. In relation to significant imbalance, Lord Bingham stated in paragraph [17] that 'the requirement of significant imbalance is met if a term is so weighted in favour of the supplier as to tilt the parties' rights and obligations under the contract significantly in his favour'. Lord Steyn in paragraph [37] held that it directed attention to the substantive unfairness of the contract but, crucially, noted that there is a 'large area of overlap' between good faith and significant imbalance. It is therefore unlikely that the courts will attempt to provide us with water-tight definitions of these concepts. The courts are more likely to adopt a much more fluid approach to the interpretation of the Regulations.

The decision of the House of Lords has been criticized on two grounds. The first is that their Lordships did not make an Article 234 reference to the European Court of Justice for a preliminary ruling on the meaning of 'unfair'. In failing to make a reference it has been argued that 'the House of Lords engaged in informed anticipatory definition, thereby infringing the interpretative monopoly of the ECJ in the area of Community law' (M Dean, 'Defining Unfair Terms in Consumer Contracts— Crystal Ball Gazing? *Director General of Fair Trading* v. *First National Bank plc*' (2002) 65 *MLR* 773). Lord Bingham addressed this issue in paragraph [17] of his speech but concluded that the language used was 'clear and not reasonably capable of differing interpretations'. The difficulty with this view is that Member States have no common concept of fairness or good faith, a point acknowledged by Lord Bingham in the same paragraph of his speech. In the absence of common concepts it can only be a matter of time before a reference is made to the European Court of Justice.

The second ground on which the decision has been criticized relates to the conclusion that the term was not an unfair term. Their Lordships did not seek to deny that there was a substantial element of unfairness in the way in which clause 8 interacted with the principal legislative provisions but they stated that the real source of the unfairness lay in the legislation and not clause 8. The basis for their conclusion that clause 8 was not an unfair term was, essentially, that the bank was simply attempting to recover the interest on the sum advanced to the customer and, as Lord Bingham remarked, 'neither party could suppose that the bank would willingly forego any part of its principal or interest'. Their Lordships accepted that many consumers felt a real sense of grievance when they discovered that they had not in fact paid off all their debts and had to meet a subsequent claim in respect of the unpaid interest but, in their view, the blame for this situation could not be laid at the door of the bank. As Lord Steyn pointed out (in para [38]), the disadvantage facing the consumer 'appears to be the consequence not of clause 8 but of the County Courts (Interest on

Judgment Debts) Order 1991'. This view is not, however, one which is universally shared. Thus Meryll Dean has concluded ((2002) 65 *MLR* 773, 780–781):

On the facts of *First National Bank* there can be little doubt that the effect of Condition 8 might reasonably be described as onerous, unexpected, disagreeable or even shocking. Nevertheless the House of Lords found that it was not unfair within the meaning of regulation 4(1). Whilst this decision will undoubtedly be welcomed by banks and lending institutions, it has done little to reassure consumers that the law really works for their protection or benefit. It is also unfortunate that the House of Lords seems to have been so confident of its interpretation of EC law that it effectively engaged in crystal ball gazing to arrive at a definition of unfair and overlooked its broader role in the development of EC consumer law.

5. ENFORCEMENT OF THE REGULATIONS

As has been noted, the primary role in the enforcement of the Regulations has been played not by the courts but by the Unfair Contracts Terms Unit of the Office of Fair Trading. An assessment of their role has been provided in the following terms:

S Bright, 'Winning the Battle Against Unfair Terms'

(2000) 20 *Legal Studies* 331, 333–338

Enforcement of the Unfair Terms in Consumer Contracts Regulations

Although the UK Regulations can be relied on in private law disputes involving consumers, it is the Unfair Contract Terms Unit that has been at the forefront of action against unfair contract terms. Private law enforcement does not provide an effective way of regulating the standard inclusion of unfair terms in adhesion contracts: it is true that success in an individual action will mean that the term is not binding upon that consumer, but its impact beyond that consumer will be limited, and there is no significant pressure on the business to discontinue future use of that term. Further, there will only ever be a trickle of private law actions as most consumers prefer to deal with matters informally, or not at all, rather than pursue complaints by formal legal mechanisms in which the costs of litigation (financial and otherwise) exceed the benefits that stand to be achieved. So far there has only been a handful of cases in which the consumer has, with mixed success, relied upon the 1994 Regulations.

The administrative model of enforcement created by the 1994 Regulations (and extended by the 1999 Regulations) is a much more effective way of preventing the continuing use of unfair terms and changing contracting practice. Investigation into allegedly unfair terms usually follows a complaint made to the Director General of Fair Trading, who is under a duty to investigate unless it is 'frivolous or vexatious'. There is a strong flow of complaints made to the Unfair Contract Terms Unit, about half of which come from local authority trading standards departments and consumer advice organisations. The Unit have adopted a pro-active response to complaints; not only will the particular term complained about be looked into, but the contract as a whole will be investigated. Indeed, investigations often spread beyond the particular contract to involve trade associations, and the Unit has initiated a number of sectoral investigations so that contracts used by traders in a similar line of business can be looked at together. So, for example, there has been notable success in securing the amendment of terms in mobile phone contracts, the sector about which there has been most complaint. By way of illustration, numerous amendments were agreed in relation to Vodafone contracts, including adjustment of the notice requirement (which had required three months notice additional to the minimum twelve month term), deletion of a clause providing for a substantial disconnection charge, and a reduction in the level of compensation payable by a consumer who terminates early. Other sectors which have been focussed upon include the home improvement industry, vehicle rental, package holidays and, most recently, the Director General of Fair Trading has announced that he is investigating conditions of airline use. Discussions with trade associations are not always a response to complaints and may be on the initiative of the Office of Fair Trading.

In practice, the vast majority of cases are dealt with by negotiation and if the contract term is found to be unfair the Unfair Contract Terms Unit will require the business to provide an undertaking to discontinue the use of the unfair term. Court action has been seen as a last resort. Although the Director General of Fair Trading has power to apply for an injunction to restrain the use of unfair terms, this has, so far, only occurred once. This is a little surprising given that the issues at stake are not insignificant. In relation to mortgages, for example, the Office of Fair Trading persuaded the City Mortgage Corporation (CMC) to reduce its dual interest rates and the manner of calculating the premium due on early redemption of the mortgage. The financial costs to CMC must be great. It is interesting to speculate just why this course of action has been so successful and why traders have, with varying degrees of willingness, complied with the requests to abandon or amend terms without forcing the issue to court. Presumably the fear of bad publicity plays a part. There is also the fact that many of the terms are fair in part—by rewriting them the trader can still secure the protection needed whilst also being fair to the consumer; if left unamended the terms may be wholly unenforceable against the consumer. Dealing with trade associations is also an efficient way of reaching businesses: as the representative figure within that sectoral activity, associations will often be anxious to present a positive public image and to maintain good working relationships with the Office of Fair Trading. Agreements reached at this level will be passed through to the trading bodies who use the association's standard contract. By way of example, the Office of Fair Trading agreed a revised model contract for use by members of The British Vehicle Rental and Leasing Association. About 85% of companies in this industry belong to this association. It is also less costly to proceed by way of undertaking than by paying the costs of going to court. However, what has been the practice over the last five years will not necessarily be the pattern of the future; if it emerges over time that the courts adopt a less consumer-oriented interpretation of the Regulations, there is the possibility that fewer cases will be settled by negotiation alone.

This administrative model of enforcement was not prescribed by the Directive. Although the Directive specifies that mechanisms must be in place to prevent the continued use of unfair terms in consumer contracts, the method deployed to achieve this end is left to Member States. States could therefore select not only to hand this role to a public official (as in the United Kingdom and in Nordic countries), but to permit consumer organisations to bring actions to prevent the continued use of unfair terms (as in Germany and France), or (possibly) to use criminal sanctions. The route chosen in the United Kingdom has proven effective, as already seen, but there were complaints that the

1994 Regulations failed to give a voice to consumer organisations. Article 7 of the Unfair Terms Directive requires Member States to ensure that 'adequate and effective means exist to prevent the continued use of unfair terms' and that the means shall 'include provisions whereby persons or organisations, having a legitimate interest under national law in protecting consumers' may take action to have terms declared unfair. In 1995, the Consumers' Association sought to have the exclusion of bodies such as theirs declared to be an unlawful implementation of the Directive. The judge, Hidden J, referred the question raised by the Consumers' Association's action to the European Court of Justice for a ruling on the Community law, but the point was never pursued as the UK government announced its intention to address their concerns through an amendment to the 1994 Regulations.

There are various models that could have been used to extend the enforcement powers beyond the Director General of Fair Trading. The approach adopted in the 1999 Regulations is to list additional specific bodies (statutory regulators, trading standards departments and the Consumers' Association) as having powers to apply for an injunction to prevent the continued use of unfair terms. With the exception of the Consumers' Association, these bodies can also notify the Director General of Fair Trading that they will investigate a complaint, and will then be under an obligation to do so. An alternative model would have been to facilitate action by any body that is able to show that it fulfils certain criteria—depending upon the criteria selected, this would have enabled organisations such as the National Consumers' Council, Citizens' Advice Bureaux and the Financial Services Authority, to apply to bring actions. This route was the preferred approach of the Department of Trade and Industry in its Consultation Paper, which set out at some length the criteria that could be used by a court in deciding whether or not to recognise bodies. Nevertheless, this route proved to be impractical. It entailed the risk of wasted expenses for traders, who could be put to the trouble and expense of defending claims from bodies who might later turn out not to fulfil the specified criteria. Implementation would also have necessitated changes to the rules of court, which would have generated further delay. There is a risk, however, that having selected the list approach, non-listed bodies might bring fresh challenges. Although the emphasis of the Consumers' Association case lay in the claim that it was unlawful to have empowered only one public body to bring actions, there must be some doubt as to whether it is within the Directive to deny this option to any body which can show that it has a 'legitimate interest under national law in protecting consumers' (Article 7). It is likely, however, that there will be a second wave of listing: the Department of Trade and Industry have invited consumer bodies who wish to have enforcement powers under the Regulations to contact them.

The extension of powers beyond the Director General of Fair Trading meant that measures had to be put in place to ensure that there would be consistent approaches taken to unfair terms, effective co-ordination between the enforcement bodies, and to protect traders from multiple challenges. To this end, if a qualifying body intends to apply for an injunction, it must give the Director General of Fair Trading notice and then, unless a shorter period is authorised, cannot commence the action within fourteen days. In addition, the qualifying body must inform the Director General of Fair Trading of all undertakings it receives and of the result of any applications for an injunction. The fact that there is only a small number of bodies authorised to act does minimise the risk of a trader being in negotiation with several 'enforcers'. The Director General of Fair Trading will remain the primary investigator and, as all investigations have to be reported to him, he will have an overview of all complaints. He retains a duty to disseminate information about the operation of the Regulations, not only about his own actions but also reporting on undertakings given to, and actions brought by, other qualifying bodies. In practice, dissemination has taken place through the issue of regular bulletins containing details of case reports, coupled with press releases reporting significant 'triumphs'.

It is anticipated that the widening of the enforcement provisions, and the ability to apply for injunctive relief in the County Court, will increase the number of cases taken to court. This may well impact upon the application of the Regulations. To date, the Office of Fair Trading has largely operated with a free hand, exercising a wide discretion to apply the Regulations in the interests of consumers. Judicial intervention may impose more checks and balances into their application. Of the few cases that have come before the courts so far, some have diverged from the approach taken by the Director General of Fair Trading. In a Northern Irish case, *Kindlance Ltd* v. *Murphy*, Master Ellison held that the dual interest rate provisions in a mortgage were exempted from the fairness test in the Regulations by the 'core terms' exclusion . . . In contrast, the Office of Fair Trading has always maintained that dual rates provisions are liable to review for fairness, an approach which also has some judicial support. There is also, however, the wider picture to consider. Although the Office of Fair Trading has largely operated in isolation, the source of the Regulations lies in the European Unfair Terms Directive. Questions of interpretation will ultimately be for the European Court of Justice, but it is unlikely that vast numbers of cases will be referred. Much of the wording of the Directive is based upon Continental notions and yet there is no obvious procedure in place to facilitate the sharing of experiences between Member States. There has been an attempt to provide for this by establishing a database which pools information from Member States about decisions, both judicial and administrative. Although the database contains information about some 6000 cases it is not easy to use and does not give sufficient information to promote deep understanding about the meaning of phrases within the Directive. Occasional conferences have been held to assess the implementation of the Unfair Terms Directive, but if the Directive is to lead to a more harmonised approach towards unfair terms in consumer contracts there needs to be a regular mechanism to ensure a consistency of approach, such as an advisory panel, spearheaded by the Directorate responsible for consumer affairs, DG XXIV.

COMMENTARY

There are at least three important lessons that we can learn from this extract. The first is that it is a mistake to focus too much attention on the courts and to assume that if there is no case-law then the legislation cannot be working. The real enforcement of the Regulations is not taking place in the courts but in the Office of Fair Trading. The second point to note is the importance of administrative regulation to the enforcement of the Regulations. As Bright observes, 'private law enforcement does not provide an effective way of regulating the standard inclusion of unfair terms in adhesion contracts'. The third point is that the extension of enforcement powers beyond the Office of Fair Trading may not necessarily operate in the interests of consumers. Much will depend on the ability of these different qualifying bodies to forge a coherent and effective enforcement strategy.

6. THE FUTURE

In August 2002, the Law Commission and the Scottish Law Commission published a consultation paper on unfair terms in contracts (Law Commission Consultation Paper No 166 and Scottish Law Commission Discussion Paper No 119). The paper proposes the introduction of legislation that will unify the Unfair Contract Terms Act 1977 (referred to in the paper as 'UCTA') and the Unfair Terms in Consumer Contracts Regulations 1999 (referred to in the paper as 'UTCCR'). They point out the various differences that exist between the two regimes and suggest that the time has come to produce a simpler, more transparent regime. In paragraphs 2.18 and 2.19 they summarize the differences between the two regimes as follows:

2.18   UCTA:

(1) applies to both consumer and business-to-business contracts, and also to terms and notices excluding certain liabilities in tort [or, in Scotland, delict];

(2) applies only to exclusion and limitation of liability clauses (and indemnity clauses in consumer contracts);

(3) makes certain exclusions or restrictions of no effect at all;

(4) subjects others to a 'reasonableness' test;

(5) contains guidelines for the application of the reasonableness test;

(6) puts the burden of proving that a term within its scope is reasonable on the party seeking to rely on the clause;

(7) applies for the most part whether the terms were negotiated or were in a 'standard form';

(8) does not apply to certain types of contract, even when they are consumer contracts;

(9) has effect only between the immediate parties; and

(10) has separate provisions for Scotland.

2.19   In contrast, UTCCR:

(1) apply only to consumer contracts;

(2) apply to any kind of term other than the definition of the main subject matter of the contract and the price;

(3) do not make any particular type of term of no effect at all;

(4) subject the terms to a 'fairness' test;

(5) do not contain detailed guidelines as to how that test should be applied, but contain a list of terms which 'may be regarded' as unfair;

(6) leave the burden of proof that the clause is unfair on the consumer;

(7) apply only to terms that have not been 'individually negotiated';

(8) apply to consumer contracts of all kinds;

(9) are not only effective between the parties but empower various bodies to take action to prevent the use of unfair terms; and

(10) apply to the UK as a whole.

The Law Commissions argue that these differences have given rise to unnecessary difficulties. They summarize these difficulties as they apply to consumer contracts in paragraph 3.124 in the following terms:

The problems caused for business in relation to 'consumer contracts' by differences between UCTA and UTCCR appear to be caused by a number of factors:

(1) The existence of two instruments is misleading. A term may not be of the type covered by UCTA yet fall foul of UTCCR.

(2) Conversely, a term may have been negotiated with the consumer and so be exempt from UTCCR, but be caught by UCTA.

(3) Terms approved by industry regulators may be exempt from UCTA but may not be exempt from UTCCR.

(4) Several important types of contract are exempt from UCTA but are subject to UTCCR.

(5) While UCTA is fairly precise in what types of exclusion or limitation of liability clause will be invalid in a consumer contract, the scope of application of section 3(2)(b) [s 17(1)(b)] is less than clear, and there are no indicative lists to give further guidance. Conversely, it is difficult to be sure which terms fall outside UTCCR because they are 'core terms'.

(6) UTCCR seem to have a plain language requirement, but it is hard to be sure to what extent either instrument really requires this or that the term be conspicuous.

(7) The burden of proof of 'fairness' seems to be different from that of 'reasonableness'.

(8) Both UTCCR and UCTA apply to consumer contracts, but the definition of 'consumer' for each purpose differs.

(9) Each regime applies only to (broadly speaking) 'business liability', but the definitions of business may differ.

But if we are to create a unified regime, which regime should prevail? Should it be the Unfair Contract Terms Act model or the Regulations? The Law Commissions come down on the side of the Regulations and, in essence, make a provisional proposal that they should, in a modified form, be extended to business-to-business contracts which are concluded on standard terms. Their provisional proposals, as set out in paragraphs 14–21 of the executive summary to their paper are as follows:

14 As far as consumers are concerned, our provisional proposals are as follows:

(1) Certain terms that under UCTA are of no effect in any circumstances, should continue to be so.

(2) All other terms that are not specifically exempted should be valid only if they are 'fair and reasonable'.

(3) The requirement that the term be fair and reasonable should apply whether or not the term was individually negotiated. (This is already the case for terms that are within UCTA. In addition, we think that consumers are unlikely to have a sufficiently full understanding of the implications of other terms, except 'core terms',

that a term can be said to be 'fair' simply because there was a degree of negotiation over it.)

(4) The 'definition of the main subject matter' of the contract should be exempt from challenge (as under UTCCR), but it should be made clear that the exemption applies only so far as the subject matter is not substantially different to what the consumer should reasonably expect. The definition must also be in plain language (transparent).

(5) Similarly the 'adequacy of the price' should be exempt from review provided that having to make the payment is not substantially different to what the consumer should reasonably expect and is not under a subsidiary term. The price must also be stated in plain language (transparent).

(6) Terms that merely reproduce what would be the law in the absence of contrary agreement should be exempt, but only if the terms are in plain language (transparent).

(7) The new legislation should provide detailed guidelines on the application of the 'fair and reasonable' test.

(8) The list of relevant factors should include not just whether the term is in 'plain and intelligible language' (as under UTCCR) but whether the term is 'transparent' in the sense that, for example, it is reasonably easy to follow and to read. (Transparency should also replace 'plain language' as a requirement of the exemptions referred to at (4)–(6) above.)

(9) The legislation should contain a list of terms that will be unfair unless the business shows otherwise. The list should not follow the list in the Annex to the Directive word for word, but rather should refer to the types of clause found in the UK, and use UK terminology. It should give examples of each type of clause, and it should list common types of unfair term that are not in the Annex to the Directive.

(10) A term which is unfair should be of no effect except to the extent that it is beneficial to the consumer.

(11) The existing powers given to the Director-General of Fair Trading and various listed bodies to act to prevent the use of unfair terms should continue. We ask who should bear the burden of proof in these cases, and whether there should be powers to prevent practices of negotiating terms that are unfair.

15 We invite views on whether the burden of proving that a term is fair should *always* rest on the business, or whether the consumer should have to show that the term is unfair unless the term in question is on the list referred to in (9) above.

BUSINESS-TO-BUSINESS CONTRACTS

16 As far as individual business-to-business contracts are concerned, we think that the somewhat wider range of terms that (for consumer contracts) are subject to UTCCR should equally be subject to control in business-to-business contracts. Terms that, for instance, make it hard for a business to cancel a long-term contract, or that commit it to paying price increases, have just as much potential for unfairness as many of the clauses already covered by UCTA. Protection should not depend on the size of the business

affected by the term, though relative size should be a factor in determining whether the term is fair and reasonable. Some of the existing, more stringent controls of UCTA should be maintained. Thus:

(1) Terms of a business-to-business contract that, under UCTA, are of no effect in any circumstances, should continue to be so.

(2) Other terms in business-to-business contracts that are 'standard' or have not been 'individually negotiated' should be subject to a 'fair and reasonable test' (with similar exceptions for the main definition of the subject matter, the adequacy of the price and terms that reflect the general 'default' law as for consumer contracts).

(3) Individually negotiated terms which, under UCTA, are subject to the requirement of reasonableness should no longer be controlled. (We think that businesses can be expected to understand the implications of individually negotiated terms and to take steps to safeguard their position.)

(4) The question should be whether the term has been 'individually negotiated' rather than whether it is 'standard'.

(5) The existing exemptions from UCTA (for example, contracts of insurance) should continue, though we invite views on whether international business-to-business contracts, and contracts subject to the law of a part of the UK only by choice of the parties, should be exempt from the controls proposed for domestic contracts.

(6) The same basic test of 'fairness and reasonableness' as for consumer contracts should apply in business-to-business contracts; and 'transparency' should be incorporated into the list of factors for business-to-business contracts.

(7) The legislation should contain the same list of factors as that for consumer contracts.

(8) There should also be a list of terms that will be treated as unfair and unreasonable unless the contrary has been shown. The list should be limited to clauses excluding and restricting liability for breach of contract or for negligence [breach of duty], but there should be power to add to the list by Ministerial Order.

(9) Where a term is not on the list, the burden of proving that it is not fair and reasonable should be on the party disputing it.

17 We invite consultees to comment on the desirability and the practicability of extending the preventive controls over unfair terms to business-to-business contracts.

SALE OR SUPPLY OF GOODS NOT RELATED TO BUSINESS

18 The existing controls over clauses excluding or restricting implied obligations as to title, etc in contracts for the sale or supply of goods should be replicated in the new legislation.

19 Clauses which exclude or restrict liability for breach of the obligations as to correspondence with description or sample should remain subject to a 'fair and reasonable' test when the sale is between private parties or is by a consumer to a business, irrespective of whether the clause has been negotiated.

NON-CONTRACTUAL NOTICES EXCLUDING BUSINESS LIABILITY FOR NEGLIGENCE OR BREACH OF DUTY

20 The existing controls over notices which might otherwise exclude a business's liability in tort [delict] to persons with whom it does not have a contractual relationship and who are killed, injured or harmed by its negligence [breach of duty] should be maintained.

21 The preventive powers should be extended to cover non-contractual notices that purport to exclude or restrict a business's liability in tort [delict].

The most contentious item in the consultation paper is the provisional proposal to extend the range of controls over business-to-business contracts. The Law Commissions give a number of examples of potentially unfair clauses against which businesses, unlike consumers, are currently not protected. The list includes deposits and forfeiture of money paid clauses, default rates of interest (unless these can be shown to be penalties), automatic extension of contract clauses, price variation clauses, entire agreement clauses, arbitration clauses, jurisdiction clauses, and termination clauses. While the consultation paper provisionally proposes to increase the protection available to businesses, it stops short of suggesting that these controls should apply to all business-to-business transactions. The provisional proposals will only apply where the term in question 'has not been individually negotiated' or is 'standard'. The Law Commissions state their preference for the former over the latter (proposal (4) above). In their provisional view 'the controls should apply to clauses that have been drafted in advance by one party and not subsequently negotiated, because this is the test which we think will be the easier one to apply when, as we think will be more and more often the case, the "standard form" will not be a printed document but an electronic one' (para 5.58). Individually negotiated terms will therefore largely cease to be the subject of legislative control (subject to proposal (1)) but the price to be paid for this exemption will be that many other contract terms will become subject to legislative control. This price may prove to be a high one.

If the provisional proposal to extend the controls over business-to-business contracts is accepted, the crucial issue will become the 'fair and reasonable' test and the way in which it is applied to commercial contracts. The Law Commissions deal with this in proposals (6)–(8) of paragraph 16 (above). These proposals are likely to draw mixed reactions. On the one hand, the proposal that commercial contracts should be subject to the same basic test of 'fairness and reasonableness' as is applicable to consumer contracts, seems not to take account of the basic differences that exist between consumer contracts and commercial contracts. On the other hand, proposal (8) does seem to recognize that there is less need for intervention in the case of commercial contracts than in the case of consumer contracts in that the list of indicatively unfair terms is much shorter.

The issues raised by this consultation paper are extremely difficult, particularly in their application to business-to-business contracts. There are two principal arguments that can be advanced in support of the proposal to extend the controls over such contracts. First, many small businesses are in a similar bargaining position to consumers and therefore stand in as much need of protection from unfair terms imposed on them by more powerful parties. Secondly, the Unfair Contract Terms Act has raised difficult jurisdictional issues as to what is, and what is not, an 'exclusion' or a 'limitation' clause (see pp. 496–498 above). The proposal radically to extend the range of terms subject to legislative control will largely, if not entirely, eliminate these threshold issues. On the other hand, the proposal to extend the range of controls will attract opposition on the ground that it will generate unnecessary uncertainty over the validity of terms that are in widespread use in commercial practice. It is argued that companies doing business in the international market-place simply do not need this level of protection. In this regard, it is important to note the question raised in proposal (5) of paragraph 16 in relation to the continuation of the exemption currently given to international business-to-business contracts and contracts subject to the law of a part of the UK only by the choice of the parties. Many international business transactions are governed by English law despite the fact that the parties to the contract have no other connection with England. Why should the terms agreed by these parties, most of whom are well able to look after themselves in the negotiating process, be subject to legislative control?

The balancing exercise that has to be conducted here is an extremely difficult one. The difficulties relate to the policy issues that are at stake and to the likely impact of these provisional proposals on the commercial community. How should the law strike the balance between freedom of contract, on the one hand, and fairness on the other hand? How much uncertainty will the Law Commissions' proposals generate in practice? The latter question, in particular, is extremely difficult to answer. Will parties in other jurisdictions stop contracting on English law if these proposals are implemented? Probably not, but they may become more hesitant if judges and regulators use their powers in a particularly interventionist manner. Legislators and courts must attempt to find a satisfactory accommodation between freedom of contract and regulation in the name of fairness. At present the Unfair Contract Terms Act 1977 strikes that balance in a rather haphazard fashion in that it only regulates certain types of contract term. The provisional proposals put forward by the Law Commissions have the great merit of providing a more coherent framework for the regulation of terms in commercial contracts that have not been individually negotiated. The question-mark over the proposals is whether or not they have gone too far, in particular whether the uncertainty which they may generate will outweigh the advantages created by the introduction of a unified regime for the regulation of unfair terms.

7. FURTHER READING

BRIGHT, S, 'Winning the Battle Against Unfair Contract Terms' (2000) 20 *Legal Studies* 331.

BRIGHT, S and BRIGHT, C, 'Unfair Terms in Land Contracts: Copy Out or Cop Out?' (1995) 111 *LQR* 655.

COLLINS, H, 'Good Faith in European Contract Law' (1994) 14 *OJLS* 229.

DEAN, M, 'Defining Unfair Terms in Consumer Contracts—Crystal Ball Gazing? *Director General of Fair Trading* v. *First National Bank plc*' (2002) 65 *MLR* 773.

HARTLEY, T, 'Five Forms of Uncertainty in European Community Law' [1996] *CLJ* 265.

LAW COMMISSION and SCOTTISH LAW COMMISSION, 'Unfair Terms in Contracts: A Joint Consultation Paper': Law Commission Consultation Paper No 166 and Scottish Law Commission Discussion Paper No 119. The report can be found at http://www.lawcom. gov.uk or http://www.scotlawcom.gov.uk.

MACDONALD, E, 'The Emperor's Old Clauses: Unincorporated Clauses, Misleading Terms and the Unfair Terms in Consumer Contracts Regulations' [1999] *CLJ* 413.

MACDONALD, E, 'Unifying Unfair Terms Legislation' (2004) 67 *MLR* 69.

TENREIRO, M, 'The Community Directive on Unfair Terms and National Legal Systems' (1995) 3 *European Review of Private Law* 273.

15

GOOD FAITH

1. CENTRAL ISSUES

1. While English contract law is influenced by notions of good faith, it does not, as yet, recognize the existence of a doctrine of good faith. In this respect English law stands out from many other legal systems in the world.

2. The fact that English law does not recognize a doctrine of good faith does not mean that the rules of contract law do not generally conform with the requirements of good faith. It would be surprising if the rules encouraged parties to behave in bad faith. The difference between English law and other legal systems is in many ways one of legal form rather than substance. Conclusions that would be reached in other legal systems by invocation of the doctrine of good faith can be reached in other ways by the English courts.

3. However now that the Unfair Terms in Consumer Contracts Regulations 1999 have introduced into English law a requirement of good faith in a significant number of consumer contracts, the question has arisen whether the influence of good faith will extend beyond the scope of the Regulations and percolate into other areas of contract law (particularly commercial contracts). In many ways there is no reason why it should. The Regulations only apply to contracts that fall within the scope of the Regulations. But there are signs of a change in both judicial and academic attitudes to good faith. Hostility or scepticism is being replaced by greater receptiveness. This being the case, it is not beyond the bounds of possibility that the English courts will in the not-too-distant future recognize the existence of a doctrine of good faith in English contract law.

4. It is therefore necessary to examine the arguments both for and against the introduction of a doctrine of good faith into English law and to consider the different forms that such a doctrine might assume.

2. INTRODUCTION

The Unfair Terms in Consumer Contracts Regulations 1999 have introduced a requirement of good faith into English law in relation to consumer contracts that fall within the scope of the Regulations (see pp. 504–521 above). When they were first enacted in 1994 this requirement excited a considerable amount of interest among English contract lawyers for the reason that English law did not then, and indeed still does not, recognize a doctrine of good faith in contract law. In the absence of such a general doctrine, how would the English courts interpret the good faith requirement in the Regulations? In the event, the courts do not seem to have experienced any particular difficulty in giving effect to the good faith requirement. They have recognized its European origins and have not sought to interpret it from a national perspective. At first instance in *Director General of Fair Trading* v. *First National Bank* [2000] 1

WLR 98, 109 Evans-Lombe J, after noting that the origin of the Regulations is a Council Directive, stated:

it is clear, therefore, that the words 'good faith' are not to be construed in the English sense of absence of dishonesty but rather in the continental civil law sense.

In the Court of Appeal Peter Gibson LJ stated ([2000] QB 672, 687) that ' "good faith" has a special meaning in the Regulations, having its conceptual roots in civil law systems'. Drawing on *Anson's Law of Contract* (27th edn, Oxford University Press, 1998), p. 293 he stated that the 'good faith' element:

seeks to promote fair and open dealing, and to prevent unfair surprise and the absence of real choice. A term to which the consumer's attention is not specifically drawn but which may operate in a way which the consumer might reasonably not expect and to his disadvantage may offend the requirement of good faith. Terms must be reasonably transparent and should not operate to defeat the reasonable expectations of the consumer. The consumer in choosing whether to enter into a contract should be put in a position where he can make an informed choice.

In the House of Lords ([2001] UKHL 52; [2002] 1 AC 481) both Lord Bingham (at para [17]) and Lord Steyn (at para [36]) recognized that good faith is an 'objective criterion' which imports the 'notion of fair and open dealing'. Two further points should be noted from the speech of Lord Bingham (which is extracted at p. 522 above). The first is his observation that the Member States of the European Union 'have no common concept of fairness or good faith'. This is an important point. While civil law systems do recognize a doctrine of good faith, their conception of good faith is not homogeneous. The second point that should be noted is Lord Bingham's remark that good faith is not a concept that is 'wholly unfamiliar to British lawyers'. Good faith had its 'champion' in Lord Mansfield in the eighteenth century and traces of his support for good faith are still to be found in English law (particularly in relation to insurance contracts). These two observations suggest that care should be taken when comparing English law with the law of our civilian counterparts. They suggest that the stark contrast that is often drawn between the common law and the civil law can be overstated both because the civil law systems are not themselves united, at least in relation to their conception of good faith, and because good faith is not in fact an unknown commodity to common lawyers.

Nevertheless, the requirement of good faith as enacted in the Regulations does present an important challenge to English lawyers and judges. It forces them to talk openly about good faith and, once they articulate a conception of good faith, the question will arise for consideration whether it should be confined to the Regulations or whether its influence should extend to contracts, such as commercial contracts, that are outside the scope of the Regulations. There is no immediate reason why the Regulations should lead to the recognition of a general doctrine of good faith. The Regulations, as we have seen (Chapter 14), are not of general application. They only apply to consumer contracts that fall within their scope. But this does not mean that they will not have a wider influence on the development of English law. Many commentators have argued that English law should recognize a doctrine of good faith and there are signs that current members of the judiciary are more receptive to the idea that good faith should have a role to play in English contract law. There is, however, a difficulty. That difficulty is the decision of the House of Lords in *Walford* v. *Miles* [1992] 2 AC 128 in which it was held that English law did not recognize the validity of an obligation to negotiate in good faith. Any recognition of a general doctrine of good faith would require re-consideration of the decision in *Walford* and that can only be done by the House of Lords.

We shall therefore start with the decision in *Walford*. It is necessary both to examine the reasons that led to the decision and also to explore its limits. Having done that we shall then consider the arguments that have been advanced in support of the refusal of English law to recognize the validity of a doctrine of good faith and then turn to the arguments that have been advanced by those who support the recognition of a doctrine of good faith.

3. WALFORD V. MILES

The leading English case on good faith is the decision of the House of Lords in *Walford* v. *Miles* [1992] 2 AC 128, where it was held that an obligation to negotiate in good faith is not valid.

Walford v. Miles

[1992] 2 AC 128, House of Lords

The defendants, Mr and Mrs Miles, were the owners of a company, PNM Laboratories Ltd. They decided to put the company up for sale in 1986. A third party offered £1.9 million for the business and its premises. The plaintiffs, the Walfords, entered into negotiations with the defendants in March 1987. The defendants were prepared to warrant that at the date of completion the cash resources in the company's bank account would not be less than £1 million and that the trading profits for the twelve months after completion would be not less than £300,000 before tax. On 12 March 1987 the parties reached agreement in principle for the sale of the business. On 18 March the plaintiffs sent a letter to the defendants which recorded an agreement reached between the parties the previous day. The letter recorded that the plaintiffs had promised to provide a comfort letter from their bank which confirmed that they were prepared to provide the finance of £2 million in order to enable the plaintiffs to acquire the company. In return the defendants agreed that if they received a letter from the bank to this effect by the end of the week they would terminate negotiations with any third party with a view to concluding an agreement with the plaintiffs. On 18 March the plaintiffs' bank duly provided a letter which stated that it had offered the plaintiffs loan facilities to enable them to acquire the company for £2 million. On 25 March the defendants confirmed that, subject to contract, they were prepared to sell the company to the plaintiffs for £2 million. On 30 March a letter was written to the plaintiffs on behalf of the defendants which stated that they had decided to sell the company to a third party.

The plaintiffs brought an action against the defendants for damages for breach of contract. They claimed damages of £1 million (on the basis that they had lost the opportunity to purchase a company worth £3 million for £2 million) and they also claimed damages for misrepresentation by the defendants in continuing to deal with third parties. The trial judge awarded the plaintiffs damages of £700 in respect of the misrepresentations made by the defendants. In relation to the claim for breach of contract, the trial judge ordered that damages for the alleged loss of opportunity be assessed but the Court of Appeal allowed the defendants' appeal. The plaintiffs appealed to the House of Lords where it was held that the agreement recorded in the defendants' letter of 18 March was unenforceable.

Lord Ackner

The Walfords relied upon an oral agreement, collateral to the negotiations which were proceeding, to purchase the company and the land it occupied 'subject to contract'. The consideration for this oral agreement was twofold—firstly the Walfords agreeing to continue the negotiations and not to withdraw and, secondly, their providing the comfort letter from their bankers in the terms requested.

For this consideration it was alleged in paragraph 5 of the statement of claim as follows:

'the first defendant on behalf of himself and the second defendant would terminate negotiations with any third party or consideration of any alternative with a view to concluding an agreement with the Plaintiffs and further that even if he received a satisfactory proposal from any third party prior to the close of business on 25 March 1987, he would not deal with that third party or give further consideration to any alternative.'

As thus pleaded, the agreement purported to be what is known as a 'lock-out' agreement, providing the plaintiffs with an exclusive opportunity to try and come to terms with the defendants, but without expressly providing any duration for such an opportunity.

For reasons which will become apparent hereafter, it was decided to amend this paragraph by the following addition:

'It was a term of the said collateral agreement necessarily to be implied to give business efficacy thereto that, so long as they continued to desire to sell the said property and shares, the first defendant on behalf of himself and the second defendant would continue to negotiate in good faith with the plaintiff.'

Thus the statement of claim alleged that, not only were the defendants 'locked-out' for some unspecified time from dealing with any third party, but were 'locked-in' to dealing with the plaintiffs, also for an unspecified period . . .

The validity of the agreement alleged in paragraph 5 of the statement of claim as amended

The justification for the implied term in paragraph 5 of the amended statement of claim was that in order to give the collateral agreement 'business efficacy', Mr Miles was obliged to 'continue to negotiate in good faith'. It was submitted to the Court of Appeal and initially to your Lordships that this collateral agreement could not be made to work, unless there was a positive duty imposed upon Mr Miles to negotiate. It was of course conceded that the agreement made no specific provision for the period it was to last. It was however contended, albeit not pleaded, that the obligation to negotiate would endure for a reasonable time, and that such time was the time which was reasonably necessary to reach a binding agreement. It was however accepted that such period of time would not end when negotiations had ceased, because all such negotiations were conducted expressly under the umbrella of 'subject to contract'. The agreement alleged would thus be valueless if the alleged obligation to negotiate ended when negotiations as to the terms of the 'subject to contract' agreement had ended, since at that stage the Miles would have been entitled at their whim to refuse to sign any contract.

Apart from the absence of any term as to the duration of the collateral agreement, it contained no provision for the Miles to determine the negotiations, albeit that such a provision was essential. It was contended by Mr Naughton [counsel for the plaintiffs] that a term was to be implied giving the Miles a right to determine the negotiations, but only if they had 'a proper reason'. However in order to determine whether a given reason was a proper one, he accepted that the test was not an objective one—would a hypothetical reasonable person consider the reason a reasonable one? The test was a subjective one— did the Miles honestly believe in the reason which they gave for the termination of the negotiations? Thus they could be quite irrational, so long as they behaved honestly.

Mr. Naughton accepted that as the law now stands and has stood for approaching 20 years, an agreement to negotiate is not recognised as an enforceable contract. This was first decided in terms in *Courtney & Fairbairn Ltd* v. *Tolaini Brothers (Hotels) Ltd* [1975] 1 WLR 297, where Lord Denning MR said, at pp. 301–302:

'If the law does not recognise a contract to enter into a contract (when there is a fundamental term yet to be agreed) it seems to me it cannot recognise a contract to negotiate. The reason is because it is too uncertain to have any binding force . . . It seems to me that a contract to negotiate, like a contract to enter into a contract, is not a contract known to the law . . . I think we must apply the general principle that where there is a fundamental matter left undecided and to be the subject of negotiation, there is no contract.'

In that case, at p. 302b, Lord Denning MR rejected as not well founded (and Lord Diplock expressly concurred with this rejection), the dictum of Lord Wright in *Hillas and Co Ltd* v. *Arcos Ltd* (1932) 147 LT 503, 515:

'There is then no bargain except to negotiate, and negotiations may be fruitless and end without any contract ensuing; yet even then, in strict theory, there is a contract (if there is good consideration) to negotiate, though in the event of repudiation by one party the damages may be nominal, unless a jury think that the opportunity to negotiate was of some appreciable value to the injured party.'

The decision in *Courtney's* case [1975] 1 WLR 297 was followed by the Court of Appeal in *Mallozzi* v. *Carapelli SpA* [1976] 1 Lloyd's Rep 407. In that case Kerr J [1975] 1 Lloyd's Rep 229 had applied the dictum of Lord Wright in *Hillas and Co Ltd* v. *Arcos Ltd*, 147 LT 503 before the *Courtney* case had been decided and held that there was an obligation on the parties at least to negotiate bona fide with a view to trying to reach an agreement. In that case a contract for the sale of grain contained a clause which provided:

'C.i.f. free out one safe port west coast Italy—excluding Genoa. First or second port to be agreed between sellers and buyers on the ship passing the Straits of Gibraltar.'

The Court of Appeal however held that it was impossible to say that the provision in the contract was legally enforceable, or that there was any legally binding obligation to negotiate.

The decision that an agreement to negotiate cannot constitute a legally enforceable contract has been followed at first instance in a number of relatively recent cases . . .

[he set out the cases and continued]

In the Court of Appeal and before your Lordships Mr Naughton submitted that the *Courtney* and the *Mallozzi* cases were distinguishable from the present case, because that which was referred to negotiation with a view to agreement in those cases was an existing difference between the parties. In the present case, so it was contended, by the end of the telephone conversation on 17 March there was no existing difference. Every point that had been raised for discussion had been agreed. However this submission overlooked that what had been 'agreed' on the telephone on 17 March was 'subject to contract'. Therefore the parties were still in negotiation even in relation to those matters. Further, there were many other matters which had still to be considered and agreed.

Before your Lordships it was sought to argue that the decision in *Courtney's* case [1975] 1 WLR 297 was wrong. Although the cases in the United States did not speak with one voice your Lordships' attention was drawn to the decision of the United States' Court of Appeal, Third Circuit, in *Channel Home Centers Division of Grace Retail Corporation* v. *Grossman* (1986) 795 F 2d 291 as being 'the clearest example' of the American cases in the appellants' favour. That case raised the issue whether an agreement to negotiate in good faith, if supported by consideration, is an enforceable contract. I do not find the decision of any assistance. While accepting that an agreement to agree is not an enforceable contract, the Court of Appeal appears to have proceeded on the basis that an agreement to negotiate in good faith is synonymous with an agreement to use best endeavours and as the latter is enforceable, so is the former. This appears to me, with respect, to be an unsustainable proposition. The reason why an agreement to negotiate, like an agreement to agree, is unenforceable, is simply because it lacks the necessary certainty. The same does not apply to an agreement to use best endeavours. This uncertainty is demonstrated in the instant case by the provision which it is said has to be implied in the agreement for the determination of the negotiations. How can a court be expected to decide whether, *subjectively*, a proper reason existed for the termination of negotiations? The answer suggested depends upon whether the negotiations have been determined 'in good faith'. However the concept of a duty to carry on negotiations in good faith is inherently repugnant to the adversarial position of the parties when involved in negotiations. Each party to the negotiations is entitled to pursue his (or her) own interest, so long as he avoids making misrepresentations. To advance that interest he must be entitled, if he thinks it appropriate, to threaten to withdraw from further negotiations or to withdraw in fact, in the hope that the opposite party may seek to reopen the negotiations by offering him improved terms. Mr Naughton, of course, accepts that the agreement upon which he relies does not contain a duty to complete the negotiations. But that still leaves the vital question—how is a vendor ever to know that he is entitled to withdraw from further negotiations? How is the court to police such an 'agreement'? A duty to negotiate in good faith is as unworkable in practice as it is inherently inconsistent with the position of a negotiating party. It is here that the uncertainty lies. In my judgment, while negotiations are in existence either party is entitled to withdraw from those negotiations, at any time and for any reason. There can be thus no obligation to continue to negotiate until there is a 'proper reason' to withdraw. Accordingly a bare agreement to negotiate has no legal content.

The validity of the agreement as originally pleaded in the statement of claim

Paragraph 5 of the statement of claim, as unamended, followed the terms of the oral agreement as recorded in the penultimate paragraph of the letter of 18 March. It alleged that for good consideration (and this certainly covered the provision by the plaintiffs of the 'comfort letter') Mr Miles on behalf of himself and his wife agreed that they:

> 'would terminate negotiations with any third party or consideration of any alternative with a view to concluding an agreement with the plaintiffs and, further, that even if he received the satisfactory proposal from any third party prior to the close of business on 20 March 1987 he would not deal with that third party or give further consideration to any alternative.'

Despite the insistence by Mr Naughton upon the implied term pleaded in the amendment involving the obligation to negotiate, Bingham LJ, in his dissenting judgment, considered that that obligation could be severed from the agreement. He concluded that the agreement, as originally pleaded was a valid and enforceable agreement and entitled the Walfords to recover whatever damages they could establish resulted in law from its repudiation.

Before considering the basis of Bingham LJ's judgment, I believe it helpful to make these observations about a so-called 'lock-out' agreement. There is clearly no reason in the English contract law why A, for good consideration, should not achieve an enforceable agreement whereby B agrees for a specified period of time not to negotiate with anyone except A in relation to the sale of his property. There are often good commercial reasons why A should desire to obtain such an agreement from B. B's property, which A contemplates purchasing, may be such as to require the expenditure of not inconsiderable time and money before A is in a position to assess what he is prepared to offer for its purchase or whether he wishes to make any offer at all. A may well consider that he is not prepared to run the risk of expending such time and money unless there is a worthwhile prospect, should he desire to make an offer to purchase, of B, not only then still owning the property, but of being prepared to consider his offer. A may wish to guard against the risk that, while he is investigating the wisdom of offering to buy B's property, B may have already disposed of it or, alternatively, may be so advanced in negotiations with a third party as to be unwilling or for all practical purposes unable, to negotiate with A. But I stress that this is a negative agreement—B by agreeing not to negotiate for this fixed period with a third party, locks himself out of such negotiations. He has in no legal sense locked himself *into* negotiations with A. What A has achieved is an exclusive opportunity, for a fixed period, to try and come to terms with B, an opportunity for which he has, unless he makes his agreement under seal, to give good consideration. I therefore cannot accept Mr Naughton's proposition, which was the essential reason for his amending paragraph 5 of the statement of claim by the addition of the implied term, that without a positive obligation on B to negotiate with A, the lock-out agreement would be futile.

The agreement alleged in paragraph 5 of the unamended statement of claim contains the essential characteristics of a basic valid lock-out agreement, save one. It does not specify for how long it is to last. Bingham LJ sought to cure this deficiency by holding that the obligation upon Mr Miles and his wife not to deal with other parties should continue to bind them 'for such time as is reasonable in all the circumstances'. He said:

> 'the time would end once the parties acting in good faith had found themselves unable to come to mutually acceptable terms ... the defendants could not ... bring the reasonable time to an end by procuring a bogus impasse, since that would involve a breach of the duty of reasonable good faith which parties such as these must, I think, be taken to owe to each other.'

However, as Bingham LJ recognised, such a duty, if it existed, would indirectly impose upon the Miles a duty to negotiate in good faith. Such a duty, for the reasons which I have given above, cannot be imposed. That it should have been thought necessary to assert such a duty helps to explain the reason behind the amendment to paragraph 5 and the insistence of Mr Naughton that without the implied term, the agreement, as originally pleaded, was unworkable—unworkable because there was no way of determining for how long the Miles were locked out from negotiating with any third party.

Thus even if, despite the way in which the Walfords' case was pleaded and argued, the severance favoured by Bingham LJ was permissible, the resultant agreement suffered from the same defect (although for different reasons), as the agreement contended for in the amended statement of claim, namely that it too lacked the necessary certainty, and was thus unenforceable.

I would accordingly dismiss this appeal with costs.

Lord Keith of Kinkel, Lord Goff of Chieveley, Lord Jauncey of Tullichettle, and **Lord Browne-Wilkinson** concurred.

COMMENTARY

There were two aspects to the agreement between the parties in *Walford*. The first was a lock-out agreement and the second was a lock-in agreement. What is the function of these agreements? Essentially, their function is to buy time in the context of a transaction such as a take-over bid. Parties often incur considerable expense when mounting a take-over bid and it may be important for them to buy a period of time in which to attempt to reach agreement or to put the deal together (in terms of putting the finance in place, etc). What is the difference between a lock-out and a lock-in agreement? The difference is that a lock-out agreement precludes a party from negotiating with any other party but does not actually require him to negotiate with the other party to the lock-out agreement, while a lock-in agreement does actually require the parties to negotiate with one another with a view to reaching agreement.

On the facts of *Walford* the House of Lords held that the lock-out agreement was unenforceable because it did not have a fixed time limit. While this was fatal to the lock-out agreement in *Walford* itself, it will not be an insuperable obstacle in other cases. It can be overcome by careful drafting. All that is required is the insertion into the lock-out agreement of a fixed point in time at which the agreement comes to an end. This was done in *Pitt* v. *PHH Asset Management Ltd* [1994] 1 WLR 327 (on which see further p. 169 above) where a fourteen day lock-out agreement was held to be enforceable. The conclusion of the House of Lords in relation to lock-in agreements is, however, more problematic because it was held that they are inherently unenforceable. Lord Ackner gave two reasons for his refusal to recognize the validity of an obligation to negotiate in good faith. The first was that such an agreement was, in his view, too uncertain to be enforced (see the discussion of the 'agreement to agree' cases at pp. 140–148 above). The second was that a duty to negotiate in good faith was 'inherently repugnant to the adversarial position of the parties involved in negotiations'. The imposition of such a duty was, in his opinion, 'inconsistent with the position of a negotiating party'.

It is the reasoning of the House of Lords in relation to the lock-in aspect of the agreement that is of primary significance for this chapter. The conclusion that English law does not recognize the validity of a duty to carry on negotiations in good faith makes it very difficult, if not impossible, for a court to recognize the existence of a doctrine of good faith in English contract law. Lord Ackner did not state expressly that in no circumstances would an English court recognize the validity of a duty of good faith, but the robust language in which he rejected the proposition that English law recognized a duty to negotiate in good faith suggests that he did not envisage any role for a doctrine of good faith in English law. However the fact that English law does not recognize the existence of a **doctrine** of good faith does not mean that good faith has no impact at all on English contract law. It does but only in the sense that it has an **influence** upon the formulation of the rules of contract law. In *First Energy (UK) Ltd* v. *Hungarian International Bank Ltd* [1993] 2 Lloyd's Rep 194 Steyn LJ stated (at p. 196) that:

a theme that runs through our law of contract is that the reasonable expectations of honest men must be protected. It is not a rule or a principle of law. It is the objective which has been and still is the principal moulding force of our law of contract. It affords no licence to a Judge to depart from binding precedent. On the other hand, if the prima facie solution to a problem runs counter to the reasonable expectations of honest men, this criterion sometimes requires a rigorous re-examination of the problem to ascertain whether the law does indeed compel demonstrable unfairness.

The limits of this principle should, however, be noted. In particular, it does not entitle a judge to 'depart from binding precedent'. The judge can only subject an argument that appears to run contrary to the reasonable expectations of honest men (or 'good faith') to 'rigorous re-examination'.

Before turning to the criticisms that have been levelled against *Walford*, it is worth noting one point which may suggest that *Walford* was on its facts correctly decided. That point relates to the measure of damages sought to be recovered by the plaintiffs. The plaintiffs brought a claim for damages of £1 million. The size of the claim might possibly have had an impact on the outcome of the case. In some legal systems a breach of an obligation to negotiate in good faith gives rise to a claim for damages, the aim of which is to entitle the claimant to recover the money wasted on the negotiations. The aim is not to give the claimant the profit which it would have made had the negotiations resulted in the conclusion of a profitable contract. In this connection it is worth noting that the plaintiffs in *Walford* recovered damages of £700 in respect of the misrepresentations made by the defendants. This sum may have represented the plaintiffs' wasted expenditure. To the extent that it did, the result of the case, albeit not the language in which it was expressed, may be consistent with that which would be reached in many other legal systems.

The decision in *Walford* has been criticized on three principal grounds. The first relates to the distinction drawn by Lord Ackner between an obligation to use 'best endeavours', which is enforceable, and an obligation to negotiate in 'good faith', which is not. Why is an obligation to use 'best endeavours' enforceable when an obligation to negotiate in 'good faith' is not? Lord Ackner does not answer this question yet he is clearly of the view that, not only is an obligation to use 'best endeavours' enforceable, but also that it is distinguishable from an obligation to negotiate in good faith. Case-law supports the validity of an obligation to use 'best endeavours' or 'reasonable endeavours' (see, for example, *Lambert* v. *HTV Cymru (Wales) Ltd, The Times*, 13 March 1998). However, such an obligation may not be enforceable in all cases. In *Phillips Petroleum Co UK Ltd* v. *Enron Europe Ltd*, unreported, Court of Appeal, 10 November 1996, Phillips LJ stated that 'it is not unknown on contracts of this kind for the parties to adopt a "best endeavours" or "reasonable endeavours" clause for the very reason that they wish to make clear a future co-operative intention without providing for an enforceable legal obligation which in negotiation one or other may have refused to agree'. While an obligation to use 'best endeavours' or 'reasonable endeavours' may not be enforceable in every case, it is probably accurate to state that it is generally valid and enforceable. Indeed, contracting parties who wish to avoid the pitfall of 'good faith' often resort to the language of 'best endeavours' or 'reasonable endeavours'. Commercial parties often negotiate with some vigour over the choice between 'best' and 'reasonable'. The case-law tends to suggest that the distinction between the two is one of degree rather than kind. 'Reasonable endeavours' clearly does not require a contractor to disregard its own commercial interests. In *Phillips Petroleum* Kennedy LJ stated that it was 'impossible to say that [the words "reasonable endeavours"] impose on the buyer a contractual obligation to disregard the financial effect on him, and indeed everything other than technical or operational practicality, when deciding how to discharge his obligation to use reasonable endeavours to agree' to a particular commissioning date. This being the case, a party subject to an obligation to use reasonable endeavours is entitled to put its own commercial interests at the forefront (contrast in this respect the dissenting judgment of Sir John Balcombe). It would therefore appear that an obligation to use 'reasonable endeavours' is not an onerous obligation and that it will impose a very limited obligation on the party subject to it; it may restrain bad faith actions but not much short of it. An obligation to use 'best endeavours' appears at first sight to impose a more onerous obligation but there is no conclusive authority on this point. It is not the equivalent of a guarantee. A party subject to an obligation to use 'best endeavours' can have regard to his own commercial interests, but probably must act reasonably and do what is 'commercially practicable' in the circumstances (*Rackham* v. *Peek Foods Ltd* [1990] BCLC 895). Given that the courts have had experience in giving effect to an obligation to use 'best endeavours' and 'reasonable endeavours' why do they refuse to give effect to an obligation to act in accordance with 'good faith'? No obvious answer to this question is apparent.

The second ground on which *Walford* has been criticized is that it does not impose a sanction on a party who negotiates in bad faith but does not make any misrepresentations. This point has been made by Lord Steyn, writing extra-judicially ('Contract

Law: Fulfilling the Reasonable Expectations of Honest Men' (1997) 113 *LQR* 433, 439), when he stated:

It is . . . surprising that the House of Lords in *Walford* v. *Miles* held that an express agreement that parties must negotiate in good faith is unenforceable. Lord Ackner observed that the concept of a duty to carry on negotiations in good faith is inherently repugnant to the adversarial position of the parties when involved in negotiations. As the Unidroit principles make clear it is obvious that a party is free to negotiate and is not liable for a failure to reach an agreement. On the other hand, where a party negotiates in bad faith not intending to reach agreement with the other party he is liable for losses caused to the other party. That is a line of reasoning not considered in *Walford* v. *Miles*. The result of the decision is even more curious when one takes into account that the House of Lords regarded a best endeavours undertaking as enforceable. If the issue were to arise again, with the benefit of fuller argument, I would hope that the concept of good faith would not be rejected out of hand.

The third criticism of *Walford* is that it takes away the parties' freedom of contract. If parties choose to assume an obligation to negotiate in good faith, why should the law deny the validity of their agreement? Contracting parties not infrequently make use of the language of good faith. Take the following two examples. The first is taken from a clause in a joint venture agreement which provides: 'the parties shall endeavour by good faith efforts to resolve by mutual agreement any dispute arising in connection with this Agreement'. Another clause that is often found in long-term contracts is a hardship clause (see pp. 439–440 above). An example of a hardship clause is the following:

Both Buyer and Seller recognise a long-term relationship requires mutual collaboration and assistance should either Buyer or Seller suffer hardship or unfairness. Both Buyer and Seller agree that they will make their best efforts to solve any problem due to any such circumstances in the spirit of mutual understanding and collaboration.

Are these clauses valid? No clear answer can be given to this question. *Walford* casts a shadow over their validity. Yet parties to long-term contracts frequently wish to preserve a degree of flexibility and co-operation so that they can adjust the contract to meet unforeseen contingencies. In order to do so they generally express themselves in co-operative language and this often entails use of the language of good faith. Where the parties expressly assume an obligation to negotiate in good faith or to act in good faith, the argument that such an obligation is too uncertain to be enforced does not trump the argument based on the parties' freedom of contract and the commercial advantages that follow from allowing parties to express their agreements in co-operative language. This being the case, it is suggested that the broad dicta in *Walford* cannot be supported and that English law should recognize an obligation to negotiate in good faith where it has been expressly (or, possibly, impliedly) assumed by the parties.

In a helpful case-note ('Promises to Negotiate in Good Faith' (2003) 119 *LQR* 357) Alan Berg supports this view and paints a more optimistic picture of the enforceability of promises to negotiate in good faith. He casts doubt on the validity of the reasoning of Lord Denning in *Courtney and Fairbairn Ltd* v. *Tolaini Brothers (Hotels) Ltd* [1975] 1 WLR 297 when Lord Denning suggested that no court could estimate the damages for a breach of a promise to negotiate in good faith because 'no one can tell whether the negotiations would be successful or would fall through; or, if successful, what the result would be'. Berg points out that the Court of Appeal in *Allied Maples Group Ltd* v. *Simmons & Simmons* [1995] 1 WLR 1602 concluded that damages can be awarded in a loss of a chance claim provided that the claimant can prove that there was a substantial chance that it would have been successful in the negotiations. This being the case, he suggests that a court 'should normally be able to assess damages for breach of a promise to negotiate which was intended to be legally binding and which was made in the context of a commercial deal the main terms of which the parties had agreed in principle'.

He then turns to the decision of the Privy Council in *Haines* v. *Carter* [2002] UKPC 49 and notes that the majority of their Lordships in that case concluded that an agreement drawn up as a result of an informal mediation which contained a clause which stated that the parties 'confirm that they have reached the agreement contained in this mediation in all good faith' was 'legally meaningful'. While he concedes that one cannot conclude that English law must recognize an obligation to *negotiate* in good faith from the existence of a good faith obligation in the context of *mediation*, he nevertheless proceeds to launch an assault on the decision of the House of Lords in *Walford* v. *Miles* [1992] 2 AC 128. He notes that the House of Lords failed adequately to consider the American case law on point (see in particular his discussion (at pp. 361–362) of the case of *Teachers Insurance and Annuity Association of America v Tribune Company* 670 F Supp 491 in which the court recognized the validity of an obligation to negotiate in good faith). He then concludes as follows (p. 362):

The fallacy of *Walford* v. *Miles* is the assumption that adversarial, competitive negotiation is the only type of negotiation. Another well-recognised type is negotiation as a problem-solving con- sensual process . . . In undertaking to negotiate in good faith, parties recognise that there are two types of negotiation—adversarial and problem-solving; and, by the expression 'in good faith', they make clear their choice of the latter. If businessmen have given such an undertaking, in terms clearly showing an intention that it should be legally binding, for the court to deny effect to the undertaking is not commercially fair.

Finally he turns to the issue of giving content to an agreement to negotiate in good faith. Drawing on a range of case-law he concludes (at p. 363) that it should be construed as 'an agreement to renounce purely adversarial negotiation' and in particular it should encompass:

(1) an obligation to commence negotiations and to have some minimum participation in them . . .

(2) an obligation to have an open mind in the sense of: (i) a willingness to consider such options for the resolution of the dispute as may be proposed by the other party, (ii) a willingness to give consideration to putting forward options for the resolution of the dispute . . .

(3) an obligation not to take advantage in the course of the negotiations of the known ignor- ance of the other party . . .

(4) an obligation not to withdraw from the negotiations without first giving a reason and a reasonable opportunity for the other party to respond; not to withdraw giving a reason which is untrue (e.g. 'I have received a higher offer', when none in fact has been received); and not to withdraw giving as the cause something which the withdrawing party knows is extremely

unreasonable (in approximately the *Wednesbury* sense), such as the other party's failure to agree a request which the withdrawing party knows that the other party could not reasonably be expected to have accepted.

4. GOOD FAITH: THE NEGATIVE VIEW

What are the reasons that have led the English courts to refuse to recognize the validity of a doctrine of good faith? The principal reasons have been summarized by Professor Brownsword in the following terms:

R Brownsword, *Contract Law: Themes for the Twenty First Century*

(Butterworths, 2000), paras 5.3–5.9

5.3 The arguments against adopting a general principle of good faith are well-rehearsed. At least five negative themes are recurrent.

5.4 First, it is objected that a doctrine of good faith, by requiring the parties to take into account the legitimate interests or expectations of one another, cuts against the essentially individualistic ethic of English contract law . . .

5.5 Secondly . . . it is said that good faith is a loose cannon in commercial contracts. Whilst everyone agrees that a doctrine of good faith represents some set of restrictions on the pursuit of self-interest, the objection is that it is not clear how far these restrictions go. In other words, good faith presupposes a set of moral standards against which contractors are to be judged, but it is not clear whose (or which) morality this is. Without a clear moral reference point, there is endless uncertainty about a number of critical questions—for example, about whether good faith requires only a clear conscience (subjective good faith) or whether it imports a standard of fair dealing independent of personal conscience (objective good faith); whether good faith applies to all phases of contracting, including pre-contractual conduct; whether good faith regulates only conduct (namely, how the parties conduct themselves during the formation of the contract and, subsequently, how they purport to rely on the contractual terms for performance, termination, and enforcement) or also the content (substance) of contracts (in other words, whether good faith regulates matters of procedure and process or also matters of contractual substance); whether a requirement of good faith adds anything to the regulation of bad faith (that is, whether good faith simply comprises so many instances of bad faith); whether good faith imposes both negative and positive requirements (covering, say, non-exploitation, non-opportunism, non-shirking as well as positive co-operation, support, and assistance); and so on.

5.6 Closely related to the second concern . . . there is a third concern, namely that a doctrine of good faith would call for difficult inquiries into contractors' states of mind. Often the literature on good faith emphasises that the question of whether a contractor has acted in good faith hinges on the contractor's reasons for action. This is not to be confused with matters of subjective honesty, but it does involve speculating about a contractor's reasons . . .

5.7 Fourthly, if good faith regulates matters of substance in a broad sense (including the remedial regime) (which it seems to do once we view it as a kind of implied term for co-operation), then this impinges on the autonomy of the contracting parties. Accordingly, even if the sceptics allow (if only for the sake of argument) that good faith may legitimately regulate the process of contracting, to ensure that agreement is genuine, they will argue that, once good faith trespasses on substance, it restricts the autonomy of the parties and is inconsistent with the fundamental philosophy of freedom of contract, with the idea that contract law should set a calculable framework for self-regulation by the parties. If we combine the thought that good faith imports an uncertain discretion with the thought that good faith challenges the autonomy of contracting parties, we have powerful reasons to be sceptical about the wisdom of adopting such a doctrine . . .

5.8 The final thread of the sceptical negative view is that a general doctrine of good faith goes wrong in failing to recognise that contracting contexts are not all alike. If contract law is to be sensitive to context, it cannot be right to apply a doctrine of good faith irrespective of context. As Michael Bridge has said:

> 'It is a fair reproach to English contract law that it unthinkingly treats the rules and principles of commodity sales, time and voyage charterparties and so on as though they could be applied without modification in very different contractual settings. Good faith theorists should avoid making the same sort of mistake. In my view, what is needed is an informed treatment of different areas of commercial contract and market activity.'

Bridge goes on to argue that it would be wholly inappropriate to introduce a doctrine of good faith into the commodities markets, where dealing is intrinsically competitive and where opportunistic behaviour is to be expected. This is not to say that, even in the commodities markets, good faith is totally rejected. However, insofar as notions of good faith are accepted, they are taken up in the standard terms of the trade and this, Bridge argues, is the way that the market best deals with new questions of fair dealing.

5.9 To sum up, the case against the adoption of a general principle of good faith is that English contract law is premised on adversarial self-interested dealing (rather than other-regarding good faith dealing); that good faith is a vague idea, threatening to import an uncertain discretion into English law; that the implementation of good faith doctrine would call for difficult inquiries into contracting parties' reasons in particular cases; that good faith represents a challenge to the autonomy of contracting parties; and that a general doctrine cannot be appropriate when contracting contexts vary so much— in particular, harking back to the first objection, a general doctrine of good faith would make little sense in those contracting contexts in which the participants regulate their dealings in a way that openly tolerates opportunism.

Some of these reasons can be identified in the speech of Lord Ackner in *Walford*, particularly the first one. The second and third objections are related in the sense that they are directed to the uncertainty that would be generated by the recognition of a doctrine of good faith. This is an objection that must be taken seriously. English lawyers tend to be hostile to broad, general principles. They are much more comfortable when reasoning incrementally and by analogy with the existing body of case-law (see E McKendrick, 'Good Faith: A Matter of Principle?' in A Forte (ed), *Good Faith in*

Contract and Property Law (Hart, 1999), p. 39). Thus the fact that there are individual rules of English contract law that are consistent with the requirements of a doctrine of good faith cannot necessarily be used to support the proposition that English law should recognize a general doctrine of good faith. Provided that the individual rules work, why abandon them in favour of a broad, general principle? The fifth objection noted by Professor Brownsword is an important one, in the sense that objections to a doctrine of good faith tend to come from particular contexts, most notably the commodity markets. It is true that these markets are competitive and that they may, to that extent, require special treatment. But not all contracts are concluded in such a competitive environment and, where they are not, the law should not necessarily be so hostile to the existence of an obligation to act in good faith.

5. GOOD FAITH: THE NEUTRAL VIEW

Professor Brownsword also identifies a neutral view of good faith. While ultimately the neutrality thesis inclines towards the negative view, it is nevertheless important to identify its existence because it is probably a view that is held by many English lawyers. Holders of the neutral view of good faith see nothing 'intrinsically objectionable about a good faith doctrine' (R Brownsword, *Contract Law: Themes for the Twenty First Century* (Butterworths, 2000), para 5.10) but point out that 'English law has its own doctrinal tools for achieving the results that are achieved via a good faith doctrine in other jurisdictions'. Professor Brownsword identifies two versions of the neutrality thesis and argues that they both incline towards scepticism for the following reasons:

R Brownsword, *Contract Law: Themes for the Twenty First Century*

(Butterworths, 2000), para. 5.11

The paradigm of neutrality holds: (i) that there is a strict equivalence between a general doctrine of good faith and the piecemeal provisions of English law that regulate fair dealing (we can call this 'the equivalence thesis') and (ii) that it makes no difference whether English law operates with a general doctrine or with piecemeal provisions (we can call this the 'indifference thesis'). Once we differentiate between the equivalence and the indifference theses, and once we distinguish between holding these theses in the abstract as against in the context of an ongoing legal system, it becomes apparent that the neutral view has a strong bias towards the negative view.

  One way in which this bias will reveal itself is if we imagine a neutral, who accepts both the equivalance and the indifference theses *in the abstract*, but who is now asked whether it would be sensible to replace the English piecemeal approach with a general doctrine of good faith. Clearly, since (ex hypothesi) nothing is to be gained by replacing one approach with the other, the neutral must take a negative view on this practical question (unless, for some bizarre reason, incurring transaction costs is judged to be a good thing).

  Suppose, though, the proposal is not to replace the English piecemeal approach with a general doctrine of good faith, but to supplement the former with the latter so that they would exist alongside one another in English law. What would the neutral say to this? Again, the neutral would have good reason to take the negative view. If, as the neutral believes, there is a strict equivalence between the piecemeal approach . . . and a general doctrine of good faith, it seems a needless duplication to supplement the former with the latter. Worse, the neutral might fear that specific doctrines, with well defined functions, are liable to become clouded once a general background standard is in play, for lawyers might be uncertain not only about whether they should found themselves on the traditional doctrines or the new general standard but also about where the boundaries of the traditional doctrines now lie.

As has been pointed out, a number of rules of English contract law can be rationalized as examples of the operation of a doctrine of good faith. Professor Clarke has pointed out ('The Common Law of Contract in 1993: Is There a General Doctrine of Good Faith?' (1993) 23 HKLJ 318, 319) that the 'foundations of a general rule of good faith can be discerned in the common law dust'. Thus far these individual instances have not been developed into a unified principle. The clearest example of the express recognition of a role for good faith is in relation to insurance contracts which are generally known as contracts of the utmost good faith or contracts '*uberrimae fidei*' (*Carter* v. *Boehm* (1766) 3 Burr 1905). It is here that Lord Mansfield has had his greatest influence, albeit that that influence is now largely confined to insurance contracts. Other examples can be found of rules which can be rationalized in terms of good faith: the rule which prevents a party snapping up a bargain which he knew was not intended by the other contracting party (*Hartog* v. *Colin and Shields* [1939] 3 All ER 566, p. 38 above), the limited duty of disclosure which English law recognizes (see, for example, *Notts Patent Brick and Tile Co* v. *Butler* (1866) 16 QBD 778, p. 675 below), the operation of the doctrines of promissory estoppel (*Central London Property Ltd* v. *High Trees House Ltd* [1947] KB 130, p. 239 above) and estoppel by convention (*Amalgamated Investment and Property Co* v. *Texas Commerce International Bank Ltd* [1982] QB 84, p. 248 above), and the willingness of the courts to imply terms into a contract in particular situations (see, for example, *Scally* v. *Southern Health and Social Services Board* [1992] 1 AC 294, p. 395 above). Yet the fact that individual rules can be rationalized in terms of good faith does not, for the reasons given above (p. 555), necessarily lead to the conclusion that English law should adopt a general doctrine of good faith. It can be taken as evidence of the fact that the law can operate satisfactorily with a series of individual rules and, this being the case, why 'cloud' their sphere of application by the adoption of a general principle of good faith?

Professor Brownsword also notes that holders of the neutral view point out that English law has its 'own doctrinal tools for achieving the results that are achieved via a good faith doctrine in other jurisdictions'. There is a considerable amount of truth in this claim. Other legal systems do use the doctrine of good faith to deal with issues which English law manages in other ways. One example of this is provided by the way in which the law responds to events which occur after the formation of the contract which have the effect of rendering performance of the contract impossible, illegal, or impracticable. English law has developed a distinct doctrine of frustration to deal with these issues, albeit that the doctrine operates within rather narrow limits (see further Chapter 23). German law, on the other hand, uses the doctrine of good faith to regulate these matters. It is not clear what English law stands to gain from abandoning a more focused doctrine such as frustration in favour of a potentially amorphous, multi-purpose doctrine of good faith. Of course, it could be argued that a doctrine of good faith might encourage English courts to develop a broader, more flexible doctrine of frustration but such a development would not necessarily be desirable and, in any event, that development could occur within the existing doctrine of frustration and does not have to wait for the creation of a doctrine of good faith. Alternatively, it could be argued that good faith is in fact the basis of the doctrine of frustration so that an analogy can indeed be drawn here between English law and German law. While it is true that English lawyers have never been able to identify the basis of the doctrine of frustration with any precision, it would not seem to be much of an advance to conclude that the foundation of the doctrine is good faith because such a conclusion would only serve to open up the debate as to what we mean by good faith. Further, it is not clear what practical consequences, if any, would follow from the conclusion that good faith was the basis of the doctrine of frustration. The disadvantages of rationalizing the doctrine of frustration in terms of good faith would therefore seem to outweigh its advantages.

6. GOOD FAITH: THE POSITIVE VIEW

Turning now to the positive side of the equation, what reasons can be advanced to support the recognition of a general doctrine of good faith in English law? Professor Brownsword has set out a positive case for a doctrine of good faith in the following terms:

R Brownsword, *Contract Law: Themes for the Twenty First Century*

(Butterworths, 2000), paras 5.15–5.19

5.15 First, to the extent, that English law already tries to regulate bad faith dealing, it may be argued that it would be more rational to address the problem directly (rather than indirectly) and openly (rather than covertly) by adopting a general principle of good faith . . .

5.16 Secondly, in the absence of a doctrine of good faith, it may be argued . . . that the law of contract is ill-equipped to achieve fair results, on occasion leaving judges 'unable to do justice at all' . . .

5.17 Thirdly, turning on its head the negative arguments against a general principle of good faith, it might be argued that, with such a principle, the courts are better equipped to respond to the varying expectations encountered in the many different contracting contexts—and, in particular, it might be argued that the courts are better able to detect co-operative dealing where it is taking place. Thus, the argument runs, if English contract law adopted a doctrine of good faith, it would pose questions of contractual interpretation and implication in a context, not only of background standards of fair dealing, but more immediately of the concrete expectations of the parties. Such concrete expectations would be based as much on the way that the parties related to one another (whether they dealt with one another in an adversarial or non-adversarial manner) as on the express provisions of the agreement. As a result, English law would recover the ability to give effect to the spirit of the deal in a way that prioritised the parties' own expectations . . .

5.18 Finally, it is arguable that the beneficial effects of a good faith doctrine go beyond (reactive) dispute-settlement, for a good faith contractual environment has the potential to give contracting parties greater security and, thus, greater flexibility about the ways in which they are prepared to do business . . . The more that contract doctrine provides a security against the risks of opportunism and exploitation to which co-operative dealing exposes a contractor, the more willing (other things being equal) contractors will be to deal in a way that optimises their interests (even though they are thereby exposed to risk). Thus, as good faith finds a place in the law, and as the contractual environment becomes more congenial to trust and risk-taking, it is possible that these reciprocal influences will work together to promote ever more co-operative thinking in both legal doctrine and contracting practice.

5.19 In sum, a good faith doctrine allows problems of bad faith to be addressed in a clean and direct fashion; it enables judges at all levels to deal in a coherent and an effective manner with cases of unfair dealing; it can bring the law much more closely into alignment with the protection of reasonable expectations (which, it must be recognised, vary from one contracting situation to another); and it can contribute to a culture of trust and co-operation that enhances the autonomy of contractors and that, on a larger scale, is an important feature of successful economies.

An illustration of the proposition that English law should attack issues of bad faith directly rather than indirectly can be provided by the law relating to the incorporation of onerous terms into a contract. As we have seen (pp. 360–363 above), the more onerous or unusual the contract term, the greater the steps that must be taken in order to draw the existence of the term to the attention of the other party before it can be incorporated into the contract. This rule is open to criticism on the ground that it fails to explain why it is that certain terms are more difficult to incorporate into a contract than others. A doctrine of good faith might more readily provide a foundation for the reluctance of the English courts to conclude that onerous or unusual terms have been incorporated into a contract (a point which was acknowledged by Bingham LJ in *Interfoto Picture Library Ltd* v. *Stiletto Visual Programmes Ltd* [1989] QB 433, 439, p. 352 above). But even if it is accepted that good faith provides a more secure conceptual foundation for the rule, this is not necessarily an argument in favour of a change in the present substantive law. Rather, it appears to be an argument that relates to the way in which we organize or classify the existing rules.

This, however, leads us on to the second argument noted by Professor Brownsword which goes beyond a reflection of the current state of the law and takes on a reforming role. This is a familiar theme in writings on good faith. Thus Professor Friedmann has argued ('Good Faith and Remedies for Breach of Contract' in J Beatson and D Friedmann (eds), *Good Faith and Fault in Contract Law* (Oxford University Press, 1995), pp. 399–400) that 'good faith may provide a unifying concept for a number of distinct rules dealt under different headings, and contribute to a greater consistency in the law by exerting pressure upon rules which are incompatible with the idea of good faith'. The first part of this quotation makes an organizational point, but the latter part goes beyond re-organization and assumes a reforming mission. The potential of good faith to bring about change and reform can also be illustrated by the experience of German law where it has been said that the 'doctrine of good faith has been used by the courts to create new causes of action where no cause of action existed in statutory law' (Ebke and Steinhauer, 'The Doctrine of Good Faith in German Contract Law' in Beatson and Friedmann (eds), *Good Faith and Fault in Contract Law*, p. 171).

So what impact might the doctrine of good faith have on the present rules of English contract law? An illustration of its potential role is provided by the decision of the Privy Council in *Union Eagle Ltd* v. *Golden Achievement Ltd* [1997] AC 514. Would this case be decided the same way if English law recognized a doctrine of good faith? The facts of the case are straightforward. The plaintiff purchaser agreed to buy a flat in Hong Kong and paid 10% of the purchase price (HK$420,000) as a deposit. The agreement specified the date, time, and place of completion and time was stated to be in every respect the essence of the agreement. Completion was to take place on or before 30 September 1991 and before 5 p.m. on that day. Clause 12 of the agreement stated that, if the purchaser failed to comply with any of the terms and conditions of the agreement, the vendor had the right to rescind the contract and forfeit the deposit. The plaintiff failed to complete by the stipulated time and tendered the purchase price ten minutes after the time for completion had passed. The vendors refused to accept late payment, rescinded the contract, and forfeited the deposit. The plaintiff refused to accept the defendants' decision to rescind the contract and brought an action seeking to have the contract specifically enforced. His attempt was unsuccessful. Lord Hoffmann stated (at p. 517) that the 'chief question' in the case was 'whether the court has, and should have exercised, an equitable power to absolve the purchaser from the contractual consequences of having been late and to decree specific performance'. The plaintiff argued that the court did have such an absolving power and that equity would intervene to restrain the enforcement of legal rights when it would be unconscionable to insist upon them. The plaintiff maintained that the element of unconscionability was present on the facts of this case: the breach was a slight one, but the consequences were, to say the least, drastic.

Lord Hoffmann rejected the plaintiff's argument and answered the chief question in the negative. He maintained that the principle invoked by the plaintiff was both contrary to the authorities and to the needs of the business world. In his view the parties should be able to know with certainty that the terms of the contract will be enforced. A jurisdiction to intervene in cases of 'unconscionability' would not produce such certainty. Indeed, the mere existence of a discretion to grant relief would be used as a negotiating tool by a defaulting purchaser. While equity will intervene to grant relief in cases of late payment of money due under a mortgage or rent due under a lease (see *G and C Kreglinger* v. *New Patagonia Meat and Cold Storage Co Ltd* [1914] AC 25, 35), this jurisdiction does not extend to the case of a contract for the sale of land. In a volatile market a vendor will want to know whether or not he can terminate the contract and deal with someone else. The law should, as far as possible, enable the vendor to know whether or not he is entitled to terminate.

The need for certainty was therefore paramount and the existence of a jurisdiction to grant relief in cases where it would be unconscionable for the vendor to exercise his right to rescind was rejected on the ground that it would detract from the need for a certain rule. This is an issue on which reasonable people will disagree and, indeed, courts in other jurisdictions take a broader view of the equitable jurisdiction to grant relief. A case can be made out that greater emphasis should have been placed upon the motive of the vendor in deciding to terminate and forfeit the deposit. Surely he behaved unreasonably in refusing to accept a ten-minute delay in receiving the purchase money? Should a vendor be entitled to act capriciously and terminate because, for example, he does not like the purchaser or because the market has moved in his favour and it has become economically advantageous for him to find a way out of the contract which he has concluded? The argument that he should not be so entitled is not without its merits. But the point of the illustration is not to debate these rival merits. It is to point out that the law cannot accept the validity of both arguments. It has to choose and English law has chosen to come down on the side of certainty.

Would the introduction of a doctrine of good faith alter that choice? This is one of the real difficulties that is likely to be caused by any recognition of a doctrine of good faith in English law, namely that it will, at least initially, enable parties to re-litigate points of law that were previously settled. In this particular case it is suggested that a doctrine of good faith should not have the effect of changing the result of the case. The result in *Union Eagle* is not as harsh as it appears at first sight. Lord Hoffmann left open the possibility that the purchaser may be able to obtain relief in extreme cases. In so far as the sum retained by the vendor exceeds a genuine pre-estimate of the loss or a reasonable deposit the court has 'a discretion to order repayment of all or part of the retained money'. And where the vendor has been unjustly enriched by improvements made at the purchaser's expense, the purchaser may have a personal restitutionary claim to recover any unjust enrichment which the vendor has obtained as a result of the work done prior to the termination. The advantage of these remedies is that they do not undermine the promotion of certainty. While the vendor should be able to know whether or not he is free to terminate the contract with the purchaser and deal with the land, it does not follow that the vendor should know with the same certainty whether or not he is entitled to retain any pre-payment made by the purchaser. In other words, while the vendor should have restored to him the 'freedom to deal with his land as he pleases', he should not have the same freedom in relation to the financial consequences of termination. This accommodation of the conflicting interests of the vendor and purchaser seems to be a reasonable one and it should not be disturbed by the creation of a doctrine of good faith.

One further argument in favour of a doctrine of good faith, which is not noted by Professor Brownsword, is that good faith is an integral component of the law of contract in other jurisdictions and is also a mandatory part of international restatements of contract law. In a global economy this is an increasingly important argument. But it is not conclusive. An examination of the role of good faith in other legal systems and in international restatements of contract law reveals that they embrace different conceptions of good faith. The most limited version of good faith is to be found in Article 7(1) of the Vienna Convention on Contracts for the International Sale of Goods which states that in the interpretation of the Convention regard is to be had, inter alia, to the 'observance of good faith in international trade'. The scope of this provision is the subject of considerable controversy. Some commentators take the view that this provision amounts to the imposition of a duty of good faith upon the parties, but this appears to ignore the fact that the role of good faith in Article 7(1) is confined to the 'interpretation' of the Convention. This being the case, it seems preferable to conclude that the Article is directed to the courts and not to the parties. In other words, the court, in the interpretation of the Convention, must have regard to the observance of good faith in international trade. A broader view of good faith is to be found in the United States of America where the Uniform Commercial Code states in s.1–203 that 'every contract or duty within this Act imposes an obligation of good faith in its performance or enforcement' and, for this purpose, s.1–201 defines good faith as 'honesty in fact in the conduct or transaction concerned'. This version of good faith is more extensive than that found in the Vienna Convention in that it is clearly directed to the parties. But it is limited in the sense that it is confined to performance and enforcement of the contract, and does not extend to the pre-contractual stage. Further, the recognition of a duty of good faith in the performance and enforcement of contracts in section 205 of the Restatement (Second) of Contracts has been hailed as a reflection of 'one of the truly major advances in American contract law during the past fifty years' (see R Summers, 'The General Duty of Good Faith—Its Recognition and Conceptualization' (1982) 67 *Cornell Law Review* 810). A still broader view of good faith is to be found in a range of national and international instruments. For example, Article 242 of the German BGB states that 'the debtor is bound to effect performance according to the requirements of good faith, giving consideration to common usage'; Article 1134 al. 3 of the French Civil Code states that contracts must be executed or performed in good faith; Article 1.7 of the Unidroit Principles of International Commercial Contracts states that 'each party must act in accordance with good faith and fair dealing in international trade'; and, finally, Article 1.106(1) of the Principles of European Contract Law states that 'in exercising his rights and performing his duties each party must act in accordance with good faith and fair dealing'. The comment to Article 1.7 of the Unidroit Principles states that 'good faith and fair dealing may be considered to be one of the fundamental ideas underlying the Principles'. The importance of 'good faith' to both the Unidroit Principles and the Principles of European Contract Law can be seen in the fact that both instruments state that the parties may not exclude or limit this duty. There is something of a paradox in the idea that one can have mandatory rules in non-binding Principles. Thus there may be no effective sanction in the event that the parties choose to incorporate the Principles into their contract but nevertheless decide to exclude good faith. But the fact that they are declared to be mandatory demonstrates the significance of good faith to both Principles.

7. GOOD FAITH: THE DIFFERENT MODELS

In practical terms it is likely that, sooner or later, English contract law will come to accept the existence of a doctrine of good faith. Since *Walford* v. *Miles* was decided there have been some signs of a more sympathetic judicial stance towards good faith (see *Timeload Ltd* v. *British Telecommunications plc* [1995] EMLR 459, *Philips Electronique Grand Publique SA* v. *British Sky Broadcasting Ltd* [1995] EMLR 472, *Balfour Beatty Civil Engineering Ltd* v. *Docklands Light Railway Ltd* (1996) 78 Build LR 42, 67–68, *Re Debtors (Nos 4449 and 4450 of 1998)* [1999] 1 All ER (Comm) 149, 157–158, *Haines* v. *Carter* [2002] UKPC 49, and *Pratt Contractors Ltd* v. *Transit New Zealand* [2003] UKPC 33). The decisive factor is likely to be the influence of other legal systems and international restatements of contract law. In a global economy England will not want to be seen to be standing almost alone. So it will have to climb on board. At that point debates about the desirability or otherwise of the recognition of a doctrine of good faith will become practically redundant. Instead the vital questions will become: (i) what does the doctrine mean? (ii) what impact will it have on the existing rules of contract law, such as the rule laid down in the *Union Eagle* case? and (iii) what is the scope of the doctrine, i.e., does it apply to pre-contractual dealings, performance, and enforcement of the contract or only to some of these? The incorporation of a doctrine of good faith is unlikely to be a painless one; it may act as an 'irritant' (G Teubner, 'Legal Irritants: Good Faith in British Law or How Unifying Law Ends Up in New Divergences' (1998) 61 *MLR* 11).

Three different possible models of good faith have been set out by Professor Brownsword in the following terms:

R Brownsword, *Contract Law: Themes for the Twenty First Century*

(Butterworths, 2000), paras 5.20–5.25

5.20 What are we to make of the arguments for and against adopting a general doctrine of good faith? This rather depends on which model of good faith we have in mind; for, essentially, there are three such models, each of which needs to be made explicit before either the negative or the positive arguments can be evaluated. The first model, 'a good faith requirement' . . . simply acts on the standards of fair dealing that are already recognised in a particular contracting context. These standards may or may not yet have crystallised into express terms commonly used, but they nevertheless represent the informal expectations of those who deal in the particular market. The second model, 'a good faith regime' . . . acts on the standards of fair dealing that are dictated by a critical morality of co-operation. Unlike the first model of good faith, this second model does not track recognised standards (although it may sometimes coincide with them) but, instead, tries to make the market in the sense of prescribing co-operative ground rules. The third model of good faith is what Michael Bridge evocatively calls 'visceral justice'. Here, judges react impressionistically to the merits of a situation and dispose of cases accordingly—all in the name of good faith. Unlike either the first or the second models of good faith, this third model is judicial licence.

5.21 On the face of it, judicial licence has little to recommend it; thus, the third model of good faith does not merit serious consideration. It follows that the only plausible choices are between the status quo and the first or second models of good faith. In this light we can reconsider the sceptical arguments, not with a view to cashing the positive case, but simply to observe where such arguments register against the adoption of a good requirement or a good faith regime.

5.22 To adopt a *good faith requirement* would be to make a relatively modest adjustment to the status quo. When, in a particular contracting context, the participants have a shared understanding of where the line is drawn between fair and unfair dealing—and, concomitantly, shared expectations about the conduct of fellow contractors—then the law simply adopts this shared view of fair dealing. On occasion, this might involve moving ahead of the standard form terms currently in circulation, but it would scarcely be vanguard law-making. Rather, a court operating with a good faith requirement would aspire simply to follow the shared sense of good faith in the particular contracting setting. Certainly, there would be no question, on this view, of good faith being employed to override clear expectations (such as those perhaps to be found in the Hong Kong property market that provided the background in the *Union Eagle* case); nor would good faith be employed to thicken up the relatively thin sense of fair dealing that one would expect to find in highly competitive contracting contexts.

What, though, would a good faith requirement signify (a) where a particular transaction does not readily fit within an identifiable context or (b) where there is an identifiable context, but there is no shared understanding of fair dealing? In cases of this kind, the law must do its best to construct the backcloth of expectation against which the parties dealt; for it cannot be emphasised too strongly that a good faith requirement is dedicated to articulating and respecting the parties' expectations. Where that backcloth involves a serious conflict of opinion about the requirements of fair dealing, the law must follow the 'better' view. Where there is a dominant view, there might well be a presumption in favour of protecting expectations that are reasonable relative to that view; where there is no such view, the law cannot avoid making an invidious choice and tie-breaking rules need to be agreed. This, however, hardly justifies condemning a good faith requirement out of hand.

5.23 The adoption of a *good faith regime* would be an altogether more ambitious, and controversial, move, inviting two lines of objection. First, if the regime is simply presented as one in which the parties should act with good faith towards one another, or should act in a way that evinces loyalty or respect for the legitimate interests of one another, the application of such an idea is likely to be unpredictable—at any rate, this is liable to be so in the absence of a developed background jurisprudence of good faith. Accordingly, if a good faith regime is not to be condemned as too vague and uncertain, it needs to be prescribed in a way that offers contractors clear guidance as to its principal requirements. Secondly, because a good faith regime is not designed to track recognised standards of fair dealing, it invites the objection that it is liable to override the intentions of the contractors. For example, it might be objected that it would be absurd to prescribe a good faith regime for a market as ruthlessly competitive as that in financial derivatives. Insofar as the good faith regime is simply a default position, which contractors can agree to displace (as, say, in commodities and derivative markets), the objection falls away—and this is largely the response to the problem. However, this assumes that a good faith regime is adopted as a facilitative measure when, to some extent, we might wish to adopt such a regime as a protective measure for the benefit of contractors who might otherwise be exploited. To bite this bullet, we certainly need to say that the good faith regime can only be displaced where there is compelling evidence of mutual agreement; and we might need to go a step further in some contracting contexts, saying that there can be no derogation from good faith.

5.24 If it is accepted that good faith as visceral justice is not an option, then where do the sceptical arguments hit home at the real targets? In the case of a *good faith requirement*, it has to be conceded that there might be some uncertainty (where the parties' expectations themselves are unclear, or where the case falls outside any recognised context); and, at various levels, there might be some difficulties of application. For example, there might be problematic inquiries into a party's reasons or motives where the recognised standards of fair dealing make such matters material. The scale of the problem should not be exaggerated, however. If there is a difficulty, it arises only where the setting in which the parties have contracted makes reasons and motives relevant factors—and, with a good faith requirement, such a setting is largely the product of the parties' own custom and practice. As for the (negative) arguments that good faith represents a challenge to the autonomy of the parties and that it does not allow for the heterogeneity of contracting contexts, these objections simply fall wide of the mark. Indeed, the positive view can turn these arguments round to claim that a good faith requirement is designed precisely to respect the autonomy of contractors—good faith, far from being a licence for visceral justice is a necessity if the contractual project is not to be eviscerated—and to do so in a way that is sensitive to the variations found in contracting contexts. In the case of a *good faith regime*, so long as this is simply the default position in contract law, there is no challenge to the parties' autonomy, and there is some allowance for variation from one contracting situation to another. However, under-prescription of such a regime will expose it to the charge of uncertainty, and, if the regime is one from which the parties are not permitted to contract-out, then the negative view strikes home unless the concept of autonomy is given a radical re-interpretation (such that, for instance, autonomous action is understood in a Kantian sense as rational moral action).

Finally, although both a good faith requirement and a good faith regime are less vulnerable to the negative view than that of good faith as visceral justice, does either have any response to the argument that English law should never be guided by anything but an adversarial ethic? The short answer is that this opening gambit on the part of the negative view is less an argument than a declaration of faith. However, if an answer is needed, supporters of good faith can point to the failure of the adversarial view to measure up to the expectations of contractors in non-adversarial contexts, as well as to the body of recent writing that holds that adversarial relations in contract are sometimes inimical to our individual and collective economic well-being.

5.25 There is an obvious symmetry in debates about the adoption of general principles of good faith and/or reasonableness. Those who advocate that English law (or, indeed, any modern common law system) should adopt such general principles must overcome two fundamental objections: first, that there is no reason why contracting should be subjected to moral constraints—it is simply a matter of parties pursuing their own self-interest; and, secondly, that if moral constraints are to be introduced, this is unworkable until agreement is reached about whose (or which) morality is to serve as the reference point for such doctrines. The first objection is easily dealt with. No one thinks that contract law is, or can be, morally neutral. Even the minimal constraints of the classical law reflect a certain kind of morality; and, even if contract is seen as essentially self-interested dealing, there are all sorts of moral (or public interest) constraints on the kind of agreements that the parties can enforce. The more serious objection, therefore, is the second one, that a moral reference point must be specified.

The second objection is undoubtedly well taken. Good faith, like reasonableness, only makes sense relative to some particular moral reference point. What is that reference point? The principal options are: (i) the standards of fair dealing recognised by the community of which the contractors are most proximately a part (as in a good faith requirement); and (ii) the standards of fair dealing and co-operation that would be prescribed by the best (i.e., most defensible) moral theory (as in a good faith regime). The former are the standards of a positive accepted morality; the latter are the standards of a critical (not necessarily accepted or recognised) morality. In the absence of philosopher kings, though, the latter option looks difficult to defend (either in terms of the practical legitimacy of judicial decisions or in terms of their theoretical justification).

Accordingly, what we might anticipate in the modern law of contract in England, in which the notion of reasonableness (if not that of good faith) abounds, is a tendency for doctrine to reflect the expectations associated with good practice (in both the field of consumer and commercial contracting). In other words, we might expect that English law will move towards the adoption of good faith as a requirement (in substance, if not in name).

This extract demonstrates that the choice that currently faces English law is not simply whether or not to recognize a doctrine of good faith. It must also consider the form which any doctrine of good faith is to assume. While English law can learn from other legal systems, these systems do not provide a uniform answer to the questions that are likely to arise. As Lord Bingham pointed out in *Director General of Fair Trading* v. *First National Bank* [2001] UKHL 52; [2002] 1 AC 481 para [17], Member States of the European Union 'have no common concept of . . . good faith'. This being the case, it is important that the English courts proceed cautiously and only recognize the existence of a doctrine of good faith where they are convinced that the harm that it will do (in terms of the uncertainty that it will bring) is outweighed by the advantages that will be brought by the open articulation of a doctrine of good faith.

8. FURTHER READING

BRIDGE, M, 'Does Anglo-Canadian Contract Law Need a Doctrine of Good Faith?' (1984) 9 *Canadian Business Law Journal* 385.

BROWNSWORD, R, ' "Good Faith in Contracts" Revisited' [1997] *CLP* 111.

CLARKE, M, 'The Common Law of Contract in 1993: Is There a General Doctrine of Good Faith?' (1993) 23 *HKLJ* 318.

McKENDRICK, E, 'Good Faith: A Matter of Principle?' in A Forte (ed), *Good Faith in Contract and Property Law* (Hart, 1999), p. 39.

NEILL, P, 'A Key to Lock-Out Agreements' (1992) 108 *LQR* 405.

STEYN, J, 'The Role of Good Faith and Fair Dealing in Contract Law: A Hair-Shirt Philosophy?' [1991] *Denning LJ* 131.

SUMMERS, R, 'The General Duty of Good Faith—Its Recognition and Conceptualization' (1982) 67 *Cornell Law Review* 810.

ZIMMERMANN, R and WHITTAKER, S (eds), *Good Faith in European Contract Law* (Cambridge University Press, 2000).

PART III

SETTING THE
CONTRACT ASIDE

16

MISTAKE

1. CENTRAL ISSUES

1. The law relating to mistake is in a state of flux. The law must strike a balance between the need for certainty in transactions (which demands a narrow doctrine of mistake) and the desire to protect a party who discovers that he has entered into an agreement which is radically different in nature from the transaction which he intended to enter (which may demand a more liberal doctrine of mistake).

2. The effect of a mistake may be to prevent the formation of a contract because, for example, the parties are at cross-purposes. But the fact that a mistake has been made is not sufficient, of itself, to set aside the contract. The reason for this is that the law adopts an objective rather than a subjective approach to agreement. One issue that has given rise to particular difficulty in the courts in this connection is the case in which the parties meet face to face and one party makes a mistake as to the identity or creditworthiness of his contracting party. The prima facie presumption which the law applies is that a person intends to contract with the person who is in front of him and the presumption will only be displaced on 'special facts'. This presumption does not apply to written contracts. Where the contract has been reduced to writing, the courts will not generally allow extrinsic evidence to be led where that evidence seeks to contradict the written terms of the contract.

3. Alternatively, the parties may reach agreement but that agreement is vitiated because the parties have made the same mistake. This is an example of 'common mistake'. Where the mistake relates to the existence, or possibly the identity, of the subject-matter of the contract, the mistake may suffice to set aside the contract where the mistake is sufficiently fundamental. More difficult is the case where the mistake is one that relates to the quality of the subject-matter of the contract. In the latter case the courts tend to be reluctant to allow a party to invoke mistake because they do not wish to provide an easy escape route for a party who has entered into a bad bargain. A mistake as to quality will only suffice to set aside a contract in the most extreme of cases.

4. The role of equity in mistake cases has proved to be extremely controversial. Lord Denning sought to enlarge the role for equity and he developed a wider, more flexible doctrine of mistake in equity than that which existed at common law. However, this wider doctrine of mistake in equity has been disapproved by the Court of Appeal, at least in the context of common mistake. The latter decision is one of the central cases in this chapter.

5. A mistake may be made when recording the agreement rather than when making it. In such a case the court may be able to rectify the document so that it is brought into conformity with the agreement that the parties actually made. But rectification is only available within narrow limits.

6. A party may not be able to understand the document that he has signed. In such a case he may be able to invoke the defence of *non est factum*. A claimant who wishes to invoke this defence must show that he was permanently or temporarily unable, through no fault of his own, to have without explanation any real understanding of the document he has signed and he must show that there was a real or substantial difference between the document which he signed and the document which he believed that he was signing.

2. INTRODUCTION

This chapter and the subsequent chapters in this Part consider the different grounds on which a contract may be set aside by the courts. In some of the cases a contract is initially formed between the parties but it is then set aside by the court, whereas in other cases the conclusion of the court is that, as a result of some defect or impediment, the parties were never actually in a contractual relationship. The words 'set aside' may not naturally encompass the latter case because it can be argued that in these cases there is no contract to 'set aside'. Such cases are nevertheless included within this Part on the basis that their exclusion would involve the creation of an artificial barrier between cases that actually have significant common elements. For example, in some cases of mistake, the effect of the mistake is to prevent a contract from coming into existence, whereas in other cases a contract does initially come into being but it is later set aside by the court on the ground of mistake. Rather than separate out the mistake cases into different chapters, they have been brought together in this chapter so that we can examine in a comprehensive manner the effect of a mistake on the validity of a contract.

The grounds on which a contract can be set aside which are considered in these chapters are mistake (the subject of the present chapter), misrepresentation (Chapter 17), duress (Chapter 18), undue influence (Chapter 19), inequality of bargaining power or unconscionability (Chapter 20), incapacity (Chapter 21), illegality or public policy (Chapter 22), and frustration (Chapter 23). There are obvious links between some of these grounds. Mistake and misrepresentation are closely linked in the sense that the law of misrepresentation is, in many ways, the law of induced mistake. Common mistake and frustration are closely linked in that they are both concerned with the situation where some common assumption shared by the parties and which is fundamental to the contract turns out to be unfounded. The difference between common mistake and frustration is a matter of timing. In the case of mistake, the common assumption is unfounded at the moment of entry into the contract, whereas in the case of frustration the common assumption is valid when the contract is concluded but turns out to be unfounded in the light of events that occur subsequent to the making of the contract. Duress, undue influence, and inequality of bargaining power (or unconscionability) are all linked in the sense that they are all concerned with the fairness of the bargain that has been concluded between the parties (although it can be argued that their focus is upon different types of fairness, in that some doctrines, such as duress, are concerned with procedural unfairness, while others, such as unconscionability, demonstrate a concern for the substantive fairness of the terms of the contract).

3. MISTAKE: THE DIFFICULTIES

The law relating to the impact of a mistake on the validity of a contract is in a mess. There are a number of reasons for this. The first is that the terminology used by the courts and commentators is inconsistent. The principal terms employed to describe the different types of mistake are unilateral, mutual, and common mistakes. 'Unilateral' mistake refers to the case in which one party only has made a mistake. 'Common' mistake refers to the case where the mistake is 'common', that is to say, the parties both made the same mistake. 'Mutual' mistake is more difficult. The word 'mutual' clearly refers to the case where both parties are mistaken but it is not clear whether the mistake must be the same one or not. It could apply to the case where both parties are mistaken but they make different mistakes (so that they are at cross-purposes) or it could apply to the case where both parties are mistaken but they make the same mistake. In the latter case they do reach agreement but their agreement is vitiated by a mistake. Given the difficulties that surround the word 'mutual' it will not be used in this chapter unless it appears (as it does appear) in the judgments which are extracted.

The second problem relates to the jurisdictional divide between law and equity. The last fifty years of the twentieth century saw the development of a wider doctrine of mistake in equity (at least in cases of common mistake) under the guiding hand of Lord Denning. This development was brought to a halt in 2002 with the decision of the Court of Appeal in *Great Peace Shipping Ltd* v. *Tsavliris Salvage (International) Ltd* [2002] EWCA Civ 1407; [2003] QB 679 where it was held that this wider doctrine of mistake in equity was inconsistent with the decision of the House of Lords in *Bell* v. *Lever Bros Ltd* [1932] AC 161. While the existence of a wider doctrine of mistake in equity has been denied in the context of common mistake, it is not the case that the role of equity has disappeared entirely in cases of mistake. It retains a role but it can no longer be used to undermine decisions that are binding on the courts, such as decisions of the House of Lords.

The third problem is that mistakes can take different forms. The different types of mistake were recently summarized by the Court of Appeal in *Great Peace Shipping Ltd* v. *Tsavliris Salvage (International) Ltd* [2002] EWCA Civ 1407; [2003] QB 679 in the following terms:

28. A mistake can be simply defined as an erroneous belief. Mistakes have relevance in the law of contract in a number of different circumstances. They may prevent the mutuality of agreement that is necessary for the formation of a contract. In order for two parties to conclude a contract binding in law each must agree with the other the terms of the contract. Whether two parties have entered into a contract in this way must be judged objectively, having regard to all the material facts. It may be that each party mistakenly believes that he has entered into such a contract in circumstances where an objective appraisal of the facts reveals that no agreement has been reached as to the terms of the contract. Such a case was *Raffles* v. *Wichelhaus* (1864) 2 H & C 906. The parties believed that they had entered into a contract for the purchase and sale of a cargo of cotton to arrive 'ex Peerless from Bombay'. That term was capable of applying equally to a cargo of cotton on two different ships, each called 'Peerless' and each having sailed from Bombay, one in [October] and one in December. The court accepted that parol evidence could be adduced to prove which shipment the parties had intended to be the subject of the contract. Had one party intended the October shipment and the other the December shipment, the agreement necessary for a binding contract would have been absent.

29.   *Raffles* v. *Wichelhaus* was a case of latent ambiguity. More commonly an objective appraisal of the negotiations between the parties may disclose that they were at cross-purposes, so that no agreement was ever reached. In such a case there will be a mutual mistake in that each party will erroneously believe that the other had agreed to his terms. This case is not concerned with the kind of mistake that prevents the formation of agreement.

30.   Another type of mistake is that where the parties erroneously spell out their contract in terms which do not give effect to an antecedent agreement that they have reached. Such a mistake can result in rectification of the contract. Again, this case is not concerned with that type of mistake.

31.   In the present case the parties were agreed as to the express terms of the contract. The defendants agreed that the '*Cape Providence*' would deviate towards the '*Great Peace*' and, on reaching her, escort her so as to be on hand to save the lives of her crew, should she founder. The contractual services would terminate when the salvage tug came up with the casualty. The mistake relied upon by the defendants is as to an assumption that they claim underlay the terms expressly agreed. This was that the '*Great Peace*' was within a few hours sailing of the '*Cape Providence*'. They contend that this mistake was fundamental in that it would take the '*Great Peace*' about 39 hours to reach a position where she could render the services which were the object of the contractual adventure.

32.   Thus what we are here concerned with is an allegation of a common mistaken assumption of fact which renders the service that will be provided if the contract is performed in accordance with its terms something different from the performance that the parties contemplated. This is the type of mistake which fell to be considered in *Bell* v. *Lever Brothers*. We shall describe it as 'common mistake', although it is often alternatively described as 'mutual mistake'.

Paragraphs 28 and 29 refer to mistakes which prevent the formation of a contract. Such mistakes are discussed in section 4. Paragraph 30 refers to mistakes made when reducing an agreement to writing. The remedy of rectification is discussed in section 7. Paragraphs 31 and 32 describe the situation in which the contracting parties enter into a contract while labouring under the same mistake. Here we can see the terminological confusion in that these mistakes are either given the label 'common' or 'mutual' mistake. The Court of Appeal in *Great Peace* preferred the label 'common' and that is the label that will be used in this chapter. 'Common' mistakes are discussed in sections 5 and 6. This list of the different types of mistake is not, however, exhaustive. A mistake may be induced by a false statement of fact made by the other party to the contract. These mistakes are discussed in Chapter 17 under the heading 'misrepresentation'. A mistake may also arise from the failure or inability of one party to understand the nature of the document which he has signed. This gives rise to a defence known as *non est factum*. This defence is discussed in section 8. *Non est factum* cases can be described as mistake cases, although they also shade into incapacity.

The fourth problem is the clash of policies that underpins this area of the law. On the one hand, we can see in some of the judgments a desire to promote certainty in commercial transactions. This policy points in favour of a narrow doctrine of mistake so that parties cannot invoke the doctrine in order to escape from what has turned out to be a bad bargain. Two policies point in the opposite direction, however. The first is a concern for fairness. In some of the cases it is clear that the judges were of the view that it was 'unfair' to hold the mistaken party to the terms of his bargain once he realized the true position. The second policy is a concern to uphold the integrity of the agreement that has been reached by the parties. Where the facts demonstrate that the parties did not actually reach agreement as a result of a mistake made by one or both of the parties then it can be argued that there is no agreement, or no contract, for the courts to enforce. The latter policy is, however, tempered in its application to English law as a result of the courts' adoption of an objective rather than a subjective approach to the existence of an agreement. Nevertheless, an emphasis on the need for '*consensus ad idem*' can be seen in some of the judgments.

The fifth problem relates to the range of factors to which the courts have regard. A number of difficult issues arise here. First, how serious must a mistake be before it suffices to set aside a contract or prevent the conclusion of a contract? Secondly, does it matter that the defendant knew of the mistake or was responsible for inducing the mistake in the mind of the claimant? Thirdly, what is the role of fault? Should the court weigh the relative blameworthiness of the parties before deciding the remedial consequences of the occurrence of a mistake? The variety of factors taken into account by the courts make it very difficult to stabilize this area of law.

Finally, mistake can have different remedial consequences. Some mistakes render a contract 'void', while others render it 'voidable'. A contract which is void is a nullity in the sense that it is set aside for all purposes and so generally produces no legal effects at all. A voidable contract, on the other hand, is valid in the sense that it is valid until the right to set it aside has been exercised. In other cases the effect of mistake is simply to deny the claimant a particular remedy, such as specific performance (see *Denny* v. *Hancock* (1870) LR 6 Ch App 1, p. 42 above). As we shall see, the difference between 'void' and 'voidable' can be crucial in relation to the rights of third parties (pp. 613–614 below).

4. MISTAKES AND FORMATION

The effect of a mistake may be to prevent the parties from reaching agreement. At this point it is necessary to recall that the courts, when deciding whether or not parties have reached agreement, adopt an objective rather than a subjective approach (see generally Chapter 2). Many of the cases discussed in Chapter 2 are, in fact, mistake cases. So the mere fact that a party has made a mistake is not enough in itself to entitle a court to conclude that the parties have not in fact entered into a contract. The effect of the adoption of an objective approach to the existence of an agreement is to narrow the scope of the doctrine of mistake. But it does not rule it out completely. Cases can be found in which the courts have concluded that the effect of the mistake was to prevent the formation of a contract between the parties.

First, a court may decide that no contract has been concluded where one party knows that the other is labouring under a mistake in relation to the terms of the agreement and fails to inform that other party of the mistake (see *Smith* v. *Hughes* (1871) LR 6 QB 597, p. 26 above). The Court of Appeal in *Smith* distinguished between the case where the plaintiff believed that the defendant thought he was buying old oats and the case where the plaintiff believed that the defendant thought he was buying oats which the plaintiff had promised were old. In the former case the defendant is liable to take the oats and must take the consequences of his own mistake, whereas in the latter he is not liable to take the oats on the ground that the parties were at cross-purposes as to the terms of the contract. Similarly, a party will not be entitled to 'snap up' an offer which he knew was not intended by the party who made the offer (see *Hartog* v. *Colin & Shields* [1939] 3 All ER 566, p. 38 above). There is also a wider category of case in which one party was at fault in failing to notice that the other party's offer contained a mistake or he was himself responsible for inducing that mistake in the other party. In such a case the party at fault may not be entitled to hold the other party to the terms of his offer (*Scriven Brothers & Co* v. *Hindley & Co* [1913] 3 KB 564, p. 45 above).

Secondly, a court may conclude that the terms of the offer and acceptance suffer from a latent ambiguity such that the parties cannot be said to have reached agreement. Such was the case in *Raffles* v. *Wichelhaus* (1864) 2 H & C 906, a case discussed by the Court of Appeal in paragraph [28] of its judgment in *Great Peace* (above). The Court of Appeal in *Great Peace* adopted the traditional understanding of *Raffles*, namely that the offer and the acceptance suffered from a 'latent ambiguity' in that, while both parties referred to the vessel 'Peerless', the buyers apparently intended to refer to the October sailing but the sellers intended to refer to the December sailing. *Raffles* is, however, an obscure case (see AWB Simpson, 'The Beauty of Obscurity: *Raffles* v. *Wichelhaus and Busch* (1864)' in *Leading Cases in the Common Law* (Oxford University Press, 1995), p. 135). The court was not asked to decide whether or not the agreement was binding on the parties. The case came before the court on a point of pleading and the issue before the court was whether or not the fact that there were two vessels of the same name was *capable* of providing the defendant buyers with a defence to the sellers' action for the price. The court concluded that it was so capable and accordingly entered judgment for the defendants. No reasons were given by the judges in support of their conclusion; they simply stated that 'there must be judgment for the defendants'. In the absence of any further reasoning it is difficult to know quite what to make of the case. Its role as a leading case is obviously not due to the significance of the judgment. Rather, its fame is attributable to the use made of it by academic writers in the late nineteenth century in the context of debates about the basis of contract law. Writers, such as Pollock, who maintained that there could be no contract without true consent, seized on *Raffles* in support of this theory, whereas writers who believed that the law was not concerned with the actual state of mind of the parties were strongly critical of the decision. But the decision of the court does not merit the significance that has subsequently been attributed to it. Professor Simpson concludes ('The Beauty of Obscurity: *Raffles* v. *Wichelhaus and Busch* (1864)' in *Leading Cases in the Common Law* (Oxford University Press, 1995), pp. 138–139):

In terms of contract law the judges seem to have thought that, once it appeared that there were two ships sailing from Bombay which answered the contractual description, and no way of telling which of the two was intended, the contract was latently ambiguous. Consequently, a jury should have been allowed to hear the evidence and decide whether the parties meant the same ship, and if so which, or different ships . . .

What would have happened if there had been no demurrer, and the case had gone to a jury? Obviously if the jury thought the agreement related to the October ship, the plaintiff would lose; if the December ship was meant, then the plaintiff would win. But what if the jury thought that the parties meant different ships, or that there was just no way of telling to which the contract related? The judge would then have the tricky task of directing them as to what consequence followed, as a matter of law, from this. But in *Raffles* v. *Wichelhaus* there was no need for the judges to reach any conclusion on what a suitable direction would have been. It was enough that the pleas, if true, *might* furnish an answer to the claim, for if so the plaintiff's legal objection to it failed. So, 'There must be judgement for the defendant'.

Suppose, however, that the case had gone to a jury, and that it had emerged at a trial that one party meant one ship, and the other the other, and there was just no way of telling which was the ship to which the *contract* related—whatever that means. What then was to be done? This has all the seductive fascination of a conundrum, and it has subsequently captured the imagination of generations of scholars and students of the law of contract. Consequently they have tried, with some desperation, to prise an answer to the conundrum out of the texts of the reports of the case.

Fortunately for the subsequent uses to which the case has been put, there is no clear answer to be found there. Mellish and Cohen [counsel for the buyers] certainly argued that, if one party meant one ship and the other party the other, there would be no contract at all; they used the expression *consensus ad idem*, agreement as to the same thing, and their argument was that, without such *consensus*, there would be no contract at all. They would know the story behind the case, and as reputable counsel would not seek to mislead the court; common sense suggests that this was indeed the situation. For some reason, which nobody explained, there had been a complete misunderstanding. Their argument was stopped at this point by the judges, but we cannot conclude from this that the judges all agreed with counsel, and even if the parties did mean different ships there might be some reason for preferring one person's understanding to the other. For example, the misunderstanding could have been the fault of one rather than the other. There was no need for the judges to grapple with this conundrum. So, although they may well have agreed with counsel, there is just no way of being sure of this. There is indeed a limit to what can be deduced from any text, or treated as consistent with it. We can, perhaps, sensibly pore over the text of *Macbeth* to determine the number of Lady Macbeth's children, but it is a waste of time to attempt to discover from it whether Macbeth suffered from athlete's foot.

While *Raffles* v. *Wichelhaus* is always discussed in the books and is cited in the courts by way of illustration, it has rarely been followed by the courts. The reason for this is that it is simply too obscure. As Chitty concludes (H Beale (ed), *Chitty on Contracts*

(29th edn, Sweet & Maxwell, 2004), para 5-060), in a modern case of similar character 'it is unlikely that the facts proved would be so sparse as not to give some ground for adopting one interpretation of the contract rather than the other'.

The third case in which a mistake may prevent the formation of a contract is where there has been a mistake as to the identity of the party with whom the contract was made. The standard case is one in which one party, A, enters into a contract with B in the mistaken belief that B is in fact C. A's mistake is typically induced by B's fraudulent representation that he is C. Does A's mistake render the contract between himself and B void (or does it merely render the contract voidable on the ground that it was entered into as a result of B's fraudulent misrepresentation, on which see p. 614 below)? This question does not admit of a simple answer. In large part, the answer depends on whether the contract between A and B has been reduced to writing. Where the contract has been reduced to writing, and the written agreement states that the parties to it are A and C, then the authorities suggest that the contract between A and B may indeed be void for mistake. But where the contract between A and B has been made orally in face-to-face dealings then A is unlikely to succeed in his claim that the contract is void for mistake because, in such a case, the law presumes that A intended to contract with the person who was actually in front of him (i.e. B) and that presumption is very difficult to rebut. Not everyone is convinced that the law should distinguish in this way between written contracts and oral contracts but the distinction was recently affirmed by the House of Lords, albeit by a bare majority, in *Shogun Finance Ltd* v. *Hudson* [2003] UKHL 62; [2004] 1 AC 919.

Given the controversy which surrounds *Shogun*, it is important to set the case in its context. There are a number of important cases which precede *Shogun* and extracts from these cases can be found on the web site which supports this book. Most of these cases are discussed in *Shogun* itself but it may be helpful to describe five of them in outline by way of introduction to *Shogun*.

The first is the decision of the House of Lords in *Cundy* v. *Lindsay* (1878) 3 App Cas 459. One Alfred Blenkarn wrote to the plaintiff linen manufacturers and ordered from them goods which included cambric handkerchiefs. The letters were written from 37 Wood Street where Blenkarn had hired a room (although he pretended to have a warehouse there). He signed his letters in such a way as to make it appear as if they had come from Blenkiron & Co. The plaintiffs knew of a respectable firm of W Blenkiron & Co which carried on business in Wood Street, albeit they did so at number 123 and not number 37. The plaintiffs sent the goods on credit to 'Messrs Blenkiron & Co., 37 Wood Street, Cheapside' where they were received by Blenkarn. Blenkarn then sold 250 dozen cambric handkerchiefs to Messrs Cundy, the defendants, who bought them in good faith. The House of Lords held that no contract had been concluded between the plaintiffs and Blenkarn for the sale of the handkerchiefs. The contract was void for mistake and, this being the case, Blenkarn had no title to the goods which he could confer on the defendants. The defendants were therefore liable to the plaintiffs for the value of the goods.

However it was not the case that every mistake made by a party to a written contract rendered the contract void. In this respect it is useful to contrast *Cundy* with *King's Norton Metal Co* v. *Edridge Merrett & Co Ltd* (1897) 14 TLR 98, where a rogue assumed the name of Hallam & Co and the plaintiffs dealt with him, through written correspondence, on this basis. The rogue, Wallis, received goods from the plaintiffs on credit and sold them on to the defendants who bought them in good faith. When Wallis' fraud was discovered the plaintiffs brought an action in conversion[1] against the defendants and relied upon the decision in *Cundy*. Their claim failed. The Court of Appeal held that the plaintiffs intended to contract with the writer of the letters. A L Smith LJ stated (at p.99) that:

[I]f it could have been shown that there was a separate entity called Hallam & Co, and another entity called Wallis then the case might have come within the decision in *Cundy* v. *Lindsay*.

But on the facts there was 'only one entity, trading it might be under an alias, and there was a contract by which the property passed to' the person who wrote the letters. The difference between *Cundy* and *King's Norton* would appear to be that the plaintiffs in *Cundy* knew of the entity with which they intended to deal, Blenkiron & Co, and that entity was different from the identity of the author of the letters, whereas the plaintiffs in *King's Norton* intended to deal with the author of the letters but were under the mistaken impression that the author was a company called Hallam & Co when in fact it was Wallis.

The remaining three cases concern contracts concluded between parties who dealt with one another face-to-face. The first of these cases is the decision of Horridge J in *Phillips* v. *Brooks* [1919] 2 KB 243. A man entered the plaintiff's shop and asked to see some pearls and some rings. He selected pearls priced at £2,550 and a ring priced at £450. He then produced a cheque book and wrote out a cheque for £3,000. As he signed the cheque he said 'You see who I am, I am Sir George Bullough' and he gave an address in St James' Square. The plaintiff knew of the existence of Sir George Bullough. Having checked the address given in a directory he said to the man 'Would you like to take the articles with you?' The man replied: 'You had better have the cheque cleared first, but I should like to take the ring as it is my wife's birthday tomorrow.' The plaintiff let him have the ring. The cheque was subsequently dishonoured. The person in the shop was not Sir George Bullough but a man called North who was later convicted of obtaining the ring by false pretences. Prior to his arrest North pledged the ring with the defendants who, in good faith and without notice, advanced £350 to him. The plaintiff brought an action for the value of the ring against the defendants. The claim failed. The contract between the plaintiff and North was not void for mistake because the plaintiff was found to have had the intention to deal with the person in front of him.

Phillips was distinguished by the Court of Appeal in the second case, *Ingram* v. *Little* [1961] 1 QB 31. The plaintiffs, two sisters, advertised their car for sale at £725 or nearest offer. They were visited by a man who said that his name was Mr Hutchinson. They agreed a price of £717 for the car. The man produced his cheque book but one of the sisters said that they would not take a cheque. He then said that he was Mr P G M

---

[1] Conversion was defined by Atkin J in *Lancashire and Yorkshire Railway* v. *MacNicholl* (1919) 88 LJKB 601 as 'dealing with goods in a manner inconsistent with the rights of the true owner . . . provided . . . there is an intention on the part of the defendant in so doing to deny the owner's right or to assert a right which is inconsistent with the owner's right.'

Hutchinson, that he lived at Stanstead House, Stanstead Road, Caterham and that he had business interests in Guildford. On being told this, one of the sisters went to a nearby Post Office and checked in a telephone directory that there was such a person living at this address. The sisters then decided that they could take a cheque. The cheque was later dishonoured but not before the rogue had sold the car to the defendant car dealer who bought the car in all good faith. The plaintiffs brought an action in conversion against the defendant and sought to recover the car or its value. The Court of Appeal held, by a majority, that the contract between the plaintiffs and the rogue was void for mistake, with the result that the plaintiffs remained the owners of the car and were entitled to bring an action in conversion against the defendant.

Ingram was further distinguished by the Court of Appeal in the third case, *Lewis* v. *Averay* [1972] 1 QB 198. The plaintiff advertised his Austin Cooper for sale for £450 in a newspaper. He was visited by a man who claimed to be Richard Greene, a well-known actor who played Robin Hood in a television series. The man agreed to pay £450 for the car and wrote a cheque for £450, signing it 'R A Green'. He wanted to take the car away immediately but the plaintiff was not willing to allow him to take the car away until the cheque had cleared. The man repeated that he wanted to take the car immediately and so the plaintiff asked him if he had anything to prove that he was Richard Greene. The man then produced a pass from Pinewood Studios, which had an official stamp on it. The pass bore the name 'Richard A Green' and included a photograph of the man. The plaintiff was satisfied at this and gave him the car, the log book, and the MOT certificate in return for a cheque for £450. The cheque turned out to be worthless, as it had been stolen. When the true situation came to light, the plaintiff brought an action in conversion against Mr Averay. The Court of Appeal held that Mr Averay was not liable to the plaintiff. The contract between the plaintiff and the rogue was held to be voidable with the result that Mr Averay acquired a good title to the car because he purchased it in good faith and for value before the plaintiff acted to set aside the contract with the rogue.

Two principal difficulties can be discerned in these cases. The first lies in the relationship between the cases involving written contracts and those involving oral contracts. The mistake made by the plaintiffs in *Cundy* v. *Lindsay* was very similar to the mistake made by the plaintiff in *Lewis* v. *Averay* (in the sense that both plaintiffs entered into the contract with one party in the belief that he was another), yet the mistake in *Cundy* rendered the contract void, whereas the mistake in *Lewis* did not. The second is that the relationship between the cases involving parties dealing with one another face-to-face is not an easy one; in particular, it is no easy task to distinguish between *Ingram* and *Lewis*. The first of these difficulties was confronted directly by the House of Lords in *Shogun*, whereas the latter was only examined incidentally. It is now time to turn to the decision of the House of Lords in *Shogun*.

Shogun Finance Ltd v. Hudson

[2003] UKHL 62; [2004] 1 AC 919, House of Lords

A motor dealer agreed a price to sell a car to a fraudster, R, who produced a stolen driving licence as proof of his identity (the driving licence belonged to a Mr Durlabh Patel). The dealer faxed a copy of this driving licence to the claimant finance company, together with a copy of a draft hire-purchase agreement which the fraudster had signed using the name of Mr Patel. The claimant ran a credit check on Mr Patel and, the check being satisfactory, it approved the sale. The fraudster paid a 10 per cent deposit in order to be able to take the car away. The next day he sold the car to the defendant who bought it from him in all good faith. When the true position came to light the claimant brought a claim in conversion against the defendant. The House of Lords, by a majority, held that the claimant was entitled to delivery up of the vehicle or damages for its conversion.

The defendant claimed that he acquired good title to the car as a result of the operation of section 27 of the Hire Purchase Act 1964 (which is set out at para [43] below). The issue to be decided in relation to this claim was whether or not the fraudster, R, was a 'debtor' under a 'hire-purchase agreement' within the meaning of the section. It was held that he was not. He was not named as the debtor under the hire purchase agreement and so was not the debtor under that agreement. Nor was evidence admissible to contradict the express terms of the agreement and to show that it was not the written agreement with Mr Patel but an agreement with R. There was no meeting of minds between the claimant and R so there was no contract between the parties, nor was there a bailment of the car by the claimant to R.

Lord Nicholls of Birkenhead (dissenting)

1. My Lords, this appeal raises a difficult problem about the effect of fraudulent misrepresentation on the formation of a contract. If a crook (C) fraudulently represents to the owner of goods (O) that he is another identifiable person (X) and on that basis O parts with goods to C by way of sale, is there in law a contract between O and C? Does the answer to this question differ according to whether O and C communicated face to face, or by correspondence, or over the telephone, or by e-mail? The law on cases involving this type of fraudulent conduct, euphemistically described as cases of 'mistaken identity', is notoriously unsatisfactory. The reported decisions are few in number and they are not reconcilable. In the present case Sedley LJ said the law has tied itself into a Gordian knot. Brooke LJ said the law is in a 'sorry condition' which only Parliament or your Lordships' House can remedy: see [2002] QB 834, 847, 855.

2. Two features are usually present when cases of this type come before the court. The first feature is that a seller of goods is concerned with the creditworthiness of the proposed buyer. The seller wants to be sure he will be paid for the goods he is handing over. Here the common law seems to have drawn a distinction between two kinds of fraudulent misrepresentation. The common law distinguished between a case (1) where a crook fraudulently asserts he is creditworthy and a case (2) where a crook fraudulently asserts he is someone else known to be creditworthy. One might suppose there is no difference of substance between these two cases. These are merely two ways a crook may assert a spurious creditworthiness. But, historically, the law seems to have been otherwise. In case (1), when the seller parts with his goods he does so pursuant to a *voidable* contract. This is said to be a case of mistake as to a person's attributes. In case (2), in some circumstances but not all, the seller has been held to part with his goods pursuant to a *void* contract, that is, no contract at all. This is said to be a case of mistake as to a person's identity.

3. The second feature usually present in cases of this type is that the crook then sells the goods to an innocent third party. This feature explains why the distinction between a voidable and a void contract matters. Having fraudulently acquired the goods from their owner, the crook then sells them to an unsuspecting third party. The rights of this innocent third party may depend upon the nice distinction between a voidable contract and a void contract. In case (1), where the crook fraudulently misrepresents his own financial standing, the loss falls on the unfortunate owner of the goods who was tricked into parting with them to the crook. *King's Norton Metal Co Ltd v. Edridge, Merrett and Co Ltd* (1897) 14 TLR 98 is an instance of this. There the crook ordered some brass rivet wire from a metal manufacturer. On his writing paper he represented he was in business in a big way, running a large factory and having several depots and agencies. The manufacturer, King's Norton, supplied the goods sought but was not paid. King's Norton was unable to recover the goods or their value from the third party to whom the crook subsequently sold them.

4. This outcome is to be contrasted with case (2), where the crook asserts he is someone else. In such a case the loss sometimes, but not always, falls upon the unfortunate third party who also was a victim of the crook's trickery. The third party paid for the goods in all honesty, but he must return them to their original owner or pay their value. Thus in *Cundy v. Lindsay* (1878) 3 App Cas 459 Cundy had to pay the linen manufacturers Lindsay & Co for the 250 dozen cambric handkerchiefs the crook acquired from Lindsay by fraudulently representing he was the respectable business firm of Blenkiron.

5. The distinction in outcome thus drawn between these two kinds of fraudulent misrepresentation, one as to 'attributes' and the other as to 'identity', is unconvincing. It has been described as a reproach to the law. To a considerable extent the distinction has now been eroded. *Cundy v. Lindsay* (1878) 3 App Cas 459 was decided over a century ago, and since then there have been significant developments in this area of case law. Unfortunately these developments have left the law in a state of disarray. The question before the House on this appeal is whether this distinction, so far as it remains, should still be regarded as good law.

FRAUDULENT MISREPRESENTATION AND INTENTION

6. The question before the House calls first for some analysis of the effect of fraudulent misrepresentation on a person's intention to enter into a contract. A contract of sale and purchase, like any other contract, requires agreement, a meeting of minds. The seller must intend, or appear to intend, to sell the goods, and the buyer must intend, or appear to intend, to buy the goods on the agreed terms. The presence of fraud does not negative the existence of such an intention on the part of either party. Fraud does not negative intention. A person's intention is a state of mind. Fraud does not negative a state of mind. The existence of a fraudulent misrepresentation means that a person's intention is formed on a false basis—a basis, moreover, known by the other party to be false. The effect of fraud is to negative legal rights or obligations otherwise flowing from an intention to enter into a contract. Fraud enables the victim of the fraud to decline to proceed with a contract into which, by reason of the fraudulent misrepresentation, he was induced to enter, and he has a claim for damages for any loss he may suffer. But fraud does not have the consequence of negativing the formation of a contract.

7. Similarly with consent . . . in this context fraud does not 'vitiate' consent. Professor

Glanville Williams rightly said that the maxim 'fraud vitiates consent' is thoroughly misleading: see 23 Canadian Bar Review (1945) 271, 291–292. Whether a person has consented to this or that is a question of fact. Fraud does not negative a fact. As with intention, so with consent, fraud negatives legal rights or obligations otherwise flowing from a person having given his consent to a particular happening. Fraud can destroy legal rights; it cannot destroy facts.

8. This distinction, between negativing intention or consent and negativing the rights otherwise flowing from intention or consent, is important. It explains why the law treats a contract induced by fraud as voidable, not void. The necessary coincidence of intention, or consensus ad idem, may exist even where the intention and consent of the victim were induced by fraud. An intention thus induced is regarded by the law as sufficient to found a contract, even though the victim may repudiate the contract as soon as he discovers the fraud.

9. Thus, if a person is induced to buy goods by a fraudulent misrepresentation that the goods are sound, in law a contract to buy the goods is created even though the goods are different from the goods the buyer intends to buy and even though the other party knows this. The fact that the goods are different in quality from the goods which, as the crook knows, the victim wishes to buy is not regarded by the law as meaning that no contract was made . . .

11. The position is similar if the owner of goods agrees to sell them to a prospective buyer on the basis of a fraudulent assertion of his financial reliability. The buyer's fraudulent statement about himself does not negative the seller's intention to sell the goods to the crook on the agreed terms. Nor does it negative the fact that, when the crook acquired the goods from the seller, he did so with the seller's consent. The fraud means only that the seller's contractual intention was formed, and his consent to hand over the goods obtained, on a fraud-induced basis. There is a contract, but it may be avoided on discovery of the fraud.

[he set out the facts of the case and continued]

FRAUDULENT MISREPRESENTATION: FACE TO FACE DEALINGS

18. I can now turn to the effect of a fraudulent misrepresentation made by a person about his identity. In cases of face to face dealings the law, as declared by the preponderance of authority, is tolerably clear. The owner of the goods believes the person in front of him is X, and in that belief he contracts with the person in front of him. The fraudulent misrepresentation by the crook C regarding his identity no more negatives O's intention to contract with C than, in my earlier example, the seller's misrepresentation about the identity of the proffered goods negatives the buyer's intention to buy the proffered goods. In each case the relevant intention is to be ascertained by looking at the position which, as a result of the misrepresentation, the other party believes to exist. On that footing there is consensus, in the relevant respect, between the parties. O believes C, the person in front of him, to be X *and he deals with C in that belief*. The fraud entitles O to avoid the contract, but it does not negative the formation of a contract with C.

19.   Thus in *Phillips* v. *Brooks Ltd* [1919] 2 KB 243 Horridge J held that the jeweller contracted to sell the ring to the crook in the shop who represented he was Sir George Bullough. The jeweller had heard of Sir George Bullough and checked he lived at the address given. The jeweller gave evidence he had no intention of making any contract with any person other than Sir George Bullough. Horridge J rightly analysed what that meant by adopting a passage from the judgment of Morton CJ in the Massachusetts case of *Edmunds* v. *Merchants' Despatch Transportation Co* 135 Mass 283, 283–284:

'The fact that the seller was induced to sell by fraud of the buyer made the sale void-able, not void. He could not have supposed that he was selling to any other person; his intention was to sell to the person present, and identified by sight and hearing; *it does not defeat the sale because the buyer assumed a false name, or practised any other deceit to induce the vendor to sell.*' (emphasis added)

20.   In *Ingram* v. *Little* [1961] 1 QB 31, another 'face to face' case, the majority of the Court of Appeal reached the contrary conclusion. A crook responded to an advertisement for a car and fraudulently introduced himself as P G M Hutchinson living at a stated address in Caterham. The owners of the car checked in the telephone directory there was a person of that name living at that address. The crook paid for the car with a cheque made out in his assumed name. Sellers and Pearce L JJ held that the owners did not enter into a contract with the crook. Sellers LJ considered the offer made by the owners of the car was capable of acceptance only by the honest P G M Hutchinson of Caterham. Pearce LJ considered that whether a party was not contracting with the physical person to whom he uttered the offer but with another individual whom he believed to be the person physically present was a question of fact.

21.   Devlin LJ disagreed. He pointed out, at p 65:

'If Miss Ingram had been asked whether she intended to contract with the man in the room or with P G M Hutchinson, the question could have no meaning for her, since she believed them both to be one and the same. The reasonable man of the law—if he stood in Miss Ingram's shoes—could not give any better answer.'

22.   Devlin LJ suggested, at p 66, that to deal with this difficulty the law should formulate a presumption that a person is intending to contract with the person to whom he is actually addressing the words of contract. That should be the starting point. Devlin LJ stressed that the presumption could not be rebutted by piling up evidence that Miss Ingram would never have contracted with the person in front of her unless she had thought him to be P G M Hutchinson. There was everything to show that Miss Ingram would never have accepted the crook's offer if she had known the truth, but nothing to rebut 'the ordinary presumption' that she was addressing her acceptance, 'in law as well as in fact', to the person to whom she was speaking.

23.   The majority decision in *Ingram* v. *Little* [1961] 1 QB 31 was doubted when the same problem came before a differently constituted Court of Appeal ten years later, in *Lewis* v. *Averay* [1972] 1 QB 198. The court comprised Lord Denning MR, Phillimore and Megaw LJJ. In the *Lewis* case a crook represented orally to the owner of a car that he was a well known actor, Richard Greene. Lord Denning MR, characteristically, enunciated a broad proposition: mistake as to identity renders an apparent contract voidable, not void. In this type of case the third party knew nothing of what passed between the seller and the rogue and he acted with complete circumspection and in good faith. It was the seller who let the rogue have the goods and thus enabled him to commit the fraud on the third party. Phillimore LJ, at p 208, considered there was nothing to displace the prima facie presumption that the car owner was dealing with the person present in the flat, the rogue: 'this case really is on all fours with *Phillips* v. *Brooks* which has been good law for over 50 years'. Megaw LJ, at p 209, based his decision on the ground that the mistake of the owner of the car went no further than a mistake as to the attributes of the rogue: it 'was simply a mistake as to the creditworthiness of the man who was there present and who described himself as Mr Green'.

24. Sometimes in these cases the transaction is evidenced in writing. This can make no difference to the outcome. Clearly there is no magic attaching to a misrepresentation made in writing rather than by word of mouth. The presence or absence of a written record of a transaction negotiated face to face, such as an invoice or receipt made out in favour of Sir George Bullough [the name assumed by the rogue in *Phillips* v. *Brooks Ltd*], with or without his address, or a cheque ostensibly signed by Sir George Bullough, is neither here nor there for present purposes. Writings such as these are no more than stark contemporary confirmation that the misrepresentation was made and that the seller believed it.

25. Similarly the contractual position between O and C must be the same if they meet face to face and the deal arranged by them is later embodied in a written agreement. This further step does not relevantly change the legal position. The written contract is expressed to be made between O and X. But C, the person with whom O was physically dealing, asserted he was X, and O believed him. So the description of C in the contract as X was a fraudulent misnomer. C used a false name and address, and the written contract is to be construed accordingly.

FRAUDULENT MISREPRESENTATION: DEALING BY CORRESPONDENCE

26. But what of the case where a fraudulent misrepresentation is made in writing but O and C do not meet each other? C writes to O saying he is X and the deal proceeds on that basis. O parts with his goods to the person with whom he is in fact dealing, namely, C, in the belief he is X.

27. At first sight it seems counter-intuitive to speak of a contract between O and C in cases of this type. It seems counter-intuitive because on its face a contract in writing or in correspondence expressed to be made between O and X is inconsistent, agency apart, with its being a contract between O and C. But this intuitive response is not a sound guide if it leaves out of account, as all too easily it may, the vitally important underlying fraudulent misrepresentation. In his dealings with O the crook C represented he was X, and O proceeded to *deal with him* (C) in that belief.

28. When this feature is kept in mind it readily becomes apparent that in principle cases of this type are no different from cases of face to face dealings. The existence of physical immediacy in one case, and the absence of it in the other, is immaterial. The physical immediacy of C in face to face cases tends to emphasise O's intention to deal with the person in front of him. With other forms of communication such as the telephone or correspondence this physical immediacy is lacking. But in each case, whatever the mode of communication, what matters is *whether* O agreed to sell his goods to the person with whom he was dealing, not *why* he did so or under what name. The latter is relevant to remedy, not to formation of a contract.

29.   In this regard mention must be made of reasoning sometimes advanced here, along the lines that the identity of the person to whom a written offer is made is a question solely of construction of the document. The offer, it is said, is made to the person identified in the document and no one else. A written offer made by O to X is not capable of acceptance by C. Hence, it is said that, whatever the position in face to face dealings, in cases of written contracts or contracts made by correspondence there can be no contract between O and C, contradicting as this would the terms of the document.

30.   The flaw in this reasoning is that it begs the crucial question: to whom was the offer made? The reasoning assumes this is a straightforward case of an offer made to the person named. Indeed the person named is X. But that is only part of the picture. O believes that X, the person to whom he is writing and to whom he addressed the offer, is one and the same as the person with whom he is dealing. In fact he is not dealing with X. He is dealing with C. O's misapprehension in this regard, induced by C's fraud, is no different in principle from a case where C's misrepresentation is made orally in the course of the face to face meeting. The legal problem is the same in both cases. The presence or absence of writing does not constitute a principled ground of distinction.

31.   Thus, when Lindsay & Co supplied linen handkerchiefs in response to a written order they were under a misapprehension regarding the identity of the person placing the order in the same way as the jeweller in the shop was under a misapprehension regarding the identity of his customer ('I am Sir George Bullough') in *Phillips* v. *Brooks Ltd* [1919] 2 KB 243. If the approach adopted in *Phillips* v. *Brooks* is correct, Lindsay's misapprehension no more negatived the formation of a contract with the person placing the written order for handkerchiefs than did the like misapprehension by the jeweller in the case of *Phillips* v. *Brooks*. The jeweller parted with his ring to the customer in his shop. Lindsay parted with their linen by sending it to the address supplied by the crook. On what terms? The answer must be, on the terms agreed between Lindsay and the person with whom they were dealing. That was a contract Lindsay could enforce, should they have wished, or repudiate on the grounds of fraudulent misrepresentation.

32.   In *Cundy* v. *Lindsay* (1878) 3 App Cas 459 the House reached the contrary conclusion. The reasoning of all their Lordships was to the same effect. Lord Cairns LC encapsulated this reasoning, at p 465:

> 'Of [the crook Blenkarn] [Lindsay] knew nothing, and of him they never thought. With him they never intended to deal. Their minds never, even for an instant of time, rested upon him, and as between him and them there was no consensus of mind which could lead to any arrangement or any contract whatever.'

Lord Hatherley and Lord Penzance left open what the position would be had the crook come into personal contact with Lindsay.

THE CHOICE

33. In my view this decision is not reconcilable with *Phillips* v. *Brooks Ltd* [1919] 2 KB 243 or with *Lewis* v. *Averay* [1972] 1 QB 198 or with the starting point 'presumption' formulated by Devlin LJ in *Ingram* v. *Little* [1961] 1 QB 31. The legal principle applicable in these cases cannot sensibly differ according to whether the transaction is negotiated face to face, or by letter, or by fax, or by e-mail, or over the telephone or by video link or video telephone. Typically today a purchaser pays for goods with a credit or debit card. He produces the card in person in a shop or provides details of the card over the telephone or by e-mail or by fax. When a credit or debit card is fraudulently misused in this way the essence of the transaction is the same in each case. It does not differ from one means of communication to the next. The essence of the transaction in each case is that the owner of the goods agrees to part with his goods on the basis of a fraudulent misrepresentation made by the other regarding his identity. Since the essence of the transaction is the same in each case, the law in its response should apply the same principle in each case, irrespective of the precise mode of communication of offer and acceptance.

34. Accordingly, if the law of contract is to be coherent and rescued from its present unsatisfactory and unprincipled state, the House has to make a choice: either to uphold the approach adopted in *Cundy* v. *Lindsay* and overrule the decisions in *Phillips* v. *Brooks Ltd* and *Lewis* v. *Averay*, or to prefer these later decisions to *Cundy* v. *Lindsay*.

35. I consider the latter course is the right one, for a combination of reasons. It is in line with the direction in which, under the more recent decisions, the law has now been moving for some time. It accords better with basic principle regarding the effect of fraud on the formation of a contract. It seems preferable as a matter of legal policy. As between two innocent persons the loss is more appropriately borne by the person who takes the risks inherent in parting with his goods without receiving payment. This approach fits comfortably with the intention of Parliament in enacting the limited statutory exceptions to the proprietary principle of *nemo dat non quod habet*. Thus, by section 23 of the Sale of Goods Act 1979 Parliament protected an innocent buyer from a seller with a voidable title. The classic instance of a person with a voidable title is a person who acquired the goods by fraud: see Bramwell LJ in *Babcock* v. *Lawson* (1880) 5 QBD 284, 286. Further, this course is supported by writers of the distinction of Sir Jack Beatson: see *Anson's Law of Contract*, 28th ed (2002), p 332. It is consistent with the approach adopted elsewhere in the common law world, notably in the United States of America in the Uniform Commercial Code, 14th edn (1995), section 2–403. And this course makes practical sense. In a case such as the present the owner of goods has no interest in the identity of the buyer. He is interested only in creditworthiness. It is little short of absurd that a subsequent purchaser's rights depend on the precise manner in which the crook seeks to persuade the owner of his creditworthiness and permit him to take the goods away with him. This ought not to be so. The purchaser's rights should not depend upon the precise form the crook's misrepresentation takes.

36. *Cundy* v. *Lindsay* has stood for a long time. But I see no reason to fear that adopting this conclusion will unsettle the law of contract. In practice the problems surrounding *Cundy* v. *Lindsay* arise only when third parties' rights are in issue. To bring the law here into line with the law already existing in 'face to face' cases will rid the law of an anomaly. Devlin LJ's starting point presumption is a workable foundation which should apply in all cases. A person is presumed to intend to contract with the person with whom he is actually dealing, whatever be the mode of communication.

37. Although expressed by Devlin LJ as a presumption, it is not easy to think of practical circumstances where, once in point, the presumption will be displaced. The factual postulate necessary to bring the presumption into operation is that a person (O) believes that the person with whom he is dealing is the person the latter has represented himself to be. Evidence that the other's identity was of importance to O, and evidence of the steps taken to check the other's identity, will lead nowhere if the transaction proceeds on the basis of the underlying factual postulate.

[He then applied these principles to the facts of the present case and concluded that the finance company had made the same mistake as the jeweller in *Phillips* v. *Brooks Ltd* but that its mistake did not negative the finance company's intention to let the car on hire to the person in the showroom on the terms set out in the hire-purchase agreement. He then concluded as follows]

41. One further point may be noted. Some time was taken up in this case with arguments on whether the dealer was an agent for the finance company and for what purposes. This was in an endeavour to bring the case within the 'face to face' principle. The need for such singularly sterile arguments underlines the practical absurdity of a principle bounded in this way. The practical reality is that in the instant case the presence or absence of a representative of the finance company in the dealer's showroom made no difference to the course of events. Had an authorised representative of the finance company been present no doubt he would have inspected the driving licence himself and himself obtained the information needed by his company. As it was, a copy of the licence, together with the necessary information, were faxed to the finance company. I can see no sensible basis on which these different modes of communication should affect the outcome of this case. I would set aside the orders of the assistant recorder and the Court of Appeal, and dismiss this action. Mr Hudson acquired a good title to the car under section 27 of the Hire-Purchase Act 1964.

Lord Hobhouse of Woodborough

42. The question at issue on this appeal is: Did Mr Hudson acquire a good title to the car when he bought the car from the rogue ('R') who himself had no title? The basic principle is *nemo dat quod non habet*: see the Sale of Goods Act 1979 s.21(1) and *Helby* v. *Matthews* [1895] AC 471 where it was held that the same rule applied to a sale by a hire-purchaser. The hire-purchaser has no title to the goods and no power to convey any title to a third party. The title to the goods and the power to transfer that title to any third party remains with the hire purchase company and with it alone. Clause 8 of the hire-purchase 'agreement' and the printed words in the form immediately below the space for the customer's signature also expressly say the same. There are common law and statutory exceptions to this rule . . .

43. In the present case, the statutory exception relied on by Mr Hudson is that in Part III of the Hire-Purchase Act 1964 as re-enacted in the Consumer Credit Act 1974:

' where a motor vehicle has been *bailed* . . . under *a hire-purchase agreement* . . . and, before the property in the vehicle has become vested in the *debtor*, he disposes of the vehicle to another person. . .[who is] a private purchaser [who has purchased] the motor vehicle in good faith without notice of the hire-purchase . . . agreement . . . that disposition shall have effect as if the creditor's title to the vehicle has been vested in the *debtor* immediately before that disposition.' (s.27(1) and (2), (emphasis supplied)

Section 29(4) adds:

' the *"debtor"* in relation to a motor vehicle which has been *bailed* . . . under *a hire-purchase agreement*. . .means the person who at the material time (whether the agreement has before that time been terminated or not) . . . is . . . the person to whom the vehicle is bailed . . . *under that agreement*.' (emphasis supplied)

44. The relevant question is therefore one of the application of this statutory provision to the facts of this case (no more, no less). Thus the question becomes: 'Was R a debtor under the hire-purchase agreement relating to the car?' Mr Hudson contends that R was; the Finance Company contends that he was not. The judge and the majority of the Court of Appeal found that he was not; Sedley LJ would have held that he was.

45. What was the 'hire-purchase' agreement relied on? It was a written agreement on a standard hire-purchase printed form purporting to be signed as the 'customer' by one Durlabh Patel, the person who lived at 45 Mayflower Rd, Leicester, to whom driving licence No.'PATEL506018DJ9FM' had been issued and with a date of birth 01/06/58. This was an accurate identification of the real Mr Durlabh Patel, but in no respect of R who was not the person who lived at that address, not the person to whom the driving licence had been issued and (one suspects) not a twin in age of the real Mr Patel. R forged Mr Patel's signature so as to make the signature on the hire-purchase 'agreement' appear to be the same as that on the driving licence. The parties to the written 'agreement' are Mr Patel (the 'customer'), and Shogun Finance Ltd (the creditor). There is also an offer and acceptance clause:

'You ["the customer named overleaf"] are offering to make a legal agreement by signing this document. We [the creditor] can reject your offer, or accept it by signing it ourselves. . . . If we sign this document it will become legally binding at once (even before we send you a signed copy) . . .'

46. The effect of this is that: (i) it re-emphasises that the customer/hirer is, and is only, the person named on the front of the document; (ii) it makes it clear that the agreement is the written agreement contained in the written document; (iii) the offer being accepted by the creditor is the offer contained in the document and that alone, that is to say, the offer of Mr Durlabh Patel of the address in Leicester and to whom the driving licence was issued; (iv) for a valid offer to be made, the form must have been signed by Mr Durlabh Patel; and, (v) most importantly of all, the question in issue becomes a question of the construction of this written document, not a question of factual investigation and evaluation. I will take these points in turn but the second and fifth are fundamental to them all and to the giving of the correct answer to this case.

47. The first point is a matter of the construction of the written document. It admits of only one conclusion. There is no mention in the document of anyone other than Mr

Durlabh Patel. The language used is clear and specific, both in the substance of the identification—name and address and driving licence number and age—and in the express words of the offer and acceptance clause—'the customer named overleaf.' The 'agreement' is a consumer credit agreement. It is unlike a mere retail sale where, although title may, indeed, will normally have already passed to the buyer, the seller is not obliged to part with the goods until he has been paid or is satisfied that he will be paid. Credit is only relevant to the release of the seller's lien and to his obligation to deliver, not to the basic transaction; the basic transaction is unaffected and will stand. Under a contract for the sale of goods, the contract has been made and, normally, the title to the goods has vested in the buyer before the time for payment has arrived. (Retention of title clauses are a modern development.) By contrast, in a consumer credit transaction, the identity of the customer is fundamental to the whole transaction because it is essential to the checking of the credit rating of the applicant borrower. All this precedes the making of any contract at all. No title to the goods is obtained by the hirer at any stage. If the finance company does not accept the proposer's offer, the proposer has acquired nothing. Unlike in the sale of goods, there is nothing—no status quo—which has to be undone. The observations of Devlin LJ in *Ingram* v. *Little* [1961] 1 QB at p.69 are not pertinent; the approach and dicta of Denning MR in *Lewis* v. *Averay* [1972] 1 QB 198 are misplaced and wrong.

48. It has been suggested that the finance company was willing to do business with anyone, whatever their name. But this is not correct: it was only willing to do business with a person who had identified himself in the way required by the written document so as to enable it to check before it enters into any contractual or other relationship that he meets its credit requirements. Mr Durlabh Patel was such an identified person and met its credit requirements so it was willing to do business with him. If the applicant had been, say, Mr B Patel of Ealing or Mr G Patel of Edgbaston, it would not have been willing to deal with them if they could not be identified or did not meet with its credit requirements. Correctly identifying the customer making the offer is an essential precondition of the willingness of the finance company to deal with that person. The rogue knew, or at least confidently expected, that the finance company would be prepared to deal with Mr Durlabh Patel but probably not with him, the rogue; and he was, in any event, not willing himself to enter into any contract with the finance company. This is not a case such as that categorised by Sedley LJ ([2002] QB at 846) as the use of a 'simple alias' to disguise the purchaser rather than to deceive the vendor—the situation which resembles that in *King's Norton Metal* v. *Edridge Merrett & Co* (14 TLR 98). But, even then, in a credit agreement it would be useless to use a pseudonym as no actual verifiable person against whom a credit check could be run would have been disclosed and the offer would never be accepted. Mr Durlabh Patel is the sole hirer under this written agreement. No one else acquires any rights under it; no one else can become the bailee of the motor car or the 'debtor' 'under the agreement'. It is not in dispute that R was not Mr Durlabh Patel nor that R had no authority from Mr Patel to enter into the agreement or take possession of the motor car.

49. Mr Hudson seeks to escape from this conclusion by saying: 'but the Rogue was the person who came into the dealer's office and negotiated a price with the dealer and signed the form in the presence of the dealer who then witnessed it.' The third and fourth points address this argument. The gist of the argument is that oral evidence may be adduced to contradict the agreement contained in a written document which is the only contract to which the finance company was a party. The agreement is a written agreement with Mr Durlabh Patel. The argument seeks to contradict this and make it an agreement with the rogue. It is argued that other evidence is always admissible to show who the parties to an agreement are. Thus, if the contents of the document are, without more, insufficient unequivocally to identify the actual individual referred to or if the identification of the party is non-specific, evidence can be given to fill any gap. Where the person signing is also acting as the agent of another, evidence can be adduced of that fact. None of this involves the contradiction of the document: *Young* v. *Schuler* 11 QBD 651, which was a case of an equivocal agency signature and it was held that evidence was admissible that the signature was also a personal signature—'evidence that he intended to sign in both capacities . . . does not contradict the document and is admissible' (per Cotton LJ at p.655). But it is different where the party is, as here, specifically identified in the document: oral or other extrinsic evidence is not admissible. Further, the Rogue was no one's agent (nor did he ever purport to be). The rule that other evidence may not be adduced to contradict the provisions of a contract contained in a written document is fundamental to the mercantile law of this country; the bargain is the document; the certainty of the contract depends on it. The relevant principle is well summarised in *Phipson on Evidence*, 15th edn (2000) pp 1165–1166, paras 42–11 and 42–12:

> 'when the parties have deliberately put their agreement into writing, it is conclusively presumed between themselves and their privies that they intend the writing to form a full and final statement of their intentions, and one which should be placed beyond the reach of future controversy, bad faith or treacherous memory.'

(See also *Bank of Australasia* v. *Palmer* [1897] AC 540, per Lord Morris at p. 545.) This rule is one of the great strengths of English commercial law and is one of the main reasons for the international success of English law in preference to laxer systems which do not provide the same certainty. The case of *Hector* v. *Lyons* 58 P&CR 156 is simply an application of this basic and long established principle. The father was claiming to be able to enforce a contract of sale of land. The father had conducted the negotiations. Woolf LJ said, at pp. 160–161:

> 'In this case there is no dispute as to who, according to the written contract, are the parties. The son was described in the contract as one of the parties. He does exist and, in so far as there was a contract at all, it was between him and the other party identified in the contract, Mrs Pamela Doris Lyons.'

Browne-Wilkinson V-C delivered to a judgment to the same effect. On p.159 he referred to the cases 'entirely concerned with transactions between two individuals face to face entering into oral agreement', saying:

> 'In my judgment the principle there enunciated has no application to a case such as the present where there is a contract and wholly in writing. There the identity of the vendor and of the purchaser is established by the names of the parties included in the written contract.'

Mr Hudson submitted, as he had to, that this decision was wrong and should be overruled. In my opinion the Court of Appeal's decision was clearly correct and correctly reasoned in accordance with well established principles.

50. The argument also fails on another ground. There was no consensus ad idem between the finance company and the rogue. Leaving on one side the fact that the rogue never had any intention himself to contract with the finance company, the hire-purchase 'agreement' to which Mr Hudson pins his argument was one purportedly made by the acceptance by the finance company, by signing the creditor's box in the form, of a written offer by Mr Durlabh Patel to enter into the hire-purchase agreement. This faces Mr Hudson with a dilemma: either the contract created by that acceptance was a contract with Mr Durlabh Patel or there was no consensus ad idem, the rogue having no honest belief or contractual intent whatsoever and the finance company believing that it was accepting an offer by Mr Durlabh Patel. On neither alternative was there a hire-purchase agreement with the rogue.

51. It is as well to digress at this stage to consider the chain of contracts or alleged contracts relied upon by Mr Hudson. First, Mr Hudson relies upon a contract of sale he made with the rogue when he agreed to buy the motor car from the rogue. He says he got a good title to it from the rogue under this contract notwithstanding that R had no title. In support of this statute-based contention he argues that there was another contract which he has to say was a contract of hire-purchase between the rogue and the finance company, the supposed contract contained in the written hire-purchase agreement. There is no dispute that the finance company had bought the motor car from the dealer and was or had become the owner of the car at the time when the finance company signed the document and thereby accepted the offer (if any) in the written hire-purchase document. (That contract of purchase was never put in evidence.) The title to the car was in the finance company. The hirer/debtor under the 'agreement'was Mr Durlabh Patel not the rogue. The rogue only comes into the picture because he was the unidentified individual who came into the dealer's office and caused the dealer to sell the motor car to the finance company and the dealer, thereafter, to deliver it to him although he was not in fact Mr Durlabh Patel. (He, of course, came into the story again later as the person who purported to sell the car to Mr Hudson.) The dealer (as his witness signature testifies) apparently believed the rogue when the rogue said his name was Mr Patel and negotiated with him, face to face, the price at which the dealer would be willing to sell the car. That negotiation enabled the dealer to fill in the appropriate finance details which the 'customer' should ask for. But the rogue never had any face to face dealings with the finance company; he dealt with it solely by submitting a written document containing an offer and acceptance clause. There is no room for the application of the 'face to face' principle between the rogue and the finance company. Nor was the dealer the agent of the finance company to enter into any contract on behalf of the finance company. The dealer is a mere facilitator serving primarily his own interests. If there could have been any doubt or room for argument about this point, it is put beyond argument or doubt by the terms of the offer and acceptance clause in the governing document. R and the dealer are not two individuals conducting negotiations in which all the terms necessary to constitute a binding contract are agreed.

52. As regards the delivery of the motor car by the dealer to the rogue, it is not in dispute that, in making that delivery, the dealer was acting as the agent of the finance company. But he was acting without authority. The dealer's authority was to deliver the car to Mr Durlabh Patel, not to anyone else. That delivery did not create any bailment of the car by the finance company to the rogue. The rogue was a thief. Albeit by an elabor-ate but effective course of action, he stole the car from the possession of the dealer just as surely as if he was a thief stealing it from the forecourt. The dealer may have acted under an innocent mistake induced by the fraud the rogue had practised on him; but it will, nevertheless, have been a tortious disposal of the motor car by the dealer. But the matter does not stop there. It would not be a delivery 'under a hire-purchase agreement'. This follows from the fact that there was no hire-purchase agreement (or any agreement or contract) between the finance company and the rogue. It further follows from the fact that the only 'debtor' under the supposed agreement was Mr Durlabh Patel. It was never the rogue and neither the finance company nor the rogue ever intended that it should be.

53.   The final point was the fact that the purported customer's signature was not in truth that of Mr Durlabh Patel. The supposed hire-purchase agreement therefore from the outset lacked an essential ingredient and within the terms of the document was never an offer eligible for acceptance. A forged signature is neither the signature of the pur-ported signatory nor of the forger. There may be an exception where the 'forger' had the authority of the actual party to sign on his behalf and in his name, in which case it probably would not be a forgery unless there was some dishonest intent to deceive. The same applies to using a 'mere pseudonym' or a trading name. But that is not this case.

54.   It follows that the appeal must be dismissed and the majority judgment of the Court of Appeal affirmed.

55.   But, before I leave this case, I should shortly summarise why the argument of the appellant's counsel was so mistaken. The first reason was that they approached the question as if it was simply a matter of sorting out the common law authorities relating to the sale of goods. They did not treat it as a matter of applying a statutory exception to the basic common law rule, *nemo dat quod non habet*. Further, they did not analyse the structure of the overall transaction and the consumer credit agreement within it. Accord-ingly, they misrepresented the role of the dealer, wrongly treating him as the contracting agent of the finance company which he was not. They never analysed the terms of the written document and had no regard at all to the offer and acceptance clause it con-tained which, if there was any contract between a 'debtor' and the finance company, governed their relationship and which expressly set out the only way in which such a contract could come into existence. They made submissions which contradicted the express written contract and were therefore contrary to principle and long established English mercantile law. They submitted that *Cundy* v. *Lindsay* (1878) 3 App Cas 459 was wrongly decided and should be overruled, substituting for it a general rule which, in disregard of the document or documents which constitute the agreement (if any), makes everything depend upon a factual enquiry into extraneous facts not known to both of the parties thus depriving documentary contracts of their certainty. They sought to convert a direct documentary contract with the finance company into a face to face oral contract made through the dealer as the contracting agent of the finance company, notwith-standing that the dealer was never such an agent of the finance company. Finally they sought, having by-passed the written contract, to rely upon authorities on oral contracts for the sale of goods, made face to face and where the title to the goods had passed to the 'buyer', notwithstanding that this was a documentary consumer credit transaction not a sale and, on any view, no title had ever passed to R. In the result they have invited a review of those authorities by reference to the particular facts of each of them. They have sought to draw your Lordships into a discussion of the evidential tools, eg rebuttable presumptions of fact and the so-called face-to-face 'principle', used by judges in those cases to assist them in making factual decisions (see also the dictum of Gresson P in *Fawcett* v. *Star Car Sales* [1960] NZLR at 413), notwithstanding that the present case concerns the construction of a written contract. They forget that the, presently relevant, fundamental principles of law to be applied—consensus ad idem, the correspondence of the contractual offer and the contractual acceptance, the legal significance of the use of a written contract—are clear and are not in dispute. Inevitably over the course of time there have been decisions on the facts of individual 'mistaken identity' cases which seem now to be inconsistent; the further learned, but ultimately unproductive, discussion of them will warm academic hearts. But what matters is the principles of law. They are clear and sound and need no revision. To cast doubt upon them can only be a disservice to English law. Similarly, to attempt to use this appeal to advocate, on the basis of continental legal systems which are open to cogent criticism, the abandonment of the soundly based *nemo dat quod non habet rule* (statutorily adopted) would be not only improper but even more damaging.

Lord Millett (dissenting)

56. My Lords, A makes an offer to B. B accepts it, believing that he is dealing with C. A knows of B's mistake, and may even have deliberately caused it. What is the result of the transaction? Is there a contract at all? There is obviously no contract with C, who is not a party to the transaction and knows nothing of it. But is there a contract with A? And if so is it void or merely voidable?

57. Generations of law students have struggled with this problem. They may be forgiven for thinking that it is contrived by their tutors to test their mettle. After all, the situation seems artificial and is one which is seldom likely to arise in practice, at least in the absence of fraud. Unfortunately fraudulent impersonation is not at all uncommon today. The growth in the number of credit transactions, often entered into electronically between persons unknown to each other, has led to a surge in what has been called 'theft of identity', that is the fraudulent assumption of another's identity by a customer in order to have the wrong account debited or to misdirect enquiries into his own creditworthiness. In the classic case A, fraudulently masquerading as C, buys goods on credit from B; B, having conducted appropriate checks to satisfy himself that C is worthy of credit and believing A to be C, lets A have possession of the goods; and A thereupon sells the goods to D, an unsuspecting purchaser, before disappearing without paying for them. Who is to bear the loss? That depends on whether D, who has paid for the goods, has obtained title to them, for if not then B can reclaim them. But D will have obtained title only if A was able to transfer title to him, and this turns on whether the transaction between A and B resulted in a voidable contract for the purchase of the goods by A (which B will have been unable to avoid in time) or no contract at all.

58. The problem is sometimes mentioned in the textbooks in the section which deals with the formation of contract, where the question is whether a contract has been concluded; but it is more usually dealt with in the section which is concerned with the effect of mistake and in particular 'mistaken identity', where the question is said to turn on whether A's identity is (i) 'fundamental' (in which case the contract is completely void) or (ii) 'material' but not 'fundamental' (in which case the contract is merely voidable). In his dissenting judgment in *Ingram* v. *Little* [1961] 1 QB 31 at p. 64 Devlin LJ distinguished between the two questions and observed that it was easy to fall into error if one did not begin with the first question, whether there is sufficient correlation between offer and acceptance to bring a contract into existence. But if there is, I question whether the contract should be held to be void for mistake rather than merely voidable.

59. As I have said, the situation is seldom likely to arise in practice in the absence of fraud, and where the fraud is not directed to the identity of the offeror the contract is only voidable, not void, for the victim of deception ought to be able to elect to affirm the contract if he chooses to do so. It seems anomalous that a mistake which is induced by fraud should have a less vitiating effect than one which is not; and it is difficult to see why a mistake induced by fraud should make a contract altogether void if it is a mistake as to the offeror's identity (whatever that may mean) and not if it is a mistake as to some other attribute of his such as his creditworthiness which may be equally or more material.

60. As Treitel observes (*The Law of Contract* 10th. ed. (1999) at p.277) it is often difficult to say precisely what mistake has been made and, even when this is clear, it is often difficult to say whether it should be classified as a mistake of identity or of attribute. As between A and B themselves, of course, it does not normally matter whether the contract is void or merely voidable; it obviously cannot be enforced by A against B's wishes in either case. The question usually assumes importance only where an innocent third party is involved, and then it is critical. Under the law as it stands at present, his title depends on whether the fraudster obtained the goods in his own name by means of a false or forged credit reference or in the name of another by means of a genuine reference relating to that other. This is indefensible. I take the view that the law should if at all possible favour a solution which protects innocent third parties by treating the contract as voidable rather than void, whether for fraud or for mistake.

61. My Lords, I think that the time has come to follow the lead given by Lord Denning MR more than thirty years ago in *Lewis* v. *Averay* [1972] 1 QB 198. He roundly rejected the theory that if a party is mistaken as to the identity of the person with whom he is contracting there is no contract, or that if there is a contract it is null and void so that no property can pass under it: see pp.206–7. He thought that the doctrine, derived from the writings of Pothier, should not be admitted as part of English law but should be 'dead and buried'. As he observed, it gives rise to fine distinctions which do no good to the law, and it is unjust that an innocent third party, who knows nothing of what passed between the rogue and his vendor, should have his title depend on such refinements.

62. But it is still necessary to answer the logically anterior and more difficult question: does the transaction result in the formation of a contract between A and B? There is clearly a transaction between them, for B has let A have possession of the goods and take them away, usually with the intention that he should be free to deal with them as owner. But is the transaction contractual?

63.   It is trite law, as Devlin LJ explained in the passage immediately following that cited above, that before a contract can come into existence there must be offer and acceptance, and these must correspond. The offer must be addressed to the offeree, either as an individual or as a member of a class or of the public. The acceptance must come from one who is so addressed and must itself be addressed to the offeror. It is not possible in law for a person to accept an offer made to someone else; or to intercept an acceptance of someone else's offer and treat it as an acceptance of his own.

64.   This is usually straightforward enough, at least in the absence of fraud. As my noble and learned friend Lord Phillips of Worth Matravers observes, there is normally no difference between the identity of the person to whom the offer or acceptance is directed and the person for whom it is intended. But what if, by reason of fraud, the two are not the same? What if A, posing as C, makes an offer to B which B purports to accept? B *directs* his acceptance to A, but *intends* it for C. It does not help to substitute the question: 'to whom was B's acceptance made?' This merely raises the question: 'what do you mean by made?'

65.   The outcome is said to depend on B's intention objectively ascertained, and this is usually treated as if it were a straightforward question of fact to be determined on the evidence. In *Ingram* v. *Little (supra)* Pearce LJ said at p. 61 that 'Each case must be decided on its own facts'. This is singularly unhelpful, since it involves asking: did B intend to contract with A believing him to be C? Or with C believing him to be A? The question is meaningless. As Devlin LJ pointed out in *Ingram* v. *Little (supra)* at p. 65:

> 'If Miss Ingram had been asked whether she intended to contract with the man in the room or with P.G.M. Hutchinson, the question could have no meaning for her, since she believed them both to be one and the same. The reasonable man of the law—if he stood in Miss Ingram's shoes—could not give any better answer . . . All that Miss Ingram or any other witness in her position can say is *that she did in fact accept the offer made to her;* and that, if she had not been tricked or deceived, she would not have accepted it' (emphasis added).

66.   In this situation the Courts have distinguished between transactions entered into in writing and transactions entered into orally between parties who are in the presence of each other. In the former case B's intention is ascertained by construing the description of the counterparty in the contract. This naturally identifies C, the person whose identity A has fraudulently assumed, and (provided that C actually exists) invariably leads to the conclusion that there is no counterparty and therefore no contract. In the latter case, the Courts have adopted a different approach. They have introduced a rebuttable presumption that, where parties deal with each other face to face, each of them intends to contract with the physical person to whom he addresses the words of contract. Unless the presumption is rebutted, this must lead to the conclusion that there is a contract with the impostor.

67.   I do not find this satisfactory. What evidence is sufficient to rebut the presumption? As Devlin LJ stressed, it cannot be rebutted by piling up evidence that B would never have accepted the offer if he had not thought that it had been made by C. Such evidence merely shows that the deception was material; it does not establish the identity of B's counterparty. There might perhaps be something to be said for making the presumption conclusive. This appears to have been the law at one time in the United States. In Corbin on Contracts (1960 ed.) at p. 619 it is stated that

'The Courts hold that if A appeared in person before B, impersonating C, an innocent purchaser from A gets property in the goods as against B.'

But there is surely nothing to be said for resorting to a rebuttable presumption in order to resolve a question of fact which is incapable of being determined by evidence. If there is no test by which the question can be answered on the evidence, there is none by which the Court can determine whether the presumption has been rebutted.

68. But the real objection to the present state of the law, in my view, is that the distinction between the face to face contract and other contracts is unrealistic. I leave aside the criticism of the face to face rule made by Corbin on Contracts (*loc. cit.*) at p. 620 that it is

'somewhat fanciful to hold that B intends to sell the goods to the physical body of A in front of him, although that body is indeed part of what we call "identity" '.

My difficulty is that I cannot see that there is any difference in principle between the two situations when it comes to identifying B's counterparty. In both cases B's acceptance is directed to the impostor but intended for the person whose identity he has assumed. Carleton Allen described the distinction as

'admittedly fine, and [one which] has always caused doubt, though not necessarily dissent, in a good many minds': see (1928) 44 *LQR* 72 at p.73.

He observed that text-book writers were divided on the subject, and that in the then most recently published treatise on Contracts the high but unhappily posthumous authority of Sir John Salmond leaned strongly against the doctrine.

69. In *Ingram v. Little (supra)* Devlin LJ said (at p.66) that

'the presumption that a person is intending to contract with the person to whom he is actually addressing the words of contract seems to me to be a simple and sensible one'.

I respectfully agree. But why should it be adopted only in the case of a contract entered into between persons who deal in the physical presence of each other? If the offeree's words of acceptance are taken to be addressed to the physical person standing in his presence who made the offer, what is the position where they deal with each other by telephone? Is the disembodied voice to be equated with physical presence? Is it sufficient that the parties are in the hearing of each other? Does it make a difference if the dealing is by televisual link, so that the parties are in the hearing and sight but not the presence of each other? New means of communication make the distinction untenable.

70. But in truth the distinction was always unsound. If the offeree's words of acceptance are taken to be addressed to the physical person standing in his presence who made the offer, why is the contract entered into by correspondence different? Why is the offeree's letter of acceptance not taken to be addressed to the physical person who made the written offer which he is accepting? The offeree addresses the offeror by his assumed name in both cases. Why should this be treated as decisive in the one case and disregarded in the other? Indeed, the correlation between offer and acceptance is likely to be greater in the case of a contract entered into by correspondence, since the offeree's letter of acceptance will either be sent to the impostor at his own address or be delivered to him personally and it will almost certainly contain internal references to his offer.

71.   In my opinion there are only two principled solutions to the problem. The law must give preference, either to the person for whom the offer or acceptance is intended, or to the person to whom it is directed, and must do so in all cases as a matter of law. The difficulty is in deciding which solution should be adopted, for there is much to commend each of them.

72.   The first solution, which gives preference to the person for whom the offer or acceptance is intended, possibly accords more closely to the existing authorities, which treat the face to face transaction as an exception to the general rule, and with the decision in *Cundy* v. *Lindsay* (1878) 3 App. Cas. 459, the only case on the subject which has come before the House. It also accords more closely with the parties' subjective intentions, for B intends to deal with C, especially if he has checked his creditworthiness, and not with A, of whom he has never heard; while A has no intention of being bound by contract at all. From his point of view the supposed contract is merely a pretence to enable him to get hold of goods without paying for them. He does not need a contract, for he is content with possession without title. In the days when the law distinguished between trickery and deception, he would have obtained possession by a trick rather than title by false pretences.

73.   The strongest argument in favour of this solution, I suppose, is that it could be said to be based on the parties' own assessment of what they mean by the counterparty's 'identity'. Ultimately this must refer to a physical person, but a physical person can only be identified by describing his or her attributes. For this purpose it is customary to refer to a person's name and address, which are usually though not always unique to one person. But names are merely identifying labels and can be assumed without any intention to deceive. A person is free to adopt whatever name suits his fancy, and may validly contract under an alias. Even if he has assumed a false name for the sole purpose of deceiving the counterparty, there is a contract so long, at least, as there is no real person of that name: see *King's Norton Metal Co Ltd* v. *Edridge, Merrett & Co Ltd* (1897) 14 TLR 98.

74.   But as Treitel observes (*loc. cit.* p.277) a person may be identified by reference to any one of his attributes. He may be identified as 'the person in the room', 'the person who spoke on the telephone', 'the person who appended the illegible signature', 'the writer of the letter under reply', or 'the person who made the offer'; but he may also be identified, and sometimes more relevantly, as 'the person whose creditworthiness has been checked and found to be satisfactory'. Any of these may be the means of identifying a unique person. An automated telling machine is programmed to identify a customer by a combination of a pin number and a number encrypted on the card which is inserted into the machine. In an increasingly electronic age we are accustomed to identifying ourselves by pin numbers and passwords; the need to eliminate fraud may in time cause us to identify ourselves by retinal imagery, which at least has the advantage of being a feature of the physical body. But even in the case of a credit card transaction there is an ambiguity. Is the customer to be identified as the person who produces the card? Or as the person whose card is produced? The whole point of a credit card fraud is that the goods should be supplied to the person who produces the card while the cost is debited to the account of the person whose card is produced.

75. Given the equivocal nature of a person's 'identity', there is something to be said for selecting those aspects of the offeror's identity which are material in causing the other party to accept the offer. In the present case, for example, Mr. Patel's name address and date of birth had no intrinsic relevance in themselves. The Respondent would have entered into the transaction with anyone, whatever his name and address or date of birth, so long as it was satisfied that he was worthy of credit. Mr. Patel's personal details were merely the information which enabled it to conduct inquiries into the credit of the person it assumed to be its customer. It makes commercial sense to treat a contract made in these circumstances as purporting to be made between the finance company and the subject of its inquiries rather than with the person who merely produced the information necessary to enable it to make them.

76. Nevertheless I have come to the conclusion that it is the second solution which ought to be adopted. All the considerations which I have mentioned, and which seem to favour the first solution, when properly analysed go to the mechanics of the deception and its materiality rather than to the identity of the offeror. They ought to come into play when consideration is given to the second question, whether the contract is voidable, rather than to the first, whether there is sufficient correlation between offer and acceptance ('*consensus ad idem*') to bring a contract into existence. Until the fraud is exposed and it is discovered that A is *not* C, the existence of a contract is not in doubt. The fraud is relevant to the question whether the contract is enforceable against B rather than its existence.

77. I regard *King's Norton Metal Co Ltd* v. *Edridge, Merrett & Co Ltd* (*supra*) as worthy of more attention than it has usually been given. In that case, where the contract was entered into by correspondence, the rogue assumed a fictitious name in order to give a spurious impression of respectability. The Court held that there was a valid (though voidable) contract. The decisive feature was thought to be that there was no one of the assumed name. A L Smith LJ is reported at p.99 as follows:

> 'The question was, With whom, upon this evidence, which was all one way, did the plaintiffs contract to sell the goods? *Clearly with the writer of the letters.* If it could have been shown that there was a separate entity called Hallam and Co [C] and another entity called Wallis [A] then the case might have come within the decision in *Cundy* v. *Lindsay.* In his opinion there was a contract by the plaintiffs with the person who wrote the letters, by which the property passed to him. There was only one entity, trading it might be under an alias, and there was a contract by which the property passed to him' (emphasis added).

78. It is unclear whether it would have made a difference if, unknown to the plaintiffs, there had been an entity called Hallam and Co; or if to the knowledge of both parties there were many such entities, as in the cases where a man used to book a hotel room for himself and a girlfriend under a common but fictitious name in order to give the impression (when such things mattered) that they were married. The case is different where the impostor assumes the name and address of a real person of substance when entering into a credit transaction. In such a case his purpose is to direct inquiries to that person's credit rather than his own. A better explanation of *King's Norton Metal Co Ltd* v. *Edridge, Merrett & Co Ltd* is that the rogue merely assumed a false name and did not go further and assume another person's identity. But the distinction is a fine one which it may not always be possible to draw, and in any case depends on the nature and purpose of the deception and is accordingly relevant to its effect on the mind of the offeree and not to the correlation between offer and acceptance.

79. The typical fraudulent credit card transaction is also illuminating. There is clearly a transaction with the impostor who produces the card and who receives cash or goods (say a cinema ticket) in exchange. If the transaction is contractual in nature (as in the case of the cinema ticket) why should the transaction be thought to be with one person and the contract with another? There is only one transaction whether the party who parts with the goods debits the right account or is deceived into debiting the wrong one. Where cash is extracted from an ATM the fraud is possible because the machine is programmed to supply the cash to the person who produces the card and to debit the account of the person whose card is produced. In the same way the staff who handled the transaction in the present case on behalf of the Respondent were instructed (programmed) to obtain the customer's personal details, run credit checks on the person whose details were produced, and authorise the dealer to deliver possession of the vehicle to the person who produced them.

80. It is noticeable that, when recounting the facts objectively, judges often find themselves obliged to describe C as having accepted A's offer. I have already cited such passages from *Ingram* v. *Little* (*supra*) and *King's Norton Metal Co Ltd* v. *Edridge, Merrett & Co Ltd* (*supra*). In the former case, where the parties dealt with each other face to face, Devlin LJ has C say

'that she did in fact accept the offer made to her; and that, if she had not been tricked or deceived, she would not have accepted it'.

In the latter, where the contract was entered into by correspondence, A.L. Smith LJ said that the offeree 'clearly' contracted with the writer of the letters which contained the offer, that is with A.

81. In my opinion, once one accepts that there are two questions involved: (i) did a contract come into existence at all? and (ii) if so was the contract vitiated by fraud or mistake? there is only one principled conclusion. Whatever the medium of communication, a contract comes into existence if, on an objective appraisal of the facts, there is sufficient correlation between offer and acceptance to make it possible to say that the impostor's offer has been accepted by the person to whom it was addressed. While a person cannot intercept and accept an offer made to some one else, he should normally be treated as intending to contract with the person with whom he is dealing. Provided that the offer is made to him, then whether his acceptance of the offer is obtained by deception or mistake, and whether his mistake is as to the identity of the offeror or some material attribute of his, the transaction should result in a contract, albeit one which is voidable.

82. This rule is easy to apply and accords with principle by distinguishing between the formation of a contract as a question of fact to be determined objectively and the consequences of mistake or fraud which depend on its effect on the mind of the person affected. It avoids undesirable refinements and gives a measure of protection to innocent third parties. Of course, someone has to bear the loss where there is fraud, but it is surely fairer that the party who was actually swindled and who had an opportunity to uncover the fraud should bear the loss rather than a party who entered the picture only after the swindle had been carried out and who had none. In the present case, the claimant could easily have exposed the fraud by writing to Mr Patel, whose address it had been given, and asking him to confirm his intention to proceed with the proposed transaction. If it had been one for which statute required a cooling off period, no doubt it would have done . . .

84. We cannot leave the law as it is. It is neither fair nor principled, and not all the authorities from which it is derived can be reconciled; some, at least, must be overruled if it is to be extricated from the present quagmire . . .

[He considered the legal solutions adopted in other jurisdictions and continued]

87. Where does this leave the authorities? Most of those which are concerned with face to face transactions can stand with the exception of the decision of the majority of the Court of Appeal in *Ingram* v. *Little* (supra), which is inconsistent with *Lewis* v. *Averay* (supra) and should be overruled. I would confirm the decision in *Phillips* v. *Brooks* [1919] 2 KB 243 . .

[He considered *Phillips, Gordon* v. *Street* [1899] 2 QB 641, *Said* v. *Butt* [1920] 3 KB 497 and *Hardman* v. *Booth* (1863) 1 H & C 803 and continued]

90. The principal obstacle which has prevented the courts from rationalising this branch of the law has been *Cundy* v. *Lindsay* . . . As an authority on the formation of contract the decision is, with respect, unconvincing. That the plaintiffs did not wish or intend to have any dealings with Blenkarn is beyond dispute; but it is far from obvious that they did not actually have such a dealing even though it was only as a result of the deception practised on them. Lord Hatherley and Lord Penzance felt unable to distinguish the case from *Hardman* v. *Booth* (1863) 1 H & C 803, although in my view the two cases are not comparable. Lord Cairns dwelt on the plaintiffs' subjective state of mind, which was of course affected by the fraud, and gave no attention to the question whether, approaching the case objectively, the plaintiffs had accepted Blenkarn's offer. Lord Penzance (at pp.471–2) initiated the unfortunate distinction between cases of persons dealing in the presence of each other and other cases, without explaining why this was material, let alone decisive.

92. The plaintiffs, indeed, 'knew nothing' of the individual named 'Blenkarn' and they addressed their letter of acceptance to 'Blenkiron & Co.' But that was because they had been deceived into believing that the offer came from Blenkiron & Co. Throughout the speeches in this House it was assumed that the plaintiffs' letter of acceptance was directed and sent, as the goods were later directed and sent, to the intended recipient (Blenkiron & Co) but at the wrong address. If the facts of that case are viewed objectively, however, with a view to ascertaining whether there was the necessary correlation between offer and acceptance and without reference to the deception, the matter wears a very different aspect. The order was placed by Blenkarn (posing as Blenkiron & Co) writing from his own address (which was not the address of Blenkiron & Co) and was duly accepted by the plaintiffs in the belief that the order came from Blenkiron & Co. They replied to Blenkarn (in his assumed name as Blenkiron & Co) at the address he had given (being his own address and not that of Blenkiron & Co) by a letter which referred to and accepted his order; and in due course they fulfilled it.

93.   In my view the proper conclusion on these facts is that the plaintiffs contracted with Blenkarn in the mistaken belief, induced by his fraud, that they were dealing with Blenkiron & Co., and that the resulting contract was voidable for fraud. If the plaintiffs' subjective state of mind, induced by the fraud, is put on one side, there is no justification for the question-begging assumption that the plaintiffs' letter of acceptance was directed to Blenkiron & Co and that it was the name which was right and the address which was wrong. Nor is there any justification for the suggestion that the signature was a forgery. Blenkarn, who signed the letter, did not claim that it was someone else's signature; he acknowledged and asserted that it was his own. Even those who consider that the case was rightly decided concede that the rogue could have been sued for the price of the goods (see Treitel *The Law of Contract* p.284). But that presupposes that there was sufficient correlation between offer and acceptance to bring a contract into existence, albeit one which was void (or voidable) at the instance of the party deceived. Yet this was the very proposition which the House rejected . . .

[He considered *Boulton* v. *Jones* (1857) 2 H & N 564 and *Hector* v. *Lyons* 58 P & CR 156 and continued]

103.   My Lords, the identification of the parties to a written instrument is . . . only partly a question of construction. That is the first step in the process, and it will often be enough. . . . But once it is established that the person whose name and other personal details are stated in the contract and the person who stated them and signed the contract are not the same, the question immediately arises: which of them should be treated as the counterparty? Do the name and other details included in the contract refer to the person to whom they belong or to the impostor who included them in order to identify himself? This is not simply a question of construction. It is partly a question of fact and partly a question of law. To say, as my noble and learned friend Lord Hobhouse of Woodborough does, that it is a question of construction which admits of only one answer, with respect simply begs the question.

104.   How should the question be answered in the present case? The case is not unlike *Hector* v. *Lyons*, with the important difference that in the present case the deception was material and induced the making of the contract. If there was a contract with the rogue, it was voidable for fraud.

105.   But was there such a contact at all? The contact came into being when the claimant executed its part of the agreement. The two parts corresponded in every material particular. They made it clear that the hirer was the person named on the front of the document and who had signed the document. This appeared to be a Mr. Durlabh Patel, with an address in Leicester, whose personal details were given. But in fact it was not Mr. Durlabh Patel at all. He knew nothing of the transaction and his driving licence had been stolen. The person who identified himself as Mr. Durlabh Patel, provided Mr. Durlabh Patel's personal details, and signed the document in Mr. Durlabh Patel's name was not Mr. Durlabh Patel but an impostor.

106. The object of the deception was to misdirect the claimant's credit enquiries. In this it succeeded. Having satisfied itself that Mr. Durlabh Patel, whom it believed to be its customer, was worthy of credit, it accepted the offer which the impostor had made, signed its part of the agreement, and authorised the dealer to deliver possession of the car to his customer as hirer under the agreement.

107. But who was his customer? It was not Mr. Durlabh Patel. In my opinion it was plainly the impostor. Any other conclusion would mean that the dealer parted with the vehicle to the impostor without authority and would, presumably, be liable in conversion if the vehicle proved to be irrecoverable. This is far removed from reality. The claimant and the dealer both believed that the customer who was hiring the car and Mr. Durlabh Patel were one and the same; but the claimant did not make that a condition of the dealer's authority to part with the car. From first to last it believed that the impostor who attended the dealer's showroom, gave his name as Mr. Durlabh Patel, and signed the agreement in that name, was indeed Mr. Durlabh Patel; in that belief it entered into a hiring agreement and authorised the dealer to deliver possession of the car to the customer who had so identified himself. In my opinion, the claimant not only took a credit risk, but also took the risk that the customer who was hiring the car was not Mr. Durlabh Patel and that its credit enquiries had been fraudulently misdirected. I would hold that there was a hiring, and the impostor was the hirer.

108. This conclusion involves a departure from *Cundy v. Lindsay*, a decision of this House which has stood for more than 120 years. But its reasoning is unsound. It is vitiated by its subjective approach to the formation of contract and the necessary correlation between offer and acceptance; which may be why textbook writers treat it as an example of unilateral mistake even though this was not the basis on which it was decided. For the same reason it cannot be regarded as authoritative on the question whether a contract otherwise properly entered into is void for mistake rather than voidable. It has had an unfortunate influence on the development of the law, leading to an unprincipled distinction between face to face transactions and others and the indefensible conclusion that an innocent purchaser's position depends on the nature of the mistake of a third party or the precise mechanics of the fraud which had been perpetrated on him. In my view it should now be discarded and the law put on a simpler and more principled and defensible basis.

109. In my opinion only the decision in *Cundy v. Lindsay* stands in the way of a rational and coherent restatement of the law. My noble and learned friend Lord Phillips of Worth Matravers has expressed the view that the conclusion to which Lord Nicholls and I have come conflicts not only with that case but with the approach in almost all the numerous cases which he has cited. If they had preceded *Cundy v. Lindsay*, that would be a strong reason for not adopting it. But they were merely following a decision of this

House by which they were bound. Far from applying it generally, they attempted to distinguish it by carving out an unprincipled exception from it which Lord Nicholls has shown cannot be supported. While departing from *Cundy* v. *Lindsay* would make obsolete the reasoning in those cases, dictated as it was by that decision, it would undermine the actual decision in very few cases. There is no long line of authority to be overruled. Indeed, only two cases need to be overruled; and neither of them can be supported even on the view that *Cundy* v. *Lindsay* was rightly decided.

110.   In my opinion *Cundy* v. *Lindsay* should no longer be followed and *Ingram* v. *Little* and *Hector* v. *Lyons* should be overruled. I would allow the appeal.

Lord Phillips of Worth Matravers
111.   This appeal is a variation on a theme that has bemused courts and commentators alike for over 150 years. Two individuals conduct negotiations in which all the terms necessary to constitute a binding contract are agreed. One of those individuals has, however, been masquerading as a third party. Does a binding contract result? Grappling with this problem in *Fawcett* v. *Star Car Sales Ltd* [1960] NZLR 406 at 413, Gresson P remarked that 'the difficulty in deciding whether a mistake of identity prevents the formation of a concluded contract is a proper assessment of the facts rather than the ascertainment of the law'. The issues that arise in this case require the facts to be set out with some particularity.

[He set out the facts of the case and the relevant statutory provisions and continued]

'WHAT'S IN A NAME?'
120.   This area of the law has developed because of confusion about names and it may be helpful at the outset to reflect on the nature of a name. Words in a language have one or more ordinary meaning, which will be known to anyone who speaks that language. Names are not those kind of words. A name is a word, or a series of words, that is used to identify a specific individual. It can be described as a label. Whenever a name is used, extrinsic evidence, or additional information, will be required in order to identify the specific individual that the user of the name intends to identify by the name—the person to whom he intends to attach the label. Almost all individuals have two or more names which they use to identify themselves and where a name is mentioned in a particular context, or a particular milieu, those who hear it may have the additional information that they need to identify to whom the speaker is referring.

121.   Where a name appears in a written document, the document itself may contain additional information which will enable the reader to identify the individual to whom the writer intended to refer when he wrote the name.

122.   Where a person introduces himself by name to someone, his intention will normally be to tell that person the name that he uses to identify himself. This may also assist that other person to identify him in the future. If a person introduces himself by a false name, that may be because he does not wish to be identified in the future. If a person introduces himself by the name of somebody else, that may be because he wishes the person to whom he introduces himself to believe that he is that other person.

FORMATION OF CONTRACT

123. A contract is normally concluded when an offer made by one party ('the offeror') is accepted by the party to whom the offer has been made ('the offeree'). Normally the contract is only concluded when the acceptance is communicated by the offeree to the offeror. A contract will not be concluded unless the parties are agreed as to its material terms. There must be 'consensus ad idem'. Whether the parties have reached agreement on the terms is not determined by evidence of the subjective intention of each party. It is, in large measure, determined by making an objective appraisal of the exchanges between the parties. If an offeree understands an offer in accordance with its natural meaning and accepts it, the offeror cannot be heard to say that he intended the words of his offer to have a different meaning. The contract stands according to the natural meaning of the words used. There is one important exception to this principle. If the offeree knows that the offeror does not intend the terms of the offer to be those that the natural meaning of the words would suggest, he cannot, by purporting to accept the offer, bind the offeror to a contract: *Hartog* v. *Colin and Shields* [1939] 3 All ER 566; *Smith* v. *Hughes* (1871) LR 6 QB 597. Thus the task of ascertaining whether the parties have reached agreement as to the terms of a contract can involve quite a complex amalgam of the objective and the subjective and involve the application of a principle that bears close comparison with the doctrine of estoppel. Normally, however, the task involves no more than an objective analysis of the words used by the parties. The object of the exercise is to determine what each party intended, or must be deemed to have intended.

124. The task of ascertaining whether the parties have reached agreement as to the terms of a contract largely overlaps with the task of ascertaining what it is that the parties have agreed. The approach is the same. It requires the construction of the words used by the parties in order to deduce the intention of the parties—see *Chitty on Contracts*, 28th edn (1999) vol 1, p 604, paras 12–042, 12–043 and the cases there cited. This is true, whether the contract is oral or in writing. The words used fall to be construed having regard to the relevant background facts and extrinsic evidence may be admitted to explain or interpret the words used. Equally, extrinsic evidence may be necessary to identify the subject matter of the contract to which the words refer.

125. Just as the parties must be shown to have agreed on the terms of the contract, so they must also be shown to have agreed the one with the other. If A makes an offer to B, but C purports to accept it, there will be no contract. Equally, if A makes an offer to B and B addresses his acceptance to C there will be no contract. Where there is an issue as to whether two persons have reached an agreement, the one with the other, the courts have tended to adopt the same approach to resolving that issue as they adopt when considering whether there has been agreement as to the terms of the contract. The court asks the question whether each intended, or must be deemed to have intended, to contract with the other. That approach gives rise to a problem where one person is mistaken as to the identity of the person with whom he is dealing, as the cases demonstrate. I propose at this point to consider those cases.

[He then turned to consider the case-law. His conclusions on the case-law were as follows. He first considered *Boulton* v. *Jones* (1857) 27 LJ Ex 117 and concluded that the result of the case was consistent with the principles he set out at paras [123]–[125], although the reasoning of the court was not fully consistent with that approach because the court focused attention on the intention of the defendant. The next case he considered was *Hardman* v. *Booth* (1863) 1 H & C 803. Here he concluded that the court 'proceeded on the simple premise that there could not be a contract between A and B if A did not intend to contract with B.' This was a case in which the courts had not begun to apply an objective test to the question of whether an agreement had been concluded between the parties. The next case was *Cundy* v. *Lindsay* (1878) 3 App Cas 459. Here he pointed out that the focus of attention was, once again, on the intention of the offeree which was to deal with the firm Blenkiron and Co and not with the person who signed the order form. Thus he concluded that 'extrinsic evidence was admitted in addition to the wording of the order in order to ascertain the intention of the plaintiffs.' Turning to *King's Norton Metal Co Ltd* v. *Edridge, Merrett & Co Ltd* (1897) 14 TLR 98 he pointed out that the case 'demonstrates that, if a person describes himself by a false name in contractual dealings, this will not, of itself, prevent the conclusion of a contract by a person who deals with him in that name.' On the facts of the case the plaintiffs could not demonstrate that their acceptance of the offer was intended for anyone other than Wallis: they intended to deal with whoever was using the name of Hallam & Co. He then came to *Phillips* v. *Brooks* and (at [138]) pointed out that it:

> 'well illustrates the conundrum that the application of the test of *intention* raises when terms are negotiated between two persons who are face to face. It arises where the two persons, A and B, are not known to each other and where A gives a name which is not his own. If B is unaware of the existence of a third person who bears that name, there will be no problem. B will clearly intend to contract with A, treating the name given by A simply as the label by which A identifies himself. Equally A will know that B intends to contract with him. The problem arises where B is aware of a third person, C, who bears the name falsely adopted by A. In that situation it is B's intention to contract both with A and with C, for he does not distinguish between the two. No sensible answer can be given to the question: does B intend to contract with A or C? Nor can any sensible answer be given to the question: does A believe that B intends to contract with him or with C?'

He noted that Horridge J solved the conundrum by drawing an 'inference' that the plaintiff intended to contract with the rogue, who was present, and not with the individual whose identity the rogue had assumed. He then noted the criticisms which have been levelled against the judgment of Viscount Haldane in *Lake* v. *Simmons* [1927] AC 487 and pointed out that no other judge dealt with the issue of mistake on the facts of that case.

When considering *Ingram* v. *Little* he noted that all three members of the Court of Appeal 'adopted the approach of identifying the intention of Miss Ingram' and that the difference between them was 'as to the manner of application of that approach where an agreement was negotiated face to face.' The majority concluded that a 'sensible answer' could be given to the question 'with whom did Miss Ingram intend to contract?' as a question of fact. Devlin LJ, by contrast, considered that 'this question could only be answered by the application of a legal presumption, which would not be rebutted where the only reason for interest in the identity of the contracting party was concern that the contracting party should be creditworthy.' Finally he considered *Lewis* v. *Averay* and pointed out the differences in the reasoning of the judges. Drawing these cases together he concluded]

153. The difficulty in applying a test of *intention* to the identification of the parties to a contract arises, so it seems to me, only where the parties conduct their dealings in some form of inter-personal contact, and where one purports to have the identity of a third party. There the innocent party will have in mind, when considering with whom he is contracting, both the person with whom he is in contact and the third party whom he imagines that person to be.

154. The same problem will not normally arise where the dealings are carried out exclusively in writing. The process of construction of the written instruments, making appropriate use of extrinsic evidence, will normally enable the court to reach a firm conclusion as to the person with whom a party intends to contract. This was the position in *Boulton* v. *Jones* 27 LJ Ex 117; *Cundy* v. *Lindsay* 3 App Cas 459 and *King's Norton Metal Co Ltd* v. *Edridge, Merrett & Co Ltd* 14 TLR 98. There is a substantial body of authority that demonstrates that the identity of a party to a contract in writing falls to be determined by a process of construction of the putative contract itself. I shall refer to some examples.

[He considered these examples and continued]

161. The effect of these authorities is that a person carrying on negotiations in writing can, by describing as one of the parties to the putative agreement an individual who is unequivocally identifiable from that description, preclude any finding that the party to the putative agreement is other than the person so described. The process of construction will lead inexorably to the conclusion that the person with whom the other party intended to contract was the person thus described.

[He considered *Hector* v. *Lyons* and continued]

THE RESULT IN THE PRESENT CASE

167. I have had the advantage of reading in draft the opinions of my noble and learned friends who have sat with me on this appeal. Lord Hobhouse of Woodborough and Lord Walker of Gestingthorpe have concluded that, as the contract was a written document, the identity of the hirer falls to be ascertained by construing that document. Adopting that approach, the hirer was, or more accurately purported to be, Mr Patel. As he had not authorised the conclusion of the contract, it was void.

168. Lord Nicholls of Birkenhead and Lord Millett have adopted a different approach. They point out the illogicality of applying a special approach to face-to-face dealings. What of dealings on the telephone, or by videolink? There also it could be said that each of the parties to the dealings is seeking to make a contract with the other party to the dealings. And this can even be said when the dealings are conducted by correspondence. If A writes to B making an offer and B writes back responding to that offer, B is intending to contract with the person who made that offer. If a contract is concluded in face-to-face dealings, notwithstanding that one party is masquerading as a third party, why should the result be different when the dealings are by letter?

169. Lord Nicholls of Birkenhead and Lord Millett propose an elegant solution to this illogicality. Where two individuals *deal with each other*, by whatever medium, and agree terms of a contract, then a contract will be concluded between them, notwithstanding that one has deceived the other into thinking that he has the identity of a third party. In such a situation the contract will be voidable but not void. While they accept that this approach cannot be reconciled with *Cundy* v. *Lindsay*, they conclude that *Cundy* v. *Lindsay* was wrongly decided and should no longer be followed.

170.   While I was strongly attracted to this solution, I have found myself unable to adopt it. *Cundy* v. *Lindsay* exemplifies the application by English law of the same approach to identifying the parties as is applied to identifying the terms of the contract. In essence this focuses on deducing the intention of the parties from their words and conduct. Where there is some form of personal contact between individuals who are conducting negotiations, this approach gives rise to problems. In such a situation I would favour the application of a strong presumption that each intends to contract with the other, with whom he is dealing. Where, however, the dealings are exclusively conducted in writing, there is no scope or need for such a presumption. This can be illustrated by a slight adaption of the facts of the present case. Assume that the rogue had himself filled in the application form and sent it and a photocopy of Mr Patel's driving licence to Shogun. Assume further that he had been authorised to do so by Mr Patel. There can be no doubt that a contract would have been concluded between Shogun and Mr Patel. Mr Patel would have intended to contract with Shogun; Shogun would have intended to contract with Mr Patel; and this would have been demonstrated by the application form.

171.   Assume now that the rogue had wrongly understood that he had been requested by Mr Patel to fill in and submit the application form on his behalf, but in fact had no authority to do so. In this situation, according to established principles of the law of agency, an apparent contract would have been concluded between Shogun and Mr Patel but, being concluded without the latter's authority, it would be a nullity. Shogun might have a claim against the rogue for breach of warranty of authority, but could not have demonstrated that a contract had been concluded with the rogue.

172.   Turning to the true position—that the rogue knew he had no authority to conclude a contract in the name of Mr Patel, but fraudulently wished to induce Shogun to believe that they were entering into such a contract—I do not see by what legal principle this change in the mental attitude of the rogue could result in a binding contract being concluded with him.

173.   The position is not, of course, as simple as that. Negotiations between the rogue and Shogun were not conducted exclusively by written correspondence. They were conducted with the aid of the dealer and the use of fax and telephone communications. Acceptance of the offer was conveyed by telephone via the dealer—and this might have been capable of concluding a contract, notwithstanding that Clause 1 of the standard terms provided for acceptance by signature—see the discussion in Chitty on Contracts 28th Ed. Vol 1 at paragraph 2–062. Sedley LJ considered that the dealings were analogous to face-to-face dealings and that the dealer was, in effect, the face of Shogun Finance Ltd. He considered that the face-to-face presumption should be applied.

174.   The majority of the Court of Appeal considered that *Hector* v. *Lyons* required them to determine the identity of the parties to the putative contract as a simple question of construction. On that basis they concluded that the putative hirer was Mr Patel and that, as the apparent contract was concluded without his authority, it was a nullity.

175. Dyson LJ considered what the result would have been had the negotiations been treated as face-to-face. He concluded that the presumption would have been displaced by the importance that Shogun attached to the identity of the person with whom they were contracting.

176. My Lords, I started this opinion by quoting Gresson P's remark that the difficulty in a case such as this is a proper assessment of the facts rather than an assessment of the law. I have not found the assessment of the law easy, but nor is the application of the law to the facts. Shogun's representatives were aware of the presence of the prospective hirer in the dealer's showrooms in Leicester. To an extent the dealings were inter-personal through the medium of the dealer. Should one treat them as comparable to face-to-face dealings and conclude that there was a presumption that Shogun intended to contract with the man with whom they were dealing? Should one treat the written agreement as no more than peripheral to the dealings and conclude that it does not override that presumption? I have concluded that the answer to these questions is 'no'.

177. Shogun had, on the evidence, set up a formal system under which contracts would be concluded in writing on a standard form. This form was designed to cater for both regulated and non-regulated hire purchase agreements. In order to be suitable for the former it had to comply with the requirements of the Consumer Credit (Agreements) Regulations 1983. Schedule 1 to these regulations, under the heading 'Parties to the agreement', requires the agreement to set out 'The name and a postal address of the creditor' and 'The name and a postal address of the debtor'. The agreement with which this appeal is concerned was not a regulated agreement, for the purchase price of the vehicle exceeded what was, at the time, the maximum to which the relevant provisions of the Consumer Credit Act 1974 applied. I do not see, however, that the approach to the identification of the parties to the putative agreement can turn on whether or not the agreement was subject to the regulations. Shogun put in place a system for concluding contracts that required both regulated and unregulated agreements to be entered into in writing in a form which provided essential information, including the identity of the parties to the agreement.

178. These considerations lead me to conclude that the correct approach in the present case is to treat the agreement as one concluded in writing and to approach the identification of the parties to that agreement as turning upon its construction. The particulars given in the agreement are only capable of applying to Mr Patel. It was the intention of the rogue that they should identify Mr Patel as the hirer. The hirer was so identified by Shogun. Before deciding to enter into the agreement they checked that Mr Patel existed and that he was worthy of credit. On that basis they decided to contract with him and with no-one else. Mr Patel was the hirer under the agreement. As the agreement was concluded without his authority, it was a nullity. The rogue took no title under it and was in no position to convey any title to Mr Hudson.

179. For these reasons I would dismiss this appeal.

Lord Walker of Gestingthorpe

[Lord Walker opened his speech by stating that he agreed with the opinion of Lord Hobhouse. He then made two observations. First, he pointed out that the difficulty which the courts face in these cases lies 'in deciding which of two innocent parties should bear the loss caused by the fraud of a third person' but warned against making an assumption that one party (whether the owner or the third party) is necessarily more deserving than the other. On the facts of *Lewis* v. *Averay* the third party purchaser was thought by the court to be more deserving of protection but in *Phillips* v. *Brooks Ltd* the third party was a pawnbroker who may not elicit the same feelings of sympathy. He stated that the court had to 'lay down a general rule to cover the generality of cases, and it would not be right to make any general assumption as to one innocent party being more deserving than the other.' The second point which he emphasised was that, when deciding whether or not an agreement has been concluded, the courts adopt an objective and not a subjective approach.

He stated that the 'right question to ask, whether the parties to an alleged contract have been negotiating face to face or at a distance, is to whom the offer is made (or to whom acceptance of an offer is made . . .).' Commencing his analysis with the case of face to face negotiations, which he characterised as the 'simplest form of oral contract', he identified the following principle which was first adopted in England in *Phillips* v. *Brooks Ltd* in the following terms (at [185]):

> 'The fact that the seller was induced to sell by fraud of the buyer made the sale voidable, but not void. He could not have supposed that he was selling to any other person; his intention was to sell to the person present, and identified by sight and hearing; it does not defeat the sale because the buyer assumed a false name, or practised any other deceit to induce the vendor to sell.'

He noted that the only case that was out of line with this principle was *Ingram* v. *Little* and he concluded that the reasoning in Devlin LJ's powerful dissenting judgment was unanswerable and that *Ingram* v. *Little* was wrongly decided. He considered whether the principle should be viewed as a presumption or as a rule of law and continued]

187. If the principle is no more than a presumption, it is a strong presumption, and exceptions to it would be rare (in *Ingram* v. *Little* Devlin LJ himself, at p 67, was content to leave this point open). I would hesitate to state it as an inflexible rule (apart from cases of agency) because the notion of one individual impersonating another covers a wide range of factual situations (broadly corresponding to the wide range of meaning conveyed by saying that one person knows, or knows of, another). At one end of the spectrum is the confidence trickster who falsely but convincingly asserts that he is a baronet (or a barrister, or a brain surgeon) in order to inspire confidence and obtain credit. Then there are cases like *Phillips* v. *Brooks Ltd* and *Ingram* v. *Little*, where the rogue falsely gives the name and address of a real person whose existence the other party can and does check (but whom the other party does not actually know by sight, or the deception would fail). The most audacious form of impersonation would be where a rogue . . . attempts, face to face, to deceive a member of the family of which he claims to be part, or someone else personally acquainted with the individual whom the rogue is impersonating. Imperson-ation of that sort must be very rare indeed, and probably limited to deception of those whose senses are impaired (as Isaac was when, according to Chapter 27 of Genesis, Jacob successfully impersonated his elder twin brother Esau). I would not exclude the possibility that impersonation of that sort might be outside the presumption. Your Lordships were shown the decision of the Court of Appeals of New York in *Morgan Munitions Supply Company* v. *Studebaker Corporation* (1919) 123 NE 146, where one brother imperson-ated his more distinguished brother in order to obtain a contract of employment; but it appears (so far as can be discerned from the report) that the contract was in writing, and that neither brother was personally known to the employer.

[He then asked himself whether the 'face-to-face principle should be applied much more generally.' On this point he concluded (at [188])]:

'It may be that it should apply to an oral contract alleged to have been made on the telephone, where the parties are identified by hearing, although not by sight. An alleged oral contract made by telephone might be a case where the presumption applied, but was rebuttable. But to extend the principle to cases where the only contract was by written communication sent by post or by e-mail would be going far beyond identification by sight and hearing. Where there is an alleged contract reached by correspondence, offer and acceptance must be found, if they are to be found at all, in the terms of the documents.'

After briefly examining *Cundy* v. *Lindsay* and *King's Norton Metal Co Ltd* v. *Edridge Merrett & Co Ltd,* Lord Walker turned to the documents in the present case and concluded at [191]):

'Shogun Finance had no doubt never heard of the real Mr Patel before the day on which the written contract was signed by the rogue, forging Mr Patel's signature. But by the time it accepted the written offer it had, by efficient information tech-nology, confirmed that Mr Patel existed and had learned a good deal of relevant information about him, including his creditworthiness. The form of contract made quite clear that Shogun Finance's intention was to accept an offer made by the real Mr Patel, and no one else. The appellant's attempt to analyse the matter as a face to face contract . . . must fail, for the reasons stated by Lord Hobhouse.']

COMMENTARY

A number of points arise out of this decision. The first is that we can see that the impact of the objective approach to the identification of an agreement is to limit the sphere within which the doctrine of mistake can operate. All of the judges applied an objective test to the facts of the case, albeit that there are differences between their versions of the objective test and the results which they reached as a result of the application of an objective test to the facts of the case and the facts of other decided cases.

The majority affirmed the validity of the distinction between a contract concluded in writing and an oral contract concluded face-to-face. The justification for the dis-tinction is said to lie in the traditional refusal of English law to allow extrinsic evi-dence to be adduced for the purpose of contradicting a term of the written contract. This justification emerges most clearly in the speech of Lord Hobhouse at [49] where the rule is stated to be 'one of the great strengths of English commercial law'. The minority, Lord Nicholls and Lord Millett, did not adopt the same approach to the sanctity of the written document. Their focus was upon the nature of the mistake made and they pointed out that the mistake made in cases such as *Cundy* v. *Lindsay* and *Phillips* v. *Brooks* was the same, in the sense that in both cases the seller entered into the transaction under the misapprehension that the person with whom he was corresponding (or, in the case of the oral contract, the person with whom he was talking) was one person, of whose name he was aware, when in fact he was a third party.

Given that a different rule is applicable to written contracts, it may be necessary to define a written contract for this purpose. In many cases this will be an easy require-ment for finance houses to satisfy because of the demands of the consumer credit legislation which require that the debtor be identified in the written documentation (although these requirements were not applicable on the facts of *Shogun* because the case fell outside the scope of the Consumer Credit Act 1974, see [177] above). *Cundy* is, perhaps, more difficult in this respect. The crucial element is that it was a contract entered into by correspondence and, for the purpose of ascertaining the identity of the parties to that contract, it was necessary to examine the correspondence which passed between the parties. In cases such as *Ingram* v. *Little* and *Lewis* v. *Averay* the contract was concluded face-to-face and the fact that payment was made by cheque (which obviously involved writing) did not suffice to turn the contract into a written contract. The point would appear to be that it is not possible to adduce evidence for the purpose of contradicting the written, express terms of the contract. This being the case, it is probably necessary to focus on the term that is in issue between the parties. If that term is in writing and one party seeks to adduce evidence for the purpose of contradicting that written term, then the evidence should not be admitted. However, it appears that it is permissible to have regard to extrinsic evidence for the purpose of ascertaining the identity of the person named in the contract (*Dumford Trading AG* v. *OAO Atlantrybflot* [2004] EWHC 1099 (Comm); [2004] 2 Lloyd's Rep 157). There is a difference between a case such as *Shogun* where the function of the extrinsic evidence is to contradict the written term of the contract and a case such as *Dumford* where extrinsic evidence is used for the purpose of identifying, and giving effect to, the intention of the parties. The former is illegitimate, while the latter is legitimate.

The arguments relating to the importance of the written terms of the contract are not all one way, however (see D W McLauchlan (2005) 121 LQR 9). The significance of the parol evidence rule has diminished greatly in recent years and it may be doubted whether Lord Hobhouse's sentiment (at [49]) reflects the drift of the modern law (see the contrasting view of Lord Millett at [103]). Difficulties are also likely to arise in the case of contracts concluded by telephone or by e-mail. Will such cases be treated as written contracts or as contracts concluded face-to-face? It is clear from *Shogun* that a contract concluded by fax falls within the definition of a written contract but it is not clear what is the position in relation to other forms of instant-aneous communication where the parties are dealing with one another at a distance.

It is also important to have regard to the transactional structure that was adopted by the parties. Hire-purchase is a technique used to provide finance for purchasers who do not have access to cash in order to acquire goods. It is important to realize that where hire purchase is used there is generally no direct contractual relationship between the car dealer and the customer in a standard hire-purchase transaction. What happens is that the car dealer sells the car to a finance company and the finance company then enters into a transaction with the customer on hire purchase terms. Hire-purchase is a contract under which the finance company agrees to hire the goods to the hirer for a period of time and the hirer in turn promises to pay rental to the finance company (often on a monthly basis). The rental is calculated in such a way that it covers the cost of the acquisition of the asset and also gives the finance company a return on the money which it has advanced to the hirer. At the end of the period of hire the hirer will be given an option to purchase the asset, generally for a nominal sum. The hirer will generally exercise the option so that he or she acquires ownership of the asset but he or she is under no legal obligation to do so. Should the hirer decide not to exercise the option then property in the goods will remain with the finance company. The fact that the contract is between the finance company and the customer and not between the dealer and the customer explains why it is that the litigation in the present case involved the finance company and not the dealer. The real interest of the finance company in the present case therefore lay in ensuring that it obtained an adequate return on its outlay and in ensuring that it had adequate security against debtor default. So it was not the case that the finance company wished to deal only with Mr Durlabh Patel; it was simply that their credit check revealed that Mr Durlabh Patel's credit history was satisfactory for the purpose of entering into the transaction. In so far as it is possible to distinguish between identity and credit-worthiness, the mistake made by the finance company in the present case can be said to be one that related to creditworthiness and not identity. It might also be worth asking the question whether or not the law ought to protect a party in the position of the finance house. After all, they can be said to have assumed the risk that their debtor would not pay and, given that they would have had to accept the risk if the debtor had told lies about the state of his finances, why should they be entitled to throw the risk on to the innocent third party purchaser in the case where the debtor tells lies, not about the state of his bank account, but about his name? This observation may lie behind the perception of Lord Nicholls and Lord Millett that the third party purchaser is generally more deserving of protection than the seller who allows the buyer to assume possession of the goods on credit terms. At the same time, one must bear in mind Lord Walker's warning about the need to produce a rule which is of general application and which is not dependent upon the sympathy evoked by one party to the particular transaction.

This leads on to a further aspect of this case which is the role of the *nemo dat quod non habet*[2] maxim. As was pointed out in this case, the litigation was conducted between two innocent parties who had been defrauded by a third party. The claim brought by the finance company was, in essence, that the defendant was in possession of their car and that he should return it to them or pay its value. In many parts of the world this would be regarded as a property claim because the claim of the finance company is one to recover property which they say belongs to them. The defendant, by contrast, refuses to return the car because he says that he is the owner of the car, having bought it in good faith from his seller. Thus we have two parties, both of whom are

---

[2] You cannot give what you do not have.

claiming ownership of the car. Legal systems strike the balance between these two claims in different ways. English law starts from the maxim *nemo dat quod non habet*; that is to say, you cannot give what you do not have. Thus if the rogue did not have ownership of the car he had no ownership to give to the defendant. It was for this reason that the distinction between a void and a voidable contract was so important. If the contract was void then the rogue at no time acquired ownership of the car and so had nothing to transfer to the defendant. On the other hand, if the contract between the finance company and the rogue was merely voidable for fraud, the rogue would acquire title to the car until such time as the contract between the rogue and the finance company was set aside and so he would have something to give to the purchaser at least before the contract with the original seller was set aside. The onus was on the defendant to prove that one of the exceptions to the *nemo dat* rule was applicable on the facts of the case and the majority concluded that no such exception was applicable. Other legal systems take a different perspective. They start from the assumption that the third party should be protected and the maxim in which this is customarily expressed is *possession vaut titre*. In essence the minority in the present case preferred the interest of the third party purchaser and so sought to carve out an additional exception to the *nemo dat* rule. But their attempt to do so failed.

One final point relates to the status of the cases where the parties deal with one another face-to-face. Lord Hobhouse found it unnecessary to consider this line of authority in any detail, given that it was not relevant to the issue which arose on the facts of the present case. The rest of their Lordships did, however, consider these cases in some detail. The general picture which emerges from the review of the cases is that they largely depend on their own facts and that there is a presumption, which is a strong one, that a contracting party intends to deal with the party who is present in front of him and that it will not suffice for a party to assert that there is no contract in existence between the parties because he believed that the person in front of him was, in fact, somebody else. Thus *Phillips* v. *Brooks* and *Lewis* v. *Averay* are cited with approval. *Ingram* v. *Little* fared rather less well. Lord Millett (at [87]) stated that it should be 'overruled' and Lord Walker (at [185]) was similarly of the view that it was 'wrongly decided.' Lord Hobhouse expressed no view on the case, simply observing (at [47]) that it was 'not pertinent' to the issue that arose on the facts of the present case. The attitude of Lord Nicholls and Lord Phillips is perhaps more difficult to discern. Lord Nicholls discussed the case at [20]–[22]. While he clearly preferred the reasoning of Devlin LJ to the reasoning of the majority (see [21]–[22]) he stopped short of saying that the case was wrongly decided. Lord Phillips discussed the case at [142]–[147] and, while he referred to the 'powerful dissenting judgment' of Devlin LJ, he too stopped short of saying that the case had been wrongly decided. Part of the difficulty here may lie in the emphasis placed by the judges on the facts of the case. If the cases ultimately depend upon their own particular facts, what useful purpose is served by stating that a particular case, decided over 40 years ago, was wrongly decided? What would appear to matter is the presumption that is applied by the court. The presumption would appear to be a presumption of fact (not law) but it is a difficult one to rebut. In particular, it will not suffice for a party to prove that he intended to deal with an identifiable third party and not with the party who was in fact in front of him. But it may be possible to rebut the presumption on certain exceptional facts. An example may be where the rogue impersonates an individual known to the claimant (as in the example of Isaac and Jacob given by Lord Walker at [187]).

The decision in *Shogun* is a difficult one and it is unlikely to be the last word on the subject. While the decision has attracted critical comment (see, for example, C Hare, 'Identity Mistakes: A Missed Opportunity?' (2004) 67 *MLR* 993), it is highly unlikely that it will be re-considered by the House of Lords. Courts will have to accept the decision and concern themselves with the rather more difficult issue of ascertaining the scope of the decision. Reform, if it is to come, will have to come from Parliament, albeit the practical likelihood of Parliament finding the time to consider this issue is low. One difficulty with the current law is its 'all-or-nothing' nature; either the claimant recovers in full or he recovers nothing. An alternative approach might be to engage in loss-splitting so that the loss occasioned by the fraud of the rogue is shared between the claimant and the defendant. Such a proposal was made by Devlin LJ in his dissenting judgment in *Ingram* v. *Little* in the following terms:

There can be no doubt, as all this difference of opinion shows, that the dividing line between voidness and voidability, between fundamental mistake and incidental deceit, is a very fine one. That a fine and difficult distinction has to be drawn is not necessarily any reproach to the law. But need the rights of the parties in a case like this depend on such a distinction? The great virtue of the common law is that it sets out to solve legal problems by the application to them of principles which the ordinary man is expected to recognise as sensible and just; their application in any particular case may produce what seems to him a hard result, but as principles they should be within his understanding and merit his approval. But here, contrary to its habit, the common law, instead of looking for a principle that is simple and just, rests on theoretical distinctions. Why should the question whether the defendant should or should not pay the plaintiff damages for conversion depend upon voidness or voidability, and upon inferences to be drawn from a conversation in which the defendant took no part? The true spirit of the common law is to override theoretical distinctions when they stand in the way of doing practical justice. For the doing of justice, the relevant question in this sort of case is not whether the contract was void or voidable, but which of two innocent parties shall suffer for the fraud of a third. The plain answer is that the loss should be divided between them in such proportion as is just in all the circumstances. If it be pure misfortune, the loss should be borne equally; if the fault or imprudence of either party has caused or contributed to the loss, it should be borne by that party in the whole or in the greater part. In saying this, I am suggesting nothing novel, for this sort of observation has often been made. But it is only in comparatively recent times that the idea of giving to a court power to apportion loss has found a place in our law. I have in mind particularly the Law Reform Acts of 1935, 1943 and 1945, that dealt respectively with joint tortfeasors, frustrated contracts and contributory negligence. These statutes, which I believe to have worked satisfactorily, show a modern inclination towards a decision based on a just apportionment rather than one given in black or in white according to the logic of the law. I believe it would be useful if Parliament were now to consider whether or not it is practicable by means of a similar act of law reform to provide for the victims of a fraud a better way of adjusting their mutual loss than that which has grown out of the common law.

This proposal was, however, considered and rejected by the Law Reform Committee in its Twelfth Report (*Transfer of Title to Chattels* Cmnd 2958 of 1966) on the ground that it would introduce too much uncertainty and complexity into the law (particularly in the case where the asset is the subject of a number of sales before the fraud is discovered).

5. COMMON MISTAKE

The law in relation to common mistake (that is to say, a mistake that is shared by both parties to the contract) is dominated by two cases. The first is the decision of the House of Lords in *Bell* v. *Lever Bros Ltd* [1932] AC 161. The second was, until relatively recently, the decision of the Court of Appeal in *Solle* v. *Butcher* [1950] 1 KB 671. But *Solle* has been overruled by the Court of Appeal in *Great Peace Shipping Ltd* v. *Tsavliris Salvage (International) Ltd* [2002] EWCA Civ 1407; [2003] QB 679. *Great Peace* has therefore dislodged *Solle* and has now assumed the role of a leading case.

The central proposition of law can be simply stated: in order to set aside a contract on the ground of common mistake, the mistake must be 'fundamental'. The difficulty is the obvious one, namely the meaning in this context of the word 'fundamental'. It would appear that the answer depends in part upon the nature of the mistake that has been made. Where the mistake is one as to the existence of the subject-matter of the contract (see section 6 of the Sale of Goods Act 1979 and *Couturier* v. *Hastie* (1856) 5 HLC 673, discussed in *Great Peace*, p. 625 below at paras [51]–[55]) or its identity (see *Diamond* v. *British Columbia Thoroughbred Breeders' Society* (1966) 52 DLR (2d) 146) then the mistake is more likely to be fundamental than in the case where the mistake is one as to the quality of the subject-matter of the contract (*Bell* v. *Lever Bros Ltd* [1932] AC 161, p. 617 below). But it is not the case that a mistake as to the existence or identity of the subject-matter of the contract will always constitute a fundamental mistake, whereas a mistake as to quality will never be fundamental. Cases can be found in which a mistake as to the existence of the subject-matter of the contract has not sufficed to set aside a contract (see *McRae* v. *Commonwealth Disposals Commission* (1951) 84 CLR 377, discussed in *Great Peace*, p. 628 below at paras [77]–[80]) and cases can also be found in which a mistake as to quality has been held to be sufficiently fundamental to set aside a contract (see *Scott* v. *Coulson* [1903] 2 Ch 349, discussed in *Great Peace*, p. 630 below at paras [87]–[88]). Prior to the decision of the Court of Appeal in *Great Peace* it was also necessary to distinguish between the test applicable at law and the test applicable in equity because the test for a fundamental mistake in equity was more relaxed than that applicable at law. *Great Peace* has, however, overruled this line of authority in equity and concluded that the answer to the question whether or not a mistake is fundamental is the same, both at law and in equity. However, given the bold and controversial nature of the step taken by the Court of Appeal, it is necessary to devote some attention to *Solle* v. *Butcher* and the line of cases which it generated. It is too soon to cast them into oblivion. The rise and fall of common mistake in equity will be considered in section 6, after we have examined the great case of *Bell* v. *Lever Bros* and its interpretation by the Court of Appeal in *Great Peace*.

Bell v. Lever Brothers Ltd

[1932] AC 161, House of Lords

Lever Brothers Ltd controlled the Niger Company. Lever Brothers agreed to employ Bell to act as the chairman, and Snelling to act as the vice-chairman, of the board of directors of Niger. Bell and Snelling secretly speculated in cocoa, a commodity in which Niger dealt. Their conduct was in breach of their contracts of employment and would have justified Lever Brothers terminating their services. Later, Niger merged with the African and Eastern Trade Corporation so that the services of Bell and Snelling were no longer required. In ignorance of their breaches of duty, Lever Brothers agreed to pay £30,000 to Bell and £20,000 to Snelling as compensation for terminating their contracts of employment.

The jury found that if Lever Brothers had known of the breaches it would have terminated the contracts of Bell and Snelling without paying compensation. When Lever Brothers discovered the breaches it brought an action claiming rescission of the compensation agreements on the grounds of fraudulent misrepresentation and unilateral mistake induced by fraud but not on the ground of 'mutual' mistake. At trial the jury found that Bell and Snelling had not acted fraudulently. However the trial judge held that the pleadings raised the issue of mutual mistake and that the compensation agreements were void, having been made under a common mistake as to the legal relations between the parties, each party believing, contrary to the truth, that the one was entitled to claim and the other was bound to pay compensation. The Court of Appeal held that if the issue of mutual mistake was not raised, the pleadings should be treated as amended in order to raise it and upheld the decision of the trial judge. On appeal the House of Lords held that the issue of mutual mistake was not raised by the pleadings and they could not be amended to raise it. However on the basis that the issue was raised, it was held by a majority (Viscount Haldane and Lord Warrington of Clyffe dissenting) that the compensation agreements were not void as the mutual mistake related not to the subject matter but to the quality of the employment contracts.

Lord Warrington of Clyffe (dissenting on the question whether the compensation agreements were void for mistake)

It is in my opinion clear that each party believed that the remunerative offices, compensation for the loss of which was the subject of the negotiations, were offices which could not be determined except by the consent of the holder thereof, and further believed that the other party was under the same belief and was treating on that footing.

The real question, therefore, is whether the erroneous assumption on the part of both parties to the agreements that the service contracts were undeterminable except by agreement was of such a fundamental character as to constitute an underlying assumption without which the parties would not have made the contract they in fact made, or whether it was only a common error as to a material element, but one not going to the root of the matter and not affecting the substance of the consideration.

With the knowledge that I am differing from the majority of your Lordships, I am unable to arrive at any conclusion except that in this case the erroneous assumption was essential to the contract which without it would not have been made.

It is true that the error was not one as to the terms of the service agreements, but it was one which, having regard to the matter on which the parties were negotiating—namely, the terms on which the service agreements were to be prematurely determined and the compensation to be paid therefor, was in my opinion as fundamental to the bargain as any error one can imagine.

Lord Atkin

Was the agreement of March 19, 1929, void by reason of a mutual mistake of Mr D'Arcy Cooper and Mr Bell? . . .

My Lords, the rules of law dealing with the effect of mistake on contract appear to be established with reasonable clearness. If mistake operates at all it operates so as to negative or in some cases to nullify consent. The parties may be mistaken in the identity of the contracting parties, or in the existence of the subject-matter of the contract at the date of the contract, or in the quality of the subject-matter of the contract. These mistakes may be by one party, or by both, and the legal effect may depend upon the class of mistake above mentioned. Thus a mistaken belief by A that he is contracting with B, whereas in fact he is contracting with C, will negative consent where it is clear that the intention of A was to contract only with B. So the agreement of A and B to purchase a specific article is void if in fact the article had perished before the date of sale. In this case, though the parties in fact were agreed about the subject-matter, yet a consent to transfer or take delivery of something not existent is deemed useless, the consent is nullified. As codified in the Sale of Goods Act the contract is expressed to be void if the seller was in ignorance of the destruction of the specific chattel. I apprehend that if the seller with knowledge that a chattel was destroyed purported to sell it to a purchaser, the latter might sue for damages for non-delivery though the former could not sue for non-acceptance, but I know of no case where a seller has so committed himself. This is a case where mutual mistake certainly and unilateral mistake by the seller of goods will prevent a contract from arising. Corresponding to mistake as to the existence of the subject-matter is mistake as to title in cases where, unknown to the parties, the buyer is already the owner of that which the seller purports to sell to him. The parties intended to effectuate a transfer of ownership: such a transfer is impossible: the stipulation is naturali ratione inutilis.[3] This is the case of *Cooper v. Phibbs* LR 2 HL 149, where A agreed to take a lease of a fishery from B, though contrary to the belief of both parties at the time A was tenant for life of the fishery and B appears to have had no title at all. To such a case Lord Westbury applied the principle that if parties contract under a mutual mistake and misapprehension as to their relative and respective rights the result is that the agreement is liable to be set aside as having proceeded upon a common mistake. Applied to the context the statement is only subject to the criticism that the agreement would appear to be void rather than voidable. Applied to mistake as to rights generally it would appear to be too wide. Even where the vendor has no title, though both parties think he has, the correct view would appear to be that there is a contract: but that the vendor has either committed a breach of a stipulation as to title, or is not able to perform his contract. The contract is unenforceable by him but is not void.

Mistake as to quality of the thing contracted for raises more difficult questions. In such a case a mistake will not affect assent unless it is the mistake of both parties, and is as to the existence of some quality which makes the thing without the quality essentially different from the thing as it was believed to be. Of course it may appear that the parties contracted that the article should possess the quality which one or other or both

---

[3] 'By natural reason (or common sense) useless'.

mistakenly believed it to possess. But in such a case there is a contract and the inquiry is a different one, being whether the contract as to quality amounts to a condition or a warranty, a different branch of the law. The principles to be applied are to be found in two cases which, as far as my knowledge goes, have always been treated as authoritative expositions of the law. The first is *Kennedy* v. *Panama Royal Mail Co* LR 2 QB 580, 586.

In that case the plaintiff had applied for shares in the defendant company on the faith of a prospectus which stated falsely but innocently that the company had a binding contract with the Government of New Zealand for the carriage of mails. On discovering the true facts the plaintiff brought an action for the recovery of the sums he had paid on calls. The defendants brought a cross action for further calls. . . . The Court came to the conclusion in that case that, though there was a misapprehension as to that which was a material part of the motive inducing the applicant to ask for the shares, it did not prevent the shares from being in substance those he applied for.

The next case is *Smith* v. *Hughes* LR 6 QB 597, 604, 606, the well known case as to new and old oats [see pp. 26–30 above]. . . . The Court ordered a new trial. It is not quite clear whether they considered that if the defendant's contention was correct, the parties were not ad idem or there was a contractual condition that the oats sold were old oats. In either case the defendant would succeed in defeating the claim.

In these cases I am inclined to think that the true analysis is that there is a contract, but that the one party is not able to supply the very thing whether goods or services that the other party contracted to take; and therefore the contract is unenforceable by the one if executory, while if executed the other can recover back money paid on the ground of failure of the consideration.

We are now in a position to apply to the facts of this case the law as to mistake so far as it has been stated. It is essential on this part of the discussion to keep in mind the finding of the jury acquitting the defendants of fraudulent misrepresentation or concealment in procuring the agreements in question. Grave injustice may be done to the defendants and confusion introduced into the legal conclusion, unless it is quite clear that in considering mistake in this case no suggestion of fraud is admissible and cannot strictly be regarded by the judge who has to determine the legal issues raised. The agreement which is said to be void is the agreement contained in the letter of March 19, 1929, that Bell would retire from the Board of the Niger Company and its subsidiaries, and that in consideration of his doing so Levers would pay him as compensation for the termination of his agreements and consequent loss of office the sum of 30,000l. in full satisfaction and discharge of all claims and demands of any kind against Lever Brothers, the Niger Company or its subsidiaries. The agreement, which as part of the contract was terminated, had been broken so that it could be repudiated. Is an agreement to terminate a broken contract different in kind from an agreement to terminate an unbroken contract, assuming that the breach has given the one party the right to declare the contract at an end? I feel the weight of the plaintiffs' contention that a contract immediately determinable is a different thing from a contract for an unexpired term, and that the difference in kind can be illustrated by the immense price of release from the longer contract as compared with the shorter. . . . But, on the whole, I have come to the conclusion that it would be wrong to decide that an agreement to terminate a definite specified contract is void if it turns out that the agreement had already been broken and could have been terminated otherwise. The contract released is the identical contract in both cases, and the party paying for release gets exactly what he bargains for. It seems immaterial that he could have got the same result in another way, or that if he had known the true facts he would not have entered into the bargain. A buys B's horse; he thinks the horse is sound and he pays the price of a sound horse; he would certainly not have bought the horse if he had known as the fact is that the horse is unsound. If B has made no representation as to soundness and has not contracted that the horse is sound, A is bound and cannot recover back the price. A buys a picture from B; both A and B believe it to be the work of an old master, and a high price is paid. It turns out to be a modern copy. A has no remedy in the absence of representation or warranty. A agrees to take on lease or to buy from B an unfurnished dwelling-house. The house is in fact uninhabitable. A would never have entered into the bargain if he had known the fact. A has no remedy, and the position is the same whether B knew the facts or not, so long as he made no representation or gave no warranty. A buys a roadside garage business from B abutting on a public thorough-fare: unknown to A, but known to B, it has already been decided to construct a byepass road which will divert substantially the whole of the traffic from passing A's garage. Again A has no remedy. All these cases involve hardship on A and benefit B, as most people would say, unjustly. They can be supported on the ground that it is of paramount importance that contracts should be observed, and that if parties honestly comply with the essentials of the formation of contracts—i.e., agree in the same terms on the same subject-matter—they are bound, and must rely on the stipulations of the contract for protection from the effect of facts unknown to them.

This brings the discussion to the alternative mode of expressing the result of a mutual mistake. It is said that in such a case as the present there is to be implied a stipulation in the contract that a condition of its efficacy is that the facts should be as understood by both parties—namely, that the contract could not be terminated till the end of the current term. The question of the existence of conditions, express or implied, is obviously one that affects not the formation of contract, but the investigation of the terms of the contract when made. A condition derives its efficacy from the consent of the parties, express or implied. They have agreed, but on what terms? One term may be that unless the facts are or are not of a particular nature, or unless an event has or has not happened, the contract is not to take effect. With regard to future facts such a condition is obviously contractual. Till the event occurs the parties are bound. Thus the condition (the exact terms of which need not here be investigated) that is generally accepted as underlying the principle of the frustration cases is contractual, an implied condition. Sir John Simon [counsel for Lever Bros] formulated for the assistance of your Lordships a proposition which should be recorded: 'Whenever it is to be inferred from the terms of a contract or its surrounding circumstances that the consensus has been reached upon the basis of a particular contractual assumption, and that assumption is not true, the contract is avoided: i.e., it is void ab initio if the assumption is of present fact and it ceases to bind if the assumption is of future fact'.

I think few would demur to this statement, but its value depends upon the meaning of 'a contractual assumption', and also upon the true meaning to be attached to 'basis', a metaphor which may mislead. When used expressly in contracts, for instance, in policies of insurance, which state that the truth of the statements in the proposal is to be the basis of the contract of insurance, the meaning is clear. The truth of the statements is made a condition of the contract, which failing, the contract is void unless the condition is waived. The proposition does not amount to more than this that, if the contract expressly or impliedly contains a term that a particular assumption is a condition of the contract, the contract is avoided if the assumption is not true. But we have not advanced far on the inquiry how to ascertain whether the contract does contain such a condition. Various words are to be found to define the state of things which make a condition. 'In the contemplation of both parties fundamental to the continued validity of the contract', 'a foundation essential to its existence', 'a fundamental reason for making it', are phrases found in the important judgment of Scrutton LJ in the present case. The first two phrases appear to me to be unexceptionable. They cover the case of a contract to serve in a particular place, the existence of which is fundamental to the service, or to procure the services of a professional vocalist, whose continued health is essential to performance. But 'a fundamental reason for making a contract' may, with respect, be misleading. The reason of one party only is presumedly not intended, but in the cases I have suggested above, of the sale of a horse or of a picture, it might be said that the fundamental reason for making the contract was the belief of both parties that the horse was sound or the picture an old master, yet in neither case would the condition as I think exist. Nothing is more dangerous than to allow oneself liberty to construct for the parties contracts which they have not in terms made by importing implications which would appear to make the contract more businesslike or more just. The implications to be made are to be no more than are 'necessary' for giving business efficacy to the transaction, and it appears to me that, both as to existing facts and future facts, a condition would not be implied unless the new state of facts makes the contract something different in kind from the contract in the original state of facts . . . We therefore get a common standard for mutual mistake, and implied conditions whether as to existing or as to future facts. Does the state of the new facts destroy the identity of the subject-matter as it was in the original state of facts? To apply the principle to the infinite combinations of facts that arise in actual experience will continue to be difficult, but if this case results in establishing order into what has been a somewhat confused and difficult branch of the law it will have served a useful purpose.

I have already stated my reasons for deciding that in the present case the identity of the subject-matter was not destroyed by the mutual mistake, if any, and need not repeat them . . .

Lord Thankerton

Turning .. to the question of mutual error or mistake, I think that the respondents' contention may be fairly stated as follows—namely, that in concluding the agreements of March, 1929, all parties proceeded on the mistaken assumption that the appellants' service agreements were not liable to immediate termination by Lever Brothers by reason of the appellants' misconduct, and that such common mistake involved the actual subject-matter of the agreements, and did not merely relate to a quality of the subject-matter.

The cases on this branch of the law are numerous, and in seeking the principle on which they rest I will at first confine my attention to those which relate to innocent mutual mistake on formation of the contract, as it appears to me that the cases relating to facts arising subsequently to the formation of the contract may be found to rest on a somewhat different principle.

But first let me define the exact position as at the date of the agreements of March, 1929. The service agreements of both appellants were then existing as binding legal contracts, although it was in the power of Lever Brothers, had they then known of the appellants' breach of contract, to have terminated the contracts; but, until the exercise of such power, the contracts remained binding. It is also clear that an essential purpose of the agreements of March, 1929, was to secure the termination of these service agreements. The mistake was not as to the existence of agreements which required termination—for such did exist—but as to the possibility of terminating them by other means.

A clear exposition of the principles to be applied in such a case as the present is to be found in the judgment of the Court of Queen's Bench (Cockburn CJ, Blackburn, Mellor and Shee JJ), in *Kennedy* v. *Panama, &c., Co* LR 2 QB 580, 586, 587, 588, delivered by Blackburn J, who, as Lord Blackburn, reaffirmed this opinion in 1881 in *Mackay* v. *Dick* 6 App Cas 251, 265. . . . Blackburn J proceeds . . where there has been an innocent misrepresentation or misapprehension, it does not authorize a rescission unless it is such as to show that there is a complete difference in substance between what was supposed to be and what was taken, so as to constitute a failure of consideration. For example, where a horse is bought under a belief that it is sound, if the purchaser was induced to buy by a fraudulent representation as to the horse's soundness, the contract may be rescinded. If it was induced by an honest misrepresentation as to its soundness, though it may be clear that both vendor and purchaser thought that they were dealing about a sound horse and were in error, yet the purchaser must pay the whole price, unless there was a warranty'. After referring to the passages in the Digest of Civil Law and the way the question is there mooted, Blackburn J says: 'The answers given by the great jurists quoted are to the effect that, if there be misapprehension as to the substance of the thing, there is no contract; but if it be only a difference in some quality or accident, even though the misapprehension may have been the actuating motive to the purchaser, yet the contract remains binding'. And he adds: 'And, as we apprehend, the principle of our law is the same as that of the civil law'. This passage makes clear that it is not enough for the purchaser to prove that the misapprehension was the inducing cause to him and that, if he had known, he would not have entered into the contract. The earlier passage as to the sale of an unsound horse also shows that it is not enough that a grossly excessive price has been paid for a bad article. . . .

The phrase 'underlying assumption by the parties', as applied to the subject-matter of a contract, may be too widely interpreted so as to include something which one of the parties had not necessarily in his mind at the time of the contract; in my opinion it can only properly relate to something which both must necessarily have accepted in their minds as an essential and integral element of the subject-matter. In the present case, however probable it may be, we are not necessarily forced to that assumption. *Cooper* v. *Phibbs* LR 2 HL 149, 170 is a good illustration. . . . There are many other cases to the same effect, but I think that it is true to say that in all of them it either appeared on the face of the contract that the matter as to which the mistake existed was an essential and integral element of the subject-matter of the contract, or it was an inevitable inference from the nature of the contract that all the parties so regarded it.

In the present case the terms of the contracts throw no light on the question, and, as already indicated, I do not find sufficient material to compel the inference that the appellants, at the time of the contract, regarded the indefeasibility of the service agreements as an essential and integral element in the subject-matter of the bargain.

Viscount Haldane agreed with the judgment of Lord Warrington of Clyffe. **Lord Blanesburgh** stated that he was in 'entire accord' with the conclusions of Lord Atkin and Lord Thankerton.

COMMENTARY

Lord Atkin uses the language of 'mutual' rather than 'common' mistake but the type
of mistake under consideration was a common mistake in that both parties entered
into the compensation agreements in the belief that Lever Bros were bound to make
the payment and that Bell and Snelling were entitled to receive it. In the first extracted
paragraph from his judgment Lord Atkin distinguishes between three different categories of mistake, namely (i) a mistake as to the identity of the contracting parties,
(ii) a mistake as the existence of the subject-matter of the contract, and (iii) a mistake
as to the quality of the subject-matter of the contract. While he acknowledges that
mistakes in the first two categories can suffice to set aside a contract, he recognizes
that mistakes in the third category raise 'more difficult questions'. It is important to
note the examples given by Lord Atkin at p. 620 above of mistakes as to the quality of
the subject-matter of the contract which would not suffice, in his opinion, to entitle a
party to set aside the contract. Particularly striking in this respect is his example of the
case of the sale of a picture which both parties mistakenly believe to be 'the work of an
old master'. In his view the buyer in such a case has no remedy in the absence of a
misrepresentation or a contractual warranty as to the provenance of the picture (see
Leaf v. *International Galleries Ltd* [1950] 2 KB 86).

Given the size of the mistake made by Lever Bros, why did the House of Lords
conclude that the mistake was not a 'fundamental' mistake? The most convincing
answer to this question has been provided by Catharine MacMillan in her detailed
historical review of the case (see C MacMillan, 'How Temptation Led to Mistake: an
Explanation of *Bell v Lever Bros. Ltd*' (2003) 119 *LQR* 625). MacMillan points out that
Lever Brothers' primary claim against Bell and Snelling was based on fraud. However
they failed to persuade the jury that Bell and Snelling had induced Lever Brothers to
enter into the termination agreements by fraudulent misrepresentation or by fraudulent concealment of their misconduct in trading in cocoa on their own account while
employed by the Niger Company. Thus she concludes (at p. 658) that the case was a
'failed case of fraudulent misrepresentation and concealment' and that 'mistake was
pleaded in the alternative and left largely unaddressed during the conduct of the trial'.
One consequence of the subsidiary nature of the mistake claim was that 'the evidence'
in relation to mistake 'was not what it could have been'.

MacMillan further points out that the facts of the case do not support many of the
explanations that have been offered in defence of the conclusion that the mistake
made by Lever Brothers was not 'fundamental'. One justification that has been offered
is that the mistake was not sufficiently fundamental because it was a mistake that
related 'primarily to cost', in the sense that Lever Brothers wished to terminate the
agreements with Bell and Snelling without paying them any compensation. But she
points out (at p. 657) that this explanation does not work because 'money . . . was not
the object of this law suit'. The law suit was brought 'upon principle and not for
profit'. The principle was the maintenance of standards of honesty and integrity in
the running of the company. The case was decided at a time when ownership of a
company was beginning to be separated from the control of the company. Bell and
Snelling were part of a 'new class of professional managers' and Lever Brothers wished

to ensure that they adhered to appropriate standards of conduct in the running of the business. Thus the litigation was not about money and any attempt to capture the essence of the case in monetary terms is doomed to failure. Secondly, it has been suggested that Lever Brothers obtained their object in that they secured the co-operation of Bell and Snelling in the corporate re-structure upon which Lever Brothers were then engaged. But, as MacMillan points out (at p. 657), this is not consistent with the facts of the case in that Bell and Snelling were not active in the negotiations that led to the amalgamation. So they did not require any inducement to agree to participate in the re-structure.

This leaves us with two principal explanations of the case. The first is that Lever Brothers 'got exactly what they bargained for', namely 'the termination of the agreements'. MacMillan rejects this explanation (at p. 658) on the ground that the mistake made by Lever Brothers did not merely make the bargain less desirable to Lever Brothers: the bargain would not have been made had Lever Brothers known the true situation. Here it must be remembered that Lever Brothers brought the claim on a point of principle and so it could not be said in any realistic sense that they had obtained what they bargained for. The final explanation for the case is 'that the principle was applied as it was because the case marks something of a high water mark for sanctity of contract'. Thus MacMillan points out (at p. 658) that the case was decided at the beginning of the Great Depression and that depression would last until the outbreak of the Second World War. At this point in history the courts did place considerable emphasis on the importance of sanctity of contract. But, as she points out, sanctity of contract 'is more of an explanation for the decision' than 'a justification for its result'.

MacMillan concludes (at p. 658) that 'an examination of the historical surrounding to the facts behind the case of *Bell v Lever Bros* reveals that the case is not the stable bedrock necessary to support a functioning doctrine of mistake'. By this it would appear that she means that regard must be had to the particular facts and circumstances of the case. These facts and circumstances include the following: (i) Lever Brothers' principal claim was based on fraud, misrepresentation and concealment and that claim failed; (ii) mistake was pleaded as an afterthought and had not been properly thought through by counsel who 'found the mistake cases difficult to reconcile and apply'; (iii) over the years Bell and Snelling had rendered 'magnificent services' to the company and had done an 'outstanding job'; (iv) the profit which Bell and Snelling had made when trading on their own account was 'comparatively small' especially when seen against the severance payments which they stood to lose; and (v) Lever Brothers had benefited considerably from their endeavours on behalf of the company. These circumstances combined to paint for their Lordships the following picture of Bell and Snelling (at pp. 651–652):

They were presented with two gentlemen who had been absolutely exonerated of fraud. These men had rendered exceptional service to the Niger; they were primarily responsible for its transformation from a failing concern to financial success. Their only error was to succumb, briefly, to temptation. They did not deny that this was a mistake. Their profits were modest, their conduct did not harm their company in any way, and when they realised their error, they made a clean breast of it to Lever Brothers. The conduct of Bell and Snelling was not exemplary, but it was not so egregiously awful as to strip them of all compensation. Bell, in failing health, would never work again. It appears that in the view of the majority, at the end of the day, the breach committed by Bell and Snelling did not justify the termination of their employment agreements. When one reads the judgments with this approach in mind, the opinions with regard to contractual mistake are understood. The majority found that the mistake was not sufficiently fundamental to vitiate the termination agreements. The problem is that while this may be the correct result in the case, it produces unfortunate law with regard to contractual mistake and also as to the standards of business conduct.

Perhaps the most appropriate conclusion to be drawn from *Bell* was summed up by MacMillan in the following passage:

the reason that the mistake was not considered sufficiently fundamental in this case was because of the peculiar and exceptional circumstances that gave rise to the termination agreements. Hard cases really do make bad law.

The circumstances in which a mistake may be held to be 'fundamental' were considered further by the Court of Appeal in:

Great Peace Shipping Ltd v. Tsavliris Salvage (International) Ltd

[2002] EWCA Civ 1407; [2003] QB 679, Court of Appeal

The defendant salvors ('the appellants') agreed to provide salvage services for a vessel, the *Cape Providence*, which was in serious difficulty in the South Indian Ocean. The defendants contacted Ocean Routes in order to discover the identity of vessels in the vicinity of the stricken vessel. They were told that the *Great Peace* was proximate to the vessel. The defendants contacted the owners of the *Great Peace*, the claimants, by telephone and an oral agreement was made under which the defendants agreed to hire the *Great Peace* for a minimum of five days. During that conversation no mention was made of the position of the *Great Peace*. The defendants believed that the vessels were thirty-five miles apart when in fact they were 410 miles apart. The defendants did not attempt immediately to set aside the agreement when they discovered the true state of affairs. They did so only when they found that another vessel was available to provide the necessary services. The claimants, the owners of the *Great Peace*, sued for the five-day hire but the defendants refused to pay on two grounds: (i) that the agreement was void at common law for fundamental mistake; and (ii) that the agreement was voidable in equity. Both defences were rejected by Toulson J and by the Court of Appeal. Judgment was entered for the claimants.

Lord Phillips of Worth Matravers [giving the judgment of the court]

50. It is generally accepted that the principles of the law of common mistake expounded by Lord Atkin in *Bell* v. *Lever Brothers* were based on the common law. . . . The first step is to identify the nature of the common law doctrine of mistake that was identified, or established, by *Bell* v. *Lever Brothers*.

51. Lord Atkin and Lord Thankerton were breaking no new ground in holding void a contract where, unknown to the parties, the subject matter of the contract no longer existed at the time that the contract was concluded. The Sale of Goods Act 1893 was a statute which set out to codify the common law. Section 6, to which Lord Atkin referred, provided:

'When there is a contract for the sale of specific goods, and the goods without the knowledge of the seller have perished at the time when the contract is made, the contract is void.'

52.   Judge Chalmers, the draftsman of the Act, commented in the first edition of his book on the Act, *The Sale of Goods Act 1893* (1894) p. 17: 'The rule may be based on the ground of mutual mistake, or on the ground of impossibility of performance.'

53.   He put at the forefront of the authorities that he cited in support *Couturier* v. *Hastie* (1856) 5 HL Cas 673. That case involved the sale of a cargo of corn which, unknown to the parties, no longer existed at the time that the contract was concluded. Other decisions where agreements were held not to be binding were *Strickland* v. *Turner* (1852) 7 Exch 208—the sale of an annuity upon the life of a person who, unknown to the parties, had died, and *Pritchard* v. *Merchants' and Tradesman's Mutual Life Assurance Society* (1858) 3 CBNS 622—an insurance policy renewed in ignorance of the fact that the assured had died.

54.   A year later, in *Huddersfield Banking Co Ltd* v. *Henry Lister & Son Ltd* [1895] 2 Ch 273, at 280–281, Lindley LJ observed, citing *Strickland* v. *Turner*:

'But I take it that an agreement founded upon a common mistake, which mistake is impliedly treated as a consideration which must exist in order to bring the agreement into operation, can be set aside, formally if necessary, or treated as set aside and as invalid without any process or proceedings to do so.'

55.   Where that which is expressly identified as the subject of a contract does not exist, the contract will necessarily be one which cannot be performed. Such a situation can readily be identified. The position is very different where there is 'a mistake as to the existence of some quality of the subject matter which makes the thing without the quality essentially different from the thing as it was believed to be' (see *Bell* v. *Lever Bros Ltd* [1932] AC 161 at 218). In such a situation it may be possible to perform the letter of the contract. In support of the proposition that a contract is void in such circumstances, Lord Atkin cited two authorities, in which he said that the principles to be applied were to be found. The first was *Kennedy* v. *Panama, New Zealand and Australian Royal Mail Co* (1867) LR 2 QB 580.

[he set out the facts of the case and extracts from the judgment of Blackburn J (see p. 622 above) and continued]

59.   *Kennedy* v. *Panama* is not an easy case to interpret. What was claimed was rescission on the grounds of fraudulent misrepresentation, or alternatively a warranty, in a prospectus. Blackburn J found that there was no more than innocent misrepresentation. He referred to principles of Roman law, but it is not clear that those principles were dealing with anything more than the circumstances in which misdescription resulted in non-performance of the contract—see Buckland *A Textbook on Roman Law* (3rd edn, 1963) p. 419. We agree with the comment in *Chitty on Contracts* 28th edn Vol. 1 p. 298 at 5–007 that it is not clear that Blackburn J was intending to say that a mistake as to substance would make a contract void at English law.

60. The other case to which Lord Atkin referred was *Smith* v. *Hughes* (1871) LR 6 QB 597. On no view did that difficult case deal with common mistake and we are not able to see how it supported the test formulated by Lord Atkin, as set out [at p. 619 above]. Indeed, Lord Atkin himself commented at p. 222:

> 'In these cases I am inclined to think that the true analysis is that there is a contract, but that the one party is not able to supply the very thing whether goods or services that the other party contracted to take; and therefore the contract is unenforceable by the one if executory, while if executed the other can recover back money paid on the ground of failure of the consideration.'

61. We conclude that the two authorities to which Lord Atkin referred provided an insubstantial basis for his formulation of the test of common mistake in relation to the quality of the subject matter of a contract. Lord Atkin advanced an alternative basis for his test: the implication of a term of the same nature as that which was applied under the doctrine of frustration, as it was then understood. In so doing he adopted the analysis of Scrutton LJ in the Court of Appeal. It seems to us that this was a more solid juris-prudential basis for the test of common mistake that Lord Atkin was proposing. At the time of *Bell* v. *Lever Brothers* the law of frustration and common mistake had advanced hand in hand on the foundation of a common principle. Thereafter frustration proved a more fertile ground for the development of this principle than common mistake, and consideration of the development of the law of frustration assists with the analysis of the law of common mistake.

[he considered the development of the law of frustration and continued]

73. What do these developments in the law of frustration have to tell us about the law of common mistake? First that the theory of the implied term is as unrealistic when considering common mistake as when considering frustration. Where a fundamental assumption upon which an agreement is founded proves to be mistaken, it is not realistic to ask whether the parties impliedly agreed that in those circumstances the contract would not be binding. The avoidance of a contract on the ground of common mistake results from a rule of law under which, if it transpires that one or both of the parties have agreed to do something which it is impossible to perform, no obligation arises out of that agreement.

74. In considering whether performance of the contract is impossible, it is necessary to identify what it is that the parties agreed would be performed. This involves looking not only at the express terms, but at any implications that may arise out of the surrounding circumstances. In some cases it will be possible to identify details of the 'contractual adventure' which go beyond the terms that are expressly spelt out, in others it will not.

75. Just as the doctrine of frustration only applies if the contract contains no provision that covers the situation, the same should be true of common mistake. If, on true construction of the contract, a party warrants that the subject matter of the contract exists, or that it will be possible to perform the contract, there will be no scope to hold the contract void on the ground of common mistake.

76. If one applies the passage from the judgment of Lord Alverstone CJ in *Hobson* v. *Pattenden & Co* (1903) 19 TLR 186 .. to a case of common mistake, it suggests that the following elements must be present if common mistake is to avoid a contract: (i) there must be a common assumption as to the existence of a state of affairs; (ii) there must be no warranty by either party that that state of affairs exists; (iii) the non-existence of the state of affairs must not be attributable to the fault of either party; (iv) the non-existence of the state of affairs must render performance of the contract impossible; (v) the state of affairs may be the existence, or a vital attribute, of the consideration to be provided or circumstances which must subsist if performance of the contractual adventure is to be possible.

77. The second and third of these elements are well exemplified by the decision of the High Court of Australia in *McRae* v. *Commonwealth Disposals Commission* (1951) 84 CLR 377. The Commission invited tenders for the purchase of 'an oil tanker lying on the Jourmaund Reef . . . said to contain oil'. The plaintiff tendered successfully for the purchase, fitted out a salvage expedition at great expense and proceeded to the reef. No tanker was to be found—it had never existed. The plaintiff claimed damages for breach of contract. The Commission argued that the contract was void because of a common mistake as to the existence of the tanker.

78. In the leading judgment Dixon and Fullagar JJ expressed doubt as to the existence of a doctrine of common mistake in contract. They considered that whether impossibility of performance discharged obligations, be the impossibility existing at the time of the contract or supervening thereafter, depended solely upon the construction of the contract. They went on, however, to consider the position if this were not correct. They observed that the common assumption that the tanker existed was one that was created by the Commission, without any reasonable grounds for believing that it was true. They held at p. 408:

> '. . . a party cannot rely on mutual mistake where the mistake consists of a belief which is, on the one hand, entertained by him without any reasonable ground, and, on the other hand, deliberately induced by him in the mind of the other party.'

79. They held (at p. 410) that, on its proper construction the contract included a promise by the Commission that the tanker existed in the position specified. Alternatively, they held that if the doctrine of mistake fell to be applied:

> 'then the Commission cannot in this case rely on any mistake as avoiding the contract, because any mistake was induced by the serious fault of their own servants, who asserted the existence of a tanker recklessly and without any reasonable ground.'

80. This seems, if we may say so, an entirely satisfactory conclusion and one that can be reconciled with the English doctrine of mistake. That doctrine fills a gap in the contract where it transpires that it is impossible of performance without the fault of either party and the parties have not, expressly or by implication, dealt with their rights and obligations in that eventuality. In *Associated Japanese Bank (International) Ltd* v. *Crédit du Nord SA* [1989] 1 WLR 255, 268 Steyn J observed:

> 'Logically, before one can turn to the rules as to mistake, whether at common law or in equity, one must first determine whether the contract itself, by express or implied condition precedent or otherwise, provides who bears the risk of the relevant mistake. It is at this hurdle that many pleas of mistake will either fail or prove to have been unnecessary. Only if the contract is silent on the point, is there scope for invoking mistake.'

81. In *William Sindall plc* v. *Cambridgeshire CC* [1994] 1 WLR 1016 at 1035, Hoffmann LJ commented that such allocation of risk can come about by rules of general law applicable to contract, such as 'caveat emptor' in the law of sale of goods or the rule that a lessor or vendor of land does not impliedly warrant that the premises are fit for any particular purpose, so that this risk is allocated by the contract to the lessee or purchaser.

82. Thus, while we do not consider that the doctrine of common mistake can be satisfactorily explained by an implied term, an allegation that a contract is void for common mistake will often raise important issues of construction. Where it is possible to perform the letter of the contract, but it is alleged that there was a common mistake in relation to a fundamental assumption which renders performance of the essence of the obligation impossible, it will be necessary, by construing the contract in the light of all the material circumstances, to decide whether this is indeed the case. In performing this exercise, the test advanced by Lord Diplock, applicable alike to both frustration and to fundamental breach, in *Hong Kong Fir Shipping Co Ltd* v. *Kawasaki Kisen Kaisha Ltd* [1962] 2 QB 26 at 65–66 can be of assistance:

> 'Every synallagmatic contract contains in it the seeds of the problem: in what event will a party be relieved of this undertaking to do that which he has agreed to do but has not yet done? The contract may itself expressly define some of these events, as in the cancellation clause in a charterparty; but, human prescience being limited, it seldom does so exhaustively and often fails to do so at all. In some classes of contracts such as sale of goods, marine insurance, contracts of affreightment evidenced by bills of lading and those between parties to bills of exchange, Parliament has defined by statute some of the events not provided for expressly in individual contracts of that class; but where an event occurs the occurrence of which neither the parties nor Parliament have expressly stated will discharge one of the parties from further performance of his undertakings, it is for the court to determine whether the event has this effect or not. The test whether an event has this effect or not has been stated in a number of metaphors all of which I think amount to the same thing: does the occurrence of the event deprive the party who has further undertakings still to perform of substantially the whole benefit which it was the intention of the parties as expressed in the contract that he should obtain as the consideration for performing those undertakings. This test is applicable whether or not the event occurs as a result of the default of one of the parties to the contract, but the consequences of the event are different in the two cases. Where the event occurs as a result of the default of one party, the party in default cannot rely upon it as relieving himself of the performance of any further undertakings on his part, and the innocent party, although entitled to, need not treat the event as relieving him of the further performance of his own undertakings? This is only a specific application of the fundamental legal and moral rule that a man should not be allowed to take advantage of his own wrong. Where the event occurs as a result of the default of neither party, each is relieved of the further performance of his own undertakings, and their rights in respect of undertakings previously performed are now regulated by the Law Reform (Frustrated Contracts) Act, 1943.'

83. This test may not, however, be adequate in the context of mistake, for there are cases where contracts have been held void for mistake, notwithstanding that the effect of the mistake was that the consideration proved to have substantially greater value than the parties had contemplated.

84. Once the court determines that unforeseen circumstances have, indeed, resulted in the contract being impossible of performance, it is next necessary to determine whether, on true construction of the contract, one or other party has undertaken responsibility for the subsistence of the assumed state of affairs. This is another way of asking whether one or other party has undertaken the risk that it may not prove possible to perform the contract, and the answer to this question may well be the same as the answer to the question of whether the impossibility of performance is attributable to the fault of one or other of the parties.

85. Circumstances where a contract is void as a result of common mistake are likely to be less common than instances of frustration. Supervening events which defeat the contractual adventure will frequently not be the responsibility of either party. Where, however, the parties agree that something shall be done which is impossible at the time of making the agreement, it is much more likely that, on true construction of the agreement, one or other will have undertaken responsibility for the mistaken state of affairs. This may well explain why cases where contracts have been found to be void in consequence of common mistake are few and far between.

86. Lord Atkin himself gave no examples of cases where a contract was rendered void because of a mistake as to quality which made 'the thing without the quality essentially different from the thing as it was believed to be'. He gave a number of examples of mistakes which did not satisfy this test, which served to demonstrate just how narrow he considered the test to be. Indeed this is further demonstrated by the result reached on the facts of *Bell* v. *Lever Brothers* itself.

87. Two cases where common mistake has been held to avoid the contract under common law call for special consideration. A case which is by no means easy to reconcile with *Bell* v. *Lever Brothers* is *Scott* v. *Coulson* [1903] 2 Ch 249. A contract for the sale of a life policy was entered into in circumstances in which both parties believed that the assured was alive. The price was paid and the policy assigned. The contract price was little more than the surrender value of the policy. In fact, the assured had died before the contract was concluded and the policy thus carried with it entitlement to the full sum assured. The vendors succeeded, in proceedings in the Chancery Court, in having the transaction set aside. In the Court of Appeal, Vaughan Williams LJ described the position as follows:

'If we are to take it that it was common ground that, at the date of the contract for the sale of this policy, both the parties to the contract supposed the assured to be alive, it is true that both parties entered into this contract upon the basis of a common affirmative belief that the assured was alive; but as it turned out that this was a common mistake, the contract was one which cannot be enforced. This is so at law; and the plaintiffs do not require to have recourse to equity to rescind the contract, if the basis which both parties recognised as the basis is not true.'

88. This case is often erroneously treated as being on all fours with *Strickland* v. *Turner*—see for example in *Bell* v. *Lever Brothers* Wright J at p. 565, Greer LJ at p. 595, and Lord Warrington at pp. 206–7. The two cases were, however, very different. An annuity on the life of someone deceased is self-evidently a nullity. The policy in *Scott* v. *Coulson* was very far from a nullity. The only way that the case can be explained is by postulating that a life policy before decease is fundamentally different from a life policy after decease, so that the contractual consideration no longer existed, but had been replaced by something quite different—ergo the contract could not be performed. Such was the explanation given by Lord Thankerton in *Bell* v. *Lever Brothers* at p. 236.

89. The other case is the decision of Steyn J in *Associated Japanese Bank* v. *Crédit du Nord SA* [1989] 1 WLR 257. The plaintiff bank entered into an agreement with a rogue under which he purported to sell and lease back four specific machines. The defendant bank agreed with the plaintiff bank to guarantee the rogue's payments under the lease-back agreement. The machines did not, in fact, exist. The rogue defaulted on his payments and the plaintiffs called on the guarantee. The defendants alleged (1) that on true construction of the agreement it was subject to an express condition precedent that the four machines existed; if this was not correct (2) that the agreement was void at law for common mistake; if this was not correct the agreement was voidable in equity on the ground of mistake and had been avoided.

90. The first head of defence succeeded. Steyn J went on, however, to consider the alternative defences founded on mistake. After reviewing the authorities on common mistake, he reached the following formulation of the law:

'The first imperative must be that the law ought to uphold rather than destroy apparent contracts. Secondly, the common law rules as to a mistake regarding the quality of the subject matter, like the common law rules regarding commercial frustration, are designed to cope with the impact of unexpected and wholly exceptional circumstances on apparent contracts. Thirdly, such a mistake in order to attract legal consequences must substantially be shared by both parties, and must relate to facts as they existed at the time the contract was made. Fourthly, and this is the point established by *Bell* v. *Lever Brothers Ltd* [1932] AC 161, the mistake must render the subject matter of the contract essentially and radically different from the subject matter which the parties believed to exist. While the civilian distinction between the substance and attributes of the subject matter of a contract has played a role in the development of our law (and was cited in speeches in *Bell* v. *Lever Brothers Ltd*), the principle enunciated in *Bell* v. *Lever Brothers Ltd* is markedly narrower in scope than the civilian doctrine. It is therefore no longer useful to invoke the civilian distinction. The principles enunciated by Lord Atkin and Lord Thankerton represent the ratio decidendi of *Bell* v. *Lever Brothers Ltd*. Fifthly, there is a requirement which was not specifically discussed in *Bell* v. *Lever Brothers Ltd*. What happens if the party, who is seeking to rely on the mistake, had no reasonable grounds for his belief? An extreme example is that of the man who makes a contract with minimal knowledge of the facts to which the mistake relates but is content that it is a good speculative risk. In my judgment a party cannot be allowed to rely on a common mistake where the mistake consists of a belief which is entertained by him without any reasonable grounds for such belief: cf *McRae* v. *Commonwealth Disposals Commission* (1951) 84 CLR 377, 408. That is not because principles such as estoppel or negligence require it, but simply because policy and good sense dictate that the positive rules regarding common mistake should be so qualified.'

91. The detailed analysis that we have carried out leads us to concur in this summary, subject to the proviso that the result in *McRae*'s case can, we believe, be explained on the basis of construction, as demonstrated above. In agreeing with the analysis of Steyn J, we recognise that it is at odds with comments that Lord Denning made on more than one occasion about *Bell* v. *Lever Brothers Ltd* to the effect that 'a common mistake, even on a most fundamental matter, does not make a contract void at law'. As to this Steyn J said at p. 267:

'With the profoundest respect to the former Master of the Rolls I am constrained to say that in my view his interpretation of *Bell* v. *Lever Brothers Ltd* does not do justice to the speeches of the majority.'

92.   We share both the respect and the conclusion. We shall shortly consider in some detail the effect of Lord Denning's treatment of the decision in *Bell* v. *Lever Brothers Ltd*.

93.   Steyn J held that the test of common mistake was satisfied. He held at p. 269:

'For both parties the guarantee of obligations under a lease with non-existent machines was essentially different from a guarantee of a lease with four machines which both parties at the time of the contract believed to exist. The guarantee is an accessory contract. The non-existence of the subject matter of the principal contract is therefore of fundamental importance. Indeed the analogy of the classic res extincta cases, so much discussed in the authorities, is fairly close. In my judgment the stringent test of common law mistake is satisfied: the guarantee is void ab initio.'

94.   Our conclusions have marched in parallel with those of Toulson J. We admire the clarity with which he has set out his conclusions, which emphasise the importance of a careful analysis of the contract and of the rights and obligations created by it as an essential precursor to consideration of the effect of an alleged mistake. We agree with him that, on the facts of the present case, the issue in relation to common mistake turns on the question of whether the mistake as to the distance apart of the two vessels had the effect that the services that the '*Great Peace*' was in a position to provide were something essentially different from that to which the parties had agreed. We shall defer answering that question until we have considered whether principles of equity provide a second string to the defendants' bow . . .

The result in this case

162.   We revert to the question that we left unanswered at paragraph 94. It was unquestionably a common assumption of both parties when the contract was concluded that the two vessels were in sufficiently close proximity to enable the '*Great Peace*' to carry out the service that she was engaged to perform. Was the distance between the two vessels so great as to confound that assumption and to render the contractual adventure impossible of performance? If so, the appellants would have an arguable case that the contract was void under the principle in *Bell* v. *Lever Brothers Ltd*.

163.   Toulson J addressed this issue in the following paragraph:

'Was the "*Great Peace*" so far away from the "*Cape Providence*" at the time of the contract as to defeat the contractual purpose—or in other words to turn it into something essentially different from that for which the parties bargained? This is a question of fact and degree, but in my view the answer is no. If it had been thought really necessary, the "*Cape Providence*" could have altered course so that both vessels were heading toward each other. At a closing speed of 19 knots, it would have taken them about 22 hours to meet. A telling point is the reaction of the defendants on learning the true positions of the vessels. They did not want to cancel the agreement until they knew if they could find a nearer vessel to assist. Evidently the defendants did not regard the contract as devoid of purpose, or they would have cancelled at once.'

164. Mr Reeder [counsel for the appellants] has attacked this paragraph on a number of grounds. He has submitted that the suggestion that the *'Cape Providence'* should have turned and steamed towards the *'Great Peace'* is unreal. We agree. The appellants were sending a tug from Singapore in an attempt to salve the *'Cape Providence'*. The *'Great Peace'* was engaged by the appellants to act as a stand-by vessel to save human life, should this prove necessary, as an ancillary aspect of the salvage service. The suggestion that the *'Cape Providence'* should have turned and steamed away from the salvage tug which was on its way towards her in order to reduce the interval before the *'Great Peace'* was in attendance is unrealistic.

165. Next Mr Reeder submitted that it was not legitimate for the Judge to have regard to the fact that the appellants did not want to cancel the agreement with the *'Great Peace'* until they knew whether they could get a nearer vessel to assist. We do not agree. This reaction was a telling indication that the fact that the vessels were considerably further apart than the appellants had believed did not mean that the services that the *'Great Peace'* was in a position to provide were essentially different from those which the parties had envisaged when the contract was concluded. The *'Great Peace'* would arrive in time to provide several days of escort service. The appellants would have wished the contract to be performed but for the adventitious arrival on the scene of a vessel prepared to perform the same services. The fact that the vessels were further apart than both parties had appreciated did not mean that it was impossible to perform the contractual adventure.

166. The parties entered into a binding contract for the hire of the *'Great Peace'*. That contract gave the appellants an express right to cancel the contract subject to the obligation to pay the 'cancellation fee' of 5 days hire. When they engaged the *'Nordfarer'* they cancelled the *'Great Peace'*. They became liable in consequence to pay the cancellation fee. There is no injustice in this result.

167. For the reasons that we have given, we would dismiss this appeal.

COMMENTARY

A number of important issues arise out of this passage. The first is the narrowness of the doctrine of mistake identified by the Court of Appeal. Examples of contracts held void in consequence of common mistake are likely to remain 'few and far between' (para [85]). But the judgment does contain a discussion of a number of cases in which contracts were held to be void for mistake, including *Couturier* v. *Hastie* (1856) 5 HL Cas 673 (para [53], although it is not entirely clear that it is properly analysed as a mistake case), *McRae* v. *Commonwealth Disposals Commission* (1951) 84 CLR 377 (para [77] and p. 635 below), *Scott* v. *Coulson* [1903] 2 Ch 249 (although doubts are expressed about the correctness of the case in paras [87] and [88]), and *Associated Japanese Bank* v. *Crédit du Nord SA* [1989] 1 WLR 257 (paras [89]–[93]). What common elements, if any, can be identified in these cases? The key factors, in the view of the Court of Appeal, are identified in paragraph [76] of their judgment. One difficulty with this paragraph, apart from the multiplicity of factors identified, is that it is not altogether easy to ascertain the relationship between the different factors. This is confirmed by the analysis in paragraphs [77]–[83] which, with respect, is not always easy to follow. Matters become clearer in paragraph [84] where a two-stage approach is advocated. At the first stage, the court must decide whether or not 'the contract has become impossible of performance' as a result of the 'unforeseen circumstances' and then, secondly, the court must decide whether 'on the true construction of the contract, one or other party has undertaken responsibility for the subsistence of the assumed state of affairs'.

The requirement that the contract must be 'impossible of performance' is likely to make it very difficult to set aside a contract on the ground of a mistake as to quality (see para [86]). Impossibility does seem to lie at the core of mistake cases. A simple example is provided by the case of *Sheikh Brothers Ltd* v. *Ochsner* [1957] AC 136. The appellants gave to the respondents a licence to cut sisal growing on land which had been leased to the appellants. The respondents undertook to manufacture and deliver to the appellants 'sisal fibre in average minimum quantities of fifty tons per month'. Lord Cohen stated (at p. 146) that 'the licence agreement provided for something of the nature of a joint adventure and was entered into on the basis that the sisal area was capable of producing sisal over the period of the agreement at the average rate of 50 tons per month'. This basis proved to be unfounded. The appellants submitted that this mistake did not go to the foundation of the contract. The Privy Council disagreed. Lord Cohen stated (at p. 147) that:

their Lordships think that it was the very basis of the contract that the sisal area should be capable of producing an average of 50 tons a month throughout the term of the licence. It follows that the mistake was as to a matter of fact essential to the agreement.

The more difficult question is whether or not impossibility should be an indispensable element in a mistake case. The cases do not, as yet, speak with one voice. Authority can be found to support the proposition that the common mistake must render performance of the contract impossible (see *Brennan* v. *Bolt Burden (a firm)* [2004] EWCA Civ 1017; [2004] 3 WLR 1321). On the other hand, the analogy with frustration suggests that the doctrine should not be so confined and that it should extend to cases where performance in the circumstances would be something radically different from what the parties had in contemplation at the time of entry into the contract (support for the latter extension can be gleaned from *Champion Investments Ltd* v. *Ahmed* [2004] All ER (D) 28 (Aug) at [32]). The merit of the latter view is that it will assist in the assimilation of the principles of common mistake and frustration and, at the same time, keep the doctrine within narrow confines and so avoid creating unnecessary uncertainty.

The second point to note is the emphasis placed by the Court of Appeal upon the importance of the construction of the contract. This approach is particularly noticeable in relation to the analysis of *McRae* v. *Commonwealth Disposals Commission* (1951) 84 CLR 377 in paragraphs [79]–[80] and of *Associated Japanese Bank* v. *Crédit du Nord SA* [1989] 1 WLR 257 in paragraphs [80] and [89]. The approval of the result in *McRae* is also significant. *McRae* has always been a problematic case as far as English law is concerned. While most commentators are of the view that *McRae* was correctly decided on its own facts, the problem lies in reconciling it with section 6 of the Sale of Goods Act 1979 which states that a contract for the sale of specific goods is void where, prior to the conclusion of the contract, the goods have perished without the knowledge of the parties. Of course, it is possible to reconcile *McRae* with section 6 on the basis that the tanker never existed and therefore could not 'perish'. While this explanation may be a satisfactory one in technical terms, it is not satisfactory in policy terms because it is does not explain why the law should distinguish between cases where the goods once existed but have perished (which are caught by section 6 and declared to be void) and cases in which the goods never existed (which may be valid under *McRae*). The preferable approach is to examine the terms of the contract in all cases in order to ascertain whether or not the rule contained in section 6 has been displaced by the terms of the contract. On this view section 6 is not a mandatory rule of law. It is a default rule and the parties can contract out of it by the simple device of making a promise to the effect that the subject-matter of the contract exists. This is the explanation given of *McRae* at paragraph [79] where it is stated that 'on its proper construction the contract included a promise by the Commission that the tanker existed in the position specified'. Equally, this exercise in construction may produce the result that no such promise was made. Such was the case in *Couturier* v. *Hastie* (1856) 5 HLC 673 (discussed at para [53]). The parties entered into a contract for the sale of a cargo of corn on what were in effect c.i.f. terms. At the time the contract was concluded the corn was believed to be in transit from Salonica to the United Kingdom. But, before the contract was made and unknown to both parties, the corn had deteriorated to such an extent that the master of the ship sold it. The seller argued that the buyer remained liable for the price of the corn because he had bought an 'interest in the adventure' or such rights as the seller had under the shipping documents. The House of Lords rejected the seller's argument, holding that the subject-matter of the contract was not the rights of the sellers under the shipping documents but the corn and that, since the corn did not exist, there was a total failure of consideration and the buyer was not liable to pay the price. The case has subsequently been rationalized as an example of a common mistake as to the existence of the subject-matter of the contract, although the word 'mistake' was nowhere mentioned in the judgment of the House of Lords. Indeed, Lord Chancellor Cranworth stated (at p. 681) that 'the whole question turns upon the construction of the contract which was entered into between the parties'. He continued: 'the contract plainly imports that there was something which was to be sold at the time of the contract, and something to be purchased'. On the facts there was nothing to be sold and accordingly there could be no liability to pay the price. It is therefore necessary to ascertain the obligations which have been assumed by the parties under the contract before deciding whether or not the contract can be set aside on the ground of mistake.

The final point of significance relates to the analogy drawn by the Court of Appeal between cases of common mistake and cases of frustration. In paragraphs [62]–[72] of their judgment (a passage which has been omitted from the extract), the Court of Appeal discuss a number of leading frustration cases which will be discussed in more detail in Chapter 23, namely *Taylor* v. *Caldwell* (1863) 3 B & S 826 (p. 869 below), *Krell* v. *Henry* [1903] 2 KB 740 (p. 896 below) and *National Carriers Ltd* v. *Panalpina (Northern) Ltd* [1981] AC 675 (p. 921 below). What lessons do we learn from the analogy? The first lesson is that the implied term technique originally used in frustration cases such as *Taylor* v. *Caldwell* is 'unrealistic' (pp. 854–855 below) and so should not be adopted in the context of common mistake (see paragraph [73]). The second point is that the doctrines of common mistake and frustration do share important common elements (see paragraphs [74], [82], and [85]). The closeness of the relationship between the two doctrines can be demonstrated by the 'coronation cases'. The leading case, *Krell* v. *Henry* [1903] 2 KB 740, is a frustration case and it is discussed in more detail in Chapter 23 (p. 896 below). The coronation procession of King Edward VII was cancelled because of the King's illness. Many rooms along the procession route had been hired for the purpose of viewing the coronation. In most of the cases (such as *Krell* v. *Henry*) the contracts were concluded before the coronation was cancelled but there is one case, *Griffith* v. *Brymer* (1903) 19 TLR 434, where the contract was entered into shortly after the decision to cancel the coronation had been made but both parties were unaware of the fact of the cancellation. The issue in these cases is the same, whether they are cases of frustration or mistake. The issue in both relates to the impact of an unforeseen event on the obligations contained in the contract. The difference between common mistake and frustration is simply one of timing. In the case of mistake the unforeseen event has, unknown to both parties, already occurred at the moment of entry into the contract, whereas in the case of frustration the event occurs after the formation of the contract. The common element is therefore that both doctrines are concerned with the allocation of risk of unforeseen events. This being the case, the courts in mistake cases should be able to draw on frustration cases and vice versa. But the difference in timing does require that care be exercised when drawing the analogy. As the Court of Appeal acknowledged in *Great Peace* (paragraph [85]), 'circumstances where a contract is void as a result of common mistake are likely to be less common than instances of frustration'. The reason for this is that the parties can, with greater diligence, find out the true position at the moment of entry into the contract, whereas they cannot discover what will happen in the future. This being the case, the law ought to be slower to relieve a party from the consequences of his failure to discover the true state of affairs at the moment of entry into the contract than from the consequences of his failure to predict the future course of events. But the difference is one of degree, not kind.

6. MISTAKE IN EQUITY

The authority of *Bell* v. *Lever Bros Ltd* was challenged by the decision of the Court of Appeal in *Solle* v. *Butcher* [1950] 1 KB 671. It was obviously not open to the Court of Appeal in *Solle* to refuse to follow *Bell*, given that *Bell* is a decision of the House of Lords. The technique used in *Solle* was to distinguish *Bell* on the ground that it was an authority on the doctrine of mistake at common law and that it did not determine the scope of the doctrine of mistake in equity. According to the Court of

Appeal in *Solle*, the doctrine of mistake in equity differed from the doctrine of mistake at common law in three respects. First the scope of the doctrine was wider. While the courts in equity also asked whether or not the mistake was 'fundamental', the definition of 'fundamental' in equity was more liberal and so encompassed a broader range of mistakes. Secondly, the effect of the mistake was different in that mistake in equity rendered a contract voidable, whereas mistake at law renders a contract void. Thirdly, and finally, the courts in equity had greater remedial flexibility when setting aside a contract, in that they could set the contract aside 'on terms'; that is to say, they could, within limits, adjust the rights and responsibilities of the parties.

Solle was decided back in 1949 and it was relied upon by the Court of Appeal and first instance judges in a handful of cases prior to the decision of the Court of Appeal in *Great Peace*. During this period the courts were aware of the uneasy relationship between *Solle* and *Bell*. The relationship between the two cases was rationalized by Steyn J in *Associated Japanese Bank* v. *Crédit du Nord SA* [1989] 1 WLR 257, 268 in the following terms:

> a narrow doctrine of common law mistake (as enunciated in *Bell* v. *Lever Bros Ltd*), supplemented by the more flexible doctrine of mistake in equity (as developed in *Solle* v. *Butcher* and later cases), seems to me to be an entirely sensible and satisfactory state of the law.

On this view the role of equitable mistake was a 'supplementary' one and Steyn J explained the relationship between common law and equitable mistake in sequential terms:

> Where common law mistake has been pleaded, the court must first consider this plea. If the contract is held to be void, no question of mistake in equity arises. But, if the contract is held to be valid, a plea of mistake in equity may still have to be considered.

The Court of Appeal in *Great Peace* took a much more robust line and held that *Solle* was inconsistent with *Bell* and should be disapproved. It is obviously an unusual step for a Court of Appeal to disapprove one of its own decisions, especially a decision that was regarded as good authority for over fifty years. It is therefore important to examine *Solle* itself before going on to consider the reasons given by the Court of Appeal for disapproving *Solle* and the cases decided in reliance upon it.

Solle v. Butcher

[1950] 1 KB 671, Court of Appeal

Solle and Butcher were partners in an estate agency. In 1947 Butcher took a lease of Maywood House, a building which contained five flats. Maywood House had been damaged by a landmine and Butcher took the lease with the intention of repairing the damage. In 1939 Flat 1 had been let for £140 per year. Solle and Butcher discussed what rent could be charged after the repairs were done. Solle told Butcher that he could charge £250 per year for Flat 1 because the rent was not restricted to the £140 charged in 1939 under the Rent Restriction Acts. Butcher relied on Solle's statement and did not attempt to calculate the additions, permitted under the Rent Restriction Acts by virtue of the repairs, to the £140 charged in 1939, on the assumption that it was the maximum rent. The additions would have brought the maximum rent to about £250. On 29 September 1947 Butcher let Flat 1 to Solle for £250 per year. Once the lease was executed no notice of intention to increase the rent could be given under the Rent Restriction Acts.

Solle sued Butcher claiming that the maximum rent was £140. Butcher claimed rescission of the lease on the ground of: (1) common mistake of fact; (2) innocent material misrepresentation; and (3) estoppel. The trial judge held that Flat 1 retained its identity notwithstanding the repairs and that the maximum rent was therefore £140 per year. He also held that there was no mistake of fact, though possibly one of law as both parties believed the Rent Restriction Acts did not apply. On appeal the Court of Appeal held, Jenkins LJ dissenting, that the lease should be set aside on terms.

Denning LJ

It is quite plain that the parties were under a mistake. They thought that the flat was not tied down to a controlled rent, whereas in fact it was. In order to see whether the lease can be avoided for this mistake it is necessary to remember that mistake is of two kinds: first, mistake which renders the contract void, that is, a nullity from the beginning, which is the kind of mistake which was dealt with by the courts of common law; and, secondly, mistake which renders the contract not void, but voidable, that is, liable to be set aside on such terms as the court thinks fit, which is the kind of mistake which was dealt with by the courts of equity. Much of the difficulty which has attended this subject has arisen because, before the fusion of law and equity, the courts of common law, in order to do justice in the case in hand, extended this doctrine of mistake beyond its proper limits and held contracts to be void which were really only voidable, a process which was capable of being attended with much injustice to third persons who had bought goods or otherwise committed themselves on the faith that there was a contract. In the well-known case of *Cundy* v. *Lindsay* (1876–8) 1 QBD 348; 3 App Cas 459, Cundy suffered such an injustice. He bought the handkerchiefs from the rogue, Blenkarn, before the Judicature Acts came into operation. Since the fusion of law and equity, there is no reason to continue this process, and it will be found that only those contracts are now held void in which the mistake was such as to prevent the formation of any contract at all.

Let me first consider mistakes which render a contract a nullity. All previous decisions on this subject must now be read in the light of *Bell* v. *Lever Bros Ltd* [1932] AC 161, 222, 224, 225–7, 236. The correct interpretation of that case, to my mind, is that, once a contract has been made, that is to say, once the parties, whatever their inmost states of mind, have to all outward appearances agreed with sufficient certainty in the same terms on the same subject matter, then the contract is good unless and until it is set aside for failure of some condition on which the existence of the contract depends, or for fraud, or on some equitable ground. Neither party can rely on his own mistake to say it was a nullity from the beginning, no matter that it was a mistake which to his mind was fundamental, and no matter that the other party knew that he was under a mistake. A fortiori, if the other party did not know of the mistake, but shared it . . .

Applying these principles, it is clear that here there was a contract. The parties agreed in the same terms on the same subject-matter. It is true that the landlord was under a mistake which was to him fundamental: he would not for one moment have considered letting the flat for seven years if it meant that he could only charge 140l. a year for it. He made the fundamental mistake of believing that the rent he could charge was not tied down to a controlled rent; but, whether it was his own mistake or a mistake common to both him and the tenant, it is not a ground for saying that the lease was from the beginning a nullity. Any other view would lead to remarkable results, for it would mean that, in the many cases where the parties mistakenly think a house is outside the Rent Restriction Acts when it is really within them, the tenancy would be a nullity, and the tenant would have to go; with the result that the tenants would not dare to seek to have their rents reduced to the permitted amounts lest they should be turned out.

Let me next consider mistakes which render a contract voidable, that is, liable to be set aside on some equitable ground. Whilst presupposing that a contract was good at law, or at any rate not void, the court of equity would often relieve a party from the consequences of his own mistake, so long as it could do so without injustice to third parties. The court, it was said, had power to set aside the contract whenever it was of opinion that it was unconscientious for the other party to avail himself of the legal advantage which he had obtained: *Torrance* v. *Bolton* (1872) LR 8 Ch 118, 124 per James LJ.

The court had, of course, to define what it considered to be unconscientious, but in this respect equity has shown a progressive development. It is now clear that a contract will be set aside if the mistake of the one party has been induced by a material misrepresentation of the other, even though it was not fraudulent or fundamental; or if one party, knowing that the other is mistaken about the terms of an offer, or the identity of the person by whom it is made, lets him remain under his delusion and concludes a contract on the mistaken terms instead of pointing out the mistake . . .

A contract is also liable in equity to be set aside if the parties were under a common misapprehension either as to facts or as to their relative and respective rights, provided that the misapprehension was fundamental and that the party seeking to set it aside was not himself at fault . . .

The principle so established by *Cooper* v. *Phibbs* (1867) LR 2 HL 149 has been repeatedly acted on: . .

Applying that principle to this case, the facts are that the plaintiff, the tenant, was a surveyor who was employed by the defendant, the landlord, not only to arrange finance for the purchase of the building and to negotiate with the rating authorities as to the new rateable values, but also to let the flats. He was the agent for letting, and he clearly formed the view that the building was not controlled. He told the valuation officer so. He advised the defendant what were the rents which could be charged. He read to the defendant an opinion of counsel relating to the matter, and told him that in his opinion he could charge 250l. and that there was no previous control. He said that the flats came outside the Act and that the defendant was 'clear'. The defendant relied on what the plaintiff told him, and authorized the plaintiff to let at the rentals which he had suggested. The plaintiff not only let the four other flats to other people for a long period of years at the new rentals, but also took one himself for seven years at 250l. a year. Now he turns round and says, quite unashamedly, that he wants to take advantage of the mistake to get the flat at 140l. a year for seven years instead of the 250l. a year, which is not only the rent he agreed to pay but also the fair and economic rent; and it is also the rent permitted by the Acts on compliance with the necessary formalities. If the rules of equity have become so rigid that they cannot remedy such an injustice, it is time we had a new equity, to make good the omissions of the old. But, in my view, the established rules are amply sufficient for this case . . .

There was clearly a common mistake, or, as I would prefer to describe it, a common misapprehension, which was fundamental and in no way due to any fault of the defendant; and *Cooper* v. *Phibbs* LR 2 HL 149 affords ample authority for saying that, by reason of the common misapprehension, this lease can be set aside on such terms as the court thinks fit.

The fact that the lease has been executed is no bar to this relief. No distinction can, in this respect, be taken between rescission for innocent misrepresentation and rescission for common misapprehension, for many of the common misapprehensions are due to innocent misrepresentation; and *Cooper* v. *Phibbs* shows that rescission is available even after an agreement of tenancy has been executed and partly performed.

In the ordinary way, of course, rescission is only granted when the parties can be restored to substantially the same position as that in which they were before the contract was made; but, as Lord Blackburn said in *Erlanger* v. *New Sombrero Phosphate Co* (1878) 3 App Cas 1218, 1278–9. 'The practice has always been for a court of equity to give this relief whenever, by the exercise of its powers, it can do what is practically just, though it cannot restore the parties precisely to the state they were in before the contract.' That indeed was what was done in *Cooper* v. *Phibbs* LR 2 HL 149. Terms were imposed so as to do what was practically just. What terms then, should be imposed here?

I think that this court should . . . impose terms which will enable the tenant to choose either to stay on at the proper rent or to go out.

The terms will be complicated by reason of the Rent Restriction Acts, but it is not beyond the wit of man to devise them. Subject to any observations which the parties may desire to make, the terms which I suggest are these: the lease should only be set aside if the defendant is prepared to give an undertaking that he will permit the plaintiff to be a licensee of the premises pending the grant of a new lease. Then, whilst the plaintiff is a licensee, the defendant will in law be in possession of the premises, and will be able to serve on the plaintiff, as prospective tenant, a notice under s. 7, sub-s. 4, of the Act of 1938 increasing the rent to the full permitted amount. The defendant must further be prepared to give an undertaking that he will serve such a notice within three weeks from the drawing up of the order, and that he will, if written request is made by the plaintiff, within one month of the service of the notice, grant him a new lease at the full permitted amount of rent, not, however, exceeding 250l. a year, for a term expiring on September 29, 1954, subject in all other respects to the same covenants and conditions as in the rescinded lease. If there is any difference of opinion about the figures stated in the notice, that can, of course, be adjusted during the currency of the lease. If the plaintiff does not choose to accept the licence or the new lease, he must go out. He will not be entitled to the protection of the Rent Restriction Acts because, the lease being set aside, there will be no initial contractual tenancy from which a statutory tenancy can spring.

In my opinion, therefore, the appeal should be allowed. The declaration that the standard rent of the flat is £140 a year should stand. An order should be made on the counterclaim that, on the defendant's giving the undertakings which I have mentioned, the lease be set aside. An account should be had to determine the sum payable for use and occupation. The plaintiff's claim for repayment of rent and for breach of covenant should be dismissed. In respect of his occupation after rescission and during the subsequent licence, the plaintiff will be liable to pay a reasonable sum for use and occupation. That sum should, prima facie, be assessed at the full amount permitted by the Acts, not, however, exceeding £250 a year. Mesne profits as against a trespasser are assessed at the full amount permitted by the Acts, even though notices of increase have not been served, because that is the amount lost by the landlord. The same assessment should be made here, because the sums payable for use and occupation are not rent, and the statutory provisions about notices of increase do not apply to them. All necessary credits must, of course, be given in respect of past payments, and so forth.

Bucknill LJ held that the lease should be set aside on the ground that there was a common mistake of fact as the repairs made such a substantial alteration to the building as to make it a different flat. **Jenkins LJ**, dissenting, held that there was no common mistake of fact but a common mistake of law as both parties believed that the Rent Restriction Acts did not have the effect of making £140 the maximum rent.

COMMENTARY

The judgment of Denning LJ in *Solle* demonstrates all three features of mistake in equity which distinguish it from its common law counterpart: (i) the nature of the mistake which entitles the court to intervene is described in more liberal terms; (ii) the mistake rendered the contract voidable rather than void; and (iii) the lease was set aside on the terms set out in the last paragraph of the judgment of Denning LJ.

Solle was followed in a number of decisions in the latter part of the twentieth century. It perhaps suffices to cite one of these cases, namely the decision of the Court of Appeal in *Magee* v. *Pennine Insurance Co Ltd* [1969] 2 QB 507. In 1961 Thomas Magee, who was then aged fifty-eight and could not drive, bought a car. The seller completed an insurance proposal form which Thomas Magee signed. The form stated that Thomas Magee held a provisional licence and that he and his elder son John Magee, then aged thirty-five and the holder of an annual licence, would drive the car in addition to his younger son. By signing the proposal Thomas Magee declared that these details were true. In fact, Thomas Magee held no licence and wanted the car for his younger son John J. Magee, then aged eighteen, to drive. Pennine Insurance Co Ltd issued a policy of insurance to Thomas Magee on the basis of the proposal. The policy was renewed each year. On 25 April 1965 John J. Magee wrecked the car. Thomas Magee claimed £600 under the policy. On 12 May 1965 Pennine offered to settle his claim for £385. Thomas Magee accepted the offer. Pennine later discovered that the details in the proposal were incorrect and refused to pay. Thomas Magee brought an action claiming £385 under the policy or the compromise agreement contained in the offer of 12 May 1965. Pennine argued that it was entitled to repudiate its liability under the policy and the agreement. The judge held that Pennine was entitled to repudiate the policy because of the incorrect details in the proposal. However the judge held that Pennine was liable to Thomas Magee for £385 under the agreement. On appeal a majority of the Court of Appeal (Winn LJ dissenting) held that in entering into the agreement both parties were under the common fundamental mistake that Thomas Magee had a valid claim under the policy and that Pennine were entitled to have the agreement set aside. This case raises, in a stark form, the problem of the relationship between the doctrine of mistake in equity and *Bell* because the mistake that was made in *Magee* was the same as that made in *Bell*. In both cases a payment was made in the belief that there was a contractual obligation to make a payment and a contractual entitlement to receive the payment, when in fact there was no such obligation to pay because of an entitlement in the payor to set aside the contract which created the payment obligation.

The tension between *Bell* and *Solle* was resolved in *Great Peace* when the Court of Appeal concluded that *Solle* should be disapproved on the ground that it was inconsistent with the decision of the House of Lords in *Bell* v. *Lever Bros.* The Court of Appeal's analysis of equitable mistake was divided into three parts. The first part consisted of an analysis of common mistake in equity prior to *Bell.* The focus of attention in this part of the judgment was upon the decision of the House of Lords in *Cooper* v. *Phibbs* (1867) LR 2 HL 149. The second part was an analysis of the effect of *Bell* on mistake in equity, while the third part consisted of a discussion of the effect of *Solle* v. *Butcher.* The extract that follows consists of the conclusion of the Court of Appeal in relation to the effect of *Bell* on mistake in equity (para [118]) and the final sections of the judgment in which the Court of Appeal set outs its conclusions in relation to the line of authority represented by *Solle* v. *Butcher* (paras [153]–[161]).

118.   These passages demonstrate that the House of Lords in *Bell* v. *Lever Brothers* considered that the intervention of equity, as demonstrated in *Cooper* v. *Phibbs*, took place in circumstances where the common law would have ruled the contract void for mistake. We do not find it conceivable that the House of Lords overlooked an equitable right in Lever Brothers to rescind the agreement, notwithstanding that the agreement was not void for mistake at common law. The jurisprudence established no such right. Lord Atkin's test for common mistake that avoided a contract, while narrow, broadly reflected the circumstances where equity had intervened to excuse performance of a contract assumed to be binding in law . . .

153.   A number of cases, albeit a small number, in the course of the last 50 years have purported to follow *Solle* v. *Butcher*, yet none of them defines the test of mistake that gives rise to the equitable jurisdiction to rescind in a manner that distinguishes this from the test of a mistake that renders a contract void in law, as identified in *Bell* v. *Lever Brothers*. This is, perhaps, not surprising, for Lord Denning, the author of the test in *Solle* v. *Butcher*, set *Bell* v. *Lever Brothers* at nought. It is possible to reconcile *Solle* v. *Butcher* and *Magee* v. *Pennine Insurance* with *Bell* v. *Lever Brothers* only by postulating that there are two categories of mistake, one that renders a contract void at law and one that renders it voidable in equity. Although later cases have proceeded on this basis, it is not possible to identify that proposition in the judgment of any of the three Lords Justices, Denning, Bucknill or Fenton Atkinson, who participated in the majority decisions in the former two cases. Nor, over 50 years, has it proved possible to define satisfactorily two different qualities of mistake, one operating in law and one in equity.

154.   In *Solle* v. *Butcher* Denning LJ identified the requirement of a common misapprehension that was 'fundamental', and that adjective has been used to describe the mistake in those cases which have followed *Solle* v. *Butcher*. We do not find it possible to distinguish, by a process of definition, a mistake which is 'fundamental' from Lord Atkin's mistake as to quality which 'makes the thing contracted for essentially different from the thing that it was believed to be'.

155.   A common factor in *Solle* v. *Butcher* and the cases which have followed it can be identified. The effect of the mistake has been to make the contract a particularly bad bargain for one of the parties. Is there a principle of equity which justifies the court in rescinding a contract where a common mistake has produced this result?

> 'Equity is . . . a body of rules or principles which form an appendage to the general rules of law, or a gloss upon them. In origin at least, it represents the attempt of the English legal system to meet a problem which confronts all legal systems reaching a certain stage of development. In order to ensure the smooth running of society it is necessary to formulate general rules which work well enough in the majority of cases. Sooner or later, however, cases arise in which, in some unforeseen set of facts, the general rules produce substantial unfairness . . .' (*Snell's Equity* (30th edn, 2000) p. 4, para 1–03).

156. Thus the premise of equity's intrusion into the effects of the common law is that the common law rule in question is seen in the particular case to work injustice, and for some reason the common law cannot cure itself. But it is difficult to see how that can apply here. Cases of fraud and misrepresentation, and undue influence, are all catered for under other existing and uncontentious equitable rules. We are *only* concerned with the question whether relief might be given for common mistake in circumstances wider than those stipulated in *Bell* v. *Lever Brothers*. But that, surely, is a question as to where the common law should draw the line; not whether, given the common law rule, it needs to be mitigated by application of some other doctrine. The common law has drawn the line in *Bell* v. *Lever Brothers*. The effect of *Solle* v. *Butcher* is not to supplement or mitigate the common law; it is to say that *Bell* v. *Lever Brothers* was wrongly decided.

157. Our conclusion is that it is impossible to reconcile *Solle* v. *Butcher* with *Bell* v. *Lever Brothers*. The jurisdiction asserted in the former case has not developed. It has been a fertile source of academic debate, but in practice it has given rise to a handful of cases that have merely emphasised the confusion of this area of our jurisprudence. In paragraphs 110 to 121 of his judgment, Toulson J has demonstrated the extent of that confusion. If coherence is to be restored to this area of our law, it can only be by declaring that there is no jurisdiction to grant rescission of a contract on the ground of common mistake where that contract is valid and enforceable on ordinary principles of contract law. That is the conclusion of Toulson J. Do the principles of case precedent permit us to endorse it? What is the correct approach where this court concludes that a decision of the Court of Appeal cannot stand with an earlier decision of the House of Lords? There are two decisions which bear on this question.

[The judgment considered two decisions in which it was held that the Court of Appeal should apply the law laid down by the House of Lords and refuse to follow the decision of the Court of Appeal and continued]

160. We have been in some doubt as to whether this line of authority goes far enough to permit us to hold that *Solle* v. *Butcher* is not good law. We are very conscious that we are not only scrutinising the reasoning of Lord Denning in *Solle* v. *Butcher* and in *Magee* v. *Pennine Insurance Co*, but are also faced with a number of later decisions in which Lord Denning's approach has been approved and followed. Further, a Division of this Court has made it clear in *West Sussex Properties Ltd* v. *Chichester DC* [2000] All ER (D) 887 that they felt bound by *Solle* v. *Butcher*. However, it is to be noticed that while junior counsel in the court below in the *West Sussex Properties* case had sought to challenge the correctness of *Solle*, in the Court of Appeal leading counsel accepted that it was good law unless and until overturned by their Lordships' House. In this case we have heard full argument, which has provided what we believe has been the first opportunity in this court for a full and mature consideration of the relation between *Bell* v. *Lever Brothers Ltd* and *Solle* v. *Butcher*. In the light of that consideration we can see no way that *Solle* v. *Butcher* can stand with *Bell* v. *Lever Brothers*. In these circumstances we can see no option but so to hold.

161. We can understand why the decision in *Bell* v. *Lever Brothers Ltd* did not find favour with Lord Denning. An equitable jurisdiction to grant rescission on terms where a common fundamental mistake has induced a contract gives greater flexibility than a doctrine of common law which holds the contract void in such circumstances. Just as the Law Reform (Frustrated Contracts) Act 1943 was needed to temper the effect of the common law doctrine of frustration, so there is scope for legislation to give greater flexibility to our law of mistake than the common law allows.

COMMENTARY

This is a bold decision. On its facts the decision appears correct. Factually, the case would have been more interesting had the 'Great Peace' been two or three days away from the stricken vessel. As it was, the impact of the mistake on the contract was probably insufficient even to satisfy the test laid down by Denning LJ in *Solle*. So, on its facts, *Great Peace* was correctly decided. The difficulty with the case lies in its formulation of the legal principles.

The conclusion that *Solle* 'cannot stand' with *Bell* is probably right in the sense that it is almost inconceivable 'that the House of Lords overlooked an equitable right in Lever Bros to rescind the agreement, notwithstanding that the agreement was not void for mistake at common law' (para [118]). A greater difficulty arises from the fact that the Court of Appeal had followed *Solle* on a number of occasions and there is a respectable case for saying that the decision to overrule *Solle* should have been left to the House of Lords. On the facts there was no need for the Court of Appeal to take the step of disapproving *Solle*. They could have held, quite simply, that the mistake in this case was, on any view, insufficient to set aside the agreement either at law or in equity. In practical terms it is likely that *Great Peace* will be the last word on the issue unless a case goes up to the House of Lords. It is probably unlikely that a subsequent Court of Appeal will depart from *Great Peace* on the ground that the Court of Appeal in *Great Peace* mistakenly concluded that *Solle* was inconsistent with *Bell* v. *Lever Bros*.

As for *Solle* itself, it would appear that it should now be regarded as having been wrongly decided. It was certainly wrong in terms of legal principle. But was it wrong on its facts? Here it is interesting to contrast the decision of the Court of Appeal in *Great Peace* with the decision of Toulson J at first instance ([2001] All ER (D) 152). He stated at paragraph [77]:

Standing back from *Solle* v. *Butcher*, the striking feature of the case on the facts is that the plaintiff himself, a surveyor, had led the defendant into his mistaken belief. It would seem unjust that he should be allowed to reap a benefit from doing so.

In his judgment (at paragraph [118]) he stated that he was 'leaving aside cases where one party's mistake is the product of fraud, misrepresentation or unconscionable dealing by the other, or where one party is aware that the other is proceeding under a mistake as to the terms of the bargain purportedly being made'. The Court of Appeal does not consider this aspect of *Solle*. To what extent is it possible to outflank the decision in *Great Peace* by submitting that there has been 'unconscionable dealing' by the party seeking to uphold the contract?

The final aspect of *Great Peace* is the reference in paragraph [161] to the flexibility which mistake in equity injected into the law. The statement that 'there is scope for legislation to give greater flexibility to our law of mistake than the common law allows' is a little surprising given that it was unnecessary for the Court of Appeal to excise the equitable jurisdiction in the way that they did. Having judicially removed the flexibility that was present in the law, they then invite Parliament to re-introduce that flexibility. The analogy drawn with the Law Reform (Frustrated Contracts) Act 1943 is also rather dubious. The 1943 Act (on which see p. 904 below) regulates the remedial consequences of a contract that has already been discharged, whereas the effect of the decision of the Court of Appeal in *Great Peace* is to hold that the contract it still binding on the parties and, if it is still binding, it is difficult to see on what basis a greater degree of flexibility should be introduced into the law.

If there is a desire to introduce a greater degree of flexibility into the law, then consideration ought to be given to Articles 4: 102–4: 105 of the Principles of European Contract Law. Articles 4: 103 and 4: 105 in particular seem to give the courts greater flexibility both in terms of the types of mistake which give rise to a claim for relief and in terms of the remedial powers available to the court.

Article 4:102—Initial impossibility

A contract is not invalid merely because at the time it was concluded performance of the obligation assumed was impossible, or because a party was not entitled to dispose of the assets to which the contract relates.

Article 4:103—Fundamental mistake as to Facts or Law

(1) A party may avoid a contract for mistake of fact or law existing when the contract was concluded if:

    (a) (i) the mistake was caused by information given by the other party; or

        (ii) the other party knew or ought to have known of the mistake and it was contrary to good faith and fair dealing to leave the mistaken party in error; or

        (iii) the other party made the same mistake, and

    (b) the other party knew or ought to have known that the mistaken party, had it known the truth, would not have entered the contract or would have done so only on fundamentally different terms.

(2) However a party may not avoid the contract if:

    (a) in the circumstances its mistake was inexcusable, or

(b) the risk of the mistake was assumed, or in the circumstances should be borne, by it.

Article 4:104—Inaccuracy in communication

An inaccuracy in the expression or transmission of a statement is to be treated as a mistake of the person who made or sent the statement and Article 4.103 applies.

Article 4:105—Adaptation of contract

(1) If a party is entitled to avoid the contract for mistake but the other party indicates that it is willing to perform, or actually does perform, the contract as it was understood by the party entitled to avoid it, the contract is to be treated as if it had been concluded as that party understood it. The other party must indicate its willingness to perform, or render such performance, promptly after being informed of the manner in which the party entitled to avoid it understood the contract and before that party acts in reliance on any notice of avoidance.

(2) After such indication or performance the right to avoid is lost and any earlier notice of avoidance is ineffective.

(3) Where both parties have made the same mistake, the court may at the request of either party bring the contract into accordance with what might reasonably have been agreed had the mistake not occurred.

7. RECTIFICATION

The mistake made by the parties may relate not to the making of the contract but to the recording of it. In such a case the parties may ask the court to rectify the document in order to make it accord with the document they intended to draw up. Rectification is a remedy that is available only within narrow limits. As Denning LJ stated in *Frederick E. Rose (London) Ltd* v. *William H. Pim Jnr & Co Ltd* [1953] 2 QB 450, 461:

Rectification is concerned with contracts and documents, not with intentions. In order to get rectification it is necessary to show that the parties were in complete agreement on the terms of their contract, but by an error wrote them down wrongly; and in this regard, in order to ascertain the terms of their contract, you do not look into the inner minds of the parties—into their intentions—any more than you do in the formation of any other contract. You look at their outward acts, that is, at what they said or wrote to one another in coming to their agreement, and then compare it with the document which they have signed. If you can predicate with certainty what their contract was, and that it is, by a common mistake, wrongly expressed in the document, then you rectify the document; but nothing less will suffice.

On the facts of the case the plaintiffs had been asked by Egyptian buyers to supply them with 'Moroccan horsebeans known here as feveroles', the defendants having assured the plaintiffs that Moroccan horsebeans were feveroles. In order to satisfy their Egyptian buyers the plaintiffs entered into a contract with the defendants under which the defendants agreed to sell 'horsebeans' to the plaintiffs. Both parties entered into the contract in the mistaken belief that 'horsebeans' were 'feveroles'. When the plaintiffs discovered that the two were not the same, they sought to have the contract rectified by the addition of the word 'feveroles' after 'horsebeans'. The Court of Appeal refused to rectify the contract. Denning LJ stated (at p. 462):

The parties, no doubt, intended that the goods should satisfy the inquiry of the Egyptian buyers, namely, 'horsebeans described in Egypt as feveroles'. They assumed that they would do so, but they made no contract to that effect. Their agreement, as outwardly expressed, both orally and in writing, was for 'horsebeans'. That is all that the sellers ever committed themselves to supply, and all they should be bound to. There was, no doubt, an erroneous assumption underlying the contract—an assumption for which it might have been set aside on the ground of misrepresentation or mistake—but that is very different from an erroneous expression of the contract, such as to give rise to rectification.

To some extent the restrictive rules on rectification can be avoided by an application of Lord Hoffmann's re-statement of the principles by which contractual documents are to be interpreted (see pp. 407–408 above). His fourth principle recognizes that it is possible to conclude that 'the parties must, for whatever reason, have used the wrong words or syntax' and his fifth principle states that 'if one would . . . conclude from the background that something must have gone wrong with the language, the law does not require judges to attribute to the parties an intention which they plainly could not have had.' These more relaxed rules of interpretation give the courts some freedom to 'rectify' the contract under the guise of interpretation. In future cases, there may be less need for parties to resort to rectification because the judge may be able to perform the necessary surgery using Lord Hoffmann's principles.

A claimant who does wish to have a document rectified must prove a number of things. First, the claimant must supply the court with convincing proof that the document fails to record the intention of the parties. Secondly, the document must generally fail to record the intention of both parties. Thirdly, the document must have been preceded by a concluded contract or by a continuing common intention. Finally, the claimant must not have been guilty of excessive delay in seeking the remedy of rectification. An example of rectification is provided by the following case:

Joscelyne v. Nissen

[1970] 2 QB 86, Court of Appeal

Mr Joscelyne was the father of Mrs Nissen. They shared a house, of which Mr Joscelyne and his wife occupied the ground floor, and Mrs Nissen and her husband the first floor. Mr Joscelyne owned a car hire business, but as a result of his wife's illness he was forced to give it up. He agreed to transfer his business to Mrs Nissen on the basis that she would, in return, pay him a weekly pension and should pay the expenses of her parents' part of the house, and that these expenses should include the gas, electricity, and coal bills and also the cost of the necessary home help. Later, their agreement was written down and signed by them. Clause 6 of the agreement provided that Mrs Nissen should discharge 'all expenses in connection with the whole premises . . . and shall indemnify [Mr Joscelyne] from and against any claim arising in respect of the same'. Clause 7 of the written agreement stated that Mr Joscelyne had the right to live in the ground floor flat 'free of all rent and outgoings of every kind in any event'.

The relationship between the parties deteriorated and Mr Joscelyne commenced proceedings in the county court against Mrs Nissen. Mrs Nissen then stopped paying the gas, electricity, and coal bills, having been advised that the contract did not require her to pay them (apparently on the basis that these bills were neither 'rent nor outgoings'). Mr Joscelyne amended his particulars of claim to raise the point that she was required to pay these expenses either as a matter of construction of the agreement or by way of rectification. The county court judge decided against the father on construction but in his favour on rectification. Mrs Nissen appealed. Dismissing the appeal the Court of Appeal held that for rectification there need not be a complete contract between the parties, and that the court has power to rectify a written instrument even when the parties were in 'common agreement' and the written instrument diverges from that agreement.

Russell LJ [giving the judgment of the court]

For the daughter it is argued that the law says that the father cannot get rectification of the written instrument save to accord with a complete antecedent concluded oral contract with the daughter, and, as was found by the judge, there was none such here. For the father it is argued that if in the course of negotiation a firm accord has been expressly reached on a particular term of the proposed contract, and both parties continue minded that the contract should contain appropriate language to embrace that term, it matters not that the accord was not part of a complete antecedent concluded oral contract.

The point of law has a curious judicial history. . . .

[he considered the development of the law and in doing so placed considerable reliance upon the following passage from the judgment of Simonds J in *Crane* v. *Hegeman-Harris Co Inc* [1939] 1 All ER 662, 664]

'Before I consider the facts and come to a conclusion whether the defendants are right in their contention, it is necessary to say a few words upon the principles which must guide me in this matter. I am clear that I must follow the decision of Clauson J, as he then was, in *Shipley Urban District Council* v. *Bradford Corpn* [1936] 1 Ch 375, the point of which is that, in order that this court may exercise its jurisdiction to rectify a written instrument, it is not necessary to find a concluded and binding contract between the parties antecedent to the agreement which it is sought to rectify. The judge held, and I respectfully concur with his reasoning and his conclusion, that it is sufficient to find a common continuing intention in regard to a particular provision or aspect of the agreement. If one finds that, in regard to a particular point, the parties were in agreement up to the moment when they executed their formal instrument, and the formal instrument does not conform with that common agreement, then this court has jurisdiction to rectify, although it may be that there was, until the formal instrument was executed, no concluded and binding contract between the parties. That is what the judge decided, and, as I say, with his reasoning I wholly concur, and I can add nothing to his authority in the matter, except that I would say that, if it were not so, it would be a strange thing, for the result would be that two parties binding themselves by a mistake to which each had equally contributed, by an instrument which did not express their real intention, would yet be bound by it. That is a state of affairs which I hold is not the law, and, until a higher court tells me it is the law, I shall continue to exercise the jurisdiction which Clauson J, as I think rightly, held might be entertained by this court.

Secondly, I want to say this upon the principle of the jurisdiction. It is a jurisdiction which is to be exercised only upon convincing proof that the concluded instrument does not represent the common intention of the parties. That is particularly the case where one finds prolonged negotiations between the parties eventually assuming the shape of a formal instrument in which they have been advised by their respective skilled legal advisers. The assumption is very strong in such a case that the instrument does represent their real intention, and it must be only upon proof which Lord Eldon, I think, in a somewhat picturesque phrase described as "irrefragable" that the court can act. I would rather, I think, say that the court can only act if it is satisfied beyond all reasonable doubt that the instrument does not represent their common intention, and is further satisfied as to what their common intention was. For let it be clear that it is not sufficient to show that the written instrument does not represent their common intention unless positively also one can show what their common intention was. It is in the light of those principles that I must examine the facts of this somewhat complicated case.'

In our judgment the law is as expounded by Simonds J in *Crane's* case with the qualification that some outward expression of accord is required. We do not wish to attempt to state in any different phrases that with which we entirely agree, except to say that it is in our view better to use only the phrase 'convincing proof' without echoing an old-fashioned word such as 'irrefragable' and without importing from the criminal law the phrase 'beyond all reasonable doubt'. Remembering always the strong burden of proof that lies on the shoulders of those seeking rectification, and that the requisite accord and continuance of accord of intention may be the more difficult to establish if a complete antecedent concluded contract be not shown, it would be a sorry state of affairs if when that burden is discharged a party to a written contract could, on discovery that the written language chosen for the document did not on its true construction reflect the accord of the parties on a particular point, take advantage of the fact.

The contention in law for the daughter would, we apprehend, involve this proposition, that if all the important terms of an agreement were set out in correspondence with clarity, but expressly 'subject to contract', and the contract by a slip of the copyist unnoticed by either party departed from what had been 'agreed', there could not be rectification . . .

We wish to stress that this is a case of rectification based on antecedent expressed accord on a point adhered to in intention by the parties to the subsequent written contract: we were in no way concerned with arguments as to collateral terms of a contract.

The actual order of the county court judge would appear to have rectified the wrong clause in the agreement, and to have omitted the reference in the accepted evidence of the father to payment of expenses being made out of the business. Counsel were able to agree the proper form of order. The order will be accordingly varied so as to provide that in lieu of rectification of clause 7 of the contract thereby ordered, clause 6 shall be rectified so as to read:

'Mrs Nissen shall until she sells the business and out of the proceeds of the business discharge Mr Joscelyne's expenses in respect of gas, coal, electricity and home help incurred by him while occupying "Martindale" . . . aforesaid or such property as may be agreed upon in pursuance of clause 7 hereof and shall indemnify Mr Joscelyne from and against any claim arising in respect of the same.'

COMMENTARY

More difficult is the case where the claimant cannot establish that the document has failed to give effect to the intention of both parties but alleges that the document does not give effect to his own intention and the other party, the defendant, knew that the document did not give effect to his intention. It is clear that unilateral mistake will not suffice of itself to entitle a claimant to rectification. In *Riverlate Properties Ltd* v. *Paul* [1975] Ch 133, 140 Russell LJ stated:

Is the lessor entitled to rescission of the lease on the mere ground that it made a serious mistake in the drafting of the lease which it put forward and subsequently executed, when (a) the lessee did not share the mistake, (b) the lessee did not know that the document did not give effect to the lessor's intention, and (c) the mistake of the lessor was in no way attributable to anything said or done by the lessee? . . . In point of principle, we cannot find that this should be so. If reference be made to principles of equity, it operates on conscience. If conscience is clear at the time of the transaction, why should equity disrupt the transaction? . . . But if equity were to enforce the views of those high-minded men, we have no doubt that it would run counter to the attitudes of much the greater part of ordinary mankind (not least the world of commerce), and would be venturing upon the field of moral philosophy in which it would soon be in difficulties.

However, a claimant who can establish that the other party knew of his mistake or sought to take advantage of it may be entitled to rectification (*A Roberts & Co Ltd* v. *Leicestershire County Council* [1961] Ch 555). In *Commissioner for the New Towns* v. *Cooper (Great Britain) Ltd* [1995] Ch 259 Stuart-Smith LJ stated (at pp. 277–280):

The commonest circumstance in which rectification is granted is where the written contract does not accurately record the parties' joint agreement. In other words, there is a mistake common to both parties. In the case of unilateral mistake, that is to say where only one party is mistaken as to the meaning of the contract, rectification is not ordinarily appropriate. This follows from the ordinary rule that it is the objective intention of the parties which determines the construction of the contract and not the subjective intention of one of them. Also, it would generally be inequitable to compel the other party to execute a contract, which he had no intention of making, simply to accord with the mistaken interpretation of the other party. . . .But the court will intervene if there are 'additional circumstances that render unconscionable reliance on the document by the party who has intended that it should have effect according to its terms'. The debate in this case turns on what amounts to unconscionable conduct. . . . It was common ground in this court that fraud, in the form of a dishonest misrepresentation, will also amount to unconscionable behaviour. . . . I would hold that where A intends B to be mistaken as to the construction of the agreement, so conducts himself that he diverts B's attention from discovering the mistake by making false and misleading statements, and B in fact makes the very mistake that A intends, then notwithstanding that A does not actually know, but merely suspects, that B is mistaken, and it cannot be shown that the mistake was induced by any misrepresentation, rectification may be granted. A's conduct is unconscionable and he cannot insist on performance in accordance to the strict letter of the contract; that is sufficient for rescission. But it may also not be unjust or inequitable to insist that the contract be performed according to B's understanding, where that was the meaning that A intended B should put upon it.

8. NON EST FACTUM

Non est factum is a defence which can be invoked by someone who does not understand a document that he has signed. However the defence operates within narrow limits, largely to protect the interests of third parties who may rely to their detriment on the validity of a signature contained in a document. A claimant who wishes to invoke the defence must establish two points. First, he must establish that he was permanently or temporarily unable through no fault of his own to have without explanation any real understanding of the document he has signed. Secondly, he must show that there was a real or substantial difference between the document which he signed and the document which he believed he was signing. However a claimant will not be able to invoke the defence when he has been careless in signing the document or has simply failed to read the document properly (*United Dominions Trust Ltd* v. *Western* [1976] QB 513). In such a case the party signing the document is bound by his signature (see pp. 343–351 above). The leading case on *non est factum* is the following decision of the House of Lords:

Saunders (Executrix of the Will of Rose Maud Gallie, dec'd) v. Anglia Building Society

[1971] AC 1004, House of Lords

Mrs Gallie was a seventy-eight year old widow. She had a leasehold interest in a house. She intended to make a gift of her interest to her nephew, Mr Parkin. She gave him the deeds knowing that he wished to raise money on the house in collaboration with his business associate, Mr Lee. In June 1962 Mr Lee asked Mrs Gallie to sign a document. As Mrs Gallie had broken her glasses and could not read the document, she asked Mr Lee to tell her what it was. He told her that it was a deed of gift of the house to her nephew. Mrs Gallie signed the document in that belief and her nephew witnessed her signature. In fact, the document was an assignment of her interest to Mr Lee for £3,000. Mr Lee never paid the £3,000 and had never intended to pay it. He mortgaged the house for £2,000 with the Anglia Building Society, used the money raised to pay his debts and subsequently defaulted on the mortgage repayments. Anglia sought possession of the house. Mrs Gallie brought an action against Mr Lee and Anglia seeking a declaration that the assignment was void on the ground of *non est factum*. The judge held that the plea of *non est factum* was made out and granted the declaration. The Court of Appeal reversed the decision. The House of Lords held that the plea of *non est factum* had not been established.

Lord Reid

The plea of non est factum obviously applies when the person sought to be held liable did not in fact sign the document. But at least since the sixteenth century it has also been held to apply in certain cases so as to enable a person who in fact signed a document to say that it is not his deed. Obviously any such extension must be kept within narrow limits if it is not to shake the confidence of those who habitually and rightly rely on signatures when there is no obvious reason to doubt their validity. Originally this extension appears to have been made in favour of those who were unable to read owing to blindness or illiteracy and who therefore had to trust someone to tell them what they were signing. I think it must also apply in favour of those who are permanently or temporarily unable through no fault of their own to have without explanation any real understanding of the purport of a particular document, whether that be from defective education, illness or innate incapacity.

But that does not excuse them from taking such precautions as they reasonably can. The matter generally arises where an innocent third party has relied on a signed document in ignorance of the circumstances in which it was signed, and where he will suffer loss if the maker of the document is allowed to have it declared a nullity. So there must be a heavy burden of proof on the person who seeks to invoke this remedy. He must prove all the circumstances necessary to justify its being granted to him, and that necessarily involves his proving that he took all reasonable precautions in the circumstances. I do not say that the remedy can never be available to a man of full capacity. But that could only be in very exceptional circumstances: certainly not where his reason for not scrutinising the document before signing it was that he was too busy or too lazy. In general I do not think he can be heard to say that he signed in reliance on someone he trusted. But, particularly when he was led to believe that the document which he signed was not one which affected his legal rights, there may be cases where this plea can properly be applied in favour of a man of full capacity.

The plea cannot be available to anyone who was content to sign without taking the trouble to try to find out at least the general effect of the document. Many people do frequently sign documents put before them for signature by their solicitor or other trusted advisers without making any inquiry as to their purpose or effect. But the essence of the plea non est factum is that the person signing believed that the document he signed had one character or one effect whereas in fact its character or effect was quite different. He could not have such a belief unless he had taken steps or been given information which gave him some grounds for his belief. The amount of information he must have and the sufficiency of the particularity of his belief must depend on the circumstances of each case.

Further, the plea cannot be available to a person whose mistake was really a mistake as to the legal effect of the document, whether that was his own mistake or that of his adviser. That has always been the law and in this branch of the law at least I see no reason for any change.

We find in many of the authorities statements that a man's deed is not his deed if his mind does not go with his pen. But that is far too wide. It would cover cases where the man had taken no precautions at all, and there was no ground for his belief that he was signing something different from that which in fact he signed. I think that it is the wrong approach to start from that wide statement and then whittle it down by excluding cases where the remedy will not be granted. It is for the person who seeks the remedy to show that he should have it.

Finally, there is the question as to what extent or in what way must there be a difference between that which in fact he signed and that which he believed he was signing. In an endeavour to keep the plea within bounds there have been many attempts to lay down a dividing line. But any dividing line suggested has been difficult to apply in practice and has sometimes led to unreasonable results. In particular I do not think that the modern division between the character and the contents of a document is at all satisfactory. Some of the older authorities suggest a more flexible test so that one can take all factors into consideration. There was a period when here, as elsewhere in the law, hard-and-fast dividing lines were sought, but I think that experience has shown that often they do not produce certainty but do produce unreasonable results.

I think that in the older authorities difference in practical result was more important than difference in legal character. If a man thinks he is signing a document which will cost him £10 and the actual document would cost him £1,000 it could not be right to deny him this remedy simply because the legal character of the two was the same. It is true that we must then deal with questions of degree, but that is a familiar task for the courts and I would not expect it to give rise to a flood of litigation.

There must, I think, be a radical difference between what he signed and what he thought he was signing—or one could use the words 'fundamental' or 'serious' or 'very substantial'. But what amounts to a radical difference will depend on all the circumstances. If he thinks he is giving property to A whereas the document gives it to B, the difference may often be of vital importance, but in the circumstances of the present case I do not think that it is. I think that it must be left to the courts to determine in each case in light of all the facts whether there was or was not a sufficiently great difference. The plea non est factum is in a sense illogical when applied to a case where the man in fact signed the deed. But it is none the worse for that if applied in a reasonable way.

I would dismiss this appeal.

Lord Wilberforce

The plea of non est factum has a long history. In medieval times, when contracts were made by deeds, and the deed had a kind of life in the law of its own, illiterate people who either could not read, or could not understand, the language in which the deed was written, were allowed this plea (that is what 'non est factum' is—a plea): the result of it, if successful, was that the deed was not their deed. I think that three things can be said about the early law. First, that no definition was given of the nature or extent of the difference which must exist between what was intended and what was done—whether such as later appeared as the distinction between 'character' and 'contents' or otherwise. . . . Secondly, the . . . cases are for the most part as between the original parties to the deed, or if a third party is concerned . . . he is a successor to the estate granted. Thirdly, there is some indication that the plea was not available where the signer had been guilty of a lack of care in signing what he did: there is no great precision in the definitions of the disabling conduct . . .

In the 19th century, the emphasis had shifted towards the consensual contract, and the courts, probably unconscious of the fact, had a choice. They could either have discarded the whole doctrine on which non est factum was based, as obsolete, or they could try to adapt it to the prevailing structure of contract. . . . They chose the course of adaptation, and, as in many other fields of the law, this process of adaptation has not been logical, or led to a logical result. The modern version still contains some fossilised elements.

We had traced, in arguments at the Bar, the emergence of the distinction, which has come to be made between a difference (of intention from result) of character, which may render a document void, and a difference of contents which at most makes it voidable. . . . It was really the language used in the second leading case of *Howatson v. Webb* [1907] 1 Ch 537 which has given rise to difficulty. There, in a judgment of Warrington J which has carried much conviction and authority, we find that, although the judgment of

Byles J in *Foster* v. *Mackinnon* (1869) LR 4 CP 704 is quoted, the use of the word 'contents' is switched to mean what the deed actually (as a matter of detail) contains, and contrasted with what is called its legal character (see p. 549: 'The misrepresentation was as to the contents of the deed, and not as to the character and class of the deed').

The distinction, as restated, is terminologically confusing and in substance illogical, as the judgments in the Court of Appeal demonstrate. On the one hand, it cannot be right that a document should be void through a mistake as to the label it bears, however little this mistake may be fundamental to what the signer intends: on the other hand, it is not satisfactory that the document should be valid if the mistake is merely as to what the document contains, however radical this mistake may be and however cataclysmic its result.

The existing test, or at least its terminology, may be criticised, but does it follow that there are no definable circumstances in which a document to which a man has put his signature may be held to be not his document, and so void rather than merely voidable? The judgment of the learned Master of the Rolls seems at first sight to suggest that there are not and that the whole doctrine ought to be discarded, but a closer reading shows that he is really confining his observations to the plainest, and no doubt commonest, cases where a man of full understanding and capacity forbears, or negligently omits, to read what he has signed. That, in the present age, such a person should be denied the non est factum plea I would accept. . . . But there remains a residue of difficult cases. There are still illiterate or senile persons who cannot read, or apprehend, a legal document; there are still persons who may be tricked into putting their signature on a piece of paper which has legal consequences totally different from anything they intended. Certainly the first class may in some cases, even without the plea, be able to obtain relief, either because no third party has become involved, or, if he has, with the assistance of equitable doctrines, because the third party's interest is equitable only and his conduct such that his rights should be postponed. . . . Certainly, too, the second class may in some cases fall under the heading of plain forgery, in which event the plea of non est factum is not needed, or indeed available . . . and in others be reduced if the signer is denied the benefit of the plea because of his negligence. But accepting all that has been said by learned judges as to the necessity of confining the plea within narrow limits, to eliminate it altogether would, in my opinion, deprive the courts of what may be, doubtless on sufficiently rare occasions, an instrument of justice.

How, then, ought the principle, on which a plea of non est factum is admissible, to be stated? In my opinion, a document should be held to be void (as opposed to voidable) only when the element of consent to it is totally lacking, that is, more concretely, when the transaction which the document purports to effect is essentially different in substance or in kind from the transaction intended. Many other expressions, or adjectives, could be used—'basically' or 'radically' or 'fundamentally' . . .

To this general test it is necessary to add certain amplifications. First, there is the case of fraud. The law as to this is best stated in the words of the judgment in *Foster* v. *Mackinnon* (1869) LR 4 CP 704, 711 where it is said that a signature obtained by fraud

> 'is invalid not merely on the ground of fraud, where fraud exists, but on the ground that the mind of the signer did not accompany the signature; in other words, that he never intended to sign, and therefore in contemplation of law never did sign, the contract to which his name is appended.'

In other words, it is the lack of consent that matters, not the means by which this result was brought about. Fraud by itself may do no more than make the contract voidable.

Secondly, a man cannot escape from the consequences, as regards innocent third parties, of signing a document if, being a man of ordinary education and competence, he chooses to sign it without informing himself of its purport and effect . . .

Thirdly, there is the case where the signer has been careless in not taking ordinary precautions against being deceived. This is a difficult area. . . . In my opinion, the correct rule, and that which in fact prevailed until *Bragg's* case [*Carlisle and Cumberland Banking Company* v. *Bragg* [1911] 1 KB 489], is that, leaving aside negotiable instruments to which special rules may apply, a person who signs a document, and parts with it so that it may come into other hands, has a responsibility, that of the normal man of prudence, to take care what he signs, which, if neglected, prevents him from denying his liability under the document according to its tenor. I would add that the onus of proof in this matter rests upon him, i.e., to prove that he acted carefully, and not upon the third party to prove the contrary. . . .

The preceding paragraphs contemplate persons who are adult and literate: the conclusion as to such persons is that, while there are cases in which they may successfully plead non est factum these cases will, in modern times, be rare.

As to persons who are illiterate, or blind, or lacking in understanding, the law is in a dilemma. On the one hand, the law is traditionally, and rightly, ready to relieve them against hardship and imposition. On the other hand, regard has to be paid to the position of innocent third parties who cannot be expected, and often would have no means, to know the condition or status of the signer. I do not think that a defined solution can be provided for all cases. The law ought, in my opinion, to give relief if satisfied that consent was truly lacking but will require of signers even in this class that they act responsibly and carefully according to their circumstances in putting their signature to legal documents.

This brings me to the present case. Mrs Gallie was a lady of advanced age, but, as her evidence shows, by no means incapable physically or mentally. It certainly cannot be said that she did not receive sympathetic consideration or the benefit of much doubt from the judge as to the circumstances in which the assignment was executed. But accepting all of this, I am satisfied, with Russell LJ, that she fell short, very far short, of making the clear and satisfactory case which is required of those who seek to have a legal act declared void and of establishing a sufficient discrepancy between her intentions and her act . . .

I would dismiss the appeal.

Lord Pearson

In my opinion, the plea of non est factum ought to be available in a proper case for the relief of a person who for permanent or temporary reasons (not limited to blindness or illiteracy) is not capable of both reading and sufficiently understanding the deed or other document to be signed. By 'sufficiently understanding' I mean understanding at least to the point of detecting a fundamental difference between the actual document and the document as the signer had believed it to be. There must be a proper case for such relief. There would not be a proper case if (a) the signature of the document was brought about by negligence of the signer in failing to take precautions which he ought to have taken, or (b) the actual document was not fundamentally different from the document as the signer believed it to be. . . .

The principle as stated is limited to a case in which it is apparent on the face of the document that it is intended to have legal consequences. . . . I wish to reserve the question whether the plea of non est factum would ever be rightly successful in a case where (1) it is apparent on the face of the document that it is intended to have legal consequences; (2) the signer of the document is able to read and sufficiently understand the document; (3) the document is fundamentally different from what he supposes it to be; (4) he is induced to sign it without reading it. It seems unlikely that the plea ought ever to succeed in such a case, but it is inadvisable to rule out the wholly exceptional and unpredictable case.

Lord Hodson and **Viscount Dilhorne** delivered concurring speeches.

COMMENTARY

The facts of the case demonstrate the conflicting interests at stake. On the one hand we have the desire to protect Mrs Gallie from being taken advantage of by her nephew and his associate, while on the other hand we can see the need to protect the building society who, as a third party, advanced money on the validity of Mrs Gallie's signature. The defence of *non est factum* is drawn by the House of Lords in narrow terms, with a view to protecting third parties, but, at the same time, there is an attempt to avoid creating arbitrary distinctions both in terms of the persons entitled to invoke the defence and in relation to the nature of the mistake that must be established in order to entitle a party to rely on the defence. The category of parties able to invoke the defence is not confined to the blind or the illiterate. It encompasses a much broader range of people but at the same time it does not extend to adults of full capacity who do not take the time to protect their own interests by reading the document they have signed. In relation to the type of mistake that entitles a party to invoke the defence, the House of Lords rejects the technical approach taken in *Howatson* v. *Webb* [1907] 1 Ch 537 (see the speech of Lord Wilberforce above) and adopts a broader approach which simply requires that the difference between the document as it was and as it was believed to be must be radical or substantial or fundamental.

9. FURTHER READING

CHANDLER, A and DEVENNEY, J, 'Mistake as to Identity and the Threads of Objectivity' (2004) 1 *Journal of Obligations and Remedies* 7.

GOODHART, A, 'Mistake as to Identity in the Law of Contract' (1941) 57 *LQR* 228.

HARE, C, 'Identity Mistakes: A Missed Opportunity' (2004) 67 *MLR* 993.

MACMILLAN, C, 'How Temptation Led to Mistake: an Explanation of *Bell v Lever Bros. Ltd*' (2003) 119 *LQR* 625.

SLADE, CJ, 'The Myth of Mistake in the English Law of Contract' (1954) 70 *LQR* 385.

SMITH, JC, 'Common Law—Mistake, Frustration and Implied Terms' (1994) 110 *LQR* 400.

17

MISREPRESENTATION

1. CENTRAL ISSUES

1. The law of misrepresentation is, in many ways, the law of induced mistake: that is to say, one party is induced to enter into a contract as a result of a false statement of fact made to him by the defendant or by a third party. The ground on which the relief is sought in these cases does not rest on the mistake made by the claimant but rather rests on the fact that the mistake was induced by the false statement of fact that was made to the claimant and which induced him to enter into the contract.

2. A claimant who wishes to seek relief on the ground of misrepresentation must, first of all, establish that a misrepresentation was made to him. A misrepresentation is an unambiguous false statement of fact, made to the claimant, which induced him to enter into a contract. This definition has given rise to a number of difficulties in the case-law. Can a statement of opinion or a statement of intention constitute a misrepresentation? Can a misrepresentation be made by conduct? Must a misrepresentation be 'material'? When will a misrepresentation be held to have induced a claimant to enter into a contract? All of these questions will be explored in this chapter.

3. English law does not generally recognize the existence of a duty of disclosure. However, in certain circumstances, a failure to disclose information may give rise to a claim for misrepresentation. These circumstances will be examined in this chapter.

4. A claimant who has been induced to enter into a contract by a misrepresentation made to him by the other party to the contract is, in principle, entitled to set aside (or 'rescind') that contract. Rescission is an extremely powerful remedy because it sets aside a contract for all purposes. There are, however, a number of 'bars' to rescission and the scope of these bars will be examined in this chapter. Rescission for misrepresentation must be distinguished from the termination of a contract for breach. Rescission for misrepresentation aims to unwind the contract so that it is set aside both retrospectively and prospectively. Termination for breach, by contrast, discharges the contract prospectively but not retrospectively.

5. Damages are also available as a remedy for misrepresentation. Prior to 1963 only a fraudulent misrepresentation gave rise to a claim for damages (in the tort of deceit). The right to claim damages for misrepresentation was extended by the House of Lords in 1963 when it was recognized that, in certain circumstances, a negligent misrepresentation could give rise to a claim for damages in tort. The final step was taken in 1967 when section 2 of the Misrepresentation Act 1967 created a statutory right to recover damages in respect of negligent misrepresentations and in respect of some innocent misrepresentations. Section 2 is now the most important source of the right to recover damages for misrepresentation. Section 2 has proved to be a controversial provision and the controversies associated with it will be examined in this chapter.

6. Attempts to exclude or restrict liability for misrepresentation are regulated by section 3 of the Misrepresentation Act 1967 which subjects such clauses to a test of reasonableness. The question whether an entire agreement

clause falls within the scope of section 3 has
proved to be a contentious issue and it has not,
as yet, been conclusively resolved. This issue
will be examined at the end of the chapter.

2. INTRODUCTION

The law of misrepresentation inhabits a borderland between contract, tort, and restitution (or unjust enrichment). A misrepresentation induces a party to enter into a
contract but is often not part of the contract itself; a fraudulent or negligent
misrepresentation can give rise to a claim for damages in tort; and a personal and
(possibly) a proprietary restitutionary claim can be brought to recover the value of
benefits conferred under a contract which has been set aside (or 'rescinded') for
misrepresentation. The role of the law of tort and the law of restitution will be
examined when discussing the remedial consequences of a misrepresentation.

The proposition that a misrepresentation induces a party to enter into a contract
but is often not part of the contract itself requires further elaboration. Not every
statement made prior to entry into a contract is incorporated into the contract as a
term. It can in fact be a difficult task to determine in any given case whether a pre-
contractual statement is simply a representation which has induced entry into the
contract but is not part of the contract or whether it is in fact a term of the contract.
The tests applied by the courts to distinguish between a term and a representation
have been examined already (see pp. 321–334 above) and it is not necessary to go over
the same ground again. Here, it suffices to state that the distinction between a term
and a representation does have remedial consequences. Where the statement is a term
of the contract, a failure to comply with it, without lawful excuse, will constitute a
breach of contract and the remedies available will be those available in a breach of
contract claim (on which see Chapters 24–26). On the other hand, where the representation is not a term of the contract then the claimant's claim will be one for misrepresentation and not for breach of contract. The remedies for misrepresentation
will be discussed in this chapter.

It is, of course, possible for a pre-contractual statement to be incorporated into the
contract as a term. In such a case the claimant will have an action for breach of
contract in the event of a breach of the term and the usual remedies for breach will be
available to him. But it may also be possible for a claimant in such a case to bring a
claim for misrepresentation and seek rescission of the contract or damages. Section
1(a) of the Misrepresentation Act 1967 provides that a party who has entered into a
contract after a misrepresentation has been made to him may rescind the contract for
misrepresentation, even in the case where the misrepresentation is subsequently
incorporated into the contract as a term, provided that he is entitled to rescind the
contract without alleging fraud. The scope of this subsection is, in some respects,
unclear but its general effect is to make provision for the survival of the right to
rescind for misrepresentation in the case where a statement of fact has been incorporated into a contract as a term but at the same time the subsection does not purport to
take away any remedies available to the claimant for breach of contract. This being the
case, the claimant would appear to have available to him the usual array of remedies

for breach of contract but also has the possibility of rescinding the contract for misrepresentation where he can establish an entitlement to do so.

The remainder of this chapter is devoted solely to liability for misrepresentation and does not deal with the complications that can arise where the statement has also been incorporated into the contract as a term. The remainder of the chapter is divided into five sections. The next section (section 3) examines the definition of a misrepresentation; section 4 deals with the extent to which English law recognizes the existence of a duty of disclosure; the subject-matter of section 5 is rescission; section 6 explores the extent to which a misrepresentation can give rise to a claim for damages; and section 7 examines the extent to which it is possible to exclude liability for misrepresentation.

3. WHAT IS A MISREPRESENTATION?

A misrepresentation can be defined as an unambiguous false statement of fact which is addressed to the party misled and which induces that party to enter into a contract. There may be further elements to the definition. One issue of controversy has been whether or not the misrepresentation must also be 'material'. The definition of a misrepresentation has proved to be surprisingly troublesome and it has given rise to a considerable amount of litigation. It is therefore necessary to examine the constituent elements of a misrepresentation in greater detail before using some cases to illustrate the difficulties that have arisen.

First, the misrepresentation must have been 'unambiguous'. An ambiguous statement will not generally give rise to a right of action for misrepresentation except in the case where a party makes an ambiguous statement intending it to convey a meaning which he knows is not true and the party to whom the statement is made reasonably understands it in the sense which is not true.

Secondly, the representation must have been 'false'. A statement which is true obviously cannot give rise to a claim for misrepresentation.

Thirdly, there must have been a 'statement'. The requirement that the misrepresentation take the form of a 'statement' draws attention to the fact that there must be some positive conduct on the part of the representor. A mere failure to disclose information will not, as a general rule, give rise to an action for misrepresentation (see pp. 673–678 below). The statement commonly takes the form of a written or an oral communication. But it need not do so. A representation can be made by conduct. Cases involving representations by conduct can give rise to acute difficulties in terms of identifying the meaning that was conveyed by the conduct.

Fourthly, the statement must be one 'of fact'. There are a number of issues here. First, this requirement serves to distinguish a representation from a promise. A promise is more than a statement of fact. It is an undertaking to do something or not to do something. A representation, by contrast, simply asserts the existence of a given state of affairs which is either true or false. The statement invites reliance upon it but it does not constitute an undertaking to bring about that state of affairs. Secondly, it has proved to be difficult to distinguish a statement of fact from other types of statement that can be made, such as statement of law, of opinion, or of intention. The distinction between these different types of statements is not as rigid as it once was because it is now clear that statements of law, opinion, and intention can, in certain circumstances, give rise to a claim for misrepresentation. Thus it is now established that a mistake of law can, in an appropriate case, entitle the mistaken party to set aside a contract entered into as a result of the mistake (*Brennan* v. *Bolt Burden (a firm)* [2004] EWCA Civ 1017; [2004] 3 WLR 1321) and that a misrepresentation of law can found a cause of action (*Pankhania* v. *London Borough of Hackney* [2002] EWHC 2441 (Ch)). Statements of opinion are more difficult. While authority can be found to support the proposition that a statement of opinion does not suffice to give a claim for mis-representation (*Bisset* v. *Wilkinson* [1927] AC 177, p. 661 below), more recent authority has held statements of opinion to be actionable where the person who makes the statement of opinion has some special skill but fails to exercise it (see *Esso Petroleum Ltd* v. *Mardon* [1976] QB 801, p. 331 above). A statement of intention, on the other hand, cannot generally constitute a misrepresentation unless the person making the statement mis-states his present intention (see *Edgington* v. *Fitzmaurice* (1885) 29 Ch D 459, p. 334 below).

Fifthly, the statement must have been 'addressed to the party misled'. This can be done in one of two ways. First, it can be made directly as in the case where one party speaks to another or writes to him. Secondly, it can be done indirectly. A statement can be addressed to a person 'indirectly' when the statement is made by the maker of the statement to a third party with the intention that the third party pass on the informa-tion to the claimant. An example is information conveyed by one bank to another with the intention that the recipient bank convey the information to one of its cus-tomers (see, for example, *Commercial Banking of Sydney* v. *R.H. Brown and Co* [1972] 2 Lloyd's Rep 360).

Sixthly, there is a debate as to whether or not the misrepresentation must have been 'material'. The judgments in *Bisset* v. *Wilkinson* [1927] AC 177 (p. 661 below), *Redgrave* v. *Hurd* (1881) 20 Ch D 1 (p. 679 below), and *Edgington* v. *Fitzmaurice* (1885) 29 Ch D 459 (p. 664 below) make frequent references to the existence or otherwise of a 'material' statement. There are two difficulties here. The first relates to the meaning of 'material'. It would appear that a 'material' statement is one that would affect the mind of a reasonable person in deciding whether or not to enter into a contract. The second difficulty relates to the role played by materiality in the case-law. Many of the references appear to be in the context of deciding whether or not the misrepresentation was an inducement to entry into the contract. But it is possible to argue that the requirement of 'materality' (if there is such a requirement) is analytic-ally distinct from the question of inducement. The difficult case is the case in which a party is induced to enter into a contract by a misrepresentation which is objectively immaterial. Such cases are unlikely to arise in practice because a court in such a case will, in all probability, find on the facts that the representation did not induce the party concerned to enter into the contract. The authorities suggest that the courts adopt the following approach: where the misrepresentation is of such a nature that it would have induced a reasonable person to enter into the contract then the court will presume that it did induce the representee to enter into the contract and the onus of proof then switches to the party who made the statement to show that the representee did not in fact rely on the representation in entering into the contract (*Museprime Properties Ltd* v. *Adhill Properties Ltd* (1991) 61 P & CR 111, 124). By contrast, in the case where the statement would not have induced a reasonable person to enter into a contract in reliance upon the statement, the onus of proof rests upon the recipient of the statement to show that the misrepresentation did in fact induce him to enter into the contract.

Seventhly, the misrepresentation must have induced the claimant to enter into the contract. The representation need not have been the only inducement to entry into the contract (*Edgington* v. *Fitzmaurice* (1885) 29 Ch D 459). It suffices that the misrepresentation was an inducement which was actively present to the claimant's mind at the time at which he entered into the contract. A misrepresentation does not induce a party to enter into a contract in the case where the claimant was unaware of the existence of the misrepresentation at the time of entry into the contract (*Horsfall* v. *Thomas* (1862) 1 H & C 90) and in the case where the claimant placed his reliance upon a third party when entering into the contract (*Atwood* v. *Small* (1838) 6 C & F 232). On the other hand, the fact that the claimant could have discovered the true position by acting in a more diligent fashion does not, of itself, prevent him from asserting that he was induced to enter into the contract in reliance upon the defendant's misrepresentation (see *Redgrave* v. *Hurd* (1881) 20 Ch D 1, p. 679 below).

These principles can be seen at work in the following three cases:

(a) STATEMENTS OF OPINION

Bisset v. Wilkinson

[1927] AC 177, Privy Council

In May 1919 Wilkinson agreed to purchase from Bisset two adjoining blocks of land in New Zealand called 'Homestead' and 'Hogan's'. Wilkinson purchased the land for the purpose of sheep farming. In accordance with the agreement Wilkinson paid part of the purchase price on the signing of the agreement. The balance was payable in May 1924 and interest was to be paid half-yearly in the meantime. Wilkinson took possession of the land but soon after experienced difficulties and did not make the interest payments when they fell due. When Bisset brought an action to recover the overdue interest payments Wilkinson sought to have the agreement rescinded, alleging that Bisset had misrepresented that the land 'had a carrying capacity of 2000 sheep if only one team were employed in the agricultural work of the land'. Bisset argued that the representation was a statement of opinion, which he honestly held, and so was not actionable. The New Zealand Court of Appeal held that the representation was an untrue statement of fact and set aside the agreement. The Privy Council allowed Bisset's appeal and held that the representation was a statement of opinion, which Bisset honestly held and was not actionable.

Lord Merrivale [delivering the judgment of the Board]
In an action for rescission, as in an action for specific performance of an executory contract, when misrepresentation is the alleged ground of relief of the party who repudiates

the contract, it is, of course, essential to ascertain whether that which is relied upon is a representation of a specific fact, or a statement of opinion, since an erroneous opinion stated by the party affirming the contract, though it may have been relied upon and have induced the contract on the part of the party who seeks rescission, gives no title to relief unless fraud is established. The application of this rule, however, is not always easy, as is illustrated in a good many reported cases, as well as in this. A representation of fact may be inherent in a statement of opinion and, at any rate, the existence of the opinion in the person stating it is a question of fact. In *Karberg's Case* [1892] 3 Ch 1, 11 Lindley LJ, in course of testing a representation which might have been, as it was said to be by interested parties, one of opinion or belief, used this inquiry: 'Was the statement of expectation a statement of things not really expected?' The Court of Appeal applied this test and rescinded the contract which was in question. In *Smith* v. *Land and House Property Corporation* (1884) 28 Ch D 7, 15 there came in question a vendor's description of the tenant of the property sold as 'a most desirable tenant'—a statement of his opinion, as was argued on his behalf in an action to enforce the contract of sale. This description was held by the Court of Appeal to be a misrepresentation of fact, which, without proof of fraud, disentitled the vendor to specific performance of the contract of purchase. 'It is often fallaciously assumed', said Bowen LJ, 'that a statement of opinion cannot involve the statement of fact. In a case where the facts are equally well known to both parties, what one of them says to the other is frequently nothing but an expression of opinion. The statement of such opinion is in a sense a statement of fact, about the condition of the man's own mind, but only of an irrelevant fact, for it is of no consequence what the opinion is. But if the facts are not equally well known to both sides, then a statement of opinion by one who knows the facts best involves very often a statement of a material fact, for he impliedly states that he knows facts which justify his opinion.' The kind of distinction which is in question is illustrated again in a well known case of *Smith* v. *Chadwick* (1884) 9 App Cas 187; (1882) 20 Ch D 27. There the words under consideration involved the inquiry in relation to the sale of an industrial concern whether a statement of 'the present value of the turnover or output' was of necessity a statement of fact that the produce of the works was of the amount mentioned, or might be and was a statement that the productive power of the works was estimated at so much. The words were held to be capable of the second of these meanings. The decisive inquiries came to be: what meaning was actually conveyed to the party complaining; was he deceived, and, as the action was based on a charge of fraud, was the statement in question made fraudulently?

In the present case, as in those cited, the material facts of the transaction, the knowledge of the parties respectively, and their relative positions, the words of representation used, and the actual condition of the subject-matter spoken of, are relevant to the two inquiries necessary to be made: What was the meaning of the representation? Was it true?

In ascertaining what meaning was conveyed to the minds of the now respondents by the appellant's statement as to the two thousand sheep, the most material fact to be remembered is that, as both parties were aware, the appellant had not and, so far as appears, no other person had at any time carried on sheep-farming upon the unit of land in question. That land as a distinct holding had never constituted a sheep-farm. The two blocks comprised in it differed substantially in character. Hogan's block was described by one of the respondents' witnesses as 'better land'. 'It might carry', he said, 'one sheep or perhaps two or even three sheep to the acre'. He estimated the carrying capacity of the land generally as little more than half a sheep to the acre. And Hogan's land had been allowed to deteriorate during several years before the respondents purchased. As was said by Sim J: 'In ordinary circumstances, any statement made by an owner who has been occupying his own farm as to its carrying capacity would be regarded as a statement of fact. . . . This, however, is not such a case. The defendants knew all about Hogan's block and knew also what sheep the farm was carrying when they inspected it. In these circumstances . . . the defendants were not justified in regarding anything said by the plaintiff as to the carrying capacity as being anything more than an expression of his opinion on the subject.' In this view of the matter their Lordships concur.

Whether the appellant honestly and in fact held the opinion which he stated remained to be considered. This involved examination of the history and condition of the property. If a reasonable man with the appellant's knowledge could not have come to the conclusion he stated, the description of that conclusion as an opinion would not necessarily protect him against rescission for misrepresentation. But what was actually the capacity in competent hands of the land the respondents purchased had never been, and never was, practically ascertained. The respondents, after two years' trial of sheep-farming, under difficulties caused in part by their inexperience, found themselves confronted by a fall in the values of sheep and wool which would have left them losers if they could have carried three thousand sheep. As is said in the judgment of Ostler J: 'Owing to sheep becoming practically valueless, they reduced their flock and went in for cropping and dairy-farming in order to make a living'.

The opinions of experts and of their neighbours, on which the respondents relied, were met by the appellant with evidence of experts admitted to be equally competent and upright with those of his opponents, and his own practical experience upon part of the land, as to which his testimony was unhesitatingly accepted by the judge of first instance. It is of dominant importance that Sim J negatived the respondents' charge of fraud.

After attending to the close and very careful examination of the evidence which was made by learned counsel for each of the parties their Lordships entirely concur in the view which was expressed by the learned judge who heard the case. The defendants failed to prove that the farm if properly managed was not capable of carrying two thousand sheep.

COMMENTARY

Bisset was narrowly interpreted by the Court of Appeal in *Esso Petroleum Ltd* v. *Mardon* [1976] QB 801 (p. 331 above). Lord Denning there distinguished *Bisset* on the ground that 'the land had never been used as a sheep farm and both parties were equally able to form an opinion as to its carrying capacity'. The key fact would therefore appear to be that the vendor was not possessed of any special skill or expertise in relation to sheep farming. The position is otherwise where, as in *Esso*, the maker of the statement does profess to have some special skill or expertise in relation to the subject-matter of his statement of opinion. In such a case the courts will readily imply that the maker of the statement is subject to a duty to make the statement with reasonable care and skill. The effect of this implication is to leave the maker of the statement potentially exposed to a claim for misrepresentation when he makes the statement without exercising reasonable care and skill. It should be noted that the Privy Council in *Bisset* did not deny the possibility that a claim for mis-representation could arise out of a statement which could be classified as one of opinion. Lord Merrivale cites with approval a passage from the judgment of Bowen LJ in *Smith* v. *Land and House Property Corporation* (1884) 28 Ch D 7, 15 where he states that:

if the facts are not equally well known to both sides, then a statement of opinion by one who knows the facts best involves very often a statement of a material fact, for he impliedly states that he knows facts which justify his opinion.

On the facts of *Smith* a vendor of property described a tenant as 'a most desirable tenant' when the vendor knew that part of the tenant's rent remained unpaid and other instalments had only been paid under the threat of legal proceedings. The vendor argued that his statement was a statement of opinion which was not action-able. His argument was rejected on the basis that his statement was held to contain an implied assertion that he knew of no facts which would lead to the conclusion that the tenant was not in fact a 'most desirable tenant'.

(b) STATEMENTS OF INTENTION AND INDUCEMENT

Edgington v. Fitzmaurice

(1885) 29 Ch D 459, Court of Appeal

The plaintiff, Mr Edgington, was a shareholder in a company of which the defendants were officers. The directors issued a prospectus which invited shareholders to subscribe to debenture bonds. It stated that the bonds were being issued for the purpose of (i) making improvements to a property recently purchased by the company, (ii) the devel-opment of a transport service for the company through the purchase of horses and vans, and (iii) the further development of their business of supplying cheap fish from the coast. The plaintiff also wrote to the company secretary and asked whether or not the deben-tures would be a first charge on the property. The company secretary confirmed that they would be.

The company was later wound up and the assets were insufficient to pay the debenture holders more than a small dividend. The plaintiff brought an action against the defend-ants to recover the sum of money advanced by him on the ground that he had been induced to pay the money by fraudulent misrepresentations for which the defendants were responsible. The defendants denied liability. The Court of Appeal held, affirming the decision of Denman J, that the plaintiff was entitled to recover the money in an action in deceit on the basis that he had been induced to pay the money to the company by the fraudulent misrepresentation of the defendants as to the purpose for which the deben-tures were issued.

Cotton LJ

I cannot doubt that the real object of the issue of debentures was to meet the pressing liabilities of the company and not to improve the property or develop the business of the company. . . . It was said, How could those who advanced the money have relied on this statement as material? I think it was material. A man who lends money reasonably wishes to know for what purpose it is borrowed, and he is more willing to advance it if he knows that it is not wanted to pay off liabilities already incurred.

But it was urged by the counsel for the Appellants that the Plaintiff himself stated that he would not have taken the debentures unless he had thought there was a charge upon the property, and that it was this mistaken notion which really induced the Plaintiff to advance his money. In my opinion this argument does not assist the Defendants if the Plaintiff really acted on the statement in the prospectus. It is true that if he had not supposed he would have a charge he would not have taken the debentures; but if he also relied on the misstatement in the prospectus, his loss none the less resulted from that misstatement. It is not necessary to shew that the misstatement was the sole cause of his acting as he did. If he acted on that misstatement, though he was also influenced by an erroneous supposition, the Defendants will be still liable.

Bowen LJ

This is an action for deceit, in which the Plaintiff complains that he was induced to take certain debentures by the misrepresentations of the Defendants, and that he sustained damage thereby. The loss which the Plaintiff sustained is not disputed. In order to sustain his action he must first prove that there was a statement as to facts which was false; and secondly, that it was false to the knowledge of the Defendants, or that they made it not caring whether it was true or false. For it is immaterial whether they made the statement knowing it to be untrue, or recklessly, without caring whether it was true or not, because to make a statement recklessly for the purpose of influencing another person is dishonest. It is also clear that it is wholly immaterial with what object the lie is told. That is laid down in Lord *Blackburn's* judgment in *Smith* v. *Chadwick* 9 App Cas 201, but it is material that the defendant should intend that it should be relied on by the person to whom he makes it. But, lastly, when you have proved that the statement was false, you must further shew that the plaintiff has acted upon it and has sustained damage by so doing: you must shew that the statement was either the sole cause of the plaintiff's act, or materially contributed to his so acting. So the law is laid down in *Clarke* v. *Dickson* 6 CB (NS) 453, and that is the law which we have now to apply.

The alleged misrepresentations were three. First, it was said that the prospectus contained an implied allegation that the mortgage for £21,500 could not be called in at once, but was payable by instalments. I think that upon a fair construction of the prospectus it does so allege; and therefore that the prospectus must be taken to have contained an untrue statement on that point; but it does not appear to me clear that the statement was fraudulently made by the Defendants. It is therefore immaterial to consider whether the Plaintiff was induced to act as he did by that statement.

[After discussing and dismissing the plaintiff's claim on the basis of the failure to mention that the mortgage might be required to be paid at once:]

Secondly, it is said that the prospectus contains an implied allegation that there was no other mortgage affecting the property except the mortgage stated therein. I think there was such an implied allegation, but I think it is not brought home to the Defendants that it was made dishonestly; accordingly, although the Plaintiff may have been damnified by the weight which he gave to the allegation, he cannot rely on it in this action: for in an action of deceit the Plaintiff must prove dishonesty. Therefore if the case had rested on these two allegations alone, I think it would be too uncertain to entitle the Plaintiff to succeed.

But when we come to the third alleged misstatement I feel that the Plaintiff's case is made out. I mean the statement of the objects for which the money was to be raised. These were stated to be to complete the alterations and additions to the buildings, to purchase horses and vans, and to develop the supply of fish. A mere suggestion of possible purposes to which a portion of the money might be applied would not have formed a basis for an action of deceit. There must be a misstatement of an existing fact: but the state of a man's mind is as much a fact as the state of his digestion. It is true that it is very difficult to prove what the state of a man's mind at a particular time is, but if it can be ascertained it is as much a fact as anything else. A misrepresentation as to the state of a man's mind is, therefore, a misstatement of fact. Having applied as careful consideration to the evidence as I could, I have reluctantly come to the conclusion that the true objects of the Defendants in raising the money were not those stated in the circular . . .

Then the question remains—Did this misstatement contribute to induce the Plaintiff to advance his money? Mr *Davey's* [counsel for the defendants'] argument has not convinced me that they did not. He contended that the Plaintiff admits that he would not have taken the debentures unless he had thought they would give him a charge on the property, and therefore he was induced to take them by his own mistake, and the misstatement in the circular was not material. But such misstatement was material if it was actively present to his mind when he decided to advance his money. The real question is, what was the state of the Plaintiff's mind, and if his mind was disturbed by the misstatement of the Defendants, and such disturbance was in part the cause of what he did, the mere fact of his also making a mistake himself could make no difference. It resolves itself into a mere question of fact. I have felt some difficulty about the pleadings, because in the statement of claim this point is not clearly put forward, and I had some doubt whether this contention as to the third misstatement was not an afterthought. But the balance of my judgment is weighed down by the probability of the case. What is the first question which a man asks when he advances money? It is, what is it wanted for? Therefore I think that the statement is material, and that the Plaintiff would be unlike the rest of his race if he was not influenced by the statement of the objects for which the loan was required. The learned Judge in the Court below came to the conclusion that the misstatement did influence him, and I think he came to a right conclusion.

Fry LJ

It is clear that their [the defendants'] object in raising the money was to meet their pressing liabilities. . . . But the statement in the prospectus was that a large sum of money had been already expended in improving the building . . . and that the directors intended to apply the money raised by the debentures in further improving the buildings. This statement was therefore false . . .

The next inquiry is whether this statement materially affected the conduct of the Plaintiff in advancing his money. He has sworn that it did, and the learned Judge who tried the action has believed him. On such a point I should not like to differ from the Judge who tried the action, even though I were not myself convinced, but in this case the natural inference from the facts is in accordance with the Judge's conclusion. The prospectus was intended to influence the mind of the reader. Then this question has been raised: the Plaintiff admits that he was induced to make the advance not merely by this false statement, but by the belief that the debentures would give him a charge on the company's property, and it is admitted that this was a mistake of the Plaintiff. Therefore it is said that the Plaintiff was the author of his own injury. It is quite true that the Plaintiff was influenced by his own mistake, but that does not benefit the Defendants' case. The Plaintiff says: I had two inducements, one my own mistake, the other the false statement of the Defendants. The two together induced me to advance the money. But in my opinion if the false statement of fact actually influenced the Plaintiff, the Defendants are liable, even though the Plaintiff may have been also influenced by other motives. I think, therefore, the Defendants must be held liable. The appeal must therefore be dismissed.

COMMENTARY

On the facts of this case, the plaintiff had no effective claim against the company (because it was insolvent) and so he brought the claim against the directors instead. Two points of significance emerge from the case. The first is that it demonstrates that a statement of intention can be actionable in a case where the maker of the statement mis-states his present intention. In Bowen LJ's memorable phrase, 'the state of a man's mind is as much a fact as the state of his digestion'. As Bowen LJ acknowledges, it can be extremely difficult to prove that a person has in fact mis-stated his present intention. A party who truly states his present intention but then changes his mind does not commit a misrepresentation. In the absence of a binding promise not to change his mind, the maker of the statement is free to change his mind without incurring any liability for doing so (*Kleinwort Benson Ltd* v. *Malaysia Mining Corporation Berhad* [1989] 1 WLR 379; *Wales* v. *Wadham* [1977] 1 WLR 199).

The second point to note is that the plaintiff advanced the money under the erroneous belief that he was entitled to a first charge on the property of the company. This was therefore not a case in which the plaintiff was relying solely upon the statements contained in the prospectus. This was held to be no barrier to the plaintiff's action. As Fry LJ stated, provided that the false statement of fact actually influenced the plaintiff he was entitled to succeed in his claim notwithstanding the fact that he was also influenced to enter into the transaction by other factors.

(c) STATEMENTS MADE BY CONDUCT

Spice Girls Ltd v. Aprilia World Service BV

[2002] EWCA Civ 15; [2002] EMLR 27, Court of Appeal

The claimants, Spice Girls Ltd ('SGL'), entered into a contract with the defendants, Aprilia World Service ('AWS'), a manufacturer of motorcycles and scooters, according to which the latter agreed to sponsor the Spice Girls' concert tour in return for promotional work carried out by the group. The contract between the parties was signed on 6 May 1998. One of the members of the Spice Girls, Ms Geri Halliwell, left the band on 27 May 1998. The defendants subsequently discovered that Ms Halliwell had informed the other members of the group of her decision to leave prior to the conclusion of the contract with the defendants. In these circumstances the defendants claimed that they had been induced to enter into the contract by a misrepresentation made by the claimants. The claimants denied that any misrepresentation had been made and, for this purpose, relied upon a clause in the contract which stated that the defendants were entitled to the 'endorsement rights of the group of individuals performing under the professional name "Spice Girls" (currently comprising . . .).' In their submission, this statement was true and it allocated to AWS the risk that one of the members of the group would decide to leave.

The misrepresentation relied upon by AWS was that SGL did not know and had no reasonable grounds to believe at or before the time of entry into the agreement that any of the Spice Girls had an existing declared intention to leave the group during the minimum term of the agreement. The trial judge, Arden J, concluded that there had been a misrepresentation by conduct in that all five members of the group participated in a commercial photo shoot on 4 May 1998 at considerable cost to the defendants at a time when they knew, but the defendants did not, that Geri Halliwell intended to leave the group. The Court of Appeal affirmed the decision of Arden J but did so on a wider basis. It relied upon a number of factors in reaching the conclusion that the claimants had, by their conduct, conveyed to the defendants the impression that all members of the group were committed to the contract with the defendants and that none of them had an existing, declared intention to leave the group.

Morritt V-C [delivering the judgment of the court]

12. [According to s 2(1) of the Misrepresentation Act 1967] liability depends on four elements: (a) a misrepresentation made by one person to another, (b) a subsequent contract between them, (c) consequential loss and (d) an absence, at the time the contract was made, of a belief or reasonable grounds therefor in the truth of the facts represented. If all those conditions are satisfied then the representor is liable to the representee for such damages as would be payable if the misrepresentation had been made fraudulently . . .

29. [In March 30, 1998 a person working for SGL's agent, KLP, sent a fax to AWS to assure the latter of the Spice Girls' commitment to the advertising campaign.] We consider that the fax of March 30, 1998 contained express representations by SGL as to the commitment of each of the Spice Girls to the future implementation of all the terms of the heads of agreement as subsequently incorporated into the formal agreement to be concluded between SGL and Aprilia. That statement was untrue because SGL knew that the term of the agreement for which provision was made in the heads of agreement was 12 months and that there was a risk that Ms Halliwell would leave after only six of them. The fact that SGL did not know of the terms of the fax and the fact that KLP did not know of the risk are not material to the question whether the fax contained a misrepresentation. The unqualified assurance as to the commitment of each Spice Girl to the entire commercial sponsorship described in the heads of agreement contained within it the implied representation that SGL did not know of any matter which might falsify the assurance. That was a representation of fact and it was false.

The representation

51. At the outset it is necessary to reiterate certain well-established principles. First, though the representation must be one of fact representations as to the future or of opinion frequently contain implied representations with regard to the present or to the knowledge of the representor. . . . Second, a representation once made is likely to have continuing effect. So if made for the purpose of an intended transaction it will continue until the transaction is completed or abandoned or the representation ceases to be operative on the mind of the representee; *With* v. *O'Flanagan* [1936] 1 Ch 575, at 585. Third, if at a time when it is continuing the representor discovers that the representation was false when made or has become false since he should correct it. The principle is most clearly expounded in the judgment of Romer LJ in *With* v. *O'Flanagan* [1936] 1 Ch 575, at 586 where he said:

'If A with a view to inducing B to enter into a contract makes a representation as to a material fact, then if at a later date and before the contract is actually entered into, owing to a change of circumstances, the representation then made would to the knowledge of A be untrue and B subsequently enters into the contract in ignorance of that change of circumstances and relying upon that representation, A cannot hold B to the bargain. There is ample authority for that statement and, indeed, I doubt myself whether any authority is necessary, it being, it seems to me, so obviously consistent with the plainest principles of equity.'

An alternative formulation, with which Romer LJ agreed, appears in the judgment of Lord Wright MR at page 583. After citing with approval the judgment of Turner LJ in *Traill* v. *Baring* 4 De GJ & S 318, at 329 he said that 'the position is based on a duty to communicate the change of circumstances'. Fourth, the meaning and effect of a state-ment or of conduct must be ascertained in the light of the circumstances pertaining at the time. Those circumstances will include the course of the negotiations and any earlier representations.

52. The representation for which AWS has contended ever since it amended its defence and counterclaim in December 1999 is that 'SGL did not know and had no reasonable grounds to believe at or before the time of entry into the agreement that any of the Spice Girls had an existing declared intention to leave the group during the min-imum term of the Agreement', *i.e.* before March 1999. This was accepted by the judge . . . but only in respect of the commercial shoot on May 4, 1998 and 'other promotional material depicting the five Spice Girls which was intended to be used at any time during the period of the agreement'.

53. In our view the judge took too limited a view of the effect of the course of the negotiations as a whole and the specific documents and conduct relied on. We have already described the course of negotiations in some detail. Accordingly at this stage it is sufficient to highlight the most salient facts and events.

54. First, shortly after the conclusion of the heads of agreement on March 4, 1998 SGL supplied the logos, images and designs depicting each of the Spice Girls which were to be used by Aprilia in the promotion of the scooters. It must have been quite obvious from all such material and the judge's finding . . . that the same five girls were required for all of them. AWS was entitled to use them throughout the period of 12 months. . . . As we understand it such material was consistently used thereafter so as to generate a connection in the public eye between the Spice Girls and the scooters. In our view the representation contended for is necessarily implicit in that conduct from early March 1998 onwards. In, seemingly, connecting such material only to the commercial shoot on May 4, 1998, in our view, the judge seriously understated its significance.

55. Second, the events of March 9, 1998 [when Geri Halliwell told the members of the group, shortly before they went on stage in Milan, that she had had enough and definitely intended to leave the group in September] were such as to bring to the attention of four of the other five directors of SGL the fact that Ms Halliwell had declared her intention to leave in September 1998. It follows that the representation implicit in the approval and use of the promotional material was false when made, or to the extent it was made before March 9, became false on March 9, 1998. The fact that the other Spice Girls mistakenly as it turned out did not take Ms Halliwell seriously is immaterial.

56. Third, the subsequent events merely served to affirm, not correct, the initial representation and its falsity. Thus, the photocalls in Madrid, Munich and Paris held on or between March 16 and 26 May have been unsatisfactory to Ms Fuzzi [AWS' manager who was responsible for the advertising and communications side of the project] but they took place and their effect was no different to the other promotional material. There were five Spice Girls each with her 'distinct and individual image, style and personality'.

57. Fourth, the fax of March 30, 1998 was sent by Mr Pettett in the light of the information given to him by Ms Halliwell and the tour manager at Arnhem on March 27, 1998 . . . we do not agree with the judge's narrow construction of that document. In our view it was an express assurance that each Spice Girl was fully committed to all the matters contained in the heads of agreement and in the draft agreement then circulating for the full term of 12 months. There is implicit in such assurance the representation for which AWS contends. That representation was false when made because of the declaration of intention made by Ms Halliwell on March 9, 1998 and never qualified or withdrawn. The fact that Mr Pettett did not consider that he was making such a representation is irrelevant. . . . Knowledge of the fax is to be attributed to SGL because KLP was its agent . . .

58. Fifth, the events of the meeting held at Wembley on April 25, 1998 [when Geri Halliwell confirmed at a meeting of the group and their legal advisors that she was going to leave the group at the end of their American tour] demonstrated quite conclusively the falsity of all the representations previously made. Whichever formulation of the principle enunciated in *With* v. *O'Flanagan* is adopted and whatever view is taken of the declaration made by Ms Halliwell on March 9, 1998 it is quite clear that SGL could no longer deal with AWS on the previous basis without disclosing Ms Halliwell's expressed intention . . .

59. Sixth, it is clear that far from correcting the previous misrepresentations SGL continued and affirmed them. There was the draft agreement originally issued on March 24 and reissued on April 30. No doubt the phrase 'currently comprising' points primarily to the present (whether at the time of the draft or as of the imminent time when the Agreement was executed) and in that limited sense was true. But to our minds, in the context of the surrounding circumstances, it was concerned with an agreement which would continue into the future, in much the same sense as the conduct of SGL in approving the promotional material or of the Spice Girls in participating in the commercial shoot, in each case, for future use. In these two latter senses there was implicit in the representation derived from the conduct of SGL in circulating the draft agreement with the phrase 'currently comprising' the representation for which AWS contends. It follows that, in that context, to say that the Spice Girls currently comprised the five named individuals without going on to say that one of them was going to leave within the period of the Agreement was false when made. What was omitted rendered that which was actually stated false or misleading in the context in which it was made: see *Chitty on Contracts* (1999, 28th ed.), Volume 1, paragraph 6–016.

60. Seventh, as the judge held, participation in the commercial shoot necessarily carried the same implication and was likewise false. It did nothing to correct the previous misrepresentations, indeed it gave them additional force.

61. SGL contended that the conduct relied on by Arden J could not give rise to the misrepresentation she found. Counsel pointed out that both the approval of the promotional material and participation in the commercial shoot on May 4 were required by the terms of the Agreement. Reliance was placed on the fact that Ms Halliwell did not appreciate that the deal with AWS could not be terminated before March 1999. It was also suggested that the description of the group as 'currently comprising' showed that there was no representation as to their future composition.

62. We do not accept those submissions. The fact that the Spice Girls were doing what the, as yet unsigned, Agreement required appears to us to support, not negate, a conclusion that the representations alleged are to be implied. The knowledge of Ms Halliwell as to the terms of the prospective Agreement is irrelevant because whether any and if so what representation is to be implied is to be determined objectively in the light of what was said and done. For the reasons we have already given we consider that the description 'currently comprising' supports the conclusions at which we have arrived.

63 Whilst it is necessary to give each episode separate consideration it is also necessary to have regard to their cumulative effect. This is not a case of an isolated representation made at an early stage of ongoing negotiations. It is the case of a series of continuing representations made throughout the two months' negotiations leading to the Agreement. Later representations gave added force to the earlier ones; earlier representations gave focus to the later ones. It is in this context, not the much more limited one the judge adopted, that the submissions for SGL as to inducement and reliance must be considered.

Inducement and reliance

64. . . . It is not disputed that [section 2(1) of the Misrepresentation Act 1967] requires the representation to have induced the representee to enter into the contract . . .

68. It is not disputed that the various misrepresentations to which we have referred were made intentionally in the sense that the express statements and conduct in which they were implicit, if not express, were not accidental. In addition they were made in the context of a commercial relationship arising from heads of agreement already concluded which both parties hoped would reach fruition in a concluded and fully performed agreement. The various representations we have found to have been made were all such as to induce a normal person to act as AWS did. In those circumstances any requisite intention on the part of the representor will be presumed; *Smith* v. *Chadwick* (1884) 9 App Cas 187 at page 190 . . .

69. It remains to consider whether the misrepresentations we have found to have been made did induce AWS to sign the Agreement . . .

70. It is sufficient that the misrepresentation is a material inducement, it does not have to be the only one. In *Smith* v. *Chadwick* (above) at page 196 Lord Blackburn said:

'I do not think it is necessary, in order to prove [damage], that the plaintiff should always be called as a witness to swear that he acted upon the inducement. At the time when *Pasley* v. *Freeman* was decided, and for many years afterwards he could not be so called. I think that if it is proved that the defendants with a view to induce the plaintiff to enter into a contract made a statement to the plaintiff of such a nature as would be likely to induce a person to enter into a contract, it is a fair inference of fact that he was induced to do so by the statement.'

Lord Blackburn went on to point out that the inference was one of fact not law and that if no evidence is given as to reliance in fact that was ground for not drawing the inference . . .

72. In our view the judge was entitled to conclude that the representations, express or implied, in both the fax of March 30, 1998, which continued, and participation in the commercial shoot on May 4, 1998 were material inducements to AWS to enter into the Agreement on May 6, 1998. Signature to the Agreement on May 6, 1998 bound AWS to pay to SGL £100,000 as the third instalment of the fee and £112,500 as the non-returnable advance against royalties on the Spice Sonic scooters. It is inconceivable, and Ms Fuzzi did not say, that AWS would have entered into those commitments had it been told of Ms Halliwell's declared intention to leave in September 1998. It might have entered into some other agreement with a view to cutting its losses but that was not alleged by SGL and is inconsistent with the evidence of Ms Fuzzi.

73. For all these reasons, while we consider that the judge took too narrow a view as to what representations were made and when, we do not accept the submissions for SGL that section 2(1) of the Misrepresentation Act 1967 is inapplicable. Subject to proof of damage, we conclude that SGL is liable to AWS under that provision.

COMMENTARY

Spice Girls neatly illustrates the problems that can arise from the fact that English law neither recognizes a duty of disclosure (below) nor a duty of good faith (Chapter 15). The source of AWS' complaint was that SGL had failed to inform them that Geri Halliwell had already decided to leave the group before the contract was concluded. But they could not plead the claim on this basis nor could they rely on a failure to act in good faith. Instead, they had to spell out from the conduct of SGL a representation which would give them a cause of action. While AWS were prepared to take the risk that one of the members of the group would decide to leave the group during the currency of the agreement (this risk seems inherent in the phrase 'currently comprising') they were not prepared to take the risk that one of the members had already decided to leave the group prior to the conclusion of the contract and told other members of the group of her decision, but did not tell the defendants. The basis on which counsel for AWS formulated the representation can be found in paragraph [52] of the judgment of the Court of Appeal. If this was the representation, when did it become a misrepresentation? Arden J took a narrow view and concluded that it became a misrepresentation at the point at which the Spice Girls, including Geri

Halliwell, participated in the commercial shoot on 4 May 1998. She stated ([2000] EMLR 479 at paragraph [112] of her judgment):

Given that the benefits of the commercial shoot could not be enjoyed by Aprilia if one of the Spice Girls left the group before March 1999, participation in the shoot in my judgment carried with it a representation by conduct that SGL did not know, and had no reasonable ground to believe, that any of the Spice Girls had an existing declared intention to leave the group before that date. Nothing was done to correct that representation which was a continuing representation. It was on the facts found material to Aprilia's decision to enter into the agreement that none of the Spice Girls was intending to leave in the contract period. Accordingly, SGL had a duty to correct its misrepresentation. What I have said about the commercial shoot must equally apply to other promotional material depicting the five Spice Girls which was intended to be used at any time during the period of the agreement.

The Court of Appeal took a broader view of the facts and relied upon a range of factors (set out in paras [54]–[60] of their judgment). While these factors, standing alone, might not have been decisive, taken together (see para [63]) they painted a picture which was false and therefore amounted to a misrepresentation.

Spice Girls would have been a much easier case for the defendants if English law had recognized a duty of disclosure or a duty of good faith. The arguments for and against the introduction of a doctrine of good faith in English law have been canvassed in Chapter 15 but here it is necessary to consider the law relating to the existence, or otherwise, of a duty of disclosure.

4. DUTY OF DISCLOSURE

English law does recognize a limited group of cases in which a duty of disclosure is imposed upon the parties to the contract. These are known as contracts of the utmost good faith or contracts '*uberrimae fidei*'. Very few contracts fall into this category. The leading example is a contract of insurance where the insured is subject to a duty to disclose all facts which a reasonable or prudent insurer would regard as material to his decision to enter into the particular contract of insurance. English law also imposes a duty of disclosure in certain categories of fiduciary relationship where one party reposes trust and confidence in the other party. The party in whom trust and confidence is reposed may be subject to a duty of disclosure.

As a general rule, however, English law does not recognize the existence of a duty to disclose material facts known to one party but not to the other (*Keates* v. *Cadogan* (1851) 10 CB 591). As Viscount Maugham stated in *Bradford Third Equitable Benefit Building Society* v. *Borders* [1941] 2 All ER 205, 211 'mere silence, however morally wrong, will not support an action of deceit'. The word 'mere' is important. Something more than silence is therefore required in order to constitute a representation of fact. But that 'something more' can take many different forms. English law does not require that the representation take the form of words. As *Spice Girls* demonstrates, the representation can be made by conduct or can be inferred from the facts and circumstances of the case. In particular, the courts have been willing to find the existence of a misrepresentation in cases where one party has actively sought to conceal a defect in the subject-matter of the contract from the other party. A number of examples can be provided of this phenomenon.

First, a misrepresentation can be made by conduct. Information can be conveyed as much by conduct as by words and the courts have generally been willing to imply representations by conduct in ordinary dealings. Thus a buyer who orders goods impliedly represents that he intends to pay for them (*Re Shackleton, ex parte Whittaker* (1875) LR 10 Ch App 446, 449 per Sir G Mellish LJ) and a person who sits down in a restaurant and orders a meal impliedly represents that he has the means to pay for the meal (*DPP* v. *Ray* [1974] AC 370). The proposition that representations can be made by conduct is also demonstrated by the *Spice Girls* case (above). Further support for the proposition that a representation can be made by conduct can be derived from the case of *Walters* v. *Morgan* (1861) 3 D F & G 718, 723–724 where Lord Campbell LC stated that, while simple reticence does not amount to a legal fraud:

a nod or a wink, or a shake of the head, or a smile from the purchaser intended to induce the vendor to believe the existence of a non-existing fact, which might influence the price of the subject to be sold

would be a sufficient ground for refusing to enforce a contract.

Secondly, a court may be prepared to infer a misrepresentation where there has been an active attempt to conceal a defect. This proposition is illustrated by the case of *Schneider* v. *Heath* (1813) 3 Camp 506 which concerned the sale of a ship 'to be taken with all faults'. The plaintiff purchased the vessel and, after taking possession of it, he took it to a shipwright to be examined, where it was discovered that the bottom of the ship was worm-eaten and the keel broken. The plaintiff brought an action to recover back the deposit paid for the purchase of the vessel on the ground that he had been induced to enter into the contract by the misrepresentation and fraud on the part of the vendor. It was held that he was entitled to recover back his deposit. Mansfield CJ stated (at p. 509) that 'it appears here that means were taken fraudulently to conceal the defect in the ship's bottom' in that the captain removed the vessel from a dry dock and kept her afloat until the sale was over. He did so for the purpose of preventing potential buyers from discovering the true state of the vessel and this was held to amount to a fraudulent misrepresentation (see to similar effect *Gordon* v. *Selico* (1985) 275 EG 899 (Goulding J) and (1986) 11 HLR 219 (CA) where it was held that the vendors had made a misrepresentation when they covered up dry rot in a flat before putting the flat up for sale).

Thirdly, a partial non-disclosure may amount to a misrepresentation (see *Spice Girls Ltd* v. *Aprilia World Service BV* (above) para [59]). In *Peek* v. *Gurney* (1873) 8 LR 6 HL 377 Lord Chancellor Chelmsford stated (at pp. 392–392) that:

It is said that the prospectus is true as far as it goes, but half a truth will sometimes amount to a real falsehood; and I go farther and say, that to my mind it contains a positive misrepresentation.

And in *Arkwright* v. *Newbold* (1881) 17 Ch D 301, 318 James LJ stated:

Supposing you state a thing partially, you may make as false a statement as much as if you misstated it altogether. Every word may be true, but if you leave out something which qualifies it you may make a false statement. For instance, if pretending to set out the report of a surveyor, you set out two passages in his report, and leave out a third passage which qualifies them, that is an actual misstatement.

Suppression of material facts can also render a statement false. In *Dimmock* v. *Hallett* (1866) LR 2 Ch App 21 a vendor of land told a purchaser that all the farms on the land were fully let but did not inform him that the tenants had given notice to quit. This was held to be a misrepresentation (see also *Central Railway Co of Venezuela* v. *Kisch* (1867) LR 2 HL 99, 114). A statement may also amount to a misrepresentation if it is literally true but it implies certain additional facts which are themselves false. In *Goldsmith* v. *Rodger* [1962] 2 Lloyd's Rep 249 a purchaser of a yacht negotiated a reduction in the price of the yacht after he told the seller that he had found defects in the yacht's keel. The statement that he had found defects in the keel was held to amount to a representation that he had taken the boat out and discovered the defect in the keel. The purchaser not having done this, it was held that his statement amounted to a misrepresentation.

Fourthly, a statement which is literally true but is nevertheless misleading because the maker of the statement has failed to disclose all the relevant information may amount to a misrepresentation. This could be regarded as another example of a partial non-disclosure. In *Notts Patent Brick and Tile Co* v. *Butler* (1866) 16 QBD 778 a purchaser of land asked the vendor's solicitors whether the land was subject to restrictive covenants. The solicitor replied that he was not aware of any, but did not say that the reason for his ignorance was that he had not bothered to check. It was held that, although the solicitor's statement was literally true, it nevertheless amounted to a misrepresentation. Lord Esher MR stated (at pp. 787–788) that:

the evidence has been read to us, and I am sorry to say that I have come to the conclusion that the defendant's solicitor allowed himself to be carried away by his zeal for his client, and that he did not act with that candour to the other side with which a solicitor is bound to act under such circumstances. He allowed himself, in his zeal for his client, to make statements which were calculated to lead the other side to believe that he was stating facts within his own knowledge, and his statements in fact misled them, so that what he said amounts to a mis-statement of facts.

Finally, a person may be held to have made a misrepresentation where he fails to correct a representation which, when made was true, but which subsequently, to his knowledge, has become false or which, at the time of making it, he believed to be true, but which he has subsequently discovered to be false. The leading example of a case in this category is the following decision of the Court of Appeal:

With v. O'Flanagan

[1936] Ch 575, Court of Appeal

In January 1934, the plaintiffs entered into negotiations for the purchase of the defendant's medical practice. Dr O'Flanagan represented that the takings of the practice were £2000 per annum. This statement was true at the time that it was made but, when Dr

O'Flanagan subsequently fell seriously ill and a number of locums ran the practice, the takings fell to an average of £5 per week. This change in circumstances was not revealed to the plaintiffs before the contract was signed in May 1934. The plaintiffs brought an action for rescission of the agreement. The trial judge refused to set aside the agreement on the basis that the representation was true when it was made and that there was no duty on the defendant to disclose the change in circumstances. The Court of Appeal allowed the plaintiffs' appeal and held that the defendant had made a misrepresentation in failing to reveal the change of circumstances and that, accordingly, the agreement between the parties should be set aside.

Lord Wright MR [set out the facts and continued]
   As to the law, which has been challenged, I want to say this. I take the law to be as it was stated by Fry J in *Davies* v. *London and Provincial Marine Insurance Co.* 8 Ch D 469. . . . The learned judge points out (at p. 474): 'Where parties are contracting with one another, each may, unless there be a duty to disclose, observe silence even in regard to facts which he believes would be operative upon the mind of the other; and it rests upon those who say that there was a duty to disclose, to shew that the duty existed'. Then the learned judge points out that in many cases there is such a duty as between persons in a confidential or a fiduciary relationship where the pre-existing relationship involves the duty of entire disclosure. Then his Lordship says: 'In the next place, there are certain contracts which have been called contracts uberrimae fidei where, from their nature, the Court requires disclosure from one of the contracting parties'. The learned judge refers to contracts of partnership and marine insurance. Then he goes on (at p. 475): 'Again, in ordinary contracts the duty may arise from circumstances which occur during the negotiation. Thus, for instance, if one of the negotiating parties has made a statement which is false in fact, but which he believes to be true and which is material to the contract, and during the course of the negotiation he discovers the falsity of that statement, he is under an obligation to correct his erroneous statement; although if he had said nothing he very likely might have been entitled to hold his tongue throughout'. Then he adds what was material in that case and what is material in this case: 'So, again, if a statement has been made which is true at the time, but which during the course of the negotiations becomes untrue, then the person who knows that it has become untrue is under an obligation to disclose to the other the change of circumstances'.
   The matter, however, may be put in another way though with the same effect, and that is on the ground that a representation made as a matter of inducement to enter into a contract is to be treated as a continuing representation. That view of the position was put in *Smith* v. *Kay* 7 HLC 750, 769 by Lord Cranworth. He says of a representation made in negotiation some time before the date of a contract: 'It is a continuing representation. The representation does not end for ever when the representation is once made; it continues on. The pleader who drew the bill, or the young man himself, in stating his case, would say, Before I executed the bond I had been led to believe, and I therefore continued to believe, that it was executed pursuant to the arrangement.'
   The underlying principle is also stated again in a slightly different application by Lord Blackburn in *Brownlie* v. *Campbell* 5 App Cas 925, 950. I need only quote a very short passage. Lord Blackburn says: 'when a statement or representation has been made in the *bonâ fide* belief that it is true, and the party who has made it afterwards comes to find out that it is untrue, and discovers what he should have said, he can no longer honestly keep

up that silence on the subject after that has come to his knowledge, thereby allowing the other party to go on, and still more, inducing him to go on, upon a statement which was honestly made at the time when it was made, but which he has not now retracted when he has become aware that it can be no longer honestly persevered in' . . .

On these grounds, with great respect to the learned judge, I think he ought to have come to the conclusion that the plaintiffs have established their case and there ought to be a declaration rescinding the contract with the consequences which follow upon such a declaration.

Romer LJ

I agree. The only principle invoked by the appellants in this case is as follows. If A with a view to inducing B to enter into a contract makes a representation as to a material fact, then if at a later date and before the contract is actually entered into, owing to a change of circumstances, the representation then made would to the knowledge of A be untrue and B subsequently enters into the contract in ignorance of that change of circumstances and relying upon that representation, A cannot hold B to the bargain. There is ample authority for that statement and, indeed, I doubt myself whether any authority is necessary, it being, it seems to me, so obviously consistent with the plainest principles of equity.

The only questions therefore that we have to decide in the present case are, first, what was the representation made on January 21, secondly, had that representation, owing to the change of circumstances to which the Master of the Rolls has referred, become untrue by May 1 when the contract was entered into? The representation was this. It was made originally by Dr O'Flanagan's agent and subsequently confirmed by Dr O'Flanagan himself that the practice was doing at the rate of 2000l. a year and he, that is Dr O'Flanagan, was asking 4000l. for it, that is to say, two years' purchase. The reference to two years', purchase makes it plain to me that the statement that the practice was doing at the rate of 2000l. a year was intended to be a statement as to an essential feature of the practice, that is to say, a representation to the proposing purchasers that if they bought the practice they would be buying what might properly be called a 2000l. a year practice. Had that statement become untrue by May 1? It appears to me plainly it had. It is stated by Dr Stern, who was the locum tenens during the last of the three periods that Dr O'Flanagan was unwell, that he only took on an average 5l. a week during three weeks and, as the Master of the Rolls pointed out, of that 15l., 10l. was received from one patient . . .

Clauson J concurred.

COMMENTARY

There are two possible bases for this decision. The first is that there was a continuing representation by the defendant and the second is that the defendant was subject to a duty to communicate to the plaintiffs the change of circumstances. In any event the principle only comes into play when the maker of the initial representation has knowledge of the fact that his representation has been falsified by later events. The principle laid down in *With* was one of the elements relied upon by the Court of Appeal in *Spice Girls* in concluding that a misrepresentation had been made on the facts of that case.

The cases examined in this section can either be explained as cases of actual misrepresentation, or as cases in which there is a duty to disclose certain facts by reason of the facts actually stated. It can be argued that they do not go far enough, particularly in cases where it is alleged that the defendant has been fraudulent. In *HIH Casualty and General Insurance Ltd* v. *Chase Manhattan Bank* [2001] EWCA Civ 1250; [2001] 2 Lloyd's Rep 483 Rix LJ stated (at para [48]):

The general rule is that mere non-disclosure does not constitute misrepresentation, and that in the absence of a duty to speak there can be no liability in fraud, however dishonest the silence. However, in certain circumstances a combination of silence together with a positive representation may itself create a misrepresentation. Such a situation may be called partial non-disclosure, and such cases may be explained as either instances of actual misrepresentation or as cases where a duty to speak arises because of matters already stated.

In terms of policy the problematic sentence is the first one. Should English law continue to hold that silence cannot amount to a misrepresentation, even when the silence is 'dishonest'? Article 4:107 of the Principles of European Contract Law states:

Article 4:107—Fraud

(1) A party may avoid a contract when it has been led to conclude it by the other party's fraudulent representation, whether by words or conduct, or fraudulent non-disclosure of any information which in accordance with good faith and fair dealing it should have disclosed.

(2) A party's representation or non-disclosure is fraudulent if it was intended to deceive.

(3) In determining whether good faith and fair dealing required that a party disclose particular information, regard should be had to all the circumstances, including:

(a) whether the party had special expertise;

(b) the cost to it of acquiring the relevant information;

(c) whether the other party could reasonably acquire the information for itself; and

(d) the apparent importance of the information to the other party.

Should English law adopt such a provision?

5. RESCISSION

(a) WHAT IS RESCISSION AND WHEN IS IT AVAILABLE?

Rescission is a remedy that is available in principle for all types of misrepresentation; that is to say, it is available whether the misrepresentation made was fraudulent, negligent, or innocent. A contract which is rescinded for misrepresentation is set aside for all purposes. It is set aside both retrospectively and prospectively with the aim of restoring the parties, as far as possible, to the position which they were in before they entered into the contract. Rescission is a potent remedy and its availability in cases of innocent misrepresentation can seem harsh. Its potential harshness is demonstrated by the following case:

Redgrave v. Hurd

(1881) 20 Ch D 1, Court of Appeal

Redgrave was an elderly solicitor due to retire. He placed an advertisement in the *Law Times* seeking a successor to his practice who would buy his house for £1600. Hurd answered the advertisement. At a meeting Redgrave stated that the business brought in about £300 a year. Hurd asked for information about the amount of business done for the last three years. At a second meeting Redgrave provided papers showing business of not quite £200 a year. When Hurd asked how the difference was made up Redgrave showed him further papers which he said related to other business. Hurd did not examine the further papers which actually showed only a small amount of business. In fact the gross returns of the business were only about £200 a year. Hurd agreed to buy Redgrave's house for £1600 and paid a deposit. Redgrave refused to include any reference to the business in the agreement. Hurd took possession of the property but on finding the business to be 'utterly worthless' refused to complete. Redgrave sought specific performance. Hurd disputed his right to specific performance and sought rescission of the contract and damages on the ground of Redgrave's misrepresentations. Fry J held that Redgrave was entitled to specific performance because Hurd, having had the opportunity to discover the truth of Redgrave's representations and not having done so, had not relied on them. On Hurd's appeal to the Court of Appeal it was held that Hurd was entitled to rescind the contract and to the return of the deposit.

Jessel MR

As regards the rescission of a contract, there was no doubt a difference between the rules of Courts of Equity and the rules of Courts of Common Law—a difference which of course has now disappeared by the operation of the Judicature Act, which makes the rules of equity prevail. According to the decisions of Courts of Equity it was not necessary, in order to set aside a contract obtained by material false representation, to prove that the party who obtained it knew at the time when the representation was made that it was false. It was put in two ways, either of which was sufficient. One way of putting the case was, 'A man is not to be allowed to get a benefit from a statement which he now admits to be false. He is not to be allowed to say, for the purpose of civil jurisdiction, that when he made it he did not know it to be false; he ought to have found that out before he made it'. The other way of putting it was this: 'Even assuming that moral fraud must be shewn in order to set aside a contract, you have it where a man, having obtained a beneficial contract by a statement which he now knows to be false, insists upon keeping that contract. To do so is a moral delinquency: no man ought to seek to take advantage of his own false statements'. The rule in equity was settled, and it does not matter on which of the two grounds it was rested. As regards the rule of Common Law there is no doubt it was not quite so wide. There were, indeed, cases in which, even at Common Law, a contract could be rescinded for misrepresentation, although it could not be shewn that the person making it knew the representation to be false. They are variously stated, but I think, according to the later decisions, the statement must have been made recklessly and without care, whether it was true or false, and not with the belief that it was true . . .

There is another proposition of law of very great importance which I think it is necessary for me to state, because, with great deference to the very learned Judge from whom this appeal comes, I think it is not quite accurately stated in his judgment. If a man is induced to enter into a contract by a false representation it is not a sufficient answer to him to say, 'If you had used due diligence you would have found out that the statement was untrue. You had the means afforded you of discovering its falsity, and did not choose to avail yourself of them'. . . . Nothing can be plainer, I take it, on the authorities in equity than that the effect of false representation is not got rid of on the ground that the person to whom it was made has been guilty of negligence. One of the most familiar instances in modern times is where men issue a prospectus in which they make false statements of the contracts made before the formation of a company, and then say that the contracts themselves may be inspected at the offices of the solicitors. It has always been held that those who accepted those false statements as true were not deprived of their remedy merely because they neglected to go and look at the contracts. Another instance with which we are familiar is where a vendor makes a false statement as to the contents of a lease, as, for instance, that it contains no covenant preventing the carrying on of the trade which the purchaser is known by the vendor to be desirous of carrying on upon the property. Although the lease itself might be produced at the sale, or might have been open to the inspection of the purchaser long previously to the sale, it has been repeatedly held that the vendor cannot be allowed to say, 'You were not entitled to give credit to my statement'. It is not sufficient, therefore, to say that the purchaser had the opportunity of investigating the real state of the case, but did not avail himself of that opportunity. It has been apparently supposed by the learned Judge in the Court below that the case of *Attwood* v. *Small* 6 Cl & F 232 conflicts with that proposition . . .

[he considered *Attwood* in some detail and continued]

In no way, as it appears to me, does the decision, or any of the grounds of decision, in *Attwood* v. *Small*, support the proposition that it is a good defence to an action for rescission of a contract on the ground of fraud that the man who comes to set aside the contract inquired to a certain extent, but did it carelessly and inefficiently, and would, if he had used reasonable diligence, have discovered the fraud.

[he then turned to the facts of the case and considered whether the defendant relied upon the statement made by the defendant and concluded]

[T]he learned Judge came to the conclusion either that the Defendant did not rely on the statement, or that if he did rely upon it he had shewn such negligence as to deprive him of his title to relief from this Court. As I have already said, the latter proposition is in my opinion not founded in law, and the former part is not founded in fact; I think also it is not founded in law, for when a person makes a material representation to another to induce him to enter into a contract, and the other enters into that contract, it is not sufficient to say that the party to whom the representation is made does not prove that he entered into the contract, relying upon the representation. If it is a material representation calculated to induce him to enter into the contract, it is an inference of law that he was induced by the representation to enter into it, and in order to take away his title to be relieved from the contract on the ground that the representation was untrue, it must be shewn either that he had knowledge of the facts contrary to the representation, or that he stated in terms, or shewed clearly by his conduct, that he did not rely on the representation. If you tell a man, 'You may enter into partnership with me, my business is bringing in between £300 and £400 a year', the man who makes that representation must know that it is a material inducement to the other to enter into the partnership, and you cannot investigate as to whether it was more or less probable that the inducement would operate on the mind of the party to whom the representation was made. Where you have neither evidence that he knew facts to shew that the statement was untrue, or that he said or did anything to shew that he did not actually rely upon the statement, the inference remains that he did so rely, and the statement being a material statement, its being untrue is a sufficient ground for rescinding the contract. For these reasons I am of opinion that the judgment of the learned Judge must be reversed and the appeal allowed.

Baggallay and Lush LJJ delivered concurring judgments.

COMMENTARY

Two points of significance emerge from *Redgrave*. The first is that it demonstrates that the availability of rescission is not confined to cases of fraudulent misrepresentation. It extends to non-fraudulent misrepresentations (that is, misrepresentations made negligently or innocently). In some ways this is surprising. The justification offered by Lord Esher MR is that 'a man is not allowed to get a benefit from a statement which he *now* admits to be false' (emphasis added). The word 'now' is important because it demonstrates that there need not have been knowledge of the falsity of the statement at the time at which it was made. Should the fact that the maker of the statement subsequently discovers that his statement was false inevitably give to the other party the right to set aside the contract? Contrast *Redgrave* with *Hart* v. *O'Connor* [1985] AC 1000 (p. 830 below) where the defendant was held to be entitled to hold the plaintiff to the terms of his contract despite the fact that the plaintiff had an inadequate understanding of the transaction into which he was entering. The Privy Council focused on the defendant's knowledge of the plaintiff's capacity *at the time of entry into* the contract, and not upon the knowledge which he gained subsequent to the making of the contract. In other words, the fact that the defendant subsequently realized that the plaintiff did not understand the nature of the transaction into which he had entered did not give to the plaintiff a right to set aside the contract. Should a similar principle not apply here so that rescission is in principle available in all cases of fraudulent and negligent misrepresentation but not in all cases of innocent misrepresentation? It can in fact be argued that English law has now reached a very similar position by virtue of the enactment of section 2(2) of the Misrepresentation Act 1967 (on which see p. 688 below).

The second point to note is that the Court of Appeal held that the defendant had relied upon the plaintiff's misrepresentation notwithstanding the fact that he failed to take the opportunity that was given to him to discover the truth. The defendant was held to be entitled to set aside the contract notwithstanding his own carelessness. At the time the defendant could not have brought a claim for damages against the plaintiff (see p. 691 below). Today the remedy of damages is more widely available and it is suggested that the carelessness of the representee can be taken into account when assessing damages (unless the misrepresentation was made fraudulently). Thus Professor Atiyah has argued (*An Introduction to the Law of Contract* (5th edn, Oxford University Press, 1995), p. 260):

It is no defence to a plea for misrepresentation to allege that the other party might have discovered the true facts by reasonable diligence. Provided that the innocent party did in part at least rely on the false statements, he is entitled to have the contract rescinded, although he might easily have discovered the falsity of the statements. It lies ill in the mouth of a person who is found to have made a false statement to say that the other person ought to have realised that it was false. However, there must be some limits to this, for an extreme want of due care by the representee would show that his reliance was unreasonable. And although the courts have not recognized a distinct principle requiring that the reliance should be reasonable, this may be implicit in the cases. Moreover it now seems possible that, where the misrepresentation is being used to found a claim for damages, it would today be possible to apportion the damages for contributory negligence, thus reducing the amount which would otherwise be payable because of the plaintiff's own share of the responsibility. Naturally the primary responsibility for a false statement must always lie with the maker of the statement but there are some circumstances in which apportionment would be wholly justified. Of course where the plaintiff's claim is for rescission of the contract, this alternative is not possible, and in that event it seems the plaintiff could only be defeated by such extreme carelessness on his own part that it could be said that the representation had no causal effect.

Redgrave therefore demonstrates that rescission is in principle available in all cases of misrepresentation. Rescission does not, however, occur automatically. A party who wishes to rescind a contract for misrepresentation must take positive steps to do so. This need not necessarily take the form of initiating legal action to set aside the contract. In *Redgrave* the point was taken by way of defence to the plaintiff's action for specific performance. The general rule is that a party who wishes to rescind a contract must bring his decision to rescind to the attention of the other party to the contract. There is one exception to this notification requirement and that arises where the representor absconds so that it is no longer possible for the party to whom the representation was made to communicate with him. In such a case it suffices for the party wishing to set aside the contract to take such steps as are reasonable to demonstrate that he is setting the contract aside (usually by notice to the police or some other official or quasi-official body).

Car and Universal Finance Co v. Caldwell

[1965] 1 QB 525, Court of Appeal

The defendant, Caldwell, was the owner of a Jaguar car. He sold the car to Norris for £975 in return for a cheque for £965 and a £10 deposit. The cheque was dishonoured the following day (13 January). The defendant immediately informed the police and the Automobile Association what had happened. Norris subsequently sold the car to Motobella Co Ltd and the car then changed hands on a number of occasions until the plaintiff bought it in all good faith. The car was later seized by police authorities, and in interpleader proceedings, one of the issues that arose was whether the defendant had validly rescinded the contract for the sale of the car on 13 January. The Court of Appeal held that he had done so.

Sellers LJ

This appeal raises a primary point in the law of contract. The question has arisen whether a contract which is voidable by one party can in any circumstances be terminated by that party without his rescission being communicated to the other party. Lord Denning MR has held in the circumstances of this case that there can be rescission without communication where the seller of a motor car, who admittedly had the right to rescind the contract of sale on the ground of fraudulent misrepresentation, terminated the contract by an unequivocal act of election which demonstrated clearly that he had elected to rescind it and to be no longer bound by it. The general rule, no doubt, is that where a party is entitled to rescind a contract and wishes to do so the contract subsists until the opposing party is informed that the contract has been terminated. The difficulty of the seller in this case was that, when he learnt of the fraud and, therefore, ascertained his right to terminate the bargain, he could not without considerable delay find either the fraudulent buyer or the car which had been sold. Such circumstances would not appear to be so rare in transactions in motor cars (or horses in earlier days) that they would not, it might be thought, have given rise to litigation and an authoritative decision, but it seems that over the years the point in issue has not been decided in any reported cases in similar or comparable circumstances . . .

An affirmation of a voidable contract may be established by any conduct which unequivocally manifests an intention to affirm it by the party who has the right to affirm or disaffirm. Communication of an acceptance of a contract after knowledge of a fundamental breach of it by the other party or of fraud affecting it is, of course, evidence establishing affirmation but it is not essential evidence. A party cannot reject goods sold and delivered if he uses them after knowledge of a right to reject, and the judgment cites a case where an instruction to a broker to re-sell was sufficient affirmation of the contract in question even though that conduct was not communicated. It may be said that a contract may be more readily approved and accepted than it can be terminated where a unilateral right to affirm or disaffirm arises. The disaffirmation or election to avoid a contract changes the relationship of the parties and brings their respective obligations to an end, whereas an affirmation leaves the contract effective though subject to a claim for damages for its breach. Where a contracting party could be communicated with, and modern facilities make communication practically world-wide and almost immediate, it would be unlikely that a party could be held to have disaffirmed a contract unless he went so far as to communicate his decision so to do. It would be what the other contracting party would normally require and unless communication were made the party's intention to rescind would not have been unequivocally or clearly demonstrated or made manifest. But in circumstances such as the present case, the other contracting party, a fraudulent rogue who would know that the vendor would want his car back as soon as he knew of the fraud, would not expect to be communicated with as a matter of right or requirement, and would deliberately, as here, do all he could to evade any such communication being made to him. In such exceptional contractual circumstances, it does not seem to me appropriate to hold that a party so acting can claim any right to have a decision to rescind communicated to him before the contract is terminated. To hold that he could would involve that the defrauding party, if skilful enough to keep out of the way, could deprive the other party to the contract of his right to rescind, a right to which he was entitled and which he would wish to exercise, as the defrauding party would well know or at least confidently suspect. The position has to be viewed, as I see it, between the two contracting parties involved in the particular contract in question. That another innocent party or parties may suffer does not in my view of the matter justify imposing on a defrauded seller an impossible task. He has to establish, clearly and unequivocally, that he terminates the contract and is no longer to be bound by it. If he cannot communicate his decision he may still satisfy a judge or jury that he had made a final and irrevocable decision and ended the contract. I am in agreement with Lord Denning MR who asked 'How is a man in the position of Caldwell ever to be able to rescind the contract when a fraudulent person absconds as Norris did here?' and answered that he can do so '. . . if he at once, on discovering the fraud, takes all possible steps to regain the goods even though he cannot find the rogue nor communicate with him'.

Upjohn LJ

Where one party to a contract has an option unilaterally to rescind or disaffirm it by reason of the fraud or misrepresentation of the other party, he must elect to do so within a reasonable time, and cannot do so after he has done anything to affirm the contract with knowledge of the facts giving rise to the option to rescind. In principle and on authority, however, he must, in my judgment, in the ordinary course communicate his intention to rescind to the other party. This must be so because the other party is entitled to treat the contractual nexus as continuing until he is made aware of the intention of the other to exercise his option to rescind. So the intention must be communicated and an uncommunicated intention, for example, by speaking to a third party or making a private note, will be ineffective . . .

Such in my view must be the general principle. Does it admit of any exception? . . .

If one party, by absconding, deliberately puts it out of the power of the other to communicate his intention to rescind which he knows the other will almost certainly want to do, I do not think he can any longer insist on his right to be made aware of the election to determine the contract. In these circumstances communication is a useless formality. I think that the law must allow the innocent party to exercise his right of rescission otherwise than by communication or repossession. To hold otherwise would be to allow a fraudulent contracting party by his very fraud to prevent the innocent party from exercising his undoubted right. I would hold that in circumstances such as these the innocent party may evince his intention to disaffirm the contract by overt means falling short of communication or repossession.

Davies LJ

On the facts of this case Norris must be taken to have known that the defendant might, on ascertaining the fraud, wish to rescind the contract. Norris disappeared; and so did the car. The defendant could, therefore, neither communicate with Norris nor retake the car. It must, therefore, I think, be taken to be implied in the transaction between Norris and the defendant that in the event of the defendant's wishing to rescind he should be entitled to do so by the best other means possible. Lex non cogit ad impossibilia.[1] It is true that it was conceivably possible that the defendant might decide not to rescind but to sue on the cheque instead; but it is most doubtful whether on the facts of this case

---

[1] The law does not compel the impossible.

such a possibility could have occurred to Norris as a real one. The fact that Norris knew that he was a rogue and that, therefore, the defendant was likely to be after him distinguishes this case from that of an innocent misrepresentor. It would not occur to the latter that the other party to the contract would have any right or desire to rescind, so that there would be no such implication as that which I have suggested arose in the present case.

COMMENTARY

The court in *Caldwell* was required to carry out the familiar exercise of deciding which of two innocent parties should bear the loss caused by the fraud of a third party. The Court of Appeal decided that the loss should be borne by the plaintiff purchaser on the basis that the seller had taken all reasonable steps to notify the fraudster of his decision to rescind the contract and on the ground that the fraudster did not wish to receive any communication from the defendant seller. A different result was reached in Scotland in *Macleod* v. *Kerr*, 1965 SC 253 where the Court of Session came down on the side of the innocent purchaser on the basis that notification given to the police by the seller did not suffice to rescind a contract with a third party (the fraudster).

  Caldwell appears to be an example of rescission operating as a proprietary restitutionary remedy in the sense that the effect of rescission was to revest ownership of the car in Mr Caldwell.

(b) LOSS OF THE RIGHT TO RESCIND

While the right to rescind is, in principle, available in all cases of misrepresentation, the right can be lost in a range of circumstances. These circumstances are generally referred to as 'bars' to rescission. There are a number of such 'bars'. The first is that a claimant cannot rescind the contract if he affirms the contract after discovering that a misrepresentation was made to him. Secondly, the right to rescind is lost if a bona fide third party purchaser for value acquires the goods which are the subject matter of the contract before the contract has been set aside. This was the principle that was invoked by the plaintiff purchaser in *Caldwell* (above) but his attempt to invoke the principle failed on the ground that the defendant had validly set aside the contract before Norris sold the car on to any bona fide third party purchaser for value. Thirdly the right to rescind can be lost by lapse of time (except in the case of a fraudulent misrepresentation). In *Leaf* v. *International Galleries* [1950] 2 KB 86 the plaintiff purchased a painting in 1944 after a representation had been made to him that it was the work of John Constable. The plaintiff attempted to sell the painting at Christies in 1949 but he was informed that the painting was not in fact a Constable. The plaintiff then returned the painting to the defendant and sought to recover from him the £85 he had paid for it. The Court of Appeal held that he was not entitled to rescind the contract on the basis that a reasonable time had elapsed since the purchase and it was no longer open to him to set aside the contract. Jenkins LJ stated (at pp. 92–93):

It is true that the plaintiff bought the picture on the faith of the representation, innocently made, that it was a painting by Constable. It is true that this was a representation of great importance, which went to the root of the contract and induced him to buy. Clearly if, before he had taken delivery of the picture, he had obtained other advice and come to the conclusion that the picture was not a Constable, it would have been open to him to rescind. It may be that if, having taken delivery of the picture on the faith of the representation and having taken it home, he had, within a reasonable time, taken other advice and satisfied himself that it was not a Constable, he might have been able to make good his claim to rescission notwithstanding the delivery. That point I propose to leave open. What in fact happened was that he took delivery of the picture, kept it for some five years, and took no steps to obtain any further evidence as to its authorship; and that, finally, when he was minded to sell the picture at the end of a matter of five years, the untruth of the representation was brought to light.

In those circumstances, it seems to me to be quite out of the question that a court of equity should grant relief by way of rescission. It is perfectly true that the county court judge held that there had been no laches, and, of course, it may be said that the plaintiff had no occasion to obtain any further evidence as to the authorship of the picture until he wanted to sell; but in my judgment contracts such as this cannot be kept open and subject to the possibility of rescission indefinitely. Assuming that completion is not fatal to his claim, I think that, at all events, it behoves the purchaser either to verify or, as the case may be, to disprove the representation within a reasonable time, or else stand or fall by it. If he is allowed to wait five, ten, or twenty years and then reopen the bargain, there can be no finality at all. I, for my part, do not think that equity will intervene in such a case, more especially as in the present case it cannot be said that, apart from rescission, the plaintiff would have been without remedy. The county court judge was of opinion, and it seems to me that he was clearly right, that the representation that the picture was a Constable amounted to a warranty. If it amounted to a warranty, and that was broken, as on the findings of the county court judge it was, then the plaintiff had a right at law in the shape of damages for breach of warranty. That remedy he did not choose to exercise, and, although he was invited at the hearing to amend his claim so as to include a claim for breach of warranty, he declined that opportunity. That being so, it seems to me that he has no justification at all for now coming to equity five years after the event and claiming rescission. Accordingly, it seems to me that this is not a case in which the equitable remedy of rescission, assuming it to be available in the absence of fraud in respect of a completed sale of chattels, should be allowed to the plaintiff. For these reasons, I agree that the appeal fails and should be dismissed.

The right to rescind is often said to be lost where it is impossible to restore the parties to their pre-contractual position. There is some confusion as to the exact basis of this requirement. Is it the case that it must be possible to restore both parties to their pre-contractual position or is the case that a claimant can obtain rescission provided that he makes restitution to the defendant for any benefit which he has obtained under the contract? The use of the phrase 'restitutio in integrum' suggests that the aim is to restore the parties to their pre-contractual position but it is suggested that the case-law is in fact consistent with the latter rationale: that is to say, the concern of the courts is to ensure that the claimant is not unjustly enriched as a result of rescission. For example, a claimant cannot get back the purchase price he has paid for the goods and keep the goods themselves. He must return the goods and may also have to make an allowance to the vendor for the use that he has made of the goods. But a defendant cannot resist rescission on the basis that he has suffered a loss which cannot be made good so that he cannot be restored to his pre-contractual position (*McKenzie* v. *Royal Bank of Canada* [1934] AC 468). The aim is therefore to prevent the unjust enrichment of the claimant and not to restore both parties to the position they were in before the contract was concluded.

The common law took an extremely restrictive view of the right of the claimant to rescind the contract. In order to be able to rescind the contract the claimant had to be able to restore to the defendant the very benefit which he had obtained from the defendant. In *Clarke* v. *Dickson* (1858) EB & E 148 Crompton J stated:

The plaintiff must rescind the contract in toto or not at all; he cannot both keep the shares and recover the whole price. That is founded on the plainest principles of justice. If he cannot return the article he must keep it, and sue for his real damage in an action on the deceit. Take the case I put in argument, of a butcher buying live cattle, killing them, and even selling the meat to his customers. If the rule of law were as the plaintiff contends, that butcher might, upon discovering a fraud on the part of the grazier who sold him the cattle, rescind the contract and get back the whole price: but how could that be consistently with justice? The true doctrine is, that a party can never repudiate a contract after, by his own act, it has become out of his power to restore the parties to their original condition.

A more flexible approach was taken in equity and that approach has prevailed. In *Erlanger* v. *New Sombrero Phosphate Co* (1878) 3 App Cas 1218 the defendants, who were promoters of the plaintiff company, sold a phosphate mine to the plaintiff for £110,000. After it had worked the mine for a period of time, the plaintiff sought to rescind the contract of sale on the ground that the defendants had breached the fiduciary duty which they owed to the plaintiff by failing to disclose that they had bought the mine for £55,000 a few days before the sale to the plaintiff. The defendants submitted that the plaintiff was not entitled to rescission because the parties could not be restored to their pre-contractual position. It was held that the plaintiff was entitled to rescind the contract and recover the purchase price on terms of giving up possession of the mine and accounting to the defendants for any profits made from working the mine. Lord Blackburn stated (at pp. 1278–1279):

It would be obviously unjust that a person who has been in possession of property under the contract which he seeks to repudiate should be allowed to throw that back on the other party's hands without accounting for any benefit he may have derived from the use of the property, or if the property, though not destroyed, has been in the interval deteriorated, without making compensation for that deterioration. But as a Court of Law has no machinery at its command for taking an account of such matters, the defrauded party, if he sought his remedy at law, must in such cases keep the property and sue in an action for deceit, in which the jury, if properly directed, can do complete justice by giving as damages a full indemnity for all that the party has lost: see *Clarke* v. *Dixon* EB & E 148 and the cases there cited.

But a Court of Equity could not give damages, and, unless it can rescind the contract, can give no relief. And, on the other hand, it can take accounts of profits, and make allowance for deterioration. And I think the practice has always been for a Court of Equity to give this relief whenever, by the exercise of its powers, it can do what is practically just, though it cannot restore the parties precisely to the state they were in before the contract. And a Court of Equity requires that those who come to it to ask its active interposition to give them relief, should use due diligence, after there has been such notice or knowledge as to make it inequitable to lie by. And any change which occurs in the position of the parties or the state of the property after such notice or knowledge should tell much more against the party *in morâ*, than a similar change before he was *in morâ* should do.

The key phrase here is 'practical justice' (see also *Spence* v. *Crawford* [1939] 3 All ER 271) and the principal issue is the extent to which the courts are willing to allow a party who wishes to rescind a contract to offer a money allowance for the benefit that he cannot physically give back. The greater the willingness of the court to allow the claimant to make a money payment in this way, the less significant this barrier to rescission will become. The courts have not recognized a right in the claimant to make a money allowance in order to rescind a contract. Instead they have emphasized their discretion and the aim of doing practical justice on the facts of the case. The position has been summed up as follows (J Beatson, *Anson's Law of Contract* (28th edn, Oxford University Press, 2002), p. 256):

> How this goal of doing 'what is practically just' may be reached depends on the circumstances of the case. For instance, the Court may think that justice requires the making of some allowance for the deterioration, or the improvement, as the case may be, of the subject-matter of the contract. Again, it may require compensation for losses incurred by the representor or recompense for services rendered to the representee. The Court will be more drastic in exercising its discretionary powers in a case of fraud than in a case where no fraud is present; it will be 'less ready to pull a transaction to pieces where the defendant is innocent, whereas in the case of fraud the Court will exercise its jurisdiction to the full in order, if possible, to prevent the defendant from enjoying the benefit of his fraud at the expense of the innocent plaintiff'. But, even in a case of fraud, rescission will not be ordered where it is not possible to achieve a broadly just result by orders for monetary adjustment to reflect benefits and detriments which have accrued under the contract since to do so would unjustly enrich the defrauded party.

The final circumstance in which the right to rescind may be lost is where the court exercises its discretion under section 2(2) of the Misrepresentation Act 1967 to award the claimant damages in lieu of rescission. At this point it is important to remember that rescission is an attractive remedy for a claimant who has entered into a bad bargain because it provides him with an exit route from his contract. This may be very harsh on a defendant, particularly a defendant who has made an innocent misrepresentation. Section 2(2) can come to the aid of such a defendant by confining the claimant to a remedy in damages. We shall return to the basis upon which the courts assess damages under section 2(2) at a later stage (see pp. 705–710 below). Here our concern is with the basis upon which the court will exercise its discretion not to grant rescission and to confine the claimant to a remedy in damages. Section 2(2) provides:

> where a person has entered into a contract after a misrepresentation has been made to him otherwise than fraudulently, and he would be entitled, by reason of the misrepresentation, to rescind the contract, then, if it is claimed in any proceedings arising out of the contract, that the contract ought to be or has been rescinded, the court or arbitrator may declare the contract subsisting and award damages in lieu of rescission, if of the opinion that it would be equitable to do so, having regard to the nature of the misrepresentation and the loss that would be caused by it if the contract were upheld, as well as to the loss that rescission would cause to the other party.

An example of the willingness of the court to use section 2(2) in order to stop a claimant escaping from a bad bargain is provided by the following case:

William Sindall plc v. Cambridgeshire County Council

[1994] 1 WLR 1016, Court of Appeal

In December 1988 William Sindall plc agreed to buy development land from Cambridge-shire County Council for £5,082,500. Before the sale was completed, Sindall made various inquiries of the council regarding rights of easement and other public rights affecting the land. The council replied on a standard form stating that, so far as it was aware, there were no rights of easement or public rights affecting the property other than those disclosed in the contract. The sale was completed in March 1989. In October 1989 Sindall discovered a private foul sewer which had been built on the land in 1970. They alleged that the existence of this foul sewer meant that the council had made a misrepresentation when they stated that there were no such matters affecting the site. By this time the value of the land had halved so Sindall brought an action for a declaration that the contract had been rescinded and for repayment of the purchase price. The judge granted the declaration. On appeal the court held that there had been no misrepresentation by the council, negligent or otherwise, but if there had been any misrepresentation, damages would be awarded under section 2(2) of the Misrepresentation Act 1967 in lieu of rescission.

Hoffmann LJ [having concluded that no misrepresentation had been made nevertheless turned to consider section 2(2) of the Act]

6. Discretion

My conclusion that there are no grounds for rescission, either for misrepresentation or mistake, mean that it is unnecessary to consider whether the judge correctly exercised his discretion under section 2(2) of the Misrepresentation Act 1967 not to award damages in lieu of rescission. But in case this case goes further, I should say that in my judgment the judge approached this question on a false basis, arising from his mistake about the seriousness of the defect. This vitiated the exercise of the discretion and would have made it necessary, if we thought that Sindall would otherwise have been entitled to rescind for misrepresentation, to exercise our own discretion under section 2(2) . . .

[he set out section 2(2) and continued]

This provision was adopted as a result of the Tenth Report of the Law Reform Committee (1962) (Cmnd. 1782) which also recommended abolishing the bar on rescission after completion. The relevant paragraphs of the report were 11 and 12:

'11.   A more fundamental objection which may be advanced against our recommendation [to abolish the bar on rescission after completion] concerns the drastic character of the remedy to which the plaintiff would be entitled. Unless the court's power to grant rescission is made more elastic than it is at present, the court will not be able to take account of the relative importance or unimportance of the facts which have been misrepresented. A car might be returned to the vendor because of a misrepresentation about the mileage done since the engine was last overhauled, or a transfer of shares rescinded on account of an incorrect statement about the right to receive the current dividend. In some cases the result could be as harsh on the representor as the absence of a right to rescind under the current law can be on the representee. Moreover, the conflict between remedies for misrepresentation and those for breach of contract would be aggravated. There is already the anomaly that a statement embodied in the contract and constituting a minor term of it is treated as a warranty, the breach of which gives only a right to damages, whereas the same statement as a representation inducing the contract enables the latter to be rescinded. Before the contract is executed and at a time when the parties can be relatively easily restored to their original positions, this anomaly may not matter very much, but the position would be different if the court had no option but to order rescission after the contract had been executed.

12.   To meet these objections we recommend that wherever the court has power to order rescission it should, as an alternative, have a discretionary power to award damages if it is satisfied that these would afford adequate compensation to the plaintiff, having regard to the nature of the misrepresentation and the fact that the injury suffered by the plaintiff is small compared with what rescission would involve. The courts were given power to award damages in addition to or in substitution for an injunction or a decree of specific performance by section 2 of Lord Cairns's Act (the Chancery Procedure Amendment Act 1858), and since the decision of the House of Lords in *Leeds Industrial Co-operative Society Ltd* v. *Slack* [1924] AC 851, the power has been exercised on principles similar to those we have just mentioned.'

The discretion conferred by section 2(2) is a broad one, to do what is equitable. But there are three matters to which the court must in particular have regard.

The first is the nature of the misrepresentation. It is clear from the Law Reform Committee's report that the court was meant to consider the importance of the representation in relation to the subject matter of the transaction. I have already said that in my view, in the context of a £5m. sale of land, a misrepresentation which would have cost £18,000 to put right and was unlikely seriously to have interfered with the development or resale of the property was a matter of relatively minor importance.

The second matter to which the court must have regard is 'the loss that would be caused by [the misrepresentation] if the contract were upheld'. The section speaks in terms of loss suffered rather than damages recoverable but clearly contemplates that if the contract is upheld, such loss will be compensated by an award of damages . . .

[he then considered the basis on which the court is to award damages under section 2(2), on which see p. 705 below]

The third matter to be taken into account under section 2(2) is the loss which would be caused to Cambridgeshire by rescission . . .

Having regard to these matters, and in particular the gross disparity between the loss which would be caused to Sindall by the misrepresentation and the loss which would be caused to Cambridgeshire by rescission, I would have exercised my discretion to award damages in lieu of rescission.

Evans LJ delivered a concurring judgment. **Russell LJ** concurred.

COMMENTARY

This case is an excellent example of a court being willing to use its discretion under section 2(2) to relegate a claimant to an award of damages. Hoffmann LJ identifies and applies the three factors identified as relevant by section 2(2), while at the same time emphasizing that the discretion given to the court under section 2(2) is a broad one. As we shall see (p. 705 below), there are difficulties in discerning the basis on which damages are to be awarded under section 2(2). Nevertheless, section 2(2) is a useful provision in so far as it enables a court to do what the Court of Appeal did on the facts of this case, namely block an attempt to use an innocent misrepresentation as a pretext to get out of what has become a bad bargain.

6. DAMAGES

Until relatively recently only a fraudulent misrepresentation gave rise to an action for damages. This point has to be borne in mind when reading cases pre-1963. Prior to the decision of the House of Lords in *Hedley Byrne & Co Ltd* v. *Heller & Partners Ltd* [1964] AC 465 the courts could not award damages for a negligent or an innocent misrepresentation. In these circumstances courts were sometimes tempted to find that what seemed to be a mere representation was in fact a term of a collateral contract so that a deserving plaintiff had a claim for damages for breach of contract (*De Lassalle* v. *Guildford* [1901] 2 KB 215, p. 322 above). The need for such subterfuge has gone. Parliament has now created a right to damages under section 2(1) of the Misrepresentation Act 1967 and the right so created is an extraordinarily generous one. We shall therefore start with the right to damages created by the Act before turning to other alternatives open to a claimant who wishes to recover damages in respect of a misrepresentation made by the defendant.

(a) SECTION 2(1) OF THE MISREPRESENTATION ACT 1967

Section 2(1) of the Misrepresentation Act 1967 provides:

Where a person has entered into a contract after a misrepresentation has been made to him by another party thereto and as a result thereof he has suffered loss then, if the person making the misrepresentation would be liable to damages in respect thereof had the misrepresentation been made fraudulently, that person shall be so liable notwithstanding that the misrepresentation was not made fraudulently, unless he proves that he had reasonable grounds to believe and did believe up to the time that the contract was made that the facts represented were true.

This subsection creates a right of action for damages where the misrepresentation has been made by the other party to the contract. Where the misrepresentation has been made by a third party, the claimant cannot rely upon section 2(1) but must bring his claim in tort. But in the case where the misrepresentation has been made by the other party to the contract then section 2(1) is the obvious remedy for a claimant who wishes to recover damages. The extraordinary advantages that can be obtained through an action for damages under section 2(1) are illustrated by the following two cases:

Royscot Trust Ltd v. Rogerson

[1991] 2 QB 297, Court of Appeal

In May 1987 Maidenhead Honda Centre Ltd, a car dealer, agreed to sell to Rogerson a car on hire-purchase terms for £7,600, £1,200 of which was payable as a deposit. Royscot Trust Ltd, a finance company, agreed to purchase the car from Maidenhead and to enter into a hire-purchase agreement with Rogerson. In its proposal to Royscot, Maidenhead innocently misrepresented the purchase price as £8,000 and the deposit as £1,600. Royscot had a policy of not entering into hire-purchase agreements unless the deposit was at least 20% of the purchase price, and on the basis of Maidenhead's misrepresentations, agreed to pay Maidenhead £6,400 for the car. Rogerson paid some of the outstanding instalments to Royscot but in August 1987 dishonestly sold the car. Rogerson informed Royscot of the sale in August 1988 and stopped making instalment payments in September 1988. Royscot brought an action against Maidenhead for damages for misrepresentation under section 2(1) of the Misrepresentation Act 1967. The trial judge awarded damages of £1,600 for the difference between the amount paid by Royscot to Maidenhead (£6,400) and the amount Royscot would have paid to Maidenhead if the deposit of £1,200 had been 20% of the purchase price (£4,800). The Court of Appeal awarded damages of £3,625.24 for the difference between the amount paid by Royscot to Maidenhead (£6,400) and the amount paid by Rogerson to Royscot (£2,774.76).

Balcombe LJ [set out the facts and continued]

So I turn to the issue on this appeal which the dealer submits raises a pure point of law: where (a) a motor dealer innocently misrepresents to a finance company the amount of the sale price of, and the deposit paid by the intended purchaser of, the car, and (b) the finance company is thereby induced to enter into a hire-purchase agreement with the purchaser which it would not have done if it had known the true facts, and (c) the purchaser thereafter dishonestly disposes of the car and defaults on the hire-purchase agreement, can the finance company recover all or part of its losses on the hire-purchase agreement from the motor dealer?

The finance company's cause of action against the dealer is based on section 2(1) of the Misrepresentation Act 1967 which reads:

[he set out the terms of the subsection and continued]

As a result of some dicta by Lord Denning MR in two cases in the Court of Appeal—*Gosling* v. *Anderson* [1972] EGD 709 and *Jarvis* v. *Swan Tours Ltd* [1973] QB 233, 237— and the decision at first instance in *Watts* v. *Spence* [1976] Ch 165, there was some doubt whether the measure of damages for an innocent misrepresentation giving rise to a cause of action under the Act of 1967 was the tortious measure, so as to put the representee in the position in which he would have been if he had never entered into the contract, or the contractual measure, so as to put the representee in the position in which he would have been if the misrepresentation had been true, and thus in some cases give rise to a claim for damages for loss of bargain. Lord Denning MR's remarks in *Gosling* v. *Anderson* were concerned with an amendment to a pleading, while his remarks in *Jarvis* v. *Swan Tours Ltd* were clearly obiter. *Watts* v. *Spence* was disapproved by this court in *Sharneyford Supplies Ltd* v. *Edge* [1987] Ch 305, 323. However, there is now a number of decisions which make it clear that the tortious measure of damages is the true one. . . . One at least,

Chesneau v. *Interhome Ltd* (1983) 134 NLJ 341; Court of Appeal (Civil Division) Transcript No 238 of 1983, is a decision of this court. The claim was one under section 2(1) of the Act of 1967 and the appeal concerned the assessment of damages. In the course of his judgment Eveleigh LJ said:

'[Damages] should be assessed in a case like the present one on the same principles as damages are assessed in tort. The subsection itself says: "if the person making the misrepresentation would be liable to damages in respect thereof had the misrepresentation been made fraudulently, that person shall be so liable . . ." By "so liable" I take it to mean liable as he would be if the misrepresentation had been made fraudulently.'

In view of the wording of the subsection it is difficult to see how the measure of damages under it could be other than the tortious measure and, despite the initial aberrations referred to above, that is now generally accepted. Indeed counsel before us did not seek to argue the contrary.

The first main issue before us was: accepting that the tortious measure is the right measure, is it the measure where the tort is that of fraudulent misrepresentation, or is it the measure where the tort is negligence at common law? The difference is that in cases of fraud a plaintiff is entitled to any loss which flowed from the defendant's fraud, even if the loss could not have been foreseen: see *Doyle* v. *Olby (Ironmongers) Ltd* [1969] 2 QB 158. In my judgment the wording of the subsection is clear: the person making the innocent misrepresentation shall be 'so liable', i.e., liable to damages as if the representation had been made fraudulently. This was the conclusion to which Walton J came in *F & B Entertainments Ltd* v. *Leisure Enterprises Ltd* (1976) 240 EG 455, 461. See also the decision of Sir Douglas Frank QC, sitting as a High Court judge, in *McNally* v. *Welltrade International Ltd* [1978] IRLR 497. In each of these cases the judge held that the basis for the assessment of damages under section 2(1) of the Act of 1967 is that established in *Doyle* v. *Olby (Ironmongers) Ltd*. This is also the effect of the judgment of Eveleigh LJ in *Chesneau* v. *Interhome Ltd* already cited: 'By "so liable" I take it to mean liable as he would be if the misrepresentation had been made fraudulently'.

This was also the original view of the academic writers. In an article, 'The Misrepresentation Act 1967' (1967) 30 *MLR* 369 by P.S. Atiyah and G.H. Treitel, the authors say, at pp. 373–374:

'The measure of damages in the statutory action will apparently be that in an action of deceit. . . . But more probably the damages recoverable in the new action are the same as those recoverable in an action of deceit . . .'

Professor Treitel has since changed his view. In Treitel, *The Law of Contract*, 7th ed. (1987), p. 278, he says:

'Where the action is brought under section 2(1) of the Misrepresentation Act 1967, one possible view is that the deceit rule will be applied by virtue of the fiction of fraud. But the preferable view is that the severity of the deceit rule can only be justified in cases of actual fraud and that remoteness under section 2(1) should depend, as in actions based on negligence, on the test of foreseeability.'

The only authority cited in support of the 'preferable' view is *Shepheard* v. *Broome* [1904] AC 342, a case under section 38 of the Companies Act 1867, which provided that in certain circumstances a company director, although not in fact fraudulent, should be 'deemed to be fraudulent'. As Lord Lindley said, at p. 346: 'To be compelled by Act of Parliament to treat an honest man as if he were fraudulent is at all times painful', but he went on to say:

'but the repugnance which is naturally felt against being compelled to do so will not justify your Lordships in refusing to hold the appellant responsible for acts for which an Act of Parliament clearly declares he is to be held liable.'

The House of Lords so held.

It seems to me that that case, far from supporting Professor Treitel's view, is authority for the proposition that we must follow the literal wording of section 2(1), even though that has the effect of treating, so far as the measure of damages is concerned, an innocent person as if he were fraudulent. *Chitty on Contracts*, 26th edn. (1989), vol. 1, p. 293, para 439, says:

'it is doubtful whether the rule that the plaintiff may recover even unforeseeable losses suffered as the result of fraud would be applied; it is an exceptional rule which is probably justified only in cases of actual fraud.'

No authority is cited in support of that proposition save a reference to the passage in Professor Treitel's book cited above.

Professor Furmston in *Cheshire, Fifoot and Furmston's Law of Contract*, 11th ed. (1986), p. 286, says:

"It has been suggested"—and the reference is to the passage in Atiyah and Treitel's article cited above—"that damages under section 2(1) should be calculated on the same principles as govern the tort of deceit". This suggestion is based on a theory that section 2(1) is based on a "fiction of fraud". We have already suggested that this theory is misconceived. On the other hand the action created by section 2(1) does look much more like an action in tort than one in contract and it is suggested that the rules for negligence are the natural ones to apply.'

The suggestion that the 'fiction of fraud' theory is misconceived occurs at p. 271, in a passage which includes:

'Though it would be quixotic to defend the drafting of the section, it is suggested that there is no such "fiction of fraud" since the section does not say that a negligent misrepresentor shall be treated for all purposes as if he were fraudulent. No doubt the wording seeks to incorporate by reference some of the rules relating to fraud but, for instance, nothing in the wording of the subsection requires the measure of damages for deceit to be applied to the statutory action.'

With all respect to the various learned authors whose works I have cited above, it seems to me that to suggest that a different measure of damage applies to an action for innocent misrepresentation under the section than that which applies to an action for fraudulent misrepresentation (deceit) at common law is to ignore the plain words of the subsection and is inconsistent with the cases to which I have referred. In my judgment, therefore, the finance company is entitled to recover from the dealer all the losses which it suffered as a result of its entering into the agreements with the dealer and the customer, even if those losses were unforeseeable, provided that they were not otherwise too remote.

[Balcombe LJ went on to consider whether Rogerson's wrongful sale of the car was a *novus actus interveniens* breaking the chain of causation between Maidenhead's innocent misrepresentations and Royscot's loss. He held that the reasonable foreseeability of the sale was relevant to this issue and that, as the sale was reasonably foreseeable, it was not a *novus actus interveniens*.]

Ralph Gibson LJ delivered a concurring judgment.

COMMENTARY

This is an extraordinary decision because its effect is to require a defendant who may not even have been negligent (in the sense that the claimant is not required to prove that the defendant had been negligent in order to recover damages under section 2(1)) to pay damages as if he had been fraudulent. The justification offered for this conclusion is the reference to 'fraud' in section 2(1). The reference had been known as the 'fiction of fraud' but the Court of Appeal held that it was no fiction as far as defendants are concerned because it requires them to pay damages on the basis that the claim brought against them is one for fraud. As Richard Hooley has pointed out ('Damages and the Misrepresentation Act 1967' (1991) 107 *LQR* 547, 549), the 'effect of the Court of Appeal's decision is to treat the foolish but honest man as if he were dishonest'. In *Smith New Court Securities Ltd* v. *Scrimgeour Vickers (Asset Management) Ltd* [1997] AC 254, 283 Lord Steyn stated:

The question is whether the rather loose wording of the statute compels the court to treat a person who was morally innocent as if he was guilty of fraud when it comes to the measure of damages. There has been trenchant academic criticism of the *Royscot* case [he refers to the article by Richard Hooley]. Since this point does not directly arise in the present case, I express no concluded view on the correctness of the decision in the *Royscot* case.

The decision in *Royscot* can be attacked on the ground that judges in other cases have not given so much weight to the 'fiction of fraud'. This can be seen in *Gran Gelato Ltd* v. *Richcliff (Group) Ltd* [1992] Ch 560 where Sir Donald Nicholls V-C, in considering whether the defence of contributory negligence was available in a case brought under section 2(1), stated (at p. 573):

In short, liability under the 1967 Act is essentially founded on negligence, in the sense that the defendant, the representor, did not have reasonable grounds to believe that the facts represented were true. (Of course, if he did not so believe the facts represented were true he will be liable for fraud.) This being so, it would be very odd if the defence of contributory negligence were not available to a claim under that Act. It would be very odd if contributory negligence were available as a defence to a claim for damages based on a breach of a duty to take care in and about the making of a particular representation, but not available to a claim for damages under the 1967 Act in respect of the same representation.

The interesting point here is that the analogy is drawn with the tort of negligence and not with the tort of deceit (where contributory negligence is not available as a defence: see *Standard Chartered Bank* v. *Pakistan National Shipping Corporation* [2002] UKHL 43; [2003] 1 AC 959). Why is it that the analogy is drawn with the tort of deceit when fixing the measure of recovery, but that the analogy is drawn with the tort of negligence when considering the defences that are available to the claim brought by the claimant? The law presently lacks coherence. While it is possible to argue that *Royscot* is wrong, it should be noted that Lord Steyn in *Smith New Court Securities* refrained from expressing a 'concluded view' on the correctness of the decision. This being the case, it must remain good law and it is a decision that is binding on the Court of Appeal and lower courts.

The primary significance of *Royscot* lies, not so much in the measure of recovery, but in the remoteness rule applicable. It is agreed that the basic measure of recovery in a claim brought under section 2(1) should aim to put the claimant in the position he would have been in had the representation not been made. This reflects the basic measure of recovery in both the tort of deceit and the tort of negligence. It is in the context of the remoteness rules that the differences become apparent. In negligence the remoteness test is based on the reasonable foreseeability of the kind of harm suffered by the claimant (see *The Wagon Mound (No 1)* [1961] AC 388), whereas in deceit the defendant is liable for all losses which flow directly from the representation whether or not they were reasonably foreseeable (*Smith New Court Securities Ltd* v. *Scrimgeour Vickers (Asset Management) Ltd* [1997] AC 254). *Royscot* almost renders the tort of deceit a dead letter in relation to a claimant who can bring his claim within the fold of section 2(1). Why should a claimant take on the arduous task of proving that a defendant was fraudulent when he can recover exactly the same amount of money by way of damages under section 2(1) by simply proving that the misrepresentation was made by the other party to the contract? Once he has demonstrated that a misrepresentation has been made he can collect damages on the basis that the defendant has been fraudulent unless the defendant can show that he had reasonable grounds to believe and did believe that his statement was true. As the next case demonstrates, it is no easy task for a defendant to discharge this burden.

Howard Marine and Dredging Co Ltd v. A Ogden & Sons (Excavations) Ltd

[1978] QB 574, Court of Appeal

The plaintiffs, Howard Marine and Dredging Co Ltd, owned two sea-going barges. The defendants, A Ogden & Sons (Excavators) Ltd, were contractors who wanted to hire the barges to carry clay out to sea for dumping. In negotiations for the hire of the barges an employee of Howard, O'Loughlin, told Ogden that the capacity of each barge was 850 cubic metres which was equivalent to 'about 1,600 tonnes deadweight carrying capacity, subject to weather, fuel load and time of year'. O'Loughlin based that figure on an entry in the Lloyd's Register. However there was a mistake in the Register and the correct figure for deadweight capacity was only 1,055 tonnes. The correct figure was stated in the ship's documents in Howard's possession. A charterparty containing an exclusion clause was agreed by Howard and Ogden but never signed. Ogden took delivery of the barges and used them for about six months. When Ogden discovered that the deadweight capacity of the barges was only 1,055 tonnes, they refused to pay the full amount for hire. Howard brought an action to recover the outstanding hire charges. Ogden counterclaimed for damages. Four issues arose at trial: (i) whether O'Loughlin's statement as to deadweight capacity was a collateral warranty which Howard had breached;

(ii) whether O'Loughlin's statement breached a common law duty of care owed by Howard to Ogden; (iii) whether O'Loughlin's statement was a misrepresentation for which Howard was liable under section 2(1) of the Misrepresentation Act 1967; and (iv) the effect of the exclusion clause. The trial judge held that Ogden were liable to pay for the hire of the barges. Ogden appealed to the Court of Appeal who, by a majority, allowed their appeal.

In the Court of Appeal all three judges held on the first issue that there was nothing in the pre-contractual negotiations which could amount to a collateral warranty. On the second issue Shaw LJ held that Howard were liable in negligence at common law as the nature of the transaction imposed on them a duty of care in giving information on matters peculiarly within their knowledge. Lord Denning MR held that Howard were under no duty of care at common law. Bridge LJ doubted whether Howard were under a duty of care at common law and, if they were, whether they had breached the duty, but expressed no concluded view. On the third issue Bridge and Shaw LJJ held that Howard were liable to Ogden for O'Loughlin's misrepresentation and had not discharged the burden in section 2(1) of the Act of 1967 of proving that O'Loughlin had a reasonable ground for believing that his representation was true. Lord Denning MR held that Howard had discharged the burden contained in section 2(1). On the fourth issue Bridge and Shaw LJJ held that Howard could not escape liability by reliance on the exclusion clause. The clause was a provision which would 'exclude or restrict . . . any liability to which a party to a contract might be subject by reason of any misrepresentation made by him' within section 3 of the Act of 1967, and it was not 'fair and reasonable' to allow Howard to rely on it. Accordingly, the clause was of no effect. Lord Denning MR held that it was 'fair and reasonable' to allow Howard to rely on the exclusion clause as the parties were of equal bargaining power and Ogden could easily have obtained advice that the barges were not fit for their purposes before concluding the contract. The extracts below concern only the second and third issues.

Lord Denning MR [dissenting]

Negligent misrepresentations

Ogdens contended . . . that the representations by Howards, as to the carrying capacity of the barges, were made negligently: and that Howards are liable in damages for negligent misrepresentation on the principles laid down in *Hedley Byrne & Co Ltd v. Heller & Partners Ltd* [1964] AC 465.

This raises the vexed question of the scope of the doctrine of *Hedley Byrne*. It was much discussed in the Privy Council in *Mutual Life and Citizens' Assurance Co Ltd v. Evatt* [1971] AC 793 and in this court in *Esso Petroleum Co Ltd v. Mardon* [1976] QB 801. To my mind one of the most helpful passages is to be found in the speech of Lord Pearce in *Hedley Byrne & Co Ltd v. Heller & Partners Ltd* [1964] AC 465, 539:

'. . . To import such a duty [of care] the representation must normally, I think, concern a business or professional transaction whose nature makes clear the gravity of the inquiry and the importance and influence attached to the answer . . . A most important circumstance is the form of the inquiry and of the answer.'

To this I would add the principle stated by Lord Reid and Lord Morris of Borth-y-Gest in the Privy Council case, *Mutual Life and Citizens' Assurance Co Ltd v. Evatt* [1971] AC 793 812, which I would adopt in preference to that stated by the majority:

'. . . when an inquirer consults a business man in the course of his business and makes it plain to him that he is seeking considered advice and intends to act on it in a particular way . . . his action in giving such advice . . . (gives rise to) . . . a legal obligation to take such care as is reasonable in the whole circumstances.'

Those principles speak of the 'gravity of the inquiry' and the seeking of 'considered advice'. Those words are used so as to exclude representations made during a casual conversation in the street; or in a railway carriage; or an impromptu opinion given off-hand; or 'off the cuff' on the telephone. To put it more generally, the duty is one of honesty and no more whenever the opinion, information or advice is given in circumstances in which it appears that it is unconsidered and it would not be reasonable for the recipient to act on it without taking further steps to check it. Some instances are to be found in the books. One is *Fish* v. *Kelly* (1864) 17 CBNS 194. The other is *Low* v. *Bouverie* [1891] 3 Ch 82, as explained by Lord Reid and Lord Morris of Borth-y-Gest in *Mutual Life and Citizens' Assurance Co Ltd* v. *Evatt* [1971] AC 793, 813. And the actual decision in *Heilbut Symons & Co Ltd* v. *Buckleton* [1913] AC 30 was that an honest answer on the telephone did not give rise to a cause of action.

Applying this test, it seems to me that at these various conversations Mr O'Loughlin was under a duty to be honest, but no more. Take the first two conversations. They were on the telephone. The callers from the north wanted to know what was the capacity of the barges. Mr O'Loughlin answered it offhand as best he could, without looking up the file. If they had wanted considered advice, they should have written a letter and got it in writing. Take the last conversation. It was on an occasion when Mr O'Loughlin went up to the north to discuss all sorts of things. In the course of it, he was asked again the capacity of the barges. He had not got the file with him, so he answered as best he could from memory. To my mind in those circumstances it was not reasonable for Ogdens to act on his answers without checking them. They ought either to have got him to put it in writing—that would have stressed the gravity and importance of it—or they ought to have got expert advice on their own behalf—especially in a matter of such importance to them. So I agree with the judge that there was not such a situation here as to give rise to a duty of care: or to make Howards liable for negligent misrepresentation at common law.

The Misrepresentation Act 1967

Alternatively Ogdens claim damages for innocent misrepresentation under the Misrepresentation Act 1967

[he set out section 2(1) of the Act and continued]

This enactment imposes a new and serious liability on anyone who makes a representation of fact in the course of negotiations for a contract. If that representation turns out to be mistaken—then however innocent he may be—he is just as liable as if he made it fraudulently. But how different from times past! For years he was not liable in damages at all for innocent misrepresentation: see *Heilbut, Symons & Co* v. *Buckleton* [1913] AC 30. Quite recently he was made liable if he was proved to have made it negligently: see *Esso Petroleum Co Ltd* v. *Mardon* [1976] QB 801. But now with this Act he is made liable—unless he proves—and the burden is on him to prove—that he had reasonable ground to believe and did in fact believe that it was true.

Section 2(1) certainly applies to the representation made by Mr O'Loughlin on July 11, 1974, when he told Ogdens that each barge could carry 1,600 tonnes. The judge found that it was a misrepresentation: that he said it with the object of getting the hire contract for Howards. They got it: and, as a result, Ogdens suffered loss. But the judge found that Mr O'Loughlin was not negligent: and so Howards were not liable for it.

The judge's finding was criticised before us: because he asked himself the question: was Mr O'Loughlin negligent? Whereas he should have asked himself: did Mr O'Loughlin have reasonable ground to believe that the representation was true? I think that criticism is not fair to the judge. By the word 'negligent' he was only using shorthand for the longer phrase contained in section 2 (1) which he had before him. And the judge, I am sure, had the burden of proof in mind: for he had come to the conclusion that Mr O'Loughlin was not negligent. The judge said in effect: 'I am satisfied that Mr O'Loughlin was not negligent': and being so satisfied, the burden need not be further considered: see *Robins* v. *National Trust Co Ltd* [1927] AC 515, 520.

It seems to me that when one examines the details, the judge's view was entirely justified. He found that Mr O'Loughlin's state of mind was this: Mr O'Loughlin had examined Lloyd's Register and had seen there that the deadweight capacity of each barge was 1,800 tonnes. That figure stuck in his mind. The judge found that 'the 1,600 tonnes was arrived at by knocking off what he considered a reasonable margin for fuel, and so on, from the 1,800 tonnes summer deadweight figure in Lloyd's Register, which was in the back of his mind'. The judge said that Mr O'Loughlin had seen at some time the German shipping documents and had seen the deadweight figure of 1,055.135 tonnes: but it did not register. All that was in his mind was the 1,800 tonnes in Lloyd's Register which was regarded in shipping circles as the Bible. That afforded reasonable ground for him to believe that the barges could each carry 1,600 tonnes pay load: and that is what Mr O'Loughlin believed.

So on this point, too, I do not think we should fault the judge. It is not right to pick his judgment to pieces—by subjecting it—or the shorthand note—to literal analysis. Viewing it fairly, the judge (who had section 2 (1) in front of him) must have been of opinion that the burden of proof was discharged.

Bridge LJ

. . . the remaining, and to my mind the more difficult, question raised in this appeal is whether Mr O'Loughlin's undoubted misrepresentation gives rise to any liability in tort either under the provisions of the Misrepresentation Act 1967 or at common law for breach of a duty of care owed to Ogdens with respect to the accuracy of the information given. I will consider first the position under the statute.

[he set out section 2(1) of the Act and continued]

The first question then is whether Howards would be liable in damages in respect of Mr O'Loughlin's misrepresentation if it had been made fraudulently, that is to say, if he had known that it was untrue. An affirmative answer to that question is inescapable. The judge found in terms that what Mr O'Loughlin said about the capacity of the barges was said with the object of getting the hire contract for Howards, in other words, with the intention that it should be acted on. This was clearly right. Equally clearly the misrepresentation was in fact acted on by Ogdens. It follows, therefore, on the plain language of the statute that, although there was no allegation of fraud, Howards must be liable unless they proved that Mr O'Loughlin had reasonable ground to believe what he said about the barges' capacity.

It is unfortunate that the judge never directed his mind to the question whether Mr O'Loughlin had any reasonable ground for his belief. The question he asked himself, in considering liability under the Misrepresentation Act 1967, was whether the innocent misrepresentation was negligent. He concluded that if Mr O'Loughlin had given the inaccurate information in the course of the April telephone conversations he would have been negligent to do so but that in the circumstances obtaining at the Otley interview in July there was no negligence. I take it that he meant by this that on the earlier occasions the circumstances were such that he would have been under a duty to check the accuracy of his information, but on the later occasions he was exempt from any such duty. I appreciate the basis of this distinction, but it seems to me, with respect, quite irrelevant to any question of liability under the statute. If the representee proves a misrepresentation which, if fraudulent, would have sounded in damages, the onus passes immediately to the representor to prove that he had reasonable ground to believe the facts represented. In other words the liability of the representor does not depend upon his being under a duty of care the extent of which may vary according to the circumstances in which the representation is made. In the course of negotiations leading to a contract the statute imposes an absolute obligation not to state facts which the representor cannot prove he had reasonable ground to believe.

[Bridge LJ considered the evidence of the grounds for O'Loughlin's belief. He noted the findings of the trial judge that: (i) O'Loughlin looked at the ship's documents and saw, but did not register, the figure of 1,055.135 tonnes; and (ii) O'Loughlin looked up the Lloyd's Register and saw the figure of 1,800 tonnes, which stayed in his mind. However Bridge LJ also noted O'Loughlin's oral evidence at trial. In particular: (i) O'Loughlin saw and understood the figure of 1,055.135 tonnes in the ship's documents and never said that the figure 'did not register' with him; and (ii) the only explanation O'Loughlin could provide for relying on the figure in the Lloyd's Register rather than the figure in the ship's documents was that the ship's documents stated the freshwater deadweight capacity rather than the saltwater cubic capacity.]

I am fully alive to the dangers of trial by transcript and it is to be assumed that Mr O'Loughlin was perfectly honest throughout. But the question remains whether his evidence, however benevolently viewed, is sufficient to show that he had an objectively reasonable ground to disregard the figure in the ship's documents and to prefer the Lloyd's Register figure. I think it is not. The fact that he was more interested in cubic capacity could not justify reliance on one figure of deadweight capacity in preference to another. The fact that the deadweight figure in the ship's documents was a freshwater figure was of no significance since, as he knew, the difference between freshwater and sea water deadweight capacity was minimal. Accordingly I conclude that Howards failed to prove that Mr O'Loughlin had reasonable ground to believe the truth of his misrepresentation to Mr Redpath.

Having reached a conclusion favourable to Ogdens on the issue of liability under the Misrepresentation Act 1967, I do not find it necessary to express a concluded view on the issue of negligence at common law. As at present advised I doubt if the circumstances surrounding the misrepresentation at the Otley interview were such as to impose on

Howards a common law duty of care for the accuracy of the statement. If there was such a duty, I doubt if the evidence established a breach of it.

Shaw LJ

I turn next to the question of liability for negligence. I would respectfully adopt what Lord Denning MR has already said in preferring the minority opinion in *Mutual Life and Citizens' Assurance Co Ltd v. Evatt* [1971] AC 793 and I would approach the problem as he has done from the standpoint of the passage he has cited from the speech of Lord Pearce in *Hedley Byrne & Co Ltd v. Heller & Partners Ltd* [1964] AC 465, 539.

Now it does seem to me that the chartering of barges for the purpose of carrying clay out to sea and there dumping it is a business transaction whose nature makes clear the importance and influence of an answer to the question: 'What is their carrying capacity in the context of the purpose of the prospective charterparties?' That the question was only asked over the telephone in April and later repeated at an interview in July does not of itself, as I see it, render the subject matter of the question less material or the impact of the answer less important. The information sought would govern the performance by Ogdens of their contract with the authority and this must have been apparent to any man of business, let alone Mr O'Loughlin. The judge so held. The information which had been asked for more than once cannot be regarded as other than important whatever the circumstances in which it was sought and given. Moreover, it was not expert advice that was sought which might honestly and reasonably have assumed different forms according to the source of it. What was asked for was a specific fact. Ogdens had not themselves any direct means of ascertaining what the fact was. Certainly they had no such ready and facile means as were available to Mr O'Loughlin. These factors in association with the relationship of the parties as owners and prospective charterers of barges to be employed for a specific purpose known to the owners did in my judgment give rise to a duty upon the owners to exercise reasonable care to be accurate in giving information of a material character which was peculiarly within their knowledge. All Mr O'Loughlin had to do was to look at documents in Howard's possession and to read them accurately. Had he done so there would have been no room for error of fact or for misconceived opinion or wrong advice. That he chose to answer an important question from mere recollection 'off the cuff' does not in my view diminish, if I may adopt the language of Lord Pearce, the 'gravity of the inquiry or the importance and influence attached to the answer'.

It is with considerable diffidence that I express this view since it is not shared by either of the other members of this court and was not held by Bristow J. None the less I would venture to hold that Ogdens have a cause of action in negligence at common law. This is not, in my judgment, affected by the exception clause which does not purport to grant absolution from the consequences of negligence on the part of the owners.

There remains the issue raised by the claim under section 2(1) of the Misrepresentation Act 1967. I do not regard the telephone conversation of April and the interview of July 11, 1974, as being so casual as to give rise to no legal consequences. Certainly I find myself unable to dismiss what was said at the interview in July as inconsequential. I share the opinion expressed in this regard in the judgment of Bridge LJ which is based on the finding of the judge. I entirely agree, furthermore, with Bridge LJ's analysis of the evidence, together with the judge's findings in this regard, and I agree also with the views expressed by Bridge LJ as to the operation and effect of the relevant provisions of the

Misrepresentation Act. I cannot do better than respectfully to adopt his reasoning without seeking to repeat it, and I agree with his conclusions.

On this ground as well as in relation to the claim based on negligence at common law I would allow the appeal.

COMMENTARY

The competition here was between a claim under section 2(1) and a claim in the tort of negligence (rather than, as in *Royscot*, a competition between section 2(1) and the tort of deceit). Once again section 2(1) emerged as the victor. The outcome of the tort claim was inconclusive in that Shaw LJ was of the opinion it would succeed, Lord Denning was of the view that it failed, while Bridge LJ doubted whether it would succeed. But the defendants did succeed in their appeal under section 2(1), albeit by a majority. The case demonstrates the significance of the shift in the onus of proof. The plaintiffs relied upon an extremely reliable source of information (which was, unusually, incorrect) but they were nevertheless unable to discharge the onus of proof because they had the correct information in their possession at the relevant time. This suggests that it will be no easy task for a representor to show that he had reasonable grounds to believe that the facts represented were true. In many ways *Howard Marine* underlines the oddity of the fiction of fraud because, on the basis of the decision of the Court of Appeal in *Royscot*, the plaintiffs in *Howard Marine* were liable to pay damages as if they had been fraudulent. Yet the defendants never even succeeded in proving that they had been negligent!

When deciding whether or not the party had reasonable grounds to believe and did believe that the facts represented were true, it is the belief of the representor that is relevant and not an agent of the representor. Thus it will not suffice for a representor to show that an agent had reasonable grounds to believe and did believe that the facts represented were true. Section 2(1) is concerned with the liability of the 'other party' to the contract (and the 'other party' for this purpose does not include the agent of that party: *Resolute Maritime Inc* v. *Nippon Kaiji Kyokai, The Skopas* [1983] 1 WLR 857). Thus, where the 'other party' is a company, it is only the belief of a party who can be identified with the company itself that is relevant (*MCI WorldCom International Inc* v. *Primus Telecommunications Inc* [2003] EWHC 2182 (Comm); [2004] 1 All ER (Comm) 138).

Section 2(1) is therefore an extraordinarily powerful weapon in the hands of a claimant. It is better than a claim in the tort of negligence because the remoteness rule is more generous, there is no need to show that the defendant owed a duty of care to the claimant, nor is it necessary for the claimant to show that the defendant has breached his duty of care. A claim under section 2(1) is also more advantageous than a claim in deceit because the claimant can recover the same measure of damages as in a deceit claim without having to prove that the defendant had been fraudulent. Are there any circumstances in which a claimant would find it preferable to invoke the tort of deceit or the tort of negligence? The obvious circumstance is where the claimant is not in a contractual relationship with the party who made the misrepresentation. In such a case the claimant must bring a claim in tort and cannot bring a claim under section 2(1). Secondly, a claimant who has himself been careless might find it advantageous to bring a claim in the tort of deceit in order to avoid the defence of contributory negligence (see p. 695 above). Thirdly, a court may hesitate to find the existence of a misrepresentation in a claim brought under section 2(1) given the Draconian consequences which can flow from the finding that there has been a misrepresentation: *Avon Insurance plc* v. *Swire Fraser Ltd* [2000] 1 All ER (Comm) 573, 633. In such a case a claimant may want to consider bringing an action in the tort of negligence.

(b) COMMON LAW NEGLIGENCE

A claimant may be able to bring an action for damages in the tort of negligence. In order to do so a claimant must prove that the defendant owes to him a duty of care and that he has breached that duty of care (in other words, that he has been careless). The decision of the House of Lords in *Hedley Byrne & Co Ltd* v. *Heller & Partners Ltd* [1964] AC 465 transformed this area of the law. A discussion of *Hedley Byrne* liability can be found in the judgments of the Court of Appeal in *Howard Marine* (p. 696 above; for more modern analysis of the scope of *Hedley Byrne* liability, see BS Markesinis and SF Deakin, *Tort Law* (5th edn, Oxford University Press, 2003), pp. 114–131). The advantages of a claim under section 2(1) over a claim in the tort of negligence are discussed above (p. 696).

(c) DECEIT

Thirdly, a claimant may be able to bring an action for damages in the tort of deceit. Prior to the decision of the House of Lords in *Hedley Byrne* a plaintiff who wished to recover damages for misrepresentation had to prove that the misrepresentation was made fraudulently and fraud is no easy matter to prove. The leading case is:

Derry v. Peek

(1889) 14 App Cas 337, House of Lords

The defendants were directors of a tramways company. They issued a prospectus stating that the company had the right to use steam power instead of horses when, in fact, under the terms of the relevant Act, the consent of the Board of Trade was required. The plaintiff subscribed for shares in the company on the strength of the prospectus. The Board of Trade subsequently refused to consent to the use of steam power and the company was wound up. The plaintiff brought an action in deceit against the directors. The trial judge found against the plaintiff, but the Court of Appeal reversed the trial judge's decision. The House of Lords reversed the decision of the Court of Appeal, on the basis that an action in deceit requires actual fraud, which is not satisfied merely by the absence of a reasonable basis for the erroneous belief. As the defendants honestly believed that their statement was true, the plaintiff's action failed.

Lord Herschell

'This action is one which is commonly called an action of deceit, a mere common law action.' This is the description of it given by Cotton LJ in delivering judgment. I think it important that it should be borne in mind that such an action differs essentially from one brought to obtain rescission of a contract on the ground of misrepresentation of a material fact. The principles which govern the two actions differ widely. Where rescission is claimed it is only necessary to prove that there was misrepresentation; then, however honestly it may have been made, however free from blame the person who made it, the contract, having been obtained by misrepresentation, cannot stand. In an action of deceit, on the contrary, it is not enough to establish misrepresentation alone; it is conceded on all hands that something more must be proved to cast liability upon the defendant, though it has been a matter of controversy what additional elements are requisite . . .

In the Court below Cotton LJ said: 'What in my opinion is a correct statement of the law is this, that where a man makes a statement to be acted upon by others which is false, and which is known by him to be false, or is made by him recklessly, or without care whether it is true or false, that is, without any reasonable ground for believing it to be true, he is liable in an action of deceit at the suit of anyone to whom it was addressed or anyone of the class to whom it was addressed and who was materially induced by the misstatement to do an act to his prejudice'. About much that is here stated there cannot, I think, be two opinions. But when the learned Lord Justice speaks of a statement made recklessly or without care whether it is true or false, *that is* without any reasonable ground for believing it to be true, I find myself, with all respect, unable to agree that these are convertible expressions. To make a statement careless whether it be true or false, and therefore without any real belief in its truth, appears to me to be an essentially different thing from making, through want of care, a false statement, which is nevertheless honestly believed to be true. And it is surely conceivable that a man may believe that what he states is the fact, though he has been so wanting in care that the Court may think that there were no sufficient grounds to warrant his belief . . .

Having now drawn attention, I believe, to all the cases having a material bearing upon the question under consideration, I proceed to state briefly the conclusions to which I have been led. I think the authorities establish the following propositions: First, in order to sustain an action of deceit, there must be proof of fraud, and nothing short of that will suffice. Secondly, fraud is proved when it is shewn that a false representation has been made (1) knowingly, or (2) without belief in its truth, or (3) recklessly, careless whether it be true or false. Although I have treated the second and third as distinct cases, I think the third is but an instance of the second, for one who makes a statement under such circumstances can have no real belief in the truth of what he states. To prevent a false statement being fraudulent, there must, I think, always be an honest belief in its truth. And this probably covers the whole ground, for one who knowingly alleges that which is false, has obviously no such honest belief. Thirdly, if fraud be proved, the motive of the person guilty of it is immaterial. It matters not that there was no intention to cheat or injure the person to whom the statement was made . . .

In my opinion making a false statement through want of care falls far short of, and is a very different thing from, fraud, and the same may be said of a false representation honestly believed though on insufficient grounds . . .

I have arrived with some reluctance at the conclusion to which I have felt myself compelled, for I think those who put before the public a prospectus to induce them to embark their money in a commercial enterprise ought to be vigilant to see that it contains such representations only as are in strict accordance with fact, and I should be very unwilling to give any countenance to the contrary idea. I think there is much to be said for the view that this moral duty ought to some extent to be converted into a legal obligation, and that the want of reasonable care to see that statements, made under such circumstances, are true, should be made an actionable wrong. But this is not a matter fit for discussion on the present occasion. If it is to be done the legislature must intervene and expressly give a right of action in respect of such a departure from duty. It ought not, I think, to be done by straining the law, and holding that to be fraudulent which the tribunal feels cannot properly be so described. I think mischief is likely to result from blurring the distinction between carelessness and fraud, and equally holding a man fraudulent whether his acts can or cannot be justly so designated.

Lord Halsbury LC, Lord Watson, Lord Bramwell, and **Lord Fitzgerald** delivered concurring judgments.

COMMENTARY

The opening paragraph from the judgment of Lord Herschell demonstrates the difference between a claim for rescission and a claim for damages. A claim to rescind a contract has never required proof of fraud, whereas an action for damages, until 1963, did require such proof. As the judgment of Lord Herschell makes clear, fraud is not an easy matter to prove and, indeed, it should not even be pleaded unless there is a substantial basis for the allegation of fraud. This being the case, section 2(1) of the 1967 Act offers a much more attractive route for a claimant who is in a contractual relationship with the defendant misrepresentor because it gives the claimant the advantages of a claim in deceit without having to assume the difficult task of alleging and proving fraud.

(d) SECTION 2(2) OF THE MISREPRESENTATION ACT 1967

Section 2(2) of the Misrepresentation Act 1967 gives the court a discretion to award damages in lieu of rescission (see p. 688 above). What is the measure of damages recoverable under section 2(2)? This issue was considered by the Court of Appeal in *William Sindall plc v. Cambridgeshire County Council* [1994] 1 WLR 1016 (p. 689 above) in the following terms:

Hoffmann LJ

The section speaks in terms of loss suffered rather than damages recoverable but clearly contemplates that if the contract is upheld, such loss will be compensated by an award of damages. Section 2(2) therefore gives a power to award damages in circumstances in which no damages would previously have been recoverable. Furthermore, such damages will be compensation for loss caused by the misrepresentation, whether it was negligent or not. This is made clear by section 2(3), which provides:

'Damages may be awarded under subsection (2) of this section whether or not he is liable to damages under subsection (1) thereof, but where he is so liable any award under subsection (2) shall be taken into account in assessing his liability under the said subsection (1).'

Damages under section 2(2) are therefore damages for the misrepresentation as such. What would be the measure of such damages? This court is not directly concerned with quantum, which would be determined at an inquiry. But since the court, in the exercise of its discretion, needs to know whether damages under section 2(2) would be an adequate remedy and to be able to compare such damages with the loss which rescission would cause to Cambridgeshire, it is necessary to decide in principle how the damages would be calculated.

The Law Reform Committee drew the analogy with Lord Cairns's Act (the Chancery Amendment Act 1858 (21 & 22 Vict. c. 27)) and in some respects this analogy is a good one. But it breaks down when one comes to decide the measure of damages. Under Lord Cairns's Act, the plaintiff who is refused specific performance or an injunction is left to his damages in contract or tort. The measure of such damages is exactly what it would be at common law: see *Johnson* v. *Agnew* [1980] AC 367, 400. The only change made by the Act was to give a remedy for purely equitable rights, such as breach of a restrictive covenant to which the plaintiff was not a party. But in such cases the common law analogy enabled a suitable measure of damages to be devised. Section 2(2), on the other hand, creates a power to award damages in a wholly new situation.

Under section 2(1), the measure of damages is the same as for fraudulent misrepresentation, i.e. all loss caused by the plaintiff having been induced to enter into the contract: *Cemp Properties (UK) Ltd* v. *Dentsply Research & Development Corporation* [1991] 2 EGLR 197. This means that the misrepresentor is invariably deprived of the benefit of the bargain (e.g. any difference between the price paid and the value of the thing sold) and may have to pay additional damages for consequential loss suffered by the representee on account of having entered into the contract. In my judgment, however, it is clear that this will not necessarily be the measure of damages under section 2(2).

First, section 2(1) provides for damages to be awarded to a person who 'has entered into a contract after a misrepresentation has been made to him by another party and as a result thereof'—[that is to say] of having entered into the contract—'he has suffered loss'. In contrast, section 2(2) speaks of 'the loss which would be caused by it'—[that is to say] the misrepresentation—'if the contract were upheld'. In my view, section 2(1) is concerned with the damage flowing from having entered into the contract, while section 2(2) is concerned with damage caused by the property not being what it was represented to be.

Secondly, section 2(3) contemplates that damages under section 2(2) may be less than damages under section 2(1) and should be taken into account when assessing damages under the latter subsection. This only makes sense if the measure of damages may be different.

Thirdly, the Law Reform Committee report makes it clear that section 2(2) was enacted because it was thought that it might be a hardship to the representor to be deprived of the whole benefit of the bargain on account of a minor misrepresentation. It could not possibly have intended the damages in lieu to be assessed on a principle which would invariably have the same effect.

The Law Reform Committee drew attention to the anomaly which already existed by which a minor misrepresentation gave rise to a right of rescission whereas a warranty in the same terms would have grounded no more than a claim for modest damages. It said that this anomaly would be exaggerated if its recommendation for abolition of the bar on rescission after completion were to be implemented. I think that section 2(2) was intended to give the court a power to eliminate this anomaly by upholding the contract and compensating the plaintiff for the loss he has suffered on account of the property not having been what it was represented to be. In other words, damages under section 2(2) should never exceed the sum which would have been awarded if the representation had been a warranty. It is not necessary for present purposes to discuss the circumstances in which they may be less.

If one looks at the matter when Sindall purported to rescind, the loss which would be caused if the contract were upheld was relatively small: the £18,000 it would have cost to divert the sewer, the loss of a plot and interest charges on any consequent delay at the rate of £2,000 a day. If one looks at the matter at the date of trial, the loss would have been nil because the sewer had been diverted.

Evans LJ

Section 2(3) makes it clear that the statutory power to award damages under section 2(2) is distinct from the plaintiff's right to recover damages under section 2(1) . . .

There is . . . much room for debate as to the 'loss that would be caused if the contract were upheld'. The subsection assumes, as I read it, that this loss will be compensated by the damages awarded, if the contract is upheld. But if the measure is the same as those awarded in respect of a fraudulent misrepresentation *(Doyle* v. *Olby (Ironmongers) Ltd* [1969] 2 QB 158) or under section 2(1) *(Cemp Properties (UK) Ltd* v. *Dentsply Research and Development Corporation* [1991] 2 EGLR 197; cf. *Royscott Trust Ltd* v. *Rogerson* [1991] 2 QB 297) in cases where the contract continues in force, then two consequences seem to follow. First damages under section 2(2) are co-extensive with those under section 2(1), whereas section 2(3) suggests that they are or may be different. Secondly, an innocent and non-negligent defendant will be liable under section 2(2) for damages which he is specifically excused under section 2(1). Furthermore, if the plaintiff recovers full compensation under section 2(2), if the contract is upheld, then he will not suffer any net loss, assuming that the damages are paid.

In my judgment, it is not correct that the measure of damages under section 2(2) for the loss that would be caused by the misrepresentation if the contract were upheld is the same measure as under section 2(1). The latter is established by the common law and it is the amount required to compensate the party to whom the misrepresentation was made for all the losses which he has sustained by reason of his acting upon it at the time when he did. But the damages contemplated by section 2(2) are damages in lieu of rescission. The starting point for the application of the sub-section is the situation where a plaintiff has established a right to rescind the contract on grounds of innocent misrepresentation: its object is to ameliorate for the innocent misrepresentor the harsh consequences of rescission for a wholly innocent (meaning, non-negligent as well as non-fraudulent) mis-representor, in a case where it is fairer to uphold the contract and award damages against him. Such an award of damages was not permitted in law or equity before 1967. The court, therefore, exercises a statutory jurisdiction and it does so having regard to the circumstances at the date of the hearing, when otherwise rescission would be ordered. (The subsection envisages that the court's order may restore a contract which has been lawfully rescinded by the innocent party at some earlier date: see *The Lucy* [1983] 1 Lloyd's Rep 188, 202, per Mustill J). When there has been a decline in market values since the date of the contract, then one party or the other will suffer that loss, depending on whether rescission is ordered or not. But that loss is not caused by the misrepresentation, except in the sense that the decline has occurred since the representation was made, and it does not measure the loss caused by the misrepresentation either when the representation was acted upon or when the court decides whether to order rescission or not. The 'loss caused by it', in my judgment, can be measured by the cost of remedying the defect or alternatively by the reduced market value attributable to the defect, together with additional compensation, if appropriate, of the kind described in *Cemp Properties (UK) Ltd* v. *Dentsply Research and Development Corporation* [1991] 2 EGLR 197.

When the court is required to form its own view of what is equitable between the parties at the date of the hearing, it is dangerous to lay down any hard-and-fast rule to the effect that no account can be taken of changed market values. Apart from the capital value of the subject matter of the contract, as here, which might rise or fall during the intervening period, there might be relevant market trading conditions which the court could properly take into account: cf. *The Lucy* [1983] 1 Lloyd's Rep. 188. Moreover, if it is right to take account of the current market value in assessing the loss which would be sustained by the council, if rescission were ordered, then it would be 'inequitable' not to have regard to this factor in the case of the builders also. But the effect of doing so is merely to restate the issue which the court has to decide: in the circumstances of the case, should the loss of market remain where it presently lies?

Viewed in this way, it would be substantially unjust, in my judgment, to deprive Cambridgeshire of the bargain which it made in 1988, albeit that the bargain was induced by a misrepresentation innocently made, but which was of little importance in relation to the contract as a whole. That misrepresentation apart, Sindall made what has proved to be so far an unfortunate bargain for them (although they remain owners of an important potential development site in what is a notoriously cyclical market). To permit them to transfer the financial consequences to Cambridgeshire, in the circumstances of this case, could properly be described as a windfall for them.

For the above reasons, and taking into account the nature of the alleged representation and the history of the matter generally, including Sindall's deliberate failure to make any serious attempt to find a solution to the difficulty which arose when the sewer was discovered, the equitable balance, in my judgment, lies in favour of upholding the contract and awarding damages in lieu of rescission in this case. If there were a live issue under section 2(2), I would award damages in lieu of rescission and order the amount of such damages to be assessed.

There remains the question of whether these damages should include the decline in the market value of the land since the contract was made. As indicated, above in my judgment they should not. This conclusion may be inconsistent with the view expressed in *McGregor on Damages*, 15th. ed. (1988), para 1752, and in deference to the distinguished author I should explain my reasons briefly. He suggests that the measure to be adopted is

'the same as the normal measure of damages in tort where the plaintiff has been induced to contract by fraudulent or negligent misrepresentation. . . . The overall result, therefore, is that the damages will be held to be the difference between the value transferred and the value received . . . no recovery being possible for consequential losses.'

If the 'value transferred' (meaning the price paid by the plaintiff, to whom the representation was made) was the market value of the property, then there is no difference between this formula and what *McGregor* calls the contract measure, that is to say, the difference between the actual value received and the value which the property would have had, if the representation had been true: see paragraph 1718. By adopting the tort measure, therefore, as he does in paragraph 1752 in the paragraph already quoted, the author impliedly rejects the contract measure, whereas in my judgment that becomes the correct measure in circumstances where the plaintiff is entitled to an order for rescission, but rescission is refused under section 2(2) of the Act. This is because the difference in value between what the plaintiff was misled into believing that he was acquiring, and the value of what he in fact received, seems to me to be the measure of the loss caused to him by the misrepresentation in a case where he cannot rescind the contract and therefore retains the property which he received.

As *McGregor on Damages* points out, the tortious measure benefits a plaintiff who made a bad bargain, that is to say, who agreed to pay more than the market value of the property in the state in which he believed it to be, more so than the contract measure would do. Conversely, it dis-benefits one who paid less than the market value, because it disentitles him from recovering the whole of the difference which the contract measure would otherwise produce. Likewise, the right to rescind benefits a plaintiff who has paid, or agreed to pay more than, with hindsight, he should have done. The period of hindsight may be short or long; where it is long, and the value has fallen in line with the market and therefore for reasons unconnected with the misrepresentation, there is no justification, in my view, for holding that the author of the misrepresentation is liable to compensate the plaintiff for that loss, in a case where rescission is refused.

It is unnecessary to explore the wider questions whether a tortious measure should ever include damages for a fall in market values, and whether this measure, as described by Lord Denning MR in *Doyle* v. *Olby (Ironmongers) Ltd* [1969] 2 QB 158, 166, is necessarily exclusive of or inconsistent with the contractual measure to the extent which has been suggested. The recovery of such damages in the present case, even if the tortious measure under section 2(2) applies, appears to be barred by the following three obstacles: (1) such damage was caused, not by the misrepresentation, but by the subsequent fall in market values, an extraneous cause; (2) the authorities suggest that the plaintiff's loss has to be assessed at the date when the property was transferred: *McGregor on Damages*, 15th ed., para 1727 citing *Waddell* v. *Blockey* (1879) 4 QBD 678; and (3) if a subsequent rise, or fall, in market values is relevant at the date of trial, then a chance element enters into the calculation, whether the contract is rescinded or not. I should add, however, that the reported authorities are sparse, as *McGregor* emphasises, and as I read them they do not purport to decide the question whether a decline in value until the time of discovery of the true facts is necessarily excluded.

It is sufficient for present purposes to say that an award of damages in lieu of rescission under section 2(2) should in my view be calculated as I have described above.

For these reasons, as well as those given by Hoffmann LJ, I would allow this appeal.

Russell LJ concurred with both judgments.

COMMENTARY

Since *William Sindall* was decided the House of Lords has held in *South Australia Asset Management Corporation* v. *York Montague Ltd* [1997] AC 191 that the scope of the duty of care owed by a valuer to a lender did not extend to a fall in the value of the property market subsequent to the valuation. The damages recoverable were held to be confined to the difference between the correct valuation of the property at the time at which the valuation was done and the valuation negligently provided by the defendant. It has been suggested (*Chitty on Contracts* (29th edn, Sweet & Maxwell

2004), para 6-098) that the same approach should be taken to a claim under section 2(2) so that damages 'should be limited to any difference between the contract price and the actual value of the property taking into account the misrepresentation but not taking into account the general fall in the value of the property'.

It should be noted that section 2(2) does not confer on a claimant a right to recover damages. It confers a *discretion* on the court to award damages in lieu of rescission. It would appear to be the case that the court only has jurisdiction to award damages under section 2(2) if it also has jurisdiction to rescind the contract at the date of the hearing (see *Zanzibar* v. *British Aerospace (Lancaster House) Ltd* [2000] 1 WLR 2333 and *Floods of Queensferry v Shand Construction Ltd* [2000] BLR 8, but contrast *Thomas Witter Ltd* v. *TBP Industries Ltd* [1996] 2 All ER 573). The discretion is one to award damages 'in lieu of' rescission so that a claimant who wishes to rescind the contract cannot invoke section 2(2) in order to recover damages.

(e) RESCISSION AND AN 'INDEMNITY'

A claimant who rescinds a contract may also be able to bring a claim for what is often referred to as an indemnity, although it is probably more accurate to describe it as a personal restitutionary claim. In *Whittington* v. *Seale-Hayne* (1900) 82 LT 49 the plaintiff entered into a lease of a farm which he intended to use for breeding prize poultry. He was induced to enter into the lease by misrepresentations made by the defendant that the premises were in a good state of repair and in a sanitary condition. The premises were not sanitary and the buildings were in a state of disrepair. As a result the plaintiff became ill and many of the pigs died. The plaintiff claimed that he was entitled to set aside the lease and recover an indemnity in respect of the losses which he had suffered in the performance of the contract before it was set aside. It was held that he was not entitled to recover an indemnity in respect of the loss of his pigs and the illness which he suffered. At the time at which the case was decided damages could only be recovered in respect of a fraudulent misrepresentation (see p. 691 above) and the plaintiff could not establish that the defendant had made the misrepresentations fraudulently. But the plaintiff was able to recover the rent paid and the cost of the repair work that had been done pursuant to an order issued by the local authority. These obligations were obligations imposed on him by the terms of the lease. The reason for his entitlement to recover these payments was that they had resulted in an enrichment to the defendant (either through the direct payment of rent or by carrying out the work ordered by the local authority) and, when the lease was set aside, the defendant became subject to a restitutionary liability to repay to the plaintiff the value of the benefits which he had received as a result of the plaintiff's performance of his obligations under the lease. But he was not subject to any wider liability to pay compensation to the plaintiff for the losses which he had suffered.

7. EXCLUSION OF LIABILITY FOR MISREPRESENTATION

A party cannot exclude liability for his own fraudulent misrepresentation (*S Pearson & Son Ltd* v. *Dublin Corporation* [1907] AC 351). The question whether English law allows a party to exclude liability for the fraud of his employee or agent is presently unclear. The Court of Appeal in *HIH Casualty and General Insurance Ltd* v. *Chase Manhattan Bank* [2001] EWCA Civ 1250; [2001] 2 Lloyd's Rep 483 at [103] held that liability for the fraud or dishonesty of employees and agents in the *performance* of a contract could be excluded but left open the question whether or not it was possible to exclude liability for the fraud of one's employee or agent in the negotiation of a contract. On appeal the House of Lords also left the latter point open (see [2003] UKHL 6; [2003] 2 Lloyd's Rep 61). Two views are possible. The first is that it is not possible as a matter of law to exclude liability for the dishonesty of one's employee or agent in the negotiation of a contract. The second is that it is possible to exclude liability for the dishonesty of one's employee or agent in the negotiation of a contract provided that sufficiently clear words are used. However, the difference between the two views may not matter a great deal in practice because of the insistence on the part of the courts that parties use clear language if they wish to exclude liability for the fraud of their agents (and the unlikelihood of a party using such clear language). Thus in *HIH Casualty and General Insurance Ltd* v. *Chase Manhattan Bank* Lord Bingham stated (at [16]):

For it is in my opinion plain beyond argument that if a party to a written contract seeks to exclude the ordinary consequences of fraudulent or dishonest misrepresentation or deceit by his agent, acting as such, inducing the making of the contract, such intention must be expressed in clear and unmistakable terms on the face of the contract. The decision of the House in *Pearson* v. *Dublin Corporation* does at least make plain that general language will not be construed to relieve a principal of liability for the fraud of an agent: see in particular the speeches of Lord Loreburn LC at page 354, Lord Ashbourne at page 360 and Lord Atkinson at page 365. General words, however comprehensive the legal analyst might find them to be, will not serve: the language used must be such as will alert a commercial party to the extraordinary bargain he is invited to make. It is no doubt unattractive for a contracting party to propose a term clearly having such effect, because of its predictable effect on the mind of the other contracting party, and this may explain why the point of principle left open in *Pearson* v. *Dublin Corporation* has remained unresolved for so long.

The ability of a contracting party to exclude liability for misrepresentation is controlled by section 3 of the Misrepresentation Act 1967 which provides:

If a contract contains a term which would exclude or restrict—

(a) any liability to which a party to a contract may be subject by reason of any misrepresentation made by him before the contract was made; or

(b) any remedy available to another party to the contract by reason of such a misrepresentation.

that term shall be of no effect except in so far as it satisfies the requirement of reasonableness as stated in section 11(1) of the Unfair Contract Terms Act 1977; and it is for those claiming that the term satisfies that requirement to show that it does.

The principles applied by the courts when deciding whether or not a clause is reasonable have been discussed above (pp. 472–478). It is probably wise not to attempt to exclude liability for 'any representation or warranty' because such a clause may, as a matter of interpretation, extend to a fraudulent misrepresentation and an attempt to exclude liability for fraudulent misrepresentation must be unreasonable (see *Thomas Witter Ltd* v. *TBP Industries Ltd* [1996] 2 All ER 573—for a contrary view see *Zanzibar* v. *British Aerospace (Lancaster House) Ltd* [2000] 1 WLR 2333, where it was held that the words 'any representation' were not apt, as a matter of construction, to encompass a fraudulent misrepresentation given that liability for fraud generally cannot be excluded, see p. 711 above). It is, however, safer to state that the exclusion or limitation applies to any representation other than one made fraudulently.

An issue which has proved to be extremely controversial is whether or not entire agreement clauses fall within the scope of section 3. As we have seen (p. 440 above) not all entire agreement clauses attempt to exclude liability for misrepresentation. But some do. An example is provided by the entire agreement clause in *Watford Electronics Ltd* v. *Sanderson CFL Ltd* [2001] All ER (D) 290 which stated:

The parties agree that these terms and conditions (together with any other terms and conditions expressly incorporated in the Contract) represent the entire agreement between the parties relating to the sale and purchase of the Equipment and that no statement or representations made by either party have been relied upon by the other in agreeing to enter into the Contract.

The effect of the first part of the entire agreement clause was to render extrinsic evidence inadmissible to prove terms other than those contained in the written contract. The second part of the clause (beginning with the words 'and that no statement ...') was directed towards liability for misrepresentation. In the past the courts insisted upon the need for clear words if liability was to be excluded for misrepresentation (see *Thomas Witter Ltd* v. *TBP Industries Ltd* [1996] 2 All ER 573, 595–597 per Jacob J). But a more relaxed approach was taken by the Court of Appeal in *E A Grimstead & Son Ltd* v. *McGarrigan*, unreported, CA, 27 October 1999 and in *Watford Electronics* itself, where it was held that the effect of the acknowledgement of non-reliance in the second part of the sentence may be to give rise to an evidential estoppel (cf *Thomas Witter* at p. 597 and *Deepak* [1998] 2 Lloyd's Rep at p. 168). The effect of the clause was not to prevent a party from proving that a representation had been made, nor from proving that the representation was false; rather its effect was to prevent the person to whom the representation was made from asserting that he relied upon it. In order to establish an evidential estoppel it is for the party who seeks to set up the acknowledgement as an evidential estoppel to plead and prove the three requirements identified by the Court of Appeal in *Lowe* v. *Lombank* [1960] 1 All ER 611, 616, namely (i) that the clause is clear and unambiguous, (ii) that the party giving the acknowledgement of non-reliance meant it to be acted on by the other party or so conducted itself that a reasonable man in the position of that other party would take the representation to be true, and (iii) that the other party in fact believed it to be true and was induced by such belief to act on it. As Chadwick LJ acknowledged in *Watford*

Electronics significant difficulties are likely to arise in seeking to set up such an evidential estoppel, 'not least because it may be impossible for a party who has made representations which he intended should be relied upon to satisfy the court that he entered into the contract in the belief that a statement by the other party that he had not relied upon those representations was true'. Given these difficulties, a party who wishes to exclude or to limit liability for misrepresentation would be well advised to say so expressly and not to rely upon the terms of an entire agreement clause.

On the assumption that the entire agreement clause is effective, as a matter of drafting to exclude liability for misrepresentation, one final issue arises, namely whether or not the entire agreement clause falls within the scope of section 3 of the Misrepresentation Act 1967. In *Watford Electronics* Chadwick LJ rejected the proposition that an acknowledgement of non-reliance is 'in substance an exclusion clause to which section 3 of the Misrepresentation Act 1967 is applicable' (see to similar effect *Overbrooke Estates Ltd* v. *Glencombe Properties Ltd* [1974] 1 WLR 1335). This appears to take entire agreement clauses, in so far as they prevent liability in misrepresentation from arising, outside the scope of the legislation on exclusion and limitation clauses. But the cases are not all one way. There are other cases in which the courts have been prepared to have regard to the substance of the clause and to subject it to the controls to be found in section 3 (see, for example, *Thomas Witter*, *Cremdean Properties Ltd* v. *Nash* (1977) 244 EG 547, *Walker* v. *Boyle* [1981] 1 WLR 495, and *South Western General Property Co Ltd* v. *Marton* (1982) 263 EG 1090). The authorities are therefore in some disarray. In the commercial context where the parties are of roughly equal bargaining power, the debate may not matter very much because the clause is likely to pass the reasonableness test but where the parties are not of equal bargaining power the debate assumes much greater significance. There is much to be said for the view that the courts should look to the substance of the clause and so subject entire agreement clauses to the controls to be found in section 3 (see further E Peel (2001) 117 *LQR* 545, 549).

8. FURTHER READING

ATIYAH, PS and TREITEL, GH, 'Misrepresentation Act 1967' (1967) 30 *MLR* 369.

CARTWRIGHT, J, *Misrepresentation* (Sweet and Maxwell, 2002).

HOOLEY, R, 'Damages and the Misrepresentation Act 1967' (1991) 107 *LQR* 547.

18

DURESS

1. CENTRAL ISSUES

1. A contract can be set aside on the ground that it has been entered into under duress. Duress can take different forms. The principal forms are duress of the person, duress of goods, and economic duress.

2. Outside the category of duress to the person, the law has been slow to develop. It was not until 1976 that the courts first recognized the existence of economic duress. A consequence of the late development of economic duress is that a number of questions remain unanswered in relation to the scope of the doctrine. There appear to be two central elements, namely (i) illegitimate pressure applied by one party which (ii) constitutes a (significant) cause inducing the other party to enter into the contract.

3. It is generally agreed that 'illegitimate pressure' includes a threat to commit a crime and a threat to commit a tort. It is also agreed that a threatened breach of contract can constitute illegitimate pressure but it is not yet clear whether all threatened breaches of contract are illegitimate for this purpose. Particularly difficult is the case where the threat is made in the bona fide belief that what has been threatened is not a breach of contract but it subsequently transpires that that belief is mistaken and that what has been threatened is, in fact, a breach of contract. On the other hand, a refusal to contract unless certain conditions are met and a refusal to waive existing contractual obligations do not constitute the application of 'illegitimate' pressure. The definition of 'illegitimacy' is one of the major issues in this chapter.

4. The test to be applied to determine whether there is a sufficient causal link between the illegitimate pressure and the entry by the claimant into the contract may depend upon the form that the duress assumes. Where it takes the form of duress of the person it would appear sufficient that the illegitimate pressure was 'a' cause of the claimant's decision to enter into the contract, whereas in the case of economic duress it would appear that the illegitimate pressure must have been a 'significant' cause of the decision to enter into the contract. If this is so, why should the law distinguish between duress of the person and economic duress in this way?

5. Other factors taken into account by the courts when deciding whether or not economic duress has been established on the facts of a case include whether the victim had any realistic practical alternative but to submit to the pressure; whether the victim protested at the time; and whether he affirmed and sought to rely on the contract. These factors would seem to be relevant to the question of whether or not there is a sufficient causal link between the illegitimate pressure and the decision of the claimant to enter into the contract but the courts appear to regard them as distinct free-standing elements which must be taken into account. While the existence of duress must ultimately depend upon a careful evaluation of the facts and circumstances of the case, the danger with a multi-factor approach is a lack of consistency as different courts place different emphasis on the different factors.

2. INTRODUCTION

Duress of the person is well-established in the authorities. By contrast duress of goods and economic duress have had a more uncertain career. Duress of goods was stunted for many years by the decision in *Skeate* v. *Beale* (1841) 11 Ad & E 983 in which it was held that the unlawful detention of goods belonging to another did not constitute duress. Economic duress (that is to say, a case in which one party uses his superior economic power in an illegitimate manner in order to compel the other party to agree to enter into a contract or to enter the contract on particular terms) was not formally recognized until the decision of Kerr J in *Occidental Worldwide Investment Corporation* v. *Skibs A/S Avanti (The Siboen and The Sibotre)* [1976] 1 Lloyd's Rep 293. The late recognition of economic duress and the problems posed for the development of a coherent doctrine of duress of goods by *Skeate* v. *Beale* meant that judges who wished to avoid giving effect to an agreement that had been procured by the application of illegitimate pressure had to find other doctrinal pegs on which to hang their decision. A classic example of this phenomenon is said to be the decision of Lord Ellenborough in *Stilk* v. *Myrick* (1809) 2 Camp 317, 6 Esp 129 (discussed in more detail at pp. 184–188 above). The argument which is advanced by some authors and judges is that, in the absence of a developed doctrine of duress, Lord Ellenborough had to make use of the doctrine of consideration in order to find that the plaintiff was not entitled to recover the promised extra pay. The obvious difficulty with this argument is that there was little evidence of duress on the facts of *Stilk*, given that the vessel was in port at the time at which the master promised to share the wages of the deserters with the remainder of the crew provided that they worked the ship back to London. However, leaving these factual difficulties to one side, it is clear that the modern trend is to regard duress as the more appropriate regulator of contract modifications (see *United States* v. *Stump Homes Specialties Manufacturing Inc*, 905 F 2d 1117 (1990), p. 200 above and *The Alev* [1989] 1 Lloyd's Rep 138, 147, p. 201 above). The desirability of this development is open to question (p. 201 above) but there can be little doubt that it is taking place. As a result duress is likely to play a greater role in the modern case-law yet judges will find that it does not provide ready-made answers to the questions that are asked of them. The consequence will be a degree of uncertainty in the case-law until the doctrine settles down and its limits are established.

There appear to be two elements to a duress claim. These two elements have been set out as follows (SA Smith, 'Contracting under Pressure: A Theory of Duress' [1997] *CLJ* 343, 344):

In a typical pressure case there are two distinct grounds upon which the impugned contract might be invalidated, one plaintiff-based and the other defendant-based. Consider the canonical example of the contract signed at gunpoint. One reason for not enforcing the 'agreement' is that the person seeking enforcement . . . is seeking to enforce an obligation by his or her own wrongdoing. A second reason for not enforcing the agreement is that the person denying the contract's validity . . . did not consent to the contract. Most, but not all, pressure cases have a similar structure.

Professor Smith argues that these two grounds are alternatives. This is in contrast to the generally accepted view which is that both elements must be present before duress can be made out on the facts of any given case; that is to say, there must be a lack of consent on the part of the party seeking to set aside the contract and there must also be some element of wrongdoing on the part of the party seeking to enforce it. The difficulty lies in defining what, for this purpose, constitutes a 'lack of consent' and what amounts to 'wrongdoing'. These elements tend to be fairly clear-cut in the case of duress to the person but they are much more difficult in cases of economic duress.

There is one further basis for duress which should be mentioned, only to be dismissed, and that is the unfairness of the terms of the contract (commonly referred to as 'substantive unfairness', on which see p. 793 below). While substantive unfairness is a common feature of duress cases it does not constitute the foundation of the doctrine. The reason for this is that the presence of substantive unfairness is not, of itself, sufficient to constitute duress, nor is its absence sufficient to negative the existence of duress. For example, if I am compelled by circumstances to sell my house quickly and forced to lower the price, the unfairness of the price will not of itself suffice to demonstrate the existence of duress. On the other hand, if a robber forces me at gunpoint to sell my house for a fair price, the fairness of the price will not prevent me from setting aside the contract on the ground of duress. What is wrong with the contract is not the fairness or the unfairness of the terms of the contract, but the nature of the threats that have been used in order to induce me to enter into it. In other words duress is an example of 'procedural unfairness' (on which see p. 793 below). It is therefore suggested that the basis of the doctrine is correctly located in the lack of consent on the part of the person seeking to set aside the contract and the wrongful or illegitimate nature of the threats made by the other party in order to induce entry into the contract. These twin elements are to be found in all cases of duress, namely duress of the person, duress of goods, and economic duress.

3. DURESS OF THE PERSON

Duress of the person is a well recognized form of duress and its operation is illustrated by the following case:

Barton v. Armstrong

[1976] AC 104, Privy Council

Armstrong and Barton were the major shareholders in a company, Landmark Corporation Ltd, which was involved in the development of a building estate which was to be known as 'Paradise Waters'. Armstrong was the chairman and Barton was the managing director. They were locked in a power struggle for control of the company which, over the years, became increasingly bitter. Barton initially succeeded in obtaining the removal of Armstrong as chairman of the company, and then negotiations began as to the terms on which Armstrong's interest was to be bought out. Armstrong demanded that

Landmark repay to him a loan of $400,000 which was stated to be payable forthwith in the event of Armstrong being removed from the chairmanship of Landmark. Barton hoped to be able to pay off Armstrong by negotiating a loan from United Dominions Corporation (Australia) Ltd (UDC) but UDC, despite initial appearances to the contrary, refused to provide the loan. In these circumstances Barton entered into negotiations with a representative of Armstrong, and these negotiations resulted in a deed of 17 January 1967 under which Barton agreed, inter alia, to repay the loan of $400,000, to pay Armstrong $140,000, and to buy his shares for $180,000. An order for the winding up of Landmark was made on 11 January 1968 but on 10 January Barton commenced a suit in equity in which he alleged that he had been coerced by Armstrong into agreeing to the terms of the deed by threats that he would be murdered and by the exertion of other unlawful pressure over him. He therefore sought a declaration that the deed was 'void' so far as it concerned him. The trial judge, Street J, found that Armstrong had indeed threatened Barton and his family, but held that Barton's primary and predominant reason for entering into the transaction was a commercial one, namely to ensure the survival of the company by ridding it of Armstrong. The Court of Appeal of New South Wales dismissed Barton's appeal. Barton appealed to the Privy Council who, by a majority (Lord Wilberforce and Lord Simon of Glaisdale dissenting), allowed the appeal on the ground that Armstrong's threats were a reason for Barton entering into the agreement and that he was entitled to relief even though he might well have entered into the contract had Armstrong not threatened him in the way in which he had done. The deeds in question were therefore declared to be void so far as they concerned Barton.

Lord Cross of Chelsea [delivering the judgment of the majority of their Lordships]
Their Lordships turn now to consider the question of law which provoked a difference of opinion in the Court of Appeal Division. It is hardly surprising that there is no direct authority on the point, for if A threatens B with death if he does not execute some document and B, who takes A's threats seriously, executes the document it can be only in the most unusual circumstances that there can be any doubt whether the threats operated to induce him to execute the document. But this is a most unusual case and the findings of fact made below do undoubtedly raise the question whether it was necessary for Barton in order to obtain relief to establish that he would not have executed the deed in question but for the threats. In answering this question in favour of Barton, Jacobs JA relied both on a number of old common law authorities on the subject of 'duress' and also—by way of analogy—on later decisions in equity with regard to the avoidance of deeds on the ground of fraud. Their Lordships do not think that the common law authorities are of any real assistance for it seems most unlikely that the authors of the statements relied on had the sort of problem which has arisen here in mind at all. On the other hand they think that the conclusion to which Jacobs JA came was right and that it is supported by the equity decisions. The scope of common law duress was very limited and at a comparatively early date equity began to grant relief in cases where the disposition in question had been procured by the exercise of pressure which the Chancellor considered to be illegitimate—although it did not amount to common law duress. Th re was a parallel development in the field of dispositions induced by fraud. At common law the only remedy available to the man defrauded was an action for deceit but equity in the same period in which it was building up the doctrine of 'undue influence' came to entertain proceedings to set aside dispositions which had been obtained by fraud: see

Holdsworth, A History of English law, vol V (1924), 328–9. There is an obvious analogy between setting aside a disposition for duress or undue influence and setting it aside for fraud. In each case—to quote the words of Holmes J in *Fairbanks* v. *Snow* (1887) 13 NE 596, 598—'the party has been subjected to an improper motive for action'. Again the similarity of the effect in law of metus and dolus in connection with dispositions of property is noted by Stair in his *Institutions of the Law of Scotland*, New edn (1832), Book IV, title 40.25. Had Armstrong made a fraudulent misrepresentation to Barton for the purpose of inducing him to execute the deed of January 17, 1967, the answer to the problem which has arisen would have been clear. If it were established that Barton did not allow the representation to affect his judgment then he could not make it a ground for relief even though the representation was designed and known by Barton to be designed to affect his judgment. If on the other hand Barton relied on the misrepresentation Armstrong could not have defeated his claim to relief by showing that there were other more weighty causes which contributed to his decision to execute the deed, for in this field the court does not allow an examination into the relative importance of contributory causes. 'Once make out that there has been anything like deception, and no contract resting in any degree on that foundation can stand': per Lord Cranworth LJ in *Reynell* v. *Sprye* (1852) 1 De GM & G 660, 708. . . . Their Lordships think that the same rule should apply in cases of duress and that if Armstrong's threats were 'a' reason for Barton's executing the deed he is entitled to relief even though he might well have entered into the contract if Armstrong had uttered no threats to induce him to do so.

It remains to apply the law to the facts. What was the state of Barton's mind when he executed the deed is, of course, a question of fact and a question the answer to which depended largely on Barton's own evidence. The judge who heard him give evidence was in a better position than anyone else to decide whether fear engendered by Armstrong's threats was 'a' reason for his executing the deed. . . . But . . . one cannot be sure that if he had applied to the facts found by him as modified by the Appeal Division what their Lordships think to be the correct principle of law he would have reached the conclusion which he did reach . . . In these circumstances their Lordships think that they can properly, and indeed should, reach their own conclusion by applying the law as they understand it to the facts found by the judge as modified by the Appeal Division. . . . If Barton had to establish that he would not have made the agreement but for Armstrong's threats, then their Lordships would not dissent from the view that he had not made out his case. But no such onus lay on him. On the contrary it was for Armstrong to establish, if he could, that the threats which he was making and the unlawful pressure which he was exerting for the purpose of inducing Barton to sign the agreement and which Barton knew were being made and exerted for this purpose in fact contributed nothing to Barton's decision to sign. The judge has found that during the 10 days or so before the documents were executed Barton was in genuine fear that Armstrong was planning to have him killed if the agreement was not signed. His state of mind was described by the judge as one of 'very real mental torment' and he believed that his fears would be at an end when once the documents were executed. It is true that the judge was not satisfied that Vojinovic [who was alleged by Barton to have been hired by Armstrong to kill him] had been employed by Armstrong but if one man threatens another with unpleasant consequences if he does not act in a particular way, he must take the risk that the impact of his threats may be accentuated by extraneous circumstances for which he is not in fact responsible. It is true that on the facts as their Lordships assume them to have been

Armstrong's threats may have been unnecessary; but it would be unrealistic to hold that they played no part in making Barton decide to execute the documents. The proper inference to be drawn from the facts found is, their Lordships think, that though it may be that Barton would have executed the documents even if Armstrong had made no threats and exerted no unlawful pressure to induce him to do so the threats and unlawful pressure in fact contributed to his decision to sign the documents and to recommend their execution by Landmark and the other parties to them. It may be, of course, that Barton's fear of Armstrong had evaporated before he issued his writ in this action but Armstrong—understandably enough—expressly disclaimed reliance on the defence of delay on Barton's part in repudiating the deed.

In the result therefore the appeal should be allowed and a declaration made that the deeds in question were executed by Barton under duress and are void so far as concerns him.

. . .

Lord Wilberforce and Lord Simon of Glaisdale [dissenting]

The reason why we do not agree with the majority decision is, briefly, that we regard the issues in this case as essentially issues of fact, issues moreover of a character particularly within the sphere of the trial judge bearing, as they do, upon motivation and credibility. On all important issues, clear findings have been made by Street J and concurred in by the Court of Appeal—either unanimously or by majority. Accepted rules of practice and, such rules apart, sound principle should, in our opinion, prevent a second court of appeal from reviewing them in the absence of some miscarriage of justice, or some manifest and important error of law or misdirection. In our view no such circumstance exists in this case. Before stating those findings of fact, which are to our mind conclusive, we think it desirable to define in our own way the legal basis on which they rest.

The action is one to set aside an apparently complete and valid agreement on the ground of duress. The basis of the plaintiff's claim is, thus, that though there was apparent consent there was no true consent to the agreement: that the agreement was not voluntary.

This involves consideration of what the law regards as voluntary, or its opposite; for in life, including the life of commerce and finance, many acts are done under pressure, sometimes overwhelming pressure, so that one can say that the actor had no choice but to act. Absence of choice in this sense does not negate consent in law: for this the pressure must be one of a kind which the law does not regard as legitimate. Thus, out of the various means by which consent may be obtained—advice, persuasion, influence, inducement, representation, commercial pressure—the law has come to select some which it will not accept as a reason for voluntary action: fraud, abuse of relation of confidence, undue influence, duress or coercion. In this the law, under the influence of equity, has developed from the old common law conception of duress—threat to life and limb—and it has arrived at the modern generalisation expressed by Holmes J—'subjected to an improper motive for action': *Fairbanks* v. *Snow*, 13 NE Reporter 596, 598.

In an action such as the present, then, the first step required of the plaintiff is to show that some illegitimate means of persuasion was used. That there were threats to Barton's life was found by the judge . . .

The next necessary step would be to establish the relationship between the illegitimate means used and the action taken. For the purposes of the present case (reserving our opinion as to cases which may arise in other contexts) we are prepared to accept, as the formula most favourable to the appellant, the test proposed by the majority, namely, that the illegitimate means used was *a* reason (not *the* reason, nor the *predominant* reason, nor the *clinching* reason) why the complainant acted as he did. We are also prepared to accept that a decisive answer is not obtainable by asking the question whether the contract would have been made even if there had been no threats because, even if the answer to this question is affirmative, that does not prove that the contract was not made because of the threats.

Assuming therefore that what has to be decided is whether the illegitimate means used was a reason why the complainant acted as he did, it follows that his reason for acting must (unless the case is one of automatism which this is not) be a conscious reason so that the complainant can give evidence of it: 'I acted because I was forced'. If his evidence is honest and accepted, that will normally conclude the issue. If, moreover, he gives evidence, it is necessary for the court to evaluate his evidence by testing it against his credibility and his actions.

In this case Barton gave evidence—his was, for practical purposes, the only evidence supporting his case. The judge rejected it in important respects and accepted it in others. The issues as to Barton's motivations were issues purely of fact (that motivation is a question of fact hardly needs authority, but see *Cox* v. *Smail* [1912] VLR 274 per Cussen J): the findings as to motivation were largely, if not entirely, findings as to credibility. It would be difficult to find matters more peculiarly than these within the field of the trial judge who saw both contestants in the box, and who dealt carefully and at length with the credibility, or lack of credibility, of each of them . . .

In our opinion the case is far from being one in which a second appellate court should reverse findings made below and endorsed by a Court of Appeal. Respect for such findings—particularly where the issues depend so much upon credibility and an estimate of rival personalities—appears to us to be a central pillar of the appellate process. It is perhaps otiose, but also fair to the judges below, to say that we have no ground for thinking that the factual conclusions which they reached after so prolonged a search did not represent the truth of the situation—or at least the nearest approximation to truth that was attainable.

We would dismiss the appeal.

COMMENTARY

The primary significance of *Barton* lies in the test applied by the court to determine whether there was a sufficient causal link between the pressure applied by Armstrong and Barton's decision to enter into the agreement on the terms on which he did. It was held that it sufficed for Barton to prove that the threats were 'a' reason which induced him to execute the deed. The threats did not have to be 'the' reason, the 'predominant' reason, or the 'clinching' reason. This is a very low threshold for a claimant to overcome. The analogy that was drawn by Lord Cross was with cases of fraudulent misrepresentation where a similar test is employed. The appropriateness of the analogy may be doubted. Fraud is a serious matter which must be clearly and distinctly proved (see *Derry* v. *Peek* (1889) 14 App Cas 337, p. 703 above). Duress, on the other hand, has different shades of wrongdoing. The degree of turpitude in cases of economic duress may be very much less than the threats to kill that were uttered in

Barton. It is therefore not surprising to find that in cases of economic duress there is authority which supports the existence of a more exacting causal requirement, namely that the threat must have been a 'significant' cause of the claimant's decision to enter into the contract (on which see further p. 744 below).

The second point that is worth noting is that the Privy Council were content to accept the submission of counsel for Barton that the effect of duress was to render the deed 'void' as far as he was concerned. This is contrary to the generally accepted view (see, for example, *Pao On* v. *Lau Yiu Long* [1980] AC 614, p. 729 below) which is that the effect of duress is to render the contract voidable (that is to say, it is valid until it has been set aside). It is not clear why the Privy Council acceded to the submission that duress rendered the deed 'void'. It may be that the point was never argued and that the assumption made that the deed was void was simply incorrect (it is certainly very difficult to reconcile with subsequent authority). There is, however, another possible view. It depends upon the conceptual foundation of duress. If it is the case that duress can rest on the absence of consent on the part of the party seeking to set aside the contract (or, as the case may be, the deed) then it becomes more plausible to argue that absence of consent can render a contract void. The difficulty with this argument is that in cases such as *Universe Tankships of Monrovia* v. *International Transport Workers Federation (The Universe Sentinel)* [1983] 1 AC 366 (p. 731 below) and *Dimskal Shipping Co SA* v. *International Transport Workers' Federation (The Evia Luck)* [1992] 2 AC 152 (p. 744 below) the House of Lords implicitly rejected the proposition that there is an absence of consent in duress cases. This being the case, it is more likely that duress renders a contract voidable rather than void.

The final point to note regarding *Barton* relates to the illegitimacy of the pressure exerted by Armstrong. It was not necessary for their Lordships to consider the meaning of 'illegitimacy' given that a threat to kill someone is self-evidently illegitimate. More difficulty has been caused in cases where the threat is not one of harm to the claimant but a threat to make use of the legal process. A threat to resort to law does not generally constitute duress. For example, there is nothing improper in threatening to sue someone for a debt in the case where there is a bona fide belief that the debt is owed. Matters are otherwise where the legal process is used for an improper purpose, for example to extract a promise of payment in return for not initiating a prosecution against someone. The ground on which such agreements tend to be set aside is not duress but undue influence (on which see Chapter 19 below). But it has to be remembered that the doctrine of duress was under-developed at the time at which many of these cases were decided and, were they to be decided today, they might be treated as cases of duress. An example is provided by the case of *Mutual Finance Ltd* v. *John Wetton & Sons Ltd* [1937] 2 KB 389. The plaintiff finance company entered into a contract of hire-purchase with a friend of Joseph Wetton. As a condition of entering into the agreement, the plaintiffs required a counter-guarantee from the defendant company. Joseph Wetton, who had previously been a director of the company, forged the signatures of his brother, Percy, and father, William (who were directors of the company), on the guarantee. When the friend defaulted the plaintiffs agreed that another purchaser could take over the contract, but insisted that the defendant company take over the guarantee. The plaintiffs did not utter any explicit threats that they would prosecute Joseph if a guarantee was not given by the company, but they knew that Percy would never have signed the guarantee on behalf of the company had it not been for the fact that his father was in very poor health and that he, Percy, believed that the shock of any such prosecution might endanger his father's life. When there was a further default on the hire-purchase contract the plaintiffs sought to enforce the guarantee against the defendant company. It was held that they could not do so and that the defendants were entitled to avoid the guarantee on the ground that it had been procured by undue influence.

4. DURESS OF GOODS

The law relating to duress of goods has struggled for recognition. For many years the courts held that the unlawful detention of another's goods did not constitute duress. The principal authority for this proposition was:

Skeate v. Beale
(1841) 11 Ad & E 983, Court of King's Bench

The plaintiff distrained for arrears of rent, claiming that £19 10s was due from the defendant. The defendant agreed that, if the distress was withdrawn, he would pay £3 7s immediately and the outstanding £16 2s 6d within a month. He failed to pay the sum so promised and the plaintiff sued to recover the outstanding amount. The defendant argued that the seizure had been wrongful as the only sum due was £3 7s 6d and that he entered into the agreement only to prevent the plaintiff from carrying out his threat to sell the goods. It was held that the defendant was not entitled to set aside the transaction and that the plaintiff was entitled to judgment for the sum claimed.

Lord Denman CJ [delivering the judgment of the court]
We consider the law to be clear, and founded on good reason, that an agreement is not void because made under duress of goods. There is no distinction in this respect between a deed and an agreement not under seal; and, with regard to the former, the law is laid down . . . and the distinction pointed out between duress of, or menace to, the person, and duress of goods. The former is a constraining force, which not only takes away the free agency, but may leave no room for appeal to the law for a remedy: a man, therefore, is not bound by the agreement which he enters into under such circumstances: but the fear that goods may be taken or injured does not deprive any one of his free agency who possesses that ordinary degree of firmness which the law requires all to exert. It is not necessary now to enter into the consideration of cases in which it has been held that money paid to redeem goods wrongfully seized, or to prevent their wrongful seizure, may be recovered back in an action for money had and received: for the distinction between those cases and the present, which must be taken to be that of an agreement, not compulsorily but voluntarily entered into, is obvious. *Lindon* v. *Hooper* (1 Cowp 414), and *Knibbs* v. *Hall* (1 Esp 84), are, however, authorities to shew that, even if the money had been paid in this case, instead of the agreement to pay it entered into, no action for money had and received could have been sustained by the now defendant. For, although

there is a difference in the circumstances, and, the distress having been made, and some rent admitted to be in arrear, no replevin could have been successfully made, yet if the plaintiff distrained goods of the value of 20l. when little more than 3l. were due, there is no doubt that, on payment of the value of the goods, or the sum claimed, an action would have lain for the excessive distress. And it is of great importance that parties should be holden to those remedies for injuries which the law prescribes, rather than allowed to enter into agreements with a view to prevent them, intending at the time not to keep their contracts. In the argument for the defendant, reliance was placed on the facts that the agreement was entered into under protest, and that the plaintiff must have known that only the smaller amount of rent was due. It is unnecessary to consider what the effect of these would have been; for neither of them is alleged in the plea. As, therefore, this plea relies solely on the menace as to the goods, under which the agreement was made, for avoiding it, we think it discloses no answer to the declaration . . .

COMMENTARY

While the unlawful detention of another's goods did not constitute duress, there was at the same time authority to support the proposition that money paid to release goods which had been unlawfully detained could be recovered. Authority for the latter proposition is *Astley* v. *Reynolds* (1731) 2 Str 915. The plaintiff pawned plate to the defendant for £20. Three years later the defendant refused to allow the plaintiff to redeem the goods unless he paid him interest of £10. The plaintiff tendered £4 but the defendant refused to accept it and refused to release the plate. The plaintiff eventually paid the £10 in order to get his goods back, and then brought an action to recover the excess which he had paid over the legal interest which the defendant was entitled to charge. It was held that the plaintiff was entitled to the recovery of the money so paid under compulsion. Holt CJ stated (at p. 916):

We think . . . that this is a payment by compulsion; the plaintiff might have such an immediate want of his goods, that an action of trover would not do his business: where the rule volenti non fit injuria is applied, it must be where the party had his freedom of exercising his will, which this man had not: we must take it he paid the money relying on his legal remedy to get it back again.

As Goff and Jones have pointed out (*The Law of Restitution* (6th edn, Sweet & Maxwell, 2002), p. 308), the decisions in *Skeate* and *Astley* require a distinction to be drawn between the following two cases:

(1) A demands a sum of money from B under duress of goods. B pays the money. He can recover it.
(2) A extracts from B under similar duress a promise to pay a sum of money. Provided there is some consideration for the promise, B is bound to pay the money.

Goff and Jones continue (at pp. 308–309):

It is difficult to support a distinction of this kind since there must have been a *scintilla temporis* when [B] must have agreed to pay before making the payment. In *Skeate* v. *Beale* Lord Denman CJ justified the rule on the ground that, whereas duress to the person is a 'constraining force', 'the fear that goods may be taken or injured does not deprive anyone of his free agency who possesses that ordinary degree of firmness which the law requires all to exert'. But this requirement of bravery has surely now been abandoned. In fact, the rule in *Skeate* v. *Beale* is in direct conflict with the modern view of duress, namely, that where a transaction has been entered into as a result of illegitimate pressure, consent has not been freely given and the transaction is voidable . . . *Skeate* v. *Beale* is no longer good law. An agreement induced by duress of goods is voidable at the instance of the coerced party, so that any money paid thereunder will be recoverable in restitution.

Authority for the proposition that *Skeate* v. *Beale* is no longer good law is to be found in the speech of Lord Goff in *Dimskal Shipping Co SA* v. *International Transport Workers' Federation (The Evia Luck)* [1992] 2 AC 152 (p. 744 below).

5. ECONOMIC DURESS

As has been noted (p. 715 above), economic duress was a late arrival in English law, not being formally recognized until the decision of Kerr J in *Occidental Worldwide Investment Corporation* v. *Skibs A/S Avanti (The Siboen and The Sibotre)* [1976] 1 Lloyd's Rep 293. Since then it has had a somewhat chequered career. One of the principal difficulties has been in identifying the elements that have to be proved in order to make out a case of economic duress. There has been a distinct change in emphasis in the case-law as it has developed. In *Pao On* v. *Lau Yiu Long* [1980] AC 614 (p. 729 below) Lord Scarman famously stated that duress 'is a coercion of the will so as to vitiate consent'. This focused attention on the party subject to the pressure rather than upon the conduct of the person applying the pressure. But in *Universe Tankships of Monrovia* v. *International Transport Workers Federation (The Universe Sentinel)* [1983] 1 AC 366 (p. 731 below) and *Dimskal Shipping Co SA* v. *International Transport Workers' Federation (The Evia Luck)* [1992] 2 AC 152 (p. 744 below) the focus of judicial attention shifted away from the thought processes of the victim towards the nature of the pressure applied by the other party. Thus the vital question became whether or not the pressure applied by the defendant was 'illegitimate'. This approach did not dispense with all inquiry into the decision-making process of the victim of the duress. It remained important to consider the position of the victim but only for the purpose of establishing whether or not there was a sufficient causal link between the pressure applied by the defendant and the decision of the claimant to enter into the contract. A third element was added to the mix by the decision in *B & S Contracts and Design Ltd* v. *Victor Green Publications Ltd* [1984] ICR 419 (p. 735 below), where the Court of Appeal examined the alternatives that were open to the party alleged to be subject to the duress. That these three elements are commonly seen to be the essential ingredients of a duress claim can be demonstrated by reference to the following passage from the judgment of Dyson J in *DSDN Subsea Ltd* v. *Petroleum Geo-Services ASA* [2000] BLR 530 when he stated (at p. 545) that:

the ingredients of actionable duress are that there must be pressure, (a) whose practical effect is that there is compulsion on, or a lack of practical choice for, the victim, (b) which is illegitimate, and (c) which is a significant cause inducing the claimant to enter into the contract.

We shall now examine the leading cases on economic duress. In doing so we shall take a chronological approach so that we can see the way in which the law has evolved. The chapter will then conclude by seeking to draw the various threads together.

North Ocean Shipping Co Ltd v. Hyundai Construction Co Ltd (The Atlantic Baron)

[1979] QB 705, Queen's Bench Division

In 1972 the defendants entered into a contract under which they agreed to construct a tanker for the plaintiffs. The contract stated that the price, which was to be paid in US dollars, was not to be subject to adjustment except in certain specific circumstances (which did not occur). In June 1983, after the devaluation of the dollar by 10% the defendants demanded that they be paid an extra 10% for the work done under the contract. The plaintiffs refused to pay the money so demanded on the ground that there was no basis in law for the demand, and they suggested that the matter be referred to arbitration. The defendants refused to agree to this suggestion and they threatened to terminate the contract if the sum was not paid. The plaintiffs were advised that the defendants were not entitled to make such a demand under the terms of the contract but, as a result of an advantageous sub-contract into which they had entered, they were anxious to obtain delivery of the tanker at the agreed time, and so they promised to pay the extra sum demanded. They paid the additional 10% on each of the remaining instalments, and the ship was delivered to the plaintiffs in November 1974. In July 1975 the plaintiffs sought to recover the extra 10% on the ground that there was no consideration for their payment and that they had agreed to make the payment only when subject to duress. The court held that there was consideration to support the agreement but that the plaintiffs had entered into the contract as a result of duress. However the plaintiffs were held not to be entitled to set aside the contract because they had affirmed the contract by making the final payments without protest and by their delay in making their claim for repayment.

Mocatta J

Having reached the conclusion that there was consideration for the agreement made on June 28 and 29, 1973, I must next consider whether even if that agreement, varying the terms of the original shipbuilding contract of April 10, 1972, was made under a threat to break that original contract and the various increased instalments were made consequently under the varied agreement, the increased sums can be recovered as money had and received. Mr Longmore [counsel for the plaintiffs] submitted that they could be, provided they were involuntary payments and not made, albeit perhaps with some grumbling, to close the transaction.

Certainly this is the well-established position if payments are made, for example, to avoid the wrongful seizure of goods where there is no prior agreement to make such payments. The best known English case to this effect is probably *Maskell* v. *Horner* [1915] 3 KB 106, where the plaintiff had over many years paid illegal tolls on his goods offered for sale in the vicinity of Spitalfields Market. The plaintiff had paid under protest, though the process was so prolonged, that the protests became almost in the nature of jokes, though the plaintiff had in fact suffered seizures of his goods when he had not paid. Lord Reading CJ did not say that express words of protest were always necessary, though they might be useful evidence to negative voluntary payments; the circumstances taken as a whole must indicate that the payments were involuntary. Buckley LJ at 124, regarded the making of a protest before paying to avoid the wrongful seizure of one's goods as 'a further factor', which went to show that the payment was not voluntary. Pickford LJ at

126 likewise regarded the fact of protest as 'some indication' that the payer intended to resist the claim.

There are a number of well-known examples in the books of English cases where the payments made have been involuntary by reason of some wrongful threatened action or inaction in relation to goods and have subsequently been recovered, but where the issue has not been complicated by the payments having been made under a contract. Some of these cases have concerned threats to seize, seizure or wrongful detention of goods, *Maskell* v. *Horner* being the best known modern example of the former two categories and *Astley* v. *Reynolds* (1731) 2 Str 915 [p. 723 above] a good example of the latter category . . .

Mr Longmore referred me to other cases decided in this country bordering upon what he called economic duress as distinct from duress to goods. Thus in *Parker* v. *Great Western Railway Co* (1844) 7 Man & G 253, approved in *Great Western Railway Co* v. *Sutton* (1869) LR 4 HL 226, it was held that the railway was not entitled to differentiate adversely between charges on goods made against one carrier or packer using the railway and others. Excess charges payable by such persons were recovered. In advising the House of Lords in the latter case, Willes J said, at 249:

'. . . I have always understood that when a man pays more than he is bound to do by law for the performance of a duty which the law says is owed to him for nothing, or for less than he has paid, there is a compulsion or concussion in respect of which he is entitled to recover the excess by condictio indebiti, or action for money had and received. This is every day's practice as to excess freight' . . .

There has been considerable discussion in the books whether, if an agreement is made under duress of goods to pay a sum of money and there is some consideration for the agreement, the excess sum can be recovered. The authority for this suggested distinction is *Skeate* v. *Beale* (1841) 11 Ad & El 983 [p. 722 above]. It was there said by Lord Denman CJ that an agreement was not void because made under duress of goods, the distinction between that case and the cases of money paid to recover goods wrongfully seized being said to be obvious in that the agreement was not compulsorily but voluntarily entered into. In the slightly later case of *Wakefield* v. *Newbon* (1844) 6 QB 276, Lord Denman CJ referred to cases such as *Skeate* v. *Beale* as 'that class where the parties have come to a voluntary settlement of their concerns, and have chosen to pay what is found due'. Kerr J in *Occidental Worldwide Investment Corporation* v. *Skibs A/S Avanti (The Siboen and The Sibotre)* [1976] 1 Lloyd's Rep 293, 335, gave strong expression to the view that the suggested distinction based on *Skeate* v. *Beale* would not be observed today. He said, though obiter, that *Skeate* v. *Beale* would not justify a decision:

'For instance, if I should be compelled to sign a lease or some other contract for a nominal but legally sufficient consideration under an imminent threat of having my house burnt down or a valuable picture slashed, though without any threat of physical violence to anyone, I do not think that the law would uphold the agreement.'

I was referred to a number of cases decided overseas . . . Isaacs J in *Smith* v. *William Charlick Ltd* (1924) 34 CLR 38, 56 . . . said:

'. . . "Compulsion" in relation to a payment of which refund is sought, and whether it is also variously called "coercion", "exaction" or "force", includes every species of duress or conduct analogous to duress, actual or threatened, exerted by or on behalf of the payee and applied to the person or the property or any right of the person who pays. . . . Such compulsion is a legal wrong, and the law provides a remedy by raising a fictional promise to repay.'

These cases do not, however, expressly deal with the position arising when the threat or compulsion result in a new or varied contract. This was, or something very like it, however, the position in *Sundell's* case, 56 SR (NSW) 323. . . . It would seem, . . . that the Australian courts would be prepared to allow the recovery of excess money paid, even under a new contract, as the result of a threat to break an earlier contract, since the threat or compulsion would be applied to the original contractual right of the party subject to the compulsion or economic duress. This also seems to be the view in the United States, where this was one of the grounds of decision in *King Construction Co* v. *WM Smith Electric Co* (1961) 350 SW 2d 940. This view also accords with what was said in *D & C Builders Ltd* v. *Rees* [1966] 2 QB 617, 625, per Lord Denning MR: 'No person can insist on a settlement procured by intimidation.' . . .

I may here usefully cite a further short passage from the valuable remarks of Kerr J in *The Siboen and The Sibotre* [1976] 1 Lloyd's Rep 293, 336, where, after referring to three of the Australian cases I have cited, he said:

'It is true that in [*D & C Builders Ltd* v. *Rees*], and in all the three Australian cases, it was held that there had been no consideration for the settlement which the courts reopened. But I do not think that it would have made any difference if the defendants in these cases had also insisted on some purely nominal but legally sufficient consideration. If the contract is void the consideration would be recoverable in quasi-contract; if it is voidable equity could rescind the contract and order the return of the consideration.'

It is also interesting at this point to quote a few sentences from an article entitled 'Duress As A Vitiating Factor in Contract' by Mr Beatson, Fellow of Merton College, Oxford in (1974) 33 *Cambridge Law Journal* 97, 108:

'It is submitted that there is no reason for making a distinction between actual payments and agreements to pay. If that is so there is nothing to prevent a court from finding that duress of goods is a ground upon which the validity of a contract can be impeached The law was accurately stated by the courts of South Carolina as early as 1795, when it was said that ". . . whenever assumpsit will lie for money extorted by duress of goods, a party may defend himself against any claim upon him for money to be paid in consequence of any contract made under similar circumstances." '

Before proceeding further it may be useful to summarise the conclusions I have so far reached. First, I do not take the view that the recovery of money paid under duress other than to the person is necessarily limited to duress to goods falling within one of the categories hitherto established by the English cases. I would respectfully follow and adopt the broad statement of principle laid down by Isaacs J cited earlier and frequently quoted and applied in the Australian cases. Secondly, from this it follows that the compulsion may take the form of 'economic duress' if the necessary facts are proved. A threat to break a contract may amount to such 'economic duress'. Thirdly, if there has been such a form of duress leading to a contract for consideration, I think that contract is a voidable one which can be avoided and the excess money paid under it recovered.

I think the facts found in this case do establish that the agreement to increase the price by 10% reached at the end of June 1973 was caused by what may be called 'economic duress'. The Yard were adamant in insisting on the increased price without having any legal justification for so doing and the owners realised that the Yard would not accept anything other than an unqualified agreement to the increase. The owners might have claimed damages in arbitration against the Yard with all the inherent unavoidable uncertainties of litigation, but in view of the position of the Yard vis-à-vis their relations with Shell it would be unreasonable to hold that this is the course they should have taken: see *Astley* v. *Reynolds* (1731) 2 Str 915. The owners made a very reasonable offer of arbitration coupled with security for any award in the Yard's favour that might be made, but this was refused. They then made their agreement, which can truly I think be said to have been made under compulsion, by the telex of June 28 without prejudice to their rights. I do not consider the Yard's ignorance of the Shell charter material. It may well be that had they known of it they would have been even more exigent.

If I am right in the conclusion reached with some doubt earlier that there was consideration for the 10 % increase agreement reached at the end of June 1973, and it be right to regard this as having been reached under a kind of duress in the form of economic pressure, then what is said in *Chitty on Contracts*, 24th edn (1977), vol 1, para 442, to which both counsel referred me, is relevant, namely, that a contract entered into under duress is voidable and not void:

> '. . . consequently a person who has entered into a contract under duress, may either affirm or avoid such contract after the duress has ceased; and if he has so voluntarily acted under it with a full knowledge of all the circumstances he may be held bound on the ground of ratification, or if, after escaping from the duress, he takes no steps to set aside the transaction, he may be found to have affirmed it' . . .

no protest of any kind was made by the owners after their telex of June 28, 1973. . . . There was . . . a delay between November 27, 1974, when the *Atlantic Baron* was delivered and July 30, 1975, before the owners put forward their claim.

The owners were, therefore, free from the duress on November 27, 1974, and took no action by way of protest or otherwise between their important telex of June 28, 1973, and their formal claim for the return of the excess 10% paid of July 30, 1975. . . . One cannot dismiss this delay as of no significance, though I would not consider it conclusive by itself. I do not attach any special importance to the lack of protest made at the time of the assignment, since the documents made no reference to the increased 10 per cent. However, by the time the *Atlantic Baron* was due for delivery in November 1974, market conditions had changed radically . . . and the owners must have been aware of this. . . . I have come to the conclusion that the important points here are that since there was no danger at this time in registering a protest, the final payments were made without any qualification and were followed by a delay until July 31, 1975, before the owners put forward their claim, the correct inference to draw, taking an objective view of the facts, is that the action and inaction of the owners can only be regarded as an affirmation of the variation in June 1973 of the terms of the original contract by the agreement to pay the additional 10 per cent. . . . I do not think that an intention on the part of the owners not to affirm the agreement for the extra payments not indicated to the Yard can avail them in their view of their overt acts. As was said in *Deacon* v. *Transport Regulation Board* [1958] VR 458, 460 in considering whether a payment was made voluntarily or not: 'No secret mental reservation of the doer is material. The question is—what would his conduct indicate to a reasonable man as his mental state'. I think this test is equally applicable to the decision this court has to make whether a voidable contract has been affirmed or not, and I have applied this test in reaching the conclusion I have just expressed.

I think I should add very shortly that having considered the many authorities cited, even if I had come to a different conclusion on the issue about consideration, I would have come to the same decision adverse to the owners on the question whether the payments were made voluntarily in the sense of being made to close the transaction.

COMMENTARY

The significance of this case lies in the acceptance of the proposition that a threatened breach of contract can constitute economic duress. In reaching this conclusion Mocatta J did not ask himself whether or not the defendants were in bad faith in demanding that the plaintiffs pay an extra 10%. The fact that he did not ask the question suggests that it is irrelevant. In any event, this case demonstrates that it is no easy task to define 'bad faith' in this context. It could be said that the defendants were in bad faith in that they knew that they were not entitled to the extra 10%. On the other hand, they had what might be called a 'good reason' for demanding the extra money on the basis that they were simply attempting to cover themselves against devaluation of the dollar: they were not seeking to exploit any vulnerability on the part of the plaintiffs. The second point which is illustrated by *The Atlantic Baron* is the need to act quickly once freed from the duress. A party who is dilatory in making a complaint of duress is likely to be held to have affirmed the contract. This leads on to the third point which is that Mocatta J concluded that duress rendered the contract voidable, and not 'void' as in *Barton* v. *Armstrong* (above). Finally, the case underlines the link between consideration and duress in that the first point taken by the plaintiffs was that there was no consideration for their promise to pay an extra 10%. Mocatta J found that consideration had been supplied but would have set the contract aside on the ground of duress had the plaintiffs not affirmed the contract. This might be said to be an example of duress being used as the more appropriate regulator of contract modifications.

Pao On v. Lau Yiu Long

[1980] AC 614, Privy Council

The facts of this case are set out at p. 227 above. The defendants' submission that the guarantee was not supported by consideration was rejected by the Privy Council. In this extract the focus is upon the defendants' submission that the guarantee was unenforceable on the ground that it had been procured by duress. The Privy Council rejected the defendants' submission and held that there had been no operative duress because the defendants could not show that their will had been coerced such as to vitiate their consent.

Lord Scarman [giving the judgment of the Board]

The third question

Duress, whatever form it takes, is a coercion of the will so as to vitiate consent. Their

Lordships agree with the observation of Kerr J in *Occidental Worldwide Investment Corporation* v. *Skibs A/S Avanti* [1976] 1 Lloyd's Rep 293, 336 that in a contractual situation commercial pressure is not enough. There must be present some factor 'which could in law be regarded as a coercion of his will so as to vitiate his consent'. This conception is in line with what was said in this Board's decision in *Barton* v. *Armstrong* [1976] AC 104, 121 by Lord Wilberforce and Lord Simon of Glaisdale—observations with which the majority judgment appears to be in agreement. In determining whether there was a coercion of will such that there was no true consent, it is material to inquire whether the person alleged to have been coerced did or did not protest; whether, at the time he was allegedly coerced into making the contract, he did or did not have an alternative course open to him such as an adequate legal remedy; whether he was independently advised; and whether after entering the contract he took steps to avoid it. All these matters are, as was recognised in *Maskell* v. *Horner* [1915] 3 KB 106, relevant in determining whether he acted voluntarily or not.

In the present case there is unanimity amongst the judges below that there was no coercion of the first defendant's will. In the Court of Appeal the trial judge's finding . . . that the first defendant considered the matter thoroughly, chose to avoid litigation, and formed the opinion that the risk in giving the guarantee was more apparent than real was upheld. In short, there was commercial pressure, but no coercion. Even if this Board was disposed, which it is not, to take a different view, it would not substitute its opinion for that of the judges below on this question of fact.

It is, therefore, unnecessary for the Board to embark upon an inquiry into the question whether English law recognises a category of duress known as 'economic duress'. But, since the question has been fully argued in this appeal, their Lordships will indicate very briefly the view which they have formed. At common law money paid under economic compulsion could be recovered in an action for money had and received: *Astley* v. *Reynolds* (1731) 2 Str 915. The compulsion had to be such that the party was deprived of 'his freedom of exercising his will' (see 916). It is doubtful, however, whether at common law any duress other than duress to the person sufficed to render a contract voidable: see *Blackstone's Commentaries*, Book 1, 12th edn 130–1 and *Skeate* v. *Beale* (1841) 11 Ad & E 983. American law (*Williston on Contracts*, 3rd edn) now recognises that a contract may be avoided on the ground of economic duress. The commercial pressure alleged to constitute such duress must, however, be such that the victim must have entered the contract against his will, must have had no alternative course open to him, and must have been confronted with coercive acts by the party exerting the pressure: *Williston on Contracts*, 3rd edn, vol. 13 (1970), section 1603. American judges pay great attention to such evidential matters as the effectiveness of the alternative remedy available, the fact or absence of protest, the availability of independent advice, the benefit received, and the speed with which the victim has sought to avoid the contract. Recently two English judges have recognised that commercial pressure may constitute duress the pressure of which can render a contract voidable: Kerr J in *Occidental Worldwide Investment Corporation* v. *Skibs A/S Avanti* [1976] 1 Lloyd's Rep 293 and Mocatta J in *North Ocean Shipping Co Ltd* v. *Hyundai Construction Co Ltd* [1979] QB 705. Both stressed that the pressure must be such that the victim's consent to the contract was not a voluntary act on his part. In their Lordships' view, there is nothing contrary to principle in recognising economic duress as a factor which may render a contract voidable, provided always that the basis of such recognition is that it must amount to a coercion of will, which vitiates consent.

It must be shown that the payment made or the contract entered into was not a voluntary act.

COMMENTARY

The significance of *Pao On* lies primarily in its adoption of the 'coercion of the will' theory. The theory has been the subject of considerable criticism on the ground that duress does not in fact 'vitiate' consent (see, for example, PS Atiyah, 'Economic Duress and the Overborne Will' (1982) 98 *LQR* 197). A party who is subject to duress does in fact choose to enter into the contract. He chooses to enter into the contract in order to avoid the greater evil presented by the threat that has been made. On the facts it was not necessary for the Privy Council to consider whether or not the pressure applied by the plaintiffs was illegitimate because the defendants failed to overcome the first hurdle of showing that they had been coerced into entering into the deed. They decided to enter into the deed for commercial reasons and they were not entitled to set it aside on the ground of duress. The conclusion of the Privy Council is unexceptional on the facts, but the reasons given in support of their conclusion are open to question, as we shall see. Once again the case illustrates the link that exists in the cases between duress and consideration (the consideration aspects of the case are discussed at pp. 227–230 above).

Universe Tankships of Monrovia v. International Transport Workers Federation (The Universe Sentinel)

[1983] 1 AC 366, House of Lords

The plaintiffs' vessel, the *Universe Sentinel*, was 'blacked' by the defendant trade union while it was docked at Milford Haven. The blacking took the form of an instruction to the tugmen at the harbour to refuse to operate their tugs. This refusal constituted a breach by the tugmen of their contracts of employment with the Harbour Authority. Negotiations then took place between the parties. The defendants demanded that the plaintiffs pay the crew of the ship $80,000 in back-pay and pay a further sum of $6,480 to the defendants' welfare fund. The plaintiffs paid the money in order to obtain the release of their vessel and then brought the present action to recover the $6,480 (but not the back-pay) which they had paid. It was conceded that the circumstances in which the payment was made amounted to economic duress but the defendants maintained that they were nevertheless entitled to retain the money because they were acting under an immunity conferred by Parliament in section 13 of the Trade Union and Labour Relations Act 1974. The House of Lords, by a majority (Lord Scarman and Lord Brandon dissenting), held that the defendants did not have the immunity which they asserted and that the money was therefore recoverable.

Lord Diplock

My Lords, I turn to the second ground on which repayment of the $6,480 is claimed, which I will call the duress point. It is not disputed that the circumstances in which ITF demanded that the shipowners should enter into the special agreement and the typescript agreement and should pay the moneys of which the latter documents acknowledge receipt, amounted to economic duress upon the shipowners; that is to say, it is conceded that the financial consequences to the shipowners of the *Universe Sentinel* continuing to be rendered off-hire under her time charter to Texaco, while the blacking continued, were so catastrophic as to amount to a coercion of the shipowners' will which vitiated their consent to those agreements and to the payments made by them to ITF. This concession makes it unnecessary for your Lordships to use the instant appeal as the occasion for a general consideration of the developing law of economic duress as a ground for treating contracts as voidable and obtaining restitution of money paid under economic duress as money had and received to the plaintiffs' use. That economic duress may constitute a ground for such redress was recognised, albeit obiter, by the Privy Council in *Pao On* v. *Lau Yiu Long* [1980] AC 614. The Board in that case referred with approval to two judgments at first instance in the commercial court which recognised that commercial pressure may constitute duress: one by Kerr J in *Occidental Worldwide Investment Corporation* v. *Skibs A/S Avanti* [1976] 1 Lloyd's Rep 293, the other by Mocatta J in *North Ocean Shipping Co Ltd* v. *Hyundai Construction Co Ltd* [1979] QB 705, which traces the development of this branch of the law from its origin in the eighteenth and early nineteenth-century cases.

It is, however, in my view crucial to the decision of the instant appeal to identify the rationale of this development of the common law. It is not that the party seeking to avoid the contract which he has entered into with another party, or to recover money that he has paid to another party in response to a demand, did not know the nature or the precise terms of the contract at the time when he entered into it or did not understand the purpose for which the payment was demanded. The rationale is that his apparent consent was induced by pressure exercised upon him by that other party which the law does not regard as legitimate, with the consequence that the consent is treated in law as revocable unless approbated either expressly or by implication after the illegitimate pressure has ceased to operate on his mind. It is a rationale similar to that which underlies the avoidability of contracts entered into and the recovery of money exacted under colour of office, or under undue influence or in consequence of threats of physical duress.

Commercial pressure, in some degree, exists wherever one party to a commercial transaction is in a stronger bargaining position than the other party. It is not, however, in my view, necessary, nor would it be appropriate in the instant appeal, to enter into the general question of the kinds of circumstances, if any, in which commercial pressure, even though it amounts to a coercion of the will of a party in the weaker bargaining position, may be treated as legitimate and, accordingly, as not giving rise to any legal right of redress. In the instant appeal the economic duress complained of was exercised in the field of industrial relations to which very special considerations apply . . .

[He then considered the relevant statutory provisions and concluded that they afforded an 'indication' which the judges should respect 'of where public policy requires that the line should be drawn between what kind of commercial pressure by a trade union upon an employer in the field of industrial relations ought to be treated as legitimised despite the fact that the will of the employer is thereby coerced, and what kind of commercial pressure in that field does amount to economic duress that entitles the employer victim to restitutionary remedies'. He concluded that the action taken by the defendants in the present case did not fall within the scope of the immunity provided by the legislation, with the consequence that the pressure was not 'legitimised' and so the defendants were liable to repay the money to the plaintiffs.]

Lord Scarman [dissenting]

It is, I think, already established law that economic pressure can in law amount to duress; and that duress, if proved, not only renders voidable a transaction into which a person has entered under its compulsion but is actionable as a tort, if it causes damage or loss: *Barton* v. *Armstrong* [1976] AC 104 and *Pao On* v. *Lau Yiu Long* [1980] AC 614. The authorities upon which these two cases were based reveal two elements in the wrong of duress: (1) pressure amounting to compulsion of the will of the victim; and (2) the illegitimacy of the pressure exerted. There must be pressure, the practical effect of which is compulsion or the absence of choice. Compulsion is variously described in the authorities as coercion or the vitiation of consent. The classic case of duress is, however, not the lack of will to submit but the victim's intentional submission arising from the realization that there is no other practical choice open to him. This is the thread of principle which links the early law of duress (threat to life or limb) with later developments when the law came also to recognize as duress first the threat to property and now the threat to a man's business or trade . . .

The absence of choice can be proved in various ways, e.g. by protest, by the absence of independent advice, or by a declaration of intention to go to law to recover the money paid or the property transferred: see *Maskell* v. *Horner* [1915] 3 KB 106. But none of these evidential matters goes to the essence of duress. The victim's silence will not assist the bully, if the lack of any practicable choice but to submit is proved. The present case is an excellent illustration. There was no protest at the time, but only a determination to do whatever was needed as rapidly as possible to release the ship. Yet nobody challenges the judge's finding that the owner acted under compulsion . . .

The real issue in the appeal is, therefore, as to the second element in the wrong duress: was the pressure applied by the ITF in the circumstances of this case one which the law recognises as legitimate? For, as Lord Wilberforce and Lord Simon of Glaisdale said in *Barton* v. *Armstrong* [1976] AC 104, 121d: 'the pressure must be one of a kind which the law does not regard as legitimate'.

As the two noble and learned Lords remarked at 121d, in life, including the life of commerce and finance, many acts are done 'under pressure, sometimes overwhelming pressure': but they are not necessarily done under duress. That depends on whether the circumstances are such that the law regards the pressure as legitimate.

In determining what is legitimate two matters may have to be considered. The first is as to the nature of the pressure. In many cases this will be decisive, though not in every case. And so the second question may have to be considered, namely, the nature of the demand which the pressure is applied to support.

The origin of the doctrine of duress in threats to life or limb, or to property, suggests strongly that the law regards the threat of unlawful action as illegitimate, whatever the demand. Duress can, of course, exist even if the threat is one of lawful action: whether it does so depends upon the nature of the demand. Blackmail is often a demand supported by a threat to do what is lawful, e.g. to report criminal conduct to the police. In many cases, therefore, 'What [one] has to justify is not the threat, but the demand . . .': see per Lord Atkin in *Thorne* v. *Motor Trade Association* [1937] AC 797, 806.

The present is a case in which the nature of the demand determines whether the pressure threatened or applied, i.e. the blacking, was lawful or unlawful. If it was unlawful, it is conceded that the owner acted under duress and can recover. If it was lawful, it is conceded that there was no duress and the sum sought by the owner is irrecoverable.

The lawfulness or otherwise of the demand depends upon whether it was an act done in contemplation or furtherance of a trade dispute. If it was, it would not be actionable in tort: section 13(1) of the Act. Although no question of tortious liability arises in this case and section 13(1) is not, therefore, directly in point, it is not possible, in my view, to say of acts which are protected by statute from suit in tort that they nevertheless can amount to duress. Parliament having enacted that such acts are not actionable in tort, it would be inconsistent with legislative policy to say that, when the remedy sought is not damages for tort but recovery of money paid, they become unlawful.

In order to determine whether the making of the demand was an act done in contemplation or furtherance of a trade dispute, it is necessary to refer to section 29 which sets out the statutory meaning of 'trade dispute'.

The issue therefore is reduced to the one question. Was the demand for contributions to the welfare fund connected with one or more of the matters specified in section 29 of the Act? It is common ground that unless the demand was connected with 'terms and conditions of employment' it was not within the section.

[After examining the relevant provisions he concluded that the demand was related to the terms and conditions of employment and so was a legitimate exercise of pressure and did not constitute duress.]

Lord Russell and **Lord Cross** delivered speeches agreeing that the appeal should be allowed. **Lord Brandon** dissented.

COMMENTARY

The importance of *The Universe Sentinel* lies in the fact that the focus of attention shifted from the 'coercion of the will' of the victim to the legitimacy of the pressure applied by the defendant. In relation to the former Lord Diplock used the language of 'apparent consent' and, while Lord Scarman referred to the 'absence of choice', he made it clear that the classic case of duress is one of 'intentional submission arising from the realisation that there is no other practical choice open to him'.

When deciding whether or not the pressure applied by the defendants was 'illegitimate', considerable emphasis was placed by their Lordships on the legislation which regulates the lawfulness of industrial action. Indeed, a large part of the speeches was taken up with an analysis of the industrial disputes legislation. In this sensitive area of the law the judges concluded that they did not have a free-hand to develop their own conception of what is or is not 'illegitimate'. Rather, they chose to reflect the standards to be found in the relevant legislation.

It seems clear from the speeches of Lord Diplock and Lord Scarman that there are two elements in any duress claim: (i) lack of consent/coercion of the will; and (ii) the illegitimacy of the pressure exerted. This combination of the two factors has been criticized by Professor Smith on the ground that 'lack of consent' and 'wrongdoing' are independent factors each of which is sufficient, on its own, to render a contract invalid. The proposition that 'wrongdoing' combined with a relevant causal link is sufficient to constitute duress is not particularly controversial. More difficult is the proposition that 'lack of consent' should suffice to render a contract invalid (a point to which we shall return, p. 744 below). In any event it is a proposition that the courts have rejected.

Finally it should be noted that the effect of economic duress was held to be to render a contract voidable (and not void). Lord Diplock added in a passage not extracted above:

The use of economic duress to induce another person to part with property or money is not a tort per se; the form that the duress takes may, or may not, be tortious. The remedy to which economic duress gives rise is not an action for damages but an action for restitution of property or money exacted under such duress and the avoidance of any contract that had been induced by it.

B & S Contracts and Design Ltd v. Victor Green Publications Ltd

[1984] ICR 419, Court of Appeal

The plaintiffs agreed to erect stands at Olympia for the defendants. The plaintiffs experienced difficulties with their workforce, who refused to erect the stands unless they were paid £9,000 severance pay. The plaintiffs offered the workmen £4,500, but this was rejected. The defendants were informed of the position and Mr Barnes, a director of the defendant company, offered to pay £4,500 as an advance payment to enable the plaintiffs to meet the claim of their workforce. This offer was rejected by the plaintiffs' financial director, Mr Fenech, who informed Mr Barnes that the plaintiffs would be unable to perform the contract unless the men could be persuaded to stay at work. Mr Barnes then said to Mr Fenech 'Well, you have me over a barrel' and so the defendants paid the extra £4,500 to the plaintiffs. The contract was duly performed but, when the plaintiffs presented the defendants with the bill, the defendants deducted the £4,500 from the contract price and paid the balance. The plaintiffs sued for £4,500 as due under the contract, and the defendants counterclaimed for the same amount as paid under duress. Sir Douglas Frank QC, sitting as a deputy judge of the High Court, dismissed the plaintiffs' claim on the ground that the money had been paid under duress. The plaintiffs appealed unsuccessfully to the Court of Appeal who also found that the money had been paid under duress.

Eveleigh LJ

For the purpose of this case it is sufficient to say that if the claimant has been influenced against his will to pay money under the threat of unlawful damage to his economic interest he will be entitled to claim that money back, and as I understand it that proposition was not dissented from.

[He considered the evidence and concluded that the defendants had been influenced against their will to pay £4,500 under the threat of unlawful damage to their economic interest.]

Griffiths LJ

I agree. The law on economic pressure creating a situation which will be recognised as duress is in the course of development, and it is clear that many difficult decisions lie ahead of the courts. Many commercial contracts are varied during their currency because the parties are faced with changing circumstances during the performance of the contract, and it is certainly not on every occasion when one of the parties unwillingly agrees to a variation that the law would consider that he had acted by reason of duress. The cases will have to be examined in the light of their particular circumstances. But two recent decisions of the highest authority—the decision of the Privy Council in *Pao On* v. *Lau Yiu Long* [1980] AC 614 and *Universe Tankships Inc of Monrovia* v. *International Transport Workers Federation* [1982] ICR 262—establish that a threatened breach of contract may impose such economic pressure that the law will recognise that a payment made as a result of the threatened breach is recoverable on the grounds of duress.

The facts of this case appear to me to be as follows. The plaintiffs intended to break their contract, subject to the effect of the force majeure clause, by allowing their workforce to walk off the job in circumstances in which they could not possibly replace it with another workforce. The defendants offered to advance the sum of £4,500 on the contract price, which would have enabled the plaintiffs to pay the men a sufficient extra sum of money to induce them to remain on the job. The plaintiffs refused this sum of money. There is no question that they refused to pay as a matter of principle. They refused to pay because they did not want to reduce the sum they would receive for the contract. They said to the defendants, 'If you will give us £4,500 we will complete the contract'. The defendants, faced with this demand, were in an impossible position. If they refused to hand over the sum of £4,500 they would not be able to erect the stands in this part of the exhibition, which would have clearly caused grave damage to their reputation and I would have thought might have exposed them to very heavy claims from the exhibitors who had leased space from them and hoped to use those stands in the ensuing exhibition. They seem to me to have been placed in the position envisaged by Lord Scarman in the Privy Council decision, *Pao On* v. *Lau Yiu Long* [1980] AC 614, in which they were faced with no alternative course of action but to pay the sum demanded of them. It was submitted to us that there was no overt demand, but it was implicit in negotiations between the parties that the plaintiffs were putting the defendants into a corner and it was quite apparent to the defendants, by reason of the plaintiffs' conduct, that unless they handed over £4,500 the plaintiffs would walk off the job. This is, in my view, a situation in which the judge was fully entitled to find in the circumstances of this case that there was duress. As the defendants' director said, he was over a barrel, he had no alternative but to pay; he had no chance of going to any other source of labour to erect the stands. That being so, the only fall-back position for the plaintiffs was the force majeure clause. Clauses of this kind have to be construed upon the basis that those relying on them will have taken all reasonable efforts to avoid the effect of the various matters set out in the clause which entitle them to vary or cancel the contract . . .

There is no doubt that the plaintiffs were faced with a strike situation and the question is, did they behave reasonably when faced with this situation? I, like Eveleigh LJ, am far from saying that whenever a contracting party with such a clause is faced with a strike situation he must give in to it in order to perform his contract. If that were the situation the clause would be absolutely worthless. But the special circumstances of this case, as I see it, are as follows. The plaintiffs were going to close down their subsidiary company; they had already dismissed the workforce and the men were working out their time. There is no question here of any ongoing industrial situation between the plaintiffs' subsidiary company and the workforce. There was no question of principle at stake; the plaintiffs were perfectly prepared to pay what the men were demanding save for the fact, they said, they did not have the money available. Well, then there came the offer of the defendants to make the money available by giving them an advance. In those circumstances I can see no reason why they should not have accepted the money and paid the workforce save their own immediate economic interests, and they chose not to do that but to put pressure on the defendants by refusing the offer and indicating that the only way out was for the defendants to hand over the £4,500 as a gift rather than as an advance.

I think that was thoroughly unreasonable behaviour, and that being so they are not entitled to rely upon the force majeure clause, and for these reasons I agree this appeal fails.

Kerr LJ

In the light of the authorities it is perhaps important to emphasise that there is no question in this case of the defendants having subsequently approbated this payment or failed to seek to avoid it, which in some cases (such as the *North Ocean Shipping Co Ltd* v. *Hyundai Construction Co Ltd* [1979] QB 705, a decision of Mocatta J, to which Eveleigh LJ has referred) would be fatal. In the present case the defendants took immediate action by deducting that £4,500 from the invoice price.

I also bear in mind that a threat to break a contract unless money is paid by the other party can, but by no means always will, constitute duress. It appears from the authorities that it will only constitute duress if the consequences of a refusal would be serious and immediate so that there is no reasonable alternative open, such as by legal redress, obtaining an injunction, etc . . . There was no other practical choice open to the defendants in the present case, and accordingly I agree that this is a case where money has been paid under duress, which was accordingly recoverable by the defendants provided they acted promptly as they did, and which they have recovered by deducting it from the contract price . . .

COMMENTARY

Griffiths and Kerr LJJ based their decision primarily upon the lack of reasonable alternatives open to the defendants. Thus Griffiths LJ stated that the defendants were in an 'impossible position' and that if they had not paid the £4,500 they would have 'caused grave damage to their reputation' and might have exposed themselves to heavy claims in damages from exhibitors who had leased space at the exhibitions. Kerr LJ stated that they had no 'reasonable alternative open, such as by legal redress'. The proposition that 'lack of reasonable alternatives' should play a dominant role in economic duress cases is a difficult one. A person who sells his house for a low price because he feels that he has no other alternative open to him cannot set aside the contract on the ground of duress. What matters is not the lack of reasonable alternatives as such, but the role of the party exerting the pressure in reducing these alternatives. However it does not follow from this that no inquiry should be made into the alternatives open to the party subject to the pressure. Consideration should be given to these alternatives but only in the context of deciding whether or not the pressure caused the party subject to the pressure to enter into the contract. The reasonableness or otherwise of the alternatives should not have a free-standing role as a separate ingredient in any test developed by the courts.

Two other points are worthy of note. First the plaintiffs denied that they had made a demand of the defendants or threatened them. The Court of Appeal rejected this submission and held that a threat to break the contract had indeed been made. There is, however, a difficulty here. A party who fears that he may be unable to perform his contractual obligations has an interest in informing the other party of this fact before the time for performance falls due so that the other party can take steps to find an alternative source of performance, if necessary. But how can a party pass on this type of information without being held to have applied economic duress to his contracting party?

The final point to note relates to the legitimacy of the threat made by the plaintiffs. There was a force majeure clause in the contract (on which see pp. 434–436 above and 893 below) which stated that:

Every effort will be made to carry out any contract based on an estimate, but the due performance of it is subject to variation or cancellation owing to an act of God, war, strikes, civil commotions, work to rule or go-slow or overtime bans, lock-out, fire, flood, drought or any other cause beyond our control, or owing to our inability to procure materials or articles except at increased prices due to any of the foregoing clauses.

The plaintiffs sought to rely on this clause for the purpose of demonstrating their entitlement to demand payment of the £4,500 but their attempt to do so failed on the ground that they had not demonstrated that they had taken 'every effort' to carry out the contract.

CTN Cash and Carry Ltd v. Gallaher

[1994] 4 All ER 714, Court of Appeal

The plaintiffs agreed to buy a consignment of cigarettes from the defendants. The defendants mistakenly delivered the cigarettes to the plaintiffs' Burnley warehouse instead of their Preston warehouse. When the mistake was discovered the defendants agreed to collect the cigarettes from Burnley and deliver them to Preston. Before they could do so, the cigarettes were stolen from the Burnley warehouse. The defendants insisted that the plaintiffs pay for the stolen cigarettes, maintaining that the cigarettes were at the plaintiffs' risk at the time they were stolen. The trial judge found that the defendants believed in all good faith that the cigarettes were at the plaintiffs' risk, but that there was no legal basis for their belief. In subsequent negotiations, the defendants made clear to the plaintiffs that, unless they paid for the cigarettes, the defendants would withdraw the credit facilities which the plaintiffs had hitherto enjoyed. The defendants were under no obligation to provide the plaintiffs with credit. The plaintiffs paid the money and then sought to recover the money on the ground that it had been paid under duress. The plaintiffs' claim failed both at first instance and in the Court of Appeal.

Steyn LJ [with whom **Farquharson LJ** agreed]
The present dispute does not concern a protected relationship. It also does not arise in the context of dealings between a supplier and a consumer. The dispute arises out of arm's length commercial dealings between two trading companies. It is true that the defendants were the sole distributors of the popular brands of cigarettes. In a sense the defendants were in a monopoly position. The control of monopolies is, however, a matter for Parliament. Moreover, the common law does not recognise the doctrine of inequality of bargaining power in commercial dealings (see *National Westminster Bank plc* v.

Morgan [1985] AC 686). The fact that the defendants were in a monopoly position cannot therefore by itself convert what is not otherwise duress into duress.

A second characteristic of the case is that the defendants were in law entitled to refuse to enter into any future contracts with the plaintiffs for any reason whatever or for no reason at all. Such a decision not to deal with the plaintiffs would have been financially damaging to the defendants, but it would have been lawful. A fortiori, it was lawful for the defendants, for any reason or for no reason, to insist that they would no longer grant credit to the plaintiffs. The defendants' demand for payment of the invoice, coupled with the threat to withdraw credit, was neither a breach of contract nor a tort.

A third, and critically important, characteristic of the case is the fact that the defendants bona fide thought that the goods were at the risk of the plaintiffs and that the plaintiffs owed the defendants the sum in question. The defendants exerted commercial pressure on the plaintiffs in order to obtain payment of a sum which they bona fide considered due to them. The defendants' motive in threatening withdrawal of credit facilities was commercial self-interest in obtaining a sum that they considered due to them.

Given the combination of these three features, I take the view that none of the cases cited to us assist the plaintiffs' case. . . . But Miss Heilbron [counsel for the plaintiffs] rightly emphasised to us that the law must have a capacity for growth in this field. I entirely agree.

I also readily accept that the fact that the defendants have used lawful means does not by itself remove the case from the scope of the doctrine of economic duress. Professor Birks, in *An Introduction to the Law of Restitution* (1989) 177, lucidly explains:

'Can lawful pressures also count? This is a difficult question, because, if the answer is that they can, the only viable basis for discriminating between acceptable and unacceptable pressures is not positive law but social morality. In other words, the judges must say what pressures (though lawful outside the restitutionary context) are improper as contrary to prevailing standards. That makes the judges, not the law or the legislature, the arbiters of social evaluation. On the other hand, if the answer is that lawful pressures are always exempt, those who devise outrageous but technically lawful means of compulsion must always escape restitution until the legislature declares the abuse unlawful. It is tolerably clear that, at least where they can be confident of a general consensus in favour of their evaluation, the courts are willing to apply a standard of impropriety rather than technical unlawfulness.'

And there are a number of cases where English courts have accepted that a threat may be illegitimate when coupled with a demand for payment even if the threat is one of lawful action (see *Thorne* v. *Motor Trade Association* [1937] AC 797 at 806–7, *Mutual Finance Ltd* v. *John Wetton & Sons Ltd* [1937] 2 KB 389 and *Universe Tankships Inc of Monrovia* v. *International Transport Workers' Federation* [1983] 1 AC 366 at 384, 401). On the other hand, Goff and Jones, *Law of Restitution* (3rd edn. 1986), 240 observed that English courts have wisely not accepted any general principle that a threat not to contract with another, except on certain terms, may amount to duress.

We are being asked to extend the categories of duress of which the law will take cognisance. That is not necessarily objectionable, but it seems to me that an extension capable of covering the present case, involving 'lawful act duress' in a commercial context in pursuit of a bona fide claim, would be a radical one with far-reaching implications.

It would introduce a substantial and undesirable element of uncertainty in the commercial bargaining process. Moreover, it will often enable bona fide settled accounts to be reopened when parties to commercial dealings fall out. The aim of our commercial law ought to be to encourage fair dealing between parties. But it is a mistake for the law to set its sights too highly when the critical inquiry is not whether the conduct is lawful but whether it is morally or socially unacceptable. That is the inquiry in which we are engaged. In my view there are policy considerations which militate against ruling that the defendants obtained payment of the disputed invoice by duress.

Outside the field of protected relationships, and in a purely commercial context, it might be a relatively rare case in which 'lawful act duress' can be established. And it might be particularly difficult to establish duress if the defendant bona fide considered that his demand was valid. In this complex and changing branch of the law I deliberately refrain from saying 'never'. But as the law stands, I am satisfied that the defendants' conduct in this case did not amount to duress.

It is an unattractive result, inasmuch as the defendants are allowed to retain a sum which at the trial they became aware was not in truth due to them. But in my view the law compels the result.

For these reasons, I would dismiss the appeal.

Sir Donald Nicholls V-C

I agree, for the reasons given by Steyn LJ, that that claim must fail. When the defendant company insisted on payment, it did so in good faith. It believed the risk in the goods had passed to the plaintiff company, so it considered it was entitled to be paid for them. The defendant company took a tough line. It used its commercial muscle. But the feature underlying and dictating this attitude was a genuine belief on its part that it was owed the sum in question. It was entitled to be paid the price for the goods. So it took the line: the plaintiff company must pay in law what it owed, otherwise its credit would be suspended.

Further, there is no evidence that the defendant's belief was unreasonable. Indeed, we were told by the defendant's counsel that he had advised his client that on the risk point the defendant stood a good chance of success. I do not see how a payment demanded and made in those circumstances can be said to be vitiated by duress.

So that must be an end to this appeal. I confess to being a little troubled at the overall outcome. At a late stage of the trial the defendant's counsel accepted that the risk in the goods had not in law passed to the plaintiff. Hence, and this must follow, the defendant company was not, and never had been, entitled to be paid for the goods. The risk remained throughout on the defendant. What also follows is that the basis on which the defendant had sought and insisted on payment was then shown to be false.

In those circumstances I confess to being a little surprised that a highly reputable tobacco manufacturer has, so far, not reconsidered the position. A claim for restitution based on wrongful retention of the money, once the risk point had been established, was not pursued before us, no doubt for good reasons. But on the sketchy facts before us, and I emphasise that we have heard argument only from the plaintiff, it does seem to me that prima facie it would be unconscionable for the defendant company to insist on retaining the money now. It demanded the money when under a mistaken belief as to its legal entitlement to be paid. It only made the demand because of its belief that it was entitled to be paid. The money was then paid to it by a plaintiff which, in practical terms, had no other option. In broad terms, in the end result the defendant may be said to have been unjustly enriched. Whether a new claim for restitution now, on the facts as they have since emerged, would succeed is not a matter I need pursue. I observe, as to that, only that the categories of unjust enrichment are not closed.

I too would dismiss this appeal.

COMMENTARY

This case provides a useful illustration of the proposition that a refusal to contract does not constitute the application of 'illegitimate pressure' for the purposes of economic duress (see also *Smith* v. *William Charlick Ltd* (1924) 34 CLR 38). However it does not provide unqualified support for this proposition because of the emphasis placed on the fact that the defendants honestly believed at the time at which they made the demand that the cigarettes were at the plaintiffs' risk. It is not entirely clear what would have been the position if the defendants had known at the time of making the demand that they were not entitled to the money. On the one hand, as Steyn LJ points out, the defendants were entitled to refuse to enter into future contracts with the plaintiffs 'for any reason whatever' and, this being the case, it is difficult to see on what basis it can be said that a refusal to contract can be illegitimate for the purposes of economic duress. On the other hand, both Steyn LJ and Nicholls V-C were careful to state that they were not deciding that a refusal to contract can 'never' constitute duress. In exceptional cases it may possibly do so.

The suggestion of Nicholls V-C that the plaintiffs might have had a claim for the return of the money paid on the ground of 'wrongful retention' is difficult to support. It frequently happens that the legal position turns out to be other than the parties originally believed but this does not generate a right to recover the money paid when the 'true' situation comes to light. Settlements of disputes would be very unstable if this was the law. So the mere fact that, with the benefit of hindsight, we know that the defendants were not entitled to the money does not remove their entitlement to keep it given that they were entitled both to make the demand and to threaten to withdraw the credit facilities.

R v. Attorney-General for England and Wales [2003] UKPC 22, Privy Council

The appellant, known simply as 'R', was a member of the SAS and, during the Gulf War of 1991, he was a member of the Bravo Two Zero patrol that was dropped behind enemy lines in Iraq in order to find Scud missiles and cut communication lines. After the war was over there was considerable concern within the SAS, and the Ministry of Defence more generally, about books written by former members of the SAS in which they gave an account (the accuracy of which was contested) of their experience as members of the Bravo Two Zero patrol. The Ministry of Defence decided to respond to this state of affairs by requiring existing SAS members to sign a confidentiality contract under which the soldiers covenanted, inter alia, not to 'disclose without express prior authority in writing from MOD any information, document or other article relating to the work of, or in support of, the United Kingdom Special Forces which is, or has been in my possession by virtue of my position as a member of any of those Forces.' The appellant signed the contract but shortly afterwards left the Army, having applied for premature voluntary release. The appellant returned to his native New Zealand and in 1998 he entered into a contract with New Zealand publishers for the publication of his own account of life as a member of the Bravo Two Zero patrol. The New Zealand publishers offered the UK rights to Hodder & Staughton, who passed a copy of the manuscript on to the Ministry of Defence. The Attorney-General, on behalf of the Crown, then commenced proceedings in the High Court of New Zealand, in which he sought an injunction to restrain publication of the book, damages, and an account of profits. The New Zealand Court of Appeal refused to grant an injunction to restrain publication of the book, but made an order for an account of profits and an assessment of damages. The appellant appealed to the Privy Council.

The appellant defended the Crown's claim for damages and an account of profits on a number of grounds, one of which was that he had entered into the contract under duress. The appellant submitted that he had signed the contract because, if he did not, he would be returned to unit ('RTU') and would no longer be a member of the SAS. Involuntary RTU was 'normally imposed as a penalty for some disciplinary offence or on grounds of professional unsuitability for the SAS' and it involved exclusion from the social life of the regiment and loss of its higher rates of pay. The Privy Council concluded that the Crown had not applied pressure on the appellant which could be described as illegitimate so that, on the facts, the doctrine of duress did not provide the appellant with a defence to the claim brought against him.

Lord Hoffmann (delivering the majority judgment of the Privy Council)

15. In *Universe Tankships Inc of Monrovia* v. *International Transport Workers Federation* [1983] 1 AC 366, 400 Lord Scarman said that there were two elements in the wrong of duress. One was pressure amounting to compulsion of the will of the victim and the second was the illegitimacy of the pressure. R says that to offer him the alternative of being returned to unit, which was regarded in the SAS as a public humiliation, was compulsion of his will. It left him no practical alternative. Their Lordships are content to assume that this was the case. But, as Lord Wilberforce and Lord Simon of Glaisdale said in *Barton* v. *Armstrong* [1976] AC 104, 121:

> 'in life . . . many acts are done under pressure, sometimes overwhelming pressure, so that one can say that the actor had no choice but to act. Absence of choice in this sense does not negate consent in law: for this the pressure must be one of a kind which the law does not regard as legitimate.'

16. The legitimacy of the pressure must be examined from two aspects: first, the nature of the pressure and secondly, the nature of the demand which the pressure is applied to support: see Lord Scarman in the *Universe Tankships* case, at p 401. Generally speaking, the threat of any form of unlawful action will be regarded as illegitimate. On the other hand, fact that the threat is lawful does not necessarily make the pressure legitimate. As Lord Atkin said in *Thorne* v. *Motor Trade Association* [1937] AC 797, 806:

> 'The ordinary blackmailer normally threatens to do what he has a perfect right to do— namely, communicate some compromising conduct to a person whose knowledge is likely to affect the person threatened . . . What he has to justify is not the threat, but the demand of money.'

17. In this case, the threat was lawful. Although return to unit was not ordinarily used except on grounds of delinquency or unsuitability and was perceived by members of the SAS as a severe penalty, there is no doubt that the Crown was entitled at its discretion to transfer any member of the SAS to another unit. Furthermore, the judge found, in para 123:

> 'The MOD could not be criticised for its motivation in introducing the contracts. They were introduced because of the concerns about the increasing number of unauthorised disclosures by former UKSF personnel and the concern that those disclosures were threatening the security of operations and personnel and were undermining the effectiveness and employability of the UKSF. Those are legitimate concerns for the MOD to have.'

18. It would follow that the MOD was reasonably entitled to regard anyone unwilling to accept the obligation of confidentiality as unsuitable for the SAS. Thus the threat was lawful and the demand supported by the threat could be justified. But the judge held that the demand was unlawful because it exceeded the powers of the Crown over a serviceman under military law. It was an attempt to restrict his freedom of expression after he had left the service and was no longer subject to military discipline.

19. The judge's reasoning was that R had signed the contract because he had been ordered to do so. The MOD could not give a serviceman an order which, as a matter of military law, he was obliged to obey after he had left the service and therefore it was an abuse of power for the MOD to try to extend the temporal reach of its orders by ordering the serviceman to sign a contract which could be enforced after he had left.

20. If R had signed the contract because as a matter of military law he had been obliged to do so, their Lordships would see much force in this reasoning. But they agree with the Court of Appeal that this was not the case. There was no order in the sense of a command which created an obligation to obey under military law. Instead, R was faced with a choice which may have constituted 'overwhelming pressure' but was not an exercise by the MOD of its legal powers over him. The legitimacy of the pressure therefore falls to be examined by normal criteria and as neither of the courts in New Zealand considered either the threat to be unlawful or the demand unreasonable, it follows that the contract was not obtained by duress.

Lord Scott dissented but not on the application of the doctrine of duress to the facts of the case.

COMMENTARY

Lord Hoffmann identified two elements to the 'wrong of duress'. The first was 'pressure amounting to compulsion of the will of the victim and the second was the illegitimacy of the pressure'. For the purposes of the hearing their Lordships were prepared to assume that the appellant had no practical alternative but to sign the contract. The crucial aspect of the case was therefore the second element of duress, namely the legitimacy or the illegitimacy of the pressure applied. Lord Hoffmann stated that the legitimacy of the pressure must be examined from 'two aspects', namely the 'nature of the pressure and . . . the nature of the demand which the pressure is applied to support'. The Privy Council thus appeared to envisage a two-stage approach to illegitimacy. First, if the threat is unlawful, it will generally amount to duress. Secondly, where the threat is lawful but is used to support a demand which is unreasonable, it may constitute duress.

6. CONCLUSION

The case-law therefore establishes that there are two elements to a duress claim, namely (i) lack of consent/coercion of the will, and (ii) the illegitimacy of the pressure exerted. Each part of the test requires further elaboration:

(a) LACK OF CONSENT

In *Barton* v. *Armstrong* (p. 716 above) the Privy Council held that the pressure need only be 'a' cause of the decision to enter into the contract. As has been noted (p. 720 above) this is a very low threshold and it is not clear that it is an appropriate test for cases of economic duress. Judicial support for the proposition that the causal test is more stringent (at least in cases of economic duress) can be derived from the following passage of the speech of Lord Goff in *Dimskal Shipping Co SA* v. *International Transport Workers' Federation (The Evia Luck)* [1992] 2 AC 152, 165:

We are here concerned with a case of economic duress. It was at one time thought that, at common law, the only form of duress which would entitle a party to avoid a contract on that ground was duress of the person. The origin for this view lay in the decision of the Court of Exchequer in *Skeate* v. *Beale* (1841) 11 Ad & El 983. However, since the decisions of Kerr J in *Occidental Worldwide Investment Corporation* v. *Skibs A/S Avanti (The Siboen and The Sibotre)* [1976] 1 Lloyd's Rep 293, of Mocatta J in *North Ocean Shipping Co Ltd* v. *Hyundai Construction Co Ltd* [1979] QB 705, and of the Judicial Committee of the Privy Council in *Pao On* v. *Lau Yiu Long* [1980] AC 614, that limitation has been discarded; and it is now accepted that economic pressure may be sufficient to amount to duress for this purpose, provided at least that the economic pressure may be characterised as illegitimate and has constituted a significant cause inducing the plaintiff to enter into the relevant contract (see *Barton* v. *Armstrong* [1976] AC 104, 121, per Lord Wilberforce and Lord Simon of Glaisdale (referred to with approval in *Pao On* v. *Lau Yiu Long* [1980] AC 614, 635, per Lord Scarman) and *Crescendo Management Pty. Ltd* v. *Westpac Banking Corporation* (1988) 19 NSWLR 40, 46, per McHugh JA). It is sometimes suggested that the plaintiff's will must have been coerced so as to vitiate his consent. This approach has been the subject of criticism; see Beatson, *The Use and Abuse of Unjust Enrichment* (1991), 113–17; and the notes by Professor Atiyah in (1982) 98 *LQR* 197–202, and by Professor Birks in [1990] 3 *LMCLQ* 342–51. I myself, like McHugh JA, doubt whether it is helpful in this context to speak of the plaintiff's will having been coerced. It is not however necessary to explore the matter in the present case. Nor is it necessary to consider the broader question of what constitutes illegitimate economic pressure, for it is accepted that blacking or a threat of blacking, such as occurred in the present case, does constitute illegitimate economic pressure in English law, unless legitimised by statute. The question which has fallen for decision by your Lordships is whether, in considering the question whether the pressure should be treated as legitimised, the

English courts should have regard to the law of Sweden (where the relevant pressure was exerted on the owners by the agents of the ITF) under which such pressure was lawful.

Two points should be noted here. The first relates to Lord Goff's comments concerning the coercion of the will theory and his apparent approval of the criticisms that have been levelled against it. The second point relates to his insertion of the word 'significant' before 'cause'. The addition of 'significant' leaves us with two problems. The first relates to the meaning of the word 'significant' and the second concerns the relationship between this test and the 'a' cause test employed by the Privy Council in *Barton*.

The relationship between *Barton* and *The Evia Luck* was considered by Mance J in *Huyton SA* v. *Peter Cremer GmbH & Co* [1999] 1 Lloyd's Rep 620, 636–639:

I start with the requirement that the illegitimate pressure must, in cases of economic duress, constitute 'a significant cause' (cf. per Lord Goff in *The Evia Luck* at p. 165). This is contrasted in Goff and Jones on *The Law of Restitution* (4th edn) p. 251, footnote 59 with the lesser requirement that it should be 'a' reason which applies in the context of duress to the person. The relevant authority in the latter context is *Barton* v. *Armstrong* [1976] AC 104 . . .

[he considered the case in some detail and continued]

The use of the phrase 'a significant cause' by Lord Goff in *The Evia Luck*, supported by the weighty observation in the footnote in Goff & Jones, suggests that this relaxed view of causation in the special context of duress to the person cannot prevail in the less serious context of economic duress. The minimum basic test of subjective causation in economic duress ought, it appears to me, to be a 'but for' test. The illegitimate pressure must have been such as actually caused the making of the agreement, in the sense that it would not otherwise have been made either at all or, at least, in the terms in which it was made. In that sense, the pressure must have been decisive or clinching. There may of course be cases where a common-sense relaxation, even of a but for requirement is necessary, for example in the event of an agreement induced by two concurrent causes, each otherwise sufficient to ground a claim of relief, in circumstances where each alone would have induced the agreement, so that it could not be said that, but for either, the agreement would not have been made. On the other hand, it also seems clear that the application of a simple 'but for' test of subjective causation in conjunction with a requirement of actual or threatened breach of duty could lead too readily to relief being granted. It would not, for example, cater for the obvious possibility that, although the innocent party would never have acted as he did, but for the illegitimate pressure, he nevertheless had a real choice and could, if he had wished, equally well have resisted the pressure and, for example, pursued alternative legal redress.

I turn therefore to consider other ingredients of economic duress. One possibility, harking back for example to a word used by the minority in *Barton*, is that the pressure should represent the 'predominant' cause. Professor Birks in *An Introduction to the Law of Restitution* (1985), pp. 182–183 has suggested that, in cases such as *Pao On* v. *Lau Yiu Long* [1980] AC 614 where relief was refused on the ground that there had been 'commercial pressure but no coercion' (p. 635), the Court was, in effect, insisting 'on a more severe test of the degree of compulsion than is found in *Barton* v. *Armstrong*', securing what he describes as 'a concealed discretion to distinguish between reasonable and unreasonable, legitimate and illegitimate applications of this species of independently unlawful pressure'. His own preference, he indicated, was for 'the simplest and more open course . . . to restrict the right to restitution to cases in which one party sought, mala fide to exploit the weakness of the other'. These comments highlight the extent to which any consideration of causation in economic duress inter-acts with consideration of the concept of legitimacy. Mr Males [counsel for the plaintiff] adopts the same approach as Professor Birks in relation to apparent contractual compromises for good consideration, suggesting that here at least bad faith ought to be a pre-condition to relief. The law will of course be cautious about re-opening an apparent compromise made in good faith on both sides. But it seems, on the one hand, questionable whether a 'compromise' achieved by one party who does not believe that he had at least an arguable case is a compromise at all—though it may be upheld if there is other consideration (cf *Occidental Worldwide Investment Corporation* v. *Skibs A/S Avanti (The Siboen and The Sibotre)* [1976] 1 Lloyd's Rep 293 at p. 334, col. 2); and, on the other hand, difficult to accept that illegitimate pressure applied by a party who believes bona fide in his case could never give grounds for relief against an apparent compromise. Another commentator, Professor Burrows, in *The Law of Restitution* (1993) pp. 181–182, has suggested that the concept of legitimacy is open to some flexibility or at least qualification, so that a threatened or actual breach of contract may not represent illegitimate pressure if there was a reasonable commercial basis for the threat or breach, e.g. because circumstances had radically changed. This suggestion too, is by no means uncontentious.

As to authority, in *The Siboen and The Sibotre*, one of the early cases on economic duress, Mr Justice Kerr indicated at p. 335, col. 1—in rejecting a contrary submission by Mr Robert Goff, QC as he was—that he did not think that bad faith had any relevance at all. On the other hand, in McHugh, JA's judgment in the Supreme Court of New South Wales in *Crescendo Management Pty Ltd* v. *Westpac Banking Corporation* (1988) 19 NSWLR 40 at p. 46, referred to by Lord Goff in *The Evia Luck*, McHugh, JA said that 'Pressure will be illegitimate if it consists of unlawful threats or amounts to unconscionable conduct'. It is also clear that illegitimate pressure may exist, although the threat is of action by itself lawful, if in conjunction with the nature of the demand, it involves potential blackmail: see *Thorn* v. *Motor Trade Association* [1937] AC 797, especially at pp. 806–807, cited in Lord Scarman's dissenting judgment in *Universe Tankships Inc* v. *International Transport Workers Federation* [1982] 1 Lloyd's Rep 537, 555 and *CTN Cash and Carry Ltd* v. *Gallagher Ltd* [1994] 4 All ER 713. And in this last case, Lord Justice Steyn, as he was, contemplated the possibility that unconscionable conduct might have a yet wider ambit. He said:

'Outside the field of protected relationships, and in a purely commercial context, it might be a relatively rare case in which "lawful act duress" can be established. And it might be particularly difficult to establish duress if the defendant bona fide considered that this demand was valid. In this complex and changing branch of the law I deliberately refrain from saying "never".'

That good or bad faith may be particularly relevant when considering whether a case might represent a rare example of 'lawful act duress' is not difficult to accept. Even in cases where the pressure relied on is an actual or threatened breach of duty, it seems to me better not to exclude the possibility that the state of mind of the person applying such pressure may in some circumstances be significant, whether or not the other innocent party correctly appreciated such state of mind. 'Never' in this context also seems too strong a word.

In *The Evia Luck*, Lord Goff did not speak in absolute terms. He said, with reference to the previous authorities, that—

'. . . it is now accepted that economic pressure may be sufficient to amount to duress for this purpose, provided at least that the economic pressure may be characterised as illegitimate and has constituted a significant cause inducing the plaintiff to enter the relevant contract.'

This description itself leaves room for flexibility in the characterization of illegitimate pressure and of the relevant causal link. Lord Goff was identifying minimum ingredients, not ingredients which, if present, would inevitably lead to liability. The recognition of some degree of flexibility is not, I think, fairly open to the reproach that it introduces a judicial 'discretion'. The law has frequently to form judgments regarding inequitability or unconscionability, giving effect in doing so to the reasonable expectations of honest persons. It is the law's function to discriminate, where discrimination is appropriate, between different factual situations—as it does, to take one example, when deciding whether or not to recognize a duty of care. The present context is intervention in relation to bargains or payments in relatively extreme situations. Lord Justice Steyn in *CTN Cash and Carry* cited, albeit in the context of threats involving no unlawful act, an aphorism of Oliver Wendell Holmes 'that general propositions do not solve concrete cases' and went on:

'It may only be a half-truth, but in my view the true part applies to this case. It is necessary to focus on the distinctive features of this case, and then to ask whether it amounts to a case of duress.'

A similar approach appears to me to be appropriate in the present context.

In older authorities, relief against economic duress was said to require illegitimate pressure coercing the innocent party's will and vitiating consent (cf. *The Siboen and The Sibotre* at p. 336 and *Pao On* v. *Lau Yiu Long* at p. 635). Lord Goff in *The Evia Luck* doubted whether it was helpful to speak in such terms, and referred to McHugh, JA's comments to that effect in the *Crescendo* case. The approach there adopted by McHugh, JA, at p. 45, was based on statements by the House of Lords in *DPP* v. *Lynch* [1975] AC 653, to the effect that, in cases of duress, 'the will [is] deflected, not destroyed'. Even on this more generous formulation, a simple enquiry whether the innocent party would have acted as he did 'but for' an actual or threatened breach of contract cannot, I think, be the hallmark of deflection of will. Whether because the specific ingredients identified by Lord Goff should be interpreted widely or because it is implicit in the flexibility of Lord Goff's formulation and the underlying rationale of the law's intervention to prevent unconscionability, relief must, I think, depend on the Court's assessment of the qualitative impact of the illegitimate pressure, objectively assessed. It is not necessary to go so far as to say that it is an inflexible third essential ingredient of economic duress that there should be no or no practical alternative course open to the innocent party. But it seems, as I have already indicated, self-evident that relief may not be appropriate, if an innocent party decides, as a matter of choice, not to pursue an alternative remedy which any and possibly some other reasonable persons in his circumstances would have pursued. Relief may perhaps also be refused, if he has made no protest and conducted himself in a way which showed that, for better or for worse, he was prepared to accept and live with the consequences, however unwelcome. Factors such as these are referred to as relevant to relief against duress in both *The Siboen and The Sibotre* and *Pao On*, although in some contexts it may also be possible to rationalize them by reference to other doctrines such as affirmation or estoppel. The emphasis, now to be discarded, in such cases on coercion of will does not, it seems to me, mean that such factors are no longer relevant. Taking, for example, *Pao On*, the complainant there was able, in the face of the illegitimate pressure, to consider its position, to take alternative steps if it wished, and to decide, as it apparently did (and however wrongly with hindsight), that the substitute arrangements proposed were of no real concern or risk to it and that it was preferable to agree to them, rather than become involved in litigation. Although there would have been no re-negotiation at all 'but for' illegitimate pressure, the relationship between the illegitimate pressure applied and the substitute arrangements made was not of a nature or quality, or sufficiently significant in objective terms in deflecting the will, to justify relief. Examination of the same relationship may also involve taking into account the extent to which the party applying illegitimate pressure intended or could reasonably foresee that pressure which he applied would lead to the agreement or payment made, or at least the extent to which factors extraneous to that party played any important role.

The onus of proof in respect of economic duress is another relatively unexplored area. McHugh, JA in *Crescendo* assumed that it would be reversed in accordance with the principle applied by the Privy Council in *Barton v. Armstrong*. That was a case of threats to kill, where the Privy Council took as an analogy dispositions induced by fraud. With such threats, as the Privy Council pointed out, it is only in the most unusual circumstances that there can be any doubt whether the threats operated to achieve their intended aim or known effect. The Privy Council's recognition of, not merely the prima facie factual inference, but of an apparent shifting of the legal onus, cannot, I think, be transposed automatically to the context of the more recently developed tort of economic duress. Threats to the person are, by definition, mala fide acts. Economic duress, as this case shows, embraces situations where the party applying what can, at least with hindsight, be shown to have been economic pressure held the view quite reasonably at the time that he was entitled to do so. There is, also, as indicated above, a major difference between the substantive test of causation in cases of threats to the person and in cases of economic duress. Leaving aside cases of fraud and fraudulent misrepresentation, mentioned in *Barton v. Armstrong*, the law normally treats the party seeking relief in respect of a breach of contract or seeking to set aside a bargain on grounds, such as innocent misrepresentation, as under a legal onus to prove his case on causation. The particular facts may give rise to an inference of loss or inducement, which may shift a factual onus to the other party, but the underlying legal onus remains at the end of the day on the party seeking relief (cf. e.g. *Marc Rich & Co v. Portman* [1996] 1 Lloyd's Rep 430 at p. 442, considering *Pan Atlantic Insurance Co v. Pine Top Insurance Co Ltd* [1994] 2 Lloyd's Rep 427 on misrepresentation and non-disclosure in relation to insurance contracts). It would seem to me, as presently advised, that this could represent the appropriate general approach in cases of economic duress. I am conscious that the question of onus of proof was only briefly touched on before me without citation of authority from outside the field of economic duress, but in view of my other conclusions I have not felt it necessary or appropriate to call for further submissions on it.

Thus the law would appear to be that, in cases of duress of the person, the illegitimate pressure need only have been 'a' cause of the decision to enter into the contract, whereas in the case of economic duress, the illegitimate pressure must have been 'a significant' cause of the decision to enter into the contract. The test for duress of goods is unknown, although presumably it is more likely to be that applicable to cases of economic duress. But, as Mance J acknowledged in *Huyton*, judicial 'consideration of causation in economic duress interacts with consideration of the concept of illegitimacy'. This suggests that it may be unwise to draw hard-and-fast lines here. The courts may prefer to apply a sliding scale according to which the causal threshold diminishes as the degree of illegitimacy increases.

It is at least clear that absence of consent is not enough in itself to entitle a party to set aside the contract. Rather, lack of consent is a threshold factor which is necessary to demonstrate the existence of a sufficient causal link between the illegitimate pressure and entry into the contract. It has been argued that this fails to take consent or autonomy seriously and that lack of consent should be sufficient to set aside the contract. The case has been made in the following terms:

SA Smith, 'Contracting Under Pressure: A Theory of Duress'

[1997] *CLJ* 343, 358–371

The ideal of freedom is widely believed to underlie not just the broad contours of the common law of contract but also the political structure of the countries in which that law is in place (and many others). Thus, it may seem self-evident that in determining if an alleged contract is valid the law is and should be concerned with whether or not the parties have consented to enter the contract . . .

The facts giving rise to a finding of no consent, like the facts giving rise to a finding of wrongdoing, need not involve pressure. Consent may be impaired where, for example, a contract is entered unintentionally or the defendant is a minor or the defendant makes a cognitive error. Our concern is solely with pressure cases. The existence of pressure makes a decision to enter a contract unfree if it (1) leaves the defendant with 'no choice' and (2) was operative in the decision-making process. A defendant has no choice, in the relevant sense, when the only alternatives to entering the contract, including doing nothing, are undesirable alternatives. Since our concern is for free choice and not for wrongdoing, the 'undesirability' of an alternative is assessed not by asking how it compares with the alternatives that would exist under an imaginary 'moral' or 'statistical' baseline, but by asking whether the defendant considers the alternative undesirable. The question is the same as that asked when defining a threat: is the relevant event unwelcome? . . .

[I]n addition to the requirement of no non-bad alternative to contracting, a further requirement must be met for a no consent defence to succeed: the defendant's lack of options must be operative in his decision to contract. Just as mere wrongdoing, standing alone, is not enough to invalidate a contract, a mere lack of options, standing alone, is insufficient. In each case, it must be shown that the relevant circumstance—wrongdoing, lack of options—was operative in the defendant's decision-making process. The test of 'causation', however, is different. Because the issue now is the defendant's responsibility for entering a contract rather than the plaintiff's responsibility for committing a wrong, the test is in effect reversed. Instead of asking whether the pressure was a necessary element of a set of actual conditions sufficient to induce the contract (the NESS test), the appropriate test is the but-for test: Would the defendant have entered the contract but-for the existence of the pressure? A party cannot disclaim responsibility for a decision that he would have made anyway, just because there exists an additional, potential excusing, reason for making that decision . . .

The consequences of taking consent seriously . . . are not as far-reaching as might be thought . . .

From the perspective of contract law, the main effect of introducing a distinct defence of no consent, and in particular a defence of necessity, would be to make it clear that contracts in which one party exploited the other party's lack of options, to adopt the usual description, are invalid. One category of cases where the necessity defence will often be relevant are contractual modification cases. Suppose that a subcontractor warns a head contractor that unless he is paid more he will be unable to complete the job. A promise to pay more that is made in response to a warning cannot be impugned on the principle of wrongdoing, but if, as is often the case, there are no alternative sub-contractors that the head contractor can hire to do the job without incurring extra expenses, and if the head contractor is working to a deadline, the head contractor may be able to plead necessity. Whether or not the plea succeeds depends primarily on whether or not the price agreed for the modification is a fair one.

A second, related example is that of a builder who runs into a serious and unexpected problem in the middle of a large construction project. Suppose that the underground cables supplying electrical power to a project have been severed. Each hour that they remain severed costs the contractor £5,000. There is one electrician available to do the job. The normal price for the job is £500 (taking into account the short notice, etc) but the electrician, realising the buyer's predicament, demands £20,000. According to the account of consent developed above, the contract is unenforceable (although the electrician should have a claim for restitution or for requested reliance if he has done the work and he may be able to recover more than £500 if his true costs, including his seller deficit, are greater than £500).

There is little support in law or academic commentary for the introduction of an explicit and general defence of necessity in contract law. Yet once the limitations on the scope of the defence are acknowledged, this reluctance is puzzling. Introducing a defence of necessity does no more than take seriously what courts have long said about the meaning of consent. In *The Universe Sentinel*, Lord Scarman defined duress as the defendant's 'intentional submission arising from the realisation that there is no other practical choice open to him'. Taken in its natural sense, this definition encompasses necessity cases. The same is true of various other judicial statements to the effect that the essence of vitiated consent is the absence of a 'reasonable alternative'. As for the general proposition that consent may be impaired without wrongdoing, this is recognised in the law regarding incapacity and minority, to mention just one example. More to the point, it is difficult to see why in principle it should matter when determining whether a contract between two ship's captains was freely entered into whether the defendant's ship was going to sink because it had sprung a leak or because the plaintiff threatened to fire a cannonball into the hull. It matters if the issue is wrongdoing, but not if the issue is autonomy. The effect on autonomy is the same even though the source of the pressure is different. In each case, the captain has no choice.

Introducing an explicit defence of necessity would change the orthodox understanding of the scope of duress. Necessity is not a recognised defence in contract law. Whether such a change would make a large difference to how cases are actually decided, as opposed to merely their reasoning, is less clear. Admiralty law enforces a rule which has the same effect as a defence of necessity in respect of rescue and salvage contracts and, while English courts do not appear to have ever applied this rule explicitly outside a maritime context, it has long been argued that courts take substantive fairness into account in assessing pleas of duress in cases involving defective markets. As for modifications, the American Restatement of Contracts holds that renegotiated terms are binding only if they are 'fair and equitable' and it can be expected that English courts would do the same although there does not yet appear to be a case in point. In short, the consent principle helps to make sense of the not-inconsiderable evidence of judicial concern for fair prices in situations of imperfect markets. The explanation of that concern, however, differs from that offered by other commentators in that it adopts the language of autonomy rather than the language of wrongdoing.

(b) ILLEGITIMACY

When is a threat 'illegitimate' for the purposes of the law relating to economic duress? In *DSDN Subsea Ltd* v. *Petroleum Geo-Services ASA* [2000] BLR 530, 545 Dyson J stated that:

In determining whether there has been illegitimate pressure, the court takes into account a range of factors. These include whether there has been an actual or threatened breach of contract; whether the person allegedly exerting the pressure has acted in good or bad faith; whether the victim had any realistic practical alternative but to submit to the pressure; whether the victim protested at the time; and whether he affirmed and sought to rely on the contract. These are all relevant factors. Illegitimate pressure must be distinguished from the rough and tumble of the pressures of normal commercial bargaining.

The difficulty with this statement is that some of the factors, such as the existence of 'any realistic practical alternative' seem more relevant to the existence of a sufficient causal link than to the legitimacy of the pressure applied. A threat to commit an unlawful act, such as a crime or a tort, is illegitimate (*The Universe Sentinel*, p. 731 above). The nature of the demand would also appear to be relevant: a threat which, though lawful in itself, is used in order to attain a goal which is unlawful, may be illegitimate (*The Universe Sentinel*, per Lord Scarman, p. 733 above). A threat to breach a contract may also be illegitimate (see *The Atlantic Baron*, p. 725 above, *The Universe Sentinel*, p. 731 above, *Atlas Express Ltd v. Kafco* [1989] QB 833 and *Carillion Construction Ltd v. Felix (UK) Ltd* [2001] BLR 1) but cases can also be found in which the courts have held that a threatened breach of contract did not constitute duress. These cases may, however, be explicable on grounds other than the illegitimacy of the threat. Thus in *Williams* v. *Roffey Bros & Nicholls (Contractors) Ltd* [1991] 1 QB 1 (p. 188 above) there does not appear to have been any 'threat' to break a contract and in *DSDN Subsea Ltd v. Petroleum Geo-Services ASA* [2000] BLR 530 the threat to break a contract did not seem to have been a significant cause of the decision to enter into the contract, given the lack of contemporaneous evidence to substantiate the claim that economic duress had been exercised. Good faith may also be a relevant factor in deciding whether or not a threatened breach of contract is illegitimate (see *DSDN Subsea Ltd* v. *Petroleum Geo-Services ASA*, above and *Huyton SA* v. *Peter Cremer GmbH & Co* p. 745 above). The relevance of good faith is, however, debatable, given that it does not seem to have been regarded as a relevant factor in cases such as *The Atlantic Baron* and English law does not generally distinguish between a good faith and a bad faith breach of contract.

A refusal to contract does not constitute the application of illegitimate pressure, at least in the absence of bad faith on the part of the person who refuses to enter into the contract (*CTN Cash and Carry Ltd* v. *Gallaher* [1994] 4 All ER 714, p. 738 above). A refusal to waive an existing contractual obligation does not amount to the application of illegitimate pressure (*Alec Lobb (Garages) Ltd* v. *Total Oil (Great Britain) Ltd* [1983] 1 WLR 87, 94) nor is it illegitimate for an owner of goods let on hire-purchase to threaten to repossess the goods when the hirer is in default and has not attempted to obtain relief against forfeiture (*Alf Vaughan & Co Ltd* v. *Royscot Trust plc* [1999] 1 All ER (Comm) 856).

7. FURTHER READING

BEATSON, J, 'Duress, Restitution and Contract Modification' in Beatson, J, *The Use and Abuse of Unjust Enrichment* (Oxford University Press, 1990) p. 95.

BIRKS, P, 'The Travails of Duress' [1990] *LMCLQ* 342.

SMITH, S, 'Contracting Under Pressure: A Theory of Duress' [1997] *CLJ* 343.

19

UNDUE INFLUENCE

1. CENTRAL ISSUES

1. Undue influence is a creature of equity and assumes many different forms. The basic distinction drawn in the cases is between actual undue influence and presumed undue influence.

2. Actual undue influence has many similarities with common law duress. It generally consists of the application of illegitimate pressure but would appear to extend to other forms of wrongdoing, such as 'overreaching' and 'cheating'.

3. Cases of presumed undue influence are more difficult to classify. The essential idea is that one party has taken advantage of a relationship of trust and confidence to the substantial detriment of the party who has reposed the trust and confidence in him. The courts have experienced considerable difficulty in identifying the circumstances which have the effect of triggering the operation of the presumption. There appear to be two principal elements: (i) there must be a relationship of sufficient trust and confidence between the parties and (ii) the transaction that has taken place between the parties must not be explicable in terms of the ordinary motives on which ordinary people act. The presumption is a rebuttable one. It can be rebutted by showing that entry into the transaction was the result of the free exercise of independent will by the party seeking to set aside the transaction.

4. The courts have generally been reluctant to attempt a comprehensive definition of undue influence. They tend to emphasize the facts and circumstances of the individual case. Thus relationships are 'infinitely various' and no description of the relevant factors is 'perfect' or 'all embracing'. The emphasis is not only on 'influence' but on the 'abuse' or the 'misuse' of that influence. In this sense undue influence has been said to have a connotation of impropriety. But it may be impropriety in an attenuated form, in that it can apparently take the form of failing to provide a claimant with access to independent advice.

2. INTRODUCTION

Cases of alleged undue influence have caused considerable difficulties for the courts in recent years. The difficulties relate, not to the existence of the doctrine, but to its scope and its relationship with other doctrines, particularly duress (on which see Chapter 18) and other cases in which courts have intervened to protect the vulnerable or those who have been exploited (on which see Chapter 20). The very words 'undue influence' give rise to difficulty. What does 'undue' mean? Does it mean 'too much', 'illegitimate' (in the sense in which that word is used in the context of duress), or 'unconscionable'? 'Influence' is not much better. Does it mean 'pressure', 'domination', 'exploitation', 'dependence', or something else? The courts have, until recently, made considerable use of a 'presumption' of undue influence. But what was it that was being presumed?

Was it illegitimate pressure, exploitation, or excessive dependence? One of the principal issues of controversy has been whether the focus of undue influence is upon the
conduct of the defendant or the state of mind of the claimant. This controversy
remains unresolved. In some recent cases (such as *R* v. *Attorney-General for England
and Wales* [2003] UKPC 22, below, p. 785, and *National Commercial Bank (Jamaica)
Ltd* v. *Hew* [2003] UKPC 51, below, p. 788) strong emphasis has been placed on the
need for some form of wrongdoing on the part of the defendant, whereas in other
cases (see, for example, *Pesticcio* v. *Huet* [2004] EWCA Civ 372; [2004] All ER (D) 36
(April), below, p. 790) the courts have stated that a finding of undue influence does
not require any wrongdoing on the part of the defendant.

The traditional approach to undue influence is to distinguish between actual and
presumed undue influence. An example of actual undue influence is provided by the
decision of the House of Lords in *Williams* v. *Bayley* (1866) LR 1 HL 200. The
plaintiff's son gave the defendant bankers promissory notes upon which he had forged
the plaintiff's signature. When the defendants discovered what had taken place they
met with the plaintiff and during the course of the meeting they informed him that
they had it within their power to prosecute his son. A solicitor was present with the
plaintiff during the meeting but he left in protest when the plaintiff was asked to meet
his son's debts. The plaintiff then agreed to enter into a mortgage to pay off the debts
of his son, which he later sought to set aside. The House of Lords held that the
plaintiff was entitled to set aside the mortgage in equity. Lord Chelmsford stated (at
p. 214) that the agreement had been 'extorted from the father by undue pressure'. In
so far as actual undue influence is based on the application of 'undue pressure' it
would appear to be the equitable counterpart of common law duress (see, for
example, *R* v. *Attorney-General for England and Wales* [2003] UKPC 22, below p. 785).
It has, however, been argued that cases of actual undue influence extend beyond cases
of the application of illegitimate pressure. Thus Professor Treitel has argued (*The Law
of Contract* (11th edn, Sweet & Maxwell, 2003), pp. 408–409):

The first group of cases in which equity gave relief on the ground of undue influence are those in
which one party had induced the other to enter into the transaction by actual pressure which
equity regarded as improper but which was formerly thought not to amount to duress at common
law because no element of violence to the person was involved. For example, a promise to pay
money can be set aside if obtained by a threat to prosecute the promisor, or his close relative, or
his spouse, for a criminal offence. Such threats might now constitute duress, but the equitable
concept of 'pressure' is still wider than that of duress at common law, for undue influence can be
exercised without making illegitimate threats or indeed any threats at all. The party who claims
relief on the ground of actual undue influence must show that such influence existed and had been
exercised, and that the transaction resulted from that influence. There is no further requirement in
cases of this kind that the transaction must be shown to be to the manifest disadvantage of the
party seeking to set it aside or that the transaction must be one that 'calls for explanation' by the
other party.

The penultimate sentence is a difficult one because it does not explain what is
involved in the 'exercise' of 'influence' and how this differs from the application of
pressure.

Cases of presumed undue influence are even more difficult. There are generally three elements to a case of presumed undue influence. First, there must have been a relationship of trust and confidence between the parties. Prior to the decision of the House of Lords in *Royal Bank of Scotland plc* v. *Etridge (No 2)* [2001] UKHL 44 (p. 763 below) it was customary to sub-divide the cases into two groups. The first group consisted of a class of relationships in which the law presumed that one party was in a position to exercise influence or dominion over the other. These relationships included parent and child, guardian and ward, doctor and patient, solicitor and client, trustee and beneficiary, and religious adviser and disciple. The second group consisted of cases in which the claimant proved that, on the facts, a relationship of trust and confidence existed between the parties. Cases in this second group were inevitably fact specific because they depended upon a finding that, *in the particular case*, a relationship of trust and confidence existed between the parties. However the future of this second category is, at best, doubtful after the decision of the House of Lords in *Etridge* (see p. 783 below).

The second element in a presumed undue influence case is that there must be something about the transaction which 'calls for an explanation'. This requirement has been expressed in different ways. In *Allcard* v. *Skinner* (1887) 36 Ch D 145 (p. 758 below) Lindley LJ stated that the gift must have been 'so large as not to be reasonably accounted for on the ground of friendship, relationship, charity, or other ordinary motives on which ordinary men act'. In *National Westminster Bank plc* v. *Morgan* [1985] AC 686 Lord Scarman stated that the transaction must be 'manifestly disadvantageous' to the person seeking to set it aside. As a result of the decision of the House of Lords in *Etridge* (p. 783 below) it would appear that the former test is the one that is to be applied in future cases.

These two elements between them suffice to trigger the presumption of undue influence. The court must then consider whether the presumption has been rebutted. This is the third element in a presumed undue influence claim. The factors relevant to the rebuttal of the presumption have been summarized by Professor Treitel (*The Law of Contract* (11th edn, Sweet & Maxwell, 2003), p. 419) as follows:

The presumption of undue influence is rebutted if the party benefiting from the transaction shows that it was 'the free exercise of independent will'. The most usual way of doing this is to show that the other party had independent advice before entering into the transaction. But the mere fact that independent advice was given will not of itself save the transaction. The advice must be competent and based on knowledge of all the relevant facts. It has been suggested that the independent adviser must also approve the transaction, and that his advice must be followed. This may be necessary where the influence is particularly strong, or where a very large gift is made; but it is not necessary in every case. There is indeed no invariable rule that independent advice is necessary to save the transaction; but the beneficiary would lack elementary prudence if he did not ensure that such advice was given.

A case, in which the presumption of undue influence was not rebutted, is *Hammond* v. *Osborn* [2002] EWCA Civ 885. A seventy-four-year-old man, Mr Pritler, who was in poor health, realized his investments and wrote out four cheques to a total value of £297,000 in favour of the defendant, Mrs Osborn, who had assumed the principal role in caring for him. This sum represented 'nearly 91.6% of his liquid assets'. Further, the consequence of the realization of his investments in this way was that 'he became prospectively liable for charges for capital gains tax and higher rate tax' amounting to almost £50,000. On the death of Mr Pritler his family sought to set aside the gifts to the defendant. The defendant conceded that there was a relationship of trust and confidence between herself and Mr Pritler and that the gift was so large as to trigger the operation of the presumption. The trial judge held that the presumption had been rebutted because he was satisfied that the donor made the gift 'only after full, free and informed thought about it'. The Court of Appeal disagreed and held that the presumption had not been rebutted. Sir Martin Nourse stated:

28. Here Mr Pritler received no advice at all, whether independent or of any other kind. I am prepared to assume that there could be a case, perhaps there has been a case, where the nature and effect of the gift was so fully explained to the donor by the donee as to satisfy the test. But there was nothing of that sort here. Mrs Osborn did not draw Mr Pritler's attention to the size of the gift, nor to the proportion of his liquid assets that it represented, nor to the relatively small amount that was left to him . . .

29. Although Mr Pritler knew that he was making a gift to Mrs Osborn and must have known that it was a substantial gift, he was never told its size, even in approximate terms. So he did not know the nature of the gift. Even more important, he was not told of its effect. . . . It is true that he was left with some £27,000 in cash, his house valued at about £130,000 and an annual income of about £14,000 net. But no consideration was given as to whether those assets would be sufficient to satisfy his future needs. Nor was any consideration given to the extremely serious fiscal consequences of the realisation of his investments. Had he lived, as he was expected to, he would have become liable to the Inland Revenue for nearly £50,000, with not much more than half that amount in cash to meet the liability. It was no answer for Mrs Osborn to say, as she consistently did, that she treated the money as still belonging to Mr Pritler and would never have left him in need. It is impossible to say that the gift was made by Mr Pritler only after full, free and informed thought about it.

30. The principal argument of Mr McCue [counsel for the defendant] in this court was that the presumption is rebutted if it is shown that the conduct of the donee has been unimpeachable, or at any rate that there has been nothing sinister in it. Such, he argued, had been the conduct of Mrs Osborn in this case . . .

32. Even if it is correct to say that Mrs Osborn's conduct was unimpeachable and that there was nothing sinister in it, that would be no answer to an application of the presumption. As Cotton LJ said in *Allcard* v. *Skinner* [p. 758 below], the court does not interfere on the ground that any wrongful act has in fact been committed by the donee but on the ground of public policy, which requires it to be affirmatively established that the donor's trust and confidence in the donee has not been betrayed or abused. In any event, I am unable to subscribe to Mr McCue's suggested view of Mrs Osborn's conduct. The judge's finding that her silence and deliberate falsehoods after Mr Pritler's death were caused by Mr Osborn ordering her to keep her mouth shut and by her fear of him, while it may to a large extent excuse her, does not make her conduct unimpeachable nor does it relieve it of its sinister appearance. What it shows is that there was still an attempted cover up, but that Mr Osborn was involved in it as well as Mrs Osborn.

33. I cannot agree with the judge's view of this question. The presumption has not been rebutted and the gift must be set aside. I would therefore allow Mrs Hammond's appeal.

3. THREE-PARTY CASES

Recent judicial exposition of undue influence has tended to take place in the context of three-party cases rather than two-party cases, that is to say, cases in which a wrong has been committed by a third party and not the defendant. The word 'wrong' has been used deliberately because one of the leading cases, *Barclays Bank plc* v. *O'Brien* [1994] 1 AC 180, did not, in the event, involve undue influence at all: it was a misrepresentation case. The facts of *Barclays Bank plc* v. *O'Brien* were as follows. Mr O'Brien negotiated an overdraft with Barclays for a company in which he had an interest. It was agreed that Mr O'Brien would guarantee the company's indebtedness and that his liability would, in turn, be secured by a second charge on the matrimonial home. The bank manager asked the branch at which the security documents were to be signed to ensure that the O'Briens were 'fully aware of the nature of the documentation to be signed and advised that if they are in any doubt they should contact their solicitor before signing'. These instructions were not complied with and Mrs O'Brien was given no explanation of the effect of the documents before she signed them, nor was she advised of the need to take independent advice. When the company's indebtedness rose to £154,000 the bank demanded that Mr O'Brien honour the guarantee. When he failed to do so, the bank sought to enforce the charge which Mrs O'Brien had signed and to obtain possession of the house. Mrs O'Brien sought to defend the claim on the ground that she had been induced to sign the charge by the undue influence of her husband and by his misrepresentation that the charge was limited to £60,000 and that its duration was to be confined to a short period of time. The claim based on undue influence was rejected in the Court of Appeal and was not pursued in the House of Lords, where the claim to set aside the transaction was based on the misrepresentation of Mr O'Brien, of which it was argued, in the event successfully, that the bank had constructive notice so that it could not enforce the charge against Mrs O'Brien.

There were three steps to the reasoning of the House of Lords in *O'Brien*. First Mrs O'Brien had to demonstrate that she was entitled to set aside 'the transaction' as against her husband. It is here that undue influence enters the arena as one of the possible grounds on which a wife may be entitled to set aside a transaction against her husband. The other ground, and the ground that was actually in issue in *O'Brien* and in many of the cases post-*O'Brien*, was misrepresentation. Secondly, the bank must have been put on notice of the possibility of wrongdoing on the part of the husband. Thirdly, once put on notice, the bank had to take certain steps to ensure that the agreement of the wife to the charge was properly obtained. It is not necessary to enter into the details of the second and third elements of this analysis because they have largely been overtaken by the decision of the House of Lords in *Etridge*. It suffices for the present purpose to note that the basis on which the claimant was held to be entitled to set aside the charge as against the defendant bank was not that the bank had committed a wrong but simply that it had notice that someone else had committed a wrong and had failed to take sufficient steps to ensure that the claimant was given adequate advice before deciding whether or not to enter into the transaction.

The leading case on undue influence is now the decision of the House of Lords in *Royal Bank of Scotland plc* v. *Etridge (No 2)* [2001] UKHL 44; [2002] 2 AC 773 (p. 763 below). It is a three-party case and it re-examines *Barclays Bank* v. *O'Brien*. It is, however, important to see the operation of undue influence at work in a standard two-party case. Thus we shall commence our analysis with the case of *Allcard* v. *Skinner* (1887) 36 Ch D 145, which, in the words of Lord Nicholls in *Etridge* (para [8]), is 'a case well known to every law student'. We shall then turn to *Etridge* itself.

4. TWO LEADING CASES

Allcard v. Skinner

(1887) 36 Ch D 145, Court of Appeal

In 1868, the plaintiff was introduced by her 'spiritual director and confessor', Rev D Nihill, to the defendant, who was the lady superior of the sisterhood of St Mary at the Cross. In July of the same year, the plaintiff became an associate of the sisterhood, and at that time promised to devote her property to the service of the poor. She subsequently became a postulant, and then a novice, before, in 1871, she joined the sisterhood. On becoming a sister the plaintiff became subject to the rules of the sisterhood. These rules demanded her implicit obedience to the lady superior, whose voice was stated to be 'the voice of God', and they also stated that she must not 'seek advice of any entern without the Superior's leave'. She also took a vow of poverty, which required her to give away all her property. Although there was no requirement that she give her property to the sisterhood, it was found that there was an expectation to that effect. The plaintiff left the sisterhood in 1879 and revoked her will under which she had left her property to the sisterhood. In 1885 the plaintiff sought to recover certain items of property which she had transferred to the sisterhood. Her claim was rejected by the Court of Appeal, affirming the decision of Kekewich J. Although she was able to show that the property had been transferred while she was under the undue influence of the defendant, it was held, Cotton LJ dissenting on this point, that her claim was barred by virtue of her delay after leaving the sisterhood in bringing proceedings (and for this purpose the majority found it unnecessary to decide whether the appropriate label for the defence was acquiesence, laches, or affirmation). The extracts which follow are concerned solely with the ground on which the plaintiff was entitled to bring her claim and not with the scope of the defences.

Cotton LJ

The question is—Does the case fall within the principles laid down by the decisions of the Court of Chancery in setting aside voluntary gifts executed by parties who at the time were under such influence as, in the opinion of the Court, enabled the donor afterwards to set the gift aside? These decisions may be divided into two classes—First, where the Court has been satisfied that the gift was the result of influence expressly used by the donee for the purpose; second, where the relations between the donor and donee have at or shortly before the execution of the gift been such as to raise a presumption that the donee had influence over the donor. In such a case the Court sets aside the voluntary gift, unless it is proved that in fact the gift was the spontaneous act of the donor acting under circumstances which enabled him to exercise an independent will and which justifies the Court in holding that the gift was the result of a free exercise of the donor's will. The first class of cases may be considered as depending on the principle that no one shall be allowed to retain any benefit arising from his own fraud or wrongful act. In the second class of cases the Court interferes, not on the ground that any wrongful act has in fact been committed by the donee, but on the ground of public policy, and to prevent the relations which existed between the parties and the influence arising therefrom being abused . . .

The question is whether the case comes within the principle of the second class, and I am of opinion that it does. At the time of the gift the Plaintiff was a professed sister, and, as such, bound to render absolute submission to the Defendant as superior of the sister-hood. She had no power to obtain independent advice, she was in such a position that she could not freely exercise her own will as to the disposal of her property, and she must be considered as being . . . 'not, in the largest and amplest sense of the term—not, in mind as well as person—an entirely free agent'. . . . In my opinion, even if there were evidence that she had, before she joined the sisterhood, advice on the question of how she should deal with her property, that would not be sufficient. The question is, I think, whether at the time when she executed the transfer she was under such influences as to prevent the gift being considered as that of one free to determine what should be done with her property . . .

Lindley LJ

. . . the fetter . . . placed on the Plaintiff was the result of her own free choice. There is no evidence that pressure was put upon her to enter upon the mode of life which she adopted. She chose it as the best for herself; she devoted herself to it, heart and soul; she was, to use her own expression, infatuated with the life and with the work. But though infatuated, there is no evidence to shew that she was in such a state of mental imbecility as to justify the inference that she was unable to take care of herself or to manage her own affairs. . . . I have examined the evidence with care in order to see whether any pressure was put upon the Plaintiff in order to induce her to give her property to the sisterhood, or whether any deception was practised upon her, or whether any unfair advantage was taken of her, or whether any of her money was applied otherwise than *bonâ fide* for the objects of the sisterhood, or for any purpose which the Plaintiff could disapprove. The result of the evidence convinces me that no pressure, except the inevitable pressure of the vows and rules, was brought to bear on the Plaintiff; that no deception was practised upon her; that no unfair advantage was taken of her; that none of her money was obtained or applied for any purpose other than the legitimate objects of the sister-hood. . . . The real truth is that the Plaintiff gave away her property as a matter of course, and without seriously thinking of the consequences to herself. She had devoted herself and her fortune to the sisterhood, and it never occurred to her that she should ever wish to leave the sisterhood or desire to have her money back. In giving away her property as she did she was merely acting up to her promise and vow and the rule of the sisterhood, and to the standard of duty which she had erected for herself under the influences and circumstances already stated . . .

Two questions are raised by the appeal, namely, 1st, Whether the gifts made by the Plaintiff to the sisterhood were revocable or irrevocable when made? 2nd, Whether, assuming them to have been revocable when made, it was competent for the Plaintiff to revoke them when she did?

The first question is one of great importance and difficulty. Its solution requires a careful consideration of the legal effect of gifts by persons of mature age who feel bound by vows and rules to give away their property, but who have taken the vows and submitted to the rules voluntarily and without pressure, and who are subject to no other coercion or influence than necessarily result from the vows and rules themselves, and from the state of their own mind. . . . There being no duress or fraud, the only ground for impeaching such gifts at law would be want of capacity on the part of the donor; and although the Plaintiff was a religious enthusiast, no one could treat her as in point of law *non compos mentis*. There is no authority whatever for saying that her gifts were invalid at law. It is to the doctrines of equity, then, that recourse must be had to invalidate such gifts, if they are to be invalidated. The doctrine relied upon by the Appellant is the doctrine of undue influence expounded and enforced in *Huguenin* v. *Baseley* (1807) 14 Ves 273 and other cases of that class. These cases may be subdivided into two groups, which, however, often overlap.

First, there are the cases in which there has been some unfair and improper conduct, some coercion from outside, some overreaching, some form of cheating, and generally, though not always, some personal advantage obtained by a donee placed in some close and confidential relation to the donor. . . . The evidence does not bring this case within this group.

The second group consists of cases in which the position of the donor to the donee has been such that it has been the duty of the donee to advise the donor, or even to manage his property for him. In such cases the Court throws upon the donee the burden of proving that he has not abused his position, and of proving that the gift made to him has not been brought about by any undue influence on his part. In this class of cases it has been considered necessary to shew that the donor had independent advice, and was removed from the influence of the donee when the gift to him was made . . .

I have not been able to find any case in which a gift has been set aside on the ground of undue influence which does not fall within one or other or both of the groups above mentioned. Nor can I find any authority which actually covers the present case. But it does not follow that it is not reached by the principle on which the Court has proceeded in dealing with the cases which have already called for decision. They illustrate but do not limit the principle applied to them.

The principle must be examined. What then is the principle? Is it that it is right and expedient to save persons from the consequences of their own folly? or is it that it is right and expedient to save them from being victimised by other people? In my opinion the doctrine of undue influence is founded upon the second of these two principles. Courts of Equity have never set aside gifts on the ground of the folly, imprudence, or want of foresight on the part of donors. The Courts have always repudiated any such jurisdiction. *Huguenin* v. *Baseley* (1807) 14 Ves 273 is itself a clear authority to this effect. It would obviously be to encourage folly, recklessness, extravagance and vice if persons could get back property which they foolishly made away with, whether by giving it to charitable institutions or by bestowing it on less worthy objects. On the other hand, to protect people from being forced, tricked or misled in any way by others into parting with their property is one of the most legitimate objects of all laws; and the equitable doctrine of undue influence has grown out of and been developed by the necessity of grappling with insidious forms of spiritual tyranny and with the infinite varieties of fraud.

As no Court has ever attempted to define fraud so no Court has ever attempted to define undue influence, which includes one of its many varieties. The undue influence which Courts of Equity endeavour to defeat is the undue influence of one person over another; not the influence of enthusiasm on the enthusiast who is carried away by it, unless indeed such enthusiasm is itself the result of external undue influence. But the influence of one mind over another is very subtle, and of all influences religious influence is the most dangerous and the most powerful, and to counteract it Courts of Equity have gone very far. They have not shrunk from setting aside gifts made to persons in a position to exercise undue influence over the donors, although there has been no proof of the actual exercise of such influence; and the Courts have done this on the avowed ground of the necessity of going this length in order to protect persons from the exercise of such influence under circumstances which render proof of it impossible. The Courts have required proof of its non-exercise, and, failing that proof, have set aside gifts otherwise unimpeachable. In this particular case I cannot find any proof that any gift made by the Plaintiff was the result of any actual exercise of power or influence on the part of the lady superior or of Mr *Nihill*, apart from the influence necessarily incidental to their position in the sisterhood. Everything that the Plaintiff did is in my opinion referable to her own willing submission to the vows she took and to the rules which she approved, and to her own enthusiastic devotion to the life and work of the sisterhood. This enthusiasm and devotion were nourished, strengthened and intensified by the religious services of the sisterhood and by the example and influence of those about her. But she chose the life and work; such fetters as bound her were voluntarily put upon her by herself; she could shake them off at any time had she thought fit, and had she had the courage so to do; and no unfair advantage whatever was taken of her. Under these circumstances it is going a long way to hold that she can invoke the doctrine of undue influence to save her from the consequences of her own acts, and to entitle her to avoid the gifts she made when in a state of mind different from that in which she now is. I am by no means insensible of the difficulty of going so far.

Nevertheless, consider the position in which the Plaintiff had placed herself. She had vowed poverty and obedience, and she was not at liberty to consult externs without the leave of her superior. She was not a person who treated her vows lightly; she was deeply religious and felt bound by her promise, by her vows, and by the rules of the sisterhood. She was absolutely in the power of the lady superior and Mr *Nihill*. A gift made by her under these circumstances to the lady superior cannot in my opinion be retained by the donee. The equitable title of the donee is imperfect by reason of the influence inevitably resulting from her position, and which influence experience has taught the Courts to regard as undue. Whatever doubt I might have had on this point if there had been no rule against consulting externs, that rule in my judgment turns the scale against the Defendant. In the face of that rule the gifts made to the sisterhood cannot be supported in the absence of proof that the Plaintiff could have obtained independent advice if she wished for it, and that she knew that she would have been allowed to obtain such advice if she had desired to do so. I doubt whether the gifts could have been supported if such proof had been given, unless there was also proof that she was free to act on the advice which might be given to her. But the rule itself is so oppressive and so easily abused that any person subject to it is in my opinion brought within the class of those whom it is the duty of the Court to protect from possible imposition. The gifts cannot be supported without proof of more freedom in fact than the Plaintiff can be supposed to have actually enjoyed.

Where a gift is made to a person standing in a confidential relation to the donor, the Court will not set aside the gift if of a small amount simply on the ground that the donor had no independent advice. In such a case, some proof of the exercise of the influence of the donee must be given. The mere existence of such influence is not enough in such a case; . . . But if the gift is so large as not to be reasonably accounted for on the ground of friendship, relationship, charity, or other ordinary motives on which ordinary men act, the burden is upon the donee to support the gift . . . in this case there was in fact no unfair or undue influence brought to bear upon the Plaintiff other than such as inevitably resulted from the training she had received, the promise she had made, the vows she had taken, and the rules to which she had submitted herself. But her gifts were in fact made under a pressure which, whilst it lasted, the Plaintiff could not resist, and were not, in my opinion, past recall when that pressure was removed. When the Plaintiff emancipated herself from the spell by which she was bound, she was entitled to invoke the aid of the Court in order to obtain the restitution from the Defendant of so much of the Plaintiff's property as had not been spent in accordance with the wishes of the Plaintiff, but remained in the hands of the Defendant.

Bowen LJ

. . . it is of essential importance to keep quite distinct two things which in their nature seem to me to be different—the rights of the donor, and the duties of the donee. . . . As to the rights of the donor in a case like the present I entertain no doubt. . . . In the present instance there was no duress, no incompetency, no want of mental power on the part of the donor. It seems to me that, so far as regards her rights, she had the absolute right to deal with her property as she chose. Passing next to the duties of the donee, . . . it is plain that equity will not allow a person who exercises or enjoys a dominant religious influence over another to benefit directly or indirectly by the gifts which the donor makes under or in consequence of such influence, unless it is shewn that the donor, at the time of making the gift, was allowed full and free opportunity for counsel and advice outside—the means of considering his or her worldly position and exercising an independent will about it. This is not a limitation placed on the action of the donor; it is a fetter placed upon the conscience of the recipient of the gift, and one which arises out of public policy and fair play . . . [The] Plaintiff . . . had vowed in the most sacred and solemn way absolute and implicit obedience to the will of the Defendant, her superior, and she was bound altogether to neglect the advice of externs—not to consult those outside the convent . . . the Plaintiff, so long as she was fettered by this vow—so long as she was under the dominant influence of this religious feeling—was a person entitled to the protection of the rule. Now, was the Defendant bound by this rule? I acquit her most entirely of all selfish feeling in the matter. I can see no sort of wrongful desire to appropriate to herself any worldly benefit from the gift; but, nevertheless, she was a person who benefited by it so far as the disposition of the property was concerned, although, no doubt, she meant to use it in conformity with the rules of the institution, and did so use it . . . the case does not turn upon the fact that the standard of duty was originally created by the Plaintiff herself, although her original intention is one of the circumstances, no doubt, which bear upon the case, and is not to be neglected. But it is not the crucial fact. We ought to look, it seems to me, at the time at which the gift was made, and to examine what was then the condition of the donor who made it. For these reasons I think that without any interference with the freedom of persons to deal with their property as they please, we can hold but one opinion, that in 1879 the Plaintiff could have set this gift aside . . .

COMMENTARY

Allcard is an interesting case for a number of reasons. First, the judges distinguish between actual and presumed undue influence. *Allcard* itself is a case of presumed undue influence. Nevertheless, the judges did give brief consideration to the scope of actual undue influence. Thus Lindley LJ stated that actual undue influence extends to cases of 'overreaching' and 'cheating'. Secondly, it is not easy to identify the basis upon which the Court of Appeal concluded that this was a case of presumed undue influence. There are passages from the judgment of Lindley LJ which suggest that 'victimization' is the basis of a finding of undue influence. This suggests that the search is for some wrongdoing on the part of the defendant. But this rationalization is difficult to reconcile with his conclusion that there was nothing to suggest that any gift made by the plaintiff was the result of the actual exercise of power or influence by the Mother Superior. This tends to suggest that the basis for the finding that this was a case of presumed undue influence had more to do with the position of the plaintiff than the behaviour of the defendant (see further p. 782 below). Thus Professors Birks and Chin ('On the Nature of Undue Influence' in J Beatson and D Friedmann (eds), *Good Faith and Fault in Contract Law* (Oxford University Press, 1995), at p. 68) suggest that:

in presuming the undue influence the Court of Appeal was not presuming recourse to threats, express or implied, either by the Mother Superior or by the clergyman who had been the co-founder of the convent. The plaintiff had been under a spell compounded of her enthusiasm for the sisterhood and devotion to its rules, which included an obligation to seek advice only within the order. Her weakness consisted in her impaired capacity *vis-à-vis* the head of the order to judge her own best interests. She was excessively dependent or, if 'dependent' is a shade wrong, she was excessively spell-bound. Either way, her autonomy was impaired to an exceptional degree.

Thirdly, it would appear that the critical factor was that the plaintiff was denied access to external, independent advice. In the absence of such independent advice there was nothing to free the plaintiff from her overwhelming sense that she was bound to give away all her property. Had she had independent advice and had nevertheless decided to give away her property, it is unlikely that the Court of Appeal would have held that the transaction could be set aside.

Royal Bank of Scotland plc v. Etridge (No 2)

[2001] UKHL 44; [2002] 2 AC 773, House of Lords

The House of Lords heard eight appeals. Each case arose out of a transaction in which a wife charged her interest in her home in favour of a bank as security for her husband's indebtedness or the indebtedness of a company through which he carried on business. In seven of the appeals the bank sought to enforce the charge signed by the wife. The wife raised a defence that the bank was on notice that her concurrence in the transaction had been procured by her husband's undue influence. In the eighth appeal the wife claimed damages from a solicitor who advised her before she entered into a guarantee obligation under the undue influence of her husband. Given the range of cases before the House of Lords it is not possible to include within the extracts the application of the legal principles to the facts of the cases. In the extracts that follow, the excerpts from the speech of Lord Nicholls cover most of the points in issue in the appeals, whereas the excerpts from the other speeches are confined to the analysis employed by their Lordships of undue influence itself.

Lord Bingham of Cornhill

3. . . . While the opinions of Lord Nicholls and Lord Scott show some difference of expression and approach, I do not myself discern any significant difference of legal principle applicable to these cases, and I agree with both opinions. But if I am wrong and such differences exist, it is plain that the opinion of Lord Nicholls commands the unqualified support of all members of the House.

Lord Nicholls of Birkenhead

5. My Lords, before your Lordships' House are appeals in eight cases. Each case arises out of a transaction in which a wife charged her interest in her home in favour of a bank as security for her husband's indebtedness or the indebtedness of a company through which he carried on business. The wife later asserted she signed the charge under the undue influence of her husband. In *Barclays Bank plc* v. *O'Brien* [1994] 1 AC 180 your Lordships enunciated the principles applicable in this type of case. Since then, many cases have come before the courts, testing the implications of the *O'Brien* decision in a variety of different factual situations. Seven of the present appeals are of this character. In each case the bank sought to enforce the charge signed by the wife. The bank claimed an order for possession of the matrimonial home. The wife raised a defence that the bank was on notice that her concurrence in the transaction had been procured by her husband's undue influence. The eighth appeal concerns a claim by a wife for damages from a solicitor who advised her before she entered into a guarantee obligation of this character.

Undue influence

6. The issues raised by these appeals make it necessary to go back to first principles. Undue influence is one of the grounds of relief developed by the courts of equity as a court of conscience. The objective is to ensure that the influence of one person over another is not abused. In everyday life people constantly seek to influence the decisions of others. They seek to persuade those with whom they are dealing to enter into transactions, whether great or small. The law has set limits to the means properly employable for this purpose. To this end the common law developed a principle of duress. Originally this was narrow in its scope, restricted to the more blatant forms of physical coercion, such as personal violence.

7. Here, as elsewhere in the law, equity supplemented the common law. Equity extended the reach of the law to other unacceptable forms of persuasion. The law will investigate the manner in which the intention to enter into the transaction was secured: 'how the intention was produced', in the oft repeated words of Lord Eldon LC, from as long ago as 1807 (*Huguenin* v. *Baseley* 14 Ves 273, 300). If the intention was produced by an unacceptable means, the law will not permit the transaction to stand. The means used is regarded as an exercise of improper or 'undue' influence, and hence unacceptable, whenever the consent thus procured ought not fairly to be treated as the expression of a person's free will. It is impossible to be more precise or definitive. The circumstances in which one person acquires influence over another, and the manner in which influence may be exercised, vary too widely to permit of any more specific criterion.

8. Equity identified broadly two forms of unacceptable conduct. The first comprises overt acts of improper pressure or coercion such as unlawful threats. Today there is much overlap with the principle of duress as this principle has subsequently developed. The second form arises out of a relationship between two persons where one has acquired over another a measure of influence, or ascendancy, of which the ascendant person then takes unfair advantage . . .

9. In cases of this latter nature the influence one person has over another provides scope for misuse without any specific overt acts of persuasion. The relationship between two individuals may be such that, without more, one of them is disposed to agree a course of action proposed by the other. Typically this occurs when one person places trust in another to look after his affairs and interests, and the latter betrays this trust by preferring his own interests. He abuses the influence he has acquired. In *Allcard* v. *Skinner* (1887) 36 Ch D 145, a case well known to every law student, Lindley LJ, at p. 181, described this class of cases as those in which it was the duty of one party to advise the other or to manage his property for him . . .

10. The law has long recognised the need to prevent abuse of influence in these 'relationship' cases despite the absence of evidence of overt acts of persuasive conduct. The types of relationship, such as parent and child, in which this principle falls to be applied cannot be listed exhaustively. Relationships are infinitely various. Sir Guenter Treitel QC has rightly noted that the question is whether one party has reposed sufficient trust and confidence in the other, rather than whether the relationship between the parties belongs to a particular type: see *Treitel, The Law of Contract,* 10th ed (1999), pp. 380–381. For example, the relation of banker and customer will not normally meet this criterion, but exceptionally it may: see *National Westminster Bank plc* v. *Morgan* [1985] AC 686, 707–709.

11. Even this test is not comprehensive. The principle is not confined to cases of abuse of trust and confidence. It also includes, for instance, cases where a vulnerable person has been exploited. Indeed, there is no single touchstone for determining whether the principle is applicable. Several expressions have been used in an endeavour to encapsulate the essence: trust and confidence, reliance, dependence or vulnerability on the one hand and ascendancy, domination or control on the other. None of these descriptions is perfect. None is all embracing. Each has its proper place.

12. In *CIBC Mortgages plc* v. *Pitt* [1994] 1 AC 200 your Lordships' House decided that in cases of undue influence disadvantage is not a necessary ingredient of the cause of action. It is not essential that the transaction should be disadvantageous to the pressurised or influenced person, either in financial terms or in any other way. However, in the nature of things, questions of undue influence will not usually arise, and the exercise of undue influence is unlikely to occur, where the transaction is innocuous. The issue is likely to arise only when, in some respect, the transaction was disadvantageous either from the outset or as matters turned out.

Burden of proof and presumptions

13.   Whether a transaction was brought about by the exercise of undue influence is a question of fact. Here, as elsewhere, the general principle is that he who asserts a wrong has been committed must prove it. The burden of proving an allegation of undue influence rests upon the person who claims to have been wronged. This is the general rule. The evidence required to discharge the burden of proof depends on the nature of the alleged undue influence, the personality of the parties, their relationship, the extent to which the transaction cannot readily be accounted for by the ordinary motives of ordinary persons in that relationship, and all the circumstances of the case.

14.   Proof that the complainant placed trust and confidence in the other party in relation to the management of the complainant's financial affairs, coupled with a transaction which calls for explanation, will normally be sufficient, failing satisfactory evidence to the contrary, to discharge the burden of proof. On proof of these two matters the stage is set for the court to infer that, in the absence of a satisfactory explanation, the transaction can only have been procured by undue influence. In other words, proof of these two facts is prima facie evidence that the defendant abused the influence he acquired in the parties' relationship. He preferred his own interests. He did not behave fairly to the other. So the evidential burden then shifts to him. It is for him to produce evidence to counter the inference which otherwise should be drawn . . .

16.   Generations of equity lawyers have conventionally described this situation as one in which a presumption of undue influence arises. This use of the term 'presumption' is descriptive of a shift in the evidential onus on a question of fact. When a plaintiff succeeds by this route he does so because he has succeeded in establishing a case of undue influence. The court has drawn appropriate inferences of fact upon a balanced consideration of the whole of the evidence at the end of a trial in which the burden of proof rested upon the plaintiff. The use, in the course of the trial, of the forensic tool of a shift in the evidential burden of proof should not be permitted to obscure the overall position. These cases are the equitable counterpart of common law cases where the principle of res ipsa loquitur is invoked. There is a rebuttable evidential presumption of undue influence.

17.   The availability of this forensic tool in cases founded on abuse of influence arising from the parties' relationship has led to this type of case sometimes being labelled 'presumed undue influence'. This is by way of contrast with cases involving actual pressure or the like, which are labelled 'actual undue influence': see *Bank of Credit and Commerce International SA* v. *Aboody* [1990] 1 QB 923, 953, and *Royal Bank of Scotland plc* v. *Etridge (No 2)* [1998] 4 All ER 705, 711–712, paras 5–7. This usage can be a little confusing. In many cases where a plaintiff has claimed that the defendant abused the influence he acquired in a relationship of trust and confidence the plaintiff has succeeded by recourse to the rebuttable evidential presumption. But this need not be so. Such a plaintiff may succeed even where this presumption is not available to him; for instance, where the impugned transaction was not one which called for an explanation.

18.   The evidential presumption discussed above is to be distinguished sharply from a different form of presumption which arises in some cases. The law has adopted a sternly protective attitude towards certain types of relationship in which one party acquires influence over another who is vulnerable and dependent and where, moreover, substantial gifts by the influenced or vulnerable person are not normally to be expected. Examples of relationships within this special class are parent and child, guardian and ward, trustee and beneficiary, solicitor and client, and medical adviser and patient. In these cases the law presumes, irrebuttably, that one party had influence over the other. The complainant need not prove he actually reposed trust and confidence in the other party. It is sufficient for him to prove the existence of the type of relationship.

19. It is now well established that husband and wife is not one of the relationships to which this latter principle applies . . . there is nothing unusual or strange in a wife, from motives of affection or for other reasons, conferring substantial financial benefits on her husband. Although there is no presumption, the court will nevertheless note, as a matter of fact, the opportunities for abuse which flow from a wife's confidence in her husband. The court will take this into account with all the other evidence in the case. Where there is evidence that a husband has taken unfair advantage of his influence over his wife, or her confidence in him, 'it is not difficult for the wife to establish her title to relief' . . .

Independent advice

20. Proof that the complainant received advice from a third party before entering into the impugned transaction is one of the matters a court takes into account when weighing all the evidence. The weight, or importance, to be attached to such advice depends on all the circumstances. In the normal course, advice from a solicitor or other outside adviser can be expected to bring home to a complainant a proper understanding of what he or she is about to do. But a person may understand fully the implications of a proposed transaction, for instance, a substantial gift, and yet still be acting under the undue influence of another. Proof of outside advice does not, of itself, necessarily show that the subsequent completion of the transaction was free from the exercise of undue influence. Whether it will be proper to infer that outside advice had an emancipating effect, so that the transaction was not brought about by the exercise of undue influence, is a question of fact to be decided having regard to all the evidence in the case.

Manifest disadvantage

21. As already noted, there are two prerequisites to the evidential shift in the burden of proof from the complainant to the other party. First, that the complainant reposed trust and confidence in the other party, or the other party acquired ascendancy over the complainant. Second, that the transaction is not readily explicable by the relationship of the parties.

22. Lindley LJ summarised this second prerequisite in the leading authority of *Allcard* v. *Skinner*, 36 Ch D 145, where the donor parted with almost all her property. Lindley LJ pointed out that where a gift of a small amount is made to a person standing in a confidential relationship to the donor, some proof of the exercise of the influence of the donee must be given. The mere existence of the influence is not enough. He continued, at p 185: 'But if the gift is so large as not to be reasonably accounted for on the ground of friendship, relationship, charity, or other ordinary motives on which ordinary men act, the burden is upon the donee to support the gift' . . .

24. . . . The second prerequisite, as expressed by Lindley LJ, is good sense. It is a necessary limitation upon the width of the first prerequisite. It would be absurd for the law to presume that every gift by a child to a parent, or every transaction between a client and his solicitor or between a patient and his doctor, was brought about by undue influence unless the contrary is affirmatively proved. Such a presumption would be too far-reaching. The law would be out of touch with everyday life if the presumption were to apply to every Christmas or birthday gift by a child to a parent, or to an agreement whereby a client or patient agrees to be responsible for the reasonable fees of his legal or medical adviser. The law would be rightly open to ridicule, for transactions such as these are unexceptionable. They do not suggest that something may be amiss. So something more is needed before the law reverses the burden of proof, something which calls for an explanation. When that something more is present, the greater the disadvantage to the vulnerable person, the more cogent must be the explanation before the presumption will be regarded as rebutted.

25. This was the approach adopted by Lord Scarman in *National Westminster Bank plc* v. *Morgan* [1985] AC 686, 703–707. He cited Lindley LJ's observations in *Allcard* v. *Skinner* 36 Ch D 145, 185, which I have set out above. He noted that whatever the legal character of the transaction, it must constitute a disadvantage sufficiently serious to require evidence to rebut the presumption that in the circumstances of the parties' relationship, it was procured by the exercise of undue influence. Lord Scarman concluded, at p. 704:

'the Court of Appeal erred in law in holding that the presumption of undue influence can arise from the evidence of the relationship of the parties without also evidence that the transaction itself was wrongful in that it constituted *an advantage taken of the person subjected to the influence which, failing proof to the contrary, was explicable only on the basis that undue influence had been exercised to procure it*.' (Emphasis added.)

26. Lord Scarman attached the label 'manifest disadvantage' to this second ingredient necessary to raise the presumption. This label has been causing difficulty. It may be apt enough when applied to straightforward transactions such as a substantial gift or a sale at an undervalue. But experience has now shown that this expression can give rise to misunderstanding. The label is being understood and applied in a way which does not accord with the meaning intended by Lord Scarman, its originator.

27. The problem has arisen in the context of wives guaranteeing payment of their husband's business debts. In recent years judge after judge has grappled with the baffling question whether a wife's guarantee of her husband's bank overdraft, together with a charge on her share of the matrimonial home, was a transaction manifestly to her disadvantage.

28. In a narrow sense, such a transaction plainly ('manifestly') is disadvantageous to the wife. She undertakes a serious financial obligation, and in return she personally receives nothing. But that would be to take an unrealistically blinkered view of such a transaction. Unlike the relationship of solicitor and client or medical adviser and patient, in the case of husband and wife there are inherent reasons why such a transaction may well be for her benefit. Ordinarily, the fortunes of husband and wife are bound up together. If the husband's business is the source of the family income, the wife has a lively interest in doing what she can to support the business. A wife's affection and self-interest run hand-in-hand in inclining her to join with her husband in charging the matrimonial home, usually a jointly-owned asset, to obtain the financial facilities needed by the business. The finance may be needed to start a new business, or expand a promising business, or rescue an ailing business.

29. Which, then, is the correct approach to adopt in deciding whether a transaction is disadvantageous to the wife: the narrow approach, or the wider approach? The answer is neither. The answer lies in discarding a label which gives rise to this sort of ambiguity. The better approach is to adhere more directly to the test outlined by Lindley LJ in *Allcard* v. *Skinner* 36 Ch D 145, and adopted by Lord Scarman in *National Westminster Bank plc* v. *Morgan* [1985] AC 686, in the passages I have cited.

30. I return to husband and wife cases. I do not think that, in the ordinary course, a guarantee of the character I have mentioned is to be regarded as a transaction which, failing proof to the contrary, is explicable only on the basis that it has been procured by the exercise of undue influence by the husband. Wives frequently enter into such transactions. There are good and sufficient reasons why they are willing to do so, despite the risks involved for them and their families. They may be enthusiastic. They may not. They may be less optimistic than their husbands about the prospects of the husbands' businesses. They may be anxious, perhaps exceedingly so. But this is a far cry from saying that such transactions as a class are to be regarded as prima facie evidence of the exercise of undue influence by husbands.

31. I have emphasised the phrase 'in the ordinary course'. There will be cases where a wife's signature of a guarantee or a charge of her share in the matrimonial home does call for explanation. Nothing I have said above is directed at such a case.

A cautionary note

32. I add a cautionary note. . . . It concerns the general approach to be adopted by a court when considering whether a wife's guarantee of her husband's bank overdraft was procured by her husband's undue influence. Undue influence has a connotation of impropriety. In the eye of the law, undue influence means that influence has been misused. Statements or conduct by a husband which do not pass beyond the bounds of what may be expected of a reasonable husband in the circumstances should not, without more, be castigated as undue influence. Similarly, when a husband is forecasting the future of his business, and expressing his hopes or fears, a degree of hyperbole may be only natural. Courts should not too readily treat such exaggerations as misstatements.

33. Inaccurate explanations of a proposed transaction are a different matter. So are cases where a husband, in whom a wife has reposed trust and confidence for the management of their financial affairs, prefers his interests to hers and makes a choice for both of them on that footing. Such a husband abuses the influence he has. He fails to discharge the obligation of candour and fairness he owes a wife who is looking to him to make the major financial decisions.

The complainant and third parties: suretyship transactions

34. The problem considered in *O'Brien's* case and raised by the present appeals is of comparatively recent origin. It arises out of the substantial growth in home ownership over the last 30 or 40 years and, as part of that development, the great increase in the number of homes owned jointly by husbands and wives. More than two-thirds of householders in the United Kingdom now own their own homes. For most home-owning couples, their homes are their most valuable asset. They must surely be free, if they so wish, to use this asset as a means of raising money, whether for the purpose of the husband's business or for any other purpose. Their home is their property. The law should not restrict them in the use they may make of it. Bank finance is in fact by far the most important source of external capital for small businesses with fewer than ten employees. These businesses comprise about 95 per cent of all businesses in the country, responsible for nearly one-third of all employment. Finance raised by second mortgages on the principal's home is a significant source of capital for the start-up of small businesses.

35   If the freedom of home-owners to make economic use of their homes is not to be frustrated, a bank must be able to have confidence that a wife's signature of the necessary guarantee and charge will be as binding upon her as is the signature of anyone else on documents which he or she may sign. Otherwise banks will not be willing to lend money on the security of a jointly owned house or flat.

36.   At the same time, the high degree of trust and confidence and emotional inter-dependence which normally characterises a marriage relationship provides scope for abuse. One party may take advantage of the other's vulnerability. Unhappily, such abuse does occur. Further, it is all too easy for a husband, anxious or even desperate for bank finance, to misstate the position in some particular or to mislead the wife, wittingly or unwittingly, in some other way. The law would be seriously defective if it did not recognise these realities.

37.   In *O'Brien's* case this House decided where the balance should be held between these competing interests . . .

38.   The jurisprudential route by which the House reached its conclusion in *O'Brien's* case has attracted criticism from some commentators. . . . Lord Browne-Wilkinson prayed in aid the doctrine of constructive notice. In circumstances he identified, a creditor is put on inquiry. When that is so, the creditor 'will have constructive notice of the wife's rights' unless the creditor takes reasonable steps to satisfy himself that the wife's agreement to stand surety has been properly obtained: see [1994] 1 AC 180, 196.

39.   Lord Browne-Wilkinson would be the first to recognise this is not a conventional use of the equitable concept of constructive notice. The traditional use of this concept concerns the circumstances in which a transferee of property who acquires a legal estate from a transferor with a defective title may nonetheless obtain a good title, that is, a better title than the transferor had. That is not the present case. The bank acquires its charge from the wife, and there is nothing wrong with her title to her share of the matrimonial home. The transferor wife is seeking to resile from the very transaction she entered into with the bank, on the ground that her apparent consent was procured by the undue influence or other misconduct, such as misrepresentation, of a third party (her husband). She is seeking to set aside her contract of guarantee and, with it, the charge she gave to the bank.

40.   The traditional view of equity in this tripartite situation seems to be that a person in the position of the wife will only be relieved of her bargain if the other party to the transaction (the bank, in the present instance) was privy to the conduct which led to the wife's entry into the transaction. Knowledge is required: . . . The law imposes no obligation on one party to a transaction to check whether the other party's concurrence was obtained by undue influence. But *O'Brien* has introduced into the law the concept that, in certain circumstances, a party to a contract may lose the benefit of his contract, entered into in good faith, if he ought to have known that the other's concurrence had been procured by the misconduct of a third party.

41. There is a further respect in which *O'Brien* departed from conventional concepts. Traditionally, a person is deemed to have notice (that is, he has 'constructive' notice) of a prior right when he does not actually know of it but would have learned of it had he made the requisite inquiries. A purchaser will be treated as having constructive notice of all that a reasonably prudent purchaser would have discovered. In the present type of case, the steps a bank is required to take, lest it have constructive notice that the wife's concurrence was procured improperly by her husband, do not consist of making inquiries. Rather, *O'Brien* envisages that the steps taken by the bank will reduce, or even eliminate, the risk of the wife entering into the transaction under any misapprehension or as a result of undue influence by her husband. The steps are not concerned to discover whether the wife has been wronged by her husband in this way. The steps are concerned to minimise the risk that such a wrong may be committed.

42. These novelties do not point to the conclusion that the decision of this House in *O'Brien* is leading the law astray. Lord Browne-Wilkinson acknowledged he might be extending the law. . . . Some development was sorely needed. The law had to find a way of giving wives a reasonable measure of protection, without adding unreasonably to the expense involved in entering into guarantee transactions of the type under consideration. The protection had to extend also to any misrepresentations made by a husband to his wife. In a situation where there is a substantial risk the husband may exercise his influence improperly regarding the provision of security for his business debts, there is an increased risk that explanations of the transaction given by him to his wife may be misleadingly incomplete or even inaccurate.

43. The route selected in *O'Brien* ought not to have an unsettling effect on established principles of contract. *O'Brien* concerned suretyship transactions. These are tripartite transactions. They involve the debtor as well as the creditor and the guarantor. The guarantor enters into the transaction at the request of the debtor. The guarantor assumes obligations. On the face of the transaction the guarantor usually receives no benefit in return, unless the guarantee is being given on a commercial basis. Leaving aside cases where the relationship between the surety and the debtor is commercial, a guarantee transaction is one-sided so far as the guarantor is concerned. The creditor knows this. Thus the decision in *O'Brien* is directed at a class of contracts which has special features of its own . . .

The threshold: when the bank is put on inquiry

44. . . . For practical reasons the level is set much lower than is required to satisfy a court that, failing contrary evidence, the court may infer that the transaction was procured by undue influence. Lord Browne-Wilkinson said [1994] 1 AC 180, 196:

'Therefore in my judgment a creditor in put on inquiry when a wife offers to stand surety for her husband's debts by the combination of two factors: (a) the transaction is on its face not to the financial advantage of the wife; and (b) there is a substantial risk in transactions of that kind that, in procuring the wife to act as surety, the husband has committed a legal or equitable wrong that entitles the wife to set aside the transaction.'

In my view, this passage, read in context, is to be taken to mean, quite simply, that a bank is put on inquiry whenever a wife offers to stand surety for her husband's debts . . .

46.   I do not understand Lord Browne-Wilkinson to have been saying that, in husband and wife cases, whether the bank is put on inquiry depends on its state of knowledge of the parties' marriage, or of the degree of trust and confidence the particular wife places in her husband in relation to her financial affairs. That would leave banks in a state of considerable uncertainty in a situation where it is important they should know clearly where they stand . . . I read (a) and (b) as Lord Browne-Wilkinson's broad explanation of the reason why a creditor is put on inquiry when a wife offers to stand surety for her husband's debts. These are the two factors which, taken together, constitute the under-lying rationale.

47.   The position is likewise if the husband stands surety for his wife's debts. Similarly, in the case of unmarried couples, whether heterosexual or homosexual, where the bank is aware of the relationship. . . . Cohabitation is not essential . . .

48.   As to the type of transactions where a bank is put on inquiry, the case where a wife becomes surety for her husband's debts is, in this context, a straightforward case. The bank is put on inquiry. On the other side of the line is the case where money is being advanced, or has been advanced, to husband and wife jointly. In such a case the bank is not put on inquiry, unless the bank is aware the loan is being made for the husband's purposes, as distinct from their joint purposes . . .

49.   Less clear cut is the case where the wife becomes surety for the debts of a company whose shares are held by her and her husband. Her shareholding may be nominal, or she may have a minority shareholding or an equal shareholding with her husband. In my view the bank is put on inquiry in such cases, even when the wife is a director or secretary of the company . . .

The steps a bank should take

50.   . . . In *O'Brien* [1994] 1 AC 180, 196–197 Lord Browne-Wilkinson said that a bank can reasonably be expected to take steps to bring home to the wife the risk she is running by standing as surety and to advise her to take independent advice. That test is applicable to past transactions. All the cases now before your Lordships' House fall into this category. For the future a bank satisfies these requirements if it insists that the wife attend a private meeting with a representative of the bank at which she is told of the extent of her liability as surety, warned of the risk she is running and urged to take independent legal advice. In exceptional cases the bank, to be safe, has to insist that the wife is separately advised . . .

53.   . . . it is plainly neither desirable nor practicable that banks should be required to attempt to discover for themselves whether a wife's consent is being procured by the exercise of undue influence of her husband. This is not a step the banks should be expected to take. Nor, further, is it desirable or practicable that banks should be expected to insist on confirmation from a solicitor that the solicitor has satisfied himself that the wife's consent has not been procured by undue influence . . .

54.   The furthest a bank can be expected to go is to take reasonable steps to satisfy itself that the wife has had brought home to her, in a meaningful way, the practical implications of the proposed transaction. This does not wholly eliminate the risk of undue influence or misrepresentation. But it does mean that a wife enters into a transaction with her eyes open so far as the basic elements of the transaction are concerned . . .

55.   . . . A bank may itself provide the necessary information directly to the wife. . . . But . . . provided a suitable alternative is available, banks ought not to be compelled to take this course. . . . It is not unreasonable for the banks to prefer that this task should be undertaken by an independent legal adviser . . .

56.   . . . Ordinarily it will be reasonable that a bank should be able to rely upon confirmation from a solicitor, acting for the wife, that he has advised the wife appropriately.

57.   The position will be otherwise if the bank knows that the solicitor has not duly advised the wife or, I would add, if the bank knows facts from which it ought to have realised that the wife has not received the appropriate advice. In such circumstances the bank will proceed at its own risk.

The content of the legal advice

. . .

61.   . . . it is not for the solicitor to veto the transaction by declining to confirm to the bank that he has explained the documents to the wife and the risks she is taking upon herself. If the solicitor considers the transaction is not in the wife's best interests, he will give reasoned advice to the wife to that effect. But at the end of the day the decision on whether to proceed is the decision of the client, not the solicitor. A wife is not to be precluded from entering into a financially unwise transaction if, for her own reasons, she wishes to do so.

62.   That is the general rule. There may, of course, be exceptional circumstances where it is glaringly obvious that the wife is being grievously wronged. In such a case the solicitor should decline to act further. . . . In identifying what are the solicitor's responsibilities the starting point must always be the solicitor's retainer. . . . As a first step the solicitor will need to explain to the wife the purpose for which he has become involved at all. He should explain that, should it ever become necessary, the bank will rely upon his involvement to counter any suggestion that the wife was overborne by her husband or that she did not properly understand the implications of the transaction. The solicitor will need to obtain confirmation from the wife that she wishes him to act for her in the matter and to advise her on the legal and practical implications of the proposed transaction.

65.   When an instruction to this effect is forthcoming, the content of the advice required from a solicitor before giving the confirmation sought by the bank will, inevitably, depend upon the circumstances of the case. Typically, the advice a solicitor can be expected to give should cover the following matters as the core minimum. (1) He will need to explain the nature of the documents and the practical consequences these will have for the wife if she signs them. She could lose her home if her husband's business does not prosper. Her home may be her only substantial asset, as well as the family's home. She could be made bankrupt. (2) He will need to point out the seriousness of the risks involved. The wife should be told the purpose of the proposed new facility, the amount and principal terms of the new facility, and that the bank might increase the amount of the facility, or change its terms, or grant a new facility, without reference to her. She should be told the amount of her liability under her guarantee. The solicitor should discuss the wife's financial means, including her understanding of the value of the property being charged. The solicitor should discuss whether the wife or her husband has any other assets out of which repayment could be made if the husband's business should fail. These matters are relevant to the seriousness of the risks involved. (3) The solicitor will need to state clearly that the wife has a choice. The decision is hers and hers alone. Explanation of the choice facing the wife will call for some discussion of the present financial position, including the amount of the husband's present indebtedness, and the amount of his current overdraft facility. (4) The solicitor should check whether the wife wishes to proceed. She should be asked whether she is content that the solicitor should write to the bank confirming he has explained to her the nature of the documents and the practical implications they may have for her, or whether, for instance, she would prefer him to negotiate with the bank on the terms of the transaction. Matters for negotiation could include the sequence in which the various securities will be called upon or a specific or lower limit to her liabilities. The solicitor should not give any confirmation to the bank without the wife's authority.

66.   The solicitor's discussion with the wife should take place at a face-to-face meeting, in the absence of the husband. It goes without saying that the solicitor's explanations should be couched in suitably non-technical language. It also goes without saying that the solicitor's task is an important one. It is not a formality.

67.   The solicitor should obtain from the bank any information he needs. If the bank fails for any reason to provide information requested by the solicitor, the solicitor should decline to provide the confirmation sought by the bank . . .

Independent advice

69.   I turn next to the much-vexed question whether the solicitor advising the wife must act for the wife alone. . . . A requirement that a wife should receive advice from a solicitor acting solely for her will frequently add significantly to the legal costs. Sometimes a wife will be happier to be advised by a family solicitor known to her than by a complete stranger. Sometimes a solicitor who knows both husband and wife and their histories will be better placed to advise than a solicitor who is a complete stranger. . . . The advantages attendant upon the employment of a solicitor acting solely for the wife do not justify the additional expense this would involve for the husband. When accepting instructions to advise the wife the solicitor assumes responsibilities directly to her, both at law and professionally. These duties, and this is central to the reasoning on this point, are owed to the wife alone. In advising the wife the solicitor is acting for the wife alone. He is concerned only with her interests. I emphasise, therefore, that in every case the solicitor must consider carefully whether there is any conflict of duty or interest and, more widely, whether it would be in the best interests of the wife for him to accept instructions from her. If he decides to accept instructions, his assumption of legal and professional responsibilities to her ought, in the ordinary course of things, to provide sufficient assurance that he will give the requisite advice fully, carefully and conscientiously. Especially so, now that the nature of the advice called for has been clarified. If at any stage the solicitor becomes concerned that there is a real risk that other interests or duties may inhibit his advice to the wife he must cease to act for her.

Agency

75. . . . The next question concerns the position when a solicitor has accepted instructions to advise a wife but he fails to do so properly . . . in advising the wife the solicitor is acting for the wife and no one else. The bank does not have, and is intended not to have, any knowledge of or control over the advice the solicitor gives the wife. The solicitor is not accountable to the bank for the advice he gives to the wife. To impute to the bank knowledge of what passed between the solicitor and the wife would contradict this essential feature of the arrangement. The mere fact that, for its own purposes, the bank asked the solicitor to advise the wife does not make the solicitor the bank's agent in giving that advice.

78. In the ordinary case, therefore, deficiencies in the advice given are a matter between the wife and her solicitor. The bank is entitled to proceed on the assumption that a solicitor advising the wife has done his job properly . . .

Obtaining the solicitor's confirmation

79. I now return to the steps a bank should take when it has been put on inquiry and for its protection is looking to the fact that the wife has been advised independently by a solicitor.

(1) . . . the bank should take steps to check *directly with the wife* the name of the solicitor she wishes to act for her. To this end, in future the bank should communicate directly with the wife, informing her that for its own protection it will require written confirmation from a solicitor, acting for her, to the effect that the solicitor has fully explained to her the nature of the documents and the practical implications they will have for her. She should be told that the purpose of this requirement is that thereafter she should not be able to dispute she is legally bound by the documents once she has signed them. She should be asked to nominate a solicitor whom she is willing to instruct to advise her, separately from her husband, and act for her in giving the necessary confirmation to the bank. She should be told that, if she wishes, the solicitor may be the same solicitor as is acting for her husband in the transaction. If a solicitor is already acting for the husband and the wife, she should be asked whether she would prefer that a different solicitor should act for her regarding the bank's requirement for confirmation from a solicitor.

The bank should not proceed with the transaction until it has received an appropriate response directly from the wife.

(2) . . . the bank must provide the solicitor with the financial information he needs. . . . What is required must depend on the facts of the case. Ordinarily this will include information on the purpose for which the proposed new facility has been requested, the current amount of the husband's indebtedness, the amount of his current overdraft facility, and the amount and terms of any new facility. If the bank's request for security arose from a written application by the husband for a facility, a copy of the application should be sent to the solicitor. The bank will, of course, need first to obtain the consent of its customer to this circulation of confidential information. If this consent is not forthcoming the transaction will not be able to proceed.

(3) Exceptionally there may be a case where the bank believes or suspects that the wife has been misled by her husband or is not entering into the transaction of her own free will. If such a case occurs the bank must inform the wife's solicitors of the facts giving rise to its belief or suspicion.

(4) The bank should in every case obtain from the wife's solicitor a written confirmation to the effect mentioned above.

80.   These steps will be applicable to future transactions. In respect of past transactions, the bank will ordinarily be regarded as having discharged its obligations if a solicitor who was acting for the wife in the transaction gave the bank confirmation to the effect that he had brought home to the wife the risks she was running by standing as surety.

A wider principle

82.   . . . the law does not regard sexual relationships as standing in some special category of their own so far as undue influence is concerned. Sexual relationships are no more than one type of relationship in which an individual may acquire influence over another individual. The *O'Brien* decision cannot sensibly be regarded as confined to sexual relationships, although these are likely to be its main field of application at present. What is appropriate for sexual relationships ought, in principle, to be appropriate also for other relationships where trust and confidence are likely to exist.

83.   The courts have already recognised this. Further application, or development, of the *O'Brien* principle has already taken place . . .

84.   The crucially important question raised by this wider application of the *O'Brien* principle concerns the circumstances which will put a bank on inquiry. A bank is put on inquiry whenever a wife stands as surety for her husband's debts. It is sufficient that the bank knows of the husband-wife relationship. That bare fact is enough. The bank must then take reasonable steps to bring home to the wife the risks involved. What, then, of other relationships where there is an increased risk of undue influence, such as parent and child? . . . a bank cannot be expected to probe the emotional relationship between two individuals, whoever they may be . . . there is no rational cut-off point, with certain types of relationship being susceptible to the *O'Brien* principle and others not . . . the only practical way forward is to regard banks as 'put on inquiry' in every case where the relationship between the surety and the debtor is non-commercial. The creditor must always take reasonable steps to bring home to the individual guarantor the risks he is running by standing as surety. As a measure of protection, this is valuable. But, in all conscience, it is a modest burden for banks and other lenders. It is no more than is reasonably to be expected of a creditor who is taking a guarantee from an individual. If the bank or other creditor does not take these steps, it is deemed to have notice of any claim the guarantor may have that the transaction was procured by undue influence or misrepresentation on the part of the debtor.

88.   Different considerations apply where the relationship between the debtor and guarantor is commercial, as where a guarantor is being paid a fee, or a company is guaranteeing the debts of another company in the same group. Those engaged in business can be regarded as capable of looking after themselves and understanding the risks involved in the giving of guarantees.

Lord Clyde

92. I question the wisdom of the practice which has grown up, . . . of attempting to make classifications of cases of undue influence. That concept is in any event not easy to define. . . . It is something which can be more easily recognised when found than exhaustively analysed in the abstract. Correspondingly the attempt to build up classes or categories may lead to confusion. The confusion is aggravated if the names used to identify the classes do not bear their actual meaning. Thus on the face of it a division into cases of 'actual' and 'presumed' undue influence appears illogical. It appears to confuse definition and proof. There is also room for uncertainty whether the presumption is of the existence of an influence or of its quality as being undue. I would also dispute the utility of the further sophistication of subdividing 'presumed undue influence' into further categories. All these classifications to my mind add mystery rather than illumination.

93. There is a considerable variety in the particular methods by which undue influence may be brought to bear on the grantor of a deed. They include cases of coercion, domination, victimisation and all the insidious techniques of persuasion. Certainly it can be recognised that in the case of certain relationships it will be relatively easier to establish that undue influence has been at work than in other cases where that sinister conclusion is not necessarily to be drawn with such ease. English law has identified certain relationships where the conclusion can prima facie be drawn so easily as to establish a presumption of undue influence. But this is simply a matter of evidence and proof. In other cases the grantor of the deed will require to fortify the case by evidence, for example, of the pressure which was unfairly applied by the stronger party to the relationship, or the abuse of a trusting and confidential relationship resulting in for the one party a disadvantage and for the other a collateral benefit beyond what might be expected from the relationship of the parties. At the end of the day, after trial, there will either be proof of undue influence or that proof will fail and it will be found that there was no undue influence. In the former case, whatever the relationship of the parties and however the influence was exerted, there will be found to have been an actual case of undue influence. In the latter there will be none . . .

Lord Hobhouse of Woodborough

(1) Presumed undue influence

103. The division between presumed and actual undue influence derives from the judgments in *Allcard* v. *Skinner*. Actual undue influence presents no relevant problem. It is an equitable wrong committed by the dominant party against the other which makes it unconscionable for the dominant party to enforce his legal rights against the other. It is typically some express conduct overbearing the other party's will. It is capable of including conduct which might give a defence at law, for example, duress and misrepresentation. . . . Actual undue influence does not depend upon some pre-existing relationship between the two parties though it is most commonly associated with and derives from such a relationship. He who alleges actual undue influence must prove it.

104. Presumed undue influence is different in that it necessarily involves some legally recognised relationship between the two parties. As a result of that relationship one party is treated as owing a special duty to deal fairly with the other. It is not necessary for present purposes to define the limits of the relationships which give rise to this duty. Typically they are fiduciary or closely analogous relationships . . .

Such legal relationships can be described as relationships where one party is legally presumed to repose trust and confidence in the other—the other side of the coin to the duty not to abuse that confidence. But there is no presumption properly so called that the confidence has been abused. It is a matter of evidence. . . . Thus, at the trial the judge will decide on the evidence whether he is in fact satisfied that there was no abuse of confidence. It will be appreciated that the relevance of the concept of 'manifest disadvantage' is evidential. It is relevant to the question whether there is any issue of abuse which can properly be raised. It is relevant to the determination whether in fact abuse did or did not occur. It is a fallacy to argue from the terminology normally used, 'presumed undue influence', to the position, not of presuming that one party reposed trust and confidence in the other, but of presuming that an abuse of that relationship has occurred; factual inference, yes, once the issue has been properly raised, but not a presumption.

105.   The Court of Appeal in *Aboody* [1990] 1 QB 923 and Lord Browne-Wilkinson [in *O'Brien*] classified cases where there was a legal relationship between the parties which the law presumed to be one of trust and confidence as 'presumed undue influence: class 2(A)'. They then made the logical extrapolation that there should be a class 2(B) to cover those cases where it was proved by evidence that one party had in fact reposed trust and confidence in the other. It was then said that the same consequences flowed from this factual relationship as from the legal class 2(A) relationship. Lord Browne-Wilkinson said [1994] 1 AC 180, 189–190:

'In a Class 2(B) case therefore, in the absence of evidence disproving undue influence, the complainant will succeed in setting aside the impugned transaction merely by proof that the complainant reposed trust and confidence in the wrongdoer without having to prove that the wrongdoer exerted actual undue influence or otherwise abused such trust and confidence in relation to the particular transaction impugned.'

There are difficulties in the literal application of this statement. It describes the other party as a 'wrongdoer' without saying why when it is expressly postulated that no wrongdoing may have occurred. He treats trust and confidence as indivisible. His actual words are: 'a relationship under which the complainant *generally* reposed trust and confidence in the wrongdoer' (emphasis supplied). But a wife may be happy to trust her husband to make the right decision in relation to some matters but not others; she may leave a particular decision to him but not other decisions. Nor is it clear why the mere 'existence of such relationship raises the presumption of undue influence'. Where the relevant question is one of fact and degree and of the evaluation of evidence, the language of presumption is likely to confuse rather than assist and this is borne out by experience.

106.   That there is room for an analogous approach to cases concerning a wife's guarantee of her husband's debts is clear and no doubt led to Lord Browne-Wilkinson saying what he did. The guarantee is given by the wife at the request of the husband. The guarantee is not on its face advantageous to the wife, doubly so where her liability is secured upon her home. The wife may well have trusted the husband to take for her the decision whether she should give the guarantee. If he takes the decision in these circum-stances, he owes her a duty to have regard to her interests before deciding. He is under a duty to deal fairly with her. He should make sure that she is entering into the obligation freely and in knowledge of the true facts. His duty may thus be analogous to that of a class 2(A) fiduciary so that it would be appropriate to require him to justify the decision. If no adequate justification is then provided, the conclusion would be that there had been an abuse of confidence. But any conclusion will only be reached after having received evidence. This evidence will inevitably cover as well whether there has in fact been an abuse of confidence or any other undue influence. The judge may have to draw inferences. He may have to decide whether he accepts the evidence of the wife and, if so, what it really amounts to, particularly if it is uncontradicted. Since there is no legal relationship of trust and confidence, the general burden of proving some form of wrongdoing remains with the wife, but the evidence which she has adduced may suffice to raise an inference of wrongdoing which the opposite party may find itself having to adduce evidence to rebut. If at the end of the trial the wife succeeds on the issue of undue influence, it will be because that is the right conclusion of fact on the state of the evidence at the end of the trial, not because of some artificial legal presumption that there must have been undue influence.

107. In agreement with what I understand to be the view of your Lordships, I consider that the so-called class 2(B) presumption should not be adopted. It is not a useful forensic tool. The wife or other person alleging that the relevant agreement or charge is not enforceable must prove her case. She can do this by proving that she was the victim of an equitable wrong. This wrong may be an overt wrong, such as oppression; or it may be the failure to perform an equitable duty, such as a failure by one in whom trust and confidence is reposed not to abuse that trust by failing to deal fairly with her and have proper regard to her interests. Although the general burden of proof is, and remains, upon her, she can discharge that burden of proof by establishing a sufficient prima facie case to justify a decision in her favour on the balance of probabilities, the court drawing appropriate inferences from the primary facts proved. sufficient to displace that conclusion. Provided it is remembered that the burden is an evidential one, the comparison with the operation of the doctrine res ipsa loquitur is useful.

Lord Scott of Foscote

Undue influence

151. Undue influence cases have, traditionally, been regarded as falling into two classes, cases where undue influence must be affirmatively proved (Class 1) and cases where undue influence will be presumed (Class 2). The nature of the two classes was described by Slade LJ in *Bank of Credit and Commerce International SA v. Aboody* [1990] 1 QB 923, 953:

'Ever since the judgments of this court in *Allcard v. Skinner* . . . clear distinction has been drawn between (1) those cases in which the court will uphold a plea of undue influence only if it is satisfied that such influence has been affirmatively proved on the evidence (commonly referred to as cases of "actual undue influence" . . . "Class 1" cases); (2) those cases (commonly referred to as cases of "presumed undue influence" . . . "Class 2" cases) in which the relationship between the parties will lead the court to presume that undue influence has been exerted unless evidence is adduced proving the contrary, eg by showing that the complaining party has had independent advice.'

152. This passage provides, if I may respectfully say so, an accurate summary description of the two classes. But, like most summaries, it requires some qualification.

153. First, the Class 2 presumption is an evidential rebuttable presumption. It shifts the onus from the party who is alleging undue influence to the party who is denying it. Second, the weight of the presumption will vary from case to case and will depend both on the particular nature of the relationship and on the particular nature of the impugned transaction. Third, the type and weight of evidence needed to rebut the presumption will obviously depend upon the weight of the presumption itself . . .

154. The onus will, of course, lie on the person alleging the undue influence to prove in the first instance sufficient facts to give rise to the presumption. The relationship relied on in support of the presumption will have to be proved.

155. In *National Westminster Bank plc v. Morgan* [1985] AC 686, 704 Lord Scarman, referring to the character of the impugned transaction in a Class 2 case, said: 'it must constitute a disadvantage sufficiently serious to require evidence to rebut the presumption that in the circumstances of the relationship between the parties it was procured by the exercise of undue influence'. Lord Scarman went on:

'In my judgment, therefore, the Court of Appeal erred in law in holding that the presumption of undue influence can arise from the evidence of the relationship of the parties without also evidence that the transaction itself was wrongful in that it consti-tuted an advantage taken of the person subjected to the influence which, failing proof to the contrary, was explicable only on the basis that undue influence had been exercised to procure it'

With respect to Lord Scarman, the reasoning seems to me to be circular. The transaction will not be 'wrongful' unless it was procured by undue influence. Its 'wrongful' character is a conclusion, not a tool by which to detect the presence of undue influence. On the other hand, the nature of the transaction, its inexplicability by reference to the normal motives by which people act, may, and usually will, constitute important evidential material.

156. Lord Browne-Wilkinson in *CIBC Mortgages plc v. Pitt* [1994] 1 AC 200 pointed out, plainly correctly, that if undue influence is proved, the victim's right to have the transaction set aside will not depend upon the disadvantageous quality of the transac-tion. Where, however a Class 2 presumption of undue influence is said to arise, the nature of the impugned transaction will always be material, no matter what the relationship between the parties. . . . It is, in my opinion, the combination of relationship and the nature of the transaction that gives rise to the presumption and, if the transaction is challenged, shifts the onus to the transferee.

157. In *Bank of Credit and Commerce International SA v. Aboody* [1990] 1 QB 923 Slade LJ split the Class 2 cases into two subdivisions. He categorised, at p. 953, the 'well established categories of relationships, such as a religious superior and inferior and doctor and patient where the relationship as such will give rise to the presumption' as Class 2A cases, and confirmed that neither a husband/wife relationship nor a banker/customer relationship would normally give rise to the presumption. (See also *National Westminster Bank plc v. Morgan* [1985] AC 686, 703 and *Barclays Bank v. O'Brien* [1994] 1 AC 180, 190.) He continued, at p 953:

'Nevertheless, on particular facts (frequently referred to in argument as "Class 2B" cases) relationships not falling within the "Class 2A" category may be shown to have become such as to justify the court in applying the same presumption.'

In *O'Brien* Lord Browne-Wilkinson adopted Slade LJ's Class 2B category for the purpose of the surety wife cases that he was considering. He said, at pp. 189–190:

'Even if there is no relationship falling within Class 2(A), if the complainant proves the de facto existence of a relationship under which the complainant generally reposed trust and confidence in the wrongdoer, the existence of such relationship raises the presumption of undue influence. In a Class 2(B) case therefore, in the absence of evidence disproving undue influence, the complainant will succeed in setting aside the impugned transaction merely by proof that the complainant reposed trust and confidence in the wrongdoer without having to prove that the wrongdoer exerted actual undue influence or otherwise abused such trust and confidence in relation to the particular transaction impugned.'

158. In my respectful opinion, this passage, at least in its application to the surety wife cases, has set the law on a wrong track. First, it seems to me to lose sight of the evidential and rebuttable character of the Class 2 presumption. The presumption arises where the combination of the relationship and the nature of the transaction justify, in the absence of any other evidence, a conclusion that the transaction was procured by the undue influence of the dominant party. Such a conclusion, reached on a balance of probabilities, is based upon inferences to be drawn from that combination. There are some relationships, generally of a fiduciary character, where, as a matter of policy, the law requires the dominant party to justify the righteousness of the transaction. These relationships do not include the husband wife relationship. In the surety wife cases, the complainant does have to prove undue influence: the presumption, if it arises on the facts of a particular case, is a tool to assist him or her in doing so. It shifts, for the moment, the onus of proof to the other side.

159. Second, the passage cited appears to regard a relationship of trust and confidence between a wife and husband as something special rather than as the norm. For my part, I would assume in every case in which a wife and husband are living together that there is a reciprocal trust and confidence between them. In the fairly common circumstance that the financial and business decisions of the family are primarily taken by the husband, I would assume that the wife would have trust and confidence in his ability to do so and would support his decisions. I would not expect evidence to be necessary to establish the existence of that trust and confidence. I would expect evidence to be necessary to demonstrate its absence. In cases where experience, probably bitter, had led a wife to doubt the wisdom of her husband's financial or business decisions, I still would not regard her willingness to support those decisions with her own assets as an indication that he had exerted undue influence over her to persuade her to do so. Rather I would regard her support as a natural and admirable consequence of the relationship of a mutually loyal married couple. The proposition that if a wife, who generally reposes trust and confidence in her husband, agrees to become surety to support his debts or his business enterprises a presumption of undue influence arises is one that I am unable to accept. To regard the husband in such a case as a presumed 'wrongdoer' does not seem to me consistent with the relationship of trust and confidence that is a part of every healthy marriage.

160. There are, of course, cases where a husband does abuse that trust and confidence. He may do so by expressions of quite unjustified over-optimistic enthusiasm about the prospects of success of his business enterprises. He may do so by positive misrepresentation of his business intentions, or of the nature of the security he is asking his wife to grant his creditors, or of some other material matter. He may do so by subjecting her to excessive pressure, emotional blackmail or bullying in order to persuade her to sign. But none of these things should, in my opinion, be presumed merely from the fact of the relationship of general trust and confidence. More is needed before the stage is reached at which, in the absence of any other evidence, an inference of undue influence can properly be drawn or a presumption of the existence of undue influence can be said to arise.

161. For my part, I doubt the utility of the Class 2B classification. Class 2A is useful in identifying particular relationships where the presumption arises. The presumption in Class 2B cases, however, is doing no more than recognising that evidence of the relationship between the dominant and subservient parties, coupled with whatever other evidence is for the time being available, may be sufficient to justify a finding of undue influence on the balance of probabilities. The onus shifts to the defendant. Unless the defendant introduces evidence to counteract the inference of undue influence that the complainant's evidence justifies, the complainant will succeed. In my opinion, the presumption of undue influence in Class 2B cases has the same function in undue influence cases as res ipsa loquitur has in negligence cases. It recognises an evidential state of affairs in which the onus has shifted.

162. In the surety wife cases it should, in my opinion, be recognised that undue influence, though a possible explanation for the wife's agreement to become surety, is a relatively unlikely one. *O'Brien* itself was a misrepresentation case. Undue influence had been alleged but the undoubted pressure which the husband had brought to bear to persuade his reluctant wife to sign was not regarded by the judge or the Court of Appeal as constituting undue influence. The wife's will had not been overborne by her husband. Nor was *O'Brien* a case in which, in my opinion, there would have been at any stage in the case a presumption of undue influence.

COMMENTARY

The decision of the House of Lords is one of enormous significance for banks and, to a lesser extent, solicitors called upon to advise non-commercial parties who agree to become guarantors. The practical significance of the case lies principally in the practical guidance given to banks and solicitors in relation to the procedures to be adopted in such cases. Our principal interest, by contrast, is in the analysis of undue influence. A number of points can be made.

The first is that their Lordships declined to provide a comprehensive definition of undue influence. The emphasis was very much on the facts and circumstances of the individual case (see, for example, para [13]). Thus relationships are 'infinitely various' (para [10]) and no description of the relevant factors is 'perfect' or 'all embracing' (para [11]). The focus of the doctrine seems to be rather more on the defendant than the claimant. Thus influence must not be 'abused' (para [6]) and undue influence is said to have 'a connotation of impropriety' (para [32]). But it may be 'impropriety' in an attenuated form, as *Allcard* v. *Skinner* suggests, where the 'impropriety' apparently took the form of not providing the plaintiff with access to independent advice before she decided to give away all her property.

Secondly, their Lordships affirmed the continued existence of the distinction between cases of actual and presumed undue influence (with the apparent exception of Lord Clyde at para [92]). Lord Nicholls seemed to conceive of actual undue influence in terms of 'improper pressure or coercion' so that there was 'much overlap with the principle of duress' (para [8]). Lord Hobhouse, on the other hand, defined actual undue influence in broader terms (see para [103]) when he said that it was an 'equitable wrong' which typically consisted of 'some express conduct overbearing the other party's will'.

Thirdly, the speeches contain much by way of discussion of presumed undue influence, although they seem to raise more questions than they answer. First, they affirm that the presumption is a rebuttable evidential presumption (see para [16]). Secondly, the future of 'the class 2B presumption' is now very doubtful. Lord Hobhouse stated that 'it should not be adopted' (para [107]), Lord Scott doubted its utility (para [161]), and Lord Clyde was generally hostile to the use of presumptions (para [92]). This being the case, there does not appear to be much point in leading evidence for the purpose of seeking to raise the presumption of undue influence. Instead, evidence should be led for the purpose of proving that undue influence has been exercised. The presumption still has a role to play in 'class 2A cases' and, indeed, Lord Nicholls stated that, in certain relationships, the law presumes 'irrebuttably' that one party had influence over the other (see para [18]).

Fourthly, 'manifest disadvantage' as a control device may have been replaced by the test originally adopted by Lindley LJ in *Allcard* v. *Skinner* (1887) 36 Ch D 145, 185, namely that the gift must have been so large that it cannot be accounted for on the grounds of friendship, relationship, charity, or other ordinary motives on which ordinary men act. This was certainly the view of Lord Nicholls (para [29]), although Lord Hobhouse referred to manifest disadvantage without apparent criticism (at para [104]). But it may be that this change will have little effect in practice. It is a change of label rather than substance. The courts are simply seeking a label to denote a transaction or a gift which calls for an explanation.

Fifthly, it was confirmed that the relationship of husband and wife does not give rise to a presumption of undue influence (paras [19], [106], and [159]–[160]).

Sixthly, it is not entirely clear what it is that is being presumed. Is it dependence? Is it exploitation? The answer would appear to be that there are different presumptions and that they operate in different ways. Thus certain relationships appear to give rise to a presumption of trust and confidence or 'influence' and, as Lord Nicholls points out, that presumption may be irrebuttable (para [18]). But this does not appear to be the same thing as the presumption of undue influence. In order to raise the presumption of undue influence it appears to be necessary to prove both the nature of the relationship between the parties and that the transaction is one that is not explicable by ordinary motives on which ordinary people act (see paras [21] and [158]). Once these two elements have been proved the law then presumes that undue influence has been exercised, unless the contrary is proved. This latter presumption may be better described as a 'factual inference' (see para [104]). Thus Lord Hobhouse states that it is the relationship of trust and confidence that is presumed and that 'there is no presumption properly so called that the confidence has been abused' (para [104]). While the court may be willing to make a 'factual inference' that abuse has taken place in certain cases, it is not the case that the law 'presumes' that abuse has taken place.

The effect of *Etridge* would appear to be to make it much more difficult for wives to establish that they have been the victims of undue influence by their husbands, at least at the trial of the action (different considerations appear to apply at the interlocutory stage, where the courts are less likely to strike out the claim as unarguable on a ground that relates to what has taken place between the husband and the wife). This is borne out by the application of the law to the facts of the various cases in the speech of Lord Scott (at paras [194]–[374]). At the trial of the action judges are encouraged to examine the facts of the case in order to decide, *on the facts*, whether or not undue influence has been exercised. Thus Lord Scott stated (at para [219]) that in a case 'where there has been a full trial . . . the judge must decide on the totality of the evidence before the court whether or not the allegation of undue influence has been proved'. Where the allegation takes the form of actual undue influence the wife must prove that she has been the subject of threats or other forms of wrongdoing by her husband. On the other hand, where she relies on the presumption of undue influence the judge must first of all decide whether or not the presumption has been triggered and, for that to happen, the wife must prove that a relationship of trust and confidence exists between the parties and that the transaction is one that is not explicable by ordinary motives on which ordinary people act. Wives are likely to find it difficult to prove the conditions necessary to trigger the operation of the presumption. This is so for two reasons. First, the relationship between husband and wife does not ordinarily trigger the presumption. However it is not impossible. In one of the appeals in *Etridge* the husband and wife were Hasidic Jews and the wife's upbringing and education 'prepared her to expect and to accept a position of subservience and obedience to the wishes of her husband' (para [283]). In this case Lord Scott concluded that the Court of Appeal had been correct to conclude that the presumption of undue influence arose on the facts of the case. Secondly, in the ordinary case, a guarantee by a wife of her husband's debts can be accounted for on the ground of their relationship and so does not give rise to an inference of undue influence. It is not a transaction that calls for an explanation or is inexplicable by reference to the ordinary motives on which ordinary people act.

Turning now to the circumstances in which the bank is put on inquiry that there is potential wrongdoing by the husband (or party in a similar position), the threshold adopted by the House of Lords is a low one. Essentially, the bank is put on inquiry whenever a wife offers to stand surety for her husband's debts or the debts of his business, even in the case where she is a shareholder and participates in the running of the company (but where the advance is made to the husband and wife jointly the bank is not put on inquiry unless the bank is aware that the loan is being made for the husband's purposes, as distinct from their joint purposes; see para [48]). The same principle applies to unmarried couples, whether heterosexual or homosexual, where the bank is aware of the relationship (see para [47]). The bank can also be put on inquiry where there is a relationship between the parties but that relationship is not sexual (see, for example, *Credit Lyonnais Bank Nederland NV v. Burch* [1997] 1 All ER 144). This extension potentially gives rise to difficulty in terms of defining the limits of the circumstances in which the bank is put on inquiry. Lord Nicholls therefore concluded (at para 84]) that the bank is put on inquiry in 'every case where the relationship between the surety and the debtor is non-commercial'. In all non-commercial cases the creditor must take reasonable steps to bring home to the individual guarantor the risks he is running by standing as surety. The line between commercial and non-commercial sureties may be indistinct at the margins. Lord Nicholls gave as examples of commercial sureties cases where the guarantor is being paid a fee or is guaranteeing the debts of another company in the same group (see para [88]). But in the vast majority of cases the distinction between a commercial and a non-commercial surety should not create difficulties in practice.

In relation to the steps to be taken by the bank once it has been put on inquiry, Lord Nicholls provided the banks with guidance at paragraph [79] of his speech. One point to note is that the bank is not required to meet with the wife and explain to her the nature of the transaction before she enters into it. It suffices for the bank to satisfy itself that the wife has been advised by her own solicitor. In many ways the obligations imposed on solicitors are more onerous than those imposed on banks. This leads us to the final issue which relates to the role of solicitors. As Lord Nicholls observed at paragraph [52] many of the difficulties that have arisen in this area 'stem from serious deficiencies, or alleged deficiencies, in the quality of the legal advice given to wives'. He concluded that independent legal advice for wives had been a 'fiction' and a 'charade'. The guidance given by Lord Nicholls in paragraphs [65] and [74] is clearly designed to provide more effective protection for wives by ensuring, as far as possible, that they have access to reliable, independent advice before they decide whether or not to act as guarantors of their husband's debts. Whether that protection will prove to be effective in the real world is, of course, another matter.

5. THE POST-*ETRIDGE* CASES

The cases post-*Etridge* continue to exhibit some uncertainty as to the basis of the doctrine of undue influence. Three cases are worthy of note. The first two (*R v. Attorney-General for England and Wales* [2003] UKPC 22 and *National Commercial Bank (Jamaica) Ltd* v. *Hew* [2003] UKPC 51) are decisions of the Privy Council, while the third (*Pesticcio* v. *Huet* [2004] EWCA Civ 372; [2004] All ER (D) 36 (April)) is a decision of the Court of Appeal. The former two cases incline towards a defendant-oriented conception of undue influence, whereas the latter very much supports a claimant-oriented perception. We shall consider each case in turn.

The first case is the decision of the Privy Council in *R* v. *Attorney-General for England and Wales* [2003] UKPC 22, the facts of which have already been set out (see p. 741 above). One of the grounds on which R sought to challenge the validity of the contract was that it had been obtained as a result of the exercise of undue influence. The Privy Council, by a majority, rejected his claim. Lord Hoffmann, giving the judgment of the majority, stated:

21. The subject of undue influence has recently been re-examined in depth by the House of Lords in *Royal Bank of Scotland plc* v. *Etridge (No 2)* [2002] AC 773. Their

Lordships summarise the effect of the judgments. Like duress at common law, undue influence is based upon the principle that a transaction to which consent has been obtained by unacceptable means should not be allowed to stand. Undue influence has concentrated in particular upon the unfair exploitation by one party of a relationship which gives him ascendancy or influence over the other.

22. The burden of proving that consent was obtained by unacceptable means is upon the party who alleges it. Certain relationships—parent and child, trustee and beneficiary, etc—give rise to a presumption that one party had influence over the other. That does not of course in itself involve a presumption that he unfairly exploited his influence. But if the transaction is one which cannot reasonably be explained by the relationship, that will be prima facie evidence of undue influence. Even if the relationship does not fall into one of the established categories, the evidence may show that one party did in fact have influence over the other. In such a case, the nature of the transaction may likewise give rise to a prima facie inference that it was obtained by undue influence. In the absence of contrary evidence, the court will be entitled to find that the burden of proving unfair exploitation of the relationship has been discharged.

23. The absence of independent legal advice may or may not be a relevant matter according to the circumstances. It is not necessarily an unfair exploitation of a relationship for one party to enter into a transaction with the other without ensuring that he has obtained independent legal advice. On the other hand, the transaction may be such as to give rise to an inference of undue influence even if the induced party was advised by an independent lawyer and understood the legal implications of what he was doing.

This summary is important for a number of reasons. First, it attempts to draw an analogy between undue influence and common law duress. Secondly, there is an emphasis on 'unacceptable means' and 'unfair exploitation' which suggests that the focus of attention is upon the conduct of the defendant rather than the state of mind of the claimant. Thirdly, the presumption to which certain relationships give rise is that 'one party had influence over the other'; it is not a 'presumption that he unfairly exploited his influence'.

For the purposes of the hearing, their Lordships were content to assume that the Army was able to exercise influence over the appellant. The vital question was whether 'the nature of the transaction was such as to give rise to an inference that it was obtained by an unfair exploitation of that relationship'. On this point Lord Hoffmann concluded (at [24]):

Like the Court of Appeal, their Lordships do not think that the confidentiality agreement can be so described. As in the case of duress, their Lordships think that the finding that it was an agreement which anyone who wished to serve or continue serving in the SAS could reasonably have been required to sign is fatal to such a conclusion. The reason why R signed the agreement was because, at the time, he wished to continue to be a member of the SAS. If facing him with such a choice was not illegitimate for the purposes of duress, their Lordships do not think that it could have been an unfair exploitation of a relationship which consisted in his being a member of the SAS. There seems to their Lordships to be some degree of contradiction between R's claim, in the context of duress, that he signed only because he was threatened with return to his unit and his claim, for the purposes of undue influence, that he signed because of the trust and confidence which he reposed in the Army or his commanding officer.

The issue which troubled the majority was 'the absence of legal advice'. But the lack of independent advice, while 'a matter for regret', did not result in the transaction being one in which the Ministry of Defence had unfairly exploited its influence over the appellant. The majority concluded that there had been no such exploitation. The appellant did not contend that he did not understand the nature of the transaction into which he had entered. Further, the absence of legal advice did not affect the fairness of the transaction. The most that the appellant could say was that a 'lawyer might have advised him to reflect upon the matter and . . . that might have led to his not signing at all' but that was a decision which he could have made without a lawyer's advice. The appellant's attempt to invoke undue influence therefore failed.

Lord Scott dissented in relation to the application of the principles of undue influence to the facts of the case. He drew heavily upon the decision of the Court of Appeal in *Allcard* v. *Skinner* (1887) 36 Ch D 145 (p. 758 above) and continued:

41. Are these principles ones that should be applied to the contract in the present case? I think they are. The appellant was not, of course, an unworldly man in a secluded religious order. He was a soldier in a highly trained and efficient fighting unit. The essence of efficiency in a military unit is obedience to orders. The Armed Services operate on a hierarchical basis. Each rank looks to the rank or ranks above for direction and, having received that direction, is expected to comply with it. It is, in my opinion, entirely artificial to draw sharp distinctions between orders from senior officers that are military orders breach of which will be an offence under military law and may attract court martial sanctions and 'orders' from senior officers couched as requests or as recommendations. It has become a music-hall joke for a sergeant-major to say to the troops under him 'I want three volunteers; you, you and you'. The hierarchical culture of the Armed Services and the deference and obedience to senior officers, both commissioned and non-commissioned, which is part of that culture are the essential background to the circumstances in which the appellant was asked to sign the contract in the present case.

42. It is to be borne in mind that members of Her Majesty's Armed Services do not, unlike ordinary employees, enter into contracts with their employers. They are engaged and can be dismissed under the Royal Prerogative. It is their agreement to serve, not any contract, that subjects them to military discipline and military law. The Board was told by counsel for the Attorney-General that there had been no other example of members of a unit of the Armed Services being asked to enter into a contract with the Ministry of Defence.

43. This background requires, in my opinion, that any contract between a member of the Armed Forces and the Ministry of Defence be looked at very carefully to see whether the benefit conferred by it on the Ministry of Defence was a benefit that the Ministry of Defence was entitled in equity to maintain.

44. The circumstances in which the contract in the present case came to be signed by the appellant were the subject of evidence at trial and the trial judge, Salmon J, formed a number of important conclusions:

(1) The judge concluded that the appellant signed because he had been ordered to do so. An analysis of the 'order' that disqualifies it from constituting a military order and regards it, no doubt correctly, merely as a recommendation or a direction is, in my opinion, of no more than marginal significance if the possibility of undue influence is being considered. What is important is how the appellant regarded it. The appellant regarded it as an order.

(2) The judge found that 'the defendant was not told the terms of the contract before signing [and] was not offered any legal advice' (para 39).

(3) He found, also, that the appellant was not permitted to show the contract to a legal adviser (para 139). The weight of this finding is not diminished by evidence from the senior officer in command of the Regiment to the effect that soldiers would have been permitted to show the contract to approved legal advisers if they had asked. What is important is the perception of the appellant, and, as to that, Salmon J's finding stands.

45. In my opinion, the relationship between the appellant and his senior officers and the circumstances, as found by the judge, in which the contract came to be signed by the appellant produced a classic 'relationship' case in which undue influence should be presumed. No evidence was introduced to rebut that presumption. Legal advice was not available to the appellant. As in *Allcard* v. *Skinner*, where no suggestion of fraud or indeed any impropriety was made against the lady superior to whom the plaintiff had transferred her assets, no such suggestion has been, or could be, made against any of the appellant's senior officers who play a part in the story. It is the relationship, produced by the background to which I have referred, between a soldier and that part of the Armed Services of which he is a member, that introduces the potentially vitiating element into the contract. If the Ministry of Defence wants to impose contractual obligations on soldiers by which they will be bound when they leave the service, it must, in my opinion, at the least make available to them independent legal advice. Fairness, in my view, requires it and I think the law requires it. In this case it was not done. I would have allowed the appeal.

The difference between the analysis of Lord Scott and that employed by the majority appears to lie in the fact that Lord Scott focused on the nature of the relationship between the parties, whereas the majority placed greater emphasis on the need for some wrongdoing on the part of the Ministry of Defence. While the majority were prepared to assume that the Army was able to exercise influence over the appellant, they found that the facts of the case 'did not give rise to an inference that [the transaction] was obtained by an unfair exploitation of that relationship.' Lord Scott, by contrast, had regard to the nature of the relationship between the appellant and the Army and, from that relationship, was prepared to infer the existence of undue influence without the need to identify specific wrongdoing on the part of the Army. In his view the nature of the relationship between the parties imposed certain obligations on the Army, for example to provide independent legal advice, and their failure to discharge these obligations, should, in his opinion, have entitled the appellant to succeed with his undue influence claim.

The second case is the decision of the Privy Council in *National Commercial Bank (Jamaica) Ltd* v. *Hew* [2003] UKPC 51. Lord Millett there described the doctrine of undue influence in the following terms:

29. Undue influence is one of the grounds on which equity intervenes to give redress where there has been some unconscionable conduct on the part of the defendant. It arises whenever one party has acted unconscionably by exploiting the influence to direct the conduct of another which he has obtained from the relationship between them. As Lord Nicholls of Birkenhead observed in *Royal Bank of Scotland plc v Etridge (No 2)* [2002] 2 AC 773 at pp. 794–5:

'Undue influence is one of the grounds of relief developed by the courts of equity as a court of conscience. The objective is to ensure that the influence of one person over another is not abused . . .

. . . [It] arises out of a relationship between two persons where one has acquired over another a measure of influence, or ascendancy, of which the ascendant person then takes unfair advantage.'

30. Thus the doctrine involves two elements. First, there must be a relationship capable of giving rise to the necessary influence. And secondly the influence generated by the relationship must have been abused.

31. The necessary relationship is variously described as a relationship 'of trust and confidence' or 'of ascendancy and dependency'. Such a relationship may be proved or presumed. Some relationships are presumed to generate the necessary influence; examples are solicitor and client and medical adviser and patient. The banker-customer relationship does not fall within this category. But the existence of the necessary relationship may be proved as a fact in any particular case . . .

33. But the second element is also necessary. However great the influence which one person may be able to wield over another equity does not intervene unless that influence has been abused. Equity does not save people from the consequences of their own folly; it acts to save them from being victimised by other people: see *Allcard v Skinner* (1887) 36 Ch D 145, 182.

34. Thus it must be shown that the ascendant party has unfairly exploited the influence he is shown or presumed to possess over the vulnerable party. It is always highly relevant that the transaction in question was manifestly disadvantageous to the person seeking to set it aside; though this is not always necessary: see *CIBC Mortgages plc v. Pitt* [1994] 1 AC 200. But 'disadvantageous' in this context means 'disadvantageous' as between the parties. Unless the ascendant party has exploited his influence to obtain some unfair advantage from the vulnerable party there is no ground for equity to intervene. However commercially disadvantageous the transaction may be to the vulnerable party, equity will not set it aside if it is a fair transaction as between the parties to it.

Once again we can see the emphasis placed on the conduct of the party who is alleged to have exercised the undue influence. It does not suffice to prove that a relationship of trust and confidence existed between the parties. Nor does it suffice to demonstrate that the transaction was a disadvantageous one for the party seeking to set it aside. It must be demonstrated that there was some advantage-taking on the part of the party who is seeking to uphold the agreement. The nature of that advantage-taking is described in various terms by Lord Millett. Thus he refers to 'abuse' (at [29]), 'victimisation' (at [33]) and 'exploitation' (at [34]). From this case, together with *Etridge* and *R* v. *Attorney-General for England and Wales*, it can be inferred that undue influence is defendant-sided in its emphasis so that some form of wrongdoing on the part of the party alleged to have exercised undue influence would appear to be an indispensable element of an undue influence claim (albeit the wrongdoing can assume different forms).

This emphasis on wrongdoing has not been universally welcomed. Professor Birks ((2004) 120 *LQR* 34) has sounded a warning in relation to the difficulties that are likely to arise from an insistence on wrongdoing in all cases. In particular, while the emphasis on wrongdoing may open the prospect of the award of compensatory damages in an undue influence claim, it may also shut out the possibility of relief in the case where the claimant cannot establish wrongdoing on the part of the defendant. *Allcard* v. *Skinner* (p. 758 above) may well come into this category (notwithstanding Lord Millett's citation of *Allcard* in support of his analysis in *Hew* at [33]). This is important where the claimant seeks relief in the form of rescission of the contract. In such a case, why does the claimant have to prove some element of wrongdoing on the part of the defendant? There is no such requirement in the law of misrepresentation where, as has been noted (see p. 678), an innocent misrepresentation gives rise to a right to rescind and innocent misrepresentation is not a wrong which attracts compensatory damages. Similarly, Professor Birks asserts that not all cases of undue influence can be regarded as cases of wrongs (an example which he cites in addition to *Allcard* is *Hammond* v. *Osborn* (on which see p. 755). He therefore maintains that English law should continue to recognise a category of 'innocent undue influence' (that is to say, the claimant is subject to too much influence in the sense that his volition is impaired but there is no advantage-taking by the defendant). He concludes (at p. 37) as follows:

As with misrepresentation, undue influence may be a wrong in aggravating circumstances. That is largely unexplored territory. It is certainly not always a wrong. A party who makes no claim to shift a loss from himself to another but merely requires that other to return to the *status quo* does not need to find and prove those extra facts. A misrepresentee can rely for that same limited purpose on an innocent misrepresentation whether because the representation really was innocent or because he does not need to and does not choose to prove the aggravating facts. The same applies to one whose autonomy is impaired by the fact that another has excessive influence over him. It would be odd if, in triggering rescission and return to the *status quo*, relational paralysis were less potent than misrepresentation.

This point was taken up in clear terms by Mummery LJ in our third case, which is the decision of the Court of Appeal in *Pesticcio* v. *Huet* [2004] EWCA Civ 372; [2004] All ER (D) 36 (April). Mummery LJ (at [20]) objected to the defendant-sided conception of undue influence in the following terms:

The insistence of [counsel] that Maureen [the person alleged to have exercised undue influence over her brother] had 'done nothing wrong' is an instance of the 'continuing misconceptions' mentioned by Sir Martin Nourse in *Hammond* about the circumstances in which gifts will be set aside on the ground of presumed undue influence. Although undue influence is sometimes described as an 'equitable wrong' or even as a species of equitable fraud, the basis of the court's intervention is not the commission of a dishonest or wrongful act by the defendant, but that, as a matter of public policy, the presumed influence arising from the relationship of trust and confidence should not operate to the disadvantage of the victim, if the transaction is not satisfactorily explained by ordinary motives: *Allcard* v. *Skinner* (1887) 36 Ch D 145 at 171. The court scrutinises the circumstances in which the transaction, under which benefits were conferred on the recipient, took place and the nature of the continuing relationship between the parties, rather than any specific act or conduct on the part of the recipient. A transaction may be set aside by the court, even though the actions and conduct of the person who benefits from it could not be criticised as wrongful. The presumption arising from the trust and confidence of their relationship made it unnecessary, for example, for Bernard [the party seeking to set aside the deed of gift] to prove that Maureen actually had influence over him in relation to the gift of the house, let alone that she in fact exercised undue influence or applied improper pressure to obtain the Deed of Gift.

Where do we stand in the light of these cases? The vast majority of undue influence cases will involve some advantage-taking on the part of the defendant (albeit that the advantage-taking will assume different forms). But we should not exclude the possibility that, exceptionally, a claimant may be able to demonstrate that he or she was so dependent upon the defendant that a finding of undue influence can be made, even in the absence of specific wrongdoing on the part of the defendant.

6. FURTHER READING

BIRKS, P and CHIN NYUK YIN, 'On the Nature of Undue Influence' in Beatson, J and Friedmann, D, *Good Faith and Fault in Contract Law* (Oxford University Press, 1995), p. 57.

BIRKS, P, 'Undue Influence as Wrongful Exploitation' (2004) 120 *LQR* 34.

O'SULLIVAN, D, 'Developing O'Brien' (2002) 118 *LQR* 337.

THOMPSON, M, 'Wives, Sureties and Banks' [2002] *Conveyancer and Property Lawyer* 174.

20

UNCONSCIONABILITY AND INEQUALITY OF BARGAINING POWER

1. CENTRAL ISSUES

1. The role of fairness in the law of contract is a matter of some controversy. It is clear that the law is concerned with matters of procedural fairness, although the extent of that concern and the meaning of procedural fairness is a matter of debate. More difficult is the role of substantive fairness. Can a court set aside a contract on the ground that it is substantively unfair or is the function of substantive unfairness confined to the provision of evidence from which some other ground of invalidity can be deduced?

2. In this chapter consideration will be given to a range of cases in which the courts were asked to set aside a contract on the ground that the contract was, in some way, unfair. An examination of the cases will reveal that the courts

have invoked a range of factors in deciding whether or not to set aside a contract. These factors include matters such as the existence of a special or serious disadvantage or disability on the part of the party seeking to set aside the contract, actual or constructive fraud on the part of the party seeking to enforce the contract, the role of independent advice, and the presence of disadvantageous terms.

3. It is also necessary to examine the role of Parliament in regulating unfair terms and the reasons why the courts have so far refused to recognize a general doctrine of unconscionability or inequality of bargaining power. The chapter will conclude by drawing on various analyses of unconscionability and the role of substantive fairness in the law of contract.

2. INTRODUCTION

There is no doubt that the law recognizes that duress and undue influence can suffice to set aside a contract (see above, Chapters 18 and 19). More difficult is the question whether or not a court can set aside a contract on the ground that it is in some way unfair. Does English law recognize a doctrine of unconscionability or inequality of bargaining power? The House of Lords in *National Westminster Bank* v. *Morgan* [1985] AC 686 (p. 815 below) saw no need for a general doctrine of inequality of bargaining power. Nevertheless, specific instances can be found of cases in which courts have intervened to set aside a contract that was, in the view of the court, unfair. The exact scope of these decisions is the subject of some debate. A further issue is whether or not the law ought to bring these disparate cases together and form one coherent doctrine. Lord Denning attempted to do this in *Lloyds Bank Ltd* v. *Bundy* [1975] QB 326 (p. 812 below) but his attempt was rejected by the House of Lords in *National Westminster Bank* v. *Morgan* [1985] AC 686.

In so far as these decisions are based on the unfairness of the procedure by which the contract was concluded they are not particularly controversial. The laws of misrepresentation and duress demonstrate that the law of contract is concerned with the fairness of the procedure by which a contract has been concluded. Much more difficulty is created by the proposition that the law of contract is concerned with the substantive fairness of the terms of the contract, particularly the adequacy or the fairness of the price. The fairness of the terms is a matter for the parties to decide, not the courts. The latter proposition is a fundamental tenet of freedom of contract. Can a commitment to the fairness of the terms be reconciled with a commitment to freedom of contract? Professor Collins, *The Law of Contract* (4th edn, Butterworths, 2003), pp. 270–271) has stated:

A system of contract law committed to freedom of contract must reject controls over the fairness of contracts. No matter that the purchaser has paid an excessive price or the seller received a gross undervalue, the principle of freedom to select the terms must prohibit intervention designed to redress the balance of obligations. At most the law can scrutinize minutely the procedures leading up to the contract to ensure that the freedom of the parties was not restricted by pressure, fraud, abuse of positions of trust, and other factors which interfered with the voluntariness of consent. Tests of procedural propriety are both compatible with and required by the principle of freedom of contract, but any examination of the fairness of the substance of the contract must be forbidden. Accordingly, texts describing the classical law of contract offered no place for a discussion of a requirement of fairness in contracts.

A reluctance to acknowledge the significance of substantive unfairness in contracts as a ground for intervention still characterises judicial decisions in the common law. A court will stress any elements of procedural impropriety that it can discover rather than address directly the unfairness of the bargain. The substantive unfairness may provide the motive for intervention, but the formal legal reason given for upsetting the contract will be couched in terms of a procedural defect, such as deception, manipulation or unfair surprise. This approach receives further support from economic analysis of law, since these procedural defects can be regarded as evidence of market failure which prevented the operation of a competitive and efficient market. To discover the real significance of substantive unfairness in the common law of contract therefore requires an investigation which digs behind the formal reasons given for decisions.

In this chapter it will be necessary to 'dig behind the formal reasons given for decisions' in order to ascertain the reason for the intervention of the court in the cases that have been extracted. The most difficult issue relates to the role of the substantive unfairness of the term or terms of the contract. What role, if any, does a concern for substantive fairness play in the cases? And what is the role of procedural fairness? Is there any one factor that predominates or do the courts rely upon a mixture of factors? Academic analyses of the cases often draw upon a mixture of factors. Thus Nicholas Bamforth (p. 816 below) identifies four factors that are consistently taken into account by the courts (namely, (i) special or serious disadvantage or disability, (ii) actual or constructive fraud, (iii) lack of independent advice, and (iv) disadvantageous terms) while David Capper (p. 818 below) identifies three factors (namely, (i) relational inequality, (ii) transactional imbalance, and (iii) unconscionable conduct). It may be that it is impossible to locate one factor which alone can explain all the cases and that the multi-factor approach is the best one to adopt. But such an approach has its dangers in that different courts can give different weight to the various factors with the consequence that the cases develop in an inconsistent and haphazard fashion.

This chapter will proceed in four stages. First, consideration will be given to a group of cases in which the courts have been asked to grant relief on the basis that the contract concluded between the parties was, in some way, unfair. Secondly, we shall turn to look at one or two examples of statutory regulation of unfair terms. Then, thirdly, consideration will be given to the arguments in favour of drawing these disparate cases together into one general doctrine before concluding the chapter by drawing on some academic reflections on the case-law and the role of fairness in the law of contract more generally.

3. UNFAIRNESS IN THE CASES

This section consists of a selection of cases in which the courts were asked to set aside a contract on the ground that it was, in some way, unfair. When reading the cases try to identify the reasons given by the judges to support their conclusion that the contract should or should not be set aside. Factors which may appear in the cases include the following: (i) the substantive unfairness of the contract, (ii) any unfairness in the negotiating process, (iii) weakness or disability on the part of the person seeking to set aside the contract, (iv) wrongdoing on the part of the person seeking to enforce the contract, and (v) lack of independent advice. The cases that follow are illustrative only. There are other examples (see, for example, *A Schroeder Music Publishing Co Ltd* v. *Macaulay* [1974] 1 WLR 1308, p. 830 below and *Hart* v. *O'Connor* [1985] AC 1000, p. 857 below). The cases have been arranged in chronological order. Given that one of the principal issues is whether or not the cases can be grouped together under any organizing principle and, if so, which principle, no attempt has been made, as yet, to classify the cases.

Earl of Aylesford v. Morris

(1873) 8 Ch App 484, Court of Appeal

The plaintiff, when he was a young man of twenty-two, had run up a large number of debts. His father was in poor health and the plaintiff stood to inherit a large amount of property on the death of his father. His creditors were pressing for payment, and the defendant money lender agreed to lend him money to pay off his debts. The plaintiff received no independent advice and the rate of interest which the defendant demanded was over 60 per cent. The plaintiff applied to have the defendant's actions for payment restrained and his action succeeded. An order for delivery up of the bills and policy which he had advanced by way of security for the loan was made on payment by the plaintiff of the sums actually advanced and interest at 5 per cent.

Lord Selborne, LC

There is hardly any older head of equity than that described by Lord Hardwicke in *Earl of Chesterfield* v. *Janssen* 2 Ves Sen 125, 157 as relieving against the fraud 'which infects catching bargains with heirs, reversioners, or expectants, in the life of the father', &c. 'These (he said) have been generally mixed cases', and he proceeded to note two characters always found in them. 'There is always fraud presumed or inferred from the circumstances or conditions of the parties contracting—weakness on one side, usury on the other, or extortion, or advantage taken of that weakness. There has been always an appearance of fraud from the nature of the bargain.' . . .

Fraud does not here mean deceit or circumvention; it means an unconscientious use of the power arising out of these circumstances and conditions; and when the relative position of the parties is such as *primâ facie* to raise this presumption, the transaction cannot stand unless the person claiming the benefit of it is able to repel the presumption by contrary evidence, proving it to have been in point of fact fair, just, and reasonable.

This is the rule applied to the analogous cases of voluntary donations obtained for themselves by the donees, and to all other cases where influence, however acquired, has resulted in gain to the person possessing at the expense of the person subject to it. Lord Cranworth, in a recent case in the House of Lords (*Smith* v. *Kay* 7 HLC 750, 751), said that no influence can be more direct, more intelligible, or more to be guarded against than that of a person who gets hold of a young man of fortune, 'and takes upon himself to supply him with means, pandering to his gross extravagance during his minority, and extorting from him, or at least obtaining from him, for every advance that he has made, a promise that the moment he comes of age it shall all be ratified, so as to make the securities good'. The circumstances of the particular case in which these words were spoken differed widely from those of the case now before us; the element of personal influence is here wanting. But it is sufficient for the application of the principle, if the parties meet under such circumstances as, in the particular transaction, to give the stronger party dominion over the weaker; and such power and influence are generally possessed, in every transaction of this kind, by those who trade upon the follies and vices of unprotected youth, inexperience, and moral imbecility.

In the cases of catching bargains with expectant heirs, one peculiar feature has been almost universally present; indeed, its presence was considered by Lord Brougham to be an indispensable condition of equitable relief, though Lord St. Leonards, with good reason, dissents from that opinion (Sug V & P 11th edn, 316). The victim comes to the snare (for this system of dealing does set snares, not, perhaps, for one prodigal more than another, but for prodigals generally as a class), excluded, and known to be excluded, by the very motives and circumstances which attract him, from the help and advice of his natural guardians and protectors, and from that professional aid which would be accessible to him, if he did not feel compelled to secrecy. He comes in the dark, and in fetters, without either the will or the power to take care of himself, and with nobody else to take care of him. Great Judges have said that there is a principle of public policy in restraining this; that this system of undermining and blasting, as it were, in the bud the fortunes of families, is a public as well as a private mischief; that it is a sort of indirect fraud upon the heads of families from whom these transactions are concealed, and who may be thereby induced to dispose of their means for the profit and advantage of strangers and usurers, when they suppose themselves to be fulfilling the moral obligation of providing for their own descendants.

Whatever weight there may be in any such collateral considerations, they could hardly prevail, if they did not connect themselves with an equity more strictly and directly personal to the Plaintiff in each particular case. But the real truth is, that the ordinary effect of all the circumstances by which these considerations are introduced, is to deliver over the prodigal helpless into the hands of those interested in taking advantage of his weakness; and we so arrive in every such case at the substance of the conditions which throw the burden of justifying the righteousness of the bargain upon the party who claims the benefit of it . . .

Sir G Mellish LJ concurred.

COMMENTARY

This case demonstrates that a concern for the fairness of the bargain is not a recent phenomenon. It has a respectable history. There is no suggestion that the plaintiff was lacking in capacity to comprehend the nature of the transaction into which he was entering. But he was young, inexperienced, and lacked access to independent advice. Furthermore, the terms of the contract were substantively unfair. The defendant certainly took advantage of the plaintiff's vulnerable position, but did he act 'wrongfully' in doing so? Further, it should be noted that the onus was put upon the defendant to prove that the transaction was fair, just, and reasonable.

Fry v. Lane

(1888) 40 Ch D 312, Chancery Division

The plaintiffs were two brothers. One (JB Fry) was a laundryman and the other (George Fry) worked for a plumber. They sold their reversionary interests in the estate of John Fry to the defendant for £170 and £270 respectively. When they entered into the transaction, the plaintiffs were advised by an inexperienced solicitor who was also acting for the defendant. The property which was the subject of their interest was later sold for £3,848, of which the plaintiffs' share would have been £730 each. The proceeds of the sale were paid into court. An actuary stated that JB Fry's contingent interest in the £730 would have been valued at £475 at the date of the transaction. The plaintiffs' claim to set aside the transaction with the defendant was successful.

Kay J

I reserved judgment that I might more carefully consider the facts of the case, and the law which is applicable to them since the passing of the statute 31 Vict c 4.[1]

Long before the passing of that Act it was settled that the Court of Chancery would relieve against a sale of or other dealing with a remainder or reversion at an undervalue on that ground alone, and this even where the remainderman was of mature age and accustomed to business.

[he listed a number of cases and continued]

In such cases it was held that the onus lay upon the purchaser to shew that he had given the 'fair' value as it was called in *Earl of Aldborough* v. *Trye* 7 Cl & F 436, 456, or 'the market value': *Talbor* v. *Staniforth* 1 J & H 484, 503.

---

[1] The Sales of Reversions Act 1867, which has since been re-enacted in section 174 of the Law of Property Act 1925. As Kay J points out, while the Act provided that a sale of a reversionary interest could not be set aside merely on the ground that the sale had taken place at an undervalue, it expressly preserved the jurisdiction of the court to set aside unconscionable bargains.

By the 31 Vict c 4, reciting that it was expedient to amend the law as administered in Courts of Equity with respect to sales of reversions, it was enacted (by sect. 1) that 'no purchase, made *bonâ fide* and without fraud or unfair dealing, of any reversionary interest in real or personal estate shall hereafter be opened or set aside merely on the ground of undervalue', and by sect 2 the word 'purchase' in the Act is to include 'every kind of contract, conveyance, or assignment, under or by which any beneficial interest in any kind of property may be acquired'. This Act came into operation on the 1st day of January, 1868.

It is obvious that the words 'merely on the ground of undervalue' do not include the case of an undervalue so gross as to amount of itself to evidence of fraud, and in *Earl of Aylesford* v. *Morris* (1873) LR 8 Ch App 484, 490 Lord Selborne said that this Act 'leaves undervalue still a material element in cases in which it is not the sole equitable ground for relief. These changes of the law have in no degree whatever altered the *onus probandi* in those cases, which, according to the language of Lord Hardwicke, raise "from the circumstances or conditions of the parties contracting—weakness on one side, usury on the other, or extortion, or advantage taken of that weakness"—a presumption of fraud. Fraud', says Lord Selborne, 'does not here mean deceit or circumvention; it means an unconscientious use of the power arising out of these circumstances and conditions; and when the relative position of the parties is such as primâ facie to raise this presumption, the transaction cannot stand unless the person claiming the benefit of it is able to repel the presumption by contrary evidence, proving it to have been in point of fact fair, just, and reasonable'.

The most common case for the interference of a Court of Equity is that of an expectant heir, reversioner, or remainderman who is just of age, his youth being treated as an important circumstance. Another analogous case is where the vendor is a poor man with imperfect education, as in *Evans* v. *Llewellin* 1 Cox 333 . . .

In the case of a poor man, in distress for money, a sale, even of property in possession, at an undervalue has been set aside in many cases.

[he discussed the cases and continued]

The result of the decisions is that where a purchase is made from a poor and ignorant man at a considerable undervalue, the vendor having no independent advice, a Court of Equity will set aside the transaction.

This will be done even in the case of property in possession, and *à fortiori* if the interest be reversionary.

The circumstances of poverty and ignorance of the vendor, and absence of independent advice, throw upon the purchaser, when the transaction is impeached, the onus of proving, in Lord Selborne's words, that the purchase was 'fair, just, and reasonable'.

Upon the evidence before me I cannot hesitate to conclude that the price of £170 in JB Fry's case and £270 in George Fry's case were both considerably below the real value. The property has been subjected to the costs of appointing new trustees, and also to part of the costs of an administration suit, and yet the net produce of one-fifth share is £730. Managed in a more careful manner it might have produced more.

Both JB Fry and his brother George were poor, ignorant men, to whom the temptation of the immediate possession of £100 would be very great. Neither of them in the transaction of the sale of his share, was, in the words of Sir J Leach, 'on equal terms' with the purchaser. Neither had independent advice. The solicitor who acted for both parties in each transaction seems, from the *Law List*, to have been admitted in March, 1877. In October, 1878, at the time of completing the sale of JB Fry's share, he had not been much more than a year and a-half on the roll. His inexperience probably in some degree accounts for his allowing himself to be put in the position of solicitor for both parties in such a case. I think in each transaction he must have been considering the purchaser's interest too much properly to guard that of the vendors . . . I regret that I must come to the conclusion that, though there was a semblance of bargaining by the solicitor in each case, he did not properly protect the vendors, but gave a great advantage to the purchasers, who had been former clients, and for whom he was then acting. The circumstances illustrate the wisdom and necessity of the rule that a poor, ignorant man, selling an interest of this kind, should have independent advice, and that a purchase from him at an undervalue should be set aside, if he has not. The most experienced solicitor, acting for both sides, if he allows a sale at an undervalue, can hardly have duly performed his duty to the vendor. To act for both sides in such a case, and permit a sale at an undervalue, is a position in which no careful practitioner would allow himself to be placed . . .

COMMENTARY

There appear to be three elements to the decision of Kay J: (i) the plaintiffs were 'poor and ignorant'; (ii) the sale was at an undervalue; and (iii) the plaintiffs were not independently advised. The justification for intervention therefore appears to be the vulnerability of the plaintiffs and the substantive unfairness of the terms of the contract. There was no express finding that the defendant had exploited the inexperience of the plaintiffs. On the other hand, the fact that the solicitor was acting for the defendant, and the fact that the sale was at a considerable undervalue might be seen as evidence of the fact that the defendant had indeed exploited the plaintiffs.

The Medina

(1876) 1 P 272, Probate Division

Sir Robert Phillimore

The circumstances of this case are very singular; but it is one in which the Court really feels no doubt as to the judgment which it ought to give. It is not necessary that I should go into an examination of the authorities which I recently referred to in the case of *The Cargo Ex Woosung* (1876) 1 P 260 and which I also referred to in the case of *The Waverley* Law Rep 3 A & E 369. But I may state the result of them to be this, that it is the practice of this Court, partly for the protection of absent owners and partly on the grounds of general policy, to control agreements made by masters when an examination of those agreements shews that they are clearly inequitable. In the present case there were upwards of five hundred pilgrims on a rock which is just six feet above water. Their ship had gone to pieces, and the plaintiffs' vessel, the *Timor*, came up close without any difficulty or danger at all; because the evidence is that the water was quite deep up to the rock; she came up and her captain, in effect, says, I will not relieve you from this situation, which a few hours of bad weather might convert into one of most imminent danger, indeed into your total destruction. I will not take you away unless you give me 4000*l*. Now, what is 4000*l*. with regard to the matter saved, which is human life? On the other hand, however, 4000*l*. is the whole sum that was to be paid for conveying the pilgrims to

Jedda, and in my opinion if the master of the *Timor* had not taken these pilgrims off the rock in the circumstances stated, and bad weather had come on, and they had lost their lives in consequence, he would hardly have been in a better position than a pirate. Nevertheless, it was certainly a valuable salvage service according to the principles upon which such services have always been considered in this Court, but I am of opinion that 4000*l*. is a great deal too much, and I shall award 1800*l*.

COMMENTARY

This is a very different case from *Earl of Aylesford* v. *Morris* and *Fry* v. *Lane*. Here the plaintiffs sought to take advantage of the imminent danger in which the master of the vessel and the pilgrims found themselves. Thus the defendants were extremely vulnerable, being in great danger, they did not appear to have any alternative open to them (other than death), and the plaintiffs sought to exploit the situation by charging an extremely high price for their services. This the court would not allow them to do and, while it held that they were entitled to recover something in respect of the services which they had rendered, they were not entitled to the sum which they had extracted from the master of the vessel. Admiralty cases do not often feature in contract textbooks probably because the rules that have evolved in Admiralty often differ in significant respects from the common law rules. But the rule laid down in *The Medina* can be reconciled with cases such as *Fry* v. *Lane*. The cause of the disadvantage may be different but the courts seem to be looking for the same elements, namely inability to look after one's own interests, lack of independent advice or alternatives, and substantively unfair terms.

The Port Caledonia and The Anna

[1903] P 184, Probate Division

The *Port Caledonia* and the *Anna* were sheltering in Holyhead Harbour from a storm when the *Port Caledonia* began to be dragged towards the *Anna*. The master of the *Port Caledonia* signalled for a tug, but the master of the tug demanded '£1,000 or no rope'. The master of the *Port Caledonia* initially objected but agreed to pay the money. The tug then towed the vessel back to its original berth. The master of the tug brought a claim to recover the £1,000. The court set aside the agreement to pay £1,000 on the ground that it was extortionate, and the plaintiffs were awarded instead the sum of £200 for the services which they had rendered.

Bucknill J

With the 1000*l*. agreement on one side, and that which I think was the value of the services on the other, I have to ask myself whether the bargain that was made was so inequitable, so unjust, and so unreasonable that the Court cannot allow it to stand?

The first question to consider is, What was the position of the two persons who made the agreement? The position was this. One man was in a position to insist upon his terms, and the other man had to put up with it. He could not help himself. He says in his letter to his owners: 'He demanded 1000*l*. to take me away. I offered him 100*l*., or to leave it to the owners; but he would not agree, so I agreed to give 1000*l*. rather than foul the *Anna*'.

He appreciated the possibility of fouling the *Anna* if the weather had remained bad, and if the wind had remained in the S.W., neither of which things happened. So he found himself obliged to give way to a person who would not move him, and who would have allowed him and the *Anna* to drift towards the rocks, and who would, I think, have seen them go there without putting a hawser on board unless he got a promise of 1000*l*.

I have expressed my opinion about the matter. This opinion is shared by the Elder Brethren, and I hold that this agreement cannot be allowed to stand, and I set it aside.

I hope that those who perform such grand services in tugs from time to time, in worse weather than this, and, in peril of their own lives, save property around the coast, will note that this Court will keep a firm hand over them if they attempt to do what has been done in this case.

This was an inequitable, extortionate, and unreasonable agreement, and I think that the services rendered will be well rewarded by the sum of 200*l*., and with county court costs.

COMMENTARY

This case is very similar to *The Medina*. There may be a difference between the two in that the ship in *The Medina* had 'gone to pieces' and the danger was to the lives of the passengers. Here the immediate danger was to the vessel itself. But the principle seems to be the same.

Cresswell v. Potter

[1978] 1 WLR 255, Chancery Division

On the break-up of her marriage to the defendant, the plaintiff, a telephonist, released and conveyed to the defendant her interest in the matrimonial home in return for an indemnity against liability under the mortgage. The defendant later sold the former matrimonial home and made a profit of £1,400 on the sale. The plaintiff sought to set aside the release on the ground that it was exercised in circumstances which amounted to unfair dealing. Her claim was successful.

Megarry J
[He considered the judgment of Kay J in *Fry* v. *Lane* and continued]

The judge thus laid down three requirements. What has to be considered is, first, whether the plaintiff is poor and ignorant; second, whether the sale was at a considerable undervalue; and third, whether the vendor had independent advice. I am not, of course, suggesting that these are the only circumstances which will suffice; thus there may be circumstances of oppression or abuse of confidence which will invoke the aid of equity. But in the present case only these three requirements are in point. Abuse of confidence, though pleaded, is no longer relied on; and no circumstances of oppression or other matters are alleged. I must therefore consider whether the three requirements laid down in *Fry* v. *Lane* are satisfied.

I think that the plaintiff may fairly be described as falling within whatever is the modern equivalent of 'poor and ignorant'. Eighty years ago, when *Fry* v. *Lane* was decided, social conditions were very different from those which exist today. I do not, however, think that the principle has changed, even though the euphemisms of the 20th century may require the word 'poor' to be replaced by 'a member of the lower income group' or the like, and the word 'ignorant' by 'less highly educated'. The plaintiff has been a van driver for a tobacconist, and is a Post Office telephonist. The evidence of her means is slender. The defendant told me that the plaintiff probably had a little saved, but not much; and there was evidence that her earnings were about the same as the defendant's, and that these were those of a carpenter. The plaintiff also has a legal aid certificate.

In those circumstances I think the plaintiff may properly be described as 'poor' in the sense used in *Fry* v. *Lane*, where it was applied to a laundryman who, in 1888, was earning £1 a week. In this context, as in others, I do not think that 'poverty' is confined to destitution. Further, although no doubt it requires considerable alertness and skill to be a good telephonist, I think that a telephonist can properly be described as 'ignorant' in the context of property transactions in general and the execution of conveyancing documents in particular. I have seen and heard the plaintiff giving evidence, and I have reached the conclusion that she satisfies the requirements of the first head.

The second question is whether the sale was at a 'considerable undervalue'. Slate Hall cost £1,500, £1,200 of the price being provided by the mortgage. The release recited that £1,196 13s. 5d remained outstanding on the mortgage, so that very little had been paid off the capital sum due. Nevertheless, all that the plaintiff was getting for giving up her half interest in Slate Hall was the release from her liability under the mortgage. If Slate Hall was worth no more than it cost, she was giving up her half share in any equity worth £300; and, after all, the mortgage was a recent mortgage to a well-known building society. If she had sought advice it is unlikely in the extreme that she would have been told that there was any real probability that the value of the property would be less than the sum due under the mortgage. There can be little doubt that she was getting virtually nothing for £150.

In fact, as is now known, within a little over two years the property fetched £3,350, so that at the time in question the plaintiff's share of the equity may have been worth appreciably more than £150. It is true, as Mr Balcombe pointed out on behalf of the defendant, that there was no valuation evidence before me, and that any valuation of the property must rest upon inferences from the prices for which the property was sold. I do not think it right to assume, without evidence, that there was a dip in the value of the property between its purchase in November 1958, and the sales in December 1960, and September 1961; and without such a dip it seems to me that the probabilities point to the property having a value in August 1959, which at all events substantially exceeded the sum due under the mortgage for £1,200. The more valuable the equity, of course, the less valuable would be the indemnity against the mortgage. It seems to me that by the release the plaintiff parted with her interest in Slate Hall at an undervalue which cannot be dismissed as being trifling or inconsiderable. In my judgment the undervalue was 'considerable'.

As for independent advice, from first to last there is no suggestion that the plaintiff had any. The defendant, his solicitor and the inquiry agent stood on one side; on the other the plaintiff stood alone. This was, of course, a conveyancing transaction, and English land law is notoriously complex. I am certainly not saying that other transactions, such as hire-purchase agreements, are free from all difficulty. But the authorities put before me on setting aside dealings at an undervalue all seem to relate to conveyancing transactions, and one may wonder whether the principle is confined to such transactions, and, if so, why. I doubt whether the principle is restricted in this way; and it may be that the explanation is that it is in conveyancing matters that, by long usage, it is regarded as usual, and, indeed, virtually essential, for the parties to have the services of a solicitor. The absence of the aid of a solicitor is thus, as it seems to me, of especial significance if a conveyancing matter is involved. The more usual it is to have a solicitor, the more striking will be his absence, and the more closely will the courts scrutinise what was done.

Mr Balcombe points out that the plaintiff was not bereft of possible legal assistance; for on or before July 28, 1959, when she was having difficulty in getting some furniture and effects from Slate Hall, she consulted a Colchester firm of solicitors, who wrote a letter dated July 28, 1959, that produced the required result. If she wanted legal advice, he said, this shows that she knew how to get it. However, what matters, I think, is not whether she could have obtained proper advice but whether in fact she had it; and she did not. Nobody, of course, can be compelled to obtain independent advice: but I do not think that someone who seeks to uphold what is, to him, an advantageous conveyancing transaction can do so merely by saying that the other party could have obtained independent advice, unless something has been done to bring to the notice of that other party the true nature of the transaction and the need for advice . . .

At the end of the day, my conclusion is that this transaction cannot stand. In my judgment the plaintiff has made out her case, and so it is for the defendant to prove that the transaction was 'fair, just, and reasonable'. This he has not done. The whole burden of his case has been that the requirements of Fry v. Lane, 40 Ch D 312, were not satisfied, whereas I have held that they were . . .

COMMENTARY

At first sight *Cresswell* appears to be a modern-day *Fry* v. *Lane* and it seeks to bring the principle up-to-date with new terminology to replace 'poor and ignorant'. Why did the court grant the plaintiff relief? Was it because she was a telephonist who did not understand conveyancing or was it because her marriage had broken up and she was dealing with the sale of the matrimonial home? In many ways it seems unnecessary to elaborate upon the meaning of 'poor and ignorant' in this way. Should it not suffice that the plaintiff was in a weak or vulnerable position, whatever the cause of her weakness or disability? *Cresswell* was followed by Balcombe J in *Backhouse* v. *Backhouse* [1978] 1 WLR 243.

Alec Lobb (Garages) Ltd v. Total Oil (Great Britain) Ltd

[1985] 1 WLR 173, Court of Appeal

The defendant oil company advanced money to the plaintiff company ('the appellants') for the purpose of its garage and petrol filling station business and took mortgages on its property as security. In 1969 the company was in financial difficulty and so it entered into fresh negotiations with the defendants. Contrary to the advice of its solicitors, the plaintiff entered into an agreement with the defendants under which the plaintiff company agreed to grant a lease of the property to the defendants for fifty-one years for a £35,000 premium and a peppercorn rent and the defendants agreed to grant the second and third plaintiffs (who were the directors of the plaintiff company) a lease-back at a rent of

£2,250 *per annum* and a tie to the defendants to supply all the petrol for the whole term of the lease-back. In 1979 the plaintiffs sought to set aside the 1969 agreement on the grounds that it was in restraint of trade and that it was an unconscionable bargain. It was held (both at first instance and in the Court of Appeal) that the lease and lease-back were not in restraint of trade, that the transaction was not unconscionable, and that, in any case, the plaintiffs' claim was barred by laches.

Dillon LJ [concluded that the lease and lease-back were not in restraint of trade and continued]

I turn therefore to the appellants' case on equitable grounds. The basis of the contention that the transaction of the lease and lease-back ought to be set aside in equity is that it is submitted, and in the court below was accepted on behalf of Total, that during the negotiations for the lease and lease-back the parties did not have equal bargaining power, and it is therefore further submitted that a contract between parties who had unequal bargaining power can only stand and be enforced by the stronger if he can prove that the contract was in point of fact fair, just and reasonable. The concept of unequal bargaining power is taken particularly from the judgment of Lord Denning MR in *Lloyds Bank Ltd* v. *Bundy* [1975] QB 326. The reference to a contract only standing if it is proved to have been in point of fact fair, just and reasonable is taken from the judgment of Lord Selborne LC in *Earl of Aylesford* v. *Morris* (1873) LR 8 Ch App 484, 490–1. Lord Selborne was not there seeking to generalise; he was dealing only with what he regarded as one of the oldest heads of equity, relieving against fraud practised on heirs or expectants, particularly fraud practised on young noblemen of great expectations, considerable extravagance and no ready money. It is none the less submitted that the logic of the development of the law leads to the conclusion that Lord Selborne LC's test should now be applied generally to any contract entered into between parties who did not have equal bargaining power.

In fact Lord Denning MR's judgment in *Lloyds Bank Ltd* v. *Bundy* merely laid down the proposition that where there was unequal bargaining power the contract could not stand if the weaker did not have legal advice. In the present case Mr Lobb and the company did have separate advice from their own solicitor. On the facts of this case, however, that does not weaken the appellants' case if the general proposition of law which they put forward is valid. Total refused to accept any of the modifications of the transaction . . . which the company's and Mr Lobb's solicitor suggested, and in the end the solicitor advised them not to proceed. Mr Lobb declined to accept that advice because his and the company's financial difficulties were so great, and, it may be said, their bargaining power was so small, that he felt he had no alternative but to accept Total's terms. Because of the existing valid tie to Total which had, as I have said, three to four years to run, he had no prospect at all of raising finance on the scale he required from any source other than Total. There is no suggestion that there was any other dealer readily available who could have bought the property from him subject to the tie. The only practical solutions open to him were to accept the terms of the lease and lease-back as put forward by Total on which Total was not prepared to negotiate, or to sell the freehold of the property to Total and cease trading. In these circumstances, it would be unreal, in my judgment, to hold that if the transaction is otherwise tainted it is cured merely because Mr Lobb and the company had independent advice.

But on the deputy judge's findings can it be said that the transaction is tainted? Lord Selborne LC dealt with the case before him as a case of fraud.

[he quoted a passage from the judgement of Lord Selborne which is set out at p. 795 above]

The whole emphasis is on extortion, or undue advantage taken of weakness, an unconscientious use of the power arising out of the inequality of the parties' circumstances, and on unconscientious use of power which the court might in certain circumstances be entitled to infer from a particular—and in these days notorious—relationship unless the contract is proved to have been in fact fair, just and reasonable. Nothing leads me to suppose that the course of the development of the law over the last 100 years has been such that the emphasis on unconscionable conduct or unconscientious use of power has gone and relief will now be granted in equity in a case such as the present if there has been unequal bargaining power, even if the stronger has not used his strength unconscionably. I agree with the judgment of Browne-Wilkinson J, in *Multiservice Bookbinding Ltd* v. *Marden* [1979] Ch 84, which sets out that to establish that a term is unfair and unconscionable it is not enough to show that it is, objectively, unreasonable.

In the present case there are findings of fact by the deputy judge that the conduct of Total was not unconscionable, coercive or oppressive. There is ample evidence to support those findings and they are not challenged by the appellants. Their case is that the judge applied the wrong test; where there is unequal bargaining power, the test is, they say, whether its terms are fair, just and reasonable and it is unnecessary to consider whether the conduct of the stronger party was oppressive or unconscionable. I do not accept the appellants' proposition of law. In my judgment the findings of the judge conclude this ground of appeal against the appellants.

Inequality of bargaining power must anyhow be a relative concept. It is seldom in any negotiation that the bargaining powers of the parties are absolutely equal. Any individual wanting to borrow money from a bank, building society or other financial institution in order to pay his liabilities or buy some property he urgently wants to acquire will have virtually no bargaining power; he will have to take or leave the terms offered to him. So, with house property in a seller's market, the purchaser will not have equal bargaining power with the vendor. But Lord Denning MR did not envisage that any contract entered into in such circumstances would, without more, be reviewed by the courts by the objective criterion of what was reasonable: see *Lloyds Bank Ltd* v. *Bundy* [1975] QB 326, 336. The courts would only interfere in exceptional cases where as a matter of common fairness it was not right that the strong should be allowed to push the weak to the wall. The concepts of unconscionable conduct and of the exercise by the stronger of coercive power are thus brought in, and in the present case they are negatived by the deputy judge's findings.

Even if, contrary to my view just expressed, the company and Mr and Mrs Lobb had initially in 1969 a valid claim in equity to have the lease and lease-back set aside as a result of the inequality of bargaining power, that claim was, in my judgment, barred by laches well before the issue of the writ in this action.

Dunn LJ

Equitable relief

Mr Cullen [counsel for the plaintiffs] conceded that he could not bring himself within any of the established categories of equitable relief, but relied on the dictum of Lord Denning MR in *Lloyds Bank Ltd* v. *Bundy* [1975] QB 326, 339 and submitted that the circumstances of this case disclosed a classic case of inequality of bargaining power of which the defendants had taken advantage by entering into the transaction, although he did not suggest any pressure or other misconduct on their part. He submitted that if it was necessary to categorise the grant of relief sought, it was an unconscionable bargain. He reminded us that the categories of unconscionable bargains are not closed (per Browne-Wilkinson J in *Multiservice Bookbinding Ltd* v. *Marden* [1979] Ch 94, 110) and sought to distinguish the instant case from that case by submitting that here the plaintiffs were under a compelling necessity to accept the loan, so that misconduct by the defendants was unnecessary. The fact of their impecuniosity, that they were already tied to the defendants by mortgages, that there was no other source of finance, and that they could not sell the equities of redemption under the mortgages without giving up trading, coupled with the knowledge of the defendants of those facts, rendered the transaction unconscionable, and placed the onus upon the defendants to show that its terms were fair and reasonable.

I find myself unable to accept those arguments. Mere impecuniosity has never been held a ground for equitable relief. In this case no pressure was placed upon the plaintiffs. On the contrary the defendants were reluctant to enter into the transaction. The plaintiffs took independent advice from their solicitors and accountants. They went into the transaction with their eyes open, and it was of benefit to them because they were enabled to continue trade from the site for a number of years. In my view the judge was right to refuse equitable relief.

Waller LJ delivered a concurring judgment.

COMMENTARY

Here we have a case in which the claim to set aside the transaction failed. Just as *Cresswell* v. *Potter* breathed new life into *Fry* v. *Lane*, so the plaintiffs in *Alec Lobb* tried to breathe new life into *Earl of Aylesford* v. *Morris*. This time the attempt failed. The plaintiffs were undoubtedly in a vulnerable economic position and, in that sense, were in a similar position to the plaintiff in *Earl of Aylesford*. But there the similarity ended. The plaintiffs in the present case had access to independent advice (which the plaintiff in *Earl of Aylesford* did not) and there was held to be no evidence of unconscionable, coercive, or oppressive conduct by the defendants on the facts of the case. In other words, there was weakness but no advantage taking. The judgment of Lord Denning in *Lloyds Bank Ltd* v. *Bundy*, which is mentioned in the judgment of Dillon LJ is discussed at p. 812 below.

Boustany v. Pigott

(1995) 69 P & CR 298, Privy Council

In 1977 Miss Pigott leased property to Mrs Boustany for a period of five years at a monthly rent of $833.33. Miss Pigott was 'quite slow', and her affairs were managed by her cousin, George Pigott. In 1980 Mrs Boustany discussed the possibility of a new lease with George Pigott but no agreement was reached. Later that year, while George Pigott was away, Mrs Boustany went to the chambers of a certain Mr Kendall and presented him with a copy of a new lease which was for ten years at a monthly rent of $1,000, renewable at the same rent at the option of Mrs Boustany. Mr Kendall demanded to see Miss Pigott together with Mr and Mrs Boustany and, during the course of the interview, he pointed out to Miss Pigott various aspects of the agreement which were not in her best interests but she insisted that he draw up the agreement. He did so. When George Pigott discovered what had happened he protested to Mrs Boustany, who was unmoved and so he asked for a declaration that the lease was an unconscionable bargain which should be declared null and void. The Privy Council, upholding the decision of the Court of Appeal of the Eastern Caribbean States, set aside the lease as an unconscionable bargain.

Lord Templeman [giving the judgment of the Privy Council]
In a careful and thoughtful submission, Mr Robertson, who appeared before the Board on behalf of Mrs Boustany, made the following submissions with which their Lordships are in general agreement:

(1) It is not sufficient to attract the jurisdiction of equity to prove that a bargain is hard, unreasonable or foolish; it must be proved to be unconscionable, in the sense that 'one of the parties to it has imposed the objectionable terms in a morally reprehensible manner, that is to say, in a way which affects his conscience': *Multiservice Bookbinding* v. *Marden* [1979] Ch 84, 110.

(2) 'Unconscionable' relates not merely to the terms of the bargain but to the behaviour of the stronger party, which must be characterised by some moral culpability or impropriety: *Lobb (Alec) (Garages) Limited* v. *Total Oil (Great Britain) Limited* [1983] 1 WLR 87, 94.

(3) Unequal bargaining power or objectively unreasonable terms provide no basis for equitable interference in the absence of unconscientious or extortionate abuse of power where exceptionally, and as a matter of common fairness, 'it was not right that the strong should be allowed to push the weak to the wall': *Lobb (Alec) (Garages) Limited* v. *Total Oil (Great Britain) Limited* [1985] 1 WLR 173, 183.

(4) A contract cannot be set aside in equity as 'an unconscionable bargain' against a party innocent of actual or constructive fraud. Even if the terms of the contract are 'unfair' in the sense that they are more favourable to one party than the other ('contractual imbalance'), equity will not provide relief unless the beneficiary is guilty of unconscionable conduct: *Hart* v. *O'Connor* [1985] AC 1000 applied in *Nichols* v. *Jessup* [1986] NZLR 226.

(5) 'In situations of this kind it is necessary for the plaintiff who seeks relief to establish unconscionable conduct, namely that unconscientious advantage has been taken of his disabling condition or circumstances': per Mason J in *Commercial Bank of Australia Ltd* v. *Amadio* (1983) 46 ALR 402, 413.

Mr Robertson submitted that Miss Pigott had received independent advice from Mr Kendall, that she had been made aware by Mr Kendall that the terms of the 1980 lease were disadvantageous to her, that Miss Pigott could not be described as poor or ignorant and that the judge did not find and could not, consistently with the evidence, have found unconscionable behaviour on the part of Mrs Boustany.

The crucial question in this case is—what brought Miss Pigott to the chambers of Mr Kendall in September 1980? That question was not answered by direct evidence because

Miss Pigott was not able to give evidence and Mrs Boustany and her husband chose not to do so. The trial judge inferred unconscionable conduct by Mrs Boustany after careful consideration of a number of features which he held were only consistent with unconscientious conduct on the part of Mrs Boustany. The management of the property had been given up by Miss Pigott because of her incapacity. The properties were managed by Mr George Pigott and there was no reason why Miss Pigott should interfere in the management of this one property leased to Mrs Boustany. There was no evidence of any personal attachment between Miss Pigott and her tenant. Mrs Boustany had negotiated with Mr George Pigott and knew that he was the representative of Miss Pigott. No advice was sought by Miss Pigott; she turned up not at her family's solicitors but to Mr Kendall who knew nothing about her save that he had prepared the 1976 lease. Miss Pigott gave to Mr Kendall, according to his evidence, absurd reasons for the grant of a new lease and no reason for the grant of a lease for 20 years on disadvantageous terms.

Miss Pigott must have been under a total misapprehension of the facts when she represented that she might be worried about the property and about the repair of the property while she was away. Mr Kendall forcibly pointed out not only to Miss Pigott but also to Mrs Boustany and her husband the disadvantages to Miss Pigott of the new lease but Mrs Boustany and her husband gave no explanation and offered no concessions. They were content to allow Miss Pigott ostensibly to insist on the unjustifiable terms which they must have already persuaded her to accept. When a writ was issued Mrs Boustany did not write to the solicitor but sought out Miss Pigott and obtained a disclaimer which the court in due course rejected. The inference which the trial judge drew, and which he was entitled to draw, was that Mrs Boustany and her husband had prevailed upon Miss Pigott to agree to grant a lease on terms which they knew they could not extract from Mr George Pigott or anyone else. When they were summoned by Mr Kendall and the unfairness of the lease was pointed out to them, they did not release Miss Pigott from the bargain which they had unfairly pressed on her. In short Mrs Boustany must have taken advantage of Miss Pigott before, during and after the interview with Mr Kendall and with full knowledge before the 1980 lease was settled that her conduct was unconscionable.

COMMENTARY

This is a curious judgment. The five 'submissions' listed by Lord Templeman are followed by a list of six factors from which unconscionable conduct was inferred. It is difficult to disagree with Nicholas Bamforth ('Unconscionability as a Vitiating Factor' [1995] *LMCLQ* 538, 543–544) when he concludes:

> *Boustany* v. *Pigott* is a prime example of the imprecise approach which must be avoided if unconscionability is to merit support as a vitiating factor. . . . There are some basic problems with the Privy Council's treatment of the facts. We are not told *why* Mrs Boustany could be said to have had full knowledge that her conduct was unconscionable, or how any of the 'submissions' were brought into play. Miss Pigott had been incapable of giving evidence at the original trial and Mrs Boustany declined to do so, explaining the need to make inferences. This cannot, however, justify the failure to explain the inferences in the light of the five 'submissions'. The Privy Council simply presented a list of 'submissions' and a list of factual findings, without connecting the two. As in other unconscionability cases, terms such as 'affects his conscience', 'moral culpability', 'unconscientious' and 'unconscionable' were used without explanation of their precise meaning . . .

The danger of using pejorative terms should be clear: precision and clarity are crucial when a court is drawing up and deploying criteria for assessing whether a transaction is unconscionable, for the court must strike a delicate balance between conflicting policy considerations. On the one hand, it is important to safeguard the certainty of commercial transactions, especially those involving real property. It is also, however, important to protect weaker parties against improper exploitation in the bargaining process. The situation is further complicated by the need, in protecting weaker parties, to avoid compromising their autonomy through excessive judicial intervention in their transactions. The chances of striking a coherent balance between those considerations are greatly reduced when courts use imprecise or ambiguous language, or fail properly to explain why transactions are upheld or struck down.

A further difficulty with *Boustany* is that Miss Pigott did have independent advice. Indeed, Lord Templeman points out that the disadvantages of the new lease were 'forcibly pointed out to her'. Why did this independent advice not suffice to negate her claim? It is not entirely clear. It may be that not enough was done to bring home to Miss Pigott the nature of the transaction she was concluding. In this sense, *Boustany* may be closer to the incapacity cases (contrast in this respect the decision in *Boustany* with *Hart* v. *O'Connor* [1985] AC 1000, p. 830 below, which is the source of 'submission' 4).

Credit Lyonnais Bank Nederland NV v. Burch

[1997] 1 All ER 144, Court of Appeal

The defendant, an eighteen-year-old, was asked by her employer, Mr Pelosi, to mortgage her flat as security for an increase in the company's overdraft (which was in the region of £250,000). She agreed to this request and she entered into a transaction with the plaintiff bank under which she gave them a second charge over the flat and gave the bank an all moneys unlimited guarantee. No attempt was made by the bank to explain to her the nature of the transaction into which she was entering. She was advised to obtain independent advice but did not do so. The company went into liquidation and the bank brought proceedings against the defendant in which they sought possession of the flat. The defendant successfully defended the proceedings. The Court of Appeal set aside the transaction on the ground of undue influence but they also gave brief consideration to the existence of a wider equitable jurisdiction to set aside the transaction.

Nourse LJ
. . . the recorder identified, although without pejorative comment, the truly astonishing feature of this case. Under the terms of the legal charge, Miss Burch was required not simply to pledge her home as security for the £20,000 extension; she was required to pledge it without limit. Worse than that, she was required to enter into a personal covenant guaranteeing not simply repayment of the additional £20,000, nor even repayment up to the new limit of £270,000; she was required to guarantee without limit repayment of all API's borrowings from the bank, present and future and of whatever kind, together with interest, commission, charges, legal and other costs, charges and expenses. All that was required as the price of extending the limit by no more than £20,000 and, be it remembered, of someone who was a mere employee of API, to whom the only detriment

in API's collapse would have been the loss of her job. It could not have helped the bank to say that it used its standard form. A mortgagee who uses such a form without regard to its impact on the individual case acts at his peril.

On that state of facts it must, I think, have been very well arguable that Miss Burch could, directly against the bank, have had the legal charge set aside as an unconscionable bargain. Equity's jurisdiction to relieve against such transactions, although more rarely exercised in modern times, is at least as venerable as its jurisdiction to relieve against those procured by undue influence.

[he considered *Fry* v. *Lane* and continued]

The decision of Megarry J in *Cresswell* v. *Potter* [1978] 1 WLR 255 at 257 where he suggested that the modern equivalent of 'poor and ignorant' might be 'a member of the lower income group . . . less highly educated', demonstrates that the jurisdiction is in good heart and capable of adaptation to different transactions entered into in changing circumstances. See also the interesting judgment of Balcombe J in *Backhouse* v. *Backhouse* [1978] 1 WLR 243 at 250–252, where he suggested that these cases may come under the general heading which Lord Denning MR referred to in *Lloyds Bank Ltd* v. *Bundy* [1975] QB 326 at 339 as 'inequality of bargaining power'.

Millett LJ
No court of equity could allow such a transaction to stand. The facts which I have recited are sufficient to entitle Miss Burch to have the transaction set aside as against Mr Pelosi and the company. Every one of those facts was known to the bank when it accepted the security. The bank must accordingly be taken to have had notice of Miss Burch's equity, and must submit to the transaction being set aside against it also.

An eighteenth century Lord Chancellor would have contented himself with saying as much. It is an extreme case. The transaction was not merely to the manifest disadvantage of Miss Burch; it was one which, in the traditional phrase, 'shocks the conscience of the court'. Miss Burch committed herself to a personal liability far beyond her slender means, risking the loss of her home and personal bankruptcy, and obtained nothing in return beyond a relatively small and possibly temporary increase in the overdraft facility available to her employer, a company in which she had no financial interest. The transaction gives rise to grave suspicion. It cries aloud for an explanation.

Miss Burch did not seek to have the transaction set aside as a harsh and unconscionable bargain. To do so she would have had to show not only that the terms of the transaction were harsh or oppressive, but that 'one of the parties to it has imposed the objectionable terms in a morally reprehensible manner, that is to say, in a way which affects his conscience' (see *Multiservice Bookbinding Ltd* v. *Marden* [1979] Ch 84 at 110 per Browne-Wilkinson J and *Alec Lobb (Garages) Ltd* v. *Total Oil GB Ltd* [1983] 1 WLR 87 at 95, where I pointed out that there must be some impropriety, both in the conduct of the stronger party and in the terms of the transaction itself, but added that 'the former may often be inferred from the latter in the absence of an innocent explanation').

Swinton Thomas LJ delivered a concurring judgment.

COMMENTARY

This is another difficult decision. Nourse LJ appears to suggest that the unfairness of the charge, combined with an inequality of bargaining power, would have been enough to set aside the transaction with the bank. The judgment of Millett LJ is more cautious in that he stated that, in order to set aside the transaction on this ground, it would have been necessary for Miss Burch to show some impropriety on the part of the bank. The Court of Appeal in *Portman Building Society* v. *Dusangh* [2000] 2 All ER (Comm) 221 distinguished *Burch* on the ground that the transaction in *Dusangh*, although improvident, was not 'overreaching and oppressive' and there was no evidence that the building society in that case had acted in 'a morally reprehensible manner'. This suggests that *Burch* will be confined within very narrow limits. In *Dusangh* the defendant, an elderly, illiterate man, living on a low income, agreed to mortgage his home in order to enable his son to acquire a supermarket. The supermarket business was not a success and the building society was held to be entitled to a declaration that it was entitled to a charge by way of a legal mortgage over the defendant's home. Ward LJ stated (at p. 232):

The salient features here are that the son had committed himself to the purchase of the small supermarket business. There is no reason to think that he did not believe that it would be a profitable venture which would turn out to his advantage. He needed money to complete the purchase. He persuaded his father to lend it. On the findings of the judge there was no undue influence and no misrepresentation. So it was a case of father coming to the assistance of his son. True it is that it was a financially unwise venture because, absent good profit from the business, there was never likely to be the income to service the borrowing and the father's home was at risk. But there was nothing, absolutely nothing, which comes close to morally reprehensible conduct or impropriety. No unconscientious advantage has been taken of the father's illiteracy, his lack of business acumen or his paternal generosity. True it may be that the son gained all the advantage and the father took all the risk, but this cannot be stigmatised as impropriety. There was no exploitation of father by son such as would prick the conscience and tell the son that in all honour it was morally wrong and reprehensible.

4. THE ROLE OF STATUTES

Parliament also has a role to play in regulating unfair terms in contracts. The most significant examples are the Unfair Terms in Consumer Contracts Regulations 1999 (see Chapter 14) and the Unfair Contract Terms Act 1977 (pp. 460–485 above). A further example of legislative regulation of unfair terms is provided by sections 137–139 of the Consumer Credit Act 1974 which gives the courts considerable powers to re-open extortionate credit bargains:

Extortionate credit bargains

137.—(1) If the court finds a credit bargain extortionate it may reopen the credit agreement so as to do justice between the parties.

When bargains are extortionate

138.—(1) A credit bargain is extortionate if it—

(a) requires the debtor or a relative of his to make payments (whether unconditionally, or on certain contingencies) which are grossly exorbitant, or

(b) otherwise grossly contravenes ordinary principles of fair dealing.

(2) In determining whether a credit bargain is extortionate, regard shall be had to such evidence as is adduced concerning—

(a) interest rates prevailing at the time it was made,

(b) the factors mentioned in subsection (3) to (5), and

(c) any other relevant considerations.

(3) Factors applicable under subsection (2) in relation to the debtor include—

(a) his age, experience, business capacity and state of health; and

(b) the degree to which, at the time of making the credit bargain, he was under financial pressure, and the nature of that pressure.

(4) Factors applicable under subsection (2) in relation to the creditor include—

(a) the degree of risk accepted by him, having regard to the value of any security provided;

(b) his relationship to the debtor; and

(c) whether or not a colourable cash price was quoted for any goods or services included in the credit bargain.

(5) Factors applicable under subsection (2) in relation to a linked transaction include the question how far the transaction was reasonably required for the protection of debtor or creditor, or was in the interest of the debtor.

Reopening of extortionate agreements

139.—(1) *[Omitted]*

(2) In reopening the agreement, the court may, for the purpose of relieving the debtor or a surety from payment of any sum in excess of that fairly due and reasonable, by order—

(a) direct accounts to be taken, or (in Scotland) an accounting to be made, between any persons,

(b) set aside the whole or part of any obligation imposed on the debtor or a surety by the credit bargain or any related agreement,

(c) require the creditor to repay the whole or part of any sum paid under the credit bargain or any related agreement by the debtor or a surety, whether paid to the creditor or any other person,

(d) direct the return to the surety of any property provided for the purposes of the security, or

(e) alter the terms of the credit agreement or any security instrument.

(3) An order may be made under subsection (2) notwithstanding that its effect is to place a burden on the creditor in respect of an advantage unfairly enjoyed by another person who is a party to a linked transaction.

(4) An order under subsection (2) shall not alter the effect of any judgment.

While statutes provide individual examples of the regulation of unfair terms, it is difficult to use statutes as building blocks in the construction of a general principle of unconscionability or inequality of bargaining power. The reason for this is that statutes and statutory instruments apply only to transactions that fall within their scope. They cannot be applied by way of analogy to cases that fall outside their scope and the courts have generally not been willing to rely on Acts of Parliament when developing the common law (see *National Westminster Bank plc* v. *Morgan* [1985] AC 686, p. 815 below, although contrast *Timeload Ltd* v. *British Telecommunications plc* [1995] EMLR 459, p. 466 above).

5. A GENERAL PRINCIPLE?

Thus far we have seen that English law has a collection of cases and statutes that seem to reflect a concern for the fairness of the bargain that has been concluded by the parties. But are they anything more than a collection of individual cases? Can they be rationalized into a principle or set of principles of general application? Lord Denning famously sought to create such a general principle in his judgment in *Lloyds Bank Ltd* v. *Bundy* [1975] QB 326. He stated (at pp. 336–339):

> Now let me say at once that in the vast majority of cases a customer who signs a bank guarantee or a charge cannot get out of it. No bargain will be upset which is the result of the ordinary interplay of forces. There are many hard cases which are caught by this rule. Take the case of a poor man who is homeless. He agrees to pay a high rent to a landlord just to get a roof over his head. The common law will not interfere. It is left to Parliament. Next take the case of a borrower in urgent need of money. He borrows it from the bank at high interest and it is guaranteed by a friend. The guarantor gives his bond and gets nothing in return. The common law will not interfere. Parliament has intervened to prevent moneylenders charging excessive interest. But it has never interfered with banks.
>
> Yet there are exceptions to this general rule. There are cases in our books in which the courts will set aside a contract, or a transfer of property, when the parties have not met on equal terms—when the one is so strong in bargaining power and the other so weak— that, as a matter of common fairness, it is not right that the strong should be allowed to push the weak to the wall. Hitherto those exceptional cases have been treated each as a separate category in itself. But I think the time has come when we should seek to find a principle to unite them. I put on one side contracts or transactions which are voidable for fraud or misrepresentation or mistake. All those are governed by settled principles. I go only to those where there has been inequality of bargaining power, such as to merit the intervention of the court.

The categories

The first category is that of 'duress of goods'. A typical case is when a man is in a strong bargaining position by being in possession of the goods of another by virtue of a legal right, such as by way of pawn or pledge or taken in distress. The owner is in a weak position because he is in urgent need of the goods. The stronger demands of the weaker more than is justly due: and he pays it in order to get the goods. Such a transaction is voidable. He can recover the excess: see *Astley* v. *Reynolds* (1731) 2 Stra 915 and *Green* v.

Duckett (1883) 11 QBD 275. To which may be added the cases of 'colore officii', where a man is in a strong bargaining position by virtue of his official position or public profession. He relies upon it so as to gain from the weaker—who is urgently in need—more than is justly due: see *Pigott's Case* cited by Lord Kenyon CJ in *Cartwright* v. *Rowley* (1799) 2 Esp 723, 723–724; *Parker* v. *Bristol and Exeter Railway Co* (1851) 6 Exch 702 and *Steele* v. *Williams* (1853) 8 Exch 625. In such cases the stronger may make his claim in good faith honestly believing that he is entitled to make his demand. He may not be guilty of any fraud or misrepresentation. The inequality of bargaining power—the strength of the one versus the urgent need of the other—renders the transaction voidable and the money paid to be recovered back: see *Maskell* v. *Horner* [1915] 3 KB 106.

The second category is that of the 'unconscionable transaction'. A man is so placed as to be in need of special care and protection and yet his weakness is exploited by another far stronger than himself so as to get his property at a gross undervalue. The typical case is that of the 'expectant heir'. But it applies to all cases where a man comes into property, or is expected to come into it—and then being in urgent need—another gives him ready cash for it, greatly below its true worth, and so gets the property transferred to him: see *Evans* v. *Llewellin* (1787) 1 Cox 333. Even though there be no evidence of fraud or misrepresentation, nevertheless the transaction will be set aside: see *Fry* v. *Lane* (1888) 40 Ch D 312, 322 where Kay J said:

> 'The result of the decisions is that where a purchase is made from a poor and ignorant man at a considerable undervalue, the vendor having no independent advice, a court of equity will set aside the transaction.'

This second category is said to extend to all cases where an unfair advantage has been gained by an unconscientious use of power by a stronger party against a weaker: see the cases cited in *Halsbury's Laws of England*, 3rd ed., vol 17 (1956), p. 682 and, in Canada, *Morrison* v. *Coast Finance Ltd* (1965) 55 DLR (2d) 710 and *Knupp* v. *Bell* (1968) 67 DLR (2d) 256.

The third category is that of 'undue influence' usually so called. These are divided into two classes as stated by Cotton LJ in *Allcard* v. *Skinner* (1887) 36 Ch D 145, 171. The first are those where the stronger has been guilty of some fraud or wrongful act—expressly so as to gain some gift or advantage from the weaker. The second are those where the stronger has not been guilty of any wrongful act, but has, through the relationship which existed between him and the weaker, gained some gift or advantage for himself. Sometimes the relationship is such as to raise a presumption of undue influence, such as parent over child, solicitor over client, doctor over patient, spiritual adviser over follower. At other times a relationship of confidence must be proved to exist. But to all of them the general principle obtains which was stated by Lord Chelmsford LC in *Tate* v. *Williamson* (1866) 2 Ch App 55, 61:

> 'Wherever two persons stand in such a relation that, while it continues, confidence is necessarily reposed by one, and the influence which naturally grows out of that confidence is possessed by the other, and this confidence is abused, or the influence is exerted to obtain an advantage at the expense of the confiding party, the person so availing himself of his position will not be permitted to retain the advantage, although the transaction could not have been impeached if no such confidential relation had existed.'

Such a case was *Tufton* v. *Sperni* [1952] 2 TLR 516.

The fourth category is that of 'undue pressure'. The most apposite of that is *Williams* v. *Bayley* (1866) LR 1 HL 200, where a son forged his father's name to a promissory note and, by means of it, raised money from the bank of which they were both customers. The bank said to the father, in effect: 'Take your choice—give us security for your son's debt. If you do take that on yourself, then it will all go smoothly: if you do not, we shall be bound to exercise pressure'. Thereupon the father charged his property to the bank with payment of the note. The House of Lords held that the charge was invalid because of undue pressure exerted by the bank. Lord Westbury said, at pp. 218–219:

> 'A contract to give security for the debt of another, which is a contract without consideration, is above all things, a contract that should be based upon the free and voluntary agency of the individual who enters into it.'

Other instances of undue pressure are where one party stipulates for an unfair advantage to which the other has no option but to submit. As where an employer—the stronger party—has employed a builder—the weaker party—to do work for him. When the builder asked for payment of sums properly due (so as to pay his workmen) the employer refused to pay unless he was given some added advantage. Stuart V-C said: 'Where an agreement, hard and inequitable in itself, has been exacted under circumstances of pressure on the part of the person who exacts it, this court will set it aside': see *Ormes* v. *Beadel* (1860) 2 Giff 166, 174 (reversed on another ground, 2 De GF & J 333) and *D & C Builders Ltd* v. *Rees* [1966] 2 QB 617, 625.

The fifth category is that of salvage agreements. When a vessel is in danger of sinking and seeks help, the rescuer is in a strong bargaining position. The vessel in distress is in urgent need. The parties cannot be truly said to be on equal terms. The Court of Admiralty have always recognised that fact. The 'fundamental rule' is

> 'if the parties have made an agreement, the court will enforce it, unless it be manifestly unfair and unjust; but if it be manifestly unfair and unjust, the court will disregard it and decree what is fair and just.'

See *Akerblom* v. *Price* (1881) 7 QBD 129, 133, per Brett LJ, applied in a striking case *The Port Caledonia and The Anna* [1903] P 184, when the rescuer refused to help with a rope unless he was paid £1,000.

The general principles

Gathering all together, I would suggest that through all these instances there runs a single thread. They rest on 'inequality of bargaining power'. By virtue of it, the English law gives relief to one who, without independent advice, enters into a contract upon terms which are very unfair or transfers property for a consideration which is grossly inadequate, when his bargaining power is grievously impaired by reason of his own needs or desires, or by his own ignorance or infirmity, coupled with undue influences or pressures brought to bear on him by or for the benefit of the other. When I use the word 'undue' I do not mean to suggest that the principle depends on proof of any wrongdoing. The one who stipulates for an unfair advantage may be moved solely by his own self-interest, unconscious of the distress he is bringing to the other. I have also avoided any reference to the will of the one being 'dominated' or 'overcome' by the other. One who is in extreme need may knowingly consent to a most improvident bargain, solely to relieve the straits in which he finds himself. Again, I do not mean to suggest that every transaction is saved by independent advice. But the absence of it may be fatal. With these explanations, I hope this principle will be found to reconcile the cases.

COMMENTARY

The choice of 'inequality of bargaining power' as the label was perhaps an unfortunate one. It appeared to suggest that a mere imbalance in bargaining power would suffice to give the court jurisdiction to intervene. But the sentence in Lord Denning's judgment immediately following the reference to 'inequality of bargaining power' makes clear that what is required is both procedural and substantive unfairness. There must be a 'grossly inadequate' consideration, a 'grievous impairment' of bargaining power, and 'undue influences or pressures'. This is hardly an easy test to satisfy. The creation of a general principle found some supporters (see, for example, S Waddams, 'Unconscionability in Contracts' (1976) 39 *MLR* 369) who saw it as a means of unifying a range of disparate cases and doctrines (for example, the penalty clause jurisdiction (p. 1124 below), the rules relating to the incorporation and interpretation of exclusion clauses (pp. 446–460 above), the rules relating to the incorporation of terms (Chapter 9 above), and the protection of weak and vulnerable parties) and as a platform for the development of the law.

However, these hopes were dashed by the House of Lords in *National Westminster Bank plc* v. *Morgan* [1985] AC 686, 707–708 when Lord Scarman stated:

Lord Denning MR [in *Bundy*] believed that the doctrine of undue influence could be subsumed under a general principle that English courts will grant relief where there has been 'inequality of bargaining power' (p. 339). He deliberately avoided reference to the will of one party being dominated or overcome by another. The majority of the court did not follow him; they based their decision on the orthodox view of the doctrine as expounded in *Allcard* v. *Skinner*, 36 Ch D 145. The opinion of the Master of the Rolls, therefore, was not the ground of the court's decision, which was to be found in the view of the majority, for whom Sir Erich Sachs delivered the leading judgment.

Nor has counsel for the respondent sought to rely on Lord Denning MR's general principle; and, in my view, he was right not to do so. The doctrine of undue influence has been sufficiently developed not to need the support of a principle which by its formulation in the language of the law of contract is not appropriate to cover transactions of gift where there is no bargain. The fact of an unequal bargain will, of course, be a relevant feature in some cases of undue influence. But it can never become an appropriate basis of principle of an equitable doctrine which is concerned with transactions 'not to be reasonably accounted for on the ground of friendship, relationship, charity, or other ordinary motives on which ordinary men act' (Lindley LJ in *Allcard* v. *Skinner*, at 185). And even in the field of contract I question whether there is any need in the modern law to erect a general principle of relief against inequality of bargaining power. Parliament has undertaken the task—and it is essentially a legislative task—of enacting such restrictions upon freedom of contract as are in its judgment necessary to relieve against the mischief: for example, the hire-purchase and consumer protection legislation, of which the Supply of Goods (Implied Terms) Act 1973, Consumer Credit Act 1974, Consumer Safety Act 1978, Supply of Goods and Services Act 1982 and Insurance Companies Act 1982 are examples. I doubt whether the courts should assume the burden of formulating further restrictions.

Two points can be made in relation to this statement. First, it depends upon a particular perception of the relationship between the common law and statute law.

According to this view, once Parliament assumes the role of protecting the weak and the vulnerable, the common law should return to its laissez-faire principles. But there is another view. The alternative view is that the common law should build upon the principles contained in these statutes: that is to say, the courts should see in these statutes a commitment to fairness which should be reflected in the law outside the immediate context of the statutes. The second point is that Lord Scarman gives priority to Lord Denning's choice of label over the substantive content of the principle he set out in *Bundy*. Greater concentration on the scope of the principle might have enabled it to survive the scrutiny of the House of Lords.

6. THE SEARCH FOR COHERENCE

If it is the case that a general principle of inequality of bargaining power or unconscionability is not acceptable to the courts, is it possible to identify the range of factors taken into account by the courts in the cases with a view to providing a structured framework within which the courts can decide whether or not to set aside a particular contract? Attempts have been made to identify these factors and, in so doing, to bring about a greater degree of coherence and predictability in the law. Two examples are set out below. The first, provided by Nicholas Bamforth, identifies 'unconscientious receipt' as the basis for intervention and further identifies four factors that are generally taken into account by the courts. Secondly, David Capper identifies three such factors, although it is important to note that his list is part of a wider project, namely to merge the doctrines of undue influence and unconscionability into one doctrine by subsuming undue influence under his wider notion of unconscionability. At the end of the extract Capper raises the question of the role of substantive unfairness in the law of contract. He suggests that it performs an evidentiary function; that is to say, it provides evidence from which other grounds of invalidity can be deduced. The last extract takes up the difficult question of the role of substantive unfairness in the law of contract. Professor Stephen A Smith argues for a more extensive role for substantive unfairness than that recognized by Capper. While he dismisses a number of reasons that are commonly put forward in support of the proposition that substantively unfair contracts are 'bad', he does identify one argument which, in his view, supports the proposition that such contracts are bad. That argument is that substantively unfair contracts make it more difficult for us to lead autonomous lives, in the sense that they make it more difficult for us to plan and direct our lives.

N Bamforth, 'Unconscionability as a Vitiating Factor'

[1995] *LMCLQ* 538, 555–557

Courts are not, in reality, acting in a wholly discretionary fashion in cases where unconscionability is invoked as a vitiating factor. Behind the imprecise language, four elements have characteristically been treated as important in assessing whether a transaction should be set aside. First, whether the weaker party was afflicted by a special or serious disadvantage or disability, mere inequality of bargaining power being insufficient.

Secondly, whether the stronger party's conduct amounted to actual or constructive fraud. Thirdly, whether the weaker party lacked independent advice. Fourthly, whether the terms of the transaction were clearly disadvantageous to the weaker party.

However, the precise weight attached to each of the four elements seems to vary. There are many views about the importance of the terms of the transaction by comparison with the other three elements, and it has even been suggested that disadvantageous terms might not always be necessary. On balance, the unconscionability cases seem to conform with Professor Atiyah's suggestion that, in judicial assessments of the propriety of transactions, 'ideas of procedural and substantive fairness feed upon each other'. The fraud element is also problematic. 'Dishonesty'—the actual fraud requirement—tends towards imprecision, and reliance on constructive fraud would take the unconscionability vitiating factor dangerously close to being the sort of general power, decried by Toohey J, to set aside bargains just because they appear at first glance to be unfair or harsh. Given the vagueness of this element, it is unsurprising that there have been differences of judicial opinion about whether the stronger party's knowledge of the other's weakness should be subjectively held or objectively assessed.

This brings us to two interconnected issues. The first—a policy issue—is whether unconscionability deserves support as a distinct vitiating factor. The second—an issue of legal principle—is to identify unconscionability's juristic basis, that is, to establish the general principle which underpins it and locates it at a particular point within the law. These two issues are interconnected because failure to identify an underpinning principle is likely to magnify any appearance of imprecision in unconscionability cases, disturbing those who believe that law should, as a matter of policy, embody a degree of certainty. A suitable underpinning principle would, by contrast, provide a way of understanding, rationalising and controlling the development of the vitiating factor's four elements, minimising the danger of palm tree justice. The identification of a suitable underpinning principle therefore affects the assessment of unconscionability's desirability, in policy terms, as a vitiating factor. The relative importance attached to the three policy factors . . . certainty in commercial transactions, protection of weaker parties from improper exploitation, and avoiding judicial intervention on a scale which deprives vulnerable persons of any bargaining autonomy—is also likely to influence the categorisation of a particular underpinning principle as suitable.

It is likely that for most lawyers the desirable policy balance will be something of a compromise—enough certainty to enable forward planning and security of receipt in transactions, but sufficient flexibility to leave room for a residual unconscionability jurisdiction according to which utterly exploitative transactions can be struck down. A variety of possible underpinning principles might fit within this balance. 'Inequality of bargaining power' has been dismissed as an underpinning principle in the case law—rightly, as it cannot explain the need for special disadvantage and the relevance of the terms of the transaction. It is also, in and of itself, too vague a principle on which to base an entire vitiating factor. Another possibility has been canvassed by John Cartwright, who argues that '[t]he key is that one party has *abused* his or her [bargaining] position *vis-à-vis* the other'. Unfortunately, the term 'abuse' does not assist us greatly, being as pejorative as much of the language used by the judiciary. This impression is confirmed by Cartwright's suggestion that misrepresentation, duress and undue influence might also be described as examples of 'abuse of bargaining position', implying that 'abuse' is a malleable concept which can simply be adjusted to fit the vitiating factor in play. A similar argument can be made against the suggestion that the basis of unconscionability is the effecting of relief in equity from fraud. Fraud is as vague a concept when deployed as an underpinning principle as it is when treated as an element which needs to be established in an unconscionability claim; and, like 'abuse of bargaining position', it appears to be capable of manipulation to fit whatever vitiating factor or rule it is said to underpin.

The most appropriate possibility, within the policy balance envisaged, is the suggestion that unconscionability works to reverse or prevent unjust enrichment ... unconscionability as a vitiating factor falls within the family of 'unjust factors' labelled 'unconscientious receipt', where 'the question for restitution is that the defendant behaved badly in receiving the value in question'.

If restitution for unconscientious receipt is the principle which underpins unconscionability as a vitiating factor, it is necessary to identify the type of behaviour which should be regarded as 'bad'. Otherwise, unconscionability will be indistinguishable from other forms of 'unconscientious receipt'. It is here that the four common elements in unconscionability cases come into play. For the purpose of 'unconscientious receipt' behaviour will be deemed to be 'bad', in the sense which justifies the intervention of unconscionability as a vitiating factor, where the stronger party exploits, in a dishonest fashion, the special disadvantage of the weaker party in concluding with them a bargain which is to their severe disadvantage, where the weaker party lacks adequate independent advice. This formulation, marrying the underpinning principle with the elements of unconscionability, is general enough to allow the vitiating factor to adapt itself to new fact-situations, but sufficiently specific that it will be kept under tight control. As 'unconscientious receipt' rests on a defendant-sided approach, it follows that the unconscionability vitiating factor should be confined to cases where there has been deliberate wrongdoing by the stronger party—in other words, where they have subjectively exploited the other's weakness rather than fallen below an objectively-assessed standard of conduct.

D Capper, 'Undue Influence and Unconscionability: A Rationalisation'

(1998) 114 *LQR* 479, 499–500

A NEW DOCTRINE OF UNCONSCIONABILITY

How would this new doctrine work? In essence, the court would have to weigh up the three elements of relational inequality, transactional imbalance, and unconscionable conduct, and come to an overall judgment as to whether a particular transaction can stand. This would not, however, be a purely impressionistic exercise. Transactional imbalance would serve an evidentiary function, that is to say a sharp case of transactional imbalance would strengthen a case for relief founded primarily on relational inequality or unconscionable conduct, and the absence of any real imbalance would point the court away from invalidity on either of these grounds. The principal grounds for relief would thus be relational inequality and unconscionable conduct. The more there was of one of these features, the less would be required of the other; and where one was not strongly in evidence transactional imbalance would be needed to bolster it. Where the parties to a transaction are on very unequal terms and the transaction is weighted strongly in favour of one party, unconscionable conduct can be inferred. Where the parties are on fairly equal terms and the defendant has clearly behaved unconscionably, the court could infer that the defendant's conduct has induced an unfair transaction if the transaction appears unbalanced. This appears to be the way that courts approach arguments of unconscionability at the moment.

The new doctrine would be neither specifically plaintiff-sided nor specifically defendant-sided. The stronger the plaintiff-sided factor the weaker the defendant-sided factor needs to be and vice versa, although a degree of unconscionable conduct would be present in all cases since the passive receipt of benefits flowing under a seriously unbalanced transaction where the plaintiff was clearly in an unequal relationship with the defendant would count as unconscionable conduct. In theory a transaction could be unconscionable where the defendant has behaved abominably and extracted benefits from a plaintiff on equal terms with himself, although it is probably unlikely that there would be many cases like this. The new doctrine would also be more concerned with procedural than with substantive unfairness. The importance of substantive unfairness as a vitiating factor in contract is acknowledged, but this tends to provide evidence from which grounds of invalidity can be deduced rather than serve as a vitiating factor of itself. Substantive unfairness is not likely to become an independent ground of invalidity so long as courts maintain the approach that they cannot make or remake a contract for the parties. If a contract is substantively unfair, the obvious solution would be to alter it to make it fair, but with some very limited exceptions, English law does not do this.

SA Smith, 'In Defence of Substantive Unfairness'

(1996) 112 *LQR* 138, 145–154

The advocate of substantive unfairness must . . . explain why substantively unfair contracts are bad. The enforcement of contracts is presumably a good thing generally, so some reason for non-enforcement must be provided. But the reason need not be along the lines that one of the parties coerced, defrauded, or manipulated the other party (though these are good reasons). All that needs to be shown, broadly speaking, is that a substantively unfair contract is not the sort of contract the law should promote. This is an easier standard to meet than the wrongfulness standard used in duress, fraud and so on. The difference is the same as the difference between deciding what sorts of activities the state should prohibit, or at least deter, and deciding what sorts of activities the state should subsidise. We may be uncertain, for example, whether prostitution should be prohibited, yet be reasonably confident that brothels should not be subsidised. Contract law—which is funded from tax revenue—subsidises certain sorts of activities.

Why, then, might a contract's price affect our valuation of the contract? Five possibilities present themselves.

Evidentiary value

The first suggestion is that prices are of evidentiary importance. Unfair prices— understood here as abnormal prices—are not always accompanied by an invalidating procedural defect, but in some circumstances they are good evidence of such a defect. If there is a high risk of duress, undue influence, or fraud and the resulting contract is at an abnormal price, then even without direct proof of wrongdoing a court might reasonably conclude that wrongdoing has occurred. . . . Evidentiary arguments . . . are of limited interest. Evidentiary arguments do not provide a reason for caring about the price per se.

At most, they merely show that in a few situations the price of a contract is evidence of something else that is valuable . . .

Distributive justice

The most common non-evidentiary, suggestion for why substantively unfair contracts should not be enforced is that they upset distributive justice. At first blush, this seems an unusual suggestion. Distributive justice is traditionally understood as requiring that common goods be distributed fairly amongst the members of a group or society. Contract law, which deals with two party interactions, appears unconcerned with the distribution of common goods.

Contract law might, however, be instrumentally important in helping to preserve a just distribution of such goods. In particular, a requirement of substantive fairness might be important in maintaining a just distribution of purchasing power. If goods are traded at fair prices—understood again as normal prices—the trading parties end up with goods of roughly equivalent value to offer in the market. If they wish, the parties can, at least in theory, return to their original pre-contract position (minus transaction costs). Their purchasing power, as determined by the normal prices of all the goods that the parties own, is unchanged. Substantively unfair contracts upset the prior pattern of purchasing power and thus, it might be argued, conflict with distributive justice.

This suggestion is largely immune to the objection that contracting parties will bargain around redistribution rules, leaving unchanged or worsened the prior distributional pattern. Substantive fairness, on a distributive justice interpretation, does not require or support redistributions of purchasing power. It calls instead for preventing redistributions. This feature of the distributive justice argument, however, is also its main weakness (leaving aside the controversial issues of the value of distributive justice generally and the extent, if any, that purchasing power is a 'common good'). The distributive justice argument calls for upholding existing entitlements and therefore it applies straightforwardly only in societies—unlike any we know of—which are already distributively just. Preserving an unjust distribution of resources does not promote distributive justice. Indeed, if resources are unjustly distributed, what are needed from the perspective of distributive justice are substantively unfair terms . . . concerns of distributive justice provide at most a very weak justification for the party-based concerns of substantive fairness.

Facilitating contracting

A third possible reason for caring about contract prices is that contract pricing can affect individuals' ability to contract. If, as seems plausible, courts should facilitate contracting, this is a legitimate concern. There are at least four ways that contract pricing might inhibit contracting. First, in monopolistic (and monopsonistic) markets non-competitive pricing causes potential contractors to be priced out of the market. Monopolistic pricing typically results in fewer contracts, but at a higher price. For whatever reason contracts are valuable, this is undesirable. Second, the pricing strategy of situational monopolists can make contracting more difficult. . . . Third, and more generally, non-competitive pricing will, even in a competitive market, reduce contracting overall. . . . Finally, in situations where one of the contracting parties is unsure of the normal price for a good, a requirement that goods be sold at normal prices can facilitate contracting . . . [I]t seems clear that the reasons these suggestions provide for caring about contract prices are not reasons based on a concern for substantive fairness. The fairness of the impugned contracts is in each case beside the point. Indeed, there is nothing actually wrong with the contracts themselves in the above examples: what is 'wrong' is that other contracts did not or will not happen. . . . In short, whatever the merits of assessing contract prices in order to facilitate contracting, such regulation is not justified by a concern for substantive fairness.

Autonomy and basic needs

One reason for not enforcing a contract is that it does not support a valuable or worthwhile activity. The rules regarding so-called immoral or illegal contracts, such as contracts to sell babies and contracts of self-enslavement, are most naturally defended (insofar as they can be defended) on this basis. The problem with substantively unfair contracts is different. A substantively unfair contract may support a perfectly worthwhile endeavour. Yet there is a connection between substantive fairness and 'non-valuable' contracts. The underlying justification for not enforcing non-valuable contracts is that the state should only lend a hand to endeavours that help individuals to achieve well-being and thus to realize fulfilling lives. Worthless activities, even if freely chosen, do not contribute to well-being. Contract prices can affect contracting parties' abilities to achieve fulfilling lives. One explanation of how this can happen draws on the importance, for well-being, of leading an autonomous, self-directed, life, and, more specifically, on the importance of having a threshold level of material wealth. It is not necessary to be rich to lead an autonomous life, but it is necessary to have one's basic physical needs met. Individuals whose every choice is dictated by the need to survive cannot lead autonomous lives. They are unable to direct their lives in any meaningful sense. A contract at abnormal prices can leave a contracting party in this position. If the magnitude of the deviation is severe enough, the wealth of the losing party may be reduced to less than the threshold level.

The problem with contracts that leave contracting parties in poverty is significant and helps to explain why some contracts at abnormal prices appear so repugnant. But, again, it is not a problem of substantive unfairness. Contracts which leave a party in poverty are like contracts of self-enslavement. They are bad, but they are not unfair (or at least only coincidentally unfair). Fairness is a relative concept: if someone has been treated unfairly, someone else has been treated differently. Yet in explaining why a contract that leaves someone in poverty is bad the situation of the other party to the contract is irrelevant. All we need to know is that one party has been left destitute. The same is true of contracts of self-enslavement: all we need to know to condemn such contracts is that someone has been made a slave. Thus, while some unfair contracts may be objectionable because they leave one of the parties in a state of poverty, the substantive unfairness of such contract is not the reason for the objection.

Autonomy and planning

The final reason for caring about contract prices is also founded on the importance, for achieving well-being, of living an autonomous life. More specifically, it is founded on the importance of being able to plan and control one's life. It is here, I suggest, that the key to understanding the value and meaning of substantive fairness is found. The problem with substantively unfair contracts is that they make it more difficult to direct our lives.

An autonomous life, in the sense I use this phrase, requires more than freedom from coercion. Autonomy is fundamentally a matter of being able to direct one's life: we lead autonomous lives, broadly speaking, when we direct our lives to a significant degree.

Autonomous individuals need not live their lives according to rigid patterns, but they must have a reasonable ability to shape and plan their lives. Contract law helps us to lead autonomous lives by helping us to achieve valuable goals and, as importantly, by helping us do this autonomously. It increases our options and lets us decide what goals to pursue. The enforcement of contracts at abnormal prices, however, can make it more difficult to lead an autonomous life. Contracts at abnormal prices upset the material foundations upon which plans and aspirations are built. Rich or poor, we plan and shape our lives upon assumptions and expectations about our purchasing power. Contracts at abnormal prices upset plans and, more generally, individuals' abilities to control and direct their lives. . . . A contract at an abnormal price is similar to an unannounced change in tax policy. It shifts the purchasing power, leaving the losing party worse-off than before the contract, and thereby making it more difficult for that party to achieve an autonomous, that is, self-directed, life. This is true regardless of the justice of the prior distribution of resources. Of course it is not possible or desirable to protect individuals from all uncertainty. But avoidable, undesired, uncertainty should not be promoted by the law.

The 'planning' justification supports a normal price standard for assessing contracts. Plans are built upon normal prices. To be sure, courts could ensure that plans were never upset by imposing fixed prices for all goods. This solution is undesirable because contracting parties are normally better able than courts to set prices at mutually attractive levels. Setting fixed prices would make contracting far less appealing, thus limiting the good that contracting can achieve.

The importance of planning and the relation between shifts in purchasing power and planning explain why courts should be concerned about contracts at abnormal prices. But these considerations do not apply equally to all contracts at abnormal prices. First, not all abnormal price contracts upset planning. In particular, contracts where either (1) the losing party was making a gift, (2) the losing party did not care about the price, or (3) the losing party was mistaken as to the nature and hence value of the good he or she was selling (for example, not realising that the painting offered was a Rembrandt) do not upset the losing party's ability to plan. In the first and third situation the losing party's expectations were not upset and in the second case the losing party had no expectations. Such contracts should therefore be enforced.

A further, more general factor, in considering to what extent planning is upset by abnormal price contracts is that if the deviation from normal price is small, either in absolute terms or relative to the contract's price, then harm to planning, though not non-existent, is relatively trivial. . . . A second reason for limiting judicial scrutiny of abnormal price contracts is that invalidating contracts itself produces uncertainty and disrupts planning. . . . Taken together the results of our inquiries into (1) the harm caused by abnormal price contracts and (2) the ease of avoiding this harm suggest, therefore, the following general rule. Contracts in which the price deviates significantly, both in absolute and relative terms, from the normal price and in which the worse-off party cared about price, was not making a gift, was not mistaken about the value of the good he or she was selling and was not in a better position than the gaining party to obtain the normal price should not be enforced.

7. FURTHER READING

Bamforth, N, 'Unconscionability as a Vitiating Factor' [1995] *LMCLQ* 538.

Capper, D, 'Undue Influence and Unconscionability: A Rationalisation' (1998) 114 *LQR* 479.

Chen-Wishart, M, 'The *O'Brien* Principle and Substantive Unfairness' [1997] *CLJ* 60.

Smith, SA, 'In Defence of Substantive Unfairness' (1996) 112 *LQR* 138.

Thal, SN 'The Inequality of Bargaining Power Doctrine: The Problem of Defining Contractual Unfairness' (1988) 8 *OJLS* 17.

Waddams, S, 'Unconscionability in Contracts' (1976) 39 *MLR* 369.

21

INCAPACITY

1. CENTRAL ISSUES

1. The law relating to incapacity seeks to strike a balance between two competing policies. The first is the desire to protect those who have limited contractual capacity and the second is the wish to protect people who deal in all good faith with those who are in some way incapacitated. The trend in the modern law is to give greater emphasis to the latter policy over the former.

2. Those who have limited contractual capacity include children, people who suffer from some mental incapacity, companies, and local authorities. The various forms of incapacity are regulated in different ways but the differences in treatment are not always easy to justify. They seem to be attributable to historical accident rather than rational development. For example, in cases of mental incapacity the contract will only be set aside where the defendant has knowledge that the claimant is suffering from an incapacity, whereas there is no such knowledge requirement in the cases where an adult concludes a contract with a child. In such cases the law does not examine the state of the adult's knowledge and, indeed, cases can be found in which the contract was held not to be binding on the child notwithstanding the fact that the child fraudulently misrepresented that he was an adult.

3. Incapacity cases are also related to some of the cases discussed in Chapter 20 (dealing with unconscionability and inequality of bargaining power). The link between the two groups of cases is particularly apparent in cases of alleged mental incapacity.

2. INTRODUCTION

Contract textbooks written in the nineteenth century and in the early part of the twentieth century gave considerable prominence to the issue of contractual capacity. The reason for this was that, during this period, over half the population had limited contractual capacity. At common law a married woman did not, as a general rule, have contractual capacity; that is to say, she could not enter into a contract on her own account. These restrictions on the contractual capacity of women have since been repealed but the process of repeal was not completed until the enactment of the Law Reform (Married Women and Tortfeasors) Act 1935 and the Married Women (Restraint upon Anticipation) Act 1949. Today the topic of contractual capacity excites far less interest. Women now have full contractual capacity. While children still have limited contractual capacity, one consequence of the reduction of the age of majority from twenty-one to eighteen has been to reduce the practical significance of the issue because many of the old cases concerned with the contractual capacity of children involved children aged between eighteen and twenty-one. Such 'children' now have full contractual capacity.

But it does not follow from the reduced practical significance of incapacity that it has lost all relevance and interest. Difficult issues can still arise in relation to the capacity of companies and public bodies. An area which also gives rise to difficulty is the contractual capacity of the elderly and the infirm. Many people in society are concerned for the welfare of their elderly parents, some of whom exhibit signs of memory loss which may or may not be associated with a form of dementia. What is the contractual capacity of people whose intellectual powers are diminishing in this way? There is an acute conflict of policy here. On the one hand, we do not wish to infantilize the elderly by depriving them of their capacity to enter into contracts. On the other hand, we do not want to leave them vulnerable to exploitation by those who are tempted to prey on their reduced capacity for their own gain. It is not uncommon now for elderly parents to confer a power of attorney on their children so that the children can contract on their behalf and relieve them of the responsibility of having to look after their own financial affairs. The difficulties associated with the contractual capacity of the elderly are likely to assume greater significance in the future, not less.

The law in this area attempts to strike a balance between two competing policies. First, there is the desire to protect those who have limited capacity. For example, in the case of children, the law wishes to protect children from their lack of understanding and experience of life. Secondly, there is the desire to protect people who deal in all good faith with those who suffer from some form of incapacity. For example, a person may enter into a contract with a seventeen-year-old, unaware of the fact that he is a child or enter into a contract with another adult unaware of the fact that that person is suffering from dementia. The balance between these two policies has proved to be a difficult one and it has resulted in the creation of a complex body of case-law.

3. CHILDREN

A child is a person who is under the age of eighteen. The word that is used in law to describe a child is a 'minor'. Children have limited contractual capacity. Unfortunately, the law has developed in a piecemeal fashion, with the result that the rules of law are unnecessarily complex. When seeking to ascertain the contractual capacity of children it is necessary to distinguish between different contracts and the different bases on which children may incur liability towards adults or be able to assert rights against adults as a result of the 'contracts' which they conclude.

(a) VALID CONTRACTS

A limited category of contracts entered into by children are valid and binding; that is to say the child can both sue and be sued on the contract. The clearest example of a contract that is valid and binding upon a child is a contract for necessaries. The definition of 'necessaries' is not a straightforward matter because regard must be had to the status in life of the particular child. What is 'necessary' for a child from a very wealthy background may well not be necessary for a child from a poorer background (contrast in this respect *Peters* v. *Fleming* (1840) 6 M & W 42 and *Nash* v. *Inman* [1908] 2 KB 1). In the case of a contract for the sale of goods 'necessaries' are defined as 'goods suitable to the condition in life of the minor or other person concerned and to his actual requirements at the time of sale and delivery' (Sale of Goods Act 1979, section 3(2)). Secondly, a contract of employment concluded by a child is binding on the child provided that the contract is a beneficial one (*Clements* v. *London and North Western Railway Company* [1894] 2 QB 482). The position is otherwise where the contract of employment is not for his benefit and is, in some way, oppressive (*De Francesco* v. *Barnum* (1890) 45 Ch D 490).

(b) VOIDABLE CONTRACTS

A second group of contracts are voidable at the instance of the child; that is to say, the child is entitled to set the contract aside provided that he does so before he reaches the age of eighteen or within a reasonable time thereafter. However, it cannot be set aside by the adult. Here we see the protective role of the law at work in that the protection is confined to the child. The child can enforce the contract as against the adult but the adult cannot, in general, enforce the contract against the child, at least where the contract has been set aside by the child. This category of voidable contracts can be sub-divided into two groups. The first, and largest category, consists of contracts that are not binding upon the child unless he ratifies them within a reasonable time of reaching majority (referred to as 'negative voidable contracts' by *Anson's Law of Contract* (28th edn, Oxford University Press, 2002), p. 220). This category of contract consists of contracts other than those that are valid (as in category (a) above) or fall within the second sub-category. That second category consists of contracts that are binding upon the minor unless he disclaims the contract either during his childhood or within a reasonable time after reaching the age of majority (referred to as 'positive voidable contracts' by *Anson's Law of Contract* (28th edn, Oxford University Press, 2002), p. 220). Contracts that are binding upon a child unless set aside by him in this way include contracts for the acquisition of an interest in land and contracts for the acquisition of shares in a company.

(c) A CHILD'S RESTITUTIONARY RIGHTS

Suppose that a child confers a benefit upon an adult in performance of a contract that is not binding upon him. Can the child recover the value of the benefit so conferred upon the adult? The answer is that the incapacity does not, of itself, entitle a child to recover the value of a benefit conferred upon an adult. In order to recover the value of a benefit conferred the child must show that he is entitled to recover its value on one of the standard grounds on which restitution is ordered, such as mistake or total failure of consideration. A case which illustrates the operation of this rule is:

Steinberg v. Scala (Leeds) Ltd

[1923] 2 Ch 452, Court of Appeal

The infant plaintiff, the respondent, bought shares in a company. She subsequently repudiated the contract and her allotment of shares was set aside. She sought the return of the money which she had paid for the shares. Her claim failed because she was unable to show that the consideration for her payment had wholly failed.

Lord Sterndale MR

I think the argument for the respondent has rather proceeded upon the assumption that the question whether she can rescind and the question whether she can recover her money back are the same. They are two quite different questions, as is pointed out by Turner LJ in his judgment in *Ex parte Taylor* 8 D M & G 254, 257, 258. He there says: 'It is clear that an infant cannot be absolutely bound by a contract entered into during his minority. He must have a right upon his attaining his majority to elect whether he will adopt the contract or not'. Then he proceeds: 'It is, however, a different question whether, if an infant pays money on the footing of a contract, he can afterwards recover it back. If an infant buys an article which is not a necessary, he cannot be compelled to pay for it, but if he does pay for it during his minority he cannot on attaining his majority recover the money back'. That seems to me to be only stating in other words the principle which is laid down in a number of other cases that, although the contract may be rescinded the money paid cannot be recovered back unless there has been an entire failure of the consideration for which the money has been paid. Therefore it seems to me that the question to which we have to address ourselves is: Has there here been a total failure of the consideration for which the money was paid?

Now the plaintiff has had the shares; I do not mean to say she had the certificates; she could have had them at any time if she had applied for them; she has had the shares allotted to her and there is evidence that they were of some value, that they had been dealt in at from 9s. to 10s. a share. Of course her shares were only half paid up and, therefore, if she had attempted to sell them she would only have obtained half of that amount, but that is quite a tangible and substantial sum.

In those circumstances is it possible to say that there was a total failure of consideration? If the plaintiff were a person of full age suing to recover the money back on the ground, and the sole ground, that there had been a failure of consideration it seems to me it would have been impossible for her to succeed, because she would have got the very thing for which the money was paid and would have got a thing of tangible value.

The argument for the respondent is I think to this effect: That it is necessary, in order to show that the consideration has not entirely failed, to prove that the plaintiff has not only had something which was worth value in the market and for which she could have obtained value, but that she has in fact received that value. It was admitted that if she had in this case sold the shares and received the 125*l*. which would have been receivable according to one of the prices mentioned in evidence she could not have recovered the money back, but it is said that as she did not in fact do that and had only an opportunity of receiving that benefit, there has been a total failure of consideration. I cannot see that. If she has obtained something which has money's worth then she has received some consideration, that is, she has received the very thing for which she paid her money, and the fact that, although it has money's worth, she has not turned that money's worth into money, does not seem to me to prevent it being some valuable consideration for the money which she has paid. I cannot see any difference when you come to consider whether there has been consideration or not between the position of a person of full age and an infant. The question whether there has been consideration or not must, I think, be the same in the two cases . . .

Warrington and Younger LJJ delivered concurring judgments.

COMMENTARY

The law therefore accords protection to a child in the sense that it allows the child to escape from the transaction but it does not then allow automatic restitution once the contract has been set aside. The child must still prove one of the standard grounds of restitution and, if he cannot do that, then he cannot recover the value of the benefit conferred. An alternative, and possibly preferable approach, would be to conclude that the child should always be entitled to recover the value of the benefit conferred provided that he restores to the adult the value of any benefit which he has received as a result of performance by the adult of his obligations under the contract before it was set aside (see *Valentini* v. *Canali* (1889) 24 QBD 166 which was, however, regarded as a case of total failure of consideration in *Pearce* v. *Brain* [1929] 1 KB 310).

(d) THE LIABILITY OF A CHILD IN RESTITUTION

Section 3 of the Minors' Contracts Act 1987 provides:

(1) Where—

(a) a person ('the plaintiff') has after the commencement of this Act entered into a contract with another ('the defendant'), and

(b) the contract is unenforceable against the defendant (or he repudiates it) because he was a minor when the contract was made,

the court may, if it is just and equitable to do so, require the defendant to transfer to the plaintiff any property acquired by the defendant under the contract, or any property representing it.

(2) Nothing in this section shall be taken to prejudice any other remedy available to the plaintiff.

This is a curiously worded provision. The liability of the child is to restore to the adult 'any property acquired . . . under the contract, or any property representing it'. The return of identifiable property will be relatively straightforward in most cases but the same cannot be said for 'property representing' the original property. What does this mean? Does it mean that the child who sells an asset and pays the proceeds into his bank account is liable to pay the proceeds out of this account at least while the account is in credit? A further difficulty which arises out of this example is whether or not the word 'property' includes 'money'. There is no authority on this point but the generally accepted view is that money ought to be included in the definition of property. Finally, it should be noted that the adult does not have a right to have the property transferred to him. Rather, the court is given a discretion to order the transfer.

Section 3(2) preserves the common law rights of the adult. The rights of adults at common law (here including equity) are, however, restricted. In *Cowern* v. *Nield* [1912] 2 KB 419 the plaintiff paid the defendant minor £35 19s for clover and hay. The defendant failed to deliver the hay and the clover which he delivered was found to be rotten. The plaintiff rejected the clover and sought to recover his pre-payment. His claim failed. Phillimore J stated that the position would have been otherwise had the money been obtained by the defendant by fraud. An example of the difference that fraud can make is provided by the case of *Stocks* v. *Wilson* [1913] 2 KB 235. The defendant child, by fraudulently misrepresenting his age, induced the plaintiff to sell and deliver to him some furniture and other goods from her house. The sale price was £300. The defendant promised to repay the value of the goods at a later date and gave the plaintiff a licence to repossess the goods in the event of his failure to pay. The defendant sold some of the goods for £30 and, with the consent of the plaintiff, granted a bill of sale of the remainder as security for an advance of £100. The defendant failed to pay the plaintiff on the appointed day and so an action was brought in equity to recover the reasonable value of the goods supplied. It was held that the defendant was liable to account to the plaintiff for the £30 and the £100 advance that he obtained as a result of the transactions into which he had entered. A different result was, however, reached in *R Leslie Ltd* v. *Sheill* [1914] 3 KB 607 where a child induced the plaintiff moneylenders to lend him £400 by fraudulently misrepresenting that he was an adult. When they discovered the true position the plaintiffs sought to recover the money they had advanced to him. It was held that they were not entitled to recover the £400. How are these cases to be reconciled? R Goff and GH Jones (*The Law of Restitution* (6th edn, Sweet & Maxwell, 2002), para 25-011) conclude as follows:

> *Stocks* v. *Wilson* . . . is reconcilable with *R Leslie Ltd* v. *Sheill*. The basis of the latter decision is, we suggest, the rule of policy that personal remedies in restitution are not to be employed indirectly to enforce contracts which are at law not binding on the minor. This rule of policy overrides the equity whereby a minor would otherwise have to pay for goods obtained by fraud or to repay money obtained fraudulently under a contract of loan. Where a minor has obtained property under a contract (other than a contract for the loan of money) induced by his fraud, he will be compelled in equity to restore such property as is still in his possession and, if he has disposed of the property, to refund the proceeds. Here the rule of policy does not bar recovery. But the minor is under no liability to pay the contract price for the property or even, it seems, a reasonable price; to require him to do so would be indirectly to enforce the contract. Similarly, if he has fraudulently obtained the money under a contract of loan, he will not be liable to repay it.

(e) THE LIABILITY OF A CHILD IN TORT

The protection afforded to a child by the law of contract is not generally to be found in the law of tort. Childhood itself does not confer a defence to an action in tort. But, where the effect of allowing a claim to succeed in tort would be to undermine the protection afforded to the child by the law of contract, then the child will, to that extent, enjoy a defence to the action in tort (*R Leslie Ltd* v. *Sheill* [1914] 3 KB 607).

4. MENTAL INCAPACITY

Section 3(2) of the Sale of Goods Act 1979 provides that 'where necessaries are sold and delivered . . . to a person who by reason of mental incapacity or drunkenness is incompetent to contract, he must pay a reasonable price for them'. In the case of contracts for the sale of things other than necessaries, the rights and liabilities of the party suffering from the incapacity depend upon whether the property of the incapacitated person is subject to the control of the court. Where it is subject to the control of the court under the provisions of Part VII of the Mental Health Act 1983, the court is given broad powers over the property of the incapacitated party and any attempt by the incapacitated person to dispose of his property will not be binding upon him because otherwise the effect of the disposition would be to oust the jurisdiction of the court.

Where the property of the incapacitated person is not subject to control by the court, then the contract is binding upon that party unless the disability was known to the other party. This rule is illustrated by the following case:

Hart v. O'Connor

[1985] AC 1000, Privy Council

The defendant, Mr Hart, agreed to purchase farm land from Mr Jack O'Connor, who was then sole trustee of his father's estate and who farmed the land in partnership with his brothers. Mr O'Connor was then aged eighty-three but, unknown to the defendant, was of unsound mind. He agreed to sell land to the defendant under an agreement which was drawn up by the defendant's solicitor. The agreement stated that the price to be paid was the market value of the land as determined by a named independent valuer. The plaintiffs, who were one of Mr O'Connor's brothers and his two sons, sought a declaration that the agreement should be set aside on the ground of the vendor's lack of capacity and also on the ground that it was an unconscionable bargain. The trial judge held that the agreement was unenforceable but that the transaction could not be set aside because the defendant was entitled to invoke the defence of laches. The Court of Appeal allowed the plaintiffs' appeal and held that laches was inapplicable. On the defendant's appeal to the Privy Council it was held that the plaintiffs were not entitled to set aside the transaction: there had been no unconscionable dealing by the defendant and the transaction could not be set aside on the ground of the vendor's lack of capacity because the defendant was unaware of the lack of capacity on the part of the vendor.

Lord Brightman

It is important to appreciate that no imputations whatever are made by the plaintiffs against the integrity of the defendant, and rightly so. The defendant's conduct leading up to the sale was above reproach . . .

Apart from questions arising out of the defendant's claim for compensation, the issues raised by the parties on this appeal are as follows: (A) Whether *Archer* v. *Cutler* [1980] 1

NZLR 386 was rightly decided; that is to say, whether a contract by a person of unsound mind, whose incapacity is unknown to the other contracting party, can be avoided (at law) on the ground that it is 'unfair' to the party lacking capacity (or those whom he represents), there being no imputations against the conduct of the other contracting party. (B) If *Archer* v. *Cutler* was rightly decided, whether the High Court and the Court of Appeal were correct in finding that the sale agreement was 'unfair' to the vendor. (C) If *Archer* v. *Cutler* was wrongly decided, whether the plaintiffs were entitled to have the contract set aside (in equity) as an 'unconscionable bargain' notwithstanding the complete innocence of the defendant. (D) If *Archer* v. *Cutler* was rightly decided, and the courts below correctly found that the sale agreement was 'unfair', whether the sale agreement would escape rescission because it was impossible to achieve restitutio in integrum.

In order to avoid unnecessary prolongation of the hearing and with a view to saving the parties expense, their Lordships invited counsel to confine their submissions to issues (A) and (C), leaving issues (B) and (D) for subsequent argument if necessary.

Their Lordships turn first to a consideration of *Archer* v. *Cutler* [1980] 1 NZLR 386. Their Lordships attach importance to three factors. First, this decision was accepted by both sides as correct when the case was argued at first instance. Secondly, the Court of Appeal in a strong judgment affirmed without hesitation that the law there set out was the law of New Zealand. Thirdly the Court of Appeal, when they gave judgment on the compensation appeal, underlined their previous statement of the law in the following important passage [1984] 1 NZLR 754, 755:

> 'In that case [*Archer* v. *Cutler*] it was held that there were no considerations of policy or principle precluding the court from holding that a contract entered into by a person of unsound mind is voidable at his option if it is proved either that the other party knew of his unsoundness of mind or, whether or not he had that knowledge, the bargain was unfair. On the basis that this principle should be adopted for New Zealand this court expressly approved *Archer* v. *Cutler*. In the result it made a declaration that the agreement for sale and purchase was rescinded.'

If *Archer* v. *Cutler* is properly to be regarded as a decision based on considerations peculiar to New Zealand, it is highly improbable that their Lordships would think it right to impose their own interpretation of the law, thereby contradicting the unanimous conclusions of the High Court and the Court of Appeal of New Zealand on a matter of local significance. If however the principle of *Archer* v. *Cutler*, if it be correct, must be regarded as having general application throughout all jurisdictions based on the common law, because it does not depend on local considerations, their Lordships could not properly treat the unanimous view of the courts of New Zealand as being necessarily decisive. In their Lordships' opinion the latter is the correct view of the decision.

Archer v. *Cutler* was a purchaser's action for specific performance of a contract for the sale of land. By way of defence the vendor pleaded first that she was of unsound mind to the knowledge of the purchaser, secondly that she was induced to enter into the agreement by the undue influence of the purchaser, and thirdly, at 388, 'that the contract should be set aside as a catching and unconscientious bargain'. The facts were briefly as follows. The vendor and the purchaser were adjoining land owners. The purchaser had a problem over access to his land, which would be solved if he acquired the vendor's land. He knew the vendor had already given a purchase option to a friend, but he made known to the vendor his interest in acquiring her land should the opportunity occur. At some later time the vendor got in touch with the purchaser, and inquired if he was still interested in buying, as her friend had decided not to exercise her option. He called on her next day to discuss the matter. The vendor suggested a price of $15,000. The purchaser thought that $17,000 would be a fairer figure and he offered to pay it subject to his being able to arrange finance. He put his offer in writing, and she wrote out her acceptance. A week later he told her that he had arranged finance and that the sale was therefore unconditional. McMullin J held that an informed vendor would have expected to receive at least $24,000; that there was however no evidence that the purchaser knew the true value of the land, and that it was understandable that two persons with no professional expertise should fix a value of $17,000 as being a fair price. He also found that the vendor was suffering from advanced senile dementia at the time of the agreement which rendered her incapable of understanding the bargain, but that the purchaser was unaware of this. The agreement represented a sale at a substantial undervalue. It was held that contractual incapacity was established; that a contract entered into by a person of unsound mind was voidable at that person's option if the other party knew of the incapacity or, whether or not he knew, if the contract was 'unfair' to the person of unsound mind; and that the contract was unfair, the indicia of unfairness being (i) a price significantly below the true value, (ii) the absence of independent legal advice for the vendor, and (iii) the difference in bargaining positions resulting from the disparity in their respective mental capacities.

If a contract is stigmatised as 'unfair', it may be unfair in one of two ways. It may be unfair by reason of the unfair manner in which it was brought into existence; a contract induced by undue influence is unfair in this sense. It will be convenient to call this 'procedural unfairness'. It may also, in some contexts, be described (accurately or inaccurately) as 'unfair' by reason of the fact that the terms of the contract are more favourable to one party than to the other. In order to distinguish this 'unfairness' from procedural unfairness, it will be convenient to call it 'contractual imbalance'. The two concepts may overlap. Contractual imbalance may be so extreme as to raise a presumption of procedural unfairness, such as undue influence or some other form of victimisation. Equity will relieve a party from a contract which he has been induced to make as a result of victimisation. Equity will not relieve a party from a contract on the ground only that there is contractual imbalance not amounting to unconscionable dealing. Of the three indicia of unfairness relied upon by the judge in *Archer* v. *Cutler* (assuming unfairness to have existed) the first was contractual imbalance and the second and third were procedural unfairness.

The judgment in *Archer* v. *Cutler* [1980] 1 NZLR 386 contains, if their Lordships may be permitted to say so, a most scholarly and erudite review by the judge of the textbook authorities and reported cases on the avoidance of a contract made by a person of unsound mind. For present purposes the key passages in the judgment are, at 400:

'From these authorities, it would seem that the English law on the subject is ill-defined. The case of *Imperial Loan Co Ltd* v. *Stone* [1892] 1 QB 599 widely accepted as being a statement of the law on avoidance of contracts made with persons of unsound mind would, save in the judgment of Lopes LJ, seem to regard unfairness of the contract as being of no moment. Proof of unsoundness of mind and the other party's knowledge of that unsoundness alone will avoid the contract. But the passage cited from the judgment of Lopes LJ and the dicta of Pollock CB in *Molton v. Camroux* (1848) 2 Exch 487, of Patteson J on appeal in the same case, of Sir Ernest Pollock MR in *York Glass Co Ltd v. Jubb* (1924) 131 LT 559 and of Sargant LJ in the same case would suggest that proof of unfairness of a bargain entered into by a person of unsound mind, even though that unsoundness be not known to the other party, will suffice to avoid it.'

And, at 401:

'I find nothing in policy or principle to prevent me from holding that a contract entered into by a person of unsound mind is voidable at his option if it is proved either that the other party knew of his unsoundness of mind or, whether or not he had that knowledge, the contract was unfair to the person of unsound mind.'

Their Lordships apprehend that in these passages the judge is dealing indifferently with procedural unfairness and contractual imbalance, either of which, or both of which in combination, may enable the contract to be avoided against a contracting party ignorant of the mental incapacity of the other.

The original rule at law, and still the rule in Scotland, was that a contract with a person of unsound mind was void, because there could be no consensus ad idem. This was later qualified by a rule that a person could not plead his own unsoundness of mind in order to avoid a contract he had made. This in turn gave way to a further rule that such a plea was permissible if it could be shown that the other contracting party knew of the insanity.

[Lord Brightman then turned to consider in some detail the three cases mentioned in the first citation from *Archer v. Cutler*, namely *Molton v. Camroux* (1848) 2 Exch 487; (1849) 4 Exch 17, *Imperial Loan Co Ltd v. Stone* [1892] 1 QB 599, and *York Glass Co Ltd v. Jubb* (1924) 131 LT 559; (1925) 134 LT 36 and continued]

In the opinion of their Lordships it is perfectly plain that historically a court of equity did not restrain a suit at law on the ground of 'unfairness' unless the conscience of the plaintiff was in some way affected. This might be because of actual fraud (which the courts of common law would equally have remedied) or constructive fraud, i.e. conduct which falls below the standards demanded by equity, traditionally considered under its more common manifestations of undue influence, abuse of confidence, unconscionable bargains and frauds on a power. (Cf. *Snell's Principles of Equity*, 27th edn. (1973), 545ff.) An unconscionable bargain in this context would be a bargain of an improvident character made by a poor or ignorant person acting without independent advice which cannot be shown to be a fair and reasonable transaction. 'Fraud' in its equitable context does not mean, or is not confined to, deceit; 'it means an unconscientious use of the power arising out of these circumstances and conditions' of the contracting parties; *Earl of Aylesford v. Morris* (1873) LR 8 Ch App 484, 491. It is victimisation, which can consist either of the active extortion of a benefit or the passive acceptance of a benefit in unconscionable circumstances.

Their Lordships have not been referred to any authority that a court of equity would restrain a suit at law where there was no victimisation, no taking advantage of another's weakness, and the sole allegation was contractual imbalance with no undertones of constructive fraud. It seems to their Lordships quite illogical to suppose that the courts of common law would have held that a person of unsound mind, whose affliction was not apparent, was nevertheless free of his bargain if a contractual imbalance could be demonstrated which would have been of no avail to him in equity. Nor do their Lordships see a sufficient foundation in the authorities brought to their attention to support any such proposition . . .

In the opinion of their Lordships, to accept the proposition enunciated in *Archer* v. *Cutler* that a contract with a person ostensibly sane but actually of unsound mind can be set aside because it is 'unfair' to the person of unsound mind in the sense of contractual imbalance, is unsupported by authority, is illogical and would distinguish the law of New Zealand from the law of Australia . . . for no good reason, as well as from the law of England from which the law of Australia and New Zealand and other 'common law' countries has stemmed. In so saying their Lordships differ with profound respect from the contrary view so strongly expressed by the New Zealand courts.

To sum the matter up, in the opinion of their Lordships, the validity of a contract entered into by lunatic who is ostensibly sane is to be judged by the same standards as a contract by a person of sound mind, and is not voidable by the lunatic or his representatives by reason of 'unfairness' unless such unfairness amounts to equitable fraud which would have enabled the complaining party to avoid the contract even if he had been sane.

Their Lordships turn finally to issue (C), whether the plaintiffs are entitled to have the contract set aside as an 'unconscionable bargain'. This issue must also be answered in the negative, because the defendant was guilty of no unconscionable conduct. Indeed, as is conceded, he acted with complete innocence throughout. He was unaware of the vendor's unsoundness of mind. The vendor was ostensibly advised by his own solicitor. The defendant had no means of knowing or cause to suspect that the vendor was not in receipt of and acting in accordance with the most full and careful advice. The terms of the bargain were the terms proposed by the vendor's solicitor, not terms imposed by the defendant or his solicitor. There was no equitable fraud, no victimisation, no taking advantage, no overreaching or other description of unconscionable doings which might have justified the intervention of equity to restrain an action by the defendant at law. The plaintiffs have in the opinion of their Lordships failed to make out any case for denying to the defendant the benefit of a bargain which was struck with complete propriety on his side.

For these reasons their Lordships have tendered to Her Majesty their humble advice that the appeal should be allowed.

COMMENTARY

Hart is a difficult and a controversial decision. It can be said to leave the infirm in a vulnerable position because their entitlement to set aside a transaction depends upon their ability to prove that the other party knew of the disability. A party who cannot demonstrate such knowledge can set aside the transaction only if he can establish a ground of relief that is also available to a person of sound mind (for example, under the rule laid down in *Fry* v. *Lane* (1888) 40 Ch D 312, p. 834 above). One consequence of the decision in *Hart* might be to tempt the courts to strain the evidence to find that the defendant did have knowledge of the claimant's incapacity. An example of the latter phenomenon is arguably provided by *Ayres* v. *Hazelgrove*, unreported, 9 February 1984 (discussed by P Birks, *Restitution—The Future* (Federation Press, 1992), pp. 50–1) in which Lady Ayres, who suffered from senile dementia, sold paintings to Hazelgrove for a fraction of their true value. He visited her at home when she was alone, but he denied that he had any knowledge of her condition. Russell J inferred that Hazelgrove must have known of her lack of capacity and he set aside the sales of the paintings. He also held that the transactions could be set aside under the rule in *Fry* v. *Lane* (1888) 40 Ch D 312.

Why is knowledge of the incapacity a vital ingredient in cases of mental incapacity but irrelevant in cases of childhood or minority? Professor Birks (*Restitution—The Future* (Federation Press, 1992), p. 52) has suggested the following:

There is a strong need to preserve the dignity and autonomy of all elderly people. If restitution were not restricted . . . old people would not be able to deal with their property in an adult, independent and unsupervised manner. The dispositions of an old person must in general stand up. Hence the strict liability has to be inhibited.

The restitutionary rights of the infirm adult must be restricted to preserve the credit and dignity of all adults, but especially the very elderly. Except in relation to necessaries, minors do not need their credit preserving. That is the crucial difference. Hence it must ultimately be decided how much the restitutionary rights arising from infirmity of mind should be restricted to prevent the infantilisation of adults and, especially, the elderly. The common law restricts restitution by saying the other must know of the infirmity. Perhaps credit and dignity would be preserved if the restriction were phrased in the alternative. Restitution would then follow if either the other knew of the infirmity of mind or the assets passed at an undervalue. This is very close to the New Zealand position which *Hart* v. *O'Connor* rejected.

It should be noted that the policy reasons identified by Professor Birks do not necessarily, as he acknowledges, lead to the result reached by the Privy Council in *Hart*. It might be possible to recognize a wider right of recovery without infantilizing the elderly. But there is another aspect to the issue which Professor Birks does not consider and that relates to the role of the relatives of the elderly and the infirm. If the law does not take sufficient steps to protect them from exploitation, it may be left to close relatives to seek a power of attorney in order to provide the protection from exploitation which the law does not provide. In other words, too great a willingness to recognize the contractual capacity of the elderly may, paradoxically, result in their effective infantilization as their children seek powers of attorney in order to control or regulate their financial affairs. A preferable rule may be that mental incapacity should of itself (that is to say, irrespective of the knowledge of the other party) suffice to give rise to a claim in restitution. This is the rule in Scots law: see *John Loudon & Co* v. *Elder's Curator Bonis*, 1923 SLT 226.

5. COMPANIES AND LOCAL AUTHORITIES

Companies and local authorities have limited contractual capacity in the sense that their powers are defined, in the case of companies, by the terms of their memorandum and articles of association, and, in the case of local authorities, by the terms of the statute which set them up. A company or a local authority which acts beyond its powers acts *ultra vires*. In *Ashbury Railway Carriage and Iron Co* v. *Riche* (1875) LR 7 HL 653 it was held that a contract which was *ultra vires* a company was void. This conclusion could have detrimental effects on third parties and statute has since intervened to protect third parties in the case of both companies and local authorities. *Ultra vires* is now of limited practical significance in the corporate context because of section 35(1) of the Companies Act 1985 which states that 'the validity of an act done by a company shall not be called into question on the ground of lack of capacity by reason of anything in the company's memorandum'. The intention behind this provision is to abrogate the *ultra vires* rule as far as third parties who deal in all good faith with the company are concerned but to leave it intact for internal purposes relating to the relationship between the shareholders and the company. In the case of local authorities, section 2(1) of the Local Government (Contracts) Act 1997 provides:

Where a local authority has entered into a contract, the contract shall, if it is a certified contract, have effect (and be deemed always to have had effect) as if the local authority had had power to enter into it (and had exercised that power properly in entering into it).

A company or a local authority which confers a benefit upon another party in the course of performance of an *ultra vires* contract may be entitled from that third party to recover the value of the benefit so conferred in a restitutionary action (see *Brougham* v. *Dwyer* (1913) 108 LT 504 (companies) and *Commonwealth of Australia* v. *Burns* [1971] VR 825 (local authorities)).

6. FURTHER READING

HUDSON, AH, 'Mental Incapacity Revisited' [1986] *Conveyancer and Property Lawyer* 178.

22

ILLEGALITY AND PUBLIC POLICY

1. CENTRAL ISSUES

1. A contract may be held to be void on the ground that it is tainted by illegality or on the ground that it is otherwise contrary to public policy. The law in this area is complex and the case-law enormous. The aim of this chapter is not to explore the rules relating to illegality in any detail. Rather, its aim is to examine a limited number of cases with a view to ascertaining the principles which are at stake.

2. Two broad issues arise. The first relates to the definitions of 'illegality' and 'public policy'. The second relates to the consequences that flow from a finding that a contract is illegal or is contrary to public policy. Neither issue is straightforward.

3. It is customary to break down the cases into different categories according to whether

the contract is 'void', 'illegal', or is 'contrary to public policy'. The difficulty is that different judges and commentators draw the boundaries between these categories in different places. There is no agreed classification of the cases. No attempt will be made to impose a classificatory scheme on the cases in this chapter.

4. Rather, an attempt will be made (in section 3) to identify the various circumstances in which the courts have concluded that a contract is illegal or contrary to public policy. We shall then consider the law in relation to restraint of trade (section 4) and then finally (in section 5) discuss the remedial consequences of a finding that a contract is illegal.

2. INTRODUCTION

A helpful introduction to this topic has been provided by Sir Jack Beatson in the following terms:

J Beatson, *Anson's Law of Contract*

(28th edn, Oxford University Press, 2002), p. 348

Public policy imposes certain limitations upon the freedom of persons to contract. An ostensibly valid contract may be tainted by illegality. The source of the illegality may arise by statute or by virtue of the principles of common law. In some instances the law prohibits the agreement itself, and the contract is then by its very nature illegal but in the majority of cases the illegality lies in the object which one or both parties have in mind or in the method of performance. As a general rule, although all the other requirements for the formation of an agreement are complied with, an agreement that is illegal in one of these ways will not be enforceable.

The subject of illegality is one of great complexity and the effects of illegality are by no means uniform. This is because the seriousness of the illegality varies. Illegal objects may range from those tainted with gross moral turpitude, e.g. murder, to those where the harm to be avoided is relatively small, e.g. breach of licensing requirements or cases in which a person commits an unlawful act in order to escape danger to his or her life. It is not surprising, therefore, that there are differences in the attitude of the judges to those who have an illegal object in view or are parties to an illegal transaction. Attempts have been made to distinguish between 'illegal' contracts and those which are 'nugatory' or 'void'. In the former case, it is said that the law will refuse to aid in any way a person whose cause of action is founded upon such a contract; in the latter case, the law simply states that the contract is not to have legal effect. While some contracts can be classified in this way, it is both impracticable and impossible to apply this classification over the whole field of the subject. Moreover, confusion is created by the fact that judges have on many occasions treated the terms as interchangeable. It seems better to use the single word 'illegality' to cover the multitude of instances where the law, for some reason of public policy or as a result of statutory prohibition, denies to one or both of the parties the rights under the contract to which he or she would otherwise be entitled.

3. ILLEGAL CONTRACTS: A SUMMARY

As Sir Jack Beatson points out, illegality can affect a contract in different ways. The contract may be illegal from the outset, as in the example of a contract to commit a murder, or the illegality may arise in the course of performance of an otherwise valid contract. An example in the latter category is a contract for the carriage of goods where the vehicle that is used to transport the goods does not have a licence and so cannot lawfully be driven. Provided that the carrier has some vehicles which are properly licensed, the contract is not illegal from the outset: it is capable of being performed lawfully. It is only when the unlicensed vehicle is used in the performance of the contract that any issue of illegality arises. The courts have tended to adopt a more sympathetic stance in cases of illegality in performance, especially in the case where the party bringing a claim for damages for breach of contract did not commit the illegal act, nor did he have any knowledge of it. The sources of illegality also differ. Statute can declare contracts to be illegal but the common law also has a significant role to play. The courts have declared a range of contracts to be illegal or contrary to public policy. Thirdly, the seriousness of the illegality varies enormously between the different cases.

A contract may be illegal for the following reasons:

(a) STATUTORY ILLEGALITY

We start with a very broad category of illegality, namely statutory illegality. Statute may declare a contract illegal, void, or unenforceable. For example, a licensing system may prohibit the making of contracts in violation of the system. In *Re Mahmoud and Ispahani* [1921] 2 KB 76 the regulations applicable to the contract were those contained in the Seeds, Oils and Fats Order 1919 which provided that 'a person shall not . . . buy or sell' linseed oil 'except under and in accordance with the terms of a licence'. The plaintiffs, who had a licence, asked the defendant if he had a licence. The defendant replied that he did when, in fact, he did not. The plaintiffs sold linseed oil to the defendant but the defendant refused to accept delivery. When sued for damages for non-acceptance the defendant took the point that the contract was illegal on account of the fact that he did not have a licence to purchase the linseed oil. The Court of Appeal held that the plaintiffs were not entitled to bring their action for damages. Atkin LJ stated (at p. 731):

When the Court has to deal with the question whether a particular contract or class of contract is prohibited by statute, it may find an express prohibition in the statute, or it may have to infer the prohibition from the fact that the statute imposes a penalty upon the person entering into that class of contract. In the latter case one has to examine very carefully the precise terms of the statute imposing the penalty upon the individual. One may find that the statute imposes a penalty upon an individual, and yet does not prohibit the contract if it is made with a party who is innocent of the offence which is created by the statute.

The Court of Appeal held that the Order expressly prohibited the making of a contract in breach of the licensing system with the consequence that the plaintiffs were not entitled to bring an action for damages. The result seems a harsh one in that the plaintiffs did inquire whether or not the defendant had a licence and the immediate cause of the illegality was the defendant's failure to answer that inquiry truthfully. The exercise in which the courts are engaged in such cases is one of statutory construction: the court must decide whether or not statute has prohibited the making of the contract. On the facts of *Mahmoud and Ispahani* the Court of Appeal concluded that the intention was to prohibit the making of the contract, whether or not the party seeking to enforce the contract was responsible for the violation of the requirements of the system.

The statutory prohibition can take different forms. In some cases statute has intervened to declare a contract void. An example is provided by section 18 of the Gaming Act 1845 which provides:

All contracts or agreements, whether by parol or in writing, by way of gaming or wagering, shall be null and void; and . . . no suit shall be brought or maintained in any court of law and equity for recovering any sum of money or valuable thing alleged to be won upon any wager, or which shall have been deposited in the hands of any person to abide the event on which any wager shall have been made: Provided always, that this enactment shall not be deemed to apply to any subscription or contribution, or agreement to subscribe or contribute, for or towards any plate, prize, or sum of money to be awarded to the winner or winners of any lawful game, sport, pastime, or exercise.

The courts have experienced particular difficulties in the case where the contravention of a statute occurs in the performance of a contract. This particular issue arose in the cases of *St John Shipping Corporation* v. *Joseph Rank Ltd* [1957] 1 QB 267 and *Archbolds (Freightage) Ltd* v. *S Spanglett Ltd* [1961] 1 QB 374. These cases are discussed in more detail on the web-site which supports this book.

(b) AGREEMENTS CONTRARY TO GOOD MORALS

We now turn to consider contracts that are illegal or contrary to public policy as a result of the application of common law principles rather than the intervention of statute. The first example in this category consists of agreements that are contrary to good morals. Such agreements are illegal and unenforceable. Contracts that have been held to fall within this category include an agreement to provide a prostitute with goods for use in her trade (see *Pearce* v. *Brooks* (1866) LR 1 Ex 213, extracted on the web-site which supports this book) and a promise by a man to pay money to a woman if she would become his mistress (see *Benyon* v. *Nettlefold* (1850) 3 Mac & G 94). In general it can be said that this category encompasses agreements the aim of which is to promote sexual immorality. Some of the old cases adopt a very conservative view of the requirements of 'good morals', particularly in relation to extra-marital cohabitation. However, public attitudes towards extra-marital cohabitation, whether heterosexual or homosexual, have changed over the years and this is reflected in the decisions of modern courts. Agreements between cohabiting parties are now enforceable provided that the parties have an intention to create legal relations (on which see Chapter 7) and provided that the subject-matter of the agreement is not exclusively related to the provision of sexual services.

(c) AGREEMENTS PREJUDICIAL TO FAMILY LIFE

An agreement which undermines the institution of marriage is illegal and unenforceable. Agreements within this category include an agreement the aim of which is to prevent or restrict the ability of a person to get married (*Lowe* v. *Peers* (1768) 4 Burr 2225) and an agreement under which one party promises to introduce a person to someone of the opposite sex with a view to marriage (*Hermann* v. *Charlesworth* [1905] 1 KB 123). It is debateable whether *Hermann* would be followed today, given the prevalence of dating and introduction agencies. This category can also encompass agreements relating to the way in which children are brought up. Thus a parent cannot in general contract out of his parental duties by transferring them to a third party (*Humphreys* v. *Polok* [1901] 2 KB 385).

(d) AGREEMENTS PREJUDICIAL TO THE ADMINISTRATION OF JUSTICE

An agreement which is prejudicial to the administration of justice is illegal and unenforceable, such as an agreement to conceal the commission of a crime (*Initial Services Ltd* v. *Putterill* [1968] 1 QB 396). Similarly, a person who accepts money in return for concealing the commission of a criminal offence may be held to have committed an offence in so doing (Criminal Law Act 1967, section 5). This category has in fact given rise to some difficulties in the courts. It suffices to note three such difficulties.

The first relates to agreements to oust the jurisdiction of the court. There is authority for the proposition that an attempt to oust the jurisdiction of the court is contrary to public policy and hence void (*Czarnikow* v. *Roth Schmidt & Co* [1922] 2 KB 478). This proposition must, however, be qualified in its application to arbitration where it is possible for the parties, within limits, to exclude the jurisdiction of the courts. Arbitration is frequently used as a means of dispute resolution in international business and the parties to arbitration agreements usually wish to ensure that their dispute is resolved privately, quickly, and as economically as possible. These purposes would be frustrated if the losing party to the arbitration could simply appeal to court for a re-hearing of the merits of the dispute. While there is a limited right to appeal to the court on a question of law arising out of an award, it is open to the parties to exclude that right of appeal, except in relation to challenges to the jurisdiction of the arbitral tribunal and allegations of serious irregularity affecting the tribunal (see sections 67 and 68 of the Arbitration Act 1996). It is also open to contracting parties to agree that the award of an arbitrator shall be a condition precedent to the right to bring an action on the contract (*Scott* v. *Avery* (1856) 5 HLC 811). Section 9 of the Arbitration Act 1996 provides that a party to an arbitration agreement against whom legal proceedings are brought in respect of a matter which under the agreement is to be referred to arbitration may apply to the court in which the proceedings have been brought to stay the proceedings so far as they concern that matter.

Secondly, the courts have experienced difficulties in defining the limits of the doctrines of 'maintenance' and 'champerty'. Maintenance is defined in H Beale (ed), *Chitty on Contracts* (29th edn, Sweet & Maxwell, 2004), para 16-050) in the following terms: 'a person is guilty of maintenance if he supports litigation in which he has no legitimate concern without just cause or excuse'. Champerty, on the other hand, has been described as an 'aggravated form of maintenance' which occurs 'when the person maintaining another stipulates for a share of the proceeds of the action or suit or other contentious proceedings where property is in dispute' (Chitty, para 16-054). These doctrines have given rise to difficulty in their application to the assignment of rights of action. Where the right assigned is a claim for a liquidated sum due under a contract it can generally be assigned irrespective of the motives of the party taking the assignment. Thus debts are generally freely assignable (*County Hotel and Wine Company* v. *London and North Western Railway* [1918] 2 KB 251). By contrast, the law in relation to the assignment of unliquidated claims is much less clear. Particular difficulty arises where the assignment takes place after the breach of contract has occurred. Where the assignment takes place prior to the breach of contract no problem generally arises: the rights of the parties are generally assignable. The traditional view of post-breach assignments was that it was not possible to assign a mere right to claim unliquidated damages for breach of contract (*May* v. *Lane* (1894) 64 LJQB 236, 237–238). That view no longer holds good in the light of modern cases such as *Trendtex Trading Corporation* v. *Credit Suisse* [1982] AC 679 and *Giles* v. *Thompson* [1994] 1 AC 142. While the law has moved from its traditional stance it has not (at least as yet) taken the stance that a right to claim unliquidated damages for breach of contract can generally be assigned. Rather it has taken what Professor Treitel (*The Law of Contract* (11th edn, Sweet & Maxwell, 2003) p. 697) has termed an 'intermediate view' namely that 'a right to unliquidated damages for breach of contract may be validly assigned, so long as the assignment does not in fact savour of maintenance or champerty'. There are at least two circumstances in which the courts have held that a right to claim unliquidated damages for breach of contract can be validly assigned. The first is where the assignee has a proprietary interest in the subject-matter of the contract (*Williams* v. *Protheroe* (1829) 5 Bing 309) and the second is where the assignee has a genuine commercial interest in the subject-matter of the contract. Thus the assignment of a right to litigate is valid if it is incidental and subsidiary to a transfer of property. So, for example, a vendor of land can assign to the purchaser the right to claim damages for breaches of covenant committed by the vendor's tenants prior to the sale. The modern origin of the 'genuine commercial interest' test is the decision of the House of Lords in *Trendtex Trading Corporation* v. *Credit Suisse* [1982] AC 679. Simplifying the facts of the case somewhat, Credit Suisse provided finance for the sale of cement by one of its customers, Trendtex. Payment was to be made under a letter of credit by the Central Bank of Nigeria ('CBN'). CBN refused to honour the letter of credit and so Trendtex brought an action against CBN. However the repudiation of the letter of credit by CBN put Trendtex in a very precarious financial position and it became heavily indebted to Credit Suisse. Eventually Trendtex assigned to Credit Suisse its right of action against CBN. Trendtex subsequently sought to set aside the assignment on the ground that it was champertous. On the facts of the case it was held that the assignment was champertous because the assignment was taken for the purpose of enabling Credit Suisse to resell Trendtex's right of action to a third party so that the profit made from the enforcement of Trendtex's right of action could be divided between the bank and the third party. Lord Roskill stated (at p. 703) that such an agreement offended against the law of champerty because 'it was a step towards the sale of a bare cause of action to a third party who had no genuine commercial interest in the claim in return for a division of the spoils'. Thus it was the fact that Credit Suisse envisaged a further onward sale of the right of action that led the House of Lords to conclude that the assignment was champertous. Had there been no onward sale in contemplation but enforcement by Credit Suisse the assignment would have been valid. Thus Lord Roskill stated (at p. 703) that:

For my part I can see no reason in English law why Credit Suisse should not have taken an assignment to themselves of Trendtex's claim against CBN for the purpose of recouping themselves for their own substantial losses arising out of CBN's repudiation of the letter of credit upon which Credit Suisse were relying to refinance their financing of the purchases by Trendtex of this cement from their German suppliers.

Thirdly, section 58 of the Courts and Legal Services Act 1990, as amended by section 27 of the Access to Justice Act 1999, permits lawyers and their clients, within certain limits, to enter into conditional fee agreements. It is probably the case that the courts cannot uphold the validity of such agreements in a wider range of circumstances than those set out in the statutory provisions (see *Awwad* v. *Geraghty & Co* [2001] QB 570, but contrast *Thai Trading Co (A Firm)* v. *Taylor* [1998] QB 781).

(e) AGREEMENTS TO COMMIT A CRIME OR A CIVIL WRONG

An agreement to commit a crime is illegal and unenforceable (*Bigos* v. *Bousted* [1951] 1 All ER 92), as is an agreement to commit a tort, such as libel or assault (*Clay* v. *Yates* (1856) 1 H & N 73) and an agreement to defraud the revenue (*Alexander* v. *Rayson* [1936] 1 KB 169). A contract is also illegal and unenforceable where it provides for money to be paid to someone as a result of the commission by him of a criminal act or a tort (see *Beresford* v. *Royal Exchange Assurance* [1938] AC 586, discussed by Devlin J in *St John Shipping Corporation* v. *Joseph Rank Ltd* [1957] 1 QB 267, on the web-site which supports this book).

(f) AGREEMENTS WHICH ARE INJURIOUS TO GOOD GOVERNMENT

A contract concluded with an enemy alien is illegal and unenforceable (*Ertel Bieber & Co* v. *Rio Tinto Co* [1918] AC 260) as is a contract which seeks to encourage action which is hostile to a friendly foreign government (*De Wûtz* v. *Hendricks* (1824) 2 Bing 314) and an agreement to sell public offices or public honours (*Parkinson* v. *College of Ambulance Ltd* [1925] 2 KB 1).

(g) AGREEMENTS WHICH ARE IN RESTRAINT OF TRADE

These agreements will be discussed in more detail in section 4 below.

(h) CAN THE COURTS DEVELOP PUBLIC POLICY?

The categories of public policy which may invalidate a contract are not fixed in stone. They are capable of adaptation to accommodate the changing values of society. But, at the same time, the courts are slow to create new heads of public policy (see *Richardson* v. *Mellish* (1824) 2 Bing 229). In general the courts leave it to Parliament to formulate new heads of public policy but at the same time cases can be found in which the courts have been prepared to develop the categories of public policy (*Enderby Town FC* v. *The Football Association Ltd* [1971] Ch 591, 606; *Nagle* v. *Fielden* [1966] 2 QB 633, 650). The current state of the law in this regard is summed up in H Beale (ed), *Chitty on Contracts* (29th edn, Sweet & Maxwell, 2004), para 16-004 in the following terms:

there is some doubt as to whether the courts can create new heads of public policy rather than merely apply existing doctrines to new situations. This is an area where the precedents hunt in packs of two. Broadly speaking, there are two conflicting positions, that have been referred to as the 'narrow view' and the 'broad view'. According to the former, the courts cannot create new heads of public policy, whereas the latter countenances judicial law-making in this area. To a large extent this debate is verbal. There is general agreement that the courts may extend existing public policy to new situations and the difference between extending an existing principle as opposed to creating a new one will often be wafer-thin. There will, however, be an understandable reluctance on the part of the courts to create completely new heads of public policy because of the existence of governmental bodies charged with the specific task of law reform and a more activist legislature. However, where Parliament has clearly articulated a principle of public policy then the courts may be willing to extend it by analogy into the field of contract.

4. RESTRAINT OF TRADE

The courts have long exercised a jurisdiction to strike down covenants which are in unreasonable restraint of trade. The justifications for the existence of the doctrine, and its scope, have been the subject of some controversy. Consider the following extract (SA Smith, 'Reconstructing Restraint of Trade' (1995) 15 *OJLS* 565–567):

The doctrine of restraint of trade is a strange beast. Its role in contract law is traditionally understood to be that of denying validity to contracts that unduly restrain the freedom of one or both of the contracting parties. The doctrine appears to place non-procedural limitations on freedom of contract and, moreover, to place these limitations because of a concern for the contracting parties' freedom. A concern for freedom is being used, it appears, to limit freedom . . .

Until relatively recently, it was thought that only three types of contractual provisions could be scrutinised under restraint of trade law: (1) post-employment covenants (such as a restriction on an employee using trade secrets in future employment); (2) sale of business covenants (such as a restraint against the seller of a business setting up business next door); and (3) horizontal restraints (restraints operating between competitors, such as an agreement to divide up the market or not to hire each other's employees). This neat categorisation was ended in *Petrofina* v. *Martin*, where Lord Denning held that a solus agreement—a type of 'vertical' restraint in which a petrol station receives guaranteed petrol at a reduced price in return for agreeing to sell only the distributor's products at recommended prices and to stay open reasonable hours—fell within the doctrine. The categories of restraint of trade, Lord Denning said, 'are not closed'. Subsequent decisions extended the doctrine to other types of exclusive dealing arrangements and to 'exclusive services' arrangements (such as the contract in *Schroeder* [p. 857 below] requiring a songwriter to hand over all his compositions to one publisher for a period of years).

The starting point for any consideration of the law relating to restraint of trade is the following passage from the judgment of Lord Macnaghten in *Nordenfelt* v. *Maxim Nordenfelt* [1894] AC 535, 565:

The public have an interest in every person's carrying on his trade freely: so has the individual. All interference with individual liberty of action in trading, and all restraints of trade of themselves, if there is nothing more, are contrary to public policy, and therefore void. That is the general rule. But there are exceptions: restraints of trade and interference with individual liberty of action may be justified by the special circumstances of a particular case. It is a sufficient justification, and indeed it is the only justification, if the restriction is reasonable—reasonable, that is, in reference to the interests of the parties concerned and reasonable in reference to the interests of the public, so framed and so guarded as to afford adequate protection to the party in whose favour it is imposed, while at the same time it is in no way injurious to the public.

From this quotation, and the passage from Professor Smith's article, it can be seen that there are three principal elements to a restraint of trade claim. The first relates to the scope of the doctrine: to which clauses or contracts does the doctrine apply? As Professor Smith makes clear, the doctrine classically applied to three particular types of contractual provisions but its scope has been extended into certain types of exclusive dealing arrangements with the result that the precise scope of the doctrine is now rather uncertain. Secondly, a clause that falls within the scope of the doctrine can be upheld if it is reasonable as between the parties and, thirdly, if it is reasonable in the public interest. The courts tend to place more emphasis on the requirement that the restraint be reasonable as between the parties than they do on the public interest requirement.

The operation of the doctrine of restraint of trade can be illustrated in its application to post-employment covenants. An employer can validly insert a post-employment restraint in a contract of employment but, in order to do so, he must demonstrate that the restraint is a reasonable one. The reasonableness requirement involves consideration of a number of issues. First, the restraint must seek to protect a legitimate interest of the employer (*Fitch* v. *Dewes* [1921] 2 AC 158). An employer does not have *carte blanche* to restrain the future employment prospects of his employees. In particular, an employer cannot legitimately restrain an employee from making use of his own skills and experience elsewhere. But he does have an interest in restraining an employee from making use of confidential information and trade secrets which he has acquired in the course of his employment and from soliciting customers of the employer. The extent to which information is confidential and hence capable of legitimate protection by a restraint of trade clause can be a difficult matter. Secondly, the restraint must be reasonable in terms of its geographical scope (*Forster and Sons* v. *Suggett* (1918) 35 TLR 87). An employer who runs a small business in a village cannot generally impose a nationwide restraint on a former employee. The restraint must be proportionate to the nature of the employer's business. Thirdly, the restraint must be reasonable in terms of its length. An indefinite restraint is highly unlikely to be reasonable, except in relation to the use of confidential information. The length of the restraint should be related to the interest that the employer is seeking to protect. An employer can restrain an employee from making use of confidential information for a far longer period of time than he can restrain an employee from soliciting customers. Fourthly, the restraint must be reasonable in relation to the nature of the employment in issue. The more senior the employee, the more likely it is that he will be the subject of a legitimate restraint. A restraint which purports to prevent the employee from taking up employment in an area of business that is unrelated to the employer's business is less likely to pass the reasonableness test (unless the restraint relates to the use by the employee of confidential information). Finally, the restraint must be reasonable in the public interest but the courts tend to be slow to invoke public interest considerations in these cases (but see *Wyatt* v. *Kreglinger and Fernau* [1933] 1 KB 793). In most cases the vital issue is whether or not the restraint is reasonable as between the employer and the employee.

A case which illustrates the application of the restraint of trade doctrine to post-employment covenants is:

Mason v. Provident Clothing & Supply Co Ltd

[1913] AC 724, House of Lords

The facts of the case are set out in the judgment of Lord Moulton. The clause that was in issue between the parties was clause 8 which was in the following terms:

'And in consideration of the premises the said William Milne Mason hereby agrees that he shall not within three years after the termination of his engagement and services with the company be in the employ of, or be engaged in any manner whatsoever whether on his own account, or as partner with, or agent, or manager, or assistant, for, any person or persons, firm or firms, company or companies, carrying on or engaged in the same or a similar business to that of "The Provident Clothing and Supply Co Ltd" carried on as aforesaid or be engaged by, or assist or help (either directly or indirectly) any person or persons who shall be employed (whether for remuneration or not) by any person or persons, firm or firms, company or companies, carrying on the same or a similar business as aforesaid, or who shall be assisting or helping (either directly or indirectly) in the carrying on of the same or a similar business, or assist or help any one in the formation of such a business, society or club as aforesaid within twenty-five miles of London aforesaid where the company carry on business or within twenty-five miles of any place where the said William Milne Mason shall have been employed by the company at any time during the continuance of this agreement. And if the said William Milne Mason shall be engaged as aforesaid he shall forfeit to the company the sum of twenty-five pounds by way of liquidated damages, and not as a penalty.'

Lord Moulton

The law as to covenants in restraint of trade was so carefully and authoritatively formulated in this House in the *Nordenfelt Case* [1894] AC 535 that I do not think it necessary to discuss the numerous authorities cited in the course of the argument in order to ascertain what is the critical question which the Court ought to put to itself in such a case as this. It is as follows: Are the restrictions which the covenant imposes upon the freedom of action of the servant after he has left the service of the master greater than are reasonably necessary for the protection of the master in his business?

The first task of the Court, therefore, is to ascertain with due particularity the nature of the master's business and of the servant's employment therein. The facts are not in dispute. The business of the respondents consists in inducing persons to become so-called "members", i.e., to subscribe for checks of various face values, say, for instance, of a value of 1l. These checks are paid for gradually by instalments at certain due dates, but they are delivered to the member when only a certain proportion of their face value has been paid by him, say, for instance, when 3s. has been paid on a 1l. check. So as soon as the check is received it is available for purchasing goods to its full face value, the company being answerable to the vendor for the price of the goods purchased, and itself collecting the instalments payable by the member. A list of firms willing to sell goods on these terms is set out in a printed list given to the members, and is therefore a matter as to which there is no secrecy, and the profits of the company are derived from the discounts given to them by the vendors of the goods.

The nature of the employment of the appellant in this business was solely to obtain members and collect their instalments. A small district in London was assigned to him, which he canvassed and in which he collected the payments due, and outside that small district he had no duties. His employment was therefore that of a local canvasser and debt collector, and nothing more.

Such being the nature of the employment, it would be reasonable for the employer to protect himself against the danger of his former servant canvassing or collecting for a rival firm in the district in which he had been employed. If he were permitted to do so before the expiry of a reasonably long interval he would be in a position to give to his new employer all the advantages of that personal knowledge of the inhabitants of the locality, and more especially of his former customers, which he had acquired in the service of the respondents and at their expense. Against such a contingency the master might reasonably protect himself, but I can see no further or other protection which he could reasonably demand. If the servant is employed by a rival firm in some district which neither includes that in which he formerly worked for the respondents, nor is immediately adjoining thereto, there is no personal knowledge which he has acquired in his former master's service which can be used to that master's prejudice. The respondents would be in no different position from that in which they would be if the appellant had acquired his experience in the service of some other company carrying on a like business.

These, then, being the limits of the protection which the master might reasonably insist on, I turn to the covenant in order to see whether it exceeds these limits. That covenant is admittedly difficult to construe, and, moreover, it is, in my opinion, vague by reason of the extraordinary generality of the language employed. But at all events it prohibits the appellant from entering into a similar employment within twenty-five miles 'of London in the county of Middlesex' for a period of three years after leaving the respondents' service. Such an area must include something like six million persons, that is to say, that on a moderate estimate it is an area a thousand times as great as the district assigned to him when in the respondents' service. Considering the strictly local character of the employment, I have no hesitation in saying that I should be prepared to hold that such an area is very far greater than could be reasonably required for the protection of his former employers.

But this is but a small portion of the restrictions imposed by the covenant. It is very arguable that it prohibits him entering into the employ of any one carrying on a similar business without any limitations of area. But assuming in favour of the respondents that we ought to give it the more limited construction which was evidently put upon it at the trial, and to which the evidence was directed, it restrains him for three years from entering into the employ of any firm which carries on a similar business within twenty-five miles of 'London in the county of Middlesex', wherever it be that his employment is located. To my mind, the employment of the appellant is in respect of its local character analogous to a milk-walk, where the servant is employed in distributing his master's goods in a certain defined district and not otherwise, and the portion of the covenant with which I am now dealing would amount in the case of a man so employed to prohibiting him from entering into the service of any milk distributing company that had a place of business within twenty-five miles of his former milk-walk no matter where it was that they proposed to employ him.

But even now we have not exhausted the extravagances of this restrictive covenant. Under it the appellant must not for a like period 'be engaged by or assist or help (either directly or indirectly) any person or persons who shall be employed (whether for remuneration or not) by any person or person, firm or firms, company or companies carrying on the same or a similar business as aforesaid, or who shall be assisting or helping either directly or indirectly in the carrying on of the same or a similar business'.

It is difficult to construe with any certainty words which are so intentionally wide and general. I doubt whether a covenant that is so intentionally unreasonable merits even the benefit of the general rule of construction that a Court should, if possible, construe language so as to give a reasonable meaning to the document. But however we construe it, the covenant is out of all measure wider than anything that can reasonably be required for the protection of the respondents in their business, and therefore the covenant is void in law and will not be enforced by the Courts.

It was suggested in the argument that even if the covenant was, as a whole, too wide, the Court might enforce restrictions which it might consider reasonable (even though they were not expressed in the covenant), provided they were within its ambit. My Lords, I do not doubt that the Court may, and in some cases will, enforce a part of a covenant in restraint of trade, even though taken as a whole the covenant exceeds what is reasonable. But, in my opinion, that ought only to be done in cases where the part so enforceable is clearly severable, and even so only in cases where the excess is of trivial importance, or merely technical, and not a part of the main purport and substance of the clause. It would in my opinion be pessimi exempli[1] if, when an employer had exacted a covenant deliberately framed in unreasonably wide terms, the Courts were to come to his assistance and, by applying their ingenuity and knowledge of the law, carve out of this void covenant the maximum of what he might validly have required. It must be remembered that the real sanction at the back of these covenants is the terror and expense of litigation, in which the servant is usually at a great disadvantage, in view of the longer purse of his master. It is sad to think that in this present case this appellant, whose employment is a comparatively humble one, should have had to go through four Courts before he could free himself from such unreasonable restraints as this covenant imposes, and the hardship imposed by the exaction of unreasonable covenants by employers would be greatly increased if they could continue the practice with the expectation that, having exposed the servant to the anxiety and expense of litigation, the Court would in the end enable them to obtain everything which they could have obtained by acting reasonably. It is evident that those who drafted this covenant aimed at making it a penal rather than a protective covenant, and that they hoped by means of it to paralyse the earning capabilities of the man if and when he left their service, and were not thinking of what would be a reasonable protection to their business, and having so acted they must take the consequences.

Viscount Haldane LC, Lord Dunedin, and **Lord Shaw of Dunfermline** delivered concurring judgments.

COMMENTARY

Mason demonstrates the need to exercise great care when drafting restraint clauses. The temptation to draft widely must be resisted because the broader the clause, the less likely it is that it will pass the reasonableness test. Further the last paragraph of Lord Moulton's judgment demonstrates the unwillingness of the courts to re-write

---

[1] A dangerous precedent.

invalid restraints. While there is a doctrine of severance (p. 863 below) it operates within very narrow limits.

A similar analysis to that conducted in the context of post-employment restraints is carried out in relation to restraint of trade covenants inserted in contracts for the sale of a business. The purchaser of the business must demonstrate that he has an interest which is capable of protection. This is generally not a difficult requirement to satisfy. A purchaser of a business will generally buy the goodwill of the business and so can take steps to protect that goodwill by, for example, restraining the vendor from soliciting his former customers. The purchaser is entitled to take steps to protect the value of the goodwill which he has purchased. As in the case of post-employment restraints, the restraint must be reasonable in terms of its geographical area, duration, and scope (*Nordenfelt* v. *Maxim Nordenfelt* [1894] AC 535). It must also be reasonable in the public interest, although, once again, the courts have been reluctant to place much reliance (at least overtly) upon public interest considerations. The primary focus is upon the reasonableness of the clause as between the parties.

The courts have also experienced some difficulty in ascertaining the scope of the doctrine of restraint of trade. This section will conclude with a consideration of two decisions of the House of Lords in which the principal issue was whether or not the doctrine of restraint of trade applied to exclusive dealing agreements. At this point we begin to enter into the regulation of anti-competitive agreements. The principal role in the regulation of such agreements is played by Article 81 of the European Community Treaty and by the Competition Act 1998. But the doctrine of restraint of trade retains a role. In the two cases that follow the House of Lords held that the doctrine of restraint of trade applied to an exclusive dealing agreement and that the restraints were, with one exception, unreasonable.

Esso Petroleum Co Ltd v. Harper's Garage (Stourport) Ltd

[1968] AC 269, House of Lords

The respondent company owned and operated two garages. The first was the Mustow Green Garage near Kidderminster and the second was the Corner Garage, Stockport. It entered into two agreements (known as 'solus agreements') with the appellants, Esso, under which it bound itself to sell Esso petrol and no other type of petrol at its garages. In the case of the Mustow Green Garage the agreement was to remain in force for four years and five months, while the duration of the agreement relating to the Corner Garage was stated to be 21 years. In the case of the Corner Garage there was also a mortgage between the parties as security for the money lent to the respondents by Esso.

When cheaper petrol came on to the market the respondents began to sell it and stopped selling Esso petrol. Esso accordingly sought injunctions to restrain the respondents from buying petrol for resale at their garages from anyone other than themselves. The respondents challenged the validity of the solus agreements on the basis that they were in unreasonable restraint of trade. Esso submitted that the ties were not in restraint of trade but that, if they were, they were nevertheless valid and reasonable. The House of Lords held that the ties were subject to the restraint of trade doctrine and that, while the tie applicable to the Mustow Green Garage was reasonable, the tie applicable to the Corner Garage was not.

Lord Reid [set out the facts and continued]

So I can now turn to the first question in this appeal—whether this agreement is to be regarded in law as an agreement in restraint of trade. The law with regard to restraint of trade is of ancient origin. There are references to it in the Year Books and it seems to have received considerable attention in the time of Queen Elizabeth I. But the old cases lie within a narrow compass. It seems to have been common for an apprentice or a crafts-man to agree with his master that he would not compete with him after leaving his service, and also for a trader who sold his business to agree that he would not thereafter compete with the purchaser of his business. But no early case was cited which did not fall within one or other of these categories. And even in recent times there have been surprisingly few reported cases falling outside these categories in which restraint of trade has been pleaded: we were informed by counsel that there are only about 40 English cases which can be traced. On the other hand, there is an immense body of authorities with regard to the two original categories. I have not found it an easy task to determine how far principles developed for the original categories have been or should be extended.

The most general statement with regard to restraint of trade is that of Lord Parker in *Attorney-General of the Commonwealth of Australia* v. *Adelaide Steamship Co Ltd* [1913] AC 781, 794 (PC). He said:

> 'Monopolies and contracts in restraint of trade have this in common, that they both, if enforced, involve a derogation from the common law right in virtue of which any member of the community may exercise any trade or business he pleases and in such manner as he thinks best in his own interests.'

But that cannot have been intended to be a definition: all contracts in restraint of trade involve such a derogation but not all contracts involving such a derogation are contracts in restraint of trade. Whenever a man agrees to do something over a period he thereby puts it wholly or partly out of his power to 'exercise any trade or business he pleases' during that period. He may enter into a contract of service or may agree to give his exclusive services to another: then during the period of the contract he is not entitled to engage in other business activities. But no one has ever suggested that such contracts are in restraint of trade except in very unusual circumstances . . .

In [t]he leading case of *Nordenfelt* v. *Maxim Nordenfelt Guns & Ammunition Co Ltd* [1894] AC 535 . . . Lord Macnaghten . . . only had in mind the two original kinds of case. There was no need in *Nordenfelt's* case to attempt to define other classes of case to which the doctrine of restraint would apply.

If a contract is within the class of contracts in restraint of trade the law which applies to it is quite different from the law which applies to contracts generally. In general unless a contract is vitiated by duress, fraud or mistake its terms will be enforced though unreasonable or even harsh and unconscionable, but here a term in restraint of trade will not be enforced unless it is reasonable. And in the ordinary case the court will not remake a contract: unless in the special case where the contract is severable, it will not strike out one provision as unenforceable and enforce the rest. But here the party who has been paid for agreeing to the restraint may be unjustly enriched if the court holds the restraint to be too wide to be enforceable and is unable to adjust the consideration given by the other party.

It is much too late now to say that this rather anomalous doctrine of restraint of trade can be confined to the two classes of case to which it was originally applied. But the cases outside these two classes afford little guidance as to the circumstances in which it should be applied. In some it has been assumed that the doctrine applies and the controversy has been whether the restraint was reasonable. And in others where one might have expected the point to be taken it was not taken, perhaps because counsel thought that there was no chance of the court holding that the restraint was too wide to be reasonable.

[he reviewed the case-law and continued]

The main argument submitted for the appellant on this matter was that restraint of trade means a personal restraint and does not apply to a restraint on the use of a particular piece of land. Otherwise, it was said, every covenant running with the land which prevents its use for all or for some trading purposes would be a covenant in restraint of trade and therefore unenforceable unless it could be shown to be reasonable and for the protection of some legitimate interest. It was said that the present agreement only prevents the sale of petrol from other suppliers on the site of the Mustow Green Garage: it leaves the respondents free to trade anywhere else in any way they choose. But in many cases a trader trading at a particular place does not have the resources to enable him to begin trading elsewhere as well, and if he did he might find it difficult to find another suitable garage for sale or to get planning permission to open a new filling station on another site. As the whole doctrine of restraint of trade is based on public policy its application ought to depend less on legal niceties or theoretical possibilities than on the practical effect of a restraint in hampering that freedom which it is the policy of the law to protect.

It is true that it would be an innovation to hold that ordinary negative covenants preventing the use of a particular site for trading of all kinds or of a particular kind are within the scope of the doctrine of restraint of trade. I do not think they are. Restraint of trade appears to me to imply that a man contracts to give up some freedom which otherwise he would have had. A person buying or leasing land had no previous right to be there at all, let alone to trade there, and when he takes possession of that land subject to a negative restrictive covenant he gives up no right or freedom which he previously had. . . . In the present case the respondents before they made this agreement were entitled to use this land in any lawful way they chose, and by making this agreement they agreed to restrict their right by giving up their right to sell there petrol not supplied by the appellants.

In my view this agreement is within the scope of the doctrine of restraint of trade as it had been developed in English law. Not only have the respondents agreed negatively not to sell other petrol but they have agreed positively to keep this garage open for the sale of the appellants' petrol at all reasonable hours throughout the period of the tie. It was argued that this was merely regulating the respondent's trading and rather promoting than restraining his trade. But regulating a person's existing trade may be a greater restraint than prohibiting him from engaging in a new trade. And a contract to take one's whole supply from one source may be much more hampering than a contract to sell one's whole output to one buyer. I would not attempt to define the dividing line between contracts which are and contracts which are not in restraint of trade, but in my view this contract must be held to be in restraint of trade. So it is necessary to consider whether its provisions can be justified . . .

Where two experienced traders are bargaining on equal terms and one has agreed to a restraint for reasons which seem good to him the court is in grave danger of stultifying itself if it says that it knows that trader's interest better than he does himself. But there may well be cases where, although the party to be restrained has deliberately accepted the main terms of the contract, he has been at a disadvantage as regards other terms: for example where a set of conditions has been incorporated which has not been the subject of negotiation—there the court may have greater freedom to hold them unreasonable.

I think that in some cases where the court has held that a restraint was not in the interests of the parties it would have been more correct to hold that the restraint was against the public interest . . . whether or not a restraint is in the personal interests of the parties, it is I think well established that the court will not enforce a restraint which goes further than affording adequate protection to the legitimate interests of the party in whose favour it is granted. This must I think be because too wide a restraint is against the public interest. It has often been said that a person is not entitled to be protected against mere competition. I do not find that very helpful in a case like the present. I think it better to ascertain what were the legitimate interests of the appellants which they were entitled to protect and then to see whether these restraints were more than adequate for that purpose.

What were the appellants' legitimate interests must depend largely on what was the state of affairs in their business and with regard to the distribution and sale of petrol generally. And those are questions of fact to be answered by evidence or common knowledge. In the present case restraint of trade was not pleaded originally and the appellants only received notice that it was to be raised a fortnight before the trial. They may have been wise in not seeking a postponement of the trial when the pleadings were amended. But the result has been that the evidence on this matter is scanty. I think however that it is legitimate to supplement it from the considerable body of reported cases regarding solus agreements and from the facts found in the Report of the Monopolies Commission of July, 1965.

When petrol rationing came to an end in 1950 the large producers began to make agreements, now known as solus agreements, with garage owners under which the garage owner, in return for certain advantages, agreed to sell only the petrol of the producer with whom he made the agreement. Within a short time three-quarters of the filling stations in this country were tied in that way and by the dates of the agreements in this case over 90 per cent. had agreed to ties. It appears that the garage owners were not at a disadvantage in bargaining with the large producing companies as there was intense competition between these companies to obtain these ties. So we can assume that both the garage owners and the companies thought that such ties were to their advantage. And it is not said in this case that all ties are either against the public interest or against the interests of the parties. The respondents' case is that the ties with which we are concerned are for too long periods. The advantage to the garage owner is that he gets a rebate on the wholesale price of the petrol which he buys and also may get other benefits or financial assistance. The main advantages for the producing company appear to be that distribution is made easier and more economical and that it is assured of a steady outlet for its petrol over a period. As regards distribution, it appears that there were some

35,000 filling stations in this country at the relevant time, of which about a fifth were tied to the appellants. So they only have to distribute to some 7,000 filling stations instead of to a very much larger number if most filling stations sold several brands of petrol. But the main reason why the producing companies want ties for five years and more, instead of ties for one or two years only, seems to be that they can organise their business better if on the average only one-fifth or less of their ties come to an end in any one year. The appellants make a point of the fact that they have invested some £200 millions in refineries and other plant and that they could not have done that unless they could foresee a steady and assured level of sales of their petrol. Most of their ties appear to have been made for periods of between five and 20 years. But we have no evidence as to the precise additional advantage which they derive from a five-year tie as compared with a two-year tie or from a 20-year tie as compared with a five-year tie.

The Court of Appeal held that these ties were for unreasonably long periods. They thought that, if for any reason the respondents ceased to sell the appellants' petrol, the appellants could have found other suitable outlets in the neighbourhood within two or three years. I do not think that that is the right test. In the first place there was no evidence about this and I do not think that it would be practicable to apply this test in practice. It might happen that when the respondents ceased to sell their petrol, the appellants would find such an alternative outlet in a very short time. But, looking to the fact that well over 90 per cent. of existing filling stations are tied and that there may be great difficulty in opening a new filling station, it might take a very long time to find an alternative. Any estimate of how long it might take to find suitable alternatives for the respondents' filling stations could be little better than guesswork.

I do not think that the appellants' interest can be regarded so narrowly. They are not so much concerned with any particular outlet as with maintaining a stable system of distribution throughout the country so as to enable their business to be run efficiently and economically. In my view there is sufficient material to justify a decision that ties of less than five years were insufficient, in the circumstances of the trade when these agreements were made, to afford adequate protection to the appellants' legitimate interests. And if that is so I cannot find anything in the details of the Mustow Green agreement which would indicate that it is unreasonable. It is true that if some of the provisions were operated by the appellants in a manner which would be commercially unreasonable they might put the respondents in difficulties. But I think that a court must have regard to the fact that the appellants must act in such a way that they will be able to obtain renewals of the great majority of their very numerous ties, some of which will come to an end almost every week. If in such circumstances a garage owner chooses to rely on the commercial probity and good sense of the producer, I do not think that a court should hold his agreement unreasonable because it is legally capable of some misuse. I would therefore allow the appeal as regards the Mustow Green agreement.

But the Corner Garage agreement involves much more difficulty. Taking first the legitimate interests of the appellants, a new argument was submitted to your Lordships that, apart from any question of security for their loan, it would be unfair to the appellants if the respondents, having used the appellants' money to build up their business, were entitled after a comparatively short time to be free to seek better terms from a competing producer. But there is no material on which I can assess the strength of this argument and I do not find myself in a position to determine whether it has any validity. A tie for 21 years stretches far beyond any period for which developments are reasonably foreseeable.

Restrictions on the garage owner which might seem tolerable and reasonable in reason-ably foreseeable conditions might come to have a very different effect in quite different conditions: the public interest comes in here more strongly. And, apart from a case where he gets a loan, a garage owner appears to get no greater advantage from a 20-year tie than he gets from a five-year tie. So I would think that there must at least be some clearly established advantage to the producing company—something to show that a shorter period would not be adequate—before so long a period could be justified. But in this case there is no evidence to prove anything of the kind. And the other material which I have thought it right to consider does not appear to me to assist the appellant here. I would therefore dismiss the appeal as regards the Corner Garage agreement.

Lord Wilberforce

The doctrine of restraint of trade (a convenient, if imprecise, expression which I continue to use) is one which has throughout the history of its subject-matter been expressed with considerable generality, if not ambiguity. The best-known general formulations, those of Lord Macnaghten in *Nordenfelt* [1894] AC 535, 565 and of Lord Parker of Waddington in *Adelaide* [1913] AC 781, 793–797, adapted and used by Diplock LJ in the Court of Appeal in the *Petrofina* case [1966] Ch 146, 180, speak generally of all restraints of trade without any attempt at a definition. Often we find the words 'restraint of trade' in a single passage used indifferently to denote, on the one hand, in a broad popular sense, any contract which limits the free exercise of trade or business, and, on the other hand, as a term of art covering those contracts which are to be regarded as offending a rule of public policy. Often, in reported cases, we find that instead of segregating two questions, (i) whether the contract is in restraint of trade, (ii) whether, if so, it is 'reasonable', the courts have fused the two by asking whether the contract is in 'undue restraint of trade' or by a compound finding that it is not satisfied that this contract is really in restraint of trade at all but, if it is, it is reasonable. A well-known text-book describes contracts in restraint of trade as those which 'unreasonably restrict' the rights of a person to carry on his trade or profession. There is no need to regret these tendencies: indeed, to do so, when consider-ation of this subject has passed through such notable minds from Lord Macclesfield onwards, would indicate a failure to understand its nature. The common law has often (if sometimes unconsciously) thrived on ambiguity and it would be mistaken, even if it were possible, to try to crystallise the rules of this, or any, aspect of public policy into neat propositions. The doctrine of restraint of trade is one to be applied to factual situations with a broad and flexible rule of reason . . .

This does not mean that the question whether a given agreement is in restraint of trade, in either sense of these words, is nothing more than a question of fact to be individually decided in each case. It is not to be supposed, or encouraged, that a bare allegation that a contract limits a trader's freedom of action exposes a party suing on it to the burden of justification. There will always be certain general categories of contracts as to which it can be said, with some degree of certainty, that the 'doctrine' does or does not apply to them. Positively, there are likely to be certain sensitive areas as to which the law will require in every case the test of reasonableness to be passed: such an area has long been and still is that of contracts between employer and employee as regards the period after the employment has ceased. Negatively, and it is this that concerns us here, there will be types of contract as to which the law should be prepared to say with some confidence that they do not enter into the field of restraint of trade at all.

How, then, can such contracts be defined or at least identified? No exhaustive test can be stated—probably no precise non-exhaustive test. But the development of the law does seem to show that judges have been able to dispense from the necessity of justification under a public policy test of reasonableness such contracts or provisions of contracts as, under contemporary conditions, may be found to have passed into the accepted and normal currency of commercial or contractual or conveyancing relations. That such contracts have done so may be taken to show with at least strong prima force that, moulded under the pressures of negotiation, competition and public opinion, they have assumed a form which satisfies the test of public policy as understood by the courts at the time, or, regarding the matter from the point of view of the trade, that the trade in question has assumed such a form that for its health or expansion it requires a degree of regulation. Absolute exemption from restriction or regulation is never obtained: circumstances, social or economic, may have altered, since they obtained acceptance, in such a way as to call for a fresh examination: there may be some exorbitance or special feature in the individual contract which takes it out of the accepted category: but the court must be persuaded of this before it calls upon the relevant party to justify a contract of this kind.

Some such limitation upon the meaning in legal practice of 'restraints of trade' must surely have been present to the minds of Lord Macnaghten and Lord Parker. They cannot have meant to say that any contract which in whatever way restricts a man's liberty to trade was (either historically under the common law, or at the time of which they were speaking) prima facie unenforceable and must be shown to be reasonable. They must have been well aware that areas existed, and always had existed, in which limitations of this liberty were not only defensible, but were not seriously open to the charge of restraining trade. Their language, they would surely have said, must be interpreted in relation to commercial practice and common sense . . .

I turn now to the agreements. In my opinion, on balance, they enter into the category of agreements in restraint of trade which require justification. They directly bear upon, and in some measure restrain, the exercise of the respondent's trade, so the question is whether they are to be treated as falling within some category excluded from the 'doctrine' of restraint of trade. The broad test, or rather approach, which I have suggested, is capable of answering this. This is not a mere transaction in property, nor a mere transaction between owners of property: it is essentially a trade agreement between traders. It is not a mere agreement for exclusive purchase of a commodity, though it contains this element: if it were nothing more, there would be a strong case for treating it as a normal commercial agreement of an accepted type. But there are other restrictive elements. There is the tie for a fixed period with no provision for determination by notice, a combination which . . . should be considered together, and there is the fetter on the terms on which the station may be sold. Admittedly Harpers could liberate themselves by finding a successor willing to take their place: admittedly, too, being a limited company, they could trade in several places simultaneously, so that even if they remained tied to these sites, and obliged to continue trading there, they could in theory set up business elsewhere. But just as in *McEllistrim's* case [1919] AC 548 the reality of the covenantor's restraint was considered more relevant than his theoretical liberty to depart, so here, in my opinion, addition of all the ingredients takes the case into the category of those which require justification. Finally the agreement is not of a character which, by the pressure of negotiation and competition, has passed into acceptance or into a balance of interest between the parties or between the parties and their customers; the solus system is both too recent and too variable for this to be said.

Lord Morris of Borth-y-Gest, **Lord Hodson**, and **Lord Pearce** delivered concurring judgments.

COMMENTARY

There were two issues at stake before the House of Lords. The first was whether the doctrine of restraint of trade applied at all. The House of Lords answered this question in the affirmative but in doing so it has given rise to some difficulties in terms of ascertaining the scope of the doctrine. Thus Professor Atiyah has stated (*An Introduction to the Law of Contract* (5th edn, Oxford University Press, 1995), pp. 325–326):

> The decision brings many problems in its wake. In particular, it now becomes necessary to decide what *is* a contract in restraint of trade. Most contracts involve *some* restriction on the freedom of the parties, for example, an employee is not free to work except for his employer during ordinary working hours, and a buyer who contracts to obtain all the supplies of some commodity which he needs from a particular seller (a common enough form of business agreement) is restricting his freedom to buy from someone else. But it would certainly be wrong to conclude that *all* contracts containing restrictions are now open to challenge as contracts in restraint of trade, and must be shown to be 'reasonable' if they are to be valid.
>
> Many customary and accepted forms of business agreement are probably still unchallengeable (at any rate under the common law rules), even though they may strictly involve some degree of business restraint. In particular, it has been held that a person who buys land (or a building) may validly enter into some restrictions on how the land is to be used without falling foul of the restraint of trade doctrine—in other words he cannot challenge the validity of the agreement on the ground that it is an unreasonable restraint. This limit on the scope of the doctrine has been justified on the ground that, if a seller could not validly demand from the buyer some restriction of this kind, he might choose not to sell at all, which would be even more restrictive of competition. But this argument is implausible: it could equally well be said of any agreement whereby a seller of a business takes an unreasonably wide restraint from the buyer.

The application of the doctrine of restraint of trade to covenants affecting land is a topic of some controversy (see *Alec Lobb (Garages) Ltd* v. *Total Oil (Great Britain) Ltd* [1985] 1 WLR 173 and GH Treitel, *The Law of Contract* (11th edn, Sweet & Maxwell, 2003), pp. 472–473). Covenants affecting land apart, the question what is or is not a restraint of trade is a matter of substance rather than form (see further *Schroeder* v. *Macaulay*, p. 857 below).

The second issue concerned the reasonableness of the restraints and here the House of Lords distinguished between the four-year and the twenty-one year restraint. Their Lordships had regard to a broad range of factors when deciding the reasonableness of the ties. Professor Bell (*Policy Arguments in Judicial Decisions* (Oxford University Press, 1983), p. 170) has pointed out that:

> Unlike the Court of Appeal, their Lordships took a wider view of what were the legitimate interests which Esso were entitled to protect. In considering this question, they had regard to the money spent on building refineries and providing other outlets, the need for overall planning to justify such expenditure and to provide a stable system of outlets, what was reasonable in return

for the advantages conferred by the agreement, what was necessary to secure the loan, and the general state of the industry. Such matters were considered questions of fact to be determined from evidence and common knowledge. Lords Reid, Hodson and Pearce relied on information provided in the report of the Monopolies Commission on Petrol and the last two used it in support of the view that a restraint of under five years was reasonable. Lords Hodson, Pearce, and Wilberforce also relied on the length of time for which Commonwealth courts had held similar agreements to be valid, and this was a major justification offered by Lord Wilberforce. Such evidence was not considered as binding upon the judges, but supported their conclusion that the restraint of four years and five months in the case of Mustow Green was not unreasonable.

The restrictions in respect of the Corner Garage were, however, held to be unreasonable in that they tied Harper's for a period which was longer than could be foreseen, and could have effect in quite different conditions, so that the public interest in preserving Harper's liberty of action applied more strongly here.

Although the arguments had centred on what tie could be reasonably imposed by [Esso] in support of their interests, the basis of the decision of the House was the injury, or potential injury, to the public of the limitations on Harper's freedom of action. If competition is to be a generally accepted way of running the economy, then restraints have to be justified in terms of their benefits to the community as well as to individuals, and for this reason the public interest figures so importantly in the considerations of the judges.

A Schroeder Music Publishing Co Ltd v. Macaulay (formerly Instone)

[1974] 1 WLR 1308, House of Lords

The respondent, a young and unknown songwriter, entered into a contract with the appellants for his exclusive services. The agreement was made on the appellants' stand-ard terms. The respondent agreed to give the appellants the copyright over all of his compositions for a five-year period and the agreement was renewable automatically for a further five years in the event that his royalties in the first five years exceeded £5,000. The contract gave the appellants the right to terminate the agreement at any time on giving one month's notice but did not give a right to terminate the agreement to the respond-ent. The appellants were entitled to assign their rights under the contract to a third party but no right to assign was given to the respondent. The appellants were under no obliga-tion to publish any of the respondent's compositions. The respondent sought a declar-ation that the agreement was void on the ground that it constituted an unreasonable restraint of trade. The appellants submitted that the doctrine of restraint of trade was not applicable to the contract and that, in any event, the terms of the contract were reason-able. The House of Lords held that the doctrine of restraint of trade was applicable to the contract and further that they were an unreasonable restraint of trade. Accordingly, the respondent was entitled to the declaration which he sought.

Lord Reid

I think that in a case like the present case two questions must be considered. Are the terms of the agreement so restrictive that either they cannot be justified at all or they must be justified by the party seeking to enforce the agreement? Then, if there is room for justification, has that party proved justification—normally by showing that the restric-tions were no more than what was reasonably required to protect his legitimate interests.

[he examined the terms of the contract and continued]

Clauses 1 and 9(a) determine the duration of the agreement. It was to last for five years in any event and for 10 years if the royalties for the first five years exceeded £5,000. There is little evidence about this extension. £5,000 in five years appears to represent a very modest success, and so if the respondent's work became well known and popular he would be tied by the agreement for 10 years. The duration of an agreement in restraint of trade is a factor of great importance in determining whether the restrictions in the agreement can be justified but there was no evidence as to why so long a period was necessary to protect the appellants' interests . . .

[he reviewed other clauses in the contract and continued]

The public interest requires in the interests both of the public and of the individual that everyone should be free so far as practicable to earn a livelihood and to give to the public the fruits of his particular abilities. The main question to be considered is whether and how far the operation of the terms of this agreement is likely to conflict with this object-ive. The respondent is bound to assign to the appellants during a long period the fruits of his musical talent. But what are the appellants bound to do with those fruits? Under the contract nothing. If they do use the songs which the respondent composes they must pay in terms of the contract. But they need not do so. As has been said they may put them in a drawer and leave them there.

No doubt the expectation was that if the songs were of value they would be published to the advantage of both parties. But if for any reason the appellants chose not to publish them the respondent would get no remuneration and he could not do anything. Inevit-ably the respondent must take the risk of misjudgment of the merits of his work by the appellants. But that is not the only reason which might cause the appellants not to publish. There is no evidence about this so we must do the best we can with common knowledge. It does not seem fanciful and it was not argued that it is fanciful to suppose that purely commercial consideration might cause a publisher to refrain from publishing and promoting promising material. He might think it likely to be more profitable to promote work by other composers with whom he had agreements and unwise or too expensive to try to publish and popularise the respondent's work in addition. And there is always the possibility that less legitimate reasons might influence a decision not to publish the respondent's work.

It was argued that there must be read into this agreement an obligation on the pub-lisher to act in good faith. I take that to mean that he would be in breach of contract if by reason of some oblique or malicious motive he refrained from publishing work which he would otherwise have published. I very much doubt this but even if it were so it would make little difference. Such a case would seldom occur and then would be difficult to prove.

I agree with the appellants' argument to this extent. I do not think that a publisher could reasonably be expected to enter into any positive commitment to publish future work by an unknown composer. Possibly there might be some general undertaking to use his best endeavours to promote the composer's work. But that would probably have to be in such general terms as to be of little use to the composer.

But if no satisfactory positive undertaking by the publisher can be devised, it appears to me to be an unreasonable restraint to tie the composer for this period of years so that his work will be sterilised and he can earn nothing from his abilities as a composer if the publisher chooses not to publish. If there had been in clause 9 any provision entitling the composer to terminate the agreement in such an event the case might have had a very different appearance [clause 9 gave a right to terminate to the publishers but not to the composer]. But as the agreement stands not only is the composer tied but he cannot recover the copyright of work which the publisher refuses to publish.

It was strenuously argued that the agreement is in standard form, that it has stood the test of time, and that there is no indication that it ever causes injustice. Reference was made to passages in the speeches of Lord Pearce and Lord Wilberforce in *Esso Petroleum Co Ltd* v. *Harper's Garage (Stourport) Ltd* [1968] AC 269 with which I wholly agree. Lord Pearce said, at p. 323:

> 'It is important that the court, in weighing the question of reasonableness, should give full weight to commercial practices and to the generality of contracts made freely by parties bargaining on equal terms,'

and Lord Wilberforce said, at pp. 332–333:

> 'But the development of the law does seem to show that judges have been able to dispense from the necessity of justification under a public policy test of reasonableness such contracts or provisions of contracts as, under contemporary conditions, may be found to have passed into the accepted and normal currency of commercial or con- tractual or conveyancing relations. That such contracts have done so may be taken to show with at least strong prima facie force that, moulded under the pressures of negotiation, competition and public opinion, they have assumed a form which satisfies the test of public policy as understood by the courts at the time, or, regarding the matter from the point of view of the trade, that the trade in question has assumed such a form that for its health or expansion it requires a degree of regulation.'

But those passages refer to contracts 'made freely by parties bargaining on equal terms' or 'moulded under the pressures of negotiation, competition and public opinion'. I do not find from any evidence in this case, nor does it seem probable, that this form of contract made between a publisher and an unknown composer has been moulded by any pressure of negotiation. Indeed, it appears that established composers who can bargain on equal terms can and do make their own contracts.

Any contract by which a person engages to give his exclusive services to another for a period necessarily involves extensive restriction during that period of the common law right to exercise any lawful activity he chooses in such manner as he thinks best. Normally the doctrine of restraint of trade has no application to such restrictions: they require no justification. But if contractual restrictions appear to be unnecessary or to be reasonably capable of enforcement in an oppressive manner, then they must be justified before they can be enforced.

In the present case the respondent assigned to the appellants 'the full copyright for the whole world' in every musical composition 'composed created or conceived' by him alone or in collaboration with any other person during a period of five or it might be 10 years. He received no payment (apart from an initial £50) unless his work was published and the appellants need not publish unless they chose to do so. And if they did not publish he had no right to terminate the agreement or to have copyrights re-assigned to him. I need not consider whether in any circumstances it would be possible to justify such a one-sided agreement. It is sufficient to say that such evidence as there is falls far short of justification. It must therefore follow that the agreement so far as unperformed is unenforceable.

I would dismiss this appeal.

Lord Diplock

My Lords, the contract under consideration in this appeal is one whereby the respondent accepted restrictions upon the way in which he would exploit his earning power as a song writer for the next ten years. Because this can be classified as a contract in restraint of trade the restrictions that the respondent accepted fell within one of those limited categories of contractual promises in respect of which the courts still retain the power to relieve the promisor of his legal duty to fulfil them. In order to determine whether this case is one in which that power ought to be exercised, what your Lordships have in fact been doing has been to assess the relative bargaining power of the publisher and the song writer at the time the contract was made and to decide whether the publisher had used his superior bargaining power to exact from the song writer promises that were unfairly onerous to him. Your Lordships have not been concerned to inquire whether the public have in fact been deprived of the fruit of the song writer's talents by reason of the restrictions, nor to assess the likelihood that they would be so deprived in the future if the contract were permitted to run its full course.

It is, in my view, salutary to acknowledge that in refusing to enforce provisions of a contract whereby one party agrees for the benefit of the other party to exploit or to refrain from exploiting his own earning power, the public policy which the court is implementing is not some 19th-century economic theory about the benefit to the general public of freedom of trade, but the protection of those whose bargaining power is weak against being forced by those whose bargaining power is stronger to enter into bargains that are unconscionable. Under the influence of Bentham and of laissez-faire the courts in the 19th century abandoned the practice of applying the public policy against unconscionable bargains to contracts generally, as they had formerly done to any contract considered to be usurious; but the policy survived in its application to penalty clauses and to relief against forfeiture and also to the special category of contracts in restraint of trade. If one looks at the reasoning of 19th-century judges in cases about contracts in restraint of trade one finds lip service paid to current economic theories, but if one looks at what they said in the light of what they did, one finds that they struck down a bargain if they thought it was unconscionable as between the parties to it and upheld it if they thought that it was not.

So I would hold that the question to be answered as respects a contract in restraint of trade of the kind with which this appeal is concerned is: 'Was the bargain fair?' The test of fairness is, no doubt, whether the restrictions are both reasonably necessary for the protection of the legitimate interests of the promisee and commensurate with the benefits secured to the promisor under the contract. For the purpose of this test all the provisions of the contract must be taken into consideration.

My Lords, the provisions of the contract have already been sufficiently stated by my noble and learned friend, Lord Reid. I agree with his analysis of them and with his conclusion that the contract is unenforceable. It does not satisfy the test of fairness as I have endeavoured to state it. I will accordingly content myself with adding some observations directed to the argument that because the contract was in a 'standard form' in common use between music publishers and song writers the restraints that it imposes upon the song writer's liberty to exploit his talents must be presumed to be fair and reasonable.

Standard forms of contracts are of two kinds. The first, of very ancient origin, are those which set out the terms upon which mercantile transactions of common occurrence are to be carried out. Examples are bills of lading, charterparties, policies of insurance, contracts of sale in the commodity markets. The standard clauses in these contracts have been settled over the years by negotiation by representatives of the commercial interests involved and have been widely adopted because experience has shown that they facilitate the conduct of trade. Contracts of these kinds affect not only the actual parties to them but also others who may have a commercial interest in the transactions to which they relate, as buyers or sellers, charterers or shipowners, insurers or bankers. If fairness or reasonableness were relevant to their enforceability the fact that they are widely used by parties whose bargaining power is fairly matched would raise a strong presumption that their terms are fair and reasonable.

The same presumption, however, does not apply to the other kind of standard form of contract. This is of comparatively modern origin. It is the result of the concentration of particular kinds of business in relatively few hands. The ticket cases in the 19th century provide what are probably the first examples. The terms of this kind of standard form of contract have not been the subject of negotiation between the parties to it, or approved by any organisation representing the interests of the weaker party. They have been dictated by that party whose bargaining power, either exercised alone or in conjunction with others providing similar goods or services, enables him to say: 'If you want these goods or services at all, these are the only terms on which they are obtainable. Take it or leave it'.

To be in a position to adopt this attitude towards a party desirous of entering into a contract to obtain goods or services provides a classic instance of superior bargaining power. It is not without significance that on the evidence in the present case music publishers in negotiating with song writers whose success has been already established do not insist upon adhering to a contract in the standard form they offered to the respondent. The fact that the appellants' bargaining power vis-a-vis the respondent was strong enough to enable them to adopt this take-it-or-leave-it attitude raises no presumption that they used it to drive an unconscionable bargain with him, but in the field of restraint of trade it calls for vigilance on the part of the court to see that they did not.

Viscount Dilhorne concurred with the speech of Lord Reid. **Lord Simon of Glaisdale** and **Lord Kilbrandon** concurred with the speeches of Lord Reid and Lord Diplock.

COMMENTARY

Schroeder is another difficult decision. It demonstrates that the doctrine of restraint of trade can apply to terms during the currency of a relationship. It also appears to link the doctrine of restraint of trade with procedural unfairness, substantive unfairness, and inequality of bargaining power (on which see Chapter 20 below). Indeed, one of the criticisms that has been levelled against the decision is that it is very difficult to locate the basis upon which the House of Lords decided to intervene. Lord Diplock, in particular, seemed to rely upon a mix of factors. Thus Professor Smith has pointed out ('Reconstructing Restraint of Trade' (1995) 15 *OJLS* 565, 583) that:

Lord Diplock suggests, at different times and in different ways, that procedural fairness, substantive fairness and the traditional notion of reasonableness are all relevant to the validity of a restraint. Lord Diplock did not attempt to reconcile his conflicting statements, although he did give a further indication that he considered 'bargaining power' relevant. Later in his judgment he said that the type of standard form contract at issue in the case was typically 'the result of the concentration of particular kinds of business in relatively few hands' and added that the ability of more 'established' singers to negotiate individualised and more favourable contracts supported a presumption of inequality of bargaining power.

Lord Diplock's assumption that the terms were presented to Mr Macaulay on a take-it-or-leave-it basis has also been challenged on the ground that it does not appear to fit the case of the music industry at the relevant time. Professor Trebilcock (*Restraint of Trade* (Carswell, 1986), p. 168) has noted that there were 428 UK music publishers in 1975–1976, 276 record and tape manufacturers/distributors/importers, and fifty-four independent record producers. He concludes that 'these numbers appear to suggest a dynamic and highly competitive music industry, probably comprising more competing firms than several of the industries cited in Lord Diplock's first category'. Professor Collins (*The Law of Contract* (4th edn, Butterworths, 2003), pp. 28–29) has concluded as follows:

If one considers this decision from the perspective of market failure, then it seems hard to justify. As Trebilcock points out, there seems to have been a competitive market operating in this instance, with many music publishers competing for young talent. Nor can it be seriously suggested that the composer did not understand the terms of the agreement because they were too complex. In the absence of such grounds to suspect market failure, economic analysis suggests that the contract should be enforced, for any interference may disrupt the market opportunities for young composers in the future.

But these arguments, although sound in themselves, miss the real objections to this contract, which concern the dimensions of power, fairness, and co-operation, not the efficiency of the market. Because the composer's career was completely dependent upon the publisher's discretion for a period up to ten years, his degree of subordination to another represented an unjustifiable form of domination. The absence of an undertaking on the part of the publisher to publish any of his songs rendered the exchange too one-sided to be fair. In addition, because the composer could not terminate the agreement during its fixed period, he had no effective sanction against the publisher to ensure that at least it made reasonable efforts to bring the venture to fruition by publishing and promoting his work.

These three themes—the concern about unjustifiable domination, the equivalence of the exchange, and the need to ensure co-operation—which seem to me to motivate the decision in *Schroeder Music Publishing Co Ltd* v. *Macaulay*, form the core of the interpretation of the law of contract presented in this book. The emphasis upon these values in the modern law signifies a new understanding and justification of the market order.

5. THE CONSEQUENCES OF ILLEGALITY

The general rule is that the courts will neither enforce an illegal contract nor will they permit the recovery of the value of benefits conferred on another party in the performance of an illegal contract. These two general rules are expressed in the maxims *ex turpi causa non oritur actio* (no action can be based on a disreputable cause) and *in pari delicto potior est conditio defendentis* (where both parties are equally at fault, the position of the defendant is stronger). Neither rule is without exceptions.

As *Archbolds (Freightage) Ltd* v. *S Spanglett Ltd* [1961] 1 QB 374 (on the web-site which supports this book) demonstrates, an innocent party, who is unaware of an illegal act committed by the defendant in the course of performance of the contract, may be entitled to enforce the contract, notwithstanding the illegality. The court may also conclude, as a matter of construction, that the effect of a statutory provision is to impose a punishment on a party who breaches the statute but not to render unenforceable a contract the performance of which involves a breach of the statute (see, for example, *St John Shipping Corporation* v. *Joseph Rank Ltd* [1957] 1 QB 267). The court may also be able to sever the illegal part of the contract from the rest of the contract and enforce the remainder of the contract (see further J Beatson, *Anson's Law of Contract* (28th edn, Oxford University Press, 2002), pp. 413–418).

While the courts will not in general enforce an illegal contract, a party to an illegal contract may be able to obtain damages for a breach of collateral warranty where the defendant is held to have warranted that he will perform the contract lawfully but fails to do so. Collateral warranties tend to arise in the licensing cases. Thus in *Archbolds (Freightage) Ltd* v. *S Spanglett Ltd* [1961] 1 QB 374 Devlin LJ stated that there was 'much to be said' for the implication of a warranty that the van was properly licensed for the service for which it was required (see also *Strongman (1945) Ltd* v. *Sincock* [1955] 2 QB 525 and *Shelley* v. *Paddock* [1980] QB 348).

The general rule that the court will not recognize the existence of a restitutionary right of recovery in the case of illegal contracts is the subject of a number of exceptions. Three distinct grounds of recovery can be identified. First, the courts will allow recovery where the parties are not *in pari delicto* (not equally guilty), secondly, where the claimant withdraws from the transaction during the *locus poenitentiae* (the space or time for repentance), and, finally, where the claimant can establish that the defendant retains his property, whether at law or in equity, without having to rely upon the illegality.

The first rule is that the claimant may recover where the parties are not *in pari delicto*. Three cases illustrate the operation of this rule. The first is the case where the claimant is unaware of the facts constituting the illegality. In *Oom* v. *Bruce* (1810) 12 East 225 the plaintiffs, acting as agents of a Russian subject, entered into a contract of insurance with the defendants in connection with the transportation of goods from St Petersburg to London. The contract was entered into the day after hostilities broke out between Russia and Great Britain, although this fact was unknown to the plaintiffs. The contract was therefore void and unenforceable. It was held that the plaintiffs were entitled to recover the premiums they had paid. Lord Ellenborough CJ stated that the plaintiffs had no knowledge of the commencement of hostilities by Russia when they effected the insurance and that, no fault being imputable to them for entering into the contract, there was no reason why they should not recover back the premiums which they had paid for an insurance from which they could never have derived any benefit. Secondly, illegality does not operate as a defence to claims for restitution based on duress. In *Smith* v. *Bromley* (1760) 2 Doug 696 the plaintiff's brother committed an act of bankruptcy. The defendant, his chief creditor, refused to sign the certificate of discharge unless he was paid £40 and given a note for a further £20. The plaintiff paid over the £40 to an agent of the defendant who, in turn, paid it over to the defendant. The defendant signed the discharge and the plaintiff's brother was discharged. The plaintiff then brought an action to recover the £40 which she had paid to the defendant. The defendant maintained that she was not entitled to recover because she had paid the money aware of the nature of the transaction into which she was entering. The plaintiff's action succeeded. The third case is on the other side of the line. In *Parkinson* v. *College of Ambulance Ltd* [1925] 2 KB 1 the plaintiff paid £3,000 to the defendant charity, after the defendant's secretary had fraudulently represented to the plaintiff that he would be able to obtain a knighthood for the plaintiff if he made a large donation to the charity. When no knighthood was forthcoming after the payment was made the plaintiff sought to recover the sum which he had paid. His claim was dismissed, notwithstanding the fact that there had been a total failure of consideration. The plaintiff could not claim that he was unware of the illegal nature of the transaction which he had concluded. He was therefore *in pari delicto* with the defendant and so not entitled to recover his payment.

Secondly, a claimant may be able to recover the value of a benefit conferred upon the other party to an illegal contract if he repudiates the contract within the *locus poenitentiae* ('the time for repentance'). While this ground of recovery is recognized in the cases, its scope is somewhat uncertain. It is uncertain in two respects. First it is not clear how much time a party has in which he can withdraw from the transaction. It is clear that he can withdraw before performance has commenced and that he cannot do so after performance has been completed. But the point in time at which, once performance has commenced, a party loses his right to withdraw and recover the value of any benefits conferred is unclear (contrast in this respect *Taylor* v. *Bowers* (1876) 1 QBD 291 and *Kearley* v. *Thomson* (1890) 24 QBD 742). Secondly, it is unclear whether the party withdrawing must genuinely repent of his decision to enter into the illegal contract. It would appear that there is no requirement that the repentance be genuine: it suffices that the claimant withdraw from the transaction (*Tribe* v. *Tribe* [1996] Ch 107, 135).

Thirdly, a claimant may be able to recover money paid or property transferred under an illegal contract if he can establish his right to the money or the property without relying upon the illegality. The law here is in a mess and the results of the cases are extremely haphazard. The principle is, however, well-established. In *Bowmakers Ltd* v. *Barnet Instruments Ltd* [1945] 1 KB 65, 71 Du Parcq LJ stated that:

in our opinion, a man's right to possess his own chattels will as a general rule be enforced against one who, without any claim of right, is detaining them, or has converted them to his own use, even though it may appear either from the pleadings, or in the course of the trial, that the chattels in question came into the defendant's possession by reason of an illegal contract between himself and the plaintiff, provided that the plaintiff does not seek, and is not forced, either to found his claim on the illegal contract or to plead its illegality in order to support his claim.

The same principle is applicable to a claimant who can establish equitable title to property without relying upon the illegality (*Tinsley* v. *Milligan* [1994] 1 AC 340). The difficulty with this principle is that it is capricious in its application because it is often entirely fortuitous whether or not a claimant can establish title to property without relying upon the illegality (see *Tribe* v. *Tribe* [1996] Ch 107, *Silverwood* v. *Silverwood* (1997) 74 P & CR 453, *Lowson* v. *Coombes* [1999] Ch 373, and *Collier* v. *Collier* [2002] EWCA Civ 1095). In *Tinsley* v. *Milligan* Lord Goff noted the unsatisfactory nature of the present law, stated that he would 'welcome an investigation' of the issue by the Law Commission and concluded that he would 'be more than happy if a new system could be evolved which was both satisfactory in its effect and capable of avoiding the kind of result which flows from the established rules of law in cases such as the present'. The Law Commission has undertaken a study of the law and has produced a consultation paper. The essence of the provisional proposals set out in the consultation paper are as follows:

Law Commission, *Illegal Transactions: The Effect of Illegality on Contracts and Trusts*

Law Com Consultation Paper No 154, (1999) paras 1.18–1.21

1.18   Our broad provisional proposal is that the present technical and complex rules governing the effect of illegality in relation to contracts and trusts should be replaced by a discretion. Under that discretion the court could decide whether or not to enforce an illegal transaction, to recognise that property rights have been transferred or created by it, or to allow benefits conferred under it to be recovered. We do not, however, recommend that the court should have an open-ended discretion to produce whatever it considers to be the 'just' solution. That is, we provisionally propose that, generally, illegality, should continue to be used only as a defence to what would otherwise be a standard claim for a contractual or restitutionary remedy or for the recognition of legal or equitable property rights. We discuss one possible exception to this general rule (withdrawal during the *locus poenitentiae*), where illegality may act as a cause of action.

1.19   We also provisionally recommend that the proposed discretion should be structured, in order to provide greater certainty and guidance. We therefore provisionally propose that, in exercising its discretion, a court should consider: (i) the seriousness of the illegality involved; (ii) the knowledge and intention of the party seeking to enforce the illegal transaction, seeking the recognition of legal or equitable rights under it, or seeking to recover benefits conferred under it; (iii) whether refusing to allow standard rights and remedies would deter illegality; (iv) whether refusing to allow standard rights and remedies would further the purpose of the rule which renders the transaction illegal; and (v) whether refusing to allow standard rights and remedies would be proportionate to the illegality involved.

1.20   Where, however, a statute has expressly provided what should be the effect of the involvement of illegality on a transaction, we provisionally recommend that our proposed discretion should not apply. That is, we do not suggest that the courts should be able to use the discretion to override the express provisions of a statute.

1.21   We consider that these provisional proposals would have two major advantages over the present law. First, a court would be able to reach its decision on the facts of a particular case using open and explicit reasoning, giving full effect to the relevance of the illegality on the transaction. Secondly, we believe that the provisional proposals would be likely to result in illegality being used less frequently to deny a plaintiff his or her usual rights or remedies. That is, under the discretion, illegality would only act as a defence where there is a clear and justifiable public interest that it should do so.

6. FURTHER READING

BUCKLEY, R, 'Illegality in Contract and Conceptual Reasoning' (1983) 12 *Anglo-American Law Review* 280.

LAW COMMISSION, Consultation Paper No 154, *Illegal Transactions: The Effect of Illegality on Contracts and Trusts.*

SMITH, S, 'Reconstructing Restraint of Trade' (1995) 15 *OJLS* 565.

23

FRUSTRATION AND FORCE MAJEURE

1. CENTRAL ISSUES

1. The doctrine of frustration operates to discharge a contract where, after the formation of the contract, something occurs which renders performance of the contract impossible, illegal, or something radically different from that which was in the contemplation of the parties at the time of entry into the contract.

2. While the doctrine of frustration is the subject of considerable analysis in textbooks, its practical significance is limited. This is so for a number of reasons. First, the doctrine does not apply where express provision has been made in the contract for the event that is alleged to have frustrated the contract. Given that force majeure and hardship clauses seek to regulate events which may impede or hinder performance of the contract, the impact of such events is more likely to be regulated by the terms of the force majeure clause or the hardship clause than by the doctrine of frustration. Secondly, the doctrine does not apply where the event alleged to have frustrated the contract was foreseeable. Thirdly, a contracting party cannot invoke the doctrine of frustration where the alleged frustrating event was caused by his own conduct rather than a supervening event. Fourthly, the consequences of the application of the doctrine are drastic in that it brings the contract automatically to an end, irrespective of the wishes of the parties. The Draconian consequences of the application of the doctrine inhibit its wider use. Finally, the courts have adopted a restrictive approach to the operation of the doctrine in order to avoid it becoming an escape route for a party who has entered into a bad bargain. As Lord Roskill once put it, the doctrine of frustration is 'not lightly to be invoked to relieve contracting parties of the normal consequences of imprudent bargains' (*The Nema* [1982] AC 724, 752).

3. This chapter has two principal aims. First, it seeks to ascertain the scope of the doctrine of frustration and to examine the relationship between the doctrine of frustration and any force majeure or hardship clause that is to be found in the contract. Secondly, it explores, albeit briefly, the reasons for the narrow scope of the doctrine of frustration and contrasts it with the more liberal regimes to be found in, for example, the Principles of European Contract Law. Should English law follow the model found in the Principles and confer broader powers on the courts, not only in relation to the circumstances in which they can intervene but also in terms of their remedial powers when they do intervene?

2. INTRODUCTION

In *J Lauritzen AS* v. *Wijsmuller BV* (*The 'Super Servant Two'*) [1990] 1 Lloyd's Rep 1 (p. 885 below), Bingham LJ stated (at p. 8) that the doctrine of frustration has evolved to 'mitigate the rigour of the common law's insistence on literal performance of absolute promises' and that its object is 'to give effect to the demands of justice, to achieve a just and reasonable result, to do what is reasonable and fair, as an expedient to escape from injustice where such would result from enforcement of a contract in its literal terms after a significant change in circumstances'. There are three elements to this statement. The first is the strict approach initially taken by the common law. Liability for breach of contract is generally strict; that is to say, liability is not dependent upon proof of fault by the party alleged to be in breach. This being the case, a party who fails to perform his contractual obligations, for whatever reason, is prima facie in breach of contract. The common law was generally reluctant to absolve a contracting party from the consequences of his failure to perform his contractual obligations. The second point is that the effect of the doctrine of frustration is to provide such an absolving power in that it brings the contract to an end without imposing a liability in damages on the party who has failed to perform his contractual obligations as a result of the supervening event. The third point is that the doctrine only applies where there has been 'a significant change in circumstances' after the making of the contract such that it would not be 'fair' to enforce the contract according to its original terms. As we shall see, the definition of a 'significant change in circumstances' has proved to be a difficult matter, but the essential point to grasp at this stage is that the doctrine of frustration operates to discharge a contract where, after the formation of the contract, something occurs which renders performance of the contract impossible, illegal, or something radically different from that which was in the contemplation of the parties at the time of entry into the contract.

The reference made by Bingham LJ to the 'common law's insistence on literal performance of absolute promises' is an important one. The original common law rule was a very strict one. As Professor Simpson has pointed out ('Innovation in Nineteenth Century Contract Law' (1975) 91 *LQR* 247, 270):

In pre-nineteenth-century law the general rule was that a change of circumstances after a promise was made did not excuse the promisor from performance, even if it made performance impossible; this view came to be known as the rule in *Paradine v. Jane* (1647) or the rule as to absolute contracts. *Paradine v. Jane* did not however deal with Acts of God, but with an Act of the King's enemies, and there remained some scope for the development of a defence of supervening impossibility through Act of God and this was allowed where death, the most dramatic Act of God, intervened.

In *Paradine* v. *Jane* (1647) Aleyn 26 a tenant of a farm was dispossessed for a period of two years as a result of an act of the King's enemies. He claimed that he was not liable to pay the rent for the period for which he had been dispossessed. It was held that he was liable: he had assumed an obligation to pay the rent and he was bound to make that obligation good. But, as Professor Simpson points out, the law did not take such an absolute approach in all cases. An example is provided by the case of the death of a party to a contract of apprenticeship. The courts held that the effect of the death of either party was to dissolve the contract without any liability being imposed for the consequences of a failure to perform the contract in accordance with its terms. Thus, while the common law approach was very strict, it would not be true to say that it was, in all cases, absolute.

The law has moved on from the strict approach taken in *Paradine* v. *Jane*. The decisive case is generally considered to be the decision in *Taylor* v. *Caldwell* (1863) 3 B

& S 826 (below). Its more liberal approach was developed in cases such as *Jackson* v. *Union Marine Insurance Co Ltd* (1874) LR 10 CP 125 and *Krell* v. *Henry* [1903] 2 KB 740 (p. 896 below). While it is true to say that the doctrine of frustration is more liberal than the common law rule to be found in *Paradine* v. *Jane*, it is important to stress that the doctrine continues to operate within very narrow limits. Twentieth century cases such as *Davis Contractors Ltd* v. *Fareham Urban District Council* [1956] AC 696 (p. 873 below), *National Carriers Ltd* v. *Panalpina (Northern) Ltd* [1981] AC 675 (p. 921 below), and *J Lauritzen AS* v. *Wijsmuller BV (The 'Super Servant Two')* [1990] 1 Lloyd's Rep 1 (p. 885 below) evince a restrictive approach to the scope of the doctrine of frustration. While it is broader than the original common law rule, it remains a very narrow doctrine.

An introduction to the scope and the basis of the doctrine of frustration can be gleaned from an examination of two cases. The first is the decision of the Court of Queen's Bench in *Taylor* v. *Caldwell* (1863) 3 B & S 826 and the second is the decision of the House of Lords in *Davis Contractors Ltd* v. *Fareham Urban District Council* [1956] AC 696. *Taylor* has been chosen because it is regarded as the origin of the modern doctrine of frustration, while *Davis* has been selected because it sets out the test that is generally applied by the modern courts when deciding whether or not a contract has been frustrated.

Taylor v. Caldwell

(1863) 3 B & S 826, Queen's Bench

The facts are set out in the judgment of Blackburn J.

Blackburn J [gave the judgment of the court]
In this case the plaintiffs and defendants had, on the 27th May, 1861, entered into a contract by which the defendants agreed to let the plaintiffs have the use of The Surrey Gardens and Music Hall on four days then to come, viz. the 17th June, 15th July, 5th August and 19th August, for the purpose of giving a series of four grand concerts, and day and night fetes at the Gardens and Hall on those days respectively; and the plaintiffs agreed to take the Gardens and Hall on those days, and pay 100l. for each day.

The parties inaccurately call this a 'letting', and the money to be paid a 'rent' but the whole agreement is such as to shew that the defendants were to retain the possession of the Hall and Gardens so that there was to be no demise of them, and that the contract was merely to give the plaintiffs the use of them on those days. Nothing however, in our opinion, depends on this. The agreement then proceeds to set out various stipulations between the parties as to what each was to supply for these concerts and entertainments, and as to the manner in which they should be carried on. The effect of the whole is to shew that the existence of the Music Hall in the Surrey Gardens in a state fit for a concert was essential for the fulfilment of the contract,—such entertainments as the parties contemplated in their agreement could not be given without it.

After the making of the agreement, and before the first day on which a concert was to be given, the Hall was destroyed by fire. This destruction, we must take it on the evidence, was without the fault of either party, and was so complete that in consequence the concerts could not be given as intended. And the question we have to decide is whether, under these circumstances, the loss which the plaintiffs have sustained is to fall upon the defendants. The parties when framing their agreement, evidently had not present to their minds the possibility of such a disaster, and have made no express stipulation with reference to it, so that the answer to the question must depend upon the general rules of law applicable to such a contract.

There seems no doubt that where there is a positive contract to do a thing, not in itself unlawful, the contractor must perform it or pay damages for not doing it, although in consequence of unforeseen accidents, the performance of his contract has become unexpectedly burthensome or even impossible. . . . But this rule is only applicable when the contract is positive and absolute, and not subject to any condition either express or implied: and there are authorities which, as we think, establish the principle that where, from the nature of the contract, it appears that the parties must from the beginning have known that it could not be fulfilled unless when the time for the fulfilment of the contract arrived some particular specified thing continued to exist, so that, when entering into the contract, they must have contemplated such continuing existence as the foundation of what was to be done; there, in the absence of any express or implied warranty that the thing shall exist, the contract is not to be construed as a positive contract, but as subject to an implied condition that the parties shall be excused in case, before breach, perform-ance becomes impossible from the perishing of the thing without default of the contractor.

There seems little doubt that this implication tends to further the great object of making the legal construction such as to fulfil the intention of those who entered into the contract. For in the course of affairs men in making such contracts in general would, if it were brought to their minds, say that there should be such a condition.

Accordingly, in the Civil law, such an exception is implied in every obligation of the class which they call obligatio de certo corpore. . . . The examples are of contracts respecting a slave, which was the common illustration of a certain subject used by the Roman lawyers, just as we are apt to take a horse; and no doubt the propriety, one might almost say necessity, of the implied condition is more obvious when the contract relates to a living animal, whether man or brute, than when it relates to some inanimate thing (such as in the present case a theatre) the existence of which is not so obviously precar-ious as that of the live animal, but the principle is adopted in the Civil law as applicable to every obligation of which the subject is a certain thing. The general subject is treated of by Pothier, who in his *Traité des Obligations*, partie 3, chap. 6, art. 3, § 668 states the result to be that the debtor corporis certi is freed from his obligation when the thing has perished, neither by his act, nor his neglect, and before he is in default, unless by some stipulation he has taken on himself the risk of the particular misfortune which has occurred.

Although the Civil law is not of itself authority in an English Court, it affords great assistance in investigating the principles on which the law is grounded. And it seems to us that the common law authorities establish that in such a contract the same condition of the continued existence of the thing is implied by English law.

There is a class of contracts in which a person binds himself to do something which requires to be performed by him in person; and such promises, e.g. promises to marry, or promises to serve for a certain time, are never in practice qualified by an express excep-tion of the death of the party; and therefore in such cases the contract is in terms broken if the promisor dies before fulfilment. Yet it was very early determined that, if the performance is personal, the executors are not liable; *Hyde* v. *The Dean of Windsor* (Cro Eliz 552, 553). See 2 Wms. Exors. 1560, 5th ed. where a very apt illustration is given. 'Thus', says the learned author, 'if an author undertakes to compose a work, and dies before completing it, his executors are discharged from this contract: for the undertaking is merely personal in its nature, and, by the intervention of the contractor's death, has become impossible to be performed'. For this he cites a dictum of Lord Lyndhurst in *Marshall* v. *Broadhurst* (1 Tyr 348, 349), and a case mentioned by Patteson J in *Wentworth* v. *Cock* (10 A & E 42, 45–46). In *Hall* v. *Wright* (E B & E 746, 749), Crompton J in his judgement, puts another case, 'Where a contract depends upon personal skill, and the act of God renders it impossible, as, for instance, in the case of a painter employed to paint a picture who is struck blind, it may be that the performance might be excused'. It seems that in those cases the only ground on which the parties or their executors, can be excused from the consequences of the breach of the contract is, that from the nature of the contract there is an implied condition of the continued existence of the life of the contractor, and, perhaps in the case of the painter of his eyesight. In the instances just given, the person, the continued existence of whose life is necessary to the fulfilment of the contract, is himself the contractor, but that does not seem in itself to be necessary to the application of the principle. . . . These, are instances where the implied condition is of the life of a human being, but there are others in which the same implication is made as to the continued existence of a thing. For example, where a contract of sale is made amounting to a bargain and sale, transferring presently the property in specific chattels, which are to be delivered by the vendor at a future day; there, if the chattels, without the fault of the vendor, perish in the interval, the purchaser must pay the price and the vendor is excused from performing his contract to deliver, which has thus become impossible. . . . It may, we think, be safely asserted to be now English law, that in all contracts of loan of chattels or bailments if the performance of the promise of the borrower or bailee to return the things lent or bailed, becomes impossible because it has perished, this impossibility (if not arising from the fault of the borrower or bailee from some risk which he has taken upon himself) excuses the borrower or bailee from the performance of his promise to redeliver the chattel. . . . The principle seems to us to be that, in contracts in which the performance depends on the continued existence of a given person or thing, a condition is implied that the impossibility of performance arising from the perishing of the person or thing shall excuse the performance. In none of these cases is the promise in words other than positive, nor is there any express stipulation that the destruction of the person or thing shall excuse the performance; but that excuse is by law implied, because from the nature of the contract it is apparent that the parties contracted on the basis of the continued existence of the particular person or chattel. In the present case, looking at the whole contract, we find that the parties contracted on the basis of the continued existence of the Music Hall at the time when the concerts were to be given; that being essential to their performance. We think, therefore, that the Music Hall having ceased to exist, without fault of either party, both parties are excused, the plaintiffs from taking the gardens and paying the money, the defendants from performing their promise to give the use of the Hall and Gardens and other things. Consequently the rule must be absolute to enter the verdict for the defendants. Rule absolute.

COMMENTARY

Taylor v. *Caldwell* is a case of enormous significance in the development of this area of the law. As Professor Treitel has stated (*Frustration and Force Majeure* (Sweet & Maxwell, 2nd edn, 2004), para 2-022):

> *Taylor* v. *Caldwell* is generally regarded as a turning point in this branch of the law, as the case in which the law moved away from the doctrine of absolute contracts to the modern doctrine of discharge by supervening events. This change was brought about by the familiar judicial technique of deducing a general principle from a series of particular examples. In his judgment in *Taylor* v. *Caldwell* Blackburn J relies on three . . . mitigations of the doctrine of absolute contracts . . .: cases in which death or permanent incapacity prevent performance of a contract for personal services, cases in which specific goods are sold and perish after the property in them has passed to the buyer, and cases in which the subject-matter of a bailment was destroyed without any default on the part of the bailee. From these examples, he deduces the general principle which applies where 'from the nature of the contract, it appears that the parties must . . . have known that it could not be fulfilled unless . . . some particular specified thing continued to exist'.

Taylor is another example of an English court drawing upon civilian influences in the development of the common law. The process of learning from other systems is no modern phenomenon.

The general principle to be found in *Taylor* is narrowly drawn. There are a number of elements to it. First the Music Hall was 'essential' to the performance of the contract; secondly, the Music Hall 'ceased to exist'; thirdly, its destruction was not attributable to the fault of either party; finally, the consequence of the destruction of the Music Hall was to 'excuse' both parties from their obligation to perform. In confining the principle to cases in which the subject-matter of the contract ceased to exist, Blackburn J was able to avoid a direct conflict with *Paradine* v. *Jane* (where the subject-matter of the contract had not ceased to exist). But this ground of distinction was not to last. While cases in which the subject-matter of the contract has ceased to exist may be at the core of the doctrine of frustration, the doctrine extends beyond such cases to cases in which, although the subject-matter of the contract still exists, it is either not available for use during the period of the contract or its use in the changed circumstances would be something radically different from that which was in the contemplation of the parties at the time of entry into the contract (*Jackson* v. *Union Marine Insurance Co Ltd* (1874) LR 10 CP 125).

The claim brought by the plaintiffs in *Taylor* was one to recover the expenses which they had incurred in advertising and making preparations for the concerts. Were the facts of *Taylor* to recur today the plaintiffs might attempt to recover these expenses from the defendants under the Law Reform (Frustrated Contracts) Act 1943 (see p. 904 below) but the claim would probably fail on the ground that the plaintiffs would not be able to establish that the defendants had obtained a 'valuable benefit' as a result of their work in advertising the concerts.

Finally, it is important to note that the technique used by the court was the implication of a condition into the contract in order to give effect to what was claimed to be the intention of the parties. As Professor Ibbetson has commented (*A Historical Introduction to the Law of Obligations* (Oxford University Press, 1999), p. 224) the nineteenth-century judges developed 'rules of law behind a façade of party intention'. He continues:

Thus in *Taylor* v. *Caldwell* it was held that no action would lie for the breach of an agreement to allow the plaintiffs the use of the defendants' music hall when the music hall burned to the ground before the contract fell due to be performed. The analysis of Blackburn J is revealing. Purporting to follow Roman texts to the effect that there would be no liability on a *stipulatio* to transfer property if it were accidentally destroyed before the due date of transfer, he held that no liability arose in English law either, on the grounds that there was an implied condition that the property should continue to exist; where Roman law had applied a rule, English law construed—or imposed—an intention.

While implication of a term was the original technique used by the court to justify the setting aside of the contract, modern courts no longer rely on this technique, as the next case demonstrates:

Davis Contractors Ltd v. Fareham Urban District Council

[1956] AC 696, House of Lords

Davis Contractors Ltd was a firm of building contractors. They submitted a tender to Fareham Urban District Council in relation to a building scheme at Gudgeheath Lane, Fareham. Attached to the tender was a letter dated 18 March 1946 which stated that the tender was subject to adequate supplies of labour being available as and when required. The tender was successful and Davis and Fareham entered into a contract in July 1946 under which Davis was to build seventy-eight houses for Fareham within eight months for £94,425. Without fault on the part of Davis or Fareham, adequate supplies of labour were not available and the work took twenty-two months to complete at a cost to Davis of £115,233. Fareham paid Davis the contract price. Davis claimed that they were entitled to be paid more than the contract price. They advanced their claim on two separate grounds. First, they submitted that the contract was subject to the conditions set out in their letter of 18 March so that the contract price was subject to the overriding condition that there would be an adequate supply of labour. Secondly, they submitted that the delay attributable to the shortage of labour had frustrated the contract. The House of Lords rejected both submissions. It held that the letter of 18 March had not been incorporated into the contract made in July 1946 and that the delay had not been sufficient to frustrate the contract. The extracts that follow do not deal with the incorporation point: they only deal with the doctrine of frustration.

Lord Reid

Frustration has often been said to depend on adding a term to the contract by implication. . . . I find great difficulty in accepting this as the correct approach because it seems to me hard to account for certain decisions of this House in this way. . . . I may be allowed to note an example of the artificiality of the theory of an implied term given by Lord Sands in *James Scott & Sons Ltd* v. *Del Sel* 1922 SC 592, 597:

'A tiger has escaped from a travelling menagerie. The milkgirl fails to deliver the milk. Possibly the milkman may be exonerated from any breach of contract; but, even so, it would seem hardly reasonable to base that exoneration on the ground that "tiger days excepted" must be held as if written into the milk contract.'

I think that there is much force in Lord Wright's criticism in *Denny, Mott & Dickson Ltd* v. *James B Fraser & Co Ltd* [1944] AC 265, 275:

'The parties did not anticipate fully and completely, if at all, or provide for what actually happened. It is not possible, to my mind, to say that, if they had thought of it, they would have said: "Well, if that happens, all is over between us." On the contrary, they would almost certainly on the one side or the other have sought to introduce reservations or qualifications or compensations.'

It appears to me that frustration depends, at least in most cases, not on adding any implied term, but on the true construction of the terms which are in the contract read in light of the nature of the contract and of the relevant surrounding circumstances when the contract was made.

Lord Radcliffe

Before I refer to the facts I must say briefly what I understand to be the legal principle of frustration. It is not always expressed in the same way, but I think that the points which are relevant to the decision of this case are really beyond dispute. The theory of frustration belongs to the law of contract and it is represented by a rule which the courts will apply in certain limited circumstances for the purpose of deciding that contractual obligations, ex facie binding, are no longer enforceable against the parties. The description of the circumstances that justify the application of the rule and, consequently, the decision whether in a particular case those circumstances exist are, I think, necessarily questions of law.

It has often been pointed out that the descriptions vary from one case of high authority to another. Even as long ago as 1918 Lord Sumner was able to offer an anthology of different tests directed to the factor of delay alone, and delay, though itself a frequent cause of the principle of frustration being invoked, is only one instance of the kind of circumstance to which the law attends (see *Bank Line Ltd* v. *Arthur Capel & Co* [1919] AC 435, pp. 457, 460). A full current anthology would need to be longer yet. But the variety of description is not of any importance so long as it is recognized that each is only a description and that all are intended to express the same general idea. I do not think that there has been a better expression of that general idea than the one offered by Lord Loreburn in *FA Tamplin Steamship Co Ltd* v. *Anglo-Mexican Petroleum Products Co Ltd* [1916] 2 AC 397, at pp. 403, 404. It is shorter to quote than to try to paraphrase it:

'. . . a court can and ought to examine the contract and the circumstances in which it was made, not of course to vary, but only to explain it, in order to see whether or not from the nature of it the parties must have made their bargain on the footing that a particular thing or state of things would continue to exist. And if they must have done so, then a term to that effect will be implied, though it be not expressed in the contract . . . no court has an absolving power, but it can infer from the nature of the contract and the surrounding circumstances that a condition which is not expressed was a foundation on which the parties contracted.'

So expressed, the principle of frustration, the origin of which seems to lie in the development of commercial law, is seen to be a branch of a wider principle which forms part of the English law of contract as a whole. But, in my opinion, full weight ought to be given to the requirement that the parties 'must have made' their bargain on the particular footing. Frustration is not to be lightly invoked as the dissolvent of a contract.

Lord Loreburn ascribes the dissolution to an implied term of the contract that was actually made. This approach is in line with the tendency of English courts to refer all the consequences of a contract to the will of those who made it. But there is something of a logical difficulty in seeing how the parties could even impliedly have provided for something which ex hypothesi they neither expected nor foresaw; and the ascription of frustration to an implied term of the contract has been criticized as obscuring the true action of the court which consists in applying an objective rule of the law of contract to the contractual obligations that the parties have imposed upon themselves. So long as each theory produces the same result as the other, as normally it does, it matters little which theory is avowed (see *British Movietonews Ltd* v. *London and District Cinemas Ltd* [1952] AC 166, 184 per Viscount Simon). But it may still be of some importance to recall that, if the matter is to be approached by way of implied term, the solution of any particular case is not to be found by inquiring what the parties themselves would have agreed on had they been, as they were not, forewarned. It is not merely that no one can answer that hypothetical question: it is also that the decision must be given 'irrespective of the individuals concerned, their temperaments and failings, their interest and circumstances' (*Hirji Mulji* v. *Cheong Yue Steamship Co Ltd* [1926] AC 497, 510). The legal effect of frustration 'does not depend on their intention or their opinions, or even knowledge, as to the event' (*ibid* at p. 509). On the contrary, it seems that when the event occurs

'the meaning of the contract must be taken to be, not what the parties did intend (for they had neither thought nor intention regarding it), but that which the parties, as fair and reasonable men, would presumably have agreed upon if, having such possibility in view, they had made express provision as to their several rights and liabilities in the event of its occurrence' (*Dahl* v. *Nelson* (1881) 6 App Cas 38 at p. 59, per Lord Watson).

By this time it might seem that the parties themselves have become so far disembodied spirits that their actual persons should be allowed to rest in peace. In their place there rises the figure of the fair and reasonable man. And the spokesman of the fair and reasonable man, who represents after all no more than the anthropomorphic conception of justice, is and must be the court itself. So perhaps it would be simpler to say at the outset that frustration occurs whenever the law recognizes that without default of either party a contractual obligation has become incapable of being performed because the circumstances in which performance is called for would render it a thing radically different from that which was undertaken by the contract. Non haec in foedera veni. It was not this that I promised to do.

There is, however, no uncertainty as to the materials upon which the court must proceed. 'The data for decision are, on the one hand, the terms and construction of the contract, read in the light of the then existing circumstances, and on the other hand the events which have occurred' (*Denny, Mott & Dickson Ltd* v. *James B Fraser & Co Ltd* [1944] AC 265, 274, 275 per Lord Wright). In the nature of things there is often no room for any elaborate inquiry. The court must act upon a general impression of what its rule requires. It is for that reason that special importance is necessarily attached to the occurrence of any unexpected event that, as it were, changes the face of things. But, even so, it is not hardship or inconvenience or material loss itself which calls the principle of frustration into play. There must be as well such a change in the significance of the obligation that the thing undertaken would, if performed, be a different thing from that contracted for.

I am bound to say that, if this is the law, the appellants' case seems to me a long way from a case of frustration. Here is a building contract entered into by a housing authority and a big firm of contractors in all the uncertainties of the post-war world. Work was begun shortly before the formal contract was executed and continued, with impediments and minor stoppages but without actual interruption, until the 78 houses contracted for had all been built. After the work had been in progress for a time the appellants raised the claim, which they repeated more than once, that they ought to be paid a larger sum for their work than the contract allowed; but the respondents refused to admit the claim and, so far as appears, no conclusive action was taken by either side which would make the conduct of one or the other a determining element in the case.

That is not in any obvious sense a frustrated contract . . .

Two things seem to me to prevent the application of the principle of frustration to this case. One is that the cause of the delay was not any new state of things which the parties could not reasonably be thought to have foreseen. On the contrary, the possibility of enough labour and materials not being available was before their eyes and could have been the subject of special contractual stipulation. It was not made so. The other thing is that, though timely completion was no doubt important to both sides, it is not right to treat the possibility of delay as having the same significance for each. The owner draws up his conditions in detail, specifies the time within which he requires completion, protects himself both by a penalty clause for time exceeded and by calling for the deposit of a guarantee bond and offers a certain measure of security to a contractor by his escalator clause with regard to wages and prices. In the light of these conditions the contractor makes his tender, and the tender must necessarily take into account the margin of profit that he hopes to obtain upon his adventure and in that any appropriate allowance for the obvious risks of delay. To my mind, it is useless to pretend that the contractor is not at risk if delay does occur, even serious delay. And I think it a misuse of legal terms to call in frustration to get him out of his unfortunate predicament.

Viscount Simonds, Lord Morton of Henryton, and **Lord Somervell of Harrow** delivered concurring opinions.

COMMENTARY

Davis is a case of alleged commercial impracticability rather than impossibility. It was clearly not impossible for Davis to carry out their contractual obligations. Indeed, they did carry them out and had been paid the contract price for so doing. Their submission was, in essence, that it was not fair to hold them to the contract price in these changed circumstances. Some jurisdictions in the world, such as the USA, recognize the existence of a doctrine of commercial impracticability. *Davis* can be interpreted as a case that is hostile to the existence of such a doctrine. But this may be to go too far. As Professor Treitel points out (*Frustration and Force Majeure* (Sweet & Maxwell, 2nd edn, 2004), para 6-025):

The case may be indicative of the English attitude towards 'impracticability' but it does not reveal any actual difference between the English and the American approaches; for in an almost contemporaneous similar American case the court reached the same result and did so for similar reasons. Moreover, the percentage by which costs had increased in the *Davis Contractors* case was relatively low: it amounted to less than 23 per cent. of the contract price and such an increase would not have come even close to bringing the American doctrine of discharge by impracticability into play.

Secondly, it is worth noting that the contractors in *Davis* did attempt to make provision for the consequences of a possible shortage of labour but failed to ensure that the term was incorporated into the contract. This demonstrates the importance not only of drafting an appropriate clause to deal with the impact of events which may make performance more onerous or difficult but also of ensuring that that term is incorporated into the contract (see further p. 352 above). The fact that labour shortages had been in the contemplation of the parties at the time of entry into the contract also made it more difficult for the contractors to argue that a shortage of labour frustrated the contract (on the significance of foreseeability, see p. 880 below).

Thirdly, it should be noted that this was a contract which had been performed according to its terms in that the contractors had done the work and the employers had paid the contract price. The reason for the reliance by the contractors on the doctrine of frustration was that it was necessary for them to set aside the original contract if they were to succeed in their aim of recovering a sum in excess of the contract price. But their attempt failed. Here one can see how frustration can be invoked by a party who wishes to escape from what has turned out to be a bad bargain. The House of Lords were, however, alert to this danger and they refused to invoke the doctrine of frustration for the purpose of enabling the contractors to escape from their original bargain.

Two final points should be noted about *Davis* and they can be taken together. The first is that the judgments demonstrate a reluctance to invoke the doctrine of frustration. Thus Lord Radcliffe stated that it was not mere hardship which caused the doctrine to be applicable and that frustration was not lightly to be invoked as the dissolvent of a contract. The second point is that the House of Lords rejected the implied term theory of frustration which had found favour with the court in *Taylor* v. *Caldwell* (p. 869 above). It was, in the view of both Lord Reid and Lord Radcliffe, unrealistic to impute the existence of the doctrine to the intention of the parties. Instead, the emphasis was placed upon the construction of the contract and whether 'the thing undertaken would, if performed, be a different thing from that contracted for'. This obviously requires the court to carry out a comparative exercise. The court must first ascertain what it is that the contract requires of the parties and then it must compare the performance in the changed circumstances with that originally undertaken. It is only in the case where there is a radical difference between the two that the doctrine of frustration comes into play.

One consequence of this narrow approach to the doctrine of frustration is that it has become a doctrine of limited practical significance. This is so for a number of reasons. First, it does not apply where express provision has been made in the contract for the event that is alleged to have frustrated the contract (see section 3). Given that force majeure and hardship clauses seek to regulate events which may impede or hinder performance of the contract, the impact of such events is more likely to be regulated by the terms of the force majeure clause or the hardship clause than by the doctrine of frustration. Secondly, the doctrine does not apply where the event alleged to have frustrated the contract was foreseeable (section 4). Thirdly, a contracting party cannot invoke the doctrine of frustration where the alleged frustrating event was caused by his own conduct rather than a supervening event (section 5). Fourthly, the courts have adopted a restrictive approach to the operation of the doctrine in order to avoid it becoming an escape route for a party who has entered into a bad bargain (section 6). As Lord Roskill once put it, the doctrine of frustration is 'not lightly to be invoked to relieve contracting parties of the normal consequences of imprudent bargains' (*The Nema* [1982] AC 724, 752). Finally, the consequences of the application of the doctrine are drastic in that it brings the contract automatically to an end, irrespective of the wishes of the parties (section 7). The Draconian consequences of the application of the doctrine inhibit its wider use.

3. CONSTRUCTION OF THE CONTRACT

The starting point in any case in which it is alleged that the contract has been frustrated must be the terms of the contract itself. This is so for two reasons. The first is that it is necessary to ascertain the extent of the obligations undertaken in the contract in order to decide whether performance in the changed circumstances is something radically different from the obligation initially assumed. The second reason is a rather different one and that is to ascertain whether or not the contract makes provision for the events which have occurred. If the contract does make provision for that event then it is the contract that will regulate the impact that the event will have on the obligations contained in the contract and not the doctrine of frustration. Many modern contracts are drafted in elaborate terms and the likelihood that the contract will make provision for the events which have occurred is rather high. This is particularly so where the contract contains a force majeure clause (see p. 434 above) or a hardship clause (see p. 439 above). In *J. Lauritzen AS* v. *Wijsmuller BV (The 'Super Servant Two')* [1990] 1 Lloyd's Rep 1 (p. 885 below) one of the events listed in the force majeure clause was 'the closure of the Suez or Panama Canal'. Suppose that performance of the contract became more onerous for one party as a result of the closure of the Suez Canal. Such an event could not frustrate the contract because the contract itself has made provision for the closure of the Suez Canal and, this being the case, it is the contract that regulates the consequences of the closure of the Suez Canal and not the doctrine of frustration.

Yet it is unlikely that the presence of a force majeure clause will suffice of itself to exclude any possibility of reliance upon the doctrine of frustration (although in *Bremer Handelsgesellschaft mbH* v. *Vanden Avenne-Izegem PVBA* [1977] 1 Lloyd's Rep 133, 163 Mocatta J thought that there was 'much to be said' for the submission that 'there was no room for the doctrine of frustration to apply' as a result of the elaborate force majeure clauses to be found in the contract). While a force majeure clause (or a hardship clause) does not suffice of itself to shut out the doctrine of frustration, the clause may be relied upon for the purpose of showing that the parties have made express provision for the event that has occurred. And, where the parties have made such provision, the contract cannot be frustrated (except in the case of subsequent illegality, p. 895 below, where overriding considerations of public policy prevent effect being given to the terms of the contract: see *Ertel Bieber and Co* v. *Rio Tinto Co Ltd* [1918] AC 260). Why does the presence of a force majeure clause not have the automatic effect of excluding the operation of the doctrine of frustration? The answer is that a force majeure clause is primarily intended to cover events which are capable of resolution within a relatively short time-frame and a court is therefore likely to conclude that it does not, as a matter of construction, extend to catastrophic events which render further performance obviously impossible.

An example is provided by *Metropolitan Water Board* v. *Dick Kerr and Co* [1918] AC 119. Contractors agreed in 1914 to construct a reservoir to be completed within six years. In 1916 the contractors were required by Government Order to stop the work and sell their plant. In these circumstances the contractors claimed that the contract had been frustrated. The Water Board denied that the contract had been frustrated and, for this purpose, placed reliance on condition 32 of the contract which, after setting out the obligations of the contractors, continued:

Provided always that if by reason of any additional works or enlargements of the works (which additions or enlargements the engineer is hereby authorised to make), or for any other just cause arising with the Board or with the engineer, or in consequence of any unusual inclemency of the weather, or general or local strikes, or combination of workmen, or for want or deficiency of any orders, drawings or directions, or by reason of any difficulties, impediments, obstructions, oppositions, doubts, disputes, or differences, whatsoever and howsoever occasioned, the contractor shall, in the opinion of the engineer (whose decision shall be final), have been unduly delayed or impeded in the completion of this contract, it shall be lawful for the engineer, if he shall so think fit, to grant from time to time, and at any time or times by writing under his hand, such extension of time either prospectively or retrospectively, and to assign such other day or days for or as for completion, as to him may seem reasonable, without thereby prejudicing or in any manner affecting the validity of the contract, or the adequacy of the contract price, or the adequacy of the sums or prices mentioned in the third schedule; and any and every such extension of time shall be deemed to be in full compensation and satisfaction for, and in respect of, any and every actual or probable loss or injury sustained or sustainable by the contractor in the premises, and shall in like manner exonerate him from any claim or demand on the part of the Board, for and in respect of the delay occasioned by the cause or causes in respect of which any and every such extension of time shall have been granted, but no further or otherwise, nor for or in respect of any delay continued beyond the time mentioned in such writing or writings respectively.

The Water Board pointed out that this condition applied to delay 'whatsoever and howsoever occasioned' and they submitted that the events which had occurred were regulated by condition 32 and not by the doctrine of frustration. The House of Lords rejected this submission and held that the contract had been frustrated. Lord Finlay LC stated (at pp. 125–126):

It is admitted that the prosecution of the works became illegal in consequence of the action of the Minister of Munitions. It became illegal on February 21, 1916, and remains illegal at the present time. This is not a case of a short and temporary stoppage, but of a prohibition in consequence of war, which has already been in force for the greater part of two years, and will, according to all appearances, last as long as the war itself, as it was the result of the necessity of preventing the diversion to civil purposes of labour and material required for purposes immediately connected with the war. Condition 32 provides for cases in which the contractor has, in the opinion of the engineer, been unduly delayed or impeded in the completion of his contract by any of the causes therein enumerated or by any other causes, so that an extension of time was reasonable. Condition 32 does not cover the case in which the interruption is of such a character and duration that it vitally and fundamentally changes the conditions of the contract, and could not possibly have been in the contemplation of the parties to the contract when it was made.

Thus the magnitude of the event was such that it took it outside the scope of the clause, notwithstanding the use of the words 'whatsoever and howsoever occasioned'. On the same reasoning, a force majeure clause which includes in the list of force majeure events 'strikes' and 'wars' may be held, as a matter of interpretation, not to cover a protracted national strike, such as a general strike, or a war of the magnitude of the first or second world war (see *Fibrosa Spolka Akcyjna* v. *Fairbairn Lawson Combe Barbour Ltd* [1943] AC 32, 40–41). Such catastrophic events are, however, comparatively rare. Most of the events that occur will fall within the scope of an appropriately drafted force majeure or hardship clause. As contracts make provision for the occurrence of a greater range of events, so the scope for the application of the doctrine of frustration diminishes. In most cases the inquiry will start and finish with the terms of the contract itself.

4. FORESEEABLE EVENTS

A further factor which limits the operation of the doctrine of frustration is the general rule that an event which was foreseeable, and therefore within the contemplation of the parties at the time of entry into the contact, does not operate to frustrate a contract. A frustrating event is one that was not foreseen and was not foreseeable by the parties. The difficulty with this formula is the obvious one, namely identifying what is and what is not foreseeable at the moment of entry into the contract. Events such as wars and earthquakes are foreseeable in the sense that we are all aware that they may take place. But in some parts of the world they are more foreseeable than in others. Take earthquakes as an example: some parts of the world are at greater risk of earthquakes than others. How foreseeable does the event have to be before it prevents reliance being placed upon the doctrine of frustration? This is a difficult question to answer because it is a question of degree. The issue was considered by the Court of Appeal in the following case:

Ocean Tramp Tankers Corporation v. V/O Sovfracht, The Eugenia

[1964] 2 QB 226, Court of Appeal

On 8 September 1956 the defendants chartered the vessel the *Eugenia* for a 'trip out to India via the Black Sea'. At the time at which they entered into the agreement both parties were aware of the possibility that the Suez Canal might be closed as a result of the build up of military activity in the area. The parties were unable to reach agreement on a clause to deal with the possibility of the Canal being closed and so the contract was silent on the point. A war clause in the contract prohibited the charterers from sailing into a zone which was 'dangerous as the result of any actual or threatened act of war' etc. The vessel arrived at Port Said at a time when Egyptian anti-aircraft guns were firing and the zone was a 'dangerous' one within the meaning of the war clause. Notwithstanding this, the vessel proceeded to enter the Suez Canal on 31 October 1956 where she became trapped and was not released until January 1957. On 4 January 1957 the charterers claimed that the charterparty had been frustrated by the events which had occurred. The owners denied that the contract had been frustrated and brought a claim for damages for breach of contract against the charterers. Their claim succeeded. It was held that the defendants were in breach of the war clause in entering the Suez Canal and that the effect of the closure of the Suez Canal had not been to frustrate the contract between the parties.

Lord Denning MR

The second question is whether the charterparty was frustrated by what took place. The arbitrator has held it was not. The judge has held that it was. Which is right? One thing that is obvious is that the charterers cannot rely on the fact that the *Eugenia* was trapped in the canal; for that was their own fault. They were in breach of the war clause in entering it. They cannot rely on a self-induced frustration, see *Maritime National Fish Ltd v. Ocean Trawlers Ltd* [1935] AC 524. But they seek to rely on the fact that the canal itself was blocked. They assert that even if the *Eugenia* had never gone into the canal, but had stayed outside (in which case she would not have been in breach of the war clause), nevertheless she would still have had to go round by the Cape. And that, they say, brings about a frustration, for it makes the venture fundamentally different from what they contracted for. The judge has accepted this view. He has held that on November 16, 1956, the charterparty was frustrated. The reason for taking November 16, 1956, was this: before November 16, 1956, mercantile men (even if she had stayed outside) would not have formed any conclusion as to whether the obstructions in the canal were other than temporary. There was insufficient information available to form a judgment. On November 16, 1956, mercantile men would conclude that the blockage of the southern end would last till March or April, 1957; so that by that time it would be clear that the only thing to do (if the ship had never entered the canal) would be to go round the Cape. The judge said: 'I hold that the adventure, involving a voyage round the Cape, is basically or fundamentally different from the adventure involving a voyage via the Suez Canal'. So he held the contract frustrated. He was comforted to find in *The Massalia*, [1961] 2 QB 278 Pearson J came to a similar conclusion.

This means that once again we have had to consider the authorities on this vexed topic of frustration. But I think the position is now reasonably clear. It is simply this: if it should happen, in the course of carrying out a contract, that a fundamentally different situation arises for which the parties made no provision—so much so that it would not be just in the new situation to hold them bound to its terms—then the contract is at an end. It was originally said that the doctrine of frustration was based on an implied term. In short, that the parties, if they had foreseen the new situation, would have said to one another: 'If that happens, of course, it is all over between us'. But the theory of an implied term has now been discarded by everyone, or nearly everyone, for the simple reason that it does not represent the truth. The parties would not have said: 'It is all over between us'. They would have differed about what was to happen. Each would have sought to insert reservations or qualifications of one kind or another. Take this very case. The parties realised that the canal might become impassable. They tried to agree on a clause to provide for the contingency. But they failed to agree. So there is no room for an implied term.

It has frequently been said that the doctrine of frustration only applies when the new situation is 'unforeseen' or 'unexpected' or 'uncontemplated', as if that were an essential feature. But it is not so. The only thing that is essential is that the parties should have made no provision for it in their contract. The only relevance of it being 'unforeseen' is this: If the parties did not foresee anything of the kind happening, you can readily infer they have made no provision for it: whereas, if they did foresee it, you would expect them to make provision for it. But cases have occurred where the parties have foreseen the danger ahead, and yet made no provision for it in the contract. Such was the case in the Spanish Civil War when a ship was let on charter to the republican government. The purpose was to evacuate refugees. The parties foresaw that she might be seized by the nationalists. But they made no provision for it in their contract. Yet, when she was seized, the contract was frustrated, see *WJ Tatem Ltd* v. *Gamboa* [1939] 1 KB 132. So here the parties foresaw that the canal might become impassable: it was the very thing they feared. But they made no provision for it. So there is room for the doctrine to apply if it be a proper case for it.

We are thus left with the simple test that a situation must arise which renders performance of the contract 'a thing radically different from that which was undertaken by the contract', see *Davis Contractors Ltd* v. *Fareham Urban District Council* [1956] AC 696, 729 by Lord Radcliffe. To see if the doctrine applies, you have first to construe the contract and see whether the parties have themselves provided for the situation that has arisen. If they have provided for it, the contract must govern. There is no frustration. If they have not provided for it, then you have to compare the new situation with the situation for which they did provide. Then you must see how different it is. The fact that it has become more onerous or more expensive for one party than he thought is not sufficient to bring about a frustration. It must be more than merely more onerous or more expensive. It must be positively unjust to hold the parties bound. It is often difficult to draw the line. But it must be done. And it is for the courts to do it as a matter of law: see *Tsakiroglou & Co Ltd* v. *Noblee Thorl GmbH* [1962] AC 93, 116, 119 by Lord Simonds and by Lord Reid.

Applying these principles to this case, I have come to the conclusion that the blockage of the canal did not bring about a 'fundamentally different situation' such as to frustrate the venture. My reasons are these: (1) The venture was the whole trip from delivery at Genoa, out to the Black Sea, there load cargo, thence to India, unload cargo, and redelivery. The time for this vessel from Odessa to Vizagapatam via the Suez Canal would be 26 days, and via the Cape, 56 days. But that is not the right comparison. You have to take the whole venture from delivery at Genoa to redelivery at Madras. We were told that the time for the whole venture via the Suez Canal would be 108 days and via the Cape 138 days. The difference over the whole voyage is not so radical as to produce a frustration. (2) The cargo was iron and steel goods which would not be adversely affected by the longer voyage, and there was no special reason for early arrival. The vessel and crew were at all times fit and sufficient to proceed via the Cape. (3) The cargo was loaded on board at the time of the blockage of the canal. If the contract was frustrated, it would mean, I suppose, that the ship could throw up the charter and unload the cargo wherever she was, without any breach of contract. (4) The voyage round the Cape made no great difference except that it took a good deal longer and was more expensive for the charterers than a voyage through the canal.

The only hesitation I have had about this case is because of the views expressed by Pearson J in *The Massalia* [1961] 2 QB 278. That case can be distingushed because there was a sentence in the charter which read 'Captain also to telegraph to "Maritsider Genoa" on passing Suez Canal'. Pearson J held that that meant there was actually an obligation to pass the Suez Canal, and hence the contract was frustrated by impossibility. I think he attached too much significance to the clause. I think that there, as here, there was no obligation to go through the Suez Canal, but only to go by the route which was customary at the time of performance; and that there is no legitimate distinction to be drawn between that case and this. That was a voyage charter and this a time charter. That makes no difference except that the burden fell on the owners and not the charterers. Pearson J held that the route via the Cape was fundamentally different from the route via the Suez Canal and that the charter was frustrated on that ground also. I am afraid I cannot take that view. It is important to notice also that since that case the House of Lords have held that, with goods sold c.i.f. Sudan to Hamburg, the contract of sale was not frustrated by the closure of the Suez Canal, see *Tsakiroglou & Co Ltd* v. *Noblee Thorl GmbH* [1962] AC 93. I know that a contract of affreightment is different from a contract for the sale of goods, but I should find it strange if, in the case of a ship loaded with cargo, the contract of affreightment was frustrated by the closure of the canal and the contract of sale was not frustrated. It would lead to endless complications.

I come, therefore, to the conclusion that the decision of Pearson J in *The Massalia* [1961] 2 QB 278 was wrong and should be overruled. It is to be noticed that both in that case and in this the arbitrators held there was no frustration. I think they were right. I would allow this appeal and hold that the contract was not frustrated.

Donovan LJ delivered a concurring judgment. **Danckwerts LJ** concurred.

COMMENTARY

The difficulty with this decision lies in Lord Denning's rejection of the proposition that the doctrine of frustration applies only to events which are 'unforeseen', 'unexpected', or 'uncontemplated'. In his view, the test to be applied is whether or not provision has been made for the event which has occurred and the foreseeability of the event is merely a factor to be taken into account when deciding whether or not one would expect parties to make provision for the event which has occurred. Professor Treitel (*Frustration and Force Majeure* (Sweet & Maxwell, 2nd edn, 2004), para 13-014) has criticized this aspect of Lord Denning's judgment on the following ground:

these remarks are *obiter* and it is respectfully submitted that this aspect of the decision can be explained on other grounds. At the time of contracting, the risk of the Canal's being closed for a *very considerable time* was not foreseen; nor was it foreseeable on the high standard of foreseeability required to exclude frustration. To the extent that the parties did foresee the risk, they seem to have allocated it by the terms of the charterparty. This took the form of a 'time charter trip', which provided that the voyage was to be paid for by the time it took, and so indicated an intention to throw the risk of delay on the charterers. There seems to be no reason why the court should, by applying the doctrine of frustration to foreseen events, reverse such an allocation of risks deliberately made by the contracting parties.

The result in *The Eugenia* seems to be correct but the reasoning is suspect. There is authority to support the proposition that a contract is not frustrated when the event which has occurred is a foreseeable one (see, for example, *Walton Harvey Ltd* v. *Walker & Homfrays Ltd* [1931] 1 Ch 274). Much is likely to turn on the meaning of 'foreseeability' in this context. Professor Treitel has suggested that foreseeability is relevant to the question whether or not a party has assumed the risk of the occurrence of the event in question. Thus he states (*Frustration and Force Majeure* (Sweet & Maxwell, 2nd edn, 2004), para 13-012) that:

'Foreseeability' will support the inference of risk-assumption only where the supervening event is one which any person of ordinary intelligence would regard as likely to occur, or . . . the contingency must be 'one which the parties could reasonably be thought to have foreseen as a real possibility'. The distinction is between cases in which parties can reasonably be expected to foresee the occurrence of the event as no more than a possibility, and those in which they can be so expected to foresee it as a real likelihood. The inference of risk assumption will be drawn only in cases of the latter kind; and even then it may be displaced by [other factors].

A second point worth noting about *The Eugenia* is the conclusion that the closure of the Suez Canal did not result in the frustration of the contract between the parties. Those responsible for the drafting of force majeure clauses have taken notice of this fact and it is now common practice to include the closure of the Suez Canal in the list of events that trigger the operation of a force majeure clause.

5. SELF-INDUCED FRUSTRATION

The doctrine of self-induced frustration has been described in *Chitty on Contracts* (29th edn, Sweet & Maxwell, 2004, para 23-059) in the following terms:

'The essence of frustration is that it should not be due to the act or election of the party seeking to rely on it'. Thus, a contracting party cannot rely on 'self-induced frustration, that is, on frustration due to his own conduct or to the conduct of those for whom he is responsible'. Although the concept of self-induced frustration is clearly established as a matter of general principle, the precise limits of the doctrine have not been clearly established. It is merely a 'label' which has been used to describe 'those situations where one party has been held by the Courts not to be entitled to treat himself as discharged from his contractual obligations'. Thus frustration has been held to be 'self-induced' where the alleged frustrating event was caused by a breach, or anticipatory breach of contract by the party claiming that the contract has been frustrated, where an act of the party claiming that the contract has been frustrated broke the chain of causation between the alleged frustrating event and the event which made performance of the contract impossible, and where the alleged frustrating event was not a supervening event or 'something altogether outside the control of the parties'. A party who has been at fault or whose act was deliberate will generally be unable to invoke frustration because of the difficulty which such a party will inevitably face in showing the existence of a supervening event which is outside his control.

The leading modern case on self-induced frustration is the decision of the Court of Appeal in *J Lauritzen AS* v. *Wijsmuller BV (The 'Super Servant Two')* [1990] 1 Lloyd's Rep 1. The case is an important one for three reasons. First, it demonstrates the width of the doctrine of self-induced frustration; second, the judgment of Bingham LJ contains a modern definition of the doctrine of frustration; and third, it demonstrates the crucial role played by force majeure clauses in commercial contracts today.

J Lauritzen AS v. Wijsmuller BV (The 'Super Servant Two')

[1990] 1 Lloyd's Rep 1, Court of Appeal

The defendants, Wijsmuller, agreed to carry the plaintiffs' drilling rig from Japan to Rotterdam. The contract, dated 7 July 1980, provided that the rig would be delivered between 20 June and 20 August 1981 and that it would be carried using either *Super Servant One* or *Super Servant Two* at Wijsmuller's option. Both of these vessels were large, self-propelled, semi-submersible barges built for carrying large loads such as the rig. Clause 17 of the contract (which is set out in full in the judgment of Bingham LJ) gave Wijsmuller the right to cancel the contract in the event of force majeure or any other circumstance which reasonably prevented the performance of the contract. The defendants claimed that by November 1980 they had made an internal decision, which they admitted was not irrevocable, to schedule *Super Servant Two* to transport the plaintiffs' rig and to allocate *Super Servant One* to the performance of other concluded contracts. On 29 January 1981 *Super Servant Two* sank while transporting another rig. On 16 February 1981 Wijsmuller told Lauritzen that it could not carry the rig using either *Super Servant One* or *Super Servant Two*. It could not use *Super Servant One* because it was required for the performance of other contracts and it could not use *Super Servant Two* because it had sunk. The plaintiffs alleged that the defendants' failure to transport the rig in the agreed manner was a breach of contract so that the defendants were liable for the additional costs that had been incurred in transporting the rig by another method. The defendants pleaded that the contract had been frustrated and they also relied on clause 17 as a defence to the claim brought by the plaintiffs.

Four issues were ordered to be tried, namely:

1. whether the defendants were entitled to cancel the contract under clause 17

(a) If the loss of the *Super Servant Two* occurred without the negligence of the Defendants, their servants or agents.

(b) If the loss of the *Super Servant Two* was caused by the negligence of the Defendants, their servants or agents.

2. whether the contract was frustrated

(a) If the loss of the *Super Servant Two* occurred without the negligence of the Defendants, their servants or agents.

(b) If the loss of the *Super Servant Two* was caused by the negligence of the Defendants, their servants or agents.

Mr Justice Hobhouse answered 'yes' to question 1(a) and 'no' to questions 1(b), 2(a) and

2(b). The defendants appealed to the Court of Appeal against the conclusion of Hobhouse J in relation to questions 1(b), 2(a) and 2(b). The Court of Appeal dismissed the appeal. Consequently the defendants were unable to invoke the doctrine of frustration and were only able to rely on clause 17 if the loss of *Super Servant Two* occurred without the negligence of the defendants.

Bingham LJ

The contract of carriage was expressly governed by English law and not many of its terms are germane to these preliminary issues. Clause 15, on which argument was founded, was in these terms:

15.   *Duty of care*

Subject to any provisions in this Contract Wijsmuller hereby agrees to do everything that a good carrier may reasonably be expected to do in order to reach the port of discharge in time and safely.

Clause 16 is of some importance and read:

16.   *Liability*

16.1.   The Principal agrees that transportation to the actual location of loading, stowage, lashing, securing, carriage, unlashing and discharge of the Cargo and the transportation to the actual location of redelivery are entirely at the Principal's risk and that in no circumstances whatsoever Wijsmuller, its employees and/or agents and/or subcontractors and/or servants and/or agents of such subcontractors shall be liable for any loss (direct or consequential) or damage to the Cargo howsoever caused unless caused by the deliberate act or omission of Wijsmuller.

16.2   The Principal will be liable for all loss and damage whatsoever sustained by any third party caused by or contributed to by the Cargo, and the Principal undertakes to indemnify Wijsmuller, its employees and/or agent and/or subcontractors and/or servants and/or agents of such subcontractors against any claims (including interest and legal costs) made against Wijsmuller, its employees and/or agents or subcontractors and/or servants and/or agents of such subcontractors by any third party in respect of such loss or damage save in the event that such loss or damage to the third party is caused by or results from the deliberate act or omission of Wijsmuller.

Clause 17 was the subject of two issues argued before the Judge, one of which remains in contention on appeal. I should recite its full terms:

17.   *Cancellation*

17.1.   Wijsmuller has the right to cancel its performance under this Contract whether the loading has been completed or not, in the event of force majeur(sic), Acts of God, perils or danger and accidents of the sea, acts of war, warlike-operations, acts of public enemies, restraint of princes, rulers or people or seizure under legal process, quarantine restrictions, civil commotions, blockade, strikes, lockout, closure of the Suez or Panama Canal, congestion of harbours or any other circumstances whatsoever, causing extraordinary periods of delay and similar events and/or circumstances, abnormal increases in prices and wages, scarcity of fuel and similar events, which reasonably may impede, prevent or delay the performance of this contract.

17.2.   In the event that Wijsmuller has the right to terminate its performance under this Contract under this clause or clause 4, and the voyage has begun, Wijsmuller shall tender redelivery of the Cargo at a convenient port or place to be determined after consultation with the Principal and when uncontactable to be determined after consultation with the authorised representative of the Principal on board the Transportation Unit, and such delivery shall constitute good delivery under the terms of this Contract.

If Wijsmuller exercises its right under this clause, all payments due to Wijsmuller under the terms of this Contract will be deemed earned by Wijsmuller and the last instalment of the Contract sum as more specifically described in the Conditions of Particular Application of this contract will be reduced or increased pro rata to the distance actually sailed or to be sailed to such convenient port or place and the distance in the normal course of the voyage i.e. between the port or place of delivery and the stated port or place of redelivery of the Cargo.

Clause 4 gave Wijsmuller a right to terminate the contract at a port of refuge which the state or condition of the cargo made it necessary to enter.

[he set out the facts of the case and the four issues ordered to be tried and continued]

Question 1(b)

The learned Judge answered question 1(a) in favour of Wijsmuller because he rejected Lauritzen's argument that cl. 17 did not apply before arrival of the carrying vessel at the loading site. It was not disputed that the loss of Super Servant Two was capable of being a circumstance which might reasonably impede or delay the performance of the contract within the meaning of cl. 17. The question for decision is whether, on a proper construction of cl. 17 read in the context of the contract as a whole and of relevant background circumstances, Wijsmuller were entitled to cancel the contract under cl. 17 if the loss of Super Servant Two was caused by their (or their servants' or agents') negligence before the time for performance had arrived. It was common ground that the Court's task is to elicit the parties' intentions from the contract they made according to familiar principles of construction . . .

[he concluded that the expression 'perils or dangers and accidents of the sea' could not be read alone but had to be read as part of the contract as a whole. He stated that, although clause 17 did not attempt to exclude liability for negligence, it conferred upon the defendants a 'right exercisable in a very wide range of circumstances to nullify the contractual bargain made between the parties at no cost to [the defendants] and regardless of the loss' to the plaintiffs. Therefore he concluded that the 'broad approach' adopted by the Privy Council in *Canada Steamship* v. *The King* [1952] AC 192 was applicable to the construction of clause 17. Applying the three rules of construction derived from *Canada Steamship* (on which see pp. 449–457 above) Bingham LJ held that clause 17.1 did not expressly cover negligence on the part of the defendants. At the second stage he held that clause 17 was wide enough on its ordinary construction to cover negligence on the part of the defendants. But at the third stage he held that clause 17 was not 'deprived of a sensible application' if it was confined to events which were not brought about by the negligence of the defendants, their employees, or agents. Almost all of the events listed in clause 17 were events which were beyond the direct or indirect control of the defendants. This being the case, clause 17 did not provide the defendants with protection in the event that *Super Servant Two* sank as a result of the negligence of the defendants.]

Question 2: general

The argument in this case raises important issues on the English law of frustration. Before turning to the specific questions I think it helpful to summarize the established law so far as relevant to this case.

The classical statement of the modern law is that of Lord Radcliffe in *Davis Contractors Ltd* v. *Fareham Urban District Council* [1956] AC 696 at p. 729.

'. . . frustration occurs whenever the law recognises that without default of either party a contractual obligation has become incapable of being performed because the circumstances in which performance is called for would render it a thing radically different from that which was undertaken by the contract. Non haec in foedera veni. It was not this that I promised to do.'

As Lord Reid observed in the same case (at p. 721):

'. . . there is no need to consider what the parties thought or how they or reasonable men in their shoes would have dealt with the new situation if they had foreseen it. The question is whether the contract which they did make is, on its true construction, wide enough to apply to the new situation: if it is not, then it is at an end.'

Certain propositions, established by the highest authority, are not open to question:

1. The doctrine of frustration was evolved to mitigate the rigour of the common law's insistence on literal performance of absolute promises (*Hirji Mulji v. Cheong Yue Steamship Co Ltd (sub. nom. Dharsi Nanji v. Cheong Yue Steamship Co Ltd)* [1926] AC 497 at p. 510; *Denny Mott and Dickson Ltd* v. *James B Fraser & Co Ltd* [1944] AC 265 at p. 275; *Joseph Constantine Steamship Line Ltd* v. *Imperial Smelting Corporation Ltd* [1942] AC 154 at p. 171). The object of the doctrine was to give effect to the demands of justice, to achieve a just and reasonable result, to do what is reasonable and fair, as an expedient to escape from injustice where such would result from enforcement of a contract in its literal terms after a significant change in circumstances (*Hirji Mulji* sup., at p. 510; *Joseph Constantine Steamship Line Ltd* (sup.), at pp. 183, 193; *National Carriers Ltd* v. *Panalpina (Northern) Ltd* [1981] AC 675 at p. 701).

2. Since the effect of frustration is to kill the contract and discharge the parties from further liability under it, the doctrine is not to be lightly invoked, must be kept within very narrow limits and ought not to be extended (*Bank Line Ltd* v. *Arthur Capel & Co* [1919] AC 435 at p. 459; *Davis Contractors Ltd* sup., at pp. 715, 727; *Pioneer Shipping Ltd* v. *BTP Tioxide Ltd (The Nema)* [1982] AC 724 at 752).

3. Frustration brings the contract to an end forthwith, without more and automatically (*Hirji Mulji*, sup. at pp. 505, 509; *Maritime National Fish Ltd* v. *Ocean Trawlers Ltd* [1935] AC 524 at p. 527; *Joseph Constantine Steamship Line Ltd* sup., at pp. 163, 170, 171, 187, 200; *Denny Mott and Dickson Ltd* sup. at p. 274).

4. The essence of frustration is that it should not be due to the act or election of the party seeking to rely on it (*Hirji Mulji*, sup., at p. 510; *Maritime National Fish Ltd* sup. at p. 530; *Joseph Constantine Steamship Ltd* sup. at p. 170; *Denny Mott and Dickson Ltd*

sup., at p. 274; *Davis Contractors Ltd* sup., at p. 728. A frustrating event must be some outside event or extraneous change of situation (*Paal Wilson & Co A/S v. Partenreederi Hannah Blumenthal (The Hannah Blumenthal)* [1983] 1 AC 854 at p. 909).

5.   A frustrating event must take place without blame or fault on the side of the party seeking to rely on it (*Bank Line Ltd* sup., at 452; *Joseph Constantine Steamship Ltd* sup. p. 171; *Davis Contractors Ltd* sup., at p. 729; *The Hannah Blumenthal* [1983] 1 AC 854 at pp. 882, 909).

Question 2(a)

Mr Clarke for Wijsmuller submitted that the extraneous supervening event necessary to found a plea of frustration occurred when Super Servant Two sank on Jan. 29, 1981. The Dan King contract was not, however, thereupon frustrated but remained alive until Wijsmuller decided a fortnight later that that contract could not be, or would not be, performed. There was, he submitted, factually, no break in the chain of causation between the supervening event and the non-performance of the contract. He acknowledged that *Maritime National Fish Ltd* sup., contained observations on their face inimical to his argument, but distinguished that as a decision on causation confined to its own peculiar facts and laying down no general rule. For authoritative support Mr Clarke relied on cases dealing with the application of force majeure clauses in commodity contracts, and in particular on an unreported judgment of Mr Justice Robert Goff, as he then was, adopted with approval by the Court of Appeal in *Bremer Handelsgesellschaft mbh* v. *Continental Grain Co* [1983] 1 Lloyd's Rep 269 at p. 292:

> '. . . the question resolves itself into a question of causation; in my judgment, at least in a case in which a seller can (as in the present case) claim the protection of a clause which protects him where fulfilment is hindered by the excepted peril, subsequent delivery of his available stock to other customers will not be regarded as an independent cause of shortage, provided that in making such delivery the seller acted reasonably in all the circumstances of the case   '

A similar approach was reflected in other cases: see, for example, *Intertradex SA v. Lesieur-Tourteaux SARL* [1977] 2 Lloyd's Rep 146 at p. 115, per Mr Justice Donaldson as he then was; [1978] 2 Lloyd's Rep 509 at p. 513, per Lord Denning, MR. Reliance was also placed on passages in *The Law of Contract* (7th ed.) by Professor Treitel, which the Judge quoted in his judgment at p. 152. Thus, Mr Clarke urged, this was a case in which Wijsmuller could not perform all their contracts once Super Servant Two was lost; they acted reasonably (as we must assume) in treating the Dan King contract as one they could not perform; so the sinking had the direct result of making that contract impossible to perform.

Mr Legh-Jones [counsel for the plaintiffs] answered that since the contract provided for the carriage to be performed by one or other vessel the loss of one did not render performance radically different, still less impossible. That apart, Wijsmuller's argument fell foul of the principles summarized above since (among other things) the frustration they sought to establish did not bring the contract to an end forthwith, without more and automatically and was not independent of the act or election of Wijsmuller. The force majeure cases were good law so far as they went, but it was one thing to construe and apply a consensual force majeure clause, another to determine whether the facts were such that the law should hold the contract to be discharged.

The doctrine of frustration depends on a comparison between circumstances as they are or are assumed to be when a contract is made and circumstances as they are when a contract is, or would be, due to be performed. It is trite law that disappointed expectations do not of themselves give rise to frustrated contracts. To frustrate, an event must significantly change—

'. . . the nature (not merely the expense or onerousness) of the outstanding contractual rights and/or obligations from what the parties could reasonably have contemplated at the time of [the contract's] execution . . .' [*National Carriers Ltd* sup., at p. 700, per Lord Simon of Glaisdale].

Had the Dan King contract provided for carriage by Super Servant Two with no alternative, and that vessel had been lost before the time for performance, then assuming no negligence by Wijsmuller (as for purposes of this question we must), I feel sure the contract would have been frustrated. The doctrine must avail a party who contracts to perform a contract of carriage with a vessel which, through no fault of his, no longer exists. But that is not this case. The Dan King contract did provide an alternative. When that contract was made one of the contracts eventually performed by Super Servant One during the period of contractual carriage of Dan King had been made, the other had not, at any rate finally. Wijsmuller have not alleged that when the Dan King contract was made either vessel was earmarked for its performance. That, no doubt, is why an option was contracted for. Had it been foreseen when the Dan King contract was made that Super Servant Two would be unavailable for performance, whether because she had been deliberately sold or accidentally sunk, Lauritzen at least would have thought it no matter since the carriage could be performed with the other. I accordingly accept Mr Legh-Jones' submission that the present case does not fall within the very limited class of cases in which the law will relieve one party from an absolute promise he has chosen to make.

But I also accept Mr Legh-Jones' submission that Wijsmuller's argument is subject to other fatal flaws. If, as was argued, the contract was frustrated when Wijsmuller made or communicated their decision on Feb. 16, it deprives language of all meaning to describe the contract as coming to an end automatically. It was, indeed, because the contract did not come to an end automatically on Jan. 29, that Wijsmuller needed a fortnight to review their schedules and their commercial options. I cannot, furthermore, reconcile Wijsmuller's argument with the reasoning or the decision in *Maritime National Fish Ltd* sup. In that case the Privy Council declined to speculate why the charterers selected three of the five vessels to be licensed but, as I understand the case, regarded the interposition of human choice after the allegedly frustrating event as fatal to the plea of frustration. If Wijsmuller are entitled to succeed here, I cannot see why the charterers lost there. The cases on frustrating delay do not, I think, help Wijsmuller since it is actual and prospective delay (whether or not recognized as frustrating by a party at the time) which frustrates the contract, not a party's election or decision to treat the delay as frustrating. I have no doubt that force majeure clauses are, where their terms permit, to be construed and applied as in the commodity cases on which Wijsmuller relied, but it is in my view inconsistent with the doctrine of frustration as previously understood on high authority that its application should depend on any decision, however reasonable and commercial, of the party seeking to rely on it.

I reach the same conclusion as the Judge for the reasons which he lucidly and persuasively gave.

Question 2(b)

The issue between the parties was short and fundamental: what is meant by saying that a frustrating event, to be relied on, must occur without the fault or default, or without blame attaching to, the party relying on it?

Mr Clarke's answer was that a party was precluded from relying on an event only when he had acted deliberately or in breach of an actionable duty in causing it. Those conditions were not met here since it was not alleged Wijsmuller sank Super Servant Two deliberately and at the material time Wijsmuller owed Lauritzen no duty of care if (as I have held) cl. 15 did not apply when the vessel sank. Mr Clarke relied on tentative doubts expressed in *Joseph Constantine Steamship Ltd* sup., whether mere negligence would render an event 'self induced' and on a statement of Lord Diplock in *Cheall* v. *Association of Professional Executive Clerical and Computer Staff* [1983] 2 AC 180 at pp. 188–189.

Mr Legh-Jones argued for a less restrictive approach. He relied on what Lord Justice Griffiths, as he then was, said in *The Hannah Blumenthal* [1983] 1 AC 854 at p. 882:

'[*Denmark Productions Ltd* v. *Boscobel Productions Ltd* [1969] 1 QB 699] best illustrates what is meant by default in the context of frustration. The essence of frustration is that it is caused by some unforeseen supervening event over which the parties to the contract have no control and for which they are therefore not responsible. To say that the supervening event occurs without the default or blame or responsibility of the parties is, in the context of the doctrine of frustration, but another way of saying it is a supervening event over which they had no control. The doctrine has no application and cannot be invoked by a contracting party when the frustrating event was at all times within his control; still less can it apply in a situation in which the parties owed a contractual duty to one another to prevent the frustrating event occurring.'

I do not pause to ask whether Lord Justice Griffith's opinion is formally binding upon us since in my judgment it clearly indicates the path which the law should follow. When, in *Bank Line Ltd* sup., at p. 452 Lord Sumner made his famous observation that 'Reliance cannot be placed on a self-induced frustration' he was contrasting a self-induced frustration with one arising 'without blame or fault on either side'. As the Judge observed (at p 156)—

'. . . in some respects the doctrine of frustration and the concept of "self-inducement" are simply opposite sides of the same coin.'

Wijsmuller's test would, in my judgment, confine the law in a legalistic strait-jacket and distract attention from the real question, which is whether the frustrating event relied upon is truly an outside event or extraneous change of situation or whether it is an event which the party seeking to rely on it had the means and opportunity to prevent but nevertheless caused or permitted to come about. A fine test of legal duty is inappropriate; what is needed is a pragmatic judgment whether a party seeking to rely on an event as discharging him from a contractual promise was himself responsible for the occurrence of that event.

Lauritzen have pleaded in some detail the grounds on which they say that Super Servant Two was lost as a result of the carelessness of Wijsmuller, their servants or agents.

If those allegations are made good to any significant extent Wijsmuller would (even if my answer to Question 2(a) is wrong) be precluded from relying on their plea of frustration.

I would answer this question also as the Judge did and would therefore dismiss the appeal.

Dillon LJ

Issues 2(a) and (b) are concerned with frustration. Was the contract frustrated by the sinking of Super Servant Two or by that event coupled with the subsequent election by the defendants to use Super Servant One on other voyages and not for carrying the Dan King? The important factor, common to both issues, is that under the contract the defendants could have satisfied their obligation by using Super Servant One to carry the rig, after Super Servant Two had sunk, but they elected not to do so.

In this respect, the present case appears to be a direct parallel to that described by Lord Wright in *Maritime National Fish Ltd* v. *Ocean Trawlers Ltd* [1935] AC 524 at pp. 529–530 where he said:

'. . . in [their Lordships] judgment the case could be properly decided on the simple conclusion that it was the act and election of the appellants which prevented the St. Cuthbert being licensed for fishing with an otter trawl. It is clear that the appellants were free to select any three of the five trawlers they were operating and could, had they willed, have selected the St. Cuthbert as one, in which event a licence would have been granted to her. It is immaterial to speculate why they preferred to put forward for licences the three trawlers which they actually selected nor is it material, as between the appellants and the respondents, that the appellants were operating other trawlers to three of which they gave the preference. What matters is that they could have got a licence for the St. Cuthbert if they had so minded. If the case be figured as one in which the St. Cuthbert was removed from the category of privileged trawlers, it was by the appellant's hand that she was so removed because it was their hand that guided the hand of the Minister in placing the licences where he did and thereby excluding the St. Cuthbert. The essence of "frustration" is that it should not be due to the act or election of the party.'

The parallel seems to be even closer, if, as some of the documents seem to suggest, the defendants, after the loss of the Super Servant Two, negotiated extra fees with the parties with whom they had other contracts of carriage before finally allocating the Super Servant One to perform those other contracts.

It is the view of Professor Treitel, expressed both in his own book on the *Law of Contract*—see the 7th ed. at pp. 674–675 and 700–701—and in the current editions of well-known textbooks of which he is editor or an editor, that where a party has entered into a number of contracts with other parties and an uncontemplated supervening event has the result that he is deprived of the means of satisfying all those contracts, he can, provided he acts 'reasonably' in making his election, elect to use such means as remains available to him to perform some of the contracts, and claim that the others, which he does not perform, have been frustrated by the supervening event. The reasoning depends on the proposition that if it is known to those concerned that the party will have entered into commitments with others and if he acts 'reasonably' in his allocation of his remaining means to his commitments, the chain of causation between the uncontemplated supervening event and the non-performance of those of his contracts which will not have been performed will not have been broken by the election to apply his remaining means in a 'reasonable' way. Similar reasoning was, as my Lord has pointed out, used by Mr Justice Robert Goff in relation to an exceptions clause in the unreported case of *Westfälische Central-Genossenschaft GmbH v. Seabright Chemicals Ltd*.

Such an approach is however inconsistent to my mind with the view expressed by Lord Wright in that passage in *Maritime National Fish* which I have already cited, where he said:

'It is immaterial to speculate why they preferred to put forward for licences the three trawlers which they actually selected.'

It is also, as my Lord has pointed out, inconsistent with the long accepted view that frustration brings the contract to an end forthwith, without more ado automatically. Plainly the sinking of Super Servant Two did not do that, since even after that sinking the defendants could have used Super Servant One to perform the contract.

We in this Court should apply *Maritime National Fish* and the other authorities to which my Lord has referred. Accordingly I agree with my Lord and the learned Judge that issues 2(a) and (b) should be answered in the negative.

COMMENTARY

The Super Servant Two is a case of considerable significance. This is so for a number of reasons. First, it demonstrates the practical significance of force majeure clauses. The defendants found some protection in clause 17 but not in the doctrine of frustration. Indeed, in many ways the narrowness of the doctrine of frustration can be explained on the basis that it is open to the parties to protect their own position by an appropriately drafted force majeure clause (see p. 878 above). Secondly, it is an important case in relation to the interpretation of force majeure clauses in that it demonstrates that the courts are unlikely to conclude, in the absence of very clear words, that a force majeure clause is apt to encompass events caused by the negligence of the party relying upon the clause. The reason for this is that the events listed in the clause are generally events that are beyond the control of the parties (such as 'acts of God', 'wars', etc) and, this being the case, the court is likely to presume that all events listed in the clause are beyond their control.

Thirdly, the case demonstrates that a party who has been at fault will generally not be entitled to invoke the doctrine of frustration. The defendants in *Super Servant Two* argued that it was only when they had acted deliberately or were in breach of a duty of care which they owed to the plaintiffs that they would be precluded from relying upon the doctrine of frustration. Bingham LJ rejected this submission on the ground that it would 'confine the law in a legalistic strait-jacket'. The view adopted by the Court of Appeal was that a frustrating event must, by definition, take place 'without blame or fault on the side of the party seeking to rely' upon the doctrine of frustration. So, if the sinking of *Super Servant Two* occurred as a result of the negligence of the defendants, that of itself would have sufficed to prevent the defendants from relying upon frustration.

The final point relates to the fact that the defendants had a choice as to the allocation of *Super Servant One*. In the view of the Court of Appeal the fact that the defendants had a choice meant that the alleged frustrating event was brought about by their own act or election and not by a supervening event. Adopting a strict approach to the interpretation of the decision of the Privy Council in *Maritime National Fish Ltd* v. *Ocean Trawlers Ltd* [1935] AC 524, the Court of Appeal held that it was irrelevant that the defendants in *Super Servant Two* had no *real* choice as to the allocation of *Super Servant One* in that it was impossible to allocate it to the performance of all concluded contracts. Cases relied upon to support the proposition that the defendants could invoke the doctrine of frustration if they had acted reasonably in their allocation of *Super Servant One* were distinguished on the ground that they were concerned with the interpretation of *force majeure* clauses and not with the doctrine of frustration. This conclusion would appear to leave a party in the position of the defendants in this case in a very difficult position. Two practical steps can be taken to mitigate the rigours of the decision. The first is to eliminate any choice on the part of the defendants. Bingham LJ stated that, had the contract been to perform the contract with *Super Servant Two*, the sinking of that vessel, without negligence on the part of the defendants, would have entitled the defendants to seek relief under the doctrine of frustration. The second step is to insert an appropriately drafted force majeure clause into the contract. This takes us back to our first point, namely the crucial role played by force majeure clauses in modern commercial contracts.

6. FRUSTRATING EVENTS

It is only in the rare case where (i) the contract does not make provision for the event that has occurred, (ii) the event was not foreseen by the parties and was not sufficiently foreseeable, and (iii) the alleged frustrating event was not 'self-induced', that a court has to decide whether or not a contract has been frustrated. Cases involving frustrated contracts can be divided into three groups.

(a) IMPOSSIBILITY

The classic example of a frustrated contract is a contract that has become impossible to perform. *Taylor* v. *Caldwell* falls into this category. *Taylor* was a case of partial rather than total impossibility in that it was still possible for the parties to make use of the Surrey Gardens. But use of the Gardens only would have been a very different contract from that which had originally been concluded by the parties. A contract of employment is frustrated on the death of the employee. More difficult is the case where the employee becomes incapacitated. Much depends upon the extent of the incapacity; the greater it is, both in extent and duration, the more likely it is that the contract of employment will be frustrated. A contract may also be frustrated where the subject-matter of the contract is unavailable for use in the performance of the contract (*Jackson* v. *Union Marine Insurance Co Ltd* (1874) LR 10 CP 125, where the charter of a ship which subsequently ran aground was held to have been frustrated as a result of the unavailability of the vessel for the contracted voyage). Where the unavailability is partial only (that is to say, it is only unavailable for a proportion of the contract period) the court must have regard to the extent of the unavailability. The greater the extent, in relation to the time-scale of the contract, the more likely it is that the contract will be frustrated (*The Nema* [1982] AC 724).

(b) ILLEGALITY

The second group of cases concerns contracts that have become illegal after the date of formation. These cases differ from the cases discussed in Chapter 22 where the illegality affected the contract from the outset. Cases that fall within this section are contracts that were valid when formed but have become illegal as a result of the occurrence of events subsequent to the making of the contract. An example is provided by the case of *Fibrosa Spolka Akcyjna* v. *Fairbairn Lawson Combe Barbour Ltd* [1943] AC 32. A contract to sell machinery to buyers in Poland was frustrated when Poland was occupied by Germany in the Second World War (it being illegal to trade with the enemy in times of war). Public policy considerations operate very strongly in this area. In cases involving subsequent illegality, the operation of the doctrine of frustration cannot be excluded by an express term of the contract (*Ertel Bieber and Co* v. *Rio Tinto Co Ltd* [1918] AC 260) nor can it be excluded on the ground that the supervening illegality was foreseen by the contracting parties. Difficult questions can arise where the supervening illegality affects part only of the contract. These cases involve questions of degree. The court must examine the impact of the illegality on the contract. Where the illegality affects the contract in a substantial or a fundamental way then the contract is likely to be frustrated (*Denny, Mott & Dickson* v. *James B Fraser & Co Ltd* [1944] AC 265). Conversely, where its impact is insubstantial the contract will not be frustrated (*Cricklewood Property & Investment Trust Ltd* v. *Leightons Investment Trust Ltd* [1945] AC 221).

(c) FRUSTRATION OF PURPOSE

The most difficult cases are those in which it is alleged that the purpose of the contract has been frustrated. The courts have exercised considerable caution in order to ensure that frustration does not become a convenient escape route for a party who discovers that he has entered into a bad bargain. More often than not, attempts to invoke the doctrine of frustration in this context have failed (see, for example, *Davis Contractors Ltd* v. *Fareham Urban District Council* [1956] AC 696, p. 873 above and *Amalgamated Investment & Property Co Ltd* v. *John Walker & Sons Ltd* [1977] 1 WLR 164). The case that gives rise to difficulty is the decision of the Court of Appeal in *Krell* v. *Henry* [1903] 2 KB 740. It gives rise to difficulty on two grounds. First, why did the Court of Appeal conclude that the contract had been frustrated? Secondly, what is the difference between *Krell* (where the contract was frustrated) and the decision of the Court of Appeal in *Herne Bay Steam Boat Company* v. *Hutton* [1903] 2 KB 683, p. 899 below (where the contract was not frustrated)? It is important to examine *Krell* and *Hutton* together (alongside the example given by Vaughan Williams LJ in *Krell* of the cab driver who agrees to take a passenger to Epsom on Derby Day). The commentary will therefore follow the decision of the Court of Appeal in *Hutton*.

Krell v. Henry

[1903] 2 KB 740, Court of Appeal

Krell owned a flat on the third floor at 56A Pall Mall. As it had been announced that the King's coronation processions would pass along Pall Mall on 26 and 27 June 1902, Henry agreed to hire Krell's flat on those days. On 20 June Krell and Henry entered into a written contract which made no reference to the coronation processions or to any other purpose for which the flat was taken. The agreement stated that Henry was to have 'the entire use of these rooms during the days (but not the nights)'. Henry paid a deposit of £25 and agreed to pay the balance of £50 on 24 June. The King became seriously ill and the coronation processions did not take place. Henry refused to pay the balance and Krell brought an action to recover it. Henry counterclaimed for the return of the £25. The trial judge held that Henry was not liable to pay the £50 and that he was entitled to the return of the £25. Krell appealed to the Court of Appeal who dismissed the appeal and held that he was not entitled to demand the balance of £50 on the ground that the contract between the parties had been frustrated.

Vaughan Williams LJ

The real question in this case is the extent of the application in English law of the principle of the Roman law which has been adopted and acted on in many English decisions, and notably in the case of *Taylor* v. *Caldwell* 3 B & S 826 . . . English law applies the principle not only to cases where the performance of the contract becomes impossible by the cessation of existence of the thing which is the subject-matter of the contract, but also to cases where the event which renders the contract incapable of performance is the cessation or non-existence of an express condition or state of things, going to the root of the contract, and essential to its performance. It is said, on the one side, that the specified thing, state of things, or condition the continued existence of which is necessary for the fulfilment of the contract, so that the parties entering into the contract must have contemplated the continued existence of that thing, condition, or state of things as the foundation of what was to be done under the contract, is limited to things which are either the subject-matter of the contract or a condition or state of things, present or anticipated, which is expressly mentioned in the contract. But, on the other side, it is said that the condition or state of things need not be expressly specified, but that it is sufficient if that condition or state of things clearly appears by extrinsic evidence to have been assumed by the parties to be the foundation or basis of the contract, and the event which causes the impossibility is of such a character that it cannot reasonably be supposed to have been in the contemplation of the contracting parties when the contract was made. In such a case the contracting parties will not be held bound by the general words which, though large enough to include, were not used with reference to a possibility of a particular event rendering performance of the contract impossible. I do not think that the principle of the civil law as introduced into the English law is limited to cases in which the event causing the impossibility of performance is the destruction or non-existence of some thing which is the subject-matter of the contract or of some condition or state of things expressly specified as a condition of it. I think that you first have to ascertain, not necessarily from the terms of the contract, but, if required, from necessary inferences, drawn from surrounding circumstances recognised by both contracting parties, what is the substance of the contract, and then to ask the question whether that substantial contract needs for its foundation the assumption of the existence of a particular state of things. If it does, this will limit the operation of the general words, and in such case, if the contract becomes impossible of performance by reason of the non-existence of the state of things assumed by both contracting parties as the foundation of the contract, there will be no breach of the contract thus limited. Now what are the facts of the present case?

[he set out the facts and continued]

In my judgment the use of the rooms was let and taken for the purpose of seeing the Royal procession. It was not a demise of the rooms, or even an agreement to let and take the rooms. It is a licence to use rooms for a particular purpose and none other. And in my judgment the taking place of those processions on the days proclaimed along the proclaimed route, which passed 56A, Pall Mall, was regarded by both contracting parties as the foundation of the contract; and I think that it cannot reasonably be supposed to have been in the contemplation of the contracting parties, when the contract was made, that the coronation would not be held on the proclaimed days, or the processions not take place on those days along the proclaimed route; and I think that the words imposing on the defendant the obligation to accept and pay for the use of the rooms for the named days, although general and unconditional, were not used with reference to the possibility of the particular contingency which afterwards occurred. It was suggested in the course of the argument that if the occurrence, on the proclaimed days, of the coronation and the procession in this case were the foundation of the contract, and if the general words are thereby limited or qualified, so that in the event of the non-occurrence of the coronation and procession along the proclaimed route they would discharge both parties from further performance of the contract, it would follow that if a cabman was engaged to take some one to Epsom on Derby Day at a suitable enhanced price for such a journey, say 10l., both parties to the contract would be discharged in the contingency of the race at Epsom for some reason becoming impossible; but I do not think this follows, for I do not think that in the cab case the happening of the race would be the foundation of the contract. No doubt the purpose of the engager would be to go to see the Derby, and the price would be proportionately high; but the cab had no special qualifications for the purpose which led to the selection of the cab for this particular occasion. Any other cab would have done as well. Moreover, I think that, under the cab contract, the hirer, even if the race went off, could have said, 'Drive me to Epsom; I will pay you the agreed sum; you have nothing to do with the purpose for which I hired the cab', and that if the cabman refused he would have been guilty of a breach of contract, there being nothing to qualify his promise to drive the hirer to Epsom on a particular day. Whereas in the case of the coronation, there is not merely the purpose of the hirer to see the coronation procession, but it is the coronation procession and the relative position of the rooms which is the basis of the contract as much for the lessor as the hirer; and I think that if the King, before the coronation day and after the contract, had died, the hirer could not have insisted on having the rooms on the days named. It could not in the cab case be reasonably said that seeing the Derby race was the foundation of the contract, as it was of the licence in this case. Whereas in the present case, where the rooms were offered and taken, by reason of their peculiar suitability from the position of the rooms for a view of the coronation procession, surely the view of the coronation procession was the foundation of the contract, which is a very different thing from the purpose of the man who engaged the cab—namely, to see the race—being held to be the foundation of the contract. Each case must be judged by its own circumstances. In each case one must ask oneself, first, what, having regard to all the circumstances, was the foundation of the contract? Secondly, was the performance of the contract prevented? Thirdly, was the event which prevented the performance of the contract of such a character that it cannot reasonably be said to have been in the contemplation of the parties at the date of the contract? If all these questions are answered in the affirmative (as I think they should be in this case), I think both parties are discharged from further performance of the contract. I think that the coronation procession was the foundation of this contract, and that the non-happening of it prevented the performance of the contract; and, secondly, I think that the non-happening of the procession, to use the words of Sir James Hannen in *Baily* v. *De Crespigny* LR 4 QB 185, was an event 'of such a character that it cannot reasonably be supposed to have been in the contemplation of the contracting parties when the contract was made, and that they are not to be held bound by general words which, though large enough to include, were not used with reference to the possibility of the particular contingency which afterwards happened' . . .

[he considered the case-law and continued]

I myself am clearly of opinion that in this case, where we have to ask ourselves whether the object of the contract was frustrated by the non-happening of the coronation and its procession on the days proclaimed, parol evidence is admissible to shew that the subject of the contract was rooms to view the coronation procession, and was so to the knowledge of both parties. When once this is established, I see no difficulty whatever in the case. It is not essential to the application of the principle of *Taylor* v. *Caldwell* 3 B & S 826 that the direct subject of the contract should perish or fail to be in existence at the date of performance of the contract. It is sufficient if a state of things or condition expressed in the contract and essential to its performance perishes or fails to be in existence at that time. In the present case the condition which fails and prevents the achievement of that which was, in the contemplation of both parties, the foundation of the contract, is not expressly mentioned either as a condition of the contract or the purpose of it; but I think for the reasons which I have given that the principle of *Taylor* v. *Caldwell* ought to be applied. This disposes of the plaintiff's claim for 50l. unpaid balance of the price agreed to be paid for the use of the rooms. The defendant at one time set up a cross-claim for the return of the 25l. he paid at the date of the contract. As that claim is now withdrawn it is unnecessary to say anything about it.

Romer LJ
With some doubt I have also come to the conclusion that this case is governed by the principle on which *Taylor* v. *Caldwell* was decided, and accordingly that the appeal must be dismissed. The doubt I have felt was whether the parties to the contract now before us could be said, under the circumstances, not to have had at all in their contemplation the risk that for some reason or other the coronation processions might not take place on the days fixed, or, if the processions took place, might not pass so as to be capable of being viewed from the rooms mentioned in the contract; and whether, under this contract, that risk was not undertaken by the defendant. But on the question of fact as to what was in the contemplation of the parties at the time, I do not think it right to differ from the conclusion arrived at by Vaughan Williams LJ.

Stirling LJ said he had an opportunity of reading the judgment delivered by Vaughan Williams LJ, with which he entirely agreed. Though the case was one of very great difficulty, he thought it came within the principle of *Taylor* v. *Caldwell.*

Herne Bay Steam Boat Company v. Hutton

[1903] 2 KB 683, Court of Appeal

The Herne Bay Steam Boat Company owned a steamboat called *Cynthia*. Early in 1902 it was announced that there would be a Royal naval review at Spithead on 28 June 1902. Hutton, the defendant, wanted to charter *Cynthia* to carry passengers to see the review. Herne Bay and Hutton signed an agreement on 23 May 1902 which stated that *Cynthia* would be at the disposal of Hutton on 28 June 'for the purpose of viewing the naval review and for a day's cruise round the fleet' and on 29 June 'for similar purposes'. Hutton paid a deposit of £50 and agreed to pay the balance of £200 before *Cynthia* left Herne Bay. On 25 June the naval review was cancelled. On the same day Herne Bay wired Hutton for instructions, stating that *Cynthia* was ready to start, but received no reply. On 28 and 29 June Herne Bay used *Cynthia* for its own purposes and made a profit of £90. On 29 June, Hutton called Herne Bay and stated that, as the naval review had been cancelled, he no longer required *Cynthia* and would not pay the balance of £200. Herne Bay brought an action to recover £110. Hutton counter-claimed for the return of his £50 deposit. The judge held that Herne Bay was not entitled to the £110 but that Hutton was not entitled to the £50. The Court of Appeal allowed Herne Bay's appeal. It held that the contract between the parties had not been frustrated and that Herne Bay was accordingly entitled to recover £110 from Hutton by way of damages for his breach of contract.

Vaughan Williams LJ
Mr Hutton, in hiring this vessel, had two objects in view: first, of taking people to see the naval review, and, secondly, of taking them round the fleet. Those, no doubt, were the purposes of Mr Hutton, but it does not seem to me that because, as it is said, those purposes became impossible, it would be a very legitimate inference that the happening of the naval review was contemplated by both parties as the basis and foundation of this contract, so as to bring the case within the doctrine of *Taylor* v. *Caldwell* 3 B & S 826. On the contrary, when the contract is properly regarded, I think the purpose of Mr Hutton, whether of seeing the naval review or of going round the fleet with a party of paying guests, does not lay the foundation of the contract within the authorities . . .

I see nothing that makes this contract differ from a case where, for instance, a person has engaged a brake to take himself and a party to Epsom to see the races there, but for some reason or other, such as the spread of an infectious disease, the races are postponed. In such a case it could not be said that he could be relieved of his bargain. So in the present case it is sufficient to say that the happening of the naval review was not the foundation of the contract.

Romer LJ
This case is not one in which the subject-matter of the contract is a mere licence to the defendant to use a ship for the purpose of seeing the naval review and going round the fleet. In my opinion, as my Lord has said, it is a contract for the hiring of a ship by the defendant for a certain voyage, though having, no doubt, a special object, namely, to see

the naval review and the fleet; but it appears to me that the object was a matter with which the defendant, as hirer of the ship, was alone concerned, and not the plaintiffs, the owners of the ship.

The case cannot, in my opinion, be distinguished in principle from many common cases in which, on the hiring of a ship, you find the objects of the hiring stated. Very often you find the details of the voyage stated with particularity, and also the nature and details of the cargo to be carried. If the voyage is intended to be one of pleasure, the object in view may also be stated, which is a matter that concerns the passengers. But this statement of the objects of the hirer of the ship would not, in my opinion, justify him in saying that the owner of the ship had those objects just as much in view as the hirer himself. The owner would say, 'I have an interest in the ship as a passenger or cargo carrying machine, and I enter into the contract simply in that capacity; it is for the hirer to concern himself about the objects'.

. . . The ship (as a ship) had nothing particular to do with the review or the fleet except as a convenient carrier of passengers to see it: any other ship suitable for carrying passengers would have done equally as well. Just as in the case of the hire of a cab or other vehicle, although the object of the hirer might be stated, that statement would not make the object any the less a matter for the hirer alone, and would not directly affect the person who was letting out the vehicle for hire. In the present case I may point out that it cannot be said that by reason of the failure to hold the naval review there was a total failure of consideration. That cannot be so. Nor is there anything like a total destruction of the subject-matter of the contract. Nor can we, in my opinion, imply in this contract any condition in favour of the defendant which would enable him to escape liability. A condition ought only to be implied in order to carry out the presumed intention of the parties, and I cannot ascertain any such presumed intention here. It follows that, in my opinion, so far as the plaintiffs are concerned, the objects of the passengers on this voyage with regard to sight-seeing do not form the subject-matter or essence of this contract.

Stirling LJ

It is said that, by reason of the reference in the contract to the 'naval review', the existence of the review formed the basis of the contract, and that as the review failed to take place the parties became discharged from the further performance of the contract, in accordance with the doctrine of *Taylor* v. *Caldwell* 3 B & S 826. I am unable to arrive at that conclusion. It seems to me that the reference in the contract to the naval review is easily explained; it was inserted in order to define more exactly the nature of the voyage, and I am unable to treat it as being such a reference as to constitute the naval review the foundation of the contract so as to entitle either party to the benefit of the doctrine in *Taylor* v. *Caldwell*. I come to this conclusion the more readily because the object of the voyage is not limited to the naval review, but also extends to a cruise round the fleet. The fleet was there, and passengers might have been found willing to go round it. It is true that in the event which happened the object of the voyage became limited, but, in my opinion, that was the risk of the defendant whose venture the taking the passengers was. For these reasons I am unable to agree with the learned judge in holding that in the contemplation of the parties the taking place of the review was the basis for the performance of the contract, and I think that the defendant is not discharged from its performance.

COMMENTARY

Krell is a difficult case: it has its supporters and its critics. It has never been over-ruled but, at the same time, the courts have been reluctant to apply it in other contexts. What is the difference between *Krell* and *Hutton*? And why is a contract to hire a room for the purpose of viewing the coronation frustrated on the cancellation of the coronation when a contract to pay a cab driver a suitably enhanced price to take a passenger to Epsom on Derby Day is not frustrated on the cancellation of the Derby? The most convincing analysis of *Krell* has been provided by Professor Treitel (*Frustration and Force Majeure* (Sweet & Maxwell, 2nd edn, 2004), para 7-014) in the following terms:

The contract in [*Krell*] was not simply one which granted a licence to use the rooms at an unusually high price. It was a contract to provide facilities for viewing the coronation processions or, as Lord Phillips MR has stated, one for a 'room with a view'. There was not, indeed, any undertaking in it that the processions would take place, or that they could be viewed from the rooms. In this respect, the contract differed from the contract that is made by buying a theatre or concert ticket: performance of such a contract would become impossible if supervening events led to the cancellation of the play or concert. In *Krell* v. *Henry* there was no such impossibility. . . . But it was the common purpose of both parties that facilities for viewing the processions should be provided: in the words of Vaughan Williams LJ, the provision of such facilities was the crucial point 'as much for the lessor as the hirer'. In the other examples, there was either no such common purpose . . . or the common purpose was not wholly defeated. The latter point reflects a recurrent feature of the cases on frustration of purpose, which shows that the approach of the law to partial frustration of purpose differs from that which it adopts to partial impossibility. In cases of partial impossibility, a contract can be discharged if its *main* purpose can no longer be achieved; but in cases of frustration of purpose the courts have applied the more rigorous test of asking whether *any* part of the contractual purpose (other than a part which was wholly trivial) could still be achieved: if so, they have refused to apply the doctrine of discharge. The *Herne Bay* case fell far short of satisfying this test. The naval review may have formed the hirer's principal inducement to enter into the contract, but the continued presence of the fleet at Spithead also provided a considerable and unusual attraction, and it was one of the purposes of the contract to give the hirer the opportunity of taking advantage of this attraction for commercial purposes. In *Krell* v. Henry, by contrast, it was no part of the contractual purpose that Mr Henry should be able to look out of the window to watch the ordinary London traffic which continued to pass down Pall Mall on the two days in question. *Krell* v. *Henry* seems, with respect, to have been correctly decided on the basis that it was the common purpose of both parties that facilities for watching the processions were to be provided under the contract, and the cancellation of the processions had prevented the achievement of that common purpose (although literal performance of the contract had not become impossible). This emphasis on the requirement that the purpose of *both* parties must be frustrated is found also in other English and American cases. It means that the supervening event must prevent one party from supplying, and the other from obtaining, what the former had contracted to provide and the latter to acquire under the contract. In this sense, formulations of the doctrine in terms of the frustration of the purpose of both parties are preferable to those (occasionally found) which refer to the frustration of the purpose of *one* party only. The point can be illustrated by supposing that, in *Krell* v. *Henry*, the coronation had taken place as planned but Mr Henry had fallen ill and so been unable to watch the processions. In that case, his purpose might have been frustrated, but the same could not have been said of Mr Krell's purpose: that purpose, being the provision of viewing facilities, would have been accomplished. Accordingly, it is submitted that, on such facts, the contract should not have been discharged.

On this basis *Krell* is a very narrow decision indeed. Provided that the focus is kept on the purpose of both parties to the contract the decision should be kept within limits and not become an escape route for parties looking for a way out of a bad bargain.

An alternative explanation of *Krell* has been provided by Posner CJ in *Northern Indiana Public Service Co* v. *Carbon County Coal Co*, 799 F 2d 265. He stated (at p. 277):

The leading case on frustration remains *Krell* v. *Henry* [1903] 2 KB 740 (CA). Krell rented Henry a suite of rooms for watching the coronation of Edward VII, but Edward came down with appendicitis and the coronation had to be postponed. Henry refused to pay the balance of the rent and the court held that he was excused from doing so because his purpose in renting had been frustrated by the postponement, a contingency outside the knowledge, or power to influence, of either party. The question was, to which party did the contract (implicitly) allocate the risk? Surely Henry had not intended to insure Krell against the possibility of the coronation's being postponed, since Krell could always relet the room, at the premium rental, for the coronation's new date. So Henry was excused.

Professor Treitel points out (para 7-012) that this rationalization of *Krell* is not 'wholly compelling'. The 'insurance' argument runs into the difficulty that neither party may have considered the possibility of insuring on the facts of the case. And the argument that Mr Krell could always have relet the room encounters the factual difficulty that the route of the procession which actually took place differed in some respects from the cancelled procession. Professor Treitel also points out that the argument in relation to the possibility of reletting the room seems to 'involve a paradox in so far as it suggests that Mr Krell's claim for the balance of £50 would have been strengthened if (to imagine the unthinkable) the coronation had been wholly cancelled because a Republic had been declared'.

7. THE EFFECTS OF FRUSTRATION

The effect of frustration is to discharge the contract automatically (*Hirji Mulji* v. *Cheong Yue Steamship Co Ltd* [1926] AC 497). Both parties are then released from their obligations to perform the contract after the date of discharge without incurring any liability for breach of contract in respect of their failure to perform these obligations. Discharge is a drastic sanction. The parties may prefer to suspend the contract while they wait to see what impact the event (such as a war) will have on the contract or they may prefer to adjust the contract so that one party does not suffer undue hardship as a result of the occurrence of the unexpected event. Parties who wish to make provision for the suspension or adjustment of the contract should insert an appropriate clause in the contract to that effect (a force majeure clause if suspension is the desired remedy and a hardship clause if adjustment of the contract is the wished-for outcome).

The law of contract does not attempt to regulate the financial consequences of the discharge of the contract on the ground of frustration. In the absence of a breach of contract, there can be no action for damages for breach. Regulation of the financial consequences of the frustration of a contract is a matter for the law of restitution (or, if one prefers, the law of unjust enrichment). The law is now to be found largely in the Law Reform (Frustrated Contracts) Act 1943. The Act has generated very little case-law. There is, however, one notable exception and that is the litigation between BP Exploration Co (Libya) Ltd and Mr Hunt. Although the case was appealed all the way up to the House of Lords, the leading judicial exposition of the Act is to be found in the judgment of the judge at first instance, Robert Goff J. Before examining the Act and the case-law it is necessary to say something about the common law rules which pre-dated the Act.

The development of the common law rules can be divided into two distinct stages. The first stage was associated with the decision of the Court of Appeal in *Chandler* v. *Webster* [1904] 1 KB 493. *Chandler* was another of the coronation cases. The principal issue in *Chandler* was the financial consequences of the frustration of the contract between the parties. The Court of Appeal held that money paid under a contract prior to it being frustrated could be recovered upon a total failure of consideration. But, crucially, they held that, in order to constitute a total failure of consideration, the contract had to be set aside *ab initio*. Frustration does not have such a consequence. The contract is set aside from the moment of the occurrence of the frustrating event but the termination is not retrospective in its effect. This being the case, the party who paid the money could not recover it because he could not demonstrate that there had been a total failure of consideration. The loss therefore lay where it fell. A similar principle was applicable in the case where services were performed prior to the frustration of the contract. In *Cutter* v. *Powell* (1795) 6 TR 320 Mr Powell employed Mr Cutter as second mate on a ship that was to sail from Jamaica to Liverpool. The level of pay offered by Mr Powell was generous but the contract stated that the money was only payable after the ship arrived in Liverpool provided that Mr Cutter had done his duty as second mate on the journey. Mr Cutter died before the ship arrived in Liverpool. His death frustrated the contract between the parties. His widow brought an action to recover the wages which she alleged were due to her deceased husband in respect of the services he performed prior to his death. Her claim failed. Mr Cutter was only entitled to payment on completion of the voyage and, having failed to do so, he was not entitled to make any claim for work done prior to the termination of the contract on his death.

The second stage in the development of the common law was the decision of the House of Lords in *Fibrosa Spolka Akcyjna* v. *Fairbairn Lawson Combe Barbour Ltd* [1943] AC 32. The House of Lords overruled *Chandler*. While they affirmed that money paid was recoverable upon a total failure of consideration, they rejected the proposition that it is necessary to set aside the contract *ab initio* in order to create such a total failure. In order to establish a total failure of consideration the payor simply has to show that the basis upon which he had paid the money has totally failed. An illustration of such a total failure is provided by the facts of *Fibrosa* itself. The respondents agreed to manufacture machines for the appellants and to deliver them to Gdynia in Poland but, before delivery could be effected, the contract was frustrated when Poland was occupied by the German army. The House of Lords held that the appellants were entitled to recover their prepayment of £1,000 on the ground that it had been paid for a consideration which had wholly failed. The money had been paid for machinery and they had not received any part of the machinery as a result of the outbreak of war. Not having received any part of the performance for which they had contracted, they were entitled to recover their money as on a total failure of consideration.

While *Fibrosa* was an improvement upon *Chandler* it still left the law in an unsatisfactory state. First, money paid was only recoverable upon a *total* failure of consideration. Had the appellants in *Fibrosa* received any part of the performance for which they had contracted they would not have been entitled to recover their prepayment. Secondly, the law did little to protect the interest of the recipient of the money. It is likely that the respondents in *Fibrosa* had acted to their detriment in manufacturing the machinery for the appellants but any such detrimental reliance did not give the respondents a claim against the appellants nor did it entitle them to set-off their expenditure against the appellants' claim to recover the prepayment they had made. Thirdly, *Fibrosa* did nothing to improve the position of the party who has performed services prior to the frustration of the contract. The House of Lords was only dealing with money claims and did not purport to deal with the case where the benefit conferred on the other party took a form other than the payment of money.

Prior to *Fibrosa* a Law Revision Committee report had been produced on the rule laid down in *Chandler*. While *Fibrosa* solved some of the problems generated by *Chandler* it did not solve them all. Parliament therefore proceeded to enact legislation in the form of the Law Reform (Frustrated Contracts) Act 1943. The text of the Act is set out below. For our purposes the principal provisions are sections 1(2) and 1(3). Section 1(2) deals with the recovery of money, while 1(3) deals with recovery in respect of non-money benefits. The Act is a short one and it is set out in full below. The Act is then followed by an extract from the judgment of Robert Goff J in *BP Exploration Co (Libya) Ltd* v. *Hunt (No 2)* [1979] 1 WLR 783. The opening part of that judgment consists of a very clear exposition of the central provisions of the Act.

Law Reform (Frustrated Contracts) Act 1943

Adjustment of rights and liabilities of parties to frustrated contracts

1.—(1) Where a contract governed by English law has become impossible of performance or been otherwise frustrated, and the parties thereto have for that reason been discharged from the further performance of the contract, the following provisions of this section shall, subject to the provisions of section two of this Act, have effect in relation thereto.

(2) All sums paid or payable to any party in pursuance of the contract before the time when the parties were so discharged (in this Act referred to as 'the time of discharge') shall, in the case of sums so paid, be recoverable from him as money received by him for the use of the party by whom the sums were paid, and, in the case of sums so payable, cease to be so payable:

Provided that, if the party to whom the sums were so paid or payable incurred expenses before the time of discharge in, or for the purpose of, the performance of the contract, the court may, if it considers it just to do so having regard to all the circumstances of the case, allow him to retain or, as the case may be, recover the whole or any part of the sums so paid or payable, not being an amount in excess of the expenses so incurred.

(3) Where any party to the contract has, by reason of anything done by any other party thereto in, or for the purpose of, the performance of the contract, obtained a valuable benefit (other than a payment of money to which the last foregoing subsection applies) before the time of discharge, there shall be recoverable from him by the said other party such sum (if any), not exceeding the value of the said benefit to the party obtaining it, as the court considers just, having regard to all the circumstances of the case and, in particular,—

(a) the amount of any expenses incurred before the time of discharge by the benefited party in, or for the purpose of, the performance of the contract, including any sums paid or payable by him to any other party in pursuance of the contract and retained or recoverable by that party under the last foregoing subsection, and

(b) the effect, in relation to the said benefit, of the circumstances giving rise to the frustration of the contract.

(4) In estimating, for the purposes of the foregoing provisions of this section, the amount of any expenses incurred by any party to the contract, the court may, without prejudice to the generality of the said provisions, include such sum as appears to be reasonable in respect of overhead expenses and in respect of any work or services performed personally by the said party.

(5) In considering whether any sum ought to be recovered or retained under the foregoing provisions of this section by any party to the contract, the court shall not take into account any sums which have, by reason of the circumstances giving rise to the frustration of the contract, become payable to that party under any contract of insurance unless there was an obligation to insure imposed by an express term of the frustrated contract or by or under any enactment.

(6) Where any person has assumed obligations under the contract in consideration of the conferring of a benefit by any other party to the contract upon any other person, whether a party to the contract or not, the court may, if in all the circumstances of the case it considers it just to do so, treat for the purposes of subsection (3) of this section any benefit so conferred as a benefit obtained by the person who has assumed the obligations as aforesaid.

Provision as to application of this Act

2.—(1) This Act shall apply to contracts, whether made before or after the commencement of this Act, as respects which the time of discharge is on or after the first day of July, nineteen hundred and forty-three, but not to contracts as respects which the time of discharge is before the said date.

(2) This Act shall apply to contracts to which the Crown is a party in like manner as to contracts between subjects.

(3) Where any contract to which this Act applies contains any provision which, upon the true construction of the contract, is intended to have effect in the event of circumstances arising which operate, or would but for the said provision operate, to frustrate the

contract, or is intended to have effect whether such circumstances arise or not, the court shall give effect to the said provision and shall only give effect to the foregoing section of this Act to such extent, if any, as appears to the court to be consistent with the said provision.

(4) Where it appears to the court that a part of any contract to which this Act applies can properly be severed from the remainder of the contract, being a part wholly performed before the time of discharge, or so performed except for the payment in respect of that part of the contract of sums which are or can be ascertained under the contract, the court shall treat that part of the contract as if it were a separate contract and had not been frustrated and shall treat the foregoing section of this Act as only applicable to the remainder of that contract.

(5) This Act shall not apply—

(a) to any charterparty, except a time charterparty or a charterparty by way of demise, or to any contract (other than a charterparty) for the carriage of goods by sea; or

(b) to any contract of insurance, save as is provided by subsection (5) of the foregoing section; or

(c) to any contract to which section 7 of the Sale of Goods Act 1979 (which avoids contracts for the sale of specific goods which perish before the risk has passed to the buyer) applies, or to any other contract for the sale, or for the sale and delivery, of specific goods, where the contract is frustrated by reason of the fact that the goods have perished.

BP Exploration Co (Libya) Ltd v. Hunt (No 2)

[1979] 1 WLR 783, Queen's Bench Division

Mr Hunt was the owner of an oil concession granted by the Libyan government. He did not have the resources to develop the concession himself, so he entered into a joint venture with BP under which BP were to carry out the exploration and development of the site and they also agreed to transfer to Mr Hunt certain 'farm-in' contributions in cash and in oil. In return Mr Hunt agreed to grant BP a half share of the concession and further agreed to repay, over a period of time, 125% of BP's 'farm-in' contributions and his half share of the expenditure incurred in the exploration and development of the fields. Payment was to be made in the form of three-eighths of Mr Hunt's share of the oil produced from the field until such time as the reimbursement was complete. A giant oil field was discovered and the field came on stream in 1967. Once the field came on stream it was agreed that the costs of production would be divided equally between the parties. In 1971 BP's interest in the oil field was expropriated by the Libyan government and, in 1973, Mr Hunt's interest was also expropriated. At this point BP had received approximately one-third of their re-imbursement oil. BP claimed that the expropriation of the interests in the oil field had frustrated the contract between the parties and that they were entitled to the award of a 'just sum' under section 1(3) of the Law Reform (Frustrated Contracts) Act 1943. The extract that follows concentrates on the analysis of the Act itself. The application of the Act to the facts of the case will be dealt with in the commentary that follows the extract.

Robert Goff J

II   The principles governing claims under the Act of 1943

The Law Reform (Frustrated Contracts) Act 1943 is described as an Act to amend the law relating to the frustration of contracts. In fact, it is concerned not with frustration itself, but with the consequences of frustration; and it creates statutory remedies, enabling the court to award restitution in respect of benefits conferred under contracts thereafter frustrated.

Section 1(1) of the Act sets out the circumstances in which the Act applies, namely, that a contract governed by English law has become impossible of performance or been otherwise frustrated, and the parties thereto have for that reason been discharged from the further performance of the contract. However, section 2(5) excludes from the operation of the Act certain contracts, which are immaterial for the purposes of the present case; and section 2(4) provides that, where part of a contract can properly be severed from the remainder, the severed part having before the time of discharge been either wholly performed or so performed except for payment of ascertained or ascertainable sums, the court shall treat the severed part as a separate contract which has not been frustrated, the Act being applicable only to the remainder.

The most important subsections are subsections (2) and (3) of section 1, which set out the statutory remedies, the former being concerned with cases where the benefit conferred under the contract consists of money, and the latter with cases where the benefit does not consist of money. These subsections are of such importance that I shall set them out in full:

[he set out the terms of the subsections and continued]

Of the remaining provisions of the Act, section 2(1) and (2) are of no materiality to the present case, nor is section 1(6). Section 1(4) provides that, in estimating expenses incurred, sums may be included for overhead expenses, and for work or services performed personally. Section 2(3) is, however, of considerable importance. I shall quote the subsection in full:

[he set out the terms of the subsection and continued]

There remains section 1(5), which is possibly related to section 2(3). This subsection provides that the court is not to take into account any sums which have by reason of the circumstances giving rise to the frustration of the contract become payable under any contract of insurance, unless there was an obligation to insure imposed by an express term of the frustrated contract or by or under any enactment.

Such, in summary, is the Act. The historical background of the Act is well known. At one time, money paid under a contract thereafter frustrated was held to be irrecoverable. This was known as the rule in *Chandler* v. *Webster* [1904] 1 KB 493. The results of this rule were so obviously harsh that, following severe criticism, the rule was referred to the Law Revision Committee which, in its seventh interim report (Rule in *Chandler* v. *Webster*) (1939) (Cmd. 6009), recommended that (with exceptions relating to freight pro rata itineris and advance freight) money paid in pursuance of a contract thereafter frustrated (or, where a severable part of such a contract had been performed, money paid in pursuance of the remainder) should be recoverable, subject to a deduction of such sum as represented a fair allowance for expenditure incurred by the payee in the performance of or for the purpose of performing the contract. However in 1942, before this recommendation had been implemented, *Chandler* v. *Webster* was overruled by the House of Lords in *Fibrosa Spolka Akcyjna* v. *Fairbairn Lawson Combe Barbour Ltd* [1943] AC 32. The effect of that decision was that money paid under a contract thereafter frustrated was recoverable, but only if the consideration for the payment had wholly failed. It was, however, considered by certain members of the House of Lords that, even with the rule in *Chandler* v. *Webster* [1904] 1 KB 493 out of the way, the common law remedy was imperfect; attention was drawn in particular to the fact that there could be no recovery if the consideration had only partially failed, and that no allowance could be made for expenses incurred by the payee: see pp. 49–50, per Viscount Simon; pp. 54–55, per Lord Atkin; and pp. 71–72 per Lord Wright. Furthermore, the *Fibrosa* case was, like the report of the Law Revision Committee, concerned only with the recovery of money. Neither touched upon the more difficult question of restitution where the benefit conferred under a contract was a benefit other than a payment of money: in such cases, the old strict common law doctrine of entire contracts provided a formidable obstacle to restitution. At all events, no doubt stimulated by the observations made in the *Fibrosa* case, in the following year the legislature enacted the Act of 1943.

It was suggested in argument that I might have regard to the report of the Law Revision Committed in construing the Act of 1943. I do not, however, consider that the report is of any assistance to me. Its terms of reference were limited to consideration of the rule in *Chandler* v. *Webster* [1904] 1 KB 493; that case was overruled by the House of Lords in the period between the date of the report and the passing of the Act, and the scope of the Act is considerably wider than that of the report.

I turn, therefore, to the construction of the Act itself. Much argument was directed towards the problem of construction, and in particular to the effect to be given to section 1(2) and (3) and section 2(3) of the Act. I shall now set out my conclusions on the effect to be given to these subsections.

(1) *The principle of recovery*

(a)   The principle, which is common to both section 1(2) and (3), and indeed is the fundamental principle underlying the Act itself, is prevention of the unjust enrichment of either party to the contract at the other's expense. It was submitted by Mr Rokison, on behalf of B.P., that the principle common to both subsections was one of restitution for net benefits received, the net benefit being the benefit less an appropriate deduction for expenses incurred by the defendant. This is broadly correct so far as section 1(2) is concerned; but under section 1(3) the net benefit of the defendant simply provides an upper limit to the award—it does not measure the amount of the award to be made to the plaintiff. This is because in section 1(3) a distinction is drawn between the plaintiff's performance under the contract, and the benefit which the defendant has obtained by reason of that performance—a distinction about which I shall have more to say later in this judgment; and the net benefit obtained by the defendant from the plaintiff's performance may be more than a just sum payable in respect of such performance, in which event a sum equal to the defendant's net benefit would not be an appropriate sum to award to the plaintiff. I therefore consider it better to state the principle underlying the Act as being the principle of unjust enrichment, which underlies the right of recovery in very many cases in English law, and indeed is the basic principle of the English law of restitution, of which the Act forms part.

(b) Although section 1 (2) and (3) is concerned with restitution in respect of different types of benefit, it is right to construe the two subsections as flowing from the same basic principle and therefore, so far as their different subject matters permit, to achieve consistency between them. Even so, it is always necessary to bear in mind the difference between awards of restitution in respect of money payments and awards where the benefit conferred by the plaintiff does not consist of a payment of money. Money has the peculiar character of a universal medium of exchange. By its receipt, the recipient is inevitably benefited; and (subject to problems arising from such matters as inflation, change of position and the time value of money) the loss suffered by the plaintiff is generally equal to the defendant's gain, so that no difficulty arises concerning the amount to be repaid. The same cannot be said of other benefits, such as goods or services. By their nature, services cannot be restored; nor in many cases can goods be restored, for example where they have been consumed or transferred to another. Furthermore the identity and value of the resulting benefit to the recipient may be debatable. From the very nature of things, therefore, the problem of restitution in respect of such benefits is more complex than in cases where the benefit takes the form of a money payment; and the solution of the problem has been made no easier by the form in which the legislature has chosen to draft section 1(3) of the Act.

(c) The Act is not designed to do certain things: (i) It is not designed to apportion the loss between the parties. There is no general power under either section 1(2) or section 1(3) to make any allowance for expenses incurred by the plaintiff (except, under the proviso to section 1(2), to enable him to enforce pro tanto payment of a sum payable but unpaid before frustration); and expenses incurred by the defendant are only relevant in so far as they go to reduce the net benefit obtained by him and thereby limit any award to the plaintiff. (ii) It is not concerned to put the parties in the position in which they would have been if the contract had been performed. (iii) It is not concerned to restore the parties to the position they were in before the contract was made. A remedy designed to prevent unjust enrichment may not achieve that result; for expenditure may be incurred by either party under the contract which confers no benefit on the other, and in respect of which no remedy is available under the Act.

(d) An award under the Act may have the effect of rescuing the plaintiff from an unprofitable bargain. This may certainly be true under section 1(2), if the plaintiff has paid the price in advance for an expected return which, if furnished, would have proved unprofitable; if the contract is frustrated before any part of that expected return is received, and before any expenditure is incurred by the defendant, the plaintiff is entitled to the return of the price he has paid, irrespective of the consideration he would have recovered had the contract been performed. Consistently with section 1(2), there is nothing in section 1(3) which necessarily limits an award to the contract consideration. But the contract consideration may nevertheless be highly relevant to the assessment of the just sum to be awarded under section 1(3); this is a matter to which I will revert later in this judgment.

(2) Claims under section 1(2)

Where an award is made under section 1(2), it is, generally speaking, simply an award for the repayment of money which has been paid to to the defendant in pursuance of the contract, subject to an allowance in respect of expenses incurred by the defendant. It is not necessary that the consideration for the payment should have wholly failed: claims under section 1(2) are not limited to cases of total failure of consideration, and cases of partial failure of consideration can be catered for by a cross-claim by the defendant under section 1(2) or section 1(3) or both. There is no discretion in the court in respect of a claim under section 1(2), except in respect of the allowance for expenses; subject to such an allowance (and, of course, a cross-claim) the plaintiff is entitled to repayment of the money he has paid. The allowance for expenses is probably best rationalised as a statutory recognition of the defence of change of position. True, the expenses need not have been incurred by reason of the plaintiff's payment; but they must have been incurred in, or for the purpose of, the performance of the contract under which the plaintiff's payment has been made, and for that reason it is just that they should be brought into account. No provision is made in the subsection for any increase in the sum recoverable by the plaintiff, or in the amount of expenses to be allowed to the defendant, to allow for the time value of money. The money may have been paid, or the expenses incurred, many years before the date of frustration; but the cause of action accrues on that date, and the sum recoverable under the Act as at that date can be no greater than the sum actually paid, though the defendant may have had the use of the money over many years, and indeed may have profited from its use. Of course, the question whether the court may award interest from the date of the accrual of the cause of action is an entirely different matter, to which I shall refer later in this judgment.

(3) *Claims under section 1(3)*

(a) General. In contrast, where an award is made under section 1(3), the process is more complicated. First, it has to be shown that the defendant has, by reason of something done by the plaintiff in, or for the purpose of, the performance of the contract, obtained a valuable benefit (other than a payment of money) before the time of discharge. That benefit has to be identified, and valued, and such value forms the upper limit of the award. Secondly, the court may award to the plaintiff such sum, not greater than the value of such benefit, as it considers just having regard to all the circumstances of the case, including in particular the matters specified in section 1(3)(a) and (b). In the case of an award under section 1(3) there are, therefore, two distinct stages—the identification and valuation of the benefit, and the award of the just sum. The amount to be awarded is the just sum, unless the defendant's benefit is less, in which event the award will be limited to the amount of that benefit. The distinction between the identification and valuation of the defendant's benefit, and the assessment of the just sum, is the most controversial part of the Act. It represents the solution adopted by the legislature of the problem of restitution in cases where the benefit does not consist of a payment of money; but the solution so adopted has been criticised by some commentators as productive of injustice, and it certainly gives rise to considerable problems, to which I shall refer in due course.

(b) Identification of the defendant's benefit. In the course of the argument before me, there was much dispute whether, in the case of services, the benefit should be identified as the services themselves, or as the end product of the services. One example canvassed (because it bore some relationship to the facts of the present case) was the example of prospecting for minerals. If minerals are discovered, should the benefit be regarded (as Mr Alexander contended) simply as the services of prospecting, or (as Mr Rokison contended) as the minerals themselves being the end product of the successful exercise? Now, I am satisfied that it was the intention of the legislature, to be derived from section 1(3) as a matter of construction, that the benefit should in an appropriate case be identified as the end product of the services. This appears, in my judgment, not only from the fact that section 1(3) distinguishes between the plaintiff's performance and the defendant's benefit, but also from section 1(3)(b) which clearly relates to the product of the plaintiff's performance. Let me take the example of a building contract. Suppose that a contract for work on a building is frustrated by a fire which destroys the building and which, therefore, also destroys a substantial amount of work already done by the plaintiff. Although it might be thought just to award the plaintiff a sum assessed on a quantum meruit basis, probably a rateable part of the contract price, in respect of the work he has done, the effect of section 1(3)(b) will be to reduce the award to nil, because of the effect, in relation to the defendant's benefit, of the circumstances giving rise to the frustration of the contract. It is quite plain that, in section 1(3)(b), the word 'benefit' is intended to refer, in the example I have given, to the actual improvement to the building, because that is what will be affected by the frustrating event; the subsection therefore contemplates that, in such a case, the benefit is the end product of the plaintiff's services, not the services themselves. This will not be so in every case, since in some cases the services will have no end product; for example, where the services consist of doing such work as surveying, or transporting goods. In each case, it is necessary to ask the question: what benefit has the defendant obtained by reason of the plaintiff's contractual performance? But it must not be forgotten that in section 1(3) the relevance of the value of the benefit is to fix a ceiling to the award. If, for example, in a building contract, the building is only partially completed, the value of the partially completed building (i.e. the product of the services) will fix a ceiling for the award; the stage of the work may be such that the uncompleted building may be worth less than the value of the work and materials that have gone into it, particularly as completion by another builder may cost more than completion by the original builder would have cost. In other cases, however, the actual benefit to the defendant may be considerably more than the appropriate or just sum to be awarded to the plaintiff, in which event the value of the benefit will not in fact determine the quantum of the award. I should add, however, that, in a case of prospecting, it would usually be wrong to identify the discovered mineral as the benefit. In such a case there is always (whether the prospecting is successful or not) the benefit of the prospecting itself, i.e. of knowing whether or not the land contains any deposit of the relevant minerals; if the prospecting is successful, the benefit may include also the enhanced value of the land by reason of the discovery; if the prospector's contractual task goes beyond discovery and includes development and production, the benefit will include the further enhancement of the land by reason of the installation of the facilities, and also the benefit of in part transforming a valuable mineral deposit into a marketable commodity.

I add by way of footnote that all these difficulties would have been avoided if the legislature had thought it right to treat the services themselves as the benefit. In the opinion of many commentators, it would be more just to do so; after all, the services in question have been requested by the defendant, who normally takes the risk that they may prove worthless, from whatever cause. In the example I have given of the building destroyed by fire, there is much to be said for the view that the builder should be paid for the work he has done, unless he has (for example by agreeing to insure to works) taken upon himself the risk of destruction by fire. But my task is to construe the Act as it stands. On the true construction of the Act, it is in my judgment clear that the defendant's benefit must, in an appropriate case, be identified as the end product of the plaintiff's services, despite the difficulties which this construction creates, difficulties which are met again when one comes to value the benefit.

(c) Apportioning the benefit.   In all cases, the relevant benefit must have been obtained by the defendant by reason of something done by the plaintiff. Accordingly, where it is appropriate to identify the benefit with an end product and it appears that the defendant has obtained the benefit by reason of work done both by the plaintiff and by himself, the court will have to do its best to apportion that benefit, and to decide what proportion is attributable to the work done by the plaintiff. That proportion will then constitute the relevant benefit for the purposes of section 1(3) of the Act.

(d) Valuing the benefit.   Since the benefit may be identified with the product of the plaintiff's performance, great problems arise in the valuation of the benefit. First, how does one solve the problem which arises from the fact that a small service may confer an enormous benefit, and conversely, a very substantial service may confer only a very small benefit? The answer presumably is that at the stage of valuation of the benefit (as opposed to assessment of the just sum) the task of the court is simply to assess the value of the benefit to the defendant. For example, if a prospector after some very simple prospecting discovers a large and unexpected deposit of a valuable mineral, the benefit to the defendant (namely, the enhancement in the value of the land) may be enormous; it must be valued as such, always bearing in mind that the assessment of a just sum may very well lead to a much smaller amount being awarded to the plaintiff. But conversely, the plaintiff may have undertaken building work for a substantial sum which is, object-ively speaking, of little or no value—for example, he may commence the redecoration, to the defendant's execrable taste, of rooms which are in good decorative order. If the contract is frustrated before the work is complete, and the work is unaffected by the frustrating event, it can be argued that the defendant has obtained no benefit, because the defendant's property has been reduced in value by the plaintiff's work; but the partial work must be treated as a benefit to the defendant, since he requested it, and valued it as such. Secondly, at what point in time is the benefit to be valued? If there is a lapse of time between the date of the receipt of the benefit, and the date of frustration, there may in the meanwhile be a substantial variation in the value of the benefit. If the benefit had simply been identified as the services rendered, this problem would not arise; the court would simply award a reasonable remuneration for the services rendered at the time when they were rendered, the defendant taking the risk of any subsequent depreciation and the benefit of any subsequent appreciation in value. But that is not what the Act provides: section 1(3)(b) makes it plain that the plaintiff is to take the risk of depreciation or destruction by the frustrating event. If the effect of the frustrating event upon the value of the benefit is to be measured, it must surely be measured upon the benefit as at the date of frustration. For example, let it be supposed that a builder does work which doubles in value by the date of frustration, and is then so severely damaged by fire that the contract is frustrated; the valuation of the residue must surely be made on the basis of the value as at the date of frustration. However, does this mean that, for the purposes of section 1(3), the benefit is always to be valued as at the date of frustration? For example, if goods are transferred and retained by the defendant till frustration when they have appreciated or depreciated in value, are they to be valued as at the date of frustration? The answer must, I think, generally speaking, be in the affirmative, for the sake of consistency. But this raises an acute problem in relation to the time value of money. Suppose that goods are supplied and sold, long before the date of frustration; does the principle that a benefit is to be valued as at the date of frustration require that allowance must be made for the use in the meanwhile of the money obtained by the disposal of the goods, in order to obtain a true valuation of the benefit as at the date of frustration? This was one of the most hotly debated matters before me, for the very good reason that in the present case it affects the valuation of the parties' respective benefits by many millions of dollars. It is very tempting to conclude that an allowance should be made for the time value of money, because it appears to lead to a more realistic valuation of the benefit as at the date of frustration; and, as will appear hereafter, an appropriate method for making such an allowance is available in the form of the net discounted cash flow system of accounting. But I have come to the conclusion that, as a matter of construction, this course is not open to me. First, the subsection limits the award to the value of the benefit obtained by the defendant; and it does not follow that, because the defendant has had the money over a period of time, he has in fact derived any benefit from it. Secondly, if an allowance was to be made for the time value of the money obtained by the defendant, a comparable allowance should be made in respect of expenses incurred by the defendant, i.e. in respect of the period between the date of incurring the expenditure and the date of frustration, and section 1(3)(a) only contemplates that the court, in making an allowance for expenses, shall have regard to the 'amount of [the] expenses.' Thirdly, as I have already indicated, no allowance for the time value of money can be made under section 1(2); and it would be inconsistent to make such an allowance under section 1(3) but not under section 1(2).

Other problems can arise from the valuation of the defendant's benefit as the end product; I shall come to these later in the consideration of the facts of the present case. But there is a further problem which I should refer to, before leaving this topic. Section 1(3)(a) requires the court to have regard to the amount of any expenditure incurred before the time of discharge by the benefited party in, or for the purpose of, the performance of the contract. The question arises—should this matter be taken into account at the stage of valuation of the benefit, or of assessment of the just sum? Take a simple example. Suppose that the defendant's benefit is valued at £150, and that a just sum is assessed at £100, but that there remain to be taken into account defendant's expenses of £75: is the award to be £75 or £25? The clue to this problem lies, in my judgment, in the fact that the allowance for expenses is a statutory recognition of the defence of change of position. Only to the extent that the position of the defendant has so changed that it would be unjust to award restitution, should the court make an allowance for expenses. Suppose that the plaintiff does work for the defendant which produces no valuable end product, or a benefit no greater in value than the just sum to be awarded in respect of the work; there is then no reason why the whole of the relevant expenses should not be set off against the just sum. But suppose that the defendant has reaped a large benefit from the plaintiff's work, far greater in value than the just sum to be awarded for the work. In such circumstances it would be quite wrong to set off the whole of the defendant's expenses against the just sum. The question whether the defendant has suffered a change of position has to be judged in the light of all the circumstances of the case.

Accordingly, on the Act as it stands, under section 1(3) the proper course is to deduct the expenses from the value of the benefit, with the effect that only in so far as they reduce the value of the benefit below the amount of the just sum which would otherwise be awarded will they have any practical bearing on the award.

Finally, I should record that the court is required to have regard to the effect, in relation to the defendant's benefit, of the circumstances giving rise to the frustration of the contract. I have already given an example of how this may be relevant, in the case of building contracts; and I have recorded the fact that this provision has been the subject of criticism. There may, however, be circumstances where it would not be just to have regard to this factor—for example if, under a building contract, it was expressly agreed that the work in progress should be insured by the building-owner against risks which include the event which had the effect of frustrating the contract and damaging or destroying the work.

(e)   Assessment of the just sum.   The principle underlying the Act is prevention of the unjust enrichment of the defendant at the plaintiff's expense. Where, as in cases under section 1(2), the benefit conferred on the defendant consists of payment of a sum of money, the plaintiff's expense and the defendant's enrichment are generally equal; and, subject to other relevant factors, the award of restitution will consist simply of an order for repayment of a like sum of money. But where the benefit does not consist of money, then the defendant's enrichment will rarely be equal to the plaintiff's expense. In such cases, where (as in the case of a benefit conferred under a contract thereafter frustrated) the benefit has been requested by the defendant, the basic measure of recovery in restitution is the reasonable value of the plaintiff's performance—in a case of services, a quantum meruit or reasonable remuneration, and in a case of goods, a quantum valebat or reasonable price. Such cases are to be contrasted with cases where such a benefit has not been requested by the defendant. In the latter class of case, recovery is rare in restitution; but if the sole basis of recovery was that the defendant had been incontrovertibly benefited, it might be legitimate to limit recovery to the defendant's actual benefit—a limit which has (perhaps inappropriately) been imported by the legislature into section 1(3) of the Act. However, under section 1(3) as it stands, if the defendant's actual benefit is less than the just or reasonable sum which would otherwise be awarded to the plaintiff, the award must be reduced to a sum equal to the amount of the defendant's benefit.

A crucial question, upon which the Act is surprisingly silent, is this: what bearing do the terms of the contract, under which the plaintiff has acted, have upon the assessment of the just sum? First, the terms upon which the work was done may serve to indicate the full scope of the work done, and so be relevant to the sum awarded in respect of such work. For example, if I do work under a contract under which I am to receive a substantial prize if successful, and nothing if I fail, and the contract is frustrated before the work is complete but not before a substantial benefit has been obtained by the defendant, the element of risk taken by the plaintiff may be held to have the effect of enhancing the amount of any sum to be awarded. Secondly, the contract consideration is always relevant as providing some evidence of what will be a reasonable sum to be awarded in respect of the plaintiff's work. Thus if a prospector, employed for a fee, discovers a gold mine before the contract under which he is employed is frustrated (for example, by illegality or by his illness or disablement) at a time when his work was incomplete, the court may think it just to make an award in the nature of a reasonable fee for what he has done (though of course the benefit obtained by the defendant will be far greater), and a rateable part of the contract fee may provide useful evidence of the level of sum to be awarded. If, however, the contract had provided that he was to receive a stake in the concession, then the just sum might be enhanced on the basis that, in all the circumstances, a reasonable sum should take account of such a factor: cf. *Way* v. *Latilla* [1937] 3 All ER 759. Thirdly, however, the contract consideration, or a rateable part of it, may provide a limit to the sum to be awarded. To take a fairly extreme example, a poor householder or a small businessman may obtain a contract for building work to be done to his premises at considerably less than the market price, on the basis that he cannot afford to pay more. In such a case, the court may consider it just to limit the award to a rateable part of the contract price, on the ground that it was the understanding of the parties that in no circumstances (including the circumstances of the contract being frustrated) should the plaintiff recover more than the contract price or a rateable part of it. Such a limit may properly be said to arise by virtue of the operation of section 2(3) of the Act. But it must not be forgotten that, unlike money, services can never be restored, nor usually can goods, since they are likely to have been either consumed or disposed of, or to have depreciated in value; and since, ex hypothesi, the defendant will only have been prepared to contract for the goods or services on the basis that he paid no more than the contract consideration, it may be unjust to compel him, by an award under the Act, to pay more than that consideration, or a rateable part of it, in respect of the services or goods he has received. It is unnecessary for me to decide whether this will always be so; but it is likely that in most cases this will impose an important limit upon the sum to be awarded—indeed it may well be the most relevant limit to an award under section 1(3) of the Act. The legal basis of the limit may be section 2(3) of the Act; but even if that subsection is inapplicable, it is open to the court, in an appropriate case, to give effect to such a limit in assessing the just sum to be awarded under section 1(3), because in many cases it would be unjust to impose upon the defendant an obligation to make restitution under the subsection at higher than the contract rate.

(4) *The effect of section 2(3) of the Act*

The court has always to bear in mind the provisions of section 2(3) of the Act. It was submitted by Mr Rokison that effect should only be given to this subsection where the relevant contractual provision was clearly intended to have effect in the event of the frustrating circumstances. I can see no good reason for so qualifying the express words of the subsection. In my judgment the effect of the subsection depends, as it expressly provides, simply upon applying the ordinary principles of construction. If the contract contains any provision which, upon the true construction of the contract, is intended to have effect in the circumstances specified in the subsection, then the court can only give effect to section 1 of the Act to such extent as is consistent with such provision.

Examples of such provisions may be terms which have the effect of precluding recovery of any award under the Act, or of limiting the amount of any such award, for example, by limiting the award to the contractual consideration or a rateable part thereof. Similarly, the parties may contract upon the terms that the plaintiff shall not be paid until the occurrence of an event, and by reason of the frustration of the contract that event does not or cannot occur; then, if upon a true construction of the contract the court concludes that the plaintiff has taken the risk of non-payment in the event of such frustration the court should make no award by virtue of section 2(3) of the Act. Such may be the

conclusion if the contract contains an express term imposing upon the plaintiff an obligation to insure against the consequences of the frustrating event. Another example considered in argument was a loan of money advanced to a businessman on the terms that it
was to be repaid out of the profits of his business. Such a term should not automatically
preclude an award in the event of frustration, for example, if the businessman is incapacitated the day after the loan is made; but if the business consists, for example, of a ship,
which strikes a reef and sinks, then it may be that the court, having regard to the terms of
the contract and the risk taken thereunder by the lender, would make no award. But in
such cases the court should only refuse to make an award if it is satisfied that the plaintiff
has, by the contract, taken the risk of the consequences of the frustrating event. The
principle is the same as in those cases where the contract consideration controls the
amount or basis of the award under the Act—the court should not act inconsistently with
the contractual intention of the parties applicable in the events which have occurred. But,
such cases apart, the court is free to make an award which differs from the anticipated
contractual performace of the defendant. I have already referred to the fact that, under
section 1(2) at least, the effect of an award under the Act may be to rescue the plaintiff
from a bad bargain. Again, the contract may provide that the plaintiff is to receive goods
or services; the court may nevertheless make an award in money. The contract may
provide for the plaintiff to receive money at a certain place or in a certain currency;
frustration may render that impossible (for example, in a case of supervening illegality),
and the court may make an award for payment which takes effect at a different place or in
a different currency. Most striking of all, in most frustrated contracts under which the
claim is made in respect of a benefit other than money, the time for payment will not yet
have come—the contract, or a severable part of it, will be 'entire' in the old strict sense of
that term; I do not, however, consider that such a provision should automatically preclude an award under section 1(3). If it were intended to do so, there would be few
awards under section 1(3), and the matter would surely be the subject of an express
provision if it was the intention that so fundamental a qualification was to be imposed
upon the power of the court under this subsection. Certainly, no such qualification is
imposed in section 1(2), and no such result can be achieved in relation to an award under
that subsection since, generally speaking, the plaintiff is entitled to the return of his
money. In my judgment, only if upon a true construction of the contract the plaintiff has
contracted on the terms that he is to receive no payment in the event which has
occurred, will the fact that the contract is 'entire' have the effect of precluding an award
under the Act.

Both parties appealed to the Court of Appeal ([1981] 1 WLR 232) on various points
and the defendants further appealed to the House of Lords ([1983] 2 AC 352). The
grounds of appeal generally concerned issues with which we are not here concerned.
But there is one passage from the judgment of Lawton LJ in the Court of Appeal
which is of considerable significance. Its importance lies in the fact that it casts doubt
upon the analytical approach adopted by Robert Goff J, in particular, his attempt to
analyse the Act in terms of an underlying principle of the prevention of unjust
enrichment. Lawton LJ stated (at pp. 237–238 and 241–243):

The Act of 1943 was passed shortly after the decision of the House of Lords in *Fibrosa
Spolka Akcyjna* v. *Fairbairn Lawson Combe Barbour Ltd* [1943] AC 32, which overruled
Chandler v. *Webster* [1904] 1 KB 493. The earlier case had been regarded as authority for

the proposition that, on the occurrence of an event which frustrates the performance of a contract, the loss lies where it falls and that money paid by one party to the contract to the other party is to be retained by the party in whose hands it is. The object of the Act was to make the operation of the law more fair when a contract governed by English law . . . has become impossible of performance and the parties to it have for that reason been discharged from further performance. This was to be done by adjusting the rights and liabilities of the parties in the ways set out: see section 1(1).

Section 1(2) dealt with payments of money. They were to be recoverable as money received for the use of the payer; but an adjustment could be made for expenses incurred by the recipient before the time of discharge in, or for the purpose of, the performance of the contract. The amount of the adjustment was to be such as the court considered just, having regard to all the circumstances of the case. In section 1(3) the Act provided for the case where one party had obtained a valuable benefit (other than a payment of money) before the time of discharge . . .

Before the court can make an award under this subsection it must be satisfied that one party to a contract has obtained a valuable benefit by reason of something done by the other. In this case the plaintiffs did a great deal for the defendant and he obtained, before the frustrating events happened, a most valuable benefit from what they had done for him, which was so great that it was incapable of any exact valuation. This part of the problem presented no difficulties for the judge. What was difficult was the assessment of the sum which the court considered just, having regard to all the circumstances of the case. Save for what is mentioned in paragraphs (a) and (b), the subsection gives no help as to how, or upon what principles, the court is to make its assessment or as to what factors it is to take into account. The responsibility lies with the judge: he has to fix a sum which he, not an appellate court, *considers* just. This word connotes the mental processes going to forming an opinion. What is just is what the trial judge thinks is just. That being so, an appellate court is not entitled to interfere with his decision unless it is so plainly wrong that it cannot be just. The concept of what is just is not an absolute one. Opinions among right thinking people may, and probably will, differ as to what is just in a particular case. No one person enjoys the faculty of infallibility as to what is just. It is with these considerations in mind that we approach this case.

The judge assessed the just sum on what can be described as a reimbursement basis, that is to say, by ensuring as far as was practicable that the plaintiffs got back what they had paid out on the defendant's behalf before the frustrating events happened . . .

Mr Rokison, on behalf of the plaintiffs, accepted that there could be more than one way of assessing a just sum. He pointed out that there was nothing in the Act to indicate that its purpose was to enable the judge to apportion losses or profits, or to put the parties in the positions which they would have been in if the contract had been fully performed or if it had never been made. This we accept. He submitted that the concept behind the Act was to prevent unjust enrichment. This is what the judge had thought. We get no help from the use of words which are not in the statute. . . . In our judgment, this court would not be justified in setting aside the judge's way of assessment merely because we thought that there were better ways. Mr Rokison tried to show that the judge's way was wrong and palpably wrong. . . . In our judgment, it cannot be said that the judge went wrong, and certainly not palpably wrong, in assessing a just sum by reference to the concept of reimbursing the plaintiffs.

COMMENTARY

Applying the principles he had set out to the complex facts of the case Robert Goff J concluded that the 'valuable benefit' which Mr Hunt obtained as a result of the work done by BP before the frustration of the contract was the 'end product' of BP's services. This Robert Goff J identified with the enhancement in the value of Mr Hunt's concession. When valuing that benefit Robert Goff J held that section 1(3)(b) required him to take account of the circumstances giving rise to the frustration of the contract which, on the facts, had the effect of reducing the value of the benefit to the value of the oil which Mr Hunt had actually obtained from the oil field and the financial settlement which he had reached with the Libyan government. In assessing the 'just sum' BP were awarded the costs and expenses which they had incurred on Mr Hunt's account plus the 'farm-in' contributions in cash and oil received by Mr Hunt less the reimbursement oil which BP had received. In essence, the just sum was the reasonable value of the services rendered and goods supplied by BP with counter-restitution being made for the value of the oil received by BP.

Leaving to one side the complex facts of the case, what issues arise out of *BP* v. *Hunt* and the interpretation placed by the judges upon the provisions of the 1943 Act? There are three principal issues to note. The first relates to the principle which under-pins the Act. Robert Goff J stated that the principle was the prevention of unjust enrichment, whereas Lawton LJ stated, somewhat dismissively, that the court derived 'no help from the use of words which are not in the statute'. This leaves the basis of the Act obscure. The analysis of Robert Goff J does, however, seem to be the preferable one. The Act is not designed to provide a flexible machinery for the adjustment of losses. Unlike legislation subsequently enacted in other parts of the Commonwealth, the 1943 Act does not empower the court to apportion losses between parties to the contract. While the Act does confer a discretion upon the court, it is not a discretion that relates explicitly to the apportionment of losses. In all cases the court must first identify the benefit which the defendant has obtained at the expense of the claimant. The discretion given to the court relates only to the proportion of that benefit which is recoverable by the claimant. It is a discretion exercisable within a framework which seeks to prevent the unjust enrichment of one party at the expense of the other.

The second point relates to the scope of section 1(2). This subsection was not directly in issue on the facts of *BP* v. *Hunt* but it was nevertheless analysed in some detail by Robert Goff J. Section 1(2) differs from *Fibrosa* in two principal respects. First, the entitlement of the payor to recover the money paid is not confined to cases in which there has been a total failure of consideration. Money paid is recoverable even upon a partial failure of consideration. Secondly, the proviso to section 1(2) gives to the court a discretion to allow the payee to retain some or all of the prepayment that has been made. Robert Goff J rationalized the proviso as a statutory recognition of the defence of change of position. A rather different approach was, however, taken by Garland J in *Gamerco SA* v. *ICM/Fair Warning (Agency) Ltd* [1995] 1 WLR 1226. A contract to promote a rock concert was held to have been frustrated when the permit to hold the concert at a sports stadium in Madrid was suddenly withdrawn because of safety fears about the stadium. The plaintiff promoters had paid the defendant group the sum of $412,500 prior to the frustration of the contract and both parties had incurred expenditure in preparing for the concert. Garland J held that the plaintiffs were entitled to the return of the prepayment which they had made under section 1(2) of the Act and that no deduction should be made under the proviso to that sub-section. The plaintiffs were therefore entitled to recover the $412,500. In so concluding Garland J stated (at pp. 1236–1237):

Various views have been advanced as to how the court should exercise its discretion and these can be categorised as follows:

1. *Total retention.* This view was advanced by the Law Revision Committee in 1939 (Cmnd 6009) on the questionable ground 'that it is reasonable to assume that in stipulating for pre-payment the payee intended to protect himself from loss under the contract'. As the editor of Chitty *on Contracts*, 27th edn, (1994) vol 1., 1141, para 23-060, note 15 (Mr EG McKendrick) comments: 'He probably intends to protect himself against the possibility of the other party's insolvency or default in payment'. To this, one can add: 'and secure his own cash flow'.

[he then considered two passages from the judgment of Robert Goff J in *BP* v. *Hunt* set out at p. 909 above and continued]

I do not derive any specific assistance from the *BP Exploration* case. There was no question of any change of position as a result of the plaintiffs' advance payment.

2. *Equal division.* This was discussed by Professor Treitel in *Frustration and Force Majeure* pp. 555–556 at paras 15–059 and 15–060 of his book. There is some attraction in splitting the loss but what if the losses are very unequal? Professor Treitel considers statutory provisions in Canada and Australia but makes the point that equal division is unnecessarily rigid and was rejected by the Law Revision Commission in the 1939 report to which reference has already been made. The parties may, he suggests, have had unequal means of providing against the loss by insurers, but he appears to overlook sub-section (5). It may well be that one party's expenses are entirely thrown away while the other is left with some realisable or otherwise usable benefit or advantage. Their losses may, as in the present case, be very unequal. Professor Treitel therefore favours the third view.

3. *Broad discretion.* It is self-evident that any rigid rule is liable to produce injustice. The words, 'if it considers it just so to do in all the circumstances of the case' clearly confer a very broad discretion. Obviously the court must not take into account anything which is not 'a circumstance of the case' or fail to take into account anything that is and then exercise its discretion rationally. I see no indication in the Act, the authorities, or the relevant literature that the court is obliged to incline either towards total retention or equal division. Its task is to do justice in a situation which the parties neither contemplated nor provided for, and to mitigate the possible harshness of allowing all loss to lie where it has fallen.

I have not found my task easy. As I have made clear, I would have welcomed assistance on the true measure of the defendants' loss and the proper treatment of overhead and non-specific expenditure. Because the defendants have plainly suffered some loss, I have made a robust assumption. In all the circumstances, and having particular regard to the plaintiffs' loss, I consider that justice is done by making no deduction under the proviso.

We can see here the same approach as that adopted by the Court of Appeal in *BP* v. *Hunt,* namely an emphasis on the discretion of the court and a refusal to confine that discretion by seeking to articulate the principles upon which the exercise of the discretion is based. One point which does, however, emerge with some clarity from *Gamerco* relates to the location of the onus of proof. Garland J stated that the onus of proof was on the defendant. The significance of this can be seen from the case of *Lobb* v. *Vasey Housing Auxiliary* [1963] VR 239. The defendants were paid £1,250 by Mrs Smith for an exclusive licence to occupy a flat in a block of flats which they were building. Mrs Smith died before her flat was completed. The defendants refused to return the £1,250. Mrs Smith's executrix sued to recover it. It was held that the death of Mrs Smith frustrated the contract between the parties and that the onus of proof was on the defendants to show that it was just in all the circumstances of the case for them to retain any part of the pre-payment. They were unable to do this. The trial judge stated that in the typical case one would expect the defendants to sell the right to occupy the flat to someone else and to recover their expenses in that way.

The third point relates to the construction of section 1(3). The most important point here is Robert Goff J's interpretation of 'valuable benefit'. He concluded that, in 'an appropriate case', the benefit is to be identified with the 'end product' of the claimant's services and not with the services themselves. This has unfortunate consequences where the effect of the frustrating event is to destroy the work of the claimant. In such a case there is no end product and so nothing to value. An example is provided by the old case of *Appleby* v. *Myers* (1867) LR 2 CP 651. The plaintiffs contracted to make and erect machinery in the defendant's factory and to maintain the machinery for a period of two years. After part of the machinery had been erected, an accidental fire destroyed the factory and the machinery and so frustrated the contract. It was held that the plaintiffs were not entitled to recover any payment in respect of the work done prior to the frustration of the contract. The same result would appear to follow under section 1(3). The result is an unfortunate one but here it must be recalled that the Act does not seek to engage in loss apportionment as such. A claimant can only recover where the defendant has received a benefit as a result of the work he has done and the consequence of identifying the benefit with the end product of the work is to narrow the concept of benefit that underpins the Act so that reliance expenditure which does not result in an end product will not be recoverable under section 1(3). An example is provided by *Taylor* v. *Caldwell* (p. 869 above) itself. The claim brought by the plaintiffs was one to recover the expenses they had incurred in advertising the concerts. It is unlikely that such expenditure would generate a claim under the Act because it does not result in a valuable benefit to the defendant.

A three-stage approach must be taken to any claim brought under section 1(3). First, the benefit itself must be identified. The benefit will generally be the goods or, in the case of the provision of services, the end product of these services. Secondly, the benefit must be valued. Thirdly, the court must decide what is a 'just sum' on the facts of the case. The 'just sum' cannot exceed the value of the benefit conferred. In *BP* v. *Hunt* Robert Goff J took a similar approach to that taken in a restitutionary claim and held that the just sum was, essentially, the reasonable value of the services rendered. But the Court of Appeal chose to place emphasis instead on the discretion of the judge at first instance. Thus Lawton LJ stated that 'what is just is what the trial judge thinks is just' and that an appellate court is not entitled to interfere with the finding of the just sum by the trial judge unless it is 'so plainly wrong that it cannot be just'. On this view the trial judge has a substantial measure of discretion and it is extremely difficult to predict what will constitute a 'just sum' in any case involving the provision of services prior to the frustration of the contract. In this respect it is perhaps fortunate that a frustrated contract is a comparative rarity in commercial practice. This being the case, the Act rarely comes into play and so the deficiencies in the Act and in the reasoning of the Court of Appeal in *BP* v. *Hunt* rarely come to light.

8. THE BASIS OF FRUSTRATION

What is the basis of the doctrine of frustration? Given that the courts do not have the power at common law to set aside a term on the basis that it is unreasonable, on what basis can the courts claim to be entitled to set aside an entire contract on the ground that the circumstances have turned out to be radically different from those which the parties had in mind when they entered into the contract? Perhaps surprisingly, these questions do not appear to have troubled the courts. The doctrine of frustration is well-established, albeit that its exact juridical basis remains uncertain. The different possible bases for the doctrine of frustration were, however, discussed by the House of Lords in *National Carriers Ltd* v. *Panalpina (Northern) Ltd* [1981] AC 675, alongside the question of whether or not a lease can be frustrated. While the House of Lords decided in clear terms that a lease could, in principle, be frustrated, they were less clear as to the basis of the doctrine of frustration.

National Carriers Ltd v. Panalpina (Northern) Ltd

[1981] AC 675, House of Lords

National Carriers, the respondents, owned a warehouse on English Street, Kingston-upon-Hull. By an agreement dated 12 July 1974 they leased the warehouse to Panalpina, the appellants, for a ten-year term. Panalpina used the warehouse for the commercial storage of goods. They agreed not to use the warehouse other than for this purpose without the consent of National Carriers. The only vehicular access to the warehouse was by Kingston Street. On 16 May 1979 the Kingston-upon-Hull City Council closed Kingston Street to allow the demolition of a derelict building nearby. Kingston Street was closed for twenty months. During this time Panalpina could not use the warehouse and stopped paying rent to National Carriers. National Carriers brought an action for unpaid rent. In its defence Panalpina claimed that the lease had been frustrated by the closure of Kingston Street. The judge held that he was bound by authority to decide that a lease could not be the subject of frustration. The House of Lords held that the doctrine of frustration was in principle applicable to leases (Lord Russell *dubitante*) but that, on the facts, the lease in this case had not been frustrated.

Lord Hailsham of St Marylebone LC

The doctrine of frustration is of comparatively recent development. The general rule of common law, laid down as early as 1647 in *Paradine v. Jane*, Aleyn 26, is that the performance of absolute promises is not excused by supervening impossibility of performance. *Paradine* v. *Jane* itself, a case arising out of the civil war, was, like the present, an action of debt based on a covenant to pay rent contained in a lease. But, since the doctrine of frustration had not at that stage come into existence, the argument turned solely on the absolute and unconditional nature of the promise to pay the rent, and the applicability to the estate in land created by the demise of any such doctrine did not arise.

It is generally accepted that the doctrine of frustration has its roots in the decision of the Court of Queen's Bench given by Blackburn J in *Taylor* v. *Caldwell* (1863) 3 B & S 826. In that case, the parties to the contract had used terms appropriate to the relationship of landlord and tenant describing the money payment as 'rent' and the transaction as a 'letting'. But, after analysing the facts, Blackburn J decided that the true nature of the transaction was not one of landlord and tenant but one of licensor and licensee. He then added at p. 832, cryptically, the words: 'Nothing, however, in our opinion, depends on this'. I am inclined to think that by these words he was in effect taking the view which I myself am about to express, but, as counsel for the respondents firmly pointed out when I put the point to him in argument, they are capable of a more neutral meaning, viz. that since the question of demise did not arise in the case before the court it did not call for decision. I am content to assume, though I am inclined to the contrary view, that this is right.

At least five theories of the basis of the doctrine of frustration have been put forward at various times, and, since the theoretical basis of the doctrine is clearly relevant to the point under discussion, I enumerate them here. The first is the 'implied term' or 'implied condition' theory on which Blackburn J plainly relied in *Taylor* v. *Caldwell*, as applying to the facts of the case before him. To these it is admirably suited. The weakness, it seems to me, of the implied term theory is that it raises once more the spectral figure of the officious bystander intruding on the parties at the moment of agreement. In the present case, had the officious bystander pointed out to the parties in July 1974 the danger of carrying on the business of a commercial warehouse opposite a listed building of doubtful stability and asked them what they would do in the event of a temporary closure of Kingston Street pending a public local inquiry into a proposal for demolition after the lease had been running for over five years, I have not the least idea what they would have said, or whether either would have entered into the lease at all. In *Embiricos v. Sydney Reid & Co* [1914] 3 KB 45, 54 Scrutton J appears to make the estimate of what constitutes a frustrating event something to be ascertained only at the time when the parties to a contract are called on to make up their minds, and this I would think to be right, both as to the inconclusiveness of hindsight which Scrutton J had primarily in mind and as to the inappropriateness of the intrusion of an officious bystander immediately prior to the conclusion of the agreement.

Counsel for the respondent sought to argue that *Taylor* v. *Caldwell*, 3 B & S 826, could as easily have been decided on the basis of a total failure of consideration. This is the second of the five theories. But *Taylor* v. *Caldwell* was clearly not so decided, and in any event many, if not most, cases of frustration which have followed *Taylor* v. *Caldwell* have occurred during the currency of a contract partly executed on both sides, when no question of total failure of consideration can possibly arise.

In *Hirji Mulji* v. *Cheong Yue Steamship Co Ltd* [1926] AC 497, 510 Lord Sumner seems to have formulated the doctrine as a '. . . device [sic], by which the rules as to absolute contracts are reconciled with a special exception which justice demands' and Lord Wright in *Denny, Mott & Dickson Ltd* v. *James B Fraser & Co Ltd* [1944] AC 265, 275 seems to prefer this formulation to the implied condition view. The weakness of the formulation, however, if the implied condition theory, with which Lord Sumner coupled it, be rejected, is that, though it admirably expresses the purpose of the doctrine, it does not provide it with any theoretical basis at all.

Hirji Mulji v. *Cheong Yue Steamship Co Ltd* is, it seems to me, really an example of the more sophisticated theory of 'frustration of the adventure' or 'foundation of the con-tract' formulation, said to have originated with *Jackson* v. *Union Marine Insurance Co Ltd* (1874) LR 10 CP 125, compare also, for example, per Goddard J in *W J Tatem Ltd* v. *Gamboa* [1939] 1 KB 132, 138. This, of course, leaves open the question of what is, in any given case, the foundation of the contract or what is 'fundamental' to it, or what is the 'adventure'. Another theory, of which the parent may have been Earl Loreburn in *F A Tamplin Steamship Co Ltd* v. *Anglo-Mexican Petroleum Products Co Ltd* [1916] 2 AC 397 is that the doctrine is based on the answer to the question: 'What in fact is the true meaning of the contract?': see p. 404. This is the 'construction theory'. In *Davis Contractors Ltd* v. *Fareham Urban District Council* [1956] AC 696, 729 Lord Radcliffe put the matter thus, and it is the formulation I personally prefer:

> '. . . frustration occurs whenever the law recognises that without default of either party a contractual obligation has become incapable or being performed because the cir-cumstances in which performance is called for would render it a thing radically differ-ent from that which was undertaken by the contract. Non haec in foedera veni. It was not this that I promised to do.'

Incidentally, it may be partly because I look at frustration from this point of view that I find myself so much in agreement with my noble and learned friends that the appellants here have failed to raise any triable issue as to frustration by the purely temporary, though prolonged, and in 1979 indefinite, interruption, then expected to last about a year, in the access to the demised premises. In all fairness, however, I must say that my approach to the question involves me in the view that whether a supervening event is a frustrating event or not is, in a wide variety of cases, a question of degree, and therefore to some extent at least of fact, whereas in your Lordships' House in *Tsakiroglou & Co Ltd* v. *Noblee Thorl GmbH* [1962] AC 93 the question is treated as one at least involving a question of law, or, at best, a question of mixed law and fact . . .

This discussion brings me to the central point at issue in this case which, in my view, is whether or not there is anything in the nature of an executed lease which prevents the doctrine of frustration, however formulated, applying to the subsisting relationship between the parties. That the point is open in this House is clear from the difference of opinion expressed in *Cricklewood Property and Investment Trust Ltd* v. *Leighton's Invest-ment Trust Ltd* [1945] AC 221 between the second Lord Russell of Killowen and Lord Goddard on the one hand, who answered the question affirmatively, and Viscount Simon LC and Lord Wright on the other, who answered it negatively, with Lord Porter reserving his opinion until the point arose definitively for consideration. The point, though one of principle, is a narrow one. It is the difference immortalised in *HMS Pinafore* between 'never' and 'hardly ever', since both Viscount Simon and Lord Wright clearly conceded that, though they thought the doctrine applicable in principle to leases, the cases in which it could properly be applied must be extremely rare.

With the view of Viscount Simon and Lord Wright I respectfully agree. . . . I conclude that the matter is not decided by authority and that the question is open to your Lordships to decide on principle. In my view your Lordships ought now so to decide it. Is there anything in principle which ought to prevent a lease from ever being frustrated? I think there is not . . .

In the result, I come down on the side of the 'hardly ever' school of thought. No doubt the circumstances in which the doctrine can apply to leases are, to quote Viscount Simon LC in the *Cricklewood* case, at p. 231, 'exceedingly rare'. Lord Wright appears to have thought the same, whilst adhering to the view that there are cases in which frustration can apply, at p. 241. But, as he said in the same passage: '. . . the doctrine of frustration is modern and flexible and is not subject to being constricted by an arbitrary formula'. To this school of thought I respectfully adhere.

Lord Wilberforce

My Lords, the arguments for and against application of [the doctrine of frustration] are fully and cogently put in the rival speeches in the *Cricklewood* case, for its possible application by Viscount Simon LC and Lord Wright, against by Lord Russell of Killowen and Lord Goddard. I can therefore give fairly briefly the reasons which have persuaded me, on the whole, that the former ought to be preferred.

1. The doctrine of frustration of contracts made its appearance in English law in answer to the proposition, . . . that an obligation expressed in absolute and unqualified terms, such as an obligation to pay rent, had to be performed and could not be excused by supervening circumstances. Since *Taylor* v. *Caldwell*, 3 B & S 826, it has been applied generally over the whole field of contract.

2. Various theories have been expressed as to its justification in law: as a device by which the rules as to absolute contracts are reconciled with a special exception which justice demands, as an implied term, as a matter of construction of the contract, as related to removal of the foundation of the contract, as a total failure of consideration. It is not necessary to attempt selection of any one of these as the true basis: my own view would be that they shade into one another and that a choice between them is a choice of what is most appropriate to the particular contract under consideration . . . the doctrine can now be stated generally as part of the law of contract; as all judicially evolved doctrines it is, and ought to be, flexible and capable of new applications.

3. In view of this generality, the onus, in my opinion, lies on those who assert that the doctrine can never apply to leases. They have at once to face the argument that it has been held to apply to demise charters of ships (and presumably by analogy could apply to hirings of other chattels), and to licences for use: *Krell* v. *Henry* [1903] 2 KB 740 and other Coronation cases. So why not to leases of land? To place leases of land beyond a firm line of exclusion seems to involve anomalies, to invite fine distinctions, or at least to produce perplexities. How, for example, is one to deal with agreement for leases? Refusal ever to apply the doctrine to leases of land must be based upon some firm legal principle which cannot be departed from . . .

4. Two arguments only by way of principle have been suggested. The first is that a lease is more than a contract: it conveys an estate in land. This must be linked to the fact

that the English law of frustration, unlike its continental counterparts, requires, when it applies, not merely adjustment of the contract, but its termination. But this argument, by itself, is incomplete as a justification for denying that frustration is possible. The argument must continue by a proposition that an estate in land once granted cannot be divested— which, as Viscount Simon LC pointed out in the *Cricklewood* case [1945] AC 221, 229, begs the whole question . . .

In the second place, if the argument is to have any reality, it must be possible to say that frustration of leases cannot occur because in any event the tenant will have that which he bargained for, namely, the leasehold estate. Certainly this may be so in many cases. . . . But there may also be cases where this is not so . . .

The second argument of principle is that on a lease the risk passes to the lessee, as on a sale it passes to the purchaser. . . . But the two situations are not parallel. Whether the risk—or any risk—passes to the lessee depends on the terms of the lease: it is not uncommon, indeed, for some risks—of fire or destruction—to be specifically allocated. So in the case of unspecified risks, which may be thought to have been mutually contemplated, or capable of being contemplated by reasonable men, why should not the court decide on whom the risks are to lie? And if it can do this and find that a particular risk falls upon the lessor, the consequence may follow that upon the risk eventuating the lessee is released from his obligation . . .

In my opinion, therefore, though such cases may be rare, the doctrine of frustration is capable of application to leases of land. It must be so applied with proper regard to the fact that a lease, that is, a grant of a legal estate, is involved. The court must consider whether any term is to be implied which would determine the lease in the event which has happened and/or ascertain the foundation of the agreement and decide whether this still exists in the light of the terms of the lease, the surrounding circumstances and any special rules which apply to leases or to the particular lease in question.

Lord Simon of Glaisdale
Frustration of a contract takes place when there supervenes an event (without default of either party and for which the contract makes no sufficient provision) which so significantly changes the nature (not merely the expense or onerousness) of the outstanding contractual rights and/or obligations from what the parties could reasonably have contemplated at the time of its execution that it would be unjust to hold them to the literal sense of its stipulations in the new circumstances; in such case the law declares both parties to be discharged from further performance.

Whether the doctrine can apply to a lease is of more than academic interest, considerable though that is . . .

The question is entirely open in your Lordships' House, as was recognised in the *Cricklewood Property* case. In my view a lease is not inherently unsusceptible to the application of the doctrine of frustration.

In the first place, the doctrine has been developed by the law as an expedient to escape from injustice where such would result from enforcement of a contract in its literal terms after a significant change in circumstances. . . . Secondly, in the words of Lord Wright in the *Cricklewood Property* case, at p. 241: '. . . the doctrine of frustration is modern and flexible and is not subject to being constricted by an arbitrary formula'. It is therefore on the face of it apt to vindicate justice wherever owing to relevant supervening circumstances the enforcement of any contractual arrangement in its literal terms would produce injustice.

Thirdly, the law should if possible be founded on comprehensive principles: compartmentalism, particularly if producing anomaly, leads to the injustice of different results in fundamentally analogous circumstances. To deny the extension of the doctrine of frustration to leaseholds produces a number of undesirable anomalies . . .

Fourthly, a number of theories have been advanced to clothe the doctrine of frustration in juristic respectability, the two most in favour being the 'implied term theory' (which was potent in the development of the doctrine and which still provides a satisfactory explanation of many cases) and the 'theory of a radical change in obligation' or 'construction theory' (which appears to be the one most generally accepted today). . . . My noble and learned friends who have preceded me have enumerated the various theories; and the matter is discussed in *Chitty on Contracts*, 24th ed. (1977), vol I, paras 1401–1411, pp. 656–663. Of all the theories put forward the only one, I think, incompatible with the application of the doctrine to a lease is that which explains it as based on a total failure of consideration. Though such may be a feature of some cases of frustration, it is plainly inadequate as an exhaustive explanation: there are many cases of frustration where the contract has been partly executed . . .

Fifthly, a lease may be prematurely determined in a considerable variety of circumstances. . . . Sixthly, it seems that authorities in some other common law jurisdictions have felt no inherent difficulty in applying the doctrine of frustration to a lease . . .

Lastly . . . 'It is no longer sensible to pretend that a commercial lease . . . is simply a conveyance and not also a contract'. The doctrine of frustration, no less than the doctrine of repudiation, is applicable to a contract. It must therefore be determined whether there is anything in a lease-as-conveyance which repels the doctrine of frustration inherent in the lease-as-contract—outweighing the demands of justice, of consistency, of juristic theory accounting for the doctrine, of analogy and of authoritative opinion in other common law jurisdictions.

I therefore turn to consider the arguments to the contrary. . . . The arguments are, I think, fourfold:

1.   The lease itself is the 'venture' or 'undertaking' on which the parties have embarked. In so far as the lease is contractual, the 'foundation' of the contract is the transfer of the landlord's possession of the demised property for a term of years in return for rent; that happens once for all on the execution of the lease; so that its contractual 'foundation' is never destroyed.

2.   The lease is more than a contract: it creates a legal estate or interest in land, and, added counsel for the respondents, it operates in rem.

3.   The contractual obligations in a lease are merely incidental to the relationship of landlord and tenant.

4.   On the conveyance the 'risk' of unforeseen events passes to the lessee, as it does to the purchaser of land.

. . . The real questions, in my respectful submission, are the second and fourth—namely, whether the fact that a legal estate or interest in land has been created makes a lease inherently unsusceptible of the application of the doctrine of frustration, and that the risk of what might otherwise be a frustrating event passes irrevocably to the lessee on execution of the lease . . .

I can for myself see nothing about the fact of creation of an estate or interest in land which repels the doctrine of frustration. . . . A fully executed contract cannot be frustrated; and a sale of land is characteristically such a contract. But a lease is partly executory: rights and obligations remain outstanding on both sides throughout its currency. Even a partly executed contract is susceptible of frustration in so far as it remains executory: there are many such cases in the books. . . . My conclusion on the first issue is therefore that the doctrine of frustration is in principle applicable to leases.

Lord Russell of Killowen

I am prepared to accept that the termination of a lease may be involved in the frustration of a commercial adventure when, as merely incidental to the overall commercial adventure, and a subordinate factor, a lease has been granted. To that extent at least I accept that there may be frustration of a lease, . . . I would reserve consideration of cases of physical destruction of flying leaseholds: and of the total disappearance of the site comprised in the lease into the sea so that it no longer existed in the form of a piece of terra firma and could not be the subject of re-entry or forfeiture. In that last case I would not need the intervention of any court to say that the term of years could not outlast the disappearance of its subject matter: the site would no longer have a freeholder lessor, and the obligation to pay rent, which issues out of the land, could not survive its substitution by the waves of the North Sea.

It will be sufficiently seen from what I have said that I am not able to go so far as do your Lordships on the potential applicability of the doctrine of frustration to leases, and would with minor qualification adhere to the views expressed in the *Cricklewood* case in this House (*Cricklewood Property and Investment Trust Ltd* v. *Leighton's Investment Trust Ltd* [1945] AC 221) by Lord Russell of Killowen and Lord Goddard . . .

Lord Roskill

On the question of principle I find it impossible to justify compartmentalisation of the law or to agree that the doctrine of frustration applies to every type of contract save a lease. I can see no logical difference between frustration of a demise charterparty and frustration of a lease. In principle the doctrine should be equally capable of universal application in all contractual arrangements. . . . But to hold that the doctrine is capable of applying to leases does not mean that it should be readily applied . . . I do not think any useful purpose would presently be served by attempting to categorise those cases where the doctrine might be successfully invoked and those where it might not. Circumstances must always vary infinitely.

COMMENTARY

Does the debate as to the jurisprudential basis of the doctrine of frustration matter? Probably not a great deal. The issue is put as follows in H Beale (ed), *Chitty on Contracts* (29th edn, Sweet & Maxwell, 2004), para 23-018):

It is . . . difficult to discern any practical consequence which flows from the different tests because, as Lord Wilberforce has stated, they appear to shade into one another. The courts have regard to the construction of the contract, the effect of the changed circumstances on the parties' contractual obligations, the intentions of the parties (objectively construed) and the demands of justice in deciding whether or not a contract has been frustrated. No one factor is conclusive: the court will balance these different factors in determining whether a contract has been frustrated. On the other hand, it must be conceded that the basis of the doctrine is not unimportant in jurisprudential terms. A test based on a fictitious or artificial assumption (such as the implied term approach) may prevent a proper understanding of the function of the doctrine and of the role of the court in applying it. And the literal application of the one theory might lead to results which are incompatible with the rules which presently make up the doctrine of frustration. For example, the implied term theory, literally applied, may suggest that the question whether a contract is frustrated is one of fact, based on the intention of the parties, but it is clear law that the question whether a contract has been frustrated is one of law. It is, however, unlikely that a modern court would apply a theory where it led to a result which was incompatible with the present rules and so it is submitted that no practical consequences flow from the debate as to the correct conceptual basis of the doctrine of frustration.

The statement that it is unlikely that practical consequences flow from the debate as to the correct conceptual basis of the doctrine plainly does not tell us what is the correct conceptual basis. It could be a concern for the fairness of the bargain made by the parties: in this sense it could be said that the courts are struggling to strike a balance between a concern for the fairness of the bargain made by the parties and the desire to hold people to the terms of their contract. On the other hand, it could be said that the courts are primarily engaged in an interpretative exercise; that is to say, they are endeavouring to ascertain whether or not the parties have made provision for the event which has occurred and, if they have not, to determine whether performance of the bargain according to its terms in the changed circumstances would be something radically different from the obligations which the parties had originally assumed under their contract.

From a comparative perspective, one of the most striking features of the doctrine of frustration in English law is the narrow scope within which it operates. There are two points here. First, the doctrine is rarely invoked and, secondly, where it is applicable, its effect is to discharge the contract. The courts are not given a power to adjust the contract to meet the changed circumstances; they must either uphold the contract according to its terms or set it aside. Parties who wish to adjust their contract must insert an express term in the contract to this effect. In other legal systems the courts do have broader powers to intervene and to adjust the contract. As far as English law is concerned, it is for the parties to protect themselves against the consequences of an improvident bargain by inserting an appropriately drafted force majeure clause or hardship clause into the contract: they cannot rely on the courts to act as their saviour. It can be argued that this approach unnecessarily increases the transaction costs of the parties because it compels them to incur the cost of drawing up an appropriate clause. On the other hand, the diversity and sophistication of the various force majeure and hardship clauses currently in use demonstrates that these are complex issues and it can be said with some justification that they are best dealt with by the parties and not by the courts. Further, a cost of giving a power to the court to adjust contracts in a wider range of circumstances is that it will generate uncertainty. The current English position may be harsh on a party who has entered into a bad bargain, but it has the merit of being clear. Once again we can see the tension between the demands of certainty and a concern for fairness.

It is interesting to compare English law with the Vienna Convention on Contracts for the International Sale of Goods, the Principles of European Contract Law, and the Unidroit Principles of International Commercial Contracts. The Vienna Convention does not make any provision for hardship or adjustment of the contract. Article 79 (below) proved to be one of the most controversial provisions in the Convention. Its scope is uncertain in that it is not clear what constitutes an 'impediment' for the purposes of Article 79(1). Further, the effect of force majeure is to protect a party against a liability in damages but it leaves other remedies, such as termination, intact. Both the Principles of European Contract Law (below) and the Unidroit Principles (below) make provision for hardship as well as force majeure. Two comments can be made here. First, it may not always be a straightforward matter to decide whether a particular case falls within the hardship/change of circumstances provisions or whether it falls within the force majeure/excuse provisions. Secondly, the hardship/ change of circumstances provisions are likely to generate some uncertainty. The commentary to Article 6:111 of the Principles of European Contract Law states that 'the mechanism reflects the modern trend towards giving the court some power to moderate the rigours of freedom and sanctity of contract'. This may be true. But in doing so it will generate considerable uncertainty. In many ways we are debating what is the most appropriate default rule. English law in principle holds the parties to their bargain and so leaves it to the parties to make their own provision for events which may make performance more onerous. The Principles of European Contract Law, by contrast, confer broader powers on the court, while leaving it open to the parties to exclude these powers should they wish to do so. Striking the most appropriate balance between these competing considerations is a difficult matter.

Vienna Convention on Contracts for the International Sale of Goods

Article 79

1.   A party is not liable for a failure to perform any of his obligations if he proves that the failure was due to an impediment beyond his control and he could not reasonably be expected to have taken the impediment into account at the time of the conclusion of the contract or to have avoided or overcome it or its consequences.

2.   If the party's failure is due to the failure by a third person whom he has engaged to perform the whole or a part of the contract, that party is exempt from liability only if:

(a) he is exempt under the preceding paragraph; and

(b) the person whom he has so engaged would be so exempt if the provisions of that paragraph were applied to him.

3.   The exemption provided by this article has effect for the period during which the impediment exists.

4.   The party who fails to perform must give notice to the other party of the impediment and its effect on his ability to perform. If the notice is not received by the other party

within a reasonable time after the party who fails to perform knew or ought to have known of the impediment, he is liable for damages resulting from such non-receipt.

5.   Nothing in this article prevents either party from exercising any right other than to claim damages under this Convention.

Principles of European Contract Law

Article 6:111—Change of Circumstances

(1) A party is bound to fulfil its obligations even if performance has become more onerous, whether because the cost of performance has increased or because the value of the performance it receives has diminished.

(2) If, however, performance of the contract becomes excessively onerous because of a change of circumstances, the parties are bound to enter into negotiations with a view to adapting the contract or terminating it, provided that:

  (a) the change of circumstances occurred after the time of conclusion of the contract,

  (b) the possibility of a change of circumstances was not one which could reasonably have been taken into account at the time of conclusion of the contract, and

  (c) the risk of the change of circumstances is not one which, according to the contract, the party affected should be required to bear.

(3) If the parties fail to reach agreement within a reasonable period, the court may:

  (a) terminate the contract at a date and on terms to be determined by the court; or

  (b) adapt the contract in order to distribute between the parties in a just and equitable manner the losses and gains resulting from the change of circumstances. In either case, the court may award damages for the loss suffered through a party refusing to negotiate or breaking off negotiations contrary to good faith and fair dealing.

Article 8:108—Excuse Due to an Impediment

(1) A party's non-performance is excused if it proves that it is due to an impediment beyond its control and that it could not reasonably have been expected to take the impediment into account at the time of the conclusion of the contract, or to have avoided or overcome the impediment or its consequences.

(2) Where the impediment is only temporary the excuse provided by this article has effect for the period during which the impediment exists. However, if the delay amounts to a fundamental non-performance, the obligee may treat it as such.

(3) The non-performing party must ensure that notice of the impediment and of its effect on its ability to perform is received by the other party within a reasonable time after the non-performing party knew or ought to have known of these circumstances. The other party is entitled to damages for any loss resulting from the non-receipt of such notice.

Unidroit Principles of International Commercial Contracts

Contract to be observed

6.2.1. (1) Where the performance of a contract becomes more onerous for one of the parties, that party is nevertheless bound to perform its obligations subject to the following provisions on hardship.

Definition of hardship

6.2.2. There is hardship where the occurrence of events fundamentally alters the equilibrium of the contract either because the cost of a party's performance has increased or because the value of the performance a party receives has diminished, and

(a) the events occur or become known to the disadvantaged party after the conclusion of the contract;

(b) the events could not reasonably have been taken into account by the disadvantaged party at the time of the conclusion of the contract;

(c) the events are beyond the control of the disadvantaged party; and

(d) the risk of the events was not assumed by the disadvantaged party.

Effects of hardship

6.2.3. (1) In case of hardship the disadvantaged party is entitled to request renegotiations. The request shall be made without undue delay and shall indicate the grounds on which it is based.

(2) The request for renegotiation does not itself entitle the disadvantaged party to withhold performance.

(3) Upon failure to reach agreement within a reasonable time either party may resort to the court.

(4) If a court finds hardship it may, if reasonable,

(a) terminate the contract at a date and on terms to be fixed; or

(b) adapt the contract with a view to restoring its equilibrium.

Force majeure

7.1.7. (1) Non-performance by a party is excused if that party proves that the non-performance was due to an impediment beyond its control and that it could not reasonably be expected to have taken the impediment into account at the time of the conclusion of the contract or to have avoided or overcome it or its consequences.

(2) When the impediment is only temporary, the excuse shall have effect for such period as is reasonable having regard to the effect of the impediment on performance of the contract.

(3) The party who fails to perform must give notice to the other party of the impediment and its effect on its ability to perform. If the notice is not received by the other party within a reasonable time after the party who fails to perform knew or ought to have known of the impediment, it is liable for damages resulting from such non-receipt.

(4) Nothing in this article prevents a party from exercising a right to terminate the contract or to withhold performance or request interest on money due.

9. FURTHER READING

McKENDRICK, E, 'The Regulation of Long-term Contracts in English Law' in Beatson, J and Friedmann, D (eds), *Good Faith and Fault in Contract Law* (Oxford University Press, 1995), p. 305.

—— 'Force Majeure and Frustration—Their Relationship and a Comparative Assessment' in McKENDRICK, E (ed), *Force Majeure and Frustration of Contract* (2nd edn, LLP, 1995), p. 33.

—— 'Frustration, Restitution and Loss Apportionment' in Burrows, A (ed), *Essays on Restitution* (Oxford University Press, 1991), p. 147.

TREITEL, GH, *Frustration and Force Majeure* (2nd edn, Sweet & Maxwell, 2004).

PART IV

REMEDIES FOR BREACH

24

BREACH OF CONTRACT
AND TERMINATION

1. CENTRAL ISSUES

1. A breach of contract consists of a failure, without lawful excuse, to perform a contractual obligation. The breach can take different forms, such as a refusal to perform, defective performance, or late performance. Breach of contract is generally a form of strict liability; that is to say, it is not usually necessary to prove fault in order to establish the existence of a breach.

2. While every breach of contract gives rise to a right to claim damages in respect of the loss occasioned by the breach, not every breach of contract gives to the innocent party the right to terminate the contract. Identification of the circumstances in which a party is entitled to terminate a contract in the event of a breach by the other party raises difficult technical questions, but it also gives rise to some difficult questions of policy. In the event of a breach should the law encourage the parties to stick together and work out their differences or should it confer upon the parties a wide right to terminate their relationship so as to enable them to find alternative performance elsewhere? English law generally attaches considerable significance to the right to terminate and it recognizes a wider right to terminate than that to be found in many other legal systems in the world. The right to terminate, as a matter of English law, depends in part upon the nature of the term broken (whether or not it is a condition) but also upon the consequences of the breach. A large part of this chapter is devoted to the identification of the circum-

stances in which the law entitles a party to terminate further performance of the contract and to the policy issues which are at stake in these cases.

3. A breach of contract does not, of itself, bring a contract to an end. The breach may give to the innocent party the right to terminate the contract but it is for the innocent party to decide whether or not to exercise that right. The innocent party has a right of election; that is to say, he can choose either to affirm the contract or to terminate it. Once he has made his decision, it is, in principle, irrevocable.

4. It is possible to breach a contract before the time for performance has arrived. This is known as an anticipatory breach of contract. An example is a case in which one party informs the other, before the time for performance, that he will not perform his obligations under the contract. In such a case the innocent party is not required to wait until the time for performance to arrive (although he is entitled to do so); he can decide immediately to terminate the contract and claim damages. The innocent party may decide to ignore the breach, continue with performance, and claim the contract price. The right of the innocent party to take the latter step was recognized by the House of Lords in *White & Carter (Councils) Ltd* v. *McGregor*. Both the existence and the scope of this right are the subject of some controversy. The controversy will be examined in the last part of this chapter.

2. INTRODUCTION

Breach of contract is a topic of some complexity. The complexity is both factual and legal. It is factually complex in the sense that the existence or otherwise of a breach of contract is often a matter of considerable dispute between the parties. In some cases both parties allege that there has been a breach of contract (for example, the buyer alleges that the seller is in breach of contract in selling goods which are not of satisfactory quality, while the seller in turn alleges that the buyer is in breach of contract in failing or refusing to pay for the goods). It is the task of the court to examine these allegations and to ascertain who has in fact broken the contract (and in some cases it may be that both parties are in breach of contract). Difficulties also arise from the complexity of the legal rules themselves. Breach is a very technical area of law, where it is necessary to proceed with caution. The need for caution is particularly apparent in the case of commercial contracts because one false step can be extremely expensive. A contracting party which purports to terminate a contract when it is not in fact entitled to do so may find itself liable for damages for wrongful termination of the contract (and the damages payable in such cases may be substantial).

The approach taken in this chapter is to proceed by asking a number of questions. These questions are as follows:

(i)   what is a breach of contract?

(ii) when does a breach of contract give rise to a right to terminate further performance of the contract?

(iii) must the innocent party exercise its right to terminate further performance of the contract?

(iv) when is the right to terminate lost?

(v)   what is an anticipatory breach of contract and what rights are generated by an anticipatory breach?

3. WHAT IS A BREACH OF CONTRACT?

Not every failure to perform amounts to a breach of contract. Take the case of a person who buys a theatre ticket, pays for it in advance but does not bother to collect the ticket or to turn up for the performance. The failure to collect the ticket or to turn up for the performance does not constitute a breach of contract for the simple reason that the purchaser of the ticket has not promised to attend the performance (unless perhaps the purchaser is a theatre critic or a celebrity who has promised to attend the play in order to generate some publicity). The contractual obligation is to pay for the ticket, not to attend the performance. Thus, in order to determine whether there has been a breach of contract it is necessary to examine the terms of the contract, both express and implied. The breach lies in the failure, without lawful excuse, to perform a contractual obligation. That failure may take many different forms, including the following: (i) an express refusal to perform the contract or a particular term of the contract (for example, a buyer of goods informs the seller that he no longer wants the goods and will not pay for them); (ii) defective performance (for example, a seller supplies the buyer with goods that do not work and so are not of satisfactory quality or not fit for the purpose for which they were sold); and (iii) incapacitating oneself from performing the contract (for example, the seller of goods sells the goods which he had agreed to sell to one buyer to another buyer so that he can no longer physically comply with his obligation to sell the goods to the first buyer).

It is, however, important to stress that not every failure to perform a contractual obligation amounts to a breach of contract. In some instances the law provides the party who fails to perform his contractual obligation with an excuse for his non-performance. Take the case of the buyer who refuses to pay for the goods which have been delivered to him on the ground that the goods are defective. The buyer who lawfully rejects the goods and refuses to pay for them is not in breach of contract in so acting. He has a lawful excuse for his actions in that the prior breach of contract by the seller and his lawful rejection of the goods discharged him from his obligation to pay for the goods. The law also provides a party with a lawful excuse for non-performance where, prior to the time for performance, the contract between the parties is frustrated (on which see Chapter 23). The effect of frustration is automatically to determine the contract between the parties and to release them from their future obligations to perform under the terms of the contract.

The existence of a breach of contract does not generally depend upon a finding that the non-performing party intentionally broke the contract or was otherwise at fault. In other words, liability for breach of contract is strict. This is not to say that liability is absolute. As we have noted, the law does on occasion relieve a contracting party of liability for a failure of performance that would otherwise amount to a breach of contract. But these exceptions operate within very narrow confines. The principal exception is the doctrine of frustration. The conclusion that liability for breach of contract is generally strict is one that is worthy of note. At first sight it may appear rather unusual. What is the justification for imposing liability on a party who has not been at fault? Liability based on fault seems much easier to justify. Thus when we turn from the law of contract to the law of tort, we find that strict liability is viewed with some suspicion by the courts (legislative examples of the imposition of strict liability are rather more common; see for example Part I of the Consumer Protection Act 1987) and that liability based on fault is the norm. A similar picture can be found when we look to the law of contract in some civilian systems where liability for breach of contract is based upon fault. The justification for the imposition of strict liability is that a defendant who has voluntarily assumed an obligation to perform should be required to perform that obligation. Thus a carrier who promises to deliver goods to their intended recipient before midday on the day after taking receipt of the goods will be liable for a failure to deliver the goods by the stipulated time even in the case where the failure to deliver is caused by an event which is not attributable to the fault of the carrier. The carrier who wishes to qualify his liability should do so by the terms of his contract. Thus he could assume an obligation to use 'best endeavours' or 'reasonable endeavours' to deliver the goods at the stated time, or he could insert an exclusion clause or a force majeure clause into the contract stating that he is not to be held liable for a failure to deliver the goods where the cause of the failure is an event which is outside his control. It would not, however, be true to say that the justification for the imposition of strict liability can be found in all cases in the voluntary assumption of such a liability. In some cases the law imposes upon one contracting party a strict obligation, irrespective of the wishes of that party. A clear example is the term implied into contracts for the sale of goods that the goods must be of satisfactory quality (see section 14 of the Sale of Goods Act 1979, discussed in more detail at p. 375 above). This obligation is imposed on a seller of goods who sells in the course of a business. The effect of this implied term is to impose liability on the seller irrespective of the wishes of the particular seller. The justification offered in support of the imposition of liability in such cases is the need to protect the buyer, in particular the consumer buyer who is assumed to be in a weaker position than the seller. In any event, the seller will, in all probability, have a claim for breach of contract against his supplier, until liability is finally chased back to the manufacturer of the defective product.

However it should not be assumed that liability for breach of contract is always strict. It is not. In some cases it is necessary to establish that the defendant was at fault. An example is provided by section 13 of the Supply of Goods and Services Act 1982 which provides that:

In a contract for the supply of a service where the supplier is acting in the course of a business, there is an implied term that the supplier will carry out the service with reasonable care and skill.

In this instance the obligation that is imposed on the supplier is one to take reasonable care so that it is only by demonstrating that the seller has failed to exercise reasonable care and skill that a breach can be established. English law recognizes the existence of a number of obligations to exercise reasonable care (for example, in relation to the obligations owed by an employer to an employee to provide a safe place and a safe system of work). But the fact that some obligations are confined to the exercise of reasonable care does not mean that the general rule is one of liability based on fault. It is not. The general rule is that liability is strict.

It should also be noted that English law has a unitary notion of breach of contract. That is to say, liability does not generally depend upon the cause of the breach of contract. In this respect English law is much simpler than some continental systems (such as that in Germany) which traditionally have distinguished between different forms of liability and thus built up an elaborate classification system. In Germany liability was, until recently, based on impossibility of performance, delay, and positive breach of contract. However on 1 January 2002 Germany introduced a very significant reform to its law of contract and the effect of that reform is to bring German law much closer to the common law model. International instruments, such as the Vienna Convention on Contracts for the International Sale of Goods (on which see p. 988 below), have tended to adopt a unitary notion of breach or non-performance and these instruments may prove to be very important in persuading other jurisdictions to adopt a unified liability system for breach of contract.

Finally, it is important to point out that, while every breach of contract gives rise to a remedy in damages (even if the claim is only for nominal damages; see further

p. 1005 below), not every breach generates a right to terminate further performance of the contract. The right to terminate further performance of the contract is only available in certain circumstances and it is the purpose of the next section of this chapter to identify the circumstances that trigger the right to terminate. Termination can be an extremely important remedy (or right) in practice because it is exercised by the parties themselves. That is to say, it is not necessary to go to court and seek an order of the court before terminating further performance of the contract. It is up to the parties to decide whether or not to terminate. However it is important to remember that the courts may be asked, after the event, to decide whether or not the party who purported to terminate the contract was in fact entitled to do so. This supervisory jurisdiction of the court assumes considerable practical significance, especially when it is borne in mind that a party who purports to terminate when it does not in fact have the right to terminate will be found to have wrongfully terminated the contract and may find itself exposed to a claim for substantial damages. It is for this reason that the lawyer must exercise great care when advising a party whether or not it should terminate further performance of the contract. Draftsmen often go to considerable lengths to draft a clause that gives a clear right to terminate (although these clauses can, on occasion, give rise to difficulties of interpretation: see, for example, *Rice* v. *Great Yarmouth District Council, The Times*, 26 July 2000, discussed in more detail at p. 977 below). It is therefore a matter of some importance to consider the circumstances in which a breach of contract gives to the innocent party the right to terminate further performance of the contract.

4. THE EXISTENCE OF A RIGHT TO TERMINATE

When considering whether or not a breach of contract entitles the innocent party to terminate further performance of the contract, one of a number of different approaches could be adopted. One approach is to leave it to the parties to decide when the right to terminate will arise. The difficulty with this approach is that the parties may not make their own provision for termination and so it is necessary for the law to provide a 'default rule' that is applicable where the parties make no provision themselves. Alternatively, one could leave it to the unfettered discretion of the court to decide whether or not there exists a right to terminate. The difficulty with this approach is that it results in too much uncertainty. Parties need to know their rights before they go to court so that they can avoid disputes or, where they do arise, settle them without incurring the cost of going to court. So there is a need for clear rules. On the other hand, clear rules can be inflexible and lead to injustice. There is therefore a need to strike a balance between the interest in certainty and the need to produce fair and just solutions when the rules are applied to individual fact situations.

English law has struggled to strike that balance in an appropriate way. But it is not alone. Other legal systems have struggled similarly. There is no one obvious solution to the problem. It is a policy issue and it is possible to strike the balance between certainty and fairness in different places. Traditionally English law is located towards the certainty end of the spectrum in that it places considerable emphasis on the need to ensure that the parties can know where they stand in the event of a breach (see, in particular, *Bunge Corporation New York* v. *Tradax Export SA, Panama* [1981] 1 WLR 711, discussed at p. 970 below). But at the same time there is a line of cases, usually associated with the recognition of intermediate or innominate terms (see *Hong Kong Fir* v. *Kawasaki Kisen Kaisha* [1962] 2 QB 26, discussed at p. 959 below) in which greater emphasis is placed on flexibility and fairness, so that the entitlement of the innocent party to terminate depends upon the seriousness of the breach which has taken place. Thus there is a tension at the heart of English law, in that it employs two apparently inconsistent strategies at the same time. The first and traditional strategy is to focus on the nature of the term broken. Thus, on this view, if the term broken is of sufficient importance, the law will confer upon the innocent party the right to terminate further performance of the contract, irrespective of the consequences of the breach. But where the term broken is of minimal significance then the right to terminate will not arise. The difficulty with this strategy is the obvious one, namely that there are many contract terms that fall into the middle: they are neither very important, nor very trivial, so how is it to be decided whether or not the breach of such a term gives rise to the right to terminate? The difficulties with this strategy have led some to argue that the focus of the law should be upon the consequences of the breach, rather than the nature of the term broken. This is the second strategy and it finds expression in the cases in which the courts have classified the term which has been broken as an innominate term so that the entitlement to terminate depends upon the consequences of the breach. The result of the adoption of this strategy is, it is said, to produce fairer outcomes to cases in that judges and arbitrators can then tailor the remedy to meet the facts of the case. But flexibility carries with it a price and that price is uncertainty in that it becomes more difficult for parties to predict the likely outcome of litigation with the result that it may become more difficult to resolve disputes.

In this section consideration will be given to the circumstances in which a breach of contract gives a right to the innocent party to terminate further performance of the contract. A right to terminate will generally arise where the term broken is a condition but not where the term broken is a warranty. Where the term broken is intermediate, or innominate, the right to terminate will depend upon the consequences of the breach. Where the consequences are serious then a right to terminate will arise. Conversely, where the consequences of the breach are not serious, a right to terminate will not arise and the innocent party will be confined to a remedy in damages. This section is therefore broken down into a number of distinct parts. Part (a) considers the right to terminate in the event of a breach of a condition. Part (b), which is extremely brief, notes that there is no right to terminate in the event of a breach of a warranty. Part (c) is devoted to intermediate terms, while Part (d) explores the problems that can arise in deciding whether a term which has not been classified by the parties is a condition, a warranty, or an intermediate term. Part (e) examines termination clauses, while Part (f) considers the significance, if any, to be attached to the good faith of the party who is alleged to have repudiated the contract. Part (g) brings this section to a close with a brief comparative discussion, in which English law will be compared with the Vienna Convention and with the Principles of European Contract Law.

(a) BREACH OF A CONDITION

It is trite law that breach of a 'condition' of the contract gives to the innocent party a right to terminate further performance of the contract. The difficulty lies in discerning whether or not a particular term amounts to a condition. As Professor Treitel has stated (' "Conditions" and "Conditions Precedent" ' (1990) 106 *LQR* 185), 'one of the most notorious sources of difficulty in the law of contract is the variety of senses in which it uses the expression "condition" '. In the first place the word 'condition' is used in different senses by the commercial community. A common example is provided by standard terms of trade which are used by businesses up and down the country. These terms are often headed 'terms and conditions of business' but it is clear in this context that not all the terms contained in the document are 'conditions' in the sense that a breach automatically generates a right to terminate further performance of the contract. In other contexts the meaning of the word 'condition' is not so clear and it can give rise to difficulties of interpretation (see, for example, *L Schuler AG* v. *Wickman Machine Tool Sales Ltd* [1974] AC 235, discussed at p. 944 below). Secondly, the word 'condition' has been used by the law in different senses and indeed its meaning has changed over time. Conditions may be either contingent or promissory. A contingent condition refers to an event that neither party has promised to bring about and upon which hinges the obligation to perform. Suppose that A promises to pay B £100 on 30 January 2010 provided that they are both still alive at that date. Neither party promises to stay alive until that date but their continued survival is a condition precedent to the entitlement of B to the £100. Contingent conditions may be either conditions precedent or subsequent. The example given is of a condition precedent. By changing the facts slightly we can create a condition subsequent. Suppose that A promises to pay B £100 per year until either of them dies. In this case death is an event that operates to bring an end to the obligation to make the payment. Again, neither party has promised not to die. Death is simply the event upon which the obligation to pay comes to an end. A promissory condition, on the other hand, is a reference to an event which one party has promised to bring about or not to bring about, as the case may be.

Our difficulties do not end here. As Professor Treitel points out ((1990) 106 *LQR* 185), 'even the concept of promissory condition is used in two senses. . . . The first relates to the *order* of performance, while the second relates to the *conformity* of the performance rendered with that promised' (emphasis in the original). It relates to the order of performance where the obligation of one party to perform is dependent upon prior performance by the other party of a particular obligation. So, for example, a builder may enter into a contract with a householder to carry out some building work. Payment is to be made on completion of the work. Completion of the work is a condition precedent to the obligation of the householder to pay for the work. The condition is a promissory one because the builder has promised to carry out the work and it is a condition that relates to an event, namely the completion of performance by the builder. But suppose that the builder completes the work defectively. In such a case the builder may have breached a promissory condition of the contract but here the condition relates not to the order of performance but to the quality of that performance.

The most important distinction for our purposes is between a promissory condition and a contingent condition. In this chapter we are only concerned with promissory conditions. More precisely, our focus is upon conditions which relate to conformity rather than to the order of performance. Nevertheless, it is not easy to maintain the distinction between the two categories, especially when reading nineteenth century case-law where the judges used the phrase 'condition precedent' to refer both to the order of performance and to the conformity of that performance with the terms of the contract (see, for example, *Bentsen* v. *Taylor Sons & Co* [1893] 2 QB 274, 281). Where the condition relates to the order of performance and the condition has not been fulfilled, the party whose performance is dependent upon the fulfilment of the condition is entitled to withhold performance until such time as the condition is fulfilled, but the failure does not necessarily entitle him to bring the contract between the parties to an end. Where, however, the condition relates to the conformity of performance, and the condition has been broken the innocent party is entitled to bring the contract between the parties to an end. So important remedial consequences can turn on the distinction between a condition precedent which relates to the order of performance and a condition precedent which relates to conformity of performance. The dual usage of 'condition precedent' creates unnecessary difficulties and, as Professor Treitel points out ((1990) 106 *LQR* 185, 186), our difficulties would be reduced if we reserved the phrase 'condition precedent' for use when discussing the order of performance or the event which gives rise to the obligation to perform and used the word condition to denote the term itself or the content of the obligation that has been assumed. In the remainder of this part we shall be concerned with conditions only in so far as they relate to the conformity of performance with the terms of the contract.

Not every term of a contract is a condition in this sense. A term may be classified as a condition in one of three ways, namely (i) by Parliament, (ii) by the courts, or (iii) by the contracting parties themselves. There are relatively few examples of classification of terms by Parliament. A rare example is provided by the Sale of Goods Act 1979 which classifies a number of terms implied into contracts of sale. The term that the seller has a right to sell the goods, that the goods must correspond with description, that the goods must be of satisfactory quality, reasonably fit for their purpose and correspond with sample are all classified as conditions (Sale of Goods Act 1979, ss 12(5A), 13(2), 14(6), and 15(3), pp. 374–376 above). The consequence of this is that any breach of one of these obligations by a seller gives to a buyer a right to reject the goods. The right of the buyer to reject the goods has, however, been qualified by section 15A(1) of the Sale of Goods Act 1979 which provides that where the buyer would, apart from this subsection, have the right to reject goods by reason of a breach on the part of a seller of a term implied by sections 13–15 of the Sale of Goods Act 1979, but the breach is so slight that it would be unreasonable for him to reject them, then, if the buyer does not deal as a consumer, the breach is not to be treated as a breach of a condition but may be treated as a breach of a warranty. The aim of this provision is to stop buyers rejecting goods for what may be termed 'technical' reasons. An infamous example of this is provided by the case of *Arcos Ltd* v. *E A Ronaasen and Son* [1933] AC 470. The parties entered into a contract for the sale of timber staves cut to a thickness of 1/2 inch. The purchasers alleged the sellers had breached the contract as the staves were of the wrong thickness, being 9/16 of an inch thick. The House of Lords held that the purchasers were entitled to reject the timber. Lord Atkin stated (at p. 479) that:

If the written contract specifies conditions of weight, measurement and the like, those conditions must be complied with. A ton does not mean about a ton, or a yard about a yard. Still less when you descend to minute measurements does 1/2 inch mean about 1/2 inch. If the seller wants a margin he must and in my experience does stipulate for it.

The buyers were held to be entitled to reject the timber notwithstanding the fact that their motive for trying to get out of the contract was that it had turned out to be a bad bargain for them as a result of a fall in the market price of timber. The House of Lords were aware of the reasons for the buyers' wish to get out of the contract but were of the view that they were irrelevant. Thus Lord Atkin stated (at pp. 479–480):

No doubt there may be microscopic deviations which business men and therefore lawyers will ignore. . . . It will be found that most of the cases that admit any deviation from the contract are cases where there has been an excess or deficiency in quantity which the Court has considered negligible. But apart from this consideration the right view is that the conditions of the contract must be strictly performed. If a condition is not performed the buyer has a right to reject. I do not myself think that there is any difference between business men and lawyers on this matter. No doubt, in business, men often find it unnecessary or inexpedient to insist on their strict legal rights. In a normal market if they get something substantially like the specified goods they may take them with or without grumbling and a claim for an allowance. But in a falling market I find that buyers are often as eager to insist on their legal rights as courts of law are ready to maintain them. No doubt at all times sellers are prepared to take a liberal view as to the rigidity of their own obligations, and possibly buyers who in turn are sellers may also dislike too much precision. But buyers are not, as far as my experience goes, inclined to think that the rights defined in the code are in excess of business needs.

Section 15A marks a distinct shift in philosophy because it restricts the right of buyers to reject the goods and, to this extent, will curtail the ability of buyers to 'insist on their strict legal rights' in a 'falling market'. But section 15A is in fact hedged around by a number of requirements. First, it only applies to buyers who do not deal as consumers; secondly the consequences of the breach must be 'slight'; thirdly it must be 'unreasonable' for the buyer to reject the goods; finally, it is open to the parties to contract out of the subsection (see s 15A(2)) so that the buyer's right to reject is not constrained in this way.

Classification by the courts is rather more difficult. The basis on which the courts decide whether a term, which has not been classified by Parliament or by the parties, is a condition, a warranty, or an intermediate term is discussed in Part (d) after we have considered the law relating to warranties and intermediate terms.

The easiest way to create a condition is for the parties themselves to agree that a particular term is to be classified as a condition. There is no finite list of conditions in English law. It is open to the parties to classify as a condition a term which would not otherwise be so classified (that is to say, the courts would not conclude that the term was a condition in the absence of express agreement to this effect by the parties). On one view, this ability to classify as a condition a clause which would not otherwise constitute a condition can generate unreasonable results, in the sense that a trivial breach of contract may confer upon the innocent party a right to terminate further performance of the contract. It is therefore necessary for contracting parties to make clear that it was their intention to classify the term as a condition. This is not as easy as it sounds given that the word 'condition' is used in different senses in the law. An example of the problems that can arise is provided by the following case:

L Schuler AG v. Wickman Machine Tool Sales Ltd

[1974] AC 235, House of Lords

The facts of the case are set out in the speech of Lord Reid.

Lord Reid

My Lords, the appellants are a German company which manufactures machine tools and other engineering products. The respondents are a selling organization. On May 1, 1963, they entered into an elaborate 'distributorship agreement' under which the appellants (whom I shall call Schuler) granted to the respondents (called Sales in the agreement but whom I shall call Wickman) the sole right to sell Schuler products in territory which included the United Kingdom. These products included '*panel presses*' defined in clause 2 and general products. The panel presses are large machine tools used by motor manufacturers. Wickman were to act as agents for Schuler in selling the panel presses but were to purchase and re-sell the general products.

Wickman's obligation with regard to the promotion of sales of Schuler products is contained in clauses 7 and 12(b) which are in the following terms:

'**7.** *Promotion by Sales*

(a) Subject to Clause 17 Sales will use its best endeavours to promote and extend the sale of Schuler products in the Territory.

(b) It shall be condition of this Agreement that:

   (i) Sales shall send its representatives to visit the six firms whose names are listed in the Schedule hereto at least once in every week for the purpose of soliciting orders for panel presses;

   (ii) that the same representative shall visit each firm on each occasion unless there are unavoidable reasons preventing the visit being made by that representative in which case the visit shall be made by an alternate representative and Sales will ensure that such a visit is always made by the same alternate representative.

Sales agrees to inform Schuler of the names of the representatives and alternate representatives instructed to make the visits required by this Clause . .

12(b) Sales undertakes, at its expense, to look after Schuler's interest carefully and will visit Schuler customers regularly, particularly those customers principally in the motor car and electrical industries whose names are set out on the list attached hereto and initialled by the parties hereto and will give all possible technical advice to customers.'

The six firms referred to in clause 7 are six of the largest motor manufacturers in this country. The agreement was to last until the end of 1967 so that clause 7(b)(i) required Wickman to make a total of some 1400 visits during the period of the agreement. Wickman failed in their obligation. At first there were fairly extensive failures to make these visits. Then there were negotiations with a view to improving the position and Schuler have been held to have waived any right arising out of those failures. Thereafter there was an improvement but there were still a considerable number of failures.

After some correspondence Schuler wrote to Wickman in October, 1964, terminating the agreement on the ground that failure to fulfil their obligation for weekly visits to the six firms entitled Schuler to treat that failure as a repudiation of the agreement by Wickman. In accordance with clause 19 of the agreement this question was referred to arbitration. In spite of the apparently simple and limited nature of the question in dispute, proceedings before the arbitrator were elaborate and protracted. Ultimately the arbitrator issued his award in the form of a special case on Oct. 6, 1969. He held that Schuler were not entitled to terminate the agreement. This finding was reversed by Mr Justice Mocatta but restored by the Court of Appeal.

In order to explain the contention of the parties, I must now set out clause 11 of the agreement.

'11. *Duration of Agreement*

(a) This Agreement and the rights granted hereunder to Sales shall commence on the First day of May 1963 and shall continue in force (unless previously determined as hereinafter provided) until the 31st day of December 1967 and thereafter unless and until determined by either party upon giving to the other not less than 12 months' notice in writing to that effect expiring on the said 31st day of December 1967 or any subsequent anniversary thereof PROVIDED that Schuler or Sales may by notice in writing to the other determine this Agreement forthwith if:

    (i) the other shall have committed a material breach of its obligations hereunder and shall have failed to remedy the same within 60 days of being required in writing so to do or

    (ii) the other shall cease to carry on business or shall enter into liquidation (other than a Members' voluntary liquidation for the purposes of reconstruction or amalgamation) or shall suffer the appointment of a Receiver of the whole or a material part of its undertaking;

and PROVIDED FURTHER that Schuler may by notice determine this Agreement forthwith if Sales shall cease to be a wholly-owned subsidiary of Wickman Limited.

(b) The termination of this Agreement shall be without prejudice to any rights or liabilities accrued due prior to the date of termination and the terms contained herein as to discount commission or otherwise will apply to any orders placed by Sales with Schuler and accepted by Schuler before such termination.'

Wickman's main contention is that Schuler were only entitled to determine the agreement for the reasons and in the manner provided in clause 11. Schuler, on the other hand, contend that the terms of clause 7 are decisive in their favour: they say that 'It shall be a condition of this agreement' in clause 7(b) means that any breach of clause 7(b)(i) or 7(b)(ii) entitles them forthwith to terminate the agreement. So as there were admittedly breaches of clause 7(b)(i) which were not waived they were entitled to terminate the contract.

I think it right first to consider the meaning of clause 11 because, if Wickman's contention with regard to this is right, then clause 7 must be construed in light of the provisions of clause 11. Clause 11 expressly provides that the agreement 'shall continue in force (unless previously determined as hereinafter provided) until' Dec. 31, 1967. That appears to imply the corollary that the agreement shall not be determined before that date in any other way than as provided in clause 11. It is argued for Schuler that those words cannot have been intended to have that implication. In the first place Schuler say that anticipatory breach cannot be brought within the scope of clause 11 and the parties cannot have intended to exclude any remedy for an anticipatory breach. And, secondly, they say that clause 11 fails to provide any remedy for an irremediable breach however fundamental such breach might be.

There is much force in this criticism. But on any view the interrelation and consequences of the various provisions of this agreement are so ill-thought out that I am not disposed to discard the natural meaning of the words which I have quoted merely because giving to them their natural meaning implies that the draftsman has forgotten something which a better draftsman would have remembered. If the terms of clause 11 are wide enough to apply to breaches of clause 7 then I am inclined to hold that clause 7 must be read subject to the provisions of clause 11.

It appears to me that clause 11(a)(i) is intended to apply to all material breaches of the agreement which are capable of being remedied. The question then is what is meant in this context by the word 'remedy'. It could mean obviate or nullify the effect of a breach so that any damage already done is in some way made good. Or it could mean cure so that matters are put right for the future. I think that the latter is the more natural meaning. The word is commonly used in connection with diseases or ailments and they would normally be said to be remedied if they were cured although no cure can remove the past effect or result of the disease before the cure took place. And in general it can only be in a rare case that any remedy of something that has gone wrong in the performance of a continuing positive obligation will, in addition to putting it right for the future, remove or nullify damage already incurred before the remedy was applied. To restrict the meaning of remedy to cases where all damage past and future can be put right would leave hardly any scope at all for this clause. On the other hand, there are cases where it would seem a misuse of language to say that a breach can be remedied. For example, a breach of clause 14 by disclosure of confidential information could not be said to be remedied by a promise not to do it again.

So the question is whether a breach of Wickman's obligation under clause 7(b)(i) is capable of being remedied within the meaning of this agreement. On the one hand, failure to make one particular visit might have irremediable consequences, e.g., a valuable order might have been lost when making that visit would have obtained it. But looking at the position broadly I incline to the view that breaches of this obligation should be held to be capable of remedy within the meaning of clause 7. Each firm had to be visited more than 200 times. If one visit is missed I think that one would normally say that making arrangements to prevent a recurrence of that breach would remedy the breach. If that is right and if clause 11 is intended to have general application then clause 7 must be read so that a breach of clause 7(b)(i) does not give to Schuler a right to rescind but only to require the breach to be remedied within 60 days under clause 11(a)(i). I do not feel at all confident that this is the true view but I would adopt it unless the provisions of clause 7 point strongly in the opposite direction, so I turn to clause 7.

Clause 7 begins with the general requirement that Wickman shall 'use its best endeavours' to promote sales of Schuler products. Then there is in clause 7(b)(i) specification of those best endeavours with regard to panel presses, and in clause 12(b) a much more general statement of what Wickman must do with regard to other Schuler products. This intention to impose a stricter obligation with regard to panel presses is borne out by the use of the word 'condition' in clause 7(b). I cannot accept Wickman's argument that condition here merely means term. It must be intended to emphasize the importance of the obligations in sub-clauses (b)(i) and (b)(ii). But what is the extent of that emphasis?

Schuler maintains that the word 'condition' has now acquired a precise legal meaning; that, particularly since the enactment of the Sale of Goods Act, 1893, its recognised meaning in English law is a term of a contract any breach of which by one party gives to the other party an immediate right to rescind the whole contract. Undoubtedly the word is frequently used in that sense. There may, indeed, be some presumption that in a formal legal document it has that meaning. But it is frequently used with a less stringent meaning. One is familiar with printed 'Conditions of Sale' incorporated into a contract, and with the words 'For conditions see back' printed on a ticket. There it simply means that the 'conditions' are terms of the contract.

In the ordinary use of the English language 'condition' has many meanings, some of which have nothing to do with agreements. In connection with an agreement it may mean a pre-condition: something which must happen or be done before the agreement can take effect. Or it may mean some state of affairs which must continue to exist if the agreement is to remain in force. The legal meaning on which Schuler relies is, I think, one which would not occur to a layman; a condition in that sense is not something which has an automatic effect. It is a term the breach of which by one party gives to the other an option either to terminate the contract or to let the contract proceed and, if he so desires, sue for damages for the breach.

Sometimes a breach of a term gives that option to the aggrieved party because it is of a fundamental character going to the root of the contract, sometimes it gives that option because the parties have chosen to stipulate that it shall have that effect. Mr Justice Blackburn said in *Bettini* v. *Gye* (1875) 1 QB 183, at p. 187: 'Parties may think some matter, apparently of very little importance, essential; and if they sufficiently express an intention to make the literal fulfilment of such a thing a condition precedent, it will be one . . .'

In the present case it is not contended that Wickman's failures to make visits amounted in themselves to fundamental breaches. What is contended is that the terms of clause 7 'sufficiently express an intention' to make any breach, however small, of the obligation to make visits a condition so that any such breach shall entitle Schuler to rescind the whole contract if they so desire.

Schuler maintains that the use of the word 'condition' is in itself enough to establish this intention. No doubt some words used by lawyers do have a rigid inflexible meaning. But we must remember that we are seeking to discover intention as disclosed by the contract as a whole. Use of the word 'condition' is an indication—even a strong indication—of such an intention but it is by no means conclusive.

The fact that a particular construction leads to a very unreasonable result must be a relevant consideration. The more unreasonable the result the more unlikely it is that the parties can have intended it, and if they do intend it the more necessary it is that they shall make that intention abundantly clear.

Clause 7(b) requires that over a long period each of the six firms shall be visited every week by one or other of two named representatives. It makes no provision for Wickman being entitled to substitute others even on the death or retirement of one of the named representatives. Even if one could imply some right to do this, it makes no provision for both representatives being ill during a particular week and it makes no provision for the possibility that one or other of the firms may tell Wickman that they cannot receive Wickman's representative during a particular week. So if the parties gave any thought to the matter at all they must have realized the probability that in a few cases out of the 1400 required visits a visit as stipulated would be impossible. But if Schuler's contention is right failure to make even one visit entitles them to terminate the contract however blameless Wickman might be. This is so unreasonable that it must make me search for some other possible meaning of the contract. If none can be found then Wickman must suffer the consequences. But only if that is the only possible interpretation.

If I have to construe clause 7 standing by itself then I do find difficulty in reaching any other interpretation. But if clause 7 must be read with clause 11 the difficulty disappears. The word 'condition' would make any breach of clause 7(b), however excusable, a material breach. That would then entitle Schuler to give notice under clause 11(a)(i) requiring the breach to be remedied. There would be no point in giving such a notice if Wickman were clearly not in fault but if it were given Wickman would have no difficulty in showing that the breach had been remedied. If Wickman were at fault then on receiving such a notice they would have to amend their system so that they could show that the breach had been remedied. If they did not do that within the period of the notice then Schuler would be entitled to rescind.

In my view, that is a possible and reasonable construction of the contract and I would therefore adopt it. The contract is so obscure that I can have no confidence that this is its true meaning but for the reasons which I have given I think that it is the preferable construction. It follows that Schuler was not entitled to rescind the contract as it purported to do. So I would dismiss this appeal.

Lord Wilberforce [dissenting]

The second legal issue which arises I would state in this way: whether it is open to the parties to a contract, not being a contract for the sale of goods, to use the word 'condition' to introduce a term, breach of which *ipso facto* entitles the other party to treat the contract as at an end.

The proposition that this may be done has not been uncriticized. It is said that this is contrary to modern trends which focus interest rather upon the nature of the breach, allowing the innocent party to rescind or repudiate whenever the breach is fundamental, whether the clause breached is called a condition or not: that the affixing of the label 'condition' cannot pre-empt the right of the Court to estimate for itself the character of the breach. Alternatively it is said that the result contended for can only be achieved if the consequences of a breach of a 'condition' (sc., that the other party may rescind) are spelt out in the contract. In support of this line of argument reliance is placed on the judgment of the Court of Appeal in *Hong Kong Fir Shipping Co Ltd* v. *Kawasaki Kisen Kaisha Ltd* [1962] 2 QB 26.

My Lords, this approach has something to commend it: it has academic support. The use as a promissory term of 'condition' is artificial, as is that of 'warranty' in some contexts. But in my opinion this use is now too deeply embedded in English law to be uprooted by anything less than a complete revision. I shall not trace the development of the term through 19th century cases, many of them decisions of Lord Blackburn, to the present time: this has been well done by academic writers. I would only add that the *Hong Kong Fir* case even if it could, did not reverse the trend. What it did decide, and I do not think that this was anything new, was that though a term (there a 'seaworthiness' term) was not a 'condition' in the technical sense, it might still be a term breach of which if sufficiently serious could go to the root of the contract. Nothing in the judgments as I read them cast any doubt upon the meaning or effect of 'condition' where that word is technically used.

The alternative argument, in my opinion, is equally precluded by authority. It is not necessary for parties to a contract, when stipulating a condition, to spell out the consequences of breach: these are inherent in the (assumedly deliberate) use of the word. (*Suisse Atlantique* v. *Rotterdamsche Kolen Centrale* [1967] AC 362, at p. 422 (per Lord Upjohn).)

It is upon this legal basis, as to which I venture to think that your Lordships are agreed, that this contract must be construed. Does clause 7(b) amount to a 'condition' or a 'term'? (to call it an important or material term adds, with all respect, nothing but some intellectual assuagement). My Lords, I am clear in my own mind that it is a condition, but your Lordships take the contrary view. On a matter of construction of a particular document, to develop the reasons for a minority opinion serves no purpose. I am all the more happy to refrain from so doing because the judgments of Mr Justice Mocatta Lord Justice Stephenson and indeed of Lord Justice Edmund Davies, on construction, give me complete satisfaction and I could in any case add little of value to their reasons. I would only add that, for my part, to call the clause arbitrary, capricious or fantastic, or to introduce as a test of its validity the ubiquitous reasonable man (I do not know whether he is English or German) is to assume, contrary to the evidence, that both parties to this contract adopted a standard of easygoing tolerance rather than one of aggressive, insistent punctuality and efficiency. This is not an assumption I am prepared to make, nor do I think myself entitled to impose the former standard upon the parties if their words indicate, as they plainly do, the latter. I note finally, that the result of treating the clause, so careful and specific in its requirements, as a term is, in effect, to deprive the appellants of any remedy in respect of admitted and by no means minimal breaches. The arbitrator's finding that these breaches were not 'material' was not, in my opinion, justified in law in the face of the parties' own characterization of them in their document: indeed the fact that he was able to do so, and so leave the appellants without remedy, argues strongly that the legal basis of his finding—that clause 7(b) was merely a term—is unsound.

I would allow this appeal.

Lord Morris of Borth-y-Gest, Lord Simon of Glaisdale, and **Lord Kilbrandon** delivered speeches dismissing the appeal.

COMMENTARY

It is of the utmost importance to pay careful attention to the details of clauses 7, 11, and 12(b). One of the problems with this case is that the contract was badly drafted and the majority used this fact in order to support their construction of the contract.

Badly drafted contracts are not an unknown phenomenon. The particular problem which arose on the facts of this case was the relationship between clauses 7 and 11. First, let us examine the clauses separately.

Clause 7(b), standing alone, does appear to create a condition. It is expressly so described. None of their Lordships doubted that the parties were entitled, by the use of clear words, to elevate clause 7(b) to the status of a condition. Thus Lord Kilbrandon stated (at p. 271) that 'it is undoubted that parties may, if they so desire, make any term whatever, unimportant as it might seem to be to an observer relying upon *a priori* reasoning of his own, a condition giving entitlement, on its breach, to rescission at the instance of the party aggrieved'. Clause 7(b) seems clear enough in this respect. Thus, had there been no clause 11 in the contract, it is suggested that it is likely that Schuler would have been entitled to terminate the contract pursuant to clause 7(b).

Clause 11, on the other hand, did not confer an immediate right to terminate. Rather, it required Schuler to give notice to Wickman and then gave Wickman a period of time in which to remedy the breach. This is a common form of clause found in commercial contracts as it strikes a balance between the competing interests of the parties by giving the defaulting party an opportunity to make good his breach but at the same time it protects the position of the innocent party by giving him an express right to terminate the contract in the event that the breach is not made good.

The problem in this case is that the events which happened appeared to fall within both clauses 7(b) and 11 but the remedial consequences appeared to differ depending upon which clause was held to govern the facts of the case. If clause 7(b) prevailed then Schuler appeared to be entitled to terminate immediately, while if clause 11 prevailed then Schuler's right to terminate could only be exercised after the expiry of the notice period without the breach being remedied. What, then, was the relationship between the two clauses? As Lord Reid stated, the inter-relationship between them was 'ill-thought out'.

Two issues arose here. The first was whether or not the events fell within the scope of clause 11 at all. There was a good argument to the effect that they did not. The breach by Wickman was a matter of past historical fact and it can be argued that it could not be 'remedied' as required by clause 11. Clauses such as clause 11 are relatively straightforward where the breach takes the form of delivery of defective goods. In such a case the breach can be remedied by the delivery of goods which conform with the terms of the contract. But it is, at first sight, not altogether easy to see how a breach of clause 7(b) could be 'remedied'. One cannot wind the clock back and make the missed visit. Lord Reid, however, looked at the position 'broadly' and concluded that the breach could be remedied by making arrangements to prevent a recurrence of the breach. This construction was, it is suggested, a rather benevolent one, at least as far as Wickman was concerned.

This led on to the second issue which was that, given that the events did appear to fall within the scope of both clauses, what remedial consequences flowed from this? Lord Reid concluded that breach of clause 7(b) did not confer upon Schuler an immediate right to terminate the contract, irrespective of the consequences of the breach. Rather, a breach of clause 7(b) was automatically a material breach for the purposes of clause 11 and thus gave to Schuler the right to invoke the machinery of clause 11. In this way, clause 7(b) did not become redundant. Its role was to assist in the definition of a material breach for the purposes of clause 11 and not to confer upon Schuler an immediate right of termination.

In many ways Wickman were rather fortunate. The key fact appears to be that the contract was badly drafted and the majority gave to Wickman the benefit of the doubt that arose in relation to the meaning of the word 'condition' in clause 7(b). There is considerable force in Lord Wilberforce's observation that the majority construction assumed, contrary to the evidence, that the parties had 'adopted a standard of easy-going tolerance rather than one of aggressive, insistent punctuality and efficiency'.

The effect of the decision was to leave Schuler exposed to a claim for damages by Wickman because they were held to have wrongfully terminated the contract between the parties. While Schuler would have a claim against Wickman for the losses that they suffered as a result of Wickman's failure to make the scheduled visits, it is unlikely that such a claim would provide them with much consolation because of the probable difficulty in proving that they had suffered any loss as a result of Wickman's failure to make a particular visit. Does this not suggest that the intention of Schuler was in fact to give themselves a right to terminate the contract in order to avoid these problems of proving that they had suffered loss as a result of the breach?

It is important to see this case in its context. It is not authority for the proposition that the word 'condition' cannot mean a condition in the sense that a breach of it gives rise to a right to terminate. The conclusion of the House of Lords was influenced heavily by the fact that the contract was badly drafted and by the difficulties caused by the relationship between clauses 7 and 11. The word 'condition' in a well-drafted contract should generally suffice to demonstrate that what is intended is that a breach of the clause should give rise to the right to terminate. An alternative is to avoid the use of the word 'condition' and use the phrase 'of the essence' instead. The efficacy of this phrase is demonstrated by the following case:

Lombard North Central plc v. Butterworth

[1987] QB 527, Court of Appeal

The plaintiff finance company leased a computer to the defendant for a period of five years. The contract stipulated, in clause 2(a), that time was of the essence with regard to payment of the quarterly rentals. Clause 5 stated that failure to make due and punctual payment entitled the plaintiffs to terminate the contract, while clause 6 provided that, on termination, the plaintiffs were entitled to recover all arrears of instalments and all future instalments that would have fallen due had the agreement not been terminated. The defendant quickly fell into arrears and, after giving due notice, the plaintiffs repossessed the computers. The plaintiffs brought an action against the defendant in order to recover the arrears as at the date of the termination and also the future instalments payable under the contract. The claim was brought both under clause 6 of the contract and for damages at common law. The Court of Appeal held that clause 6 was unenforceable as a penalty clause but that the plaintiffs were entitled to recover the arrears and the future instalments as damages at common law following upon the defendant's repudiatory breach of contract.

Mustill LJ

The hiring agreement contained the following material provisions:

'The lessee . . . agrees:

2.(a)   to pay to the lessor: (i) punctually and without previous demand the rentals set out in Part 3 of the Schedule together with value added tax thereon punctual payment of each which shall be of the essence of this lease: . . .

5.   In the event that (a) the lessee shall (i) make default in the due and punctual payment of any of the rentals or of any sum of money payable to the lessor hereunder or any part thereof . . . then upon the happening of such event . . . the lessor's consent to the lessee's possession of the goods shall determine forthwith without any notice being given by the lessor, and the lessor may terminate this lease either by notice in writing, or by taking possession of the goods . . .

6.   In the event that the lessor's consent to the lessee's possession of the goods shall be determined under clause 5 hereof (a) the lessee shall pay forthwith to the lessor (i) all arrears of rentals; (ii) all further rentals which would but for the determination of the lessor's consent to the lessee's possession of the goods have fallen due to the end of the fixed period of this lease less a discount thereon for accelerated payment at the rate of 5 per cent per annum; and (iii) damages for any breach of this lease and all expenses and costs incurred by the lessor in retaking possession of the goods and/or enforcing the lessor's rights under this lease together with such value added tax as shall be legally payable thereon; (b) the lessor shall be entitled to exercise any one or more of the rights and remedies provided for in clause 5 and sub-clause (a) of this clause and the determination of the lessor's consent to the lessee's possession of the goods shall not affect or prejudice such rights and remedies and the lessee shall be and remain liable to perform all outstanding liabilities under this lease notwithstanding that the lessor may have taken possession of the goods and/or exercised one or more of the rights and remedies of the lessor; (c) any right or remedy to which the lessor is or may become entitled under this lease or in consequence of the lessee's conduct may be enforced from time to time separately or concurrently with any other right or remedy given by this lease or now or hereinafter provided for or arising by operation of law so that such rights and remedies are not exclusive of the other or others of them but are cumulative.' . . .

Three issues were canvassed before us . . .

[he set out the first two issues and continued]

3.   Does the provision in clause 2(a) of the agreement that time for payment of the instalments was of the essence have the effect of making the defendant's late payment of the outstanding instalments a repudiatory breach? . . .

I would, however, wish to deal with the third point. . . . The reason why I am impelled to hold that the plaintiffs' contentions are well-founded can most conveniently be set out in a series of propositions.

1.   Where a breach goes to the root of the contract, the injured party may elect to put an end to the contract. Thereupon both sides are relieved from those obligations which remain unperformed.

2. If he does so elect, the injured party is entitled to compensation for (a) any breaches which occurred before the contract was terminated and (b) the loss of his opportunity to receive performance of the promisor's outstanding obligations.

3. Certain categories of obligation, often called conditions, have the property that any breach of them is treated as going to the root of the contract. Upon the occurrence of any breach of condition, the injured party can elect to terminate and claim damages, whatever the gravity of the breach.

4. It is possible by express provision in the contract to make a term a condition, even if it would not be so in the absence of such a provision.

5. A stipulation that time is of the essence, in relation to a particular contractual term, denotes that timely performance is a condition of the contract. The consequence is that delay in performance is treated as going to the root of the contract, without regard to the magnitude of the breach.

6. It follows that where a promisor fails to give timely performance of an obligation in respect of which time is expressly stated to be of the essence, the injured party may elect to terminate and recover damages in respect of the promisor's outstanding obligations, without regard to the magnitude of the breach.

7. A term of the contract prescribing what damages are to be recoverable when a contract is terminated for a breach of condition is open to being struck down as a penalty, if it is not a genuine covenanted pre-estimate of the damage, in the same way as a clause which prescribes the measure for any other type of breach. No doubt the position is the same where the clause is ranked as a condition by virtue of an express provision in the contract.

8. A clause expressly assigning a particular obligation to the category of condition is not a clause which purports to fix the damages for breaches of the obligation, and is not subject to the law governing penalty clauses.

9. Thus, although in the present case clause 6 is to be struck down as a penalty, clause 2(a)(i) remains enforceable. The plaintiffs were entitled to terminate the contract independently of clause 5, and to recover damages for loss of the future instalments. This loss was correctly computed by the master.

These bare propositions call for comment. The first three are uncontroversial. The fourth was not, I believe, challenged before us, but I would in any event regard it as indisputable. That there exists a category of term, in respect of which any breach whether large or small entitles the promisee to treat himself as discharged, has never been doubted in modern times, and the fact that a term may be assigned to this category by express agreement has been taken for granted for at least a century: see, by way of example only, *Bettini v. Gye* (1876) 1 QBD 183, 187; *Hong Kong Fir Shipping Co Ltd v. Kawasaki Kisen Kaisha Ltd* [1962] 2 QB 26, 70; *Financings Ltd v. Baldock* [1963] 2 QB 104; *Photo Production Ltd v. Securicor Transport Ltd* [1980] AC 827, 849E; *Bunge Corporation, New York v. Tradax Export SA, Panama* [1981] 1 WLR 711, 715, 719; Cheshire & Fifoot, Law of Contract, 11th ed (1986), p. 148.

The fifth proposition is a matter of terminology, and has been more taken for granted than discussed. That making time of the essence is the same as making timely performance a condition was, however, expressly stated by Megaw and Browne LJJ in *Bunge Corporation, New York* v. *Tradax Export SA, Panama* [1980] 1 Lloyd's Rep 294, 305, 307, 309 and 310, and the same proposition is implicit in the leading speeches of Lords Wilberforce and Roskill in the House of Lords [1981] 1 WLR 711.

The sixth proposition is a combination of the first five. There appears to be no direct authority for it, and it is right to say that most of the cases on the significance of time being of the essence have been concerned with the right of the injured party to be discharged, rather than the principles upon which his damages are to be computed. Nevertheless, it is axiomatic that a person who establishes a breach of condition can terminate and claim damages for loss of the bargain, and I know of no authority which suggests that the position is any different where late performance is made into a breach of condition by a stipulation that time is of the essence.

In this connection, it is useful to refer to *Bunge Corporation, New York* v. *Tradax Export SA, Panama*. An f.o.b. contract for the sale of goods required the buyers to give notice of the probable readiness of the ships on which the goods were to be carried. The notice was given four days too late. The sellers declared the buyers in default and claimed damages for default on the basis that the term as to notice was a condition. The damages claimed were the difference between the contract price and the market price, the classical measure for wrongful non-acceptance, by which the seller recovers on the basis that the buyer's repudiation has cost him the benefit of the buyer's future obligation to pay the price. The sellers did not contend that, if the term was not a condition, the delay of four days amounted to a repudiation: see p. 303. Most of the attention given to the dispute, in its passage through two levels of arbitration and three hearings in the courts, was devoted to consideration of whether the term was a condition. There was, however, a subsidiary question whether the damages should be computed in accordance with a particular contractual term (which the House of Lords [1981] 1 WLR 711 held that they should not), and if not, whether at common law they should be computed on the basis of the contract quantity. If the defendant's argument in the present case is right, the whole of this discussion was misconceived. Yet it was never suggested by counsel or by any of the arbitrators and judges who heard the case that the comparative triviality of the breach made any difference to the seller's right, if the term was properly to be regarded as a condition, to recover damages in respect of the buyer's unperformed obligations. If they were right in making this assumption, in a case where time was of the essence by implication, how much more should this be so where the parties have made an express stipulation to this effect.

I return to the propositions stated above. The seventh is uncontroversial, and I would add only the rider that when deciding upon the penal nature of a clause which prescribes a measure of recovery for damages resulting from a termination founded upon a breach of condition, the comparison should be with the common law measure: namely, with the loss to the promisee resulting from the loss of his bargain. If the contract permits him to treat the contract as repudiated, the fact that the breach is comparatively minor should in my view play no part in the equation.

I believe that the real controversy in the present case centres upon the eighth proposition. I will repeat it: a clause expressly assigning a particular obligation to the category of conditions is not a clause which purports to fix the damages for breach of the obligation, and is not subject to the law governing penalty clauses. I acknowledge, of course, that by promoting a term into the category where all breaches are ranked as breaches of condition, the parties indirectly bring about a situation where, for breaches which are relatively small, the injured party is enabled to recover damages as on the loss of the bargain, whereas without the stipulation his measure of recovery would be different. But I am unable to accept that this permits the court to strike down as a penalty the clause which brings about this promotion. To do so would be to reverse the current of more than 100 years' doctrine, which permits the parties to treat as a condition something which would not otherwise be so. I am not prepared to take this step . . .

For these reasons I conclude that the plaintiffs are entitled to retain the damages which the master has awarded. This is not a result which I view with much satisfaction: partly because the plaintiffs have achieved by one means a result which the law of penalties might have prevented them from achieving by another, and partly because if the line of argument under clause 2 had been developed from the outset, the defendant might have found an answer based on waiver which the court is now precluded from assessing, for want of the necessary facts. Nevertheless, it is the answer to which, in my view, the authorities clearly point. Accordingly, I would dismiss the appeal.

Nicholls LJ

Thus far I have reached my conclusion regarding repudiation [his conclusion being that the facts did not justify a finding of repudiation] without giving any weight or effect to the provision in clause 2(a) of the lease, that punctual payment of each rental instalment was of the essence of the lease.

I must now consider a further submission advanced by the plaintiffs that, time of payment having been made of the essence by this provision, it was open to the plaintiffs, once default in payment of any one instalment on the due date had occurred, to treat the agreement as having been repudiated by the defendant, and claim damages for loss of the whole transaction, even though in the absence of this provision such a default would not have had that consequence. On this, the question which arises is one of construction: on the true construction of the clause, did the 'time of the essence' provision have the effect submitted by the plaintiffs? In my view, the answer to that question is 'Yes'. The provision in clause 2(a) has to be read and construed in conjunction with the other provisions in the agreement, including clauses 5 and 6. So read, it is to be noted that failure to pay any instalment triggers a right for the plaintiffs to terminate the agreement by re-taking possession of the goods (clause 5), with the expressed consequence that the defendant becomes liable to make payments which assume that the defendant is liable to make good to the plaintiffs the loss by them of the whole transaction (clause 6). Given that context, the 'time of the essence' provision seems to me to be intended to bring about the result that default in punctual payment is to be regarded (to use a once fashionable term) as a breach going to the root of the contract and, hence, as giving rise to the consequences in damages attendant upon such a breach. I am unable to see what other purpose the 'time of the essence' provision in clause 2(a) can serve or was intended to serve or what other construction can fairly be ascribed to it.

If that construction of the agreement is correct then, as at present advised, it seems to me that the legal consequence is that the plaintiffs are entitled to claim damages for loss of the whole transaction. I say 'as at present advised', because on this no argument to the contrary was advanced on behalf of the defendant, and Mustill LJ's illuminating analysis leaves no escape from the conclusion that parties are free to agree that a particular provision in their contract shall be a condition such that a breach of it is to be regarded as going to the root of the contract and entitling the innocent party (1) to accept that breach as a repudiation, and (2) to be paid damages calculated upon that footing.

I have to say that I view the impact of that principle in this case with considerable dissatisfaction, for this reason . . . the principle applied in *Financings Ltd* v. *Baldock* [1963] 2 QB 104 was that when an owner determines a hire purchase agreement in exercise of a power so to do given him by the agreement on non-payment of instalments, he can recover damages for any breaches up to the date of termination but (in the absence of repudiation) not thereafter. There is no practical difference between (1) an agreement containing such a power and (2) an agreement containing a provision to the effect that time for payment of each instalment is of the essence, so that any breach will go to the root of the contract. The difference between these two agreements is one of drafting form, and wholly without substance. Yet under an agreement drafted in the first form, the owner's damages claim arising upon his exercise of the power of termination is confined to damages for breaches up to the date of termination, whereas under an agreement drafted in the second form the owner's damages claim, arising upon his acceptance of an identical breach as a repudiation of the agreement, will extend to damages for loss of the whole transaction.

Nevertheless, as at present advised, I can see no escape from the conclusion that such is the present state of the law. This conclusion emasculates the decision in *Financings Ltd* v. *Baldock*, for it means that a skilled draftsman can easily side-step the effect of that decision. Indeed, that is what has occurred here.

I add only that I can see nothing in *Financings Ltd* v. *Baldock* itself that would assist the defendant on this point. Each member of the court emphasised that in that case there had been no repudiation of the agreement, and Diplock LJ observed, at p. 118, that in that case time of payment was not of the essence of the contract and, at p. 120, that 'in the absence of any express provision to the contrary in the contract' the failure to pay two instalments on the due date did not of themselves go to the root of the contract.

For these reasons, I too would dismiss this appeal.

Lawton LJ concurred.

COMMENTARY

The result of this case is particularly striking because the finance company first attempted to recover the arrears as at the date of the termination and the future instalments (subject to a discount for accelerated receipt) under clause 6 but it was held that they could not do so because clause 6 was a penalty clause (on which see further pp. 1124–1131 below). But they were able to recover the same sum by way of an action for damages, using clause 2(a) to demonstrate that the defendant had repudiated the contract. Thus the plaintiffs were able to obtain by one method (a common law claim for damages) something which they were unable to obtain by another method (a claim brought under clause 6 of the contract).

Lombard should be contrasted with the earlier decision of the Court of Appeal in *Financings Ltd* v. *Baldock* [1963] 2 QB 104 where a hirer failed to pay the first two instalments on the hire-purchase of a lorry. The contract stipulated that:

should the hirer fail to pay the initial instalments . . . or any subsequent instalment . . . within ten days after the same shall have become due or if he shall die . . . the owner may . . . by written notice . . . forthwith and for all purposes terminate the hiring.

The Court of Appeal held that this clause gave the owners the right to terminate the contract but that they were only entitled to recover by way of damages the unpaid instalments as at the date of the termination of the contract (and not the loss of the future instalments). The vital difference between *Baldock* and *Lombard* is that clause 2(a) of the contract in *Lombard* stated that time of payment was of the essence of the contract. The effect of this was to turn a failure to pay into a breach of a condition so that the breach was repudiatory and the plaintiffs were in consequence entitled to recover loss of bargain damages. By contrast, the owners in *Baldock* were unable to demonstrate that the defendant had repudiated the contract. Breach of the clause relating to payment was not in itself repudiatory and they could not show that the hirer had evinced an intention no longer to be bound by the terms of the contract. This being the case, they were only entitled to recover the loss of rentals as at the date of termination. Thus elevation of a term to the status of a condition can be important not only in relation to the right to terminate but also for the damages recoverable upon the termination of the contract.

The decision in *Lombard* has its critics (see GH Treitel, 'Damages on Rescission for Breach of Contract' [1987] *LMCLQ* 143 and W Bojczuk, 'When is a Condition not a Condition?' [1987] *JBL* 353) and its supporters (B Opeskin, 'Damages for Breach of Contract Terminated under Express Terms' (1990) 106 *LQR* 293). Professor Treitel argues that it is only where the breach is repudiatory under the general law, that is apart from the express agreement of the parties, that the owner is entitled to recover loss of bargain damages. In his view, loss of bargain damages should not be available where the owner 'rescinds for a minor breach under an express contractual provision entitling him to do so'. The difficulty with this argument is that the law does not generally distinguish between a condition that arises under the general law and a condition which has been created by an express provision in the contract (see *Stellar Chartering and Brokerage Inc* v. *Efibanca-Ente Finanziaro Interbancario Spa (The Span Terza, No 2)* [1984] 1 WLR 27, 33). It is therefore suggested that *Lombard*, harsh though it appears, was correctly decided.

Lombard further demonstrates that parties are free to classify as a condition a term which would not otherwise amount to a condition. Freedom of contract here prevails. This stands in contrast with the approach operative in some other jurisdictions where the question whether or not a breach is sufficiently fundamental to entitle a party to terminate is a question for the law (or the courts) and not for the parties themselves.

When considering the policy issues at stake in *Lombard* it is important to remember that the Consumer Credit Act 1974 enacts substantial protection for individuals who enter into hire-purchase and other credit agreements where the value of the credit advanced is less than £25,000. A consumer who falls within the scope of this Act receives considerable protection; in particular the Act places substantial limits on the ability of the owner to retake possession of the goods. The problem case is the one, such as *Lombard*, which falls outside the scope of the Consumer Credit Act 1974 because, once one is outside the scope of the Act, the unfortunate hirer is left exposed to the chill winds of the common law.

(b) BREACH OF A WARRANTY

A warranty is a lesser, subsidiary term of the contract. Breach of a warranty gives rise to a claim for damages but it does not, it is suggested, give an innocent party the right to terminate further performance of the contract. The Sale of Goods Act 1979 classifies certain obligations of a seller of goods as warranties. Thus the term that the goods are free from any charge or encumbrance not disclosed or known to the buyer before the contract is made and that the buyer will enjoy quiet possession of the goods except in so far as it may be disturbed by the owner or other person entitled to the benefit of any charge or encumbrance so disclosed or known is classified as a warranty (s. 12(5A)).

The view that breach of a warranty cannot give rise to a right to terminate further performance of the contract has been challenged by Professor Treitel who maintains (*Some Landmarks of Twentieth Century Contract Law* (Oxford University Press, 2002), p. 124) that:

there is the possibility that the breach of a term which is a warranty because it is . . . 'collateral to the main purpose of the contract' may, in exceptional circumstances, have unexpectedly serious effects; and there is some support in the judgment of Ormrod LJ in *The Hansa Nord* for the view that, if a seller's breach of warranty does have such effects, or if the breach is one which is deliberate in the sense that the seller could easily put it right but refuses to do so, then the buyer could reject. It is quite hard to think of a realistic sale of goods example since the ambit of the statutorily implied terms as to quality or fitness for a particular purpose is now so wide and since all these terms are classified by the Sale of Goods Act as conditions. Perhaps we might take the case of a contract for the hire of a car in which the owner 'warranted' to make the car available at 8 am on Derby Day and then the previous day told the hirer that it would not be available until 8 pm. In all probability, the court would conclude that the word 'warranty' was not here used in its technical sense but meant 'condition'. But if for some reason the drafting precluded this line of reasoning, the court might well hold that in such a case it was not appropriate to require the hirer to pay the agreed hire and then to claim damages; and that the breach, though one of 'warranty', justified his immediate cancellation of the contract.

The problem which concerns Professor Treitel is the case where the breach has serious consequences for the innocent party but the term broken has been classified by the parties as a 'warranty'. In many ways, this is the flip-side of *Schuler* v. *Wickman* (p. 944 above). If the court is not satisfied that the word 'warranty' was used in its technical sense then use of the word 'warranty' should not act as a barrier to a party terminating the contract where the consequences of the breach are serious. On the other hand, in the case where the parties do use the word 'warranty' in its technical sense, then it is submitted that there should be no right to terminate. Just as it is open to the parties to agree that any term is a condition (in its technical sense) so it should be open to the parties to agree that any term is a warranty (in its technical sense) and, in such a case, the breach of the warranty should not give rise to a right to terminate but only a right to recover damages.

(c) BREACH OF AN INTERMEDIATE TERM

The origin of intermediate terms (as we know them today) is to be found in the decision of the Court of Appeal in *Hong Kong Fir* v. *Kawasaki Kisen Kaisha* [1962] 2 QB 26. The origin of this category may, perhaps, be doubtful but there is no doubt that the category of intermediate or innominate terms exists and that they are rather prevalent. The main contribution which they have made is that they give to the courts a degree of remedial flexibility in that they can decide whether or not the breach was repudiatory by having regard to the consequences of the breach rather than the nature of the term broken. The difficulty which the existence of intermediate terms poses for legal advisors is that they give rise to a degree of uncertainty in that it can be very difficult to predict whether or not the judge will conclude that the breach was sufficiently serious to entitle the innocent party to terminate the contract.

Hong Kong Fir Shipping Co Ltd v. Kawasaki Kisen Kaisha Ltd
[1962] 2 QB 26, Court of Appeal

By a time charter (that is to say, the hire of a ship for a period of time) the shipowners agreed to deliver the vessel, the *Hong Kong Fir*, to the charterers for a period of twenty-four months. Clause 1 of the time charter stated that the vessel was 'in every way fitted for ordinary cargo service' and the shipowners further undertook in clause 3 to 'maintain her in a thoroughly efficient state in hull and machinery during service'. Hire was not, however, payable in respect of any period exceeding 24 hours lost as a result of the vessel undergoing repairs. Such 'off-hire time' was, at the charterers' option, to be added to the hire period.

The ship was delivered to the charterers on 13 February 1957 and set sail for Virginia. At the date of delivery the ship was unseaworthy because her engine rooms were under-manned and the engine-room staff were incompetent. The ship immediately set sail for Osaka. She arrived in Osaka on 25 May 1957 but, in that period, had been off-hire for some 30 days because of the need to carry out repairs to her engine. When she arrived in Osaka it was discovered that the ship would be off-hire for a further period of fifteen weeks in order to carry out repairs to the engine. During the period between February and June 1957 there was a considerable fall in the freight market (this meant that the charter was no longer an attractive one from the perspective of the charterers because they could obtain a ship at a lower rate of hire elsewhere). On 6 June 1957 (and again on 11 September 1957) the charterers wrote to the shipowners to inform them that they were terminating the charter and seeking damages for breach of contract. On 13 September 1957 the shipowners formally accepted that the contract was at an end. The shipowners then brought an action against the charterers in which they claimed damages on the ground that the charterers had wrongfully repudiated the contract.

At first instance Salmon J held that the ship was unseaworthy but that the charterers were not entitled to terminate the charter on account of the unseaworthiness of the ship. The charterers appealed to the Court of Appeal but their appeal was dismissed on the ground that the breach of contract by the shipowners was not sufficiently serious to entitle the charterers to terminate further performance of the contract.

Sellers LJ [stated the facts and continued]

By clause 1 of the charterparty the shipowners contracted to deliver the vessel at

Liverpool 'she being in every way fitted for ordinary cargo service'. She was not fit for ordinary cargo service when delivered because the engine room staff was incompetent and inadequate and this became apparent as the voyage proceeded. It is commonplace language to say that the vessel was unseaworthy by reason of this inefficiency in the engine room. Ships have been held to be unseaworthy in a variety of ways and those who have been put to loss by reason thereof (in the absence of any protecting clause in favour of a shipowner) have been able to recover damages as for a breach of warranty. It would be unthinkable that all the relatively trivial matters which have been held to be unseaworthiness could be regarded as conditions of the contract or conditions precedent to a charterer's liability and justify in themselves a cancellation or refusal to perform on the part of the charterer . . .

[he considered the authorities and continued]

In my judgment authority over many decades and reason support the conclusion in this case that there was no breach of a condition which entitled the charterers to accept it as a repudiation and to withdraw from the charter. It was not contended that the maintenance clause is so fundamental a matter as to amount to a condition of the contract. It is a warranty which sounds in damages.

Upjohn LJ

Why is this apparently basic and underlying condition of seaworthiness not, in fact, treated as a condition? It is for the simple reason that the seaworthiness clause is breached by the slightest failure to be fitted 'in every way' for service. Thus, to take examples from the judgments in some of the cases I have mentioned above, if a nail is missing from one of the timbers of a wooden vessel or if proper medical supplies or two anchors are not on board at the time of sailing, the owners are in breach of the seaworthiness stipulation. It is contrary to common sense to suppose that in such circumstances the parties contemplated that the charterer should at once be entitled to treat the contract as at an end for such trifling breaches.

A condition, or a condition precedent, to give it its proper title under the old system of pleading, was a condition performance of which had to be averred by the plaintiff in the declaration in order to establish his claim against the defendant. It was decided in the great plantation case of *Boone* v. *Eyre*, 1 H Bl 273 however, that it was only necessary to aver as a condition precedent a condition which went to the whole consideration of both sides. The rule is, I think, best stated by Lord Ellenborough CJ in *Davidson* v. *Gwynne* 12 East 380, 389:

'The principle laid down in *Boone* v. *Eyre* 1 H Bl 273 has been recognised in all the subsequent cases, that unless the non-performance alleged in breach of the contract goes to the whole root and consideration of it, the covenant broken is not to be considered as a condition precedent, but as a distinct covenant, for the breach of which the party injured may be compensated in damages.'

It is open to the parties to a contract to make it clear either expressly or by necessary implication that a particular stipulation is to be regarded as a condition which goes to the root of the contract, so that it is clear that the parties contemplate that any breach of it entitles the other party at once to treat the contract as at an end. That matter has to be determined as a question of the proper interpretation of the contract. Bramwell B in

Tarrabochia v. *Hickie* 1 H & N 183 has warned against the dangers of too ready an implication of such a condition. He said *Ibid*. 188:

> 'No doubt it is competent for the parties, if they think fit, to declare in express terms that any matter shall be a condition precedent, but when they have not so expressed themselves, it is necessary for those who construe the instrument to see whether they intended to do it. Since, however, they could have done it, those who construe the instrument should be chary in doing for them that which they might, but have not done for themselves.'

Where, however, upon the true construction of the contract, the parties have not made a particular stipulation a condition, it would in my judgment be unsound and misleading to conclude that, being a warranty, damages is necessarily a sufficient remedy.

In my judgment the remedies open to the innocent party for breach of a stipulation which is not a condition strictly so called, depend entirely upon the nature of the breach and its foreseeable consequences. Breaches of stipulation fall, naturally, into two classes. First there is the case where the owner by his conduct indicates that he considers himself no longer bound to perform his part of the contract; in that case, of course, the charterer may accept the repudiation and treat the contract as at an end. The second class of case is, of course, the more usual one and that is where, due to misfortune such as the perils of the sea, engine failures, incompetence of the crew and so on, the owner is unable to perform a particular stipulation precisely in accordance with the terms of the contract try he ever so hard to remedy it. In that case the question to be answered is, does the breach of the stipulation go so much to the root of the contract that it makes further commercial performance of the contract impossible, or in other words is the whole contract frustrated? If yea, the innocent party may treat the contract as at an end. If nay, his claim sounds in damages only.

If I have correctly stated the principles, then as the stipulation as to the seaworthiness is not a condition in the strict sense the question to be answered is, did the initial unseaworthiness as found by the judge, and from which there has been no appeal, go so much to the root of the contract that the charterers were then and there entitled to treat the charterparty as at an end? The only unseaworthiness alleged, serious though it was, was the insufficiency and incompetence of the crew, but that surely cannot be treated as going to the root of the contract for the parties must have contemplated that in such an event the crew could be changed and augmented. In my judgment, on this part of his case counsel for the charterers necessarily fails.

Diplock LJ

Every synallagmatic contract contains in it the seeds of the problem: in what event will a party be relieved of his undertaking to do that which he has agreed to do but has not yet done? The contract may itself expressly define some of these events, as in the cancellation clause in a charterparty; but, human prescience being limited, it seldom does so exhaustively and often fails to do so at all. In some classes of contracts such as sale of goods, marine insurance, contracts of affreightment evidenced by bills of lading and those between parties to bills of exchange, Parliament has defined by statute some of the events not provided for expressly in individual contracts of that class; but where an event occurs the occurrence of which neither the parties nor Parliament have expressly stated will discharge one of the parties from further performance of his undertakings, it is for the court to determine whether the event has this effect or not.

The test whether an event has this effect or not has been stated in a number of metaphors all of which I think amount to the same thing: does the occurrence of the event deprive the party who has further undertakings still to perform of substantially the whole benefit which it was the intention of the parties as expressed in the contract that he should obtain as the consideration for performing those undertakings?

This test is applicable whether or not the event occurs as a result of the default of one of the parties to the contract, but the consequences of the event are different in the two cases. Where the event occurs as a result of the default of one party, the party in default cannot rely upon it as relieving himself of the performance of any further undertakings on his part, and the innocent party, although entitled to, need not treat the event as relieving him of the further performance of his own undertakings. This is only a specific application of the fundamental legal and moral rule that a man should not be allowed to take advantage of his own wrong. Where the event occurs as a result of the default of neither party, each is relieved of the further performance of his own undertakings, and their rights in respect of undertakings previously performed are now regulated by the Law Reform (Frustrated Contracts) Act, 1943.

This branch of the common law has reached its present stage by the normal process of historical growth, and the fallacy in counsel for the charterers' contention that a different test is applicable when the event occurs as a result of the default of one party from that applicable in cases of frustration where the event occurs as a result of the default of neither party lies, in my view, from a failure to view the cases in their historical context. The problem: in what event will a party to a contract be relieved of his undertaking to do that which he has agreed to do but has not yet done? has exercised the English courts for centuries, probably ever since assumpsit emerged as a form of action distinct from covenant and debt and long before even the earliest cases which we have been invited to examine; but until the rigour of the rule in *Paradine* v. *Jane* (1647) Aleyn 26 was mitigated in the middle of the last century by the classic judgments of Blackburn J in *Taylor* v. *Caldwell* (1863) 3 B & S 826 and Bramwell B in *Jackson* v. *Union Marine Insurance Co Ltd* (1874) LR 10 CP 125 it was in general only events resulting from one party's failure to perform his contractual obligations which were regarded as capable of relieving the other party from continuing to perform that which he had undertaken to do . . .

[he considered the historical development of the law and continued]

Once it is appreciated that it is the event and not the fact that the event is a result of a breach of contract which relieves the party not in default of further performance of his obligations, two consequences follow. (1) The test whether the event relied upon has this consequence is the same whether the event is the result of the other party's breach of contract or not, as Devlin J pointed out in *Universal Cargo Carriers Corporation* v. *Citati* [1957] 2 QB 401, 434. (2) The question whether an event which is the result of the other party's breach of contract has this consequence cannot be answered by treating all contractual undertakings as falling into one of two separate categories: 'conditions' the breach of which gives rise to an event which relieves the party not in default of further performance of his obligations, and 'warranties' the breach of which does not give rise to such an event.

Lawyers tend to speak of this classification as if it were comprehensive, partly for the historical reasons which I have already mentioned and partly because Parliament itself adopted it in the Sale of Goods Act, 1893, as respects a number of implied terms in contracts for the sale of goods and has in that Act used the expressions 'condition' and 'warranty' in that meaning. But it is by no means true of contractual undertakings in general at common law.

No doubt there are many simple contractual undertakings, sometimes express but more often because of their very simplicity ('It goes without saying') to be implied, of which it can be predicated that every breach of such an undertaking must give rise to an event which will deprive the party not in default of substantially the whole benefit which it was intended that he should obtain from the contract and such a stipulation, unless the parties have agreed that breach of it shall not entitle the non-defaulting party to treat the contract as repudiated, is a 'condition'. So too there may be other simple contractual undertakings of which it can be predicated that no breach can give rise to an event which will deprive the party not in default of substantially the whole benefit which it was intended that he should obtain from the contract; and such a stipulation, unless the parties have agreed that breach of it shall entitle the non-defaulting party to treat the contract as repudiated, is a 'warranty'.

There are, however, many contractual undertakings of a more complex character which cannot be categorised as being 'conditions' or 'warranties', if the late nineteenth-century meaning adopted in the Sale of Goods Act 1893, and used by Bowen LJ in *Bentsen* v. *Taylor, Sons & Co* [1893] 2 QB 274, 280 be given to those terms. Of such undertakings all that can be predicated is that some breaches will and others will not give rise to an event which will deprive the party not in default of substantially the whole benefit which it was intended that he should obtain from the contract; and the legal consequences of a breach of such an undertaking, unless provided for expressly in the contract, depend upon the nature of the event to which the breach gives rise and do not follow automatically from a prior classification of the undertaking as a 'condition' or a 'warranty'. For instance, to take Bramwell B's example in *Jackson* v. *Union Marine Insurance Co Ltd* LR 10 CP 125, 142 itself, breach of an undertaking by a shipowner to sail with all possible dispatch to a named port does not necessarily relieve the charterer of further performance of his obligation under the charterparty, but if the breach is so prolonged that the contemplated voyage is frustrated it does have this effect . . .

In 1874 when the doctrine of frustration was being foaled by 'impossibility of performance' out of 'condition precedent' it is not surprising that the explanation given by Bramwell B should give full credit to the dam by suggesting that in addition to the express warranty to sail with all possible dispatch there was an implied condition precedent that the ship should arrive at the named port in time for the voyage contemplated. In *Jackson* v. *Union Marine Insurance Co Ltd* LR 10 CP 125, 142 there was no breach of the express warranty; but if there had been, to engraft the implied condition upon the express warranty would have been merely a more complicated way of saying that a breach of a shipowner's undertaking to sail with all possible dispatch may, but will not necessarily, give rise to an event which will deprive the charterer of substantially the whole benefit which it was intended that he should obtain from the charter. Now that the doctrine of frustration has matured and flourished for nearly a century and the old technicalities of pleading 'conditions precedent' are more than a century out of date, it does not clarify, but on the contrary obscures, the modern principle of law where such an event has occurred as a result of a breach of an express stipulation in a contract, to continue to add the now unnecessary colophon. 'Therefore it was an implied condition of the contract that a particular kind of breach of an express warranty should not occur'.

The common law evolves not merely by breeding new principles but also, when they are fully grown, by burying their progenitors.

As my brethren have already pointed out, the shipowners' undertaking to tender a seaworthy ship has, as a result of numerous decisions as to what can amount to 'unseaworthiness', become one of the most complex of contractual undertakings. It embraces obligations with respect to every part of the hull and machinery, stores and equipment and the crew itself. It can be broken by the presence of trivial defects easily and rapidly remediable as well as by defects which must inevitably result in a total loss of the vessel. Consequently the problem in this case is, in my view, neither solved nor soluble by debating whether the shipowner's express or implied undertaking to tender a seaworthy ship is a 'condition' or a 'warranty'. It is like so many other contractual terms an undertaking one breach of which may give rise to an event which relieves the charterer of further performance of his undertakings if he so elects and another breach of which may not give rise to such an event but entitle him only to monetary compensation in the form of damages. It is, with all deference to counsel for the charterers' skilful argument, by no means surprising that among the many hundreds of previous cases about the shipowner's undertaking to deliver a seaworthy ship there is none where it was found profitable to discuss in the judgments the question whether that undertaking is a 'condition' or a 'warranty'; for the true answer, as I have already indicated, is that it is neither, but one of that large class of contractual undertakings one breach of which may have the same effect as that ascribed to a breach of 'condition' under the Sale of Goods Act, 1893, and a different breach of which may have only the same effect as that ascribed to a breach of 'warranty' under that Act.

What the learned judge had to do in the present case, as in any other case where one party to a contract relies upon a breach by the other party as giving him a right to elect to rescind the contract, and the contract itself makes no express provision as to this, was to look at the events which had occurred as a result of the breach at the time at which the charterers purported to rescind the charterparty and to decide whether the occurrence of those events deprived the charterers of substantially the whole benefit which it was the intention of the parties as expressed in the charterparty that the charterers should obtain from the further performance of their own contractual undertakings.

One turns therefore to the contract, the Baltime 1939 charter, of which Sellers LJ has already cited the relevant terms. Clause 13, the 'due diligence' clause, which exempts the shipowners from responsibility for delay or loss or damage to goods on board due to unseaworthiness, unless such delay or loss or damage has been caused by want of due diligence of the owners in making the vessel seaworthy and fitted for the voyage, is in itself sufficient to show that the mere occurrence of the events that the vessel was in some respect unseaworthy when tendered or that such unseaworthiness had caused some delay in performance of the charterparty would not deprive the charterer of the whole benefit which it was the intention of the parties he should obtain from the performance of his obligations under the contract—for he undertakes to continue to perform his obligations notwithstanding the occurrence of such events if they fall short of frustration of the contract and even deprives himself of any remedy in damages unless such events are the consequence of want of due diligence on the part of the shipowner.

The question which the learned judge had to ask himself was, as he rightly decided, whether or not at the date when the charterers purported to rescind the contract, namely, June 6, 1957, or when the shipowners purported to accept such rescission, namely, August 8, 1957, the delay which had already occurred as a result of the incompetence of the engine-room staff, and the delay which was likely to occur in repairing the engines of the vessel and the conduct of the shipowners by that date in taking steps to remedy these two matters, were, when taken together, such as to deprive the charterers of substantially the whole benefit which it was the intention of the parties they should obtain from further use of the vessel under the charterparty.

In my view, in his judgment—on which I would not seek to improve—the judge took into account and gave due weight to all the relevant considerations and arrived at the right answer for the right reasons.

COMMENTARY

The vital factor in persuading the Court of Appeal to conclude that the obligation to provide a seaworthy ship was an intermediate term was that the term could have been broken in a trivial manner (which could be remedied adequately by an award of damages) or in a way that was so fundamental that it would have undermined the purpose which the parties had in mind in entering into the contract. The conclusion that either every breach gave rise to a right to terminate further performance of the contract or that no breach gave rise to a right to terminate was too stark a choice for the court. The common law was capable of providing a more proportionate and calibrated approach. That approach was to have regard to the consequences of the breach (although it is not entirely clear that the judges intended to create a new category of intermediate terms in so deciding).

Intermediate terms are now well-established in the case-law. Their introduction has generated two difficulties. The first lies in distinguishing an intermediate term from a condition and a warranty (an issue which is discussed in the next section). The second difficulty is one of ascertaining how serious the consequences of the breach must be before an innocent party is entitled to terminate. In other words, how 'serious' is 'serious'? The best answer one can give is that it must be very serious. Diplock LJ drew an analogy with frustration, in the sense that the breach must be such as to deprive the innocent party substantially of the benefit that he intended to obtain from performance. Case-law demonstrates that the courts have regard to a range of factors in deciding whether or not the breach is sufficiently serious. Factors to which the courts have regard include the losses caused by the breach, the cost of making performance comply with the terms of the contract, the value of the performance that has been received by the innocent party, the willingness of the party in breach to make good the consequences of the breach, the likelihood of a further breach by the party in breach, and the adequacy of damages as a remedy to the innocent party. Given the range of factors to which the courts have regard and their generality, the balancing of these factors must, at the end of the day, depend to a large extent upon the facts of the individual case. This uncertainty can cause difficulty in practice. Suppose a case in which the consequences of the breach are serious but not disastrous and the innocent party has substantial doubts about the ability of his contracting party to perform in the future (although he is unlikely to be able to prove that he will not be able to perform in the future). What advice should be given to the innocent party who informs his lawyer that he wishes to terminate the contract? At this point it is important to recall that a party who purports to terminate a contract when not in fact entitled to do so will be held to have repudiated the contract. This being the case, advisors to the innocent party are likely to err on the side of caution: that is to say, they are likely to advise him that a decision to terminate carries with it a risk that a court may subsequently decide that he was not entitled to terminate and hold him liable in damages for the loss suffered by the other party as a result of any wrongful termination. On the other hand, if he contents himself with a claim for damages for the loss that he has suffered as a result of the breach, he should be compensated for the loss that he has suffered and will eliminate the risk of incurring any liability to the other party. A risk-averse party is unlikely to terminate in such a case. In this way, classification of a term as an intermediate term may operate in practice to inhibit use of termination as a remedy.

(d) MAKING THE CHOICE

It is not easy to ascertain how prevalent intermediate terms are in fact. Some authors assume (see, for example, H Beale (ed), *Chitty on Contracts* (29th edn, Sweet & Maxwell, 2004), para 12-040) that a term will be held to be intermediate unless a judge is compelled by statute, binding authority, or the choice of the parties to conclude that the term is a condition. It is clear that the courts must respect the intention of Parliament and they must follow binding authority (at least where the contract term in issue is identical to the term that was in issue in the previous case). Subject to the considerations which influenced the House of Lords in *Schuler* v. *Wickman*, the courts will generally respect the choice of the parties.

But what do the courts do in the case where the term has not been previously classified? Is it the case that the courts will assume that the clause is intermediate? A study of the cases reveals that there is no such assumption. In fact, the cases reveal a significant level of disagreement as to the approach to be adopted in such cases. Indeed it is not unknown for the Court of Appeal to adopt a different classification from that adopted by the trial judge (and for the House of Lords in turn to adopt a different classification from the one adopted by the Court of Appeal). When deciding whether a term is a condition, a warranty, or an innominate term, the courts have regard to a range of factors and the exercise in which they are engaged is very much a balancing exercise as the following cases demonstrate.

In *Maredelanto Compania Naviera SA* v. *Bergbau-Handel GmbH (The Mihalis Angelos)* [1971] 1 QB 164 the owners chartered the vessel *Mihalis Angelos* to the charterers for a voyage from Haiphong in North Vietnam to Hamburg. Clause 1 of the charterparty stated that the vessel was 'expected ready to load under this charter about 1 July 1965'. The owners had no reasonable basis for this expectation. The *Mihalis Angelos* was in use on another voyage and was not expected to arrive at Haiphong until the 13 or 14 of July. Meanwhile the charterers discovered that they had problems of their own. They had chartered the vessel in order to transport a cargo of apatite to Europe but they discovered that there was no apatite ore available in North Vietnam. They believed that the lack of apatite was attributable to the war then taking place in Vietnam and so they purported to cancel the contract on the ground of force majeure.

The shipowners interpreted this as a repudiation of the contract by the charterers and sought to recover damages from the shipowners. One of the issues before the court was whether or not clause 1 of the contract was a condition or a warranty. The Court of Appeal held that it was a condition with the result that the charterers were entitled to terminate the charter, notwithstanding the fact that they had initially sought to justify their decision to terminate the contract on a completely different ground. Megaw LJ reached the conclusion that clause 1 was a condition for 'four inter-related reasons'. These were:

First, it tends towards certainty in the law. One of the essential elements of law is some measure of uniformity. One of the important elements of the law is predictability. At any rate in commercial law, there are obvious and substantial advantages in having, where possible, a firm and definite rule for a particular class of legal relationship: for example, as here, the legal categorisation of a particular, definable type of contractual clause in common use. It is surely much better, both for shipowners and charterers (and, incidentally, for their advisers), when a contractual obligation of this nature is under consideration, and still more when they are faced with the necessity for an urgent decision as to the effects of a suspected breach of it, to be able to say categorically: 'If a breach is proved, then the charterer can put an end to the contract', rather than that they should be left to ponder whether or not the courts would be likely, in the particular case, when the evidence has been heard, to decide that in the particular circumstances the breach was or was not such as 'to go to the root of the contract'. Where justice does not require greater flexibility, there is everything to be said for, and nothing against, a degree of rigidity in legal principle.

Second, it would, in my opinion, only be in the rarest case, if ever, that a shipowner could legitimately feel that he had suffered an injustice by reason of the law having given to a charterer the right to put an end to the contract because of the breach by the shipowner of a clause such as this. If a shipowner has chosen to assert contractually, but dishonestly or without reasonable grounds, that he expects his vessel to be ready to load on such-and-such a date, wherein does the grievance lie?

Third, it is, as Mocatta J held, clearly established by authority binding on this court that where a clause 'expected ready to load' is included in a contract for the sale of goods to be carried by sea, that clause is a condition, in the sense that any breach of it enables the buyer to reject the goods without having to show that the dishonest or unreasonable expectation of the seller has in fact been prejudicial to the buyer. The judgment of Bankes LJ, in which Warrington LJ and Atkin LJ concurred, in *Finnish Government* v. *H Ford & Co Ltd* (1921) 6 Ll L Rep 188 is in point. The clause there was 'Steamers expected ready to load February and/or March 1920'. Bankes LJ said, at p. 189: 'I come to the conclusion . . . that this clause is one containing a contract. It is a contract which is in its nature a condition. . . .' That authority is not only binding on this court, but is, I think, completely and desirably in conformity with the line of cases which have decided—and the law in that respect is now accepted as being beyond dispute—that a statement in a contract of sale as to the loading period is a condition in the sense which I have indicated. If the contract says 'loading to be during July', the buyer can reject the goods if the loading was not complete until midday on August 1. He is not limited to claiming damages; he is not obliged to show that he has suffered any damage.

It would, in my judgment, produce an undesirable anomaly in our commercial law if such a clause—'expected ready to load'—were to be held to have a materially different legal effect where it is contained in a charterparty from that which it has when it is contained in a sale of goods contract. True, in the latter case the relevant 'expectation' is that of the seller of the goods, who may himself be the charterer; whereas in the former case the relevant 'expectation' is that of the shipowner. But I do not see that that fact is sufficient to warrant the making of a distinction between the two. True, also, as was stressed by counsel for the owners, the charterparty will almost invariably include a cancelling clause; and it is argued that that fact justifies the drawing of a distinction. Again, I think not, for various reasons. One of them is that the date before which the cancelling clause cannot be exercised . . . is itself normally fixed by reference to the date of expected readiness to load, and on the assumption that that is an honest and reasonable expectation.

The fourth reason why I think that the clause should be regarded as being a condition when it is found in a charterparty is that that view was the view of Scrutton LJ so expressed in his capacity as the author of *Scrutton on Charterparties*.

The Mihalis Angelos can be contrasted with the later decision of the Court of Appeal in *Cehave NV* v. *Bremer Handelsgesellschaft mbH (The Hansa Nord)* [1976] QB 44 where the judicial pendulum appeared to swing significantly in favour of construction as an intermediate term. The parties entered into two contracts for the sale of citrus pulp pellets. Clause 7 of the contract stated: 'Shipment to be made in good condition . . . each shipment shall be considered a separate contract'. The buyers paid the price of approximately £100,000 in exchange for the shipping documents. However they rejected the entire cargo on its arrival in Rotterdam on the ground that part of the cargo in one of the holds was found to be damaged. The goods were then sold pursuant to a court order and, through a third party, the buyers were able to purchase them for some £30,000. In these circumstances the buyers sought to recover the purchase price from the sellers. They claimed that they were entitled to reject the goods and recover the price on two grounds. The first was that there had been a breach by the sellers of clause 7 of the contract and the second was that the goods were not of 'merchantable quality' so that the sellers were in breach of section 14(2) of the Sale of Goods Act 1893. The buyers succeeded in their arguments before a trade arbitration panel and before Mocatta J but the sellers appealed successfully to the Court of Appeal. In relation to the buyers' submission that there had been a breach of section 14(2) of the Sale of Goods Act, the Court of Appeal held that the goods were in fact of merchantable quality on the basis that they remained fit for their intended purpose and were, indeed, used by the buyers for that purpose. In relation to the breach of clause 7 of the contract, the Court of Appeal concluded that the buyers were entitled to damages but that the breach did not entitle them to terminate the contract. Clause 7 had not been expressly classified by the parties as a condition, nor was the court bound by authority to conclude that it was a condition. In the absence of party stipulation and binding authority, the court concluded that clause 7 was an intermediate term and not a condition. Thus Lord Denning MR stated that small-scale deviations from the contractual standard should be met by a price allowance and that 'buyers should not have a right to reject the whole cargo unless [the deficiency] was serious and substantial'. To similar effect is the following passage from the judgment of Roskill LJ (at pp. 70–71):

In my view, a court should not be over ready, unless required by statute or authority to do so, to construe a term in a contract as a 'condition' any breach of which gives rise to a right to reject rather than as a term any breach of which sounds in damages. . . . In principle, contracts are made to be performed and not to be avoided according to the whims of market fluctuation and where there is free choice between two possible constructions I think the court should tend to prefer that construction which will ensure performance, and not encourage avoidance of contractual obligations.

The reference to 'whims of market fluctuation' is surely significant here. At the time of the arrival of the goods the market price of the goods had already dropped to approximately £86,000 so that the buyers had an economic interest in finding a way out of the contract so that they could purchase alternative goods in the market-place at a lower price. The fact that they were able to purchase the goods for £30,000 simply added, albeit significantly, to their windfall. In the words of Professor Brownsword ('Retrieving Reasons, Retrieving Rationality? A New Look at the Right to Withdraw for Breach of Contract' (1992) 5 *Journal of Contract Law* 83, 91) the Court of Appeal took a stand not only against 'bad faith' but 'more generally, against economic opportunism within a contractual relationship'.

This leads on to another point which is that English law presently does not examine the motivations of the party seeking to exercise a right to terminate. The law focuses on the existence or otherwise of the entitlement to terminate, not the reasons behind the decision to terminate. It can be argued that this leads to unfairness. An alternative approach is to focus attention on the reasons for the decision to terminate. Such an analysis has been put forward by Professor Brownsword ('Retrieving Reasons, Retrieving Rationality? A New Look at the Right to Withdraw for Breach of Contract' (1992) 5 *Journal of Contract Law* 83, 92–93) in the following terms:

If the innocent party's reasons for withdrawal were to be treated as a focal consideration, in what circumstances would there be a right to withdraw for breach? Basically, a right to withdraw would be available where it was conferred by legislation or case law, or where it was so agreed by the parties; but, failing such special provision, the right to withdraw would depend upon the innocent party having good reasons for claiming the option of release from the contract, as opposed to settling for damages . . .

The fact that there has been a breach of contract raises the possibility that the innocent party might have the right to withdraw. The mere fact of breach, however, is not sufficient reason. Breach warrants compensatory damages, but not necessarily the option of withdrawal. What kind of reasons, then, might an innocent party advance to support an argument in favour of the right to withdraw? Without any claim to being exhaustive of possible good reasons, six arguable grounds for the right to withdraw may be suggested as follows:

(1) the contract breaker evinces, through the breach, a lack of commitment to the contract as a source of obligation (for example, the breach is intentional/calculating, or fraud/dishonesty is involved);

(2) the breach raises concerns about the competence of the contract-breaker (for example, the breach involves negligence);

(3) the breach, although unintentional and non-negligent, renders performance under the contract radically different from that envisaged at formation;

(4) proving (or quantifying) losses flowing from the breach gives rise to difficulties which put the innocent party at risk;

(5) the breach gives rise to concern about the contract-breaker's ability to meet future claims; and

(6) the breach gives rise to concern about the *innocent party's* own ability to perform either the contract in question or another's associated contract.

Without arguing the point, let us suppose that an innocent party claiming a right to withdraw for good reason must make out a prima facie case under any one of these heads. Further, let us suppose that the right to withdraw only obtains where the innocent party (i) acts in good faith, and (ii) has reasonable grounds for believing that the particular supporting reason applies. Accordingly, once a prima facie case has been made out, the onus shifts to the contract-breaker to rebut the innocent party's claim. This could be done by showing either a lack of good faith or a lack of reasonable grounds. The former might involve dishonesty or the like, but, crucially, if the innocent party has relied on collateral economic reasons—and, thus, is not seeking withdrawal '*for* breach'—this would constitute a lack of good faith and would disqualify withdrawal.

The obvious merit of this proposal is that it holds out the possibility of fairer results and it gives the court in a case such as *Hansa Nord* a direct route to a solution. But in other respects the proposal gives rise to significant difficulties. It can be attacked as a matter of principle. Why should a party who has a right to terminate the contract lose that right simply because he was unaware of the existence of the right at the moment of termination? Secondly, the proposal may increase the cost of litigation in that it requires the court to scrutinize the motivations of the contracting parties; a difficult evidential inquiry. Thirdly, it does not remove all our difficulties. Even on this view *The Mihalis Angelos* remains a difficult case because both parties may have acted in bad faith. The shipowners were probably acting in bad faith (if not dishonestly) in putting forward a date of expected readiness to load which they knew would not be complied with, but the charterers equally may have been acting in bad faith in relying initially on force majeure and only relying on the breach of clause 1 at a later point in time.

However the next swing of the judicial pendulum was back in the direction of certainty. The decision of the House of Lords in *Bunge Corporation New York* v. *Tradax Export SA* [1981] 1 WLR 711 is an important one and it requires more detailed treatment.

Bunge Corporation New York v. Tradax Export SA

[1981] 1 WLR 711, House of Lords

The parties entered into a contract which incorporated the terms of GAFTA 119 (an industry-wide standard-form contract). The dispute between the parties related to the June shipment of goods. The responsibilities of the parties in relation to the shipment of the goods were divided as follows. The time of shipment was at the buyer's option but the sellers had the option as to the port of shipment. Clause 7 of the contract further provided that the 'buyers shall give at least 15 consecutive days' notice of probable readiness of vessel(s)'. The last day of the delivery period for the June shipment was 30 June 1975 and so, counting back from that date, the last day on which the buyers could give notice consistently with their obligation under clause 7 was 12 June. The buyers in fact gave notice on 17 June. The sellers refused to accept the notice as a valid notice, declared the buyers to be in default and claimed damages on the basis that the buyers had repudiated the contract through their failure to comply with the terms of clause 7.

The buyers argued that their breach of clause 7 of the contract was not a repudiatory breach of contract. They submitted that clause 7 was an intermediate or an innominate term and that the consequences of the breach were not sufficiently serious to entitle the sellers to terminate the contract because the breach had not deprived them of 'substantially the whole benefit which it was intended that they should obtain from the contract'. Further, the buyers argued that clause 7 was not a condition because, in order to amount to a condition, the sellers had to show that every breach of the clause would result in a loss to the sellers of substantially the whole benefit of the contract. The buyers' arguments were rejected by the House of Lords. It was held that clause 7 of the contract was, on its true construction, a condition of the contract so that the sellers were entitled to terminate further performance of the contract and claim damages from the buyers on the basis that the buyers had repudiated the contract.

Lord Wilberforce

The appeal depends upon the construction to be placed upon cl. 7 of GAFTA 119 as completed by the special contract. It is not expressed as a 'condition' and the question is whether, in its context and in the circumstances it should be read as such.

Apart from arguments on construction which have been fully dealt with by my noble and learned friend, the main contention of Mr Buckley QC [counsel for the appellants] was based on the decision of the Court of Appeal in *Hong Kong Fir Shipping Co Ltd* v. *Kawasaki Kisen Kaisha Ltd* [1962] 2 QB 26, as it might be applied to cl. 7. Lord Justice Diplock, as he then was, in his seminal judgment illuminated the existence in contracts of terms which were neither, necessarily, conditions nor warranties, but, in terminology which has since been applied to them, intermediate or innominate terms capable of operating, according to the gravity of the breach, as either conditions or warranties. Relying on this, Mr Buckley's submission was that the buyer's obligation under the clause, to—

'. . . give at least [15] consecutive days' notice of probable readiness of vessel(s) and of the approximate quantity required to be loaded . . .'

is of this character. A breach of it, both generally and in relation to this particular case might be, to use [counsel's] expression, 'inconsequential', i.e., not such as to make performance of the seller's obligation impossible. If this were so it would be wrong to treat it as a breach of condition: *Hong Kong Fir* would require it to be treated as a warranty.

This argument, in my opinion, is based upon a dangerous misunderstanding, or misapplication, of what was decided and said in *Hong Kong Fir*. That case was concerned with an obligation of seaworthiness, breaches of which had occurred during the course of the voyage. The decision of the Court of Appeal was that this obligation was not a condition, a breach of which entitled the charterer to repudiate. It was pointed out that, as could be seen in advance the breaches, which might occur of it, were various. They might be extremely trivial, the omission of a nail; they might be extremely grave, a serious defect in the hull or in the machinery; they might be of serious but not fatal gravity, incompetence or incapacity of the crew. The decision, and the judgments of the Court of Appeal, drew from these facts the inescapable conclusion that it was impossible to ascribe to the obligation, in advance, the character of a condition.

Lord Justice Diplock then generalized this particular consequence into the analysis which has since become classical. The fundamental fallacy of the appellant's argument lies in attempting to apply this analysis to a time clause such as the present in a mercantile contract, which is totally different in character. As to such a clause there is only one kind of breach possible, namely, to be late, and the questions which have to be asked are, first, what importance have the parties expressly ascribed to this consequence, and secondly, in the absence of expressed agreement, what consequence ought to be attached to it having regard to the contract as a whole.

The test suggested by the appellants was a different one. One must consider, they said, the breach actually committed and then decide whether that default would deprive the party not in default of substantially the whole benefit of the contract. They invoked even certain passages in the judgment of Lord Justice Diplock in *Hong Kong Fir* to support it. One may observe in the first place that the introduction of a test of this kind would be commercially most undesirable. It would expose the parties, after a breach of one, two, three, seven and other numbers of days to an argument whether this delay would have left time for the seller to provide the goods. It would make it, at the time, at least difficult, and sometimes impossible, for the supplier to know whether he could do so. It would fatally remove from a vital provision in the contract that certainty which is the most indispensable quality of mercantile contracts, and lead to a large increase in arbitrations. It would confine the seller—perhaps after arbitration and reference through the Courts— to a remedy in damages which might be extremely difficult to quantify. These are all serious objections in practice. But I am clear that the submission is unacceptable in law. The judgment of Lord Justice Diplock does not give any support and ought not to give any encouragement to any such proposition; for beyond doubt it recognizes that it is open to the parties to agree that, as regards a particular obligation, any breach shall entitle the party not in default to treat the contract as repudiated. Indeed, if he were not doing so he would, in a passage which does not profess to be more than clarificatory, be discrediting a long and uniform series of cases—at least from *Bowes* v. *Shand* (1877) 2 App Cas 455 onwards which have been referred to by my noble and learned friend, Lord Roskill. It remains true, as Lord Roskill has pointed out in *Cehave NV* v. *Bremer Handelsgesellschaft mbH* [1976] 1 QB 44, that the Courts should not be too ready to interpret contractual clauses as conditions. And I have myself commended, and continue to commend, the greater flexibility in the law of contracts to which *Hong Kong Fir* points the way (*Reardon Smith Line Ltd* v. *Hansen-Tangen* [1976] 1 WLR 989, at p. 998). But I do not doubt that, in suitable cases, the Courts should not be reluctant, if the intentions of the parties as shown by the contract so indicate, to hold that an obligation has the force of a condition, and that indeed they should usually do so in the case of time clauses in mercantile contracts. To such cases the 'gravity of the breach' approach of *Hong Kong Fir* would be unsuitable.

[He concluded that on the facts of the case it was 'clearly essential' that both buyer and seller should know precisely what their rights were and that the clause was therefore a condition.]

Lord Scarman

I read the *Hong Kong Fir* case as being concerned as much with the construction of the contract as with the consequences and effect of breach. The first question is always, therefore, whether, upon the true construction of a stipulation and the contract of which it is part, it is a condition, an innominate term, or only a warranty. If the stipulation is one, which upon the true construction of the contract the parties have not made a condition, and breach of which may be attended by trivial, minor, or very grave consequences, it is innominate, and the Court (or an arbitrator) will, in the event of dispute, have the task of deciding whether the breach that has arisen is such as the parties would have said, had they been asked at the time they made their contract: 'it goes without saying that, if that happens, the contract is at an end'.

Where, therefore, as commonly happens, the parties do not identify a stipulation as a condition, innominate term, or warranty, the Court will approach the problem of construction in the way outlined by Lord Justice Upjohn at pp. 63 and 64 of the reports. As the Lord Justice put it:

> 'Where, however, upon the true construction of the contract, the parties have not made a particular stipulation a condition, it would in my judgment be unsound and misleading to conclude that, being a warranty, damages is necessarily a sufficient remedy.'

Unless the contract makes it clear, either by express provision or by necessary implication arising from its nature, purpose, and circumstances ('the factual matrix' as spelt out, for example, by Lord Wilberforce in his speech in the *Reardon Smith* case [1976] 1 WLR 989 at pp. 995E-997D), that a particular stipulation is a condition or only a warranty, it is an innominate term, the remedy for a breach of which depends upon the nature, consequences, and effect of the breach.

[On the present facts he concluded that it made 'commercial sense' to treat the clause as a condition.]

Lord Lowry

The law having been established, why should we regard the term here in question as a condition? I start by expressing my full agreement with the reasons given in your Lordships' speeches. Among the points which have weighed with me are the following:—

1.   There are enormous practical advantages in certainty, not least in regard to string contracts where today's buyer may be tomorrow's seller.

2.   Most members of the string will have many ongoing contracts simultaneously and they must be able to do business with confidence in the legal results of their actions.

3.   Decisions would be too difficult if the term were innominate, litigation would be rife and years might elapse before the results were known.

4.   The difficulty of assessing damages is an indication in favour of condition: *McDougall* v. *Aeromarine of Emsworth Ltd* [1958] 1 WLR 1126, 1133.

5.   One can at least say that recent litigation has provided indications that the term is a condition. Parties to similar contracts should (failing a strong contra-indication) be able to rely on this: *The Mihalis Angelos* [1971] 1 QB 164 at p. 199F per Lord Justice Edmund-Davies.

6.   To make 'total loss' the only test of a condition is contrary to authority and experience, when one recalls that terms as to the date of sailing, deviation from a voyage and the date of delivery are regarded as conditions, but that failure to comply with them does not always have serious consequences.

7.   Nor need an implied condition pass the total loss test: see 6 above.

8.   If the consequences of breach of condition turn out to be slight, the innocent party may treat the condition as an innominate term or a warranty.

9.   While the sellers could have made time of the essence, if it were not so already, this would require reasonable notice, which might well not be practical either in a string contract or at all.

10.   In *Tarrabochia* v. *Hickie* (1856) 1 H & N 183; 156 ER 1168, upon which the appellants strongly relied, Baron Bramwell said:

'No doubt it is competent for the parties, if they think fit, to declare in express terms that any matter shall be a condition precedent, but when they have not so expressed themselves, it is necessary for those who construe the instrument to see whether they intend to do it. Since, however, they could have done it, those who construe the instrument should be chary in doing for them that which they might, but have not done for themselves.'

But in that very case both Chief Baron Pollock and Baron Bramwell, without the benefit of any express term, said that, where the agreement was that a ship should sail on a particular day, that was a condition precedent.

11.   To accept the argument that conditions ought not to be implied 'because the parties themselves know how to describe a term' would logically condemn the entire doctrine of implied terms.

12.   Arbitrators and Courts might, if the term were innominate, give different answers concerning the effect of a breach in very similar transactions, and parties could never learn by experience what was likely to happen in a given situation. So-called string contracts are not made, or adjudicated on, in strings.

The only arguments against treating the term as a condition appear to me to be based on generalities, whereas the considerations which are peculiar to this contract and similar contracts tell in favour of its being a condition.

For these reasons, and for the reasons given by my noble and learned friends, I would concur in dismissing both the appeal and the cross-appeal.

Lord Roskill

My Lords, it is beyond question that there are many cases in the books where terms, the breach of which do not deprive the innocent party of substantially the whole of the benefit which he was intended to receive from the contract, were nonetheless held to be conditions any breach of which entitled the innocent party to rescind. . . . Parties to commercial transactions should be entitled to know their rights at once and should not, when possible, be required to wait upon events before those rights can be determined. Of course, in many cases of alleged frustration or of alleged repudiatory delay it may be necessary to await events upon the happening or non-happening of which rights may well crystallize. But your Lordships' House has recently reiterated in a series of cases arising from the withdrawal of ships on time charter for non-payment of hire the need for certainty where punctual payment of hire is required and has held that the right to rescind automatically follows a breach of any such condition . . .

My Lords, the judgment of Lord Justice Diplock in the *Hong Kong Fir* case is, if I may respectfully say so, a landmark in the development of one part of our law of contract in the latter part of this century. The learned Lord Justice showed by reference to detailed historical analysis, contrary to what had often been thought previously, that there was no complete dichotomy between conditions and warranties and that there was a third class of term, the innominate term. But I do not believe the learned Lord Justice ever intended his judgment to afford an easy escape route from the normal consequences of rescission to a contract breaker who had broken what was, upon its true construction, clearly a condition of the contract by claiming that he had only broken an innominate term . . .

In short, while recognizing the modern approach and not being over ready to construe terms as conditions unless the contract clearly requires the Court so to do, none the less the basic principles of construction for determining whether or not a particular term is a condition remain as before, always bearing in mind on the one hand the need for certainty and on the other the desirability of not, when legitimate, allowing rescission where the breach complained of is highly technical and where damages would clearly be an adequate remedy. It is therefore in my opinion wrong to use the language employed by Lord Justice Diplock in the *Hong Kong Fir* case as directed to the determination of the question which terms of a particular contract are conditions and which are only innominate terms . . .

To my mind the most important single factor in favour of [counsel for the respondent's] submission is that until the requirement of the 15 day consecutive notice was fulfilled, the respondents could not nominate the 'one Gulf port' as the loading port, which under the instant contract it was their sole right to do. I agree with Mr Staughton that in a mercantile contract when a term has to be performed by one party as a condition precedent to the ability of the other party to perform another term, especially an essential term such as the nomination of a single loading port, the term as to time for the performance of the former obligation will in general fall to be treated as a condition. Until the 15 consecutive days' notice had been given, the respondents could not know for certain which loading port they should nominate so as to ensure that the contract goods would be available for loading on the ship's arrival at that port before the end of the shipment period.

It follows that in my opinion the umpire, the Board of Appeal and the Court of Appeal all reached the correct conclusion and for the reasons I have given I would dismiss the appellants' appeal.

Lord Fraser of Tullybelton agreed with the speeches of Lord Wilberforce and Lord Roskill.

COMMENTARY

It should be noted that the parties did not expressly classify clause 7 of the contract as a 'condition'. But English law has generally taken a strict approach to time stipulations in commercial contracts (with the exception of the time of payment) so that, a breach of a time stipulation, no matter how small, entitles the innocent party to bring the contract to an end.

In deciding the status of clause 7 it can be seen that the judges had regard to a number of factors and balanced them against one another. The combination of a number of factors persuaded the House of Lords to conclude that the term was a condition. The first, emphasized by Lord Roskill, was the need for certainty in commerial transactions. Secondly, as Lord Lowry pointed out, buyers and sellers operate in a market where one day they may be buyers and on another day they will be sellers. In such a market there is evidently a need for clear rules so that parties can decide whether or not they are entitled to terminate further performance of the contract. Thirdly, the judges had regard to the fact that the obligations of the parties were interdependent (until the buyer gave the requisite notice the sellers could not exercise their right to nominate the port of shipment). Fourthly, the experience of businessmen was thought to support the conclusion that clause 7 was a condition. Fifthly, the fact that damages for breach of clause 7 would have been very difficult to assess was a further factor which suggested that termination was the remedy which the parties had in mind for a breach of clause 7. Finally, their Lordships rejected the submission made by counsel for the buyers that, in order to amount to a condition, the breach must be such as to deprive the innocent party of substantially the whole benefit which it was intended that he should receive from the contract. A similar balancing exercise to that undertaken in *Bunge* was adopted by the House of Lords in *Compagnie Commerciale Sucres et Denrees* v. *C Czarnikow Ltd (The Naxos)* [1990] 1 WLR 1337 where it was held that the sellers had breached a condition of the contract in failing to have the goods ready to be delivered on the arrival of the vessel into port.

One other point should be noted about *Bunge* by way of a footnote. Were the facts of the case to recur today, its result would not be affected in any way by section 15A of the Sale of Goods Act 1979 (p. 942 above) because the breach in issue between the parties was a breach by the buyer, whereas section 15A applies only to a breach by the seller of one of the terms implied into contracts of sale by sections 13–15 of the Sale of Goods Act 1979. Indeed, this is one of the criticisms that can be levelled against section 15A, namely that it does not operate in an even-handed way. It curbs buyer opportunism, but not opportunism by sellers.

On one view *Bunge* stands as authority for the proposition that a clause should be classified as a condition where this is required by the demands of commerce but that otherwise a term should be classified as intermediate. This is probably an over-simplification. The reality is more complex. The courts in each case are engaged in a delicate balancing exercise and the demands of commerce and certainty are but one factor, albeit an important factor, in that balancing exercise. The uncertainty can be demonstrated by our final example. The issue before the Court of Appeal in *BS & N Ltd (BVI)* v. *Micado Shipping Ltd (Malta) (The 'Seaflower')* [2001] 1 Lloyd's Rep 341 turned on whether or not part of the following clause was a condition or an intermediate term:

Vessel is presently MOBIL (expiring 27/1/98), CONOCO (expiring 3/2/98), BP (expiring 28/1/98) and SHELL (expiring 14/1/98) acceptable. Owners guarantee to obtain within 60 (sixty) days EXXON' approval in addition to present approvals. On delivery date rate will be discounted USD250 (two hundred and fifty) for each approval missing, ie MOBIL, CONOCO, BP, SHELL, EXXON.

If for any reason, during the time-charter period. Owners would loose (sic) even one of such acceptances they must advise Charterers at once and they must reinstate same within 30 (thirty) days from such occurrence (sic) failing which Charterers will be at liberty to cancel charterparty or to maintain same at reduced rate stipulated above. Hire rate will be reinstated once Owners will show written evidence of approvals from Major Oil Companies.

The owners failed to obtain Exxon approval within sixty days. Aikens J, the judge at first instance, held that this was a breach of an intermediate term but the Court of Appeal held that it was in fact a breach of a condition. One difficulty in the way of concluding that the clause was a condition was that the second paragraph of the clause provided for an express right of termination (thereby suggesting that this was the only circumstance in which a right to terminate was granted) but Waller LJ attached greater significance to the fact that the parties should be assumed to have intended to be consistent about the importance of obtaining and maintaining majors' approvals (that is approval from Mobil, Conoco, BP, Shell, and Exxon). He did have some difficulty in fitting the clause together, particularly in the context of an approval which was withdrawn after the contract was made but before the charter began, but the Court of Appeal was prepared to smooth over the rough edges of the contract. The Court of Appeal put forward a number of arguments in support of the conclusion that the clause was a condition. They included: (i) the need for certainty in commercial transactions, (ii) the attitude to time stipulations adopted by the House of Lords in *Bunge* v. *Tradax*, (iii) the need for consistency in relation to approvals by the majors, (iv) the use of the word 'guarantee' in the second sentence in paragraph one, and (v) the use of 'even one' in the second paragraph. That said, the arguments were not all one way. There were some arguments against the conclusion that the term was a condition: (i) the parties had not classified it as a condition, (ii) paragraph 2 contained an express right of termination, but no such right had been attached by the parties to the second sentence in paragraph one, (iii) the slightest infringement would give rise to a right to terminate, and (iv) the analogy with seaworthiness which is an intermediate term (see *Hong Kong Fir*). *The Seaflower* neatly illustrates the problems that arise when parties fail to make clear whether a term is a condition, a warranty, or an intermediate term. In the absence of party stipulation it can be extremely difficult for the courts to ascertain the true status of the clause and judges can and do differ when carrying out this interpretative exercise.

(e) TERMINATION CLAUSES

Rather than have to classify the nature of each and every term of the contract, commercial parties sometimes insert into their contracts a termination clause which confers on the parties (or one of them) an express right to terminate the contract in certain defined circumstances. These clauses can be drafted in very broad terms but, as the next case demonstrates, judges can, by a process of construction, cut down the apparent scope of a termination clause.

Rice (t/a Garden Guardian) v. Great Yarmouth Borough Council

The Times, 26 July 2000, Court of Appeal

The claimant entered into two contracts with the defendant local authority. The first contract was for the maintenance and management of the local authority's sport facilities (such as its cricket and football pitches) and the second was for the maintenance of the local authority's parks, gardens and children's playgrounds. The contracts were dated 14 February 1996 and their duration was stated to be four years from 1 January 1996. Between 9 May 1996 and July 1996 the local authority served a number of default notices on the claimant and on 5 August 1996 letters were hand delivered to the claimant informing him that the local authority had decided to terminate the contract. The claimant sought to recover from the defendant damages for wrongful termination of the contract. The defendant claimed that it was entitled to terminate the contract under clause 23.2.1 which stated that

'if the contractor commits a breach of any of its obligations under the Contract; . . . the Council may, without prejudice to any accrued rights or remedies under the Contract, terminate the Contractor's employment under the Contract by notice in writing having immediate effect.'

Clause 27 of the contract also entitled the defendant to issue against the claimant a notice of default, which specified the misconduct and the time allowed for rectification. The Court of Appeal held that the defendant had not been entitled to terminate the contract and further held that the claimant was entitled to recover damages in respect of the loss which he had suffered as a result of the defendant's wrongful termination of the contract.

Hale LJ [having set out the facts and the relevant contract clauses continued]

17. The council argued first that clause 23.2.1 should be applied literally so as to give them the right to terminate the contract for the breach of any of the obligations contained in it, other than the trivial. The judge was referred to a number of well-known authorities. On the one hand, 'it is open to the parties to agree that, as regards a particular obligation, any breach shall entitle the party not in default to treat the contract as repudiated': see *Bunge Corporation* v. *Tradax Export SA* [1981] 1 WLR 711, per Lord Wilberforce at 715E. On the other hand '. . . if detailed semantic and syntactical analysis of words in a commercial contract is going to lead to a conclusion that flouts business commonsense, it must yield to business commonsense': see *Antaios Compania SA* v. *Salen Rederierna* [1985] AC 191, per Lord Diplock at p. 201D.

18. The judge pointed out that none of these authorities

'. . . dealt with commercial circumstances having many parallels to those of a local authority and a contractor who is contractually required for a period of years to provide a wide variety of services on a repetitive basis.'

He continued:

'There has long been a tension in the world of contract between an attachment to literal meaning that makes for certainty with all in black and white and the parties knowing exactly where they are and little room for the relative unpredictability of judicial intervention, and a desire to avoid consequences seen as unfair or seen as offending commercial commonsense.'

As to which line of authority should apply, he concluded:

'In the context of a contract intended to last for four years, involving substantial investment or at least substantial undertaking of financial obligations by one party and involving a myriad of obligations of differing importance and varying frequency, I have no hesitation in holding that the common sense interpretation should be imposed upon the strict words of the contract and that a repudiatory breach or an accumulation of breaches that as a whole can properly be described as repudiatory are a precondition to termination pursuant to clause 23.2.1.'

Another point in favour of a commercial, common sense interpretation was

'. . . that ephemeral breaches, even where substantial and not trivial, are subject to substantial contractual disciplines, default notices, deductions, performance by others at the contractor's expense and so on.'

19. Mr Martin Mann QC [counsel for the local authority], in challenging this conclusion, repeats essentially the same arguments as were put before the judge. These depend upon some basic principles of the law of contract, easy to state but not always easy to apply in practice.

20. As is well-known, the classic position in English (but not Scottish) contract law was that the consequences of breach depended upon the importance of the term broken. A minor breach of an important term, a condition, could entitle the innocent party to terminate the contract. Breach of a less important term, a warranty, would sound only in damages. Then along came the seminal case of *Hong Kong Fir Shipping Co Ltd* v. *Kawasaki Kisen Kaisha Ltd* [1962] 2 QB 26, in which Diplock LJ, in the words of Lord Wilberforce in *Bunge* v. *Tradax*, above, at p. 714G,

'. . . illuminated the existence in contracts of terms which are neither, necessarily, conditions nor warranties, but in terminology which has since been applied to them, intermediate or innominate terms capable of operating, according to the gravity of the breach, as either conditions or warranties.'

21. Lord Wilberforce emphasised, in the words already quoted in paragraph [17] above, that it is still open to the parties to agree that a term is so important to them that it should have that effect. He continued:

'It remains true, as Lord Roskill has pointed out in *Cehave NV* v. *Bremer Handelsgesellshaft mbH (The Hansa Nord)* [1976] QB 44, that courts should not be too ready to interpret contractual clauses as conditions. . . . But I do not doubt that, in suitable cases, the courts should not be reluctant, if the intentions of the parties as shown by the contract so indicate, to hold that an obligation has the force of a condition.'

22. The problem with the council's argument in this case is that clause 23.2.1 does not characterise any particular term as a condition or indicate which terms are to be considered so important that any breach will justify termination. It appears to visit the same draconian consequences upon any breach, however small, of any obligation, however small. In this it is unlike cases, such as Bunge, which concerned an obviously vital time clause that can only be broken in one way, and much closer to the cases, such as *Hong Kong Fir Shipping* and *The Antaios*, concerning multi-faceted obligations, which can be broken in many different ways.

23. The comparable term in *The Antaios* provided that 'on any breach of this charterparty, the owners shall be at liberty to withdraw the vessel . . .' The owners sought to do so on discovering that inaccurate bills of lading had been issued. As Lord Diplock observed, the dispute

'was a typical case of a shipowner seeking to find an excuse to bring a long term time charter to a premature end in a rising market. Stripped to its essentials the shipowners were seeking to rely upon the charterers breach of an innominate term in the charter-party relating to the charterer's rights . . . to issue bills of lading . . . as constituting "any other breach of this charterparty" . . .'

Lord Diplock agreed entirely with the arbitrators' view that

'the owner's construction is wholly unreasonable, totally uncommercial and in total contradiction to the whole purpose of the NYPE time charter form.'

The contract should not be interpreted in such a way as to defeat its commercial purpose.

24.   Mr Mann seeks to distinguish clause 23.2.1 from the clause in *The Antaios* on the basis that the latter referred to 'any breach of this charterparty', while clause 23.2.1 refers to the 'breach of any of its obligations under this contract'. While the *Antaios* term might be limited to a breach defeating the whole contract, the term here might refer to any material or non-trivial breach. The judge characterised this distinction as a semantic one and I agree with him. For the reasons which the judge gave, the notion that this term would entitle the council to terminate a contract such as this at any time for any breach of any term flies in the face of commercial common sense.

25.   However, Mr Mann also argues that the judge should first have considered which terms of the contract had been broken and whether they were such important terms as to give rise to a right to terminate. He identified a core obligation in each contract, either in the exact terms of clause 6.1 or something very similar to it:

'During the contract period the contractor shall provide the Service in a proper skilful and workmanlike manner, to the contract standard and to the entire satisfaction of the authorised officer.'

26.   The difficulty with that argument is that this is a classic example of an innominate term: one which can be broken in so many different ways and with such varying con-sequences that the parties cannot be taken to have intended that any breach should entitle the innocent party to terminate the whole contract. In the words of Diplock LJ in the *Hong Kong Fir Shipping* case, at p. 71:

'It is like so many other contractual terms an undertaking one breach of which may give rise to an event which relieves the charterer of further performance of his under-takings if he so elects and another breach of which may not give rise to such an event but entitle him only to monetary compensation in the form of damages.'

27.   Alternatively, Mr Mann argues that clause 23.2.1 has to be read with clause 27.6, which provided a mechanism for identifying those breaches which the council con-sidered serious. That cannot be right. Clause 27.6 is primarily aimed at remedying breaches as they occur rather than identifying repudiatory breaches. No distinction is drawn between more and less serious matters. The £140 charge is manifestly not liquid-ated damages: it bears no relationship at all to any damage which might be suffered as a result of the particular default notified. It was explained in evidence as a charge to cover the administrative costs of the procedure: otherwise it would undoubtedly be a penalty. In any event, the notices are primarily a way of securing proper performance under the contract rather than a way of bringing it to an end.

28. In my view the judge was entirely right to reach the conclusion he did on this aspect of the case and for the reasons he gave.

The second issue

29. The council argued that, in any event, the totality of breaches found by the judge were sufficient to justify it in terminating the contract. It was argued on behalf of the contractor that the appropriate test of a repudiatory breach was that derived from the *Hong Kong Fir Shipping* case, at p. 66:

'. . . does the occurrence of the event deprive the party who has further undertakings still to perform of substantially the whole benefit which it was the intention of the parties as expressed in the contract that he should obtain as the consideration for performing those undertakings?'

The judge later stated that, had he felt able to accept this proposition, his task would have been an easy one:

'Just as it is plain as can be that many of the breaches cannot be brushed aside as trivial, so it is plain as can be that even cumulatively the breaches relied upon cannot be said to have substantially deprived the defendant of the whole benefit for which it contracted.'

30. However, he had taken the view that that test was 'apt for what one may call contracts of single obligation', but:

'In the case of contracts of multiple, separate obligations, such as those under consideration in this case it seems to me, again invoking the doctrines of commercial common sense, that a breach which deprived the innocent party of substantially the whole benefit of substantially any aspect of the contract should be regarded as repudiatory.'

He later identified three categories of repudiatory breach:

'Cumulative breaches that justify an inference that the contractor would continue to deliver a substandard performance in relation to substantial portions of the contract could, in my judgment, be assessed as repudiatory. In short such breaches would show that the contractor was not up to the job. Likewise, breaches that evinced an intention by the contractor to render a continuing substandard performance in respect of a defined and significant part of the works could be repudiatory. . . . Thirdly, breaches of such significance as to be individually repudiatory, being substantial in themselves and not truly compensated for by contractual remedies, likewise could justify the termination of the contract.'

31. There were no breaches in the second, intentional, category. Some breaches might fall within the third category, particularly those relating to the delayed start to the football season at two recreation grounds and the delay in the summer bedding. But the thrust of the council's case was directed at the first category. The judge then considered the effect of all the breaches admitted or proved in relation to each contract. He was invited by counsel to step back and form an overall view to see the wood from the trees. In relation to the Grounds Maintenance II contract, 'if the wood to be considered is a wood of breach trees alone, then the defendant's case . . . is overwhelming'. In relation to the Leisure Management Contract, he was 'just persuaded that the breaches . . . cumulatively would be sufficient to be treated as repudiatory'.

32.   However, both had to be considered in context. That context included three important elements: first, it was an exceptionally dry summer; secondly, there was a discrepancy in the contractual documents as to the period allowed for the summer bedding to be completed, a discrepancy for which the council had to take responsibility; and thirdly, the council had issued a flurry of default notices on 24 June 1996, requiring the summer bedding to be completed within five days (ie within the shorter of the timescales envisaged in the documents), thus impelling the contractor to move men off other work and proceed at a faster rate than planned in order to avoid further financial levies under clause 27.6. This had had a knock on effect upon other work. The judge concluded that

'. . . had these breaches stood by themselves I would in relation to both contracts, more hesitantly in one case, have concluded that they were indeed repudiatory. In the event, those matters to which I have referred as having to be taken into consideration have led me to the conclusion that the repudiatory breaches have not been shown.'

33.   Mr Mann QC for the council argues that the judge was wrong, as a matter of law, to discount the repudiatory effect of the breaches he had found by reference to these factors. He appeared, in the first of the three categories of breach described in paragraph 30 above, to be applying some concept of anticipatory breach. Having found that the cumulative effect of the existing breaches was repudiatory he could not then go back on that finding. Once a breach has been found, it is irrelevant that there may be excuses for it.

34.   Mr Smith for the contractor, on the other hand, complains that the judge applied a test too generous to the council. He should have applied the *Hong Kong Fir Shipping* test as it stands. Further, whichever test he applied, the judge had to take all the circumstances into account. The drought was relevant because the contract provided for it: indeed, in the case of the football pitches, there was no breach at all, because the renovation had to be done when conditions allowed, it could not have been done at the expected time because the ground was baked hard, and the council's own expert accepted that irrigation was not practicable. The drought conditions were also relevant to the substandard quality of the bedding display before 7 August, by which time it was passable. The judge had to ask himself what the real causes of that were. Preparation had been affected by the flurry of default notices requiring three weeks' work to be done in five days. This was the council's fault because it was their responsibility to resolve discrepancies. They knew of this discrepancy but did nothing about it until serving those default notices.

35.   The question for the court (and indeed the contracting parties) in any case like this is whether the cumulative effect of the breaches of contract complained of is so serious as to justify the innocent party in bringing the contract to a premature end. The technical term is 'repudiatory' but that is just a label to describe the consequence which may flow. It is is not always an entirely satisfactory label, if it implies that the conduct itself must always be such as to demonstrate an intention to abandon contractual obligations: while this will sometimes be so it is not an invariable requirement. As the judge indicated, there are in effect three catefories: (1) those cases in which the parties have agreed either that the term is so important that any breach will justify termination or that the particular breach is so important that it will justify termination; (2) those contractors who simply walk away from their obligations thus clearly indicating an intention no longer to be bound; and (3) those cases in which the cumulative effect of the breaches which have taken place is sufficiently serious to justify the innocent party in bringing the contract to a premature end.

36. It is clear that the test of what is sufficiently serious to bring the case within the third of these categories is severe. No case has been cited to us which addresses this question in the context of a long running contract to provide public services such as this. There are some parallels with a charterparty, but that is a somewhat less complex under-taking than these. There are also some parallels with building contracts, in the number and variety of the obligations involved and the varying gravity of the breaches which may be committed, some of which may be remediable and some not. In *Sutcliffe* v. *Chippendale and Edmundson* (1971) 18 BLR 157, at p. 161, His Honour Judge Sir William Stabb QC said this:

'I take the view that the whole combination of circumstances that then existed and to which I have already alluded did justify the plaintiff in ordering the contractors off the site. I think that their manifest inability to comply with the completion date require-ments, the nature and number of complaints received from sub-contractors and [the architect's] own admission that in May and June the quality of work was deteriorating and the number of defects was multiplying, many of which he had tried unsuccessfully to have put right, all point to the truth of the plaintiff's expressed view that the con-tractors had neither the ability, competence or the will by this time to complete the work in the manner required by the contract.'

37. Building contracts differ from these contracts in that there will, it is hoped, be an end product. Defects may or should be remedied during or, in some cases, after comple-tion. Delay in completion can be compensated. These contracts contemplated a multi-tude of different results at different times, from cricket pitches ready for the summer season, football pitches ready for the autumn, flower beds in full bloom at the appropri-ate times, properly mown grass on lawns and bowling greens, raked bunkers in a pitch and putt course, edged and weeded rose beds, pruned shrubs, cleared litter, and so on and so on. Mr Smith accepted that in the case of a four year contract such as this, the court is entitled to look at the contractor's performance over a year, the most important part of which is the spring and summer, but it must still ask itself whether the council was deprived of substantially the whole benefit of what it had contracted for during that period.

38. These contracts are, however, like building contracts in that the accumulation of past breaches is relevant, not only for its own sake, but also for what it shows about the future. In my view, the judge was right to ask himself whether the cumulative breaches were such as to justify an inference that the contractor would continue to deliver a substandard performance. However, I would agree with Mr Smith that the inference should be that the council would thereby be deprived of a substantial part of the totality of that which it had contracted for that year, subject to the additional possibility that some aspects of the contract were so important that the parties are to be taken to have intended that depriving the council of that part of the contract would be sufficient in itself. That is not what the judge found in this case.

39. Once it is accepted that the proven breaches are relevant to show what will happen in the future, it is clear that the judge was entitled to take both the drought and the knock on effect of the council's own behaviour in relation to the summer bedding into account. He examined the facts of this case in great detail over a trial lasting some 13 days. He was well placed to evaluate the true importance of the proven breaches in the context of the contracts as a whole and all the circumstances of the case. He had a judgment to make. If anything, the test which he applied was somewhat more favourable to the council than the test which, in my judgment, he should have applied. He was undoubtedly entitled to reach the conclusion that he did.

40. I would dismiss this appeal.

May LJ and **Peter Gibson LJ** concurred.

COMMENTARY

Two points of significance emerge from this case. The first is that, in deciding whether or not there has been a repudiatory breach of contract, it is permissible to take a cumulative approach and have regard to the range of breaches committed by the party in breach. The second and much more important point relates to the interpretation of clause 23.2.1 adopted by the Court of Appeal. It held that it gave the council the right to terminate the contract only on the occurrence of a repudiatory breach of contract. There are two substantial objections to this interpretation. First, the council had a right to terminate under the general law on the occurrence of a repudiatory breach so why insert a clause into the contract if its only effect was to replicate a right that already existed under the general law? Secondly, the Court of Appeal failed to give sufficient weight to the word 'any' in the clause ('if the contractor commits a breach of *any* of its obligations under the contract, the Council may . . . terminate the Contractor's employment'). The response of the Court of Appeal to this objection was that the notion that this term entitled the council to terminate the contract at any time for any breach of any term flew in the face of commercial common sense. It is difficult to resist the conclusion that the Court of Appeal allowed its perception of 'commercial common sense' to override the ordinary meaning of the words in the contract. Further, the effect of doing so was to expose the council to a claim for substantial damages for wrongful termination.

This decision gives rise to significant drafting difficulties. Termination clauses are regularly used in practice and this decision has caused a degree of consternation among practitioners. Is it possible to draft a clause which gives a right to terminate the contract when the breach is not a repudiatory breach at common law? Many practitioners rely on phrases such as 'material breach' (see *National Power plc* v. *United Gas Co Ltd*, unreported, 3 July 1998, Coleman J) or 'substantial breach' (see *Crane Co* v. *Wittenborg A/S*, unreported, Court of Appeal, 21 December 1999) but it is difficult to see on what basis the insertion of the words 'material' or 'substantial' can improve matters. In many ways it seems rather odd to suggest, as some have done, that a party can be better off by the inclusion of the words 'material' or 'substantial' because the clause in *Great Yarmouth* purported to entitle the council to terminate the contract if the contractor commited a breach of 'any' of its obligations under the contract. A party who wishes to have the benefit of a wide right to terminate might be better advised to stipulate that the right to terminate arises in the event of 'any breach (whether or not that breach is repudiatory)'. *Great Yarmouth* is an important case because it demonstrates the importance of drafting issues and the important role that interpretation of clauses can play in the development of the law. Judges can wield significant power through the process of interpretation and *Great Yarmouth* has certainly caused commercial parties to exercise caution both in the drafting of termination clauses and in the use that is made of them.

(f) THE RELEVANCE OF GOOD FAITH

The point has been made that the existence of a breach of contract is not generally dependent upon a finding that the party said to be in breach has been at fault. Liability for breach of contract is, in principle, strict. But there is a line of cases in which the courts appear to have had regard to the good faith of the party in breach when deciding whether or not the breach of contract was a repudiatory breach which entitled the other party to terminate the contract. An example of such a case is:

Vaswani v. Italian Motors (Sales and Services) Ltd

[1996] 1 WLR 270, Privy Council

The defendant sellers entered an agreement to sell a Ferrari motor car to the plaintiff. The contract provided for the payment of a deposit, with the balance being payable on delivery. Condition 8 of the contract stipulated that the deposit would be forfeited if, having been informed by the seller that the car was ready for delivery, the buyer did not pay the due balance within seven days. In addition, conditions 4 and 5 of the contract allowed the seller to vary the price according to set criteria. The sellers informed the plaintiff that the car was ready and requested payment of an increased price but, due to their own innocent mistake, demanded payment of a price which was too high. The buyer refused to pay the higher price, asserting he was only willing to pay such increases as were justified by conditions 4 and 5. After a month, no payment being forthcoming, the seller rescinded the contract. The buyer sued for the return of his deposit.

Two issues arose before the Privy Council. The first, the question of construction, was whether or not the sellers were entitled to demand that the plaintiff pay the increased sum. The second was, on the assumption that the sellers were not so entitled, whether they had repudiated the contract by demanding that the plaintiff pay a sum of money which he was not, by the terms of his contract, obliged to pay.

Lord Woolf [giving the judgment of the Privy Council, set out the facts and concluded that, as a matter of construction, the defendants were not entitled to demand that the plaintiff pay them the sum demanded. He then continued]

The repudiation issue

... There are here features of this case which make this issue by no means straight-forward. There is the fact that the sellers were acting bona fide in seeking the higher price although they did not initially put forward the claim on the basis that the price in their price list was conclusive under the contract. The other feature is that it appears to be reasonably clear that even if the sellers had demanded the correct balance of the purchase price this would not have been paid by the buyer.

The sellers were given the right to forfeit the deposit under condition 8.

[he set out condition 8 and continued]

If the sellers had demanded the payment of the correct sum then they would have had the right to forfeit the deposit and resell the car. The sellers having demanded a sum in excess of that due their primary argument is based on the proposition that it does not amount to a repudiation of a contract to assert a genuinely held but erroneous view as to the effect of the contract. That this can be the position is good sense and already subject to considerable judicial support. The position is accurately set out by Lord Wilberforce in *Woodar Investment Development Ltd* v. *Wimpey Construction UK Ltd* [1980] 1 WLR 277, 283, where he also warned that: 'Repudiation is a drastic conclusion which should only be held to arise in clear cases of a refusal, in a matter going to the root of the contract, to perform contractual obligations.'

While therefore here the request for the payment of an excessive price would not in itself amount to a repudiation, if the conduct relied on went beyond the assertion of a genuinely held view of the effect of the contract the conduct could amount to a repudiation. This is the position if the conduct is inconsistent with the continuance of the contract. Then the bona fide motives of the party responsible do not prevent the conduct being repudiatory. Again the position is clearly expressed by Lord Wilberforce, this time in a case concerning a charterparty, *Federal Commerce & Navigation Co Ltd* v. *Molena Alpha Inc* [1979] AC 757. Lord Wilberforce, having described how the owners subjected the charterers to irresistible pressure to pay over sums of money that the charterers had deducted pending the outcome of an arbitration, states the position in these terms, at p 780:

'It is thirdly irrelevant that it was in the owners' real interest to continue the charters rather than to put an end to them. If a party's conduct is such as to amount to a threatened repudiatory breach, his subjective desire to maintain the contract cannot prevent the other party from drawing the consequences of his actions. The two cases relied on by the buyers (*James Shaffer Ltd* v. *Findlay Durham & Brodie* [1953] 1 WLR 106 and *Sweet & Maxwell Ltd* v. *Universal News Services Ltd* [1964] 2 QB 699) do not support a contrary proposition, and would only be relevant here if the owners' action had been confined to asserting their own view—possibly erroneous—as to the effect of the contract. They went, in fact, far beyond this when they threatened a breach of the contract with serious consequences.'

Nor is conduct, if it is repudiatory, excused because it occurs in consequence of legal advice as may be the case with the sellers' actions in this case. The position is correctly set out by Lord Denning MR in the *Federal Commerce* case in the Court of Appeal [1978] QB 927, 979, in a passage of his judgment cited by Lord Scarman in *Woodar Investment*

Development Ltd v. *Wimpey Construction UK Ltd* [1980] 1 WLR 277, 298, which is in these terms:

> ' "I have yet to learn that a party who breaks a contract can excuse himself by saying that he did it on the advice of his lawyers: or that he was under an honest misapprehension. . . . I would go by the principle . . . that if the party's conduct" ["contract" must be a misprint] "—objectively considered in its impact on the other party—is such as to evince an intention no longer to be bound by his contractual obligations, then it is open to the other party to accept his repudiation and treat the contract as discharged from that time onwards." '

In this case while the sellers did indicate to the buyer that he should pay a sum which was excessive or the deposit would be forfeited they never went so far as to indicate to the buyer that it would be purposeless to pay the correct sum as required by condition 8. This was not therefore a case like *The Norway* (1865) 3 Moo PCCNS 245 where the sellers had made it clear that it was pointless to tender a lesser sum. All they had done was to put forward their calculation which had gone unchallenged. There was nothing to prevent the buyer paying the sum he calculated was due. Until he at least tendered the sum he considered was due the sellers were not required to deliver the vehicle. However in fact the buyer never called for delivery by the sellers. This was no doubt because he had made no further payment and never intended to attempt to test their willingness to deliver. The sellers did not threaten 'a breach of the contract with serious consequences' as in *Federal Commerce & Navigation Co Ltd* v. *Molena Alpha Inc* [1979] AC 757, 780, and there was no conduct by them which was totally inconsistent with the continuance of the contract until after the buyer had made it clear that he was not going to make any further payment. This being the situation their Lordships are of the opinion the sellers did not repudiate the contract.

COMMENTARY

The effect of *Vaswani* is to put the buyer in a difficult position when faced with threatened non-performance by the seller. If he refuses to pay when faced with an erroneous but good faith demand by the seller, he may not be able to show that the seller has repudiated the contract. So he must, apparently, go further and tender performance of the sum which he believes is the sum due and thereby hope to persuade a court that, when the seller refused to accept that performance, he thereby repudiated the contract.

Cases such as *Vaswani* demonstrate a certain reluctance to conclude that a party who has acted in good faith has repudiated the contract. This stance is not altogether easy to reconcile with the general rule that bad faith is not an essential element of a breach of contract. A breach is a breach whether it is committed in good faith or in bad faith. It may be possible to reconcile the cases on the basis that it is not a repudiation for one party to put forward his genuine and bona fide interpretation of what the contract requires of him (*Woodar Investment Development Ltd* v. *Wimpey Construction UK Ltd* [1980] 1 WLR 277; *James Shaffer Ltd* v. *Findlay Durham and Brodie* [1953] 1 WLR 106; *Sweet and Maxwell Ltd* v. *Universal News Services Ltd* [1964] 2 QB 699; and *Vaswani* v. *Italian Motors (Sales) Ltd* [1996] 1 WLR 270) but where that party performs in a manner which is not consistent with the terms of the contract, it is no defence for that party to show that he acted in good faith (*Federal Commerce & Navigation Co Ltd* v. *Molena Alpha Inc* [1979] AC 757). In other words, a distinction should be drawn in this respect between actual breach and anticipatory breach (on which see pp. 993–1004 below). Where the breach is anticipatory only and consists of the assertion of an interpretation of the contract which turns out, subsequently, to have been erroneous, the courts should be slow to infer that there has been a repudiatory breach. Were the law otherwise, it would be very difficult to conduct negotiations about the meaning of a contract without running the risk of repudiating the contract. But when it comes to the time for performance, and a party performs his contract in a manner that is inconsistent with the terms of the contract, he should not be able to rely on his good faith for the purpose of demonstrating that the breach was not repudiatory.

(g) SOME COMPARATIVE REFLECTIONS

English law in relation to termination for breach can be said to stand out from other jurisdictions in two respects. First, it appears to place considerable emphasis upon the importance of termination as a remedy. It is a significant remedy in practice (albeit not as important as damages). In this respect it has a more prominent status than in other systems where termination is seen as a secondary remedy or even as a remedy of last resort. There is a difficult policy issue at stake here. What should be the aim of a remedial regime for breach of contract? Should it be to encourage parties to continue their relationship and resolve their difficulties or should it encourage parties to walk away from a deal when things go wrong and seek performance elsewhere? English law appears to tend towards the latter model (although it should be noted that a number of the cases discussed in this chapter are shipping cases or cases of commodity sales where the parties are often speculating on the movement of prices in the market-place and, in such a case, termination appears to be a more widely used remedy). Secondly, English law places considerable emphasis on freedom of contract in the sense that it gives to contracting parties considerable freedom to decide for themselves when the right to terminate will arise (for example, it is open to the parties to classify any term they like as a condition). Again, this is in contrast with some other systems where it is for the court to decide whether or not the breach justifies termination.

Two instruments have been chosen for comparative purposes. The first is the Vienna Convention on Contracts for the International Sale of Goods and the second is the Principles of European Contract Law.

Article 25 of the Vienna Convention provides:

A breach of contract committed by one of the parties is fundamental if it results in such detriment to the other party as substantially to deprive him of what he is entitled to expect under the contract, unless the party in breach did not foresee and a reasonable person of the same kind in the same circumstances would not have foreseen such a result.

This provision appears to be similar to an intermediate term (although it is not identical). As such it presents a difficulty for English lawyers because it appears to deny to the parties the right to agree that any breach of a particular term shall give rise to a right to terminate (in other words it appears not to recognize the existence of conditions, at least party-created conditions). One reason for this may be that termination appears to play a less important role in the remedial structure of the Convention. The remedial regime is much more complex than that found in English law and it appears to give greater emphasis to remedies that enable the parties to maintain their relationship (such as the right to cure the breach and price reduction). It also places much more emphasis on notification obligations before exercising the right to terminate the contract. For example, in the case of non-delivery of the goods by the seller the buyer is given the right to fix an additional period of time of reasonable length for performance by the seller of his obligations and, in the event that the seller fails to deliver the goods within that additional period of time, the buyer is entitled to terminate the contract (see Articles 47(1) and 49(1)). The difference between English law and the Convention is, essentially, that English law makes greater provision for immediate termination upon breach, whereas under the Convention a party may have to fix an additional period of time for performance before resorting to the more drastic remedy of termination. The difference between the two regimes is very much an issue of policy: should termination be seen as a primary remedy or as a secondary remedy, only to be resorted to when other remedies are unavailable or will not work?

The provisions of the Principles of European Contract Law appear to be somewhat closer to English law. Article 9:301 deals with the right to terminate the contract and it provides:

(1) A party may terminate the contract if the other party's non-performance is fundamental.
(2) In the case of delay the aggrieved party may also terminate the contract under Article 8:106(3).

Article 8:103 defines fundamental non-performance in the following terms:

A non-performance of an obligation is fundamental to the contract if:

(a) strict compliance with the obligation is of the essence of the contract; or
(b) the non-performance substantially deprives the aggrieved party of what it was entitled to expect under the contract, unless the other party did not foresee and could not reasonably have foreseen that result;
(c) the non-performance is intentional and gives the aggrieved party reason to believe that it cannot rely on the other party's future performance.

To English eyes, this provision is very different from the Vienna Convention. The vital difference is paragraph (a) which seems to approximate to a condition. It thus appears to preserve the right of the parties to classify the status of the terms of their contract. Paragraph (b) is much closer to an intermediate term, while paragraph (c) distinguishes between intentional and unintentional non-performance (a distinction which is not generally drawn in English law).

The Principles also contain a number of other provisions on the subject of breach (or non-performance). Articles 8:104–8:106 provide:

8:104 Cure by non-performing party

A party whose tender of performance is not accepted by the other party because it does not conform to the contract may make a new and conforming tender where the time for performance has not yet arrived or the delay would not be such as to constitute fundamental non-performance.

8:105 Assurance of Performance

(1) A party which reasonably believes that there will be a fundamental non-performance by the other party may demand adequate assurance of due performance and meanwhile may withhold performance of its own obligations so long as such reasonable belief continues.

(2) Where this assurance is not provided within a reasonable time, the party demanding it may terminate the contract if it still reasonably believes that there will be a fundamental non-performance by the other party and gives notice of termination without delay.

8:106 Notice Fixing Additional Period for Performance

(1) In any case of non-performance the aggrieved party may by notice to the other party allow an additional period of time for performance.

(2) During the additional period the aggrieved party may withhold performance of its own reciprocal obligations and may claim damages, but it may not resort to any other remedy. If it receives notice from the other party that the latter will not perform within that period, or if upon expiry of that period due performance has not been made, the aggrieved party may resort to any of the remedies that may be available under chapter 9.

(3) If in a case of delay in performance which is not fundamental the aggrieved party has given notice fixing an additional period of time of reasonable length, it may terminate the contract at the end of the period of notice. The aggrieved party may in its notice provide that if the other party does not perform within the period fixed by the notice the contract shall terminate automatically. If the period stated is too short, the aggrieved party may terminate, or, as the case may be, the contract shall terminate automatically, only after a reasonable period from the time of the notice.

Article 8:105 is a helpful provision which English law could usefully adopt. The right to demand an assurance of performance is a useful right in the not uncommon case where a contracting party has reason to believe that the other party will not perform his contractual obligations.

5. ELECTION

Must an innocent party exercise its right to terminate further performance of the contract? The answer is that there is no obligation to exercise the right. A breach of contract, even where it is repudiatory, does not of itself operate to bring the contract to an end. What it does is to confer on the innocent party a choice. The innocent party can either choose to bring the contract to an end or he can choose to affirm the contract and continue with performance of the contract. This choice on the part of the innocent party is known as an election.

A party who wishes to exercise his right to terminate further performance of the contract must generally notify the party in breach that he is doing so. This is known as 'acceptance of the repudiation'. In *Vitol SA* v. *Norelf Ltd* [1996] AC 800, 810 Lord Steyn stated:

An act of acceptance of a repudiation requires no particular form: a communication does not have to be couched in the language of acceptance. It is sufficient that the communication or conduct clearly and unequivocally conveys to the repudiating party that the aggrieved party is treating the contract as at an end.

As a general rule acceptance cannot take the form of silence, unless the only construction that can be put upon the conduct of the parties is that one party has accepted the other's repudiatory breach of contract. For example, a contractor who does not turn up for work after having been told by the employer, in breach of contract, to get off the site is likely to be held to have accepted the employer's repudiatory breach. However, even in such a case, a contractor who sought legal advice would be told to communicate to the employer his acceptance of the latter's repudiatory breach. Given the general rule that silence does not amount to acceptance, a party in the position of the contractor would be advised to avoid any doubt and make his acceptance of the repudiation explicit.

Acceptance of a repudiatory breach of contract operates to bring the contract between the parties to an end. Termination operates prospectively, but not retrospectively. Thus termination operates to release both parties from their future obligations to perform their primary obligations under the contract, but it leaves intact rights which have accrued prior to the termination of the contract (*Photo Production Ltd* v. *Securicor Transport Ltd* [1980] AC 827). In this sense termination for breach differs from rescission of the contract for misrepresentation (see pp. 678–691 above). Rescission for misrepresentation sets aside a contract for all purposes (that is to say, the contract is set aside both retrospectively and prospectively). Termination for breach, by contrast, does not have retrospective effect: there is no attempt to unwind the contract. Indeed, it is possible for a term in a clause to survive termination. Where the parties intend the clause to survive termination then the courts will generally give effect to that intention. Clauses that generally survive termination are arbitration clauses (see *Heyman* v. *Darwins Ltd* [1942] AC 356) and, possibly, confidentiality clauses (*Campbell* v. *Frisbee* [2002] EWCA Civ 1374; [2003] ICR 141).

6. LOSS OF THE RIGHT TO TERMINATE

The right to terminate the contract will generally be lost if the innocent party decides to affirm the contract. Affirmation must generally be unequivocal. The mere fact that the innocent party has called on the party in breach to perform his contractual obligations does not necessarily constitute affirmation. As Moore-Bick J stated in *Yukong Line Ltd of Korea* v. *Rendsberg Investments Corpn of Liberia* [1996] 2 Lloyd's Rep 604, 608, 'the law does not require an injured party to snatch at a repudiation and he does not automatically lose his right to treat the contract as discharged merely by calling on the other to reconsider his position and recognize his obligation'. But the innocent party must proceed with great caution because the choice between affirmation and termination, once made, is, in principle, irrevocable. As a general rule a party will not be held to have affirmed the contract unless he had knowledge of the facts giving rise to the breach and he knew of his right to choose between affirmation and termination.

It is sometimes said that there is no 'middle way' or 'third choice' open to the innocent party (*Bentsen* v. *Taylor* [1893] 2 QB 274, 279 and *Fercometal SARL* v. *Mediterranean Shipping Co SA* [1989] AC 788, 799–801): he must make his choice between termination and affirmation. This is true in the sense that there is no 'third choice, as a sort of via media, to affirm the contract and yet be absolved from tendering further performance unless and until [the breaching party] gives reasonable notice that he is once again able and willing to perform' (*Fercometal SARL* v. *Mediterranean Shipping Co SA* [1989] AC 788, 801). But the proposition that there is no middle way can be over-stated. There is a sense in which there is a middle way open to the innocent party in that it is given a period of time in which to make up its mind whether it is going to affirm the contract or terminate it. The Court of Appeal so concluded in *Stocznia Gdanska SA* v. *Latvian Shipping Company (No 2)* [2002] EWCA Civ. 889 [2002] 2 Lloyd's Rep 436.

The decision in *Stocznia Gdanska SA* is a welcome recognition of the fact that a repudiatory breach of contract can often put the innocent party in a difficult position. He may well be reluctant to terminate the contract as a result of the breach given the extent of his commitment to the relationship. On the other hand, he may be reluctant to affirm the contract given that an affirmation, once communicated, is, in principle, irrevocable. The Court of Appeal in *Stocznia Gdanska* recognized that there is, in effect, a third option open to the innocent party in the sense that he has a period of time in which to decide whether or terminate or affirm. Rix LJ stated (at para [87]):

In my judgment, there is of course a middle ground between acceptance of repudiation and affirmation of the contract, and that is the period when the innocent party is making up his mind what to do. If he does nothing for too long, there may come a time when the law will treat him as having affirmed. If he maintains the contract in being for the moment, while reserving his right to treat it as repudiated if his contract partner persists in his repudiation, then he has not yet elected. As long as the contract remains alive, the innocent party runs the risk that a merely anticipatory repudiatory breach, a thing 'writ in water' until acceptance, can be overtaken by another event which prejudices the innocent party's rights under the contract—such as frustration or even his own breach. He also runs the risk, if that is the right word, that the party in repudiation will resume performance of the contract and thus end any continuing right in the innocent party to elect to accept the former repudiation as terminating the contract.

This is a welcome recognition of commercial reality, namely that parties do require a period of time in which to make up their minds. The length of that period will very much depend upon the facts of the case. The period may not be a long one because, as Rix LJ points out, a party who does nothing for too long may be held to have affirmed the contract. The decision does nothing to encourage dilatoriness but it performs a useful function in so far as it recognizes that an innocent party has a period of time in which to decide whether to terminate the contract or affirm it.

A party who wishes to call upon the other party to perform but who does not wish such action to be construed as an affirmation of the contract would be well advised expressly to reserve his contractual rights. The innocent party in *Stocznia Gdanska* did not do so and this almost persuaded Rix LJ to conclude that it had affirmed the contract. But, at the end of the day, he was prepared to uphold the finding of the trial judge to the effect that there had been no affirmation.

There is one major exception to the general rule that an election, once made, is irrevocable. This exception arises in the context of continuing repudiatory conduct by the party in breach. In such a case an innocent party who has elected to affirm the contract after the first breach of contract may be able to treat the continued non-performance as a fresh act of repudiation (see *Johnson* v. *Agnew* [1980] AC 367 and *Safehaven* v. *Springbok* (1998) 71 P & CR 59). Once a repudiation is spent there cannot be an acceptance of the breach but if there is a continued refusal to perform by the party in breach and that continued refusal amounts to further repudiatory conduct, the innocent party is entitled to bring the contract to an end notwithstanding the initial affirmation. Were the law otherwise an innocent party would have to continue performing his obligations even in the case where it is clear from the continued refusal to perform that the party in breach would never do so.

7. ANTICIPATORY BREACH

It sometimes happens that, before the time fixed for performance under the contract, one party informs the other that he will not or cannot perform his obligations under the contract or that he intends to carry out his obligations in a way that is not consistent with the terms of the contract. This is known as an anticipatory breach of contract. What is the effect in law of an anticipatory breach of contract? One response would be to say that it has no effect at all. The time for performance has not yet arisen and one cannot be in breach of contract prior to the time for performance. But such a view presents difficulties for both parties. As far as the innocent party is concerned it leaves him in a state of some uncertainty. Will he receive the promised performance? Should he seek alternative performance elsewhere? The party who has committed the anticipatory breach also has an interest in effect being given to his renunciation. One reason why a party who is unable to perform may inform the other party prior to the time for performance is that he wishes to give the other party the opportunity to find alternative performance elsewhere. The effect of advance notice may well be to reduce the losses of the innocent party and the non-performing party has an obvious interest in reducing his potential exposure to a damages claim. The alternative response is to regard the intimation of the refusal to perform in accordance with the terms of the contract as a breach of contract which immediately gives the innocent party access to the usual array of remedies for breach.

The choice was made by the English courts in *Hochster* v. *De la Tour* (1853) 2 E & B 678. The defendant entered into an agreement with the plaintiff under which he agreed to employ the plaintiff as his courier for three months. The commencement date was agreed as 1 June 1852. On 11 May 1852 the defendant wrote to the plaintiff, informing him that his services were no longer required. On 22 May the plaintiff brought an action for damages against the defendant. The claim succeeded notwith-standing the fact that the claim was brought before the time fixed for performance under the contract. *Hochster* was followed some years later in *Frost* v. *Knight* (1872) LR 7 Ex 111. The defendant promised to marry the plaintiff on the death of his father (his father objected to the marriage). The defendant broke off the engagement while his father was still alive. The plaintiff brought an action against the defendant for breach of his promise to marry her (at this time promises to marry were legally enforceable). The defendant defended the claim on the ground that no claim for breach of contract could be brought while his father was still alive. The plaintiff succeeded in her claim. Cockburn CJ stated (at p. 114) that:

It is true . . . that there can be no actual breach of a contract by reason of non-performance so long as the time for performance has not yet arrived. But, on the other hand, there is—and the decision in *Hochster* v. *De la Tour* proceeds on that assumption—a breach of the contract when the promisor repudiates it and declares he will no longer be bound by it. The promisee has an inchoate right to the performance of the bargain, which becomes complete when the time for performance has arrived. In the mean time he has a right to have the contract kept open as a subsisting and effective contract. Its unimpaired and unimpeached efficacy may be essential to his interests. His rights acquired under it may be dealt by him in various ways for his benefit and advantage. Of such advantage the repudiation of the contract by the other party, and the announcement that it never will be fulfilled, must of course deprive him. It is therefore quite right to hold that such an announcement amounts to a violation of the contract in omnibus, and that upon it the promisee, if so minded, may at once treat it as a breach of the entire contract, and bring his action accordingly.

It is therefore clear law that an anticipatory breach of contract gives to the innocent party an immediate cause of action; he is not required to wait for the time for performance. The innocent party can seek a remedy immediately or can choose to affirm the contract and wait for the time for performance. The remedies available to the innocent party at the time of the anticipatory breach will depend upon the nature of the breach. If the anticipatory breach is a repudiatory breach of contract then the innocent party can terminate the contract and seek damages to compensate him for the loss of his bargain. Most anticipatory breaches are repudiatory breaches because they take the form of a clear and unequivocal statement that performance will not be forthcoming. It is clear that such a renunciation amounts to a repudiatory breach. In other cases the position may not be so clear. For example, in the case where the parties disagree as to the true construction of the contract and, prior to the time for perform-ance, one party puts forward a construction of the contract which is contrary to the 'true' interpretation of the contract, the courts have been reluctant to conclude that such a mistake is inevitably a repudiatory breach (see *Woodar Investment Development Ltd* v. *Wimpey Construction UK Ltd* [1980] 1 WLR 277, p. 987 above).

Where the innocent party decides to terminate further performance of the contract on account of the anticipatory breach, he must 'accept' the breach and inform the other party of his decision to terminate. But he need not accept the breach. He can elect to affirm the contract and to wait for the time for performance. In such a case the contract remains alive for the benefit of both parties so that the innocent party must continue with the performance of his own obligations under the contract (see *Ferco-metal SARL* v. *Mediterranean Shipping Co SA* [1989] AC 788). Similarly, the innocent party has no cause of action where he chooses to affirm the contract and, prior to the time for performance, the contract is frustrated. In such a case the contract remains alive after the anticipatory breach and is terminated not by the breach but by the operation of the doctrine of frustration (*Avery* v. *Bowden* (1855) 5 E & B 714).

The right of the innocent party to affirm the contract and continue with perform-ance is, however, a source of considerable controversy. The source of the controversy can be traced back to the following decision of the House of Lords:

White and Carter (Councils) Ltd v. McGregor

[1962] AC 413, House of Lords

In 1954 the parties entered into a contract under which the appellant advertising con-tractors agreed to display advertisements on local authority litter bins for the respond-ent's garage for a three-year period. The contract was renewed for a further three-year period in 1957. On the day that the renewal contract was concluded the respondent wrote to the appellants, seeking to cancel the contract on the ground that his sales manager, who concluded the contract on the respondent's behalf, had no specific authority to make the contract. The appellants refused to accept the respondent's cancel-lation and continued with performance of the contract and they displayed the advert-isements on the litter bins in accordance with the terms of the contract. The respondent refused to pay for the advertisements. The appellants sued for the full sum due under the contract for the period of three years. The claim was brought pursuant to clause 8 of the contract which provided:

'In the event of an instalment or part thereof being due for payment, and remaining unpaid for a period of four weeks or in the event of the advertiser being in any way in breach of this contract then the whole amount due for the 156 weeks or such part of the said 156 weeks as the advertiser shall not yet have paid shall immediately become due and payable.'

The respondent maintained that he was not liable to pay the sum alleged to be due on the ground that he had repudiated the contract before anything had been done under it so that the appellants were not entitled to continue with performance and sue for the price.

The House of Lords held by a majority (Lord Morton of Henryton and Lord Keith of Avonholm dissenting) that the appellants were entitled to recover the contract price on the ground that the respondent's unaccepted repudiation of the contract had not oper-ated to terminate the contract between the parties. The appellants were therefore entitled to continue with performance of the contract and recover the contract price.

Lord Reid [set out the facts and, having set out the terms of clause 8, continued]

A question was debated whether this clause provides a penalty or liquidated damages, but on the view which I take of the case it need not be pursued. The clause merely provides for acceleration of payment of the stipulated price if the advertiser fails to pay an instalment timeously. As the respondent maintained that he was not bound by the contract he did not pay the first instalment within the time allowed. Accordingly, if the appellants were entitled to carry out their part of the contract notwithstanding the respondent's repudiation, it was hardly disputed that this clause entitled them to sue immediately for the whole price and not merely the first instalment.

The general rule cannot be in doubt. It was settled in Scotland at least as early as 1848 and it has been authoritatively stated time and again in both Scotland and England. If one party to a contract repudiates it in the sense of making it clear to the other party that he refuses or will refuse to carry out his part of the contract, the other party, the innocent party, has an option. He may accept that repudiation and sue for damages for breach of contract, whether or not the time for performance has come; or he may if he chooses disregard or refuse to accept it and then the contract remains in full effect.

[he considered the case of *Howie* v. *Anderson* (1848) 10 D 355 and continued]

I need not refer to the numerous authorities. They are not disputed by the respondent but he points out that in all of them the party who refused to accept the repudiation had no active duties under the contract. The innocent party's option is generally said to be to *wait* until the date of performance and then to claim damages estimated as at that date. There is no case in which it is said that he may, in face of the repudiation, go on and incur useless expense in performing the contract and then claim the contract price. The option, it is argued, is merely as to the date as at which damages are to be assessed.

Developing this argument, the respondent points out that in most cases the innocent party cannot complete the contract himself without the other party doing, allowing or accepting something, and that it is purely fortuitous that the appellants can do so in this case. In most cases by refusing co-operation the party in breach can compel the innocent party to restrict his claim to damages. Then it was said that, even where the innocent party can complete the contract without such co-operation, it is against the public interest that he should be allowed to do so. An example was developed in argument. A company might engage an expert to go abroad and prepare an elaborate report and then repudiate the contract before anything was done. To allow such an expert then to waste thousands of pounds in preparing the report cannot be right if a much smaller sum of damages would give him full compensation for his loss. It would merely enable the expert to extort a settlement giving him far more than reasonable compensation.

[he then considered the case of *Langford & Co* v. *Dutch*, 1952 SC 15 in some detail and continued]

We must now decide whether that case was rightly decided. In my judgment it was not. It could only be supported on one or other of two grounds. It might be said that, because in most cases the circumstances are such that an innocent party is unable to complete the contract and earn the contract price without the assent or co-operation of the other party, therefore in cases where he can do so he should not be allowed to do so. I can see no justification for that.

The other ground would be that there is some general equitable principle or element of public policy which requires this limitation of the contractual rights of the innocent party. It may well be that, if it can be shown that a person has no legitimate interest, financial or otherwise, in performing the contract rather than claiming damages, he ought not to be allowed to saddle the other party with an additional burden with no benefit to himself. If a party has no interest to enforce a stipulation, he cannot in general enforce it: so it might be said that, if a party has no interest to insist on a particular remedy, he ought not to be allowed to insist on it. And, just as a party is not allowed to enforce a penalty, so he ought not to be allowed to penalise the other party by taking one course when another is equally advantageous to him. If I may revert to the example which I gave of a company engaging an expert to prepare an elaborate report and then repudiating before anything was done, it might be that the company could show that the expert had no substantial or legitimate interest in carrying out the work rather than accepting damages: I would think that the de minimis principle would apply in determining whether his interest was substantial, and that he might have a legitimate interest other than an immediate financial interest. But if the expert had no such interest then that might be regarded as a proper case for the exercise of the general equitable jurisdiction of the court. But that is not this case. Here the respondent did not set out to prove that the appellants had no legitimate interest in completing the contract and claiming the contract price rather than claiming damages; there is nothing in the findings of fact to support such a case, and it seems improbable that any such case could have been proved. It is, in my judgment, impossible to say that the appellants should be deprived of their right to claim the contract price merely because the benefit to them, as against claiming damages and re-letting their advertising space, might be small in comparison with the loss to the respondent: that is the most that could be said in favour of the respondent. Parliament has on many occasions relieved parties from certain kinds of improvident or oppressive contracts, but the common law can only do that in very limited circumstances. Accordingly, I am unable to avoid the conclusion that this appeal must be allowed and the case remitted so that decree can be pronounced as craved in the initial writ.

Lord Morton of Henryton [dissenting]
My Lords, I think that this is a case of great importance, although the claim is for a comparatively small sum. If the appellants are right, strange consequences follow in any case in which, under a repudiated contract, services are to be performed by the party who has not repudiated it, so long as he is able to perform these services without the co-operation of the repudiating party. Many examples of such contracts could be given. One, given in the course of the argument and already mentioned by my noble and learned friend, Lord Reid, is the engagement of an expert to go abroad and write a report on some subject for a substantial fee plus his expenses. If the appellants succeed in the present case, it must follow that the expert is entitled to incur the expense of going abroad, to write his unwanted report, and then to recover the fee and expenses, even if the other party has plainly repudiated the contract before any expense has been incurred.

It is well established that repudiation by one party does not put an end to a contract. The other party can say 'I hold you to your contract, which still remains in force'. What then is his remedy if the repudiating party persists in his repudiation and refuses to carry out his part of the contract? The contract has been broken. The innocent party is entitled to be compensated by damages for any loss which he has suffered by reason of the breach, and in a limited class of cases the court will decree specific implement. The law of Scotland provides no other remedy for a breach of contract and there is no reported case which decides that the innocent party may act as the appellants have acted. The present case is one in which specific implement could not be decreed, since the only obligation of the respondent under the contract was to pay a sum of money for services to be rendered by the appellants. Yet the appellants are claiming a kind of inverted specific implement of the contract. They first insist on performing their part of the contract, against the will of the other party, and then claim that he must perform his part and pay the contract price for unwanted services. In my opinion, my Lords, the appellants' only remedy was damages, and they were bound to take steps to minimise their loss, according to a well-established rule of law. Far from doing this, having incurred no expense at the date of the repudiation, they made no attempt to procure another advertiser, but deliberately went on to incur expense and perform unwanted services with the intention of creating a money debt which did not exist at the date of the repudiation . . .

In my opinion, the appellants' alternative claim for the same sum of £196 4s. as liquidated damages should be rejected for the reasons which will shortly be given by my noble and learned friend, Lord Keith of Avonholm.

I would dismiss the appeal.

Lord Tucker
My Lords, I have had the advantage of reading the opinion prepared by my noble and learned friend, Lord Hodson. I am in complete agreement with the reasons he gives for allowing the appeal.

Lord Keith of Avonholm [dissenting]
I find the argument advanced for the appellants a somewhat startling one. If it is right it would seem that a man who has contracted to go to Hong Kong at his own expense and make a report, in return for remuneration of £10,000, and who, before the date fixed for the start of the journey and perhaps before he has incurred any expense, is informed by the other contracting party that he has cancelled or repudiates the contract, is entitled to set off for Hong Kong and produce his report in order to claim in debt the stipulated sum. Such a result is not, in my opinion, in accordance with principle or authority, and cuts across the rule that where one party is in breach of contract the other must take steps to minimise the loss sustained by the breach.

There remains for consideration the alternative case made for the appellants upon condition 8 of the contract. Their claim is, that in respect of the defender's repudiation and breach of contract he is liable in damages, and that under the clause the damages are fixed at three years' rent which, they say, is liquidated damages, and not a penalty. But the clause, in my opinion, is only intended to take effect after the contract comes into operation. This is clear in the first event mentioned in the clause, because there can be no failure of payment until the advertising plates have been displayed in terms of the agreement. This could not happen on the hypothesis, which must be accepted on this part of the case, that the pursuers were not entitled to go on with the contract. The clause is, in my opinion, just a debt clause ancillary to the conditions for the payment of rent and providing for instant payment of the whole rent in the event of failure in punctual payment of the instalments. No very convincing suggestions were given as to what was meant to be covered by the second event. But, in my opinion, this also must refer to some breaches in the course of performance of the contract, which will again involve instant payment of the full rent. I fail to see how the clause can be at one and the same time a contractual clause sounding in payment of debt and a damages clause for repudiation of the contract. The clause accordingly has, in my opinion, no operation here, and I find it unnecessary to consider whether, if it had, it is a clause for liquidated damages, or for a penalty.

I would dismiss the appeal.

Lord Hodson

It is settled as a fundamental rule of the law of contract that repudiation by one of the parties to a contract does not itself discharge it. See Viscount Simon's speech in *Heyman v. Darwins Ltd* [1942] AC 356, 361, citing with approval the following sentence from a judgment of Scrutton LJ in *Golding* v. *London and Edinburgh Insurance Co Ltd* (1932) 43 Ll L Rep 487, 488: 'I have never been able to understand what effect the repudiation of one party has unless the other party accepts the repudiation'.

In *Howard* v. *Pickford Tool Co Ltd* [1951] 1 KB 417, 421 Asquith LJ said: 'An unaccepted repudiation is a thing writ in water and of no value to anybody: it confers no legal rights of any sort or kind'. These are English cases but that the law of Scotland is the same is, I think, clear from the authorities, of which I need only refer to one, namely, *Howie* v. *Anderson*, 10 D 355 where language to the same effect is to be found in the opinions of the Lord President and Lord Moncrieff.

It follows that, if, as here, there was no acceptance, the contract remains alive for the benefit of both parties and the party who has repudiated can change his mind but it does not follow that the party at the receiving end of the proffered repudiation is bound to accept it before the time for performance and is left to his remedy in damages for breach.

Counsel for the respondent did not seek to dispute the general proposition of law to which I have referred but sought to argue that if at the date of performance by the innocent party the guilty party maintains his refusal to accept performance and the innocent party does not accept the repudiation, although the contract still survives, it does not survive so far as the right of the innocent party to perform it is concerned but survives only for the purpose of enforcing remedies open to him by way of damages or specific implement. This produces an impossible result; if the innocent party is deprived of some of his rights it involves putting an end to the contract except in cases, unlike this, where, in the exercise of the court's discretion, the remedy of specific implement is available.

The true position is that the contract survives and does so not only where specific implement is available. When the assistance of the court is not required the innocent party can choose whether he will accept repudiation and sue for damages for anticipatory breach or await the date of performance by the guilty party. Then, if there is failure in performance, his rights are preserved.

It may be unfortunate that the appellants have saddled themselves with an unwanted contract causing an apparent waste of time and money. No doubt this aspect impressed the Court of Session but there is no equity which can assist the respondent. It is trite that equity will not rewrite an improvident contract where there is no disability on either side. There is no duty laid upon a party to a subsisting contract to vary it at the behest of the other party so as to deprive himself of the benefit given to him by the contract. To hold otherwise would be to introduce a novel equitable doctrine that a party was not to be held to his contract unless the court in a given instance thought it reasonable so to do. In this case it would make an action for debt a claim for a discretionary remedy. This would introduce an uncertainty into the field of contract which appears to be unsupported by authority either in English or Scottish law save for the one case upon which the Court of Session founded its opinion and which must, in my judgment, be taken to have been wrongly decided.

The appellants were given leave to amend their claim by praying in the alternative for the same sum, namely, £196 4s. as liquidated damages for breach of contract on the footing that the repudiation must be treated as if accepted. The respondent resisted the alternative claim on the ground that the sum sued for being a penalty and not liquidated damages the appellants were not entitled to decree therefor.

The only material obligation which the respondent was bound to fulfil was to pay the sum of money claimed and it is difficult to see how damages should be assessed for breach of this obligation. It is, however, unnecessary in view of the opinion I have expressed to consider the question whether the sum claimed is recoverable as a genuine pre-estimate of probable or possible interest in the due performance of the contract or is irrecoverable as a penalty.

I would allow the appeal.

COMMENTARY

A vital key to understanding the issue in *White & Carter* is the distinction between a claim in debt and a claim in damages. A claim in debt is a claim that the debtor owes to the creditor a liquidated sum of money. Such a claim is not subject to the require-ment that the creditor must have mitigated his loss. Either the debtor owes the sum of money to the creditor or he does not. A claim in damages, on the other hand, is an unliquidated claim to be compensated for the loss that the innocent party has suffered as a result of the breach of contract. A claimant who brings a claim for damages is under a 'duty' to mitigate his loss, in the sense that he cannot recover that portion of his loss that is attributable to his failure to mitigate (see further p. 1099). Thus the classification of the claim, as either a claim in debt or in damages, was crucial to the outcome of the case. Had it been a claim in damages, the appellants would have been subject to a requirement that they take reasonable steps to mitigate their loss (through seeking to find other people to take over the advertising space vacated by the respond-ent). But the claim was held to be one in debt. Clause 8 of the contract was critical in reaching the conclusion that the claim was one in debt because the effect of the clause was to declare that the entire price for the three-year period was 'immediately due and payable'. The claim was therefore for a debt that was owed rather than for the loss of an entitlement to an income stream over a period of years. The obligation to mitigate was therefore not in play.

The majority comprised Lord Hodson, Lord Tucker, and Lord Reid. For Lord Hodson this was a claim in debt and a claim in debt could not be turned into a discretionary remedy. It should be noted that Lord Tucker agreed with Lord Hodson and did not express his agreement with the speech of Lord Reid. Lord Reid's speech differed from that of Lord Hodson in that he introduced the 'legitimate interest' test (in that he held that it was open to the respondent to seek to show that the appellants had no legitimate interest in continuing with performance of the contract). The question which then arose was whether or not this was part of the ratio of the case. In *Hounslow London Borough Council* v. *Twickenham Garden Developments Ltd* [1971] Ch 233, 254 Megarry J stated that 'it seems to me that the ratio of the *White* case involves acceptance of Lord Reid's limitations, even though Lord Tucker and Lord Hodson said nothing of them: for without Lord Reid there was no majority for the decision of the House. Under the doctrine of precedent, I do not think that it can be said that a majority of a bare majority is itself the majority'.

The decision in *White & Carter* has proved to be an extremely controversial one. It has been attacked on the ground that it was unfair to the respondent in that it saddled him with a performance which he did not want. It has also been argued that it leads to a result which is economically inefficient in that performance was a waste (although on the facts it could be argued that the respondent did derive at least some benefit from the advertisement of his garage on the litter bins). In subsequent cases courts have generally chosen to interpret the case narrowly. They have done so in two different ways. The first exception is that the rule does not apply where the innocent party is dependent upon the co-operation of the party in breach in order to be able to continue with performance. The second exception arises where the innocent party has no legitimate interest in performance of the contract.

First, the rule in *White & Carter* does not apply where the innocent party is dependent upon the co-operation of the party in breach in order to be able to continue with performance. The innocent party cannot get an order of the court requiring the party in breach to co-operate with a performance which he no longer wants. In such a case the innocent party must be content with a claim in damages which, of course, is subject to the mitigation rule. Further, the courts have adopted a broad notion of co-operation so that the innocent party can neither require the active nor the passive co-operation of the party in breach. In *Hounslow London Borough Council* v. *Twickenham Garden Developments Ltd* Megarry J stated (at pp. 253–254):

Suppose that A, who owns a large and valuable painting, contracts with B, a picture restorer, to restore it over a period of three months. Before the work is begun, A receives a handsome offer from C to purchase the picture, subject to immediate delivery of the picture in its unrestored state, C having grave suspicions of B's competence. If the work of restoration is to be done in A's house, he can effectually exclude B by refusing to admit him to the house; without A's 'co-operation' to this extent B cannot perform his contract. But what if the picture stands in A's locked barn, the key of which he has lent to B so that he may come and go freely, or if the picture has been removed to B's premises? Can B insist in these cases in performing his contract, even though this makes it impossible for A to accept C's offer? In the case of the barn A's co-operation may perhaps be said to be requisite to the extent of not barring B's path to the barn or putting another lock on the door; but if the picture is on B's premises, no active co-operation by A is needed. Nevertheless, the picture is A's property, and I find it difficult to believe that Lord Reid intended to restrict the concept of 'co-operation' to active co-operation. In the *White* case, no co-operation by the proprietor, either active or passive, was required; the contract could be performed by the agent wholly without reference to the proprietor or his property. The case was far removed from that of a property owner being forced to stand impotently aside while a perhaps ill-advised contract is executed on property of his which he has delivered into the possession of the other party, and is powerless to retrieve.

The principle underlying the co-operation exception was further considered by Nicholas Strauss QC, sitting as a Deputy Judge of the High Court, in *Ministry of Sound (Ireland) Ltd* v. *World Online Ltd* [2003] EWHC 2178 (Ch); [2003] 2 All ER (Comm) 823. He stated (at [49]) that:

in essence, the principle is that the breach of contract does not convert a dependent obligation into an independent one; if the right to the payment claimed is dependent upon the performance of contractual obligations, the prevention of performance by the other party's breach of contract does not alter the position.

It is therefore crucial to examine the precise scope of the contractual right to payment. Where the right to payment is dependent upon performance by the innocent party of his contractual obligations, and the innocent party has been unable to perform these obligations as a result of the lack of co-operation from the breaching party, the innocent party will not be entitled to claim payment under the contract because the right to payment has not arisen. On the other hand, where the right to payment is not dependent upon performance by the innocent party of his contractual obligations, then the innocent party should be entitled to claim payment in accordance with the contract provided that any conditions which entitle him to payment have been satisfied.

The other exception is the 'legitimate interest' requirement to be found in the speech of Lord Reid in *White & Carter*. Lord Reid stated that the exception was inapplicable on the facts of *White & Carter* on the ground that the respondent had not set out to prove that the appellants had no legitimate interest in completing the contract and claiming the contract price rather than claiming damages. It is hardly surprising that the respondent did not make such an attempt given that he presumably did not know that he had such an option open to him until Lord Reid told him that he did. But breaching parties in later cases have been quick to seize on the exception and exploit it to the full. They have generally found the courts to be receptive to arguments based on the exception.

In *Attica Sea Carriers Corporation* v. *Ferrostaal Poseidon Bulk Reederei GmbH (The Puerto Buitrago)* [1976] 1 Lloyd's Rep 250 charterers chartered a vessel from shipowners for seventeen months. After six months the vessel required substantial repairs. The cost of these repairs was some $2 million. But the vessel was not worth repairing because, even when it was fully repaired, it would be worth only $1 million. In these circumstances the charterers terminated the charter hire and re-delivered the vessel. The charterers admitted liability for $400,000 of the repairs but the shipowners refused to accept the re-delivery of the vessel, contending that the charterers were liable under the contract to pay the hire until the repairs had been carried out. The Court of Appeal rejected the shipowner's argument, holding that the obligation to repair the vessel was not a condition precedent to the entitlement of the charterer to redeliver the vessel. It was therefore not necessary for the Court of Appeal to decide whether or not the shipowners were entitled to recover the hire until such time as the repairs were done. But the court nevertheless gave brief consideration to the issue. It was held that *White & Carter* was distinguishable. Lord Denning MR expressed himself in characteristically robust terms. After noting that the decision in *White & Carter* had been said by one leading textbook writer to give rise to a 'grotesque' result, he continued as follows (at p. 255):

Even though it was a Scots case, it would appear that the House of Lords, as at present constituted, would expect us to follow it in any case that is precisely on all fours with it. But I would not follow it otherwise. It has no application whatever in a case where the plaintiff ought, in all reason, to accept the repudiation and sue for damages—provided that damages would provide an adequate remedy for any loss suffered by him. The reason is because, by suing for the money, the plaintiff is seeking to enforce specific performance of the contract –and he should not be allowed to do so when damages would be an adequate remedy. Take a servant, who has a contract for six months certain, but is dismissed after one month. He cannot sue for his wages for each of the six months by alleging that he was ready and willing to serve. His only remedy is damages. Take a finance company which lets a machine or motor-car on hire purchase, but the hirer refuses to accept it. The finance company cannot sue each month for the instalments. Its only remedy is in damages. . . . So here, when the charterers tendered redelivery at the end of the period of the char-ter—in breach of the contract to repair—the shipowners ought in all reason to have accepted it. They cannot sue for specific performance—either of the promise to pay the charter hire, or of the promise to do the repairs—because damages are an adequate remedy for the breach.

Orr LJ was rather more circumspect. He distinguished *White & Carter* on the ground that the shipowners could not fulfil the contract without any co-operation from the charterers and also because the charterers had set out to show that the shipowners had no legitimate interest in continuing with performance of the contract. Browne LJ concurred with both judgments.

In *Gator Shipping Corporation* v. *Trans-Asiatic Oil Ltd SA and Occidental Shipping Establishment (The Odenfield)* [1978] 2 Lloyd's Rep 357, 373–374 Kerr J adopted a less restrictive approach to the scope of *White & Carter.* He considered *The Puerto Buitrago* and stated (at p. 373) that he did not

regard the case as any authority for a general proposition to the effect that whenever a charterer repudiates a time or demise charter, for whatever reason and in whatever circumstances, the owners are always bound to take the vessel back, because a refusal to do so would be equivalent to seeking an order for specific performance. The consequences of such a proposition would be extremely serious in many cases, and no trace of such a doctrine is to be found in our shipping law. But no such general proposition was laid down. . . . It follows that any fetter on the innocent party's right of election whether or not to accept a repudiation will only be applied in extreme cases, viz where damages would be an adequate remedy *and* where an election to keep the contract alive would be *wholly unreasonable* [emphasis in the original].

The next case is the decision of Lloyd J in *Clea Shipping Corporation* v. *Bulk Oil International Ltd (The Alaskan Trader)* [1984] 1 All ER 129. The defendant shipowners chartered a vessel to the plaintiff charterers for approximately twenty-four months. After almost a year of largely trouble-free use, the vessel suffered a serious engine breakdown which necessitated repairs that would take several months to complete. In these circumstances the plaintiffs informed the defendants that they had no further use for the vessel but the defendants nevertheless proceeded to carry out the repairs at a cost of some £800,000. On completion of the repairs the defendants informed the plaintiffs that the vessel was once again at their disposal. However the plaintiffs were of the view that the charterparty had come to an end and so they refused to give any directions to the master of the vessel. The defendants nevertheless refused to accept that the charter was at an end and kept the vessel, fully-manned, at the disposal of the plaintiffs. The plaintiffs, having paid the hire for the entire period, sought to recover the hire paid for the period after the breakdown of the vessel. It was held that the plaintiffs were entitled to recover the hire subject to their liability in damages for the loss caused by their refusal to take the vessel. On the facts Lloyd J concluded that the owners had no legitimate interest in claiming the hire rather than pursuing a claim for damages. He considered the authorities and concluded (at pp. 136–137):

Whether one takes Lord Reid's language, which was adopted by Orr and Browne LJJ in *The Puerto Buitrago*, or Lord Denning's language in that case ('in all reason'), or Kerr J's language in *The Odenfield* ('wholly unreasonable . . . quite unrealistic, unreasonable and untenable') there comes a point at which the court will cease, on general equitable principles, to allow the innocent party to enforce his contract according to its strict legal terms. How one defines that point is obviously a matter of some difficulty, for it involves drawing a line between conduct which is merely unreasonable . . . and conduct which is *wholly* unreasonable. . . . But however difficult it may be to define the point, that there is such a point seems to me to have been accepted both by the Court of Appeal in *The Puerto Buitrago* and by Kerr J in *The Odenfield*.

The final case is the decision of Simon J in *Ocean Marine Navigation Ltd* v. *Koch Carbon Inc (The 'Dynamic')* [2003] EWHC 1936 (Comm); [2003] 2 Lloyd's Rep 693. He concluded that the 'qualifying word *wholly* in the expression *wholly unreasonable* in *The Odenfield* properly emphasises that the rule is general and the exception only applies in extreme cases' and 'adds nothing to the test'. He sought to summarize the current state of the law in the following propositions:

These cases establish the following exception to the general rule that the innocent party has an option whether or not to accept a repudiation: (i) The burden is on the *contract-breaker* to show that the innocent party has no legitimate interest in performing the contract rather than claiming damages. (ii) This burden is not discharged merely by showing that the benefit to the other party is small in comparison to the loss to the contract breaker. (iii) The exception to the general rule applies only in extreme cases where damages would be an adequate remedy and where an election to keep the contract alive would be unreasonable.

8. FURTHER READING

BROWNSWORD, R, 'Retrieving Reasons, Retrieving Rationality? A New Look at the Right to Withdraw for Breach of Contract' (1992) 5 *Journal of Contract Law* 83.

SMITH, JC, 'Anticipatory Breach of Contract' in Lomnicka, E and Morse, CJG (eds), *Contemporary Issues in Commercial Law: Essays in Honour of A. G. Guest* (Sweet & Maxwell, 1994), p. 175.

TREITEL, GH, ' "Conditions" and "Conditions Precedent" ' (1990) 106 *LQR* 185.

—— *Some Landmarks of Twentieth Century Contract Law* (Oxford University Press, 2002), Chapter 3.

25

DAMAGES

1. CENTRAL ISSUES

1. The aim of an award of damages is generally to put the claimant in the position which he would have been in had the contract been performed according to its terms. The aim is thus to protect the claimant's 'expectation interest', or his 'performance interest'. The scope of the claimant's expectation or performance interests is a major focus of this chapter. Is the claimant's expectation defined by reference to the financial value of performance or by reference to the performance itself? How are damages to be assessed in the case in which the claimant does not appear to have a direct financial interest in the performance of the contract? When is the claimant entitled to recover the cost of making performance conform to the terms of the contract and when is he entitled to recover the difference in value between the performance which he has received and the performance which he was promised? These questions will all be explored in this chapter.

2. The courts have also experienced difficulty in deciding when a claimant is entitled to recover damages for non-pecuniary losses suffered as a result of a breach of contract. Can damages be recovered for the disappointment of not receiving the contractual performance which the defendant promised to provide? What is the appropriate measure of damages

in the case where, for example, the contract is one for the provision of pleasure such as a holiday and the defendant breaches the contract?

3. The law must place some limits on the liability of the defendant, otherwise liability could prove to be endless. Doctrines, such as remoteness of damage, are used by the courts to keep liability within acceptable bounds. These doctrines will be examined in this chapter. Consideration will also be given to the responsibility of the claimant not to take unreasonable steps to increase the loss and to take reasonable steps to reduce the loss caused by the breach.

4. Exceptionally damages may be assessed by reference to the gain which the defendant has made from his breach of contract. The circumstances in which English law allows a claimant to recover damages assessed by reference to the defendant's gain will be examined in this chapter.

5. Finally, consideration will be given to the extent to which it is open to the parties to make their own provision for the financial consequences of a breach of contract. The courts have long exercised a jurisdiction to control agreed damages clauses, although the extent of the jurisdiction, and the justifications for its existence, are a source of some controversy.

2. INTRODUCTION

The aim of this chapter is to examine the entitlement of a claimant to recover damages in respect of a breach of contract committed by the defendant. Every breach of contract gives rise to a claim for damages. In the case where the claimant has not suffered any loss as a result of the breach, he is still entitled to recover damages but damages will be nominal. The word 'damages', as used in this chapter, is not tied to compensatory damages. As Dr Edelman suggests in his book *Gain-Based Damages: Contract, Tort, Equity and Intellectual Property* (Hart, 2002), p. 22, the word '"damages" can only mean money awards which respond to wrongs'. On this view the word 'damages' is not tied to any particular measure of recovery. There is a range of measures available to the court, all of which can be described as different types of damages. Thus we have nominal damages, compensatory damages, restitutionary (or disgorgement) damages, and exemplary (or punitive) damages. This chapter will focus on compensatory damages but it will also explore the circumstances in which a claimant can recover 'restitutionary damages', 'disgorgement damages', or 'an account of profits' (the three labels being synonymous for present purposes). Exemplary damages make only a fleeting appearance. English law does not, as yet, recognize an entitlement to recover exemplary damages for a breach of contract.

The chapter is divided into the following sections. The bulk of it is devoted to compensatory damages, given that they are the most commonly awarded form of damages. It opens (in section 3) with a discussion of the different measures of damages that can be awarded and concludes that the aim of an award of damages is generally to protect the claimant's performance (or expectation) interest. The next section (section 4) is devoted to an analysis of the performance interest and it consists largely of an analysis of two recent decisions of the House of Lords. Section 5 examines the circumstances in which a claimant can seek damages based on his 'reliance' losses rather than his performance interest, while section 6 discusses the circumstances in which damages may be awarded to protect the claimant's 'restitution' interest. Section 7 examines the entitlement of a claimant to recover damages in respect of non-pecuniary losses, particularly 'mental distress'. Section 8 then turns to a consideration of the various doctrines that the courts use in order to keep liability within acceptable bounds. Doctrines examined in this section include remoteness, mitigation, and contributory negligence. Section 9 considers the circumstances in which a defendant can be ordered to account to a claimant for the profits which he has made from his breach of contract. Section 10 examines, albeit briefly, the possibility that exemplary damages might have a role to play in breach of contract cases. The chapter concludes, in sections 11 and 12, with a discussion of agreed damages clauses (and related clauses) and their legal regulation.

3. DAMAGES: THE DIFFERENT MEASURES

The most cited article ever written on the law of contract is Fuller and Perdue's article entitled 'The Reliance Interest in Contract Damages' which was published in two parts in the *Yale Law Journal* in 1936 and 1937. This article has been hailed as a classic and its influence on a number of contract scholars has been immense (see, for example, the preface to PS Atiyah, *The Rise and Fall of Freedom of Contract* (Oxford University Press, 1979)). Its major impact has been on the terminology which we use when describing the different measures of damages that can be recovered on a breach of contract. In this, the opening section of their essay, they set out the three different interests that the law of contract might protect. The principal points to note are the ranking of these three interests, their relegation of the significance of the expectation interest (or performance interest) which, at the time, was the generally accepted measure of recovery, and their championing of the cause of the reliance interest.

LL Fuller and William R Perdue Jr, 'The Reliance Interest in Contract Damages'

(1936) 46 *Yale LJ* 52, 53–62

It is convenient to distinguish three principal purposes which may be pursued in awarding contract damages. These purposes, and the situations in which they become appropriate, may be stated briefly as follows:

First, the plaintiff has in reliance on the promise of the defendant conferred some value on the defendant. The defendant fails to perform his promise. The court may force the defendant to disgorge the value he received from the plaintiff. The object here may be termed the prevention of gain by the defaulting promisor at the expense of the promisee; more briefly, the prevention of unjust enrichment. The interest protected may be called the *restitution interest* . . .

Secondly, the plaintiff has in reliance on the promise of the defendant changed his position. For example, the buyer under a contract for the sale of land has incurred expense in the investigation of the seller's title, or has neglected the opportunity to enter other contracts. We may award damages to the plaintiff for the purpose of undoing the harm which his reliance on the defendant's promise has caused him. Our object is to put him in as good a position as he was in before the promise was made. The interest protected in this case may be called the *reliance interest.*

Thirdly, without insisting on reliance by the promisee or enrichment of the promisor, we may seek to give the promisee the value of the expectancy which the promise created. We may in a suit for specific performance actually compel the defendant to render the promised performance to the plaintiff, or, in a suit for damages, we may make the defendant pay the money value of this performance. Here our object is to put the plaintiff in as good a position as he would have occupied had the defendant performed his promise. The interest protected in this case we may call the *expectation interest.*

It will be observed that what we have called the *restitution interest* unites two elements: (1) reliance by the promisee, (2) a resultant gain to the promisor. It may for some purposes be necessary to separate these elements. In some cases a defaulting promisor may after his breach be left with an unjust gain which was not taken from the promisee (a third party furnished the consideration), or which was not the result of reliance by the promisee (the promisor violated a promise not to appropriate the promisee's goods). Even in those cases where the promisor's gain results from the promisee's reliance it may happen that damages will be assessed somewhat differently, depending on whether we take the promisor's gain or the promisee's loss as the standard of measurement. Generally, however . . . gain by the promisor will be accompanied by a corresponding and, so far as its legal measurement is concerned, identical loss to the promisee, so that for our purposes the most workable classification is one which presupposes in the restitution interest a correlation of promisor's gain and promisee's loss. If, as we shall assume, the gain involved in the restitution interest results from and is identical with the plaintiff's loss through reliance, then the restitution interest is merely a special case of the reliance interest; all of the cases coming under the restitution interest will be covered by the reliance interest, and the reliance interest will be broader than the restitution interest only to the extent that it includes cases where the plaintiff has relied on the defendant's promise without enriching the defendant.

It should not be supposed that the distinction here taken between the reliance and expectation interests coincides with that sometimes taken between 'losses caused' . . . and 'gains prevented'. In the first place, though reliance ordinarily results in 'losses' of an affirmative nature (expenditures of labor and money) it is also true that opportunities for gain may be foregone in reliance on a promise. Hence the reliance interest must be interpreted as at least potentially covering 'gains prevented' as well as 'losses caused'. . . . On the other hand, it is not possible to make the expectation interest entirely synonymous with 'gains prevented'. The disappointment of an expectancy often entails losses of a positive character.

It is obvious that the three 'interests' we have distinguished do not present equal claims to judicial intervention. It may be assumed that ordinary standards of justice would regard the need for judicial intervention as decreasing in the order in which we have listed the three interests. The 'restitution interest', involving a combination of unjust impoverishment with unjust gain, presents the strongest case for relief. If, following Aristotle, we regard the purpose of justice as the maintenance of an equilibrium of goods among members of society, the restitution interest presents twice as strong a claim to judicial intervention as the reliance interest, since if A not only causes B to lose one unit but appropriates that unit to himself, the resulting discrepancy between A and B is not one unit but two.

On the other hand, the promisee who has actually relied on the promise, even though he may not thereby have enriched the promisor, certainly presents a more pressing case for relief than the promisee who merely demands satisfaction for his disappointment in not getting what was promised him. In passing from compensation for change of position to compensation for loss of expectancy we pass, to use Aristotle's terms again, from the realm of corrective justice to that of distributive justice. The law no longer seeks merely to heal a disturbed status quo, but to bring into being a new situation. It ceases to act defensively or restoratively, and assumes a more active role. With the transition, the justification for legal relief loses its self-evident quality. It is as a matter of fact no easy thing to explain why the normal rule of contract recovery should be that which measures damages by the value of the promised performance. Since this 'normal rule' throws its shadow across our whole subject it will be necessary to examine the possible reasons for its existence. It may be said parenthetically that the discussion which follows, though directed primarily to the normal measure of recovery where damages are sought, also has relevance to the more general question, why should a promise which has not been relied on ever be enforced at all, whether by a decree of specific performance or by an award of damages? . . .

WHY SHOULD THE LAW EVER PROTECT THE EXPECTATION INTEREST?

Perhaps the most obvious answer to this question is one which we may label 'psychological'. The answer would run something as follows: The breach of a promise arouses in the promisee a sense of injury. This feeling is not confined to cases where the promisee has relied on the promise. Whether or not he has actually changed his position because of the promise, the promisee has formed an attitude of expectancy such that a breach of the promise causes him to feel that he has been 'deprived' of something which was 'his'. Since this sentiment is a relatively uniform one, the law has no occasion to go back to it. It accepts it as a datum and builds its rule about it.

The difficulty with this explanation is that the law does in fact go back on the sense of injury which the breach of promise engenders. No legal system attempts to invest with juristic sanction all promises. Some rule or combination of rules effects a sifting out for enforcement of those promises deemed important enough to society to justify the law's concern with them. Whatever the principles which control this sifting out process may be, they are not convertible into terms of the degree of resentment which the breach of a particular kind of promise arouses. Therefore, though it may be assumed that the impulse to assuage disappointment is one shared by those who make and influence the law, this impulse can hardly be regarded as the key which solves the whole problem of the protection accorded by the law to the expectation interest.

A second possible explanation for the rule protecting the expectancy may be found in the much-discussed 'will theory' of contract law. This theory views the contracting parties as exercising, so to speak, a legislative power, so that the legal enforcement of a contract becomes merely an implementing by the state of a kind of private law already established by the parties. . . . It is enough to note here that while the will theory undoubtedly has some bearing on the problem of contract damages, it cannot be regarded as dictating in all cases a recovery of the expectancy. If a contract represents a kind of private law, it is a law which usually says nothing at all about what shall be done when it is violated. A contract is in this respect like an imperfect statute which provides no penalties, and which leaves it to the courts to find a way to effectuate its purposes. There would, therefore, be no necessary contradiction between the will theory and a rule which limited damages to the reliance interest. Under such a rule the penalty for violating the norm established by the contract would simply consist in being compelled to compensate the other party for detrimental reliance. Of course there may be cases where the parties have so obviously anticipated that a certain form of judicial relief will be given that we can, without stretching things, say that by implication they have 'willed' that this relief should be given. This attitude finds a natural application to promises to pay a definite sum of money. But certainly as to most types of contracts it is vain to expect from the will theory a ready-made solution for the problem of damages.

A third and more promising solution to our difficulty lies in an economic or institutional approach. The essence of a credit economy lies in the fact that it tends to eliminate the distinction between present and future (promised) goods. Expectations of future values become, for purposes of trade, present values. In a society in which credit has become a significant and pervasive institution, it is inevitable that the expectancy created by an enforceable promise should be regarded as a kind of property, and breach of the promise as an injury to that property . . .

The most obvious objection which can be made to the economic or institutional explanation is that it involves a *petitio principii*. A promise has present value, why? Because the law enforces it. 'The expectancy' regarded as a present value, is not the cause of legal intervention but the consequence of it. This objection may be reinforced by a reference to legal history. Promises were enforced long before there was anything corresponding to a general system of 'credit', and recovery was from the beginning measured by the value of the promised performance, the 'agreed price'. It may therefore be argued that the 'credit system' when it finally emerged was itself in large part built on the foundations of a juristic development which preceded it.

The view just suggested asserts the primacy of law over economics; it sees law not as the creature but as the creator of social institutions. The shift of emphasis thus implied suggests the possibility of a fourth explanation for the law's protection of the unrelied-on expectancy, which we may call *juristic*. This explanation would seek a justification for the normal rule of recovery in some policy consciously pursued by courts and other law-makers. It would assume that courts have protected the expectation interest because they have considered it wise to do so, not through a blind acquiescence in habitual ways of thinking and feeling, or through an equally blind deference to the individual will. Approaching the problem from this point of view, we are forced to find not a mere explanation for the rule in the form of some sentimental, volitional, or institutional datum, but articulate reasons for its existence.

What reasons can be advanced? In the first place, even if our interest were confined to protecting promisees against out-of-pocket loss, it would still be possible to justify the rule granting the value of the expectancy, both as a cure for, and as a prophylaxis against, losses of this sort.

It is a cure for these losses in the sense that it offers the measure of recovery most likely to reimburse the plaintiff for the (often very numerous and very difficult to prove) individual acts and forbearances which make up his total reliance on the contract. If we take into account 'gains prevented' by reliance, that is, losses involved in foregoing the opportunity to enter other contracts, the notion that the rule protecting the expectancy is adopted as the most effective means of compensating for detrimental reliance seems not at all far-fetched. Physicians with an extensive practice often charge their patients the full office call fee for broken appointments. Such a charge looks on the face of things like a claim to the promised fee; it seems to be based on the 'expectation interest'. Yet the physician making the charge will quite justifiably regard it as compensation for the loss of the opportunity to gain a similar fee from a different patient. This foregoing of other opportunities is involved to some extent in entering most contracts, and the impossibility of subjecting this type of reliance to any kind of measurement may justify a categorical rule granting the value of the expectancy as the most effective way of compensating for such losses.

The rule that the plaintiff must after the defendant's breach take steps to mitigate damages tends to corroborate the suspicion that there lies hidden behind the protection of the expectancy a concern to compensate the plaintiff for the loss of the opportunity to enter other contracts. Where after the defendant's breach the opportunity remains open to the plaintiff to sell his services or goods elsewhere, or to fill his needs from another source, he is bound to embrace that opportunity. Viewed in this way the rule of 'avoidable harms' is a qualification on the protection accorded the expectancy, since it means that the plaintiff, in those cases where it is applied, is protected only to the extent that he has in reliance on the contract foregone other equally advantageous opportunities for accomplishing the same end.

But, as we have suggested, the rule measuring damages by the expectancy may also be regarded as a prophylaxis against the losses resulting from detrimental reliance. Whatever tends to discourage breach of contract tends to prevent the losses occasioned through reliance. Since the expectation interest furnishes a more easily administered measure of recovery than the reliance interest, it will in practice offer a more effective sanction against contract breach. It is therefore possible to view the rule measuring damages by the expectancy in a quasi-criminal aspect, its purpose being not so much to compensate the promisee as to penalize breach of promise by the promisor. The rule enforcing the unrelied-on-promise finds the same justification, on this theory, as an ordinance which fines a man for driving through a stop-light when no other vehicle is in sight.

In seeking justification for the rule granting the value of the expectancy there is no need, however, to restrict ourselves by the assumption hitherto made, that the rule can only be intended to cure or prevent the losses caused by reliance. A justification can be developed from a less negative point of view. It may be said that there is not only a policy in favor of preventing and undoing the harms resulting from reliance, but also a policy in favor of promoting and facilitating reliance on business agreements. As in the case of the stop-light ordinance we are interested not only in preventing collisions but in speeding traffic. Agreements can accomplish little, either for their makers or for society, unless they are made the basis for action. When business agreements are not only made but are also acted on, the division of labor is facilitated, goods find their way to the places where they are most needed, and economic activity is generally stimulated. These advantages would be threatened by any rule which limited legal protection to the reliance interest. Such a rule would in practice tend to discourage reliance. The difficulties in proving reliance and subjecting it to pecuniary measurement are such that the business man knowing, or sensing, that these obstacles stood in the way of judicial relief would hesitate to rely on a promise in any case where the legal sanction was of significance to him. To encourage reliance we must therefore dispense with its proof. For this reason it has been found wise to make recovery on a promise independent of reliance, both in the sense that in some cases the promise is enforced though not relied on (as in the bilateral business agreement) and in the sense that recovery is not limited to the detriment incurred in reliance.

The juristic explanation in its final form is then twofold. It rests the protection accorded to the expectancy on (1) the need for curing and preventing the harms occasioned by reliance, and (2) on the need for facilitating reliance on business agreements. From this spelling out of a possible juristic explanation, it is clear that there is no incompatibility between it and the economic or institutional explanation. The essence of both of them lies in the word 'credit'. The economic justification views credit from its institutional side; the juristic explanation views it from its rational side. The economic view sees credit as an accepted way of living; the juristic view invites us to explore the considerations of utility which underlie this mode of living; and the part which conscious human direction has played in bringing it into being.

At the end of the day Fuller and Perdue do not seriously challenge the courts' practice of awarding expectation damages. Rather, they challenge the theoretical justifications for making such awards. The justification, in their view, lies not in the need to protect the 'interest' created by a binding promise but in the desire to provide a cure for, and prophylaxis against, reliance losses. Other jurists, building on the work of Fuller and Perdue, went further and openly questioned the justifications for awarding damages to protect the claimant's expectation interest, particularly in the case where the contract remained executory. The courts have, however, remained stubbornly resistant to Fuller and Perdue's analysis and have not demonstrated a willingness to abandon their commitment to the protection of the expectation or the performance interest (see S Macauley, 'The Reliance Interest and the World Outside the Laws Schools' Doors' [1991] *Wisc LR* 247, esp. pp. 266–287).

Fuller and Perdue's analysis has recently been challenged, in what is suggested is a convincing fashion, by Professor Friedmann in the following terms:

D Friedmann, 'The Performance Interest in Contract Damages'

(1995) 111 *LQR* 628, 629–639, 646–650 and 654

The essence of contract is performance. Contracts are made in order to be performed. This is usually the one and only ground for their formation. Ordinarily, a person enters into a contract because he is interested in getting that which the other party has to offer and because he places a higher value on the other party's performance than on the cost and trouble he will incur to obtain it. This interest in getting the promised performance (hereafter the 'performance interest') is the only pure contractual interest. The performance interest is protected by specific remedies which aim at getting the innocent party the very performance promised to him, and by substitutional remedies. The specific remedies are:

(1) Specific performance and injunction, originally equitable and, therefore, discretionary remedies.

(2) The recovery of a debt . . .

The substitutional remedies are:

(1) Compensating damages or 'loss of bargain' damages. It is also possible to term them 'performance damages', since they are intended to put the plaintiff in as good a position as that in which he would have been, had the contract been performed.

(2) Recovery of the 'substitute' which relates to the situation in which the promisor can no longer perform but has obtained a substitute for the promised performance. Examples of such a 'substitute' include insurance proceeds for a loss, and damages or price paid by a third party . . .

(3) Recovery in restitution of profits made by the other party through the breach. This remedy partly overlaps the right to the substitute . . . but the extent of its availability has been much debated . . .

The performance interest is also protected against third parties by means of the tort of inducement of breach of contract and also by equitable and restitutionary remedies.

THE RANKING OF INTERESTS AND THE NEW TERMINOLOGY

Fuller and Perdue . . . identified three interests: the expectation interest, the reliance interest and the restitution interest. These interests were ranked in accordance with the strength of their claim for judicial intervention. Restitution arrived first and reliance second. The expectation interest ended at the bottom of the list.

The expectation interest is simply an inappropriate term describing the performance interest. The other two have acquired the title 'interest' probably under the influence of

German law. Whatever is the nature of reliance and restitution, they are certainly not contractual interests. Thus, the interest of a person who made a payment in order to get a house, a car or even a pizza is to get the house, the car or the pizza. Such a person will be greatly surprised to learn that upon contracting to purchase a house, he acquired an interest in getting his payment back (restitution interest). In all probability he is likely to protest that this is not what he wanted. Had he preferred the money to the house he would not have made the contract in the first place. He would need a lot of coaching in an American course on contracts to learn that his interest in getting his payment back ranks higher in the hierarchy than his interest in getting the house . . .

The greatest terminological innovation of Fuller and Perdue and the most inappropriate one, was the invention of the 'expectation' or 'expectancy'. This term . . . was used to describe the normal measure of contractual damages, namely the measure based upon the right to get the promised performance . . . one can hardly conceive of a term that is less appropriate than 'expectancy' or 'expectation'. 'Expectancy' is often used to describe a prospect or a probability of receiving a benefit in the future, *when this possibility is not supported by a legal right* . . . Indeed, the term 'expectation' may be more appropriate in this context, in which the expectation is not based upon a legal right, than in the contractual context, in which the plaintiff has a legal right to receive that which was promised to him.

THE MARGINALISATION OF THE PERFORMANCE INTEREST

The next step in Fuller and Perdue's derogation of the right to performance comes in the process of the ranking of interests, in which the performance interest (now already diminished to a mere 'expectancy') is outclassed by both restitution and reliance. That being accomplished, there comes a question which casts doubt upon the very legitimacy of the right to performance. The subtitle on page 57 of the article reads: 'Why Should the Law Ever Protect the Expectation Interest?' This is followed by a rather detailed discussion in which expectation again does not fare too well. In essence, three explanations are offered . . .

The third and only justification which Fuller and Perdue find for what they term 'expectation' damages lies in the 'difficulties in proving reliance and subjecting it to pecuniary measurement . . . To encourage reliance we must therefore dispense with its proof'. Performance damages, thus, receive an additional blow. They are not justified in their own right. They are merely parasitic and exist because of the difficulties in measuring the 'real' interest, namely reliance.

The argument is most unconvincing. The proof of reliance losses is by no means more difficult than proof of performance (or 'expectation') losses, even if they are to include 'loss of opportunity'. . . . In fact, reliance damages are sometimes awarded on the ground that it is impossible to appraise the performance, or 'loss of bargain', damages. This, of course, is the very opposite of the argument made by Fuller and Perdue.

The difficulties with Fuller and Perdue's reasoning are, however, more fundamental . . . they accept the 'will theory' and the premise that a contractual promise is legally binding. They assume, however, that the question of the remedy is completely divorced from the nature of the right. It is, therefore, open to prefer the reliance measure of damages to that of the performance (in their terminology 'expectation'). The reasoning is, however, most unconvincing. It is, of course, legitimate to examine the grounds for recognizing the binding effect of contracts. . . . However, Fuller and Perdue avoided this question. They accepted the validity of the contractual obligation but erroneously assumed that it entails few consequences as to the remedy.

It is, of course, true that the mere recognition of a specific right does not provide answers to all issues regarding the remedies available for its protection. Thus, the fact that the legal system recognizes the right of ownership does not tell us whether the owner, whose property was misappropriated, will be entitled to restitution *in specie* or merely to damages. The rules on remoteness of damages are similarly not self-evident. It is, however, an unwarranted jump to conclude that the right tells us nothing about the remedy and that rights and remedies raise totally unrelated issues.

It is submitted that the very recognition of a legal right entails some consequences regarding the remedy, one of which relates to the initial point of inquiry. This initial point relates to the value of legal right, at least where such value can be ascertained. The right of recovery may be qualified or subject to exceptions. The initial point is, however, clear.

Thus, suppose that P acquired for $300 shares which are now worth $1000. The shares have been misappropriated by D. In Fuller and Perdue's terminology the $300 represents 'reliance loss' whereas the $1000 represents 'expectation damages'. After all, P never had the $1000. He had shares which he could expect to sell. This expectation, if realised, would yield him $1000. However, the translation of the situation into Fuller and Perdue's terminology merely confuses the issue. The historical expenditure or the reliance interest (in the above example, $300) is irrelevant, except where it serves as evidence of existing value. Recovery is based upon the present value of the shares. The recognition of P's right of property suffices to justify such recovery.

It is clearly legitimate to question the justification of private property. However, once private ownership is recognized, it follows as a matter of course that the owner whose property has been misappropriated will either recover it *in specie* or will get damages reflecting its value. In order to justify this result, there is no need to resort to the 'lost opportunity' explanation (the owner could have brought other shares that might have similarly appreciated in value) or to some other fiction.

Let us now revert to the contract situation. Suppose that in consideration of $300 D undertook to transfer to P, within 6 months, certain shares. After 5 months, when the price of the shares reaches $1000, D reneges. If we assume that the contract was valid so that it vested in P the right to the promised performance, it follows that P would be entitled either to specific performance (the value of which is $1000) or to the substitutionary remedy of damages, which will be based upon the value of the promised performance, namely $1000.

This argument, as well as the analogy to property, is strengthened by the possibility of assignment. In the property example P could sell the shares for $1000. In the contract example he could have assigned his contractual right to receive the shares for a similar amount. In both instances, the measure of recovery ought, therefore, to be similar. To claim that the contract was binding, i.e. that P was entitled to D's performance, and yet that recovery can be confined to P's expenditure ($300), is a contradiction in terms.

Fuller and Perdue feel, however, that the obvious result needs explanation. The superfluous explanation is based upon the lost opportunity theory, which forms part of the reliance loss. Because P entered into contract no. 1 with D, he gave up the possibility of another potential contract (contract no. 2) with a third party (T) which would have yielded him similar gains. The argument is doubly flawed. First, if P's gains from the actual contract (no. 1) with D are not recoverable in their own right as part of his performance (or 'expectation') interest, why do these very gains become recoverable when attributed to another potential contract (contract no. 2)? Is it because they have changed denomination and appear under the guise of reliance? Second, the whole argument is based on circular reasoning. If it is assumed that the entitlement to recover performance (expectation) damages in contract no. 1 derives solely from the lost opportunity (potential contract no. 2), we have to examine the value of this opportunity. This is obviously dependent upon the nature of the entitlement and the ensuing measure of damages in potential contract no. 2. If there is no justification for performance damages (other than lost opportunity) then the value of contract no.2 was not $1000, but a mere $300, unless we assume that the recovery will again be based on lost opportunity (potential contract no. 3) and so *ad infinitum*.

THE VALUE OF THE LEGAL RIGHT AND THE MEASURE OF DAMAGES IN CONTRACT AND TORT

Fuller and Perdue raise the question whether broad adoption in contracts of the so called 'tort principle', namely, the reliance interest, would not 'blur the lines of division separating the different branches of the law'. In their view the breaking of the barriers between the branches of the law of obligations 'would represent a distinct service to legal thinking'.

The basic assumption that there exists, on this specific point, such a barrier between tort and contract damages is, however, erroneous. It is assumed that tort damages look backwards and aim at returning the plaintiff to the *status quo ante* whereas contract damages look forward and strive to put the plaintiff in the position in which he would have been in had the contract been performed. Reliance damages are, thus, akin to the tort principle since they are meant to put the plaintiff in his pre-contract position, whereas performance damages reflect the contract principle.

This analysis is based on a misconception which derives from the failure to adequately distinguish between rights and remedies. It is submitted that the *basic principle as to damages is identical in contract and tort*, though there may be some variations in its application. The principle provides in essence that the purpose of damages is to put the plaintiff, in economic terms, in the position in which he would have been had the wrong (either a tort or breach of contract) not been committed. *The different results reached in tort and contract derive from the fact that they are usually called on to protect different rights*. Where, however, they are invoked to protect the same right, the calculation of damages, which reflect the value of this right, either in tort or in contract, will be similar . . .

THE IMPACT OF FULLER AND PERDUE—TERMINOLOGY AND SUBSTANCE

(a) *Terminological impact*

As already pointed out, the most significant effect of Fuller and Perdue lies in the introduction of new terminology. No student is likely to complete an American course on contracts without reciting 'expectation interest' and 'reliance interest'. In recent years the new terminology has spread to England and to other Commonwealth jurisdictions . . .

(b) *Substantive impact*

. . . Fuller and Perdue did not expressly advocate the curtailment of the protection granted to the performance interest. However, much of the article consists of an attempt to question its justification, to describe it as an 'expectancy' and to suggest its legitimacy depends on reliance. They also hinted at the possibility of limiting recovery to reliance losses in certain cases in which a binding contract has been concluded, notably in situations that are not within the credit system. Professor Atiyah went a step further. He was 'troubled and uncertain about the extent to which executory contracts should be enforced, and the extent to which the expectation damages measure is appropriate . . .' He also considered that 'it would not be surprising if future developments tend to show a still further whittling down of expectation damages'.

Modern law hardly reflects any traces of this approach . . . Notwithstanding *The Reliance Interest* there are no signs of weakening of the performance interest. On the contrary, one of the major trends in modern contract law is the strengthening of the protection accorded to the performance interest. Traditional limitations upon the availability of specific performance and upon the recovery of performance damages have either been removed or severely curtailed . . .

The scope of specific performance has spread beyond real estate cases to many other types of contracts. . . . The law of damages shows similar signs of expanding the protection granted to the performance interest. The fundamental principle under which, so far as money can do it, the injured party should be placed in the same situation as if the contract had been performed, is constantly applied. Furthermore, legal rules that have in the past limited the prospect of obtaining full performance damages seem to lose at least part of their effect . . . Another development which reflects the strengthening of the performance interest relates to the measure of recovery where the defendant renders a defective performance or a performance which is not in line with contract requirements. The cost of curing the defect is usually higher than the difference in market value between the performance as rendered and the value of the performance had it conformed to the terms of the contract. In this type of situation recovery was often confined to the difference in value, if the cost of cure was disproportionate to the difference in value. However, the present tendency is to award the plaintiff the cost of repair even where there is a large disparity between this cost and the difference in value, provided that it is reasonable for the plaintiff to insist on reinstatement. Furthermore, circumstances are conceivable in which the costs of repair are unreasonable while the difference in value is small or even nil. Under the traditional approach, in such a case, the plaintiff might have been left without a remedy. The recent decision of the House of Lords in *Ruxley Electronics Ltd* [p. 1018 below] indicates that these two measures of recovery are not exhaustive, and that damages might be awarded by reference to the fact that the plaintiff's performance interest has been frustrated by the defendant's breach. The court may, thus, be required to appraise an element that has no market price in order to provide an adequate remedy. Needless to say, this development is predicated on the approach that *pacta sunt servanda* and that the plaintiff's performance interest should be respected.

The expansion of the protection afforded to the performance interest is also reflected in the rules relating to non-economic losses. Traditionally, recovery of damages for such losses, resulting from breach of contract, has not been allowed. But this rule is becoming the subject of ever-increasing exceptions . . .

There is a great discrepancy between *The Reliance Interest's* intellectual appeal and its effect on substantive law. The article made a deep impact on academic thinking, upon the language and discourse of contracts and led to the adoption of new terminology, which in the case of 'expectation' was an unhappy development. Its effect on substantive law is at best secondary. The attack upon the performance interest goes against the grain. This interest constitutes the very core of contract law. Its ample protection is likely to be maintained and possibly expanded as long as the essence of contract law as we know it remains.

4. THE PERFORMANCE INTEREST

As Professor Friedmann notes, the courts remain committed to the protection of the claimant's performance interest (to use Professor Friedmann's phrase in preference to the language of the 'expectation' interest employed by Fuller and Perdue). In his article Professor Friedmann argues that 'one of the major trends in modern contract law is the strengthening of the protection afforded to the performance interest'. It is certainly true that the courts' commitment to the protection of the performance interest has been tested in the courts recently but it is suggested that their commitment to the performance interest can be seen to be less than whole-hearted.

It is the case that the starting point for the courts' analysis is a commitment to the protection of the performance interest. This was classically expressed by Parke B in *Robinson* v. *Harman* (1848) 1 Ex 850, 855 when he stated that the

rule of the common law is, that where a party sustains a loss by reason of a breach of contract, he is, so far as money can do it, to be placed in the same situation, with respect to damages, as if the contract had been performed.

This commitment to the performance interest expressed by Parke B has been challenged in the courts recently in two different ways. The first relates to the method chosen by the court to fulfil the performance interest. There are two principal methods. The first is to award the claimant the difference in value between the performance for which he contracted and the performance which he received. This measure is committed to putting the claimant in the financial position which he would have been in had the contract been performed according to its terms (in the sense that the expected increase in his wealth will be protected). The alternative is to award the claimant damages assessed on a 'cost of cure' basis. On this basis, the claimant is given the sum of money needed in order to enable him to obtain the performance for which he contracted. This measure is committed to enabling the claimant to obtain performance itself rather than the economic value of performance (as is the case in the diminution in value measure). In many cases the difference between the two measures is relatively trivial and it does not give rise to litigation. But in some cases the difference can be substantial. One such case is the decision of the House of Lords in *Ruxley Electronics and Construction Ltd* v. *Forsyth* [1996] AC 344, to which we shall shortly turn.

The second issue that has arisen relates to the case in which the claimant has no direct financial interest in the performance of the contract. The classic example is a case in which the claimant enters into a contract under which he agrees to pay for repair work to be done on the property of a third party. What is the measure of the claimant's recovery in the event that the repair work is carried out defectively? Can the party who carried out the work maintain that the claimant is only entitled to nominal damages on the basis that he has suffered no loss as a result of the fact that work on someone else's property has been done defectively? This is the principal issue that arose in our second case, the recent, and extremely difficult, decision of the House of Lords in *Alfred McAlpine Construction Ltd* v. *Panatown Ltd* [2001] 1 AC 518. We shall turn to *Panatown* after examining *Ruxley*.

Ruxley Electronics and Construction Ltd v. Forsyth

[1996] AC 344, House of Lords

The plaintiffs entered into a contract with the defendant under which they agreed to build a swimming pool for the defendant in his garden. It was agreed that the pool would be built to a depth of seven feet six inches. In breach of contract the plaintiffs built the swimming pool to a depth of six feet nine inches. When he eventually discovered this fact the defendant refused to pay the contract price. The plaintiffs sued him for the price. The trial judge held that the defendant was liable to pay the price for the work done on the basis that the plaintiffs had 'substantially performed' their obligations under the contract. The defendant was therefore left to his counterclaim for damages for breach of contract.

At trial, two points were established via expert evidence. The first was that the difference in value between a pool built to a depth of seven feet six inches and one built to a depth of six feet was nil. The second was that the only practicable way to increase the depth was to rebuild the pool at a cost of £21,560. The trial judge also found that the difference in depth did not in any way impair the defendant's use of the pool.

The trial judge refused to award the defendant damages assessed on a cost of cure basis and instead awarded him 'loss of amenity' damages of £2,500. The Court of Appeal allowed the defendant's appeal and held that he was entitled to cost of cure damages of £21,560. The plaintiffs appealed to the House of Lords. The appeal was allowed. It was held that the defendant (the respondent in the appeal) was not entitled to recover damages assessed on a cost of cure basis on the ground that the cost of carrying out the work was out of all proportion to the benefit which he would receive from full performance. There being no challenge by the plaintiffs to the trial judge's award of £2,500 damages for 'loss of amenity', it was held that this fixed the measure of the defendant's recovery.

Lord Jauncey of Tullichettle

Damages are designed to compensate for an established loss and not to provide a gratuitous benefit to the aggrieved party from which it follows that the reasonableness of an award of damages is to be linked directly to the loss sustained. If it is unreasonable in a particular case to award the cost of reinstatement it must be because the loss sustained does not extend to the need to reinstate. A failure to achieve the precise contractual objective does not necessarily result in the loss which is occasioned by a total failure . . .

I take the example suggested during argument by my noble and learned friend, Lord Bridge of Harwich. A man contracts for the building of a house and specifies that one of the lower courses of brick should be blue. The builder uses yellow brick instead. In all other respects the house conforms to the contractual specification. To replace the yellow bricks with blue would involve extensive demolition and reconstruction at a very large cost. It would clearly be unreasonable to award to the owner the cost of reconstructing because his loss was not the necessary cost of reconstruction of his house, which was entirely adequate for its design purpose, but merely the lack of aesthetic pleasure which he might have derived from the sight of blue bricks. Thus in the present appeal the respondent has acquired a perfectly serviceable swimming pool, albeit one lacking the specified depth. His loss is thus not the lack of a useable pool with consequent need to construct a new one. Indeed were he to receive the cost of building a new one and retain the existing one he would have recovered not compensation for loss but a very substantial gratuitous benefit, something which damages are not intended to provide.

What constitutes the aggrieved party's loss is in every case a question of fact and degree. Where the contract breaker has entirely failed to achieve the contractual object-ive it may not be difficult to conclude that the loss is the necessary cost of achieving that objective. Thus if a building is constructed so defectively that it is of no use for its designed purpose the owner may have little difficulty in establishing that his loss is the necessary cost of reconstructing. Furthermore in taking reasonableness into account in determining the extent of loss it is reasonableness in relation to the particular contract and not at large. Accordingly if I contracted for the erection of a folly in my garden which shortly thereafter suffered a total collapse it would be irrelevant to the determination of my loss to argue that the erection of such a folly which contributed nothing to the value of my house was a crazy thing to do. As Oliver J said in *Radford* v. *De Froberville* [1977] 1 WLR 1262, 1270:

> 'If he contracts for the supply of that which he thinks serves his interests—be they commercial, aesthetic or merely eccentric—then if that which is contracted for is not supplied by the other contracting party I do not see why, in principle, he should not be compensated by being provided with the cost of supplying it through someone else or in a different way, subject to the proviso, of course, that he is seeking compensation for a genuine loss and not merely using a technical breach to secure an uncovenanted profit.'

However where the contractual objective has been achieved to a substantial extent the position may be very different.

It was submitted that where the objective of a building contract involved satisfaction of a personal preference the only measure of damages available for a breach involving failure to achieve such satisfaction was the cost of reinstatement. In my view this is not the case. Personal preference may well be a factor in reasonableness and hence in deter-mining what loss has been suffered but it cannot per se be determinative of what that loss is.

My Lords, the trial judge found that it would be unreasonable to incur the cost of demolishing the existing pool and building a new and deeper one. In so doing he impli-citly recognized that the respondent's loss did not extend to the cost of reinstatement. He was, in my view, entirely justified in reaching that conclusion. It therefore follows that the appeal must be allowed.

It only remains to mention two further matters. The appellant argued that the cost of reinstatement should only be allowed as damages where there was shown to be an intention on the part of the aggrieved party to carry out the work. Having already decided that the appeal should be allowed I no longer find it necessary to reach a conclusion on this matter. However I should emphasise that in the normal case the court has no concern with the use to which a plaintiff puts an award of damages for a loss which has been established. Thus irreparable damage to an article as a result of a breach of contract will entitle the owner to recover the value of the article irrespective of whether he intends to replace it with a similar one or to spend the money on something else. Intention, or lack of it, to reinstate can have relevance only to reasonableness and hence to the extent of the loss which has been sustained. Once that loss has been established intention as to the subsequent use of the damages ceases to be relevant.

The second matter relates to the award of £2,500 for loss of amenity made by the trial judge. The respondent argued that he erred in law in making such award. However as the appellant did not challenge it, I find it unnecessary to express any opinion on the matter.

Lord Mustill

My Lords, I agree that this appeal should be allowed for the reasons stated by my noble and learned friends, Lord Jauncey of Tullichettle and Lord Lloyd of Berwick. I add some observations of my own on the award by the trial judge of damages in a sum intermediate between, on the one hand, the full cost of reinstatement, and on the other the amount by which the malperformance has diminished the market value of the property on which the work was done: in this particular case, nil. This is a question of everyday practical importance to householders who have engaged contractors to carry out small building works, and then find (as often happens) that performance has fallen short of what was promised. I think it proper to enter on the question here, although there is no appeal against the award, because the possibility of such a recovery in a suitable case sheds light on the employer's claim that reinstatement is the only proper measure of damage.

The proposition that these two measures of damage represent the only permissible bases of recovery lie at the heart of the employer's case. From this he reasons that there is a presumption in favour of the cost of restitution, since this is the only way in which he can be given what the contractor had promised to provide. Finally, he contends that there is nothing in the facts of the present case to rebut this presumption.

The attraction of this argument is its avoidance of the conclusion that, in a case such as the present, unless the employer can prove that the defects have depreciated the market value of the property the householder can recover nothing at all. This conclusion would be unacceptable to the average householder, and it is unacceptable to me. It is a common feature of small building works performed on residential property that the cost of the work is not fully reflected by an increase in the market value of the house, and that comparatively minor deviations from specification or sound workmanship may have no direct financial effect at all. Yet the householder must surely be entitled to say that he chose to obtain from the builder a promise to produce a particular result because he wanted to make his house more comfortable, more convenient and more conformable to his own particular tastes; not because he had in mind that the work might increase the amount which he would receive if, contrary to expectation, he thought it expedient in the future to exchange his home for cash. To say that in order to escape unscathed the builder has only to show that to the mind of the average onlooker, or the average potential buyer, the results which he has produced seem just as good as those which he had promised would make a part of the promise illusory, and unbalance the bargain. In the valuable analysis contained in *Radford* v. *De Froberville* [1977] 1 WLR 1262, Oliver J emphasised, at p. 1270, that it was for the plaintiff to judge what performance he required in exchange for the price. The court should honour that choice. *Pacta sunt servanda*. If the appellant's argument leads to the conclusion that in all cases like the present the employer is entitled to no more than nominal damages, the average householder would say that there must be something wrong with the law.

In my opinion there would indeed be something wrong if, on the hypothesis that cost of reinstatement and the depreciation in value were the only available measures of recovery, the rejection of the former necessarily entailed the adoption of the latter; and the court might be driven to opt for the cost of reinstatement, absurd as the consequence might often be, simply to escape from the conclusion that the promisor can please himself whether or not to comply with the wishes of the promise which, as embodied in the contract, formed part of the consideration for the price. Having taken on the job the contractor is morally as well as legally obliged to give the employer what he stipulated to obtain, and this obligation ought not to be devalued. In my opinion however the hypothesis is not correct. There are not two alternative measures of damage, at opposite poles, but only one; namely, the loss truly suffered by the promisee. In some cases the loss cannot be fairly measured except by reference to the full cost of repairing the deficiency in performance. In others, and in particular those where the contract is designed to fulfil a purely commercial purpose, the loss will very often consist only of the monetary detriment brought about by the breach of contract. But these remedies are not exhaustive, for the law must cater for those occasions where the value of the promise to the promisee exceeds the financial enhancement of his position which full performance will secure. This excess, often referred to in the literature as the 'consumer surplus' (see for example the valuable discussion by Harris, Ogus and Phillips (1979) 95 *LQR* 581) is usually incapable of precise valuation in terms of money, exactly because it represents a personal, subjective and non-monetary gain. Nevertheless where it exists the law should recognize it and compensate the promisee if the misperformance takes it away. The lurid bathroom tiles, or the grotesque folly instanced in argument by my noble and learned friend, Lord Keith of Kinkel, may be so discordant with general taste that in purely economic terms the builder may be said to do the employer a favour by failing to install them. But this is too narrow and materialistic a view of the transaction. Neither the contractor nor the court has the right to substitute for the employer's individual expectation of performance a criterion derived from what ordinary people would regard as sensible. As my Lords have shown, the test of reasonableness plays a central part in determining the basis of recovery, and will indeed be decisive in a case such as the present when the cost of reinstatement would be wholly disproportionate to the non-monetary loss suffered by the employer. But it would be equally unreasonable to deny all recovery for such a loss. The amount may be small, and since it cannot be quantified directly there may be room for difference of opinion about what it should be. But in several fields the judges are well accustomed to putting figures to intangibles, and I see no reason why the imprecision of the exercise should be a barrier, if that is what fairness demands.

My Lords, once this is recognized the puzzling and paradoxical feature of this case, that it seems to involve a contest of absurdities, simply falls away. There is no need to remedy the injustice of awarding too little, by unjustly awarding far too much. The judgment of the trial judge acknowledges that the employer has suffered a true loss and expresses it in terms of money. Since there is no longer any issue about the amount of the award, as distinct from the principle, I would simply restore his judgment by allowing the appeal.

Lord Lloyd of Berwick [after setting out the facts in considerable detail continued]

Reasonableness

The starting point is *Robinson* v. *Harman*, 1 Exch 850, where Parke B said, at p. 855:

> 'The rule of the common law is, that where a party sustains a loss by reason of a breach of contract, he is, so far as money can do it, to be placed in the same situation, with respect to damages, as if the contract had been performed.'

This does not mean that in every case of breach of contract the plaintiff can obtain the monetary equivalent of specific performance. It is first necessary to ascertain the loss the plaintiff has in fact suffered by reason of the breach. If he has suffered no loss, as sometimes happens, he can recover no more than nominal damages. For the object of damages is always to compensate the plaintiff, not to punish the defendant.

This was never more clearly stated than by Viscount Haldane LC in the first of the two broad principles which he formulated in *British Westinghouse Electric and Manufacturing Co Ltd* v. *Underground Electric Railways* Co *of London Ltd* [1912] AC 673, 689:

> 'The first is that, as far as possible, he who has proved a breach of a bargain to supply what he contracted to get is to be placed, as far as money can do it, in as good a situation as if the contract had been performed. The fundamental basis is thus compensation for pecuniary loss naturally flowing from the breach . . .'

Note that Lord Haldane does not say that the plaintiff is always to be placed in the same situation physically as if the contract had been performed, but in as good a situation financially, so far as money can do it. This necessarily involves measuring the pecuniary loss which the plaintiff has in fact sustained.

In building cases, the pecuniary loss is almost always measured in one of two ways; either the difference in value of the work done or the cost of reinstatement. Where the cost of reinstatement is less than the difference in value, the measure of damages will invariably be the cost of reinstatement. By claiming the difference in value the plaintiff would be failing to take reasonable steps to mitigate his loss. In many ordinary cases, too, where reinstatement presents no special problem, the cost of reinstatement will be the obvious measure of damages, even where there is little or no difference in value, or where the difference in value is hard to assess. This is why it is often said that the cost of reinstatement is the ordinary measure of damages for defective performance under a building contract.

But it is not the only measure of damages. Sometimes it is the other way round. This was first made clear in the celebrated judgment of Cardozo J giving the majority opinion in the Court of Appeals of New York in *Jacob & Youngs* v. *Kent*, 129 NE 889. In that case the building owner specified that the plumbing should be carried out with galvanized piping of 'Reading manufacture'. By an oversight, the builder used piping of a different manufacture. The plaintiff builder sued for the balance of his account. The defendant, as in the instant case, counter-claimed the cost of replacing the pipe work even though it would have meant demolishing a substantial part of the completed structure, at great expense. Cardozo J pointed out, at p. 891, that there is 'no general license to install whatever, in the builder's judgment, may be regarded as 'just as good'. But he went on to consider the measure of damages in the following paragraph:

'In the circumstances of this case, we think the measure of the allowance is not the cost of replacement, which would be great, but the difference in value, which would be either nominal or nothing. . . . It is true that in most cases the cost of replacement is the measure. . . . The owner is entitled to the money which will permit him to complete, unless the cost of completion is grossly and unfairly out of proportion to the good to be attained. When that is true, the measure is the difference in value. Specifications call, let us say, for a foundation built of granite quarried in Vermont. On the completion of the building, the owner learns that through the blunder of a sub-contractor part of the foundation has been built of granite of the same quality quarried in New Hampshire. The measure of allowance is not the cost of reconstruction. There may be omissions of that which could not afterwards be supplied exactly as called for by the contract without taking down the building to its foundations, and at the same time the omission may not affect the value of the building for use or otherwise, except so slightly as to be hardly appreciable.'

Cardozo J's judgment is important, because it establishes two principles, which I believe to be correct, and which are directly relevant to the present case; first, the cost of reinstatement is not the appropriate measure of damages if the expenditure would be out of all proportion to the benefit to be obtained, and, secondly, the appropriate measure of damages in such a case is the difference in value, even though it would result in a nominal award.

The first of these principles is contrary to Staughton LJ's view that the plaintiff is entitled to reinstatement, however expensive, if there is no cheaper way of providing what the contract requires. The second principle is contrary to the whole thrust of Mr Jacob's argument [Mr Jacob was counsel for the defendant] that the judge had no alternative but to award the cost of reinstatement, once it became apparent that the difference in value produced a nil result . . .

[he turned to examine the case-law and continued]

If the court takes the view that it would be unreasonable for the plaintiff to insist on reinstatement, as where, for example, the expense of the work involved would be out of all proportion to the benefit to be obtained, then the plaintiff will be confined to the difference in value. If the judge had assessed the difference in value in the present case at, say, £5,000, I have little doubt that the Court of Appeal would have taken that figure rather than £21,560. The difficulty arises because the judge has, in the light of the expert evidence, assessed the difference in value as nil. But that cannot make reasonable what he has found to be unreasonable.

So I cannot accept that reasonableness is confined to the doctrine of mitigation. It has a wider impact. . . . How then does Mr Jacob seek to support the majority judgment? It can only be, I think, by attacking the judge's finding of fact that the cost of rebuilding the pool would have been out of all proportion to the benefit to be obtained. Mr Jacob argues that this was not an ordinary commercial contract but a contract for a personal preference. . . . I am far from saying that personal preferences are irrelevant when choosing the appropriate measure of damages ('predilections' was the word used by Ackner LJ in *G.W. Atkins Ltd* v. *Scott*, 7 Const LJ 215, 221, adopting the language of Oliver J in *Radford* v. *De Froberville* [1977] 1 WLR 1262). But such cases should not be elevated into a separate category with special rules. If, to take an example mentioned in the course of argument, a landowner wishes to build a folly in his grounds, it is no answer to a claim for defective workmanship that many people might regard the presence of a well built folly as reducing the value of the estate. The eccentric landowner is entitled to his whim, provided the cost of reinstatement is not unreasonable. But the difficulty of that line of argument in the present case is that the judge, as is clear from his judgment, took Mr Forsyth's personal preferences and predilections into account. Nevertheless, he found as a fact that the cost of reinstatement was unreasonable in the circumstances. The Court of Appeal ought not to have disturbed that finding.

Staughton LJ was much influenced by the decision in *Radford v. De Froberville* [1977] 1 WLR 1262. The defendant in that case was in breach of covenant to build a wall between two properties. The plaintiff claimed as damages the cost of building the wall on his own land. The defendant argued that a prefabricated fence would do just as well. Oliver J rejected that argument. He asked himself whether 'the carrying out of the work on his own land [was] a reasonable thing for the plaintiff to do?' He answered that question in favour of the plaintiff, and one can see why. It was a case that fell clearly on the other side of the factual line. It throws no light on the question of fact which the judge had to decide in the present case. Indeed, the question which Oliver J asked himself affords further support for Judge Diamond's approach . . .

Intention

I fully accept that the courts are not normally concerned with what a plaintiff does with his damages. But it does not follow that intention is not relevant to reasonableness, at least in those cases where the plaintiff does not intend to reinstate. Suppose in the present case Mr Forsyth had died, and the action had been continued by his executors. Is it to be supposed that they would be able to recover the cost of reinstatement, even though they intended to put the property on the market without delay?. . . In the present case the judge found as a fact that Mr Forsyth's stated intention of rebuilding the pool would not persist for long after the litigation had been concluded. In these circumstances it would be 'mere pretence' to say that the cost of rebuilding the pool is the loss which he has in fact suffered. . . . Does Mr Forsyth's undertaking to spend any damages which he may receive on rebuilding the pool make any difference? Clearly not. He cannot be allowed to create a loss, which does not exist, in order to punish the defendants for their breach of contract. The basic rule of damages, to which exemplary damages are the only exception, is that they are compensatory not punitive.

Loss of amenity

I turn last to the head of damages under which the judge awarded £2,500. . . . In the Court of Appeal Mr Forsyth sought to increase the award under this head. According to Staughton LJ this led to an interesting argument. But the Court of Appeal did not find it necessary to deal with the point.

Before your Lordships, Mr Jacob abandoned the point altogether, for what Mr McGuire [counsel for the plaintiffs] described as forensic reasons. It undermined the main theme of his argument that since difference in value gave Mr Forsyth nothing by way of damages, he must be entitled to the cost of reinstatement. So Mr Jacob was contending that the judge's award of £2,500 was without precedent in the field of damages, and was fundamentally inconsistent with the decision of this House in *Addis v. Gramophone Co Ltd* [1909] AC 488. For obvious reasons, Mr McGuire did not press the contrary argument.

So your Lordships are placed in something of a difficulty. The House does not have the benefit of the views of the Court of Appeal on the point, and the submissions before your Lordships have been artificially restricted.

Addis v. *Gramophone Co Ltd* established the general rule that in claims for breach of contract, the plaintiff cannot recover damages for his injured feelings. But the rule, like most rules, is subject to exceptions. One of the well established exceptions is when the object of the contract is to afford pleasure, as, for example, where the plaintiff has booked a holiday with a tour operator. If the tour operator is in breach of contract by failing to provide what the contract called for, the plaintiff may recover damages for his disappointment: see *Jarvis* v. *Swans Tours Ltd* [1973] QB 233 and *Jackson* v. *Horizon Holidays Ltd* [1975] 1 WLR 1468.

This was, as I understand it, the principle which Judge Diamond applied in the present case. He took the view that the contract was one 'for the provision of a pleasurable amenity.' In the event, Mr Forsyth's pleasure was not so great as it would have been if the swimming pool had been 7 feet 6 inches deep. This was a view which the judge was entitled to take. If it involves a further inroad on the rule in *Addis* v. *Gramophone Co Ltd* [1909] AC 488, then so be it. But I prefer to regard it as a logical application or adaptation of the existing exception to a new situation. I should, however, add this note of warning. Mr Forsyth was, I think, lucky to have obtained so large an award for his disappointed expectations. But as there was no criticism from any quarter as to the quantum of the award as distinct from the underlying principle, it would not be right for your Lordships to interfere with the judge's figure.

That leaves one last question for consideration. I have expressed agreement with the judge's approach to damages based on loss of amenity on the facts of the present case. But in most cases such an approach would not be available. What is then to be the position where, in the case of a new house, the building does not conform in some minor respect to the contract, as, for example, where there is a difference in level between two rooms, necessitating a step. Suppose there is no measurable difference in value of the complete house, and the cost of reinstatement would be prohibitive. Is there any reason why the court should not award by way of damages for breach of contract some modest sum, not based on difference in value, but solely to compensate the buyer for his disappointed expectations? Is the law of damages so inflexible, as I asked earlier, that it cannot find some middle ground in such a case? I do not give a final answer to that question in the present case. But it may be that it would have afforded an alternative ground for justifying the judge's award of damages. And if the judge had wanted a precedent, he could have found it in Sir David Cairns's judgment in *G.W. Atkins Ltd* v. *Scott*, 7 Const LJ 215, where, it will be remembered, the Court of Appeal upheld the judge's award of £250 for defective tiling. Sir David Cairns said, at p. 221:

> 'There are many circumstances where a judge has nothing but his common sense to guide him in fixing the quantum of damages, for instance, for pain and suffering, for loss of pleasurable activities or for inconvenience of one kind or another.'

If it is accepted that the award of £2,500 should be upheld, then that at once disposes of Mr Jacob's argument that Mr Forsyth is entitled to the cost of reinstatement, because he must be entitled to something. But even if he were entitled to nothing for loss of amenity, or for difference in value, it would not follow as Mr Jacob argued that he was entitled to the cost of reinstatement. There is no escape from the judge's finding of fact that to insist on the cost of reinstatement in the circumstances of the present case was unreasonable.

I would therefore allow the appeal and restore the judgment of Judge Diamond.

Lord Keith of Kinkel concurred and **Lord Bridge of Harwich** delivered a concurring speech.

COMMENTARY

There are a number of points to note here. The first is that the defendant's claim for damages was made by way of a counterclaim. The initial point taken by the defendant by way of defence was that he was not liable to pay at all. The rule invoked by the defendant is often known as the 'entire contracts' rule, although the subject-matter of the rule is generally entire obligations rather than entire contracts. A claimant who has partially performed an obligation which is entire is generally not entitled to payment for his part performance (see *Cutter* v. *Powell* (1795) 6 TR 320, p. 903 above). The defendant is entitled to maintain that his obligation to pay does not arise until the claimant has fully performed his obligation in accordance with the contract. This rule is well-established in the books, although it has been the subject of some criticism on the basis of its tendency to produce harsh results (see, for example, *Sumpter* v. *Hedges* [1898] 1 QB 673, although for a recent defence of the case see B McFarlane and R Stevens, 'In Defence of *Sumpter* v. *Hedges*' (2002) 118 *LQR* 569). The rule is the subject of some exceptions, one of which is known as the doctrine of substantial performance. The effect of this exception is to entitle a claimant who has substantially performed his obligations to recover the contract price subject to the defendant's claim for damages for the loss he has suffered as a result of the claimant's breach of contract. This rule was applied by the trial judge in *Ruxley* so that the plaintiffs were held to be entitled to recover the contract price subject to the defendant's counterclaim for damages. It was the counterclaim that was the subject-matter of the appeal to the Court of Appeal and then to the House of Lords.

The second point to note is a tactical one. Technically, the award of £2,500 loss of amenity damages by the trial judge was not in issue in the House of Lords. The decision that was the subject-matter of the appeal to the House of Lords was the Court of Appeal's decision that the plaintiffs were liable to pay cost of cure damages of £21,560. The plaintiffs did not seek to challenge the decision of the trial judge that they were liable for loss of amenity damages of £2,500. In many ways it was not in their interests to do so. This being the case, the decision in *Ruxley* should not be taken as an authority on the amount of damages payable in a loss of amenity case. Lord Lloyd clearly thought that £2,500 was high but, given that the plaintiffs did not dispute the amount, he did not intervene. The fact that the plaintiffs did not contest their liability to pay £2,500 made their submission to the House of Lords seem more reasonable in that it enabled them to submit that their liability was to pay loss of amenity damages but not cost of cure damages. This tactic pushed counsel for the defendant into an extreme position in which he, in essence, argued that the judge was not entitled to award loss of amenity damages, and that the choice which faced the House of Lords was one between diminution in value (which was zero) and cost of cure. Their Lordships refused to be boxed into a corner in this way and concluded that it was not the case that they had to award the defendant everything or nothing at all. They were attracted by the 'third way' which enabled them to hold that the plaintiffs were liable to pay the defendant damages for the loss of amenity which he suffered in not getting the swimming pool for which he had contracted. Thus, although it was not technically in issue between the parties, the award of damages for loss of amenity played a critical role in the reasoning of their Lordships.

This leads us on to the award of damages for 'loss of amenity'. Lord Mustill and Lord Lloyd adopted different approaches in relation to this aspect of the claim. Lord Lloyd took the narrower approach and linked the claim for loss of amenity damages with a line of cases (to be discussed at pp. 1062–1077 below) where damages were awarded against a defendant who failed to provide the plaintiff with the pleasure that he had promised (for example, a holiday which turned into a disaster as a result of the defendant's breach of contract). Lord Mustill adopted a broader approach which did not confine the recovery of loss of amenity damages to pleasurable amenity cases. His adoption of the concept of the 'consumer surplus' has a broader impact in that it would appear to be applicable in any case in which a consumer puts a higher value on performance than the market value. Particularly important in this regard is Lord Mustill's statement that 'the law must cater for those occasions where the value of the promise to the promisee exceeds the financial enhancement of his position which full performance will secure'. This is an explicit recognition of the fact that parties can and do enter into contracts for reasons other than to make money and that the law ought to reflect that fact in the approach which it adopts to the assessment of damages. There is one further question here and that relates to the nature of an award of damages for 'loss of amenity'. What exactly is it? Is it a species of non-pecuniary loss? What is the 'amenity' which the claimant must have lost? We shall return to this point after examining the speech of Lord Millett in *McAlpine* v. *Panatown* where this issue is explored in greater detail.

The fourth point relates to the reasons which led the House of Lords to conclude that cost of cure damages were unreasonable on the facts of the case. It would appear that the unreasonableness was attributable to a combination of two factors. First, the cost of carrying out the repair work was high; second, the work would not have been of benefit to the defendant. If the defendant had had the pool built to enable him to engage in his favourite hobby of diving into a swimming pool from a diving board then the result of the case would, in all probability, have been different. In such a case the difference in depth would have been material and, indeed, on such facts the defendant might have been able to resist the plaintiffs' action for the price on the ground that they had not substantially performed their obligations under the contract. This balancing exercise is a difficult one. On the one hand the law does not wish to encourage contractors to render a performance which is different from that which they agreed to supply and then deny the existence of a liability to pay damages, other than loss of amenity damages. For this reason, some consumer groups have been critical of the decision in *Ruxley*—it gives to contractors a licence to provide a different performance and then offer a trifling sum by way of loss of amenity damages as compensation. On the other hand, the law does not generally wish to over-compensate claimants by giving them cost of cure damages in cases where they do not appear to have any intention of carrying out the repair work. This in turn raises the difficult question of the role of intention. Their Lordships were unwilling to allow the defendant in *Ruxley* to turn an undertaking to use the damages in effecting the repairs into a passport to a claim for substantial damages. Intention was but one factor to be considered when deciding whether or not it was unreasonable to allow the party claiming damages to recover damages assessed on a cost of cure basis.

However, the courts may be slow to conclude that the award of cost of cure damages is unreasonable. In *McLaren Murdoch & Hamilton Ltd* v. *The Abercromby Motor Group Ltd* 2003 SCLR 323, a Scottish case, Lord Drummond Young held that a pursuer (or claimant) is entitled to recover the cost of making works conform to the contract unless the cost involved is manifestly disproportionate to any benefit that will be obtained from it. Further, he held that, in deciding whether or not there is a sufficient degree of disproportion, the balance between cost and benefit should not be weighed too finely. The reason for this is that the innocent party is the victim of the breach of contract and the party in breach is not in a position to 'place unreasonable obstacles' in the way of the innocent party's recovery of damages.

Three final points can be noted about *Ruxley*. First, the plaintiffs did not profit as a result of their breach of contract. If *Ruxley* had been a case in which the plaintiffs had built a shallow pool in order to make a bigger profit, the defendant might possibly have had a claim to recover the profits made by the plaintiffs as a result of their breach (see the discussion of the 'skimped performance' cases in *Attorney-General* v. *Blake* [2001] 1 AC 268, p. 1113 below, where Lord Nicholls was sceptical of the claim that these cases fell within the scope of the remedy of account of profits). Secondly, *Ruxley* has been the subject of subsequent judicial analysis by the House of Lords in *McAlpine* v. *Panatown*, (p. 1029 below) and in *Farley* v. *Skinner* [2001] UKHL 49 (p. 1063 below) and so we shall have cause to return to the case. The third point relates to the question of whether or not the effect of the decision was to protect the defendant's performance interest. Professor Friedmann (p. 1016 above) suggests that it does. He states that *Ruxley* is 'predicated on the approach that *pacta sunt servanda* and that the [defendant's] performance interest should be protected'. On the other hand, it can be argued that the House of Lords failed adequately to protect the defendant's performance interest. The basis for this argument is that the award did not enable him to obtain the pool for which he contracted. He had to put up with something less and was given an award of damages to reflect the disappointment or loss of amenity which he suffered as a result of not getting the promised contractual performance. In this sense, his full performance interest was not protected. Against this, it can be argued that English law is not committed to ensuring that an innocent party receives the actual performance for which he contracted. This is demonstrated by its reluctance to order a party in breach specifically to perform his contractual obligations (specific performance is discussed in more detail in Chapter 26). It is clear that the defendant in *Ruxley* would not have been granted a specific performance order requiring the plaintiffs to build a pool in accordance with the contractual specifications. Does the fact that a court would have refused to make a specific performance order not suggest that the innocent party's interest is not in actual performance of the contract but in the financial equivalent of performance, which can be measured by the diminution or difference in value? Of course it can be argued that it does not follow from the fact that the innocent party is not entitled to performance from the party in breach that he is not entitled to recover by way of damages the cost of obtaining performance from another party, but the fact that the law is not prepared to commit itself to specific performance as the primary remedy does suggest that its commitment to ensuring that performance (rather than the economic end-result of performance) is achieved is less than whole-hearted. In this sense it has been argued that English law has failed to recognize the value of the right to performance itself rather than the consequences of performance or the economic end-result of performance (see generally B Coote, 'Contract Damages, *Ruxley* and the Performance Interest' [1997] *CLJ* 537).

The question of the extent to which the law protects the performance interest of a claimant was directly in issue in our next case. The case is one of great complexity. It is therefore necessary to set out the factual and legal background to the case in some detail. The speeches of their Lordships deserve to be read in full, notwithstanding the fact that they run to some seventy-four pages of the law reports. The extracts that follow are no more than an outline of the issues at stake in the case.

Alfred McAlpine Construction Ltd v. Panatown Ltd

[2001] 1 AC 518, House of Lords

Panatown entered into a construction contract with Alfred McAlpine for the construction of a new building in Cambridge. The building was to be constructed on land owned by UIPL, a member of the same corporate group ('the Unex group') as Panatown. For tax reasons the contract with McAlpine was made by Panatown rather than UIPL. The Unex group of companies wished to avoid payment of VAT on the construction works and this made it necessary for the contract to be concluded by Panatown rather than UIPL. The sum of £7.5 million was paid to Panatown by another member of the Unex group of companies in late March 1989. The exact basis on which the money was paid was the subject of a dispute but it was found by Judge Thornton QC that, in return for the payment, Panatown accepted an obligation to procure the construction of the development works. A construction contract for the works was entered into between Panatown and McAlpine on 2 November 1989. A number of related transactions were concluded on the same day, one of which was a duty of care deed ('DCD') entered into between McAlpine and UIPL. The deed consisted of a short, four-page document under which McAlpine warranted, among other things, that it had and would continue to exercise all reasonable skill, care, and attention; that it owed a duty of care to UIPL; that UIPL was entitled to rely on McAlpine's professional skill and judgment in respect of certain matters and that McAlpine would use all reasonable endeavours to maintain in force professional indemnity insurance. The deed also contained a clause which entitled UIPL to assign the benefit of the deed to its successors in title or to any other party with the consent of McAlpine, which consent was not to be unreasonably withheld.

The project proved to be a disaster. Panatown alleged that there were substantial defects in the works and, by the time of the hearing before the House of Lords, they estimated the cost of repairs at £40 million (this sum included damages for the delay in completion of the works and the claim for the consequences of delay constituted a significant part of the claim). In these circumstances two possible courses of action were open to the Unex group; either UIPL could bring proceedings against McAlpine under the duty of care deed or Panatown could sue McAlpine under the construction contract. For essentially procedural reasons it was decided within the Unex group of companies that Panatown would bring the claim against McAlpine.

Panatown issued a notice of arbitration on 8 July 1992. McAlpine took, by way of defence, the point that Panatown had not suffered any loss as a result of any breach of contract it had committed. The arbitrator ordered the following preliminary issue to be tried:

'Do Panatown's claims for (a) liquidated damages for delay, (b) unliquidated damages for delay and failure to complete and (c) damages for defective and/or incomplete work (or any and if so which of them) fail (insofar as they relate to greater than nominal damages) because Panatown is not the owner of the property?'

The arbitrator answered these three questions in the negative. McAlpine then sought to set aside the arbitrator's award on the ground that it contained errors of law. Judge Thornton held that Panatown was not entitled to recover substantial damages from McAlpine on any of the bases identified by the arbitrator but he did not dismiss the claim. Rather, he remitted it to the arbitrator because he was able to identify three possible bases upon which Panatown's claim for substantial damages might succeed, none of which had been answered by the arbitrator. Meanwhile Panatown appealed to the Court of Appeal who held that Panatown was entitled in principle to recover substantial damages in relation to all three claims. McAlpine then appealed to the House of Lords.

Before the House of Lords Panatown sought to recover damages on two grounds. First, it claimed that it was entitled to recover damages in respect of the loss suffered by a third party, namely UIPL (being the owner of the land). In advancing its claim on this basis Panatown relied upon the decision of the House of Lords in *Linden Gardens Trust Ltd* v. *Lenesta Sludge Disposals Ltd* [1994] 1 AC 85 and the decision of the Court of Appeal in *Darlington Borough Council* v. *Wiltshier Northern Ltd* [1995] 1 WLR 68. Secondly, it submitted that it had suffered a loss which entitled it to recover substantial damages, notwithstanding the fact that it was not any worse off financially as a result of the breach. In relation to the latter claim Panatown relied upon what has become known as the 'broad ground' which can be traced back to the speech of Lord Griffiths in *Linden Gardens*. The critical passage from the speech of Lord Griffiths was the following (at pp. 96–97):

'I cannot accept that in a contract of this nature, namely for work, labour and the supply of materials, the recovery of more than nominal damages for breach of contract is dependent upon the plaintiff having a proprietary interest in the subject matter of the contract at the date of breach. In everyday life contracts for work and labour are constantly being placed by those who have no proprietary interest in the subject matter of the contract. To take a common example, the matrimonial home is owned by the wife and the couple's remaining assets are owned by the husband and he is the sole earner. The house requires a new roof and the husband places a contract with a builder to carry out the work. The husband is not acting as agent for his wife, he makes the contract as principal because only he can pay for it. The builder fails to replace the roof properly and the husband has to call in and pay another builder to complete the work. Is it to be said that the husband has suffered no damage because he does not own the property? Such a result would in my view be absurd and the answer is that the husband has suffered loss because he did not receive the bargain for which he had contracted with the first builder and the measure of damages is the cost of securing the performance of that bargain by completing the roof repairs properly by the second builder.'

The House of Lords allowed McAlpine's appeal and held, by a majority of 3–2 (Lord Goff and Lord Millett dissenting), that Panatown was not entitled to recover substantial damages on either of the two grounds advanced by it. It was held that Panatown could not recover substantial damages in respect of the loss suffered by UIPL because UIPL had its own right of action against McAlpine under the duty of care deed and there was therefore no justification for holding that Panatown was entitled to recover damages on UIPL's behalf. Secondly, the majority held that Panatown could not recover substantial damages under Lord Griffiths' broad ground because it had not in fact incurred any expenditure in making good the defects in the construction works (or was found to have had no intention of carrying out such works) and, given that UIPL had its own claim under the duty of care deed, there was no loss to Panatown because its interest in performance lay in the provision of a service to UIPL and that interest was protected by the direct right of action given to UIPL by the duty of care deed. There was therefore no need to confer on Panatown an additional right to recover substantial damages, given that the effect of recognizing such a claim would be to add to the complexity of the case by opening up potential problems such as double liability.

The extracts that follow focus largely upon the second ground. The first ground will be examined in more detail in Chapter 27 in the context of a discussion of the extent to which English law allows a contracting party to sue and recover damages in respect of a loss suffered by a third party (see pp. 1195–1202 below).

Lord Clyde
My Lords, Panatown employed McAlpine to build a building on land owned by UIPL. The work was defective. Panatown has sought to terminate the contract on the ground of McAlpine's failure in performance. Panatown has suffered no loss. UIPL owns a defective building, which requires a significant expenditure for its repair, and has been unable for a considerable period to put the building to a profitable use. Panatown now seeks to recover, by way of an arbitration, from McAlpine the loss which UIPL has suffered. The appeal thus concerns the circumstances in which the employer in a contract of services may claim from the contractor on the ground of breach of contract damages in respect of a loss which has been suffered by a third party.

I find no reason to question the general principle that a plaintiff may only recover damages for a loss which he has himself suffered. But there are exceptions to that principle. One is where the one party expressly enters a contract as agent or trustee for another. The existence of this category of case was recognized in *Woodar Investment Development Ltd* v. *Wimpey Construction UK Ltd* [1980] 1 WLR 277. In such a case the contracting party may be entitled to recover damages for all the loss which his principal has suffered. But a solution along the lines of a formal agency is not available in the present case. Although the duty of care deed expressly records that Panatown was acting on behalf of the building owner, that is UIPL, any relationship of agency was disowned by the respondents. The precise analysis of the relationships which may have existed between the companies associated with the employer remains obscure. The issue in the case has required to be resolved against the unsatisfactory background of that obscurity.

The exception which is invoked by the respondents, Panatown, is the one which was identified in *The Albazero* [1977] AC 774 . . .

[he considered whether or not the claim could be brought within the principle laid down in *The Albazero* (on which see further p. 1202 below). He concluded that it could not and continued]

I turn accordingly to what was referred to in the argument as the broader ground. But the label requires more careful definition. . . . What it proposes is that the innocent party to the contract should recover damages for himself as a compensation for what is seen to be his own loss. In this context no question of accounting to anyone else arises. This approach however seems to me to have been developed into two formulations.

The first formulation, and the seeds of the second, are found in the speech of Lord Griffiths in the *St Martins* case [1994] 1 AC 85, 96. At the outset his Lordship expressed the opinion that Corporation, faced with a breach by McAlpine of their contractual duty to perform the contract with sound materials and with all reasonable skill and care, would be entitled to recover from McAlpine the cost of remedying the defect in the work as the normal measure of damages. He then dealt with two possible objections. First, it should not matter that the work was not being done on property owned by Corporation. Where a husband instructs repairs to the roof of the matrimonial home it cannot be said that he has not suffered damage because he did not own the property. He suffers the damage measured by the cost of a proper completion of the repair:

> 'In cases such as the present the person who places the contract has suffered financial loss because he has to spend money to give him the benefit of the bargain which the defendant had promised but failed to deliver.' (See p. 97.)

The second objection, that Corporation had in fact been reimbursed for the cost of the repairs was answered by the consideration that the person who actually pays for the repairs is of no concern to the party who broke the contract. But Lord Griffiths added, at p. 97:

> 'The court will of course wish to be satisfied that the repairs have been or are likely to be carried out but if they are carried out the cost of doing them must fall upon the defendant who broke his contract.'

In the first formulation this approach can be seen as identifying a loss upon the innocent party who requires to instruct the remedial work. That loss is, or may be measured by, the cost of the repair. The essential for this formulation appears to be that the repair work is to be, or at least is likely to be, carried out. This consideration does not appear to be simply relevant to the reasonableness of allowing the damages to be measured by the cost of repair. It is an essential condition for the application of the approach, so as to establish a loss on the part of the plaintiff. Thus far the approach appears to be consistent with principle, and in particular with the principle of privity. It can cover the case where A contracts with B to pay a sum of money to C and B fails to do so. The loss to A is in the necessity to find other funds to pay to C and provided that he is going to pay C, or indeed has done so, he should be able to recover the sum by way of damages for breach of contract from B. If it was evident that A had no intention to pay C, having perhaps changed his mind, then he would not be able to recover the amount from B because he would have sustained no loss, and his damages would at best be nominal.

But there can also be found in Lord Griffiths's speech the idea that the loss is not just constituted by the failure in performance but indeed consists in that failure. This is the 'second formulation'. In relation to the suggestion that the husband who instructs repair work to the roof of his wife's house and has to pay for another builder to make good the faulty repair work has sustained no damage Lord Griffiths observed, at p. 97:

> 'Such a result would in my view be absurd and the answer is that the husband has suffered loss because he did not receive the bargain for which he had contracted with the first builder and the measure of damages is the cost of securing the performance of that bargain by completing the roof repairs properly by the second builder.'

That is to say that the fact that the innocent party did not receive the bargain for which he contracted is itself a loss. As Steyn LJ put it in *Darlington Borough Council* v. *Wiltshier Northern Ltd* [1995] 1 WLR 68, 80: 'He suffers a loss of bargain or of expectation interest'. In this more radical formulation it does not matter whether the repairs are or are not carried out, and indeed in the *Darlington* case that qualification is seen as unnecessary. In that respect the disposal of the damages is treated as *res inter alios acta*.[1] Nevertheless on this approach the intention to repair may cast light on the reasonableness of the measure of damages adopted. In order to follow through this aspect of the second formulation in Lord Griffiths's speech it would be necessary to understand his references to the carrying out of the repairs to be relevant only to that consideration.

I find some difficulty in adopting the second formulation as a sound way forward. First, if the loss is the disappointment at there not being provided what was contracted for, it seems to me difficult to measure that loss by consideration of the cost of repair. A more apt assessment of the compensation for the loss of what was expected should rather be the difference in value between what was contracted for and what was supplied. Secondly, the loss constituted by the supposed disappointment may well not include all the loss which the breach of contract has caused. It may not be able to embrace consequential losses, or losses falling within the second head of *Hadley* v. *Baxendale* 9 Exch 341. The inability of the wife to let one of the rooms in the house caused by the inadequacy of the repair, does not seem readily to be something for which the husband could claim as his loss. Thirdly, there is no obligation on the successful plaintiff to account to anyone who may have sustained actual loss as a result of the faulty performance. Some further mechanism would then be required for the court to achieve the proper disposal of the monies awarded to avoid a double jeopardy. Alternatively, in order to achieve an effective solution, it would seem to be necessary to add an obligation to account on the part of the person recovering the damages. But once that step is taken the approach begins to approximate to *The Albazero* exception. Fourthly, the 'loss' constituted by a breach of contract has usually been recognized as calling for an award of nominal damages, not substantial damages.

The loss of an expectation which is here referred to seems to me to be coming very close to a way of describing a breach of contract. A breach of contract may cause a loss, but is not in itself a loss in any meaningful sense. When one refers to a loss in the context of a breach of contract, one is in my view referring to the incidence of some personal or patrimonial damage. A loss of expectation might be a loss in the proper sense if damages were awarded for the distress or inconvenience caused by the disappointment. Professor

---

[1] A thing done among strangers.

Coote ('Contract Damages, *Ruxley* and the Performance Interest' [1997] *CLJ* 537) draws a distinction between benefits in law, that is bargained-for contractual rights, and benefits in fact, that is the enjoyment of the fruits of performance. Certainly the former may constitute an asset with a commercial value. But while frustration may destroy the rights altogether so that the contract is no longer enforceable, a failure in the obligation to perform does not destroy the asset. On the contrary it remains as the necessary legal basis for a remedy. A failure in performance of a contractual obligation does not entail a loss of the bargained-for contractual rights. Those rights remain so as to enable performance of the contract to be enforced, as by an order for specific performance. If one party to a contract repudiates it and that repudiation is accepted, then, to quote Lord Porter in *Heyman* v. *Darwins Ltd* [1942] AC 356, 399, 'By that acceptance he is discharged from further performance and may bring an action for damages, but the contract itself is not rescinded'. The primary obligations under the contract may come to an end, but secondary obligations then arise, among them being the obligation to compensate the innocent party. The original rights may not then be enforced. But a consequential right arises in the innocent party to obtain a remedy from the party who repudiated the contract for his failure in performance.

Both of these two formulations seek to remedy the problem of the legal black hole. At the heart of the problem is the doctrine of privity of contract which excludes the ready development of a solution along the lines of a *jus quaesitum tertio*[2] . . .

It seems to me that a more realistic and practical solution is to permit the contracting party to recover damages for the loss which he and a third party has suffered, being duly accountable to them in respect of their actual loss, than to construct a theoretical loss in law on the part of the contracting party, for which he may be under no duty to account to anyone since it is to be seen as his own loss. The solution is required where the law will not tolerate a loss caused by a breach of contract to go uncompensated through an absence of privity between the party suffering the loss and the party causing it. In such a case, to avoid the legal black hole, the law will deem the innocent party to be claiming on behalf of himself and any others who have suffered loss. It does not matter that he is not the owner of the property affected, nor that he has not himself suffered any economic loss. He sues for all the loss which has been sustained and is accountable to the others to the extent of their particular losses. While it may be that there is no necessary right in the third party to compel the innocent employer to sue the contractor, in the many cases of the domestic or familial situation that consideration should not be a realistic problem. In the commercial field, in relation to the interests of such persons as remoter future proprietors who are not related to the original employer, it may be that a solution by way of collateral warranty would still be required. If there is an anxiety lest the exception would permit an employer to receive excessive damages, that should be set at rest by the recognition of the basic requirement for reasonableness which underlies the quantification of an award of damages.

The problem which has arisen in the present case is one which is most likely to arise in the context of the domestic affairs of a family group or the commercial affairs of a group of companies. How the members of such a group choose to arrange their own affairs among themselves should not be a matter of necessary concern to a third party who has undertaken to one of their number to perform services in which they all have

---

[2] Right accruing to a third party.

some interest. It should not be a ground of escaping liability that the party who instructed the work should not be the one who sustained the loss or all of the loss which in whole or part has fallen on another member or members of the group. But the resolution of the problem in any particular case has to be reached in light of its own circumstances. In the present case the decision that Panatown should be the employer under the building contract although another company in the group owned the land was made in order to minimise charges of VAT. No doubt thought was given as to the mechanics to be adopted for the building project in order to achieve the course most advantageous to the group. Where for its own purposes a group of companies decides which of its members is to be the contracting party in a project which is of concern and interest to the whole group I should be reluctant to refuse an entitlement to sue on the contract on the ground simply that the member who entered the contract was not the party who suffered the loss on a breach of the contract. But whether such an entitlement is to be admitted must depend upon the arrangements which the group and its members have decided to make both among themselves and with the other party to the contract. In the present case there was a plain and deliberate course adopted whereby the company with the potential risk of loss was given a distinct entitlement directly to sue the contractor and the professional advisers. In the light of such a clear and deliberate course I do not consider that an exception can be admitted to the general rule that substantial damages can only be claimed by a party who has suffered substantial loss.

I agree that the appeal should be allowed.

Lord Goff of Chieveley [dissenting]
I wish to state that I find persuasive the reasoning and conclusion expressed by Lord Griffiths in his opinion in the *St Martins case* [1994] 1 AC 85 that the employer under a building contract may in principle recover substantial damages from the building contractor, because he has not received the performance which he was entitled to receive from the contractor under the contract, notwithstanding that the property in the building site was vested in a third party. The example given by Lord Griffiths of a husband contracting for repairs to the matrimonial home which is owned by his wife is most telling. It is not difficult to imagine other examples, not only within the family, but also, for example, where work is done for charitable purposes—as where a wealthy man who lives in a village decides to carry out at his own expense major repairs to, or renovation or even reconstruction of, the village hall, and himself enters into a contract with a local builder to carry out the work to the existing building which belongs to another, for example to trustees, or to the parish council. Nobody in such circumstances would imagine that there could be any legal obstacle in the way of the charitable donor enforcing the contract against the builder by recovering damages from him if he failed to perform his obligations under the building contract, for example because his work failed to comply with the contract specification.

At this stage I find it necessary to return to the opinion of Lord Griffiths in the *St Martins* case. In the passage from his opinion . . . he gave the example of a husband placing a contract with a builder for the replacement of the roof of the matrimonial home which belonged to his wife. The work proved to be defective. Lord Griffiths expressed the opinion that, in such a case, it would be absurd to say that the husband has suffered no damage because he does not own the property. I wish now to draw attention to the fact that, in his statement of the facts of his example, Lord Griffiths included the fact that the husband had to call in and pay another builder to complete the work. It might perhaps be thought that Lord Griffiths regarded that fact as critical to the husband's cause of action against the builder, on the basis that the husband only has such a cause of action in respect of defective work on another person's property if he himself has actually sustained financial loss, in this example by having paid the second builder. In my opinion, however, such a conclusion is not justified on a fair reading of Lord Griffiths's opinion. This is because he stated the answer to be that

> 'the husband has suffered loss because he did not receive the bargain for which he had contracted with the first builder and the measure of damages is the cost of securing the performance of that bargain by completing the roof repairs properly by the second builder.'

It is plain, therefore, that the payment to the second builder was not regarded by Lord Griffiths as essential to the husband's cause of action.

The point can perhaps be made more clearly by taking a different example, of the wealthy philanthropist who contracts for work to be done to the village hall. The work is defective; and the trustees who own the hall suggest that he should recover damages from the builder and hand the damages over to them, and they will then instruct another builder, well known to them, who, they are confident, will do the work well. The philanthropist agrees, and starts an action against the first builder. Is it really to be suggested that his action will fail, because he does not own the hall, and because he has not incurred the expense of himself employing another builder to do the remedial work? Echoing the words of Lord Griffiths, I regard such a conclusion as absurd. The philanthropist's cause of action does not depend on his having actually incurred financial expense; as Lord Griffiths said of the husband in his example, he 'has suffered loss because he did not receive the bargain for which he had contracted with the first builder' . . .

[Lord Goff cited a number of academic writings and examined the case-law, including the judgment of Oliver J in *Radford* v. *De Froberville* [1977] 1 WLR 1262 and the decision of the House of Lords in *Ruxley Electronics and Construction Ltd* v. *Forsyth* [1996] AC 344 and continued]

I do not regard Lord Griffiths's broader ground as a departure from existing authority, but as a reaffirmation of existing legal principle. Indeed, I know of no authority which stands in its way. On the contrary, there have been statements in the cases which provide support for his view. Thus in *Darlington Borough Council* v. *Wiltshier Northern Ltd* [1995] 1 WLR 68, 80, Steyn LJ described Lord Griffiths's broader ground as based on classic contractual theory, a statement with which I respectfully agree. Moreover, Lord Griffiths's reasoning was foreshadowed in the opinions of members of the Appellate Committee in *Woodar Investment Development Ltd* v. *Wimpey Construction UK Ltd* [1980] 1 WLR 277; see especially the opinion of Lord Keith of Kinkel, at pp. 297–298, and in addition the more tentative statements of Lord Salmon, at p. 291, and Lord Scarman, at pp. 300–301. Furthermore, as I have just indicated, full recognition of the importance of the performance interest will open the way to principled solution of other well-known problems in the law of contract, notably those relating to package holidays which are booked by one person for the benefit not only of himself but of others, normally members of his family (as to which see *Jackson* v. *Horizon Holidays Ltd* [1975] 1 WLR 1468[3]), and other cases of a similar kind referred to by Lord Wilberforce in his opinion in the *Woodar Investment* case [1980] 1 WLR 277, 283[4]—cases of an everyday kind which are calling out for a sensible solution on a principled basis. Even if it is not thought, as I think, that the solution which I prefer is in accordance with existing principle, nevertheless it is surely within the scope of the type of development of the common law which, especially in the law of obligations, is habitually undertaken by appellate judges as part of their ordinary judicial function . . .

The present case provides, in my opinion, a classic example of a case which falls properly within the judicial province. I, for my part, have therefore no doubt that it is desirable, indeed essential, that the problem in the present case should be the subject of judicial solution by providing proper recognition of the plaintiff 's interest in the performance of the contractual obligations which are owed to him . . .

The DCD

I now turn to the second issue in the case, which relates to the possible impact of the DCD on Panatown's remedy against McAlpine in damages.

It was the submission of McAlpine that the existence of the building owner's remedy under the DCD had the effect of precluding Panatown from recovering damages from McAlpine under the building contract. I have to say that this is, on its face, a remarkable submission; it is a strange conclusion indeed that the effect of providing a subsidiary remedy for the owner of the land (UIPL), on a restricted basis (breach of a duty of care), is that the building employer, who has furnished the consideration for the building, is excluded from pursuing his remedy in damages under the main contract, which makes elaborate provision, under a standard form specially adapted for this particular develop-ment, for the terms upon which the contractor has agreed to design and construct the buildings in question.

[he considered *The Albazero* where the fact that the third party has his own claim prevents the contracting party from recovering damages on behalf of the third party and continued]

This reasoning has, however, no application to Lord Griffiths's broader ground, under which the employer is seeking to recover damages for his own account in respect of his own loss, i.e. the damage to his interest in the performance of the building contract to which he, as employer, is party and under which he has contracted to pay for the build-ing. The mere fact that the building contractor, McAlpine, has entered into a separate contract in different terms with another party with regard to possible defects in the building which is the subject of the building contract cannot of itself detract from its obligations to the employer under the building contract itself. In other words, it is plain that the exception identified by Lord Diplock in *The Albazero* [1977] AC 774 is confined to the circumstances of the special rule in *Dunlop* v. *Lambert* as formulated by him. There is no basis for extending it to the circumstances of the present case.

For the reasons I have given, I would dismiss McAlpine's appeal from the decision of the Court of Appeal.

---

[3] The case is extracted below at p. 1196.   [4] The case is extracted below at p. 1199.

Lord Jauncey of Tullichettle

The greater part of Lord Griffiths's reasoning was directed to reject the proposition that entitlement to more than nominal damages was dependent upon the plaintiff having a proprietary interest in the subject matter. His examples predicated that the husband/ employer required to pay for repairs rendered necessary by the breach. He did not require to address the situation where, as here, Panatown has neither spent money in entering into the contract nor intends to do so in remedying the breach and has there- fore suffered no loss thereby. Had he had to do so I very much doubt whether he would have expressed the same views in relation thereto.

Since writing this speech, I have had the advantage of reading in draft the speech of my noble and learned friend, Lord Goff of Chieveley. I respectfully agree with his rejection of the proposition that the employer under a building contract is unable to recover substantial damages for breach of the contract if the work in question is to be performed on land or buildings which are not his property. In such a case the employer's right to substantial damages will, in my view, depend upon whether he has made good or intends to make good the effects of the breach. . . . This produces a sensible result and avoids the recovery of an 'uncovenanted' profit by an employer who does not intend to take steps to remedy the breach.

However, there is a further matter to be considered in this case, namely the DCD in favour of UIPL. This, in my view, is equally relevant to the broader as to the narrow ground. The former as does the latter seeks to find a rational way of avoiding the 'black hole'. What is the justification for allowing A to recover from B as his own a loss which is truly that of C when C has his own remedy against B? I would submit none. . . . I therefore consider that Panatown is not entitled to recover under [the] broader ground not only because they have suffered no financial loss but also because UIPL have a direct right of action against McAlpine under the DCD. As I have come to the conclusion that neither the narrow nor the broader ground is applicable to the facts of this case I would allow the appeal.

Lord Browne-Wilkinson

In my judgment the direct cause of action which UIPL has under the DCD is fatal to any claim to substantial damages made by Panatown against McAlpine based on the narrower ground . . .

I will assume that the broader ground is sound in law and that in the ordinary case where the third party (C) has no direct cause of action against the building contractor (B) A can recover damages from B on the broader ground. Even on that assumption, in my judgment Panatown has no right to substantial damages in this case because UIPL (the owner of the land) has a direct cause of action under the DCD.

The essential feature of the broader ground is that the contracting party A, although not himself suffering the physical or pecuniary damage sustained by the third party C, has suffered his own damage being the loss of his performance interest, i.e. the failure to provide C with the benefit that B had contracted for C to receive. In my judgment it follows that the critical factor is to determine what interest A had in the provision of the service for the third party C. If, as in the present case, the whole contractual scheme was designed, inter alia, to give UPIL and its successors a legal remedy against McAlpine for failure to perform the building contract with due care, I cannot see that Panatown has suffered any damage to its performance interests: subject to any defence based on limitation of actions, the physical and pecuniary damage suffered by UPIL can be redressed by UPIL exercising its own cause of action against McAlpine. It is not clear to me why this has not occurred in the present case: but, subject to questions of limitation which were not explored, there is no reason even now why UPIL should not be bringing the proceedings against McAlpine. The fact that the DCD may have been primarily directed to ensuring that UPIL's successors in title should enjoy a remedy in tort against McAlpine is nothing to the point: the contractual provisions were directed to ensuring that UPIL and its successors in title did have the legal right to sue McAlpine direct. So long as UPIL enjoys this right Panatown has suffered no failure to satisfy its performance interest.

The theoretical objection to giving the contracting party A substantial damages for breach of the contract by B for failing to provide C with a benefit which C itself can enforce against B is further demonstrated by great practical difficulties which such a view would entail. Let me illustrate this by postulating a case where, before the breach occurred, UPIL had with consent assigned the benefit of the DCD to a purchaser of the site, X. What if Panatown itself was entitled to, and did, sue for and recover damages from McAlpine? Presumably McAlpine could not in addition be liable to X for breach of the DCD: yet Panatown would not be liable to account to X for the damages it had recovered from McAlpine. The result would therefore be another piece of legal nonsense: the party who had suffered real, tangible damage, X, could recover nothing but Panatown which had suffered no real loss could recover damages. Again, suppose that X agrees with McAlpine certain variations of McAlpine's liability under the building contract. What rights would Panatown then have against McAlpine? The Law Commission in its Report, Privity of Contract: Contracts for the Benefit of Third Parties (1996) (Law Com No 242), considered at length questions like these (see in particular paragraphs 11.14, 11.21 and 11.22) and many other problems such as set-off and counter-claims. The Law Commission recommended that in certain defined circumstances third parties should be entitled to enforce the contract. But in the draft Bill annexed to the Report and in the Act of Parliament which enacted the recommendations, the Contracts (Rights of Third Parties) Act 1999, specific statutory provisions were included to deal with the difficulties arising. Although both the Law Commission's Report (paragraphs 5.10 and 5.11) and sections 4 and 6(1) of the Act make it clear that the Act is not intended to discourage the courts from developing the rights of third parties when it is appropriate to do so, in my judgment there is little inducement in a case such as the present where a third party has himself the right to enforce the contract against the contract breaker, to extend the law so as to give both the promisee and the third party concurrent rights of enforcement.

For these reasons I would allow the appeal.

Lord Millett [dissenting]
My Lords, Lord Griffiths was not proposing to depart from the general rule that a plaintiff can only recover compensatory damages for breach of contract in respect of a loss which he has himself sustained. He was insisting that, in certain kinds of contract at least, the right to performance has a value which is capable of being measured by the cost of obtaining it from a third party . . .

[he considered the academic literature in which Lord Griffiths' approach was analysed and continued]

To my mind the most significant feature of the academic literature is that no one has suggested that the adoption of the broad ground would have any adverse consequences on commercial arrangements. Nor, despite every incentive to do so, has McAlpine been able to suggest a situation in which it would cause difficulties or defeat the commercial expectations of the parties. In my view it would help to rationalise the law and provide a sound basis for decisions like *Ruxley Electronics and Construction Ltd* v. *Forsyth* [1996] AC 344 and *Jackson* v. *Horizon Holidays Ltd* [1975] 1 WLR 1468. If it is adopted, it will be for future consideration whether it would provide the better solution in cases such as *St Martins* also.

In the *Ruxley* case your Lordships' House refused to allow the full costs of reinstatement on the well-recognized ground that reinstatement would be an unreasonable course to take. But it was not constrained to withhold substantial damages on the ground that the value of the property was unaffected by the breach. It expressly rejected the view that these were the only two possible measures of damage in a building case. It awarded an intermediate sum for 'loss of amenity'. The evidence, however, showed that, viewed objectively, there was no loss of amenity either. The amenity in question was entirely subjective to the plaintiff; and its loss could equally well, and perhaps more accurately, be described as a defeated expectation.

In *Woodar Investment Development Ltd* v. *Wimpey Construction UK Ltd* [1980] 1 WLR 277 Lord Wilberforce was prepared to support the *Jackson* case [1975] 1 WLR 1468 either as a broad decision on the measure of damages or as an example of a type of contract calling for special treatment. Other examples which he instanced were persons contracting for family holidays, ordering meals in restaurants for a party, or hiring a taxi for a group. He observed that there are many situations of daily life which do not fit neatly into conceptual analysis but which require some flexibility in the law of contract.

It must be wrong to adopt a Procrustean approach which leaves parties without a remedy for breach of contract because their arrangements do not fit neatly into some precast contractual formula. When such arrangements have been freely entered into and are of an everyday character or are commercially advantageous to the parties, it is surely time to re-examine the position.

This is the product of the narrow accountants' balance sheet quantification of loss which measures the loss suffered by the promisee by the diminution in his overall financial position resulting from the breach. One of the consequences of this approach is to produce an artificial distinction between a contract for the supply of goods to a third party and a contract for the supply of services to a third party. A man who buys a car for his wife is entitled to substantial damages if an inferior car is supplied, on the assumption (not necessarily true) that the property in the car is intended to vest momentarily in him before being transferred to his wife, whereas a man who orders his wife's car to be repaired is entitled to nominal damages only if the work is imperfectly carried out. This is surely indefensible; the reality of the matter is that in both cases the man is willing to undertake a contractual liability in order to be able to provide a benefit to his wife.

The idea that a contracting party is entitled to damages measured by the value of his own defeated interest in having the contract performed was not new in 1994. A strong case for its adoption in the case of consumer contracts was made in an important article 'Contract Remedies and the Consumer Surplus' (1979) 95 *LQR* 581, in which the authors explained that this would make a significant difference only in a minority of cases. As I shall show, the language of defeated expectation has been employed in the context of building contracts, at least in ordinary two-party cases like *Ruxley*, since the 19th century. As for three-party cases like the present, Lord Keith adverted to it as a possible solution in the *Woodar* case [1980] 1 WLR 277, and in the same case both Lord Salmon and Lord Scarman expressed the view that the question required consideration by the House. Lord Scarman said, at pp. 300–301:

'Likewise, I believe it open to the House to declare that, in the absence of evidence to show that he has suffered no loss, A, who has contracted for a payment to be made to C, may rely on the fact that he required the payment to be made as prima facie evidence that the promise for which he contracted was a benefit to him and that the measure of his loss in the event of non-payment is the benefit which he intended for C but which has not been received. Whatever the reason, he must have desired the payment to be made to C and he must have been relying on B to make it. If B fails to make the payment, A must find the money from other funds if he is to confer the benefit which he sought by his contract to confer upon C. Without expressing a final opinion on a question which is clearly difficult, I think the point is one which does require consideration by your Lordships' House.'

Whether the law should take account of the performance interest when considering the measure of damages for breach of contract arose clearly in the seminal case of *Radford v. De Froberville* [1977] 1 WLR 1262. The landlord of premises let to tenants had obtained a covenant from the owner of neighbouring land to build a garden wall on the neighbour's side of the boundary. The wall was not built. The landlord sued on the covenant for damages, claiming the cost of building a similar wall on his own side of the boundary. Oliver J found that the absence of the wall caused no reduction in value to the landlord's reversionary interest, and that the landlord (as opposed to his tenants) would derive no amenity or other advantage from having the wall built. The defendant contended that, since the landlord had suffered no loss, he was entitled to nominal damages only. The judge found that the landlord intended to apply the damages in building the wall in order to provide his tenants with the amenity which the promised wall would have done, and that this was a reasonable course for him to take. On these findings Oliver J awarded the landlord the cost of building the wall. He said, at p. 1270:

'Now, it may be that, viewed objectively, it is not to the plaintiff's financial advantage to be supplied with the article or service which he has stipulated. It may be that another person might say that what the plaintiff has stipulated for will not serve his commercial interests so well as some other scheme or course of action. And that may be quite right. But that, surely, must be for the plaintiff to judge. Pacta sunt servanda. If he contracts for the supply of that which he thinks serves his interests—be they commercial, aesthetic or merely eccentric—then if that which is contracted for is not supplied by the other contracting party I do not see why, in principle, he should not be compensated by being provided with the cost of supplying it through someone else or in a different way, subject to the proviso, of course, that he is seeking compensation for a genuine loss and not merely using a technical breach to secure an uncovenanted profit.'

This is the language of Lord Griffiths's broad ground. Moreover, Oliver J raised the question of the tenants' interest, recalling the defendant's argument that the landlord was merely a landlord with an investment property and that he was not entitled to damages for a loss suffered by his tenants who were strangers to the contract. He dealt with the point, at p. 1285:

'Whilst I see the force of this, I do not think that it really meets the point that, whatever his status, the plaintiff had a contractual right to have the work done and does in fact want to do it. I refrain from expressing any view about what the position would be if his motives were merely capricious, for there is no suggestion of anything of that sort. As it seems to me, the fact that his motive may be to confer what he conceives to be a benefit on persons who have no contractual rights to demand it cannot alter the genuineness of his intentions. The recent case of *Jackson* v. *Horizon Holidays Ltd* [1975] 1 WLR 1468 demonstrates that the plaintiff may obtain damages for breach of a contract entered into for the benefit of himself and other persons not parties to the contract.'

This is the language of defeated expectation with substantial damages being awarded for the loss of the performance interest.

My Lords, Oliver J's judgment has been very influential. His test of reasonableness was approved and applied by your Lordships' House in *Ruxley Electronics and Construction Ltd* v. *Forsyth* [1996] AC 344. I believe that it provides the key to the present case. The similarity of the two cases is striking. Both are concerned with building contracts in circumstances where performance would benefit a third party to the contract but not the promisee. I would draw particular attention to the fact that in *Radford* v. *De Froberville* [1977] 1 WLR 1262 the proper measure of damages was taken to be the cost of doing the promised work (i.e. fulfilling the landlord's contractual expectation) and not the tenants' loss of amenity. No independent attempt was made to evaluate this.

The seed was planted more than 20 years ago. It has been long in germination, but it has been watered and nurtured by favourable judicial and academic commentators in the meantime. I think the time has come to give it the imprimatur of your Lordships' House. I am not impressed by the argument that such a radical change, with the attendant risk of opening the floodgates to capricious and complex claims to damages in unforeseen situations of every kind, should be left to Parliament. In the first place, I do not think that it is a radical change. I respectfully agree with Steyn LJ in *Darlington Borough Council* v. *Wiltshier Northern Ltd* [1995] 1 WLR 68 that it is based on orthodox contractual principles. And in the second place, the development of the remedial response to civil wrongs and the appropriate measure of damages are matters which have traditionally been the province of the judiciary. For the present I would restrict the broad ground to building contracts and other contracts for the supply of work and materials where the claim is in respect of defective or incomplete work or delay in completing it. I would not exclude the claim for damages for delay, since the performance interest extends to having the work done timeously as well as properly. There is no difficulty in quantifying the loss due to delay, at least in the family or group context. In the case of building contracts the broad ground is in line with the principle that the prima facie measure of damages is the cost of repair rather than the reduction in the market value of the property or any loss of amenity, even where the cost of repair is substantially greater, subject only to the qualification that the carrying out of the repairs must be a reasonable course to adopt . . .

The rationale which underlies this measure of damages is instructive. It is best summed up in a passage in the judgment of Wetmore J in an old Canadian case (*Allen* v. *Pierce* (1895) 3 Terr LR 319, 323) cited with approval in Hudson's Building and Engineering Contracts, 11th ed. (1995) vol. 1, p. 1047:

'It is not a mere matter of difference between the value of the material supplied and that contracted for, or of the work done and that which ought to have been done, or of the house as it stands and that which ought to have been built under the contract. If these were the standards of damages, there would be no point in a man contracting for the best materials. The owner of the building is, therefore, entitled to recover such damages as will put him in a position to have the building he contracted for.'

Again this is the language of defeated expectation. Of course, as the last sentence cited shows, Wetmore J was speaking of the ordinary two-party case where the building employer is also the building owner. But his reasoning applies equally, and perhaps with even greater force, to the case where the building employer is not the building owner. If it did not, there would be no point in the building employer entering into the contract at all. It would be strange logic to allow the building employer to recover the cost of achieving his contractual expectations even where these do not affect the value of his land, and insist at the same time that he must own the land in question if he is to recover more than nominal damages. In my opinion, it is not a departure from orthodoxy to say, adapting Wetmore J's words, that the building employer, whether or not he is also the owner of the building, is entitled to recover such damages as will put him in a position to have the building he contracted for.

Moreover, the question must be considered from a wider perspective than merely defective work. As my noble and learned friend, Lord Goff, observes, unless the law recognizes the performance interest it can provide no remedy to the building employer if the contractor repudiates the contract before he has done any work at all, and the building employer has to engage another contractor to do the work at a higher price. This would be manifestly unjust, and to defend it by saying that the loss is suffered by the building owner (who in fact has suffered none) and not by the building employer is nothing short of absurd.

The broad ground may be more readily applicable where the contracting party had a legitimate interest, though not necessarily a commercial one, in placing the order for the services to be supplied to the third party. Where there is a family or commercial relationship between them, as in the present case, any such requirement is easily satisfied, though it would not be right to limit the application of the principle to cases where such a relationship exists. The charitable donor has a legitimate interest in the object of his charity. But I do not think that the existence of such an interest should be seen as a separate or necessary requirement. It is rather an aspect of the test adopted by Oliver J., that is to say, reasonableness. There is much to be said for the view expressed by Lord Scarman in the *Woodar* case that the fact that a contracting party has required services to be supplied at his own cost to a third party is at least prima facie evidence of the value of those services to the party who placed the order.

Must the building employer intend to carry out the work?

Where the broad ground applies, the plaintiff recovers damages for his own loss, and accordingly in my opinion there can be no question of requiring him to account for them to the third party. In the *St Martins* case Lord Griffiths drew attention to the fact that the person who places the contract suffers loss because he has to spend money to obtain the benefit of the bargain which the defendant had promised but failed to deliver. He added that the court would wish to be satisfied that the repairs had been or would be carried out. Professor Treitel has argued that Lord Griffiths was merely saying that the plaintiff could recover damages in respect of his own loss in making alternative arrangements. I do not think that this can be right. If the making of such arrangements were a precondition of recovery, it would follow that in their absence no such damages would be recoverable. But a plaintiff is bound to mitigate his loss. He cannot increase it by entering into other arrangements. I respectfully agree with Steyn LJ in the *Darlington Borough Council* case [1995] 1 WLR 68 that what the plaintiff proposes to do with his damages is of no more concern to the party in breach in a three-party case than it is in a two-party case. In my opinion, it may be evidence of the reasonableness or otherwise of the plaintiff's claim to damages, but it cannot be conclusive.

In the present case, the development of the site was a group project financed by group money. Panatown was chosen to be the building employer, but it did not use its own money to fund the cost. This was provided to it from within the group, almost certainly (if implicitly) on terms that it should be applied in paying for the works and for no other purpose. UIPL was the building owner, and must be taken to have known and approved of the works and allowed Panatown to grant McAlpine permission to enter the land and carry out the works, presumably on the basis that they would be carried out properly and in accordance with the building contract. It would be inconsistent with these arrangements if Panatown were simply to retain the damages for its own benefit. They will almost certainly be held on trust to apply them at the direction of the group company which provided the building finance . . .

Does the existence of the DCD bar recovery?

. . . I agree with the Court of Appeal that the existence of the DCD does not demonstrate an intention that any damages caused by defective or incomplete performance of McAlpine's obligations under the building contract should be recoverable by UIPL under the DCD and not by Panatown under the building contract. I do not, however, agree with their formulation of the question: whether the parties contemplated that the DCD would 'replace' the more detailed provisions of the building contract. It is not correct to ask whether Panatown would have had a claim under the building contract if there had been no DCD and then ask whether the parties intended to replace that claim by a claim by UIPL under the DCD. If it be relevant to impute intention to the parties, the correct approach is to examine the whole complex of contracts and ask whether they contemplated that the building contract could be enforced by Panatown.

But the broad ground does not rest on imputed intention . . . [It] is based on ordinary contractual principles. It has nothing to do with the privity rule. The plaintiff is a contracting party who recovers for his own loss, not that of a third party. Whatever arrangements the third party may have entered into, these do not concern the plaintiff and cannot deprive him of his contractual rights. He is not accountable for the damages to anyone else, and he cannot be denied a remedy because 'it is not needed'. I respectfully agree with my noble and learned friend, Lord Goff of Chieveley, that the exception identified by Lord Diplock in *The Albazero* [1977] AC 774 is confined to the narrow ground and that it is inappropriate to apply it to the broad ground.

The real significance of the DCD is different. By giving the third party a cause of action, it raises the spectre of double recovery. Even though the plaintiff recovers for his own loss, this obviously reflects the loss sustained by the third party. The case is, therefore, an example, not unknown in other contexts, where breach of a single obligation creates a liability to two different parties. Since performance of the primary obligation to do the work would have discharged the liability to both parties, so must performance of the secondary obligation to pay damages. Payment of damages to either must *pro tanto* discharge the liability to both. The problem, in my view, is not one of double recovery, but of ensuring that the damages are paid to the right party.

There can be no complaint by the building employer if the damages are recovered by the building owner, since he was the intended beneficiary of the arrangements in the first place. The building employer's performance interest will be satisfied by carrying out the remedial work or by providing the building owner with the means to pay for it to be done. This provides the key to the proper approach in the converse case like the present where the action is brought by the building employer despite the existence of a cause of action in the building owner. Since the building employer's expectation loss reflects and cannot exceed the loss suffered by the building owner, and would be satisfied by any award of damages to the latter, his claim should normally be subordinated to any claim made by the building owner. While, therefore, I do not accept that Panatown's claim to substantial damages is excluded by the existence of the DCD, I think that an action like the present should normally be stayed in order to allow the building owner to bring his own proceedings. The court will need to be satisfied that the building owner is not proposing to make his own claim and is content to allow his claim to be discharged by payment to the building employer before allowing the building employer's action to proceed.

My noble and learned friend, Lord Browne-Wilkinson, has postulated the case where the breach does not occur (or the defects are not discovered) until after completion of the work and sale of the building to a purchaser who has taken an assignment of a collateral warranty.

I do not share his concern that such a case will cause difficulty in practice. The position will be the same as in the ordinary case where the building owner and the building employer are one and the same. In such a case, the building employer/owner suffers no financial loss if he disposes of the building before the breach occurs or the defects are discovered. It cannot make any difference that the building owner and the building employer are different. The purchaser will have a cause of action under the collateral warranty. Whether this bars the remedy of the building employer depends on whether the *St Martins* case is properly regarded as covered by the narrow ground or, now that it is available, the broad ground. If the former, it is an exception to the privity rule, and the building owner's action is barred (because it is not needed) by the existence of the purchaser's cause of action. If the latter, then the building owner is in theory entitled to bring proceedings in respect of his own defeated expectation interest, but they are likely to be stayed since in practice the purchaser will normally prefer to bring his own.

All the supposed difficulties disappear once it is grasped that the building employer's performance interest merely reflects the interest of the building owner and that his loss cannot exceed that of the building owner.

Conclusion

In the present case UIPL is fully aware of the present proceedings and supports Panatown's claim to substantial damages. It has no wish to be forced to invoke its own subsidiary and inferior remedy under the DCD. There is no need to join it in the proceedings or require it to enter into a formal waiver of its claim under the DCD. Any claim it may have under the DCD will be satisfied by the payment of damages to Panatown.

I would dismiss the appeal.

COMMENTARY

This is an extremely difficult case. In terms of the resolution of the case, the vital document was the duty of care deed. The conclusion that the duty of care deed prevented Panatown from recovering damages in respect of the loss suffered by UIPL seems correct. Given that UIPL had its own claim, why allow Panatown to bring an action in respect of UIPL's loss? More difficult is the proposition that the duty of care deed operated to take away Panatown's right to recover substantial damages in respect of its own loss. In many ways the fundamental question raised on the facts of the case was whether or not Panatown had a claim for substantial damages given that it did not suffer any financial loss as a result of the breach. It did not suffer a financial loss because it was not the owner of the property, it had paid less to McAlpine than it had received from the Unex group (it had been paid £7.5 million and had paid McAlpine £7.4 million) and it could not prove that McAlpine's breach of contract resulted in it incurring any liability to UIPL or to any member of the Unex group.

The central issue of principle raised by *Panatown* relates to the rights conferred on a promisee by an enforceable promise. This question of principle arises whether the promise made by the promisor is one to benefit the promisee or to benefit a third party. Is it a right to recover the economic value to the promisee of the promised performance? Or is the entitlement of the claimant one that relates to the promised performance itself and not simply to the economic value of that performance? In other words, must a claimant show that it is worse off either physically or financially as a result of the defendant's breach of contract in order to be entitled to recover other than nominal damages in respect of the breach? This was the view of Lord Clyde in *Panatown* when he said:

when one refers to a loss in the context of a breach of contract, one is in my view referring to the incidence of some personal or patrimonial damage.

On the other hand, Lord Millett was critical of this approach which he stated was a 'product of the narrow accountants' balance sheet quantification of loss which measures the loss suffered by the promisee by the diminution of his overall financial position resulting from the breach'. Which view is correct? It is suggested that Lord Millett is right and that he is right as a matter of principle and as a matter of authority.

He is right as a matter of principle because an enforceable promise confers on the promisee an entitlement to the promised performance, not simply the economic value of that performance. This entitlement is reflected in the remedy of specific performance (on which see Chapter 26) and it should also be reflected in the law relating to the assessment of damages. In other words, the aim of an award of damages should be to provide the claimant with a substitute for the performance which he was promised. The reason why the conception of loss adopted by the law of contract should extend beyond physical damage and financial loss is that many people in society enter into contracts with a view other than to make money. Consumers frequently do so. Take the example of the homeowner who enters into a contract to have a new kitchen fitted or to have the dining room re-decorated. If supplied with the wrong kitchen or the wrong wallpaper he is unlikely to be impressed by the argument that he has suffered no loss because the alternative supplied is of the same or greater value than the performance for which he contracted. Increasingly we enter into contracts in pursuit of our leisure interests or to obtain services which promote the quality of our lives but do not directly enhance our financial position. These are interests which our society values and they should be reflected in our law of contract. Contracts may also be concluded for altruistic reasons, for example to confer a benefit upon a third party. Take the example of a daughter who enters into a contract to have a central heating system installed in her elderly parents' home or, to use Lord Goff's example, the wealthy philanthropist who contracts for work to be done on the local village hall. And the likelihood of parties contracting for reasons other than to make money will increase as the horizons of the law of contract extend into new areas, such as public services (for example, the national health service and education) and possibly even into family life (see pp. 304–305 above). If contract's empire is to be expanded in this way, it must not take the form of an impoverished conception of contract that conceives of all relationships in society in purely economic terms. There is more to life than money and there is more to the law of contract than the protection of economic interests. This should be reflected both in the conception of loss adopted by the law of contract and in the rules applicable to the assessment of damages.

It is a more difficult task to demonstrate, as a matter of authority, that the law of contract recognizes a conception of loss that does not require the promisee to have suffered some diminution of his overall financial position as a result of the breach. On this particular issue the decision in *Panatown* cannot be said to be conclusive. Their Lordships did not speak with one voice. Lord Goff and Lord Millett, the dissentients, did not impose a requirement that the promisee must have suffered such a diminution in his overall financial position. Lord Clyde, on the other hand, did (indeed, as the opening paragraphs of his speech make clear, he conceived of this case as one in which Panatown was seeking to recover damages in respect of UIPL's loss and not its own loss). Lord Jauncey also appeared to impose such a requirement but his willingness to award cost of cure damages where the promisee intends to make good the effects of the breach may, in practice, take him close to the position adopted by Lords Goff and Millett. Lord Browne Wilkinson stated that he was prepared to assume that Panatown would have been entitled to recover substantial damages from McAlpine had it not been for the duty of care deed between UIPL and McAlpine but his endorsement of the broader principle was distinctly lukewarm. The duty of care deed cast a long shadow over the reasoning of their Lordships and made it unnecessary for them to determine the precise scope of Panatown's entitlement to damages in the absence of such a deed. In this state of affairs, as Lord Cooke of Thorndon subsequently acknowledged when delivering the judgment of the Privy Council in *The Bay Hotel and Resort Ltd* v. *Cavalier Construction Co Ltd* [2001] UKPC 34, there is little likelihood of *Panatown* being the last word on this particular issue. We must therefore look beyond *Panatown* for the answer to our question.

The difficulty we find, however, is that this judicial division of opinion extends beyond *Panatown* and can also be found in a number of recent decisions of the House of Lords, namely *Ruxley* v. *Forsyth* (p. 1018 above), *Farley* v. *Skinner* [2001] UKHL 49; [2002] 2 AC 732, (p. 1063 below), and *Attorney-General* v. *Blake* [2001] 1 AC 268, 298

(p. 1108 below). Different judges have adopted different conceptions of loss. The analysis of Lord Clyde can claim the support of a number of judicial dicta in which it has been stated that the aim of an award of damages is to put the claimant in the financial position which he would have been in had the contract been performed according to its terms (see, for example, *White Arrow Express Ltd* v. *Lamey's Distribution Ltd* [1996] Trading Law Reports 69 and *Ford* v. *White* [1964] 1 WLR 885). Nevertheless the proposition that damages cannot be recovered unless the claimant has suffered a diminution in his overall financial position cannot stand in the light of cases such as *Ruxley* v. *Forsyth* (p. 1018 above) where, notwithstanding the fact that Mr Forsyth did not suffer a diminution in his overall financial position, all the judges who heard the case concluded that Mr Forsyth was entitled to recover damages, albeit that there was disagreement as to the measure of damages to which he was entitled. In the end he was awarded £2,500 for his 'loss of amenity'. Once again, we return to the question of the nature of this claim for 'loss of amenity' damages.

What is it? One answer is that it is a species of non-pecuniary loss. The law of contract recognizes that, in certain circumstances, damages may be awarded for non-pecuniary losses suffered as a result of a breach of contract, albeit that the precise scope of the entitlement to recover such damages remains uncertain (see p. 1062 below). One view of *Ruxley* is that it falls into this category (see p. 1075 below). But there is a broader view of *Ruxley*. In *Panatown* Lord Millett stated that, viewed objectively, there was no loss of amenity in *Ruxley* and that the loss could be described, more accurately, as a 'defeated expectation'. A similar view was expressed by Lord Scott in *Farley* v. *Skinner* (p. 1073 below, at para [88]). And in *Ruxley* itself Lord Mustill explicitly stated that the law of contract must recognize that the value of a promise can exceed the enhancement of the financial position of the promisee that will follow from performance of the promise.

The use of the language of 'defeated expectations' to describe the loss of the claimant was criticized by Lord Clyde in *Panatown* on the ground that it came 'very close to a way of describing a breach of contract' and, as he pointed out, a 'breach of contract may cause a loss, but is not in itself a loss in any meaningful sense'. The use of the word 'expectation' in this context is unfortunate. The claimant does not have a mere expectation of performance; he has, as Professor Friedmann has acknowledged (p. 1013 above), an entitlement to performance. It follows that a breach of contract has the effect of depriving him of the performance to which he was entitled. The law of contract has at its disposal a range of remedies, such as specific performance, the claim in debt, and the action for damages, all of which have as their aim the protection of the claimant's entitlement to performance in accordance with the terms of the contract. These remedies must be seen as a coherent whole because the aim of each remedy should be identical, namely to provide the claimant with a substitute for the performance for which he contracted. That substitute may take the form of an order of the court that the defendant specifically perform his obligations under the contract. Or it may take the form of a monetary award but the aim of the monetary award should be the same, namely to provide the claimant with a substitute for performance. Judicial support for this conception of the function of the damages award can be found in the dissenting judgment of Lord Hobhouse in *Attorney-General* v. *Blake*

(p. 1116 below) when he stated that the claim for damages for breach of contract is one to 'put the plaintiff in the same position as if the contract had been performed. It is a *substitute* for performance'. As he pointed out, the error which is often made is 'to describe compensation as relating to a loss as if there has to be some identified physical or monetary loss to the plaintiff'. On this view the damages award is seen very much as a monetary equivalent of specific performance and, in many cases, the monetary equivalent of specific performance is cost of cure damages. This was recognized by Lord Hobhouse in *Blake* as he went on to refer to *Ruxley* v. *Forsyth* and observed that 'the *prima facie* measure of damages' was the cost of cure but that on the facts of *Ruxley* 'this sum was so disproportionate' that the courts refused to award it.

This linkage between damages and specific performance is not one that is universally shared. Indeed, it was expressly rejected in Scotland by Lord Drummond Young in *McLaren Murdoch & Hamilton Ltd* v. *The Abercromby Motor Group Ltd* 2003 SCLR 323. He stated that damages was a 'fundamentally different' remedy from specific implement (the Scottish equivalent of specific performance). In Scotland specific implement is the primary remedy for breach of contract and is accordingly 'available on the mere occurrence of a breach'. Damages, by contrast, 'requires more' because it is a 'secondary, substitutional remedy' to which 'notions of loss and financial redress' are central. A party who wishes to recover damages must therefore assume the burden of proving that it has suffered loss that can be 'measured in financial terms'. Lord Drummond Young further suggested that the minority in *Panatown* may have been influenced by the fact that damages is regarded as the primary remedy for breach of contract in England. Here he appears to be suggesting that the damages remedy in England is, in some sense, being required to perform the work that in Scotland is done by specific implement so that Scots law, with its conception of specific implement as a primary remedy, has no need to go down the path taken by Lord Goff and Lord Millett in *Panatown*. But this reasoning can be pressed too far. While it is true that Scots law and English law differ in relation to the role that each system accords to the remedy of specific implement or specific performance (see below p. 1162), it does not follow that this should result in a different approach to the assessment of damages. Nor does it require a dislocation between specific performance and damages. The principal aim of the two remedies is the same, namely to provide the claimant with a substitute for the performance which he was promised. However, it is true to say that there are concerns which attach to the remedy of specific performance that do not apply to the remedy of damages. In the case of specific performance, the court must balance the claim of the party seeking the remedy against the impact of the remedy on the liberty of the defendant. But these libertarian considerations do not arise in relation to the damages remedy. In the case of damages, the problem that confronts the court is one of fashioning a remedy that gives the claimant an appropriate substitute for the performance which he was promised. The breach of contract causes a loss to the claimant in the sense that it deprives him of the performance to which he was entitled. But that does not of itself entitle the claimant to recover substantial damages. He must then quantify the loss that he has suffered as a result of the loss of the performance to which he was entitled. Ordinarily, that will be the cost of providing him with the performance to which he was entitled. The fundamental point to note here relates to the shift in the aim of an award of damages. On the view advanced here, it should no longer be tied to putting the claimant into the financial position which he would have been in had the contract been performed, but instead should aim to give the claimant an appropriate substitute for the performance to which he was entitled. This broader conception of the aim of the damages remedy should not expose defendants to fears of indeterminate liability. Rather, it requires the courts to focus carefully upon the nature of the claimant's interest in performance. Where that interest is purely financial, then the aim of the damages remedy will generally be fulfilled by putting the claimant in the financial position he would have been in had the contract been performed. But where the claimant's interest lies, not in the economic end result of performance, but in performance of the quality, type, or standard promised by the defendant the court ought to look beyond the claimant's financial interest in performance and provide a level of compensation which enables the claimant to obtain performance of the same quality, type, or standard as that promised by the defendant.

It cannot be said that the cases recognize with any clarity the proposition that the law of contract recognizes a conception of loss that does not require the promisee to have suffered some diminution of his overall financial position as a result of the breach. *Panatown* is ambivalent, *Ruxley* susceptible to different interpretations, and Lord Hobhouse's speech in *Blake* is a dissenting speech, albeit that the majority did not find it necessary to consider this particular issue. Cases post-*Panatown* have done little to clarify the issue. Some first instance decisions have been hostile to any broadening of the conception of loss (see, for example, *Rolls-Royce Power Engineering plc* v. *Allen Power Engineering plc and Ricardo Consulting Engineers Ltd* [2003] EWHC 2871 (TCC) and (in Scotland) *McLaren Murdoch & Hamilton Ltd* v. *The Abercromby Motor Group Ltd*, 2003 SCLR 323), while others have been more receptive (see, for example, *Bovis Lend Lease Ltd* v. *R D Fire Protection Ltd* [2003] EWHC 939 (TCC); (1993) 89 Con LR 169 and *Earl Terrace Properties Ltd* v. *Nilsson Design Ltd and Charter Construction plc* [2004] EWHC 136; [2004] BLR 273). In this situation, where the authorities do not speak with one voice, the issue must be resolved as one of principle and here, it is suggested, that principle points, for the reasons already given, unequivocally in the direction of the recognition of a principle that the existence of a loss should no longer be dependent upon the claimant establishing that he has suffered some identifiable physical or financial loss as a result of the breach and that damages should now be conceived as a remedy, the aim of which is to give the claimant a substitute for the performance for which he contracted. In the case where the claimant has suffered no physical or monetary loss as a result of the breach, the loss to the claimant will generally consist of the cost to him of obtaining the performance for which he contracted. Thus the principal consequence that will flow from a recognition of the fact that the aim of an award of damages is to provide the claimant with a substitute for performance should be the wider availability of cost of cure damages as courts give to claimants the financial means to enable them to obtain from a third party the performance for which they contracted.

Recognition of the principle that the aim of an award of damages is to provide the claimant with a substitute for the performance for which he contracted will not bring an end to all of our problems. On the contrary, it will create new problems. Once we depart unequivocally from the proposition that the claimant must demonstrate that he has suffered some physical or monetary loss as a result of the breach, we can expect claimants to test out the limits of the new principle. It will be important to proceed cautiously if the floodgates are not to be opened and in this connection it is important to bear in mind the following points. The first is that the courts have at their disposal a range of remedies, all of which have as their aim the protection of the claimant's entitlement to performance in accordance with the terms of the contract. The court need not award cost of cure damages. It could award specific performance or damages assessed on a diminution in value basis. Principles will have to be worked out to guide the courts when seeking to select the remedy that is most appropriate on the facts of the case. The second issue is that various rules of the law of contract demonstrate that the claimant's entitlement to the performance for which he contracted is not an unqualified one. Thus we find that there are limits, and significant limits, on the ability of a claimant to obtain the remedy of specific performance. Equally, we find in the context of a claim for damages rules that limit the ability of a claimant to claim the full protection of his entitlement to performance (see, for example, the discussion of mitigation and remoteness, pp. 1078–1101 below). There is a need to bring some coherence to these rules. They are dealing with the same issue, namely the qualification or limitation of the claimant's entitlement to claim the performance for which he contracted.

Some idea of the difficulties that lie ahead can be gleaned by returning to the facts of *Panatown* itself. Here it is necessary to distinguish between the claim in respect of the defective work and the claim for delay in completion (here leaving to one side the duty of care deed which was held to exclude Panatown's entitlement to substantial damages). At first sight the claim in respect of the defects in the work appears to be straightforward. But initial appearances can be deceptive. Starting from the proposition that the loss to the claimant will generally consist of the cost to him of obtaining the performance for which he contracted, it seems clear that Panatown would prima facie be entitled to recover cost of cure damages. However we know from *Ruxley* and from the speeches of Lord Goff and Lord Millett in *Panatown* that the claimant does not have an unfettered right to claim cost of cure damages. The courts have reserved to themselves the power to limit that right in the name of reasonableness or proportionality. There appear to be two principal circumstances in which the courts may refuse to award cost of cure damages. The first is where the court is not satisfied that the claimant will use the money to carry out the repair work. The legitimacy of this concern is in issue. Ordinarily, one would not expect a court to concern itself with the use which the claimant makes of the damages awarded. Damages are awarded in respect of a loss that the claimant has suffered and it is for the claimant himself to decide how to spend his damages. But in this particular context it is suggested that it is legitimate for the court to concern itself with the use which the claimant is likely to make of the damages award. The choice which the court has in many of these cases is between awarding damages on a cost of cure basis or on a diminution in value basis. Where it is apparent on the evidence that the claimant has no intention of carrying out the repair work, damages assessed on a difference in value basis will generally suffice to give the claimant the performance for which he contracted. On the other hand, where the claimant genuinely intends to carry out the repair work so that he can thereby obtain the performance for which he contracted, then his claim for cost of cure damages becomes a much stronger one. This point may be important on the facts of *Panatown* because Lord Jauncey stated that Panatown had no intention of spending money in remedying the breach (no other judge in the House of Lords commented on this issue). This finding is, however, a questionable one. At first instance, Judge Thornton QC (1998) 58 Con LR 46, 71 recorded that the arbitrator 'made no findings of fact in relation to the question of whether or not Panatown has spent money, or intends to spend money, in consequence of McAlpine's breaches.' However, if it was the case that Panatown did not intend to carry out the repair work, it is suggested that such a finding would, of itself, suffice to preclude an award of substantial damages. The second situation where the court may decline to award cost of cure damages is where it would cause unnecessary hardship to the defendant. *Ruxley* itself may be an example in this category, although it is close to the limit. This concern for the position of the defendant is not confined to claims for damages. It can also be found in the context of claims for specific performance. English law appears to accept the proposition that severe hardship to the defendant is a ground on which a court can refuse to order specific performance (see p. 1147 below). Thus Professor Treitel states (*The Law of Contract* (11th edn, Sweet & Maxwell, 2003), p. 1026) that 'specific performance may . . . be refused where the cost of performance to the defendant is wholly out of proportion to the benefit which performance will confer on the claimant'. This principle seems very similar to the one invoked by the House of Lords on the facts of *Ruxley*. If severe hardship to the defendant constitutes a ground on which a court can refuse to make a specific performance order, should it not also be a ground on which a court can refuse to grant cost of cure damages, given the fact that the latter is, in essence, the monetary equivalent of specific performance? However neither of these grounds appears to be applicable to the facts of *Panatown*.

Care must also be taken to ensure that double liability is not imposed on the defendant. Thus McAlpine argued that it should not be exposed to a claim for substantial damages because that would leave it vulnerable to potential double liability (if it had been sued by UIPL under the duty of care deed). The law must obviously take steps to ensure that the defendant is not liable to pay damages twice in respect of the same loss but it should be possible for English law to devise a procedure which ensures that this does not in fact occur (see in particular the analysis of Lord Millett in the closing paragraphs of his speech).

There is a more serious difficulty in relation to Panatown's claim for damages for delay (although both Lord Goff and Lord Millett would have allowed Panatown's claim to succeed in this respect). The claim for delay is more difficult than the claim in respect of the defects in the work because delay is a matter of past historical fact and it cannot be undone by giving to Panatown a sum of money to enable it to purchase substitute, timely performance. This being the case, how can we identify the loss suffered by Panatown as a result of any delay in performance by McAlpine? There does not appear to be any loss other than the loss to UIPL caused by the delay in being able to make use of the building on their land. But this is a loss suffered by the third party and not the contracting party. This point becomes clearer if we return to the example of the daughter who enters into a contract to have central heating installed in the home of her elderly parents. Time may well be of the essence in such a contract because it may be important that the work is completed before the onset of winter. Suppose however that the heating engineer fails to complete the work on time. The conclusion that the heating engineer is not liable in damages appears an unattractive one in that it appears to deny one of the most important terms of the contract, the time stipulation, of an effective means of enforcement. So what loss does the daughter suffer as a result of this breach of contract by the heating engineer? She could try to argue that she has suffered a loss in that she would have paid a lower price for the work to be done had she known that the heating engineer would not complete the work on time. But that is a difficult argument to advance on the facts given that, in all probability, she would not have contracted with him at all had she known that he was not going to complete the work before the onset of winter. The reality surely is that, in such a case, the loss is in fact suffered by a third party, namely her parents, and the question which then arises is whether or not the daughter should be entitled to recover in respect of the losses suffered by her parents (on which see pp. 1195–1202 below).

One final problem should be mentioned. It did not arise on the facts of *Panatown* but it has been raised by some commentators who doubt the wisdom of the broader approach to the identification of loss. The example given is a variant of Lord Goff's illustration of the philanthropist who enters into a contract to repair the village hall and the work is done defectively by the contractors. What is to be done in the case where the villagers subsequently decide to carry out the repair work themselves? In such a case can the philanthropist nevertheless recover cost of cure damages from the contractor? The problem here does not relate to the initial existence of the loss. Rather, it arises because the initial loss has been made good by a third party. Thus, had the villagers not carried out the repair work themselves, the philanthropist would have had a prima facie claim for cost of cure damages. Where the loss has been made good by a third party or by the claimant himself, the law must consider whether the fact that the loss has been made good has the effect of denying to the claimant a claim for substantial damages. In the philanthropist example, the question is: who should take the benefit of the voluntary intervention of the villagers? Should it be the philanthropist or the builder? There is a temptation to conclude that it should be the philanthropist and not the builder on the basis that, as between the two of them, the philanthropist is the innocent party. But the fact that the philanthropist is an innocent party should not entitle him to recover in respect of a loss that he has not suffered.

This is another difficult issue and it is one that concerns collateral benefits. The law of contract currently lacks a coherent set of rules to deal with this particular problem. It is submitted that the general rule should be that, where the loss has been made good, the claimant no longer has a claim for substantial damages. But the claimant's loss may be made good in a number of different ways. It may be made good by the intervention of the claimant himself or by the intervention of a third party. Where the claimant acts in such a way as to eliminate his loss, whether by obtaining a substitute at a price lower than the contract price or by selling the defective item supplied by the defendant at full market price, the effect should generally be to deny to the claimant a claim for substantial damages. The claimant has, by his own actions, eliminated the loss and there is no longer a loss to compensate. However the authorities do not speak with one voice on this issue, particularly in the context of contracts for the sale of goods (in this respect contrast the decisions of the Court of Appeal in *Slater* v. *Hoyle & Smith Ltd* [1920] 2 KB 11 and *Bence Graphics International Ltd* v. *Fasson UK Ltd* [1998] QB 87). Where the intervention is by a third party once again the general effect of the intervention should be to reduce or to eliminate the loss initially suffered by the claimant, unless, perhaps, the intervention of the third party is as a result of charity. It is this latter point that makes the philanthropist example a difficult one because it can be said that the intervention of the villagers is an act of charity with the result that, consistently with the policy adopted elsewhere in the law, the effect of the charitable donation should not be to eliminate the loss initially suffered by the claimant. However, in the absence of a charitable donation, it is suggested that the general rule should be that intervention by a third party should operate to reduce or eliminate the loss suffered by the contracting party.

5. THE RELIANCE INTEREST

Rather than seek to protect his performance interest, a claimant may choose to bring a claim for damages to protect his reliance interest. As Fuller and Perdue demonstrate, the reliance interest is a somewhat elusive concept. They adopt an expansive conception of the reliance interest which encompasses 'losses involved in foregoing the opportunity to enter other contracts' (p. 1008 above). In practice this takes the reliance interest very close to the performance interest (in that the claimant is able to recover his loss of profits on any substitute transaction he would have concluded, rather than his loss of profit on the actual transaction). However, the more widely used conception of the reliance interest is that it enables the claimant to recover his out-of-pocket expenditure incurred in the course of performance of the contract.

As Professor Friedmann points out (p. 1013 above), a party does not enter into a contract in order to obtain the return of the expenditure which he incurs in the course of performance of the contract. He enters into a contract in order to obtain the promised performance. Of course, in most cases the protection of the claimant's performance interest will include the protection of his reliance interest on the basis that, in most cases, contracting parties expect to recoup their outlay and, in addition, make a profit on the transaction. The performance interest will therefore include the reliance expenditure plus the net profit on the transaction. This being the case, a claimant will have an obvious interest in bringing a claim to protect his performance interest rather than confine himself to his reliance interest (which will not include net profit, unless, as per Fuller and Perdue, we allow the claimant to recover his net profit on a substitute transaction into which he would have entered but for the contract concluded with the defendant).

In principle claimants have a right to choose between the reliance measure of damages and the performance interest (see *CCC Films* v. *Impact Quadrant Films Ltd* [1985] QB 16). Generally speaking, however, claimants will wish to bring a claim for damages to protect their performance interest. The reason for this is that a reliance loss claim will generally be lower than a claim to protect the performance interest because the former will not include a claim for loss of profit. When will a claimant wish to bring a claim for his reliance losses (meaning here, his out-of-pocket expenditure)? There are three principal situations. The first is where he cannot prove his loss of profit. The second is where he wishes to recover damages in respect of his pre-contract expenditure. The third is where he has entered into a losing bargain. We shall take each case in turn.

The first example is the case of an extremely speculative transaction. In such a case the claimant may have to content himself with a claim for his reliance expenditure (see, for example, *McRae* v. *Commonwealth Disposals Commission* (1951) 84 CLR 377, p. 635 above). But the courts will generally strive to put a value on the claimant's performance interest. In *Chaplin* v. *Hicks* [1911] 2 KB 786 the plaintiff, an aspiring actress, entered into a competition organized by the defendant, a theatre manager. The prize for the competition winners was a term of employment with the defendant. The plaintiff won the first stage of the competition, being selected as one of fifty out of 6,000 entrants to proceed to the second stage. The second stage involved an interview with each of the fifty successful entrants by the defendant, who would then select twelve eventual winners. In breach of contract the defendant deprived the plaintiff of a reasonable opportunity of attending the interview. The plaintiff sued for breach of contract, claiming damages for the loss of a chance of winning the competition. The defendant argued that the plaintiff was only entitled to recover nominal damages. The jury awarded the plaintiff damages of £100. The defendant appealed to the Court of Appeal but they dismissed the appeal. Fletcher Moulton LJ stated (at pp. 798–799) that:

Where by contract a man has a right to belong to a limited class of competitors, he is possessed of something of value, and it is the duty of the jury to estimate the pecuniary value of that advantage, if it is taken from him. The present case is a typical one. From a body of six thousand, who sent in their photographs, a smaller body of fifty was formed, of which the plaintiff was one, and among that smaller body twelve prizes were allotted for distribution; by reason of the defendant's breach of contract she has lost all the advantage of being in the limited competition, and she is entitled to have her loss estimated. I cannot lay down any rule as to the measure of damages in such a case; this must be left to the good sense of the jury. They must of course give effect to the consideration that the plaintiff's chance is only one out of four and that they cannot tell whether she would have ultimately proved to be the winner. But having considered all this they may well think that it is of considerable pecuniary value to have got into so small a class, and they must assess the damages accordingly.

The courts will generally strive to overcome valuation difficulties and will relegate a claimant to reliance loss damages only in the case where there is no objective basis for the award of damages designed to protect his performance interest.

The second situation in which a claimant will wish to bring a claim for reliance loss damages is in the case in which he wishes to recover damages in respect of his pre-contractual expenditure. An example in this category is provided by the following case:

Anglia Television v. Reed

[1972] 1 QB 60, Court of Appeal

The facts are set out in the judgment of Lord Denning MR.

Lord Denning MR

Anglia Television Ltd, the plaintiffs, were minded in 1968 to make a film of a play for television entitled 'The Man in the Wood'. It portrayed an American man married to an English woman. The American has an adventure in an English wood. The film was to last for 90 minutes. Anglia Television made many arrangements in advance. They arranged for a place where the play was to be filmed. They employed a director, a designer and a stage manager, and so forth. They involved themselves in much expense. All this was done before they got the leading man. They required a strong actor capable of holding the play together. He was to be on the scene the whole time. Anglia Television eventually found the man. He was Mr Robert Reed, the defendant, an American who has a very high reputation as an actor. He was very suitable for this part. By telephone conversation on August 30, 1968, it was agreed by Mr Reed through his agent that he would come to England and be available between September 9 and October 11, 1968, to rehearse and play in this film. He was to get a performance fee of £1,050, living expenses of £100 a week, his first class fares to and from the United States, and so forth. It was all subject to the permit of the Ministry of Labour for him to come here. That was duly given on September 2, 1968. So the contract was concluded. But unfortunately there was some muddle with the bookings. It appears that Mr Reed's agents had already booked him in America for some other play. So on September 3, 1968, the agent said that Mr Reed would not come to England to perform in this play. He repudiated his contract. Anglia Television tried hard to find a substitute but could not do so. So on September 11 they accepted his repudiation. They abandoned the proposed film. They gave notice to the people whom they had engaged and so forth.

Anglia Television then sued Mr Reed for damages. He did not dispute his liability, but a question arose as to the damages. Anglia Television do not claim their profit. They cannot say what their profit would have been on this contract if Mr Reed had come here and performed it. So, instead of claim for loss of profits, they claim for the wasted expenditure. They had incurred the director's fees, the designer's fees, the stage manager's and assistant manager's fees, and so on. It comes in all to £2,750. Anglia Television say that all that money was wasted because Mr Reed did not perform his contract.

Mr Reed's advisers take a point of law. They submit that Anglia Television cannot recover for expenditure incurred *before* the contract was concluded with Mr Reed. They can only recover the expenditure *after* the contract was concluded. They say that the expenditure *after* the contract was only £854.65, and that is all that Anglia Television can recover.

The master rejected that contention: he held that Anglia Television could recover the whole £2,750; and now Mr Reed appeals to this court.

Mr Butler, for Mr Reed, has referred us to the recent case of *Perestrello & Companhia*

Limitada v. *United Paint Co Ltd, The Times*, April 16, 1969, in which Thesiger J quoted the words of Tindal CJ in *Hodges* v. *Earl of Litchfield* (1835) 1 Bing NC 492, 498:

> 'The expenses preliminary to the contract ought not to be allowed. The party enters into them for his own benefit at a time when it is uncertain whether there will be any contract or not.'

Thesiger J applied those words, saying: 'In my judgment pre-contract expenditure, though thrown away, is not recoverable'.

I cannot accept the proposition as stated. It seems to me that a plaintiff in such a case as this has an election: he can either claim for loss of profits; or for his wasted expenditure. But he must elect between them. He cannot claim both. If he has not suffered any loss of profits—or if he cannot prove what his profits would have been—he can claim in the alternative the expenditure which has been thrown away, that is, wasted, by reason of the breach. That is shown by *Cullinane* v. *British 'Rema' Manfacturing Co Ltd* [1954] 1 QB 292, 303, 308.

If the plaintiff claims the wasted expenditure, he is not limited to the expenditure incurred *after* the contract was concluded. He can claim also the expenditure incurred *before* the contract, provided that it was such as would reasonably be in the contemplation of the parties as likely to be wasted if the contract was broken. Applying that principle here, it is plain that, when Mr Reed entered into this contract, he must have known perfectly well that much expenditure had already been incurred on director's fees and the like. He must have contemplated—or, at any rate, it is reasonably to be imputed to him—that if he broke his contract, all that expenditure would be wasted, whether or not it was incurred before or after the contract. He must pay damages for all the expenditure so wasted and thrown away. This view is supported by the recent decision of Brightman J in *Lloyd* v. *Stanbury* [1971] 1 WLR 535. There was a contract for the sale of land. In anticipation of the contract—and before it was concluded—the purchaser went to much expense in moving a caravan to the site and in getting his furniture there. The seller afterwards entered into a contract to sell the land to the purchaser, but afterwards broke his contract. The land had not increased in value, so the purchaser could not claim for any loss of profit. But Brightman J held, at p. 547, that he could recover the cost of moving the caravan and furniture, because it was 'within the contemplation of the parties when the contract was signed'. That decision is in accord with the correct principle, namely, that wasted expenditure can be recovered when it is wasted by reason of the defendant's breach of contract. It is true that, if the defendant had never entered into the contract, he would not be liable, and the expenditure would have been incurred by the plaintiff without redress; but, the defendant having made his contract and broken it, it does not lie in his mouth to say he is not liable, when it was because of his breach that the expenditure has been wasted.

I think the master was quite right and this appeal should be dismissed.

Phillimore and **Megaw LJJ** concurred.

COMMENTARY

Three points of interest arise from this case. First, one of the reasons why the plaintiffs brought a claim for reliance loss damages was that they could not prove what their loss of profit would have been. Secondly, the decision has been criticized in so far as it enables a claimant to recover damages in respect of pre-contractual expenditure. Professor Ogus ('Damages for Pre-Contract Expenditure' (1972) 35 *MLR* 423, 424) stated that the proposition that such damages are recoverable is a 'doubtful proposition'. He continued:

The measure of damages so envisaged would not put the plaintiffs in the position they would have been in if the contract had not been made, for the expenses would still have been incurred. The expenses were incurred not in reliance on the defendant's promise to perform—they were incurred merely in the hope that agreement with the defendant would be secured. There was indeed no causal connection between the loss (the wasted expenses) and either the making of the contract or its breach. In the United States of America these theoretical objections have proved decisive: all attempts to recover pre-contract expenditure (where there was no special agreement binding the defaulting party to pay) have failed.

Now it may be conceded that dogmatically to insist that there may be recovery of expenditure incurred only from the moment that the contract was complete may lead to artificial results. If the parties have clearly reached agreement on the substance of the contract and all that remains is for their legal advisers to draft and execute the contract, it would be unfair to the plaintiff to disallow a claim for expenses incurred at this stage. On the other hand, the doctrine of *restitutio in integrum* which lies at the heart of the reliance interest award surely dictates that while a contract is still being negotiated a party who incurs expenditure does so at his own risk. Perhaps the best solution would be for the reliance interest award to comprise those expenses incurred as from the time when there was *substantial agreement between the parties*.

Thirdly, Lord Denning MR suggested that a claimant must elect between a claim for reliance loss damages and damages to protect his performance interest: he cannot claim both. It is certainly the case that a claimant cannot recover both his reliance loss and his gross profit because that would involve an element of double recovery. It is less clear whether a claimant can combine a claim for his reliance loss with a claim for net profit. In such a case there is no element of double recovery. Professor Treitel suggests that it should be possible to combine such a claim (*The Law of Contract* (11th edn, Sweet & Maxwell, 2003), pp. 942–943).

The third situation in which a claimant may wish to bring a claim for reliance loss damages is where he has entered into a bad bargain. However the courts will not, in general, allow a claimant to use a claim for reliance losses as an escape route from what has turned out to be a bad bargain. This is demonstrated by the following case:

C & P Haulage v. Middleton

[1983] 1 WLR 1461, Court of Appeal

The plaintiffs granted the defendant a contractual licence to use the plaintiffs' premises for the defendant's business on a renewable six-month basis. The licence provided that any fixtures added to the premises by the licence holder could not be removed upon the termination of the licence. Despite this, the defendant incurred expense in making improvements to the premises in order to make them suitable for his business. Ten weeks before the end of a six-month period, the defendant was unlawfully ejected from the premises by the plaintiffs. The defendant secured temporary permission from the local authority to use the garage of his home as his place of work. The defendant used his home in this manner until well after the six-month period would have expired. The plaintiffs brought an action against the defendant in relation to a cheque that had been stopped by the defendant. The defendant counterclaimed for damages for the cost of the improvements he had made to the premises and the appeal to the Court of Appeal was solely concerned with the counterclaim. At first instance, it was held that the defendant had suffered no loss as he had been able to move the business into his home where he did not have to pay any rent and the cost of improvements to the premises would have been lost in any event when the licence lawfully terminated after six months. The defendant appealed to the Court of Appeal who dismissed his appeal.

Ackner LJ [set out the facts of the case, considered the decision of the Court of Appeal in *Anglia Television* v. *Reed* (p. 1056 above) and continued]

The case which I have found of assistance—and I am grateful to counsel for their research—is a case in the British Columbia Supreme Court: *Bowlay Logging Ltd* v. *Domtar Ltd* [1978] 4 WWR 105. Berger J, in a very careful and detailed judgment, goes through various English and American authorities and refers to the leading textbook writers, and I will only quote a small part of his judgment. At the bottom of p. 115 he refers to the work of Professor LL Fuller and William R Perdue, Jr, in 'The Reliance Interest in Contract Damages: 1' (1936), 46 *Yale Law Journal* 52 and their statement, at p. 79:

'We will not in a suit for reimbursement for losses incurred in reliance on a contract knowingly put the plaintiff in a better position than he would have occupied had the contract been fully performed.'

Berger J, at p. 116, then refers to *L Albert & Son* v. *Armstrong Rubber Co* (1949) 178 F 2d 182 in which Learned Hand CJ, speaking for the Circuit Court of Appeals, Second Circuit:

'held that on a claim for compensation for expenses in part performance the defendant was entitled to deduct whatever he could prove the plaintiff would have lost if the contract had been fully performed.'

What Berger J had to consider was this, p. 105:

'The parties entered into a contract whereby the plaintiff would cut timber under the defendant's timber sale, and the defendant would be responsible for hauling the timber away from the site of the timber sale. The plaintiff claimed the defendant was in breach of the contract as the defendant had not supplied sufficient trucks to make the plaintiff's operation, which was losing money, viable, and claimed not for loss of profits but for compensation for expenditures. The defendant argued that the plaintiff's operation lost money not because of a lack of trucks but because of the plaintiff's inefficiency, and, further, that even if the defendant had breached the contract the plaintiff should not be awarded damages because its operation would have lost money in any case.'

This submission was clearly accepted because the plaintiff was awarded only nominal damages, and Berger J said, at p. 117:

'The law of contract compensates a plaintiff for damages resulting from the defendant's breach; it does not compensate a plaintiff for damages resulting from his making a bad bargain. Where it can be seen that the plaintiff would have incurred a loss on the contract as a whole, the expenses he has incurred are losses flowing from entering into the contract, not losses flowing from the defendant's breach. In these circumstances, the true consequence of the defendant's breach is that the plaintiff is released from his obligation to complete the contract—or in other words, he is saved from incurring further losses. If the law of contract were to move from compensating for the consequences of breach to compensating for the consequences of entering into contracts, the law would run contrary to the normal expectations of the world of commerce. The burden of risk would be shifted from the plaintiff to the defendant. The defendant would become the insurer of the plaintiff's enterprise. Moreover, the amount of the damages would increase not in relation to the gravity or consequences of the breach but in relation to the inefficiency with which the plaintiff carried out the contract. The greater his expenses owing to inefficiency, the greater the damages. The fundamental principle upon which damages are measured under the law of contract is restitutio in integrum. The principle contended for here by the plaintiff would entail the award of damages not to compensate the plaintiff but to punish the defendant.'

It is urged here that the garage itself was merely an element in the defendant's business; it was not a profit-making entity on its own. Nevertheless, if as a result of being kept out of these premises the defendant had found no other premises to go to for a period of time, his claim would clearly have been a claim for such loss of profit as he could establish his business suffered.

In my judgment, the approach of Berger J is the correct one. It is not the function of the courts where there is a breach of contract knowingly, as this would be the case, to put a plaintiff in a better financial position than if the contract had been properly performed. In this case the defendant who is the plaintiff in the counterclaim, if he was right in his claim, would indeed be in a better position because, as I have already indicated, had the contract been lawfully determined as it could have been in the middle of December, there would have been no question of his recovering these expenses.

This is a case, let it be stressed, where there was no question of the defendant being able to establish that he was a tenant; but had he been a tenant, then the compensation for the improvements which he had carried out would have been regulated by the Landlord and Tenant Act 1927. That would have involved him in complying with the various conditions which the Act lays down before a valid claim for compensation for improvements can be made; but even when such a claim is open to a tenant, there is a ceiling put to what can be recovered, namely the net addition to the value of the holding which may be far less than the money actually expended on the improvements.

So the approach which the judge in the county court was asked to follow, and which we have also been invited to follow, would not only put this licensee in a better position as a result of the breach than if the licence had been lawfully determined, but would put him in a better position than if he had achieved the superior status in law of being a tenant and not a licensee.

I do not consider that a plaintiff is entitled in an action for damages for breach of contract to ask to be put in the position in which he would have been if the contract had never been made. Accordingly, save in the respect to which I have already made reference, namely that there should be judgment for the defendant for nominal damages of £10, I would dismiss the appeal.

Fox LJ

The present case seems to me to be quite different both from *Anglia Television Ltd* v. *Reed* [1972] 1 QB 60 and from *Lloyd* v. *Stanbury* [1971] 1 WLR 535 in that while it is true that the expenditure could in a sense be said to be wasted in consequence of the breach of contract, it was equally likely to be wasted if there had been no breach, because the plaintiffs wanted to get the defendant out and could terminate the licence at quite short notice. A high risk of waste was from the very first inherent in the nature of the contract itself, breach or no breach. The reality of the matter is that the waste resulted from what was, on the defendant's side, a very unsatisfactory and dangerous bargain.

I agree with Ackner LJ that the appeal must be dismissed.

COMMENTARY

The Court of Appeal held that the defendant's loss flowed, not from the breach of contract, but from the fact that he had entered into a bad bargain. The court refused to re-distribute the contractual allocation of risk on the ground that the plaintiffs had committed a repudiatory breach of contract. But it is important to note that it is the party in breach who bears the burden of proving that the bargain was a losing one for the innocent party. The law of contract presumes that a party will recoup his expenditure and so throws on to the party in breach the burden of proving that this was not, in fact, the case (see *Commonwealth of Australia* v. *Amann Aviation Pty Ltd* (1991) 66 ALJR 123). This burden is not an easy one for the party in breach to discharge and, this being the case, the innocent party will generally be able to recover his wasted expenditure (unless, as was the case in *C & P Haulage*, it is clear from the facts that the innocent party would not have been able to recoup his expenditure).

6. THE RESTITUTION INTEREST

Fuller and Perdue conclude (p. 1008 above) that the restitution interest presents the strongest claim for protection because there is both a benefit to the defendant and a loss to the claimant. But in fact the law of restitution plays a residual role in breach of contract claims. In particular, it has no role to play unless and until the contract between the parties is set aside. In the case where the contract has not been set aside, the contract governs the rights and remedies of the parties.

Where the contract is set aside as a result of the claimant's acceptance of the defendant's repudiatory breach, the claimant may have a claim to recover the value of any benefit conferred upon the defendant in the course of performance prior to the termination of the contract. But the right is only available within narrow confines. Where the claim is one to recover money paid to the defendant, it is only available where there has been a total failure of consideration, that is to say, where the claimant has received no part of the performance for which he contracted (*Giles* v. *Edwards* (1797) 7 Term Rep 181). Where he has received part of the promised performance, he is confined to a claim for contractual damages (that is, the protection of his performance interest or, if appropriate, his reliance interest). The situation in which a claimant will particularly wish to recover his money back is in the case where he has entered into a bad bargain. Suppose a party enters into a contract under which he pays £500 for goods that are worth only £300. In breach of contract, the defendant fails to supply the goods. In such a case the claimant is not confined to the protection of his performance interest (£300) but can claim the return of his £500 on the ground that it was paid for a consideration which totally failed. In this way the claim to recover upon a total failure of consideration has the effect of rescuing the claimant from his bad bargain. The rule that money paid can only be recovered upon a total failure of consideration has been criticized by many academic commentators on the law of restitution (see, for example, P Birks, 'Failure of Consideration' in FD Rose (ed), *Consensus Ad Idem: Essays on the Law of Contract* (Sweet & Maxwell, 1996), p. 179). The generally accepted view among restitution scholars today is that money paid should be recoverable upon a failure of consideration, whether that failure is total or partial. But, despite the occasional judicial hint that the courts will allow a claim to recover based on a partial failure of consideration (see, for example, *Goss* v. *Chilcott* [1996] AC 788, 798), the total failure requirement remains part of the law.

In the case where the innocent party has supplied goods or services to the party in breach prior to the termination of the contract, there is no total failure requirement. Total failure of consideration applies only to claims to recover money paid to the defendant. A claimant who wishes to recover the reasonable value of goods or services supplied prior to termination can either pursue a contractual claim or bring a restitutionary claim (usually referred to as a *quantum meruit* or a *quantum valebat* claim) for the reasonable value of the services provided or goods supplied (see, for example, *Planché* v. *Colburn* (1831) 8 Bing 14). The vital issue in this connection is not the existence of the restitutionary claim but the measure of recovery, in particular the question whether the contract price acts as a ceiling on the value of the claimant's restitutionary claim. There is much to be said for the view that the claimant should not be entitled to rely on the defendant's breach of contract for the purpose of reversing the contractual allocation of risk and recovering a sum in excess of the contract price, but the authorities, such as they are, appear to lend some support for the proposition that the claimant can, in a restitutionary claim, recover a sum in excess of the contract price (*Lodder* v. *Slowey* [1904] AC 442 and *Rover International Ltd* v. *Cannon Film Sales Ltd (No 3)* [1989] 1 WLR 912).

One final point remains to be made. The cases discussed in this section are cases in which there is a precise correlation between the gain to the defendant and the loss to the claimant; the one is the mirror image of the other. A separate issue arises in the case where the defendant makes a profit from his breach of contract and that profit exceeds the loss that has been suffered by the claimant. The question of the extent to which a claimant can recover such a gain from a party in breach of contract is discussed in section 9 below.

7. NON-PECUNIARY LOSSES

It is clear law that damages can be recovered for physical injury suffered by the claimant as a result of the defendant's breach of contract provided that the loss is not too remote a consequence of the breach of contract (see, for example, *Grant* v. *Australian Knitting Mills Ltd* [1936] AC 85). More difficult is the case in which the claimant suffers physical inconvenience or 'mental distress' as a result of the breach. Until recently, the leading authority on the latter issue was the decision of the Court of Appeal in *Watts* v. *Morrow* [1991] 1 WLR 1421, where it was held that damages for such non-pecuniary losses could be recovered in two situations. The first consisted of cases where 'the very object of a contract is to provide pleasure, relaxation, peace of mind or freedom from molestation'. The second category consisted of cases in which the claim was one for damages for 'physical inconvenience and discomfort caused by the breach and mental suffering directly related to that inconvenience and discomfort'. *Watts* has now been replaced as the leading authority by the following decision of the House of Lords:

Farley v. Skinner

[2001] UKHL 49; [2002] 2 AC 732, House of Lords

The plaintiff employed the defendant surveyor to survey a 'gracious country residence' which the plaintiff was contemplating buying as a weekend residence. Given that the property was situated some fifteen miles from Gatwick airport, the plaintiff expressly asked the defendant to report on whether or not aircraft noise was likely to be a problem. The defendant did so and reported that it was 'unlikely that the property will suffer greatly from such noise, although some planes will inevitably cross the area, depending on the direction of the wind and the positioning of the flight paths'. The plaintiff purchased the house and, after spending in excess of £100,000 in carrying out improvements, he discovered that aircraft noise was indeed a problem for him and that it interfered with his enjoyment of the house. The house was not far from Mayfield Stack where aeroplanes waiting to land at Gatwick are stacked until a landing slot becomes available (the stacking tends to take place during busy periods, namely in the morning, early evening, and at weekends). The plaintiff sued the defendant for damages, alleging that he had been negligent in carrying out his obligations under the contract. The trial judge found that the defendant was in breach of contract. He held that the plaintiff was not entitled to recover damages on a diminution in value basis because he found that the property was not worth any less as a result of the defendant's failure to point out to the plaintiff the true position in relation to aircraft noise. Instead, he awarded the plaintiff damages of £10,000 for the distress and inconvenience caused to him by the aircraft noise. The defendant appealed to the Court of Appeal where it was held that the plaintiff had not suffered any physical discomfort and inconvenience as a result of the defendant's breach of contract and that the object of the contract between the parties was not to provide enjoyment or relief from stress so that the claim did not fall within the class of case in respect of which it was appropriate to award damages for distress and inconvenience. The defendant's appeal was therefore allowed and it was held that he was entitled to recover nominal damages only. The plaintiff appealed to the House of Lords. His appeal was allowed and he was held to be entitled to damages of £10,000.

Lord Steyn

14. The judgments in the Court of Appeal and the arguments before the House took as their starting point the propositions enunciated by Bingham LJ in *Watts* v. *Morrow* [1991] 1 WLR 1421. In that case the Court of Appeal had to consider a claim for damages for distress and inconvenience by a buyer of a house against his surveyor who had negligently failed to report defects in the house. Bingham LJ observed, at p. 1445:

'(1) A contract-breaker is not in general liable for any distress, frustration, anxiety, dis-pleasure, vexation, tension or aggravation which his breach of contract may cause to the innocent party. This rule is not, I think, founded on the assumption that such reactions are not foreseeable, which they surely are or may be, but on considerations of policy.

(2) But the rule is not absolute. Where the very object of a contract is to provide pleasure, relaxation, peace of mind or freedom from molestation, damages will be awarded if the fruit of the contract is not provided or if the contrary result is procured instead. If the law did not cater for this exceptional category of case it would be defective. A contract to survey the condition of a house for a prospective purchaser does not, however, fall within this exceptional category.

(3) In cases not falling within this exceptional category, damages are in my view recoverable for physical inconvenience and discomfort caused by the breach and mental suffering directly related to that inconvenience and discomfort. If those effects are foreseeably suffered during a period when defects are repaired I am prepared to accept that they sound in damages even though the cost of the repairs is not recoverable as such. But I also agree that awards should be restrained, and that the awards in this case far exceeded a reasonable award for the injury shown to have been suffered.' (Numbering introduced) . . .

15. But useful as the observations of Bingham LJ undoubtedly are, they were never intended to state more than broad principles. In *Broome* v. *Cassell & Co Ltd* [1972] AC 1027 Lord Reid commented, at p. 1085:

'experience has shown that those who have to apply the decision [*Rookes* v. *Barnard* [1964] AC 1129] to other cases and still more those who wish to criticise it seem to find it difficult to avoid treating sentences and phrases in a single speech as if they were provisions in an Act of Parliament. They do not seem to realise that it is not the function of . . . judges to frame definitions or to lay down hard and fast rules. It is their function to enunciate principles and much that they say is intended to be illustrative or explana-tory and not to be definitive.'

Bingham LJ would have had this truth about judicial decision making well in mind. So interpreted the passage cited is a helpful point of departure for the examination of the issues in this case. Specifically, it is important to bear in mind that *Watts* v. *Morrow* [1991] 1 WLR 1421 was a case where a surveyor negligently failed to discover defects in a property. The claim was not for breach of a specific undertaking to investigate a matter important for the buyer's peace of mind. It was a claim for damages for inconvenience and discomfort resulting from breach. In *Watts* v. *Morrow* [1991] 1 WLR 1421 therefore there was no reason to consider the case where a surveyor is in breach of a distinct and important contractual obligation which was intended to afford the buyer information confirming the presence or absence of an intrusive element before he committed himself to the purchase.

V. Recovery of non-pecuniary damages

16. The examination of the issues can now proceed from a secure foothold. In the law of obligations the rules governing the recovery of compensation necessarily distinguish between different kinds of harm. . . . In contract law distinctions are made about the kind of harm which resulted from the breach of contract. The general principle is that compensation is only awarded for financial loss resulting from the breach of contract: *Livingstone* v. *Rawyards Coal Co* (1880) 5 App Cas 25, 39, per Lord Blackburn. In the words of Bingham LJ in *Watts* as a matter of legal policy 'a contract breaker is not *in general* liable for any distress, frustration, anxiety, displeasure, vexation, tension or aggravation which his breach of contract may cause to the innocent party' (my emphasis). There are, however, limited exceptions to this rule. One such exception is damages for pain, suffering and loss of amenities caused to an individual by a breach of contract: see McGregor *on Damages*, 16th ed, para 96, pp. 56–57. It is not material in the present case. But the two exceptions mentioned by Bingham LJ, namely where the very object of the contract is to provide pleasure (proposition (2)) and recovery for physical inconvenience caused by the breach (proposition (3)), are pertinent. The scope of these exceptions is in issue in the present case. It is, however, correct, as counsel for the surveyor submitted, that the entitlement to damages for mental distress caused by a breach of contract is not established by mere foreseeability: the right to recovery is dependent on the case falling fairly within the principles governing the special exceptions. So far there is no real disagreement between the parties.

VI. The very object of the contract: The framework

17. I reverse the order in which the Court of Appeal considered the two issues. I do so because the issue whether the present case falls within the exceptional category governing cases where the very object of the contact is to give pleasure, and so forth, focuses directly on the terms actually agreed between the parties. It is concerned with the reasonable expectations of the parties under the specific terms of the contract. Logically, it must be considered first.

18. It is necessary to examine the case on a correct characterisation of the plaintiff's claim. Stuart-Smith LJ [2000] Lloyd's Rep PN 516, 521 thought that the obligation undertaken by the surveyor was 'one relatively minor aspect of the overall instructions'. What Stuart-Smith and Mummery LJJ would have decided if they had approached it on the basis that the obligation was a major or important part of the contract between the plaintiff and the surveyor is not clear. But the Court of Appeal's characterisation of the case was not correct. The plaintiff made it crystal clear to the surveyor that the impact of aircraft noise was a matter of importance to him. Unless he obtained reassuring information from the surveyor he would not have bought the property. That is the tenor of the evidence. It is also what the judge found. The case must be approached on the basis that the surveyor's obligation to investigate aircraft noise was a major or important part of the contract between him and the plaintiff. It is also important to note that, unlike in *Addis* v. *Gramophone Co Ltd* [1909] AC 488, the plaintiff's claim is not for injured feelings caused by the breach of contract. Rather it is a claim for damages flowing from the surveyor's failure to investigate and report, thereby depriving the buyer of the chance of making an informed choice whether or not to buy resulting in mental distress and disappointment.

19. The broader legal context of *Watts* v. *Morrow* [1991] 1 WLR 1421 must be borne in mind. The exceptional category of cases where the very object of a contract is to provide pleasure, relaxation, peace of mind or freedom from molestation is not the product of Victorian contract theory but the result of evolutionary developments in case-law from the 1970s. Several decided cases informed the description given by Bingham LJ of this category. The first was the decision of the sheriff court in *Diesen* v. *Samson* 1971 SLT (Sh Ct) 49. A photographer failed to turn up at a wedding, thereby leaving the couple without a photographic record of an important and happy day. The bride was awarded damages for her distress and disappointment. In the celebrated case of *Jarvis* v. *Swans Tours Ltd* [1973] QB 233, the plaintiff recovered damages for mental distress flowing from a disastrous holiday resulting from a travel agent's negligent representations: compare also *Jackson* v. *Horizon Holidays Ltd* [1975] 1 WLR 1468. In *Heywood* v. *Wellers* [1976] QB 446, the plaintiff instructed solicitors to bring proceedings to restrain a man from molest-ing her. The solicitors negligently failed to take appropriate action with the result that the molestation continued. The Court of Appeal allowed the plaintiff damages for mental distress and upset. While apparently not cited in *Watts* v. *Morrow* [1991] 1 WLR 1421, *Jackson* v. *Chrysler Acceptances Ltd* [1978] RTR 474 was decided before *Watts* v. *Morrow*. In *Jackson's* case the claim was for damages in respect of a motor car which did not meet the implied condition of merchantability in section 14 of the Sale of Goods Act 1893. The buyer communicated to the seller that one of his reasons for buying the car was a forthcoming touring holiday in France. Problems with the car spoilt the holiday. The disappointment of a spoilt holiday was a substantial element in the award sanctioned by the Court of Appeal.

20. At their Lordships' request counsel for the plaintiff produced a memorandum based on various publications which showed the impact of the developments already described on litigation in the county courts. Taking into account the submissions of counsel for the surveyor and making due allowance for a tendency of the court some-times not to distinguish between the cases presently under consideration and cases of physical inconvenience and discomfort, I am satisfied that in the real life of our lower courts non-pecuniary damages are regularly awarded on the basis that the defendant's breach of contract deprived the plaintiff of the very object of the contract, viz pleasure, relaxation, and peace of mind. The cases arise in diverse contractual contexts, eg the supply of a wedding dress or double glazing, hire purchase transactions, landlord and tenant, building contracts, and engagements of estate agents and solicitors. The awards in such cases seem modest. For my part what happens on the ground casts no doubt on the utility of the developments since the 1970s in regard to the award of non-pecuniary damages in the exceptional categories. But the problem persists of the precise scope of the exceptional category of case involving awards of non-pecuniary damages for breach of contract where the very object of the contract was to ensure a party's pleasure, relaxation or peace of mind.

21. An important development for this branch of the law was *Ruxley Electronics and Construction Ltd* v. *Forsyth* [1996] AC 344 . . .

[he set out the facts and continued]

Lord Mustill and Lord Lloyd of Berwick justified the award in carefully reasoned judg-ments which carried the approval of four of the Law Lords. It is sufficient for present purposes to mention that for Lord Mustill, at p. 360, the principle of pacta sunt servanda would be eroded if the law did not take account of the fact that the consumer often demands specifications which, although not of economic value, have value to him. This is sometimes called the 'consumer surplus': see Harris, Ogus and Philips, 'Contract Remedies and the Consumer Surplus' (1979) 95 *LQR* 581. Lord Mustill rejected the idea that 'the promisor can please himself whether or not to comply with the wishes of the promisee which, as embodied in the contract, formed part of the consideration for the price'. Lords Keith of Kinkel and Bridge of Harwich agreed with Lord Mustill's judgment and with Lord Lloyd of Berwick's similar reasoning. Labels sometimes obscure rather than illuminate. I do not therefore set much store by the description 'consumer surplus'. But the controlling principles stated by Lord Mustill and Lord Lloyd are important. It is difficult to reconcile this decision of the House with the decision of the Court of Appeal [2000] Lloyd's Rep PN 516 in the present case. I will in due course return to the way in which the majority attempted to distinguish *Ruxley Electronics and Construction Ltd* v. *Forsyth* [1996] AC 344. At this stage, however, I draw attention to the fact that the majority in the Court of Appeal, at p. 521, regarded the relevant observations of Lord Mustill and Lord Lloyd as obiter dicta. I am satisfied that the principles enunciated in *Ruxley*'s case in support of the award of £2,500 for a breach of respect of the provision of a pleasurable amenity have been authoritatively established.

VII. The very object of the contract: The arguments against the plaintiff's claim

22. Counsel for the surveyor advanced three separate arguments each of which he said was sufficient to defeat the plaintiff's claim. First, he submitted that even if a major or important part of the contract was to give pleasure, relaxation and peace of mind, that was not enough. It is an indispensable requirement that the object of the entire contract must be of this type. Secondly, he submitted that the exceptional category does not extend to a breach of a contractual duty of care, even if imposed to secure pleasure, relaxation and peace of mind. It only covers cases where the promiser guarantees achievement of such an object. Thirdly, he submitted that by not moving out of Riverside House the plaintiff forfeited any right to recover non-pecuniary damages.

23. The first argument fastened onto a narrow reading of the words 'the very object of [the] contract' as employed by Bingham LJ in *Watts* v. *Morrow* [1991] 1 WLR 1421, 1445. Cases where a major or important part of the contract was to secure pleasure, relaxation and peace of mind were not under consideration in *Watts* v. *Morrow*. It is difficult to see what the principled justification for such a limitation might be. After all, in 1978 the Court of Appeal allowed such a claim in *Jackson* v. *Chrysler Acceptances Ltd* [1978] RTR 474 in circumstances where a spoiled holiday was only one object of the contract.

[he considered the decision of the Court of Appeal in *Knott* v. *Bolton* (1995) 11 Const LJ 375 and continued]

There is no reason in principle or policy why the scope of recovery in the exceptional category should depend on the object of the contract as ascertained from all its constituent parts. It is sufficient if a major or important object of the contract is to give pleasure, relaxation or peace of mind. In my view *Knott* v. *Bolton* 11 Const LJ 375 was wrongly decided and should be overruled. To the extent that the majority in the Court of Appeal relied on *Knott* v. *Bolton* their decision was wrong.

25. That brings me to the second issue, namely whether the plaintiff's claim is barred by reason of the fact that the surveyor undertook an obligation to exercise reasonable care and did not guarantee the achievement of a result. This was the basis upon which Hale LJ after the first hearing in the Court of Appeal thought that the claim should be disallowed. This reasoning was adopted by the second Court of Appeal and formed an essential part of the reasoning of the majority. This was the basis on which they distinguished *Ruxley Electronics and Construction Ltd* v. *Forsyth* [1996] AC 344. Against the broad sweep of differently framed contractual undertakings, and the central purpose of contract law in promoting the observance of contractual promises, I am satisfied that this distinction ought not to prevail. It is certainly not rooted in precedent. I would not accept the suggestion that it has the pedigree of an observation of Ralph Gibson LJ in *Watts* v. *Morrow* [1991] 1 WLR 1421, 1442B–D: his emphasis appears to have been on the fact that the contract did not serve to provide peace of mind, and so forth. As far as I am aware the distinction was first articulated in the present case. In any event, I would reject it. I fully accept, of course, that contractual guarantees of performance and promises to exercise reasonable care are fundamentally different. The former may sometimes give greater protection than the latter. Proving breach of an obligation of reasonable care may be more difficult than proving breach of a guarantee. On the other hand, a party may in practice be willing to settle for the relative reassurance offered by the obligation of reasonable care undertaken by a professional man. But why should this difference between an absolute and relative contractual promise require a distinction in respect of the recovery of non-pecuniary damages? Take the example of a travel agent who is consulted by a couple who are looking for a golfing holiday in France. Why should it make a difference in respect of the recoverability of non-pecuniary damages for a spoiled holiday whether the travel agent gives a guarantee that there is a golf course very near the hotel, represents that to be the case, or negligently advises that all hotels of the particular chain of hotels are situated next to golf courses? If the nearest golf course is in fact 50 miles away a breach may be established. It may spoil the holiday of the couple. It is difficult to see why in principle only those plaintiffs who negotiate guarantees may recover non-pecuniary damages for a breach of contract. It is a singularly unattractive result that a professional man, who undertakes a specific obligation to exercise reasonable care to investigate a matter judged and communicated to be important by his customer can in Lord Mustill's words in *Ruxley Electronics and Construction Ltd* v. *Forsyth* [1996] AC 344, 360 'please himself whether or not to comply with the wishes of the promisee which, as embodied in the contract, formed part of the consideration for the price'. If that were the law it would be seriously deficient. I am satisfied that it is not the law. In my view the distinction drawn by Hale LJ and by the majority in the Court of Appeal between contractual guarantees and obligations of reasonable care is unsound.

26. The final argument was that by failing to move out the plaintiff forfeited a right to claim non-pecuniary damages. This argument was not advanced in the Court of Appeal. It will be recalled that the judge found as a fact that the plaintiff had acted reasonably in making 'the best of a bad job'. The plaintiff's decision also avoided a larger claim against the surveyor. It was never explained on what legal principle the plaintiff's decision not to move out divested him of a claim for non-pecuniary damages . . . The third argument must also be rejected.

27. While the dicta of Bingham LJ are of continuing usefulness as a starting point, it will be necessary to read them subject to the three points on which I have rejected the submissions made on behalf of the surveyor.

VIII. Quantum

28. In the surveyor's written case it was submitted that the award of £10,000 was excessive. It was certainly high. Given that the plaintiff is stuck indefinitely with a position which he sought to avoid by the terms of his contract with the surveyor I am not prepared to interfere with the judge's evaluation on the special facts of the case. On the other hand, I have to say that the size of the award appears to be at the very top end of what could possibly be regarded as appropriate damages. Like Bingham LJ in *Watts* v. *Morrow* [1991] 1 WLR 1421, 1445H I consider that awards in this area should be restrained and modest. It is important that logical and beneficial developments in this corner of the law should not contribute to the creation of a society bent on litigation.

IX. Conclusion

29. In agreement with the reasoning of Clarke LJ I would therefore hold that the decision of the majority in the Court of Appeal was wrong . . .

X. Inconvenience and discomfort

30. It is strictly unnecessary to discuss the question whether the judge's decision can be justified on the ground that the breach of contract resulted in inconvenience and discomfort. It is, however, appropriate that I indicate my view. The judge had a great deal of evidence on aircraft noise at Riverside House. It is conceded that noise can produce a physical reaction and can, depending on its intensity and the circumstances, constitute a nuisance. Noise from aircraft is exempted from the statutory nuisance system and in general no action lies in common law nuisance by reason only of the flight of aircraft over a property: see section 6(1) of the Civil Aviation Act 1982 and McCracken, Jones, Pereira and Payne, *Statutory Nuisance*, 2001, 10.33. The existence of the legislation shows that aircraft noise could arguably constitute a nuisance. In any event, aircraft noise is capable of causing inconvenience and discomfort within the meaning of Bingham LJ's relevant proposition. It is a matter of degree whether the case passes the threshold. It is sufficient to say that I have not been persuaded that the judge's decision on this point was not open to him on the evidence which he accepted. For this further reason, in general agreement with Clarke LJ, I would rule that the decision of the Court of Appeal was wrong.

XI. Disposal

31. I would allow the appeal and restore the judge's decision.

Lord Clyde

35. . . . The expression 'physical inconvenience' may be traced at least to the judgment of *Hobbs* v. *London and South Western Railway Co* (1875) LR 10 QB 111, 122, where in that case damages were awarded for the inconvenience suffered by the plaintiffs for having to walk between four and five miles home as a result of the train on which they had taken tickets to Wimbledon travelling instead to Esher. They had tried to obtain a conveyance but found that there was none to be had . . . It does not seem to me that there is any particular magic in the word 'physical'. It served in *Hobbs's* case to emphasise the exclusion of matters purely sentimental, but it should not require detailed analysis or definition. As matter of terminology I should have thought that 'inconvenience' by itself sufficiently covered the kinds of difficulty and discomfort which are more than mere matters of sentimentality, and that 'disappointment' would serve as a sufficient label for those mental reactions which in general the policy of the law will exclude.

36.   In *Hobbs's* case the defendants were prepared to compensate the plaintiffs for the cost of a conveyance, even although they had not been able to find any. In the present case the defendant would be prepared to pay for the costs of sale and removal if the plaintiff had decided to sell because of the noise. It is said by the respondent that since he has decided to keep the house he is not entitled to any damages at all. But in *Hobbs* the plaintiffs were entitled to damages in respect of the inconvenience. It is hard to understand why a corresponding result should not follow here. That an award may be made in such circumstances is to my mind in line with the thinking of this House in *Ruxley Electronics and Construction Ltd v. Forsyth* [1996] AC 344 . . .

37.   The judge found that the plaintiff was not a man of excessive susceptibility and he refers to the inconvenience he was suffering as 'real discomfort'. I do not consider it appropriate to explore the detail of the inconvenience as being 'physical', either because it impacts upon his eardrums, or because it has some geographical element, such as the relative locations of the aircraft and the property, or the obviously greater audibility of their movements when the plaintiff is seeking to enjoy the amenity of the terrace and the gardens than when he is inside the house. In my view the real discomfort which the judge found to exist constituted an inconvenience to the plaintiff which is not a mere matter of disappointment or sentiment. It is unnecessary that the noise should be so great as to make it impossible for the plaintiff to sit at all on his terrace. Plainly it significantly interferes with his enjoyment of the property and in my view that inconvenience is something for which damages can and should be awarded . . .

38.   . . . In my view the appeal can be allowed on the foregoing basis.

39.   But it is possible to approach the case as one of the exceptional kind in which the claim would be for damages for disappointment. If that approach was adopted so as to seek damages for disappointment, I consider that it should also succeed.

40.   It should be observed at the outset that damages should not be awarded, unless perhaps nominally, for the fact of a breach of contract as distinct from the consequences of the breach. That was a point which I sought to stress in *Panatown Ltd v. Alfred McAlpine Construction Ltd* [2001] 1 AC 518. For an award to be made a loss or injury has to be identified which is a consequence of the breach but not too remote from it, and which somehow or other can be expressed and quantified in terms of a sum of money. So disappointment merely at the fact that the contract has been breached is not a proper ground for an award. The mere fact of the loss of a bargain should not be the subject of compensation. But that is not the kind of claim which the plaintiff is making here. What he is seeking is damages for the inconvenience of the noise, the invasion of the peace and quiet which he expected the property to possess and the diminution in his use and enjoyment of the property on account of the aircraft noise.

41.   The critical factor on this approach, as it seems to me, is that the plaintiff made the specific request of the defendant to discover whether the property might be affected by aircraft noise . . .

42. . . . The present case is not an 'ordinary surveyor's contract'. The request for the report on aircraft noise was additional to the usual matters expected of a surveyor in the survey of a property and could properly have attracted an extra fee if he had spent extra time researching that issue. It is the specific provision relating to the peacefulness of the property in respect of aircraft noise which makes the present case out of the ordinary . . .

44. The object of the request to consider the risk of aircraft noise was very plainly to enable the plaintiff to determine the extent of the peace and quiet which he could enjoy at the property. It would be within the contemplation of the defendant that if the noise was such as to interfere with the occupier's peaceful enjoyment of the property the plaintiff would either not buy it at all or live there deprived of his expectation of peace and quiet. Each of these consequences seems to me to flow directly from the breach of contract so as to enable an award of damages to be made on one or other basis. The present case can in my view qualify as one of the exceptional cases where a contract for peace or pleasure has been made and breached, thereby entitling the injured party to claim damages for the disappointment occasioned by the breach.

45. For the foregoing reasons I would allow the appeal and restore the judge's award.

Lord Scott of Foscote

75. In my opinion, the issue can and should be resolved by applying the well known principles laid down in *Hadley* v. *Baxendale* (1854) 9 Exch 341 (as restated in *Victoria Laundry Ltd* v. *Newman Industries Ltd* [1949] 2 KB 528) in the light of the recent guidance provided by Bingham LJ in *Watts* v. *Morrow* [1991] 1 WLR 1421 and by this House in *Ruxley Electronics and Construction Ltd* v. *Forsyth* [1996] AC 344.

76. The basic principle of damages for breach of contract is that the injured party is entitled, so far as money can do it, to be put in the position he would have been in if the contractual obligation had been properly performed. He is entitled, that is to say, to the benefit of his bargain: see *Robinson* v. *Harman* (1848) 1 Exch 850, 855.

[he considered the decision of the House of Lords in *Ruxley Electronics and Construction Ltd* v. *Forsyth* [1996] AC 344 and continued]

79. *Ruxley's* case establishes, in my opinion, that if a party's contractual performance has failed to provide to the other contracting party something to which that other was, under the contract, entitled, and which, if provided, would have been of value to that party, then, if there is no other way of compensating the injured party, the injured party should be compensated in damages to the extent of that value. Quantification of that value will, in many cases be difficult and may often seem arbitrary. In *Ruxley's* case the value placed on the amenity value of which the pool owner had been deprived was £2,500. By that award, the pool owner was placed, so far as money could do it, in the position he would have been in if the diving area of the pool had been constructed to the specified depth.

80. In *Ruxley's* case the breach of contract by the builders had not caused any consequential loss to the pool owner. He had simply been deprived of the benefit of a pool built to the depth specified in the contract. It was not a case where the recovery of damages for consequential loss consisting of vexation, anxiety or other species of mental distress had to be considered.

81. In *Watts* v. *Morrow* [1991] 1 WLR 1921, however, that matter did have to be considered . . .

[he set out the facts of the case and quoted the passage from the judgment of Bingham LJ set out at paragraph [14] above and continued]

82. In the passage I have cited, Bingham LJ was dealing with claims for consequential damage consisting of the intangible mental states and sensory experiences to which he refers. Save for the matters referred in the first paragraph, all of which reflect or are brought about by the injured party's disappointment at the contract breaker's failure to carry out his contractual obligations, and recovery for which, if there is nothing more, is ruled out on policy grounds, Bingham LJ's approach is, in my view, wholly consistent with established principles for the recovery of contractual damages.

83. There are, however, two qualifications that I would respectfully make to the proposition in the final paragraph of the cited passage that damages 'for physical inconvenience and discomfort caused by the breach' are recoverable.

84. First, there will, in many cases, be an additional remoteness hurdle for the injured party to clear. Consequential damage, including damage consisting of inconvenience or discomfort, must, in order to be recoverable, be such as, at the time of the contract, was reasonably foreseeable as liable to result from the breach: see McGregor *on Damages*, 16th ed. (1997), para 250, pp. 159–160.

85. Second, the adjective 'physical', in the phrase 'physical inconvenience and discomfort', requires, I think, some explanation or definition. The distinction between the 'physical' and the 'non-physical' is not always clear and may depend on the context. Is being awoken at night by aircraft noise 'physical'? If it is, is being unable to sleep because of worry and anxiety 'physical'? What about a reduction in light caused by the erection of a building under a planning permission that an errant surveyor ought to have warned his purchaser-client about but failed to do so? In my opinion, the critical distinction to be drawn is not a distinction between the different types of inconvenience or discomfort of which complaint may be made but a distinction based on the cause of the inconvenience or discomfort. If the cause is no more than disappointment that the contractual obligation has been broken, damages are not recoverable even if the disappointment has led to a complete mental breakdown. But, if the cause of the inconvenience or discomfort is a sensory (sight, touch, hearing, smell etc) experience, damages can, subject to the remoteness rules, be recovered.

86. In summary, the principle expressed in *Ruxley Electronics and Construction Ltd* v. *Forsyth* [1996] AC 344 should be used to provide damages for deprivation of a contractual benefit where it is apparent that the injured party has been deprived of something of value but the ordinary means of measuring the recoverable damages are inapplicable. The principle expressed in *Watts* v. *Morrow* [1991] 1 WLR 1421 should be used to determine whether and when contractual damages for inconvenience or discomfort can be recovered.

87. These principles, in my opinion, provide the answer, not only to the issue raised in the present case, but also to the issues raised in the authorities which were cited to your Lordships.

88. In *Hobbs* v. *London and South Western Railway Co* (1875) LR 10 QB 111 the claim was for consequential damage caused by the railway company's breach of contract. Instead of taking the plaintiff, his wife and two children to Hampton Court, their train dumped them at Esher and they had to walk five miles or so home in the rain. The plaintiff's wife caught a cold as a result of the experience. The plaintiff was awarded damages for the inconvenience and discomfort of his and his family's walk home but his wife's cold was held to be too remote a consequence. The plaintiff's recovery of damages attributable, in part, to the discomfort suffered by his wife and children was in accordance with principle. The contractual benefit to which he was entitled was the carriage of himself and his family to Hampton Court. It was reasonable in my opinion, to value that benefit, of which he had been deprived by the breach of contract, by reference to the discomfort to the family of the walk home. This was, in my view, a *Ruxley Electronics and Construction Ltd* v. *Forsyth* [1996] AC 344 case . . .

[he applied the principles set out in paragraph [86] to a range of cases and continued]

105. It is time for me to turn to the present case and apply the principles expressed in *Ruxley Electronics and Construction Ltd* v. *Forsyth* [1996] AC 344 and *Watts* v. *Morrow* [1991] 1 WLR 1421. In my judgment, Mr Farley is entitled to be compensated for the 'real discomfort' that the judge found he suffered. He is so entitled on either of two alternative bases.

106. First, he was deprived of the contractual benefit to which he was entitled. He was entitled to information about the aircraft noise from Gatwick bound aircraft that Mr Skinner, through negligence, had failed to supply him with. If Mr Farley had, in the event, decided not to purchase Riverside House, the value to him of the contractual benefit of which he had been deprived would have been nil. But he did buy the property. And he took his decision to do so without the advantage of being able to take into account the information to which he was contractually entitled. If he had had that information he would not have bought. So the information clearly would have had a value to him. Prima facie, in my opinion, he is entitled to be compensated accordingly.

107. In these circumstances, it seems to me, it is open to the court to adopt a *Ruxley Electronics and Construction Ltd* v. *Forsyth* [1996] AC 344 approach and place a value on the contractual benefit of which Mr Farley has been deprived. In deciding on the amount, the discomfort experienced by Mr Farley can, in my view, properly be taken into account. If he had had the aircraft noise information he would not have bought Riverside House and would not have had that discomfort.

108. Alternatively, Mr Farley can, in my opinion, claim compensation for the discomfort as consequential loss. Had it not been for the breach of contract, he would not have suffered the discomfort. It was caused by the breach of contract in a causa sine qua non sense. Was the discomfort a consequence that should reasonably have been contemplated by the parties at the time of contract as liable to result from the breach? In my opinion, it was. It was obviously within the reasonable contemplation of the parties that, deprived of the information about aircraft noise that he ought to have had, Mr Farley would make a decision to purchase that he would not otherwise have made. Having purchased, he would, having become aware of the noise, either sell—in which case at least the expenses of the re-sale would have been recoverable as damages—or he would keep the property and put up with the noise. In the latter event, it was within the reasonable contemplation of the parties that he would experience discomfort from the noise of the aircraft. And the discomfort was 'physical' in the sense that Bingham LJ in *Watts* v. *Morrow* [1991] 1 WLR 1421, 1445 had in mind. In my opinion, the application of *Watts* v. *Morrow* principles entitles Mr Farley to damages for discomfort caused by the aircraft noise.

109.   I would add that if there had been an appreciable reduction in the market value of the property caused by the aircraft noise, Mr Farley could not have recovered both that difference in value and damages for discomfort. To allow both would allow double recovery for the same item.

110.   Whether the approach to damages is on *Ruxley Electronics and Construction Ltd* v. *Forsyth* [1996] AC 344 lines, for deprivation of a contractual benefit, or on *Watts* v. *Morrow* [1991] 1 WLR 1421 lines, for consequential damage within the applicable remoteness rules, the appropriate amount should, in my opinion, be modest. The degree of discomfort experienced by Mr Farley, although 'real', was not very great. I think £10,000 may have been on the high side. But in principle, in my opinion, the judge was right to award damages and I am not, in the circumstances, disposed to disagree with his figure.

111.   For the reasons I have given and for the reasons contained in the opinion of my noble and learned friend, Lord Steyn, I would allow the appeal and restore the judge's order.

Lord Browne-Wilkinson concurred. **Lord Hutton** delivered a concurring speech.

COMMENTARY

A number of points should be noted about this decision (see further E McKendrick and M Graham, 'The Sky's the Limit: Contractual Damages for Non-Pecuniary Loss' [2002] *LMCLQ* 161). The first relates to the conclusion that it is no longer necessary that the 'object of the contract' be the provision of pleasure or peace of mind. It now suffices that the object of the term broken is to provide pleasure or freedom from distress and that the term is an important one in the context of the contract as a whole. While this is a welcome development, it may not always be easy to ascertain whether this requirement has been satisfied on the facts of any given case. Some cases are likely to be relatively straightforward: for example, a contract to take photographs at a wedding (*Diesen* v. *Samson*, 1971 SLT (Sh Ct) 49) or to provide a holiday (*Jarvis* v. *Swans Tours Ltd* [1973] QB 233). But others are likely to prove more difficult. An example is provided by *Hamilton Jones* v. *David & Snape (a firm)* [2003] EWHC 3147 (Ch); [2004] 1 All ER 657 where Neuberger J had some difficulty in deciding whether a contract with a solicitor could fall within this category. The claimant, who was concerned that her husband might remove their children from the jurisdiction, instructed the defendant solicitors. As a result of their negligence, her husband was able to abduct their sons to Tunisia, where he was awarded custody. Neuberger J held that the claimant was entitled to recover damages of £20,000 in respect of the distress which she had suffered. The claimant had, and was perceived by the defendants to have had, 'her own peace of mind and pleasure in the company of her children as an important factor' when entering into the contract with the defendants. Contracts with surveyors have also given rise to difficulty in this respect. There appears to be a distinction between an 'ordinary surveyor's contract', which the House of Lords in *Farley* held does not fall within this category, and the contract in *Farley*, which did (see para [42]). The distinction between the two cases would appear to rest on the fact that the plaintiff in *Farley* specifically asked the surveyor to investigate noise levels from aircraft (see para [15]). Yet why should the plaintiff have to ask for peace of mind in this respect? Is it not implicit in every contract with a surveyor that the houseowner is seeking peace of mind? *Ruxley* v. *Forsyth* (p. 1018 above) may also fall within this category (see further below).

The second point relates to the recovery of damages for inconvenience and discomfort. Lord Clyde held that the plaintiff was entitled to recover damages on the basis of the inconvenience and discomfort that he suffered as a result of the defendant's breach. This was Lord Clyde's primary ground for his decision (see paras [37]– [39]), whereas for the others it was their secondary ground. The difficulty here relates to the scope of the category. How far does it extend and how does one distinguish between inconvenience (which falls within its scope) and disappointment (which does not)? Inconvenience is not easy to define. The definition adopted by Lord Scott, which places emphasis on the existence of a 'sensory' cause of the inconvenience or discomfort (see para [85]), may prove to be a workable definition in many cases. Further, Lord Steyn's reference to the law of nuisance (in para [30]) has the advantage of tapping into an established body of case-law. On the other hand, Lord Clyde found it unnecessary (para [35]) to provide a 'detailed analysis or definition' of inconvenience. For him, 'inconvenience' was to be distinguished from the 'purely sentimental'. The aircraft noise fell into the former category since it 'significantly interfered' with the plaintiff's use of his property. Of the four speeches, only Lord Scott purported to draw a principled distinction between disappointment and inconvenience, the others being prepared only to identify 'inconvenience' on the facts of the particular case.

A related difficulty is that inconvenience and discomfort are highly subjective in nature. In this respect *Farley* may be close to the line. As Lord Scott observed (at para [68]), there was 'evidence that many, perhaps most, of the residents in the area were not troubled by the noise'. But the test for the existence of discomfort does not appear to be an objective one: it contains a significant subjective element in that regard must be had to the plaintiff's mode of life. In the present case the plaintiff was in the habit of enjoying 'a quiet, reflective breakfast, a morning stroll in his garden', and pre-dinner drinks on the terrace and all three activities were interfered with by the noise from the aircraft. Will this subjective approach to the identification of inconvenience open the floodgates to claims of this type? Probably not. Liability will be contained by the remoteness rules (on which see pp. 1078–1099 below). Had the plaintiff not made clear to the defendant the importance that he attached to not being troubled by aircraft noise, the defendant would not have been liable on the ground that the loss suffered by the plaintiff would not have been within the contemplation of both parties at the time of entry into the contract.

The third point relates to the scope of *Ruxley*. The speeches in *Farley* contain three different explanations for Mr Forsyth's entitlement to recover £2,500. Lords Steyn (at para [21]) and Hutton (at para [49]) classified the contract in *Ruxley* as one for the provision of a pleasurable amenity, thus the damages reflected Mr Forsyth's disappointment at the loss of this amenity. By contrast Lord Clyde, while he made reference to the fact that the contract was one for the provision of a pleasurable amenity, analysed *Ruxley* in the section of his speech devoted to the award of damages for inconvenience (para [35]). However Lord Lloyd in his speech in *Ruxley* records that the trial judge awarded Mr Forsyth damages of £750 for 'general inconvenience and disturbance' separately from the award of £2,500 in respect of his 'loss of amenity'. It therefore seems at best doubtful whether the award of £2,500 in *Ruxley* can also be regarded as compensation for inconvenience. The third and most radical analysis of *Ruxley* was adopted by Lord Scott (at para [79]). This takes us back to the discussison of Lord Millett's analysis of *Ruxley* in *Panatown* (p. 1039 above).

The fourth point relates to Lord Scott's division of the cases into two distinct groups (see para [86]). The first group, represented by *Ruxley*, consists of cases where the claim is one to recover the value of the promised performance which has not been supplied by the party in breach. The second group, represented by *Watts v. Morrow*, consists of claims to recover consequential loss. In theory, the distinction has merit. But in practice it is likely to be difficult to distinguish between the two categories. A case that illustrates the difficulty is *Hobbs* v. *London and South Western Rly Co* (1875) LR 10 QB 111 (discussed by Lord Scott at para [88]). Does this case fall within Lord Scott's first category or his second? Lord Scott himself put it in the first category on the basis that the damages were awarded to compensate the plaintiff for the loss of the contractual benefit to which he was entitled, namely carriage of him and his family to Hampton Court. On the other hand, Lord Clyde (at paras [35]–[36]) clearly regarded it as a case where damages were awarded to compensate the plaintiff for the inconvenience suffered (and, on this basis, it would appear to fall within Lord Scott's second category). The difficulty in distinguishing between the two categories lies in part in the fact that damages are assessed in a category one case in a manner which may resemble the approach taken in a category two case. Thus Lord Scott classified *Hobbs* as a category one case but, in relation to the assessment of damages, stated (at para [88]) that it was reasonable to value the contractual benefit to which the plaintiff was entitled 'by reference to the discomfort to the family of the walk home'. This very much mirrors the approach that would be taken in a category two case and so, in practice, tends to blur the distinction between the two categories.

Nevertheless, Lord Scott's analysis is useful in so far as it demonstrates that there is more than one way of framing a claim for damages. One of the difficulties with *Hobbs* lies in explaining the basis on which damages were recovered for the inconvenience suffered by the members of the plaintiff's family, given the general rule that a contracting party cannot sue and recover damages in respect of a loss that has been suffered by a third party (on which see p. 1195 below). Thus if the claim was a category two case, only the plaintiff should have been compensated for his inconvenience and discomfort. On the other hand, if the claim is properly classified as a category one case then it becomes possible to argue that the performance for which the plaintiff contracted was the carriage of himself and his family to Hampton Court.

An alternative analysis (see E McKendrick and K Worthington, 'Damages for Non-Pecuniary Loss' in N Cohen and E McKendrick (eds), *Comparative Remedies for Breach of Contract* (Hart, Oxford, 2004), p. 274), which is similar to that adopted by Lord Scott, is to distinguish those cases in which the claimant seeks damages in respect of the defendant's failure to confer on the claimant a promised non-pecuniary benefit from those cases in which the claimant seeks damages to compensate her for the non-pecuniary loss which she has suffered as a result of, or as a consequence of, the defendant's breach of contract. The first category consists of cases in which the defendant, expressly or impliedly, promises to confer a non-pecuniary benefit on the claimant or the effect of the breach was to deny the claimant the non-pecuniary benefit which she would have obtained from performance in accordance with the terms of the contract. This category encompasses the holiday cases (such as *Jarvis* v. *Swans Tours Ltd* [1973] QB 233) but it can also extend to cases such as *Ruxley* where the defendant did not promise, either expressly or impliedly, to confer a non-pecuniary benefit on the claimant but the contractual specification broken, of no intrinsic financial value in itself, was accorded 'added value' by the claimant. The second category consists of cases in which the claimant has attempted to recover damages in respect of non-pecuniary losses which she has suffered as a consequence of the defendant's breach of contract. These consequential non-pecuniary losses can be divided into different categories, although the categories are not watertight. The types of consequential non-pecuniary losses that have been recognized in the cases include physical injury, psychiatric injury or illness, embarrassment and loss of reputation (physical) inconvenience, and mental distress or disappointment. The courts have been much more willing to allow damages to be recovered in respect of physical injuries suffered as a result of a breach of contract than they have been in the case where the claimant suffers mental distress or disappointment. The latter appear to be recoverable only within the limits recognized by the House of Lords in *Farley*, although it is suggested that most of the cases in which damages have been awarded for distress and loss of enjoyment are better seen within the first category; that is to say they are cases in which the defendant expressly or impliedly promised to provide the claimant with pleasure or relief from distress or the claimant was deprived, as a result of the breach, of performance to which she attached 'added value'.

The final point regarding *Farley* relates to the assessment of damages. In this respect *Farley* resembles *Ruxley* (above) in that all the reasoned speeches in the House of Lords recognized that £10,000 was at the top end of the scale but they were not prepared to deem it to be excessive on the facts of the case. Fears that this case will open the floodgates seem misplaced. Rather, the effect of the decision is more likely to be to bring the law formally into line with practice in the lower courts, particularly the county courts, which, as Lord Steyn pointed out (at para [20]), regularly award damages on a modest scale for non-pecuniary losses in the 'diverse contractual contexts' to which he makes reference. This practice has been legitimated by the House of Lords but the decision in *Farley* should not be seen as a green light for the increase in the level of damages awarded. It is not. Damages should continue to be awarded on a modest scale.

8. LIMITING THE PROTECTION OF THE PERFORMANCE INTEREST

A claimant cannot in all circumstances claim the full protection of his performance interest. The law places various limits upon his ability to do so. These limits are sometimes inherent in the ordinary rules of proof. For example, a claimant must prove that the defendant has breached the terms of the contract and that the breach has caused him the loss in respect of which he brings his claim for damages. In some cases it can be a difficult task for a claimant to show that the breach has caused that loss (see, for example, *Chaplin* v. *Hicks* [1911] 2 KB 786, p. 1055 above and *Monarch Steamship Co Ltd* v. *Karlshamns Oljefabriker (A/B)* [1949] AC 196). In this section three doctrines will be examined. Each doctrine demonstrates that the law is not committed to the full protection of the claimant's performance interest (albeit that the reasons for limiting the extent of the claim differ in each category).

(a) REMOTENESS

A claimant cannot recover damages in respect of a loss which is too remote a consequence of the defendant's breach of contract. As has been pointed out (p. 444 above), claims for consequential losses are extremely significant in practice, largely because of their size. The remoteness rules are therefore extremely important because, the greater the extent of the liability that is imposed at common law, the greater the steps that have to be taken to draft clauses, such as exclusion and limitation clauses, which aim to keep liability within acceptable bounds.

It is in fact no easy task to discern the point at which the courts draw the line between losses that are too remote and hence irrecoverable and losses that are recoverable. The difference between a loss that is too remote and one that is not appears to be one of degree, and not kind. The leading case is *Hadley* v. *Baxendale* (1854) 9 Exch 341. The rule there laid down was that the losses are recoverable if they flow naturally from the breach or if they are in the contemplation of both parties at the time of entry into the contract. In the twentieth century the principal issue of controversy was the relationship between the decisions of the Court of Appeal in *Victoria Laundry (Windsor)* v. *Newman Industries* [1949] 2 KB 528 and *Parsons (Livestock) Ltd* v. *Uttley Ingham & Co Ltd* [1978] QB 791. The tension between these two cases remains largely unresolved. But certain things are clear. First, the nature of the breach is irrelevant; that is to say, the courts do not distinguish between intentional, careless and inadvertent breaches of contract (although in tort the law does distinguish in this respect between intentional and unintentional torts). Secondly, the recoverability of damages does not depend upon the nature of the loss suffered, although Lord Denning sought to draw such a distinction in *Parsons*. Rather, the recoverability of damages depends upon the knowledge or the contemplation of the parties at the time of entry into the contract and, in particular, the knowledge of the party in breach.

There are three distinct parts to this section. The first part consists of an analysis of *Hadley* v. *Baxendale*, the second part examines the relationship between *Victoria*

Laundry and *Parsons*, together with the decision of the House of Lords in *The Heron II*, while the final part consists of some concluding thoughts.

Hadley v. Baxendale

(1854) 9 Exch 341, Court of Exchequer

The plaintiff, a mill owner, entered into a contract with the defendant, a carrier, under which the defendant agreed to carry a broken crank shaft from the plaintiff's mill to a third party engineer for repair and then to deliver the crank shaft back to the plaintiff once the repairs had been completed. In breach of contract, the defendant delayed in the delivery of the crank shaft to the third party engineer and this resulted in a complete loss of production at the mill for five extra days. The plaintiff claimed damages for the loss of profit for the five days that the mill was shut down as a consequence of the defendant's breach but it was held that the loss of profits was too remote a consequence of the breach and was therefore not recoverable.

Alderson B

Now we think the proper rule in such a case as the present is this:—Where two parties have made a contract which one of them has broken, the damages which the other party ought to receive in respect of such breach of contract should be such as may fairly and reasonably be considered either arising naturally, i.e. according to the usual course of things, from such breach of contract itself, or such as may reasonably be supposed to have been in the contemplation of both parties, at the time they made the contract, as the probable result of the breach of it. Now, if the special circumstances under which the contract was actually made were communicated by the plaintiffs to the defendants, and thus known to both parties, the damages resulting from the breach of such a contract, which they would reasonably contemplate, would be the amount of injury which would ordinarily follow from a breach of contract under these special circumstances so known and communicated. But, on the other hand, if these special circumstances were wholly unknown to the party breaking the contract, he, at the most, could only be supposed to have had in his contemplation the amount of injury which would arise generally, and in the great multitude of cases not affected by any special circumstances, from such a breach of contract. For, had the special circumstances been known, the parties might have specially provided for the breach of contract by special terms as to the damages in that case; and of this advantage it would be very unjust to deprive them. Now the above principles are those by which we think the jury ought to be guided in estimating the damages arising out of any breach of contract. It is said, that other cases such as breaches of contract in the nonpayment of money, or in the not making a good title to land, are to be treated as exceptions from this, and as governed by a conventional rule. But as, in such cases, both parties must be supposed to be cognisant of that well-known rule, these cases may, we think, be more properly classed under the rule above enunciated as to cases under known special circumstances, because there both parties may reasonably be presumed to contemplate the estimation of the amount of damages according to the conventional rule. Now, in the present case, if we are to apply the principles above laid down, we find that the only circumstances here communicated by the plaintiffs to the defendants at the time the contract was made, were, that the article to be carried was the broken shaft of a mill, and that the plaintiffs were the millers of that mill. But how do these circumstances shew reasonably that the profits of the mill must be stopped by an unreasonable delay in the delivery of the broken shaft by the carrier to the third person? Suppose the plaintiffs had another shaft in their possession put up or putting up at the time, and that they only wished to send back the broken shaft to the engineer who made it; it is clear that this would be quite consistent with the above circumstances, and yet the unreasonable delay in the delivery would have no effect upon the intermediate profits of the mill. Or, again, suppose that, at the time of the delivery to the carrier, the machinery of the mill had been in other respects defective, then, also, the same results would follow. Here it is true that the shaft was actually sent back to serve as a model for a new one, and that the want of a new one was the only cause of the stoppage of the mill, and that the loss of profits really arose from not sending down the new shaft in proper time, and that this arose from the delay in delivering the broken one to serve as a model. But it is obvious that, in the great multitude of cases of millers sending off broken shafts to third persons by a carrier under ordinary circumstances, such consequences would not, in all probability, have occurred; and these special circumstances were here never communicated by the plaintiffs to the defendants. It follows, therefore, that the loss of profits here cannot reasonably be considered such a consequence of the breach of contract as could have been fairly and reasonably contemplated by both the parties when they made this contract. For such loss would neither have flowed naturally from the breach of this contract in the great multitude of such cases occurring under ordinary circumstances, nor were the special circumstances, which, perhaps, would have made it a reasonable and natural consequence of such breach of contract, communicated to or known by the defendants. The Judge ought, therefore, to have told the jury, that, upon the facts then before them, they ought not to take the loss of profits into consideration at all in estimating the damages. There must therefore be a new trial in this case.

Rule absolute.

COMMENTARY

Hadley was decided at a critical point in the development of English contract law. It was decided at a time when the judges were assuming a greater role in the formulation of legal principle and, in consequence, the role of the jury was diminishing. The judgment thus aims to lay down principles to be applied by the jury when assessing the damages payable upon a breach of contract.

The rule laid down in *Hadley* is sometimes required to do work for which it was not intended. In some cases it is cited as authority for the basic measure of recovery (see, for example, *Bence Graphics International Ltd* v. *Fasson UK Ltd* [1998] QB 87, 102) when in fact the function of the rule laid down in the case is to *limit* the liability of the party in breach. It does so by stating that the innocent party cannot be put in the position which he would have been in had the contract been performed according to its terms if the losses sought to be recovered do not flow naturally from the breach or were not within the reasonable contemplation of both parties at the time of entry into the contract. The rules relating to the interpretation of a clause which purports to exclude liability for 'indirect or consequential loss' have also become inter-twined with *Hadley* v. *Baxendale* (see pp. 458–460 above). The reason for this is that the courts have held that the effect of such a clause is to exclude liability for losses falling within the second limb of *Hadley* (that is to say, losses that are within the contemplation of both parties at the time of entry into the contract) but not losses that fall within the first (losses that flow naturally from the breach). The use of *Hadley* in this latter context seems doubly unfortunate. First, it is unlikely that the court in *Hadley* intended such a result and it also seems unlikely that parties to a contract containing such an exclusion clause intended to produce this result. Secondly, it is a matter of some doubt whether there are two rules in *Hadley* or only one and it seems unfortunate that the courts in the context of the interpretation of an exclusion clause insist that there are two rules when in the remoteness cases the drift of judicial opinion appears to be in the direction of there being only one test (see, for example, the judgment of Asquith LJ in *Victoria Laundry (Windsor)* v. *Newman Industries* [1949] 2 KB 528, p. 1083 below).

Why was the loss not recoverable on the facts of the case? First, the loss did not flow naturally from the breach; the mill owner might have had a spare mill shaft. Secondly, it was not within the contemplation of both parties at the time of entry into the contract because the defendants did not have knowledge of the loss likely to be suffered by the plaintiffs. Three points should be noted here. First, it is important to note that the relevant time is the time of entry into the contract and not the time of breach. What the courts are doing is to examine the contractual allocation of risk. A defendant who knows at the time of entry into the contract that he is potentially exposed to a claim for substantial damages will either insert a clause into the contract in order to exclude or limit that liability or he will increase the price in order to reflect the increased risk he must bear. What the law does not allow a claimant to do is to say nothing about the extent of any special loss he is likely to suffer as a result of the breach, and so avoid the possibility of being asked to pay more in return for the defendant agreeing to accept responsibility for that loss, and then seek to recover in respect of that loss. In this sense, the remoteness rules encourage parties to disclose special losses likely to be suffered as a result of the breach. The price of failing to do so is that the innocent party may be unable to recover in respect of that loss.

The second relates to the knowledge of the defendants on the facts of *Hadley*. This proved to be an issue of some controversy on the facts of the case itself. The headnote to the case states that the defendant's clerk was told, prior to the conclusion of the contract, that the mill was stopped and that the shaft must be delivered immediately. The Court of Appeal in *Victoria Laundry (Windsor)* v. *Newman Industries* [1949] 2 KB 528 (p. 1082 below) concluded that the headnote was, in this respect, misleading on the basis that the court must have rejected the evidence adduced on behalf of the plaintiffs on this issue because Alderson B concluded (above) that:

we find that the only circumstances here communicated by the plaintiffs to the defendants at the time the contract was made, were, that the article to be carried was the broken shaft of a mill, and that the plaintiffs were the millers of that mill.

Thus *Hadley* is a case in which the defendants did not have knowledge of the fact that the mill would be shut until the crank shaft had been repaired and returned to the mill.

This leads us to the third point which relates to the matters that the plaintiffs in *Hadley* would have had to prove in order to hold the defendants liable for the losses which they suffered. There are two possible tests. One view is that it would suffice for the plaintiffs to prove that the defendants had knowledge of the fact that the mill was shut. A second view is that knowledge is not enough of itself and that it must be demonstrated that the defendant has, in some way, accepted that he will bear responsibility for the loss should it eventuate. In *British Columbia Saw Mill Co* v. *Nettleship* (1868) LR 3 CP 499 Willes J stated that the knowledge must be brought home to the defendant under such circumstances that he knows that the person with whom he contracts reasonably believes that he accepts responsibility for the special loss (to similar effect see *Horne* v. *Midland Railway Co* (1873) LR 8 CP 131 where there are suggestions that the notice must amount to an agreement to accept liability before the loss can be recovered). On the other hand, a more liberal approach was adopted by the court in *Simpson* v. *London and North Western Railway Co* (1876) 1 QBD 274 where the stipulation that samples 'must be at Newcastle on Monday certain' was held to be sufficient to impose a liability on the defendant for the loss of profit suffered by the plaintiff as a result of the defendant's failure to deliver the goods to the showground in time for an agricultural show. It is suggested that a great deal turns on the circumstances in which the information is conveyed to the defendant. If it is given to him in the context of pre-contractual negotiations then it is suggested that the defendant will be fixed with liability for the loss unless he makes clear to the other party that he does not accept responsibility for the loss in question. Where, however, the defendant acquires the information fortuitously (that is to say, it is not acquired in the context of pre-contractual negotiations) then mere knowledge of the loss will not suffice to impose liability on the defendant. The claimant will have to show that the defendant in some way assented to the assumption of responsibility in respect of that loss.

Victoria Laundry (Windsor) v. Newman Industries

[1949] 2 KB 528, Court of Appeal

The plaintiffs entered into a contract with the defendants under which they agreed to buy from the defendants a large boiler for use in their business as launderers and dyers. At the time at which the contract was concluded the boiler was installed on the defendants' premises. It was therefore necessary to dismantle the boiler before it could be delivered to the plaintiffs. The boiler was badly damaged while it was being dismantled and the consequence was that there was a delay of some five months in delivering it to the plaintiffs. The defendants knew that the plaintiffs were launderers and dyers and that they wanted the boiler for use in their business. During the negotiations the plaintiffs expressed their intention to put the boiler 'into use in the shortest possible space of time'. The plaintiffs brought an action for damages for the losses they had suffered as a result of the defendants' breach of contract.

   The trial judge, Streatfeild J, gave judgment for the plaintiffs for damages of £110 under certain minor heads, but held that the plaintiffs were not entitled to recover damages in respect of their loss of profit during the period of delay. He concluded that the boiler was not a whole plant capable of being used by itself as a profit-making machine, that the case fell within the second limb of the rule laid down in *Hadley* v. *Baxendale* and that the defendants were not liable for the plaintiffs' loss of profit because the special object for which the plaintiffs were acquiring the boiler had not been drawn to the defendants' attention. The plaintiffs appealed to the Court of Appeal who allowed the appeal and held that the plaintiffs were entitled to recover damages for their general loss of profits but not for the loss of profits which they suffered on the lucrative contracts that they had concluded with the Ministry of Supply.

Asquith LJ [delivering the judgment of the court]
The authorities on recovery of loss of profits as a head of damage are not easy to reconcile. At one end of the scale stand cases where there has been non-delivery or delayed delivery of what is on the face of it obviously a profit-earning chattel; for instance, a merchant or passenger ship: see *Fletcher* v. *Tayleur* (1855) 17 CB 21. . . . In such cases loss of profit has rarely been refused. A second and intermediate class of case in which loss of profit has often been awarded is where ordinary mercantile goods have been sold to a merchant with knowledge by the vendor that the purchaser wanted them for resale; at all events, where there was no market in which the purchaser could buy similar goods against the contract on the seller's default, see, for instance, *Borries* v. *Hutchinson* (1865) 18 CB (NS) 445. At the other end of the scale are cases where the defendant is not a vendor of the goods, but a carrier, see, for instance, *Hadley* v. *Baxendale* 9 Exch 341. . . . In such cases the courts have been slow to allow loss of profit as an item of damage. This was not, it would seem, because a different principle applies in such cases, but because the application of the same principle leads to different results. A carrier commonly knows less than a seller about the purposes for which the buyer or consignee needs the goods, or about other 'special circumstances' which may cause exceptional loss if due delivery is withheld.

Three of the authorities call for more detailed examination.

[he examined *Hadley* v. *Baxendale, British Columbia Sawmills* v. *Nettleship* LR 3 CP 409, and *Cory* v. *Thames Ironworks Company* LR 3 QB 181 and continued]

What propositions applicable to the present case emerge from the authorities as a whole, including those analysed above? We think they include the following:—

(1.) It is well settled that the governing purpose of damages is to put the party whose rights have been violated in the same position, so far as money can do so, as if his rights had been observed: (*Sally Wertheim* v. *Chicoutimi Pulp Company* [1911] AC 301). This purpose, if relentlessly pursued, would provide him with a complete indemnity for all loss de facto resulting from a particular breach, however improbable, however unpredictable. This, in contract at least, is recognized as too harsh a rule. Hence,

(2.) In cases of breach of contract the aggrieved party is only entitled to recover such part of the loss actually resulting as was at the time of the contract reasonably forseeable as liable to result from the breach.

(3.) What was at that time reasonably so foreseeable depends on the knowledge then possessed by the parties or, at all events, by the party who later commits the breach.

(4.) For this purpose, knowledge 'possessed' is of two kinds; one imputed, the other actual. Everyone, as a reasonable person, is taken to know the 'ordinary course of things' and consequently what loss is liable to result from a breach of contract in that ordinary course. This is the subject matter of the 'first rule' in *Hadley* v. *Baxendale* 9 Exch 341. But to this knowledge, which a contract-breaker is assumed to possess whether he actually possesses it or not, there may have to be added in a particular case knowledge which he actually possesses, of special circumstances outside the 'ordinary course of things', of such a kind that a breach in those special circumstances would be liable to cause more loss. Such a case attracts the operation of the 'second rule' so as to make additional loss also recoverable.

(5.) In order to make the contract-breaker liable under either rule it is not necessary that he should actually have asked himself what loss is liable to result from a breach. As has often been pointed out, parties at the time of contracting contemplate not the breach of the contract, but its performance. It suffices that, if he had considered the question, he would as a reasonable man have concluded that the loss in question was liable to result (see certain observations of Lord du Parcq in the recent case of *A/B Karl-shamns Oljefabriker* v. *Monarch Steamship Company Limited* [1949] AC 196).

(6.) Nor, finally, to make a particular loss recoverable, need it be proved that upon a given state of knowledge the defendant could, as a reasonable man, foresee that a breach must necessarily result in that loss. It is enough if he could foresee it was likely so to result. It is indeed enough, to borrow from the language of Lord du Parcq in the same case, at page 158, if the loss (or some factor without which it would not have occurred) is a 'serious possibility' or a 'real danger'. For short, we have used the word 'liable' to result. Possibly the colloquialism 'on the cards' indicates the shade of meaning with some approach to accuracy.

If these, indeed, are the principles applicable, what is the effect of their application to the facts of this case? We have, at the beginning of this judgment, summarized the main relevant facts. The defendants were an engineering company supplying a boiler to a laundry. We reject the submission for the defendants that an engineering company knows no more than the plain man about boilers or the purposes to which they are commonly put by different classes of purchasers, including laundries. The defendant company were not, it is true, manufacturers of this boiler or dealers in boilers, but they gave a highly technical and comprehensive description of this boiler to the plaintiffs by letter of January 19, 1946, and offered both to dismantle the boiler at Harpenden and to re-erect it on the plaintiffs' premises. Of the uses or purposes to which boilers are put, they would clearly know more than the uninstructed layman. Again, they knew they were supplying the boiler to a company carrying on the business of laundrymen and dyers, for use in that business. The obvious use of a boiler, in such a business, is surely to boil water for the purpose of washing or dyeing. A laundry might conceivably buy a boiler for some other purpose; for instance, to work radiators or warm bath water for the comfort of its employees or directors, or to use for research, or to exhibit in a museum. All these purposes are possible, but the first is the obvious purpose which, in the case of a laundry, leaps to the average eye. If the purpose then be to wash or dye, why does the company want to wash or dye, unless for purposes of business advantage, in which term we, for the purposes of the rest of this judgment, include maintenance or increase of profit, or reduction of loss? (We shall speak henceforward not of loss of profit, but of 'loss of business'.) No commercial concern commonly purchases for the purposes of its business a very large and expensive structure like this—a boiler 19 feet high and costing over

2,000l.—with any other motive, and no supplier, let alone an engineering company, which has promised delivery of such an article by a particular date, with knowledge that it was to be put into use immediately on delivery, can reasonably contend that it could not foresee that loss of business (in the sense indicated above) would be liable to result to the purchaser from a long delay in the delivery thereof. The suggestion that, for all the supplier knew, the boiler might have been needed simply as a 'standby', to be used in a possibly distant future, is gratuitous and was plainly negatived by the terms of the letter of April 26, 1946.

Since we are differing from a carefully reasoned judgment, we think it due to the learned judge to indicate the grounds of our dissent.

[he set out the reasoning of the trial judge and continued]

First, . . . the learned judge appears to infer that because certain 'special circumstances' were, in his view, not 'drawn to the notice of' the defendants and therefore, in his view, the operation of the 'second rule' was excluded, ergo nothing in respect of loss of business can be recovered under the 'first rule.' This inference is, in our view, no more justified in the present case than it was in the case of Cory v. Thames Ironworks Company (1868) LR 3 QB 181. Secondly, that while it is not wholly clear what were the 'special circumstances' on the non-communication of which the learned judge relied, it would seem that they were, or included, the following:— (a) the 'circumstance' that delay in delivering the boiler was going to lead 'necessarily' to loss of profits. But the true criterion is surely not what was bound 'necessarily' to result, but what was likely or liable to do so, and we think that it was amply conveyed to the defendants by what was communicated to them (plus what was patent without express communication) that delay in delivery was likely to lead to 'loss of business'; (b) the 'circumstance' that the plaintiffs needed the boiler 'to extend their business'. It was surely not necessary for the defendants to be specifically informed of this, as a precondition of being liable for loss of business. Reasonable persons in the shoes of the defendants must be taken to foresee without any express intimation, that a laundry which, at a time when there was a famine of laundry facilities, was paying 2,000l. odd for plant and intended at such a time to put such plant 'into use' immediately, would be likely to suffer in pocket from five months' delay in delivery of the plant in question, whether they intended by means of it to extend their business, or merely to maintain it, or to reduce a loss; (c) the 'circumstance' that the plaintiffs had the assured expectation of special contracts, which they could only fulfil by securing punctual delivery of the boiler. Here, no doubt, the learned judge had in mind the particularly lucrative dyeing contracts to which the plaintiffs looked forward and which they mention in . . . [their] statement of claim. We agree that in order that the plaintiffs should recover specifically and as such the profits expected on these contracts, the defendants would have had to know, at the time of their agreement with the plaintiffs, of the prospect and terms of such contracts. We also agree that they did not in fact know these things. It does not, however, follow that the plaintiffs are precluded from recovering some general (and perhaps conjectural) sum for loss of business in respect of dyeing contracts to be reasonably expected, any more than in respect of laundering contracts to be reasonably expected.

Thirdly, the other point on which Streatfeild J largely based his judgment was that there is a critical difference between the measure of damages applicable when the defendant defaults in supplying a self-contained profit-earning whole and when he defaults in supplying a part of that whole. In our view, there is no intrinsic magic, in this connexion, in the whole as against a part. The fact that a part only is involved is only significant in so far as it bears on the capacity of the supplier to foresee the consequences of non-delivery. If it is clear from the nature of the part (or the supplier of it is informed) that its non-delivery will have the same effect as non-delivery of the whole, his liability will be the same as if he had defaulted in delivering the whole. The cases of *Hadley* v. *Baxendale* . . ., *British Columbia Sawmills* v. *Nettleship* LR 3 CP 499 . . ., which were so strongly relied on for the defence and by the learned judge, were all cases in which, through want of a part, catastrophic results ensued, in that a whole concern was paralysed or sterilized; a mill stopped, a complex of machinery unable to be assembled, a threshing machine unable to be delivered in time for the harvest and therefore useless. In all three cases the defendants were absolved from liability to compensate the plaintiffs for the resulting loss of business, not because what they had failed to deliver was a part, but because there had been nothing to convey to them that want of that part would stultify the whole business of the person for whose benefit the part was contracted for. There is no resemblance between these cases and the present, in which, while there was no question of a total stoppage resulting from non-delivery, yet there was ample means of knowledge on the part of the defendants that business loss of some sort would be likely to result to the plaintiffs from the defendants' default in performing their contract.

We are therefore of opinion that the appeal should be allowed and the issue referred to an official referee as to what damage, if any, is recoverable in addition to the 110l. awarded by the learned trial judge. The official referee would assess those damages in consonance with the findings in this judgment as to what the defendants knew or must be taken to have known at the material time, either party to be at liberty to call evidence as to the quantum of the damage in dispute.

COMMENTARY

This is another case in which the plaintiffs' claim did not succeed (at least in respect of the claim to recover the loss of profit on the contracts with the Ministry of Supply). The defendant did not have knowledge of these lucrative contracts and so was not liable for the exceptional loss of profits suffered by the plaintiffs. The distinction between ordinary losses of profit and exceptional losses of profit is a difficult one. It is a distinction of degree rather than kind and elsewhere in the law the extent of the loss need not be foreseeable provided that the kind of loss is foreseeable. We shall return to the case after a brief detour in order to consider the rather difficult decision of the House of Lords in:

The Heron II C. Czarnikow Ltd v. Koufos

[1969] 1 AC 350, House of Lords

The plaintiff chartered the defendant's vessel to carry 3,000 tons of sugar to Basrah. In breach of contract, the vessel arrived at its destination nine days late. The plaintiff intended to sell the sugar at Basrah. However, by the time the vessel arrived the market for sugar had fallen from £32 10s per ton to £31 2s 9d per ton. The plaintiff sued the defendant for breach of contract, claiming the difference in price as damages. At trial, it was found that, although the defendant *did not* know what the plaintiff intended to do with the sugar, the defendant *did* know that there was a market for sugar in Basrah.

However, the judge found that it was impossible to say that it was reasonably foreseeable to the defendant that delay in delivery would result in that kind of loss. The Court of Appeal reversed this decision, and held that loss due to the fall in market prices was not too remote. The House of Lords unanimously affirmed the decision of the Court of Appeal.

Lord Reid

It is generally sufficient that that event would have appeared to the defendant as not unlikely to occur. It is hardly ever possible in this matter to assess probabilities with any degree of mathematical accuracy. But I do not find . . . any warrant for regarding as within the contemplation of the parties any event which would not have appeared to the defendant, had he thought about it, to have a very substantial degree of probability.

But then it has been said that the liability of defendants has been further extended by *Victoria Laundry (Windsor) Ltd.* v. *Newman Industries Ltd.* I do not think so.

[He set out the facts of the case and considered the six propositions of law to be found in the judgment of Asquith LJ (see p. 1083 above) and continued]

But what is said to create a 'landmark' is the statement of principles by Asquith LJ This does to some extent go beyond the older authorities and in so far as it does so, I do not agree with it. In paragraph (2) it is said that the plaintiff is entitled to recover 'such part of the loss actually resulting as was at the time of the contract reasonably foreseeable as liable to result from the breach.' To bring in reasonable foreseeability appears to me to be confusing measure of damages in contract with measure of damages in tort. A great many extremely unlikely results are reasonably foreseeable: it is true that Lord Asquith may have meant foreseeable as a likely result, and if that is all he meant I would not object further than to say that I think that the phrase is liable to be misunderstood. For the same reason I would take exception to the phrase 'liable to result' in paragraph (5). Liable is a very vague word but I think that one would usually say that when a person foresees a very improbable result he foresees that it is liable to happen.

I agree with the first half of paragraph (6). For the best part of a century it has not been required that the defendant could have foreseen that a breach of contract must necessarily result in the loss which has occurred. But I cannot agree with the second half of that paragraph. It has never been held to be sufficient in contract that the loss was foreseeable as 'a serious possibility' or 'a real danger' or as being 'on the cards.' It is on the cards that one can win £100,000 or more for a stake of a few pence—several people have done that. And anyone who backs a hundred to one chance regards a win as a serious possibility—many people have won on such a chance. And the *Wagon Mound (No 2)* [1967] AC 617 could not have been decided as it was unless the extremely unlikely fire should have been foreseen by the ship's officer as a real danger. It appears to me that in the ordinary use of language there is wide gulf between saying that some event is not unlikely or quite likely to happen and saying merely that it is a serious possibility, a real danger, or on the cards. Suppose one takes a well-shuffled pack of cards, it is quite likely or not unlikely that the top card will prove to be a diamond: the odds are only 3 to 1 against. But most people would not say that it is quite likely to be the nine of diamonds for the odds are then 51 to 1 against. On the other hand I think that most people would say that there is a serious possibility or a real danger of its being turned up first and of course it is on the cards. If the tests of 'real danger' or 'serious possibility' are in future to be authoritative then the *Victoria Laundry* case would indeed be a landmark because it would mean that *Hadley* v. *Baxendale* would be differently decided today. I certainly could not understand any court deciding that, on the information available to the carrier in that case, the stoppage of the mill was neither a serious possibility nor a real danger. If those tests are to prevail in future then let us cease to pay lip service to the rule in *Hadley* v. *Baxendale*. But in my judgment to adopt these tests would extend liability for breach of contract beyond what is reasonable or desirable. From the limited knowledge which I have of commercial affairs I would not expect such an extension to be welcomed by the business community and from the legal point of view I can find little or nothing to recommend it . . .

It appears to me that, without relying in any way on the *Victoria Laundry* case, and taking the principle that had already been established, the loss of profit claimed in this case was not too remote to be recoverable as damages.

Lord Morris of Borth-y-Gest

I think it is clear that the loss need not be such that the contract-breaker could see that it was certain to result. The question that arises concerns the measure of prevision which should fairly and reasonably be ascribed to him.

My Lords, in applying the guidance given in *Hadley* v. *Baxendale* I would hope that no undue emphasis would be placed upon any one word or phrase . . . The result in any particular case need not depend upon giving pride of place to any one of such phrases as 'liable to result' or 'not unlikely to result.' Each one of these phrases may be of help but so may many others . . .

My Lords, the words, phrases and passages to which I have referred are useful and helpful indications of the application of the rule in *Hadley* v. *Baxendale*. But they neither add to the rule nor do they modify it. I regard the illuminating judgment of the Court of Appeal in *Victoria Laundry (Windsor) Ltd.* v. *Newman Industries Ltd.* as a most valuable analysis of the rule. It was there pointed out that in order to make a contract-breaker liable under what was called 'either rule' in *Hadley* v. *Baxendale* it is not necessary that he should actually have asked himself what loss is liable to result from a breach but that it suffices that if he had considered the question he would as a reasonable man have concluded that the loss in question was liable to result. Nor need it be proved, in order to recover a particular loss, that upon a given state of knowledge he could, as a reasonable man, foresee that a breach must necessarily result in that loss. Certain illustrative phrases are employed in that case. They are valuable by way of exposition but for my part I doubt whether the phrase 'on the cards' has a sufficiently clear meaning or possesses such a comparable shade of meaning as to qualify it to take its place with the various other phrases which line up as expositions of the rule.

If the problem in the present case is that of relating accepted principle to the facts which have been found, I entertain no doubt that if at the time of their contract the parties had considered what the consequence would be if the arrival of the ship at Basrah was delayed they would have contemplated that some loss to the respondents was likely or was liable to result. The appellant at the time that he made his contract must have known that if in breach of contract his ship did not arrive at Basrah when it ought to arrive he would be liable to pay damages. He would not know that a loss to the respondents was certain or inevitable but he must, as a reasonable business man, have contemplated that the respondents would very likely suffer loss, and that it would be or would be likely to be a loss referable to market price fluctuations at Basrah. I cannot think that he should escape liability by saying that he would only be aware of a possibility of loss but not of a probability of certainty of it. He might have used any one of many phrases. He might have said that a loss would be likely; or that a loss would not be unlikely; or that a loss was liable to result; or that the risk that delay would cause loss to the respondents was a serious possibility; or that there would be a real danger of a loss; or that the risk of his being liable to have to pay for the loss was one that he ought commercially to take into account. As a practical business man he would not have paused to reflect on the possible nuances of meaning of any one of these phrases. Nor would he have sent for a dictionary . . .

Lord Hodson

A close study of the [remoteness] rule was made by the Court of Appeal in the case of the *Victoria Laundry (Windsor) Ltd.* v. *Newman Industries Ltd.* The judgment of the court . . . was delivered by Asquith LJ, who referred to the *Monarch Steamship* case [1949] AC 196 and suggested the phrase 'liable to result' as appropriate to describe the degree of probability required. This may be a colourless expression but I do not find it possible to improve on it. If the word 'likelihood' is used it may convey the impression that the chances are all in favour of the thing happening, an idea which I would reject.

Lord Pearce

[T]he case of *Victoria Laundry (Windsor) Ltd.* v. *Newman Industries Ltd* . . . represented (in felicitous language) the approximate view of *Hadley v. Baxendale* taken by many judges in trying ordinary cases of breach of contract.

It is argued that it was an erroneous departure from *Hadley* v. *Baxendale* in that it allowed damages where the loss was 'a serious possibility' or 'a real danger' instead of maintaining that the loss must be 'probable,' in the sense that it was more likely to result than not . . . in my opinion the expressions used in the *Victoria Laundry* case were right. I do not however accept the colloquialism 'on the cards' as being a useful test because I am not sure just what nuance it has either in my own personal vocabulary or in that of others. I suspect that it owes its attraction, like many other colloquialisms, to the fact that one may utter it without having the trouble of really thinking out with precision what one means oneself or what others will understand by it, a spurious attraction which in general makes colloquialism unsuitable for definition, though it is often useful as shorthand for a collection of definable ideas. It was in this latter convenient sense that the judgment uses the ambiguous words 'liable to result.' They were not intended as a further or different test from 'serious possibility' or 'real danger.'

Lord Upjohn

Asquith LJ in *Victoria Laundry* used the words 'likely to result' and he treated that as synonymous with a serious possibility of a real danger. He went on to equate that with the expression 'on the cards' but like all your Lordships I deprecate the use of that phrase which is far too imprecise and to my mind is capable of denoting a most improbable and unlikely event, such as winning a prize on a premium bond on any given drawing.

But in my opinion Asquith LJ was not attempting to do more than explain the rule in the light of the observations made in this House in *The Monarch* [1949] AC 196 . . .

It is clear that on the one hand the test of foreseeability as laid down in the case of tort is not the test for breach of contract; nor on the other hand must the loser establish that the loss was a near certainty or an odds-on probability. I am content to adopt as the test a 'real danger' or a 'serious possibility.' There may be a shade of difference between these two phrases but the assessment of damages is not an exact science and what to one judge or jury will appear a real danger may appear to another judge or jury to be a serious possibility.

COMMENTARY

The decision of the House of Lords has attracted some criticism, not so much in terms of the result of the case but in relation to the length of the speeches and the variety of phrases used to express the outcome. Two American commentators stated that their Lordships 'gave speeches which restated each others' views at great length in a stunning display of polixity' (Dawson and Harvey, *Contracts: Cases and Comment* (3rd edn, 1977), p. 70). The reasoning of their Lordships has been summarized as follows (H Beale (ed), *Chitty on Contracts* (29th edn, 2004, para 26-052):

What was in the contemplation of reasonable men obviously depends on the relevant degree of likelihood that a particular kind of loss may occur, and this issue was extensively discussed in *The Heron II*. Lord Reid used 'the words "not unlikely" as denoting a degree of probability considerably less than an even chance but nevertheless not very unusual and easily foreseeable.' Although Lord Morris thought it unnecessary to choose any one phrase he used 'not unlikely to occur', with 'liable to result' as an alternative; Lord Hodson accepted the latter phrase. Both Lords Pearce and Upjohn adopted the words 'a real danger' or 'a serious possibility' which were the phrases used in the House of Lords in 1991 (four of their Lordships in *The Heron II* agreed that the colloquialism 'on the cards' should not be used).

A more concise summary of the case has been offered by Professor Burrows in the following terms (A Burrows, 'Limitations on Compensation' in A Burrows and E Peel (eds), *Commercial Remedies: Current Issues and Problems* (Oxford University Press, 2003), 27, 33): 'perhaps the clearest way of expressing the essence of their Lordships' reasoning is that, while a slight possibility of the loss occurring is required in tort, a serious possibility of the loss occurring is required in contract.' Not unsurprisingly, the decision in *Heron II* has not been the last word on the subject of remoteness of damage. The next important case to consider the topic was the following decision of the Court of Appeal:

Parsons (Livestock) Ltd v. Uttley Ingham & Co Ltd

[1978] QB 791, Court of Appeal

The defendant company contracted to supply and install a large cylindrical metal hopper on the plaintiffs' pig farm, in which the plaintiffs intended to store pig feed. When they erected the hopper the defendants failed to notice that the ventilator at the top of the hopper was closed. The plaintiffs then filled the hopper with pignuts and subsequently fed them to the pigs. As a result of the lack of ventilation the nuts began to turn mouldy over a period of time. The plaintiffs continued to feed the nuts to the pigs because mouldy nuts do not generally cause harm to pigs. Over time the pigs began to show signs of illness and the plaintiffs eventually discovered the lack of ventilation in the hopper. The plaintiffs alleged that a large number of their pigs contracted E coli as a result of eating the mouldy nuts. They alleged that 254 pigs had died as a result of the outbreak, that they had incurred considerable expense in combating it, and that they had suffered a substantial loss of profit.

The defendants denied that they were liable for the loss of profit suffered by the plaintiffs on the basis that it was too remote a consequence of their breach of contract. The Court of Appeal held that they were liable for the illness and death of the pigs, albeit that the judges gave different reasons for allowing the claim.

Lord Denning MR

The law as to remoteness

Remoteness of damage is beyond doubt a question of law. In *C Czarnikow Ltd* v. *Koufos* [1969] AC 350 the House of Lords said that, in remoteness of damage, there is a difference between contract and tort. In the case of a *breach of contract*, the court has to consider whether the consequences were of such a kind that a reasonable man, at the time of making the contract, would *contemplate* them as being of a very substantial degree of probability. (In the House of Lords various expressions were used to describe this degree of probability, such as, not merely 'on the cards' because that may be too low: but as being 'not unlikely to occur' (see pp. 383 and 388); or 'likely to result or at least not unlikely to result' (see p. 406); or 'liable to result' (see p. 410); or that there was a 'real danger' or 'serious possibility' of them occurring (see p. 415).)

In the case of a *tort*, the court has to consider whether the consequences were of such a kind that a reasonable man, at the time of the tort committed, would *foresee* them as being of a much lower degree of probability. (In the House of Lords various expressions were used to describe this, such as, it is sufficient if the consequences are 'liable to happen in the most unusual case' (see p. 385); or in a 'very improbable' case (see p. 389); or that 'they may happen as a result of the breach, however unlikely it may be, unless it can be brushed aside as far-fetched' (see p. 422).)

I find it difficult to apply those principles universally to all cases of contract or to all cases of tort: and to draw a distinction between what a man 'contemplates' and what he 'foresees'. I soon begin to get out of my depth. I cannot swim in this sea of semantic exercises—to say nothing of the different degrees of probability—especially when the cause of action can be laid either in contract or in tort. I am swept under by the conflicting currents. I go back with relief to the distinction drawn in legal theory by Professors Hart and Honorè in their book *Causation in the Law* (1959), at pp. 281–287. They distinguish between those cases in contract in which a man has suffered no damage to person or property, but only *economic loss*, such as, loss of profit or loss of opportunities for gain in some future transaction: and those in which he claims damages for an *injury actually done* to his person or *damage actually done* to his property (including his livestock) or for ensuing expense (damnum emergens) to which he has actually been put. In the law of tort, there is emerging a distinction between economic loss and physical damage: see *Spartan Steel & Alloys Ltd* v. *Martin & Co (Contractors) Ltd* [1973] QB 27, 36–37. It underlies the words of Lord Wilberforce in *Anns* v. *Merton London Borough Council* [1978] AC 728, recently, where he classified the recoverable damage as 'material, physical damage'. It has been much considered by the Supreme Court of Canada in *Rivtow Marine Ltd* v. *Washington Iron Works and Walkem Machinery & Equipment Ltd* [1973] 6 WWR 692 and by the High Court of Australia in *Caltex Oil (Australia) Pty Ltd* v. *Dredge Willemstad* (1976) 51 ALGR 270.

It seems to me that in the law of contract, too, a similar distinction is emerging. It is between loss of profit consequent on a breach of contract and physical damage consequent on it.

Loss of profit cases

I would suggest as a solution that in the former class of case—loss of profit cases—the defaulting party is only liable for the consequences if they are such as, at the time of the contract, he ought reasonably to have *contemplated* as a *serious* possibility or real danger. You must assume that, at the time of the contract, he had the very kind of breach in mind—such a breach as afterwards happened, as for instance, delay in transit—and then you must ask: ought he reasonably to have *contemplated* that there was a *serious* possibility that such a breach would involve the plaintiff in loss of profit? If yes, the contractor is liable for the loss unless he has taken care to exempt himself from it by a condition in the contract—as, of course, he is able to do if it was the sort of thing which he could reasonably contemplate. The law on this class of case is now covered by the three leading cases of *Hadley* v. *Baxendale*, 9 Exch 341; *Victoria Laundry (Windsor) Ltd* v. *Newman Industries Ltd* [1949] 2 KB 528; and *C Czarnikow Ltd* v. *Koufos* [1969] 1 AC 350. These were all 'loss of profit' cases: and the test of 'reasonable contemplation' and 'serious possibility' should, I suggest, be kept to that type of loss or, at any rate, to economic loss.

Physical damage cases

In the second class of case—the physical injury or expense case—the defaulting party is liable for any loss or expense which he ought reasonably to have *foreseen* at the time of the breach as a possible consequence, even if it was only a *slight* possibility. You must assume that he was aware of his breach, and then you must ask: ought he reasonably to have foreseen, at the time of the breach, that something of this kind might happen in consequence of it? This is the test which has been applied in cases of tort ever since *The Wagon Mound* cases [1961] AC 388 and [1967] 1 AC 617. But there is a long line of cases which support a like test in cases of contract.

One class of case which is particularly apposite here concerns latent defects in goods: in modern words 'product liability'. In many of these cases the manufacturer is liable in contract to the immediate party for a breach of his duty to use reasonable care and is liable in tort to the ultimate consumer for the same want of reasonable care. The ultimate consumer can either sue the retailer in contract and pass the liability up the chain to the manufacturer, or he can sue the manufacturer in tort and thus by-pass the chain. The liability of the manufacturer ought to be the same in either case. In nearly all these cases the defects were outside the range of anything that was in fact contemplated, or could reasonably have been contemplated, by the manufacturer or by anyone down the chain to the retailers. Yet the manufacturer and others in the chain have been held liable for the damage done to the ultimate user, as for instance the death of the young pheasants in *Hardwick Game Farm* v. *Suffolk Agricultural Poultry Producers Association* [1969] 2 AC 31 and of the mink in *Christopher Hill Ltd* v. *Ashington Piggeries Ltd* [1972] AC 441. Likewise, the manufacturers and retailers were held liable for the dermatitis caused to the wearer in the woollen underwear case of *Grant* v. *Australian Knitting Mills Ltd* [1936] AC 85, even though they had not the faintest suspicion of any trouble. So were the manufacturers down the chain to the sub-contractors for the disintegrating roofing tiles in *Young & Marten Ltd* v. *McManus Childs Ltd* [1969] 1 AC 454 . . .

Instances could be multiplied of injuries to persons or damage to property where the defendant is liable for his negligence to one man in contract and to another in tort. Each suffers like damage. The test of remoteness is, and should be, the same in both.

Coming to the present case, we were told that in some cases the makers of these hoppers supply them direct to the pig farmer under contract with him, but in other cases they supply them through an intermediate dealer—who buys from the manufacturer and resells to the pig farmer on the self-same terms—in which the manufacturer delivers direct to the pig farmer. In the one case the pig farmer can sue the manufacturer in contract. In the other in tort. The test of remoteness should be the same. It should be the test in tort.

Conclusion

The present case falls within the class of case where the breach of contract causes physical damage. The test of remoteness in such cases is similar to that in tort. The contractor is liable for all such loss or expense as could reasonably have been foreseen, at the time of the breach, as a possible consequence of it. Applied to this case, it means that the makers of the hopper are liable for the death of the pigs. They ought reasonably to have foreseen that, if the mouldy pignuts were fed to the pigs, there was a possibility that they might become ill. Not a serious possibility. Nor a real danger. But still a slight possibility. On that basis the makers were liable for the illness suffered by the pigs. They suffered from diarrhoea at the beginning. This triggered off the deadly E. coli. That was a far worse illness than could then be foreseen. But that does not lessen this liability. The type or kind of damage was foreseeable even though the extent of it was not: see *Hughes* v. *Lord Advocate* [1963] AC 837. The makers are liable for the loss of the pigs that died and of the expenses of the vet and such like, but not for loss of profit on future sales or future opportunities of gain: see *Simon* v. *Pawson and Leafs Ltd* (1932) 38 Com Cas 151.

So I reach the same result as the judge, but by a different route. I would dismiss the appeal.

Orr LJ

I agree with Lord Denning MR and also with Scarman LJ, whose judgment I have had the opportunity of reading, that this appeal should be dismissed, but with respect to Lord Denning MR I would dismiss it for the reasons to be given by Scarman LJ and not on the basis that a distinction is to be drawn for the present purposes between loss of profits and physical damage cases. I have not been satisfied that such a distinction is sufficiently supported by the authorities.

For the present purposes the crucial passages in the judgment of Swanwick J are those to be quoted by Scarman LJ and also, in my judgment, the passage where the learned Judge says:

'How far must his (the defendant's) contemplation coincide with the damage that occurs? It is in my view right that his assumed contemplation should be limited to the type of damage that occurs but that he is liable if the quantum is greater than he may be presumed to anticipate. Obviously the principle may be difficult of appreciation in some cases, but I need not elaborate it here because I agree with Mr Bathurst that E. Coli is not different in type from the digestive upset that might trigger it off. It is simply the proliferation of an organism naturally occurring in the bowel which then upsets the excretory system still further and admittedly much worse.'

On this basis, in my judgment correct in law, it was sufficient to establish liability for the damage in question that physical injury to the pigs was a serious possibility if in breach of contract the hopper was unfit for storing nuts suitable to be fed to them and I do not think it matters for this purpose whether there was only one contract, or were two contracts, though I agree with Lord Justice Scarman that there was only one.

For these reasons and in complete agreement with the judgment to be delivered by Scarman LJ, I would dismiss this appeal and I would add my tribute to the manner in which the case was dealt with by the trial Judge.

Scarman LJ

My conclusion in the present case is the same as that of Lord Denning MR but I reach it by a different route. I would dismiss the appeal. I agree with him in thinking it absurd that the test for remoteness of damage should, in principle, differ according to the legal classification of the cause of action, though one must recognize that parties to a contract have the right to agree on a measure of damages which may be greater, or less, than the law would offer in the absence of agreement. I also agree with him in thinking that, notwithstanding the interpretation put on some dicta in C Czarnikow Ltd v. Koufos [1969] AC 350, the law is not so absurd as to differentiate between contract and tort save in situations where the agreement, or the factual relationship, of the parties with each other requires it in the interests of justice. I differ from him only to this extent: the cases do not, in my judgment, support a distinction in law between loss of profit and physical damage. Neither do I think it necessary to develop the law judicially by drawing such a distinction. Of course (and this is a reason for refusing to draw the distinction in law) the type of consequence—loss of profit or market or physical injury—will always be an important matter of fact in determining whether in all the circumstances the loss or injury was of a type which the parties could reasonably be supposed to have in contemplation.

In C Czarnikow Ltd v. Koufos [1969] 1 AC 350 (a case of a contract of carriage of goods by sea) the House of Lords resolved some of the difficulties in this branch of the law. The law which the House in that case either settled or recognized as already settled may be stated as follows. (1) The general principle regulating damages for breach of contract is that 'where a party sustains a loss by reason of a breach of contract, he is, so far as money can do it, to be placed in the same situation . . . as if the contract had been performed': see per Lord Pearce, at p. 414, quoting Parke B in Robinson v. Harman (1848) 1 Exch 850, 855. (2) The formulation of the remoteness test is not the same in tort and in contract because the relationship of the parties in a contract situation differs from that in tort: see per Lord Reid, at pp. 385–386. (3) The two rules formulated by Alderson B in Hadley v. Baxendale, 9 Exch. 341 are but two aspects of one general principle—that to be recoverable in an action for damages for breach of contract the plaintiff's loss must be such as may reasonably be supposed would have been in the contemplation of the parties as a serious possibility had their attention been directed to the possibility of the breach which has, in fact, occurred.

Two problems are left unsolved by C Czarnikow Ltd v. Koufos: (1) the law's reconciliation of the remoteness principle in contract with that in tort where, as, for instance, in some product liability cases, there arises the danger of differing awards, the lesser award going to the party who has a contract, even though the contract is silent as to the measure of damages and all parties are, or must be deemed to be, burdened with the same knowledge, or enjoying the same state of ignorance; and (2) what is meant by 'serious possibility' or its synonyms: is it a reference to the type of consequence which the parties might be supposed to contemplate as possible though unlikely, or must the chance of it happening appear to be likely? (see the way Lord Pearce puts it, at pp. 416–417).

As to the first problem, I agree with Lord Denning MR in thinking that the law must be such that, in a factual situation where all have the same actual or imputed knowledge and the contract contains no term limiting the damages recoverable for breach, the amount of damages recoverable does not depend upon whether, as a matter of legal classification, the plaintiff's cause of action is breach of contract or tort. It may be that the necessary reconciliation is to be found, notwithstanding the strictures of Lord Reid at pp. 389–390, in holding that the difference between 'reasonably foreseeable' (the test in tort) and 'reasonably contemplated' (the test in contract) is semantic, not substantial. Certainly, Asquith LJ, in *Victoria Laundry (Windsor) Ltd* v. *Newman Industries Ltd* [1949] 2 KB 528, 535 and Lord Pearce in *C Czarnikow Ltd* v. *Koufos* [1969] 1 AC 350, 414 thought so; and I confess I think so too.

The second problem—what is meant by a 'serious possibility'—is, in my judgment, ultimately a question of fact. I shall return to it, therefore, after analysing the facts, since I believe it requires of the judge no more—and no less—than the application of common sense in the particular circumstances of the case.

Finally, there are two legal rules relevant to the present case which were not considered in *C Czarnikow Ltd* v. *Koufos*. The first relates to sale of goods. Section 53(2) of the Sale of Goods Act 1893 provides that 'The measure of damages for breach of warranty is the estimated loss directly and naturally resulting, in the ordinary course of events, from the breach of warranty'. The subsection, clearly a statutory formulation of the first rule in *Hadley* v. *Baxendale*, is not, however, intended to oust the second rule, where appropriate: see section 54. Nevertheless, it vindicates the judge's approach to this case, always assuming that the facts are such as to make the application of the first rule appropriate.

Secondly, the breach does not have to be foreseen, or contemplated. In a breach of warranty case the point may be put in this way: it does not matter if the defect is latent. It may be unknown, even unknowable: see *Grant* v. *Australian Knitting Mills Ltd* [1936] AC 85. The court has to assume, though it be contrary to the fact, that the parties had in mind the breach that has occurred. Thus, whenever a question of remoteness of damage arises in a contract case, its solution involves the court in making a hypothesis, which may, or may not, correspond with fact.

The court's task, therefore, is to decide what loss to the plaintiffs it is reasonable to suppose would have been in the contemplation of the parties as a serious possibility had they had in mind the breach when they made their contract.

I now turn to the facts of the case . . .

I would agree with *McGregor on Damages*, 13th ed. (1972), pp. 131–132 that

'. . . in contract as in tort, it should suffice that, if physical injury or damage is within the contemplation of the parties, recovery is not to be limited because the degree of physical injury or damage could not have been anticipated.'

This is so, in my judgment, not because there is, or ought to be, a specific rule of law governing cases of physical injury but because it would be absurd to regulate damages in such cases upon the necessity of supposing the parties had a prophetic foresight as to the exact nature of the injury that does in fact arise. It is enough if upon the hypothesis predicated physical injury must have been a serious possibility. Though in loss of market or loss of profit cases the factual analysis will be very different from cases of physical injury, the same principles, in my judgment, apply. Given the situation of the parties at the time of contract, was the loss of profit, or market, a serious possibility, something that would have been in their minds had they contemplated breach?

It does not matter, in my judgment, if they thought that the chance of physical injury, loss of profit, loss of market, or other loss as the case may be, was slight, or that the odds were against it, provided they contemplated as a serious possibility the type of consequence, not necessarily the specific consequence, that ensued upon breach. Making the assumption as to breach that the judge did, no more than common sense was needed for them to appreciate that food affected by bad storage conditions might well cause illness in the pigs fed upon it.

As I read the judgment under appeal, this was how the judge, whose handling of the issues at trial was such that none save one survives for our consideration, reached this decision. In my judgment, he was right, upon the facts as found, to apply the first rule in *Hadley* v. *Baxendale*, 9 Exch 341 or, if the case be one of breach of warranty, as I think it is, the rule in section 53(2) of the Sale of Goods Act 1893 without inquiring as to whether, upon a juridical analysis, the rule is based upon a presumed contemplation. At the end of a long and complex dispute the judge allowed common sense to prevail. I would dismiss the appeal.

COMMENTARY

Parsons is a difficult case because the Court of Appeal gave different reasons for reaching the decision which it did. Lord Denning distinguished between physical damage cases and economic loss cases but this distinction did not commend itself to Scarman and Orr LJJ. The majority phrased the question at a high level of generality. The question which they asked was not whether it was reasonably contemplated at the time of contracting as a serious possibility that supplying a hopper with inadequate ventilation would make the pigs ill. Rather they asked whether it was reasonably contemplated at the time of contracting as a serious possibility that supplying a hopper that was unfit for the purpose of storing food for pigs would make the pigs ill. As Professor Burrows has pointed out (*Remedies for Torts and Breach of Contract* (3rd edn, Oxford University Press, 2004), p. 91):

Scarman LJ's approach shows that, by defining the breach more generally, the loss is less likely to be judged too remote. Thus it would appear that the courts enjoy a measure of discretion in relation to the level of generality at which a breach is described and that this discretion can have a profound impact on the outcome of cases.

Professor Atiyah has concluded (*An Introduction to the Law of Contract* (5th edn, Oxford University Press, 1995), pp. 467–468):

There does seem to be an air of unreality about the foreseeability test in cases of this nature. In one sense, everything that happens (except perhaps for voluntary human action) occurs according to the laws of the physical universe, and in so far as these are known (and for practical purposes, they are after all pretty well known today), virtually any result is foreseeable as possible from a base which supposes knowledge of the initial breach of contract. Thus, the only consequences that come to be regarded as unforeseeable are those where the train of events that come to be regarded as unforeseeable are those where the train of events has been interrupted by conscious human interventions. This seems to go much too far. It would surely be more sensible in a case of this nature to ask whether losses from pig disease ought to be treated as part of the risks of farming, or of the manufacture and sale of animal food hoppers.

A further difficulty with *Parsons* lies in ascertaining its relationship with *Victoria Laundry*. Professor Burrows has noted (*Remedies for Torts and Breach of Contract* (3rd edn, Oxford University Press, 2004), p. 90) that the majority in *Parsons* 'did not say how types of loss are to be divided up'. He continues:

One could argue, for example, that since illness and death of pigs were regarded as the same type of loss, and merely differed in extent, the majority's approach is irreconcilable with *Victoria Laundry*; for one could argue that the type of loss in issue there was loss of profits, and that the exceptional profits were merely a greater extent of that same type of loss. Presumably, the majority's answer to this would be that its test allows the courts a discretion as to how to divide up types of loss, and that *Victoria Laundry* is reconcilable by regarding the ordinary loss of profits as a different type of loss from the exceptional loss of profits. But such discretion and flexibility in the test is only achieved at the expense of certainty.

The continuing uncertainty in the law can be seen in the following two cases. The first is the decision of the Court of Appeal in *Brown* v. *KMR Services Ltd* [1995] 4 All ER 598. The plaintiff brought an action against the defendants in which he alleged that the defendants had acted negligently and in breach of contract in failing to warn him of the dangers of excess of loss syndicates. The issue with which we are concerned relates to the defendants' submission that they were not liable for the losses on the basis that their scale was unprecedented and unforeseeable. In this respect the defendants relied upon *Victoria Laundry*. The Court of Appeal in *Brown* distinguished *Victoria Laundry*. Stuart Smith LJ stated (at p. 621) that, while he accepted that difficulties can arise in practice in categorizing the loss which the plaintiff has suffered (especially where that loss assumes the form of economic loss), he did not 'see any difficulty in holding that loss of ordinary business profits is different in kind from that flowing from a particular contract which gives rise to very high profits, the existence of which is unknown to the other contracting party who therefore does not accept the risk of such loss occurring'. Hobhouse LJ adopted a different approach. He distinguished (at p. 642) *Victoria Laundry* on the ground that it was a case concerned with indirect or consequential losses, whereas *Brown* was concerned with a direct and wholly foreseeable loss.

The second case is the decision of the House of Lords in *Balfour Beatty Construction (Scotland) Ltd* v. *Scottish Power plc*, 1994 SLT 807. The pursuers were the main contractors for the construction of a section of the Edinburgh bypass. In order to carry out their contractual obligations, it was necessary for them to install a concrete batching plant a few miles away from the site. The pursuers entered into a contract with the defenders for the supply of electricity to the plant. The supply of electricity failed after the fuses supplied by the defenders ruptured. The power failed late in the evening and at a vital moment in the performance of the contract. The pursuers were constructing an aqueduct which required a continuous pour of concrete over a period of time. It was necessary for the pursuers to knock down the work done and recommence the construction of the aqueduct. The cost of doing so amounted to £230,000 and the pursuers sought to recover this sum from the defenders. Their claim failed. The trial judge held that the demolition and reconstruction of the aqueduct was not within the reasonable contemplation of the defenders at the moment of entry into the contract. Lord Jauncey concluded (at p. 810):

It must always be a question of circumstances what one contracting party is presumed to know about the business activities of the other. No doubt the simpler the activity of the one, the more readily can it be inferred that the other would have reasonable knowledge thereof. However, when the activity of A involves complicated construction or manufacturing techniques, I can see no reason why B who supplies a commodity that A intends to use in the course of those techniques should be assumed, merely because of the order for the commodity, to be aware of the details of all the techniques undertaken by A and the effect thereupon of any failure of or deficiency in that commodity.

On the facts, the defenders were held to be unaware of the loss which the pursuers would suffer as a result of the demolition and reconstruction of the aqueduct and so were not liable for the loss. *Balfour Beatty* seems to be closer to *Victoria Laundry* than *Parsons*. The decision in *Balfour Beatty* underlines the importance of disclosing special losses before the time of entry into the contract because a failure to do so may result in the loss being held to be irrecoverable.

The law therefore remains in an uncertain state. The decision in *Balfour Beatty* is not easy to reconcile with *Parsons* v. *Uttley Ingham* and, indeed, Lord Jauncey in *Balfour Beatty* left open the question whether *Parsons* had been correctly decided. Further, it is no easy task to reconcile *Brown* v. *KMR Services* and *Victoria Laundry* or *Parsons* and *Victoria Laundry*. However it may that it is not possible to state the applicable rules with any precision because the courts in these cases are in fact seeking to identify the agreement of the parties in relation to the allocation of responsibility for the consequences of breach and any such agreement must depend heavily on the facts of the individual case. Thus Kramer has argued (A Kramer, 'An Agreement-Centred Approach to Remoteness and Contract Damages' in N Cohen and E McKendrick (eds), *Comparative Remedies for Breach of Contract* (Hart, 2004), p. 240) that:

the allocation of responsibility for the consequences of breach is one of the matters that is determined by contractual agreement, even when it is not covered by the express terms of those agreements. According to this view, the central rule restricting awards of damages, the foreseeability requirement, is not a strict rule originating outside the contract for reasons of efficiency, fairness or proportionality, but is a rule of thumb that is justified when and to the extent that it indicates what the parties wanted. The foreseeability rule, and many of the other rules governing damages, should thus be understood as a framework for discovering what was agreed, not a default rule to operate when nothing was agreed.

He identifies a number of norms which he maintains that the courts take into account when seeking to ascertain the implied agreement that the parties have made in terms of allocating responsibility for the consequences of the breach. These norms include the following:

- It may be that the promisor can *prima facie* be assumed to be taking responsibility for all consequences with regard to which the promisee considered the promise significant;

- It may be that a promisee is less likely to accept the risk of suffering physical harm than to accept the risk of suffering economic loss;

- A promisee usually accepts the risk of suffering idiosyncratic non-economic losses due to disappointment or lack of pleasure;

- Often the party that can most easily or cheaply avert the consequences can be assumed to have taken responsibility for them; and

- A party is unlikely to take responsibility for losses caused by the fault of the other party.

Having set out a list of norms, Kramer concludes as follows (p. 250):

[t]he foreseeability test should be reconceived . . . as being [an application] of one basic principle that looks to the scope of the implied assumption of responsibility (and the orientation of the obligation, if that metaphor is thought to be helpful). Foreseeability should be seen as a good but inconclusive indication of an assumption of responsibility, and the label remoteness may be applied to this new approach or discarded, according to taste. Problems of determining *how likely* a forseeable loss must be, and *how precisely* it must be foreseeable, will then fall away as mere indications of what responsibility reasonably appears to have been assumed.

(b) MITIGATION

The claimant must take reasonable steps to minimize the loss suffered by a breach of contract (*British Westinghouse Electric and Manufacturing Co Ltd* v. *Underground Electric Railways Co of London Ltd* [1912] AC 673). This is commonly expressed in the formula that a claimant is under a 'duty' to mitigate his loss. This terminology is, however, misleading. A claimant is not under a duty to mitigate his loss, in the sense that he can be sued if he fails to do so. The sanction for a failure to mitigate is that a claimant cannot recover damages in respect of losses attributable to his failure to do so. As Professor Bridge notes ('Mitigation of Damages in Contract and the Meaning of Avoidable Loss' (1989) 105 *LQR* 398, 399), the language of 'duty' is misleading, but it is 'well entrenched and difficult to substitute'.

There are two aspects to the mitigation doctrine. The first is that the claimant must not unreasonably increase the loss suffered as a result of the breach (*Banco de Portugal* v. *Waterlow & Sons Ltd* [1932] AC 452). The second is that the claimant must take reasonable steps to minimize his loss. The claimant need only take *reasonable* steps and, in this respect, the law does not make onerous demands of a claimant (*Pilkington* v. *Wood* [1953] Ch 770). The defendant, as a contract-breaker, is not in a position to ask the court to make onerous demands. As Tomlinson J observed in *Britvic Soft*

Drinks Ltd v. *Messer UK Ltd* [2002] 1 Lloyd's Rep 20, 46 the law of contract adopts a 'tender approach to those who have been placed in a predicament by a breach of contract'. Whether or not an innocent party has taken reasonable steps is a question of fact.

Three points should be noted about the doctrine of mitigation. The first is that it amounts to a substantial qualification to the protection which the law affords to the claimant's performance interest. It means that, in the case where the claimant can reasonably obtain substitute performance in the market-place, the claimant must go out and obtain that performance: he cannot sit back and wait for the defendant to perform in accordance with the terms of the contract. Of course, the law does not actually compel the claimant to go out into the market-place and purchase substitute performance but the fact that the claimant cannot recover damages in respect of losses attributable to his failure to mitigate gives him a substantial incentive to do so. The claimant who goes out into the market-place and purchases substitute performance will be entitled to recover as damages the difference between the price under the substitute transaction and the contract price. In this way the claimant can obtain performance at the price which was agreed in the contract but not from the party who promised to provide it.

Secondly, the doctrine of mitigation can have the effect of requiring the innocent party to consider, and possibly accept, an offer of alternative performance by the party in breach. Such was the case in one of the leading mitigation cases, *Payzu Ltd* v. *Saunders* [1919] 2 KB 581. The defendants entered into a contract with the plaintiffs under which they agreed to sell to the plaintiffs a quantity of silk, to be delivered in instalments. The contract provided that payment was to be made within one month following delivery of each instalment. The plaintiffs failed to pay the first instalment on time. This led the defendants to the erroneous conclusion that the plaintiffs were unable to pay at all (when in fact the cause of late payment was simply that they had had difficulty in getting the cheque signed by one of their directors). Fearing that the plaintiffs were facing insolvency, the defendants wrote to the plaintiffs and informed them that they would not make any further deliveries unless the plaintiffs paid for each instalment in cash on delivery. The plaintiffs refused to accept these terms. They brought an action for damages and sought to recover the difference between the contract price and the market price of the silk (at the time the market price was rising). It was held that the plaintiffs were not entitled to recover the difference in price on the ground that their rejection of the defendants' offer to supply the silk on cash terms constituted a failure to mitigate their loss. Scrutton LJ stated that, in a case involving a commercial contract, it is generally reasonable to expect a party to consider and accept a reasonable offer made by the party in breach of contract (the position is otherwise in the case of a contract for personal services: see *Clayton-Greene* v. *De Courville* (1920) 36 TLR 790).

Payzu was taken a step further in *Sotiros Shipping Inc* v. *Sameiet Solholt (The Solholt)* [1983] 1 Lloyd's Rep 605 (CA); [1981] 2 Lloyd's Rep 574 (Staughton J). The buyers of a ship lawfully terminated a contract on the ground that the sellers were late in tendering delivery of the vessel. The contract price was $5 million. At the time of the breach the market price had risen to $5.5 million and the sellers later sold the vessel for $5.8 million. The buyers' claim for damages assessed by reference to the difference between the contract price and the market price was rejected on the ground that they had failed to mitigate their loss. There was no evidence that the sellers had offered to sell the ship to the buyers for $5 million after the termination of the contract but Staughton J, the judge at first instance, held that the buyers had failed to mitigate because they should have offered to buy the vessel for $5 million rather than claim $500,000 in damages. The Court of Appeal dismissed the buyers' appeal. While they clearly had doubts about the decision of Staughton J, they decided that they were not prepared to interfere with the finding of the trial judge that the buyers had failed to act reasonably. While the result in *The Solholt* has received support on the basis that it recognizes the value of the re-negotiation of contracts, it can be criticized on three substantial grounds. First, it rendered the buyer's right to reject the vessel illusory. There seems to be no point in exercising a right to reject if the buyer then has to make an offer to purchase the rejected goods at the contract price (at least in the case of a rising market). Secondly, it entitled the sellers to retain the profits attributable to the rise in the market price of the vessel. They were able to keep the difference between the contract price of $5 million and the price of $5.8 million for which they eventually sold the vessel when they should have been entitled to retain the difference between the market price at the date of the breach ($5.5 million) and the price for which they sold the vessel ($5.8 million). In effect, they were enriched to the extent of $500,000 by their breach of contract. Third, mitigation relates to the avoidance of losses and, on the facts of *The Solholt*, the loss had already occurred at the date of breach (in the sense that the market price had already moved) and the question for the court was which party was to take the benefit of the rise in the market price. On the facts it was held that it was the sellers, the party in breach, who were entitled to retain the rise in the market price. As Professor Bridge has observed ((1989) 109 *LQR* 389, 421–422):

if one had to speculate on the failure to recognise principle in *Payzu* and *The Solholt*, it would be on the ground that the law's insistence upon treating the possibility of mitigation as a question of fact, together with a preoccupation with the reasonableness of the plaintiff's conduct, has created an intellectual vacuum.

The final point to be noted in relation to the doctrine of mitigation is that it can be seen as part of a broader principle that a claimant must act reasonably. This principle can be seen at work in *Ruxley* (p. 1018 above) where Lord Lloyd stated he did not accept the submission that 'reasonableness is confined to the doctrine of mitigation'. The 'obligation' to act reasonably can extend into matters such as the measure of recovery to which the claimant is entitled (i.e., whether it is cost of cure or difference in value).

(c) CONTRIBUTORY NEGLIGENCE

A controversial issue in recent years has been the question whether or not it is possible to reduce the damages payable to the claimant on the ground that the claimant's carelessness has contributed to the losses that he has suffered. The problem here relates to the application of the Law Reform (Contributory Negligence) Act 1945 to contractual claims. The Act seems to have been drafted with tort claims in mind, particularly claims in the tort of negligence, and the consequence is that the concepts that it employs, particularly the notion of 'fault', do not translate easily into a contractual context. In determining whether or not contributory negligence can be invoked as a defence by a defendant who is sued for damages for breach of contract, the courts in England and Wales distinguish between three different types of claim. The first is a case in which the defendant's liability arises from a breach of a contractual provision which does not depend on a failure to take reasonable care; that is to say, the breach of a strict contractual duty. Contributory negligence is not available as a defence to such a claim. The second is a case in which liability arises from an express contractual obligation to take care which does not correspond to any duty which would exist independently of the contract. Once again, contributory negligence is not available as a defence to such a claim. The third case is one in which the liability for breach of contract is the same as, and coextensive with, a liability in tort independently of the existence of a contract. Contributory negligence is available as a defence to such a claim. The operation of these rules is illustrated by the following case:

Barclays Bank plc v. Fairclough Building Ltd

[1995] QB 214, Court of Appeal

The defendant contractors, Fairclough, agreed to carry out work for the plaintiff, Barclays Bank, at Millbrook Industrial Estate, Wythenshaw. A significant part of that work required the defendant to clean and treat some asbestos cement sheets. The contract did not specify the method by which the work was to be done but it was a condition of the contract that all roofing work should be executed by a specialist firm of roofing contractors or by the defendant's own craftsmen if properly experienced in such work. The defendant sub-contracted the work to a sub-contractor who used high-pressure hoses to jet clean the sheets. As a result of the way in which the work was done the building became heavily contaminated with asbestos dust which necessitated extensive remedial works at a cost of approximately £4m. Neither the defendant, nor the sub-contractor, had taken any of the recommended precautions when using the high pressure hose method of cleaning the asbestos roofs. The defendant accepted that it was seriously in breach of the terms of the contract. The defendant breached two of the main obligations under the contract. First, there was a clear breach of the defendant's obligation to carry out the work in accordance with the specification and to achieve the standard specified. The defendant's failure in this respect was a breach of a strict obligation and not simply a failure to exercise reasonable care and skill. Second, the defendant's failure to comply with the requirements of the Asbestos Regulations of 1987 was a breach of condition 5.1 and was also a breach of a strict contractual term. The defendant alleged that the plaintiff had been guilty of contributory negligence in that, through its safety officer and its supervising officer, it should have drawn the defendant's attention to the dangers and the supervising officer could and should have insisted on compliance with the terms of the contract.

The plaintiff brought an action to recover damages for the losses that it had suffered. The trial judge awarded the plaintiff substantial damages but reduced the award by 40%

under sections 1(1) and 4 of the Law Reform (Contributory Negligence) Act 1945 on the ground that the plaintiff had been guilty of contributory negligence. The plaintiff appealed to the Court of Appeal who allowed the appeal and held that the damages payable to the plaintiff did not fall to be reduced under the 1945 Act.

Beldam LJ

Breach of contract and contributory negligence

The common law rule that in an action in tort a plaintiff whose own fault contributed with the defendant's to cause his damage could recover nothing was perceived to be unfair and, as a result of the Law Revision Committee's Eighth Report (Contributory Negligence) (1939) (Cmd. 6032), the Law Reform (Contributory Negligence) Act 1945 was passed. Its purpose was to enable a court in actions of tort to apportion responsibility for the damage suffered by the plaintiff where there had been fault by both parties. It is the definition of 'fault' under section 4 which has since 1945 given rise to continuing debate and uncertainty whether the court's ability to apportion damages applies to a case in which the plaintiff's cause of action lies in contract. After nearly half a century of extensive academic analysis, inconclusive discussion in a number of decided cases and conflicting Commonwealth decisions, the position remained uncertain and in 1989 the Law Commission published Working Paper No 114, Contributory Negligence as a Defence in Contract. In this consultation paper the competing arguments based on the interpretation of section 4 and the state of the law as it then appeared to be were fully examined. After consultation the Commission reported its recommendations in December 1993, Contributory Negligence as a Defence in Contract (Law Com. No 219). In the light of this extensive review of the law, a short summary of the position is in my view sufficient for the purposes of the present case.

Section 4 of the Act defines 'fault':

'"fault" means negligence, breach of statutory duty or other act or omission which gives rise to a liability in tort or would, apart from this Act, give rise to the defence of contributory negligence;. . .'

It is generally agreed that the first part of the definition relates to the defendant's fault and the second part to the plaintiff's but debate has focused on the words 'or other act or omission which gives rise to a liability in tort' in the first part and 'other act or omission which . . . would, apart from this Act, give rise to the defence of contributory negligence' in the second part. It has been argued that, merely because the plaintiff frames his cause of action as a breach of contract, if the acts or omissions on which he relies could equally well give rise to a liability in tort the defendant is entitled to rely on the defence of contributory negligence. Examples frequently cited are claims for damages against an employer or by a passenger against a railway or bus company where the plaintiff may frame his action either in tort or in contract and the duty relied on in either case is a duty to take reasonable care for the plaintiff's safety. Contributory negligence has been a defence in such actions for many years. So it is argued that, in all cases in which the contractual duty broken by a defendant is the same as and is coextensive with a similar duty in tort, the defendant may now rely on the defence. An opposing view based on the second part of the definition is that, if the plaintiff framed his action for breach of contract, contributory negligence at common law was never regarded as a defence to his claim and so cannot be relied on under the Act of 1945.

Under the first part of the definition, if the plaintiff claims damages for breach of a contractual term which does not correspond with a duty in tort to take reasonable care, the defendant's acts or omissions would not give rise to a liability in tort and accordingly no question of contributory negligence could arise.

These arguments have led courts to classify contractual duties under three headings: (i) where a party's liability arises from breach of a contractual provision which does not depend on a failure to take reasonable care; (ii) where the liability arises from an express contractual obligation to take care which does not correspond to any duty which would exist independently of the contract; (iii) where the liability for breach of contract is the same as, and coextensive with, a liability in tort independently of the existence of a contract. This analysis was adopted by Hobhouse J in *Forsikringsaktieselskapet Vesta* v. *Butcher* [1986] 2 All ER 488 and by the Court of Appeal in the same case [1989] AC 852, 860, 862, 866–867. The judgments in the Court of Appeal in that case assert that in category (iii) cases the Court of Appeal is bound by the decision in *Sayers* v. *Harlow Urban District Council* [1958] 1 WLR 623 to admit the availability of the defence.

Since I do not regard the case before the court as being in that category, I am content to accept that decision. To regard the definition of fault in section 4 as extending to cases such as employer's liability places no great strain on the construction of the words used . . .

On the other hand, in category (i) cases there is no decision in which contributory negligence has been held to be a partial defence. There are powerful dicta to the effect that it cannot be: see the judgment of the court in *Tennant Radiant Heat Ltd* v. *Warrington Development Corporation* [1988] 1 EGLR 41, in *Bank of Nova Scotia* v. *Hellenic Mutual War Risks Association (Bermuda) Ltd* [1990] 1 QB 818, 904, and the observations of Nolan LJ in *Schering Agrochemicals Ltd* v. *Resibel NV SA* (unreported), 26 November 1992; Court of Appeal (Civil Division) Transcript No 1298 of 1992, noted in (1993) 109 *LQR* 175, 177.

The defendant's argument that, because the plaintiff owed duties to its employees it was therefore under a duty in its own interest to see that the defendant fulfilled its obligations under the contract, is inconsistent with many cases in which it has been held that employers and others liable to third parties for failure of plant or equipment are entitled to rely on warranties given by their suppliers . . .

The present case

I have already stated my conclusion that in the present case the defendant was in breach of two conditions which required strict performance and did not depend on a mere failure to take reasonable care. Nevertheless it was argued by Mr Butcher [counsel for the defendant] in support of the respondent's notice that the defendant could have been held liable in tort for the same acts or omissions. By creating the asbestos dust it was guilty of nuisance. Further the settling of the dust on the storage racks and floors of the plaintiff's building amounted to trespass. I would reject these submissions.

On the other hand, Mr Elliott [counsel for the plaintiff] addressed arguments to the court that the defendant would not have been found liable to the plaintiff in negligence, for the only damage proved was economic loss. These arguments amply justified the fears expressed by the Law Commission in its 1993 report (Law Com. No 219) that actions for breach of a strict contractual obligation would become unduly complex if contributory negligence were admitted as a partial defence by introducing an element of uncertainty into many straightforward commercial disputes and increasing the issues to be determined.

In my judgment therefore in the present state of the law contributory negligence is not a defence to a claim for damages founded on breach of a strict contractual obligation. I do not believe the wording of the Law Reform (Contributory Negligence) Act 1945 can reasonably sustain an argument to the contrary. Even if it did, in the present case the nature of the contract and the obligation undertaken by the skilled contractor did not impose on the plaintiff any duty in its own interest to prevent the defendant from committing the breaches of contract. To hold otherwise would, I consider, be equivalent to implying into the contract an obligation on the part of the plaintiff inconsistent with the express terms agreed by the parties. The contract clearly laid down the extent of the obligations of the plaintiff as architect and of the defendant. It was the defendant who was to provide appropriate supervision on site, not the architect . . .

For the reasons I have given, I would allow the appeal.

Simon Brown LJ

The central issue raised by this appeal is clearly one of some importance: when does section 1(1) of the Law Reform (Contributory Negligence) Act 1945 apply to actions in contract? Although I agree entirely with the judgment of Beldam LJ, I wish, in deference to the skilful arguments presented on both sides, to indicate something of my own approach . . . The argument by which Mr Butcher seeks to uphold the judge's finding that the plaintiff here was 40 per cent. contributorily negligent proceeded, as I understand it, essentially as follows. (i) There is no challenge (save only as to the sufficiency of the defendant's pleading) to the judge's finding that the damage suffered by the plaintiff was the result partly of its own fault. (ii) Accepting, as the judge found, that the defendant's liability for that damage arose from breaches of one or more strict contractual terms, i.e. provisions which did not depend on negligence on the defendant's part, and so fall into category 1 of the three categories identified by Hobhouse J in *Forsikringsaktie-selskapet Vesta* v. *Butcher* [1986] 2 All ER 488, 508, nevertheless the defendant was entitled to the benefit of apportionment under section 1(1) provided only and always that it established that the damage resulted not only from its contractual breach but also from some 'fault,' i.e. tortious liability, on its part. (iii) Such tortious 'fault' here consisted in (a) its own breach of a duty of care at common law, (b) its own nuisance, (c) its own trespass.

Although Mr Butcher's argument is clearly vulnerable at all three stages—stage (i) the pleading point, for the reasons given by Beldam LJ; stage (iii) because of the various technical difficulties which arise with regard to each of the suggested causes of action, such as that the plaintiff's loss was exclusively economic so that there could be no liability in negligence—I prefer to focus on stage (ii) because it is there that I believe as a matter of principle the argument should fail.

Why should it fail? Not, let me acknowledge, for any failure to bring the defendant's case within the language of section 1(1). I for my part would accept that the defendant here—assuming it could make good stage (iii) of its argument—would thereby establish that the relevant damage was the result equally and concurrently of its tortious fault as of its breaches of contract . . . I would . . . reject its claim to be entitled to apportionment. I would, however, do so by reference rather to the proper construction of the contract than of the statute itself.

I for my part would accept Hobhouse J's view expressed in *Forsikringsaktieselskapet Vesta* v. *Butcher* [1986] 2 All ER 488, 509–510, that apportionment of blame and liability is open to the court in any ordinary category (iii) case, unless the parties by their contract have varied that position, because, as he explained:

'there is independently of contract a status or common law relationship which exists between the parties and which can then give rise to tortious liabilities which fall to be adjusted in accordance with the Act of 1945.'

In short, the contract in such cases really adds nothing to the common law position . . .

But when, as in a category (i) case, the contractual liability is by no means immaterial, when rather it is a strict liability arising independently of any negligence on the defendant's part, then there *seem* to me compelling reasons why the contract, even assuming it is silent as to apportionment, should be construed as excluding the operation of the Act of 1945. The very imposition of a strict liability on the defendant is to my mind inconsistent with an apportionment of the loss. And not least because of the absurdities that the contrary approach carries in its wake. Assume a defendant, clearly liable under a strict contractual duty. Is his position to be improved by demonstrating that besides breaching that duty he was in addition negligent? Take this very case. Is this contract really to be construed so that the defendant is advantaged by an assertion of its own liability in nuisance or trespass as well as in contract? Are we to have trials at which the defendant calls an expert to implicate him in tortious liability, whilst the plaintiff's expert seeks paradoxically to exonerate him? The answer to all these questions is surely 'No'. Whatever arguments exist for apportionment in other categories of case—and these are persuasively deployed in the 1993 Law Commission Report (Law Com. No 219)—to my mind there are none in the present type of case and I for my part would construe the contract accordingly. For these reasons in addition to those given by Beldam LJ, I, too, would allow this appeal.

Nourse LJ delivered a concurring judgment.

COMMENTARY

In many ways, the litigation in *Fairclough* demonstrates the controversies that currently exist in this area of law. The law currently compels the parties to take up unusual positions. For example, it was the defendant in *Fairclough* who argued that it was liable to the plaintiff in tort and it did so for the purpose of seeking to invoke the defence of contributory negligence. By contrast, the plaintiff argued that the defendant was not liable in tort so that it could avoid the application of the defence. It is, to say the least, very odd to give an incentive to a defendant to admit a liability for the purpose of seeking to reduce his liability (or, to view the same issue from the perspective of the claimant, to put the claimant in the position of denying that he has a particular claim for the purpose of increasing the size of his claim against the defendant). But this is the position that English law has currently reached. If the law is to change, which direction should the change take? One approach would be to conclude that contributory negligence should always be available as a defence to a claim in contract so as to give to claimants an incentive to take steps to ensure that losses are not unreasonably increased. It can also be argued that the wider availability of contributory negligence as a defence will enable courts to reach fairer results on the facts of the cases that come before them. Contributory negligence is typically a partial defence and so it can be tailored to meet the facts of the individual case. Doctrines of mitigation and break in the chain of causation, by contrast, operate in an all-or-nothing fashion. As Professor Burrows has observed ('Limitations on Compensation' in A Burrows and E Peel (eds), *Commercial Remedies: Current Issues and Problems* (Oxford University Press, 2003), 27, 41):

it seems wrong in terms of policy for the law to be that a claimant may be wholly barred from receiving damages because of the claimant's own fault, through the application of the duty to mitigate or intervening cause, while there is no mis-position where damages may be merely reduced. The denial of contributory negligence unsatisfactorily forces the courts to choose between the blameworthy claimant recovering 100 per cent damages or no damages for the particular loss in question.

The alternative is to conclude that contributory negligence should not have a role to play in contractual claims on the ground that the claimant has paid for the performance by the defendant of his contractual duties and, provided that the loss to the claimant is caused by the defendant's breach of contract, the law should not impose upon a claimant an obligation to take reasonable steps to ensure that the defendant is performing his contractual obligations or to take reasonable care to ensure that loss is not suffered as a result of the defendant's failure to perform his contractual obligations. The latter approach was taken by the High Court of Australia in *Astley* v. *Austrust Limited* (1999) 197 CLR 1, 31, 36–37, where Gleeson CJ, McHugh, Gummow, and Hayne JJ concluded as follows:

In our opinion, those decisions which have applied apportionment legislation, based on the Law Reform (Contributory Negligence) Act (UK), to breaches of contract are wrong and should not be followed in this country. The interpretation of the legislation adopted by those courts which have applied the legislation to contract claims is strained, to say the least . . . when the nature of an action for breach of a contractual term to take reasonable care and the nature of an action in tort for breach of a general law duty of care are examined, it is by no means evident that there is anything anomalous or unfair in a plaintiff who sues in contract being outside the scope of the apportionment legislation. Tort obligations are imposed on the parties; contractual obligations are voluntarily assumed . . .

In contract, the plaintiff gives consideration, often very substantial consideration, for the defendant's promise to take reasonable care. The terms of the contract allocate responsibility for the risks of the parties' enterprise including the risk that the damage suffered by one party may arise partly from the failure of that party to take reasonable care for the safety of that person's property or person. Ordinarily, that risk is borne by the party whose breach of contract is causally connected to the damage. Rarely do contracts apportion responsibility for damage on the basis of the respective fault of the parties. Commercial people in particular prefer the certainty of fixed rules to the vagueness of concepts such as 'just and equitable'. That is why it is commonplace for contracts to contain provisions regulating liability for breach of a duty to take reasonable care, whether by excluding liability altogether or limiting it in some other way.

Absent some contractual stipulation to the contrary, there is no reason of justice or sound legal policy which should prevent the plaintiff in a case such as the present recovering for all the damage that is causally connected to the defendant's breach even if the plaintiff's conduct has contributed to the damage which he or she has suffered. By its own voluntary act, the defendant has accepted an obligation to take reasonable care and, subject to remoteness rules, to pay damages for any loss or damage flowing from a breach of that obligation. If the defendant wishes to reduce its liability in a situation where the plaintiff's own conduct contributes to the damage suffered, it is open to the defendant to make a bargain with the plaintiff to achieve that end. Of course, the result of such a bargain may be that the defendant will have to take a reduced consideration for its promise to take reasonable care. But the bargain will be the product of the parties' voluntary agreement to subject themselves to their respective obligations. . . .

It is one thing to apportion the liability for damage between a person who has been able to obtain the gratuitous services of a defendant where the negligence of each has contributed to the plaintiff's loss. It is another matter altogether to reduce the damages otherwise payable to a plaintiff who may have paid a very large sum to the defendant for a promise of reasonable care merely because the plaintiff's own conduct has also contributed to the suffering of the relevant damage.

9. ACCOUNT OF PROFITS

There may be cases in which the defendant makes a profit from his breach of contract and that profit exceeds the loss suffered by the claimant. In such a case, can the claimant recover the profit made by the defendant? This issue was considered by the House of Lords in the following case:

Attorney-General v. Blake

[2001] 1 AC 268, House of Lords

On 4 May 1989 George Blake entered into a contract with the publishers Jonathan Cape Ltd under which he granted to Jonathan Cape Ltd an exclusive right to publish his autobiography. Mr Blake had been a member of the security and intelligence services for a number of years but during that period he had betrayed his country by acting as an agent for the Soviet Union. In his book, entitled 'No Other Choice', Blake recounted some of his activities as a secret intelligence officer. The information disclosed in the book was, by the time of publication, no longer confidential, nor was its disclosure damaging to the public interest. Nevertheless, its disclosure was in breach of contract. On entry to the security and intelligence services Blake signed an Official Secrets Act declaration which included the following:

'I undertake not to divulge any official information gained by me as a result of my employment, either in the press or in book form. I also understand that those provisions apply not only during the period of service but also after employment has ceased.'

In failing to submit his manuscript for clearance prior to its publication Blake committed a breach of this undertaking. The House of Lords held that Blake was accountable to the Crown for all of the profit he made as a result of his breach of contract.

Lord Nicholls of Birkenhead [set out the facts of the case and then turned to consider some 'established, basic principles, of law by way of background to the central point of law in issue between the parties. He considered three such basic principles. First, he considered the law relating to interference with rights of property, where the law does recognize that, in the case of trespass to land and wrongful detention of goods, damages may be assessed by reference to the benefit received by the wrongdoer. Similarly he noted the role of account of profits as a remedy in intellectual property cases. Secondly, he noted that equity requires a trustee or fiduciary to account for any profits he derives from his office or position. Thirdly, he noted that an award of damages under what used to be known as Lord Cairns' Act may include damages measured by reference to the benefits likely to be obtained in the future, by the defendant. He continued]

Breach of contract

Against this background I turn to consider the remedies available for breaches of contract. The basic remedy is an award of damages. In the much quoted words of Baron Parke, the rule of the common law is that where a party sustains a loss by reason of a breach of contract, he is, so far as money can do it, to be placed in the same position as if the contract had been performed: *Robinson* v. *Harman* (1848) 1 Exch 850, 855. Leaving aside the anomalous exception of punitive damages, damages are compensatory. That is axiomatic. It is equally well established that an award of damages, assessed by reference to financial loss, is not always 'adequate' as a remedy for a breach of contract. The law recognises that a party to a contract may have an interest in performance which is not readily measurable in terms of money. On breach the innocent party suffers a loss. He fails to obtain the benefit promised by the other party to the contract. To him the loss may be as important as financially measurable loss, or more so. An award of damages, assessed by reference to financial loss, will not recompense him properly. For him a financially assessed measure of damages is inadequate.

The classic example of this type of case, as every law student knows, is a contract for the sale of land. The buyer of a house may be attracted by features which have little or no impact on the value of the house. An award of damages, based on strictly financial criteria, would fail to recompense a disappointed buyer for this head of loss. The primary response of the law to this type of case is to ensure, if possible, that the contract is performed in accordance with its terms. The court may make orders compelling the party who has committed a breach of contract, or is threatening to do so, to carry out his contractual obligations. To this end the court has wide powers to grant injunctive relief. The court will, for instance, readily make orders for the specific performance of contracts for the sale of land, and sometimes it will do so in respect of contracts for the sale of goods. In *Beswick* v. *Beswick* [1968] AC 58 the court made an order for the specific performance of a contract to make payments of money to a third party. The law recognised that the innocent party to the breach of contract had a legitimate interest in having the contract performed even though he himself would suffer no financial loss from its breach. Likewise, the court will compel the observance of negative obligations by granting injunctions. This may include a mandatory order to undo an existing breach, as where the court orders the defendant to pull down building works carried out in breach of covenant.

All this is trite law. In practice, these specific remedies go a long way towards providing suitable protection for innocent parties who will suffer loss from breaches of contract which are not adequately remediable by an award of damages. But these remedies are not always available. For instance, confidential information may be published in breach of a non-disclosure agreement before the innocent party has time to apply to the court for urgent relief. Then the breach is irreversible. Further, these specific remedies are discretionary. Contractual obligations vary infinitely. So do the circumstances in which breaches occur, and the circumstances in which remedies are sought. The court may, for instance, decline to grant specific relief on the ground that this would be oppressive.

An instance of this nature occurred in *Wrotham Park Estate Co Ltd* v. *Parkside Homes Ltd* [1974] 1 WLR 798. For social and economic reasons the court refused to make a mandatory order for the demolition of houses built on land burdened with a restrictive covenant. Instead, Brightman J made an award of damages under the jurisdiction which originated with Lord Cairns's Act. The existence of the new houses did not diminish the value of the benefited land by one farthing. The judge considered that if the plaintiffs were given a nominal sum, or no sum, justice would manifestly not have been done. He assessed the damages at 5% of the developer's anticipated profit, this being the amount of money which could reasonably have been demanded for a relaxation of the covenant.

In reaching his conclusion the judge applied by analogy the cases mentioned above concerning the assessment of damages when a defendant has invaded another's property rights but without diminishing the value of the property. I consider he was right to do so. Property rights are superior to contractual rights in that, unlike contractual rights, property rights may survive against an indefinite class of persons. However, it is not easy to see why, as between the parties to a contract, a violation of a party's contractual rights should attract a lesser degree of remedy than a violation of his property rights. As Lionel D. Smith has pointed out in his article 'Disgorgement of the profits of Breach of Contract: Property, Contract and "Efficient Breach"' (1995) 24 *Can BLJ* 121, it is not clear why it should be any more permissible to expropriate personal rights than it is permissible to expropriate property rights.

I turn to the decision of the Court of Appeal in *Surrey County Council* v. *Bredero Homes Ltd* [1993] 1 WLR 1361. A local authority had sold surplus land to a developer and obtained a covenant that the developer would develop the land in accordance with an existing planning permission. The sole purpose of the local authority in imposing the covenant was to enable it to share in the planning gain if, as happened, planning permission was subsequently granted for the erection of a larger number of houses. The purpose was that the developer would have to apply and pay for a relaxation of the covenant if it wanted to build more houses. In breach of covenant the developer completed the development in accordance with the later planning permission, and the local authority brought a claim for damages. The erection of the larger number of houses had not caused any financial loss to the local authority. The judge awarded nominal damages of £2, and the Court of Appeal dismissed the local authority's appeal.

This is a difficult decision. It has attracted criticism from academic commentators and also in judgments of Sir Thomas Bingham MR and Millett LJ in *Jaggard* v. *Sawyer* [1995] 1 WLR 269. I need not pursue the detailed criticisms. In the *Bredero* case Dillon LJ himself noted, at p. 1364, that had the covenant been worded differently, there could have been provision for payment of an increased price if a further planning permission were forthcoming. That would have been enforceable. But, according to the *Bredero* decision, a covenant not to erect any further houses without permission, intended to achieve the same result, may be breached with impunity. That would be a sorry reflection on the law. Suffice to say, in so far as the *Bredero* decision is inconsistent with the approach adopted in the *Wrotham Park* case, the latter approach is to be preferred.

The *Wrotham Park* case, therefore, still shines, rather as a solitary beacon, showing that in contract as well as tort damages are not always narrowly confined to recoupment of financial loss. In a suitable case damages for breach of contract may be measured by the benefit gained by the wrongdoer from the breach. The defendant must make a reasonable payment in respect of the benefit he has gained. In the present case the Crown seeks to go further. The claim is for all the profits of Blake's book which the publisher has not yet paid him. This raises the question whether an account of profits can ever be given as a remedy for breach of contract. The researches of counsel have been unable to discover any case where the court has made such an order on a claim for breach of contract. In *Tito* v. *Waddell (No 2)* [1977] Ch 106, 332, a decision which has proved controversial, Sir Robert Megarry V-C said that, as a matter of fundamental principle, the question of damages was 'not one of making the defendant disgorge' his gains, in that case what he had saved by committing the wrong, but 'one of compensating the plaintiff'. In *Occidental Worldwide Investment Corporation* v. *Skibs A/S Avanti* [1976] 1 Lloyd's Rep 293, 337, Kerr J summarily rejected a claim for an account of profits when ship owners withdrew ships on a rising market.

There is a light sprinkling of cases where courts have made orders having the same effect as an order for an account of profits, but the courts seem always to have attached a different label. A person who, in breach of contract, sells land twice over must surrender his profits on the second sale to the original buyer. Since courts regularly make orders for the specific performance of contracts for the sale of land, a seller of land is, to an extent, regarded as holding the land on trust for the buyer: *Lake* v. *Bayliss* [1974] 1 WLR 1073. In *Reid-Newfoundland Co* v. *Anglo-American Telegraph Co Ltd* [1912] AC 555 a railway company agreed not to transmit any commercial messages over a particular telegraph wire except for the benefit and account of the telegraph company. The Privy Council held that the railway company was liable to account as a trustee for the profits it wrongfully made from its use of the wire for commercial purposes. In *British Motor Trade Association* v. *Gilbert* [1951] 2 All ER 641 the plaintiff suffered no financial loss but the award of damages for breach of contract effectively stripped the wrongdoer of the profit he had made from his wrongful venture into the black market for new cars.

These cases illustrate that circumstances do arise when the just response to a breach of contract is that the wrongdoer should not be permitted to retain any profit from the breach. In these cases the courts have reached the desired result by straining existing concepts. Professor Peter Birks has deplored the 'failure of jurisprudence when the law is forced into this kind of abusive instrumentalism'; see 'Profits of Breach of Contract' (1993) 109 *LQR* 518, 520. Some years ago Professor Dawson suggested there is no inherent reason why the technique of equity courts in land contracts should not be more widely employed, not by granting remedies as the by-product of a phantom 'trust' created by the contract, but as an alternative form of money judgment remedy. That well known ailment of lawyers, a hardening of the categories, ought not to be an obstacle: see 'Restitution or Damages' (1959) 20 *Ohio SLJ* 175.

My conclusion is that there seems to be no reason, in principle, why the court must in all circumstances rule out an account of profits as a remedy for breach of contract. I prefer to avoid the unhappy expression 'restitutionary damages'. Remedies are the law's response to a wrong (or, more precisely, to a cause of action). When, exceptionally, a just response to a breach of contract so requires, the court should be able to grant the discretionary remedy of requiring a defendant to account to the plaintiff for the benefits he has received from his breach of contract. In the same way as a plaintiff's interest in performance of a contract may render it just and equitable for the court to make an order for specific performance or grant an injunction, so the plaintiff's interest in performance may make it just and equitable that the defendant should retain no benefit from his breach of contract.

The state of the authorities encourages me to reach this conclusion, rather than the reverse. The law recognises that damages are not always a sufficient remedy for breach of contract. This is the foundation of the court's jurisdiction to grant the remedies of specific performance and injunction. Even when awarding damages, the law does not adhere slavishly to the concept of compensation for financially measurable loss. When the circumstances require, damages are measured by reference to the benefit obtained by the wrongdoer. This applies to interference with property rights. Recently, the like approach has been adopted to breach of contract. Further, in certain circumstances an account of profits is ordered in preference to an award of damages. Sometimes the injured party is given the choice: either compensatory damages or an account of the wrongdoer's profits. Breach of confidence is an instance of this. If confidential information is wrongfully divulged in breach of a non-disclosure agreement, it would be nothing short of sophistry to say that an account of profits may be ordered in respect of the equitable wrong but not in respect of the breach of contract which governs the relationship between the parties. With the established authorities going thus far, I consider it would be only a modest step for the law to recognise openly that, exceptionally, an account of profits may be the most appropriate remedy for breach of contract. It is not as though this step would contradict some recognised principle applied consistently throughout the law to the grant or withholding of the remedy of an account of profits. No such principle is discernible.

The main argument against the availability of an account of profits as a remedy for breach of contract is that the circumstances where this remedy may be granted will be uncertain. This will have an unsettling effect on commercial contracts where certainty is important. I do not think these fears are well founded. I see no reason why, in practice, the availability of the remedy of an account of profits need disturb settled expectations in the commercial or consumer world. An account of profits will be appropriate only in exceptional circumstances. Normally the remedies of damages, specific performance and injunction, coupled with the characterisation of some contractual obligations as fiduciary, will provide an adequate response to a breach of contract. It will be only in exceptional cases, where those remedies are inadequate, that any question of accounting for profits will arise. No fixed rules can be prescribed. The court will have regard to all the circumstances, including the subject matter of the contract, the purpose of the contractual provision which has been breached, the circumstances in which the breach occurred, the consequences of the breach and the circumstances in which relief is being sought. A useful general guide, although not exhaustive, is whether the plaintiff had a legitimate interest in preventing the defendant's profit-making activity and, hence, in depriving him of his profit.

It would be difficult, and unwise, to attempt to be more specific. In the Court of Appeal [1998] Ch 439 Lord Woolf MR suggested there are at least two situations in which justice requires the award of restitutionary damages where compensatory damages would be inadequate: see p. 458. Lord Woolf MR was not there addressing the question of when an account of profits, in the conventional sense, should be available. But I should add that, so far as an account of profits is concerned, the suggested categorisation would not assist. The first suggested category was the case of 'skimped' performance, where the defendant fails to provide the full extent of services he has contracted to provide. He should be liable to pay back the amount of expenditure he saved by the breach. This is a much discussed problem. But a part refund of the price agreed for services would not fall within the scope of an account of profits as ordinarily understood. Nor does an account of profits seem to be needed in this context. The resolution of the problem of cases of skimped performance, where the plaintiff does not get what was agreed, may best be found elsewhere. If a shopkeeper supplies inferior and cheaper goods than those ordered and paid for, he has to refund the difference in price. That would be the outcome of a claim for damages for breach of contract. That would be so, irrespective of whether the goods in fact served the intended purpose. There must be scope for a similar approach, without any straining of principle, in cases where the defendant provided inferior and cheaper services than those contracted for.

The second suggested category was where the defendant has obtained his profit by doing the very thing he contracted not to do. This category is defined too widely to assist. The category is apt to embrace all express negative obligations. But something more is required than mere breach of such an obligation before an account of profits will be the appropriate remedy.

Lord Woolf MR [1998] Ch 439, 457, 458, also suggested three facts which should not be a sufficient ground for departing from the normal basis on which damages are awarded: the fact that the breach was cynical and deliberate; the fact that the breach enabled the defendant to enter into a more profitable contract elsewhere; and the fact that by entering into a new and more profitable contract the defendant put it out of his power to perform his contract with the plaintiff. I agree that none of these facts would be, by itself, a good reason for ordering an account of profits.

The present case

The present case is exceptional. The context is employment as a member of the security and intelligence services. Secret information is the lifeblood of these services. In the 1950s Blake deliberately committed repeated breaches of his undertaking not to divulge official information gained as a result of his employment. He caused untold and immeasurable damage to the public interest he had committed himself to serve. In 1990 he published his autobiography, a further breach of his express undertaking. . . . When he joined the Secret Intelligence Service Blake expressly agreed in writing that he would not disclose official information, during or after his service, in book form or otherwise. He was employed on that basis. That was the basis on which he acquired official information. The Crown had and has a legitimate interest in preventing Blake profiting from the disclosure of official information, whether classified or not, while a member of the service and thereafter. Neither he, nor any other member of the service, should have a financial incentive to break his undertaking. It is of paramount importance that members of the service should have complete confidence in all their dealings with each other, and that those recruited as informers should have the like confidence. Undermining the willingness of prospective informers to co-operate with the services, or undermining the morale and trust between members of the services when engaged on secret and dangerous operations, would jeopardise the effectiveness of the service. An absolute rule against disclosure, visible to all, makes good sense.

In considering what would be a just response to a breach of Blake's undertaking the court has to take these considerations into account. The undertaking, if not a fiduciary obligation, was closely akin to a fiduciary obligation, where an account of profits is a standard remedy in the event of breach. Had the information which Blake has now disclosed still been confidential, an account of profits would have been ordered, almost as a matter of course. In the special circumstances of the intelligence services, the same conclusion should follow even though the information is no longer confidential. That would be a just response to the breach. I am reinforced in this view by noting that most of the profits from the book derive indirectly from the extremely serious and damaging breaches of the same undertaking committed by Blake in the 1950s. As already mentioned, but for his notoriety as an infamous spy his autobiography would not have commanded royalties of the magnitude Jonathan Cape agreed to pay.

As a footnote I observe that a similar conclusion, requiring the contract breaker to disgorge his profits, was reached in the majority decision of the United States Supreme Court in *Snepp* v. *United States* (1980) 444 US 507. The facts were strikingly similar. A former employee of the Central Intelligence Agency, whose conditions of employment included a promise not to divulge any information relating to the agency without pre-publication clearance, published a book about the agency's activities in Vietnam. None of the information was classified, but an agent's violation of his non-disclosure obligation impaired the agency's ability to function properly. The court considered and rejected various forms of relief. The actual damage was not quantifiable, nominal damages were a hollow alternative, and punitive damages after a jury trial would be speculative and unusual. Even if recovered they would bear no relation to either the government's irreparable loss or Snepp's unjust gain. The court considered that a remedy which required Snepp 'to disgorge the benefits of his faithlessness', was swift and sure, tailored to deter those who would place sensitive information at risk and, since the remedy reached only funds attributable to the breach, it could not saddle the former agent with exemplary damages out of all proportion to his gain. In order to achieve this result the court 'imposed' a constructive trust on Snepp's profits. In this country, affording the plaintiff the remedy of an account of profits is a different means to the same end.

The form of the order

The Attorney General's entitlement to an account of Blake's profits does not, in this case, confer on the Crown any proprietary interest in the debt due to Blake from Jonathan Cape. The Crown is entitled, on the taking of the account, to a money judgment which can then be enforced by attachment of the debt in the usual way. These formal steps may be capable of being short-circuited. Despite the niceties and formalities once associated with taking an account, the amount payable under an account of profits need not be any more elaborately or precisely calculated than damages. But in this case there is a complication. Blake has brought third party proceedings against Jonathan Cape, seeking payment of £90,000 (less tax). In the third party proceedings Jonathan Cape has sought to deduct legal expenses incurred in resisting a defamation claim and in resisting the Crown's claim. Accordingly, the appropriate form of order on this appeal is a declaration that the Attorney General is entitled to be paid a sum equal to whatever amount is due and owing to Blake from Jonathan Cape under the publishing agreement of 4 May 1989. The injunction granted by the Court of Appeal will remain in force until Jonathan Cape duly makes payment to the Attorney General. I would dismiss this appeal.

Lord Steyn

My Lords, in law classification is important. Asking the right questions in the right order reduces the risk of wrong decisions. This truth is illustrated by the case before the House . . .

[he set out the facts and continued]

In the Court of Appeal in *Surrey County Council* v. *Bredero Homes Ltd* [1993] 1 WLR 1361 I discussed some of the difficulties inherent in creating a general remedy for the recovery of restitutionary damages for breach of contract. On that occasion I remarked that it is not traditional to describe a claim for restitution following a breach of contract as damages. The terminology is however less important than the substance: under consideration are claims for the disgorgement of profits against a contract breaker. There has been a substantial academic debate on the merits of the actual decision in the *Bredero* case. Since this issue has not been directly debated in the present case I propose to express no view on it. But it is right to acknowledge that the academic comment has been critical of the decision in the *Bredero* case. I would, however, respectfully offer a comment on the valuable academic debate. On the one hand, there is no or virtually no support for a general action for disgorgement of profits made by a contract breaker by reason of his breach. On the other hand, there is significantly absent from the post-*Bredero* academic comment a reasoned statement of the particular circumstances when such a remedy should be available. That is not surprising because it is a notoriously difficult subject. But the Court of Appeal has been bold [he set out the two situations in which the Court of Appeal held that the remedy should be available and noted academic criticisms of the reasoning of the Court of Appeal and continued] . . . I am not at present willing to endorse the broad observations of the Court of Appeal. Exceptions to the general principle that there is no remedy for disgorgement of profits against a contract breaker are best hammered out on the anvil of concrete cases.

In the hearing before the House Mr Ross Cranston, the Solicitor General, in a thoughtful and careful speech argued for a recognition of an action for disgorgement of profits against a contract breaker where four conditions are fulfilled. (1) There has been a breach of a negative stipulation. (2) The contract breaker has obtained the profit by doing the very thing which he promised not to do. (3) The innocent party (in this case the Crown as represented by the Attorney General) has a special interest over and above the hope of a benefit to be assessed in monetary terms. (4) Specific performance or an injunction is an ineffective or virtually ineffective remedy for the breach. The Solicitor General persuaded me that in the case of Blake each of these conditions is satisfied. But since I recognise that it would be wrong to create a remedy simply to cover this case, it is right that I should explain the specific considerations which lead me to conclude that it is right on a principled basis to develop the law in a way which covers this case and other cases sharing materially similar features.

My Lords, it has been held at first instance and in the Court of Appeal that Blake is not a fiduciary. This is not an issue before the House. But, as my noble and learned friend, Lord Nicholls of Birkenhead, has observed, the present case is closely analogous to that of fiduciaries: compare *Reading* v. *Attorney General* [1951] AC 507. If the information was still confidential, Blake would in my view have been liable as a fiduciary. That would be so despite the fact that he left the intelligence services many years ago. The distinctive feature of this case is, however, that Blake gave an undertaking not to divulge any information, confidential or otherwise, obtained by him during his work in the intel-ligence services. This obligation still applies to Blake. He was, therefore in regard to all information obtained by him in the intelligence services, confidential or not, in a very similar position to a fiduciary. The reason of the rule applying to fiduciaries applies to him. Secondly, I bear in mind that the enduring strength of the common law is that it has been developed on a case-by-case basis by judges for whom the attainment of practical justice was a major objective of their work. It is still one of the major moulding forces of judicial decision-making. . . . For my part practical justice strongly militates in favour of granting an order for disgorgement of profits against Blake. The decision of the United States Supreme Court in *Snepp* v. *United States*, 444 US 507 is instructive. On very similar facts the Supreme Court imposed a constructive trust on the intelligence officer's profits. Our law is also mature enough to provide a remedy in such a case but does so by the route of the exceptional recognition of a claim for disgorgement of profits against the contract breaker. In my view therefore there is a valid claim vesting in the Attorney General against Blake for disgorgement of his gain . . .

My Lords, for these reasons, as well as the detailed and far more compelling reasons given by Lord Nicholls of Birkenhead, I would make the order which he has proposed.

Lord Hobhouse of Woodborough [dissenting]

I cannot join your Lordships in [the conclusion that the Crown's private law claim should succeed]. I have two primary difficulties. The first is the facts of the present case. The speech of my noble and learned friend explores what is the 'just response' to the defend-ant's conduct. The 'just response' visualised in the present case is, however it is formu-lated, that Blake should be punished and deprived of any fruits of conduct connected with his former criminal and reprehensible conduct. The Crown have made no secret of this. It is not a commercial claim in support of any commercial interest. It is a claim relating to past criminal conduct. The way it was put by the Court of Appeal [1998] Ch 439, 464 was:

> 'The ordinary member of the public would be shocked if the position was that the courts were powerless to prevent [Blake] profiting from his criminal conduct.'

The answer given by my noble and learned friend does not reflect the essentially punitive nature of the claim and seeks to apply principles of law which are only appropriate where commercial or proprietary interests are involved. Blake has made a financial gain but he has not done so at the expense of the Crown or making use of any property of or commercial interest of the Crown either in law or equity.

My second difficulty is that the reasoning of my noble and learned friend depends upon the conclusion that there is some gap in the existing state of the law which requires to be filled by a new remedy. He accepts that the term 'restitutionary damages' is unsatis-factory but, with respect, does not fully examine why this is so, drawing the necessary conclusions . . .

Where the plaintiff has failed to obtain or failed to apply for an injunction, he has to be content with a remedy in damages. What has happened in such cases is that there has either actually or in effect been a compulsory purchase of the plaintiff's right of refusal. . . . What the plaintiff has lost is the sum which he could have exacted from the defendant as the price of his consent to the development. This is an example of compen-satory damages. They are damages for breach. They do not involve any concept of restitution and so to describe them is an error. The error comes about because of the assumption that the only loss which the plaintiff can have suffered is a reduction in the value of the dominant tenement. It is for this reason that I agree with my noble and learned friend, Lord Nicholls, that the decision in *Wrotham Park Estate Co Ltd* v. *Parkside Homes Ltd* [1974] 1 WLR 798 is to be preferred to that in *Surrey County Council* v. *Bredero Homes Ltd* [1993] 1 WLR 1361: see also *Jaggard* v. *Sawyer* [1995] 1 WLR 269. I would however add that the order proposed by your Lordships does not reflect this principle; it goes further. It does not award to the Crown damages for breach of contract assessed by reference to what would be the reasonable price to pay for permission to publish. It awards the Crown damages which equal the whole amount owed by Jonathan Cape to Blake. That is a remedy based on proprietary principles when the necessary proprietary rights are absent.

The principle of compensation is both intellectually sound as the remedy for breach and provides the just answer. The examples discussed in my noble and learned friend's speech do not on the correct analysis disclose the supposed need to extend the boundaries of remedies for breach of contract. The reason why the Crown should not recover damages in the present case derives from the exceptional public law nature of the undertaking which Blake gave. If the relationship had been a commercial one it is probable that by 1989 the undertaking would be regarded as spent or no longer enforceable, but if still enforcible the breach of it would have supported compensatory damages on the 'compulsory purchase' basis.

The examples given by my noble and learned friend are examples of compensatory damages. Lord Halsbury's dining-room chair is no different unless the error which I have identified is made. He would have lost the use of the chair and it, like other such amenity-value assets, can be assessed by reference to the sum which has been expended on its acquisition and/or maintenance or interest upon its capital value during the period of deprivation. The supposed problem arises from asking the wrong question not from receiving the wrong answer.

I must also sound a further note of warning that if some more extensive principle of awarding non-compensatory damages for breach of contract is to be introduced into our commercial law the consequences will be very far reaching and disruptive. I do not believe that such is the intention of your Lordships but if others are tempted to try to extend the decision of the present exceptional case to commercial situations so as to introduce restitutionary rights beyond those presently recognised by the law of restitution, such a step will require very careful consideration before it is acceded to . . .

I would allow the appeal and dismiss the cross-appeal.

Lord Goff of Chieveley and **Lord Browne-Wilkinson** agreed with the speech of Lord Nicholls.

COMMENTARY

Once again, a number of points arise out of this case (see further E McKendrick, 'Breach of Contract, Restitution for Wrongs and Punishment' in A Burrows and E Peel (eds), *Commercial Remedies: Current Issues and Problems* (Oxford University Press, 2003), p. 95). The first relates to the choice of label. Lord Nicholls preferred 'account of profits' to the 'unhappy expression "restitutionary damages" '. The difficulty with the choice of label is that it has a very strong bias towards cases decided in equity and it does not seem apt to encompass the case in which the defendant makes his profit by saving expenditure which he otherwise would have incurred. It may therefore prove to be necessary to abandon the language of account of profits in favour of some more neutral term, such as restitutionary damages or gain-based damages.

Secondly, it is clear that the remedy is an exceptional one. The key paragraph in the speech of Lord Nicholls is the paragraph which begins 'The main argument against the availability of an account of profits' at p. 1112 above. The essence of the guidance given by Lord Nicholls in that paragraph can be summarized in three statements. First, the remedy of an account of profits will be available only where other contractual remedies are inadequate. Secondly, the claimant must generally have a 'legitimate interest' in preventing the defendant making or retaining his profit. Thirdly the court must have regard to 'all the circumstances of the case'.

Thirdly, the decision in *Blake* has been criticized on the ground that it will generate too much uncertainty in commercial transactions. Evidence of this uncertainty is provided by the following two contrasting decisions. The first is the decision of Morritt V-C in *Esso* v. *Niad*, unreported, Chancery Division, 22 November 2001. The defendant, Niad, sold petrol as a franchisee of the claimant, Esso. The parties had concluded an agreement whereby, as part of a national marketing campaign ('Pricewatch'), Niad undertook not to sell petrol above the maximum price recommended by Esso. In return, Esso paid Niad certain price support payments. In breach of this contract, Niad repeatedly sold petrol at prices above the instructed maxima. Esso brought a claim for compensatory damages but the difficulty with this claim lay in establishing the value of the sales lost as a result of the defendant's failure to charge at or below the recommended price. So it advanced an alternative claim. Relying upon the decision of the House of Lords in *Blake*, it sought an account of the profits earned by the defendant as a result of selling petrol at the inflated price. Morritt V-C held that Esso was in principle entitled to an account of profits. He relied upon four factors in reaching this conclusion, namely (i) compensatory damages was an inadequate remedy for Esso, (ii) the obligation to implement and maintain the recommended pump prices was fundamental to Pricewatch, (iii) complaint was made of the defendant on four occasions and the defendant gave the appearance of complying with Esso's complaint when notified of it, and (iv) Esso had a legitimate interest in preventing the defendant from profiting from its breach of obligation.

On the other side of the line is *AB Corporation* v. *CD Company (The 'Sine Nomine')*, [2002] 1 Lloyd's Rep 805, an arbitral award which, unusually, has been published in part in an English law report. The case concerned the wrongful withdrawal of a vessel from a charterparty by its owners ('the respondents'). The charterers sought to recover any profits made by the respondents from the alternative use made of the vessel and relied upon *Blake* to bolster their submission. The arbitrators rejected the claim for wrongful profits and did so in forthright language. They stated:

It is by no means uncommon for commercial contracts to be broken deliberately because a more profitable opportunity has arisen. Or the contract-breaker takes an over-generous view of his rights, knowing that the law may ultimately be against him. In such a case he may have little or nothing to lose by taking a chance; the downside at worst is that he will have to pay the costs of both sides. International commerce on a large scale is red in tooth and claw. We do not say that the Respondents' action was either deliberate or cynical wrongdoing in this case; they had a respectable argument on liability, although a commercial judge refused their application for leave to appeal.

Our solution to the present problem is that there should not be an award of wrongful profits where both parties are dealing with a marketable commodity—the services of a ship in this case—for which a substitute can be found in the market place. In the ordinary way the damages which the claimant suffers by having to buy in at the market price will be equal to the profit which the wrongdoer makes by having his goods or his ships' services to sell at a higher price. It is in the nature of things unlikely that the wrongdoer will make a greater profit than that. And if he does, it is an adventitious benefit which he can keep. The commercial law of this country should not make moral judgments, or seek to punish contract-breakers; we do not, for example, award triple damages, as in the USA.

The contrast between these two decisions is sharp. The arbitral award attempts, as far as possible, to confine the scope of *Blake*, whereas *Esso* v. *Niad* demonstrates that an account of profits may be recovered in the case of a breach of an ordinary commercial contract. Of the two decisions it is submitted that it is the decision in *Esso* v. *Niad* that is the troublesome one.

Most of the elements relied upon by Morritt V-C to support his finding that Esso was entitled to an account of profits are a source of some concern. The first concern relates to his finding that damages were inadequate. The reason given for the inadequacy was that it was 'almost impossible to attribute lost sales to a breach by one out of several hundred dealers who operated Pricewatch'. It is not obvious that problems of proof should lead to the conclusion that damages are not an adequate remedy. Secondly, Esso's loss could have been quantified by means other than lost sales, for example, damage to reputation or loss of goodwill. Placing a figure on such a loss would undoubtedly involve an element of arbitrariness, but no more so than when the courts award sums for loss of life or limb. It is hard to see why such an award would not have been adequate to compensate Esso. Thirdly, it appears that Morritt V-C confined his consideration to the adequacy of compensatory damages and did not consider the adequacy of the range of remedies, as stated by Lord Nicholls.

The fourth point relates to the measure of recovery. It is clear that, had Blake been subject to the jurisdiction of the court, he would have been accountable for the whole of his profit. In this respect *Blake* should be contrasted with *Wrotham Park Estate Co Ltd* v. *Parkside Homes Ltd* [1974] 1 WLR 798 (discussed at p. 1110 above) where the defendant was required to account for only 5% of its anticipated profits. The Court of Appeal in *Experience Hendrix LLC* v. *PPX Enterprises Inc* [2003] EWCA Civ 323; [2003] All ER (D) 328 (Mar) held that the *Wrotham Park* measure will have greater application than the *Blake* measure; in other words, a court is more likely to require defendants to account for a proportion of the profit made by the breach than it is to order the defendant to account for the whole of the profit so made. The Court of Appeal recognized that *Blake* was an exceptional case. As Mance LJ pointed out, *Blake* concerned matters of national security, the profits derived by Blake from the publishing contract were derived from his prior breaches of secrecy and Blake was in a position which was analogous to that of a fiduciary. These distinctive features of *Blake* suggest that it will be a rare case in which a defendant will be held accountable to a claimant for the entirety of the profit made from his breach of contract. These 'exceptional' factors were not present on the facts of *Wrotham Park* and consequently the latter decision is of much wider application.

The claimant in *Experience Hendrix* was successor in title to the estate of the rock musician Jimi Hendrix. A settlement agreement was concluded between the defendants and the estate of Hendrix in 1973. The agreement provided that the defendants were entitled to the masters of various recordings made by Hendrix (the 'Schedule A masters') provided that they paid royalties to the estate of Hendrix. In breach of the settlement agreement the defendants granted licences in respect of masters which were not listed in Schedule A to various parties. The claimant brought proceedings against the defendants in respect of their breaches of the settlement agreement. The trial judge granted the claimant an injunction to restrain future breaches of the settlement agreement but held that the claimant was only entitled to nominal damages in respect of past breaches. The claimant appealed to the Court of Appeal and the appeal was allowed.

Mance LJ stated that it would be both anomalous and unjust if the defendants could, by breaching the terms of the settlement agreement, avoid paying royalties or any sum when they would have had to pay royalties in respect of the use of Schedule A masters. The case was not so exceptional as to demand that the court should 'order a full account of all profits which have been or may be made by' the defendants as a result of their breaches. Mance LJ concluded that the defendants should pay to the claimants 'a reasonable sum' for their use of the material in breach of the settlement agreement. He stated that that sum could properly be described as 'such sum as might reasonably have been demanded' by Jimi Hendrix's estate 'as a quid pro quo for agreeing to permit the two licences into which PPX entered in breach of the settlement agreement.' He acknowledged that there was an element of artificiality in this process in that it requires the court to overlook the fact that the claimant might never have given permission for the licences. But he held that the approach nevertheless had 'the merit of directing the court's attention to the commercial value of the right infringed and of enabling it to assess the sum payable by reference to the fees that might in other contexts be demanded and paid between willing parties.' Thus on the facts of the case the court ordered that the defendants should pay over, by way of damages, a proportion of each of the advances received to date and (subject to deduction of such proportion) an appropriate royalty rate on retail selling prices. Further, the Court of Appeal held that the fact that the claimant had obtained an injunction in respect of future use of the recordings did not, of itself, act as a barrier to the recovery of a reasonable sum in respect of past breaches. Thus Mance LJ stated that:

Since *Blake* I see no reason why, if the beneficiary of a restrictive covenant is unaware of its infringement in time to obtain an injunction immediately, but is able to obtain an injunction for the future after the defendant by the infringement has obtained some benefit, the appellant should be precluded from obtaining an injunction and, if justice requires, a reasonable sum to compensate for the past infringement, even though he may not be able to show any financial loss to himself.

Are cases such as *Wrotham Park* and *Blake* governed by the same principle? Lord

Nicholls seemed to be of the view that they are (contrast in this respect the view of Lord Hobhouse who stated that *Wrotham Park Estates* was 'an example of compensatory damages'). Lord Nicholls cited *Wrotham Park Estates* as an example of a case in which damages were measured by reference to the 'benefit gained by the wrongdoer from the breach'. If they are governed by the same principle, how should courts decide whether the claimant is entitled to recover a percentage of the defendant's profit or all of it? One answer is to leave it to the discretion of the court. An alternative view is that there are two distinct principles at work here which ought to be disentangled. Dr Edelman argues that a distinction should be drawn between 'restitutionary damages' and 'disgorgement damages' (*Gain-Based Damages: Contract, Tort, Equity and Intellectual Property* (Hart, 2002), Chapter 3). 'Restitutionary damages' are defined (at p. 68) as 'damages which reverse wrongful transfers of wealth from a claimant by subtracting the objective benefit received by the defendant'. 'Disgorgement damages', by contrast, are measured not by reference to what has been transferred by the claimant but by 'the actual profit accruing to the defendant from the wrong' (see p. 72). In Dr Edelman's view *Wrotham Park Estates* is an example of the award of restitutionary damages, while *Blake* is an example of disgorgement damages. Further, he argues that the rationales which underpin the two measures of recovery are different. He argues (at p. 80) that restitutionary damages 'should in theory always be available for wrongs' and their rationale is to reverse a wrongful transfer of wealth. Disgorgement damages, on the other hand, aim to deter wrongdoing and so should only be available where compensatory damages are an inadequate deterrent (see pp. 83–85). Dr Edelman's thesis does appear to offer a better alternative to leaving the matter to the discretion of the court, although in favour of the latter approach it can be said that a discretionary approach, which has regard to the 'justice of the case' and to all the circumstances of the case, is more in keeping with the general tenor of Lord Nicholls' speech.

There is a further problem with the *Wrotham Park* line of cases and that it is that they are susceptible to analysis in terms of compensation for loss; that is to say, the courts are in fact compensating the claimant for the loss of his opportunity to sell his property (or other right) at a price of his own choosing. A case which seems to be based on this type of reasoning is *Lane* v. *O'Brien Homes* [2004] EWHC 303 (QB) where David Clarke J held that a vendor of land was entitled to recover a share of the potential profits made by the buyer of the land as a result of a breach by the buyer of a collateral contract not to build more than three new houses on the land acquired. It was held that the proper approach to apply was to consider the price which would have been offered by the buyer and accepted by the seller at the time when the release from the contractual prohibition was being sought. On the facts, David Clarke J, after stating that 'the assessment of this form of damages is not a precise mathematical process' upheld the award of damages of £150,000 to the vendor. It has been objected that this loss is a fiction in so far as it overlooks the fact that the claimant may not have wished to sell his property at any price. But the same fiction is present in *Experience Hendrix* where Mance LJ openly acknowledged the artificiality involved in valuing the right which the defendant had obtained. It would therefore seem that these cases can be explained on two different grounds. First, some of them may be cases in which damages were awarded in order to compensate the claimant for the loss of the opportunity to sell his property at a price of his own choosing. Secondly, they may be explained on the ground that the aim of the award is to strip the defendant of the gain which he has made and which can be attributed to his breach of contract.

The fifth point arising out of *Blake* is that the courts will have to develop rules in order to limit the liability of defendants in such cases. There are a number of issues here. What are the rules that will determine whether or not profit is attributable to the defendant's breach of contract? For example, is it open to a defendant to argue that the profit was attributable to his skill and enterprise and that there is no justification for awarding the profit, or a share of the profit, to the claimant on the sole ground that the defendant's breach provided the defendant with the opportunity of making the profit? When will the profit be too remote a consequence of the breach of contract? Can a defendant deduct from the profit which he must disgorge to the claimant the profit he would have made in an alternative business or occupation in which he would have become involved had he not been involved in his wrongful conduct? As yet, no clear answer can be given to these questions.

Finally, it is important to note the dissenting speech of Lord Hobhouse in *Blake*. His broader conception of loss, which has been noted in the context of analysing the decision of the House of Lords in *McAlpine* v. *Panatown* (p. 1048 above), enabled him to reach the conclusion that the Crown was entitled to recover compensatory damages for the loss that it had suffered and that there was therefore no need to create uncertainty in commercial transactions by recognizing that a court could order an account of profits in a breach of contract claim.

10. PUNITIVE DAMAGES

It was held by the House of Lords in 1909 that punitive damages cannot be recovered for a breach of contract (*Addis* v. *Gramophone Co Ltd* [1909] AC 488). This absolute ban on the recovery of punitive damages for breach of contract is likely to come under some pressure as a result of the decision of the House of Lords in *Kuddus* v. *Chief Constable of Leicestershire Constabulary* [2001] 2 WLR 1789 where it was held that, in order to recover punitive damages, it is no longer necessary for a claimant in a tort action to establish that exemplary damages had been awarded in respect of that particular cause of action prior to the decision of the House of Lords in *Rookes* v. *Barnard* [1964] AC 1129. Instead, the entitlement of a claimant to recover punitive damages in the future is likely to turn on whether or not they fall within the two categories of case recognized by Lord Devlin in *Rookes*, namely oppressive, arbitrary, or unconstitutional action by servants of the government and cases in which the defendant's conduct has been calculated by him to make a profit for himself which may well exceed the compensation payable to the claimant. The scope of these categories may change slightly over time but they are likely to form the foundation for the modern law.

There are two issues here for contract law. The first is whether or not the courts will take the step of recognizing that a breach of contract can, in principle, give rise to a claim for punitive damages. The second issue only arises if it is decided that the law should take the step of recognizing that punitive damages can be recovered in a breach of contract claim; this issue relates to the circumstances in which a claim for exemplary damages should be available.

As to the first question it can be argued that it is not at all obvious that the courts should take the step of recognizing that the courts can award punitive damages for a breach of contract. Breach of contract was never the subject of the arbitrary constraints imposed by *Rookes* because the source of the conclusion that punitive damages could not be recovered was not *Rookes* but the decision of the House of Lords back in *Addis*. It was the product of a considered decision, not the consequence of an arbitrary freezing of the law in 1964. On this basis contract can be distinguished from other wrongs. The pressure to recognize that a breach of contract can, in principle, give rise to a claim for punitive damages is building. The Supreme Court of Canada has now recognized that punitive damages may be awarded in respect of a breach of contract upon proof of an independent actionable wrong arising out of the same facts as the breach (see *Royal Bank of Canada* v. *W Got & Associates Electric Ltd* (2000) 178 DLR (4th) 385 and *Whiten* v. *Pilot Insurance Co* [2002] SCC 18 and, more generally, J Edelman, 'Exemplary Damages for Breach of Contract' (2001) 117 LQR 539). Will the English courts eventually reach this conclusion? It is suggested that in time they will. If torts and equitable wrongs can generate a claim for punitive damages, why should a breach of contract never give rise to such a claim? As Lord Nicholls stated in *A* v. *Bottrill* [2002] UKPC 44; [2003] 1 AC 449, paragraph [26], in recognizing that punitive damages can, in principle, be recovered in a case where the wrong committed by the defendant was neither intentional nor reckless, ' "Never say never" is a sound judicial admonition'. A refusal to recognize that a breach of contract can give rise to punitive damages will simply encourage claimants to characterize the breach as some other cause of action for the purpose of seeking punitive damages. This subterfuge will bring little credit to the law. The logic behind the abolition of the 'cause of action' test will eventually bring down the rule that a breach of contract can never give rise to a claim for punitive damages.

This leads us on to the second question. When will punitive damages be available in a breach of contract case? The answer, it is suggested, will be very rarely. There are essentially two reasons for this. The first is that, as both Lord Nicholls and Lord Scott pointed out in *Kuddus* (at paras [67] and [109] respectively), the effect of *Attorney-General* v. *Blake* may well be to undermine Lord Devlin's second category in *Rookes* on the basis that 'the profit made by a wrongdoer can be extracted from him without the need to rely on . . . exemplary damages' (para [109]). This being the case, punitive damages are only likely to be available where the breach of contract by the defendant is 'so outrageous, his disregard of the plaintiff's rights so contumelious, that something more is needed to show that the law will not tolerate such behaviour' (para [63]). Such cases are likely to be few and far between. In particular, the mere fact that the defendant has broken his contract with the claimant in order to pursue a more profitable relationship with another party will not suffice to entitle the claimant to punitive damages. Much more will be required before a finding is made that a defendant has behaved in an 'outrageous' fashion.

11. AGREED DAMAGES CLAUSES

It is open to contracting parties to make their own provision for the consequences of a breach of contract. Thus they can insert into the contract a clause which quantifies, or liquidates, the sum payable on the occurrence of a breach of contract. However, the courts have reserved to themselves the power to regulate these provisions. If the term in the contract making provision for the payment of damages is held to be a penalty clause, it will not be enforced and the innocent party will be confined to a claim for damages assessed on the basis of the principles applied by the courts in the earlier sections of this chapter (see, in particular, section 4). On the other hand, if the term is held to be a liquidated damages clause then the clause will be valid and it will fix the liability of the party in breach, in the sense that the sum stipulated in the clause will be the sum that must be paid, irrespective of the loss that is actually suffered on the facts of the case.

Dunlop Pneumatic Tyre Ltd v. New Garage and Motor Co Ltd

[1915] AC 79, House of Lords

The appellants agreed to supply the respondents with car tyres and inner tubes and that the respondents in turn would sell the goods on to their customers. The contract between the parties provided that the respondents would not sell the goods on for a price which was lower than the list price. Further clause 5 of the agreement provided:

> 'We [that is the respondents] agree to pay to the Dunlop Pneumatic Tyre Co Ltd, the sum of 5l. for each and every tyre, cover or tube sold or offered in breach of this agreement, as and by way of liquidated damages and not as a penalty, but without prejudice to any other rights or remedies you or the Dunlop Pneumatic Tyre Co Ltd, may have hereunder.'

The plaintiffs discovered that on 4 May 1911 the respondents committed a breach of the agreement by selling to the Motorists' Mutual Co-operative Society a tyre cover at a price less than the current list price. The appellants brought an action against the respondents in which they sought an injunction and damages. The respondents defended the claim for damages on the ground that clause 5 was a penalty clause. The trial judge held that the clause was a valid liquidated damages clause but the Court of Appeal held that it was a penalty clause and that the appellants were entitled to recover nominal damages only. The appellants appealed to the House of Lords where it was held that clause 5 was a liquidated damages clause and not a penalty clause with the result that the appellants were entitled to enforce the clause according to its terms.

Lord Dunedin

My Lords, we had the benefit of a full and satisfactory argument, and a citation of the very numerous cases which have been decided on this branch of the law. The matter has been handled, and at no distant date, in the Courts of highest resort. I particularly refer to the *Clydebank* Case [1905] AC 6 in your Lordships' House and the cases of *Public Works Commissioner* v. *Hills* [1906] AC 368 and *Webster* v. *Bosanquet* [1912] AC 394 in the Privy Council. In both of these cases many of the previous cases were considered. In view of that fact, and of the number of the authorities available, I do not think it advisable to attempt any detailed review of the various cases, but I shall content myself with stating succinctly the various propositions which I think are deducible from the decisions which rank as authoritative:—

1.   Though the parties to a contract who use the words 'penalty' or 'liquidated damages' may prima facie be supposed to mean what they say, yet the expression used is not conclusive. The Court must find out whether the payment stipulated is in truth a penalty or liquidated damages. This doctrine may be said to be found passim in nearly every case.

2.   The essence of a penalty is a payment of money stipulated as in terrorem of the offending party; the essence of liquidated damages is a genuine covenanted pre-estimate of damage (*Clydebank Engineering and Shipbuilding Co* v. *Don Jose Ramos Yzquierdo y Castaneda* [1905] AC 6).

3.   The question whether a sum stipulated is penalty or liquidated damages is a question of construction to be decided upon the terms and inherent circumstances of each particular contract, judged of as at the time of the making of the contract, not as at the time of the breach (*Public Works Commissioner* v. *Hills* [1906] AC 368 and *Webster* v. *Bosanquet* [1912] AC 394).

4.   To assist this task of construction various tests have been suggested, which if applicable to the case under consideration may prove helpful, or even conclusive. Such are:

(a) It will be held to be penalty if the sum stipulated for is extravagant and unconscionable in amount in comparison with the greatest loss that could conceivably be proved to have followed from the breach. (Illustration given by Lord Halsbury in the *Clydebank* Case [1905] AC 6.)

(b) It will be held to be a penalty if the breach consists only in not paying a sum of money, and the sum stipulated is a sum greater than the sum which ought to have been paid (*Kemble* v. *Farren* 6 Bing 141). This though one of the most ancient instances is truly a corollary to the last test. Whether it had its historical origin in the doctrine of the common law that when A. promised to pay B. a sum of money on a certain day and did not do so, B. could only recover the sum with, in certain cases, interest, but could never recover further damages for non-timeous payment, or whether it was a survival of the time when equity reformed unconscionable bargains merely because they were unconscionable,—a subject which much exercised Jessel MR in *Wallis* v. *Smith* 21 Ch D 243—is probably more interesting than material.

(c) There is a presumption (but no more) that it is penalty when 'a single lump sum is made payable by way of compensation, on the occurrence of one or more or all of several events, some of which may occasion serious and others but trifling damage' (Lord Watson in *Lord Elphinstone* v. *Monkland Iron and Coal Co* 11 App Cas 332).

On the other hand:

(d) It is no obstacle to the sum stipulated being a genuine pre-estimate of damage, that the consequences of the breach are such as to make precise pre-estimation almost an impossibility. On the contrary, that is just the situation when it is probable that pre-estimated damage was the true bargain between the parties (*Clydebank* Case [1905] AC 6, 11, Lord Halsbury; *Webster* v. *Bosanquet* [1912] AC 394, 398, Lord Mersey).

Turning now to the facts of the case, it is evident that the damage apprehended by the appellants owing to the breaking of the agreement was an indirect and not a direct damage. So long as they got their price from the respondents for each article sold, it could not matter to them directly what the respondents did with it. Indirectly it did. Accordingly, the agreement is headed 'Price Maintenance Agreement', and the way in which the appellants would be damaged if prices were cut is clearly explained in evidence by Mr Baisley [the appellants' manager], and no successful attempt is made to controvert that evidence. But though damage as a whole from such a practice would be certain, yet damage from any one sale would be impossible to forecast. It is just, therefore, one of those cases where it seems quite reasonable for parties to contract that they should estimate that damage at a certain figure, and provided that figure is not extravagant there would seem no reason to suspect that it is not truly a bargain to assess damages, but rather a penalty to be held in terrorem.

The argument of the respondents was really based on two heads. They overpressed, in my judgment, the dictum of Lord Watson in *Lord Elphinstone's* Case 11 App Cas 332, 342, reading it as if he had said that the matter was conclusive, instead of saying, as he did, that it raised a presumption, and they relied strongly on the case of *Willson* v. *Love* [1896] 1 QB 626.

Now, in the first place, I have considerable doubt whether the stipulated payment here can fairly be said to deal with breaches, 'some of which'—I am quoting Lord Watson's words—'may occasion serious and others but trifling damage'. As a mere matter of construction, I doubt whether clause 5 applies to anything but sales below price. But I will assume that it does. None the less the mischief, as I have already pointed out, is an indirect mischief, and I see no data on which, as a matter of construction, I could settle in my own mind that the indirect damage from selling a cover would differ in magnitude from the indirect damage from selling a tube; or that the indirect damage from a cutting-price sale would differ from the indirect damage from supply at a full price to a hostile, because prohibited, agent. You cannot weigh such things in a chemical balance. The character of the agricultural land which was ruined by slag heaps in *Elphinstone's* Case 11 App Cas 332 was not all the same, but no objection was raised by Lord Watson to applying an overhead rate per acre, the sum not being in itself unconscionable.

I think *Elphinstone's* Case, or rather the dicta in it, do go this length, that if there are various breaches to which one indiscriminate sum to be paid in breach is applied, then the strength of the chain must be taken at its weakest link. If you can clearly see that the loss on one particular breach could never amount to the stipulated sum, then you may come to the conclusion that the sum is penalty. But further than this it does not go; so, for the reasons already stated, I do not think the present case forms an instance of what I have just expressed.

As regards *Willson's* Case [1896] 1 QB 626, I do not think it material to consider whether it was well decided on the facts. For it was decided on the view of the facts that the manurial value of straw and of hay were known ascertainable quantities as at the time of the bargain, and radically different, so that the damage resulting from the want of one could never be the same as the damage resulting from the want of the other.

Added to that, the parties there had said 'penalty', and the effort was to make out that that really meant liquidated damages; and lastly, if my view of the facts in the present case is correct, then Rigby LJ would have agreed with me, for the last words of his judgment are as follows: 'On the other hand it is stated that, when the damages caused by a breach of contract are incapable of being ascertained, the sum made by the contract payable on such a breach is to be regarded as liquidated damages. The question arises, What is meant in this statement by the expression "incapable of being ascertained"? In their proper sense the words appear to refer to a case where no rule or measure of damages is available for the guidance of a jury as to the amount of the damages, and a judge would have to tell them they must fix the amount as best they can'. To arrive at the indirect damage in this case, supposing no sum had been stipulated, that is just what a judge would, in my opinion, have had to do.

On the whole matter, therefore, I go with the opinion of Kennedy LJ, and I move your Lordships that the appeal be allowed, and judgment given for the sum as brought out by the Master, the appellants to have their costs in this House and in the Courts below.

Lord Atkinson, Lord Parker of Waddington, and **Lord Parmoor** delivered concurring judgments.

COMMENTARY

Lord Dunedin's judgment is important because it attempts to rationalize the case-law up to that point in time. Prior to *Dunlop* the cases were in some disarray. This judgment succeeded in consolidating that case-law and in providing the foundation for the modern law. Each of Lord Dunedin's four propositions requires further comment.

The first proposition is that the label used by the parties is not conclusive. Thus the courts can override the label used by the parties if satisfied that it does not reflect the 'true' nature of the transaction that has been concluded by the parties. It was not always so. In the nineteenth century, the courts viewed their task as being to give effect to the agreement of the parties and they would give effect to the label chosen by the parties. The turning point was the case of *Kemble* v. *Farren* (1829) 6 Bing 141 where a contractual term expressed to be a 'liquidated and ascertained damages' clause and not a penalty was nevertheless held to be a penalty clause. The question whether a clause is penal or not is a question of substance, not form. The courts will not be dictated to by a clause which states that it is 'liquidated damages and not a penalty'. It does not, however, follow from this that the parties' choice of label is irrelevant. It is relevant but it is not conclusive.

The second proposition defines the essence of a liquidated damages clause and a penalty clause. However the 'dichotomy between a genuine pre-estimate of damages and a penalty does not necessarily cover all the possibilities' (*Cine Bes Filmcilik ve Yapimcilik* v. *United International Pictures* [2003] EWCA Civ 1669; [2004] 1 CLC 401). There may be clauses which operate on breach, 'but which fall into neither category, and they may be commercially perfectly justifiable' (see *Lordsvale Finance Ltd* v. *Bank of Zambia* [1996] QB 752, 763–764). That is to say, there may be exceptional cases in which the clause is not a 'genuine' pre-estimate of the loss, in the sense that both parties to the contract realize that the sum stipulated is likely to be in excess of the loss which will be occasioned by the breach, but the courts will nevertheless not classify the term as a penalty clause because it has been accepted by the parties and is, in the opinion of the court, commercially justifiable.

The essence of a liquidated damages clause is that it must be a 'genuine' or a 'bona fide' pre-estimate of the loss. The test is not whether it is a 'reasonable' pre-estimate of the loss. This is not to say that the reasonableness of the clause is irrelevant. It is relevant in the sense that the more unreasonable the clause, the less likely it is that the pre-estimate is 'genuine'. The parties have greater latitude in the case where the obligation of the party in breach is to perform a service given that, in the latter case, it can be difficult to assess the damages payable (see *Philips Hong Kong Ltd* v. *Attorney General of Hong Kong* (1993) 61 BLR 41, p. 1129 below).

But the latitude given to the parties has its limits. Thus a clause which is drafted from the perspective of one party only, and which fails to give any consideration to the position of the breaching party, may fall foul of the penalty clause rule (see, for example, *Cine Bes Filmcilik ve Yapimcilik* v. *United International Pictures* (above) where it was held that the clause was arguably penal on the ground that it failed to give the breaching party any credit for the benefits which were restored to the innocent party on the termination of the contract). The drafting of a clause making provision for the financial consequences of a breach of contract 'requires care' and ought to involve a balancing of the benefits lost and received as a result of the breach.

The third proposition is that the court must focus attention on the time of entry into the contract and not the time of breach, nor the date of the hearing. This enables the parties to know where they stand in the sense that the validity of the clause does not hinge upon future, unknown events. Thus the fact that, with the benefit of hindsight, we can see that the figure chosen by the parties was incorrect does not lead to the conclusion that the clause must be penal. It is the intention of the parties at the moment of entry into the contract that is decisive. Nevertheless, there may be cases in which the courts will have regard to events subsequent to the making of the contract for the purpose of ascertaining the intended scope of the clause. In *Philips Hong Kong Ltd* v. *Attorney General of Hong Kong* (1993) 61 BLR 41 Lord Woolf stated (at p. 59) that what actually happened can 'provide valuable evidence as to what could reasonably be expected to be the loss at the time the contract was made'.

The fourth proposition consists of a number of 'presumptions'. The weight of these presumptions is variable: some are 'helpful', while others are 'conclusive'. The first presumption deals with a clause that requires the payment of a sum of money which is 'extravagant and unconscionable in amount in comparison with the greatest loss that could conceivably be proved to have followed from the breach'. This is no easy requirement to satisfy. In *Clydebank Engineering and Shipbuilding Co* v. *Don Jose Ramos Yzquierdo y Castaneda* [1905] AC 6, the defendants agreed to supply the plaintiffs with four torpedo boats. The defendants were late in delivering the vessels. The contract provided that a 'penalty' of £500 per week was payable for each week of delay. The plaintiffs sued to enforce the clause and their claim succeeded. It is clear from the speeches of their Lordships that a finding of 'unconscionability' will only be made in the clearest of cases. Lord Dunedin in *Dunlop* refers to Lord Halsbury's illustration in *Clydebank* where he gave the example of a contract to build a house for £50 which contained a clause to the effect that, if the builder failed to complete the work, he would pay one million pounds as a penalty. The difficulty with this illustration is that it is too extreme. But it does give an indication of the extent of the courts' reluctance to intervene.

The second presumption deals with a failure to pay money and it is linked to the common law rule that interest was not recoverable upon a failure to pay a debt on time (but see now the Late Payment of Commercial Debts (Interest) Act 1998). A party who seeks to recover a sum of money in excess of the sum that is actually owed to him runs the risk of the clause being held to be penal.

The third presumption is a tricky one and it has caused a number of difficulties in practice. It was the presumption invoked by the respondents in *Dunlop*, albeit without success. An example of the successful invocation of the presumption is provided by *Lombard North Central plc* v. *Butterworth* [1987] QB 527 (p. 951 above) where clause 6 of the contract of hire was held to be penal because it failed to distinguish between serious and trifling breaches by the hirer.

The final presumption was also in issue in *Dunlop* in that it was extremely difficult, if not impossible, to pre-estimate the loss likely to be caused to the appellants by a breach of clause 5. In these circumstances the courts tend to be slow to second-guess the parties. A further example of the reluctance of the courts to engage in such second-guessing is provided by the decision of the Privy Council in *Philips Hong Kong Ltd* v. *Attorney General of Hong Kong* (1993) 61 BLR 41 where Lord Woolf stated (at pp. 55 and 61):

> Although there is a good deal of disagreement as to how the penalty jurisdiction grew up . . . it is recorded in the judgment of Kay LJ in *Law* v. *Local Board of Redditch* [1892] 1 QB 127 at page 133 that originally it was by the Courts of Equity that relief was granted. They did so where a sum of money was agreed to be paid as a penalty for non-performance of a collateral contract where the actual damage which would be sustained could be estimated. In such circumstances the Courts would limit the sum recoverable to the actual loss suffered. The principle would be applied in particular where the penalty was agreed to be paid for the non-payment of a sum of money under a bond. This limited application of the principle was subsequently extended to other situations by the courts of common law, but the principle was always recognised as being subject to fairly narrow constraints and the courts have always avoided claiming that they have any general jurisdiction to rewrite the contracts that the parties have made . . .
>
> Except possibly in the case of situations where one of the parties to the contract is able to dominate the other as to the choice of the terms of a contract, it will normally be insufficient to establish that a provision is objectionably penal to identify situations where the application of the provision could result in a larger sum being recovered by the injured party than his actual loss. Even in such situations so long as the sum payable in the event of non-compliance with the contract is not extravagant, having regard to the range of losses that it could reasonably be anticipated it would have to cover at the time the contract was made, it can still be a genuine pre-estimate of the loss that would be suffered and so a perfectly valid liquidated damage provision.

The use in argument of unlikely illustrations should therefore not assist a party to defeat a provision as to liquidated damages. As the Law Commission stated in Working Paper No 61 (page 30):—

> 'The fact that in certain circumstances a party to a contract might derive a benefit in excess of his loss does not . . . outweigh the very definite practical advantages of the present rule upholding a genuine estimate, formed at the time the contract was made of the probable loss.'

A difficulty can arise where the range of possible loss is broad. Where it should be obvious that, in relation to part of the range, the liquidated damages are totally out of proportion to certain of the losses which may be incurred, the failure to make special provision for those losses may result in the 'liquidated damages' not being recoverable. . . . However the court has to be careful not to set too stringent a standard and bear in mind that what the parties have agreed should normally be upheld. Any other approach will lead to undesirable uncertainty especially in commercial contracts.

This case helps us to get our perspective right. Freedom of contract is the norm and the penalty clause jurisdiction is the exception. This being the case, the onus is upon the party seeking to set aside the clause to show that it is a penalty and *Philips Hong Kong* suggests that that burden will not easily be discharged, at least in the case where both parties are of roughly equal bargaining power and the loss likely to follow from the breach of contract cannot easily be ascertained.

It is, however, possible to evade the penalty clause rule completely. Firstly, it does not apply to an acceleration clause of the type that we saw at work in *White & Carter (Councils) Ltd* v. *McGregor* [1962] AC 413 (p. 995 above). An acceleration clause does not impose a new liability on the debtor. Acceleration clauses are classically found in contracts of hire or in finance leases. The clause provides that in the event of a failure to pay a single instalment on the due date the sum which was always owed becomes immediately payable. In this way the existing liability to pay is accelerated and, in law, this acceleration does not constitute a penalty, albeit that, from the perspective of the debtor, the acceleration of the liability to pay can constitute a very real hardship.

Secondly, the penalty clause rule only applies to sums that are payable on a breach of contract. Thus it is possible to evade the application of the rule by making the sum payable on an event which is not a breach of contract (see *Alder* v. *Moore* [1961] 2 QB 57, *Export Credit Guarantee Department* v. *Universe Oil Products Ltd* [1983] 1 WLR 399). In some cases it can be difficult to ascertain whether the sum is payable on a breach of contract or not. An example is provided by *Interfoto Picture Library Ltd* v. *Stiletto Visual Programmes Ltd* [1989] QB 433 (p. 352 above) where condition 2 of the plaintiffs' terms and conditions provided:

All transparencies must be returned to us within 14 days from the date of posting/delivery/collection. A holding fee of £5 plus VAT per day will be charged for each transparency which is retained by you longer than the said period of 14 days save where a copyright licence is granted or we agree a longer period in writing with you.

Bingham LJ suggested that condition 2 might have been susceptible to challenge on the ground that it was a 'disguised penalty clause'. The application of the penalty clause rule to condition 2 would turn on whether or not the hirer was in breach of

contract in retaining the transparencies beyond fourteen days. If condition 2 conferred upon the hirer an option to retain the transparencies beyond fourteen days on
payment of a greater sum the penalty clause rule would not be in play because of the
absence of a breach of contract by the hirer. If, however, the hirer was in breach of
contract in retaining the transparencies beyond the initial fourteen-day period then
the penalty clause would be in play. Thus the applicability of the penalty clause rule to
condition 2 would depend upon the meaning of the words 'all transparencies must be
returned to us within 14 days'. Do these words mean that the hirer is in breach of
contract if he fails to return the transparencies within fourteen days? Paradoxically, it
is the hirer who would have an interest in arguing that he was in breach of contract so
that he could claim the protection of the penalty clause rule, whereas the plaintiff
owners might wish to argue that there was no breach so that the clause was not open
to challenge on the ground that it was penal. As Lord Denning noted in *Campbell
Discount Ltd* v. *Bridge* [1962] AC 600, equity commits itself to the paradox that it will
protect the party who breaks his contract but not the party who honestly admits his
inability to perform his obligations under the contract and exercises his contractual
right to bring the contract to an end.

In many ways cases such as *Interfoto* and *Campbell Discount* demonstrate the
unsatisfactory state of the present law in that it can be evaded by careful draftsman-
ship. The problem is that the law has chosen to regulate the particular term rather
than the contract as a whole and, this being the case, jurisdictional questions can arise
as to whether or not the particular term falls within the scope of the rule or not. It is
not surprising that the penalty clause rule has been attacked on the ground that it is
haphazard in terms of its application. But, if we accept this criticism, the question
which then arises is which direction the law should take. Should it follow the path of
freedom of contract and leave the parties free to decide for themselves the remedial
consequences of a breach of contract, without fear of judicial intervention, or should
we broaden the scope of the jurisdiction so as to reduce the possibility for evasion
through devices such as making the sum payable on an event which is not a breach of
contract? This is a difficult policy question and its resolution depends upon the
balance to be struck between freedom of contract, on the one hand, and a concern for
fairness (both in procedural and substantive terms) on the other. In this respect it will
be important to observe the fate of the Consultation Paper produced by the Law
Commission and the Scottish Law Commission on unfair terms in contracts (Law
Commission Consultation Paper No 166 and Scottish Law Commission Discussion
Paper No 119, pp. 535–540 above). Their provisional proposal to extend the range of
controls over business-to-business contracts where the term in question 'has not been
individually negotiated' or is 'standard' may provide the opportunity to put the law
on a more coherent basis through the creation of a more general power of review
which is not so dependent upon the identification of particular clauses that are
susceptible to regulation in this way. On the other hand, it may be that the Law
Commission's provisional proposal will not find acceptance because it will create too
much uncertainty.

12. DEPOSITS AND PART PAYMENTS

Rather than include in the contract a provision to the effect that a particular sum is payable on a breach of contract, the contract may provide that a sum of money is to be paid up front and that it will not be returned in the event of a failure by the party making the payment to perform his contractual obligations. One obvious advantage of this type of clause is that it is not necessary to initiate legal proceedings in order to recover the agreed sum because it is paid in advance. The onus is put on the party who has paid the money to take steps to recover the prepayment. The entitlement of the party in breach to recover his prepayment will depend upon the nature of the prepayment that has been made. Where the money has been paid by way of a deposit, it is less likely to be recoverable than in the case where it is a part payment of the contract price.

A deposit is a security and is generally irrecoverable, whereas a part payment is simply a part payment of the price and is recoverable by the party in breach in the event of termination of the contract. Whether a payment is made by way of deposit or part payment of the price is a question of construction and, in cases of doubt, it will generally be regarded as a part payment (*Dies* v. *British and International Mining and Finance Co* [1939] 1 KB 715).

The general rule is that a part payment is recoverable by the party in breach subject to his liability in damages for the loss caused to the innocent party by his breach of contract (see *Dies*, above). However, the right of the party in breach to recover his prepayment is not unqualified. In a case where it is clear from the contract that the payee will have to incur reliance expenditure before completing his performance of the contract, then, in the absence of a stipulation in the contract to the contrary, the part payment will generally be irrecoverable (*Hyundai Shipbuilding and Heavy Industries Ltd* v. *Papadopoulos* [1980] 1 WLR 1129). Indeed, it may be the case that a prepayment is only recoverable where the payor can demonstrate that it has been paid for a consideration that has totally failed.

The general rule in relation to deposits is that they are not recoverable by the party in breach. The function of a deposit is to serve as a security against a breach of contract and so, were it to be recoverable upon a breach, it would defeat its function as a security. The right of the recipient to retain the deposit is not, however, unqualified. The right of a payee to retain a deposit was qualified by the Privy Council in the following case:

Workers Trust and Merchant Bank Ltd v. Dojap Investments Ltd

[1993] AC 573, Privy Council

The facts are set out in the judgment of Lord Browne-Wilkinson.

Lord Browne-Wilkinson

On 5 October 1989 Workers Trust & Merchant Bank Ltd ('the bank') as second mortgagee sold certain premises at auction to Dojap Investments Ltd ('the purchaser') at a price of

Jamaican $11,500,000. Clause 4 of the contract provided for the payment of a deposit of 25 per cent. of the contract price and a deposit of $2,875,000 was duly paid by the purchaser to the bank's solicitors. The contract provided that the remainder of the purchase money should be paid within 14 days of the date of the auction whereupon the bank was to execute a transfer of the property to the purchaser and lodge such transfer for registration. Clause 15 of the contract provided that time should be of the essence of all time limits contained in the contract. Clause 13 of the contract provided:

'If the purchaser shall fail to observe or comply with any of the foregoing stipulation on his part his deposit shall be forfeited to the vendor who shall be at liberty (without tendering any transfer) to resell the property either by public auction or private contract at such time and in such manner and subject to such conditions as the vendor may think fit and any deficiency in price which may result on and all charges costs and expenses attending a resale or attempted resale, together or rendered useless by such default, shall be made good and paid by the defaulting purchaser at the present sale and be recoverable from him by the vendor as liquidated damages. Any increase of price on a resale shall belong to the vendor.'

On the date fixed for completion (19 October 1989) the purchaser's attorney, Mr Clough, sent to the bank a letter of undertaking from the Jamaica Citizens Bank Ltd to pay the balance of the purchase price, subject to certain conditions. The bank's attorney, Miss Eaton, rejected this and gave the purchaser 24 hours to provide a satisfactory undertaking. The purchaser attempted to do so on 20 October 1989, but the bank again rejected it. On 23 October, the bank wrote to the purchaser rescinding the contract and purporting to forfeit the deposit. The purchaser refused to accept this, and on 26 October 1989 tendered to the bank the balance of the purchase price with interest. The bank returned the cheque the next day.

On 24 November 1989 the purchaser started proceedings claiming specific performance or alternatively relief from forfeiture of the deposit. The case was heard by Zacca CJ before whom a number of different issues arose for decision on the claim for specific performance. These are no longer in issue before the Board. The judge gave judgment on 25 June 1990, rejecting the purchaser's claim for specific performance and its claim for return of the deposit.

On 12 November 1990 the purchaser arranged to purchase the same piece of land from the first mortgagee, Jamaica Citizens Bank Ltd, as a result of which the claim to specific performance of the contract of the bank became largely academic. The purchaser appealed to the Court of Appeal but did not pursue its claim for specific performance. On the purchaser's alternative claim for relief from forfeiture and the return of the deposit, the Court of Appeal (Rowe P, Forte and Downer JJA) held that the purchaser was entitled to relief from forfeiture to the extent that the deposit exceeded 10 per cent. of the price but did not award any interest on that sum. The bank appeals to the Board against the decision of the Court of Appeal to give such relief against forfeiture. The purchaser cross-appeals claiming that it should have been awarded relief against forfeiture as to the whole of the 25 per cent. deposit and should also have been awarded interest.

In general, a contractual provision which requires one party in the event of his breach of the contract to pay or forfeit a sum of money to the other party is unlawful as being a penalty, unless such provision can be justified as being a payment of liquidated damages being a genuine pre-estimate of the loss which the innocent party will incur by reason of the breach. One exception to this general rule is the provision for the payment of a deposit by the purchaser on a contract for the sale of land. Ancient law has established that the forfeiture of such a deposit (customarily 10 per cent. of the contract price) does not fall within the general rule and can be validly forfeited even though the amount of the deposit bears no reference to the anticipated loss to the vendor flowing from the breach of contract.

This exception is anomalous and at least one textbook writer has been surprised that the courts of equity ever countenanced it: see Farrand, Contract and Conveyance, 4th ed. (1983), p. 204. The special treatment afforded to such a deposit derives from the ancient custom of providing an earnest for the performance of a contract in the form of giving either some physical token of earnest (such as a ring) or earnest money. The history of the law of deposits can be traced to the Roman law of arra, and possibly further back still: see Howe v. Smith (1884) 27 Ch D 89, 101–102, per Fry LJ. Ever since the decision in Howe v. Smith, the nature of such a deposit has been settled in English law. Even in the absence of express contractual provision, it is an earnest for the performance of the contract: in the event of completion of the contract the deposit is applicable towards payment of the purchase price; in the event of the purchaser's failure to complete in accordance with the terms of the contract, the deposit is forfeit, equity having no power to relieve against such forfeiture.

However, the special treatment afforded to deposits is plainly capable of being abused if the parties to a contract, by attaching the label 'deposit' to any penalty, could escape the general rule which renders penalties unenforceable. There are two authorities which indicate that this cannot be done. In Stockloser v. Johnson [1954] 1 QB 476, Denning LJ in considering the power of the court to relieve against forfeiture said, obiter, at p. 491:

'Again, suppose that a vendor of property, in lieu of the usual 10 per cent. deposit, stipulates for an initial payment of 50 per cent. of the price as a deposit and part payment; and later, when the purchaser fails to complete, the vendor resells the property at a profit and in addition claims to forfeit the 50 per cent. deposit. Surely the court will relieve against the forfeiture. The vendor cannot forestall this equity by describing an extravagant sum as a deposit, any more than he can recover a penalty by calling it liquidated damages.'

In Linggi Plantations Ltd v. Jagatheesan [1972] 1 MLJ 89 Lord Hailsham of St Marylebone LC delivered the judgment of the Board which upheld the claim to forfeit a normal 10 per cent. deposit even though the vendor had in fact suffered no loss. He referred on a number of occasions to a requirement that the amount of a deposit should be 'reasonable' and said, at p. 94:

'It is also no doubt possible that in a particular contract the parties may use language normally appropriate to deposits properly so-called even to forfeiture which turn out on investigation to be purely colourable and that in such a case the real nature of the transaction might turn out to be the imposition of a penalty, by purporting to render forfeit something which is in truth part payment. This no doubt explains why in some cases the irrecoverable nature of a deposit is qualified by the insertion of the adjective "reasonable" before the noun. But the truth is that a reasonable deposit has always been regarded as a guarantee of performance as well as a payment on account, and its forfeiture has never been regarded as a penalty in English law or common English usage.'

In the view of their Lordships these passages accurately reflect the law. It is not possible for the parties to attach the incidents of a deposit to the payment of a sum of money unless such sum is reasonable as earnest money. The question therefore is whether or not the deposit of 25 per cent. in this case was reasonable as being in line with the traditional concept of earnest money or was in truth a penalty intended to act in terrorem.

Zacca CJ tested the question of 'reasonableness' by reference to the evidence before him that it was of common occurrence for banks in Jamaica selling property at auction to demand deposits of between 15 per cent. and 50 per cent. He held that, since this was a common practice, it was reasonable. Like the Court of Appeal, their Lordships are unable to accept this reasoning. In order to be reasonable a true deposit must be objectively operating as 'earnest money' and not as a penalty. To allow the test of reasonableness to depend upon the practice of one class of vendor, which exercises considerable financial muscle, would be to allow them to evade the law against penalties by adopting practices of their own.

However although their Lordships are satisfied that the practice of a limited class of vendors cannot determine the reasonableness of a deposit, it is more difficult to define what the test should be. Since a true deposit may take effect as a penalty, albeit one permitted by law, it is hard to draw a line between a reasonable, permissible amount of penalty and an unreasonable, impermissible penalty. In their Lordships' view the correct approach is to start from the position that, without logic but by long continued usage both in the United Kingdom and formerly in Jamaica, the customary deposit has been 10 per cent. A vendor who seeks to obtain a larger amount by way of forfeitable deposit must show special circumstances which justify such a deposit.

[he considered the evidence advanced to support the validity of a deposit of 25% and concluded]

Their Lordships agree with the Court of Appeal that this evidence falls far short of showing that it was reasonable to stipulate for a forfeitable deposit of 25 per cent. of the purchase price or indeed any deposit in excess of 10 per cent . . .

The question therefore arises whether the court has jurisdiction to relieve against the express provision of the contract that the deposit of 25 per cent. was to be forfeited. Although there is no doubt that the court will not order the payment of a sum contracted for (but not yet paid) if satisfied that such sum is in reality a penalty, it was submitted that the court could not order, by way of relief, the repayment of sums already paid to the defendant in accordance with the terms of the contract which, on breach, the contract provided should be forfeit. The basis of this submission was the view expressed in a considered obiter dictum of Romer LJ in *Stockloser v. Johnson* [1954] 1 QB 476.

In that case there was a contract for the sale of quarry machinery to the plaintiff, the purchase price to be paid by instalments. The contract provided that in the event of a default in payment of the instalments, the vendor could retake the machinery and all instalments of the price previously paid should be forfeit. Pursuant to the contract, the plaintiff took possession and used the machinery but defaulted in payment of an instalment. The defendant forfeited the instalments already paid. In the action, the plaintiff sought to recover the instalments, alleging that their forfeiture was a penalty. The Court of Appeal unanimously held that the forfeiture did not constitute a penalty on the facts of that case but went on to express conflicting views, obiter, as to whether, if the forfeiture had been a penalty, the court had jurisdiction to order repayment. Somervell LJ and

Denning LJ expressed the view that there was such jurisdiction. Romer LJ held that there was no general right in equity to mend the parties' bargain and that, even where there was jurisdiction to relieve from forfeiture, that could only be exercised by allowing a late completion to a party who was in default in performance but willing and able to carry out the terms of the contract belatedly.

Their Lordships do not find it necessary to decide which of those two views is correct in a case where a party is seeking relief from forfeiture for breach of contract to pay a price by instalments, the party in default having been let into possession in the mean-time. This is not such a case. In the view of their Lordships, since the 25 per cent. deposit was not a true deposit by way of earnest, the provision for its forfeiture was a plain penalty. There is clear authority that in a case of a sum paid by one party to another under the contract as security for the performance of that contract, a provision for its forfeiture in the event of non-performance is a penalty from which the court will give relief by ordering repayment of the sum so paid, less any damage actually proved to have been suffered as a result of non-completion: *Commissioner of Public Works* v. *Hills* [1906] AC 368. Accordingly, there is jurisdiction in the court to order repayment of the 25 per cent. deposit.

The Court of Appeal took a middle course by ordering the repayment of 15 per cent. out of the 25 per cent. deposit, leaving the bank with its normal 10 per cent. deposit which it was entitled to forfeit. Their Lordships are unable to agree that this is the correct order. The bank has contracted for a deposit consisting of one globular sum, being 25 per cent. of the purchase price. If a deposit of 25 per cent. constitutes an unreasonable sum and is not therefore a true deposit, it must be repaid as a whole. The bank has never stipulated for a reasonable deposit of 10 per cent.: therefore it has no right to such a limited payment. If it cannot establish that the whole sum was truly a deposit, it has not contracted for a true deposit at all.

COMMENTARY

Three points should be noted about this decision. First, it may begin the process of bringing the law relating to deposits closer to the law relating to liquidated damages clauses. The rules are not yet identical. It cannot be said that a 'reasonable' deposit must be a 'genuine pre-estimate of the loss' but it would appear that a genuine pre-estimate of the loss will be a reasonable deposit. The reason it cannot be said that a deposit must be a genuine pre-estimate of the loss is that, in the case of contracts for the sale of land, a 10 per cent deposit is reasonable even in the case where it is not a genuine pre-estimate of the loss. The second point relates to the role of market practice in determining whether a deposit is reasonable. In the case of the sale of land, market practice is a substantial factor in support of the conclusion that a 10 per cent deposit is reasonable but market practice is not determinative (as can be seen from the reluctance of the Privy Council to concede that 25 per cent was a reasonable deposit because there was some evidence of a practice of taking such a deposit). Thirdly, the case underlines the danger of asking for too big a deposit. The court will not re-write the terms of the deposit. Instead it will strike down an unreasonable deposit and relegate the claimant to a claim for damages. This being the case, it is better to err on the side of caution. One view is to say that a party should not ask for more than a genuine pre-estimate of his loss because, if he does so, he runs the risk that the deposit will be unreasonable. If this is the case, the law relating to liquidated damages clauses and deposits may be closer in substance than we are often led to believe.

13. FURTHER READING

BRIDGE, M, 'Mitigation of Damages in Contract and the Meaning of Avoidable Loss' (1989) 105 *LQR* 398.

BURROWS, A, 'Limitations on Compensation' in Burrows, A and Peel, E (eds), *Commercial Remedies: Current Issues and Problems* (Oxford University Press, 2003), p. 27.

CARTWRIGHT, J, 'Remoteness of Damage in Contract and Tort: A Reconsideration' [1996] *CLJ* 488.

COOTE, B, 'Contract Damages, *Ruxley* and the Performance Interest' [1997] *CLJ* 537.

FAUST, F, '*Hadley* v. *Baxendale*: An Understandable Miscarriage of Justice' (1994) 15 *Journal of Legal History* 41.

FRIEDMANN, D, 'The Performance Interest in Contract Damages' (1995) 111 *LQR* 628.

FULLER, L and PERDUE, W, 'The Reliance Interest in Contract Damages' (1936) 46 *Yale LJ* 52 and (1937) 46 *Yale LJ* 373.

GOETZ, GE and SCOTT, RE, 'Liquidated Damages, Penalties and the Just Compensation Principle' (1977) 77 *Columbia Law Review* 554.

KRAMER, A, 'An Agreement-Centred Approach to Remoteness and Contract Damages' in Cohen, N and McKendrick, E (eds), *Comparative Remedies for Breach of Contract* (Hart, 2004), p. 249.

McKENDRICK, E, 'Breach of Contract and the Meaning of Loss' [1999] *Current Legal Problems* 53.

—— 'Breach of Contract, Restitution for Wrongs and Punishment' in Burrows, A and Peel, E (eds), *Commercial Remedies: Current Issues and Problems* (Oxford University Press, 2003), 95.

—— 'The Common Law at Work: The Saga of Panatown Ltd v Alfred McAlpine Construction Ltd' (2003) 3 *Oxford University Commonwealth Law Journal* 145.

—— and GRAHAM, M, 'The Sky's the Limit: Contractual Damages for Non-Pecuniary Loss' [2002] *LMCLQ* 161.

—— and WORTHINGTON, K 'Damages for Non-Pecuniary Loss' in Cohen, N and McKendrick, E (eds), *Comparative Remedies for Breach of Contract* (Hart, 2004), p. 274.

26

SPECIFIC PERFORMANCE

1. CENTRAL ISSUES

1. Specific performance is a remedy which orders the defendant to perform his obligations under the contract. It is an equitable remedy which is available in the discretion of the court.

2. Traditionally, specific performance has been perceived as a secondary remedy, only available where damages would be inadequate. This restrictive perception of the role of specific performance has come under challenge recently. An alternative perception of specific performance is that it is available when it is the most appropriate remedy on the facts of the case. One of the aims of this chapter is to examine the circumstances in which the courts will make a specific performance order. Particular attention will be paid to the decision of the House of Lords in *Co-operative Insurance Society Ltd* v. *Argyll Stores (Holdings) Ltd* [1998] AC 1.

3. Finally, the chapter concludes with a consideration of the question whether English law should develop a more liberal approach to the availability of specific performance and recognize the existence of a general right to specific performance.

2. WHAT IS SPECIFIC PERFORMANCE?

The term 'specific performance' in English law is used to denote 'the remedy available in equity to compel a person actually to perform a contractual obligation' (H Beale (ed), *Chitty on Contracts* (29th edn, Sweet & Maxwell, 2004), para 27-004). This definition requires qualification in two respects. In the first place it can be argued that specific performance is not 'specific' at all in that, in the vast majority of cases, the defendant is not ordered 'specifically' to perform a contractual obligation. The obligation that the defendant is ordered to perform generally differs in some way from the initial obligation that was undertaken in the contract. Most claimants do not seek specific performance until the defendant has already broken the contract, although it is not strictly necessary for a claimant seeking a specific performance order to demonstrate that the defendant has already broken the terms of the contract between the parties. In such a case, the defendant obviously cannot perform exactly in accordance with the original contractual obligation in that, at the least, performance will take place at a different time from that originally agreed. On this basis it can be argued that specific performance is a *substitutionary* and not a specific remedy. This point is not an unimportant one in that, if it is correct, it enables a more direct comparison to be made with the damages remedy which clearly aims to provide the claimant with a substitute (in the form of a monetary award) for the performance originally promised. Secondly, not every action to compel a person to perform a contractual obligation falls under the rubric of 'specific performance'. Thus where the obligation sought to be enforced is one to pay money, it is usually described as an action for the price or a claim in debt, not a claim for specific performance. The latter proposition has been thrown into some doubt by *Ministry of Sound (Ireland) Ltd* v. *World Online Ltd* [2003] EWHC 2178 (Ch); [2003] 2 All ER (Comm) 823 where Nicholas Strauss QC, sitting as a Deputy Judge of the High Court, accepted (at [67]) the submission that the claim for payment advanced by the claimant was 'a claim for specific performance.' The consequence of accepting this submission was to make it 'appropriate to consider whether there are discretionary reasons why [the claim for payment] might be refused.' It is suggested that this analysis is inconsistent with the decision of the House of Lords in *White & Carter (Councils) Ltd* v. *McGregor* [1962] AC 413 (p. 995 above), where their Lordships refused to apply equitable principles to a claim in debt, and should not be followed in subsequent cases. 'Specific performance' is therefore used in a rather restricted sense in English law in comparison with some civilian legal systems where, for example, the remedy of repair or replacement of the goods is sometimes described as a form of specific performance.

In English law specific performance is an equitable remedy. The common law did not specifically enforce a contract, except the obligation to pay money. The equitable origins of the remedy continue to have an impact on the modern law. In the first place, specific performance is a discretionary remedy. It is not available as of right, unlike the action for damages at common law. However it does not follow from this that one can never predict when specific performance will be ordered by the courts. There are 'well-established principles' that govern the exercise of the court's discretion (see, for example, the speech of Lord Hoffmann in *Co-operative Insurance Society Ltd* v. *Argyll Stores (Holdings) Ltd* [1998] AC 1 p. 1148 below). Thus one can find situations where specific performance is either routinely available (for example, in favour of a purchaser under a contract for the sale of land) or generally unavailable (for example, contracts for 'personal services', on which see p. 1143 below). The discretion is therefore a structured one. However, in the final analysis, the remedy lies in the discretion of the court and it is always necessary to pay careful attention to the facts and circumstances of the individual case. Secondly, the courts have had to work out the relationship between the equitable remedy of specific performance and the common law remedies. The traditional formula used by the courts is that 'specific performance will not be ordered when damages are an adequate remedy'. This formula requires further elaboration.

3. SPECIFIC PERFORMANCE AND THE ADEQUACY OF DAMAGES

The statement that specific performance will not be ordered when damages are an adequate remedy prompts two questions. First, when are damages an adequate remedy? Second, must a court refuse to make a specific performance order where damages are an adequate remedy?

The courts tend not to answer the first question directly; that is to say, they do not spell out the circumstances in which damages are an adequate remedy. Rather, they identify the circumstances in which damages are inadequate. Damages may be inadequate where the loss which the claimant has suffered is either difficult to quantify or to prove (*Adderley* v. *Dixon* (1824) 1 Sim & St 607, cf *Fothergill* v. *Rowland* (1873) LR 17 Eq 132) or where the claimant is only entitled to recover nominal damages in respect of the defendant's breach (as in *Beswick* v. *Beswick* [1968] AC 58, discussed at p. 1181 below). The case that is usually cited by way of illustration of the 'inadequacy of damages' rule is the case of the contract for the sale of unique goods. Thus the contract in *Falcke* v. *Gray* (1859) 4 Drew 651 was for the sale of two china jars. Although the court refused to make a specific performance order on the facts of the case, the Vice-Chancellor stated that:

> In the present case the contract is for the purchase of articles of unusual beauty, rarity and distinction, so that damages would not be an adequate compensation for non-performance; and I am of opinion that a contract for articles of such description is such a contract as this Court will enforce; and, in the absence of all other objection, I should have no hesitation in decreeing specific performance.

It is an unresolved question whether uniqueness includes goods that are commercially unique, in the sense that there are no other goods with the same characteristics available in the market. Support for the proposition that 'uniqueness' encompasses commercial uniqueness can be gleaned from *Behnke* v. *Bede Shipping Co Ltd* [1927] 1 KB 649. The plaintiffs sought an order for specific performance of a contract for the purchase of a ship named *City*. Wright J made the order sought. He stated (at p. 661):

> In the present case there is evidence that the *City* was of peculiar and practically unique value to the plaintiff. She was a cheap vessel, being old, having been built in 1892, but her engines and boilers were practically new and such as to satisfy the German regulations, and hence the plaintiff could, as a German shipowner, have her at once put on the German register. A very experienced ship valuer has said that he knew of only one other comparable ship, but that may now have been sold. The plaintiff wants the ship for immediate use, and I do not think damages would be an adequate compensation. I think he is entitled to the ship and a decree of specific performance in order that justice may be done.

A different result was, however, reached in *Société des Industries Metallurgiques SA* v. *The Bronx Engineering Co Ltd* [1975] 1 Lloyd's Rep 465 where the Court of Appeal held that the fact that the buyers would have to wait between nine and twelve months for a replacement delivery did not of itself establish that the goods were unique. Lord Edmund Davies quoted from the judgment of Wright J in *Benhke* and continued (at p. 468):

> By way of contrast with that case, the real substance of the plaintiffs' claim here is that were they now obliged to go to another manufacturer they would probably have to wait another 9–12 months before they could get delivery of such new machinery and that, by reason of that delay and other factors, they would stand to lose a substantial sum. There has been no suggestion of financial inability in the defendants to satisfy such a money judgment (whatever its dimensions) as might be awarded against them to cover all such items of damages as the plaintiffs could legitimately rely upon. While sympathising with the dilemma in which the plaintiffs finds themselves, I see

nothing which removes this case from the ordinary run of cases arising out of commercial contracts where damages are claimed.

The reason for making a specific performance order in cases such as *Benhke* is that the lack of an available substitute makes it extremely difficult for a court to assess the damages payable with any degree of accuracy and these problems of assessment can be avoided by making a specific performance order. On the other hand, damages are likely to be an adequate remedy where the claimant can obtain the promised perform- ance from another source and then recover the difference in the cost of the alternative performance from the defaulting party. It is important to note that the fact that damages are inadequate does not of itself entitle the claimant to a specific perform- ance order. A court may nevertheless, in its discretion, refuse to make such an order. Thus inadequacy of damages is a necessary but not a sufficient condition for the making of a specific performance order.

The proposition that inadequacy of damages is a necessary condition for the mak- ing of a specific performance order has, however, come under some challenge in recent years. That challenge was led by the House of Lords in *Beswick* v. *Beswick* [1968] AC 58 (see p. 1181 below) where emphasis was placed on the appropriateness of specific performance on the facts of the case or the justice of making the order rather than on the inadequacy of the damages remedy (see to similar effect *Tito* v. *Waddell (No 2)* [1977] Ch 106, 322). This was most explicit in the speech of Lord Pearce. He alone of the judges was of the view that the plaintiff was entitled to substantial damages but he stated (at p. 88) that it was not 'necessary to consider the amount of damages more closely, since this is a case in which . . . the more appropri- ate remedy is that of specific performance'. The point being made by Lord Pearce is not that the adequacy, or inadequacy, of the damages remedy should be disregarded entirely. Rather, it is that it should remain a relevant factor but that it should no longer be a necessary ingredient of a claim for specific performance. Disquiet with the traditional 'adequacy of damages' formula is based on a number of grounds. The first is that a claimant, as the innocent party, should be entitled to choose the remedy that is most appropriate to the facts of the case and should not have his choice constrained by an unnecessary restriction. Secondly, a claimant runs an inevitable risk in arguing that the damages to which he is otherwise entitled are inadequate. Should the court in its discretion decide not to make the specific performance order, then he will be left with a measure of damages which, by his own admission, is inadequate. A claimant should not be put in the position of having to make the potentially damaging conces- sion that damages are inadequate in order to substantiate his claim to a completely different remedy, namely specific performance. Thirdly, to the extent that the courts continue to develop the remedy of damages in order to further the goal of ensuring that claimants receive full compensation for the losses suffered as a result of a breach of contract (on which see pp. 1017–1054 above), this will result, on the traditional formula, in a reduction in the availability of specific performance because claimants will find it increasingly difficult to demonstrate that damages are an inadequate rem- edy. Reform of the law of damages should not carry with it, as a necessary by-product, a reduction in the availability of specific performance.

The law is therefore in a state of flux. The judges are no longer confined to asking themselves whether or not damages would be an adequate remedy on the facts of the case. They can take account of a broader range of factors when deciding whether or not to make a specific performance order. The adequacy of damages to the claimant remains a very important factor in making this decision but it is no longer decisive. Nevertheless, in the vast majority of cases, one would expect a court to refuse to make a specific performance order where damages would be an adequate remedy for the claimant. In this respect it may be said that the modern emphasis on the 'appropriateness' of the remedy on the facts of the case is no more than a change of label. Thus in *Rainbow Estates Ltd* v. *Tokenhold Ltd* [1998] 2 All ER 860, 868 Lawrence Collins QC, sitting as a deputy judge of the High Court, stated that 'the remedy should be available when damages are not an adequate remedy or, in the more modern formulation, when specific performance is the appropriate remedy'. But it would perhaps be premature to write this change off as one that is devoid of substance. It widens the field of inquiry and it relieves the claimant of the need positively to establish that damages would not be an adequate remedy (albeit that the adequacy of damages remains an important factor in deciding whether or not to make the specific performance order).

4. THE RANGE OF FACTORS TO WHICH THE COURTS WILL HAVE REGARD

The proposition that specific performance should be available when damages are not an adequate remedy or when it is the most appropriate remedy on the facts of the case does not, however, tell the whole story. The cases reveal that there are a number of circumstances in which the courts will refuse to make a specific performance order. The weight to be attached to these different 'circumstances' is variable. Some weigh much more heavily on the scales than others and are sometimes described as 'bars to specific performance'. Thus Professor Treitel (*The Law of Contract* (11th edn, Sweet & Maxwell, 2003), pp. 1026–1037), while acknowledging that there are exceptions of varying scope in each case, states that the following are not specifically enforceable, namely (i) contracts involving personal service, (ii) contracts requiring constant supervision, (iii) contracts which are too vague, (iv) building contracts, (v) contracts sought to be enforced in part only, (vi) a contract which the defendant is entitled to terminate in any event or which is subject to a condition precedent not within the control of the party seeking specific performance, and (vii) promises made without consideration. He also lists the following as factors that are taken into account by the courts in the exercise of their discretion when deciding not to make a specific performance order, namely (i) the order would cause 'severe hardship to the defendant', (ii) the contract has been procured 'by means that are unfair, even though they do not amount to grounds on which the contract can be invalidated', (iii) the consideration for the defendant's promise to perform is inadequate (although Professor Treitel concedes at p. 1027 that the legitimacy of taking this factor into account is now doubtful given that it is clear that '*mere* inadequacy of consideration is not a ground for refusing specific performance'), (iv) the conduct of the claimant, in the sense that if the claimant has himself acted unfairly or improperly this may be used as a basis for denying the remedy on the ground that the claimant has not come to court 'with clean hands', and (v) the fact that it is impossible for the defendant to comply with the terms of the order. This list of factors does not purport to be exhaustive and, indeed, other authors have drawn up a list in slightly different terms (see, for example, A Burrows, *Remedies for Torts and Breach of Contract* (3rd edn, Oxford University Press, 2004) pp. 458–505). For present purposes these differences can be put to one side; they are largely matters of detail into which it is not necessary for us to enter. The list performs the function of indicating, in broad terms, the range of factors taken into consideration by the courts when deciding whether or not to make a specific performance order.

The more difficult points relate to, firstly, the weight to be given to some of the factors that have been relied upon in the past to justify a decision not to order specific performance and, secondly, the scope of some of the acknowledged 'bars' to specific performance. The cause of these difficulties is that some of the bars are of some antiquity and they are, to modern eyes, reflective of an unduly restrictive approach to the availability of specific performance. In order to illustrate this point we shall examine three of the grounds on which the courts have refused to order specific performance. In the first two instances (namely, personal service contracts and mutuality) we can see the courts gradually cutting back on the scope of the bar to specific performance. The third example, namely hardship to the defendant, demonstrates that this more liberal approach is not without its limits and that the courts continue to take account of the interests of defendants when deciding whether or not it is appropriate to make a specific performance order. We shall then move on in the next section to consider the leading modern authority on specific performance, namely the decision of the House of Lords in *Co-operative Insurance Society Ltd* v. *Argyll Stores (Holdings) Ltd* [1998] AC 1.

(a) PERSONAL SERVICE CONTRACTS

A contract involving personal service (for example, a contract of employment) will not generally be specifically enforced. Thus section 236 of the Trade Union and Labour Relations (Consolidation) Act 1992 provides:

No court shall, whether by way of—

   (a) an order of specific performance or specific implement of a contract of employment, or

   (b) an injunction or interdict restraining a breach or threatened breach of such a contract,

compel an employee to do any work or attend at any place for the doing of any work.

It should be noted that section 236 applies both to specific performance orders and to injunctions, although, as we shall see, the courts have, in fact, been willing in certain cases to grant an injunction, the effect of which is to restrain the employer from terminating the contract of employment with the claimant employee. In so far as the law wishes to avoid turning a contract of employment into a form of slavery, the proposition that the courts should not make a specific performance order or grant an injunction is readily understandable (see, for example, *De Francesco* v. *Barnum* (1890) 45 Ch D 430, 438). And, from an employer's perspective, one can see that an employer may well wish not to continue to employ a worker in whom he no longer has any trust and confidence. But it does not follow from this that the courts should never have the power at common law to restrain an employer from terminating a contract of employment. As Lord Hoffmann acknowledged in *Johnson* v. *Unisys Ltd* [2001] UKHL 13; [2003] 1 AC 518, paragraph [35], it is now recognized that 'a person's employment is usually one of the most important things in his or her life. It gives not only a livelihood but an occupation, an identity and a sense of self-esteem'. Consistently with this, the unfair dismissal legislation, first introduced in 1971, provides for the remedies of re-instatement and re-engagement (see now ss. 113–117 of the Employment Rights Act 1996) as well as compensation. This commitment in principle to re-instatement as a remedy has not, however, been reflected in practice. As Lord Steyn observed in *Johnson* (para [23]), the level of re-instatement may be as low as 3% of all unfair dismissal applicants. The reasons for the low take up of re-instatement are complex. Many employees prefer to be compensated rather than be faced with the prospect of returning to their old place of work; employment tribunals appear to be reluctant to make use of the remedy; and an employer can ultimately resist a re-instatement order provided that it is prepared to pay an enhanced level of compensation (s. 117 of the Employment Rights Act 1996). Of course, it does not follow from the fact that employment tribunals have been given a statutory power to order re-instatement that the courts should have such a power at common law. On the contrary, section 236 of the Trade Union and Labour Relations (Consolidation) Act 1992 states that they have no such power.

However, one can find modern examples of cases in which the courts have been prepared to grant an injunction, the effect of which was to restrain the employer from terminating the contract of employment with the employee. One such case is *Irani* v. *Southampton and South West Hampshire Health Authority* [1985] ICR 590. The defendant employer purported to terminate the plaintiff's contract of employment in breach of a statutory appeal procedure that was applicable to the plaintiff. The plaintiff sought, and obtained, an interlocutory injunction restraining the defendant from terminating his contract of employment without first exhausting the procedure laid down in section 33 of the Whitley Council's Conditions of Service. It is, however, important to note the terms of the injunction proposed by Warner J, namely:

Injunction restraining defendant until trial or further order from implementing notice dated 8 June 1984 purporting to determine plaintiff's employment with defendant as from 23 July 1984 before carrying out procedure under section 33 of Whitley Council's Conditions of Service.

Plaintiff undertaking not to present himself for work at any establishment of defendant's pending trial.

An important feature of this injunction is that it refrains from ordering the defendant to provide the plaintiff with work. On the contrary, the plaintiff expressly undertook not to turn up for work. The plaintiff was protected in so far as his status as an employee was preserved and the employer remained liable to pay his salary, but he could not compel the employer to provide him with work (see also *Robb* v. *Hammersmith and Fulham LBC* [1991] ICR 514, where the terms of the injunction were similarly limited). The limited nature of the injunction granted may simply reflect the reality that the law should be slow to require parties to co-operate with each other in the face of evidence that the trust and confidence which once existed between them has evaporated. Conversely, where it appears that the relationship of trust and confidence continues to subsist between the employer and the employee, the court may not require the employee to give an undertaking that he will not present himself for work: see, for example, *Hill* v. *C A Parsons Ltd* [1972] Ch 305 where the cause of the dismissal was the intervention of a trade union and the relationship between the employer and employee appeared to remain a strong one.

Thus we can conclude from cases such as *Irani*, *Robb*, and *Hill* that there is no longer an absolute bar to a court granting an injunction to restrain the termination of an employment relationship, at least where the party seeking the injunction is an employee. Further evidence in support of the existence of a more liberal approach can be gleaned from the expansion in recent years of public law remedies which has enabled a number of workers to obtain judicial review of the decision to dismiss them (see, for example, *Stevenson* v. *United Road Transport Union* [1977] ICR 893 and *R* v. *BBC, ex p Lavelle* [1983] 1 WLR 23 but contrast the more restrictive stance adopted in *R.* v. *East Berkshire Health Authority, ex p Walsh* [1985] QB 152).

In the light of these cases it may now be appropriate to re-consider the justifications for the proposition that the courts should not specifically enforce a contract for personal services. The case for (limited) reform was best put by Megarry J in *C H Giles & Co Ltd* v. *Morris* [1972] 1 WLR 307, 318 when he stated:

One day, perhaps, the courts will look again at the so-called rule that contracts for personal services or involving the continuous performance of services will not be specifically enforced. Such a rule is plainly not absolute and without exception, nor do I think that it can be based on any narrow consideration such as difficulties of constant superintendence by the court. Mandatory injunctions are by no means unknown, and there is normally no question of the court having to send its officers to supervise the performance of the order of the court. Prohibitory injunctions are common, and again there is no direct supervision by the court. Performance of each type of injunction is normally secured by the realisation of the person enjoined that he is liable to be punished for contempt if evidence of his disobedience to the order is put before the court; and if the injunction is prohibitory, actual committal will usually, so long as it continues, make disobedience impossible. If instead the order is for specific performance of a contract for personal services, a similar machinery of enforcement could be employed, again without there being any question of supervision by any officer of the court. The reasons why the court is reluctant to decree specific performance of a contract for personal services (and I would regard it as a strong reluctance rather than a rule) are, I think, more complex and more firmly bottomed on human nature. If a singer contracts to sing, there could no doubt be proceedings for committal if, ordered to sing, the singer remained obstinately dumb. But if instead the singer sang flat, or sharp, or too fast, or too slowly, or too loudly, or too quietly, or resorted to a dozen of the manifestations of temperament traditionally associated with some singers, the threat of committal would reveal itself as a most unsatisfactory weapon; for who could say whether the imperfections of performance were natural or self-induced? To make an order with such possibilities of evasion would be vain; and so the order will not be made. However, not all contracts of personal service or for the continuous performance of services are as dependent as this on matters of opinion and judgment, nor do all such contracts involve the same degree of the daily impact of person on person. In general, no doubt, the inconvenience and mischief of decreeing specific performance of most of such contracts will greatly outweigh the advantages and specific performance will be refused. But I do not think that it should be assumed that as soon as any element of personal service or continuous services can be discerned in a contract the court will, without more, refuse specific performance.

(b) MUTUALITY

Sir Edward Fry in the first edition of his book *Specific Performance*, published in 1858, stated that:

A contract to be specifically enforced by the Court must, as a general rule, be mutual,—that is to say, such that it might, at the time it was entered into, have been enforced by either of the parties against the other of them.

This proposition was subject to much academic criticism but it did not receive sustained judicial consideration until 1977 in the form of the decision of the Court of Appeal in *Price* v. *Strange* [1978] Ch 337. A number of criticisms were levelled against Fry's proposition, of which it suffices to mention two. The first was that it was not supported by the cases cited by Fry and the cases also demonstrated that there were a number of exceptions to the rule. Secondly, it was argued that the focus of attention should not be on the time at which the contract was concluded but on the position of the parties at the time of judgment. At the time at which it gives judgment the court ought to consider the relative positions of the parties; and, to the extent that there are obligations of the claimant that remain unperformed, the court should consider the remedies available to the defendant to ensure that it is adequately compensated in the event of non-performance by the claimant. In the light of these criticisms Buckley LJ in *Price* v. *Strange* [1978] Ch 337, 367–368 concluded:

I can discover nothing in principle to recommend the Fry proposition, and authority seems to me to be strongly against it. Accordingly in my judgment it should be regarded as wrong. The time at which the mutual availability of specific performance and its importance must be considered is, in my opinion, the time of judgment, and the principle to be applied can I think be stated simply as follows: the court will not compel a defendant to perform his obligations specifically if it cannot at the same time ensure that any unperformed obligations of the plaintiff will be specifically performed, unless, perhaps, damages would not be an adequate remedy to the defendant for any default on the plaintiff's part.

Subsequent courts have followed the lead given by Buckley LJ. In *Rainbow Estates Ltd* v. *Tokenhold Ltd* [1998] 2 All ER 860, 865–866 Lawrence Collins QC, stated that:

as regards the requirement of mutuality, it is now clear that it does not follow from the fact that specific performance is not available to one party that it is not available to the other; want of mutuality is a discretionary, and not an absolute, bar to specific performance. The court will grant specific performance if it can be done without injustice or unfairness to the defendant.

The importance of the judgment of Lawrence Collins QC lies in its recognition of the fact that want of mutuality is no longer, if it ever was, an absolute bar to making a specific performance order; it is simply a factor to be taken into account by the court in the exercise of its discretion. The modern position is perhaps best summed up by Sir Jack Beatson (*Anson's Law of Contract* (28th edn, Oxford University Press 2002) p. 635) in the following way:

lack of mutuality is now only relevant if, at the date of the hearing, the claimant has not performed its obligations under the contract and could not be compelled for some reason to perform its unperformed obligations specifically. Even where mutuality in this sense does not exist, the Court may possibly, in the exercise of its discretion, order specific performance if damages would be an adequate remedy to the defendant for any default on the claimant's part.

(c) UNDUE HARDSHIP

A court may refuse to make a specific performance order on the ground that it will cause severe hardship to the defendant. The difficulty which the courts face here lies in discerning what constitutes 'severe hardship' for this purpose. The hardship need not be of sufficient severity to entitle the defendant to set aside the contract (in such a case the defendant could attack the validity of the contract rather than merely rely on a defence to the application for specific performance). But how far below the threshold for the validity of a contract can the court go? It is impossible to produce a hard-and-fast rule here. Much depends on the facts of the individual case. A modern illustration of a court considering a defence based on hardship is provided by the decision of Goulding J in *Patel* v. *Ali* [1984] Ch 283. The defendant and a Mr Ahmed entered into a contract to sell the defendant's matrimonial home to the plaintiff (the property was registered in the name of Mr Ahmed). The contract was concluded in July 1979, with a completion date of 28 August 1979. Completion did not, however, take place on 28 August. The plaintiff issued a writ seeking specific performance of the contract on 11 August 1980 but did not apply for summary judgment until 4 July 1983. The reasons for the delay were not conclusively established, but appeared to be caused by two principal factors. The first was that the defendant's husband had been adjudicated bankrupt in May 1979 and his trustee in bankruptcy succeeded in obtaining an injunction restraining completion of the sale. Her husband was not released from that injunction until 21 July 1980. Secondly, the plaintiffs had difficulty in effecting service of proceedings on Mr Ahmed, as he had returned to Pakistan. However, in this intervening period the defendant suffered considerable misfortune. In July 1979 she was twenty-three years old, had one child, was in apparent good health and spoke very little English. But in 1980 it was discovered that she had bone cancer in her right thigh which led to the amputation of her right leg at the hip joint in July of that year. At that time she was heavily pregnant and she gave birth to her second child in August 1980. Then in 1981 her husband was sent to prison for a year and she gave birth to her third child in 1983, after her husband's release from prison. In these circumstances the defendant asked the court to refuse the plaintiffs' application for specific performance and to leave the plaintiffs to their remedy in damages. After considering the authorities Goulding J concluded that his discretion was wide enough to entitle him to refuse to make a specific performance order on the ground of 'hardship subsequent to the contract and not caused by the plaintiff'. He acknowledged that 'mere pecuniary difficulties . . . afford no excuse from performance of a contract' and continued (at p. 288):

> The important and true principle, in my view, is that only in extraordinary and persuasive circumstances can hardship supply an excuse for resisting performance of a contract for the sale of immovable property. A person of full capacity who sells or buys a house takes the risk of hardship to himself and his dependants, whether arising from existing facts or unexpectedly supervening in the interval before completion. This is where, to my mind, great importance attaches to the immense delay in the present case, not attributable to the defendant's conduct. Even after issue of the writ, she could not complete, if she had wanted to, without the concurrence of the absent Mr Ahmed. Thus, in a sense, she can say she is being asked to do what she had never bargained for, namely to complete the sale after more than four years, after all the unforeseeable changes that such a period entails. I think that in this way she can fairly assert that specific performance would inflict on her a 'hardship amounting to injustice' to use the phrase employed by James LJ, in a different but comparable context, in *Tamplin* v. *James* (1880) 15 Ch D 215 at 221. Equitable relief may, in my view, be refused because of an unforeseen change of circumstances not amounting to legal frustration, just as it may on the ground of mistake insufficient to avoid a contract at law.
>
> In the end, I am satisfied that it is within the court's discretion to accede to the defendant's prayer if satisfied that it is just to do so. And, on the whole, looking at the position of both sides after the long unpredictable delay for which neither seeks to make the other responsible, I am opinion that it *is* just to leave the plaintiffs to their remedy in damages if that can indeed be effective.

An important feature of *Patel* was the plaintiffs' delay in seeking a specific performance order. It was thus the *combination* of hardship to the defendant and delay by the plaintiffs (although the two were strongly linked on the facts) that led Goulding J to conclude that it would not be just to make the order. It is a more difficult question whether or not hardship alone would have sufficed to justify a refusal to make a specific performance order. It is suggested that it would not. Hardship is a factor which the courts will consider alongside other factors but it is unlikely on its own to have sufficient weight to justify a decision to refuse to make an order for specific performance.

5. CO-OPERATIVE INSURANCE SOCIETY LTD V. ARGYLL STORES (HOLDINGS) LTD

The leading modern authority on specific performance is the decision of the House of Lords in *Co-operative Insurance Society Ltd* v. *Argyll Stores (Holdings) Ltd* [1998] AC 1. The case is particularly important for its consideration of, and re-characterization of, the 'constant supervision' bar to the making of a specific performance order. But the significance of the case transcends this particular issue. In the course of a broad-ranging speech Lord Hoffmann surveyed the nature and extent of the discretion exercised by the court when deciding whether or not to make a specific performance order, the supposed contrast between common law and civil law systems in their approach to specific performance, and the impact which the sanction of contempt of court has on the willingness of the court to make a specific performance order. Given its significance, the speech of Lord Hoffmann is extracted in full. The commentary which follows the extract explores the issues largely in the order in which they are raised by Lord Hoffmann and it may be useful to have regard to the commentary when reading the case.

Co-operative Insurance Society Ltd v. Argyll Stores (Holdings) Ltd

[1998] AC 1, House of Lords

The facts of the case are set out in the speech of Lord Hoffmann.

Lord Hoffmann
My Lords,

In 1955 Lord Goddard CJ said:

'No authority has been quoted to show that an injunction will be granted enjoining a person to carry on a business, nor can I think that one ever would be, certainly not where the business is a losing concern': *Attorney-General* v. *Colchester Corporation* [1955] 2 QB 207, 217.

In this case his prediction has been falsified. The appellant defendants, Argyll Stores (Holdings) Ltd ('Argyll'), decided in May 1995 to close their Safeway supermarket in the Hillsborough Shopping Centre in Sheffield because it was losing money. This was a breach of a covenant in their lease, which contained in clause 4(19) a positive obligation to keep the premises open for retail trade during the usual hours of business. Argyll admitted the breach and, in an action by the landlord, Co-operative Insurance Society Ltd ('C.I.S.') consented to an order for damages to be assessed. But the Court of Appeal [1996] Ch 286, reversing the trial judge, ordered that the covenant be specifically performed. It made a final injunction ordering Argyll to trade on the premises during the remainder of the term (which will expire on 3 August 2014) or until an earlier subletting or assignment. The Court of Appeal suspended its order for three months to allow time for Argyll to complete an assignment which by that time had been agreed. After a short agreed extension, the lease was assigned with the landlord's consent. In fact, therefore, the injunction never took effect. The appeal to your Lordships is substantially about costs. But the issue remains of great importance to landlords and tenants under other commercial leases.

2.   The facts

A decree of specific performance is of course a discretionary remedy and the question for your Lordships is whether the Court of Appeal was entitled to set aside the exercise of the judge's discretion. There are well-established principles which govern the exercise of the discretion but these, like all equitable principles, are flexible and adaptable to achieve the ends of equity, which is, as Lord Selborne LC once remarked, to 'do more perfect and complete justice' than would be the result of leaving the parties to their remedies at common law: *Wilson* v. *Northampton and Banbury Junction Railway Co* (1874) LR 9

Ch App 279, 284. Much therefore depends upon the facts of the particular case and I shall begin by describing these in more detail.

The Hillsborough Shopping Centre consists of about 25 shops. Safeway was by far the largest shop and the greatest attraction. Its presence was a commercial benefit to the smaller shops nearby. The lease was for a term of 35 years from 4 August 1979 with five-yearly rent reviews. Clause 4(12)(a) contained a negative covenant as to the user of the premises:

'Not to use or suffer to be used the demised premises other than as a retail store for the sale of food groceries provisions and goods normally sold from time to time by a retail grocer food supermarkets and food superstores . . .'

Clause 4(19) was the positive covenant enforced in this case:

'To keep the demised premises open for retail trade during the usual hours of business in the locality and the display windows properly dressed in a suitable manner in keeping with a good class parade of shops.'

Competition in the supermarket business is fierce and in 1994 Argyll undertook a major review of its business and decided to reduce the scale of its operations. The management was to be reorganised, 27 loss-making or less profitable supermarkets closed and thousands of employees made redundant. Hillsborough, which according to Argyll's management accounts had made a loss of about £70,000 in the previous year, was on the list for closure. For administrative reasons, as well as to avoid the demoralising effect of successive closure announcements, it was decided to close all the supermarkets at once and try to negotiate the disposal of their sites as a package. In early April 1995 Argyll announced that Hillsborough and the other supermarkets would close on 6 May 1995.

As soon as C.I.S. heard of the impending closure, it protested. On 12 April 1995 Mr Wightman, the regional surveyor of the investment department, wrote to Mr Jefferies of Safeway:

'Whilst obviously there is little point in trying to influence your corporate decision with regard to the closure of this unit I am dismayed at the short period of notice given which will undoubtedly have immediate impact on the Centre and all the other tenants trading therein.'

He drew attention to the covenant to keep open, invited Safeway to agree to continue trading until a suitable assignee had been found, offered to negotiate a temporary rent concession and asked for a reply by return of post.

Unfortunately he received no answer. Mr Jefferies had himself fallen victim to the reorganisation; he had been made redundant. No one else dealt with the letter. On Saturday, 6 May 1995 the supermarket closed and over the next two weeks its fittings were stripped out. On 22 May 1995 C.I.S. issued a writ claiming specific performance of the covenant to keep open and damages.

3. The trial

C.I.S. issued a summons for judgment under R.S.C., Ord. 14 but when the matter came before Judge Maddocks, sitting as a judge of the High Court on 1 August 1995, it was agreed that, since the material facts were not in dispute, the hearing should be treated as the trial of the action. The judge was therefore invited by C.I.S. to make a final order that the covenant be performed for the remainder of the lease or until an earlier assignment or subletting. By this time Argyll were already in serious negotiation with another supermarket chain for an assignment but no contract had yet been signed.

The judge refused to order specific performance. He said that there was on the authorities a settled practice that orders which would require a defendant to run a business would not be made. He was not content, however, merely to follow authority. He gave reasons why he thought that specific performance would be inappropriate. Two such reasons were given by way of justification for the general practice. An order to carry on a business, as opposed to an order to perform a 'single and well-defined act', was difficult to enforce by the sanction of committal. And where a business was being run at a loss, specific relief would be 'too far-reaching and beyond the scope of control which the court should seek to impose.' The other two related to the particular case. A resumption of business would be expensive (refitting the shop was estimated to cost over £1m) and although Argyll had knowingly acted in breach of covenant, it had done so 'in the light of the settled practice of the court to award damages'. Finally, while the assessment of damages might be difficult, it was the kind of exercise which the courts had done in the past.

4.   The settled practice

There is no dispute about the existence of the settled practice to which the judge referred. It is sufficient for this purpose to refer to *Braddon Towers Ltd* v. *International Stores Ltd* [1987] 1 EGLR 209, 213, where Slade J said:

> 'Whether or not this may be properly described as a rule of law, I do not doubt that for many years practitioners have advised their clients that it is the settled and invariable practice of this court never to grant mandatory injunctions requiring persons to carry on business.'

But the practice has never, so far as I know, been examined by this House and it is open to C.I.S. to say that it rests upon inadequate grounds or that it has been too inflexibly applied.

Specific performance is traditionally regarded in English law as an exceptional remedy, as opposed to the common law damages to which a successful plaintiff is entitled as of right. There may have been some element of later rationalisation of an untidier history, but by the 19th century it was orthodox doctrine that the power to decree specific performance was part of the discretionary jurisdiction of the Court of Chancery to do justice in cases in which the remedies available at common law were inadequate. This is the basis of the general principle that specific performance will not be ordered when damages are an adequate remedy. By contrast, in countries with legal systems based on civil law, such as France, Germany and Scotland, the plaintiff is prima facie entitled to specific performance. The cases in which he is confined to a claim for damages are regarded as the exceptions. In practice, however, there is less difference between common law and civilian systems than these general statements might lead one to suppose. The principles upon which English judges exercise the discretion to grant specific performance are reasonably well settled and depend upon a number of considerations, mostly of a practical nature, which are of very general application. I have made no investigation of civilian systems, but *a priori* I would expect that judges take much the same matters into account in deciding whether specific performance would be inappropriate in a particular case.

The practice of not ordering a defendant to carry on a business is not entirely dependent upon damages being an adequate remedy. In *Dowty Boulton Paul Ltd* v. *Wolverhampton Corporation* [1971] 1 WLR 204, Sir John Pennycuick V-C refused to order the corporation to maintain an airfield as a going concern because: 'It is very well established that the court will not order specific performance of an obligation to carry on a business': see p. 211. He added: 'It is unnecessary in the circumstances to discuss whether damages would be an adequate remedy to the company': see p. 212. Thus the reasons which underlie the established practice may justify a refusal of specific performance even when damages are not an adequate remedy.

The most frequent reason given in the cases for declining to order someone to carry on a business is that it would require constant supervision by the court. In *J C Williamson Ltd* v. *Lukey and Mulholland* (1931) 45 CLR 282, 297–298, Dixon J said flatly: 'Specific performance is inapplicable when the continued supervision of the court is necessary in order to ensure the fulfilment of the contract'.

There has, I think, been some misunderstanding about what is meant by continued superintendence. It may at first sight suggest that the judge (or some other officer of the court) would literally have to supervise the execution of the order. In *CH Giles & Co Ltd* v. *Morris* [1972] 1 WLR 307, 318 Megarry J said that 'difficulties of constant superintendence' were a 'narrow consideration' because:

> 'there is normally no question of the court having to send its officers to supervise the performance of the order. . . . Performance . . . is normally secured by the realisation of the person enjoined that he is liable to be punished for contempt if evidence of his disobedience to the order is put before the court; . . .'

This is, of course, true but does not really meet the point. The judges who have said that the need for constant supervision was an objection to such orders were no doubt well aware that supervision would in practice take the form of rulings by the court, on applications made by the parties, as to whether there had been a breach of the order. It is the possibility of the court having to give an indefinite series of such rulings in order to ensure the execution of the order which has been regarded as undesirable.

Why should this be so? A principal reason is that, as Megarry J pointed out in the passage to which I have referred, the only means available to the court to enforce its order is the quasi-criminal procedure of punishment for contempt. This is a powerful weapon; so powerful, in fact, as often to be unsuitable as an instrument for adjudicating upon the disputes which may arise over whether a business is being run in accordance with the terms of the court's order. The heavy-handed nature of the enforcement mechanism is a consideration which may go to the exercise of the court's discretion in other cases as well, but its use to compel the running of a business is perhaps the paradigm case of its disadvantages and it is in this context that I shall discuss them.

The prospect of committal or even a fine, with the damage to commercial reputation which will be caused by a finding of contempt of court, is likely to have at least two undesirable consequences. First, the defendant, who ex hypothesi did not think that it was in his economic interest to run the business at all, now has to make decisions under a sword of Damocles which may descend if the way the business is run does not conform to the terms of the order. This is, as one might say, no way to run a business. In this case the Court of Appeal made light of the point because it assumed that, once the defendant had been ordered to run the business, self-interest and compliance with the order would thereafter go hand in hand. But, as I shall explain, this is not necessarily true.

Secondly, the seriousness of a finding of contempt for the defendant means that any application to enforce the order is likely to be a heavy and expensive piece of litigation. The possibility of repeated applications over a period of time means that, in comparison with a once-and-for-all inquiry as to damages, the enforcement of the remedy is likely to be expensive in terms of cost to the parties and the resources of the judicial system.

This is a convenient point at which to distinguish between orders which require a defendant to carry on an activity, such as running a business over a more or less extended period of time, and orders which require him to achieve a result. The possibility of repeated applications for rulings on compliance with the order which arises in the former case does not exist to anything like the same extent in the latter. Even if the achievement of the result is a complicated matter which will take some time, the court, if called upon to rule, only has to examine the finished work and say whether it complies with the order. This point was made in the context of relief against forfeiture in *Shiloh Spinners Ltd* v. *Harding* [1973] AC 691. If it is a condition of relief that the tenant should have complied with a repairing covenant, difficulty of supervision need not be an objection. As Lord Wilberforce said, at p. 724:

> 'what the court has to do is to satisfy itself, ex post facto, that the covenanted work has been done, and it has ample machinery, through certificates, or by inquiry, to do precisely this.'

This distinction between orders to carry on activities and orders to achieve results explains why the courts have in appropriate circumstances ordered specific performance of building contracts and repairing covenants: see *Wolverhampton Corporation* v. *Emmons* [1901] 1 KB 515 (building contract) and *Jeune* v. *Queens Cross Properties Ltd* [1974] Ch 97 (repairing covenant). It by no means follows, however, that even obligations to achieve a result will always be enforced by specific performance. There may be other objections, to some of which I now turn.

One such objection, which applies to orders to achieve a result and a fortiori to orders to carry on an activity, is imprecision in the terms of the order. If the terms of the court's order, reflecting the terms of the obligation, cannot be precisely drawn, the possibility of wasteful litigation over compliance is increased. So is the oppression caused by the defendant having to do things under threat of proceedings for contempt. The less precise the order, the fewer the signposts to the forensic minefield which he has to traverse. The fact that the terms of a contractual obligation are sufficiently definite to escape being void for uncertainty, or to found a claim for damages, or to permit compliance to be made a condition of relief against forfeiture, does not necessarily mean that they will be sufficiently precise to be capable of being specifically enforced. So in *Wolverhampton Corporation* v. *Emmons*, Romer LJ said, at p. 525, that the first condition for specific enforcement of a building contract was that

> 'the particulars of the work are so far definitely ascertained that the court can sufficiently see what is the exact nature of the work of which it is asked to order the performance.'

Similarly in *Morris* v. *Redland Bricks Ltd* [1970] AC 652, 666, Lord Upjohn stated the following general principle for the grant of mandatory injunctions to carry out building works:

'the court must be careful to see that the defendant knows exactly in fact what he has to do and this means not as a matter of law but as a matter of fact, so that in carrying out an order he can give his contractors the proper instructions.'

Precision is of course a question of degree and the courts have shown themselves willing to cope with a certain degree of imprecision in cases of orders requiring the achievement of a result in which the plaintiffs' merits appeared strong; like all the reasons which I have been discussing, it is, taken alone, merely a discretionary matter to be taken into account: see Spry, *Equitable Remedies*, 4th ed. (1990), p. 112. It is, however, a very important one.

I should at this point draw attention to what seems to me to have been a misreading of certain remarks of Lord Wilberforce in *Shiloh Spinners Ltd* v. *Harding*, at p. 724. He pointed out, as I have said, that to grant relief against forfeiture subject to compliance with a repairing covenant involves the court in no more than the possibility of a retro-spective assessment of whether the covenanted work has been done. For this reason, he said:

'Where it is necessary, and, in my opinion, right, to move away from some 19th century authorities, is to reject as a reason against granting relief, the impossibility for the courts to supervise the doing of work.'

This is plainly a remark about cases involving the achievement of a result, such as doing repairs, and, within that class, about making compliance a condition of relief against forfeiture. But in *Tito* v. *Waddell (No 2)* [1977] Ch 106, 322 Sir Robert Megarry V-C took it to be a generalisation about specific performance and, in particular, a rejection of dif-ficulty of supervision as an objection, even in cases of orders to carry on an activity. Sir Robert Megarry V-C regarded it as an adoption of his own views (based, as I have said, on incomplete analysis of what was meant by difficulty of supervision) in *C H Giles & Co Ltd* v. *Morris* [1972] 1 WLR 307, 318. In the present case [1996] Ch 286, 292–293, Leggatt LJ took this claim at face value. In fact, Lord Wilberforce went on to say that impossibility of supervision 'is a reality no doubt, and explains why specific performance cannot be granted of agreements to this effect . . .' Lord Wilberforce was in my view drawing atten-tion to the fact that the collection of reasons which the courts have in mind when they speak of difficulty of supervision apply with much greater force to orders for specific performance, giving rise to the possibility of committal for contempt, than they do to conditions for relief against forfeiture. While the paradigm case to which such objections apply is the order to carry on an activity, they can also apply to an order requiring the achievement of a result.

There is a further objection to an order requiring the defendant to carry on a business, which was emphasised by Millett LJ in the Court of Appeal. This is that it may cause injustice by allowing the plaintiff to enrich himself at the defendant's expense. The loss which the defendant may suffer through having to comply with the order (for example, by running a business at a loss for an indefinite period) may be far greater than the plaintiff would suffer from the contract being broken. As Professor R J Sharpe explains in 'Specific Relief for Contract Breach', ch. 5 of *Studies in Contract Law* (1980), edited by Reiter and Swan, p. 129:

'In such circumstances, a specific decree in favour of the plaintiff will put him in a bargaining position vis-à-vis the defendant whereby the measure of what he will receive will be the value to the defendant of being released from performance. If the plaintiff bargains effectively, the amount he will set will exceed the value to him of performance and will approach the cost to the defendant to complete.'

This was the reason given by Lord Westbury LC in *Isenberg* v. *East India House Estate Co Ltd* (1863) 3 De GJ & S 263, 273 for refusing a mandatory injunction to compel the defendant to pull down part of a new building which interfered with the plaintiff's light and exercising instead the Court of Chancery's recently-acquired jurisdiction under Lord Cairns's Act 1858 (21 & 22 Vict. c. 27) to order payment of damages:

'I hold it . . . to be the duty of the court in such a case as the present not, by granting a mandatory injunction, to deliver over the defendants to the plaintiff bound hand and foot, in order to be made subject to any extortionate demand that he may by possibility make, but to substitute for such mandatory injunction an inquiry before itself, in order to ascertain the measure of damage that has been actually sustained.'

It is true that the defendant has, by his own breach of contract, put himself in such an unfortunate position. But the purpose of the law of contract is not to punish wrongdoing but to satisfy the expectations of the party entitled to performance. A remedy which enables him to secure, in money terms, more than the performance due to him is unjust. From a wider perspective, it cannot be in the public interest for the courts to require someone to carry on business at a loss if there is any plausible alternative by which the other party can be given compensation. It is not only a waste of resources but yokes the parties together in a continuing hostile relationship. The order for specific performance prolongs the battle. If the defendant is ordered to run a business, its conduct becomes the subject of a flow of complaints, solicitors' letters and affidavits. This is wasteful for both parties and the legal system. An award of damages, on the other hand, brings the litigation to an end. The defendant pays damages, the forensic link between them is severed, they go their separate ways and the wounds of conflict can heal.

The cumulative effect of these various reasons, none of which would necessarily be sufficient on its own, seems to me to show that the settled practice is based upon sound sense. Of course the grant or refusal of specific performance remains a matter for the judge's discretion. There are no binding rules, but this does not mean that there cannot be settled principles, founded upon practical considerations of the kind which I have discussed, which do not have to be re-examined in every case, but which the courts will apply in all but exceptional circumstances. As Slade J said, in the passage which I have quoted from *Braddon Towers Ltd* v. *International Stores Ltd* [1987] 1 EGLR 209, 213, lawyers have no doubt for many years advised their clients on this basis. In the present case, Leggatt LJ [1996] Ch 286, 294 remarked that there was no evidence that such advice had been given. In my view, if the law or practice on a point is settled, it should be assumed that persons entering into legal transactions will have been advised accordingly. I am sure that Leggatt LJ would not wish to encourage litigants to adduce evidence of the particular advice which they received. Indeed, I doubt whether such evidence would be admissible.

5.   The decision of the Court of Appeal

I must now examine the grounds upon which the majority of the Court of Appeal [1996] Ch 286 thought it right to reverse the judge. In the first place, they regarded the practice which he followed as outmoded and treated Lord Wilberforce's remarks about relief against forfeiture in *Shiloh Spinners Ltd* v. *Harding* [1973] AC 691, 724 as justifying a rejection of the arguments based on the need for constant supervision. Even Millett LJ, who dissented on other grounds, said, at p. 303, that such objections had little force today. I do not agree. As I have already said, I think that Lord Wilberforce's remarks do not support this proposition in relation to specific performance of an obligation to carry on an activity and that the arguments based on difficulty of supervision remain powerful.

The Court of Appeal said that it was enough if the contract defined the tenant's obligation with sufficient precision to enable him to know what was necessary to comply with the order. Even assuming this to be right, I do not think that the obligation in clause 4(19) can possibly be regarded as sufficiently precise to be capable of specific performance. It is to 'keep the demised premises open for retail trade'. It says nothing about the level of trade, the area of the premises within which trade is to be conducted, or even the kind of trade, although no doubt the tenant's choice would be restricted by the need to comply with the negative covenant in clause 4(12)(a) not to use the premises 'other than as a retail store for the sale of food groceries provisions and goods normally sold from time to time by a retail grocer food supermarkets and food superstores. . . .' This language seems to me to provide ample room for argument over whether the tenant is doing enough to comply with the covenant.

The Court of Appeal thought that once Argyll had been ordered to comply with the covenant, it was, as Roch LJ said, at p. 298, 'inconceivable that they would not operate the business efficiently'. Leggatt LJ said, at p. 292, that the requirement

> 'was quite intelligible to the defendants, while they were carrying on business there. . . . If the premises are to be run as a business, it cannot be in the defendants' interest to run it half-heartedly or inefficiently . . .'

This treats the way the tenant previously conducted business as measuring the extent of his obligation to do so. In my view this is a non sequitur: the obligation depends upon the language of the covenant and not upon what the tenant has previously chosen to do. No doubt it is true that it would not be in the interests of the tenant to run the business inefficiently. But running the business efficiently does not necessarily mean running it in the way it was run before. Argyll had decided that, from its point of view, the most efficient thing to do was to close the business altogether and concentrate its resources on achieving better returns elsewhere. If ordered to keep the business open, it might well decide that the next best strategy was to reduce its costs as far as was consistent with compliance with its obligations, in the expectation that a lower level of return would be more than compensated by higher returns from additional expenditure on more profitable shops. It is in my view wrong for the courts to speculate about whether Argyll might voluntarily carry on business in a way which would relieve the court from having to construe its order. The question of certainty must be decided on the assumption that the court might have to enforce the order according to its terms.

C.I.S. argued that the court should not be concerned about future difficulties which might arise in connection with the enforcement of the order. It should simply make the order and see what happened. In practice Argyll would be likely to find a suitable assignee (as it in fact did) or conduct the business so as to keep well clear of any possible enforcement proceedings or otherwise come to terms with C.I.S. This may well be true, but the likelihood of Argyll having to perform beyond the requirements of its covenant or buy its way out of its obligation to incur losses seems to me to be in principle an objection to such an order rather than to recommend it. I think that it is normally undesirable for judges to make orders in terrorem, carrying a threat of imprisonment, which work only if no one inquires too closely into what they mean.

The likelihood that the order would be effective only for a short time until an assignment is an equivocal argument. It would be burdensome to make Argyll resume business only to stop again after a short while if a short stoppage would not cause any substantial damage to the business of the shopping centre. On the other hand, what would happen if a suitable assignee could not be found? Would Argyll then have to carry on business until 2014? Mr Smith, who appeared for C.I.S., said that if the order became oppressive (for example, because Argyll were being driven into bankruptcy) or difficult to enforce, they could apply for it to be varied or discharged. But the order would be a final order and there is no case in this jurisdiction in which such an order has been varied or discharged, except when the injuncted activity has been legalised by statute. Even assuming that there was such a jurisdiction if circumstances were radically changed, I find it difficult to see how this could be made to apply. Difficulties of enforcement would not be a change of circumstances. They would have been entirely predictable when the order was made. And so would the fact that Argyll would suffer unquantifiable loss if it was obliged to continue trading. I do not think that such expedients are an answer to the difficulties on which the objections to such orders are based.

Finally, all three judges in the Court of Appeal took a very poor view of Argyll's conduct. Leggatt LJ said [1996] Ch 286, 295, that they had acted 'with gross commercial cynicism'; Roch LJ began his judgment by saying that they had 'behaved very badly' and Millett LJ said, at p. 301, that they had no merits. The principles of equity have always had a strong ethical content and nothing which I say is intended to diminish the influence of moral values in their application. I can envisage cases of gross breach of personal faith, or attempts to use the threat of non-performance as blackmail, in which the needs of justice will override all the considerations which support the settled practice. But although any breach of covenant is regrettable, the exercise of the discretion as to whether or not to grant specific performance starts from the fact that the covenant has been broken. Both landlord and tenant in this case are large sophisticated commercial organisations and I have no doubt that both were perfectly aware that the remedy for breach of the covenant was likely to be limited to an award of damages. The interests of both were purely financial: there was no element of personal breach of faith, as in the Victorian cases of railway companies which refused to honour obligations to build stations for landowners whose property they had taken: compare *Greene* v. *West Cheshire Railway Co* (1871) LR 13 Eq 44. No doubt there was an effect on the businesses of other traders in the Centre, but Argyll had made no promises to them and it is not suggested that C.I.S. warranted to other tenants that Argyll would remain. Their departure, with or without the consent of C.I.S., was a commercial risk which the tenants were able to deploy in negotiations for the next rent review. On the scale of broken promises, I can think of worse cases, but the language of the Court of Appeal left them with few adjectives to spare.

It was no doubt discourteous not to have answered Mr Wightman's letter. But to say, as Roch LJ did, at p. 299, that they had acted 'wantonly and quite unreasonably' by removing their fixtures seems to me an exaggeration. There was no question of stealing a march, or attempting to present C.I.S. with a fait accompli, because Argyll had no reason to believe that C.I.S. would have been able to obtain a mandatory injunction whether the fixtures had been removed or not. They had made it perfectly clear that they were closing the shop and given C.I.S. ample time to apply for such an injunction if so advised.

6. Conclusion

I think that no criticism can be made of the way in which Judge Maddocks exercised his discretion. All the reasons which he gave were proper matters for him to take into account. In my view the Court of Appeal should not have interfered and I would allow the appeal and restore the order which he made.

Lords Browne-Wilkinson, Slynn, Hope, and **Clyde** agreed with the speech of Lord Hoffmann.

COMMENTARY

Lord Hoffmann sought to strike a balance between certainty and flexibility. The emphasis which he placed on the fact that there are 'well-established principles which govern the exercise of the discretion' and his evident reluctance to disturb a 'settled practice', especially where parties have entered into transactions on the basis of legal advice as to the existence of such a 'settled practice', reflect a concern for certainty. On the other hand, the emphasis on the need to have regard to the facts of the individual case and the statement that there are no 'binding rules' in this area demonstrate his awareness of the need to preserve a significant degree of flexibility so that the judge is able to do justice on the facts of the individual case.

Lord Hoffmann relied upon a number of factors in reaching his conclusion: (i) there was a settled practice that a specific performance order would not be made the effect of which would be to require a defendant to run a business, (ii) an order compelling the defendants to trade could have exposed them to enormous losses, (iii) the task of framing the order was not an easy one, (iv) there was the possibility of wasteful litigation over compliance, (v) it was oppressive to the defendants to have to run a business under the threat of proceedings for contempt, and (vi) it was not in the public interest to require someone to carry on a business at a loss if there was a plausible alternative by which the other party could be compensated for the loss it had suffered. Cumulatively these factors demonstrated that the settled practice not to make a specific performance order was based on 'sound sense' and that the trial judge had acted within his discretion in refusing to grant the order that the plaintiffs sought. This balancing exercise is a feature of cases concerned with specific performance. The factors taken into account by the courts overlap (to some extent) and they can point in different directions. For example, in *Co-operative Retail* itself, the lack of precision pointed against making the order, whereas the wilful conduct of the defendants (on which see below) could be said to have pointed in favour of making the order. The task of the judge is to have regard to the relevant factors and to balance them and this, in the final analysis, depends, to a large extent, upon the facts of the individual case.

Lord Hoffmann stated that in practice there may be less difference between common law and civil law systems in this area than one might suppose (a point developed in more detail at p. 1162 below). This statement does not command universal assent. Thus Lord Clyde, while he stated that he agreed that the appeal should be allowed for the reasons given by Lord Hoffmann, was careful to add a reservation in relation to the approach that might be adopted by 'civilian systems'. This reservation was clearly made with Scots law in mind. Lord Clyde's reservation proved to be well judged. The Inner House of the Court of Session has since refused to follow *Co-operative Retail Insurance* in *Highland and Universal Properties Ltd* v. *Safeway Properties Ltd*, 2000 SLT 414, where it was held that a covenant to keep retail trading premises open for a significant period of time was specifically enforceable. The case underlines the different approach that is applicable to specific performance in civilian systems and it demonstrates that the differences in emphasis between common law systems and civilian systems can have practical consequences. As Lord President Rodger stated in his judgment:

legal advisers of prospective developers and tenants will have little difficulty in identifying any relevant difference between the two systems and in handling any resulting problems in either system. The mere fact that the two systems may come to different results in particular cases is not in my view a sufficient reason for saying that this court should remould our law so as to reach the same result as would be reached under English law in a particular situation.

The courts have traditionally refused to grant a specific performance order that would require 'constant supervision' by the court (see, for example, *Ryan* v. *Mutual Tontine Association* [1893] 1 Ch 116). This objection or bar must be re-cast in the light of Lord Hoffmann's speech. He noted that there has been 'some misunderstanding' as to the meaning of this phrase and pointed out that the supervision is undertaken by the parties and not by the courts. The role of the court is to rule on applications made to it and it is the prospect of a court being required to give an 'indefinite series of such rulings' that lies at the heart of the desire to restrict the availability of specific performance in these cases.

Lord Hoffmann then turned to the role of contempt of court as a sanction. The problem here is that contempt of court is too Draconian a sanction, involving, as it does, the possibility of imprisonment. If contempt were to be removed as a sanction (and emphasis placed on other means of enforcement, as in many civilian systems) one might expect the courts to become more willing to make a specific performance order.

The distinction drawn between an obligation to carry on an activity and an obligation to achieve a result is obviously of crucial significance for Lord Hoffmann. In many cases it will not be difficult to distinguish the two categories. But in some cases it will be. *Posner* v. *Scott-Lewis* [1987] Ch 25 provides an illustration of the problems that might lie ahead. In *Posner* the plaintiff tenants sought specific performance of a covenant (cl. 3.11) by the defendant landlord to:

employ . . . a resident porter for the following purposes and for no other purposes:- (a) To keep clean the common staircases and entrance hall landings and passages and lift (b) To be responsible for looking after and stoking the central heating and domestic hot water boilers (c) To carry down rubbish from the properties to the dustbins outside the building every day.

The defendants admitted that they did not employ a resident porter but they contended that they were not in breach of clause 3.11 because the duties were being discharged by a non-resident porter. Mervyn Davies J rejected this submission on the ground that clause 3.11 clearly required the employment of a 'resident' porter and the defendants had, on their own admission, not employed a resident porter. Turning to the remedy, Mervyn Davies J concluded that clause 3.11 was a provision susceptible of specific performance. The defendants relied on the factually similar case of *Ryan* v. *Mutual Tontine Association* [1893] 1 Ch 116 but Mervyn Davies J dismissed the objection based on constant supervision. He stated that:

I do not see that such an order will occasion any protracted superintendence by the court. If the defendants without good cause fail to comply with the order in due time, then the plaintiffs can take appropriate enforcement proceedings against the defendants.

It is not easy to tell on which side of Lord Hoffmann's line *Posner* falls. Is it an example of a breach of an obligation to carry on an activity or a breach of an obligation to achieve a result?

One consequence of the decision is that it is now extremely unlikely that a court will make an order which requires a defendant to run a business. Lord Hoffmann gave a number of reasons in support of his conclusion that such an order should not be made. One of them was that one effect of making an order requiring the defendant to carry on a business might be to 'enable the plaintiff to enrich himself at the defend-ant's expense'. This is not a straightforward proposition. Had a specific performance order been made on the facts C.I.S. would only have received the performance for which it had contracted and what is wrong with that?

Lord Hoffmann concluded that clause 4(19) was insufficiently precise to be capable of specific performance. Two points should be noted here. The first is the link drawn between the vagueness of the obligation imposed by the contract upon the defendant and the 'constant supervision' as re-characterized by Lord Hoffmann. The two issues are linked on the basis that, if the terms of the court's order cannot be precisely drawn, the possibility of wasteful litigation over compliance is increased and the likelihood of the court making a specific performance order diminishes. Secondly, it is important to note the disagreement between the Court of Appeal and the House of Lords in relation to the precision of clause 4(19). The Court of Appeal held that the clause was sufficiently precise to be specifically enforceable and relied on the fact that the parties had operated the lease for a number of years without apparent difficulty. But, as Lord Hoffmann stated, past practice is not necessarily a good guide to future problems. In his view, the court must examine the language of the contract and not focus upon what the tenant had previously chosen to do. The question of the certainty of the term sought to be enforced must therefore be decided on the assumption that the court might have to enforce the order according to its terms. The court should not shut its eyes to future difficulties.

Lord Hoffmann attached far less significance to the conduct of the defendants than did the Court of Appeal. Is the effect of his speech to encourage commercial parties to engage in cynical, non-co-operative behaviour? Should the law of contract not do more in terms of encouraging commercial parties to behave in a more ethical manner?

The effect of the decision was to confine the plaintiffs to a claim for damages. Yet there is a question here as to the adequacy of the damages remedy. Suppose that the departure of the defendants led to such a loss of trade that other tenants were forced to close. Would the plaintiffs have been entitled to recover the loss of rent from such tenants from the defendants? Should the House of Lords not have held that the plaintiffs were entitled to the remedy of specific performance in order to avoid these problems of proof of loss? Assume that you are acting for the landlord of a major shopping centre. What steps can you take to ensure that, as far as possible, the anchor tenant does not terminate its tenancy before the end of the period of the lease? Alternatively, how do you ensure that an adequate remedy is available in the event of the tenant leaving the site early?

6. FUTURE DIRECTIONS

Should English law continue to develop a more liberal approach to the availability of specific performance and recognize the existence of a general right to specific performance? Professor Schwartz ('The Case for Specific Performance' (1979) 89 *Yale LJ* 271, 277) has argued that the law should develop in this direction. In his view the

restrictions on the availability of specific performance cannot be justified on the basis that damage awards are usually compensatory. On the contrary, the compensation goal implies that specific performance should be routinely available. This is because damage awards actually are undercompensatory in more cases than is commonly supposed; the fact of a specific performance request is itself good evidence that damages would be inadequate; and courts should delegate to promisees the decision of which remedy best satisfies the compensation goal.

Others have been more hesitant (see, for example, A Burrows, *Remedies for Torts and Breach of Contract* (3rd edn, Oxford University Press, 2004), pp. 472–475, A Kronman, 'Specific Performance' (1978) 45 *U Chicago L Rev* 351, and SA Smith, 'Performance, Punishment and the Nature of Contractual Obligation' (1997) 60 *MLR* 360). The principal arguments against the recognition of a general right to specific performance are that the present law is congruent with the intention of contracting parties and so reduces transaction costs (Kronman), the fact that the mitigation rule does not apply to claims for specific performance so that a general right to specific performance would not encourage claimants to take reasonable steps to minimize their loss (Burrows), that specific performance constitutes a greater infringement of individual liberty than a remedy in damages to the extent that it requires the defendant to carry out an act that he is no longer willing to perform (Burrows), and that forced performance is 'self-defeating' because the bonds created by the voluntary undertakings contained in the contract can only be realized by performance that is itself voluntary (Smith).

It is difficult to strike a balance between these competing arguments. The argument that specific performance amounts to an infringement of individual liberty can be countered by the argument that the initial promise was voluntarily given so that there is, in fact, no violation of individual liberty because the defendant is only being ordered to do that which he had already promised to do. The argument that mitigation does not apply to specific performance is true but against that must be weighed the argument that claimants have a strong incentive not to seek specific performance in practice because 'a breaching promisor is reluctant to perform and may be hostile' (Schwartz, above p. 277). This incentive to seek performance elsewhere from a willing contracting party should counter the temptation not to take reasonable steps to mitigate loss.

The argument that the present law is congruent with the intention of the contracting parties is more difficult to assess, largely because of the lack of empirical evidence as to the intentions of contracting parties. However, it has been argued (Kronman, 'Specific Performance' (1978) 45 *U Chicago L Rev* 351) that the present rules relating to specific performance do reflect the wishes of contracting parties as to the availability of the remedy and hence reduce the cost of negotiating contracts. Professor Kronman notes that the 'most important common feature' of the cases where specific performance is available is that the subject-matter of the contract is unique and he argues that it is only where the goods are unique that the parties will wish to contract for specific performance. This reasoning has been convincingly criticized by Professor Schwartz ('The Case for Specific Performance' (1979) 89 *Yale LJ* 271). It is likely that no one factor can be identified that conclusively determines the parties' remedial preferences; they are, in large part, context dependent. This being the case, it is very difficult to rely on the intention of the parties either in support of the current rule or as part of an attempt to widen the availability of specific performance.

Nevertheless, it may be the case that English law should, in fact, pay greater attention to the wishes of the contracting parties, at least where that intention is expressed in the terms of the contract. At present the decision whether or not to order specific performance lies in the discretion of the court: the parties cannot exercise that discretion on behalf of the court. In *Quadrant Visual Communications Ltd* v. *Hutchison Telephone UK Ltd* [1993] BCLC 442, 451 Stocker LJ stated that 'once the court is asked for the equitable remedy of specific performance, its discretion cannot be fettered' by the stipulation of the parties. The parties could not, by the terms of their contract, confine the role of the court to that of a 'rubber stamp'. While it is right that the courts should not be bound by the stipulation of the parties it can be argued that they should treat it with considerable respect, particularly where the parties are of equal bargaining power, and only refuse to give effect to it where there are strong countervailing policy considerations. In this respect, the facts of *Quadrant Visual Communications* might provide an illustration of such countervailing policy considerations. The plaintiff was held not to be entitled to specific performance on the ground that it was guilty of some 'trickery' in failing to disclose to the defendants an agreement which the court held that it should have disclosed to them.

A further factor fuelling the demand for a more liberal availability of specific performance is the impact of comparative law. The secondary role accorded to specific performance in English law is said to contrast with civilian systems where specific performance (or specific implement, as it is known in Scotland) is a primary remedy. In the *Co-operative Insurance Society* case (above) Lord Hoffmann suggested that the difference between common law and civilian systems can be overplayed. Support for this proposition can be gleaned from the fact that there appears to be a high degree of correlation between the situations in which the different legal systems refuse to order specific performance. Courts in most jurisdictions are reluctant to order specific performance where performance of the contract would be impossible, unlawful, or expose the performing party to severe hardship. The difference between the different systems lies, not so much in the circumstances in which the courts generally refuse to order specific performance, but in the starting point for the reasoning of the court. In most civilian jurisdictions specific performance is a primary remedy so that the court will assume that the claimant is entitled to the remedy unless the defendant can show that, for some reason, the claimant is not entitled to it. In England, on the other hand, it is for the claimant to establish his entitlement to specific performance. It could be said that this is no more than a difference in the location of the burden of proof. In England it is the claimant who bears the burden of establishing his entitlement to specific performance, whereas in civilian systems it is for the defendant to show that the claimant is not entitled to the remedy. On the other hand, it can be argued that the difference is a matter of substance and not simply a matter relating to the burden of proof. Thus it has proved to be very difficult to bring common law and civilian systems together when drafting international conventions. Article 28 of the Vienna Convention on Contracts for the International Sale of Goods states:

If, in accordance with the provisions of this Convention, one party is entitled to require performance of any obligation by the other party, a court is not bound to enter a judgement for specific performance unless the court would do so under its own law in respect of similar contracts of sale not governed by this Convention.

This provision is clearly a compromise between common law and civil law systems in that it leaves it to domestic law to determine the entitlement of a seller or a buyer of goods to specific performance. It does not attempt to bridge the gap between the common law and civil law: rather, it draws attention to that gap by leaving the problem to national law.

Rather more progress was, however, made by those responsible for drafting the Principles of European Contract Law. Article 9:102 states:

Non-monetary Obligations

(1) The aggrieved party is entitled to specific performance of an obligation other than one to pay money, including the remedying of a defective performance.

(2) Specific performance cannot, however, be obtained where:

(a) performance would be unlawful or impossible; or

(b) performance would cause the obligor unreasonable effort or expense; or

(c) the performance consists in the provision of services or work of a personal character or depends upon a personal relationship; or

(d) the aggrieved party may reasonably obtain performance from another source.

(3) The aggrieved party will lose the right to specific performance if it fails to seek it within a reasonable time after it has or ought to have become aware of the non-performance.

This provision also represents a compromise but it is a rather more elaborate one than that found in the Vienna Convention (a similar compromise is to be found in Article 7.2.2 of the Unidroit Principles of International Commercial Contracts).

Paragraph (1) recognizes the existence of a general entitlement to specific perform-ance (thus reflecting the approach taken in civil law systems) while paragraphs (2) and (3) take account of (at least some of) the concerns of English lawyers by provid-ing that, in certain circumstances, specific performance is not to be ordered (although it should be noted that it is difficult to tell how far these concerns have been taken into account because much depends on the meaning of phrases such as 'unreasonable effort or expense' and the weight to be given to these factors—for example, how would the *Co-operative Insurance Society* case have been decided under Article 9:102?).

Article 9:102 attempts to strike a balance between the competing interests at stake and the reality is that a balance must be struck between these interests in all legal systems (whether common law or civilian). On the one hand, we have the interest of the claimant in obtaining the performance for which he contracted and to which he claims to be entitled. On the other hand, to require the defendant to perform his contractual obligations may cause him unnecessary hardship or result in an inefficient use of resources. It is no easy task to strike the right balance. While English law has moved some way from its original, restrictive approach to specific performance, it still has some way to go before it can be said to have struck the right balance. As cases such as *Co-operative Insurance Society* demonstrate, the courts can still, on occasion, give insufficient emphasis to the performance interest of the claimant.

7. FURTHER READING

KRONMAN, A, 'Specific Performance' (1978) 45 *U Chicago L Rev* 351.

SCHWARTZ, G, 'The Case for Specific Performance' (1979) 89 *Yale LJ* 271.

SMITH, SA, 'Performance, Punishment and the Nature of Contractual Obligation' (1997) 60 *MLR* 360.

PART V

THIRD PARTY RIGHTS

27

THIRD PARTIES

1. CENTRAL ISSUES

1. The general rule at common law in England is that a third party cannot acquire rights under a contract to which he is not a party nor can he be subject to a burden by a contract to which he is not a party. These rules are known as the doctrine of privity of contract.

2. The rule that a third party cannot acquire rights under a contract to which he is not a party has proved to be a controversial one and the courts over time have created a number of exceptions to it. But the exceptions are of limited scope and they did not bring to an end the demands for reform of this rule.

3. Reform was eventually implemented in the form of the Contracts (Rights of Third Parties) Act 1999. The 1999 Act provides a relatively simple mechanism by which contracting parties can confer upon a third party a right to enforce a term of their contract. The dominant philosophy which underpins the 1999 Act is one of freedom of contract, so it is possible for the contracting parties to define for themselves the scope of the third party right of action.

4. The 1999 Act has not, however, escaped criticism. Some have questioned the justifications put forward in support of the proposition that a third party should be entitled to enforce a term of a contract to which he is not a party. The principal objections put forward are that the third party is not a promisee, nor has he provided any consideration for the promise, and so he ought not to be entitled to a remedy in his own right. The competing arguments for and against recognition of a third party right of action are considered in this chapter.

5. The 1999 Act does not abolish the exceptions to the doctrine of privity that pre-dated the Act. However it is likely that the practical significance of these exceptions will diminish over time. Contracting parties who wish to confer an enforceable right of action upon a third party are more likely to use the 1999 Act than the pre-Act exceptions.

6. A contracting party who, in breach of contract, fails to confer a benefit on a third party will incur a liability towards the other party to the contract. The remedies available to the latter party are not affected by the 1999 Act and, in certain circumstances, he may be able to obtain a remedy, such as a specific performance order, which will be of benefit to the third party. The circumstances in which a contracting party can sue and recover damages on behalf of a third party is an issue of some controversy that is discussed in this chapter.

7. As a general rule parties to a contract cannot impose an obligation on a third party without the latter's consent. The existence of this general rule is widely accepted. While it is the subject of some exceptions, neither the general rule nor its exceptions are affected by the 1999 Act.

2. INTRODUCTION

A contract creates rights and obligations as between the parties to the contract. But what impact does it have on third parties, that is to say, those who are not party to the contract? Broadly speaking, there are two questions to be answered here. The first is whether or not a third party can acquire any rights under the contract, and the second is whether or not the contract can impose upon him obligations or liabilities. The general rule which English law has adopted is that the contract creates rights and imposes obligations only between the parties to the contract: the third party thus neither acquires rights under the contract nor is he subject to liabilities. This general rule is known as the doctrine of privity of contract. The rule is the subject of a number of exceptions and the scope of these exceptions, particularly in relation to the acquisition of contractual rights by third parties, has been a source of considerable controversy. Indeed, Professor Treitel has stated (*Some Landmarks of Twentieth Century Contract Law* (Oxford University Press, 2002), p. 47) that the 'most significant doctrinal development in English contract law in the twentieth century was no doubt the outcome of what I shall call the battle over privity'. The outcome of that battle was the enactment of the Contracts (Rights of Third Parties) Act 1999 (generally referred to in this chapter as 'the 1999 Act'). This Act is now the most important source of the law relating to third party rights in that it provides a relatively simple means by which contracting parties can, if they so desire, confer upon a third party the right to enforce a term of the contract. It is, however, important to note that the Act does not purport to abolish the doctrine of privity with the consequence that, in a case that falls outside the scope of the Act, the doctrine of privity remains applicable. On the other hand, it can be said that the Act introduces into English law a limited third party right of action.

The bulk of this chapter will be devoted to the topic of the acquisition of contractual rights by third parties. The reason for this is that it has proved to be the most contentious aspect of the doctrine of privity. By contrast, the rule that the parties to a contract cannot impose a contractual liability upon a third party is generally accepted, although it too is a rule that is subject to some exceptions. The reason for the general acceptance of the latter rule is that it would be an 'unwarranted infringement of a third party's liberty if contracting parties were able, as a matter of course, to impose burdens on a third party without his or her consent' (Law Commission, *Privity of Contract: Contracts for the Benefit of Third Parties*, Law Com No 242, 1996, para 2.1). Before examining the dual aspects of the doctrine of privity, it is important to examine the relationship between third party rights of action and the contract structures that are commonly adopted in commercial practice.

3. CONTRACT STRUCTURES

An impression that is often gained from a reading of contract cases is that all contracts have two parties to them and that each contract is separate and distinct from every other contract. Any such impression is misleading. Contracts can and frequently do involve more than two parties. But that is not our present concern. Rather our concern is with the proposition that each contract is separate and distinct from every other contract. This proposition is simply not true. Contracts are linked in many complex ways. Two hypotheticals will illustrate the point, one drawn from the commercial sphere and the other based on a more commonplace example involving a consumer. In the case of the commercial transaction the initial assumption that will be made is that the law does not entitle two contracting parties to confer a right on a third party to enforce a term of their contract.

The commercial example is based loosely on the facts of the case of *Junior Books Ltd* v. *Veitchi Co Ltd* [1983] 1 AC 520. A company (X) wishes to have a new factory built and, for this purpose, enters into a contract with another company (Y) which agrees to design and build the factory. Y cannot provide all of the necessary services itself and so, to the knowledge of X, it plans to sub-contract some of the work to company Z. X is content to allow Y to sub-contract the work in this way and is also generally satisfied with the quality of Z's work but it nevertheless harbours a concern that an employee of Z might, through his negligence, cause damage to the works and thereby inflict loss on X. How can X take steps to protect itself in this situation? One possibility is to resort to a claim in tort in the event of negligence on the part of an employee of Z. The problem with this strategy is that X is likely to encounter severe difficulties in bringing a claim in tort in the event that it suffers economic loss as a result of the negligence of Z (the courts being extremely reluctant to find liability in tort in the case of economic loss: see *D & F Estates Ltd* v. *Church Commissioners for England and Wales* [1989] AC 177).

What contractual routes of redress are open to X? The obvious claim is against Y, its contracting party. Here it is important for X to ensure that Y assumes a contractual responsibility for the quality of the works that includes the work to be carried out by Z. Then, in the event of a breach of duty by Z, X can sue Y for breach of contract and then leave Y to seek redress from Z. This is a commonly used structure, although the risk inherent in it is that Y will become insolvent, leaving X with no obvious means of redress against Z. An alternative strategy is for X to require that Z enter into a contract with it under which Z promises to exercise reasonable care and skill in the performance of its obligations. Such a warranty, commonly known as a collateral warranty (an example of which is to be found in *Alfred McAlpine Construction Ltd* v. *Panatown Ltd* [2001] 1 AC 518, discussed in more detail at p. 1029 above), will generally be entered into in the form of a deed in order to avoid any argument about whether or not X has provided consideration for Z's promise to exercise reasonable care and skill.

We can look at the same transaction from the perspective of Z. Z may be concerned about its exposure to a claim by X. For example, it may have a very good working relationship with Y and prefer to assume responsibility only to Y. It may therefore be unwilling to provide a collateral warranty to X (although it may not in practice have the bargaining power to resist such a demand).

We can see that there are two principal structural options open to the parties in this case. The first is for Z to assume a contractual responsibility towards Y and for Y to assume contractual responsibility to X but Z does not assume such a responsibility towards X. In this example (subject to the possibility of a claim in tort) liability will be left to flow down the chain of contracts. Thus in the event of a breach by Z which results in loss to X, X will sue Y and Y will then sue Z but X cannot sue Z directly. The second is for Z to assume a direct contractual responsibility to X in addition to Y's contractual responsibilities to X. The point to grasp here is that the parties have a choice to make and (at least in the case of parties who are legally advised) they will have their reasons for choosing one type of contract structure in preference to another and, further, they will expect the courts to respect and give effect to the distribution of rights and obligations set out by the particular contract structure they have chosen.

Now let us feed into the equation the possibility of a third party right of action. The obvious advantage of a third party right of action is that it provides another means by which X can protect its position. X could insist that Y insert a clause into its contract with Z the effect of which would be to confer on X a right to enforce the term of the contract by which Z assumed an obligation to exercise reasonable care and skill in the performance of its duties. The ability to confer an enforceable right of action on the third party appears to perform a useful function (although not everyone accepts this, see p. 1233–1236 below) in that it provides a means by which contracting parties can give effect to their intention to confer an enforceable right of action upon a third party. But the parties will obviously not want the courts to imply the existence of a third party right of action in the case where the parties have chosen to structure their transaction in such a way that Z does not assume a direct contractual responsibility to X but only to Y. In such a case recognition of a direct third party right of action in X would cut across the contract structure adopted by the parties and could result in a distribution of liability other than that intended by the parties. It must be stressed at this point that such a result is not an inevitable consequence of the introduction of a third party right of action. But this example does underline the need for any third party right of action to be sensitive to the contract structure that has been adopted by the parties.

Our second example is a consumer transaction and can be dealt with more quickly. Suppose that a consumer wishes to buy a car on credit but the car dealer cannot provide the credit facilities himself. A finance house is, however, prepared to provide the finance. How can these three parties structure their transaction? They have a range of possibilities open to them but these possibilities can be divided into two broad groups. The first and most commonly adopted structure is for the car dealer to sell the car to the finance house which will then supply the car to the consumer on credit terms. Very often consumers are unaware of the fact that this is the structure which they have agreed. As far as they are concerned they are purchasing a car from the dealer. But in law there are two transactions taking place, not one. The first is the sale by the car dealer to the finance house and the second is the transaction between the finance house and the consumer. One drawback to this structure is that, in the absence of a collateral contract (which the courts may be prepared to imply, see *Andrews* v. *Hopkinson* [1957] 1 QB 229), there is no direct contractual relationship between the dealer and the consumer. This may be a problem in the event that the car proves to be defective. The consumer wants a claim against the dealer, not the finance house and, for that matter, the finance house does not want to involve itself in the repair of the car. Its intention is to provide the finance, not the services of a mechanic. But in legal theory (at least as far as the common law is concerned) the consumer has a claim against the finance house and the finance house has a claim against the dealer, but the consumer does not have a direct claim against the dealer, albeit in practice the problem will be resolved by the consumer dealing directly with the dealer.

The second alternative is for the dealer to sell the car to the consumer and then either the consumer or the dealer enter into a credit transaction with the finance house. Thus the dealer may agree to sell the car to the consumer and then assign its contractual rights against the consumer to the finance house in return for an immediate payment by the finance house. Suppose that the consumer has agreed to pay the dealer £5,500 for the car over a two-year period (this sum being known as a receivable). In return for assigning to the finance house its rights against the consumer the dealer may be able to obtain immediate payment from the finance house of a percentage of the sum due to it from the consumer, say £5,000. The dealer may even have an agreement with the finance house under which the dealer agrees to sell all its receivables to the finance house in return for immediate payment. Alternatively, the dealer may sell the car to the consumer and the consumer can then enter into a transaction with the finance house in order to obtain the credit necessary to pay the dealer (such as a sale and lease-back). In both of these alternatives there is a direct contractual relationship between the dealer and the consumer so that this time the consumer will have a direct claim against the dealer in the event that the car proves to be defective. But, once again, the point to be made is that contracting parties (at least in the case of the dealer and the finance house) frequently give a great deal of thought to the contractual structures which they adopt and they take into account a broad range of factors in making a decision about the contract structure that is most beneficial to them (these factors include matters such as liability for defects and tax and accounting considerations). As was the case in the example drawn from the commercial sphere, any introduction of a third party right of action must be sensitive to this fact and not produce a right of action which cuts across, or undermines, the distribution of rights and obligations that has been agreed by the parties.

4. THIRD PARTIES AND THE ACQUISITION OF CONTRACTUAL RIGHTS

The enactment of the 1999 Act constitutes a watershed in any discussion of the contractual rights of third parties. Given its importance today it should be the first item for discussion. Yet it is very difficult, if not impossible, to appreciate the significance of the Act without an understanding of the way in which the law has evolved. The Act must be placed in its context. In order to do this it is necessary to examine the cases which established the general rule at common law that a third party does not have a right to enforce a term of a contract to which he is not a party, the various exceptions to the general rule that were recognized prior to the enactment of the 1999 Act, and the arguments that were advanced both in support of, and in opposition to, the reform of the law that culminated in the 1999 Act.

The discussion of the acquisition of contractual rights by third parties will therefore be divided into six parts. The first part will focus upon the two leading cases in which the doctrine of privity of contract was established at common law. The second part shifts attention to the position of the contracting parties themselves. It may seem out of place to analyse the rights of the contracting parties in the context of a discussion of the rights of the third party. But this is not so. Take the case of a contract between A and B under which B promises to do some work for A and A promises, in return, to pay a sum of money to C. Assume that B does the work for A but that A refuses in breach of contract to pay any money to C. In this situation B (generally referred to as 'the promisee') has a claim against A for breach of contract and the question which falls for consideration is whether or not B can obtain a remedy from A the effect of which will be to give C the promised performance. The third part returns to the position of the third party and considers the exceptions to the doctrine of privity that were recognized at common law and by statute prior to the enactment of the 1999 Act. The fourth part is devoted to the subject of third parties, exclusion clauses, and exclusive jurisdiction clauses. In many ways this line of cases could have been accommodated within part three but they raise issues of some difficulty and so merit separate discussion. The fifth part is concerned with the debate over the reform of the doctrine of privity that preceded the enactment of the 1999 Act. The final part is devoted to the 1999 Act itself. The principal provisions of the Act are analysed and consideration will also be given to the impact of the Act on some of the cases that pre-dated the 1999 Act.

(a) THE GENERAL RULE AT COMMON LAW: THIRD PARTIES HAVE NO RIGHT OF ACTION

Professor Ibbetson states (*A Historical Introduction to the Law of Obligations* (Oxford University Press, 1999), p. 241) that the 'rule that a third party could not enforce rights arising under a contract has been a feature of English law since at least the thirteenth century'. English law was not alone in adopting this stance. According to classical Roman law a contract created rights and obligations only between the parties to it and did not have any effect, whether in terms of the acquisition of rights or the imposition of liabilities, upon third parties. Over time the influence of classical Roman law on the continent of Europe waned. The influence of natural lawyers, such as Grotius, and the emphasis which they placed on the importance of the will of the parties and upon consensus or agreement led to the gradual recognition of the contract in favour of a third party. Thus Professor Zimmermann concludes (*The Law of Obligations* (Oxford University Press, 1996), p. 42) that in 'the 17th century the great breakthrough towards the recognition of the contract in favour of the third party had taken place and the prevailing new attitude had already influenced many of the codes of that time'. For a time it appeared that English law might follow the lead taken on the continent of Europe. Cases could be found which appeared to support the existence of a third party right of action (see, for example, *Dutton* v. *Poole* (1678) 2 Lev 210; 83 ER 523, *Pigott* v. *Thompson* (1802) 3 Bos & Pul 98; 126 ER 799, and *Carnegie* v. *Waugh* (1823) 1 LJ (KB) 89). But, equally, there were cases which were hostile to the existence of such a third party right of action (see, for example, *Crow* v. *Rogers* (1724) 1 Str 591; 93 ER 719 and *Price* v. *Easton* (1833) 4 B & Ad 433; 110 ER 518). The cases thus appeared to be in some disarray. The case which is credited with resolving the conflict and committing English law to the rule that a third party cannot acquire contractual rights under a contract to which he is not a party is the decision of the Court of Queen's Bench in *Tweddle* v. *Atkinson* (1861) 1 B & S 393, as subsequently confirmed by the House of Lords in the leading case of *Dunlop Pneumatic Tyre Co Ltd* v. *Selfridge and Co Ltd* [1915] AC 847. These two cases established the doctrine of privity of contract as a 'fundamental' principle of English contract law and it is therefore necessary to examine them in more detail.

Tweddle v. Atkinson

(1861) 1 B & S 393; 121 ER 762, Court of Queen's Bench

William Tweddle married the daughter of William Guy. Prior to the wedding William Guy entered into a verbal agreement with John Tweddle, William Tweddle's father, under which both promised to give their children marriage portions. After the wedding had taken place, they entered into a written agreement which was intended to give effect to their verbal promises under which William Guy agreed to pay £200 to William Tweddle and John Tweddle agreed to pay him £100. The agreement contained the following sentence: 'it is hereby further agreed by the aforesaid William Guy and the said John Tweddle that the said William Tweddle has full power to sue the said parties in any Court of law or equity for the aforesaid sums hereby promised and specified'. William Guy failed to pay the promised amount and so William Tweddle brought an action against the executor of William Guy's estate for the sum of £200. His claim failed.

Wightman J

Some of the old decisions appear to support the proposition that a stranger to the consideration of a contract may maintain an action upon it, if he stands in such a near relationship to the party from whom the consideration proceeds, that he may be considered a party to the consideration. The strongest of those cases is that cited in *Bourne* v. *Mason* 1 Ventr 6, in which it was held that the daughter of a physician might maintain assumpsit upon a promise by her father to give her a sum of money if he performed a certain cure. But there is no modern case in which the proposition has been supported. On the contrary, it is now established that no stranger to the consideration can take advantage of a contract, although made for his benefit.

Crompton J

... The modern cases have, in effect, overruled the old decisions; they shew that the consideration must move from the party entitled to sue upon the contract. It would be a monstrous proposition to say that a person was a party to the contract for the purpose of suing upon it for his own advantage, and not a party to it for the purpose of being sued . . .

Blackburn J

. . . Mr Mellish [counsel for the plaintiff] admits that in general no action can be maintained upon a promise, unless the consideration moves from the party to whom it is made. But he says that there is an exception; namely, that when the consideration moves from a father, and the contract is for the benefit of his son, the natural love and affection between the father and son gives the son the right to sue as if the consideration had proceeded from himself. And *Dutton and Wife* v. *Poole* was cited for this. We cannot overrule a decision of the Exchequer Chamber; but there is a distinct ground on which that case cannot be supported. The cases . . . shew that natural love and affection are not a sufficient consideration whereon an action of assumpsit may be founded.

COMMENTARY

Why did William Tweddle's claim fail? Two possible reasons can be given. The first is that he was not a party to the contract concluded between his father and his father-in-law. The second is that he did not provide any consideration for William Guy's promise to pay him £200. Which reason was invoked by the judges in *Tweddle*? It would appear that their focus was on the latter rule. Counsel for the defendant submitted that 'it is now settled that an action for breach of contract must be brought by the person from whom the consideration moved' and cited *Price* v. *Easton* (1833) 4 B & Ad 433 in support of his submission. Counsel for the plaintiff, Mr Mellish, accepted that there was such a general rule but submitted that there was an exception to it 'in the case of contracts made by parents for the purpose of providing for their children'. Thus battle was joined on the issue whether or not William Tweddle was a 'stranger' to the consideration provided by his father. The acceptance by Mr Mellish of this general rule has been criticized (see R Flannigan, 'Privity—The End of an Era (Error)' (1987) 103 *LQR* 564, 571) on the basis that 'it seems entirely unsatisfactory that the general third party right of action should be lost on an unnecessary concession'. This criticism is not without foundation. As we have noted, the cases did not all point one way (although one would scarcely guess this from the tenor of the judgments in *Tweddle*) and in 1859 the New York Court of Appeals had taken a step in the opposite direction in *Lawrence* v. *Fox*, 20 NY 268 (1859) when it recognized the existence of a third party right of action (although the case did not even merit a mention either in argument or in the judgments in *Tweddle*). On the other hand, it could be said that the criticism misses the point in that the reason given by the judges for the failure of William Tweddle's claim was not that he was a third party but that he had not provided any consideration for the promise made by William Guy.

Two further points should be noted about *Tweddle*. The first is that it underlines the fact that there is a close relationship between the rule that consideration must move from the promisee (on which see p. 230 above) and the doctrine of privity. In many cases the former rule renders consideration of the latter unnecessary. *Tweddle* itself illustrates this point. The judges found that William Tweddle had not provided any consideration. His claim was therefore doomed to fail and it was not necessary for them to consider whether or not his claim was also bound to fail on the ground that he was a third party. It is therefore only in the rare case where the third party has provided consideration but is not party to the agreement that the need for a distinct third party rule emerges. Such cases are likely to be very rare. Professor Treitel gives the following example (*The Law of Contract* (11th edn, Sweet & Maxwell, 2003), p. 587):

A father might, for example, promise his daughter to pay £1,000 to anyone who married her. A man who married the daughter with knowledge of and in reliance on such a promise might provide consideration for it, but could not enforce it, as it was not addressed to him.

In this example the doctrines of consideration and privity do appear to be separate and distinct (unless one takes the view advocated by Professor Smith (JC Smith and JAC Thomas, *A Casebook on Contract* (11th edn, Sweet & Maxwell, 2000) pp. 279–280) that, 'only an offeree can give consideration to the offeror so as to make a contract' in which case there would be no contract at all on the facts of Professor Treitel's hypothetical and so no contract for anyone to be privy to).

The second point to note about *Tweddle* relates to the position of William Tweddle's father, John Tweddle. Why did he not bring a claim against William Guy's executor? One reason might have been that he had not paid his son the promised £100. Lord Denning in *Beswick* v. *Beswick* [1966] Ch 538, 553–554 offered the following analysis of *Tweddle*:

The action failed for the very good reason that the husband's father had not done his part. He had not paid his promised £100. The son could not himself be sued for his father's failure to pay the £100: for he was no party to the contract. So he could not be allowed to sue his wife's father for the £200. . . . But if the husband's father had paid his £100 and thus wholly performed his part, then the husband's father in his lifetime, or his executor after his death, could have sued the wife's father or his executor for the £200. As Wightman J observed 1 B & S 393, 397:

'If the father of the plaintiff had paid the £100 which he promised, might not he have sued the father of the plaintiff's wife on his express promise?'

To which the answer would undoubtedly be: 'Yes, he could sue and recover the £200', but he would recover it not for his own benefit, or for the benefit of the estate, but for the benefit of the son.

The difficulty with this view is that no reference is made in the judgments to the position of John Tweddle. Lord Denning's reference to the observation of Wightman J is to an observation made by him in the course of argument and it does not amount to a categorical statement that the promised £100 had not in fact been paid. The point is, however, one of some significance and we shall return to it when we come to apply the 1999 Act to the facts of *Tweddle* (p. 1240 below). Nevertheless, it is not possible to confine the rule laid down in *Tweddle* in such a narrow way. The reason for this is to be found in the next case, a decision of the House of Lords.

Dunlop Pneumatic Tyre Co Ltd v. Selfridge and Co Ltd

[1915] AC 847, House of Lords

In 1911, Messrs Dew, motor accessory agents, agreed to buy a quantity of tyres and other goods from Dunlop (the appellants) who carried on business as motor tyre manufacturers. Dunlop agreed to give Dew certain discounts off their list price and Dew in return agreed not to sell Dunlop's goods to any person at less than the list prices. However, it was also agreed that Dew could give genuine trade customers a limited discount off Dunlop's list prices if, as agents of Dunlop, Dew obtained from the trader a similar written undertaking that it would observe the list prices. On 2 January 1912, the respondents, Selfridge, large storekeepers who sold tyres by retail to the public, ordered Dunlop tyres from Dew. Dew agreed to give Selfridge certain discounts off Dunlop's list prices and Selfridge agreed not to sell any Dunlop tyres to private customers at less than the list prices. Dunlop sued Selfridge for breach of this undertaking when Selfridge sold Dunlop tyres to private customers for less than the list prices. The trial judge gave judgment for Dunlop. The Court of Appeal reversed this decision on the ground that the agreement of 2 January 1912 was not a contract between Dunlop and Selfridge but between Dew and Selfridge. The House of Lords dismissed Dunlop's appeal.

Viscount Haldane LC

My Lords, in the law of England certain principles are fundamental. One is that only a person who is a party to a contract can sue on it. Our law knows nothing of a jus quaesitum tertio[1] arising by way of contract. Such a right may be conferred by way of property, as, for example, under a trust, but it cannot be conferred on a stranger to a contract as a right to enforce the contract in personam. A second principle is that if a person with whom a contract not under seal has been made is to be able to enforce it consideration must have been given by him to the promisor or to some other person at the promisor's request. These two principles are not recognized in the same fashion by the jurisprudence of certain Continental countries or of Scotland, but here they are well established. A third proposition is that a principal not named in the contract may sue upon it if the promisee really contracted as his agent. But again, in order to entitle him so to sue, he must have given consideration either personally or through the promisee, acting as his agent in giving it.

My Lords, in the case before us, I am of opinion that the consideration, the allowance of what was in reality part of the discount to which Messrs Dew, the promisees, were entitled as between themselves and the appellants, was to be given by Messrs Dew on their own account, and was not in substance, any more than in form, an allowance made by the appellants. The case for the appellants is that they permitted and enabled Messrs Dew, with the knowledge and by the desire of the respondents, to sell to the latter on the terms of the contract of January 2, 1912. But it appears to me that even if this is so the answer is conclusive. Messrs Dew sold to the respondents goods which they had a title to obtain from the appellants independently of this contract. The consideration by way of discount under the contract of January 2 was to come wholly out of Messrs Dew's pocket, and neither directly nor indirectly out of that of the appellants. If the appellants enabled

---

[1] A *jus quaesitum tertio* is a third party right of action.

them to sell to the respondents on the terms they did, this was not done as any part of the terms of the contract sued on.

No doubt it was provided as part of these terms that the appellants should acquire certain rights, but these rights appear on the face of the contract as jura quaesita tertio, which the appellants could not enforce. Moreover, even if this difficulty can be got over by regarding the appellants as the principals of Messrs Dew in stipulating for the rights in question, the only consideration disclosed by the contract is one given by Messrs Dew, not as their agents, but as principals acting on their own account.

The conclusion to which I have come on the point as to consideration renders it unnecessary to decide the further question as to whether the appellants can claim that a bargain was made in this contract by Messrs Dew as their agents; a bargain which, apart from the point as to consideration, they could therefore enforce. If it were necessary to express an opinion on this further question, a difficulty as to the position of Messrs Dew would have to be considered. Two contracts—one by a man on his own account as principal, and another by the same man as agent—may be validly comprised in the same piece of paper. But they must be two contracts, and not one as here. I do not think that a man can treat one and the same contract as made by him in two capacities. He cannot be regarded as contracting for himself and for another uno flatu.

My Lords, the form of the contract which we have to interpret leaves the appellants in this dilemma, that, if they say that Messrs Dew contracted on their behalf, they gave no consideration, and if they say they gave consideration in the shape of a permission to the respondents to buy, they must set up further stipulations, which are neither to be found in the contract sued upon nor are germane to it, but are really inconsistent with its structure. That contract has been reduced to writing, and it is in the writing that we must look for the whole of the terms made between the parties. These terms cannot, in my opinion consistently with the settled principles of English law, be construed as giving to the appellants any enforceable rights as against the respondents.

I think that the judgment of the Court of Appeal was right, and I move that the appeal be dismissed with costs.

Lord Dunedin

My Lords, I confess that this case is to my mind apt to nip any budding affection which one might have had for the doctrine of consideration. For the effect of that doctrine in the present case is to make it possible for a person to snap his fingers at a bargain deliberately made, a bargain not in itself unfair, and which the person seeking to enforce it has a legitimate interest to enforce. Notwithstanding these considerations I cannot say that I have ever had any doubt that the judgment of the Court of Appeal was right.

My Lords, I am content to adopt from a work of Sir Frederick Pollock, to which I have often been under obligation, the following words as to consideration: 'An act or forbearance of one party, or the promise thereof, is the price for which the promise of the other is bought, and the promise thus given for value is enforceable'. (Pollock on Contracts, 8th ed., p. 175.)

Now the agreement sued on is an agreement which on the face of it is an agreement between Dew and Selfridge. But speaking for myself, I should have no difficulty in the circumstances of this case in holding it proved that the agreement was truly made by Dew as agent for Dunlop, or in other words that Dunlop was the undisclosed principal, and as such can sue on the agreement. None the less, in order to enforce it he must show consideration, as above defined, moving from Dunlop to Selfridge.

In the circumstances, how can he do so? The agreement in question is not an agreement for sale. It is only collateral to an agreement for sale; but that agreement for sale is an agreement entirely between Dew and Selfridge. The tyres, the property in which upon the bargain is transferred to Selfridge, were the property of Dew, not of Dunlop, for Dew under his agreement with Dunlop held these tyres as proprietor, and not as agent. What then did Dunlop do, or forbear to do, in a question with Selfridge? The answer must be, nothing. He did not do anything, for Dew, having the right of property in the tyres, could give a good title to any one he liked, subject, it might be, to an action of damages at the instance of Dunlop for breach of contract, which action, however, could never create a vitium reale in the property of the tyres. He did not forbear in anything, for he had no action against Dew which he gave up, because Dew had fulfilled his contract with Dunlop in obtaining, on the occasion of the sale, a contract from Selfridge in the terms prescribed.

To my mind, this ends the case. That there are methods of framing a contract which will cause persons in the position of Selfridge to become bound, I do not doubt. But that has not been done in this instance; and as Dunlop's advisers must have known of the law of consideration, it is their affair that they have not so drawn the contract.

I think the appeal should be dismissed.

Lords Atkinson, Parker of Waddington, Sumner, and **Parmoor** delivered concurring judgments.

COMMENTARY

Dunlop is a case of great significance largely because of Viscount Haldane's statement (in the first extracted paragraph of his judgment) to the effect that the rule that only a person who is a party to a contract can sue upon it is separate and distinct from the requirements of the doctrine of consideration (a point subsequently affirmed by the Privy Council in *Kepong Prospecting Ltd* v. *Schmidt* [1968] AC 810). But the fact that they have their separate existence does not remove the fact that they are closely related in the sense that the 'rule that only a party to the agreement can enforce it will often lead to the same result as the rule that consideration must move from the promisee' (GH Treitel, *The Law of Contract* (11th edn, Sweet & Maxwell, 2003), p. 587). The close connection between the two doctrines can be seen in *Dunlop* itself in that the greater part of the judgments was taken up with the doctrine of consideration. Indeed, it was the doctrine of consideration that was the object of Lord Dunedin's wrath. However Lord Dunedin may not have been correct in his assertion that the doctrine of consideration made it possible for Selfridge to snap their fingers at a bargain deliberately made. While the contract was not enforceable by Dunlop, it does not follow that it could not have been enforced by Dew. Had Dew sought an injunction to restrain further breaches of contract by Selfridge it probably would have been successful (although it would have been more difficult for Dew to have sued Selfridge for damages because it did not appear to have suffered any loss as a result of the breach and it is unlikely that, in the state of the law as it was then, it could have recovered damages for the loss suffered by Dunlop, a third party (on which see p. 1195)).

Two further points should be noted about *Dunlop*. The first is that the aim of

Dunlop in setting up this scheme was to fix the price of its products by setting minimum prices at which they could be sold. Such price maintenance agreements are now regulated by statute in the public interest (see generally the Competition Act 1998). But it is important to note that no point was taken before their Lordships to the effect that the agreements were invalid on the ground that they were contrary to public policy. On the contrary, their Lordships assumed that price maintenance agreements were in principle valid and enforceable at common law. It is therefore not possible to confine *Dunlop* on the basis that the case was concerned with 'the maintenance of prices to the public disadvantage' (as Denning LJ appeared to suggest in *Smith and Snipes Hall Farm* v. *River Douglas Catchment Board* [1949] 2 KB 500, 519). As far as their Lordships were concerned, the failure of Dunlop's claim had nothing to do with the fact that the public might have been disadvantaged in any way by Dunlop's attempt to fix the prices of its products.

The second point is that Viscount Haldane recognizes that the principle that only a person who is a party to a contract can sue is not absolute. Two exceptions are apparent from his judgment (and from the judgment of Lord Dunedin). The first is that it is possible to confer a right of action upon a third party via a trust. This is an important point and the device of a trust of a promise has become a recognized exception to the doctrine of privity, albeit that it operates within narrow limits (on which see p. 1203 below). The second exception is the doctrine of agency. Thus Viscount Haldane states that 'a principal not named in the contract may sue upon it if the promisee really contracted as his agent'. On the facts of the case, Dunlop was not able to avail itself of the agency exception because of the finding that the consideration had been supplied by Dew on its own account and not as agent for Dunlop. But, had Dew acted within the scope of its authority as an agent for Dunlop in concluding the contract with Selfridge, it would have resulted in the creation of a contract between Dunlop and Selfridge with the consequence that Dunlop would have been entitled to bring a claim against Selfridge (agency is discussed in slightly more detail at p. 1207 below).

(b) THE RIGHTS OF THE PROMISEE

In both *Tweddle* and *Dunlop* the temptation is to focus attention exclusively on the position of the third party and the defendant and thereby ignore the position of the defendant's contracting party (John Tweddle and Messrs Dew respectively). The emphasis on the position of the third party and the defendant is understandable given that they were the parties to the litigation. Nevertheless, sight must not be lost of the position of the defendant's contracting party ('the promisee'). There are at least three reasons why attention must be paid to the position of the promisee. The first is that the promisee has paid for the defendant's promise of performance, whereas the third party is generally no more than a gratuitous beneficiary of that promise. On this basis it can be argued that the law's primary concern should be for the position of the promisee, not the third party. Secondly, the defendant may have a defence to any claim brought by the promisee and this defence should also be available to the claim brought by the third party. *Tweddle* itself may be an example in this category (on the

assumption that Lord Denning was correct in stating that the promisee, John Tweddle, had not carried out his obligation to pay £100 to his son). Thirdly, there is a
temptation to assume that a failure to provide the third party with a remedy will
enable the defendant to break his contract with impunity. This is not necessarily the
case. Proper consideration of the position of the promisee may lead us to the conclusion that the more appropriate way of providing redress in respect of the breach is via
an action by the promisee rather than by conferring a right of action on the third
party. This is not the place to debate the merits of conferring a right of action upon
the third party (that will come later: pp. 1229–1236). It suffices here to make the point
that the rights of the promisee are important and could even be said to be of greater
importance than the rights of the third party.

The rights of the promisee can be broken down into two broad categories. The first
relates to the entitlement of the promisee to a 'specific remedy', namely a remedy
which requires the defendant specifically to comply with its obligations under the
contract. The form of the remedy will depend upon the nature of the obligation
which has been assumed by the defendant. If the obligation is a positive one, namely
to perform a particular act, the remedy is likely to take the form of a specific performance order (on which see Chapter 26), that is to say, an order of the court that the
defendant perform his obligations in accordance with the terms of the contract.
Where, however, the obligation of the defendant is one not to do a particular thing
(for example not to compete with the third party), the remedy is likely to take the
form of an injunction, namely an order of the court that restrains the defendant from
doing the act that he has contracted not to do (although it may also take the form of
a stay of proceedings, discussed in more detail at pp. 1192–1194 below). It is vital to
note that the specific remedies are of importance to the third party as well as to the
promisee. Where the promise made by the defendant is one to confer a benefit on a
third party, the effect of the specific performance order will be to require the defendant to confer the benefit on the third party. In this way the position of both the
promisee and the third party will be protected. The second right of the promisee
relates to its entitlement to recover damages in respect of the promisor's breach of
contract. The damages remedy may or not may not be of significance to the third
party. Where damages are awarded to compensate the promisee for his own loss then
the remedy will be of little significance to the third party. But where damages are
awarded to compensate the promisee for the loss which has been suffered by the third
party, then the remedy is of obvious significance for the third party. As we shall see,
the question whether or not (and, if so, in what circumstances) English law entitles a
contracting party to sue and recover damages in respect of a loss suffered by a third
party is one of some controversy that remains largely unresolved.

Any consideration of the rights of the promisee must therefore distinguish between
the various remedies that are potentially available to the promisee. We shall focus
attention on three of the principal remedies, namely (i) specific performance, (ii) a
stay of proceedings, and (iii) damages.

(I) SPECIFIC PERFORMANCE
The leading case on the entitlement of the promisee to the remedy of specific

performance is the decision of the House of Lords in *Beswick* v. *Beswick* [1968] AC 58. However the significance of *Beswick* transcends this particular issue. The case is of importance for a number of reasons. First, it evidences the judicial assault that Lord Denning launched on the doctrine of privity in the middle of the twentieth century. It is for this reason that an extract has been included from Lord Denning's judgment in the Court of Appeal. Secondly, the case illustrates the attitude of the House of Lords to the doctrine of privity during the same period. While they spoke of the doctrine in critical terms they did not attempt to abrogate it. Thirdly, Mrs Beswick brought her action in a dual capacity: first, as the personal representative of her husband (who was the promisee) and secondly in her own capacity (as third party). The case therefore neatly illustrates the difference between the legal position of the promisee and the legal position of the third party. Finally the case evidences the range of doctrines and statutory provisions that have been used in the attempt to outflank the doctrine of privity. A significant part of the judgments in the House of Lords was taken up with an analysis of section 56(1) of the Law of Property Act 1925. The precise scope of this subsection has never been established. But the point which was established by the House of Lords, and which can be seen in the extract from the speech of Lord Reid, is that the section cannot be used as the foundation for a full-scale assault on the doctrine of privity in the way that Lord Denning had envisaged in the Court of Appeal.

Beswick v. Beswick

[1966] Ch 538, Court of Appeal; [1968] AC 58, House of Lords

In March 1962 Peter Beswick, who was then aged 70 and in poor health, agreed to sell his coal delivery business to his nephew, John Beswick. On 14 March they visited a solicitor who drew up an agreement to give effect to their intentions. John Beswick agreed to employ Peter Beswick as a consultant to the business at £6 10s a week for the rest of his life and to pay his wife an annuity of £5 a week for her life, after his death. Peter Beswick's wife, Ruth, was not a party to the agreement. In November 1963 Peter Beswick died. John Beswick made one payment of £5 to Mrs Beswick but refused to make any further payments. Mrs Beswick brought an action against John Beswick for specific performance of the agreement of March 1962 in her capacity as administratrix of Peter Beswick's estate and in her personal capacity. The trial judge refused to make an order for specific performance. The Court of Appeal allowed her appeal and held that Mrs Beswick was entitled to enforce the March 1962 agreement by way of specific performance both in her capacity as administratrix of her husband's estate and also, by virtue of section 56(1) of the Law of Property Act 1925, in her personal capacity.

Lord Denning MR

We have here the standard pattern of a contract for the benefit of a third person. A man has a business or other assets. He transfers them to another and, instead of taking cash, takes a promise by that other that he will pay an annuity or other sum to his widow or children. Can the transferee take the assets and reject the promise? I think not. In my opinion a contract such as this, for the benefit of widow and children, is binding. The party who makes the promise must honour it, unless he has some good reason why he should not do so. He may, for instance, be able to say that the contract should be rescinded as being induced by fraud or misrepresentation, or that it was varied or rescinded by agreement between the parties, before the widow or children knew about it and adopted it. But unless he has some good reason, he is bound. The executor of the dead man can sue to enforce it on behalf of the widow and children. The widow and children can join with the executor as plaintiffs in the action. If he refuses to sue, they may sue in their own names joining him as a defendant. In this way they have a right which can be enforced. I will prove this by reference to the common law, reinforced by equity, and now by statute.

1. THE COMMON LAW

[He considered *Dutton* v. *Poole* (1678) 8 T Raym 302; 2 Lev 210; 1 Vent 318, 332; 3 Keb 786; T Jo 102 and *Tweddle* v. *Atkinson* (1861) 1 B & S 393 and continued]

Those two cases give the key at common law to the whole problem of contracts for the benefit of a third person. Although the third person cannot as a rule sue alone in his own name, nevertheless there is no difficulty whatever in the one contracting party suing the other party for breach of the promise. The third person should, therefore, bring the action in the name of the contracting party, just as an assignee used to do. Face to face with the contracting party, the defaulter has no defence. He is sued by one who has provided consideration and to whom he has given his promise to pay the third person. He has broken his promise and must pay damages. The defaulter sometimes seeks to say that the contracting party can only recover nominal damages because it is not he but the third person who has suffered the damage. The common law has never allowed the defaulter to escape by such a shifty means. It holds that the contracting party can recover the money which should have been paid to the third person. He can get judgment for the sum and issue a writ of fi. fa. or other machinery to enforce payment: but when he recovers it, he holds the proceeds for the benefit of the third person. He cannot retain the money himself because it belongs to the third person and not to him: see *In re Schebsman, Ex parte the Official Solicitor, the Trustee. Cargo Superintendents (London) Ltd v. Schebsman* [1944] Ch 83 CA. It is money had and received to the use of the third person. In *Robertson* v. *Wait* (1853) 8 Exch 299, 301 Martin B said: 'If a person makes a contract whereby another obtains a benefit, why may not the former sue for it?' And in *Lloyd's* v. *Harper* Lush LJ said (1880) 16 Ch D 290, 321, CA:

> 'I consider it to be an established rule of law that where a contract is made with A for the benefit of B, A can sue on the contract for the benefit of B and recover all that B could have recovered if the contract had been made with B himself.'

Such was the position at common law if the action was brought in the name of the contracting party by himself alone. But nowadays when joinder of parties is freely permissible, it is far better for the contracting party and the third person to join as co-plaintiffs. Judgment will be given for the plaintiffs for the amount: and on payment, it will go at once to the third person who is entitled to it.

2. EQUITY

Sometimes one of the contracting parties makes the contract on trust for the third person, in this sense, that from the very beginning the right to sue is vested in him as trustee for the third person as beneficiary. Such a contract is different from those we are considering. It cannot be rescinded or varied except with the consent of the third person beneficiary: see *In re Empress Engineering Co* (1880) 16 Ch D 125. In such a case it is clearly established that the third person himself can sue in equity to enforce the contract: see *Tomlinson* v. *Gill* (1756) Amb 330 and *Gregory* v. *Williams* (1817) 3 Mer 582; but even so, he ought as a rule to join the trustee as a party. Here we have a case where there is admittedly no trust of the contractual right. Peter Beswick and his nephew might by agreement before his death have rescinded or varied the agreement, if they so wished. Nevertheless, although there is no trust, I do not think equity is powerless. It has in its hands the potent remedy of ordering a party specifically to perform his contract. If a party makes a promise to pay money to a third person, I see no reason why a court of equity should not order him to perform his promise. The action must be brought, of course, in the name of the other contracting party; but, that being done, there is no bar to a decree for specific performance being made. True it is for the payment of money, but a court of equity often decrees specific performance of a promise to pay money. It can enforce it by the appointment of a receiver, or other appropriate machinery . . .

These cases in equity fit in exactly with the common law. The contracting party is entitled by himself alone, or jointly with the third person, to have the contract performed according to its terms, and the court will decree specific performance of it.

3. STATUTE

Section 56(1) of the Law of Property Act, 1925, says that

'A person may take an immediate or other interest in land or other property, or the benefit of any condition, right of entry, covenant or agreement over or respecting land or other property, although he may not be named as a party to the conveyance or other instrument':

and by section 205(1)(xx) ' "Property" includes any thing in action, and any interest in real or personal property'. Apply that section to this case. The promise of the nephew to pay the widow £5 a week was a 'thing in action': for the simple reason that it could be enforced by action, namely, an action by the contracting party. This section says, as clearly as can be, that the widow can take the benefit of the agreement, although she is not named as a party to it. Seeing that she is to take the benefit of it, she must be able to sue for it, if not by herself alone, at least jointly with the contracting party. Otherwise the section is made of no effect. Ubi jus, ibi remedium.[2] If there was, therefore, any doubt as to her ability to sue at common law or equity, that doubt is removed by this section.

4. CONCLUSION

The general rule undoubtedly is that 'no third person can sue, or be sued, on a contract to which he is not a party': but at bottom that is only a rule of procedure. It goes to the form of remedy, not to the underlying right. Where a contract is made for the benefit of a third person who has a legitimate interest to enforce it, it can be enforced by the third person in the name of the contracting party or jointly with him or, if he refuses to join, by adding him as a defendant. In that sense, and it is a very real sense, the third person has a right arising by way of contract. He has an interest which will be protected by law. . . . It is different when a third person has no legitimate interest, as when he is seeking to enforce

---

[2] Where there is a right, there is a remedy.

the maintenance of prices to the public disadvantage, as in *Dunlop Pneumatic Tyre Co Ltd v. Selfridge & Co Ltd* [1915] AC 847, 853, HL(E): or when he is seeking to rely, not on any right given to him by the contract, but on an exemption clause seeking to exempt himself from his just liability. He cannot set up an exemption clause in a contract to which he was not a party: see *Midland Silicones Ltd* v. *Scruttons Ltd* [1962] AC 446, HL(E).

The widow here sues in her capacity as executrix of her husband's estate (and therefore as contracting party), and also in her personal capacity (and therefore as a third person). This joint claim is clearly good. She is entitled to an order for specific performance of the agreement, by ordering the defendant to pay the arrears of £175, and the instalments of £5 a week as they fall due. The order for paying the arrears of £175 is equivalent to a judgment for that sum and can be enforced by fi. fa. or other appropriate machinery: see R.S.C. Ord. 42, r. 3. When the money is recovered, it will go to the widow for her own benefit, and not to her husband's estate.

Danckwerts LJ delivered a concurring judgment while **Salmon LJ** agreed that Mrs Beswick was entitled to a specific performance order in her capacity as administratrix of her husband's estate but left open the question of her entitlement to a remedy under section 56(1) of the 1925 Act.

John Beswick appealed to the House of Lords. The House of Lords affirmed the decision of the Court of Appeal in so far as it held that Mrs Beswick ('the respondent') was entitled to enforce the March 1962 agreement in her capacity as administratrix of her husband's estate. But their Lordships held that she was not entitled to enforce the agreement in her personal capacity under section 56(1) of the Law of Property Act 1925.

Lord Reid [set out the facts and continued]
For clarity I think it best to begin by considering a simple case where, in consideration of a sale by A to B, B agrees to pay the price of £1,000 to a third party X. Then the first question appears to me to be whether the parties intended that X should receive the money simply as A's nominee so that he would hold the money for behoof of A and be accountable to him for it, or whether the parties intended that X should receive the money for his own behoof and be entitled to keep it. That appears to me to be a question of construction of the agreement read in light of all the circumstances which were known to the parties. There have been several decisions involving this question. I am not sure that any conflicts with the view which I have expressed. . . . I think that *In Re Schebsman* [1944] Ch 83 was rightly decided and that the reasoning of Uthwatt J and the Court of Appeal supports what I have just said. In the present case I think it clear that the parties to the agreement intended that the respondent should receive the weekly sums of £5 in her own behoof and should not be accountable to her deceased husband's estate for them. Indeed the contrary was not argued.

Reverting to my simple example the next question appears to me to be: Where the intention was that X should keep the £1,000 as his own, what is the nature of B's obligation and who is entitled to enforce it? It was not argued that the law of England regards B's obligation as a nullity, and I have not observed in any of the authorities any suggestion that it would be a nullity. There may have been a time when the existence of a right depended on whether there was any means of enforcing it, but today the law would be sadly deficient if one found that, although there is a right, the law provides no means for enforcing it. So this obligation of B must be enforceable either by X or by A. I shall leave aside for the moment the question whether section 56(1) of the Law of Property Act, 1925, has any application to such a case, and consider the position at common law.

Lord Denning's view, expressed in this case not for the first time, is that X could enforce this obligation. But the view more commonly held in recent times has been that such a contract confers no right on X and that X could not sue for the £1,000. Leading counsel for the respondent based his case on other grounds, and as I agree that the respondent succeeds on other grounds, this would not be an appropriate case in which to solve this question. It is true that a strong Law Revision Committee recommended so long ago as 1937 (Cmd 5449):

'That where a contract by its express terms purports to confer a benefit directly on a third party it shall be enforceable by the third party in his own name . . .' (p. 31).

And, if one had to contemplate a further long period of Parliamentary procrastination, this House might find it necessary to deal with this matter. But if legislation is probable at any early date I would not deal with it in a case where that is not essential. So for the purposes of this case I shall proceed on the footing that the commonly accepted view is right.

What then is A's position? I assume that A has not made himself a trustee for X, because it was not argued in this appeal that any trust had been created. So, if X has no right, A can at any time grant a discharge to B or make some new contract with B. If there were a trust the position would be different. X would have an equitable right and A would be entitled and, indeed, bound to recover the money and account for it to X. And A would have no right to grant a discharge to B. If there is no trust and A wishes to enforce the obligation, how does he set about it? He cannot sue B for the £1,000 because under the contract the money is not payable to him, and, if the contract were performed according to its terms, he would never have any right to get the money. So he must seek to make B pay X.

The argument for the appellant is that A's only remedy is to sue B for damages for B's breach of contract in failing to pay the £1,000 to X. Then the appellant says that A can only recover nominal damages of 40s. because the fact that X has not received the money will generally cause no loss to A: he admits that there may be cases where A would suffer damage if X did not receive the money but says that the present is not such a case.

Applying what I have said to the circumstances of the present case, the respondent in her personal capacity has no right to sue, but she has a right as administratrix of her husband's estate to require the appellant to perform his obligation under the agreement. He has refused to do so and he maintains that the respondent's only right is to sue him for damages for breach of his contract. If that were so, I shall assume that he is right in maintaining that the administratrix could then only recover nominal damages because his breach of contract has caused no loss to the estate of her deceased husband.

If that were the only remedy available the result would be grossly unjust. It would mean that the appellant keeps the business which he bought and for which he has only paid a small part of the price which he agreed to pay. He would avoid paying the rest of the price, the annuity to the respondent, by paying a mere 40s. damages.

The respondent's first answer is that the common law has been radically altered by section 56(1) of the Law of Property Act, 1925, and that that section entitles her to sue in her personal capacity and recover the benefit provided for her in the agreement although she was not a party to it. Extensive alterations of the law were made at that time but it is necessary to examine with some care the way in which this was done. That Act was a consolidation Act and it is the invariable practice of Parliament to require from those who have prepared a consolidation Bill an assurance that it will make no substantial change in the law and to have that checked by a committee [he considered the legislative history of the section and continued] . . . it is therefore quite certain that those responsible for the preparation of this legislation must have believed and intended that section 56 would make no substantial change in the earlier law, and equally certain that Parliament passed section 56 in reliance on an assurance that it did make no substantial change.

In construing any Act of Parliament we are seeking the intention of Parliament and it is quite true that we must deduce that intention from the words of the Act. If the words of the Act are only capable of one meaning we must give them that meaning no matter how they got there. But if they are capable of having more than one meaning we are, in my view, well entitled to see how they got there. . . . I can see no objection to investigating in the present case the antecedents of section 56.

Section 56 was obviously intended to replace section 5 of the Real Property Act, 1845 (8 and 9 Vict. c. 106). That section provided:

> 'That, under an indenture, executed after October 1, 1845, an immediate estate or interest, in any tenements or hereditaments, and the benefit of a condition or covenant, respecting any tenements or hereditaments, may be taken, although the taker thereof be not named a party to the same indenture . . .'

Section 56 (1) now provides:

> 'A person may take an immediate or other interest in land or other property, or the benefit of any condition, right of entry covenant or agreement over or respecting land or other property, although he may not be named as a party to the conveyance or other instrument: . . .'

If the matter stopped there it would not be difficult to hold that section 56 does not substantially extend or alter the provisions of section 5 of the Act of 1845. But more difficulty is introduced by the definition section of the Act of 1925 (section 205) which provides:

> '(1) In this Act unless the context otherwise requires, the following expressions have the meanings hereby assigned to them respectively, that is to say:- . . . (xx) "Property" includes any thing in action, and any interest in real or personal property.'

Before further considering the meaning of section 56(1) I must set out briefly the views which have been expressed about it in earlier cases . . . [he considered the case-law and continued]

I can now return to consider the meaning and scope of section 56. It refers to any 'agreement over or respecting land or other property'. If 'land or other property' means the same thing as 'tenements or hereditaments' in the Act of 1845 then this section simply continues the law as it was before the Act of 1925 was passed, for I do not think that the other differences in phraseology can be regarded as making any substantial change. So any obscurities in section 56 are obscurities which originated in 1845. But if its scope is wider, then two points must be considered. The section refers to agreements 'over or respecting land or other property'. The land is something which existed before and independently of the agreement and the same must apply to the other property. So an agreement between A and B that A will use certain personal property for the benefit of

X would be within the scope of the section, but an agreement that if A performs certain services for B, B will pay a sum to X would not be within the scope of the section. Such a capricious distinction would alone throw doubt on this interpretation.

Perhaps more important is the fact that the section does not say that a person may take the benefit of an agreement although he was not a party to it: it says that he may do so although he was not named as a party in the instrument which embodied the agreement. It is true that section 56 says 'although he may not be named'; but section 5 of the Act of 1845 says although he 'be not named a party'. Such a change of phraseology in a consolidation Act cannot involve a change of meaning . . .

But it may be that additional difficulties would arise from the application to section 56 of the definition of property in the definition section. If so, it becomes necessary to consider whether that definition can be applied to section 56. By express provision in the definition section a definition contained in it is not to be applied to the word defined if in the particular case the context otherwise requires. If application of that definition would result in giving to section 56 a meaning going beyond that of the old section, then, in my opinion, the context does require that the definition of 'property' shall not be applied to that word in section 56. The context in which this section occurs is a consolidation Act. If the definition is not applied the section is a proper one to appear in such an Act because it can properly be regarded as not substantially altering the pre-existing law. But if the definition is applied the result is to make section 56 go far beyond the pre-existing law. Holding that the section has such an effect would involve holding that the invariable practice of Parliament has been departed from *per incuriam* so that something has got into this consolidation Act which neither the draftsman nor Parliament can have intended to be there. I am reinforced in this view by two facts. The language of section 56 is not at all what one would have expected if the intention had been to bring in all that the application of the definition would bring in. And, secondly, section 56 is one of 25 sections which appear in the Act under the cross-heading 'Conveyances and other Instruments'. The other twenty-four sections come appropriately under that heading and so does section 56 if it has a limited meaning: but, if its scope is extended by the definition of property, it would be quite inappropriately placed in this part of the Act. For these reasons I am of opinion that section 56 has no application to the present case.

The respondent's second argument is that she is entitled in her capacity of administratrix of her deceased husband's estate to enforce the provision of the agreement for the benefit of herself in her personal capacity, and that a proper way of enforcing that provision is to order specific performance. That would produce a just result, and, unless there is some technical objection, I am of opinion that specific performance ought to be ordered. For the reasons given by your Lordships I would reject the arguments submitted for the appellant that specific performance is not a possible remedy in this case.

Lord Pearce

My Lords, if the annuity had been payable to a third party in the lifetime of Beswick senior and there had been default, he could have sued in respect of the breach. His administratrix is now entitled to stand in his shoes and to sue in respect of the breach which has occurred since his death.

It is argued that the estate can only recover nominal damages and that no other remedy is open, either to the estate or to the personal plaintiff. Such a result would be wholly repugnant to justice and commonsense. And if the argument were right it would show a very serious defect in the law.

In the first place, I do not accept the view that damages must be nominal. Lush LJ in *Lloyd's* v. *Harper* (1880) 16 Ch D 290, 321 said:

'Then the next question which, no doubt, is a very important and substantial one, is, that Lloyd's, having sustained no damage themselves, could not recover for the losses sustained by third parties by reason of the default of Robert Henry Harper as an underwriter. That, to my mind, is a startling and alarming doctrine, and a novelty, because I consider it to be an established rule of law that where a contract is made with A for the benefit of B, A can sue on the contract for the benefit of B, and recover all that B could have recovered if the contract had been made with B himself.'

. . . I agree with the comment of Windeyer J in the case of *Coulls* v. *Bagot's Executor and Trustee Co Ltd* (1967) 40 ALJR 471, 486 in the High Court of Australia that the words of Lush LJ cannot be accepted without qualification and regardless of context and also with his statement:

'I can see no reason why in such cases the damages which A would suffer upon B's breach of his contract to pay C $500 would be merely nominal: I think that in accordance with the ordinary rules for the assessment of damages for breach of contract they could be substantial. They would not necessarily be $500; they could I think be less or more.'

In the present case I think that the damages, if assessed, must be substantial. It is not necessary, however, to consider the amount of damages more closely since this is a case in which, as the Court of Appeal rightly decided, the more appropriate remedy is that of specific performance.

The administratrix is entitled, if she so prefers, to enforce the agreement rather than accept its repudiation, and specific performance is more convenient than an action for arrears of payment followed by separate actions as each sum falls due. Moreover, damages for breach would be a less appropriate remedy since the parties to the agreement were intending an annuity for a widow; and a lump sum of damages does not accord with this. And if (contrary to my view) the argument that a derisory sum of damages is all that can be obtained be right, the remedy of damages in this case is manifestly useless.

The present case presents all the features which led the equity courts to apply their remedy of specific performance. The contract was for the sale of a business. The defendant could on his part clearly have obtained specific performance of it if Beswick senior or his administratrix had defaulted. Mutuality is a ground in favour of specific performance.

Moreover, the defendant on his side has received the whole benefit of the contract and it is a matter of conscience for the court to see that he now performs his part of it. . . . What, then, is the obstacle to granting specific performance?

It is argued that since the widow personally had no rights which she personally could enforce the court will not make an order which will have the effect of enforcing those rights. I can find no principle to this effect. The condition as to payment of an annuity to the widow personally was valid. The estate (though not the widow personally) can enforce it. Why should the estate be barred from exercising its full contractual rights merely because in doing so it secures justice for the widow who, by a mechanical defect of our law, is unable to assert her own rights? Such a principle would be repugnant to justice and fulfil no other object than that of aiding the wrongdoer. I can find no ground on which such a principle should exist . . .

In my opinion, the plaintiff as administratrix is entitled to a decree of specific performance.

[He then considered the widow's claim at common law and under section 56(1) of the Law of Property Act 1925 and concluded that the widow had a claim on neither basis].

Lord Upjohn

As it is necessary to keep clear and distinct the rights of the widow as administratrix of her husband and personally, I think it will be convenient to use letters: letter A represents the deceased and A1 the widow, as personal representative, B the widow in her personal capacity and C the appellant. And in other examples I shall give, these letters will serve the same purpose.

Much is common ground between the parties: (1) B was not a party to the agreement; (2) A did not enter into the agreement as trustee for B in relation to the annuity to be paid to her, (3) A1 stands for all relevant purposes in the shoes of A and is entitled to sue C for breach of his admitted repudiation of the agreement . . ., but the parties differ fundamentally as to the remedy to which A1 is entitled in such an action.

Counsel for the respondent has not felt able to support the view, expressed by Lord Denning MR, that apart from section 56 of the Law of Property Act, 1925, B is entitled to sue C at common law. I think that he was right to make this concession, for whatever may have been the state of the law before *Tweddle* v. *Atkinson* (1861) 1 B & S 393 it is difficult to see how your Lordships can go back over 100 years in view of the decisions in this House of *Dunlop Pneumatic Tyre Co Ltd* v. *Selfridge & Co Ltd* [1915] AC 847 and *Scruttons Ltd* v. *Midland Silicones Ltd* [1962] AC 496.

Leaving section 56 out of account, there was no real dispute between the parties as to their respective rights (as distinct from remedies) under the agreement. (*a*) B has no rights thereunder. But it was clear from the whole tenor of the agreement that the annuity was to be paid to her for her own beneficial enjoyment, so if C paid it to her she could keep it and did not hold it as a constructive trustee for A1; (*b*) C would completely perform his obligation under the contract by continuing to pay the annuity to B during her life. Neither A nor A1 could compel C to pay it to A or A1, but (*c*) A or A1 and C could, if they pleased, agree to modify, compromise or even discharge further performance of the contract by C, and B would have no right to complain. . . . Admittedly A1 can sue from time to time for damages at common law on failure to pay each instalment of the annuity. But surely on a number of grounds this is a case for specific performance.

First, here is the sale of a business for full consideration wholly executed on A's part who has put C into possession of all the assets. C is repudiating the obligations to be performed by him . . .

The fact that A by the agreement was to render such services as consultant as he might find convenient or at his own absolute discretion should decide may be ignored as de minimis and the contrary was not argued. In any event the fact that there is a small element of personal service in a contract of this nature does not destroy that quality of mutuality (otherwise plainly present) want of which may in general terms properly be a ground for refusing a decree of specific performance.

In the courts below, though not before your Lordships, it was argued that the remedy of specific performance was not available when all that remained was the obligation to make a money payment. Danckwerts LJ rightly demolished this contention as untenable for the reasons he gives [1967] Ch 538, 560–561.

But when the money payment is not made once and for all but in the nature of an annuity there is an even greater need for equity to come to the assistance of the common law. Equity is to do true justice to enforce the true contract that the parties have made and to prevent the trouble and expense of a multiplicity of actions. This has been well settled for over a century . . .

It is in such common sense and practical ways that equity comes to the aid of the common law and it is sufficiently flexible to meet and satisfy the justice of the case in the many different circumstances that arise from time to time.

To sum up this matter: had C repudiated the contract in the lifetime of A the latter would have had a cast iron case for specific performance. Can it make any difference that by the terms of the agreement C is obliged to pay the annuity after A's death to B? Of course not. On the principle I have just stated it is clear that there can be nothing to prevent equity in A's specific performance action making an appropriate decree for specific performance directing payment of the annuity to A but during his life and thereafter to B for her life . . .

But when A dies and his rights pass to A1, it is said that the remedy of specific performance is no longer appropriate against C. The argument was first that the estate of A suffered no damage by reason of C's failure to pay B; so A1 is entitled to nominal damages but as she is not otherwise interested in the agreement as such it would be wrong to grant specific performance; for that remedy is available only where damages will be an inadequate remedy. Here nominal damages are adequate. Further, it was argued, to do so would really be to confer upon B a right which she does not have in law or equity to receive the annuity. Then, secondly, it was said that if the remedy of specific performance is granted it might prejudice creditors of A so that the parties ought to be left to their strict rights at law. Thirdly, it is said that there are procedural difficulties in the way of enforcing an order for specific performance in favour of a third party. I will deal with these points, though in reverse order.

As to procedural difficulties, I fear I do not understand the argument. The point if valid applies to an action for specific performance by A just as much as by A1 yet in the authorities I have quoted no such point was ever taken; . . .

Then as to the second point. Let me assume (contrary to the fact) that A died with substantial assets but also many creditors. The legal position is that prima facie the duty of A1 is to carry out her intestate's contracts and compel C to pay B; but the creditors may be pressing and the agreement may be considered onerous; so it may be her duty to try and compromise the agreement with C and save something for the estate even at the expense of B. . . . So be it, but how can C conceivably rely upon this circumstance as a defence by him to an action for specific performance by A1? Of course not; he, C, has no interest in the estate; he cannot plead a possible jus tertii which is no concern of his. It is his duty to fulfil his contract by paying C. A1 alone is concerned with the creditors, beneficiaries or next of kin of A and this point therefore can never be a defence by C if A1 in fact chooses to sue for specific performance rather than to attempt a compromise in the interest of the estate. This point seems to me misconceived. In any event, on the facts of this case there is no suggestion that there are any unpaid creditors and B is sole next of kin, so the point is academic.

Then, as to the first point. On this question we were referred to the well-known dictum of Lush LJ in *Lloyd's v. Harper* 16 Ch D 290, 321:

'I consider it to be an established rule of law that where a contract is made with A for the benefit of B, A can sue on the contract for the benefit of B and recover all that B could have recovered if the contract had been made with B himself.'

While in the circumstances it is not necessary to express any concluded opinion thereon, if the learned Lord Justice was expressing a view on the purely common law remedy of damages, I have some difficulty in going all the way with him. If A sues for damages for breach of contract by reason of the failure to pay he must prove his loss; that may be great or nominal according to circumstances.

I do not see how A can, in conformity with clearly settled principle in assessing damages for breach of contract, rely at common law on B's loss. . . . I incline to the view that on the facts of this case damages are nominal for it appears that A died without any assets save and except the agreement which he hoped would keep him and then his widow for their lives. At all events let me assume that damages are nominal. So it is said nominal damages are adequate and the remedy of specific performance ought not to be granted. That is, with all respect, wholly to misunderstand that principle. Equity will grant specific performance when damages are inadequate to meet the justice of the case.

But in any event quantum of damages seldom affects the right to specific performance. If X contracts with Y to buy Blackacre or a rare chattel for a fancy price because the property or chattel has caught his fancy he is entitled to enforce his bargain and it matters not that he could not prove any damage.

In this case the court ought to grant a specific performance order all the more because damages *are* nominal. C has received all the property; justice demands that he pay the price and this can only be done in the circumstances by equitable relief. It is a fallacy to suppose that B is thereby obtaining additional rights; A1 is entitled to compel C to carry out the terms of the agreement . . .

My Lords, in my opinion the Court of Appeal were clearly right to grant a decree of specific performance.

[He then proceeded to consider the true scope of section 56 of the Law of Property Act, 1925 and concluded that the section did 'not help' the plaintiff].

Lord Hodson and **Lord Guest** delivered concurring speeches in which they held that Mrs Beswick was entitled to a specific performance order in her capacity as administratrix of her husband's estate but not in her personal capacity.

COMMENTARY

A number of points of significance emerge from the decision of the House of Lords in *Beswick*. The first group of points relates to the failure of Mrs Beswick's claim in her personal capacity. It should be noted that in the House of Lords counsel for Mrs Beswick did not attempt to support Lord Denning's view that Mrs Beswick was entitled to succeed in her claim at common law, apart from section 56 of the Law of Property Act 1925. Their Lordships were therefore not asked to engage in a re-examination of the doctrine of privity. In relation to section 56, their Lordships held that it did not have the effect which Lord Denning attributed to it. But its precise scope remains uncertain. Professor Treitel comments (*The Law of Contract* (11th edn, Sweet & Maxwell, 2003), p. 670):

there is support in *Beswick* v. *Beswick* for four limitations on its scope: namely, that it applies only (1) to real property, (2) to covenants running with the land; (3) to cases where the instrument is not merely for the benefit of the third party but purports to contain a grant to or covenant with him; and (4) to deeds strictly *inter partes*. But there is no clear majority in the speeches in favour of all, some or even one of these limitations, so that the scope of the subsection remains obscure.

The conclusion that Mrs Beswick was not entitled to a specific performance order in her own capacity gives rise to apparent anomalies. Had the executor of Peter Beswick's estate been someone other than Mrs Beswick, she would not have been entitled to a specific performance order, nor would she have been able to compel the executor to seek a specific performance order. It would have been for the executor himself to decide whether or not to seek a remedy and, if so, which remedy. On the other hand, it can be argued that there is no anomaly here. The remedy belonged to the estate (on the ground that Peter Beswick provided the consideration for the promise of his nephew), not Mrs Beswick, and the same remedies would have been available whoever happened to be the administrator of the estate.

The second group of points relates to the conclusion that Mrs Beswick was entitled to a specific performance order in her capacity as administratrix of her husband's estate. What factors were relied upon by Lord Pearce and Lord Upjohn to support the conclusion that a specific performance order was the most appropriate remedy on the facts of the case? Lord Upjohn stated that damages were 'inadequate to meet the justice of the case'. Why was this so? Damages may have been an inadequate remedy to protect the interests of Mrs Beswick in her own capacity but she was not suing in that capacity. She was suing as the representative of the estate and on what basis could it be said that damages were an inadequate or inappropriate remedy for the estate?

Finally, what would have been the position if the contract had not been specifically enforceable? It was not necessary for their Lordships to decide this particular point given that they concluded that the contract was specifically enforceable. But it is worth noting that Lord Pearce was of the view that the estate would have been entitled to substantial damages, while the rest of their Lordships were content to assume that damages would have been nominal. Which view is the correct one?

(II) STAY OF PROCEEDINGS

Where the promise made by the promisor is a promise not to sue a third party, the promisee may be able to seek a stay of the promisor's action against the third party under section 49(3) of the Supreme Court Act 1981 which states:

Nothing in this Act shall affect the power of the Court of Appeal or the High Court to stay any proceedings before it, where it thinks fit to do so, either of its own motion or on the application of any person, whether or not a party to the proceedings.

In order to obtain a stay the promisee must demonstrate that the promisor has promised not to sue the third party and that the promisee has a sufficient interest in the enforcement of the promisor's promise to justify the grant of a stay. A case in which these requirements were not satisfied is *Gore* v. *Van Der Lann* [1967] 2 QB 31. The plaintiff fell when attempting to board a bus operated by Liverpool Corporation. She brought an action in negligence against the bus conductor who was an employee of the corporation. The corporation applied to stay her action. The basis for their application was that the plaintiff had applied for a free bus pass from the corporation and in doing so had signed an application form which stated that the pass was issued 'subject to the conditions that neither the Liverpool Corporation nor any of their servants or agents responsible for the driving, management, control or working of their bus system, are to be liable to the holder . . . for . . . injury . . . however caused'. It was held that the corporation was not entitled to the stay. The Court of Appeal held that the condition relied upon by the corporation was caught by section 151 of the Road Traffic Act 1960 and was consequently invalid.[3] But in any event it was held that the corporation was not entitled to the stay because (i) the plaintiff had not promised not to sue the bus conductor (although one might wish to argue that the exemption clause in the bus pass ought to have been treated as a promise not to sue) and (ii) the corporation did not have a sufficient interest in the enforcement of any such promise (had it been made) because it was not under an obligation to indemnify its employee against his liability to the plaintiff in negligence.

A different result was reached in *Snelling* v. *John G Snelling Ltd* [1973] 1 QB 87. Three brothers were directors of a family company and they were all owed substantial sums of money by the company. Differences arose between the brothers and, in an attempt to resolve these differences, they entered into an agreement under which they agreed that if one of them resigned his directorship he should 'forfeit' all monies due to him from the company. The plaintiff resigned his directorship and brought an action to recover the sums owed to him by the company. The company sought to rely on the terms of the agreement between the brothers as a defence to the claim. The plaintiff's two brothers then applied to be joined as defendants to the claim and they adopted the defence of the company and counterclaimed for a declaration that the sum due to the plaintiff by the company had been forfeited. Ormrod J dismissed the plaintiff's claim and gave judgment for the two brothers on their counterclaim. On what basis did he dismiss the plaintiff's claim? It is important to distinguish here between the position of the company and the position of the two brothers who were joined as defendants. The company was, as Ormrod J stated (at p. 96), 'not entitled to rely directly on the terms of the contract'. But the brothers were entitled to judgment on their counterclaim against the plaintiff. This being the case, Ormrod J continued (at pp. 96–97).

to give judgment for the plaintiff against the defendant company for the amount claimed in the statement of claim and judgment for the second and third defendants on the counterclaim would be absurd, unless, which is clearly not the case here, the second and third defendants could be adequately compensated in damages. So far as they are concerned a judgment against the company would frustrate the very purpose for which their agreement with the plaintiff was made. The next problem is to consider the relief to which they are entitled. They have claimed a declaration that the amount shown in the plaintiff's loan account has been forfeited to the defendant company and is now applicable in accordance with the resolution of the board of directors of the defendant company passed on May 22, 1969, but I feel some doubt whether this is the appropriate form of declaration. They are certainly entitled to a declaration that the provisions in the agreement of March 22, 1968, are binding on the plaintiff. Had these provisions been worded positively and not negatively, e.g., as a promise by the resigning director to release the company from its indebtedness to him, I think that, on the authority of *Beswick* v. *Beswick* [1968] AC 58, this would have been an appropriate case on the facts in which to order specific performance of that promise in

[3] Section 151 invalidated any clause in a contract for the conveyance of a passenger in a public service vehicle which purported to exempt a person from liability in respect of death or personal injury suffered while being carried in, entering, or alighting from the vehicle.

whatever was the appropriate form. Similarly, had the second and third defendants themselves taken proceedings, before the plaintiff issued his writ, to restrain the anticipated breach they would have been entitled to an injunction restraining him from demanding payment by the company of his loan account. Had he subsequently started an action against the company it would, presumably, have been stayed as an abuse of the process of the court. But what is the appropriate form of order when the second and third defendants have been joined in the plaintiff's action, and succeeded on the counterclaim? . . . In my judgment . . . the second and third defendants have made out an unambiguous case and have shown that the interests of justice require that the plaintiff be not permitted to recover against the defendant company. It follows that this is a proper case in which to grant a stay of all further proceedings in the plaintiff's action against the company.

[Counsel for the defendants], however, has submitted that he is entitled to go further and ask for the plaintiff's claim against the company to be dismissed . . . [he considered the submission and concluded] . . . I am inclined to the view that in a case such as this where the promisees under the agreement and the party to be benefited by the agreement are all before the court and the promisees have succeeded against the plaintiff on their counterclaim, the right view is that the plaintiff's claim should be dismissed. . . . If the action was left with no more than an order staying further proceedings on the claim, the plaintiff could start another action only to have it also stayed and so on ad infinitum. The reality of the matter is that the plaintiff's claim fails and the order of the court ought, if possible, clearly to reflect that fact.

Accordingly, I think the plaintiff's claim should be dismissed and that there should be judgment for the second and third defendants on the counterclaim, together with a declaration in appropriate terms.

The approach of Ormrod J is less restrictive than that adopted by the Court of Appeal in *Gore* in that he dismissed the plaintiff's claim notwithstanding the fact the two brothers were not under any obligation to indemnify the company in respect of its liability to the plaintiff. Ormrod J took a broad view of the situation and concluded that the interest which the brothers had in the running of the family company was sufficient to give them an interest in obtaining a stay (and, indeed, the dismissal of the plaintiff's claim).

(III) DAMAGES

Finally, the promisee may seek a remedy in damages from the promisor. The promisee is clearly entitled to sue and recover damages in respect of the loss that he has suffered as a result of the breach. Take the case where the promisee is a debtor of the third party and the promisor has promised to pay a sum of money to the third party in order to discharge the promisee's liability to the third party. The promisor fails to make the promised payment to the third party. The consequence is that the promisee remains indebted to the third party and, to that extent, the promisee does suffer loss as a result of the failure of the promisor to make the payment to the third party. But in other cases the promisee is likely to find it difficult to prove that he has suffered loss as a result of the promisor's breach. *Beswick* v. *Beswick* [1968] AC 58 is a case in point. It was assumed by all of their Lordships, with the exception of Lord Pearce, that Mrs Beswick only had a claim for nominal damages in her capacity as administratrix of her husband's estate. The reason for this was that the estate did not appear to have suffered any loss as a result of John Beswick's breach of contract. Lord Pearce made no such assumption: in his opinion the estate was entitled to 'substantial' damages. It is not necessary for us to resolve this point here. It has already been discussed in the chapter on damages (see pp. 1017–1054 above). It suffices to note that the ability of the promisee to recover damages for his own loss depends on whether or not he has suffered a loss as a result of the promisor's breach of contract.

The party who is more likely to have suffered loss as a result of the breach is the third party. Can the promisee sue and recover damages in respect of the third party's loss? The general rule is that he cannot. He can only recover damages in respect of his own loss. The existence of this general rule was affirmed by the House of Lords in *Alfred McAlpine Construction Ltd* v. *Panatown Ltd* [2001] 1 AC 518. The three judges in the majority all accepted the existence of the general rule (see Lord Clyde at p. 522, Lord Jauncey at p. 563, and Lord Browne-Wilkinson at p. 575), but it is in the speeches of the dissentients, Lord Goff and Lord Millett, that we find more extended analysis of both the basis for the general rule and the criticisms that have been levelled against it. Lord Millett (at p. 580) defended the general rule in the following terms:

Compensation is compensation for loss; its object is to make good a loss. It is inherent in the concept of compensation that only the person who has suffered the loss is entitled to have it made good by compensation. Compensation for a third party's loss is a contradiction in terms. It is impossible on any logical basis to justify the recovery of compensatory damages by a person who has not suffered the loss in respect of which they are awarded unless he is accountable for them to the person who has.

Lord Goff, on the other hand, was more sceptical. He doubted the existence of the general rule. He stated (at pp. 538–539 and p. 544):

It would be an extraordinary defect in our law if, where (for example) A enters into a contract with B that B should carry out work for the benefit of a third party, C, A should have no remedy in damages against B if B should perform his contract in a defective manner. Contracts in this form are a commonplace of everyday life, very often in the context of the family; but, as the present case shows, they may also occur in a commercial context. It is not surprising therefore to discover that the authority for the supposed rule which excludes such a right to damages is very thin, and that its existence has been doubted by distinguished writers. . . . Plainly it is right that a contracting party should not use the remedy of damages to recover what has been described by Oliver J in a notable judgment in *Radford* v. *De Froberville* [1977] 1 WLR 1262, 1270 as 'an uncovenanted profit', or indeed to impose on the other contracting party an uncovenanted burden. But if the supposed rule exists, it could deprive a contracting party of any effective remedy in the case of a contract which is intended to confer a benefit on a third party but not to confer on the third party an enforceable right. It is not surprising therefore to discover increasing concern on the part of scholars specialising in the law of contract that the supposed rule, if rigidly applied, can have the effect of depriving parties of the fulfilment of their reasonable contractual expectations, and to read of doubts on their part whether any such rule exists.

Given that the majority in *Panatown* accepted the existence of the general rule, Lord Millett's view would appear to be the correct one as a matter of authority. Nevertheless, the concerns of Lord Goff are reflected in the exceptions to the general rule and in the case-law more generally. He points out that the general rule can cause problems both in the family and in the commercial context. Before giving brief consideration to the exceptions to the general rule it may be useful to examine two cases in which the general rule has given rise to difficulty. The first case, *Jackson* v. *Horizon Holidays Ltd* [1975] 1 WLR 1468, is drawn from the family context, while the second, *Woodar Investment Development Ltd* v. *Wimpey Construction UK Ltd* [1980] 1 WLR 277 is a commercial case.

Jackson v. Horizon Holidays Ltd

[1975] 1 WLR 1468, Court of Appeal

Julian Jackson booked a holiday for himself, his wife, and his three-year-old sons at the Pegasus Reef Hotel, Sri Lanka through Horizon Holidays Ltd, a travel company. Before making the booking Jackson set out his precise requirements regarding accommodation, food, amenities, and facilities in a letter to Horizon and was assured by Horizon that they would be met. The price payable was £1,432. Soon afterwards, Horizon informed Jackson that the Pegasus Reef Hotel would not be ready in time and offered him accommodation at the Brown's Beach Hotel for £1,200 instead. Jackson agreed after an assurance from Horizon that the hotel would be up to his expectation. The accommodation, food, amenities, and facilities at the Brown's Beach Hotel were unsatisfactory and the whole family suffered distress and inconvenience. Jackson brought an action against Horizon claiming damages for misrepresentation and breach of contract. Judge Edgar Fay QC awarded Jackson damages of £1,100. Horizon appealed on the ground that the damages awarded were excessive. The Court of Appeal refused to interfere with Judge Fay's award and dismissed the appeal.

Lord Denning MR [set out the facts and continued]
The judge did not divide up the £1,100. Counsel has made suggestions about it. Counsel for Horizon Holidays suggests that the judge gave £100 for diminution in value and £1,000 for the mental distress. But counsel for Mr Jackson suggested that the judge gave £600 for the diminution in value and £500 for the mental distress. If I were inclined myself to speculate, I think the suggestion of counsel for Mr Jackson may well be right. The judge took the cost of the holidays at £1,200. The family only had about half the value of it. Divide it by two and you get £600. Then add £500 for the mental distress.

On this question a point of law arises. The judge said that he could only consider the mental distress to Mr Jackson himself, and that he could not consider the distress to his wife and children. He said:

'The damages are the plaintiff's. . . . I can consider the effect upon his mind of the wife's discomfort, vexation, and the like, although I cannot award a sum which represents her own vexation.'

We have had an interesting discussion as to the legal position when one person makes a contract for the benefit of a third party. In this case it was a husband making a contract for the benefit of himself, his wife and children. Other cases readily come to mind. A host makes a contract with a restaurant for a dinner for himself and his friends. The vicar makes a contract for a coach trip for the choir. In all these cases there is only one person who makes the contract. It is the husband, the host or the vicar, as the case may be. Sometimes he pays the whole price himself. Occasionally he may get a contribution from the others. But in any case it is he who makes the contract. It would be a fiction to say that the contract was made by all the family, or all the guests, or all the choir, and that he was only an agent for them. Take this very case. It would be absurd to say that the twins of three years old were parties to the contract or that the father was making the contract on their behalf as if they were principals. It would equally be a mistake to say that in any of these instances there was a trust. The transaction bears no resemblance to a trust. There was no trust fund and no trust property. No, the real truth is that in each instance, the father, the host or the vicar, was making a contract himself for the benefit of the whole party. In short, a contract by one for the benefit of third persons.

What is the position when such a contract is broken? At present the law says that the only one who can sue is the one who made the contract. None of the rest of the party can sue, even though the contract was made for their benefit. But when that one does sue, what damages can he recover? Is he limited to his own loss? Or can he recover for the others? Suppose the holiday firm puts the family into a hotel which is only half built and the visitors have to sleep on the floor? Or suppose the restaurant is fully booked and the guests have to go away, hungry and angry, having spent so much on fares to get there? Or suppose the coach leaves the choir stranded halfway and they have to hire cars to get home? None of them individually can sue. Only the father, the host or the vicar can sue. He can, of course, recover his own damages. But can he not recover for the others? I think he can. The case comes within the principle stated by Lush LJ in *Lloyd's* v. *Harper* (1880) 16 Ch D 290, 321:

'I consider it to be an established rule of law that where a contract is made with *A* for the benefit of *B*, *A* can sue on the contract for the benefit of *B*, and recover all that *B* could have recovered if the contract had been made with *B* himself.'

It has been suggested that Lush LJ was thinking of a contract in which A was trustee for B. But I do not think so. He was a common lawyer speaking of common law. His words were quoted with considerable approval by Lord Pearce in *Beswick* v. *Beswick* [1968] AC 58, 88. I have myself often quoted them. I think they should be accepted as correct, at any rate so long as the law forbids the third persons themselves from suing for damages. It is the only way in which a just result can be achieved. Take the instance I have put. The guests ought to recover from the restaurant their wasted fares. The choir ought to recover the cost of hiring the taxis home. Then is no one to recover for them except the one who made the contract for their benefit? He should be able to recover the expense to which he has been put, and pay it over to them. Once recovered, it will be money had and received to their use. (They might even, if desired, be joined as plaintiffs.) If he can recover for the expense, he should also be able to recover for the discomfort, vexation and upset which the whole party have suffered by reason of the breach of contract, recompensing them accordingly out of what he recovers.

Applying the principles to this case, I think that the figure of £1,100 was about right. It would, I think, have been excessive if it had been awarded only for the damage suffered by Mr Jackson himself. But when extended to his wife and children, I do not think it is excessive. People look forward to a holiday. They expect the promises to be fulfilled. When it fails, they are greatly disappointed and upset. It is difficult to assess in terms of money; but it is the task of the judges to do the best they can. I see no reason to interfere with the total award of £1,100. I would therefore dismiss the appeal.

Orr LJ

I agree.

James LJ

In this case Mr Jackson, as found by the judge on the evidence, was in need of a holiday at the end of 1970. He was able to afford a holiday for himself and his family. According to the form he completed, which was the form of Horizon Holidays Ltd, he booked what was a family holiday. The wording of that form might in certain circumstances give rise to a contract in which the person signing the form is acting as his own principal and as agent for others. In the circumstances of this case, as indicated by Lord Denning MR, it would be wholly unrealistic to regard this contract as other than one made by Mr Jackson for a family holiday. The judge found that he did not get a family holiday. The costs were some £1,200. When he came back he felt no benefit. His evidence was to the effect that, without any exaggeration, he felt terrible. He said: 'The only thing, I was pleased to be back, very pleased, but I had nothing at all from that holiday'. For my part, on the issue of damages in this matter, I am quite content to say that £1,100 awarded was the right and proper figure in those circumstances. I would dismiss the appeal.

COMMENTARY

The Court of Appeal held that Mr Jackson was entitled to £1,100 by way of damages. But on what basis? Lord Denning was clearly of the view that £1,100 was excessive if it was awarded solely in respect of the loss suffered by Mr Jackson but that it was nevertheless justifiable on the basis that Mr Jackson was entitled to recover damages on behalf of his family in respect of the loss which they had all suffered. Thus in his view Mr Jackson's claim was not one for his own loss but for the loss suffered by third parties (namely the members of his family). The judgment of James LJ is short but it would appear that he was content to uphold the award of the trial judge who awarded damages on the basis that the sum awarded was solely in respect of the loss suffered by Mr Jackson. So it would appear that James LJ was of the view that damages were awarded in respect of Mr Jackson's loss and not the loss suffered by members of his family. Given this apparent judicial division of opinion as to the basis on which damages were awarded to Mr Jackson, the judgment of Orr LJ assumes considerable significance. But what is the meaning to be ascribed to his two-word judgment? Did he agree with the substance of Lord Denning's judgment or did he simply agree with his conclusion that the appeal should be dismissed? It is impossible to give a definitive answer to this question and, this being the case, *Jackson* cannot be regarded as un-equivocal authority for the proposition that a contracting party can sue and recover damages in respect of a loss suffered by a third party to the contract. Although the basis of the decision is a matter of debate (were damages awarded to compensate Mr Jackson for his loss or to compensate Mr Jackson for the loss which he and his family suffered?), the decision (in terms of its result) is not. It was accepted by the House of Lords in *Woodar Investment Development Ltd* v. *Wimpey Construction UK Ltd* [1980] 1 WLR 277 (below) and by Lord Goff and Lord Millett in *Panatown*.

One final point should be noted about *Jackson*. A common concern that emerges from the speeches of Lords Goff and Millett in *Panatown* (at p. 544) is that the contracting party should not be entitled to recover an 'uncovenanted profit'. In so far as damages are awarded to the claimant in respect of the loss suffered by the third party, the claimant should be required to account for them to the third party. Lord Denning was alive to this problem. Thus he stated that the contracting party was accountable to the third parties by means of an action for 'money had and received to their use' (in other words, a personal restitutionary claim) for the damages received in respect of the loss suffered by the third parties.

Turning now to the commercial context, our illustrative case is:

Woodar Investment Development Ltd v. Wimpey Construction UK Ltd

[1980] 1 WLR 277, House of Lords

Wimpey agreed to buy land from Woodar. The contract stated that the purchase price was £850,000 but it further provided that upon completion of the purchase Wimpey should pay a further £150,000 to Transworld Trade Ltd ('Transworld'). Woodar alleged that Wimpey had committed a repudiatory breach of the contract and they claimed damages from Wimpey which included the £150,000 that Wimpey had agreed to pay to Transworld. The House of Lords held that Wimpey had not repudiated the contract and, this being the case, it was not necessary to decide whether or not Woodar were entitled to recover damages in respect of the money payable to Transworld. Nevertheless, their Lordships did consider the entitlement of Woodar to recover damages in the following terms.

Lord Wilberforce [referred to the decision of the Court of Appeal in *Jackson* v. *Horizon Holidays Ltd* and continued]
I am not prepared to dissent from the actual decision in that case. It may be supported either as a broad decision on the measure of damages (per James LJ) or possibly as an example of a type of contract, examples of which are persons contracting for family holidays, ordering meals in restaurants for a party, hiring a taxi for a group, calling for special treatment. As I suggested in *New Zealand Shipping Co Ltd* v *A M Satterthwaite & Co Ltd (The Eurymedon)* [1975] AC 154, 167, there are many situations of daily life which do not fit neatly into conceptual analysis, but which require some flexibility in the law of contract. *Jackson's* case may well be one.

I cannot however agree with the basis on which Lord Denning MR put his decision in that case. The extract on which he relied from the judgment of Lush LJ in *Lloyd's* v. *Harper* . . . was part of a passage in which the Lord Justice was stating as an 'established rule of law' that an agent . . . may sue on a contract made by him on behalf of the principal . . . if the contract gives him such a right, and is no authority for the proposition required in *Jackson's* case, still less for the proposition, required here, that, if Woodar made a contract for a sum of money to be paid to Transworld, Woodar can, without showing that it has itself suffered loss or that Woodar was agent or trustee for Transworld, sue for damages for non-payment of that sum . . .

Whether in a situation such as the present—viz, where it is not shown that Woodar was agent or trustee for Transworld, or that Woodar itself sustained any loss, Woodar can recover any damages at all, or any but nominal damages, against Wimpey, and on what principle, is, in my opinion, a question of great doubt and difficulty—no doubt open in this House—but one on which I prefer to reserve my opinion.

Lord Keith of Kinkel [referred to the decision of the Court of Appeal in *Jackson* v. *Horizon Holidays Ltd* and continued]

That case is capable of being regarded as rightly decided upon a reasonable view of the measure of damages due to the plaintiff as the original contracting party, and not as laying down any rule of law regarding the recovery of damages for the benefit of third parties. There may be a certain class of cases where third parties stand to gain indirectly by virtue of a contract, and where their deprivation of that gain can properly be regarded as no more than a consequence of the loss suffered by one of the contracting parties. In that situation there may be no question of the third parties having any claim to damages in their own right, but yet it may be proper to take into account in assessing the damages recoverable by the contracting party an element in respect of expense incurred by him in replacing by other means benefits of which the third parties have been deprived or in mitigating the consequences of that deprivation. The decision in *Jackson* v. *Horizon Holidays Ltd* is not, however . . . capable of being supported upon the basis of the true ratio decidendi in *Lloyd's* v. *Harper* 16 Ch D 290, which rested entirely on the principles of agency.

Lord Scarman

I believe it open to the House to declare that, in the absence of evidence to show that he has suffered no loss, A, who has contracted for a payment to be made to C, may rely on the fact that he required the payment to be made as prima facie evidence that the promise for which he contracted was a benefit to him and that the measure of his loss in the event of non-payment is the benefit which he intended for C but which has not been received. Whatever the reason, he must have desired the payment to be made to C and he must have been relying on B to make it. If B fails to make the payment, A must find the money from other funds if he is to confer the benefit which he sought by his contract to confer upon C. Without expressing a final opinion on a question, which is clearly difficult, I think the point is one which does require consideration by your Lordships' House.

Lord Salmon agreed with Lord Wilberforce, but added that, in his opinion, 'the law as it stands at present in relation to damages of this kind is most unsatisfactory: and I can only hope that your Lordships' House will soon have an opportunity of reconsidering it unless in the meantime it is altered by statute'. **Lord Russell of Killowen** was critical of the reasoning of Lord Denning in *Jackson's* case and pointed out 'that the order of the Court of Appeal as drawn up did not suggest that any part of the damages awarded to [Mr Jackson] were "for the use and benefit of" any member of his family'. He was therefore of the opinion that Woodar were only entitled to recover nominal damages in respect of the £150,000 payable to Transworld.

COMMENTARY

One point which does emerge with clarity from the judgments in *Woodar* is their Lordships' disapproval of the reasoning of Lord Denning in *Jackson*. Matters are more difficult in relation to the scope of the right of recovery recognized by their Lordships. The fact that their analysis was all *obiter*, and hence rather tentative, does not help. If Woodar had acted as agent or trustee for Transworld, it seems clear that Woodar would have been entitled to recover substantial damages. But in the absence of agency or trust, and assuming that Woodar had not itself suffered any loss as a result of the failure to make the payment to Transworld, it seems that Woodar's claim would have failed in the absence of judicial re-consideration of the underlying general rule that a party can only recover in respect of his own loss. But, as we have noted (p. 1195 above), the general rule was recently re-affirmed by the House of Lords in *Alfred McAlpine Construction Ltd* v. *Panatown Ltd* [2001] 1 AC 518. Indeed, *Woodar* would appear to emerge unscathed from *Panatown*. Lord Clyde cited it (at p. 522) for its recognition of the agency and trustee exception to the general rule, although (at p. 535) he also cited with approval Lord Wilberforce's observation that 'there are many situations of daily life which do not fit neatly into conceptual analysis, but which require some flexibility in the law of contract'. Lord Jauncey summarized the judgments in *Woodar* (at pp. 572–573) and, while he noted the reservations of Lords Salmon and Scarman, did not suggest that Woodar should have been entitled to recover. Lord Browne-Wilkinson made no mention of the case. Of the dissentients, Lord Goff (at p. 553) was of the view that broader recognition of the plaintiff's performance interest (discussed in more detail at pp. 1046–1054 above) would encompass some of the examples given by Lord Wilberforce in his judgment but he did not state expressly whether or not he would have held that Woodar was entitled to recover damages in respect of the £150,000 payable to Transworld. Lord Millett (at p. 589) cited the passage extracted above from the speech of Lord Scarman with apparent approval and his broad conception of the plaintiff's performance interest would appear to lead him to the conclusion that Woodar should have been entitled to recover substantial damages in respect of Wimpey's failure to pay Transworld but, again, he did not say so expressly.

Why should Woodar not be entitled to recover damages in respect of the £150,000 payable to Transworld? Even assuming that there is a general rule to the effect that a contracting party cannot recover damages in respect of a loss suffered by a third party, should the parties not be able to contract out of it? If A and B enter into a contract and they agree that any breach by A will have a detrimental effect on C and that B should be entitled to sue and recover damages on behalf of C, why should the law refuse to give effect to that agreement? This hypothetical example is not very far away from the fact situation in *Woodar*. Wimpey agreed to pay £150,000 to Transworld and it is unlikely that the parties intended that Wimpey should be able to break its promise with impunity. Is it not more likely that the parties intended that Woodar should be entitled to sue for damages subject to its duty to account for the sum so received to Transworld? It may be that the parties did not make their intention in this regard sufficiently explicit (and they also failed to make use of agency or the trust which would have protected Woodar's claim in relation to the £150,000) but, assuming that such was their intention, should the courts not have given effect to it? In other words, the law should recognize that the parties are entitled to contract out of the rule that a party to a contract cannot sue and recover damages in respect of a loss suffered by a third party.

As it is, the law recognizes various exceptions to the general rule that a party can only recover damages in respect of its own loss, albeit that the exceptions do not appear to go as far as to suggest that it is open to the parties to contract out of the general rule. The principal exceptions which have been recognized are as follows.

First, a trustee can sue and recover damages even though the loss is suffered by the beneficiary. Secondly, an agent can recover damages notwithstanding the fact that the loss has been suffered by his principal. A further exception was recognized by Lord Diplock in *The Albazero* [1977] AC 774, 847 when he stated:

in a commercial contract concerning goods where it is in the contemplation of the parties that the proprietary interests in the goods may be transferred from one owner to another after the contract has been entered into and before the breach which causes loss or damage to the goods, an original party to the contract, if such be the intention of them both, is to be treated in law as having entered into the contract for the benefit of all persons who have or may acquire an interest in the goods before they are lost or damaged, and is entitled to recover by way of damages for breach of contract the actual loss sustained by those for whose benefit the contract is entered into.

The scope of this exception is a matter of some doubt. This principle originated in the context of contracts for the carriage of goods but it is clear that it is no longer so confined. It has been applied by the House of Lords to building contracts (see *Linden Gardens Trust Ltd* v. *Lenesta Sludge Disposals Ltd* [1994] 1 AC 85). It is clear that the exception cannot be invoked where the third party is given its own right of action against the party in breach (*Alfred McAlpine Construction Ltd* v. *Panatown Ltd* [2001] 1 AC 518). One particularly troublesome issue is whether or not it is confined to the case where it was in the contemplation of the parties that the ownership of the property would or might in the ordinary course of business be transferred by the contracting party to a successor in title during the currency of the contract. Lord Diplock clearly thought it was so confined and his view was endorsed by Lord Millett in *Panatown* (at p. 583). On the other hand, Lord Clyde stated in *Panatown* (at p. 531) that a change of ownership was not a necessary ingredient of the exception and the Court of Appeal so decided in *Darlington Borough Council* v. *Wiltshier Northern Ltd* [1995] 1 WLR 68.

(c) THE EXCEPTIONS TO PRIVITY

The rule that a third party cannot sue on a contract to which he is not party was never absolute. The law always recognized some exceptions to, or qualifications of, the rule. The source of these exceptions is to be found both at common law and in various statutes. The principal exceptions, prior to the enactment of the 1999 Act, are as follows:

(i) COLLATERAL CONTRACTS

The first is to find that the third party is not in fact a third party but is a party to a contract with the party who has failed to carry out his promise. The device that the courts can employ to this effect is the collateral contract. It can be seen at work in the case of *Shanklin Pier Ltd* v. *Detel Products Ltd* [1951] 2 KB 854. The defendant paint manufacturers represented to the plaintiffs, the owners of a pier, that the paint which they manufactured was suitable for use in the re-painting of the pier and would have a life of seven to ten years. In reliance upon the defendant's representation the plaintiffs instructed the contractors they had employed to re-paint the pier that they should use the defendant's paint. The paint proved to be unsuitable for use on the pier and its life span was considerably less than the promised seven to ten years. The plaintiffs brought an action against the defendants. The defendants denied that they had provided any warranty but the trial judge, McNair J, held that such a warranty had been given. He then turned to the defendants' second line of defence which was that the warranty did not give to the plaintiffs a cause of action. McNair J stated (at p. 856):

Counsel for the defendants submitted that in law a warranty can give rise to no enforceable cause of action except between the same parties as the parties to the main contract in relation to which the warranty is given. In principle, this submission seems to me to be unsound. If, as is elementary, the consideration for the warranty in the usual case is the entering into of the main contract in relation to which the warranty is given, I see no reason why there may not be an enforceable warranty between A and B supported by the consideration that B should cause C to enter into a contract with A or that B should do some act for the benefit of A.

He therefore held that the plaintiffs were entitled to recover damages from the defendant.

The principal problem likely to confront any claimant who wishes to rely upon the existence of a collateral contract is that it must adduce evidence to support the existence of such a contract (in terms of offer, acceptance, intention to create legal relations, and consideration). In some cases the courts have found that there was no intention to create a collateral contract (see, for example, *Independent Broadcasting Authority* v. *EMI Electronics* (1980) 14 Build LR 1). However examples can be found of cases in which the courts have adopted a very flexible approach to the identification of offer, acceptance, and consideration (see, in particular, *New Zealand Shipping Co Ltd* v. *AM Satterthwaite & Co Ltd (The Eurymedon)* [1975] AC 154, at p. 1223 below).

The status of the collateral contract device as an exception to the doctrine of privity is open to question on the basis that it is not in fact an exception because it rests on a finding by the court that the third party is not a third party but is a party to a contract. Nevertheless, it is customary to treat the collateral contract device as an exception to the doctrine of privity on the basis that some of the cases adopt a rather strained analysis of the relationship between the parties in order to find that the claimant and the defendant were in fact contracting parties (see, in particular, *The Eurymedon*).

(ii) TRUST OF A CONTRACTUAL RIGHT

In *Dunlop Pneumatic Tyre Company Ltd* v. *Selfridge and Company Ltd* [1915] AC 847 (p. 1176 above) Viscount Haldane LC stated that, while English law does not recognize a third party right of action arising by way of contract, such a 'right may be conferred by way of property, as, for example, under a trust'. In other words a promisee may agree to hold his contractual right to sue the promisor on trust for the third party and, as a beneficiary under a trust, the third party acquires a property right which he can assert against someone, such as the promisor, who interferes with it. Cases can be found in which the courts have found the existence of a trust of a contractual right (see, for example, *Les Affreteurs Reunis* v. *Walford* [1919] AC 801) and, for a time, it appeared that the trust might prove to be a suitable vehicle for out-flanking privity and conferring enforceable rights of action on third parties. But it was not to be. By the time we get to *Beswick* v. *Beswick* in 1967 (p. 1181 above) we find that it was 'common ground' between the parties that Peter Beswick did not enter into the agreement with his nephew as trustee for his wife in relation to the annuity to be paid to her.

With the benefit of hindsight we can see that the turning point was the decision of the Court of Appeal in *Re Schebsman* [1944] Ch 83. John Schebsman (referred to as 'the debtor') worked for a Swiss company and its subsidiary, an English company, until his contract was terminated in 1940. On 20 September 1940 Schebsman entered into an agreement with the two companies under which, in consideration of the termination of his employment, the companies agreed to pay him £5,500 in six instalments. The agreement provided that, in the event that Schebsman died before all six payments had been made to him, the money was to be paid to his wife and, if she died, his daughter. Schebsman was adjudicated bankrupt on 5 March 1942 and died on 12 May 1942. His trustee in bankruptcy sought a declaration that the sums payable to Schebsman's widow and, possibly, his daughter formed part of Schebsman's estate with the result that they should be gathered in by the trustee in bankruptcy and distributed among Schebsman's creditors rather than paid to his widow or daughter. The basis on which the trustee in bankruptcy sought this declaration was the submission that Schebsman had a right to intercept the money payable to his widow and that that right now resided in the trustee in bankruptcy. The Court of Appeal held that Schebsman had no such right of interception and that the trustee in bankruptcy was not entitled to the declaration sought. Our interest in the case lies in the submission advanced by counsel for the defendant, Mr Denning KC, that the contract between the companies and Schebsman created a trust in favour of Schebsman's widow and daughter. Uthwatt J and the Court of Appeal held that no such trust had been created. In the Court of Appeal Lord Greene MR stated (at p. 89) that:

The first question which arises is whether or not the debtor was a trustee for his wife and daughter of the benefit of the undertaking given by the English company in their favour. An examination of the decided cases does, it is true, show that the courts have on occasions adopted what may be called a liberal view on questions of this character, but in the present case I cannot find in the contract anything to justify the conclusion that a trust was intended. It is not legitimate to import into the contract the idea of a trust when the parties have given no indication that such was their intention. To interpret this contract as creating a trust would, in my judgment, be to disregard the dividing line between the case of a trust and the simple case of a contract made between two persons for the benefit of a third. That dividing line exists, although it may not always be easy to determine where it is to be drawn. In the present case I find no difficulty.

To similar effect is the judgment of du Parcq LJ. He stated (at p. 104):

It was argued by Mr Denning that one effect of the agreement of September 20, 1940, was that a trust was thereby created, and that the debtor constituted himself trustee for Mrs Schebsman of the benefit of the covenant under which payments were to be made to her. Uthwatt J rejected this contention, and the argument has not satisfied me that he was wrong. It is true that, by the use possibly of unguarded language, a person may create a trust, as Monsieur Jourdain talked prose, without knowing it, but unless an intention to create a trust is clearly to be collected from the language used and the circumstances of the case, I think that the court ought not to be astute to discover indications of such an intention. I have little doubt that in the present case both parties (and certainly the debtor) intended to keep alive their common law right to vary consensually the terms of the obligation undertaken by the company, and if circumstances had changed in the debtor's life-time injustice might have been done by holding that a trust had been created and that those terms were accordingly unalterable. On this point, therefore, I agree with Uthwatt J.

The demise of the trust in this context can be attributed to two related factors. The first is that the courts now take seriously the requirement that the parties must have had an intention to create a trust. At first instance in *Re Schebsman* [1943] Ch 366, 368 Mr Denning KC referred Uthwatt J to a famous article by Professor Corbin ('Contracts for the Benefit of Third Parties' (1930) 46 *LQR* 12) in support of his submission that a trust had been created on the facts of the case. Uthwatt J referred to the article by Corbin, considered the cases referred to in the article, and continued (at p. 370):

I am unable to see that they justify the conclusion at which he arrived that in some cases of the class now under consideration a fiction has been resorted to in order to raise a trust. The cases, no doubt, are hard to reconcile, but, to my mind, the explanation of them is that different minds may reach differing conclusions on the question whether the circumstances sufficiently show an intention to create a trust. Inferences as to intent may vary. . . . In the present case there can be no question of any estoppel, and there is nothing, except the terms of the contract itself, on which to ground an inference that there was an intention to create a trust and that the intent was duly put into effect . . . I do not think any such inference can properly be drawn. The only inference I draw is the obvious one, that the parties thought the contract would be carried out.

In most cases (*Schebsman* being an example) the intention of the parties is simply to enter into a contract and they will have given no thought to the creation of a trust. This being the case, there will be no intention to create a trust and so no trust. The second, and related factor is that a trust, once recognized, is irrevocable. This protects the position of the third party, in that he acquires an irrevocable right, but it deprives the parties to the contract of the freedom to change their minds. As du Parcq LJ noted in *Schebsman* (above) the contracting parties are likely to be slow to give up their freedom in this respect and, this being the case, the courts can be expected to be slow to infer the existence of a trust.

It would, however, be a mistake to dismiss the trust as a modern day irrelevance in this context. Parties who wish to create a trust of a contractual right are free to do so and it is not a difficult task for a lawyer to draw up a document that makes clear the parties' intention to create a trust. The principal drawback is that the trust, once constituted, is irrevocable. This being the case, it is necessary to think carefully before setting up a trust. But contracting parties who are certain that they want to confer an irrevocable right of action upon the third party can make use of the trust device in order to give effect to their intention.

(III) ASSIGNMENT

The doctrine of privity prevents A and B from conferring upon C, a third party, a right to enforce a term of their contract. But the law does allow a contracting party to transfer, or assign, his rights under a contract to a third party. This process, known as assignment, is an important feature of commercial practice. Assignment is particularly common in relation to debts (although it is not confined to debts). Suppose that A owes a sum of money to B and that the debt is repayable over a three-year period. B decides that he does not want to wait for three years for repayment in full and so he sells to C his rights against A in return for a cash payment from C. B, the creditor, will sell his rights against A by assigning them to C. The amount paid by C will generally be a percentage of the debt. In this way B gets access to instant cash and C makes his profit by paying to B a percentage (say 85 per cent) of the debt owed by A and by recovering the debt from A over the three-year period. The law relating to assignment is complex but it suffices for our purposes to note five points.

The first is that a distinction must be drawn between the assignment of contractual rights and the assignment of liabilities. As a general rule liabilities cannot be assigned without the consent of the party to whom the liability is owed. Contractual rights are more freely assignable and the extent to which they can be assigned is discussed in points two, three, and four.

The second point relates to the legal basis of an assignment. Assignments are either equitable or statutory in nature (the common law having largely set its face against the assignment of contractual rights). A statutory assignment generally takes effect under section 136 of the Law of Property Act 1925 provided that the requirements of the section have been satisfied. There are a number of requirements: (i) the assignment must be absolute and not by way of charge; (ii) the assignment must be unconditional so that it cannot, for example, take effect upon the occurrence of a future, uncertain event; (iii) the assignment must be in writing and signed by the assignor; (iv) express notice in writing must be given to the debtor; and (v) the assignment must be of 'any debt or other legal thing in action'. A statutory assignee is entitled to sue the debtor without having to join the assignor as a party to the action. Equity generally takes a more flexible approach to the validity of assignments so that an assignment that fails to comply with the requirements of section 136 may nevertheless take effect as an equitable assignment. Thus an equitable assignment may be valid notwithstanding the fact that it is not in writing (unless statute, such as s. 53(1)(c) of the Law of Property Act 1925, provides otherwise) and notice has not been given to the debtor (although good practice usually dictates that notice is given to the debtor). An equitable assignee must generally join the assignor as a party to the action. In the case of a statutory assignment the assignee need not have provided consideration, although, in the case of an equitable assignment, the point is more doubtful (the safest course being to ensure that consideration is provided).

The third point relates to the extent to which contractual rights are assignable. Not all contractual rights are assignable. In the first place the contract may prohibit assignment or place limits on the extent to which rights under the contract can be assigned. A purported assignment which breaches a prohibition upon assignment will not be effective to confer rights upon the assignee, at least as between the assignee and the debtor (see *Linden Gardens Trust Ltd* v. *Lenesta Sludge Disposals Ltd* [1994] 1 AC 85). Secondly, a mere right to sue for damages (or, as it is sometimes put, a bare right to litigate) is not assignable unless the assignee has a genuine commercial or financial interest in taking the assignment (*Trendtex Trading Corporation* v. *Credit Suisse* [1982]

AC 679). Thirdly, where the relationship between the parties to the original contract is a personal one, the law may not give effect to an assignment of the rights under that contract (so, for example, the benefit of a car insurance policy is not assignable nor is any contractual right involving personal skill on the part of the creditor). In *Tolhurst* v. *Associated Portland Cement Manufacturers Ltd* [1902] 2 KB 660, 668 Collins MR summed up the position when he stated that the benefit of a contract is only assignable in cases 'where it can make no objective difference to the person on whom the obligation lies to which of two persons he is to discharge it'.

The fourth point is that an assignment takes effect 'subject to equities', that is to say, the assignee acquires the contractual rights of the assignor subject to all the defences that would have prevailed against the assignor. A related rule is that an assignee cannot generally recover more by way of damages than the assignor would have recovered had there been no assignment (see *Dawson* v. *Great Northern & City Railway Co* [1905] 1 KB 260).

The final point is that the burden of a contract cannot be assigned without the consent of the other party to the contract. The requirement that consent be obtained to the transfer of liabilities is necessary to protect the right of contracting parties to choose their contracting parties. Were the law otherwise a party could enter into a contract with one party, only to find that performance is provided by another party and that he has no right to object and no means of redress. It is, however, important to note that the law does allow liabilities to be transferred provided that consent is obtained. This process is known as novation. The law relating to novation was summarized by David Steel J in *The Tychy (No 2)* [2001] 1 Lloyd's Rep 10, 24 in the following terms:

(a) Novation involves the creation of a new contract where an existing party is replaced by a new party. (b) Thus, novation requires the consent of all parties, including in particular the party which is thereby accepting a new person as his debtor or as his counterpart under an executory contract. (c) The consent may be apparent from express words or inferred from conduct. (d) The consent must be clearly established on the evidence as being only consistent with the intent of achieving a novation.

Novation provides a means by which one contracting party can drop out of the contract and be replaced by another party who will acquire the rights and obligations of the party who drops out of the contract. So, for example, novation provides the means by which a third party can be substituted as a lender under a loan agreement. Novation thus assumes an important role in commercial practice in that it enables the parties to restructure transactions and it also facilitates the transfer of financial assets.

(IV) AGENCY

The relationship between the law of agency and the doctrine of privity is an uneasy one. Parts of the law of agency can be explained in terms which are consistent with privity, but other parts, particularly the rules relating to undisclosed principals, are very difficult to reconcile with privity. As we have noted (p. 1179 above) Viscount Haldane in *Dunlop Pneumatic Tyre Company Ltd* v. *Selfridge and Company Ltd* [1915]

AC 847 stated that a principal not named in a contract may sue upon it if the promisee really contracted as his agent provided that the principal has given consideration either personally or through the promisee acting as his agent.

An agent is a person who has authority from another party, his principal, to act on the principal's behalf in such a way as to affect the principal's legal relations with third parties. Suppose that company X appoints a number of independent brokers to act on its behalf in selling the company's products. Company X limits the authority of its brokers in various ways (for example, no broker can offer a customer a discount greater than 10% without first obtaining approval from head office). One of the brokers, after disclosing that he is acting as an agent for X, concludes a contract with a third party under which the third party agrees to buy products from company X. Who are the parties to the contract for the purchase of these products? The answer is that it is company X and the third party. The general rule is that once an agent, acting within the scope of his authority, has concluded a contract with a third party, the agent 'drops out of the picture' so that he can neither sue nor be sued upon the contract (*Wakefield* v. *Duckworth* [1915] 1 KB 218). More difficult is the case where the agent acts in excess of his authority in concluding the contract. Suppose that the broker offers the third party a discount of 15% without first obtaining approval from head office. Is X bound by this contract? The answer depends on whether or not the agent was acting within the scope of his authority in entering into the contract on these terms. Obviously the broker did not have actual authority to conclude the contract but the prohibition or limitation placed on his authority by X does not necessarily bind the third party. In order to protect the position of third parties the law adopts a more extensive conception of authority that extends beyond actual authority to implied authority, apparent authority, and usual authority. It is not necessary to analyse these concepts in any detail here. It suffices to state that, where the principal holds out the agent as having certain authority or a party in the position of the agent would customarily have a certain amount of authority, the third party is not generally bound by any narrower limit on the authority of the agent unless the third party has notice of such a limitation. This branch of the law of agency can generally be explained in terms that are consistent with the doctrine of privity. In these cases the principal is not a third party intervening on a contract which he did not make. The agent disclosed to the third party that he was acting on behalf of the principal and the agent's function was to bring about a contractual relationship between the principal and the third party. In these circumstances the proposition that the principal is a party to, or privy to, the contract is an acceptable one.

Much more difficult to explain is the doctrine of the undisclosed principal. The law relating to the undisclosed principal was summarized by Lord Lloyd in *Siu Yin Kwan* v. *Eastern Insurance Co Ltd* [1994] 2 AC 199, 207 in the following terms:

(1) An undisclosed principal may sue and be sued on a contract made by an agent on his behalf, acting within the scope of his actual authority. (2) In entering into the contract, the agent must intend to act on the principal's behalf. (3) The agent of an undisclosed principal may also sue and be sued on the contract. (4) Any defence which the third party may have against the agent is available against his principal. (5) The terms of the contract may, expressly or by implication,

exclude the principal's right to sue, and his liability to be sued. The contract itself, or the circumstances surrounding the contract, may show that the agent is the true and only principal.

In this instance the third party is unaware of the existence of the principal but the principal is nevertheless entitled to sue, and can be sued, on the contract. As Professor Reynolds points out (*Bowstead and Reynolds on Agency*, (17th edn, Sweet & Maxwell, 2001), para 8-071), 'it is difficult to deny that the undisclosed principal is really a third party intervening on a contract which he did not make'. This point was conceded by Lord Lloyd in *Siu Yin Kwan* when he stated that 'it seems to be generally accepted that, while the development of this branch of the law may have been anomalous, since it runs counter to fundamental principles of privity of contract, it is justified on grounds of commercial convenience'. The 'commercial convenience' of the doctrine has been disputed on the ground that it can cause hardship to a third party who finds himself bound by a contract with a party of whose existence he was unaware and to whose presence he may object (although it should be noted that, where the benefit of the contract is assignable, the third party does not have the right to choose his contracting party). True, the law has imposed limits on the entitlement of the principal to intervene on the contract (see, for example, *Said* v. *Butt* [1920] 3 KB 497) but these limits are of uncertain scope and may leave the third party bound by a contract with a principal with whom the third party would never knowingly have contracted (*Dyster* v. *Randall & Sons* [1926] Ch 932). Some of the cases in this area of the law are extremely difficult, if not impossible to reconcile with the doctrine of privity (see, for example, *Watteau* v. *Fenwick* [1893] 1 QB 346). It seems odd that a principal can intervene on a contract when he is not named and one of the parties objects to his participation in the contract while the doctrine of privity prevents a third party from intervening on a contract when the two parties to the contract have expressly stated that the third party is to have the right to intervene and enforce the contract (as was the case in *Tweddle* v. *Atkinson* p. 1173 above).

(V) NEGOTIABLE INSTRUMENTS

A negotiable instrument has been defined by Professor Goode (*Commercial Law* (Penguin, 3rd edn, 2004), p. 477) as an instrument 'which, by statute or mercantile usage, may be transferred by delivery and indorsement to a bona fide purchaser for value in such circumstances that he takes free from defects in the title of prior parties'. It is important to note that this 'bona fide purchaser', known as a holder in due course, takes 'free from defects' and so is in a better position than an assignee because an assignment takes effect 'subject to equities'. A cheque is a negotiable instrument. A person who writes a cheque is known as 'the drawer'. The cheque is essentially an instruction by the drawer to his bank, the drawee, to pay a third party a given sum of money. The third party recipient of the cheque can then present the cheque and demand payment from the drawer's bank. Cheques, together with other negotiable instruments (such as bills of exchange and promissory notes) have for many years played an important role in the economy and their commercial success has depended, in large part, upon the third party being given a secure right to demand payment from the bank. While the significance of cheques is likely to diminish in the future, with the development of new electronic methods of payment, it is important not to lose sight of the benefits that can be obtained by the use of a negotiable instrument.

(VI) TORT

A claimant who suffers loss as a result of the negligence of the defendant in the performance of a contract with another party may have a claim against the defendant in the tort of negligence. This proposition does not excite much controversy where the loss which the claimant suffers is physical injury or property damage. In the great case of *Donoghue* v. *Stevenson* [1932] AC 562 the pursuer (the term used to describe the claimant in Scotland) alleged that she became ill after drinking ginger beer out of a bottle which contained the remains of a decomposed snail. The ginger beer was purchased at a café by the pursuer's friend and so she did not have a claim in contract against the café proprietor. So she brought an action in delict (tort) against the manufacturer of the ginger beer. The manufacturer defended the claim and submitted that the duty which it owed was to its contracting party and that it could not owe a duty to a third party with whom it was not in a contractual relationship. The House of Lords rejected the defender's submission and held that it could be liable to the pursuer (provided that she could establish the factual basis of her claim). Lord Atkin stated that:

A manufacturer of products, which he sells in such a form as to show that he intends them to reach the ultimate consumer in the form in which they left him with no reasonable possibility of intermediate examination, and with the knowledge that the absence of reasonable care in the preparation or putting up of the products will result in an injury to the consumer's life or property, owes a duty to the consumer to take that reasonable care.

More difficult is the case where the claimant suffers economic loss as a result of the negligence of the defendant in the performance of his contract with a third party. Cases can be found in which the courts have imposed a duty of care in favour of the claimant in this situation, although the cases themselves have proved to be extremely controversial. The most controversial case is the decision of the House of Lords in *Junior Books Ltd* v. *Veitchi Co Ltd* [1983] 1 AC 520. The pursuers entered into a contract with main contractors for the construction of a factory and the defenders were employed as sub-contractors by the main contractors (although they were nominated by the pursuers). The pursuers alleged that the floor had been laid defectively and they brought an action in delict (tort) against the defenders. Their claim succeeded in the House of Lords. Normally such claims would be brought in contract: the pursuer would sue the main contractor and the main contractor would then sue the sub-contractor and so liability would flow down the chain of contracts. But the effect of *Junior Books* was to enable the pursuers to jump down the chain of contracts and bring an action directly against the sub-contractors. The case is open to criticism in so far as it rests on a finding that the defenders had assumed a responsibility towards the pursuers. The normal construction (and the one adopted in cases such as *Simaan General Contracting Co* v. *Pilkington Glass Ltd (No 2)* [1988] QB 758) is that the responsibility assumed by the party in the position of the defender is a contractual one owed to its immediate contracting party and not in tort to a remoter party down the chain of contracts.

The second case is *White* v. *Jones* [1995] 2 AC 207, a case which the Law Commission in their Report on Privity of Contract (at para 2.14) state is best analysed as 'allowing a third party to enforce a contract by pursuing an action in tort'. The defendant solicitor was instructed by a testator to draw up a new will. The defendant failed to do so before the testator's death. The intended beneficiaries under the new will brought an action in negligence against the defendant on the basis that his negligent failure to draw up the will had caused them to lose their bequests. By a majority of 3–2 the House of Lords held that the claimants were entitled to bring an action in negligence against the defendants. One factor which weighed heavily with their Lordships was that the beneficiaries were the parties who had suffered the loss and, if they did not have a claim against the solicitor, there would be a lacuna in the law because, although the estate (as the contracting party) had a claim against the solicitor, it had suffered no loss and so had no effective claim. The remedy which their Lordships fashioned in order to avoid such a lacuna was tortious in form but has the features of a contractual claim in that, as Lord Goff acknowledged, the solicitor is entitled to rely on any term of the contract with his client in order to limit or exclude his liability to the beneficiaries in tort. It is therefore a claim in tort that is subject to the terms of the contract between the solicitor and his client.

While a claim in tort thus has the potential to outflank the doctrine of privity in this way it is subject to the obvious limitation that the claimant, in order to succeed, must prove that the defendant was negligent.

(VII) STATUTORY EXCEPTIONS

Prior to the enactment of the Contracts (Rights of Third Parties) Act 1999 there were a number of statutory exceptions to the doctrine of privity. We have already seen, in *Beswick* v. *Beswick* (p. 1181 above) the use that was made by Lord Denning of section 56(1) of the Law of Property Act 1925 in an attempt to outflank the doctrine of privity of contract. The attempt failed because their Lordships could not discern any intention in section 56 to effect such a radical change to common law doctrine. But in other contexts Parliament has intervened with the express purpose of recognizing third party rights. The significance of these legislative interventions should not be underestimated. The contracts regulated are important commercial transactions where tri-partite relationships are common (particularly insurance and shipping contracts). Thus section 11 of the Married Women's Property Act 1882 provides:

A policy of assurance effected by any man on his own life and expressed to be for the benefit of his wife, or of his children, or of his wife and children, or any of them, or by any woman on her own life, and expressed to be for the benefit of her husband, or of her children, or of her husband and children, or any of them, shall create a trust in favour of the objects therein named, and the moneys payable under any such policy shall not, so long as any object of the trust remains unperformed, form part of the estate of the insured, or be subject to his or her debts.

And section 14(2) of the Marine Insurance Act 1906 provides:

A mortgagee, consignee, or other person having an interest in the subject-matter insured may insure on behalf and for the benefit of other persons interested as well as for his own benefit.

Section 148(7) of the Road Traffic Act 1988 provides:

Notwithstanding anything in any enactment, a person issuing a policy of insurance under section
145 of this Act shall be liable to indemnify the persons or classes of persons specified in the policy
in respect of any liability which the policy purports to cover in the case of those persons or classes
of persons.

Finally section 2 of the Carriage of Goods by Sea Act 1992 provides that a person who
becomes the lawful holder of a bill of lading shall, by virtue of becoming the holder of
the bill, have transferred to and vested in him all rights of suit under the contract of
carriage as if he had been a party to that contract from the outset. The significance
of section 2 is explained in greater detail below.

(d) THIRD PARTIES, EXCLUSION CLAUSES, AND EXCLUSIVE
JURISDICTION CLAUSES

An issue which has given rise to great difficulty in the case-law is the question
whether, and if so to what extent, a third party may take the benefit of an exclusion or
limitation clause in a contract to which it is not a party. A related issue is whether or
not a claimant can be bound by an exclusion or limitation clause in a contract to
which the defendant is a party but the claimant is not. As we shall see this issue is not
confined to exclusion or limitation clauses: it can arise in the context of other clauses,
notably exclusive jurisdiction clauses. The cases are both long and complex. Yet their
practical significance has diminished as a result of the enactment of the Contracts
(Rights of Third Parties) Act 1999 which provides a much simpler mechanism by
which contracting parties can extend the sphere of application of these clauses. Nevertheless, the Act will not catch all cases and, in such cases, the courts will have to fall
back on the common law rules as set out in these cases.

The approach that will be adopted in this section is to use one case, *The Mahkutai*
[1996] AC 650, as the vehicle for discussion of these issues. At the outset it must be
acknowledged that there is one drawback in this approach which is that the case
involves an exclusive jurisdiction clause (that is, a clause which requires that legal
proceedings be brought in a particular jurisdiction) rather than an exclusion clause
and exclusive jurisdiction clauses raise one or two additional complexities in comparison with exclusion clauses. But this disadvantage is more than outweighed by the
clarity and the elegance of Lord Goff's analysis of the leading cases (such as *Elder
Dempster & Co* v. *Paterson Zochonis & Co* [1924] AC 522, *Scruttons Ltd* v. *Midland
Silicones Ltd* [1962] AC 446, *New Zealand Shipping Co Ltd* v *AM Satterthwaite & Co
Ltd (The Eurymedon)* [1975] AC 154, *Port Jackson Stevedoring Pty Ltd* v. *Salmond &
Spraggon (Australia) Pty Ltd (The New York Star)* [1981] 1 WLR 138, and *The Pioneer
Container* [1994] 2 AC 324). Discussion of these cases follows the extract from Lord
Goff's judgment but you may wish to resort to the commentary section after reading
Lord Goff's analysis of each leading case. Before turning to Lord Goff's judgment
three preliminary comments must be made.

The first relates to the technicality of the language that is used in the judgments.
Three phrases merit further discussion at this point: (i) bill of lading, (ii) bailment on

terms, and (iii) vicarious immunity. A bill of lading and its functions have been described in A Guest (ed), *Benjamin's Sale of Goods* (6th edn, Sweet & Maxwell, 2003), para 18-008 in the following terms:

A bill of lading is a document issued by or on behalf of a carrier of goods by sea to the person (usually known as the shipper) with whom he has contracted for the carriage of goods. Such a document has three functions. First, it is a receipt: i.e. it is evidence that the goods described in it have been received by the carrier, or actually shipped; secondly, it is a contractual document: i.e. it is evidence of, or contains, a contract of carriage and it provides a mechanism for the transfer of rights arising under that contract to, and for the imposition of liabilities arising under it on, persons who were not original parties to that contract; and thirdly. . .it is a document of title to the goods . . .

Of these three functions, it is the second one that is important for our purposes. Bailment on terms is a little more difficult to describe and indeed the precise meaning of this phrase is the subject of some debate. Bailment is the term used to describe the situation where one person (the bailee) is voluntarily in possession of goods that belong to another (the bailor). Bailment on terms arises where the bailor entrusts goods to the bailee and, either expressly or impliedly, authorizes the bailee to entrust the goods to a third party. In such a case the bailor will be bound by the terms of the sub-bailment to which he has consented or has authorized. Vicarious immunity, on the other hand, means that an employee or agent who performs a contract is entitled to rely on any immunity from liability which the contract confers on his employer or principal.

The second point is that it is vital to distinguish the case in which the clause at issue between the parties is to be found in the main contract from the case in which the clause at issue is to be found in the sub-contract. These two cases raise different issues, although it is possible to have a case in which there are two clauses in issue between the parties, one in the main contract and one in the sub-contract but the claimant and the defendant are not in a direct contractual relationship (*Scruttons Ltd* v. *Midland Silicones Ltd* [1962] AC 446 being such a case).

The third point relates to the policy issues at stake. The policy issues in the exclusion clause cases differ from those that arise in the context of exclusive jurisdiction clauses. The policy issues in relation to exclusive jurisdiction clauses are raised in Lord Goff's judgment in *The Mahkutai* (below) and so here it suffices to mention the conflicting policy issues that arise in the exclusion clause cases. On the one hand, the courts have, as we have seen (Chapter 13), generally adopted a restrictive approach towards exclusion clauses. This suggests that they are likely to apply privity strictly and refuse to extend the benefit of an exclusion clause to a third party. On the other hand, in some of the cases it seems clear that the intention of all the parties was that the benefit of the exclusion clause should be enjoyed by the third party (such as an employee) and, in such cases, the judges are generally unwilling to frustrate the intention of the parties, particularly in commercial transactions which have been negotiated at arm's length. This conflict of policies has been reflected in the different approaches taken by the judiciary over the years, a point noted by Lord Goff in *The Mahkutai*.

The Mahkutai

[1996] AC 650, Privy Council

Indonesian shipowners chartered their vessel to an Indonesian corporation ('the carrier') who, in turn sub-chartered it to Indonesian timber merchants ('the shippers') for the carriage of a cargo of plywood from Jakarta to Shantou in the People's Republic of China. The master of the vessel authorized the carrier's agent to sign a bill of lading which provided, in condition 4, that, every servant, agent or subcontractor of the carrier was to have the benefit of all 'exceptions, limitations, provision, conditions and liberties herein benefiting the carrier as if such provisions were expressly made for their benefit'. Condition 19 of the bill of lading further provided that:

> 'the contract evidenced by the bill of lading shall be governed by the law of Indonesia and any dispute arising hereunder shall be determined by the Indonesian courts according to that law to the exclusion of the jurisdiction of the courts of any other country.'

When the vessel arrived in Shantou it was discovered that the plywood in one of the holds had been damaged by sea water. The vessel then proceeded to Hong Kong for the purpose of discharging other cargo. On arrival of the vessel in Hong Kong the cargo owners issued a writ against the shipowners claiming damages for breach of contract, breach of duty, or negligence. The shipowners sought to stay the proceedings in Hong Kong on the ground that the proceedings had been brought in breach of condition 19, the exclusive jurisdiction clause. Sears J held that the shipowners were entitled to invoke the exclusive jurisdiction clause and he ordered that the proceedings in Hong Kong be stayed. The cargo owners appealed to the Court of Appeal who allowed the appeal. The shipowners then appealed to the Privy Council. They submitted that they were entitled to rely on the exclusive jurisdiction clause on the basis of two principles: (i) that established by the Privy Council in *New Zealand Shipping Co Ltd v. A M Satterthwaite & Co Ltd (The Eurymedon)* [1975] AC 154 and *Port Jackson Stevedoring Pty Ltd v. Salmond & Spraggon (Australia) Pty Ltd (The New York Star)* [1981] 1 WLR 138 and (ii), in the alternative, on the basis of the principle of bailment on terms, the origins of which are to be found in the speech of Lord Sumner in *Elder Dempster & Co v. Paterson Zochonis & Co* [1924] AC 522. The Privy Council held that the shipowners were not entitled to invoke the exclusive jurisdiction clause against the cargo owners, that the cargo owners were entitled to bring the action in Hong Kong against the shipowners and that the stay had been properly set aside.

Lord Goff of Chieveley [giving the judgment of the Privy Council set out the facts and continued]

The pendulum of judicial opinion

The two principles which the shipowners invoke are the product of developments in English law during the present century. During that period, opinion has fluctuated about the desirability of recognising some form of modification of, or exception to, the strict doctrine of privity of contract to accommodate situations which arise in the context of carriage of goods by sea, in which it appears to be in accordance with commercial expectations that the benefit of certain terms of the contract of carriage should be made available to parties involved in the adventure who are not parties to the contract. These cases have been concerned primarily with stevedores claiming the benefit of exceptions and limitations in bills of lading, but also with shipowners claiming the protection of such terms contained in charterers' bills. At first there appears to have been a readiness on the part of judges to recognise such claims, especially in *Elder Dempster & Co v. Paterson, Zochonis & Co Ltd*, [1924] AC 522, concerned with the principle of bailment on terms. Opinion however hardened against them in the middle of the century as the pendulum swung back in the direction of orthodoxy in *Midland Silicones Ltd v. Scruttons Ltd* [1962] AC 446; but in more recent years it has swung back again to recognition of their commercial desirability, notably in the two leading cases concerned with claims by stevedores to the protection of a Himalaya clause—*New Zealand Shipping Co Ltd v. A M Satterthwaite & Co Ltd (The Eurymedon)* [1975] AC 154 and *Port Jackson Stevedoring Pty Ltd v. Salmond & Spraggon (Australia) Pty Ltd (The New York Star)* [1981] 1 WLR 138.

In the present case shipowners carrying cargo shipped under charterers' bills of lading are seeking to claim the benefit of a Himalaya clause in the time charterers' bills of lading, or in the alternative to invoke the principle of bailment on terms. However they are seeking by these means to invoke not an exception or limitation in the ordinary sense of those words, but the benefit of an exclusive jurisdiction clause. This would involve a significantly wider application of the relevant principles; and, to judge whether this extension is justified, their Lordships consider it desirable first to trace the development of the principles through the cases.

The Elder Dempster case [1924] AC 522

The principle of bailment on terms finds its origin in the *Elder Dempster* case. That case was concerned with a damage to cargo claim in respect of a number of casks of palm oil which had been crushed by heavy bags of palm kernels stowed above them in a ship with deep holds but no 'tween decks to take the weight of the cargo stowed above. The main question in the case was whether such damage was to be classified as damage arising from unseaworthiness of the ship due to absence of 'tween decks, or as damage arising from bad stowage; in the latter event, no claim lay under the bills of lading, which contained an exception excluding claims for bad stowage. The bills of lading were time charterers' bills, the vessel having been chartered in by the time charterers as an additional vessel for their West African line. The House of Lords (on this point differing from a majority of the Court of Appeal) held that the damage was to be attributed to bad stowage, and as a result the time charterers were protected by the bill of lading exception; but the cargo owners had also sued the shipowners in tort, and the question arose whether the shipowners too were protected by the exception contained in the bill of lading, to which they were not parties. In the Court of Appeal [1923] 1 KB 420, 441–442, Scrutton LJ (who alone considered that the damage was to be attributed to bad stowage rather than unseaworthiness) rejected the claim against the shipowners on a suggested principle of vicarious immunity. This principle was relied on by the shipowners in argument before the House of Lords [1924] AC 522 and was accepted, at p. 534, by Viscount Cave (with whom Lord Carson, at p. 565, agreed), and apparently also by Viscount Finlay, at p. 548. But the preferred reason given by Lord Sumner, at p. 564 (with whom Lord Dunedin, at p. 548, and Lord Carson, at p. 565, agreed) was that:

'in the circumstances of this case the obligations to be inferred from the reception of the cargo for carriage to the United Kingdom amount to a bailment upon terms, which include the exceptions and limitations of liability stipulated in the known and contemplated form of bill of lading.'

The Midland Silicones case [1962] AC 446

This was a test case in which it was sought to establish a basis upon which stevedores could claim the protection of exceptions and limitations contained in the bill of lading contract. Here the stevedores had negligently damaged a drum of chemicals after discharge at London, to which the goods had been shipped from New York under a bill of lading incorporating the United States Carriage of Goods by Sea Act 1936, which contained the Hague Rules limitation of liability to £500 per package or unit. The stevedores sought to claim the benefit of this limit as against the receivers. They claimed to rely on the principle of bailment on terms derived from the *Elder Dempster* case [1924] AC 522. But they also sought a contractual basis for their contention on various grounds—that they had contracted with the receivers through the agency of the shipowners; that they could rely on an implied contract independent of the bill of lading; or that they could as an interested third party take the benefit of the limit in the bill of lading contract. All these arguments failed. The principle of bailment on terms was given a restrictive treatment; and the various contractual arguments foundered on the doctrine of privity of contract, Viscount Simonds in particular reasserting that doctrine in its orthodox form: [1962] AC 446, 467–468. For present purposes, however, three features can be selected as important.

First, the case revealed, at least on the part of Viscount Simonds (here reflecting the view expressed by Fullagar J in *Wilson v. Darling Island Stevedoring and Lighterage Co Ltd* (1956) 95 CLR 43, 78), a remarkable shift from the philosophy which informed the decision in the *Elder Dempster* case [1924] AC 522. There the point in question was treated very briefly by the members of the Appellate Committee, apparently because it seemed obvious to them that the cargo owners' alternative claim against the shipowners should fail. It was perceived, expressly by Viscount Finlay, at p. 548, and, it seems, implicitly by the remainder, that:

'It would be absurd that the owner of the goods could get rid of the protective clauses of the bill of lading, in respect of all stowage, by suing the owner of the ship in tort.'

By contrast Fullagar J, in the *Darling Island* case, 95 CLR 43, 71, condemned 'a curious, and seemingly irresistible, anxiety to save grossly negligent people from the normal consequences of their negligence', a sentiment to be echoed by Viscount Simonds in the concluding sentence of his speech in the *Midland Silicones* case [1962] AC 446, 472.

Second, the *Elder Dempster* case [1924] AC 522 was kept within strict bounds. Viscount Simonds [1962] AC 446, 470, quoted with approval the interpretation adopted by Fullagar J (with whom Dixon CJ agreed) in the High Court of Australia in the *Darling Island* case, 95 CLR 43, 78 where he said:

'In my opinion, what the *Elder Dempster* case decided, and all that it decided, is that in such a case, the master having signed the bill of lading, the proper inference is that the shipowner, when he receives the goods into his possession, receives them on the terms of the bill of lading. The same inference might perhaps be drawn in some cases even if the charterer himself signed the bill of lading, but it is unnecessary to consider any such question.'

This approach is consistent with that of Lord Sumner in the *Elder Dempster* case [1924] AC 522. In the *Midland Silicones* case [1962] AC 446, Lord Keith of Avonholm, at p. 481, and Lord Morris of Borth-y-Gest, at p. 494, spoke in similar terms. Lord Reid, at p. 479, treated the decision on the point as: 'an anomalous and unexplained exception to the general principle that a stranger cannot rely for his protection on provisions in a contract to which he is not a party'. Lord Denning dissented, at pp. 481–492.

It has to be recognised that this reception did not enhance the reputation of the *Elder Dempster* case [1924] AC 522, as witness certain derogatory descriptions later attached to it, for example by Donaldson J in *Johnson Matthey & Co Ltd* v. *Constantine Terminals Ltd* [1976] 2 Lloyd's Rep 215, 219—'something of a judicial nightmare'—and by Ackner LJ in *The Forum Craftsman* [1985] 1 Lloyd's Rep 291, 295—'heavily comatosed, if not long-interred'.

Third, however, and most important, Lord Reid in the *Midland Silicones* case [1962] AC 446, while rejecting the agency argument on the facts of the case before him, neverthe- less indicated how it might prove successful in a future case. He said, at p. 474:

> 'I can see a possibility of success of the agency argument if (first) the bill of lading makes it clear that the stevedore is intended to be protected by the provisions in it which limit liability, (secondly) the bill of lading makes it clear that the carrier, in addition to contracting for these provisions on his own behalf, is also contracting as agent for the stevedore that these provisions should apply to the stevedore, (thirdly) the carrier has authority from the stevedore to do that, or perhaps later ratification by the stevedore would suffice, and (fourthly) that any difficulties about consideration moving from the stevedore were overcome.'

It was essentially on this passage that the Himalaya clause (called after the name of the ship involved in *Adler* v. *Dickson* [1955] 1 QB 158) was later to be founded.

The pendulum swings back again

In more recent years the pendulum of judicial opinion has swung back again, as recogni- tion has been given to the undesirability, especially in a commercial context, of allowing plaintiffs to circumvent contractual exception clauses by suing in particular the servant or agent of the contracting party who caused the relevant damage, thereby undermining the purpose of the exception, and so redistributing the contractual allocation of risk which is reflected in the freight rate and in the parties' respective insurance arrange- ments. Nowadays, therefore, there is a greater readiness, not only to accept something like Scrutton LJ's doctrine of vicarious immunity (as to which see, e.g., article 4 bis of the Hague-Visby Rules scheduled to the Carriage of Goods by Sea Act 1971) but also to rehabilitate the *Elder Dempster* case [1924] AC 522 itself, which has been described by Bingham LJ, in *Dresser UK Ltd* v. *Falcongate Freight Management Ltd* [1992] QB 502, 511F as 'a pragmatic legal recognition of commercial reality'. Even so, the problem remains how to discover, in circumstances such as those of the *Elder Dempster* case [1924] AC 522, the factual basis from which the rendering of the bailment subject to such a provi- sion can properly be inferred. At all events the present understanding, based on Lord Sumner's speech, is that in the circumstances of that case the shippers may be taken to have impliedly agreed that the goods were received by the shipowners, as bailees, sub- ject to the exceptions and limitations contained in the known and contemplated form of bill of lading: see *The Pioneer Container* [1994] 2 AC 324, 339–340. Their Lordships will

however put on one side for later consideration the question how far the principle of
bailment on terms may be applicable in the present case, and will turn first to consider the
principle developed from Lord Reid's observations in the *Midland Silicones* case [1962] AC
446, 474, in *The Eurymedon* [1975] AC 154 and *The New York Star* [1981] 1 WLR 138.

The Eurymedon and The New York Star

Their Lordships have already quoted the terms of clause 4 (the Himalaya clause) of the bill
of lading in the present case. For the purposes of this aspect of the case, the essential
passage reads as follows:

> 'Without prejudice to the foregoing, every such servant, agent and subcontractor shall
> have the benefit of all exceptions, limitations, provision, conditions and liberties herein
> benefiting the carrier as if such provisions were expressly made for their benefit, and, in
> entering into this contract, the carrier, to the extent of these provisions, does so not
> only on [his] own behalf, but also as agent and trustee for such servants, agents and
> subcontractors.'

The effectiveness of a Himalaya clause to provide protection against claims in tort by
consignees was recognised by the Privy Council in *The Eurymedon* [1975] AC 154 and *The
New York Star* [1981] 1 WLR 138. In both cases, stevedores were sued by the consignees
for damages in tort, in the first case on the ground that the stevedores had negligently
damaged a drilling machine in the course of unloading, and in the second on the ground
that they had negligently allowed a parcel of goods, after unloading onto the wharf, to
be removed by thieves without production of the bill of lading. In both cases, the bill of
lading contract incorporated a one year time bar, and a Himalaya clause which extended
the benefit of defences and immunities to independent contractors employed by the
carrier. The stevedores relied upon the Himalaya clause to claim the benefit of the time
bar as against the consignees.

In *The Eurymedon* [1975] AC 154 the Privy Council held, by a majority of three to two,
that the stevedores were entitled to rely on the time bar. The leading judgment was
delivered by Lord Wilberforce, at pp. 164–183. He referred to clause 1 of the bill of lading
under which the carrier stipulated for certain exemptions and immunities, among them
the one year time bar in article III, rule 6, of the Hague Rules, and in addition (in the
Himalaya clause) the carrier, as agent for (among others) independent contractors, stipulated for the same exemptions. Referring to Lord Reid's four criteria in the *Midland
Silicones* case [1962] AC 446, 474, he considered it plain that the first three were satisfied,
the only question being whether the requirement of consideration was fulfilled. He was
satisfied that it was. He observed, at p. 167B, that 'If the choice, and the antithesis, is
between a gratuitous promise, and a promise for consideration . . . there can be little
doubt which, in commercial reality, this is'. He then proceeded to analyse the transaction
in a way which showed a preference by him for what is usually called a unilateral contract,
though he recognised that there might be more than one way of analysing the
transaction.

In *The New York Star* [1981] 1 WLR 138, the Privy Council again upheld (on this occasion unanimously) the efficacy of a Himalaya clause to confer upon the stevedores the
benefit of defences and immunities contained in the bill of lading, including a one year
time bar. The judgment of the Judicial Committee was again given by Lord Wilberforce.
In the course of his judgment, he stressed, at p. 143:

'It may indeed be said that the significance of Satterthwaite's case lay not so much in the establishment of any new legal principle, as in the finding that in the normal situation involving the employment of stevedores by carriers, accepted principles enable and require the stevedore to enjoy the benefit of contractual provisions in the bill of lading.'

He continued, at p. 144:

'Although, in each case, there will be room for evidence as to the precise relationship of carrier and stevedore and as to the practice at the relevant port, the decision does not support, and their Lordships would not encourage, a search for fine distinctions which would diminish the general applicability, in the light of established commercial practice, of the principle.'

Lord Wilberforce in particular expressed the Board's approval of the reasoned analysis of the relevant legal principles in the judgment of Barwick CJ, which in his opinion substantially agreed with, and indeed constituted a powerful reinforcement of, one of the two possible bases put forward in the Board's judgment in *The Eurymedon* [1975] AC 154. In his judgment in the court below (the High Court of Australia), Barwick CJ saw no difficulty in finding that the carrier acted as the authorised agent of the stevedores in making an arrangement with the consignor for the protection of the stevedores: see [1979] 1 Lloyd's Rep 298, 304–305. By later accepting the bill of lading the consignee became party to that arrangement. He could not read the clauses in the bill of lading as an unaccepted but acceptable offer by the consignor to the stevedores. However the consignor and the stevedores were ad idem through the carrier's agency, upon the acceptance by the consignor of the bill of lading, as to the protection the stevedores should have in the event that they caused loss of or damage to the consignment. But that consensus lacked consideration. He continued, at p. 305:

'To agree with another that, in the event that the other acts in a particular way, that other shall be entitled to stated protective provisions only needs performance by the doing of the specified act or acts to become a binding contract. . . . The performance of the act or acts at the one moment satisfied the test for consideration and enacted the agreed terms.'

Such a contract Barwick CJ was prepared, with some hesitation, to describe as a bilateral contract.

Critique of the Eurymedon principle

In *The New York Star* [1981] 1 WLR 138, 144, Lord Wilberforce discouraged 'a search for fine distinctions which would diminish the general applicability, in the light of established commercial practice, of the principle'. He was there, of course, speaking of the application of the principle in the case of stevedores. It has however to be recognised that, so long as the principle continues to be understood to rest upon an enforceable contract as between the cargo owners and the stevedores entered into through the agency of the shipowner, it is inevitable that technical points of contract and agency law will continue to be invoked by cargo owners seeking to enforce tortious remedies against stevedores and others uninhibited by the exceptions and limitations in the relevant bill of lading contract. Indeed, in the present case their Lordships have seen such an exercise being legitimately undertaken by Mr Aikens on behalf of the cargo owners. In this connection their Lordships wish to refer to the very helpful consideration of the principle in *Palmer on Bailment*,

2nd ed. (1991), at pp. 1610–1625, which reveals many of the problems which may arise, and refers to a number of cases, both in England and in Commonwealth countries, in which the courts have grappled with those problems. In some cases, notably but by no means exclusively in England, courts have felt impelled by the established principles of the law of contract or of agency to reject the application of the principle in the particular case before them. In others, courts have felt free to follow the lead of Lord Wilberforce in *The Eurymedon* [1975] AC 154, and of Lord Wilberforce and Barwick CJ in *The New York Star* [1981] 1 WLR 138; [1979] 1 Lloyd's Rep 298, and so to discover the existence of a contract (nowadays a bilateral contract of the kind identified by Barwick CJ) in circumstances in which lawyers of a previous generation would have been unwilling to do so.

Nevertheless there can be no doubt of the commercial need of some such principle as this, and not only in cases concerned with stevedores; and the bold step taken by the Privy Council in *The Eurymedon* [1975] AC 154, and later developed in *The New York Star* [1981] 1 WLR 138, has been widely welcomed. But it is legitimate to wonder whether that development is yet complete. Here their Lordships have in mind not only Lord Wilberforce's discouragement of fine distinctions, but also the fact that the law is now approaching the position where, provided that the bill of lading contract clearly provides that (for example) independent contractors such as stevedores are to have the benefit of exceptions and limitations contained in that contract, they will be able to enjoy the protection of those terms as against the cargo owners. This is because (1) the problem of consideration in these cases is regarded as having been solved on the basis that a bilateral agreement between the stevedores and the cargo owners, entered into through the agency of the shipowners, may, though itself unsupported by consideration, be rendered enforceable by consideration subsequently furnished by the stevedores in the form of performance of their duties as stevedores for the shipowners; (2) the problem of authority from the stevedores to the shipowners to contract on their behalf can, in the majority of cases, be solved by recourse to the principle of ratification[4]; and (3) consignees of the cargo may be held to be bound on the principle in *Brandt* v. *Liverpool, Brazil and River Plate Steam Navigation Co Ltd* [1924] 1 KB 575. Though these solutions are now perceived to be generally effective for their purpose, their technical nature is all too apparent; and the time may well come when, in an appropriate case, it will fall to be considered whether the courts should take what may legitimately be perceived to be the final, and perhaps inevitable, step in this development, and recognise in these cases a fully-fledged exception to the doctrine of privity of contract, thus escaping from all the technicalities with which courts are now faced in English law. It is not far from their Lordships' minds that, if the English courts were minded to take that step, they would be following in the footsteps of the Supreme Court of Canada: see *London Drugs Ltd* v. *Kuehne & Nagel International Ltd* (1992) 97 DLR (4th) 261 and, in a different context, the High Court of Australia: see *Trident General Insurance Co Ltd* v. *McNiece Bros Pty Ltd* (1988) 165 CLR 107. Their Lordships have given consideration to the question whether they should face up to this question in the present appeal. However, they have come to the conclusion that it would not be appropriate for them to do so, first, because they have not heard argument specifically directed towards this fundamental question, and second because, as will become clear in due course, they are satisfied that the appeal must in any event be dismissed.

[4] An act done by one party for the benefit of another party, but without the latter's authority, can be ratified or confirmed by the party for whose benefit the act was performed in such a way as to render it his act.

Application of the Eurymedon principle in the present case

Their Lordships now turn to the application of the principle in *The Eurymedon* [1975] AC 154 to the facts of the present case. Two questions arose in the course of argument which are specific to this case. The first is whether the shipowners qualify as 'subcontractors' within the meaning of the Himalaya clause (clause 4 of the bill of lading). The second is whether, if so, they are entitled to take advantage of the exclusive jurisdiction clause (clause 19). Their Lordships have come to the conclusion that the latter question must be answered in the negative. It is therefore unnecessary for them to answer the first question; and they will proceed to address the question of the exclusive jurisdiction clause on the assumption that the shipowners can be regarded as subcontractors for this purpose.

The exclusive jurisdiction clause

The Himalaya clause provides that, among others, subcontractors shall have the benefit of 'all exceptions, limitations, provision, conditions and liberties herein benefiting the carrier as if such provisions were expressly made for their benefit'. The question therefore arises whether the exclusive jurisdiction clause (clause 19) falls within the scope of this clause.

In *The Eurymedon* [1975] AC 154, 169 and *The New York Star* [1981] 1 WLR 138, 143 Lord Wilberforce stated the principle to be applicable, in the case of stevedores, to respectively 'exemptions and limitations' and 'defences and immunities' contained in the bill of lading . . .

It however by no means follows that the same can be said of an exclusive jurisdiction clause . . . the exclusive jurisdiction clause itself creates serious problems. Such a clause can be distinguished from terms such as exceptions and limitations in that it does not benefit only one party, but embodies a mutual agreement under which both parties agree with each other as to the relevant jurisdiction for the resolution of disputes. It is therefore a clause which creates mutual rights and obligations. Can such a clause be an exception, limitation, provision, condition or liberty benefiting the carrier within the meaning of the clause?

First of all, it cannot in their Lordships' opinion be an exception, limitation, condition or liberty. But can it be a provision? That expression has, of course, to be considered in the context of the Himalaya clause; and so the question is whether an exclusive jurisdiction clause is a provision benefiting the carrier, of which servants, agents and subcontractors of the carrier are intended to have the benefit, as if the provision was expressly made for their benefit. Moreover, the word 'provision' is to be found at the centre of a series of words, viz. 'exceptions, limitations . . . conditions and liberties', all of which share the same characteristic, that they are not as such rights which entail correlative obligations on the cargo owners.

In considering this question, their Lordships are satisfied that some limit must be placed upon the meaning of the word 'provision' in this context. In their Lordships' opinion the word 'provision' must have been inserted with the purpose of ensuring that any other provision in the bill of lading which, although it did not strictly fall within the description 'exceptions, limitations, . . . conditions and liberties', nevertheless benefited the carrier in the same way in the sense that it was inserted in the bill for the carrier's protection, should enure for the benefit of the servants, agents and subcontractors of the carrier. It cannot therefore extend to include a mutual agreement, such as an exclusive jurisdiction clause, which is not of that character.

Their Lordships draw support for this view from the function of the Himalaya clause. That function is, as revealed by the authorities, to prevent cargo owners from avoiding the effect of contractual defences available to the carrier (typically the exceptions and limitations in the Hague-Visby Rules) by suing in tort persons who perform the contractual services on the carrier's behalf. To make available to such a person the benefit of an exclusive jurisdiction clause in the bill of lading contract does not contribute to the solution of that problem . . .

Furthermore, it is of some significance to observe how adventitious would have been the benefit of the exclusive jurisdiction clause to the shipowners in the present case. Such a clause generally represents a preference by the carrier for the jurisdiction where he carries on business. But the same cannot necessarily be said of his servants, agents or subcontractors . . .

In the opinion of their Lordships, all these considerations point strongly against the exclusive jurisdiction clause falling within the scope of the Himalaya clause. However in support of his submission that the exclusive jurisdiction clause fell within the scope of the Himalaya clause in the present case [counsel] for the shipowners invoked the decision of the Privy Council in *The Pioneer Container* [1994] 2 AC 324. That case was however concerned with a different situation, where a carrier of goods subcontracted part of the carriage to a shipowner under a 'feeder' bill of lading, and that shipowner sought to enforce an exclusive jurisdiction clause contained in that bill of lading against the owners of the goods. The Judicial Committee held that the shipowner was entitled to do so, because the goods owner had authorised the carrier so to subcontract 'on any terms', with the effect that the shipowner as sub-bailee was entitled to rely on the clause against the goods owner as head bailor. The present case is however concerned not with a question of enforceability of a term in a *sub-bailment* by the sub-bailee against the head bailor, but with the question whether a subcontractor is entitled to take the benefit of a term in the *head contract*. The former depends on the scope of the *authority* of the intermediate bailor to act on behalf of the head bailor in agreeing on his behalf to the relevant term in the *sub-bailment*; whereas the latter depends on the scope of the *agreement* between the head contractor and the subcontractor, entered into by the intermediate contractor as agent for the subcontractor, under which the benefit of a term in the *head contract* may be made available by the head contractor to the subcontractor. It does not follow that a decision in the former type of case provides any useful guidance in a case of the latter type; and their Lordships do not therefore find *The Pioneer Container* of assistance in the present case.

In the event, for the reasons they have already given, their Lordships have come to the conclusion that the Himalaya clause does not have the effect of enabling the shipowners to take advantage of the exclusive jurisdiction clause in the bill of lading in the present case.

Application of the principle of bailment on terms in the present case

In the light of the principle stated by Lord Sumner in the *Elder Dempster* case [1924] AC 522, 564, as interpreted by Fullagar J in the *Darling Island* case, 95 CLR 43, 78, the next question for consideration is whether the shipowners can establish that they received the goods into their possession on the terms of the bill of lading, including the exclusive jurisdiction clause (clause 19)—i.e., whether the shipowners' obligations as bailees were effectively subjected to the clause as a term upon which the shipowners implicitly received the goods into their possession: see *The Pioneer Container* [1994] 2 AC 324, 340, per Lord Goff of Chieveley . . .

Their Lordships feel able to deal with this point very briefly, because they consider that in the present case there is an insuperable objection to the argument of the shipowners. This is that the bill of lading under which the goods were shipped on board contained a Himalaya clause under which the shipowners as subcontractors were expressed to be entitled to the benefit of certain terms in the bill of lading but, as their Lordships have held, those terms did not include the exclusive jurisdiction clause. In these circumstances their Lordships find it impossible to hold that, by receiving the goods into their possession pursuant to the bill of lading, the shipowners' obligations as bailees were effectively subjected to the exclusive jurisdiction clause as a term upon which they implicitly received the goods into their possession. Any such implication must, in their opinion, be rejected as inconsistent with the express terms of the bill of lading.

COMMENTARY

When describing the fluctuations in judicial opinion that have taken place Lord Goff makes reference to four leading cases, namely *Elder Dempster, Midland Silicones, The Eurymedon,* and *The New York Star.* One or two additional points can be made in relation to each case.

Elder Dempster was always a troublesome case and, as Lord Goff notes, it received a distinctly frosty judicial reception in the latter half of the twentieth century. Lord Goff points out that the case could be explained either on the basis of vicarious immunity or as an example of bailment on terms. The former doctrine was rejected by the House of Lords in *Midland Silicones* with the consequence that the case must now be regarded as an example of bailment on terms.

Midland Silicones is a case in which the defendant stevedores sought to rely both on a limitation clause in the contract between themselves and the carriers and on a limitation clause in the contract between the cargo owners and the carriers. Two further aspects of *Midland Silicones* are worthy of note. The first is Lord Denning's dissent. He held that the cargo owners were bound by the terms of the contract between the carriers and the stevedores on the basis that they impliedly authorized the carrier to employ the stevedores on the terms that their liability would be limited. The second is Lord Reid's four-stage test (on p. 474 set out at p. 1217 above) which in many ways formed the basis for future developments in *The Eurymedon.*

The Eurymedon is an important case because the Privy Council there held, albeit by a 3–2 majority, that the stevedores were entitled to rely on the time bar in order to defeat the claim brought by the consignors. In both *The Eurymedon* and *The New York Star* the leading judgment was given by Lord Wilberforce and in both cases he adopted a rather broad brush approach in finding the existence of a contract between the stevedores and the consignors which entitled the stevedores to rely on the time bar. The dissentients in *The Eurymedon,* while not denying that 'a suitably drawn document could bring a consignor and a stevedore into a relationship of obligation' (p. 183) were not prepared to paint with such a broad brush. Thus Viscount Dilhorne stated (at p. 175) that:

clause 1 of the bill of lading was obviously not drafted by a layman but by a highly qualified lawyer.

It is a commercial document but the fact that it is of that description does not mean that to give it efficacy, one is at liberty to disregard its language and read into it that which it does not say and could have said or construe the English words it contains as having a meaning which is not expressed and which is not implied.

The clause does not in my opinion either expressly or impliedly contain an offer by the shipper to the carrier to enter into an agreement whereby if the appellant performed services in relation to the goods the shipper would give it the benefit of every exemption from and limitation of liability contained in the bill of lading.

So on what basis did Lord Wilberforce conclude that the stevedores and consignors/shippers were contracting parties? As Lord Goff notes there are two possible analyses: a unilateral contract or a bilateral contract. Lord Wilberforce himself adopted a unilateral contract analysis in the following terms (at pp. 167–168):

[The present contract] is one of carriage from Liverpool to Wellington. The carrier assumes an obligation to transport the goods and to discharge at the port of arrival. The goods are to be carried and discharged, so the transaction is inherently contractual. It is contemplated that a part of this contract, viz. discharge, may be performed by independent contractors—viz. the appellant. By clause 1 of the bill of lading the shipper agrees to exempt from liability the carrier, his servants and independent contractors in respect of the performance of this contract of carriage. Thus, if the carriage, including the discharge, is wholly carried out by the carrier, he is exempt. If part is carried out by him, and part by his servants, he and they are exempt. If part is carried out by him and part by an independent contractor, he and the independent contractor are exempt. The exemption is designed to cover the whole carriage from loading to discharge, by whomsoever it is performed: the performance attracts the exemption or immunity in favour of whoever the performer turns out to be. There is possibly more than one way of analysing this business transaction into the necessary components; that which their Lordships would accept is to say that the bill of lading brought into existence a bargain initially unilateral but capable of becoming mutual, between the shipper and the appellant, made through the carrier as agent. This became a full contract when the appellant performed services by discharging the goods. The performance of these services for the benefit of the shipper was the consideration for the agreement by the shipper that the appellant should have the benefit of the exemptions and limitations contained in the bill of lading. The conception of a 'unilateral' contract of this kind was recognised in *Great Northern Railway Co* v. *Witham* (1873) LR 9 CP 16 and is well established. This way of regarding the matter is very close to if not identical to that accepted by Beattie J in the Supreme Court: he analysed the transaction as one of an offer open to acceptance by action such as was found in *Carlill* v. *Carbolic Smoke Ball Co* [1893] 1 QB 256. But whether one describes the shipper's promise to exempt as an offer to be accepted by performance or as a promise in exchange for an act seems in the present context to be a matter of semantics. The words of Bowen LJ in *Carlill* v. *Carbolic Smoke Ball Co* [1893] 1 QB 256, 268: 'why should not an offer be made to all the world which is to ripen into a contract with anybody who comes forward and performs the condition?' seem to bridge both conceptions: he certainly seems to draw no distinction between an offer which matures into a contract when accepted and a promise which matures into a contract after performance, and, though in some special contexts (such as in connection with the right to withdraw) some further refinement may be needed, either analysis may be equally valid.

The bilateral contract analysis adopted by Barwick CJ in *The New York Star* [1979] 1 Lloyd's Rep 298, 304–305 was in the following terms:

For my part, I find no difficulty in interpreting the arrangement made by the bill of lading and its acceptance by the consignor as providing that if, in fact the appellant stevedored the cargo, leaving aside for the moment what the stevedoring involved, the appellant should have the benefit of the clauses of the bill including the benefit of the time limitation expressed in cl. 17 of the bill of lading. I am unable to treat the clauses of the bill of lading as in any respect an unaccepted but acceptable offer by consignor to stevedore. Indeed, I do not think the bill can be interpreted as containing an offer at large by the consignor. The consignor and the appellant as stevedore were ad idem through the carrier's agency upon the acceptance by the consignor of the bill of lading as to the protection the stevedore should have in the event that it stevedored the consignment. But this consensus lacked the essential of consideration. The appellant through the bill of lading made no promise to stevedore the cargo. Thus, while I would not analyse the situation obtaining on the acceptance of the bill of lading as an exchange of promises, I would not analyse it as merely the making of an offer susceptible of acceptance by an act of the stevedore done in purported acceptance of the offer. For this reason I have described the bill of lading in so far as the carrier there purports to act for the appellant as an arrangement. To agree with another that, in the event that the other acts in a particular way, that other shall be entitled to stated protective provisions only needs performance by the doing of the specified act or acts to become a binding contract. Whether or not the arrangement is susceptible of unilateral disavowal before the stated act is done need not be discussed. Here the act was done. The performance of the act or acts at the one moment satisfied the test for consideration and enacted the agreed terms. For myself and with due respect to those who find comfort in them, I find the descriptions 'unilateral and bilateral' or 'mutual' unhelpful in the resolution of this case. Indeed, the use of them seems to assume that they are mutually exclusive terms and together cover all possibilities. But I do not think they do. Indeed, this bill of lading, as I read it, indicates in my opinion that they do not. As I see it, we have here an arrangement, a compact with agreed conditions to attend the performance of certain acts, which are not promised to be done. True enough that, until such performance, the consensus has nothing upon which to operate. But that is its essential characteristic, to provide an agreed consequence to future action should that action take place: to attach conditions to a relationship arising from conduct. If one desires to use the terms, it could be said that the arrangement is mutual: it is bilateral: to it there are two parties both agreeing to the terms of the intended consequence, on the one hand the consignor and on the other the stevedore acting through its authorised agent, the carrier. The performance of the contemplated act both supplies the occasion for those conditions to operate and the consideration which makes the arrangement contractual.

Neither solution is free from technical difficulties and, notwithstanding Lord Wilberforce's attempt in *The New York Star* to discourage parties from taking technical points, Lord Goff was surely correct in *The Mahkutai* to state that it is 'inevitable that technical points of contract law and agency will continue to be taken' while this line of authority remains binding. The unilateral contract analysis is problematic for the following reasons: (i) it may not be easy to identify the existence of the offer of immunity by the consignor (the stumbling block for the minority in *The Eurymedon* and for Barwick CJ in *The New York Star*); (ii) the third party may not be aware of the existence of the offer at the time that it performs the act that constitutes the acceptance (an acceptance performed in ignorance of the offer is not generally valid: see p. 128 above); and (iii) the third party does not enjoy the immunity when it damages the goods when preparing to undertake the task set out in the main contract (*Raymond Burke Motors Ltd* v. *Mersey Docks and Harbour Co* [1986] 1 Lloyd's Rep

155). The latter problem also arises in the context of the bilateral contract analysis. A further difficulty with the bilateral contract analysis lies in ascertaining the precise moment in time at which the contract is concluded. Finally, Professor Treitel states (*Some Landmarks of Twentieth Century Contract Law* (Oxford University Press, 2002), p. 67) that he prefers Lord Wilberforce's analysis 'since it avoids the consequence of the stevedore's being in breach of a separate contract with the cargo-owner if he has justifiably terminated his contract with the carrier on account of the latter's breach and consequently refused to unload the goods'.

Given these (and other) technical problems with the solutions adopted in *The Eurymedon* and *The New York Star*, Lord Goff states in *The Mahkutai* that the time may come when the courts will develop 'a fully-fledged exception to the doctrine of privity of contract, thus escaping from all the technicalities with which courts are now faced in English law' (see further *Homburg Houtimport BV* v. *Agrosin Private Ltd (The Starsin)* [2003] UKHL 12; [2004] 1 AC 715, where the House of Lords once again discussed these issues in some detail but stopped short of creating a fully fledged exception to the doctrine of privity). One of the cases to which Lord Goff makes reference in this context is the decision of the Supreme Court of Canada in *London Drugs Ltd* v. *Kuehne & Nagel International Ltd* (1992) 97 DLR (4th) 261. London Drugs delivered an electrical transformer to Kuehne & Nagel for storage in a warehouse. The contract between them contained a limitation clause which stated that 'the warehouseman's liability on any one package is limited to $40 unless the holder has declared in writing a valuation in excess of $40 and paid the additional charge specified to cover warehouse liability'. The transformer was damaged as a result of the negligence of two of Kuehne & Nagel's employees. London Drugs brought a claim against Kuehne & Nagel and their two employees. In relation to the claim against the employees the issue before the Supreme Court was whether or not the employees were entitled to rely on the limitation clause, notwithstanding the fact the clause made no express mention of them. It was held that they were entitled to invoke the benefit of the limitation clause. The basis for this conclusion was later summarized by Iacobucci J, giving the judgment of the Supreme Court of Canada in *Fraser River Pile & Dredge Ltd* v. *Can-Dive Services Ltd* [2000] 1 Lloyd's Rep 199, 205–206 in the following terms:

In order to distinguish mere strangers to a contract from those in the position of third-party beneficiaries, the Court first established a threshold requirement whereby the parties to the contract must have intended the relevant provision to confer a benefit on the third party. In other words, an employer and its customer may agree to extend, either expressly or by implication, the benefit of any limitation of liability clause to the employees. In the circumstances of London Drugs, the customer had full knowledge that the storage services contemplated by the contract would be provided not only by the employer, but by the employees as well. In the absence of any clear indication to the contrary, the Court held that the necessary intention to include coverage for the employees was implied in the terms of the agreement. The employees, therefore, as third-party beneficiaries, could seek to rely on the limitation clause to avoid liability for the loss to the customer's property.

The Court further held, however, that the intention to extend the benefit of a contractual provision to the actions of a third-party beneficiary was irrelevant unless the actions in question came within the scope of agreement between the initial parties. Accordingly, the second aspect of the functional inquiry was whether the employees were acting in the course of their employment when the loss occurred, and whether in so acting they were performing the very services specified in the contract between their employer and its customer. Based on uncontested findings of fact, it was clear that the damage to the customer's transformer occurred when the employees were acting in the course of their employment to provide the very storage services specified in the contract.

Taking all of these circumstances into account, the Court interpreted the term 'warehouseman' in the limitation of liability clause to include coverage for the employees, thereby absolving them of any liability in excess of Can$40 for the loss that occurred. The Court concluded that the departure from the traditional doctrine of privity was well within its jurisdiction representing, as it did, an incremental change to the common law rather than a wholesale abdication of existing principles. Given that the exception was dependent on the intention stipulated in the contract, relaxing the doctrine of privity in the given circumstances did not frustrate the expectations of the parties.

The effect of *London Drugs* is, essentially, to introduce into Canadian law a form of vicarious immunity, a principle rejected, as far as English law is concerned, by the House of Lords in *Midland Silicones*. Nevertheless, English cases can be found which reach a similar result to that reached in *London Drugs*, albeit by a different route. One such case is *Norwich City Council* v. *Harvey* [1989] 1 WLR 828. Norwich City Council employed contractors to construct an extension to a swimming pool. Clause 20(c) of the contract provided that the building was at the sole risk of the employer as regards loss or damage by fire and that the employer would maintain adequate insurance against those risks. The contractors sub-contracted the roofing work to the defendants on the same terms as those contained in the main contract. The property suffered extensive damage as a result of a fire caused by the negligence of one of the defendants' employees. Norwich City Council sued the defendants in tort. The Court of Appeal held, having regard to the contract structure adopted by the parties, that the defendants did not owe a duty of care to the council. May LJ stated (at p. 837):

approaching the question on the basis of what is just and reasonable I do not think that the mere fact that there is no strict privity between the employer and the subcontractor should prevent the latter from relying upon the clear basis upon which all of the parties contracted in relation to damage to the employer's building caused by fire, even when due to the negligence of the contractors or subcontractors.

Earlier in his judgment May LJ stated (at p. 834) that 'if in principle the subcontractor owed no specific duty to the building owner in respect of damage by fire, then neither in my opinion can any of its employees have done so'. It therefore followed that both the defendants and their employees were absolved from responsibility for the consequences of their negligence. The case differs from *The Eurymedon* in that reliance was placed on the contract structure, not for the purpose of finding the existence of a contract between the defendants and the council, but for the purpose of negating the duty of care that otherwise would have been owed by the defendants to the council. The difficulty with *Norwich City Council* is that in substance, but not in form, it appears to undermine the House of Lords' rejection of vicarious immunity in *Midland Silicones*. It is therefore difficult to ascertain the limits of the case. On the one hand it could be confined to its own facts. On the other hand, it is possible that it could, in combination with cases such as *London Drugs*, form the building blocks for the construction of a broader exception to the doctrine of privity. The merits of such a development are open to question. The difficult case is a case such as *Adler* v. *Dickson* [1955] 1 QB 158 where the plaintiff suffered severe injuries when the gangway of a ship which she was boarding moved and she fell from a height of sixteen feet. She brought an action in negligence against the members of the crew. They sought to rely on the terms of an exclusion clause contained in the ticket issued by the carrier. The Court of Appeal held that they were not entitled to do so. The company had excluded its own liability and had not acted as an agent for its employees. Further, the contract did not expressly exempt the employees from the consequences of their negligence and the Court of Appeal refused to imply such an exemption. But how would a case such as *Adler* be decided on the basis of the principle laid down in *London Drugs*? The difference between the two cases may lie in the position of the two plaintiffs. In *London Drugs* the plaintiffs were found to have accepted that the employees were entitled to rely on the limitation clause, whereas the Court of Appeal in *Adler* formed the view that the plaintiff had no such intention. If this is the case the ability of the employees to take the benefit of the exclusion or limitation clause will hinge upon the state of knowledge of their employer's customer, which seems, at least from their perspective, to be a less than satisfactory conclusion. But it is preferable to the alternative which is to deprive claimants of their rights of action without their knowledge or assent. This being the case *Adler* would probably be decided the same way even if *London Drugs* were subsequently to be imported into English law.

Two other points remain to be made in relation to the judgment of Lord Goff in *The Mahkutai*. The first relates to his reference to *The Pioneer Container*. The latter case is distinguishable from *The Mahkutai* because there the exclusive jurisdiction clause was to be found in the sub-contract not the main contract. Thus the issue before the court in *The Pioneer Container* was not whether the sub-bailee could take the benefit of a clause in a contract to which he was not a party (as it was in *The Mahkutai*) but whether the head bailor was bound by the terms of a clause in a contract to which he was not a party. As Lord Goff points out, the latter question must be answered by reference to the authority given by the head bailor to the intermediate bailor to act on his behalf when agreeing to the term in the sub-bailment (on which see further GH Treitel, *The Law of Contract* (11th edn, Sweet & Maxwell, 2003), pp. 640–642).

The final point relates to Lord Goff's conclusion that the shipowners could not invoke the exclusive jurisdiction clause on the facts of *The Mahkutai*. His reason for reaching this conclusion was, essentially, that the exclusive jurisdiction clause, unlike an exclusion clause, was not a term that operated only for the benefit of the shipowner. It was a term which created mutual rights and obligations and, while the shipowners, being Indonesian, were content to be bound by it on the facts of the case, this would not be so in every case. This being the case, the exclusive jurisdiction clause did not fall within the scope of the Himalaya clause (whether the case would be decided differently under the 1999 Act is discussed at p. 1249 below).

(e) THE CASE FOR REFORM

Having considered the doctrine of privity of contract and the various exceptions to it, we are now in a position to weigh up the arguments advanced both for and against further reform of the law. The case for reform of the law was put forward by the Law Commission and their report formed the basis of the 1999 Act. They concluded as follows:

Law Commission, *Privity of Contract: Contracts for the Benefit of Third Parties*

(Law Com No 242, 1996) paras 3.1–3.28

1. The Intention of the Original Contracting Parties are Thwarted

3.1   A first argument in favour of reform . . . is that the third party rule prevents effect being given to the intention of the contracting parties. If the theoretical justification for the enforcement of contracts is seen as the realisation of the promises or the will or the bargain of the contracting parties, the failure of the law to afford a remedy to the third party where the contracting parties intended that it should have one frustrates their intentions, and undermines the general justifying theory of contract.

2. The Injustice to the Third Party

3.2   A second argument focuses on the injustice to the third party where a valid contract, albeit between two other parties, has engendered in the third party reasonable expectations of having the legal right to enforce the contract particularly where the third party has relied on that contract to regulate his or her affairs. In most circumstances this argument complements the above argument based on the intentions of the contracting parties. For in most circumstances the intentions of the contracting parties and the reasonable expectations of the third party are consistent with each other. However, one of the most difficult issues that we face is the extent to which the contracting parties can vary or discharge the contract. That issue can be presented as raising the conflict between these two fundamental arguments for reform. In other words, should the injustice to the third party trump the intentions of the parties *where those intentions change*? As will become clear, we believe that where the injustice to the third party is sufficiently 'strong' (that is, where the third party has not merely had expectations engendered by knowledge of the contract but has relied on the contract or has accepted it by communicating its assent to the promisor) it should trump the changed intentions of the contracting parties. That is, the original parties' right to change their minds and vary the contract should be overridden once the third party has relied on, or accepted, the contractual promise.

3. The Person Who Has Suffered the Loss Cannot Sue, While the Person Who Has Suffered No Loss Can Sue.

3.3   In a standard situation, the third party rule produces the perverse, and unjust, result that the person who has suffered the loss (of the intended benefit) cannot sue, while the person who has suffered no loss can sue. This can be illustrated by reference to *Beswick* v. *Beswick*. In that case . . . the House of Lords held that the widow could not enforce the promise in her personal capacity, since the contract was one to which she was not privy. However, as administratix of her husband's estate, she was able to sue as promisee, albeit that she could only recover nominal damages because the uncle, and hence his estate, had suffered no loss from the nephew's breach. Hence we see that the widow in her personal capacity, who had suffered the loss of the intended benefit, had no right to sue, while the estate, represented by the widow in her capacity as administratrix, who had suffered no loss, had that right. As it was, a just result was achieved by their Lordships' decision that nominal damages were, in this three party situation, inadequate so that specific performance of the nephew's obligation to pay the annuity to the widow should be ordered in respect of the claim by the administratrix. But where specific performance is not available (for example, where the contract is not one supported by valuable consideration or where the contract is one for personal service) the standard result is both perverse and unjust.

4. Even if the Promisee Can Obtain a Satisfactory Remedy for the Third Party, the Promisee May not be Able to, or Wish to, Sue

3.4 In *Beswick* v. *Beswick*, the promisee, as represented by the widow as administratrix, clearly wanted to sue to enforce the contract made for her personal benefit. However, in many other situations in which contracts are made for the benefit of third parties, the promisee may not be able to, or wish to, sue, even if specific performance or substantial damages could be obtained. Clearly the stress and strain of litigation and its cost will deter many promisees who might fervently want their contract enforced for the benefit of third parties. Or the contracting party may be ill or outside the jurisdiction. And if the promisee has died, his or her personal representatives may reasonably take the view that it is not in the interests of the estate to seek to enforce a contract for the benefit of the third party.

5. The Development of Non-Comprehensive Exceptions

3.5 A number of statutory and common law exceptions to the third party rule exist. . . . Where an exception to the third party rule has been either recognised by case-law or created by statute, the rule may now not cause difficulty. Self-evidently, this is not the case where the situation is a novel one in which devices to overcome the third party rule have not yet been tested. We believe that the existence of exceptions to the third party rule is a strong justification for reform. This is for two reasons. First, the existence of so many legislative and common law exceptions to the rule demonstrates its basic injustice. Secondly, the fact that these exceptions continue to evolve and to be the subject of extensive litigation demonstrates that the existing exceptions have not resolved all the problems.

6. Complexity, Artificiality and Uncertainty

3.6 The existence of this rule, together with the exceptions to it, has given rise to a complex body of law and to the use of elaborate and artificial stratagems and structures in order to give third parties enforceable rights. Reform would enable the artificiality and some of the complexity to be avoided. The technical hurdles which must be overcome if one is to circumvent the rule in individual cases also lead to uncertainty, since it will often be possible for a defendant to raise arguments that a technical requirement has not been fulfilled. Such uncertainty is commercially inconvenient.

7.   Widespread Criticism Throughout the Common Law World

3.7   . . . we saw that there had been criticism of the third party rule and calls for its reform from academics, law reform bodies and the judiciary. We shall see . . . that the rule has been abrogated throughout much of the common law world, including the United States, New Zealand, and parts of Australia. The extent of the criticism and reform elsewhere is itself a strong indication that the privity doctrine is flawed.

8.   The Legal Systems of Most Member States of the European Union Allow Third Parties to Enforce Contracts

3.8   A further factor in support of reforming the third party rule in English law is the fact that the legal systems of most of the member states of the European Union recognise and enforce the rights of third party beneficiaries under contracts. In France, for example, the general principle that contracts have effect only between the parties to them is qualified by Art 1121 of the *Code Civil*, which permits a stipulation for the benefit of a third party as a condition of a stipulation made for oneself or of a gift made to another. The French courts interpreted this as permitting the creation of an enforceable stipulation for a person in whose welfare the stipulator had a moral interest. In so doing, they widened the scope of the Article so as to permit virtually any stipulation for a third person to be enforced by him or her, where the agreement between the stipulator and the promisor was intended to confer a benefit on the third person. In Germany, contractual rights for third parties are created by Art 328 of the *Burgerliches Gesetzbuch* permitting stipulations in contracts for performances to third parties with the effect that the latter requires the direct right to demand performance, although the precise scope of these rights depends on the terms and circumstances of the contract itself. Surveying the member states of the European Union, we are aware that the laws of France, Germany, Italy, Austria, Spain, Portugal, Netherlands, Belgium, Luxembourg, and Greece recognise such rights (as does Scotland), whereas only the laws of England and Wales (and Northern Ireland) and the Republic of Ireland do not. With the growing recognition of the need for harmonisation of the commercial law of the states of the European Union   illustrated most importantly by the work being carried out by the Commission on European Contract Law under the chairmanship of Professor Ole Lando— it seems likely that there will be ever increasing pressure on the UK to bring its law on privity of contract into line with that predominantly adopted in Europe.

9.   The Third Party Rule Causes Difficulties in Commercial Life

3.9   Lest it be erroneously thought that the third party rule nowadays causes no real difficulties in commercial life, or that the case for reform is purely theoretical rather than practical, we have chosen two types of contracts—construction contracts and insurance contracts—to illustrate some of the difficulties caused by the rule . . .

10. Conclusion

3.28   For the reasons articulated above, we believe that a reform of the third party rule is necessary. Contracting parties may not, under the present law, create provisions in their contracts which are enforceable directly by a third party unless they can take advantage of one of the exceptions to the third party rule. Our basic philosophy for reform is that it should be straightforwardly possible for contracting parties to confer on third parties the right to enforce the contract.

The arguments are not all one way, however. While most commentators have accepted the validity of the arguments advanced by the Law Commission, there have been some critical voices. The most sustained critical analysis of the Law Commission's arguments has been provided by Robert Stevens (R Stevens, 'The Contracts (Rights of Third Parties) Act 1999' (2004) 120 *LQR* 292). Stevens provides a point-by-point response to the arguments advanced by the Law Commission. In summary his views are as follows.

First, he points out that it is not entirely accurate to state that the denial of a third party action has the consequence of thwarting the intentions of the original contracting parties. The promisor's intention is only thwarted in the sense that he has refused to carry out the terms of his promise. It is the intention of the promisee which has not been fulfilled but, as Stevens points out, this lack of fulfilment does not require that the third party be provided with a remedy. Rather, it demands that the law fashion an effective remedy for the promisee, to the extent that it has not done so already. He also points out that 'intentions have the unfortunate habit of changing' and that the effect of conferring a right of action on the third party may be to deny to the original contracting parties the right to change their minds by taking away the entitlement of the third party.

Secondly, he disputes the proposition that the common law rule results in injustice to the third party. In his view, 'it may be queried how deserving of sympathy a party who relies upon a promise made to someone else is'. The party who has a legitimate expectation that the promise will be kept is the party to whom the promise was made, namely the promisee. This is a point to which we shall return.

Thirdly, he challenges the validity of the claim that the person who has suffered the loss cannot sue, while the person who has suffered no loss can sue. Here his argument turns in large part on the decision of the House of Lords in *Alfred McAlpine Construction Ltd* v. *Panatown Ltd* [2001] 1 AC 518 (see p. 1029 above) and the extent to which that decision plugs any gaps that exist in the law. He notes that the 'weight of authority would seem to favour allowing the promisee to recover substantial damages for his own loss in the situation where the lacuna is said to exist' and that the 'keenest supporters of the [Contracts (Rights of Third Parties) Act 1999] are strongly critical of this approach'. Further, he points out that, even if there is a lacuna in the law, it does not justify conferring a cause of action on the third party: it suffices to 'reform the remedies available to the promisee.'

Fourthly, while he accepts that the promisee may not be able to sue or wish to sue, he points out that it is for the promisee to decide whether or not to enforce his rights and, if he chooses not to do so or is unable to do so, that does not justify the conferral of a right of action on a third party. It is for the promisee to decide what is to be done with his rights.

Fifthly, Stevens claims that some of the alleged exceptions to the privity rule are not in fact true exceptions and, to the extent that they are exceptions, the existence of the present exceptions does not justify the creation of a further exception.

Sixthly, in so far as the common law is said to be complex, artificial and uncertain, he points out that the Contracts (Rights of Third Parties) Act 1999 has not simplified the law; on the contrary, it has made the law more complex. Further, to the extent that the common law solutions in cases such as *The Eurymedon* [1975] AC 154 can be said to be artificial, Stevens' response is to advocate the adoption of a solution which is less artificial and 'more readily defensible'. Finally, he points to a number of uncertainties in the Act itself so that, once again, it cannot be said that the Act has reduced the uncertainty in the law.

Seventhly, while the existence of widespread criticism of the privity rule throughout the common law world should give us 'pause for thought', it does not 'necessarily demonstrate that English law is wrong and other systems are right'.

Eighthly, in relation to the claim that the legal systems of most Member States of the European Union allow third parties to enforce contracts, he points out that Roman law did not recognize third party rights arising from contracts and that it is necessary to see the third party rule in modern European legal systems in their context. In particular, some European legal systems look to the law of contract to do work which in English law is done by the law of tort. The reality is that English law, French law and German Law (for example) recognize the existence of third party rights in different situations so that it is not true to say that there is a 'European consensus with which English law is out of line'.

Finally, he doubts the validity of the claim that privity causes difficulties in commercial life. He examines the claim that the privity rule causes difficulties in the context of construction contracts and insurance contracts. In the case of construction contracts, he concludes that 'it is unlikely that the Act will have significant impact in the construction industry' and in the case of insurance contracts he claims that the Act 'fails to address the real source of difficulty' in that it is likely to be of 'little assistance to third party beneficiaries under insurance contracts when in competition with the creditors or the estate of the insured'.

The heart of the debate relates to the justice of giving a right of action to the third party. Two principal arguments have been advanced in support of the proposition that justice does not demand the recognition of a third party right of action. The first is that the third party is not a promisee and the second is that the third party has not provided any consideration for the promisor's promise. The first argument is developed in the following extract:

SA Smith, 'Contracts for the Benefit of Third Parties: In Defence of the Third-Party Rule'

(1997) 7 *OJLS* 643, 645–646

Defending the Third Party Rule

A simplified example is helpful in discussing the third-party rule. I will refer to the following case as the 'gardening contract':

A agrees with B that in return for B paying A £100, A will do C's gardening for one year

(C is B's sister). A receives the money, does C's gardening for one month, and then goes on holiday for the rest of the year.

The effect of the third-party rule is to preclude C (the third party) from successfully suing A (the promisor) for the value (to C) of A's promise to B: in other words, the third-party rule prevents C from enforcing the contract.

How can this result be justified? The justification, it is suggested, flows from the nature of contractual obligations as voluntary obligations. The specific type of voluntary obligation (promise, agreement, consent, etc.) to which contractual obligations give rise is not important for our purposes: for ease of expression I will adopt conventional terminology and refer to contractual obligations as promissory obligations. What is important is that voluntary obligations, of whatever stripe, do not exist in the air: they are obligations undertaken to particular persons, extending to and only to those persons. A promise is formed by communicating an intention to undertake an obligation. The communication must be addressed to (and received by) the person to whom the obligation is undertaken. This is a general feature of voluntary obligations. In the case of a vow the obligation is addressed to and undertaken to oneself. In the case of a promise the obligation is undertaken to the addressee of the promise. The promissory obligation thus created is an obligation between the person undertaking it, the promisor, and the person to whom the obligation was given, the promisee. Thus the reason that C in our example should not be able to enforce A's promise is the simple but profound fact that A did not make a promise to C. The promisor A has a duty to perform his promise, but the duty is owed to B, the promisee, not to C.

That promisees and non-promisees are in a different position *vis-à-vis* the enforcement of a promise is a well-recognised feature of ordinary moral reasoning. Few would dispute that there is a difference between B in our example saying 'but you promised me you would do it' and C saying, 'but I heard you promise B that you would do it'. It is because of this difference that we get more upset, and with good reason, at promise-breakers when the promise broken was made to us than when it was made to someone else, even if the practical consequences are the same in each case. Indeed, that promisees and non-promisees are in a different position regarding the enforceability of a promise is accepted by even the strongest critics of the third-party rule. No one suggests that just anyone should be able to sue on a (legally valid) promise and no legal system allows just anyone to sue. Only some third parties should be able to sue. But if there is a difference between third parties and promisees, what is it? The difference cannot be merely that third parties have not provided consideration . . . no one supposes that were consideration abolished then just anyone would be able to sue on a promise and in legal systems without a requirement of consideration this clearly is not the case. Nor can the difference be that promisees are more likely than third parties to rely on the promise . . . the short response to this suggestion is that reliance is not relevant to the existence of promissory obligation. Promises may bind even when they have not been relied upon. The only possible significance of the distinction is the most obvious one: the promisee alone is the person to whom the promissory duty is owed. Thus only the promisee can complain of the promise *qua* promise being broken. This is what is means to be a promisee; and it is why contractual rights have always been understood, correctly, as personal rights.

The distinction that is drawn here by Smith is between a promisee and a third party. Thus a third party is a party to whom a promise of performance has not been made. It follows from this that a third party to whom a promise of performance is made must have a right to enforce that promise. Thus Smith continues (at p. 648):

in some privity cases one or both of the contracting parties may have communicated to the third party an intention to undertake an obligation to that party . . . where such an intention has been communicated the third-party rule is not a bar to the third party bringing an action in contract (the primary bar is consideration). This is because where one or both of the contracting parties communicate to the third party an intention to be bound to that party, the requirements for promissory obligation are satisfied. A promise has been made to the third party. Thus, the third party is not a third party to the agreement made with her, but only to the agreement made between the other two parties. It remains to add only that it is crucial to distinguish this sort of intention (the intention to undertake an obligation) from a mere intent to benefit another or to grant another person legal rights. If X says 'it is my desire and intention to give Y £100 on 1 December' no contract has been created (even ignoring consideration). The same is true if X says 'I grant Y the right to cross over my property'. Assuming that X's words were intended to be understood in their ordinary sense, the reason no contract is created is that while X has intended to do something (to pay a sum of money, to grant a legal right), he has not communicated an intention to put himself under an obligation to do something for Y.

The Law Commission respond to this argument in a footnote located at the end of paragraph 3.1 (above). They refer to an article by Kincaid (1994) 8 JCL 51 where Kincaid argues in similar terms that only a promisee can enforce the promise. The Law Commission respond by stating that 'in our view, this is to take an unnecessarily narrow view of the morality of promise-keeping where a promise is intended to benefit a third party'. Does this answer the points made by Smith and Kincaid?

The second objection is that the third party has not provided any consideration. Thus P Kincaid has argued ('Third Parties: Rationalising A Right to Sue' [1989] *CLJ* 243, 244–245):

Although frequently no coherent justification is offered for the proposition that it is unjust not to allow third parties to sue, when one is given it is usually that the promisor should not be allowed to get away with breaking his promise. My view is that such an approach is inconsistent with the common-law attitude to civil liability generally. The common law's concern in civil liability is to give redress to the plaintiff, not to punish the defendant. This attitude may be contrasted with the moral flavour of the criminal law, where the focus is on the wrongdoing of the defendant. To use such a focus as the rationale for third-party rights is to depart radically from the common law's approach to promissory liability. If such a departure is desirable, it should be the result of a conscious choice.

Bargain is the common law's present general theory which answers the question, who should be able to enforce promises. The answer is, anyone to whom a promise was made and who has paid the price for it requested of him by the promisor. The plaintiff establishes his right by showing a change in his 'condition' (suffering a detriment as the consideration) and by showing a 'link' to the defendant (the request) which makes it just that the defendant should be responsible for loss suffered by the plaintiff as the result of these two factors.

Clearly the third party cannot qualify as a plaintiff under the bargain theory. He has suffered no detriment at the request of the promisor . . .

Kincaid's point is not that the third party should not have a right to sue but that recognition of such a right would entail the development of a new theory of promissory liability and that theory would have to encompass gratuitous promisees as well as third parties. But is it the case that the third party is in the same position as a gratuitous promisee? Does the fact that the promisee has provided consideration not make a difference? The third party is not seeking to enforce a wholly gratuitous promise. While it may be gratuitous as far as the third party is concerned the promisee has paid for the promise. But this argument would appear to lead to the conclusion that the right of action belongs in truth to the promisee and not to the third party. However that may be, the arguments of the Law Commission won the day and their report led to the enactment of the Contracts (Rights of Third Parties) Act 1999.

(f) CONTRACTS (RIGHTS OF THIRD PARTIES) ACT 1999

The Contracts (Rights of Third Parties) Act 1999 can now be said to be the principal source of the law relating to third party rights of action. The Act aims to provide a simple mechanism by which two contracting parties can give to a third party the right to enforce a term of their contract. However the Act is not a straightforward piece of legislation and it requires careful analysis. It will therefore be set out section by section and brief comments will follow most sections.

Right of third party to enforce contractual term

1.—(1) Subject to the provisions of this Act, a person who is not a party to a contract (a 'third party') may in his own right enforce a term of the contract if—

(a) the contract expressly provides that he may, or

(b) subject to subsection (2), the term purports to confer a benefit on him.

(2) Subsection (1)(b) does not apply if on a proper construction of the contract it appears that the parties did not intend the term to be enforceable by the third party.

(3) The third party must be expressly identified in the contract by name, as a member of a class or as answering a particular description but need not be in existence when the contract is entered into.

(4) This section does not confer a right on a third party to enforce a term of a contract otherwise than subject to and in accordance with any other relevant terms of the contract.

(5) For the purpose of exercising his right to enforce a term of the contract, there shall be available to the third party any remedy that would have been available to him in an action for breach of contract if he had been a party to the contract (and the rules relating to damages, injunctions, specific performance and other relief shall apply accordingly).

(6) Where a term of a contract excludes or limits liability in relation to any matter references in this Act to the third party enforcing the term shall be construed as references to his availing himself of the exclusion or limitation.

(7) In this Act, in relation to a term of a contract which is enforceable by a third party—

'the promisor' means the party to the contract against whom the term is enforceable by the third party, and 'the promisee' means the party to the contract by whom the term is enforceable against the promisor.

COMMENTARY

Section 1 establishes two separate tests of enforceability, the first to be found in section 1(1)(a) and section 1(3) and the second in section 1(1)(b) and section 1(3). The scope of these two tests has been set out by Professor Burrows, the Law Commissioner primarily responsible for the Law Commission report on which the Act was based, in the following terms:

A Burrows, 'The Contracts (Rights of Third Parties) Act and its Implications for Commercial Contracts'

[2000] *LMCLQ* 540, 542–546

The first, and simplest [test of enforceability], is in s.1(1)(a) and s.1(3). By s.1(1)(a) a third party has a right to enforce a term of the contract where the contract expressly provides that he may. This is satisfied where the contract contains words such as 'and C shall have the right to enforce the contract' or 'C shall have the right to enforce terms 25, 26 and 27 of the contract' or 'C shall have the right to sue'. Section 1(3) makes clear that the third party does not have to be named (e.g. Joe Smith or X Co). Rather it is sufficient if the third party is expressly identified in the contract as a member of a class (eg, stevedores, subsequent owners, subsequent tenants) or as answering a particular description (eg, 'person living at 3 Coronation Street' or 'B's nominee'). And the third party does not need to be in existence when the contract is made, so that contracting parties may confer rights on an unborn child, a future spouse, or a company that has not yet been incorporated.

The first test—as clarified in s.1(6)—also covers 'negative rights' (ie, exclusion and limitation clauses) conferred on expressly identified third parties. So, for example, in a head building contract between an employer and head-contractor, if there is a term excluding liability on the part of all subcontractors, and the employers sue a subcontractor in the tort of negligence for damage to the building, the subcontractor will be able to rely on the exclusion clause by reason of s. 1(1)(a). Additional words, such as 'and the third party shall be entitled to rely on that exclusion or limitation clause', over and above words clarifying that the clause is for the third party's benefit, seem unnecessary. This is because, by definition, an exclusion or limitation clause is intended to affect the legal rights of beneficiaries of such clauses. The Act therefore provides a solution to the problems raised by cases in the construction industry on exclusion clauses, such as . . . *Norwich City Council* v. *Harvey*. It also produces a solution to the even-better known 'Himalaya clause' difficulties in contracts for the carriage of goods by sea where stevedores wish to take advantage of exclusion clauses in the main contract of carriage to protect them against claims by the owner for negligent damage to the goods in unloading them. . . .

Less straightforward, and less clear-cut, is the second test of enforceability, which is in section 1(1)(b) and 1(3). If s.1(1)(a) is concerned with the *express* conferral of rights on a third party, we can say that the second test is concerned with the *implied* conferral of rights on a third party.

The Act has been criticised in some quarters for including this second test. It has been argued that everything would have been much more certain if there had just been the first test. But there are a number of important justifications for including the second test. I mention here three of them.

(i) Contractual rights as between two parties are not merely a matter of express rights. Rather they include implied rights through the concept of implied terms. Just as the normal law of contract would be artificially restricted if one confined it to express terms, so the same applies to third party rights. Put another way, if one is seeking to effect parties' intentions, these are not necessarily expressed intentions.

(ii) Examination of past cases coming before the courts where privity has caused problems shows that a reform confined to an express conferral of rights would not solve many of the problems. For example, cases concerning A contracting with B to pay money to C, such as *Beswick* v. *Beswick* and *Woodar* v. *Wimpey*; the booking of a holiday for family members or friends, as in *Jackson* v. *Horizon Holidays*; or the taking out of liability insurance designed to protect third parties to the contract, as in *Trident General Insurance Co Ltd* v. *McNiece Bros*. In all of these well-known cases, unless the parties included a magic formula so as to fall within the first test (eg, 'and the third party shall have the right to enforce the term'), the 1999 Act would not have improved the position of the third parties.

(iii) Closely linked to the second point is that a magic formula within the first test will only be used in well-drafted contracts. But not all contracts are well drafted, and in the consumer sphere good legal advice may not be affordable.

For those sorts of reasons the Act contains a second test of enforceability according to which a third party will have a right to enforce a term if three conditions are satisfied: first, the term purports to confer a benefit on him (s.1(1)(b)); secondly, he is expressly identified by name, class or description (s.1(3)); unless, on a proper construction of the contract the parties did not intend the term to be enforceable by him (s.1(2)).

The second test therefore uses a rebuttable presumption of intention.... It is this rebuttable presumption that provides the essential balance between sufficient certainty for contracting parties and the flexibility required for the reform to deal fairly with a huge range of different situations. The presumption is based on the idea that, if you ask yourself, 'When is it that parties are likely to have intended to confer rights on a third party to enforce a term, albeit that they have not expressly conferred that right', the answer will be: 'Where the term purports to confer a benefit on an expressly identified third party'. That then sets up the presumption. But the presumption can be rebutted if, as a matter of ordinary contractual interpretation, there is something else indicating that the parties did not intend such a right to be given.

So, if money is to be paid by A not to B but to an expressly identified third party C, the presumption is that C has the right to enforce that term. But that presumption can be rebutted. For example, there may be an express term of the contract laying down that C shall have no right of enforceability. Or the rebuttal may occur because of other inconsistent terms. For example, the contract may prohibit assignment to C of B's right to enforce the payment without A's written consent. That would indicate that the parties did not intend to confer on C an immediate right of enforceability.

There are two main additional points to make on this second test. First ... the words 'purport to confer a benefit on' the third party are designed to ensure that the presumption is triggered only where the third party is to receive a benefit directly from the promisor. They are not designed to cover consequential or incidental benefits stemming from the promisor's performance. Professor Treitel gives a very good example. If A were employed by B to 'cut my (B's) hedge adjoining C's land', performance by A might benefit C but the term would not purport to confer a benefit on C. Similarly, a solicitor's contractual obligation to use reasonable care in drawing up a will would not, *vis-à-vis*, the beneficiaries of that will, fall within s.1(1)(b) because the term does not purport to confer a benefit on the beneficiaries of the will; the benefit to them derives from the testator not from the solicitor, whose role is to enable his client, at the client's discretion, to confer a benefit on the beneficiaries . . .

Secondly, what material can be used in determining the proper construction of the contract under s.1(2)? The idea was that the normal objective approach to contractual interpretation should be applied, subject to there being a reversed burden of proof . . .

So much, then, for the two tests of enforceability. It can be seen that a contract draftsman can make the position absolutely certain; either by giving identified third parties express rights to enforce particular terms so as to fall within the first test; or by saying that third parties shall not have the right to enforce particular terms or indeed any terms. If a contract draftsman does not want anything to do with the 1999 Act, a simple standard term, such as the following, can be included: 'A person who is not a party to this agreement shall have no right under the Contracts (Rights of Third Parties) Act 1999 to enforce any of its terms [except and to the extent that this agreement expressly provides for such Act to apply to any of its terms]'.

It should be noted that that term seems preferable, generally speaking, to merely saying: 'A person who is not a party to this agreement shall have no right to enforce any of its terms'. This formulation would exclude any right of a third party which exists apart from the 1999 Act (eg, by assignment or trust of the promise or existing statutory exceptions) and this may not be what is intended.

The concern has been expressed that, if the contract draftsman does not say anything expressly one way or the other, the 1999 Act can lead to unintended liabilities being imposed on the parties. If that were the case it would certainly contradict the purpose of the second test, which is to give effect to the parties' intentions, albeit by using a presumption. If applying normal objective rules of construction, including implied terms, neither contracting party intended to confer a right on a third party, the presumption would be rebutted and no right would be conferred on the third party. The real concern, I would suggest, is that *one* party (the promisor) might conceivably find itself landed with an obligation to a third party that *it* subjectively did not intend to undertake; but unintended liabilities in that sense are a risk of any contract, given objective interpretation . . .

What does the right of enforceability mean? This is laid down in s. 1(5). The third party has the same remedies for breach of the contractual term as if he had been a party to the contract. He can therefore recover expectation (or reliance) damages *for his own loss* (subject to normal restrictions, for example, remoteness or the duty to mitigate). Or applying analogous rules to those normally applied, the third party may be awarded specific performance or an injunction.

The first reported case to consider section 1 of the Act is the decision of Colman J in *Nisshin Shipping Co Ltd* v. *Cleaves & Co Ltd* [2003] EWHC 2602 (Comm); [2004] 1 Lloyd's Rep 38. Cleaves negotiated time charters on behalf of Nisshin, the owners of the vessels. Each charterparty contained an arbitration clause. A dispute arose as to whether or not Cleaves was entitled to its commission under the charterparties. The relevant clause stated:

A commission of two per cent for equal division is payable by the vessel and owners to Messrs Ifchor S.A.Lausanne and Messrs Cleaves and Company Ltd, London on hire earned and paid under this Charter.

Nisshin disputed the entitlement of Cleaves to recover its commission on the ground that it alleged that Cleaves was in breach of the agency agreement. Cleaves purported to refer the issue to arbitration. While there was no arbitration agreement in the contract between Nisshin and Cleaves, Cleaves sought to rely on the arbitration clause to be found in the time charters and, in doing so, relied upon the 1999 Act. The arbitrators ruled that they did have jurisdiction and Nisshin brought a challenge to that conclusion under section 67 of the Arbitration Act 1996. Nisshin submitted that Cleaves was not entitled to rely on sections 1 and 8 of the 1999 Act with the result that the arbitrators lacked jurisdiction. Colman J rejected these submissions and held that Cleaves was entitled to rely on the 1999 Act with the consequence that the arbitrators did have jurisdiction. There were a number of steps in the reasoning of Colman J.

The first question was whether a term in the time charter purported to confer a benefit on Cleaves so as to bring the case within section 1(1)(b) of the Act. Colman J held that the clause entitling Cleaves to a commission of 1% did confer a benefit on Cleaves so that the requirement of section 1(1)(b) was satisfied.

The second question was whether the effect of section 1(2) was to deprive Cleaves of the right to enforce the term. As Colman J pointed out, the onus is put on the party seeking to allege that section 1(1)(b) has been disapplied. Thus, if the contract is neutral, section 1(1)(b) is not disapplied. On the facts, he held that section 1(1)(b) had not been disapplied.

Thirdly, it was argued on behalf of the owners that the fact that the agents had a claim by virtue of the operation of a trust of the promise (on which see pp. 1203–1205 above) operated to deny to Cleaves a direct right of action under the 1999 Act. Colman J rejected this submission and held that the 1999 Act provided a much simpler method by which Cleaves could enforce its rights and, this being the case, it could not be inferred that the parties had intended to confine the rights of Cleaves to those arising under the trust and to deny them the right to rely on the 1999 Act. This point, combined with the previous point, underlines the need for parties who wish to avoid the application of the Act to make their intention clear: they are unlikely to be able to rely on the availability of an alternative remedy in order to defeat the claim of the third party to rely on the Act. Parties who remain silent may find, perhaps to their surprise, that the Act is applicable and that it operates to confer a right of action on the third party.

In the absence of further case law, one way of attempting to ascertain the limits of section 1 is to apply it to the facts of decided cases. This is not always an easy task because the parties, at the time of these cases, were operating on the assumption that the law did not recognize a third party right of action of the type contained in the 1999 Act. *Tweddle* v. *Atkinson* (p. 1173 above) would appear to fall within the scope of section 1(1)(a) because the contract between John Tweddle and William Guy expressly stated that William Tweddle was to have the right to enforce the contract. On the other hand, *White* v. *Jones* (p. 1211 above) satisfies neither test. The wording of section 1(1)(b) will not stretch to the *White* v. *Jones* fact situation because the undertaking of the solicitor to exercise reasonable care and skill does not purport to confer a benefit on the beneficiary. Section 1(6) deals with exclusion and limitation clauses and provides a much simpler mechanism by which the benefit of such clauses can be extended to third parties (and so would appear to cover *The Eurymedon* type case).

Slightly more difficult are cases such as *Beswick* v. *Beswick* (p. 1181 above) and *Jackson* v. *Horizon Holidays Ltd* (p. 1196 above). Professor Burrows implies that they would now fall within the scope of the 1999 Act and this is confirmed by the Law Commission report at paragraphs 7.46 and 7.40 respectively. In relation to *Beswick* the Law Commission state (at para 7.46):

the provision of old Mr Beswick's contract with his nephew providing for payment of an annuity to Mrs Beswick would give Mrs Beswick a presumed right of enforceability under our second limb. The nephew promised to confer the benefit (the annuity payments) on Mrs Beswick, who was expressly named. The presumption could only be rebutted if the nephew could demonstrate that, on the proper construction of the contract, he and old Mr Beswick had no intention at the time of contracting that Mrs Beswick should have the right to enforce the provision. In our view, the nephew would not be able to satisfy the onus of proof so that Mrs Beswick would have the right of enforcement.

It is certainly the case that the 1999 Act makes it easier for the parties to confer an enforceable right of action on the third party. But it does not necessarily follow that *Beswick* would now fall within the scope of the Act. Professor Treitel has expressed his doubts on this score. He points out (*Some Landmarks of Twentieth Century Contract Law* (Oxford University Press, 2002), p. 87) that the agreement concluded between Peter and John Beswick was drawn up by a solicitor and that 'it would have been so easy for the solicitor to have drawn up the agreement so as to confer enforceable rights on Ruth [i.e., Mrs Beswick]'. It could have been done by, for example, making her a party to the agreement. Why did the solicitor not confer enforceable rights on Ruth? One possible answer, which Professor Treitel is reluctant to adopt in the absence of any evidence, is that the solicitor was negligent. The other possibility suggested by Professor Treitel is that:

he was simply carrying out his instructions. We have no way of knowing what passed between him and his clients on 14 March 1962; but there is a possibility of his having told Peter and John (1) that they could create legally enforceable rights in favour of Ruth but (2) that if they did so, their right to vary their contract would be lost or limited. Peter and John might not have liked that idea and instructed him accordingly.

This latter possibility is significant in terms of the application of the Act. As Professor Treitel points out, the requirements of section 1(1)(a) were not satisfied, in that the agreement did not expressly provide that Mrs Beswick was to have the right to enforce any term of the contract. But she would have a prima facie right of action under section 1(1)(b) unless the presumption was rebutted under section 1(2). At this point it would be necessary to discover what was said by the parties in the solicitor's office on the fateful day in question and to explore the reasons for the failure of the solicitor to confer an enforceable right of action upon Mrs Beswick. If he was acting on instructions not to confer a right of action upon Mrs Beswick then the presumption that she was intended to have a right of enforcement would be rebutted. Of course, as Professor Treitel points out, we will never know the reason for the failure to confer an enforceable right of action upon Mrs Beswick but his careful examination of the facts of the case serves as a helpful reminder of the point that we should not lightly assume that the intention of two contracting parties is inevitably to confer a right of action on the third party.

Cases such as *Jackson* v. *Horizon Holidays Ltd* probably fall within the scope of section 1(1)(b) provided that the members of the holiday party are identified at the time of entry into the contract. Thus Professor Treitel states (*The Law of Contract* (11th edn, Sweet & Maxwell, 2003), p. 655):

> If the person making the booking supplied the names of other members of the family when the contract was made, those other members would probably acquire rights under subsection 1(1); but no such rights are likely to be acquired if a person simply rented a holiday cottage without giving any information as to the number or names of the persons with whom he proposed to share the accommodation.

Professor Burrows also suggests that a third party, C, will not acquire a right to enforce a term of the contract where the contract between A and B contains a term which prohibits the assignment to C of B's right to enforce the payment without A's written consent. But can one go even further and suggest that a clause that entitles B to assign his rights to C operates to deny to C the right to enforce the term of the contract under section 1 of the Act? In such a case C acquires rights as the assignee of B. What useful purpose is served by conferring on C an additional right of action under the 1999 Act? Might it not be the case that the intention of the parties in such a case was to confer upon C one right of action, namely his rights as assignee of B and so negative the intention to confer a right of action under the Act? Obviously much will depend upon the facts of the individual case but there must at least be the possibility that a court would reach such a conclusion.

Section 1 gives to contracting parties an incentive to make their intention clear. They can do so either by conferring a right of action upon the third party or by making it clear that the third party has no such right of action. The initial reaction in commercial practice, particularly in the construction industry, was to insert into contracts a clause the effect of which was to exclude the application of the 1999 Act. This negative response to the Act is still to be found in standard form contracts in the construction industry (see D Cornes and R Winward, *Winward Fearon on Collateral Warranties* (2nd edn, Blackwell, 2002), pp. 58–59). The attitude within commercial practice more generally remains cautious but the initial hostility is perhaps being replaced by a realization that the Act is beneficial where the contracting parties do intend to create an enforceable right of action in the third party. As this realization dawns, one might expect that greater use will be made of the Act.

Three other points can be made in relation to section 1. First, the section makes no mention of the doctrine of consideration but the effect of the statement that the third party 'may in his own right enforce a term of the contract' is sufficient to make it clear that the third party has a right to enforce the term notwithstanding the fact that he has not provided any consideration.

Secondly, as Professor Burrows points out, the third party has the same remedies for breach of the contractual term as if he had been a party to the contract. Neil Andrews illustrates the point in the following way ('Strangers to Justice No Longer: The Reversal of the Privity Rule Under the Contracts (Rights of Third Parties) Act 1999' [2001] *CLJ* 353, 360):

Suppose A promises B that A will pay C £100,000, and C relies on this promise to the extent of £5,000. The court must decide whether C is entitled on the facts to £5,000 (the amount of his reliance) or the sum of £100,000, the latter award fully vindicating C's expectation of performance by A . . . The Law Commission clearly wished third parties to gain satisfaction of their 'expectation interest' and not to be fobbed off with protection of their reliance loss . . . It seems likely that the courts will give effect generally to the third party's expectation interest unless, in exceptional circumstances, this will lead to injustice. Here we can peer at the future only through a glass, darkly.

How much do you think C should be entitled to recover in this hypothetical case?

Thirdly, section 1 refers to 'contracts' and it is therefore a matter of some doubt whether or not the Act applies to a deed. The Act is silent on this point. This is unfortunate and is in marked contrast with section 4 of the New Zealand Contracts (Privity) Act 1982 which states that 'where a promise contained in a deed or contract confers, or purports to confer, a benefit on a person . . .'

Variation and rescission of contract

2.—(1) Subject to the provisions of this section, where a third party has a right under section 1 to enforce a term of the contract, the parties to the contract may not, by agreement, rescind the contract, or vary it in such a way as to extinguish or alter his entitlement under that right, without his consent if—

(a) the third party has communicated his assent to the term to the promisor,

(b) the promisor is aware that the third party has relied on the term, or

(c) the promisor can reasonably be expected to have foreseen that the third party would rely on the term and the third party has in fact relied on it.

(2) The assent referred to in subsection (1)(a)—

(a) may be by words or conduct, and

(b) if sent to the promisor by post or other means, shall not be regarded as communicated to the promisor until received by him.

(3) Subsection (1) is subject to any express term of the contract under which—

(a) the parties to the contract may by agreement rescind or vary the contract without the consent of the third party, or

(b) the consent of the third party is required in circumstances specified in the contract instead of those set out in subsection (1)(a) to (c).

(4) Where the consent of a third party is required under subsection (1) or (3), the court

or arbitral tribunal may, on the application of the parties to the contract, dispense with his consent if satisfied—

(a) that his consent cannot be obtained because his whereabouts cannot reasonably be ascertained, or

(b) that he is mentally incapable of giving his consent.

(5) The court or arbitral tribunal may, on the application of the parties to a contract, dispense with any consent that may be required under subsection (1)(c) if satisfied that it cannot reasonably be ascertained whether or not the third party has in fact relied on the term.

(6) If the court or arbitral tribunal dispenses with a third party's consent, it may impose such conditions as it thinks fit, including a condition requiring the payment of compensation to the third party.

(7) The jurisdiction conferred on the court by subsections (4) to (6) is exercisable by both the High Court and a County court.

COMMENTARY

The aim of section 2 is to strike a balance between the rights of the third party and the rights of the original contracting parties. It does so by limiting the right of the parties to the contract to rescind or to vary the rights of the third party without the latter's consent. In this sense the right of the third party may trump the rights of the parties to the initial contract. The point at which the contracting parties lose the right to rescind or vary the terms of their contract is either when the third party communicates his assent to the term to the promisor (s. 2(1)(a)) or where he relies on that term and the promisor is aware of that reliance or ought to have foreseen that reliance (s. 2(1)(b), (c)). From the perspective of the third party, the safest course of action is expressly to communicate his assent to the promisor. More difficult is the case where the third party alleges that he has relied on the term. As Andrews has pointed out ([2001] *CLJ* 353, 366) it 'seems inevitable' that sections 2(1)(b) and 2(1)(c) 'will excite litigation'.

But it is important to note that it is open to the contracting parties to reserve to themselves the right to rescind or vary their contract without obtaining the consent of the third party provided that they reserve such a power to themselves in their contract (s. 2(3)). In this way the Act preserves the freedom of contract of the contracting parties. They remain entitled to define for themselves the scope of the right which the third party will acquire but, in the event of their failure to specify the scope of that right in their contract, they may lose their right to rescind or vary their contract if the third party satisfies the requirements of section 2(1).

What is the meaning of the word 'rescind' in section 2(1)? It clearly encompasses a case where the two parties to the contract attempt consensually to terminate their contract. But what happens in the case where the promisor wishes to set aside the contract because of a repudiatory breach committed by the promisee? Can the promisor terminate the contract notwithstanding the fact that the third party has satisfied the requirements of section 2(1)? The word 'rescind' was inserted into the Bill by way of an amendment made in the House of Lords (the word used in the Law Commission draft Bill being 'cancel'). Moving the amendment the Lord Chancellor stated that 'we would not want a contracting party to be prevented from accepting a repudiation because of the interests of the third party' (HL Deb, vol 601, col 1055, 27 May 1999). This being the case, it would appear that the promisor can elect to terminate the contract in the event that the promisee commits a repudiatory breach and that the effect of the termination will be to deprive the third party of his right to enforce the term. This point is of significance with regard to *Tweddle* v. *Atkinson* (p. 1173 above). In *Beswick* v. *Beswick* (p. 1181 above) Lord Denning pointed out that it would appear that the reason for the failure of William Tweddle's claim was that his father had not paid the promised £100. Would this failure on his father's part also prevent William Tweddle from bringing a claim under the Act? It appears that it would. His claim would fail either because William Guy made a conditional promise to pay William Tweddle (that is, he would pay provided that John Tweddle also paid) and that condition was never fulfilled or because John Tweddle's failure to make the payment was a repudiatory breach of contract which William Guy accepted, thereby terminating the contract and with it any third party right previously enjoyed by William Tweddle. A similar result would appear to follow both in the case where the promisor has a right to set aside the contract against the promisee on a ground such as misrepresentation, undue influence, etc. and in the case where the contract is brought to an end as a result of the application of the doctrine of frustration. This result can be justified either on the ground that the contract has not been rescinded 'by agreement' within the meaning of section 2 or on the ground that section 3 (below) entitles the promisor to invoke against the third party any defences that he would have had to the claim had it been brought by the promisee.

Can the contracting parties confer on the third party a right which is irrevocable from the moment of its creation? The Law Commission concluded that they could not. They stated at paragraph 9.46 of their report:

We do not see the attraction, nor the justification, for holding the contracting parties to a contract which the third party has neither relied upon nor accepted. In our view this would be an unreasonable fetter on the contracting parties' freedom of contract which could not be justified by reference to any injustice to another party. In any event, this would cut across the standard contractual principle that the parties are free to vary any term of the contract, even a 'no-variation' term. We therefore consider that any provision of a contract for the benefit of a third party which purports to render that contract irrevocable should be as open to variation or discharge as any other contractual term. Similarly if the parties have expressly laid down a crystallisation test different from reliance or acceptance, they should be free to vary it prior to reliance or acceptance by the third party.

Professor Burrows has since stated that this passage is 'misleading' ([2000] *LMCLQ* 540, 547 fn. 22) and he concludes that it must give way to the 'broad wording' of section 2(3)(b) which, in his view, entitles 'the parties by an express term to make the contract irrevocable', that is to say they can give 'the third party absolute security irrespective of the third party's reliance or communication of intent'. As Andrews has pointed out ([2001] *CLJ* 353, 362) it would be 'unfortunate if the Law Commission's view were to prevail because this would create a trap for the third party. Faced by such an ostensibly irrevocable term, C might wrongly suppose that his rights under A and B's contract are indefeasible even if he neither assents to the relevant term nor relies upon it'. In the absence of case-law, and given this conflict of opinion, the matter must be regarded as one of some doubt. This being the case, parties who wish to confer on the third party a right that is irrevocable from the moment of its creation would be better advised to create a trust of the contractual right (on which see p. 1203 above).

Defences etc. available to promisor

3.—(1) Subsections (2) to (5) apply where, in reliance on section 1, proceedings for the enforcement of a term of a contract are brought by a third party.

(2) The promisor shall have available to him by way of defence or set-off any matter that—

    (a) arises from or in connection with the contract and is relevant to the term, and

    (b) would have been available to him by way of defence or set-off if the proceedings had been brought by the promisee.

(3) The promisor shall also have available to him by way of defence or set-off any matter if—

    (a) an express term of the contract provides for it to be available to him in proceedings brought by the third party, and

    (b) it would have been available to him by way of defence or set-off if the proceedings had been brought by the promisee.

(4) The promisor shall also have available to him—

    (a) by way of defence or set-off any matter, and

    (b) by way of counterclaim any matter not arising from the contract,

that would have been available to him by way of defence or set-off or, as the case may be, by way of counterclaim against the third party if the third party had been a party to the contract.

(5) Subsections (2) and (4) are subject to any express term of the contract as to the matters that are not to be available to the promisor by way of defence, set-off or counterclaim.

(6) Where in any proceedings brought against him a third party seeks in reliance on section 1 to enforce a term of a contract (including, in particular, a term purporting to exclude or limit liability), he may not do so if he could not have done so (whether by reason of any particular circumstances relating to him or otherwise) had he been a party to the contract.

COMMENTARY

The effect of this section is to protect the position of the promisor in so far as it entitles the promisor to rely, in an action brought by the third party, on the defences that would have been available to the promisor had he been sued on the contract by the promisee. This provision further demonstrates the fact that the third party right of action cannot be described as a right to enforce the promise of performance in that his right is subject to such rights as the promisor has against the promisee.

However the entitlement of the promisor to bring into account matters relevant between himself and the promisee is limited by the terms of section 3(2). First, the promisor is entitled to rely on a 'defence or set-off' but cannot bring into account a counterclaim against the promisee. The reason for this is essentially to protect the position of the third party. The effect of a defence or set-off may be to reduce the third party's claim to zero but it cannot leave the third party with a liability to the promisor. However, had the promisor been entitled to rely on a counterclaim which he had against the promisee, and the size of that counterclaim had exceeded the amount claimed by the third party, the effect might have been to leave the third party liable to the promisor. Secondly the matter must have arisen 'from or in connection with the contract' and be 'relevant to the term'.

Section 3(4) takes into account the equities as between the third party and the promisor in that the third party's claim is subject to the defences, counterclaims (not arising from the contract), and set-offs that would have been available to the promisor had the third party been a party to the contract. This time the promisor is entitled to bring any counterclaim against the third party into account: the reason for this is that, if the promisor does have a counterclaim against the third party, the third party cannot be made worse off by allowing the promisor to bring that counterclaim into account in the proceedings.

Once again the contracting parties can contract out of this provision either by providing that the promisor may not raise any defence or set-off that would have been available against the promisee or by making the third party's claim subject to all defences and set-offs that the promisor would have had against the promisee whether or not they arose from or in connection with the contract and were relevant to the term.

Enforcement of contract by promisee

4. Section 1 does not affect any right of the promisee to enforce any term of the contract.

COMMENTARY

The effect of this section is to preserve the rights of the promisee. It therefore follows that the rights of the promisee (discussed at pp. 1179–1202 above) are unaffected by the enactment of the 1999 Act. This being the case, the promisor is now potentially exposed to liability both to the promisee and the third party. Section 5 of the Act seeks to protect the promisor against the possibility of double liability.

Protection of promisor from double liability

5. Where under section 1 a term of a contract is enforceable by a third party, and the promisee has recovered from the promisor a sum in respect of—

(a) the third party's loss in respect of the term, or

(b) the expense to the promisee of making good to the third party the default of the promisor, then, in any proceedings brought in reliance on that section by the third party, the court or arbitral tribunal shall reduce any award to the third party to such extent as it thinks appropriate to take account of the sum recovered by the promisee.

COMMENTARY

Section 5 deals with the case where the third party brings an action against the promisor after the promisee has brought an action against the promisor and has recovered from the promisor a sum of money in respect of the third party's loss. In such a case the court or tribunal shall reduce any award to the third party to the extent that it thinks appropriate taking account of the sum recovered by the promisee. The section does not deal with the case where the promisee brings an action against the promisor after the third party has sued the promisor and recovered damages in respect of its loss. In such a case the promisee will not be entitled to recover damages in respect of the loss that has already been made good and will be confined to a claim for its own loss (which is likely to be nominal in most cases).

Exceptions

6.—(1) Section 1 confers no rights on a third party in the case of a contract on a bill of exchange, promissory note or other negotiable instrument.

(2) Section 1 confers no rights on a third party in the case of any contract binding on a company and its members under section 14 of the Companies Act 1985.

(2A) Section 1 confers no rights on a third party in the case of any incorporation document of a limited liability partnership or any limited liability partnership agreement as defined in the Limited Liability Partnerships Regulations 2001 (SI No 2001/1090).[5]

(3) Section 1 confers no right on a third party to enforce—

(a) any term of a contract of employment against an employee,

(b) any term of a worker's contract against a worker (including a home worker), or

(c) any term of a relevant contract against an agency worker.

(4) In subsection (3)—

(a) 'contract of employment', 'employee', 'worker's contract', and 'worker' have the meaning given by section 54 of the National Minimum Wage Act 1998,

(b) 'home worker' has the meaning given by section 35(2) of that Act,

(c) 'agency worker' has the same meaning as in section 34(1) of that Act, and

(d) 'relevant contract' means a contract entered into, in a case where section 34 of that Act applies, by the agency worker as respects work falling within subsection (1)(a) of that section.

(5) Section 1 confers no rights on a third party in the case of—

(a) a contract for the carriage of goods by sea, or

(b) a contract for the carriage of goods by rail or road, or for the carriage of cargo by air, which is subject to the rules of the appropriate international transport convention,

---

[5] Inserted by the Limited Liability Partnerships Regulations 2001 (SI No 2001/1090).

except that a third party may in reliance on that section avail himself of an exclusion or limitation of liability in such a contract.

(6) In subsection (5) 'contract for the carriage of goods by sea' means a contract of carriage—

(a) contained in or evidenced by a bill of lading, sea waybill or a corresponding electronic transaction, or

(b) under or for the purposes of which there is given an undertaking which is contained in a ship's delivery order or a corresponding electronic transaction.

(7) For the purposes of subsection (6)—

(a) 'bill of lading', 'sea waybill' and 'ship's delivery order' have the same meaning as in the Carriage of Goods by Sea Act 1992, and

(b) a corresponding electronic transaction is a transaction within section 1(5) of that Act which corresponds to the issue, indorsement, delivery or transfer of a bill of lading, sea waybill or ship's delivery order.

(8) In subsection (5) 'the appropriate international transport convention' means—

(a) in relation to a contract for the carriage of goods by rail, the Convention which has the force of law in the United Kingdom under section 1 of the International Transport Conventions Act 1983,

(b) in relation to a contract for the carriage of goods by road, the Convention which has the force of law in the United Kingdom under section 1 of the Carriage of Goods by Road Act 1965, and

(c) in relation to a contract for the carriage of cargo by air—

(i) the Convention which has the force of law in the United Kingdom under section 1 of the Carriage by Air Act 1961, or

(ii) the Convention which has the force of law under section 1 of the Carriage by Air (Supplementary Provisions) Act 1962, or

(iii) either of the amended Conventions set out in Part B of Schedule 2 or 3 to the Carriage by Air Acts (Application of Provisions) Order 1967.

COMMENTARY

The aim of this section is to exclude certain types of contract from the scope of the Act. In the case of subsections (1), (5), (6), (7), and (8) the aim was to avoid a clash with existing legislative schemes which conferred rights of action upon third parties. In the case of subsections (2)–(4) the aim was rather different, namely to ensure that the third party did not have a right of action in the specified circumstances. Section 6(5) provides that the Act applies to contracts for the carriage of goods by sea only if the relevant term is an exclusion or limitation clause (s. 1(6) is similarly confined to terms which exclude or limit liability) and this may suggest that an exclusive jurisdiction clause does not fall within the scope of the Act on the ground that the Privy Council in *The Mahkutai* (p. 1214 above) concluded that an exclusive jurisdiction clause was not an exception clause or a limitation clause because it was a clause which created mutual rights and obligations between the parties.

Supplementary provisions relating to third party

7.—(1) Section 1 does not affect any right or remedy of a third party that exists or is available apart from this Act.

(2) Section 2(2) of the Unfair Contract Terms Act 1977 (restriction on exclusion etc. of liability for negligence) shall not apply where the negligence consists of the breach of an obligation arising from a term of a contract and the person seeking to enforce it is a third party acting in reliance on section 1.

(3) In sections 5 and 8 of the Limitation Act 1980 the references to an action founded on a simple contract and an action upon a specialty shall respectively include references to an action brought in reliance on section 1 relating to a simple contract and an action brought in reliance on that section relating to a specialty.

(4) A third party shall not, by virtue of section 1(5) or 3(4) or (6), be treated as a party to the contract for the purposes of any other Act (or any instrument made under any other Act).

COMMENTARY

Section 7(1) preserves the existing exceptions to the doctrine of privity. In this sense the Act does not reduce the complexity of the law. That said, the practical significance of some of these exceptions is likely to reduce as use is made of the Act. Is it open to the judiciary to develop further exceptions to the doctrine of privity? The Law Commission concluded that it was. In their report they stated (at para 5.10):

We should emphasise that we do not wish our proposed legislation . . . to hamper the judicial development of third party rights. Should the House of Lords decide that in a particular sphere our reform does not go far enough and that, for example, a measure of imposed consumer protection is required or that employees (even though not mentioned in the contract) should be able to rely on exclusion clauses that protect their employers under a doctrine of vicarious immunity, we would not wish our proposed legislation to be construed as hampering that development.

It therefore remains open to the judiciary (at least at the level of the House of Lords) to take the step mentioned by Lord Goff in *The Mahkutai* (p. 1214 above) of recognizing a 'fully-fledged exception to the doctrine of privity of contract', perhaps by following the lead of the Supreme Court of Canada in *London Drugs Ltd* v. *Kuehne & Nagel International Ltd* (p. 1226 above). The Act has reduced the practical need for the courts to take such a step but the possibility cannot be ruled out.

Section 7(2) is a controversial provision. Its effect is to entitle a promisor to exclude his liability to the third party for a breach of the promisor's contractual duty of care without fear of challenge under section 2(2) of the Unfair Contract Terms Act 1977 (except where the third party suffers personal injury or death in which case s. 2(1) of the Unfair Contract Terms Act 1977 continues to offer protection to the third party). The effect of section 7(2) is therefore to put the third party in an inferior position in comparison with the promisee in that the promisee can invoke section 2(2) of the Unfair Contract Terms Act 1977 to challenge the validity of the promisor's exclusion or limitation clause but the third party cannot.

Arbitration provisions

8.—(1) Where—

(a) a right under section 1 to enforce a term ('the substantive term') is subject to a term providing for the submission of disputes to arbitration ('the arbitration agreement'), and

(b) the arbitration agreement is an agreement in writing for the purposes of Part I of the Arbitration Act 1996,

the third party shall be treated for the purposes of that Act as a party to the arbitration agreement as regards disputes between himself and the promisor relating to the enforcement of the substantive term by the third party.

(2) Where—

(a) a third party has a right under section 1 to enforce a term providing for one or more descriptions of dispute between the third party and the promisor to be submitted to arbitration ('the arbitration agreement'),

(b) the arbitration agreement is an agreement in writing for the purposes of Part I of the Arbitration Act 1996, and

(c) the third party does not fall to be treated under subsection (1) as a party to the arbitration agreement,

the third party shall, if he exercises the right, be treated for the purposes of that Act as a party to the arbitration agreement in relation to the matter with respect to which the right is exercised, and be treated as having been so immediately before the exercise of the right.

COMMENTARY

The Law Commission recommended (para 14.19 of their report) that 'a third party shall have no rights of enforceability under our proposed reform in respect of an arbitration agreement or a jurisdiction agreement'. The Act does not give effect to this recommendation. In the first place, it makes no express provision for exclusive jurisdiction clauses at all (although it can be argued that they do not fall within the scope of the Act in any event, see p. 1249 above). Secondly section 8 departs from the Law Commission's recommendation in relation to arbitration clauses. The Act is concerned with the acquisition of rights by third parties, not the imposition of liabilities on third parties. Arbitration clauses straddle that divide in that, like exclusive jurisdiction clauses, they carry burdens as well as confer benefits. Section 8(1) deals with the more common situation and it provides that where a third party is given a right of enforceability under section 1 and the contract provides that all rights, including the right of the third party, must be referred to arbitration then the third party must resort to arbitration if he wishes to enforce his substantive right under the contract. In this situation, in order to obtain the benefit of his third party right of action, he must submit to the condition that he assert it in arbitral proceedings rather than litigation.

Section 8 was considered by Colman J in *Nisshin Shipping Co Ltd* v. *Cleaves & Co Ltd* [2003] EWHC 2602 (Comm); [2004] 1 Lloyd's Rep 38 (above p. 1239). One of the issues between the parties was whether or not the enforcement of Cleaves's rights was subject to the arbitration agreement in the charterparties. Colman J held that Cleaves were entitled to and were in fact obliged to refer the disputes to arbitration and that the arbitrators had jurisdiction to determine them. This conclusion is a difficult one. It depends in large part on the analogy drawn by Colman J with the law of assignment. He held that the arbitration clause was wide enough to embrace a dispute between owners and charterers about the payment of commission and, this being the case, Cleaves had to stand in the shoes of the promisee as regards enforcement of the term. This approach may not, however, be consistent with the intention of Parliament in enacting section 8. The difficulty with the approach adopted by Colman J is that it treats the third party as if it were a party to the contract, whereas the intention behind the Act was to confer on the third party a right to enforce a term of the contract and not to make it party to the contract. This being the case, the preferable approach would appear to be to adopt the analysis which was rejected by Colman J, namely to conclude that the arbitration clause can only be invoked by (or against) the third party if, on its true construction, the intention of the parties was that an issue relating to the rights of third parties should in fact be referred to arbitration. The difference in reasoning can be important because the arbitration clause in the present case clearly operated as between the owners and the charterers and did not, in its face, extend to a claim by the third party. The upshot of the case is that care must be taken when drafting arbitration clauses and consideration should be given to whether or not it is intended to encompass the third party within an arbitration clause (see further Ambrose [2001] *Journal of Business Law* 415).

Northern Ireland

9.—(1) In its application to Northern Ireland, this Act has effect with the modifications specified in subsections (2) and (3).

(2) In section 6(2), for 'section 14 of the Companies Act 1985' there is substituted 'Article 25 of the Companies (Northern Ireland) Order 1986'.

(3) In section 7, for subsection (3) there is substituted—

'(3) In Articles 4(a) and 15 of the Limitation (Northern Ireland) Order 1989, the references to an action founded on a simple contract and an action upon an instrument under seal shall respectively include references to an action brought in reliance on section 1 relating to a simple contract and an action brought in reliance on that section relating to a contract under seal.'

(4) In the Law Reform (Husband and Wife) (Northern Ireland) Act 1964, the following provisions are hereby repealed—

(a) section 5, and

(b) in section 6, in subsection (1)(a), the words 'in the case of section 4' and 'and in the case of section 5 the contracting party' and, in subsection (3), the words 'or section 5'.

Short title, commencement and extent

10.—(1) This Act may be cited as the Contracts (Rights of Third Parties) Act 1999.

(2) This Act comes into force on the day on which it is passed but, subject to subsection (3), does not apply in relation to a contract entered into before the end of the period of six months beginning with that day.

(3) The restriction in subsection (2) does not apply in relation to a contract which—

(a) is entered into on or after the day on which this Act is passed, and

(b) expressly provides for the application of this Act.

(4) This Act extends as follows—

(a) section 9 extends to Northern Ireland only;

(b) the remaining provisions extend to England and Wales and Northern Ireland only.

COMMENTARY

The Act does not have retrospective effect. It applies to contracts entered into on or after 11 May 2000. Given the inevitable time lag between the formation of a contract, the occurrence of a dispute, and the resultant litigation it is not surprising that there has not, as yet, been any litigation under the Act. But the Act is in force and can be used in commercial practice.

5. THIRD PARTIES AND THE IMPOSITION
OF LIABILITIES

As a general rule parties to a contract cannot impose an obligation on a third party without the latter's consent. The existence of this general rule is widely accepted and consequently this area of law has not witnessed the upheaval we have seen in the context of the acquisition of rights by third parties. The general rule is subject to a number of exceptions and it is important to note that neither the rule nor its exceptions are affected by the 1999 Act (the Law Commission expressly stated in their report (para 2.1) that their proposed reforms 'do not . . . seek to change the "burden" aspect of the privity doctrine or the exceptions to it'). Three exceptions to the rule require further comment.

The first is that the existence of a contract imposes an obligation upon third parties in the sense that it is a tort to induce one party to a contract to break that contract. In this respect it can be said that third parties must respect the sanctity of contracts to which they are not a party. Take the case where A and B conclude a contract under which A agrees to work for B for a period of two years. C wishes to procure the services of A during that two-year period and so he offers to double A's salary if A terminates his contract with B. Does C commit a tort in seeking to persuade A to terminate his contract with B? The answer depends on whether or not C persuaded A to terminate the contract lawfully. If C offered A an increase in salary and A gave notice of termination in accordance with the terms of the contract then C would incur no liability towards B. But the position is different in the case where C persuades A to breach his contract with B. In such a case C may be liable in tort to B. Authority for this proposition is to be found in the case of *Lumley* v. *Gye* (1853) 2 El & Bl 216. The plaintiff and the defendant were rival theatre owners. Miss Wagner, a famous opera singer, had entered into a contract with the plaintiff under which she agreed to sing at his theatre for a period of time. The defendant induced her to break her contract with the plaintiff by promising to pay her more if she sang at his theatre. The plaintiff brought an action against the defendant. He succeeded on the ground that the defendant had committed a tort in inducing Miss Wagner to break her contract with the plaintiff. The case has been a source of some controversy on the ground that it can be argued that the plaintiff should have brought his claim against Miss Wagner (who had, after all, broken her contract with the plaintiff) and not against the defendant. According to this view, it should be for a contracting party to decide whether or not to perform her obligations under the contract and she must decide whether or not to resist the inducement to breach her contract. But this is not the view that the courts have taken. Instead they have concluded that it is a tort to induce one party to a contract to break it and thereby cause loss to the other contracting party. More broadly, the courts have also recognized the existence of a tort of interference with contractual rights by unlawful means (see, for example, *Torquay Hotel Co Ltd* v. *Cousins* [1969] 2 Ch 106).

A second exception is the doctrine of bailment on terms, to which reference has already been made (see p. 1213 above). The effect of this doctrine is to bind an owner of goods to the terms of a sub-bailment provided that certain conditions are satisfied (see *The Pioneer Container* [1994] 2 AC 324 (discussed at p. 1228 above) and *Morris* v. *C W Martin & Sons Ltd* [1966] 1 QB 716).

The third and most controversial exception is the extent to which a purchaser of land or goods is affected by a contract relating to the land or the goods which was entered into by the vendor prior to the sale of the land or goods to the purchaser. On what basis can the purchaser be affected by a contract to which he was not a party? One view is that he is affected because he has notice of the existence of the contract at the time of acquisition of the land or goods. Authority to this effect can be found in the judgment of Knight Bruce LJ in *De Mattos* v. *Gibson* (1858) 4 De G & J 276 when he stated (at p. 282):

Reason and justice seem to prescribe that, at least as a general rule, where a man, by gift or purchase, acquires property from another, with knowledge of a previous contract, lawfully and for valuable consideration made by him with a third person, to use and employ the property for a particular purpose in a specified manner, the acquirer shall not, to the material damage of the third person, in opposition to the contract and inconsistently with it, use and employ the property in a manner not allowable to the giver or seller. This rule, applicable alike in general as I conceive to moveable and immoveable property, and recognised and adopted, as I apprehend, by the English law, may, like other general rules, be liable to exceptions arising from special circumstances; but I see at present no room for any exception in the instance before us.

This statement is open to challenge. The right of the third party is a personal right which is exercisable against the vendor; it is not a property right which can be asserted and enforced against third parties, such as the purchaser. And the fact that the purchaser has notice of the third party's contractual right against the vendor ought not to be able to transform the third party's personal right against the vendor into a property right binding on the purchaser. Yet the authorities appear to say otherwise.

In relation to the acquisition of land there is long-standing authority to the effect that a party who acquires property that is, to his knowledge, subject to a restrictive covenant is bound by the terms of that covenant and may be restrained from acting inconsistently with the terms of the covenant (*Tulk* v. *Moxhay* (1848) 2 Ph 774). But this principle operates within narrow limits. In particular, the person seeking to enforce the covenant must show that the covenant was imposed for the benefit of neighbouring land owned by him.

The position is more complex in relation to the acquisition of goods or chattels. Here we encounter the statement of principle made by Knight-Bruce LJ in *De Mattos* v. *Gibson* (above). This statement of principle has given rise to difficulty, particularly in the cases of *Lord Strathcona Steamship Co Ltd* v. *Dominion Coal Co Ltd* [1926] AC 108 and *Port Line Ltd* v. *Ben Line Steamers Ltd* [1958] 2 QB 146. These cases were summarized and then analysed by Browne-Wilkinson J in *Swiss Bank Corporation* v. *Lloyd's Bank Ltd* [1979] Ch 548, 572–575 in the following terms:

In *De Mattos* v. *Gibson*, 4 De G & J 276, the plaintiff had chartered a ship from its owner Curry. Curry had subsequently charged the ship to Gibson, who had actual notice of the charterparty. Curry got into financial difficulties and was unable to continue the voyage. Gibson was proposing to sell the ship of which he had taken possession. In the action the plaintiff claimed an injunction against Gibson restraining him from interfering with the charterparty. The plaintiff applied for an interim injunction which was granted, on appeal. The ground for the decision of Knight Bruce LJ were those set out at p. 282, in the passage I have already read. The decision of Turner LJ at p. 284 was founded entirely on balance of convenience, but one of the three questions he said would have to be decided at the trial was whether the plaintiff, even if not entitled to specific performance of the charterparty, was entitled to an injunction to restrain a breach of the charterparty. In due course the action came on for trial before Page Wood V-C from whose decision there was an appeal to Lord Chelmsford LC. The Lord Chancellor held that no injunction should be granted against Gibson. He referred expressly to the three questions posed by Turner LJ, at p. 294, and after holding that the charterparty could not be specifically performed, said, at p. 299, that Gibson having taken with full knowledge of the charter could be restrained from doing any act which would have the immediate effect of preventing its performance. But Lord Chelmsford LC went on to show that on the facts there was no real possibility of Curry performing the charterparty whatever Gibson did, and therefore there was no question of any act by Gibson constituting an interference by Gibson with the plaintiff's contractual rights. In my judgment that case is an authority binding on me that a person taking a charge on property which he knows to be subject to a contractual obligation can be restrained from exercising his rights under the charge in such a way as to interfere with the performance of that contractual obligation: in my judgment the *De Mattos* v. *Gibson* principle is merely the equitable counterpart of the tort. But two points have to be emphasised about the decision in *De Mattos* v. *Gibson*: first, the ship was acquired with actual knowledge of the plaintiff's contractual rights, secondly, that no such injunction will be granted against the third party if it is clear that the original contracting party cannot in any event perform his contract. It is this second point which in my judgment accounts for the fact that the *De Mattos* v. *Gibson* principle is not applicable to restrictive covenants: the original contracting party—even if traceable— could not carry out his contract relating to the land or the chattel once he had parted with it.

In *Lord Strathcona Steamship Co Ltd* v. *Dominion Coal Co Ltd* [1926] AC 108, the facts were that a ship which was the subject matter of a charterparty to Dominion was sold to Strathcona expressly subject to the rights of Dominion under the charterparty. The Privy Council held that an injunction could be granted restraining Strathcona from inter- fering with Dominion's rights under the charterparty. It will be noted that the *Strathcona* case is of the type I considered under category (b) above, i.e. Strathcona bought expressly subject to Dominion's rights, and certainly one ground of decision is that, in the circumstances, Strathcona was a constructive trustee: see pp. 124–125. It is not clear to me whether this was the only ground of decision since the passages in the judgment dealing with *De Mattos* v. *Gibson*, 4 De G & J 276—which was held to be good law—certainly seem to proceed on the basis of knowing interference with another's contract: see p. 119. The Privy Council accepted that, in order to get an injunction the plaintiff had to have a continuing interest in the property but undoubtedly held that a bare contractual right, as opposed to a property interest, was a sufficient interest for this purpose.

There are parts of the judgment in the *Strathcona* case [1926] AC 108 which I find difficult to follow but in my judgment it certainly decides (a) that *De Mattos* v. *Gibson*, 4 De G & J 276, is good law and (b) that an injunction can be granted to restrain a subsequent purchaser of a chattel from using it so as to cause a breach of a contract of which he has express notice.

In *Port Line Ltd* v. *Ben Line Steamers Ltd* [1958] 2 QB 146 Diplock J—sitting as a judge of first instance—stated that he thought the *Strathcona* case [1926] AC 108 was wrongly decided and refused to follow it. In that case Port had chartered a vessel from Silver. Silver then sold to Ben but subject to an immediate re-charter by Ben to Silver. Under the charterparty between Port and Silver the requisitioning of the vessel did not determine the charter: under the charterparty between Ben and Silver it did. The vessel was requisi- tioned and Port was claiming from Ben compensation received by Ben for the requisition. It is important to notice that Port could only succeed if it showed either that it had a positive right to possession of the vessel or that Ben was accountable for the compensa- tion as constructive trustee. Diplock J was not concerned with the question whether Port was entitled to a negative injunction to restrain the tort.

It is not necessary for me to express any view as to whether the *Strathcona* case was rightly decided so far as it was a decision based on constructive trusteeship, which was all that Diplock J was concerned with: the *Strathcona* case itself decided that there was no right to specific performance of the charterparty. However, although I of course differ from Diplock J with diffidence, in my judgment the *Strathcona* case was rightly decided on the basis that Dominion was entitled to an injunction against Strathcona to prevent Strathcona from interfering with the contract between Dominion and the original char- terer. Diplock J at p. 165, explained *De Mattos* v. *Gibson*, 4 De G & J 276, on that ground, and at p. 168, gave as an alternative ground for his decision that actual, as opposed to constructive, notice was necessary in such a case. To that extent his decision supports my own view.

In my judgment there is in any event a decision of the Court of Appeal which is binding upon me, namely, *Manchester Ship Canal Co* v. *Manchester Racecourse Co* [1901] 2 Ch 37. In that case the Racecourse Co had granted the Canal Co a right of first refusal over certain land. The Racecourse Co, without giving proper effect to such a right of first refusal, had entered into a contract to sell the land to a third party, Trafford. The Court of Appeal held—whether rightly or wrongly does not for this purpose matter—that the right of first refusal did not create any property interest in the land, but even so granted an injunction against Trafford restraining them from completing their contract to purchase. The Court of Appeal founded its decision expressly on the basis that Trafford, having full knowledge, was proposing to do some thing which would cause a breach of the contract between the Canal Co and the Racecourse Co, i.e. to commit the tort. In my judgment this is a decision of the Court of Appeal that the court will restrain a person from enforcing his contractual rights so as to cause a breach of another contract of which he had full knowledge when he entered into his own contract. As such, it covers the present case. But it is to be noted that Trafford in that case had actual knowledge, as opposed to constructive notice, of the contract between the Canal Co and the Racecourse Co.

In *Binion* v. *Evans* [1972] Ch 359, 371, Megaw LJ indicated that he thought the case could properly have been decided on the basis that an injunction to restrain the tort should be granted. This again supports the existence of the jurisdiction.

What then are the authorities which suggest that the *De Mattos* v. *Gibson* principle is not good law? In my judgment apart from the *Port Line* case [1958] 2 QB 146 they are all cases falling within category (a) above [namely cases involving restrictive covenants affecting land and resale price maintenance conditions affecting chattels]; that is to say not cases in which the plaintiff sought an injunction to restrain the defendant from committing the tort but cases where the plaintiff was seeking to make the defendant positively perform a contract to which he was not a party. In particular, it is in my judgment clear that the remarks of Scrutton LJ in *London County Council* v. *Allen* [1914] 3 KB 642 and *Barker* v. *Stickney* [1919] 1 KB 121 are to be read in their context as cases where the plaintiff was seeking to enforce performance of the contract against the defendant who was not a party to the contract. So far as I can see, in neither of those cases was there any consideration of the rights of the plaintiff to a negative injunction restraining the defendant from causing someone else to breach the contract with the plaintiff.

Therefore, in my judgment the authorities establish the following propositions. (1) The principle stated by Knight Bruce LJ in *De Mattos* v. *Gibson*, 4 De G & J 276, is good law and represents the counterpart in equity of the tort of knowing interference with contractual rights. (2) A person proposing to deal with property in such a way as to cause a breach of a contract affecting that property will be restrained by injunction from so doing if when he acquired that property he had actual knowledge of that contract. (3) A plaintiff is entitled to such an injunction even if he has no proprietary interest in the property: his right to have his contract performed is a sufficient interest. (4) There is no case in which such an injunction has been granted against a defendant who acquired the property with only constructive, as opposed to actual, notice of the contract. In my judgment constructive notice is not sufficient, since actual knowledge of the contract is a requisite element in the tort.

COMMENTARY

This line of cases has generated a considerable academic literature (see, for example, S Gardner (1982) 98 *LQR* 279, A Tettenborn [1982] *CLJ* 58, N Cohen-Grabelsky (1982) 45 *MLR* 241, and W Swadling in N Palmer and E McKendrick (eds), *Interests in Goods* (2nd edn, LLP, 1998), Chapter 20). The cases give rise to two principal difficulties. The first is one of principle: what principle is it that demands that the purchaser should be affected by a contract that had been concluded by the vendor with a third party? The second relates to the scope of the doctrine. When will the purchaser be affected by the contract and with what effect? It would appear that the principle can only be invoked where the purchaser has actual knowledge of the existence of the contract at the time of acquisition. Further, the only remedy to which the third party is entitled is an injunction to restrain the purchaser from acting inconsistently with the terms of the contract between the third party and the vendor. In particular, the third party is not entitled to a specific performance order requiring the purchaser to give effect to the contract between the vendor and the third party.

6. CONCLUSION

The importance of the 1999 Act should not be underestimated. It provides a relatively simple mechanism by which contracting parties can confer upon a third party a right to enforce a term of their contract. The dominant philosophy that underpins the 1999 Act is one of freedom of contract and, this being the case, the success of the Act in practice will depend upon contracting parties themselves. At the moment they, or, perhaps more accurately their lawyers, appear to be reluctant to make use of the Act. But this may change over time. While the 1999 Act expressly preserves the exceptions to the doctrine of privity that pre-dated the Act, it is likely that the significance of these exceptions will diminish over time. Contracting parties who wish to confer a right of action upon a third party are probably more likely to make use of the 1999 Act than to rely upon one of the common law or other statutory exceptions to the doctrine of privity. In many ways the 1999 Act has given contracting parties an incentive to make their intention clear in relation to the creation of third party rights of action. Where they make that intention clear, whether in favour or against the existence of a third party right of action, the court must respect and give effect to their choice.

More difficult is the case where the contracting parties do not make their intention clear. In such a case a court must first decide whether or not the third party has acquired a right to enforce a term of the contract under section 1(1)(b) of the 1999 Act. Where the requirements of that subsection are satisfied the Act will determine the rights of the third party. In the case where the requirements of section 1(1)(b) have not been satisfied, the court must go on to consider whether the third party has acquired rights by virtue of one of the common law exceptions to the doctrine of privity or one of the other statutory exceptions to the doctrine. While the Act expressly preserves the existence of these exceptions, and indeed preserves the ability of the judiciary to develop still further exceptions to the doctrine of privity, the willingness of the judges to make use of these exceptions in the light of the enactment of the 1999 Act remains to be tested. It is possible that they will be more reluctant to make use of the common law exceptions to the doctrine of privity on the basis that the parties could have made use of the 1999 Act but have chosen, for one reason or another, not to do so. On the other hand, they are directed by the Act itself to continue, where appropriate, to make use of these exceptions. The precise role of these exceptions, following the Act, remains to be seen but it is suggested that the fundamental point that has to be grasped is that the 1999 Act is now the first port of call in any case concerned with third party rights of action and, in many cases, it is also likely to be the last port of call.

7. FURTHER READING

ANDREWS, N, 'Strangers to Justice No Longer: The Reversal of the Privity Rule Under the Contracts (Rights of Third Parties) Act 1999' [2001] *CLJ* 353.

BURROWS, A, 'The Contracts (Rights of Third Parties) Act and its Implications for Commercial Contracts' [2000] *LMCLQ* 540.

COHEN-GRABELSKY, N, 'Interference with Contractual Relations and Equitable Doctrines' (1982) 45 *MLR* 241.

CORBIN, A, 'Contracts for the Benefit of Third Parties' (1930) 46 *LQR* 12.

FLANNIGAN, R, 'Privity—The End of an Era (Error)' (1987) 103 *LQR* 564.

GARDNER, S, 'The Proprietary Effect of Contractual Obligations under *Tulk* v. *Moxhay* and *De Mattos* v. *Gibson*' (1982) 98 *LQR* 279.

KINCAID, P, 'Privity Reform in England' (2000) 116 *LQR* 43.

—— 'Third Parties: Rationalising A Right to Sue' [1989] *CLJ* 243.

LAW COMMISSION, *Privity of Contract: Contracts for the Benefit of Third Parties*: Law Com No 242, 1996.

MACMILLAN, C, 'A Birthday Present for Lord Denning: The Contracts (Rights of Third Parties) Act 1999' (2000) 63 *MLR* 721.

MERKIN, R (ed), *Privity of Contract* (LLP, 2000).

PHANG, A, 'On Justification and Method in Law Reform—The Contracts (Rights of Third Parties) Act 1999' (2002) 18 *Journal of Contract Law* 32.

SMITH, SA, 'Contracts for the Benefit of Third Parties: In Defence of the Third-Party Rule' (1997) 7 *OJLS* 643.

STEVENS, R, 'The Contracts (Rights of Third Parties) Act 1999' (2004) 120 *LQR* 292.

SWADLING, W, 'The Proprietary Effect of a Hire of Goods' in Palmer, N and McKendrick, E (eds), *Interests in Goods* (2nd edn, LLP, 1998), Chapter 20.

TETTENBORN, A, 'Contracts, Privity of Contract and the Purchaser of Personal Property' [1982] *CLJ* 58.

TREITEL, GH, *Some Landmarks of Twentieth Century Contract Law* (Oxford University Press, 2002), Chapter 2.

INDEX